W9-BPL-257

2019-2020

OFFICIAL CONGRESSIONAL DIRECTORY

116TH CONGRESS

CONVENED JANUARY 3, 2019

JOINT COMMITTEE ON PRINTING
UNITED STATES CONGRESS

Lanham • Boulder • New York • London

Published by Bernan Press
An imprint of The Rowman & Littlefield Publishing Group, Inc.
4501 Forbes Boulevard, Suite 200, Lanham, Maryland 20706
www.rowman.com

86-90 Paul Street, London EC2A 4NE

ISBN 978-1-64143-468-3 (cloth)
ISBN 978-1-64143-469-0 (paperback)

™ The paper used in this publication meets the minimum requirements of American National Standard for Information Sciences—Permanence of Paper for Printed Library Materials, ANSI/NISO Z39.48-1992.

NOTES

Closing date for compilation of the Congressional Directory was July 22, 2020.

SENATORS

[Republicans in roman, Democrats in *italic*.]

REPRESENTATIVES

[Democrats in roman, Republicans in *italic*.]

The following changes have occurred in the membership of the 116th Congress since the election of November 6, 2018:

Name	Resigned, [Died], 【Term Ended】, or (Interim Vacant Status)	Successor	Elected or [Appointed]	Sworn in
SENATORS				
Johnny Isakson, GA ...	Dec. 31, 2019	Kelly Loeffler	[Jan. 1, 2020] ...	Jan. 6, 2020
REPRESENTATIVES				
Robert Pittenger, 9th NC	Jan. 3, 2019	*Dan Bishop*	Sept. 10, 2019 ..	Sept. 17, 2019
Tom Marino, 12th PA	Jan. 23, 2019	*Fred Keller*	May 22, 2019 ..	June 3, 2019
Walter B. Jones, Jr., 3d NC	[Feb. 10, 2019]	*Gregory F. Murphy*	Sept. 10, 2019 ..	Sept. 17, 2019
Sean Duffy, 7th WI	Sept. 23, 2019	*Thomas P. Tiffany*	May 12, 2020 ..	May 19, 2020
Chris Collins, 27th NY	Oct. 1, 2019	*Chris Jacobs*	June 23, 2020 ..	July 21, 2020
Elijah E. Cummings, 7th MD	[Oct. 17, 2019]	Kweisi Mfume	April 28, 2020	May 5, 2020
Katie Hill, 25th CA	Nov. 3, 2019	*Mike Garcia*	May 12, 2020 ..	May 19, 2020
Duncan Hunter,[1] 50th CA	(Jan. 13, 2020)	....	....	
Mark Meadows,[2] 11th NC	(Mar. 30, 2020)	....	....	
John Ratcliffe,[3] 4th TX	(May 22, 2020)	....	....	
John Lewis,[4] 5th GA	[July 17, 2020]	....	....	

[1] This seat is in interim vacant status. It will remain so until the general election on November 3, 2020.

[2] This seat is in interim vacant status. Mark Meadows resigned to become White House Chief of Staff. The seat will remain vacant until the general election on November 3, 2020.

[3] This seat is in interim vacant status. John Ratcliffe resigned to become Director of National Intelligence. The seat will remain vacant until the general election on November 3, 2020.

[4] This seat is in interim vacant status. John Lewis died on July 17, 2020. The seat will remain vacant until the general election on November 3, 2020.

[Republicans in roman, Democrats in *italic.*]

The following changes have occurred in the membership of the 115th Congress since the election of November 8, 2016:

Name	Resigned, [Died], 【Term Ended】, or (Interim Vacant Status)	Successor	Elected or [Appointed]	Sworn in
SENATORS				
Luther Strange, AL	【Jan. 3, 2018】	*Doug Jones*	Dec. 12, 2017 ..	Jan. 3, 2018
Al Franken, MN	Jan. 3, 2018	*Tina Smith*	[Jan. 2, 2018] ...	Jan. 3, 2018
Thad Cochran, MS	Apr. 1, 2018	Cindy Hyde-Smith	[Apr. 2, 2018] ..	Apr. 9, 2018
REPRESENTATIVES				
Mike Pompeo,[1] 4th KS	Jan. 23, 2017	Ron Estes	Apr. 11, 2017 ..	Apr. 25, 2017
Xavier Becerra, 34th CA	Jan. 24, 2017	*Jimmy Gomez*	June 6, 2017	July 11, 2017
Tom Price,[2] 6th GA	Feb. 10, 2017	Karen C. Handel	June 20, 2017 ..	June 26, 2017
Mick Mulvaney,[3] 5th SC	Feb. 16, 2017	Ralph Norman	June 20, 2017 ..	June 26, 2017
Ryan K. Zinke,[4] At Large MT	Mar. 1, 2017	Greg Gianforte	May 25, 2017 ..	June 21, 2017
Jason Chaffetz, 3d UT	June 30, 2017	John R. Curtis	Nov. 7, 2017	Nov. 13, 2017
Tim Murphy, 18th PA	Oct. 21, 2017	*Conor Lamb*	Mar. 13, 2018 ..	Apr. 12, 2018
John Conyers, Jr.,[5] 13th MI	(Dec. 5, 2017)	....	....	
Trent Franks, 8th AZ	Dec. 8, 2017	Debbie Lesko	Apr. 24, 2018 ..	May 7, 2018
Patrick J. Tiberi,[6] 12th OH	(Jan. 15, 2017)	....	....	
Louise McIntosh Slaughter,[7] 25th NY	[Mar. 16, 2018]	....	....	
Blake Farenthold 27th TX	Apr. 6, 2018	Michael Cloud	June 30, 2018 ..	July 10, 2018
Jim Bridenstine,[8] 1st OK	(Apr. 23, 2018)	....	....	
Patrick Meehan,[9] 7th PA	(Apr. 27, 2018)	....	....	
Charles W. Dent,[10] 15th PA	(May 12, 2018)	....	....	

[1] Mike Pompeo resigned to become Director of the Central Intelligence Agency.

[2] Tom Price resigned to become Secretary of the Department of Health and Human Services.

[3] Mick Mulvaney resigned to become Director of the Office of Management and Budget.

[4] Ryan K. Zinke resigned to become Secretary of the Department of the Interior.

[5] This seat is in interim vacant status. A special election for a new U.S. Representative will be held on November 6, 2018.

[6] This seat is in interim vacant status. A special election for a new U.S. Representative will be held on August 7, 2018, to serve the remainder of Representative Tiberi's term until January 3, 2019.

[7] This seat is in interim vacant status. Louise Slaughter died on March 16, 2018. A special election, concurrent with the general election, will be held on November 6, 2018, for a new U.S. Representative to serve the remainder of Representative Slaughter's term.

[8] Jim Bridenstine resigned to become Administrator of the National Aeronautics and Space Administration.

[9] This seat is in interim vacant status. A special election for a new U.S. Representative for the 7th District will be held on November 6, 2018. The special election coincides with the general election for the newly redrawn 7th District made up of the old 15th, 17th, and 10th Districts. The old 7th District will no longer exist on December 31, 2018.

[10] This seat is in interim vacant status. The Supreme Court of Pennsylvania redrew the district in February 2018. Boundaries of the old 15th District will be compressed, becoming the 7th District. The old 5th District will have its boundaries adjusted to become the 15th district for the 2018 election.

FOREWORD

The *Congressional Directory* is one of the oldest working handbooks within the United States Government. While there were unofficial directories for Congress in one form or another beginning with the 1st Congress in 1789, the *Congressional Directory* published in 1847 for the 30th Congress is considered by scholars and historians to be the first official edition because it was the first to be ordered and paid for by Congress. With the addition of biographical sketches of legislators in 1867, the *Congressional Directory* attained its modern format.

The *Congressional Directory* is published by the United States Congress in partnership with the Government Publishing Office, at the direction of the Joint Committee on Printing under the authority of Title 44, Section 721 of the U.S. Code.

JOINT COMMITTEE ON PRINTING

Zoe Lofgren, Representative from California, *Chairperson*

Roy Blunt, Senator from Missouri, *Vice Chair*

House

Jamie Raskin, of Maryland.
Susan A. Davis, of California.
Rodney Davis, of Illinois.
Barry Loudermilk, of Georgia.

Senate

Pat Roberts, of Kansas.
Roger F. Wicker, of Mississippi.
Amy Klobuchar, of Minnesota.
Tom Udall, of New Mexico.

The 2019–20 *Congressional Directory* was compiled by the Government Publishing Office, under the direction of the Joint Committee on Printing by:

Project Manager.—Mary C. Forschler.

Editor.—Cameron G. Matthews.

Typographers / Editors: Connie Gaulding, Greg Matiasevich.

Proofreader / Editor.—Tom Young.

State District Maps.—Election Data Services, Inc.

Representatives' Zip Codes.—House Office of Mailing Services / U.S. Postal Service.

For sale by the Superintendent of Documents, U.S. Government Publishing Office
Phone: toll free (866) 512–1800; DC area (202) 512–1800
Fax: (202) 512–2250
Mail: Stop SSOP, Washington, DC 20402–0001
Internet: https://bookstore.gpo.gov

Paper Cover ISBN–978–0–16–095386–6

Casebound ISBN–978–0–16–095391–0

CONTENTS

Name Index on page 1157

116th Congress*

THE VICE PRESIDENT

MIKE PENCE, Republican, of Columbus, IN; born in Columbus, June 7, 1959; education: Hanover College, 1981; J.D., Indiana University School of Law, 1986; professional: former Republican nominee for the U.S. House of Representatives, 2nd District in 1988 and 1990; president, Indiana Policy Review Foundation, 1991–93; radio broadcaster: the Mike Pence Show, syndicated statewide in Indiana; married: Karen; children: Michael, Charlotte, and Audrey; elected to the 107th Congress on November 7, 2000; reelected to the 108th through 112th Congress, 2000–13; Governor, State of Indiana, 2013–17; elected 48th Vice President of the United States on November 8, 2016; took the oath of office on January 20, 2017.

The Office of the Vice President is S–212 in the Capitol. The Vice President has offices in the Dirksen Senate Office Building, the Eisenhower Executive Office Building (EEOB), and the White House (West Wing).

Assistant to the President and Chief of Staff to the Vice President.—Marc Short.

Assistant to the President and National Security Advisor to the Vice President.—Keith Kellogg.

Deputy Assistant to the President and Deputy Chief of Staff and Counsel to the Vice President.—Matthew Morgan.

Deputy Assistant to the President and Chief of Staff to Mrs. Karen Pence.—Jana Toner.

Deputy Assistant to the President and Deputy National Security Advisor to the Vice President.—Stephen Pinkos.

Deputy Assistant to the President and Director of Advance to the Vice President.—Aaron Chang.

Deputy Assistant to the President and Director of Policy for the Vice President.—John Gray.

Deputy Assistant to the President and Director of Public Liaison and Intergovernmental Affairs for the Vice President.—Sarah Makin.

Special Assistant to the President and Deputy Director of Public Liaison and Intergovernmental Affairs.—Andeliz Castillo.

Special Assistant to the President and Press Secretary to the Vice President.—Katie Waldman.

Assistant to the Vice President and Director of Legislative Affairs.—Christopher Hodgson.

Deputy Director of Legislative Affairs.—Benjamin Cantrell.

Deputy Assistant to the Vice President and Director of Administration and Finance.—Katherine Purucker.

Deputy Assistant to the Vice President and Director of Scheduling.—Bethany Scully.

Special Assistant to the Vice President.—Zach Bauer.

*Biographies are based on information furnished or authorized by the respective Senators and Representatives.

ALABAMA

(Population 2010, 4,779,736)

SENATORS

RICHARD C. SHELBY, Republican, of Tuscaloosa, AL; born in Birmingham, AL, May 6, 1934; education: attended the public schools; B.A., University of Alabama, 1957; LL.B., University of Alabama School of Law, 1963; professional: attorney; admitted to the Alabama Bar in 1961 and commenced practice in Tuscaloosa; member, Alabama State Senate, 1970–78; law clerk, Supreme Court of Alabama, 1961–62; city prosecutor, Tuscaloosa, 1963–71; U.S. Magistrate, Northern District of Alabama, 1966–70; Special Assistant Attorney General, State of Alabama, 1969–71; chairman, Legislative Council of the Alabama Legislature, 1977–78; former president, Tuscaloosa County Mental Health Association; member, Alabama Code Revision Committee, 1971–75; member, Phi Alpha Delta legal fraternity, Tuscaloosa County; Alabama and American Bar Associations; First Presbyterian Church of Tuscaloosa; Exchange Club; American Judicature Society; Alabama Law Institute; married: the former Annette Nevin in 1960; children: Richard C., Jr., and Claude Nevin; committees: chair, Appropriations; Banking, Housing, and Urban Affairs; Environment and Public Works; Rules and Administration; Joint Committee on the Library; elected to the 96th Congress on November 7, 1978; reelected to the three succeeding Congresses; elected to the U.S. Senate on November 4, 1986; reelected to each succeeding Senate term.

Office Listings

https://shelby.senate.gov https://facebook.com/RichardShelby
twitter: @SenShelby https://instagram.com/senatorshelby

304 Russell Senate Office Building, Washington, DC 20510 .... (202) 224–5744
Chief of Staff.—Dayne Cutrell.
Personal Secretary / Appointments.—Anne Caldwell.
Communications Director.—Blair Taylor.
The Federal Building, 2005 University Boulevard, Suite 2100, Tuscaloosa, AL 35401 .... (205) 759–5047
Vance Federal Building, Room 321, 1800 5th Avenue North, Birmingham, AL 35203 .... (205) 731–1384
John A. Campbell Federal Courthouse, Suite 445, 113 St. Joseph Street, Mobile, AL 36602 .... (251) 694–4164
Frank M. Johnson Federal Courthouse, Suite 208, 15 Lee Street, Montgomery, AL 36104 (334) 223–7303
Huntsville International Airport, 1000 Glenn Hearn Boulevard, Box 20127, Huntsville, AL 35824 .... (256) 772–0460

* * *

DOUG JONES, Democrat, of Birmingham, AL; born in Fairfield, AL, May 4, 1954; education: University of Alabama, Tuscaloosa, AL, 1976; Cumberland School of Law, 1979; honored for his work by the Southern Christian Leadership Conference, the NAACP, the Federal Bureau of Investigation, the SCLC / Women, Inc., and the Community Affairs Committee of Operation New Birmingham, among many others; religion: Christian; family: wife, Louise; children, Carson and Christopher; committees: Armed Services; Banking, Housing, and Urban Affairs; Health, Education, Labor, and Pensions; Special Committee on Aging; elected to the U.S. Senate, by special election, on December 12, 2017, to fill the vacancy caused by the resignation of Senator Jefferson Sessions for the term ending January 3, 2021, and took the oath of office on January 3, 2018.

Office Listings

https://jones.senate.gov

330 Hart Senate Office Building, Washington, DC 20510 .... (202) 224–4124
Chief of Staff.—Dana Gresham.
Deputy Chief of Staff.—Mark Libel.
Scheduler.—Brenda Strickland.
Press Secretary.—Heather Fluit.
Vance Federal Building, 1800 Fifth Avenue North, Birmingham, AL 35203 .... (205) 731–1500
BB&T Centre, Suite 2300–A, 41 West I–65 Service Road North, Mobile, AL 36608.
200 Clinton Avenue West, Suite 802, Huntsville, AL 35801.
Frank M. Johnson Jr. Federal Courthouse, 1 Church Street, Suite 500–B, Montgomery, AL 36104.

REPRESENTATIVES

FIRST DISTRICT

BRADLEY BYRNE, Republican, of Fairhope, AL; born in Mobile, AL, February 16, 1955; education: B.A. in public policy and history, Duke University, 1977; J.D., the University of Alabama, 1980; professional: Alabama State Board of Education; Chancellor of two-year college system; Alabama State Senate / Organizations: Leadership Alabama; Alabama PTA; U.S. Supreme Court Bar; Alabama State Workforce Planning Council; chair / awards: Council for Leaders in Alabama Schools Legislative Leadership Award, 2007; Alabama Wildlife Foundation Legislator of the Year Award, 2005; South Alabama Literacy Champion Award, 2006; religion: Episcopalian; wife: Rebecca; children: Patrick, Laura, Kathleen, and Colin; committees: Armed Services; Education and Labor; elected, by special election, to the 113th Congress on December 17, 2013, to fill the vacancy caused by the resignation of U.S. Representative Jo Bonner; reelected to each succeeding Congress.

Office Listings

https://byrne.house.gov https://facebook.com/RepByrne https://twitter.com/RepByrne

119 Cannon House Office Building, Washington, DC 20515 .... (202) 225–4931
Chief of Staff.—Chad Carlough. FAX: 225–0562
Legislative Director.—Mitch Relfe.
Communications Director.—Bradley Jaye.
Scheduler.—Jordan Howard.
11 North Water Street, Suite 15290, Mobile, AL 36602 .... (251) 690–2811
502 West Lee Street, Summerdale, AL 36580 .... (251) 989–2664

Counties: BALDWIN, CLARKE (part), ESCAMBIA, MOBILE, MONROE, AND WASHINGTON. Population (2010), 687,841.

ZIP Codes: 36033 (part), 36401 (part), 36420 (part), 36425, 36426 (part), 36432 (part), 36439, 36441, 36444–45, 36451 (part), 36460 (part), 36470, 36471 (part), 36475 (part), 36480, 36481 (part), 36482 (part), 36483 (part), 36502 (part), 36505, 36507, 36509, 36511–13, 36518, 36521–23, 36525–30, 36532, 36535, 36538–39, 36541–45, 36548–51, 36553, 36555–56, 36558 (part), 36559–62, 36564, 36567–69, 36571–72, 36574–76, 36578–85, 36587, 36590, 36602–13, 36615–19, 36688, 36693, 36695, 36751 (part), 36753 (part), 36768 (part), 36919 (part)

* * *

SECOND DISTRICT

MARTHA ROBY, Republican, of Montgomery, AL; born in Montgomery, July 26, 1976; education: B.M., New York University, New York, NY, 1998; J.D., Cumberland School of Law at Samford University, Birmingham, AL, 2001; professional: attorney, Copeland, Franco, Screws, and Gill, P.A.; Councilor, District 7, City of Montgomery; religion: Christian (Presbyterian); family: husband, Riley; children: Margaret and George; committees: Appropriations; Judiciary; elected to the 112th Congress on November 2, 2010; reelected to each succeeding Congress.

Office Listings

https://roby.house.gov https://twitter.com/RepMarthaRoby

504 Cannon House Office Building, Washington, DC 20515 .... (202) 225–2901
Chief of Staff.—Mike Albares.
Legislative Director.—David Allen.
Communications Director.—Emily Johnson.
Director of Scheduling.—Kate Hollis.
401 Adams Avenue, Suite 160, Montgomery, AL 36104 .... (334) 262–7718
217 Graceland Drive, Suite 5, Dothan, AL 36305 .... (334) 794–9680
505 East Three Notch Street, Andalusia City Hall, Room 322, Andalusia, AL 36420 .... (334) 428–1129

Counties: AUTAUGA, BARBOUR, BULLOCK, BUTLER, COFFEE, CONECUH, COVINGTON, CRENSHAW, DALE, ELMORE, GENEVA, HENRY, HOUSTON, MONTGOMERY (part), AND PIKE. Population (2010), 673,887.

ZIP Codes: 35010, 36003, 36005–06, 36009–10, 36016–17, 36020, 36022, 36024–30, 36032–38, 36041–43, 36046–49, 36051–54, 36064, 36066–67, 36069, 36071, 36078–82, 36089, 36091–93, 36104–13, 36115–17, 36301, 36303, 36305, 36310–14, 36316–23, 36330, 36340, 36343–46, 36350–53, 36360, 36362, 36370–71, 36373–76, 36401, 36420–21, 36426, 36432, 36442, 36453–56, 36460, 36467, 36471, 36473–77, 36483, 36502, 36703, 36749, 36758, 36860

* * *

THIRD DISTRICT

MIKE ROGERS, Republican, of Saks, AL; born in Hammond, IN, July 16, 1958; education: B.A., Jacksonville State University, 1981; M.P.A., Jacksonville State University, 1984; J.D., Birmingham School of Law, 1991; professional: attorney; awards: Anniston Star Citizen of the Year, 1998; public service: Calhoun County Commissioner, 1987–91; Alabama House of Representatives, 1994–2002; family: married to Beth; children: Emily, Evan, and Elliot; committees: ranking member, Homeland Security; Armed Services, elected to the 108th Congress on November 5, 2002; reelected to each succeeding Congress.

Office Listings

https://mikerogers.house.gov https://facebook.com/CongressmanMikeDRogers
twitter: @RepMikeRogersAL

2184 Rayburn House Office Building, Washington, DC 20515 .... (202) 225–3261
Chief of Staff.—Chris Brinson. FAX: 226–8485
Legislative Director.—Whitney Verett.
Press Secretary.—Shea Miller.
Scheduler.—Alexis Barranca.
1129 Noble Street, 104 Federal Building, Anniston, AL 36201 .... (256) 236–5655
District Director.—Sheri Rollins.
G.W. Andrews Building, 701 Avenue A, Suite 300, Opelika, AL 36801 .... (334) 745–6221
Field Representatives: Alvin Lewis, Lee Vanoy.

Counties: CALHOUN, CHAMBERS, CHEROKEE, CLAY, CLEBURNE, LEE, MACON, MONTGOMERY (part), RANDOLPH, RUSSELL, ST. CLAIR, TALLADEGA, AND TALLAPOOSA. Population (2010), 682,819.

ZIP Codes: 30165, 31905, 35004, 35010, 35014, 35032, 35044, 35052, 35054, 35072, 35082, 35089, 35094, 35096, 35112, 35120–21, 35125, 35128, 35131, 35133, 35135, 35146, 35149–51, 35160, 35173, 35178, 35901, 35903, 35905, 35953, 35959–61, 35967, 35972–73, 35983, 35987, 36013, 36027, 36029, 36031, 36039, 36052, 36064, 36075, 36078, 36083, 36088–89, 36116–17, 36201, 36203, 36205–07, 36250–51, 36255–56, 36258, 36260, 36262–69, 36271–74, 36276–80, 36801, 36804, 36830, 36832, 36849–50, 36852–56, 36858–63, 36865–67, 36869–71, 36874–75, 36877, 36879

* * *

FOURTH DISTRICT

ROBERT B. ADERHOLT, Republican, of Haleyville, AL; born in Haleyville, July 22, 1965; education: graduate, Birmingham Southern University; J.D., Cumberland School of Law, Samford University; professional: attorney; assistant legal advisor to Governor Fob James, 1995–96; Haleyville municipal judge, 1992–96; George Bush delegate, Republican National Convention, 1992; Republican nominee for the 17th District, Alabama House of Representatives, 1990; married: Caroline McDonald; children: Mary Elliott and Robert Hayes; committees: Appropriations; elected to the 105th Congress; reelected to each succeeding Congress.

Office Listings

https://aderholt.house.gov twitter: @Robert_Aderholt

1203 Longworth House Office Building, Washington, DC 20515 .... (202) 225–4876
Chief of Staff.—Brian Rell. FAX: 225–5587
Legislative Director.—Mark Dawson.
Communications Directors / Press Secretaries: Carson Clark, Brian Rell.
Administrative Director.—Chris Lawson.
Carl Elliott Building, 1710 Alabama Avenue, Room 247, Jasper, AL 35501 .... (205) 221–2310
District Field Director.—Paul Housel.
205 Fourth Avenue, Northeast, Suite 104, Cullman, AL 35055 .... (256) 734–6043
Director of Constituent Services.—Jennifer Taylor.
600 Broad Street, Suite 107, Gadsden, AL 35901 .... (256) 546–0201
Field Representative.—James Manasco.
1011 George Wallace Boulevard, Suite 146, Tuscumbia, AL 35674 .... (256) 381–3450
Field Representative.—Kreg Kennedy.

Counties: BLOUNT (part), CHEROKEE (part), COLBERT, CULLMAN, DEKALB, ETOWAH, FAYETTE, FRANKLIN, JACKSON (part), LAMAR, LAWRENCE, MARION, MARSHALL, TUSCALOOSA (part), WALKER, AND WINSTON. Population (2010), 682,029.

ZIP Codes: 35006, 35013, 35016, 35019, 35031, 35033, 35049, 35053, 35055, 35057–58, 35062–63, 35070, 35077, 35079, 35083, 35087, 35097–98, 35121, 35126, 35130, 35133, 35146, 35172, 35175, 35179–80, 35447, 35461, 35481, 35501, 35503–04, 35540–46, 35548–50, 35552–55, 35563–65, 35570–72, 35574–82, 35584–87, 35592–94, 35601, 35603, 35619,

35621–22, 35640, 35653–54, 35670, 35673, 35747, 35754–55, 35760, 35765, 35769, 35771, 35775–76, 35901, 35903–07, 35950–54, 35956–57, 35961–64, 35966–68, 35971–72, 35974–76, 35978–81, 35984, 35986–90, 36272

* * *

FIFTH DISTRICT

MO BROOKS, Republican, of Huntsville, AL; born in Charleston, SC, April 29, 1954; education: B.A., Duke University, Durham, NC, 1975; J.D., University of Alabama School of Law, Tuscaloosa, AL, 1978; professional: lawyer, private practice, partner in Leo and Brooks law firm; prosecutor, Office of the District Attorney, Tuscaloosa County, AL, 1978–80; clerk, Circuit Court Judge John Snodgrass, 1980–82; member of the Alabama State House of Representatives, 1983–91; district attorney, Office of the District Attorney, Madison County, AL, 1991–93; special assistant attorney general, State of Alabama, 1995–2002; commissioner, Madison County, AL, board of commissions, 1996–2010; religion: Christian; married: Martha; four children; 10 grandchildren; committees: Armed Services; Science, Space, and, Technology; elected to the 112th Congress on November 2, 2010; reelected to each succeeding Congress.

Office Listings

https://brooks.house.gov https://facebook.com/RepMoBrooks https://twitter.com/RepMoBrooks

2246 Rayburn House Office Building, Washington, DC 20515 .... (202) 225–4801
Chief of Staff / Legislative Director.—Mark Pettitt.
Scheduler / Office Manager.—Madison Engelking.
2101 West Clinton Avenue, Suite 302, Huntsville, AL 35805 .... (256) 551–0190
District Director.—Tiffany Noel.
Field Representative and Grants Coordinator.—Kathy Murray.
Caseworkers: Debi Echols, Timothy Jackson.
302 Lee Street, Room 86, Decatur, AL 35601 .... (256) 355–9400
District Field Representative and Caseworker.—Johnny Turner.
102 South Court Street, Suite 310, Florence, AL 35630 .... (256) 718–5155
District Field Representative and Caseworker.—Laura Smith.

Counties: JACKSON, LAUDERDALE, LIMESTONE, MADISON, AND MORGAN. Population (2010), 718,724.

ZIP Codes: 35016, 35601–03, 35609–15, 35617, 35619–22, 35630–34, 35640, 35645, 35647–49, 35652, 35670–71, 35673, 35677, 35699, 35739–42, 35744–46, 35748–52, 35754–69, 35756–63, 35767, 35771–76, 35801–16, 35824, 35893–94, 35896, 35898–99, 35958, 35966, 35978–79

* * *

SIXTH DISTRICT

GARY PALMER, Republican, of Hoover, AL; born in Hackleburg, AL, May 14, 1954; education: B.S., University of Alabama, Tuscaloosa, 1977; professional: president, Alabama Policy Institute; founding member, State Policy Network; member, Briarwood Presbyterian Church; spouse: Ann; children: Claire, Kathleen, and Rob; committees: Oversight and Reform; Transportation and Infrastructure; Select Committee on the Climate Crisis; elected to the 114th Congress on November 4, 2014; reelected to each succeeding Congress.

Office Listings

https://palmer.house.gov https://facebook.com/CongressmanGaryPalmer twitter: @USRepGaryPalmer
https://youtube.com/channel/UCYZfP-cNIvlJY3AcAc9OPpQ

207 Cannon House Office Building, Washington, DC 20515 .... (202) 225–4921
Chief of Staff.—William Smith. FAX: 225–2082
Deputy Chief of Staff.—Cari Fike.
Communications Director.—Elizabeth Hance.
Legislative Director.—Hunter Hobart.
Scheduler.—Ashley Sills.
3535 Grandview Parkway, Suite 525, Birmingham, AL 35243 .... (205) 968–1290
703 Second Avenue North, P.O. Box 502, Clanton, AL 35045 .... (205) 280–6846
220 2nd Avenue East, Oneonta, AL 35121 .... (205) 274–2136

Counties: BIBB, BLOUNT (part), CHILTON, COOSA (part), JEFFERSON (part), AND SHELBY. CITIES AND TOWNSHIPS: Adamsville, Allgood, Altoona, Argo, Bessemer, Birmingham, Blountsville, Brantleyville, Brent, Brook Highland, Brookside, Calera, Cardiff, Center Point, Centreville, Chelsea, Clanton, Clay, Cleveland, Columbiana, Concord, County Line, Dunnavant, Forestdale, Fultondale, Garden City, Gardendale, Goodwatter, Graysville, Harpersville, Hayden, Helena, Highland Lake, Hissop, Homewood, Hoover, Hueytown, Indian Springs Village, Irondale, Jemison, Kellyton, Kimberly, Leeds, Locust

Fork, Maplesville, Maytown, McDonald Chapel, Meadowbrook, Montevallo, Morris, Mount Olive, Mountain Brook, Mulga, Nectar, North Johns, Oneonta, Pelham, Pinson, Pleasant Grove, Rock Creek, Rockford, Rosa, Shelby, Shoal Creek, Smoke Rise, Snead, Sterrett, Susan Moore, Sylvan Springs, Tarrant, Thorsby, Trafford, Trussville, Vance, Vandiver, Vestavia Hills, Vincent, Warrior, West Blocton, West Jefferson, Westover, Wilsonville, Wilton, and Woodstock. Population (2010), 682,819.

ZIP Codes: 35004–07, 35015, 35022–23, 35035, 35040, 35043, 35046, 35048, 35051–52, 35054, 35060, 35062–63, 35068, 35071, 35073–74, 35078–80, 35085, 35091, 35094, 35096, 35111–12, 35114–20, 35123–28, 35130–31, 35133, 35135, 35137, 35139, 35142–44, 35146–48, 35151, 35171–73, 35175–76, 35178, 35180–88, 35201–03, 35205–07, 35209–10, 35212–17, 35219, 35222–26, 35230, 35233, 35235–37, 35240, 35242–46, 35249, 35253–55, 35259–61, 35266, 35277–83, 35285, 35287–99, 35402–03, 35406–07, 35444, 35446, 35452, 35456–58, 35466, 35468, 35473, 35475–76, 35480, 35482, 35490, 35546, 35579, 35953, 35987, 36006, 36051, 36064, 36091, 36750, 36758, 36790, 36792–93

* * *

SEVENTH DISTRICT

TERRI A. SEWELL, Democrat, of Birmingham, AL; born in Selma, AL, January 1, 1965; education: graduated from Selma High School, Selma, AL; B.A., *cum laude*, Princeton University, Princeton, NJ, 1986; master's degree, first class honors, Oxford University, Oxford, UK, 1988; J.D., Harvard Law School, Cambridge, MA, 1992; professional: attorney; judicial law clerk to the Honorable Chief Judge U.W. Clemon, U.S. District Court, Northern District of Alabama, Birmingham; memberships and boards: treasurer of the board and chair of the finance committee, St. Vincent's Foundation; Girl Scouts of Cahaba Council; community advisory board for the DAB Minority Health and Research Center; governing board of the Alabama Council on Economic Education; Corporate Partners Council for the Birmingham Art Museum; Alpha Kappa Alpha Sorority, Inc.; professional affiliations: American Bar Association; National Bar Association; Alabama Bar Association; religion: African Methodist Episcopal; Chief Deputy Whip; committees: Ways and Means; Permanent Select Committee on Intelligence; elected to the 112th Congress on November 2, 2010; reelected to each succeeding Congress.

Office Listings

https://sewell.house.gov https://facebook.com/RepSewell twitter: @RepTerriSewell

2201 Rayburn House Office Building, Washington, DC 20515 .... (202) 225–2665
Chief of Staff.—Cachavious English.
Communications Director.—Jackie McGuiness.
Senior Policy Advisor.—Hillary Beard.
Tax and Economic Policy Advisor.—Evan Giesemann.
Legislative Assistant.—Robert Nuttall.
Legislative Aide / Scheduler.—Perry Hamilton.
Staff Assistant / Legislative Correspondent.—Scott Harris.
Two 20th Street North, Suite 1130, Birmingham, AL 35203 .... (205) 254–1960
District Director.—Melinda Williams. FAX: 254–1974
Federal Building, 908 Alabama Avenue, Suite 112, Selma, AL 36701 .... (334) 877–4414
FAX: 877–4489
2501 7th Street, Suite 300, Tuscaloosa, AL 35401 .... (205) 752–5380
FAX: 752–5899
101 South Lawrence Street, Montgomery, AL 36104 .... (334) 262–1919
FAX: 262–1921

Counties: CHOCTAW, CLARKE (part), DALLAS, GREENE, HALE, JEFFERSON (part), LOWNDES, MARENGO, MONTGOMERY (part), PERRY, PICKENS (part), SUMTER, TUSCALOOSA (part), AND WILCOX. Population (2010), 682,742.

ZIP Codes: 35005–06, 35020–23, 35034, 35036, 35041–42, 35061, 35064, 35068, 35071, 35073–74, 35079, 35111, 35117, 35126–27, 35173, 35175, 35184, 35188, 35203–15, 35217–18, 35221–22, 35224, 35228–29, 35233–35, 35238, 35243, 35401, 35404–06, 35440–44, 35446–49, 35452–53, 35456, 35459–60, 35462–64, 35466, 35469–71, 35473–78, 35480–81, 35485–87, 35490–91, 35546, 35601, 35603, 35640, 35754, 36030, 36032, 36040, 36064, 36105, 36435–36, 36451, 36482, 36524, 36540, 36545, 36558, 36701–03, 36720, 36722–23, 36726–28, 36732, 36736, 36738, 36740–42, 36744–45, 36748–54, 36756, 36758–59, 36761–69, 36773, 36775–76, 36782–86, 36790, 36792–93, 36901, 36904, 36906–08, 36910, 36912–13, 36915–16, 36919, 36921–22, 36925

ALASKA

(Population 2010, 710,231)

SENATORS

LISA MURKOWSKI, Republican, of Anchorage, AK; born in Ketchikan, AK, May 22, 1957; education: Willamette University, 1975–77; Georgetown University, 1978–80, B.A., economics; Willamette College of Law, 1982–85, J.D.; professional: attorney; private law practice; Alaska and Anchorage Bar Associations; public service: Anchorage Equal Rights Commission; Anchorage District Court Attorney, 1987–89; Task Force on the Homeless, 1990–91; Alaska State Representative, 1999–2002; family: married to Verne Martell; children: Nicholas and Matthew; committees: chair, Energy and Natural Resources; Appropriations; Health, Education, Labor, and Pensions; Indian Affairs; appointed to the U.S. Senate on December 20, 2002; elected to the U.S. Senate for a full term on November 2, 2004; reelected as a write-in candidate to the U.S. Senate on November 2, 2010; reelected to the U.S. Senate on November 8, 2016.

Office Listings

https://murkowski.senate.gov https://facebook.com/senlisamurkowski
https://twitter.com/lisamurkowski https://instagram.com/senlisamurkowski

522 Hart Senate Office Building, Washington, DC 20510 .... (202) 224–6665
Chief of Staff.—Michael Pawlowski. FAX: 224–5301
Legislative Director.—Garrett Boyle.
Scheduler.—Kristen Daimler-Nothdurft.
510 L Street, Suite 600, Anchorage, AK 99501 .... (907) 271–3735
250 Cushman Avenue, Suite 2D, Fairbanks, AK 99701 .... (907) 456–0233
1900 First Avenue, Suite 225, Ketchikan, AK 99901 .... (907) 225–6880
851 East Westpoint Drive, Suite 307, Wasilla, AK 99654 .... (907) 376–7665
44539 Sterling Highway, Suite 203, Soldotna, AK 99669 .... (907) 262–4220
800 Glacier Avenue, Suite 101, Juneau, AK .... (907) 586–7277

* * *

DAN SULLIVAN, Republican, of Anchorage, AK; born in Fairview Park, OH, November 13, 1964; education: B.A., economics, Harvard University, 1987; joint masters of science in foreign service and J.D., Georgetown University, 1993; military: U.S. Marine Corps, 1993–97; U.S. Marine Corps Reserve, 1997–present, attaining rank of Colonel; professional: attorney, private law practice, 1997–2001; public service: director, National Security Council Staff, 2002–04; U.S. Assistant Secretary of State for Economic, Energy and Business Affairs, 2006–09; Attorney General, State of Alaska, 2009–10; commissioner, Alaska Department of Natural Resources, 2011–13; chairman, International Republican Institute (IRI), 2018–present; awards: National Security Council Outstanding Service Award; Defense Meritorious Service Medal; religion: Catholic; family: married to Julie Fate Sullivan; children: Meghan, Isabella, and Laurel; committees: Armed Services; Commerce, Science, and Transportation; Environment and Public Works; Veterans' Affairs; elected to the U.S. Senate on November 4, 2014.

Office Listings

https://sullivan.senate.gov https://facebook.com/SenDanSullivan https://twitter.com/SenDanSullivan

302 Hart Senate Office Building, Washington, DC 20510 .... (202) 224–3004
Chief of Staff.—Larry Burton. FAX: 224–6501
Legislative Director.—Erik Elam.
Scheduling Director.—Avery Fogels.
510 L Street, Suite 750, Anchorage, AK 99501 .... (907) 271–5915
101 12th Avenue, Room 328, Fairbanks, AK 99701 .... (907) 456–0261
851 East Westpoint Drive, Suite 309, Wasilla, AK 99654 .... (907) 357–9956
800 Glacier Avenue, Suite 101, Juneau, AK 99801 .... (907) 586–7277
44539 Sterling Highway, Suite 204, Soldotna, AK 99669 .... (907) 262–4040
1900 First Avenue, Suite 225, Ketchikan, AK 99901 .... (907) 225–6880

REPRESENTATIVE

AT LARGE

DON YOUNG, Republican, of Fort Yukon, AK; born in Meridian, CA, June 9, 1933; education: A.A., Yuba Junior College; B.A., Chico State College, Chico, CA; honorary doctorate of laws, University of Alaska, Fairbanks; professional: State House of Representatives, 1966–70; U.S. Army, 41st Tank Battalion, 1955–57; elected member of the State Senate, 1970–73; served on the Fort Yukon City Council for 6 years, serving 4 years as Mayor; educator for 9 years; river boat captain; member: National Education Association; Elks; Lions; Jaycees; spouse: Anne Garland Walton of Fairbanks; widowed: Lula Fredson of Fort Yukon; children: Joni and Dawn; committees: Natural Resources; Transportation and Infrastructure; elected to the 93rd Congress, by special election, on March 6, 1973, to fill the vacancy created by the death of Congressman Nick Begich; reelected to each succeeding Congress.

Office Listings

https://donyoung.house.gov https://facebook.com/RepDonYoung https://twitter.com/RepDonYoung

2314 Rayburn House Office Building, Washington, DC 20515 .... (202) 225–5765
FAX: 225–0425
Chief of Staff.—Pamela Day.
Executive Assistant / Office Manager.—Paula Conru.
Legislative Director.—Alex Ortiz.

471 West 36th Avenue, Suite 201, Anchorage, AK 99503 .... (907) 271–5978
FAX: 271–5950

100 Cushman Street, Suite 307, Fairbanks, AK 99701 .... (907) 456–0210

Population (2010), 710,231.

ZIP Codes: 99501–24, 99540, 99546–59, 99561, 99563–69, 99571–81, 99583–91, 99599, 99602–15, 99619–22, 99624–41, 99643–45, 99647–72, 99674–95, 99697, 99701–12, 99714, 99716, 99720–27, 99729–30, 99732–34, 99736–86, 99788–89, 99791, 99801–03, 99811, 99820–21, 99824–27, 99829–30, 99832–33, 99835–36, 99840–41, 99850

ARIZONA

(Population 2010, 6,392,017)

SENATORS

KYRSTEN SINEMA, Democrat, of Phoenix, AZ; born in Tucson, AZ, July 12, 1976; education: B.A., social work, Brigham Young University, Provo, UT, 1995; M.A., social work, Arizona State University, Tempe, AZ, 1999; J.D., Arizona State University, Tempe, AZ, 2004; Ph.D., social justice, social inquiry, Arizona State University, Tempe, AZ, 2012; M.B.A., Arizona State University, Tempe, AZ, 2018; professional: member of the Arizona House of Representatives, 2005–11; Aspen-Rodel Public Leadership Fellow, 2008; assistant minority leader, Arizona House of Representatives, 2009–11; *Time* Magazine's Top 40 Under 40, 2010; member of the Arizona State Senate, 2011–12; TED Fellow, 2012; committees: Banking, Housing, and Urban Affairs; Commerce, Science, and Transportation; Homeland Security and Governmental Affairs; Veterans' Affairs; Special Committee on Aging; elected to the 113th Congress on November 6, 2012 and reelected to each succeeding Congress; elected to the U.S. Senate on November 6, 2018.

Office Listings

https://sinema.senate.gov https://facebook.com/SenatorSinema twitter: @SenatorSinema

317 Hart Senate Office Building, Washington, DC 20510 .... (202) 224–4521
Chief of Staff.—Meg Joseph. FAX: 228–0461
Legislative Director.—Michael Brownlie.
Communications Director.—John LaBombard.
Scheduler.—Jamie Lynch.
3333 East Camelback Road, Suite 200, Phoenix, AZ 85016 .... (602) 598–7327
Deputy Chief of Staff, State.—Michelle Davidson.

* * *

MARTHA MCSALLY, Republican, of Tucson, AZ; born in Warwick, RI, March, 22, 1966; education: St. Mary Academy-Bay View, Riverside, RI, 1984; United States Air Force Academy, Colorado Springs, CO, 1988; master of public policy, Harvard, Cambridge, MA, 1990; master of strategic studies, United States Air War College, Montgomery, AL, 2007; professional: U.S. Air Force officer with various assignments, 1988–2010; T–37 Instructor Pilot, 1991–94; A–10 pilot / Instructor Pilot, 1994–99; Air Force Legislative Fellowship Program, 1999–2000; director of Joint Search and Rescue Center, 2000–01; Flight Commander / Operation Officer, 612th Combat Operations Squadron, 2002–04; 354th Fighter Squadron Commander, 2004–06; Chief of Current Operations, United States Africa Command, 2007–10; professor of national security studies, George C. Marshall European Center for Security Studies, 2010–12; leadership development and inspirational speaker, 2012–14; military: Bronze Star and six Air Medals; Defense Superior Service Medal; Defense and Air Force Meritorious Service Medal; Air Force Association David C. Schilling Award for the most outstanding contribution in the field of flight in 2006 (awarded to 354th Fighter Squadron under McSally's command); religion: Christian; committees: Armed Services; Banking, Housing, and Urban Affairs; Energy and Natural Resources; Indian Affairs; Special Committee on Aging; elected to the 114th Congress on December 17, 2014; reelected to the 115th Congress on November 8, 2016; appointed to the U.S. Senate on December 18, 2018.

Office Listings

https://mcsally.senate.gov https://facebook.com/SenMarthaMcSally twitter: @SenMcSallyAZ

404 Russell Senate Office Building, Washington, DC 20510 .... (202) 224–2235
Chief of Staff.—Justin Roth.
Scheduler.—Alana Wilson.
Legislative Director.—Pace McMullan.
Communications Director.—Katie Waldman.
2201 East Camelback Road, Suite 115, Phoenix, AZ 85016 .... (602) 952–2410
407 West Congress Street, Suite 103, Tucson, AZ 85701 .... (520) 670–6334

REPRESENTATIVES

FIRST DISTRICT

TOM O'HALLERAN, Democrat, of the Village of Oak Creek, AZ; born in Chicago, IL, January 24, 1946; education: graduated from St. Mel High School, Chicago, IL, 1964; attended Lewis University, Romeoville, IL, 1965–66; attended DePaul University, Chicago, 1991–92; professional: police officer, Chicago, 1966–79; bond trader; business owner; member of the Arizona House of Representatives, 2001–07; member of the Arizona Senate, 2007–09; religion: Catholic; family: spouse, Pat O'Halleran; caucuses: Congressional Native American Caucus; Labor and Working Families Caucus; Law Enforcement Caucus; Problem Solvers Caucus; committees: Agriculture; Energy and Commerce; elected to the 115th Congress on November 8, 2016; reelected to the 116th Congress on November 6, 2018.

Office Listings

https://ohalleran.house.gov

324 Cannon House Office Building, Washington, DC 20515 .... (202) 225–3361
Chief of Staff.—Jeremy Nordquist. FAX: 225–3462
Legislative Director.—Sally Adams.
Communications Director.—Cody Uhing.
Digital Director.—Kaitlin Hooker.
Scheduler.—Charlie Burgin.
Legislative Assistants: Paul Babbitt, Lucas LaRose, Edgar Rivas.
405 North Beaver Street, Suite 6, Flagstaff, AZ 86001 .... (928) 286–5338
Northern District Director.—Chip Davis.
Constituent Services Manager.—Judy Burns-Sulltrop.
Northern Office Manager.—Keith Brekhus.
211 North Florence Street, Suite 1, Casa Grande, AZ 85122 .... (520) 316–0839
Southern District Director.—Blanca Varela.
Veterans Service Representative.—JoAnna Mendoza.
3037 West Ina Road, Suite 101, Tucson, AZ 85741 .... (928) 304–0131
Constituent Services Representative.—Max Dell'Oliver. MOBILE: (202) 225–3361
Director of Tribal Engagement.—Jack Jackson.
Tribal Engagement Representative.—Luther Lee.
Constituent Services Representative.—Rochelle Lacapa.

Counties: APACHE, COCONINO, GILA (part), GRAHAM, GREENLEE, MARICOPA (part), NAVAJO, PIMA (part), PINAL (part), AND YAVAPAI (part). Population (2010), 724,868.

ZIP Codes: 85122–23, 85128, 85130–32, 85135, 85137–39, 85141–42, 85145, 85172–73, 85191–94, 85226, 85248, 85339, 85501–02, 85530–36, 85539–40, 85542–43, 85545–46, 85548, 85550–52, 85618, 85623, 85631, 85643, 85652–54, 85658, 85704, 85718, 85737, 85739, 85741–43, 85755, 85901–02, 85911–12, 85920, 85922–42, 86001–04, 86011, 86015, 86017–18, 86020, 86022–25, 86028, 86030–33, 86035–36, 86038–40, 86042, 86044–47, 86052–54, 86322, 86325–26, 86335–36, 86339–42, 86351, 86434–35, 86502–08, 86510–12, 86514–15, 86520, 86535, 86538, 86540, 86544–45, 86547, 86556

* * *

SECOND DISTRICT

ANN KIRKPATRICK, Democrat, of Tucson, AZ; born in McNary, AZ, March 24, 1950; education: B.A., University of Arizona, Tucson, 1972; J.D., University of Arizona College of Law, Tucson, 1979; professional: Coconino Deputy County Attorney, 1980–81; Pima Deputy County Attorney, 1981–85; Sedona City Attorney, 1990–91; partner, Kirkpatrick & Harris, Law Firm P.C., 1991–2008; instructor, Business Law & Ethics, Coconino Community College, 2004; Representative, Arizona State House, District 2, 2005–07; Representative, 111th United States Congress, District 1, 2009–10; caucuses: Academic Medicine; Afterschool; Anti–Bullying; Career and Technical Education; Congressional Academic Medicine Caucus; Congressional Diabetes; Congressional Gaming; Congressional Tennis Caucus; General Aviation; Healthcare Innovation Caucus; Healthy Forests Caucus; Hidden Heroes; High Performance Building Caucus; Mental Health; Native American; P3 Caucus; Small Brewers; Small Business; Tourism and Travel; United Solutions; Veterans' Jobs; Writers; Youth Drug Prevention; religion: Catholic; married: husband, Roger Curley, two children; committees: Agriculture; Appropriations; elected to the 111th Congress to represent the 1st District on November 4, 2008; elected to the 113th Congress to represent the 1st District on November 6, 2012; reelected to the 114th Congress on November 4, 2014; elected to represent the 2nd District in the 116th Congress on November 6, 2018.

Office Listings

https://kirkpatrick.house.gov https://facebook.com/RepKirkpatrick
https://twitter.com/RepKirkpatrick https://instagram.com/RepAnnKirkpatrick

309 Cannon House Office Building, Washington, DC 20515 .... (202) 225–2542
Chief of Staff.—Carmen Gallus.
Legislative Director.—Christian Walker.
Communications Director.—Abigail O'Brien.
Scheduler.—Matt Lubisich.
Legislative Assistants: Emily Cummins, Lisa Walker.
1636 North Swan Road, Suite 200, Tucson, AZ 85712 .... (520) 881–3588
District Director.—Ron Barber.
Casework Manager.—Kendra Johnson.
Caseworkers: Alesia Ash, Rosa Garza, Travonne Smith.
77 Calle Portal, Suite B160, Sierra Vista, AZ 85635 .... (520) 459–3115
Deputy Communications Director.—Alex Alvarez.
Community Outreach Director.—Billy Kovacs.
Operations Director.—Karla Avalos.

Counties: COCHISE AND PIMA (part). Population (2010), 713,631.

ZIP Codes: 85602–03, 85605–11, 85613–17, 85619–20, 85622, 85625–27, 85629–30, 85632, 85635–38, 85641, 85643–45, 85650, 85655, 85670, 85704–08, 85710–13, 85715–19, 85728, 85730–33, 85738, 85740–45, 85747–52

* * *

THIRD DISTRICT

RAÚL M. GRIJALVA, Democrat, of Tucson, AZ; born in Tucson, February 19, 1948; education: Sunnyside High School, Tucson, AZ; B.A., University of Arizona; professional: former Assistant Dean for Hispanic Student Affairs, University of Arizona; former Director of the El Pueblo Neighborhood Center; public service: Tucson Unified School District Governing Board 1974–86; Pima County Board of Supervisors, 1989–2002; family: married to Ramona; three daughters; committees: chair, Natural Resources; Education and Labor; elected to the 108th Congress on November 5, 2002; reelected to each succeeding Congress.

Office Listings

https://grijalva.house.gov https://facebook.com/Rep.Grijalva twitter: @RepRaulGrijalva

1511 Longworth House Office Building, Washington, DC 20515 .... (202) 225–2435
Chief of Staff.—Amy Emerick. FAX: 225–1541
Legislative Director.—Norma Salazar.
Communications Director.—Geoff Nolan.
Scheduler.—Cristina Villa.
101 West Irvington Road, Tucson, AZ 85714 .... (520) 622–6788
146 North State Avenue, Somerton, AZ 85350 .... (928) 343–7933
1412 North Central Avenue, Suite B, Avondale, AZ 85323 .... (623) 536–3388

Counties: LA PAZ (part), MARICOPA (part), PIMA (part), PINAL (part), SANTA CRUZ (part), and YUMA. Population (2010), 710,224.

ZIP Codes: 85033 (part), 85037 (part), 85043 (part), 85123 (part), 85139 (part), 85193 (part), 85305 (part), 85307 (part), 85321–22, 85323 (part), 85326 (part), 85333 (part), 85336–37, 85338–40 (part), 85341, 85343, 85347 (part), 85349–50, 85353–54 (part), 85364–65 (part), 85392 (part), 85395 (part), 85396, 85601, 85611 (part), 85621, 85622 (part), 85624, 85629 (part), 85633–34, 85637 (part), 85640, 85645 (part), 85646, 85648, 85653 (part), 85701, 85705–06 (part), 85713–14 (part), 85719 (part), 85723–24, 85726, 85735–36, 85743 (part), 85745 (part), 85746, 85756 (part), 85757

* * *

FOURTH DISTRICT

PAUL GOSAR, Republican, of Prescott, AZ; born in Rock Springs, WY, November 27, 1958; education: graduated, Pinedale High School, Pinedale, WY; B.S., Creighton University, Omaha, NE, 1981; D.D.S., Creighton University, Omaha, 1985; religion: Catholic; family: wife, Maude; children: Elle, Gaston, and Isabelle; caucuses: chairman, Western Caucus; Coal Caucus; Conservative Opportunity Society; GOP Doctor's Caucus; House Freedom Caucus; Immigration Reform Caucus; committees: Natural Resources; Oversight and Reform; elected to the 112th Congress on November 2, 2010; reelected to each succeeding Congress.

Office Listings

https://gosar.house.gov https://facebook.com/repgosar twitter: @RepGosar
https://instagram.com/repgosar https://youtube.com/repgosar https://flickr.com/photos/repgosar

2057 Rayburn House Office Building, Washington, DC 20515 .... (202) 225–2315
Chief of Staff.—Thomas Van Flein.
Legislative Director.—Rory Burke.
Communications Director.—Ben Goldey.
Scheduler / Office Manager.—Leslie Foti.
District Director.—Penny Pew.
6499 South Kings Ranch Road, #4, Gold Canyon, AZ 85118 .... (480) 882–2697
122 North Cortez Street, Suite 104, Prescott, AZ 86301 .... (928) 445–1683

Counties: GILA, LA PAZ, MARICOPA, MOHAVE, PINAL, YAVAPAI, AND YUMA. CITIES AND TOWNSHIPS: Apache Junction, Arcosanti, Arizona Village, Ash Fork, Bagdad, Beaver Dam, Big Park, Black Canyon City, Blackwater, Bouse, Buckeye, Bullhead City, Central Heights-Midland City, Chino Valley, Chloride, Chuichu, Cibola, Clarkdale, Colorado City, Cordes Lakes, Cornville, Cottonwood-Verde Village, Dateland, Desert Hills, Dewey-Humboldt, Dolan Springs, Dudleyville, Ehrenberg, Florence, Fort Mohave, Fortuna Foothills, Gisela, Globe, Gold Canyon, Golden Valley, Hackberry, Hope, Jerome, Kaibab, Kearny, Kingman, Kohls Ranch, Lake Havasu City, Lake Montezuma, Litchfield Park, Littlefield, Mayer, Meadview, Mesquite Creek, Mohave Valley, Mojave Ranch Estates, New Kingman-Butler, New River, Nothing, Oatman, Parker, Parker Strip, Paulden, Payson, Peeples Valley, Peoria, Pine-Strawberry, Poston, Prescott Valley, Quartzsite, Queen Creek, Queen Valley, Salome, San Tan Valley, Santan, Scenic, Seligman, Spring Valley, Stanfield, Star Valley, Superior, Tacna, Topock, Top-of-the-World, Valentine, Wellton, Wendon, Wickenburg, Wikieup, Wilhoit, Williamson, Willow Valley, Winkelman, Yarnell, Young, Yucca, and Yuma. Population (2010), 707,750.

ZIP Codes: 85087 (part), 85117–19, 85120 (part), 85128 (part), 85132 (part), 85140, 85142 (part), 85143, 85173 (part), 85178, 85190, 85212 (part), 85215 (part), 85262 (part), 85320, 85324–26, 85328, 85331 (part), 85332, 85333 (part), 85334, 85340 (part), 85342, 85344, 85346–48, 85352, 85354, 85355 (part), 85356–60, 85361 (part), 85362, 85364, 85366–67 (part), 85371, 85383, 85387, 85390, 85396, 85538, 85541, 85544, 85545 (part), 85547, 85553–54, 86021–22, 86046 (part), 86301–05, 86312–15, 86320–21, 86323, 86325–26 (part), 86327, 86329, 86331–34, 86337–38, 86343, 86401–06, 86409, 86411, 86412 (part), 86413, 86426–27, 86429–33, 86436 (part), 86437, 86438 (part), 86439–40, 86441 (part), 86442–43, 86444 (part), 86445–46

* * *

FIFTH DISTRICT

ANDY BIGGS, Republican, of Gilbert, AZ; born in Tucson, AZ; education: B.A. in Asian studies, Brigham Young, Provo, UT, 1982; M.A. in political science, Arizona State University, Phoenix, AZ, 1999; J.D., Arizona State University, Phoenix, 1984; professional: licensed attorney; member of the Arizona Legislature, 1999–2016; president, Arizona State Senate, 2012–16; awards: ''Champion of the Taxpayer'' from Americans for Prosperity; ''Friend of Liberty'' from Goldwater Institute; religion: Church of Jesus Christ of Latter-Day Saints; family: wife, Cindy; six children; four grandchildren; committees: Judiciary; Science, Space, and Technology; elected to the 115th Congress on November 8, 2016; reelected to the 116th Congress on November 6, 2018.

Office Listings

https://biggs.house.gov https://facebook.com/RepAndyBiggs twitter: @RepAndyBiggsAZ

1318 Longworth House Office Building, Washington, DC 20515 .... (202) 225–2635
Chief of Staff.—Kate LaBorde. FAX: 226–4386
Director of Operations / Scheduler.—Carolyn Busse.
Communications Director.—Daniel Stefanski.
2509 South Power Road, Suite 204, Mesa, AZ 85209 .... (480) 699–8239

Counties: MARICOPA (part) AND PINAL (part). CITIES AND TOWNSHIPS: Apache Junction, Chandler, Gilbert, Mesa, and Queen Creek. Population (2010), 710,224.

ZIP Codes: 85120–21, 85127, 85142, 85147, 85201, 85203–10, 85212–13, 85215–16, 85224–25, 85233–34, 85236, 85249, 85275, 85277, 85286, 85295–97

* * *

SIXTH DISTRICT

DAVID SCHWEIKERT, Republican, of Fountain Hills, AZ; born March 3, 1962; education: B.A., Arizona State University, Tempe, AZ, 1988; M.B.A., Arizona State University, Tempe, AZ, 2005; professional: business owner of a real estate company; realtor; financial consultant; member of the Arizona State House of Representatives, 1989–94; member of the Arizona State Board of Equalization, 1995–2003; former Treasurer, Maricopa County, AZ, 2004–06; religion:

Catholic; married: Joyce Schweikert; committees: Ways and Means; Joint Economic Committee; elected to the 112th Congress on November 2, 2010; reelected to each succeeding Congress.

Office Listings

https://schweikert.house.gov https://facebook.com/repdavidschweikert twitter: @RepDavid

1526 Longworth House Office Building, Washington, DC 20515 .... (202) 225–2190
Chief of Staff.—Katherina Dimenstein.
Scheduler.—Ashley Sylvester.
Legislative Director.—Katherine Duveneck.
Communications Director.—Grace White.
14500 North Northsight Boulevard, Suite 221, Scottsdale, AZ 85260 .... (480) 946–2411
FAX: 946–2446

Counties: MARICOPA (part). CITIES AND TOWNSHIPS: Carefree, Cave Creek, Fountain Hills, Paradise Valley, Phoenix (part), Rio Verde, Scottsdale, Salt River Pima Maricopa Indian Community, and Yavapai Nation. Population (2010), 754,482.

ZIP Codes: 85020, 85022–24, 85027–29, 85032, 85050, 85054, 85201, 85250–51, 85253–56, 85258–60, 85264, 85268

* * *

SEVENTH DISTRICT

RUBEN GALLEGO, Democrat, of Phoenix, AZ; born in Chicago, IL, November 20, 1979; education: A.B., Harvard University, Cambridge, MA, 2004; professional: delegate, Democratic National Convention, 2008; Chief of Staff to Phoenix Councilman Michael Nowakowski, 2008–10; vice chair, Arizona Democratic Party, 2009; member of the Arizona House of Representatives, 2011–14; Assistant Democratic Leader for the Arizona House of Representatives, 2013–14; military: U.S. Marine Corps, 2000–06; awards: Combat Action Ribbon; religion: Catholic; caucuses: Congressional Hispanic Caucus; Congressional LGBT Equality Caucus; Congressional Progressive Caucus; Medicaid Expansion Caucus; Post 9/11 Veterans Caucus; Quiet Skies Caucus; committees: Armed Services; Natural Resources; elected to the 114th Congress on November 4, 2014; reelected to each succeeding Congress.

Office Listings

https://rubengallego.house.gov https://facebook.com/RepRubenGallego twitter: @RepRubenGallego

1131 Longworth House Office Building, Washington, DC 20515 .... (202) 225–4065
Scheduler.—Allison Childress.
1601 North 7th Street, Suite 310, Phoenix, AZ 85006 .... (602) 256–0551
District Director.—Luis Heredia.

Counties: MARICOPA (part). Population (2010), 725,197.

ZIP Codes: 85001–10, 85012–19, 85021, 85025–26, 85030–31, 85033–38, 85040–44, 85048, 85051, 85061–64, 85066–67, 85072, 85074–75, 85079, 85082, 85098, 85282–83, 85301, 85303, 85305, 85311, 85318, 85323, 85339, 85353

* * *

EIGHTH DISTRICT

DEBBIE LESKO, Republican, of Peoria, AZ; born November 14, 1958; education: B.B.A., University of Wisconsin, Madison, WI; professional/awards: business owner; Arizona State Representative, Legislative District 21, 2008–12 (Majority Whip, 2011–12); Arizona State Senator, Legislative District 21, 2015–18 (President Pro Tempore, 2017–18; chair, Appropriations Committee); Republican Chairman, Legislative District 9; voter registration chair, Maricopa County Republican Party; Senator of the Year Award, Arizona Chamber of Commerce; religion: Christian; married; three children; caucuses: Republican Study Committee; committees: Homeland Security; Judiciary; Rules; elected to the 115th Congress, by special election, on April 24, 2018, to fill the vacancy caused by the resignation of Representative Trent Franks; reelected to the 116th Congress on November 6, 2018.

Office Listings

https://lesko.house.gov https://facebook.com/RepDebbieLesko twitter: @RepDLesko

1113 Longworth House Office Building, Washington, DC 20515 .... (202) 225–4576

Office Listings—Continued

Chief of Staff.—Matthew Simon. FAX: 225–6328
Legislative Director.—Ronald Donado.
7121 West Bell Road, Suite 200, Glendale, AZ 85308 .... (623) 776–7911
District Director.—Lisa Gray.

Counties: GLENDALE, MARICOPA, NEW RIVER, NEW VILLAGE, NORTH GATEWAY, PEORIA, SUN CITY, SUN CITY WEST, AND SURPRISE (part). Population (2014), 741,374.

ZIP Codes: 85083, 85085–87, 85301–10, 85312, 85318, 85331, 85335, 85338, 85340, 85345, 85351, 85361, 85363, 85372–76, 85378–83, 85385, 85387–88, 85395

* * *

NINTH DISTRICT

GREG STANTON, Democrat, of Phoenix, AZ; born in Long Island, New York, March 8, 1970; education: B.A., Marquette University, Milwaukee, WI, 1992; J.D., University of Michigan, Ann Arbor, MI, 1995; professional: lawyer, private practice; member, Phoenix City Council, 2000–09, Deputy Attorney General, State of Arizona Attorney General's Office, 2009–11; Mayor, City of Phoenix, AZ, 2012–18; religion: Catholic; family: wife, Nicole; two children; committees: Judiciary; Transportation and Infrastructure; elected to the 116th Congress on November 6, 2018.

Office Listings

https://stanton.house.gov https://facebook.com/repgregstanton twitter: @RepGregStanton

128 Cannon House Office Building, Washington, DC 20515 .... (202) 225–9888
Chief of Staff / General Counsel.—Seth Scott.
Deputy Chief of Staff / Legislative Director.—Tracee Sutton.
Communications Director / Policy Advisor.—Nicole Pasteur.
Executive Assistant / Media Assistant.—Ashley Zafaranlou.
2944 North 44th Street, Suite 150, Phoenix, AZ 85018 .... (602) 956–2463
Senior District Advisor.—Eric Chalmers.

Counties: MARICOPA COUNTY (part). CITIES: Ahwatukee, Chandler, Guadalupe, Mesa, Phoenix, and Tempe. Population (2010), 722,896.

ZIP Codes: 85008 (part), 85012–14 (part), 85016 (part), 85018 (part), 85020–21 (part), 85034 (part), 85040 (part), 85044 (part), 85045, 85048 (part), 85051 (part), 85201 (part), 85202, 85203–04 (part), 85210 (part), 85224–26 (part), 85233 (part), 85251 (part), 85253 (part), 85256–57 (part), 85281–83 (part), 85284

ARKANSAS

(Population 2010, 2,915,918)

SENATORS

JOHN NICHOLS BOOZMAN, Republican, of Rogers, AR; born in Shreveport, LA, December 10, 1950; education: Southern College of Optometry, Memphis, TN, 1977; also attended University of Arkansas, Fayetteville, AR; professional: doctor of optometry; business owner; rancher; religion: Southern Baptist; married: Cathy Boozman; children: three daughters; committees: Agriculture, Nutrition, and Forestry; Appropriations; Environment and Public Works; Veterans' Affairs; elected to the U.S. House of Representatives 2001–11; elected to the U.S. Senate on November 2, 2010; reelected to each succeeding Senate term.

Office Listings

https://boozman.senate.gov https://facebook.com/JohnBoozman twitter: @JohnBoozman

141 Hart Senate Office Building, Washington, DC 20510 .... (202) 224–4843
Chief of Staff.—Toni-Marie Higgins.
Deputy Chief of Staff / Counsel.—Susan Olson.
Legislative Director.—Mackensie Burt.
Communications Director.—Sara Lasure.
Scheduler.—Holly Lewis.
Senior Communications Advisor.—Patrick Creamer.
106 West Main Street, Suite 104, El Dorado, AR 71730 870–863–4641
1120 Garrison Avenue, Suite 2B, Fort Smith, AR 72901 479–573–0189
Constituent Services Director.—Kathy Watson.
300 South Church Street, Suite 400, Jonesboro, AR 72401 870–268–6925
1401 West Capitol Avenue, Suite 155, Little Rock, AR 72201 501–372–7153
213 West Monroe, Suite N, Lowell, AR 72745 479–725–0400
State Director.—Stacey McClure.
1001 Highway 62 East, Suite 11, Mountain Home, AR 72653 870–424–0129
620 East 22nd Street, Suite 204, Stuttgart, AR 72160 870–672–6941

* * *

TOM COTTON, Republican, of Dardanelle, AR; born in Dardanelle, AR, May 13, 1977; education: graduated Dardanelle High School; B.A., Harvard University, 1999; J.D., Harvard University, 2002; professional: attorney; management consultant; military service: U.S. Army Infantry Officer, 2005–09; awards: graduated *magna cum laude*, Harvard University; Ranger Tab Recipient; Army Commendation Medal; Combat Infantryman Badge; Iraq Campaign Medal; Bronze Star Medal; committees: Armed Services; Banking, Housing, and Urban Affairs; Joint Economic Committee; Select Committee on Intelligence; elected to the 113th Congress on November 6, 2012; elected to the U.S. Senate on November 4, 2014.

Office Listings

https://cotton.senate.gov

326 Russell Senate Office Building, Washington, DC 20510 .... (202) 224–2353
Chief of Staff.—Doug Coutts. FAX: 228–0908
Legislative Director.—Aaron MacLean.
Communications Director.—Caroline Tabler.
1401 West Capitol Avenue, Suite 235, Little Rock, AR 72201 .... (501) 223–9081
State Director.—Vanessa Moody.
1108 South Old Missouri Road, Suite B, Springdale, AR 72764 .... (479) 751–0879
300 South Church, Suite 338, Jonesboro, AR 72401 .... (870) 933–6223
106 West Main Street, Suite 410, El Dorado, AR 71730 .... (870) 864–8582

REPRESENTATIVES

FIRST DISTRICT

RICK CRAWFORD, Republican, of Jonesboro, AR; born in Homestead AFB, FL, January 22, 1966; education: graduated, Alvirne High School; B.A., agricultural business and economics, Arkansas State University, 1996; professional: bomb disposal technician, U.S. Army, 1985–89; professional rodeo announcer; news anchor, KAIT–TV Jonesboro; farm director, KFIN–FM; producer and anchor, Delta Farm Roundup TV Show; marketing manager, John Deere; owner and operator, Agwatch; member: National Association of Farm Broadcasting; 4–H Foundation Board of Arkansas; recipient of the NAFB Newscast Award, 2006 and 2008; married: Stacy; children: Will and Delaney; caucuses: Republican Study Committee; committees: Agriculture; Transportation and Infrastructure; Permanent Select Committee on Intelligence; elected to the 112th Congress on November 2, 2010; reelected to each succeeding Congress.

Office Listings

https://crawford.house.gov twitter: @RepRickCrawford
https://instagram.com/reprickcrawford

2422 Rayburn House Office Building, Washington, DC 20515 .... (202) 225–4076
Chief of Staff.—Jonah Shumate.
Press Secretary.—Sara Robertson.
Legislative Director.—Ashley Shelton.
112 South First Street, Cabot, AR 72023 .... (501) 843–3043
2400 East Highland Drive, Suite 300, Jonesboro, AR 72401 .... (870) 203–0540
1001 Highway 62 East, Suite 9, Mountain Home, AR 72653 .... (870) 424–2075
101 East Waterman Street, Dumas, AR 71639 .... (870) 337–5571

Counties: ARKANSAS, BAXTER, CHICOT, CLAY, CLEBURNE, CRAIGHEAD, CRITTENDEN, CROSS, DESHA, FULTON, GREENE, INDEPENDENCE, IZARD, JACKSON, JEFFERSON (part), LAWRENCE, LEE, LINCOLN, LONOKE, MISSISSIPPI, MONROE, PHILLIPS, POINSETT, PRAIRIE, RANDOLPH, SAINT FRANCIS, SEARCY, SHARP, STONE, AND WOODRUFF. Population (2017), 722,287.

ZIP Codes: 71601, 71603, 71630, 71638–40, 71644, 71653–54, 71662, 71666, 71667, 71670, 71674–75, 71678, 72003, 72005–07, 72014, 72017, 72020–21, 72023–24, 72026, 72029, 72031, 72036–38, 72040–44, 72046, 72048, 72051, 72055, 72059–60, 72064, 72067, 72069, 72072–76, 72083, 72086, 72101–02, 72108, 72112, 72121, 72123, 72130–31, 72134, 72137, 72139–40, 72142–43, 72153, 72160, 72165–66, 72169–70, 72175–76, 72179, 72189, 72301, 72303, 72310–13, 72315–16, 72319–22, 72324–33, 72335–36, 72338–42, 72346–48, 72350–55, 72358–60, 72364–70, 72372–74, 72376–77, 72383–84, 72386–87, 72389–92, 72394–96, 72401–04, 72410–17, 72419, 72421–22, 72424–45, 72447, 72449–51, 72453–62, 72464–67, 72469–76, 72478–79, 72482, 72501, 72503, 72512–13, 72515, 72517, 72519–34, 72536–40, 72542–46, 72550, 72553–56, 72560–62, 72564–69, 72571–73, 72575–79, 72581, 72583–85, 72587, 72610, 72613, 72617, 72623, 72626, 72629, 72631, 72633, 72635–36, 72639, 72642, 72645, 72650–51, 72653–54, 72658, 72663, 72669, 72675, 72679–80, 72686

* * *

SECOND DISTRICT

J. FRENCH HILL, Republican, of Little Rock, AR; born in Little Rock, December 5, 1956; education: B.S., economics, Vanderbilt University, Nashville, TN, 1979, graduated *magna cum laude* ; professional: senior financial analyst, InterFirst Corporation, 1979–82; legislative assistant, assistant to the chairman, Subcommittee on Housing and Urban Development, the Honorable John Tower (R–TX), Senate Committee on Banking, Housing, and Urban Affairs, 1982–84; director, Mason Best Company, 1984–89; Deputy Assistant Secretary (Corporate Finance), U.S. Department of the Treasury, 1989–91; Special Assistant to the President, Executive Office of the White House, 1991–93; executive officer, Regions West, 1993–99; chief executive officer, Delta Trust & Banking Corp., 1999–2014; religion: Roman Catholic; family: married, two children; caucuses: Bipartisan Congressional Arts Caucus; Congressional Air Force Caucus; Congressional Army Caucus; Congressional Boating Caucus; Congressional Caucus on Fitness; Congressional Caucus on Foster Youth; Congressional Caucus on India and Indian-Americans; Congressional Chicken Caucus; Congressional Congenital Heart Caucus; Congressional Caucus on India and Indian-Americans; Congressional Diabetes Caucus; Congressional French Caucus; Congressional Historic Preservation Caucus; Congressional International Conservation Caucus; Congressional Israel Allies Caucus; Congressional Kidney Caucus; Congressional Missile Defense Caucus; Congressional Natural Gas Caucus; Congressional Prayer Caucus; Congressional Scouting Caucus; Congressional Sportsmen's Caucus; Congressional Wine Caucus; House Republican Israel Caucus; House Small Brewers Caucus; National Guard and Reserve Components Caucus (NGRCC); Science, Technology, Engineering, and Math (STEM) Education Caucus; U.S.-Japan Caucus; committees: Financial Services; elected to the 114th Congress on November 4, 2014; reelected to each succeeding Congress.

Office Listings

https://hill.house.gov https://facebook.com/RepFrenchHill
https://twitter.com/repfrenchhill https://youtube.com/channel/UCT8uWroJtkwSsCJlVg0IKvQ

1533 Longworth House Office Building, Washington, DC 20515 .... (202) 225–2506

Office Listings—Continued

Chief of Staff.—A. Brooke Bennett. FAX: 225–5903
Communications Director.—Steven Smith.
Legislative Director.—Dylan Frost.
Senior Adviser.—Ashley Gunn.
Legislative Assistants: Lesley Hill, Matt Karvelas.
Legislative Correspondent/Legislative Assistant.—Anna Wilbourn.
Executive Assistant.—Mary Grace Munson.
Staff Assistant.—Mitchell Whalen.
1501 North University, Suite 630, Little Rock, AR 72207 .... (501) 324–5941
District Representatives: Chloe Maxwell, Leigh Anna Gildner. FAX: 324–6029
District Representatives for Military/Veterans Affairs: David L. Carnahan, Richard E. Maxwell.
Staff Assistant.—Anna Reckling.
1105 Deer Street, Suite 12, Conway, AR 72032 .... (501) 358–3481
District Representative.—Anushree Jumde. FAX: 358-3494

Counties: CONWAY, FAULKNER, PERRY, PULASKI, SALINE, VAN BUREN, AND WHITE. Population (2010), 751,377.

ZIP Codes: 71772, 71909, 72001–02, 72010–13, 72015–18, 72020, 72022–23, 72025, 72027–28, 72030–35, 72039, 72045–47, 72052–53, 72057–61, 72063, 72065–68, 72070, 72076, 72078–82, 72085, 72087–89, 72099, 72102–04, 72106–08, 72110–11, 72113–22, 72124–27, 72131, 72135–37, 72139, 72141–43, 72145, 72149, 72153, 72156–57, 72164, 72167, 72173, 72178, 72180–81, 72183, 72190, 72199, 72201–07, 72209–12, 72214–17, 72219, 72221–23, 72225, 72227, 72231, 72260, 72295, 72419, 72568, 72629, 72645, 72679, 72823

* * *

THIRD DISTRICT

STEVE WOMACK, Republican, of Rogers, AR; born in Russellville, AR, February 18, 1957; education: Russellville High School, Russellville, AR; B.A., Arkansas Tech University, 1979; professional: radio station manager; financial consultant; Mayor of Rogers, AR; military: retired colonel, National Guard; awards: Legion of Merit; Meritorious Service Medal; Army Commendation Medal; Army Achievement Medal; Global War on Terror Expeditionary and Service Medals; religion: Southern Baptist; family: married the former Terri Williams of DeWitt, AR; three sons; caucuses: Congressional Chicken Caucus; committees: ranking member, Budget; Appropriations; elected to the 112th Congress on November 2, 2010; reelected to each succeeding Congress.

Office Listings

https://womack.house.gov twitter: @rep_stevewomack

2412 Rayburn House Office Building, Washington, DC 20515 .... (202) 225–4301
Chief of Staff.—Beau Walker. FAX: 225–5713
Scheduler.—Madison Nash.
Legislative Director.—Geoff Hempelmann.
Communications Director.—Alexia Sikora.
Legislative Assistants: Katie Morley, Jessica Powell.
Military Fellow.—Levi Hofts.
Military Legislative Assistant.—Nick Runkel.
Legislative Correspondent.—Brett Dieringer.
Staff Assistant.—Zach Deatherage.
3333 Pinnacle Hills Parkway, Suite 120, Rogers, AR 72758 .... (479) 464–0446
District Director.—Bootsie Ackerman. FAX: 464–0063
Constituent Service Manager.—Janet Foster.
Field Representative.—Jeff Thacker.
Projects Director.—Kyle Weaver.
Caseworker.—Gillie Brandolini.
6101 Phoenix Avenue, Suite 4, Fort Smith, AR 72903 .... (479) 424–1146
Caseworker.—Chris Bader. FAX: 424–2737
Field Representative.—Janice Scaggs.
400 North Main Street, Suite 3, Harrison, AR 72601 .... (870) 741–6900
Field Representative.—Teri Garrett. FAX: 741–7741

Counties: BENTON, BOONE, CARROLL, CRAWFORD, MARION, NEWTON (part), POPE, SEARCY (part), SEBASTIAN (part), AND WASHINGTON. Population (2010), 754,704.

ZIP Codes: 65729, 65733, 65761, 72063, 72080, 72601, 72611, 72616, 72619, 72624, 72630–34, 72638, 72640–41, 72644, 72648, 72653, 72655, 72660–62, 72668–69, 72672, 72675, 72677, 72679, 72682–83, 72685, 72687, 72701, 72703–04, 72712, 72714–15, 72717–19, 72722, 72727, 72729–30, 72732, 72734, 72736, 72738–40, 72744–45, 72747, 72749, 72751, 72753, 72756, 72758, 72761–62, 72764, 72768–69, 72773–74, 72801–02, 72823, 72837, 72839, 72843, 72846–

47, 72856, 72858, 72901, 72903–04, 72908, 72916, 72921, 72923, 72927, 72932–34, 72936–37, 72940–41, 72945–46, 72948, 72952, 72955–56, 72959

* * *

FOURTH DISTRICT

BRUCE WESTERMAN, Republican, of Hot Springs, AR; born in Hot Springs, November 18, 1967; education: graduated, Fountain Lake High School, 1986; B.S., University of Arkansas, 1990; M.F., Yale University, 2001; professional: engineer; forester; past elected office: Arkansas House of Representatives Majority Leader, 2013; Arkansas House of Representatives Minority Leader, 2012; Arkansas State Representative, 2011–15; Fountain Lake School Board President, 2009–10; Fountain Lake School Board, 2006–10; awards: University of Arkansas College of Engineering, Outstanding Young Alumni Award, 2005; University of Arkansas College of Engineering, Distinguished Alumni Award, 2012; Engineer of the Year by the Arkansas Society of Professional Engineers, 2013; committees: Natural Resources; Transportation and Infrastructure; elected to the 114th Congress on November 4, 2014; reelected to each succeeding Congress.

Office Listings

https://westerman.house.gov https://facebook.com/RepWesterman
https://twitter.com/RepWesterman

209 Cannon House Office Building, Washington, DC 20515 .... (202) 225–3772
Chief of Staff.—Vivian Moeglein. FAX: 225–1314
Legislative Director.—Jefferson Deming.
Communications Director.—Rebekah Hoshiko.
National Parks Service Headquarters, 101 Reserve Street, Suite 200, Hot Springs, AR 71901 .... (501) 609–9796
District Director.—Jason McGehee.
George Howard Jr. Federal Building, 100 East 8th Avenue, Room 2521, Pine Bluff, AR 71601 .... (870) 536–8178
Franklin County Courthouse, 211 West Commercial Street, Ozark, AR 72949 .... (479) 667–0075
Union County Courthouse, 101 North Washington Avenue, Suite 406, El Dorado, AR 71730 .... (870) 864–8946

Counties: Ashley, Bradley, Calhoun, Clark, Cleveland, Columbia, Crawford, Dallas, Drew, Franklin, Garland, Grant, Hempstead, Hot Spring, Howard, Jefferson, Johnson, Lafayette, Little River, Logan, Madison, Miller, Montgomery, Nevada, Newton (part), Ouachita, Pike, Polk, Scott, Sebastian, Sevier, Union, and Yell. Population (2010), 717,926.

ZIP Codes: 71601–03, 71631, 71635, 71638, 71642, 71644, 71646–47, 71651–52, 71655, 71658–61, 71663, 71665, 71667, 71670–71, 71675–77, 71701, 71711, 71720, 71722, 71724–26, 71730, 71740, 71742–45, 71747, 71751–53, 71758–59, 71762–66, 71770, 71772, 71801, 71820, 71822–23, 71825–27, 71832–39, 71841–42, 71845–47, 71851–55, 71857–62, 71865–66, 71901, 71909, 71913, 71921–23, 71929, 71933, 71935, 71937, 71940–41, 71943–45, 71949–50, 71952–53, 71956–62, 71964–65, 71968–73, 71998–99, 72004, 72015, 72025, 72046, 72057, 72065, 72079, 72084, 72087, 72104, 72128–29, 72132, 72150, 72152, 72167–68, 72175, 72601, 72624, 72628, 72632, 72638, 72641, 72648, 72655, 72666, 72670, 72703, 72721, 72727, 72738, 72740, 72742, 72752, 72756, 72760, 72773, 72776, 72821, 72824, 72826–28, 72830, 72832–35, 72838–42, 72845–47, 72851–57, 72860, 72863, 72865, 72921, 72926–28, 72930, 72933–38, 72940–41, 72943–47, 72949–51, 72956, 72958–59

CALIFORNIA

(Population 2010, 37,253,956)

SENATORS

DIANNE FEINSTEIN, Democrat, of San Francisco, CA; born in San Francisco, June 22, 1933; education: B.A., Stanford University, 1955; professional: elected to San Francisco Board of Supervisors, 1970–78; president of Board of Supervisors, 1970–71, 1974–75, 1978; Mayor of San Francisco, 1978–88; candidate for governor of California, 1990; recipient: Achievement Award, Business and Professional Women's Club, 1970; Golden Gate University, California, LL.D. (hon.), 1979; University of Santa Clara, D.P.S. (hon.); University of Manila, D.P.A. (hon.), 1981; Antioch University, LL.D. (hon.), 1983; French Legion d'Honneur from President Mitterand, 1984; Mills College, LL.D. (hon.), 1985; U.S. Army Commander's Award for Public Service, 1986; Brotherhood/Sisterhood Award, National Conference of Christians and Jews, 1986; Paulist Fathers Award, 1987; Episcopal Church Award for Service, 1987; U.S. Navy Distinguished Civilian Award, 1987; All Pro Management Team Award for No. 1 Mayor, *City and State* Magazine, 1987; Community Service Award Honoree for Public Service, 1987; American Jewish Congress, 1987; Coro Investment in Leadership Award, 1988; President's Medal, University of California at San Francisco, 1988; University of San Francisco, D.H.L. (hon.), 1988; Hubert H. Humphrey Humanitarian Award, National Jewish Democratic Council, 1995; Woodrow Wilson Award for Public Service, Wilson Center, 2001; Funding Hero Award, Breast Cancer Research Foundation, 2004; Guardian Award, Partnership for a Drug-Free America, 2004; Outstanding Member of the United States Senate, National Narcotic Officers' Associations' Coalition, 2005; Congressional Leader of the Year Award, League of California Cities, 2006; Voice for Choice Award, Planned Parenthood, 2006; Religious and Political Hall of Fame Induction, Black American Political Association of California, 2006; Distinguished Public Service Award, American Legion, 2007; Congressional Leadership Award, Alliance of Dedicated Cancer Centers, 2007; Leadership Award, Environmental Protection Agency, 2009; Champion Award for Public Service, Endangered Species Coalition, 2009; Publius Award, Center for the Study of the Presidency and Congress, 2009; Courageous Leadership Award, Women Against Gun Violence, 2011; Friend of the National Parks Award, National Parks Conservation Association, 2011; Outstanding International Public Service Award, World Affairs Council, 2012; Distinguished Honoree Award, Law Center to Prevent Gun Violence, 2013; We Are EMILY Award, EMILY's List, 2014; Lifetime Legacy and Service Award, Federal City Council, 2015; Constitutional Champion Award, The Constitution Project, 2016; Ansel Adams Award, The Wilderness Society, 2016; Legislative Leadership Award, Association of California Water Agencies, 2017; member: Coro Foundation, Fellowship, 1955–56; California Women's Board of Terms and Parole, 1960–66, executive committee; U.S. Conference of Mayors, 1983–88; Mayor's Commission on Crime, San Francisco; Bank of California, director, 1988–89; San Francisco Education Fund's Permanent Fund, 1988–89; Japan Society of Northern California, 1988–89; Inter-American Dialogue, 1988–present; chair, U.S. Senate Caucus on International Narcotics Control; married: Dr. Bertram Feinstein (dec.); married on January 20, 1980, to Richard C. Blum; children: one child; three stepchildren; religion: Jewish; committees: ranking member, Judiciary; Appropriations; Rules and Administration; Select Committee on Intelligence; elected to the U.S. Senate, by special election, on November 3, 1992, to fill the vacancy caused by the resignation of U.S. Senator Pete Wilson; reelected to each succeeding Senate term.

Office Listings

https://feinstein.senate.gov twitter: @senfeinstein

331 Hart Senate Office Building, Washington, DC 20510 .... (202) 224–3841
Chief of Staff.—David Grannis. FAX: 228–3954
Legislative Director.—Josh Esquivel.
Director of Communications.—Tom Mentzer.
880 Front Street, Suite 4236, San Diego, CA 92101 .... (619) 231–9712
2500 Tulare Street, Suite 4290, Fresno, CA 93721 .... (559) 485–7430
One Post Street, Suite 2450, San Francisco, CA 94104 .... (415) 393–0707
11111 Santa Monica Boulevard, Suite 915, Los Angeles, CA 90025 .... (310) 914–7300

* * *

KAMALA D. HARRIS, Democrat, of Los Angeles, CA; born in Oakland, CA; October 20, 1964; education: B.A., Howard University, Washington, DC; J.D., University of California Hastings College of Law, San Francisco, CA; professional: attorney, Alameda County District Attorney's Office, 1990–98; attorney, San Francisco District Attorney's Office, 1998–2000; attorney, San Francisco City Attorney's Office, 2000–04; elected District Attorney, San Francisco,

2004–10; elected Attorney General, California, 2011–17; married: Douglas Emhoff, 2014; children: Cole and Ella; committees: Budget; Homeland Security and Governmental Affairs; Judiciary; Select Committee on Intelligence; elected to the U.S. Senate on November 8, 2016.

Office Listings

https://harris.senate.gov

112 Hart Senate Office Building, Washington, DC 20510 .... (202) 224–3553
Chief of Staff.—Rohini Kosoglu. FAX: 228–2382
Legislative Director.—Deanne Millison.
Director of Scheduling.—Michelle Rothblum.
Communications Director.—Chris Harris.
11845 Olympic Boulevard, Suite 1250W, Los Angeles, CA 90064 .... (213) 894–5000
333 Bush Street, Suite 3225, San Francisco, CA 94104 .... (415) 981–9369
501 I Street, Suite 7–600, Sacramento, CA 95814 .... (916) 448–2787
600 B Street, Suite 2240, San Diego, CA 92101 .... (619) 239–3884
2500 Tulare Street, Suite 5290, Fresno, CA 93721 .... (559) 497–5109

REPRESENTATIVES

FIRST DISTRICT

DOUG LAMALFA, Republican, of Richvale, CA; born in Oroville, CA, July 2, 1960; education: graduated from Oroville High School; B.S., California Polytechnic State University, San Luis Obispo, CA, 1982; professional: rice farmer; California State Assemblyman, 2002–08; California State Senator, 2010–12; married: Jill; children: four; caucuses: Cement Caucus; Congressional Sportsmen's Caucus; Congressional Western Caucus; Congressional Wine Caucus; National Guard and Reserve Components Caucus; Natural Gas Caucus; PORTS Caucus; Prayer Caucus; Republican Study Committee; Rice CALIFORNIA 115th Congress 21 Caucus; Sikh Caucus; Small Business Caucus; Values Action Team; committees: Agriculture; Transportation and Infrastructure; elected to the 113th Congress on November 6, 2012; reelected to each succeeding Congress.

Office Listings

https://lamalfa.house.gov https://facebook.com/RepLaMalfa twitter: @replamalfa

322 Cannon House Office Building, Washington, DC 20515 .... (202) 225–3076
Chief of Staff.—Mark Spannagel. FAX: 226–0852
Scheduler.—Haley Slaybaugh.
Legislative Director.—Jack Lincoln.
Communications Director.—Parker Williams.
120 Independence Circle, Suite B, Chico, California 95973 .... (530) 343–1000
FAX: 534–7800
2885 Churn Creek Road, Suite C, Redding, CA 96002 .... (530) 223–5898
FAX: 605–4342
2399 Rickenbacker Way, Auburn, CA 95602 .... (530) 878–5035
FAX: 878–5037

Counties: BUTTE, GLENN, LASSEN, MODOC, NEVADA, PLACER, PLUMAS, SHASTA, SIERRA, SISKIYOU, AND TEHAMA. Population (2010), 702,905.

ZIP Codes: 95568, 95602–03, 95712–13, 95728, 95910, 95914–17, 95923–24, 95926–30, 95934, 95936, 95938, 95940–42, 95944–49, 95954, 95956–60, 95965–66, 95968–69, 95971, 95973–78, 95980, 95983–84, 95986, 96001, 96006–09, 96011, 96013–17, 96019–23, 96025, 96027–29, 96031–35, 96037–40, 96044, 96047, 96050–51, 96054–59, 96061–62, 96064–65, 96067–71, 96073–75, 96078–80, 96084–90, 96092, 96094–97, 96101, 96104–06, 96108–19, 96121–30, 96132, 96134–37, 96161, 97635

* * *

SECOND DISTRICT

JARED W. HUFFMAN, Democrat, of San Rafael, CA; born in Independence, MO, February 18, 1964; education: B.A., University of California, Santa Barbara, CA, 1986; J.D., Boston College, Newton, MA, 1990; professional: California Assembly, 2006–12; senior lawyer, Natural Resources Defense Council, 2001–06; board member, Marin Municipal Water District, 1994–2006; public interest attorney, 1990–2001; family: married, Susan Huffman; two children; caucuses: co-chair, Congressional Freethought Caucus; co-chair, Wild Salmon Caucus; Congressional Animal Protection Caucus; Congressional Labor and Working Families Caucus; Congressional Progressive Caucus; Congressional Rare Disease Caucus; Congressional Shellfish Caucus; Congressional Wine Caucus; House Rural Education Caucus; National Marine Sanctuary Caucus; Native American Caucus; Sensible Drug Policy Working Group; Sustainable Energy & Environment Coalition; committees: Natural Resources; Transportation and Infrastructure; Select Committee on the Climate Crisis; elected to the 113th Congress on November 6, 2012; reelected to each succeeding Congress.

Office Listings

https://huffman.house.gov https://facebook.com/rephuffman twitter: @rephuffman

1527 Longworth House Office Building, Washington, DC 20515 .... (202) 225–5161
Chief of Staff.—Benjamin Miller. FAX: 225–5163
Executive Assistant / Scheduler.—Steven Mion.
999 Fifth Avenue, Suite 290, San Rafael, CA 94901 .... (415) 258–9657
District Director.—Jeannine Callaway.
430 North Franklin Street, P.O. Box 2208, Fort Bragg, CA 95437 .... (707) 962–0933
Field Representative.—Sheba Brown.
317 Third Street, Suite 1, Eureka, CA 95501 .... (707) 407–3585
District Representative.—John Driscoll.

Counties: DEL NORTE, HUMBOLDT, MARIN, MENDOCINO, SONOMA (part), AND TRINITY. CITIES AND TOWNSHIPS: Arcata, Cloverdale, Crescent City, Eureka, Fort Bragg, Garberville, Healdsburg, Mendocino, Mill Valley, Novato, Petaluma, San Rafael, Sebastopol, Ukiah, Willits, and Windsor. Population (2010), 708,596.

ZIP Codes: 94946–50, 94952–54, 94956–57, 94960, 94963–66, 94970–79, 94998–99, 95401, 95403–04, 95410, 95412, 95415, 95417–18, 95420–21, 95425, 95427–30, 95432, 95436–37, 95441, 95444–46, 95448–51, 95454, 95456, 95459–60, 95462–63, 95465–66, 95468–73, 95480–82, 95486, 95488, 95490, 95492, 95494, 95497, 95501–03, 95511, 95514, 95518–19, 95521, 95524–28, 95531–32, 95534, 95536–38, 95540, 95542–43

* * *

THIRD DISTRICT

JOHN GARAMENDI, Democrat, of Walnut Grove, CA; born in Camp Blanding, FL, January 24, 1945; raised in Mokelumne Hill, CA; education: B.A., business, University of California-Berkeley, Berkeley, CA, 1966; M.B.A., Harvard University, Cambridge, MA, 1974; professional: small business owner; Peace Corps volunteer, 1966–68; California State Assembly member, 1974–76; member of the California State Senate, 1976–90; California Insurance Commissioner, 1991–94, and 2002–06; Deputy Secretary of the U.S. Interior Department, 1995–98; previously California Lieutenant Governor, 2007–09; regent, University of California; trustee, California State University; religion: Christian; family: married to Patricia Garamendi; six children; thirteen grandchildren; caucuses: co-chair, American Sikh Caucus; co-chair, Coast Guard Caucus; co-chair, Mobility Air Forces Caucus; member of Make It in America Working Group; Deputy Whip; committees: Armed Services; Transportation and Infrastructure; elected, by special election, to the 111th Congress on November 3, 2009, to fill the vacancy caused by the resignation of U.S. Representative Ellen Tauscher; reelected to each succeeding Congress.

Office Listings

https://garamendi.house.gov https://facebook.com/repgaramendi
https://twitter.com/RepGaramendi https://instagram.com/repgaramendi

2368 Rayburn House Office Building, Washington, DC 20515 .... (202) 225–1880
Chief of Staff.—Bradley Bottoms. FAX: 225–5914
Legislative Director.—Iain Hart.
Deputy Chief of Staff / District Director.—Debbi Gibbs.
Digital Director / Scheduler.—Tessa Browne.
Communications Director.—Eric Olsen.
412 G Street, Davis, CA 95616 .... (530) 753–5301
FAX: 753–5614
1261 Travis Boulevard, Suite 180, Fairfield, CA 94533 .... (707) 438–1822
FAX: 438–0523

Counties: COLUSA, GLENN (part), LAKE (part), SACRAMENTO (part), SOLANO (part), SUTTER, YOLO (part), AND YUBA. Population (2010), 712,075.

ZIP Codes: 94503, 94510, 94512, 94533–35, 94558, 94571, 94585, 94591, 95422–24, 95443, 95451, 95453, 95457–58, 95464, 95485, 95493, 95606–07, 95612, 95615–18, 95620, 95625–27, 95632, 95637, 95639, 95641, 95645, 95653–

54, 95659–60, 95668, 95673–74, 95676, 95679–80, 95687–88, 95690–92, 95694–98, 95757–59, 95776, 95823, 95834–37, 95843, 95901, 95903, 95912–14, 95918–19, 95922, 95925, 95932, 95935, 95937, 95939, 95941, 95950–51, 95953, 95955, 95957, 95960–63, 95966, 95970, 95972, 95977, 95979, 95982, 95987–88, 95991–93

* * *

FOURTH DISTRICT

TOM McCLINTOCK, Republican, of Granite Bay, CA; born in Bronxville, NY, July 10, 1956; education: B.A., *cum laude,* political science, UCLA, Los Angeles, CA, 1978; professional: member, California State Assembly, 1982–92 and 1996–2000; member, California State Senate, 2000–08; director, Center for the California Taxpayer, National Tax Limitation Foundation, 1992–94; director, Economic and Regulatory Affairs, Claremont Institute, 1994–96; married: Lori; two children; committees: Judiciary; Natural Resources; elected to the 111th Congress on November 4, 2008; reelected to each succeeding Congress.

Office Listings

https://mcclintock.house.gov https://facebook.com/Congressman-Tom-McClintock-81125319109
twitter: @repmcclintock

2312 Rayburn House Office Building, Washington, DC 20515 .... (202) 225–2511
Chief of Staff.—Rocky Deal. FAX: 225–5444
Executive Assistant.—Hannah Cooke.
DC Chief of Staff.—Chris Tudor.
Deputy Chief of Staff / Legislative Director.—Steve Koncar.
Senior Legislative Assistant.—Andrew Marcel-Keyes.
Legislative Correspondent.—Kyle Campbell.
2200A Douglas Boulevard, Suite 240, Roseville, CA 95661 .... (916) 786–5560
Office Director.—Matt Reed.

Counties: ALPINE, AMADOR, CALAVERAS, EL DORADO, FRESNO (part), MADERA (part), MARIPOSA, NEVADA (part), PLACER (part), AND TUOLUMNE. Population (2010), 760,078.

ZIP Codes: 35251, 59223, 85252, 92532, 93601–02, 93604–05, 93610–11, 93614, 93619, 93621, 93623, 93626, 93628, 93633–34, 93636, 93638, 93641, 93643–45, 93649, 93651, 93653, 93657, 93664, 93667, 93669, 93675, 93701, 94248, 95147, 95221–26, 95228–30, 95232–33, 95236, 95245–49, 95251–52, 95254–57, 95305–06, 95309–11, 95318, 95321, 95325, 95327, 95329, 95333, 95335, 95338, 95345–47, 95364, 95369–70, 95372–73, 95379, 95383, 95389, 95601, 95603, 95613–14, 95619, 95623, 95626, 95629, 95631, 95633–36, 95640, 95642, 95644, 95646, 95648, 95650–51, 95656, 95658, 95661, 95663–69, 95672, 95675, 95678, 95681–82, 95684–85, 95689, 95699, 95709, 95713, 95715, 95720–21, 95724, 95726, 95728, 95735, 95746–47, 95762, 95765, 95945–46, 95949, 95959, 96120, 96140–43, 96145–46, 96148, 96150, 96161–62

* * *

FIFTH DISTRICT

MIKE THOMPSON, Democrat, of Napa Valley, CA; born in St. Helena, CA, January 24, 1951; education: graduated, St. Helena High School, St. Helena, CA; B.A., Chico State University, 1982; M.A., Chico State University, 1996; professional: U.S. Army, 1969–72; Purple Heart; teacher at San Francisco State University, and Chico State University; elected to the California State Senate, 2nd District, 1990–98; former chairman of the California State Senate Budget Committee; family: married to Janet; two children: Christopher and Jon; committees: Ways and Means; elected to the 106th Congress; reelected to each succeeding Congress.

Office Listings

https://mikethompson.house.gov https://facebook.com/RepMikeThompson twitter: @repthompson

406 Cannon House Office Building, Washington, DC 20515 .... (202) 225–3311
Chief of Staff.—Melanie Rhinehart Van Tassell. FAX: 225–4335
Deputy Chief of Staff.—Jennifer Goedke.
Communications Director.—Alex Macfarlane.
2721 Napa Valley Corporate Drive, Napa, CA 94558 .... (707) 226–9898
420 Virginia Street, Suite 1C, Vallejo, CA 94590 .... (707) 645–1888
2300 County Center Drive, Suite A100, Santa Rosa, CA 95403 .... (707) 542–7182

Counties: CONTRA COSTA. CITIES AND TOWNSHIPS: Christie, Crockett, Glen Frazer, Hercules, Martinez, Pinole, Port Costa, Rodeo, Selby, Tara Hills, Tormey, and Vine Hill. LAKE COUNTY. CITIES AND TOWNSHIPS: Cobb, Kelseyville, Lakeport, and Middletown. SONOMA COUNTY. CITIES AND TOWNSHIPS: Boyes Hot Springs, Cotati, El Verano, Eldridge, Fetters Hot Springs, Fulton, Glen Ellen, Kenwood, Mark West, Rohnert Park, Santa Rosa, Sonoma, and Vineburg. NAPA COUNTY. CITIES AND TOWNSHIPS: American Canyon, Angwin, Aetna Springs, Calistoga, Deer Park, Oakville, Pope

Valley, Rutherford, and St. Helena. SOLANO COUNTY. CITIES AND TOWNSHIPS: Benicia, Tiara, and Vallejo. Population (2011), 547,495.

ZIP Codes: 94508, 94510, 94515, 94525, 94547, 94553, 94558–59, 94562, 94564, 94567, 94569, 94572–74, 94576, 94581, 94587, 94589–92, 94599, 94806, 94926–28, 94931, 95401, 95409, 95416, 95426, 95431, 95433, 95435, 95439, 95442, 95451–53, 95461, 95476, 95492, 95621

* * *

SIXTH DISTRICT

DORIS OKADA MATSUI, Democrat, of Sacramento, CA; born in Poston, AZ, September 25, 1944; education: B.A., University of California, Berkeley, CA, 1966; professional: staff, White House, 1992–98; private advocate; previous organizations: Meridian International Center Board of Trustees; Woodrow Wilson Center Board of Trustees; California Institute Board of Directors; current organizations: Smithsonian Institution Board of Regents; National Symphony Orchestra Board of Directors; married: Robert Matsui, 1966; children: Brian Robert; grandchildren: Anna Elizabeth and Robert Thomas; committees: Energy and Commerce; Rules; elected to the 109th Congress, by special election, on March 8, 2005, to fill the vacancy caused by the death of her husband, Representative Robert Matsui; reelected to each succeeding Congress.

Office Listings

https://matsui.house.gov https://facebook.com/doris.matsui https://twitter.com/dorismatsui

2311 Rayburn House Office Building, Washington, DC 20515 .... (202) 225–7163
Chief of Staff.—Kyle Victor. FAX: 225–0566
Executive Assistant.—Mckinley Edelman.
Legislative Director.—Vacant.
Communications Director.—Kyle Morse.
501 I Street, 12–600, Sacramento, CA 95814 .... (916) 498–5600
District Director.—Glenda Corcoran.

Counties: SACRAMENTO COUNTY (part) AND YOLO COUNTY (part). CITIES: Sacramento and West Sacramento. Population (2010), 702,905.

ZIP Codes: 95605, 95621, 95652, 95660, 95673, 95691, 95758, 95811, 95814–26, 95828–29, 95831–35, 95837–38, 95841–43, 95864

* * *

SEVENTH DISTRICT

AMI BERA, Democrat, of Elk Grove, CA; born in La Palma, CA, March 2, 1965; education: B.S., University of California, Irvine, CA; M.D., University of California, Irvine, CA, 1991; professional: medical director for care management, Mercy Hospital, Sacramento, CA; chief medical officer, Sacramento, CA; associate dean of admissions for University of California, Davis Medical School, 2004–07; religion: Unitarian; married: Janine Bera (also a physician); children: Sydra; committees: Foreign Affairs; Science, Space, and Technology; elected to the 113th Congress on November 6, 2012; reelected to each succeeding Congress.

Office Listings

https://bera.house.gov https://facebook.com/RepAmiBera
https://twitter.com/repbera https://instagram.com/repbera

1727 Longworth House Office Building, Washington, DC 20515 .... (202) 225–5716
Chief of Staff.—Chad Obermiller. FAX: 226–1298
Scheduler.—Kellie Karney.
Legislative Director.—Kelvin Lum.
Communications Director.—Travis Horne.
Senior Policy Advisor.—Colleen Nguyen.
Legislative Assistants: Emma Bruce, Ryan Uyehara.
Legislative Correspondent / Legislative Aide.—Stephanie Perera.
Staff Assistant / Press Assistant.—Elena Radding.
APAICS Congressional Fellow.—Ariel Higuchi.
8950 Cal Center Drive, Building 3, Suite 100, Sacramento, CA 95826 .... (916) 635–0505
District Director.—Matthew Ceccato.

Counties: EASTERN HALF OF SACRAMENTO COUNTY. CITIES: Citrus Heights, Elk Grove, Folsom, and Rancho Cordova. UNINCORPORATED COMMUNITIES: Arden Arcade (part), Carmichael, Fair Oaks, Florin, Herald, La Riviera, Orangevale, Rancho Murieta, Rosemont, Sloughhouse, Vineyard, Vintage Park, and Wilton. Population (2010), 710,607.

ZIP Codes: 95608–09, 95610 (part), 95611, 95621 (part), 95624, 95628, 95630, 95632 (part), 95638, 95655, 95661 (part), 95662, 95670–71, 95678 (part), 95683, 95693, 95741–42, 95757–58 (part), 95759, 95763, 95821 (part), 95823 (part), 95825–26 (part), 95827, 95828–29 (part), 95830, 95841–42 (part), 95860 (part), 95864–66 (part)

* * *

EIGHTH DISTRICT

PAUL COOK, Republican, of Yucca Valley, CA; born in Meriden, CT, March 3, 1943; education: B.S., Southern Connecticut University, New Haven, CT, 1966; M.P.A., California State University San Bernardino, San Bernardino, CA, 1996; M.A., University of California Riverside, Riverside, CA, 2000; professional: U.S. Marine Corps, 1966–92; professor; member, Yucca Valley California Town Council, 1998–2006; California State Assemblyman, 2006–12; married: Jeanne; committees: Armed Services; Natural Resources; elected to the 113th Congress on November 6, 2012; reelected to each succeeding Congress.

Office Listings

https://cook.house.gov twitter: @RepPaulCook

1027 Longworth House Office Building, Washington, DC 20515 .... (202) 225–5861
Chief of Staff.—John Sobel. FAX: 225–6498
14955 Dale Evans Parkway, Apple Valley, CA 92307 .... (760) 247–1815
District Director.—Timothy Itnyre.

Counties: INYO, MONO, AND SAN BERNARDINO (part). CITIES AND TOWNSHIPS: Adelanto, Angelus Oaks, Apple Valley, Arrowbear, Arrowhead Farms, Baker, Baldy Mesa, Barstow, Bear Valley, Benton, Big Bear City, Big Bear Lake, Big Pine, Big River, Bishop, Bridgeport, Bums Canyon, Cartago, Cedar Glen, Cedar Pines Park, Coleville, Crestline, Daggett, Darwin, El Mirage, Erwin Lake, Fawnskin, Flamingo Heights, Forest Falls, Furnace Creek, Green Valley Lake, Helendale, Hesperia, Highland, Hinkley, Independence, Joshua Tree, June Lake, Keeler, Lake Arrowhead, Landers, Lee Vining, Lenwood, Lytle Creek, Mono City, Morongo Valley, Mount Baldy, Needles, Newberry Springs, Oak Glen, Oak Hills, Oro Grande, Paradise, Phelan, Pinon Hills, Pioneertown, Red Mountain, Rimrock, Running Springs, Skyforest, Sugarloaf, Topaz, Trona, Twentynine Palms, Twin Peaks, Victorville, Walker, Wrightwood, Yucaipa, and Yucca Valley. Population (2010), 708,578.

ZIP Codes: 91759, 92242, 92252, 92256, 92268, 92277–78, 92284–86, 92301, 92304–05, 92307–12, 92314–15, 92317, 92320–23, 92325, 92327–29, 92332–33, 92338–42, 92344–47, 92352, 92356, 92358–59, 92363–65, 92368–69, 92372, 92382, 92385–86, 92388–89, 92391–95, 92397–99, 92407, 93512–15, 93522, 93526, 93529–30, 93541, 93549, 93558, 93562–92, 95223, 95967, 95969, 96107, 96133

* * *

NINTH DISTRICT

JERRY MCNERNEY, Democrat, of Stockton, CA; born in Albuquerque, NM, June 18, 1951; education: attended the U.S. Military Academy, West Point, NY, 1969–71; B.S., University of New Mexico, Albuquerque, NM, 1973; M.S., University of New Mexico, 1975; Ph.D. in Mathematics, University of New Mexico, 1981; professional: wind engineer; entrepreneur; business owner; married: Mary; children: Michael, Windy, and Greg; committees: Energy and Commerce; Science, Space, and Technology; elected to the 110th Congress on November 7, 2006; reelected to each succeeding Congress.

Office Listings

https://mcnerney.house.gov https://facebook.com/jerrymcnerney twitter: @repmcnerney

2265 Rayburn House Office Building, Washington, DC 20515 .... (202) 225–1947
Chief of Staff.—Nicole Damasco Alioto. FAX: 225–4060
Scheduler.— Trevor Jones.
Communications Director.—Nikki Cannon.
Legislative Director.—Rishi Sahgal.
District Director.—Alisa Alva.
2222 Grand Canal Boulevard, #7, Stockton, CA 95207 .... (209) 476–8552
4703 Lone Tree Way, Antioch, CA 94531 .... (925) 754–0716

Counties: CONTRA COSTA (part), SACRAMENTO (part), AND SAN JOAQUIN (part). CITIES AND TOWNSHIPS: Antioch, Brentwood, Discovery Bay, Galt, Lathrop, Lodi, Oakley, and Stockton. Population (2010), 648,766.

ZIP Codes: 94505, 94509, 94511, 94513–14, 94531, 94548, 94561, 95201–15, 95219–20, 95227, 95230–31, 95234, 95236–37, 95240–42, 95253, 95258, 95267, 95269, 95296, 95304, 95320, 95330, 95336–37, 95361, 95366, 95391, 95632, 95686, 95690, 95757

* * *

TENTH DISTRICT

JOSH HARDER, Democrat, of Turlock, CA; born in Turlock, Stanislaus County, CA, August 1, 1986; education: graduated from Modesto Public High School, Modesto, CA; B.A., Stanford University, Stanford, CA; M.B.A., Harvard University, Cambridge, MA; M.P.P., Harvard University, Cambridge, MA; professional: entrepreneur; consultant; educator; caucuses: Assyrian Caucus; Religious Minorities Caucus; committees: Agriculture; Education and Labor; elected to the 116th Congress on November 6, 2018.

Office Listings

https://harder.house.gov https://facebook.com/RepJoshHarder https://twitter.com/repjoshharder

131 Cannon House Office Building, Washington, DC 20515 .... (202) 225–4540
Chief of Staff.—Rachael Goldenberg. FAX: 225–3402
Deputy Chief of Staff / Legislative Director.—Adela Amador.
Communications Director.—Ian Lee.
Director of Operations / Scheduler.—Claris Chang.
4701 Sisk Road, Suite 202, Modesto, CA 95356 .... (209) 579–5458
District Director.—Karen Warner.

Counties: SAN JOAQUIN COUNTY (part) AND STANISLAUS COUNTY (part). CITIES AND TOWNSHIPS: Airport, Bret Harte, Bystrom, Ceres, Cowan, Cowan Landing, Del Rio, Denair, Diablo Grande, East Oakdale, Empire, Escalon, Grayson, Hickman, Hughson, Keyes, Manteca, Modesto, Monterey Park Tract, Newman, Oakdale, Parklawn, Patterson, Ripon, Riverbank, Riverdale Park, Rouse, Salida, Shackelford, Tracy, Turlock, Valley Home, Waterford, Westley, West Modesto, Westport, and Woodbridge. Population (2010), 714,750.

ZIP Codes: 94550, 95230, 95304, 95307, 95313, 95316, 95319–20, 95322–23, 95326, 95328–30, 95336–37, 95350–51, 95354–58, 95360–61, 95363, 95366–68, 95376–77, 95380, 95382, 95385–87

* * *

ELEVENTH DISTRICT

MARK DESAULNIER, Democrat, of Concord, CA; born in Lowell, MA, March 31, 1952; education: B.A., history, College of the Holy Cross, Worcester, MA, 1974; professional: deputy probation officer, 1970–74; hotel service employee, 1975–76; restaurant general manager, 1978; restaurant owner, 1978–2006; Concord Mayor, 1993; Concord City Council, 1991–94; Contra Costa County Supervisor, 1994–2006; California Area Resources Board, 1997–2006; California Assembly, 2006–08; California Senate, 2008–15; religion: Catholic; children: Tristan and Tucker; committees: Education and Labor; Oversight and Reform; Rules; Transportation and Infrastructure; elected to the 114th Congress on November 4, 2014; reelected to each succeeding Congress.

Office Listings

https://desaulnier.house.gov twitter: @RepDeSaulnier

503 Cannon House Office Building, Washington, DC 20515 .... (202) 225–2095
Chief of Staff.—Betsy Arnold Marr. FAX: 225–5609
Scheduler.—Bambi Yingst.
3100 Oak Road, Suite 110, Walnut Creek, CA 94597 .... (925) 933–2660
District Director.—Shanelle Scales Preston.
440 Civic Center Plaza, Second Floor, Richmond, CA 94804 .... (510) 620–1000
Scheduler.—Jessica Angulo.

Counties: CONTRA COSTA (part). CITIES AND TOWNSHIPS: Alamo, Antioch, Bay Point, Clayton, Concord, Danville, Diablo, El Cerrito, El Sobrante, Kensington, Lafayette, Martinez, Moraga, Orinda, Pacheco, Pittsburg, Pleasant Hill, Richmond, San Pablo, and Walnut Creek. Population (2014), 773,916.

ZIP Codes: 94506–07, 94509, 94517–24, 94526–30, 94549, 94553, 94556, 94563, 94565, 94595–98, 94708, 94801–08, 94820, 94850

* * *

TWELFTH DISTRICT

NANCY PELOSI, Democrat, of San Francisco, CA; born in Baltimore, MD, March 26, 1940; daughter of the late Representative Thomas D'Alesandro, Jr., of MD; education: graduated, Institute of Notre Dame High School, 1958; B.A., Trinity College, Washington, DC (major, political science; minor, history), 1962; professional: northern chair, California Democratic Party, 1977–81; state chair, California Democratic Party, 1981–83; chair, 1984 Democratic National Convention Host Committee; finance chair, Democratic Senatorial Campaign Committee, 1985–86; member: Democratic National Committee; California Democratic Party Executive Committee; San Francisco Library Commission; Board of Trustees, LSB Leakey Foundation; married: Paul F. Pelosi, 1963; children: Nancy Corinne, Christine, Jacqueline, Paul, Jr., and Alexandra; nine grandchildren; elected by special election, June 2, 1987, to the 100th Congress to fill the vacancy caused by the death of U.S. Representative Sala Burton; reelected to each succeeding Congress; elected Democratic Whip in the 107th Congress; Democratic Leader in the 108th and 109th Congresses; elected Speaker of the House in the 110th and 111th Congresses; elected Democratic Leader in the 112th, 113th, 114th, and 115th Congresses; elected Speaker of the House in the 116th Congress.

Office Listings

https://speaker.gov https://pelosi.house.gov twitter: @SpeakerPelosi

1236 Longworth House Office Building, Washington, DC 20515 .... (202) 225–4965
Chief of Staff.—Robert Edmonson (California). FAX: 225–8259
90 7th Street, Suite 2–800, San Francisco, CA 94103 .... (415) 556–4862
District Chief of Staff.—Dan Bernal.

County: SAN FRANCISCO COUNTY (part). CITY: San Francisco. Population (2010), 702,905.

ZIP Codes: 94014, 94102–05, 94107–12, 94114–18, 94121–24, 94127, 94129–34, 94158, 94164

* * *

THIRTEENTH DISTRICT

BARBARA LEE, Democrat, of Oakland, CA; born in El Paso, TX, July 16, 1946; education: graduated, San Fernando High School; B.A., Mills College, 1973; MSW, University of California, Berkeley, 1975; professional: congressional aide and social worker; senior advisor and Chief of Staff to Congressman Ronald V. Dellums in Washington, DC, and Oakland, CA, 1975–87; California State Assembly, 1990–96; California State Senate, 1996–98; Assembly committees: Housing and Land Use; Appropriations; Business and Professions; Industrial Relations; Judiciary; Revenue and Taxation; board member, California State Coastal Conservancy, District Export Council, and California Defense Conversion Council; committees: Appropriations; Budget; elected to the 105th Congress on April 7, 1998, by special election, to fill the remaining term of retiring U.S. Representative Ronald V. Dellums; reelected to each succeeding Congress.

Office Listings

https://lee.house.gov https://facebook.com/RepBarbaraLee twitter: @repbarbaralee

2470 Rayburn House Office Building, Washington, DC 20515 .... (202) 225–2661
Chief of Staff.—Julie Nickson. FAX: 225–9817
Scheduler.—Aisling Martin.
Communications Director.—David Stephen.
Legislative Director.—Emma Mehrabi.
1301 Clay Street, Suite 1000–N, Oakland, CA 94612 .... (510) 763–0370

Counties: ALAMEDA COUNTY. CITIES: Alameda, Albany, Berkeley, Emeryville, Oakland, Piedmont, and San Leandro. Population (2015), 755,776.

ZIP Codes: 94501–02, 94530 (part), 94577–78 (part), 94579, 94580 (part), 94601–10, 94611 (part), 94612–15, 94617–18, 94619 (part), 94620–21, 94623–24, 94649, 94661–62, 94666, 94701–05, 94706–08 (part), 94709–10, 94712, 94720

* * *

FOURTEENTH DISTRICT

JACKIE SPEIER, Democrat, of Hillsborough, CA; born in San Francisco, CA, May 14, 1950; education: B.A., University of California at Davis; J.D., University of California, Hastings College of the Law, 1976; professional: legislative counsel, Congressman Leo J. Ryan; member, San Mateo County Board of Supervisors; member, California State Assembly; senator, California State Senate; married: Barry Dennis; two children: Jackson Sierra and Stephanie Sierra; committees: Armed Services; Oversight and Reform; Permanent Select Committee on Intelligence; elected, by special election, on April 8, 2008, to fill the vacancy caused by the death of U.S. Representative Thomas P. Lantos; elected to the 111th Congress on November 4, 2008; reelected to each succeeding Congress.

Office Listings

https://speier.house.gov https://facebook.com/jackiespeier twitter: @repspeier
https://youtube.com/user/jackiespeierCA12 instagram: @jackiespeier

2465 Rayburn House Office Building, Washington, DC 20515 .... (202) 225–3531
Chief of Staff.—Josh Connolly. FAX: 226–4183
Legislative Director.—Yana Mayayeva.
155 Bovet Road, Suite 780, San Mateo, CA 94402 .... (650) 342–0300
District Representative.—Brian Perkins. FAX: 375–8270

Counties: SAN MATEO COUNTY (part). CITIES: Belmont, Brisbane, Burlingame, Colma, Daly City, East Palo Alto, Foster City, Half Moon Bay, Hillsborough, Menlo Park, Millbrae, Montara, Moss Beach, Pacifica, Redwood City, San Bruno, San Carlos, San Gregorio, San Mateo, South San Francisco, and Woodside. SAN FRANCISCO COUNTY (part). CITIES: San Francisco. Population (2012), 726,958.

ZIP Codes: 94002, 94005, 94010–11, 94013–15, 94019, 94025, 94030, 94038, 94044, 94061–66, 94070, 94074, 94080, 94083, 94099, 94112, 94116–17, 94127–28, 94131–32, 94134, 94143, 94303, 94401–04, 94497

* * *

FIFTEENTH DISTRICT

ERIC SWALWELL, Democrat, of Dublin, CA; born in Sac City, IA, November 16, 1980; education: graduated, Dublin High School, Dublin, CA, 1999; B.A., University of Maryland, College Park, College Park, MD, 2003; J.D., University of Maryland School of Law, Baltimore, MD, 2006; professional: former city councilman at City of Dublin City Council; former Deputy District Attorney at Alameda County District Attorney's Office; Planning Commissioner at City of Dublin; Heritage & Cultural Arts Commissioner at City of Dublin; law clerk at Alameda County District Attorney's Office; commission: Tom Lantos Human Rights; caucuses: Ad Hoc Congressional Committee for Irish Affairs; Congressional Anti-Bullying Caucus; Congressional Asian Pacific American Caucus; Congressional Autism Caucus; Congressional Caucus on India and Indian Americans; Congressional Cyber Security Caucus; Congressional Diabetes Caucus; Congressional Dyslexia Caucus; Congressional Friends of Ireland Caucus; Congressional High Tech Caucus; Congressional Internet Caucus; Congressional LGBT Equality Caucus; Congressional PORTS Caucus; Congressional Pro-Choice Caucus; Congressional Soccer Caucus; Congressional Victims' Rights Caucus; Congressional Wine Caucus; Democratic Whip's Task Force on Poverty and Opportunity; House Science and National Labs Caucus; International Religious Freedom Caucus; committees: Judiciary; Permanent Select Committee on Intelligence; elected to the 113th Congress on November 6, 2012; reelected to each succeeding Congress.

Office Listings

https://swalwell.house.gov https://facebook.com/CongressmanEricSwalwell twitter: @repswalwell

407 Cannon House Office Building, Washington, DC 20515 .... (202) 225–5065
Chief of Staff.—Michael Reed. FAX: 226–3805
3615 Castro Valley Boulevard, Castro Valley, CA 94546 .... (510) 370–3322

Counties: ALAMEDA COUNTY (part) AND CONTRA COSTA (part). CITIES AND TOWNSHIPS: Ashland, Castro Valley, Danville (part), Dublin, Fairview, Fremont (part), Hayward, Pleasanton, San Leandro (part), San Lorenzo, San Ramon, Sunol, and Union City. Population (2010), 732,515.

ZIP Codes: 94505–06, 94514, 94526, 94536, 94538–39, 94541–42, 94544–46, 94550–52, 94555, 94566, 94568, 94577–78

* * *

SIXTEENTH DISTRICT

JIM COSTA, Democrat, of Fresno, CA; born in Fresno, April 13, 1952; education: B.A., California State University, Fresno, 1974; professional: special assistant, Congressman John Krebs, 1975–76; administrative assistant, California Assemblyman Richard Lehman, 1976–78;

California State Assembly, 1978–94; California State Senate, 1994–2002; chief executive officer, Costa Group, 2002–03; religion: Catholic; caucuses: co-chair, Victims' Rights Caucus; Blue Dog Coalition; Congressional Hispanic Caucus; Transatlantic Legislators' Dialogue; committees: Agriculture; Foreign Affairs; Natural Resources; elected to the 109th Congress on November 2, 2004; reelected to each succeeding Congress.

Office Listings

https://costa.house.gov https://facebook.com/repjimcosta https://twitter.com/repjimcosta https://youtube.com/user/repjimcostaca20

2081 Rayburn House Office Building, Washington, DC 20515 .... (202) 225–3341
Chief of Staff.—Juan López. FAX: 225–9308
Legislative Director.—Jared Feldman.
Press Secretary.—Tammy Johnson (CA).
Schedulers: Christy Bourbon (CA), Elina Karapetyan (DC).
Deputy Chief of Staff.—Kathy Mahan (CA).
855 M Street, Suite 940, Fresno, CA 93721 .... (559) 495–1620
2222 M Street, Suite 305, Merced, CA 95340 .... (209) 384–1620

Counties: FRESNO (part), MADERA (part), and MERCED. Population (2011), 714,214.

ZIP Codes: 93606, 93610 (part), 93620 (part), 93622 (part), 93626 (part), 93630 (part), 93635, 93636 (part), 93637, 93638 (part), 93639, 93661, 93665, 93701–03, 93704–06 (part), 93707–09, 93711 (part), 93712, 93714–18, 93720 (part), 93721, 93722–23 (part), 93724, 93725–27 (part), 93728, 93741, 93744–45, 93747, 93750, 93755, 93760–61, 93764, 93771–79, 93786, 93790–94, 93844, 93888, 95301, 95303, 95312, 95315, 95316 (part), 95317, 95322 (part), 95324–25 (part), 95333–34, 95340–41, 95343–44, 95348, 95360 (part), 95365, 95369 (part), 95374, 95380 (part), 95388

* * *

SEVENTEENTH DISTRICT

RO KHANNA, Democrat, of Fremont, CA; born in Philadelphia, PA, September 13, 1976; education: B.A., economics, University of Chicago, 1998; J.D., Yale Law, 2001; professional: taught economics at Stanford University, law at Santa Clara University, and American Jurisprudence at San Francisco State University; author, *Entrepreneurial Nation: Why Manufacturing is Still Key to America's Future*;. lawyer, specializing in intellectual property law; Deputy Assistant Secretary at the U.S. Department of Commerce, 2009–11; appointed by California Governor Jerry Brown in 2012 to the California Workforce Investment Board; religion: Hindu; married: Ritu Ahuja Kanna; caucuses: vice chair, Progressive Caucus; committees: Armed Services; Budget; Oversight and Reform; elected to the 115th Congress on November 8, 2016; reelected to the 116th Congress on November 8, 2018.

Office Listings

https://khanna.house.gov https://facebook.com/RepRoKhanna twitter: @RepRoKhanna

221 Cannon House Office Building, Washington, DC 20515–0517 .... (202) 225–2631
Chief of Staff.—Pete Spiro. FAX: 225–2699
Legislative Director.—Chris Schloesser.
Communications Director.—Heather Purcell.
3150 De La Cruz Boulevard, Suite 240, Santa Clara, CA 95054 .... (408) 436–2720
District Director.—Tom Pyke. FAX: 436–2721

Counties: ALAMEDA (part), SANTA CLARA (part). CITIES AND TOWNSHIPS: Cupertino, Fremont, Milpitas, Newark, North San Jose, Santa Clara, and Sunnyvale. Population (2014), 724,244.

ZIP Codes: 94024, 94040, 94043, 94085–89, 94536, 94538–39, 94555, 94560, 95002, 95014–15, 95035–36, 95050–56, 95070, 95101, 95110, 95112, 95116–17, 95126–29, 95131–34, 95140

* * *

EIGHTEENTH DISTRICT

ANNA G. ESHOO, Democrat, of Menlo Park, CA; born in New Britain, CT, December 13, 1942; education: A.A., Cañada College, Redwood City, CA, 1975; professional: chairwoman, San Mateo County Democratic Party, 1978–82; chief of staff to Speaker of the California State Assembly, 1981–82; member of the Democratic National Commission on Presidential Nominations, 1982; member of the San Mateo County, California Board of Supervisors, 1983–92, president, 1986; committees: Energy and Commerce; elected on November 3, 1992, to the 103rd Congress; reelected to each succeeding Congress.

Office Listings

https://eshoo.house.gov https://facebook.com/RepAnnaEshoo twitter: @RepAnnaEshoo

202 Cannon House Office Building, Washington, DC 20515 .... (202) 225–8104
Chief of Staff.—Matthew McMurray. FAX: 225–8890
Press Secretary.—Michael Brady.
Executive Assistant / Scheduler.—Noor Shah.
698 Emerson Street, Palo Alto, CA 94301 .... (650) 323–2984
District Chief of Staff.—Karen Chapman.

Counties: SAN MATEO COUNTY. CITIES AND TOWNS: Atherton, La Honda, Ladera, Loma Mar, Menlo Park, Pescadero, Portola Valley, Redwood City, and Woodside. SANTA CLARA COUNTY. CITIES AND TOWNS: Cambrian Park, Campbell, Fruitdale, Lexington Hills, Los Altos, Los Altos Hills, Los Gatos, Monte Sereno, Mountain View, Palo Alto, San Jose (part), Saratoga, and Stanford. SANTA CRUZ COUNTY. CITIES AND TOWNS: Ben Lomond, Bonny Doon, Boulder Creek, Brookdale, Davenport, Felton, Lompico, Scotts Valley, and Zayante. Population (2017), 742,728.

ZIP Codes: 94020–28, 94035, 94039–43, 94060–63, 94074, 94301–06, 94309, 95005–09, 95011, 95014, 95017–18, 95026, 95030–33, 95041–42, 95044, 95050, 95060, 95065–67, 95070–71, 95073, 95076, 95117–18, 95120, 95123–26, 95128–30, 95141, 95154, 95157–58, 95160, 95170

* * *

NINETEENTH DISTRICT

ZOE LOFGREN, Democrat, of San Jose, CA; born in San Mateo, CA, December 21, 1947; education: graduated, Gunn High School, 1966; B.A., Stanford University, Stanford, CA, 1970; J.D., Santa Clara Law School, Santa Clara, CA, 1975; professional: admitted to the California Bar, 1975; District of Columbia Bar, 1981; U.S. Supreme Court Bar, 1986; member: board of trustees, San Jose Evergreen Community College District, 1979–81; board of supervisors, Santa Clara County, CA, 1981–94; married: John Marshall Collins, 1978; children: Sheila and John; committees: chair, House Administration; chair, Joint Committee on Printing; vice chair, Joint Committee on the Library; Judiciary; Science, Space, and Technology; Select Committee on the Modernization of Congress; elected to the 104th Congress; reelected to each succeeding Congress.

Office Listings

https://lofgren.house.gov https://facebook.com/zoelofgren twitter: @repzoelofgren

1401 Longworth House Office Building, Washington, DC 20515 .... (202) 225–3072
Chief of Staff.—Stacey Leavandosky. FAX: 225–3336
Communications Director.—Yianni Varonis.
Executive Assistant / Scheduler.—Andrew DeLuca.
635 North First Street, Suite B, San Jose, CA 95112 .... (408) 271–8700
District Chief of Staff.—Sandra Soto.

Counties: SANTA CLARA (part). CITIES AND TOWNSHIPS: Gilroy, San Jose, San Martin, and unincorporated portions of southern SANTA CLARA COUNTY. Population (2010), 702,904.

ZIP Codes: 94550, 95013, 95020, 95023, 95033, 95035, 95037–38, 95046, 95050, 95076, 95103, 95106, 95108–13, 95115–16, 95118–28, 95132–33, 95135–36, 95138–41, 95148, 95150–53, 95155–56, 95159, 95172–73, 95191–92, 95196

* * *

TWENTIETH DISTRICT

JIMMY PANETTA, Democrat, of Carmel Valley, CA; born in Washington, DC, October 1, 1969; education: A.A., Monterey Peninsula College, Monterey, CA, 1989; bachelor's in international relations, University of California at Davis, Davis, CA, 1991; law degree, Santa Clara University, Santa Clara, CA, 1996; professional: clerk, United States Department of State, 1992; ordinary seaman, National Oceanic and Atmospheric Association NOAA Ship Rainier, 1992; Alameda County, CA, deputy district attorney, 1996–2010; Monterey County, CA, deputy district attorney, 2010–16; Monterey County, CA, central Democratic committee vice chairman, 2012–16; military: United States Navy Reserve, 2003–11; Afghanistan War Veteran, 2007–08, Operation Enduring Freedom; medals: awarded Bronze Star for Meritorious Service; Joint Meritorious Unit Award Ribbon; Meritorious Unit Commendation Ribbon; National Defense Service Medal; Afghanistan Campaign Medal; Global War on Terrorism Expeditionary Medal; Global War on Terrorism Service Medal; Navy Armed Services Reserve Deployment Medal; Navy Expert Rifle Military Medal; Navy Expert Pistol Military Medal; religion: Catholic; married:

Carrie McIntyre Panetta; two daughters; Siri and Gia; committees: Agriculture; Budget; Ways and Means; elected to the 115th Congress on November 8, 2016; reelected to the 116th Congress on November 6, 2018.

Office Listings

https://panetta.house.gov https://facebook.com/RepJimmyPanetta
twitter: @RepJimmyPanetta https://instagram.com/repjimmypanetta
https://youtube.com/channel/UCmw-aERG51C96edMDPN7fXQ

212 Cannon House Office Building, Washington, DC 20515 .... (202) 225–2861
Chief of Staff.—Joel Bailey.
Legislative Director.—Matthew Manning.
Press Secretary.—Sarah Davey.
701 Ocean Street, Room 318C, Santa Cruz, CA 95060 .... (831) 429–1976
100 West Alisal Street, Salinas, CA 93901 .... (831) 424–2229

Counties: MONTEREY, SAN BENITO, SANTA CRUZ (southern half), AND SANTA CLARA (southern portion). Population (2010), 744,350.

ZIP Codes: 93426, 93450–51, 93901–02, 93905–08, 93912, 93915, 93920–28, 93930, 93932–33, 93940, 93942–44, 93950, 93953–55, 93960, 93962, 95001, 95003–04, 95010, 95012, 95019, 95020–21, 95023–24, 95039, 95043, 95045, 95060–65, 95073, 95075–77

* * *

TWENTY-FIRST DISTRICT

TJ COX, Democrat, of Fresno, CA; born in Walnut Creek, CA, July 18, 1963; education: B.S., chemical engineering, University of Nevada, Reno, NV, 1986; M.B.A., Southern Methodist University, Dallas, TX, 1999; professional: registered professional engineer, CA; religion: Catholic; married: Kathleen Murphy, M.D.; children: four; committees: Agriculture; Natural Resources; elected to the 116th Congress on November 6, 2018.

Office Listings

https://cox.house.gov https://facebook.com/RepTJCox https://twitter.com/RepTjCox
https://instagram.com/RepTjCox https://youtube.com/reptjcox

1728 Longworth House Office Building, Washington, DC 20515 .... (202) 225–4695
Chief of Staff.—Francois Genard. FAX: 225–3196
Legislative Director.—Jared Henderson.
Communications Director.—Drew Godinich.
Legislative Assistant / Press Secretary.—Fabiola Rodriguez.
2700 M Street, Suite 250B, Bakersfield, CA 93301 .... (661) 864–7736
District Director.—Gilbert Felix.

Counties: FRESNO (part), KERN (part), KINGS, AND TULARE (part). Population (2010), 714,164.

ZIP Codes: 93201–04, 93206, 93210, 93212, 93215, 93218–19, 93227, 93230, 93234, 93237, 93239, 93241–43, 93245, 93249–51, 93256–57, 93261, 93263, 93266, 93270, 93272, 93274–75, 93278–80, 93290–91, 93304–07, 93311–12, 93314, 93607–09, 93616, 93620, 93622, 93624–25, 93627, 93631, 93640, 93648, 93652, 93654, 93656–57, 93660, 93662, 93668, 93706, 93723, 93725

* * *

TWENTY-SECOND DISTRICT

DEVIN NUNES, Republican, of Tulare, CA; born in Tulare County, CA, October 1, 1973; education: A.A., College of the Sequoias; B.S., agricultural business, and a master's degree in agriculture, from California Polytechnic State University, San Luis Obispo; graduate, California Agriculture Leadership Fellowship Program; professional: farmer and businessman; elected, College of the Sequoias Board of Trustees, 1996, reelected, 2000; appointed by President George W. Bush to serve as California State Director of the U.S. Department of Agriculture Rural Development Office, 2001; religion: Catholic; married: the former Elizabeth Tamariz, 2003; three children; committees: Ways and Means; Joint Committee on Taxation; Permanent Select Committee on Intelligence; elected to the 108th Congress on November 5, 2002; reelected to each succeeding Congress.

Office Listings

https://nunes.house.gov

1013 Longworth House Office Building, Washington, DC 20515 .... (202) 225–2523
Chief of Staff.—Jilian Plank. FAX: 225–3404
Legislative Director.—Ian Foley.
Communications Director.—Jack Langer.
Scheduler.—Jennifer Morrow.
113 North Church Street, Suite 208, Visalia, CA 93291 .... (559) 733–3861
264 Clovis Avenue, Suite 206, Clovis, CA 93612 .... (559) 323–5235

Counties: FRESNO (part) AND TULARE. Population (2010), 702,904.

ZIP Codes: 93201, 93207–08, 93212, 93215, 93218–19, 93221, 93223, 93227, 93235, 93237, 93242, 93244, 93247, 93256–58, 93260–62, 93265, 93267, 93270–72, 93274–75, 93277–79, 93286, 93290–92, 93602–03, 93605, 93609, 93611–13, 93615–16, 93618, 93621, 93625–26, 93628, 93631, 93633–34, 93641–42, 93646–49, 93651, 93654, 93656–57, 93662, 93664, 93666–67, 93670, 93673, 93675, 93703, 93710, 93720, 93726–27, 93740, 93747

* * *

TWENTY-THIRD DISTRICT

KEVIN McCARTHY, Republican, of Bakersfield, CA; born in Bakersfield, January 26, 1965; education: graduated, Bakersfield High School, 1983; B.S., business administration, CSU-Bakersfield, 1989; M.B.A., CSU-Bakersfield, 1994; professional: intern, worked up to District Director for U.S. Congressman Bill Thomas, 1987–2002; served as trustee, Kern Community College District, 2000–02; served in the California State Assembly, 2002–06; elected, California Assembly Republican Leader, 2003–06; married to the former Judy Wages, 1992; two children: Connor and Meghan; elected, House Majority Whip, 2011–14; elected, House Majority Leader, 2014–19; elected, House Republican Leader, 2019–present; committees: Financial Services (on leave); elected to the 110th Congress on November 7, 2006; reelected to each succeeding Congress.

Office Listings

https://kevinmccarthy.house.gov https://facebook.com/RepKevinMcCarthy twitter: @GOPleader

2468 Rayburn House Office Building, Washington, DC 20515 .... (202) 225–2915
Chief of Staff.—James Min. FAX: 225–2908
Scheduler.—Alexandra Gourdikian.
Legislative Director.—Kyle Lombardi.
Senior Legislative Assistant.—Trevor Smith.
Press Secretary.—Brittany Martinez.
4100 Empire Drive, Suite 150, Bakersfield, CA 93309 .... (661) 327–3611
District Administrator.—Robin Lake Foster.
District Scheduler.—Christiana Duncan.

Counties: KERN COUNTY (part). CITIES AND TOWNSHIPS: Arvin, Bakersfield, Bodfish, Boron, Caliente, California City, Cantil, China Lake, Edison, Edwards, Fellows, Frazier Park, Glennville, Havilah, Inyokern, Keene, Kernville, Lake Isabella, Lebec, Maricopa, McKittrick, MojAvenue, Monolith, North Edwards, Onyx, Randsburg, Ridgecrest, Rosamond, Taft, Tehachapi, Tupman, Weldon, Willow Springs, Wofford Heights, and Woody. TULARE COUNTY (part). CITIES AND TOWNSHIPS: Badger, California Hot Springs, Exeter, Lemon Cove, Lindsay, Orosi, Porterville, Posey, Springville, Strathmore, Terra Bella, Three Rivers, Visalia, and Woodlake. LOS ANGELES COUNTY (part). CITIES AND TOWNSHIPS: Lancaster. Population (2012), 707,345.

ZIP Codes: 93203, 93205, 93207–08, 93221–22, 93224–26, 93238, 93240, 93243–44, 93247, 93251–52, 93255, 93257, 93260, 93262, 93265, 93267–68, 93270–71, 93276, 93283, 93285–87, 93292, 93301, 93304–07, 93309, 93311–14, 93501, 93505, 93516, 93518–19, 93523, 93527–28, 93531, 93534, 93536, 93554–55, 93560–61, 93603, 93633, 93647

* * *

TWENTY-FOURTH DISTRICT

SALUD O. CARBAJAL, Democrat, of Santa Barbara, CA; born in Moroleón, Mexico, November 11, 1956; education: B.A., Iberian studies, University of California, Santa Barbara, 1990; M.A., organizational management, Fielding University, 2004; military: U.S. Marine Corps Reserve veteran; religion: Catholic; wife: Gina Carbajal; children: Natasha and Michael; caucuses: Congressional Hispanic Caucus; New Democratic Coalition; Problem Solvers Caucus; committees: Agriculture; Armed Services; Transportation and Infrastructure; elected to the 115th Congress on November 8, 2016; reelected to the 116th Congress on November 6, 2018.

Office Listings

https://carbajal.house.gov https://facebook.com/repsaludcarbajal twitter: @RepCarbajal

1431 Longworth House Office Building, Washington, DC 20515 .... (202) 225–3601
Chief of Staff.—Jeremy Tittle.
Executive Assistant.—Erin Sandlin.
Legislative Director.—Nancy Juarez.
Communications Director.—Tess Whittlesey.
Senior Defense Policy Advisor.—Annie Yea.
Legislative Assistant.—Johanna Montiel.
Legislative Correspondent.—Max Hokit.
Press / Staff Assistant.—Leila Miller.
1411 Marsh Street, Suite 205, San Luis Obispo, CA 93401 .... (805) 546–8348
District Representatives: Caitlin Cox, Greg Haas, Erica Reyes.
360 South Hope Avenue, Suite C–301, Santa Barbara, CA 93105 .... (805) 730–1710
District Director.—Christopher Henson.
District Scheduler.—Diana Villanueva.
District Representatives: Jesse Ebadi, Blanca Figueroa, Wendy Motta.
1619 South Thornburg Street, Santa Maria, CA 93458.

Counties: SAN LUIS OBISPO COUNTY (all). CITIES AND TOWNSHIPS: Arroyo Grande, Atascadero, Baywood-Los Osos, Cambria, Cayucos, Grover Beach, Morro Bay, Nipomo, Oceano, Paso Robles, Pismo Beach, and San Luis Obispo. SANTA BARBARA COUNTY (all). CITIES AND TOWNSHIPS: Carpinteria, Goleta, Guadalupe, Isla Vista, Mission Canyon, Montecito, Santa Barbara, Santa Maria, Summerland, and Toro Canyon. VENTURA COUNTY (part). CITIES AND TOWNSHIPS: Ventura. Population (2010), 708,744.

ZIP Codes: 93001, 93013–14, 93067, 93101–21, 93130, 93140, 93150, 93160, 93190, 93199, 93254, 93401–12, 93420–24, 93427–30, 93432–37, 93440–49, 93451–58, 93460–61, 93463–65, 93475, 93483, 94338

* * *

TWENTY-FIFTH DISTRICT

MIKE GARCIA, Republican, of Santa Clarita, CA; born in Granada Hills, CA, April 24, 1976; graduated from Saugus High School, Santa Clarita, CA, 1994; B.S., political science, U.S. Naval Academy, Annapolis, MD, 1998; M.A., National Security Studies, Georgetown University, Washington, DC, 1998; U.S. Navy, 1999–2009; U.S. Navy Reserve, 2009–12; business executive, Raytheon Company, 2009–18; real estate developer; married, Rebecca Garcia; two children; committees: Homeland Security; Science, Space, and Technology; Transportation and Infrastructure; elected to the 116th Congress by special election on May 12, 2020 to fill the vacancy caused by the resignation of U.S. Representative Katie Hill.

Office Listings

https://mikegarcia.house.gov

1130 Longworth House Office Building, Washington, DC 20515 .... (202) 225–1956
Chief of Staff.—Morris Thomas.
23734 Valencia Boulevard, Suite 206, Santa Clarita, CA 91355 .... (661) 568–4855
District Director.—Angela Giacchetti.
1008 West Avenue, M–14, Suite E, Palmdale, CA 93551 .... (661) 839–0532
1445 East Los Angeles Avenue, Suite 206, Simi Valley, CA 93065 .... (661) 802–0244

Counties: NORTHERN LOS ANGELES (part) AND VENTURA (part). CITIES: Lancaster, Northern San Fernando Valley (part), Palmdale, Santa Clarita, and Simi Valley. Population (2010), 702,904.

ZIP Codes: 91304, 91311, 91321, 91326, 91344, 91350–51, 91354–55, 91381, 91384, 91387, 91390, 93063, 93065, 93243, 93510, 93532, 93534–36, 93543–44, 93550–53, 93563, 93591

* * *

TWENTY-SIXTH DISTRICT

JULIA BROWNLEY, Democrat, of Westlake Village, CA; born in Aiken, SC, August 28, 1952; education: B.A., Mount Vernon College at George Washington University, 1975; M.B.A., American University, 1979; professional: product manager, Steelcase, 1984–92; sales manager, Pitney Bowes, 1981–84; sales manager, Burroughs Corporation, 1976–81; Santa Monica-Malibu School Board, 1994–2006; California State Assembly, 2007–12; chair of California State Assembly Committee on Education; children: Fred and Hannah; committees: Transportation and Infrastructure; Veterans' Affairs; Select Committee on the Climate Crisis; elected to the 113th Congress on November 6, 2012; reelected to each succeeding Congress.

Office Listings

https://juliabrownley.house.gov https://facebook.com/RepBrownley twitter: @RepBrownley

2262 Rayburn House Office Building, Washington, DC 20515 .... (202) 225–5811
Chief of Staff.—Lenny Young. FAX: 225–1100
Legislative Director.—Sharon Wagener.
Communications Director.—Carina Armenta.
Scheduler.—Ryan Dillon.
201 East Fourth Street, Suite 209B, Oxnard, CA 93030 .... (805) 379–1779
223 East Thousand Oaks Boulevard, Suite 220, Thousand Oaks, CA 91360 .... (805) 379–1779
District Director.—Nina Moussavi. FAX: 379–1799

Counties: LOS ANGELES (part) AND VENTURA (part). Population (2010), 702,905.

ZIP Codes: 91320, 91360–62, 91377, 93003–04, 93010, 93012, 93015, 93021–23, 93030, 93033, 93035–36, 93040–41, 93060, 93065–66

* * *

TWENTY-SEVENTH DISTRICT

JUDY M. CHU, Democrat, of Pasadena, CA; born in Los Angeles, CA, July 7, 1953; education: B.A., math, UCLA, Los Angeles, CA, 1974; Ph.D., psychology, California School of Professional Psychology, 1979; professional: Garvey School District Board member, 1985–88; Monterey Park City Council and Mayor, 1988–2001; California State Assembly, 2001–06; California State Board of Equalization, 2006–09; first Chinese-American woman elected to Congress; family: married to former Assemblymember Mike Eng in 1978; caucuses: chair, Congressional Asian Pacific American Caucus; co-chair, Creative Rights Caucus; committees: Small Business; Ways and Means; elected to the 111th Congress on July 14, 2009, by special election, to fill the vacancy caused by the resignation of U.S. Representative Hilda Solis; reelected to each succeeding Congress.

Office Listings

https://chu.house.gov https://twitter.com/repjudychu

2423 Rayburn House Office Building, Washington, DC 20515 .... (202) 225–5464
Chief of Staff.—Linda Shim. FAX: 225–5467
Legislative Director.—Sonali Desai.
Congressional Asian Pacific American Caucus (CAPAC):
Executive Director.—Krystal Ka'ai.
Policy Advisor / Press Assistant.—Anisah Assim.
Senior Legislative Assistant.—Ellen Hamilton.
Legislative Counsel.—Rricha Mathur.
Legislative Aide.—David Silberberg.
Communications Director.—Ben Suarato.
Scheduler.—Alyssa Giammarella.
Staff Assistant.—Nell Menefee-Libey.
527 South Lake Avenue, Suite 250, Pasadena, CA 91101 .... (626) 304–0110
District Director.—Becky Cheng. FAX: 304–0132
Deputy District Director.—Enrique Robles.
Field Representative / Case Worker.—Maile Plan.
Constituent Services Representatives: Lauren Jacobs, Cindy Lee.
District Scheduler.—Lindsay Plake.
Staff Assistant.—Jonathan Horton.
415 West Foothill Boulevard, Suite 122, Claremont, CA 91711 .... (909) 625–5394
FAX: 399–0198

Counties: LOS ANGELES COUNTY (part). CITIES: Alhambra, Altadena (unincorporated), Arcadia, Bradbury, Claremont, East Pasadena (unincorporated), Glendora, Monrovia, Monterey Park, Pasadena, Rosemead, San Antonio Heights (unincorporated), San Gabriel, San Marino, Sierra Madre, South Pasadena, South San Gabriel (unincorporated), Temple City, and Upland. Population (2017), 717,980.

ZIP Codes: 91001, 91003, 91006–07, 91010, 91016–17, 91024–25, 91030–31, 91066–77, 91101–10, 91114–18, 91121, 91123–26, 91129, 91131, 91175, 91182, 91184–89, 91191, 91711, 91740–41, 91754–56, 91770–72, 91775–76, 91778, 91780, 91784–86, 91801–04, 91841, 91896, 91899

* * *

TWENTY-EIGHTH DISTRICT

ADAM B. SCHIFF, Democrat, of Burbank, CA; born in Framingham, MA, June 22, 1960; education: B.A., Stanford University, 1982; J.D., Harvard University, 1985; professional: attorney; U.S. Attorney's Office, served as a criminal prosecutor; public service: elected to the California State Senate, 1996; involved in numerous community service activities; family: married: Eve; children: Alexa and Elijah; committees: chair, Permanent Select Committee on Intelligence; on leave from Appropriations Committee; elected to the 107th Congress on November 7, 2000; reelected to each succeeding Congress.

Office Listings

https://schiff.house.gov https://facebook.com/RepAdamSchiff twitter: @repadamschiff

2269 Rayburn House Office Building, Washington, DC 20515 .... (202) 225–4176
Chief of Staff.—Jeff Lowenstein. FAX: 225–5828
Communications Director.—Patrick Boland.
Executive Assistant.—Christopher Hoven.
245 East Olive Avenue, #200, Burbank, CA 91502 .... (818) 450–2900
District Director.—Ann Peifer.

Counties: LOS ANGELES (part). CITIES: Burbank, Glendale, La Canada-Flintridge, La Crescenta, Los Angeles, Pasadena, and West Hollywood. Population (2010), 702,904.

ZIP Codes: 90004, 90026–29, 90031, 90036, 90038–39, 90046, 90048, 90068–69, 91011, 91020, 91040, 91042 (part), 91103, 91105, 91201–08, 91214, 91352 (part), 91501–02, 91504–06

* * *

TWENTY-NINTH DISTRICT

ANTONIO CÁRDENAS, Democrat, of San Fernando Valley, CA; born in Pacoima, CA, March 31, 1963; education: B.A., University of California at Santa Barbara, 1986; professional: businessman; public service: California State Assembly, 1996–2002; Los Angeles City Council, 2002–13; religion: Christian; family: married to Norma Sanchez; children: Andres, Alina, Vanessa, and Cristian; committees: Energy and Commerce; elected to the 113th Congress on November 6, 2012; reelected to each succeeding Congress.

Office Listings

https://cardenas.house.gov https://facebook.com/CongressmanCardenas twitter: @RepCardenas
https://instagram.com/repcardenas https://youtube.com/repcardenas

2438 Rayburn House Office Building, Washington, DC 20515 .... (202) 225–6131
Chief of Staff.—Miguel Franco. FAX: 225–0819
Deputy Chief of Staff / Legislative Director.—Tejasi Thatte.
Communications Director.—Bryan Doyle.
9612 Van Nuys Boulevard, Suite 201, Panorama City, CA 91402 .... (818) 221–3718
District Director.—Gabriela Marquez.

Counties: LOS ANGELES. Population (2017), 713,745.

ZIP Codes: 91040, 91321, 91331, 91340, 91342–45, 91352, 91387, 91401–02, 91405–06, 91411, 91504–05, 91601–02, 91605–07

* * *

THIRTIETH DISTRICT

BRAD SHERMAN, Democrat, of Sherman Oaks, CA; born in Los Angeles, CA, October 24, 1954; education: B.A., *summa cum laude,* UCLA, 1974; J.D., *magna cum laude,* Harvard Law School, 1979; professional: admitted to the California Bar in 1979 and began practice in Los Angeles; attorney; CPA; certified tax law specialist; elected to the California State Board of Equalization, 1990, serving as chairman, 1991–95; committees: Financial Services; Foreign Affairs; Science, Space, and Technology; elected to the 105th Congress; reelected to each succeeding Congress.

Office Listings

https://sherman.house.gov https://facebook.com/CongessmanBradSherman twitter: @bradsherman

2181 Rayburn House Office Building, Washington, DC 20515 .... (202) 225–5911
Chief of Staff.—Don MacDonald. FAX: 225–5879
5000 Van Nuys Boulevard, Suite 420, Sherman Oaks, CA 91403 .... (818) 501–9200

Office Listings—Continued

District Director.—Scott Abrams.

Counties: LOS ANGELES (part). Population (2013), 744,617.

ZIP Codes: 90046, 90049, 90068, 90077, 90210, 90290, 91302–09, 91311, 91313, 91316, 91324–30, 91335, 91337, 91342–45, 91356–57, 91364–65, 91367, 91371, 91381, 91394, 91396, 91401, 91403, 91406, 91411, 91413, 91416, 91423, 91426, 91436, 91505–06, 91522–23, 91601–02, 91604, 91607–08, 91610, 91614, 91617, 93063

* * *

THIRTY-FIRST DISTRICT

PETE AGUILAR, Democrat, of Redlands, CA; born in Fontana, San Bernardino County, CA, June 19, 1979; education: B.S., University of Redlands, Redlands, CA, 2001; professional: business owner; interim director and deputy director, Inland Empire Regional Office of the Governor of California, 2001; member of the Redlands, California City Council, 2006–14; Mayor of Redlands, CA, 2010–14; married: Alisha; children: Evan and Palmer; committees: Appropriations, House Administration; elected to the 114th Congress on November 4, 2014; reelected to each succeeding Congress.

Office Listings

https://aguilar.house.gov https://facebook.com/reppeteaguilar twitter: @RepPeteAguilar

109 Cannon House Office Building, Washington, DC 20515 .... (202) 225–3201
District Chief of Staff.—Boris Medzhibovsky. FAX: 226–6962
DC Chief of Staff.—Becky Cornell.
Legislative Director.—Stephanie Cuevas.
Communications Director.—Parker Dorrough.
685 East Carnegie Drive, Suite 100, San Bernardino, CA 92408 .... (909) 890–4445
District Director.—Teresa Valdez. FAX: 890–9643

Counties: SAN BERNARDINO (part). CITIES AND TOWNSHIPS: Colton, Fontana, Grand Terrace, Loma Linda, Rancho Cucamonga, Redlands, Rialto, San Bernardino, and Upland. Population (2011), 727,523.

ZIP Codes: 91701, 91730, 91737, 91739, 91785–86, 92313, 92316, 92324, 92335–36, 92346, 92350, 92354, 92357, 92359, 92373–74, 92376–77, 92399, 92401, 92404–05, 92407–08, 92410–11

* * *

THIRTY-SECOND DISTRICT

GRACE F. NAPOLITANO, Democrat, of Los Angeles, CA; born in Brownsville, TX, December 4, 1936; education: Brownsville High School, Brownsville, TX; Cerritos College, Norwalk, CA; Texas Southmost College, Brownsville, TX; professional: transportation coordinator, Ford Motor Company; elected to Norwalk, California, City Council, 1986; became Mayor of Norwalk, 1989; elected to the California Assembly, 58th District, 1992–98; organizations: Norwalk Lions Club; Veterans of Foreign Wars (auxiliary); American Legion (auxiliary); Soroptimist International; past director, Cerritos College Foundation; director, Community Family Guidance Center; League of United Latin American Citizens; director, Los Angeles County Sanitation District; director, Los Angeles County Vector Control (Southeast District); director, Southeast Los Angeles Private Industry Council; director, Los Angeles County Sheriff's Authority; National Women's Political Caucus; past national board secretary, United States-Mexico Sister Cities Association; caucuses: co-chair, Congressional Mental Health Caucus; Congressional Hispanic Caucus; maiden name: Flores; widowed: Frank Napolitano (deceased); children: Yolanda Louwers (deceased), Fred Musquiz, Edward Musquiz, Michael Musquiz, and Cynthia Dowling; committees: Natural Resources; Transportation and Infrastructure; elected to the 106th Congress; reelected to each succeeding Congress.

Office Listings

https://napolitano.house.gov https://facebook.com/repgracenapolitano
https://twitter.com/gracenapolitano https://youtube.com/repgracenapolitano

1610 Longworth House Office Building, Washington, DC 20515 .... (202) 225–5256

Office Listings—Continued

Chief of Staff.—Daniel Chao. FAX: 225–0027
Legislative Director.—Joe Sheehy.
Press Secretary.—Jerry O'Donnell.
Scheduler.—Joseph Ciccone.
4401 Santa Anita Avenue, Suite 201, El Monte, CA 91731 .... (626) 350–0150
District Director.—Perla Hernandez.

Counties: LOS ANGELES (part). Population (2010), 702,905.

ZIP Codes: 91009–10, 91016–17, 91702, 91706, 91714–16, 91722–24, 91731–32, 91734–35, 91744, 91746–47, 91749–50, 91773, 91790–93, 91797

* * *

THIRTY-THIRD DISTRICT

TED LIEU, Democrat, of Torrance, CA; born in Taipei, Taiwan, March 29, 1969; education: B.A., political science, Stanford University, 1991; B.S., computer science, Stanford University, CA, 1991; J.D., Georgetown University Law Center, 1994; professional: admitted to the California State Bar, 1994; U.S. Air Force, 1995–99; United States Air War College, 2012; U.S. Air Force Reserve, 2000–present; Air Force Humanitarian Service Medal; Air Force Commendation Medal; Air Force Meritorious Service Medal; Torrance City Council member, 2002–05; California State Assemblyman, 2005–10; California State Senator, 2011–14; married to Betty Chim; children: Brennan and Austin; elected as president of the Democratic Freshman Class, 2015–16; committees: Foreign Affairs; Judiciary; elected to the 114th Congress on November 4, 2014; reelected to each succeeding Congress.

Office Listings

https://lieu.house.gov https://facebook.com/tedlieu twitter: @reptedlieu

403 Cannon House Office Building, Washington, DC 20515 .... (202) 225–3976
Chief of Staff.—Marc Cevasco.
Legislative Director.—Corey Jacobson.
Communications Director.—Jenna Bushnell.
Scheduler.—Harshitha Teppala.
1645 Corinth Avenue, Suite 101, Los Angeles, CA 90025 .... (323) 651–1040
1600 Rosecrans Avenue, 4th Floor, Manhattan Beach, CA 90266 .... (310) 321–7664
District Director.—Nicolas Rodriquez.

Counties: LOS ANGELES COUNTY (part). CITIES AND TOWNSHIPS: Agoura Hills, Bel-Air, Beverly Hills, Brentwood, Calabasas, El Segundo, Hermosa Beach, Malibu, Manhattan Beach, Marina Del Rey, Pacific Palisades, Palos Verdes Estates, Rancho Palos Verdes, Redondo Beach, Rolling Hills, Rolling Hills Estates, Santa Monica, Topanga, Venice, and Vista Del Mar. The 33rd Congressional District also includes a portion of the COMMUNITIES of Hancock Park, Harbor City, San Pedro, Torrance, West Los Angeles, and Westwood. Population (2010), 707,854.

ZIP Codes: 90004 (part), 90020 (part), 90024 (part), 90036, 90048–49, 90073, 90077, 90095, 90209, 90211–13, 90245, 90254, 90263–67, 90272, 90274–75, 90277–78, 90290–95, 90401–08 (part), 90409–11, 90503 (part), 90505 (part), 90710 (part), 90731–32 (part), 90744 (part), 91301–02, 91376

* * *

THIRTY-FOURTH DISTRICT

JIMMY GOMEZ, Democrat, of Los Angeles, CA; born in Fullerton, CA, November 25, 1974; education: graduated, Ramona High School, Riverside, 1993; attended Riverside Community College, 1993–96; B.A., University of California Los Angeles, 1999; M.P.P., Harvard John F. Kennedy School of Government, Cambridge, MA, 2003; professional: Assemblyman, California State Legislature, Sacramento, CA, 2012–17; political director, United Nurses Association of California, Los Angeles, CA, 2009–12; political representative, American Federation of State, County and Municipal Employees, Los Angeles, 2006–09; field operations assistant, National League of Cities, Washington, DC, 2005–06; married to Mary Hodge; caucuses: Congressional Asian Pacific American Caucus; Congressional Hispanic Caucus; Congressional LGBT Equality Caucus; Congressional Progressive Caucus; Future Forum; committees: Oversight and Reform; Ways and Means; elected, by special election, to the 115th Congress on June 6, 2017, to fill the vacancy caused by the resignation of U.S. Representative Xavier Becerra; reelected to the 116th Congress on November 6, 2018.

Office Listings

https://gomez.house.gov https://facebook.com/RepJimmyGomez twitter: @RepJimmyGomez

1530 Longworth House Office Building, Washington, DC 20515 .... (202) 225–6235
Chief of Staff.—Bertha Alisia Guerrero.
Counsel and Legislative Director.—Samuel Negatu.
Senior Advisor and Communications Director.—Eric Harris.
Senior Legislative Assistant.—Charlie Arnowitz.
Legislative Assistant.—Diana Rios.
Legislative Correspondent.—Maria Martirosyan.
350 South Bixel Street, #120, Los Angeles, CA 90017 .... (213) 481–1425
District Director.—Marcella Cortez.
Office Manager.—Michael Nielsen.
Senior Field Deputy.—Roberto Gama.
Field Deputy.—Rolando Chavez.
Caseworker.—Cindy Muro.
Digital Content Manager.—Daniel Santa Cruz.

Counties: LOS ANGELES COUNTY (part). CITIES: Los Angeles. Population (2010), 698,741.

ZIP Codes: 90004–07, 90010, 90012–15, 90017–23, 90026, 90030–33, 90038, 90041–42, 90053, 90057, 90063, 90065, 90071, 90079, 90086, 90090

* * *

THIRTY-FIFTH DISTRICT

NORMA J. TORRES, Democrat, of Pomona, CA; born in Escuintla, Guatemala; education: B.A., labor studies, National Labor College, Silver Spring, MD, 2012; professional: 9–1–1 dispatcher; Pomona City Council, 2000–06; Mayor of Pomona, 2006–08; member of the California State Assembly, 2008–13; member of the California State Senate, 2013–14; married: Louis; children: Robert, Matthew, and Christopher; one grandchild; caucuses: chair, Central America Caucus; chair, New American Caucus; Ahmadiyya Caucus; Animal Protection Caucus; Arthritis Caucus; Cancer Prevention Caucus; Caucus for Effective Foreign Assistance; Congressional Hispanic Caucus; Congressional Human Trafficking Caucus; Congressional Law Enforcement Caucus; Congressional Native American Caucus; Diabetes Caucus; Former Mayor's Caucus; Foster Youth Caucus; Hospitality Caucus; Job Corps Caucus; Manufacturing Caucus; NextGen 9–1–1 Caucus; PORTS Caucus; Primary Care Caucus; Gun Violence Prevention Task Force; Poverty Income Inequality, and Opportunity Task Force; Tom Lantos Human Rights Commission; committees: Appropriations; Rules; elected to the 114th Congress on November 4, 2014; reelected to each succeeding Congress.

Office Listings

https://torres.house.gov https://facebook.com/repnormatorres twitter: @normajtorres

2444 Rayburn House Office Building, Washington, DC 20515 .... (202) 225–6161
Chief of Staff.—James Cho. FAX: 225–8671
Legislative Director.—Clay Boggs.
Legislative Assistant.—Mariah Carray.
Legislative Correspondent.—Sophie Wellen.
Communications Director.—Veronica Bonilla.
Deputy Press Secretary.—Edgar Rodriguez.
Executive Assistant / Scheduler.—Leah Carey.
Staff Assistant.—Maru Vazquez.
3200 Inland Empire Boulevard, Suite 200B, Ontario, CA 91764 .... (909) 481–6474
Deputy District Directors: Daniel Enz, Marisol Guerra. FAX: 941–1362

Counties: SAN BERNARDINO COUNTY (part). CITIES: Bloomington, Chino, Fontana, Montclair, Ontario, and Rialto. LOS ANGELES COUNTY (part). CITIES: Pomona. Population (2015), 739,819.

ZIP Codes: 91708–11, 91730, 91739, 91743, 91750, 91752, 91758, 91761–69, 91786, 91789, 92316, 92324, 92331, 92334–37, 92509, 92880

* * *

THIRTY-SIXTH DISTRICT

RAUL RUIZ, M.D., Democrat, of Palm Springs, CA; born in Coachella, CA, August 25, 1972; education: B.S., University of California, Los Angeles, 1994; M.D., Harvard University,

2001; M.P.P., Harvard University, 2001; M.P.H., Harvard University, 2007; professional: emergency physician, Eisenhower Medical Center; founder, Coachella Valley Healthcare Initiative, 2010; senior associate dean, School of Medicine at University of California Riverside, 2011; caucuses: Friends of Canada Caucus; Government Efficiency Caucus; Law Enforcement Caucus; LGBT Caucus; Native American Caucus; No Labels-Problem Solvers; Renewable Energy Caucus; Seniors Task Force; Small Business Caucus; Specialty Crop Caucus; Veterans Job Caucus; committees: Energy and Commerce; elected to the 113th Congress on November 6, 2012; reelected to each succeeding Congress.

Office Listings

https://ruiz.house.gov https://facebook.com/CongressmanRaulRuizMD twitter: @CongressmanRuiz

2342 Rayburn House Office Building, Washington, DC 20515 .... (202) 225–5330
FAX: 225–1238
Chief of Staff.—Tim Del Monico.
Legislative Director.—Erin Doty.
Press Secretary.—Hernan Quintas.
Scheduler.—Lauren Heasley.
43875 Washington Street, Suite F, Palm Desert, CA 92211 .... (760) 424–8888
District Director.—Jacqueline Lopez.
445 East Florida Avenue, 2nd Floor, Hemet, CA 92543 .... (951) 765–2304

Counties: RIVERSIDE COUNTY. CITIES: Cathedral City, Coachella, Desert Hot Springs, Indian Wells, Indio, Palm Desert, Palm Springs, and Rancho Mirage. Population (2010), 714,975.

ZIP Codes: 92201–03, 92210–11, 92220, 92230, 92234, 92236, 92240–41, 92253–54, 92258, 92260, 92262, 92264, 92270, 92276, 92282, 92539, 92549, 92561, 92583

* * *

THIRTY-SEVENTH DISTRICT

KAREN R. BASS, Democrat, of Los Angeles, CA; born in Los Angeles, October 3, 1953; education: B.S., health sciences, California State University, Dominguez Hills, CA, 1990; Master of Social Work, USC, 2015; P.A., University of Southern California School of Medicine, Los Angeles; professional: elected first Democratic woman Speaker of the California Assembly; founded and served as Executive Director of the nonprofit organization Community Coalition, Los Angeles; physician assistant, Los Angeles County General Hospital; religion: Baptist; family: daughter, Emilia Bass-Lechuga, son-in-law, Michael Wright; stepchildren: Scythia, Omar, and Yvette Lechuga; awards: JFK Profile in Courage Award; Congressional Black Caucus Phoenix Award; committees: Foreign Affairs; Judiciary; elected to the 112th Congress on November 2, 2010; reelected to each succeeding Congress.

Office Listings

https://bass.house.gov https://facebook.com/RepKarenBass
https://twitter.com/RepKarenBass https://instagram.com/RepKarenBass

2059 Rayburn House Office Building, Washington, DC 20515 .... (202) 225–7084
FAX: 225–2422
Chief of Staff.—Caren Street.
Legislative Director.—Janice Bashford.
Scheduler/Executive Assistant.—Lauren Radice.
Communications Director.—Zach Seidl.
4929 Wilshire Boulevard, Suite 650, Los Angeles, CA 90010 .... (323) 965–1422
District Director.—Darryn Harris.

Counties: LOS ANGELES (part). CITIES: Culver City and Los Angeles. COMMUNITIES: Ladera Heights and View Park-Windsor Hills. Population (2010), 702,904.

ZIP Codes: 90004–08, 90010–11, 90016, 90018–20, 90022, 90026–29, 90033–39, 90043–45, 90047–48, 90053, 90056–58, 90062–64, 90066, 90068, 90070, 90078, 90083, 90093, 90099, 90103, 90230–33

* * *

THIRTY-EIGHTH DISTRICT

LINDA T. SÁNCHEZ, Democrat, of Lakewood, CA; born in Orange, CA, January 28, 1969; education: B.A., University of California, Berkeley; J.D., UCLA Law School; passed bar exam in 1995; professional: attorney; has practiced in the areas of appellate, civil rights, and employment law; International Brotherhood of Electrical Workers Local 441; National Electrical Contractors Association; Orange County Central Labor Council Executive Secretary, AFL–CIO; religion: Catholic; caucuses: co-founder and co-chair, Congressional Labor and Working Families Caucus; vice chair, LGBT Equality Caucus; Congressional Hispanic Caucus; Congressional Progressive Caucus; committees: Ways and Means; elected to the 108th Congress on November 5, 2002; reelected to each succeeding Congress.

Office Listings

https://lindasanchez.house.gov twitter: @RepLindaSanchez

2329 Rayburn House Office Building, Washington, DC 20515 .... (202) 225–6676
Chief of Staff.—Lea Sulkala. FAX: 226–1012
Legislative Director.—Melissa Kiedrowicz.
Press Secretary.—Jacob Abbott.
12440 East Imperial Highway, Suite 140, Norwalk, CA 90650 .... (562) 860–5050
District Director.—Yvette Shahinian.

Counties: Los Angeles (part). Population (2010), 715,745.

ZIP Codes: 90601–06, 90623, 90638, 90701, 90703, 90706, 90716, 90712–13, 90715, 90640, 90650, 90660, 90670, 91733

* * *

THIRTY-NINTH DISTRICT

GILBERT R. CISNEROS, Jr., Democrat, of Yorba Linda, CA; born in Torrance, CA, February 12, 1971; education: B.A., George Washington University, Washington, DC, 1994; M.B.A., Regis University, Denver, CO, 2002; M.A., Brown University, Providence, RI, 2015; professional: small business owner; corporate manager; nonprofit executive; Lieutenant Commander, United States Navy, 1994–2004; member: American Legion Post 277; Los Angeles Chamber of Commerce; awards: Hispanic Scholarship Fund Hall of Fame; religion: Catholic; married: Jacki Wells, 2005; children: Christopher and Alexander; caucuses: Congressional Asian Pacific American Caucus; Congressional Hispanic Caucus; Congressional Progressive Caucus; For Country Caucus; LGBT Equality Caucus; New Democrats; Sustainable Energy and Environment Coalition; committees: Armed Services; Veterans' Affairs; elected to the 116th Congress on November 6, 2018.

Office Listings

https://cisneros.house.gov https://facebook.com/RepGilCisneros
https://twitter.com/RepGilCisneros https://instagram.com/repgilcisneros
https://youtube.com/channel/UC9Z5B59ZgKD-JPZ7_BSAZMA

431 Cannon House Office Building, Washington, DC 20515 .... (202) 225–4111
Chief of Staff.—Nic Jordan.
Communications Director.—Michael Quibuyen.
Legislative Director.—Emma Norvell.
Scheduler.—Annie Campbell.
1440 North Harbor Boulevard, Suite 601, Fullerton, CA 92835 .... (714) 459–4575
District Director.—Marc Hanson.
20995 Pathfinder Road, Suite 330, Diamond Bar, CA 91765.

Counties: California's 39th District encompasses cities in northern Orange County, eastern Los Angeles County, and southwestern San Bernardino County. Cities: Brea, Buena Park, Chino Hills, Diamond Bar, Fullerton, Hacienda Heights, La Habra, Placentia, Rowland Heights, Walnut, and Yorba Linda. Population (2013), 721,014.

ZIP Codes: 90603, 90620–22, 90624, 90631–33, 90638, 91709–10, 91745–46, 91748–49, 91765–66, 91768, 91788–89, 92801, 92806–07, 92811, 92817, 92821–23, 92831–38, 92865, 92867, 92870–71, 92885–87, 92899

* * *

FORTIETH DISTRICT

LUCILLE ROYBAL-ALLARD, Democrat, of Los Angeles, CA; born in Los Angeles, June 12, 1941; education: B.A., California State University, Los Angeles, 1965; professional: served in the California State Assembly, 1987–92; the first Mexican-American woman elected to Congress on November 3, 1992 to the 103rd Congress; the first woman to serve as the chair of the California Democratic Congressional Delegation in the 105th Congress; in the 106th Congress, she became the first woman to chair the Congressional Hispanic Caucus, and the first Latina in history to be appointed to the House Appropriations Committee; in the 114th Congress, she became the first Latina to serve as ranking member of a House Appropriations subcommittee; and in the 116th Congress, she became the first Latina to serve as chairwoman of a House Appropriations subcommittee; appointed to the Smithsonian Institution Board of Regents in 2019; married: Edward T. Allard III; two children: Lisa Marie and Ricardo; two stepchildren: Angela and Guy Mark; committees: Appropriations; elected to the 103rd Congress; reelected to each succeeding Congress.

Office Listings

https://roybal-allard.house.gov https://facebook.com/RepRoybalAllard
https://twitter.com/RepRoybalAllard https://instagram.com/RepRoybalAllard
https://youtube.com/RepRoybalAllard

2083 Rayburn House Office Building, Washington, DC 20515–0534 .... (202) 225–1766
Chief of Staff.—Victor G. Castillo. FAX: 226–0350
Legislative Director.—Josh Caplan.
Executive Assistant.—Christine C. Ochoa.
500 Citadel Drive, Suite 320, Commerce, CA 90040–1572 .... (323) 721–8790
District Director.—Ana Figueroa. FAX: 721–8789

Counties: LOS ANGELES COUNTY (part). CITIES: Bell, Bell Gardens, Bellflower (part), Commerce, Cudahy, Downey, East Los Angeles (part), Florence-Firestone (part), Huntington Park, Maywood, Paramount, South Los Angeles (part), and Vernon. Population (2010), 694,514.

ZIP Codes: 90001, 90003, 90007, 90011, 90015, 90021–23, 90037, 90040, 90052, 90058–59, 90063, 90082, 90091, 90201–02, 90239–42, 90255, 90270, 90280, 90640, 90660, 90706, 90723, 91754

* * *

FORTY-FIRST DISTRICT

MARK TAKANO, Democrat, of Riverside, CA; born in Riverside, December 10, 1960; education: B.A. in government, Harvard College, 1983; M.A. in fine arts, University of California Riverside, 2010; professional: public school teacher; Riverside Community College District Board Trustee; awards: chairman of the Asian Pacific Islander Caucus of the California Democratic Party; charter member of the Association of Latino Community College Trustees; member of the Association of California Asian American Trustees; member of Asian Pacific Americans in Higher Education; recipient of Martin Luther King Visionaries Award; religion: Methodist; committees: chair, Veterans' Affairs; Education and Labor; elected to the 113th Congress on November 6, 2012; reelected to each succeeding Congress.

Office Listings

https://takano.house.gov https://twitter.com/repmarktakano

420 Cannon House Office Building, Washington, DC 20515 .... (202) 225–2305
Chief of Staff.—Richard Kirk McPike. FAX: 225–7018
Legislative Director.—Justin Maturo.
3403 10th Street, Suite 610, Riverside, CA 92501 .... (951) 222–0203
District Director.—Rafael Elizalde.

Counties: RIVERSIDE (part). CITIES: Jurupa Valley, Moreno Valley, Perris, and Riverside. Population (2010), 797,133.

ZIP Codes: 91572, 92324, 92373, 92501, 92503–09, 92518, 92551, 92553, 92555, 92557, 92570–71, 92880

* * *

FORTY-SECOND DISTRICT

KEN CALVERT, Republican, of Corona, CA; born in Corona, June 8, 1953; education: A.A., Chaffey College, CA, 1973; B.A. in economics, San Diego State University, 1975; professional: congressional aide to Representative Victor V. Veysey, CA; general manager, Jolly Fox Restaurant, Corona, 1975–79; Marcus W. Meairs Co., Corona, 1979–81; president and general manager, Ken Calvert Real Properties, 1981–92; County Youth Chairman, Representative Veysey's District, 1970–72; Corona/Norco Youth Chairman for Nixon, 1968 and 1972; Reagan-Bush campaign worker, 1980; co-chairman, Wilson for Senate Campaign, 1982; chairman, Riverside

Republican Party, 1984–88; co-chairman, George Deukmejian election, 1978, 1982, and 1986; co-chairman, George Bush election, 1988; co-chairman, Pete Wilson Senate elections, 1982 and 1988; co-chairman, Pete Wilson for Governor election, 1990; chairman and charter member, Lincoln Club of Riverside County, 1986–90; past president, Corona Rotary Club; Corona Elks; Navy League of Corona/Norco; Corona Chamber of Commerce; past chairman, Norco Chamber of Commerce; County of Riverside Asset Leasing; past chairman, Corona/Norco Board of Realtors; Monday Morning Group; Corona Group; executive board, Economic Development Partnership; charter member, Corona Community Hospital Corporate 200 Club; Silver Eagles (March AFB Support Group); Corona Airport Advisory Commission; committees: Appropriations; elected on November 3, 1992 to the 103rd Congress; reelected to each succeeding Congress.

Office Listings

https://calvert.house.gov https://facebook.com/RepKenCalvert twitter: @kencalvert

2205 Rayburn House Office Building, Washington, DC 20515 .... (202) 225–1986
Chief of Staff.—Dave Kennett. FAX: 225–2004
Chief of Staff/Operations.—Tricia Evans.
Chief of Staff/Policy and Appropriations.—Rebecca Keightley.
400 South Vicentia Avenue, Suite 125, Corona, CA 92882 .... (951) 277–0042
District Director.—Jolyn Murphy.
Senior Advisor/Press Secretary.—Jason Gagnon.

Counties: RIVERSIDE COUNTY. CITIES AND TOWNSHIPS: Canyon Lake, Corona, Eastvale, Lake Elsinore, Menifee, Murrieta, Norco, a portion of Temecula, and Wildomar. Population (2010), 710,617.

ZIP Codes: 91752, 92028, 92223, 92503–04, 92506–08, 92530–32, 92536, 92544–45, 92548, 92555, 92562–63, 92567, 92570–71, 92582, 92584–87, 92590–92, 92595–96, 92860, 92877–83

* * *

FORTY-THIRD DISTRICT

MAXINE WATERS, Democrat, of Los Angeles, CA; born in St. Louis, MO, August 15, 1938; education: B.A., California State University; honorary degrees: Harris-Stowe State College, St. Louis, MO; Central State University, Wilberforce, OH; Spelman College, Atlanta, GA; North Carolina A&T State University; Howard University; Central State University; Bishop College; and Morgan State University; professional: elected to California State Assembly, 1976; reelected every 2 years thereafter; member: California State Assembly Democratic Caucus; Board of TransAfrica Foundation, National Women's Political Caucus; chair, Democratic Caucus Special Committee on Election Reform; chair, Ways and Means Subcommittee on State Administration; chair, Joint Committee on Public Pension Fund Investments; founding member, National Commission for Economic Conversion and Disarmament; member of the board, Center for National Policy; Clara Elizabeth Jackson Carter Foundation (Spelman College); Minority AIDS Project; married to Sidney Williams, former U.S. Ambassador to the Commonwealth of the Bahamas; two children: Karen and Edward; committees: chair, Financial Services; elected to the 102nd Congress on November 6, 1990; reelected to each succeeding Congress.

Office Listings

https://waters.house.gov twitter: @RepMaxineWaters

2221 Rayburn House Office Building, Washington, DC 20515 .... (202) 225–2201
Chief of Staff.—Twaun Samuel. FAX: 225–7854
Legislative Director.—Patrick Fergusson.
Communications Director.—Rykia Dorsey Craig.
10124 South Broadway, Suite 1, Los Angeles, CA 90003 .... (323) 757–8900
District Director.—Blanca Jimenez.

Counties: LOS ANGELES COUNTY (part). CITIES: Gardena, Hawthorne, Inglewood, Lawndale, Lomita, Los Angeles, Playa Del Ray, and Torrance. Population (2010), 702,983.

ZIP Codes: 90007, 90009, 90044–45, 90047, 90052, 90056, 90059, 90061, 90066, 90082, 90094, 90189, 90247–51, 90260–61, 90293, 90301–13, 90397–98, 90504, 90506, 90717

* * *

FORTY-FOURTH DISTRICT

NANETTE DIAZ BARRAGÁN, Democrat, of San Pedro, CA; born in Harbor City, CA, September 15, 1976; education: J.D., University of Southern California, Los Angeles, CA, 2005; caucuses: Congressional Hispanic Caucus; Congressional Progressive Caucus; committees: Energy and Commerce; Homeland Security; elected to the 115th Congress on November 8, 2016; reelected to the 116th Congress on November 6, 2018.

Office Listings

https://barragan.house.gov

1030 Longworth House Office Building, Washington, DC 20515 .... (202) 225–8220
Chief of Staff.—Robert Primus. FAX: 226–7290
Legislative Director.—Ernesto Rodriguez.
Scheduler.—Jenae Jackson.
302 West 5th Street, Suite 201, San Pedro, CA 90731 .... (310) 831–1799
8650 California Avenue, South Gate, CA 90280 .... (323) 563–9562
701 East Carson Street, Carson, CA 90745 .... (310) 233–4811
205 South Willowbrook Avenue, Compton, CA 90220 .... (310) 831–1799

Counties: LOS ANGELES (part). CITIES AND COMMUNITIES: Carson, Compton, Lynwood, North Long Beach, Rancho Dominguez, San Pedro, South Gate, Walnut Park, Watts, Willowbrook, and Wilmington.

ZIP Codes: 90001–05 (part), 90007 (part), 90011 (part), 90015 (part), 90018 (part), 90020–23 (part), 90025–26 (part), 90031 (part), 90037–38 (part), 90058–59 (part), 90061 (part), 90063–64 (part), 90089 (part), 90220, 90221 (part), 90222, 90223 (part), 90230 (part), 90248 (part), 90255 (part), 90262 (part), 90280, 90291–92 (part), 90302 (part), 90405 (part), 90503–05 (part), 90631 (part), 90640 (part), 90706 (part), 90710 (part), 90712 (part), 90717 (part), 90731–32 (part), 90733–34, 90744 (part), 90746–48, 90802 (part), 90805 (part), 90810–11 (part), 90895, 91016 (part), 91030 (part), 91103 (part), 91105 (part), 91124 (part), 91321 (part), 91344 (part), 91505 (part), 91702 (part), 91711 (part), 91724 (part), 91731–32 (part), 91740 (part), 91745 (part), 91754 (part), 91768 (part), 91770 (part), 91773 (part), 91789 (part), 93550–51 (part)

* * *

FORTY-FIFTH DISTRICT

KATIE PORTER, Democrat, of Irvine, CA; born in Fort Dodge, Webster County, IA, January 3, 1974; education: B.A., Yale University, New Haven, CT, 1996; J.D., Harvard University, Cambridge, MA, 2001; professional: law professor; staff, Office of the Attorney General, California State Department of Justice, 2012–14; faculty, University of California, Irvine, CA, 2011–18; children: Luke, Paul, Betsey; committees: Financial Services; Oversight and Reform; elected to the 116th Congress on November 6, 2018.

Office Listings

https://porter.house.gov https://facebook.com/repkatieporter
https://twitter.com/RepKatiePorter

1117 Longworth House Office Building, Washington, DC 20515 .... (202) 225–5611
Chief of Staff.—Amanda Fischer.
Legislative Director.—Brieana Marticorena.
Communications Director.—Jordon Wong.
Scheduler.—Elizabeth Murray.
2151 Michelson Drive, Suite 195, Irvine, CA 92612 .... (949) 668–6600
District Director.—Kelly Jones.

Counties: ORANGE COUNTY (part). CITIES: Anaheim Hills, Irvine, Laguna Hills, Lake Forest, Mission Viejo, North Tustin, Rancho Santa Margarita, Tustin, and Villa Park.

ZIP Codes: 92602–04, 92606, 92609–10, 92612, 92614, 92617–18, 92620, 92630, 92637, 92653, 92656, 92676–79, 92688, 92691–92, 92701, 92705, 92780, 92782, 92807–08, 92861, 92865, 92867, 92869, 92887

* * *

FORTY-SIXTH DISTRICT

J. LUIS CORREA, Democrat, of Santa Ana, CA; born in East Los Angeles, CA, January 24, 1958; education: graduate of California State University, Fullerton; J.D. and M.B.A., University of California Los Angeles; religion: member of Christ Cathedral Catholic Church; married: Esther Correa; four children; caucuses: Blue Dog Coalition; Congressional Hispanic Caucus; New Democrat Caucus; committees: Homeland Security; Judiciary; elected to the 115th Congress on November 8, 2016; reelected to the 116th Congress on November 6, 2018.

Office Listings

https://correa.house.gov https://facebook.com/RepLouCorrea twitter: @reploucorrea

1039 Longworth House Office Building, Washington, DC 20515 .... (202) 225–2965
Chief of Staff.—Laurie Saroff. FAX: 225–5859
Scheduler.—Julia Kermott.
Legislative Director.—Emilio Mendez.
Communications Director.—Andrew Scibetta.
Staff Assistant.—Tony Flores.
2323 North Broadway, Third Floor, Santa Ana, CA 92706.
Acting District Director.—Claudio Gallegos.

Counties: ORANGE COUNTY (part). CITIES: Anaheim, Garden Grove, Orange, and Santa Ana. Population (2010), 648,663.

ZIP Codes: 90620–21, 92606, 92614, 92701, 92703–07, 92780, 92801–07, 92840, 92843, 92865–68, 92870

* * *

FORTY-SEVENTH DISTRICT

ALAN S. LOWENTHAL, Democrat, of Long Beach, CA; born in Manhattan, New York County, NY, March 8, 1941; education: Baldwin High School, Baldwin, NY, 1958; B.A., Hobart College, Geneva, NY, 1962; M.A., Ohio State University, Columbus, OH, 1965; Ph.D., Ohio State University, Columbus, OH, 1967; professional: psychology professor, California State University, Long Beach, 1969–98; president, Long Beach Area Citizens Involved, 1989–92; member of the Long Beach, CA, City Council, 1992–98; member of the California State Assembly, 1998–2004; member of the California State Senate, 2004–12; caucuses: chair, Congressional Safe Climate Caucus; chair, Green Schools Caucus; co-chair, Cambodia Caucus; co-chair, Congressional Caucus on Vietnam; co-chair, Ports Caucus; co-chair, STARBASE Caucus; vice chair, House LGBT Equality Caucus; vice chair, Sustainable Energy and Environment Coalition; committees: Natural Resources; Transportation and Infrastructure; elected to the 113th Congress on November 6, 2012; reelected to each succeeding Congress.

Office Listings

https://lowenthal.house.gov https://facebook.com/RepLowenthal twitter: @replowenthal

108 Cannon House Office Building, Washington, DC 20515 .... (202) 225–7924
Chief of Staff.—Tim Hysom. FAX: 225–7926
Legislative Director.—Chris Gorud.
Communications Director.—Keith Higginbotham.
Scheduler.—Anthony Pham.
100 West Broadway Street, West Tower, Suite 600, Long Beach, CA 90802 .... (562) 436–3828
Deputy Chief of Staff.—Mark Pulido.

Counties: LOS ANGELES COUNTY (part). CITIES: Avalon, Lakewood, Long Beach, and Signal Hill. ORANGE COUNTY (part). CITIES: Anaheim, Buena Park, Cypress, Garden Grove, Los Alamitos, Midway City, Rossmoor, Stanton, and Westminster. Population (2013), 719,805.

ZIP Codes: 90620, 90623, 90630, 90680, 90704, 90712–13, 90716, 90720–21, 90731, 90740, 90744, 90755, 90801–10, 90813–15, 90831–35, 90840, 90842, 90844, 90846–48, 90853, 92647, 92655, 92683–85, 92703, 92801–02, 92804, 92840–46

* * *

FORTY-EIGHTH DISTRICT

HARLEY ROUDA, Democrat, of Laguna Beach, CA; born in Columbus, Franklin County, OH, December 10, 1961; education: B.A., University of Kentucky, Lexington, KY, 1984; J.D., Capital University, Columbus, OH, 1986; M.B.A., Ohio State University, Columbus, OH, 2002; professional: realtor; lawyer, private practice; business executive; married: Kaira Rouda; children: four; committees: Oversight and Reform; Transportation and Infrastructure; elected to the 116th Congress on November 6, 2018.

Office Listings

https://rouda.house.gov https://facebook.com/RepHarley twitter: @RepHarley
https://instagram.com/repharleyrouda

2300 Rayburn House Office Building, Washington, DC 20515 .... (202) 225–2415
Chief of Staff.—Emily Crerand. FAX: 226–2263
Deputy Chief of Staff / Legislative Director.—Andrew Noh.
Communications Director.—Zach Helder.
Administrative Director / Scheduler.—Caroline Bovair.
4000 Westerly Place, #270, Newport Beach, CA 92660 .... (714) 960–6483
District Director.—Laura Oatman. FAX: (833) 298–8465

Counties: ORANGE COUNTY (part). COMMUNITIES: Aliso Viejo, Corona del Mar, Costa Mesa, Fountain Valley, Garden Grove (part), Huntington Beach, Laguna Beach, Laguna Niguel, Midway City (part), Newport Beach, Santa Ana (part), Seal Beach, Sunset Beach, Surfside, and Westminster (part). Population (2010), 702,905.

ZIP Codes: 90740, 90742–43, 92625–27, 92646–49, 92651, 92655 (part), 92656–57, 92660–63, 92677, 92683 (part), 92703–04 (part), 92708, 92843–44 (part)

* * *

FORTY-NINTH DISTRICT

MIKE LEVIN, Democrat, of San Juan Capistrano, CA; born in Inglewood, CA, October 20, 1978; education: graduated from Loyola High School, Los Angeles, CA, 1997; B.A., Stanford University, Stanford, CA, 2001; J.D., Duke University, Raleigh, NC, 2005; professional: lawyer, private practice; business executive; married: Chrissy; children: Jonathan and Elizabeth; caucuses: Congressional Hispanic Caucus; Congressional Progressive Caucus; Gun Violence Prevention Taskforce; Sustainable Energy and Environment Coalition; committees: Natural Resources; Veterans' Affairs; Select Committee on the Climate Crisis; elected to the 116th Congress on November 6, 2018.

Office Listings

https://mikelevin.house.gov https://facebook.com/RepMikeLevin
https://twitter.com/RepMikeLevin https://instagram.com/RepMikeLevin
https://youtube.com/channel/UCYFDRohyZgoPy5rXOaVZO-A/featured

1626 Longworth House Office Building, Washington, DC 20515 .... (202) 225–3906
Chief of Staff.—Kara Van Stralen.
Scheduler.—Mark Foley.
2204 El Camino Real, Suite 314, Oceanside, CA 92054 .... (760) 599–5000
District Director.—Francine Busby.
33282 Golden Lantern, Suite 102, Dana Point, CA 92629 .... (949) 281–2449

Counties: ORANGE (part) AND SAN DIEGO (part). Population (2010), 702,906.

ZIP Codes: 92003, 92007–14, 92018, 92023–24, 92028–29, 92037, 92049, 92051–52, 92054–58, 92067–69, 92075, 92078, 92081, 92083–85, 92091–93, 92121, 92127, 92130, 92624, 92629, 92672–75, 92677, 92688, 92690–94

* * *

FIFTIETH DISTRICT

VACANT

Counties: SAN DIEGO COUNTY (part). CITIES AND TOWNSHIPS: Alpine, Barona I.R., Bonsall, Borrego Springs, Boulevard, Descanso, El Cajon, Escondido, Fallbrook, Guatay, Jamul, Julian, La Mesa, Lakeside, Mount Laguna, Pala, Palamar Mountain, Pauma Valley, Pine Valley, Potrero, Poway, Ramona, Ranchita, San Marcos, Santa Ysabel, Santee, Spring Valley, Temecula, Valley Center, Vista, and Warner Springs. Population (2010), 724,472.

ZIP Codes: 91901, 91903, 91916, 91931, 91935, 91941, 91948, 91962, 91978, 92003–04, 92019–21, 92025–30, 92033, 92036, 92040, 92046, 92059–61, 92064–66, 92069–72, 92078–79, 92082, 92084, 92086, 92088, 92589–93

* * *

FIFTY-FIRST DISTRICT

JUAN VARGAS, Democrat, of San Diego, CA; born in National City, CA, March 7, 1961; education: B.A., University of San Diego, San Diego, CA, 1983; M.A., Fordham University,

New York, NY, 1987; J.D., Harvard University, Cambridge, MA, 1991; professional: lawyer; business executive; member of the San Diego, CA, City Council, 1993–2000; member of the California State Assembly, 2000–06; member of the California State Senate, 2010–12; religion: Roman Catholic; spouse: Adrienne Vargas; children: Rosa Celina Vargas and Helena Jeanne Vargas; committees: Financial Services; Foreign Affairs; elected to the 113th Congress on November 6, 2012; reelected to each succeeding Congress.

Office Listings

https://vargas.house.gov https://facebook.com/RepJuanVargas https://twitter.com/repjuanvargas

2244 Rayburn House Office Building, Washington, DC 20515 ..... (202) 225–8045
Chief of Staff.—Tim Walsh. FAX: 225–2772
Scheduler / Executive Assistant.—Beth Farvour.
Legislative Director.—Scott Hinkle.
333 F Street, Suite A, Chula Vista, CA 91910 ..... (619) 422–5963
District Director.—Janine Bryant. FAX: 422–7290
380 North 8th Street, Suite 14, El Centro, CA 92243 ..... (760) 312–9900
Senior Field Representative.—Tomas Oliva. FAX: 312–9664

Counties: SAN DIEGO (part) AND IMPERIAL COUNTY. CITIES: Bombay Beach, Bonita, Boulevard, Brawley, Calexico, Calipatria, Campo, Chula Vista, Desert Shores, Dulzura, El Centro, Heber, Holtville, Imperial, Imperial Beach, Jacumba, National City, Niland, Ocotillo, Palo Verde, Potrero, Salton City, Salton City Beach, San Diego, Seeley, Westmorland, and Winterhaven. Population (2010), 702,906.

ZIP Codes: 91901–02, 91905–06, 91909–12, 91915, 91917, 91932–35, 91945, 91950–51, 91962–63, 91980, 91987, 92019, 92101–02, 92104–05, 92113–15, 92136, 92139, 92143, 92153–54, 92158, 92165, 92170, 92173–74, 92179, 92222, 92225, 92227, 92231–33, 92243–44, 92249–51, 92257, 92259, 92266, 92273–74, 92281, 92283

* * *

FIFTY-SECOND DISTRICT

SCOTT PETERS, Democrat, of La Jolla, CA; born in Springfield, OH, June 17, 1958; education: *magna cum laude*, Phi Beta Kappa, Duke University; New York University School of Law; professional: Environmental Protection Agency economist; environmental lawyer; City Council President; San Diego Port Commissioner; religion: Lutheran; wife, Lynn; two children; committees: Budget; Energy and Commerce; elected to the 113th Congress on November 6, 2012; reelected to each succeeding Congress.

Office Listings

https://scottpeters.house.gov https://facebook.com/RepScottPeters twitter: @repscottpeters

2338 Rayburn House Office Building, Washington, DC 20515 ..... (202) 225–0508
DC Chief of Staff.—Daniel Zawitoski.
Scheduler.—Hannah Stern.
Legislative Director.—Sterling McHale.
Press Secretary.—Martha Spieker.
Digital Media Director.—Quin LaCapra.
4350 Executive Drive, Suite 105, San Diego, CA 92121 ..... (858) 455–5550
Chief of Staff.—MaryAnne Pintar.

Counties: SAN DIEGO COUNTY (part). CITIES AND TOWNSHIPS: Carmel Valley, Coronado, Downtown San Diego, La Jolla, Point Loma, and Poway. Population (2010), 704,565.

ZIP Codes: 92025, 92027, 92037, 92064, 92101, 92106–07, 92109–11, 92117–18, 92121–24, 92126–31, 92137, 92140, 92145, 92155

* * *

FIFTY-THIRD DISTRICT

SUSAN A. DAVIS, Democrat, of San Diego, CA; born in Cambridge, MA, April 13, 1944; education: B.S., University of California at Berkeley; M.A., University of North Carolina; public service: served three terms in the California State Assembly; served 9 years on the San Diego City School Board; former president of the League of Women Voters of San Diego; awards: California School Boards Association Legislator of the Year; League of Middle Schools Legislator of the Year; family: married to Steve; children: Jeffrey and Benjamin; grandsons: Henry and Theo; granddaughter: Jane; committees: Armed Services; Education and Labor;

House Administration; Joint Committee on Printing; elected to the 107th Congress on November 7, 2000; reelected to each succeeding Congress.

Office Listings

https://susandavis.house.gov https://facebook.com/RepSusanDavis
https://twitter.com/RepSusanDavis https://instagram.com/repsusandavis
https://youtube.com/RepSusanADavis

1214 Longworth House Office Building, Washington, DC 20515 .... (202) 225–2040
Chief of Staff.—Lisa Sherman. FAX: 225–2948
Press Secretary.—Aaron Hunter.
Scheduler.—Cynthia Patton.
2700 Adams Avenue, Suite 102, San Diego, CA 92116 .... (619) 280–5353
District Director.—Jessica Mier. FAX: 280–5311

Counties: SAN DIEGO COUNTY (part). Population (2010), 639,008.

ZIP Codes: 91902, 91908, 91910–11, 91913–15, 91921, 91941–46, 91976–79, 92019–22, 92101–05, 92108, 92110–11, 92114–16, 92119–20, 92123–24, 92134, 92139, 92149, 92154, 92160, 92163–64, 92168, 92171, 92175–76, 92182, 92190, 92193, 92195

COLORADO

(Population 2010, 5,029,196)

SENATORS

MICHAEL F. BENNET, Democrat, of Denver, CO; born in New Delhi, India, November 28, 1964; education: B.A., Wesleyan University, 1987; J.D., Yale Law School, 1993; editor-in-chief of the *Yale Law Journal*; professional: Counsel to U.S. Deputy Attorney General, 1995–97; special assistant, U.S. Attorney, CT, 1997; managing director, Anschutz Investment Co., 1997–2003; Chief of Staff to Mayor of Denver, CO, 2003–05; superintendent, Denver Public Schools, 2005–09; married: Susan D. Daggett; children: Caroline, Halina, and Anne; committees: Agriculture, Nutrition, and Forestry; Finance; Select Committee on Intelligence; appointed January 21, 2009, to the U.S. Senate for the term ending January 3, 2011; elected for a full Senate term on November 2, 2010; reelected to the U.S. Senate on November 8, 2016.

Office Listings

https://bennet.senate.gov https://facebook.com/senbennetco https://twitter.com/SenatorBennet

261 Russell Senate Office Building, Washington, DC 20510–0606 .... (202) 224–5852
Chief of Staff.—Jonathan Davidson.
Legislative Director.—Brian Appel.
Communications Director.—Courtney Gidner.
Scheduler.—Kristin Mollet.
1244 Speer Boulevard, Denver, CO 80204 .... (303) 455–7600
FAX: 455–8851
129 West B Street, Pueblo, CO 81003 .... (719) 542–7550
FAX: 542–7555
609 Main Street, Suite 110, Alamosa, CO 81101 .... (719) 587–0096
FAX: 587–0098
409 North Tejon, Suite 107, Colorado Springs, CO 80903 .... (719) 328–1100
FAX: 328–1129
1200 South College Avenue, Suite 211, Fort Collins, CO 80524 .... (970) 224–2200
FAX: 224–2205
225 North 5th Street, Suite 511, Grand Junction, CO 81501 .... (970) 241–6631
FAX: 241–8313
835 East 2nd Avenue, Suite 206, Durango, CO 81301 .... (970) 259–1710
FAX: 259–9789

* * *

CORY GARDNER, Republican, of Yuma, CO; born in Yuma, CO, August 22, 1974; education: B.A., political science, Colorado State University, Fort Collins, CO, 1997; J.D., University of Colorado, Boulder, CO, 2001; professional: agricultural advocate; staff, U.S. Senator Wayne Allard of Colorado, 2002–05; member of the Colorado State House of Representatives, 2005–10; member of the U.S. House of Representatives, 2011–14; committees: Commerce, Science, and Transportation; Energy and Natural Resources; Foreign Relations; elected to the U.S. Senate on November 4, 2014.

Office Listings

https://gardner.senate.gov https://facebook.com/SenCoryGardner
https://twitter.com/sencorygardner https://instagram.com/sencorygardner

354 Russell Senate Office Building, Washington, DC 20510 .... (202) 224–5941
Chief of Staff.—Curtis Swager.
Deputy Chief of Staff.—Alex Siciliano.
Communications Director.—Annalyse Keller.
Director of Scheduling.—Amy Barrera.
1961 Stout Street, Suite 12–300, Denver, CO 80294 .... (303) 391–5777
400 Rood Avenue, Suite 220, Grand Junction, CO 81501 .... (970) 245–9553
801 8th Street, Suite 140A, Greeley, CO 80631 .... (970) 352–5546
529 North Albany Street, Suite 1220, Yuma, CO 80759 .... (970) 848–3095
503 North Main Street, Suite 426, Pueblo, CO 81003 .... (719) 543–1324
2001 South Shields Street, Building H, Suite 104, Fort Collins, CO 80526 .... (970) 484–3502
329 South Camino Del Rio, Suite I, Durango, CO 81303 .... (970) 259–1231

REPRESENTATIVES

FIRST DISTRICT

DIANA DEGETTE, Democrat, of Denver, CO; born in Tachikawa, Japan, July 29, 1957; education: B.A., political science, *magna cum laude,* The Colorado College, 1979; J.D., New York University School of Law, 1982 (Root Tilden Scholar); professional: attorney with McDermott, Hansen, and Reilly; Colorado Deputy State Public Defender, Appellate Division, 1982–84; Colorado House of Representatives, 1992–96; member and formerly on board of governors, Colorado Bar Association; member, Colorado Women's Bar Association; past memberships: board of trustees, The Colorado College; Denver Women's Commission; board of directors, Colorado Trial Lawyers Association; former editor, *Trial Talk* magazine; listed in 1994–96 edition of *Who's Who in America;* committees: Energy and Commerce; Natural Resources; elected to the 105th Congress; reelected to each succeeding Congress.

Office Listings

https://degette.house.gov https://facebook.com/DianaDeGette twitter: @RepDianaDeGette

2111 Rayburn House Office Building, Washington, DC 20515 .... (202) 225–4431
Chief of Staff.—Lisa B. Cohen. FAX: 225–5657
Scheduler.—Diana Gambrel.
Communications Director.—Ryan Brown.
600 Grant Street, Suite 202, Denver, CO 80203 .... (303) 844–4988
District Director.—Joeana Middleton.

Counties: ARAPAHOE (part), DENVER, AND JEFFERSON (part). Population (2010), 718,457.

ZIP Codes: 80012 (part), 80014 (part), 80110–11 (part), 80113 (part), 80120–21 (part), 80123 (part), 80127–28 (part), 80202–07, 80209–11, 80212 (part), 80214 (part), 80216 (part), 80218–19, 80220–21 (part), 80222–23, 80224 (part), 80226–27 (part), 80230, 80231–32 (part), 80235 (part), 80236–38, 80239 (part), 80246, 80247 (part), 80249, 80264, 80290, 80293–94.

* * *

SECOND DISTRICT

JOSEPH NEGUSE, Democrat, of Lafayette, CO; born in Bakersfield, CA, May 13, 1984; education: B.A., political science and economics, University of Colorado, Boulder, CO, 2005; J.D., University of Colorado Law School, Boulder, CO, 2009; professional: associate attorney, Holland and Hart, Denver, CO, 2009–15; regent, University of Colorado Board of Regents, 2009–15; executive director, Colorado State Department of Regulatory Agencies, Denver, CO, 2015–17; counsel, Snell and Wilmer, Denver, CO, 2017–19; family: wife, Andrea, one daughter; committees: Judiciary; Natural Resources; Select Committee on the Climate Crisis; elected to the 116th Congress on November 6, 2018.

Office Listings

https://neguse.house.gov

1419 Longworth House Office Building, Washington, DC 20515 .... (202) 225–2161
Chief of Staff.—Lisa Bianco.
Legislative Director.—Bo Morris.
2503 Walnut Street, Suite 300, Boulder, CO 80302 .... (303) 335–1045
Communications Director.—Sally Tucker.
1220 South College Avenue, Unit 100A, Fort Collins, CO 80524 .... (970) 372–3971

Counties: BOULDER (part), BROOMFIELD, CLEAR CREEK, EAGLE (part), GILPIN, GRAND, JEFFERSON (part), LARIMER, PARK (part), AND SUMMIT. Population (2010), 732,658.

ZIP Codes: 80007 (part), 80020–21 (part), 80023 (part), 80025–27, 80127, 80128 (part), 80135 (part), 80228 (part), 80234 (part), 80301–05, 80310, 80401 (part), 80403 (part), 80421 (part), 80422, 80423 (part), 80424–25, 80427, 80433, 80435–36, 80438–39, 80442–44, 80446–47, 80448 (part), 80451–55, 80457, 80459, 80465 (part), 80466, 80468, 80470–71, 80475–76, 80478, 80481–82, 80497–98, 80503–04 (part), 80510–12, 80513 (part), 80515, 80516 (part), 80517, 80521, 80524 (part), 80525–26, 80528, 80532, 80534 (part), 80535–36, 80537 (part), 80538, 80540, 80544–45, 80547, 80549–50 (part), 80612 (part), 81620 (part), 81632 (part), 81645 (part), 81649, 81655 (part), 81657, 82063

* * *

THIRD DISTRICT

SCOTT TIPTON, Republican, of Cortez, CO; born in Espanola, NM, November 9, 1956; education: graduated, B.S., political science, Ft. Lewis College, Durango, CO, 1978; professional: owner/president of Mesa Verde Pottery, Cortez, CO; public service: elected to Colorado House of Representatives, 2008–10; religion: Anglican; married: Jean Tipton; children: Liesl (married to Chris Ross) and Elizabeth (married to Jace Weber); caucuses: chair, Small Business Caucus; vice chair, Western Caucus; Aerospace; Beef; Coal; Dairy; Forestry; Heroin Task Force; Israel; NASA; Native American; Natural Gas; Rural Broadband; Rural Housing; Rural Veterans; Sportsmen's; Steel; Travel and Tourism; committees: Financial Services; elected to the 112th Congress on November 2, 2010; reelected to each succeeding Congress.

Office Listings

https://tipton.house.gov

218 Cannon House Office Building, Washington, DC 20515 .... (202) 225–4761
Chief of Staff.—Joshua Green. FAX: 226–9669
Legislative Director.—Liz Payne.
Executive Assistant.—Agustina Pardal.
225 North 5th Street, Suite 702, Grand Junction, CO 81501 .... (970) 241–2499
District Director.—Brian McCain.
609 Main Street, Suite 105, Box 11, Alamosa, CO 81101 .... (719) 587–5105
503 North Main Street, Suite 658, Pueblo, CO 81003 .... (719) 542–1073
835 East Second Avenue, Suite 230, Durango, CO 81301 .... (970) 259–1490

Counties: Alamosa, Archuleta, Conejos, Costilla, Custer, Delta, Dolores, Eagle (part), Garfield, Gunnison, Hinsdale, Huerfano, Jackson, La Plata, Lake, Mesa, Mineral, Moffat, Montezuma, Montrose, Ouray, Pitkin, Pueblo, Rio Blanco, Rio Grande, Routt, Saguache, San Juan, and San Miguel. Population (2010), 718,457.

ZIP Codes: 80423 (part), 80426, 80428, 80434, 80461, 80463, 80467, 80469, 80473, 80477, 80479–80, 80483, 80487–88, 81001, 81003–07, 81008 (part), 81019, 81022–23, 81025, 81039 (part), 81040, 81055, 81069, 81089, 81101, 81120–26, 81128–33, 81136–38, 81140–41, 81143–44, 81146–49, 81151–52, 81154–55, 81210, 81220, 81224–25, 81230–31, 81235, 81237, 81239, 81241, 81243, 81248, 81251–52, 81253 (part), 81301, 81303, 81320–21, 81323–28, 81330–32, 81334–35, 81401, 81403, 81410–11, 81413, 81415–16, 81418–19, 81422–35, 81501, 81503–07, 81520–27, 81601, 81610–12, 81615, 81620 (part), 81621, 81623–25, 81630–31, 81632 (part), 81633, 81635, 81637–43, 81645 (part), 81646–48, 81650, 81652–54, 81655 (part), 81656

* * *

FOURTH DISTRICT

KEN BUCK, Republican, of Windsor, CO; born February 16, 1959; education: undergraduate, Princeton University, Princeton, NJ, 1980; J.D., University of Wyoming, Laramie, WY, 1983; professional: prosecutor; U.S. Department of Justice, Washington, DC, 1985–95; U.S. Attorney's Office, CO, 1995–2000; District Attorney, Weld County, CO, 2004–14; corporate counsel, Hensel Phelps Construction, 2002–04; committees: Foreign Affairs; Judiciary; elected to the 114th Congress on November 4, 2014; reelected to each succeeding Congress.

Office Listings

https://buck.house.gov

2455 Rayburn House Office Building, Washington, DC 20515 .... (202) 225–4676
Chief of Staff.—Garrett Ventry.
Legislative Director.—James Hampson.
Communications Director.—Lindsey Curnutte.
Scheduling/Office Administrator.—Ansley Braden.
1023 39th Avenue, Unit B, Greeley, CO 80634 .... (970) 702–2136
900 Castleton Road, Meadows Crossing, Suite 112, Castle Rock, CO 80109 .... (720) 639–9165

Counties: Adams (part), Arapahoe (part), Baca, Bent, Boulder (part), Cheyenne, Crowley, Douglas (part), Elbert, Kiowa, Kit Carson, Las Animas, Lincoln, Logan, Morgan, Otero, Phillips, Prowers, Sedgwick, Washington, Weld, and Yuma.

ZIP Codes: 80101–09, 80112, 80116–18, 80124–27, 80130–31, 80134–38, 80501–04, 80514, 80520, 80530, 80534, 80542–43, 80546, 80550–51, 80603, 80610–12, 80615, 80620–24, 80631–34, 80638–39, 80642–46, 80648–54, 80701, 80705, 80720–23, 80726–29, 80731–37, 80740–47, 80749–51, 80754–55, 80757–59, 80801–02, 80804–05, 80807, 80810, 80812, 80815, 80818, 80821–26, 80828, 80830, 80832–36, 80861–62, 81020–21, 81024, 81027, 81029–30, 81033–34, 81036,

81038–39, 81041, 81043–47, 81049–50, 81052, 81054, 81057–59, 81062–64, 81067, 81071, 81073, 81076–77, 81084, 81087, 81090–92

* * *

FIFTH DISTRICT

DOUG LAMBORN, Republican, of Colorado Springs, CO; born in Leavenworth, KS, May 24, 1954; education: B.S., University of Kansas, Lawrence, 1978; J.D., University of Kansas, Lawrence, 1985; professional: lawyer, private practice (business and real estate); Colorado State House of Representatives, 1995–98; Colorado State Senate, 1998–2006; married: Jeanie; five children; committees: Armed Services; Natural Resources; elected to the 110th Congress on November 7, 2006; reelected to each succeeding Congress.

Office Listings

https://lamborn.house.gov https://facebook.com/CongressmanDougLamborn twitter: @RepDLamborn

2371 Rayburn House Office Building, Washington, DC 20515 .... (202) 225–4422
Chief of Staff.—Dale Anderson.
Legislative Director.—James Thomas.
Director of Communications.—Cassandra Sebastian.
Scheduler / Executive Assistant.—Kate Morgan.
1125 Kelly Johnson Boulevard, Suite 330, Colorado Springs, CO 80920 .... (719) 520–0055

Counties: CHAFFEE, EL PASO, FREMONT, PARK (part), AND TELLER. Population (2010), 718,457.

ZIP Codes: 80106 (part), 80132, 80133 (part), 80420, 80421 (part), 80432, 80440, 80448 (part), 80449, 80456, 80808 (part), 80809, 80813–14, 80816–17, 80819–20, 80827, 80829, 80831–33 (part), 80840, 80860, 80863–64, 80902–11, 80913–30, 80938–39, 80951, 81008 (part), 81201, 81211–12, 81221–23, 81226–27, 81232–33, 81236, 81240, 81242, 81244, 81253 (part)

* * *

SIXTH DISTRICT

JASON CROW, Democrat, of Aurora, CO; born in Madison, WI, March 15, 1979; education: B.A., University of Wisconsin, Madison, WI, 2002; J.D., University of Denver Sturm College of Law, 2009; military: United States Army, 2002–06; Bronze Star; professional: attorney, Holland & Hart LLP, 2009–19; committees: Armed Services; Small Business; elected to the 116th Congress on November 6, 2018.

Office Listings

https://crow.house.gov https://facebook.com/RepJasonCrow https://twitter.com/repjasoncrow

1229 Longworth House Office Building, Washington, DC 20515 .... (202) 225–7882
Chief of Staff.—Alex Ball.
Scheduler.—Liz Natonski.
3300 South Parker Road, Suite 100, Aurora, CO 80014 .... (720) 748–7514

Counties: ADAMS (part), ARAPAHOE (part), AND DOUGLAS (part). Population (2010), 718,456.

ZIP Codes: 80010–11, 80012–16 (part), 80017, 80018 (part), 80019, 80022–23 (part), 80045, 80102 (part), 80110–13 (part), 80120–21 (part), 80122, 80123–26 (part), 80128 (part), 80129, 80130 (part), 80137–38 (part), 80220 (part), 80224 (part), 80231 (part), 80241 (part), 80247 (part), 80601–03 (part), 80640 (part), 80642–43 (part)

* * *

SEVENTH DISTRICT

ED PERLMUTTER, Democrat, of Arvada, CO; born in Denver, CO, May 1, 1953; education: B.A., University of Colorado, 1975; J.D., University of Colorado, 1978; professional: former partner at the law firm Berenbaum Weinshienk, specializing in bankruptcy law; served as a member of the Board of Governors of the Colorado Bar Association; served on the Board of Trustees and Judicial Performance Commission for the First Judicial District; Trustee, Midwest Research Institute, the primary operator of the National Renewable Energy Laboratory; board member, National Jewish Medical and Research Center; elected to two 4-year terms to represent central Jefferson County as a Colorado State Senator, 1995–2003; served on numerous committees in the State Senate, including Water, Finance, Judiciary, Child Welfare, Telecommunication, Transportation, Legal Services, and Oil and Gas; also served as chair of the Public Policy and Planning Committee, chair of the Bi-Partisan Renewable Energy Caucus, and President Pro Tem, 2001–02 session; married to Nancy Perlmutter; between them they have six adult children; committees: Financial Services; Rules; Science, Space, and Technology; elected to the 110th Congress on November 7, 2006; reelected to each succeeding Congress.

Office Listings

https://perlmutter.house.gov https://facebook.com/RepPerlmutter
https://twitter.com/RepPerlmutter

1226 Longworth House Office Building, Washington, DC 20515 .... (202) 225–2645
Chief of Staff.—Danielle Radovich Piper (CO).
Legislative Director.—Jeff O'Neil.
Chief of Operations / Scheduler.—Alison Wright.
Staff Assistant.—John McInerney.
12600 West Colfax Avenue, Suite B400, Lakewood, CO 80215 .... (303) 274–7944

Counties: ADAMS (part) AND JEFFERSON (part). CITIES AND TOWNSHIPS: Arvada, Commerce City, Edgewater, Federal Heights, Golden, Lakewood, Northglenn, Thornton, Westminster, and Wheat Ridge. Population (2010), 718,456.

ZIP Codes: 80002, 80003–05, 80007 (part), 80020–23 (part), 80024, 80030–31, 80033, 80123 (part), 80127 (part), 80212 (part), 80214 (part), 80215, 80216 (part), 80221 (part), 80226–28 (part), 80229, 80232 (part), 80233, 80234–35 (part), 80239 (part), 80241 (part), 80260, 80401 (part), 80403 (part), 80419, 80465 (part), 80601–03 (part), 80640 (part)

CONNECTICUT

(Population 2010, 3,574,097)

SENATORS

RICHARD BLUMENTHAL, Democrat, of Greenwich, CT; born in Brooklyn, NY, February 13, 1946; son of Martin and Jane Rosenstock Blumenthal; education: graduated, Riverdale Country School, Riverdale, NY, 1963; B.A., government, Harvard College, Cambridge, MA, 1967; J.D., Yale Law School, New Haven, CT, 1973; professional: admitted to Connecticut Bar, 1976; admitted to District of Columbia Bar, 1977; appointed U.S. Attorney for the District of Connecticut, 1977–81; Connecticut State House of Representatives, 1984–87; Connecticut State Senate, 1987–90; elected Attorney General for the State of Connecticut, 1990, reelected in 1994, 1998, 2002, and 2006; military: served in the U.S. Marine Corps Reserve, 1970–76, honorably discharged as Sergeant; married: Cynthia M. Blumenthal; children: Matthew, Michael, David, and Claire; committees: Armed Services; Commerce, Science, and Transportation; Judiciary; Veterans' Affairs; Special Committee on Aging; elected to the U.S. Senate on November 2, 2010; reelected to the U.S. Senate on November 8, 2016.

Office Listings

https://blumenthal.senate.gov

706 Hart Senate Office Building, Washington, DC 20510 .... (202) 224–2823
Chief of Staff.—Joel Kelsey. FAX: 224–9673
Legislative Director.—Colleen Bell.
Scheduling Director.—Michael Lawson.
Communications Director.—Maria McElwain.
90 State House Square, 10th Floor, Hartford, CT 06103 .... (860) 258–6940
State Director.—Rich Kehoe. FAX: 258–6958
915 Lafayette Boulevard, Suite 304, Bridgeport, CT 06604 .... (203) 330–0598
FAX: 330–0608

* * *

CHRISTOPHER S. MURPHY, Democrat, of Wethersfield, CT; born in White Plains, Westchester County, NY, August 3, 1973; education: attended Exeter College, Oxford, England, 1994–95; graduated with honors with a double major in history and political science, Williams College, Williamstown, MA, 1996; J.D., University of Connecticut, Hartford, CT, 2002; professional: lawyer, private practice; Southington, CT, planning and zoning commission, 1997–99; practiced real estate and banking law from 2002–06, with the firm of Ruben, Johnson & Morgan in Hartford; member of the Connecticut State House of Representatives, 1999–2003; member of the Connecticut State Senate, 2003–06; married: Cathy Holahan, a legal aid attorney who represents children in need in New Britain and Waterbury; children: Chris, Cathy, and their sons Owen and Rider; committees: Appropriations; Foreign Relations; Health, Education, Labor, and Pensions; elected as a Democrat to the 110th Congress and to the two succeeding Congresses, January 3, 2007–January 3, 2013; elected to the U.S. Senate on November 6, 2012; reelected to the U.S. Senate on November 6, 2018.

Office Listings

https://murphy.senate.gov

136 Hart Senate Office Building, Washington, DC 20510 .... (202) 224–4041
Chief of Staff.—Allison Herwitt. FAX: 224–9750
Executive Assistant.—Liam McEnroe.
Legislative Director.—David Bonine.
120 Huyshope Avenue, Suite 401, Hartford, CT 06106 .... (860) 549–8463
State Director.—Kenny Curran.

REPRESENTATIVES

FIRST DISTRICT

JOHN B. LARSON, Democrat, of East Hartford, CT; born in Hartford, July 22, 1948; education: Mayberry Elementary School, East Hartford, CT; East Hartford High School; B.A., Central Connecticut State University; Senior Fellow, Yale University, Bush Center for Child Development and Social Policy; professional: high school teacher, 1972–77; insurance broker, 1978–98; president, Larson and Lysik; public service: Connecticut State Senate, 12 years, President Pro Tempore, 8 years; married: Leslie Larson; children: Carolyn, Laura, and Raymond; committees: Ways and Means; elected to the 106th Congress; reelected to each succeeding Congress.

Office Listings

https://larson.house.gov

1501 Longworth House Office Building, Washington, DC 20515 .... (202) 225–2265
Washington, DC, Chief of Staff.—Scott Stephanou.
Communications Director.—Mary Yatrousis.
221 Main Street, Hartford, CT 06106–1864 .... (860) 278–8888
District Chief of Staff.—Maureen Moriarty.
District Deputy Chief of Staff.—Conor Quinn.

Counties: HARTFORD (part), LITCHFIELD (part), AND MIDDLESEX (part). Population (2010), 714,820.

ZIP Codes: 06002, 06010, 06013, 06016, 06021, 06023, 06026–27, 06033, 06035, 06037, 06040, 06042, 06052, 06057–63, 06065, 06067, 06073–74, 06088, 06090–91, 06095–96, 06098, 06103, 06105–12, 06114, 06117–20, 06160, 06416, 06444, 06451, 06457, 06467, 06479–80, 06489, 06759, 06790

* * *

SECOND DISTRICT

JOE COURTNEY, Democrat, of Vernon, CT; born in Hartford, CT, April 6, 1953; education: B.A., Tufts University, 1971–75; University of Connecticut Law School, 1975–78; public service: Connecticut State Representative, 1987–94; Vernon Town Attorney, 2003–06; professional: attorney, Courtney, Boyan, and Foran, LLC, 1978–2006; religion: Roman Catholic; married: Audrey Courtney; children: Robert and Elizabeth; committees: Armed Services; Education and Labor; elected to the 110th Congress on November 7, 2006; reelected to each succeeding Congress.

Office Listings

https://courtney.house.gov https://facebook.com/joecourtney https://twitter.com/repjoecourtney

2332 Rayburn House Office Building, Washington, DC 20515 .... (202) 225–2076
Chief of Staff.—Neil McKiernan. FAX: 225–4977
Communications Director.—Patrick Cassidy.
Scheduler.—Kathleen Corcoran.
Legislative Director.—Alexa Combelic.
55 Main Street, Suite 250, Norwich, CT 06360 .... (860) 886–0139
District Director.—Ayanti Grant. FAX: 886–2974
77 Hazard Avenue, Unit J, Enfield, CT 06082 .... (860) 741–6011
FAX: 741–6036

Counties: HARTFORD (part), MIDDLESEX (part), NEW HAVEN (part), NEW LONDON, TOLLAND, AND WINDHAM. Population (2010), 714,819.

ZIP Codes: 06029, 06033, 06043, 06066, 06071, 06076, 06078, 06082, 06084, 06093, 06226, 06231–32, 06234–35, 06237–39, 06241–43, 06247–50, 06254–56, 06259–60, 06262–64, 06266, 06268–69, 06277–82, 06320, 06330–36, 06339–40, 06350–51, 06353–55, 06357, 06359–60, 06365, 06370–71, 06373–80, 06382, 06384–85, 06387, 06389, 06409, 06412–15, 06417, 06419–20, 06423–24, 06426, 06438, 06441–43, 06447, 06456, 06469, 06475

* * *

THIRD DISTRICT

ROSA L. DELAURO, Democrat, of New Haven, CT; born in New Haven, March 2, 1943; education: graduated, Lauralton Hall High School; attended London School of Economics, Queen Mary College, London, 1962–63; B.A., *cum laude*, history and political science, Marymount College, NY, 1964; M.A., international politics, Columbia University, NY, 1966; professional: executive assistant to Mayor Frank Logue, city of New Haven, 1976–77; executive assistant/development administrator, city of New Haven, 1977–78; chief of staff, Senator Christopher Dodd, 1980–87; executive director, Countdown '87, 1987–88; executive director, Emily's List, 1989–90; religion: Catholic; family: married, Stanley Greenberg; children: Anna, Kathryn, and Jonathan; co-chair, Democratic Steering and Policy Committee; committees: Appropriations;

Budget; elected to the 102nd Congress on November 6, 1990; reelected to each succeeding Congress.

Office Listings

https://delauro.house.gov https://facebook.com/CongresswomanRosaDeLauro
https://twitter.com/rosadelauro

2413 Rayburn House Office Building, Washington, DC 20515 .... (202) 225–3661
Chief of Staff.—Leticia Mederos. FAX: 225–4890
Scheduler.—Ryann Kinney.
59 Elm Street, New Haven, CT 06510 .... (203) 562–3718
District Director.—Jennifer Lamb.
District Scheduler.—Samantha Palumbo.

Counties: FAIRFIELD (part), MIDDLESEX (part), AND NEW HAVEN (part). CITIES AND TOWNSHIPS: Ansonia, Beacon Falls, Bethany, Branford, Derby, Durham, East Haven, Guilford, Hamden, Middlefield, Middletown (part), Milford, Naugatuck, New Haven, North Branford, North Haven, Orange, Prospect, Seymour, Shelton (part), Stratford, Wallingford, Waterbury (part), West Haven, and Woodbridge. Population (2011), 718,549.

ZIP Codes: 06401, 06403, 06405, 06410, 06418, 06422, 06437, 06450, 06455, 06457, 06460, 06471–73, 06477, 06481, 06483–84, 06492–94, 06501–21, 06524–25, 06530–38, 06540, 06607, 06614–15, 06706, 06708, 06712, 06762, 06770

* * *

FOURTH DISTRICT

JAMES A. HIMES, Democrat, of Cos Cob, CT; born in Lima, Peru, to American parents, July 5, 1966; education: B.A., Harvard University, Cambridge, MA, 1988; M.Phil, Oxford University, Oxford, England, 1990; professional: vice president, Goldman Sachs & Co., 1990–2002; vice president, Enterprise Community Partners, 2002–07; Commissioner, Greenwich Housing Authority; chair, Greenwich Democratic Town Committee; religion: Presbyterian; married: Mary Himes, 1994; children: Emma and Linley; committees: Financial Services; Permanent Select Committee on Intelligence; elected to the 111th Congress on November 4, 2008; reelected to each succeeding Congress.

Office Listings

https://himes.house.gov https://facebook.com/RepJimHimes https://twitter.com/jahimes

1227 Longworth House Office Building, Washington, DC 20515 .... (202) 225–5541
Chief of Staff.—Mark Henson. FAX: 225–9629
Scheduler.—Emily Fritcke.
888 Washington Boulevard, Stamford, CT 06901–2927 .... (203) 353–9400
211 State Street, 2nd Floor, Bridgeport, CT 06604–4223 .... (203) 333–6600
District Director.—Cara Pavlock.

Counties: FAIRFIELD (part) AND NEW HAVEN (part). CITIES AND TOWNSHIPS: Bridgeport, Darien, Easton, Fairfield, Greenwich, Monroe, New Canaan, Norwalk, Oxford, Redding, Ridgefield, Shelton, Stamford, Trumbull, Weston, Westport, and Wilton. Population (2010), 714,819.

ZIP Codes: 06468, 06478, 06604–08, 06610–12, 06807, 06820, 06824–25, 06830–31, 06840, 06850–51, 06853–56, 06870, 06877–78, 06880, 06883, 06890, 06896–97, 06901–03, 06905–07

* * *

FIFTH DISTRICT

JAHANA HAYES, Democrat, of Wolcott, CT; born in Waterbury, CT, March 8, 1973; education: B.A., Southern Connecticut State University, New Haven, CT, 2005; M.A., University of Saint Joseph, West Hartford, CT, 2012; Sixth-Year Certificate in Educational Leadership, University of Bridgeport, Bridgeport, CT, 2014; professional: teacher, government and history; public school administrator; awards: 2015 John F. Kennedy Teacher of the Year; 2015 Waterbury School District Educator of the Year; 2016 Connecticut Teacher of the Year; 2016 National Teacher of the Year; religion: Methodist; family: married to Detective Milford Hayes; four children; caucuses: Autism Caucus; Congressional Black Caucus; Pro-Choice Caucus; committees: Agriculture; Education and Labor; elected to the 116th Congress on November 6, 2018 (the first African-American woman and the first African-American Democrat to ever represent the state of CT in Congress).

Office Listings

https://hayes.house.gov https://facebook.com/RepJahanaHayes
https://twitter.com/RepJahanaHayes https://instagram.com/repjahanahayes

1415 Longworth House Office Building, Washington, DC 20515 .... (202) 225–4476
Chief of Staff.—Acacia Salatti.
Scheduler.—Annmarie Goyzueta.
Legislative Director.—Alex Ginis.
Press Secretary.—Sam Dorn.
108 Bank Street, 2nd Floor, Waterbury, CT 06702 .... (860) 223–8412

Counties: FAIRFIELD (part), HARTFORD (part), LITCHFIELD, AND NEW HAVEN (part). CITIES: Danbury, Meriden, New Britain, Torrington, and Waterbury. Population (2010), 714,820.

ZIP Codes: 06001, 06013, 06018–20, 06022, 06024, 06030–32, 06034, 06039, 06050–53, 06058–59, 06062, 06068–70, 06079, 06081, 06085, 06087, 06089, 06092, 06107, 06404, 06408, 06410–11, 06440, 06450–51, 06454, 06470, 06482, 06487–88, 06701–06, 06708, 06710, 06716, 06720–26, 06749–59, 06762–63, 06776–79, 06781–87, 06790–91, 06793–96, 06798, 06801, 06804, 06810–14, 06816–17

DELAWARE

(Population 2010, 897,934)

SENATORS

THOMAS R. CARPER, Democrat, of Wilmington, DE; born in Beckley, WV, January 23, 1947; education: B.A., Ohio State University, 1968; M.B.A., University of Delaware, 1975; military service: U.S. Navy, served during Vietnam War; public service: Delaware State Treasurer, 1977–83; U.S. House of Representatives, 1983–93; Governor of Delaware, 1993–2001; organizations: Third Way; New Democrat Network; former National Governors' Association chair; religion: Presbyterian; family: married to the former Martha Ann Stacy; children: Ben and Christopher; committees: ranking member, Environment and Public Works; Finance; Homeland Security and Governmental Affairs; elected to the U.S. Senate on November 7, 2000; reelected to each succeeding Senate term.

Office Listings

https://carper.senate.gov https://facebook.com/tomcarper twitter: @SenatorCarper

513 Hart Senate Office Building, Washington, DC 20510 .... (202) 224–2441
Chief of Staff.—Emily Spain. FAX: 228–2190
Legislative Director.—Jan Beukelman.
Administrative Director.—Madge Farooq.
500 West Loockerman Street, Suite 470, Dover, DE 19904 .... (302) 674–3308
301 North Walnut Street, Suite 102 L–1, Wilmington, DE 19801 .... (302) 573–6291
12 The Circle, Georgetown, DE 19947 .... (302) 856–7690

* * *

CHRISTOPHER A. COONS, Democrat, of Wilmington, DE; born in Greenwich, CT, September 9, 1963; education: B.A., Amherst College, 1985; M.A.R., Yale University, 1992; J.D., Yale University, 1992; professional: associate (legal counsel), W.L. Gore & Associates, 1996–2004; president of New Castle County Council, 2000–04; county executive, New Castle County, 2005–10; religion: Presbyterian; married: Annie; children: Michael, Jack, and Maggie; committees: vice chair, Select Committee on Ethics; Appropriations; Foreign Relations; Judiciary; Small Business and Entrepreneurship; elected on November 2, 2010, to the U.S. Senate to fill the remainder of the vacancy caused by the unfinished term of Joseph R. Biden, Jr., and took the oath of office on November 15, 2010; reelected to the U.S. Senate on November 4, 2014.

Office Listings

https://coons.senate.gov https://facebook.com/senatorchriscoons https://twitter.com/ChrisCoons

218 Russell Senate Office Building, Washington, DC 20510 .... (202) 224–5042
Chief of Staff.—Jonathan Stahler. FAX: 228–3075
Legislative Director.—Brian Winseck.
Communications Director.—Sean Coit.
Administrative Director.—Trinity Hall.
1105 North Market Street, Suite 100, Wilmington, DE 19801–1233 .... (302) 573–6345
State Director.—Jim Paoli.
500 West Loockerman Street, Suite 450, Dover, DE 19904 .... (302) 736–5601
Kent / Sussex County Director.—Kate Rohrer.

REPRESENTATIVE

AT LARGE

LISA BLUNT ROCHESTER, Democrat, of Wilmington, DE; born in Philadelphia, PA, February 10, 1962; education: graduated from Padua Academy, Wilmington, DE, 1980; B.A., Fairleigh Dickinson University, Rutherford, NJ, 1985; M.A., University of Delaware, Newark, DE, 2003; professional: staff, U.S. Representative Thomas Richard Carper of Delaware; Deputy Secretary, Delaware Department of Health and Social Services, 1993–98; Delaware State Secretary of Labor, 1998–2001; Personnel Director, State of Delaware, 2001–04; chief executive officer, Metropolitan Wilmington Urban League, 2004–07; senior fellow, University of Massachusetts Boston, 2012–15; caucuses: Congressional Black Caucus; Congressional Progressive Caucus; Equality Caucus; New Democrat Coalition; committees: Energy and Commerce; elected to the 115th Congress on November 8, 2016; reelected to the 116th Congress on November 6, 2018.

Office Listings

https://bluntrochester.house.gov https://facebook.com/RepLBR https://twitter.com/RepLBR

1519 Longworth House Office Building, Washington, DC 20515 .... (202) 225–4165
Chief of Staff.—Jacqueline Sanchez.
Legislative Director.—Kevin Diamond.
DC Scheduler.—Kalila Hines.
1105 North Market Street, Suite 400, Wilmington, DE 19801 .... (302) 830–2330
State Director.—Courtney McGregor.
DE Scheduler.—Kim Jones.

Counties: KENT, NEW CASTLE, AND SUSSEX. CITIES AND TOWNSHIPS: Bethany Beach, Bethel, Bellefonte, Blades, Bowers, Bridgeville, Camden, Cheswold, Dagsboro, Delmar, Delaware City, Dewey Beach, Dover, Ellendale, Elsmere, Farmington, Felton, Fenwick Island, Frankford, Frederica, Georgetown, Greenwood, Harrington, Hartly, Henlopen Acres, Houston, Kenton, Laurel, Lewes, Little Creek, Leipsic, Magnolia, Middletown, Milford, Millsboro, Millville, Milton, New Castle, Newark, Newport, Ocean View, Odessa, Rehoboth Beach, Seaford, Selbyville, Slaughter Beach, South Bethany, Smyrna, Townsend, Viola, Wilmington, Woodside, and Wyoming. Population (2010), 897,934.

ZIP Codes: 19701–03, 19706–18, 19720–21, 19725–26, 19730–36, 19801–10, 19850, 19880, 19884–87, 19890–99, 19901–06, 19930–31, 19933–34, 19936, 19938–41, 19943–47, 19950–56, 19958, 19960–64, 19966–71, 19973, 19975, 19977, 19979–80

FLORIDA

(Population 2010, 18,801,310)

SENATORS

MARCO A. RUBIO, Republican, of West Miami, FL; born in Miami, May 28, 1971; education: South Miami Senior High School, 1989; B.S., political science, University of Florida, 1993; J.D., *cum laude,* University of Miami, 1996; professional: Florida House of Representatives, 2000–08; served as Majority Whip, Majority Leader, and Speaker of the House; attorney, Broad and Cassel; Marco Rubio, P.A.; lecturer and senior fellow at Florida International University, 2009–present; Bob Dole for President, 1996, Miami-Dade County Director; religion: Roman Catholic; married: Jeanette; children: Amanda, Daniella, Anthony, and Dominick; Commission on Security and Cooperation in Europe; committees: chair, Small Business and Entrepreneurship; chair, Select Committee on Intelligence; Appropriations; Foreign Relations; Special Committee on Aging; elected to the U.S. Senate on November 2, 2010; reelected on November 8, 2016.

Office Listings

https://rubio.senate.gov https://facebook.com/SenatorMarcoRubio twitter: @SenRubioPress

284 Russell Senate Office Building, Washington, DC 20510 .... (202) 224–3041
Chief of Staff.—Michael Needham. FAX: 228–0285
Legislative Director.—Lauren Reamy.
201 South Orange Avenue, Suite 350, Orlando, FL 32801 .... (407) 254–2573
700 South Palafox Street, Suite 125, Pensacola, FL 32502 .... (850) 433–2603
7400 Southwest 87th Avenue, Suite 270, Miami, FL 33173 .... (305) 596–4224
402 South Monroe Street, Suite 2105E, Tallahassee, FL 32399 .... (850) 599–9100
4580 PGA Boulevard, Suite 201, Palm Beach Gardens, FL 33418 .... (561) 775–3360
2120 Main Street, Room 200, Fort Myers, FL 33901 .... (866) 630–7106
300 North Hogan Street, Suite 8–111, Jacksonville, FL 32202 .... (904) 354–4300

* * *

RICK SCOTT, Republican, of Naples, FL; born in Bloomington, IL, December 1, 1952; military: active duty, U.S. Navy radar man, USS *Glover*; education: B.S., business administration, University of Missouri-Kansas City; J.D., Southern Methodist University, Dallas, TX; professional: attorney, Johnson & Swanson, Dallas, TX; founder of Columbia Hospital Corporation, the world's largest health care company; public service: Governor, State of Florida, 2011–19; married: wife, Ann; family: two daughters, Allison and Jordan; six grandsons: Auguste, Quinton, Sebastian, Eli, Louie, and Jude; committees: Armed Services; Budget; Commerce, Science, and Transportation; Homeland Security and Governmental Affairs; Special Committee on Aging; elected to the U.S. Senate on November 6, 2018.

Office Listings

https://rickscott.senate.gov twitter: @SenRickScott

716 Hart Senate Office Building, Washington, DC 20510 .... (202) 224–5274
Chief of Staff.—Jackie Schutz Zeckman.
U.S. Courthouse Annex, 111 North Adams Street, Suite 208, Tallahassee, FL 32301 .... (850) 942–8415
FAX: 942–8450
801 North Florida Avenue, 4th Floor, Tampa, FL 33602 .... (813) 225–7040

REPRESENTATIVES

FIRST DISTRICT

MATT GAETZ, Republican, of Fort Walton Beach, FL; born in Hollywood, FL, May 7, 1982; education: B.S., political science, Florida State University, Tallahassee, FL, 2003; J.D., College of William and Mary, Williamsburg, VA, 2007; professional: Florida House of Representatives, 2010–16; attorney with the Keefe, Anchors & Gordon law firm; religion: Baptist; family: Don Gaetz, father; Vicky Gaetz, mother; and Erin Gaetz, sister; committees: Armed Services; Judiciary; elected to the 115th Congress on November 8, 2016; reelected to the 116th Congress on November 6, 2018.

Office Listings

https://gaetz.house.gov https://facebook.com/CongressmanMattGaetz twitter: @RepMattGaetz

1721 Longworth House Office Building, Washington, DC 20515 .... (202) 225–4136
Chief of Staff.—Jillian Lane Wyant. FAX: 225–3414
Legislative Director.—Devin Murphy.
Scheduler.—Alison Thomas.
22 South Palafox Place, 6th Floor, Pensacola, FL 32502 .... (850) 479–1183
District Director.—Dawn McArdle.

Counties: ESCAMBIA (all). CITIES AND TOWNSHIPS: Bellview, Brent, Century, Ensley, Ferry Pass, Gonzalez, Goulding, Molino, Myrtle Grove, Pensacola, Warrington, and West Pensacola. HOLMES (part). CITIES AND TOWNSHIPS: Esto, Noma, Ponce de Leon, and Westville. OKALOOSA (all). CITIES AND TOWNSHIPS: Cinco Bayou, Crestview, Destin, Eglin, Fort Walton Beach, Lake Lorraine, Laurel Hill, Mary Esther, Niceville, Ocean City, Shalimar, Valparaiso, and Wright. SANTA ROSA (all). CITIES AND TOWNSHIPS: Allentown, Avalon, Bagdad, Berrydale, Brownsdale, Chumuckla, Cobbtown, Dickerson City, Dixonville, East Milton, Fidelis, Floridatown, Garcon Point, Gulf Breeze, Harold, Holley, Jay, Midway, Milton, Mount Carmel, Mulat, Munson, Navarre, Navarre Beach, Oriole Beach, Pace, Pea Ridge, Pine Level, Point Baker, Roeville, Springhill, Tiger Point, Wallace, and Woodlawn Beach. WALTON (all). CITIES AND TOWNSHIPS: De Funiak Springs, Freeport, Miramar Beach, and Paxton. Population (2010), 687,856.

ZIP Codes: 32413 (part), 32425 (part), 32433, 32435, 32439, 32440 (part), 32455, 32459, 32461, 32462 (part), 32464, 32501–09, 32511, 32514, 32526, 32530, 32531, 32533–36, 32539, 32541–42, 32544, 32547–48, 32550, 32561, 32563–71, 32577–80, 32583

* * *

SECOND DISTRICT

NEAL P. DUNN, Republican, of Panama City, FL; born in New Haven, CT, February 16, 1953; education: B.A., Washington and Lee University, Lexington, VA; M.D., George Washington University Medical School, Washington, DC; residency, Walter Reed Army Medical Center; professional: founding president, Advanced Urology Institute, Panama City, FL; founding chair, Summit Bank, Panama City, FL; member, board of governors, Florida Medical Association; military: Major, U.S. Army (Ret.); religion: Roman Catholic; married, Leah Ott Dunn; three children; committees: Agriculture; Veterans' Affairs; elected to the 115th Congress on November 8, 2016; reelected to the 116th Congress on November 6, 2018.

Office Listings

https://dunn.house.gov https://facebook.com/DrNealDunnFL2 https://twitter.com/drnealdunnfl2

316 Cannon House Office Building, Washington, DC 20515 .... (202) 225–5235
Chief of Staff.—Michael Lowry.
Communications Director.—Shelby Hodgkins.
Legislative Director.—Matt Blackwell.
Legislative Assistants: Danielle Houser, Courtney Veatch.
Legislative Correspondent.—Emily Hadden.
Scheduler.—Marissa Mullen.
300 South Adams Street, Suite A–3, Tallahassee, FL 32301 .... (850) 891–8610
District Director.—Will Kendrick.
840 West 11th Street, Suite 2250, Panama City, FL 32401 .... (850) 785–0812

Counties: BAY, CALHOUN, COLUMBIA (part), DIXIE, FRANKLIN, GILCHRIST, GULF, HOLMES (part), JACKSON, JEFFERSON (part), LAFAYETTE, LEON (part), LEVY, LIBERTY, MARION (part), SUWANNEE, TAYLOR, WAKULLA, AND WASHINGTON. Population (2010), 737,519.

ZIP Code: 32008, 32024–25, 32038, 32055, 32060–62, 32064, 32066, 32071, 32094, 32096, 32301, 32303–05, 32308–12, 32317, 32320–23, 32327–28, 32331, 32334, 32336, 32344, 32346–48, 32355–56, 32358–59, 32361, 32399, 32401, 32403–05, 32407–10, 32413, 32420–21, 32423–28, 32430–32, 32437–38, 32440, 32442–49, 32456, 32460, 32462–63, 32465–66, 32618–19, 32621, 32625–26, 32628, 32639, 32643, 32648, 32668–69, 32680, 32683, 32692–93, 32696, 34431–32, 34449, 34474, 34476, 34481–82, 34498

* * *

THIRD DISTRICT

TED S. YOHO, D.V.M., Republican, of Gainesville, FL; born in Minneapolis, MN, April 13, 1955; education: graduated from Deerfield Beach High School, Deerfield Beach, FL, 1973; attended Florence State University (University of North Alabama), Florence, AL; A.A., Broward Community College, Fort Lauderdale, FL, 1977; B.S.A., University of Florida, Gainesville, FL, 1979; D.V.M., University of Florida, Gainesville, FL, 1983; professional: large animal veterinarian; religion: Christian; married: the former Carolyn Sue Marlin; children: Katie, Tyler, and

Lauren; caucuses: Congressional Cystic Fibrosis Caucus; Congressional Sportsmen's Caucus; Florida Ports Caucus; Freshman Regulatory Reform Working Group; House Liberty Caucus; Republican Study Committee; Veterinary Medicine Caucus; committees: Agriculture; Foreign Affairs; elected to the 113th Congress on November 6, 2012; reelected to each succeeding Congress.

Office Listings

https://yoho.house.gov https://facebook.com/CongressmanTedYoho
twitter: @RepTedYoho https://instagram.com/RepTedYoho

1730 Longworth House Office Building, Washington, DC 20515 .... (202) 225–5744
Chief of Staff.—Larry Calhoun. FAX: 225–3973
Scheduler.—Allison Turk.
Legislative Director.—James Walsh.
Communications Director.—Brian Kaveney.
5000 Northwest 27th Court, Suite A, Gainesville, FL 32606 .... (352) 505–0838
Deputy Chief of Staff.—Kat Cammack.
District Director.—Jessica Norfleet.
35 Knight Boxx Road, Suite 1, Orange Park, FL 32065 .... (904) 276–9626
Constituent Advocacy Manager.—Dorothy Richardson.
2509 Crill Avenue, Suite 200, Palatka, FL 32177 .... (386) 326–7221

Counties: ALACHUA, BRADFORD, CLAY, MARION (part), AND PUTNAM. Population (2015), 726,720.

ZIP Codes: 32003, 32008, 32024–26, 32038, 32043–44, 32052–55, 32058–62, 32064–66, 32068, 32071, 32073, 32079, 32083, 32091, 32094, 32096, 32234, 32331, 32340, 32350, 32359, 32601, 32603, 32605–09, 32612, 32615–16, 32618–19, 32621–22, 32625–26, 32628, 32631, 32639–41, 32643, 32648, 32653, 32656, 32658, 32664, 32666–69, 32680, 32683, 32686, 32692–94, 32696–97, 34431–32, 34449, 34474–76, 34481–82, 34498

* * *

FOURTH DISTRICT

JOHN H. RUTHERFORD, Republican, of Jacksonville, FL; born in Omaha, NE, September 2, 1952; education: B.S., criminology, at Florida State University; FBI National Academy in Quantico, VA, graduated in session 171; professional: law enforcement officer with the Jacksonville Sheriff's Office and Duval County Sheriff from 2003–15; religion: Catholic; family, married: Patricia; children: Alicia and Michael; grandchildren: Michela, Hannah, Maria Vittoria, Kiera, and John-Carlo; committees: Appropriations; elected to the 115th Congress on November 8, 2016; reelected to the 116th Congress on November 6, 2018.

Office Listings

https://rutherford.house.gov https://facebook.com/RepRutherfordFL twitter: @RepRutherfordFL

1711 Longworth House Office Building, Washington, DC 20515 .... (202) 225–2501
Chief of Staff.—Kelly Simpson.
Legislative Director.—Jenifer Bradley.
Communications Director.—Alex Lanfranconi.
4130 Salisbury Road, Suite 2500, Jacksonville, FL 32216 .... (904) 831–5205
District Director.—Chris Miller.

Counties: DUVAL (part), NASSAU AND ST. JOHNS. CITIES AND TOWNSHIPS: Atlantic Beach, Callahan, Fernandina Beach, Jacksonville, Jacksonville Beach, Neptune Beach, and St. Augustine.

ZIP Codes: 32004, 32009, 32011, 32033 (part), 32034–35, 32040 (part), 32041, 32046, 32073 (part), 32080–82 (part), 32084 (part), 32085, 32086–87 (part), 32092 (part), 32095 (part), 32097 (part), 32099, 32145 (part), 32202 (part), 32204–05 (part), 32207 (part), 32209–12 (part), 32214, 32216–19 (part), 32220, 32221–22 (part), 32223, 32224–25 (part), 32226–29, 32233, 32234–35 (part), 32237, 32240–41, 32244–46 (part), 32250, 32254 (part), 32255–58, 32259 (part), 32260, 32266, 32277 (part)

* * *

FIFTH DISTRICT

AL LAWSON, JR., Democrat, of Tallahassee, FL; born in Midway, FL, September 23, 1948; education: B.S., Florida A&M University, 1970; M.P.A., Florida State University, 1973; professional: insurance executive, Northwestern Mutual; public service: former member, Florida House of Representatives and Florida State Senate; Dean, Florida Legislature, 2008–10; Senate

Democratic Leader, 2008–10; chair, Environmental Preservation and Conservation Committee; chair, Florida Conference of Black State Legislators; chair, Government Oversight and Accountability Committee; chair, Health & Life Insurance and General Insurance Regulation Committee; vice chair, General Government Appropriations; religion: Episcopal; married: Delores Brooks Lawson; committees: Agriculture; Financial Services; elected to the 115th Congress on November 8, 2016; reelected to the 116th Congress on November 6, 2018.

Office Listings

https://lawson.house.gov https://facebook.com/RepAlLawsonJr twitter: @RepAlLawsonJr

1406 Longworth House Office Building, Washington, DC 20515 .... (202) 225–0123
Chief of Staff.—Tola Thompson. FAX: 225–2256
Special Assistant / Scheduler.—Vincent Evans.
Legislative Director.—Margaret Franklin.
District Directors: Deborah Fairhurst (Tallahassee), Kortney Wesley (Jacksonville).
117 West Duval Street, Suite 240, Jacksonville, FL 32202 .... (904) 354–1652
435 North Macomb Street, Tallahassee, FL 32301 .... (850) 558–9450

Counties: BAKER, COLUMBIA (part), DUVAL (part), GADSDEN, HAMILTON, JEFFERSON (part), LEON (part), AND MADISON. Population (2010), 696,345.

ZIP Codes: 32003 (part), 32043 (part), 32073 (part), 32102 (part), 32113 (part), 32134 (part), 32140 (part), 32148 (part), 32177 (part), 32202 (part), 32204–05 (part), 32206, 32207 (part), 32208–09, 32210–12 (part), 32216 (part), 32218–22 (part), 32244 (part), 32254 (part), 32277 (part), 32601 (part), 32609 (part), 32631 (part), 32640–41 (part), 32664 (part), 32666–67 (part), 32681, 32686 (part), 32702–03 (part), 32712 (part), 32736 (part), 32746 (part), 32751 (part), 32757 (part), 32767, 32771 (part), 32773 (part), 32776 (part), 32784 (part), 32798, 32801 (part), 32804–06 (part), 32808, 32809–11 (part), 32818–19, 32835, 32839, 34734, 34761

* * *

SIXTH DISTRICT

MICHAEL WALTZ, Republican, of St. Augustine, FL; born in Boynton Beach, Palm Beach County, FL, January 31, 1974; education: graduated from Stanton High School, Jacksonville, FL, 1992; B.A., Virginia Military Institute, Lexington, VA, 1996; professional: Office of Secretary of Defense 2007–09; Office of Vice President Richard B. Cheney, 2007–09; Chief Executive Officer; television commentator; author; military: Green Beret, United States Army, 1996-2017; United States Army Reserve, 2017–present; religion: Episcopalian; children: Anderson; caucuses: vice chair, For Country Caucus; Congressional Shipbuilding Caucus; Congressional Veterans Jobs Caucus; Friends of a Free, Stable and Democratic Syria Caucus; House Republican Study Committee; Republican Main Street Partnership; committees: Armed Services; Science, Space, and Technology; elected to the 116th Congress on November 6, 2018.

Office Listings

https://waltz.house.gov https://facebook.com/repmichaelwaltz twitter: @RepMichaelWaltz
https://instagram.com/RepMichaelWaltz https://youtube.com/RepMichaelWaltz

216 Cannon House Office Building, Washington, DC 20515 .... (202) 225–2706
Chief of Staff.—Micah Ketchel. FAX: 226–6299
Legislative Director.—Walker Barrett.
Communications Director.—Allison Nielsen.
Scheduler.—Deborah Hansen.
1000 City Center Circle, 2nd Floor, Port Orange, FL 32129 .... (386) 238–9711
District Director.—Ernest Audino.
31 Lupi Court, Suite 130, Palm Coast, FL 32137 .... (386) 302–0442
120 South Florida Avenue, Suite 324, DeLand, FL 32720 .... (386) 279–0707

Counties: FLAGLER, ST. JOHNS, AND VOLUSIA (part). CITIES: Daytona Beach, Deltona, and Palm Coast. Population (2015), 755,981.

ZIP Codes: 32033, 32080–82, 32084, 32086, 32092, 32095, 32102 (part), 32110, 32112, 32114, 32117–19, 32124, 32127–32, 32134 (part), 32136–37, 32139, 32140 (part), 32141, 32145, 32147, 32148 (part), 32157, 32164, 32168 (part), 32169, 32174, 32176, 32177 (part), 32180–81, 32187, 32189–90, 32193, 32224 (part), 32259, 32640 (part), 32720 (part), 32724 (part), 32738 (part), 32744 (part), 32759, 32763–64 (part)

* * *

SEVENTH DISTRICT

STEPHANIE N. MURPHY, Democrat, of Winter Park, FL; born in Ho Chi Minh City, Vietnam, September 16, 1978; education: B.A., economics and international relations, College of

William and Mary, Williamsburg, VA, 2000; M.S., foreign service, Georgetown University, Washington, DC, 2004; professional: strategy and operations consultant, Deloitte, 2000–02; multiple roles at the U.S. Department of Defense, 2004–08, including national security specialist, Office of the Under Secretary of Defense for Policy; executive, SunGate Capital LLC, 2008–16; instructor, Rollins College, 2014–16; awards: Secretary of Defense Medal for Exceptional Civilian Service; married: Sean Murphy; children: Liem and Maya; appointments: U.S. Military Academy West Point Board of Visitors; caucuses: chair, Future Forum; co-chair, Blue Dog Coalition; Climate Solutions Caucus; Congressional Asian Pacific American Caucus; Equality Caucus; Gun Violence Prevention Task Force; Modeling, Simulation, and Training Caucus; New Democrat Coalition; Problem Solvers Caucus; committees: Ways and Means; elected to the 115th Congress on November 8, 2016; reelected to the 116th Congress on November 6, 2018.

Office Listings

https://stephaniemurphy.house.gov https://facebook.com/RepStephMurphy
https://twitter.com/RepStephMurphy https://instagram.com/RepStephMurphy

1710 Longworth House Office Building, Washington, DC 20515 .... (202) 225–4035
Chief of Staff.—Brad Howard. FAX: 226–0821
District Director.—Lauren Allen.
Deputy Chief of Staff / Legislative Director.—John Laufer.
Communications Director.—Jonathan Uriarte.
Scheduler.—Alli Everton.
225 East Robinson Street, Suite 525, Orlando, FL 32801 .... (888) 205–5421
110 West First Street, Suite 210, Sanford, FL 32771 .... (888) 205–5421

Counties: ORANGE COUNTY (part). CITIES AND TOWNSHIPS: Maitland, Orlando, and Winter Park. SEMINOLE COUNTY. CITIES AND TOWNSHIPS: Altamonte Springs, Casselberry, Lake Mary, Longwood, Oviedo, Sanford, and Winter Springs. Population (2010), 702,203.

ZIP Codes: 32168 (part), 32701, 32703 (part), 32707–08, 32712 (part), 32714, 32730, 32732, 32738 (part), 32744 (part), 32746 (part), 32750, 32751 (part), 32754 (part), 32765–66, 32771 (part), 32773 (part), 32779, 32789, 32792 (part), 32803–04 (part), 32807 (part), 32810 (part), 32814 (part), 32817 (part), 32820 (part), 32826 (part), 32833 (part)

* * *

EIGHTH DISTRICT

BILL POSEY, Republican, of Rockledge, FL; born in Washington, DC, December 18, 1947; education: graduated, Cocoa High School, 1966; A.A., Eastern Florida State College; professional: realtor; Rockledge City Council, 1976–86; Florida House of Representatives, 1992–2000; Florida Senate, 2000–08; National Legislator of the Year by the American Legislative Exchange Council; married: Katie Posey; children: Pamela and Catherine; caucuses: chair, Congressional Automotive Performance and Motorsports Caucus; chair, Congressional Estuary Caucus; chair, Congressional Motorsports Caucus; Congressional Autism Caucus; Congressional Kidney Caucus; House Aerospace Caucus; Military Veterans Caucus; committees: Financial Services; Science, Space, and Technology; elected to the 111th Congress on November 4, 2008; reelected to each succeeding Congress.

Office Listings

https://posey.house.gov https://facebook.com/bill.posey15 twitter: @congbillposey

2150 Rayburn House Office Building, Washington, DC 20515 .... (202) 225–3671
Chief of Staff.—Stuart Burns. FAX: 225–3516
Legislative Director.—Valentina Valenta.
Communications Director / Deputy Chief of Staff.—George Cecala.
Scheduler.—Grace Reid.
2725 Judge Fran Jamieson Way, Building C, Melbourne, FL 32940 .... (321) 632–1776
Indian River County .... (772) 226–1701
Titusville .... (321) 383–6090
District Director.—Patrick Gavin.
Directors of Community Relations: David Jackson, Rob Medina, Cheryl Moore.

Counties: BREVARD, INDIAN RIVER, AND ORANGE (part). Population (2010), 696,344.

ZIP Codes: 32709, 32754 (part), 32780, 32796, 32820 (part), 32828 (part), 32831 (part), 32833 (part), 32901, 32903–05, 32907–09, 32920, 32922, 32925–27, 32931, 32934–35, 32937, 32940, 32948–53, 32955, 32958, 32960, 32962–63, 32966–68, 32970, 32976

* * *

NINTH DISTRICT

DARREN SOTO, Democrat, of Kissimmee, FL; born in Ringwood, NJ, February 25, 1978; education: B.A., economics, Rutgers University, New Brunswick, NJ, 2000; J.D., George Washington University Law School, Washington, DC, 2004; professional: founder of Darren Soto Law Firm; served for 4 years in the Florida Senate; served for 5 years in the Florida House of Representatives; former member of the Civil Service Board for the City of Orlando; former treasurer of the Orange County Democrats; former vice president of communications for the Orange County Young Democrats; awards: Champion of Northern Everglades, the Audobon Society of Florida; religion: Roman Catholic; married to Amanda Soto; leadership: Democratic Steering and Policy, Assistant Regional Whip; caucuses: chair, Civil Rights and Voting Rights Task Force; Congenital Heart Caucus; Congressional #FutureForum; Congressional Hispanic Caucus; Japan Caucus; New Democrat Coalition; Problem Solvers Caucus; Turkey Caucus; committees: Energy and Commerce; Natural Resources; elected to the 115th Congress on November 8, 2016; reelected to the 116th Congress on November 6, 2018.

Office Listings

https://soto.house.gov https://facebook.com/CongressmanDarrenSoto
twitter: @RepDarrenSoto https://instagram.com/RepDarrenSoto

1507 Longworth House Office Building, Washington, DC 20515 .... (202) 225–9889
Chief of Staff.—Christine Biron. FAX: 225–9742
Deputy Chief of Staff / Scheduler.—Liana Guerra.
Legislative Director.—Mike Nichola.
Communications Director.—Oriana Pina.
Legislative Aides: Nicole McLaren, Martin Rivera, Bill Rockwood.
Staff Assistant.—Andrea Valdes.
804 Bryan Street, Kissimmee, FL 34741 .... (407) 452–1171
District Director.—Michelle Martinez.
Outreach Director.—Vivian Rodriguez.
13800 Veterans Way, Suite 1F806, Orlando, FL 32827 .... (202) 322–4476
Director of Constituent Services.—Shasta Shaffer.
620 East Main Street, Haines City, FL 33844 .... (202) 600–0843
FAX: 615–1308
451 3rd Street, NW., Winter Haven, FL 33881 .... (202) 600–0843
FAX: 615–1308

Counties: ORANGE (part), OSCEOLA, AND POLK (part). Population (2010), 753,549.

ZIP Codes: 32792 (part), 32803 (part), 32806–07 (part), 32809 (part), 32812 (part), 32814 (part), 32817 (part), 32821–22 (part), 32824–25, 32826 (part), 32827, 32828 (part), 32829, 32831 (part), 32832, 32837 (part), 33837–38 (part), 33844 (part), 33848, 33851, 33881 (part), 33896 (part), 34739, 34741, 34743–44, 34746, 34747 (part), 34758–59, 34769, 34771–73, 34972 (part)

* * *

TENTH DISTRICT

VAL BUTLER DEMINGS, Democrat, of Orlando, FL, born in Jacksonville, FL, March, 12, 1957; education: B.S., criminology, Florida State University; M.A., public administration, Webster University; professional: former Orlando Police Detective, Detective Sergeant, Police Chief; caucuses: vice chair, House Gun Violence Prevention Task Force; Congressional Black Caucus; Congressional Caucus for Women's Issues; Congressional Caucus on Black Women and Girls; Congressional Cybersecurity Caucus; Congressional Florida Ports Caucus; Congressional Pro-Choice Caucus; Congressional Travel and Tourism Caucus; Law Enforcement Caucus; New Democrat Coalition; committees: Homeland Security; Judiciary; Permanent Select Committee on Intelligence; elected to the 115th Congress on November 8, 2016; reelected to the 116th Congress on November 6, 2018.

Office Listings

https://demings.house.gov https://facebook.com/RepValDemings twitter: @RepValDemings

217 Cannon House Office Building, Washington, DC 20515 .... (202) 225–2176

Office Listings—Continued

Chief of Staff.—Wendy Anderson.
Legislative Director.—Aimee Collins-Mandeville.
Communications Director.—Daniel Gleick.
Senior Legislative Aide.—Stuart Styron.
Legislative Correspondent.—Brittan Robinson.
Staff Assistant.—Kathrin Bowyer.
Scheduler / Executive Assistant.—Wendy Featherson.
District Director.—Sonja White.
Director of Community and Economic Development.—Erin Waldron.
District Outreach Coordinator.—Mark Hinson.
Constituent Services Caseworker.—Chester Glover.
Staff Assistant.—Kathrin Bowyer.
District Outreach Coordinator / Constituent Services Caseworker.—Peggy Gustave.
Constituent Services Caseworker.—David Sanchez.
Wounded Warrior Fellow.—Natalia Romero Roman.

Counties: ORANGE (part).

ZIP Codes: 32703 (part), 32704, 32710, 32712, 32751, 32757 (part), 32768, 32776–77, 32789 (part), 32798, 32801 (part), 32802, 32803–06 (part), 32808, 32809 (part), 32810, 32811–12 (part), 32815, 32818–19 (part), 32821–22 (part), 32824, 32827, 32830, 32835 (part), 32836, 32837 (part), 32839 (part), 32854–55, 32858–62, 32868–69, 32877, 32885–86, 32891, 32896, 34734 (part), 34736–37, 34740, 34744, 34747 (part), 34760, 34761 (part), 34777–78, 34786–87

* * *

ELEVENTH DISTRICT

DANIEL WEBSTER, Republican, of Clermont, FL; born in Charleston, WV, April 27, 1949; education: graduated from Evans High School, Orlando, FL; B.S., Georgia Institute of Technology, Atlanta, GA, 1971; professional: president, Webster Air Conditioning & Heating, Inc., Orlando, FL; Florida House of Representatives, 1980–98; Speaker, Florida House of Representatives, 1996–98; Florida Senate, 1998–2008; Senate Majority Leader, Florida Senate, 2006–08; married: Sandy Jordan; father of six children and grandfather of 18; committees: Natural Resources; Transportation and Infrastructure; elected to represent the 8th District in the 112th Congress on November 2, 2010; elected to represent the 10th District in the 113th Congress on November 6, 2012, and reelected to the 114th Congress on November 4, 2014; elected to represent the 11th District in the 115th Congress on November 8, 2016; reelected to the 116th Congress on November 6, 2018.

Office Listings

https://webster.house.gov https://facebook.com/RepWebster twitter: @RepWebster

1210 Longworth House Office Building, Washington, DC 20515 .... (202) 225–1002
Chief of Staff / Communications Director.—Jaryn Emhof. FAX: 225–0999
Legislative Director.—Scott Mackenzie.
Legislative Assistant.—Jessica Thompson.
Communications Assistant.—Adam Pakledinaz.
Staff Assistant.—Vacant.
318 South 2nd Street, Suite A, Leesburg, FL 34748 .... (352) 241–9220
Constituent Services Director.—Stephen Shylkofski.
Scheduler.—Natali Knight.
Community Relations Representative.—Pam Jones.
Constituent Services Representatives: Sam Green, Debbie Warren.
Staff Assistant.—Natasha Dobrowski.
15 North Main Street, Suite B, Brooksville, FL 34601 .... (352) 241–9230
District Director.—Christa Pearson.
212 West Main Street, Suite 208A, Inverness, FL 34450 .... (352) 241–9204
Community Relations Associate.—Victoria White.
8015 East County Road 466, Suite B, The Villages, FL 32162 .... (352) 383–3552
Community Relations Representative.—Cindy Brown.

Counties: CITRUS, HERNANDO, LAKE (part), MARION (part), AND SUMTER. CITIES AND TOWNSHIPS: Brooksville, Ocala, and The Villages. Population (2010), 696,345.

ZIP Codes: 32111, 32133, 32158–59, 32162–63, 32179, 32183, 32195, 32702 (part), 32726 (part), 32735 (part), 32757 (part), 32778 (part), 32784 (part), 33513–14, 33521, 33523 (part), 33538, 33585, 33597 (part), 34420–21, 34423, 34428–29, 34432 (part), 34433–34, 34436, 34441–42, 34445–48, 34449 (part), 34450–53, 34460–61, 34464–65, 34470–71 (part), 34472, 34473–74 (part), 34476 (part), 34480–81 (part), 34483–84, 34487, 34488 (part), 34491–92, 34601–03, 34604 (part), 34605–09, 34611, 34613–14, 34636, 34661, 34705, 34711 (part), 34715 (part), 34729, 34731, 34736–37 (part), 34748–49, 34753 (part), 34755–56, 34762, 34785, 34787–88 (part), 34789, 34797

* * *

TWELFTH DISTRICT

GUS M. BILIRAKIS, Republican, of Palm Harbor, FL; born in Gainesville, FL, February 8, 1963; raised in Tarpon Springs, FL; education: B.A., University of Florida, 1986; J.D., Stetson University, 1989; son of former Representative Michael Bilirakis (1983–2006); professional: volunteered on his father's congressional campaigns; interned for President Ronald Reagan and the National Republican Congressional Committee; worked for former Representative Don Sundquist (R–TN); ran the Bilirakis Law Group in Holiday, FL; taught government classes at St. Petersburg College; member of the Florida House of Representatives, 1998–2006; chaired several prominent panels in the State House, including Crime Prevention, Public Safety Appropriations, and the Economic Development, Trade, and Banking Committee; married: Eva; children: Michael, Teddy, Manuel, and Nicholas; committees: Energy and Commerce; Veterans' Affairs; elected to the 110th Congress on November 7, 2006; reelected to each succeeding Congress.

Office Listings

https://bilirakis.house.gov https://facebook.com/gusbilirakis https://twitter.com/repgusbilirakis

2227 Rayburn House Office Building, Washington, DC 20515 .... (202) 225–5755
Chief of Staff.—Elizabeth Hittos. FAX: 225–4085
Legislative Director.—Jonathan Vecchi.
Deputy Chief of Staff / Communications Director.—Summer Robertson.
7132 Little Road, New Port Richey, FL 34654 .... (727) 232–2921
FAX: 232–2923
38500 U.S. Highway 19 North, Room BB–038, Tarpon Springs, FL 34689 .... (727) 940–5860
FAX: 940–5861

Counties: HILLSBOROUGH (part): Lutz and Odessa. PASCO: Aripeka, Bayonet Point, Crystal Springs, Dade City, Elfers, Holiday, Hudson, Lacoochee, Land O'Lakes, New Port Richey, Port Richey, San Antonio, Shady Hills, Spring Hill, St. Leo, Tilby, Trinity, Wesley Chapel, and Zephyrhills. PINELLAS (part): Dunedin, Clearwater, East Lake, Oldsmar, Ozona, Palm Harbor, Safety Harbor, and Tarpon Springs. Population (2015), 740,955.

ZIP Codes: 33523 (part), 33525, 33540 (part), 33541–45, 33548–49 (part), 33556, 33558, 33559 (part), 33574, 33576, 33597 (part), 33612–13 (part), 33618 (part), 33624–26 (part), 33647 (part), 33761 (part), 34610, 34637–39, 34652–55, 34667–69, 34677 (part), 34679 (part), 34681, 34683–84 (part), 34685, 34688–91, 34695 (part), 34698 (part)

* * *

THIRTEENTH DISTRICT

CHARLIE CRIST, Democrat, of St. Petersburg, FL; born in Altoona, PA, July 24, 1956; education: graduated from St. Petersburg High School, 1974; B.A., Florida State University, Tallahassee, FL, 1978; J.D., Samford University Cumberland School of Law, Birmingham, AL, 1981; professional: former Florida State Senator; former Education Commissioner of Florida; former Attorney General of Florida; Florida's 44th Governor; religion: Methodist; committees: Appropriations; Science, Space, and Technology; elected to the 115th Congress on November 8, 2016; reelected to the 116th Congress on November 6, 2018.

Office Listings

https://crist.house.gov https://facebook.com/RepCharlieCrist twitter: @RepCharlieCrist

215 Cannon House Office Building, Washington, DC 20515 .... (202) 225–5961
Chief of Staff.—Austin Durrer. FAX: 225–9764
Legislative Director.—Christopher Fisher.
Legislative Assistant.—Ryan McGuire.
Senior Legislative Assistant.—Sarah Hanson.
Legislative Assistant.—Virginia Poe.
Legislative Correspondent.—David Thompson.
Scheduler.—Jonathan Pekkala.
Press Assistant.—Samantha Ramirez.
Staff Assistant.—Justin Oh.
696 1st Avenue North, Suite #203, St. Petersburg, FL 33701 .... (727) 318–6770
District Director.—Steven Cary. FAX: 623–0619
Deputy District Director.—Gershom Faulkner.
Constituent Services Manager / District Press Assistant.—Chloe Kessock.
Constituent Services Representatives: Michael Batista, Dillion Stafford.
District Operations and Outreach Manager.—Kendrick Lewis.

Counties: PINELLAS COUNTY (part). CITIES AND TOWNSHIPS: Bardmoor, Bay Pines, Bear Creek, Belleair, Belleair Beach, Belleair Bluffs, Belleair Shore, Clearwater, Dunedin, Feather Sound, Greenbriar, Gulfport, Harbor Bluffs, Indian Rocks Beach, Indian Shores, Kenneth City, Largo, Lealman, Madeira Beach, North Redington Beach, Olsmar, Pinellas Park, Redington Beach, Redington Shores, Ridgecrest, Safety Harbor, Seminole, South Highpoint, South Pasadena, St. Pete Beach, St. Petersburg, Tierra Verde, Treasure Island, and West Lealman. Population (2012), 702,203.

ZIP Codes: 33701 (part), 33702–03, 33704–05 (part), 33706, 33707 (part), 33708–09, 33710–11 (part), 33713 (part), 33714–16, 33744, 33755–56, 33759–60, 33761 (part), 33762–65, 33767, 33770–74, 33776–78, 33781–82, 33785–86, 34677 (part), 34683–84 (part), 34695 (part), 34698

* * *

FOURTEENTH DISTRICT

KATHY CASTOR, Democrat, of Tampa, FL; born in Miami, FL, August 20, 1966; education: B.A., political science, Emory University, 1988; J.D., Florida State University, 1991; professional: Assistant General Counsel, State of Florida, Department of Community Affairs, 1991–94; attorney, Icard Merrill, 1994–95; partner, Broad and Cassel, 1995–2000; ran for Florida State Senate, 2000; Hillsborough County Commissioner, 2002–06; religion: member of Palma Ceia Presbyterian Church; married: William Lewis; children: two; committees: chair, Select Committee on the Climate Crisis; Energy and Commerce; elected to the 110th Congress on November 7, 2006; reelected to each succeeding Congress.

Office Listings

https://castor.house.gov https://facebook.com/USRepKathyCastor https://twitter.com/USRepKCastor

2052 Rayburn House Office Building, Washington, DC 20515 .... (202) 225–3376
Chief of Staff.—Clay Phillips. FAX: 225–5652
Deputy Chief of Staff / Scheduler.—Lara Hopkins.
Legislative Director.—Elizabeth Brown.
4144 North Armenia Avenue, Suite 300, Tampa, FL 33607 .... (813) 871–2817
District Director.—Marcia Mejia.
Press Secretary.—Steven Angotti.

Counties: HILLSBOROUGH. CITIES: East Lake-Orient Park, Egypt Lake-Leto, Gibsonton, Lake Magdalene, Northdale, Palm River-Clair Mel, Tampa, Town 'n' Country, University of South Florida, and Westchase. Population (2015), 757,440.

ZIP Codes: 33510–11 (part), 33534 (part), 33549 (part), 33570 (part), 33572, 33578 (part), 33584 (part), 33602–07, 33609, 33610 (part), 33611, 33612–13 (part), 33614–16, 33617–18 (part), 33619, 33621, 33624–26 (part), 33629, 33634–35, 33637 (part), 33701 (part), 33704–05 (part), 33707 (part), 33710–11 (part), 33712, 33713 (part)

* * *

FIFTEENTH DISTRICT

ROSS SPANO, Republican, of Dover, FL; born in Tampa, Hillsborough County, FL, July 16, 1966; education: graduated from Brandon High School, Brandon, FL, 1984; B.A., Hillsborough Community College, University of South Florida, Tampa, FL, 1994; J.D., Florida State University, Tallahassee, FL, 1998; professional: lawyer, private practice; member of the Florida State House of Representatives, 2012–18; religion: Christianity; married: Amie Spano; children: four; committees: Small Business; Transportation and Infrastructure; elected to the 116th Congress on November 6, 2018.

Office Listings

https://spano.house.gov https://facebook.com/RepRossSpano twitter: @RepRossSpano

224 Cannon House Office Building, Washington, DC 20515 .... (202) 225–1252
Chief of Staff.—Jamie Robinette. FAX: 226–0585
Legislative Director.—Gus Ashton.
Scheduler.—Naomi Hilton.
124 South Florida Avenue, Suite 304, Lakeland, FL 33801 .... (863) 644–8215
District Director.—Blaine Gravitt.

Counties: HILLSBOROUGH (part). CITIES AND TOWNSHIPS: Bloomingdale, Brandon, Dover, East Lake-Orient Park, Fish Hawk, Lake Magdalene, Mango, Pebble Creek, Plant City, Riverview, Seffner, Tampa, Temple Terrace, Thonotosassa, and Valrico. POLK (part). CITIES AND TOWNSHIPS: Combee Settlement, Crystal Lake, Fussels Corner, Highland City, Kathleen, Lakeland Highlands, Lakeland, and Medulla. LAKE (part). CITIES AND TOWNSHIPS: Clermont, Four Corners, Groveland, Orange Mountain, Polk City, Skytop, and South Clermont. Population (2010), 813,570.

ZIP Codes: 33510–11 (part), 33527, 33540 (part), 33547–49 (part), 33559 (part), 33563, 33565–67, 33569 (part), 33578 (part), 33584 (part), 33592, 33594, 33596 (part), 33610 (part), 33612–13 (part), 33617–18 (part), 33620, 33637 (part),

33647 (part), 33801, 33803, 33805 (part), 33809 (part), 33810–13, 33815, 33823 (part), 33830 (part), 33849, 33860 (part), 33868 (part), 33880 (part)

* * *

SIXTEENTH DISTRICT

VERN BUCHANAN, Republican, of Longboat Key, FL; born in Detroit, MI, May 8, 1951; education: B.B.A., business administration, Cleary University; M.B.A., University of Detroit; honorary degree: Doctorate of Science in Business Administration, Cleary University; professional: founder and chairman, Buchanan Enterprises; founder and chairman, Buchanan Automotive Group, 1992; operations include Sarasota Ford and 18 auto franchises in the southeastern United States; experience in real estate including home building and property development and management; awards: One of America's Ten Outstanding Young Men, U.S. Jaycees; Entrepreneur of the Year, *Inc.* Magazine and Arthur Young; Entrepreneur of the Year, Harvard Business School, Club of Detroit; One of Michigan's Five Outstanding Young Men, Michigan Jaycees; President's Award, Ford Motor Company; Certified Retailer Award, J.D. Power and Associates; Outstanding Citizen Award, United Negro College Fund; Outstanding Philanthropic Corporation Award, National Society of Fund Raising Executives; Freedom Award for Business and Industry, NAACP; The American Jewish Committee Civic Achievement Award; Tampa Bay Business Hall of Fame Award; married: Sandy Buchanan; children: James and Matt; committees: Ways and Means; elected to the 110th Congress on November 7, 2006; reelected to each succeeding Congress.

Office Listings

https://buchanan.house.gov https://facebook.com/CongressmanBuchanan twitter: @VernBuchanan

2427 Rayburn House Office Building, Washington, DC 20515 .... (202) 225–5015
Chief of Staff.—Dave Karvelas. FAX: 226–0828
Deputy Chief of Staff/Legislative Director.—Sean Brady.
Senior Policy Counsel.—Ashley Rose.
Communications Director.—Anthony Cruz.
Scheduler.—Jaclyn Knight.
111 South Orange Avenue, Suite 202W, Sarasota, FL 34236 .... (941) 951–6643
District Director.—Sally Dionne.
1051 Manatee Avenue West, Suite 305, Bradenton, FL 34205 .... (941) 747–9081

Counties: MANATEE AND SARASOTA. Population (2010), 639,345.

ZIP Codes: 33834, 34211–12, 34219, 34221, 34223, 34240–41, 34251, 34287–88, 34292–93

* * *

SEVENTEENTH DISTRICT

W. GREGORY STEUBE, Republican, of Sarasota, FL; born in Bradenton, Manatee County, FL, May 19, 1978; graduated from Southeast High School, Bradenton, FL, 1996; B.A., University of Florida, Gainesville, 2000; J.D., University of Florida, Gainesville, FL, 2003; professional: attorney; member of the Florida State House of Representatives, 2010–16; member of the Florida State Senate, 2016–18; military: United States Army Airborne Infantry Officer and Judge Advocate General's Corps, Captain, 2004–08; awards: Commendation Medal; National Defense Service Medal; Global War on Terrorism Service Medal; Iraq Campaign Medal; Army Service Ribbon; Overseas Service Bar; Parachutist Badge; religion: Christian; married: Jennifer; children: Ethan; committees: Judiciary; Oversight and Reform; Veterans' Affairs; elected to the 116th Congress on November 6, 2018.

Office Listings

https://steube.house.gov https://facebook.com/RepGregSteube
twitter: @RepGregSteube https://instagram.com/repgregsteube

521 Cannon House Office Building, Washington, DC 20515 .... (202) 225–5792
Chief of Staff.—Alex Blair. FAX: 225–3132
Legislative Director.—Reginald Darby.
Communications Director.—Rachel Harris.
Legislative Counsel.—Justin Tamayo.
Scheduler.—Gabrielle Cirenza.
226 Taylor Street, Suite 230, Punta Gorda, FL 33950 .... (941) 499–3214

Office Listings—Continued

304 Northwest 2nd Street, Okeechobee, FL 34972 .... (941) 499–3214
4507 George Boulevard, Sebring, FL 33875 .... (941) 499–3214
District Director.—Sydney Gruters.

Counties: CHARLOTTE, DESOTO, GLADES, HARDEE, HIGHLANDS, LEE (part), OKEECHOBEE, POLK (part), AND SARASOTA (part). Population (2010), 696,344.

ZIP Codes: 33471, 33503, 33511 (part), 33534 (part), 33547 (part), 33569–70 (part), 33573, 33578 (part), 33579, 33596 (part), 33598 (part), 33825, 33827, 33830 (part), 33834, 33838 (part), 33839, 33841, 33843, 33844 (part), 33847, 33852–59, 33860 (part), 33865, 33867, 33870, 33872–73, 33875–77, 33880–81 (part), 33884 (part), 33890, 33898, 33903 (part), 33905 (part), 33917 (part), 33920, 33921 (part), 33935–36 (part), 33944, 33946–48, 33950, 33952–54, 33955 (part), 33960, 33971 (part), 33972, 33974 (part), 33980–83, 34219 (part), 34223–24 (part), 34251 (part), 34266 (part), 34268–69, 34972 (part), 34974 (part)

* * *

EIGHTEENTH DISTRICT

BRIAN J. MAST, Republican, of Palm City, FL; born in Grand Rapids, MI, July 10, 1980; education: bachelor's degree in extension studies with a concentration in economics and minors in government and environmental studies, Harvard Extension School, Cambridge, MA, 2016; professional: analyst in NA–42 Office of Emergency Response, National Nuclear Security Administration, Department of Energy; instructor in post-blast analysis and homemade explosives, Bureau of Alcohol, Tobacco, and Firearms; explosive specialist under the Department of Homeland Security; military: 12-year Army veteran, including under the elite Joint Special Operations Command; awards: Bronze Star Medal; Army Commendation Medal for Valor; Purple Heart Medal; Defense Meritorious Service Medal; religion: Christian; family: wife, Brianna; children: Magnum, Maverick, and Madeline; committees: Foreign Affairs; Transportation and Infrastructure; elected to the 115th Congress on November 8, 2016; reelected to the 116th Congress on November 6, 2018.

Office Listings

https://mast.house.gov https://facebook.com/RepBrianMast twitter: @RepBrianMast
https://instagram.com/RepBrianMast

2182 Rayburn House Office Building, Washington, DC 20515 .... (202) 225–3026
Chief of Staff.—James Langenderfer. FAX: 225–8398
Deputy Chief of Staff.—Brad Stewart.
Legislative Director.—Barry Smith.
Director of Operations.—Jaclyn Neuman.
Press Secretary.—Kyle VonEnde.
Legislative Assistants: Sarah Miller, Michael Weglein.
Legislative Aide.—Julian Fleischman.
Legislative Correspondent.—Stephanie Cope.
171 Southwest Flagler Avenue, Stuart, FL 34994 .... (772) 403–0900
Deputy Chief of Staff.—Stephen Leighton.
Constituent Services Representative.—Amy Galante.
Field Representative.—John Haddox.
121 Southwest Port St. Lucie Boulevard, Room 187, Port St. Lucie, FL 34984 .... (772) 336–2877
Constituent Services Director.—Kalene Rowley.
Constituent Services Representative.—Derek Hankerson.
Outreach Coordinator.—Angel Robertson.
420 U.S. Highway 1, Suite 19, North Palm Beach, FL 33408 .... (561) 530–7778
District Director.—Nick Ciotti.
Constituent Services Representatives: Kyle Morgan, John South.

Counties: MARTIN, PALM BEACH (northern part), AND ST. LUCIE. CITIES: Eden, Fort Pierce, Hobe Sound, Hutchinson Island, Indian River Estates, Indiantown, Jensen Beach, Juno Beach, Jupiter, Jupiter Inlet Colony, Jupiter Island, Lakewood Park, Loxahatchee, North Palm Beach, Palm Beach Gardens, Palm Beach Shores, Palm City, Port Salerno, Port St. Lucie, Riviera Beach, Royal Palm Beach, Sewall's Point, Singer Island (part), Stuart, Tequesta, Tradition, and West Palm Beach (part). Population (2010), 696,345.

ZIP Codes: 33403–04, 33407–12, 33417–18, 33420, 33422, 33438, 33455, 33458, 33468–70, 33475, 33477–78, 34945–54, 34956–58, 34972, 34974, 34979, 34981–88, 34990–92, 34994–97

* * *

NINETEENTH DISTRICT

FRANCIS ROONEY, Republican, of Naples, FL; born in Tulsa, OK, December 4, 1953; education: A.B., English, Georgetown University, Washington, DC, 1975; J.D., Georgetown University, Washington, DC, 1978; professional: former CEO of an international investment company; U.S. Ambassador to the Holy See, 2005–08; religion: Catholic; family: wife, Kathleen C. Rooney; three children: Larry, married to Porscha; Michael, married to Frances; and Kathleen, married to Rob; one grandson, Beckett, and one granddaughter, Bergen; committees: Foreign Affairs; Science, Space, and Technology; elected to the 115th Congress on November 8, 2016; reelected to the 116th Congress on November 6, 2018.

Office Listings

https://francisrooney.house.gov https://facebook.com/RepRooney twitter: @RepRooney

120 Cannon House Office Building, Washington, DC 20515 .... (202) 225–2536
Chief of Staff.—Jessica Carter.
Legislative Director.—Corey Schrodt.
Communications Director.—Chris Berardi.
Scheduler.—Chloe Wick.
3299 Tamiami Trail East, Suite 105, Naples, FL 34112 .... (239) 252–6225
1039 Southeast 9th Avenue, Suite 308, Cape Coral, FL 33990 .... (239) 599–6033

Counties: COLLIER (part) AND LEE (part). Population (2010), 696,345.

ZIP Codes: 33901, 33903 (part), 33904, 33905 (part), 33907–09, 33912–14, 33916, 33917 (part), 33919, 33921 (part), 33922, 33924, 33928, 33931, 33936 (part), 33945, 33955 (part), 33956–57, 33965–67, 33971 (part), 33973, 33974 (part), 33976, 33990–91, 33993, 34101–03, 34104–05 (part), 34108, 34109 (part), 34110, 34112 (part), 34113, 34114 (part), 34119 (part), 34134–35, 34140, 34145

* * *

TWENTIETH DISTRICT

ALCEE L. HASTINGS, Democrat, of Delray Beach, FL; born in Altamonte Springs, FL, September 5, 1936; education: graduated, Crooms Academy, Sanford, FL, 1954; B.A., Fisk University, Nashville, TN, 1958; Howard University, Washington, DC; J.D., Florida A&M University, Tallahassee, 1963; professional: attorney; admitted to the Florida bar, 1963; Circuit Judge, U.S. District Court for the Southern District of Florida; member: NAACP; Miami-Dade Chamber of Commerce; Family Christian Association; ACLU; Southern Poverty Law Center; National Organization for Women; Planned Parenthood; Women and Children First, Inc.; Sierra Club; Cousteau Society; Broward County Democratic Executive Committee; Dade County Democratic Executive Committee; Lauderhill Democratic Club; Hollywood Hills Democratic Club; Pembroke Pines Democratic Club; Urban League; National Bar Association; Florida Chapter of the National Bar Association; T.J. Reddick Bar Association; National Conference of Black Lawyers; Simon Wiesenthal Center; The Furtivist Society; Progressive Black Police Officers Club; International Black Firefighters Association; co-chair, Florida Delegation; religion: member, African Methodist Episcopal Church; family: three children: Alcee Lamar II, Chelsea, and Leigh; ranking Democratic member, Helsinki Commission; Senior Democratic Whip; committees: Rules; elected on November 3, 1992, to the 103rd Congress; reelected to each succeeding Congress.

Office Listings

https://alceehastings.house.gov https://facebook.com/RepHastingsFL https://twitter.com/RepHastingsFL

2353 Rayburn House Office Building, Washington, DC 20515 .... (202) 225–1313
Chief of Staff.—Lale Morrison. FAX: 225–1171
Legislative Director / Senior Counsel.—Tom Carnes.
Counsel / Rules Associate.—Lindsey Garber.
Senior Legislative Assistant.—Evan Polisar.
Legislative Assistant / Communications Director.—Katrina Martell.
Director of Operations.—DeBorah Posey.
5701 Northwest 88th Avenue, Suite 200, Tamarac, FL 33321 .... (954) 733–2800
District Director.—Patricia Williams.
5725 Corporate Way, Suite 208, West Palm Beach, FL 33407 .... (561) 469–7048

Counties: BROWARD (part) AND PALM BEACH (part). Population, 713,165.

ZIP Codes: 33060 (part), 33063–64 (part), 33066 (part), 33068, 33069 (part), 33071 (part), 33301 (part), 33304–05 (part), 33309 (part), 33311–12 (part), 33313, 33317 (part), 33319, 33321, 33322 (part), 33326–27 (part), 33334 (part), 33351, 33401 (part), 33403–11 (part), 33413–15 (part), 33417–18 (part), 33426 (part), 33428 (part), 33430, 33435 (part), 33438 (part), 33440–42 (part), 33449 (part), 33460 (part), 33462 (part), 33470 (part), 33472 (part), 33476, 33493, 34142 (part)

* * *

TWENTY-FIRST DISTRICT

LOIS FRANKEL, Democrat, of West Palm Beach, FL; born in New York City, NY, May 16, 1948; education: B.A., Boston University, Boston, MA, 1970; J.D., Georgetown University Law Center, Washington, DC, 1973; professional: elected State Representative in the 83rd District of the Florida House of Representatives, 1986; first female Florida House Minority Leader from 1995–2003; elected Mayor of West Palm Beach from 2003–11; religion: Jewish; caucuses: co-chair, Democratic Women's Caucus; Bipartisan Congressional Task Force on Alzheimer's Disease; Bipartisan Task Force for Combating Anti-Semitism; Congressional Animal Protection Caucus; Congressional Arts Caucus; Congressional Boating Caucus; Congressional Everglades Caucus; Congressional Human Trafficking Caucus; Congressional LGBT Equality Caucus; Congressional Military Sexual Assault Prevention Caucus; Congressional Ports Caucus; Congressional Pro-Choice Caucus; Congressional Progressive Caucus; Congressional Travel and Tourism Caucus; Democratic Israel Working Group; Safe Climate Caucus; committees: Appropriations; Joint Economic Committee; elected to the 113th Congress on November 6, 2012; reelected to each succeeding Congress.

Office Listings

https://frankel.house.gov https://facebook.com/RepLoisFrankel https://twitter.com/RepLoisFrankel

2305 Rayburn House Office Building, Washington, DC 20515 .... (202) 225–9890
Chief of Staff.—Kelsey Moran. FAX: 225–1224
Legislative Director.—Ian Wolf.
Legislative Assistants: Daniel Bleiberg, MiQuel Davies, Bradley Solyan.
Communications Director.—Rachel Huxley-Cohen.
Press Secretaries: Olivia Hodge, Gillian Spolarich.
Scheduler.—Kate Regan.
Staff Assistant.—Nisha Thanawala.
2500 North Military Trail, Suite 490, Boca Raton, FL 33431 .... (561) 998–9045
District Director.—Felicia Goldstein. FAX: 998–9048

Counties: PALM BEACH. CITIES: Boynton Beach, Delray Beach, Greenacres, Lake Worth, Wellington, and West Palm Beach. Population (2010), 738,875.

ZIP Codes: 33400–01, 33411, 33414, 33422, 33424, 33426, 33435, 33437, 33444, 33448–49, 33460, 33467, 33472, 33474, 33482, 33484

* * *

TWENTY-SECOND DISTRICT

THEODORE DEUTCH, Democrat, of Fort Lauderdale, FL; born in Bethlehem, PA, May 7, 1966; education: graduate of Liberty High School; B.A., University of Michigan, Ann Arbor, MI, 1988; J.D., University of Michigan Law School, Ann Arbor, 1990; admitted to the Florida Bar, 1991; professional: attorney; Florida State Senator, 2006–10; member: Florida Bar Association; Jewish Federation of South Palm Beach County; League of Women Voters; married to the former Jill Weinstock; three children; committees: chair, Ethics; Foreign Affairs; Judiciary; elected, by special election, to the 111th Congress on April 13, 2010, to fill the vacancy caused by the resignation of U.S. Representative Robert Wexler; reelected to each succeeding Congress.

Office Listings

https://teddeutch.house.gov https://facebook.com/CongressmanTedDeutch
twitter: @RepTedDeutch https://instagram.com/repteddeutch

2447 Rayburn House Office Building, Washington, DC 20515 .... (202) 225–3001
Chief of Staff.—Joshua Rogin. FAX: 225–5974
Deputy Chief of Staff.—Ellen McLaren.
Press Secretary.—Jason Attermann.
7900 Glades Road, Suite 250, Boca Raton, FL 33434 .... (561) 470–5440
District Director.—Wendi Lipsich. FAX: 470–5446

Counties: BROWARD (part). CITIES: Broadview Park, Coconut Creek, Deerfield Beach, Fort Lauderdale, Hillsboro Beach, Lauderdale-by-the-Sea, Lighthouse Point, Oakland Park, Pompano Beach, Sea Ranch Lakes, and Wilton Manors. PALM BEACH (part). CITIES: Boca Raton and Highland Beach. Population (2010), 696,345.

ZIP Codes: 33060 (part), 33062, 33064 (part), 33069 (part), 33301 (part), 33304–05 (part), 33306, 33308, 33309 (part), 33311–12 (part), 33315–17 (part), 33322–25 (part), 33334 (part), 33401 (part), 33404–07 (part), 33415 (part), 33426 (part), 33431–32, 33433–36 (part), 33441 (part), 33444–45, 33460 (part), 33461, 33462–63 (part), 33480, 33483, 33484 (part), 33486–87, 33496 (part)

* * *

TWENTY-THIRD DISTRICT

DEBBIE WASSERMAN SCHULTZ, Democrat, of Weston, FL; born in Forest Hills, Queens County, NY, September 27, 1966; education: B.A., University of Florida, Gainesville, FL, 1988; M.A., University of Florida, 1990; professional: public policy curriculum specialist, Nova Southeastern University; adjunct instructor, political science, Broward Community College; aide to Florida State House of Representatives member Peter Deutsch, 1989–92; member, Florida State House of Representatives, 1992–2000; member, Florida State Senate, 2000–04; organizations: board of trustees, Westside Regional Medical Center; Outstanding Freshman Legislator, Florida Women's Political Caucus; board of directors, American Jewish Congress; member, Broward National Organization for Women; board of directors, National Safety Council, South Florida Chapter; religion: Jewish; married: Steve; children: Rebecca, Jake, and Shelby; Chief Deputy Democratic Whip; chair, Democratic National Committee, 2011–16; committees: Appropriations; Oversight and Reform; elected to the 109th Congress on November 2, 2004; reelected to each succeeding Congress.

Office Listings

https://wassermanschultz.house.gov https://facebook.com/RepDWS twitter: @repDWStweets

1114 Longworth House Office Building, Washington, DC 20515 .... (202) 225–7931
Chief of Staff.—Tracie Pough. FAX: 226–2052
District Director.—Vivian Piereschi.
Communications Director.—David Damron.
Legislative Director.—Lauren Wolman.
Scheduler / Executive Assistant.—Lauren Mylott.
777 Sawgrass Corporate Parkway, Sunrise, FL 33325 .... (954) 845–1179
19200 West Country Club Drive, Third Floor, Aventura, FL 33180 .... (305) 936–5724

Counties: BROWARD COUNTY (part). CITIES: Cooper City, Dania Beach, Davie, Fort Lauderdale, Hallandale Beach, Hollywood, Pembroke Pines, Plantation, Southwest Ranches, Sunrise, and Weston. MIAMI-DADE COUNTY (part). CITIES: Aventura, Bal Harbour, Bay Harbor Islands, Golden Beach, Indian Creek, Sunny Isles Beach, and Surfside. Population (2010), 703,594.

ZIP Codes: 33004, 33009 (part), 33019–20, 33021 (part), 33023–25 (part), 33026, 33027 (part), 33028, 33029 (part), 33109 (part), 33132 (part), 33139 (part), 33140, 33141 (part), 33154 (part), 33160 (part), 33179–81 (part), 33312 (part), 33314, 33315–17 (part), 33323–27 (part), 33328, 33330–31, 33332 (part)

* * *

TWENTY-FOURTH DISTRICT

FREDERICA S. WILSON, Democrat, of Miami, FL; born in Miami, November 5; education: B.S., Fisk University; M.S., University of Miami; honorary doctorate of humane letters, Florida Memorial University and Bethune-Cookman University; professional: executive director, Office of Alternative Education and Dropout Prevention, Miami-Dade County Schools; member, Miami-Dade County School Board, 1992–98; Minority Whip, Florida State House of Representatives, 1998–2002; Democratic Whip, Florida State Senate, 2002–04; Minority Leader Pro Tempore, Florida State Senate, 2002–10; Minority Whip, Florida State Senate, 2008–10; organizations: regional director, Alpha Kappa Alpha Sorority, Inc., 1986–present; founder / member, 5000 Role Models of Excellence, Inc., 1993–present; founder, Stop Day Enough is Enough, 1996–present; Miami delegate, President's Summit for America's Future, 1997; State of Florida "STOP DAY", Enough is Enough, founder, 1996; President's Summit for America's Future, 1997; founder, Miami-Dade County "Keep Me Safe" summit, march, and candlelight vigil; board member, Women's Action for New Directions Educational Fund, 2004; current member, National Association of Black School Educators; current member, the Links, Inc.; honors and awards: Southern Living, Outstanding Southerner, May 1993; Macedonia Missionary Baptist Church, Image Maker, 1993; South Florida Association of Black Journalists, Kuumba Award, 1994; St. Petersburg Junior College, In Recognition, 1996; American Red Cross, Spectrum Award, 1998; African-American Achiever Award for Education, 1998; Peace Education Foundation, Peacemaker of the Year, 1998; Youth Crime Watch / Citizens Crime Watch, a Champion for All Poor and Minority Students, 1998; Imperial Daughters of Isis Miami Beach, Florida Hall of Fame, 1999; NAACP, Florida Chapter, Morris Milton Memorial Award, 2001; Zeta Phi Beta Sorority, Inc., Leadership Award, 2001; Florida A&M University, National Alumni Association Expresses Gratitude, 2001; The Florida HIV-AIDS Ministries, Inc., Honors State Representative Frederica S. Wilson, 2001; Florida AIDS Action, Outstanding Leadership and Support for HIV/AIDS and Health Care, 2002; Alpha Kappa Alpha Sorority, Inc., In Appreciation, 2002; Western Union, L'Union Fait la Force Award, 2003; Community Action Agency, Citizen of the Year Award, 2004; American Cancer Society, Florida Chapter, Legislative Leadership Award, 2004; Florida Education Association, Educator of the Year, 2004; Association of Black Health-System Pharmacists, Legislator Achievement Award, 2004; Easter Seals of Miami-Dade, Legislator of the Year Award, 2004; Northside Seventh Day Adventist Church (Miami), Distinguished Community Leader Award, 2004; The Black Archives, History and Research Foundation of South Florida, Inc., Chairman's Award, 2004; Sierra Club, Florida Chapter, Legislative Recognition Award, 2004; Network Miami Magazine, One of Miami's 50 Most Influential Black Business Professionals, 2004; Millennium Movers, Inc., Shaker Award, 2004; Alpha Kappa Alpha Sorority, Ft. Pierce, Florida Chapter, Soror of the Year, 2005; Alpha Kappa Alpha Sorority, Ft. Walton Beach, Florida Chapter, Soror of the Year, 2005; Alpha Kappa Alpha Sorority, Thomasville, GA Chapter, Soror of the Year, 2005; Carrie P. Meek Education Leadership Achievement Award, 2005; Miami Gardens Jaycees, Distinguished Service Award, 2005; Alpha Kappa Alpha, Inc., Emerald Service Award, 2005; The Links, Inc., Links of Gold Award, 2005; Belafonte TACOLCY Center, Inc., U.S. Department of Justice/Drug Enforcement Administration in Recognition of State Senator Frederica S. Wilson, 2005; SEIU Florida Healthcare Union, Legislative Hero Award, 2006; Barry University, SGA Acknowledgement of Florida's Residents Access Grant Award, 2006; City of Miami, Women Builders of Community Dreams Award, 2006; Florida Memorial University, SGA Leadership Character and Service Award, 2006; Holy Faith Missionary Baptist Church, Participation Award, 2006; Miami-Dade Police Department, Appreciation Award, 2006; The Historic St. Agnes Episcopal Church, 108th Anniversary Appreciation Award, 2006; FAU, Small Business Development Appreciation Award, 2006; Day of the Child, Mentoring Award, 2006; Project H.O.P.E., Katrina Humanitarian Award, 2006; South Florida Chapter of the Coalition of Black Trade Unionists, Audrey McCollum Scholarship Award, 2006; CEO Magazine, Legislative Action Recognition, 2006; Community Action Agency, Youth Leadership Award, 2006; I.B.P.O.E. of W., Antlers Temple #39, Legislative Excellence Award, 2006; Community Health of South Dade, Inc., Health Hero Award, 2006; Health Council of South Florida, Inc., Health Leadership Award, 2006; National Coalition of 100 Black Women, Inc., Greater Miami Chapter, Candace Award, 2006; Kiwanis Club of Miami Shores, North Dade Exemplary Service Award, 2006; Academy of Florida Trial Lawyers, Rosemary Barkett Award, 2006; National Pan Hellenic Council, Inc., Celebration of Excellence, 2006; NAACP Milton Morris Award, 2007; Jessie C. Trice Humanitarian Award, 2007; Liberty City's Community Action Agency, Community Service Award, 2007; Miami Dade College, Pathway to Opportunity Appreciation Award, 2007; Florida Association of School Administrators, Legislator of the Year, 2007; Florida Association of Women Lawyers, Legislative Recognition Award, 2007; Florida Health Center, Jessie C. Trice Humanitarian Award, 2007; Miami Dade Community Action Agency, Liberty City Advisor Committee in Recognition of State Senator Frederica S. Wilson June 2007; The National Medical Association, Scroll of Merit for Public Education Advocacy, 2008; American School Health Association, Legislator of the Year, 2008; Alpha Kappa Alpha Sorority International, Rosa Parks Coretta Scott King Award, 2008; Florida Association of Counties (FAC), County Partner Award, 2008; Florida Cable Telecommunications Association, Leaders in Learning Award, 2008; AKA Educational Advancement Foundation, The Green Diamond Award, 2008; Bethune-Cookman University, In Tribute, 2009; Alpha Kappa Alpha Sorority, Inc., With Appreciation, 2009; The Links, Inc., In Appreciation, 2010 Alpha Kappa Alpha Sorority, Inc., Timeless Service to Mankind, 2011; Miami Dade Chamber of Commerce, H.T. Smith Lifetime Achievement Award, 2011; ICABA, Salutes South Florida's 100 Accomplished Caribbean Americans, 2012; TheGrio.com, The Grio's 100, 2012; Louie Bing Scholarship Fund, Inc., Award of Excellence, 2012; National Voices for Equality Education and Enlightenment Voices of Leadership Award, Congresswoman Wilson, April 2012; First Focus Campaign for Children, Defender of Children, 2012; Youth Power Movement, First Annual Humanitarian Award, 2012; I Am Empowered for Jobs Award, National Urban League, 2013; Broward Black Elected Officials Inaugural Lifetime Achievement Community Service Award; The Links, Inc., Services to Youth Award, 2013; City of North Miami, In Recognition, 2013; Honorary Nigerian Chieftaincy title of "Jagunmolu," which means The People's Warrior in the Yoruba language, October 2016; Appreciation Trophy, City of Miami Gardens, 2016; Appreciation Trophy, City of North Miami, 2016; Visionary Honoree, Little Haiti Cultural Complex Women's International Month, 2016; Community Service Award, Word of life Bible Ministry, 2016; Matron, Word of life Bible Ministry, 2016; David Lawrence Jr. Champion for Children Award by The Children's Trust, July 2017; caucuses: founder and chair, Florida Ports Caucus; committees: Education and Labor; Transportation and Infrastructure; elected to the 112th Congress on November 2, 2010; reelected to each succeeding Congress.

Office Listings

https://wilson.house.gov https://facebook.com/RepWilson https://twitter.com/RepWilson
https://instagram.com/repwilson https://youtube.com/user/RepFredericaWilson

2445 Rayburn House Office Building, Washington, DC 20515 .... (202) 225–4506
Chief of Staff.—Chasseny Lewis. FAX: 226–0777
Deputy Chief of Staff.—Jean Roseme.
Communications Director.—Joyce Jones.
Legislative Assistant.—David Simon.
Press Assistant.—Max Wolf-Johnson.
Staff Assistant.—Devin Wilcox.
Special Assistant / Scheduler.—Cheyenne Range.
18425 Northwest 2nd Avenue, Suite 355, Miami, FL 33169 .... (305) 690–5905
District Chief of Staff.—Alexis Snyder.
District Office Director.—Joyce Postell.
Directors of Field Operations: Quincy Cohen, Shirlee Moreau-Lafleur.
Director of Special Community Relations.—Nikki Austin-Shipp.
District Policy Director.—Jessica Sinkfield.
Director of Special Projects.—Delvin Thomas.
Director of Special Community Outreach.—Charles C. Scott II.
Congressional Aide.—Jakaria Williams.
2600 Hollywood Boulevard, Old Library 1st Floor, Hollywood, FL 33020 .... (954) 921–3682
West Park City Hall, 1965 South State Road 7, West Park, FL 33023 .... (954) 989–2688

Counties: BROWARD (part) AND MIAMI-DADE (part). Population (2010), 725,282.

ZIP Codes: 33009, 33013–14, 33021, 33023–25, 33027, 33054–56, 33101, 33109, 33125, 33127–28, 33130–32, 33136–39, 33141–42, 33147, 33150, 33154, 33160–62, 33167–69, 33179–81

* * *

TWENTY-FIFTH DISTRICT

MARIO DIAZ-BALART, Republican, of Miami, FL; born in Ft. Lauderdale, FL, September 25, 1961; education: University of South Florida; professional: president, Gordon Diaz-Balart and Partners (public relations and marketing business); public service: administrative assistant to the Mayor of Miami, 1985–88; Florida House of Representatives, 1988–92, and 2000–02; Florida State Senate, 1992–2000; religion: Catholic; committees: Appropriations; elected Representative of the 25th District to the 108th Congress on November 5, 2002; reelected to each succeeding Congress; elected Representative of the 21st District to the 112th Congress on November 2, 2010; elected Representative of the 25th District to the 113th Congress on November 6, 2012; reelected to each succeeding Congress.

Office Listings

https://mariodiazbalart.house.gov https://facebook.com/mdiazbalart
https://twitter.com/MarioDB https://youtube.com/MarioDiazBalart
https://instagram.com/repmariodb

404 Cannon House Office Building, Washington, DC 20515 .... (202) 225–4211
Chief of Staff.—Cesar A. Gonzalez. FAX: 226–8576
Legislative Director.—Christopher Sweet.
8669 Northwest 36th Street, Suite 100, Doral, FL 33166 .... (305) 470–8555
Deputy Chief of Staff.—Miguel Otero. FAX: 470–8575
District Director.—Gloria Oliveros.
4715 Golden Gate Parkway, Suite 1, Naples, FL 34116 .... (239) 348–1620
Southwest Florida Director.—Enrique Padron. FAX: 348–3569

Counties: COLLIER (part). CITIES AND TOWNSHIPS: Chokoloskee, Everglades, Everglades City, Golden Gate, Immokalee, Island Walk, Orangetree, Plantation Island, Verona Walk, and Vineyards. HENDRY. CITIES AND TOWNSHIPS: Clewiston, Fort Denaud, LaBelle, Montura, Pioneer, and Port LaBelle. MIAMI-DADE COUNTY (part). CITIES AND TOWNSHIPS: Country Club, Doral, Fountainebleau, Hialeah, Hialeah Gardens, Medley, Miami Lakes, Palm Springs North, Sweetwater, Tamiami, Virginia Gardens, and West Little River. Population (2015), 754,595.

ZIP Codes: 33010 (part), 33012–14 (part), 33015–16, 33018, 33027 (part), 33029 (part), 33054 (part), 33122 (part), 33126 (part), 33147 (part), 33166 (part), 33172, 33174 (part), 33178, 33182, 33184 (part), 33194 (part), 33332 (part), 33440 (part), 33930, 33935–36 (part), 34104–05 (part), 34109 (part), 34112 (part), 34114 (part), 34116–17, 34119 (part), 34120, 34137–39, 34141, 34142 (part)

* * *

TWENTY-SIXTH DISTRICT

DEBBIE MUCARSEL-POWELL, Democrat, of Miami, FL; born in Guayaquil, Ecuador, January 18, 1971; education: graduated from Pomona Catholic High School, Pomona, CA, 1988; B.S., Pitzer College, Claremont, CA, 1992; M.A., Claremont Graduate University, Claremont, CA, 1996; professional: consultant; faculty, Florida International University, Miami, FL, 2003–11; married with two children; caucuses: Congressional Animal Protection Caucus; Congressional Hispanic Caucus (Education and Labor Task Force; Health Care and Mental Health Task Force; chair, Women's Task Force); Congressional Progressive Caucus; Everglades Caucus; Future Forum; Gun Violence Prevention Task Force; House Oceans Caucus; Mental Health Caucus; New Democrat Coalition; Women's Caucus; committees: Judiciary; Transportation and Infrastructure; elected to the 116th Congress on November 6, 2018.

Office Listings

https://mucarsel-powell.house.gov https://facebook.com/RepDMP twitter: @RepDMP
https://instagram.com/repdmp

114 Cannon House Office Building, Washington, DC 20515 .... (202) 225–2778
Chief of Staff.—Laura Rodriguez.
Legislative Director.—Courtney Fogwell.
Scheduler.—Patrick Sullivan.
Communications Director.—Sebastian Silva.
12851 Southwest 42nd Street, Suite 131, Miami, FL 33175 .... (305) 222–0160
District Director.—Natalia Vanegas.
1100 Simonton Street, Suite 1–213, Key West, FL 33040 .... (305) 292–4485
404 West Palm Drive, Florida City, FL 33034.

Counties: MIAMI-DADE (part). CITIES AND TOWNSHIPS: Country Walk, Florida City, Goulds, Homestead, Kendall, Kendale Lakes, Kendall West, Leisure City, Naranja, Olympia Heights, Palmetto Estates, Princeton, Richmond Heights, Richmond West, South Miami Heights, Sunset, Tamiami, The Crossings, The Hammocks, Three Lakes, University Park, West Perrine, Westchester, and Westwood Lakes. MONROE (all): Big Coppitt Key, Big Pine Key, Cudjoe Key, Duck Key, Islamorada, Village of Islands, Key Colony Beach, Key Largo, Key West, Layton, Marathon, North Key Largo, Stock Island, and Tavernier. Population (2014), 728,285.

ZIP Codes: 33001, 33030 (part), 33031, 33032–33 (part), 33034, 33035 (part), 33036–37, 33040, 33042–43, 33050–51, 33070, 33157, 33165, 33170, 33173 (part), 33175, 33176 (part), 33177, 33183, 33184 (part), 33185–87, 33189 (part), 33193, 33194 (part), 33196, 34141 (part)

* * *

TWENTY-SEVENTH DISTRICT

DONNA E. SHALALA, Democrat, of Miami, FL; born in Cleveland, Cuyahoga County, OH, February 14, 1941; education: graduated from West Technical High School, Cleveland, OH, 1958; A.B., Western College for Women, Oxford, OH, 1962; Ph.D., Syracuse University, Syracuse, NY, 1970; professional: United States Peace Corps, 1962–64; professor, Teachers College, Columbia University, 1972–77; assistant secretary, Department of Housing and Urban Development, 1977–80; professor and president, Hunter College of the City University of New York, New York City, NY, 1980–87; professor and chancellor, University of Wisconsin-Madison, Madison, WI, 1987–93; Secretary of Health and Human Services in the Cabinet of President William J. Clinton, 1993–2001; president, University of Miami, Miami, FL, 2001–15; president and CEO, The Clinton Foundation, 2015–17; religion: Catholic; committees: Education and Labor; Rules; elected to the 116th Congress on November 6, 2018.

Office Listings

https://shalala.house.gov https://facebook.com/RepShalala
https://twitter.com/repshalala https://instagram.com/repshalala

1320 Longworth House Office Building, Washington, DC 20515 .... (202) 225–3931
Chief of Staff.—Jessica Killin. FAX: 225–5620
Legislative Director.—Carla McGarvey.
Scheduler.—Nicole Marquez.
7700 North Kendall Drive, #605, Miami, FL 33156 .... (305) 668–2285
District Director.—Raul Martinez, Jr.

Counties: MIAMI-DADE (part). CITIES AND TOWNSHIPS: Coral Gables, Cutler Bay, Fountainebleau, Gladeview, Glenvar Heights, Kendall, Key Biscayne, Miami, Miami Beach, Olympia Heights, Palmetto Bay, Pinecrest, South Miami, Virginia Gardens, West Little River, West Miami, and Westchester. Population (2010), 696,345.

ZIP Codes: 33010 (part), 33012–13 (part), 33030 (part), 33032–33 (part), 33035 (part), 33039, 33109 (part), 33122 (part), 33125–26 (part), 33128 (part), 33129, 33130–31 (part), 33133–35, 33136 (part), 33142 (part), 33143–46, 33147 (part), 33149, 33155–56, 33157 (part), 33158, 33165–66 (part), 33170 (part), 33173–74 (part), 33176 (part), 33189 (part), 33190

GEORGIA

(Population 2010, 9,687,653)

SENATORS

DAVID PERDUE, Republican, of Glynn County, GA; born in Macon, GA, December 10, 1949; education: graduated, Northside High School, Warner Robins, GA, 1968; bachelor's degree in industrial engineering, Georgia Institute of Technology, 1972; master's degree in operations research, Georgia Institute of Technology, 1975; professional: senior vice president of operations for Sara Lee Corporation, 1992–94; senior vice president of Haggar Corporation, 1994–98; CEO of Reebok, 2001–02; CEO of Pillowtex, 2002–03; CEO of Dollar General, 2003–07; religion: United Methodist; married: the former Bonnie Dunn, 1972; children: David A. Perdue III and Blake Perdue; committees: Armed Services; Banking, Housing, and Urban Affairs; Budget; Foreign Relations; elected to the U.S. Senate on November 4, 2014.

Office Listings

https://perdue.senate.gov https://facebook.com/SenatorDavidPerdue twitter: @sendavidperdue

455 Russell Senate Office Building, Washington, DC 20510 .... (202) 224–3521
Chief of Staff.—Megan Whittemore. FAX: 228–1031
Director of Operations.—Caleb Moore.
Legislative Director.—John Eunice.
Communications Director.—Cherie Gillan.
Scheduler.—Gabriele Forsyth.
State Director.—PJ Waldrop.
3280 Peachtree Road, NE., Suite 2640, Atlanta, GA 30305 .... (404) 865–0087
FAX: 861–3435

* * *

KELLY LOEFFLER, Republican, of Atlanta, GA; born in Bloomington, IL, November 27, 1970; education: B.S., University of Illinois, Urbana-Champaign, IL, 1992; M.B.A., international finance and marketing, Kellstadt Graduate School of Business, DePaul University, Chicago, IL, 1999 professional: district account manager, Toyota North America, 1992–96; equity research associate (Citi Global Asset Management, Stamford, CT, 1999 and William Blair, Chicago, IL, 1999-2001; manager, investor relations, Crossroads Investment Advisers, L.P., Dallas, TX, 2001–02; chief communications and marketing officer, head of investor relations, Intercontinental Exchange, Atlanta, GA, 2002–18; first chief executive officer of Bakkt, a cryptocurrency exchange firm, 2018–19; co-owner, Atlanta Dream WNBA team, 2011–present; board member, Atlanta Sports Council, 2012–14; board of directors, Grady Memorial Hospital Corporation, 2015–present; member, board of directors, Georgia Power Company, 2019; married: Jeffrey Sprecher; committees: Agriculture, Nutrition, and Forestry; Health, Education, Labor, and Pensions; Veterans' Affairs; Joint Economic Committee; appointed as a Republican to the United States Senate to fill the vacancy caused by the resignation of Johnny Isakson, and took the oath of office on January 6, 2020.

Office Listings

https://loeffler.senate.gov

131 Russell Senate Office Building, Washington, DC 20510 .... (202) 224–3643
Chief of Staff.—Joan Kirchner Carr. FAX: 228–0724
Deputy Chief of Staff.—Edward Tate.
Scheduler.—Stefanie Mohler.
One Overton Park, 3625 Cumberland Boulevard, Suite 970, Atlanta, GA 30339 .... (770) 661–0999

REPRESENTATIVES

FIRST DISTRICT

EARL L. "BUDDY" CARTER, Republican, of Pooler, GA; born in Port Wentworth, GA, September, 6, 1957; education: Young Harris College, 1977; University of Georgia, 1980; professional: pharmacist; small business owner; Mayor of Pooler, GA, 1996–2004; Georgia State Legislature, 2006–14; married: Amy Carter, 1979; children: Joel, Barrett, and Travis; committees: Energy and Commerce; Select Committee on the Climate Crisis; elected to the 114th Congress on November 4, 2014; reelected to each succeeding Congress.

Office Listings

https://buddycarter.house.gov https://facebook.com/CongressmanBuddyCarter
twitter: @RepBuddyCarter

2432 Rayburn House Office Building, Washington, DC 20515 .... (202) 225–5831
Chief of Staff.—Chris Crawford. FAX: 226–2269
Legislative Director.—Nick Schemmel.
Legislative Assistants: Jay Gulshen, Hart Thompson.
Legislative Correspondent.—Caroline Holden.
Communications Director.—Mary Carpenter.
Scheduler.—Brooke Miller.
Staff Assistant.—SK Bowen.
6602 Abercorn Street, Suite 105–B, Savannah, GA 31405 .... (912) 352–0101
Caseworkers: Bruce Bazemore, Tracy Dowdy.
Staff Assistant.—Lee Ann Powell.
Field Representative.—Hunter Hall.
District Director.—Brooke Childers.
1510 Newcastle Street, Suite 200, Brunswick, GA 31520 .... (912) 265–9010
Field Representative.—Emmitt Nolan.

Counties: BACON, BRANTLEY, BRYAN, CAMDEN, CHARLTON, CHATHAM, CLINCH, ECHOLS, EFFINGHAM (part), GLYNN, LIBERTY, LONG, LOWNDES (part), MCINTOSH, PIERCE, WARE, AND WAYNE. Population (2017), 747,334.

ZIP Codes: 30427–28, 31300–01, 31305, 31308–09, 31313–16, 31319–21, 31323–24, 31327–28, 31331–33, 31401–12, 31414–16, 31418–21, 31501–03, 31520–21, 31523–25, 31542, 31553, 31605–24, 31630–32, 31634–36

* * *

SECOND DISTRICT

SANFORD D. BISHOP, JR., Democrat, of Albany, GA; born in Mobile, AL, February 4, 1947; education: attended Mobile County public schools; B.A., Morehouse College, 1968; J.D., Emory University, 1971; professional: attorney; admitted to the Georgia and Alabama Bars; Georgia House of Representatives, 1977–91; Georgia Senate, 1991–93; former member: Executive Board, Boy Scouts of America; YMCA; Sigma Pi Phi Fraternity; Kappa Alpha Psi Fraternity; 32nd Degree Mason, Shriner; member: Mt. Zion Baptist Church, Albany, GA; married: Vivian Creighton Bishop; child: Aayesha Reese; committees: Appropriations; elected to the 103rd Congress; reelected to each succeeding Congress.

Office Listings

https://bishop.house.gov https://facebook.com/sanfordbishop twitter: @SanfordBishop

2407 Rayburn House Office Building, Washington, DC 20515 .... (202) 225–3631
Chief of Staff.—Michael Reed. FAX: 225–2203
Scheduler/Office Manager.—Lauren Hughes.
Legislative Director.—Jonathan Halpern.
Legislative Assistant/Social Media Manager.—N'Dea Rackard.
Legislative Assistant.—Jonathan Black.
Communications Director.—Owen Dodd.
323 Pine Avenue, Suite 400, Albany, GA 31701 .... (229) 439–8067
District Director.—Kenneth Cutts.
Office Manager/Constituent Services.—Toni Pickel.
Field Representatives: Michael Bryant, Paul Fryer, Tammye Pettyjohn Jones.
Constituent Services.—Tameka Wimbush.
Staff Assistant.—Krystal Pickett.
18 Ninth Street, Suite 201, Columbus, GA 31901 .... (706) 320–9477
Constituent Services: Arnez Cherry, Lenzie Jones, Peggy Sagul.
Field Representative.—Elaine Gillispie.
Staff Assistant.—Gerald Washington.
300 Mulberry Street, Suite 502, Macon, GA 31201 .... (478) 803–2631
Deputy District Director.—Shavonda Hill.
Constituent Services/Colleges and Universities Liaison.—Elizabeth Kringer.
Staff Assistant.—Haleigh Apple.

Counties: BAKER, BIBB, CALHOUN, CHATTAHOOCHEE, CLAY, CRAWFORD, CRISP, DECATUR, DOOLY, DOUGHERTY, EARLY, GRADY, LEE, MACON, MARION, MILLER, MITCHELL, MUSCOGEE, PEACH, QUITMAN, RANDOLPH, SCHLEY, SEMINOLE, STEWART, SUMTER, TALBOT, TAYLOR, TERRELL, AND WEBSTER. Population (2010), 631,973.

ZIP Codes: 31006–08, 31015–16, 31020, 31030, 31039, 31041, 31050–52, 31057–58, 31063, 31066, 31068–70, 31072, 31076, 31078, 31081, 31091–92, 31201, 31204, 31206–07, 31210–11, 31213, 31216–17, 31220, 31701, 31705, 31707,

31709, 31711–12, 31716, 31719, 31721, 31730, 31735, 31743–44, 31763–65, 31773, 31779–80, 31784, 31787, 31791–92, 31801, 31803, 31805–06, 31810, 31812, 31814–16, 31820–21, 31824–27, 31829, 31831–32, 31836, 31901, 31903–07, 31909, 39813, 39815, 39817, 39819, 39823–28, 39834, 39836–37, 39840–42, 39845–46, 39851, 39854, 39859, 39861–62, 39866–67, 39870, 39877, 39885–86, 39897

* * *

THIRD DISTRICT

A. DREW FERGUSON IV, Republican, of West Point, GA; born in Langdale, AL, November 15, 1966; education: D.M.D., Medical College of Georgia, Augusta, GA, 1992; professional: dentist; public service: Mayor of West Point, 2008–16; religion: Christian; children: Drew, Lucy, Mary Parks, and Thad; committees: Ways and Means; elected to the 115th Congress on November 8, 2016; reelected to the 116th Congress on November 6, 2018.

Office Listings

https://ferguson.house.gov https://facebook.com/RepDrewFerguson https://twitter.com/RepDrewFerguson

1032 Longworth House Office Building, Washington, DC 20515 .... (202) 225–5901
Chiefs of Staff: Bobby Saparow, David Sours. FAX: 225–2515
Communications Director.—Amy Timmerman.
Legislative Director.—Allie White.
Office Manager / Scheduler.—Jenna Heard.
1601 East Highway 34, Suite B, Newnan, GA 30265 .... (770) 683–2033

Counties: CARROLL. CITIES AND TOWNSHIPS: Bowdon, Carrollton, Mount Zion, Roopville, Temple, Villa Rica, and Whitesburg. COWETA (part). CITIES AND TOWNSHIPS: Grantville, Haralson, Lone Oak, Luthersville, Meriwether, Moreland, Newnan, Palmetto, Senoia, Sharpsburg, and Turin. FAYETTE. CITIES AND TOWNSHIPS: Brooks, Fayetteville, Peachtree City, Tyrone, and Woolsey. HARRIS. CITIES AND TOWNSHIPS: Cataula, Ellerslie, Fortson, Hamilton, Midland, Pine Mountain, Pine Mountain Valley, Shiloh, Waverly Hall, and West Point. HENRY (part). CITIES AND TOWNSHIPS: Hampton, Locust Grove, McDonough, and Stockbridge. LAMAR. CITIES AND TOWNSHIPS: Aldora, Barnesville, and Milner. MUSCOGEE (part). CITIES AND TOWNSHIPS: Columbus. PIKE. CITIES AND TOWNSHIPS: Concord, Meansville, Molena, Williamson, and Zebulon. SPALDING. CITIES AND TOWNSHIPS: Griffin, Orchard Hill, and Sunny Side. TROUP. CITIES AND TOWNSHIPS: Hogansville and LaGrange. UPSON. CITIES AND TOWNSHIPS: Thomaston and Yatesville. Population (2010), 757,344.

ZIP Codes: 30257–59, 30263, 30265, 30268–69, 30275–77, 30285–86, 30290, 30292–93, 30295, 31016, 31029, 31066, 31097, 31800, 31804, 31807–08, 31811, 31816, 31820, 31822–23, 31826, 31829–31, 31833, 31901, 31904, 31906, 31909

* * *

FOURTH DISTRICT

HENRY C. "HANK" JOHNSON, JR., Democrat, of Lithonia, GA; born in Washington, DC, October 2, 1954; education: B.A., Clark College (Clark Atlanta University), Atlanta, GA, 1976; J.D., Thurgood Marshall School of Law, Texas Southern University, Houston, TX, 1979; professional: partner, Johnson & Johnson Law Group LLC, 1980–2007; judge, magistrate court, 1989–2001; DeKalb County Commissioner, 2001–06; married: Mereda, 1979; two children: Randi and Alex; committees: Judiciary; Transportation and Infrastructure; elected to the 110th Congress on November 7, 2006; reelected to each succeeding Congress.

Office Listings

https://hankjohnson.house.gov https://facebook.com/RepHankJohnson
twitter: @RepHankJohnson https://instagram.com/RepHankJohnson

2240 Rayburn House Office Building, Washington, DC 20515 .... (202) 225–1605
Chief of Staff.—Arthur D. Sidney. FAX: 226–0691
Legislative Director.—Jacqui Kappler.
Office Manager / Scheduler.—Brianne Sparkman.
5240 Snapfinger Park Drive, Suite 140, Decatur, GA 30035 .... (770) 987–2291
District Director.—Kathy Register.

Counties: DEKALB (part), GWINNETT (part), NEWTON (part), AND ROCKDALE. CITIES: Atlanta (part), Avondale Estates (part), Clarkston, Conyers, Covington, Decatur (part), Lilburn (part), Lithonia, Norcross, Oxford, Pine Lake, Snellville, Stonecrest, Stone Mountain, and Tucker (part). Population (2010), 691,976.

ZIP Codes: 30002–03, 30012–17, 30021, 30030–39, 30047, 30052, 30054, 30058, 30070, 30072, 30074, 30078–79, 30083–84, 30086–88, 30252, 30281, 30294, 30329, 30340, 30345, 30359

* * *

FIFTH DISTRICT

VACANT

Counties: CLAYTON (part), DEKALB (part), AND FULTON (part). Population (2012), 691,975.

ZIP Codes: 30030 (part), 30032 (part), 30034 (part), 30236 (part), 30260 (part), 30273–74 (part), 30281 (part), 30288, 30294 (part), 30296–97 (part), 30303, 30305 (part), 30306–19 (part), 30322, 30324 (part), 30326–27 (part), 30331–32, 30334, 30336, 30337 (part), 30342 (part), 30344 (part), 30349 (part), 30354, 30363

* * *

SIXTH DISTRICT

LUCIA ''LUCY'' KAY McBATH, Democrat, of Marietta, GA; born in Joliet, IL, June 1, 1960; education: B.A., political science, Virginia State University, Petersburg, VA, 1982; professional: American gun violence prevention advocate; national spokesperson for Everytown for Gun Safety and Moms Demand Action for Gun Sense in America (in November 2012, Lucy's 17-year-old son, Jordan Davis, was shot and killed at a gas station); flight attendant for Delta Air Lines (for 30 years); family: married to Curtis; caucuses: vice chair, Gun Violence Prevention Task Force; founding member, Black Maternal Health Caucus; Congressional Black Caucus; New Democrat Coalition; committees: Education and Labor; Judiciary; elected to the 116th Congress on November 6, 2018.

Office Listings

https://mcbath.house.gov https://facebook.com/replucymcbath https://twitter.com/RepLucyMcBath

1513 Longworth House Office Building, Washington, DC 20515 .... (202) 225–4501
Chief of Staff.—Rebecca Walldorff.
5775 Glenridge Drive, Building B, Suite 380, Atlanta, GA 30328 .... (470) 773–6330
District Director.—Antrell Tyson.

Counties: COBB (part), DEKALB (part), AND FULTON (part). CITIES AND TOWNSHIPS: Alpharetta, Brookhaven, Chamblee, Doraville, Dunwoody, Johns Creek, Milton, Roswell, Sandy Springs, and Tucker. Population (2010), 699,103.

ZIP Codes: 30004–07, 30009, 30022–24, 30033, 30062, 30065–68, 30075–77, 30084–85, 30092–93, 30097–98, 30102, 30144, 30188, 30319, 30324, 30326, 30328–29, 30338–42, 30345–46, 30350, 30356, 30358, 30360, 30362, 30366, 31119, 31141, 31145–46, 31150, 31156

* * *

SEVENTH DISTRICT

W. ROBERT WOODALL, Republican, of Lawrenceville, GA; born in Athens, GA, February 11, 1970; education: undergraduate, B.A., Furman University, Greenville, SC, 1992; J.D., University of Georgia, Athens, GA, 1997; awards: co-author of *The New York Times* bestselling book *Fair Tax: The Truth;* religion: Methodist; committees: Budget; Rules; Transportation and Infrastructure; Select Committee on the Modernization of Congress; elected to the 112th Congress on November 2, 2010; reelected to each succeeding Congress.

Office Listings

https://woodall.house.gov https://facebook.com/RepRobWoodall https://twitter.com/RepRobWoodall

1724 Longworth House Office Building, Washington, DC 20515 .... (202) 225–4272
Chief of Staff.—Derick Corbett. FAX: 225–4696
Legislative Director.—Janet Rossi.
District Director.—Debra Poirot.
75 Langley Drive, Lawrenceville, GA 30046 .... (770) 232–3005
(No mail accepted at this address.) FAX: 232–2909

Counties: FORSYTH (part) AND GWINNETT (part). Population (2010), 691,975.

ZIP Codes: 30004–05, 30017, 30019, 30024, 30040–41, 30043–49, 30052, 30071, 30078, 30091–93, 30095–97, 30099, 30340, 30360, 30518–19

* * *

EIGHTH DISTRICT

AUSTIN SCOTT, Republican, of Tifton, GA; born in Augusta, GA, December 10, 1969; education: B.B.A., University of Georgia, 1993; professional: business owner; member of the Georgia State House of Representatives, 1997–2010; member, National Association of Insurance and Financial Advisors; Coastal Plains Chapter of the American Red Cross; awards: American Cancer Society's Outstanding Legislative Leadership Award, 2003 and 2004; Georgia Association of Emergency Medical Services Star of Life Legislative Award, 2007 and 2008; religion: Southern Baptist; married: wife, Vivien; son, Wells; daughter, Carmen Gabriela; son, John Philip; Republican Freshman Class President; committees: Agriculture; Armed Services; elected to the 112th Congress on November 2, 2010; reelected to each succeeding Congress.

Office Listings

https://austinscott.house.gov https://facebook.com/RepAustinScott
twitter: @AustinScottGA08 https://youtube.com/user/RepAustinScott

2417 Rayburn House Office Building, Washington, DC 20515 .... (202) 225–6531
Chief of Staff.—Jason Lawrence.
Legislative Director / Military Legislative Assistant.—Michael Tehrani.
Press Secretary.—Rachel Ledbetter.
Legislative Assistants: Craig Anderson, Mark Sanders.
Legislative Correspondent.—Zach Roberts.
Scheduler.—Crawford Pierson.
127–B North Central Avenue, Tifton, GA 31794 .... (229) 396–5175
FAX: 396–5179
230 Margie Drive, Suite 500, Warner Robins, GA 31088 .... (478) 971–1776
FAX: 971–1778

Counties: ATKINSON, BEN HILL, BERRIEN, BIBB (part), BLECKLEY, BROOKS, COLQUITT, COOK, DODGE, HOUSTON, IRWIN, JONES, LANIER, LOWNDES (part), MONROE, PULASKI, TELFAIR, THOMAS, TIFT, TURNER, TWIGGS, WILCOX, WILKINSON, AND WORTH. Population (2011), 693,640.

ZIP Codes: 30233, 31001, 31033–35, 31008, 31011–17, 31020–21, 31023, 31028–33, 31035–38, 31042, 31044, 31046–47, 31054–55, 31060–61, 31065–66, 31069, 31071–72, 31077, 31079, 31083–84, 31086, 31088, 31090–93, 31095, 31098–99, 31204, 31209–11, 31217, 31220–21, 31297, 31512, 31544, 31549, 31601–66, 31620, 31622, 31624–27, 31629, 31632, 31635–39, 31641–45, 31647, 31649–50, 31698, 31705, 31712, 31714, 31720, 31722, 31727, 31733, 31738, 31744, 31747, 31749–50, 31753, 31756–58, 31760, 31765, 31768–69, 31771–79, 31781, 31783–84, 31788–96, 31798–99

* * *

NINTH DISTRICT

DOUGLAS COLLINS, Republican, of Gainesville, GA; born in Gainesville, August 16, 1966; education: B.S., political science, criminal law, University of North Georgia, Dahlonega, GA, 1988; master of divinity, New Orleans Baptist Theological Seminary, New Orleans, LA, 1996; juris doctorate, John Marshall Law School, Atlanta, GA, 2008; professional: preacher; business owner; Chaplain, U.S. Air Force Reserve; lawyer; Georgia State House of Representatives, 2007–13; religion: Baptist; married: Lisa Collins; children: Jordan, Copelan, and Cameron; committees: ranking member, Judiciary; elected, by regular election, to the 113th Congress on November 6, 2012, to fill the vacancy caused by the redistricting of District 9; reelected to each succeeding Congress.

Office Listings

https://dougcollins.house.gov https://facebook.com/RepresentativeDougCollins
twitter: @RepDougCollins

1504 Longworth House Office Building, Washington, DC 20515 .... (202) 225–9893
Chief of Staff.—Joel Katz. FAX: 226–1224
Communications Director.—Amanda Gonzalez-Thompson.
Deputy Chief of Staff.—Sally Rose Larson.
Scheduler.—Erin Wall.
Counsel.—Dan Ashworth.
Senior Legislative Assistant.—Erica Barker.
Legislative Assistant.—William Smith.
Legislative Correspondent.—Jacob Rogers.
Special Assistant.—Cooper Mullinax.
Staff Assistant.—Raymond Sweney.
210 Washington Street Northwest, Suite 202, Gainesville, GA 30501 .... (770) 297–3388

Counties: BANKS, CLARKE (part), DAWSON, ELBERT, FANNIN, FORSYTH (part), FRANKLIN, GILMER, HABERSHAM, HALL, HART, JACKSON, LUMPKIN, MADISON, PICKENS (part), RABUN, STEPHENS, TOWNS, UNION, AND WHITE. CITIES AND TOWNSHIPS: Alto, Arcade, Baldwin, Blairsville, Blue Ridge, Bowersville, Bowman, Braselton, Canon, Carlton, Carnesville, Clarkesville, Clayton, Clermont, Cleveland, Colbert, Comer, Commerce, Cornelia, Cumming, Dahlonega, Danielsville, Dawsonville, Demorest, Dillard, Elberton, Elijay, Flowery Branch, Franklin Springs, Gainesville, Gillsville, Hartwell, Helen, Hiawassee, Homer, Hoschton, Hull, Ila, Jasper, Jefferson, Lavonia, Lula, Martin, McCaysville, Morganton, Mount Airy, Mountain City, Nelson, Nicholson, Oakwood, Pendergrass, Royston, Sky Valley, Talking Rock, Tallulah Falls, Talmo, Toccoa, and Young Harris. Population (2010), 691,975.

ZIP Codes: 30028 (part), 30040–41 (part), 30107 (part), 30143 (part), 30148, 30151, 30175 (part), 30177, 30501, 30504, 30506–07, 30510–13, 30516, 30517–19 (part), 30520–23, 30525, 30527–31, 30533, 30534 (part), 30535–38, 30540–43, 30545–47, 30548 (part), 30549, 30552–55, 30557–60, 30562–68, 30571–73, 30575–77, 30581–82, 30601 (part), 30605 (part), 30607 (part), 30622 (part), 30624, 30627–29 (part), 30633–35, 30643, 30646, 30662, 30666 (part), 30680 (part), 30683 (part)

* * *

TENTH DISTRICT

JODY B. HICE, Republican, of Greensboro, GA; born in Atlanta, GA, April 22, 1960; education: graduated, Tucker High School, Tucker, GA, 1978; B.A., ministry, Asbury University, Wilmore, KY, 1982; M.Div., Southwestern Baptist Theological Seminary, Fort Worth, TX, 1986; D.Min., Luther Rice College and Seminary, Lithonia, GA, 1988; professional: pastor; religion: Southern Baptist; married: Dee Dee Crocker Hice; children: Anna and Sara; grandchildren: Peter, Margaret, Alyssa, and Felix; committees: Natural Resources; Oversight and Reform; elected to the 114th Congress on November 4, 2014; reelected to each succeeding Congress.

Office Listings

https://hice.house.gov https://facebook.com/CongressmanJodyHice
https://twitter.com/congressmanhice

409 Cannon House Office Building, Washington, DC 20515 .... (202) 225–4101
Chief of Staff.—Tim Reitz.
Director of Scheduling and Operations.—Taylor Ford.
Communications Director.—Nadgey Louis-Charles.
Legislative Director.—Nicholas R. Brown.
Legislative Assistant.—Kaitlyn Dwyer.
Legislative Assistant / Deputy Press Assistant.—Elizabeth Gentry.
Legislative Correspondent.—Nathan Barker.
Staff Assistant.—Hannah Arvey Funk.
100 Court Street, Monroe, GA 30655 .... (770) 207–1776
Senior Field Coordinator.—Ben Stout.
Constituent Services Representative / Grants Coordinator.—Keri Gardner.
Constituent Services and Field Representative.—Carolyn Dallas.
3015 Heritage Road, Suite 6, Milledgeville, GA 31061 .... (478) 457–0007
Field Representative.—Daniel T. Lentz.
Constituent Services Representative.—Domenick A. Riviezzo.
Special Assistant.—Lt. Col. R. Edward Shelor, USMC (Ret.).
210 Railroad Street, Thomson-McDuffie County Government Center, Room 2401, Thomson, GA 30824 .... (770) 207–1776
Deputy Chief of Staff / District Director.—Jessica Hayes.
Director of Constituent Services.—Beth Goolsby.

Counties: BALDWIN, BARROW, BUTTS, CLARKE (part), COLUMBIA (part), GLASCOCK, GREENE, GWINNETT (part), HANCOCK, HENRY (part), JASPER, JEFFERSON, JOHNSON, LINCOLN, MCDUFFIE, MORGAN, NEWTON (part), OCONEE, OGLETHORPE, PUTNAM, TALIAFERRO, WALTON, WARREN, WASHINGTON, AND WILKES. Population (2010), 691,976.

ZIP Codes: 30011–12, 30014, 30016, 30019, 30025, 30043, 30045, 30052, 30054–56, 30216, 30233–34, 30248, 30252–53, 30413, 30434, 30477, 30517, 30519, 30548, 30601–02, 30605–07, 30609, 30619–23, 30625, 30627–31, 30641–42, 30648, 30650, 30655–56, 30660, 30663–69, 30773, 30677–78, 30680, 30683, 30802–03, 30807–10, 30814, 30816–18, 30820–21, 30823–24, 30828, 30833, 31002, 31018, 31024, 31029, 31031, 31033, 31035, 31038, 31045, 31049, 31061–62, 31064, 31067, 31082, 31085, 31087, 31089, 31094, 31096

* * *

ELEVENTH DISTRICT

BARRY LOUDERMILK, Republican, of Cassville, GA; born in Riverdale, GA, December 22, 1963; education: A.A. in telecommunications technology, Community College of the Air Force, Maxwell AFB, AL, 1987; B.S. in occupational education and information systems technology, Wayland Baptist University, Plainview, TX, 1992; professional: former small business owner, Innovative Network Systems, Inc. and Freedom Flight Center; founder of nonprofit, Firm Reliance; served in Georgia State House, 2005–10; Georgia State Senate, 2011–13; member, NRA; Aircraft Owners and Pilots Association; American Legion; served in the U.S. Air Force, 1984–92; Civil Air Patrol member, official auxiliary of the U.S. Air Force, 2005–present; Republican Study Committee (RSC); religion: Protestant; married to Desiree since 1983; three grown children; committees: Financial Services; House Administration; Joint Committee on the Library; Joint Committee on Printing; elected to the 114th Congress on November 4, 2014; reelected to each succeeding Congress.

Office Listings

https://loudermilk.house.gov https://facebook.com/RepLoudermilk https://twitter.com/reploudermilk

422 Cannon House Office Building, Washington, DC 20515 .... (202) 225–2931
Chief of Staff.—Robert Adkerson. FAX: 225–2944
Legislative Director.—Colin Carr.
District Director.—Wayne Dodd.
9898 Highway 92, Suite 100, Woodstock, GA 30188 .... (770) 429–1776
135 West Cherokee Avenue, Suite 122, Cartersville, GA 30120 .... (770) 429–1776
600 Galleria Parkway Southeast, Suite 120, Atlanta, GA 30339 .... (770) 429–1776

Counties: BARTOW, CHEROKEE, COBB (part), AND FULTON (part). Population (2010), 794,969.

ZIP Codes: 30004, 30008, 30040, 30060, 30062, 30064, 30066–68, 30075, 30080, 30082, 30101–04, 30107, 30114–15, 30120–21, 30127, 30132, 30137, 30139, 30143–45, 30152–53, 30157, 30161, 30171, 30178, 30183–84, 30188–89, 30305, 30318–19, 30326–27, 30339, 30342

* * *

TWELFTH DISTRICT

RICK W. ALLEN, Republican, of Augusta, GA; born in Augusta, November 7, 1951; education: graduated, Evans High School, Evans, GA, 1969; B.S., in building construction, Auburn University, Auburn, AL, 1973; professional: founder and owner of R.W. Allen & Associates construction company, Augusta, GA, and Athens, GA, founded in 1976; awards: Augusta Metro Chamber of Commerce Small Business Person of the Year, 2008; CSRA Business Hall of Fame Inductee, 2011; religion: Methodist; married: wife, Robin; children: Jennifer Allen Green, Andy Allen, Molly Allen Hargather, and Robin Anne Allen Wills; grandchildren: Hadley Green, Wyche Green, Hutton Green, Collier Green, Hammond Hargather, Delle Hargather, Riley Kate Wills, Ellis Wills, Elsie Allen, Luke Hargarther, Mills Hargarther, Hampton Wills, and R.W. Allen; committees: Agriculture; Education and Labor; elected to the 114th Congress on November 4, 2014; reelected to each succeeding Congress.

Office Listings

https://allen.house.gov https://facebook.com/CongressmanRickAllen https://twitter.com/RepRickAllen

2400 Rayburn House Office Building, Washington, DC 20515 .... (202) 225–2823
Chief of Staff.—Tim Baker. FAX: 225–3377
Deputy Chief of Staff.—Lauren Hodge.
Legislative Director.—Katie Hunter.
Press Secretary.—Carlton Norwood.
2743 Perimeter Parkway, Building 200, Suite 105, Augusta, GA 30909 .... (706) 228–1980
Statesboro City Hall, 50 East Main Street, Statesboro, GA 30458 .... (912) 243–9452
100 South Church Street, Dublin, GA 31021 .... (478) 272–4030
Vidalia Community Center, 107 Old Airport Road, Suite A, Vidalia, GA 30474 .... (912) 403–3311

Counties: APPLING, BULLOCH, BURKE, CANDLER, COFFEE, COLUMBIA (part), EFFINGHAM (part), EMANUEL, EVANS, JEFF DAVIS, JENKINS, LAURENS, MONTGOMERY, RICHMOND, SCREVEN, TATTNALL, TOOMBS, TREUTLEN, AND WHEELER. Population (2010), 701,142.

ZIP Codes: 30401, 30410–12, 30415, 30417, 30420–21, 30423, 30425–29, 30434, 30436, 30438–39, 30441–42, 30445–46, 30448–58, 30460–61, 30464, 30467, 30470–71, 30473–75, 30802, 30805, 30809, 30812–16, 30822, 30830, 30901, 30903–07, 30909, 30912, 31002, 31009, 31019, 31021–22, 31027, 31037, 31049, 31065, 31075, 31083, 31303, 31308, 31312, 31321, 31326, 31329, 31510, 31512–13, 31518–19, 31532–33, 31535, 31539, 31549, 31552, 31554–55, 31563, 31567, 31624, 31650, 31798

* * *

THIRTEENTH DISTRICT

DAVID SCOTT, Democrat, of Atlanta, GA; born in Aynor, SC, June 27, 1945; education: Florida A&M University, graduated with honors, 1967; M.B.A., graduated with honors, University of Pennsylvania Wharton School of Finance, 1969; professional: businessman; owner and CEO, Dayn-Mark Advertising; public service: Georgia House of Representatives, 1974–82; Georgia State Senate, 1983–2002; married: Alfredia Aaron, 1969; children: Dayna and Marcye; committees: Agriculture; Financial Services; elected to the 108th Congress on November 5, 2002; reelected to each succeeding Congress.

Office Listings

https://davidscott.house.gov https://facebook.com/RepDavidScott twitter: @repdavidscott

225 Cannon House Office Building, Washington, DC 20515 .... (202) 225–2939
Chief of Staff.—Gary Woodward. FAX: 225–4628
Scheduler and Office Manager.—Gerard Henderson.
173 North Main Street, Jonesboro, GA 30236 .... (770) 210–5073
888 Concord Road, Suite 100, Smyrna, GA 30080 .... (770) 432–5405

Counties: CLAYTON, COBB, DOUGLAS, FAYETTE, FULTON, AND HENRY. Population (2010), 707,070.

ZIP Codes: 30252–53, 30260, 30268, 30273–74, 30281, 30290–91, 30294, 30296–97, 30331, 30337, 30344, 30349

* * *

FOURTEENTH DISTRICT

TOM GRAVES, Republican, of Ranger, GA; born in St. Petersburg, FL, February 3, 1970; education: B.A.A., finance, University of Georgia, Athens, GA, 1993; professional: business owner; Georgia State House of Representatives, 2003–10; religion: Baptist: married: Julie Howard Graves; children: JoAnn, John, and Janey; committees: vice chair, Select Committee on the Modernization of Congress; Appropriations; elected to the 111th Congress on June 8, 2010, by special election, to fill the vacancy caused by the resignation of U.S. Representative John Nathan Deal; elected to the 112th Congress on November 2, 2010; reelected to each succeeding Congress.

Office Listings

https://tomgraves.house.gov https://facebook.com/reptomgraves https://twitter.com/RepTomGraves

2078 Rayburn House Office Building, Washington, DC 20515 .... (202) 225–5211
Chief of Staff.—John Donnelly. FAX: 225–8272
Legislative Director.—Jason Murphy.
Communications Director.—Danielle Stewart.
Scheduler.—Kristin Fillingim.
702 South Thornton Avenue, Dalton, GA 30720 .... (706) 226–5320
FAX: 278–0840
600 East First Street, Suite 301, Rome, GA 30161 .... (706) 290–1776
FAX: 232–7864

Counties: CATOOSA, CHATTOOGA, DADE, FLOYD, GORDON, HARALSON, MURRAY, PAULDING, PICKENS (part), POLK, WALKER, AND WHITFIELD. Population (2010), 619,974.

ZIP Codes: 30101, 30103–05, 30110, 30113, 30120, 30124–25, 30127, 30129, 30132, 30134, 30138–41, 30143

HAWAII

(Population 2010, 1,360,301)

SENATORS

BRIAN SCHATZ, Democrat, of Hawaii; born in Ann Arbor, MI, October 20, 1972; education: graduated from Punahou School, Honolulu, HI, 1990; B.A., Pomona College, Claremont, CA, 1994; professional: chairman, Democratic Party of Hawaii, 2008–10; CEO, Helping Hands Hawaii, 2002–10; Hawaii House of Representatives, 1998–2006; Lieutenant Governor of Hawaii, 2010–12; married: Linda Schatz; committees: Appropriations; Banking, Housing, and Urban Affairs; Commerce, Science, and Transportation; Indian Affairs; Select Committee on Ethics; appointed to the U.S. Senate on December 26, 2012, and took the oath of office on December 27, 2012; subsequently elected to the U.S. Senate, by special election, on November 4, 2014; reelected to the U.S. Senate on November 8, 2016.

Office Listings

https://schatz.senate.gov https://facebook.com/SenBrianSchatz twitter: @SenBrianSchatz

722 Hart Senate Office Building, Washington, DC 20510 .... (202) 224–3934
Chief of Staff.—Eric Einhorn. FAX: 228–1153
Scheduler.—Diane Miyasato.
Legislative Director.—Arun Revana.
Communications Director.—Michael Inacay.
300 Ala Moana Boulevard, Room 7–212, Honolulu, HI 96850 .... (808) 523–2061
FAX: 523–2065

* * *

MAZIE HIRONO, Democrat, of Hawaii; born in Fukushima, Japan, November 3, 1947; education: graduated from Kaimuki High School, Honolulu, HI; B.A., University of Hawaii, Manoa, HI, 1970; J.D., Georgetown University, Washington, DC, 1978; professional: lawyer, private practice; member of the Hawaii State House of Representatives, 1981–94; Hawaii Lieutenant Governor, 1994–2002; elected to the U.S. House of Representatives as a Democrat to the 110th, 111th, and 112th Congresses; was not a candidate for reelection to the U.S. House of Representatives for the 113th Congress; committees: Armed Services; Energy and Natural Resources; Judiciary; Small Business and Entrepreneurship; Veterans' Affairs; elected to the U.S. Senate on November 6, 2012; reelected to the U.S. Senate on November 6, 2018.

Office Listings

https://hirono.senate.gov https://facebook.com/senatorhirono
twitter: @maziehirono https://instagram.com/maziehirono

713 Hart Senate Office Building, Washington, DC 20510 .... (202) 224–6361
Chief of Staff.—Alan Yamamoto.
DC Deputy Chief of Staff.—Coti Haia.
Prince Kuhio Federal Building, 300 Ala Moana Boulevard, Room 3–106, Honolulu, HI 96850 .... (808) 522–8970
Hawaii Deputy Chief of Staff.—Kehau Yap. FAX: 545–4683

REPRESENTATIVES

FIRST DISTRICT

ED CASE, Democrat, of Kāne'ohe, HI; born in Hilo, HI, September 27, 1952; education: Hawai'i Preparatory Academy, 1970; B.A., Williams College, Williamstown, MA, 1975; J.D., University of California/Hastings College of Law, San Francisco, CA, 1981; professional: attorney, private practice; employment: law clerk, Hawai'i Supreme Court Chief Justice William Richardson, 1981–82; Carlsmith Ball (law firm), 1983–2002 (partner, 1989–2002; managing partner, 1992–94); Bays Lung Rose & Holma (law firm), 2007–13; Outrigger Hotels Hawai'i, senior vice president/chief legal officer, 2013–18; public service: legislative assistant, U.S. Representative/Senator Spark Matsunaga, 1975–78; Mānoa Neighborhood Board, 1985–89; Hawai'i State House of Representatives, 1994–2002, Majority Leader, 1999–2000; candidate, Governor of Hawai'i, 2002; religion: Episcopal; family: married to the former Audrey

Nakamura; children: James, David, Megan, and David; committees: Appropriations; Natural Resources; elected to the 107th Congress, by special election, on November 30, 2002, to fill the vacancy caused by the death of U.S. Representative Patsy Mink; reelected to the 108th Congress, by special election, on January 4, 2003; reelected to the 109th Congress on November 2, 2004; reelected to the 116th Congress on November 6, 2018.

Office Listings

https://case.house.gov https://facebook.com/RepEdCase twitter: @RepEdCase

2443 Rayburn House Office Building, Washington, DC 20515 .... (202) 225–2726
Chief of Staff / Legislative Director.—Tim Nelson. FAX: 255–0688
Scheduler.—Shanise Ka'aikala.
Communications Director.—Nestor Garcia.
1132 Bishop Street, Suite 1910, Honolulu, HI 96813 .... (808) 650–6688

Counties: HONOLULU (part). CITIES AND TOWNSHIPS: 'Aiea, 'Ewa Beach, Honolulu, Kāhala, Kaimukī, Kalihi, Kapolei (part), Mānoa, Mililani, Pālolo, Pearl City, Waikīkī, and Waipahu. Population (2010), ~700,000.

ZIP Codes: 96701, 96706–07, 96782, 96789, 96797, 96813–19, 96821–22, 96825–26, 96850, 96853, 96859–60

* * *

SECOND DISTRICT

TULSI GABBARD, Democrat, of Hawai'i; born in Leloaloa, American Samoa, April 12, 1981; education: B.S.B.A., Hawai'i Pacific University, Honolulu, HI, 2009; Officer Candidate School, Army; professional: member of the Hawai'i House of Representatives from the 42nd District, 2002–04; member of the Honolulu City Council from the 6th District, 2011–12; member of the Hawai'i Army National Guard, 2003–present; committees: Armed Services; Financial Services; elected to the 113th Congress on November 6, 2012; reelected to each succeeding Congress.

Office Listings

https://gabbard.house.gov https://facebook.com/RepTulsiGabbard https://twitter.com/tulsipress

1433 Longworth House Office Building, Washington, DC 20515 .... (202) 225–4906
Legislative Director.—Guido Weiss.
300 Ala Moana Boulevard, Room 5–104, Prince Kuhio Federal Building, Honolulu, HI 96850 .... (808) 541–1986
Chief of Staff.—Kainoa Penaroza.

Counties: HAWAI'I. CITIES: Hawi, Hilo, Honoka'a, Kailua-Kona, Kealakekua, Na'alehu, Ocean View, Pahoa, Volcano, Waikoloa, and Waimea. HONOLULU COUNTY (part). CITIES: Hale'iwa, Honolulu, Kailua, Kane'ohe, Kapolei, La'ie, Makakilo, Nanakuli, Wahiawa, Waialua, Wai'anae, and Waimanalo. KALAWAO COUNTY. CITY: Kalaupapa. KAUA'I COUNTY. CITIES: Hanalei, Hanapepe, Kalaheo, Kapa'a, Kekaha, Kilauea, Koloa, Lihue, Pu'uwai, and Waimea. MAUI COUNTY. CITIES: Hana, Kahului, Kaunakakai, Lahaina, Lana'i City, Makawao, and Wailuku. NORTHWESTERN HAWAIIAN ISLANDS. Islands of: Becker, French Frigate Shoals, Gardener Pinnacles, Hermes and Kure Atolls, Laysan, Lisianski, Maro Reef, Nihoa, and Pearl. Population (2010), 679,805.

ZIP Codes: 96703–05, 96707–08, 96710, 96712–14, 96716–17, 96719–20, 96722, 96725–32, 96734, 96737–38, 96740–44, 96746–57, 96759–66, 96768–74, 96776–81, 96783, 96785–86, 96789–93, 96795–97, 96825, 96857, 96863

IDAHO

(Population 2010, 1,567,582)

SENATORS

MIKE CRAPO, Republican, of Idaho Falls, ID; born in Idaho Falls, May 20, 1951; education: graduated, Idaho Falls High School, 1969; B.A., Brigham Young University, Provo, UT, 1973; J.D., Harvard University Law School, Cambridge, MA, 1977; professional: attorney; admitted to the California Bar, 1977; admitted to the Idaho Bar, 1979; law clerk, Hon. James M. Carter, Judge of the U.S. Court of Appeals for the 9th Circuit, San Diego, CA, 1977–78; associate attorney, Gibson, Dunn, and Crutcher, San Diego, 1978–79; attorney, Holden, Kidwell, Hahn and Crapo, 1979–92; partner, 1983–92; Idaho State Senate, 1984–92; Assistant Majority Leader, 1987–89, President Pro Tempore, 1989–92; member: American Bar Association; Boy Scouts of America; Idaho Falls Rotary Club, 1984–88; married: the former Susan Diane Hasleton, 1974; children: Michelle, Brian, Stephanie, Lara, and Paul; caucuses: co-chair, COPD Caucus; co-chair, Western Water Caucus; Sportsmen's Caucus; Majority Chief Deputy Whip; committees: chair, Banking, Housing, and Urban Affairs; Budget; Finance; Judiciary; Joint Committee on Taxation; elected on November 3, 1992, to the 103rd Congress; reelected to each succeeding Congress; elected to the U.S. Senate on November 3, 1998; reelected to each succeeding Senate term.

Office Listings

https://crapo.senate.gov https://facebook.com/mikecrapo twitter: @MikeCrapo

239 Dirksen Senate Office Building, Washington, DC 20510 .... (202) 224–6142
Chief of Staff.—Susan Wheeler. FAX: 228–1375
Legislative Director.—Scott Riplinger.
251 East Front Street, Suite 205, Boise, ID 83702 .... (208) 334–1776
Chief of Staff.—John Hoehne.
Communications Director.—Lindsay Nothern.
610 Hubbard Street, Suite 209, Coeur d'Alene, ID 83814 .... (208) 664–5490
Director.—Karen Roetter.
313 D Street, Suite 105, Lewiston, ID 83501 .... (208) 743–1492
Director.—Tony Snodderly.
275 South 5th Avenue, Suite 100, Pocatello, ID 83201 .... (208) 236–6775
Director.—Farhanna Hibbert.
410 Memorial Drive, Suite 204, Idaho Falls, ID 83402 .... (208) 522–9779
Director.—Kathryn Hitch.
202 Falls Avenue, Suite 2, Twin Falls, ID 83301 .... (208) 734–2515
Director.—Samantha Marshall.

* * *

JAMES E. RISCH, Republican, of Boise, ID; born in Milwaukee, WI, May 3, 1943; education: St. Johns Cathedral High School, Milwaukee; B.S., forestry, University of Idaho, Moscow, ID, 1965; J.D., University of Idaho, Moscow, 1968; Law Review, College of Law Advisory Committee; professional: Ada County Prosecuting Attorney, 1970–74; president, Idaho Prosecuting Attorneys Association, 1973; Idaho State Senate, 1974–88, 1995–2003; Assistant Majority Leader, 1996; Majority Leader, 1976–82, 1997–2002; President Pro Tempore, 1983–88; Lieutenant Governor of Idaho, 2003–06, 2007–09; Governor of Idaho, 2006; small business owner; rancher/farmer; former partner, Risch, Goss, Insinger, Gustavel law firm; member, National Cattle Association; Idaho Cattle Association; American, Idaho and Boise Valley Angus Associations; National Rifle Association; Ducks Unlimited; Rocky Mountain Elk Foundation; married: Vicki; children: James, Jason, and Jordan; three daughters-in-law; nine grandchildren; caucuses: Aerospace Caucus; Air Force Caucus; Caucus on Foster Youth; Caucus on International Narcotics Control; Caucus on Poland; Congressional Arthritis Caucus; Congressional Caucus on Parkinson's Disease; Congressional Caucus on the Deadliest Cancers; Congressional Coalition on Adoption; Congressional Heart and Stroke Coalition; Congressional Semiconductor Caucus; Congressional Sportsmen's Caucus; Congressional TRIO Caucus; Diabetes Caucus; Foreign Service Caucus; Former Governors Caucus; General Aviation Caucus; Impact Aid Coalition; Multiple Sclerosis Caucus; National Guard Caucus; National Laboratory Caucus; Ocean's Caucus; Outdoor Recreation Caucus; Paper and Packaging Caucus; Rare Disease Caucus; Recycling Caucus; Western Caucus; Working Forests Caucus; committees: chair, Foreign Relations; Energy and Natural Resources; Small Business and Entrepreneurship; Select Committee on Ethics; Select Committee on Intelligence; elected to the U.S. Senate on November 4, 2008; reelected to the U.S. Senate on November 4, 2014.

Office Listings

https://risch.senate.gov twitter: @SenatorRisch

483 Russell Senate Office Building, Washington, DC 20510 .... (202) 224–2752
Chief of Staff.—John Insinger. FAX: 224–2573
Communications Director.—Vacant.
Executive Assistant / Scheduler.—Alexa Green.
Legislative Director.—Charles Adams.
350 North Ninth Street, Suite 302, Boise, ID 83702 .... (208) 342–7985

REPRESENTATIVES

FIRST DISTRICT

RUSS FULCHER, Republican, of Meridian, ID; born in Boise, ID, March 9, 1962; education: B.B.A., Boise State University, 1984; M.B.A., Boise State University, 1988; certified, electrical engineering, Micron Technology, 1993; certified, energy policy planning, University of Idaho, 2012; professional: realtor; technology executive; started at Micron Technology as a production-line worker and advanced to director of sales and marketing for the manufacturing division (he conducted business in all 50 states and worked on-site in 36 countries); member of the Idaho State Senate, 2005–14 (elected by his colleagues to be the Senate Republican Caucus Leader for 6 of the 10 years he served); delegate, Republican National Convention, 2016; religion: Christian; family: three children, Meghan, Benjamin, and Nicole; committees: Education and Labor; Natural Resources; elected to the 116th Congress on November 6, 2018.

Office Listings

https://fulcher.house.gov https://facebook.com/RepRussFulcher twitter: @RepRussFulcher
https://instagram.com/RepRussFulcher https://www.youtube.com/channel/UCx2AS0O5frzPB8D6TqJ3Mqg

1520 Longworth House Office Building, Washington, DC 20515 .... (202) 225–6611
Chief of Staff.—Cliff Bayer.
Scheduler.—Daniel Tellez.
Legislative Director.—Andrew Neill.
Communications Director.—Alexah Rogge.
33 East Broadway Avenue, Suite 251, Meridian, ID 83642 .... (208) 888–3188
313 D Street, Suite 107, Lewiston, ID 83501 .... (208) 743–1388
1250 West Ironwood Drive, Suite 200, Coeur d'Alene, ID 83814 .... (208) 667–0127

Counties: ADA (part), ADAMS, BENEWAH, BOISE, BONNER, BOUNDARY, CANYON, CLEARWATER, GEM, IDAHO, KOOTENAI, LATAH, LEWIS, NEZ PERCE, OWYHEE, PAYETTE, SHOSHONE, VALLEY, AND WASHINGTON. Population (2010), 784,132.

ZIP Codes: 59847, 83302, 83316, 83501, 83520, 83522–26, 83530, 83533, 83535–37, 83539–49, 83552–55, 83602, 83604–05, 83607, 83610–12, 83615–17, 83619, 83622, 83624, 83626–29, 83631–32, 83634, 83636–39, 83641–46, 83650–51, 83654–57, 83660–61, 83666, 83669–72, 83676–77, 83686–87, 83702, 83705, 83709, 83713–14, 83716, 83801–06, 83808–15, 83821–27, 83830, 83832–37, 83839–52, 83854–58, 83860–61, 83864, 83866–74, 83876, 89832, 97910, 97913, 99128

* * *

SECOND DISTRICT

MICHAEL K. SIMPSON, Republican, of Blackfoot, ID; born in Burley, ID, September 8, 1950; education: graduated, Blackfoot High School, 1968; Utah State University, 1972; Washington University School of Dental Medicine, 1977; professional: dentist, private practice; Blackfoot, ID, City Council, 1981–85; Idaho State Legislature, 1985–98; Idaho Speaker of the House, 1992–98; married: Kathy Simpson; committees: Appropriations; elected to the 106th Congress; reelected to each succeeding Congress.

Office Listings

https://simpson.house.gov https://facebook.com/Mike-Simpson-96007744606
https://twitter.com/CongMikeSimpson

2084 Rayburn House Office Building, Washington, DC 20515 .... (202) 225–5531
Chief of Staff.—Lindsay Slater. FAX: 225–8216
Scheduler.—Jocelyn Bryant.
Legislative Director.—Sarah Cannon.
Communications Director.—Nikki Wallace.
802 West Bannock, Suite 600, Boise, ID 83702 .... (208) 334–1953

Office Listings—Continued

650 Addison Avenue West, #1078, Twin Falls, ID 83301 .... (208) 734–7219
410 Memorial Drive, Suite 203, Idaho Falls, ID 83402 .... (208) 523–6701

Counties: ADA (Part), BANNOCK, BEAR LAKE, BINGHAM, BLAINE, BONNEVILLE, BUTTE, CAMAS, CARIBOU, CASSIA, CLARK, CUSTER, ELMORE, FRANKLIN, FREMONT, GOODING, JEFFERSON, JEROME, LEMHI, LINCOLN, MADISON, MINIDOKA, ONEIDA, POWER, TETON, AND TWIN FALLS. Population (2010), 793,109.

ZIP Codes: 83201–06, 83209–15, 83217–18, 83220–21, 83223, 83226–30, 83232–39, 83241, 83243–46, 83250–56, 83261–63, 83271–72, 83274, 83276–78, 83281, 83283, 83285–87, 83301–03, 83311–14, 83316, 83318, 83320–25, 83327–28, 83330, 83332–38, 83340–44, 83346–50, 83352–55, 83401–06, 83415, 83420–25, 83427–29, 83431, 83433–36, 83438, 83440–46, 83448–52, 83454–55, 83460, 83462–69, 83601–02, 83604, 83623–24, 83627, 83633–34, 83647–48, 83701–09, 83712, 83714–17, 83720–33, 83735, 83744, 83756

ILLINOIS

(Population 2010, 12,830,632)

SENATORS

RICHARD J. DURBIN, Democrat, of Springfield, IL; born in East St. Louis, IL, November 21, 1944; son of William and Ann Durbin; education: graduated, Assumption High School, East St. Louis; B.S., foreign service and economics, Georgetown University, Washington, DC, 1966; J.D., Georgetown University Law Center, 1969; professional: attorney; admitted to the Illinois Bar in 1969; began practice in Springfield; legal counsel to Lieutenant Governor Paul Simon, 1969–72; legal counsel to Illinois Senate Judiciary Committee, 1972–82; parliamentarian, Illinois Senate, 1969–82; adjunct professor, Southern Illinois University School of Medicine; married: the former Loretta Schaefer, 1967; children: Christine (deceased), Paul, and Jennifer; committees: Agriculture, Nutrition, and Forestry; Appropriations; Judiciary; Rules and Administration; elected to the 98th Congress on November 2, 1982; reelected to each succeeding Congress; elected to the U.S. Senate on November 5, 1996; reelected to each succeeding Senate term; elected as Democratic Whip, 2004; reelected for each succeeding Congress.

Office Listings

https://durbin.senate.gov https://facebook.com/SenatorDurbin https://twitter.com/SenatorDurbin

711 Hart Senate Office Building, Washington, DC 20510 .... (202) 224–2152
Chief of Staff.—Patrick Souders.
Legislative Director.—Corey Tellez.
Communications Director.—Emily Hampsten.
Director of Scheduling.—Claire Reuschel.
230 South Dearborn, Kluczynski Building, 38th Floor, Chicago, IL 60604 .... (312) 353–4952
Chicago Director.—Clarisol Duque.
525 South Eighth Street, Springfield, IL 62703 .... (217) 492–4062
State Director.—Bill Houlihan.
1504 Third Avenue, Suite 227, Rock Island, IL 61201 .... (309) 786–5173
250 West Cherry Street, Suite 115D, Carbondale, IL 62901 .... (618) 351–1122

* * *

TAMMY DUCKWORTH, Democrat, of Hoffman Estates, IL; born in Bangkok, Thailand; education: B.A., political science, University of Hawaii, 1989; M.A., George Washington University, Washington, DC, 1992; Ph.D., in human services at Capella University, 2014; professional: Rotary International; Illinois Department of Veterans' Affairs; U.S. Department of Veterans Affairs; military: lieutenant colonel, Illinois National Guard; combat veteran, Operation Iraqi Freedom; married: Bryan Bowlsbey; committees: Armed Services, Commerce, Science, and Transportation; Environment and Public Works; Small Business and Entrepreneurship; elected to the 113th Congress on November 6, 2012; reelected to the 114th Congress on November 4, 2014; elected to the U.S. Senate on November 8, 2016.

Office Listings

https://duckworth.senate.gov https://facebook.com/SenDuckworth
https://twitter.com/SenDuckworth https://instagram.com/SenDuckworth
https://youtube.com/SenDuckworth

524 Hart Senate Office Building, Washington, DC 20510 .... (202) 224–2854
Chief of Staff.—Kaitlin Fahey. FAX: 228–0618
Deputy Chief of Staff.—Kalina Bakalov.
Legislative Director.—Ben Rhodeside.
Communications Director.—Ben Garmisa.
Administrative Director.—Paul Kohnstamm.
Scheduling Director.—Kelsey Becker.
230 South Dearborn Street, Suite 3900, Chicago, IL 60604 .... (312) 886–3506
Chicago Director.—Marina Faz-Huppert.
8 South Old State Capitol Plaza, Springfield, IL 62701 .... (217) 528–6124
State Director.—Cameron Joost.
Downstate Director.—Randy Sikowski.
Eurma C. Hayes Center, 441 East Willow Street, Carbondale, IL 62901 .... (618) 677–7000
1823 2nd Avenue, Suite 2, Rock Island, IL 61201 .... (309) 606–7060
23 Public Square, Suite 460, Belleville, IL 62220 .... (618) 722–7070

REPRESENTATIVES

FIRST DISTRICT

BOBBY L. RUSH, Democrat, of Chicago, IL; born in Albany, GA, November 23, 1946; education: attended Marshall High School, Marshall, IL; B.A., Roosevelt University, Chicago, IL, 1974; M.A., University of Illinois, Chicago, 1994; M.A., McCormick Theological Seminary, Chicago, 1998; professional: U.S. Army, 1963–68; insurance agent; alderman, Chicago, IL, City Council, 1983–93; deputy chairman, Illinois Democratic Party, 1990; unsuccessful candidate for Mayor of Chicago, 1999; minister; wife: Paulette; five children; committees: Energy and Commerce; elected on November 3, 1992 to the 103rd Congress; reelected to each succeeding Congress.

Office Listings

https://rush.house.gov https://facebook.com/congressmanbobbyrush https://twitter.com/RepBobbyRush

2188 Rayburn House Office Building, Washington, DC 20515 .... (202) 225–4372
Chief of Staff / Counsel.—Yardly Pollas. FAX: 226–0333
Legislative Director.—Nishith Pandya.
Director of Administration and Operations.—N. Lenette Myers.
Communications Director.—Ryan Johnson.
11750 South Western Avenue, Chicago, IL 60643 .... (773) 779–2400
District Director.—Robyn Wheeler Grange.

Counties: COOK COUNTY (part) AND WILL COUNTY (part). CITIES AND TOWNSHIPS: Alsip, Blue Island, Bremen Township, Calumet Park, Calumet Township, Chicago, Country Club Hills, Crestwood, Dixmoor, Elwood, Evergreen Park, Frankfort, Frankfort Square, Frankfort Township, Green Garden Township, Harvey, Jackson Township, Manhattan, Manhattan Township, Markham, Merrionette Park, Midlothian, Mokena, New Lenox, New Lenox Township, Oak Forest, Oak Lawn, Orland Hills, Orland Park, Orland Township, Palos Heights, Palos Township, Posen, Rich Township, Riverdale, Robbins, Thornton Township, Tinley Park, Will County, Worth, and Worth Township. Population (2012), 711,982.

ZIP Codes: 60406, 60418, 60421, 60423, 60426, 60428, 60442, 60445, 60448–49, 60451–53, 60462–64, 60467–69, 60472, 60477–78, 60482, 60487, 60609, 60615–17, 60619–21, 60628–29, 60636–37, 60643, 60649, 60652–53, 60655, 60803, 60805, 60827

* * *

SECOND DISTRICT

ROBIN L. KELLY, Democrat, of Matteson, IL; born in New York, NY, April 30, 1956; education: B.A. in psychology, Bradley University, IL, 1977; M.A., counseling, Bradley University, 1982; Ph.D., political science, Northern Illinois University, IL, 2004; professional: counselor; community affairs director, Matteson, IL, 1992–2006; member, Illinois State House of Representatives, 2003–07; Chief of Staff, Illinois State Treasurer, 2007–10; Chief Administrative Officer, Cook County, IL, 2010–12; caucuses: co-chair, Diversifying Tech Caucus; vice chair, Gun Violence Prevention Task Force; member, Congressional Black Caucus; Congressional Caucus on Black Women and Girls; married: Dr. Nathaniel Horn; two children; committees: Energy and Commerce; Oversight and Reform; elected to the 113th Congress on April 9, 2013, by special election, to fill the vacancy caused by the resignation of U.S. Representative Jesse L. Jackson, Jr.; reelected to each succeeding Congress.

Office Listings

https://robinkelly.house.gov https://facebook.com/reprobinkelly https://twitter.com/reprobinkelly

2416 Rayburn House Office Building, Washington, DC 20515 .... (202) 225–0773
Chief of Staff.—Julius West.
Legislative Director.—Matt McMurray.
Communications Director.—James Lewis.
Legislative Assistants: Charles Bolden, Nicole Varner.
Director of Advance / Scheduler.—Tony Presta.
600 Holiday Plaza Drive, Suite 505, Matteson, IL 60443 .... (708) 679–0078
District Director.—Cynthia DeWitt.

Counties: COOK (part), KANKAKEE, AND WILL (part). CITIES AND TOWNSHIPS: Beecher, Blue Island, Bonfield, Bourbonnais, Bradley, Buckingham, Cabery, Calumet City, Chebanse, Chicago, Chicago Heights, Country Club Hills, Crete, Custer Park, Dixmoor, Dolton, Essex, Flossmoor, Ford Heights, Frankfort, Gardner, Glenwood, Grant Park, Harvey, Hazel Crest, Herscher, Homewood, Hopkins Park, Kankakee, Lansing, Lynwood, Manhattan, Manteno, Markham, Matteson, Momence, Monee, Olympia Fields, Park Forest, Pembroke Township, Peotone, Phoenix, Reddick, Richton Park, Riverdale, Saint Anne, Sauk Village, South Chicago Heights, South Holland, Steger, Tinley Park, Thornton, Union Hill, University Park, and Wilmington. Population (2010), 718,507.

ZIP Codes: 60401, 60406, 60409, 60411–12, 60417, 60419, 60422–23, 60425–26, 60428–30, 60438, 60443, 60449, 60461, 60466, 60468, 60471, 60473, 60475–78, 60481, 60484, 60615, 60617, 60628, 60633, 60637, 60649, 60827, 60901, 60913–15, 60917, 60919, 60922, 60935, 60940–42, 60944, 60950, 60954, 60958, 60961, 60964, 60969

* * *

THIRD DISTRICT

DANIEL LIPINSKI, Democrat, of Chicago, IL; born in Chicago, July 15, 1966; son of former Congressman William Lipinski, 1983–2004; education: B.S., mechanical engineering, *magna cum laude,* Northwestern University, 1988; M.S., engineering-economic systems, Stanford University, 1989; Ph.D., political science, Duke University, 1998; professional: aide to U.S. Representative George Sangmeister, 1993–94; aide to U.S. Representative Jerry Costello, 1995–96; aide to U.S. Representative Rod Blagojevich, 1999–2000; professor, James Madison University Washington Program, Washington, DC, 2000; professor, University of Notre Dame, South Bend, IN, 2000–01; professor, University of Tennessee, Knoxville, TN, 2001–04; married: Judy; committees: Science, Space, and Technology; Transportation and Infrastructure; elected to the 109th Congress on November 2, 2004; reelected to each succeeding Congress.

Office Listings

https://lipinski.house.gov https://facebook.com/repdanlipinski twitter: @RepLipinski

2346 Rayburn House Office Building, Washington, DC 20515 .... (202) 225–5701
Chief of Staff.—Brian Oszakiewski. FAX: 225–1012
Office Administrator.—Jennifer Sypolt.
Legislative Director.—Sofya Leonova.
6245 South Archer Avenue, Chicago, IL 60638 .... (773) 948–6223
District Director.—Joe Bonomo.
222 East 9th Street, Suite 109, Lockport, IL 60441 .... (815) 838–1990
Communications Director.—Philip Davidson.
5210 West 95th Street, Suite 104, Oak Lawn, IL 60453 .... (708) 424–0853
14700 South Ravinia Avenue, 1st Floor, Orland Park, IL 60462 .... (708) 403–4379

Counties: COOK (part), DUPAGE (part), AND WILL (part). CITIES AND TOWNSHIPS: Alsip, Bedford Park, Berwyn, Bridgeview, Brookfield, Burbank, Burr Ridge, Chicago, Chicago Ridge, Cicero, Countryside, Crest Hill, Forest Park, Forest View, Hickory Hills, Hillside, Hinsdale, Homer Glen, Hometown, Hodgkins, Indian Head Park, Justice Burbank, La Grange, Lemont, Lockport, Lyons, McCook, Merrionette Park, North Riverside, Oak Lawn, Oak Park, Palos Heights, Palos Hills, Palos Park, Proviso, Riverside, Romeoville, Stickney, Summit Brookfield, Western Springs, Willow Springs, and Worth. Population (2012), 704,438.

ZIP Codes: 60402 (part), 60406, 60415, 60432 (part), 60435 (part), 60439 (part), 60441 (part), 60446 (part), 60448 (part), 60451 (part), 60463 (part), 60455, 60456 (part), 60457–58, 60459 (part), 60462–65 (part), 60467 (part), 60477 (part), 60480 (part), 60482 (part), 60501, 60513 (part), 60521 (part), 60425–26 (part), 60534 (part), 60544 (part), 60546 (part), 60558 (part), 60561 (part), 60608–09 (part), 60616 (part), 60620 (part), 60629 (part), 60632 (part), 60636 (part), 60638 (part), 60643 (part), 60652 (part), 60655 (part), 60803 (part), 60804 (part), 60805 (part)

* * *

FOURTH DISTRICT

JESÚS G. ''CHUY'' GARCÍA, Democrat, of Chicago, IL; born in Durango, Mexico, April 12, 1956; education: graduated from St. Rita High School, Chicago, IL, 1974; B.A., University of Illinois, Chicago, IL, 1999; M.A., University of Illinois, Chicago, IL, 2002; professional: Alderman, Chicago City Council, 1986–93; Illinois State Senator, 1993–98; founder of Enlace Chicago, 1999–2009; Cook County Board Commissioner, 2010–18; married: Evelyn; children: Jesús, Samuel, and Rosa; caucuses: Congressional Caucus to End the Youth Vaping Epidemic; Congressional Hispanic Caucus; Congressional LGBT Equality Caucus; Congressional Progressive Caucus; Future of Transportation Caucus; New Americans Caucus; committees: Financial Services; Natural Resources; Transportation and Infrastructure; elected to the 116th Congress on November 6, 2018.

Office Listings

https://chuygarcia.house.gov https://facebook.com/RepChuyGarcia
twitter: @RepChuyGarcia https://instagram.com/repchuygarcia

530 Cannon House Office Building, Washington, DC 20515 .... (202) 225–8203
Chief of Staff.—Kari Moe. FAX: 225–7810
Legislative Director.—Don Andres.
Communications Director.—Fabiola Rodriguez-Ciampoli.
Scheduler.—Julissa Santoy.
5624 West Diversey Avenue, Chicago, IL 60639 .... (773) 342–0774

Office Listings—Continued

4376 South Archer Avenue, Chicago, IL 60632 .... (773) 475–0833
District Director.—Patty Garcia.

Counties: COOK COUNTY (part). CITIES: Berkeley, Berwyn, Brookfield, Chicago, Cicero, Elmwood Park, Forest Park, Hillside, La Grange Park, Lyons, Maywood, Melrose Park, North Riverside, Northlake, Oak Park, Riverside, Stickney, Stone Park, and Westchester. Population (2012), 724,644.

ZIP Codes: 60126, 60154, 60160, 60162–64, 60304–05, 60402, 60513, 60546, 60608–09, 60616, 60618, 60622–23, 60625, 60629–30, 60632, 60634, 60639, 60641, 60647, 60651, 60707, 60804

* * *

FIFTH DISTRICT

MIKE QUIGLEY, Democrat, of Chicago, IL; born in Indianapolis, IN, October 17, 1958; education: B.A., political science, Roosevelt University, 1981; M.P.P., University of Chicago, 1985; J.D., Loyola University, 1989; professional: Chicago aldermanic aide, 1983–89; practicing attorney, 1990–2009; Cook County Commissioner, 1998–2009; adjunct professor, Roosevelt University, 2006–07; adjunct professor, Loyola University, 2002–09; married: Barbara; children: Meghan and Alyson; committees: Appropriations; Permanent Select Committee on Intelligence; elected to the 111th Congress on April 7, 2009, by special election, to fill the vacancy caused by the resignation of U.S. Representative Rahm Emanuel; reelected to each succeeding Congress.

Office Listings

https://quigley.house.gov https://facebook.com/repmikequigley https://twitter.com/RepMikeQuigley

2458 Rayburn House Office Building, Washington, DC 20515 .... (202) 225–4061
Chief of Staff.—Juan Hinojosa. FAX: 225–5603
Communications Director.—Victoria Oms.
Scheduler.—Isabella Spinozzi.
Legislative Director.—Allison Jarus.
4345 North Milwaukee Avenue, Chicago, IL 60641 .... (773) 267–5926
FAX: 267–6583
3223 North Sheffield Avenue, Chicago, IL 60657 .... (773) 267–5926

Counties: COOK COUNTY (part). Population (2010), 648,610.

ZIP Codes: 60018, 60106, 60126, 60131, 60154, 60160, 60162, 60164, 60171, 60176, 60181, 60191, 60521, 60523, 60525–26, 60558, 60610, 60612–14, 60618, 60622, 60625, 60630–31, 60634, 60640–42, 60645–47, 60656–57, 60659, 60706–07, 60714

* * *

SIXTH DISTRICT

SEAN CASTEN, Democrat, of Downers Grove, IL; born in Dublin, Ireland, November 23, 1971; education: graduated from Woodlands High School, Hartsdale, NY, 1989; B.A., Middlebury College, Middlebury, VT, 1993; M.S., Dartmouth College, Hanover, NH, 1998; M.E.M., Dartmouth College, Hanover, NH, 1998; professional: cancer researcher, 1993–95; biofuels researcher, 1995–98; technology consultant, 1998–2000; clean energy entrepreneur/CEO, 2000–16; founding chairman, Northeast Combined Heat & Power Initiative, 2001; U.S. Clean Heat & Power Association board member; awards: Chicago Council of Global Affairs Emerging Leader, Class of 2009; USCHPA CHP Champion, 2005; Casten Family Foundation Contributing author, Grist.org, 2008–12; married to Kara Casten; two children: Audrey and Gwen; caucuses: New Democratic Coalition Caucus; committees: Financial Services; Science, Space, and Technology; Select Committee on the Climate Crisis; elected to the 116th Congress on November 6, 2018.

Office Listings

https://casten.house.gov https://facebook.com/RepSeanCasten
twitter: @RepCasten https://instagram.com/repseancasten

429 Cannon House Office Building, Washington, DC 20515 .... (202) 225–4561

Office Listings—Continued

Chief of Staff.—Ann Adler. FAX: 225–1166
Legislative Director.—Calli Shapiro.
Communications Director.—Maddie Carlos.
Scheduler.—Sameer Chintamani.
2700 International Drive, Suite 304, West Chicago, IL 60185 .... (630) 520–9450
District Director.—Anne Wick.

Counties: COOK (part), DUPAGE (part), LAKE (part), AND MCHENRY (part). CITIES AND TOWNSHIPS: Algonquin, Barrington, Barrington Hills, Bartlett, Carol Stream, Carpentersville, Cary, Clarendon Hills, Crystal Lake, Darien, Deer Park, Downers Grove, Dundee, East Dundee, Elgin, Fox River Grove, Gilberts, Glen Ellyn, Hanover Park, Hawthorne Woods, Hinsdale, Hoffman Estates, Huntley, Inverness, Kildeer, Lake Barrington, Lake in the Hills, Lake Zurich, Lakewood, Lisle, Lombard, Long Grove, Naperville, North Barrington, Oak Brook, Oakbrook Terrace, Oakwood Hills, Palatine, Port Barrington, Rolling Meadows, Saint Charles, Schaumburg, Sleepy Hollow, South Barrington, South Elgin, Tower Lakes, Trout Valley, Warrenville, Wayne, West Chicago, West Dundee, Westmont, Wheaton, Willowbrook, and Winfield. Population (2010), 712,813.

ZIP Codes: 60008, 60010–11, 60013–14, 60021, 60039, 60047, 60055, 60060, 60067, 60074, 60078, 60094, 60102–03, 60107, 60110, 60118, 60120, 60122–24, 60133, 60136–39, 60142, 60148, 60156, 60169, 60173–75, 60177, 60179, 60181, 60184–85, 60187–90, 60192, 60195, 60197, 60199, 60514–16, 60521, 60523, 60527, 60532, 60540, 60555, 60559, 60561, 60563–65

* * *

SEVENTH DISTRICT

DANNY K. DAVIS, Democrat, of Chicago, IL; born in Parkdale, AR, September 6, 1941; education: B.A., Arkansas AM&N College, 1961; M.A., Chicago State University; Ph.D., Union Institute, Cincinnati, OH; professional: educator and health planner-administrator; board of directors, National Housing Partnership; Cook County Board of Commissioners, 1st District, 1990–96; Chicago City Council, 29th Ward, 1979–90; recipient of the Independent Voters of Illinois' Best Alderman Award for 1980–82 and 1989–90; co-chair, Clinton-Gore-Braun '92; founder and past president, Westside Association for Community Action; past president, National Association of Community Health Centers; recipient of the Leon M. Despres Award, 1987; married to Vera G. Davis; two sons: Jonathan and Stacey (deceased); committees: Ways and Means; elected to the 105th Congress; reelected to each succeeding Congress.

Office Listings

https://davis.house.gov https://facebook.com/CongressmanDKDavis twitter: @RepDannyDavis

2159 Rayburn House Office Building, Washington, DC 20515 .... (202) 225–5006
Chief of Staff.—Yul Edwards. FAX: 225–5641
Deputy Chief of Staff.—Jill Hunter-Williams.
Director of Issues and Communications.—Ira Cohen.
2815 West 5th Avenue, Chicago, IL 60612 .... (773) 533–7520

Counties: COOK. CITIES AND TOWNSHIPS: Berwyn, Chicago, Oak Park, Proviso, River Forest, and Riverside. Population (2010), 712,812.

ZIP Codes: 60104, 60130, 60141, 60153–55, 60160, 60162–63, 60301–12, 60614–16, 60621–24, 60629, 60632, 60636–37, 60639, 60642, 60644, 60651, 60653–54, 60661, 60707, 60804

* * *

EIGHTH DISTRICT

RAJA KRISHNAMOORTHI, Democrat, of Schaumburg, IL; born in New Delhi, India, July 19, 1973; education: B.S.E., mechanical engineering and certificate in public policy, Princeton University, 1995; J.D., Harvard Law School, 2000; professional: private law practice; Special Assistant Illinois Attorney General; Deputy Illinois Treasurer; president of research-oriented small businesses; religion: Hindu; married to Priya; three children: Vijay, Vikram, and Sonia; committees: Oversight and Reform; Permanent Select Committee on Intelligence; elected to the 115th Congress on November 8, 2016; reelected to the 116th Congress on November 6, 2018.

Office Listings

https://krishnamoorthi.house.gov https://facebook.com/CongressmanRaja
https://twitter.com/congressmanraja https://instagram.com/congressmanraja
https://youtube.com/c/CongressmanRaja

115 Cannon House Office Building, Washington, DC 20515 .... (202) 225–3711

Office Listings—Continued

Chief of Staff.—Mark Schauerte. FAX: 225–7830
Legislative Director.—Brian Kaissi.
Communications Director.—Wilson Baldwin.
Scheduler.—Amol Shalia.
1701 East Woodfield Road, Suite 704, Schaumburg, IL 60173 .... (847) 413–1959
District Director.—Sabey Abraham. FAX: 413–1965

Counties: COOK COUNTY (part). TOWNSHIPS: Arlington Heights, Barrington Hills, Buffalo Grove, Chicago (part), Des Plaines, Elk Grove, Hoffman Estates, Mount Prospect, Palatine, Rolling Meadows, Rosemont, Schaumburg, Streamwood, and Wheeling. DUPAGE COUNTY (part). TOWNSHIPS: Addison, Bartlett, Bensenville, Bloomingdale, Carol Stream, Elmhurst, Glen Ellyn, Glendale, Hanover Park, Itasca, Lombard, Oak Brook, Oakbrook Terrace, Roselle, Villa Park, and Wheaton. KANE COUNTY (part). TOWNSHIPS: Algonquin, Carpentersville, East Dundee, and Elgin. Population (2010), 726,418.

ZIP Codes: 60004–05, 60007–10, 60016, 60018, 60038, 60056, 60067, 60074, 60089–90, 60101–03, 60106–08, 60110, 60116–18, 60120–21, 60123–24, 60126, 60131–33, 60137, 60139, 60143, 60148, 60157, 60168–70, 60172–73, 60177, 60179, 60181, 60187–88, 60191–95, 60399, 60523

* * *

NINTH DISTRICT

JANICE D. SCHAKOWSKY, Democrat, of Evanston, IL; born in Chicago, IL, May 26, 1944; education: B.A., University of Illinois, 1965; professional: consumer advocate; program director, Illinois Public Action; executive director, Illinois State Council of Senior Citizens, 1985–90; State Representative, 18th District, Illinois General Assembly, 1991–99; served on Labor and Commerce, Human Service Appropriations, Health Care, and Electric Deregulation Committees; religion: Jewish; married: Robert Creamer; children: Ian, Mary, and Lauren; Chief Deputy Whip; Steering and Policy Committee; committees: Budget; Energy and Commerce; elected to the 106th Congress; reelected to each succeeding Congress.

Office Listings

https://schakowsky.house.gov https://facebook.com/janschakowsky https://twitter.com/janschakowsky

2367 Rayburn House Office Building, Washington, DC 20515 .... (202) 225–2111
Chief of Staff.—Robert Marcus. FAX: 226–6890
Communications Director.—Miguel Ayala.
Legislative Director.—Syd Terry.
Deputy Chief of Staff/Executive Assistant.—Kim Muzeroll.
5533 North Broadway, Chicago, IL 60640 .... (773) 506–7100
District Director.—Leslie Combs.
1852 Johns Drive, Glenview, IL 60025 .... (847) 328–3409

Counties: COOK COUNTY (part). CITIES: Arlington Heights, Chicago, Des Plaines, Evanston, Glenview, Golf, Kenilworth, Lincolnwood, Morton Grove, Mount Prospect, Niles, Northbrook, Northfield, Park Ridge, Prospect Heights, Skokie, Wheeling, Wilmette, and Winnetka. Population (2010), 712,813.

ZIP Codes: 60004–05, 60016, 60018–19, 60025–26, 60029, 60043, 60053, 60056, 60062, 60068, 60070, 60076–77, 60090–91, 60093, 60176, 60201–03, 60613, 60626, 60630, 60640, 60645–46, 60656–57, 60659–60, 60706, 60712, 60714

* * *

TENTH DISTRICT

BRADLEY SCOTT SCHNEIDER, Democrat, of Deerfield, IL; born in Denver, CO, August 20, 1961; education: Cherry Creek High School, Greenwood Village, CO, 1979; B.A., Northwestern University, Evanston, IL, 1983; M.B.A., Kellogg School of Management, Evanston, IL, 1988; professional: owner, Cadence Consulting Group, LLC; director of Family Business Center, Blackman Kallick, LLP; managing principal, Davis Dann Adler Schneider, LLC; family: wife, Julie Dann; children: Adam and Daniel; committees: Small Business; Ways and Means; elected to the 113th Congress on November 6, 2012; unsuccessful candidate for reelection to the 114th Congress in 2014; elected to the 115th Congress on November 8, 2016; reelected to the 116th Congress on November 6, 2018.

Office Listings

https://schneider.house.gov https://facebook.com/CongressmanBradSchneider
https://twitter.com/repschneider

1432 Longworth House Office Building, Washington, DC 20515 .... (202) 225–4835

Office Listings—Continued

Chief of Staff.—Casey O'Shea. FAX: 225–0837
111 Barclay Boulevard, Suite 200, Lincolnshire, IL 60069 .... (847) 383–4870
District Director.—Magen Ryan. FAX: 793–0677

Counties: COOK (part) AND LAKE (part). Population (2010), 709,209.

ZIP Codes: 60004, 60015–16, 60020, 60022, 60025–26, 60030–31, 60035, 60037, 60040–41, 60044–48, 60050–51, 60053, 60056, 60060–62, 60064, 60068–70, 60073, 60081, 60083, 60085, 60087–90, 60093, 60096, 60099, 60714

* * *

ELEVENTH DISTRICT

BILL FOSTER, Democrat, of Naperville, IL; born in Madison, WI, October 7, 1955; education: B.S., University of Wisconsin-Madison, 1976; Ph.D., Harvard University, 1983; professional: small business owner; physicist; committees: Financial Services; Science, Space, and Technology; elected to the 113th Congress on November 6, 2012; reelected to each succeeding Congress.

Office Listings

https://foster.house.gov https://facebook.com/CongressmanBillFoster
https://twitter.com/RepBillFoster

2366 Rayburn House Office Building, Washington, DC 20515 .... (202) 225–3515
Chief of Staff.—Scott Shewcraft. FAX: 225–9420
2711 East New York Street, Suite 204, Aurora, IL 60502 .... (630) 585–7672
815 North Larkin Avenue, Suite 206, Joliet, IL 60435 .... (815) 280–5876
District Director.—Hilary Denk.

Counties: COOK (part), DUPAGE (part), KANE (part), KENDALL (part), AND WILL (part). Population (2010), 722,173.

ZIP Codes: 60403–04, 60410, 60421, 60431–36, 60439–42, 60446–48, 60451, 60480, 60490, 60502–06, 60512, 60515–17, 60519, 60525, 60527, 60532, 60538, 60540, 60542–44, 60559–65, 60586

* * *

TWELFTH DISTRICT

MIKE BOST, Republican, of Murphysboro, IL; born in Murphysboro, December 30, 1960; education: University of Illinois Certified Firefighter II Academy; professional: state representative; small business owner; firefighter; military: U.S. Marine Corps, 1979–82; religion: Christian, non-denominational; married: Tracy Stanton, 1980; children: Steven, Kasey, and Kaitlin; committees: Agriculture; Transportation and Infrastructure; Veterans' Affairs; elected to the 114th Congress on November 4, 2014; reelected to each succeeding Congress.

Office Listings

https://bost.house.gov https://facebook.com/RepBost https://twitter.com/repBost

1440 Longworth House Office Building, Washington, DC 20515 .... (202) 225–5661
Chief of Staff.—Matt McCullough. FAX: 225–0285
Scheduler.—Tyler Cianciotti.
Legislative Director.—Mark Ratto.
Communications Director.—George O'Connor.
District Director.—Dave Tanzyus.
302 West State Street, O'Fallon, IL 62269 .... (618) 622–0766
FAX: 233–8765
300 East Main Street, Suite 4, Carbondale, IL 62901 .... (618) 457–5787
FAX: 457–2990
200 Potomac Boulevard, Mt. Vernon, IL 62864 .... (618) 513–5294

Counties: ALEXANDER, FRANKLIN, JACKSON, JEFFERSON, MADISON (part), MONROE, PERRY, PULASKI, RANDOLPH, ST. CLAIR, UNION, AND WILLIAMSON. Population (2010), 712,813.

ZIP Codes: 62002, 62010, 62018, 62024–25, 62035, 62040, 62048, 62059–60, 62067, 62084, 62087, 62090, 62095, 62201, 62203–08, 62217, 62220–21, 62223, 62225–26, 62232–34, 62236–44, 62248, 62254–55, 62257–58, 62260–61, 62263–

65, 62268–69, 62272, 62274, 62277–80, 62282, 62285–86, 62288–89, 62292–95, 62297–98, 62801, 62808, 62810, 62812, 62814, 62816, 62819, 62822, 62825, 62830–32, 62836, 62841, 62846, 62851, 62856, 62860, 62864–65, 62872, 62874, 62877, 62883–84, 62888–91, 62893–94, 62896–98, 62901–03, 62905–07, 62912, 62914–18, 62920–24, 62926–27, 62932–33, 62939–42, 62948–52, 62956–59, 62961–64, 62966, 62969–70, 62974–76, 62983, 62987–88, 62990, 62992, 62994, 62996–99

* * *

THIRTEENTH DISTRICT

RODNEY DAVIS, Republican, of Taylorville, IL; born in Des Moines, IA, January 5, 1970; education: graduated from Taylorville High School, 1988; B.A., Millikin University, IL, 1992; professional: congressional aide, 1999–2012; has served on numerous local civic and community organizations and groups; religion: Catholic; married: Shannon R. Davis; children: Toryn, Clark, and Griffin; committees: ranking member, House Administration; Agriculture; Transportation and Infrastructure; Joint Committee on the Library; Joint Committee on Printing; Select Committee on the Modernization of Congress; elected to the 113th Congress on November 6, 2012; reelected to each succeeding Congress.

Office Listings

https://rodneydavis.house.gov https://facebook.com/RepRodneyDavis https://twitter.com/RodneyDavis

1740 Longworth House Office Building, Washington, DC 20515 .... (202) 225–2371
Chief of Staff.—Bret Manley.
Legislative Director.—Jimmy Ballard.
Scheduler.—Brianna Nagle.
Communications Director.—Aaron DeGroot.
243 South Water Street, Suite 100, Decatur, IL 62523 .... (217) 791–6224
District Director.—Helen Albert.
2004 Fox Drive, Champaign, IL 61820 .... (217) 403–4690
2833 South Grand Avenue East, Springfield, IL 62703 .... (217) 791–6224
104 West North Street, Normal, IL 61761 .... (309) 252–8834
108 West Market Street, Taylorville, IL 62568 .... (217) 824–5117
15 Professional Park Drive, Maryville, IL 62062 .... (618) 205–8660

Counties: BOND (part), CALHOUN, CHAMPAIGN (part), CHRISTIAN, DEWITT, GREENE, JERSEY, MACON, MACOUPIN, MADISON (part), MCLEAN (part), MONTGOMERY, PIATT, AND SANGAMON (part). Population (2010), 710,784.

ZIP Codes: 60481, 61252, 61701–02, 61704–05, 61709–10, 61727, 61735, 61745, 61749, 61756, 61761, 61772, 61777–78, 61790–91, 61799, 61801–03, 61813, 61815, 61818, 61820–22, 61824, 61826, 61830, 61839, 61842, 61854–56, 61864, 61872, 61874, 61880, 61882, 61884, 61913, 61929, 61936, 62002, 62006, 62009, 62013–17, 61719, 61721–23, 61725–28, 62031–37, 62044–45, 62049–54, 62056, 62058, 62060, 62062–63, 62065, 62069–70, 62074–77, 62079, 62081–83, 62086, 62088–89, 62091–94, 62097, 62234, 62262, 62355, 62501, 62510, 62513, 62517, 62521–26, 62531, 62533, 62535, 62538, 62540, 62544–47, 62549–51, 62554–58, 62560, 62563, 62567–68, 62570, 62572–73, 62626, 62629–30, 62640, 62649, 62667, 62670, 62672, 62674, 62685–86, 62690, 62701–04, 62707, 62711–12

* * *

FOURTEENTH DISTRICT

LAUREN UNDERWOOD, Democrat, of Naperville, IL; born in Mayfield Heights, Cuyahoga County, OH, October 4, 1986; education: graduated Neuqua Valley High School, Naperville, IL, 2004; B.S.N., University of Michigan, Ann Arbor, MI, 2008; M.S.N./M.P.H., Johns Hopkins University, Baltimore, MD, 2009; professional: nurse; professor; senior advisor, United States Department of Health and Human Services, 2014–17; awards: American Association of Colleges of Nursing, Government Affairs Fellow; National Institutes of Health, Post Baccalaureate Intramural Research Training Award Fellow; committees: Education and Labor; Homeland Security; Veterans' Affairs; elected to the 116th Congress on November 6, 2018.

Office Listings

https://underwood.house.gov https://facebook.com/repunderwood twitter: @RepUnderwood

1118 Longworth House Office Building, Washington, DC 20515 .... (202) 225–2976

Office Listings—Continued

Chief of Staff.—Andrea Harris. FAX: 225–0697
Deputy Chief of Staff.—Kirsten Hartman.
Legislative Director.—Caroline Paris-Behr.
Scheduler.—Ashley Clayton.
Press Secretary / Digital Director.—Amanda Roberts.
Legislative Correspondent.—Chloe Grainger.
Legislative Assistant.—Donald Pollard.
Fellow.—Leith Daghistani.
Staff Assistant.—Quristin Walker.
490 East Roosevelt Road, Suite 202, West Chicago, IL 60185 .... (630) 549–2190
District Director.—Michelle Thimios.
Outreach Director.—Jacqueline Muhammad.
Caseworkers: Aditya Banerji, Rebecca Hooper.
Staff Assistant.—Jake Girmscheid.

Counties: DEKALB (part), DUPAGE (part), KANE (part), KENDALL (part), LAKE (part), MCHENRY (part), AND WILL (part). CITIES AND TOWNSHIPS: Alden, Algonquin, Antioch, Aurora, Batavia, Beach Park, Big Grove, Big Rock, Blackberry, Bolingbrook, Boulder Hill, Bristol, Bull Valley, Burlington, Burton, Campton, Campton Hills, Channahon, Channel Lake, Chemung, Coral, Cortland, Crystal Lake, DeKalb, Dorr, Dunham, Elburn, Elgin, Fox, Fox Lake, Fox Lake Hills, Fremont, Geneva, Grafton, Grandwood Park, Greenwood, Gurnee, Hampshire, Hartland, Harvard, Hawthorn Woods, Hebron, Hinckley, Holiday Hills, Huntley, Island Lake, Johnsburg, Joliet, Kaneville, Kendall, Lake Barrington, Lake Catherine, Lake in the Hills, Lake Villa, Lakemoor, Lakewood, Lily Lake, Lindenhurst, Lisbon, Little Rock, Maple Park, Marengo, McCullom Lake, McHenry, Millbrook, Millington, Minooka, Montgomery, Mundelein, Na-Au-Say, Naperville, Newark, Newport, North Aurora, North Barrington, Nunda, Oakwood Hills, Old Mill Creek, Oswego, Pierce, Pingree Grove, Pistakee Highlands, Pittsfield, Plainfield, Plano, Plato, Plattville, Port Barrington, Prairie Grove, Prestbury, Richmond, Riley, Ringwood, Romeoville, Rutland, St. Charles, Sandwich, Seneca, Seward, Shorewood, Somonauk, Spring Grove, Squaw Grove, Sugar Grove, Sycamore, Troy, Union, Virgil, Volo, Wadsworth, Warren, Warrenville, Wauconda, Waukegan, West Chicago, Wheatland, Winfield, Wonder Lake, Woodstock, and Yorkville. Population (2010), 721,774.

ZIP Codes: 60001–02, 60010, 60012–14, 60020, 60030–31, 60033–34, 60042, 60046–48, 60050–51, 60060, 60071–73, 60075, 60081, 60083–84, 60087, 60097–99, 60102, 60109, 60112, 60115, 60119, 60124, 60134–36, 60140, 60142, 60144, 60147, 60151–52, 60156, 60174–75, 60178, 60180, 60183, 60185–86, 60189–90, 60404, 60410, 60431, 60447, 60450, 60490, 60502–03, 60506, 60510–12, 60520, 60536–39, 60541–45, 60548, 60552, 60554–56, 60560, 60563–65, 60585, 61012, 61038

* * *

FIFTEENTH DISTRICT

JOHN SHIMKUS, Republican, of Collinsville, IL; born in Collinsville, February 21, 1958; education: graduated from Collinsville High School; B.S., United States Military Academy, West Point, NY, 1980; teaching certificate, Christ College, Irvine, CA, 1990; M.B.A., Southern Illinois University, Edwardsville, IL, 1997; professional: U.S. Army, 1980–85; U.S. Army Reserve, 1985–2008; government and history teacher, Metro East Lutheran High School, Edwardsville; Collinsville Township trustee, 1989; Madison County Treasurer, 1990–96; married: the former Karen Muth, 1987; children: David, Daniel, and Joshua; committees: Energy and Commerce; elected to the 105th Congress; reelected to each succeeding Congress.

Office Listings

https://shimkus.house.gov https://facebook.com/repshimkus

2217 Rayburn House Office Building, Washington, DC 20515 .... (202) 225–5271
Chief of Staff.—Craig Roberts. FAX: 225–5880
15 Professional Park Drive, Maryville, IL 62062 .... (618) 288–7190
District Director.—Debra Fansler.
201 North Vermillion Street, Suite 325, Danville, IL 61832 .... (217) 446–0664
101 North 4th Street, Suite 303, Effingham, IL 62401 .... (217) 347–7947
110 East Locust Street, Room 12, Harrisburg, IL 62946 .... (618) 252–8271

Counties: BOND, CHAMPAIGN, CLARK, CLAY, COLES, CRAWFORD, CUMBERLAND, DOUGLAS (part), EDGAR, EDWARDS, EFFINGHAM, FAYETTE, FORD, GALLATIN, HAMILTON, HARDIN, JASPER, JOHNSON, LAWRENCE, MADISON (part), MARION, MASSAC, MOULTRIE, POPE, RICHLAND, SALINE (part), SHELBY, VERMILLION, WABASH, WASHINGTON, WAYNE, AND WHITE. Population (2011), 715,066.

ZIP Codes: 60932–33, 60936 (part), 60942 (part), 60949, 60957, 60960, 60963, 61802 (part), 61810–11, 61814, 61816–17, 61822 (part), 61832–34, 61840–41, 61843–44, 61845 (part), 61846–50, 61852, 61853 (part), 61857–59, 61863 (part), 61864 (part), 61865–66, 61870–73, 61875 (part), 61876–78, 61880 (part), 61883, 61910–12, 61913 (part), 61914 (part), 61917, 61919–20, 61924, 61925 (part), 61928, 61929 (part), 61930–33, 61937 (part), 61938, 61940–44, 61949, 61951, 61953, 61955–57, 62001 (part), 62002, 62011–12, 62025 (part), 62032 (part), 62034 (part), 62035, 62040, 62046, 62061–62, 62074 (part), 62075 (part), 62080 (part), 62086 (part), 62097 (part), 62214, 62231–32, 62234 (part), 62237 (part), 62246 (part), 62249, 62253, 62255 (part), 62257 (part), 62262 (part), 62263, 62265 (part), 62266, 62268 (part), 62271, 62273, 62275, 62281 (part), 62284 (part), 62292, 62293 (part), 62294 (part), 62401, 62410–11, 62414,

62417–22, 62424, 62426–28, 62431–33, 62435–36, 62439–43, 62445–52, 62454, 62458–68, 62471, 62473–76, 62479–81, 62510 (part), 62534, 62544 (part), 62550 (part), 62553 (part), 62557 (part), 62565, 62571, 62801 (part), 62803, 62806–07, 62808 (part), 62809, 62810 (part), 62811, 62814 (part), 62815, 62817–18, 62820–21, 62823–24, 62827–28, 62830 (part), 62831 (part), 62835, 62836 (part), 62837–39, 62842–44, 62848–50, 62851 (part), 62852–54, 62858–59, 62860 (part), 62861–63, 62867–71, 62875–76, 62877 (part), 62879–82, 62886–87, 62889 (part), 62890 (part), 62892, 62893 (part), 62895, 62899 (part), 62908, 62910 (part), 62912 (part), 62917 (part), 62919, 62922 (part), 62923 (part), 62928, 62930–31, 62934–35, 62938, 62939 (part), 62941 (part), 62946, 62953–54, 62956 (part), 62960, 62965, 62967, 62977, 62979, 62982, 62984–85, 62987 (part), 62995, 62215, 62216, 62218, 62219, 62230, 62231, 62245, 62250, 62253, 62265 (part), 62266, 62293 (part)

* * *

SIXTEENTH DISTRICT

ADAM KINZINGER, Republican, of Channahon, IL; born in Kankakee, IL, February 27, 1978; education: graduated, Normal Community West High School, 1996; B.S., Illinois State University, 2000; professional: McLean County Board, 1998–2003; sales representative, STL Technologies, 2000–03; U.S. Air National Guard, 2003–present, current rank: Major; religion: Protestant; single; Deputy Republican Whip; committees: Energy and Commerce; Foreign Affairs; elected to the 112th Congress on November 2, 2010; reelected to each succeeding Congress.

Office Listings

https://kinzinger.house.gov https://facebook.com/RepKinzinger https://twitter.com/RepKinzinger

2245 Rayburn House Office Building, Washington, DC 20515 .... (202) 225–3635
Chief of Staff.—Austin Weatherford.
628 Columbus Street, Suite 507, Ottawa, IL 61350 .... (815) 431–9271
District Director.—Bonnie Walsh.
Deputy District Director.—Patrick Doggett.
Legislative Director.—Michael Mansour.
Communications Director.—Maura Gillespie.

Counties: BOONE, BUREAU, DEKALB (part), FORD (part), GRUNDY, IROQUOIS, LASALLE, LEE, LIVINGSTON, OGLE, PUTNAM, STARK (part), WILL (part), AND WINNEBAGO (part). Population (2010), 712,813.

ZIP Codes: 60033, 60111, 60113, 60115, 60129, 60135, 60140, 60145–46, 60150, 60152, 60178, 60407–08, 60410, 60416, 60420–21, 60424, 60437, 60442, 60444, 60447, 60450, 60460, 60470, 60474, 60479, 60481, 60518, 60520, 60530–31, 60537, 60541, 60548–53, 60556–57, 60911–12, 60917–22, 60924, 60926–31, 60934, 60936, 60938, 60941–42, 60945–46, 60948, 60950–53, 60955–56, 60959–62, 60964, 60966, 60968, 60970, 60973–74, 61006–08, 61010–12, 61015–16, 61019–21, 61024, 61030–31, 61038–39, 61042–43, 61047, 61049, 61051–52, 61054, 61057, 61061, 61063–65, 61068, 61071–73, 61078–81, 61084, 61088, 61091, 61101–04, 61107–09, 61111–12, 61114–15, 61283, 61301, 61310–38, 61340–42, 61344–46, 61348–50, 61353–54, 61356, 61358–64, 61367–68, 61370–74, 61376–79, 61421, 61443, 61483, 61491, 61537, 61560, 61726, 61731, 61739–41, 61743–44, 61764, 61769, 61773, 61775, 61845

* * *

SEVENTEENTH DISTRICT

CHERI BUSTOS, Democrat, of Moline, IL; born in Springfield, IL, October 17, 1961; education: graduated B.A., University of Maryland, College Park, MD, 1983; M.A., University of Illinois at Springfield, 1985; religion: Roman Catholic; married: Gerry; children: Tony, Nick, and Joseph; committees: Agriculture; Appropriations; elected to the 113th Congress on November 6, 2012; reelected to each succeeding Congress.

Office Listings

https://bustos.house.gov https://facebook.com/RepCheri twitter: @RepCheri

1233 Longworth House Office Building, Washington, DC 20515 .... (202) 225–5905
Chief of Staff.—Jon Pyatt.
Deputy Chief of Staff.—Trevor Reuschel.
Communications Director.—Vacant.
Scheduler.—Ashley Williams.
Legislative Assistants: Leighton Huch, Liam Steadman.
Legislative Correspondent.—Yusuf Nekzad.
Director of Member Services.—Gabby Miller.
Press Secretary.—Sean Sibley.
Staff Assistant.—Tammy Zapata.
2401 4th Avenue, Rock Island, IL 61201 .... (309) 786–3406
District Director.—Kate Jennings.
Deputy District Director.—Lucie VanHecke.
Director of Constituent Services and Casework.—Miranda French.
Constituent Advocate.—Ellie LaBotte.
820 Southwest Adams Street, Peoria, IL 61602 .... (309) 966–1813

Office Listings—Continued

Field Representative.—Luke Headley.
Constituent Advocate.—Laura Rude.
119 North Church Street, Suite 101, Rockford, IL 61101 .... (815) 968–8011
Field Representative.—Ricardo Montoya-Picazo.
Constituent Advocate.—Gabrielle Torina.

Counties: CARROLL, FULTON, HENDERSON, HENRY, JO DAVIESS, KNOX, MERCER, PEORIA (part), ROCK ISLAND, STEPHENSON, TAZEWELL (part), WARREN, WHITESIDE, AND WINNEBAGO (part). Population (2010), 712,813.

ZIP Codes: 61001, 61007, 61013–14, 61018–20, 61025, 61027–28, 61032, 61036–37, 61039, 61041, 61044, 61046–48, 61050–51, 61053, 61059–60, 61062–64, 61067, 61070–71, 61074–75, 61077–78, 61081, 61084–85, 61087–89, 61101–10, 61125, 61201, 61204, 61230–44, 61250–52, 61254, 61256–66, 61270, 61272–79, 61281–85, 61299, 61344, 61361, 61401–02, 61410, 61412–15, 61417–19, 61422–23, 61425, 61427–28, 61430–37, 61439, 61441–43, 61447–50, 61453–54, 61458–60, 61462, 61465–78, 61480, 61482, 61484–86, 61488–90, 61501, 61519–20, 61524, 61529, 61531, 61533–34, 61536, 61539, 61542–47, 61553–55, 61558, 61563–64, 61569, 61572, 61601–07, 61610–11, 61613–16, 61625, 61629–30, 61633–34, 61636–37, 61641, 61650–56, 62330, 62644

* * *

EIGHTEENTH DISTRICT

DARIN LAHOOD, Republican, of Peoria, IL; born in Peoria, July 5, 1968; education: B.A., Loras College, Dubuque, IA, 1990; juris doctorate, John Marshall Law School, 1997; professional: Illinois State Senate, 2011–15; Miller, Hall, & Triggs, 2006–15; Assistant U.S. Attorney, 2001–06; religion: Roman Catholic; married: Kristen; children: McKay, Lucas, and Teddy; committees: Ways and Means; Joint Economic Committee; elected, by special election, to the 114th Congress on September 10, 2015, to fill the vacancy caused by the resignation of U.S. Representative Aaron Schock; reelected to each succeeding Congress.

Office Listings

https://lahood.house.gov https://facebook.com/replahood https://twitter.com/RepLaHood

1424 Longworth House Office Building, Washington, DC 20515 .... (202) 225–6201
Chief of Staff.—Steven Pfrang. FAX: 225–9249
Legislative Director.—Ashley Antoskiewicz.
Communications Director.—John Rauber.
Scheduler.—Alexis "Alex" Alavi.
Legislative Assistants: Samantha Dybas, Mary Ellen Richardson.
Legislative Correspondent.—Eric Anderson.
100 Northeast Monroe Street, Room 100, Peoria, IL 61602 .... (309) 671–7027
District Director.—Brad Stotler.
Office Manager.—Lester Davis.
Military Affairs Advisor.—Michael Gilmore.
Constituent Services Representatives: Lester Davis, Autum Greeson.
201 West Morgan Street, Jacksonville, IL 62650 .... (217) 245–1431
Constituent Services Representative.—Barb Baker.
235 South 6th Street, Springfield, IL 62701 .... (217) 670–1653
Field Representative.—Jay Bergles.
3004 G.E. Road, Suite 1B, Bloomington, IL 61704 .... (309) 205–9556

Counties: ADAMS, BROWN, CASS, HANCOCK, LOGAN, MARSHALL, MASON, MCDONOUGH, MCLEAN (part), MENARD, MORGAN, PEORIA (part), PIKE, SANGAMON (part), SCHUYLER, SCOTT, STARK (part), TAZEWELL (part), AND WOODFORD. Population (2010), 712,813.

ZIP Codes: 61321, 61358, 61369, 61375, 61377, 61411, 61415–16, 61420–22, 61424, 61426, 61434, 61438, 61440, 61449–52, 61455, 61459, 61470, 61473, 61475, 61479, 61482–84, 61489, 61491, 61516–17, 61523, 61525–26, 61528–37, 61540–41, 61545–48, 61550, 61552, 61554, 61559, 61561–62, 61565, 61567–71, 61603–04, 61607, 61610–12, 61614–16, 61635, 61638, 61643, 61701–02, 61704–05, 61709–10, 61720–26, 61728–34, 61736–38, 61742, 61744–45, 61747–49, 61751–55, 61758–61, 61770–71, 61774, 61776, 61791, 61799, 61842–43, 62082, 62301, 62305–06, 62311–14, 62316, 62319–21, 62323–26, 62329–30, 62334, 62336, 62338–41, 62343–49, 62351–63, 62365–67, 62370, 62373–76, 62378–80, 62512, 62515, 62518–20, 62530, 62536, 62539, 62541, 62543, 62545, 62548, 62558, 62561, 62563, 62601, 62610–13, 62615, 62617–18, 62621–22, 62624–25, 62627–29, 62631, 62633–35, 62638–39, 62642–44, 62650–51, 62655–56, 62659–68, 62670–71, 62673, 62675, 62677, 62681–82, 62684, 62688–95, 62702–04, 62707, 62711–12

INDIANA

(Population 2010, 6,483,802)

SENATORS

TODD C. YOUNG, Republican, of Bloomington, IN; born in Indianapolis, IN, August 24, 1972; education: B.S., political science, United States Naval Academy, Annapolis, MD, 1995; M.B.A., University of Chicago, Chicago, IL, 2000; M.A., American history, School of Advanced Study, University of London, UK, 2001; J.D., Indiana University, Bloomington, 2005; professional: legislative assistant, U.S. Senate, 2002–03; management consultant, Crowe Chizek, 2003–05; attorney, Tucker and Tucker, PC, in Paoli, IN, 2005–09; military: U.S. Navy, 1990–95; U.S. Marine Corps, 1995–2000; member: Sherwood Oaks Christian Church, Bloomington, IN; married: Jennifer Tucker Hill; children: Tucker, Annalise, Abigail, and Ava; committees: Commerce, Science, and Transportation; Finance; Foreign Relations; Small Business and Entrepreneurship; elected to the 112th Congress on November 2, 2010; reelected to each succeeding Congress; elected to the U.S. Senate on November 8, 2016.

Office Listings

https://toddyoung.senate.gov twitter: @SenToddYoung

185 Dirksen Senate Office Building, Washington, DC 20510 .... (202) 224–5623
Chief of Staff.—John Connell.
Deputy Chief of Staff.—Jim Durrett.
Legislative Director.—Adam Hechavarria.
Communications Director.—Amy Graham.
Scheduler.—Lindsay McDonough.
101 Martin Luther King Jr. Boulevard, Suite 110, Evansville, IN 47708 .... (812) 465–6500
1300 South Harrison Street, Suite 3161, Fort Wayne, IN 46802 .... (260) 426–3151
251 North Illinois Street, Suite 120, Indianapolis, IN 46204 .... (317) 226–6700
3602 Northgate Court, New Albany, IN 47150 .... (812) 542–4820

* * *

MIKE BRAUN, Republican, of Jasper, IN; born in Jasper, March 24, 1954; education: B.A., economics, Wabash College, Crawfordsville, IN; M.B.A., Harvard University Business School, Boston, MA, 1978; professional: co-founder, Crystal Farms, Inc., Jasper, IN; founder, president and CEO of Meyer Distributing, Jasper, IN; public service: Jasper, IN, School Board, 2004–14; Representative, District 63, Indiana State House of Representatives, 2014–17; religion: Roman Catholic; married: Maureen, 1979; four children: Jason, Jeff, Ashley, Kristen; committees: Agriculture, Nutrition and Forestry; Budget; Environment and Public Works; Health, Education, Labor, and Pensions; Special Committee on Aging; elected to the U.S. Senate on November 6, 2018.

Office Listings

https://braun.senate.gov https://facebook.com/SenatorBraun https://twitter.com/SenatorBraun

374 Russell Senate Office Building, Washington, DC 20510 .... (202) 224–4814
Chief of Staff.—Joshua Kelley.
Scheduler.—Jessica Wedgewood.
Legislative Director.—Katie Bailey.
Communications Director.—Jahan Wilcox.
115 North Pennsylvania Street, Suite 100, Indianapolis, IN 46204 .... (317) 822–8240
205 West Colfax Avenue, South Bend, IN 46601 .... (574) 288–6302
5400 Federal Plaza, Suite 3200, Hammond, IN 46320 .... (219) 937–9650
203 East Berry Street, Suite 702B, Fort Wayne, IN 46802 .... (260) 427–2167

REPRESENTATIVES

FIRST DISTRICT

PETER J. VISCLOSKY, Democrat, of Gary, IN; born in Gary, IN, August 13, 1949; education: graduated, Andrean High School, Merrillville, IN, 1967; B.S., accounting, Indiana University Northwest, Gary, 1970; J.D., University of Notre Dame Law School, Notre Dame, IN, 1973; LL.M., international and comparative law, Georgetown University Law Center, Washington, DC, 1982; professional: attorney; admitted to the Indiana State Bar, 1974, the District of Columbia Bar, 1978, and the U.S. Supreme Court Bar, 1980; associate staff, U.S. House of Representatives, Committee on Appropriations, 1977–80; Committee on the Budget, 1980–82; practicing attorney, Merrillville law firm, 1983–84; wife: Joanne Royce; children: John Daniel and Timothy Patrick; committees: Appropriations; elected to the 99th Congress on November 6, 1984; reelected to each succeeding Congress.

Office Listings

https://visclosky.house.gov https://facebook.com/repvisclosky twitter: @RepVisclosky

2328 Rayburn House Office Building, Washington, DC 20515 .... (202) 225–2461
Chief of Staff.—Mark Lopez. FAX: 225–2493
Deputy Chief of Staff / Communications Director.—Kevin Spicer.
Executive Assistant.—Korry Baack.
7895 Broadway, Suite A, Merrillville, IN 46410 .... (219) 795–1844
District Directors: Gregory Gulvas, Elizabeth Johnson. FAX: 795–1850
(888) 423–7383

Counties: LAKE, LAPORTE (part), AND PORTER. Population (2010), 720,422.

ZIP Codes: 46301–04, 46307–08, 46310–12, 46319–25, 46327, 46341–42, 46345, 46347–49, 46350, 46355–56, 46360, 46368, 46373, 46375–77, 46379–85, 46390, 46392–94, 46401–11

* * *

SECOND DISTRICT

JACKIE WALORSKI, Republican, of Elkhart, IN; born in South Bend, IN, August 17, 1963; education: B.A., communications, Taylor University, Upland, IN, 1985; professional: served in the Indiana General Assembly from 2005–10; religion: Christian; married: Dean; committees: Ethics; Ways and Means; elected to the 113th Congress on November 6, 2012; reelected to each succeeding Congress.

Office Listings

https://walorksi.house.gov https://facebook.com/RepJackieWalorski https://twitter.com/RepWalorski

419 Cannon House Office Building, Washington, DC 20515 .... (202) 225–3915
Chief of Staff.—Mike Dankler. FAX: 225–6798
Legislative Director.—Martin Schultz.
Scheduler.—Faith Ammen.
Communications Director.—Jack Morrissey.
202 Lincolnway East, Suite 101, Mishawaka, IN 46544 .... (574) 204–2645
709 Main Street, Rochester, IN 46975 .... (574) 223–4373

Counties: ELKHART, FULTON, KOSCIUSKO (part), LAPORTE (part), MARSHALL, MIAMI, PULASKI, ST. JOSEPH, STARKE, AND WABASH. CITIES: Elkhart, Goshen, Knox, La Porte, Mishawaka, Peru, Plymouth, Rochester, South Bend, Syracuse, Wabash, and Winamac. Population (2010), 718,237.

ZIP Codes: 46340, 46345–46, 46348, 46350, 46352, 46365–66, 46374, 46382, 46501–02, 46504, 46506–08, 46510–11, 46513–17, 46524, 46526–28, 46530–32, 46534, 46536–39, 46540, 46542–46, 46550, 46552–56, 46561, 46563, 46565, 46567, 46570, 46572–74, 46580, 46582, 46595, 46601, 46613–17, 46619, 46624, 46626, 46628, 46634–35, 46637, 46660, 46680, 46702, 46732, 46750, 46767, 46787, 46901, 46910–12, 46914, 46919, 46921–22, 46926, 46931–32, 46939, 46940–41, 46943, 46945–46, 46950–51, 46958–59, 46960, 46962, 46968, 46970–71, 46974–75, 46978, 46980, 46982, 46984–85, 46988, 46990, 46992, 46996, 47946, 47957, 47959, 47960

* * *

THIRD DISTRICT

JIM BANKS, Republican, of Columbia City, IN; born in Columbia City, July 16, 1979; education: B.A., Indiana University, Bloomington, IN, 2004; M.B.A, Grace College, Winona Lake, IN, 2013; professional: commercial construction and real estate industry, 2008–10; member of the Whitley County Council, 2008–10; Indiana State Senate, 2010–16; military: U.S. Navy Reserve, Supply Corps Officer, 2012–15; deployed to Afghanistan, 2014–15; awards: Defense Meritorious Service Medal; Afghanistan Campaign Medal; ISAF NATO Medal; American Legion's Distinguished Public Service Award, 2013, 2014, and 2016; religion: Evangelical; family: wife, Amanda; daughters: Lillian, Elizabeth, and Joann; caucuses: 115th Class Caucus; Air Force Caucus; Army Caucus; Automotive Caucus; Caucus on Macedonia and Macedonian-Americans; Congressional Sportsmen's Caucus; Israel Caucus; Long Range Strike Caucus; Medical Technology Caucus; National Guard and Reserve Components Caucus; Navy–USMC Caucus; Pro-Life Caucus; Republican Study Committee; School Choice Caucus; Shipbuilding Caucus; Steel Caucus; Submarine Caucus; Taiwan Caucus; Warrior Caucus; committees: Armed Services; Education and Labor; Veterans' Affairs; elected to the 115th Congress on November 8, 2016; reelected to the 116th Congress on November 6, 2018.

Office Listings

https://banks.house.gov https://facebook.com/RepJimBanks
twitter: @RepJimBanks https://instagram.com/RepJimBanks

1713 Longworth House Office Building, Washington, DC 20515 .... (202) 225–4436
Chief of Staff.—David Keller.
Deputy Chief of Staff / Legislative Director.—Amy Surber.
Scheduler.—Garrett Serstad.
Communications Director.—Mitchell Hailstone.
1300 South Harrison Street, Fort Wayne, IN 46802 .... (260) 702–4750
District Director.—Tinisha Weigelt.

Counties: ADAMS, ALLEN, BLACKFORD (part), DEKALB, HUNTINGTON, JAY, KOSCIUSKO (part), LAGRANGE, NOBLE, STEUBEN, WELLS, AND WHITLEY. Population (2010), 723,633.

ZIP Codes: 46538, 46555, 46562, 46565, 46571, 46580, 46582, 46590, 46701–03, 46705–06, 46710–11, 46714, 46721, 46723, 46725, 46730–33, 46737–38, 46740–43, 46745–48, 46750, 46755, 46759–60, 46762–67, 46770, 46772–74, 46776–77, 46779, 46781, 46783–85, 46787–88, 46791–95, 46797–98, 46802–09, 46814–16, 46818–19, 46825, 46835, 46845, 47326, 47359, 47369, 47371, 47373, 47381

* * *

FOURTH DISTRICT

JIM BAIRD, Republican, of Greencastle, IN; born in Fountain County, IN, June 4, 1945; education: B.S., 1967, and M.S., animal sciences, 1969, Purdue University, West Lafayette, IN; Ph.D., monogastric nutrition, University of Kentucky, Lexington, KY, 1975; military: First Lieutenant, U.S. Army, 1969–72; awards: Bronze Star with V(valor) Device; two Purple Hearts; Army Commendation Medal with V Device (Oak Leaf Cluster); National Defense Service Medal; Meritorious Unit Citation; Vietnam Service Medal; Vietnam Campaign Medal with 60 device; Vietnam Cross of Gallantry with Palm; Republic of Vietnam Civil Actions Award and U.S. Army Transportation Unit Hall of Fame; professional: farmer, Baird Family Farms; small business owner, Indiana Home Care Plus; member, Putnam County Commission, Greencastle, IN, 2006–10; member, Indiana House of Representatives, Indianapolis, IN, 2010–18; religion: United Methodist; family: wife, Danise; three children; committees: Agriculture; Science, Space and Technology; elected to the 116th Congress on November 6, 2018.

Office Listings

https://baird.house.gov https://facebook.com/RepJimBaird twitter: @RepJimBaird

532 Cannon House Office Building, Washington, DC 20515 .... (202) 225–5037
Chief of Staff.—Ashlee Vinyard. FAX: 226–0544
Legislative Director.—Sarah Czufin.
Communications Director.—Heather Douglass.
Scheduler.—Alyssa Jennings.
355 South Washington Street, Suite 210, Danville, IN 46122 .... (317) 563–5567
Indiana Chief of Staff.—Quincy Cunningham.

Counties: BENTON, BOONE (part), CARROLL, CASS, CLINTON, FOUNTAIN, HENDRICKS, HOWARD (part), JASPER, MONTGOMERY, MORGAN (part), NEWTON, PUTNAM, TIPPECANOE, WARREN, AND WHITE. Population (2010), 774,798.

ZIP Codes: 46035, 46039, 46041, 46049–50, 46052, 46057–58, 46065, 46069, 46071, 46075, 46077, 46103, 46105, 46112–13, 46118, 46120–23, 46125, 46128, 46135, 46147, 46149, 46151, 46157–58, 46165–68, 46171–72, 46175, 46180, 46231, 46234, 46278, 46310, 46349, 46374, 46379, 46381, 46392, 46901–02, 46913, 46915, 46917, 46920, 46923, 46926, 46929, 46932, 46947, 46950, 46961, 46967, 46970, 46978–79, 46985, 46988, 46994, 46996, 46998, 47456, 47840, 47868, 47872, 47901, 47904–07, 47909, 47916–18, 47920–26, 47929–30, 47932–33, 47940–44, 47946, 47948–52, 47954–55, 47957–60, 47963–65, 47967–71, 47975, 47977–78, 47980–83, 47987, 47989–95, 47997

* * *

FIFTH DISTRICT

SUSAN W. BROOKS, Republican, of Carmel, IN; born in Fort Wayne, IN, August 25, 1960; education: graduated, Homestead High School, 1978; Miami University, Oxford, OH, 1982; J.D.

from the Indiana University Robert H. McKinney School of Law, 1985; professional: criminal defense attorney, 1985–97; Deputy Mayor of Indianapolis, 1998–99; Ice Miller Government Affairs, 1999–2001; U.S. Attorney for the Southern District of Indiana, 2001–07; Ivy Tech Community College Senior Vice President and General Counsel, 2007–11; married: David; children: Jessica and Conner; committees: Energy and Commerce; Select Committee on the Modernization of Congress; elected to the 113th Congress on November 6, 2012; reelected to each succeeding Congress.

Office Listings

https://susanwbrooks.house.gov https://facebook.com/CongresswomanSusanWBrooks
https://twitter.com/SusanWBrooks

2211 Rayburn House Office Building, Washington, DC 20515 .... (202) 225–2276
Chief of Staff.—Megan Savage. FAX: 225–0016
Legislative Director.—Rob Hicks.
Communications Director.—Becky Card.
Scheduler / Executive Assistant.—Natalie Goodwin.
District Director.—Karen Glaser.
11611 North Meridian Street, Suite 415, Carmel, IN 46032 .... (317) 848–0201
120 East 8th Street, Suite 101, Anderson, IN 46016 .... (765) 640–5115

Counties: BLACKFORD, BOONE, GRANT, HAMILTON, HOWARD, MADISON, MARION, AND TIPTON. Population (2010), 720,423.

ZIP Codes: 4 6001, 46011–13, 46016–17, 46030–34, 46036–38, 46040, 46044–45, 46047–52, 46055–56, 46060, 46062–64, 46068–70, 46072, 46074–77, 46112, 46205, 46208, 46216, 46220, 46226, 46228, 46234–36, 46240, 46250, 46254, 46256, 46260, 46268, 46278, 46280, 46290–02, 46919, 46928, 46930, 46933, 46936, 46938, 46940, 46952–53, 46957, 46986–87, 46989, 46991, 47336, 47348, 47356

* * *

SIXTH DISTRICT

GREG PENCE, Republican, of Columbus, IN; born in Columbus, November 13, 1956; education: B.A., theology and philosophy, 1979, M.B.A., 1985, Loyola University of Chicago; military: U.S. Marine Corps, 1979–83; professional: president, Kiel Brothers Oil Company, 1998–2004; owner/operator, antique malls; committees: Foreign Affairs; Transportation and Infrastructure; elected to the 116th Congress on November 6, 2018.

Office Listings

https://pence.house.gov https://facebook.com/RepGregPence
twitter: @repgregpence https://youtube.com/channel/UCL2cxXwzTek7uXLOdwbJ3Ag

222 Cannon House Office Building, Washington, DC 20515 .... (202) 225–3021
Chief of Staff.—Kyle Robertson. FAX: 225–3382
Legislative Director.—Hillary Lassiter.
Communications Director.—Milly Lothian.
Scheduler/Office Manager.—Alana McRaney.
555 1st Street, Suite B, Columbus, IN 47201 .... (812) 799–5230
Deputy Chief of Staff for Indiana.—Ryan Jarmula.
Deputy District Director.—Liz Dessauer.
2810 West Ethel Avenue, Suite 9, Muncie, IN 47304 .... (765) 702–2434
50 North 5th Street, 2nd Floor, Richmond, IN 47374 .... (765) 660–1083
18 East Main Street, Suite 210, Greenfield, IN 46140 .... (812) 799–5233

Counties: BARTHOLOMEW, DEARBORN, DECATUR, DELAWARE, FAYETTE, FRANKLIN, HANCOCK, HENRY, JEFFERSON, JENNINGS, OHIO, RANDOLPH, RIPLEY, RUSH, SCOTT (part), SHELBY, SWITZERLAND, UNION, AND WAYNE. Population (2018), 719,771.

ZIP Codes: 45003, 45030, 45053, 45056, 45347, 45390, 46001, 46012, 46017, 46040, 46055–56, 46064, 46070, 46104, 46110, 46115, 46117, 46124, 46126–27, 46130–31, 46133, 46140, 46144, 46146, 46148, 46150, 46154–56, 46161–63, 46173, 46176, 46182, 46186, 46229, 46235–36, 46239, 46259, 46725, 46989, 46994, 47001, 47003, 47006, 47010–12, 47016–18, 47020, 47022–25, 47030–32, 47034–38, 47040–43, 47060, 47102, 47138, 47141, 47147, 47170, 47177, 47201–03, 47223–27, 47229–32, 47234, 47236, 47240, 47243–47, 47250, 47261, 47263, 47265, 47270, 47272–74, 47280, 47282–83, 47302–05, 47307–08, 47320, 47322, 47324–25, 47327, 47330–31, 47334–42, 47344–46, 47351–58, 47360–62, 47366–68, 47370, 47373–75, 47380, 47382–88, 47390, 47392–94, 47396, 47448, 47546

* * *

SEVENTH DISTRICT

ANDRÉ CARSON, Democrat, of Indianapolis, IN; born in Indianapolis, October 16, 1974; education: graduated, Arsenal Technical High School, Indianapolis, IN; B.A. in criminal justice management, Concordia University Wisconsin, Mequon, WI; M.B.A., Indiana Wesleyan University, Marion, IN; professional: investigative officer for the Indiana State Excise Police, 1997–2006; Indiana Department of Homeland Security's Intelligence Fusion Center, 2006; City County Councilor, Marion County, 2007; religion: Muslim; children: Salimah; Senior Whip; caucuses: first vice chair, Congressional Black Caucus; New Democrat Coalition; Progressive Caucus; committees: Transportation and Infrastructure; Permanent Select Committee on Intelligence; elected to the 110th Congress on March 11, 2008, by special election, to fill the vacancy caused by the death of U.S. Representative Julia Carson; reelected to each succeeding Congress.

Office Listings

https://carson.house.gov https://facebook.com/CongressmanAndreCarson
https://twitter.com/repandrecarson

2135 Rayburn House Office Building, Washington, DC 20515 .... (202) 225–4011
Chief of Staff.—Kim Rudolph. FAX: 225–5633
Legislative Director.—Nathan Bennett.
Legislative Assistants: Andrea Martin, Zachary Wilkinson.
Communications Director.—Copeland Tucker.
Scheduler.—Holly Woytcke.
300 East Fall Creek Parkway North Drive, Suite 300, Indianapolis, IN 46205 .... (317) 283–6516
District Director.—Megan Sims. FAX: 283–6567
Staff Assistant / Legislative Correspondent.—Hadeel Said.

Counties: MARION. City of Indianapolis, township of Center, parts of the townships of Decatur, Lawrence, Perry, Pike, Warren, Washington, and Wayne, included are the cities of Beech Grove and Lawrence. Population (2010), 676,351.

ZIP Codes: 46107, 46160, 46201–09, 46211, 46214, 46216–22, 46224–31, 46234–35, 46237, 46239–42, 46244, 46247, 46249, 46251, 46253–55, 46260, 46266, 46268, 46274–75, 46277–78, 46282–83, 46285, 46291, 46295–96, 46298

* * *

EIGHTH DISTRICT

LARRY BUCSHON, Republican, of Evansville, IN; born in Kincaid, IL, May 31, 1962; education: graduated from South Fork High School, Kincaid, IL, 1980; B.S., with a concentration in chemistry, University of Illinois, Urbana-Champaign, IL, 1984; M.D., University of Illinois, Chicago, 1988; professional: residency, Medical College of Wisconsin in Milwaukee, 1988–95; cardiothoracic surgeon, 1995–2010; commissioned lieutenant, U.S. Navy Reserve, 1989; promoted, lieutenant commander, 1994; honorable discharge, 1998; married: Kathryn; children: Luke, Alec, Blair, and Zoe; committees: Energy and Commerce; elected to the 112th Congress on November 2, 2010; reelected to each succeeding Congress.

Office Listings

https://bucshon.house.gov twitter: @RepLarryBucshon

2313 Rayburn House Office Building, Washington, DC 20515 .... (202) 225–4636
Chief of Staff.—Kyle Jackson. FAX: 225–3284
Deputy Chief of Staff / Legislative Director.—Sarah Killeen.
Communications Director.—Andrew Hansen.
Scheduler.—Jessica Graff.
420 Main Street, Suite 1402, Evansville, IN 47708 .... (812) 465–6484
District Director.—Carol Jones.
901 Wabash Avenue, Suite 140, Terre Haute, IN 47807 .... (812) 232–0523

Counties: CLAY, CRAWFORD (part), DAVIESS, DUBOIS, GIBSON, GREENE, KNOX, MARTIN, OWEN, PARKE, PERRY, PIKE, POSEY, SPENCER, SULLIVAN, VANDERBURGH, VERMILLION, VIGO, AND WARRICK. Population (2010), 694,398.

ZIP Codes: 46105, 46120–21, 46128, 46135, 46165–66, 46170–72, 46175, 47403–04, 47424, 47427, 47429, 47431–33, 47438–39, 47441, 47443, 47445–46, 47449, 47453, 47455–57, 47459–60, 47462, 47465, 47469–71, 47501, 47512, 47516, 47519, 47522–24, 47527–29, 47535, 47537, 47541–42, 47553, 47557–58, 47561–62, 47564, 47567–68, 47573, 47578, 47581, 47584–85, 47590–91, 47596–98, 47601, 47610–14, 47616, 47618–20, 47629–31, 47633, 47637–40, 47647–49, 47654, 47660, 47665–66, 47670, 47683, 47701–06, 47708, 47710–16, 47719–22, 47724–25, 47727–28, 47730–37, 47739–41, 47744, 47747, 47750, 47801–05, 47807–09, 47811–12, 47830–34, 47836–38, 47840–42, 47845–66, 47868–72, 47874–76, 47878–82, 47884–85, 47917–18, 47921, 47928, 47932, 47952, 47966, 47969–70, 47974–75, 47982, 47987, 47989, 47991–93

* * *

NINTH DISTRICT

TREY HOLLINGSWORTH, Republican, of Jeffersonville, IN; born in Clinton, TN, September 12, 1983; education: business degree, Wharton School, University of Pennsylvania, Philadelphia, PA, 2004; master's degree, Georgetown University, Washington, DC, 2014; wife: Kelly; committees: Financial Services; elected to 115th Congress on November 8, 2016; re-elected to the 116th Congress on November 6, 2018.

Office Listings

https://hollingsworth.house.gov

1641 Longworth House Office Building, Washington, DC 20515 .... (202) 225–5315
Washington, DC, Chief of Staff.—Rebecca Shaw. FAX: 226–6866
Communications Director.—Katie Webster.
Legislative Director.—Connor Lentz.
Scheduler.—Marie Policastro.
321 Quartermaster Court, Jeffersonville, IN 47130 .... (812) 288–3999
Indiana Chief of Staff.—Rachel Jacobs.
100 East Jefferson Street, Franklin, IN 46131 .... (317) 851–8710

Counties: BROWN, CLARK, CRAWFORD (part), FLOYD, HARRISON, JACKSON, JOHNSON, LAWRENCE, MONROE, MORGAN (part), ORANGE, SCOTT (part), AND WASHINGTON. Population (2010), 726,570.

ZIP Codes: 46106, 46110–11, 46113, 46124, 46131, 46140, 46142–43, 46151, 46158, 46160, 46162, 46164, 46166, 46181, 46184, 46229, 46259, 47019, 47021, 47033, 47039, 47102, 47104, 47106–08, 47110–12, 47114–20, 47122–26, 47129–38, 47140–47, 47150–51, 47160–67, 47170, 47172, 47175, 47177, 47190, 47199, 47201, 47220, 47228–29, 47235, 47249, 47260, 47264, 47274, 47281, 47401–08, 47420–21, 47426, 47429, 47432–37, 47446, 47448, 47451–52, 47454, 47458, 47460, 47462–64, 47467–70

IOWA

(Population 2010, 3,046,355)

SENATORS

CHUCK GRASSLEY, Republican, of New Hartford, IA; born in New Hartford, September 17, 1933; education: graduated, New Hartford Community High School, 1951; B.A., University of Northern Iowa, 1955; M.A., University of Northern Iowa, 1956; doctoral studies, University of Iowa, 1957–58; professional: farmer; member: Iowa State Legislature, 1959–74; Farm Bureau; Butler County and State of Iowa Historical Societies; Masons; Baptist Church; and International Association of Machinists, 1962–71; International Narcotics Control Caucus; married: the former Barbara Ann Speicher, 1954; children: Lee, Wendy, Robin, Michele, and Jay; committees: chair, Finance; chair, Joint Committee on Taxation; Agriculture, Nutrition, and Forestry; Budget; Judiciary; elected to the 94th Congress, November 5, 1974; reelected to the 95th and 96th Congresses; elected to the U.S. Senate, November 4, 1980; reelected to each succeeding Senate term.

Office Listings

https://grassley.senate.gov https://facebook.com/grassley
https://twitter.com/chuckgrassley https://instagram.com/senatorchuckgrassley

135 Hart Senate Office Building, Washington, DC 20510 .... (202) 224–3744
Chief of Staff.—Aaron Cummings. FAX: 224–6020
Legislative Director.—James Rice.
721 Federal Building, 210 Walnut Street, Des Moines, IA 50309 .... (515) 288–1145
State Administrator.—Carol Olson.
111 7th Avenue, Southeast, Suite 6800, Cedar Rapids, IA 52401 .... (319) 363–6832
120 Federal Courthouse Building, 320 Sixth Street, Sioux City, IA 51101 .... (712) 233–1860
210 Waterloo Building, 531 Commercial Street, Waterloo, IA 50701 .... (319) 232–6657
201 West 2nd Street, Suite 720, Davenport, IA 52801 .... (563) 322–4331
307 Federal Building, 8 South Sixth Street, Council Bluffs, IA 51501 .... (712) 322–7103

* * *

JONI ERNST, Republican, of Red Oak, IA; born in Red Oak, July 1, 1970; education: graduated Stanton High School, Stanton, IA; B.S., Iowa State University, Ames, IA, 1992; M.P.A., Columbus State University, 1995; military service: U.S. Army Reserve, 1993–2001; Iowa Army National Guard, 1992–2015; professional: auditor of Montgomery County, IA, 2005–11; member of the Iowa State Senate, 2011–14; child: Elizabeth; committees: Agriculture, Nutrition, and Forestry; Armed Services; Environment and Public Works; Judiciary; Small Business and Entrepreneurship; elected to the U.S. Senate on November 4, 2014.

Office Listings

https://ernst.senate.gov https://facebook.com/senjoniernst
https://twitter.com/SenJoniErnst https://instagram.com/senjoniernst

730 Hart Senate Office Building, Washington, DC 20510 .... (202) 224–3254
Chief of Staff.—Lisa Goeas.
Legislative Director.—Jena McNeil.
National Communications Director.—Kelsi Daniell.
Iowa Communications Director.—Brendan Conley.
733 Federal Building, 210 Walnut Street, Des Moines, IA 50309 .... (515) 284–4574
111 7th Avenue, Southeast, Suite 480, Cedar Rapids, IA 52401 .... (319) 365–4504
201 West Second Street, Suite 806, Davenport, IA 52801 .... (563) 322–0677
194 Federal Building, 320 Sixth Street, Room 110, Sioux City, IA 51101 .... (712) 252–1550
221 Federal Building, 8 South Sixth Street, Council Bluffs, IA 51501 .... (712) 352–1167

REPRESENTATIVES

FIRST DISTRICT

ABBY FINKENAUER, Democrat, of Dubuque, IA; born in Dubuque, December 27, 1988; education: B.A., Drake University, Des Moines, IA, 2011; professional: communications professional; Congressional Page for the U.S. House of Representatives, 2006; Speaker's Page for the Iowa House of Representatives, 2007; State of Iowa volunteer coordinator for Vice President

Joe Biden's presidential campaign, 2007; legislative assistant in the Iowa House of Representatives for Representative Todd Taylor, 2012–13; board member, Greater Dubuque Development Corporation; member, District 99, Iowa House of Representatives, 2015–19; committees: Small Business; Transportation and Infrastructure; elected to the 116th Congress on November 6, 2018.

Office Listings

https://finkenauer.house.gov https://facebook.com/RepAbbyFinkenauer https://twitter.com/RepFinkenauer

124 Cannon House Office Building, Washington, DC 20515 .... (202) 225–2911
Chief of Staff.—Tyler Wilson.
308 3rd Street, Southeast, Suite 200, Cedar Rapids, IA 52401 .... (319) 364–2288
District Director.—Jared Mullendore.
1050 Main Street, Dubuque, IA 52001 .... (563) 557–7789
521A Lafayette Street, Waterloo, IA 50703 .... (319) 266–6925

Counties: ALLAMAKEE, BENTON, BLACK HAWK, BREMER, BUCHANAN, CLAYTON, DELAWARE, DUBUQUE, FAYETTE, HOWARD, IOWA, JACKSON, JONES, LINN, MARSHALL, MITCHELL, POWESHIEK, TAMA, WINNESHIEK, AND WORTH. Population (2010), 761,548.

ZIP Codes: 50005, 50027, 50051, 50078, 50106, 50112, 50120, 50136, 50141–42, 50148, 50153, 50157–58, 50162, 50171, 50173, 50206–07, 50234, 50239, 50242, 50247, 50258, 50434, 50440, 50444, 50446, 50448, 50450, 50454–56, 50458–61, 50464, 50466, 50471–72, 50476, 50603, 50606–07, 50609, 50612–13, 50621–22, 50626, 50628–30, 50632, 50634–35, 50641, 50643–45, 50647–48, 50650–52, 50654–55, 50662, 50664, 50666–71, 50674–77, 50681–82, 50701–03, 50707, 52001–03, 52030–33, 52035, 52037–50, 52052–54, 52057, 52060, 52064–66, 52068–70, 52072–74, 52076–79, 52101, 52132–36, 52140–42, 52144, 52146–47, 52151, 52154–66, 52168–72, 52175, 52201–03, 52205–25, 52227–29, 52232–33, 52236–37, 52249, 52251, 52253, 52257, 52301–02, 52305–16, 52318, 52320–21, 52323–26, 52328–30, 52332, 52334, 52336, 52338–39, 52341–42, 52345–49, 52351–52, 52354–56, 52361–62, 52401–05, 52411, 52731

* * *

SECOND DISTRICT

DAVID LOEBSACK, Democrat, of Iowa City, IA; born in Sioux City, IA, December 23, 1952; education: graduated, East High School, 1970; B.A., Iowa State University, 1974; M.A., Iowa State University, 1976; Ph.D., political science, University of California, Davis, 1985; professional: professor, political science, Cornell College, 1982–2006; married: Teresa Loebsack; four children; committees: Energy and Commerce; elected to the 110th Congress on November 7, 2006; reelected to each succeeding Congress.

Office Listings

https://loebsack.house.gov https://facebook.com/DaveLoebsack https://twitter.com/daveloebsack

1211 Longworth House Office Building, Washington, DC 20515 .... (202) 225–6576
Chief of Staff.—Eric Witte.
Office Manager / Scheduler.—Sean Dempsey.
209 West 4th Street, Suite 104, Davenport, IA 52801 .... (563) 323–5988
District Director.—Rob Sueppel. FAX: 323–5231
125 South Dubuque Street, Iowa City, IA 52240–4003 .... (319) 351–0789
(866) 914–4692

Counties: APPANOOSE, CEDAR, CLARKE, CLINTON, DAVIS, DECATUR, DES MOINES, HENRY, JASPER, JEFFERSON, JOHNSON, KEOKUK, LEE, LOUISA, LUCAS, MAHASKA, MARION, MONROE, MUSCATINE, SCOTT, VAN BUREN, WAPELLO, WASHINGTON, AND WAYNE. Population (2010), 761,624.

ZIP Codes: 50008, 50027–28, 50044, 50049, 50052, 50054, 50057, 50060, 50062, 50065, 50067–68, 50103–04, 50108, 50116, 50119, 50123, 50127, 50135–38, 50140, 50143–44, 50147, 50150–51, 50153, 50163, 50165, 50168, 50170, 50174, 50207–08, 50213–14, 50219, 50225, 50228, 50232, 50238, 50251–52, 50255–56, 50262, 50264, 50268, 50272, 50275, 52037, 52201, 52216, 52231, 52235, 52240–48, 52254–55, 52306, 52317, 52319, 52322, 52327, 52333, 52335, 52337–38, 52340, 52353, 52355–56, 52358–59, 52531, 52533–35, 52537–38, 52540, 52542–44, 52549–52, 52555–57, 52560–63, 52565, 52567–74, 52576–77, 52580–81, 52583–86, 52588, 52590–91, 52593–95, 52601, 52619–21, 52623–27, 52630–32, 52635, 52637–42, 52644–60, 52701, 52720–22, 52726–34, 52736–39, 52742, 52745–61, 52765–69, 52771–74, 52776–78, 52801–09

* * *

THIRD DISTRICT

CINDY AXNE, Democrat, of West Des Moines, IA; born in Des Moines, IA, April 20, 1965; education: B.A., University of Iowa, 1987; M.B.A., Northwestern University, 2002; professional: State of Iowa, 2005–14; small business owner; committees: Agriculture; Financial Services; elected to the 116th Congress on November 6, 2018.

Office Listings

https://axne.house.gov   https://facebook.com/RepCindyAxne   twitter: @RepCindyAxne

330 Cannon House Office Building, Washington, DC 20515 .... (202) 225–5476
Chief of Staff.—Joseph Diver.
400 East Court Avenue, Suite 346, Des Moines, IA 50309 .... (515) 400–8180
District Director.—Kaitryn Patchett.
Caseworker.—Chloe Gearhart.
208 West Taylor Street, Creston, IA 50801 .... (641) 278–1828
Caseworker.—John Riemenschneider.
501 5th Avenue, Council Bluffs, IA 51503 .... (712) 890–3117
Caseworker.—Kyle McGlade.

Counties: ADAIR, ADAMS, CASS, DALLAS, FREMONT, GUTHRIE, MADISON, MILLS, MONTGOMERY, PAGE, POLK, POTTAWATTAMIE, RINGGOLD, TAYLOR, UNION, AND WARREN. Population (2010), 761,612.

ZIP Codes: 50001–03, 50007, 50009, 50020–23, 50026, 50029, 50032–33, 50035, 50038–39, 50047–48, 50061, 50063, 50066, 50069–70, 50072–74, 50109, 50111, 50115, 50118, 50125, 50128, 50131, 50133, 50139, 50145–46, 50149, 50155, 50160, 50164, 50166–67, 50169, 50210–11, 50216, 50218, 50220, 50222, 50226, 50229, 50233, 50237, 50240–41, 50243, 50250, 50254, 50257, 50261, 50263, 50265–66, 50273–74, 50276–77, 50301–25, 50327–36, 50339–40, 50359–64, 50367–69, 50380–81, 50391–96, 50398, 50801, 50830–31, 50833, 50835–37, 50839–43, 50845–49, 50851, 50853–54, 50857–64, 50936, 50940, 50947, 50950, 50980–83, 51501–03, 51510, 51521, 51525–26, 51532–36, 51540–42, 51544, 51548–49, 51551–54, 51559–61, 51566, 51571, 51573, 51575–77, 51591, 51601, 51603, 51630–32, 51636–40, 51645–54, 51656

* * *

FOURTH DISTRICT

STEVE KING, Republican, of Kiron, IA; born in Storm Lake, IA, May 28, 1949; education: graduated, Denison Community High School; attended Northwest Missouri State University, Maryville, MO, 1967–70; professional: agri-businessman; owner and operator of King Construction Company; public service: Iowa State Senate, 1996–2002; religion: Catholic; family: married to Marilyn; children: David, Michael, and Jeff; elected to the 108th Congress on November 5, 2002; reelected to each succeeding Congress.

Office Listings

https://steveking.house.gov   https://facebook.com/SteveKingIA   twitter: @SteveKingIA

2210 Rayburn House Office Building, Washington, DC 20515 .... (202) 225–4426
Chief of Staff.—Sarah Stevens. FAX: 225–3193
Legislative Director.—Suanne Edmiston.
Scheduler.—Vacant.
Communications Director.—John Kennedy.
320 6th Street, Room 112, Sioux City, IA 51101 .... (712) 224–4692
202 1st Street, SE., Suite 126, Mason City, IA 50401 .... (641) 201–1624
723 Central Avenue, Fort Dodge, IA 50501 .... (515) 573–2738
306 North Grand Avenue, Spencer, IA 51301 .... (712) 580–7754
1421 South Bell Avenue, Suite 102, Ames, IA 50010 .... (515) 232–2885

Counties: AUDUBON, BOONE, BUENA VISTA, BUTLER, CALHOUN, CARROLL, CERRO GORDO, CHEROKEE, CHICKASAW, CLAY, CRAWFORD, DICKINSON, EMMET, FLOYD, FRANKLIN, GREENE, GRUNDY, HAMILTON, HANCOCK, HARDIN, HARRISON, HUMBOLDT, IDA, KOSSUTH, LYON, MONONA, O'BRIEN, OSCEOLA, PALO ALTO, PLYMOUTH, POCAHONTAS, SAC, SHELBY, SIOUX, STORY, WEBSTER, WINNEBAGO, WOODBURY, AND WRIGHT. Population (2010), 761,571.

ZIP Codes: 50006, 50010–12, 50014, 50020, 50022, 50025–26, 50029, 50034, 50036, 50040–42, 50046, 50050, 50055–56, 50058, 50064, 50071, 50075–76, 50101–02, 50105, 50107, 50117, 50122, 50124, 50126, 50128–30, 50132, 50134, 50154, 50156, 50161, 50201, 50206, 50212, 50217, 50220, 50223, 50227, 50230–31, 50235–36, 50243–44, 50246–49, 50258, 50269, 50271, 50276, 50278, 50401, 50420–21, 50423–24, 50428, 50430–36, 50438–39, 50441, 50444, 50446, 50449–53, 50457–58, 50460–61, 50464–65, 50467–71, 50473, 50475, 50477–80, 50482–84, 50501, 50510–11, 50514–25, 50527–33, 50535–36, 50538–46, 50548, 50551, 50554, 50556–63, 50565–71, 50573–79, 50581–83, 50585–86, 50588, 50590–95, 50597–99, 50601–05, 50609, 50611, 50613, 50616, 50619–21, 50624–25, 50627, 50630, 50633, 50636, 50638, 50642–43, 50645, 50653, 50657–60, 50665–66, 50669–70, 50672–74, 50680, 51001–12, 51014, 51016, 51018–20, 51022–31, 51033–41, 51044–56, 51058, 51060–63, 51101, 51103–06, 51108–09, 51111, 51201, 51230–32, 51234–35, 51237–50, 51301, 51331, 51333–34, 51338, 51340–43, 51345–47, 51350–51, 51354–55, 51357–58, 51360, 51363–66, 51401, 51430–31, 51433, 51436, 51439–55, 51458–59, 51460–63, 51465–67, 51520–21, 51523, 51527–31, 51537, 51543, 51545–46, 51550, 51552, 51555–59, 51562–65, 51570, 51572, 51577–79, 52154, 52171

KANSAS

(Population 2010, 2,853,118)

SENATORS

PAT ROBERTS, Republican, of Dodge City, KS; born in Topeka, KS, April 20, 1936; education: graduated, Holton High School, Holton, KS, 1954; B.S., journalism, Kansas State University, Manhattan, KS, 1958; professional: captain, U.S. Marine Corps, 1958–62; editor and reporter, Arizona newspapers, 1962–67; aide to Senator Frank Carlson, 1967–68; aide to Representative Keith Sebelius, 1969–80; U.S. House of Representatives, 1980–96; married: the former Franki Fann, 1969; children: David, Ashleigh, and Anne-Wesley; committees: chair, Agriculture, Nutrition, and Forestry; Finance; Health, Education, Labor, and Pensions; Rules and Administration; Joint Committee on the Library; Joint Committee on Printing; Select Committee on Ethics; elected to the U.S. Senate in November, 1996; reelected to each succeeding Senate term.

Office Listings

https://roberts.senate.gov https://facebook.com/SenPatRoberts twitter: @SenPatRoberts

109 Hart Senate Office Building, Washington, DC 20510 .... (202) 224–4774
Chief of Staff.—Jackie Cottrell. FAX: 224–3514
Legislative Director.—Amber Kirchhoefer.
Scheduler.—Jensine Moyer.
Communications Director.—Sarah Little.
100 Military Plaza, P.O. Box 550, Dodge City, KS 67801 .... (620) 227–2244
District Director.—Martha Ruiz-Martinez.
125 North Market Street, Suite 1120, Wichita, KS 67202 .... (316) 263–0416
District Director.—Tamara Woods.
Frank Carlson Federal Building, 444 Southeast Quincy, Room 392, Topeka, KS 66683 ..... (785) 295–2745
District Director.—Gilda Lintz.
11900 College Boulevard, Suite 203, Overland Park, KS 66210 .... (913) 451–9343
State Director.—Chad Tenpenny.

* * *

JERRY MORAN, Republican, of Manhattan, KS; born in Plainville, KS, May 29, 1954; education: B.S., University of Kansas, Lawrence, KS, 1976; J.D., University of Kansas School of Law, Lawrence, KS, 1981; M.B.A., candidate, Fort Hays State University, Hays, KS; professional: banker; attorney; U.S. House of Representatives, 1997–2010; Kansas State Senate, 1989–97, served as vice president, 1993–95, Majority Leader, 1995–97; Kansas State Special Assistant Attorney General, 1982–85; deputy attorney, Rooks County, KS, 1987–95; University of Kansas School of Law Board of Governors, served as vice president, 1993–94, president, 1994–95; volunteering: Fort Hays State University Endowment Foundation, Board of Trustees; Coronado Area Council of the Boy Scouts of America, Executive Committee; former trustee, Eisenhower Foundation; Lions Club member; Rotary Club member; and Sons of The American Legion member; religion: Christian; family: married, Robba; two daughters, Kelsey and Alex; caucuses: co-founder, Economic Mobility Caucus; co-founder, Senate Community Pharmacy Caucus; co-founder, Senate Competitiveness Caucus; co-founder, Senate Hunger Caucus; co-founder, Senate NIH Caucus; co-chair, Congressional Task Force on Down Syndrome; co-chair, Senate Aerospace Caucus; co-chair, Senate Defense Communities Caucus; committees: chair, Veterans' Affairs; Appropriations; Banking, Housing, and Urban Affairs; Commerce, Science, and Transportation; Indian Affairs; elected to the U.S. Senate on November 2, 2010; reelected to the U.S. Senate on November 8, 2016.

Office Listings

https://moran.senate.gov https://facebook.com/jerrymoran https://twitter.com/jerrymoran

521 Dirksen Senate Office Building, Washington, DC 20510 .... (202) 224–6521
Chief of Staff.—Brennen Britton. FAX: 228–6966
Legislative Director.—Tom Bush.
Scheduler.—Emily Whitfield.
Communications Director.—Tom Brandt.
1200 Main Street, Suite 402, Hays, KS 67601 .... (785) 628–6401
State Casework Director.—Chelsey Ladd. FAX: 628–3791
23600 College Boulevard, Suite 201, Olathe, KS 66061 .... (913) 393–0711
Kansas State Scheduler.—Lisa Dethloff. FAX: 768–1366
306 North Broadway, Suite 125, P.O. Box 1372, Pittsburg, KS 66762 .... (620) 232–2286
FAX: 232–2284
1880 Kimball Avenue, Suite 270, Manhattan, KS 66502 .... (785) 539–8973

Office Listings—Continued

FAX: 587–0789

100 North Broadway, Suite 210, Wichita, KS 67202 .... (316) 269–9257
State Director.—Alex Richard. FAX: 269–9259
Deputy State Director.—Mike Zamrzla.

REPRESENTATIVES

FIRST DISTRICT

ROGER W. MARSHALL, Republican, of Great Bend, KS; born in El Dorado, KS, August 9, 1960; education: A.S., Butler Community College, El Dorado, 1980; B.S., biochemistry, Kansas State University, Manhattan, KS; M.D., University of Kansas School of Medicine, Kansas City, KS, 1987; professional: former board chairman of Great Bend Regional Hospital; board member of Farmers Bank and Trust; former Rotary district governor; military: Captain, U.S. Army Reserve; awards: Teacher of the Year during residency in St. Petersburg, FL; Resident Research Award in St. Petersburg; religion: Christian; family: wife; children: four; grandchildren: two; committees: Agriculture; Science, Space, and Technology; elected to the 115th Congress on November 8, 2016; reelected to the 116th Congress on November 6, 2018.

Office Listings

https://marshall.house.gov https://facebook.com/RogerMarshallMD https://twitter.com/RogerMarshallMD

312 Cannon House Office Building, Washington, DC 20515 .... (202) 225–2715
Chief of Staff.—Brent Robertson.
Legislative Director.—Michael Brooks.
Senior Legislative Assistant.—Katie Moore.
Health Policy Advisor.—Charlotte Pineda.
Legislative Assistant.—Zach Lowry.
Scheduler.—Solvi Pollack.
Press Assistant.—Michael Rogenmoser.
Legislative Correspondent.—Bill Birsic.
200 East Iron Avenue, Salina, KS 67401 .... (785) 829–9000
District Director.—Katie Sawyer.
Communications Assistant.—Eric Pahls.
816 Campus Drive, Suite 500, Garden City, KS 67846 .... (620) 765–7800
Deputy District Director.—Rebecca Swender.

Counties: BARBER, BARTON, CHASE, CHEYENNE, CLARK, CLAY, CLOUD, COMANCHE, DECATUR, DICKINSON, EDWARDS, ELLIS, ELLSWORTH, FINNEY, FORD, GEARY (part), GOVE, GRAHAM, GRANT, GRAY, GREELEY, GREENWOOD (part), HAMILTON, HASKELL, HODGEMAN, JEWELL, KEARNY, KIOWA, LANE, LINCOLN, LOGAN, LYON, MCPHERSON, MARION (part), MARSHALL, MEADE, MITCHELL, MORRIS, MORTON, NEMAHA (part), NESS, NORTON, OSBORNE, OTTAWA, PAWNEE, PHILLIPS, PRATT, RAWLINS, RENO, REPUBLIC, RICE, ROOKS, RUSH, RUSSELL, SALINE, SCOTT, SEWARD, SHERIDAN, SHERMAN, SMITH, STAFFORD, STANTON, STEVENS, THOMAS, TREGO, WABAUNSEE, WALLACE, WASHINGTON, AND WICHITA. Population (2010), 713,278.

ZIP Codes: 66401, 66403 (part), 66406 (part), 66407, 66411–13 (part), 66422 (part), 66423, 66427 (part), 66431–32 (part), 66438 (part), 66441–42, 66449, 66501–03, 66506–07, 66508 (part), 66514, 66517–18, 66520, 66521 (part), 66523 (part), 66526, 66531, 66535, 66536 (part), 66547, 66548 (part), 66549, 66554, 66614–15 (part), 66801, 66830, 66833–35, 66838, 66840 (part), 66843, 66845–46, 66849–51, 66854 (part), 66858–59, 66860 (part), 66861–62, 66864 (part), 66865, 66866 (part), 66868 (part), 66869, 66872–73, 66901, 66930, 66932–33, 66935–46, 66948–49, 66951–53, 66955–56, 66958–60, 66962–64, 66966–68, 66970, 67020 (part), 67025 (part), 67035 (part), 67053, 67062 (part), 67063, 67068 (part), 67073, 67107–08 (part), 67114 (part), 67127 (part), 67151 (part), 67401, 67410, 67416–18, 67420, 67422–23, 67425, 67427–28, 67430–32, 67436–39, 67441–52, 67454–60, 67464, 67466–68, 67470, 67473–75, 67478, 67480–85, 67487, 67490–92, 67501–02, 67505, 67510–16, 67518, 67519 (part), 67520–21, 67522–23 (part), 67524–25, 67526 (part), 67529–30 (part), 67543–44, 67546, 67547 (part), 67548, 67550 (part), 67553–54, 67556, 67557 (part), 67559–61, 67563 (part), 67564–66, 67567 (part), 67568, 67570 (part), 67572–73, 67574 (part), 67575, 67579, 67581, 67583 (part), 67584, 67601, 67621–23, 67625–26, 67628–29, 67631–32, 67634–35, 67637–40, 67642–51, 67653–54, 67656–61, 67663–65, 67667, 67669, 67671–75, 67701, 67730–41, 67743–45, 67747–49, 67751–53, 67756–58, 67761–62, 67764, 67801, 67831, 67834–44, 67846, 67849–51, 67853–55, 67857, 67859–65, 67867–71, 67876–80, 67882, 67901, 67951–54

* * *

SECOND DISTRICT

STEVE WATKINS, Republican, of Topeka, KS; born at Lackland Air Force Base, San Antonio, TX, September 18, 1976; education: B.S., engineering, United States Military Academy, West Point, NY, 1995; M.S.R.E.D., Massachusetts Institute of Technology, Cambridge, MA,

2010; M.C./M.P.A., Harvard University, Cambridge, MA, 2017; military: United States Army, 1994–2004; professional: independent security contractor in Iraq, Afghanistan, and Central Asia for 10 years, U.S. Department of Defense; business consultant; religion: Methodist; family: married to Fong Liu; committees: Education and Labor; Foreign Affairs; Veterans' Affairs; elected to the 116th Congress on November 6, 2018.

Office Listings

https://watkins.house.gov https://facebook.com/CongressmanSteveWatkins
https://twitter.com/Rep_Watkins

1205 Longworth House Office Building, Washington, DC 20515 .... (202) 225–6601
Chief of Staff.—Colin Brainard. FAX: 225–7986
Scheduler.—Kayla Herron.
Legislative Director.—Adam York.
Communications Director.—Jim Joice.
3550 Southwest 5th Street, Topeka, KS 66606 .... (785) 234–5966
402 North Broadway Street, Suite B, Pittsburg, KS 66762 .... (620) 231–5966

Counties: ALLEN, ANDERSON, ATCHISON, BOURBON, BROWN, CHEROKEE, COFFEY, CRAWFORD, DONIPHAN, DOUGLAS, FRANKLIN, JACKSON, JEFFERSON, LABETTE, LEAVENWORTH, LINN, MARSHALL (part), MIAMI (part), MONTGOMERY, NEMAHA, NEOSHO, OSAGE, SHAWNEE, WILSON, AND WOODSON. Population (2010), 713,272.

ZIP Codes: 66002, 66006–08, 66010, 66012, 66014–17, 66020–21, 66023–27, 66032–33, 66035, 66039–50, 66052–54, 66056, 66058, 66060, 66064, 66066–67, 66070–73, 66075–76, 66078–80, 66083, 66086–88, 66090–95, 66097, 66109, 66402–04, 66406, 66408–09, 66411–19, 66422, 66424–25, 66427–29, 66431–32, 66434, 66436, 66438–40, 66451, 66508–10, 66512, 66515–16, 66521–24, 66527–28, 66532–34, 66536–44, 66546, 66548, 66550, 66552, 66603–12, 66614–19, 66621–22, 66701, 66710–14, 66716–17, 66720, 66724–25, 66728, 66732–36, 66738–41, 66743, 66746, 66748–49, 66751, 66753–58, 66760–63, 66767, 66769–73, 66775–83, 66839, 66852, 66854, 66856–57, 66864, 66868, 66871, 67047, 67301, 67330, 67332–33, 67335–37, 67340–42, 67344, 67347, 67351, 67354, 67356–57, 67363–64

* * *

THIRD DISTRICT

SHARICE DAVIDS, Democrat, of Roeland Park, KS; born in Frankfurt, West Germany, May 22, 1980; education: attended Haskell Indian Nations University, Lawrence, KS; attended University of Kansas, Lawrence, KS; A.A., Johnson County Community College, Overland Park, KS, 2003; B.A., University of Missouri, Kansas City, MO, 2007; J.D., Cornell University, Ithaca, NY, 2010; professional: nonprofit executive at Pine Ridge Reservation; lawyer; business owner; teacher; school administrator; professional competitor, Mixed Martial Arts; White House Fellow, U.S. Department of Transportation, Washington, DC, 2016–17; committees: Small Business; Transportation and Infrastructure; one of the first two Native American women to serve in Congress; elected to the 116th Congress on November 6, 2018.

Office Listings

https://davids.house.gov https://facebook.com/RepDavids https://twitter.com/RepDavids
https://instagram.com/repdavids https://youtube.com/channel/UCNUfpXQeUVdh6oKWVmq3xxQ

1541 Longworth House Office Building, Washington, DC 20515 .... (202) 225–2865
Chief of Staff.—Allison Teixeira Sulier.
Director of Operations.—Christina Jones.
Legislative Director.—Brandon Naylor.
7325 West 79th Street, Overland Park, KS 66204 .... (913) 621–0832
753 State Avenue, Suite 460, Kansas City, KS 66101 .... (913) 766–3993
District Director.—Danielle Robinson.

Counties: JOHNSON, MIAMI (part), AND WYANDOTTE. Population (2010), 713,272.

ZIP Codes: 66012–13, 66018–19, 66021, 66025, 66030–31, 66053, 66061–62, 66071, 66083, 66085, 66101–06, 66109, 66111–12, 66115, 66118, 66202–21, 66223–24, 66226–27

* * *

FOURTH DISTRICT

RON ESTES, Republican, of Wichita, KS; born in Topeka, KS; education: B.A., civil engineering, Tennessee Technological University, Cookeville, TN, 1973; M.B.A., Tennessee Technological University, 1983; professional: engineer; Sedgwick County (Kansas) Treasurer; Kansas State Treasurer; married: Susan Estes; children: Brent, Laura, and Grace; committees: Ways and Means; elected to the 115th Congress on April 11, 2017, by special election, to fill the vacancy caused by the resignation of U.S. Representative Mike Pompeo; reelected to the 116th Congress on November 6, 2018.

Office Listings

https://estes.house.gov https://facebook.com/RepRonEstes https://twitter.com/RepRonEstes

1524 Longworth House Office Building, Washington, DC 20515 .... (202) 225–6216
Chief of Staff.—Josh Bell.
Deputy Chief of Staff.—Nicholas O'Boyle.
Communications Director.—Greg Steele.
Scheduler.—Grace Davis.
Legislative Assistants: Katarina DeFilippo, Elizabeth Diohep, Daniel Martin.
Legislative Correspondent.—Nicole Harrison.
Staff Assistant.—Collin Harrison.
7701 East Kellogg, Suite 510, Wichita, KS 67207 .... (316) 262–8992

Counties: BARBER, BUTLER, CHAUTAUQUA, COMANCHE, COWLEY, EDWARDS, ELK, GREENWOOD, HARPER, HARVEY, KINGMAN, KIOWA, PAWNEE (part), PRATT, SEDGWICK, STAFFORD, AND SUMNER. Population (2010), 715,456.

ZIP Codes: 66736 (part), 66777 (part), 66840 (part), 66842, 66852 (part), 66853, 66860 (part), 66863, 66866 (part), 66870, 67001–05, 67008–10, 67012–13, 67016–19, 67020 (part), 67021–24, 67025 (part), 67026, 67028–31, 67035 (part), 67036–39, 67041–42, 67045, 67047 (part), 67049–52, 67054–61, 67062 (part), 67065–67, 67068 (part), 67070–72, 67074, 67101, 67103–06, 67107–08 (part), 67109–12, 67114 (part), 67117–20, 67122–24, 67127 (part), 67131–35, 67137–38, 67140, 67142–44, 67146–47, 67149–50

KENTUCKY

(Population 2010, 4,339,367)

SENATORS

MITCH McCONNELL, Republican, of Louisville, KY; born in Colbert County, AL, February 20, 1942; education: graduated, Manual High School, Louisville, 1960, president of the student body; B.A. with honors, University of Louisville, 1964, president of the student council, president of the student body of the College of Arts and Sciences; J.D., University of Kentucky Law School, 1967, president of student bar association, outstanding oral advocate; professional: attorney, admitted to the Kentucky Bar, 1967; Chief Legislative Assistant to U.S. Senator Marlow Cook, 1968–70; Deputy Assistant U.S. Attorney General, 1974–75; Judge/Executive of Jefferson County, KY, 1978–84; chairman, National Republican Senatorial Committee, 1997–2000; chairman, Joint Congressional Committee on Inaugural Ceremonies, 1999–2001; Senate Majority Whip, 2002–06; Senate Republican Leader, 2007–14, Senate Majority Leader, 2015–present; married to Secretary Elaine L. Chao on February 6, 1993; children: Elly, Claire, and Porter; committees: Agriculture, Nutrition, and Forestry; Appropriations; Rules and Administration; ex officio, Select Committee on Intelligence; elected to the U.S. Senate on November 6, 1984; reelected to each succeeding Senate term.

Office Listings

https://mcconnell.senate.gov https://facebook.com/mitchmcconnell https://twitter.com/McConnellPress

317 Russell Senate Office Building, Washington, DC 20510 .... (202) 224–2541
Chief of Staff.—Phil Maxson.
Executive Assistant and Director of Scheduling.—Sarah Fairchild.
Legislative Director.—Katelyn Bunning.
Communications Director.—Robert Steurer.
601 West Broadway, Suite 630, Louisville, KY 40202 .... (502) 582–6304
State Director.—Terry Carmack.
Federal Building, 241 East Main Street, Room 102, Bowling Green, KY 42101 .... (270) 781–1673
1885 Dixie Highway, Suite 345, Fort Wright, KY 41011 .... (859) 578–0188
771 Corporate Drive, Suite 108, Lexington, KY 40503 .... (859) 224–8286
300 South Main Street, Suite 310, London, KY 40741 .... (606) 864–2026
100 Fountain Avenue, Suite 300, Paducah, KY 42001 .... (270) 442–4554

* * *

RAND PAUL, Republican, of Bowling Green, KY; born in Pittsburgh, PA, January 7, 1963; education: undergraduate, Baylor University, Waco, Texas, 1981–84; M.D., Duke University School of Medicine, 1988; religion: Methodist; family: married to the former Kelley Ashby; three sons: William, Duncan, and Robert; committees: Foreign Relations; Health, Education, Labor, and Pensions; Homeland Security and Governmental Affairs; Small Business and Entrepreneurship; elected to the U.S. Senate on November 2, 2010; reelected to the U.S. Senate on November 8, 2016.

Office Listings

https://paul.senate.gov https://facebook.com/SenatorRandPaul twitter: @RandPaul

167 Russell Senate Office Building, Washington, DC 20510 .... (202) 224–4343
Chief of Staff.—William Henderson.
Deputy Chief of Staff of Communications.—Sergio Gor.
Press Secretary.—Matthew Hawes.
Scheduler.—Drake Henle.
State Director.—Jim Milliman.
1029 State Street, Bowling Green, KY 42101 .... (270) 782–8303

REPRESENTATIVES

FIRST DISTRICT

JAMES COMER, Republican, of Tompkinsville, KY; born in Carthage, TN, August 19, 1972; education: B.S., agriculture, Western Kentucky University, Bowling Green, KY, 1993; professional: businessman; farmer; member, Kentucky House of Representatives, 2001–12; Kentucky Commissioner of Agriculture, 2012–15; religion: Baptist; spouse: Tamara Jo; children: Reagan, Harlan, and Aniston; committees: Agriculture; Education and Labor; Oversight and Reform; elected simultaneously to the 114th and 115th Congresses, by special election, on November 8, 2016, to fill the vacancy caused by the resignation of U.S. Representative Ed Whitfield; reelected to the 116th Congress on November 6, 2018.

Office Listings

https://comer.house.gov

1037 Longworth House Office Building, Washington, DC 20515 .... (202) 225–3115
Chief of Staff.—Caroline Cash.
Director of Operations.—Kaity Wolfe.
Communications Director.—Michael Gossum.
200 North Main, Suite F, Tompkinsville, KY 42167 .... (270) 487–9509
District Director.—Sandy Simpson.
67 North Main Street, Madisonville, KY 42431 .... (270) 487–9509
Field Representatives: Corey Elder, Amelia Wilson.
300 South 3rd Street, Paducah, KY 42003 .... (270) 408–1865
Field Representative.—Martie Wiles.

Counties: ADAIR, ALLEN, BALLARD, CALDWELL, CALLOWAY, CARLISLE, CASEY, CHRISTIAN, CLINTON, CRITTENDEN, CUMBERLAND, FULTON, GRAVES, HENDERSON, HICKMAN, HOPKINS, LIVINGSTON, LOGAN, LYON, MARION, MARSHALL, MCCRACKEN, MCLEAN, METCALF, MONROE, MUHLENBERG, OHIO, RUSSELL, SIMPSON, TAYLOR, TODD, TRIGG, UNION, WASHINGTON, AND WEBSTER. Population (2010), 725,929.

ZIP Codes: 40009, 40033, 40037, 40040, 40049, 40052, 40060–63, 40069, 40078, 40119, 40328, 40330, 40437, 40442, 40448, 40464, 40468, 40484, 40489, 42001–03, 42020–25, 42027–29, 42031–33, 42035–41, 42044–45, 42047–51, 42053–56, 42058, 42060–61, 42063–64, 42066, 42069–71, 42076, 42078–79, 42081–88, 42101, 42104, 42120, 42122–24, 42129, 42133–35, 42140–41, 42150–51, 42153–54, 42164, 42166–67, 42170, 42201–04, 42206, 42209–11, 42214–17, 42219–21, 42223, 42232, 42234, 42236, 42240–41, 42251–52, 42254, 42256, 42262, 42265–67, 42274, 42276, 42280, 42283, 42286–88, 42301, 42320–28, 42330, 42332–34, 42337–38, 42344–45, 42347, 42349–50, 42352, 42354, 42356, 42361, 42367–69, 42370–72, 42374–76, 42378, 42402–04, 42406, 42408–11, 42413, 42419–20, 42431, 42436–37, 42440–42, 42444–45, 42450–53, 42455–64, 42516, 42528, 42539, 42541, 42544, 42565–67, 42602–03, 42629, 42642, 42711, 42715–16, 42718–20, 42728, 42731, 42733, 42735, 42740–43, 42746, 42749, 42753, 42758–59, 42786

* * *

SECOND DISTRICT

BRETT GUTHRIE, Republican, of Bowling Green, KY; born in Florence, AL, February 18, 1964; education: B.S., United States Military Academy, West Point, NY, 1987; M.P.M., Yale University, New Haven, CT, 1997; military service: U.S. Army, Field Artillery Office, 101st Airborne Division, 1987–90; professional: vice president, Trace Die Cast, 1991–2009; member: Kentucky Senate, 1998–2009; married: Beth; children: Caroline, Robby, and Elizabeth; committees: Education and Labor; Energy and Commerce; elected to the 111th Congress on November 4, 2008; reelected to each succeeding Congress.

Office Listings

https://guthrie.house.gov https://facebook.com/CongressmanGuthrie twitter: @RepGuthrie

2434 Rayburn House Office Building, Washington, DC 20515 .... (202) 225–3501
Chief of Staff.—Eric Bergren.
Legislative Director.—Sophie Trainor.
Communications Director.—Lauren Gaydos.
Scheduler.—Jennifer Beil.
996 Wilkinson Trace, Suite B2, Bowling Green, KY 42103 .... (270) 842–9896
District Director.—Mark Lord.

Counties: BARREN, BOYLE, BRECKINRIDGE, BULLITT, BUTLER, DAVIESS, EDMONSON, GARRARD, GRAYSON, GREEN, HANCOCK, HARDIN, HART, JESSAMINE (part), LARUE, MEADE, MERCER, NELSON, SPENCER (part), WARREN, AND WASHINGTON (part). Population (2010), 723,137.

ZIP Codes: 40004, 40008, 40012–13, 40020, 40037 (part), 40040, 40046 (part), 40047–48, 40051, 40052 (part), 40069 (part), 40071 (part), 40078, 40104, 40107–11, 40115, 40117, 40119 (part), 40121, 40140, 40142–46, 40150, 40152, 40155, 40157, 40160–62, 40165, 40170–71, 40175–76, 40177 (part), 40178, 40229 (part), 40272 (part), 40299, 40310, 40328 (part), 40330, 40339, 40356 (part), 40372 (part), 40383 (part), 40390 (part), 40403 (part), 40419 (part), 40422 (part), 40440 (part), 40444 (part), 40461 (part), 40464 (part), 40468 (part), 40484 (part), 42101–03, 42104 (part), 42122 (part), 42123, 42127, 42130, 42133 (part), 42141, 42154 (part), 42156, 42159–60, 42163, 42166 (part), 42170 (part), 42171, 42206 (part), 42207, 42210, 42214 (part), 42256 (part), 42259, 42261, 42273, 42274 (part), 42275, 42285, 42301 (part), 42303, 42320 (part), 42327 (part), 42333 (part), 42339 (part), 42343 (part), 42348, 42349 (part), 42351, 42355–56, 42361 (part), 42366 (part), 42368 (part), 42376 (part), 42378 (part), 42701, 42712–13, 42716 (part), 42718 (part), 42721–22, 42724, 42726, 42729, 42732, 42740, 42743 (part), 42746 (part), 42748, 42749 (part), 42754, 42757, 42762, 42764–65, 42776, 42782, 42784, 42788

* * *

THIRD DISTRICT

JOHN A. YARMUTH, Democrat, of Louisville, KY; born in Louisville, November 4, 1947; education: graduated, Atherton High School, Louisville, 1965; graduated, Yale University, New Haven, CT, 1969; professional: legislative aide for Kentucky Senator Marlow Cook, 1971–74; publisher, *Louisville Today Magazine,* 1976–82; Associate Vice President of University Relations at the University of Louisville, 1983–86; vice president of a local healthcare firm, 1986–90; founder, editor, and writer, *LEO Newsweekly,* 1990–2005; television host and commentator, 2003–05; awards: 2007 Spirit of Enterprise Award; Louisville Alzheimer's Association Person of the Year; named Outstanding New Member of Congress by the Committee for Education and Funding; 16 Metro Louisville Journalism Awards for editorial and column writing; married: Cathy Yarmuth, 1981; child: Aaron; committees: chair, Budget; elected to the 110th Congress on November 7, 2006; reelected to each succeeding Congress.

Office Listings

https://yarmuth.house.gov https://facebook.com/RepJohnYarmuth https://twitter.com/RepJohnYarmuth

402 Cannon House Office Building, Washington, DC 20515 .... (202) 225–5401
Chief of Staff.—Julie Carr. FAX: 225–5776
Legislative Director.—Katy Rowley.
Press Secretary.—Christopher Schuler.
Scheduler.—Claire Elliott.
600 Martin Luther King, Jr. Place, Suite 216, Louisville, KY 40202 .... (502) 582–5129
District Director.—Nicole Yates.

Counties: JEFFERSON. Population (2010), 741,096.

ZIP Codes: 40025, 40027, 40041, 40047, 40059 (part), 40118, 40177 (part), 40201–22, 40223 (part), 40224–25, 40228, 40229 (part), 40231–33, 40241 (part), 40242–43, 40245 (part), 40250–53, 40255–59, 40261, 40266, 40268–70, 40272 (part), 40280–83, 40285, 40289–90, 40291 (part), 40292–93, 40295, 40297–98, 40299 (part)

* * *

FOURTH DISTRICT

THOMAS MASSIE, Republican, of Garrison, KY; born in Huntington, WV, January 13, 1971; education: graduated from Lewis County High School; B.S., electrical engineering / economics, Massachusetts Institute of Technology, 1993; M.S., mechanical engineering, Massachusetts Institute of Technology, 1996; professional: inventor / engineer; founder of SensAble Devices, Inc.; farmer; Lewis County Judge Executive; married: Rhonda; four children; committees: Oversight and Reform; Transportation and Infrastructure; elected simultaneously to the 112th and 113th Congresses on November 6, 2012, by special election, to fill the vacancy caused by the resignation of U.S. Representative Geoffrey C. (Geoff) Davis; reelected to each succeeding Congress.

Office Listings

https://massie.house.gov https://facebook.com/RepThomasMassie
https://twitter.com/RepThomasMassie

2453 Rayburn House Office Building, Washington, DC 20515 .... (202) 225–3465
Chief of Staff.—John Ferland.
Legislative Director / Deputy Chief of Staff.—Seana Cranston.
Legislative Assistants: Nino Marchese, Patrick O'Grady.
Press Secretary.—Laura Lington.
Scheduler.—Megan Buckham.
Staff Assistant.—William Wadsworth.
541 Buttermilk Pike, Suite 208, Crescent Springs, KY 41017 .... (859) 426–0080
District Director.—Chris McCane. FAX: 426–0061
District Office Manager / Scheduler.—Mary Troutman.
District of Constituent Services.—Carrie Porter.
District Field Director.—Bob Porter.
Staff Assistant.—Kevin Kreft.
1700 Greenup Avenue, R–505, Ashland, KY 41101 .... (606) 324–9898
Eastern District Field Representative.—J.R. Reed.
110 West Jefferson Street, Suite 100, La Grange, KY 40031 .... (502) 265–9119
Western District Field Representative.—Stacie Rockaway. FAX: 265–9126

Counties: BOONE, BOYD, BRACKEN, CAMPBELL, CARROLL, GALLATIN, GRANT, GREENUP, HARRISON, HENRY, JEFFERSON, KENTON, LEWIS, MASON, OLDHAM, OWEN, PENDLETON, SHELBY, SPENCER, AND TRIMBLE. Population (2010), 723,450.

ZIP Codes: 40003 (part), 40006–07, 40010–11, 40014, 40019, 40022–23, 40026, 40031, 40036, 40045, 40046 (part), 40050, 40055–58, 40059 (part), 40065, 40067–68, 40070, 40071 (part), 40075, 40076 (part), 40077, 40241 (part), 40245 (part), 40291 (part), 40299 (part), 40359, 40363, 40370 (part), 40379 (part), 40601 (part), 41001–03, 41004 (part), 41005–08, 41010 (part), 41011, 41014–18, 41030, 41031 (part), 41033–35, 41040, 41042–43, 41044 (part), 41045–46, 41048, 41051–52, 41055 (part), 41056, 41059, 41062–63, 41064 (part), 41071, 41073–76, 41080, 41083, 41085–86, 41091–92, 41093 (part), 41094–95, 41097–99, 41101, 41102 (part), 41121, 41129 (part), 41135, 41139, 41141, 41143 (part), 41144, 41164 (part), 41166, 41169, 41174–75, 41179, 41183, 41189

* * *

FIFTH DISTRICT

HAROLD ROGERS, Republican, of Somerset, KY; born in Barrier, KY, December 31, 1937; education: graduated, Wayne County High School, 1955; attended Western Kentucky University, 1956–57; A.B., University of Kentucky, 1962; LL.B., University of Kentucky Law School, 1964; professional: lawyer; admitted to the Kentucky State Bar, 1964; commenced practice in Somerset; member, North Carolina and Kentucky National Guard, 1957–64; associate, Smith and Blackburn, 1964–67; private practice, 1967–69; Commonwealth Attorney, Pulaski and Rockcastle Counties, KY, 1969–80; delegate, Republican National Convention, 1972, 1976, 1980, 1984, and 1988; Republican nominee for Lieutenant Governor, KY, 1979; past president, Kentucky Commonwealth Attorneys Association; member and past president, Somerset-Pulaski County Chamber of Commerce and Pulaski County Industrial Foundation; founder, Southern Kentucky Economic Development Council, 1986; member, Chowder and Marching Society, 1981–present; married: the late former Shirley McDowell, 1957; three children: Anthony, Allison, and John Marshall; married: the former Cynthia Doyle Stewart, 1999; committees: Appropriations; elected to the 97th Congress, November 4, 1980; reelected to each succeeding Congress.

Office Listings

https://halrogers.house.gov

2406 Rayburn House Office Building, Washington, DC 20515 .... (202) 225–4601
FAX: 225–0940

Chief of Staff.—Megan O'Donnell Bell.
Office Manager.—Chelsea Jarrett.
Legislative Correspondent.—Will Tenner.
Staff Assistant.—Giulia DiGuglielmo.
Legislative Assistants: Austin Gage, Rebekah Smith.
Legislative Director.—Jake Johnson.
Scheduler.—Sarah Brown.
District Director.—Karen Kelly.

551 Clifty Street, Somerset, KY 42503 .... (606) 679–8346
FAX: 678–4856

48 South Kentucky Highway 15, Hazard, KY 41701 .... (606) 439–0794
FAX: 439–4647

110 Resource Court, Suite A, Prestonsburg, KY 41653–1842 .... (606) 886–0844
FAX: 889–0371

Counties: BELL, BOYD, BREATHITT, CARTER, CLAY, ELLIOTT, FLOYD, HARLAN, JACKSON, JOHNSON, KNOTT, KNOX, LAUREL, LAWRENCE, LEE, LESLIE, LETCHER, LINCOLN, MAGOFFLIN, MARTIN, MCCREARY, MORGAN, OWSLEY, PERRY, PIKE, PULASKI, ROCKCASTLE, ROWAN, WAYNE, AND WHITLEY. Population (2010), 723,228.

ZIP Codes: 40313, 40351, 40393, 40402, 40409, 40434, 40445, 40447–48, 40456, 40460, 40481, 40486, 40701, 40729, 40734, 40737, 40740–41, 40743–44, 40759, 40763, 40769, 40771, 40801, 40806–08, 40813, 40815–16, 40818–20, 40823–24, 40826–31, 40840, 40843–45, 40847, 40849, 40854–56, 40858, 40862–63, 40865, 40868, 40870, 40873–74, 40902–03, 40906, 40913–15, 40921, 40923, 40927, 40935, 40940–41, 40943, 40946, 40949, 40953, 40958, 40962, 40964–65, 40972, 40977, 40979, 40982–83, 40988, 40995, 40997, 41124, 41132, 41142, 41146, 41149, 41159, 41168, 41171, 41180, 41201, 41203–04, 41214, 41216, 41219, 41222, 41224, 41226, 41230–32, 41234, 41238, 41240, 41250, 41254–57, 41260, 41262–65, 41267–68, 41271, 41274, 41311, 41314, 41317, 41339, 41348, 41352, 41366–67, 41385, 41390, 41397, 41408, 41421, 41425, 41464–65, 41472, 41501, 41503, 41512–14, 41517, 41519, 41522, 41526, 41527–28, 41531, 41534–35, 41537–40, 41544, 41547–48, 41553–55, 41557–60, 41562–64, 41566–68, 41571, 41601–07, 41612, 41615–16, 41619, 41621–22, 41630–32, 41635–36, 41640, 41642–43, 41645, 41647, 41649–50, 41653, 41659–60, 41663, 41666–67, 41669, 41701, 41712–14, 41719, 41721–23, 41725, 41727, 41729, 41731, 41735, 41739–40, 41745–46, 41749, 41751, 41754, 41759–60, 41762–64, 41766, 41772–77, 41804, 41810, 41815, 41817, 41819, 41822, 41824–26, 41828, 41831–37, 41840, 41843–45, 41847–49, 41855, 41858, 41861–62, 42501, 42503, 42518–19, 42533, 42567, 42631, 42634–35, 42638, 42649, 42653

* * *

SIXTH DISTRICT

ANDY BARR, Republican, of Lexington, KY; born in Lexington, July 24, 1973; education: B.A. degree in government and philosophy from the University of Virginia in Charlottesville,

VA, 1996, graduating with *magna cum laude* and Phi Beta Kappa honors; J.D., from the University of Kentucky College of Law, in Lexington, KY, 2001; religion: Episcopal; wife: the former Eleanor Carol Leavell of Georgetown, Kentucky (deceased); together, they are the proud parents of two daughters; caucuses: chair, Congressional Horse Caucus; Bipartisan Prescription Drug Caucus; Can Caucus; Congressional Arthritis Caucus; Congressional Automotive Caucus; Congressional Bourbon Caucus; Congressional Coal Caucus; Congressional Diabetes Caucus; Congressional Down Syndrome Caucus; Congressional Kurdish American Caucus; Congressional Natural Gas Caucus; Congressional Peace Corps Caucus; Congressional Prayer Caucus; Congressional Recycling Caucus; Congressional Sportsmen's Caucus; Congressional United Solutions Caucus; Congressional Veterans Job Caucus; Historic Preservation Caucus; House Army Caucus; House Baltic Caucus; House General Aviation Caucus; House Manufacturing Caucus; House Military Depot, Arsenal, Ammunition Plant, and Industrial Facilities Caucus; Military Sexual Assault Prevention Caucus; National Guard and Reserves Components Caucus; National Guard Youth Challenge Caucus; Pro-Life Caucus; USO Congressional Caucus; US-Japan Caucus; Republican Study Committee; committees: Financial Services; Veterans' Affairs; elected to the 113th Congress on November 6, 2012; reelected to each succeeding Congress.

Office Listings

https://barr.house.gov https://facebook.com/RepAndyBarr
https://twitter.com/RepAndyBarr https://youtube.com/user/RepAndyBarr

2430 Rayburn House Office Building, Washington, DC 20515 .... (202) 225–4706
Chief of Staff.—Mary Rosado.
Legislative Director.—Joseph "Hunt" VanderToll.
Press Secretary.—Alex Bellizzi.
Communications Director.—Jodi Whitaker.
Scheduler.—Madeline Gale.
2709 Old Rosebud Road, Suite 100, Lexington, KY 40509 .... (859) 219–1366

Counties: ANDERSON, BATH, BOURBON, CLARK, ESTILL, FAYETTE, FLEMING, FRANKLIN, HARRISON (part), JESSAMINE (part), MADISON, MENIFEE, MONTGOMERY, NICHOLAS, POWELL, ROBERTSON, SCOTT, WOLFE, AND WOODFORD. Population (2010), 723,203.

ZIP Codes: 40003, 40046, 40076, 40311–13, 40316, 40322, 40324, 40334, 40336–37, 40340, 40342, 40346–48, 40350, 40353, 40356, 40358, 40360–61, 40370–72, 40374, 40376, 40379–80, 40383, 40385, 40387, 40390–91, 40403–04, 40461, 40472, 40475, 40502–11, 40513–17, 40601, 40604, 41004, 41010, 41031, 41039, 41041, 41044, 41049, 41055, 41064, 41093, 41301, 41332, 41360, 41365

LOUISIANA

(Population 2010, 4,553,762)

SENATORS

BILL CASSIDY, Republican, of Baton Rouge, LA; born in Highland Park, IL, September 28, 1957; education: graduated, Tara High School; B.S., Louisiana State University, Baton Rouge, 1979; M.D., Louisiana State University Medical School, New Orleans, LA, 1983; professional: medical doctor, Baton Rouge; associate professor of medicine with LSU Health Sciences Center; member of the Louisiana State Senate; married: Laura Layden Cassidy, M.D.; children: Will, Meg, and Kate; committees: Energy and Natural Resources; Finance; Health, Education, Labor, and Pensions; Veterans' Affairs; Joint Economic Committee; elected to the 111th Congress; reelected to the 112th and 113th Congresses; won the runoff election to the U.S. Senate on December 6, 2014.

Office Listings

https://cassidy.senate.gov https://facebook.com/SenBillCassidy https://twitter.com/SenBillCassidy

520 Hart Senate Office Building, Washington, DC 20510 .... (202) 224–5824
Chief of Staff.—James Quinn. FAX: 224–9735
Deputy Chief of Staff.—Allison Kapsner.
Communications Director.—Ty Bofferding.
Press Secretary.—Cole Avery.
5555 Hilton Avenue, Suite 100, Baton Rouge, LA 70808 .... (225) 929–7711
3421 North Causeway Boulevard, Suite 204, Metairie, LA 70002 .... (504) 838–0130
101 La Rue France, Suite 505, Lafayette, LA 70508 .... (337) 261–1400
1651 Louisville Avenue, Suite 123, Monroe, LA 71201 .... (318) 324–2111

* * *

JOHN KENNEDY, Republican, of Madisonville, LA; born in Centreville, MS, November 21, 1951; education: B.A., Vanderbilt University, Nashville, TN, 1973; J.D., University of Virginia, Charlottesville, VA, 1977; BCL, Magdalen College, Oxford University, 1979; professional: special counsel to Louisiana Governor Buddy Roemer, 1988–92; secretary in the governor's cabinet, 1990–92; secretary of the Louisiana Department of Revenue, 1996–99; Louisiana State Treasurer, 2000–17; religion: Methodist; wife: Rebecca Stulb; child: Preston; committees: Appropriations; Banking, Housing, and Urban Affairs; Budget; Judiciary; Small Business and Entrepreneurship; won the runoff election to the U.S. Senate on December 10, 2016.

Office Listings

https://kennedy.senate.gov https://facebook.com/SenatorJohnKennedy
https://twitter.com/SenJohnKennedy

416 Russell Senate Office Building, Washington, DC 20510 .... (202) 224–4623
Chief of Staff.—David Stokes. FAX: 228–5061

REPRESENTATIVES

FIRST DISTRICT

STEVE SCALISE, Republican, of Jefferson, LA; born in New Orleans, LA, October 6, 1965; education: B.S., Louisiana State University, Baton Rouge, LA, 1989; professional: computer programmer; Louisiana House of Representatives, 1995–2007; Louisiana Senate, 2007–08; religion: Catholic; married to the former Jennifer Letulle; children: Madison and Harrison; elected, Chairman of the Republican Study Committee, 2013–14; elected, House Majority Whip, 2014–18; elected, House Republican Whip, 2019–present; committees: Energy and Commerce; elected to the 110th Congress, by special election, on May 3, 2008; reelected to each succeeding Congress.

Office Listings

https://scalise.house.gov https://facebook.com/RepSteveScalise https://twitter.com/SteveScalise

H–148, the Capitol, Washington, DC 20515 .... (202) 225–0197

Office Listings—Continued

Chief of Staff.—Brett Horton.
Policy Director.—Bill Hughes.
Communications Director.—Lauren Fine.
2049 Rayburn House Office Building, Washington, DC 20515 .... (202) 225–3015
Chief of Staff.—Megan Miller.
Legislative Director.—Claire Trokey.
Scheduler.—Jacqueline Battaglia.
110 Veterans Memorial Boulevard, Suite 500, Metairie, LA 70005 .... (504) 837–1259
21454 Koop Drive, Suite 2C, Mandeville, LA 70471 .... (985) 893–9064
1514 Martens Drive, Suite 10, Hammond, LA 70401 .... (985) 340–2185
8026 Main Street, Suite 700, Houma, LA 70360 .... (985) 879–2300

Parishes (all or part of): JEFFERSON, LAFOURCHE, ORLEANS, PLAQUEMINES, ST. BERNARD, ST. TAMMANY, TANGIPAHOA, AND TERREBONNE. Population (2010), 758,994.

ZIP Codes: 70001–06, 70009–11, 70033, 70038, 70041, 70055–56, 70060, 70062, 70064–65, 70083, 70091, 70115, 70118–19, 70121–24, 70160, 70181, 70183–84, 70343–45, 70353–54, 70357–58, 70360–61, 70363–64, 70373–74, 70377, 70401–04, 70420, 70427, 70431, 70433–38, 70445, 70447–48, 70452, 70454–67, 70469–71, 70764–65

* * *

SECOND DISTRICT

CEDRIC L. RICHMOND, Democrat, of New Orleans, LA; born in New Orleans, September 13, 1973; education: B.A., Morehouse College, Atlanta, GA, 1995; J.D., Tulane School of Law, New Orleans, 1998; Harvard University Executive Education Program at the John F. Kennedy School of Government, Cambridge, MA; professional: member of the Louisiana State House of Representatives, 1999–2010; awards: *Time* magazine's 2010 40 Under 40; Innocence Project Legislative Champion Award; religion: Baptist; commissions, caucuses: Congressional Black Caucus; New Democrat Coalition; committees: Homeland Security; Judiciary; elected to the 112th Congress on November 2, 2010; reelected to each succeeding Congress.

Office Listings

https://richmond.house.gov https://facebook.com/RepRichmond twitter: @RepRichmond

506 Cannon House Office Building, Washington, DC 20515 .... (202) 225–6636
Chief of Staff.—Kwabena Nsiah. FAX: 225–1988
Senior Advisor.—Kemah Dennis-Morial.
Legislative Director.—Peter Hunter.
Communications Director.—Jalina Porter.
2021 Lakeshore Drive, Suite 309, New Orleans, LA 70122 .... (504) 288–3777
Deputy Chief of Staff.—Enix Smith.
200 Derbigny Street, Suite 3200, Gretna, LA 70053 .... (504) 365–0390
1520 Thomas H. Delpit Drive, Suite 126, Baton Rouge, LA 70802 .... (225) 636–5600

Parishes: ASCENSION (part), ASSUMPTION (part), EAST BATON ROUGE (part), IBERVILLE (part), JEFFERSON (part), ORLEANS (part), ST. CHARLES (part), ST. JAMES, ST. JOHN THE BAPTIST (part), AND WEST BATON ROUGE (part). Population (2010), 755,538.

ZIP Codes: 70001, 70003, 70030, 70031, 70039, 70047, 70049, 70051–53, 70056–58, 70062, 70065, 70068, 70070–72, 70076, 70080, 70084, 70086, 70087, 70090, 70094, 70112–19, 70121–31, 70139, 70163, 70301, 70341, 70346, 70372, 70390, 70391, 70393, 70710, 70714, 70719, 70721, 70723, 70725, 70734, 70737, 70743, 70763, 70764, 70767, 70776, 70780, 70788, 70791, 70802, 70805–07, 70811, 70812, 70814, 70815

* * *

THIRD DISTRICT

CLAY HIGGINS, Republican, of Lafayette, LA; born in New Orleans, LA, August 24, 1961; education: Covington High School, Covington, LA; attended Louisiana State University, Baton Rouge, LA; professional: Lafayette City Marshal Deputy; Deputy Sheriff, St. Landry Parish; officer, Port Barre Police Department; reserve officer, Opelousas Police Department; manager, auto dealership; military: Military Police Corps, Louisiana National Guard; religion: Catholic; married: Rebecca; children: Daniella (deceased), Haley, Heather, and Joseph; committees: Homeland Security; Oversight and Reform; elected to the 115th Congress on December 10, 2016; reelected to the 116th Congress on November 6, 2018.

Office Listings

https://clayhiggins.house.gov https://facebook.com/CongressmanClayHiggins

424 Cannon House Office Building, Washington, DC 20515 .... (202) 225–2031
Chief of Staff.—Kathee Facchiano. FAX: 225–5724
Legislative Director.—Ward Cormier.
Scheduler.—Jordan Lane.
Communications Director.—Andrew David.
600 Jefferson Street, Suite 808, Lafayette, LA 70501 .... (337) 703–6105
One Lakeshore Drive, Suite 1670, Lake Charles, LA 70629 .... (337) 656–2833

Parishes: ACADIA, CALCASIEU, CAMERON, IBERIA, JEFFERSON DAVIS, LAFAYETTE, ST. MARTIN, ST. MARY, AND VERMILION. Population (2010), 760,696.

ZIP Codes: 70339–40, 70342, 70380, 70392, 70501, 70503, 70506–08, 70510, 70512–20, 70523, 70525–26, 70528–29, 70531–35, 70537–38, 70542–44, 70546, 70548–49, 70552, 70555–56, 70558–60, 70563, 70575, 70578, 70581–84, 70591–92, 70601, 70605, 70607, 70611, 70615, 70630–33, 70640, 70643, 70645–48, 70650, 70657, 70661, 70663, 70665, 70668–69, 70757

* * *

FOURTH DISTRICT

MIKE JOHNSON, Republican, of Benton, LA; born in Shreveport, LA, January 30, 1972; education: J.D., Paul M. Hebert Law Center, Louisiana State University, Baton Rouge, LA, 1998; religion: Southern Baptist; family: wife, Kelly; children: Hannah, Abigail, Jack, and Will; committees: Judiciary; Natural Resources; elected to the 115th Congress on December 10, 2016; reelected to the 116th Congress on November 6, 2018.

Office Listings

https://mikejohnson.house.gov https://facebook.com/RepMikeJohnson twitter: @RepMikeJohnson

418 Cannon House Office Building, Washington, DC 20515 .... (202) 225–2777
Chief of Staff.—Hayden Haynes. FAX: 225–8039
Legislative Director.—Brad Morris.
Scheduler.—Ruth Ward.
Communications Director.—Vacant.
2250 Hospital Drive, Suite 248, Bossier City, LA 71111 .... (318) 840–0309
Deputy Chief of Staff.—Chip Layton.
3329 University Parkway, Building 552, Room 24, Leesville, LA 71446 .... (337) 423–4232
444 Caspari Drive, South Hall Room 224, Natchitoches, LA 71497 .... (318) 951–4316

Parishes: ALLEN, BEAUREGARD, BIENVILLE, BOSSIER, CADDO, CLAIBORNE, DESOTO, EVANGELINE, NATCHITOCHES, RED RIVER, SABINE, ST. LANDRY, UNION, VERNON, AND WEBSTER. Population (2010), 667,109.

ZIP Codes: 70515, 70524, 70535, 70541, 70570, 70576, 70584–86, 70589, 70634, 70637–39, 70644, 70648, 70651–60, 70662, 71001–09, 71016, 71018–19, 71021, 71023–24, 71027–34, 71037–40, 71043–52, 71055, 71058, 71060–61, 71063–73, 71075, 71078–80, 71082, 71101–13, 71115, 71118–20, 71129–30, 71133–38, 71148, 71156, 71161, 71163–66, 71171–72, 71222, 71234, 71241, 71256, 71260, 71277, 71403, 71406, 71411, 71414, 71416, 71419, 71426, 71429, 71434, 71438–39, 71443, 71446–47, 71449–50, 71456–63, 71468–69, 71474–75, 71486, 71496–97, 71526

* * *

FIFTH DISTRICT

RALPH LEE ABRAHAM, Republican, of Alto, LA; born in Monroe, LA, September 16, 1954; education: studied biochemistry as an undergraduate at Louisiana State University, Baton Rouge, LA, 1972–76; D.V.M., Louisiana State University School of Veterinary Medicine, Baton Rouge, 1980; M.D., Louisiana State University School of Medicine, Shreveport, LA, 1994; professional: general family practitioner; military: Army National Guard; religion: Baptist; married: Dianne; three children, nine grandchildren; committees: Agriculture; Armed Services; elected to the 114th Congress on December 6, 2014 in a run-off election; reelected to each succeeding Congress.

Office Listings

https://abraham.house.gov https://facebook.com/CongressmanRalphAbraham
https://twitter.com/RepAbraham

417 Cannon House Office Building, Washington, DC 20515 .... (202) 225–8490

Office Listings—Continued

Chief of Staff.—Luke Letlow. FAX: 225–5639
Legislative Director.—Ted Verrill.
Communications Director.—Cole Avery.
Scheduler.—Emma Herrock.
North Louisiana Office, 426 DeSiard Street, Monroe, LA 71201 .... (318) 322–3500
Central Louisiana Office, 2003 MacArthur Drive, Building 5, Alexandria, LA 71301 .... (318) 445–0818
South Louisiana Office, 5934 Commerce Street, St. Francisville, LA 70775 .... (985) 516–5858

Parishes: AVOYELLES, CALDWELL, CATAHOULA, CONCORDIA, EAST CARROLL, EAST FELICIANA (part), FRANKLIN, JACKSON, LASALLE, LINCOLN, MADISON, MOREHOUSE, OUACHITA, RAPIDES, RICHLAND, ST. LANDRY (part), ST. HELENA (part), TANGIPAHOA (part), TENSAS, WASHINGTON, WEST CARROLL, WEST FELICIANA, AND WINN. Population (2010), 758,851.

ZIP Codes: 70401, 70422, 70426–27, 70431, 70435–38, 70441–44, 70446, 70450–51, 70455–56, 70465–66, 70512, 70570, 70577, 70589, 70656, 70712, 70722, 70730, 70748, 70750, 70761, 70775, 70782, 70787, 70789, 71001, 71031, 71201–03, 71209, 71219–20, 71223, 71225–27, 71229, 71232–35, 71237, 71238, 71243, 71245, 71247, 71250–51, 71253–54, 71259, 71261, 71263–64, 71266, 71268–70, 71272, 71275–76, 71279–80, 71282, 71286, 71291–92, 71295, 71301–03, 71316, 71322–23, 71325–28, 71331, 71333–34, 71336, 71339–43, 71345–46, 71350–51, 71353–58, 71360, 71362, 71366–69, 71371, 71373, 71375, 71377–78, 71401, 71404–05, 71407, 71409–10, 71417, 71418, 71422–25, 71427, 71430, 71432–33, 71435, 71438, 71441, 71447, 71454–55, 71457, 71463, 71465–67, 71472–73, 71479–80, 71483, 71485

* * *

SIXTH DISTRICT

GARRET GRAVES, Republican, of Baton Rouge, LA; born in Baton Rouge, January 31, 1972; education: graduated, Catholic High School; studied at Louisiana Tech, University of Alabama, and the American University; professional: coastal preservation; served as an aide for the U.S. Senate Committee on Commerce, Science, and Transportation; staff director for the U.S. Senate Subcommittee on Climate Change and Impacts; chief legislative aide to the U.S. Senate Committee on Environment and Public Works; served as the head of the Louisiana Coastal Protection and Restoration Authority; married: Carissa Vanderleest Graves; children: Ralston, Calla, and Kulshan; committees: Natural Resources; Transportation and Infrastructure; Select Committee on the Climate Crisis; elected to the 114th Congress in a runoff election on December 6, 2014; reelected to each succeeding Congress.

Office Listings

https://garretgraves.house.gov https://facebook.com/CongressmanGarrettGraves
https://twitter.com/RepGarretGraves

2402 Rayburn House Office Building, Washington, DC 20515 .... (202) 225–3901
Chief of Staff.—Paul Sawyer. FAX: 225–7313
Press Secretary.—Kevin Roig.
2351 Energy Drive, Suite 1200, Baton Rouge, LA 70808 .... (225) 442–1731
29261 Frost Road, Livingston, LA 70754 .... (225) 686–4413
908 East 1st Street NSU, Candies Hall, Suite 405, Thibodaux, LA 70301 .... (985) 448–4103

Parishes: ASCENSION, ASSUMPTION, EAST BATON ROUGE, EAST FELICIANA, IBERVILLE, LAFOURCHE, LIVINGSTON, POINTE COUPEE, ST. CHARLES, ST. HELENA, ST. JOHN THE BAPTIST, TERREBONNE, AND WEST BATON ROUGE. Population (2010), 755,607.

ZIP Codes: 70030, 70047, 70068–69, 70079, 70087, 70301–02, 70339, 70341, 70352, 70356, 70359–61, 70364, 70371–72, 70375, 70380, 70390, 70394–95, 70403, 70422, 70436, 70441, 70443, 70449, 70453, 70456, 70462, 70466, 70704, 70706–07, 70710–11, 70714–15, 70718–19, 70722, 70725–30, 70732–34, 70736–37, 70739–40, 70744, 70747–49, 70752–57, 70759–60, 70762, 70764–65, 70767, 70769–70, 70772–74, 70777–78, 70783, 70785–86, 70788, 70791, 70801–02, 70806–11, 70814–21, 70825–27, 70831, 70835–37, 70874, 70879, 70884, 70893–96, 70898

MAINE

(Population, 2010 1,328,361)

SENATORS

SUSAN M. COLLINS, Republican, of Bangor, ME; born in Caribou, ME, December 7, 1952; education: graduated, Caribou High School, 1971; B.A., *magna cum laude*, Phi Beta Kappa, St. Lawrence University, Canton, NY, 1975; Outstanding Alumni Award, St. Lawrence University, 1992; professional: staff director, Senate Subcommittee on the Oversight of Government Management, 1981–87; for 12 years, principal advisor on business issues to former Senator William S. Cohen; Commissioner of Professional and Financial Regulation for Maine Governor John R. McKernan, Jr., 1987; New England administrator, Small Business Administration, 1992–93; appointed Deputy Treasurer of Massachusetts, 1993; executive director, Husson College Center for Family Business, 1994–96; committees: chair, Special Committee on Aging; Appropriations; Health, Education, Labor, and Pensions; Select Committee on Intelligence; elected to the U.S. Senate on November 5, 1996; reelected to each succeeding Senate term.

Office Listings

https://collins.senate.gov https://facebook.com/susancollins twitter: @senatorcollins

413 Dirksen Senate Office Building, Washington, DC 20510 .... (202) 224–2523
Chief of Staff.—Steve Abbott. FAX: 224–2693
Communications Director.—Annie Clark.
Legislative Director.—Olivia Kurtz.
202 Harlow Street, Suite 20100, Bangor, ME 04401 .... (207) 945–0417
State Representative.—Carol Woodcock.
68 Sewall Street, Room 507, Augusta, ME 04330 .... (207) 622–8414
State Representative.—Mark Winter.
160 Main Street, Biddeford, ME 04005 .... (207) 283–1101
State Representative.—Alex Pelczar.
55 Lisbon Street, Suite 1100, Lewiston, ME 04240 .... (207) 784–6969
State Representative.—Carlene Tremblay.
25 Sweden Street, Suite A, Caribou, ME 04736 .... (207) 493–7873
State Representative.—Trisha House.
One Canal Plaza, Suite 802, Portland, ME 04101 .... (207) 780–3575
State Representative.—Kate Simson.

* * *

ANGUS S. KING, JR., Independent, of Brunswick, ME; born in Alexandria, VA, March 31, 1944; education: graduated, Dartmouth College, 1966; J.D., University of Virginia Law School, 1969; professional: Chief Counsel to U.S. Senate Subcommittee on Alcoholism and Narcotics for former Maine Senator William Hathaway; founded Northeast Energy Management, Inc., 1989; elected Maine's 71st Governor, 1994; reelected 1998 by one of the largest margins in Maine's history; Maine's first Independent U.S. Senator; committees: Armed Services; Energy and Natural Resources; Rules and Administration; Select Committee on Intelligence; elected to the U.S. Senate on November 6, 2012; reelected to the U.S. Senate on November 6, 2018.

Office Listings

https://king.senate.gov https://facebook.com/SenatorAngusSKingJr twitter: @SenAngusKing

133 Hart Senate Office Building, Washington, DC 20510 .... (202) 224–5344
Chief of Staff.—Kathleen Connery Dawe. FAX: 224–1946
Personal Assistant.—Joe Newlin.
DC Scheduler/Executive Assistant.—Claire Bridgeo.
Communications Director.—Matthew Felling.
State Scheduler.—Marielle Thete.
Legislative Director.—Chad Metzler.
Administrative Director.—Patrick Doak.
4 Gabriel Drive, Suite 3, Augusta, ME 04330 .... (207) 622–8292
202 Harlow Street, Suite 20350, Bangor, ME 04401 .... (207) 945–8000
169 Academy Street, Suite A, Presque Isle, ME 04769 .... (207) 764–5124
Regional Representatives: Sharon Campbell, Gail Kezer, Bonnie Pothier, Chris Rector, Edie Smith, Ben Tucker, Scott Wilkinson.

REPRESENTATIVES

FIRST DISTRICT

CHELLIE PINGREE, Democrat, of North Haven, ME; born in Minneapolis, MN, April 2, 1955; education: B.A., College of the Atlantic, Bar Harbor, ME, 1979; professional: farmer; businesswoman; religion: Lutheran; family: three children; caucuses: co-chair, Arts Caucus; Bicycle Caucus; House Oceans Caucus; House Trade Working Group; Humanities Caucus; National Guard and Reserve Component Caucus; Philanthropy Caucus; Progressive Caucus; Sustainable Energy and Environment Coalition; Women's Caucus; committees: Agriculture; Appropriations; elected to the 111th Congress on November 4, 2008; reelected to each succeeding Congress.

Office Listings

https://pingree.house.gov

2162 Rayburn House Office Building, Washington, DC 20515 .... (202) 225–6116
Chief of Staff.—Jesse Connolly. FAX: 225–5590
Scheduler.—Karen Sudbay.
2 Portland Fish Pier, Suite 304, Portland, ME 04101 .... (207) 774–5019
1 Silver Street, Waterville, ME 04901 .... (207) 873–5713

Counties: CUMBERLAND, KENNEBEC (part), KNOX, LINCOLN, SAGADAHOC, AND YORK. Population (2010), 668,515.

ZIP Codes: 03901–11, 04001–11, 04013–15, 04017, 04019–21, 04024, 04027–30, 04032–34, 04038–40, 04042–43, 04046–50, 04053–57, 04061–64, 04066, 04069–79, 04082–87, 04090–98, 04101–10, 04112, 04116, 04122–24, 04259–60, 04265, 04284, 04287, 04330, 04332–33, 04336, 04338, 04341–55, 04357–60, 04363–64, 04530, 04541, 04543–44, 04547–48, 04551, 04553–56, 04558, 04562–65, 04567–68, 04570–76, 04578–79, 04841, 04843, 04846–56, 04858–65, 04901, 04910, 04917–18, 04922, 04926–27, 04935, 04937, 04941, 04949, 04952, 04962–63

* * *

SECOND DISTRICT

JARED F. GOLDEN, Democrat, of Lewiston, ME; born in Lewiston, July 25, 1982; education: B.A., Bates College, Lewiston, ME, 2011; professional: staff, United States Senate Committee on Homeland Security and Governmental Affairs, 2011–12; staff, U.S. Senator Susan Collins of Maine, 2013; staff, Maine State House of Representatives, 2013–14; member of the Maine State House of Representatives, 2014–19 (chosen by his peers to serve as the Democratic Assistant Majority Leader in 2016); military: U.S. Marine Corps; infantryman, deploying to Afghanistan in 2004 and Iraq in 2005–06; family: married to Isobel (who served as city councilor in Lewiston, 2016–18); committees: Armed Services; Small Business; elected to the 116th Congress on November 6, 2018.

Office Listings

https://golden.house.gov

1223 Longworth House Office Building, Washington, DC 20515 .... (202) 225–6306
Chief of Staff.—Aisha Woodward. FAX: 225–2943
Scheduler.—Ainsley Jamieson.
Communications Director.—Nick Zeller.
Legislative Director.—Eric Kanter.
6 State Street, Suite 101, Bangor, ME 04401 .... (207) 249–7400
7 Hatch Drive, Suite 230, Caribou, ME 04736 .... (207) 492–6009
179 Lisbon Street, Lewiston, ME 04240 .... (207) 241–6767
FAX: 241–6770

Counties: ANDROSCOGGIN, AROOSTOOK, FRANKLIN, HANCOCK, KENNEBEC (part), OXFORD, PENOBSCOT, PISCATAQUIS, SOMERSET, WALDO, AND WASHINGTON. Population (2010), 664,180.

ZIP Codes: 04010, 04016, 04022, 04037, 04041, 04051, 04068, 04088, 04210–12, 04216–17, 04219–28, 04230–31, 04234, 04236–41, 04243, 04250, 04252–58, 04261–63, 04266–68, 04270–71, 04274–76, 04278, 04280–83, 04285–86, 04288–92, 04294, 04354, 04401–02, 04406, 04408, 04410–24, 04426–31, 04434–35, 04438, 04441–44, 04448–51, 04453–57, 04459–64, 04467–69, 04471–76, 04478–79, 04481, 04485, 04487–93, 04495–97, 04549, 04605–07, 04609, 04611–17, 04619, 04622–31, 04634–35, 04637, 04640, 04642–46, 04648–50, 04652–58, 04660, 04662, 04664, 04666–69, 04671–77, 04679–81, 04683–86, 04691, 04693–94, 04730, 04732–47, 04750–51, 04756–66, 04768–70, 04772–77, 04779–81, 04783, 04785–88, 04848–51, 04857, 04903, 04911–12, 04915, 04920–25, 04928–30, 04932–33, 04936–45, 04947, 04949–58, 04961, 04964–67, 04969–76, 04978–79, 04981–88, 04992

MARYLAND

(Population 2010, 5,773,552)

SENATORS

BENJAMIN L. "BEN" CARDIN, Democrat, of Baltimore, MD; born in Baltimore, October 5, 1943; education: graduated, City College High School, 1961; B.A., *cum laude*, University of Pittsburgh, 1964; L.L.B., 1st in class, University of Maryland School of Law, 1967; professional: attorney, Rosen and Esterson, 1967–78; elected to the Maryland House of Delegates in November 1966, served from 1967–87; Speaker of the House of Delegates, youngest Speaker at the time, 1979–87; elected to the U.S. House of Representatives in November 1986, Maryland 3rd Congressional District, served from 1987–2007; member: Associated Jewish Charities and Welfare Fund, 1985–89; trustee, Baltimore Council on Foreign Affairs, 1999–2007; trustee, Goucher College, 1999–2008; trustee, St. Mary's College, 1988–99; lifetime member, NAACP, since 1990; Board of Visitors, University of Maryland Law School, 1998–present; President's Board of Visitors, UMBC, 1993–present; Johns Hopkins University Institute for Policy Studies' National Advisory Board, 2003–present; Board of Visitors, U.S. Naval Academy, 2007–present; Board of Trustees, The James Madison Memorial Fellowship, 2010–present; awards: Congressional Award, Small Business Council of America, 1993, 1999, 2005; Public Sector Distinguished Award, Tax Foundation, 2003; Congressional Voice for Children Award, National PTA, 2009; Congressional Leadership Award, American College of Emergency Physicians, 2010; Whitney M. Young Award, Baltimore Urban League, 2011; Chesapeake Conservation Hero, Chesapeake Conservancy, 2012; commissioner, Commission on Security and Cooperation in Europe (CSCE), since 1993; co-chair, CSCE, 2007–08; chair, CSCE, 2009–10; co-chair, CSCE, 2011–13; chair, CSCE, 2013–14; ranking Senate Democrat, CSCE, 2018–present; vice president, Organization for Security and Cooperation in Europe (OSCE) Parliamentary Assembly, 2006–14; Special Representative on Anti-Semitism, Racism, and Intolerance for the OSCE Parliamentary Assembly, 2015–present; member, U.S. Holocaust Memorial Council, 2018–present; religion: Jewish; married: Myrna Edelman of Baltimore, 1964; two children (one deceased); two grandchildren; committees: ranking member, Small Business and Entrepreneurship; Environment and Public Works; Finance; Foreign Relations; elected to the U.S. Senate on November 7, 2006; reelected to each succeeding Senate term.

Office Listings

https://cardin.senate.gov https://facebook.com/senatorbencardin twitter: @SenatorCardin

509 Hart Senate Office Building, Washington, DC 20510 .... (202) 224–4524
Chief of Staff.—Chris Lynch. FAX: 224–1651
Floor Director.—Gray Maxwell.
Scheduler.—Debbie Yamada.
Communications Director.—Sue Walitsky.
State Director.—Carleton Atkinson.
100 South Charles Street, Tower I, Suite 1710, Baltimore, MD 21201 .... (410) 962–4436
FAX: 962–4256
10201 Martin Luther King Jr. Highway, Suite 210, Bowie, MD 20720 .... (301) 860–0414
451 Hungerford Drive, Suite 230, Rockville, MD 20850 .... (301) 762–2974
212 West Main Street, Suite 301C, P.O. Box 11, Salisbury, MD 21801 .... (410) 546–4250
13 Canal Street, Room 305, Cumberland, MD 21502 .... (301) 777–2957

* * *

CHRIS VAN HOLLEN, Democrat, of Kensington, MD; born in Karachi, Pakistan, January 10, 1959; education: B.A., Swarthmore College, 1982; master's in public policy, Harvard University, 1985; J.D., Georgetown University, 1990; professional: attorney; legislative assistant to former Senator Charles McC. Mathias, Jr., of Maryland; staff member, U.S. Senate Committee on Foreign Relations; senior legislative advisor to former Maryland Governor William Donald Schaefer; public service: elected, Maryland House of Delegates, 1990; elected, Maryland State Senate, 1994; married: Katherine; children: Anna, Nicholas, and Alexander; committees: Appropriations; Banking, Housing, and Urban Affairs; Budget; Environment and Public Works; elected to the 108th Congress on November 5, 2002; reelected to each succeeding Congress through 2016; elected to the U.S. Senate on November 8, 2016.

Office Listings

https://vanhollen.senate.gov

110 Hart Senate Office Building, Washington, DC 20510 .... (202) 224–4654

Office Listings—Continued

Chief of Staff.—Karen Robb.
Legislative Director.—Sarah Schenning.
Communications Director.—Bridgett Frey.
111 Rockville Pike, Suite 960, Rockville, MD 20850 .... (301) 545–1500
State Director.—Joan Kleinman.
32 West Washington Street, Suite 203, Hagerstown, MD 21740 .... (301) 797–2826
1900 North Howard Street, Suite 100, Baltimore, MD 21218 .... (667) 212–4610
60 West Street, Suite 107, Annapolis, MD 21401 .... (410) 263–1325
1101 Mercantile Lane, Suite 210, Largo, MD 20774 .... (301) 322–6560
204 Cedar Street, Suite 200C, Cambridge, MD 21613 .... (410) 221–2074

REPRESENTATIVES

FIRST DISTRICT

ANDY HARRIS, Republican, of Cockeysville, MD; born in Brooklyn, NY, January 25, 1957; education: B.S., Johns Hopkins University, Baltimore, MD, 1977; M.D., Johns Hopkins University, Baltimore, 1980; M.H.S., Johns Hopkins University, 1995; professional: anesthesiologist, as an associate professor of anesthesiology and critical care medicine; member of the Maryland State Senate, 1998–2010; Minority Whip, Maryland State Senate; military: Commander, Johns Hopkins Medical Naval Reserve Primus Unit P0605C; religion: Catholic; married: Nicole; five children; four grandchildren; committees: Appropriations; elected to the 112th Congress on November 2, 2010; reelected to each succeeding Congress.

Office Listings

https://harris.house.gov https://facebook.com/AndyHarrisMD https://twitter.com/repandyharrismd

2334 Rayburn House Office Building, Washington, DC 20515 .... (202) 225–5311
Chief of Staff.—John Dutton. FAX: 225–0254
Legislative Director.—Tim Daniels.
Press Secretary.—Julia Nista.
Scheduler.—Victoria Cesaro.
100 Olde Point Village, Suite 101, Chester, MD 21619 .... (410) 643–5425
15 Churchville Road, Suite 102B, Bel Air, MD 21014 .... (410) 588–5670
100 East Main Street, Suite 702, Salisbury, MD 21801 .... (443) 944–8624

Counties: BALTIMORE (part), CAROLINE, CARROLL (part), CECIL, DORCHESTER, KENT, HARFORD (part), QUEEN ANNE'S, SOMERSET, TALBOT, WICOMICO, AND WORCESTER. Population (2010), 721,529.

ZIP Codes: 21001, 21009, 21013–15, 21018, 21023, 21028, 21030–32, 21034, 21040, 21047–48, 21050–51, 21053, 21057, 21074, 21078, 21082, 21084–85, 21087–88, 21102, 21111, 21120, 21128, 21131–32, 21136, 21154–57, 21160–62, 21234, 21236, 21286, 21601, 21606–07, 21609–10, 21612–13, 21617, 21619–20, 21622–29, 21631–32, 21634–36, 21638–41, 21643–45, 21647–73, 21675–79, 21681–85, 21687, 21690, 21757, 21784, 21787, 21791, 21801–04, 21810–11, 21813–14, 21817, 21821–22, 21824, 21826, 21829–30, 21835–38, 21840–43, 21849–53, 21856–57, 21861–67, 21869, 21871–72, 21874–75, 21890, 21901–04, 21911–22, 21930

* * *

SECOND DISTRICT

C. A. DUTCH RUPPERSBERGER, Democrat, of Cockeysville, MD; born in Baltimore, MD, January 31, 1946; education: Baltimore City College; University of Maryland, College Park; J.D., University of Baltimore Law School, 1970; professional: attorney; partner, Ruppersberger, Clark, and Mister (law firm); public service: Baltimore County Assistant State's Attorney, 1972–80; Baltimore County Council, 1985–94; Baltimore County Executive, 1994–2002; married: the former Kay Murphy; children: Cory and Jill; committees: Appropriations; elected to the 108th Congress on November 5, 2002; reelected to each succeeding Congress.

Office Listings

https://dutch.house.gov https://facebook.com/RepDutchRuppersberger
https://twitter.com/CallMeDutch https://instagram.com/dutchruppersberger

2206 Rayburn House Office Building, Washington, DC 20515 .... (202) 225–3061
Chief of Staff.—Tara Oursler. FAX: 225–3094
Deputy Chief of Staff.—Walter Gonzales.
Scheduler.—Victoria Graham.
The Atrium, 375 West Padonia Road, Suite 200, Timonium, MD 21093 .... (410) 628–2701

Office Listings—Continued

District Director.—Cori Duggins. FAX: 628–2708
Communications Director.—Jaime Lennon.

Counties: ANNE ARUNDEL (part), BALTIMORE CITY (part), BALTIMORE COUNTY (part), HARFORD (part), AND HOWARD (part). Population (2016), 763,156.

ZIP Codes: 20701, 20723–24, 20755, 20763, 20794, 21001, 21005, 21009–10, 21015, 21017, 21022, 21027, 21030–31, 21040, 21043, 21052, 21057, 21062, 21071, 21075–78, 21085, 21090, 21093–94, 21113, 21117, 21128, 21130, 21133, 21136, 21139, 21144, 21162–63, 21204, 21206, 21208, 21212–14, 21219–22, 21224–27, 21230–31, 21234, 21236–37, 21239, 21240, 21244, 21252, 21281, 21284, 21286

* * *

THIRD DISTRICT

JOHN P. SARBANES, Democrat, of Baltimore, MD; born in Baltimore, May 22, 1962; education: A.B., *cum laude*, Woodrow Wilson School of Public and International Affairs, Princeton University, 1984; Fulbright Scholar, Greece, 1985; J.D., Harvard University School of Law, 1988; professional: law clerk to Judge J. Frederick Motz, U.S. District Court for the District of Maryland, 1988–89; admitted to Maryland Bar, 1988; member: American Bar Association; Maryland State Bar Association; attorney, Venable, LLP, 1989–2006 (chair, health care practice); founding member, board of trustees, Dunbar Project, 1990–94; board of directors, Public Justice Center, 1991–2006 (president, 1994–97); Institute for Christian and Jewish Studies, 1991–2018 (past chair, membership committee); Special Assistant to State Superintendent of Schools, State Department of Education, 1998–2005; awards: Unsung Hero Award, Maryland Chapter of the Association of Fundraising Professionals, 2006; Arthur W. Machen, Jr. Award, Maryland Legal Services Corp., 2006; married to Dina Sarbanes; three children; committees: Energy and Commerce; Oversight and Reform; elected to the 110th Congress on November 7, 2006; reelected to each succeeding Congress.

Office Listings

https://sarbanes.house.gov

2370 Rayburn House Office Building, Washington, DC 20510 .... (202) 225–4016
Chief of Staff.—Dvora Lovinger. FAX: 225–9219
Deputy Chief of Staff / Legislative Director.—Raymond O'Mara.
Scheduler.—Kelly Moura.
Legislative Assistants: Timia Crisp, Peter Gelman, Jordan Wolfe.
Communications Director.—Daniel Jacobs.
600 Baltimore Avenue, Suite 303, Towson, MD 21204 .... (410) 832–8890
44 Calvert Street, Suite 349, Annapolis, MD 21401 .... (410) 295–1679

Counties: ANNE ARUNDEL (part), BALTIMORE (part), BALTIMORE CITY (part), HOWARD (part), AND MONTGOMERY (part). Population (2010), 720,094.

ZIP Codes: 20705, 20707, 20723–24, 20759, 20777, 20783, 20832–33, 20853, 20855, 20860–62, 20866, 20868, 20882, 20901, 20903–06, 21012, 21022, 21029, 21037, 21043–46, 21054, 21056, 21060–61, 21075–77, 21090, 21093, 21108, 21113, 21117, 21122, 21128, 21136, 21139, 21144, 21153, 21201–15, 21218, 21223–27, 21229–31, 21234, 21236–37, 21239, 21252, 21281–82, 21285–86, 21401–03, 21409, 21412, 21797

* * *

FOURTH DISTRICT

ANTHONY G. BROWN, Democrat, of Bowie, MD; born in Huntington, NY, November 21, 1961; education: A.B. in government, Harvard University, Cambridge, MA, 1984; J.D., Harvard University, Cambridge MA, 1992; professional: clerkship for Chief Judge Eugene Sullivan of the United States Courts of Appeals for the Armed Forces, 1992–94; associate attorney, Wilmer, Cutler & Pickering, Washington, DC, 1994–98; Of Counsel, Gibbs & Haller, 2000–07; delegate, Maryland House of Delegates, 1999–2007; Lt. Governor of Maryland, 2007–14; co-chair, Agency Review Team for U.S. Department of Veterans' Affairs, Obama-Biden Transition, 2008–09; chair, National Lieutenant Governors Association, 2010–11; military: U.S. Army, Commissioned Aviation Officer (Captain), 1984–89; U.S. Army Reserve, 1989–2014: Colonel in Judge Advocate General's Corps, 2007–14; served in Iraq with 353rd Civil Affairs Command as senior consultant to Iraqi Ministry of Displacement and Migration, 2004–05; Commander, 153rd Legal Support Organization, 2008–11; medals and honors (partial list): Bronze Star Medal; Legion of

Merit; Meritorious Service Medal; Army commendation with 2 Oak Leaf Clusters; Iraq Campaign Medal; awards: Public Officials of the Year, *Governing* magazine, 2013; Nathan Davis Award, American Medical Association, 2013; Congressional Leadership Award, Congressional Black Caucus, 2012; Morris H. Blum Humanitarian Award, Dr. Martin Luther King, Jr., Committee, 2012; honorary doctor of laws, Hood College, 2011; Policymaker/Elected Official of the Year, Association of Defense Communities, 2011; Toll Fellow, Council of State Governments, 2000; religion: Catholic; member, St. Joseph Catholic Church, Largo, MD; family: married: Karmen Walker-Brown; three children; caucuses: Parliamentarian, Congressional Black Caucus; New Democrat Coalition; committees: Armed Services; Ethics; Natural Resources; Transportation and Infrastructure; elected to the 115th Congress on November 8, 2016; reelected to the 116th Congress on November 6, 2018.

Office Listings

https://anthonybrown.house.gov https://facebook.com/RepAnthonyBrown
https://twitter.com/RepAnthonyBrown

1323 Longworth House Office Building, Washington, DC 20515 .... (202) 225–8699
Chief of Staff.—Maia Estes.
Legislative Director.—James DeAtley.
Deputy Chief of Staff/Communications Director.—Matthew Verghese.
District Director.—Nichelle Schoultz.
Director of Operations.—Lindsey Cox.
Deputy District Director.—Ben Wolff.
9701 Apollo Drive, Suite 103, Largo, MD 20774 .... (301) 458–2600
2666 Riva Road, Suite 120, Annapolis, MD 21401 .... (410) 266–3249

Counties: ANNE ARUNDEL (part) AND PRINCE GEORGE'S (part). CITIES AND TOWNSHIPS: Andrews Air Force Base, Annapolis, Arnold, Beltsville, Bladensburg, Bowie, Brentwood, Capitol Heights, Clinton, College Park, Crofton, Crownsville, Davidsonville, District Heights, Edgewater, Fort Washington, Gambrills, Glen Burnie, Glenn Dale, Hyattsville, Lanham, Laurel, Millersville, Mount Rainier, Odenton, Oxon Hill, Pasadena, Riva, Riverdale, Severn, Severna Park, Sherwood Forest, Silver Spring, Suitland, Takoma Park, Temple Hills, and Upper Marlboro. Population (2010), 720,065.

ZIP Codes: 20705–08, 20710, 20712, 20720–22, 20724, 20735, 20737, 20740, 20743–48, 20762, 20769, 20772, 20774, 20781–85, 20903–04, 20912, 21012, 21032, 21035, 21037, 21054, 21061, 21108, 21113–14, 21122, 21140, 21144, 21146, 21401, 21405, 21409

* * *

FIFTH DISTRICT

STENY H. HOYER, Democrat, of Mechanicsville, MD; born in New York, NY, June 14, 1939; education: graduated, Suitland High School; B.S., University of Maryland, 1963; J.D., Georgetown University Law Center, 1966; honorary doctor of public service, University of Maryland, 1988; admitted to the Maryland Bar Association, 1966; professional: practicing attorney, 1966–90; Maryland State Senate, 1967–79; vice chairman, Prince George's County, MD, Senate delegation, 1967–69; chairman, Prince George's County, MD, Senate delegation, 1969–75; president, Maryland State Senate, 1975–79; member, State Board for Higher Education, 1978–81; married: Judith Pickett, deceased, February 6, 1997; children: Susan, Stefany, and Anne; Democratic Steering Committee; Democratic Whip, 108th and 109th Congresses; House Majority Leader, 110th, 111th, and 116th Congresses; Democratic Whip, 112th, 113th, 114th, and 115th Congresses; elected to the 97th Congress on May 19, 1981, by special election; reelected to each succeeding Congress.

Office Listings

https://hoyer.house.gov https://facebook.com/LeaderHoyer twitter: @LeaderHoyer

1705 Longworth House Office Building, Washington, DC 20515 .... (202) 225–4131
Chief of Staff.—Alexis Covey-Brandt. FAX: 226–0663
Maryland Chief of Staff.—Jim Notter.
U.S. Federal Courthouse, 6500 Cherrywood Lane, Suite 310, Greenbelt, MD 20770 .... (301) 474–0119
4475 Regency Place, Suite 203, White Plains, MD 20695 .... (301) 843–1577

Counties: ANNE ARUNDEL (part), CALVERT, CHARLES, PRINCE GEORGE'S (part), AND ST. MARY'S. Population (2012), 721,529.

ZIP Codes: 20601–03, 20606–09, 20611–13, 20615–26, 20628–30, 20632, 20634, 20636–37, 20639–40, 20645–46, 20650, 20653, 20657–60, 20662, 20664, 20667, 20670, 20674–76, 20678, 20680, 20684–90, 20692–93, 20695, 20705–08, 20711, 20714–16, 20720–21, 20732–33, 20735–37, 20740, 20742, 20744, 20746, 20748, 20751, 20754, 20758, 20762, 20764–65, 20769–70, 20772, 20774, 20776, 20778–79, 20781–84, 21035, 21037, 21054, 21113–14

* * *

SIXTH DISTRICT

DAVID J. TRONE, Democrat, of Potomac, MD; born in Cheverly, MD, September 21, 1955; education: B.A., Furman University, Greenville, SC, 1977, *magna cum laude*, Phi Beta Kappa; M.B.A., University of Pennsylvania, Philadelphia, PA, 1985; professional: business owner, co-founder and co-owner of Total Wine & More, the largest privately owned beer, wine, and spirits retailer in the U.S., along with his brother; awards: Distinguished Service Award, 2012, for his many contributions to the KEEN (Kids Enjoy Exercise Now) Greater DC organization, which provides recreational programs for children with developmental and physical disabilities; honored at the 2014 Ernst & Young Entrepreneur of the Year Awards Greater Washington, in the "large company" category; awarded the Anti-Defamation League's annual achievement award, 2016; Furman University's Carl F. Kohrt Distinguished Alumni Award, 2017; religion: raised Lutheran; attends Temple Beth Ami in Rockville, MD; family: married to June; four children: Michelle, Julie, Natalie, and Rob; committees: Education and Labor; Foreign Affairs; Joint Economic Committee; elected to the 116th Congress on November 6, 2018.

Office Listings

https://trone.house.gov https://facebook.com/repdavidtrone https://twitter.com/repdavidtrone

1213 Longworth House Office Building, Washington, DC 20515 .... (202) 225–2721
Chief of Staff.—Andy Flick. FAX: 225–2193
Director of Operations and Scheduling.—Jeri Sparling.
Legislative Director.—Christina Tsafoulias.
Communications Director.—Hannah Muldavin.
9801 Washingtonian Center, Gaithersburg, MD 20878 .... (301) 926–0300
1850 Dual Highway, Suite 101, Hagerstown, MD 21740 .... (240) 382–6464
217 Glenn Street, Suite 500, Cumberland, MD 21502.

Counties: ALLEGANY, FREDERICK (part), GARRETT, MONTGOMERY (part), AND WASHINGTON. CITIES AND TOWNSHIPS: Boonsboro, Boyds, Clarksburg, Cumberland, Darnestown, Frederick, Frostburg, Funkstown, Gaithersburg, Germantown, Hagerstown, Hancock, Montgomery Village, Oakland, Poolesville, Potomac, Rockville, Sharpsburg, Smithburg, Urbana, and Williamsport. Also includes Antietam National Battlefield. Population (2010), 728,400.

ZIP Codes: 20837–39, 20841–42, 20850, 20852–55, 20859, 20871–72, 20874–80, 20882, 20884–86, 20898–99, 20906, 21501–05, 21520–24, 21528–30, 21531–32, 21536, 21538–43, 21545, 21550, 21555–57, 21560–62, 21701–05, 21709–11, 21713, 21715–17, 21719–22, 21733–34, 21740–42, 21746–50, 21754–56, 21758, 21766–67, 21769, 21774, 21777, 21779–83, 21790, 21795

* * *

SEVENTH DISTRICT

KWEISI MFUME, Democrat, of Baltimore, MD; born in Baltimore, October 24, 1948; attended Baltimore City Public Schools; B.S. (*magna cum laude*), Morgan State University, Baltimore, 1976; M.A., Johns Hopkins University, Baltimore, 1984; member, Baltimore City Council, 1979–86; assistant professor, Morgan State University; program director, WEAA-FM Radio; member: Pi Sigma Alpha National Political Honor Society; NAACP; Baltimore Council on Foreign Affairs; very active in civil affairs and recipient of numerous community awards; married: Tiffany McMillian; five sons: Donald, Kevin, Keith, Ronald, and Michael; committees: Oversight and Reform; Small Business; elected to the 100th Congress, November 4, 1986; reelected to the 101st through 104th Congresses; elected to the 116th Congress, by special election, on April 28, 2020, to fill the vacancy caused by the death of U.S. Representative Elijah E. Cummings.

Office Listings

https://mfume.house.gov

2163 Rayburn House Office Building, Washington, DC 20515 .... (202) 225–4741
Chief of Staff.—Vacant.
1010 Park Avenue, Suite 105, Baltimore, MD 21201 .... (410) 951–2450
754 Frederick Road, Catonsville, MD 21228 .... (410) 818–2120
8267 Main Street, Room 102, Ellicott City, MD 21043 .... (443) 364–5413

Counties: BALTIMORE (part), BALTIMORE CITY (part), AND HOWARD (part). Population (2010), 660,523.

ZIP Codes: 20777 (part), 20833 (part), 21013 (part), 21020, 21029–31 (part), 21036, 21041–42, 21043–45 (part), 21048, 21051 (part), 21057 (part), 21065, 21074–75 (part), 21082 (part), 21092, 21093 (part), 21102 (part), 21104 (part),

21111 (part), 21117 (part), 21120 (part), 21131 (part), 21133 (part), 21136 (part), 21152, 21155 (part), 21161 (part), 21163 (part), 212101 (part), 21203, 21205 (part), 21207, 21208–15, 21216–17, 21218 (part), 21223–25 (part), 21227 (part), 21228, 21229–31 (part), 21233, 21235, 21239–40 (part), 21241, 21244 (part), 21250–51, 21263–64, 21270, 21273, 21275, 21278–79, 21286–87 (part), 21289–90, 21297, 21701, 21723, 21737–38, 21765, 21771 (part), 21784 (part), 21794, 21797 (part)

* * *

EIGHTH DISTRICT

JAMIE RASKIN, Democrat, of Takoma Park, MD; born in Washington, DC, December 13, 1962; education: B.A., *magna cum laude*, government, Harvard University, Cambridge, MA, 1983; J.D., *magna cum laude*, Harvard Law School, Cambridge, 1987; professional: teaching fellow, Harvard University Government Department, 1985–87; Assistant Attorney General, Commonwealth of Massachusetts, 1987–89; general counsel, National Rainbow Coalition, 1989–90; professor of law, Washington College of Law, American University, 1990–2016; founder, Marshall-Brennan Fellowship Program, American University, 1999–2016; Senator, Maryland State Legislature, 2007–16; religion: Jewish; member, Temple Sinai; married: Sarah Bloom Raskin; children: Hannah, Tommy, and Tabitha; caucuses: elected Caucus Leadership Representative to House Democratic Leadership; House Democratic Steering and Policy Committee; Congressional Progressive Caucus; committees: vice chair, House Administration; Judiciary; Oversight and Reform; Rules; Joint Committee on Printing; elected to the 115th Congress on November 8, 2016; reelected to the 116th Congress on November 6, 2018.

Office Listings

https://raskin.house.gov https://facebook.com/RepRaskin twitter: @RepRaskin

412 Cannon House Office Building, Washington, DC 20515 .... (202) 225–5341
Chief of Staff.—Julie Tagen.
Legislative Director.—Vacant.
Communications Director.—Samantha Brown.
51 Monroe Street, Suite 503, Rockville, MD 20850 .... (301) 354–1000
District Director.—Kathleen Connor.

Counties: CARROLL (part), FREDERICK (part), AND MONTGOMERY (part). Population (2015), 761,778.

ZIP Codes: 20810–11, 20812 (part), 20813–16, 20817 (part), 20818, 20824–25, 20827 (part), 20832–33 (part), 20847–49, 20850 (part), 20851, 20852–55 (part), 20857, 20859–60 (part), 20871–72 (part), 20877–78 (part), 20882 (part), 20889, 20894–96, 20901 (part), 20902, 20903–06 (part), 20907–08, 20910–11, 20912 (part), 20913, 20914 (part), 20915–16, 20918, 20993, 21048 (part), 21104 (part), 21157–58 (part), 21701–04 (part), 21713 (part), 21714, 21718, 21727, 21754–55 (part), 21757 (part), 21759, 21762, 21765 (part), 21769 (part), 21770, 21771 (part), 21773, 21774 (part), 21775–76, 21778, 21780 (part), 21788, 21791 (part), 21793, 21794 (part), 21797 (part), 21798

MASSACHUSETTS

(Population 2010, 6,547,629)

SENATORS

ELIZABETH WARREN, Democrat, of Cambridge, MA; born in Oklahoma City, OK, June 22, 1949; education: B.A., University of Houston, Houston, TX, 1970; J.D., Rutgers Law School, Newark, NJ, 1976; professional: Leo Gottlieb Professor of Law, Harvard Law School, 1995–2012; chief advisor, National Bankruptcy Review Commission, 1995–97; chair, Congressional Oversight Panel, 2008–10; Assistant to the President and Special Advisor to the Secretary of the Treasury for the Consumer Financial Protection Bureau, 2010–11; married: Bruce Mann; two children; three grandchildren; committees: Armed Services; Banking, Housing, and Urban Affairs; Health, Education, Labor, and Pensions; Special Committee on Aging; elected to the U.S. Senate on November 6, 2012; reelected to the U.S. Senate on November 6, 2018.

Office Listings

https://warren.senate.gov https://facebook.com/senatorelizabethwarren twitter: @SenWarren

309 Hart Senate Office Building, Washington, DC 20510 .... (202) 224–4543
Chief of Staff.—Anne Morris Reid.
Deputy Chief of Staff.—Bruno Freitas.
Legislative Director.—Beth Pearson.
2400 JFK Federal Building, 15 New Sudbury Street, Boston, MA 02203 .... (617) 565–3170
State Director.—Nikko Mendoza.
1550 Main Street, Suite 406, Springfield, MA 01103 .... (413) 788–2690

* * *

EDWARD J. MARKEY, Democrat, of Malden, MA; born in Malden, July 11, 1946; education: B.A., Boston College, Boston, MA, 1968; J.D., Boston College, Boston, 1972; U.S. Army Reserve, 1968–73; professional: member, Massachusetts House of Representatives, 1973–76; U.S. House of Representatives, 1976–2013; ranking member, Natural Resources Committee, 2011–13; chair, Select Committee on Energy Independence and Global Warming, 2007–11; chair, Subcommittee on Energy and the Environment, 2009–11; chair, Subcommittee on Telecommunications and the Internet, 2007–09; married: Dr. Susan Blumenthal; committees: Commerce, Science, and Transportation; Environment and Public Works; Foreign Relations; Small Business and Entrepreneurship; elected to the U.S. Senate, by special election, on June 25, 2013, to fill the vacancy caused by the resignation of U.S. Senator John F. Kerry to become Secretary of State; reelected to the U.S. Senate on November 4, 2014.

Office Listings

https://markey.senate.gov https://facebook.com/EdJMarkey twitter: @SenMarkey

255 Dirksen Senate Office Building, Washington, DC 20510 .... (202) 224–2742
Chief of Staff.—Paul Tencher.
Scheduler.—Sarah Butler.
Communications Director.—Giselle Barry.
JFK Federal Building, 15 New Sudbury Street, Suite 975, Boston, MA 02203 .... (617) 565–8519
222 Milliken Boulevard, Suite 312, Fall River, MA 02721 .... (508) 677–0523
1550 Main Street, 4th Floor, Springfield, MA 01103 .... (413) 785–4610

REPRESENTATIVES

FIRST DISTRICT

RICHARD E. NEAL, Democrat, of Springfield, MA; born in Springfield, February 14, 1949; education: graduated, Springfield Technical High School, 1968; B.A., American International College, Springfield, 1972; M.A., University of Hartford Barney School of Business and Public Administration, West Hartford, CT, 1976; professional: instructor and lecturer; assistant to Mayor of Springfield, 1973–78; Springfield City Council, 1978–84; Mayor, City of Springfield, 1983–89; member: Massachusetts Mayors Association; Adult Education Council; American International College Alumni Association; Boys Club Alumni Association; Emily Bill Athletic Association; Cancer Crusade; John Boyle O'Reilly Club; United States Conference of Mayors;

Valley Press Club; Solid Waste Advisory Committee for the State of Massachusetts; Committee on Leadership and Government; Mass Jobs Council; trustee: Springfield Libraries and Museums Association, Springfield Red Cross, Springfield YMCA; married: Maureen; children: Rory Christopher, Brendan Conway, Maura Katherine, and Sean Richard; committees: chair, Ways and Means; vice chair, Joint Committee on Taxation; elected on November 8, 1988 to the 101st Congress; reelected to each succeeding Congress.

Office Listings

https://neal.house.gov

2309 Rayburn House Office Building, Washington, DC 20515 .... (202) 225–5601
Chief of Staff / Press Secretary.—William Tranghese.
Scheduler / Legislative Assistant.—Tim Ranstrom.
300 State Street, Suite 200, Springfield, MA 01105 .... (413) 785–0325
District Manager.—William Powers.
78 Center Street, Pittsfield, MA 01201 .... (413) 442–0946
Office Manager.—Cynthia Clark.

Counties: BERKSHIRE, FRANKLIN (part), HAMPDEN (part), HAMPSHIRE (part), AND WORCESTER (part). Population (2010), 727,515.

ZIP Codes: 01001, 01008–13, 01020–22, 01026–30, 01032–34, 01036, 01039–40, 01050, 01056–57, 01069–71, 01073, 01075, 01077, 01079–81, 01083–86, 01089, 01092, 01095–98, 01103–09, 01118–19, 01128–29, 01151, 01199, 01201, 01220, 01222–26, 01229–30, 01235–38, 01240, 01242–45, 01247, 01253–60, 01262, 01264, 01266–67, 01270, 01301, 01330, 01337–41, 01343, 01346, 01350, 01367, 01370, 01506–07, 01515, 01518, 01521, 01550, 01566, 01571, 01585

* * *

SECOND DISTRICT

JAMES P. McGOVERN, Democrat, of Worcester, MA; born in Worcester, November 20, 1959; education: B.A., M.P.A., American University; professional: legislative director and senior aide to Congressman Joe Moakley (D-South Boston); led the 1989 investigation into the murders of six Jesuit priests and two laywomen in El Salvador; interned for and managed Senator George McGovern's (D-SD) 1984 presidential campaign in Massachusetts and delivered his nomination speech at the Democratic National Convention; board of directors, Congressional Hunger Center; married: Lisa Murray McGovern; chair: Congressional-Executive Commission on China; Democratic co-chair: Tom Lantos Human Rights Commission; caucuses: House Hunger Caucus; committees: chair, Rules; Agriculture; elected to the 105th Congress; reelected to each succeeding Congress.

Office Listings

https://mcgovern.house.gov https://facebook.com/RepJimMcGovern twitter: @RepMcGovern

408 Cannon House Office Building, Washington, DC 20515 .... (202) 225–6101
Chief of Staff.—Jennifer Chandler. FAX: 225–5759
Legislative Director.—Cindy Buhl.
Communications Director.—Matthew Bonaccorsi.
12 East Worcester Street, Suite 1, Worcester, MA 01604 .... (508) 831–7356
District Director.—Jon Niedzielski.
24 Church Street, Suite 27, Leominster, MA 01543 .... (978) 466–3552
Regional Manager.—Eladia Romero.
94 Pleasant Street, Northampton, MA 01060 .... (413) 341–8700
Regional Manager.—Jon Niedzielski.

Counties: FRANKLIN (part), HAMPDEN (part), HAMPSHIRE (part), NORFOLK (part), AND WORCESTER (part). CITIES AND TOWNSHIPS: Amherst, Athol, Auburn, Barre, Belchertown, Bellingham, Blackstone, Boylston, Deerfield, Douglas, Erving, Gill, Grafton, Greenfield, Hadley, Hardwick, Hatfield, Holden, Hubbardston, Leicester, Leominster, Leverett, Mendon, Millbury, Millville, Montague, New Braintree, New Salem, North Brookfield, Northampton, Northborough, Northbridge, Northfield, Oakham, Orange, Oxford, Palmer, Paxton, Pelham, Petersham, Phillipston, Princeton, Royalston, Rutland, Shrewsbury, Shutesbury, Spencer, Sterling, Sunderland, Sutton, Templeton, Upton, Uxbridge, Ware, Warwick, Webster, Wendell, West Boylston, West Brookfield, Westborough, Whately, Winchendon, and Worcester. Population (2010), 727,514.

ZIP Codes: 01002–03, 01005, 01007, 01031, 01035, 01037–39, 01053–54, 01060, 01062–63, 01066, 01068–69, 01072, 01074, 01082, 01088, 01093–94, 01301, 01331, 01342, 01344, 01347, 01349, 01351, 01354–55, 01360, 01364, 01366, 01368, 01370, 01373, 01375–76, 01378–79, 01420, 01436, 01438, 01440, 01452–53, 01468, 01475, 01501, 01504–05, 01516, 01519–20, 01522, 01524–25, 01527, 01529, 01531–32, 01534–37, 01540–43, 01545, 01560, 01562, 01564, 01568–70, 01581, 01583, 01585, 01588, 01590, 01602–12, 01756–57, 02019

* * *

THIRD DISTRICT

LORI TRAHAN, Democrat, of Westford, MA; born in Lowell, MA, October 27, 1973; education: B.S., regional and comparative studies, Georgetown University, Washington, DC, 1995; played NCAA Division I volleyball on a 4-year scholarship; attended Harvard Business School, Boston, MA, 2013; professional: staffer to former U.S. Representative Marty Meehan (MA-5), 1995–2005; consulting executive; software executive; married: husband David; five children: young daughters, Grace and Caroline; three grown stepsons, Thomas, Dean, and Christian; caucuses: Congressional Hispanic Caucus; Congressional Progressive Caucus; New Dems; committees: Armed Services; Education and Labor; elected to the 116th Congress on November 6, 2018.

Office Listings

https://trahan.house.gov https://facebook.com/RepLoriTrahan twitter: @RepLoriTrahan

1616 Longworth House Office Building, Washington, DC 20515 .... (202) 225–3411
Chief of Staff.—Alicia Molt West.
Deputy Chief of Staff.—Jackie Bart.
Legislative Director.—Ron Carlton.
Communications Director.—Mark McDevitt.
Scheduler.—Lisa Degou.
126 John Street, Suite 12, Lowell, MA 01852 .... (978) 459–0101
District Director.—Emily Byrne.

Counties: ESSEX, MIDDLESEX, AND WORCESTER. Population (2010), 732,090.

ZIP Codes: 01432, 01450–51, 01460, 01464, 01503, 01523, 01718–20, 01740–42, 01749, 01754, 01775–76, 01778, 01810, 01821, 01824, 01826–27, 01830, 01840–44, 01850–54, 01862–63, 01876, 01879, 01886

* * *

FOURTH DISTRICT

JOSEPH P. KENNEDY III, Democrat, of Newton, MA; born in Brighton, MA, October 4, 1980; education: graduated, Buckingham, Browne & Nichols, 1999; B.S., Stanford University, 2003; J.D., Harvard University, 2009; professional: Peace Corps, 2004–06; Assistant District Attorney, Cape and Islands Office, 2009–11; Assistant District Attorney, Middlesex Office, 2011–12; committees: Energy and Commerce; elected to the 113th Congress on November 6, 2012; reelected to each succeeding Congress.

Office Listings

https://kennedy.house.gov

304 Cannon House Office Building, Washington, DC 20515 .... (202) 225–5931
Chief of Staff.—Greg Mecher. FAX: 225–0182
Deputy Chief of Staff/Legislative Director.—Eric Fins.
Scheduler.—Nate Matteson.
8 North Main Street, Suite 200, Attleboro, MA 02703 .... (508) 431–1110
29 Crafts Street, Suite 375, Newton, MA 02458 .... (617) 332–3333
District Director.—Lisa Nelson.
Communications Director.—Dan Black.

Counties: BRISTOL (part), MIDDLESEX (part), NORFOLK (part), PLYMOUTH (part), AND WORCESTER (part). CITIES AND TOWNSHIPS: Attleboro, Bellingham, Berkley, Brookline, Dighton, Dover, Easton, Fall River, Foxboro, Franklin, Freetown, Hopedale, Hopkinton, Lakeville, Mansfield, Medfield, Medway, Milford, Millis, Needham, Newton, Norfolk, North Attleborough, Norton, Plainville, Raynham, Rehoboth, Seekonk, Sharon, Somerset, Swansea, Taunton, Wellesley, and Wrentham. Population (2010), 727,514.

ZIP Codes: 01747–48, 01757, 02019, 02030–31, 02035, 02038, 02048, 02052–54, 02056, 02067, 02070, 02093, 02171, 02334, 02347–48, 02356–57, 02375, 02445–47, 02456–62, 02464–68, 02481–82, 02492, 02494–95, 02702–03, 02712, 02715, 02718, 02725–26, 02760–63, 02766–69, 02771, 02777, 02779–80

* * *

FIFTH DISTRICT

KATHERINE M. CLARK, Democrat, of Melrose, MA; born in New Haven, CT, July 17, 1963; education: B.A., Saint Lawrence University, 1985; J.D., Cornell School of Law, 1989;

M.P.A., Harvard University, 1997; professional: admitted to the Massachusetts Bar, 1997; served as general counsel for the Massachusetts Office of Child Care Services; Chief of the Policy Division for the Massachusetts Attorney General and prosecutor; elected in March 2008 to the Massachusetts House of Representatives; elected to the Massachusetts State Senate in November 2010; religion: Protestant; married: Rodney Dowell; children: Addison, Jared, and Nathaniel; Democratic Steering and Policy Committee; committees: Appropriations; elected to the 113th Congress, by special election, on December 10, 2013; reelected to each succeeding Congress.

Office Listings

https://katherineclark.house.gov https://facebook.com/CongresswomanKatherineClark
twitter: @RepKClark

2448 Rayburn House Office Building, Washington, DC 20515 .... (202) 225–2836
Chief of Staff.—Brooke Scannell. FAX: 226–0092
Legislative Director.—Steve Thornton.
District Director.—Kelsey Perkins.
157 Pleasant Street, Suite 4, Malden, MA 02148 .... (617) 354–0292
116 Concord Street, Suite 1, Framingham, MA 01702 .... (508) 319–9757

Counties: Middlesex (part), Suffolk (part), and Worcester (part). Cities and Townships: Arlington, Ashland, Belmont, Cambridge, Framingham, Holliston, Lexington, Lincoln, Malden, Medford, Melrose, Natick, Revere, Sherborn, Southborough, Stoneham, Sudbury, Waltham, Watertown, Wayland, Weston, Winchester, Winthrop, and Woburn. Population (2010), 727,515.

ZIP Codes: 01701–05, 01721, 01746, 01760, 01770, 01772–73, 01776, 01778, 01890, 02138–42, 02148, 02151–53, 02155, 02176, 02180, 02238, 02420–21, 02451–54, 02471–72, 02474, 02476–78, 02493

* * *

SIXTH DISTRICT

SETH MOULTON, Democrat, of Salem, MA; born in Salem, October 24, 1978; education: Phillips Academy Andover, 1997; A.B., Harvard College, 2001; M.B.A., Harvard Business School, 2011; M.P.A., Harvard Kennedy School of Government, 2011; professional: U.S. Marine Corps, 2002–08; business manager; committees: Armed Services; Budget; elected to the 114th Congress on November 4, 2014; reelected to each succeeding Congress.

Office Listings

https://moulton.house.gov https://facebook.com/RepMoulton twitter: @sethmoulton, @teammoulton

1127 Longworth House Office Building, Washington, DC 20515 .... (202) 225–8020
Chief of Staff.—Alexis L'Heureux.
Communications Director.—Tim Biba.
Legislative Assistants: Olivia Hussey, Jim Miner.
Senior Foreign Policy Advisor.—Christine Wagner.
Legislative Director.—Julio Lainez.
Staff Assistant.—Ananda Bhatia.
Scheduler.—Asher MacDonald.
Department of Defense Fellow.—Billy Quinn.
Digital Director.—Peter Roby.
21 Front Street, Salem, MA 01970 .... (978) 531–1669
District Director.—Rick Jakious.
Director of Constituent Services.—Anne Meeker.
Regional Directors: Kelly Bovio, Mike Devin.
District Aides / Caseworkers: Marven Hyppolite, Neesha Suarez.
Staff Assistant.—Isis Patterson.

Counties: Essex and Middlesex. Cities and Townships: Amesbury, Andover, Bedford, Beverly, Billerica, Boxford, Burlington, Danvers, Essex, Georgetown, Gloucester, Groveland, Hamilton, Ipswich, Lynn, Lynnfield, Manchester-by-the-Sea, Marblehead, Merrimac, Middletown, Nahant, Newbury, Newburyport, North Andover, North Reading, Peabody, Reading, Rockport, Rowley, Salem, Salisbury, Saugus, Swampscott, Tewksbury, Topsfield, Wenham, West Newbury, Wakefield, and Wilmington. Population (2010), 731,681.

ZIP Codes: 01730–31, 01801, 01803, 01805, 01810, 01821–22, 01833–34, 01845, 01860, 01864, 01867, 01876, 01880, 01885, 01887, 01889, 01901–08, 01910, 01913, 01915, 01921–23, 01929–31, 01936–38, 01940, 01944–45, 01949–52, 01960–61, 01965–66, 01969–71, 01982–85

* * *

SEVENTH DISTRICT

AYANNA PRESSLEY, Democrat, of Boston, MA; born in Cincinnati, OH, February 3, 1974; education: attended Boston University, 1992–94; professional: staff, Office of U.S. Representative Joseph Kennedy II (MA-8), constituency director, scheduler, district representative, 1994–97; staff, Office of U.S. Senator John Kerry, constituency director, senior aide, scheduler, 1997–2009; member, Boston City Council, 2010–18; married: Conan Harris; committees: Financial Services; Oversight and Reform; elected to the 116th Congress on November 6, 2018.

Office Listings

https://pressley.house.gov https://facebook.com/RepAyannaPressley twitter: @RepPressley

1108 Longworth House Office Building, Washington, DC 20515 .... (202) 225–5111
Chief of Staff.—Sarah Groh.
Scheduler.—Lona Watts.
Legislative Director.—Aissa Canchola.
Communications Director.—Lina Francis.
1700 Dorchester Avenue, Boston, MA, 02122 .... (617) 850–0040
District Director.—Eric White.

Counties: MIDDLESEX (part), NORFOLK (part), AND SUFFOLK (part). CITIES AND TOWNSHIPS: Boston (part), Cambridge (part), Chelsea, Everett, Milton (part), Randolph, and Somerville. Population (2010), 727,514.

ZIP Codes: 02111, 02115–26, 02128–32, 02134–36, 02138–45, 02149–50, 02163, 02186, 02199, 02368

* * *

EIGHTH DISTRICT

STEPHEN F. LYNCH, Democrat, of South Boston, MA; born in South Boston, March 31, 1955; education: South Boston High School, 1973; B.S., Wentworth Institute of Technology; J.D., Boston College Law School; master in public administration, John F. Kennedy School of Government, Harvard University; professional: attorney; former president of Ironworkers Local #7; organizations: South Boston Boys and Girls Club; Colonel Daniel Marr Boys and Girls Club; public service: elected to the Massachusetts House of Representatives in 1994, and the State Senate in 1996; family: married to Margaret; one child: Victoria; committees: Financial Services; Oversight and Reform; Transportation and Infrastructure; elected to the 107th Congress, by special election, on October 16, 2001; reelected to each succeeding Congress.

Office Listings

https://lynch.house.gov https://facebook.com/repstephenlynch twitter: @RepStephenLynch

2109 Rayburn House Office Building, Washington, DC 20515 .... (202) 225–8273
Chief of Staff.—Kevin Ryan. FAX: 226–6513
Legislative Director.—Bruce Fernandez.
Scheduler.—Megan Hollingshead.
Communications Director.—Molly Rose Tarpey.
1 Harbor Place, Suite 304, Boston, MA 02210 .... (617) 428–2000
37 Belmont Street, Suite 3, Brockton, MA 02301 .... (508) 586–5555
1245 Hancock Street, Suite 41, Quincy, MA 02169 .... (617) 657–6305

Counties: BRISTOL (part), NORFOLK (part), PLYMOUTH (part), AND SUFFOLK (part). Population (2010), 732,884.

ZIP Codes: 02021, 02025–26, 02032, 02043, 02045, 02047, 02050, 02062, 02066, 02071–72, 02081, 02090, 02108–10, 02113–14, 02118, 02122, 02124–25, 02127, 02130–32, 02136, 02169–71, 02184, 02186, 02188–91, 02203, 02210, 02301–02, 02322, 02324, 02333, 02343, 02351, 02368, 02379, 02382, 02467, 02767

* * *

NINTH DISTRICT

WILLIAM "BILL" KEATING, Democrat, of Bourne, MA; born in Norwood, MA, September 6, 1952; education: B.A., Boston College, MA, 1974; M.B.A., Boston College, 1982; J.D., Suffolk University Law School, MA, 1985; professional: admitted to the Massachusetts

Bar in 1985 and began practice in Stoughton, MA; Massachusetts House of Representatives, 1977–84; vice chairman, Massachusetts State House Committee on Criminal Justice; Massachusetts State House Committee on Election Laws; Massachusetts State Senate, 1985–98; chairman, Joint Committee on the Judiciary; State Senate Committee on Taxation; Joint Committee on Public Safety; State Senate Steering and Policy Committee; Norfolk County District Attorney, 1999–2011; religion: Roman Catholic; family: wife, Tevis; two children, Kristen and Patrick; committees: Armed Services; Foreign Affairs; elected to the 112th Congress on November 2, 2010; reelected to each succeeding Congress.

Office Listings

https://keating.house.gov

2351 Rayburn House Office Building, Washington, DC 20515 .... (202) 225–3111
Chief of Staff.—Garrett Donovan. FAX: 225–5658
Deputy Chief of Staff / Communications Director.—Lauren Amendolara McDermott.
Legislative Director.—Michael Wertheimer.
Director of Operations.—David Oleksak.
District Director.—Michael Jackman.
50 Resnik Road, Suite 103, Plymouth, MA 02360 .... (508) 746–9000
259 Stevens Street, Suite E, Hyannis, MA 02601 .... (508) 771–6868
128 Union Street, Suite 103, New Bedford, MA 02740 .... (508) 999–6462

Counties: BARNSTABLE, BRISTOL (part), DUKES, NANTUCKET, AND PLYMOUTH. Population (2010), 727,514.

ZIP Codes: 02050, 02061, 02330, 02332, 02338–39, 02341, 02344–46, 02349, 02359–60, 02364, 02367, 02370, 02532, 02534–40, 02542–43, 02553–54, 02556–59, 02561–63, 02568, 02571, 02574–76, 02601, 02631, 02633, 02635–39, 02641–53, 02655, 02657, 02659–64, 02666–73, 02675, 02713–14, 02719–24, 02738–48, 02770, 02790

MICHIGAN

(Population 2010, 9,883,640)

SENATORS

DEBBIE STABENOW, Democrat, of Lansing, MI; born in Gladwin, MI, April 29, 1950; education: Clare High School; B.A., Michigan State University, 1972; M.S.W., Michigan State University, 1975; public service: Ingham County, MI, Commissioner, 1975–78, chairperson for 2 years; Michigan State House of Representatives, 1979–90; Michigan State Senate, 1991–94; religion: Methodist; children: Todd and Michelle; committees: ranking member, Agriculture, Nutrition, and Forestry; Budget; Energy and Natural Resources; Finance; Joint Committee on Taxation; elected to the U.S. House of Representatives in 1996 and 1998; elected to the U.S. Senate on November 7, 2000; reelected to each succeeding Senate term.

Office Listings

https://stabenow.senate.gov https://facebook.com/SenatorStabenow twitter: @SenStabenow

731 Hart Senate Office Building, Washington, DC 20510 .... (202) 224–4822
Chief of Staff.—Matt VanKuiken. FAX: 228–0325
Legislative Director.—Emily Carwell.
Scheduler.—Anne Stanski.
221 West Lake Lansing Road, Suite 100, East Lansing, MI 48823 .... (517) 203–1760
719 Griswold Street, Suite 700, Detroit, MI 48226 .... (313) 961–4330
432 North Saginaw Street, Suite 301, Flint, MI 48502 .... (810) 720–4172
3335 South Airport Road West, Suite 6B, Traverse City, MI 49684 .... (231) 929–1031
3280 East Beltline Court, NE., Suite 400, Grand Rapids, MI 49525 .... (616) 975–0052
1901 West Ridge, Suite 7, Marquette, MI 49855 .... (906) 228–8756

* * *

GARY C. PETERS, Democrat, of Bloomfield Township, MI; born in Pontiac, MI, December 1, 1958; education: B.A., Alma College, Alma, MI, 1980; M.B.A. in finance, University of Detroit, Detroit, MI, 1984; J.D., Wayne State University Law School, Detroit, 1989; M.A. in philosophy, Michigan State University, East Lansing, MI, 2007; professional: assistant vice president, Merrill Lynch, 1980–89; vice president, UBS/Paine Webber, 1989–2003; former arbitrator, Financial Industry Regulatory Authority; At-Large City Councilman, Rochester Hills, MI, 1991–93; Lieutenant Commander, Seabee Combat Warfare Specialist, U.S. Navy Reserve, 1993–2000, 2001–05; Michigan State Senator, 1995–2002; Chief Administrative Officer for the Bureau of Investments, State of Michigan, 2003; Lottery Commissioner, State of Michigan, 2003–07; former instructor, Oakland University and Wayne State University; Griffin Endowed Chair in American Government, Central Michigan University, 2007–08; member, Michigan Bar Association; religion: Episcopalian; married: Colleen Ochoa Peters; three children: Gary, Jr., Madeleine, and Alana; committees: ranking member, Homeland Security and Governmental Affairs; Armed Services; Commerce, Science, and Transportation; Joint Economic Committee; elected to the U.S. House of Representatives in 2008, 2010, and 2012; elected to the U.S. Senate on November 4, 2014.

Office Listings

https://peters.senate.gov https://facebook.com/SenGaryPeters
twitter: @SenGaryPeters instagram: @sengarypeters

724 Hart Senate Office Building, Washington, DC 20510 .... (202) 224–6221
Chief of Staff.—Eric Feldman. FAX: 224–7387
Deputy Chief of Staff.—Caitlyn Stephenson.
Legislative Director.—Zephranie Buetow.
Communications Director.—Sarah Schakow.
Scheduling Director.—Angeli Chawla.
State Director.—Elise Lancaster.
Patrick V. McNamara Federal Building, 477 Michigan Avenue, Suite 1837, Detroit, MI 48226 .... (313) 226–6020
124 West Allegan Street, Suite 1400, Lansing, MI 48933 .... (517) 377–1508
Gerald R. Ford Federal Building, 110 Michigan Street, NW., Suite 720, Grand Rapids, MI 49503 .... (616) 233–9150
407 6th Street, Suite C, Rochester, MI 48307 .... (248) 608–8040
515 North Washington Avenue, Suite 401, Saginaw, MI 48607 .... (989) 754–0112
818 Red Drive, Suite 40, Traverse City, MI 49684 .... (231) 947–7773
857 West Washington Street, Suite 308, Marquette, MI 49855 .... (906) 226–4554

REPRESENTATIVES

FIRST DISTRICT

JACK BERGMAN, Republican, of Watersmeet, MI; born in Savage, MN, on February 2, 1947; education: B.A., Gustavus Adolphus College, 1969; M.B.A., University of West Florida; military education: Naval Aviation Flight Training; Marine Corps Command and Staff College; Combined Forces Air Component Command; professional: commercial pilot for 22 years; Lieutenant General, USMC (Ret.); former Commander of Marine Forces Reserve / Marine Forces North; awards: Air Medal; Defense Meritorious Service Medal; Joint Meritorious Service Medal; Navy Distinguished Service Medal; and numerous unit awards; religion: Lutheran; family: wife, Cindy; five children; eight grandchildren; caucuses: Freshman Caucus; Great Lakes Taskforce; Native American Caucus; Pro-Life Caucus; Republican Study Committee; Sportsmen's Caucus; Working Forests Caucus; committees: Armed Services; Veterans' Affairs; elected to the 115th Congress on November 8, 2016; reelected to the 116th Congress on November 6, 2018.

Office Listings

https://bergman.house.gov https://facebook.com/RepJackBergman twitter: @RepJackBergman

414 Cannon House Office Building, Washington, DC 20515 .... (202) 225–4735
Chief of Staff.—Tony Lis. FAX: 225–4710
Deputy Chief of Staff / Legislative Director.—Michelle Jelnicky.
Scheduler / Director of Operations.—Amelia Burns.
1396 Douglas Drive, Suite 22B, Traverse City, MI 49696 .... (231) 944–7633
Director of Michigan Operations.—Melanie Collinsworth.
Communications Director.—James Hogge.
1500 West Washington Street, Suite 2, Marquette, MI 49855 .... (906) 273–2227

Counties: ALCONA, ALGER, ALPENA, ANTRIM, BARAGA, BENZIE, CHARLEVOIX, CHEBOYGAN, CHIPPEWA, CRAWFORD, DELTA, DICKINSON, EMMET, GRAND TRAVERSE, HOUGHTON, IRON, KALKASKA, KEWEENAW, LEELANAU, LUCE, MACKINAC, MANISTEE, MARQUETTE, MASON (part), MENOMINEE, MONTMORENCY, ONTONAGON, OSCODA, OTSEGO, PRESQUE ISLE, AND SCHOOLCRAFT. Population (2010), 650,222.

ZIP Codes: 48621, 48636, 48705, 48721, 48740, 48742, 49402, 49405, 49410–11, 49431, 49610–11, 49614–15, 49617, 49619, 49621–22, 49626–29, 49634–37, 49645–46, 49648, 49650, 49653–54, 49660, 49664, 49666, 49670, 49673–75, 49680, 49682, 49685–86, 49696, 49705, 49709–11, 49715, 49717, 49719, 49722–26, 49728, 49734–37, 49739–40, 49743–45, 49748–49, 49752–53, 49757, 49759–62, 49764, 49766, 49768, 49775, 49779, 49781–86, 49788, 49791–93, 49796–97, 49799, 49802, 49805–06, 49808, 49812, 49814–16, 49819–21, 49826–27, 49829, 49833–35, 49837–41, 49845, 49847–49, 49852, 49858, 49862–66, 49868, 49870–72, 49874, 49876–77, 49881, 49886–87, 49891, 49893–94, 49896, 49901–03, 49905, 49908, 49910–12, 49915–19, 49921–22, 49925, 49927, 49929–31, 49934–35, 49938, 49942, 49946, 49948, 49950, 49952–53, 49955, 49959–64, 49968–71

* * *

SECOND DISTRICT

BILL HUIZENGA, Republican, of Zeeland, MI; born in Zeeland, January 31, 1969; education: graduated, Holland Christian High School; B.A., Calvin College, Grand Rapids, MI, 1987; professional: co-owner, Huizenga Gravel Company, Jenison, MI; formerly licensed realtor and developer; married: the former Natalie Tiesma; children: Garrett, Adrian, Alexandra, William, and Sieger; committees: Financial Services; elected to the 112th Congress on November 2, 2010; reelected to each succeeding Congress.

Office Listings

https://huizenga.house.gov https://facebook.com/rephuizenga https://twitter.com/RepHuizenga

2232 Rayburn House Office Building, Washington, DC 20515 .... (202) 225–4401
Chief of Staff.—Jon DeWitte. FAX: 226–0779
Deputy Chief of Staff.—Marliss McManus.
Communications Director.—Brian Patrick.
Scheduler.—Emily Zajac.
District Director of Policy.—Matt Kooiman.
4555 Wilson Avenue Southwest, Suite 3, Grandville, MI 49418 .... (616) 570–0917
1 South Harbor Avenue, Suite 6B, Grand Haven, MI 49417 .... (616) 414–5516

Counties: ALLEGAN (part), KENT (part), LAKE, MASON (part), MUSKEGON, NEWAYGO, OCEANA, AND OTTAWA. Population (2010), 705,975.

ZIP Codes: 49303–04, 49307, 49309, 49312, 49315–16, 49318, 49321, 49323, 49327, 49329–30, 49337–38, 49343, 49345, 49349, 49401–05, 49409–10, 49412–13, 49415, 49417–18, 49420–31, 49434–37, 49440–46, 49448–49, 49451–52, 49454–

61, 49463–64, 49504, 49508–09, 49512, 49519, 49534, 49544, 49546, 49548, 49601, 49623, 49642, 49644, 49655–56, 49677, 49688

* * *

THIRD DISTRICT

JUSTIN A. AMASH, Libertarian, of Cascade, MI; born in Grand Rapids, MI, April 18, 1980; education: attended Kelloggsville Christian School and Grand Rapids Christian High School; B.A., economics, *magna cum laude*, University of Michigan, Ann Arbor, MI, 2002; J.D., University of Michigan Law School, Ann Arbor, MI, 2005; professional: small business owner; attorney; member: State Bar of Michigan, Grand Rapids Bar Association; State Representative, Michigan's 72nd District, 2009–10; religion: member, St. Nicholas Antiochian Orthodox Christian Church; married: Kara; three children; elected to the 112th Congress on November 2, 2010; reelected to each succeeding Congress.

Office Listings

https://amash.house.gov https://twitter.com/amashoffice

106 Cannon House Office Building, Washington, DC 20515 .... (202) 225–3831
Chief of Staff.—Poppy Nelson. FAX: 225–5144
Legislative Director.—Carolyn Iodice.
Scheduler.—Grace Gumina.
110 Michigan Street, NW., Suite 460, Grand Rapids, MI 49503 .... (616) 451–8383
District Director.—Matt Weibel.
70 West Michigan Avenue, Suite 212, Battle Creek, MI 49017 .... (269) 205–3823

Counties: BARRY, CALHOUN, IONIA, KENT (part), AND MONTCALM (part). CITIES: Albion, Battle Creek, Belding, Cedar Springs, East Grand Rapids, Grand Rapids, Hastings, Ionia, Lowell, Marshall, Portland, Rockford, and Springfield. Population (2010), 707,973.

ZIP Codes: 48809, 48813, 48815, 48834, 48838, 48845–46, 48849, 48851, 48860–61, 48865, 48873, 48875, 48881, 48890, 48894, 48897, 49011–12, 49014–15, 49017, 49021, 49029, 49033–34, 49037, 49046, 49050–52, 49058, 49060, 49068, 49073, 49076, 49080, 49083, 49092, 49094, 49224, 49237, 49245, 49252, 49284, 49301–03, 49306, 49315–16, 49318–19, 49321, 49323, 49325–27, 49330–31, 49333, 49341, 49343–45, 49347–48, 49403, 49418, 49435, 49501, 49503–09, 49512, 49525, 49534, 49544, 49546, 49548, 49560

* * *

FOURTH DISTRICT

JOHN MOOLENAAR, Republican, of Midland, MI; born in Midland, May 8, 1961; education: graduated from Herbert Henry Dow High School, Midland; B.S., Hope College, Holland, MI, 1983; M.P.A., Harvard University, Cambridge, MA, 1989; professional: chemist; businessman; school administrator; member of the Midland, MI, City Council, 1997–2000; member of the Michigan House of Representatives, 2003–08; member of the Michigan State Senate, 2011–14; committees: Appropriations; elected to the 114th Congress on November 4, 2014; reelected to each succeeding Congress.

Office Listings

https://moolenaar.house.gov https://facebook.com/RepMoolenaar twitter: @RepMoolenaar

117 Cannon House Office Building, Washington, DC 20515 .... (202) 225–3561
Chief of Staff.—Lindsay Ryan. FAX: 225–9679
Legislative Director.—Jayson Schimmenti.
Communications Director.—David Russell.
Executive Assistant.—Alexa Williams.
200 East Main Street, Suite 230, Midland, MI 48640 .... (989) 631–2552
District Chief of Staff.—Ashton Bortz.
201 North Mitchell Street, Suite 301, Cadillac, MI 49601 .... (231) 942–5070

Counties: CLARE COUNTY. CITIES: Clare, Farwell, Harrison, Lake, and Lake George. CLINTON COUNTY. CITIES: Dewitt, East Lansing (part), Grand Ledge (part), and St. Johns. GLADWIN COUNTY. CITIES: Beaverton and Gladwin. GRATIOT COUNTY. CITIES: Alma, Ashley, Bannister, Breckenridge, Elm Hall, Elwell, Ithaca, Middleton, North Star, Perrinton, Pompeii, Riverdale, Sumner, St. Louis, and Wheeler. ISABELLA COUNTY. CITIES: Blanchard, Millbrook, Mt. Pleasant, Rosebush, Shepherd, Weidman, and Winn. MECOSTA COUNTY. CITIES: Barryton, Big Rapids, Canadian Lakes, Chippewa Lakes, Mecosta, Morley, Paris, Remus, and Stanwood. MIDLAND COUNTY. CITIES: Coleman, Edenville, Hope, Laporte, Midland, North Bradley, Poseyville, and Sanford. MISSAUKEE COUNTY. CITIES: Falmouth, Lake City, McBain, Merritt, and Moorestown. MONTCALM COUNTY. CITIES: Alger, Butternut, Carson City, Cedar Lake, Coral, Crystal, Edmore, Entrican, Fenwick, Gowen, Greenville, Howard City, Lakeview, Langston, Maple Hill, McBride, Pierson, Sand Lake,

Sheridan, Sidney, Six Lakes, Stanton, Trufant, Vestaburg, and Vickeryville. OGEMAW COUNTY. CITIES: Rose City and West Branch. OSCEOLA COUNTY. CITIES: Evart, Hersey, LeRoy, Marion, Reed City, Sears, and Tustin. ROSCOMMON COUNTY. CITIES: Higgins Lake, Houghton Lake, Houghton Lake Heights, Prudenville, Roscommon, and St. Helen. SAGINAW COUNTY (part). CITIES: Birch Run, Brant, Burt, Carrollton, Chesaning, Frankenmuth, Freeland, Fremont, Hemlock, Merrill, Oakley, St. Charles, and University Center. SHIAWASSEE COUNTY. CITIES: Bancroft, Caledonia, Chapin, Corunna, Durand, Henderson, Laingsburg, Morrice, New Haven, New Lothrup, Owosso, Perry, Shaftsburg, Venice, and Vernon. WEXFORD COUNTY. CITIES: Cadillac and Manton. Population (2010), 705,974.

ZIP Codes: 48048, 48050, 48264, 48414–15, 48417–18, 48429, 48449, 48460, 48476, 48601, 48609–10, 48612, 48614–18, 48620, 48622–23, 48625–30, 48632–33, 48637, 48642, 48648–49, 48651, 48653–57, 48661–63, 48670, 48674, 48686, 48710, 48722, 48724, 48734, 48756, 48801, 48804, 48806–07, 48811–12, 48817–18, 48820, 48822, 48829–32, 48834–35, 48838, 48841, 48847–48, 48850, 48852, 48856–59, 48862, 48866–67, 48871–72, 48874, 48877–80, 48882–86, 48888–89, 48891, 48893–94, 48896, 49083, 49305, 49307, 49310, 49316, 49320, 49322, 49326, 49329, 49332, 49334, 49336, 49338–40, 49343, 49346–47, 49412–13, 49601, 49620, 49631–32, 49638–40, 49651, 49653, 49655, 49657, 49665, 49667–68, 49677, 49679, 49688, 49886

* * *

FIFTH DISTRICT

DANIEL T. KILDEE, Democrat, of Flint Township, MI; born in Flint, August 11, 1958; education: graduated, Northern High School, 1976; B.S., administration, Central Michigan University, 2011; married: Jennifer, 1988; children: Ryan, Kenneth, and Katy; two grandchildren, Caitlin and Colin; Chief Deputy Whip; Democratic Steering and Policy Committee; committees: Budget; Ways and Means; elected to the 113th Congress, November 6, 2012; reelected to each succeeding Congress.

Office Listings

https://dankildee.house.gov https://facebook.com/RepDanKildee twitter: @RepDanKildee

203 Cannon House Office Building, Washington, DC 20515 .... (202) 225–3611
Chief of Staff.—Mitchell Rivard. FAX: 225–6393
Deputy Chief of Staff.—Ghada Alkiek.
Legislative Director.—Troy Nienberg.
Scheduler / Executive Assistant.—Elizabeth Virga.
601 South Saginaw Street, Suite 403, Flint, MI 48502 .... (810) 238–8627
District Director.—Chris Flores. FAX: 238–8658

Counties: ARENAC, BAY, GENESEE, IOSCO, SAGINAW (part), AND TUSCOLA (part). Population (2010), 705,975.

ZIP Codes: 48411, 48415, 48418, 48420–21, 48423, 48429–30, 48433, 48436–39, 48442, 48449, 48451, 48457–58, 48462–64, 48473, 48480, 48501–07, 48509, 48519, 48529, 48531–32, 48550–57, 48601–08, 48610–11, 48613, 48623, 48631, 48634, 48638, 48642, 48650, 48652, 48658–59, 48663, 48703, 48706–08, 48710, 48722, 48724, 48730, 48732–34, 48737–39, 48743, 48745–50

* * *

SIXTH DISTRICT

FRED UPTON, Republican, of St. Joseph, MI; born in St. Joseph, April 23, 1953; education: graduated, Shattuck School, Fairbault, MN, 1971; B.A., journalism, University of Michigan, Ann Arbor, 1975; professional: field manager, Dave Stockman Campaign, 1976; staff member, Congressman Dave Stockman, 1976–80; legislative assistant, Office of Management and Budget, 1981–83; deputy director of Legislative Affairs, 1983–84; director of Legislative Affairs, 1984–85; member: First Congregational Church, Emil Verbin Society; married: the former Amey Rulon-Miller; committees: Energy and Commerce; elected to the 100th Congress on November 4, 1986; reelected to each succeeding Congress.

Office Listings

https://upton.house.gov https://facebook.com/RepFredUpton twitter: @RepFredUpton

2183 Rayburn House Office Building, Washington, DC 20515 .... (202) 225–3761
Chief of Staff.—Joan Hillebrands. FAX: 225–4986
720 Main Street, St. Joseph, MI 49085 .... (269) 982–1986
350 East Michigan Avenue, Suite 130, Kalamazoo, MI 49007 .... (269) 385–0039

Counties: ALLEGAN (part), BERRIEN, CASS, KALAMAZOO, ST. JOSEPH, AND VAN BUREN. CITIES AND TOWNSHIPS: Allegan, Augusta, Bangor, Baroda, Benton Harbor, Berrien Center, Berrien Springs, Bloomingdale, Breedsville, Bridgman, Buchanan, Burr Oak, Cassopolis, Centreville, Climax, Coloma, Colon, Comstock, Constantine, Covert, Decatur, Delton, Douglas, Dowagiac, Eau Claire, Edwardsburg, Fulton, Galesburg, Galien, Gobles, Grand Junction, Hagar Shores, Harbert,

Hartford, Hickory Corners, Holland, Jones, Kalamazoo, Lakeside, Lawrence, Lawton, Leonidas, Marcellus, Mattawan, Mendon, Nazareth, New Buffalo, New Troy, Niles, Nottawa, Oshtemo, Otsego, Paw Paw, Plainwell, Portage, Pullman, Richland, Riverside, Saugatuck, Sawyer, Schoolcraft, Scotts, Sodus, South Haven, St. Joseph, Stevensville, Sturgis, Three Oaks, Three Rivers, Union, Union Pier, Vandalia, Vicksburg, Watervliet, and White Pigeon. Population (2010), 705,974.

ZIP Codes: 49001–13, 49015, 49019, 49022–24, 49026–27, 49030–32, 49034, 49038–43, 49045, 49047–48, 49052–53, 49055–57, 49060–67, 49070–72, 49074–75, 49077–81, 49083–85, 49087–88, 49090–91, 49093, 49095, 49097–99, 49101–04, 49106–07, 49111–13, 49115–17, 49119–20, 49125–30, 49311, 49314–16, 49323, 49328, 49333, 49335, 49344, 49348, 49406, 49408, 49416, 49419, 49423, 49426, 49450, 49453, 49464

* * *

SEVENTH DISTRICT

TIMOTHY L. WALBERG, Republican, of Tipton, MI; born in Chicago, IL, April 12, 1951; education: studied forestry at Western Illinois University, Macomb, IL; graduated from Moody Bible Institute, Chicago, IL; B.A., religious education, Fort Wayne Bible College, 1975; M.A., communications, Wheaton College Graduate School, Wheaton, IL, 1978; professional: minister, New Haven Baptist Church, 1973–77; minister, Union Gospel Church, 1978–82; member of the Michigan House of Representatives, 1983–99; president, Warren Reuther Center for Education and Community Impact, 1999–2000; division manager, Moody Bible Institute, 2000–06; married: Susan; three adult children; committees: Education and Labor; Energy and Commerce; elected to the U.S. House of Representatives for the 110th Congress, 2007–09; elected to the 112th Congress on November 2, 2010; reelected to each succeeding Congress.

Office Listings

https://walberg.house.gov   https://facebook.com/RepWalberg   twitter: @RepWalberg

2266 Rayburn House Office Building, Washington, DC 20515 .... (202) 225–6276
Chief of Staff.—R.J. Laukitis. FAX: 225–6281
Deputy Chief of Staff / Communications Director.—Dan Kotman.
Legislative Director.—Joanna Brown.
401 West Michigan Avenue, Jackson, MI 49201 .... (517) 780–9075

Counties: BRANCH, EATON, HILLSDALE, JACKSON, LENAWEE, MONROE, AND WASHTENAW (part). Population (2010), 705,974.

ZIP Codes: 48103, 48105, 48108, 48111, 48117–18, 48130–31, 48133–34, 48137, 48140, 48144–45, 48157–62, 48164, 48166–70, 48176–79, 48182, 48189–91, 48197, 48813, 48821, 48827, 48837, 48849, 48861, 48876, 48890, 48897, 48906, 48911, 48917, 49011, 49021, 49028, 49030, 49036, 49040, 49073, 49076, 49082, 49089, 49092, 49094, 49096, 49201–03, 49220–21, 49224, 49227–30, 49232–38, 49240–42, 49245–56, 49259, 49261–72, 49274, 49276–77, 49279, 49282–89

* * *

EIGHTH DISTRICT

ELISSA SLOTKIN, Democrat, of Holly, MI; born on July 10, 1976; education: A.B., Cornell University, 1998; M.A., Columbia University, 2003; professional: analyst, Central Intelligence Agency; director for Iraq, National Security Council, The White House; senior advisor on Iraq, U.S. Department of State; senior advisor on Middle East Transition, Office of the Undersecretary of Defense for Policy; Acting Assistant Secretary of Defense for International Security Affairs, Office of the Secretary of Defense; married: David Moore; committees: Armed Services; Homeland Security; elected to the 116th Congress on November 6, 2018.

Office Listings

https://slotkin.house.gov

1531 Longworth House Office Building, Washington, DC 20515 .... (202) 225–4872
Chief of Staff.—Mela Louise Norman. FAX: 225–5820
Legislative Director.—Danielle Most.
Press Secretary.—Hannah Lindow.
Scheduler.—Megan Birleson.
1100 West Saginaw Street, Suite 3A, Lansing, MI 48915 .... (517) 993–0510
Deputy Chief of Staff.—Alexa Stanard.
Deputy District Director.—Samantha Woll.
445 South Livernois Road, Suite 316, Rochester Hills, MI 48307 .... (517) 993–0510

Counties: INGHAM, LIVINGSTON, AND OAKLAND (part). CITIES AND TOWNSHIPS: Addison Township, Brandon Township, Brighton, Cohoctah, Dansville, East Lansing, Fenton, Fowlerville, Gregory, Groveland Township, Hamburg, Hartland,

Haslett, Hell, Holly Township, Holt, Howell, Independence Township, Lakeland, Lansing, Leslie, Mason, Meridian Township, Oak Grove, Oakland Township, Okemos, Onondaga, Orion Township, Oxford Township, Pinckney, Rochester, Rochester Hills (part), Rose Township, Springfield Township, Stockbridge, Unadilla, Village of Clarkston, Webberville, and Williamston. Population (2010), 705,974.

ZIP Codes: 48114, 48116, 48139, 48143, 48306–07, 48309, 48346, 48350, 48359–60, 48362–63, 48366–67, 48370–71, 48430, 48442, 48462, 48805, 48816, 48819, 48824–26, 48842–44, 48854–55, 48864, 48895, 48901, 48909–10, 48912–13, 48915–16, 48918–19, 48921–22, 48924, 48929–30, 48933, 48937, 48951, 48956, 48980, 49251

* * *

NINTH DISTRICT

ANDY LEVIN, Democrat, of Bloomfield Hills, MI; born in Detroit, Wayne County, MI, August 10, 1960; education: attended Berkley High School, Berkley, MI, and graduated from Bethesda-Chevy Chase High School, Bethesda, MD, 1978; B.A., Williams College, Williamstown, MA, 1983; M.A., University of Michigan, Ann Arbor, MI, 1990; J.D., Harvard University, Cambridge, MA, 1994; professional: union organizer, SEIU, 1983–88; staff attorney, U.S. Commission on the Future of Worker-Management; trade union director; chief workforce officer, state of Michigan, 2007–10; acting director, Michigan Department of Energy, Labor, and Economic Growth, 2007–11; business executive; religion: Judaism; married: Mary; children: Jacob, Saul, Ben, and Molly; committees: Education and Labor; Foreign Affairs; elected to the 116th Congress on November 6, 2018.

Office Listings

https://andylevin.house.gov https://facebook.com/repandylevin
https://twitter.com/RepAndyLevin https://instagram.com/RepAndyLevin

228 Cannon Office House Building, Washington, DC 20515 .... (202) 225–4961
Chief of Staff.—Ven Neralla. FAX: 225–3227
Legislative Director.—Catherine Rowland.
Communications Director.—Austin Laufersweiler.
30500 Van Dyke Avenue, Suite 306, Warren, MI 48093 .... (586) 498–7122
District Director.—Walt Herzig.
Constituent Services Director.—Zeenath Hussain.

Counties: MACOMB (part) AND OAKLAND (part). CITIES: Berkley, Beverly Hills, Bingham Farms, Bloomfield Township, Clawson (part), Center Line, Clinton Township, Eastpointe, Ferndale, Franklin, Fraser, Lake Township, Hazel Park, Huntington Woods, Madison Heights, Mount Clemens, Pleasant Ridge, Roseville, Royal Oak, St. Clair Shores, Southfield Township, Sterling Heights (part), and Warren. Population (2010), 705,975.

ZIP Codes: 48009 (part), 48015, 48017 (part), 48021, 48025 (part), 48026, 48030, 48034–36, 48038, 48043, 48045 (part), 48066–67, 48069–73, 48080–82, 48084 (part), 48088–89, 48091–93, 48220 (part), 48236–37 (part), 48301–02 (part), 48304 (part), 48310 (part), 48312–13 (part), 48320 (part), 48323 (part), 48341 (part)

* * *

TENTH DISTRICT

PAUL MITCHELL, Republican, of Dryden, MI; born in Boston, MA, November 14, 1956; education: attended James Madison College at Michigan State University, East Lansing, MI, 1978; professional: owned and operated Ross Medical Education Center; married: Sherry Mitchell; children: Brendan, Meghann, Luke, Claire, Emma, and Declan; committees: Armed Services; Transportation and Infrastructure; elected to the 115th Congress on November 8, 2016; reelected to the 116th Congress on November 6, 2018.

Office Listings

https://mitchell.house.gov https://facebook.com/reppaulmitchell
https://twitter.com/RepPaulMitchell

211 Cannon House Office Building, Washington, DC 20515 .... (202) 225–2106
Chief of Staff.—Kyle Kizzier. FAX: 226–1169
Legislative Director.—Pat Pelletier.
Communications Director.—Alex Davidson.
Scheduler.—Molly Harrington.
48701 Van Dyke Avenue, Shelby Township, MI 48317 .... (586) 997–5010

Counties: HURON, LAPEER, MACOMB (part), SAINT CLAIR, SANILAC, AND TUSCOLA (part). Population (2010), 719,712.

ZIP Codes: 48001–03, 48005–06, 48014, 48022–23, 48027–28, 48032, 48035, 48039–42, 48044–45, 48047–51, 48054, 48059–60, 48062–65, 48074, 48079, 48094–97, 48306, 48312–17, 48367, 48371, 48401, 48412–13, 48416, 48419,

48421–23, 48426–28, 48432, 48435, 48438, 48441, 48444–46, 48450, 48453–56, 48461–72, 48475, 48720, 48725–27, 48729, 48731, 48735, 48759–60, 48767

* * *

ELEVENTH DISTRICT

HALEY M. STEVENS, Democrat, of Rochester Hills, MI; born in Rochester Hills, Oakland County, MI, June 24, 1983; education: graduated from Ernest W. Seaholm High School, Birmingham, MI, 2001; B.A., American University, Washington, DC, 2005; M.A., American University, Washington, DC, 2007; professional: presidential campaign aide; chief of staff, U.S. Auto Rescue Task Force, 2009–11; business executive; caucuses: Automotive Caucus; Future of Work Task Force; Gun Violence Prevention Task Force; India Caucus; Manufacturing Caucus; New Democrat Coalition; PFAS Task Force; committees: Education and Labor; Science, Space, and Technology; elected to the 116th Congress on November 6, 2018.

Office Listings

https://stevens.house.gov https://facebook.com/RepHaleyStevens
https://twitter.com/RepHaleyStevens https://instagram.com/rephaleystevens

227 Cannon House Office Building, Washington, DC 20515 .... (202) 225–8171
Chief of Staff.—Justin German. FAX: 225–2667
Legislative Director.—Sarah Reingold.
Press Secretary.—Blake McCarren.
Scheduler.—John Martin.
37695 Pembroke Avenue, Livonia, MI 48152 .... (734) 853–3040
District Director.—Colleen Pobur.
Deputy District Director.—Eli Isaguirre.

Counties: WAYNE COUNTY. CITIES: Caton Township, Livonia, Northville, Northville Township, Plymouth, and Plymouth Township. OAKLAND COUNTY. CITIES: Auburn Hills, Birmingham, Bloomfield Hills, Clawson, Commerce Township, Farmington, Highland, Lake Angelus, Lyon Township, Milford, Novi, Rochester Hills, South Lyon, Troy, Walled Lake, Waterford, West Bloomfield, White Lake, Wixom, and Wolverine Lake. Population (2010), 705,974.

ZIP Codes: 48009, 48017, 48073, 48083–85, 48098, 48150, 48152, 48154, 48165, 48167–68, 48170, 48178, 48187–88, 48304, 48309, 48320, 48323–24, 48326–29, 48335–36, 48341, 48346, 48356–57, 48359, 48374–75, 48377, 48380–83, 48386, 48390, 48393, 48442

* * *

TWELFTH DISTRICT

DEBBIE DINGELL, Democrat, of Dearborn, MI; born in Detroit, MI, November 23, 1953; education: B.S., Georgetown University, 1975; M.S., Georgetown University, 1998; professional: president, General Motors Foundation; executive director of Global Community Relations and Government Relations, GM; president, D2 Strategies; electoral: Wayne State University Board of Governors; married: former Congressman John D. Dingell (deceased); co-chair, House Democratic Policy and Communications Committee (DPCC); committees: Energy and Commerce; Natural Resources; elected to the 114th Congress on November 4, 2014; reelected to each succeeding Congress.

Office Listings

https://debbiedingell.house.gov https://facebook.com/RepDebbieDingell
https://twitter.com/RepDebDingell

116 Cannon House Office Building, Washington, DC 20515 .... (202) 225–4071
Chief of Staff.—Greg Sunstrum.
Legislative Director.—Kevin Rambosk.
Scheduler.—Bobby Mainville.
Communications Director.—Maggie Rousseau.
19855 West Outer Drive, Suite 103–E, Dearborn, MI 48124 .... (313) 278–2936
District Administrator.—Kelly Tebay.
301 West Michigan Avenue, Ypsilanti, MI 48197 .... (734) 481–1100
Office Manager.—Katy Jesaitis.

Counties: WAYNE COUNTY (part). CITIES AND TOWNSHIPS: Allen Park, Belleville, Brownstone Township, Brownstown, Dearborn, Dearborn Heights (part), Flat Rock, Gibraltar, Grosse Ile Township, Huron Township, Lincoln Park, Riverview, Rockwood, Southgate, Sumpter Township, Taylor, Trenton, Van Buren Township, Woodhaven, and Wyandotte. WASHTENAW COUNTY (part). CITIES AND TOWNSHIPS: Ann Arbor, Ann Arbor Township, Pittsfield Township, Scio Township, Ypsilanti, and Ypsilanti Township. Population (2018), 709,832.

ZIP Codes: 48101, 48103–05, 48108–09, 48111, 48114, 48120, 48122, 48124–28, 48130, 48134, 48139, 48146, 48164, 48173–74, 48176, 48180, 48183–84, 48188, 48192–93, 48195, 48197–98, 48127, 48229

* * *

THIRTEENTH DISTRICT

RASHIDA TLAIB, Democrat, of Detroit, MI; born in Detroit, Wayne County, July 24, 1976; education: graduated from Southwestern High School, Detroit, 1994; B.A., Wayne State University, Detroit, 1998; J.D., Cooley Law School, Lansing, MI, 2004; professional: lawyer; staff, Michigan State House of Representatives, 2007–08; member of the Michigan State House of Representatives, 2009–14; religion: Islam; children: two; commissions, caucuses: Auto Caucus; Black Maternal Healthcare Caucus; Congressional Freethought Caucus; Congressional Progressive Caucus; Democratic Women's Caucus; Free Syria Caucus; Great Lakes-St. Lawrence Legislative Caucus; Historically Black Colleges and Universities Caucus; House Manufacturing Caucus; LGBT Equality Caucus; Medicare for All Caucus; Pro-Choice Caucus; Small Brewers Caucus; committees: Financial Services; Oversight and Reform; elected to the 116th Congress on November 6, 2018.

Office Listings

https://tlaib.house.gov https://facebook.com/RepRashida twitter: @RepRashida

1628 Longworth House Office Building, Washington, DC 20515 .... (202) 225–5126
Chief of Staff.—Ryan Anderson. FAX: 225–0072
Legislative Director.—Vacant.
Counsel.—Andrew Goddeeris.
Communications Director.—Denzel McCampbell.
Press Secretary.—Adrienne Salazar.
Office Manager / Scheduler.—Sara Maaiki.
7700 2nd Avenue, Detroit, MI 48202 .... (313) 463–6220
District Director.—Larissa Richardson.

Counties: WAYNE COUNTY (part). CITIES AND TOWNSHIPS: Dearborn Heights, Detroit, Ecorse, Garden City, Highland Park, Inkster, Melvindale, Redford, River Rouge, Romulus, Wayne, and Westland. Population (2010), 699,214.

ZIP Codes: 48122 (part), 48125–26 (part), 48127, 48135, 48141, 48174 (part), 48184 (part), 48185–86, 48201–02, 48203 (part), 48204, 48206, 48207 (part), 48208, 48209–17 (part), 48218–19, 48221 (part), 48223, 48226–27 (part), 48228, 48229 (part), 48235 (part), 48238 (part), 48239–40, 48242

* * *

FOURTEENTH DISTRICT

BRENDA L. LAWRENCE, Democrat, of Bloomfield, MI; born in Detroit, MI, October 18, 1954; education: attended University of Detroit; B.S., public administration, Central Michigan University; professional: U.S. Postal Service, letter carrier to human relations executive, 1978–2008; Mayor of Southfield, 2001–15; Southfield City Council, 1996–2000; South Field City Council President, 1999; Southfield Public School Board of Education President, Vice President, Secretary, 1992–96; religion: Christian, non-denominational; married: M. McArthur Lawrence; children: Michael and Michelle; granddaughter, Aysa; caucuses: Congressional Black Caucus; Congressional Caucus on Foster Youth; Congressional Progressive Caucus; Democratic Women's Caucus; Former Mayors Caucus; New Democratic Coalition; Skilled Workforce Caucus; committees: Appropriations; Oversight and Reform; elected to the 114th Congress on November 4, 2014; reelected to each succeeding Congress.

Office Listings

https://lawrence.house.gov https://facebook.com/Rep.BLawrence https://twitter.com/RepLawrence

2463 Rayburn House Office Building, Washington, DC 20515 .... (202) 225–5802
Chief of Staff.—Ryan Hedgepeth. FAX: 226–2356
Legislative Director.—Varun Krovi.
Communications Director.—Denise Tolliver.
26700 Lahser Road, Suite 330, Southfield, MI 48033 .... (248) 356–2052
District Office Director.—Rose Dady.

Counties: OAKLAND (part) AND WAYNE (part). CITIES AND TOWNSHIPS: Detroit, Farmington Hills, Grosse Pointe, Grosse Pointe Farms, Grosse Pointe Park, Grosse Pointe Woods, Hamtramck, Harper Woods, Keego Harbor, Lathrup Village, Oak Park, Orchard Lake, Pointe Shores, Pontiac, Royal Oak Township, Southfield, Sylvan Lake, Village of Grosse Pointe Shores, and West Bloomfield. Population (2010), 706,429.

ZIP Codes: 48033–34, 48075–76, 48203, 48205, 48207, 48209, 48212, 48214, 48216, 48221, 48224–26, 48230, 48233–35, 48237, 48243, 48320–23, 48325, 48331, 48334, 48336, 48340–43

MINNESOTA

(Population 2010, 5,303,925)

SENATORS

AMY KLOBUCHAR, Democrat, of Minneapolis, MN; born in Plymouth, MN, May 25, 1960; education: B.A., *magna cum laude*, Yale University, 1982; J.D., *magna cum laude*, University of Chicago Law School, 1985; professional: attorney at law firm Dorsey & Whitney, 1985–93, partner in 1993; partner at law firm Gray, Plant, Mooty, Mooty & Bennett, 1993–98; public service: City of Minneapolis Prosecutor, 1988; elected Hennepin County Attorney, 1998, reelected, 2002; religion: Congregationalist; married: John; child: Abigail; committees: ranking member, Rules and Administration; Agriculture, Nutrition, and Forestry; Commerce, Science, and Transportation; Judiciary; Joint Committee on the Library; Joint Committee on Printing; Joint Economic Committee; elected to the U.S. Senate on November 7, 2006; reelected to each succeeding Senate term.

Office Listings

https://klobuchar.senate.gov twitter: @SenAmyKlobuchar

425 Dirksen Senate Office Building, Washington, DC 20510 .... (202) 224–3244
Chief of Staff.—Elizabeth ''Lizzy'' Peluso.
Legislative Director.—Elizabeth Farrar.
Deputy Chief of Staff.—Hannah Hankins.
Communications Director.—Jonathan Beeton.
Scheduler.—Blair Mallin.
Director of Operations.—Devan Cayea.
1200 Washington Avenue South, Suite 250, Minneapolis, MN 55415 .... (612) 727–5220
State Director.—Ben Hill.
1130½ 7th Street, Northwest, Suite 212, Rochester, MN 55901 .... (507) 288–5321
121 4th Street South, Moorhead, MN 56560 .... (218) 287–2219
Olcott Plaza, 820 9th Street North, Suite 105, Virginia, MN 55792 .... (218) 741–9690

* * *

TINA SMITH, Democrat, of Minneapolis, MN; born March 4, 1958; education: B.A., Stanford University, Stanford, CA, 1980; M.B.A., Tuck School of Business at Dartmouth College, Hanover, NH, 1984; professional: began working at Minnesota-based General Mills in 1984; later opened her own small business; went on to serve as vice president for external affairs at Planned Parenthood Minnesota, North Dakota, South Dakota (PPMNS); served as chief of staff to both Minneapolis Mayor R.T. Rybak and Governor Mark Dayton; in 2014, Tina was elected to serve as Minnesota's 48th Lieutenant Governor; married: Archie Smith, for more than 30 years; two sons and two daughters-in-law; committees: Agriculture, Nutrition, and Forestry; Banking, Housing, and Urban Affairs; Health, Education, Labor, and Pensions; Indian Affairs; appointed to the U.S. Senate on December 13, 2017, to fill the vacancy caused by the resignation of Senator Al Franken; took the oath of office on January 3, 2018; subsequently elected to the U.S. Senate in a special election on November 6, 2018, for the remainder of the term ending January 3, 2021.

Office Listings

https://smith.senate.gov https://facebook.com/USSenTinaSmith twitter: @SenTinaSmith

720 Hart Senate Office Building, Washington, DC 20510 .... (202) 224–5641
Chief of Staff.—Jeff Lomonaco. FAX: 224–0044
Deputy Chief of Staff/Communications Director.—Ed Shelleby.
State Director.—Sara Silvernail.
Legislative Director.—Gohar Sedighi.
Scheduler.—Michael Weiss.
Press Secretary.—Molly Morrissey.
60 East Plato Boulevard, Suite 220, St. Paul, MN 55107 .... (651) 221–1016
FAX: 221–1078
1210½ Seventh Street, NW., Suite 218, Rochester, MN 55901 .... (507) 288–2003
FAX: 288–2217
515 West First Street, Suite 104, Duluth, MN 55802 .... (218) 722–2390
FAX: 722–4131
819 Center Avenue, Suite 2A, Moorhead, MN 56560 .... (218) 284–8721
FAX: 284–8722

REPRESENTATIVES

FIRST DISTRICT

JIM HAGEDORN, Republican, of Blue Earth, MN; born in Blue Earth, August 4, 1962; education: B.A., government and politics, George Mason University, Fairfax, VA, 1993; professional: Legislative Assistant to U.S. Representative Arlan Stangeland (MN-7), 1984–91; Director of Legislative and Public Affairs, Financial Management Service, 1991–98, and Congressional Affairs Officer, Bureau of Engraving and Printing, U.S. Treasury Department; committees: Agriculture; Small Business; elected to the 116th Congress on November 6, 2018.

Office Listings

https://hagedorn.house.gov https://facebook.com/RepHagedorn twitter: @RepHagedorn

325 Cannon House Office Building, Washington, DC 20515 .... (202) 225–2472
Chief of Staff.—Peter Su. FAX: 225–3433
Legislative Director.—Jim Hahn.
Scheduler.—Karin Mantor.
11 Civic Center Plaza, Suite 301, Mankato, MN 56001 .... (507) 323–6090
1530 Greenview Drive, SW., Suite 207, Rochester, MN 55902 .... (507) 323–6090

Counties: BLUE EARTH COUNTY. CITIES: Amboy, Eagle Lake, Garden City, Good Thunder, Lake Crystal, Madison Lake, Mankato, Mapleton, Pemberton, St. Clair, and Vernon Center. BROWN COUNTY. CITIES: Cobden, Comfrey (part), Evan, Hanska, New Ulm, Sleepy Eye, and Springfield. COTTONWOOD COUNTY (part). CITIES: Bingham Lake, Mountain Lake, and Windom. DODGE COUNTY. CITIES: Claremont, Dodge Center, Hayfield, Kasson, Mantorville, and West Concord. FARIBAULT COUNTY. CITIES: Blue Earth, Bricelyn, Delavan, Easton, Elmore, Frost, Huntley, Kiester, Minnesota Lake, Walters, Wells, and Winnebago. FILLMORE COUNTY. CITIES: Canton, Chatfield (part), Fountain, Harmony, Lanesboro, Mabel, Ostrander, Peterson, Preston, Rushford, Rushford Village, Spring Valley, Whalan, and Wykoff. FREEBORN COUNTY. CITIES: Albert Lea, Alden, Clarks Grove, Conger, Emmons, Freeborn, Geneva, Glenville, Hartland, Hayward, Hollandale, London, Manchester, Myrtle, Oakland, and Twin Lakes. HOUSTON COUNTY. CITIES: Brownsville, Caledonia, Eitzen, Hokah, Houston, La Crescent (part), and Spring Grove. JACKSON COUNTY. CITIES: Alpha, Heron Lake, Jackson, Lakefield, Okabena, and Wilder. LE SUEUR COUNTY. CITIES: Cleveland, Elysian, Heidelberg, Kasota, Kilkenny, Le Center, Le Sueur, Montgomery, New Prague, and Waterville. MARTIN COUNTY. CITIES: Ceylon, Dunnell, Fairmount, Granada, Northrop, Sherburn, Truman, and Welcome. MOWER COUNTY. CITIES: Adams, Austin, Brownsdale, Dexter, Elkton, Grand Meadow, Le Roy, Lyle, Racine, Rose Creek, Sargeant, Taopi, and Waltham. NICOLLET COUNTY. CITIES: Courtland, Lafayette, North Mankato, and St. Peter. NOBLES COUNTY. CITIES: Adrian, Bigelow, Brewster, Dundee, Ellsworth, Kinbrae, Lismore, Round Lake, Rushmore, Wilmont, and Worthington. OLMSTED COUNTY. CITIES: Byron, Chatfield (part), Dover, Eyota, Oronoco, Pine Island, Rochester, and Stewartville. RICE COUNTY (PART). CITIES: Faribault, Lorisdale, Morristown, Shieldsville, Walcott, Warsaw, Webster, and Wheatland. ROCK COUNTY. CITIES: Beaver Creek, Hardwick, Hills, Jasper, Kenneth, Luverne, Magnolia, and Steen. STEELE COUNTY. CITIES: Blooming Prairie, Ellendale, Medford, and Owatonna. WASECA COUNTY. CITIES: Janesville, New Richland, Waldorf, and Waseca. WATONWAN COUNTY. CITIES: Butterfield, Darfur, La Salle, Lewisville, Madelia, Oden, Ormsby, and St. James. WINONA COUNTY. CITIES: Altura, Dakota, Elba, Goodview, Lewiston, Minneiska, Minnesota City, Rollingstone, St. Charles, Stockton, Utica, and Winona. Population (2010), 644,787.

ZIP Codes: 51360, 55019 (part), 55021 (part), 55046, 55049 (part), 55052, 55057 (part), 55060, 55087, 55088 (part), 55332–35 (part), 55901–02, 55904–05, 55906 (part), 55909, 55910 (part), 55912, 55917–27, 55929, 55931, 55932 (part), 55933–36, 55939–41, 55943–44, 55947, 55949–55, 55956 (part), 55959, 55960 (part), 55961–62, 55963–64 (part), 55965, 55967, 55969–77, 55979, 55982, 55985 (part), 55987, 55990, 55991, 56001, 56003, 56007, 56009–10, 56011 (part), 56013–14, 56016–17, 56019–29, 56031–37, 56039, 56041–43, 56044 (part), 56045–48, 56050–52, 56054 (part), 56055–58, 56060, 56062–63, 56065, 56068–69, 56071 (part), 56072–75, 56078, 56080–82, 56083 (part), 56085 (part), 56087 (part), 56088–91, 56093, 56096–98, 56101 (part), 56110–11, 56116–21, 56122 (part), 56127, 56128 (part), 56129, 56131, 56134, 56137 (part), 56138, 56141, 56143, 56144 (part), 56145 (part), 56146–47, 56150, 56153, 56155–56, 56158–62, 56165, 56167–68, 56171, 56173, 56176, 56181, 56185, 56187, 56266, 57030, 57068

* * *

SECOND DISTRICT

ANGIE CRAIG, Democrat, of Eagan, MN; born in West Helena, AR, February 14, 1972; education: B.A., journalism, University of Memphis, Memphis, TN, 1994; professional: St. Jude Medical, human resources and communications, 2005–17; religion: Lutheran; family: married to Cheryl Greene, with four sons; committees: Agriculture; Small Business; Transportation and Infrastructure; elected to the 116th Congress on November 6, 2018.

Office Listings

https://craig.house.gov https://facebook.com/RepAngieCraig https://twitter.com/RepAngieCraig

1523 Longworth House Office Building, Washington, DC 20515 .... (202) 225–2271
Chief of Staff.—Mara Kunin.
Communications Director.—Jen Gates.
Scheduler.—Maria Ferrara.
12940 Harriet Avenue South, Suite 238, Burnsville, MN 55337 .... (651) 846–2120
District Director.—Nick Coe.

Counties: DAKOTA COUNTY. CITIES: Apple Valley, Burnsville, Eagan, Farmington, Hastings, Inver Grove Heights, Lakeville, Rosemount, South St. Paul, and West St. Paul. GOODHUE COUNTY. CITIES: Cannon Falls, Pine Island, Red Wing, and Zumbrota. RICE COUNTY (part). CITIES: Northfield. SCOTT COUNTY. CITIES: Belle Plaine, Jordan, New Prague, Prior Lake, Savage, and Shakopee. WABASHA COUNTY. WASHINGTON COUNTY (part). CITIES: Cottage Grove and St. Paul Park. Population (2010), 668,891.

ZIP Codes: 55001 (part), 55009, 55016, 55018, 55019 (part), 55020, 55021 (part), 55024, 55026–27, 55031, 55033, 55041, 55044, 55049 (part), 55053–54, 55057 (part), 55065–66, 55068, 55071 (part), 55075–77, 55085, 55088 (part), 55089, 55118 (part), 55120–24, 55150, 55306, 55337, 55352, 55372, 55378–79, 55906 (part), 55910 (part), 55932 (part), 55945–46, 55956 (part), 55957, 55960 (part), 55963 (part), 55964 (part), 55968, 55981, 55983, 55985 (part), 55991 (part), 55992, 56011 (part), 56071 (part)

* * *

THIRD DISTRICT

DEAN PHILLIPS, Democrat, of Deephaven, MN; born in St. Paul, MN, January 20, 1969; education: B.A., urban studies, Brown University, Providence, RI, 1991; M.B.A., Carlson School of Management, University of Minnesota, Minneapolis, MN, 2000; professional: President/CEO, 1993–2012, former chair of the board, 2014–17, Phillips Distilling Company; former chair, Talenti Gelato; co-founder, Penny's Coffee, 2016; committees: Ethics, Financial Services, Foreign Affairs; elected to the 116th Congress on November 6, 2018.

Office Listings

https://phillips.house.gov https://facebook.com/RepDeanPhillips
twitter: @RepDeanPhillips https://instagram.com/repdeanphillips

1305 Longworth House Office Building, Washington, DC 20515 .... (202) 225–2871
Chief of Staff.—Tim Bertocci.
Legislative Director.—Imani Augustus.
Press Secretary.—Samantha Anderson.
Scheduler.—Sophie Mirviss.
13911 Ridgedale Drive, Suite 200, Minnetonka, MN 55305 .... (952) 656–5176
District Chief of Staff.—Zach Rodvold.
District Scheduler.—Mae Hougo.

Counties: ANOKA (part), CARVER (part), AND HENNEPIN (part). CITIES AND TOWNSHIPS: Bloomington, Brooklyn Park, Champlin, Chanhassen, Chaska, Coon Rapids, Corcoran, Dahlgren Township, Dayton, Deephaven, Eden Prairie, Edina (part), Excelsior, Greenfield, Greenwood, Hassan Township, Independence, Laketown Township, Long Lake, Loretto, Maple Grove, Maple Plain, Medina, Medicine Lake, Minnetonka, Minnetonka Beach, Minnetrista, Mound, Orono, Osseo, Plymouth, Rogers, St. Bonifacius, Shorewood, Spring Park, Tonka Bay, Victoria, Wayzata, and Woodland. Population (2010), 650,185.

ZIP Codes: 55304–05 (part), 55311, 55316–17, 55318 (part), 55327–28 (part), 55331, 55340, 55343 (part), 55344–47, 55356, 55357 (part), 55359, 55364, 55369, 55373–75 (part), 55384, 55386, 55387–88 (part), 55391, 55420, 55423 (part), 55425, 55426 (part), 55428–30 (part), 55431, 55433, 55435, 55436 (part), 55437–39, 55441 (part), 55442–43, 55444 (part), 55445–47, 55448 (part)

* * *

FOURTH DISTRICT

BETTY MCCOLLUM, Democrat-Farmer-Labor Party, of St. Paul, MN; born in Minneapolis, MN, July 12, 1954; education: A.A., Inver Hills Community College; B.S., College of St. Catherine; professional: teacher and sales manager; public service: North St. Paul City Council, 1986–92; Minnesota House of Representatives, 1992–2000; organizations: Girl Scouts of America; VFW Ladies Auxiliary; American Legion Ladies Auxiliary; awards: Friend of the National Parks Award, National Parks Conservation Association, 2013; Congressional Leadership Award, National Council of Urban Indian Health, 2013; Groundwater Protector Award, National Ground Water Association, 2012; Bruce Vento Hope-Builder Award, Mesothelioma Applied Research Foundation, 2014; Champion of the Endangered Species Act, International Fund for Animal Welfare, 2016; Bruce Vento Public Service Award, National Park Trust, 2016; Joan and Walter Mondale Award for Public Service, 2017; International Institute of Minnesota's Olga Zoltai Award for Service to New Americans, 2017; Churches for Middle East Peace Congressional Award, 2018; Academy of Nutrition and Dietetics Public Policy Leadership Award, 2018; Sidney R. Yates Award, 2019; Champion of Historic Preservation, 2019; children: Sean and Katie; appointments: National Council on the Arts; caucuses: founder, Congressional Global Health Caucus; co-chair emeritus, Congressional Native American Caucus; co-chair, Friends of Norway Caucus; co-chair, International Conservation Caucus; committees: Appropriations; elected to the 107th Congress on November 7, 2000; reelected to each succeeding Congress.

Office Listings

https://mccollum.house.gov https://facebook.com/repbettymccollum
https://twitter.com/BettyMcCollum04

2256 Rayburn House Office Building, Washington, DC 20515 .... (202) 225–6631
Chief of Staff.—Bill Harper. FAX: 225–1968
Legislative Director.—Ben Peterson.
Communications Director.—Amanda Yanchury.
Scheduler.—Mia Hartley.
661 LaSalle Street, Suite 110, St. Paul, MN 55114 .... (651) 224–9191
District Director.—Joshua Straka.

Counties: RAMSEY (part) AND WASHINGTON (part). Population (2010), 614,624.

ZIP Codes: 55001 (part), 55003, 55038 (part), 55042–43, 55055, 55071 (part), 55082 (part), 55090, 55101–09, 55110 (part), 55112 (part), 55113–17, 55118 (part), 55119, 55125, 55126 (part), 55127–30, 55155, 55418 (part), 55432 (part), 55449 (part)

* * *

FIFTH DISTRICT

ILHAN OMAR, Democrat-Farmer-Labor, of Minneapolis, MN; born in Mogadishu, Somalia, October 4, 1982; education: B.A., political science and international studies, North Dakota State University, Fargo, ND, 2011; professional: community nutrition educator, University of Minnesota, Greater Minneapolis-St. Paul area, 2006–09; manager, Kari Dzeidzic's Campaign for Minnesota State Senate, 2012; child nutrition outreach coordinator, Minnesota State Department of Education, 2012–13; manager, Andrew Johnson's Campaign for Minneapolis City Council seat, 2013; senior policy aide, Office of Minneapolis City Councilman Andrew Johnson, 2013–15; member, District 60B and Assistant Minority Leader, Minnesota State House of Representatives, 2017–19; committees: Budget; Education and Labor; Foreign Affairs; elected to the 116th Congress on November 6, 2018.

Office Listings

https://omar.house.gov https://facebook.com/RepIlhan https://twitter.com/Ilhan

1517 Longworth House Office Building, Washington, DC 20515 .... (202) 225–4755
Chief of Staff.—Connor McNutt.
Legislative Director.—Kelly Misselwitz.
Communications Director.—Jeremy Slevin.
Scheduler.—Philip Bennett.
404 3rd Avenue North, Suite 203, Minneapolis, MN 55401 .... (612) 333–1272
Deputy District Director.—Ali Isse.

Counties: ANOKA (part), HENNEPIN (part), AND RAMSEY (part). CITIES: Minneapolis and the surrounding suburbs of Brooklyn Center, Columbia Heights, Crystal, Edina (part), Fridley, Golden Valley, Hilltop, Hopkins, New Hope, Richfield, Robbinsdale, St. Anthony, and St. Louis Park. Population (2010), 677,196.

ZIP Codes: 55111, 55112 (part), 55305 (part), 55343 (part), 55401–17, 55418 (part), 55419, 55421–22, 55424, 55426 (part), 55427, 55428–30 (part), 55432 (part), 55436 (part), 55441 (part), 55444 (part), 55450, 55454–55

* * *

SIXTH DISTRICT

TOM EMMER, Republican, of Delano, MN; born in South Bend, IN, March 3, 1961; education: B.A., political science, from the University of Alaska-Fairbanks, Fairbanks, AK, 1984; J.D. from William Mitchell College of Law, St. Paul, MN, 1988; professional: practiced insurance, banking, and equity law through his own practice; served in the Minnesota House of Representatives from 2004–08; was a radio host on Twin Cities News Talk AM 1130; married: Jacquie; children: Thomas Earl III "Tripp", Jack, Bobby, Joey, Billy, and Johnny (sons), and Katie (daughter); House Republican Steering Committee; committees: Financial Services; elected to the 114th Congress on November 4, 2014; reelected to each succeeding Congress.

Office Listings

https://emmer.house.gov https://facebook.com/reptomemmer twitter: @RepTomEmmer

315 Cannon House Office Building, Washington, DC 20515 .... (202) 225–2331

Office Listings—Continued

Chief of Staff.—Christopher Maneval. FAX: 225–6475
Legislative Director.—Landon Zinda.
Press Secretary.—Abby Rime.
9201 Quaday Avenue, NE., Suite 206, Otsego, MN 55330 .... (763) 241–6848

Counties: ANOKA (part), BENTON, CARVER (part), HENNEPIN (part), SHERBURNE, STEARNS (part), WASHINGTON (PART), AND WRIGHT. Population (2010), 662,990.

ZIP Codes: 55005, 55011, 55014, 55025, 55038 (part), 55047, 55070 (part), 55073 (part), 55079 (part), 55082 (part), 55092 (part), 55110 (part), 55126 (part), 55301–03, 55304 (part), 55308–09, 55313, 55315, 55318 (part), 55319–22, 55327–29 (part), 55330, 55339 (part), 55341, 55349, 55353 (part), 55357 (part), 55358, 55360, 55362–63, 55367–68, 55371 (part), 55373–75 (part), 55376, 55382 (part), 55387–90 (part), 55395 (part), 55397–98 (part), 55434, 55448–49 (part), 56011 (part), 56301, 56303–04, 56307 (part), 56310 (part), 56314 (part), 56320–21, 56329–30 (part), 56340 (part), 56357 (part), 56362 (part), 56367, 56368 (part), 56369, 56373 (part), 56374–75, 56377, 56379, 56387

* * *

SEVENTH DISTRICT

COLLIN C. PETERSON, Democrat, of Detroit Lakes, MN; born in Fargo, ND, June 29, 1944; education: graduated from Glyndon (MN) High School, 1962; B.A., business administration and accounting, Moorhead State University, 1966; professional: U.S. Army National Guard, 1963–69; CPA, owner and partner; Minnesota State Senator, 1976–86; member: AOPA, Safari Club, Ducks Unlimited, American Legion, Sea Plane Pilots Association, Pheasants Forever, Benevolent Protective Order of Elks, and Cormorant Lakes Sportsman's Club; three children: Sean, Jason, and Elliott; committees: chair, Agriculture; Veterans' Affairs; elected to the 102nd Congress on November 6, 1990; reelected to each succeeding Congress.

Office Listings

https://collinpeterson.house.gov https://facebook.com/RepCollinPeterson

2204 Rayburn House Office Building, Washington, DC 20515 .... (202) 225–2165
Chief of Staff.—Allison Stock. FAX: 225–1593
Deputy Chief of Staff/Legislative Director.—Adam Durand.
Assistants: Chelsea Cornett, Cody Hollerich, Richard Lee, Zach Martin, Rebekah Solem, Rylee Stirn.
Lake Avenue Plaza Building, 714 Lake Avenue, Suite 101, Detroit Lakes, MN 56501 .... (218) 847–5056
1700 Technology Drive, Suite 119, Willmar, MN 56201 .... (320) 235–1061
1420 East College Drive, Suite 800, Marshall, MN 56258 .... (507) 537–2299
13892 Airport Drive, Suite 3, Thief River Falls, MN 56701 .... (218) 683–5405

Counties: BECKER, BELTRAMI (part), BIG STONE, CHIPPEWA, CLAY, CLEARWATER, COTTONWOOD (part), DOUGLAS, GRANT, KANDIYOHI, KITTSON, LAC QUI PARLE, LAKE OF THE WOODS, LINCOLN, LYON, MAHNOMEN, MARSHALL, MCLEOD, MEEKER, MURRAY, NORMAN, OTTER TAIL, PENNINGTON, PIPESTONE, POLK, POPE, RED LAKE, REDWOOD, RENVILLE, ROSEAU, SIBLEY, STEARNS (part), STEVENS, SWIFT, TODD, TRAVERSE, WILKIN, AND YELLOW MEDICINE. Population (2010), 662,991.

ZIP Codes: 55307, 55310, 55312, 55314, 55324–25, 55329 (part), 55332–35 (part), 55336, 55338, 55339 (part), 55342, 55350, 55353 (part), 55354–55, 55366, 55370, 55381, 55382 (part), 55385, 55389 (part), 55395 (part), 55396, 55397 (part), 56011 (part), 56044 (part), 56054 (part), 56058 (part), 56083 (part), 56085 (part), 56087 (part), 56101 (part), 56113–15, 56122 (part), 56123, 56125, 56128 (part), 56131 (part), 56132, 56136, 56137 (part), 56139–40, 56141 (part), 56142, 56144–45 (part), 56149, 56151–52, 56157, 56164, 56166, 56169–70, 56172, 56174–75, 56177–78, 56180, 56183, 56186, 56201, 56207–12, 56214–16, 56218–32, 56235–37, 56239–41, 56243–45, 56248–49, 56251–53, 56255–58, 56260, 56262–65, 56266 (part), 56267, 56270–71, 56273–74, 56276–85, 56287–89, 56291–97, 56307–09, 56310 (part), 56311–12, 56315–16, 56318 (part), 56319, 56323–27, 56331–32, 56334–36, 56339, 56340 (part), 56343, 56347, 56349, 56352, 56354–56, 56360–61, 56362 (part), 56368 (part), 56371, 56376, 56378, 56381, 56382 (part), 56385, 56389, 56434 (part), 56437–38, 56440, 56443 (part), 56446, 56453, 56464 (part), 56466 (part), 56470 (part), 56477 (part), 56479 (part), 56481–82 (part), 56501, 56510–11, 56514–25, 56527–29, 56531, 56533–37, 56540–54, 56556–57, 56560, 56565–81, 56583–94, 56601 (part), 56621, 56623 (part), 56630 (part), 56634, 56644, 56646, 56650 (part), 56652, 56666, 56667 (part), 56670 (part), 56671, 56673, 56676, 56678 (part), 56684–87, 56701, 56710–11, 56713–16, 56720–29, 56731–38, 56741–42, 56744, 56748, 56750–51, 56754–63, 57026, 58225

* * *

EIGHTH DISTRICT

PETE STAUBER, Republican, of Hermantown, MN; born in Duluth, MN, May 10, 1966; education: B.S., Lake Superior State University, Sault Sainte Marie, MI, 1990; professional: professional hockey player, Detroit Red Wings organization, National Hockey League, 1990–93; police officer, Duluth, MN Police Department, 1995–2017; member, Hermantown, MN

Town Council, 2001–05 and 2011–13; member, St. Louis County, MN Board of Commissioners, Duluth, MN, 2013–19; committees: Small Business; Transportation and Infrastructure; elected to the 116th Congress on November 6, 2018.

Office Listings

https://stauber.house.gov https://facebook.com/RepPeteStauber
https://twitter.com/RepPeteStauber https://instagram.com/reppetestauber

126 Cannon House Office Building, Washington, DC 20515 .... (202) 225–6211
Chief of Staff.—Desiree Koetzle.
Legislative Director.—Jeff Bishop.
Communications Director.—Kelsey Mix.
Scheduler.—Linnea Melbye.
5094 Miller Trunk Highway, Suite 900, Hermantown, MN 55811 .... (218) 481–6396
District Director.—Isaac Schultz.
501 Laurel Street, Brainerd, MN 56401 .... (218) 355–0862
300 3rd Avenue, NE., Cambridge, MN 55008 .... (763) 552–3359
316 West Lake Street, Room 7, Chisholm, MN 55719 .... (218) 355–0726

Counties: AITKIN, BELTRAMI (part), CARLTON, CASS, CHISAGO, COOK, CROW WING, HUBBARD, ISANTI, ITASCA, KANABEC, KOOCHICHING, LAKE, MILLE LACS, MORRISON, PINE, ST. LOUIS, AND WADENA. CITIES: Aitkin, Baxter, Brainerd, Cambridge, Carlton, Center City, Chisago City, Chisholm, Cloquet, Duluth, Ely, Eveleth, Grand Marais, Grand Rapids, Hermantown, Hibbing, International Falls, Isanti, Lindstrom, Little Falls, Milaca, Moose Lake, Mora, North Branch, Orr, Park Rapids, Pine City, Princeton, Proctor, Rush City, Silver Bay, Two Harbors, Virginia, Wadena, Walker, and Wyoming. Population (2010), 660,347.

ZIP Codes: 55006–08, 55012–13, 55017, 55025, 55029–30, 55032, 55036–37, 55040, 55045, 55051, 55056, 55063, 55069, 55070 (part), 55072, 55073 (part), 55074, 55079 (part), 55080, 55084, 55092 (part), 55371 (part), 55398 (part), 55601–07, 55609, 55612–16, 55702–13, 55716–26, 55731–36, 55738, 55741–42, 55744, 55746, 55748–53, 55756–58, 55760, 55763–69, 55771–72, 55775, 55779–87, 55790, 55792–93, 55795, 55797–98, 55802–08, 55810–12, 55814, 56313, 56314 (part), 56318 (part), 56328, 56329–30 (part), 56338, 56340 (part), 56342, 56345, 56350, 56353, 56357–59, 56363–64, 56373 (part), 56382 (part), 56384, 56386, 56401, 56425, 56431, 56433, 56434 (part), 56435–36, 56441–42, 56443 (part), 56444, 56447–50, 56452, 56455–56, 56458, 56461, 56464 (part), 56465, 56466 (part), 56467–69, 56470 (part), 56472–75, 56477 (part), 56479 (part), 56481–82 (part), 56484, 56601 (part), 56623 (part), 56626–29, 56330 (part), 56633, 56636–37, 56639, 56641, 56647, 56649, 56650 (part), 56653–55, 56657–63, 56667 (part), 56668–69, 56670 (part), 56672, 56678 (part), 56680–81, 56683, 56688

MISSISSIPPI

(Population 2010, 2,967,297)

SENATORS

ROGER F. WICKER, Republican, of Tupelo, MS; born in Pontotoc, MS, July 5, 1951; education: graduated, Pontotoc High School; B.A., University of Mississippi, 1973; J.D., University of Mississippi, 1975; president, Associated Student Body, 1972–73; *Mississippi Law Journal*, 1973–75; Air Force ROTC; professional: U.S. Air Force, 1976–80; U.S. Air Force Reserve, 1980–2004 (retired with rank of Lieutenant Colonel); U.S. House of Representatives Rules Committee staff for Representative Trent Lott, 1980–82; private law practice, 1982–94; Lee County Public Defender, 1984–87; Tupelo City Judge Pro Tempore, 1986–87; Mississippi State Senate, 1988–94, chairman: Elections Committee, 1992, Public Health and Welfare Committee, 1993–94; member: Lions Club, University of Mississippi Hall of Fame, Sigma Nu Fraternity Hall of Fame, Omicron Delta Kappa, Phi Delta Phi; religion: Southern Baptist, deacon, adult choir of First Baptist Church, Tupelo, MS; married: Gayle Long Wicker; children: Margaret (Manning) McPhillips, Caroline (Kirk) Sims, and McDaniel (Kellee) Wicker; grandchildren: Caroline McPhillips, Henry McPhillips, Maury Beth McPhillips, Virginia McPhillips, Evelyn Sims, and Joseph Sims; co-chairman of the U.S. Helsinki Commission and a vice president of the OSCE's Parliamentary Assembly; committees: chair, Commerce, Science, and Transportation; Armed Services; Environment and Public Works; Rules and Administration; Joint Committee on Printing; elected to the 104th Congress, November 8, 1994; president, Republican freshman class, 1995; reelected to each succeeding Congress; appointed by the Governor, December 31, 2007, to fill the vacancy caused by the resignation of Senator Trent Lott; elected to the U.S. Senate on November 4, 2008; reelected to each succeeding Senate term.

Office Listings

https://wicker.senate.gov https://facebook.com/SenatorWicker twitter: @SenatorWicker

555 Dirksen Senate Office Building, Washington, DC 20510 .... (202) 224–6253
Chief of Staff.—Michelle Barlow Richardson. FAX: 228–0378
Legislative Director.—Rob Murray.
Communications Director.—Rick VanMeter.
Scheduler.—Jen Jett.
U.S. Federal Courthouse, 501 East Court Street, Suite 3–500, Jackson, MS 39201 .... (601) 965–4644
FAX: 965–4007
2909 13th Street, Suite 303, Gulfport, MS 39501 .... (228) 871–7017
FAX: 871–7196
330 West Jefferson Street, Suite B, Tupelo, MS 38804 .... (662) 844–5010
321 Losher Street, Hernando, MS 38632 .... (662) 429–1002
FAX: 429–6002

* * *

CINDY HYDE-SMITH, Republican, of Brookhaven, MS; born in Brookhaven, May 10, 1959; education: graduated from Copiah-Lincoln Community College, Wesson, MS; B.A., University of Southern Mississippi, 1981; professional: cattle farmer; Mississippi State Senator, 2000–12; first woman elected as Commissioner of Agriculture and Commerce, State of Mississippi, 2012–18; awards: Agriculture Legislator of the Year Award from the Mississippi Association of Conservation Districts; Ambassador Award from the Mississippi Farm Bureau Federation; Achievement Award from the Delta Council; Outstanding Service to Small Farmers Award from Alcorn State University; religion: Baptist; family: husband, Michael; daughter, Anna-Michael; committees: Agriculture, Nutrition, and Forestry; Appropriations; Energy and Natural Resources; Rules and Administration; appointed to the U.S. Senate to fill the vacancy caused by the resignation of U.S. Senator Thad Cochran; took the oath of office on April 9, 2018, to serve until a special election on November 6, 2018; elected in a runoff election on November 27, 2018, for the remainder of the term ending January 3, 2021; first woman elected to represent Mississippi in Congress.

Office Listings

https://hydesmith.senate.gov https://facebook.com/SenatorCindyHydeSmith
twitter: @SenHydeSmith https://instagram.com/sencindyhydesmith
youtube: U.S. Senator Cindy Hyde-Smith

702 Hart Senate Office Building, Washington, DC 20510 .... (202) 224–5054

Office Listings—Continued

Chief of Staff.—Brad White. FAX: 224–5321
Deputy Chief of Staff.—Daniel Ulmer.
Legislative Director.—Tim Wolverton.
Scheduler.—Alexandra Calhoon.
State Director.—Umesh Sanjanwala.

190 East Capitol Street, Suite 550, Jackson, MS 39201 .... (601) 965–4459
FAX: 965–4919

911 East Jackson Avenue, Suite 249, Oxford, MS 38655 .... (662) 236–1018
FAX: 236–7618

2012 15th Street, Suite 451, Gulfport, MS 39501 .... (228) 867–9710
FAX: 867–9789

REPRESENTATIVES

FIRST DISTRICT

TRENT KELLY, Republican, of Saltillo, MS; born in Union, MS, March 1, 1966; education: Union High School, Union, MS, 1984; associate of arts, East Central Community College, Decatur, MS, 1986; bachelor of business administration, marketing, University of Mississippi, Oxford, MS, 1989; juris doctor, University of Mississippi, Oxford, MS, 1994; master's in strategic studies, United States Army War College, Carlisle, PA, 2010; professional: private law practice, Saltillo, MS, 1995–99; City Prosecutor, Tupelo, MS, 1999–2011; forfeiture attorney, North Mississippi Narcotics Unit, 2000–11; District Attorney for Lee, Pontotoc, Alcorn, Monroe, Itawamba, Prentiss, and Tishomingo Counties, 2012–June 2015; military: 31 years in the Mississippi Army National Guard as an engineer; currently serving as a Brigadier General; mobilized for Desert Storm as an Engineer Second Lieutenant, 1990; deployed as a Major to Iraq with the 155th Brigade as the operations officer of the 150th Engineer Battalion, 2005; deployed as a Lieutenant Colonel to Iraq as the battalion commander of Task Force Knight of the 155th Brigade Combat Team and commanded over 670 troops from Mississippi, Ohio, and Kentucky, 2009–10; awards: two Bronze Stars; Combat Action Badge; DeFleury Medal, and numerous other federal and state awards; religion: Methodist; married: Sheila Stephens Kelly; children: John Forrest, Morgan, and Jackson; committees: Agriculture; Armed Services; elected to the 114th Congress on June 2, 2015, by special election, to fill the vacancy caused by the death of U.S. Representative Alan S. Nunnelee; reelected to each succeeding Congress.

Office Listings

https://trentkelly.house.gov https://facebook.com/RepTrentKelly twitter: @RepTrentKelly

1005 Longworth House Office Building, Washington, DC 20515 .... (202) 225–4306
Chief of Staff.—Paul Howell.
Scheduler.—Reed Craddock.

431 West Main Street, Suite 450, Tupelo, MS 38804 .... (662) 841–8808
District Director.—Darren Herring. FAX: 841–8845

318 Seventh Street North, Suite D, Columbus, MS 39701 .... (662) 327–0748
Mailing: P.O. Box 1012, Columbus, MS 39703 .... FAX: 328–5982

2565 Caffey Street, #200, Hernando, MS 38632 .... (662) 449–3090
Mailing: P.O. Box 218, Hernando, MS 38632 .... FAX: 449–4836

855 South Dunn Street, Eupora, MS 39744 .... (662) 258–1545
FAX: 258–7240

4135 County Road 200, Corinth, MS 38844 .... (662) 687–1525

Counties: Alcorn, Benton, Calhoun, Chickasaw, Choctaw, Clay, Desoto, Itawamba, Lafayette, Lee, Lowndes, Marshall, Monroe, Pontotoc, Prentiss, Tate, Tippah, Tishomingo, Union, Webster, Winston, and Oktibbeha (part). Population (2013), 756,459.

ZIP Codes: 38601, 38603, 38606 (part), 38610–11, 38618, 38619 (part), 38625, 38627, 38629, 38632–33, 38635, 38637, 38641–42, 38647, 38650–52, 38654–55, 38659, 38661, 38663, 38665, 38668, 38671–74, 38677, 38680, 38683, 38685, 38801, 38804, 38821, 38824, 38826–29, 38833–34, 38838, 38841, 38843–44, 38846–52, 38855–60, 38862–66, 38868–71, 38873, 38876, 38878–79, 38913–16, 38929 (part), 38949, 38951, 38965 (part), 39108 (part), 39339, 39346 (part), 39354 (part), 39701–02, 39705, 39730, 39735–37, 39740–41, 39743 (part), 39744, 39745 (part), 39746, 39750 (part), 39751–52, 39755 (part), 39756, 39766–67, 39769 (part), 39771, 39772 (part), 39773, 39776

* * *

SECOND DISTRICT

BENNIE G. THOMPSON, Democrat, of Bolton, MS; born in Bolton, January 28, 1948; education: graduated, Hinds County Agriculture High School; B.A., Tougaloo College, 1968; M.S.,

Jackson State University, 1972; professional: teacher; Bolton Board of Aldermen, 1969–73; Mayor of Bolton, 1973–79; Hinds County Board of Supervisors, 1980–93; Housing Assistance Council; NAACP 100 Black Men of Jackson, MS; Southern Regional Council; Kappa Alpha Psi Fraternity; married to the former London Johnson, Ph.D.; one daughter: BendaLonne; caucuses: Congressional Black Caucus; Congressional Gaming Caucus; Congressional Sportsmen's Caucus; House Education Caucus; Progressive Caucus; Rural Caucus; committees: chair, Homeland Security; elected to the 103rd Congress by special election; reelected to each succeeding Congress.

Office Listings

https://benniethompson.house.gov https://facebook.com/CongressmanBennieGThompson
twitter: @BennieGThompson https://instagram.com/benniegthompson

2466 Rayburn House Office Building, Washington, DC 20515 .... (202) 225–5876
Chief of Staff.—Andrea Lee. FAX: 225–5898
Legislative Director.—Claytrice Henderson.
Legislative Assistant / Press Secretary.—Tyron James.
Scheduler.—Earvin Miers.
Staff Assistant / Legislative Assistant.—Meco Shoulders.
107 West Madison Street, P.O. Box 610, Bolton, MS 39041–0610 .... (601) 866–9003
Director of Administration.—Fannie Ware.
3607 Medgar Evers Boulevard, Jackson, MS 39213 .... (601) 946–9003
263 East Main Street, P.O. Box 356, Marks, MS 38646 .... (662) 326–9003
Mound Bayou City Hall, 106 Green Avenue, P.O. Box 679, Suite 106, Mound Bayou, MS 38762 .... (662) 741–9003
728 Main Street, Suite A, Greenwood, MS 38930 .... (662) 455–9003
910 Courthouse Lane, Greenville, MS 38701 .... (662) 335–9003

Counties: ATTALA, BOLIVAR, CARROLL, CLAIBORNE, COAHOMA, COPIAH, GRENADA, HINDS (part), HOLMES, HUMPHREYS, ISSAQUENA, JEFFERSON, LEAKE, LEFLORE, MADISON (part), MONTGOMERY, PANOLA, QUITMAN, SHARKEY, SUNFLOWER, TALLAHATCHIE, TUNICA, WARREN, WASHINGTON, YALOBUSHA, AND YAZOO. Population (2010), 741,862.

ZIP Codes: 38606, 38614, 38617, 38619–23, 38626, 38630–31, 38639, 38643–46, 38658, 38664–66, 38670, 38676, 38701–04, 38720–23, 38725–26, 38730–32, 38736–38, 38740, 38744–46, 38748–49, 38751, 38753–54, 38756, 38759–62, 38764–65, 38767–69, 38771–74, 38778, 38781, 38901, 38914, 38917, 38920–25, 38927–30, 38940–41, 38943–48, 38950, 38952–54, 38957–58, 38961–67, 39038–41, 39045–46, 39051, 39054, 39056, 39059, 39061, 39063, 39066–67, 39069, 39071, 39078–79, 39083, 39086, 39088, 39090, 39094–97, 39108, 39110, 39113, 39115, 39120, 39144, 39146, 39150, 39154, 39156–57, 39159–60, 39162, 39166, 39169–70, 39174–77, 39179–80, 39183, 39189, 39191–92, 39194, 39201–04, 39206, 39209, 39211–13, 39216–17, 39272, 39365, 39653, 39668, 39745, 39747, 39767

* * *

THIRD DISTRICT

MICHAEL GUEST, Republican, of Brandon, MS; born in Woodberry, NJ, February 4, 1970; education: B.A., accounting, Mississippi State University, Starkville, MS, 1992; J.D., University of Mississippi, Oxford, MS, 1995; professional: attorney; member of both the Rankin County and Mississippi Bar Associations; Assistant District Attorney for Madison and Rankin counties, 1994–2008, and District Attorney, 2008–19; religion: Southern Baptist; member, Sunday school teacher, and deacon at Brandon Baptist Church; family: married to the former Haley Kennedy; two children: Kennedy and Patton; committees: Ethics (the only first-term Member of Congress to be selected to this panel); Foreign Affairs; Homeland Security; elected to the 116th Congress on November 6, 2018.

Office Listings

https://guest.house.gov https://facebook.com/RepMichaelGuest
https://twitter.com/RepMichaelGuest https://instagram.com/repmichaelguest

230 Cannon House Office Building, Washington, DC 20515 .... (202) 225–5031
Chief of Staff.—Jordan Downs. FAX: 225–5797
Policy Director.—Elizabeth Joseph.
Communications Director.—Rob Pillow.
600 Russell Street, Suite 160, Starkville, MS 39759 .... (662) 324–0007
Deputy District Director.—Kyle Jordan.
308 B East Government Street, Brandon, MS 39042 .... (769) 241–6120
District Director.—Brady Stewart.
Director of Scheduling.—Debra Boutwell.
2214 5th Street, Suite 2170, Meridian, MS 39301 .... (601) 693–6681
Special Assistant.—Frances White.
230 South Whitworth Avenue, Brookhaven, MS 39601 .... (601) 823–3400
(Call for Appointment)

Counties: ADAMS, AMITE, CLARKE (part), COVINGTON, FRANKLIN, HINDS (part), JASPER, JEFFERSON DAVIS, KEMPER, LAUDERDALE, LAWRENCE, LINCOLN, MADISON (part), NESHOBA, NEWTON, NOXUBEE, OKTIBBEHA (part), PIKE, RANKIN, SCOTT, SIMPSON, SMITH, WALTHALL, AND WILKINSON. Population (2014), 711,115.

ZIP Codes: 39042, 39044, 39046–47, 39051, 39057, 39062, 39071, 39073–74, 39082, 39092, 39094, 39110–11, 39114, 39116–17, 39119–20, 39410, 39145, 39149, 39152–53, 39157, 39167–68, 39189, 39191, 39193, 39201, 39203–04, 39206, 39208–09, 39211–13, 39216, 39218, 39232, 39269, 39301, 39305, 39307, 39309, 39320, 39323, 39325–28, 39330, 39332, 39335–38, 39341–42, 39345–48, 39350, 39352, 39354–56, 39358–61, 39363–66, 39401–02, 39421–22, 39428–29, 39439, 39443, 39474, 39478–83, 39601, 39629–31, 39633, 39635, 39638, 39641, 39643, 39645, 39647–48, 39652–54, 39657, 39661–63, 39666–69, 39743, 39750, 39759–60, 39762, 39769

* * *

FOURTH DISTRICT

STEVEN M. PALAZZO, Republican, of Biloxi, MS; born in Gulfport, MS, February 21, 1970; education: B.S., University of Southern Mississippi, Hattiesburg, MS, 1994; M.P.A., University of Southern Mississippi, Hattiesburg, 1996; professional: accountant; military: U.S. Marine Corps Reserve, 1988–96; Mississippi Army National Guard, 2007–present; member of Mississippi State House of Representatives, 2007–10; children: Barrett, Aubrey, and Bennett; caucuses: Aerospace Caucus; Congressional Sportsmen's Caucus; Gulf Coast Caucus; Home Protection Caucus; National Guard Caucus; Shipbuilding Caucus; committees: Appropriations; elected to the 112th Congress on November 2, 2010; reelected to each succeeding Congress.

Office Listings

https://palazzo.house.gov https://facebook.com/stevenpalazzo https://twitter.com/congpalazzo

2349 Rayburn House Office Building, Washington, DC 20515 .... (202) 225–5772
Chief of Staff.—Hunter Lipscomb. FAX: 225–7074
Legislative Director.—Patrick Large.
Scheduler.—Vacant.
84 48th Street, Gulfport, MS 39507 .... (228) 864–7670
641 Main Street, Suite 142, Hattiesburg, MS 39401 .... (601) 582–3246
3118 Pascagoula Street, Suite 181, Pascagoula, MS 39567 .... (228) 202–8104
FAX: 202–8105

Counties: CLARKE (part), FORREST, GEORGE, GREENE, HANCOCK, HARRISON, JACKSON, JONES, LAMAR, MARION, PEARL RIVER, PERRY, STONE, AND WAYNE. CITIES AND TOWNSHIPS: Biloxi, Gulfport, Hattiesburg, Laurel, and Pascagoula. Population (2010), 741,776.

ZIP Codes: 39301, 39307, 39322, 39324, 39330, 39332, 39347–48, 39355–56, 39360, 39362–63, 39366–67, 39401–04, 39406, 39422–23, 39425–26, 39429, 39436–37, 39439–43, 39451–52, 39455–57, 39459, 39461–66, 39470, 39475–78, 39480–82, 39501–03, 39505–07, 39520–22, 39525, 39529–35, 39540, 39552–53, 39555–56, 39558, 39560–69, 39571–74, 39576–77, 39581, 39595

MISSOURI

(Population 2010, 5,988,927)

SENATORS

ROY BLUNT, Republican, of Springfield, MO; born in Niangua, MO, January 10, 1950; education: B.A., Southwest Baptist University, 1970; M.A., Missouri State University, 1972; professional: county clerk and chief election official of Greene County, MO, 1973–84; Secretary of State of Missouri, 1985–92; president of Southwest Baptist University, 1993–96; member, U.S. House of Representatives, for Missouri's 7th District, 1997–2010; married: Abigail Blunt; children: Governor Matthew Blunt, Amy Blunt, Andrew Blunt, and Alexander Charles Blunt; committees: chair, Rules and Administration; chair, Joint Committee on the Library; vice chair, Joint Committee on Printing; Appropriations; Commerce, Science, and Transportation; Select Committee on Intelligence; elected to the U.S. Senate on November 2, 2010; reelected to the U.S. Senate on November 8, 2016.

Office Listings

https://blunt.senate.gov

260 Russell Senate Office Building, Washington, DC 20510 .... (202) 224–5721
Chief of Staff.—Stacy McBride.
Deputy Chief of Staff.—Richard Eddings.
Legislative Director.—Daniel Burgess.
Communications Director.—Katie Boyd.
Director of Scheduling.—Richard Eddings.
2740B East Sunshine, Springfield, MO 65804 .... (417) 877–7814
1000 Walnut Street, Suite 1560, Kansas City, MO 64106 .... (816) 471–7141
111 South 10th Street, Suite 23.305, St. Louis, MO 63102 .... (314) 725–4484
1123 Wilkes Boulevard, Suite 320, Columbia, MO 65201 .... (573) 442–8151
Deputy Chief of Staff, State.—Derek Coats.
338 Broadway, Suite 303, Cape Girardeau, MO 63701 .... (573) 334–7044

* * *

JOSH HAWLEY, Republican, of Lexington, MO; born in Springdale, AR, December 31, 1979; education: B.A., history, with highest honors, Stanford University, Stanford, CA, 2002; J.D., Yale University Law School, New Haven, CT, 2006; professional: clerk for Appeals Court Judge Michael McConnell, 10th Circuit, U.S. Court of Appeals, Denver, CO, 2006–07; clerk for U.S. Supreme Court Chief Justice John Roberts, Washington, DC, 2007–08; attorney, Hogan Lovells, US LLP, Washington, DC, 2008–11; Of counsel, Becket Fund for Religious Liberty, Washington, DC, 2011–15; associate professor, University of Missouri School of Law, Columbia, MO, 2011–16; Attorney General, State of Missouri, Jefferson City, MO, 2017–19; married: Erin, 2002; children: two sons; committees: Armed Services; Homeland Security and Governmental Affairs; Judiciary; Small Business and Entrepreneurship; Special Committee on Aging; elected to the U.S. Senate on November 6, 2018.

Office Listings

https://hawley.senate.gov https://facebook.com/SenatorHawley https://twitter.com/SenHawleyPress

212 Russell Senate Office Building, Washington, DC 20510 .... (202) 224–6154
Chief of Staff.—Kyle Plotkin. FAX: 228–0526
Deputy Chief of Staff.—Corey Messervy.
Legislative Director.—Ryan Leavitt.
Communications Director.—Kelli Ford.
Director of Scheduling.—Ellen James.
111 South 10th Street, Suite 23.366, St. Louis, MO 63102 .... (314) 354–7060
District Director.—Sam Saffa.
4141 Pennsylvania Avenue, Suite 101, Kansas City, MO 64111 .... (816) 960–4694
Constituent Services Director.—Shawn Cowing.
Field Representative.—Elizabeth Johnson.
Caseworker.—Chris Naylor.
555 Independence Street, Suite 1600, Cape Girardeau, MO 63703 .... (573) 334–5995
District Director.—Matt Bain.
1123 Wilkes Boulevard, Suite 220, Columbia, MO 65201 .... (202) 860–5207
State Director.—Daniel Hartman.
Deputy State Director.—Ray Bozarth.
324 Park Central West, Suite 101, Springfield, MO 65806 .... (417) 869–4433
District Director.—Clayton Campbell.

REPRESENTATIVES

FIRST DISTRICT

WM. LACY CLAY, Democrat, of St. Louis, MO; born in St. Louis, July 27, 1956; education: Springbrook High School, Silver Spring, MD, 1974; B.A., University of Maryland, College Park, MD, 1983; public service: Missouri House of Representatives, 1983–91; Missouri State Senate, 1991–2000; nonprofit organizations: St. Louis Gateway Classic Sports Foundation; Mary Ryder Homes; William L. Clay Scholarship and Research Fund; religion: Catholic; married: Patricia Clay; children: Carol and William III; committees: Financial Services; Natural Resources; Oversight and Reform; elected to the 107th Congress on November 7, 2000; reelected to each succeeding Congress.

Office Listings

https://lacyclay.house.gov https://facebook.com/CongressmanClayMO1

2428 Rayburn House Office Building, Washington, DC 20515 .... (202) 225–2406
Chief of Staff.—Yvette P. Cravins. FAX: 226–3717
Scheduler.—Karyn Long.
Legislative Assistants: Darrell Doss, Erica Powell.
Thomas F. Eagleton U.S. Courthouse, 111 South 10th Street, Suite 24–344, St. Louis, MO 63102 .... (314) 367–1970
FAX: 367–1341
6830 Gravois, St. Louis, MO 63116 .... (314) 669–9393
FAX: 669–9398
1281 Graham Road, Suite 202, Florissant, MO 63031 .... (314) 383–5240

Counties: ST. LOUIS COUNTY (part). CITIES: St. Louis. Population (2010), 748,616.

ZIP Codes: 63031, 63033–34, 63042–45, 63074, 63101–25, 63130, 63132–41, 63143–44, 63146–47, 63155

* * *

SECOND DISTRICT

ANN L. WAGNER, Republican, of Ballwin, MO; born in St. Louis, MO, September 13, 1962; education: B.A.B.S., University of Missouri, Columbia, 1984; professional: businesswoman; Hallmark Cards; Ralston Purina; public service: committeewoman for Lafayette Township; chair of Missouri Republican Party, 1999–2005; co-chair of the Republican National Committee, 2001–05; U.S. Ambassador to Luxembourg, 2005–09; family: married to Raymond, Jr.; children: Raymond III, Stephen, and Mary Ruth; committees: Financial Services; Foreign Affairs; elected to the 113th Congress on November 6, 2012; reelected to each succeeding Congress.

Office Listings

https://wagner.house.gov https://facebook.com/RepAnnWagner https://twitter.com/RepAnnWagner

2350 Rayburn House Office Building, Washington, DC 20515 .... (202) 225–1621
Chief of Staff.—Charlie Keller.
Scheduler.—Emily Ann Smith.
301 Sovereign Court, Suite 201, St. Louis, MO 63011 .... (636) 779–5449
District Director.—Miriam Stonebraker.

Counties: JEFFERSON (part), ST. CHARLES (part), AND ST. LOUIS (part). Population (2010), 706,622.

ZIP Codes: 63005, 63010–11, 63017, 63021, 63025–26, 63038, 63040, 63043–44, 63049, 63069, 63074, 63088, 63105, 63114, 63117, 63119, 63122–32, 63141, 63144, 63146, 63301, 63303–04, 63341, 63366, 63368, 63376

* * *

THIRD DISTRICT

BLAINE LUETKEMEYER, Republican, of St. Elizabeth, MO; born in Jefferson City, MO, May 7, 1952; education: graduate of Lincoln University, Jefferson City, MO, 1974, where he earned a degree with distinction in political science and a minor in business administration; professional: served as Missouri State Representative, 1999–2005, and after leaving office was appointed by the Governor to serve as director of the Missouri Division of Tourism; religion: life-long member of St. Lawrence Catholic Church; married: Jackie, three children; committees: Financial Services; elected to the 111th Congress on November 4, 2008; reelected to each succeeding Congress.

Office Listings

https://luetkemeyer.house.gov https://facebook.com/BlaineLuetkemeyer
twitter: @RepBlaine https://instagram.com/repblaine

2230 Rayburn House Office Building, Washington, DC 20515 .... (202) 225–2956
Chief of Staff.—Chad Ramey.
Senior Policy Advisor.—Lucas West.
Legislative Director.—Meghan Schmedtlein.
Communications Director.—Georgeanna Sullivan.
Director of Operations.—Ann Vogel.
Legislative Assistant.—Josiah Boman.
Legislative Aide.—Jordan Wood.
Staff Assistant.—Shawnda Turner.
2117 Missouri Boulevard, Jefferson City, MO 65109 .... (573) 635–7232
Deputy Chief of Staff.—Jeremy Ketterer.
Director of Constituent Affairs.—Keri Stuart.
Constituent Liaison.—Lori Boyken.
Special Assistant.—Taylor Gibbs.
516 Jefferson Street, Washington, MO 63090 .... (636) 239–2276
District Office Director.—Jim McNichols.
113 East Pearce Boulevard, Wentzville, MO 63385 .... (573) 327–7055
District Office Director.—Christa Montgomery.

Counties: CALLAWAY, CAMDEN (part), COLE, FRANKLIN, GASCONADE, JEFFERSON (part), LINCOLN, MARIES, MILLER, MONTGOMERY, OSAGE, ST. CHARLES (part), AND WARREN. Population (2010), 748,615.

ZIP Codes: 63005 (part), 63010 (part), 63012 (part), 63013–14, 63015–16 (part), 63019 (part), 63023 (part), 63025–26 (part), 63028 (part), 63037, 63039, 63041 (part), 63048, 63049–50 (part), 63051–53, 63055, 63057, 63060–61, 63068, 63069–70 (part), 63072 (part), 63073, 63077, 63079, 63080 (part), 63084, 63089–91, 63301 (part), 63302, 63303 (part), 63332–33, 63334 (part), 63341 (part), 63342, 63343–44 (part), 63346–51, 63352 (part), 63357, 63359 (part), 63361–63, 63365, 63366 (part), 63367, 63368 (part), 63369–70, 63373, 63376 (part), 63377–79, 63381, 63383, 63384 (part)

* * *

FOURTH DISTRICT

VICKY HARTZLER, Republican, of Harrisonville, MO; born in Archie, MO, October 13, 1960; education: B.S., in education, *summa cum laude*, University of Missouri-Columbia, Columbia, MO, 1983; M.S., in education, Central Missouri State University (now University of Central Missouri), Warrensburg, MO, 1992; professional: served as State spokesperson for the Coalition to Protect Marriage, 2004; member of the Missouri State House of Representatives, 124th District, 1995–2001; appointed chair, Missouri Women's Council, 2005; teacher of family and consumer sciences for 11 years in Lebanon and Belton, MO; religion: Evangelical Christian; family: married to Lowell Hartzler; one child: Tiffany; caucuses: Air Force Caucus; Army Caucus; China Caucus; Congressional Coalition on Adoption; EMP Caucus; General Aviation Caucus; Human Trafficking Caucus; International Religious Freedom Caucus; Israel Allies Caucus; Job Creators' Caucus; Long-Range Strike Caucus; Military Family Caucus; Missile Defense Caucus; Prayer Caucus; Pro-Life Caucus; Republican Study Committee; Rural Caucus; Small Business Caucus; Taiwan Caucus; committees: Agriculture; Armed Services; elected to the 112th Congress on November 2, 2010; reelected to each succeeding Congress.

Office Listings

https://hartzler.house.gov https://facebook.com/Congresswoman.Hartzler https://twitter.com/rephartzler

2235 Rayburn House Office Building, Washington, DC 20515 .... (202) 225–2876
Chief of Staff.—Chris Connelly. FAX: 225–0148
Legislative Director.—Chrissi Lee.
Communications Director.—Anna Swick.
Scheduler.—Jillian Vogl.
2415 Carter Lane, Suite 4, Columbia, MO 65201 .... (573) 442–9311
1909 North Commercial Street, Harrisonville, MO 64701 .... (816) 884–3411
219 North Adams Street, Lebanon, MO 65536 .... (417) 532–5582

Counties: AUDRAIN (part), BARTON, BATES, BENTON, BOONE, CAMDEN, CASS, CEDAR, COOPER, DADE, DALLAS, HENRY, HICKORY, HOWARD, JOHNSON, LACLEDE, MONITEAU, MORGAN, PULASKI, RANDOLPH, ST. CLAIR, VERNON, AND WEBSTER (part). Population (2010), 748,616.

ZIP Codes: 63352, 64011–12, 64019–20, 64030, 64034, 64037, 64040, 64061, 64070–71, 64076, 64078, 64080, 64082–83, 64090, 64093, 64147, 64149, 64701, 64720, 64722–26, 64728, 64730, 64733–35, 64738–48, 64750, 64752, 64755–56, 64759, 64761–63, 64765–67, 64769–72, 64776, 64778–81, 64783–84, 64788, 64790, 64832, 64855, 65010–11, 65018, 65020, 65023, 65025–26, 65034, 65037–39, 65042, 65046, 65050, 65055, 65064, 65068, 65072, 65074, 65078–79, 65081, 65084, 65201–03, 65205, 65211–12, 65215–18, 65230–33, 65237, 65239–40, 65243–44, 65247–48, 65250, 65254–57, 65259–60, 65264–65, 65270, 65274, 65276, 65278–80, 65284–85, 65287, 65299, 65301–02, 65305, 65322–26, 65329, 65332–38, 65340, 65345, 65347–48, 65350–51, 65354–55, 65360, 65452, 65457, 65459, 65461, 65463, 65470, 65473, 65534, 65536, 65543, 65550, 65552, 65556, 65567, 65583–84, 65590–91, 65603–04, 65607, 65622, 65632, 65634–36, 65644, 65646, 65648–50, 65652, 65661–62, 65668, 65674, 65682, 65685, 65706, 65713, 65722, 65724, 65732, 65735, 65742, 65746, 65752, 65757, 65764, 65767, 65770, 65774, 65779, 65783, 65785–87

* * *

FIFTH DISTRICT

EMANUEL CLEAVER II, Democrat, of Kansas City, MO; born in Waxahachie, TX, October 26, 1944; education: M.Div., Saint Paul School of Theology, MO, 1974; B.S., Prairie View A&M University, TX, 1972; professional: senior pastor, St. James United Methodist Church, 1973–2009; City Councilman, Kansas City, MO, 5th District, 1979–91; founder, Harmony in a World of Difference, 1991; founder, Southern Christian Leadership Conference, Kansas City Chapter; Mayor of Kansas City, MO, 1991–99; member, President-elect Bill Clinton's transitional team, 1992; host, Under the Clock, KCUR radio, 1999–2004; chairman of the Congressional Black Caucus, 2010–12; member, National Co-Chair of President Barack Obama Campaign Committee, 2012; married: Dianne; four children; four grandchildren; committees: Financial Services; Homeland Security; Select Committee on the Modernization of Congress; elected to the 109th Congress on November 2, 2004; reelected to each succeeding Congress.

Office Listings

https://cleaver.house.gov https://facebook.com/emanuelcleaverii
https://twitter.com/repcleaver https://instagram.com/repcleaver

2335 Rayburn House Office Building, Washington, DC 20515 .... (202) 225–4535
Chief of Staff.—Jennifer Taft. FAX: 225–4403
Legislative Director.—Christina Mahoney.
Scheduler.—Herline Mathieu.
101 West 31st Street, Kansas City, MO 64108 .... (816) 842–4545
Communications Director.—Matt Helfant.
411 West Maple Avenue, Suite F, Independence, MO 64050 .... (816) 833–4545
1923 Main Street, Higginsville, MO 64037 .... (660) 584–7373

Counties: CLAY COUNTY (part), JACKSON COUNTY (part), LAFAYETTE, RAY, AND SALINE COUNTIES. CITIES AND TOWNSHIPS: Blue Springs, Claycomo, Concordia, Gladstone, Grain Valley, Grandview, Higginsville, Independence, Kansas City, Lawson, Lee's Summit, Lexington, Marshall, North Kansas City, Oak Grove, Odessa, Raytown, Richmond, Slater Sugar Creek, and Sweet Springs. Population (2010), 747,573.

ZIP Codes: 64001, 64011, 64017, 64020–22, 64024, 64029, 64035–37, 64062, 64067, 64071, 64074–77, 64084–85, 64096–97, 64747–48, 65320, 65327, 65330, 65339–40, 65344, 65347, 65349, 65351

* * *

SIXTH DISTRICT

SAM GRAVES, Republican, of Tarkio, MO; born in Fairfax, MO, November 7, 1963; education: B.S., University of Missouri-Columbia, 1986; professional: farmer; organizations: Missouri Farm Bureau; Northwest Missouri State University Agriculture Advisory Committee; University Extension Council; Rotary Club; awards: Associated Industries Voice of Missouri Business Award; Tom Henderson Award; Tarkio Community Betterment Award; Missouri Physical Therapy Association Award; Outstanding Young Farmer Award, 1997; Hero of the Taxpayer Award; NFIB Guardian of Small Business Award; public service: elected to the Missouri House of Representatives, 1992; elected to the Missouri State Senate, 1994; religion: Baptist; committees: Armed Services; Transportation and Infrastructure; elected to the 107th Congress on November 7, 2000; reelected to each succeeding Congress.

Office Listings

https://graves.house.gov https://facebook.com/RepSamGraves https://twitter.com/RepSamGraves

1135 Longworth House Office Building, Washington, DC 20515 .... (202) 225–7041
Chief of Staff.—Tom Brown.
Legislative Director.—Julie Devine.
Communications Director.—Bryan Nichols.
Scheduler.—Amanda Sollazzo.
411 Jules Street, Suite 111, St. Joseph, MO 64501 .... (816) 749–0800

Office Listings—Continued

11724 Northwest Plaza Circle, Suite 900, Kansas City, MO 64153 .... (816) 792–3976
FAX: 792–0694
906 Broadway, P.O. Box 364, Hannibal, MO 63401 .... (573) 221–3400

Counties: ADAIR, ANDREW, ATCHISON, AUDRAIN (part), BUCHANAN, CALDWELL, CARROLL, CHARITON, CLARK, CLAY (part), CLINTON, DAVIESS, DEKALB, GENTRY, GRUNDY, HARRISON, HOLT, JACKSON (part), KNOX, LEWIS, LINN, LIVINGSTON, MACON, MARION, MERCER, MONROE, NODAWAY, PIKE, PLATTE, PUTNAM, RALLS, SCHUYLER, SCOTLAND, SHELBY, SULLIVAN, AND WORTH. Population (2010), 748,616.

ZIP Codes: 63119, 63330, 63334, 63336, 63339, 63343–45, 63352–53, 63359, 63382, 63384, 63401, 63430–43, 63445–48, 63450–54, 63456–69, 63471–74, 63501, 63530–41, 63543–49, 63551–52, 63555–61, 63563, 63565–67, 64013–16, 64018, 64024, 64028–30, 64048, 64051, 64055–58, 64060, 64062–64, 64066, 64068–69, 64072, 64074–75, 64077, 64079, 64085–86, 64088–89, 64092, 64098, 64106, 64112, 64116, 64118–19, 64134, 64150–58, 64163–68, 64188, 64190, 64195, 64401–02, 64420–24, 64426–34, 64436–46, 64448–49, 64451, 64453–59, 64461, 64463, 64465–71, 64473–77, 64479–87, 64489–94, 64496–99, 64501–08, 64601, 64620, 64622–25, 64628, 64630–33, 64635–61, 64664, 64667–68, 64670–74, 64676, 64679, 64681–83, 64686, 64688–89, 64701, 65065, 65202, 65205, 65230, 65232, 65236, 65240, 65243–44, 65246–47, 65254–55, 65258, 65260–61, 65263–65, 65270, 65275, 65280–83, 65286

* * *

SEVENTH DISTRICT

BILLY LONG, Republican, of Springfield, MO; born in Springfield, August 11, 1955; education: attended University of Missouri, Columbia, MO, 1973–74; Missouri Auction School, Kansas City, MO, 1979; Certified Auctioneer Institute designation, University of Indiana, Bloomington, IN, 1983; professional: owner, Billy Long Auctions, LLC; radio talk show host, KWTO AM 560, 1999–2006; former president, Missouri Professional Auctioneers Association; past board member, National Auctioneers Association; past member, Southeast Rotary Club, Springfield; awards: Missouri Professional Auctioneers' Hall of Fame; Outstanding Young Alumni Award, Greenwood Lab School; religion: Presbyterian; family: wife, Barbara Long;.two daughters; caucuses: Republican Conference, 2011–present; committees: Energy and Commerce; elected to the 112th Congress on November 2, 2010; reelected to each succeeding Congress.

Office Listings

https://long.house.gov https://facebook.com/Rep.Billy.Long https://twitter.com/USRepLong

2454 Rayburn House Office Building, Washington, DC 20515 .... (202) 225–6536
FAX: 225–5604
Chief of Staff.—Joe Lillis.
Legislative Director.—Ben Elleson.
Scheduler.—Colton Huthsing.
Communications Director.—Hannah Smith.
3232 East Ridgeview Street, Springfield, MO 65804 .... (417) 889–1800
FAX: 889–4915
2727 East 32nd Street, Suite 2, Joplin, MO 64804 .... (417) 781–1041
FAX: 781–2832

Counties: BARRY, CHRISTIAN, GREENE, JASPER, LAWRENCE, MCDONALD, NEWTON, POLK, STONE, TANEY, AND WEBSTER (part). Population (2010), 721,754.

ZIP Codes: 64748, 64755–56, 64766, 64769, 64801–04, 64830–36, 64840–44, 64847–50, 64853–59, 64861–70, 64873–74, 65603–05, 65608–20, 65622–27, 65629–31, 65633, 65635, 65637–38, 65640–41, 65645–50, 65652–58, 65661, 65663–64, 65666, 65669, 65672–76, 65679–82, 65686, 65702, 65705, 65707–08, 65710, 65712, 65714–15, 65720–21, 65723, 65725–30, 65733–34, 65737–42, 65744–45, 65747, 65752–57, 65759–62, 65765–73, 65781, 65784–85, 65801–10, 65814, 65817, 65890, 65898–99

* * *

EIGHTH DISTRICT

JASON T. SMITH, Republican, of Salem, MO; born in St. Louis, MO, June 16, 1980; education: graduate of Salem High School; received B.S. degrees, agricultural economics and business administration, with an emphasis in finance, University of Missouri, Columbia; earned law degree from Oklahoma City University School of Law; Trinity College, Cambridge, England; professional: attorney; real estate agent; small business owner and fourth generation owner of the family farm; NRA; Missouri Farm Bureau; former president, current member of the Salem FFA Alumni Association; holds an American FFA degree; elected to the Missouri State House of Representatives, 2005 (special election), 2006, and 2008; leadership: served as Majority Whip in the 96th General Assembly; youngest Speaker Pro Tem in the 97th General Assembly; religion: Assemblies of God; committees: Budget; Ways and Means; elected, by special election, to the 113th Congress on June 4, 2013, to fill the vacancy caused by the resignation of U.S. Representative Jo Ann Emerson; reelected to each succeeding Congress.

Office Listings

https://jasonsmith.house.gov https://facebook.com/repjasonsmith
https://twitter.com/RepJasonSmith

2418 Rayburn House Office Building, Washington, DC 20515 .... (202) 225–4404
Chief of Staff.—Mark Roman. FAX: 226–0326
Executive Assistant / Scheduler.—Marshall Stallings.
2502 Tanner Drive, Suite 205, Cape Girardeau, MO 63703 .... (573) 335–0101
830A South Bishop, Rolla, MO 65401 .... (573) 364–2455
22 East Columbia Street, Farmington, MO 63640 .... (573) 756–9755
35 Court Square, Suite 300, West Plains, MO 65775 .... (417) 255–1515
2725 North Westwood Boulevard, Suite 5A, Poplar Bluff, MO 63901 .... (573) 609–2996

Counties: Bollinger, Butler, Cape Girardeau, Carter, Crawford, Dent, Douglas, Dunklin, Howell, Iron, Jefferson (part), Madison, Mississippi, New Madrid, Oregon, Ozark, Pemiscot, Perry, Phelps, Reynolds, Ripley, St. Francois, Ste. Genevieve, Scott, Shannon, Stoddard, Texas, Washington, Wayne, and Wright. Population (2010), 748,616.

ZIP Codes: 63036, 63071, 63601, 63620–26, 63628–33, 63636–38, 63640, 63648, 63650–51, 63653–56, 63660, 63662–66, 63674–75, 63701–03, 63730, 63732, 63735–40, 63742–48, 63750–52, 63755, 63758, 63760, 63763–64, 63766–67, 63769–72, 63774–76, 63779–85, 63787, 63801, 63820–30, 63833–34, 63837, 63839–41, 63845–53, 63855, 63857, 63860, 63862–63, 63866–70, 63873–82, 63901–02, 63931–45, 63950–57, 63960–67, 65401–02, 65409, 65436, 65438–41, 65444, 65446, 65449, 65453, 65456, 65459, 65461–62, 65464, 65466, 65468, 65479, 65483–84, 65501, 65529, 65532, 65541–42, 65546, 65548, 65550, 65552, 65555, 65557, 65564–66, 65570–71, 65586, 65588–89, 65606, 65608–09, 65614, 65616, 65618, 65620, 65626–27, 65629, 65637–38, 65652–53, 65655, 65660, 65662, 65666–67, 65676, 65679–80, 65688–90, 65692, 65701–02, 65704, 65711, 65713, 65715, 65717, 65720, 65729, 65731, 65733, 65740–41, 65744, 65746, 65753, 65755, 65759–62, 65766, 65768, 65773, 65775, 65777–78, 65784, 65788–91, 65793

MONTANA

(Population 2010, 989,415)

SENATORS

JON TESTER, Democrat, of Big Sandy, MT; born in Havre, MT, August 21, 1956; education: graduated, Big Sandy High School, 1974; B.S., music, University of Great Falls, 1978; professional: farmer, T-Bone Farms, Big Sandy, 1978–present; teacher, Big Sandy School District, 1978–80; member, Big Sandy Soil Conservation Service Committee, 1980–83; chairman, Big Sandy School Board of Trustees, 1983–92; past master, Treasure Lodge #95 of the Masons; member, Chouteau County Agricultural Stabilization and Conservation Service Committee, 1990–95; member, Organic Crop Improvement Association, 1996–97; served in Montana Senate, 1999–2007; Montana Senate Democratic Whip, 2001–03; Montana Senate Democratic Leader, 2003–05; Montana Senate President, 2005–07; vice chair, Congressional Sportsmen's Caucus; married: Sharla Tester; two children: Christine and Shon; committees: ranking member, Veterans' Affairs; Appropriations; Banking, Housing, and Urban Affairs; Commerce, Science, and Transportation; Indian Affairs; elected to the U.S. Senate on November 7, 2006; reelected to each succeeding Senate term.

Office Listings

https://tester.senate.gov https://facebook.com/senatortester twitter: @SenatorTester

311 Hart Senate Office Building, Washington, DC 20510 .... (202) 224–2644
Chief of Staff.—Dylan Laslovich. FAX: 224–8594
Legislative Director.—Justin Folsom.
Communications Director.—Sarah Feldman.
Director of Scheduling.—Trecia McEvoy.
State Director.—Pamela Haxby-Cote.
2900 4th Avenue North, Suite 201, Billings, MT 59101 .... (406) 252–0550
FAX: 252–7768
1 East Main Street, Suite 202, Bozeman, MT 59715 .... (406) 586–4450
125 West Granite, Suite 200, Butte, MT 59701 .... (406) 723–3277
119 First Avenue North, Suite 102, Great Falls, MT 59401 .... (406) 452–9585
208 North Montana Avenue, Suite 202, Helena, MT 59601 .... (406) 449–5401
8 3rd Street East, Kalispell, MT 59901 .... (406) 257–3360
130 West Front Street, Missoula, MT 59802 .... (406) 728–3003

* * *

STEVE DAINES, Republican, of Bozeman, MT; born in Van Nuys, CA, August 20, 1962; education: B.S., Montana State University, Bozeman, MT, 1984; professional: businessman; public service: Republican National Convention delegate, 1984; U.S. Representative, 2013–15; married: Cindy; children: David, Annie, Michael, and Caroline; committees: Appropriations; Energy and Natural Resources; Finance; Indian Affairs; elected to the 113th Congress on November 6, 2012; elected to the U.S. Senate on November 4, 2014.

Office Listings

https://daines.senate.gov https://facebook.com/SteveDainesMT

320 Hart Senate Office Building, Washington, DC 20510 .... (202) 224–2651
Chief of Staff.—Jason Thielman.
Deputy Chief of Staff.—Wally Hsueh.
Legislative Director.—Darin Thacker.
Communications Director.—Katie Schoettler.
State Director.—Liz Dellwo.
Scheduler.—Caitlin Affolter.
Press Secretary.—Julia Doyle.
13 South Willson Avenue, Suite 8, Bozeman, MT 59715 .... (406) 587–3446
30 West 14th Street, Suite 206, Helena, MT 59601 .... (406) 443–3189
222 North 32nd Street, Suite 100, Billings, MT 59101 .... (406) 245–6822
218 East Front Street, Suite 103, Missoula, MT 59802 .... (406) 549–8198
104 4th Street North, Suite 302, Great Falls, MT 59401 .... (406) 453–0148
609 South Central Avenue, Suite #4 (Central Plaza Building), Sidney, MT 59270 .... (406) 482–9010
40 2nd Street East, Suite 211 (KM Building), Kalispell, MT 59901 .... (406) 257–3765

REPRESENTATIVE

AT LARGE

GREG GIANFORTE, Republican, of Bozeman, MT; born April 17, 1961; education: M.S. and B.E., Stevens Institute of Technology, Hoboken, NJ, 1983; professional: co-founder, Brightwork Development Inc.; founder, RightNow Technologies; religion: nondenominational Christian, Grace Bible Church; married: Susan; children: Richard, David, Adam, and Rachel; committees: Energy and Commerce; elected to the 115th Congress, by special election, on May 25, 2017, to fill the vacancy caused by the resignation of U.S. Representative Ryan Zinke; reelected to the 116th Congress on November 6, 2018.

Office Listings

https://gianforte.house.gov https://facebook.com/RepGianforte

1222 Longworth House Office Building, Washington, DC 20515 .... (202) 225–3211
Chief of Staff.—Christine Heggem. FAX: 225–5687
Communications Director.—Travis Hall.
Legislative Director.—Will Carraco.
Scheduler.—Alissa Knight.
222 North 32nd Street, Suite 900, Billings, MT 59101 .... (406) 969–1736
District Director.—Lesley Robinson.
7 West 6th Avenue, Suite 3B, Helena, MT 59601 .... (406) 502–1435
710 Central Avenue, Great Falls, MT 59401 .... (406) 952–1280

Counties: BEAVERHEAD, BIG HORN, BLAINE, BROADWATER, CARBON, CARTER, CASCADE, CHOUTEAU, CUSTER, DANIELS, DAWSON, DEER LODGE, FALLON, FERGUS, FLATHEAD, GALLATIN, GARFIELD, GLACIER, GOLDEN VALLEY, GRANITE, HILL, JEFFERSON, JUDITH BASIN, LAKE, LEWIS AND CLARK, LIBERTY, LINCOLN, MADISON, MCCONE, MEAGHER, MINERAL, MISSOULA, MUSSELLSHELL, PARK, PETROLEUM, PHILLIPS, PONDERA, POWDER RIVER, POWELL, PRAIRIE, RAVALLI, RICHLAND, ROOSEVELT, ROSEBUD, SANDERS, SHERIDAN, SILVER BOW, STILLWATER, SWEET GRASS, TETON, TOOLE, TREASURE, VALLEY, WHEATLAND, WIBAUX, AND YELLOWSTONE. Population (2010), 989,415.

ZIP Codes: 59001–04, 59006–08, 59010–16, 59018–20, 59022, 59024–39, 59041, 59043–44, 59046–47, 59050, 59052–55, 59057–59, 59061–72, 59074–79, 59081–89, 59101–08, 59201, 59211–15, 59217–19, 59221–23, 59225–26, 59230–31, 59240–44, 59247–48, 59250, 59252–63, 59270, 59273–76, 59301, 59311–19, 59322–24, 59326–27, 59330, 59332–33, 59336–39, 59341, 59343–45, 59347, 59349, 59351, 59353–54, 59401–06, 59410–12, 59414, 59416–22, 59424–25, 59427, 59430, 59432–36, 59440–48, 59450–54, 59456–57, 59460–69, 59471–72, 59474, 59477, 59479–80, 59482–87, 59489, 59501, 59520–32, 59535, 59537–38, 59540, 59542, 59544–47, 59601–02, 59604, 59620, 59623–24, 59626, 59631–36, 59638–45, 59647–48, 59701–03, 59710–11, 59713–22, 59724–25, 59727–33, 59735–36, 59739–41, 59743, 59745–52, 59754–56, 59758–62, 59771–73, 59801–04, 59806–08, 59812, 59820–21, 59823–35, 59837, 59840–48, 59851, 59853–56, 59858–60, 59863–68, 59870–75, 59901, 59903–04, 59910–23, 59925–37

NEBRASKA

(Population 2010, 1,826,341)

SENATORS

DEB FISCHER, Republican, of Valentine, NE; born in Lincoln, NE, March 1, 1951; education: B.S., University of Nebraska-Lincoln, Lincoln, NE, 1988; professional: rancher; Senator in the Nebraska Unicameral, 2005–13; president of the Nebraska Association of School Boards; commissioner on the Coordinating Commission for Post-Secondary Education; Valentine Rural High School Board of Education; awards: BILLD Fellow, Midwest Council of State Governments Bowhay Institute for Legislative Leadership, 2005; NRD Farm and Ranch Conservation Award, 1999; Nebraska Association of School Boards Lifetime Achievement Award, 1999; Nebraska Rural Community Schools Association Outstanding Board Member Award, 1998–99; Nebraska Cattlemen Environmental Stewardship Award, 1995; Rangeman's Award, Nebraska Section Society for Range Management, 1994; NRD State Grasslands Conservation Award, 1993; Kellogg Fellow, National Center for Food and Policy Research, Resources for the Future, Washington, DC, 1991; LEAD VIII Fellow, Nebraska Leadership Program, 1988–90; religion: Presbyterian; married: Bruce Fischer; three children; three grandchildren; caucuses: co-chair, Sportsmen's Caucus; National Guard Caucus; Pro-Life Caucus; Senate Western Caucus; committees: Agriculture, Nutrition, and Forestry; Armed Services; Commerce, Science, and Transportation; Rules and Administration; elected to the U.S. Senate on November 6, 2012; reelected to the U.S. Senate on November 6, 2018.

Office Listings

https://fischer.senate.gov https://facebook.com/senatordebfischer https://twitter.com/SenatorFischer

454 Russell Senate Office Building, Washington, DC 20510 .... (202) 224–6551
Chief of Staff.—Joe Hack. FAX: 228–1325
Legislative Director.—Emily Leviner.
Communications Director.—Brianna Puccini.
Administrative Director.—Sherri Hupart.
11819 Miracle Hills Drive, Suite 205, Omaha, NE 68154 .... (402) 391–3411
State Director.—Holly Baker. FAX: 391–4725
440 North 8th Street, Suite 120, Lincoln, NE 68508 .... (402) 441–4600
FAX: 476–8753
120 East 16th Street, Suite 203, Scottsbluff, NE 69361 .... (308) 630–2329
FAX: 630–2321
20 West 23rd Street, Kearney, NE 68847 .... (308) 234–2361
FAX: 234–3684
P.O. Box 1021, Norfolk, NE 68702 .... (402) 200–8816

* * *

BEN SASSE, Republican, of Fremont, NE; born in Plainview, NE, February 22, 1972; education: B.A., Harvard University, Cambridge, MA, 1994; M.A., St. John's College, Annapolis, MD, 1998; M.A., M.Phil., and Ph.D., Yale University, New Haven, CT, 2004; professional: management strategist; policy strategist; historian; college president; religion: Presbyterian/Evangelical; married: Melissa McLeod Sasse; three children: Elizabeth, Alexandra, and Breck; committees: Banking, Housing, and Urban Affairs; Finance; Judiciary; Select Committee on Intelligence; elected to the U.S. Senate on November 4, 2014.

Office Listings

https://sasse.senate.gov https://facebook.com/SenatorSasse https://twitter.com/SenSasse

107 Russell Senate Office Building, Washington, DC 20510 .... (202) 224–4224
Chief of Staff.—Raymond Sass.
Deputy Chiefs of Staff: Shelly Blake, Tyler Grassmeyer.
Legislative Director.—Patrick Lehman.
1128 Lincoln Mall, Suite 305, Lincoln, NE 68508 .... (402) 476–1400
4111 Fourth Avenue, Suite 26, Kearney, NE 68845 .... (308) 233–3677
115 Railway Street, Suite C102, Scottsbluff, NE 69361 .... (308) 632–6032
304 North 168th Circle, Suite 213, Omaha, NE 68118 .... (402) 550–8040

REPRESENTATIVES

FIRST DISTRICT

JEFF FORTENBERRY, Republican, of Lincoln, NE; born in Baton Rouge, LA, December 27, 1960; education: B.A., Louisiana State University, 1982; M.P.P., Georgetown University, Washington, DC, 1986; M.Div., Franciscan University, Steubenville, Ohio, 1996; professional: Lincoln City Council, 1997–2001; publishing executive; worked as economist; managed a public relations firm; congressional aide for the Senate Subcommittee on Intergovernmental Relations; family: married to Celeste Gregory; children: five; committees: Appropriations; elected to the 109th Congress on November 2, 2004; reelected to each succeeding Congress.

Office Listings

https://fortenberry.house.gov https://facebook.com/jefffortenberry twitter: @JeffFortenberry

1514 Longworth House Office Building, Washington, DC 20515 .... (202) 225–4806
Chief of Staff.—Reyn Archer. FAX: 225–5686
Legislative Director.—Alan Feyerherm.
Communications Director.—James Crotty.
Executive Assistant.—Mariel Bailey.
301 South 13th Street, Suite 100, Lincoln, NE 68508 .... (402) 438–1598
641 North Broad Street, Fremont, NE 68025.
506 West Madison Avenue, Suite 2, Norfolk, NE 68701 .... (402) 379–2064

Counties: BURT, BUTLER, CASS, COLFAX, CUMING, DIXON, DODGE, LANCASTER, MADISON, OTOE, PLATTE, POLK, SARPY, SAUNDERS, SEWARD, STANTON, THURSTON, AND WASHINGTON. Population (2015), 638,320.

ZIP Codes: 68001–05, 68007 (part), 68008–09, 68014–20, 68023 (part), 68025–26, 68029, 68031, 68033–34, 68036–42, 68044–45, 68047 (part), 68048, 68050, 68055–58, 68061–63, 68064 (part), 68065–67, 68068 (part), 68070–73, 68112 (part), 68113, 68122–23 (part), 68133 (part), 68142 (part), 68147 (part), 68152 (part), 68157 (part), 68301 (part), 68304, 68307, 68313 (part), 68314, 68316 (part), 68317, 68324 (part), 68329 (part), 68330, 68333 (part), 68336, 68339 (part), 68341 (part), 68343 (part), 68344, 68346–47, 68349, 68358–59 (part), 68360, 68364, 68366, 68367–68 (part), 68372, 68379 (part), 68382, 68402–03, 68404–05 (part), 68407, 68409–10, 68413, 68417–19, 68421 (part), 68423, 68428, 68430, 68431 (part), 68434, 68438–39, 68443 (part), 68446, 68448 (part), 68454–56, 68460 (part), 68461–63, 68465 (part), 68501–10, 68512, 68514, 68516–17, 68520–24, 68526–29, 68531–32, 68542, 68583, 68588, 68601 (part), 68602, 68621, 68624, 68626, 68628 (part), 68629, 68631–35, 68640 (part), 68641–44, 68647–49, 68651, 68653, 68654 (part), 68658–59, 68660 (part), 68661–62, 68663 (part), 68664, 68666 (part), 68667, 68669, 68701 (part), 68702, 68710 (part), 68714 (part), 68715–16, 68733 (part), 68738 (part), 68740 (part), 68748, 68752 (part), 68758 (part), 68761 (part), 68768 (part), 68778 (part), 68779, 68781 (part), 68784 (part), 68788, 68791 (part)

* * *

SECOND DISTRICT

DON BACON, Republican, of Papillion, NE; born in Momence, IL, August 16, 1963; education: B.A., political science, Northern Illinois University, 1984; M.A. management, University of Phoenix, 1995; M.A., national security strategy, National War College, 2004; professional: U.S. Air Force, 1985–2014; retired Brigadier General; Air Force Distinguished Service Medal, two Bronze Stars, two Legion of Merits, five Meritorious Service Medals, and Aerial Achievement Medal; military advisor to Congressman Jeff Fortenberry, 2014–15; professor, Bellevue University, 2015–16; candidate for Congress, 2015–16; religion: Christian; family: married to Angie Bacon; children: four; caucuses: Airborne ISR Caucus; Air Force Caucus; Climate Solutions Caucus; Congressional Army Caucus; Congressional Humanities Caucus; Congressional Long-Range Strike Caucus; Congressional Soccer Caucus; Congressional Taiwan Caucus; For Country Caucus; Foster Youth Caucus; GPS Caucus; House Indian Caucus; Military Family Caucus; Problem Solvers Caucus; Republican Study Group; Task Force for Combating Anti-Semitism; Task Force to End Sexual Violence; U.S.-Japan Caucus; U.S.-Philippine Friendship Caucus; Value Action Team; committees: Agriculture; Armed Services; elected to the 115th Congress on November 8, 2016; reelected to the 116th Congress on November 6, 2018.

Office Listings

https://bacon.house.gov https://facebook.com/RepDonBacon twitter: @RepDonBacon

1024 Longworth House Office Building, Washington, DC 20515 .... (202) 225–4155
Chief of Staff.—Mark Dreiling.
Policy Director.—Jeff Kratz.
Executive Assistant.—Claire London.
Communications Director.—Danielle Jensen.
13906 Gold Circle, Suite 101, Omaha, NE 68144 .... (402) 938–0300
Deputy Chief of Staff / District Director.—Ben Ungerman.

Counties: DOUGLAS AND SARPY (part). **CITIES:** Bennington, Boys Town, Elkhorn, Gretna, La Vista, Omaha, Papillion, Ralston, Springfield, Valley, and Waterloo. Population (2010), 608,781.

ZIP Codes: 68010, 68022, 68028, 68046, 68059, 68069, 68102, 68104–06, 68108, 68110–11, 68114, 68116–18, 68124, 68127–28, 68130–32, 68134–38, 68144, 68154, 68164, 68178

* * *

THIRD DISTRICT

ADRIAN SMITH, Republican, of Gering, NE; born in Scottsbluff, NE, December 19, 1970; education: graduated from Gering High School, Gering, 1989; B.S., University of Nebraska, 1993; professional: business owner; education coordinator; Gering, NE, City Council, 1994–98; member of the Nebraska State Legislature, 1999–2007; married: Andrea McDaniel Smith; committees: Ways and Means; elected to the 110th Congress on November 7, 2006; reelected to each succeeding Congress.

Office Listings

https://adriansmith.house.gov twitter: @RepAdrianSmith

502 Cannon House Office Building, Washington, DC 20515 .... (202) 225–6435
Chief of Staff.—Monica Didiuk. FAX: 225–0207
Legislative Director.—Josh Jackson.
Communications Director.—Matthew Goulding.
District Director.—Jena Hoehne.
Scheduler.—Becca Salter.
416 Valley View Drive, Suite 600, Scottsbluff, NE 69361 .... (308) 633–6333
1811 West Second Street, Suite 275, Grand Island, NE 68803 .... (308) 384–3900

Counties: ADAMS, ANTELOPE, ARTHUR, BANNER, BLAINE, BOONE, BOX BUTTE, BOYD, BROWN, BUFFALO, CEDAR, CHASE, CHERRY, CHEYENNE, CLAY, CUSTER, DAKOTA, DAWES, DAWSON, DEUEL, DIXON, DUNDY, FILLMORE, FRANKLIN, FRONTIER, FURNAS, GAGE, GARDEN, GARFIELD, GOSPER, GRANT, GREELEY, HALL, HAMILTON, HARLAN, HAYES, HITCHCOCK, HOLT, HOOKER, HOWARD, JEFFERSON, JOHNSON, KEARNEY, KEITH, KEYA PAHA, KIMBALL, KNOX, LINCOLN, LOGAN, LOUP, MCPHERSON, MERRICK, MORRILL, NANCE, NEMAHA, NUCKOLLS, PAWNEE, PERKINS, PHELPS, PIERCE, RED WILLOW, RICHARDSON, ROCK, SALINE, SCOTTSBLUFF, SHERIDAN, SHERMAN, SIOUX, THAYER, THOMAS, VALLEY, WAYNE, WEBSTER, WHEELER, AND YORK. Population (2010), 608,438.

ZIP Codes: 60902, 68030, 68305, 68309–10, 68315, 68318, 68320–21, 68326, 68328, 68330, 68337, 68340, 68350, 68352, 68355, 68361–62, 68375, 68377, 68380, 68401, 68406, 68414–15, 68422, 68429, 68431, 68433, 68440, 68444–45, 68450, 68457, 68467, 68620, 68622, 68710–11, 68713, 68717–18, 68720, 68722–24, 68727–28, 68731, 68736, 68738, 68741–43, 68749, 68751, 68753, 68756, 68760–61, 68763, 68765–66, 68774, 68776, 68778, 68780, 68783, 68787, 68789–90, 68802, 68810, 68812, 68814, 68816, 68818, 68820–22, 68824–27, 68837–38, 68841–44, 68846–50, 68852–54, 68861–62, 68865, 68870–71, 68873, 68879, 68881, 68901, 68920, 68923, 68925–26, 68929, 68932–33, 68939–40, 68946, 68950, 68952, 68954, 68956, 68959, 68961, 68966, 68969–71, 68973, 68975–76, 69020–21, 69023, 69032, 69034, 69036–37, 69041–42, 69046, 69103, 69121, 69123, 69125, 69131–33, 69140–44, 69150–52, 69154, 69160, 69162, 69170, 69171, 69190, 69211, 69218–21, 69331, 69339, 69345–46, 69354, 69361, 69363, 69366–67, 69855

NEVADA

(Population 2010, 2,700,551)

SENATORS

CATHERINE CORTEZ MASTO, Democrat, of Las Vegas, NV; born in Las Vegas, March 29, 1964; education: graduated Clark High School, Las Vegas; B.S., finance, University of Nevada, Reno, 1986; J.D., Gonzaga University, Spokane, WA, 1990; admitted to the Nevada State Bar in 1990; professional: Chief of Staff to Nevada Governor Bob Miller; Criminal Prosecutor, U.S. Attorney's Office, Washington, DC; elected Nevada Attorney General, 2007–15; executive vice chancellor for the Nevada System of Higher Education; committees: Banking, Housing, and Urban Affairs; Energy and Natural Resources; Finance; Indian Affairs; Rules and Administration; elected to the U.S. Senate on November 8, 2016.

Office Listings

https://cortezmasto.senate.gov https://facebook.com/SenatorCortezMasto twitter: @SenCortezMasto

516 Hart Senate Office Building, Washington, DC 20510 .... (202) 224–3542
Chief of Staff.—Reynaldo Benitez.
Legislative Director.—Joleen Rivera.
Communications Director.—Ryan King.
Scheduler.—Anaisy Tolentino.
333 Las Vegas Boulevard South, Suite 8016, Las Vegas, NV 89101 .... (702) 388–5020
State Director.—Zach Zaragoza.
400 South Virginia Street, Suite 902, Reno, NV 89501 .... (775) 686–5750
Northern Nevada Director.—Jennifer Crowe.

* * *

JACKY ROSEN, Democrat, of Henderson, NV; born in Chicago, IL; August 2, 1957; education: B.A., University of Minnesota, Twin Cities, in Minneapolis, MN, 1979; professional: computer programmer, software developer and designer for Summa Corporation; Citibank; Southwest Gas Company; awards: President of Congregation Ner Tamid; religion: Jewish; married: Larry Rosen; children: one; caucuses: Artificial Intelligence Caucus; Comprehensive Care Caucus; Congressional Asian Pacific American Caucus; Congressional Coalition on Adoption; Congressional TRIO Caucus; Cybersecurity Caucus; Cystic Fibrosis Caucus; Senate Cancer Coalition; Senate Caucus on International Narcotics Control; Senate Recycling Caucus; committees: Commerce, Science, and Transportation; Health, Education, Labor, and Pensions; Homeland Security and Governmental Affairs; Small Business and Entrepreneurship; Special Committee on Aging; elected to the 115th Congress on November 8, 2016; elected to the U.S. Senate on November 6, 2018.

Office Listings

https://rosen.senate.gov https://facebook.com/SenJackyRosen
twitter: @SenJackyRosen https://instagram.com/senjackyrosen

144 Russell Senate Office Building, Washington, DC 20510 .... (202) 224–6244
Chief of Staff.—Dara Cohen. FAX: 228–2937
Scheduler.—Nicole Echeto.
Legislative Director.—Grant Dubler.
Communications Director.—Jorge Silva.
Administrative Director.—John Fossum.
Lloyd D. George Federal Courthouse, 333 Las Vegas Boulevard South, Suite 8203, Las Vegas, NV 89101 .... (702) 388–0205
State Director.—Nelson Araujo.
Bruce R. Thompson U.S. Courthouse, 400 South Virginia Street, Suite 738, Reno, NV 89501 .... (775) 337–0110
Northern Nevada Director.—Emily Lande-Rose.

REPRESENTATIVES

FIRST DISTRICT

DINA TITUS, Democrat, of Las Vegas, NV; born in Thomasville, Thomas County, GA, May 23, 1950; education: B.A., College of William and Mary, Williamsburg, VA, 1970; M.A., University of Georgia, Athens, GA, 1973; Ph.D., Florida State University, Tallahassee, FL, 1976; professional: professor, University of Nevada, Las Vegas, NV, 1977–2011; UNLV professor emeritus, 2011–present; member of Nevada State Senate, 1989–2008; Minority Leader of Nevada State Senate, 1993–2008; married: Thomas C. Wright, Ph.D.; committees: Foreign Affairs; Homeland Security; Transportation and Infrastructure; elected to the 3rd District in the 111th Congress on November 4, 2008; elected to the 1st District on November 6, 2012 in the 113th Congress; reelected to each succeeding Congress.

Office Listings

https://titus.house.gov https://facebook.com/CongresswomanTitus https://twitter.com/RepDinaTitus

2464 Rayburn House Office Building, Washington, DC 20515 .... (202) 225–5965
Chief of Staff.—Jay Gertsema. FAX: 225–3119
Legislative Director.—Ben Rosenbaum.
Communications Director.—Kevin Gerson.
Scheduler.—Colleen Hearin.
495 South Main Street, 3rd Floor, Las Vegas, NV 89101 .... (702) 220–9823
District Director.—Vinny Spotleson. FAX: 220–9841

Counties: CLARK COUNTY (part). CITIES: Las Vegas and North Las Vegas. Population (2010), 659,962.

ZIP Codes: 89030, 89087, 89101–04, 89106–22, 89125–26, 89128, 89132, 89142, 89145–47, 89150–53, 89155–58, 89160, 89162, 89169–70, 89173, 89177, 89180, 89193

* * *

SECOND DISTRICT

MARK E. AMODEI, Republican, of Carson City, NV; born in Carson City, June 12, 1958; education: B.A., University of Nevada, Reno, NV, 1980; J.D., University of the Pacific, McGeorge School of Law, Sacramento, CA, 1983; professional: lawyer, Allison, MacKenzie et al., 1987–present; lawyer, U.S. Army Judge Advocate General Corps, 1983–87; Nevada State Assembly, 1996–98; Senator, Nevada State Senate, 1998–2010; President Pro Tempore, Nevada State Senate, 2003–08; member of Carson City Master Plan Advisory Committee; member of Education Commission of the States; vice chair of Governor's Task Force on Access to Public Health Care; member of Nevada Supreme Court's Committee on Court Funding; member of Tahoe Regional Planning Agency Legislative Oversight Committee; committees: Appropriations; elected, by special election, to the 112th Congress on September 13, 2011; reelected to each succeeding Congress.

Office Listings

https://amodei.house.gov https://facebook.com/MarkAmodeiNV2 twitter: @MarkAmodeiNV2

104 Cannon House Office Building, Washington, DC 20515 .... (202) 225–6155
Chief of Staff.—Bruce Miller. FAX: 225–5679
905 Railroad Street, Suite 104 D, Elko, NV 89801 .... (775) 777–7705
FAX: 753–9984
5310 Kietzke Lane, Suite 103, Reno, NV 89511. ....

Counties: CARSON CITY, CHURCHILL, DOUGLAS, ELKO, HUMBOLDT, LANDER, LYON (part), PERSHING, STOREY, AND WASHOE. Population (2010), 679,147.

ZIP Codes: 89310, 89316, 89402–06, 89408, 89410–14, 89418–19, 89421, 89423–26, 89428–29, 89431, 89433–34, 89436, 89438–42, 89444–51, 89460, 89501–03, 89506, 89508–12, 89519, 89521, 89523, 89701–06, 89801, 89815, 89820–23, 89825–26, 89828, 89830–35, 89883

* * *

THIRD DISTRICT

SUSIE LEE, Democrat; of Las Vegas, NV; born in Canton, OH, November 7, 1966; education: B.A., 1989, and M.P.M., 1990, Carnegie Mellon University, Pittsburgh, PA; professional: nonprofit executive; committees: Education and Labor; Veterans' Affairs; elected to the 116th Congress on November 6, 2018.

Office Listings

https://susielee.house.gov https://facebook.com/RepSusieLee https://twitter.com/RepSusieLee

522 Cannon House Office Building, Washington, DC 20515 .... (202) 225–3252

Office Listings—Continued

Chief of Staff.—Brandon Cox. FAX: 225–2185
Scheduler.—Sreyashe Dhar.
Legislative Director.—Sam Morgante.
Communications Director.—Sarah Abel.
District Director.—Mike Vannozzi.
8872 South Eastern Avenue, Suite 220, Las Vegas, NV 89123 .... (702) 963–9500

Counties: CLARK COUNTY (part). Population (2010), 675,138.

ZIP Codes: 89002, 89004–05 (part), 89011 (part), 89012, 89014 (part), 89015, 89019, 89026, 89029, 89039, 89044, 89046, 89052, 89054, 89074, 89113 (part), 89117–20 (part), 89122 (part), 89123, 89124 (part), 89134 (part), 89135, 89138–39, 89141, 89144–45 (part), 89147 (part), 89148, 89156 (part), 89161, 89178–79, 89183

* * *

FOURTH DISTRICT

STEVEN HORSFORD, Democrat, of North Las Vegas, NV; born in Las Vegas, NV, April 29, 1973; education: attended University of Nevada, Reno; professional: CEO, Culinary Training Academy; member of the Nevada State Senate, 2004–12; majority leader, Nevada State Senate, 2009–12; Representative, 113th United States Congress, District 4, 2013–15; religion: Baptist; married: Dr. Sonya Horsford; caucuses: Black Men and Boys Caucus; Congressional Asian Pacific American Caucus; Congressional Black Caucus; Congressional Progressive Caucus; Gun Violence Prevention Task Force; Men's Health Caucus; New Democrats Coalition; Pro-Choice Caucus; committees: Budget, Natural Resources, Ways and Means; elected to the 113th Congress on November 6, 2012; elected to the 116th Congress on November 6, 2018.

Office Listings

https://horsford.house.gov https://facebook.com/RepHorsford twitter: @RepHorsford

1330 Longworth House Office Building, Washington, DC 20515 .... (202) 225–9894
Chief of Staff.—Asha Jones. FAX: 225–9783
Deputy Chief of Staff.—Jason Rodriguez.
Legislative Director.—Josie Villanueva.
Communications Director.—Shelbie Bostedt.
Scheduler.—Oscar Dunham.
2250 Las Vegas Boulevard North, Suite 500, North Las Vegas, NV 89030 .... (702) 963–9360

Counties: CLARK COUNTY (most of the northern part), ESMERALDA, LINCOLN, LYON (part), MINERAL, NYE, AND WHITE PINE. Population (2010), 680,935.

ZIP Codes: 89001, 89003, 89007–08, 89010, 89013–14, 89017–18, 89020–23, 89025, 89027, 89030–32, 89034, 89040–43, 89045, 89047–49, 89060–61, 89081, 89084–86, 89101, 89103, 89106–10, 89115, 89124, 89128–31, 89134–35, 89142–43, 89149, 89156, 89158, 89161, 89166, 89191, 89301, 89310–11, 89314–19, 89409, 89415, 89420, 89422, 89427, 89430, 89444, 89447, 89833, 89883

NEW HAMPSHIRE

(Population 2010, 1,316,470)

SENATORS

JEANNE SHAHEEN, Democrat, of Madbury, NH; born in Saint Charles, MO, January 28, 1947; education: graduated, Selinsgrove Area High School, Selinsgrove, PA, 1965; B.A., Shippensburg University, Shippensburg, PA, 1969; M.S.S., University of Mississippi, 1973; professional: high school teacher; co-owner of a small retail business; consultant; New Hampshire State Senator; Governor of New Hampshire; director of Harvard's Institute of Politics; married: William Shaheen; three children: Stefany, Stacey, and Molly; Commission on Security and Cooperation in Europe; committees: Appropriations; Armed Services; Foreign Relations; Small Business and Entrepreneurship; Select Committee on Ethics; elected to the 111th U.S. Senate on November 4, 2008; reelected to the U.S. Senate on November 4, 2014.

Office Listings

https://shaheen.senate.gov https://facebook.com/SenatorShaheen
https://twitter.com/SenatorShaheen https://instagram.com/senatorshaheen

506 Hart Senate Office Building, Washington, DC 20510 .... (202) 224–2841
Chief of Staff.—Chad Kreikemeier.
Deputy Chief of Staff.—Jennifer MacLellan.
Legislative Director.—Robert Diznoff.
Communications Director.—Ryan Nickel.
Press Secretary.—Sarah Weinstein.
Scheduler.—Meaghan D'Arcy.
2 Wall Street, Suite 220, Manchester, NH 03101 .... (603) 647–7500
60 Main Street, Suite 217, Nashua, NH 03060 .... (603) 883–0196
340 Central Avenue, Suite 205, Dover, NH 03820 .... (603) 750–3004
50 Opera House Square, Claremont, NH 03743 .... (603) 542–4872
961 Main Street, Berlin, NH 03570 .... (603) 752–6300
12 Gilbo Avenue, Suite C, Keene, NH 03431 .... (603) 358–6604

* * *

MARGARET "MAGGIE" WOOD HASSAN, Democrat, of Newfields, NH; born in Boston, MA, February 27, 1958; education: B.A., Brown University, Providence, RI, 1980; J.D., Northeastern University School of Law, Boston, MA, 1985; professional: attorney; New Hampshire State Senator, 2004–10, serving as Majority Leader, 2008–10; Governor of New Hampshire, 2013–16; married: Thomas Hassan; two children: Ben and Meg; committees: Finance; Health, Education, Labor, and Pensions; Homeland Security and Governmental Affairs; Joint Economic Committee; elected to the U.S. Senate on November 8, 2016.

Office Listings

https://hassan.senate.gov https://facebook.com/SenatorHassan https://twitter.com/senatorhassan

324 Hart Senate Office Building, Washington, DC 20510 .... (202) 224–3324
Chief of Staff.—Marc Goldberg. FAX: 224–4952
Deputy Chief of Staff.—Kelly Boyer.
Legislative Director.—Dave Christie.
Communications Director.—Aaron Jacobs.
Scheduler.—Catherine George.
1589 Elm Street, Third Floor, Manchester, NH 03101 .... (603) 622–2204
14 Manchester Square, Suite 140, Portsmouth, NH 03801 .... (603) 433–4445

REPRESENTATIVES

FIRST DISTRICT

CHRIS PAPPAS, Democrat, of Manchester, NH; born in Manchester, June 4, 1980; education: graduated from Manchester Central High School, Manchester, NH, 1998; A.B., government, Harvard University, Cambridge, MA, 2002; professional: fourth generation owner of a family restaurant business, The Puritan Backroom, that opened in 1917; member, New Hampshire State House of Representatives, 2003–07; Hillsborough County, NH, treasurer, 2007–11; member, New Hampshire Executive Council, 2013–18; religion: Greek Orthodox; caucuses: co-chair, Congressional LGBT Equality Caucus; New Democrat Coalition; Tom Lantos Human Rights Commission; committees: Transportation and Infrastructure; Veterans' Affairs; the first openly gay person representing NH in Congress; elected to the 116th Congress on November 6, 2018.

Office Listings

https://pappas.house.gov https://facebook.com/RepChrisPappas
https://twitter.com/RepChrisPappas https://instagram.com/repchrispappas

323 Cannon House Office Building, Washington, DC 20515 .... (202) 225–5456
Chief of Staff.—Matt Lee.
Scheduler.—Liz Kulig.
Legislative Director.—Steven Carlson.
Communications Director.—Collin Gately.
889 Elm Street, Manchester, NH 03101 .... (603) 935–6710
660 Central Avenue, Suite 101, Dover, NH 03820 .... (603) 285–4300

Counties: BELKNAP (part), CARROLL, GRAFTON (part), HILLSBOROUGH (part), MERRIMACK (part), ROCKINGHAM (part), AND STRAFFORD. CITIES AND TOWNS: Bedford, Derry, Dover, Durham, Goffstown, Londonderry, Manchester, Merrimack, Portsmouth, and Rochester. Population (2015), 671,640.

ZIP Codes: 03031–32, 03034, 03036, 03038, 03040–42, 03044–45, 03051, 03053–54, 03077, 03101–06, 03108–11, 03215, 03217–18, 03220, 03223, 03225–27, 03235, 03237, 03245–47, 03249, 03252–54, 03256, 03259, 03261, 03269, 03276, 03285, 03289–91, 03299, 03801–04, 03809–27, 03830, 03832–33, 03835–62, 03864–75, 03878, 03882–87, 03890, 03894, 03896–97

* * *

SECOND DISTRICT

ANN McLANE KUSTER, Democrat, of Hopkinton, NH; born in Concord, NH, September 5, 1956; education: B.A., Dartmouth College, Hanover, NH, 1978; J.D., Georgetown University Law Center, Washington, DC, 1984; professional: consultant and owner, Newfound Strategies LLC; lawyer and partner, Rath, Young and Pignatelli; married: Brad Kuster; children: Zach and Travis; committees: Energy and Commerce; elected to the 113th Congress on November 6, 2012; reelected to each succeeding Congress.

Office Listings

https://kuster.house.gov

320 Cannon House Office Building, Washington, DC 20515 .... (202) 225–5206
Chief of Staff.—Pat Devney. FAX: 225–2946
Legislative Director.—Travis Krogman.
Scheduler.—Maria Ewing.
Communications Director.—Jen Fox.
18 North Main Street, 4th Floor, Concord, NH 03301 .... (603) 226–1002
District Director.—Nick Brown. FAX: 226–1010
184 Main Street, Nashua, NH 03060 .... (603) 595–2006
FAX: 595–2016
33 Main Street, Suite 202, Littleton, NH 03561 .... (603) 444–7700

Counties: BELKNAP (part), CHESHIRE, COOS, GRAFTON (part), HILLSBOROUGH (part), MERRIMACK (part), ROCKINGHAM (part), AND SULLIVAN. Population (2013), 658,237.

ZIP Codes: 03031, 03033–34, 03037–38, 03043, 03045–49, 03051–52, 03054–55, 03057, 03060–64, 03070–71, 03073, 03076, 03079, 03082, 03084, 03086–87, 03110, 03215–17, 03220–24, 03226, 03229–31, 03233–35, 03237–38, 03240–45, 03251, 03253, 03255–58, 03260–64, 03266, 03268, 03272–73, 03275–76, 03278–82, 03284–85, 03287, 03293, 03301–05, 03307, 03431, 03435, 03440–52, 03455–58, 03461–62, 03464–70, 03561, 03570, 03574–76, 03579–86, 03588–90, 03592–93, 03595, 03597–98, 03601–05, 03607–09, 03740–41, 03743, 03745–46, 03748–56, 03765–66, 03768–71, 03773–74, 03777, 03779–82, 03784–85, 03811, 03825, 03841

NEW JERSEY

(Population 2010 8,791,894)

SENATORS

ROBERT MENENDEZ, Democrat, of North Bergen, NJ; born in New York City, NY, January 1, 1954; education: graduated, Union Hill High School, 1972; B.A., St. Peter's College, Jersey City, NJ, 1976; J.D., Rutgers Law School, Newark, NJ, 1979; professional: attorney; elected to the Union City Board of Education, 1974–78; admitted to the New Jersey Bar, 1980; Mayor of Union City, 1986–92; member: New Jersey Assembly, 1987–91; New Jersey State Senate; Alliance Civic Association; U.S. House of Representatives, 1993–2006; vice chair, Democratic Caucus, 1998–99; chair, Democratic Caucus, 2003–06; chair, Democratic Senatorial Campaign Committee, 2009–10; chairman, Senate Committee on Foreign Relations, 2013–15; children: Alicia and Robert; committees: ranking member, Foreign Relations; Banking, Housing, and Urban Affairs; Finance; elected on November 3, 1992, to the 103rd Congress; reelected to each succeeding Congress; appointed to the U.S. Senate on January 17, 2006, by Governor Jon S. Corzine; elected to the 110th Congress for a full Senate term on November 7, 2006; reelected to each succeeding Senate term.

Office Listings

https://menendez.senate.gov https://facebook.com/senatormenendez https://twitter.com/SenatorMenendez

528 Hart Senate Office Building, Washington, DC 20510 .... (202) 224–4744
Chief of Staff.—Fred L. Turner. FAX: 228–2197
Administrative Director.—Robert Kelly.
Legislative Director.—Rebecca Schatz.
One Gateway Center, 11th Floor, Newark, NJ 07102 .... (973) 645–3030
208 White Horse Pike, Suite 18, Barrington, NJ 08007 .... (856) 757–5353

* * *

CORY A. BOOKER, Democrat, of Newark, NJ; born in Washington, DC, April 27, 1969; education: graduated, Northern Valley Regional High School at Old Tappan, 1987; B.A., political science, Stanford University, 1991; M.A., sociology, Stanford University, 1992; Oxford University Rhodes Scholar, 1994; J.D., Yale Law School, 1997; professional: staff attorney, Urban Justice Center, New York, NY, 1997; member, Newark City Council, 1998–2002; partner, Booker, Rabinowitz, Trenk, Lubetkin, Tully, DiPasquale & Webster, P.C., 2002–06; Mayor, City of Newark, 2006–13; religion: Baptist; committees: Environment and Public Works; Foreign Relations; Judiciary, Small Business and Entrepreneurship; elected, by special election, to the U.S. Senate on October 16, 2013, to fill the vacancy caused by the death of U.S. Senator Frank R. Lautenberg; reelected to the U.S. Senate on November 4, 2014.

Office Listings

https://booker.senate.gov twitter: @senbooker

717 Hart Senate Office Building, Washington, DC 20510 .... (202) 224–3224
Chief of Staff.—Tricia Russell. FAX: 224–8378
Legislative Director.—Veronica Duron.
Scheduler.—Jane Wiesenberg.
Communications Director.—Kristin Lynch.
One Gateway Center, 11–43 Raymond Plaza West, Suite 2300, Newark, NJ 07102 .... (973) 639–8700
One Port Center, 2 Riverside Drive, Suite 505, Camden, NJ 08101 .... (856) 338–8922

REPRESENTATIVES

FIRST DISTRICT

DONALD NORCROSS, Democrat, of Camden, NJ; born in Camden, December 13, 1958; education: graduated, Pennsauken High School, Pennsauken, NJ, 1977; associate's degree, criminal justice, Camden County College, Blackwood, NJ, 1979; professional: vice president of United Building Trades Council of Southern New Jersey, 2004–13; electrician at IBEW Local 351, 1979–93; United Way board member, 1992–2014; Union Organization for Social Service, president and CEO, 1993–98; business agent / assistant business manager of IBEW Local 351, 1998–2014; president of the Southern New Jersey AFL–CIO Central Labor Council, 1995–2011; New Jersey General Assembly, 2010; New Jersey State Senate, 2010–14; married: Andrea

Doran; children: Donald Jr., Corey, and Greg; committees: Armed Services; Education and Labor; elected simultaneously to the 113th and 114th Congresses on November 4, 2014, by special election, to fill the vacancy caused by the resignation of U.S. Representative Robert Andrews; reelected to each succeeding Congress.

Office Listings

https://norcross.house.gov https://facebook.com/DonaldNorcrossNJ https://twitter.com/DonaldNorcross

2437 Rayburn House Office Building, Washington, DC 20515 .... (202) 225–6501
Chief of Staff.—Michael J. Maitland.
Legislative Director.—Ryan Ehly.
Communications Director.—Allyson Kehoe.
10 Melrose Avenue, Suite 210, Cherry Hill, NJ 08003 .... (856) 427–7000
District Director.—Mary Campbell Cruz.

Counties: BURLINGTON COUNTY. CITIES AND TOWNSHIPS: Maple Shade Township and Palmyra. CAMDEN COUNTY. CITIES AND TOWNSHIPS: Audubon, Audubon Park, Barrington, Bellmawr, Berlin, Berlin Township, Brooklawn, Camden, Cherry Hill, Chesilhurst, Clementon, Collingswood, Gibbsboro, Gloucester City, Gloucester Township, Haddon Heights, Haddon Township, Hi-Nella, Laurel Springs, Lawnside, Lindenwold, Magnolia, Merchantville, Mt. Ephraim, Oaklyn, Pennsauken Township, Pine Hill, Pine Valley, Runnemede, Somerdale, Stratford, Tavistock, Voorhees Township, Winslow Township, and Woodlynne. GLOUCESTER COUNTY. CITIES AND TOWNSHIPS: Deptford, East Greenwich, Greenwich, Logan Township, Monroe, National Park, Paulsboro, Washington Township, Wenonah, West Deptford Township, Westville, Woodbury, and Woodbury Heights. Population (2015), 727,496.

ZIP Codes: 08002–04, 08007, 08009, 08012, 08014, 08020–21, 08026–33, 08037, 08043, 08045, 08049, 08051–52, 08056, 08059, 08061–63, 08065–66, 08077–78, 08080–81, 08083–86, 08089–91, 08093–94, 08096–97, 08099, 08101–05, 08107–10

* * *

SECOND DISTRICT

JEFFERSON VAN DREW, Republican, of Dennis Township, NJ; born in New York City, NY, February 23, 1953; education: B.S., Rutgers University, New Brunswick, NJ; D.D.S., Fairleigh Dickinson University, Teaneck, NJ; professional: retired dentist; Dennis Township Fire Commissioner, 1983–86; Cape May County Board of Freeholders, 1994–97; Mayor, Dennis Township, 1994–95 and 1997–2003; member, New Jersey General Assembly, 2002–07; Assistant Majority Leader, 2006–07; New Jersey State Senator, 2008–19; committees: Education and Labor; Homeland Security; elected to the 116th Congress on November 6, 2018.

Office Listings

https://vandrew.house.gov https://facebook.com/CongressmanJVD https://twitter.com/CongressmanJVD

331 Cannon House Office Building, Washington, DC 20515 .... (202) 225–6572
Chief of Staff.—Allison Murphy.
5914 Main Street, Mays Landing, NJ 08330 .... (609) 625–5008
District Director.—John Kirk.

Counties: BURLINGTON (part). CITIES AND TOWNSHIPS: Bass River and Washington. CAMDEN COUNTY (part) AND ATLANTIC COUNTY. CITIES AND TOWNSHIPS: Absecon, Atlantic City, Brigantine, Buena, Cardiff, Collings Lake, Cologne, Corbin City, Dorothy, Egg Harbor, Estell Manor, Galloway, Hammonton, Landisville, Leeds Point, Linwood, Longport, Margate, Mays Landing, Milmay, Minotola, Mizpah, Newtonville, Northfield, Oceanville, Pleasantville, Pomona, Port Republic, Richland, Somers Point, and Ventnor. CAPE MAY COUNTY. CITIES AND TOWNSHIPS: Avalon, Bargaintown, Beesley's, Belleplain, Burleigh, Cape May, Cape May C.H., Cape May Point, Cold Springs, Del Haven, Dennisville, Dias Creek, Eldora, Erma, Fishing Creek, Goshen, Green Creek, Marmora, Ocean City, Ocean View, Rio Grande, Sea Isle, South Dennis, South Seaville, Stone Harbor, Strathmere, Tuckahoe, Villas, Whitesboro, Wildwood, and Woodbine. CUMBERLAND COUNTY. CITIES AND TOWNSHIPS: Bridgeton, Cedarville, Deerfield, Delmont, Dividing Creek, Dorchester, Fairton, Fortescue, Greenwich, Heislerville, Hopewell, Leesburg, Mauricetown, Millville, Newport, Port Elizabeth, Port Norris, Rosenhayn, Shiloh, and Vineland. GLOUCESTER COUNTY (part). CITIES AND TOWNSHIPS: Clayton, East Greenwich, Ewan, Franklinville, Harrisonville, Malaga, Mantua, Mickleton, Mullica Hill, Newfield, Pitman, Richwood, Swedesboro, and Williamstown. OCEAN COUNTY (part). CITIES AND TOWNSHIPS: Barnegat Light, Harvey Cedars, Stafford Township, Eagleswood, Tuckerton, Little Egg Harbor, Loveladies, Surf City, Ship Bottom, Long Beach Township, and Beach Haven. SALEM COUNTY. CITIES AND TOWNSHIPS: Alloway, Carney's Point, Daretown, Deepwater, Elmer, Elsinboro, Hancocks Bridge, Monroeville, Norma, Pedricktown, Penns Grove, Pennsville, Quinton, Salem, and Woodstown. Population (2010), 736,397.

ZIP Codes: 08001, 08004–06, 08008–09, 08019–20, 08023, 08028, 08037–39, 08050–51, 08056, 08062, 08067, 08069–72, 08074, 08079–80, 08085, 08087, 08089, 08092, 08094, 08098, 08201–05, 08210, 08212, 08215, 08217, 08221, 08223–26, 08230, 08232, 08234, 08240–44, 08251, 08260, 08270, 08302, 08310–12, 08316–24, 08326–30, 08332, 08340–41, 08343–46, 08348–50, 08352–53, 08360–61, 08401–03, 08406

* * *

THIRD DISTRICT

ANDY KIM, Democrat, of Bordentown, NJ; born in Boston, MA, July 12, 1982; education: B.A., political science, University of Chicago, Chicago, IL, 2004; master's, 2007, Ph.D., 2010, international relations, Rhodes Scholar, Truman Scholar, Oxford University, Oxford, United Kingdom; professional: conflict management specialist, U.S. Agency for International Development, 2005; foreign affairs officer, U.S. Department of State, 2009–13; strategic adviser to the Commander, North Atlantic Treaty Organization, International Security Assistance Force, 2011; Iraq Country Director, Office of the Secretary of Defense, U.S. Department of Defense, 2013; director for Iraq, National Security Council, Executive Office of the President of the United States, 2013–15; married: wife, Kammy Lai; two children; committees: Armed Services; Small Business; elected to the 116th Congress on November 6, 2018.

Office Listings

https://kim.house.gov https://facebook.com/RepAndyKimNJ https://twitter.com/RepAndyKimNJ

1516 Longworth House Office Building, Washington, DC 20515 .... (202) 225–4765
Chief of Staff.—Amy Pfeiffer. FAX: 225–0778
John F. Kennedy Center, 429 John F. Kennedy Way, P.O. Box 9, Willingboro, NJ 08046 (856) 703–2700
FAX: 369–8988
Township of Toms River Town Hall, 33 Washington Street, P.O. Box 728, Toms River, NJ 08753 .... (732) 504–0490
New Jersey District Director.—Ben Giovine. FAX: 714–4244

Counties: BURLINGTON (part) AND OCEAN (part). Population (2010), 732,658.

ZIP Codes: 08005–06, 08008, 08010–11, 08015–16, 08019, 08022, 08036, 08041–42, 08046, 08048, 08050, 08052–55, 08057, 08060, 08064–65, 08068, 08073, 08075, 08077, 08087–88, 08092, 08501, 08505, 08511, 08515, 08518, 08554, 08562, 08610, 08620, 08640–41, 08701, 08721–24, 08731–32, 08734–35, 08738, 08740–42, 08751–53, 08755, 08757–59

* * *

FOURTH DISTRICT

CHRISTOPHER H. SMITH, Republican, of Hamilton, NJ; born in Rahway, NJ, March 4, 1953; education: attended Worcester College, England, 1974; B.A., Trenton State College, 1975; professional: executive director, New Jersey Right to Life Committee, Inc.; businessman; religion: Catholic; married to the former Marie Hahn, 1977; four adult children; six grandchildren; caucuses and commissions: co-chair, Congressional Pro-Life Caucus; co-chair, Tom Lantos Human Rights Commission; ranking member, Congressional-Executive Commission on China; former chair, House Veterans' Affairs Committee; Bicameral Congressional Task Force on Alzheimer's Disease; Bi-Partisan Coalition for Combating Anti-Semitism; Coalition on Autism Research and Education (CARE); Congressional Human Trafficking Caucus; Lyme Disease Caucus; U.S. Helsinki Commission; committees: Foreign Affairs; elected to the 97th Congress on November 4, 1980; reelected to each succeeding Congress.

Office Listings

https://chrissmith.house.gov https://facebook.com/RepChrisSmith https://twitter.com/RepChrisSmith

2373 Rayburn House Office Building, Washington, DC 20515 .... (202) 225–3765
Chief of Staff.—Mary McDermott Noonan. FAX: 225–7768
District Director.—Jo Schloeder.
Legislative Director.—Kelsey Griswold.
112 Village Center Drive, 2nd Floor, Freehold, NJ 07728 .... (732) 780–3035
4573 South Broad Street, First Floor, Hamilton, NJ 08620 .... (609) 585–7878
405 Route 539, Plumsted, NJ 08514 .... By Appointment

Counties: MERCER. MUNICIPALITIES: Hamilton and Robbinsville. MONMOUTH. MUNICIPALITIES: Allentown, Avon-by-the-Sea, Belmar, Bradley Beach, Brielle, Colts Neck, Eatontown, Englishtown, Fair Haven, Farmingdale, Freehold Borough, Freehold Township, Homdel, Howell, Lake Como, Little Silver, Manalapan, Manasquan, Middletown (part), Millstone, Neptune City, Neptune Township, Ocean Township, Red Bank, Roosevelt, Rumson, Sea Girt, Shrewsbury Borough, Shrewsbury Township, Spring Lake, Spring Lake Heights, Tinton Falls, Upper Freehold, and Wall. OCEAN. MUNICIPALITIES: Bay Head, Jackson, Lakehurst, Lakewood, Manchester, Plumsted, Point Pleasant (part), and Point Pleasant Beach. Population (2010), 732,657.

ZIP Codes: 07701 (part), 07702, 07703 (part), 07704, 07711–12 (part), 07717, 07719–20, 07722, 07723 (part), 07724, 07726 (part), 07727–28, 07730 (part), 07731, 07733 (part), 07738–39, 07740 (part), 07748 (part), 07753, 07755–

56, 07760 (part), 07762, 08501, 08510, 08514, 08520 (part), 08527, 08533, 08535, 08555, 08561, 08609 (part), 08610–11 (part), 08619, 08620 (part), 08629 (part), 08638 (part), 08690 (part), 08691, 08701 (part), 08720, 08724 (part), 08730, 08733, 08736, 08742 (part), 08750, 08757 (part), 08759

* * *

FIFTH DISTRICT

JOSH GOTTHEIMER, Democrat, of Wyckoff, NJ; born in Livingston, NJ, March 8, 1975; education: bachelor's in history, University of Pennsylvania, PA, 1997; J.D., Harvard Law School, Boston, MA, 2004; Thouron Fellow; professional: speechwriter to President Bill Clinton; senior advisor to the chair, U.S. Commission on Civil Rights; senior counselor to the chairman of the Federal Communications Commission; director of strategic communications at Ford Motor Company; general manager for corporate strategy at Microsoft; religion: Jewish; wife: Marla; two children: Ben and Ellie; caucuses: co-chair, Problem Solvers Caucus; committees: Financial Services; elected to the 115th Congress on November 8, 2016; reelected to the 116th Congress on November 6, 2018.

Office Listings

https://gottheimer.house.gov

213 Cannon House Office Building, Washington, DC 20515 .... (202) 225–4465
Chief of Staff.—Ashley Lantz.
Legislative Director.—Hannah Berner.
Communications Director.—James Adams.
65 Harristown Road, Suite 104, Glen Rock, NJ 07452 .... (201) 389–1100
District Director.—Vacant.
93 Spring Street, Suite 408, Newton, NJ 07860 .... (973) 940–1117

Counties: BERGEN (part), PASSAIC (part), SUSSEX (part), AND WARREN (part). Population (2010), 731,055.

ZIP Codes: 07401, 07410, 07416–19, 07422–23, 07428, 07430, 07432, 07436, 07446, 07450–52, 07456, 07458, 07461–63, 07466, 07480–81, 07495, 07508, 07601–04, 07607, 07620–22, 07624, 07626–28, 07630–31, 07640–49, 07652–53, 07656, 07660–61, 07663, 07666, 07675–77, 07820–23, 07825–27, 07832–33, 07838–39, 07844, 07846, 07848, 07851, 07855, 07860, 07863, 07865, 07874–75, 07877, 07879–80, 07882, 07890

* * *

SIXTH DISTRICT

FRANK PALLONE, JR., Democrat, of Long Branch, NJ; born in Long Branch, October 30, 1951; education: B.A., Middlebury College, Middlebury, VT, 1973; M.A., Fletcher School of Law and Diplomacy, 1974; J.D., Rutgers University School of Law, 1978; professional: member of the bar: Florida, New York, Pennsylvania, and New Jersey; attorney, Marine Advisory Service; assistant professor, Cook College, Rutgers University Sea Grant Extension Program; counsel, Monmouth County, NJ, Protective Services for the Elderly; instructor, Monmouth College; Long Branch City Council, 1982–88; New Jersey State Senate, 1983–88; married the former Sarah Hospodor, 1992; committees: chair, Energy and Commerce; elected to the 100th Congress, by special election, on November 8, 1988, to fill the vacancy caused by the death of U.S. Representative James J. Howard; reelected to each succeeding Congress.

Office Listings

https://pallone.house.gov https://facebook.com/RepFrankPallone twitter: @FrankPallone

2107 Rayburn House Office Building, Washington, DC 20515 .... (202) 225–4671
Chief of Staff.—Liam Fitzsimmons. FAX: 225–9665
Legislative Director.—Roberto Sada.
Communications Director.—Mary Werden.
504 Broadway, Long Branch, NJ 07740 .... (732) 571–1140
67/69 Church Street, Kilmer Square, New Brunswick, NJ 08901–1242 .... (732) 249–8892

Counties: MIDDLESEX COUNTY. CITIES AND TOWNSHIPS: Avenel, Carteret, Colonia, Edison, Fords, Highland Park, Hopelawn, Iselin, Keasbey, Menlo Park Terrace, Metuchen, New Brunswick, Old Bridge, Perth Amboy, Piscataway, Port Reading, Sayreville, Sewaren, South Amboy, South Plainfield, and Woodbridge. MONMOUTH COUNTY. CITIES AND TOWNSHIPS: Aberdeen, Allenhurst, Asbury Park, Atlantic Highlands, Deal, Hazlet, Highlands, Interlaken, Keansburg, Keyport, Loch Arbor, Long Branch, Marlboro, Matawan, Middletown, Monmouth Beach, Oceanport, Sea Bright, Union Beach, and West Long Branch. Population (2010), 732,657.

ZIP Codes: 07001, 07008, 07060, 07064–65, 07067, 07077, 07080, 07095, 07701, 07703, 07711–12, 07716, 07718, 07721–23, 07726, 07728, 07730, 07732–35, 07737, 07740, 07746–48, 07750–53, 07755, 07757–58, 07760, 07764–65, 08812,

08817–18, 08820, 08830, 08832, 08837, 08840, 08846, 08854–55, 08857, 08859, 08861–63, 08871–73, 08879, 08899, 08901–04, 08906, 08933, 08989

* * *

SEVENTH DISTRICT

TOM MALINOWSKI, Democrat, of Rocky Hill, NJ; born in Slupsk, Poland, September 23, 1965; education: B.A., University of California, Berkeley, CA, 1987; Rhodes Scholar, M.Phil., Oxford University, Oxford England, 1991; professional: research assistant, Ford Foundation, 1992–93; speechwriter, Policy Planning Staff, U.S. Department of State, Washington, DC, 1994–98; senior director, Foreign Policy Speechwriting, White House, Washington, DC, 1998–2001; Washington director, Human Rights Watch, 2001–13; Assistant Secretary of State for Democracy, Human Rights, and Labor, Washington, DC, 2014–17; caucuses: Building Trades Caucus; Cancer Prevention Caucus; Congressional Animal Protection Caucus; Congressional Arts Caucus; Congressional Caucus on Poland; Congressional Caucus on the Association of Southeast Asian Nations; Congressional Community College Caucus; Congressional Hazards Caucus; Congressional Public Transportation Caucus; Fire Services Caucus; Law Enforcement Caucus; LGBT Equality Caucus; New Americans Caucus; New Democrat Coalition; Rare Disease Caucus; Small Brewers Caucus; Task Force for Combating Anti-Semitism; Task Force to End Sexual Violence; committees: Foreign Affairs; Transportation and Infrastructure; elected to the 116th Congress on November 6, 2018.

Office Listings

https://malinowski.house.gov https://facebook.com/RepTomMalinowski
https://twitter.com/RepMalinowski

426 Cannon House Office Building, Washington, DC 20515 .... (202) 225–5361
Chief of Staff.—Colston Reid.
Communications Director.—Amanda Osborne.
Scheduler.—D'Andre Carter.
75–77 North Bridge Street, Somerville, NJ 00876 .... (908) 547–3307
District Director.—Mitchelle Drulis.

Counties: UNION COUNTY. MUNICIPALITIES: Berkeley Heights, Clark, Cranford, Garwood, Kenilworth, Linden, Mountainside, New Providence, Springfield, Summit, Union, Westfield, and Winfield. HUNTERDON COUNTY. MUNICIPALITIES: Alexandria, Bethlehem, Bloomsbury, Califon, Clinton, Clinton Township, Delaware Township, East Amwell, Flemington, Frenchtown, Glen Gardner, Hampton, High Bridge, Holland, Kingwood, Lambertville, Lebanon, Lebanon Township, Milford, Oldwick, Raritan, Readington, Stockton, Tewksbury, Union, West Amwell, and Whitehouse Station. SOMERSET COUNTY. MUNICIPALITIES: Bedminster, Bernards, Bernardsville, Branchburg, Bridgewater, Far Hills, Green Brook, Hillsborough, Montgomery Township, Millstone, North Plainfield, Peapack-Gladstone, Raritan, Rocky Hill, Somerville, Warren, and Watchung. MORRIS COUNTY. MUNICIPALITIES: Chester, Dover, Long Hill, Mine Hill, Mount Arlington, Mount Olive, Netcong, Roxbury, Washington, and Wharton. WARREN COUNTY. MUNICIPALITIES: Alpha, Franklin, Greenwich, Harmony, Lopatcong, and Phillipsburg. ESSEX COUNTY. MUNICIPALITIES: Millburn. Population (2010), 733,961.

ZIP Codes: 07016, 07027, 07033, 07036, 07041, 07059–60, 07066, 07069, 07081, 07083, 07090, 07092, 07416, 07676, 07801–03, 07806, 07828, 07830, 07836, 07856–57, 07869, 07885, 07901, 07920–22, 07930–31, 07933–34, 07974, 07977–78, 08323, 08502, 08504, 08530, 08540, 08551, 08553, 08557–59, 08801–04, 08807, 08809, 08812, 08821–22, 08825–27, 08829, 08833, 08836, 08844, 08848, 08853, 08858, 08865, 08867, 08869–70, 08876, 08889

* * *

EIGHTH DISTRICT

ALBIO SIRES, Democrat, of West New York, NJ; born in Bejucal, Provincia de la Habana, Cuba, January 26, 1951; education: graduated, Memorial High School; B.A., St. Peter's College, 1974; M.A., Middlebury College, Middlebury, VT, 1985; studied Spanish in Madrid, Spain; professional: businessman; teacher; part-owner, A.M. Title Agency, Union Township; Mayor, West New York, NJ, 1995–2006; member: New Jersey General Assembly, 1999–2006; Speaker, New Jersey General Assembly, 2002–05; family: wife, Adrienne; stepdaughter, Tara Kole; committees: Budget; Foreign Affairs; Transportation and Infrastructure; elected to the 109th Congress, by special election, to fill the vacancy caused by the resignation of U.S. Representative Robert Menendez; reelected to each succeeding Congress.

Office Listings

https://sires.house.gov https://facebook.com/RepAlbioSires https://twitter.com/RepSires

2268 Rayburn House Office Building, Washington, DC 20515 .... (202) 225–7919

Office Listings—Continued

Chief of Staff.—Gene Martorony. FAX: 226–0792
Administrative Director / Scheduler.—Judi Wolford.
Legislative Director.—Clare Plassche.
257 Cornelison Avenue, Suite 4408, Jersey City, NJ 07302 .... (201) 309–0301
Communications Director.—Erica Daughtrey. FAX: 309–0384
5500 Palisade Avenue, Suite A, West New York, NJ 07093 .... (201) 558–0800
800 Anna Street, Elizabeth, NJ 07201 .... (908) 820–0692
FAX: 820–0694

Counties: BERGEN (part), ESSEX (part), HUDSON (part), and UNION (part). CITIES AND TOWNSHIPS: Bayonne, Belleville, East Newark, Elizabeth, Fairview, Guttenberg, Harrison, Hoboken, Jersey City, Kearny, Newark, North Bergen, Union City, Weehawken, and West New York. Population (2010), 732,658.

ZIP Codes: 07002–03 (part), 07017 (part), 07022, 07029–30, 07032 (part), 07047, 07083 (part), 07086–87, 07093, 07102, 07104–05 (part), 07107 (part), 07109 (part), 07114 (part), 07201–02, 07206, 07208 (part), 07302 (part), 07304–06 (part), 07307, 07310–11

* * *

NINTH DISTRICT

BILL PASCRELL, JR., Democrat, of Paterson, NJ; born in Paterson, January 25, 1937; education: B.A., journalism, and M.A., philosophy, Fordham University; veteran, U.S. Army and Army Reserve; professional: educator; elected Minority Leader Pro Tempore, New Jersey General Assembly, 1988–96; Mayor of Paterson, 1990–96; named Mayor of the Year by bipartisan NJ Conference of Mayors, 1996; started Paterson's first Economic Development Corporation; married the former Elsie Marie Botto; three children: William III, Glenn, and David; caucuses: co-chair, Congressional Fire Services Caucus; co-chair, Italian-American Delegation; co-chair, Law Enforcement Caucus; co-chair, Traumatic Brain Injury Task Force; committees: Ways and Means; elected to the 105th Congress; reelected to each succeeding Congress.

Office Listings

https://pascrell.house.gov https://facebook.com/pascrell twitter: @BillPascrell

2409 Rayburn House Office Building, Washington, DC 20515 .... (202) 225–5751
Chief of Staff.—Ben Rich. FAX: 225–5782
Legislative Director.—Elaina House.
Senior Legislative Assistant.—Dylan Sodaro.
200 Federal Plaza, Suite 500, Paterson, NJ 07505 .... (973) 523–5152
District Director.—Ritzy Morales.
Communications Director.—Mark Greenbaum.
2–10 North Van Brunt Street, Englewood, NJ 07631 .... (201) 935–2248
367 Valley Brook Avenue, Lyndhurst, NJ 07071 .... (201) 935–2248
330 Passaic Street, Passaic, NJ 07055 .... (973) 472–4510

Counties: BERGEN COUNTY. CITIES: Carlstadt, Cliffside Park, Cresskill, East Rutherford, Edgewater, Elmwood Park, Englewood, Englewood Cliffs, Fort Lee, Garfield, Hasbrouck Heights, Leonia, Little Ferry, Lyndhurst, Moonachie, North Arlington, Palisades Park, Ridgefield, Ridgefield Park, Rutherford, Saddle Brook, South Hackensack, Teaneck (part), Tenafly, Teterboro, Wallington, and Wood-Ridge. HUDSON COUNTY. CITIES: Kearny (part) and Secaucus. PASSAIC COUNTY. CITIES: Clifton, Haledon, Hawthorne, Passaic, Paterson, and Prospect Park. Population (2010), 742,508.

ZIP Codes: 07010–15, 07020, 07024, 07026, 07031–32, 07055, 07057, 07070–75, 07094, 07096, 07099, 07407, 07501–14, 07522, 07524, 07533, 07538, 07543–44, 07604–06, 07608, 07626, 07631–32, 07643, 07650, 07657, 07660, 07663, 07666, 07670

* * *

TENTH DISTRICT

DONALD M. PAYNE, JR., Democrat, of Newark, NJ; born in Newark, December 17, 1958; education: graduated from Hillside High School; attended Kean College (now Kean University), Union, NJ; professional: elected to Newark Municipal Council, president, 2006–12; elected to Essex County Board of Chosen Freeholders, 2006–12; director of Student Transportation for the Essex County Educational Services Commission; married: wife, Beatrice; three children: Jack, Yvonne, and Donald III (triplets); caucuses: co-founder, PAD Caucus; Addiction, Treatment, and Recovery Caucus; Congressional Animal Protection Caucus; Congressional Black Caucus; Congressional Caucus on Sudan and South Sudan; Congressional Diabetes Caucus; Congressional Down Syndrome Caucus; Congressional Full Employment Caucus; Congressional

LGBT Equality Caucus; Congressional Library of Congress Caucus; Congressional Men's Health Caucus; Congressional Small Business Caucus; Congressional Taiwan Caucus; Congressional TRIO Caucus; Democratic Whip Task Force on Poverty, Income Equality, and Opportunity; Fire Services Caucus; Foster Care Youth Caucus; Homeland Security Task Force; House Medical Technology Caucus; Indian and American Indian Caucus; Ports, Opportunity, Renewable, Trade, and Security (PORTS) Caucus; U.S. Senate International Conservation Caucus; U.S. Senate Oceans Caucus; committees: Homeland Security; Transportation and Infrastructure; elected simultaneously to the 112th and 113th Congresses, by special election, on November 6, 2012, to fill the vacancy caused by the death of U.S. Representative Donald Milford Payne; reelected to each succeeding Congress.

Office Listings

https://payne.house.gov https://facebook.com/DonaldPayneJr
twitter: @RepDonaldPayne https://instagram.com/repdonaldpaynejr

103 Cannon House Office Building, Washington, DC 20515 .... (202) 225–3436
Chief of Staff.—LaVerne Alexander.
Communications Director.—Patrick Wright.
60 Nelson Place, 14th Floor, Newark, NJ 07102 .... (973) 645–3213
253 Martin Luther King Drive, Jersey City, NJ 07305 .... (201) 369–0392
1455 Liberty Avenue, Hillside, NJ 07205 .... (862) 229–2994

Counties: ESSEX, HUDSON, AND UNION. CITIES AND TOWNSHIPS: Bayonne, Bloomfield, East Orange, Glen Ridge, Hillside, Irvington, Jersey City, Linden, Maplewood, Montclair, Newark, Orange, Rahway, Roselle, Roselle Park, South Orange, Union, and West Orange. Population (2010), 732,658.

ZIP Codes: 07002–03 (part), 07017 (part), 07018, 07028, 07036 (part), 07040, 07041 (part), 07042, 07043–44 (part), 07050, 07052 (part), 07065, 07079, 07083 (part), 07088, 07102 (part), 07103, 07104–05 (part), 07106, 07107 (part), 07108, 07111–12, 07114 (part), 07203–05, 07208 (part), 07302 (part), 07304–06 (part)

* * *

ELEVENTH DISTRICT

MIKIE SHERRILL, Democrat, of Montclair, NJ; born in Alexandria, VA, January 19, 1972; education: B.S., U.S. Naval Academy, Annapolis, MD, 1994; M.Sc., Global History, London School of Economics and Political Science, London, England, 2003; J.D., Georgetown University, Washington, DC, 2007; military: served, U.S. Navy; professional: attorney; Office of the U.S. Attorney, New Jersey; committees: Armed Services; Science, Space, and Technology; elected to the 116th Congress on November 6, 2018.

Office Listings

https://sherrill.house.gov

1208 Longworth House Office Building, Washington, DC 20515 .... (202) 225–5034
Chief of Staff.—Jean Roehrenbeck. FAX: 225–3186
Communications Director.—Jackie Burns.
Legislative Director.—Tom Stewart.
Scheduler.—Julie Jochem.
8 Wood Hollow Road, Suite 203, Parsippany, NJ 07054 .... (973) 526–5668

Counties: ESSEX COUNTY. CITIES AND TOWNSHIPS: Bloomfield, Caldwell, Cedar Grove, Essex Fells, Fairfield Township, Livingston, Montclair, North Caldwell, Nutley, Roseland, Verona, West Caldwell, and West Orange. MORRIS COUNTY. CITIES AND TOWNSHIPS: Boonton, Boonton Township, Butler, Chatham Borough, Chatham Township, Denville, East Hanover, Florham Park, Hanover, Harding, Jefferson Township, Kinnelon, Lincoln Park, Madison, Mendham Borough, Mendham Township, Montville, Morris Plains, Morris Township, Morristown, Mountain Lakes, Parsippany-Troy Hills, Pequannock, Randolph, Riverdale, Rockaway Borough, Rockaway Township, and Victory Gardens. PASSAIC COUNTY. CITIES: Bloomingdale, Little Falls, North Haledon, Pompton Lakes, Totowa, Wanaque, Wayne, and Woodland Park. SUSSEX COUNTY. CITIES AND TOWNSHIPS: Byram, Hopatcong, Ogdensburg, Sparta Township, and Stanhope. Population (2010), 732,658.

ZIP Codes: 07003–07, 07009, 07021, 07028, 07034–39, 07042–46, 07052, 07054, 07058, 07068, 07082, 07110, 07403, 07405, 07420, 07424, 07435, 07438–40, 07442, 07444, 07457, 07465, 07470, 07474, 07508, 07512, 07806, 07821, 07834, 07837, 07842–43, 07845, 07848–49, 07866, 07869, 07871, 07874, 07878, 07920, 07926–28, 07930, 07932, 07935–36, 07940, 07945, 07950, 07960–63, 07976

* * *

TWELFTH DISTRICT

BONNIE WATSON COLEMAN, Democrat, of Ewing Township, NJ; born in Camden, NJ, February 6, 1945; first African-American woman ever elected to Congress from New Jersey;

education: B.A., Thomas Edison State College; professional: former Assistant Commissioner, New Jersey Department of Community Affairs; former Bureau Chief, New Jersey Division on Civil Rights; eight-term member of the New Jersey General Assembly; first African-American woman to serve as Majority Leader of the New Jersey General Assembly; first African-American woman to chair the New Jersey Democratic State Committee; religion: Baptist; married: Rev. William E. Coleman; children: William, Jared, and Troy; two grandchildren: Kamryn and William; committees: Appropriations; Homeland Security; elected to the 114th Congress on November 4, 2014; reelected to each succeeding Congress.

Office Listings

https://watsoncoleman.house.gov https://facebook.com/RepBonnie
twitter: @RepBonnie https://instagram.com/repbonnie

2442 Rayburn House Office Building, Washington, DC 20515 .... (202) 225–5801
Chief of Staff.—James Gee. FAX: 225–6025
Legislative Director.—Kevin Block.
Communications Director.—Courtney Cochran.
Scheduler.—Jaimee Gilmartin.
850 Bear Tavern Road, Suite 201, Ewing, NJ 08628 .... (609) 883–0026
District Director.—Kari Osmond.

Counties: MERCER COUNTY. CITIES AND TOWNSHIPS: East Windsor, Ewing, Hightstown, Hopewell Borough, Hopewell Township, Lawrence, Pennington, Princeton, Trenton, and West Windsor. MIDDLESEX COUNTY. CITIES AND TOWNSHIPS: Cranbury, Dunellen, East Brunswick, Helmetta, Jamesburg, Middlesex, Milltown, Monroe, North Brunswick, Old Bridge, Plainsboro, South Brunswick, South River, and Spotswood. SOMERSET COUNTY. CITIES AND TOWNSHIPS: Bound Brook, Franklin, Manville, and South Bound Brook. UNION COUNTY. CITIES AND TOWNSHIPS: Fanwood, Plainfield, and Scotch Plains. Population (2010), 732,658.

ZIP Codes: 07023, 07060–63, 07076, 07747, 08512, 08520, 08525, 08528, 08530, 08534, 08536, 08540–44, 08550, 08560, 08608–11, 08618–19, 08628–29, 08638, 08648, 08691, 08805, 08810, 08812, 08816, 08823–24, 08828, 08831, 08835, 08846, 08850, 08852, 08857, 08859, 08873, 08875, 08880, 08882, 08884, 08890, 08902

NEW MEXICO

(Population 2010, 2,059,179)

SENATORS

TOM UDALL, Democrat, of Santa Fe, NM; born in Tucson, AZ, May 18, 1948; education: graduate of McLean High School, 1966; B.A., Prescott College, Prescott, AZ, 1970; LL.B., Cambridge University, Cambridge, England, 1975; J.D., University of New Mexico, Albuquerque, NM, 1977; professional: admitted to the New Mexico Bar, 1978; served as New Mexico Attorney General, 1990–98; served as U.S. Representative for New Mexico's 3rd Congressional District, 1998–2008; married: Jill Z. Cooper; children: Amanda; member of the Commission on Security and Cooperation in Europe; committees: vice chair, Indian Affairs; Appropriations; Commerce, Science, and Transportation; Foreign Relations; Rules and Administration; Joint Committee on Printing; elected to the U.S. Senate on November 4, 2008; reelected to the U.S. Senate on November 4, 2014.

Office Listings

https://tomudall.senate.gov https://facebook.com/senatortomudall https://twitter.com/SenatorTomUdall

531 Hart Senate Office Building, Washington, DC 20510 .... (202) 224–6621
Chief of Staff.—Bianca Ortiz Wertheim. FAX: 228–3261
Legislative Director.—Andrew Wallace.
Communications Director.—Ned Adriance.
Executive Assistant.—Cara Gilbert.
400 Gold Avenue, SW., Suite 300, Albuquerque, NM 87102 .... (505) 346–6791
201 North Church Street, Suite 201B, Las Cruces, NM 88001 .... (575) 526–5475
120 South Federal Place, Suite 302, Santa Fe, NM 87501 .... (505) 988–6511
102 West Hagerman, Suite A, Carlsbad, NM 88220 .... (575) 234–0366
100 South Avenue A, Suite 113, Portales, NM 88130 .... (505) 356–6811

* * *

MARTIN HEINRICH, Democrat, of Albuquerque, NM; born in Fallon, NV, October 17, 1971; education: B.S., mechanical engineering, University of Missouri, Columbia, MO, 1995; professional: executive director of the Cottonwood Gulch Foundation, 1996–2001; Albuquerque City Council, 2003–07; State of New Mexico Natural Resources Trustee, 2006–07; served as U.S. Representative for New Mexico's First Congressional District, 2009–12; married: Julie Heinrich; children: Carter Heinrich and Micah Heinrich; caucuses, commissions: Artificial Intelligence Caucus; Congressional Dietary Supplement Caucus; Congressional Sportsmen's Caucus; Migratory Bird Conservation Commission; National Service Congressional Caucus; Senate Climate Action Task Force; Senate Democratic Hispanic Task Force; committees: Armed Services; Energy and Natural Resources; Joint Economic Committee; Select Committee on Intelligence; elected to the U.S. Senate on November 6, 2012; reelected to the U.S. Senate on November 6, 2018.

Office Listings

https://heinrich.senate.gov https://facebook.com/MartinHeinrich twitter: @MartinHeinrich

303 Hart Senate Office Building, Washington, DC 20510 .... (202) 224–5521
Chief of Staff.—Joe Britton. FAX: 228–2841
Deputy Chief of Staff.—Whitney Potter.
Legislative Director.—Virgilio Barrera.
Director of Scheduling.—Caitlin Terry.
400 Gold Avenue Southwest, Suite 1080, Albuquerque, NM 87102 .... (505) 346–6601
7450 East Main Street, Suite A, Farmington, NM 87402 .... (505) 325–5030
505 South Main Street, Suite 148, Las Cruces, NM 88001 .... (575) 523–6561
200 East 4th Street, Suite 300, Roswell, NM 88201 .... (575) 622–7113
123 East Marcy Street, Suite 103, Santa Fe, NM 87501 .... (505) 988–6647

REPRESENTATIVES

FIRST DISTRICT

DEBRA A. HAALAND, Democrat, of Albuquerque, NM; born in Winslow, AZ, December 2, 1960; education: B.A., English, University of New Mexico, Albuquerque, NM, 1994; attended University of California, Los Angeles, CA, 2000; J.D., Indian law, University of New Mexico, Albuquerque, NM, 2006; professional: business executive (running her own small business producing and canning Pueblo Salsa); first Chairwoman elected to the Laguna Development Corporation Board of Directors, overseeing business operations of the second largest tribal gaming enterprise in NM; delegate, Democratic National Convention, 2008; tribal administrator, San Felipe Pueblo, 2013–15; chair, New Mexico Democratic Party, 2015–17; first Native American woman to be elected to lead a State Party; starting in 2016, Haaland has served as an Honorary Commander of Kirtland Air Force Base; religion: Catholic; family: one daughter; caucuses: co-chair, Congressional Native American Caucus; Congressional Progressive Caucus; committees: vice chair, Natural Resources; Armed Services; elected to the 116th Congress on November 6, 2018.

Office Listings

https://haaland.house.gov https://facebook.com/RepDebHaaland https://twitter.com/RepDebHaaland
https://instagram.com/RepDebHaaland https://youtube.com/channel/UCbRtULGdCu5N3NytJUyve3A

1237 Longworth House Office Building, Washington, DC 20515 .... (202) 225–6316
Chief of Staff.—Jennifer Van der Heide. FAX: 225–4975
Scheduler.—Christopher Garcia.
Legislative Director.—Eric Werwa.
Communications Director.—Felicia Salazaar.
400 Gold Avenue Southwest, Suite 680, Albuquerque, NM 87102 .... (505) 346–6781

Counties: BERNALILLO (part), SANDOVAL (part), SANTA FE (part), TORRANCE, AND VALENCIA (part). CITIES AND TOWNSHIPS: Albuquerque, Bernalillo, Edgewood, Estancia, Moriarty, Mountainair, Rio Rancho, and South Valley. Population (2010), 693,772.

ZIP Codes: 87004, 87008, 87015, 87026, 87035–36, 87047–48, 87059, 87063, 87067, 87102, 87104–14, 87116–17, 87120–24, 87131, 87144, 88321

* * *

SECOND DISTRICT

XOCHITL TORRES SMALL, Democrat, of Las Cruces, NM; born November 15, 1984; education: B.S.F.S., Georgetown University, Washington, DC, 2007; J.D., University of New Mexico, Albuquerque, NM, 2015; professional: lawyer, private practice; federal law clerk, New Mexico District Court, 2015–16; field representative, Senator Tom Udall of New Mexico, 2009–12; attorney specializing in water and natural resources, Kemp Smith law firm; caucuses: Congressional Caucus for Women's Issues; Blue Dog Coalition; Congressional Hispanic Caucus; New Democrat Coalition; religion: Evangelical Lutheran; married: Nathan Small (New Mexico House of Representatives, District 36); committees: Agriculture; Armed Services; Homeland Security; elected to the 116th Congress on November 6, 2018.

Office Listings

https://torressmall.house.gov https://facebook.com/RepTorresSmall
https://twitter.com/RepTorresSmall https://instagram.com/reptorressmall

430 Cannon House Office Building, Washington, DC 20515 .... (202) 225–2365
Chief of Staff.—Brian Sowyrda.
Scheduler.—Rachelle Holdridge.
Communications Director.—Paloma Perez.
Legislative Director.—Brooke Stuedell.
240 South Water Street, Las Cruces, NM 88001 .... (575) 323–6384
719 South Main Street, Room 1, Belen, NM 87002 .... (505) 966–2751
101 North Halagueno, Carlsbad, NM 88220.

Counties: BERNALILLO (part), CATRON, CHAVES, CIBOLA, DEBACA, DONA ANA, EDDY, GRANT, GUADALUPE, HIDALGO, LEA, LINCOLN, LUNA, MCKINLEY (part), OTERO, ROOSEVELT (part), SIERRA, SOCORRO, AND VALENCIA (part). Population (2010), 702,936.

ZIP Codes: 79821, 79835, 79922, 79932, 79934, 85534, 87002, 87005–07, 87011, 87014, 87020–23, 87026, 87028, 87031, 87034, 87038, 87040, 87045, 87049, 87051, 87062, 87068, 87105, 87121, 88024–34, 88036, 88038–49, 88051–56, 88058, 88061–63, 88065, 88072, 88081, 88113–16, 88118–19, 88123–26, 88130, 88132, 88134, 88136, 88201–03, 88210–11, 88213, 88220–21, 88230–32, 88240–42, 88250, 88252–56, 88260, 88262–65, 88267–68, 88301, 88310–12, 88314, 88316–18, 88323–25, 88330, 88336–55, 88417, 88431, 88435

* * *

THIRD DISTRICT

BEN RAY LUJÁN, Democrat, of Santa Fe, NM; born in Nambe, NM, June 7, 1972; education: B.B.A., New Mexico Highlands University, Las Vegas, NM, 2007; professional: elected to the New Mexico Public Regulation Commission, 2005–08; caucuses: co-chair, Nuclear Cleanup Caucus; co-chair, Science and National Labs Caucus; co-chair, Technology Transfer Caucus; Hispanic Caucus; Native American Caucus; committees: Energy and Commerce; Select Committee on the Climate Crisis; elected to the 111th Congress on November 4, 2008; reelected to each succeeding Congress.

Office Listings

https://lujan.house.gov https://facebook.com/RepBenRayLujan twitter.com/repbenraylujan

2323 Rayburn House Office Building, Washington, DC 20515 .... (202) 225–6190
Chief of Staff.—Angela Ramirez. FAX: 226–1528
Communications Director.—Lauren French.
Deputy Chief of Staff / Legislative Director.—Graham Mason.
Scheduler.—Matthew Hoeck.
1611 Calle Lorca, Suite A, Santa Fe, NM 87505 .... (505) 984–8950
District Director.—Jennifer Catechis.
3200 Civic Center Circle, NE., Suite 330, Rio Rancho, NM 87144 .... (505) 994–0499
District Scheduler.—Juan Abeyta.
Constituent Services Representative / Veterans Liaison.—Brian Lee.
110 West Aztec Avenue, Suite 102, Gallup, NM 87301 .... (505) 863–0582
Field Representative and Navajo Nation Liaison.—Brian Lee.
404 West Route 66 Boulevard, Tucumcari, NM 88401 .... (575) 461–3029
Field Representative.—Ron Wilmot.

Counties: BERNALILLO (part), COLFAX, CURRY, HARDING, LOS ALAMOS, MCKINLEY (part), MORA, NAVAJO NATION, QUAY, RIO ARRIBA, ROOSEVELT (part), SANDOVAL (part), SAN JUAN, SAN MIGUEL, SANTA FE, TAOS, AND UNION. Population (2010), 686,393.

ZIP Codes: 87001, 87004, 87010, 87012–13, 87015, 87017–18, 87024–25, 87027, 87029, 87037, 87041, 87044–48, 87052–53, 87056, 87064, 87072, 87083, 87114, 87120, 87123–24, 87144, 87174, 87301–02, 87305, 87310–13, 87316–17, 87319–23, 87325–26, 87328, 87347, 87364–65, 87375, 87401–02, 87410, 87412–13, 87415–21, 87455, 87461, 87499, 87501–25, 87527–33, 87535, 87537–40, 87543–45, 87548–49, 87551–54, 87556–58, 87560, 87562, 87564–67, 87569, 87571, 87573–83, 87592, 87594, 87701, 87710, 87712–15, 87718, 87722–23, 87728–36, 87740, 87742–43, 87745–47, 87749–50, 87752–53, 88101–03, 88112–13, 88115–16, 88118, 88120–26, 88130, 88132–35, 88401, 88410–11, 88414–16, 88418–19, 88421–22, 88424, 88426–27, 88430, 88433–34, 88436–37, 88439

NEW YORK

(Population 2010, 19,378,102)

SENATORS

CHARLES E. SCHUMER, Democrat, of Brooklyn and Queens, NY; born in Brooklyn, November 23, 1950; education: graduated valedictorian, Madison High School; Harvard University, *magna cum laude,* 1971; J.D. with honors, Harvard Law School, 1974; professional: admitted to the New York State Bar in 1975; elected to the New York State Assembly, 1974; served on Judiciary, Health, Education, and Cities committees; chairman, subcommittee on City Management and Governance, 1977; chairman, Committee on Oversight and Investigation, 1979; reelected to each succeeding legislative session until December 1980; married: Iris Weinshall, 1980; children: Jessica Emily and Alison Emma; committees: Rules and Administration; Select Committee on Intelligence; elected to the 97th Congress on November 4, 1980; reelected to each succeeding Congress; elected to the U.S. Senate on November 3, 1998; reelected to each succeeding Senate term; Minority Leader, 2017 to present.

Office Listings

https://schumer.senate.gov https://facebook.com/senschumer https://twitter.com/SenSchumer

322 Hart Senate Office Building, Washington, DC 20510 .... (202) 224–6542
Chief of Staff.—Mike Lynch. FAX: 228–3027
Deputy Chief of Staff.—Erin Sager Vaughn.
Communications Director.—Justin Goodman.
Legislative Director.—Meghan Taira.
780 Third Avenue, Suite 2301, New York, NY 10017 .... (212) 486–4430
Leo O'Brien Building, Room 420, Albany, NY 12207 .... (518) 431–4070
130 South Elmwood Avenue, #660, Buffalo, NY 14202 .... (716) 846–4111
100 State Street, Room 3040, Rochester, NY 14614 .... (585) 263–5866
100 South Clinton, Room 841, Syracuse, NY 13261–7318 .... (315) 423–5471
Federal Office Building, 15 Henry Street, #100A–F, Binghamton, NY 13901 .... (607) 772–6792
145 Pine Lawn Road, #300N, Melville, NY 11747 .... (631) 753–0978
One Park Place, Suite 100, Peekskill, NY 10566 .... (914) 734–1532

* * *

KIRSTEN E. GILLIBRAND, Democrat, of Brunswick, NY; born in Albany, NY, December 9, 1966; education: B.A., Dartmouth College, Hanover, NH, 1988; J.D., UCLA, Los Angeles, CA, 1991; professional: attorney; Special Counsel to the U.S. Secretary of Housing and Urban Development Andrew Cuomo; private legal practice; religion: Catholic; married: Jonathan Gillibrand, 2001; two sons: Theodore, 2004, and Henry, 2008; committees: Agriculture, Nutrition, and Forestry; Armed Services; Environment and Public Works; Special Committee on Aging; appointed to the 111th Congress on January 23, 2009, to fill the vacancy caused by the resignation of U.S. Senator Hillary Clinton; subsequently elected on November 2, 2010, for the remaining two years of the unexpired term; reelected to each succeeding Senate term.

Office Listings

https://gillibrand.senate.gov https://facebook.com/SenKirstenGillibrand https://twitter.com/gillibrandny

478 Russell Senate Office Building, Washington, DC 20510 .... (202) 224–4451
Chief of Staff.—Joi Chaney. FAX: 228–0282
Legislative Director.—Brooke Jamison.
Communications Director.—Whitney Brennan.
Scheduler.—Angelica Annino.
780 Third Avenue, Suite 2601, New York, NY 10017 .... (212) 688–6262
Federal Office Building, 1 Clinton Square, Room 821, Albany, NY 12207 .... (518) 431–0120
Larkin at Exchange, 726 Exchange Street, Suite 511, Buffalo, NY 14210 .... (716) 854–9725
155 Pinelawn Road, Suite 250 North, Melville, NY 11747 .... (631) 249–2825
P.O. Box 273, Lowville, NY 13367 .... (315) 376–6118
Federal Office Building, 100 State Street, Room 4195, Rochester, NY 14614 .... (585) 263–6250
Federal Office Building, 100 South Clinton Street, Room 1470, P.O. Box 7378, Syracuse, NY 13261 .... (315) 448–0470
Lower Hudson Valley Office, P.O. Box 893, Mahopac, NY 10541 .... (845) 875–4585
Westchester County Office .... (914) 725–9294

REPRESENTATIVES

FIRST DISTRICT

LEE M. ZELDIN, Republican, of Shirley, NY; born in East Meadow, NY, January 30, 1980; education: William Floyd High School; University at Albany, SUNY; Albany Law School; religion: Jewish; married: Diana Zeldin; children: Mikayla and Arianna; committees: Financial Services; Foreign Affairs; elected to the 114th Congress on November 4, 2014; reelected to each succeeding Congress.

Office Listings

https://zeldin.house.gov https://facebook.com/RepLeeZeldin
https://twitter.com/RepLeeZeldin https://instagram.com/repleezeldin

2441 Rayburn House Office Building, Washington, DC 20515 .... (202) 225–3826
Chief of Staff.—Eric Amidon.
Executive Assistant / Scheduler.—Andrea Grace.
Legislative Director.—Kevin Dowling.
Communications Director.—Kathleen Vincentz.
31 Oak Street, Suite 20, Patchogue, NY 11772 .... (631) 289–1097
District Director.—Mark Woolley.
Director of Constituent Services.—William Doyle.
30 West Main Street, Suite 201, Riverhead, NY 11901 .... (631) 209–4235

Counties: SUFFOLK COUNTY (part). TOWNS: Brookhaven, East Hampton, Islip, Riverhead, Shelter Island, Smithtown, Southampton, and Southold. Population (2010), 717,707.

ZIP Codes: 00501, 00544, 11713, 11715, 11719–20, 11727, 11733, 11738, 11741–42, 11745, 11754–55, 11763–64, 11766–68, 11772, 11776–80, 11784, 11786–90, 11792, 11794, 11901, 11930–35, 11937, 11939–42, 11944, 11946–65, 11967–73, 11975–78, 11980

* * *

SECOND DISTRICT

PETER T. KING, Republican, of Seaford, NY; born in Manhattan, NY, April 5, 1944; education: B.A., St. Francis College, NY, 1965; J.D., University of Notre Dame Law School, IN, 1968; military service: served, U.S. Army Reserve National Guard, Specialist 5, 1968–73; professional: attorney; admitted to New York Bar, 1969; Deputy Nassau County Attorney, 1972–74; executive assistant to the Nassau County Executive, 1974–76; general counsel, Nassau Off-Track Betting Corporation, 1977; Hempstead Town Councilman, 1978–81; Nassau County Comptroller, 1981–92; member: Ancient Order of Hiberians; Sons of Italy; Knights of Columbus; 69th Infantry Veterans Corps; American Legion; married: Rosemary Wiedl King, 1967; children: Sean and Erin; two grandchildren; committees: Homeland Security; elected on November 3, 1992 to the 103rd Congress; reelected to each succeeding Congress.

Office Listings

https://peteking.house.gov

302 Cannon House Office Building, Washington, DC 20515 .... (202) 225–7896
Chief of Staff / Press Secretary.—Kevin Fogarty. FAX: 226–2279
Legislative Director.—Deena Tauster.
1003 Park Boulevard, Massapequa Park, NY 11762 .... (516) 541–4225
District Director.—Anne Rosenfeld.
Suffolk County .... (631) 541–4225

Counties: NASSAU (part) AND SUFFOLK (part). CITIES AND TOWNSHIPS: Amityville, Babylon, Bayport, Bay Shore, Bethpage, Bohemia, Brentwood, Brightwaters, Copiague, Central Islip, Deer Park, East Islip, Farmingdale, Great River, Holbrook, Islip, Islip Terrace, Levittown, Lindenhurst, Massapequa, Massapequa Park, North Babylon, North Lindenhurst, Oakdale, Patchogue, Seaford, Wantagh, West Babylon, West Islip, and Wyandanch. Population (2010), 724,053.

ZIP Codes: 11701–06, 11714, 11716–18, 11722, 11726, 11730, 11735, 11739, 11741, 11751–53, 11756–58, 11762, 11769, 11772, 11779, 11782, 11793, 11795, 11798

* * *

THIRD DISTRICT

THOMAS R. SUOZZI, Democrat, of Glen Cove, NY; born in Glen Cove, August 31, 1962; education: B.S., accounting, Boston College 1984; J.D., Fordham Law School, 1989; professional: certified public accountant; attorney; Glen Cove Mayor, 1994–2002; Nassau County executive, 2002–10; religion: Catholic; family: married, wife: Helene; three children; caucuses: co-chair, Long Island Sound Caucus; co-chair, Quiet Skies Caucus; vice chair, Problem Solvers Caucus; committees: Ways and Means; elected to the 115th Congress on November 8, 2016; reelected to the 116th Congress on November 6, 2018.

Office Listings

https://suozzi.house.gov

214 Cannon House Office Building, Washington, DC 20515 .... (202) 225–3335
Chief of Staff.—Mike Florio. FAX: 225–4669
Communications Director.—Jay Bhargava.
Deputy Chief of Staff/Legislative Director.—Diane Shust.
Scheduler.—Samantha Smith.
478A Park Avenue, Huntington, NY 11743 .... (631) 923–4100
250–02 Northern Boulevard, Little Neck, NY 11362 .... (718) 631–0400
District Director.—Cindy Rogers. (631) 923–4102

Counties: NASSAU COUNTY (part) AND SUFFOLK COUNTY (part). CITIES: Asharoken, Bay Shore, Bayport, Bayside, Bayville, Centerport, Cold Springs Harbor, Commack, Deer Park, Dix Hills, Douglaston, East Hills, East Northport, East Williston, Eaton's Neck, Elwood, Farmingdale, Flushing, Fort Salonga, Glen Cove, Great Neck, Greenlawn, Greenvale, Halesite, Hauppauge, Herricks, Hicksville, Huntington, Huntington Station, Jericho, King's Park, Kings Point, Lake Success, Little Neck, Lloyd Harbor, Manhasset, Melville, Mill Neck, Mineola, Muttontown, North Hills, Northport, Old Bethpage, Old Brookville, Old Westbury, Oyster Bay, Plandome, Plainview, Port Washington, Queens Village, Roslyn, Roslyn Harbor, Roslyn Heights, Saddle Rock, Sands Point, Sea Cliff, Smithtown, South Huntington, Syosset, West Hills, Whitestone, Williston Park, Woodbury, and Wyandanch. Population (2013), 724,490.

ZIP Codes: 11101, 11004–05, 11020–21, 11023–24, 11030, 11040, 11042, 11050, 11357–63, 11426–28, 11507, 11542, 11545, 11547–48, 11560, 11577, 11579, 11590, 11596, 11709, 11714, 11721, 11724–25, 11729, 11731–32, 11739, 11743, 11746–47, 11753–54, 11756, 11765, 11768, 11771, 11787–88, 11791, 11797, 11801, 11803–04

* * *

FOURTH DISTRICT

KATHLEEN M. RICE, Democrat, of Garden City, NY; born in New York City, NY, February 15, 1965; education: graduated, Garden City High School, 1983; B.A., The Catholic University of America, Washington, DC, 1987; J.D., Touro Law Center, Long Island, NY, 1991; professional: Assistant District Attorney, Kings County, NY (Brooklyn), 1992–99; Assistant U.S. Attorney, U.S. Department of Justice, Philadelphia, PA, 1999–2005; elected District Attorney of Nassau County, NY, 2006–14; president, District Attorneys Association of the State of New York, 2013–14; awards: Mothers Against Drunk Driving (MADD) Lifetime Achievement Award; Governors Highway Safety Association (GHSA) James J. Howard Highway Safety Trailblazer Award; U.S. Inspector General's Integrity Award; U.S. Attorney General's Director's Award for Superior Performance as an Assistant U.S. Attorney; religion: Catholic; caucuses: Bipartisan Taskforce for Combating Anti-Semitism; Bipartisan Working Group; Congressional Caucus for Women's Issues; Congressional Coalition on Autism Research and Education; Congressional Diabetes Caucus; Congressional Fire Services Caucus; Congressional Long Island Sound Caucus; Congressional Pro-Choice Caucus; Congressional Stop DUI Caucus; Congressional Taiwan Caucus; Congressional Tourette Caucus; Democracy Task Force; Democratic Israel Working Group; New Democrat Coalition; NY Defense Working Group; Quiet Skies Caucus; U.S.-Philippines Friendship Caucus; committees: Homeland Security; Veterans' Affairs; elected to the 114th Congress on November 4, 2014; reelected to each succeeding Congress.

Office Listings

https://kathleenrice.house.gov

2435 Rayburn House Office Building, Washington, DC 20515 .... (202) 225–5516
Chief of Staff.—Nell Reilly. FAX: 225–5758
District Director.—Amanda Walsh.
Scheduler.—Landy Wade.
Communications Director.—Michael Aciman.
229 7th Street, Suite 300, Garden City, NY 11530 .... (516) 739–3008

Counties: NASSAU (part). CITIES AND TOWNSHIPS: Atlantic Beach, Baldwin, Bellerose, Carle Place, Cedarhurst, East Meadow, East Rockaway, East Williston, Elmont, Floral Park, Franklin Square, Freeport, Garden City, Garden City Park, Hempstead, Hewlett, Inwood, Lakeview, Lawrence, Lynbrook, Malverne, Merrick, Mineola, New Cassel, New Hyde Park, North Bellmore, North New Hyde Park, Oceanside, Rockville Centre, Roosevelt, Salisbury, Stewart Manor, South Floral Park, South Valley Stream, Uniondale, Valley Stream, West Hempstead, Westbury, Williston Park, Woodmere, and Woodsburgh. Population (2010), 717,708.

ZIP Codes: 11003, 11010, 11040, 11096, 11501, 11509–10, 11514, 11516, 11518, 11520, 11530, 11549–50, 11552–54, 11556–59, 11561, 11563, 11565–66, 11569–70, 11572, 11575, 11580–81, 11590, 11596, 11598, 11710, 11793, 11801

* * *

FIFTH DISTRICT

GREGORY W. MEEKS, Democrat, of Southern Queens, NY; born in Harlem, NY, September 25, 1953; education: P.S. 183; Robert F. Wagner Junior High School; Julia Richman High School, New York, NY; B.A., Adelphi University, 1971–75; J.D., Howard University School of Law, 1975–78; professional: lawyer, admitted to bar, 1979; Queens District Attorney's Office, 1978–83, Assistant Specialist Narcotics Prosecutor, 1981–83; Assistant Counsel to State Investigation Commission, 1983–85; served as Assistant District Attorney; Supervising Judge, New York State Workers' Compensation Board; public service: New York State Assemblyman, 1992–97; organizations: Alpha Phi Alpha Fraternity; National Bar Association; caucuses: co-chair, Congressional Services Caucus; co-chair, European Union Caucus; co-chair, Malaria Caucus; co-chair, Organizations of American States; active member, Congressional Black Caucus; married: Simone-Marie Meeks, 1997; children: Aja, Ebony, and Nia-Ayana; committees: Financial Services; Foreign Affairs; elected to the 105th Congress on February 3, 1998; reelected to each succeeding Congress.

Office Listings

https://meeks.house.gov

2310 Rayburn House Office Building, Washington, DC 20515 .... (202) 225–3461
Chief of Staff.—Sophia Lafargue. FAX: 226–4169
Legislative Director.—Vacant.
Office Manager / Scheduler.—Reginald Belon.
153–01 Jamaica Avenue, 2nd Floor, Jamaica, NY 11432 .... (718) 725–6000
District Chief of Staff.—Robert Simmons.
67–12 Rockaway Beach Boulevard, Arverne, NY 11692 .... (347) 230–4032
Executive Director.—Joseph Edwards.

Counties: QUEENS COUNTY (part). CITIES AND TOWNSHIPS: Belmont, Cambria Heights, Elmont, Floral Park, Glen Oaks, Hollis, Howard Beach, Jamaica, Jamaica Estates, Kew Gardens, Laurelton, New Hyde Park, Ozone Park, Queens Village, Richmond Hill, the Rockaway Peninsula, Rosedale, St. Albans, South Jamaica, South Ozone Park, Springfield Gardens, Valley Stream (North and South), and Woodhaven. Population (2015), 779,896.

ZIP Codes: 11001 (part), 11003 (part), 11010 (part), 11096 (part), 11366 (part), 11411–13, 11416–18 (part), 11419–20, 11422–23, 11426–28 (part), 11429–30, 11432 (part), 11433–34, 11435 (part), 11436, 11451, 11559 (part), 11580–81 (part), 11691–94, 11697

* * *

SIXTH DISTRICT

GRACE MENG, Democrat, of Queens, NY; born in Elmhurst, NY, October 1, 1975; education: Stuyvesant High School; B.A., University of Michigan, 1997; J.D., Yeshiva University's Benjamin Cardozo School of Law, 2002; attorney, 2003–08; New York State Assembly, 2008–12; religion: Christian; husband, Wayne Kye; children: Brandon and Tyler; caucuses: Congressional Asian Pacific American Caucus; Congressional Bangladesh Caucus; Congressional Caucus for Women's Issues; Congressional Caucus on India and Indian Americans; Congressional Caucus on Korea; Congressional Caucus on Sikh Americans; Congressional Creative Rights Caucus; Congressional Equality Caucus; Congressional Hellenic Caucus; Congressional Hellenic-Israel Caucus; Congressional Kids Safety Caucus; Congressional Oral Health Caucus; Congressional Pro-Choice Caucus; Congressional Quiet Skies Caucus; Congressional Taiwan Caucus; Gun Violence Prevention Task Force; United Solutions Caucus; U.S.-Philippines Friendship Caucus; Women's Working Group on Immigration Reform; committees: Appropriations; Ethics; elected to the 113th Congress on November 6, 2012; reelected to each succeeding Congress.

Office Listings

https://meng.house.gov https://facebook.com/repgracemeng https://twitter.com/RepGraceMeng

2209 Rayburn House Office Building, Washington, DC 20515 .... (202) 225–2601
Chief of Staff.—Justin Oswald. FAX: 225–1589
Executive Assistant / Scheduler.—Brenda Connolly.
40–13 159th Street, Suite A, Flushing, NY 11358 .... (718) 358–6364
FAX: 445–7868
118–15 Queens Boulevard, 17th Floor, Forest Hills, NY 11375 .... (718) 358–6364

Office Listings—Continued

District Director.—Anthony Lemma.
Communications Director.—Jordan Goldes.

Counties: QUEENS COUNTY (part). CITIES AND TOWNSHIPS: Auburndale, Bayside, Briarwood, Electchester-Pomonok, Elmhurst, Flushing, Forest Hills, Fresh Meadows, Glendale, Jamaica, Kew Gardens, Kew Gardens Hills, Maspeth, Middle Village, Oakland Gardens, Rego Park, Ridgewood, and Woodside. Population (2010), 724,352.

ZIP Codes: 11352, 11354–55, 11357–58, 11360–61, 11364–67, 11373–75, 11377–81, 11385, 11415, 11418, 11421, 11423–24, 11427, 11432, 11435

* * *

SEVENTH DISTRICT

NYDIA M. VELÁZQUEZ, Democrat, of New York, NY; born in Yabucoa, PR, March 28, 1953; education: B.A. in political science, University of Puerto Rico, 1974; M.A. in political science, New York University, 1976; professional: faculty member, University of Puerto Rico, 1976–81; adjunct professor, Hunter College of the City University of New York, 1981–83; special assistant to Congressman Ed Towns, 1983; member, City Council of New York, 1984–86; national director of Migration Division Office, Department of Labor and Human Resources of Puerto Rico, 1986–89; director, Department of Puerto Rican Community Affairs in the United States, 1989–92; committees: chair, Small Business; Financial Services; Natural Resources; elected on November 3, 1992, to the 103rd Congress; reelected to each succeeding Congress.

Office Listings

https://velazquez.house.gov https://facebook.com/RepNydiaVelazquez
https://twitter.com/NydiaVelazquez

2302 Rayburn House Office Building, Washington, DC 20515 .... (202) 225–2361
Chief of Staff.—Adam Minehardt. FAX: 226–0327
Communications Director.—Alex Haurek.
Scheduler.—Richard Bruno.
Legislative Director.—Justin Pelletier.
266 Broadway, Suite 201, Brooklyn, NY 11211 .... (718) 599–3658
500 Pearl Street, Suite 973, New York, NY 10007 .... (212) 619–2606

Counties: KINGS (part), NEW YORK (part), AND QUEENS (part). Population (2010), 717,708.

ZIP Codes: 10002, 10004, 10007, 10009, 10012–13, 10038, 11201, 11205–08, 11211, 11215, 11217–21, 11231–32, 11237, 11378–79, 11385, 11416–18, 11421

* * *

EIGHTH DISTRICT

HAKEEM S. JEFFRIES, Democrat, of New York, NY; born in Brooklyn, NY, August 4, 1970; education: graduated from Midwood High School, 1988; B.A., State University of New York at Binghamton, 1992; M.P.P., Georgetown University, 1994; J.D., New York University Law School, 1997; professional: member, New York State Assembly, 2007–13; religion: Baptist; married; two children; leadership: elected Democratic Caucus Chair in the 116th Congress; committees: Budget; Judiciary; elected to the 113th Congress on November 6, 2012; reelected to each succeeding Congress.

Office Listings

https://jeffries.house.gov https://facebook.com/RepJeffries twitter: @RepJeffries

2433 Rayburn House Office Building, Washington, DC 20515 .... (202) 225–5936
Chief of Staff.—Tasia Jackson. FAX: 225–1018
Scheduler.—Lauren Milnes.
Legislative Director.—Zoë Oreck.
District Director.—Maron Alemu.
55 Hanson Place, Suite 603, Brooklyn, NY 11217 .... (718) 237–2211
445 Neptune Avenue, 1st Floor, Brooklyn, NY 11224 .... (718) 373–0033

Counties: KINGS (part) AND QUEENS (part). Population (2010), 713,512.

ZIP Codes: 11201, 11205–08, 11210, 11212–13, 11216–17, 11221, 11224, 11229, 11233–36, 11238–39, 11243, 11245, 11247, 11256, 11414, 11416–17

* * *

NINTH DISTRICT

YVETTE D. CLARKE, Democrat, of Brooklyn, NY; born in Brooklyn, November 21, 1964; education: attended Edward R. Murrow High School; graduated from Oberlin College; professional: legislative aide to New York State Senator Velmanette Montgomery; executive assistant to New York Assemblywoman Barbara Clark; staff assistant, New York State Workers' Compensation Board Chair Barbara Patton; Director of Youth Programs, Hospital League/Local 1199 Training and Upgrading Fund; Director of Business Development for the Bronx Empowerment Zone (BOEDC); member of City Council of New York, 2001–06; committees: Energy and Commerce; Homeland Security; elected to the 110th Congress on November 7, 2006; reelected to each succeeding Congress.

Office Listings

https://clarke.house.gov https://facebook.com/repyvettedclarke twitter: @RepYvetteClarke

2058 Rayburn House Office Building, Washington, DC 20515 .... (202) 225–6231
Chief of Staff.—Charlyn Stanberry. FAX: 226–0112
Legislative Director.—David Dorfman.
222 Lenox Road, Suites 1&2, Brooklyn, NY 11226 .... (718) 287–1142

Counties: KINGS (part). Population (2010), 717,708.

ZIP Codes: 11203, 11210, 11212–13, 11216–18, 11225–26, 11229–30, 11233–36, 11238

* * *

TENTH DISTRICT

JERROLD NADLER, Democrat, of New York, NY; born in Brooklyn, NY, June 13, 1947; education: graduated from Stuyvesant High School, 1965; B.A., Columbia University, 1969; J.D., Fordham University, 1978; professional: New York State Assembly, 1977–92; member: ACLU; NARAL Pro-Choice America; AIPAC; National Organization for Women; married: 1976; one child; Assistant Whip; committees: chair, Judiciary; elected to the 102nd Congress on November 3, 1992, to fill the vacancy caused by the death of U.S. Representative Ted Weiss; at the same time elected to the 103rd Congress; reelected to each succeeding Congress.

Office Listings

https://nadler.house.gov

2132 Rayburn House Office Building, Washington, DC 20515 .... (202) 225–5635
Director.—John Doty. FAX: 225–6923
201 Varick Street, Suite 669, New York, NY 10014 .... (212) 367–7350
Chief of Staff.—Amy Rutkin.
6605 Fort Hamilton Parkway, NY 11219 .... (718) 373–3198

Counties: KINGS (part) AND NEW YORK (part). Population (2010), 716,172.

ZIP Codes: 10001, 10003 (part), 10004–06, 10007 (part), 10008, 10011–13 (part), 10014, 10018–19 (part), 10021–22 (part), 10023, 10024–25 (part), 10027–28 (part), 10032 (part), 10036 (part), 10038 (part), 10041, 10043, 10045, 10065 (part), 10069, 10080–81, 10087 (part), 10101, 10107 (part), 10108, 10115, 10116 (part), 10119 (part), 10121–22, 10123 (part), 10128 (part), 10129, 10185 (part), 10199, 10249, 10256, 10268–69, 10271–72, 10274–75, 10277, 10278 (part), 10279–82, 10285–86, 10204, 11214–15 (part), 11218–20 (part), 11223 (part), 11228 (part), 11230–32 (part)

* * *

ELEVENTH DISTRICT

MAX ROSE, Democrat, of Staten Island, NY; born in Brooklyn, Kings County, NY, November 28, 1986; education: graduated from Poly Prep Country Day School, Brooklyn, NY, 2004; B.A., Wesleyan University, Middletown, CT, 2008; M.A., London School of Economics, London, England, 2009; attended Oxford University, Oxford, England; professional: staff, Office of Brooklyn District Attorney Ken Thompson; nonprofit healthcare executive; military: United States Army, 2010–14; New York Army National Guard, 2014–present; awards: Bronze Star, Purple Heart, and Combat Infantry Badge; religion: Jewish; married: Leigh Rose; committees: Homeland Security; Veterans' Affairs; elected to the 116th Congress on November 6, 2018.

Office Listings

https://maxrose.house.gov https://facebook.com/RepMaxRose
twitter: @RepMaxRose https://youtube.com/c/repmaxrose

1529 Longworth House Office Building, Washington, DC 20515 .... (202) 225–3371
Chief of Staff.—Anne Sokolov. FAX: 226–1272
Legislative Director.—Erin Meegan.
Communications Director.—Jonas Edwards-Jenks.
Scheduler.—Lily Wacker.
265 New Dorp Lane, 2nd Floor, Staten Island, NY 10306 .... (718) 667–3313
District Director.—Kevin Elkins.
8203 3rd Avenue, Brooklyn, NY 11209 .... (978) 306–5500

Counties: KINGS (part) AND RICHMOND. Population (2010), 717,707.

ZIP Codes: 10301–10, 10312–14, 11204, 11209, 11214, 11219–20, 11223, 11228, 11252

* * *

TWELFTH DISTRICT

CAROLYN B. MALONEY, Democrat, of New York City, NY; born in Greensboro, NC, February 19, 1946; education: B.A., Greensboro College, Greensboro, NC, 1968; professional: various positions, New York City Board of Education, 1970–77; legislative aide, New York State Assembly, senior program analyst, 1977–79; executive director of advisory council, 1979–82; director of special projects, New York State Senate Office of the Minority Leader; New York City Council member, 1982–93; chairperson, New York City Council Committee on Contracts; member: Council Committee on Aging; National Organization of Women; Common Cause; Sierra Club; Americans for Democratic Action; New York City Council Committee on Housing and Buildings; Citizens Union; Grand Central Business Improvement District; Harlem Urban Development Corporation, 1982–91; Commission on Early Childhood Development Programs; Council of Senior Citizen Centers of New York City, 1982–87; widowed: Clifton H.W. Maloney; children: Virginia Marshall Maloney and Christina Paul Maloney; committees: chair, Oversight and Reform; Financial Services; Joint Economic Committee; elected on November 3, 1992, to the 103rd Congress; reelected to each succeeding Congress.

Office Listings

https://maloney.house.gov https://facebook.com/RepCarolynMaloney twitter: @repmaloney

2308 Rayburn House Office Building, Washington, DC 20515 .... (202) 225–7944
Chief of Staff.—Michael Iger. FAX: 225–4709
Legislative Director.—Christina Parisi.
Executive Assistant.—Rebecca Tulloch.
1651 Third Avenue, Suite 311, New York, NY 10128 .... (212) 860–0606
31–19 Newtown Avenue, Astoria, NY 11102 .... (718) 932–1804
619 Lorimer Street, Brooklyn, NY 11211 .... (718) 349–5972

Counties: KINGS (part), NEW YORK (part), AND QUEENS (part). CITIES AND NEIGHBORHOODS: Astoria, Brooklyn, Greenpoint, Long Island City, Manhattan, Queens, Roosevelt Island, and Williamsburg. Population (2010), 712,053.

ZIP Codes: 10001–03, 10009, 10010–12, 10016–19, 10020–22, 10028–29, 10035–36, 10044, 10055, 10065, 10075, 10087, 10103–07, 10110–13, 10118–19, 10120–21, 10123–24, 10128, 10130–31, 10150–56, 10158–59, 10162–69, 10170–79, 10199, 10259, 10261, 10276, 11101–13, 11106, 11109, 11206, 11211, 11222, 11249, 11377–78

* * *

THIRTEENTH DISTRICT

ADRIANO ESPAILLAT, Democrat, of Manhattan, New York City, NY; born in Santiago, Dominican Republic, September 27, 1954; education: B.A., Queens College, 1979; professional: Manhattan Court Services coordinator for the NYC Criminal Justice Agency, 1980; director of the Washington Heights Victims Services Community Office, 1992; New York State Assembly,

1996; chair, New York State Black, Puerto Rican, Hispanic and Asian Legislative Caucus, 2002; New York State Assembly committees: Environmental Conservation; Economic Development; Codes; Insurance; Judiciary; New York State Senate, 2010; ranking member of the New York State Senate Housing, Construction, and Community Development Committee; chair of the Senate Puerto Rican/Latino Caucus; religion: Catholic; children: Adriano Espaillat, Jr., and Natalia Espaillat; caucuses: Whip, Congressional Hispanic Caucus (CHC); committees: Foreign Affairs; Small Business; Transportation and Infrastructure; elected to the 115th Congress on November 8, 2016; reelected to the 116th Congress on November 6, 2018.

Office Listings

https://espaillat.house.gov https://facebook.com/RepEspaillat
https://twitter.com/RepEspaillat https://instagram.com/repadrianoespaillat

1630 Longworth House Office Building, Washington, DC 20515 .... (202) 225–4365
Chief of Staff.—Aneiry Batista.
Deputy Chief of Staff.—Candance Randle Person.
Harlem Office: 163 West 125th Street, Room 508, New York, NY 10027 .... (212) 663–3900
Deputy District Director.—Cynthia Rodriguez.
Bronx Office: 2530 Grand Concourse, Ground Floor, Bronx, NY 10458 .... (718) 450–8241

Counties: BRONX (part) AND NEW YORK (part). Population (2012), 738,943.

ZIP Codes: 10025 (part), 10026–27, 10029–35, 10037, 10039–40, 10453, 10458, 10463, 10467–68

* * *

FOURTEENTH DISTRICT

ALEXANDRIA OCASIO-CORTEZ, Democrat, of The Bronx, NY; born in New York City, Bronx County, NY, October 13, 1989; education: graduated from Yorktown High School, Yorktown Heights, NY, 2007; B.A., Boston University, Boston, MA, 2011; professional: community organizer; organizer, Bernie Sanders for President; educational director, National Hispanic Institute; founder, Brook Avenue Press; Foreign Affairs and Immigration Liaison/Constituent Services, Office of U.S. Senator Ted Kennedy; bartender; waitress/front of house manager; religion: Christian; committees: Financial Services; Oversight and Reform; elected to the 116th Congress on November 6, 2018.

Office Listings

https://ocasio-cortez.house.gov https://facebook.com/repAOC twitter: @RepAOC

229 Cannon House Office Building, Washington, DC 20515 .... (202) 225–3965
Chief of Staff.—Ariel Eckblad. FAX: 225–1909
Deputy Director of Operations.—Tanushri Shankar.
Press Secretary.—Anika Legrand-Wittich.
Legislative Director.—Gerardo Bonilla Chavez.
Senior Counsel and Policy Advisor.—Dan Riffle.
Legislative Assistants: Randy Abreu, Claudia Pagon Marchena, Klarissa Reynoso.
Staff Assistant.—Taseen Anwar.
74–09 37th Avenue, Suite 305, Jackson Heights, NY 11372 .... (718) 662–5970
District Director.—Maribel Hernandez Rivera.
Deputy District Director.—Naureen Akhter.

Counties: BRONX (part) AND QUEENS (part). Population (2010), 717,708.

ZIP Codes: 10458, 10460–62, 10464–67, 10469, 10475, 11101–05, 11354, 11356–57, 11368–73, 11375, 11377–78

* * *

FIFTEENTH DISTRICT

JOSÉ E. SERRANO, Democrat, of Bronx, NY; born in Mayagüez, PR, October 24, 1943; education: Dodge Vocational High School, Bronx, NY; attended Lehman College, City University of New York, NY; professional: served with the U.S. Army Medical Corps, 1964–66; employed by the Manufacturers Hanover Bank, 1961–69; Community School District 7, 1969–74; New York State Assemblyman, 1974–90; chairman, Consumer Affairs Committee, 1979–83; chairman, Education Committee, 1983–90; religion: Roman Catholic; committees: Appropriations; elected to the 101st Congress, by special election, March 28, 1990, to fill the vacancy caused by the resignation of U.S. Representative Robert Garcia; reelected to each succeeding Congress.

Office Listings

https://serrano.house.gov https://facebook.com/RepJoseSerrano https://twitter.com/RepJoseSerrano
https://instagram.com/repjoseserrano https://youtube.com/user/congressmanserrano

2354 Rayburn House Office Building, Washington, DC 20515 .... (202) 225–4361
Chief Administrator.—Idalia Domínguez de Marty. FAX: 225–6001
Chief of Staff.—Matthew Alpert.
Legislative Aide / Scheduler.—Alexis Philbrick.
Communications Director.—Paola Amador.
Legislative Director and Counsel.—Angel Nigaglioni.
Legislative Assistant / Press Assistant.—Valentin Castillo.
Senior Legislative Assistant.—Marcus Garza.
1231 Lafayette Street, 4th Floor, Bronx, NY 10474 .... (718) 620–0084
District Director.—Anthony Jordan.
Deputy District Director.—Ramon Cabral.
Community Liason.—Hatou Camara.

Counties: BRONX COUNTY (part). CITIES AND TOWNSHIPS: Bronx. Population (2013), 747,271.

ZIP Codes: 10451–60, 10462, 10468, 10472–74

* * *

SIXTEENTH DISTRICT

ELIOT L. ENGEL, Democrat, of Bronx, NY; born in Bronx, February 18, 1947; education: B.A., Hunter-Lehman College, 1969; M.A., City University of New York, 1973; J.D., New York Law School, 1987; professional: teacher and guidance counselor in the New York City public school system, 1969–77; elected to the New York Legislature, 1977–88; chaired the Assembly Committee on Alcoholism and Substance Abuse and Subcommittee on Mitchell-Lama Housing (12 years prior to his election to Congress); married: Patricia Ennis, 1980; three children; caucuses: co-chairman, Albanian Issues Caucus; co-chair, Task Force on Anti-Semitism; board member, Congressional Ad Hoc Committee on Irish Affairs; Allergy and Asthma Caucus; Animal Protection Caucus; Arts Caucus; Congressional Human Rights Caucus; Congressional LGBT Equality Caucus; Diabetes Caucus; EU Caucus; Fragile X Caucus; HIV / AIDS Caucus; Long Island Sound Caucus; Medicare for All Caucus; New Democrat Coalition; Oil and National Security Caucus; Pro-Choice Caucus; Renewable and Energy Efficiency Caucus; Tuberculosis Elimination Caucus; committees: chair, Foreign Affairs; Energy and Commerce; elected on November 8, 1988 to the 101st Congress; reelected to each succeeding Congress.

Office Listings

https://engel.house.gov

2426 Rayburn House Office Building, Washington, DC 20515 .... (202) 225–2464
Administrative Assistant.—E.H. ''Ned'' Michalek. FAX: 225–5513
Office Manager.—Darlene Murray.
Legislative Director.—Brian Skretny.
3655 Johnson Avenue, Bronx, NY 10463 .... (718) 796–9700
Chief of Staff.—William F. Weitz. FAX: 796–5134
District Manager.—Lori Copland.
Communications and Deputy District Director.—Bryant Daniels.
6 Gramatan Avenue, Suite 205, Mt. Vernon, NY 10550 .... (914) 699–4100
FAX: 699–3646
177 Dreiser Loop, Room 3, Bronx, NY 10475 .... (718) 320–2314
FAX: 320–2047

Counties: BRONX (part) AND WESTCHESTER (part). CITIES AND TOWNSHIPS: Parts of Bronx, Eastchester, Greenburgh, Mamaroneck, Mount Vernon, New Rochelle, Pelham, Rye, Scarsdale, and Yonkers. Population (2010), 717,707.

ZIP Codes: 10463, 10466–67, 10469–71, 10475, 10502, 10528, 10530, 10538, 10543, 10550–53, 10557–58, 10580, 10583, 10701–05, 10707–10, 10801–02, 10804–05

* * *

SEVENTEENTH DISTRICT

NITA M. LOWEY, Democrat, of Harrison, NY; born in New York, NY, July 5, 1937; education: graduated, Bronx High School of Science, 1955; B.A., Mount Holyoke College, 1959; professional: assistant to the Secretary of State for Economic Development and Neighborhood Preservation, and deputy director, Division of Economic Opportunity, 1975–85; Assistant Secretary of State, 1985–87; member: boards of directors, Close-Up Foundation; Effective Parenting Information for Children; Windward School, Downstate (New York Region); Westchester Jewish Conference; Westchester Opportunity Program; National Committee of the Police Corps; Women's Network of the YWCA; Legal Awareness for Women; National Women's Political Caucus of Westchester; American Jewish Committee of Westchester; married: Stephen Lowey, 1961; children: Dana, Jacqueline, and Douglas; committees: chair, Appropriations; elected on November 8, 1988 to the 101st Congress; reelected to each succeeding Congress.

Office Listings

https://lowey.house.gov https://facebook.com/RepLowey https://twitter.com/NitaLowey

2365 Rayburn House Office Building, Washington, DC 20515 .... (202) 225–6506
Chief of Staff.—Elizabeth Stanley. FAX: 225–0546
Deputy Chief of Staff.—Kelly Healton.
Executive Assistant and Scheduler.—Matt Pastore.
Legislative Director.—Dana Acton.
Communications Director.—Katelynn Thorpe.
222 Mamaroneck Avenue, Suite 312, White Plains, NY 10605 .... (914) 428–1707
67 North Main Street, Suite 101, New City, NY 10956 .... (845) 639–3485
District Director.—Patricia Keegan.

Counties: ROCKLAND (all) AND WESTCHESTER (part). CITIES AND TOWNSHIPS: Briarcliff Manor, Buchanan, Chappaqua, Cortlandt, Cortlandt Manor, Crompond, Croton-on-Hudson, Dobbs Ferry, East Irvington, Elmsford, Fairview, Harrison, Hartsdale, Haverstraw, Hawthorne, Irvington, Jefferson Valley, Millwood, Mohegan Lake, Mount Kisco, Mount Pleasant, New City, North White Plains, Ossining, Peekskill, Pleasantville, Pocantico Hills, Port Chester, Purchase, Rye Brook, Scarborough, Sleepy Hollow, Tarrytown, Thornwood, Valhalla, Verplanck, West Harrison, West Haverstraw, White Plains, and Yorktown Heights. Population (2010), 717,708.

ZIP Codes: 10510–11, 10514, 10517, 10520, 10522–23, 10528, 10530, 10532–33, 10535, 10546–49, 10562, 10566–67, 10570, 10573, 10577, 10580, 10588, 10591, 10594–96, 10598, 10601, 10603–07, 10901, 10913, 10920, 10923, 10927, 10931, 10952, 10954, 10956, 10960, 10964–65, 10968, 10970, 10974, 10976–77, 10980, 10982–84, 10986, 10989, 10993–94

* * *

EIGHTEENTH DISTRICT

SEAN PATRICK MALONEY, Democrat, of Cold Spring, NY; born in Sherbrooke, Quebec, July 30, 1966; education: graduated, Hanover High School, Hanover, NH, 1984; B.A., University of Virginia, 1988; J.D., University of Virginia, 1992; professional: White House Deputy Staff Secretary, 1997–99; White House Staff Secretary and Assistant to the President of the United States, 1999–2000; chief operating officer, Kiodex, Inc., 2000–03; First Deputy Secretary to the Governor of New York, 2007–08; corporate partner, Kirkland & Ellis LLP, 2009–11; partner, Orrick, Herrington & Sutcliffe LLP; husband: Randy Florke, 1992–present; children: Jesus, Daley, and Essie; committees: Agriculture; Transportation and Infrastructure; Permanent Select Committee on Intelligence; elected to the 113th Congress on November 6, 2012; reelected to each succeeding Congress.

Office Listings

https://seanmaloney.house.gov https://facebook.com/repseanmaloney
https://twitter.com/repseanmaloney https://instagram.com/repseanpatrickmaloney

2331 Rayburn House Office Building, Washington, DC 20515 .... (202) 225–5441
Chief of Staff.—Timothy Persico.
Deputy Chief of Staff.—Ryan Lehman.
Communications Director.—Aaron White.
Legislative Director.—Molly Carey.
Director of Scheduling.—Kevin Golden.
Digital Director.—Libbie Wilcox.
123 Grand Street, 2nd Floor, Newburgh, NY 12550 .... (845) 561–1259
Director of Constituent Services.—Gerardo Alvarez.

Counties: NORTHERN WESTCHESTER (part), ORANGE, PUTNAM, AND SOUTHERN DUTCHESS (part). CITIES AND TOWNSHIPS: Arlington, Balmville, Beacon, Beaver Dam Lake, Bedford, Bedford Hills, Brewster, Brewster Hill, Brinckerhoff, Carmel Hamlet, Chester, Cold Spring, Cornwall-on-Hudson, Crown Heights, Fairview, Firthcliffe, Fishkill, Florida, Fort Montgomery, Gardnertown, Golden's Bridge, Goshen, Greenwood Lake, Harriman, Heritage Hills, Highland Falls, Hillside Lake, Hopewell Junction, Katonah, Kiryas Joel, Lake Carmel, Lincolndale, Mahopac, Maybrook, Mechanicstown, Merritt Park, Middletown, Monroe, Montgomery, Mountain Lodge Park, Myers Corner, Nelsonville, New Windsor, Newburgh, Orange Lake, Otisville, Peach Lake, Pine Bush, Port Jervis, Poughkeepsie, Putnam Lake, Red Oaks Mill, Salisbury Mills, Scotchtown, Scotts Corners, Shenorock, South Blooming Grove, Spackenkill, Titusville, Tuxedo Park, Vails Gate, Walden, Walton Park, Wappingers Falls, Warwick, Washington Heights, Washingtonville, West Point, and Woodbury. Population (2010), 717,707.

ZIP Codes: 10501, 10504–07, 10509, 10512, 10516, 10518–19, 10524, 10526–27, 10536–37, 10540–42, 10549, 10560, 10562, 10576, 10578–79, 10587, 10589–90, 10597–98, 10910, 10912, 10914–19, 10921–22, 10924–26, 10928, 10930, 10932–33, 10940–41, 10949–50, 10953, 10958–59, 10963, 10969, 10973–75, 10979, 10981, 10985, 10987–88, 12508, 12511–12, 12518, 12520, 12524, 12527, 12531, 12533, 12537–38, 12540, 12542–43, 12549–53, 12555, 12563–64, 12566, 12569, 12575, 12577, 12582, 12584, 12586, 12589–90, 12601–04, 12721, 12729, 12746, 12771, 12780, 12785

* * *

NINETEENTH DISTRICT

ANTONIO DELGADO, Democrat, of Rhinebeck, NY; born in Schenectady, Schenectady County, NY, January 28, 1977; education: graduated from Notre Dame-Bishop Gibbons High School, Schenectady, NY, 1995; B.A., Colgate University, Hamilton, NY, 1999; Rhodes Scholar, B.A. (M.A. Oxon), Oxford University, Oxford, England, 2001; J.D., Harvard University, Cambridge, MA, 2005; professional: musician; lawyer, private practice; married: Lacey Schwartz Delgado; children: Maxwell and Coltrane; caucuses: Affordable Prescription Drug Task Force; Bipartisan Heroin and Opioids Task Force; Congressional Black Caucus; Dairy Farmers Caucus; Democracy Reform Task Force; Expand Social Security Caucus; Freshmen Working Group on Addiction; Future Forum Caucus; House Small Brewers Caucus; LGBT Equality Caucus; Lyme Disease Caucus; PFAS Task Force; Rural Broadband Caucus; Rural Broadband Task Force; Ski and Snowboard Caucus; Task Force on Alzheimer's Disease; committees: Agriculture; Small Business; Transportation and Infrastructure; elected to the 116th Congress on November 6, 2018.

Office Listings

https://delgado.house.gov https://facebook.com/RepAntonioDelgado
twitter: @repdelgado https://instagram.com/repantoniodelgado

1007 Longworth House Office Building, Washington, DC 20515 .... (202) 225–5614
Chief of Staff.—John Bivona.
Deputy Chief of Staff/Legislative Director.—Jessie Andrews.
Communications Director.—Margaret Mulkerrin.
Scheduler.—Christina Ives.
256 Clinton Avenue, Kingston, NY 12401 .... (845) 443–2930
District Director.—Amanda Boomhower.
Deputy Director.—Victoria Perry.
111 Main Street, Delhi, NY 13753.
59 North Main Street, #301, Liberty, NY 12754.
189 Main Street, #500, Oneonta, NY 13820.

Counties: COLUMBIA, DELAWARE, GREENE, OTSEGO, SCHOHARIE, SULLIVAN, ULSTER, and parts of BROOME, DUTCHESS, MONTGOMERY, AND RENSSELAER COUNTIES.

ZIP Codes: 12015, 12017, 12022–24, 12029, 12031, 12033, 12035–37, 12042–43, 12050–53, 12057–58, 12060–63, 12110, 12115–16, 12118, 12121, 12153–57, 12160, 12165–68, 12172–76, 12180–82, 12184–85, 12187, 12189, 12192, 12194–98, 12401, 12404–05, 12407, 12409–21, 12435–36, 12438, 12451–61, 12463–75, 12481–82, 12485–87, 12489–96, 12498, 12501–04, 12506–07, 12561, 12563–65, 12592, 12594, 12601, 12603, 12701, 12719–27, 12732–34, 12736–38, 12740–45, 12747, 12749–52, 12754, 12758–60, 12762–64, 12766–67, 12776–79, 12781, 12783–92, 12816, 13315, 13317, 13459, 13468, 13475, 13482, 13485, 13755–57, 13774, 13786, 13788, 13796, 13804, 13806–10

* * *

TWENTIETH DISTRICT

PAUL D. TONKO, Democrat, of Amsterdam, NY; born in Amsterdam, June 18, 1949; education: graduated, Amsterdam High School, Amsterdam, NY, 1967; B.S., mechanical and industrial engineering, Clarkson University, Potsdam, NY, 1971; professional: engineer, NYS Department of Transportation; engineer, NYS Department of Public Service; Montgomery County Board of Supervisors, 1976–83; chairman, Montgomery County Board of Supervisors, 1981–83; NYS Assembly, 1983–2007; chairman, NYS Assembly Standing Committee on Energy,

1992–2007; president and CEO, NYS Energy Research and Development Authority, 2007–08; caucuses: co-chair, Congressional Horse Caucus; co-chair, Sustainable Energy and Environment Coalition; committees: Energy and Commerce; Natural Resources; Science, Space, and Technology; elected to the 111th Congress on November 4, 2008; reelected to each succeeding Congress.

Office Listings

https://tonko.house.gov https://facebook.com/reppaultonko twitter: @RepPaulTonko

2369 Rayburn House Office Building, Washington, DC 20515 .... (202) 225–5076
Chief of Staff.—Clinton Britt. FAX: 225–5077
Communications Director.—Matt Sonneborn.
Legislative Director.—Jeff Morgan.
Director of Operations.—David Mastrangelo.
Legislative Assistants: Brendan Larkin, Emily Silverberg, Noor Teebi.
Legislative Correspondent.—Katie Greenberg.
19 Dove Street, Suite 302, Albany, NY 12210 .... (518) 465–0700
105 Jay Street (Schenectady City Hall), Room 15, Schenectady, NY 12305 .... (518) 374–4547
61 Church Street (Amsterdam City Hall), Room 309, Amsterdam, NY 12010 .... (518) 843–3400

Counties: ALBANY, MONTGOMERY (part), RENSSELAER (part), SARATOGA (part), AND SCHENECTADY. Population (2010), 720,133.

ZIP Codes: 12007–10, 12016, 12019–20, 12023, 12027, 12033, 12041, 12045–47, 12053–56, 12059, 12061, 12065–70, 12072, 12074, 12077, 12083–87, 12095, 12107, 12110, 12118, 12120, 12122–23, 12128, 12137, 12141, 12143–44, 12147–48, 12150–51, 12157–61, 12166, 12170, 12177, 12180–83, 12186, 12188–89, 12193, 12196, 12198, 12201–12, 12220, 12222–24, 12226–50, 12252, 12255–57, 12260–61, 12288, 12301–09, 12325, 12345, 12460, 12469, 12866

* * *

TWENTY-FIRST DISTRICT

ELISE M. STEFANIK, Republican, of Willsboro, NY; born in Albany, NY, July 2, 1984; education: graduated from Albany Academy for Girls, Albany, NY, 2002; B.A., Harvard University, Cambridge, MA, 2006; professional: staff, President George W. Bush administration, 2006–09; campaign aide; businesswoman; committees: Armed Services; Education and Labor; Permanent Select Committee on Intelligence; elected to the 114th Congress on November 4, 2014; reelected to each succeeding Congress.

Office Listings

https://stefanik.house.gov https://facebook.com/RepEliseStefanik https://twitter.com/RepStefanik

318 Cannon House Office Building, Washington, DC 20515 .... (202) 225–4611
Chief of Staff.—Anthony Pileggi.
Communications Director.—Maddie Anderson.
Legislative Director.—Julia Angelotti.
District Director.—Michael Ostrander.
5 Warren Street, Suite 4, Glens Falls, NY 12801 .... (518) 743–0964
23 Durkee Street, Suite C, Plattsburgh, NY 12901 .... (518) 561–2324
88 Public Square, Suite A, Watertown, NY 13601 .... (315) 782–3150

Counties: CLINTON, ESSEX, FRANKLIN, FULTON, HAMILTON, HERKIMER, JEFFERSON, LEWIS, ST. LAWRENCE, SARATOGA, WARREN, AND WASHINGTON. Population (2015), 716,340.

Zip Codes: 12010 (part), 12020 (part), 12025, 12028 (part), 12032, 12057 (part), 12068 (part), 12070 (part), 12074 (part), 12078, 12086 (part), 12094–95 (part), 12108, 12117, 12118 (part), 12134, 12139, 12154 (part), 12164, 12170 (part), 12185 (part), 12190, 12801, 12803–04, 12808–12, 12814–17, 12819, 12821–24, 12827–28, 12831–32, 12833 (part), 12834–39, 12841–47, 12849–53, 12855–65, 12866 (part), 12870–74, 12878, 12883–87, 12901, 12903, 12910–14, 12916–24, 12926–30, 12932–37, 12939, 12941–46, 12950, 12952–53, 12955–62, 12964–67, 12969–70, 12972–81, 12983, 12985–87, 12989, 12992–93, 12996–98, 13305, 13312, 13316 (part), 13324 (part), 13325, 13327, 13329, 13331, 13338–39 (part), 13343, 13345, 13353, 13360, 13367–68, 13404, 13420, 13431 (part), 13433, 13436–38, 13452 (part), 13454, 13470–73, 13489 (part), 13601–03, 13605–08, 13612–26, 13628, 13630, 13633–43, 13646–48, 13650–52, 13654–56, 13658–62, 13664–70, 13672–82, 13684–85, 13687, 13690–97

* * *

TWENTY-SECOND DISTRICT

ANTHONY BRINDISI, Democrat, of Utica, NY; born in Utica, NY, November 22, 1978; education: B.A., Siena College, Loudonville, NY, 2000; J.D., Albany Law School of Union

University, Albany, NY, 2004; professional: lawyer, private practice; member, Utica School Board, 2009–12; member, New York State Assembly, 2012–18; married: Erica McGovern Brindisi; children: two, Anthony, Jr., and Lily; committees: Agriculture; Veterans' Affairs; elected to the 116th Congress on November 6, 2018.

Office Listings

https://brindisi.house.gov https://facebook.com/RepBrindisi
twitter: @RepBrindisi https://instagram.com/repbrindisi

329 Cannon House Office Building, Washington, DC 20515 .... (202) 225–3665
Chief of Staff.—Macey Matthews.
Legislative Director.—Robert Dougherty.
Communications Director.—Luke Jackson.
Scheduler.—Caroline Ehlich.
430 Court Street, Suite 102, Utica, NY 13502 .... (315) 732–0713
District Director.—Sarah Bormann.
49 Court Street, Suite 210, Binghamton, NY 13901 .... (607) 242–0200

Counties: BROOME (part), CHENANGO, CORTLAND, HERKIMER, MADISON, ONEIDA, OSWEGO (part), TIOGA (part), AND TOMPKINS (part). CITIES, TOWNS, AND VILLAGES: Binghamton, Camden, Cortland, Cortlandville, Forestport, Little Falls, Mexico, New Berlin, Norwich, Oneida, Sandy Creek, Sherrill, Sullivan, Utica, Vestal, and Windsor. Population (2010), 717,708.

ZIP Codes: 13028, 13030, 13032, 13035–37, 13040, 13042, 13044–45, 13052–54, 13061, 13072, 13076–77, 13082–83, 13087, 13101, 13103–04, 13114, 13122–24, 13126, 13131–32, 13134, 13136, 13141–42, 13144–45, 13155, 13157–59, 13162–63, 13167, 13301–04, 13308–10, 13313–14, 13316, 13318–19, 13321–24, 13328, 13332, 13334, 13338–41, 13346, 13350, 13352, 13354–55, 13357, 13361–65, 13402–03, 13406–09, 13411, 13413, 13416–18, 13421, 13424–25, 13431, 13435, 13437–41, 13456, 13460–61, 13464, 13469, 13471, 13475–78, 13480, 13483–86, 13489–95, 13501–02, 13661, 13730, 13732–33, 13736, 13744, 13746, 13748, 13760, 13777–78, 13780, 13784, 13787, 13790, 13794–95, 13797, 13801–03, 13809, 13811–13, 13815, 13826–27, 13830, 13832–33, 13835, 13841, 13843–44, 13850, 13862–63, 13865, 13901–05

* * *

TWENTY-THIRD DISTRICT

TOM REED, Republican, of Corning, NY; born in Joliet, IL, November 18, 1971; education: graduated, B.A., Alfred University, Alfred, NY, 1993; J.D., Ohio Northern University College of Law, Ada, OH, 1996; professional: lawyer, private practice, Law Office of Thomas W. Reed II; business owner; Mayor of Corning, NY, 2008–09; religion: Catholic; family: wife, Jean; children: Autumn and Will; caucuses: co-chair, Problem Solvers Caucus; committees: Ways and Means; elected to the 111th Congress, by special election, on November 2, 2010, to fill the vacancy caused by the resignation of U.S. Representative Eric J.J. Massa; subsequently elected to a full term in the 112th Congress on November 2, 2010; reelected to each succeeding Congress.

Office Listings

https://reed.house.gov https://facebook.com/RepTomReed
https://twitter.com/RepTomReed https://instagram.com/reptomreed

2263 Rayburn House Office Building, Washington, DC 20515 .... (202) 225–3161
Chief of Staff.—Joe Rizzo. FAX: 226–6599
Legislative Director.—Logan Hoover.
Communications Director.—Nathaniel Sizemore.
District Director.—Alison Hunt.
89 West Market Street, Corning, NY 14830 .... (607) 654–7566
433 Exchange Street, Geneva, NY 14456 .... (315) 759–5229
2 East 2nd Street, Suite 208, Jamestown, NY 14701 .... (716) 708–6369
One Bluebird Square, Olean, NY 14760 .... (716) 379–8434

Counties: ALLEGANY, CATTARAUGUS, CHAUTAUQUA, CHEMUNG, ONTARIO (part), SCHUYLER, SENECA, STEUBEN, TIOGA (part), TOMPKINS, AND YATES. Population (2010), 717,707.

ZIP Codes: 13053, 13062, 13068, 13073, 13102, 13734, 13736, 13743, 13811–12, 13827, 13835, 13840, 13845, 13864, 14029, 14041–42, 14048, 14060, 14062–63, 14065, 14070, 14081, 14101, 14129, 14133, 14135–36, 14168, 14171, 14173, 14415, 14418, 14424, 14432, 14441, 14453, 14456, 14461, 14463, 14478, 14504, 14507, 14512, 14518, 14527, 14529, 14532, 14537, 14544, 14547–48, 14561, 14572, 14701–02, 14706–24, 14726–45, 14747–48, 14750–58, 14760, 14766–67, 14769–70, 14772, 14774–75, 14777–79, 14781–88, 14801–10, 14812–27, 14830, 14837–43, 14845, 14850, 14854–59, 14861, 14863–65, 14867, 14869–74, 14876–87, 14889, 14891–95, 14897–98, 14901–05, 14925

* * *

TWENTY-FOURTH DISTRICT

JOHN KATKO, Republican, of Camillus, NY; education: graduated from Bishop Ludden High School; B.A., Niagara University, *cum laude*; J.D., Syracuse University College of Law, *cum laude*; professional: Federal Prosecutor (most recently as Assistant U.S. Attorney with the Northern District of New York) for over 20 years; married: wife of over 27 years, Robin; three sons; committees: Homeland Security; Transportation and Infrastructure; elected to the 114th Congress on November 4, 2014; reelected to each succeeding Congress.

Office Listings

https://katko.house.gov

2457 Rayburn House Office Building, Washington, DC 20515 .... (202) 225–3701
Chief of Staff.—Zach Howell.
Executive Assistant.—Emily Bazydlo.
440 South Warren Street, 7th Floor, Suite 711, Syracuse, NY 13202 .... (315) 423–5657
FAX: 423–5604
71 Genesee Street, Auburn, NY 13021 .... (315) 253–4068
FAX: 253–2435
7376 State Route 31, Lyons, NY 14489 (open Wednesdays, 10 a.m. until 4 p.m.).
13 West Oneida Street, 2nd Floor, Oswego, NY 13126 (open Wednesdays, 10 a.m. until 3 p.m.).

Counties: CAYUGA, ONONDAGA, OSWEGO (part), AND WAYNE. Population (2010), 717,707.

ZIP Codes: 13020–21, 13024, 13026–31, 13033–37, 13039, 13041, 13045, 13051–52, 13057, 13060, 13063–64, 13066, 13069, 13071, 13073–74, 13077–78, 13080–84, 13088, 13090, 13092, 13102, 13104, 13108, 13110–18, 13120, 13122, 13126, 13131–32, 13135, 13138, 13140–41, 13143, 13146–47, 13152–53, 13156, 13158–60, 13164, 13166, 13202–12, 13214–15, 13219, 13224, 13290, 14433, 14450, 14489, 14502, 14505, 14551, 14555, 14568, 14580, 14589, 14590

* * *

TWENTY-FIFTH DISTRICT

JOSEPH D. MORELLE, Democrat, of Irondequoit, NY; born in Utica, Oneida County, NY, April 29, 1957; education: graduated from Eastridge High School, Irondequoit, NY, 1975; B.A., SUNY Geneseo, Geneseo, NY, 1986; professional: Monroe County Legislature, 1984–90; member, New York State Assembly, 1990–2018; Majority Leader New York State Assembly, 2013–18; married: Mary Beth Morelle; children: three; grandchildren: three; committees: Budget; Education and Labor; Rules; elected simultaneously to the 115th and 116th Congresses, by special election, on November 6, 2018, to fill the vacancy caused by the death of U.S. Representative Louise Slaughter.

Office Listings

https://morelle.house.gov https://facebook.com/RepJoeMorelle twitter: @RepJoeMorelle

1317 Longworth House Office Building, Washington, DC 20515 .... (202) 225–3615
Chief of Staff.—Nicholas Weatherbee. FAX: 225–7822
Legislative Director.—Abbie Sorrendino.
Scheduler.—Daniel Lemire.
3120 Federal Building, 100 State Street, Rochester, NY 14614 .... (585) 232–4850
District Director.—Kristin McCann. FAX: 232–1954
Communications Director.—Sean Hart.
Counsel.—Robert Bergin.
Press Secretary.—Dana Vernetti.

Counties: MONROE (majority). CITIES AND TOWNSHIPS: Brighton, Brockport, Chili, Churchville, Clarkson, East Rochester, Fairport, Gates, Greece, Hamlin, Henrietta, Hilton, Irondequoit, Ogden, Parma, Penfield, Perinton, Pittsford, Riga, Rochester, Rush, Scottsville, Spencerport, Sweden, and Webster. Population (2013), 724,587.

ZIP Codes: 14416, 14420, 14428, 14445, 14450, 14464, 14467–68, 14502, 14514, 14519, 14526, 14534, 14543, 14546, 14559, 14564, 14580, 14586, 14604–10, 14612–13, 14615–18, 14620–26

* * *

TWENTY-SIXTH DISTRICT

BRIAN HIGGINS, Democrat, of Buffalo, NY; born in Buffalo, October 6, 1959; education: B.A., Buffalo State College, NY, 1984; M.P.A., Harvard University, Cambridge, MA, 1996;

professional: lecturer, Buffalo State College; member of the Buffalo Common Council, 1988–93; member of the New York State Assembly, 1999–2004; married: Mary Jane Hannon; two children: John and Maeve; committees: Budget; Ways and Means; elected to the 109th Congress on November 2, 2004; reelected to each succeeding Congress.

Office Listings

https://higgins.house.gov https://facebook.com/repbrianhiggins twitter: @RepBrianHiggins

2459 Rayburn House Office Building, Washington, DC 20515 .... (202) 225–3306
Chief of Staff.—Chuck Eaton. FAX: 226–0347
DC Chief of Staff.—Matthew Fery.
Legislative Director.—Kayla Williams.
Communications Director.—Theresa Kennedy.
Larkin at Exchange, 726 Exchange Street, Suite 601, Buffalo, NY 14210 .... (716) 852–3501
800 Main Street, Suite 3C, Niagara Falls, NY 14301 .... (716) 282–1274

Counties: ERIE (part) AND NIAGARA (part). CITIES AND TOWNSHIPS: Amherst (part), Buffalo, Cheektowaga, Grand Island, Lackawanna, Niagara Falls (part), North Tonawanda, Tonawanda (city), Tonawanda (township), and West Seneca. Population (2010), 717,707.

ZIP Codes: 14043, 14051, 14068, 14072, 14120, 14150, 14201–28, 14261, 14301–05

* * *

TWENTY-SEVENTH DISTRICT

CHRIS JACOBS, Republican, of Orchard Park, NY; born in Buffalo, November 28, 1966; education: B.A., Boston College, M.B.A., American University, Washington, DC; J.D., State University of New York at Buffalo; professional: co-founder, BISON scholarship fund, 1995; Deputy Commissioner, Erie County Office of Planning and Economic Development, 2000–02; founder and owner, Avalon Development real estate development company, 2002; member, Buffalo Public Schools Board of Education, 2004–11; 62nd Secretary of the State of New York 2006–07; County Clerk, Erie County, 2012–17; New York State Senator, 60th District, 2017–20; married, Martina Jacobs; daughter, Anna; committees: Agriculture; Budget; elected to the 116th Congress, by special election, on June 23, 2020, to fill the vacancy caused by the resignation of U.S. Representative Chris Collins.

Office Listings

https://jacobs.house.gov

2243 Rayburn House Office Building, Washington, DC 20515 .... (202) 225–5265
Chief of Staff.—Michael Hook.
Staff Assistant.—Elizabeth Murphy.
Legislative Director.—Erynn Hook.
Communications Director.—Sarah Minkel.
8203 Main Street, Suite 2, Williamsville, NY 14221 .... (716) 634–2324
District Director.—Michael Kracker.
128 Main Street, Geneseo, NY 14454 .... (585) 519–4002

Counties: ERIE (part), GENESEE, LIVINGSTON, MONROE (part), NIAGARA (part), ONTARIO (part), ORLEANS, AND WYOMING. Population (2010), 717,707.

ZIP Codes: 14001, 14004–06, 14008–13, 14020–21, 14024–28, 14030–40, 14043, 14047, 14051–52, 14054–59, 14061, 14066–67, 14069–70, 14075, 14080–83, 14085–86, 14091–92, 14094–95, 14098, 14102–03, 14105, 14107–13, 14120, 14125–27, 14130–32, 14134, 14139–41, 14143–45, 14167, 14169–70, 14172, 14174, 14218–19, 14221, 14224, 14228, 14304–05, 14411, 14414, 14416, 14420, 14422–25, 14427–29, 14435, 14437, 14443, 14452–54, 14462, 14464, 14466–72, 14475–77, 14479–82, 14485–88, 14506, 14508, 14510–12, 14517, 14522, 14525, 14530, 14533–34, 14536, 14539, 14543, 14545–46, 14548–50, 14556–58, 14560, 14564, 14569, 14571–72, 14585–86, 14591–92, 14735, 14822, 14836, 14846, 14884

NORTH CAROLINA

(Population 2010, 9,535,483)

SENATORS

RICHARD BURR, Republican, of Winston-Salem, NC; born in Charlottesville, VA, November 30, 1955; education: R.J. Reynolds High School, Winston-Salem, NC, 1974; B.A., communications, Wake Forest University, Winston-Salem, NC, 1978; professional: sales manager, Carswell Distributing; member: Reynolds Rotary Club; board member, Brenner Children's Hospital; public service: U.S. House of Representatives, 1995–2005; served as vice-chairman of the Energy and Commerce Committee; married: Brooke Fauth, 1984; children: two sons; committees: Finance; Health, Education, Labor, and Pensions; Select Committee on Intelligence; Special Committee on Aging; elected to the U.S. Senate on November 2, 2004; reelected to each succeeding Senate term.

Office Listings

https://burr.senate.gov https://facebook.com/SenatorRichardBurr twitter: @SenatorBurr

217 Russell Senate Office Building, Washington, DC 20510 .... (202) 224–3154
Office Manager.—Polly Walker. FAX: 228–2981
Chief of Staff.—Natasha Hickman.
Legislative Director.—Christopher Toppings.
Scheduler.—Michael Sorensen.
2000 West First Street, Suite 508, Winston-Salem, NC 27104 .... (336) 631–5125
State Director and Deputy Chief of Staff.—Dean Myers.
100 Coast Line Street, Room 210, Rocky Mount, NC 27804 .... (252) 977–9522
201 North Front Street, Suite 809, Wilmington, NC 28401 .... (910) 251–1058
151 Patton Avenue, Suite 204, Asheville, NC 28801 .... (828) 350–2437

* * *

THOM TILLIS, Republican, of Huntersville, NC; born in Jacksonville, FL, August 30, 1960; education: B.S., University of Maryland University College, 1997; professional: partner, IBM Global Business Services, 2002–09; partner, PricewaterhouseCoopers, 1990–2002; public service: North Carolina State House Speaker, 2011–15, North Carolina State House, 2009–15; religion: Catholic; married: Susan Tillis; children: one daughter, one son; committees: Armed Services; Banking, Housing, and Urban Affairs; Judiciary; Veterans' Affairs; elected to the U.S. Senate on November 4, 2014.

Office Listings

https://tillis.senate.gov https://facebook.com/SenatorThomTillis twitter: @SenThomTillis

113 Dirksen Senate Office Building, Washington, DC 20510 .... (202) 224–6342
Chief of Staff.—Ted Lehman.
Communications Director.—Daniel Keylin.
State Director.—Kim Canady Barnes.
1694 East Arlington Boulevard, Suite B, Greenville, NC 27858 .... (252) 329–0371
310 New Bern Avenue, Suite 122, Raleigh, NC 27601 .... (919) 856–4630
9300 Harris Corners Parkway, Suite 170, Charlotte, NC 28269 .... (704) 509–9087
1840 Eastchester Drive, Suite 200, High Point, NC 27265 .... (336) 885–0685
1 Historic Courthouse Square, Suite 112, Hendersonville, NC 28972 .... (828) 693–8750
FAX: 693–9724

REPRESENTATIVES

FIRST DISTRICT

G. K. BUTTERFIELD, Democrat, of Wilson County, NC; born, April 27, 1947; education: North Carolina Central University, graduated in 1971, with degrees in sociology and political science; North Carolina Central University School of Law, graduated in 1974, with a juris doctor degree; military service: U.S. Army, 1968–70; served as a Personnel Specialist; discharged with the rank of Specialist E–4; professional: attorney; private practice, 1974–88; public service: elected to the North Carolina Superior Court bench in November, 1988; appointed on February 8, 2001, by Governor Michael F. Easley to the North Carolina Supreme Court; after leaving the Supreme Court, following the 2002 election, Governor Easley appointed Justice Butterfield as a Special Superior Court Judge; served until his retirement on May 7, 2004; organizations:

North Carolina Bar Association; North Carolina Association of Black Lawyers; Wilson Opportunities Industrialization Center; religion: Baptist; appointed Chief Deputy Whip, 110th Congress; chair, Congressional Black Caucus, 114th Congress; committees: Energy and Commerce; House Administration; Joint Committee on the Library; elected to the 108th Congress, by special election, on July 20, 2004; elected to the 109th Congress on November 2, 2004; reelected to each succeeding Congress.

Office Listings

https://butterfield.house.gov https://facebook.com/congressmangkbutterfield
https://twitter.com/GKButterfield

2080 Rayburn House Office Building, Washington, DC 20515 .... (202) 225–3101
Chief of Staff.—Vacant.
Communications Director.—Nicole Julius.
Scheduler.—Lindsey Bowen.
216 Northeast Nash Street, Suite B, Wilson, NC 27893 .... (252) 237–9816
2741 Campus Walk Avenue, Building 400, Suite 300, Durham, NC 27705 .... (919) 908–0164

Counties: BERTIE, DURHAM (part), EDGECOMBE, GATES, GRANVILLE, HALIFAX, HERTFORD, MARTIN, NORTHAMPTON, PITT (part), VANCE, WARREN, WASHINGTON, AND WILSON (part). Estimated Population (2016), 750,278.

ZIP Codes: 27278, 27503, 27507, 27509, 27517, 27522, 27525, 27536–37, 27544, 27551, 27553, 27556, 27560, 27563, 27565, 27572, 27581–82, 27587, 27589, 27596, 27613, 27617, 27701, 27703–05, 27707, 27712–13, 27801, 27803, 27805, 27809, 27812, 27818–20, 27822–23, 27825, 27829, 27831–32, 27834, 27839–47, 27849–50, 27852–53, 27855, 27857–58, 27860–62, 27864, 27866, 27869–74, 27876, 27878, 27881, 27883–84, 27886, 27888–93, 27896–97, 27910, 27922, 27924, 27926, 27928, 27935, 27937–38, 27942, 27946, 27957, 27962, 27967, 27970, 27979, 27983, 27986, 28590

* * *

SECOND DISTRICT

GEORGE HOLDING, Republican, of Raleigh, NC; born in Raleigh, April 17, 1968; education: B.A., classics, Wake Forest University, Winston-Salem, NC, 1991; J.D., Wake Forest University Law School, Winston-Salem, NC, 1996; professional: law clerk for U.S. District Judge Terrence Boyle; practiced law in Raleigh with Kilpatrick Stockton; served as legislative counsel to U.S. Senator Jessie Helms, 1998–2002; joined the U.S. Attorney's office for the Eastern District of North Carolina, 2002–06; confirmed by U.S. Senate as the U.S. Attorney for Eastern North Carolina, 2006–11; religion: Baptist; committees: Budget; Ethics; Ways and Means; elected to the 113th Congress on November 6, 2012; reelected to each succeeding Congress.

Office Listings

https://holding.house.gov https://facebook.com/CongressmanGeorgeHolding
https://twitter.com/RepHolding

1110 Longworth House Office Building, Washington, DC 20515 .... (202) 225–3032
Chief of Staff.—Katie Smith. FAX: 225–0181
Legislative Director.—Rich Sheedy.
Communications Director.—William Glenn.
Scheduler.—Carly Kilgore.
7200 Falls of Neuse Road, Suite 204, Raleigh, NC 27615 .... (919) 782–4400

Counties: FRANKLIN, HARNETT, JOHNSTON (part), NASH, WAKE (part), AND WILSON (part).

ZIP Codes: 27203, 27205, 27207–09, 27215, 27233, 27242, 27248, 27252, 27260, 27263, 27281, 27283, 27298, 27312–13, 27316–17, 27325, 27330, 27332, 27341, 27344, 27349–50, 27355–56, 27360, 27370–71, 27376, 27501–02, 27504–05, 27511, 27513, 27517, 27519, 27521, 27523, 27526, 27539–40, 27546, 27559–60, 27562, 27592, 27607, 27713, 28301, 28303–08, 28310–12, 28314–15, 28323, 28326–27, 28334, 28339, 28342, 28344, 28347–48, 28350, 28356–57, 28371, 28373–74, 28376, 28386–87, 28390–91, 28394–95

* * *

THIRD DISTRICT

GREGORY F. MURPHY, M.D., Republican, of Greenville, NC; born in 1963; education: B.S., pre-medical studies, religion, Davidson College, Davidson, NC, 1985; M.D., University of North Carolina School of Medicine, Chapel Hill, NC, 1989; Chief of Staff, Vidant Medical Center, 3-year term; Division Chief of Urology, Department of Surgery, East Carolina University School of Medicine, Greenville, NC; President and Senior Management Partner, Eastern Urological Associates, P.A., Greenville, NC; married: Wendy; 3 children; committees: Education and Labor; Science, Space, and Technology; elected to the 116th Congress, by special election, on September 10, 2019, to fill the vacancy caused by the death of Walter B. Jones.

Office Listings

https://gregmurphy.house.gov https://facebook.com/RepGregMurphy https://twitter.com/RepGregMurphy

2333 Rayburn House Office Building, Washington, DC 20515 .... (202) 225–3415
Chief of Staff.—Glen Downs. FAX: 225–3286
Office Manager.—Maggie Ayrea.
Communications Director.—Maria Jeffrey.
1105–C Corporate Drive, Greenville, NC 27858 .... (252) 931–1003
District Constituent Outreach Director.—Catherine Jordan.

Counties: BEAUFORT, CAMDEN, CARTERET, CHOWAN, CRAVEN, CURRITUCK, DARE, GREENE, HYDE, JONES, LENOIR, ONSLOW, PAMLICO, PASQUOTANK, PERQUIMANS, PITT (PART), AND TYRRELL. CITIES: Atlantic Beach, Ayden, Beaufort, Belhaven, Emerald Isle, Greenville, Havelock, Jacksonville, Kill Devil Hills, Kinston, Kitty Hawk, Morehead City, Nags Head, New Bern, Newport, River Bend, Trent Woods, Washington, and Winterville. Population (2010), 749,823.

ZIP Codes: 27534 (part), 27806, 27808, 27810–11, 27814, 27817, 27821, 27824, 27826–28, 27829 (part), 27834 (part), 27837 (part), 27852 (part), 27858 (part), 27860 (part), 27863 (part), 27865 (part), 27871 (part), 27875, 27879, 27883 (part), 27885 (part), 27888–89 (part), 27906–07, 27909, 27915–17, 27919 (part), 27920–21, 27923, 27925, 27927, 27928 (part), 27929, 27932, 27936, 27939, 27941, 27943–44, 27946 (part), 27947–50, 27953–54, 27956, 27958–60, 27962 (part), 27964–66, 27968, 27972–74, 27976, 27978, 27980–82, 27985, 28501–04, 28445 (part), 28454 (part), 28460, 28509–13, 28515–16, 28518 (part), 28519–20, 28521 (part), 28522–24, 28525 (part), 28526–33, 28537–47, 28551 (part), 28552–57, 28560–64, 28570–71, 28572 (part), 28573, 28574 (part), 28575, 28577, 28578 (part), 28579–87, 28589, 28590 (part), 28594

* * *

FOURTH DISTRICT

DAVID E. PRICE, Democrat, of Chapel Hill, NC; born in Erwin, TN, August 17, 1940; education: B.A., Morehead Scholar, University of North Carolina; bachelor of divinity, 1964, and Ph.D., political science, 1969, Yale University; professional: professor of political science and public policy, Duke University; past chairman and executive director, North Carolina Democratic Party; author of four books and numerous book chapters, essays, and scholarly articles on Congress and the American political system; leadership roles: chairman, House Democracy Partnership; co-chair, Democratic Policy Group; Assistant Democratic Whip; legislative accomplishments: Home Equity Loan Consumer Protection Act (100th Congress); Scientific and Technical Education Act (102nd Congress); Education Affordability Act (105th Congress); Stand By Your Ad Act (107th Congress); Teaching Fellows Act (110th Congress); Credit Card Minimum Payment Warning Act (111th Congress); selected awards: Hubert Humphrey Public Service Award, American Political Science Association, 1990; Champion of Science Award, The Science Coalition, 2002; Charles Dick Medal of Merit, North Carolina National Guard, 2002; William Sloane Coffin Award for Peace and Justice, Yale Divinity School, 2006; Legislator of the Year, Biotechnology Industry Association, 2011; John Tyler Caldwell Award for the Humanities, North Carolina Humanities Council, 2011; past chairman of the board and Sunday School teacher, Binkley Memorial Baptist Church; married: Lisa Price; children: Karen and Michael; committees: Appropriations; Budget; elected to the 100th–103rd Congresses; elected to the 105th Congress; reelected to each succeeding Congress.

Office Listings

https://price.house.gov https://facebook.com/RepDavidEPrice twitter: @RepDavidEPrice

2108 Rayburn House Office Building, Washington, DC 20515 .... (202) 225–1784
Chief of Staff.—Justin Wein. FAX: 225–2014
Legislative Director.—Sean Maxwell.
Executive Assistant.—Janssen White.
Systems Manager.—Elizabeth Adkins.
436 North Harrington Street, Suite 100, Raleigh, NC 27603 .... (919) 859–5999
Communications Director.—Katelynn Vogt.
1777 Fordham Boulevard, Suite 204, Chapel Hill, NC 27514 .... (919) 967–7924

Counties: DURHAM (part), ORANGE (all), AND WAKE (part). CITIES: Apex, Carrboro, Cary, Cedar Grove, Chapel Hill, Durham, Efland, Garner, Hillsborough, Knightdale, Morrisville, Raleigh, Research Triangle Park, and Zebulon. Population (2017), 856,104.

ZIP Codes: 27231, 27243, 27278, 27502–03, 27510–19, 27523, 27529, 27539–40, 27545, 27560, 27587–88, 27591–92, 27599

* * *

FIFTH DISTRICT

VIRGINIA FOXX, Republican, of Banner Elk, NC; born in New York, NY, June 29, 1943; education: A.B., University of North Carolina, Chapel Hill, NC, 1968; M.A.C.T., University of North Carolina, Chapel Hill, 1972; Ed.D., University of North Carolina, Greensboro, NC, 1985; professional: instructor, Caldwell Community College, Hudson, NC; instructor, Appalachian State University, Boone, NC; assistant dean, Appalachian State University, Boone, NC; president, Mayland Community College, Spruce Pine, NC, 1987–94; nursery operator; deputy secretary for management, North Carolina Department of Administration; organizations: member, Watauga County Board of Education, 1967–88; member, North Carolina State Senate, 1994–2004; Executive Committee of North Carolina Citizens for Business and Industry; Z. Smith Reynolds Foundation Advisory Panel; National Advisory Council for Women's Educational Programs; Board of Directors of the NC Center for Public Research; UNC-Chapel Hill Board of Visitors; National Conference of State Legislatures' Blue Ribbon Advisory Panel on Child Care; Foscoe-Grandfather Community Center Board; family: married to Tom Foxx; one daughter; elected House GOP Conference Secretary in the 113th and 114th Congresses; committees: ranking member, Education and Labor; Oversight and Reform; elected to the 109th Congress on November 2, 2004; reelected to each succeeding Congress.

Office Listings

https://foxx.house.gov

2462 Rayburn House Office Building, Washington, DC 20515 .... (202) 225–2071
Chief of Staff.—Cyrus Artz. FAX: 225–2995
Legislative Director.—Carson Middleton.
Press Secretary.—Sara Werner.
400 Shadowline Drive, Suite 205, Boone, NC 28607 .... (828) 265–0240
FAX: 265–0390
3540 Clemmons Road, Suite 125, Clemmons, NC 27012 .... (336) 778–0211
FAX: 778–2290

Counties: ALEXANDER, ALLEGHANY, ASHE, AVERY, CATAWBA, FORSYTH, STOKES, SURRY, WATAUGA, WILKES, AND YADKIN. CITIES: Ararat, Banner Elk, Beech Mountain, Belews Creek, Bethania, Blowing Rock, Boomer, Boone, Boonville, Clemmons, Creston, Crumpler, Danbury, Deep Gap, Dobson, East Bend, Eden, Elk Park, Elkin, Ennice, Ferguson, Fleetwood, Germanton, Glade Valley, Glendale Springs, Grassy Creek, Hamptonville, Hays, Hickory, Hiddenite, Jefferson, Jonesville, Kernersville, King, Lansing, Laurel Springs, Lawsonville, Lewisville, Lowgap, Madison, McGrady, Millers Creek, Moravian Falls, Mount Airy, Newland, North Wilkesboro, Pfafftown, Pilot Mountain, Pine Hall, Piney Creek, Pinnacle, Purlear, Roaring Gap, Roaring River, Ronda, Rural Hall, Sandy Ridge, Scottville, Siloam, Sparta, State Road, Stony Point, Sugar Grove, Taylorsville, Thurmond, Toast, Tobaccoville, Todd, Traphill, Valle Crucis, Vilas, Walkertown, Walnut Cove, Warrensville, West Jefferson, Westfield, White Plains, Wilkesboro, Winston-Salem, Yadkinville, and Zionville. Population (2010), 741,095.

ZIP Codes: 27007, 27009–13, 27016–19, 27021–25, 27030, 27284, 28604–08, 28615–18, 28621–24, 28626–27, 28629–30, 28634–36, 28640, 28642–44, 28646, 28649, 28652–53, 28657, 28731, 28734

* * *

SIXTH DISTRICT

MARK WALKER, Republican, of Greensboro, NC; born in Dothan, Houston County, AL, May 20, 1969; education: attended Trinity Baptist College, Jacksonville, FL, 1987–88; B.A., Piedmont International University, Winston-Salem, NC, 1999; professional: businessman; minister; caucuses: chair, Republican Study Committee; committees: Education and Labor; Homeland Security; House Administration; elected to the 114th Congress on November 4, 2014; reelected to each succeeding Congress.

Office Listings

https://walker.house.gov https://facebook.com/RepMarkWalker
twitter: @RepMarkWalker https://instagram.com/repmarkwalker

1725 Longworth House Office Building, Washington, DC 20515 .... (202) 225–3065

Office Listings—Continued

Chief of Staff.—Scott Luginbill. FAX: 225–8611
Scheduler.—Emily Cambon.
Legislative Director.—Ryan Walker.
Communications Director.—Jack Minor.
809 Green Valley Road, Suite 104, Greensboro, NC 27408 .... (336) 333–5005
219 B West Elm Street, P.O. Box 812, Graham, NC 27253 .... (336) 229–0159
District Director.—Julie Scott Emmons. FAX: 350–9514
Director of Constituent Services.—Janine Osborne.
222 Sunset Avenue, Suite 101, Asheboro, NC 27203 .... (336) 626–3060
FAX: 629–7819

Counties: ALAMANCE, CASWELL, CHATHAM, GUILFORD (part), LEE, PERSON, RANDOLPH, AND ROCKINGHAM. Population (2010), 762,758.

ZIP Codes: 27025, 27027, 27048, 27201–05, 27207–08, 27212–17, 27220, 27228, 27230, 27235, 27237, 27244, 27248–49, 27252–53, 27256, 27258, 27283–84, 27288–89, 27291, 27298, 27301–02, 27305, 27310–12, 27314–17, 27320–23, 27326, 27330–32, 27340–41, 27343–44, 27349–50, 27355, 27357–59, 27370, 27375, 27377, 27379, 27395, 27409–10, 27455, 27505, 27541, 27559, 27573–74, 27583, 28355

* * *

SEVENTH DISTRICT

DAVID ROUZER, Republican, of McGee's Crossroads, NC; born at Landstuhl Army Medical Center in Landstuhl, Germany, February 16, 1972; education: B.S. in agriculture business management, agricultural economics; B.A. in chemistry; professional: legislative assistant, Office of U.S. Senator Jesse Helms; senior policy advisor, U.S. Senator Jesse Helms; assistant to the Dean and Director of Commodity Relations, College of Agriculture and Life Sciences, NC State University; senior advisor, U.S. Senator Elizabeth Dole; Associate Administrator, Rural Business-Cooperative Programs/Director, Legislative and Public Affairs, U.S. Department of Agriculture; principal, The Rouzer Company; committees: Agriculture; Transportation and Infrastructure; elected to the 114th Congress on November 4, 2014; reelected to each succeeding Congress.

Office Listings

https://rouzer.house.gov https://facebook.com/RepRouzer https://twitter.com/RepDavidRouzer

2439 Rayburn House Office Building, Washington, DC 20515 .... (202) 225–2731
Chief of Staff.—Melissa Murphy. FAX: 225–5773
Communications Director.—John Elizandro.
Legislative Director.—Jason Cooke.
District Director.—Chance Lambeth.
201 North Front Street, Suite 502, Wilmington, NC 28401 .... (910) 395–0202
310 Government Center Drive, Unit 1, Bolivia, NC 28422 .... (910) 253–6111
4001 U.S. Highway 301 South, Suite 106, Four Oaks, NC 27524 .... (919) 938–3040

Counties: BLADEN, BRUNSWICK, COLUMBUS, DUPLIN, JOHNSTON, NEW HANOVER, PENDER, SAMPSON, AND WAYNE. Population (2013), 762,540.

ZIP Codes: 27501, 27504, 27524, 27530–31, 27534, 27542, 27568–69, 27576–77, 27592, 27603, 27830, 27863, 27883, 28318, 28320, 28325, 28328, 28333–34, 28337, 28341, 28344, 28349, 28365–66, 28382, 28385, 28393, 28398, 28401, 28403, 28405, 28409, 28411, 28412, 28420–25, 28428–36, 28438–39, 28441–45, 28447–58, 28461–70, 28472, 28478–80, 28508, 28518, 28521, 28525, 28551, 28572, 28574, 28578

* * *

EIGHTH DISTRICT

RICHARD HUDSON, Republican, of Concord, NC; born in Franklin, VA, November 4, 1971; education: B.A. in history and political science, University of North Carolina at Charlotte, 1996; professional: served as District Director for 8th District Congressman Robin Hayes; served as Chief of Staff for Congresswoman Virginia Foxx, Congressman John Carter, and Congressman Mike Conaway; religion: Christian; married: Renee; caucuses: Agriculture and Rural America Task Force; Agriculture Policy Group; Atlantic Offshore Energy Caucus; Carbonated and Non-alcoholic (CAN) Caucus; Congressional Army Aviation Caucus; Congressional Chicken Caucus; Congressional General Aviation Caucus; Congressional Peanut Caucus; Congressional Prayer Caucus; Congressional Sportsmen's Caucus; Congressional Textile Caucus; House

National Guard and Reserve Components Caucus; House Republican Israel Caucus; House Special Operations Forces Caucus; Pediatric Trauma Caucus; Republican Policy Committee; Republican Study Committee; committees: Energy and Commerce; elected to the 113th Congress on November 6, 2012; reelected to each succeeding Congress.

Office Listings

https://hudson.house.gov

2112 Rayburn House Office Building, Washington, DC 20515 .... (202) 225–3715
Chief of Staff.—Chris Carter.
Communications Director.—Tatum Gibson.
Legislative Director.—Preston Bell.
Scheduler.—Kristine Bieniek.
325 McGill Avenue, NW., Suite 500, Concord, NC 28027 .... (704) 786–1612
225 Green Street, Suite 202, Fayetteville, NC 28301 .... (910) 997–2070

Counties: CABARRUS, CUMBERLAND (part), HOKE, MONTGOMERY, MOORE, ROWAN (part), AND STANLY. Population (2010), 701,000.

ZIP Codes: 27205, 27208–09, 27229, 27239, 27281, 27292, 27306, 27325, 27330, 27341, 27356, 27360, 27370–71, 27376, 28001–02, 28009, 28023, 28025–27, 28036, 28039, 28041, 28071–72, 28075, 28078–79, 28081–83, 28088, 28097, 28103, 28107, 28109–10, 28112, 28115, 28124–25, 28127–29, 28137–38, 28144, 28146–47, 28159, 28170, 28174, 28213, 28215, 28227, 28262, 28269, 28301–11, 28314–15, 28326–27, 28331, 28334, 28338, 28342, 28344, 28347–48, 28350–52, 28356–58, 28360, 28364, 28370–74, 28376–77, 28379, 28383–84, 28386–88, 28390, 28394–96

* * *

NINTH DISTRICT

DAN BISHOP, Republican, of Charlotte, NC; born in Charlotte, July 1, 1964; education: B.S., business administration, 1986, J.D., 1990, University of North Carolina at Chapel Hill, NC; professional: attorney, Robinson, Bradshaw, and Hinson, Charlotte, NC, 1990–96; attorney, Erwin, Bishop, Capitano, and Moss, Charlotte, NC, 1996–present; Commissioner, District 5, Mecklenburg County Board of Commissioners, Charlotte, NC, 2004–08; Representative, 104th District, North Carolina House of Representatives, Raleigh, NC, 2015–16; Senator, 39th District, North Carolina Senate, Raleigh, NC, 2017–19; religion: Methodist; family: wife, Jo; one child: Jack; committees: Homeland Security; Small Business; elected to the 116th Congress, by special election, on September 10, 2019, to fill a vacancy in the district.

Office Listings

https://danbishop.house.gov https://facebook.com/repdanbishop twitter: @RepDanBishop

132 Cannon House Office Building, Washington, DC 20515 .... (202) 225–1976
Chief of Staff.—Peter Barnes.
Legislative Director.—Mark Rusthoven.
Legislative Assistant: Vacant.
Legislative Correspondent.—John Wynne.
Executive Assistant.—Conley Lowrance.
Staff Assistant.—Abigail Michos.
300 North Main Street, Monroe, NC 28112 .... (704) 218–5300
District Director.—Chris Maples.
Outreach Director.—Chris Sullivan.
Caseworker.—Linda Ferster.

Counties: ANSON, BLADEN (part), CUMBERLAND (part), MECKLENBURG (part), RICHMOND, ROBESON, SCOTLAND, AND UNION. Population (2010), 733,498.

ZIP Codes: 27229 (part), 27281 (part), 28007, 28079, 28091, 28102–04, 28105 (part), 28107 (part), 28110, 28112, 28119, 28133, 28135, 28170, 28173–74, 28204 (part), 28207 (part), 28209–11 (part), 28226–27 (part), 28270 (part), 28274, 28277 (part), 28301 (part), 28305–06 (part), 28312, 28318 (part), 28320 (part), 28330, 28332, 28337–38 (part), 28340, 28343, 28345, 28347–48 (part), 28351–52, 28357 (part), 28358, 28360, 28362–63, 28364 (part), 28367, 28369, 28371 (part), 28372, 28375, 28377 (part), 28378–79, 28382 (part), 28383–84, 28386 (part), 28391 (part), 28392, 28395 (part), 28396, 28399, 28433 (part), 28438 (part), 28441 (part), 28444 (part), 28448 (part)

* * *

TENTH DISTRICT

PATRICK T. McHENRY, Republican, of Denver, NC; born in Gastonia, NC, October 22, 1975; education: graduated Ashbrook High School, Gastonia, NC; attended North Carolina State

University, Raleigh, NC; B.A., Belmont Abbey College, Belmont, NC, 1999; professional: realtor; media executive; appointed special assistant to the U.S. Secretary of Labor by President George W. Bush in 2001; member, North Carolina House of Representatives, 2002–04; organizations: Gaston Chamber of Commerce; Gastonia Rotary Club; the National Rifle Association; Saint Michael Church; board of directors, United Way's Success by Six Youth Program; married: Giulia, 2010; daughter Cecelia born in 2014; daughter Rese born in 2018; served as Chief Deputy Whip from June of 2014 to December of 2018; committees: ranking member, Financial Services; elected to the 109th Congress on November 2, 2004; reelected to each succeeding Congress.

Office Listings

https://mchenry.house.gov https://facebook.com/CongressmanMcHenry twitter: @PatrickMcHenry

2004 Rayburn House Office Building, Washington, DC 20515 .... (202) 225–2576
Chief of Staff.—Jeff Butler. FAX: 225–0316
Legislative Director.—Doug Nation.
Scheduler.—Grace Tricomi.
1990 Main Avenue, SE., P.O. Box 1830, Hickory, NC 28603 .... (828) 327–6100
Constituent Services Director.—David McCrary. FAX: 327–8311
128 West Main Avenue, Suite 115, Gastonia, NC 28052 .... (704) 833–0096
District Director.—Brett Keeter. FAX: 833–0887
160 Midland Avenue, Black Mountain, NC 28711 .... (828) 669–0600
Regional Director.—Roger Kumpf.

Counties: BUNCOMBE (part), CATAWBA (part), CLEVELAND, GASTON, IREDELL (part), LINCOLN, POLK, AND RUTHERFORD. CITIES AND TOWNSHIPS: Asheville, Gastonia, Hickory, Lincolnton, and Shelby. Population (2010), 733,499.

ZIP Codes: 28006, 28012, 28016–21, 28032–34, 28037, 28040, 28043, 28052, 28054, 28056, 28073, 28076–77, 28080, 28086, 28089–90, 28092, 28098, 28101, 28114, 28117, 28120, 28139, 28150, 28152, 28160, 28164, 28167–69, 28601–02, 28609–10, 28612–13, 28650, 28658, 28673, 28682, 28704, 28709, 28711, 28720, 28722, 28730, 28732, 28746, 28756–57, 28773, 28778, 28782, 28787, 28792, 28801, 28803–06

* * *

ELEVENTH DISTRICT

VACANT

Counties: BUNCOMBE (part), BURKE, CALDWELL, CHEROKEE, CLAY, GRAHAM, HAYWOOD, HENDERSON, JACKSON, MACON, MADISON, MCDOWELL, MITCHELL, SWAIN, TRANSYLVANIA, AND YANCEY. CITIES AND TOWNSHIPS: Franklin, Hayesville, Hendersonville, Lenoir, Morganton, Murphy, and Waynesville. Population (2017), 759,358.

ZIP Codes: 28604, 28645, 28655, 28657, 28701–02, 28704–05, 28707–08, 28712–13, 28715, 28717–19, 28721, 28723, 28730, 28734, 28736, 28739–43, 28747, 28751–54, 28759, 28763, 28765, 28771, 28774–75, 28779, 28781, 28783, 28786–87, 28789–91, 28901–02, 28904–06, 28909

* * *

TWELFTH DISTRICT

ALMA S. ADAMS, Democrat, of Charlotte, NC; born in High Point, NC, May 27, 1946; education: art education, North Carolina A&T State University, Greensboro, NC, 1968; master's degree in art education, North Carolina A&T State University, Greensboro, 1972; Ph.D. in art education and multicultural education from The Ohio State University in Columbus, Ohio, 1981; professional: Greensboro City School Board, 1984–86; Greensboro City Council, 1987–94; Bennett College art professor, curator, and administrator; North Carolina State House, 1994–2014; family: two children, Linda Jeanelle Lindsay and Billy Eugene Adams II; four grandchildren; caucuses: founder, Congressional Bipartisan HBCU Caucus; Agriculture Research Caucus; AIDS/HIV Caucus; Animal Protection Caucus; Art Caucus; Autism Caucus; Black Maternal Health Caucus; Blue Collar Worker Caucus; Congressional Black Caucus; Congressional Humanities Caucus; Congressional Progress Caucus; Congressional Safe Climate Caucus; CTE Caucus; Diabetes Caucus; Friends of Switzerland Caucus; Friends of Turkey Caucus; Historic Preservation Caucus; Hunger Caucus; Manufacturing Caucus; Medicare Expansion Caucus; Pro Choice Caucus; Progressive Education Caucus; STEAM Caucus; Women's Congressional Caucus on Women's Issues; committees: Agriculture; Education and Labor; Financial Services; elected to the 113th Congress, by special election, to fill the vacancy caused by the resignation of U.S. Representative Mel Watt, while simultaneously elected to the 114th Congress on November 4, 2014, to serve a full two-year term; reelected to each succeeding Congress.

Office Listings

https://adams.house.gov https://facebook.com/CongresswomanAdams twitter: @RepAdams

2436 Rayburn House Office Building, Washington, DC 20515 .... (202) 225–1510
Chief of Staff.—Monica Cloud. FAX: 225–1512
Legislative Director.—John Christie.
Deputy Chief of Staff / Communications Director.—Sam Spencer.
801 East Morehead Street, Suite 150, Charlotte, NC 28202 .... (704) 344–9950
District Director.—Phanalphie Rhue.
Director of Operations / Scheduler.—Sandra Brown.

Counties: MECKLENBURG (part). Population (2015), 830,225.

ZIP Codes: 28031, 28036 (part), 28078 (part), 28105 (part), 28134 (part), 28202–03, 28204 (part), 28205–06, 28207 (part), 28208, 28209–11 (part), 28212, 28213 (part), 28214, 28215 (part), 28216–17, 28226–27 (part), 28244, 28262 (part), 28269–70 (part), 28273, 28277 (part), 28278, 28280, 28282

* * *

THIRTEENTH DISTRICT

TED BUDD, Republican, of Advance, NC; born in Winston-Salem, NC, October 21, 1971; education: B.S.B.A., business management, Appalachian State University; M.B.A., Wake Forest University; masters, educational leadership and family life, Dallas Theological Seminary; professional: executive vice president, The Budd Group; owner, ProShots Indoor Range & Training; religion: Christian; family: spouse, Amy Kate Budd; three children; committees: Financial Services; elected to the 115th Congress on November 8, 2016; reelected to the 116th Congress on November 6, 2018.

Office Listings

https://budd.house.gov

118 Cannon House Office Building, Washington, DC 20515 .... (202) 225–4531
Chief of Staff.—Andrew Bell.
Legislative Director.—Alex Vargo.
Press Secretary.—Melissa Brown.
Director of Operations.—Elizabeth Dews.
Communications Director.—Chase Jennings.
128 Peachtree Lane, Suite A, Advance, NC 27006 .... (336) 998–1313
1208 Eastchester Drive, Suite 203, High Point, NC 27265 .... (336) 858–5013

Counties: DAVIDSON, DAVIE, GUILFORD (part), IREDELL, AND ROWAN (part). Population (2010), 732,434.

ZIP Codes: 27006, 27012 (part), 27013–14, 27020 (part), 27028, 27054, 27055 (part), 27104 (part), 27107 (part), 27114–16 (part), 27127 (part), 27202 (part), 27233 (part), 27235 (part), 27239 (part), 27260 (part), 27261, 27262–65 (part), 27268 (part), 27284 (part), 27292 (part), 27293–94, 27295 (part), 27299, 27310 (part), 27313 (part), 27317 (part), 27351, 27360 (part), 27261, 27373–74, 27401 (part), 27402–04, 27405–06 (part), 27407, 27408–10 (part), 27412, 27413 (part), 27415 (part), 27416–17, 27419–20, 27425 (part), 27427 (part), 27429, 27435, 27438, 27455 (part), 27495, 27497 (part), 27498–99, 28010, 28036 (part), 28115 (part), 28117 (part), 28123, 28125 (part), 28127 (part), 28144–47 (part), 28159 (part), 28166 (part), 28625 (part), 28634 (part), 28636 (part), 28660, 28677–78 (part), 28687–88, 28689 (part), 28699

NORTH DAKOTA

(Population 2010, 675,591)

SENATORS

JOHN HOEVEN, Republican, of Bismarck, ND; born in Bismarck, March 13, 1957; education: B.A., Dartmouth College, Hanover, NH, 1979; M.B.A., Northwestern University, Chicago, IL, 1981; professional: executive vice president, First Western Bank, Minot, 1986–93; president and CEO, Bank of North Dakota, 1993–2000; Governor of North Dakota, 2000–10; religion: Catholic; family: married to Mikey; two children; caucuses: Air Force Caucus; Congressional Sportsmen's Caucus; E–911 Caucus; General Aviation Caucus; Hydrogen Fuel Cell Caucus; ICBM Coalition; Impact Aid Coalition; National Guard Caucus; Norway Caucus; Port-to-Plains Caucus; Rural Education Caucus; Rural Health Caucus; Senate Republican High-Tech Task Force; Senate Veterans Jobs Caucus; Senate Western Caucus; UAS Integration Working Group; Unmanned Aerial Systems Caucus; committees: chair, Indian Affairs; Agriculture, Nutrition, and Forestry; Appropriations; Energy and Natural Resources; elected to the U.S. Senate on November 2, 2010; reelected to the U.S. Senate on November 8, 2016.

Office Listings

https://hoeven.senate.gov https://facebook.com/SenatorJohnHoeven https://twitter.com/SenJohnHoeven

338 Russell Senate Office Building, Washington, DC 20510 .... (202) 224–2551
Chief of Staff.—Tony Eberhard. FAX: 224–7999
Legislative Director.—Daniel Auger.
Communications Director.—Kami Capener.
U.S. Federal Building, 220 East Rosser Avenue, Room 312, Bismarck, ND 58501 .... (701) 250–4618
State Director.—Jessica Lee. FAX: 250–4484
123 Broadway North, Suite 201, Fargo, ND 58102 .... (701) 239–5389
Federal Building, 102 North Fourth Street, Room 108, Grand Forks, ND 58203 .... (701) 746–8972
100 1st Street Southwest, Suite 107, Minot, ND 58701 .... (701) 838–1361
Watford City, ND .... (701) 609–2727

* * *

KEVIN CRAMER, Republican, of Bismarck, ND; born in Rolette, ND, January 21, 1961; education: B.A., social work, Concordia College, Moorhead, MN, 1983; M.A., management, University of Mary, Bismarck, ND, 2003; professional: chairman, North Dakota Republican Party, 1991–93; North Dakota Tourism Director, 1993–97; State Economic Development and Finance Director, 1997–2000; Executive Director, Harold Schafer Leadership Foundation, 2000–03; North Dakota Public Service Commissioner, 2003–12; married: Kris Cramer; children: Ian, Isaac, Rachel "Cale" Wegner, Annie "Nick" Senne, and Abel; grandchildren: Lila, Beau, Nico, and Chet; committees: Armed Services; Banking, Housing, and Urban Affairs; Budget; Environment and Public Works; Veterans' Affairs; elected to the 113th Congress on November 6, 2012, and reelected to the two succeeding Congresses; elected to the U.S. Senate on November 6, 2018.

Office Listings

https://cramer.senate.gov https://facebook.com/SenatorKevinCramer https://twitter.com/SenKevinCramer

400 Russell Senate Office Building, Washington, DC 20510 .... (202) 224–2043
Chief of Staff.—Mark Gruman.
Deputy Chief of Staff.—Jason Stverak.
Communications Director.—Jake Wilkins.
Legislative Director.—Micah Chambers.
328 Federal Building, 220 East Rosser Avenue, Bismarck, ND 58501 .... (701) 699–7020
306 Federal Building, 657 Second Avenue North, Fargo, ND 58102 .... (701) 232–5094
State Director.—Lisa Gibbens.
105 Federal Building, 100 First Street Southwest, Minot, ND 58701 .... (701) 837–6141
114 Federal Building, 102 North 4th Street, Grand Forks, ND 58203 .... (701) 699–7030

REPRESENTATIVE

AT LARGE

KELLY ARMSTRONG, Republican, of Dickinson, ND; born in Dickinson, October 8, 1976; education: B.A., psychology, University of North Dakota, Grand Forks, ND; J.D., University of North Dakota Law School, Grand Forks, ND; professional: partner, Reichert Armstrong law firm; vice president, Armstrong Corporation; volunteer fireman, 2004–12; president, Dickinson Baseball Club, 2006–12; chairman, North Dakota Republican Party, 2015–18; North Dakota State Senator, 2013–18; married: Kjersti Armstrong; children: Anna and Eli; committees: Judiciary; Oversight and Reform; Select Committee on the Climate Crisis; elected to the 116th Congress on November 6, 2018.

Office Listings

https://armstrong.house.gov https://facebook.com/RepArmstrongND
https://twitter.com/RepArmstrongND

1004 Longworth House Office Building, Washington, DC 20515 .... (202) 225–2611
Chief of Staff.—Roz Leighton.
Legislative Director.—Casey Fitzpatrick.
Communications Director.—Brandon VerVelde.
Federal Building, 220 East Rosser Avenue, Room 228, Bismarck, ND 58501 .... (701) 354–6700
3217 Fiechtner Drive South, Suite B, Fargo, ND 58103 .... (701) 353–6665
State Director.—Jeff Rustvang.

Population (2018), 760,077.

ZIP Codes: 58001–02, 58004–09, 58011–13, 58015–18, 58021, 58027, 58029, 58030–33, 58035–36, 58038, 58040–43, 58045–49, 58051–54, 58056–65, 58067–69, 58071–72, 58074–79, 58081, 58102–09, 58121–22, 58124–26, 58201–06, 58208, 58210, 58212, 58214, 58216, 58218–20, 58222–25, 58227–31, 58233, 58235–41, 58243–44, 58249–51, 58254–62, 58265–67, 58269–78, 58281–82, 58301, 58310–11, 58313, 58316–19, 58321, 58323–25, 58327, 58329–32, 58335, 58338–39, 58341, 58343–46, 58348, 58351–53, 58355–57, 58359, 58361–63, 58365–70, 58372, 58374, 58377, 58379–82, 58384–86, 58401–02, 58405, 58413, 58415–16, 58418, 58420–26, 58428–31, 58433, 58436, 58438–45, 58448, 58451–52, 58454–56, 58458, 58460–61, 58463–64, 58466–67, 58472, 58474–84, 58486–88, 58490, 58492, 58494–97, 58501–07, 58520–21, 58523–24, 58528–33, 58535, 58538, 58540–42, 58544–45, 58549, 58552, 58554, 58558–66, 58568–73, 58575–77, 58579–81, 58601–02, 58620–23, 58625–27, 58630–32, 58634, 58636, 58638–47, 58649–56, 58701–05, 58707, 58710–13, 58716, 58718, 58721–23, 58725, 58727, 58730–31, 58733–37, 58740–41, 58744, 58746–48, 58750, 58752, 58755–63, 58765, 58768–73, 58775–76, 58778–79, 58781–85, 58787–90, 58792–95, 58801–02, 58830–31, 58833, 58835, 58838, 58843–45, 58847, 58849, 58852–54, 58856

OHIO

(Population 2010, 11,536,504)

SENATORS

SHERROD BROWN, Democrat, of Cleveland, OH; born in Mansfield, OH, November 9, 1952; education: B.A., Yale University, New Haven, CT, 1974; M.A., education, Ohio State University, Columbus, OH, 1979; M.A., public administration, Ohio State University, Columbus, 1981; professional: Ohio House of Representatives, 1975–82; Ohio Secretary of State, 1983–91; U.S. House of Representatives, 1992–2006; member: Eagle Scouts of America; married: Connie Schultz; children: Emily, Elizabeth, Andrew, and Caitlin; committees: ranking member, Banking, Housing, and Urban Affairs; Agriculture, Nutrition, and Forestry; Finance; Veterans' Affairs; elected to the 103rd Congress on November 3, 1992; reelected to each succeeding Congress; elected to the U.S. Senate on November 7, 2006; reelected to each succeeding Senate term.

Office Listings

https://brown.senate.gov https://facebook.com/SenatorSherrodBrown https://twitter.com/SenSherrodBrown

503 Hart Senate Office Building, Washington, DC 20510 .... (202) 224–2315
Chief of Staff.—Sarah Benzing. FAX: 228–6321
Legislative Director.—Jeremy Hekhuis.
Communications Director.—Jennifer Donohue.
Press Secretary.—Rachael Hartford.
801 West Superior Avenue, Suite 1400, Cleveland, OH 44113 .... (216) 522–7272
State Director.—John Ryan.
425 Walnut Street, Suite 2310, Cincinnati, OH 45202 .... (513) 684–1021
200 North High Street, Room 614, Columbus, OH 43215 .... (614) 469–2083
200 West Erie Avenue, Suite 312, Lorain, OH 44052 .... (440) 242–4100

* * *

ROBERT J. PORTMAN, Republican, of Terrace Park, OH; born in Cincinnati, OH, December 19, 1955; education: B.A., Dartmouth College, Hanover, NH, 1979; J.D., University of Michigan Law School, Ann Arbor, MI, 1984; professional: associate counsel to George H.W. Bush, 1989; Deputy Assistant and Director, White House Office of Legislative Affairs, 1989–91; member of the U.S. House of Representatives, 1993–2005; U.S. Trade Representative, 2005–06; Director of the Office of Management and Budget, 2006–07; religion: Methodist; married: Jane Portman; three children: Jed, Will, and Sally; committees: Finance; Foreign Relations; Homeland Security and Governmental Affairs; Joint Economic Committee; elected to the U.S. Senate on November 2, 2010; reelected to the U.S. Senate on November 8, 2016.

Office Listings

https://portman.senate.gov https://facebook.com/senrobportman twitter: @senrobportman

448 Russell Senate Office Building, Washington, DC 20510 .... (202) 224–3353
Chief of Staff.—Kevin Smith.
Communications Director.—Emily Benavides.
Legislative Director.—Pam Thiessen.
Scheduler.—Angie Youngen.
37 West Broad Street, Suite 300, Columbus, OH 43215 .... (614) 469–6774
State Director.—Kevin Hoggatt.
District Director.—Jason Knox.
District Representative.—Vacant.
312 Walnut Street, Suite 3425, Cincinnati, OH 45202 .... (513) 684–3265
District Director.—Nan Cahall.
District Representative.—Sam Bain.
1240 East 9th Street, Room 3061, Cleveland, OH 44199 .... (216) 522–7095
District Director.—Caryn Candisky.
District Representative.—Josh Prest.
420 Madison Avenue, Room 1210, Toledo, OH 43604 .... (419) 259–3895
District Representative.—Cayla Shreffler.

REPRESENTATIVES

FIRST DISTRICT

STEVE CHABOT, Republican, of Cincinnati, OH; born in Cincinnati, January 22, 1953; education: graduated from LaSalle High School in Cincinnati; B.A., College of William and Mary, Williamsburg, VA, 1975; J.D., Salmon P. Chase College of Law, Highland Heights, KY, 1978; professional: teacher, 1975–76; member of the City Council, Cincinnati, OH, 1985–90; commissioner, Hamilton County, OH, 1990–94; family: wife, Donna; two children: Erica and Randy; elected as a Republican to the 104th–110th Congresses, January 3, 1995–January 3, 2009; served as ranking member on the Committee on Small Business, 110th Congress; committees: ranking member, Small Business; Foreign Affairs; Judiciary; elected to the 112th Congress on November 2, 2010; reelected to each succeeding Congress.

Office Listings

https://chabot.house.gov https://facebook.com/RepSteveChabot twitter: @RepSteveChabot

2408 Rayburn House Office Building, Washington, DC 20515 .... (202) 225–2216
Chief of Staff.—Stacy Palmer Barton. FAX: 225–3012
Legislative Director.—Jonathan Lowe.
Scheduler.—Lisa Feldman.
Carew Tower, 441 Vine Street, Room 3003, Cincinnati, OH 45202 .... (513) 684–2723
District Director.—Joe Abner. FAX: 421–8722
Communications Director.—Brian Griffith.
11 South Broadway Street, Third Floor, Lebanon, OH 45036 .... (513) 421–8704

Counties: HAMILTON (part) AND WARREN. Population (2010), 721,032.

ZIP Codes: 45001–02, 45005, 45030, 45033–34, 45036, 45039–40, 45052, 45054, 45065–66, 45068, 45111, 45140, 45152, 45162, 45202–07, 45210–11, 45214–17, 45219–21, 45223–25, 45229, 45232–33, 45237–43, 45246–49, 45251–52

* * *

SECOND DISTRICT

BRAD WENSTRUP, Republican, of Cincinnati, OH; born in Cincinnati, June 17, 1958; education: B.A., University of Cincinnati, 1980; B.S. and D.P.M., William M. Scholl College of Podiatric Medicine, Chicago, IL, 1985; professional: private practice physician/surgeon, 1986–2012; U.S. Army Reserve, 1998–present; religion: Catholic; married: Monica; children: Brad R. Wenstrup, Jr. and Sophia Marie Wenstrup; committees: Ways and Means; Permanent Select Committee on Intelligence; elected to the 113th Congress on November 6, 2012; reelected to each succeeding Congress.

Office Listings

https://wenstrup.house.gov https://facebook.com/RepBradWenstrup twitter: @RepBradWenstrup

2419 Rayburn House Office Building, Washington, DC 20515 .... (202) 225–3164
Chief of Staff.—Derek Harley. FAX: 225–1992
Deputy Chief of Staff/Legislative Director.—Greg Brooks.
Communications Director.—Ann Tumolo.
Scheduler.—Abbie Sumbrum.
7954 Beechmont Avenue, Suite 200, Cincinnati, OH 45255 .... (513) 474–7777
District Director.—Alex Scharfetter.
170 North Main Street, Peebles, OH 45660 .... (513) 605–1380
4350 Aicholtz Road, Cincinnati, OH 45245 .... (513) 605–1389

Counties: ADAMS, BROWN, CLERMONT, HAMILTON (part), HIGHLAND, PIKE, SCIOTO (part), AND ROSS (part). CITIES AND TOWNSHIPS: Anderson Township, Batavia, Blue Ash, Cincinnati (part), Chillicothe, Georgetown, Hillsboro, Loveland, Manchester, Milford, Mount Orab, New Richmond, Norwood, Peebles, Piketon, Portsmouth, Ripley, Sardinia, and Union Township. Population (2010), 721,031.

ZIP Codes: 45101–03, 45106–07, 45112, 45115, 45118, 45120–22, 45130–31, 45133, 45140, 45142, 45144, 45150, 45153–54, 45156–57, 45160, 45162, 45167–68, 45171, 45174, 45176, 45202, 45206, 45208–09, 45212–13, 45226–27, 45230, 45236, 45241–46, 45255, 45601, 45612–13, 45616, 45624, 45642, 45646, 45648, 45650, 45652, 45657, 45660–63, 45671, 45679, 45684, 45690, 45693, 45697

* * *

THIRD DISTRICT

JOYCE BEATTY, Democrat, of Blacklick, OH; born in Dayton, OH, March 12, 1950; education: B.A., Central State University, Wilberforce, OH, 1972; M.S., Wright State University, Fairborn, OH, 1974; attended University of Cincinnati, Cincinnati, OH; professional: executive director, Montgomery County, OH; human services; professor; businesswoman; member, Ohio State House of Representatives, 1999–2008, Minority Leader, 2006–08; senior vice-president, The Ohio State University, 2008–12; Delta Sigma Theta Sorority, Inc. (life member) and The Links, Inc.; House Region 10 Whip; named one of the 150 most powerful African Americans, *Ebony Magazine*, 2008; recipient, YWCA Women of Achievement Award, 2002; NAACP Freedom Award; United Way Key Club Community Leadership Award, 2014; married: Otto; stepchildren: Laurel and Otto; Tom Lantos Human Rights Commission; caucuses: Brain Injury Taskforce; CBC Taskforce on Economic Development and Wealth Creation; Financial Literacy Caucus; Heart and Stroke Coalition; House Human Trafficking Caucus; Women's Caucus; committees: Financial Services; Joint Economic Committee; elected to the 113th Congress on November 6, 2012; reelected to each succeeding Congress.

Office Listings

https://beatty.house.gov https://facebook.com/RepJoyceBeatty twitter: @RepBeatty

2303 Rayburn House Office Building, Washington, DC 20515 .... (202) 225–4324
Chief of Staff / Chief Counsel.—Kimberly Ross. FAX: 225–1984
Legislative Director.—Nicholas Semanko.
Scheduler / Executive Assistant.—Leila M. Diallo.
Communications Director.—Dominic Manecke.
471 East Broad Street, Suite 1100, Columbus, OH 43215 .... (614) 220–0003
District Director.—Ernie Davis. FAX: 220–5640

Counties: FRANKLIN (part). Population (2010), 732,258.

ZIP Codes: 43004, 43026, 43054, 43068, 43081, 43085, 43109–10, 43119, 43123, 43125, 43137, 43201–07, 43209–15, 43217, 43219, 43221–24, 43227–32

* * *

FOURTH DISTRICT

JAMES D. "JIM" JORDAN, Republican, of Urbana, OH; born in Troy, OH, February 17, 1964; education: graduated, Graham High School, St. Paris, OH, 1982; B.S. in economics, University of Wisconsin, Madison, WI, 1986; M.A. in education, The Ohio State University, Columbus, OH, 1991; J.D., Capital University School of Law, Columbus, 2001; professional: assistant wrestling coach, The Ohio State University, 1987–95; State Representative, Ohio House of Representatives, 85th District, 1995–2001; State Senator, Ohio State Senate, 12th District, 2001–06; awards: four-time high school wrestling champion (Ohio), 1979–82; two-time NCAA Division I National Wrestling Champion, 1985–86; three-time All-American, 1984–86; Wisconsin Badgers Hall of Fame; third place, Olympic Trials in Wrestling, 1988; Friend of the Taxpayer, Americans for Tax Reform, 1997; Leadership in Government Award from the Ohio Roundtable and Freedom Forum, 2001; awards from the United Conservatives of Ohio: Outstanding Freshman Legislator Award, 1996; Watchdog of the Treasury, 1996, 2000, 2004; Pro-Life Legislator of the Year, 1998; Outstanding Legislator Award, 2004; Hero of the Taxpayer, Americans for Tax Reform, 2007; National Legislator of the Year, Coalitions for America, 2012; Freedom Fighter Award, Freedom Works, 2012; activities: Grace Bible Church, Springfield; Local and National Right to Life organizations; Champaign County Republican Executive Committee; married: Polly (Stickley) Jordan; parents: John and Shirley Jordan; children: Rachel, Benjamin, Jessie, and Isaac; committees: Judiciary; Oversight and Reform; elected to the 110th Congress on November 7, 2006; reelected to each succeeding Congress.

Office Listings

https://jordan.house.gov https://facebook.com/repjimjordan https://twitter.com/jim_jordan

2056 Rayburn House Office Building, Washington, DC 20515 .... (202) 225–2676
Chief of Staff.—Kevin Eichinger. FAX: 226–0577
Legislative Director.—Jared Dilley.
Executive Assistant.—Emma Summers.
3121 West Elm Plaza, Lima, OH 45805 .... (419) 999–6455

Office Listings—Continued

13B East Main Street, Norwalk, OH 44857 .... (419) 663–1426
District Director.—Cameron Warner.

Counties: ALLEN, AUGLAIZE, CHAMPAIGN, CRAWFORD, ERIE (part), HURON (part), LOGAN, LORAIN (part), MARION (part), MERCER (part), SANDUSKY, SENECA, SHELBY, AND UNION. Population (2017), 710,603.

ZIP Codes: 43007, 43009, 43029, 43036, 43040, 43044–45, 43047, 43060, 43067, 43070, 43072, 43077, 43078, 43083–84, 43301–02, 43310–11, 43314, 43316, 43318–19, 43322–24, 43326, 43331–33, 43336–37, 43340–45, 43347–48, 43357–58, 43360, 43407, 43410, 43420, 43431, 43435, 43442, 43464, 43469, 44001, 44035–36, 44039, 44044, 44050, 44052–55, 44074, 44089, 44090, 44802, 44807, 44809, 44811, 44814–16, 44818, 44820, 44824–28, 44830, 44833, 44836, 44839, 44841, 44845–47, 44849, 44853–54, 44856–57, 44860–61, 44865, 44867, 44870, 44875, 44881, 44883, 44887, 44889, 45302, 45306, 45312, 45317, 45326, 45333–34, 45336, 45340, 45344, 45353, 45356, 45360, 45363, 45365, 45367, 45380, 45388–89, 45502, 45801–02, 45804–10, 45812, 45817, 45819–20, 45822, 45830, 45833, 45845, 45850, 45854, 45862, 45865–66, 45869–71, 45877, 45884–85, 45887–88, 45894–96

* * *

FIFTH DISTRICT

ROBERT E. ''BOB'' LATTA, Republican, of Bowling Green, OH; born in Bluffton, OH, April 18, 1956; education: graduated, Bowling Green High School, Bowling Green, OH, 1974; B.A., history, Bowling Green State University, Bowling Green, 1978; J.D., University of Toledo College of Law, Toledo, OH, 1981; professional: legislator; lawyer; elected Wood County Commissioner, 1990, reelected 1994; elected to the Ohio Senate, 1996; elected to the Ohio House of Representatives in 2000, reelected to successive terms in 2002, 2004, and 2006; awards: Ohio Farm Bureau, Friend of Farm Bureau Award; U.S. Chamber of Commerce, Spirit of Enterprise Award; American Conservative Union, ACU Conservative Award; United Conservatives of Ohio, Watchdog of the Treasury; U.S. Sportsmen's Alliance, Patriot Award; Ohio National Guard, Major General Charles Dick Award for Legislative Excellence; President's Award; National Federation of Independent Business's (NFIB) Guardian of Small Business Award; National Association of Manufacturer's Manufacturing Legislative Excellence Award; Prism Propane Award; National Grocer's Association, Spirit of America Award; Family Research Council's True Blue Award; National Retail Federation's Hero of Main Street Award; Healthcare Distribution Management Association's (HDMA) Rx Safety and Leadership Award (Rx Award); Safari Club International's Federal Legislator of the Year; the National Shooting Sports Foundation's Legislator of the Year; member, Bowling Green Noon Kiwanis; Bowling Green Chamber of Commerce; Wood County Farm Bureau; caucuses: co-chair, Congressional French Caucus; co-chair, Grid Innovation Caucus; co-chair, Propane Caucus; co-chair, Rural Broadband Caucus; co-chair, Wi-Fi Caucus; former co-chair, Congressional Sportsmen's Caucus; previous committees: Agriculture, Transportation and Infrastructure; committees: Energy and Commerce; elected to the 110th Congress, by special election, on December 11, 2007 to fill the vacancy caused by the death of U.S. Representative Paul Eugene Gillmor; reelected to each succeeding Congress.

Office Listings

https://latta.house.gov https://facebook.com/boblatta twitter: @boblatta

2467 Rayburn House Office Building, Washington, DC 20515 .... (202) 225–6405
Chief of Staff.—Drew Griffin. FAX: 225–1985
Legislative Director.—Madeline Vey.
Scheduler.—Erin Partee.
1045 North Main Street, Suite 6, Bowling Green, OH 43402 .... (419) 354–8700
101 Clinton Street, Suite 1200, Defiance, OH 43512 .... (419) 782–1996
318 Dorney Plaza, Room 302, Findlay, OH 45840 .... (419) 422–7791

Counties: DEFIANCE, FULTON, HANCOCK, HARDIN, HENRY, LUCAS (part), MERCER (part), OTTAWA, PAULDING, PUTNAM, VAN WERT, WILLIAMS, WOOD, AND WYANDOT. Population (2010), 726,090.

ZIP Codes: 43310, 43316, 43323, 43326, 43330–32, 43337, 43340, 43345, 43347, 43351, 43359, 43402–03, 43406, 43408, 43412–13, 43416, 43430, 43432, 43437, 43443, 43445, 43447, 43449–52, 43457–58, 43460, 43462–63, 43465–69, 43501–02, 43504–06, 43511–12, 43515–19, 43521–29, 43531–37, 43540–43, 43545, 43547–49, 43551, 43553–58, 43560, 43565–67, 43569–71, 43605–06, 43613–15, 43617, 43619, 43623, 44802, 44804, 44817, 44830, 44844, 44849, 44882, 45810, 45812–14, 45816–17, 45821–22, 45827–28, 45830, 45831–33, 45835–36, 45838, 45840–41, 45843–44, 45846, 45849–51, 45853, 45855–56, 45858–59, 45861–64, 45867–68, 45872–77, 45879–82, 45886–87, 45889–91, 45894, 45896–99

* * *

SIXTH DISTRICT

WILLIAM L. ''BILL'' JOHNSON, Republican, of Marietta, OH; born in Roseboro, NC, November 10, 1954; raised in Roseboro, NC; education: B.A., graduated *summa cum laude* at Troy University, Troy, AL, 1979; M.A., computer science, Georgia Tech, Atlanta, GA, 1984; professional: co-founder of Johnson-Schley Management Group, Inc.; founder of J2 Business Solutions, Inc.; chief information officer of a global manufacturer of highly electronic components for the transportation industry; military: retired as Lieutenant Colonel; distinguished graduate from the Air Force Reserve Officer Training Corps, Squadron Officers School, and Air Command and Staff College; religion: Protestant; family: married to LeeAnn Johnson; children: Nathan, Joshua, Julie, and Jessica; awards: recipient of Air Force Meritorious Service Medal; Air Force Commendation Medal; National Defense Service Medal; caucuses: Air Force Caucus; Aluminum Caucus; Army Aviation Caucus; Automotive Caucus; Baseball Caucus; China Caucus; Cybersecurity Caucus; Diabetes Caucus; Dyslexia Caucus; E-Learning Caucus; Ethnic and Religious Freedom in Sri Lanka Caucus; Fire Services Caucus; General Aviation Caucus; Hellenic Issues Caucus; House Law Enforcement Caucus; Invisible Wounds Caucus; Israel Allies Caucus; Joint Strike Fighter Caucus; Military Sexual Assault Prevention Caucus; Military Veterans Caucus; Mobility Air Forces Caucus; Natural Gas Caucus; Ohio River Basin Congressional Caucus; Prayer Caucus; Problem Solvers Caucus; Pro-Israel Caucus; Republican Israel Caucus; Rock and Roll Caucus; Sportsmen's Caucus; Steel Caucus; U.S.-Turkish Relations and Turkish Americans Caucus; USO Congressional Caucus; Veterans Jobs Caucus; Congressional Vision Caucus; committees: Budget; Energy and Commerce; elected to the 112th Congress on November 2, 2010; reelected to each succeeding Congress.

Office Listings

https://billjohnson.house.gov

2336 Rayburn House Office Building, Washington, DC 20515 .... (202) 225–5705
Chief of Staff.—Mike Smullen.
Legislative Director.—David Rardin.
Communications Director.—Ben Keeler.
Scheduler / Office Manager.—Katherine Gwyn.
246 Front Street, Marietta, OH 45750 .... (740) 376–0868
192 East State Street, Salem, OH 44460 .... (330) 337–6951
202 Park Avenue, Suite C, Ironton, OH 45638 .... (740) 534–9431
116 Southgate Parkway, Cambridge, OH 43725 .... (740) 432–2366

Counties: ATHENS (part), BELMONT, CARROLL, COLUMBIANA, GALLIA, GUERNSEY, HARRISON, JACKSON, JEFFERSON, LAWRENCE, MAHONING (part), MEIGS, MONROE, MUSKINGUM (part), NOBLE, SCIOTO (part), TUSCARAWAS (part), AND WASHINGTON. Population (2010), 721,032.

ZIP Codes: 43701, 43711, 43713, 43716–19, 43722–25, 43732–33, 43736, 43747, 43749–50, 43754–55, 43759, 43762, 43767–68, 43772–73, 43778–80, 43786–88, 43793, 43802, 43812, 43821–22, 43830, 43832, 43837, 43842, 43901–08, 43910, 43912–15, 43917, 43920, 43925–28, 43930–35, 43938–40, 43942–48, 43950–53, 43961–64, 43967–68, 43970–74, 43976–77, 43983, 43985–86, 43988, 44401, 44406, 44408, 44413, 44423, 44427, 44431–32, 44441–45, 44449, 44451–52, 44454–55, 44460, 44493, 44514, 44601, 44607, 44609, 44615, 44620–21, 44625, 44629, 44634, 44643–44, 44651, 44653, 44656–57, 44663, 44672, 44675, 44682–83, 44688, 44693, 44695, 44699, 44730, 45601, 45613–14, 45619–21, 45623, 45629, 45631, 45634, 45636, 45638, 45640, 45645, 45648, 45650, 45652, 45653, 45656, 45658–59, 45662–63, 45669, 45672, 45674, 45678, 45680, 45682, 45685–86, 45688, 45692, 45694, 45696, 45701, 45710–11, 45714–15, 45721, 45723–24, 45727, 45729, 45734–35, 45741–46, 45750, 45760, 45767–73, 45775–76, 45779, 45784, 45786–89

* * *

SEVENTH DISTRICT

ROBERT B. GIBBS, Republican, of Lakeville, OH; born in Peru, IN, June 14, 1954; education: graduated from Bay Village Senior High School, Bay Village, OH; A.A.S., Ohio State University Agricultural Technical Institute, Wooster, OH, 1974; professional: technician; farmer; business owner; president, Ohio Farm Bureau Federation; member of the Ohio State House of Representatives, 2003–09; member of the Ohio State Senate, 2009–10; married: Jody Gibbs; children: Adam, Amy, and Andrew; grandchildren: Luke; committees: Oversight and Reform; Transportation and Infrastructure; elected to the 112th Congress on November 2, 2010; reelected to each succeeding Congress.

Office Listings

https://gibbs.house.gov https://facebook.com/RepBobGibbs twitter: @RepBobGibbs

2446 Rayburn House Office Building, Washington, DC 20515 .... (202) 225–6265

Office Listings—Continued

Chief of Staff.—Hillary Gross. FAX: 225–3394
Scheduler.—Rachael Van Mersbergen.
Legislative Director.—Alex Briggs.
Legislative Aides: Brian Bates, Ryan Dilworth.
Deputy Chief of Staff/Communications Director.—Dallas Gerber.
110 Cottage Street, Ashland, OH 44805 .... (419) 207–0650
District Director.—Tim Ross. FAX: 207–0655

Counties: ASHLAND, COSHOCTON (part), HOLMES, HURON (part), KNOX, LORAIN (part), MEDINA (part), RICHLAND (part), STARK (part), AND TUSCARAWAS (part). Population (2010), 726,076.

ZIP Codes: 43005–06, 43011, 43014, 43019, 43022, 43028, 43037, 43050, 43080, 43749, 43804, 43811–12, 43821–22, 43824, 43832, 43836, 43843–45, 44011, 44028, 44035, 44039, 44044, 44050, 44090, 44149, 44212, 44214–15, 44235, 44253–54, 44256, 44273, 44275, 44280, 44287, 44601, 44608, 44610–13, 44618, 44624, 44626–28, 44632–34, 44637–38, 44641, 44643, 44646–47, 44652, 44654, 44657, 44661–62, 44666, 44669–70, 44676, 44681, 44685, 44687–90, 44702–10, 44714, 44718, 44720–21, 44805, 44807, 44811, 44813, 44822, 44826–27, 44833, 44837–38, 44840, 44842–43, 44847–48, 44850–51, 44855, 44857, 44859, 44864–66, 44874–75, 44878, 44880–90, 44903, 44905–07

* * *

EIGHTH DISTRICT

WARREN DAVIDSON, Republican, of Troy, OH; born in Sidney, OH, March 1, 1970; education: B.S., American history, United States Military Academy, West Point, NY, 1995; M.B.A., University of Notre Dame, South Bend, Indiana, 2005; professional: managing director, West Troy, 2000–15; president, Global Source Manufacturing, 2002–15; founder, Factory Techs, 2008–15; managing director, RK Metals, 2014–15; managing director, Integral Manufacturing, 2015–16; religion: Christian; family: married, two children; committees: Financial Services; elected to the 114th Congress, by special election, on June 7, 2016, to fill the vacancy caused by the resignation of U.S. Representative John Andrew Boehner; sworn in on June 9, 2016; reelected to each succeeding Congress.

Office Listings

https://davidson.house.gov https://facebook.com/CongressmanWarrenDavidson
https://twitter.com/WarrenDavidson

1107 Longworth House Office Building, Washington, DC 20515 .... (202) 225–6205
Chief of Staff.—Adam Hewitt.
Press Secretary.—Matthew Henderson.
8857 Cincinnati-Dayton Road, Suite 102, West Chester, OH 45069 .... (513) 779–5400
20 Dotcom Drive, Troy, Ohio 45373 .... (937) 339–1524
76 East High Street, 3rd Floor, Springfield, OH 45502 .... (937) 322–1120

Counties: BUTLER, CLARK, DARKE, MERCER (part), MIAMI, AND PREBLE. Population (2010), 721,032.

ZIP Codes: 43010, 43044, 43153, 45003–04, 45011–15, 45018, 45042, 45044, 45050, 45053, 45055–56, 45061–64, 45067, 45069–71, 45241, 45246, 45303–04, 45308, 45310–12, 45317–26, 45328, 45330–32, 45337–39, 45341, 45344, 45346–49, 45361–62, 45368–69, 45371–74, 45378, 45380–83, 45387–88, 45390, 45501–06, 45822, 45826, 45828, 45846, 45860, 45862, 45866, 45869, 45882–83, 45894, 45898

* * *

NINTH DISTRICT

MARCY KAPTUR, Democrat, of Toledo, OH; born in Toledo, June 17, 1946; education: graduated, St. Ursula Academy, Toledo, 1964; B.A., University of Wisconsin, Madison, 1968; master of urban planning, University of Michigan, Ann Arbor, 1974; attended University of Manchester, England, 1974; professional: urban planner; Assistant Director for Urban Affairs, Domestic Policy Staff, White House, 1977–79; American Planning Association and American Institute of Certified Planners Fellow; member: National Center for Urban Ethnic Affairs Advisory Committee; University of Michigan Urban Planning Alumni Association; NAACP Urban League; Polish Museum; Polish American Historical Association; Lucas County Democratic Party Executive Committee; Democratic Women's Campaign Association; Little Flower Parish Church; religion: Roman Catholic; caucuses: co-chair, Congressional Great Lakes Caucus; co-chair, 4–H Caucus; co-chair, House Auto Caucus; co-chair, House Auto Parts Task Force; co-chair, Hungarian Caucus; co-chair, Poland Caucus; co-chair and co-founder, Ukraine Caucus; committees: Appropriations; elected on November 2, 1982, to the 98th Congress; reelected to each succeeding Congress.

Office Listings

https://kaptur.house.gov https://facebook.com/RepMarcyKaptur twitter: @RepMarcyKaptur

2186 Rayburn House Office Building, Washington, DC 20515 .... (202) 225–4146
Chief of Staff.—Steve Katich.
Office Manager / Scheduler.—Courtney Hruska.
Legislative Director.—Jenny Perrino.
One Maritime Plaza, Suite 600, Toledo, OH 43604 .... (419) 259–7500
17021 Lorain Avenue, Cleveland, OH 44114 .... (216) 767–5933
200 West Erie Avenue, Room 310, Lorain, OH 44052 .... (440) 288–1500
FAX: (419) 225–9623

Counties: CUYAHOGA COUNTY (part). CITIES AND TOWNSHIPS: Bay Village, Berea, Brook Park, Brooklyn, Brooklyn Heights, Cleveland, Lakewood, Linndale, Parma, and Rocky River. ERIE COUNTY (part). CITIES AND TOWNSHIPS: Castalia, Huron, and Sandusky. LORAIN COUNTY (part). CITIES AND TOWNSHIPS: Amherst, Avon Lake, Elyria, Grafton, Lorain, North Eaton, Oberlin, Ridgeville, Rochester, Sheffield Lake, South Amherst, and Vermilion. LUCAS COUNTY (part). CITIES AND TOWNSHIPS: Curtice, Gypsum, Harbor View, Oregon, Reno Beach, Toledo, and Washington. OTTAWA COUNTY. CITIES AND TOWNSHIPS: Bay Shore, Bono, Catawba Island, Danbury, Eagle Beach, Gem Beach, Graytown, Hessville, Isle St. George, Kelleys Island, Lacarne, Lakeside, Lindsey, Marblehead, Martin, Middle Bass, Oak Harbor, Port Clinton, Portage, Put-in-Bay, Rocky Ridge, Vickery, Whites Landing, and Williston. Population (2010), 721,032.

ZIP Codes: 43412, 43433–34, 43436, 43438–40, 43445–46, 43449, 43452, 43456, 43464, 43601–16, 43620, 43635, 43697, 43699, 44001, 44012, 44017, 44052–55, 44089, 44102, 44107, 44109, 44111, 44116, 44129–30, 44134–35, 44140, 44142, 44144, 44181, 44824, 44839, 44870–71

* * *

TENTH DISTRICT

MICHAEL R. TURNER, Republican, of Dayton, OH; born in Dayton, January 11, 1960; education: B.A., Ohio Northern University, 1982; J.D., Case Western Reserve University Law School, 1985; M.B.A., University of Dayton, 1992; professional: attorney; Ohio Bar Association; California Bar Association; Bar of the Supreme Court of the United States; public service: Mayor of Dayton, 1994–2002; children: Jessica and Carolyn; committees: Armed Services; Permanent Select Committee on Intelligence; elected to the 108th Congress on November 5, 2002; reelected to each succeeding Congress.

Office Listings

https://turner.house.gov https://facebook.com/RepMikeTurner twitter: @RepMikeTurner

2082 Rayburn House Office Building, Washington, DC 20515 .... (202) 225–6465
Chief of Staff.—Adam Howard. FAX: 225–6754
Legislative Director.—Jeffrey Wilson.
Scheduler.—Kate Pietkiewicz.
120 West Third Street, Suite 305, Dayton, OH 45402 .... (937) 225–2843
District Director.—Frank DeBrosse.

Counties: FAYETTE (northern part), GREENE, AND MONTGOMERY. Population (2010), 721,032.

ZIP Codes: 43106, 43128, 43142–43, 43145, 43153, 43160, 45005, 45066, 45068–69, 45301, 45305, 45307, 45309, 45314–16, 45322, 45324, 45327, 45335, 45342, 45344–45, 45354, 45368, 45370–71, 45381, 45384–85, 45387, 45402–06, 45409–10, 45414–20, 45424, 45426, 45428–34, 45439–40, 45449, 45458–59

* * *

ELEVENTH DISTRICT

MARCIA L. FUDGE, Democrat, of Warrensville Heights, OH; born in Cleveland, OH, October 29, 1952; education: B.S., Ohio State University, 1975; J.D., Cleveland Marshall College of Law, 1983; professional: Director of Budget and Finance, Cuyahoga County Prosecutor's Office; chief administrator for Cuyahoga County Prosecutor; Mayor of Warrensville Heights, OH; committees: Agriculture; Education and Labor; House Administration; elected to the 110th Congress, by special election, to fill the vacancy caused by the death of U.S. Representative Stephanie Tubbs Jones; reelected to each succeeding Congress.

Office Listings

https://fudge.house.gov https://facebook.com/RepMarciaLFudge
twitter: @RepMarciaFudge https://instagram.com/repmarciafudge

2344 Rayburn House Office Building, Washington, DC 20515 .... (202) 225–7032

Office Listings—Continued

Chief of Staff.—Veleter Mazyck.
Deputy Chief of Staff / Legislative Director.—Eyang Garrison.
Communications Director.—Bernadine Stallings.
Scheduler / Office Manager.—Imani Edwards.
4834 Richmond Road, Suite 150, Warrensville Heights, OH 44128 .... (216) 522–4900
District Director.—Clifton Williams.
Scheduler / Office Manager.—Linda Matthews.
1225 Lawton Street, Akron, OH 44320 .... (330) 835–4758
Outreach Coordinator.—Joan Williams.

Counties: CUYAHOGA COUNTY (part) AND SUMMIT COUNTY (part). CITIES: Akron, Bath Township, Beachwood, Bedford, Bedford Heights, Bratenahl, Broadview Heights, Brooklyn Heights, Cleveland, Cleveland Heights, Cuyahoga Heights, East Cleveland, Euclid, Fairlawn, Garfield Heights, Glenwillow, Highland Hills, Maple Heights, Newburgh Heights, North Randall, Oakwood Village, Orange, Pepper Pike, Richfield Township, Richfield Village, Richmond Heights, Seven Hills, Shaker Heights, South Euclid, University Heights, Warrensville Heights, and Woodmere. Population (2010), 705,659.

ZIP Codes: 44022, 44101–15, 44117–25, 44127–28, 44131–33, 44137, 44139, 44141, 44143, 44146–47, 44256, 44264, 44286, 44301–08, 44310–14, 44319–21, 44333

* * *

TWELFTH DISTRICT

TROY BALDERSON, Republican, of Zanesville, OH; born in Zanesville, January 16, 1962; education: attended Muskingum College, Muskingum, OH, 1980–82; attended The Ohio State University, Columbus, OH, 1982–83; professional: worked on the family farm; automotive dealer at his family owned automobile dealership; member of the Ohio State House of Representatives, 2009–11; member of the Ohio State Senate, representing the 20th District, 2011–18, where he served as chairman of the Committee on Energy and Natural Resources and as member of the Finance Committee; religion: Christian; has served as an elder at the First Christian Church in Zanesville; family: one son, Joshua; caucuses: Air Cargo Caucus; ALS Caucus; Apprenticeship Caucus; Army Caucus; Auto Care Caucus; Auto Performance and Motorsports Caucus; Beef Caucus; Boating Caucus; Civility & Respect Caucus; Community College Caucus; Community Health Centers Caucus; Congressional Appalachian National Scenic Trail Caucus; Congressional Grid Innovation Caucus; Congressional Motorcycle Caucus; Congressional Motorsports Caucus; Congressional Ohio River Basin Caucus; Congressional Rural Caucus; Congressional Second Amendment Caucus; Congressional Small Business Caucus; Congressional Study Group on Japan; CTE Caucus; General Aviation Caucus; House Automotive Caucus; Main Street; Manufacturing Caucus; RSC; Smart Cities; Suburban Caucus; Taiwan Caucus; Travel & Tourism Caucus; Tuesday Group; Vision Caucus; committees: Science, Space, and Technology; Small Business; Transportation and Infrastructure; elected, by special election, to the 115th Congress on August 7, 2018, to fill the vacancy caused by the resignation of U.S. Representative Patrick Tiberi; reelected to the 116th Congress on November 6, 2018.

Office Listings

https://balderson.house.gov https://facebook.com/RepTroyBalderson
https://twitter.com/RepBalderson https://youtube.com/channel/UCm6vJzx-mu4Xr56FnQKRz0w

1221 Longworth House Office Building, Washington, DC 20515 .... (202) 225–5355
Chief of Staff.—Teri Geiger. FAX: 226–4523
Scheduler.—Kim Waskowsky.
Legislative Director.—Brittany Madni.
Communications Director.—Erin Collins.
Deputy Communications Director.—Clark Siddle.
250 East Wilson Bridge Road, Suite 100, Worthington, OH 43085 .... (614) 523–2555

Counties: DELAWARE, FRANKLIN (part), LICKING, MARION (part), MORROW, MUSKINGUM (part), AND RICHLAND (part). Population (2010), 728,420.

ZIP Codes: 43001–04, 43008, 43011, 43013, 43015–19, 43021, 43023, 43025–27, 43030–33, 43035, 43040, 43046, 43050, 43054–56, 43058, 43061–62, 43065–66, 43068–69, 43071, 43073–74, 43076, 43080–82, 43085–86, 43093, 43105, 43147, 43201–02, 43214, 43217–21, 43226, 43229–30, 43235–36, 43240, 43302, 43314–15, 43317, 43320–21, 43334, 43338, 43342, 43344, 43356, 43701–02, 43720–21, 43727, 43731–32, 43734–35, 43738–40, 43746, 43756, 43760, 43762, 43767, 43771, 43777, 43791, 43822, 43830, 44813, 44822, 44833, 44862, 44864, 44901–07

* * *

THIRTEENTH DISTRICT

TIM RYAN, Democrat, of Howland, OH; born in Niles, OH, July 16, 1973; education: B.S., Bowling Green University, 1995; J.D., University of New Hampshire School of Law (formerly Franklin Pierce Law Center), 2000; professional: legislative aide, Washington, DC; married: Andrea Ryan; committees: Appropriations; Joint Committee on the Library; elected to the 108th Congress on November 5, 2002; reelected to each succeeding Congress.

Office Listings

https://timryan.house.gov https://facebook.com/timryan twitter: @RepTimRyan

1126 Longworth House Office Building, Washington, DC 20515 .... (202) 225–5261
Chief of Staff.—Ron Grimes. FAX: 225–3719
Scheduler.—Erin Isenberg.
Legislative Director.—Ryan Keating.
197 West Market Street, Warren, OH 44481 .... (330) 373–0074
241 West Federal Street, Youngstown, OH 44503 .... (330) 740–0193
1030 East Tallmadge Avenue, Akron, OH 44310 .... (330) 630–7311

Counties: MAHONING (part), PORTAGE (part), STARK (part), SUMMIT (part), AND TRUMBULL (part). Population (2010), 723,713.

ZIP Codes: 44141, 44201, 44203, 44221, 44223–24, 44231, 44236, 44240, 44241, 44243, 44255, 44260, 44262, 44264, 44266, 44272, 44278, 44285, 44288, 44301–08, 44310–14, 44319–20, 44333, 44401–06, 44410–12, 44418, 44420, 44425, 44429–30, 44436–38, 44440, 44444, 44446, 44449, 44451, 44470–71, 44473, 44481, 44483–85, 44491, 44502–07, 44509–12, 44514–15, 44601, 44640

* * *

FOURTEENTH DISTRICT

DAVID JOYCE, Republican, of Geauga, OH; born in Cleveland, OH, March 17, 1957; education: B.S., University of Dayton, Dayton, OH, 1979; J.D., University of Dayton, 1982; professional: prosecuting attorney, Geauga County, 1988–2012; married: Kelly Joyce; children: Trenton, Keighle, and Bridey; committees: Appropriations; elected to the 113th Congress on November 6, 2012; reelected to each succeeding Congress.

Office Listings

https://joyce.house.gov https://facebook.com/RepDaveJoyce twitter: @RepDaveJoyce

1124 Longworth House Office Building, Washington, DC 20515 .... (202) 225–5731
Chief of Staff.—Anna Alburger.
Scheduler.—Kelsi Brogan.
Legislative Director.—Charles Castagna.
Communications Director.—Katherine Sears.
8500 Station Street, Suite 390, Mentor, OH 44060 .... (440) 352–3939
FAX: 266–9004
10075 Ravenna Road, Twinsburg, OH 44087 .... (330) 357–4139
FAX: 425–7071

Counties: ASHTABULA, CUYAHOGA (part), GEAUGA, LAKE, PORTAGE (part), SUMMIT (part), AND TRUMBULL (part). Population (2010), 721,032.

ZIP Codes: 44003–04, 44010, 44021–24, 44026, 44030, 44032, 44040–41, 44045–48, 44056–57, 44060, 44062, 44064–65, 44067, 44072, 44076–77, 44080–82, 44084–87, 44092–95, 44099, 44122, 44124–25, 44131, 44139, 44141, 44143, 44146–47, 44202, 44221, 44223–24, 44231, 44234, 44236, 44240–41, 44255, 44262, 44264, 44266, 44278, 44313, 44402, 44404, 44410, 44417–18, 44428, 44439, 44450, 44473, 44481, 44491

* * *

FIFTEENTH DISTRICT

STEVE STIVERS, Republican, of Columbus, OH; born in Cincinnati, OH, March 24, 1965; education: B.A., Ohio State University, Columbus, OH, 1989; M.B.A., Ohio State University, 1996; M.A., United States Army War College; professional: military; colonel, Ohio Army National Guard, 1988–present; Ohio Company and Bank One; member of the Ohio State Senate,

2003–08; married: Karen Stivers; children: Sarah and Samuel; committees: Financial Services; elected to the 112th Congress on November 2, 2010; reelected to each succeeding Congress.

Office Listings

https://stivers.house.gov https://facebook.com/RepSteveStivers twitter: @RepSteveStivers

2234 Rayburn House Office Building, Washington, DC 20515	(202) 225–2015
Chief of Staff.—Courtney Whetstone.	FAX: 225–3529
Scheduler.—Sara Donlon.	
Legislative Director.—Nick Bush.	
Communications Director.—AnnMarie Graham.	
3790 Municipal Way, Hilliard, OH 43026	(614) 771–4968
	FAX: 771–3990
Fairfield County District Office, 104 East Main Street, Lancaster, OH 43130	(740) 654–2654
	FAX: 654–2482
Clinton County District Office, 69 North South Street, Wilmington, OH 45177	(937) 283–7049
	FAX: 283–7052

Counties: ATHENS (part), CLINTON, FAIRFIELD, FAYETTE (part), FRANKLIN (part), HOCKING, MADISON, MORGAN, PERRY, PICKAWAY, ROSS (part), AND VINTON. Population (2010), 721,031.

ZIP Codes: 43002, 43016–17, 43026, 43029, 43044, 43046, 43062, 43064, 43068, 43076, 43101–03, 43105, 43107, 43110–13, 43115–17, 43119, 43123, 43125–27, 43130, 43135–38, 43140, 43143–58, 43160, 43162, 43164, 43201, 43204, 43206–07, 43210, 43212, 43215, 43217, 43220–23, 43228, 43235, 43724, 43728, 43730–31, 43739, 43748, 43756, 43758, 43760–61, 43764, 43766, 43777, 43782–83, 43787, 45068, 45107, 45113, 45123, 45135, 45142, 45146, 45148, 45159, 45164, 45166, 45169, 45177, 45335, 45369, 45601, 45622, 45628, 45634, 45644, 45647, 45651, 45654, 45672, 45681, 45686, 45695, 45698, 45701, 45710–11, 45715–16, 45719, 45723, 45732, 45735, 45740, 45761, 45764, 45766, 45776, 45778, 45780, 45782

* * *

SIXTEENTH DISTRICT

ANTHONY GONZALEZ, Republican, of Rocky River, OH; born in Avon Lake, OH, November 18, 1984; education: B.A., Ohio State University, Columbus, OH, 2007; M.B.A., Stanford University, Stanford, CA, 2014; professional: professional athlete, National Football League, New England Patriots, 2012, Indianapolis Colts, 2007–11; business developer and former COO; religion: Catholic; family: married to Elizabeth; one son: Alexander; committees: Financial Services; Science, Space, and Technology; elected to the 116th Congress on November 6, 2018 (becoming the first Hispanic American to represent Ohio in Congress).

Office Listings

https://anthonygonzalez.house.gov https://facebook.com/RepAGonzalez
https://twitter.com/RepAGonzalez https://instagram.com/repagonzalez
https://youtube.com/channel/UC1GnxY58Cx2F47ULByqT0oA

1023 Longworth House Office Building, Washington, DC 20515	(202) 225–3876
Chief of Staff.—Tim Lolli.	FAX: 225–3059
Scheduler.—Carol Kresse.	
Legislative Director.—Stephen Hostelley.	
Communications Director.—Emily Carlin.	
4150 Belden Village Street, Suite 607, Canton, OH 44718	(330) 599–7037
13477 Prospect Road, Suite 212, Strongsville, OH 44149	(440) 783–3696

Counties: CUYAHOGA (part), MEDINA (part), PORTAGE (part), STARK (part), SUMMIT (part), AND WAYNE. Population (2010), 724,108.

ZIP Codes: 44017, 44070, 44116, 44126, 44129–30, 44133–34, 44136, 44138, 44145, 44149, 44201, 44203, 44212, 44214–17, 44230, 44233, 44235, 44240, 44250–51, 44254, 44256, 44260, 44265–66, 44270, 44272–74, 44276, 44278, 44280–81, 44287, 44306, 44312, 44319–21, 44333, 44601, 44606, 44611, 44614, 44618, 44624, 44627, 44632, 44636, 44638, 44645–47, 44659, 44662, 44666–67, 44676–77, 44685, 44691, 44703, 44706, 44708–10, 44718, 44720–21, 44840

OKLAHOMA

(Population 2010, 3,751,351)

SENATORS

JAMES M. INHOFE, Republican, of Tulsa, OK; born in Des Moines, IA, November 17, 1934; education: graduated, Central High School, Tulsa, OK, 1953; B.A., University of Tulsa, OK, 1959; military service: served in the U.S. Army, private first class, 1957–58; professional: businessman; active pilot; president, Quaker Life Insurance Company; Oklahoma House of Representatives, 1967–69; Oklahoma State Senate, 1969–77; Mayor of Tulsa, OK, 1978–84; religion: member, First Presbyterian Church of Tulsa; married: Kay Kirkpatrick; children: Jim, Perry, Molly, and Katy; twelve grandchildren; committees: chair, Armed Services; Environment and Public Works; Small Business and Entrepreneurship; Select Committee on Intelligence; elected to the 100th Congress on November 4, 1986; reelected to each succeeding Congress; elected to the U.S. Senate on November 8, 1994, finishing the unexpired term of Senator David Boren; reelected to each succeeding Senate term.

Office Listings

https://inhofe.senate.gov https://facebook.com/jiminhofe https://twitter.com/InhofePress

205 Russell Senate Office Building, Washington, DC 20510 .... (202) 224–4721
Chief of Staff.—Luke Holland. FAX: 228–0380
Legislative Director.—Andrew Forbes.
Communications Director.—Leacey Burke.
Scheduler.—Wendi Price.
1924 South Utica, Suite 530, Tulsa, OK 74104–6511 .... (918) 748–5111
3817 Northwest Expressway, Suite 780, Oklahoma City, OK 73112 .... (405) 208–8841
302 North Independence, Suite 104, Enid, OK 73701 .... (580) 234–5105
215 East Choctaw, Suite 106, McAlester, OK 74501 .... (918) 426–0933

* * *

JAMES LANKFORD, Republican, of Oklahoma City, OK; born in Dallas, TX, March 4, 1968; education: B.S., secondary education, University of Texas, 1990; master of divinity, Southwestern Baptist Theological Seminary, 1994; professional: Baptist General Convention of Oklahoma, youth ministry specialist and director of the Falls Creek Youth Camp, 1995–2009; public service: U.S. House of Representatives, 2011–14; elected House Republican Policy Committee Chair, 2012–14; married: Cindy, 1992; children: Hannah and Jordan; religion: Christian; committees: chair, Select Committee on Ethics; Appropriations; Finance; Homeland Security and Governmental Affairs; Indian Affairs; elected to the U.S. Senate on November 4, 2014, to complete the unexpired term of U.S. Senator Tom Coburn; reelected to the U.S. Senate on November 8, 2016.

Office Listings

https://lankford.senate.gov https://facebook.com/SenatorLankford
https://twitter.com/SenatorLankford https://instagram.com/senatorlankford

316 Hart Senate Office Building, Washington, DC 20510 .... (202) 224–5754
Chief of Staff.—Michelle Altman.
Legislative Director.—Sarah Seitz.
Scheduler.—Jaclyn O'Neil.
Communications Director.—Aly Beley.
State Director.—Mona Taylor.
1015 North Broadway Avenue, Suite 310, Oklahoma City, OK 73102 .... (405) 231–4941
401 South Boston Avenue, Suite 2150, Tulsa, OK 74103 .... (918) 581–7651

REPRESENTATIVES

FIRST DISTRICT

KEVIN HERN, Republican, of Tulsa, OK; born in Belton, MO, December 4, 1961; education: B.S., Arkansas Tech University, Russellville, AR, 1986; M.B.A., University of Arkansas, Little Rock, AR, 1999; attended the Georgia Institute of Technology, studying for a Ph.D. in astronautical engineering; professional: McDonald's franchisee; chairman, Finance Committee, 2011–15, Oklahoma Turnpike Authority, Oklahoma City, OK; religion: Protestant, member of the Church at Battle Creek; family: married to Tammy; three children; committees: Budget; Natural Resources; Small Business; appointed to the 115th Congress by the Governor of Oklahoma under the provisions of Oklahoma Statute, Section 26–12–101 (B) to fill the vacancy caused by the resignation of U.S. Representative Jim Bridenstine; elected to the 116th Congress on November 6, 2018.

Office Listings

https://hern.house.gov https://facebook.com/repkevinhern https://twitter.com/repkevinhern

1019 Longworth House Office Building, Washington, DC 20515 .... (202) 225–2211
Chief of Staff.—Cameron Foster. FAX: 225–9187
Scheduler.—Courtney Ballenger.
Communications Director.—Miranda Dabney.
Legislative Director.—Michael Martin.
2448 East 81st Street, Suite 5150, Tulsa, OK 74137 .... (918) 935–3222

Counties: CREEK (part), ROGERS (part), TULSA, WAGONER, AND WASHINGTON. Population (2010), 750,270.

ZIP Codes: 74003–06, 74008, 74011–12, 74014–15, 74021–22, 74029, 74033, 74036–37, 74041, 74047, 74050–51, 74055, 74061, 74063, 74066, 74070, 74073, 74080, 74082–83, 74103–08, 74110, 74112, 74114–17, 74119–20, 74126–37, 74145–46, 74337, 74352, 74403, 74429, 74434, 74436, 74446, 74454, 74458, 74467, 74477

* * *

SECOND DISTRICT

MARKWAYNE MULLIN, Republican, of Westville, OK; born in Tulsa, OK, July 26, 1977; education: attended Missouri Valley College, Marshall, MO, 1996; A.A.S., Oklahoma State University Institute of Technology, Okmulgee, OK, 2010; professional: business owner; plumber; rancher; married on June 14, 1997; children: father of six; committees: Energy and Commerce; elected to the 113th Congress on November 6, 2012; reelected to each succeeding Congress.

Office Listings

https://mullin.house.gov https://facebook.com/RepMullin twitter: @RepMullin

2421 Rayburn House Office Building, Washington, DC 20515 .... (202) 225–2701
DC Chief of Staff.—Kayla Priehs.
Communications Director.—Meredith Blanford.
Legislative Director.—Miranda Moorman.
Executive Assistant / Scheduler.—Vacant.
223 West Patti Page Boulevard, Claremore, OK 74017 .... (918) 283–6262
811–A North York Street, Muskogee, OK 74403 .... (918) 687–2533
1 East Choctaw, Suite 175, McAlester, OK 74501 .... (918) 423–5951

Counties: ADAIR, ATOKA, BRYAN, CHEROKEE, CHOCTAW, COAL, CRAIG, DELAWARE, HASKELL, HUGHES, JOHNSTON, LATIMER, LEFLORE, MARSHALL, MAYES, MCCURTAIN, MCINTOSH, MUSKOGEE, NOWATA, OKFUSKEE, OKMULGEE, OTTAWA, PITTSBURGH, PUSHMATAHA, ROGERS, AND SEQUOYAH. Population (2010), 750,270.

ZIP Codes: 73432, 73439–40, 73446–47, 73449–50, 73455, 73460–61, 74016–19, 74027, 74042, 74048, 74053, 74072, 74301, 74330–33, 74338–40, 74342–44, 74346–47, 74349–50, 74354, 74358–70, 74401, 74421–23, 74425–28, 74430–32, 74435, 74437–38, 74441–42, 74445, 74447, 74450–52, 74455–57, 74459–60, 74462–64, 74468–72, 74501, 74521–23, 74525, 74528, 74530–31, 74533–36, 74538, 74540, 74543, 74546–47, 74549, 74552–53, 74556, 74560–63, 74565, 74569–72, 74576, 74578, 74701, 74720, 74723, 74726–30, 74733, 74735–36, 74740–41, 74743, 74745, 74747–48, 74750, 74756, 74759, 74764, 74766, 74829, 74833, 74839, 74845, 74848, 74850, 74856, 74859–60, 74880, 74883, 74885, 74901–02, 74930, 74932, 74935–37, 74940–42, 74944–46, 74948, 74951, 74953–56, 74959–60, 74962, 74964–66

* * *

THIRD DISTRICT

FRANK D. LUCAS, Republican, of Cheyenne, OK; born in Cheyenne, January 6, 1960; education: B.S., agricultural economics, Oklahoma State University, 1982; professional: rancher and farmer; served in Oklahoma State House of Representatives, 1989–94; secretary, Oklahoma House Republican Caucus, 1991–94; member: Oklahoma Farm Bureau, Oklahoma Cattlemen's Association, and Oklahoma Shorthorn Association; married: Lynda Bradshaw Lucas; children: Jessica, Ashlea, and Grant; committees: ranking member, Science, Space, and Technology; Financial Services; elected to the 103rd Congress, by special election, in May 1994; reelected to each succeeding Congress.

Office Listings

https://lucas.house.gov https://facebook.com/RepFrankLucas
https://twitter.com/repfranklucas https://instagram.com/repfranklucas

2405 Rayburn House Office Building, Washington, DC 20515 .... (202) 225–5565
Senior Advisor.—Nicole Scott. FAX: 225–8698
Communications Director.—Patrick Bond.
Legislative Director.—Alison Slagell.
Scheduler / Office Manager.—Meg Wagner.
Legislative Assistants: Dillon Johnson, Mitchell Wilkinson.
10952 Northwest Expressway, Suite B, Yukon, OK 73099 .... (405) 373–1958
Chief of Staff.—Stacey Glasscock.

Counties: ALFALFA, BEAVER, BECKHAM, BLAINE, CADDO, CANADIAN (part), CIMARRON, CREEK (part), CUSTER, DEWEY, ELLIS, GARFIELD, GRANT, GREER, HARMON, HARPER, JACKSON, KAY, KINGFISHER, KIOWA, LINCOLN, LOGAN, MAJOR, NOBLE, OSAGE, PAWNEE, PAYNE, ROGER MILLS, TEXAS, WASHITA, WOODS, AND WOODWARD. CITIES: Altus, Clinton, El Reno, Elk City, Enid, Guthrie, Guymon, Oklahoma City, Perry, Ponce City, Sapulpa, Stillwater, Tulsa, Weatherford, Woodward, and Yukon. Population (2010), 745,941.

ZIP Codes: 73001, 73005–07, 73009, 73014–17, 73021–22, 73024, 73027–29, 73033–34, 73036, 73038, 73040–45, 73047–48, 73050, 73053–54, 73056, 73058–59, 73061–64, 73073, 73077–79, 73085, 73090, 73096–97, 73099, 73127, 73521–23, 73526, 73532, 73537, 73539, 73544, 73547, 73549–50, 73554, 73556, 73559–60, 73564, 73566, 73571, 73601, 73620, 73622, 73624–28, 73632, 73638–39, 73641–42, 73644–48, 73650–51, 73654–55, 73658–64, 73666–69, 73673, 73701–03, 73705–06, 73716–20, 73722, 73724, 73726–31, 73733–39, 73741–44, 73746–47, 73749–50, 73753–64, 73766, 73768, 73770–73, 73801–02, 73832, 73834–35, 73838, 73840–44, 73848, 73851–53, 73855, 73857–60, 73901, 73931–33, 73937–39, 73942, 73944–47, 73949–51, 74001–03, 74010, 74020, 74023, 74026, 74028, 74030, 74032, 74034–35, 74038–39, 74044–47, 74051–52, 74054, 74056, 74058–60, 74062–63, 74066–68, 74070–71, 74073–79, 74081, 74084–85, 74106, 74126–27, 74131–32, 74601–02, 74604, 74630–33, 74636–37, 74640–41, 74643–44, 74646–47, 74650–53, 74824, 74832, 74834, 74851, 74855, 74864, 74869, 74875, 74881

* * *

FOURTH DISTRICT

TOM COLE, Republican, of Moore, OK; born in Shreveport, LA, April 28, 1949; education: B.A., Grinnell College, 1971; M.A., Yale University, 1974; Ph.D., University of Oklahoma, 1984; Watson Fellow, 1971–72; Fulbright Fellow, 1977–78; professional: former college professor of history and politics; president, Cole Hargrave Snodgrass & Associates (political consulting firm); public service: Oklahoma State Senate, 1988–91; Oklahoma Secretary of State, 1995–99; has served as chairman, and executive director, of the Oklahoma Republican Party; former chairman of the National Republican Congressional Committee; and chief of staff of the Republican National Committee; family: married to Ellen; one child: Mason; religion: United Methodist; committees: ranking member, Rules; Appropriations; elected to the 108th Congress on November 5, 2002; reelected to each succeeding Congress.

Office Listings

https://cole.house.gov https://facebook.com/TomColeOK04 twitter: @TomColeOK04

2207 Rayburn House Office Building, Washington, DC 20515 .... (202) 225–6165
Chief of Staff.—Joshua Grogis. FAX: 225–3512
Deputy Chief of Staff / Legislative Director.—Maria Bowie.
Communications Director.—Sarah Corley.
Scheduler.—Sabrina Parker.
2424 Springer Drive, Suite 201, Norman, OK 73069 .... (405) 329–6500
711 Southwest D Avenue, Suite 201, Lawton, OK 73501 .... (580) 357–2131
Sugg Clinic Office Building, 100 East 13th Street, Suite 213, Ada, OK 74820 .... (580) 436–5375

Counties: CANADIAN (part), CARTER, CLEVELAND, COMANCHE, COTTON, GARVIN, GRADY, JEFFERSON, LOVE, MCCLAIN, MURRAY, OKLAHOMA (part), PONTOTOC, STEPHENS, AND TILLMAN. Population (2010), 750,270.

ZIP Codes: 73002, 73004, 73006, 73010–11, 73017–20, 73026, 73030, 73032, 73051–52, 73055, 73057, 73059, 73064–69, 73071–72, 73074–75, 73079–80, 73082, 73086, 73089, 73092–93, 73095, 73098, 73110, 73130, 73135, 73139, 73141, 73145, 73149–50, 73159–60, 73165, 73169–70, 73173, 73401, 73425, 73430, 73433–34, 73437–38, 73441–44, 73448, 73453, 73456, 73458–59, 73463, 73481, 73487, 73491, 73501, 73503, 73505, 73507, 73520, 73527–31, 73533, 73538, 73540–43, 73546, 73548, 73551–53, 73555, 73557, 73559, 73562, 73564–70, 73572–73, 74572, 74820, 74825, 74831, 74842–44, 74852, 74856–57, 74865, 74871–72, 74878

* * *

FIFTH DISTRICT

KENDRA S. HORN, Democrat, of Oklahoma City, OK; born in Chickasha, OK, June 9, 1976; education: B.A., political science, University of Tulsa, Tulsa, OK, 1998; J.D., Southern Methodist University, Dedman School of Law, Dallas, TX, 2001; professional: lawyer, private practice; opened a solo practice in 2002; political consultant; press secretary, U.S. Representative Brad Carson of Oklahoma, 2004–05; manager of government affairs and communications, Space Foundation; campaign manager for ''Joe Dorman for Oklahoma'' in 2014; nonprofit executive, Sally's List; co-founder, Women Lead Oklahoma, a nonpartisan, nonprofit that trains and supports women to encourage community and civic action; religion: Episcopalian; caucuses: co-chair, NASA Caucus; co-chair, Space Power Caucus; Blue Dog Coalition; Career and Technical Education Caucus; Freshman Working Group on Addiction; House Impact Aid Coalition; House Space Caucus; Library of Congress Caucus; Native American Caucus; New Democrat Coalition; Servicewomen and Women Veterans Caucus; Special Forces Operations Caucus; TRiO Caucus; Women's Caucus; committees: Armed Services, Science, Space, and Technology; elected to the 116th Congress on November 6, 2018 (to become the first Democratic congresswoman to represent Oklahoma).

Office Listings

https://horn.house.gov https://facebook.com/RepKendraHorn https://twitter.com/RepKendraHorn

415 Cannon House Office Building, Washington, DC 20515 .... (202) 225–2132
Chief of Staff.—Brady King. FAX: 226–1463
Deputy Chief of Staff.—Amanda McLain-Snipes.
Scheduler.—Kyle Dunn.
Legislative Director.—Rayshon Payton.
Communications Director.—Catherine Sweeney.
Director of Constituent Services.—Jay Williams.
400 North Walker Avenue, Suite 210, Oklahoma City, OK 73102 .... (405) 602–3074

Counties: OKLAHOMA (part), POTTAWATOMIE, AND SEMINOLE. CITIES: Arcadia, Asher, Aydelotte, Bethany, Bethel Acres, Bowlegs, Brooksville, Choctaw, Cromwell, Del City, Earlsboro, Edmond, Forest Park, Harrah, Johnson, Jones, Konawa, Lake Aluma, Lima, Luther, Macomb, Maud, McLoud, Midwest City, Newalla, Nichols Hills, Nicoma Park, Oklahoma City, Pink, Prague, Sasakwa, Seminole, Shawnee, Smith Village, Spencer, St. Louis, Tecumesh, The Village, Tribbey, Valley Brook, Wanette, Warr Acres, Wewoka, and Woodlawn Park. Population (2010), 750,271.

ZIP Codes: 73003, 73007–08, 73013, 73020, 73034, 73045, 73049, 73054, 73066, 73083–84, 73101–32, 73134–37, 73139, 73141–49, 73151–52, 73154–57, 73159–60, 73162, 73164, 73169, 73172–73, 73178–79, 73184–85, 73190, 73194–96, 73198, 74587, 74801–02, 74804, 74818, 74826, 74830, 74837, 74840, 74849, 74851–52, 74854, 74857, 74866–68, 74873, 74878, 74884

OREGON

(Population 2010, 3,831,074)

SENATORS

RON WYDEN, Democrat, of Portland, OR; born in Wichita, KS, May 3, 1949; education: graduated from Palo Alto High School, 1967; B.A. in political science, with distinction, Stanford University, 1971; J.D., University of Oregon Law School, 1974; professional: attorney; member, American Bar Association; former director, Oregon Legal Services for the Elderly; former public member, Oregon State Board of Examiners of Nursing Home Administrators; cofounder and codirector, Oregon Gray Panthers, 1974–80; married: Nancy Bass Wyden; children: Adam David, Lilly Anne, Ava Rose, William Peter, and Scarlett Willa; committees: ranking member, Finance; Budget; Energy and Natural Resources; Joint Committee on Taxation; Select Committee on Intelligence; elected to the 97th Congress, November 4, 1980; reelected to each succeeding Congress; elected to the U.S. Senate on February 6, 1996, to fill the unexpired term of Senator Bob Packwood; reelected to each succeeding Senate term.

Office Listings

https://wyden.senate.gov https://twitter.com/RonWyden

221 Dirksen Senate Office Building, Washington, DC 20510 .... (202) 224–5244
Chief of Staff.—Jeff Michels.
Legislative Director.—Isaiah Akin.
Director of Scheduling.—Montana Judd.
911 Northeast 11th Avenue, Suite 630, Portland, OR 97232 .... (503) 326–7525
405 East Eighth Avenue, Suite 2020, Eugene, OR 97401 .... (541) 431–0229
The Federal Courthouse, 310 West Sixth Street, Room 118, Medford, OR 97501 .... (541) 858–5122
The Jamison Building, 131 Northwest Hawthorne Avenue, Suite 107, Bend, OR 97701 ..... (541) 330–9142
SAC Annex Building, 105 Fir Street, Suite 201, La Grande, OR 97850 .... (541) 962–7691
707 Thirteenth Street, SE., Suite 285, Salem, OR 97310 .... (503) 589–4555

* * *

JEFF MERKLEY, Democrat, of Portland, OR; born in Myrtle Creek, OR, October 24, 1956; education: graduated from David Douglas High School; B.A., international relations, Stanford University, 1979; M.P.P., Woodrow Wilson School, Princeton University, 1982; professional: Presidential Fellow at the Office of the Secretary of Defense, 1982–85; Policy Analyst at the Congressional Budget Office, 1985–89; Executive Director of Portland Habitat for Humanity, 1991–94; Director of Housing Development at Human Solutions, 1995–96; President of World Affairs Council of Oregon, 1996–2003; elected to Oregon House of Representatives, 1999; Democratic Leader of the Oregon House of Representatives, 2003; elected Speaker of the Oregon House of Representatives, 2007; married: Mary Sorteberg; children: Brynne and Jonathan; committees: Appropriations; Budget; Environment and Public Works; Foreign Relations; elected to the U.S. Senate on November 4, 2008; reelected to the U.S. Senate on November 4, 2014.

Office Listings

https://merkley.senate.gov https://facebook.com/jeffmerkley twitter: @SenJeffMerkley

313 Hart Senate Office Building, Washington, DC 20510 .... (202) 224–3753
Chief of Staff.—Michael Zamore. FAX: 228–3997
Legislative Director.—Laura Updegrove.
Deputy Chief of Staff of Operations.—Jennifer Piorkowski.
Communications Director.—Ray Zaccaro.
One World Trade Center, 121 Southwest Salmon Street, Suite 1400, Portland, OR 97204 .. (503) 326–3386
Jamison Building, 131 Northwest Hawthorne Avenue, Suite 208, Bend, OR 97703 .... (541) 318–1298
Wayne Morse Federal Courthouse, 405 East 8th Avenue, Suite 2010, Eugene, OR 97401 .. (541) 465–6750
10 South Bartlett Street, Suite 201, Medford, OR 97501 .... (541) 608–9102
500 Liberty Street, SE., Suite 320, Salem, OR 97301 .... (503) 362–8102
310 Southeast Second Street, Suite 105, Pendleton, OR 97801 .... (541) 278–1129

REPRESENTATIVES

FIRST DISTRICT

SUZANNE MARIE BONAMICI, Democrat, of Beaverton, OR; born in Michigan, October 14, 1954; education: J.D., University of Oregon, Eugene, OR, 1983; B.A., journalism, University of Oregon, Eugene, 1980; A.A., Lane Community College, Eugene, 1978; professional: lawyer, Federal Trade Commission, Washington, DC; lawyer, private practice; staff, Oregon State House, 2001–06; served in the Oregon State House from 2007–08; served in the Oregon State Senate from 2008–11; married: husband, Michael Simon; children: son, Andrew Simon; daughter, Sara Simon; caucuses: co-founder and co-chair of the STEAM Caucus; co-chair of the Oceans Caucus; committees: Education and Labor; Science, Space, and Technology; Select Committee on the Climate Crisis; elected to the 112th Congress, by special election, on January 31, 2012; reelected to each succeeding Congress.

Office Listings

https://bonamici.house.gov https://facebook.com/CongresswomanBonamici
https://twitter.com/RepBonamici https://instagram.com/RepBonamici

2231 Rayburn House Office Building, Washington, DC 20515 .... (202) 225–0855
Chief of Staff.—Rachael Bornstein. FAX: 225–9497
Legislative Director.—Allison Smith.
Scheduler.—Ethan Rank.
Press Secretary.—Natalie Crofts.
12725 Southwest Millikan Way, Suite 220, Beaverton, OR 97005 .... (503) 469–6010
District Director.—Sarah Baessler. FAX: 469–6018
District Scheduler.—Joyce Fleming.

Counties: CLATSOP, COLUMBIA, MULTNOMAH (part), WASHINGTON, AND YAMHILL. Population (2010), 766,216.

ZIP Codes: 97005–08, 97016, 97018, 97048, 97051, 97053–54, 97056, 97064, 97103, 97106, 97109–11, 97113–17, 97119, 97121, 97123–25, 97127–28, 97133, 97138, 97144–46, 97148, 97208, 97223–24, 97229, 97231

* * *

SECOND DISTRICT

GREG WALDEN, Republican, of Hood River, OR; born in The Dalles, OR, January 10, 1957; education: B.S., journalism, University of Oregon, 1981; member: Associated Oregon Industries; Oregon Health Sciences Foundation; Hood River Rotary Club; Hood River Elk's Club; National Federation of Independent Business; Hood River Chamber of Commerce; Hood River Memorial Hospital; Columbia Bancorp; Oregon State House of Representatives, 1989–95, and Majority Leader, 1991–93; Assistant Majority Leader, Oregon State Senate, 1995–97; awards: Oregon Jaycees Outstanding Young Oregonian, 1991; National Republican Legislators Association Legislator of the Year, 1993; married: Mylene Walden; one child: Anthony David Walden; committees: ranking member, Energy and Commerce; elected to the 106th Congress on November 3, 1998; reelected to each succeeding Congress.

Office Listings

https://walden.house.gov https://facebook.com/repgregwalden https://twitter.com/repgregwalden

2185 Rayburn House Office Building, Washington, DC 20515 .... (202) 225–6730
Chief of Staff.—Lorissa Bounds. FAX: 225–5774
Scheduler.—Brooke Starr.
Communications Director.—Molly Jenkins.
14 North Central Avenue, Suite 112, Medford, OR 97504 .... (541) 776–4646
1211 Washington Avenue, La Grande, OR 97850 .... (541) 624–2400
FAX: 624–2402
1051 Northwest Bond Street, Suite 400, Bend, OR 97701 .... (541) 389–4408
FAX: 389–4452

Counties: BAKER, CROOK, DESCHUTES, GILLIAM, GRANT, HARNEY, HOOD RIVER, JACKSON, JEFFERSON, JOSEPHINE (part), KLAMATH, LAKE, MALHEUR, MORROW, SHERMAN, UMATILLA, UNION, WALLOWA, WASCO, AND WHEELER. Population (2010), 766,215.

ZIP Codes: 89421, 97001, 97014, 97021, 97029, 97031, 97033, 97037, 97039–41, 97050, 97057–58, 97063, 97065, 97497, 97501–04, 97520, 97522, 97524–27, 97530, 97535–37, 97539–41, 97601, 97603–04, 97620–27, 97630, 97632–41, 97701–02, 97707, 97710–12, 97720–22, 97730–39, 97741, 97750–56, 97758–61, 97801, 97810, 97812–14, 97817–20, 97823–28, 97830, 97833–46, 97848, 97850, 97856–57, 97859, 97862, 97864–65, 97867–70, 97873–77, 97880, 97882–86, 97901, 97903–11, 97913–14, 97918, 97920, 99362

* * *

THIRD DISTRICT

EARL BLUMENAUER, Democrat, of Portland, OR; born in Portland, August 16, 1948; education: graduated from Centennial High School; B.A., Lewis and Clark College; J.D., Northwestern School of Law; professional: assistant to the president, Portland State University; served in Oregon State Legislature, 1973–78; chaired Revenue and School Finance Committee; Multnomah County Commissioner, 1978–85; Portland City Commissioner, 1986–96; served on Governor's Commission on Higher Education; National League of Cities Transportation Committee; National Civic League Board of Directors; member of the board of directors, Portland Community College; married: Margaret Kirkpatrick; children: Jon and Anne; committees: Ways and Means; elected to the U.S. House of Representatives, by special election, on May 21, 1996, to fill the vacancy caused by Representative Ron Wyden's election to the U.S. Senate; reelected to each succeeding Congress.

Office Listings

https://blumenauer.house.gov

1111 Longworth House Office Building, Washington, DC 20515 .... (202) 225–4811
Chief of Staff.—Willie Smith. FAX: 225–8941
Deputy Chief of Staff / Legislative Director.—Laura Thrift.
Scheduler.—Kyle King.
Communications Director.—Sean Ryan.
911 Northeast 11th Avenue, Suite 200, Portland, OR 97232 .... (503) 231–2300
District Director.—Aisling Coghlan.

Counties: CLACKAMAS (part) AND MULTNOMAH (part). Population (2010), 766,215.

ZIP Codes: 97004, 97009, 97011, 97014–15, 97017, 97019, 97022–24, 97028, 97030, 97035, 97045, 97049, 97055, 97060, 97067, 97080, 97124, 97133, 97202–03, 97206, 97210–18, 97220, 97222, 97227, 97229–33, 97236, 97238, 97242, 97256, 97266–67, 97269, 97282–83, 97286, 97290, 97292–94, 97299

* * *

FOURTH DISTRICT

PETER A. DEFAZIO, Democrat, of Springfield, OR; born in Needham, MA, May 27, 1947; education: B.A., Tufts University, 1969; M.S., University of Oregon, 1977; professional: aide to Representative Jim Weaver, 1977–82; commissioner, Lane County, 1983–86; married: Myrnie Daut; committees: chair, Transportation and Infrastructure; elected to the 100th Congress, November 4, 1986; reelected to each succeeding Congress.

Office Listings

https://defazio.house.gov https://facebook.com/RepPeterDeFazio https://twitter.com/RepPeterDeFazio

2134 Rayburn House Office Building, Washington, DC 20515 .... (202) 225–6416
Chief of Staff.—Kristie Greco Johnson.
Legislative Director.—Kris Pratt.
Scheduler.—Matt Leasure.
405 East Eighth Avenue, Suite 2030, Eugene, OR 97401 .... (541) 465–6732
District Director.—Dan Whelan.
125 Central Avenue, Room 350, Coos Bay, OR 97420 .... (541) 269–2609
612 Southeast Jackson Street, Room 9, Roseburg, OR 97470 .... (541) 440–3523

Counties: BENTON (part), COOS, CURRY, DOUGLAS, JOSEPHINE (part), LANE, AND LINN. CITIES: Eugene, Roseburg, and Coos Bay. Population (2010), 766,214.

ZIP Codes: 97321–22, 97324, 97326–27, 97329–31, 97333, 97345–46, 97348, 97350, 97352, 97355, 97358, 97360–61, 97370, 97374, 97377, 97383, 97386, 97389–90, 97401–06, 97408, 97410–17, 97419–20, 97423–24, 97426, 97429–31, 97434–39, 97446–59, 97461–63, 97465–67, 97469–71, 97476–81, 97484, 97486–90, 97492–99, 97523, 97526–27, 97531–32, 97534, 97538, 97543–44, 97731, 97759

* * *

FIFTH DISTRICT

KURT SCHRADER, Democrat, of Canby, OR; born in Bridgeport, CT, October 19, 1951; education: B.A., Cornell University, 1973; D.V.M., University of Illinois, 1977; professional:

small business owner; veterinarian; farmer; past member: Oregon State Senate; Oregon House of Representatives; Canby Planning Commission; religion: Episcopalian; spouse: Susan Mora; children: Clare, Maren, Steven, Travis, R.J., Michael, Marie, and Renee; committees: Energy and Commerce; elected to the 111th Congress on November 4, 2008; reelected to each succeeding Congress.

Office Listings

https://schrader.house.gov https://facebook.com/repschrader twitter: @RepSchrader

2431 Rayburn House Office Building, Washington, DC 20515 .... (202) 225–5711
Chief of Staff.—Paul Gage. FAX: 225–5699
Deputy Chief of Staff.—Chris Huckleberry.
Executive Assistant / Scheduler.—Larkin Parker.
530 Center Street, NE., Suite 415, Salem, OR 97301 .... (503) 588–9100
621 High Street, Oregon City, OR 97045 .... (503) 557–1324
District Director.—Suzanne Kunse.

Counties: BENTON (part), CLACKAMAS (part), LINCOLN, MARION, MULTNOMAH (part), POLK, AND TILLAMOOK. CITIES: Lincoln City, Lake Oswego, Oregon City, Salem, and Tillamook. Population (2010), 766,214.

ZIP Codes: 97002, 97013, 97015, 97017, 97020, 97023, 97026–27, 97032, 97034–36, 97038, 97042, 97045, 97062, 97068, 97070–71, 97086, 97101, 97107–08, 97112, 97118, 97122, 97130–32, 97135–37, 97140–41, 97143, 97147, 97149, 97201–02, 97206, 97219, 97222, 97236, 97239, 97266–69, 97301–12, 97314, 97317, 97321, 97324–26, 97338, 97341–44, 97346–47, 97350–52, 97357–58, 97360–62, 97364–71, 97373, 97375–76, 97378, 97380–81, 97383–85, 97388, 97390–92, 97394, 97396, 97498

PENNSYLVANIA

(Population 2010, 12,702,379)

SENATORS

ROBERT P. CASEY, Jr., Democrat, of Scranton, PA; born in Scranton, April 13, 1960; education: A.B., English, College of the Holy Cross, 1982; J.D., Catholic University of America, 1988; professional: lawyer; Pennsylvania State Auditor General, 1997–2005; Pennsylvania State Treasurer, 2005–07; married: Terese; four daughters: Elyse, Caroline, Julia, and Marena; committees: ranking member, Special Committee on Aging; Agriculture, Nutrition, and Forestry; Finance; Health, Education, Labor, and Pensions; elected to the U.S. Senate on November 7, 2006; reelected to each succeeding Senate term.

Office Listings

https://casey.senate.gov https://facebook.com/SenatorBobCasey
https://twitter.com/SenBobCasey https://youtube.com/SenatorBobCasey

393 Russell Senate Office Building, Washington, DC 20510 .... (202) 224–6324
Chief of Staff.—Kristen Gentile. (866) 802–2833
Legislative Director.—Derek Miller. FAX: 228–0604
Communications Director.—John Rizzo.

200 North Third Street, Suite 14A, Harrisburg, PA 17101 .... (717) 231–7540
(866) 461–9159
FAX: 231–7542

2000 Market Street, Suite 610, Philadelphia, PA 19103 .... (215) 405–9660
FAX: 405–9669

Grant Building, 310 Grant Street, Suite 2415, Pittsburgh, PA 15219 .... (412) 803–7370
FAX: 803–7379

409 Lackawanna Avenue, Suite 303, Scranton, PA 18503 .... (570) 941–0930
FAX: 941–0937

817 East Bishop Street, Suite C, Bellefonte, PA 16823 .... (814) 357–0314
FAX: 357–0318

17 South Park Row, Suite B–150, Erie, PA 16501 .... (814) 874–5080
FAX: 874–5084

840 Hamilton Street, Suite 301, Allentown, PA 18101 .... (610) 782–9470
FAX: 782–9474

* * *

PAT TOOMEY, Republican, of Zionsville, PA; born in East Providence, RI, November 17, 1961; education: graduated as valedictorian from La Salle Academy in 1980; B.A., political science, *cum laude*, Harvard University, Cambridge, MA, 1984; professional: worked for Chemical Bank and Morgan Grenfell in New York City; has deep experience in the financial services sector, culminating with building a community bank from the ground up; founded several restaurants in Allentown, PA, with his two brothers, Steve and Michael Toomey, 1990–97; member of the Allentown Government Study Commission, 1994; elected to the U.S. House of Representatives in 1998, winning two reelections, 2000–02; president, Club for Growth, 2005; co-chairman of the Board of Directors of Team Capital Bank, 2005–09; married: Kris Duncan, 1997; children: Bridget, Patrick, and Duncan; committees: Banking, Housing, and Urban Affairs; Budget; Finance; elected to the U.S. Senate on November 2, 2010; reelected to the U.S. Senate on November 8, 2016.

Office Listings

https://toomey.senate.gov https://facebook.com/senatortoomey
https://twitter.com/SenToomey https://youtube.com/sentoomey

248 Russell Senate Office Building, Washington, DC 20510 .... (202) 224–4254
Chief of Staff.—Daniel Brandt. FAX: 228–0284
Legislative Director.—Brad Grantz.
Director of Operations.—Laurel Edmondson.
Communications Director.—Steve Kelly.

1150 South Cedar Crest Boulevard, Suite 101, Allentown, PA 18103 .... (610) 434–1444
(855) 552–1831
FAX: (202) 228–2727

Federal Building, 17 South Park Row, Suite B–120, Erie, PA 16501 .... (814) 453–3010
FAX: 455–9925

Strawberry Square, 320 Market Street, Suite 475E, Harrisburg, PA 17101 .... (717) 782–3951
FAX: 782–4920

Richland Square III, Suite 302, 1397 Eisenhower Boulevard, Johnstown, PA 15904 .... (814) 266–5970

FAX: 266–5973
U.S. Custom House, 200 Chestnut Street, Suite 600, Philadelphia, PA 19106 .... (215) 241–1090
FAX: (202) 224–4442
310 Grant Street, Suite 1440, Pittsburgh, PA 15219 .... (412) 803–3501
FAX: 803–3504
7 North Wilkes-Barre Boulevard, Suite 406, Wilkes-Barre, PA 18702 .... (570) 820–4088
FAX: 820–6442

REPRESENTATIVES

FIRST DISTRICT

BRIAN K. FITZPATRICK, Republican, of Middletown Township, PA; born in Philadelphia, December 17, 1973; education: B.S., LaSalle University, Philadelphia, PA, 1996; J.D., Pennsylvania State University Dickinson School of Law, 2001; M.B.A., Pennsylvania State University, 2001; professional: FBI Supervisory Special Agent; Special Assistant U.S. Attorney; certified public accountant; emergency medical technician; religion: Roman Catholic; caucuses: Animal Protection Caucus; Bipartisan Heroin Task Force; Climate Solutions Caucus; Congressional Citizen Legislature Caucus; Problem Solvers Caucus; committees: Foreign Affairs; Transportation and Infrastructure; elected to represent the 8th District in the 115th Congress on November 8, 2016; elected to represent the 1st District in the 116th Congress on November 6, 2018.

Office Listings

https://fitzpatrick.house.gov https://facebook.com/RepBrianFitzpatrick twitter: @RepBrianFitz

1722 Longworth House Office Building, Washington, DC 20515 .... (202) 225–4276
Chief of Staff.—Joseph Knowles. FAX: 225–9511
1717 Langhorne Newtown Road, Suite 400, Langhorne, PA 19047 .... (215) 579–8102
District Director.—Sue Simon. FAX: 579–8109

Counties: BUCKS (all) AND MONTGOMERY (part). CITIES AND TOWNSHIPS: Franconia Township, Horsham Township, Montgomery Township, and the BOROUGHS of Hatfield, Lansdale, Souderton and Telford. Population (2010), 705,688.

ZIP Codes: 18036 (part), 18041 (part), 18054–55 (part), 18073 (part), 18077 (part), 18081, 18901–02, 18912–15, 18917, 18920, 18923, 18925, 18929–30, 18932, 18935–36, 18938, 18940, 18942, 18944, 18947, 18950 (part), 18954–55, 18960, 18962, 18964 (part), 18966, 18969 (part), 18970, 18972, 18974, 18976–77, 18980, 19002 (part), 19006 (part), 19007, 19020–21, 19030, 19040 (part), 19044 (part), 19047, 19053–57, 19067, 19440 (part), 19446 (part), 19454 (part)

* * *

SECOND DISTRICT

BRENDAN F. BOYLE, Democrat, of Philadelphia, PA; born in the Olney section of Philadelphia, PA, February 6, 1977; education: graduated from the Cardinal Dougherty High School in Philadelphia, PA, 1995; B.A., University of Notre Dame, South Bend, IN, 1999; M.P.P., John F. Kennedy School of Government, Harvard University, Cambridge, MA, 2005; professional: Representative, Pennsylvania House of Representatives, 170th District, 2009–15; married: Jennifer Boyle; children: Abigail; committees: Budget; Ways and Means; elected to represent the 13th District in the 114th Congress on November 4, 2014 and reelected to the 115th Congress on November 8, 2016; elected to represent the 2nd District in the 116th Congress on November 6, 2018.

Office Listings

https://boyle.house.gov https://facebook.com/CongressmanBoyle twitter: @CongBoyle

1133 Longworth House Office Building, Washington, DC 20515 .... (202) 225–6111
Chief of Staff.—John McCarthy. FAX: 226–0611
Legislative Director.—Vacant.
Communications Director.—Sean Tobin.
District Director.—Scott Heppard.
8572 Bustleton Avenue, Philadelphia, PA 19152 .... (215) 335–3355
2630 Memphis Street, Philadelphia, PA 19125 .... (215) 426–4616
5675 North Front Street, Suite 180, Philadelphia, PA 19120 .... (267) 335–5643

County: PHILADELPHIA (part). CITY: Philadelphia (part). Population (2010), 705,688.

ZIP Codes: 19106 (part), 19111, 19114–16, 19120, 19122, 19123 (part), 19124–25, 19126 (part), 19132 (part), 19133–37, 19140–41 (part), 19149, 19152, 19154

* * *

THIRD DISTRICT

DWIGHT EVANS, Democrat, of Philadelphia, PA; born in Philadelphia, May 16, 1954; education: graduate of the Community College of Philadelphia; B.A., La Salle University, Philadelphia, PA, 1975; professional: Pennsylvania House of Representatives, representing 203rd District, Philadelphia County; elected Democratic Chairman of House Appropriations Committee in 1990 and served in this role until November 2010; caucuses: Congressional Black Caucus; Congressional Progressive Caucus; LGBT Equality Caucus; committees: vice chair, Small Business; Ways and Means; elected simultaneously to represent the 2nd District in the 114th and the 115th Congresses, by special election, on November 8, 2016 to fill the vacancy caused by the resignation of United States Representative Chaka Fattah; elected to represent the 3rd District on November 6, 2018.

Office Listings

https://evans.house.gov https://facebook.com/RepDwightEvans twitter: @RepDwightEvans

1105 Longworth House Office Building, Washington, DC 20515 .... (202) 225–4001
Chief of Staff.—Kimberly Turner-Dixon. FAX: 225–5392
Legislative Director.—Jayme Holliday.
Communications Director.—Ben Turner.
7174 Ogontz Avenue, Philadelphia, PA 19138 .... (215) 276–0340

County: PHILADELPHIA (part). CITY: Philadelphia (part). Population (2010), 705,688.

ZIP Codes: 19102–04, 19106 (part), 19107, 19109, 19118 (part), 19119, 19121, 19123 (part), 19126 (part), 19127–31, 19132 (part), 19138–39, 19140–41 (part), 19143 (part), 19144, 19145 (part), 19146–47, 19148 (part), 19150 (part), 19151

* * *

FOURTH DISTRICT

MADELEINE DEAN, Democrat, of Jenkintown, PA; born June 6, 1959; education: Abington High School, 1977; B.A., La Salle University, 1981; J.D., Widener University School of Law, 1984; professional: associate, A. Harold Datz P.C., 1984; in-house counsel, Cunnane Bicycle Company; co-founder, general law practice, Dean, Homicki & DeVita; assistant professor, English, La Salle University, 2001–12; op-ed writer, The Philadelphia Daily News, The Philadelphia Inquirer, 2012–18; elected, commissioner, Abington Township, Ward 7, 2011; Member, Pennsylvania House of Representatives, 2012–18; appointed, Pennsylvania Commission on Women, 2015–present; committees: Financial Services; Judiciary; elected to the 116th Congress on November 6, 2018.

Office Listings

https://dean.house.gov https://facebook.com/RepMadeleineDean https://twitter.com/RepDean

129 Cannon House Office Building, Washington, DC 20515 .... (202) 225–4731
Chief of Staff.—Koh Chiba.
Legislative Director.—Colleen Carlos.
Director of Operations.—Yodit Tewelde.
Communications Director.—Tim Mack.
Legislative Assistants: Damiyal Ahmed, Chris McCann.
Legislative Correspondent.—Rina Patel.
Staff Assistant.—Megan Ruane.
115 East Glenside Avenue, Suite 1, Glenside, PA 19038 .... (215) 884–4300
District Director.—Kathleen Joyce. FAX: 884–3640
District Scheduler and Events Coordinator.—Meghan Janoson.
Veteran and Military Affairs Representative.—Dave Corrigan.
Casework Manager.—Michael Tucker.
Staff Assistant.—Emanuel Wilkerson.
101 East Main Street, Suite A, Norristown, PA 19401 .... (610) 382–1250
Caseworkers: Shae Ashe, Valerie Cooper. FAX: 275–1759

Counties: BERKS (part). TOWNSHIPS: Colebrookdale (part), Douglass, and Washington. BOROUGHS: Bally, Bechtelsville, and Boyertown. MONTGOMERY (part). TOWNSHIPS: Abington, Cheltenham, Douglass, East Norriton, Franconia (part), Horsham (part), Limerick, Lower Frederick, Lower Gwynedd, Lower Merion (part), Lower Moreland, Lower Pottsgrove, Lower Providence, Lower Salford, Marlborough, New Hanover, Perkiomen, Plymouth, Salford, Sippack, Springfield, Towamencin, Upper Dublin, Upper Frederick; Upper Gwynedd, Upper Hanover, Upper Merion, Upper Moreland, Upper

Pottsgrove, Upper Providence, Upper Salford, West Norriton, West Pottsgrove, Whitemarsh, Whitpain, and Worcester. BOROUGHS: Ambler, Bridgeport, Bryn Athyn, Collegeville, Conshohocken, East Greenville, Green Lane, Hatboro, Jenkintown, Narberth, Norristown, North Wales, Pennsburg, Pottstown, Red Hill, Rockledge, Royersford, Schwenksville, Trappe, and West Conshohocken. Population (2010), 705,687.

ZIP Codes: 18041 (part), 18054 (part), 18070 (part), 18073 (part), 18074, 18076, 18964 (part), 18969 (part), 19001, 19002 (part), 19004, 19006 (part), 19009, 19010 (part), 19012, 19025, 19027, 19031, 19034, 19035 (part), 19038, 19040 (part), 19044 (part), 19046, 19066 (part), 19072, 19075, 19085 (part), 19087 (part), 19090, 19095, 19096 (part), 19118 (part), 19150 (part), 19401, 19403, 19405–06, 19422, 19426, 19428, 19435–38, 19440 (part), 19444, 19446, 19453, 19454 (part), 19456, 19460 (part), 19462, 19464, 19468, 19472–74, 19477, 19492, 19503–05 (part), 19512 (part), 19518 (part), 19525, 19545

* * *

FIFTH DISTRICT

MARY GAY SCANLON, Democrat, of Swarthmore, PA; born August 30, 1959 in Watertown, NY; education: B.A., Colgate University, Hamilton, NY, 1980; J.D., University of Pennsylvania Law School, Philadelphia, PA, 1984; professional: attorney, Education Law Center, Philadelphia, PA; pro bono counsel, Ballard Spahr, LLP, Philadelphia, PA; appointed vice chair of Wallingford-Swarthmore Tax Commission, 2006–07; elected member, Wallingford-Swarthmore School Board (2009–11, President), 2007–15; family: husband Mark Stewart; three children: Casey, Daniel, and Matthew; committees: vice chair, Judiciary; Rules; Select Committee on the Modernization of Congress; elected simultaneously, by special election, on November 6, 2018 to represent the Seventh District in the 115th and the Fifth District in the 116th Congresses to fill the vacancy caused by the resignation of U.S. Representative Patrick Meehan.

Office Listings

https://scanlon.house.gov https://facebook.com/RepMGS twitter: @RepMGS

1535 Longworth House Office Building, Washington, DC 20515 .... (202) 225–2011
Chief of Staff.—Roddy Flynn. FAX: 226–0280
Legislative Director.—Armita Pedramrazi.
Scheduler.—Faith Wilcox.
Communications Director.—Gabby Richards.
927 East Baltimore Avenue, East Lansdowne, PA 19050 .... (610) 626–2020
District Director.—Heather Boyd.

Counties: CHESTER (part). TOWNSHIP: Birmingham (part). DELAWARE AND MONTGOMERY (part). TOWNSHIP: Lower Merion (part). PHILADELPHIA (part). CITY: Philadelphia (part). Population (2010), 705,688.

ZIP Codes: 19003, 19008, 19010 (part), 19013–15, 19017–18, 19022–23, 19026, 19029, 19032–33, 19035–36, 19041, 19043, 19050, 19060–61, 19063–64, 19066 (part), 19070, 19073 (part), 19074, 19076, 19078–79, 19081–83, 19085 (part), 19086, 19087 (part), 19094, 19096 (part), 19112–13, 19142, 19143 (part), 19145 (part), 19148 (part), 19153, 19312, 19317 (part), 19319 (part), 19342 (part), 19373, 19382 (part)

* * *

SIXTH DISTRICT

CHRISSY HOULAHAN, Democrat, of Devon, PA; born in Patuxent River, MD, June 5, 1967; education: B.S., industrial engineering, U.S. Air Force ROTC scholarship, Stanford University, Stanford, CA, 1989; M.S., technology and policy, Massachusetts Institute of Technology, Cambridge, MA, 1994; professional: research assistant, Massachusetts Institute of Technology, Cambridge, MA, 1992–94; AND1 footwear and clothing company, Director of Distribution and Information Systems, 1996–2000, Chief Operating Officer, 2000–05, Vice President of Retail, 2004–05; Founder and Chief Operating Officer, B-Lab non-profit, 2008–11; chemistry teacher, Teach for America Program, Simon Gratz High School, Philadelphia, PA, 2011–12; President and Chief Financial Officer/Chief Operating Officer, Springboard Collaborative, non-profit, Philadelphia, PA, 2012–16; military: active duty, project manager, air and space defense technologies, Hanscom Air Force Base, Bedford, MA, 1989–92; U.S. Air Force Reserve, 1992–2006; family: husband, Bart; children: two adult daughters, Molly and Carly; caucuses: Congressional LGBT Equality Caucus; For Country; Freshman Working Group on Addiction; Gun Violence Prevention Task Force; New Democrats; Servicewomen and Women Veterans; Sustainable Energy & Environment Coalition; committees: Armed Services, Foreign Affairs, Small Business; elected to the 116th Congress on November 6, 2018.

Office Listings

https://houlahan.house.gov https://facebook.com/RepChrissyHoulahan twitter: @RepHoulahan

1218 Longworth House Office Building, Washington, DC 20515 .... (202) 225–4315

Office Listings—Continued

Chief of Staff.—Michelle Dorothy.
Legislative Director.—Caitlin Frazer.
Communications Director.—Connor Lounsbury.
709 East Gay Street, Suite 4, West Chester, PA 19380 .... (610) 883–5050
815 Washington Street, Reading, PA 19601 .... (610) 295–0815

Counties: BERKS (part). CITY: Reading. TOWNSHIPS: Adamstown, Brecknock, Caernarvon, Cumru, Exeter (part), Lower Alsace, Robeson, Spring, and Union. BOROUGHS: Birdsboro, Kenhorst, Mohnton, Mount Penn, New Morgan, Shillington, Sinking Spring, St. Lawrence, West Reading, and Wyomissing. CHESTER (part). CITY: Coatesville. TOWNSHIPS: Birmingham (part), Britain, Caln, Charlestown, East Bradford, East Brandywine, East Caln, East Coventry, East Fallowfield, East Goshen, East Marlborough, East Nantmeal, East Nottingham, East Pikeland, East Vincent, East Whiteland, Easttown, Elk, Franklin, Highland, Honey Brook, Kennett, London, London Grove, Londonderry, Lower Oxford, New Garden, New London, Newlin, North Coventry, Penn, Pennsbury, Pocopson, Sadsbury, Schuylkill, South Coventry, Thornbury, Tredyffrin, Upper Oxford, Upper Uwchlan, Valley, Wallace, Warwick, West Bradford, West Brandywine, West Caln, West Fallowfield, West Goshen, West Marlborough, West Nantmeal, West Nottingham, West Pikeland, West Sadsbury, West Vincent, West Whiteland, Westtown, and Willistown. BOROUGHS: Atglen, Avondale, Downingtown, Elverson, Honey Brook, Kennett Square, Malvern, Modena, Oxford, Parkesburg, Phoenixville, South Coatesville, Spring City, West Chester, and West Grove. Population (2010), 720,487.

ZIP Codes: 17527 (part), 17555 (part), 17569 (part), 19073 (part), 19087 (part), 19301, 19310 (part), 19311, 19312 (part), 19316, 19317 (part), 19319 (part), 19320, 19330, 19333 (part), 19335, 19341, 19342 (part), 19343, 19344 (part), 19345, 19348, 19350, 19352, 19355, 19358, 19362–63 (part), 19365, 19367, 19372, 19374–75, 19380, 19382 (part), 19383, 19390, 19425, 19442, 19457, 19460 (part), 19465, 19475, 19508 (part), 19518 (part), 19520, 19523, 19540 (part), 19543 (part), 19601 (part), 19602, 19604–06 (part), 19607, 19608 (part), 19609–11

* * *

SEVENTH DISTRICT

SUSAN WILD, Democrat, of Allentown, PA; born June 7, 1957 in Wiesbaden, Germany; education: B.A., political science/psychology, American University, Washington, DC, 1978; J.D., George Washington University, Washington, DC, 1982; professional: partner, Post and Schell, P.C., 1988–99; partner, Gross, McGinley, LLP; Appointed Solicitor, Allentown, PA, 2015–17; family: two children, Clay and Addie; committees: Education and Labor; Ethics; Foreign Affairs; elected simultaneously to the 115th and the 116th Congresses, by special election, on November 6, 2018, to fill the vacancy caused by the resignation of U.S. Representative Charles W. Dent.

Office Listings

https://wild.house.gov https://facebook.com/repsusanwild https://twitter.com/RepSusanWild

1607 Longworth House Office Building, Washington, DC 20515 .... (202) 225–6411
Chief of Staff.—Jed Ober.
840 Hamilton Street, Suite 303, Allentown PA 18101 .... (484) 781–6000
District Chief of Staff.—Megan Beste. FAX: (877) 347–4103
637 Main Street, Suite 316, Stroudsburg, PA 18360 .... (570) 807–0333
400 Northampton Street, Suite 503, Easton, PA .... (610) 333–1170
FAX: (877) 561–7520

Counties: LEHIGH (all) AND MONROE (part). TOWNSHIPS: Eldred, Hamilton, Ross, Smithfield (part), and Stroud. BOROUGHS: Delaware Water Gap, East Stroudsburg, and Stroudsburg. NORTHAMPTON (all). Population (2010), 705,688.

ZIP Codes: 18011 (part), 18013–18, 18020, 18031 (part), 18032, 18034–35, 18036 (part), 18037–38, 18040, 18041 (part), 18042, 18045–46, 18049, 18051–53, 18055 (part), 18058 (part), 18059, 18062 (part), 18063–64, 18066–69, 18071 (part), 18072, 18077 (part), 18078–80, 18083, 18085–88, 18091, 18092 (part), 18101–06, 18109, 18195, 18301–02 (part), 18321 (part), 18327, 18343, 18351, 18353–54 (part), 18356, 18360 (part), 18951 (part), 19529–30 (part), 19539 (part)

* * *

EIGHTH DISTRICT

MATT CARTWRIGHT, Democrat, of Moosic, PA; born in Erie, PA, May 1, 1961; education: B.A., history, Hamilton College, Clinton, NY, 1983; J.D., University of Pennsylvania, Philadelphia, PA, 1986; professional: attorney, Munley, Munley and Cartwright, 1987–2012; religion: Roman Catholic; family: wife, Marion; two sons, Jack and Matt; caucuses: Academic Medicine Caucus; Ad-Hoc Committee for Irish Affairs; Admadiyya Muslim Caucus; Adult Literacy Caucus; Aluminum Caucus; Appalachian National Scenic Trail Caucus; Animal Protection Caucus; Autism Caucus; Baseball Caucus; Battlefield Caucus; Bike Caucus; Bipartisan Climate

Solutions Caucus; Bipartisan Congressional Watchdog Caucus; Bipartisan Disaster Relief Caucus; Bipartisan Peace Corps Caucus; Bipartisan Taskforce for Combating Anti-Semitism; Blue Collar Caucus; Brain Injury Task Force; Cement Caucus; Chesapeake Bay Watershed Caucus; Childhood Cancer Caucus; Clean Water Caucus; Coal Caucus; Cybersecurity Caucus; Cystic Fibrosis Caucus; Defense Communities Caucus; Democratic Caucus; Diabetes Caucus; Energy Savings Performance Caucus; Financial and Economic Literacy Caucus; Fire Services Caucus; Foster Youth Caucus; Free File Caucus; Friends of Ireland Caucus; Friends of Thailand Caucus; Full Employment Caucus; General Aviation Caucus; German-American Caucus; Hazards Caucus; Hearing Health Caucus; Historic Preservation Caucus; History Caucus; House Manufacturing Caucus; House Renewable Energy and Energy Efficiency Caucus; International Conservation Caucus; Iran Human Rights and Democracy Caucus; Kidney Caucus; LGBT Equality Caucus; Maker Caucus; Men's Health Caucus; Military Depot Caucus; Military Families Caucus; Military Mental Health Caucus; Military Sexual Assault Prevention Caucus; Military Veterans; Motorsports Caucus; National Parks Caucus; NASA Caucus; Nursing Caucus; Organ and Tissue Donation Awareness Caucus; P3 Caucus; Parkinson's Disease Caucus; Philanthropy Caucus; Pilots Caucus; Planetary Science Caucus; Poland Caucus; Pollinator Protection Caucus; Prescription Drug Abuse Caucus; Progressive Caucus; Public Broadcasting Caucus; Public Service Caucus; Public Transportation Caucus; Recycling Caucus; Safe Climate Caucus; Savings and Ownership Caucus; School Health & Safety Caucus; Seniors Task Force; Scouting Caucus; Ski and Snowboard Caucus; Skin Cancer Caucus; Small Brewers Caucus; Small Business Caucus; Soils Caucus; STEAM Caucus; Steel Caucus; Structured Settlements Caucus; Submarine Caucus; Sustainable Energy and Environment Coalition (SEEC); Taiwan Caucus; Travel and Tourism Caucus; Ukrainian Caucus; USO Caucus; Veterans Job Caucus; Veterinary Medicine Caucus; Whip's Task Force on Poverty and Opportunity; Wildlife Refuge Caucus; Writers Caucus; committees: Appropriations; Natural Resources; elected to represent the 17th District in the 113th Congress on November 7, 2012; reelected to each succeeding Congress; elected to represent the 8th District in the 116th Congress on November 6, 2018.

Office Listings

https://cartwright.house.gov https://facebook.com/CongressmanMattCartwright
https://twitter.com/RepCartwright

1034 Longworth House Office Building, Washington, DC 20515	(202) 225–5546
Chief of Staff.—Hunter Ridgway.	FAX: 226–0996
Deputy Chief of Staff.—Jeremy Marcus.	
Legislative Director.—Stephen Coffey.	
Scheduler.—Kaylee Robinson.	
226 Wyoming Avenue, Scranton, PA 18503	(570) 341–1050
	FAX: 341–1055
20 North Pennsylvania Avenue, Suite 213, Wilkes-Barre, PA 18711	(570) 371–0317
1 South Church Street, Suite 100, Hazleton, PA 18201	(570) 751–0050
2959 Route 611, Suite 105, Tannersville, PA 18372	(570) 355–1818
8 Silk Mill Drive, Suite 213, Hawley, PA 18428	(570) 576–8005

Counties: LACKAWANNA AND LUZERNE (part). CITIES: Hazleton, Nanticoke, Pittston, and Wilkes-Barre. TOWNSHIPS: Bear Creek, Buck, Butler, Dallas, Dennison, Exeter, Fairview, Foster, Franklin, Hanover, Hazle (part), Jackson, Jenkins, Kingston, Pittston, Plains, Plymouth, Rice, Wilkes-Barre, and Wright. BOROUGHS: Ashley, Avoca, Bear Creek Village, Courtdale, Dupont, Duryea, Edwardsville, Exeter, Forty Fort, Freeland, Hughestown, Jeddo, Kingston, Laflin, Larksville, Laurel Run, Luzerne, Nuangola, Penn Lake Park, Plymouth, Pringle, Sugar Notch, Swoyersville, Warrior Run, West Hazleton, West Pittston, West Wyoming, White Haven, Wyoming, and Yatesville. MONROE (part). TOWNSHIPS: Barrett, Chestnuthill, Coolbaugh, Jackson, Middle Smithfield, Paradise, Pocono, Polk, Price, Smithfield (part), Tobyhanna, and Tunkhannock. BOROUGH: Mount Pocono. PIKE AND WAYNE. Population (2010), 705,687.

ZIP Codes: 18058 (part), 18071 (part), 18201–02 (part), 18210 (part), 18216 (part), 18221, 18222 (part), 18223–25, 18234, 18239, 18247, 18249 (part), 18255 (part), 18301–02 (part), 18321 (part), 18322–26, 18328, 18330–32, 18333 (part), 18334, 18336–37, 18340, 18342, 18344, 18346–50, 18352, 18353–54 (part), 18355, 18357, 18360 (part), 18370–72, 18403, 18405, 18407 (part), 18410–11, 18414 (part), 18415–17, 18419 (part), 18420, 18421 (part), 18424 (part), 18425–28, 18430 (part), 18431, 18433–40, 18443–45, 18446 (part), 18447–49, 18451–61, 18462 (part), 18463–64, 18465 (part), 18466, 18469, 18470 (part), 18471–73, 18501–05, 18507–10, 18512, 18515, 18517–19, 18602, 18610, 18612 (part), 18615 (part), 18618 (part), 18621 (part), 18626–27 (part), 18634 (part), 18640–44, 18651, 18653, 18661 (part), 18701–06, 18707–08 (part), 18709–11, 18762, 18764–67, 18769, 18773, 18847 (part)

* * *

NINTH DISTRICT

DAN MEUSER, Republican, of Dallas, PA; born in Flushing, New York, NY, February 10, 1964; education: attended Maritime College, New York, NY, majored in maritime transportation/business, 1982–83; B.A., economics/government studies, on U.S. Navy ROTC scholarship, Cornell University, 1986; professional: 20 years of experience at Pride Mobility Products, Exeter, PA, Regional Manager, 1988–89, National Sales Manager, 1989–92, Vice

President of Sales, 1992–95, Senior Vice President, Sales and Marketing, 1995–2001, and President, 2001–08; Pennsylvania State Secretary, Revenue Department, Harrisburg, PA, 2011–15; committees: Budget; Education and Labor; Veterans' Affairs; elected to the 116th Congress on November 6, 2018.

Office Listings

https://meuser.house.gov

326 Cannon House Office Building, Washington, DC 20515 .... (202) 225–6511
Chief of Staff.—Patrick Rooney.
Legislative Director.—Eli Woerpel.
1044 East Main Street, Palmyra, PA 17078 .... (717) 473–5375
121 Progress Avenue, Suite 110, Losch Plaza, Pottsville, PA 17901 .... (570) 871–6370
Reading Regional Airport, 2501 Bernville Road, Reading, PA 19605 .... (610) 568–9959

Counties: BERKS (part). TOWNSHIPS: Albany, Alsace, Amity, Bern, Bethel, Centre, District (part), Earl, Exeter (part), Greenwich, Heidelberg, Hereford, Jefferson, Longswamp, Lower Heidelberg, Maidencreek, Marion, Maxatawny, Muhlenberg, North Heidelberg, Oley, Ontelaunee, Penn, Perry, Pike, Richmond, Rockland, Ruscombmanor, South Heidelberg, Tilden, Tulpehocken, Upper Bern, Upper Tulpehocken, and Windsor. BOROUGHS: Bernville, Centerport, Fleetwood, Hamburg, Kutztown, Laureldale, Leesport, Lenhartsville, Lyons, Robesonia, Shoemakersville, Strausstown, Topton, Wernersville, and Womelsdorf. CARBON (all), COLUMBIA (all), LEBANON (all), AND LUZERNE (part). TOWNSHIPS: Black Creek, Conyngham, Dorrance, Fairmount, Hazle (part), Hollenback, Hunlock, Huntington, Lake, Lehman, Nescopeck, Newport, Ross, Salem, Slocum, Sugarloaf, and Union. BOROUGHS: Conyngham, Dallas, Harveys Lake, Nescopeck, New Columbus, and Shickshinny. MONTOUR (all) AND NORTHUMBERLAND (part). CITY: Shamokin. TOWNSHIPS: Coal, East Cameron, Mount Carmel, Ralpho, and Upper Mahanoy (part). BOROUGHS: Kulpmont, Marion Heights, and Mount Carmel. SCHUYLKILL (all). Population, 705,687.

ZIP Codes: 17003, 17010, 17016, 17026, 17028 (part), 17033 (part), 17038–39, 17041–42, 17046, 17064, 17067, 17073 (part), 17077, 17078 (part), 17083, 17087–88, 17545 (part), 17569 (part), 17756 (part), 17772 (part), 17774 (part), 17777 (part), 17814 (part), 17815, 17820, 17821 (part), 17822, 17824, 17832, 17834, 17836 (part), 17840, 17846–47 (part), 17851, 17859, 17860 (part), 17866, 17872 (part), 17878, 17884, 17888, 17901, 17920–23, 17925, 17929–31, 17933–36, 17938, 17941 (part), 17943–46, 17948–49, 17951–54, 17957, 17959–61, 17963, 17964 (part), 17965, 17967–68, 17970, 17972, 17974, 17976, 17978–79, 17980 (part), 17981–83, 17985, 18011 (part), 18030, 18031 (part), 18041 (part), 18056, 18058 (part), 18062 (part), 18070–71 (part), 18092 (part), 18201–02 (part), 18210 (part), 18211–12, 18214, 18216 (part), 18220, 18222 (part), 18229–32, 18235, 18237, 18240–42, 18244 (part), 18245–46, 18248, 18249 (part), 18250–52, 18254, 18255 (part), 18256, 18603, 18610 (part), 18612 (part), 18617, 18618 (part), 18621 (part), 18622, 18624, 18631, 18634 (part), 18635, 18636 (part), 18655–56, 18660, 18661 (part), 18707–08 (part), 19503–05 (part), 19506–07, 19508 (part), 19510–11, 19512 (part), 19518 (part), 19519, 19522, 19526, 19529–30 (part), 19533–36, 19538, 19539 (part), 19541–42, 19544, 19547, 19549–50, 19551 (part), 19554–55, 19559–60, 19562, 19564–65, 19567, 19601 (part), 19604–06 (part), 19608 (part)

* * *

TENTH DISTRICT

SCOTT PERRY, Republican, of York County, PA; born in San Diego, CA, May 27, 1962; education: Northern York High School, 1980; B.S., business administration management, Pennsylvania State University, 1991; M.S. in strategic studies, United States Army War College, 2012; professional: small business owner, Hydrotech Mechanical Services; military: Brigadier General (Ret.), Pennsylvania Army National Guard; organizations: former president of Pennsylvania Young Republicans; former regional director for Pennsylvania Chapter of Jaycees; Dillsburg Legion Post #2; Dillsburg VFW Post #6771; public service: Pennsylvania House of Representatives, 2006–12; married: Christy; children: two daughters; committees: Foreign Affairs; Transportation and Infrastructure; elected to represent the 4th District in the 113th Congress on November 6, 2012; reelected to the two succeeding Congresses; elected on November 6, 2018 to represent the 10th District in the 116th Congress.

Office Listings

https://perry.house.gov https://facebook.com/repscottperry twitter: @RepScottPerry

1207 Longworth House Office Building, Washington, DC 20515 .... (202) 225–5836
Chief of Staff.—Lauren Muglia. FAX: 226–1000
Legislative Director.—Jared Culver.
Communications Director.—Brandy Brown.
Legislative Assistants: Laura Detter, Patrick Schilling.
Legislative Correspondent.—Christopher Fernandez.
Staff Assistant.—Mike Maiale.
800 Corporate Circle, Suite 202, Harrisburg, PA 17110 .... (717) 603–4980
District Director.—Jay Ostrich.
Director of Constituent Services.—Tyra Wallace.
Scheduler.—Carol Wiest.
Constituent Service Representative.—Jodi Marsico.
2501 Catherine Street, Suite 11, York, PA 17408 .... (717) 893–7868
Constituent Service Representative.—Donna Austin.
730 North Front Street, Wormleysburg, PA 17043 .... (717) 635–9504

Office Listings—Continued

Field Representative.—Holly Sutphin.
Staff Assistant.—Ceason Stroud.

Counties: CUMBERLAND (part). TOWNSHIPS: East Pennsboro, Hampden, Lower Allen, Middlesex, Monroe, North Middleton (part), Silver Spring, South Middleton, and Upper Allen. BOROUGHS: Camp Hill, Carlisle, Lemoyne, Mechanicsburg, Mount Holly Springs, New Cumberland, Shiremanstown, and Wormleysburg. DAUPHIN AND YORK (part). CITIES: York. TOWNSHIPS: Carroll, Conewago, Dover, East Manchester, Fairview, Franklin, Manchester, Monaghan, Newberry, Spring Garden, Springettsbury, Warrington, Washington, West Manchester, and York (part). BOROUGHS: Dillsburg, Dover, Franklintown, Goldsboro, Lewisberry, Manchester, Mount Wolf, North York, Wellsville, West York, Yoe, and York Haven. Population (2010), 705,687.

ZIP Codes: 17005, 17007, 17011, 17013 (part), 17015 (part), 17017 (part), 17018, 17019–20 (part), 17022 (part), 17023, 17025, 17027, 17028 (part), 17030, 17032, 17033 (part), 17034, 17036, 17043, 17048, 17050, 17053 (part), 17055, 17057, 17061, 17065 (part), 17070, 17072, 17078 (part), 17080, 17093, 17097–98, 17101–04, 17109–13, 17120, 17313 (part), 17315–16 (part), 17318–19, 17324 (part), 17339, 17345, 17347 (part), 17356 (part), 17364 (part), 17365, 17370, 17372 (part), 17401, 17402–03 (part), 17404, 17406 (part), 17408 (part), 17980 (part)

* * *

ELEVENTH DISTRICT

LLOYD SMUCKER, Republican, of West Lampeter Township, PA; born in Lancaster, January 23, 1964; education: Lancaster Mennonite High School, Lancaster, 1981; attended Franklin & Marshall College, Lancaster; professional: small business owner, Smucker Company; religion: Lutheran; family: wife Cindy; children: Paige, Regan, and Nicholas; caucuses: Problem Solvers Caucus; Republican Policy Committee; Republican Study Committee; committees: Education and Labor; Transportation and Infrastructure; elected to the 115th Congress on November 8, 2016; reelected to the 116th Congress on November 6, 2018.

Office Listings

https://smucker.house.gov https://facebook.com/RepSmucker https://twitter.com/RepSmucker

127 Cannon House Office Building, Washington, DC 20515 .... (202) 225–2411
Chief of Staff.—Greg Facchiano. FAX: 225–2013
Deputy Chief of Staff/Legislative Director.—Andrew Robreno.
Administrative Director.—Elizabeth Butler.
51 South Duke Street, Suite 201, Lancaster, PA 17602 .... (717) 393–0667
118 Carlisle Street, Hanover, PA 17331 .... (717) 969–6132
100 Redco Avenue, Red Lion, PA 17356 .... (717) 969–6133

Counties: LANCASTER (all) AND YORK (part). TOWNSHIPS: Chanceford, Codorus, East Hopewell, Fawn, Heidelberg, Hellam, Hopewell, Jackson, Lower Chanceford, Lower Windsor, Manheim, North Codorus, North Hopewell, Paradise, Peach Bottom, Penn, Shrewsbury, Springfield, West Manheim, Windsor, and York (part). BOROUGHS: Cross Roads, Dallastown, Delta, East Prospect, Fawn Grove, Felton, Glen Rock, Hallam, Hanover, Jacobus, Jefferson, Loganville, New Freedom, New Salem, Railroad, Red Lion, Seven Valleys, Shrewsbury, Spring Grove, Stewartstown, Windsor, Winterstown, Wrightsville, and Yorkana. Population (2010), 705,688.

ZIP Codes: 17022 (part), 17073 (part), 17301 (part), 17302, 17309, 17311, 17313 (part), 17314, 17315–16 (part), 17317, 17321–22, 17327, 17329, 17331 (part), 17347 (part), 17349, 17352, 17355, 17356 (part), 17360–63, 17364 (part), 17366, 17368, 17371, 17402–03 (part), 17406 (part), 17408 (part), 17501–02, 17505, 17507–09, 17512, 17516–20, 17522, 17527 (part), 17529, 17532, 17535–36, 17538, 17540, 17543, 17545 (part), 17547, 17550–52, 17554, 17555 (part), 17557, 17560, 17562, 17563 (part) 17565–66, 17569 (part), 17570, 17572, 17576, 17578–79, 17581–82, 17584, 17601–03, 17606, 19310 (part), 19344 (part), 19362–63 (part), 19501, 19540 (part), 19543 (part), 19551 (part)

* * *

TWELFTH DISTRICT

FRED KELLER, Republican, of Middleburg, PA; born in Page, AZ, October 23, 1965; education: graduated from Shikellamy High School, Sunbury, PA, 1984; graduated from Don Paul Shearer Real Estate School, Wormleysburg, PA, 1985; professional: business manager; business owner; member of the Pennsylvania State House of Representatives, 2010–19; religion: Protestant; family: wife, Kay; two children; committees: Education and Labor; Oversight and Reform; elected to the 116th Congress, by special election, on May 21, 2019, to fill the vacancy caused by the resignation of United States Representative Thomas A. Marino.

Office Listings

https://keller.house.gov https://facebook.com/CongressmanFredKeller
https://twitter.com/RepFredKeller

1717 Longworth House Office Building, Washington, DC 20515 .... (202) 225–3731

Office Listings—Continued

Chief of Staff.—Jonathan Anzur.
Office Manager / Scheduler.—Monica Zagame.
Legislative Director.—Erin Wilson.
Communications Director.—Jason Gottesman.
Legislative Assistant.—Kevin O'Keefe.
Press Assistant / Legislative Correspondent.—Nicholas Barley.
Staff Assistant.—Jonathan Hayes.
1020 Commerce Park Drive, Suite 1A, Williamsport, PA 17701 .... (570) 322–3961
District Director.—Ann Kaufman. FAX: 322–3965
Constituent Casework Manager.—Jacqueline Bell.
District Representative.—Benjamin Ranck.
713 Bridge Street, Room 29, Selinsgrove, PA 17870 .... (570) 374–9469
Constituent Caseworker.—Amiee Snyder. FAX: 374–9589
Veterans Affairs Liaison.—Michael Knouse.
181 West Tioga Street, Suite 2, Tunkhannock, PA 18657 .... (570) 996–6550
Constituent Caseworker / Field Representative.—Thomas Cahill.
District Representative.—David Broadwell.

Counties: BRADFORD AND CENTRE (part). TOWNSHIPS: College, Ferguson, Gregg, Haines, Halfmoon (part), Harris, Miles, Penn, and Potter. BOROUGHS: Centre Hall, Millheim, and State College. CLINTON, JUNIATA, LYCOMING, MIFFLIN, AND NORTHUMBERLAND (part). CITY: SUNBURY. TOWNSHIPS: Delaware, East Chillisquaque, Jackson, Jordan, Lewis, Little Mahanoy, Lower Augusta, Lower Mahanoy, Point, Rockefeller, Rush, Shamokin, Turbot, Upper Augusta, Upper Mahanoy (part), Washington, West Cameron, West Chillisquaque, and Zerbe. BOROUGHS: Herndon, McEwensville, Milton, Northumberland, Riverside, Snydertown, Turbotville, and Watsontown. PERRY, POTTER, SNYDER, SULLIVAN, SUSQUEHANNA, TIOGA, UNION, AND WYOMING. Population (2010), 700,573.

ZIP Codes: 16720 (part), 16743 (part), 16746, 16748 (part), 16801 (part), 16802, 16803 (part), 16820, 16822–23 (part), 16827, 16828 (part), 16832, 16841 (part), 16848, 16851–52, 16854, 16865 (part), 16868, 16870–72, 16875, 16877 (part), 16882, 16901, 16911–12, 16914–15, 16917, 16920–23, 16925–30, 16932–33, 16935–41, 16943, 16946–48, 16950, 17002 (part), 17004, 17006, 17009, 17017 (part), 17020–21 (part), 17024, 17029, 17035, 17037, 17040, 17044–45, 17047, 17049, 17051, 17053 (part), 17056, 17058–59, 17062–63, 17066 (part), 17068–69, 17071, 17074–76, 17082, 17084, 17086, 17090, 17094, 17099, 17243 (part), 17701–02, 17721, 17723–24, 17727–31, 17737, 17739–40, 17742, 17744–45, 17747–52, 17754, 17756 (part), 17758, 17760, 17762–65, 17767–68, 17771, 17772 (part), 17774 (part), 17776, 17777 (part), 17778–79, 17801, 17810, 17812–13, 17814 (part), 17820, 17821 (part), 17823, 17827, 17829–30, 17835, 17836 (part), 17837, 17841–42, 17844–45, 17846–47 (part), 17850, 17853, 17855–57

* * *

THIRTEENTH DISTRICT

JOHN JOYCE, Republican, of Hollidaysburg, PA; born in Altoona, PA, February 8, 1957; education: B.S., biology, Pennsylvania State University, University Park, 1979; M.D., Temple University, Philadelphia, PA, 1983; medical residency, Johns Hopkins Hospital, Baltimore, MD; military: served as physician, U.S. Naval Hospital, Portsmouth, VA; professional: co-founder and physician, Altoona Dermatology Associates; married: wife, Alice; three children; committees: Homeland Security; Small Business; elected to the 116th Congress on November 6, 2018.

Office Listings

https://johnjoyce.house.gov https://facebook.com/RepJohnJoyce https://twitter.com/RepJohnJoyce

1337 Longworth House Office Building, Washington, DC 20515 .... (202) 225–2431
Chief of Staff.—Jeremy Shoemaker. FAX: 225–2486
Legislative Director.—Matthew Tucker.
Communications Director.—Emma Thomson.
100 Lincoln Way East, Suite B, Chambersburg, PA 17201 .... (717) 753–6344
District Office Director.—Chad Reichard.
5414 6th Avenue, Altoona, PA 16602 .... (814) 656–6081
District Office Director.—Jennifer Mearkle.
451 Stoystown Road, Suite 102, Somerset, PA 15501 .... (814) 485–6020
District Office Director.—Ellen Stephens.
282 West King Street, Abbottstown, PA 17301 .... (717) 357–6320
District Office Director.—Nancy Bull.

Counties: ADAMS, BEDFORD, BLAIR, AND CAMBRIA (part). CITY: Johnstown. TOWNSHIPS: Conemaugh, East Taylor (part), Lower Yoder, Middle Taylor, Stonycreek, Upper Yoder, and West Taylor. BOROUGHS: Brownstown, Daisytown, Dale, East Conemaugh, Ferndale, Franklin, Lorain, Southmont, and Westmont. CUMBERLAND (part). TOWNSHIPS: Cooke, Dickinson, Hopewell, Lower Frankford, Lower Mifflin, North Middleton (part), North Newton, Penn, Shippensburg, South Newton, Southampton, Upper Frankford, Upper Mifflin, and West Pennsboro. BOROUGHS: Newburg, Newville, and Shippensburg. FRANKLIN, FULTON, HUNTINGDON, SOMERSET, AND WESTMORELAND (part). TOWNSHIPS: Derry, Donegal, Fairfield, Ligonier, St. Clair, and Unity (part). BOROUGHS: Bolivar, Derry, Donegal, Laurel Mountain, Ligonier, New Alexandria, New Florence, Seward, and Youngstown. Population (2010), 705,688.

ZIP Codes: 15411, 15424 (part), 15501–02, 15510, 15520–22, 15530–42, 15544–47, 15550–52, 15554–55, 15557 (part), 15558–64, 15610 (part), 15620, 15622 (part), 15627–28, 15638, 15646, 15650, 15655, 15658, 15661, 15670 (part),

15671, 15677, 15687, 15693, 15696, 15717 (part), 15779, 15901, 15902 (part), 15904 (part), 15905, 15906 (part), 15909 (part), 15923–24, 15926, 15928, 15935–37, 15942 (part), 15944 (part), 15946 (part), 15953, 15954 (part), 15963 (part), 16601–02, 16611, 16613 (part), 16617, 16621–23, 16625, 16631, 16633–35, 16636 (part), 16637–38, 16641 (part), 16647–48, 16650, 16652, 16655, 16657, 16659, 16662, 16664–65, 16667, 16669–70, 16672–74, 16678–79, 16682–83, 16685, 16686 (part), 16689, 16691, 16693–95, 16865 (part), 16877 (part), 17002 (part), 17013 (part), 17015 (part), 17019 (part), 17021 (part), 17052, 17060, 17065 (part), 17066 (part), 17081, 17201–02, 17210–15, 17217, 17219–25, 17228–29, 17733, 17735–41, 17243 (part), 17244, 17246–47, 17249–57, 17260–68, 17270–72, 17301 (part), 17304, 17306–07, 17316 (part), 17320, 17324 (part), 17325, 17331 (part), 17340, 17343–44, 17350, 17353, 17372

* * *

FOURTEENTH DISTRICT

GUY RESCHENTHALER, Republican, of Peters Township, PA; born April 17, 1983; education: B.A., political science, Pennsylvania State University Erie, the Behrend College, 2004; J.D., Duquesne University School of Law, Pittsburgh, PA, 2007; military: Judge Advocate General Corps, U.S. Navy, 2007–12; professional: lawyer, Brennan, Robins & Daley, P.C., Pittsburgh, PA; elected Allegheny County Magisterial District Judge, 2013–15; Representative, District 37, Senate, Commonwealth of Pennsylvania, Harrisburg, PA, 2015–19; committees: Foreign Affairs; Judiciary; elected to the 116th Congress on November 6, 2018.

Office Listings

https://reschenthaler.house.gov https://facebook.com/GReschenthaler
https://twitter.com/GReschenthaler

531 Cannon House Office Building, Washington, DC 20515 .... (202) 225–2065
Chief of Staff.—Aaron Bonnaure.
Legislative Director.—Emily Ackerman.
Scheduler.—Ashlee Bierworth.
700 Pellis Road, Suite 1, Greensburg, PA 15601 .... (724) 219–4200
14 South Main Street, Washington, PA 15301 .... (724) 206–4800

Counties: FAYETTE, GREENE, WASHINGTON, AND WESTMORELAND (part). CITIES: Arnold, Greensburg, Jeannette, Latrobe, Lower Burrell, Monessen, and New Kensington. TOWNSHIPS: Allegheny, Bell, East Huntingdon, Hempfield, Loyalhanna, Mount Pleasant, North Huntingdon, Penn, Rostraver, Salem, Sewickley, South Huntingdon, Unity (part), Upper Burrell, and Washington. BOROUGHS: Adamsburg, Arona, Avonmore, Delmont, East Vandergrift, Export, Hunker, Hyde Park, Irwin, Madison, Manor, Mount Pleasant, Murrysville, New Stanton, North Belle Vernon, North Irwin, Oklahoma, Penn, Scottdale, Smithton, South Greensburg, Southwest Greensburg, Sutersville, Trafford, Vandergrift, West Leechburg, West Newton, and Youngwood. Population (2010), 705,688.

ZIP Codes: 15004, 15012, 15017 (part), 15019, 15021–22, 15025–26 (part), 15033, 15038, 15053–55, 15057 (part), 15060, 15062, 15063 (part), 15067, 15068 (part), 15072, 15078, 15083, 15085 (part), 15087, 15089 (part), 15126 (part), 15129 (part), 15131 (part), 15137 (part), 15146 (part), 15241 (part), 15301, 15310–17, 15320–25, 15327, 15329–31, 15332 (part), 15333–34, 15337–38, 15340–42, 15344–53, 15357–64, 15366–68, 15370, 15378–80, 15401, 15410, 15412–13, 15417, 15419–23, 15424 (part), 15425, 15427–38, 15440, 15442–51, 15454–56, 15458–64, 15466–70, 15472–80, 15482–84, 15486, 15489–90, 15492, 15557 (part), 15601, 15610 (part), 15611–12, 15613 (part), 15615–17, 15618 (part), 15621, 15622 (part), 15623–26, 15629, 15631–37, 15639–41, 15642 (part), 15644, 15647, 15650 (part), 15656 (part), 15660, 15662–63, 15665–66, 15668 (part), 15670 (part), 15672, 15675–76, 15678–80, 15681 (part), 15683–84, 15688–89, 15690 (part), 15691–92, 15695, 15697–98, 16229 (part)

* * *

FIFTEENTH DISTRICT

GLENN ''GT'' THOMPSON, Republican, of Howard Township, PA; born in Bellefonte, PA, July 27, 1959; education: B.S., therapeutic recreation, Pennsylvania State University, 1981; M.Ed., health science / therapeutic recreation, Temple University, 1998; NHA / L, nursing home administrator, Marywood University, 2006; professional: rehabilitation services manager for Susquehanna Health Services, adjunct faculty for Cambria County Community College; chief recreational therapist for the Williamsport Hospital; residential services aid for Hope Enterprises; orderly for Centre Crest Nursing Home; organization / awards: past president / fire fighter / EMT / rescue technician for Howard VFD; former, Howard Boy Scout Master; former, president and senior VP for Juniata Valley Boy Scout Council; International Advisory Council member for the Accreditation of Rehabilitation Facilities Commission; board member / vice chair of the Private Industry Council of Central Corridors; political career: Centre County Republican chair, Pennsylvania Republican State Committee, alternate delegate for the Republican National Convention; candidate for the Pennsylvania House of Representatives, 1998 and 2000; member, Bald Eagle Area School District Board of Education; religion: Protestant; married to Penny Ammerman-Thompson; three sons, Parker, Logan, and Kale; committees: Agriculture; Education and Labor; elected to represent the 5th District in the 111th Congress on November 4, 2008; reelected to each succeeding Congress; elected to represent the 15th District in the 116th Congress on November 6, 2018.

Office Listings

https://thompson.house.gov https://facebook.com/CongressmanGT twitter: @CongressmanGT

400 Cannon House Office Building, Washington, DC 20515 .... (202) 225–5121
FAX: 225–5796
Chief of Staff.—Matthew Brennan.
Legislative Director.—John Busovsky.
Scheduler.—Lindsay Reusser.
Communications Director.—Taylor McCarty.
217 Elm Street, Suite B, Oil City, PA 16301 .... (814) 670–0432
District Director.—Brad Moore.
107 South Center Street, Ebensburg, PA 15931 .... (814) 419–8583
3555 Benner Pike, Suite 101, Bellefonte, PA 16823 .... (814) 353–0215

Counties: ARMSTRONG AND BUTLER (part). TOWNSHIPS: Allegheny, Buffalo, Clearfield, Concord, Donegal, Fairview, Jefferson (part), Oakland, Parker, Summit, Venango, Washington, and Winfield. BOROUGHS: Bruin, Cherry Valley, Chicora, East Butler, Eau Claire, Fairview, Karns City, and Petrolia. Cambria (part). TOWNSHIPS: Adams, Allegheny, Barr, Blacklick, Cambria, Chest, Clearfield, Cresson, Croyle, Dean, East Carroll, East Taylor (part), Elder, Gallitzin, Jackson, Munster, Portage, Reade, Richland, Summerhill, Susquehanna, Washington, West Carroll, and White. BOROUGHS: Ashville, Carrolltown, Cassandra, Chest Springs, Cresson, Ebensburg, Ehrenfeld, Gallitzin, Geistown, Hastings, Lilly, Loretto, Nanty Glo, Northern Cambria, Patton, Portage, Sankertown, Scalp Level, South Fork, Summerhill, Tunnelhill, Vintondale, and Wilmore. CAMERON AND CENTRE (part). TOWNSHIPS: Benner, Boggs, Burnside, Curtin, Halfmoon (part), Howard, Huston, Liberty, Marion, Patton, Rush, Snow Shoe, Spring, Taylor, Union, Walker, and Worth. BOROUGHS: Bellefonte, Howard, Milesburg, Philipsburg, Port Matilda, Snow Shoe, and Unionville. CLARION, CLEARFIELD, ELK, FOREST, INDIANA, JEFFERSON, MCKEAN, VENANGO, AND WARREN. Population (2010), 705,688.

ZIP Codes: 15613 (part), 15618 (part), 15656 (part), 15673, 15681 (part), 15686, 15690 (part), 15701, 15710–16, 15717 (part), 15721–25, 15727–34, 15736–39, 15741–42, 15744–48, 15750, 15752–54, 15756–57, 15759–62, 15764–65, 15767, 15770–78, 15780–81, 15783–84, 15801, 15821, 15823–25, 15827–29, 15832, 15834, 15840–41, 15845–49, 15851, 15853, 15856–57, 15860–61, 15863–66, 15868, 15870, 15902 (part), 15904 (part), 15906 (part), 15909, 15920–22, 15925, 15927, 15929–31, 15934, 15938, 15940, 15942 (part), 15943, 15944–46 (part), 15948–49, 15951–52, 15954 (part), 15955–58, 15960–62, 15963 (part), 16001–02 (part), 16020 (part), 16022, 16023 (part), 16025, 16028–30, 16034, 16036, 16038 (part), 16040 (part), 16041, 16048–50, 16054, 16055–56 (part), 16061 (part), 16127 (part), 16153 (part), 16201, 16210–14, 16217–18, 16222–24, 16226, 16228, 16229 (part), 16230, 16232–33, 16235–36, 16238–40, 16242, 16244–46, 16248–50, 16253–56, 16258–60, 16262–63, 16301, 16311 (part), 16314 (part), 16312–13, 16317 (part), 16319, 16321–23, 16326, 16329, 16331–34, 16340–41, 16342 (part), 16343–47, 16350–53, 16354 (part), 16361, 16362 (part), 16364–65, 16370–74, 16402, 16405, 16407 (part), 16416, 16420, 16434 (part), 16436, 16613 (part), 16616, 16619–20, 16624, 16627, 16630, 16636 (part), 16639–40, 16641 (part), 16645–46, 16651, 16656, 16661, 16666, 16668, 16671, 16677, 16680, 16686 (part), 16692, 16699, 16701, 16720 (part), 16724–35, 16738, 16740, 16743 (part), 16744–45, 16748 (part), 16749–50, 16801 (part), 16803 (part), 16821, 16822–23 (part), 16825–26, 16828 (part), 16829–30, 16833–40, 16841 (part), 16843–45, 16847, 16849, 16853, 16855, 16858–61, 16863, 16866, 16870–71 (part), 16874, 16876, 16877 (part), 16878–79, 16881

* * *

SIXTEENTH DISTRICT

MIKE KELLY, Republican, of Butler, PA; born in Pittsburgh, PA, May 10, 1948; education: B.A., sociology with a minor in philosophy and theology, University of Notre Dame, South Bend, IN, 1970; professional: owner of Kelly Automotive Cadillac, Chevrolet, Hyundai, and Kia car dealership; married 45 years: Victoria Kelly; four children; committees: Ways and Means; elected to represent the 3rd District in the 112th Congress on November 2, 2010; re-elected to each succeeding Congress; elected to represent the 16th District in the 116th Congress on November 6, 2018.

Office Listings

https://kelly.house.gov https://facebook.com/MikeKellyPA https://twitter.com/MikeKellyPA

1707 Longworth House Office Building, Washington, DC 20515 .... (202) 225–5406
FAX: 225–3103
Chief of Staff.—Matthew Stroia.
Policy Director / Tax Counsel.—Lori Prater.
Director of Communications.—Andrew Eisenberger.
Director of Administration.—James Marsh.
Legislative Assistants: Parker Bennett, Kevin Dawson.
Legislative Correspondent.—Anna McCleaf.
Staff Assistant.—Juliet Long.
208 East Bayfront Parkway, Suite 102, Erie, PA 16507 .... (814) 454–8190
District Director.—Tim Butler.
101 East Diamond Street, Suite 210, Butler, PA 16001 .... (724) 282–2557
FAX: 282–3682
33 Chestnut Avenue, Sharon, PA 16146 .... (724) 342–7170
FAX: 342–7242

Counties: BUTLER (part). CITY: Butler. TOWNSHIPS: Adams, Brady, Butler, Center, Cherry, Clay, Clinton, Connoquenessing, Cranberry (part), Forward, Franklin, Jackson, Jefferson (part), Lancaster, Marion, Mercer, Middlesex, Muddycreek, Penn, Slippery Rock, and Worth. BOROUGHS: Callery, Connoquenessing, Evans City, Harmony, Harrisville, Mars, Portersville, Prospect, Saxonburg, Seven Fields, Slippery Rock, Valencia, West Liberty, West Sunbury, and Zelienople. CRAWFORD, ERIE, LAWRENCE, AND MERCER. Population (2010), 705,688.

ZIP Codes: 15044, 16001–02 (part), 16020 (part), 16023 (part), 16024, 16027, 16033, 16035, 16037–38 (part), 16040 (part), 16045–46, 16051–53, 16055–56 (part), 16057, 16059 (part), 16061 (part), 16063 (part), 16066 (part), 16101–02, 16105, 16110–14, 16116, 16117 (part), 16120 (part), 16121, 16123 (part), 16124–25, 16127 (part), 16130–34, 16137, 16140, 16141 (part), 16142–43, 16145–46, 16148, 16150–51, 16153 (part), 16154–56, 16157 (part), 16159–61, 16311 (part), 16314 (part), 16316, 16317 (part), 16327–28, 16335, 16342, 16354 (part), 16360, 16362 (part), 16401, 16403–04, 16406, 16407 (part), 16410–12, 16415, 16417, 16421–24, 16426–28, 16433, 16434 (part), 16435, 16438, 16440–44, 16501–11, 16546, 16563

* * *

SEVENTEENTH DISTRICT

CONOR LAMB, Democrat, of Mt. Lebanon, PA; born in Washington, DC, June 27, 1984; education: graduated from Pittsburgh Central Catholic High School, 2002; University of Pennsylvania, Philadelphia, PA, 2006; J.D., University of Pennsylvania Law School, 2009; Captain, active duty U.S. Marine Corps, 2009–13; continues to serve as a Major in the U.S. Marine Corps Reserve; Assistant U.S. Attorney, Pittsburgh, PA, 2014–17; committees: Science, Space, and Technology; Veterans' Affairs; elected by special election on March 13, 2018 to represent the 18th District in the 115th Congress; elected to represent the 17th District in the 116th Congress on November 6, 2018.

Office Listings

https://lamb.house.gov https://facebook.com/RepConorLamb https://twitter.com/RepConorLamb

1224 Longworth House Office Building, Washington, DC 20515 .... (202) 225–2301
Chief of Staff.—Craig Kwiecinski.
Legislative Director.—Chris Bowman.
Scheduler.—Carly Krystyniak.
Senior Advisor.—Abby Murphy.
Director of Communications.—Reenie Kuhlman.
504 Washington Road, Pittsburgh, PA 15228 .... (412) 344–5583
3468 Brodhead Road, Suite #1, Monaca, PA 15061 .... (724) 206–4860

Counties: ALLEGHENY (part). TOWNSHIPS: Aleppo, Baldwin, Collier, Crescent, East Deer, Fawn, Findlay, Frazer, Hampton, Harmar, Harrison, Indiana, Kennedy, Kilbuck, Leet, Marshall, McCandless, Moon, Mount Lebanon, Neville, North Fayette, O'Hara, Ohio, Penn Hills (part), Pine, Reserve, Richland, Robinson, Ross, Scott, Shaler, South Fayette (part), Springdale, Stowe, and West Deer. BOROUGHS: Aspinwall, Avalon, Bell Acres, Bellevue, Ben Avon, Ben Avon Heights, Blawnox, Brackenridge, Bradford Woods, Carnegie, Castle Shannon, Cheswick, Coraopolis, Crafton, Dormont, Edgeworth, Emsworth, Etna, Fox Chapel, Franklin Park, Glen Osborne, Glenfield, Green Tree, Haysville, Heidelberg, Ingram, Leetsdale, McDonald, McKees Rocks, Millvale, Oakdale, Oakmont, Pennsbury Village, Rosslyn Farms, Sewickley, Sewickley Heights, Sewickley Hills, Sharpsburg, Springdale, Tarentum, Thornburg, Verona, and West View. BEAVER (all) AND BUTLER (part). TOWNSHIP: Cranberry (part). Population (2010), 705,688.

ZIP Codes: 15001, 15003, 15005–07, 15009–10, 15014–15, 15017 (part), 15024, 15026 (part), 15027, 15030, 15031 (part), 15042–43, 15044 (part), 15046, 15049–52, 15056, 15057 (part), 15059, 15061, 15064 (part), 15065–66, 15071 (part), 15074–77, 15081–82, 15084, 15086, 15090, 15101, 15106 (part), 15108, 15116, 15126 (part), 15136, 15139 (part), 15142–44, 15147 (part), 15202, 15204–05 (part), 15208 (part), 15209, 15212 (part), 15214–16 (part), 15220–21 (part), 15223, 15225, 15226 (part), 15228 (part), 15229, 15234–35 (part), 15237, 15238 (part), 15241 (part), 15243 (part), 16037 (part), 16046 (part), 16055 (part), 16059 (part), 16063 (part), 16066 (part), 16115, 16117 (part), 16120 (part), 16123 (part), 16136, 16141 (part), 16157

* * *

EIGHTEENTH DISTRICT

MIKE DOYLE, Democrat, of Forest Hills, PA; born in Swissvale, PA, August 5, 1953; education: graduated, Swissvale Area High School, 1971; B.S., Pennsylvania State University, 1975; professional: co-owner, Eastgate Insurance Agency, Inc., 1983; elected and served as finance and recreation chairman, Swissvale Borough Council, 1977–81; member: Ancient Order of the Hibernians; Italian Sons and Daughters of America; Leadership Pittsburgh Alumni Association; Lions Club; National Italian-American Foundation; Penn State Alumni Association; Pennsylvania Democratic Delegation; caucuses: Ad Hoc Committee on Irish Affairs; Congressional Steel Caucus; Democratic Caucus; Democratic Study Group; Travel and Tourism CMO; married: Susan Beth Doyle, 1975; children: Michael, David, Kevin, and Alexandra; committees: Energy and Commerce; elected to represent the 14th District in the 104th Congress, November 8, 1994; reelected to each succeeding Congress; elected to the 116th Congress to represent the 18th District on November 6, 2018.

Office Listings

https://doyle.house.gov https://facebook.com/usrepmikedoyle https://twitter.com/usrepmikedoyle

306 Cannon House Office Building, Washington, DC 20515 .... (202) 225–2135

Office Listings—Continued

Chief of Staff.—David Lucas. FAX: 225–3084
Legislative Director.—Phil Murphy.
Office Manager / Scheduler.—Ellen Young.
2637 East Carson Street, Pittsburgh, PA 15203 .... (412) 390–1499
District Director.—Paul D'Alesandro.
4705 Library Road, Bethel Park, PA 15102 .... (412) 283–4451
627 Lysle Boulevard, McKeesport, PA 15132 .... (412) 664–4049

Counties: ALLEGHENY (part). CITIES: Clairton, Duquesne, McKeesport, and Pittsburgh. TOWNSHIPS: Elizabeth, Forward, North Versailles, Penn Hills (part), South Fayette (part), South Park, South Versailles, Upper St. Clair, and Wilkins. BOROUGHS: Baldwin, Bethel Park, Braddock, Braddock Hills, Brentwood, Bridgeville, Chalfant, Churchill, Dravosburg, East McKeesport, East Pittsburgh, Edgewood, Elizabeth, Forest Hills, Glassport, Homestead, Jefferson Hills, Liberty, Lincoln, Monroeville, Mount Oliver, Munhall, North Braddock, Pitcairn, Pleasant Hills, Plum, Port Vue, Rankin, Swissvale, Trafford, Turtle Creek, Versailles, Wall, West Elizabeth, West Homestead, West Mifflin, Whitaker, White Oak, Whitehall, Wilkinsburg, and Wilmerding. Population (2010), 705,688.

ZIP Codes: 15017 (part), 15018, 15020, 15025, 15028, 15031 (part), 15034–35, 15037, 15045, 15047, 15057 (part), 15063–64 (part), 15068 (part), 15071 (part), 15085 (part), 15088, 15089 (part), 15102, 15104, 15106 (part), 15110, 15112, 15120, 15122, 15129 (part), 15131–33, 15135, 15137 (part), 15139 (part), 15140, 15145, 15146–47 (part), 15148, 15201, 15203 (part), 15204–05 (part), 15206–07, 15208 (part), 15210–11, 15212 (part), 15213, 15214–16 (part), 15217–19, 15220–21 (part), 15222, 15224, 15226 (part), 15227, 15228 (part), 15232–33, 15234–35 (part), 15236, 15238 (part), 15239, 15241 (part), 15243 (part), 15260, 15290, 15332 (part), 15642 (part), 15668 (part)

RHODE ISLAND

(Population 2010, 1,052,567)

SENATORS

JACK REED, Democrat, of Jamestown, RI; born in Providence, RI, November 12, 1949; graduated, La Salle Academy, Providence, RI, 1967; B.S., U.S. Military Academy, West Point, NY, 1971; M.P.P., Kennedy School of Government, Harvard University, 1973; J.D., Harvard Law School, 1982; professional: served in the U.S. Army, 1967–79; platoon leader, company commander, battalion staff officer, 1973–77; associate professor, Department of Social Sciences, U.S. Military Academy, West Point, NY, 1978–79; 2nd BN (Abn) 504th Infantry, 82nd Airborne Division, Fort Bragg, NC; lawyer, admitted to the Washington, DC Bar, 1983; military awards: Army Commendation Medal with Oak Leaf Cluster, ranger, senior parachutist, jumpmaster, expert infantryman's badge; elected to the Rhode Island State Senate, 1985–90; ex officio member of the Select Committee on Intelligence; committees: ranking member, Armed Services; Appropriations; Banking, Housing, and Urban Affairs; elected to the 102nd Congress on November 6, 1990; served three terms in the U.S. House of Representatives; elected to the U.S. Senate, November 5, 1996; reelected to each succeeding Senate term.

Office Listings

https://reed.senate.gov https://facebook.com/SenJackReed https://twitter.com/SenJackReed

728 Hart Senate Office Building, Washington, DC 20510 .... (202) 224–4642
Chief of Staff.—Neil Campbell. FAX: 224–4680
Press Secretary.—Chip Unruh.
1000 Chapel View Boulevard, Suite 290, Cranston, RI 02920 .... (401) 943–3100
Chief of Staff.—Raymond Simone.
U.S. District Courthouse, One Exchange Terrace, Suite 408, Providence, RI 02903 .... (401) 528–5200

* * *

SHELDON WHITEHOUSE, Democrat, of Newport, RI; born in New York City, NY, October 20, 1955; education: B.A., Yale University, New Haven, CT, 1978; J.D., University of Virginia, Charlottesville, VA, 1982; professional: director, Rhode Island Department of Business Regulation, 1992–94; United States Attorney, 1994–98; Attorney General, Rhode Island State, 1999–2003; committees: Budget; Environment and Public Works; Finance; Judiciary; elected to the U.S. Senate on November 7, 2006; reelected to each succeeding Senate term.

Office Listings

https://whitehouse.senate.gov

530 Hart Senate Office Building, Washington, DC 20510 .... (202) 224–2921
Chief of Staff.—Sam Goodstein. FAX: 228–6362
Legislative Director.—Josh Karetny.
Communications Director.—Richard Davidson.
170 Westminster Street, Suite 1100, Providence, RI 02903 .... (401) 453–5294
State Director.—George Carvalho.

REPRESENTATIVES

FIRST DISTRICT

DAVID N. CICILLINE, Democrat, of Providence, RI; born in Providence, July 15, 1961; education: graduated, Narragansett High School, Narragansett, RI; B.A., Brown University, Providence, 1983; J.D., Georgetown University Law Center, Washington, DC, 1986; professional: public defender, Washington, DC, 1986–87; lawyer, private practice; lawyer, American Civil Liberties Union; faculty, Roger Williams Law School, Bristol, RI; member of the Rhode Island State House of Representatives, 1995–2003; Mayor of Providence, RI, 2003–11; committees: Foreign Affairs; Judiciary; elected to the 112th Congress on November 2, 2010; reelected to each succeeding Congress.

Office Listings

https://cicilline.house.gov https://facebook.com/CongressmanDavidCicilline
https://twitter.com/repcicilline

2233 Rayburn House Office Building, Washington, DC 20515 .... (202) 225–4911

Office Listings—Continued

Chief of Staff.—Peter Karafotas. FAX: 225–3290
Legislative Director.—Sarah Trister.
Legislative Assistant / Scheduler.—Zan Guendert.
Communications Director.—Richard Luchette.
1070 Main Street, Suite 300, Pawtucket, RI 02860 .... (401) 729–5600

Counties: BRISTOL, NEWPORT, AND PROVIDENCE (part). CITIES AND TOWNSHIPS: Barrington, Bristol, Burrillville, Central Falls, Cumberland, East Providence, Jamestown, Lincoln, Little Compton, Middleton, Newport, North Providence, North Smithfield, Providence, Pawtucket, Portsmouth, Smithfield, Tiverton, Warren, and Woonsocket. Population (2010), 526,283.

ZIP Codes: 02802, 02806, 02809, 02828, 02835, 02837, 02838, 02840–42, 02860–61, 02863–65, 02871–72, 02876, 02878, 02885, 02895–96, 02903–12, 02914–17, 02919

* * *

SECOND DISTRICT

JAMES R. LANGEVIN, Democrat, of Warwick, RI; born in Providence, RI, April 22, 1964; education: B.A., double major in political science and public administration, Rhode Island College, 1990; M.P.A., Harvard University, 1994; community service: American Red Cross; March of Dimes; Lions Club of Warwick; PARI Independent Living Center; Knights of Columbus; public service: secretary, Rhode Island Constitutional Convention, 1986; Rhode Island State Representative, 1989–95; Rhode Island Secretary of State, 1995–2000; committees: Armed Services; Homeland Security; elected to the 107th Congress; reelected to each succeeding Congress.

Office Listings

https://langevin.house.gov https://facebook.com/CongressmanJimLangevin twitter: @JimLangevin

2077 Rayburn House Office Building, Washington, DC 20515 .... (202) 225–2735
Chief of Staff.—Todd Adams. FAX: 225–5976
Legislative Director.—Nick Leiserson.
Office Manager.—Stu Rose.
The Summit South, 300 Centerville Road, Suite 200, Warwick, RI 02886 .... (401) 732–9400
District Director.—Seth Klaiman.

Counties: KENT, PROVIDENCE (part), AND WASHINGTON. CITIES AND TOWNSHIPS: Burrillville, Charlestown, Coventry, Cranston, Exeter, Foster, Glocester, Greenwich (East and West), Hopkinton, Johnston, Kingstown (North and South), Narragansett, New Shoreham, Providence, Richmond, Scituate, Warwick, West Warwick, and Westerly. Population (2010), 516,587.

ZIP Codes: 02804, 02807–08, 02812–18, 02822–23, 02825, 02826–33, 02836, 02839, 02852, 02857–58, 02873–75, 02877, 02879–83, 02886–89, 02891–94, 02898, 02901–05, 02907–11, 02917, 02919–21

SOUTH CAROLINA

(Population 2010, 4,625,364)

SENATORS

LINDSEY GRAHAM, Republican, of Seneca, SC; born in Seneca, July 9, 1955; education: graduated, Daniel High School, Central, SC; B.A., University of South Carolina, 1977; awarded J.D., 1981; military service: joined the U.S. Air Force, 1982; Base Legal Office and Area Defense Counsel, Rhein Main Air Force Base, Germany, 1984; circuit trial counsel, U.S. Air Force; Base Staff Judge Advocate, McEntire Air National Guard Base, SC, 1989–94; retired as a Colonel in the U.S. Air Force Reserve, 2015; awards: Meritorious Service Medal for Outstanding Service; Meritorious Service Medal for Active Duty Tour in Europe; professional: established private law practice, 1988; former member, South Carolina House of Representatives; Assistant County Attorney for Oconee County, 1988–92; City Attorney for Central, SC, 1990–94; member: Walhalla Rotary; American Legion Post 120; appointed to the Judicial Arbitration Commission by the Chief Justice of the Supreme Court; religion: attends Corinth Baptist Church; committees: chair, Judiciary; Appropriations; Budget; Foreign Relations; elected to the 104th Congress on November 8, 1994; reelected to each succeeding Congress; elected to the U.S. Senate on November 5, 2002; reelected to each succeeding Senate term.

Office Listings

https://lgraham.senate.gov

290 Russell Senate Office Building, Washington, DC 20510 .... (202) 224–5972
Chief of Staff.—Richard Perry. FAX: 224–3808
Legislative Director.—Mathew Rimkunas.
Scheduler/Press Secretary.—Alice James.
Deputy Communications Director.—Taylor Reidy.
130 South Main Street, Suite 700, Greenville, SC 29601 .... (864) 250–1417
State Director.—Van Cato.
Communications Director.—Kevin Bishop.
Upstate Regional Director.—Angela Omer.
State Scheduler.—Edward Mercer.
530 Johnnie Dodds Boulevard, Suite 202, Mt. Pleasant, SC 29464 .... (843) 849–3887
Low Country Regional Director.—Dan Head.
508 Hampton Street, Suite 202, Columbia, SC 29201 .... (803) 933–0112
Midlands Regional Director.—Yvette Rowland.
John L. McMillan Federal Building, 401 West Evans Street, Suite 111, Florence, SC 29501 .... (843) 669–1505
Pee Dee Regional Director.—Celia Urquhart.
235 East Main Street, Suite 100, Rock Hill, SC 29730 .... (803) 366–2828
Piedmont Regional Outreach Director.—Theresa Thomas.
124 Exchange Street, Suite A, Pendleton, SC 29670 .... (864) 646–4090
Senior Advisor.—Denise Bauld.

* * *

TIM SCOTT, Republican, of North Charleston, SC; born in North Charleston, September 19, 1965; education: R.B. Stall High School; B.S., Charleston Southern University, Charleston, SC, 1988; professional: former owner of Tim Scott Allstate and partner of Pathway Real Estate Group; served on Charleston County Council, 1995–2008; four terms as chair of the Charleston County Council; member of the South Carolina State House of Representatives, 2009–10; member of the U.S. House of Representatives, 2010–12; committees: Banking, Housing, and Urban Affairs; Finance; Health, Education, Labor, and Pensions; Small Business and Entrepreneurship; Special Committee on Aging; appointed by the Governor, January 2, 2013, to fill the vacancy caused by the resignation of Senator James DeMint; appointment took effect upon his resignation from the House of Representatives on January 2, 2013; took the oath of office on January 3, 2013; elected, by special election, on November 4, 2014, for the final two years of Senator DeMint's second term; reelected to the U.S. Senate on November 8, 2016.

Office Listings

https://scott.senate.gov https://facebook.com/SenatorTimScott https://twitter.com/SenatorTimScott

104 Hart Senate Office Building, Washington, DC 20510 .... (202) 224–6121
Chief of Staff.—Jennifer DeCasper. FAX: 228–5143
Legislative Director.—Chuck Cogar.
Communications Director.—Sean Smith.
Scheduler.—Brie Kelly.
2500 City Hall Lane, 3rd Floor Suite, North Charleston, SC 29406 .... (843) 727–4525

Office Listings—Continued

State Director.—Joe McKeown. FAX: (855) 802–9355
104 South Main Street, Suite 803, Greenville, SC 29601 .... (864) 233–5366
1901 Main Street, Suite 1425, Columbia, SC 29201 .... (803) 771–6112

REPRESENTATIVES

FIRST DISTRICT

JOE CUNNINGHAM, Democrat, of Charleston, SC; born in Caldwell County, KY, May 26, 1982; Eagle Scout; education: B.S. in ocean engineering, Florida Atlantic University, Boca Raton, FL, 2005; J.D., Northern Kentucky University, Highland Heights, KY, 2014; professional: ocean engineer; attorney; business owner; religion: Christian; family: married to Amanda; one child: Boone; caucuses: Auto Care Caucus; Beer Caucus; Black Maternal Health; Blue Dog Coalition; Congressional Alzheimer's Caucus; New Democrat Coalition; Problem Solvers; committees: Natural Resources; Veterans' Affairs; elected to the 116th Congress on November 6, 2018.

Office Listings

https://cunningham.house.gov https://facebook.com/RepJoeCunningham
https://twitter.com/RepCunningham

423 Cannon House Office Building, Washington, DC 20515 .... (202) 225–3176
Chief of Staff.—Lane Lofton. FAX: 225–3407
Scheduler.—Jesse Mayer.
Legislative Director.—Rashawn Mitchell.
Communications Director.—Rebecca Drago.
710 Boundary Street, #1D, Beaufort, SC 29902 .... (843) 521–2530
530 Johnnie Dodds Boulevard, Suite 201, Mt. Pleasant, SC 29464 .... (843) 352–7572

Counties: BEAUFORT (part), BERKELEY (part), CHARLESTON (part), COLLETON (part), AND DORCHESTER (part). Population (2010), 660,766.

ZIP Codes: 29401–03, 29405–07, 29410, 29412, 29414, 29417–18, 29420, 29422, 29424–25, 29429, 29430–31, 29438–39, 29445, 29450, 29453, 29455–58, 29461, 29464–66, 29469–70, 29472, 29479, 29482–85, 29487, 29492, 29901–07, 29909–10, 29915, 29920, 29925–26, 29928, 29935–36, 29938

* * *

SECOND DISTRICT

JOE WILSON, Republican, of Springdale, SC; born in Charleston, SC, July 31, 1947; education: graduated, B.A., Washington & Lee University, Lexington, VA; J.D., University of South Carolina School of Law; professional: attorney; Kirkland, Wilson, Moore, Taylor; former Deputy General Counsel, U.S. Department of Energy; former judge of the town of Springdale, SC; military service: U.S. Army Reserve, 1972–75; retired Colonel in the South Carolina Army National Guard as a Staff Judge Advocate for the 218th Mechanized Infantry Brigade, 1975–2003; organizations: Cayce-West Columbia Rotary Club; Sheriff's Department Law Enforcement Advisory Council; Reserve Officers Association; Lexington County Historical Society; Columbia Home Builders Association; County Community and Resource Development Committee; American Heart Association; Mid-Carolina Mental Health Association; Cayce-West Columbia Jaycees; Kidney Foundation; South Carolina Lung Association; Alston-Wilkes Society; Cayce-West Metro Chamber of Commerce; Columbia World Affairs Council; Fellowship of Christian Athletes, Sinclair Lodge 154; Jamil Temple; Woodmen of the World; Sons of Confederate Veterans; Military Order of the World Wars; Lexington, Greater Irmo, Chapin, Columbia, West Metro, and Batesburg-Leesville Chambers of Commerce; West Metro and Dutch Fork Women's Republican Clubs; Executive Council of the Indian Waters Council, Boy Scouts of America; awards: U.S. Chamber of Commerce, Spirit of Enterprise Award; Americans for Tax Reform, Friend of the Taxpayer Award; National Taxpayers' Union, Taxpayers' Friend Award; Americans for Prosperity, Friend of the American Motorist Award; public service: South Carolina State Senate, 1984–2001; family: married to Roxanne Dusenbury McCrory; four sons; Assistant GOP Whip; member, Republican Policy Committee; committees: Armed Services; Foreign Affairs; elected to the 107th Congress, by special election, on December 18, 2001; reelected to each succeeding Congress.

Office Listings

https://joewilson.house.gov https://facebook.com/JoeWilson twitter: @RepJoeWilson

1436 Longworth House Office Building, Washington, DC 20515 .... (202) 225–2452
Chief of Staff.—Jonathan Day. FAX: 225–2455
Communications Director.—McLaurine Klingler.
Legislative Director.—Oren Adaki.
1930 University Parkway, Suite 1600, Aiken, SC 29801 .... (803) 642–6416
1700 Sunset Boulevard (U.S. 378), Suite 1, West Columbia, SC 29169 .... (803) 939–0041

Counties: AIKEN, BARNWELL, LEXINGTON, ORANGEBURG (part), AND RICHLAND (part). CITIES AND TOWNSHIPS: Aiken, Arcadia Lakes, Ballentine, Barnwell, Batesburg-Leesville (part), Bath, Beech Island, Belvedere, Blackville, Blythewood, Bowman, Boyden Arbor, Branchville, Burnettown, Capitol View, Cayce, Chapin, Clearwater, Columbia (part), Cope, Cordova, Dentsville, Eastover, Eau Claire, Elko, Fairwood Acres, Gadsden, Gaston, Gilbert, Gloverville, Graniteville, Harbison, Hilda, Hilton, Hopkins, Horrell Hill, Irmo (part), Jackson, Killian, Kingville, Kline, Lake Murray, Langley, Lexington (county seat), Livingston, Lykes, Monetta, Montmorenci, Mountain Brook, Neeses, New Ellenton, North, North Augusta, Norway, Oak Grove, Pelion, Perry, Pine Ridge, Pontiac, Red Bank, Ridge Spring, Rowesville, Salley, Santee, Seven Oaks, Snelling, South Congaree, Springdale, Springfield, St. Andrews, State Park, Summit, Swansea, Vance, Vaucluse, Wagener, Warrenville, Wateree, West Columbia, Williston, Windsor, Windsor Estates, White Rock, and Woodford. Population (2010), 670,436.

ZIP Codes: 29002, 29006, 29016, 29033, 29036, 29038–39, 29044–45, 29053–54, 29061, 29063, 29070–73, 29075, 29078, 29105, 29107, 29112–13, 29115, 29123, 29129–30, 29137, 29146, 29160, 29164, 29169–72, 29177, 29180, 29203–07, 29209–10, 29212, 29219, 29223, 29229, 29260, 29801–05, 29808–09, 29812–13, 29816–17, 29822, 29826, 29898, 29829, 29831–32, 29834, 29836, 29839, 29841–43, 29847, 29849–51, 29853, 29856, 29860–61

* * *

THIRD DISTRICT

JEFF DUNCAN, Republican, of Laurens, SC; born in Greenville, SC, January 7, 1966; education: B.A., political science, Clemson University, 1988; professional: small business owner; public service: South Carolina House of Representatives, 2002–10; religion: Southern Baptist, attends Clinton First Baptist Church; married: Melody; children: Graham, John Philip, and Parker; committees: Energy and Commerce; elected to the 112th Congress on November 2, 2010; reelected to each succeeding Congress.

Office Listings

https://jeffduncan.house.gov https://facebook.com/RepJeffDuncan twitter: @RepJeffDuncan

2229 Rayburn House Office Building, Washington, DC 20515 .... (202) 225–5301
Chief of Staff.—Allen Klump. FAX: 225–3216
Legislative Director.—Joshua Gross.
303 West Beltline Boulevard, Anderson, SC 29625 .... (864) 224–7401
Deputy Chief of Staff.—Rick Adkins.
100 Plaza Circle, Suite A1, Clinton, SC 29325 .... (864) 681–1028

Counties: ABBEVILLE, ANDERSON, EDGEFIELD, GREENWOOD, LAURENS, MCCORMICK, OCONEE, PICKENS, SALUDA, NEWBERRY (part), GREENVILLE (part). Population (2010), 660,767.

ZIP Codes: 29006, 29037, 29070, 29105, 29108, 29127, 29129, 29138, 29145, 29166, 29178, 29325, 29332, 29335, 29351, 29355, 29360, 29370, 29384, 29388, 29605, 29611, 29620–21, 29624–28, 29630–35, 29638–46, 29649, 29653–59, 29661, 29664–67, 29669–73, 29675–78, 29680, 29682, 29684–86, 29689, 29691–93, 29695–97, 29801, 29803, 29805, 29808, 29819, 29821–22, 29824, 29832, 29835, 29838, 29840, 29844–45, 29847–48, 29853, 29860, 29899

* * *

FOURTH DISTRICT

WILLIAM R. TIMMONS IV, Republican, of Greenville, SC; born in Greenville, April 30, 1984; education: B.A., George Washington University, Washington, DC, 2006; M.A., University of South Carolina, Columbia, SC, 2009; J.D., University of South Carolina, 2010; professional: staff, U.S. Senator William H. Frist of Tennessee, 2006–07; prosecutor, South Carolina's 13th Circuit Solicitor's Office, 2011–15; owner, Timmons & Company, LLC, 2012–present; member, South Carolina State Senate, 2016–18; owner, Swamp Rabbit CrossFit, 2012–present; military: First Lieutenant, South Carolina Air National Guard, 2018–present; religion: Christian; committees: Financial Services; Select Committee on the Modernization of Congress; Freshman Representative, Republican Steering Committee; elected to the 116th Congress on November 6, 2018.

Office Listings

https://timmons.house.gov https://facebook.com/RepTimmons
https://twitter.com/reptimmons https://instagram.com/reptimmons

313 Cannon House Office Building, Washington, DC 20515 .... (202) 225–6030
Chief of Staff.—Moutray McLaren.
Legislative Director.—Hilary Ranieri.
Communications Director.—Joshua Goodwin.
104 South Main Street, Suite 801, Greenville, SC 29601 .... (864) 241–0175
101 West St. John Street, Suite 303, Spartanburg, SC 29306 .... (864) 583–3264
District Director.—Hope Blackley.
Constituent Services Director.—Seth Blanton.
Outreach Director.—Freddie Gault.

Counties: GREENVILLE (part) AND SPARTANBURG (part). Population (2010), 660,766.

ZIP Codes: 29301–07, 29316, 29319–20, 29322–24, 29329–31, 29333–36, 29346, 29348–49, 29356, 29365, 29369, 29372–79, 29385–86, 29388, 29395, 29601–17, 29635–36, 29650–52, 29661–62, 29673, 29680–81, 29683, 29687–88, 29690

* * *

FIFTH DISTRICT

RALPH NORMAN, Republican, of Rock Hill, SC; born in Rock Hill, June 20, 1953; education: graduated from Rock Hill High School in 1971; B.S., business, Presbyterian College, Clinton, SC, 1975; professional: real estate developer; member of South Carolina State House of Representatives, 2005–06 and 2009–17; family: married to Elaine Rice Norman; four children: Ralph Warren, Anne, Mary Catherine, and Caroline; 16 grandchildren; committees: Budget; Oversight and Reform; Science, Space, and Technology; elected to the 115th Congress, by special election, on June 20, 2017, to fill the vacancy caused by the resignation of U.S. Representative Mick Mulvaney; reelected to the 116th Congress on November 6, 2018.

Office Listings

https://norman.house.gov https://facebook.com/RepRalphNorman
twitter: @RepRalphNorman https://instagram.com/repralphnorman

319 Cannon House Office Building, Washington, DC 20515 .... (202) 225–5501
Chief of Staff.—Mark Piland.
Communications Director.—Austin Livingston.
454 South Anderson Road, Suite 302 B, Rock Hill, SC 29730 .... (803) 327–4330
District Director.—David O'Neal.
Cherokee Administration Building, 110 Railroad Avenue, Gaffney, SC 29340.

Counties: CHEROKEE, CHESTER, FAIRFIELD, KERSHAW, LANCASTER, LEE, NEWBERRY (part), SPARTANBURG (part), SUMTER (part), UNION, AND YORK. Population (2013), 675,124.

ZIP Codes: 29009 (part), 29010, 29014–15, 29016 (part), 29020, 29031–32, 29036 (part), 29040, 29045 (part), 29046, 29055, 29058, 29062, 29065, 29067, 29069 (part), 29074, 29075 (part), 29078 (part), 29080 (part), 29104 (part), 29108 (part), 29122, 29125 (part), 29126, 29127 (part), 29128, 29130 (part), 29150 (part), 29152, 29153 (part), 29154, 29168, 29175, 29178 (part), 29180 (part), 29303 (part), 29307 (part), 29316 (part), 29321, 29322 (part), 29323, 29330 (part), 29335 (part), 29338, 29340–41, 29349 (part), 29353, 29355 (part), 29364, 29368, 29372 (part), 29374 (part), 29379, 29550 (part), 29702, 20704, 29706–08, 29710, 29712, 29714–15, 29717, 29718 (part), 29720, 29724, 29726, 29729, 29730, 29732–33, 29742–43, 29745

* * *

SIXTH DISTRICT

JAMES E. CLYBURN, Democrat, of Columbia, SC; born in Sumter, SC, July 21, 1940; education: graduated, Mather Academy, Camden, SC, 1957; B.S., South Carolina State University, Orangeburg, 1962; attended University of South Carolina Law School, Columbia, 1972–74; professional: South Carolina State Human Affairs Commissioner; assistant to the Governor for Human Resource Development; executive director, South Carolina Commission for Farm Workers, Inc.; director, Neighborhood Youth Corps and New Careers; counselor, South Carolina Employment Security Commission; member: lifetime member, NAACP; Southern Regional Council; Omega Psi Phi Fraternity, Inc.; Arabian Temple, No. 139; Nemiah Lodge No. 51 F&AM; married: the former Emily England; children: Mignon, Jennifer, and Angela; elected vice chair, Democratic Caucus, 2002; chair, Democratic Caucus, 2006; Majority Whip; Assistant Democratic Leader, 2010 and 2012; elected on November 3, 1992, to the 103rd Congress; reelected to each succeeding Congress.

Office Listings

https://clyburn.house.gov

200 Cannon House Office Building, Washington, DC 20515 .... (202) 225–3315
Chief of Staff.—Yelberton Watkins. FAX: 225–2313
Deputy Chief of Staff / Scheduler.—Lindy Birch Kelly.
1225 Lady Street, Suite 200, Columbia, SC 29201 .... (803) 799–1100
District Director.—Robert Nance.
District Scheduler.—Bre Maxwell.
130 West Main Street, Kingstree, SC 29556 .... (843) 355–1211

Counties: ALLENDALE COUNTY. CITIES AND TOWNS: Allendale, Appleton, Barton, Cave, Fairfax, Martin, Millett, Ulmer, and Sycamore. BAMBERG COUNTY. CITIES AND TOWNSHIPS: Bamberg, Denmark, Erhardt, and Olar. BEAUFORT COUNTY. CITIES AND TOWNS: Corner, Dale, Gardens, Lobeco, Sheldon, and Yemasee. BERKELEY COUNTY (part). CITIES AND TOWNSHIPS: Bethera, Cross, Daniel Island, Huger, Jamestown, Pineville, Russellville, Saint Stephen, and Wando. CALHOUN COUNTY (part). CITY: Cameron, Creston, Fort Motte, and St. Matthews. CHARLESTON COUNTY (part). CITIES AND TOWNSHIPS: Adams Run, Charleston, Edisto Island, Hollywood, Johns Island, Ravenel, and Wadmalaw Island. CLARENDON COUNTY. CITIES AND TOWNSHIPS: Alcolu, Davis Station, Gable, Manning, New Zion, Rimini, Summerton, and Turbeville. COLLETON COUNTY. CITIES AND TOWNSHIPS: Ashton, Cottageville, Green Pond, Hendersonville, Islandton, Jacksonboro, Lodge, Ritter, Round O, Smoaks, Walterboro, and Williams. DORCHESTER COUNTY (part). CITIES AND TOWNSHIPS: Dorchester, Harleyville, Reevesville, Ridgeville, Rosinville, and Saint George. HAMPTON COUNTY. CITIES AND TOWNS: Brunson, Crockettville, Cummings, Early Branch, Estill, Furman, Garnett, Gifford, Hampton, Luray, Miley, Scotia, Varnville, and Yemasee. JASPER COUNTY. CITIES AND TOWNS: Coosawhatchie, Gillisonville, Grays, Hardeeville, Pineland, Pocotaligo, Ridgeland, Robertville, Switzerland, Tarboro, and Tillman. ORANGEBURG COUNTY (part). CITIES AND TOWNSHIPS: Bowman, Branchville, Elloree, Eutawville, Holly Hill, Norway, Orangeburg, Rowesville, Santee, and Vance. RICHLAND COUNTY (part). CITIES AND TOWNSHIPS: Blythewood, Columbia, Eastover, Gadsden, and Hopkins. SUMTER COUNTY (part). CITIES AND TOWNSHIPS: Mayesville and Sumter. WILLIAMSBURG COUNTY. CITIES AND TOWNSHIPS: Cades, Greeleyville, Hemingway, Kingstree, Lane, Nesmith, Salters, and Trio. Population (2010), 660,766.

ZIP Codes: 29001, 29003, 29016, 29018, 29030, 29039, 29042, 29044, 29047–48, 29051–53, 29056, 29059, 29061, 29078, 29080–82, 29102, 29104, 29107, 29111–12, 29114–15, 29117–18, 29125, 29133, 29135, 29142, 29147–48, 29150, 29153, 29160, 29162–63, 29201–06, 29208–10, 29212, 29223, 29225, 29229, 29401, 29403–06, 29409–10, 29418, 29420, 29426, 29431–32, 29434–37, 29445–46, 29448–50, 29452–53, 29456, 29461, 29464, 29468–72, 29474–75, 29477, 29479, 29481, 29483, 29487–88, 29492–93, 29510, 29518, 29530, 29554–56, 29560, 29564, 29580, 29583, 29590–91, 29810, 29812, 29817, 29827, 29836, 29843, 29849, 29906–07, 29909, 29911–12, 29916, 29918, 29921–24, 29927, 29929, 29932, 29934, 29936, 29939, 29940–41, 29943–45

* * *

SEVENTH DISTRICT

TOM RICE, Republican, of South Carolina; born in Charleston County, SC, August 4, 1957; education: attended high school in Myrtle Beach, SC; B.S., University of South Carolina, Columbia, SC, 1979; M.A., University of South Carolina, Columbia, 1982; J.D., University of South Carolina, Columbia, 1982; professional: lawyer, private practice; accountant; chairman of the Horry County Council, 2010–12; committees: Ways and Means; elected to the 113th Congress on November 6, 2012; reelected to each succeeding Congress.

Office Listings

https://rice.house.gov https://facebook.com/reptomrice https://twitter.com/reptomrice

512 Cannon House Office Building, Washington, DC .... (202) 225–9895
Chief of Staff.—Jennifer Watson. FAX: 225–9690
Legislative Director.—Walker Truluck.
2411 North Oak Street, Suite 405, Myrtle Beach, SC 29577 .... (843) 445–6459
1831 West Evans Street, Suite 300, Florence, SC 29501 .... (843) 679–9781

Counties: CHESTERFIELD, DARLINGTON, DILLON, FLORENCE (part), GEORGETOWN, HORRY, MARION, AND MARLBORO. Population (2010), 660,767.

ZIP Codes: 28112, 29009, 29069, 29101, 29114, 29161, 29440, 29442, 29501, 29505–06, 29510–12, 29516, 29519–20, 29525–27, 29530, 29532, 29536, 29540–41, 29543–47, 29550, 29554–55, 29560, 29563, 29565–72, 29574–77, 29579, 29581–85, 29588–89, 29591–94, 29596, 29709, 29718, 29727–28, 29741

SOUTH DAKOTA

(Population 2010, 814,180)

SENATORS

JOHN THUNE, Republican, of Murdo, SD; born in Pierre, SD, January 7, 1961; education: Jones County High School, 1979; B.S., business administration, Biola University, CA; M.B.A., University of South Dakota, 1984; professional: executive director, South Dakota Municipal League; board of directors, National League of Cities; executive director, South Dakota Republican Party, 1989–91; appointed, State Railroad Director, 1991; former congressional legislative assistant and deputy staff director; elected, U.S. House of Representatives, 1997–2003; married: Kimberly Weems, 1984; two children; four grandchildren; committees: Agriculture, Nutrition, and Forestry; Commerce, Science, and Transportation; Finance; serves as Senate Majority Whip; elected to the U.S. Senate on November 2, 2004; reelected to each succeeding Senate term.

Office Listings

https://thune.senate.gov https://facebook.com/SenJohnThune twitter: @SenJohnThune

511 Dirksen Senate Office Building, Washington, DC 20510 .... (202) 224–2321
Chief of Staff.—Ryan Nelson. FAX: 228–5429
Deputy Chief of Staff and Legislative Director.—Jessica McBride.
Communications Director.—Ryan Wrasse.
5015 South Bur Oak, Sioux Falls, SD 57108 .... (605) 334–9596
246 Founders Park Drive, Suite 102, Rapid City, SD 57701 .... (605) 348–7551
320 South First Street, Suite 101, Aberdeen, SD 57401 .... (605) 225–8823

* * *

MIKE ROUNDS, Republican, of Fort Pierre, SD; born in Huron, SD, October 24, 1954; education: South Dakota State University, B.S., political science, 1977; professional: elected to South Dakota Senate in 1990 and reelected in 1992, 1994, 1996, and 1998; committees: Commerce; Education; Legislative Procedure; Local Government; Retirement; State Affairs; Taxation; became Senate Minority Whip in 1993; selected as Senate Majority Leader in 1995; elected as Governor of South Dakota in 2002; reelected in 2006; religion: Roman Catholic; married: Jean Vedvei, 1978; children: Christopher, Brian, Carrie, and John; committees: Armed Services; Banking, Housing, and Urban Affairs; Environment and Public Works; Veterans' Affairs; elected to the U.S. Senate on November 4, 2014.

Office Listings

https://rounds.senate.gov https://facebook.com/SenatorMikeRounds
https://twitter.com/senatorrounds https://instagram.com/senatorrounds

502 Hart Senate Office Building, Washington, DC 20510 .... (202) 224–5842
Chief of Staff.—Rob Skjonsberg.
DC Chief of Staff.—Mark Johnston.
Legislative Director.—Gregg Rickman.
Communications Director.—Natalie Krings.
320 North Main Avenue, Suite B, Sioux Falls, SD 57104 .... (605) 336–0486
1313 West Main Street, Rapid City, SD 57701 .... (605) 343–5035
111 West Capitol Avenue, Suite 210, P.O. Box 309, Pierre, SD 57501 .... (605) 244–1450
514 South Main Street, Suite 100, Aberdeen, SD 57401 .... (605) 225–0366

REPRESENTATIVE

AT LARGE

DUSTY JOHNSON, Republican, of Mitchell, SD; born in Pierre, SD, September 30, 1976; education: B.A., University of South Dakota, Vermillion, SD, 1999; M.P.A., University of Kansas, Lawrence, KS, 2002; professional: vice president of consulting, Vantage Point Solutions (a South Dakota-based engineering and consulting firm specializing in rural telecommunications to help rural providers design, build, and operate broadband systems in 40 states, 2014–18); chief of staff, Office of Governor Daugaard of South Dakota, 2011–14; South Dakota Public Utilities Commissioner, 2005–11 (the youngest utilities commissioner in the nation); senior policy advisor, Office of Governor Mike Rounds of South Dakota, 2003–05; family: married to Jacquelyn; children: three sons, Max, Benjamin, and Owen; committees: Agriculture; Education and Labor; elected to the 116th Congress on November 6, 2018.

Office Listings

https://dustyjohnson.house.gov https://facebook.com/RepDustyJohnson
twitter: @RepDustyJohnson https://instagram.com/repdustyjohnson

1508 Longworth House Office Building, Washington, DC 20515 .... (202) 225–2801
Chief of Staff.—Andrew Christianson.
Legislative Director.—Darren Hedlund.
Communications Director.—Jazmine Kemp.
Scheduler.—Alana Lomis.
300 North Dakota Avenue, Suite 314, Sioux Falls, SD 57104 .... (605) 275–2868
State Director.—Courtney Heitkamp.
State Operations Manager.—Chelsea Schull.
304 6th Avenue, SE., Aberdeen, SD 57401 .... (605) 622–1060
Northeast Director.—Aimee Kamp.
2525 West Main Street, Suite 310, Rapid City, SD 57702 .... (605) 646–6454
West River Director.—Katie Murray.

Population (2010), 814,180.

ZIP Codes: 57001–07, 57010, 57012–18, 57020–22, 57024–59, 57061–73, 57075–79, 57101, 57103–10, 57117–18, 57186, 57188–89, 57192–98, 57201, 57212–14, 57216–21, 57223–27, 57231–39, 57241–43, 57245–49, 57251–53, 57255–66, 57268–74, 57276, 57278–79, 57301, 57311–15, 57317, 57319, 57321–26, 57328–32, 57334–35, 57337, 57339–42, 57344–46, 57348–50, 57353–56, 57358–59, 57361–71, 57373–76, 57379–86, 57399, 57401–02, 57420–22, 57424, 57426–30, 57432–42, 57445–46, 57448–52, 57454–57, 57460–61, 57465–77, 57479, 57481, 57501, 57520–23, 57528–29, 57531–34, 57536–38, 57540–44, 57547–48, 57551–53, 57555, 57559–60, 57562–64, 57566–72, 57574, 57576–77, 57579–80, 57584–85, 57601, 57620–23, 57625–26, 57630–34, 57636, 57638–42, 57644–46, 57648–52, 57656–61, 57701–03, 57706, 57709, 57714, 57716–20, 57722, 57724–25, 57730, 57732, 57735, 57737–38, 57741, 57744–45, 57747–48, 57750–52, 57754–56, 57758–64, 57766–67, 57769–70, 57772–73, 57775–77, 57779–80, 57782–83, 57785, 57787–88, 57790–94, 57799

TENNESSEE

(Population 2010, 6,346,105)

SENATORS

LAMAR ALEXANDER, Republican, of Maryville, TN; born in Maryville, July 3, 1940; only Tennessean ever popularly elected both Governor and U.S. Senator; 2008 general election vote total of 1,579,477 is the largest ever received by a statewide candidate; in October 2019, will have served more combined years (24 years, 9 months) as Governor and U.S. Senator than any other Tennessean; education: graduated with honors in Latin American history, Phi Beta Kappa, Vanderbilt University; New York University Law School; served as *Law Review* editor; professional: clerk to Judge John Minor Wisdom, U.S. Court of Appeals in New Orleans; legislative assistant to Senator Howard Baker (R–TN), 1967; staff assistant to Bryce Harlow, counselor to President Nixon, 1969; manager of Winfield Dunn's general election campaign, 1970; president, University of Tennessee, 1988–91; co-founded Nashville's Dearborn & Ewing law firm, 1972, and two successful businesses: Blackberry Farm, Inc., 1976, and Corporate Child Care Inc., 1987, which merged with Bright Horizons, becoming the largest provider of worksite day care; public service: Republican nominee for Governor of Tennessee, 1974; Governor of Tennessee, 1979–87; chairman of the National Governors Association, 1985–86; chairman, President Reagan's Commission on Americans Outdoors, 1986; U.S. Secretary of Education under President George H.W. Bush, 1991–93; candidate for President of the United States, 1995–96 and 1999–2000; professor of practice in public service, Harvard's Kennedy School of Government, 2001–02; community service: chairman, Salvation Army Red Shield Family Initiative; chairman, Museum of Appalachia in Norris, TN; received Tennessee Conservation League Conservationist of the Year Award; family: married to Honey Alexander; four children; nine grandchildren; chair, Senate Republican Conference, 2007–12; committees: chair, Health, Education, Labor, and Pensions; Appropriations; Energy and Natural Resources; Rules and Administration; elected to the U.S. Senate on November 5, 2002; reelected to each succeeding Senate term.

Office Listings

https://alexander.senate.gov https://facebook.com/senatorlamaralexander twitter: @SenAlexander

455 Dirksen Senate Office Building, Washington, DC 20510 .... (202) 224–4944
Chief of Staff.—David Cleary. FAX: 228–3398
Legislative Director.—Lindsay Garcia.
Counsel.—Allison Martin.
Communications Directors: Ashton Davies, Taylor Haulsee.
Executive Assistant / Scheduler.—Sarah Fairchild.
3322 West End Avenue, Suite 120, Nashville, TN 37203 .... (615) 736–5129
Howard H. Baker, Jr., U.S. Courthouse, 800 Market Street, Suite 112, Knoxville, TN 37902 .... (865) 545–4253
Federal Building, 167 North Main Street, Suite 1068, Memphis, TN 38103 .... (901) 544–4224
111 Murray Guard Drive, Suite D, Jackson, TN 38305 .... (731) 664–0289
Joel E. Solomon Federal Building, 900 Georgia Avenue, Suite 260, Chattanooga, TN 37402 .... (423) 752–5337
Tri-Cities Regional Airport, Terminal Building, P.O. Box 1113, 2525 Highway 75, Suite 101, Blountville, TN 37617 .... (423) 325–6240

* * *

MARSHA BLACKBURN, Republican, of Franklin, TN; born in Laurel, MS, June 6, 1952; education: B.S., Mississippi State University, 1973; professional: retail marketing; public service: American Council of Young Political Leaders; executive director, Tennessee Film, Entertainment, and Music Commission; chairman, Governor's Prayer Breakfast; Tennessee State Senate, 1998–2002; Minority Whip; founding member of the Republican Women's Policy Committee, U.S. House of Representatives; community service: Rotary Club; Chamber of Commerce; Arthritis Foundation; Nashville Symphony Guild Board; Tennessee Biotechnology Association; March of Dimes; American Lung Association; awards: Chi Omega Alumnae Greek Woman of the Year, 1999; Middle Tennessee 100 Most Powerful People, 1999–2002; *More* magazine, ''Women Run The World'' honoree, April 2013; married: Chuck; children: Mary Morgan Ketchel and Chad; two grandchildren; committees: Armed Services; Commerce, Science, and Transportation; Judiciary; Veterans' Affairs; elected to the 108th Congress on November 5, 2002 and reelected to seven succeeding Congresses; elected to the U.S. Senate on November 6, 2018.

Office Listings

https://blackburn.senate.gov https://facebook.com/marshablackburn twitter: @MarshaBlackburn

357 Dirksen Senate Office Building, Washington, DC 20510 .... (202) 224–3344
Chief of Staff.—Chuck Flint. FAX: 228–0566
Legislative Director.—Sean Farrell.
Executive Assistant.—Grace Burch.
10 West Martin Luther King Boulevard, 6th Floor, Chattanooga, TN 37402 .... (423) 541–2939
FAX: 541–2944
91 Stonebridge Boulevard, Suite 103, Jackson, TN 38305 .... (731) 660–3971
FAX: 660–3978
800 Market Street, Suite 121, Knoxville, TN 37902 .... (865) 540–3781
FAX: 540–7952
100 Peabody Place, Suite 1125, Memphis, TN 38103 .... (901) 527–9199
State Director.—Nick Kistenmacher. FAX: 527–9515
3322 West End Avenue, Suite 610, Nashville, TN 37203 .... (629) 800–6600
FAX: 298–2148
1105 East Jackson Boulevard, Suite 4, Jonesborough, TN 37659 .... (423) 753–4009
FAX: 788–0250

REPRESENTATIVES

FIRST DISTRICT

DAVID "PHIL" ROE, Republican, of Johnson City, TN; born in Clarksville, TN; July 21, 1945; education: B.S., Austin Peay State University, Clarksville, TN, 1967; M.D., University of Tennessee, Knoxville, TN, 1970; professional: U.S. Army Medical Corps, 1970–72; Vice Mayor of Johnson City, 2003–07; Mayor of Johnson City, 2007–09; religion: member of Munsey United Methodist Church; spouse: Clarinda; children: David C. Roe, John Roe, and Whitney Larkin; caucuses: Academic Medicine Caucus; Doctors Caucus; committees: ranking member, Veterans' Affairs; Education and Labor; elected to the 111th Congress; reelected to each succeeding Congress.

Office Listings

https://roe.house.gov https://facebook.com/DrPhilRoe https://twitter.com/drphilroe

102 Cannon House Office Building, Washington, DC 20515 .... (202) 225–6356
Chief of Staff.—Matt Meyer. FAX: 225–5714
Press Secretary.—Whitley Alexander.
Scheduler.—Courtney Eubanks.
Legislative Director.—Aaron Bill.
Legislative Staff: Kyle Jacobs, John Witherspoon.
Legislative Correspondent.—Liam MacDonald.
Staff Assistant.—Hannah King.
205 Revere Street, Kingsport, TN 37660 .... (423) 247–8161
District Director.—Bill Darden. FAX: 247–0119
Administrative Assistant.—Sheila Houser.
Caseworkers: Sandra Barfield, Carolyn Ferguson, Tracie O'Hara.
1609 Walters State CC Drive, Suite 4, Morristown, TN 37813 .... (423) 254–1400
District Representative.—Daryl Brady. FAX: 254–1403
Caseworkers: Cheryl Bennett, Angie Jarnagin.
Fellow.—Terry Harris.

Counties: Carter, Cocke, Greene, Hamblen, Hancock, Hawkins, Jefferson, Johnson, Sevier, Sullivan, Unicoi, and Washington. Population (2010), 705,123.

ZIP Codes: 37601, 37604, 37614–18, 37620, 37640–43, 37645, 37650, 37656–60, 37663–65, 37681–83, 37686–88, 37690–92, 37694, 37711, 37713, 37722, 37725, 37727, 37731, 37738, 37743, 37745, 37748, 37753, 37760, 37764–65, 37809–11, 37813–14, 37818, 37821, 37843, 37857, 37860, 37862–63, 37865, 37869, 37871, 37873, 37876–77, 37879, 37881, 37890, 37891

* * *

SECOND DISTRICT

TIM BURCHETT, Republican, of Knoxville, TN; born August 25, 1964 in Knoxville; education: B.S., University of Tennessee, 1988; professional: small businessman; member, District 18, Tennessee State House of Representatives, 1995–98, Nashville, TN; Tennessee State Senator, District 7, 1999–2010, Knoxville, TN; Mayor, Knox County, Knoxville, TN, 2010–18; religion: Presbyterian; committees: Budget; Foreign Affairs; Small Business; elected to the 116th Congress on November 6, 2018.

Office Listings

https://burchett.house.gov https://facebook.com/reptimburchett
https://twitter.com/reptimburchett https://instagram.com/reptimburchett

1122 Longworth House Office Building, Washington, DC 20515 .... (202) 225–5435
Chief of Staff.—Michael Grider. FAX: 225–6440
Legislative Director.—Kelsey Wolfgram.
Scheduler.—Denise Lambert.
Assistant Scheduler / Staff Assistant.—Canon Woodward.
Legislative Staff.—Will Strother.
Legislative Correspondent.—Rachel Partlow.
Press Secretary.—Will Bensur.
800 Market Street, Suite 110, Knoxville, TN 37902 .... (865) 523–3772
District Director / Communications Director.—Jennifer Linginfelter.
Community Outreach.—Sarah Fansler.
Senior Caseworker.—Jennifer Stansberry.
Caseworkers: Pat Gibson, Madison Heinsohn.
331 Court Street, Blount County Courthouse, Maryville, TN 37804 .... (865) 984–5464

Counties: BLOUNT, CAMPBELL, CLAIBORNE, GRAINGER, JEFFERSON, KNOX, AND LOUDON. CITIES AND TOWNSHIPS: Alcoa, Farragut, Halls (Knox Co.), Harrogate, Jefferson City, Jellico, Knoxville, Lenoir City, Loudon, Maryville, Powell, and Seymour. Population (2010), 714,622.

ZIP Codes: 37701, 37709, 37721 (part), 37725 (part), 37737, 37742 (part), 37754 (part), 37764 (part), 37771 (part), 37772, 37774 (part), 37777, 37779 (part), 37801 (part), 37802–04, 37806, 37807 (part), 37820 (part), 37830 (part), 37846 (part), 37849 (part), 37853, 37865 (part), 37871 (part), 37874 (part), 37876 (part), 37878, 37882, 37884, 37885 (part), 37886, 37901–02, 37909, 37912, 37914–19, 37920 (part), 37921–24, 37927–30, 37931 (part), 37932–33, 37938 (part), 37939–40, 37950, 37995–98

* * *

THIRD DISTRICT

CHUCK FLEISCHMANN, Republican, of Ooltewah, TN; born in New York City, NY, October 11, 1962; education: graduated from Elk Grove High School, Elk Grove Village, IL, 1980; B.A., political science, University of Illinois, Urbana-Champaign, IL, 1983; J.D., University of Tennessee College of Law, Knoxville, TN, 1986; professional: attorney; small business owner; former president of the Chattanooga Bar Association, 1996; former chairman of the Chattanooga Lawyers Pro Bono Committee; religion: Catholic; married: Brenda Fleischmann; three children; committees: Appropriations; elected to the 112th Congress on November 2, 2010; reelected to each succeeding Congress.

Office Listings

https://fleischmann.house.gov https://facebook.com/repchuck
https://twitter.com/RepChuck https://instagram.com/repchuck

2410 Rayburn House Office Building, Washington, DC 20515 .... (202) 225–3271
Chief of Staff.—Jim Hippe.
Legislative Director.—Daniel Tidwell.
Communications Director.—Kasey Lovett.
Legislative Assistant / Scheduler.—Holly Hendrix.
900 Georgia Avenue, Suite 126, Chattanooga, TN 37402 .... (423) 756–2342
District Director.—Bob White.
200 Administration Road, Suite 100, Oak Ridge, TN 37830 .... (865) 576–1976
6 East Madison Avenue, Athens, TN 37303 .... (423) 745–4671

Counties: ANDERSON, BRADLEY (part), CAMPBELL (part), HAMILTON, MCMINN, MONROE, MORGAN, POLK, ROANE, SCOTT, AND UNION. Population (2010), 711,391.

ZIP Codes: 37302–03, 37307–11, 37315, 37317, 37322–23, 37325–26, 37329, 37331, 37333, 37336, 37338, 37341, 37343, 37350–51, 37353–54, 37361–63, 37369–70, 37373, 37377, 37379, 37385, 37391, 37402–12, 37415, 37419, 37421, 37705, 37710, 37714, 37716, 37719, 37721, 37729, 37732–33, 37754–57, 37763, 37766, 37769, 37770–71, 37774, 37779, 37801, 37807, 37825–26, 37828–30, 37840–41, 37845–49, 37852, 37854, 37866, 37870, 37872, 37874, 37880, 37885, 37887–88, 37892, 37931, 38504

* * *

FOURTH DISTRICT

SCOTT DESJARLAIS, Republican, of South Pittsburg, TN; born in Sturgis, SD, February 21, 1964; education: B.S., chemistry and psychology, University of South Dakota, 1987; M.D., University of South Dakota School of Medicine, Vermillion, 1991; professional: general practitioner, Grand View Medical Center, Jasper, TN; religion: member, Epiphany Episcopalian Church, Sherwood, TN; married: Amy; children: Tyler, Ryan, and Maggie; committees: Agriculture; Armed Services; elected to the 112th Congress on November 2, 2010; reelected to each succeeding Congress.

Office Listings

https://desjarlais.house.gov https://facebook.com/ScottDesJarlaisTN04 https://twitter.com/DesJarlaisTN04

2301 Rayburn House Office Building, Washington, DC 20515 .... (202) 225–6831
Chief of Staff.—Richard Vaughn. FAX: 226–5172
Legislative Director.—Vacant.
Communications Director.—Brendan Thomas.
301 Keith Street, SW., Suite 212, Cleveland, TN 37311 .... (423) 472–7500
808 South Garden Street, 2nd Floor, Columbia, TN 38401 .... (931) 381–9920
200 South Jefferson Street, Suite 311, Federal Building, Winchester, TN 37398 .... (931) 962–3180
305 West Main Street, Murfreesboro, TN 37130 .... (615) 896–1986

Counties: BEDFORD, BLEDSOE, BRADLEY (part), FRANKLIN, GRUNDY, LINCOLN, MARION, MARSHALL, MAURY (part), MOORE, RHEA, RUTHERFORD, SEQUATCHIE, VAN BUREN (part), AND WARREN. Population (2010), 705,123.

ZIP Codes: 37014, 37018–20, 37025, 37034, 37037, 37046–47, 37060, 37063–64, 37085–86, 37090–91, 37110–11, 37118, 37122, 37127–30, 37132, 37135, 37144, 37149, 37153, 37160, 37166–67, 37174, 37180, 37183, 37190, 37301, 37305–06, 37308–13, 37318, 37321–24, 37327–28, 37330, 37332, 37334–40, 37345, 37347–49, 37352–53, 37356–57, 37359–60, 37365–67, 37373–83, 37387–89, 37394, 37396–98, 37405, 37419, 37773, 37778, 37826, 37880, 38402, 38449, 38451, 38453, 38459, 38472, 38474, 38483, 38488, 38550, 38555, 38557, 38559, 38572, 38581, 38583, 38585, 39401

* * *

FIFTH DISTRICT

JIM COOPER, Democrat, of Nashville, TN; born in Nashville, June 19, 1954; education: B.A., history and economics, University of North Carolina at Chapel Hill, 1975; Rhodes Scholar, Oxford University, 1977; J.D., Harvard Law School, 1980; admitted to Tennessee Bar, 1980; professional: attorney; Waller, Lansden, Dortch, and Davis (law firm), 1980–82; managing director, Equitable Securities, 1995–99; adjunct professor, Vanderbilt University Owen School of Management, 1995–2002 and 2006–18; partner, Brentwood Capital Advisors LLC, 1999–2002; married: Martha Hays; three children; caucuses: Blue Dog Coalition; New Democrat Coalition; committees: Armed Services; Budget; Oversight and Reform; elected to the U.S. House of Representatives, 1982–95; elected to the 108th Congress on November 5, 2002; reelected to each succeeding Congress.

Office Listings

https://cooper.house.gov https://facebook.com/JimCooper https://twitter.com/repjimcooper

1536 Longworth House Office Building, Washington, DC 20515 .... (202) 225–4311
Chief of Staff.—Lisa Quigley. FAX: 226–1035
Legislative Director / Deputy Chief of Staff.—Jason Lumia.
605 Church Street, Nashville, TN 37219 .... (615) 736–5295

Counties: CHEATHAM (part), DAVIDSON, AND DICKSON. Population (2010), 713,990.

ZIP Codes: 37011, 37013, 37015, 37024–25, 37027, 37029, 37032, 37035–36, 37043, 37051–52, 37055–56, 37062, 37064, 37070, 37072–73, 37076, 37080, 37082, 37086, 37101, 37115–16, 37122, 37135, 37138, 37143, 37146, 37165, 37171, 37181, 37187, 37189, 37201–22, 37224, 37227–30, 37232, 37234–36, 37238, 37240–44, 37246, 37250

* * *

SIXTH DISTRICT

JOHN W. ROSE, Republican, of Cookeville, TN; born in Cookeville, February 23, 1965; education: B.S., agribusiness economics, Tennessee Technological University, 1988; M.S., agricultural economics, Purdue University, West Lafayette, IN, 1990; J.D., Vanderbilt University Law School, Nashville, TN, 1993; professional: co-founder and president, IT certification company, Transcender Corporation, 1992–2000; owner/operator, Rose Farm, 1999–present; president, Boson Software LLC (assists in training of IT professionals), 2005–present; Tennessee State Commissioner of Agriculture, 2002–03; married: wife, Chelsea; one child; committees: Financial Services; elected to the 116th Congress on November 6, 2018.

Office Listings

https://johnrose.house.gov https://facebook.com/repjohnrose twitter: @RepJohnRose

1232 Longworth House Office Building, Washington, DC 20515 .... (202) 225–4231
Chief of Staff.—Van Hilleary.
Scheduler.—Leah Bane.
321 East Spring Street, Suite 301, Cookeville, TN 38501 .... (931) 854–9430
355 North Belvedere Drive, Suite 308, Gallatin, TN 37066 .... (615) 206–8204
District Director.—Rebecca Foster.

Counties: CANNON, CHEATHAM (part), CLAY, COFFEE, CUMBERLAND, DEKALB, FENTRESS, JACKSON, MACON, OVERTON, PICKETT, PUTNAM, ROBERTSON, SMITH, SUMNER, TROUSDALE, VAN BUREN, WHITE, AND WILSON. Population (2010), 705,123.

ZIP Codes: 37010, 37012, 37015–16, 37018, 37022, 37030–32, 37034–36, 37048–49, 37059, 37066, 37072–75, 37077, 37080, 37082–83, 37085, 37087, 37090, 37095, 37143, 37155, 37118–19, 37122, 37141, 37146, 37150, 37152, 37166, 37172, 37183–84, 37186–88, 37190, 37337, 37342, 37355, 37357, 37360, 37388, 37723, 37726, 37854, 38501–06, 38543–44, 38547–49, 38551, 38553, 38555–56, 38558–59, 38562, 38565, 38570–74, 38577, 38579, 38581, 38583, 38585, 38587, 38589

* * *

SEVENTH DISTRICT

MARK GREEN, Republican, of Clarksville, TN; born November 8, 1964 in Jacksonville, FL; education: B.S., business quantitative, West Point, 1986; masters certificate, systems management, University of Southern California; M.D., Wright State University, Dayton, OH, 1999; military: U.S. Army Infantry officer, Fort Knox, KY: rifle platoon leader, scout platoon leader, battalion adjutant, infantry battalion; airborne battalion supply officer and rifle company commander, 82nd Airborne Division, Fort Bragg, NC; medical residency, Fort Hood, TX; flight surgeon, 160th Special Operations Aviation Regiment (tour of duty in the Afghanistan War and two tours of duty in the Iraq War); awards and honors: Bronze Star; Meritorious Service Medal with two oak clusters; Air Medal with ''V'' Device; Achievement Medal with three oak leaf clusters; Army Commendation Medal with two oak clusters; Flight Surgeon of the Year; Combat Medical Badge; Air Assault Badge; Flight Surgeon Badge; Army Ranger Tab; Senior Parachutist Badge; professional: chief of emergency medicine, Gateway Medical Center, Clarksville, TN, 2004–07; president, Emergency Services Network, a hospital staffing company, 2006–08; chief of emergency medicine, Jennie Stuart Medical Center, Hopkinsville, KY, 2007–08; founder and president, Align MD, hospital staffing company, 2008–15 and CEO and chairman of the Board, 2015–16; Tennessee State Senator, District 22, Nashville, TN, 2013–19; family: wife, Camie; children, Mitchell and Alexa; religion: member, LifePoint Church, Clarksville, TN; committees: Homeland Security; Oversight and Reform; elected to the 116th Congress on November 6, 2018.

Office Listings

https://markgreen.house.gov https://facebook.com/RepMarkGreenTN https://twitter.com/repmarkgreen

533 Cannon House Office Building, Washington, DC 20515 .... (202) 225–2811
Chief of Staff.—Stephen Siao. FAX: 225–3004
Legislative Director.—Jay Kronzer.
Communications Director.—Sydney Thomas.
Scheduler.—Jerrica Proferes.
305 Public Square, Suite 212, Franklin, TN 37064 .... (629) 223–6050
District Director.—Steve Allbrooks.
128 North 2nd Street, Suite 104, Clarksville, TN 37040 .... (931) 266–4483

Counties: BENTON (part), CHESTER, DECATUR, GILES, HARDEMAN, HARDIN, HENDERSON, HICKMAN, HOUSTON, HUMPHREYS, LAWRENCE, LEWIS, MAURY (part), MCNAIRY, MONTGOMERY, PERRY, STEWART, WAYNE, AND WILLIAMSON. Population (2010), 705,192.

ZIP Codes: 37010, 37014–15, 37023, 37025, 37027–28, 37032, 37037, 37040, 37042–43, 37046–47, 37050–52, 37055, 37059–62, 37067, 37078–79, 37096–98, 37101, 37134–35, 37137, 37140, 37142, 37144, 37171, 37174–79, 37181,

37185, 37191, 37214–15, 37220, 38008, 38039, 38042, 38044, 38052, 38061, 38067, 38075, 38221, 38310, 38463–64, 38468–69, 38471–78, 38481–83, 38485–87, 42223

* * *

EIGHTH DISTRICT

DAVID KUSTOFF, Republican, of Germantown, TN; born in Memphis, TN, October 8, 1966; education: undergraduate degree, University of Memphis, Memphis, TN; law degree, University of Memphis Cecil C. Humphreys School of Law, 1992; professional: opened a law firm in Memphis, in 1998; chairman, Shelby County GOP, 1995–99; Tennessee chairman of both Bush/Cheney presidential campaigns in 2000 and 2004; appointed U.S. Attorney for the Western District of Tennessee by President Bush in 2006; served on the board of BankTennessee, 2010–16; appointed to the Tennessee Higher Education Commission by Tennessee Governor Bill Haslam in 2015; religion: Jewish; married: Roberta Kustoff; children: two; caucuses: ProTENNESSEE Israel Caucus, Sportsmen's Caucus; committees: Financial Services; elected to the 115th Congress on November 8, 2016; reelected to the 116th Congress on November 6, 2018.

Office Listings

https://kustoff.house.gov https://facebook.com/RepDavidKustoff twitter: @RepDavidKustoff

523 Cannon House Office Building, Washington, DC 20515 .... (202) 225–4714
Chief of Staff.—Tyler Threadgill.
Deputy Chief of Staff.—Justin Melvin.
Communications Director.—Kate Kelly.
Legislative Director.—Andrew Hogin.
Legislative Correspondent.—John Newman.
Legislative Assistant.—Eliana Goodman.
Scheduler.—Anderson Briggs.
Staff Assistant.—William Courtney.
425 West Court Street, Dyersburg, TN 38024 .... (731) 412–1037
117 North Liberty Street, Jackson, TN 38301 .... (731) 423–4848
5900 Poplar Avenue, Suite 202, Memphis, TN 38119 .... (901) 682–4422

Counties: BENTON (part), CARROLL, CROCKETT, DYER, FAYETTE, GIBSON, HAYWOOD, HENRY, LAKE, LAUDERDALE, MADISON, OBION, SHELBY (part), TIPTON, AND WEAKLEY. Population (2010), 705,122.

ZIP Codes: 38001–02, 38004, 38006–07, 38011–12, 38015–19, 38021, 38023–24, 38028–30, 38034, 38036–37, 38039–42, 38046–47, 38049–50, 38053–54, 38057–60, 38063, 38066, 38068–70, 38075–77, 38079–80, 38111, 38117, 38119–20, 38125, 38128, 38133–35, 38138–39, 38141, 38152, 38201, 38220–22, 38224–26, 38229–33, 38235, 38237, 38240–42, 38251, 38253–61, 38301, 38305, 38313, 38316–18, 38326, 38330, 38337, 38341–44, 38348, 38351, 38355–56, 38358, 38362, 38366, 38369, 38382, 38387, 38390–92, 38401

* * *

NINTH DISTRICT

STEPHEN IRA "STEVE" COHEN, Democrat, of Memphis, TN; born in Memphis, May 24, 1949; education: attended Pasadena, CA, Polytechnic School, 1964–66; graduated from Coral Gables, FL, Senior High School, 1967; B.A., Vanderbilt University, Nashville, TN, 1971; J.D., University of Memphis, 1973; professional: attorney, Memphis Police Department, 1975–78; lawyer, private practice; vice president, Tennessee State Constitutional Convention, 1977; Shelby County, TN, commissioner, 1978–80; member of the Tennessee State Senate, 1982–2006; delegate to the Democratic National Convention, 1980, 1992, 2004, 2008, 2012, 2016; Helsinki Commission (Commission on Security and Cooperation in Europe); committees: Judiciary; Science, Space, and Technology; Transportation and Infrastructure; elected to the 110th Congress on November 7, 2006; reelected to each succeeding Congress.

Office Listings

https://cohen.house.gov https://facebook.com/CongressmanSteveCohen
https://twitter.com/repcohen https://instagram.com/repcohen

2104 Rayburn House Office Building, Washington, DC 20515 .... (202) 225–3265
Chief of Staff.—Marilyn Dillihay. FAX: 225–5663
Scheduler.—Hannah Ryans.
Legislative Director.—Reisha Buster.
Communications Director.—Bartholomew Sullivan.
167 North Main Street, Suite 369, Memphis, TN 38103 .... (901) 544–4131
FAX: 544–4329

County: SHELBY COUNTY (part). CITY: Memphis. Population (2010), 705,123.

ZIP Codes: 37501, 38016, 38018, 38053, 38101, 38103–09, 38111–20, 38122–28, 38130–36, 38138, 38141, 38146, 38148, 38151–52, 38159, 38167–68, 38173–75, 38181–82, 38186, 38188, 38190, 38193–94

TEXAS

(Population 2010, 25,145,561)

SENATORS

JOHN CORNYN, Republican, of Austin, TX; born in Houston, TX, February 2, 1952; education: graduated, Trinity University, and St. Mary's School of Law, San Antonio, TX; master of laws, University of Virginia, Charlottesville, VA; professional: attorney; Bexar County District Court Judge; Presiding Judge, Fourth Administrative Judicial Region; Texas Supreme Court, 1990–97; Texas Attorney General, 1999–2002; community service: Salvation Army Adult Rehabilitation Council; World Affairs Council of San Antonio; Lutheran General Hospital Board; chair, National Republican Senatorial Committee, 2009–13; committees: Finance; Judiciary; Select Committee on Intelligence; elected to the U.S. Senate on November 5, 2002, for the term beginning January 3, 2003; appointed to the Senate on December 2, 2002, to fill the vacancy caused by the resignation of Senator Phil Gramm; reelected to each succeeding Senate term.

Office Listings

https://cornyn.senate.gov https://facebook.com/SenJohnCornyn

517 Hart Senate Office Building, Washington, DC 20510 .... (202) 224–2934
Chief of Staff.—Beth Jafari. FAX: 224–5220
Legislative Director.—Stephen Tausend.
5300 Memorial Drive, Suite 980, Houston, TX 77007 .... (713) 572–3337
Providence Tower, 5001 Spring Valley Road, #1125E, Dallas, TX 75244 .... (972) 239–1310
100 East Ferguson Street, Suite 1004, Tyler, TX 75702 .... (903) 593–0902
221 West Sixth Street, Suite 1530, Austin, TX 78701 .... (512) 469–6034
Wells Fargo Center, 1500 Broadway, #1230, Lubbock, TX 79401 .... (806) 472–7533
222 East Van Buren, Suite 404, Harlingen, TX 78550 .... (956) 423–0162
600 Navarro Street, Suite 210, San Antonio, TX 78205 .... (210) 224–7485

* * *

TED CRUZ, Republican, of Houston, TX; born December 22, 1970; raised in Houston, TX; education: graduated *cum laude* from Princeton University with a B.A. from the Woodrow Wilson School of Public and International Affairs in 1992 and *magna cum laude* from Harvard Law School with a J.D. in 1995; professional: domestic policy advisor of the 2000 Bush-Cheney campaign; director of the Office of Policy Planning at the Federal Trade Commission; Associate Deputy Attorney General at the U.S. Department of Justice; adjunct professor of law at the University of Texas School of Law; Solicitor General of the State of Texas; partner at Morgan, Lewis & Bockius LLP; religion: Southern Baptist; married: Heidi Cruz; committees: Commerce, Science, and Transportation; Foreign Relations; Judiciary; Rules and Administration; Joint Economic Committee; elected to the U.S. Senate on November 6, 2012; reelected to the U.S. Senate on November 6, 2018.

Office Listings

https://cruz.senate.gov https://facebook.com/SenatorTedCruz https://twitter.com/SenTedCruz

127A Russell Senate Office Building, Washington, DC 20510 .... (202) 224–5922
Chief of Staff.—Steve Chartan.
Deputy Chief of Staff.—Sam Cooper.
Legislative Director.—Sean McLean.
State Director.—Carl Mica.
300 East 8th Street, Suite 961, Austin, TX 78701 .... (512) 916–5834
The Mickey Leland Federal Building, 1919 Smith Street, Suite 9047, Houston, TX 77002 (713) 718–3057
Lee Park Tower II, 3626 North Hall Street, Suite 410, Dallas, TX 75219 .... (214) 599–8749
9901 IH–10 West, Suite 950, San Antonio, TX 78230 .... (210) 340–2885
305 South Broadway Avenue, Suite 501, Tyler, TX 75702 .... (903) 593–5130
200 South 10th Street, Suite 1603, McAllen, TX 78501 .... (956) 686–7339

REPRESENTATIVES

FIRST DISTRICT

LOUIE GOHMERT, Republican, of Tyler, TX; born in Pittsburg, TX, August 18, 1953; education: B.A., Texas A&M University, 1975; J.D., Baylor University, Waco, TX, 1977; professional: U.S. Army, 1978–82; District Judge, Smith County, 1992–2002; appointed by Governor Rick Perry to complete an unexpired term as Chief Justice of the 12th Court of Appeals, 2002–03; Brigade Commander of the Corps of Cadets, Texas A&M; organizations: president of the South Tyler Rotary Club; Boy Scout District Board of Directors; religion: deacon of Green Acres Baptist Church; director of Leadership Tyler; director of Centrepoint Ministries; married: Kathy; children: Katy, Caroline, and Sarah; committees: Judiciary; Natural Resources; elected to the 109th Congress on November 2, 2004; reelected to each succeeding Congress.

Office Listings

https://gohmert.house.gov https://facebook.com/RepLouieGohmert twitter: @replouiegohmert

2267 Rayburn House Office Building, Washington, DC 20515 .... (202) 225–3035
Chief of Staff.—Connie Hair. FAX: 226–1230
Legislative Director.—Caralee Conklin.
Communications Director.—Kimberly Willingham.
1121 East Southeast Loop 323, Suite 206, Tyler, TX 75701 .... (903) 561–6349

Counties: ANGELINA, GREGG, HARRISON, NACOGDOCHES, PANOLA, RUSK, SABINE, SAN AUGUSTINE, SHELBY, SMITH, UPSHUR (part), AND WOOD (part). Population (2010), 710,704.

ZIP Codes: 75140, 75451, 75480, 75494, 75601–08, 75615, 75631, 75633, 75637, 75639–47, 75650–54, 75657–63, 75666–67, 75669–72, 75680–85, 75687–89, 75691–94, 75701–13, 75750, 75755, 75757, 75760, 75762, 75765, 75771, 75773, 75783–84, 75788–89, 75790–92, 75798–99, 75901–04, 75915, 75925–26, 75929–31, 75934–39, 75941–44, 75946, 75948–49, 75954, 75958–65, 75968–69, 75972–76, 75978, 75980

* * *

SECOND DISTRICT

DAN CRENSHAW, Republican, of Houston, TX; born in Aberdeen, Scotland, to American parents, March 14, 1984; education: B.A., foreign relations, Tufts University, Medford, MA, 2006; M.P.A., John F. Kennedy School of Government at Harvard University, Cambridge, MA, 2017; military: United States Navy, Navy SEAL, Lieutenant Commander USN (Ret.), 2006–16; awards: two Bronze Stars (one with Valor), Purple Heart, Navy Commendation Medal with Valor, among others; married: Tara Crenshaw; committees: Budget; Homeland Security; elected to the 116th Congress on November 6, 2018.

Office Listings

https://crenshaw.house.gov https://facebook.com/RepDanCrenshaw https://twitter.com/repdancrenshaw
https://youtube.com/channel/UC2XDiCjAHtJqnSEzrHAY5IQ

413 Cannon House Office Building, Washington, DC 20515 .... (202) 225–6565
Chief of Staff.—Eliza Baker.
Legislative Director.—Matthew Hodge.
Communications Director.—Kerry Rom.
Administrative Director.—Daniel Walden.
1849 Kingwood Drive, Suite 100, Kingwood, TX 77339 .... (713) 860–1330
District Director.—Sue Walden.
Field Representative.—Kaaren Cambio.
9720 Cypresswood Drive, Suite 206, Houston, Texas 77070 .... (281) 640–7720

Counties: HARRIS. Population (2010), 698,488.

ZIP Codes: 77002, 77004–08, 77018–19, 77024–25, 77030, 77040–41, 77043–44, 77055, 77064–66, 77069–70, 77079–80, 77084, 77086, 77088, 77092, 77095, 77098, 77336, 77338–39, 77345–46, 77357, 77365, 77373, 77375, 77377, 77379, 77388, 77396, 77429, 77532

* * *

THIRD DISTRICT

VAN TAYLOR, Republican, of Plano, TX; born in Dallas, Dallas County, TX, August 1, 1972; education: A.B., Harvard University, Cambridge, MA, 1995; M.B.A., Harvard University, Cambridge, MA, 2001; professional: businessman; member of the Texas House of Representatives, 2010–15; member of the Texas State Senate, 2015–19; military: United States Marine Corps, Officer 2nd Lieutenant-Major, Marine Officer, Captain; awards: Combat Action Ribbon; Navy Commendation Medal with ''V'' for valor; Presidential Unit Citation; religion: Episcopalian; married: 2002; children: three; caucuses: founding member, For Country Caucus; co-chair,

Carbonated and Non-Alcoholic (C.A.N.) Caucus; co-chair, Congressional Caucus on Innovation and Entrepreneurship; Bipartisan Task Force for Combating Anti-Semitism; Congressional Future of Work Caucus; Congressional Veteran Jobs Caucus; Financial Security Caucus; Freshman Working Group on Addiction; House Automotive Caucus; Men's Health Caucus; Navy and Marine Corps Caucus; Servicewomen and Women Veterans Caucus; committees: Financial Services; elected to the 116th Congress on November 6, 2018.

Office Listings

https://vantaylor.house.gov https://facebook.com/RepVanTaylor
twitter: @RepVanTaylor https://instagram.com/repvantaylor

1404 Longworth House Office Building, Washington, DC 20515 .... (202) 225–4201
Chief of Staff.—Lonnie Dietz. FAX: 225–1485
Deputy Chief of Staff and Communications Director.—Anna McCormack.
Legislative Director.—Jett Thompson.
Financial Administrator.—Margaret Wetherald.
5600 Tennyson Parkway, #275, Plano, TX 75024 .... (972) 202–4150
District Director.—Sable Coleman-Jones.

Counties: The 3rd District of Texas encompasses the majority of COLLIN COUNTY, including all or part of the CITIES of Allen, Anna, Blue Ridge, Dallas, Fairview, Frisco, Lavon, Lowry Crossing, Lucas, McKinney, Melissa, Murphy, New Hope, Parker, Plano, Princeton, Prosper, Richardson, St. Paul, Wylie, and portions of unincorporated land in COLLIN COUNTY. Population (2010), 747,284.

ZIP Codes: 75002 (part), 75009 (part), 75013, 75023, 75024 (part), 75025, 75035, 75044 (part), 75048 (part), 75069–70, 75071 (part), 75074–75, 75078 (part), 75080 (part), 75082 (part), 75093–94 (part), 75098 (part), 75166 (part), 75173 (part), 75248 (part), 75252 (part), 75287 (part), 75407, 75409 (part), 75424 (part), 75442 (part), 75454

* * *

FOURTH DISTRICT

VACANT

Counties: BOWIE COUNTY. CITIES AND TOWNSHIPS: DeKalb, Hooks, Leary, Maud, Nash, New Boston, Red Lick, Redwater, Texarkana, and Wake Village. CAMP COUNTY. CITIES AND TOWNSHIPS: Pittsburg and Rocky Mound. CASS COUNTY. CITIES AND TOWNSHIPS: Atlanta, Avinger, Bloomburg, Domino, Douglassville, Hughes Springs, Linden, Marietta, and Queen City. COLLIN COUNTY. CITIES AND TOWNSHIPS: Anna, Blue Ridge, Celina, Farmersville, Josephine, Lavon, Nevada, Royse City, Van Alstyne, Westminster, Weston, and Wylie. DELTA COUNTY. CITIES AND TOWNSHIPS: Cooper and Pecan Gap. FANNIN COUNTY. CITIES AND TOWNSHIPS: Bailey, Bonham, Dodd City, Ector, Honey Grove, Ladonia, Leonard, Pecan Gap, Ravenna, Savoy, Trenton, Whitewright, and Windom. FRANKLIN COUNTY. CITIES AND TOWNSHIPS: Mount Vernon and Winnsboro. GRAYSON COUNTY. CITIES AND TOWNSHIPS: Bells, Collinsville, Denison, Dorchester, Gunter, Howe, Knollwood, Pottsboro, Sadler, Sherman, Southmayd, Tioga, Tom Bean, Van Alstyne, Whitesboro, and Whitewright. HOPKINS COUNTY. CITIES AND TOWNSHIPS: Como, Cumby, Sulphur Springs, and Tira. HUNT COUNTY. CITIES AND TOWNSHIPS: Caddo Mills, Campbell, Celeste, Commerce, Greenville, Hawk Cove, Josephine, Lone Oak, Neylandville, Quinlan, West Tawakoni, and Wolfe City. LAMAR COUNTY. CITIES AND TOWNSHIPS: Blossom, Deport, Paris, Reno, Roxton, Sun Valley, and Toco. MARION COUNTY. CITIES AND TOWNSHIPS: Jefferson City and Pine Harbor. MORRIS COUNTY. CITIES AND TOWNSHIPS: Daingerfield, Hughes Springs, Lone Star, Naples, and Omaha. RAINS COUNTY. CITIES AND TOWNSHIPS: Alba, East Tawakoni, Emory, and Point. RED RIVER COUNTY. CITIES AND TOWNSHIPS: Annona, Avery, Bogata, Clarksville, Deport, and Detroit. ROCKWALL COUNTY. CITIES AND TOWNSHIPS: Fate, Garland, Heath, Mclendon-Chisholm, Mobile City, Rockwall, Rowlett, Royse City, and Wylie. TITUS COUNTY. CITIES AND TOWNSHIPS: Miller's Cove, Mount Pleasant, and Talco. UPSHUR COUNTY. CITIES AND TOWNSHIPS: Clarksville City, East Mountain, Gilmer, Gladewater, Ore City, Union Grove, and Warren City. Population (2010), 705,523.

ZIP Codes: 75002, 75009, 75013, 75019, 75030, 75032, 75034–35, 75040–41, 75058, 75069, 75071, 75074, 75076, 75078, 75087–88, 75090, 75094, 75097–98, 75132, 75135, 75164, 75166, 75173, 75189, 75407, 75409, 75413–14, 75416–18, 75422–24, 75426, 75428–29, 75431–33, 75435–36, 75438–40, 75442, 75446, 75449, 75452–55, 75457, 75459, 75460, 75462, 75469, 75472–74, 75476–77, 75479, 75482, 75486–87, 75489, 75490–95, 75501, 75550–51, 75554, 75556, 75559–61, 75563, 75566–73, 75572, 75630, 75638, 75644–47, 75656–57, 75668, 75683, 75686, 75855, 76233, 76264, 76268, 76271, 76273

* * *

FIFTH DISTRICT

LANCE GOODEN, Republican, of Terrell, TX; born in Nashville, TN, December 1, 1982; education: graduated from Terrell High School, Terrell, TX, 2001; B.A., University of Texas, Austin, TX, 2004; B.B.A., University of Texas, Austin, TX, 2004; professional: insurance; member of the Texas House of Representatives, 2011–15, 2017–19; religion: Church of Christ; married: Alexa; children: Liam; committees: Financial Services; elected to the 116th Congress on November 6, 2018.

Office Listings

https://gooden.house.gov https://facebook.com/RepGooden twitter: @RepLanceGooden
https://youtube.com/channel/UCaEs0pYlL_1cLlPBHfl0RIg

425 Cannon House Office Building, Washington, DC 20515 .... (202) 225–3484
Chief of Staff.—Aaron Harris. FAX: 226–4888
Legislative Director.—Ryan Ethington.
Communications Director.—Will Martin.
Deputy Chief of Staff.—Mehgan Perez-Acosta.
18601 LBJ Freeway, Suite 725, Mesquite, TX 75150 .... (214) 765–6789
District Director.—Ed McCain.

Counties: ANDERSON, CHEROKEE, DALLAS (part), HENDERSON, KAUFMAN, VAN ZANDT, AND WOOD. Population (2010), 698,498.

ZIP Codes: 75041–43, 75103, 75114, 75117–18, 75124, 75126–27, 75140, 75142–43, 75147–50, 75156–61, 75163, 75169, 75180–82, 75185, 75187, 75214, 75217–18, 75227–28, 75231, 75238, 75243, 75253, 75336, 75355, 75382, 75389, 75410, 75431, 75440, 75444, 75474, 75494, 75497, 75751–52, 75754, 75756–59, 75763–64, 75766, 75770, 75772–73, 75778–80, 75782–85, 75789–90, 75801–03, 75832, 75839, 75844, 75853, 75861, 75880, 75882, 75884, 75886, 75925, 75976

* * *

SIXTH DISTRICT

RON WRIGHT, Republican, of Arlington, TX; born in Cherokee County, TX, April 8, 1953; education: graduated from Azle High School, Azle, TX, 1971; attended University of Texas, Austin, TX; professional: sales executive; business manager; newspaper columnist; member of the Arlington, TX, City Council, 2000–08; Mayor Pro Tempore, Arlington, TX, City Council, 2004–08; staff, U.S. Representative Joe Linus Barton of Texas, 2000–11; tax assessor-collector, Tarrant County, TX, 2011–17; religion: Catholic; married to Susan Wright for 18 years; three children and six grandchildren; committees: Education and Labor; Foreign Affairs; elected to the 116th Congress on November 6, 2018.

Office Listings

https://wright.house.gov https://facebook.com/Congressman-Ron-Wright-594717754318936
twitter: @RepRonWright

428 Cannon House Office Building, Washington, DC 20515 .... (202) 225–2002
Chief of Staff.—Ryan Thompson. FAX: 225–3052
Deputy Chief of Staff.—Micah Cavanaugh.
Legislative Director.—Blair Rotert.
Scheduler.—Caroline Waller.
5840 West Ronald Reagan Memorial Highway, Suite 115, Arlington, TX 76017.
District Director.—Andy Hguyen.

Counties: ELLIS, NAVARRO, AND TARRANT. CITIES AND TOWNSHIPS: Alma, Angus, Arlington, Bardwell, Barry, Blooming Grove, Burleson, Cedar Hill, Corsicana, Crowley, Dawson, Emhouse, Ennis, Eureka, Ferris, Fort Worth, Frost, Garrett, Glenn Heights, Goodlow, Grand Prairie, Italy, Kennedale, Kerens, Mansfield, Maypearl, Midlothian, Milford, Mustang, Navarro, Oak Leaf, Oak Valley, Ovilla, Palmer, Pecan Hill, Powell, Red Oak, Rendon, Retreat, Rice, Richland, Venus, and Waxahachie. Population (2010), 720,861.

ZIP Codes: 75050, 75052, 75054, 75101–02, 75104–06, 75109–10, 75119–20, 75125, 75144, 75146, 75151–55, 75165, 75167–68, 75859, 76001–04, 76006, 76010–19, 76028, 76036, 76041, 76050, 76060, 76094, 76096, 76119–20, 76123, 76133–34, 76140, 76623, 76626, 76639, 76641, 76651, 76670, 76679, 76681

* * *

SEVENTH DISTRICT

LIZZIE PANNILL FLETCHER, Democrat, of Harris County, TX; born in Houston, TX, February 13, 1975; education: graduated from St. John's School, Houston, TX, 1993; B.A., Kenyon College, Gambier, OH; 1997; J.D., College of William & Mary, Williamsburg, VA, 2006; professional: lawyer; married: Scott Fletcher, 2010; committees: Science, Space, and Technology; Transportation and Infrastructure; elected to the 116th Congress on November 6, 2018.

Office Listings

https://fletcher.house.gov https://facebook.com/RepFletcher twitter: @RepFletcher
https://instagram.com/repfletcher https://youtube.com/channel/UCIWDLoDPvawP118TNWi-9rg

1429 Longworth House Office Building, Washington, DC 20515 .... (202) 225–2571

Office Listings—Continued

Chief of Staff.—Sarah Kaplan Feinmann. FAX: 225–4381
Legislative Director.—Ben Jackson.
Communications Director.—Alaina Berner.
Scheduler.—Olivia Cox.
5599 San Felipe Road, Suite 950, Houston, TX 77056 .... (713) 353–8680
District Director.—Brooke Boyett.

County: HARRIS (part). Population (2010), 717,354.

ZIP Codes: 77005, 77019, 77024–25, 77027, 77035–36, 77040–42, 77046, 77055–57, 77063–65, 77074, 77077, 77079, 77080–82, 77084, 77094–96, 77098, 77401–02, 77429, 77433, 77449–50

* * *

EIGHTH DISTRICT

KEVIN BRADY, Republican, of The Woodlands, TX; born in Vermillion, SD, April 11, 1955; education: B.S., mass communications, University of South Dakota; professional: Rapid City Common Council, 1982; served in Texas House of Representatives, 1991–96, the second Republican to capture the 8th District seat since the district's creation; chair, Council of Chambers of Greater Houston; president, East Texas Chamber Executive Association; president, South Montgomery County Woodlands Chamber of Commerce, 1985–96; director, Texas Chamber of Commerce Executives; Rotarian; awards: Achievement Award, Texas Conservative Coalition; Outstanding Young Texan (one of five), Texas Jaycees; Ten Best Legislators for Families and Children, State Bar of Texas; Legislative Standout, Dallas Morning News; Scholars Achievement Award for Excellence in Public Service, North Harris Montgomery Community College District; Victims' Rights Equalizer Award, Texans for Equal Justice Center; Support for Family Issues Award, Texas Extension Homemakers Association; True Blue Award; Family Research Council; Conservative Achievement Award, American Conservative Union; Hero of Mainstreet Award, National Retail Federation; Champion for Healthy Seniors Award, Partnership to Fight Chronic Disease; Defender of Small Business Award, Job Creators Network; Manufacturing Legislative Excellence Award, National Association of Manufacturers; religion: attends Saints Simon and Jude Catholic Church; married: Cathy Brady; committees: ranking member, Ways and Means; Joint Committee on Taxation; elected to the 105th Congress; reelected to each succeeding Congress.

Office Listings

https://kevinbrady.house.gov https://facebook.com/kevinbrady https://twitter.com/repkevinbrady

1011 Longworth House Office Building, Washington, DC 20515 .... (202) 225–4901
Chief of Staff.—David Davis.
Legislative Director.—Jonathan Porter.
Communications Director / Senior Advisor.—Shana Teehan.
Director of Scheduling.—Laura Cureton.
Deputy Press Secretary / Washington.—Isabelle Gwozdz.
200 River Pointe Drive, Suite 304, Conroe, TX 77304 .... (936) 441–5700
District Director.—Heather Washburn.
1300 11th Street, Suite 400, Huntsville, TX 77340 .... (936) 439–9532

Counties: GRIMES, HARRIS (part), HOUSTON, LEON, MADISON, MONTGOMERY, SAN JACINTO, TRINITY, AND WALKER. CITIES AND TOWNSHIPS: Anderson, Augusta, Bedias, Centerville, Conroe, Crockett, Decker Prairie, Grapeland, Groveton, Huntsville, Madisonville, Magnolia, Maynard, Midway, Montgomery, Navasota, New Caney, Normangee, Pinehurst, Plantersville, Point Blank, Porter Springs, Roans Prairie, Shepherd, Splendora, Spring, The Woodlands, Todd Mission, Tomball, Trinity, Weches, Willis, and Woodlake. Population (2010), 743,782.

ZIP Codes: 75833, 75835, 75844–45, 75847, 75852, 75856, 75858, 75862, 75849–51, 75926, 77070, 77301–06, 77316, 77318, 77320, 77328, 77331, 77333–34, 77340–42, 77353–59, 77365, 77367, 77371–73, 77375, 77377–89, 77393, 77447, 77830–31, 77855, 77861, 77864, 77868, 77876

* * *

NINTH DISTRICT

AL GREEN, Democrat, of Houston, TX; born in New Orleans, LA, September 1, 1947; raised in Florida; education: Florida A&M University, Tallahassee, FL, 1966–71; attended Tuskegee University, Tuskegee, AL; J.D., Texas Southern University, Houston, TX, 1974; professional: co-founded and co-managed the law firm of Green, Wilson, Dewberry and Fitch; Justice of the Peace, Precinct 7, Position 2, 1977–2004; organizations: former president of the Houston NAACP; Houston Citizens Chamber of Commerce; awards: NAACP Houston Branch Mickey Leland Humanitarian Award, 2018; Memorial Foundation's Leader of Democracy Award, 2014; VetsFirst Congressional Bronze Star; Texas Association of Realtors' Legacy Award, 2011; Texas Black Democrats' Profiles of Courage Award, 2007; AFL–CIO MLK Drum Major Award for Service, 2007; *Ebony* Magazine's 100 Most Influential Black People, 2006; NAACP Missouri City and Vicinity Branch Mickey Leland Humanitarian Award, 2006; committees: Financial Services; Homeland Security; elected to the 109th Congress on November 2, 2004; reelected to each succeeding Congress.

Office Listings

https://algreen.house.gov https://facebook.com/repalgreen twitter: @RepAlGreen

2347 Rayburn House Office Building, Washington, DC 20515 .... (202) 225–7508
Chief of Staff / Legislative Director.—Amena Ross. FAX: 225–2947
3003 South Loop West, Suite 460, Houston, TX 77054 .... (713) 383–9234
District Director.—Rachael Rodriguez. FAX: 383–9202
District Manager of Administration.—Crystal Webster.
Press Secretary.—Kwentoria A. Williams.

Counties: FORT BEND (part) AND HARRIS (part). Population (2010), 698,488.

ZIP Codes: 77004, 77025, 77030–31, 77033, 77035–36, 77042, 77045, 77047–48, 77051, 77053–54, 77061, 77063, 77071–72, 77074, 77077, 77082–83, 77085, 77087, 77096, 77099, 77407, 77459, 77477, 77489, 77498, 77545

* * *

TENTH DISTRICT

MICHAEL T. McCAUL, Republican, of Austin, TX; born in Dallas, TX, January 14, 1962; education: B.S., Trinity University, San Antonio, TX, 1984; J.D., St. Mary's University, San Antonio, TX, 1987; professional: lawyer, private practice; Deputy Attorney General, Office of Texas State Attorney General; committees: ranking member, Foreign Affairs; Homeland Security; elected to the 109th Congress on November 2, 2004; reelected to each succeeding Congress.

Office Listings

https://mccaul.house.gov https://facebook.com/michaeltmccaul https://twitter.com/RepMcCaul

2001 Rayburn House Office Building, Washington, DC 20515 .... (202) 225–2401
Chief of Staff.—Chris Del Beccaro. FAX: 225–5955
Legislative Director.—Thomas Rice.
Communications Director.—Rachel Walker.
Director of Operations.—Kelly Cotner.
Special Assistant / DC Scheduler.—Emma Cunningham.
District Director.—Matthew Conner.
3301 Northland Drive, Suite 212, Austin, TX 78731 .... (512) 473–2357
Rosewood Professional Building, 990 Village Square, Suite B, Tomball, TX 77375 .... (281) 255–8372
1526 Katy Gap Road, Suite 803, Katy, TX 77494 .... (281) 505–6130
401 South Austin Street, Brenham, TX 77833 .... (979) 830–8497

Counties: AUSTIN, BASTROP, COLORADO, FAYETTE, HARRIS, LEE, TRAVIS, WALLER, AND WASHINGTON. Population (2010), 698,487.

ZIP Codes: 77070, 77355, 77363, 77375, 77377, 77389, 77412, 77418, 77423, 77426, 77428–29, 77433–35, 77442, 77445–47, 77449–50, 77460, 77466, 77470, 77473–75, 77484–85, 77493–94, 77833, 77835, 77868, 77880, 77964, 78602, 78612–13, 78621, 78641, 78645, 78650, 78653, 78703, 78705, 78723–24, 78726, 78730–32, 78746, 78751–54, 78756–59, 78931–35, 78938, 78940–51, 78954, 78956–57, 78959, 78962–63

* * *

ELEVENTH DISTRICT

K. MICHAEL CONAWAY, Republican, of Midland, TX; born in Borger, TX, June 11, 1948; education: B.B.A., Texas A&M-Commerce, 1970; professional: Spec 5, U.S. Army, 1970–72; tax manager, Price Waterhouse & Company, 1972–80; chief financial officer, Keith D. Graham & Lantern Petroleum Company, 1980–81; chief financial officer, Bush Exploration Company,

1982–84; chief financial officer, Spectrum 7 Energy Corporation, 1984–86; senior vice president/chief financial officer, United Bank, 1987–90; senior vice president, Texas Commerce Bank, 1990–92; owner, K. Conaway CPA, 1993–present; religion: Baptist; married: Suzanne; children: Brian, Erin, Kara, and Stephanie; Deputy Republican Whip; committees: ranking member, Agriculture; Armed Services; Permanent Select Committee on Intelligence; elected to the 109th Congress on November 2, 2004; reelected to each succeeding Congress.

Office Listings

https://conaway.house.gov https://facebook.com/mikeconaway twitter: @ConawayTX11

2469 Rayburn House Office Building, Washington, DC 20515 .... (202) 225–3605
Chief of Staff.—Mark Williams. FAX: 225–1783
Legislative Director.—Matthew Russell.
Scheduler.—Maggie Mullins.
6 Desta Drive, Suite 2000, Midland, TX 79705 .... (432) 687–2390
Regional Director.—Evan Thomas.

Counties: ANDREWS, BROWN, CALLAHAN, COKE, COLEMAN, COMANCHE, CONCHO, DAWSON, EASTLAND, ECTOR, ERATH, GLASSCOCK, HOOD, IRION, KIMBLE, LLANO, MARTIN, MASON, MCCULLOCH, MENARD, MIDLAND, MILLS, MITCHELL, PALO PINTO, RUNNELS, SAN SABA, STEPHENS, STERLING, AND TOM GREEN. Population (2010), 698,488.

ZIP Codes: 76033, 76035, 76048–49, 76066–67, 76087, 76401, 76424, 76429, 76432–33, 76435–37, 76442–46, 76448–50, 76452–55, 76462–64, 76466, 76469–72, 76474–76, 76484, 76486, 76531, 76801–02, 76820–21, 76823, 76825, 76827–28, 76831–32, 76834, 76836–37, 76841–42, 76844–45, 76848–49, 76852–54, 76856–59, 76861–62, 76864–66, 76869–75, 76877–78, 76882, 76884–85, 76887–88, 76890, 76901, 76903–05, 76908, 76930, 76933–35, 76937, 76939–41, 76945, 76949, 76951, 76953, 76955, 76957–58, 78607, 78609, 78618, 78631, 78639, 78643, 78657, 78672, 79331, 79351, 79377, 79504, 79506, 79510, 79512, 79519, 79532, 79538, 79541, 79565–67, 79601–02, 79701, 79703, 79705–07, 79713–14, 79720, 79739, 79741, 79748–49, 79758–59, 79761–66, 79782–83

* * *

TWELFTH DISTRICT

KAY GRANGER, Republican, of Fort Worth, TX; born in Greenville, TX, January 18, 1943; education: B.S., *magna cum laude*, 1965, and honorary doctorate of humane letters, 1992, Texas Wesleyan University; professional: owner, Kay Granger Insurance Agency, Inc.; former public school teacher; elected Mayor of Fort Worth, 1991, serving three terms; during her tenure, Fort Worth received All-America City Award from the National Civic League; former Fort Worth Councilwoman; past chair, Fort Worth Zoning Commission; past board member: Dallas-Fort Worth International Airport; North Texas Commission; Fort Worth Convention and Visitors Bureau; U.S. Conference of Mayors Advisory Board; Business and Professional Women's Woman of the Year, 1989; three grown children: J.D., Brandon, and Chelsea; first woman Republican to represent Texas in the U.S. House of Representatives; first woman Republican to serve as Ranking Member on House Appropriations Committee; Republican Whip; committees: ranking member, Appropriations; elected to the 105th Congress; reelected to each succeeding Congress.

Office Listings

https://granger.house.gov https://facebook.com/RepKayGranger https://twitter.com/RepKayGranger

1026 Longworth House Office Building, Washington, DC 20515 .... (202) 225–5071
Chief of Staff.—Krister Holladay. FAX: 225–5683
Legislative Director/Deputy Chief of Staff.—Vacant.
Staff Assistant.—Alex Dunn.
Scheduler.—Holly Warden.
1701 River Run Road, Suite 407, Fort Worth, TX 76107 .... (817) 338–0909
District Director.—Charlie Cripliver. FAX: 335–5852

Counties: PARKER, TARRANT (part), AND WISE. Population (2010), 728,142.

ZIP Codes: 76008, 76020, 76023 (part), 76035 (part), 76049 (part), 76052 (part), 76066 (part), 76071, 76078 (part), 76082 (part), 76085, 76098, 76101, 76104 (part), 76106 (part), 76113, 76121, 76126, 76129, 76147, 76161, 76177 (part), 76179, 76185, 76191, 76195, 76234 (part), 76244 (part), 76246 (part), 76439, 76462 (part), 76485, 76490

* * *

THIRTEENTH DISTRICT

MAC THORNBERRY, Republican, of Clarendon, TX; born in Clarendon, July 15, 1958; education: graduate, Clarendon High School; B.A., Texas Tech University; law degree, University of Texas; professional: rancher; attorney; admitted to the Texas Bar, 1983; member: Joint Forces Command Transformation; Republican Study Committee; married: Sally Adams, 1986; children: Will and Mary Kemp; committees: ranking member, Armed Services; elected to the 104th Congress; reelected to each succeeding Congress.

Office Listings

https://thornberry.house.gov https://facebook.com/repmacthornberry
https://twitter.com/mactxpress https://youtube.com/repmacthornberry
https://instagram.com/macthornberry

2208 Rayburn House Office Building, Washington, DC 20515 .... (202) 225–3706
Chief of Staff.—Jessica Sunday. FAX: 225–3486
Deputy Chief of Staff / Legislative Director.—Kamal Patel.
Press Secretary.—Jessica Graff.
Executive Assistant / Scheduler.—Aimee Pitchford.
Staff Assistant.—Travis Stedje.
District Director.—Sandra Ross.
Deputy District Director.—Paul Simpson.
2525 Kell Boulevard, Suite 406, Wichita Falls, TX 76308 .... (940) 692–1700
620 South Taylor Street, Suite 200, Amarillo, TX 79101 .... (806) 371–8844

Counties: Archer, Armstrong, Baylor, Briscoe, Carson, Childress, Clay, Collingsworth, Cooke, Cottle, Dallam, Deaf Smith, Dickens, Donley, Floyd, Foard, Gray, Hall, Hansford, Hardeman, Hartley, Hemphill, Hutchinson, Jack, King, Knox, Lipscomb, Montague, Moore, Motley, Ochiltree, Oldham, Potter, Randall, Roberts, Sherman, Swisher, Wheeler, Wichita, Wilbarger, and Wise (part). Population (2010), 703,835.

ZIP Codes: 73448, 73539, 73562, 73848–49, 76023, 76073, 76078, 76082, 76225, 76228, 76230, 76233–34, 76238–40, 76250–52, 76255, 76259, 76261, 76263, 76265–66, 76270–73, 76301–02, 76305–06, 76308–11, 76351, 76354, 76357, 76360, 76363–67, 76371, 76373–74, 76377, 76379–80, 76384, 76389, 76426–27, 76431, 76458–59, 76486–87, 79001, 79005, 79007, 79011, 79014–16, 79018–19, 79022, 79029, 79034, 79036, 79039–40, 79042, 79044–46, 79052, 79056–59, 79061–62, 79065, 79068, 79070, 79079–81, 79083–84, 79086–88, 79092, 79094–98, 79101–04, 79106–11, 79118–19, 79121, 79124, 79178, 79201, 79220, 79225–27, 79229–30, 79234–35, 79237, 79239–41, 79243–45, 79247–48, 79251–52, 79255–57, 79259, 79261, 79370, 79529

* * *

FOURTEENTH DISTRICT

RANDY WEBER, Republican, of Friendswood, TX; born in Pearland, TX, July 2, 1953; education: B.S., University of Houston, Clear Lake, 1977; professional: owner, Weber's Air and Heat, 1981–2017; married: 1976; children: Kristin, Keith, and Kyle; grandchildren: eight; committees: Science, Space, and Technology; Transportation and Infrastructure; elected to the 113th Congress on November 6, 2012; reelected to each succeeding Congress.

Office Listings

https://weber.house.gov https://facebook.com/txrandy14 https://twitter.com/txrandy14

107 Cannon House Office Building, Washington, DC 20515 .... (202) 225–2831
Chief of Staff.—Chara McMichael. FAX: 225–0271
Legislative Director.—William Christian.
Communications Director.—Emma Polefko.
350 Pine Street, Suite 730, Beaumont, TX 77701 .... (409) 835–0108
122 West Way Street, Suite 301, Lake Jackson, TX 77566 .... (979) 285–0231
174 Calder Road, Suite 150, League City, TX 77573 .... (281) 316–0231

Counties: Brazoria (part), Galveston, and Jefferson. Population (2010), 705,051.

ZIP Codes: 77510, 77517–18, 77539, 77546, 77549–55, 77563, 77565, 77568, 77573–74, 77590–92, 77617, 77623, 77650

* * *

FIFTEENTH DISTRICT

VICENTE GONZALEZ, Democrat, of McAllen, TX; born in Corpus Christi, TX, September 4, 1967; education: G.E.D., 1985; associate degree in banking and finance, Del Mar College, Corpus Christi, TX, 1990; bachelor's degree in aviation business administration, Embry Riddle University, Corpus Christi, TX, 1992; J.D., Texas Wesleyan University School of Law (now Texas A&M School of Law), Fort Worth, TX, 1996; professional: lawyer; private practice, V. Gonzalez & Associates, PC, 1997–present; religion: Roman Catholic; married: Lorena Saenz

Gonzalez; committees: Financial Services; Foreign Affairs; elected to the 115th Congress on November 8, 2016; reelected to the 116th Congress on November 6, 2018.

Office Listings

https://gonzalez.house.gov https://facebook.com/USCongressmanVicenteGonzalez
https://twitter.com/RepGonzalez

113 Cannon House Office Building, Washington, DC 20515 .... (202) 225–2531
Chief of Staff.—Jose Borjon. FAX: 225–5688
1305 West Hackberry Avenue, McAllen, TX 78501 .... (956) 682–5545
District Director.—Stephanie Toscano. FAX: 682–0141
North District .... (956) 682–5545
North District Director.—Albert Martinez.

Counties: BROOKS, DUVALL, GUADALUPE, HIDALGO, JIM HOGG, KARNES, LIVE OAK (part), AND WILSON. CITIES AND TOWNSHIPS: Alamo, Alton, Cibolo, Edinburg, Hidalgo, McAllen, Mercedes, Mission, New Braunfels, Pharr, San Juan, Schertz, Seguin, Taft, Three Rivers, Weslaco, and Whitsett. Population (2011), 722,529.

ZIP Codes: 78008, 78022, 78060, 78071, 78108, 78111, 78113–19, 78121, 78123–24, 78130, 78132, 78140–41, 78143–44, 78151, 78154–56, 78160, 78164, 78332, 78341, 78349–50, 78353, 78355, 78357, 78360–61, 78368, 78372, 78376, 78383–84, 78501–05, 78516, 78537–43, 78549, 78557–59, 78562–63, 78569–70, 78572–74, 78577, 78589, 78596, 78599, 78638, 78648, 78655, 78666, 78670

* * *

SIXTEENTH DISTRICT

VERONICA ESCOBAR, Democrat, of El Paso, TX; born in El Paso, September 15, 1969; education: B.A., University of Texas at El Paso, El Paso, 1991; M.A., New York University, New York City, NY, 1993; professional: college professor; nonprofit executive; communications director; El Paso County Commissioner, 2006–10; El Paso County Judge, 2011–17; committees: Armed Services; Judiciary; elected to the 116th Congress on November 6, 2018.

Office Listings

https://escobar.house.gov https://facebook.com/RepEscobar https://twitter.com/RepEscobar
https://youtube.com/channel/UC46TX2P8K0CA_4gZv8_R2Og

1505 Longworth House Office Building, Washington, DC 20515 .... (202) 225–4831
Chief of Staff.—Eduardo Lerma. FAX: 225–2016
Legislative Director.—Jacqueline Sanchez.
Communications and Special Projects Director.—Elizabeth Lopez-Sandoval.
Scheduler.—Jessica Andino.
Wells Fargo Plaza, 221 North Kansas Street, Suite 1500, El Paso, TX 79901 .... (915) 541–1400

Counties: EL PASO (part). Population (2010), 698,488.

ZIP Codes: 79901–06, 79908, 79911–12, 79915–16, 79920, 79922, 79924–25, 79930, 79932, 79934–36

* * *

SEVENTEENTH DISTRICT

WILLIAM H. ''BILL'' FLORES, Republican, of Bryan, TX; born at Warren Air Force Base, Cheyenne, WY, February 25, 1954; education: graduated, Stratford High School, Stratford, TX, 1972; B.B.A., *cum laude,* Texas A&M University, College Station, TX, 1976; M.B.A., Houston Baptist University, Houston, TX, 1985; Texas Certified Public Accountant (CPA), 1978–present; commissioner, Texas Real Estate Commission (appointed by Governor Perry), 2004–09; CEO and president, Phoenix Exploration Company, 2006–09; Texas A&M University Distinguished Alumnus, 2010; Houston Baptist University Distinguished Alumnus, 2013; married: the former Gina Bass; children: Will and John; daughter-in-law, Aimee; four grandchildren; committees: Budget; Energy and Commerce; elected to the 112th Congress on November 2, 2010; reelected to each succeeding Congress.

Office Listings

https://flores.house.gov https://facebook.com/RepBillFlores https://twitter.com/RepBillFlores

2228 Rayburn House Office Building, Washington, DC 20515 .... (202) 225–6105

Office Listings—Continued

Chief of Staff.—Jon Oehmen. FAX: 225–0350
Legislative Director.—Eric Gustafson.
Communications Director.—Andre Castro.
400 Austin Avenue, Suite 302, Waco, TX 76701 .... (254) 732–0748
District Director.—Jana Hixson.
14205 Burnet Road, Suite 230, Austin, TX 78728 .... (512) 373–3378
3000 Briarcrest Drive, Suite 406, Bryan, TX 77802 .... (979) 703–4037
FAX: 691–8939

Counties: BRAZOS, BURLESON, FALLS, FREESTONE, LEE, LEON, LIMESTONE, MCLENNAN, MILAM, ROBERTSON, AND TRAVIS (part). Population (2010), 710,793.

ZIP Codes: 75833, 75840, 75848, 75850, 75860, 76518, 76520, 76523, 76632, 76635, 76638, 76640, 76643, 76654, 76656, 76661, 76678, 76680, 76684, 76686, 76701–05, 76707–08, 76710–12, 76714–16, 76797–99, 77801–03, 77805–06, 77837–38, 77840–45, 77850, 77852–53, 77855–57, 77862–63, 77865–67, 77870, 77878–79, 77881–82, 78660, 78691, 78727–28, 78753, 78948

* * *

EIGHTEENTH DISTRICT

SHEILA JACKSON LEE, Democrat, of Houston, TX; born in Queens, NY, January 12, 1950; education: graduated, Jamaica High School; B.A., Yale University, New Haven, CT, 1972; J.D., University of Virginia Law School, 1975; professional: practicing attorney for 12 years; AKA Sorority; Houston Area Urban League; American Bar Association; staff counsel, U.S. House Select Committee on Assassinations, 1977–78; admitted to the Texas Bar, 1975; City Council (at large), Houston, 1990–94; Houston Municipal Judge, 1987–90; married: Dr. Elwyn Cornelius Lee, 1973; two children: Erica Shelwyn and Jason Cornelius Bennett; two grandchildren; U.S. Helsinki Commission; committees: Budget; Homeland Security; Judiciary; elected to the 104th Congress; reelected to each succeeding Congress.

Office Listings

https://jacksonlee.house.gov twitter: @JacksonLeeTX18 https://instagram.com/repjacksonlee

2079 Rayburn House Office Building, Washington, DC 20515 .... (202) 225–3816
Chief of Staff.—Glenn Rushing. FAX: 225–3317
Chief Counsel.—Gregory Berry.
Senior Policy Director.—Leon Buck.
Policy Director.—Lillie Coney.
Legislative Counsel / Communications Director.—Vacant.
Scheduler.—LaDedra Drummond.
Special Assistant / Legislative Assistant.—Remmington Belford.
1919 Smith Street, Suite 1180, Houston, TX 77002 .... (713) 655–0050
District Director.—Larry Freeman.
District Counsel.—Booker Morris.
Executive Assistant.—Martha Hernandez.
Field Representatives and Caseworkers: Edward Howard, Michael Nyugen, Alma Vazquez.
Account and Finance.—Dexter Ingram.
420 West 19th Street, Houston, TX 77008 .... (713) 861–4070
6719 West Montgomery, Suite 204, Houston, TX 77091 .... (713) 691–4882

Counties: HARRIS COUNTY (part). CITY: Houston. Population (2010), 698,488.

ZIP Codes: 77001–10, 77013, 77016, 77018–24, 77026, 77028–30, 77033, 77035, 77038, 77040–41, 77045, 77047–48, 77051–52, 77054–55, 77064, 77066–67, 77076, 77078, 77080, 77086–88, 77091–93, 77097–98, 77201–06, 77208, 77210, 77212, 77216, 77219, 77221, 77226, 77230, 77233, 77238, 77240–41, 77251–53, 77255, 77265–66, 77277, 77288, 77291–93, 77297–99

* * *

NINETEENTH DISTRICT

JODEY C. ARRINGTON, Republican, of Lubbock, TX; born in Kansas City, MO, March 9, 1972; education: B.A. in political science, Texas Tech University, Lubbock, 1994; master of public administration, Texas Tech University, 1997; Certificate of International Business Management, McDonough School of Business at Georgetown University, Washington, DC, 2004; professional: appointments manager for Governor George W. Bush, Austin, TX, 1996–

2000; Special Assistant to the President and Associate Director of Presidential Personnel during the George W. Bush administration, Washington, DC, 2000–01; Chief of Staff to the Chairman of the FDIC, Washington, DC, 2001–05; Deputy Federal Coordinator and Chief Operating Officer at the Office of the Federal Coordinator for Gulf Coast Rebuilding, Washington, DC, 2005–06; chief of staff to the chancellor of the Texas Tech University System, Lubbock, TX, 2006–11; vice chancellor for research and commercialization at Texas Tech University System, Lubbock, TX, 2011–14; president, Scott Laboratories, Lubbock, TX, 2014–16; awards: 2003 Distinguished Public Service Award as part of the 22nd annual Center for Public Service Symposium in Lubbock, TX; religion: Presbyterian; married: Anne; three children; committees: Ways and Means; elected to the 115th Congress on November 7, 2016; reelected to the 116th Congress on November 6, 2018.

Office Listings

https://arrington.house.gov https://facebook.com/JodeyArrington
https://twitter.com/reparrington https://instagram.com/repjodeyarrington

1029 Longworth House Office Building, Washington, DC 20515 .... (202) 225–4005
Chief of Staff.—Chelsea Brown. FAX: 225–9615
Deputy Chief of Staff.—Tim Cummings.
Communications Director.—Sam Taylor.
Legislative Director.—Dominique Spadavecchia.
Legislative Assistant.—Kaley Mathis.
Scheduler.—Marisa Burleson.
Communications Assistant.—Andrew Brennan.
Staff Assistant.—Jessica Weiner.
1312 Texas Avenue, Suite 219, Lubbock, TX 79401 .... (806) 763–1611
District Director.—Lindley Herring.
Constituent Services Representatives: McKenzie Hammonds, Sarah Moses.
500 Chestnut Street, #819, Abilene, TX 79602 .... (325) 675–9779
Regional Director.—Glen Pugh.
Constituent Services Representative.—Sarah Conley.

Counties: BAILEY, BORDEN, CASTRO, COCHRAN, CROSBY, FISHER, FLOYD (part), GAINES, GARZA, HALE, HASKELL, HOCKLEY, HOWARD, JONES, KENT, LAMB, LUBBOCK, LYNN, NOLAN, PARMER, SCURRY, SHACKELFORD, STEPHENS (part), STONEWALL, TAYLOR, TERRY, THROCKMORTON, YOAKUM, AND YOUNG.. Population (2010), 707,772.

ZIP Codes: 76372, 76374 (part), 76388, 76424 (part), 76429 (part), 76430, 76450 (part), 76460, 76464 (part), 76481, 76483, 76491, 79009, 79021, 79027, 79031–32, 79035 (part), 79041, 79042 (part), 79043, 79045 (part), 79052 (part), 79053, 79063–64, 79072 (part), 79082, 79085, 79088 (part), 79231, 79235 (part), 79241 (part), 79250, 79311–14, 79316, 79322–26, 79329–30, 79331 (part), 79336, 79339, 79342–47, 79350, 79351 (part), 79353, 79355–60, 79363–64, 79366–67, 79369, 79370 (part), 79371–73, 79376, 79378–82, 79401, 79403–04, 79406–07, 79410–16, 79423–24, 79501–03, 79504 (part), 79506 (part), 79508, 79511, 79512 (part), 79517–18, 79520–21, 79525–28, 79529 (part), 79530, 79532 (part), 79533–37, 79539, 79540, 79541 (part), 79543–49, 79553, 79556, 79560–63, 79566 (part), 79567 (part), 79601 (part), 79602 (part), 79603, 79605–07, 79699, 79713 (part), 79720 (part), 79733, 79738, 79748 (part)

* * *

TWENTIETH DISTRICT

JOAQUIN CASTRO, Democrat, of San Antonio, TX; born in San Antonio, September 16, 1974; education: Thomas Jefferson High School, 1992; B.A., Stanford University, CA, 1996; J.D., Harvard University, Cambridge, MA, 2000; professional: attorney; law instructor; religion: Catholic; family: wife, Anna Flores; caucuses: Congressional Caucus on ASEAN; Congressional Hispanic Caucus; Congressional Pre-K Caucus; New Democrat Coalition; U.S.-Japan Caucus; committees: Education and Labor; Foreign Affairs; Permanent Select Committee on Intelligence; elected to the 113th Congress on November 6, 2012; reelected to each succeeding Congress.

Office Listings

https://castro.house.gov https://facebook.com/joaquincastrotx twitter: @joaquincastrotx

2241 Rayburn House Office Building, Washington, DC 20515 .... (202) 225–3236
Chief of Staff.—Danny Meza.
Legislative Director.—Ben Thomas.
Legislative Assistant.—Kaitlyn Montan.
Legislative Correspondent.—Christian Krueger.
Communications Director.—Vacant.
Scheduler.—Danielle Moon.
Press Secretary.—Katherine Schneider.
727 East Cesar E. Chavez Boulevard, Suite B–128, San Antonio, TX 78206 .... (210) 348–8216
District Director.—Antonietta Hernandez-Serna.

Counties: BEXAR (part). CITIES: Alamo Heights, Balcones Heights, Lackland AFB, Helotes, Leon Valley, and San Antonio. Population (2010), 716,759.

ZIP Codes: 78023, 78073, 78201, 78204, 78207, 78209, 78211–14, 78216, 78221, 78224–31, 78236–38, 78240, 78242, 78245, 78249–57

* * *

TWENTY-FIRST DISTRICT

CHIP ROY, Republican, of Austin, TX; born in Bethesda, Montgomery County, MD, August 7, 1972; education: graduated from Loudoun Valley High School, Purcellville, VA, 1990; B.S., University of Virginia, Charlottesville, VA, 1994; M.S., University of Virginia, Charlottesville, VA, 1995; J.D., University of Texas, Austin, TX, 2003; professional: banking executive; staff, U.S. Senator John Cornyn of Texas, 2002–06; Special Assistant District Attorney for the U.S. Attorney for the Eastern District of Texas; staff, Governor Rick Perry of Texas; director, Texas Office of State-Federal Relations, 2011–12; staff, U.S. Senator Ted Cruz of Texas, 2012–14; First Assistant Attorney General, Office of the Attorney General, state of Texas, 2014–16; professional advocate; nonprofit executive; married: Carrah Roy; children: Charlie and Virginia; caucuses: House Freedom Caucus; committees: Budget; Oversight and Reform; Veterans' Affairs; elected to the 116th Congress on November 6, 2018.

Office Listings

https://roy.house.gov https://facebook.com/RepChipRoy twitter: @RepChipRoy

1319 Longworth House Office Building, Washington, DC 20515 .... (202) 225–4236
Chief of Staff.—Wade Miller. FAX: 225–8628
Legislative Director.—Maggie Harrell.
Communications Director.—Robert Donachie.
Executive Scheduler.—Caroline Brennan.
1100 Northeast Loop 410, Suite 640, San Antonio, TX 78209 .... (210) 821–5024
District Director.—Nathan McDaniel. FAX: 821–5947
5900 Southwest Parkway, Building 2, Suite 201a, Austin, TX 78735 .... (512) 871–5959
125 Lehmann Drive, Suite 201, Kerrville, TX 78028 .... (830) 896–0154

Counties: BANDERA, BEXAR (part), BLANCO, COMAL (part), KENDALL, KERR, REAL, TRAVIS (part), GILLESPIE, AND HAYS (part). Population (2010), 698,488.

ZIP Codes: 78003, 78006, 78010, 78013, 78015, 78024–25, 78027–29, 78055, 78058, 78063, 78070, 78130–33, 78135, 78148, 78163, 78209, 78212–13, 78216–18, 78230–33, 78239, 78241, 78247, 78258–59, 78261, 78265–66, 78270, 78606, 78610, 78618–20, 78623–24, 78631, 78635–36, 78641, 78645, 78652, 78663, 78666, 78669, 78675–76, 78726, 78730–39, 78741, 78746, 78748–50, 78759, 78883, 78885

* * *

TWENTY-SECOND DISTRICT

PETE OLSON, Republican, of Sugar Land, TX; born in Fort Lewis, WA, December 9, 1962; education: B.A., Rice University, Houston, TX, 1985; law degree, University of Texas, Austin, TX, 1988; professional: U.S. Navy, 1988–98; U.S. Senate, 1998–2007; Naval Aviator wings, 1991; Naval Liaison, U.S. Senate; religion: United Methodist; married: Nancy Olson; children: Kate and Grant; committees: Energy and Commerce; elected to the 111th Congress on November 4, 2008; reelected to each succeeding Congress.

Office Listings

https://olson.house.gov https://facebook.com/Rep.PeteOlson
https://twitter.com/reppeteolson https://instagram.com/reppeteolson

2133 Rayburn House Office Building, Washington, DC 20515 .... (202) 225–5951
Chief of Staff.—Melissa Kelly.
Legislative Director.—Rich England.
Communications Director.—Cate Cullen.
Scheduler.—Keeley Tenney.
2277 Plaza Drive, Suite 195, Sugar Land, TX 77479 .... (281) 494–2690
District Director.—Christian Bionat.
6117 Broadway Street, Pearland, TX 77581 .... (281) 485–4855

Counties: BRAZORIA, FORT BEND, AND HARRIS (part). CITIES: Alvin, Arcola, Beasley, Brookside Village, Friendswood, Fulshear, Katy, Manvel, Meadows Place, Missouri City, Needville, Orchard, Pearland, Pleak, Richmond, Rosenberg, Simonton, Stafford, Sugar Land, Village of Fairchilds, Webster, and Weston Lakes. Population (2010), 698,504.

ZIP Codes: 77406–07, 77417, 77441, 77450, 77461, 77464, 77469, 77471, 77476–79, 77487, 77489, 77493–94, 77511–12, 77545–46, 77578, 77581, 77583–84, 77588, 77598

* * *

TWENTY-THIRD DISTRICT

WILL HURD, Republican, of San Antonio, TX; born in San Antonio, August 19, 1977; education: attended public schools in San Antonio, TX; B.S., computer science, Texas A&M University, College Station, TX, 1999; professional: cybersecurity consultant; CIA officer; religion: Christian; committees: Appropriations; Permanent Select Committee on Intelligence; elected to the 114th Congress on November 4, 2014; reelected to each succeeding Congress.

Office Listings

https://hurd.house.gov https://facebook.com/hurdonthehill https://twitter.com/hurdonthehill

317 Cannon House Office Building, Washington, DC 20515 .... (202) 225–4511
Chief of Staff.—John Byers. FAX: 225–2237
Legislative Director.—Austin Agrella.
Deputy Chief of Staff / Scheduler.—Nancy Pack.
Communications Director.—Katie Thompson.
Press Secretary.—Callie Strock.
Senior Legislative Assistant.—Christopher Malen.
Legislative Assistants: Anton Castaneda, Connor Pfeiffer.
Legislative Correspondent.—Rachel Thompson.
Staff Assistant.—Jon Murphy.
727 East Cesar E. Chavez Boulevard, San Antonio, TX 78206 .... (210) 921–3130
District Director.—Justin Hollis. FAX: 927–4903
124 South Horizon Boulevard, Socorro, TX 79927 .... (915) 235–6421
1104 West 10th Street, Del Rio, TX 78840 .... (830) 422–2040
100 South Monroe Street, Eagle Pass, TX 78852 .... (210) 921–3130
103 West Callaghan, First Floor, Fort Stockton, TX 79735 .... (210) 245–1961

Counties: BEXAR (part), BREWSTER, CRANE, CROCKETT, CULBERSON, DIMMIT, EDWARDS, EL PASO (part), FRIO, HUDSPETH, JEFF DAVIS, KINNEY, LA SALLE (part), LOVING, MAVERICK, MEDINA, PECOS, PRESIDIO, REAGAN, REEVES, SCHLEICHER, SUTTON, TERRELL, UPTON, UVALDE, VAL VERDE, WARD, WINKLER, AND ZAVALA. Population (2014), 725,874.

ZIP Codes: 76841, 76932, 76935–36, 76943, 76950, 78001–03, 78005–06, 78009, 78014–17, 78019, 78021, 78023, 78039, 78052, 78056–57, 78059, 78061, 78066, 78069, 78073, 78112, 78211, 78214, 78220–24, 78227, 78230–32, 78236, 78245, 78248–49, 78251–58, 78260, 78264, 78801–02, 78827–30, 78832–34, 78836–40, 78843, 78850–52, 78860–61, 78870–73, 78877, 78879–81, 78884, 78886, 79718–19, 79730–31, 79734–35, 79739, 79742–45, 79752, 79754–56, 79766, 79770, 79772, 79777–78, 79780–81, 79785, 79788–89, 79830–31, 79834, 79836–39, 79842–43, 79845–49, 79851–55, 79907, 79927–28, 79938, 79942, 88220

* * *

TWENTY-FOURTH DISTRICT

KENNY MARCHANT, Republican, of Coppell, TX; born in Bonham, TX, February 23, 1951; education: B.A., Southern Nazarene University, Bethany, OK, 1974; attended Nazarene Theological Seminary, Kansas City, MO, 1975–76; professional: real estate developer; member of the Carrollton, TX, City Council, 1980–84; Mayor of Carrollton, TX, 1984–87; member of the Texas State House of Representatives, 1987–2004; member, Advisory Board of Children's Medical Center; married: Donna; four children; committees: ranking member, Ethics; Ways and Means; Joint Economic Committee; elected to the 109th Congress on November 2, 2004; reelected to each succeeding Congress.

Office Listings

https://marchant.house.gov https://facebook.com/repkennymarchant https://twitter.com/repkenmarchant

2304 Rayburn House Office Building, Washington, DC 20515 .... (202) 225–6605
Chief of Staff.—Brian Thomas. FAX: 225–0074
Deputy Chief of Staff, Washington.—Scott Cunningham.
Legislative Director.—John Deoudes.
Communications Director.—Luke Bunting.
Legislative Assistant.—Nicholas Smith.
Deputy Communications Director / Legislative Correspondent.—Ryan Hamilton.
Legislative Assistant / Scheduler.—Lindsay Hurley.
Staff Assistant.—Cesar Prieto.
9901 East Valley Ranch Parkway, Suite 2060, Irving, TX 75063 .... (972) 556–0162
Deputy Chief of Staff, District.—Susie Miller.
Military and Veterans Liaison.—John Hayes.
Director of District Affairs.—Todd Martin.
Communications and Outreach Representative.—Rhett Gum.
Constituent Services Representative.—Chelsea Payne.

Counties: DALLAS (part), DENTON (part), AND TARRANT (part). CITIES AND TOWNSHIPS: Addison, Bedford, Carrollton, Colleyville, Coppell, Dallas (part), Euless, Farmer's Branch, Fort Worth (part), Grapevine, Hurst, Irving (part), Lewisville (part), Plano (part), Southlake, and The Colony. Population (2010), 698,488.

ZIP Codes: 75001, 75006–07, 75010–11, 75014, 75016, 75019, 75022, 75024, 75028, 75038–39, 75056, 75061–63, 75067, 75093, 75099, 75209, 75220, 75229–30, 75234, 75240, 75244, 75248, 75252, 75254, 75261, 75287, 75354, 75368, 75379–81, 75391, 76021–22, 76034, 76039–40, 76051, 76053–54, 76092, 76095, 76099, 76118, 76120, 76155, 76180, 76182, 76248, 76262

* * *

TWENTY-FIFTH DISTRICT

ROGER WILLIAMS, Republican, of Austin, TX; born in Evanston, IL, September 13, 1949; education: graduated, Arlington Heights High School; B.S., Texas Christian University, Fort Worth, TX, 1972; professional: drafted by the Atlanta Braves Organization; owner Roger Williams Car Dealerships; 105th Secretary of State of Texas, 2004–07; regional finance chair for Governor Bush, 1994, 1998; North Texas chairman for the Bush / Cheney 2000 campaign; North Texas finance chairman and national grassroots fundraising chairman for Bush / Cheney 2004, Inc.; appointed chairman of the Republican National Finance Committee's Eagles Program by President George W. Bush, 2001; state finance chair for John Cornyn for U.S. Senate, Inc., 2002; chief liaison for Texas Border and Mexican Affairs, 2005; chair of the Texas Base Realignment and Closure Response Strike Force; boards: Texas Christian University Board of Trustees; National Football Foundation; College Football Hall of Fame; religion: member, University Christian Church; married: Patty Williams; children: Sabrina and Jaclyn; committees: Financial Services; elected to the 113th Congress on November 6, 2012; reelected to each succeeding Congress.

Office Listings

https://williams.house.gov https://facebook.com/RepRogerWilliams https://twitter.com/RepRWilliams

1708 Longworth House Office Building, Washington, DC 20515 .... (202) 225–9896
Chief of Staff.—John Etue. FAX: 225–9692
Deputy Chief / Legislative Director.—Pat Arlantico.
Legislative Assistants: Zack Barth, Benjamin Johnson.
Legislative Correspondent.—Katie Crane.
Staff Assistant.—Colton Teis.
Press Secretary.—Sara Broadwater.
Scheduler.—Courtney Butler.
1005 Congress Avenue, Suite 925, Austin, TX 78701 .... (512) 473–8910
Deputy District Director.—Aaron Helton. FAX: 473–8946
115 South Main Street, Suite 206, Cleburne, TX 76033 .... (817) 774–2575
District Director.—Robyn Parker. FAX: 774–2577
Deputy Director of Constituent Services / Case Worker.—Ruth Zachary.

Counties: BELL (part), BOSQUE, BURNET, CORYELL, ERATH (part), HAMILTON, HAYS (part), HILL, JOHNSON, LAMPASAS, SOMERVELL, TARRANT (part), AND TRAVIS (part). Population (2010), 698,478.

ZIP Codes: 76009, 76028, 76031, 76033, 76035–36, 76043–44, 76048–49, 76050, 76055, 76058–59, 76063, 76070, 76077, 76084, 76093, 76401–02, 76433, 76436, 76446, 76457, 76522, 76525–28, 76531, 76538–39, 76544, 76549–50, 76557, 76561, 76565–66, 76621–22, 76627, 76631, 76633–34, 76636–38, 76645, 76648–49, 76652, 76657, 76660, 76665–66, 76671, 76673, 76676, 76689–90, 76692, 76853, 76877, 76880, 78605, 78608, 78610–11, 78613, 78619–20, 78623, 78639, 78641–42, 78645, 78652, 78654, 78657, 78666, 78669, 78676, 78701–03, 78705, 78712, 78721–25, 78730–34, 78736–39, 78745–46, 78749–50

* * *

TWENTY-SIXTH DISTRICT

MICHAEL C. BURGESS, Republican, of Denton County, TX; born, December 23, 1950; education: B.A., biology, North Texas State University; M.S., physiology, North Texas State University; M.D., University of Texas Medical School, Houston; M.S., medical management, University of Texas, Dallas; completed medical residency programs, Parkland Hospital in Dallas; professional: founder, Private Practice Specialty Group for Obstetrics and Gynecology; former Chief of Staff and Chief of Obstetrics, Lewisville Medical Center; organizations: former president, Denton County Medical Society; Denton County delegate, Texas Medical Association; alternate delegate, American Medical Association; married: Laura; three children; committees: Energy and Commerce; Rules; elected to the 108th Congress on November 5, 2002; reelected to each succeeding Congress.

Office Listings

https://burgess.house.gov https://facebook.com/michaelcburgess twitter: @michaelcburgess

2161 Rayburn House Office Building, Washington, DC 20515 .... (202) 225–7772
Chief of Staff.—James Decker. FAX: 225–2919
Legislative Director.—Rachel Huggins.
Press Secretary.—Emma Thompson.
Scheduler.—Amanda Baldwin.
2000 South Stemmons Freeway, Suite 200, Lake Dallas, TX 75065 .... (940) 497–5031

Counties: DALLAS (part), DENTON (part), AND TARRANT (part). Population (2010), 698,488.

ZIP Codes: 75009, 75019, 75022, 75027–29, 75033–34, 75056–57, 75065, 75067–68, 75077–78, 76034, 76052, 76065, 76078, 76092, 76117, 76137, 76148, 76177, 76180, 76182, 76201–10, 76226–27, 76234, 76244, 76247–49, 76258–59, 76262

* * *

TWENTY-SEVENTH DISTRICT

MICHAEL CLOUD, Republican, of Victoria, TX; born in Baton Rouge, LA, May 13, 1975; education: graduated from Miamisburg High School, Miamisburg, OH, 1993; B.S., Oral Roberts University, Tulsa, OK, 1997; professional: communications director; business owner; committees: Oversight and Reform; Science, Space, and Technology; elected to the 115th Congress, by special election, on June 30, 2018, to fill the vacancy caused by the resignation of U.S. Representative Blake Farenthold; reelected to the 116th Congress on November 6, 2018.

Office Listings

https://cloud.house.gov https://facebook.com/RepCloudTX https://twitter.com/RepCloudTX

1314 Longworth House Office Building, Washington, DC 20515 .... (202) 225–7742
Chief of Staff.—Adam Magary. FAX: 226–1134
Deputy Chief of Staff / Legislative Director.—Hugh Fike.
Communications Director.—Savannah Frasier.
Executive Assistant / Scheduler.—Emily Helms.
101 North Shoreline Boulevard, Suite 306, Corpus Christi, TX 78401 .... (361) 884–2222
District Director.—JD Kennedy.
111 North Glass Street, Victoria, TX 77901 .... (361) 894–6446

Counties: ARANSAS, BASTROP, CALDWELL, CALHOUN, GONZALES, JACKSON, LAVACA, MATAGORDA, NUECES, REFUGIO, SAN PATRICIO, VICTORIA, AND WHARTON. Population (2010), 702,804.

ZIP Codes: 77404, 77414–15, 77419–20, 77428, 77432, 77435–37, 77440, 77443, 77448, 77453–58, 77465, 77467–68, 77482–83, 77488, 77901–05, 77950–51, 77957, 77961–62, 77964, 77968–71, 77973, 77975–79, 77982–84, 77986–88, 77990–91, 77995, 78330, 78335–36, 78339–40, 78343, 78347, 78351–52, 78358–59, 78362, 78368, 78370, 78373–74, 78377, 78380–82, 78387, 78390, 78393, 78401–19, 78426–27, 78460, 78463, 78465–69, 78472, 78480, 78602, 78612, 78614, 78616, 78629, 78632, 78648, 78655–56, 78658, 78661–62, 78953, 78957

* * *

TWENTY-EIGHTH DISTRICT

HENRY CUELLAR, Democrat, of Laredo, TX; born in Laredo, September 19, 1955; education: associate's degree from Laredo Community College, Laredo, TX, 1976 (then known as Laredo Junior College); B.S., *cum laude*, foreign service, from the Edmund A. Walsh School of Foreign Service at Georgetown University, Washington, DC, 1978; J.D., University of Texas, Austin, TX, 1981; M.B.A., international trade, Texas A&M University, Laredo, TX, 1982; Ph.D., government, University of Texas, Austin, 1998; with a total of five advanced degrees, Congressman Cuellar is the most degreed member of Congress; professional: lawyer, private practice; attorney, Law Office of Henry Cuellar, 1981–present; instructor, Department of Government, Laredo Community College, Laredo, TX, 1982–86; licensed U.S. Customs broker, 1983–present; adjunct professor, international commercial law, Texas A&M International, 1984–86; Representative, Texas State House of Representatives, 1986–2001; Secretary of State, State of Texas, 2001; public and civic organizations: board of directors, Kiwanis Club of Laredo, TX, 1982–83; co-founder / president, Laredo Volunteer Lawyers Program, Inc., 1982–83; board of directors, United Way, 1982–83; co-founder / treasurer, Stop Child Abuse and Neglect, 1982–83, and advisory board member, 1984; president, board of directors, Laredo Legal Aid Society, Inc., 1982–84; president, board of directors, Laredo Young Lawyers Association, 1983–84; sustaining member, Texas Democratic Party, 1984; legal advisor, American GI, local chapter,

1986–87; International Trade Association, Laredo State University, 1988; Texas Delegate, National Democratic Convention, 1992; president, board of directors, International Good Neighbor Council; member, the College of the State Bar of Texas, 1994; Texas Lyceum, 1997; policy board of advisors, *Texas Hispanic Journal of Law,* University of Texas Law School, 2002; member: American Bar Association; Inter-American Bar Association; Texas Bar Association; Webb/Laredo Bar Association; recipient of various awards; religion: Catholic; married: wife, Imelda; two daughters, Christina Alexandra and Catherine Ann; Senior Whip; vice chairman of the Steering and Policy Committee; caucuses: co-chair of the Blue Dog Coalition; Congressional Unmanned Systems Caucus; committees: Appropriations; elected to the 109th Congress on November 2, 2004; reelected to each succeeding Congress.

Office Listings

https://cuellar.house.gov https://facebook.com/repcuellar
twitter: @RepCuellar https://instagram.com/repcuellar

2372 Rayburn House Office Building, Washington, DC 20515 .... (202) 225–1640
Chief of Staff.—Catherine Edmonson. FAX: 225–1641
Legislative Director.—Travis Knight.
District Press Secretary.—Leslie Martinez.
Scheduler.—Amelia Dal Pra.
602 East Calton Road, Suite 2, Laredo, TX 78041 .... (956) 725–0639
FAX: 725–2647
615 East Houston Street, Suite 563, San Antonio, TX 78205 .... (210) 271–2851
FAX: 277–6671
117 East Tom Landry, Mission, TX 78572 .... (956) 424–3942
FAX: 424–3936
100 North F.M. 3167, Suite 208, Rio Grande City, Texas 78582 .... (956) 487–5603
FAX: 488–0952

Counties: ATASCOSA, BEXAR (part), HIDALGO (part), LA SALLE (part), MCMULLEN, STARR, WEBB, WILSON (part), AND ZAPATA. Population (2010), 698,488.

ZIP Codes: 78002, 78007–08, 78011–12, 78019, 78026, 78040–46, 78050, 78052, 78062, 78065, 78067, 78072–73, 78076, 78101, 78109, 78112, 78121, 78147–48, 78150, 78152, 78160–61, 78209, 78218–20, 78222–23, 78233, 78239, 78244, 78263–64, 78344, 78369, 78371, 78501, 78536, 78541, 78545, 78547–48, 78560, 78563–65, 78572, 78582, 78584–85, 78588, 78591, 78595

* * *

TWENTY-NINTH DISTRICT

SYLVIA R. GARCIA, Democrat, of Houston, TX; born in Palito Blanco, Jim Wells County, TX, September 6, 1950; education: graduated from Ben Bolt-Palito Blanco High School, Palito Blanco, TX; B.S.W., Texas Women's University, Denton, TX, 1972; J.D., Texas Southern University, Houston, TX, 1978; professional: lawyer; social worker; director and presiding judge, Houston, TX, municipal court system, 1983–98; Houston, TX, city controller, 1998–2003; member of the Harris County, TX, commissioners court, 2003–10; member of the Texas State Senate, 2013–19; religion: Catholic; committees: Financial Services; Judiciary; elected to the 116th Congress on November 6, 2018.

Office Listings

https://sylviagarcia.house.gov https://facebook.com/RepSylviaGarcia twitter: @RepSylviaGarcia
https://instagram.com/repsylviagarcia

1620 Longworth House Office Building, Washington, DC 20515 .... (202) 225–1688
Chief of Staff.—John Chapa Gorczynski. FAX: 225–9903
Legislative Director.—Patrick Bond.
Communications Director.—Don Shaw.
Scheduler.—Evan Dale.
11811 East Freeway, Suite 430, Houston, TX 77029 .... (832) 325–3150
District Director.—Claudia Hogue.

Counties: HARRIS (part). CITIES AND TOWNSHIPS: Channelview, Galena Park, Houston, Humble, Jacinto City, Pasadena, and South Houston. Population (2013), 729,827.

ZIP Codes: 77003, 77009, 77011–13, 77015–17, 77020, 77022–23, 77026, 77029, 77032, 77034, 77037, 77039, 77044, 77049–50, 77060–61, 77075–76, 77087, 77089, 77091, 77093, 77396, 77502–06, 77530, 77536, 77547, 77587

* * *

THIRTIETH DISTRICT

EDDIE BERNICE JOHNSON, Democrat, of Dallas, TX; born in Waco, McLennan County, TX, December 3, 1935; education: graduated from A.J. Moore High School, Waco, TX, 1952; nursing certificate, St. Mary's College at the University of Notre Dame, Notre Dame, IN, 1955; B.S., Texas Christian University, Fort Worth, TX, 1967; M.P.A., Southern Methodist University, Dallas, TX, 1976; professional: chief psychiatric nurse and psychotherapist, Veterans Administration Hospital, Dallas, TX; member of the Texas State House of Representatives, 1972–77; administrator, United States Department of Health, Education and Welfare, 1977–81; business owner; member of the Texas State Senate, 1986–92; awards: NABTP Mickey Leland Award for Excellence in Diversity, 2000; National Association of School Nurses, Inc., Legislative Award, 2000; the State of Texas Honorary Texan issued by the Governor of Texas, 2000; Links, Inc., Co-Founders Award, 2000; 100 Black Men of America, Inc., Woman of the Year, 2001; National Black Caucus of State Legislators Image Award, 2001; National Conference of Black Mayors, Inc. President's Award, 2001; Alpha Kappa Alpha Trailblazer, 2002; Thurgood Marshall Scholarship Community Leader, 2002; Phi Beta Sigma Fraternity Woman of the Year, 2002; CBCF Outstanding Leadership, 2002; member: St. John Baptist Church, Dallas; children: Dawrence Kirk; grandchildren: Kirk, Jr., David, and James; congressional caucuses: co-chair, Task Force on International HIV / AIDS; Airpower; Asian-Pacific; Army; Arts; Biomedical Research; Children's Working Group; chair (107th Congress), Congressional Black Caucus; Fire Services; Human Rights Caucus; Korean Caucus; Livable Communities Task Force; Medical Technology; Oil and Gas Educational Forum; Singapore Caucus; Study Group on Japan; TX-21 Transportation Caucus; Urban; Women's Caucus; Women's Issues; committees: chair, Science, Space, and Technology; Transportation and Infrastructure; elected on November 3, 1992 to the 103rd Congress; reelected to each succeeding Congress.

Office Listings

https://ebjohnson.house.gov https://facebook.com/CongresswomanEBJtx30 https://twitter.com/RepEBJ

2306 Rayburn House Office Building, Washington, DC 20515 .... (202) 225–8885
Chief of Staff.—Murat Gokcigdem. FAX: 226–1477
Communications Director.—Sameer Assanie.
Legislative Director.—Ken Nealy.
Legislative Assistants: Jonathan Jackson, Nawaid Ladak, Tonia Wu.
Staff Assistant.—Zachary Mitchiner.
1825 Market Center Boulevard, Suite 440, Dallas, TX 75207 .... (214) 922–8885
District Director of Operations.—Dominique Brown.

Counties: DALLAS (part). CITIES AND TOWNSHIPS: Downtown Dallas, Fair Park, Kessler Park, Old East Dallas, Pleasant Grove, South Dallas, and South Oak Cliff; all of Cedar Hill, DeSoto, Duncanville, Hutchins, Lancaster, and Wilmer and parts of Ferris, Glenn Heights, South Grand Prairie, Oak Lawn, Ovilla, Uptown / Victory Park, and West Dallas. Population (2010), 698,487.

ZIP Codes: 75051–52, 75054, 75115–16, 75125, 75134, 75137, 75141, 75146, 75149–50, 75154, 75159, 75172, 75180, 75201–04, 75207–12, 75214–20, 75223–28, 75232–33, 75235–37, 75241, 75246–47, 75249, 75253, 75270

* * *

THIRTY-FIRST DISTRICT

JOHN R. CARTER, Republican, of Round Rock, TX; born in Houston, TX, November 6, 1941; education: Texas Tech University, 1964; University of Texas Law School, 1969; professional: attorney; private law practice; public service: appointed and elected a Texas District Court Judge, 1981–2001; awards: recipient and namesake of the Williamson County ''John R. Carter Lifetime Achievement Award''; family: married to Erika Carter; children: Gilianne, John, Theodore, and Danielle; committees: Appropriations; elected to the 108th Congress on November 5, 2002; reelected to each succeeding Congress.

Office Listings

https://carter.house.gov https://facebook.com/judgecarter https://twitter.com/JudgeCarter

2110 Rayburn House Office Building, Washington, DC 20515 .... (202) 225–3864
Chief of Staff.—Jonas Miller. FAX: 225–5886
Communications Director.—Emily Dowdell.
Schedulers: Marie Alvarado (District), Evan Bender (DC).
1717 North IH 35, Suite 303, Round Rock, TX 78664 .... (512) 246–1600

Office Listings—Continued

6544B South General Bruce Drive, Temple, TX 76502 .... (254) 933–1392

Counties: BELL AND WILLIAMSON. Population (2010), 739,975.

ZIP Codes: 76501, 76504, 76511, 76513, 76527, 76530, 76534, 76537, 76542–43, 76548–49, 76557, 76559, 76569, 76571, 76574, 76578, 78613, 78615, 78621, 78628, 78633–34, 78641–42, 78664–65, 78681, 78717, 78728–29

* * *

THIRTY-SECOND DISTRICT

COLIN Z. ALLRED, Democrat, of Dallas, TX; born in Dallas, Dallas County, TX, April 15, 1983; education: graduated from Hillcrest High School, Dallas, TX, 2001; B.A., Baylor University, Waco, TX, 2005; J.D., University of California, Berkeley, CA, 2014; professional: professional athlete; lawyer; staff, United States Department of Housing and Urban Development, 2016–17; Perkins Coie LLP Political Law Group, associate; Battleground Texas, Regional Director of Voter Protection; United States Attorney's Office, law clerk; married: Alexandra Eber; children: one son; caucuses: Congressional Black Caucus; New Democrat Coalition; committees: Foreign Affairs; Transportation and Infrastructure; Veterans' Affairs; elected to the 116th Congress on November 6, 2018.

Office Listings

https://allred.house.gov https://facebook.com/RepColinAllred twitter: @RepColinAllred
https://instagram.com/repcolinallred https://youtube.com/channel/UCm3l7ZntoH0EI2vIsvxeVqg

328 Cannon House Office Building, Washington, DC 20515 .... (202) 225–2231
Chief of Staff.—Paige Hutchinson. FAX: 225–5878
Legislative Director.—Janelle McClure.
Communications Director.—Josh Stewart.
Scheduler.—Mina Pulitzer.
100 North Central Expressway, Suite 602, Richardson, TX 75080 .... (972) 972–7949
District Director.—Judith Tankel. FAX: (888) 671–0539

County: DALLAS (part) AND COLLIN (part). CITIES AND TOWNSHIPS: Dallas, Richardson, University Park, Highland Park, Mesquite, Garland, Sachse, Rowlett, and Wylie. Population (2010), 698,488.

ZIP Codes: 75002, 75040–44, 75048, 75080–82, 75088–89, 75094, 75098, 75150, 75166, 75182, 75201, 75204–06, 75209, 75214, 75218–19, 75223, 75225–26, 75229–31, 75235, 75238, 75243–46, 75248, 75251–52

* * *

THIRTY-THIRD DISTRICT

MARC A. VEASEY, Democrat, of Fort Worth, TX; born in Fort Worth, January 3, 1971; education: B.S., Texas Wesleyan University, Fort Worth, 1995; professional: journalist; staff, U.S. Representative J. Martin Frost of Texas; real estate; Texas State Representative, 2004–12; religion: Christian; married: Tonya Veasey; children: Adam Veasey; caucuses: Blue Collar Caucus; Congressional Black Caucus; Congressional Voting Rights Caucus; committees: Energy and Commerce; elected to the 113th Congress on November 6, 2012; reelected to each succeeding Congress.

Office Listings

https://veasey.house.gov https://facebook.com/congressmanmarcveasey
twitter: @repveasey instagram: @repveasey

2348 Rayburn House Office Building, Washington, DC 20515 .... (202) 225–9897
Chief of Staff.—Askia Suruma. FAX: 225–9702
Scheduler.—Jane Phipps.
Legislative Director.—Nicole Varner.
Senior Legislative Assistant.—Thaddeus Woody.
Legislative Assistant.—Zahraa Saheb.
Communications Director.—Emily Druckman.
Press Secretary / Digital Director.—Antonio DeLoera.
Staff Assistant / Legislative Correspondent.—Luke Dube.
6707 Brentwood Stair Road, Suite 200, Fort Worth, TX 76112 .... (817) 920–9086
District Director.—Anne Hagan.
1881 Sylvan Avenue, Suite 108, Dallas, TX 75208 .... (214) 741–1387

Counties: DALLAS (part) AND TARRANT (part). CITIES AND TOWNSHIPS: Arlington, Cockrell Hill, parts of Dallas, Everman, Forest Hill, Fort Worth, Grand Prairie, Haltom City, Irving, Saginaw, and Sansom Park. Population (2010), 698,488.

ZIP Codes: 75050–52, 75060–62, 75203, 75208, 75211–12, 75216, 75220, 75224, 75229, 75233–36, 75247, 76006, 76010–12, 76014, 76040, 76053, 76103–06, 76109–12, 76114–15, 76117–20, 76133–34, 76137, 76140, 76155, 76164, 76179

* * *

THIRTY-FOURTH DISTRICT

FILEMON VELA, Democrat, of Brownsville, TX; born in Harlingen, TX, February 13, 1963; education: B.A., Georgetown University, 1985; J.D., University of Texas at Austin School of Law, 1987; professional: attorney; admitted, Texas Bar and U.S. District Court, Western and Southern Districts of Texas, 1988; married: Rose Rivera, February 3, 1990; caucuses: co-chair, Border Caucus; co-chair, Citrus Caucus; co-chair, Zika Caucus; Career and Technical Education Caucus; Coastal Communities Caucus; Community College Caucus; Community Health Center Caucus; Congressional Friends of the National Park Service; Congressional Hispanic Caucus; Diabetes Caucus; Disaster Relief Caucus; Friends of Job Corps Congressional Caucus; General Aviation Caucus; I–69 Caucus; Ports Caucus; Pre-K Caucus; Texas Caucus on Shale Oil and Gas; Texas Maritime Caucus; TX-21 Transportation Congressional Caucus; U.S.-Mexico Friendship Caucus; committees: Agriculture; Armed Services; elected to the 113th Congress on November 6, 2012; reelected to each succeeding Congress.

Office Listings

https://vela.house.gov https://facebook.com/UsCongressmanFilemonVela
https://twitter.com/repfilemonvela

307 Cannon House Office Building, Washington, DC 20515 .... (202) 225–9901
Chief of Staff.—Sandra Alcala.
Deputy Chief of Staff.—Karen De Los Santos.
Chief Counsel.—Perry Brody.
Director of Operations.—Liza Lynch.
Scheduler.—Jill Caress.
Legislative Director.—Leigh Maiden.
Senior Defense Advisor.—Julie Merberg.
Legislative Assistants: Gabrielle Howard, Keith Timmer.
Military Fellow.—Bob Muchow.
800 North Expressway 77–83, Suite 9, Brownsville, TX 78521 .... (956) 544–8352
District Director.—Marisela Cortez.
Senior Caseworker.—Maria Barrera Jaross.
District Press Secretary / Caseworker.—Brenda Rangel.
500 East Main Street, Alice, TX 78332 .... (361) 230–9776
District Director.—Jose Pereida.
1390 West Expressway 83, San Benito, TX 78586 .... (956) 276–4497
Office Manager / Caseworker.—Sally Lara.
301 West Railroad Avenue, Weslaco, TX 78596 .... (956) 520–8273
Caseworker.—Anissa Guajardo.

Counties: BEE, CAMERON, DEWITT, GOLIAD, GONZALES, HIDALGO, JIM WELLS, KENEDY, KLEBERG, SAN PATRICIO, AND WILLACY. Population (2010), 716,416.

ZIP Codes: 77954, 77960, 77963, 77993–94, 78104, 78107, 78122, 78125, 78142, 78145–46, 78159, 78162, 78164, 78338, 78342, 78363, 78375, 78379, 78385, 78389, 78391, 78520–21, 78526, 78535, 78550, 78552, 78559, 78561, 78566–67, 78575, 78578–80, 78583, 78586, 78590, 78592–94, 78597–98, 78614, 78677

* * *

THIRTY-FIFTH DISTRICT

LLOYD DOGGETT, Democrat, of Austin, TX; born in Austin, October 6, 1946; education: graduated, Austin High School; B.B.A., University of Texas, Austin, 1967; J.D., University of Texas, 1970; president, University of Texas student body; associate editor, *Texas Law Review;* professional: Outstanding Young Lawyer, Austin Association of Young Lawyers; president, Texas Consumer Association; admitted to the Texas State Bar, 1971; Texas State Senate, 1973–85, elected at age 26; Senate author of 124 state laws and Senate sponsor of 63 House bills enacted into law; elected President Pro Tempore of Texas Senate; served as acting governor; named Outstanding Young Texan by Texas Jaycees; Arthur B. DeWitty Award for outstanding achievement in human rights, Austin NAACP; honored for work by Austin Rape Crisis Center, Planned Parenthood of Austin; Austin chapter, American Institute of Architects; Austin Council on Alcoholism; Disabled American Veterans; Save the Children Congressional Champion for Real and Lasting Change; AARP Legislative Achievement Award; Justice on Texas Supreme Court, 1989–94; chairman, Supreme Court Task Force on Judicial Ethics, 1992–94; Outstanding Judge (Mexican-American Bar of Texas), 1993; adjunct professor, University of Texas School of Law, 1989–94; James Madison Award, Texas Freedom of Information Foundation, 1990; First Amendment Award, National Society of Professional Journalists, 1990; religion: member, First United Methodist Church; married: Libby Belk Doggett, 1969; children: Lisa and Cathy; caucuses: co-founder and co-chair, House Affordable Prescription Drug Task Force; Congressional Task Force on Tobacco and Health; Democratic Caucus Task Force on Child Care; committees: Budget; Ways and Means; Joint Committee on Taxation; elected to the 104th Congress; reelected to each succeeding Congress.

Office Listings

https://doggett.house.gov https://facebook.com/RepLloydDoggett https://twitter.com/replloyddoggett

2307 Rayburn House Office Building, Washington, DC 20515 .... (202) 225–4865
Chief of Staff.—Michael J. Mucchetti. FAX: 225–3073
Communications Director.—Kate Stotesbery.
Staff Assistant / Scheduler.—Luis Guerrero.
217 West Travis Street, San Antonio, TX 78205 .... (210) 704–1080
District Director.—MaryEllen Veliz.
300 East 8th Street, Suite 763, Austin, TX 78701 .... (512) 916–5921
District Director.—Erin Gurak.

Counties: BEXAR, CALDWELL, COMAL, GUADALUPE, HAYS, AND TRAVIS. Population (2010), 698,488.

ZIP Codes: 78108, 78130, 78132, 78154, 78201–05, 78207–08, 78210, 78212, 78214–15, 78217–20, 78222–23, 78228, 78233–35, 78239, 78244, 78247, 78266, 78610, 78612, 78617, 78622, 78640, 78644, 78653, 78655–56, 78666, 78702, 78704, 78719, 78721, 78725, 78741–42, 78744–45, 78747–48, 78753–54, 78758

* * *

THIRTY-SIXTH DISTRICT

BRIAN BABIN, Republican, of Woodville, TX; born in Port Arthur, TX, March 23, 1948; education: B.S., Lamar University; D.D.S., University of Texas; professional: dentist; Mayor of Woodville, 1982–84; Woodville City Councilman, 1984–89; Woodville Independent School Board, 1992–95; director of Tyler County Chamber of Commerce; president of Texas State Board of Dental Examiners, 1981–87; Deep East Texas Council of Governments member, 1982–84; Texas Historical Commission, 1989–95; Appointee to Lower Neches Valley Authority, 1999–2014; caucuses: Air Force Caucus; Autism Caucus; Boating Caucus; Border Security Caucus; Congressional Aerospace Caucus; Congressional Sportsmen's Caucus; Diabetes Caucus; Foster Youth Caucus; GOP Doctors Caucus; House Republican Israel Caucus; Israel Allies Caucus; Military Veterans Caucus; Oral Health Caucus; Ports Caucus; Pro Life Caucus; Refinery Caucus; Republican Study Committee; committees: Science, Space, and Technology; Transportation and Infrastructure; elected to the 114th Congress on November 4, 2014; reelected to each succeeding Congress.

Office Listings

https://babin.house.gov https://facebook.com/repbrianbabin https://twitter.com/repbrianbabin

2236 Rayburn House Office Building, Washington, DC 20515 .... (202) 225–1555
Chief of Staff.—Ben Couhig. FAX: 226–0396
Legislative Director.—Steve Janushkowsky.
Press Secretary.—Sarah Reese.
Legislative Staff: Avery Littrell, Lauren Zigler.
Staff Assistant.—Ben Taylor.
Scheduler.—Beth Barber.
203 Ivy Avenue, Suite 600, Deer Park, TX 77536 .... (832) 780–0966
1201 South Childers Road, Orange, TX 77630 .... (409) 883–8075
100 West Bluff Drive, Woodville, TX 75979 .... (844) 303–8934
2004 North Cleveland Street, Dayton, TX 77535 .... (832) 780–0966

Counties: CHAMBERS, HARDIN, HARRIS (part), JASPER, LIBERTY, NEWTON, ORANGE, POLK, AND TYLER. Population (2010), 712,433.

ZIP Codes: 75326–27, 75335, 75350, 75360, 75368, 75928, 75932–39, 75942, 75951, 75956, 75960, 75966, 75977, 75979, 77369, 77374, 77376, 77505, 77507, 77514, 77519, 77520–21, 77523, 77533, 77535, 77538, 77560–62, 77564, 77571, 77575, 77580, 77585–86, 77597, 77611–12, 77614–16, 77624–25, 77630, 77632, 77656–57, 77659–64

UTAH

(Population 2010, 2,763,885)

SENATORS

MICHAEL S. LEE, Republican, of Alpine, UT; born in Mesa, AZ, June 4, 1971; education: B.S., Brigham Young University, Provo, UT, 1994; J.D., Brigham Young University, 1997; professional: law clerk to Judge Dee Benson of the U.S. District Court for the District of Utah; law clerk to Judge Samuel A. Alito, Jr. on the U.S. Court of Appeals for the Third Circuit Court; attorney with the law firm Sidley & Austin; Assistant U.S. Attorney in Salt Lake City; general counsel to the Governor of Utah; law clerk to Supreme Court Justice Samuel A. Alito; partner at Howrey law firm; religion: Church of Jesus Christ of Latter-Day Saints; married: Sharon Burr of Provo, UT; children: James, John, and Eliza; committees: chair, Joint Economic Committee; Commerce, Science, and Transportation; Energy and Natural Resources; Judiciary; elected to the U.S. Senate on November 2, 2010; reelected to the U.S. Senate on November 8, 2016.

Office Listings

https://lee.senate.gov https://facebook.com/senatormikelee
https://twitter.com/SenMikeLee https://youtube.com/senatormikelee

361A Russell Senate Office Building, Washington, DC 20510 .... (202) 224–5444
Chief of Staff.—Allyson Bell. FAX: 228–1168
Legislative Director.—Christy Woodruff.
Communications Director.—Conn Carroll.
Press Secretary.—Erik Kujanpaa.
Administrative Director.—Alyssa Burleson.
State Director.—Robert Axson.
Federal Building, 125 South State, Suite 4225, Salt Lake City, UT 84138 .... (801) 524–5933
Federal Building, 324 25th Street, Suite 1410, Ogden, UT 84401 .... (801) 392–9633
285 West Tabernacle Street, Suite 200, St. George, UT 84770 .... (435) 628–5514

* * *

MITT ROMNEY, Republican, of Holladay, UT; born in Bloomfield Hills, MI, March 12, 1947; education: B.A., Brigham Young University, Provo, UT, 1971; M.B.A., Harvard Business School and J.D., Harvard Law School, 1975; professional: vice president, Bain and Company, Inc. (management consulting firm), Boston, MA, 1978–84; founder of Bain Capital (investment company); president, Salt Lake Organizing Committee for 2002 Winter Olympic Games; Governor, Commonwealth of Massachusetts, 2003–07; married: Ann; five sons; committees: Foreign Relations; Health, Education, Labor, and Pensions; Homeland Security and Governmental Affairs; Small Business and Entrepreneurship; elected to the U.S. Senate on November 6, 2018.

Office Listings

https://romney.senate.gov https://facebook.com/senatorromney
https://twitter.com/SenatorRomney

124 Russell Senate Office Building, Washington, DC 20510 .... (202) 224–5251
Chief of Staff.—Matt Waldrip. FAX: 228–0836
Legislative Director.—Chris Barkley.
Communications Director.—Liz Johnson.
Scheduler.—Meagan Shepherd.
Federal Building, Suite 8402, 125 South State Street, Salt Lake City, UT 84138 .... (801) 524–4380
State Director.—Adam Gardiner.

REPRESENTATIVES

FIRST DISTRICT

ROB BISHOP, Republican, of Brigham City, UT; born in Kaysville, UT, July 13, 1951; education: B.A., political science, *magna cum laude,* University of Utah, 1974; professional: high school teacher; public service: Utah House of Representatives, 1979–94, Speaker of the House during his last 2 years; elected, chair, Utah Republican Party, 1997 (served two terms); religion: Church of Jesus Christ of Latter-Day Saints; family: married to Jeralynn Hansen; children: Shule, Jarom, Zenock, Maren, and Jashon; committees: ranking member, Natural Resources;

Armed Services; elected to the 108th Congress on November 5, 2002; reelected to each succeeding Congress.

Office Listings

https://robbishop.house.gov

123 Cannon House Office Building, Washington, DC 20515 .... (202) 225–0453
Chief of Staff.—Devin Wiser. FAX: 225–5857
Legislative Assistants: Paul Johnson, Lee Lonsberry, D. Murphy, Adam Stewart.
Scheduler.—Barbara Andrade.
6 North Main Street, Brigham City, UT 84302.
152 East 100 North, Vernal, UT 84078.
324 25th Street, 1017 Federal Building, Ogden, UT 84401 .... (801) 625–0107

Counties: BOX ELDER, CACHE, DAGGETT, DAVIS (part), DUCHESNE, MORGAN, RICH, SUMMIT, UINTAH, AND WEBER. Population (2010), 690,971.

ZIP Codes: 82930, 83312, 83342, 84001–02, 84007, 84015, 84017–18, 84021, 84023–28, 84031, 84033, 84035–41, 84046, 84050–53, 84055–56, 84060–61, 84063–64, 84066–67, 84072–73, 84075–76, 84078, 84083, 84085–86, 84098, 84301–02, 84304–21, 84324–41, 84401, 84403–05, 84414, 84526, 84540

* * *

SECOND DISTRICT

CHRIS STEWART, Republican, of Farmington, UT; born in Logan, UT, July 15, 1960; education: B.S., economics, Utah State University; professional: president and CEO, Shipley Group; independent author; military: pilot, U.S. Air Force; religion: Church of Jesus Christ of Latter-Day Saints; married: Evie; children: Sean, Dane, Lance, Kayla, Bryce, and Megan; committees: Appropriations; Budget; Permanent Select Committee on Intelligence; elected to the 113th Congress on November 6, 2012; reelected to each succeeding Congress.

Office Listings

https://stewart.house.gov https://facebook.com/RepChrisStewart
https://twitter.com/repchrisstewart https://instagram.com/repChrisStewart
https://youtube.com/RepChrisStewart

2242 Rayburn House Office Building, Washington, DC 20515 .... (202) 225–9730
Chief of Staff.—Clay White. FAX: 225–9627
Executive Assistant.—Mark Coffield.
Communications Director.—Madi Shupe.
420 East South Temple, #390, Salt Lake City, UT 84111 .... (801) 364–5550
District Director.—Gary Webster. FAX: 364–5551
253 West St. George Boulevard, Suite 100, St. George, UT 84770 .... (435) 627–1500
Southern Utah Director.—Adam Snow. FAX: 627–1911

Counties: BEAVER, DAVIS (part), GARFIELD, IRON, JUAB (part), KANE, MILLARD, PIUTE, SALT LAKE (part), SANPETE (part), SEVIER, TOOELE, WASHINGTON, AND WAYNE. CITIES: Alton Town, Annabella Town, Antimony Town, Apple Valley Town, Aurora City, Beaver City, Beryl Junction, Bicknell Town, Big Water Town, Boulder Town, Bountiful City, Brian Head Town, Bryce Canyon, Cannonville Town, Cedar City, Centerfield Town, Centerville City, Central, Central Valley Town, Circleville Town, Dammeron Valley, Delta City, Deseret, Dugway, Elsinore Town, Emigration Canyon, Enoch City, Enterprise City, Ephraim City, Erda, Escalante City, Eureka City, Farmington City (part), Fayette Town, Fillmore City, Fremont, Fruit Heights City (part), Glendale Town, Glenwood Town, Grantsville City, Gunnison City, Hanksville Town, Hatch Town, Henrieville Town, Hildale City, Hinckley Town, Holden Town, Hurricane City, Ivins City, Joseph Town, Junction Town, Kanab City, Kanarraville Town, Kanosh Town, Kaysville City (part), Kearns (part), Kingston Town, Koosharem Town, La Verkin City, Leamington Town, Leeds Town, Loa Town, Lyman Town, Lynndyl Town, Magna, Manti City, Marysvale Town, Mayfield Town, Meadow Town, Milford City, Minersville Town, Monroe City, New Harmony Town, Newcastle, North Salt Lake City, Oak City Town, Oasis, Ophir Town, Orderville Town, Panguitch City, Paragonah Town, Parowan City, Pine Valley, Redmond Town, Richfield City, Rockville Town, Rush Valley Town, Salina City, Salt Lake City (part), Santa Clara City, Scipio Town, Sigurd Town, Springdale Town, St. George City, Stansbury Park, Sterling Town, Stockton Town, Summit, Sutherland, Teasdale, Tooele City, Toquerville Town, Torrey Town, Tropic Town, Vernon Town, Veyo, Virgin Town, Washington City, Wendover City, West Bountiful City, West Valley City (part), and Woods Cross City. Population (2010), 690,971.

ZIP Codes: 84010, 84014, 84022, 84025, 84029, 84034, 84037, 84044, 84054, 84069, 84071, 84074–75, 84080–81, 84083, 84087, 84101–06, 84108–09, 84111–13, 84115–16, 84118–20, 84128, 84144, 84180, 84533, 84620–24, 84627–28, 84630–31, 84634–38, 84640, 84642–43, 84648–49, 84652, 84654, 84656–57, 84662, 84665, 84701, 84710–16, 84718–26, 84728–47, 84749–67, 84770, 84772–76, 84779–84, 84790

* * *

THIRD DISTRICT

JOHN CURTIS, Republican, of Provo, UT; born in Salt Lake City, UT, May 10, 1960; education: B.S., business management, Brigham Young University, Provo, UT, 1985; professional: Mayor, Provo City, 2010–17; COO and part-owner, Action Target, 1999–2010; manager, O.C. Tanner Co., 1989–99; overseas lead buyer, Brazil International, 1987–88; territory representative, Citizen Watch Co., 1984–86; missionary, Church of Jesus Christ of Latter-Day Saints, Taiwan, 1979–81; religion: Church of Jesus Christ of Latter-Day Saints; married: Sue; children: Kirsten, Zane, Jacob, Sarah Jane, Emily, and Nicole; grandchildren: Jet, Jane, Clare, Sage, Hazel, and Genevieve; caucuses: Dietary Supplement Caucus; Friends of Wales Caucus; Republican Main Street Partnership; Western Caucus; committees: Foreign Affairs; Natural Resources; elected, by special election, to the 115th Congress on November 17, 2017, to fill the vacancy caused by the resignation of U.S. Representative Jason Chaffetz; reelected to the 116th Congress on November 6, 2018.

Office Listings

https://curtis.house.gov https://facebook.com/RepJohnCurtis https://twitter.com/RepJohnCurtis

125 Cannon House Office Building, Washington, DC 20515 .... (202) 225–7751
Chief of Staff.—Corey Norman.
Legislative Director.—Jake Bornstein.
Scheduler.—Stephanie Heinrich.
Press Secretary.—Ally Riding.
Legislative Assistants: Troy Dougall, Rebekah Rodriquez.
Counsel.—Liz Whitlock.
Staff Assistant.—Ray Phillips.
3549 North University Avenue, Suite 275, Provo, UT 84604 .... (801) 922–5400
District Director.—Lorie Fowlke.

Counties: CARBON, EMERY, GRAND, SALT LAKE (part), SAN JUAN, UTAH (part), AND WASATCH. Population (2010), 708,809.

ZIP Codes: 84003–04, 84020, 84032, 84036 (part), 84042, 84043 (part), 84047 (part), 84049, 84057–59, 84060 (part), 84062, 84070 (part), 84082, 84090–94, 84097, 84109, 84117 (part), 84121 (part), 84124 (part), 84171, 84501, 84510–13, 84515–16, 84518, 84520–23, 84525–26, 84528–37, 84539–40, 84542, 84601–06, 84651 (part), 84653, 84655 (part), 84660 (part), 84663 (part), 84664

* * *

FOURTH DISTRICT

BEN MCADAMS, Democrat, of Salt Lake City, UT; born in West Bountiful, UT, December 5, 1974; education: B.A., political science, University of Utah, Salt Lake City, UT, 2000; J.D., with honors, Columbia University, New York, NY, 2003; professional: associate, law firm Dorsey & Whitney in Salt Lake City, working in securities law; lawyer in New York and Utah, assisting businesses with federal securities regulation compliance; volunteer adjunct faculty member, University of Utah College of Law; Senior Advisor to Salt Lake City Mayor Ralph Becker, 2008–12; Utah State Senator, 2009–12; Mayor of Salt Lake County, 2013–19; religion: The Church of Jesus Christ of Latter-day Saints; served a mission to Brazil in the mid-1990s; family: married to Julie; four children; caucuses: Blue Dog Coalition; New Democrat Coalition; committees: Financial Services; Science, Space, and Technology; elected to the 116th Congress on November 6, 2018.

Office Listings

https://mcadams.house.gov https://facebook.com/RepBenMcAdams
https://twitter.com/RepBenMcAdams https://instagram.com/repbenmcadams

130 Cannon House Office Building, Washington, DC 20515 .... (202) 225–3011
Chief of Staff.—Nichole Dunn. FAX: 225–5638
Scheduler.—Stephanie Withers.
Communications Director.—Alyson Heyrend.
Legislative Director.—Eric May.
9067 South 1300 West, Suite 101, West Jordan, UT 84088 .... (801) 999–9801

Counties: JUAB (part), SALT LAKE (part), SANPETE (part), AND UTAH (part). Population (2010), 690,971.

ZIP Codes: 84003 (part), 84005–06, 84013, 84020 (part), 84043 (part), 84045, 84047 (part), 84065, 84070 (part), 84081 (part), 84084, 84088, 84095–96, 84106 (part), 84107, 84109 (part), 84115 (part), 84117–21 (part), 84123, 84124 (part), 84129, 84141, 84157, 84165, 84170, 84184, 84623, 84626, 84629, 84632–33, 84639, 84645–48, 84651 (part), 84655 (part), 84660 (part), 84662, 84663 (part), 84667

VERMONT

(Population 2010, 625,741)

SENATORS

PATRICK LEAHY, President Pro Tempore Emeritus; Democrat, of Middlesex, VT; born in Montpelier, VT, March 31, 1940, son of Howard and Alba Leahy; education: graduate of St. Michael's High School, Montpelier, 1957; B.A., St. Michael's College, 1961; J.D., Georgetown University, 1964; professional: attorney, admitted to the Vermont Bar, 1964; admitted to the District of Columbia Bar, 1979; admitted to practice before: the Vermont Supreme Court, 1964; the Federal District Court of Vermont, 1965; the Second Circuit Court of Appeals in New York, 1966; and the U.S. Supreme Court, 1968; State's Attorney, Chittenden County, 1966–74; vice president, National District Attorneys Association, 1971–74; member, Smithsonian Board of Regents; married: the former Marcelle Pomerleau, 1962; children: Kevin, Alicia, and Mark; first Democrat and youngest person in Vermont to be elected to the U.S. Senate; committees: ranking member, Appropriations; Agriculture, Nutrition, and Forestry; Judiciary; Rules and Administration; Joint Committee on the Library; elected to the Senate on November 5, 1974; reelected to each succeeding Senate term.

Office Listings

https://leahy.senate.gov https://facebook.com/SenatorPatrickLeahy
twitter: @SenatorLeahy instagram: @senatorleahy

437 Russell Senate Office Building, Washington, DC 20510 .... (202) 224–4242
Chief of Staff.—John P. Dowd. FAX: 224–3479
Deputy Chief of Staff.—Ann Berry.
Legislative Director.—Erica Chabot.
Communications Director.—David Carle.
87 State Street, Room 338, Montpelier, VT 05602 .... (802) 229–0569
199 Main Street, Courthouse Plaza, Burlington, VT 05401 .... (802) 863–2525

* * *

BERNARD SANDERS, Independent, of Burlington, VT; born in Brooklyn, NY, September 8, 1941; education: graduated, Madison High School, Brooklyn; B.S., political science, University of Chicago, 1964; professional: carpenter; writer; college professor; Mayor of Burlington, VT, 1981–89; married: the former Jane O'Meara, 1988; children: Levi, Heather, Carina, and David; committees: ranking member, Budget; Energy and Natural Resources; Environment and Public Works; Health, Education, Labor, and Pensions; Veterans' Affairs; elected to the 102nd Congress on November 6, 1990; reelected to each succeeding Congress; elected to the U.S. Senate on November 7, 2006; reelected to each succeeding Senate term.

Office Listings

https://sanders.senate.gov https://facebook.com/senatorsanders https://twitter.com/sensanders

332 Dirksen Senate Office Building, Washington, DC 20510 .... (202) 224–5141
Chief of Staff.—Caryn Compton. FAX: 228–0776
Legislative Director.—Lori Kearns.
Communications Director.—Keane Bhatt.
1 Church Street, Third Floor, Burlington, VT 05401 .... (800) 339–9834

REPRESENTATIVE

AT LARGE

PETER WELCH, Democrat, of Norwich, VT; born in Springfield, MA, May 2, 1947; education: Cathedral High School, Springfield, MA, 1969; B.A., *magna cum laude*, College of the Holy Cross, 1969; J.D., University of California at Berkeley, 1973; professional: attorney; Vermont State Senate, 1981–89, 2001–07; Minority Leader, 1983–85; President Pro Tempore, 1985–89, 2003–07; member, Vermont Public Utility Commission; spouse: Margaret Cheney; three stepchildren: James, Catherine, Peter; wife: Joan Smith (deceased 2004); son: Michael; stepchildren: Beth, Mary, Bill, John; committees: Energy and Commerce; Oversight and Reform; Permanent Select Committee on Intelligence; elected to the 110th Congress on November 7, 2006; reelected to each succeeding Congress.

Office Listings

https://welch.house.gov https://facebook.com/PeterWelch
twitter: @PeterWelch https://instagram.com/reppeterwelch

2187 Rayburn House Office Building, Washington, DC 20515 .... (202) 225–4115
Chief of Staff.—Bob Rogan.
Director of Scheduling & Operations.—Patrick Etka.
Legislative Director.—Patrick Satalin.
Communications Director.—Lincoln Peek.
128 Lakeside Avenue, Suite 235, Burlington, VT 05401 .... (802) 652–2450
State Director.—Rebecca Ellis.

Population (2014), 626,562.

ZIP Codes: 05001, 05009, 05030–43, 05045–56, 05058–62, 05065, 05067–77, 05079, 05081, 05083–86, 05088–89, 05091, 05101, 05141–43, 05146, 05148–56, 05158–59, 05161, 05201, 05250–55, 05257, 05260–62, 05301–04, 05340–46, 05350–63, 05401–07, 05439–66, 05468–74, 05476–79, 05481–83, 05485–92, 05494–95, 05601–04, 05609, 05620, 05633, 05640–41, 05647–58, 05660–67, 05669–82, 05701–02, 05730–48, 05750–51, 05753, 05757–70, 05772–78, 05819–30, 05832–33, 05836–43, 05845–51, 05853, 05855, 05857–63, 05866–68, 05871–75, 05901–07

VIRGINIA

(Population 2010, 8,001,024)

SENATORS

MARK R. WARNER, Democrat, of Alexandria, VA; born in Indianapolis, IN, December 15, 1954; son of Robert and Marge Warner of Vernon, CT; education: B.A., political science, George Washington University, 1977; J.D., Harvard Law School, 1980; professional: Governor, Commonwealth of Virginia, 2002–06; chairman of the National Governor's Association, 2004–05; religion: Presbyterian; wife: Lisa Collis; children: Madison, Gillian, and Eliza; committees: vice chair, Select Committee on Intelligence; Banking, Housing, and Urban Affairs; Budget; Finance; Rules and Administration; elected to the U.S. Senate on November 4, 2008; reelected to the U.S. Senate on November 4, 2014.

Office Listings

https://warner.senate.gov

703 Hart Senate Office Building, Washington, DC 20510 .... (202) 224–2023
Chief of Staff.—Mike Harney.
Legislative Director.—Elizabeth Falcone.
Communications Director.—Rachel Cohen.
Press Secretary.—Nelly Decker.
Scheduler.—Malcolm Fouhy.
8000 Towers Crescent Drive, Suite 200, Vienna, VA 22182 .... (703) 442–0670
FAX: 442–0408
180 West Main Street, Abingdon, VA 24210 .... (276) 628–8158
FAX: 628–1036
101 West Main Street, Suite 7771, Norfolk, VA 23510 .... (757) 441–3079
FAX: 441–6250
919 East Main Street, Richmond, VA 23219 .... (804) 775–2314
FAX: 775–2319
110 Kirk Avenue, Southwest, Roanoke, VA 24011 .... (540) 857–2676
FAX: 857–2800

* * *

TIM KAINE, Democrat, of Richmond, VA; born in St. Paul, MN, February 26, 1958; education: B.A., University of Missouri, 1979; J.D., Harvard University, 1983; professional: worked with the Jesuit order as a Catholic missionary in Honduras, 1980–81; civil rights lawyer; professor, University of Richmond, 1987–2013; Richmond City Council, 1994–98; Mayor of Richmond, VA, 1998–2001; Lieutenant Governor of Virginia, 2002–06; Governor of Virginia, 2006–10; married: Anne Holton, interim president, George Mason University; one of the Senate's few members who speak fluent Spanish; one of 30 Senators in history to have also served as a mayor and governor; 51st chair of the Democratic National Committee, 2009–11; caucuses: co-chair, Military Families Caucus; co-chair, Senate Career and Technical Education (CTE) Caucus; committees: Armed Services; Budget; Foreign Relations; Health, Education, Labor, and Pensions; elected to the U.S. Senate on November 6, 2012; reelected to the U.S. Senate on November 6, 2018.

Office Listings

https://kaine.senate.gov https://facebook.com/SenatorKaine

231 Russell Senate Office Building, Washington, DC 20510 .... (202) 224–4024
FAX: 228–6363
Chief of Staff.—Mike Henry.
Communications Director.—Sarah Peck.
Legislative Director.—Nick Barbash.
Scheduler.—Kate McCarroll.
State Director.—Keren Dongo.
222 Central Park Avenue, Suite 120, Virginia Beach, VA 23462 .... (757) 518–1674
919 East Main Street, Suite 970, Richmond, VA 23219 .... (804) 771–2221
611 South Jefferson, Suite 5B, Roanoke, VA 24011 .... (540) 682–5693
121 Russell Road, Suite 2, Abingdon, VA 24210 .... (276) 525–4790
9408 Grant Avenue, Suite 202, Manassas, VA 20110 .... (703) 361–3192

REPRESENTATIVES

FIRST DISTRICT

ROBERT J. WITTMAN, Republican, of Montross, VA; born in Washington, DC, February 2, 1959; education: B.S., biology, Virginia Polytechnic Institute and State University, 1981; M.P.H., health policy and administration, University of North Carolina at Chapel Hill, 1989; Ph.D., Virginia Commonwealth University, Richmond, VA, 2002; professional: field director for the Virginia Health Department's Division of Shellfish Sanitation; public service: Montross Town Council, 1986–96; public policy and administration, 1992; Mayor of Montross, 1992–96; Westmoreland County Board of Supervisors, 1995–2003, and chairman, 2003–05; Virginia House of Delegates, 2005–07; religion: Episcopalian; married: Kathryn Wittman; children: Devon and Joshua; committees: Armed Services; Natural Resources; elected to the 110th Congress, by special election, on December 11, 2007; elected to the 111th Congress; reelected to each succeeding Congress.

Office Listings

https://wittman.house.gov https://facebook.com/RepRobWittman twitter: @RobWittman

2055 Rayburn House Office Building, Washington, DC 20515 .... (202) 225–4261
Chief of Staff.—Carolyn King. FAX: 225–4382
Legislative Director.—Brent Robinson.
Communications Director.—Kathleen Gayle.
Scheduler / Office Manager.—Jordan Wilson.
6501 Mechanicsville Turnpike, Suite 102, Mechanicsville, VA 23111 .... (804) 730–6595
District Director.—Joe Schumacher.
95 Dunn Drive, Suite 201, Stafford, VA 22556 .... (540) 659–2734
508 Church Lane, Tappahannock, VA 22560 .... (804) 443–0668

Counties: ALL OF CAROLINE, ESSEX, GLOUCESTER, HANOVER, KING AND QUEEN, KING GEORGE, KING WILLIAM, LANCASTER, MATHEWS, MIDDLESEX, NEW KENT, NORTHUMBERLAND, RICHMOND, STAFFORD, AND WESTMORELAND COUNTIES; all of the City of Fredericksburg; part of FAUQUIER COUNTY comprised of the Bealeton (303), Catlett (102), Lois (104), and Morrisville (301) Precincts and part of the Remington (302) Precinct; part of JAMES CITY COUNTY comprised of the Berkeley A Part 1 (101), Berkeley B Part 1 (1012), Berkeley B Part 2 (1022), Berkeley C (103), Powhatan A (301), Powhatan B (302), Powhatan C (303), Powhatan D (304), Stonehouse A (401), Stonehouse B (402), and Stonehouse C (403) Precincts and part of the Jamestown A (201), Jamestown B (202) Precincts; part of PRINCE WILLIAM COUNTY comprised of the Victory (108), Piney Branch (109), Buckland Mills (110), Bristow Run (111), Burke-Nickens (112), Marshall (202), Bennett (203), Ellis (204), Coles (206), Spriggs (207), Hylton (208), Independent Hill (209), Penn (210), Saratoga (213), Lucasville (214), Quantico (304), Pattie (305), Washington-Reid (306), Henderson (307), Montclair (308), Ashland (309), Forest Park (310), Triangle (312), Cardinal (313), Cabin Branch (314), Ben Lomond (404), Stonewall (405), Sudley (408), Mullen (411), Lake Ridge (501), Mohican (505), Springwoods (508), Mc Coart (509), Westridge (511), and King (609) Precincts; part of SPOTSYLVANIA COUNTY comprised of the Travelers Rest (103), Massaponax (104), Summit (401), Parkside (402), Lee Hill (403), Battlefield (701), Brents Mill (702), Fairview (703), and Gayle (704) Precincts. Population (2010), 727,366.

ZIP Codes: 20109–12 (part), 20119 (part), 20136, 20181 (part), 22025, 22026 (part), 22134 (part), 22172 (part), 22401, 22405–06, 22407–08 (part), 22427, 22432, 22435–38, 22443, 22448, 22454, 22460, 22469, 22473, 22476, 22480, 22482, 22485, 22488, 22503–04, 22509, 22511, 22514, 22520, 22529–30, 22535, 22538–39, 22546, 22548, 22551 (part), 22554, 22556, 22560, 22572, 22576, 22578–79, 22580 (part), 22712 (part), 22720, 22728 (part), 22734 (part), 22742, 23005, 23009, 23011, 23015 (part), 23021, 23023, 23024 (part), 23025, 23032, 23035, 23043, 23045, 23047, 23050, 23056, 23059 (part), 23061–62, 23064, 23066, 23068–72, 23076, 23079, 23085–86, 23089, 23091–92, 23102 (part), 23106, 23108–11, 23115–16, 23119, 23124–26, 23128, 23130, 23138, 23140 (part), 23141, 23146 (part), 23148–49, 23156, 23161, 23163, 23168–69, 23175–77, 23180–81, 23185 (part), 23188 (part), 23192 (part)

* * *

SECOND DISTRICT

ELAINE G. LURIA, Democrat, of Norfolk, VA; born in Birmingham, Jefferson County, AL, August 15, 1975; education: B.S., United States Naval Academy, Annapolis, MD, 1997; attended United States Naval Nuclear Power School, Goose Creek, SC, 2000; M.S., Old Dominion University, Norfolk, VA, 2004; professional: small business owner; military: United States Navy, 1997–2017; religion: Jewish; married: Robert Blondin; children: Violette Blondin, Chloe Blondin, Clay Blondin; caucuses: American Flood Coalition; Bipartisan Task Force Combating Anti-Semitism; Chesapeake Bay Task Force; Congressional HBCU Caucus; Congressional Military Families Caucus; Congressional Small Business Caucus; For Country Caucus; Gun Safety Task Force; House Oceans Caucus; National Guard and Reserve Component Caucus; New Democrats Climate Change Task Force; New Democrats Coalition; Problem Solvers Caucus; Shipbuilding Caucus, LGBT Equality Caucus; Solar Caucus; committees: Armed Services; Veterans' Affairs; elected to the 116th Congress on November 6, 2018.

Office Listings

https://luria.house.gov https://facebook.com/RepElaineLuria twitter: @RepElaineLuria

534 Cannon House Office Building, Washington, DC 20515 .... (202) 225–4215
Chief of Staff.—Kathryn Sorenson.
Legislative Director.—Tyrone Bratton.
Communications Director.—Chris Carroll.
Scheduler.—Kate Fegley.
283 Constitution Drive, One Columbus Center, Suite 900, Virginia Beach, VA 23462 .... (757) 364-7650
District Director.—Dave Wickersham. FAX: 687–8298
25020 Shore Parkway, Suite 1B, Onley, VA 23418 .... (757) 364–7631
105 Professional Parkway, Suite 1512, Yorktown, VA 23693 .... (757) 364–7634

Counties: ACCOMACK, NORTHAMPTON, JAMES CITY (part), AND YORK. CITIES: Hampton (part), Norfolk (part), Poquoson City, Virginia Beach, and Williamsburg. Population (2010), 721,969.

ZIP Codes: 23185 (part), 23187, 23188 (part), 23301–03, 23306–08, 23310, 23313, 23316, 23336–37, 23347, 23350, 23354, 23356–59, 23389, 23395, 23398, 23401, 23405, 23407–10, 23413–18, 23420–23, 23440–42, 23451–57, 23459–62, 23464, 23480, 23486, 23488, 23502 (part), 23503, 23505 (part), 23509 (part), 23511 (part), 23513 (part), 23518 (part), 23551, 23602 (part), 23603 (part), 23651, 23662, 23663–64 (part), 23665, 23666 (part), 23669 (part), 23690–93, 23696

* * *

THIRD DISTRICT

ROBERT C. "BOBBY" SCOTT, Democrat, of Newport News, VA; born in Washington, DC, April 30, 1947; education: graduated, Groton High School; B.A., Harvard University; J.D., Boston College Law School; professional: served in the Massachusetts National Guard and U.S. Army Reserve; attorney; admitted to the Virginia Bar; Virginia House of Delegates, 1978–83; Senate of Virginia, 1983–92; member: Alpha Phi Alpha Fraternity; NAACP; Sigma Pi Phi Fraternity; committees: chair, Education and Labor; Budget; elected on November 3, 1992 to the 103rd Congress; reelected to each succeeding Congress.

Office Listings

https://bobbyscott.house.gov https://facebook.com/repbobbyscott https://twitter.com/bobbyscott

1201 Longworth House Office Building, Washington, DC 20515 .... (202) 225–8351
Chief of Staff.—David Dailey. FAX: 225–8354
Deputy Chief of Staff.—Randi Petty.
Press Secretary.—Austin Barbera.
Senior Legislative Assistant.—Paige Schwartz.
2600 Washington Avenue, Suite 1010, Newport News, VA 23607 .... (757) 380–1000
District Director.—Gisele Russell.
Director of District Operations & Constituent Services.—Demontre Boone.

Counties: ISLE OF WIGHT. CITIES: Chesapeake (part), Franklin, Hampton (part), Newport News, Norfolk (part), Portsmouth, and Suffolk (part). Population (2015), 737,635.

ZIP Codes: 23011 (part), 23030 (part), 23075 (part), 23089 (part), 23111 (part), 23124 (part), 23140–41 (part), 23150 (part), 23168 (part), 23181 (part), 23185 (part), 23219–25 (part), 23227 (part), 23230–31 (part), 23234–35 (part), 23250 (part), 23284 (part), 23298 (part), 23304, 23314–15, 23320–21 (part), 23323–25 (part), 23397 (part), 23424 (part), 23430, 23432–33, 23434 (part), 23435–36, 23487, 23502 (part), 23504, 23505 (part), 23507–08, 23509 (part), 23510, 23511 (part), 23513 (part), 23517, 23518 (part), 23523, 23601, 23602–03 (part), 23604–08, 23661, 23663–64 (part), 23666 (part), 23667–68, 23669 (part), 23693 (part), 23701–04, 23707–09, 23801 (part), 23803 (part), 23805 (part), 23839 (part), 23842 (part), 23846 (part), 23851 (part), 23860 (part), 23866 (part), 23875 (part), 23881 (part), 23883 (part), 23888 (part), 23890 (part), 23898–99 (part)

* * *

FOURTH DISTRICT

A. DONALD MCEACHIN, Democrat, of Henrico County, VA; born in Nuremberg, Germany, October 10, 1961; education: B.S., political history, American University, Washington, DC, 1982; J.D., University of Virginia, Charlottesville, VA; M.Div., Virginia Union University, Richmond, VA, 2008; leadership: co-president of Freshman Class; Democratic Leadership's Environmental Messaging Team; Regional Whip; religion: Episcopal; married: Colette McEachin; three adult children; commissions: Franking Commission; caucuses: Chesapeake Bay Watershed Caucus; Congressional Black Caucus; Congressional PORTS Caucus; Congressional Ship-Building Caucus; House Democratic Caucus; House Pro-Choice Caucus; LGBT Equality Caucus;

Sustainable Energy and Environment Coalition; taskforces: United for Climate Environmental Justice Congressional Taskforce (co-founder); Community Based Special Needs Taskforce; committees: Energy and Commerce; Natural Resources; Select Committee on the Climate Crisis; elected to the 115th Congress on November 8, 2016; reelected to the 116th Congress on November 6, 2018.

Office Listings

https://mceachin.house.gov

314 Cannon House Office Building, Washington, DC 20515 .... (202) 225–6365
Chief of Staff.—Abbi Easter. FAX: 226–1170
DC Chief of Staff.—Keenan Austin Reed.
Legislative Director.—Corey Solow.
Communications Director.—Ariana Valderrama.
District Director.—Tara Rountree.
110 North Robinson Street, Suite 403, Richmond, VA 23220 .... (804) 486–1840
131 North Saratoga Street, Suite B, Suffolk, VA 23434.

Counties: CHARLES CITY, CHESAPEAKE (part), CHESTERFIELD (part), COLONIAL HEIGHTS, DINWIDDIE, EMPORIA, GREENSVILLE, HENRICO (part), HOPEWELL, PETERSBURG, PRINCE GEORGE, RICHMOND, SOUTHAMPTON, SUFFOLK (part), SURRY, AND SUSSEX. Population (2010), 881,217.

ZIP Codes: 22402–04 (part), 22555 (part), 22901 (part), 23030, 23058 (part), 23075, 23113 (part), 23140 (part), 23147, 23150, 23173, 23185 (part), 23187 (part), 23218–21, 23222 (part), 23223, 23224–27 (part), 23229–32, 23234–35 (part), 23237, 23241, 23242 (part), 23249–50, 23255 (part), 23260–61, 23269, 23273 (part), 23274, 23276, 23278, 23282, 23284–86, 23290–93, 23294 (part), 23298, 23315, 23320–23 (part), 23327–28 (part), 23430 (part), 23434, 23437–38, 23439 (part), 23450 (part), 23454 (part), 23457 (part), 23464 (part), 23466–67 (part), 23471 (part), 23487 (part), 23612 (part), 23801, 23803–05, 23822, 23824 (part), 23827–31, 23832–33 (part), 23834, 23836–37, 23838 (part), 23839–42 (part), 23844, 23846, 23847 (part), 23850–51 (part), 23856 (part), 23860, 23866 (part), 23867, 23870, 23872, 23874–75, 23878–79, 23881–85, 23887 (part), 23888, 23890–91, 23894 (part), 23897, 23898 (part), 23899

* * *

FIFTH DISTRICT

DENVER RIGGLEMAN, Republican, of Afton, VA; born in Manassas, VA, March 17, 1970; education: graduated from Stonewall Jackson High School, Manassas, VA, 1988; A.A., Burlington County College, Mount Laurel, NJ, 1996; A.A.S., Community College of the Air Force, Maxwell Air Force Base, AL, 1996; B.A., University of Virginia, Charlottesville, VA, 1998; military: United States Air Force, 1992–2007; professional: federal contractor; small business owner; distillery operator; religion: Christian; married: Christine Riggleman; children: Lauren, Lilly, and Abigail Riggleman; committees: Financial Services; elected to the 116th Congress on November 6, 2018.

Office Listings

https://riggleman.house.gov https://facebook.com/RepRiggleman
twitter: @RepRiggleman https://instagram.com/repriggleman

1022 Longworth House Office Building, Washington, DC 20515 .... (202) 225–4711
Chief of Staff.—David Natonski. FAX: 225–5681
Legislative Director.—Borden Hoskins.
Communications Director.—Joseph Chelak.
Scheduler.—Haley Brady.
308 Craghead Street, Suite 102–D, Danville, VA 24541 .... (434) 791–2596
District Director.—Denise Van Valkenburg.
686 Berkmar Circle, Charlottesville, VA 22901 .... (434) 973–9631

Counties: ALBEMARLE (all). CITIES AND TOWNSHIPS: Barboursville, Batesville, Charlotteville, Covesville, Crozet, Earlysville, Esmont, Free Union, Greenwood, Hatton, Ivy, Keene, Keswick, North Garden, and Scottsville. APPOMATTOX (all). CITIES AND TOWNSHIPS: Appomattox, Evergreen, Pamplin, and Spout Spring. BEDFORD (part). CITIES AND TOWNSHIPS: Bedford, Big Island, Coleman Falls, Forest, Goode, Goodview, Hardy, Huddleston, Lowry, Moneta, and Thaxton. BRUNSWICK (all). CITIES AND TOWNSHIPS: Alberta, Brodnax, Gasburg, Lawrenceville, and White Plains. BUCKINGHAM. CITIES AND TOWNSHIPS: Andersonville, Arvonia, Buckingham, Dillwyn, and New Canton. CAMPBELL (all). CITIES AND TOWNSHIPS: Altavista, Brookneal, Concord, Evington, Gladys, Long Island, Lynch Station, Naruna, and Rustburg. CHARLOTTE (all). CITIES AND TOWNSHIPS: Barnesville, Charlotte Court House, Cullen, Drakes Branch, Keysville, Phenix, Randolph, Red House, Red Oak, Saxe, and Wylliesburg. CHARLOTTESVILLE CITY: Charlottesville. CUMBERLAND (all). CITIES AND TOWNSHIPS: Cartersville, Cumberland, and Tamworth. DANVILLE CITY: Danville. FAUQUIER (part). CITIES AND TOWNSHIPS: Airlie, Bealeton, Belle Meade, Belvoir, Broad Run, Calverton, Casanova, Delaplane, Germantown, Halfway, Hume, Linden (part), Markham, Marshall, Midland (part), Morrisville, New Baltimore, Old Tavern, Opal (part), Orlean, Paris, Rectortown, Remington, The Plains, Upperville, and Warrenton. FLUVANNA (all). CITIES AND TOWNSHIPS: Bremo Bluff, Bybee, Carysbrook, Columbia, Fork Union, Kents Store, Palmyra, and Troy. FRANKLIN (all). CITIES AND TOWNSHIPS: Boones Mill, Callaway, Ferrum, Gladehill, Henry, Redwood, Penhook, Rocky Mount, Union Hall, Waidsboro, and Wirtz. GREENE (all). CITIES AND TOWNSHIPS: Amicus, Barnes, Burtonville, Dawsonville, Dyke, Geer, Haneytown, Lydia, McMullen, Midway, Newton, Pirkey, Quinque, Ruckersville, Stanardsville, St. George, Shady Grove, Simmons

Gap, Twin Lakes, Upper Pocosin, and Williams Fork. HALIFAX (all). CITIES AND TOWNSHIPS: Alton, Clover, Cluster Springs, Crystal Hill, Denniston, Halifax, Ingram, Lennig, Mayo, Nathalie, Republican Grove, Scottsburg, Turbeville, Vernon Hill, and Virgilina. HENRY (part). CITIES AND TOWNSHIPS: Axton, Chatmoss, and Ridgeway. LUNENBURG (all). CITIES AND TOWNSHIPS: Dundas, Fort Mitchell, Kenbridge, Lunenburg, Rehoboth, and Victoria. MADISON (all). CITIES AND TOWNSHIPS: Achash, Aroda, Aylor, Banco, Beaver Park, Big Meadows, Burnt Tree, Criglersville, Decapolis, Duet, Elly, Etlan, Five Forks, Fletcher, Fordsville, Graves Mill, Haywood, Hood, Kinderhook, Leon, Locust Dale, Madison, Madison Mills, Nethers, Novum, O'Neal, Oakpark, Oldrag, Pratts, Radiant, Repton Mills, Rochelle, Ruth, Shelby, Shifflet Corner, Syria, Tanners, Tryme, Twymans Mill, Uno, Wolftown, and Zeus. MECKLENBURG (all). CITIES AND TOWNSHIPS: Baskerville, Blackridge, Boydton, Bracey, Buffalo Junction, Chase City, Clarksville, Forksville, LaCrosse, Nelson, Palmer Springs, Skipwith, South Hill, and Union Level. NELSON (all). CITIES AND TOWNSHIPS: Afton, Arrington, Faber, Gladstone, Lovingston, Massies Mill, Montebello, Nellysford, Norwood, Piney River, Roseland, Schuyler, Shipman, Tye River, Tyro, and Wingina. PITTSYLVANIA (all). CITIES AND TOWNSHIPS: Blairs, Callands, Cascade, Chatham, Dry Fork, Gretna, Hurt, Java, Keeling, Pittsville, Ringgold, Sandy Level, and Sutherlin. PRINCE EDWARD (all). CITIES AND TOWNSHIPS: Darlington Heights, Farmville, Green Bay, Hampden-Sydney, Meherrin, Prospect, and Rice. RAPPAHANNOCK (all). CITIES AND TOWNSHIPS: Amissville, Castleton, Chester Gap, Flint Hill, Huntly, Laurel Mills, Massies Corner, Peola Mills, Revercombs Corner, Sperryville, Wakefield Manor, Washington, and Woodville. Population (2010), 727,365.

ZIP Codes: 20106 (part), 20115, 20117 (part), 20119 (part), 20130 (part), 20137 (part), 20139, 20144, 20181 (part), 20184 (part), 20186 (part), 20187, 20198, 22623 (part), 22627, 22630 (part), 22639–40, 22642 (part), 22643, 22701 (part), 22709, 22711, 22712–13 (part), 22715–16, 22719, 22722–23, 22727, 22728 (part), 22730–32, 22733–35 (part), 22738, 22740 (part), 22743, 22747, 22749, 22835 (part), 22901–04, 22911, 22920 (part), 22922–23 (part), 22931–32, 22935–38, 22940, 22942 (part), 22943, 22946, 22947 (part), 22948–49, 22958 (part), 22959, 22960 (part), 22963–64, 22967 (part), 22968–69, 22971, 22973, 22974 (part), 22976, 22989, 23004, 23022, 23027, 23038 (part), 23040, 23055, 23084 (part), 23093 (part), 23123, 23139 (part), 23821, 23824 (part), 23843, 23845, 23847 (part), 23856 (part), 23857, 23868, 23876, 23887, 23889, 23893, 23901, 23909, 23915, 23917, 23919–21, 23922 (part), 23923–24, 23927, 23934, 23936–38, 23942–44, 23947, 23950, 23952, 23954, 23958–60, 23962–64, 23966 (part), 23967–68, 23970, 23974, 23976, 24054–55 (part), 24059 (part), 24064–65 (part), 24067, 24069, 24079 (part), 24088 (part), 24091 (part), 24092, 24095, 24101, 24102 (part), 24104, 24112 (part), 24121, 24122 (part), 24137, 24139, 24148 (part), 24151, 24161, 24174 (part), 24176, 24179 (part), 24184, 24464, 24501–02 (part), 24504 (part), 24517, 24520, 24521 (part), 24522, 24523 (part), 24527–31, 24534, 24538–41, 24549, 24550–51 (part), 24553 (part), 24554, 24557–58, 24562–63, 24565–66, 24569–71, 24577, 24580–81, 24586, 24588–90, 24592–94, 24597–99

* * *

SIXTH DISTRICT

BEN CLINE, Republican, of Lexington, VA; born in Stillwater, Payne County, OK, February 29, 1972; education: graduated from Lexington High School, Lexington, VA, 1990; B.A., Bates College, Lewiston, ME, 1994; J.D., University of Richmond Law School, Richmond, VA, 2007; professional: staff, U.S. Representative Bob Goodlatte of VA, 1994–2002; marketing consultant; assistant commonwealth's attorney, Rockingham County, VA, 2007–13; member of the Virginia House of Delegates, 2002–18; religion: Catholic; married: Elizabeth; caucuses: Republican Policy Committee; committees: Education and Labor; Judiciary; elected to the 116th Congress on November 6, 2018.

Office Listings

https://cline.house.gov https://facebook.com/RepBenCline twitter: @RepBenCline
https://instagram.com/RepBenCline

1009 Longworth House Office Building, Washington, DC 20515 .... (202) 225–5431
Chief of Staff.—Matt Miller. FAX: 225–9681
Legislative Director.—Nicole Manley.
Communications Director.—Ryan Saylor.
Scheduler.—Beth Kaczmarek.

117 South Lewis Street, Suite 215, Staunton, VA 24401 .... (540) 885–3861
District Director.—Debbie Garrett. FAX: 885–3930

70 North Mason Street, Suite 110, Harrisonburg, VA 22802 .... (540) 432–2391
FAX: 432–6593

916 Main Street, Suite 300, Lynchburg, VA 24504 .... (434) 845–8306
FAX: 845–8245

10 Franklin Road Southeast, Suite 510, Roanoke, VA 24011 .... (540) 857–2672
FAX: 857–2675

Counties: AMHERST, AUGUSTA, BATH, BEDFORD (part), BOTETOURT, HIGHLAND, PAGE, ROANOKE (part), ROCKBRIDGE, ROCKINGHAM, SHENANDOAH, AND WARREN. CITIES: Buena Vista, Harrisonburg, Lexington, Lynchburg, Roanoke, Staunton, and Waynesboro. Population (2010), 737,755.

ZIP Codes: 22610, 22623, 22630, 22641–42, 22644–45, 22650, 22652, 22654–55, 22657, 22660, 22664, 22801–02, 22807, 22810–12, 22815, 22820–21, 22824, 22827, 22830–32, 22834–35, 22840–47, 22849–51, 22853, 22920, 22922, 22939, 22952, 22958, 22967, 22980, 24011–20, 24064–66, 24077, 24083, 24085, 24090, 24122, 24130, 24153, 24174–75, 24179, 24401, 24411–13, 24415–16, 24421–22, 24430–33, 24435, 24437, 24439–42, 24445, 24450, 24458–60, 24465, 24467, 24471–73, 24476–77, 24479, 24482–87, 24501–04, 24521, 24523, 24526, 24536, 24550–51, 24553, 24555–56, 24572, 24574, 24578–79, 24595

* * *

SEVENTH DISTRICT

ABIGAIL DAVIS SPANBERGER, Democrat, of Glen Allen, VA; born in Red Bank, Monmouth County, NJ, August 7, 1979; education: graduated from J.R. Tucker High School, Henrico, VA; United States Capitol Page School, 1996; B.A., University of Virginia, Charlottesville, VA, 2001; M.B.A., Purdue University, West Lafayette, IN, 2002; professional: teacher; postal inspector, United States Postal Service; case officer, Central Intelligence Agency, 2006–14; consultant; married: Adam; children: three; caucuses: Blue Dog Coalition; Freshman Working Group on Addiction; Gun Violence Prevention Task Force; LGBT Equality Caucus; New Democrat Coalition; Rural Broadband Caucus; Servicewomen and Women Veterans Congressional Caucus; Women's Caucus; committees: Agriculture; Foreign Affairs; elected to the 116th Congress on November 6, 2018.

Office Listings

https://spanberger.house.gov https://facebook.com/RepSpanberger twitter: @RepSpanberger
https://instagram.com/repspanberger

1239 Longworth House Office Building, Washington, DC 20515 .... (202) 225–2815
Chief of Staff.—Roscoe Jones.
Legislative Director.—Maryam Janani.
Press Secretary.—Connor Joseph.
Scheduler.—Emma Carl.
4201 Dominion Boulevard, Suite 110, Glen Allen, VA 23060 .... (804) 401–4110
District Director.—Karen Mask.
9104 Courthouse Road, Room 249, Spotsylvania, VA 22553 .... (540) 321–6130

Counties: AMELIA, CHESTERFIELD (part), CULPEPER, GOOCHLAND, HENRICO (part), LOUISA, NOTTOWAY, ORANGE, POWHATAN, AND SPOTSYLVANIA (part). Population (2010), 727,366.

ZIP Codes: 20106, 20186, 22407–08, 22433, 22508, 22534, 22542, 22551, 22553, 22565, 22567, 22580, 22701, 22713–14, 22718, 22724, 22726, 22729, 22733–37, 22740–41, 22923, 22942, 22947, 22957, 22960, 22972, 22974, 23002, 23015, 23024, 23038–39, 23058–60, 23063, 23065, 23067, 23083–84, 23093, 23102–03, 23112–14, 23117, 23120, 23129, 23139, 23146, 23153, 23160, 23222, 23224–30, 23233–38, 23294, 23297, 23824, 23832–33, 23838, 23850, 23922, 23930, 23955, 23966

* * *

EIGHTH DISTRICT

DONALD S. BEYER, JR., Democrat, of Alexandria, VA; born in the Free Territory of Trieste, June 20, 1950; education: B.A., Williams College, MA, 1972; professional: Ambassador to Switzerland and Liechtenstein, 2009–13; 36th Lieutenant Governor of Virginia, 1990–98; co-founder of the Northern Virginia Technology Council; former chair of Jobs for Virginia Graduates; served on Board of the D.C. Campaign to Prevent Teen Pregnancy; former chair of the Virginia Economic Recovery Commission; spouse: Megan; children: Don, Stephanie, Clara, and Grace; caucuses: Congressional Progressive Caucus; New Democrat Coalition; committees: vice chair, Joint Economic Committee; Science, Space, and Technology; Ways and Means; elected to the 114th Congress on November 4, 2014; reelected to each succeeding Congress.

Office Listings

https://beyer.house.gov https://facebook.com/repdonbeyer https://twitter.com/repdonbeyer

1119 Longworth House Office Building, Washington, DC 20515 .... (202) 225–4376
Chief of Staff.—Tanya Bradsher. FAX: 225–0017
Legislative Director.—Zach Cafritz.
Communications Director.—Aaron Fritschner.
Scheduler.—Sophia Rubio.
1901 North Moore Street, Suite 1108, Arlington, VA 22209 .... (703) 658–5403
District Director.—Noah Simon.

Counties: ARLINGTON AND FAIRFAX (part). CITIES: Alexandria and Falls Church. Population (2010), 767,596.

ZIP Codes: 22003 (part), 22041–44 (part), 22046, 22060, 22079 (part), 22101–02 (part), 22150–51 (part), 22153 (part), 22201–07, 22209, 22211, 22213–14, 22301–12, 22314–15

* * *

NINTH DISTRICT

H. MORGAN GRIFFITH, Republican, of Salem, VA; born March 15, 1958; education: graduated, Andrew Lewis High School, 1976; B.A., Emory and Henry College, 1980; J.D., Washington and Lee University School of Law, 1983; professional: attorney, private practice, 1983–2011; partner, Albo & Oblon, LLP, 2008–11; Virginia House of Delegates, 1994–2011; Majority Leader, Virginia House of Delegates, 2001–11; married: Hilary; children: Abby, Davis, and Starke; committees: Energy and Commerce; Select Committee on the Climate Crisis; elected to the 112th Congress on November 2, 2010; reelected to each succeeding Congress.

Office Listings

https://morgangriffith.house.gov https://facebook.com/repmorgangriffith twitter: @repmgriffith

2202 Rayburn House Office Building, Washington, DC 20515 .... (202) 225–3861
Chief of Staff.—Kelly Lungren McCollum. FAX: 225–0076
Legislative Director.—Emily Michael.
Communications Director.—Kevin Baird.
323 West Main Street, Abingdon, VA 24210 .... (276) 525–1405
District Director.—John Bebber.
District Scheduler.—Kacie Crosswhite.
17 West Main Street, Christiansburg, VA 24073 .... (540) 381–5671

Counties: ALLEGHANY, BLAND, BUCHANAN, CARROLL, CRAIG, DICKENSON, FLOYD, GILES, GRAYSON, HENRY (part), LEE, MONTGOMERY, PATRICK, PULASKI, ROANOKE (part), RUSSELL, SCOTT, SMYTH, TAZEWELL, WASHINGTON, WISE, AND WYTHE. ITIES: Bristol, Covington, Galax, Martinsville, Norton, Radford, and Salem. Population (2010), 727,366.

ZIP Codes: 24019 (part), 24053, 24055 (part), 24058, 24059 (part), 24060, 24070, 24072–73, 24076, 24078, 24079 (part), 24082, 24084, 24085 (part), 24086–87, 24088 (part), 24089, 24091 (part), 24093, 24102 (part), 24105, 24112 (part), 24120, 24124, 24127–28, 24131–34, 24136, 24138, 24141–42, 24147, 24148 (part), 24149–50, 24153 (part), 24162, 24165, 24167–68, 24171, 24175 (part), 24185, 24201–02, 24210–11, 24216–17, 24219–21, 24224–26, 24228, 24230, 24236–37, 24239, 24243–46, 24248, 24250–51, 24256, 24258, 24260, 24263, 24265–66, 24269–73, 24277, 24279–83, 24290, 24292–93, 24301, 24311–19, 24322–26, 24328, 24330, 24333, 24340, 24343, 24347–48, 24350–52, 24360–61, 24363, 24366, 24368, 24370, 24374–75, 24377–78, 24380–82, 24422 (part), 24426, 24445 (part), 24448, 24457, 24474, 24601–07, 24609, 24612–14, 24620, 24622, 24628, 24630–31, 24634–35, 24637, 24639, 24641, 24646, 24649, 24651, 24656–57

* * *

TENTH DISTRICT

JENNIFER WEXTON, Democrat, of Leesburg, VA; born in Washington, DC, May 27, 1968; education: B.A., University of Maryland, College Park, MD, 1992; J.D., College of William and Mary Law School, Williamsburg, VA, 1995; professional: lawyer, private practice; Assistant Commonwealth's Attorney, Loudoun County, VA, 2001–05; substitute judge, Loudoun, VA, 2010–11; member of the Virginia State Senate, 2014–18; married: Andrew; children: Jamie and Matthew; caucuses: Animal Protection Caucus; Chesapeake Bay Task Force; Freshman Working Group on Addiction; LGBT Equality Caucus; Pro-Choice Caucus; SEEC Caucus; Small Brewers Caucus; Transgender Equality Task Force; committees: Financial Services; Science, Space, and Technology; elected to the 116th Congress on November 6, 2018.

Office Listings

https://wexton.house.gov https://facebook.com/CongresswomanWexton
twitter: @RepWexton https://instagram.com/repwexton

1217 Longworth House Office Building, Washington, DC 20515 .... (202) 225–5136
Chief of Staff.—Abigail Carter. FAX: 225–0437
Legislative Director.—Mike Lucier.
Communications Director.—Amir Avin.
Scheduler.—Meaghan Johnson.
21351 Gentry Drive, Suite 140, Sterling, VA 20166 .... (703) 234–3800
District Director.—Erica Constance.

Counties: CLARKE, FAIRFAX (part), FREDERICK, LOUDOUN, AND PRINCE WILLIAM (part). CITIES: Manassas, Manassas Park, and Winchester. Population (2010), 758,321.

ZIP Codes: 20105, 20109–12 (part), 20117 (part), 20118, 20120–21 (part), 20124 (part), 20129, 20130 (part), 20132, 20135, 20137 (part), 20141, 20143, 20147–48, 20151 (part), 20152, 20155, 20158, 20164–66, 20169, 20170–71 (part), 20175–76, 20180, 20184 (part), 20190–91 (part), 20194 (part), 20197, 22015 (part), 22030 (part), 22033 (part), 22039 (part), 22066, 22079 (part), 22101–02 (part), 22124 (part), 22153 (part), 22182 (part), 22601–03, 22611, 22620, 22624–25, 22630 (part), 22637, 22645–46, 22654–55 (part), 22656, 22663

* * *

ELEVENTH DISTRICT

GERALD E. CONNOLLY, Democrat, of Fairfax, VA; born in Boston, MA, March 30, 1950; education: B.A., Maryknoll College; M.A., public administration, Harvard University, 1979; professional: member, Fairfax County Board of Supervisors, 1995–2003, chairman, 2003–08; religion: Roman Catholic; married: Cathy; children: Caitlin; committees: Foreign Affairs; Oversight and Reform; elected to the 111th Congress on November 4, 2008; reelected to each succeeding Congress.

Office Listings

https://connolly.house.gov

2238 Rayburn House Office Building, Washington, DC 20515 .... (202) 225–1492
Chief of Staff / Communications Director.—Jamie Smith.
Legislative Director.—Collin Davenport.
4115 Annandale Road, Suite 103, Annandale, VA 22003 .... (703) 256–3071
District Director.—Sharon Stark.
2241–D Tackett's Mill Drive, Woodbridge, VA 22192 .... (571) 408–4407
Prince William Director.—Marlon Dubuisson.

Counties: FAIRFAX (part) AND PRINCE WILLIAM (part). CITIES: Annandale, Burke, Centreville, Dale City, Fairfax, Fairfax Station, Herndon, Lorton, Manassas, Oakton, Occoquan, Reston, Springfield, Vienna, and Woodbridge. Population (2010), 770,944.

ZIP Codes: 20112, 20120–21, 20124, 20151, 20170–71, 20190–91, 20194, 22003, 22015, 22026–27, 22030–33, 22035, 22039, 22041–44, 22079, 22102, 22124–25, 22134, 22150–53, 22172, 22180–82, 22185, 22191–93

WASHINGTON

(Population 2010, 6,724,540)

SENATORS

PATTY MURRAY, Democrat, of Seattle, WA; born in Seattle, October 11, 1950; education: B.A., Washington State University, 1972; professional: teacher, Shoreline Community College; citizen lobbyist for environmental and educational issues, 1983–88; parent education instructor for Crystal Springs, 1984–87; school board member, 1985–89; elected board of directors, Shoreline School District, 1985–89; Washington State Senate, 1988–92; Democratic Whip, 1990–92; State Senate committees: chair, School Transportation Safety Task Force; Commerce and Labor; Domestic Timber Processing Select Committee; Education; Open Government Select Committee; Ways and Means; award: Washington State Legislator of the Year, 1990; married: Rob Murray; children: Randy and Sara; committees: ranking member, Health, Education, Labor, and Pensions; Appropriations; Budget; Veterans' Affairs; elected to the U.S. Senate on November 3, 1992; reelected to each succeeding Senate term.

Office Listings

https://murray.senate.gov

154 Russell Senate Office Building, Washington, DC 20510 .... (202) 224–2621
Chief of Staff.—Mindi Linquist. FAX: 224–0238
Legislative Director.—Ben Merkel. TDD: 224–4430
Communications Director.—Helen Hare.
2988 Jackson Federal Building, 915 Second Avenue, Seattle, WA 98174 .... (206) 553–5545
State Director.—Shawn Bills.
The Marshall House, 1323 Officer's Row, Vancouver, WA 98661 .... (360) 696–7797
District Director.—Bryan Stebbins.
10 North Post Street, Suite 600, Spokane, WA 99201 .... (509) 624–9515
District Director.—John Culton.
2930 Wetmore Avenue, Suite 9D, Everett, WA 98201 .... (425) 259–6515
District Director.—Ann Larson.
402 East Yakima Avenue, Suite 420, Yakima, WA 98901 .... (509) 453–7462
District Director.—Raquel Crowley.
950 Pacific Avenue, Room 650, Tacoma, WA 98402 .... (253) 572–3636
District Director.—Christine Nhan.

* * *

MARIA CANTWELL, Democrat, of Edmonds, WA; born in Indianapolis, IN, October 13, 1958; education: B.A., Miami University, Miami, OH, 1980; professional: businesswoman; RealNetworks, Inc.; organizations: South Snohomish County Chamber of Commerce; Alderwood Rotary; Mountlake Terrace Friends of the Library; public service: Washington State House of Representatives, 1987–92; U.S. House of Representatives, 1992–94; religion: Roman Catholic; committees: ranking member, Commerce, Science, and Transportation; Energy and Natural Resources; Finance; Indian Affairs; Small Business and Entrepreneurship; elected to the U.S. Senate on November 7, 2000; reelected to each succeeding Senate term.

Office Listings

https://cantwell.senate.gov https://facebook.com/senatorcantwell twitter: @senatorcantwell

511 Hart Senate Office Building, Washington, DC 20510 .... (202) 224–3441
Chief of Staff.—Jami Burgess.
Legislative Director/Deputy Chief of Staff.—Vacant.
Administrative Director.—Michael Hill.
915 Second Avenue, Suite 3206, Seattle, WA 98174 .... (206) 220–6400
The Marshall House, 1313 Officers Row, Vancouver, WA 98661 .... (360) 696–7838
950 Pacific Avenue, Suite 615, Tacoma, WA 98402 .... (253) 572–2281
U.S. Federal Courthouse, 920 West Riverside Avenue, Suite 697, Spokane, WA 99201 .... (509) 353–2507
825 Jadwin Avenue, Suite 206, Richland, WA 99352 .... (509) 946–8106
2930 Wetmore Avenue, Suite 9B, Everett, WA 98201 .... (425) 303–0114

REPRESENTATIVES

FIRST DISTRICT

SUZAN K. DELBENE, Democrat, of Medina, WA; born in Selma, Dallas County, AL, February 17, 1962; education: B.A., Reed College, Portland, OR, 1983; M.B.A., University of

Washington, Seattle, WA, 1990; professional: business executive; director, Washington State Department of Revenue, 2010–12; married: Kurt; two children: Becca and Zach; committees: Ways and Means; Select Committee on the Modernization of Congress; elected simultaneously as a Democrat to the 112th Congress and 113th Congress, by special election, to fill the vacancy caused by the resignation of U.S. Representative Jay Inslee; reelected to each succeeding Congress.

Office Listings

https://delbene.house.gov https://facebook.com/RepDelBene twitter: @RepDelBene

2330 Rayburn House Office Building, Washington, DC 20515 .... (202) 225–6311
Chief of Staff.—Aaron Schmidt. FAX: 226–1606
Legislative Director.—Kyle Hill.
Communications Director.—Lou Wasson.
Scheduler.—Mary Kate McTague.
Canyon Park Business Center, 22121 17th Avenue Southeast, Suite 220, Bothell, WA 98021 .... (425) 485–0085
204 West Montgomery Street, Mount Vernon, WA 98273 .... (360) 417–7879
District Director.—Dennis Sills.

Counties: KING (part), SKAGIT (part), SNOHOMISH (part), AND WHATCOM (part). CITIES AND TOWNSHIPS: Blaine, Bothell, Carnation, Concrete, Darrington, Duvall, Everson, Ferndale, Gold Bar, Granite Falls, Hamilton, Hunts Point, Index, Kenmore, Kirkland, Lake Stevens, Lyman, Lynden, Medina, Mill Creek, Monroe, Mount Vernon, Nooksack, Point Roberts, Redmond, Skykomish, Snohomish, Sultan, Sumas, Woodinville, and Yarrow Point. Population (2010), 691,738.

ZIP Codes: 98004 (part), 98007–08 (part), 98011, 98012 (part), 98014, 98019, 98021 (part), 98024 (part), 98028, 98033–34, 98036 (part), 98039, 98041, 98045 (part), 98052 (part), 98053, 98065 (part), 98072–73, 98074 (part), 98077, 98082–83, 98155 (part), 98201 (part), 98208 (part), 98220, 98223 (part), 98224, 98225–26 (part), 98230–31, 98233 (part), 98235, 98237, 98240–41, 98244, 98247–48, 98251–52, 98255–56, 98258 (part), 98262–64, 98266–67, 98270 (part), 98272, 98273–74 (part), 98276, 98281, 98283, 98284 (part), 98288, 98290–91, 98293–96

* * *

SECOND DISTRICT

RICK LARSEN, Democrat, of Everett, WA; born in Arlington, WA, June 15, 1965; education: B.A., Pacific Lutheran University; M.P.A., University of Minnesota; professional: economic development official at the Port of Everett; director of public affairs for a health provider association; public service: Snohomish County Council; religion: Methodist; married: Tiia Karlen; children: Robert and Per; committees: Armed Services; Transportation and Infrastructure; elected to the 107th Congress on November 7, 2000; reelected to each succeeding Congress.

Office Listings

https://larsen.house.gov https://facebook.com/RepRickLarsen https://twitter.com/RepRickLarsen

2113 Rayburn House Office Building, Washington, DC 20515 .... (202) 225–2605
Chief of Staff.—Terra Sabag. FAX: 225–4420
Legislative Director.—J.Z. Golden.
Communications Director.—Amanda Munger.
2930 Wetmore Avenue, Suite 9F, Everett, WA 98201 .... (425) 252–3188
119 North Commercial Street, Suite 275, Bellingham, WA 98225 .... (360) 733–4500

Counties: ISLAND, SAN JUAN, SKAGIT (part), SNOHOMISH (part), AND WHATCOM (part). CITIES AND TOWNSHIPS: Anacortes, Arlington, Bellingham, Blakely Island, Bow, Burlington, Clinton, Conway, Coupeville, Deer Harbor, Eastsound, Everett, Freeland, Friday Harbor, Greenbank, Guemes Island, La Conner, Langley, Lopez Island, Lynnwood, Marysville, Mountlake Terrace, Mukilteo, Oak Harbor, Olga, Orcas Island, San Juan Island, Sedro-Woolley, Shaw Island, Silvana, Stanwood, Tulalip, and Waldron. Population (2015), 726,951.

ZIP Codes: 98012, 98021, 98026–27, 98036–37, 98043, 98046, 98087, 98201–08, 98221–23, 98225–26, 98229, 98232–33, 98236, 98239, 98245, 98249–50, 98253, 98257, 98259–61, 98270–72, 98274–75, 98277–78, 98280, 98282, 98284, 98290

* * *

THIRD DISTRICT

JAIME HERRERA BEUTLER, Republican, of Battle Ground, WA; born in Glendale, CA, November 3, 1978; education: communications, University of Washington, Seattle, WA, 2004;

religion: Christian; family: married to Daniel Beutler; committees: Appropriations; Joint Economic Committee; elected to the 112th Congress on November 2, 2010; reelected to each succeeding Congress.

Office Listings

https://jhb.house.gov · https://facebook.com/herrerabeutler twitter: @HerreraBeutler

2352 Rayburn House Office Building, Washington, DC 20515 .... (202) 225–3536
Chief of Staff.—Casey Bowman.
Deputy Chief of Staff / Legislative Director.—Jordan Evich.
Legislative Assistants: Ben Bruns, Rachel Thompson.
Communications.—Craig Wheeler.
Executive Assistant / Scheduler.—Krystal Thomas.
Legislative Correspondent.—Rachel Nepomuceno.
Staff Assistant.—Reilly Lamp.
750 Anderson Street, Suite B, Vancouver, WA 98661 .... (360) 695–6292
District Director.—Pam Peiper.
Caseworkers: Rachel Katz, David Perez.
District Staff Assistant.—Kole Musgrove.

Counties: CLARK, COWLITZ, KLICKITAT, LEWIS, PACIFIC, SKAMANIA, THURSTON (part), AND WAHKIAKUM. Population (2010), 672,448.

ZIP Codes: 98304 (part), 98330 (part), 98336, 98355–56, 98361, 98377, 98522, 98527, 98530–33, 98537 (part), 98538–39, 98542, 98544, 98547 (part), 98554, 98561, 98564–65, 98568 (part), 98570, 98572, 98576 (part), 98577, 98579 (part), 98581–82, 98585–86, 98589 (part), 98590–91, 98593, 98596, 98597 (part), 98601–07, 98609–14, 98616–17, 98619–26, 98628–29, 98631–32, 98635, 98637–45, 98647–51, 98660–66, 98668, 98670–75, 98682–87, 98935 (part), 99322 (part), 99350 (part), 99356

* * *

FOURTH DISTRICT

DAN NEWHOUSE, Republican, of Sunnyside, WA; born in Sunnyside, July 10, 1955; education: graduated, Sunnyside High School, 1973; B.S., Washington State University, 1977; graduated, Washington Agriculture and Forestry Leadership Program, 1981; member: Washington State House of Representatives, 2003–09; Assistant Whip; Assistant Floor Leader; Floor Leader; Water Caucus; Drought Committee Chairman; CSG Leadership Academy; director, Washington State Department of Agriculture, 2009–13; married: Carol Hammond, 1982–2017 (deceased 2017); children: Jensena and Devon; married: Joan Galvin, 2018; committees: Appropriations; Select Committee on the Modernization of Congress; elected to 114th Congress on November 4, 2014; reelected to each succeeding Congress.

Office Listings

https://newhouse.house.gov https://facebook.com/RepNewhouse
twitter: @RepNewhouse https://instagram.com/repnewhouse

1414 Longworth House Office Building, Washington, DC 20515 .... (202) 225–5816
Chief of Staff.—Carrie Meadows.
Scheduler / Office Manager.—Lacey Wallace.
Communications Director.—Will Boyington.
3100 George Washington Way, #130, Richland, WA 99354 .... (509) 713–7374
402 East Yakima Avenue, Suite 1000, Yakima, WA 98901 .... (509) 452–3243
P.O. Box 823, Twisp, WA 98856 .... (509) 433–7760

Counties: ADAMS COUNTY. CITIES: Othello and Ritzville. BENTON COUNTY. CITIES AND TOWNSHIPS: Benton City, Kennewick, Paterson, Plymouth, Prosser, Richland, and West Richland. DOUGLAS COUNTY. CITIES AND TOWNSHIPS: Bridgeport, East Wenatchee, Leahy, Mansfield, Orondo, Palisades, Rock Island, and Waterville. FRANKLIN COUNTY. CITIES AND TOWNSHIPS: Basin City, Connell, Eltopia, Kahlotus, Mesa, Pasco, and Windust. GRANT COUNTY. CITIES AND TOWNSHIPS: Beverly, Coulee City, Desert Aire, Electric City, Ephrata, George, Grand Coulee, Hartline, Marlin, Mattawa, Moses Lake, Quincy, Royal City, Soap Lake, Stratford, Warden, and Wilson Creek. OKANOGAN COUNTY. CITIES: Brewster, Nespelem, Okanogan, Omak, Oroville, Tonasket, and Twisp. WALLA WALLA COUNTY (part). CITIES: Burbank. YAKIMA COUNTY. CITIES AND TOWNSHIPS: Brownstown, Buena, Carson, Cowiche, Grandview, Granger, Harrah, Mabton, Moxee, Naches, Outlook, Parker, Selah, Sunnyside, Tieton, Toppenish, Underwood, Wapato, White Swan, Yakima, and Zillah. Population (2010), 695,040.

ZIP Codes: 98068, 98602, 98605, 98610, 98613, 98617, 98619–20, 98623, 98628, 98635, 98648, 98650–51, 98670, 98672–73, 98801–02, 98807, 98811–13, 98815–17, 98819, 98821–24, 98826, 98828–32, 98834, 98836–37, 98840–45, 98847–48, 98850–53, 98855–58, 98860, 98901–04, 98907–09, 98920–23, 98925–26, 98929–30, 98932–44, 98946–48, 98950–53, 99103, 99115–16, 99123–24, 99133, 99135, 99155, 99169, 99301–02, 99320–23, 99326, 99330, 99335–38, 99343–46, 99349–50, 99352–54, 99356–57

* * *

FIFTH DISTRICT

CATHY McMORRIS RODGERS, Republican, of Spokane, WA; born in Salem, OR, May 22, 1969; education: graduated from Kettle Falls High School, Kettle Falls, WA, 1986; B.A., Pensacola Christian College, Pensacola, FL, 1990; M.B.A., University of Washington, Seattle, WA, 2002; professional: family orchard business; member, Washington State House of Representatives, 1994–2004; Minority Leader, 2002–03; chair, House Republican Conference, 2013–19; committees: Energy and Commerce; elected to the 109th Congress on November 2, 2004; reelected to each succeeding Congress.

Office Listings

https://mcmorris.house.gov https://facebook.com/mcmorrisrodgers https://twitter.com/cathymcmorris

1035 Longworth House Office Building, Washington, DC 20515 .... (202) 225–2006
Chief of Staff.—Nate Hodson. FAX: 225–3392
Deputy Chief of Staff.—Olivia Hnat.
Scheduler.—Emily King.
Legislative Director.—Michael Taggart.
Communications Director.—Jared Powell.
Legislative Counsel.—Matt Neighbors.
Legislative Coordinator.—Kendall Dehnel.
Deputy Press Secretary.—Michael Cameron.
10 North Post Street, Suite 625, Spokane, WA 99201 .... (509) 353–2374
District Director.—Traci Couture.
Deputy District Director.—Patrick Bell.
Manager, Constituent Relations.—Paige Blackburn.
District Scheduler.—Collin Tracy.
555 South Main Street, Colville, WA 99114 .... (509) 684–3481
Northern Regional Representative.—Andrew Engall.
26 East Main Street, Suite 2, Walla Walla, WA 99362 .... (509) 529–9358
Southern Regional Representative.—Victor Valerio.

Counties: Asotin, Columbia, Ferry, Garfield, Lincoln, Pend Oreille, Spokane, Stevens, Walla Walla, and Whitman. Population (2015), 696,416.

ZIP Codes: 98832, 99001, 99003–06, 99008–09, 99011–13, 99016–23, 99025–27, 99029–34, 99036–37, 99039–40, 99101–03, 99109–11, 99113–14, 99117–19, 99121–22, 99125–26, 99128–31, 99133–34, 99136–41, 99143–44, 99146–61, 99163–64, 99166–67, 99169–71, 99173–74, 99176, 99179–81, 99185, 99201–08, 99212, 99216–18, 99223–24, 99324, 99328–29, 99333, 99347–48, 99359–62, 99401–03

* * *

SIXTH DISTRICT

DEREK KILMER, Democrat, of Gig Harbor, WA; born in Port Angeles, January 1, 1974; education: graduated, Port Angeles High School, 1992; B.A., public affairs, Princeton University, 1996; Ph.D., University of Oxford, 1999; professional: worked as a consultant with McKinsey & Company from 1999–2002; worked for the Economic Development Board for Tacoma-Pierce County; elected to be a Washington State Representative in 2004; served in the Washington State Senate from 2007–12; Rotary; married: the former Jennifer Saunders; children: Sophie and Tess; caucuses: chair, New Democrat Coalition; co-chair, Puget Sound Recovery Caucus; Democratic Caucus; committees: chair, Select Committee on the Modernization of Congress; Appropriations; elected to the 113th Congress on November 6, 2012; reelected to each succeeding Congress.

Office Listings

https://kilmer.house.gov https://facebook.com/derek.kilmer https://twitter.com/RepDerekKilmer

1410 Longworth House Office Building, Washington, DC 20515 .... (202) 225–5916
Chief of Staff.—Rachel Kelly. FAX: 226–3575
Communications Director.—Andrew Wright.
Legislative Director.—Katie Allen.
Scheduler.—Tony Scordato.
950 Pacific Avenue, Suite 1230, Tacoma, WA 98402 .... (253) 272–3515
District Director.—Andrea Roper.
345 Sixth Street, Suite 500, Bremerton, WA 98337 .... (360) 373–9725
322 East Fifth Street, Port Angeles, WA 98362 .... (360) 797–3623

Counties: Clallam. Cities and Townships: Blyn, Forks, Joyce, LaPush, Neah Bay, Port Angeles, Sequim, and Sieku. Grays Harbor. Cities and Townships: Aberdeen, Amanda Park, Cosmopolis, Elma, Hoquiam, McCleary, MoClips,

Montesano, Oakville, Ocean City, Ocean Shores, Quinault, Seabrook, Taholah, and Westport. JEFFERSON. CITIES AND TOWNSHIPS: Chimicum, Nordland, Port Hadlock, Port Ludlow, Port Townsend, and Quilcene. KITSAP. CITIES AND TOWNSHIPS: Bainbridge Island, Bremerton, Hansville, Indianola, Kingston, Manchester, Olalla, Port Orchard, Poulsbo, Seabeck, Silverdale, and Southworth. MASON (part). CITIES AND TOWNSHIPS: Allyn, Belfair, Grapeview, Harstine Island, Shelton, Skokomish, and Union. PIERCE (part). CITIES AND TOWNSHIPS: Fox Island, Gig Harbor, Key Center, Lakebay, Longbranch, Purdy, Tacoma, Vaughn, and Wauna. Population (2010), 687,387.

ZIP Codes: 98061, 98110, 98305, 98310–12, 98315, 98320, 98322, 98324–26, 98329, 98331–33, 98335, 98337, 98339–40, 98342–43, 98345–46, 98349–51, 98353, 98357–59, 98362–68, 98370, 98376, 98378, 98380–84, 98386, 98392–95, 98401–03, 98405–09, 98411–13, 98415, 98417–19, 98421, 98444, 98465–67, 98471, 98499, 98502, 98520, 98524, 98526, 98528, 98535–37, 98541, 98546–48, 98550, 98552, 98555, 98557, 98559–60, 98562–63, 98566, 98568–69, 98571, 98575, 98583–84, 98587–88, 98592, 98595

* * *

SEVENTH DISTRICT

PRAMILA JAYAPAL, Democrat, of Seattle, WA; born in Chennai, Tamil Nadu, India, September, 21, 1965; education: B.A., Georgetown University, Washington, DC; M.B.A, Northwestern University, Evanston, IL; professional: director of technology transfer, Program for Appropriate Technology in Health (PATH); founder, OneAmerica (originally Hate Free Zone), 2004–12; White House Champion of Change, 2013; married: Steven Williamson; mother of Janak and stepmother of Michael; dog owner: Otis the Labradoodle; Senior Whip; caucuses: co-chair, Congressional Progressive Caucus; co-chair, Women's Working Group on Immigration; vice chair, LGBT Equality Caucus; executive board member, Congressional Asian Pacific American Caucus; Democratic Caucus; committees: Budget; Education and Labor; Judiciary; elected to the 115th Congress on November 8, 2016; reelected to the 116th Congress on November 6, 2018.

Office Listings

https://jayapal.house.gov https://facebook.com/RepJayapal
twitter: @RepJayapal https://instagram.com/repjayapal

1510 Longworth House Office Building, Washington, DC 20515 .... (202) 225–3106
Chief of Staff.—Gautam Raghavan.
Deputy Chief of Staff / Legislative Director.—Lindsay Owens.
Press Secretary.—Mary Hurrell.
Scheduler.—Kate Brescia.
1904 Third Avenue, Suite 510, Seattle, WA 98101–1313 .... (206) 674–0040
District Director.—Rachel Berkson.

Counties: KING (part) AND SNOHOMISH (part). CITIES AND TOWNSHIPS: Included in the district (in whole or in part): Burien, Des Moines, Edmonds, Lake Forest Park, Normandy Park, Seattle, Shoreline, Vashon, and Woodway. Population (2010), 672,455.

ZIP Codes: 98013, 98020, 98026, 98037, 98043, 98070, 98101–09, 98111–13, 98115–17, 98119, 98121–22, 98125–27, 98129, 98133–34, 98136, 98139, 98141, 98146, 98148, 98154–55, 98161, 98164–66, 98168, 98174–75, 98177, 98181, 98185, 98191, 98194–95, 98198–99

* * *

EIGHTH DISTRICT

KIM SCHRIER, M.D., Democrat, of Sammamish, WA; born in Los Angeles, CA, August 23, 1968; education: B.A., University of California, Berkeley, CA, 1991 (graduated Phi Beta Kappa with a degree in astrophysics); M.D., University of California Davis School of Medicine, Davis, CA, 1997; professional: pediatric residency, Lucile Packard Children's Hospital at Stanford University, Palo Alto, CA, 2000; pediatrician; Virginia Mason Medical Center, Issaquah, WA, 2001; awards: Best Pediatrician in the Greater Seattle Area, 2013, by Parents Map Magazine; religion: Jewish; family: married to David; one son: Sam; caucuses: New Democrat Coalition; committees: Agriculture; Education and Labor; elected to the 116th Congress on November 6, 2018 (becoming the only woman doctor in Congress and the first pediatrician).

Office Listings

https://schrier.house.gov https://facebook.com/RepKimSchrier
https://twitter.com/repkimschrier https://instagram.com/repkimschrier

1123 Longworth House Office Building, Washington, DC 20515 .... (202) 225–7761

Office Listings—Continued

Chief of Staff.—Erin O'Quinn.
Scheduler.—Shanley Miller.
Legislative Director.—Alex Payne.
Communications Director.—Elizabeth Carlson.
1445 Northwest Mall Street, Suite 4, Issaquah, WA 98027 .... (425) 657–1001

Counties: KING COUNTY (part). CITIES AND TOWNSHIPS: Auburn, Black Diamond, Bonney Lake, Covington, Enumclaw, Federal Way, Issaquah, North Bend, Sammamish, and Snoqualmie. CHELAN COUNTY. CITIES AND TOWNSHIPS: Cashmere, Chelan, Leavenworth, and Wenatchee. KITTITAS. CITIES AND TOWNSHIPS: Cle Elum, Easton, Ellensburg, Kittitas, Roslyn, Snoqualmie Pass, and Thorp. DOUGLAS. CITIES AND TOWNSHIPS: East Wenatchee. PIERCE COUNTY (part). CITIES AND TOWNSHIPS: Ashfort, Bonney Lake, Buckley, Eatonville, Graham, Orting, and Sumner. Population (2010), 690,250.

ZIP Codes: 98001–03, 98010, 98022, 98024, 98027, 98029–32, 98038, 98042, 98045, 98047, 98050–51, 98058–59, 98065, 98068, 98074–75, 98092, 98304, 98321, 98323, 98328, 98330, 98338, 98354, 98360, 98372, 98374–75, 98385, 98387, 98390–91, 98396, 98424, 98558, 98580, 98801–02, 98811, 98815–17, 98821–22, 98826, 98828, 98831, 98836, 98847, 98852, 98901, 98922, 98925–26, 98934, 98937, 98940–41, 98943, 98946, 98950

* * *

NINTH DISTRICT

ADAM SMITH, Democrat, of Tacoma, WA; born in Washington, DC, June 15, 1965; education: graduated, Tyee High School, 1983; graduated, Fordham University, NY, 1987; law degree, University of Washington, 1990; admitted to the Washington Bar in 1991; professional: Prosecutor for the city of Seattle; Washington State Senate, 1990–96; member: Kent Drinking Driver Task Force; board member, Judson Park Retirement Home; married: Sara Smith, 1993; committees: chair, Armed Services; elected to the 105th Congress; reelected to each succeeding Congress.

Office Listings

https://adamsmith.house.gov https://facebook.com/RepAdamSmith twitter: @RepAdamSmith

2264 Rayburn House Office Building, Washington, DC 20515 .... (202) 225–8901
Chief of Staff.—Shana Chandler. FAX: 225–5893
Communications Director.—Vacant.
101 Evergreen Building, 15 South Grady Way, Renton, WA 98057 .... (425) 793–5180
District Director.—Sarah Servin.
Office Manager.—Caitlyn Cole.

Counties: KING (part) AND PIERCE (part). CITIES: Bellevue, Burien, Des Moines, Federal Way, Kent, Mercer Island, Newcastle, Renton, SeaTac, Seattle, Tacoma, and Tukwila. Population (2010), 672,460.

ZIP Codes: 98001 (part), 98003–04 (part), 98005–06, 98007–08 (part), 98009, 98015, 98023, 98027 (part), 98030–33 (part), 98035 (part), 98040, 98042 (part), 98055–57, 98058–59 (part), 98063, 98089 (part), 98093, 98102 (part), 98104 (part), 98108–09 (part), 98112 (part), 98114, 98118, 98122 (part), 98124 (part), 98131, 98134 (part), 98138, 98141 (part), 98144, 98148 (part), 98155 (part), 98158, 98168 (part), 98178, 98188 (part), 98190, 98198 (part), 98354 (part), 98402 (part), 98421 (part), 98422, 98424 (part)

* * *

TENTH DISTRICT

DENNY HECK, Democrat, of Olympia, WA; born in Vancouver, WA, July 29, 1952; education: graduated, Columbia River High School, WA, 1970; graduated, The Evergreen State College, WA, 1973; professional: small business owner; president and co-founder of TVW, Washington's statewide public affairs cable channel, 1993–2003; Chief of Staff to Governor Booth Gardner, 1989–93; elected to five consecutive terms in the Washington State House of Representatives, starting in 1976; religion: member, The Lutheran Church of The Good Shepherd; former trustee, Washington State Historical Society; former trustee, The Evergreen State College; married: Paula Heck, 1976; committees: Financial Services; Joint Economic Committee; Permanent Select Committee on Intelligence; elected to the 113th Congress on November 6, 2012; reelected to each succeeding Congress.

Office Listings

https://dennyheck.house.gov https://facebook.com/CongressmanDennyHeck
https://twitter.com/RepDennyHeck

2452 Rayburn House Office Building, Washington, DC 20515 .... (202) 225–9740

Office Listings—Continued

Chief of Staff.—Jami Burgess. FAX: 225–0129
Legislative Director.—Brendan Woodbury.
Communications Director.—Kati Rutherford.
420 College Street Southeast, Suite 3000, Lacey, WA 98503 .... (360) 459–8514
6000 Main Street, SW., Suite 3B, Lakewood, WA 98499 .... (253) 533–8332
District Director.—Phil Gardner.

Counties: MASON (part), PIERCE (part), AND THURSTON (part). CITIES: Chehalis Indian Reservation (part), DuPont, Edgewood, Fife, Fircrest, Joint Base Lewis-McChord, Lacey, Lakewood, Nisqually Indian Reservation, Olympia, Puyallup, Puyallup Indian Reservation (part), Rainier, Roy, Shelton, Squaxin Island Indian Reservation (part), Steilacoom, Sumner, Tacoma (part), Tenino, Tumwater, University Place, and Yelm. Population (2010), 672,455.

ZIP Codes: 98047, 98303, 98327, 98338, 98354, 98371–75, 98387–88, 98390–91, 98404, 98408, 98418, 98421, 98424, 98430, 98433, 98438–39, 98443–47, 98466–67, 98498–99, 98501–03, 98506, 98512–13, 98516, 98558, 98576, 98579–80, 98584, 98589, 98597

WEST VIRGINIA

(Population 2010, 1,852,994)

SENATORS

JOE MANCHIN III, Democrat, of Fairmont, WV; born in Farmington, WV, August 24, 1947; education: graduated, Farmington High School, Farmington, 1965; B.A., West Virginia University, WV, 1970; professional: businessman; member of the West Virginia House of Delegates, 1982–86; member of the West Virginia State Senate, 1986–96; Secretary of State, West Virginia, 2000–04; elected Governor of West Virginia in 2004 and reelected in 2008; chairman of the National Governors Association, 2010; religion: Catholic; married: Gayle Conelly; three children: Heather, Joseph IV, and Brooke; seven grandchildren; committees: ranking member, Energy and Natural Resources; Appropriations; Armed Services; Veterans' Affairs; elected to the 111th U.S. Senate, by special election, on November 2, 2010, for the term ending January 3, 2013, to fill the seat previously held by Senator Carte Goodwin, and took the oath of office on November 15, 2010; reelected to each succeeding Senate term.

Office Listings

https://manchin.senate.gov https://facebook.com/joemanchinIII https://twitter.com/Sen_JoeManchin

306 Hart Senate Office Building, Washington, DC 20510 .... (202) 224–3954
Chief of Staff.—Pat Hayes. FAX: 228–0002
Legislative Director.—Wes Kungel.
Communications Director.—Jonathan Kott.
900 Pennsylvania Avenue, Suite 629, Charleston, WV 25302 .... (304) 342–5855
State Director.—Mara Boggs.
261 Aikens Center, Suite 305, Martinsburg, WV 25404 .... (304) 264–4626
230 Adams Street, Fairmont, WV 26554 .... (304) 368–0567

* * *

SHELLEY MOORE CAPITO, Republican, of Charleston, WV; born in Glen Dale, WV, November 26, 1953; education: B.S., Duke University; M.Ed., University of Virginia; professional: career counselor, West Virginia State College; West Virginia Board of Regents; organizations: Community Council of Kanawha Valley; YWCA; West Virginia Interagency Council for Early Intervention; Habitat for Humanity; public service: elected to the West Virginia House of Delegates, 1996; reelected in 1998; awards: Coalition for a Tobacco-Free West Virginia Legislator of the Year; elected to the 107th Congress on November 7, 2000; served in the U.S. House of Representatives from 2001–14; religion: Presbyterian; married: Charles L. Capito, Jr.; three children; six grandchildren; first woman elected to the U.S. Senate from West Virginia; committees: Appropriations; Commerce, Science, and Transportation; Environment and Public Works; Rules and Administration; elected to the U.S. Senate on November 4, 2014.

Office Listings

https://capito.senate.gov https://facebook.com/senshelley https://twitter.com/sencapito

172 Russell Senate Office Building, Washington, DC 20510 .... (202) 224–6472
Chief of Staff.—Joel Brubaker. FAX: 224–7665
Legislative Director.—Adam Tomlinson.
Communications Director.—Tyler Hernandez.
Office Manager.—Shay Kelly.
State Director.—Mary Elisabeth Eckerson.
500 Virginia Street East, Suite 950, Charleston, WV 25301 .... (304) 347–5372
300 Foxcroft Avenue, Suite 202A, Martinsburg, WV 25401 .... (304) 262–9285
48 Donley Street, Suite 504, Morgantown, WV 26501 .... (304) 292–2310
220 North Kanawha Street, Suite 1, Beckley, WV 25801 .... (304) 347–5372

REPRESENTATIVES

FIRST DISTRICT

DAVID B. MCKINLEY, Republican, of Wheeling, WV; born in Wheeling, March 28, 1947; education: B.S.C.E., civil engineering, Purdue University, West Lafayette, IN, 1969; professional: engineer (started McKinley and Associates with offices in Wheeling and Charleston, WV, and Washington, PA); member of West Virginia State House of Representatives, 1981–94; chairman, West Virginia Republican Party, 1990–94; religion: Episcopalian; married: Mary

McKinley; children: David, Amy, Elizabeth, and Bennett; committees: Energy and Commerce; elected to the 112th Congress on November 2, 2010; reelected to each succeeding Congress.

Office Listings

https://mckinley.house.gov

2239 Rayburn House Office Building, Washington, DC 20515 .... (202) 225–4172
Chief of Staff.—Mike Hamilton. FAX: 225–7564
Executive Assistant.—Mary Galey.
Legislative Director.—Vacant.
Communications Director.—Vacant.
709 Beechurst Avenue, Suite 29, Morgantown, WV 26505 .... (304) 284–8506
Horne Building, 1100 Main Street, Suite 101, Wheeling, WV 26003 .... (304) 232–3801
408 Market Street, Parkersburg, WV 26101 .... (304) 422–5972

Counties: BARBOUR, BROOKE, DODDRIDGE, GILMER, GRANT, HANCOCK, HARRISON, MARION, MARSHALL, MINERAL, MONONGALIA, OHIO, PLEASANTS, PRESTON, RITCHIE, TAYLOR, TUCKER, TYLER, WETZEL, AND WOOD. CITIES AND TOWNSHIPS: Albright, Alma, Alvy, Anmoore, Arthur, Arthurdale, Auburn, Aurora, Baldwin, Barrackville, Baxter, Bayard, Beech Bottom, Belington, Belleville, Bellview, Belmont, Bens Run, Benwood, Berea, Bethany, Big Run, Blacksville, Blandville, Booth, Brandonville, Bretz, Bridgeport, Bristol, Brownton, Bruceton Mills, Burlington, Burnt House, Burton, Cabins, Cairo, Cameron, Carolina, Cassville, Cedarville, Center Point, Central Station, Century, Chester, Clarksburg, Coburn, Colfax, Colliers, Core, Corinth, Cove, Coxs Mills, Cuzzart, Dallas, Davis, Davisville, Dawmont, Dellslow, Dorcas, Eglon, Elk Garden, Ellenboro, Elm Grove, Enterprise, Eureka, Everettville, Fairmont, Fairview, Farmington, Flemington, Flower, Follansbee, Folsom, Fort Ashby, Fort Neal, Four States, Friendly, Galloway, Gilmer, Glen Dale, Glen Easton, Glenville, Goffs, Gormania, Grafton, Grant Town, Granville, Greenwood, Gypsy, Hambleton, Harrisville, Hastings, Haywood, Hazelton, Hebron, Hendricks, Hepzibah, Highland, Hundred, Idamay, Independence, Industrial, Jacksonburg, Jere, Jordan, Junior, Keyser, Kingmont, Kingwood, Knob Fork, Lahmansville, Letter Gap, Lima, Linn, Littleton, Lockney, Lost Creek, Lumberport, MacFarlan, Mahone, Maidsville, Mannington, Masontown, Maysville, McMechen, McWhorter, Meadowbrook, Medley, Metz, Middlebourne, Mineral Wells, Moatsville, Monongah, Montana Mines, Morgantown, Moundsville, Mount Clare, Mount Storm, Mountain, New Creek, New Cumberland, New England, New Manchester, New Martinsville, New Milton, Newberne, Newburg, Newell, Normantown, North Parkersburg, Nutter Fort, Osage, Owings, Paden City, Parkersburg, Parsons, Pennsboro, Pentress, Perkins, Petersburg, Petroleum, Philippi, Piedmont, Pine Grove, Porters Falls, Proctor, Pullman, Pursglove, Rachel, Reader, Red Creek, Reedsville, Reynoldsville, Ridgeley, Rivesville, Rocket Center, Rockport, Rosedale, Rosemont, Rowlesburg, Saint George, Saint Marys, Salem, Sand Fork, Shinnston, Shirley, Shocks, Short Creek, Simpson, Sistersville, Smithburg, Smithfield, Smithville, Spelter, Stonewood, Stouts Mill, Stumptown, Tanner, Terra Alta, Thomas, Thornton, Toll Gate, Troy, Triadelphia, Tunnelton, Valley Grove, Vienna, Volga, Wadestown, Walker, Wallace, Wana, Warwood, Washington, Watson, Waverly, Weirton, Wellsburg, Wendel, West Liberty, West Milford, West Union, Westover, Wheeling, Wick, Wilbur, Wiley Ford, Wileyville, Williamstown, Wilson, Wilsonburg, Windsor Heights, Wolf Summit, Worthington, and Wyatt. Population (2010), 615,991.

ZIP Codes: 25267, 26003, 26030–41, 26047, 26050, 26055–56, 26059–60, 26062, 26070, 26074–75, 26101, 26104–05, 26133–34, 26136–37, 26142–43, 26146, 26148–50, 26155, 26159, 26161, 26164, 26167, 26169–70, 26175, 26178, 26180–81, 26184, 26187, 26201, 26238, 26250, 26260, 26263, 26267, 26269, 26271, 26275–76, 26283, 26287, 26292, 26301, 26320, 26323, 26325, 26327, 26330, 26335, 26337, 26339, 26342, 26346–49, 26351, 26354, 26361–62, 26366, 26369, 26374, 26377–78, 26384–86, 26404–05, 26408, 26410–12, 26415–16, 26419, 26421–22, 26424–26, 26430–31, 26435–38, 26440, 26443–44, 26448, 26451, 26456, 26501, 26505, 26508, 26519–21, 26525, 26534, 26537, 26541–43, 26547, 26554, 26559–60, 26562–63, 26568, 26570–72, 26574–76, 26581–82, 26585–88, 26590–91, 26611, 26636, 26638, 26705, 26707, 26710, 26716–17, 26719–20, 26726, 26731, 26739, 26743, 26750, 26753, 26763–64, 26767, 26833, 26847, 26855

* * *

SECOND DISTRICT

ALEXANDER X. MOONEY, Republican, of Charles Town, WV; born in Washington, DC, June 7, 1971; education: B.A., philosophy, Dartmouth College, 1993; professional: owner, AXM Consulting, LLC; executive director, The National Journalism Center (a program of Young America's Foundation), 2005–12; State Senator, Maryland State Senate, 1999–2010; religion: Roman Catholic; married: Dr. Grace Gonzalez Mooney, Ph.D., M.D.; three children; committees: Financial Services; elected to the 114th Congress on November 4, 2014; reelected to each succeeding Congress.

Office Listings

https://mooney.house.gov https://facebook.com/CongressmanAlexMooney twitter: @RepAlexMooney

2440 Rayburn House Office Building, Washington, DC 20515 .... (202) 225–2711
Chief of Staff.—Michael Hough. FAX: 225–7856
Legislative Director.—Brandon Steinmann.
Communications Director.—Vacant.
405 Capitol Street, Suite 306, Charleston, WV 25301 .... (304) 925–5964
300 Foxcroft Avenue, Suite 101, Martinsburg, WV 25401 .... (304) 264–8810

Counties: BERKELEY, BRAXTON, CALHOUN, CLAY, HAMPSHIRE, HARDY, JACKSON, JEFFERSON, KANAWHA, LEWIS, MORGAN, PENDLETON, PUTNAM, RANDOLPH, ROANE, UPSHUR, AND WIRT. Population (2010), 654,275.

ZIP Codes: 25002–03, 25005, 25011, 25015, 25019, 25025–26, 25030, 25033, 25035, 25039, 25043, 25045–46, 25054, 25059, 25061, 25063–64, 25067, 25070–71, 25075, 25079, 25081–83, 25085–86, 25088, 25102–03, 25106–07, 25109–

13, 25123–26, 25132–34, 25136, 25139, 25141, 25143, 25147, 25150, 25156, 25159–60, 25162, 25164, 25168, 25177, 25187, 25201–02, 25211, 25213–14, 25231, 25234–35, 25239, 25241, 25243–45, 25247–48, 25251–53, 25259–62, 25264–68, 25270–71, 25275–76, 25279, 25281, 25285–87, 25301–06, 25309, 25311–15, 25317, 25320–39, 25350, 25356–58, 25360–62, 25364–65, 25375, 25392, 25396, 25401–02, 25410–11, 25413–14, 25419–23, 25425, 25427–32, 25434, 25437–38, 25440–44, 25446, 25502–03, 25510, 25515, 25520, 25523, 25526, 25541, 25550, 25560, 25569, 26133, 26136–38, 26141, 26143, 26147, 26151–52, 26160–61, 26164, 26173, 26180, 26201–02, 26205, 26210, 26215, 26218, 26224, 26228–30, 26234, 26236–38, 26241, 26253–54, 26257, 26259, 26261, 26263, 26267–68, 26270, 26273, 26276, 26278, 26280, 26282–83, 26285, 26293–94, 26296, 26321, 26335, 26338, 26342–43, 26351, 26372, 26376, 26378, 26384–85, 26412, 26430, 26443, 26447, 26452, 26546, 26590, 26601, 26610–11, 26615, 26617, 26619, 26621, 26623–24, 26627, 26629, 26631, 26636, 26638–39, 26641, 26651, 26656, 26660, 26662, 26667, 26671, 26675–76, 26678–79, 26681, 26684, 26690–91, 26704–05, 26707, 26710–11, 26714, 26717, 26722, 26731, 26739, 26743, 26750, 26755, 26757, 26761, 26763–64, 26801–02, 26804, 26807–08, 26810, 26812, 26814–15, 26817–18, 26823–24, 26836, 26838, 26845, 26847, 26851–52, 26865–66, 26884, 26886

* * *

THIRD DISTRICT

CAROL D. MILLER, Republican, of Huntington, WV; born in Columbus, OH, November 4, 1950; daughter of U.S. Representative Samuel L. Devine; education: B.S., history and political science, Columbia College, Columbia, SC, 1972; professional: member, West Virginia House of Delegates, 2007–19 (rising to become the first female Majority Whip); owner/operator, Swann Ridge Bison Farm; real estate manager; religion: Baptist; family: married to Matt; two children: Chris and Sam; five grandchildren; committees: Oversight and Reform; Transportation and Infrastructure; Select Committee on the Climate Crisis; elected to the 116th Congress on November 6, 2018.

Office Listings

https://miller.house.gov https://facebook.com/RepCarolMiller
https://twitter.com/RepCarolMiller https://instagram.com/repcarolmiller

1605 Longworth House Office Building, Washington, DC 20515 .... (202) 225–3452
Chief of Staff.—Matt Donnellan. FAX: 225–9061
Deputy Chief of Staff / Communications Director.—Tom Moran.
Legislative Director.—Lauren Billman.
Scheduler.—Bronti Viskovich.
Press Secretary.—Samantha Cantrell.
307 Prince Street, Beckley, WV 25801 .... (304) 250–6177
601 Federal Street, Elizabeth Kee Federal Building, Bluefield, WV 24701.
845 5th Avenue, Sidney L. Christie Federal Building, Huntington, WV 25701 .... (304) 522–2201

Counties: BOONE, CABELL, FAYETTE, GREENBRIER, LINCOLN, LOGAN, MASON, MCDOWELL, MERCER, MINGO, MONROE, NICHOLAS, POCAHONTAS, RALEIGH, SUMMERS, WAYNE, WEBSTER, AND WYOMING. Population (2010), 613,376.

ZIP Codes: 24701, 24712, 24714–16, 24719, 24724, 24726, 24729, 24731–33, 24736–40, 24747, 24751, 24801, 24808, 24811, 24813, 24815–18, 24820–31, 24834, 24836, 24839, 24842–57, 24859–62, 24866–74, 24878–82, 24884, 24887–88, 24892, 24894–99, 24901–02, 24910, 24915–18, 24920, 24924–25, 24927, 24931, 24934–36, 24938, 24941, 24943–46, 24950–51, 24954, 24957, 24961–63, 24966, 24970, 24974, 24976–77, 24981, 24983–86, 24991, 24993, 25002–04, 25007–10, 25021–22, 25024, 25028, 25031, 25036, 25040, 25043–44, 25047–49, 25051, 25053, 25057, 25059–60, 25062, 25076, 25081–83, 25085, 25090, 25093, 25106, 25108, 25114–15, 25118–19, 25121, 25123, 25130, 25136, 25139–40, 25142, 25148–49, 25152, 25154, 25161, 25165, 25169, 25173–74, 25180–81, 25183, 25185–86, 25193, 25202–06, 25208–09, 25213, 25239, 25241, 25247, 25253, 25260, 25264–65, 25287, 25501–08, 25510–12, 25514, 25517, 25520–21, 25523–24, 25526, 25529–30, 25534–35, 25537, 25540–41, 25544–45, 25547, 25550, 25555, 25557, 25559, 25562, 25564–65, 25567, 25570, –73, 25601, 25606–08, 25611–12, 25614, 25617, 25621, 25624–25, 25628, 25630, 25632, 25634–39, 25644, 25646–47, 25649–54, 25661, 25665–67, 25669–72, 25674, 25676, 25678, 25682, 25685–88, 25690–92, 25694, 25696, 25699, 25701–29, 25755, 25770–79, 25801–02, 25810–13, 25816–18, 25820, 25823, 25825–27, 25831–33, 25836–37, 25839–41, 25843–49, 25851, 25853–57, 25859–60, 25862, 25864–66, 25868, 25870–71, 25873, 25875–76, 25878–80, 25882, 25901–02, 25904, 25906–09, 25911, 25913–22, 25927–28, 25931–32, 25934, 25936, 25938, 25942–43, 25951, 25958, 25961–62, 25965–67, 25969, 25971–72, 25976–79, 25981, 25984–86, 25989, 26202–03, 26205–06, 26208–09, 26217, 26222, 26230, 26234, 26261, 26264, 26266, 26288, 26291, 26294, 26298, 26610, 26617, 26639, 26651, 26656, 26660, 26662, 26674, 26676, 26678–81, 26684, 26690–91

WISCONSIN

(Population 2010, 5,686,986)

SENATORS

RONALD H. JOHNSON, Republican, of Oshkosh, WI; born in Mankato, MN, April 8, 1955; education: B.A., business administration, University of Minnesota, Twin Cities, MN, 1977; professional: CEO Pacur, LLC; married: wife, Jane; three children: daughters, Carey and Jenna; son, Ben; committees: chair, Homeland Security and Governmental Affairs; Budget; Commerce, Science, and Transportation; Foreign Relations; elected to the U.S. Senate on November 2, 2010; reelected to the U.S. Senate on November 8, 2016.

Office Listings

https://ronjohnson.senate.gov https://facebook.com/SenRonJohnson twitter: @SenRonJohnson

328 Hart Senate Office Building, Washington, DC 20510 .... (202) 224–5323
Chief of Staff.—Tony Blando. FAX: 228–6965
Deputy Chief of Staff / Administration.—Marlo Meuli.
Deputy Chief of Staff / Operations.—Jen O'Neil.
Legislative Director.—Sean Riley.
Communications Director.—Ben Voelkel.
5315 Wall Street, Suite 110, Madison, WI 53718 .... (608) 240–9629
517 East Wisconsin Avenue, Room 408, Milwaukee, WI 53202 .... (414) 276–7282
219 Washington Avenue, Suite 100, Oshkosh, WI 54901 .... (920) 230–7250
Deputy Chief of Staff, Wisconsin.—Julie Leschke.

* * *

TAMMY BALDWIN, Democrat, of Madison, WI; born in Madison, February 11, 1962; education: graduated, Madison West High School, Madison, 1980; A.B., Smith College, Northampton, MA, 1984; J.D., University of Wisconsin Law School, Madison, 1989; professional: appointed to Madison Common Council, Madison, 1986; elected to Dane County Board of Supervisors, Madison, served 1986–94; elected to the Wisconsin State Assembly, Madison, served 1992–98; elected to the U.S. House of Representatives, served 1998–2012; Democratic Conference Secretary, 2017–present; committees: Appropriations; Commerce, Science, and Transportation; Health, Education, Labor, and Pensions; elected to the U.S. Senate on November 6, 2012; reelected to the U.S. Senate on November 6, 2018.

Office Listings

https://baldwin.senate.gov https://facebook.com/senatortammybaldwin twitter: @SenatorBaldwin

709 Hart Senate Office Building, Washington, DC 20510 .... (202) 224–5653
Chief of Staff.—Bill Murat.
Legislative Director.—Dan McCarthy.
Communications Director.—John Kraus.
Executive Assistant.—Carolyn Walser.
30 West Mifflin Street, Suite 700, Madison, WI 53703 .... (608) 264–5338
State Director.—Janet Piraino.
633 West Wisconsin Avenue, Suite 1920, Milwaukee, WI 53203 .... (414) 297–4451
205 5th Avenue South, Room 216, La Crosse, WI 54601 .... (608) 796–0045
P.O. Box 61, Ashland, WI 54806 .... (715) 450–3754
1039 West Mason Street, Suite 119, Green Bay, WI 54303 .... (920) 498–2668
500 South Barstow Street, Suite LL2, Eau Claire, WI 54701 .... (715) 832–8424

REPRESENTATIVES

FIRST DISTRICT

BRYAN STEIL, Republican, of Janesville, WI; born in Janesville, March 3, 1981; education: Joseph A. Craig High School; B.S., business administration, Georgetown University, Washington, DC, 2003; J.D., University of Wisconsin School of Law, Madison, WI, 2007; professional: legal counsel, Regal Beloit; attorney for Milton, WI-based plastics manufacturer Charter NEX Film; member, University of Wisconsin Board of Regents, 2016–18; committees: Financial Services; elected to the 116th Congress on November 6, 2018.

Office Listings

https://steil.house.gov https://facebook.com/RepBryanSteil
https://twitter.com/repbryansteil https://instagram.com/repbryansteil
https://youtube.com/repbryansteil

1408 Longworth House Office Building, Washington, DC 20515 .... (202) 225–3031
DC Chief of Staff.—Ryan Carney.
Scheduler.—Matthew Brown.
Communications Director.—Sally Fox.
Legislative Director.—David Goldfarb.
20 South Main Street, Suite 10, Janesville, WI 53545 .... (608) 752–4050
Wisconsin Chief of Staff.—Rich Zipperer.
Somers Village / Town Hall, 7511 12th Street, Somers, WI 53171 .... (262) 654–1901
Racine County Courthhouse, Room 101, 730 Wisconsin Avenue, Racine, WI 53403 .... (262) 637–0510

Counties: KENOSHA, MILWAUKEE (part), RACINE, ROCK (part), WALWORTH, AND WAUKESHA (part). Population (2010), 728,042.

ZIP Codes: 53018 (part), 53066 (part), 53101–05, 53108–09, 53114–15, 53118–19 (part), 53120–21, 53125–30, 53132, 53138–44, 53146 (part), 53147–49, 53150–51 (part), 53152–53, 53154 (part), 53157–59, 53167–68, 53170–71, 53176–77, 53179, 53181–82, 53183 (part), 53184–85, 53188–90 (part), 53191–92, 53194–95, 53220 (part), 53221, 53228 (part), 53401–08, 53505, 53511 (part), 53525, 53538 (part), 53545–46 (part), 53547, 53548 (part), 53563 (part), 53585

* * *

SECOND DISTRICT

MARK POCAN, Democrat, of the Town of Vermont, WI; born in Kenosha, WI, August 14, 1964; education: graduated from Bradford High School, 1982; journalism, University of Wisconsin, 1986; professional: small business owner, 1986–present; elected to the Dane County Board of Supervisors, 1991–96; elected to the State Assembly from the 78th District, 1999–2013; married: Philip Frank in 2006; committees: Appropriations; Select Committee on the Modernization of Congress; elected to the 113th Congress on November 6, 2012; reelected to each succeeding Congress.

Office Listings

https://pocan.house.gov https://facebook.com/repmarkpocan https://twitter.com/repmarkpocan

1421 Longworth House Office Building, Washington, DC 20515 .... (202) 225–2906
Chief of Staff.—Glenn Wavrunek. FAX: 225–6942
Legislative Director.—David Bagby.
Scheduler.—Kelly McCone.
Communications Director.—Ron Boehmer.
10 East Doty Street, Suite 405, Madison, WI 53703 .... (608) 258–9800
District Director.—Dane Varese.
100 State Street, 3rd Floor, Beloit, WI 53511 .... (608) 365–8001

Counties: DANE, GREEN, IOWA, LAFAYETTE, RICHLAND (part), ROCK (part), and SAUK. Population (2010), 729,417.

ZIP Codes: 53501–04, 53506–08, 53510–11, 53515–17, 53520–23, 53526–37, 53540–46, 53548, 53553–56, 53558–63, 53565–66, 53569–78, 53580–83, 53586–90, 53593–94, 53597–99, 53703–06, 53711, 53713–19, 53726, 53792, 53803, 53807, 53811, 53818, 53911, 53913, 53924–25, 53937, 53941, 53943–44, 53951, 53959, 53961, 53965, 53968

* * *

THIRD DISTRICT

RON KIND, Democrat, of La Crosse, WI; born in La Crosse, March 16, 1963; education: B.A., Harvard University, 1985; M.A., London School of Economics, 1986; J.D., University of Minnesota Law School, 1990; professional: admitted to the Wisconsin Bar, 1990; State Prosecutor, La Crosse County District Attorney's Office; board of directors, La Crosse Boys and Girls Club; Coulee Council on Alcohol and Drug Abuse; Wisconsin Harvard Club; Wisconsin Bar Association; La Crosse County Bar Association; married: Tawni Zappa in 1994; two sons: Jonathan and Matthew; committees: Ways and Means; elected to the 105th Congress; reelected to each succeeding Congress.

Office Listings

https://kind.house.gov

1502 Longworth House Office Building, Washington, DC 20515 .... (202) 225–5506

Office Listings—Continued

Chief of Staff.—Hana Greenberg.
Press Secretary.—Sarah Abel.
Legislative Director.—Alex Eveland.
Scheduler.—Hannah Pierce.
205 Fifth Avenue South, Suite 400, La Crosse, WI 54601 .... (608) 782–2558
District Director.—Loren Kannenberg.
131 South Barstow Street, Suite 301, Eau Claire, WI 54701 .... (715) 831–9214
Congressional Aide.—Mark Aumann.

Counties: ADAMS, BUFFALO, CHIPPEWA, CRAWFORD, DUNN, EAU CLAIRE, GRANT, JACKSON, JUNEAU, LA CROSSE, MONROE, PEPIN, PIERCE, PORTAGE, RICHLAND, TREMPEALEAU, VERNON, AND WOOD. Population (2010), 710,873.

ZIP Codes: 53518, 53543, 53554, 53556, 53569, 53573, 53581, 53801–02, 53804, 53805–11, 53813, 53816–18, 53820–21, 53825–27, 53910, 53920, 53924, 53929, 53934, 53936–37, 53941, 53944, 53948, 53950, 53952, 53964–65, 53968, 54003, 54005, 54010–11, 54013–14, 54021–22, 54406–07, 54410, 54412–13, 54423, 54443, 54454–55, 54457–58, 54466–67, 54469, 54473, 54475, 54481–82, 54489, 54494–95, 54499, 54601, 54603, 54610–16, 54618–19, 54621–32, 54634–39, 54642–45, 54648, 54650–61, 54664–67, 54669–70, 54701, 54703, 54720–27, 54729–30, 54734, 54736–42, 54747, 54749–51, 54754–63, 54765, 54767–70, 54772–73, 54909, 54921, 54930, 54943, 54945, 54966, 54977, 54981, 54984

* * *

FOURTH DISTRICT

GWENDOLYNNE S. "GWEN" MOORE, Democrat, of Milwaukee, WI; born in Racine, WI, April 18, 1951; education: graduated, Northern Division High School, Milwaukee, WI, 1969; B.A., Marquette University, Milwaukee, WI, 1978; professional: housing officer, Wisconsin Housing and Development Authority; member: Wisconsin State Assembly, 1989–92; Wisconsin State Senate, 1993–2004; president pro tempore, 1997–98; three children; committees: Ways and Means; elected to the 109th Congress on November 2, 2004; reelected to each succeeding Congress.

Office Listings

https://gwenmoore.house.gov https://facebook.com/GwenSMoore https://twitter.com/RepGwenMoore

2252 Rayburn House Office Building, Washington, DC 20515 .... (202) 225–4572
Chief of Staff.—Sean Gard.
250 East Wisconsin Avenue, Suite 950, Milwaukee, WI 53202 .... (414) 297–1140
District Administrator.—Shirley Ellis. FAX: 297–1086

Counties: MILWAUKEE (part). CITIES AND TOWNSHIPS: Bayside, Brown Deer, Fox Point, Glendale, Milwaukee, Shorewood, South Milwaukee, St. Francis, West Milwaukee, and Whitefish Bay. Population (2016), 715,895.

ZIP Codes: 53051, 53110, 53154, 53172, 53201–28, 53233, 53235, 53295

* * *

FIFTH DISTRICT

F. JAMES SENSENBRENNER, JR., Republican, of Menomonee Falls, WI; born in Chicago, IL, June 14, 1943; education: graduated, Milwaukee Country Day School, 1961; A.B., Stanford University, 1965; J.D., University of Wisconsin Law School, 1968; admitted to the Wisconsin Bar, 1968; commenced practice in Cedarburg, WI; admitted to practice before the U.S. Supreme Court in 1972; professional: attorney; staff member of former U.S. Congressman J. Arthur Younger of California, 1965; elected to the Wisconsin Assembly, 1968, reelected in 1970, 1972, and 1974; elected to Wisconsin Senate in a special election, 1975, reelected in 1976 (Assistant Minority Leader); member: Waukesha County Republican Party; Wisconsin Bar Association; American Philatelic Society; awards: Schuman Medal; Order of the Rising Sun; married: the former Cheryl Warren, 1977; children: Frank James III and Robert Alan; grandchild: Kevin Vartan; committees: Foreign Affairs; Judiciary; elected to the 96th Congress on November 7, 1978; reelected to each succeeding Congress.

Office Listings

https://sensenbrenner.house.gov https://facebook.com/RepSensenbrenner https://twitter.com/JimPressOffice

2449 Rayburn House Office Building, Washington, DC 20515–4905 .... (202) 225–5101

Office Listings—Continued

Chief of Staff.—Matt Bisenius.
Legislative Director.—Amy Bos.
Communications Director.—Chris Krepich.
Scheduler / Office Manager.—Nathan Cobb.
120 Bishops Way, Room 154, Brookfield, WI 53005–6294 .... (262) 784–1111
Chief of Staff.—Loni Hagerup.

Counties: JEFFERSON, MILWAUKEE (part), DODGE (part), WASHINGTON, AND WAUKESHA (part). Population (2010), 716,218.

ZIP Codes: 53005, 53007, 53018, 53022, 53029, 53032, 53035–40, 53045–46, 53051–52, 53056, 53058, 53066, 53072, 53076, 53078, 53089–90, 53094–95, 53098, 53122, 53137, 53146, 53151, 53156, 53178, 53186, 53188–90, 53210, 53213–14, 53219–21, 53226–28, 53538, 53549, 53551, 53579, 53594

* * *

SIXTH DISTRICT

GLENN GROTHMAN, Republican, of Glenbeulah, WI; born in Milwaukee, WI, July 3, 1955; education: graduated, Homestead High School, 1973; B.B.A., University of Wisconsin, 1978; J.D., University of Wisconsin, 1983; professional: admitted to the Wisconsin State Bar Association; lawyer, Schloemer Law Firm; elected to the Wisconsin State Assembly, 1993; elected to the Wisconsin State Senate, 2004, served until 2015; committees: Education and Labor; Oversight and Reform; elected to the 114th Congress on November 4, 2014; reelected to each succeeding Congress.

Office Listings

https://grothman.house.gov https://facebook.com/RepGrothman https://twitter.com/REPGROTHMAN

1427 Longworth House Office Building, Washington, DC 20515 .... (202) 225–2476
Chief of Staff.—Rachel Ver Velde.
Legislative Director.—Ryan Croft.
Communications Director.—Timothy Svoboda.
Scheduler.—Megan Prangley.
24 West Pioneer Road, Fond du Lac, WI 54935 .... (920) 907–0624
District Director.—Alan Ott.
Deputy District Director / Operations Director.—Sadie Parafiniuk.

Counties: COLUMBIA, DODGE (part), FOND DU LAC, GREEN LAKE, MANITOWOC, MILWAUKEE (part), OZAUKEE, SHEBOYGAN, WAUSHARA, AND WINNEBAGO (part). Population (2010), 709,482.

ZIP Codes: 53001, 53004, 53006, 53010–15, 53019–21, 53023–24, 53031–32, 53035, 53040, 53042, 53044, 53048–50, 53057, 53061–63, 53065, 53070, 53073–75, 53079–85, 53090–93, 53095, 53097, 53217, 53532, 53555, 53561, 53578, 53583, 53901, 53911–23, 53925–28, 53930–33, 53935, 53939, 53946–47, 53949, 53952–56, 53960, 53963–65, 53969, 54110, 54126, 54207–08, 54214, 54220–28, 54230–32, 54241–47, 54901–09, 54914–15, 54923, 54930, 54932, 54934–41, 54943, 54947, 54952–60, 54963–74, 54979–86

* * *

SEVENTH DISTRICT

THOMAS P. TIFFANY, Republican, of Minocqua, WI; born December 30, 1957, Wabasha, MN; education: graduate, Elmwood High School, Elmwood, WI, 1976; B.S. in agricultural economics, University of Wisconsin-River Falls, 1980; professional: dam tender, Wisconsin Valley Improvement Company; supervisor, Town of Little Rice, WI, 2009–13; Wisconsin State Assembly, 2010–12; Wisconsin State Senator, 2012–20; married; three children; committees: Judiciary; Science, Space, and Technology; elected to the 116th Congress, by special election, to fill the vacancy caused by the resignation of U.S. Representative Sean Duffy.

Office Listings

https://tiffany.house.gov https://facebook.com/RepTiffany https://twitter.com/RepTiffany

1714 Longworth House Office Building, Washington, DC 20515 .... (202) 225–3365
Chief of Staff.—Jason Bauknecht.
Deputy Chief of Staff.—Mac Zimmerman.
Press Secretary.—Brigid Nealon.
Scheduler.—Mary Galey.
2620 Stewart Avenue, Suite 312, Wausau, WI 54401 .... (715) 298–9344

Counties: ASHLAND, BARRON, BAYFIELD, BURNETT, CHIPPEWA (part), CLARK, DOUGLAS, FLORENCE, FOREST, IRON, JACKSON (part), JUNEAU (part), LANGLADE, LINCOLN, MARATHON, MONROE (part), ONEIDA, POLK, PRICE, RUSK, ST. CROIX, SAWYER, TAYLOR, VILAS, WASHBURN, AND WOOD (part). Population (2010), 710,873.

ZIP Codes: 53950, 54001–02, 54004–07, 54009, 54013, 54015–17, 54020, 54022–28, 54082, 54103–04, 54120–21, 54125, 54151, 54175, 54401, 54403, 54405, 54408–14, 54417–18, 54420–22, 54424–28, 54430, 54433, 54435–37, 54440–43, 54446–49, 54451–52, 54454–57, 54459–60, 54462–63, 54465–66, 54470–71, 54473–74, 54476, 54479–80, 54484–85, 54487–91, 54493, 54495, 54498–99, 54501, 54511–15, 54517, 54519–21, 54524–27, 54529–31, 54534, 54536–42, 54545–48, 54550, 54552, 54554–66, 54568, 54611, 54615–16, 54618, 54635, 54641, 54646, 54660, 54666, 54724, 54726–34, 54741, 54745–46, 54748–49, 54754, 54757, 54762–63, 54765–68, 54771, 54801, 54805–06, 54810, 54812–14, 54817, 54819–22, 54824, 54826–30, 54832, 54835–50, 54853–59, 54861–62, 54864–65, 54867–68, 54870–76, 54880, 54888–89, 54891, 54893, 54895–96

* * *

EIGHTH DISTRICT

MIKE GALLAGHER, Republican, of Green Bay, WI; born in Green Bay, March 3, 1984; education: A.B., Princeton University, Princeton, NJ, 2006; M.S., National Intelligence University, Washington, DC, 2010; M.A., Georgetown University, Washington, DC, 2012, 2013; Ph.D., Georgetown University, Washington, DC, 2015; professional: U.S. Marine Corps, 2006–13; staff, U.S. Senate Foreign Relations Committee, 2013–15; Scott Walker presidential campaign staff, 2015; businessman; religion: Catholic; committees: Armed Services; Transportation and Infrastructure; elected to the 115th Congress on November 8, 2016; reelected to the 116th Congress on November 6, 2018.

Office Listings

https://gallagher.house.gov https://facebook.com/RepMikeGallagher https://twitter.com/RepGallagher

1230 Longworth House Office Building, Washington, DC 20515 .... (202) 225–5665
Chief of Staff.—Taylor Andreae.
Scheduler.—Naomi Villaca.
Communications Director.—Jordan Dunn.
1702 Scheuring Road, Suite B, De Pere, WI 54115 .... (920) 301–4500
District Director.—Rick Sense.

Counties: BROWN, CALUMET, DOOR, KEWAUNEE, MARINETTE, MENOMINEE, OCONTO, OUTAGAMIE (part), SHAWANO, WAUPACA, AND WINNEBAGO (part). Population (2010), 706,840.

ZIP Codes: 53014 (part), 53020 (part), 53042 (part), 53049 (part), 53061 (part), 53088, 54101–02, 54103–04 (part), 54106–07, 54110 (part), 54111–15, 54119, 54120 (part), 54123–24, 54125–26 (part), 54127–30, 54135–41, 54143, 54149–50, 54151 (part), 54153–57, 54159–62, 54165–66, 54169–71, 54173–74, 54175 (part), 54177, 54180, 54201–02, 54204–05, 54208 (part), 54209–13, 54216–17, 54229, 54234–35, 54246, 54301–04, 54307, 54311, 54313, 54408–09 (part), 54414 (part), 54416, 54427 (part), 54450, 54486, 54491 (part), 54499 (part), 54904 (part), 54911, 54913, 54914–15 (part), 54922, 54927–29, 54931, 54933, 54940 (part), 54942, 54944, 54945 (part), 54946, 54947 (part), 54948–50, 54952 (part), 54956 (part), 54961–62, 54963 (part), 54965 (part), 54977 (part), 54981 (part), 54983 (part), 54986 (part)

WYOMING

(Population 2010, 563,626)

SENATORS

MICHAEL B. ENZI, Republican, of Gillette, WY; born in Bremerton, WA, February 1, 1944; education: B.A., accounting, George Washington University, 1966; M.B.A., Denver University, 1968; professional: served in Wyoming National Guard, 1967–73; accounting manager and computer programmer, Dunbar Well Service, 1985–97; director, Black Hills Corporation, a New York Stock Exchange company, 1992–96; member, founding board of directors, First Wyoming Bank of Gillette, 1978–88; owner, with wife, of NZ Shoes; served in Wyoming House of Representatives, 1987–91, and in Wyoming State Senate, 1991–96; Mayor of Gillette, 1975–82; commissioner, Western Interstate Commission for Higher Education, 1995–96; served on the Education Commission of the States, 1989–93; president, Wyoming Association of Municipalities, 1980–82; president, Wyoming Jaycees, 1973–74; member: Lions Club; Eagle Scout; elder, Presbyterian Church; married: Diana Buckley, 1969; children: Amy, Brad, and Emily; committees: chair, Budget; Finance; Health, Education, Labor, and Pensions; Homeland Security and Governmental Affairs; Joint Committee on Taxation; elected to the U.S. Senate in November, 1996; reelected to each succeeding Senate term.

Office Listings

https://enzi.senate.gov https://facebook.com/mikeenzi https://twitter.com/senatorenzi

379–A Russell Senate Office Building, Washington, DC 20510 .... (202) 224–3424
Chief of Staff.—Coy Knobel. FAX: 228–0359
Legislative Director.—Doug Dziak.
Press Secretary.—Rachel Vliem.
Office Manager.—Christen Thompson.
Federal Center, Suite 2007, 2120 Capitol Avenue, Cheyenne, WY 82001 .... (307) 772–2477
222 South Gillette Avenue, Suite 503, Gillette, WY 82716 .... (307) 682–6268
100 East B Street, Room 3201, P.O. Box 33201, Casper, WY 82602 .... (307) 261–6572
1110 Maple Way, Suite G, P.O. Box 12470, Jackson, WY 83002 .... (307) 739–9507
1285 Sheridan Avenue, Suite 210, Cody, WY 82414 .... (307) 527–9444

* * *

JOHN BARRASSO, Republican, of Casper, WY; born in Reading, PA, July 21, 1952; education: B.S., Georgetown University, Washington, DC, 1974; M.D., Georgetown University, Washington, DC, 1978; professional: Casper Orthopaedic Associates, 1983–2007; chief of staff, Wyoming Medical Center, 2003–05; president, Wyoming Medical Society; president, National Association of Physician Broadcasters, 1988–89; member, Wyoming State Senate, 2002–06; wife: Bobbi; children: Peter, Emma, and Hadley; chair, Senate Republican Conference; committees: chair, Environment and Public Works; Energy and Natural Resources; Foreign Relations; Indian Affairs; appointed to the U.S. Senate on June 22, 2007; sworn in by Vice President Cheney on June 25, 2007 to the 110th Congress to fill the vacancy caused by the death of Senator Craig Thomas; elected to the U.S. Senate on November 4, 2008; reelected to each succeeding Senate term.

Office Listings

https://barrasso.senate.gov https://facebook.com/johnbarrasso
https://twitter.com/senjohnbarrasso https://instagram.com/senjohnbarrasso

307 Dirksen Senate Office Building, Washington, DC 20510 .... (202) 224–6441
Chief of Staff.—Dan Kunsman. FAX: 224–1724
Legislative Director.—Bryn Stewart.
Communications Director.—Bronwyn Lance.
Office Manager.—Amber Moyerman.
100 East B Street, Suite 2004, Casper, WY 82602 .... (307) 261–6413
FAX: 265–6706
2120 Capitol Avenue, Suite 2013, Cheyenne, WY 82001 .... (307) 772–2451
FAX: 638–3512
324 East Washington Avenue, Riverton, WY 82501 .... (307) 856–6642
FAX: 856–5901
1575 Dewar Drive, Suite 218, Rock Springs, WY 82901 .... (307) 362–5012
FAX: 362–5129
51 Coffeen Avenue, Suite 202, Sheridan, WY 82801 .... (307) 672–6456
FAX: 672–8227

REPRESENTATIVE

AT LARGE

LIZ CHENEY, Republican, of Wilson, WY; born in Madison, WI, July 28, 1966; education: B.A., Colorado College, 1988; J.D., University of Chicago Law School, 1996; religion: Methodist; married: Philip Perry; children: five; chair, House Republican Conference; Whip team; caucuses: Congressional Air Force Caucus; Congressional Army Caucus; Congressional Coal Caucus; Congressional Navy and Marine Corps Caucus; Congressional Western Caucus; Republican Study Committee; committees: Armed Services; Natural Resources; elected to the 115th Congress on November 8, 2016; reelected to the 116th Congress on November 6, 2018.

Office Listings

https://cheney.house.gov https://facebook.com/replizcheney https://twitter.com/RepLizCheney

416 Cannon House Office Building, Washington, DC 20515 .... (202) 225–2311
Chief of Staff.—Kara Ahern. FAX: 225–3057
Deputy Chief of Staff/Legislative Director.—Scott Hughes.
Press Secretary.—Ali Pardo.
Scheduler.—Elizabeth Pearce.
100 East B Street, Suite 4003, Casper, WY 82602 .... (307) 261–6595
FAX: 261–6597
2120 Capitol Avenue, Suite 8005, Cheyenne, WY 82001 .... (307) 772–2595
FAX: 772–2597
325 West Main Street, Unit B, Riverton, WY 82501 .... (307) 463–0482
300 South Gillette Avenue, Suite 2001, Gillette, WY 82716 .... (307) 414–1677
FAX: 414–1711

Population (2010), 563,626.

ZIP Codes: 82001, 82003, 82005–10, 82050–55, 82058–61, 82063, 82070–73, 82081–84, 82190, 82201, 82210, 82212–15, 82217–19, 82221–25, 82227, 82229, 82240, 82242–44, 82301, 82310, 82321–25, 82327, 82329, 82331–32, 82334–36, 82401, 82410–12, 82414, 82420–23, 82426, 82428, 82430–35, 82440–43, 82450, 82501, 82510, 82512–16, 82520, 82523–24, 82601–02, 82604–05, 82609, 82615, 82620, 82630, 82633, 82635–40, 82642–44, 82646, 82648–49, 82701, 82710–12, 82714–18, 82720–21, 82723, 82725, 82727, 82729–32, 82801, 82831–40, 82842, 82844–45, 82901–02, 82922–23, 82925, 82929–39, 82941–45, 83001–02, 83011–14, 83025, 83101, 83110–16, 83118–24, 83126–28

AMERICAN SAMOA

(Population 2010, 67,380)

DELEGATE

AUMUA AMATA COLEMAN RADEWAGEN, Republican, of Pago Pago, AS; born in Washington, DC, December 29, 1947; holds the orator (talking chief) title of Aumua from the village of Pago Pago, AS; education: graduate of Sacred Hearts High School in Hawaii; B.A. from University of Guam; professional: executive assistant to the first Delegate-at-Large to Washington from American Samoa; scheduling director for U.S. House of Representatives Majority Leadership for 8 years; scheduling director for U.S. Representative Philip Crane of Illinois; appointed by President George W. Bush in 2001 as a White House Commissioner for Asian Americans and Pacific Islanders (AAPI), chairman of the Community Security Committee; member: American Council of Young Political Leaders, 1986; ACYPL Alumni Council in 1987; Business and Professional Women and board member of Goodwill Industries; Field House 100 American Samoa, a non-profit organization devoted to finding athletic scholarships for high school athletes in American Samoa; spokesperson for the Samoan Women's Health Project; liaison to the National Breast Cancer Coalition since 1993; married: Fred Radewagen; three children and two grandchildren; committees: Natural Resources; Small Business; Veterans' Affairs; elected to the 114th Congress on November 4, 2014; reelected to each succeeding Congress.

Office Listings

https://radewagen.house.gov https://facebook.com/aumuaamata https://twitter.com/repamata

1339 Longworth House Office Building, Washington, DC 20515 .... (202) 225–8577
Chief of Staff.—Leafaina O. Yahn. FAX: 225–8757
Scheduler/Office Manager.—Nancy Dehlinger.
Legislative Director.—Richard Stanton.
P.O. Box 5859, Pago Pago, AS 96799 .... (684) 633–3601

ZIP Codes: 96799

* * *

DISTRICT OF COLUMBIA

(Population 2010, 601,723)

DELEGATE

ELEANOR HOLMES NORTON, Democrat, of Washington, DC; born in Washington, DC, June 13, 1937; education: graduated, Dunbar High School, 1955; B.A., Antioch College, 1960; M.A., Yale Graduate School, 1963; J.D., Yale Law School, 1964; honorary degrees: Cedar Crest College, 1969; Bard College, 1971; Princeton University, 1973; Marymount College, 1974; City College of New York, 1975; Georgetown University, 1977; New York University, 1978; Howard University, 1978; Brown University, 1978; Wilberforce University, 1978; Wayne State University, 1980; Gallaudet College, 1980; Denison University, 1980; Syracuse University, 1981; Yeshiva University, 1981; Lawrence University, 1981; Emanuel College, 1981; Spelman College, 1982; University of Massachusetts, 1983; Smith College, 1983; Medical College of Pennsylvania, 1983; Tufts University, 1984; Bowdoin College, 1985; Antioch College, 1985; Haverford College, 1986; Lesley College, 1986; New Haven University, 1986; University of San Diego, 1986; Sojourner-Douglas College, 1987; Salem State College, 1987; Rutgers University, 1988; St. Joseph's College, 1988; University of Lowell, 1988; Colgate University, 1989; Drury College, 1989; Florida International University, 1989; St. Lawrence University, 1989; University of Wisconsin, 1989; University of Hartford, 1990; Ohio Wesleyan University, 1990; Wake Forest University, 1990; Fisk University, 1991; Tougalvo University, 1992; University of Southern Connecticut, 1992; professional: professor of law, Georgetown University, 1982–90; past/present member: chair, New York Commission on Human Rights, 1970–2017; chair, Equal Employment Opportunity Commission, 1977–81; board, Community Foundation of Greater Washington; Yale Corporation, 1982–88; trustee, Rockefeller Foundation, 1982–90; Executive Assistant to the Mayor of New York City (concurrent appointment); law clerk, Judge A. Leon Higginbotham, Federal District Court, 3rd Circuit; attorney, admitted to practice by examination in the District of Columbia, Pennsylvania, and in the U.S. Supreme Court; Council on

Foreign Relations; Overseas Development Council; honors and awards: Harper Fellow, Yale Law School, 1976, (for ''a person . . . who has made a distinguished contribution to the public life of the nation . . .''); Yale Law School Association Citation of Merit Medal to the Outstanding Alumnus of the Law School, 1980; visiting fellow, Harvard University, John F. Kennedy School of Government, spring 1984; Ralph E. Shikes Bicentennial Fellow, Harvard Law School, 1987; One Hundred Most Important Women (*Ladies Home Journal*, 1988); One Hundred Most Powerful Women in Washington (*Washingtonian* magazine, September 1989); divorced; two children: John and Katherine; committees: Oversight and Reform; Transportation and Infrastructure; elected to the 102nd Congress on November 6, 1990; reelected to each succeeding Congress.

Office Listings

https://norton.house.gov https://facebook.com/CongresswomanNorton
https://twitter.com/eleanornorton

2136 Rayburn House Office Building, Washington, DC 20515 .... (202) 225–8050
Chief of Staff.—Raven Reeder. FAX: 225–3002
Legislative Director.—Bradley Truding.
Communications Director.—Jack Miller.

ZIP Codes: 20001–13, 20015–20, 20024, 20026–27, 20029–30, 20032–33, 20035–45, 20047, 20049–53, 20055–71, 20073–77, 20080, 20088, 20090–91, 20099, 20201–04, 20206–08, 20210–13, 20215–24, 20226–33, 20235, 20237, 20239–42, 20244–45, 20250, 20254, 20260, 20268, 20270, 20277, 20289, 20301, 20303, 20306–07, 20310, 20314–15, 20317–19, 20330, 20340, 20350, 20370, 20372–76, 20380, 20388–95, 20398, 20401–16, 20418–29, 20431, 20433–37, 20439–42, 20444, 20447, 20451, 20453, 20456, 20460, 20463, 20469, 20472, 20500, 20503–10, 20515, 20520–27, 20530–36, 20538–44, 20546–49, 20551–55, 20557, 20559–60, 20565–66, 20570–73, 20575–77, 20579–81, 20585–86, 20590–91, 20593–94, 20597, 20599

* * *

GUAM

(Population 2010, 159,358)

DELEGATE

MICHAEL SAN NICOLAS, Democrat, of Dededo, Guam; born on January 30, 1981 in Talofofo, Guam; education: B.A., University of Guam, Mangilao, Guam, 2004; professional: former high school teacher and financial adviser; Senator, Guam Legislature, 2013–18; committees: Financial Services; Natural Resources; elected to the 116th Congress on November 6, 2018.

Office Listings

https://sannicolas.house.gov https://facebook.com/CongressmanMichaelF.Q.SanNicolas

1632 Longworth House Office Building, Washington, DC 20515 .... (202) 225–1188
District Deputy Chief of Staff.—Jennifer S. Winn.
Scheduler.—T'Nelta Mori.
330 Hernan Cortez Avenue, Suite 300, Hagåtña, GU 96910 .... (671) 475–6453

ZIP Codes: 96910, 96912–13, 96915–17, 96919, 96921, 96923, 96926, 96928–29, 96931–32

* * *

NORTHERN MARIANA ISLANDS

(Population 2010, 53,883)

DELEGATE

GREGORIO KILILI CAMACHO SABLAN, Democrat, of Saipan, MP; born in Saipan, January 19, 1955; education: University of Hawaii, Manoa Honolulu, HI; 1989–90; professional: member, Northern Mariana Islands Commonwealth Legislature, 1982–86 (two terms); special assistant to Senator Daniel Inouye; special assistant for OMB to Northern Mariana Islands Governor Froilan C. Tenorio; special assistant to Northern Mariana Islands Governor Pedro P.

Tenorio; executive director of the Commonwealth Election Commission; family: married to Andrea C. Sablan; son: Jesse; daughters: Sharlene, Barbara Jean, Diane, Patricia, and Madonna; caucuses: American Citizens Abroad Caucus; Bipartisan Disabilities Caucus; Community College Caucus; Congressional Asian Pacific American Caucus; Congressional Hispanic Caucus; Democratic Caucus; Friends of New Zealand Caucus; International Conservation Caucus; National Marine Sanctuary Caucus; committees: Education and Labor; Natural Resources; Veterans' Affairs; elected to the 111th Congress on November 4, 2008; reelected to each succeeding Congress.

Office Listings

https://sablan.house.gov https://facebook.com/congressmansablan
https://twitter.com/Kilili_Sablan https://instagram.com/kilili_sablan

2411 Rayburn House Office Building, Washington, DC 20515 .... (202) 225–2646
Chief of Staff.—Robert J. Schwalbach. FAX: 226–4249
Scheduler.—John R.P. Del Rosario.
JCT II Building, Susupe, P.O. Box 504879, Saipan, MP 96950 .... (670) 323–2647
Dolores Plaza Building, Songsong, P.O. Box 1361, Rota, MP 96951 .... (670) 532–2647
Villagomez Ent. Building, San Jose, P.O. Box 520394, Tinian, MP 96952 .... (670) 433–2647
District Office Director.—Mike Tenorio. FAX: 323–2649

ZIP Codes: 96950–52

* * *

PUERTO RICO

(Population 2010, 3,725,789)

RESIDENT COMMISSIONER

JENNIFFER GONZÁLEZ-COLÓN, Republican, of San Juan, PR; born in San Juan, August 5, 1976; education: B.A., political science, University of Puerto Rico, Rio Piedras, PR, 2001; J.D., Inter-American University of Puerto Rico, San Juan, PR, 2010; LL.M., Inter-American University of Puerto Rico, San Juan, PR, 2014; professional: member of the Puerto Rico House of Representatives, 2002–16; Speaker of the Puerto Rico House of Representatives, 2009–12; Minority Leader of the Puerto Rico House of Representatives, 2013–16; vice president of the PNP of Puerto Rico, 2008–present; chair of the Puerto Rico Republican Party, 2015–present; religion: Catholic; committees: Natural Resources; Transportation and Infrastructure; elected on November 8, 2016, to serve a four-year term in the 115th and 116th Congresses.

Office Listings

https://gonzalez-colon.house.gov https://facebook.com/RepJenniffer https://twitter.com/RepJenniffer
https://instagram.com/RepJenniffer https://youtube.com/channel/UCZj99h3-GNKjGGeyp7AJeXw

1609 Longworth House Office Building, Washington, DC 20515 .... (202) 225–2615
Chief of Staff.—Gabriella Boffelli. FAX: 225–2154
Deputy Chief of Staff and Legal Counsel.—Veronica Ferraiuoli.
Communications Director.—Marieli Padró-Raldiris.
Scheduler / DC Press Secretary.—Natasha Marquez.
Legislative Director.—Ross Dietrich.
Senior Policy Advisor.—José Díaz Marrero.
Legislative Assistants: Gabriel Bravo, Natalia Gandía.
Legislative Aide.—Jeronimo Naranjo.
Press Assistant.—Linoshka Luna.
157 Avenida de la Constitución Antiguo Edificio de Medicina Tropical, Ala de la Enfermería 2ndo Piso, San Juan, PR 00901 .... (787) 723–6333
District Office Director.—Narel Colón-Torres. FAX: 729–7738
Deputy District Director and District Scheduler.—Ciary Perez-Pena.
Office Manager.—Allison Rodriguez-Arroyo.
Immigration Caseworker.—John Olivari-Cruz.
Caseworker.—Camilie Rivera-Dueño.
Veterans' Caseworker.—Norma Miranda.
Receptionist.—Francisco Laureano-Miranda.

ZIP Codes: 00601–06, 00610–14, 00616–17, 00622–24, 00627, 00631, 00636–38, 00641, 00646–47, 00650, 00652–53, 00656, 00659–60, 00662, 00664, 00667, 00669–70, 00674, 00676–78, 00680–83, 00685, 00687–88, 00690, 00692–94, 00698, 00703–05, 00707, 00714–21, 00723, 00725–42, 00744–45, 00751, 00754, 00757, 00765–67, 00769, 00771–

73, 00775, 00777–78, 00780, 00782–86, 00791–92, 00794–95, 00901–02, 00906–31, 00933–37, 00939–40, 00949–63, 00965–66, 00968–71, 00975–79, 00981–88

* * *

VIRGIN ISLANDS

(Population 2010, 106,405)

DELEGATE

STACEY E. PLASKETT, Democrat, of St. Croix, VI; born in New York, NY, May 13, 1966; education: B.S.F.S, Georgetown University, Washington, DC, 1988; J.D., American University School of Law, Washington, DC, 1994; professional: Bronx Assistant District Attorney; counsel on U.S. House of Representatives' Committee on Ethics; Senior Counsel to the Deputy Attorney General at U.S. Department of Justice; Deputy General Counsel at United Health Group; General Counsel, Virgin Islands Economic Development Authority; family: spouse, Jonathan Buckney-Small; children: Jeremiah, Christian, Ariel, Israel Duffy, and Taliah Buckney-Small; caucuses: Congressional Black Caucus; Congressional Caribbean Caucus; Congressional Caucus on Public-Private Partnerships; Congressional Coastal Communities Caucus; Congressional Historically Black Colleges and Universities (HBCU) Caucus; Congressional Liquefied Natural Gas (LNG) Export Caucus; Congressional Women's Caucus; House National Guard and Reserve Components Caucus; committees: Agriculture; Oversight and Reform; Transportation and Infrastructure; elected to the 114th Congress on November 4, 2014; reelected to each succeeding Congress.

Office Listings

https://plaskett.house.gov https://facebook.com/repstaceyplaskett https://twitter.com/staceyplaskett

2404 Rayburn House Office Building, Washington, DC 20515 .... (202) 225–1790
Chief of Staff.—Erik Prince. FAX: 225–5517
Director of Operations.—Lewis H. Meyers III.
District Director.—Cletis Clendinen.
60 King Street, Frederiksted, St. Croix, VI 00840 .... (340) 778–5900
9100 Havensight Port of Sale Mall, St. Thomas, VI 00802 .... (340) 774–4408
Case Worker/Field Representative.—Mae-Louise Williams.

ZIP Codes: 00801–05, 00820–24, 00830–31, 00840–41, 00850–51

STATE DELEGATIONS

Number before names designates Congressional district.

Senate Republicans in roman; Senate Democrats in *italic*; Senate Independents in SMALL CAPS; House Democrats in roman; House Republicans in *italic*; House Libertarians in SMALL CAPS; Resident Commissioner and Delegates in **boldface**.

ALABAMA

SENATORS
Richard C. Shelby
Doug Jones

REPRESENTATIVES
[Democrat 1, Republicans 6]

1. *Bradley Byrne*
2. *Martha Roby*
3. *Mike Rogers*
4. *Robert B. Aderholt*
5. *Mo Brooks*
6. *Gary J. Palmer*
7. Terri A. Sewell

ALASKA

SENATORS
Lisa Murkowski
Dan Sullivan

REPRESENTATIVE
[Republican 1]
At Large - *Don Young*

ARIZONA

SENATORS
Kyrsten Sinema
Martha McSally

REPRESENTATIVES
[Democrats 5, Republicans 4]

1. Tom O'Halleran
2. Ann Kirkpatrick
3. Raúl M. Grijalva
4. *Paul A. Gosar*
5. *Andy Biggs*
6. *David Schweikert*
7. Ruben Gallego
8. *Debbie Lesko*
9. Greg Stanton

ARKANSAS

SENATORS
John Boozman
Tom Cotton

REPRESENTATIVES
[Republicans 4]

1. *Eric A. "Rick" Crawford*
2. *J. French Hill*
3. *Steve Womack*
4. *Bruce Westerman*

CALIFORNIA

SENATORS
Dianne Feinstein
Kamala D. Harris

REPRESENTATIVES
[Democrats 45, Republicans 7, Vacant 1]

1. *Doug LaMalfa*
2. Jared Huffman
3. John Garamendi
4. *Tom McClintock*
5. Mike Thompson
6. Doris O. Matsui
7. Ami Bera

8. *Paul Cook*
9. Jerry McNerney
10. Josh Harder
11. Mark DeSaulnier
12. Nancy Pelosi
13. Barbara Lee
14. Jackie Speier
15. Eric Swalwell
16. Jim Costa
17. Ro Khanna
18. Anna G. Eshoo
19. Zoe Lofgren
20. Jimmy Panetta
21. TJ Cox
22. *Devin Nunes*
23. *Kevin McCarthy*
24. Salud O. Carbajal
25. *Mike Garcia* [1]
26. Julia Brownley
27. Judy Chu
28. Adam B. Schiff
29. Tony Cárdenas
30. Brad Sherman
31. Pete Aguilar
32. Grace F. Napolitano
33. Ted Lieu
34. Jimmy Gomez
35. Norma J. Torres
36. Raul Ruiz
37. Karen Bass
38. Linda T. Sánchez
39. Gilbert Ray Cisneros, Jr.
40. Lucille Roybal-Allard
41. Mark Takano
42. *Ken Calvert*
43. Maxine Waters
44. Nanette Diaz Barragán
45. Katie Porter
46. J. Luis Correa
47. Alan S. Lowenthal
48. Harley Rouda
49. Mike Levin
50. —— [2]
51. Juan Vargas
52. Scott H. Peters
53. Susan A. Davis

COLORADO

SENATORS
Michael F. Bennet
Cory Gardner

REPRESENTATIVES
[Democrats 4, Republicans 3]

1. Diana DeGette
2. Joe Neguse
3. *Scott R. Tipton*
4. *Ken Buck*
5. *Doug Lamborn*
6. Jason Crow
7. Ed Perlmutter

CONNECTICUT

SENATORS
Richard Blumenthal
Christopher Murphy

REPRESENTATIVES
[Democrats 5]

1. John B. Larson
2. Joe Courtney
3. Rosa L. DeLauro
4. James A. Himes
5. Jahana Hayes

DELAWARE

SENATORS
Thomas R. Carper
Christopher A. Coons

REPRESENTATIVE
[Democrat 1]
At Large – Lisa Blunt Rochester

FLORIDA

SENATORS
Marco Rubio
Rick Scott

REPRESENTATIVES
[Democrats 13, Republicans 14]

1. *Matt Gaetz*
2. *Neal P. Dunn*
3. *Ted S. Yoho*
4. *John H. Rutherford*
5. Al Lawson, Jr.
6. *Michael Waltz*
7. Stephanie N. Murphy
8. *Bill Posey*
9. Darren Soto
10. Val Butler Demings
11. *Daniel Webster*
12. *Gus M. Bilirakis*
13. Charlie Crist
14. Kathy Castor

15. *Ross Spano*
16. *Vern Buchanan*
17. *W. Gregory Steube*
18. *Brian J. Mast*
19. *Francis Rooney*
20. Alcee L. Hastings
21. Lois Frankel
22. Theodore E. Deutch
23. Debbie Wasserman Schultz
24. Frederica S. Wilson
25. *Mario Diaz-Balart*
26. Debbie Mucarsel-Powell
27. Donna E. Shalala

GEORGIA

SENATORS
David Perdue
Kelly Loeffler

REPRESENTATIVES
[Democrats 4, Republicans 9, Vacant 1]

1. *Earl L. ''Buddy'' Carter*
2. Sanford D. Bishop, Jr.
3. *A. Drew Ferguson IV*
4. Henry C. ''Hank'' Johnson, Jr.
5. ——[3]
6. Lucy McBath
7. *Rob Woodall*
8. *Austin Scott*
9. *Doug Collins*
10. *Jody B. Hice*
11. *Barry Loudermilk*
12. *Rick W. Allen*
13. David Scott
14. *Tom Graves*

HAWAII

SENATORS
Brian Schatz
Mazie K. Hirono

REPRESENTATIVES
[Democrats 2]

1. Ed Case
2. Tulsi Gabbard

IDAHO

SENATORS
Mike Crapo
James E. Risch

REPRESENTATIVES
[Republicans 2]

1. *Russ Fulcher*
2. *Michael K. Simpson*

ILLINOIS

SENATORS
Richard J. Durbin
Tammy Duckworth

REPRESENTATIVES
[Democrats 13, Republicans 5]

1. Bobby L. Rush
2. Robin L. Kelly
3. Daniel Lipinski
4. Jesús G. ''Chuy'' García
5. Mike Quigley
6. Sean Casten
7. Danny K. Davis
8. Raja Krishnamoorthi
9. Janice D. Schakowsky
10. Bradley Scott Schneider
11. Bill Foster
12. *Mike Bost*
13. *Rodney Davis*
14. Lauren Underwood
15. *John Shimkus*
16. *Adam Kinzinger*
17. Cheri Bustos
18. *Darin LaHood*

INDIANA

SENATORS
Todd Young
Mike Braun

REPRESENTATIVES
[Democrats 2, Republicans 7]

1. Peter J. Visclosky
2. *Jackie Walorski*
3. *Jim Banks*
4. *James R. Baird*
5. *Susan W. Brooks*
6. *Greg Pence*
7. André Carson
8. *Larry Bucshon*
9. *Trey Hollingsworth*

IOWA

SENATORS
Chuck Grassley
Joni Ernst

REPRESENTATIVES
[Democrats 3, Republican 1]
1. Abby Finkenauer
2. David Loebsack
3. Cynthia Axne
4. *Steve King*

KANSAS

SENATORS
Pat Roberts
Jerry Moran

REPRESENTATIVES
[Democrat 1, Republicans 3]
1. *Roger W. Marshall*
2. *Steve Watkins*
3. Sharice Davids
4. *Ron Estes*

KENTUCKY

SENATORS
Mitch McConnell
Rand Paul

REPRESENTATIVES
[Democrat 1, Republicans 5]
1. *James Comer*
2. *Brett Guthrie*
3. John A. Yarmuth
4. *Thomas Massie*
5. *Harold Rogers*
6. *Andy Barr*

LOUISIANA

SENATORS
Bill Cassidy
John Kennedy

REPRESENTATIVES
[Democrat 1, Republicans 5]
1. *Steve Scalise*
2. Cedric L. Richmond
3. *Clay Higgins*
4. *Mike Johnson*
5. *Ralph Lee Abraham*
6. *Garret Graves*

MAINE

SENATORS
Susan M. Collins
ANGUS S. KING, JR.

REPRESENTATIVES
[Democrats 2]
1. Chellie Pingree
2. Jared F. Golden

MARYLAND

SENATORS
Benjamin L. Cardin
Chris Van Hollen

REPRESENTATIVES
[Democrats 7, Republican 1]
1. *Andy Harris*
2. C. A. Dutch Ruppersberger
3. John P. Sarbanes
4. Anthony G. Brown
5. Steny H. Hoyer
6. David J. Trone
7. Kweisi Mfume [4]
8. Jamie Raskin

MASSACHUSETTS

SENATORS
Elizabeth Warren
Edward J. Markey

REPRESENTATIVES
[Democrats 9]

1. Richard E. Neal
2. James P. McGovern
3. Lori Trahan
4. Joseph P. Kennedy III
5. Katherine M. Clark
6. Seth Moulton
7. Ayanna Pressley
8. Stephen F. Lynch
9. William R. Keating

MICHIGAN

SENATORS
Debbie Stabenow
Gary C. Peters

REPRESENTATIVES
[Democrats 7, Republicans 6, Libertarian 1]

1. *Jack Bergman*
2. *Bill Huizenga*
3. JUSTIN AMASH
4. *John R. Moolenaar*
5. Daniel T. Kildee
6. *Fred Upton*
7. *Tim Walberg*
8. Elissa Slotkin
9. Andy Levin
10. *Paul Mitchell*
11. Haley M. Stevens
12. Debbie Dingell
13. Rashida Tlaib
14. Brenda L. Lawrence

MINNESOTA

SENATORS
Amy Klobuchar
Tina Smith

REPRESENTATIVES
[Democrats 5, Republicans 3]

1. *Jim Hagedorn*
2. Angie Craig
3. Dean Phillips
4. Betty McCollum
5. Ilhan Omar
6. *Tom Emmer*
7. Collin C. Peterson
8. *Pete Stauber*

MISSISSIPPI

SENATORS
Roger F. Wicker
Cindy Hyde-Smith

REPRESENTATIVES
[Democrat 1, Republicans 3]

1. *Trent Kelly*
2. Bennie G. Thompson
3. *Michael Guest*
4. *Steven M. Palazzo*

MISSOURI

SENATORS
Roy Blunt
Josh Hawley

REPRESENTATIVES
[Democrats 2, Republicans 6]

1. Wm. Lacy Clay
2. *Ann Wagner*
3. *Blaine Luetkemeyer*
4. *Vicky Hartzler*
5. Emanuel Cleaver
6. *Sam Graves*
7. *Billy Long*
8. *Jason Smith*

MONTANA

SENATORS
Jon Tester
Steve Daines

REPRESENTATIVE
[Republican 1]

At Large – *Greg Gianforte*

NEBRASKA

SENATORS
Deb Fischer
Ben Sasse

REPRESENTATIVES
[Republicans 3]
1. *Jeff Fortenberry*
2. *Don Bacon*
3. *Adrian Smith*

NEVADA

SENATORS
Catherine Cortez Masto
Jacky Rosen

REPRESENTATIVES
[Democrats 3, Republican 1]
1. Dina Titus
2. *Mark E. Amodei*
3. Susie Lee
4. Steven Horsford

NEW HAMPSHIRE

SENATORS
Jeanne Shaheen
Margaret Wood Hassan

REPRESENTATIVES
[Democrats 2]
1. Chris Pappas
2. Ann M. Kuster

NEW JERSEY

SENATORS
Robert Menendez
Cory A. Booker

REPRESENTATIVES
[Democrats 10, Republicans 2]
1. Donald Norcross
2. *Jefferson Van Drew*
3. Andy Kim
4. *Christopher H. Smith*
5. Josh Gottheimer
6. Frank Pallone, Jr.
7. Tom Malinowski
8. Albio Sires
9. Bill Pascrell, Jr.
10. Donald M. Payne, Jr.
11. Mikie Sherrill
12. Bonnie Watson Coleman

NEW MEXICO

SENATORS
Tom Udall
Martin Heinrich

REPRESENTATIVES
[Democrats 3]
1. Debra A. Haaland
2. Xochitl Torres Small
3. Ben Ray Luján

NEW YORK

SENATORS
Charles E. Schumer
Kirsten E. Gillibrand

REPRESENTATIVES
[Democrats 21, Republicans 6]
1. *Lee M. Zeldin*
2. *Peter T. King*
3. Thomas R. Suozzi
4. Kathleen M. Rice
5. Gregory W. Meeks
6. Grace Meng
7. Nydia M. Velázquez
8. Hakeem S. Jeffries
9. Yvette D. Clarke
10. Jerrold Nadler

11. Max Rose
12. Carolyn B. Maloney
13. Adriano Espaillat
14. Alexandria Ocasio-Cortez
15. José E. Serrano
16. Eliot L. Engel
17. Nita M. Lowey
18. Sean Patrick Maloney
19. Antonio Delgado
20. Paul Tonko
21. *Elise M. Stefanik*
22. Anthony Brindisi
23. *Tom Reed*
24. *John Katko*
25. Joseph D. Morelle
26. Brian Higgins
27. *Chris Jacobs*[5]

NORTH CAROLINA

SENATORS
Richard Burr
Thom Tillis

REPRESENTATIVES
[Democrats 3, Republicans 9, Vacant 1]

1. G. K. Butterfield
2. *George Holding*
3. *Gregory F. Murphy*[6]
4. David E. Price
5. *Virginia Foxx*
6. *Mark Walker*
7. *David Rouzer*
8. *Richard Hudson*
9. *Dan Bishop*[7]
10. *Patrick T. McHenry*
11. ——[8]
12. Alma S. Adams
13. *Ted Budd*

NORTH DAKOTA

SENATORS
John Hoeven
Kevin Cramer

REPRESENTATIVE
[Republican 1]

At Large – *Kelly Armstrong*

OHIO

SENATORS
Sherrod Brown
Rob Portman

REPRESENTATIVES
[Democrats 4, Republicans 12]

1. *Steve Chabot*
2. *Brad R. Wenstrup*
3. Joyce Beatty
4. *Jim Jordan*
5. *Robert E. Latta*
6. *Bill Johnson*
7. *Bob Gibbs*
8. *Warren Davidson*
9. Marcy Kaptur
10. *Michael R. Turner*
11. Marcia L. Fudge
12. *Troy Balderson*
13. Tim Ryan
14. *David P. Joyce*
15. *Steve Stivers*
16. *Anthony Gonzalez*

OKLAHOMA

SENATORS
James M. Inhofe
James Lankford

REPRESENTATIVES
[Democrat 1, Republicans 4]

1. *Kevin Hern*
2. *Markwayne Mullin*
3. *Frank D. Lucas*
4. *Tom Cole*
5. Kendra S. Horn

OREGON

SENATORS
Ron Wyden
Jeff Merkley

REPRESENTATIVES
[Democrats 4, Republican 1]

1. Suzanne Bonamici

2. *Greg Walden*
3. Earl Blumenauer
4. Peter A. DeFazio
5. Kurt Schrader

PENNSYLVANIA

SENATORS
Robert P. Casey, Jr.
Patrick J. Toomey

REPRESENTATIVES
[Democrats 9, Republicans 9]

1. *Brian K. Fitzpatrick*
2. Brendan F. Boyle
3. Dwight Evans
4. Madeleine Dean
5. Mary Gay Scanlon
6. Chrissy Houlahan
7. Susan Wild
8. Matt Cartwright
9. *Daniel Meuser*
10. *Scott Perry*
11. *Lloyd Smucker*
12. *Fred Keller*[9]
13. *John Joyce*
14. *Guy Reschenthaler*
15. *Glenn Thompson*
16. *Mike Kelly*
17. Conor Lamb
18. Michael F. Doyle

RHODE ISLAND

SENATORS
Jack Reed
Sheldon Whitehouse

REPRESENTATIVES
[Democrats 2]

1. David N. Cicilline
2. James R. Langevin

SOUTH CAROLINA

SENATORS
Lindsey Graham
Tim Scott

REPRESENTATIVES
[Democrats 2, Republicans 5]

1. Joe Cunningham
2. *Joe Wilson*
3. *Jeff Duncan*
4. *William R. Timmons IV*
5. *Ralph Norman*
6. James E. Clyburn
7. *Tom Rice*

SOUTH DAKOTA

SENATORS
John Thune
Mike Rounds

REPRESENTATIVE
[Republican 1]

At Large – *Dusty Johnson*

TENNESSEE

SENATORS
Lamar Alexander
Marsha Blackburn

REPRESENTATIVES
[Democrats 2, Republicans 7]

1. *David P. Roe*
2. *Tim Burchett*
3. *Charles J. ''Chuck'' Fleischmann*
4. *Scott DesJarlais*
5. Jim Cooper
6. *John W. Rose*
7. *Mark E. Green*
8. *David Kustoff*
9. Steve Cohen

TEXAS

SENATORS
John Cornyn
Ted Cruz

REPRESENTATIVES
[Democrats 13, Republicans 22, Vacant 1]

1. *Louie Gohmert*
2. *Dan Crenshaw*
3. *Van Taylor*
4. ——[10]
5. *Lance Gooden*
6. *Ron Wright*
7. Lizzie Fletcher
8. *Kevin Brady*
9. Al Green
10. *Michael T. McCaul*
11. *K. Michael Conaway*
12. *Kay Granger*
13. *Mac Thornberry*
14. *Randy K. Weber, Sr.*
15. Vicente Gonzalez
16. Veronica Escobar
17. *Bill Flores*
18. Sheila Jackson Lee
19. *Jodey C. Arrington*
20. Joaquin Castro
21. *Chip Roy*
22. *Pete Olson*
23. *Will Hurd*
24. *Kenny Marchant*
25. *Roger Williams*
26. *Michael C. Burgess*
27. *Michael Cloud*
28. Henry Cuellar
29. Sylvia R. Garcia
30. Eddie Bernice Johnson
31. *John R. Carter*
32. Colin Z. Allred
33. Marc A. Veasey
34. Filemon Vela
35. Lloyd Doggett
36. *Brian Babin*

UTAH

SENATORS
Mike Lee
Mitt Romney

REPRESENTATIVES
[Democrat 1, Republicans 3]

1. *Rob Bishop*
2. *Chris Stewart*
3. *John R. Curtis*
4. Ben McAdams

VERMONT

SENATORS
Patrick J. Leahy
BERNARD SANDERS

REPRESENTATIVE
[Democrat 1]

At Large – Peter Welch

VIRGINIA

SENATORS
Mark R. Warner
Tim Kaine

REPRESENTATIVES
[Democrats 7, Republicans 4]

1. *Robert J. Wittman*
2. Elaine G. Luria
3. Robert C. "Bobby" Scott
4. A. Donald McEachin
5. *Denver Riggleman*
6. *Ben Cline*
7. Abigail Davis Spanberger
8. Donald S. Beyer, Jr.
9. *H. Morgan Griffith*
10. Jennifer Wexton
11. Gerald E. Connolly

WASHINGTON

SENATORS
Patty Murray
Maria Cantwell

REPRESENTATIVES
[Democrats 7, Republicans 3]

1. Suzan K. DelBene
2. Rick Larsen
3. *Jaime Herrera Beutler*
4. *Dan Newhouse*
5. *Cathy McMorris Rodgers*
6. Derek Kilmer
7. Pramila Jayapal
8. Kim Schrier
9. Adam Smith
10. Denny Heck

WEST VIRGINIA

SENATORS
Joe Manchin III
Shelley Moore Capito

REPRESENTATIVES
[Republicans 3]

1. *David B. McKinley*
2. *Alexander X. Mooney*
3. *Carol D. Miller*

WISCONSIN

SENATORS
Ron Johnson
Tammy Baldwin

REPRESENTATIVES
[Democrats 3, Republicans 5]

1. *Bryan Steil*
2. Mark Pocan
3. Ron Kind
4. Gwen Moore
5. *F. James Sensenbrenner, Jr.*
6. *Glenn Grothman*
7. *Thomas P. Tiffany* [11]
8. *Mike Gallagher*

WYOMING

SENATORS
Michael B. Enzi
John Barrasso

REPRESENTATIVE
[Republican 1]
At Large – *Liz Cheney*

AMERICAN SAMOA

DELEGATE
[Republican 1]
Aumua Amata Coleman Radewagen

DISTRICT OF COLUMBIA

DELEGATE
[Democrat 1]
Eleanor Holmes Norton

GUAM

DELEGATE
[Democrat 1]
Michael F. Q. San Nicolas

NORTHERN MARIANA ISLANDS

DELEGATE
[Democrat 1]
Gregorio Kilili Camacho Sablan

PUERTO RICO

RESIDENT COMMISSIONER
[Republican 1]
Jenniffer González-Colón

VIRGIN ISLANDS

DELEGATE
[Democrat 1]
Stacey E. Plaskett

[1] Elected May 12, 2020, to fill the vacancy due to the resignation of Katie Hill, November 3, 2019.
[2] Vacancy due to the resignation of Duncan Hunter, January 13, 2020.
[3] Vacancy due to the death of John Lewis on July 17, 2020.
[4] Elected April 28, 2020, to fill the vacancy due to the death of Elijah E. Cummings, October 17, 2019.
[5] Elected June 23, 2020, to fill the vacancy due to the resignation of Chris Collins, September 30, 2019.
[6] Elected September 10, 2019, to fill the vacancy due to the death of Walter B. Jones, February 10, 2019.
[7] Elected September 10, 2019, in a new election ordered by the North Carolina State Board of Elections on February 21, 2019.
[8] Vacancy due to the resignation of Mark Meadows, March 30, 2020.
[9] Elected May 21, 2019, to fill the vacancy due to the resignation of Tom Marino, January 23, 2019.
[10] Vacancy due to the resignation of John Ratcliffe, May 22, 2020.
[11] Elected May 12, 2020, to fill the vacancy due to the resignation of Sean P. Duffy, September 23, 2019.

ALPHABETICAL LIST

SENATORS

Alphabetical list of Senators, Representatives, Delegates, and Resident Commissioner. Republicans in roman (53); Democrats in *italic* (45); Independents in SMALL CAPS (2).

Alexander, Lamar, TN
Baldwin, Tammy, WI
Barrasso, John, WY
Bennet, Michael F., CO
Blackburn, Marsha, TN
Blumenthal, Richard, CT
Blunt, Roy, MO
Booker, Cory A., NJ
Boozman, John, AR
Braun, Mike, IN
Brown, Sherrod, OH
Burr, Richard, NC
Cantwell, Maria, WA
Capito, Shelley Moore, WV
Cardin, Benjamin L., MD
Carper, Thomas R., DE
Casey, Robert P., Jr., PA
Cassidy, Bill, LA
Collins, Susan M., ME
Coons, Christopher A., DE
Cornyn, John, TX
Cortez Masto, Catherine, NV
Cotton, Tom, AR
Cramer, Kevin, ND
Crapo, Mike, ID
Cruz, Ted, TX
Daines, Steve, MT
Duckworth, Tammy, IL
Durbin, Richard J., IL
Enzi, Michael B., WY
Ernst, Joni, IA
Feinstein, Dianne, CA
Fischer, Deb, NE
Gardner, Cory, CO
Gillibrand, Kirsten E., NY
Graham, Lindsey, SC
Grassley, Chuck, IA
Harris, Kamala D., CA
Hassan, Margaret Wood, NH
Hawley, Josh, MO
Heinrich, Martin, NM
Hirono, Mazie K., HI
Hoeven, John, ND
Hyde-Smith, Cindy, MS
Inhofe, James M., OK
Johnson, Ron, WI
Jones, Doug, AL
Kaine, Tim, VA
Kennedy, John, LA
KING, ANGUS S., JR., ME
Klobuchar, Amy, MN
Lankford, James, OK
Leahy, Patrick J., VT
Lee, Mike, UT
Loeffler, Kelly, GA
Manchin, Joe, III, WV
Markey, Edward J., MA
McConnell, Mitch, KY
McSally, Martha, AZ
Menendez, Robert, NJ
Merkley, Jeff, OR
Moran, Jerry, KS
Murkowski, Lisa, AK
Murphy, Christopher, CT
Murray, Patty, WA
Paul, Rand, KY
Perdue, David, GA
Peters, Gary C., MI
Portman, Rob, OH
Reed, Jack, RI
Risch, James E., ID
Roberts, Pat, KS
Romney, Mitt, UT
Rosen, Jacky, NV
Rounds, Mike, SD
Rubio, Marco, FL
SANDERS, BERNARD, VT
Sasse, Ben, NE
Schatz, Brian, HI
Schumer, Charles E., NY
Scott, Rick, FL
Scott, Tim, SC
Shaheen, Jeanne, NH
Shelby, Richard C., AL
Sinema, Kyrsten, AZ
Smith, Tina, MN
Stabenow, Debbie, MI
Sullivan, Dan, AK
Tester, Jon, MT
Thune, John, SD
Tillis, Thom, NC
Toomey, Patrick J., PA
Udall, Tom, NM
Van Hollen, Chris, MD
Warner, Mark R., VA
Warren, Elizabeth, MA
Whitehouse, Sheldon, RI
Wicker, Roger F., MS
Wyden, Ron, OR
Young, Todd, IN

REPRESENTATIVES, RESIDENT COMMISSIONER, AND DELEGATES

Democrats in roman (232); Republicans in *italic* (198); Libertarians in SMALL CAPS (1); Vacancies (4); Resident Commissioner and Delegates in **boldface** (6); total, 441.

Abraham, Ralph Lee, LA (5th)
Adams, Alma S., NC (12th)
Aderholt, Robert B., AL (4th)
Aguilar, Pete, CA (31st)
Allen, Rick W., GA (12th)
Allred, Colin Z., TX (32d)
AMASH, JUSTIN, MI (3d)
Amodei, Mark E., NV (2d)
Armstrong, Kelly, ND (At Large)
Arrington, Jodey C., TX (19th)
Axne, Cynthia, IA (3d)
Babin, Brian, TX (36th)
Bacon, Don, NE (2d)
Baird, James R., IN (4th)
Balderson, Troy, OH (12th)
Banks, Jim, IN (3d)
Barr, Andy, KY (6th)
Barragán, Nanette Diaz, CA (44th)
Bass, Karen, CA (37th)
Beatty, Joyce, OH (3d)
Bera, Ami, CA (7th)
Bergman, Jack, MI (1st)
Beyer, Donald S., Jr., VA (8th)
Biggs, Andy, AZ (5th)
Bilirakis, Gus M., FL (12th)
Bishop, Dan, NC (9th)
Bishop, Rob, UT (1st)
Bishop, Sanford D., Jr., GA (2d)
Blumenauer, Earl, OR (3d)
Blunt Rochester, Lisa, DE (At Large)
Bonamici, Suzanne, OR (1st)
Bost, Mike, IL (12th)
Boyle, Brendan F., PA (2d)
Brady, Kevin, TX (8th)
Brindisi, Anthony, NY (22d)
Brooks, Mo, AL (5th)
Brooks, Susan W., IN (5th)
Brown, Anthony G., MD (4th)
Brownley, Julia, CA (26th)
Buchanan, Vern, FL (16th)
Buck, Ken, CO (4th)
Bucshon, Larry, IN (8th)
Budd, Ted, NC (13th)
Burchett, Tim, TN (2d)
Burgess, Michael C., TX (26th)
Bustos, Cheri, IL (17th)
Butterfield, G. K., NC (1st)
Byrne, Bradley, AL (1st)
Calvert, Ken, CA (42d)
Carbajal, Salud O., CA (24th)
Cárdenas, Tony, CA (29th)
Carson, André, IN (7th)
Carter, Earl L. ''Buddy'', GA (1st)
Carter, John R., TX (31st)
Cartwright, Matt, PA (8th)
Case, Ed, HI (1st)
Casten, Sean, IL (6th)
Castor, Kathy, FL (14th)
Castro, Joaquin, TX (20th)
Chabot, Steve, OH (1st)
Cheney, Liz, WY (At Large)
Chu, Judy, CA (27th)
Cicilline, David N., RI (1st)
Cisneros, Gilbert Ray, Jr., CA (39th)
Clark, Katherine M., MA (5th)
Clarke, Yvette D., NY (9th)
Clay, Wm. Lacy, MO (1st)
Cleaver, Emanuel, MO (5th)
Cline, Ben, VA (6th)
Cloud, Michael, TX (27th)
Clyburn, James E., SC (6th)
Cohen, Steve, TN (9th)
Cole, Tom, OK (4th)
Collins, Doug, GA (9th)
Comer, James, KY (1st)
Conaway, K. Michael, TX (11th)
Connolly, Gerald E., VA (11th)
Cook, Paul, CA (8th)
Cooper, Jim, TN (5th)
Correa, J. Luis, CA (46th)
Costa, Jim, CA (16th)
Courtney, Joe, CT (2d)
Cox, TJ, CA (21st)
Craig, Angie, MN (2d)
Crawford, Eric A. ''Rick'', AR (1st)
Crenshaw, Dan, TX (2d)
Crist, Charlie, FL (13th)
Crow, Jason, CO (6th)
Cuellar, Henry, TX (28th)
Cunningham, Joe, SC (1st)
Curtis, John R., UT (3d)
Davids, Sharice, KS (3d)
Davidson, Warren, OH (8th)
Davis, Danny K., IL (7th)
Davis, Rodney, IL (13th)
Davis, Susan A., CA (53d)
Dean, Madeleine, PA (4th)
DeFazio, Peter A., OR (4th)
DeGette, Diana, CO (1st)
DeLauro, Rosa L., CT (3d)
DelBene, Suzan K., WA (1st)
Delgado, Antonio, NY (19th)
Demings, Val Butler, FL (10th)
DeSaulnier, Mark, CA (11th)
DesJarlais, Scott, TN (4th)
Deutch, Theodore E., FL (22d)
Diaz-Balart, Mario, FL (25th)
Dingell, Debbie, MI (12th)
Doggett, Lloyd, TX (35th)
Doyle, Michael F., PA (18th)
Duncan, Jeff, SC (3d)
Dunn, Neal P., FL (2d)
Emmer, Tom, MN (6th)
Engel, Eliot L., NY (16th)
Escobar, Veronica, TX (16th)
Eshoo, Anna G., CA (18th)
Espaillat, Adriano, NY (13th)
Estes, Ron, KS (4th)

Evans, Dwight, PA (3d)
Ferguson, A. Drew, IV, GA (3d)
Finkenauer, Abby, IA (1st)
Fitzpatrick, Brian K., PA (1st)
Fleischmann, Charles J. "Chuck", TN (3d)
Fletcher, Lizzie, TX (7th)
Flores, Bill, TX (17th)
Fortenberry, Jeff, NE (1st)
Foster, Bill, IL (11th)
Foxx, Virginia, NC (5th)
Frankel, Lois, FL (21st)
Fudge, Marcia L., OH (11th)
Fulcher, Russ, ID (1st)
Gabbard, Tulsi, HI (2d)
Gaetz, Matt, FL (1st)
Gallagher, Mike, WI (8th)
Gallego, Ruben, AZ (7th)
Garamendi, John, CA (3d)
García, Jesús G. "Chuy", IL (4th)
Garcia, Mike, CA (25th)
Garcia, Sylvia R., TX (29th)
Gianforte, Greg, MT (At Large)
Gibbs, Bob, OH (7th)
Gohmert, Louie, TX (1st)
Golden, Jared F., ME (2d)
Gomez, Jimmy, CA (34th)
Gonzalez, Anthony, OH (16th)
Gonzalez, Vicente, TX (15th)
Gooden, Lance, TX (5th)
Gosar, Paul A., AZ (4th)
Gottheimer, Josh, NJ (5th)
Granger, Kay, TX (12th)
Graves, Garret, LA (6th)
Graves, Sam, MO (6th)
Graves, Tom, GA (14th)
Green, Al, TX (9th)
Green, Mark E., TN (7th)
Griffith, H. Morgan, VA (9th)
Grijalva, Raúl M., AZ (3d)
Grothman, Glenn, WI (6th)
Guest, Michael, MS (3d)
Guthrie, Brett, KY (2d)
Haaland, Debra A., NM (1st)
Hagedorn, Jim, MN (1st)
Harder, Josh, CA (10th)
Harris, Andy, MD (1st)
Hartzler, Vicky, MO (4th)
Hastings, Alcee L., FL (20th)
Hayes, Jahana, CT (5th)
Heck, Denny, WA (10th)
Hern, Kevin, OK (1st)
Herrera Beutler, Jaime, WA (3d)
Hice, Jody B., GA (10th)
Higgins, Brian, NY (26th)
Higgins, Clay, LA (3d)
Hill, J. French, AR (2d)
Himes, James A., CT (4th)
Holding, George, NC (2d)
Hollingsworth, Trey, IN (9th)
Horn, Kendra S., OK (5th)
Horsford, Steven, NV (4th)
Houlahan, Chrissy, PA (6th)
Hoyer, Steny H., MD (5th)
Hudson, Richard, NC (8th)
Huffman, Jared, CA (2d)
Huizenga, Bill, MI (2d)
Hurd, Will, TX (23d)
Jackson Lee, Sheila, TX (18th)
Jacobs, Chris, NY (27th)
Jayapal, Pramila, WA (7th)
Jeffries, Hakeem S., NY (8th)
Johnson, Bill, OH (6th)
Johnson, Dusty, SD (At Large)
Johnson, Eddie Bernice, TX (30th)
Johnson, Henry C. "Hank", Jr., GA (4th)
Johnson, Mike, LA (4th)
Jordan, Jim, OH (4th)
Joyce, David P., OH (14th)
Joyce, John, PA (13th)
Kaptur, Marcy, OH (9th)
Katko, John, NY (24th)
Keating, William R., MA (9th)
Keller, Fred, PA (12th)
Kelly, Mike, PA (16th)
Kelly, Robin L., IL (2d)
Kelly, Trent, MS (1st)
Kennedy, Joseph P., III, MA (4th)
Khanna, Ro, CA (17th)
Kildee, Daniel T., MI (5th)
Kilmer, Derek, WA (6th)
Kim, Andy, NJ (3d)
Kind, Ron, WI (3d)
King, Peter T., NY (2d)
King, Steve, IA (4th)
Kinzinger, Adam, IL (16th)
Kirkpatrick, Ann, AZ (2d)
Krishnamoorthi, Raja, IL (8th)
Kuster, Ann M., NH (2d)
Kustoff, David, TN (8th)
LaHood, Darin, IL (18th)
LaMalfa, Doug, CA (1st)
Lamb, Conor, PA (17th)
Lamborn, Doug, CO (5th)
Langevin, James R., RI (2d)
Larsen, Rick, WA (2d)
Larson, John B., CT (1st)
Latta, Robert E., OH (5th)
Lawrence, Brenda L., MI (14th)
Lawson, Al, Jr., FL (5th)
Lee, Barbara, CA (13th)
Lee, Susie, NV (3d)
Lesko, Debbie, AZ (8th)
Levin, Andy, MI (9th)
Levin, Mike, CA (49th)
Lieu, Ted, CA (33d)
Lipinski, Daniel, IL (3d)
Loebsack, David, IA (2d)
Lofgren, Zoe, CA (19th)
Long, Billy, MO (7th)
Loudermilk, Barry, GA (11th)
Lowenthal, Alan S., CA (47th)
Lowey, Nita M., NY (17th)
Lucas, Frank D., OK (3d)
Luetkemeyer, Blaine, MO (3d)
Luján, Ben Ray, NM (3d)
Luria, Elaine G., VA (2d)
Lynch, Stephen F., MA (8th)
Malinowski, Tom, NJ (7th)
Maloney, Carolyn B., NY (12th)
Maloney, Sean Patrick, NY (18th)
Marchant, Kenny, TX (24th)
Marshall, Roger W., KS (1st)

Massie, Thomas, KY (4th)
Mast, Brian J., FL (18th)
Matsui, Doris O., CA (6th)
McAdams, Ben, UT (4th)
McBath, Lucy, GA (6th)
McCarthy, Kevin, CA (23d)
McCaul, Michael T., TX (10th)
McClintock, Tom, CA (4th)
McCollum, Betty, MN (4th)
McEachin, A. Donald, VA (4th)
McGovern, James P., MA (2d)
McHenry, Patrick T., NC (10th)
McKinley, David B., WV (1st)
McNerney, Jerry, CA (9th)
Meeks, Gregory W., NY (5th)
Meng, Grace, NY (6th)
Meuser, Daniel, PA (9th)
Mfume, Kweisi, MD (7th)
Miller, Carol D., WV (3d)
Mitchell, Paul, MI (10th)
Moolenaar, John R., MI (4th)
Mooney, Alexander X., WV (2d)
Moore, Gwen, WI (4th)
Morelle, Joseph D., NY (25th)
Moulton, Seth, MA (6th)
Mucarsel-Powell, Debbie, FL (26th)
Mullin, Markwayne, OK (2d)
Murphy, Gregory F., NC (3d)
Murphy, Stephanie N., FL (7th)
Nadler, Jerrold, NY (10th)
Napolitano, Grace F., CA (32d)
Neal, Richard E., MA (1st)
Neguse, Joe, CO (2d)
Newhouse, Dan, WA (4th)
Norcross, Donald, NJ (1st)
Norman, Ralph, SC (5th)
Nunes, Devin, CA (22d)
Ocasio-Cortez, Alexandria, NY (14th)
O'Halleran, Tom, AZ (1st)
Olson, Pete, TX (22d)
Omar, Ilhan, MN (5th)
Palazzo, Steven M., MS (4th)
Pallone, Frank, Jr., NJ (6th)
Palmer, Gary J., AL (6th)
Panetta, Jimmy, CA (20th)
Pappas, Chris, NH (1st)
Pascrell, Bill, Jr., NJ (9th)
Payne, Donald M., Jr., NJ (10th)
Pelosi, Nancy, CA (12th)
Pence, Greg, IN (6th)
Perlmutter, Ed, CO (7th)
Perry, Scott, PA (10th)
Peters, Scott H., CA (52d)
Peterson, Collin C., MN (7th)
Phillips, Dean, MN (3d)
Pingree, Chellie, ME (1st)
Pocan, Mark, WI (2d)
Porter, Katie, CA (45th)
Posey, Bill, FL (8th)
Pressley, Ayanna, MA (7th)
Price, David E., NC (4th)
Quigley, Mike, IL (5th)
Raskin, Jamie, MD (8th)
Reed, Tom, NY (23d)
Reschenthaler, Guy, PA (14th)
Rice, Kathleen M., NY (4th)
Rice, Tom, SC (7th)
Richmond, Cedric L., LA (2d)
Riggleman, Denver, VA (5th)
Roby, Martha, AL (2d)
Rodgers, Cathy McMorris, WA (5th)
Roe, David P., TN (1st)
Rogers, Harold, KY (5th)
Rogers, Mike, AL (3d)
Rooney, Francis, FL (19th)
Rose, John W., TN (6th)
Rose, Max, NY (11th)
Rouda, Harley, CA (48th)
Rouzer, David, NC (7th)
Roy, Chip, TX (21st)
Roybal-Allard, Lucille, CA (40th)
Ruiz, Raul, CA (36th)
Ruppersberger, C. A. Dutch, MD (2d)
Rush, Bobby L., IL (1st)
Rutherford, John H., FL (4th)
Ryan, Tim, OH (13th)
Sánchez, Linda T., CA (38th)
Sarbanes, John P., MD (3d)
Scalise, Steve, LA (1st)
Scanlon, Mary Gay, PA (5th)
Schakowsky, Janice D., IL (9th)
Schiff, Adam B., CA (28th)
Schneider, Bradley Scott, IL (10th)
Schrader, Kurt, OR (5th)
Schrier, Kim, WA (8th)
Schweikert, David, AZ (6th)
Scott, Austin, GA (8th)
Scott, David, GA (13th)
Scott, Robert C. "Bobby", VA (3d)
Sensenbrenner, F. James, Jr., WI (5th)
Serrano, José E., NY (15th)
Sewell, Terri A., AL (7th)
Shalala, Donna E., FL (27th)
Sherman, Brad, CA (30th)
Sherrill, Mikie, NJ (11th)
Shimkus, John, IL (15th)
Simpson, Michael K., ID (2d)
Sires, Albio, NJ (8th)
Slotkin, Elissa, MI (8th)
Smith, Adam, WA (9th)
Smith, Adrian, NE (3d)
Smith, Christopher H., NJ (4th)
Smith, Jason, MO (8th)
Smucker, Lloyd, PA (11th)
Soto, Darren, FL (9th)
Spanberger, Abigail Davis VA (7th)
Spano, Ross, FL (15th)
Speier, Jackie, CA (14th)
Stanton, Greg, AZ (9th)
Stauber, Pete, MN (8th)
Stefanik, Elise M., NY (21st)
Steil, Bryan, WI (1st)
Steube, W. Gregory, FL (17th)
Stevens, Haley M., MI (11th)
Stewart, Chris, UT (2d)
Stivers, Steve, OH (15th)
Suozzi, Thomas R., NY (3d)
Swalwell, Eric, CA (15th)
Takano, Mark, CA (41st)
Taylor, Van, TX (3d)
Thompson, Bennie G., MS (2d)
Thompson, Glenn, PA (5th)

Thompson, Mike, CA (5th)
Thornberry, Mac, TX (13th)
Tiffany, Thomas P., WI (7th)
Timmons, William R., IV, SC (4th)
Tipton, Scott R., CO (3d)
Titus, Dina, NV (1st)
Tlaib, Rashida, MI (13th)
Tonko, Paul, NY (20th)
Torres, Norma J., CA (35th)
Torres Small, Xochitl, NM (2d)
Trahan, Lori, MA (3d)
Trone, David J., MD (6th)
Turner, Michael R., OH (10th)
Underwood, Lauren, IL (14th)
Upton, Fred, MI (6th)
Van Drew, Jefferson, NJ (2d)
Vargas, Juan, CA (51st)
Veasey, Marc A., TX (33d)
Vela, Filemon, TX (34th)
Velázquez, Nydia M., NY (7th)
Visclosky, Peter J., IN (1st)
Wagner, Ann, MO (2d)
Walberg, Tim, MI (7th)
Walden, Greg, OR (2d)
Walker, Mark, NC (6th)
Walorski, Jackie, IN (2d)
Waltz, Michael, FL (6th)
Wasserman Schultz, Debbie, FL (23d)
Waters, Maxine, CA (43d)
Watkins, Steve, KS (2d)
Watson Coleman, Bonnie, NJ (12th)
Weber, Randy K., Sr., TX (14th)
Webster, Daniel, FL (11th)
Welch, Peter, VT (At Large)
Wenstrup, Brad R., OH (2d)
Westerman, Bruce, AR (4th)
Wexton, Jennifer, VA (10th)
Wild, Susan, PA (7th)
Williams, Roger, TX (25th)
Wilson, Frederica S., FL (24th)
Wilson, Joe, SC (2d)
Wittman, Robert J., VA (1st)
Womack, Steve, AR (3d)
Woodall, Rob, GA (7th)
Wright, Ron, TX (6th)
Yarmuth, John A., KY (3d)
Yoho, Ted S., FL (3d)
Young, Don, AK (At Large)
Zeldin, Lee M., NY (1st)

RESIDENT COMMISSIONER
González-Colón, Jenniffer, PR

DELEGATES
Radewagen, Aumua Amata Coleman, AS
Norton, Eleanor Holmes, DC
San Nicolas, Michael F. Q., GU
Sablan, Gregorio Kilili Camacho, MP
Plaskett, Stacey E., VI

116th Congress
Nine-Digit Postal ZIP Codes

Senate Post Office (20510): The four-digit numbers in these tables were assigned by the Senate Committee on Rules and Administration. Mail to all Senate offices is delivered by the main Post Office in the Dirksen Senate Office Building.

Senate Committees

Committee on Agriculture, Nutrition, and Forestry	–6000
Committee on Appropriations	–6025
Committee on Armed Services	–6050
Committee on Banking, Housing, and Urban Affairs	–6075
Committee on the Budget	–6100
Committee on Commerce, Science, and Transportation	–6125
Committee on Energy and Natural Resources	–6150
Committee on Environment and Public Works	–6175
Committee on Finance	–6200
Committee on Foreign Relations	–6225
Committee on Health, Education, Labor and Pensions	–6300
Committee on Homeland Security and Governmental Affairs	–6250
Committee on Indian Affairs	–6450
Committee on the Judiciary	–6275
Committee on Rules and Administration	–6325
Committee on Small Business and Entrepreneurship	–6350
Committee on Veterans' Affairs	–6375
Committee on Aging (Special)	–6400
Committee on Ethics (Select)	–6425
Committee on Intelligence (Select)	–6475

Joint Committee Offices, Senate Side

Joint Economic Committee	–6602
Joint Committee on the Library	–6625
Joint Committee on Printing	–6650
Joint Committee on Taxation	–6675

Senate Leadership Offices

President Pro Tempore	–7000
Chaplain	–7002
Majority Leader	–7010
Assistant Majority Leader	–7012
Secretary for the Majority	–7014
Minority Leader	–7020
Assistant Minority Leader	–7022
Secretary for the Minority	–7024
Democratic Policy Committee	–7050
Republican Conference	–7060
Secretary to the Republican Conference	–7062
Republican Policy Committee	–7064
Republican Steering Committee	–7066
National Security Working Group	–7070

Senate Officers

Secretary of the Senate	–7100
Curator	–7102
Disbursing Office	–7104
Printing and Document Service	–7106
Historical Office	–7108
Human Resources	–7109
Interparliamentary Services	–7110
Senate Library	–7112
Office of Senate Security	–7114
Office of Public Records	–7116
Office of Official Reporters of Debates	–7117
Stationery Room	–7118
U.S. Capitol Preservation Commission	–7122
Office of Conservation and Preservation	–7124
Information Systems	–7125
Web Technology Office	–7126
Legislative Systems	–7127
Senate Gift Shop	–7128
Senate Legal Counsel	–7130
Emergency Terror Response (COOP)	–7131
Chief Counsel for Employment	–7132
Senate Sergeant at Arms	–7200
General Counsel	–7201
Finance Division	–7205
Budget	–7205
Accounting	–7205
Hair Care Services	–7206
Procurement	–7207
Capitol Guide Service	–7209
Employee Assistance Program Office	–7211
Human Resources	–7212
Safety Program	–7212
Health Promotion / Seminars	–7213
Placement Office	–7214
Workman's Compensation	–7214
Joint Office of Education and Training	–7215
Capitol Police	–7218
Congressional Special Services Office	–7228
Office Support Services	–7230
Customer Support	–7231
IT Request Processing	–7232
Chief Information Officer	–7233
State Liaison	–7285
Periodical Press Gallery	–7234
Press Gallery	–7238
Press Photo Gallery	–7242
Radio and TV Gallery	–7246
Webster Hall	–7248
Office of Protective Services and Continuity (OPSAC)	–7249
Law Enforcement Support Office	–7249
Intelligence & Protective Services	–7249
State Office Readiness Program	–7249
Police Operations Security Emergency Preparedness (POSEP)	–7249
Office of Continuity & Emergency Preparedness (CEPO)	–7249

Other Offices on the Senate Side

Senate Legal Counsel	–7250
Central Operations—Administration	–7260
Parking / ID	–7262
Printing Graphics and Direct Mail—PSQ	–7264
Printing Graphics and Direct Mail—Capitol Hill	–7266
Facilities	–7204
Furniture Shop	–7204
Framing Shop	–7204

Cabinet Shop	–7204
Photo Studio	–7216
Post Office	–7220
Recording Studio	–7222
Senate Legislative Counsel	–7275
Program Management	–7276
IT Support Services—Administration	–7280
Telecom Support	–7281
Equipment Services	–7282
Desktop/LAN Support	–7284
IT Research/Deployment	–7292
Technology Development—Administration	–7290
Systems Architecture	–7277
Information Security	–7278
Applications Development	–7291
Network Engineering and Management	–7293
Enterprise IT Systems	–7294
Inter/Intranet Services	–7296
Architect of the Capitol	–8000
Superintendent of Senate Buildings	–8002
Restaurant	–8050
Amtrak Ticket Office	–9010
Airlines Ticket Office (CATO)	–9014
Child Care Center	–9022
Credit Union	–9026
Veterans' Liaison	–9054
Social Security Liaison	–9064
Caucus of International Narcotics Control	–9070
Army Liaison	–9082
Air Force Liaison	–9083
Coast Guard Liaison	–9084
Navy Liaison	–9085
Marine Liaison	–9087

House Post Office (20515): Mail to all House offices is delivered by the House Postal Operations.

House Committees Leadership

U.S. House of Representatives	–0001
Cannon House Office Building	–0002
Rayburn House Office Building	–0003
Longworth House Office Building	–0004
Ford House Office Building	–0006
The Capitol	–0007
Committee on Agriculture	–6001
Committee on Appropriations	–6015
Committee on Armed Services	–6035
Committee on the Budget	–6065
Committee on Education and the Workforce	–6100
Committee on Energy and Commerce	–6115
Committee on Ethics	–6328
Committee on Financial Services	–6050
Committee on Foreign Affairs	–6128
Committee on Homeland Security	–6480
Committee on House Administration	–6157
Committee on the Judiciary	–6216
Committee on Natural Resources	–6201
Committee on Oversight and Government Reform	–6143
Committee on Rules	–6269
Committee on Science, Space, and Technology	–6301
Committee on Small Business	–6315
Committee on Transportation and Infrastructure	–6256
Committee on Veterans' Affairs	–6335
Committee on Ways and Means	–6348
Permanent Select Committee on Intelligence	–6415

Joint Committee Offices, House Side

Joint Economic Committee	–6432
Joint Committee on the Library	–6439
Joint Committee on Printing	–6446
Joint Committee on Taxation	–6453

House Leadership Offices

Office of the Speaker	–6501
Office of the Majority Leader	–6502
Office of the Majority Whip	–6503
Democratic Caucus	–6524
Democratic Congressional Campaign Committee	–6525
Democratic Steering and Policy Committee	–6527
Democratic Cloakroom	–6528
Office of the Democratic Leader	–6537
Office of the Democratic Whip	–6538
House Republican Conference	–6544
Republican Congressional Committee, National	–6547
Republican Policy Committee	–6545
Republican Cloakroom	–6650

House Officers

Office of the Clerk	–6601
Office of Art and Archives	–6612
Office of Employment and Counsel	–6622
Legislative Computer Systems	–6618
Office of Legislative Operations	–6602
Legislative Resource Center	–6612
Official Reporters	–6615
Office of Communications	–6611
Office of Interparliamentary Affairs	–6579
Office of the Chaplain	–6655
Office of the House Historian	–6701
Office of the Parliamentarian	–6731
Chief Administrative Officer	–6860
First Call	–6660
Administrative Counsel	–6660
Periodical Press Gallery	–6624
Press Gallery	–6625
Radio/TV Correspondents' Gallery	–6627
HIR Call Center	–6165
HIR Information Systems Security	–6165
Outplacement Services	–9920
Office of Employee Assistance	–6619
ADA Services	–6860
Personnel and Benefits	–9980
Child Care Center	–0001
Payroll and Benefits	–6604
Financial Counseling	–6604
Members' Services	–9970
Office Supply Service	–6860
House Gift Shop	–6860
Mail List/Processing	–6860
Mailing Services	–6860
Contractor Management	–6860
Photography	–6623
House Recording Studio	–6613
Furniture Support Services	–6610
House Office Service Center	–6860
Budget	–6604
Financial Counseling	–6604
Procurement Management	–9940
Office of the Sergeant at Arms	–6634

House Commissions and Offices

Congressional Executive Commission on China	–6481
Commission on Security and Cooperation in Europe	–6460
Commission on Congressional Mailing Standards	–6461
Office of the Law Revision Counsel	–6711
Office of Emergency Management	–6462
Office of the Legislative Counsel	–6721
General Counsel	–6532
Architect of the Capitol	–6906
Attending Physician	–6907
Congressional Budget Office	–6925

Liaison Offices

Air Force	–6854
Army	–6855
Coast Guard	–6856
Navy	–6857
Office of Personnel Management	–6858
Veterans' Administration	–6859

TERMS OF SERVICE

EXPIRATION OF THE TERMS OF SENATORS

CLASS II.—SENATORS WHOSE TERMS OF SERVICE EXPIRE IN 2021

[33 Senators in this group: Republicans, 21; Democrats, 12]

Name	Party	Residence
Alexander, Lamar	R.	Maryville, TN.
Booker, Cory A.[1]	D.	Newark, NJ.
Capito, Shelley Moore	R.	Charleston, WV.
Cassidy, Bill	R.	Baton Rouge, LA.
Collins, Susan M.	R.	Bangor, ME.
Coons, Christopher A.[2]	D.	Wilmington, DE.
Cornyn, John	R.	Austin, TX.
Cotton, Tom	R.	Dardanelle, AR.
Daines, Steve	R.	Bozeman, MT.
Durbin, Richard J.	D.	Springfield, IL.
Enzi, Michael B.	R.	Gillette, WY.
Ernst, Joni	R.	Red Oak, IA.
Gardner, Cory	R.	Yuma, CO.
Graham, Lindsey	R.	Seneca, SC.
Hyde-Smith, Cindy[3]	R.	Brookhaven, MS.
Inhofe, James M.[4]	R.	Tulsa, OK.
Jones, Doug[5]	D.	Birmingham, AL.
McConnell, Mitch	R.	Louisville, KY.
Markey, Edward J.[6]	D.	Malden, MA.
Merkley, Jeff	D.	Portland, OR.
Perdue, David	R.	Glynn County, GA.
Peters, Gary C.	D.	Bloomfield Township, MI.
Reed, Jack	D.	Jamestown, RI.
Risch, James E.	R.	Boise, ID.
Roberts, Pat	R.	Dodge City, KS.
Rounds, Mike	R.	Fort Pierre, SD.
Sasse, Ben	R.	Fremont, NE.
Shaheen, Jeanne	D.	Madbury, NH.
Smith, Tina[7]	D.	Minneapolis, MN.
Sullivan, Dan	R.	Anchorage, AK.
Tillis, Thom	R.	Huntersville, NC.
Udall, Tom	D.	Santa Fe, NM.
Warner, Mark R.	D.	Alexandria, VA.

[1] Senator Booker won the special election on October 16, 2013, for the term ending January 3, 2015, to fill the vacancy caused by the death of Senator Frank Lautenberg and took the oath of office on October 31, 2013, replacing appointed Senator Jeffrey Chiesa; elected to a full term on November 4, 2014.

[2] Senator Coons won the special election on November 2, 2010, for the term ending January 3, 2015, to fill the vacancy caused by the resignation of Senator Joseph R. Biden, Jr., and took the oath of office on November 15, 2010, replacing appointed Senator Ted Kaufman; elected to a full term on November 4, 2014.

[3] Senator Hyde-Smith was appointed on April 2, 2018, to fill the vacancy caused by the resignation of Senator Thad Cochran and took the oath of office on April 9, 2018; won the special election on November 27, 2018, for the term ending January 3, 2021.

[4] Senator Inhofe won the special election on November 8, 1994, for the term ending January 3, 1997, to fill the vacancy caused by the resignation of Senator David Boren and took the oath of office on November 17, 1994; elected to a full term on November 5, 1996.

[5] Senator Jones won the special election on December 12, 2017, for the term ending January 3, 2021, to fill the vacancy caused by the resignation of Senator Jeff Sessions, and took the oath of office on January 3, 2018, replacing appointed Senator Luther Strange.

[6] Senator Markey won the special election on June 25, 2013, for the term ending January 3, 2015, to fill the vacancy caused by the resignation of Senator John F. Kerry, and took the oath of office on July 16, 2013, replacing appointed Senator William Cowan; elected to a full term on November 4, 2014.

[7] Senator Smith was appointed on January 2, 2018, to fill the vacancy caused by the resignation of Senator Al Franken, and took the oath of office on January 3, 2018; won the special election on November 6, 2018, for the term ending January 3, 2021.

CLASS III.—SENATORS WHOSE TERMS OF SERVICE EXPIRE IN 2023

[34 Senators in this group: Republicans, 22; Democrats, 12]

Name	Party	Residence
Bennet, Michael F.[1]	D.	Denver, CO.
Blumenthal, Richard	D.	Greenwich, CT.
Blunt, Roy	R.	Springfield, MO.
Boozman, John	R.	Rogers, AR.
Burr, Richard	R.	Winston-Salem, NC.
Cortez Masto, Catherine	D.	Las Vegas, NV.
Crapo, Mike	R.	Idaho Falls, ID.
Duckworth, Tammy	D.	Hoffman Estates, IL.
Grassley, Chuck	R.	New Hartford, IA.
Harris, Kamala D.	D.	Los Angeles, CA.
Hassan, Margaret Wood	D.	Newfields, NH.
Hoeven, John	R.	Bismarck, ND.
Johnson, Ron	R.	Oshkosh, WI.
Kennedy, John	R.	Madisonville, LA.
Lankford, James[2]	R.	Oklahoma City, OK.
Leahy, Patrick J.	D.	Middlesex, VT.
Lee, Mike	R.	Alpine, UT.
Loeffler, Kelly[3]	R.	Atlanta, GA.
McSally, Martha[4]	R.	Tucson, AZ.
Moran, Jerry	R.	Manhattan, KS.
Murkowski, Lisa[5]	R.	Anchorage, AK.
Murray, Patty	D.	Seattle, WA.
Paul, Rand	R.	Bowling Green, KY.
Portman, Rob	R.	Terrace Park, OH.
Rubio, Marco	R.	West Miami, FL.
Schatz, Brian[6]	D.	Honolulu, HI.
Schumer, Charles E.	D.	Brooklyn, NY.
Scott, Tim[7]	R.	North Charleston, SC.
Shelby, Richard C.[8]	R.	Tuscaloosa, AL.
Thune, John	R.	Murdo, SD.
Toomey, Patrick J.	R.	Zionsville, PA.
Van Hollen, Chris	D.	Kensington, MD.
Wyden, Ron[9]	D.	Portland, OR.
Young, Todd	R.	Bloomington, IN.

[1] Senator Bennet was appointed on January 21, 2009, to fill the vacancy caused by the resignation of Senator Kenneth L. Salazar and took the oath of office on January 22, 2009; elected to a full term on November 2, 2010.

[2] Senator Lankford won the special election on November 4, 2014, for the term ending January 3, 2017, to fill the vacancy caused by the resignation of Senator Tom Coburn and took the oath of office on January 3, 2015; elected to a full term on November 8, 2016.

[3] Senator Loeffler was appointed on January 1, 2020, to fill the vacancy caused by the resignation of Senator Johnny Isakson and took the oath of office on January 6, 2020, to serve until a special election is held on November 3, 2020, for the remainder of the term ending January 3, 2023.

[4] Senator McSally was appointed on January 3, 2019, to fill the vacancy caused by the death of John McCain, a seat previously held by appointed Senator Jon Kyl, to serve until a special election is held on November 3, 2020, for the remainder of the term ending January 3, 2023.

[5] Senator Murkowski was appointed on December 20, 2002, to fill the vacancy caused by the resignation of her father, Senator Frank Murkowski, and took the oath of office on January 4, 2003; elected to a full term on November 2, 2004.

[6] Senator Schatz was appointed on December 26, 2012, to fill the vacancy caused by the death of Senator Daniel Inouye and took the oath of office on December 27, 2012; won the special election on November 4, 2014, for the term ending January 3, 2017; elected to a full term on November 8, 2016.

[7] Senator Scott was appointed on January 2, 2013, to fill the vacancy caused by the resignation of Senator James DeMint and took the oath of office on January 3, 2013; won the special election on November 4, 2014, for the term ending January 3, 2017; elected to a full term on November 8, 2016.

[8] Senator Shelby changed party affiliation from Democrat to Republican on November 5, 1994.

[9] Senator Wyden won the special election on January 30, 1996, for the term ending January 3, 1999, to fill the vacancy caused by the resignation of Senator Robert Packwood and took the oath of office on February 6, 1996; elected to a full term on November 3, 1998.

CLASS I.—SENATORS WHOSE TERMS OF SERVICE EXPIRE IN 2025

[33 Senators in this group: Republicans, 10; Democrats, 21; Independents, 2]

Name	Party	Residence
Baldwin, Tammy	D.	Madison, WI.
Barrasso, John [1]	R.	Casper, WY.
Blackburn, Marsha	R.	Franklin, TN.
Braun, Mike	R.	Jasper, IN.
Brown, Sherrod	D.	Cleveland, OH.
Cantwell, Maria	D.	Edmonds, WA.
Cardin, Benjamin L.	D.	Baltimore, MD.
Carper, Thomas R.	D.	Wilmington, DE.
Casey, Robert P., Jr.	D.	Scranton, PA.
Cramer, Kevin	R.	Bismarck, ND.
Cruz, Ted	R.	Houston, TX.
Feinstein, Dianne [2]	D.	San Francisco, CA.
Fischer, Deb	R.	Valentine, NE.
Gillibrand, Kirsten E. [3]	D.	Brunswick, NY.
Hawley, Josh	R.	Ashland, MO.
Heinrich, Martin	D.	Albuquerque, NM.
Hirono, Mazie K.	D.	Honolulu, HI.
Kaine, Tim	D.	Richmond, VA.
King, Angus S., Jr.	I.	Brunswick, ME.
Klobuchar, Amy	D.	Minneapolis, MN.
Manchin, Joe, III [4]	D.	Fairmont, WV.
Menendez, Robert [5]	D.	Paramus, NJ.
Murphy, Christopher	D.	Cheshire, CT.
Romney, Mitt	R.	Holladay, UT.
Rosen, Jacky	D.	Henderson, NV.
Sanders, Bernard	I.	Burlington, VT.
Scott, Rick	R.	Naples, FL.
Sinema, Kyrsten	D.	Phoenix, AZ.
Stabenow, Debbie	D.	Lansing, MI.
Tester, Jon	D.	Big Sandy, MT.
Warren, Elizabeth	D.	Cambridge, MA.
Whitehouse, Sheldon	D.	Newport, RI.
Wicker, Roger F. [6]	R.	Tupelo, MS.

[1] Senator Barrasso was appointed on June 22, 2007, to fill the vacancy caused by the death of Senator Craig Thomas and took the oath of office on June 25, 2007; won the special election on November 4, 2008, for the term ending January 3, 2013; elected to a full term on November 6, 2012.

[2] Senator Feinstein won the special election on November 3, 1992, for the term ending January 3, 1995, to fill the vacancy caused by the resignation of Senator Pete Wilson and took the oath of office on November 10, 1992, replacing appointed Senator John Seymour; elected to a full term on November 8, 1994.

[3] Senator Gillibrand was appointed on January 23, 2009, to fill the vacancy caused by the resignation of Senator Hillary Rodham Clinton and took the oath of office on January 27, 2009; won the special election on November 2, 2010, for the term ending January 3, 2013; elected to a full term on November 6, 2012.

[4] Senator Manchin won the special election on November 2, 2010, for the term ending January 3, 2013, to fill the vacancy caused by the death of Senator Robert C. Byrd and took the oath of office on November 15, 2010, replacing appointed Senator Carte P. Goodwin; elected to a full term on November 6, 2012.

[5] Senator Menendez was appointed on January 17, 2006, to fill the vacancy caused by the resignation of Senator Jon S. Corzine and took the oath of office on January 18, 2006; elected to a full term on November 7, 2006.

[6] Senator Wicker was appointed on December 31, 2007, to fill the vacancy caused by the resignation of Senator Trent Lott and took the oath of office on December 31, 2007; won the special election on November 4, 2008, for the term ending January 3, 2013; elected to a full term on November 6, 2012.

CONTINUOUS SERVICE OF SENATORS

[Republicans in roman (53); Democrats in *italic* (45); Independents in SMALL CAPS (2); total, 100]

Rank	Name	State	Beginning of present service
1	*Leahy, Patrick J.*	Vermont	Jan. 3, 1975.
2	Grassley, Chuck †	Iowa	Jan. 3, 1981.
3	McConnell, Mitch	Kentucky	Jan. 3, 1985.
4	Shelby, Richard C.†	Alabama	Jan. 3, 1987.
5	*Feinstein, Dianne* [1]	California	Nov. 10, 1992.‡
6	*Murray, Patty*	Washington	Jan. 3, 1993.
7	Inhofe, James M. † [2]	Oklahoma	Nov. 17, 1994.‡
8	*Wyden, Ron* † [3]	Oregon	Feb. 6, 1996.‡
9	Collins, Susan M.	Maine	Jan. 3, 1997.
	Durbin, Richard J. †	Illinois	
	Enzi, Michael B.	Wyoming	
	Reed, Jack †	Rhode Island	
	Roberts, Pat †	Kansas	
10	Crapo, Mike †	Idaho	Jan. 3, 1999.
	Schumer, Charles E. †	New York	
11	*Cantwell, Maria* †	Washington	Jan. 3, 2001.
	Carper, Thomas R.†	Delaware	
	Stabenow, Debbie †	Michigan	
12	Cornyn, John [4]	Texas	Dec. 2, 2002.
13	Murkowski, Lisa [5]	Alaska	Dec. 20, 2002.
14	Alexander, Lamar	Tennessee	Jan. 3, 2003.
	Graham, Lindsey †	South Carolina	
15	Burr, Richard †	North Carolina	Jan. 3, 2005.
	Thune, John †	South Dakota	
16	*Menendez, Robert* † [6]	New Jersey	Jan. 17, 2006.
17	*Brown, Sherrod* †	Ohio	Jan. 3, 2007.
	Cardin, Benjamin L. †	Maryland	
	Casey, Robert P., Jr.	Pennsylvania	
	Klobuchar, Amy	Minnesota	
	SANDERS, BERNARD †	Vermont	
	Tester, Jon	Montana	
	Whitehouse, Sheldon	Rhode Island	
18	Barrasso, John [7]	Wyoming	June 22, 2007.
19	Wicker, Roger F. † [8]	Mississippi	Dec. 31, 2007.
20	*Merkley, Jeff*	Oregon	Jan. 3, 2009.
	Risch, James E.	Idaho	
	Shaheen, Jeanne	New Hampshire	
	Udall, Tom †	New Mexico	
	Warner, Mark R.	Virginia	
21	*Bennet, Michael F.* [9]	Colorado	Jan. 21, 2009.
22	*Gillibrand, Kirsten E.*† [10]	New York	Jan. 26, 2009.
23	*Coons, Christopher A.* [11]	Delaware	Nov. 15, 2010.‡
	Manchin, Joe, III [12]	West Virginia	‡
24	*Blumenthal, Richard*	Connecticut	Jan. 3, 2011.
	Blunt, Roy	Missouri	
	Boozman, John †	Arkansas	
	Hoeven, John	North Dakota	
	Johnson, Ron	Wisconsin	
	Lee, Mike	Utah	
	Moran, Jerry	Kansas	
	Paul, Rand	Kentucky	
	Portman, Rob	Ohio	
	Rubio, Marco	Florida	
	Toomey, Patrick J.	Pennsylvania	

CONTINUOUS SERVICE OF SENATORS—CONTINUED

[Republicans in roman (53); Democrats in *italic* (45); Independents in SMALL CAPS (2); total, 100]

Rank	Name	State	Beginning of present service
25	*Schatz, Brian* [13]	Hawaii	Dec. 26, 2012.
26	Scott, Tim † [14]	South Carolina	Jan. 2, 2013.
27	*Baldwin, Tammy*	Wisconsin	Jan. 3, 2013.
	Cruz, Ted	Texas	
	Fischer, Deb	Nebraska	
	Heinrich, Martin	New Mexico	
	Hirono, Mazie K.	Hawaii	
	Kaine, Tim	Virginia	
	KING, ANGUS S., JR.	Maine	
	Murphy, Christopher	Connecticut	
	Warren, Elizabeth	Massachusetts	
28	*Markey, Edward J.* † [15]	Massachusetts	July 16, 2013. ‡
29	*Booker, Cory A.* [16]	New Jersey	Oct. 31, 2013. ‡
30	Capito, Shelley Moore †	West Virginia	Jan. 3, 2015.
	Cassidy, Bill †	Louisiana	
	Cotton, Tom †	Arkansas	
	Daines, Steve †	Montana	
	Ernst, Joni	Iowa	
	Gardner, Cory †	Colorado	
	Lankford, James †	Oklahoma	
	Perdue, David	Georgia	
	Peters, Gary C. †	Michigan	
	Rounds, Mike	South Dakota	
	Sasse, Ben	Nebraska	
	Sullivan, Dan	Alaska	
	Tillis, Thom	North Carolina	
31	*Cortez Masto, Catherine*	Nevada	Jan. 3, 2017.
	Duckworth, Tammy †	Illinois	
	Harris, Kamala D.	California	
	Hassan, Margaret Wood	New Hampshire	
	Kennedy, John †	Louisiana	
	Van Hollen, Chris †	Maryland	
	Young, Todd †	Indiana	
32	*Smith, Tina* [17]	Minnesota	Jan. 3, 2018.
	Jones, Doug [18]	Alabama	‡
33	Hyde-Smith, Cindy [19]	Mississippi	April 9, 2018.
34	Blackburn, Marsha	Tennessee	Jan. 3, 2019.
	Sinema, Kyrsten	Arizona	
	Cramer, Kevin	North Dakota	
	McSally, Martha [20]	Arizona	
	Rosen, Jacky	Nevada	
	Romney, Mitt	Utah	
	Braun, Mike	Indiana	
	Hawley, Josh	Missouri	
35	Scott, Rick	Florida	Jan. 8, 2019.
36	Loeffler, Kelly [21]	Georgia	Jan. 6, 2020.

† Served in the House of Representatives previous to service in the Senate.

‡ Senators elected to complete unexpired terms typically begin their terms on the day following the election, but individual cases may vary.

[1] Senator Feinstein won the special election on November 3, 1992, for the term ending January 3, 1995, to fill the vacancy caused by the resignation of Senator Pete Wilson and took the oath of office on November 10, 1992, replacing appointed Senator John Seymour; elected to a full term on November 8, 1994.

[2] Senator Inhofe won the special election on November 8, 1994, for the term ending January 3, 1997, to fill the vacancy caused by the resignation of Senator David Boren and took the oath of office on November 17, 1994; elected to a full term on November 5, 1996.

[3] Senator Wyden won the special election on January 30, 1996, for the term ending January 3, 1999, to fill the vacancy caused by the resignation of Senator Robert Packwood and took the oath of office on February 6, 1996; elected to a full term on November 3, 1998.

[4] Senator Cornyn was elected on November 5, 2002, for the 6-year term commencing January 3, 2003; subsequently appointed on December 2, 2002, to fill the vacancy caused by the resignation of Senator Phil Gramm.

[5] Senator Murkowski was appointed on December 20, 2002, to fill the vacancy caused by the resignation of her father, Senator Frank Murkowski and took the oath of office on January 4, 2003; elected to a full term on November 2, 2004.

[6] Senator Menendez was appointed on January 17, 2006, to fill the vacancy caused by the resignation of Senator Jon S. Corzine and took the oath of office on January 18, 2006; elected to a full term on November 7, 2006.

[7] Senator Barrasso was appointed on June 22, 2007, to fill the vacancy caused by the death of Senator Craig Thomas and took the oath of office on June 25, 2007; won the special election on November 4, 2008, for the term ending January 3, 2013; elected to a full term on November 6, 2012.

[8] Senator Wicker was appointed on December 31, 2007, to fill the vacancy caused by the resignation of Senator Trent Lott and took the oath of office on December 31, 2007; won the special election on November 4, 2008, for the term ending January 3, 2013; elected to a full term on November 6, 2012.

[9] Senator Bennet was appointed on January 21, 2009, to fill the vacancy caused by the resignation of Senator Kenneth L. Salazar and took the oath of office on January 22, 2009; elected to a full term on November 2, 2010.

[10] Senator Gillibrand was appointed on January 23, 2009, to fill the vacancy caused by the resignation of Senator Hillary Rodham Clinton and took the oath of office on January 27, 2009; won the special election on November 2, 2010, for the term ending January 3, 2013; elected to a full term on November 6, 2012.

[11] Senator Coons won the special election on November 2, 2010, for the term ending January 3, 2015, to fill the vacancy caused by the resignation of Senator Joseph R. Biden, Jr., and took the oath of office on November 15, 2010, replacing appointed Senator Ted Kaufman; elected to a full term on November 4, 2014.

[12] Senator Manchin won the special election on November 2, 2010, for the term ending January 3, 2013, to fill the vacancy caused by the death of Senator Robert C. Byrd and took the oath of office on November 15, 2010, replacing appointed Senator Carte P. Goodwin; elected to a full term on November 6, 2012.

[13] Senator Schatz was appointed on December 26, 2012, to fill the vacancy caused by the death of Senator Daniel Inouye and took the oath of office on December 27, 2012; won the special election on November 4, 2014, for the term ending January 3, 2017; elected to a full term on November 8, 2016.

[14] Senator Scott was appointed on January 2, 2013, to fill the vacancy caused by the resignation of Senator James DeMint and took the oath of office on January 3, 2013; won the special election on November 4, 2014, for the term ending January 3, 2017; elected to a full term on November 8, 2016.

[15] Senator Markey won the special election on June 25, 2013, for the term ending January 3, 2015, to fill the vacancy caused by the resignation of Senator John F. Kerry, and took the oath of office on July 16, 2013, replacing appointed Senator William Cowan; elected to a full term on November 4, 2014.

[16] Senator Booker won the special election on October 16, 2013, for the term ending January 3, 2015, to fill the vacancy caused by the death of Senator Frank Lautenberg and took the oath of office on October 31, 2013, replacing appointed Senator Jeffrey Chiesa; elected to a full term on November 4, 2014.

[17] Senator Smith was appointed on January 2, 2018, to fill the vacancy caused by the resignation of Senator Al Franken and took the oath of office on January 3, 2018; won the special election on November 6, 2018, for the term ending January 3, 2021.

[18] Senator Jones won the special election on December 12, 2017, for the term ending January 3, 2021, to fill the vacancy caused by the resignation of Senator Jeff Sessions, and took the oath of office on January 3, 2018, replacing appointed Senator Luther Strange.

[19] Senator Hyde-Smith was appointed on April 2, 2018, to fill the vacancy caused by the resignation of Senator Thad Cochran and took the oath of office on April 9, 2018; won the special election on November 27, 2018, for the term ending January 3, 2021.

[20] Senator McSally was appointed on January 3, 2019, to fill the vacancy caused by the death of Senator John McCain and took the oath of office on January 3, 2019, replacing appointed Senator John Kyl.

[21] Senator Loeffler was appointed on January 1, 2020, to fill the vacancy caused by the resignation of Senator Johnny Isakson and took the oath of office on January 6, 2020.

CONGRESSES IN WHICH REPRESENTATIVES, RESIDENT COMMISSIONER, AND DELEGATES HAVE SERVED WITH BEGINNING OF PRESENT SERVICE

[* Elected to fill a vacancy; Democrats in roman (232); Republicans in *italic* (198); Libertarians in SMALL CAPS (1); Vacancies (4); Resident Commissioner and Delegates in **boldface** (6); total, 441]

Name	State	Congresses (inclusive)	Beginning of present service
		24 terms, consecutive	
Young, Don	AK	*93d to 116th	Mar. 6, 1973
		21 terms, consecutive	
Sensenbrenner, F. James, Jr.	WI	96th to 116th	Jan. 3, 1979
		20 terms, consecutive	
Hoyer, Steny H.	MD	*97th to 116th	May 19, 1981
Rogers, Harold	KY	97th to 116th	Jan. 3, 1981
Smith, Christopher H.	NJ	97th to 116th	Jan. 3, 1981
		19 terms, consecutive	
Kaptur, Marcy	OH	98th to 116th	Jan. 3, 1983
		18 terms, consecutive	
Visclosky, Peter J.	IN	99th to 116th	Jan. 3, 1985
		17 terms, consecutive	
DeFazio, Peter A.	OR	100th to 116th	Jan. 3, 1987
Pallone, Frank, Jr.	NJ	*100th to 116th	Nov. 8, 1988
Pelosi, Nancy	CA	*100th to 116th	June 2, 1987
Upton, Fred	MI	100th to 116th	Jan. 3, 1987
		16 terms, consecutive	
Engel, Eliot L.	NY	101st to 116th	Jan. 3, 1989
Lowey, Nita M.	NY	101st to 116th	Jan. 3, 1989
Neal, Richard E.	MA	101st to 116th	Jan. 3, 1989
Serrano, José E.	NY	*101st to 116th	Mar. 20, 1990
		16 terms, not consecutive	
Price, David E.	NC	100th to 103d and 105th to 116th.	Jan. 3, 1997
		15 terms, consecutive	
DeLauro, Rosa L.	CT	102d to 116th	Jan. 3, 1991
Nadler, Jerrold	NY	*102d to 116th	Nov. 3, 1992
Peterson, Collin C.	MN	102d to 116th	Jan. 3, 1991
Waters, Maxine	CA	102d to 116th	Jan. 3, 1991
		15 terms, not consecutive	
Cooper, Jim	TN	98th to 103d and 108th to 116th.	Jan. 3, 2003
		14 terms, consecutive	
Bishop, Sanford D., Jr.	GA	103d to 116th	Jan. 3, 1993
Calvert, Ken	CA	103d to 116th	Jan. 3, 1993
Clyburn, James E.	SC	103d to 116th	Jan. 3, 1993
Eshoo, Anna G.	CA	103d to 116th	Jan. 3, 1993
Hastings, Alcee L.	FL	103d to 116th	Jan. 3, 1993

CONGRESSES IN WHICH REPRESENTATIVES, RESIDENT COMMISSIONER, AND DELEGATES HAVE SERVED WITH BEGINNING OF PRESENT SERVICE—CONTINUED

[* Elected to fill a vacancy; Democrats in roman (232); Republicans in *italic* (198); Libertarians in SMALL CAPS (1); Vacancies (4); Resident Commissioner and Delegates in **boldface** (6); total, 441]

Name	State	Congresses (inclusive)	Beginning of present service
Johnson, Eddie Bernice	TX	103d to 116th	Jan. 3, 1993
King, Peter T.	NY	103d to 116th	Jan. 3, 1993
Lucas, Frank D.	OK	* 103d to 116th	May 10, 1994
Maloney, Carolyn B.	NY	103d to 116th	Jan. 3, 1993
Roybal-Allard, Lucille	CA	103d to 116th	Jan. 3, 1993
Rush, Bobby L.	IL	103d to 116th	Jan. 3, 1993
Scott, Robert C. "Bobby"	VA	103d to 116th	Jan. 3, 1993
Thompson, Bennie G.	MS	* 103d to 116th	Apr. 13, 1993
Velázquez, Nydia M.	NY	103d to 116th	Jan. 3, 1993
13 terms, consecutive			
Blumenauer, Earl	OR	* 104th to 116th	May 21, 1996
Doggett, Lloyd	TX	104th to 116th	Jan. 3, 1995
Doyle, Michael F.	PA	104th to 116th	Jan. 3, 1995
Jackson Lee, Sheila	TX	104th to 116th	Jan. 3, 1995
Lofgren, Zoe	CA	104th to 116th	Jan. 3, 1995
Thornberry, Mac	TX	104th to 116th	Jan. 3, 1995
12 terms, consecutive			
Aderholt, Robert B.	AL	105th to 116th	Jan. 3, 1997
Brady, Kevin	TX	105th to 116th	Jan. 3, 1997
Davis, Danny K.	IL	105th to 116th	Jan. 3, 1997
DeGette, Diana	CO	105th to 116th	Jan. 3, 1997
Granger, Kay	TX	105th to 116th	Jan. 3, 1997
Kind, Ron	WI	105th to 116th	Jan. 3, 1997
Lee, Barbara	CA	* 105th to 116th	Apr. 7, 1998
McGovern, James P.	MA	105th to 116th	Jan. 3, 1997
Meeks, Gregory W.	NY	* 105th to 116th	Feb. 3, 1998
Pascrell, Bill, Jr.	NJ	105th to 116th	Jan. 3, 1997
Sherman, Brad	CA	105th to 116th	Jan. 3, 1997
Shimkus, John	IL	105th to 116th	Jan. 3, 1997
Smith, Adam	WA	105th to 116th	Jan. 3, 1997
12 terms, not consecutive			
Chabot, Steve	OH	104th to 110th and 113th to 116th.	Jan. 3, 2011
11 terms, consecutive			
Larson, John B.	CT	106th to 116th	Jan. 3, 1999
Napolitano, Grace F.	CA	106th to 116th	Jan. 3, 1999
Schakowsky, Janice D.	IL	106th to 116th	Jan. 3, 1999
Simpson, Michael K.	ID	106th to 116th	Jan. 3, 1999
Thompson, Mike	CA	106th to 116th	Jan. 3, 1999
Walden, Greg	OR	106th to 116th	Jan. 3, 1999
10 terms, consecutive			
Clay, Wm. Lacy	MO	107th to 116th	Jan. 3, 2001
Davis, Susan A.	CA	107th to 116th	Jan. 3, 2001
Graves, Sam	MO	107th to 116th	Jan. 3, 2001

CONGRESSES IN WHICH REPRESENTATIVES, RESIDENT COMMISSIONER, AND DELEGATES HAVE SERVED WITH BEGINNING OF PRESENT SERVICE—CONTINUED

[* Elected to fill a vacancy; Democrats in roman (232); Republicans in *italic* (198); Libertarians in SMALL CAPS (1); Vacancies (4); Resident Commissioner and Delegates in **boldface** (6); total, 441]

Name	State	Congresses (inclusive)	Beginning of present service
Langevin, James R.	RI	107th to 116th	Jan. 3, 2001
Larsen, Rick	WA	107th to 116th	Jan. 3, 2001
Lynch, Stephen F.	MA	* 107th to 116th	Oct. 16, 2001
McCollum, Betty	MN	107th to 116th	Jan. 3, 2001
Schiff, Adam B.	CA	107th to 116th	Jan. 3, 2001
Wilson, Joe	SC	* 107th to 116th	Dec. 18, 2001
9 terms, consecutive			
Bishop, Rob	UT	108th to 116th	Jan. 3, 2003
Burgess, Michael C.	TX	108th to 116th	Jan. 3, 2003
Butterfield, G. K.	NC	* 108th to 116th	July 20, 2004
Carter, John R.	TX	108th to 116th	Jan. 3, 2003
Cole, Tom	OK	108th to 116th	Jan. 3, 2003
Diaz-Balart, Mario	FL	108th to 116th	Jan. 3, 2003
Grijalva, Raúl M.	AZ	108th to 116th	Jan. 3, 2003
King, Steve	IA	108th to 116th	Jan. 3, 2003
Nunes, Devin	CA	108th to 116th	Jan. 3, 2003
Rogers, Mike	AL	108th to 116th	Jan. 3, 2003
Ruppersberger, C. A. Dutch	MD	108th to 116th	Jan. 3, 2003
Ryan, Tim	OH	108th to 116th	Jan. 3, 2003
Sánchez, Linda T.	CA	108th to 116th	Jan. 3, 2003
Scott, David	GA	108th to 116th	Jan. 3, 2003
Turner, Michael R.	OH	108th to 116th	Jan. 3, 2003
8 terms, consecutive			
Cleaver, Emanuel	MO	109th to 116th	Jan. 3, 2005
Conaway, K. Michael	TX	109th to 116th	Jan. 3, 2005
Costa, Jim	CA	109th to 116th	Jan. 3, 2005
Cuellar, Henry	TX	109th to 116th	Jan. 3, 2005
Fortenberry, Jeff	NE	109th to 116th	Jan. 3, 2005
Foxx, Virginia	NC	109th to 116th	Jan. 3, 2005
Gohmert, Louie	TX	109th to 116th	Jan. 3, 2005
Green, Al	TX	109th to 116th	Jan. 3, 2005
Higgins, Brian	NY	109th to 116th	Jan. 3, 2005
Lipinski, Daniel	IL	109th to 116th	Jan. 3, 2005
Marchant, Kenny	TX	109th to 116th	Jan. 3, 2005
Matsui, Doris O.	CA	* 109th to 116th	Mar. 8, 2005
McCaul, Michael T.	TX	109th to 116th	Jan. 3, 2005
McHenry, Patrick T.	NC	109th to 116th	Jan. 3, 2005
Moore, Gwen	WI	109th to 116th	Jan. 3, 2005
Rodgers, Cathy McMorris	WA	109th to 116th	Jan. 3, 2005
Sires, Albio	NJ	* 109th to 116th	Nov. 7, 2006
Wasserman Schultz, Debbie	FL	109th to 116th	Jan. 3, 2005
7 terms, consecutive			
Bilirakis, Gus M.	FL	110th to 116th	Jan. 3, 2007
Buchanan, Vern	FL	110th to 116th	Jan. 3, 2007
Carson, André	IN	* 110th to 116th	Mar. 11, 2008
Castor, Kathy	FL	110th to 116th	Jan. 3, 2007
Clarke, Yvette D.	NY	110th to 116th	Jan. 3, 2007

CONGRESSES IN WHICH REPRESENTATIVES, RESIDENT COMMISSIONER, AND DELEGATES HAVE SERVED WITH BEGINNING OF PRESENT SERVICE—CONTINUED

[* Elected to fill a vacancy; Democrats in roman (232); Republicans in *italic* (198); Libertarians in SMALL CAPS (1); Vacancies (4); Resident Commissioner and Delegates in **boldface** (6); total, 441]

Name	State	Congresses (inclusive)	Beginning of present service
Cohen, Steve	TN	110th to 116th	Jan. 3, 2007
Courtney, Joe	CT	110th to 116th	Jan. 3, 2007
Fudge, Marcia L.	OH	* 110th to 116th	Nov. 18, 2008
Johnson, Henry C. "Hank", Jr.	GA	110th to 116th	Jan. 3, 2007
Jordan, Jim	OH	110th to 116th	Jan. 3, 2007
Lamborn, Doug	CO	110th to 116th	Jan. 3, 2007
Latta, Robert E.	OH	* 110th to 116th	Dec. 11, 2007
Loebsack, David	IA	110th to 116th	Jan. 3, 2007
McCarthy, Kevin	CA	110th to 116th	Jan. 3, 2007
McNerney, Jerry	CA	110th to 116th	Jan. 3, 2007
Perlmutter, Ed	CO	110th to 116th	Jan. 3, 2007
Sarbanes, John P.	MD	110th to 116th	Jan. 3, 2007
Scalise, Steve	LA	* 110th to 116th	May 3, 2008
Smith, Adrian	NE	110th to 116th	Jan. 3, 2007
Speier, Jackie	CA	* 110th to 116th	Apr. 8, 2008
Welch, Peter	VT	110th to 116th	Jan. 3, 2007
Wittman, Robert J.	VA	* 110th to 116th	Dec. 11, 2007
Yarmuth, John A.	KY	110th to 116th	Jan. 3, 2007
6 terms, consecutive			
Chu, Judy	CA	* 111th to 116th	July 14, 2009
Connolly, Gerald E.	VA	111th to 116th	Jan. 3, 2009
Deutch, Theodore E.	FL	* 111th to 116th	Apr. 13, 2010
Garamendi, John	CA	* 111th to 116th	Nov. 3, 2009
Graves, Tom	GA	* 111th to 116th	June 8, 2010
Guthrie, Brett	KY	111th to 116th	Jan. 3, 2009
Himes, James A.	CT	111th to 116th	Jan. 3, 2009
Luetkemeyer, Blaine	MO	111th to 116th	Jan. 3, 2009
Luján, Ben Ray	NM	111th to 116th	Jan. 3, 2009
McClintock, Tom	CA	111th to 116th	Jan. 3, 2009
Olson, Pete	TX	111th to 116th	Jan. 3, 2009
Pingree, Chellie	ME	111th to 116th	Jan. 3, 2009
Posey, Bill	FL	111th to 116th	Jan. 3, 2009
Quigley, Mike	IL	* 111th to 116th	Apr. 7, 2009
Reed, Tom	NY	* 111th to 116th	Nov. 2, 2010
Roe, David P.	TN	111th to 116th	Jan. 3, 2009
Schrader, Kurt	OR	111th to 116th	Jan. 3, 2009
Thompson, Glenn	PA	111th to 116th	Jan. 3, 2009
Tonko, Paul	NY	111th to 116th	Jan. 3, 2009
6 terms, not consecutive			
Foster, Bill[1]	IL	* 110th to 111th and 113th to 116th.	Jan. 3, 2013
Mfume, Kweisi	MD	* 100th to 104th and 116th.	May 5, 2020
Walberg, Tim	MI	* 110th and 112th to 116th.	Jan. 3, 2011

CONGRESSES IN WHICH REPRESENTATIVES, RESIDENT COMMISSIONER, AND DELEGATES HAVE SERVED WITH BEGINNING OF PRESENT SERVICE—CONTINUED

[* Elected to fill a vacancy; Democrats in roman (232); Republicans in *italic* (198); Libertarians in SMALL CAPS (1); Vacancies (4); Resident Commissioner and Delegates in **boldface** (6); total, 441]

Name	State	Congresses (inclusive)	Beginning of present service
		5 terms, consecutive	
AMASH, JUSTIN	MI	112th to 116th	Jan. 3, 2011
Amodei, Mark E.	NV	* 112th to 116th	Sept. 13, 2011
Bass, Karen	CA	112th to 116th	Jan. 3, 2011
Bonamici, Suzanne	OR	* 112th to 116th	Jan. 31, 2012
Brooks, Mo	AL	112th to 116th	Jan. 3, 2011
Bucshon, Larry	IN	112th to 116th	Jan. 3, 2011
Cicilline, David N.	RI	112th to 116th	Jan. 3, 2011
Crawford, Eric A. ''Rick''	AR	112th to 116th	Jan. 3, 2011
DelBene, Suzan K.	WA	* 112th to 116th	Nov. 6, 2012
DesJarlais, Scott	TN	112th to 116th	Jan. 3, 2011
Duncan, Jeff	SC	112th to 116th	Jan. 3, 2011
Fleischmann, Charles J. ''Chuck''	TN	112th to 116th	Jan. 3, 2011
Flores, Bill	TX	112th to 116th	Jan. 3, 2011
Gibbs, Bob	OH	112th to 116th	Jan. 3, 2011
Gosar, Paul A.	AZ	112th to 116th	Jan. 3, 2011
Griffith, H. Morgan	VA	112th to 116th	Jan. 3, 2011
Harris, Andy	MD	112th to 116th	Jan. 3, 2011
Hartzler, Vicky	MO	112th to 116th	Jan. 3, 2011
Herrera Beutler, Jaime	WA	112th to 116th	Jan. 3, 2011
Huizenga, Bill	MI	112th to 116th	Jan. 3, 2011
Johnson, Bill	OH	112th to 116th	Jan. 3, 2011
Keating, William R.	MA	112th to 116th	Jan. 3, 2011
Kelly, Mike	PA	112th to 116th	Jan. 3, 2011
Kinzinger, Adam	IL	112th to 116th	Jan. 3, 2011
Long, Billy	MO	112th to 116th	Jan. 3, 2011
Massie, Thomas	KY	* 112th to 116th	Nov. 6, 2012
McKinley, David B.	WV	112th to 116th	Jan. 3, 2011
Palazzo, Steven M.	MS	112th to 116th	Jan. 3, 2011
Payne, Donald M., Jr.	NJ	* 112th to 116th	Nov. 6, 2012
Richmond, Cedric L.	LA	112th to 116th	Jan. 3, 2011
Roby, Martha	AL	112th to 116th	Jan. 3, 2011
Schweikert, David	AZ	112th to 116th	Jan. 3, 2011
Scott, Austin	GA	112th to 116th	Jan. 3, 2011
Sewell, Terri A.	AL	112th to 116th	Jan. 3, 2011
Stivers, Steve	OH	112th to 116th	Jan. 3, 2011
Tipton, Scott R.	CO	112th to 116th	Jan. 3, 2011
Webster, Daniel	FL	112th to 116th	Jan. 3, 2011
Wilson, Frederica S.	FL	112th to 116th	Jan. 3, 2011
Womack, Steve	AR	112th to 116th	Jan. 3, 2011
Woodall, Rob	GA	112th to 116th	Jan. 3, 2011
		5 terms, not consecutive	
Titus, Dina	NV	111th and 113th to 116th.	Jan. 3, 2013
		4 terms, consecutive	
Adams, Alma S.	NC	* 113th to 116th	Nov. 4, 2014
Barr, Andy	KY	113th to 116th	Jan. 3, 2013
Beatty, Joyce	OH	113th to 116th	Jan. 3, 2013

CONGRESSES IN WHICH REPRESENTATIVES, RESIDENT COMMISSIONER, AND DELEGATES HAVE SERVED WITH BEGINNING OF PRESENT SERVICE—CONTINUED

[* Elected to fill a vacancy; Democrats in roman (232); Republicans in *italic* (198); Libertarians in SMALL CAPS (1); Vacancies (4); Resident Commissioner and Delegates in **boldface** (6); total, 441]

Name	State	Congresses (inclusive)	Beginning of present service
Bera, Ami	CA	113th to 116th	Jan. 3, 2013
Brooks, Susan W.	IN	113th to 116th	Jan. 3, 2013
Brownley, Julia	CA	113th to 116th	Jan. 3, 2013
Bustos, Cheri	IL	113th to 116th	Jan. 3, 2013
Byrne, Bradley	AL	* 113th to 116th	Dec. 17, 2013
Cárdenas, Tony	CA	113th to 116th	Jan. 3, 2013
Cartwright, Matt	PA	113th to 116th	Jan. 3, 2013
Castro, Joaquin	TX	113th to 116th	Jan. 3, 2013
Clark, Katherine M.	MA	* 113th to 116th	Dec. 10, 2013
Collins, Doug	GA	113th to 116th	Jan. 3, 2013
Cook, Paul	CA	113th to 116th	Jan. 3, 2013
Davis, Rodney	IL	113th to 116th	Jan. 3, 2013
Frankel, Lois	FL	113th to 116th	Jan. 3, 2013
Gabbard, Tulsi	HI	113th to 116th	Jan. 3, 2013
Heck, Denny	WA	113th to 116th	Jan. 3, 2013
Holding, George	NC	113th to 116th	Jan. 3, 2013
Hudson, Richard	NC	113th to 116th	Jan. 3, 2013
Huffman, Jared	CA	113th to 116th	Jan. 3, 2013
Jeffries, Hakeem S.	NY	113th to 116th	Jan. 3, 2013
Joyce, David P.	OH	113th to 116th	Jan. 3, 2013
Kelly, Robin L.	IL	* 113th to 116th	Apr. 9, 2013
Kennedy, Joseph P., III	MA	113th to 116th	Jan. 3, 2013
Kildee, Daniel T.	MI	113th to 116th	Jan. 3, 2013
Kilmer, Derek	WA	113th to 116th	Jan. 3, 2013
Kuster, Ann M.	NH	113th to 116th	Jan. 3, 2013
LaMalfa, Doug	CA	113th to 116th	Jan. 3, 2013
Lowenthal, Alan S.	CA	113th to 116th	Jan. 3, 2013
Maloney, Sean Patrick	NY	113th to 116th	Jan. 3, 2013
Meng, Grace	NY	113th to 116th	Jan. 3, 2013
Mullin, Markwayne	OK	113th to 116th	Jan. 3, 2013
Norcross, Donald	NJ	* 113th to 116th	Nov. 4, 2014
Perry, Scott	PA	113th to 116th	Jan. 3, 2013
Peters, Scott H.	CA	113th to 116th	Jan. 3, 2013
Pocan, Mark	WI	113th to 116th	Jan. 3, 2013
Rice, Tom	SC	113th to 116th	Jan. 3, 2013
Ruiz, Raul	CA	113th to 116th	Jan. 3, 2013
Smith, Jason	MO	* 113th to 116th	June 4, 2013
Stewart, Chris	UT	113th to 116th	Jan. 3, 2013
Swalwell, Eric	CA	113th to 116th	Jan. 3, 2013
Takano, Mark	CA	113th to 116th	Jan. 3, 2013
Vargas, Juan	CA	113th to 116th	Jan. 3, 2013
Veasey, Marc A.	TX	113th to 116th	Jan. 3, 2013
Vela, Filemon	TX	113th to 116th	Jan. 3, 2013
Wagner, Ann	MO	113th to 116th	Jan. 3, 2013
Walorski, Jackie	IN	113th to 116th	Jan. 3, 2013
Weber, Randy K., Sr.	TX	113th to 116th	Jan. 3, 2013
Wenstrup, Brad R.	OH	113th to 116th	Jan. 3, 2013
Williams, Roger	TX	113th to 116th	Jan. 3, 2013
Yoho, Ted S.	FL	113th to 116th	Jan. 3, 2013

CONGRESSES IN WHICH REPRESENTATIVES, RESIDENT COMMISSIONER, AND DELEGATES HAVE SERVED WITH BEGINNING OF PRESENT SERVICE—CONTINUED

[* Elected to fill a vacancy; Democrats in roman (232); Republicans in *italic* (198); Libertarians in SMALL CAPS (1); Vacancies (4); Resident Commissioner and Delegates in **boldface** (6); total, 441]

Name	State	Congresses (inclusive)	Beginning of present service
4 terms, not consecutive			
Case, Ed	HI	* 107th to 109th and 116th.	Jan. 3, 2019
Kirkpatrick, Ann	AZ	111th, 113th to 114th, and 116th.	Jan. 3, 2019
3 terms, consecutive			
Abraham, Ralph Lee	LA	114th to 116th	Jan. 3, 2015
Aguilar, Pete	CA	114th to 116th	Jan. 3, 2015
Allen, Rick W.	GA	114th to 116th	Jan. 3, 2015
Babin, Brian	TX	114th to 116th	Jan. 3, 2015
Beyer, Donald S., Jr.	VA	114th to 116th	Jan. 3, 2015
Bost, Mike	IL	114th to 116th	Jan. 3, 2015
Boyle, Brendan F.	PA	114th to 116th	Jan. 3, 2015
Buck, Ken	CO	114th to 116th	Jan. 3, 2015
Carter, Earl L. ''Buddy''	GA	114th to 116th	Jan. 3, 2015
Comer, James	KY	* 114th to 116th	Nov. 8, 2016
Davidson, Warren	OH	* 114th to 116th	June 7, 2016
DeSaulnier, Mark	CA	114th to 116th	Jan. 3, 2015
Dingell, Debbie	MI	114th to 116th	Jan. 3, 2015
Emmer, Tom	MN	114th to 116th	Jan. 3, 2015
Evans, Dwight	PA	* 114th to 116th	Nov. 8, 2016
Gallego, Ruben	AZ	114th to 116th	Jan. 3, 2015
Graves, Garret	LA	114th to 116th	Jan. 3, 2015
Grothman, Glenn	WI	114th to 116th	Jan. 3, 2015
Hice, Jody B.	GA	114th to 116th	Jan. 3, 2015
Hill, J. French	AR	114th to 116th	Jan. 3, 2015
Hurd, Will	TX	114th to 116th	Jan. 3, 2015
Katko, John	NY	114th to 116th	Jan. 3, 2015
Kelly, Trent	MS	* 114th to 116th	June 2, 2015
LaHood, Darin	IL	* 114th to 116th	Sept. 10, 2015
Lawrence, Brenda L.	MI	114th to 116th	Jan. 3, 2015
Lieu, Ted	CA	114th to 116th	Jan. 3, 2015
Loudermilk, Barry	GA	114th to 116th	Jan. 3, 2015
Moolenaar, John R.	MI	114th to 116th	Jan. 3, 2015
Mooney, Alexander X.	WV	114th to 116th	Jan. 3, 2015
Moulton, Seth	MA	114th to 116th	Jan. 3, 2015
Newhouse, Dan	WA	114th to 116th	Jan. 3, 2015
Palmer, Gary J.	AL	114th to 116th	Jan. 3, 2015
Rice, Kathleen M.	NY	114th to 116th	Jan. 3, 2015
Rouzer, David	NC	114th to 116th	Jan. 3, 2015
Stefanik, Elise M.	NY	114th to 116th	Jan. 3, 2015
Torres, Norma J.	CA	114th to 116th	Jan. 3, 2015
Walker, Mark	NC	114th to 116th	Jan. 3, 2015
Watson Coleman, Bonnie	NJ	114th to 116th	Jan. 3, 2015
Westerman, Bruce	AR	114th to 116th	Jan. 3, 2015
Zeldin, Lee M.	NY	114th to 116th	Jan. 3, 2015

CONGRESSES IN WHICH REPRESENTATIVES, RESIDENT COMMISSIONER, AND DELEGATES HAVE SERVED WITH BEGINNING OF PRESENT SERVICE—CONTINUED

[* Elected to fill a vacancy; Democrats in roman (232); Republicans in *italic* (198); Libertarians in SMALL CAPS (1); Vacancies (4); Resident Commissioner and Delegates in **boldface** (6); total, 441]

Name	State	Congresses (inclusive)	Beginning of present service
3 terms, not consecutive			
Schneider, Bradley Scott	IL	113th and 115th to 116th.	Jan. 3, 2017
2 terms			
Arrington, Jodey C.	TX	115th to 116th	Jan. 3, 2017
Bacon, Don	NE	115th to 116th	Jan. 3, 2017
Balderson, Troy	OH	* 115th to 116th	Aug. 7, 2018
Banks, Jim	IN	115th to 116th	Jan. 3, 2017
Barragán, Nanette Diaz	CA	115th to 116th	Jan. 3, 2017
Bergman, Jack	MI	115th to 116th	Jan. 3, 2017
Biggs, Andy	AZ	115th to 116th	Jan. 3, 2017
Blunt Rochester, Lisa	DE	115th to 116th	Jan. 3, 2017
Brown, Anthony G.	MD	115th to 116th	Jan. 3, 2017
Budd, Ted	NC	115th to 116th	Jan. 3, 2017
Carbajal, Salud O.	CA	115th to 116th	Jan. 3, 2017
Cheney, Liz	WY	115th to 116th	Jan. 3, 2017
Cloud, Michael	TX	* 115th to 116th	June 30, 2018
Correa, J. Luis	CA	115th to 116th	Jan. 3, 2017
Crist, Charlie	FL	115th to 116th	Jan. 3, 2017
Curtis, John R.	UT	* 115th to 116th	Nov. 13, 2017
Demings, Val Butler	FL	115th to 116th	Jan. 3, 2017
Dunn, Neal P.	FL	115th to 116th	Jan. 3, 2017
Espaillat, Adriano	NY	115th to 116th	Jan. 3, 2017
Estes, Ron	KS	* 115th to 116th	Apr. 11, 2017
Ferguson, A. Drew, IV	GA	115th to 116th	Jan. 3, 2017
Fitzpatrick, Brian K.	PA	115th to 116th	Jan. 3, 2017
Gaetz, Matt	FL	115th to 116th	Jan. 3, 2017
Gallagher, Mike	WI	115th to 116th	Jan. 3, 2017
Gianforte, Greg	MT	* 115th to 116th	May 25, 2017
Gomez, Jimmy	CA	* 115th to 116th	June 6, 2017
Gonzalez, Vicente	TX	115th to 116th	Jan. 3, 2017
Gottheimer, Josh	NJ	115th to 116th	Jan. 3, 2017
Hern, Kevin	OK	* 115th to 116th	Nov. 13, 2018
Higgins, Clay	LA	115th to 116th	Jan. 3, 2017
Hollingsworth, Trey	IN	115th to 116th	Jan. 3, 2017
Jayapal, Pramila	WA	115th to 116th	Jan. 3, 2017
Johnson, Mike	LA	115th to 116th	Jan. 3, 2017
Khanna, Ro	CA	115th to 116th	Jan. 3, 2017
Krishnamoorthi, Raja	IL	115th to 116th	Jan. 3, 2017
Kustoff, David	TN	115th to 116th	Jan. 3, 2017
Lamb, Conor	PA	* 115th to 116th	Mar. 13, 2018
Lawson, Al, Jr.	FL	115th to 116th	Jan. 3, 2017
Lesko, Debbie	AZ	* 115th to 116th	May 7, 2018
Marshall, Roger W.	KS	115th to 116th	Jan. 3, 2017
Mast, Brian J.	FL	115th to 116th	Jan. 3, 2017
McEachin, A. Donald	VA	115th to 116th	Jan. 3, 2017
Mitchell, Paul	MI	115th to 116th	Jan. 3, 2017
Morelle, Joseph D.	NY	* 115th to 116th	Nov. 13, 2018
Murphy, Stephanie N.	FL	115th to 116th	Jan. 3, 2017
Norman, Ralph	SC	* 115th to 116th	June 20, 2017

CONGRESSES IN WHICH REPRESENTATIVES, RESIDENT COMMISSIONER, AND DELEGATES HAVE SERVED WITH BEGINNING OF PRESENT SERVICE—CONTINUED

[* Elected to fill a vacancy; Democrats in roman (232); Republicans in *italic* (198); Libertarians in SMALL CAPS (1); Vacancies (4); Resident Commissioner and Delegates in **boldface** (6); total, 441]

Name	State	Congresses (inclusive)	Beginning of present service
O'Halleran, Tom	AZ	115th to 116th	Jan. 3, 2017
Panetta, Jimmy	CA	115th to 116th	Jan. 3, 2017
Raskin, Jamie	MD	115th to 116th	Jan. 3, 2017
Rooney, Francis	FL	115th to 116th	Jan. 3, 2017
Rutherford, John H.	FL	115th to 116th	Jan. 3, 2017
Scanlon, Mary Gay	PA	*115th to 116th	Nov. 13, 2018
Smucker, Lloyd	PA	115th to 116th	Jan. 3, 2017
Soto, Darren	FL	115th to 116th	Jan. 3, 2017
Suozzi, Thomas R.	NY	115th to 116th	Jan. 3, 2017
Wild, Susan	PA	*115th to 116th	Nov. 27, 2018
2 terms, not consecutive			
Horsford, Steven	NV	114th and 116th	Jan. 3, 2019
1 term			
Allred, Colin Z.	TX	116th	Jan. 3, 2019
Armstrong, Kelly	ND	116th	Jan. 3, 2019
Axne, Cynthia	IA	116th	Jan. 3, 2019
Baird, James R.	IN	116th	Jan. 3, 2019
Bishop, Dan	NC	*116th	Sept. 10, 2019
Brindisi, Anthony	NY	116th	Jan. 3, 2019
Burchett, Tim	TN	116th	Jan. 3, 2019
Casten, Sean	IL	116th	Jan. 3, 2019
Cisneros, Gilbert Ray, Jr.	CA	116th	Jan. 3, 2019
Cline, Ben	VA	116th	Jan. 3, 2019
Cox, TJ	CA	116th	Jan. 3, 2019
Craig, Angie	MN	116th	Jan. 3, 2019
Crenshaw, Dan	TX	116th	Jan. 3, 2019
Crow, Jason	CO	116th	Jan. 3, 2019
Cunningham, Joe	SC	116th	Jan. 3, 2019
Davids, Sharice	KS	116th	Jan. 3, 2019
Dean, Madeleine	PA	116th	Jan. 3, 2019
Delgado, Antonio	NY	116th	Jan. 3, 2019
Escobar, Veronica	TX	116th	Jan. 3, 2019
Finkenauer, Abby	IA	116th	Jan. 3, 2019
Fletcher, Lizzie	TX	116th	Jan. 3, 2019
Fulcher, Russ	ID	116th	Jan. 3, 2019
García, Jesús G. "Chuy"	IL	116th	Jan. 3, 2019
Garcia, Mike	CA	*116th	May 19, 2020
Garcia, Sylvia R.	TX	116th	Jan. 3, 2019
Golden, Jared F.	ME	116th	Jan. 3, 2019
Gonzalez, Anthony	OH	116th	Jan. 3, 2019
Gooden, Lance	TX	116th	Jan. 3, 2019
Green, Mark E.	TN	116th	Jan. 3, 2019
Guest, Michael	MS	116th	Jan. 3, 2019
Haaland, Debra A.	NM	116th	Jan. 3, 2019
Hagedorn, Jim	MN	116th	Jan. 3, 2019
Harder, Josh	CA	116th	Jan. 3, 2019
Hayes, Jahana	CT	116th	Jan. 3, 2019
Horn, Kendra S.	OK	116th	Jan. 3, 2019
Houlahan, Chrissy	PA	116th	Jan. 3, 2019

CONGRESSES IN WHICH REPRESENTATIVES, RESIDENT COMMISSIONER, AND DELEGATES HAVE SERVED WITH BEGINNING OF PRESENT SERVICE—CONTINUED

[* Elected to fill a vacancy; Democrats in roman (232); Republicans in *italic* (198); Libertarians in SMALL CAPS (1); Vacancies (4); Resident Commissioner and Delegates in **boldface** (6); total, 441]

Name	State	Congresses (inclusive)	Beginning of present service
Jacobs, Chris	NY	* 116th	July 21, 2020
Johnson, Dusty	SD	116th	Jan. 3, 2019
Joyce, John	PA	116th	Jan. 3, 2019
Keller, Fred	PA	* 116th	May 21, 2019
Kim, Andy	NJ	116th	Jan. 3, 2019
Lee, Susie	NV	116th	Jan. 3, 2019
Levin, Andy	MI	116th	Jan. 3, 2019
Levin, Mike	CA	116th	Jan. 3, 2019
Luria, Elaine G.	VA	116th	Jan. 3, 2019
Malinowski, Tom	NJ	116th	Jan. 3, 2019
McAdams, Ben	UT	116th	Jan. 3, 2019
McBath, Lucy	GA	116th	Jan. 3, 2019
Meuser, Daniel	PA	116th	Jan. 3, 2019
Miller, Carol D.	WV	116th	Jan. 3, 2019
Mucarsel-Powell, Debbie	FL	116th	Jan. 3, 2019
Murphy, Gregory F.	NC	* 116th	Sept. 10, 2019
Neguse, Joe	CO	116th	Jan. 3, 2019
Ocasio-Cortez, Alexandria	NY	116th	Jan. 3, 2019
Omar, Ilhan	MN	116th	Jan. 3, 2019
Pappas, Chris	NH	116th	Jan. 3, 2019
Pence, Greg	IN	116th	Jan. 3, 2019
Phillips, Dean	MN	116th	Jan. 3, 2019
Porter, Katie	CA	116th	Jan. 3, 2019
Pressley, Ayanna	MA	116th	Jan. 3, 2019
Reschenthaler, Guy	PA	116th	Jan. 3, 2019
Riggleman, Denver	VA	116th	Jan. 3, 2019
Rose, John W.	TN	116th	Jan. 3, 2019
Rose, Max	NY	116th	Jan. 3, 2019
Rouda, Harley	CA	116th	Jan. 3, 2019
Roy, Chip	TX	116th	Jan. 3, 2019
Schrier, Kim	WA	116th	Jan. 3, 2019
Shalala, Donna E.	FL	116th	Jan. 3, 2019
Sherrill, Mikie	NJ	116th	Jan. 3, 2019
Slotkin, Elissa	MI	116th	Jan. 3, 2019
Spanberger, Abigail Davis	VA	116th	Jan. 3, 2019
Spano, Ross	FL	116th	Jan. 3, 2019
Stanton, Greg	AZ	116th	Jan. 3, 2019
Stauber, Pete	MN	116th	Jan. 3, 2019
Steil, Bryan	WI	116th	Jan. 3, 2019
Steube, W. Gregory	FL	116th	Jan. 3, 2019
Stevens, Haley M.	MI	116th	Jan. 3, 2019
Taylor, Van	TX	116th	Jan. 3, 2019
Tiffany, Thomas P.	WI	* 116th	May 19, 2020
Timmons, William R., IV	SC	116th	Jan. 3, 2019
Tlaib, Rashida	MI	116th	Jan. 3, 2019
Torres Small, Xochitl	NM	116th	Jan. 3, 2019
Trahan, Lori	MA	116th	Jan. 3, 2019
Trone, David J.	MD	116th	Jan. 3, 2019
Underwood, Lauren	IL	116th	Jan. 3, 2019
Van Drew, Jefferson	NJ	116th	Jan. 3, 2019
Waltz, Michael	FL	116th	Jan. 3, 2019

CONGRESSES IN WHICH REPRESENTATIVES, RESIDENT COMMISSIONER, AND DELEGATES HAVE SERVED WITH BEGINNING OF PRESENT SERVICE—CONTINUED

[* Elected to fill a vacancy; Democrats in roman (232); Republicans in *italic* (198); Libertarians in SMALL CAPS (1); Vacancies (4); Resident Commissioner and Delegates in **boldface** (6); total, 441]

Name	State	Congresses (inclusive)	Beginning of present service
Watkins, Steve	KS	116th	Jan. 3, 2019
Wexton, Jennifer	VA	116th	Jan. 3, 2019
Wright, Ron	TX	116th	Jan. 3, 2019
RESIDENT COMMISSIONER			
González-Colón, Jenniffer	PR	115th to 116th	Jan. 3, 2017
DELEGATES			
Norton, Eleanor Holmes	DC	102d to 116th	Jan. 3, 1991
Sablan, Gregorio Kilili Camacho	MP	111th to 116th	Jan. 3, 2009
Plaskett, Stacey E.	VI	114th to 116th	Jan. 3, 2015
Radewagen, Aumua Amata Coleman.	AS	114th to 116th	Jan. 3, 2015
San Nicolas, Michael F. Q.	GU	116th	Jan. 3, 2019

[1] Special Election, March 8, 2008.

NOTE: Members elected by special election are considered to begin service on the date that they were sworn in, except for those elected after a sine die adjournment. If elected after the Congress has adjourned for the session, Members are considered to begin their service on the day after the election.

STANDING COMMITTEES OF THE SENATE

[Republicans in roman; Democrats in *italic*; Independents in SMALL CAPS]

[Room numbers beginning with SD are in the Dirksen Building, SH in the Hart Building, SR in the Russell Building, and S in The Capitol]

Agriculture, Nutrition, and Forestry

328A Russell Senate Office Building 20510–6000

phone 224–2035, fax 228–2125, TTY / TDD 224–2587

https://agriculture.senate.gov

meets first and third Wednesdays of each month

Pat Roberts, of Kansas, *Chair*

Mitch McConnell, of Kentucky.
John Boozman, of Arkansas.
John Hoeven, of North Dakota.
Joni Ernst, of Iowa.
Cindy Hyde-Smith, of Mississippi.
Mike Braun, of Indiana.
Chuck Grassley, of Iowa.
John Thune, of South Dakota.
Deb Fischer, of Nebraska.
Kelly Loeffler, of Georgia.

Debbie Stabenow, of Michigan.
Patrick J. Leahy, of Vermont.
Sherrod Brown, of Ohio.
Amy Klobuchar, of Minnesota.
Michael F. Bennet, of Colorado.
Kirsten E. Gillibrand, of New York.
Robert P. Casey, Jr., of Pennsylvania.
Tina Smith, of Minnesota.
Richard J. Durbin, of Illinois.

SUBCOMMITTEES

[The chair and ranking minority member are ex officio (non-voting) members of all subcommittees on which they do not serve.]

Commodities, Risk Management, and Trade

John Boozman, of Arkansas, *Chair*

Mitch McConnell, of Kentucky.
John Hoeven, of North Dakota.
Cindy Hyde-Smith, of Mississippi.
Chuck Grassley, of Iowa.

Sherrod Brown, of Ohio.
Michael F. Bennet, of Colorado.
Kirsten E. Gillibrand, of New York.
Tina Smith, of Minnesota.
Richard J. Durbin, of Illinois.

Conservation, Forestry, and Natural Resources

Mike Braun, of Indiana, *Chair*

John Boozman, of Arkansas.
Cindy Hyde-Smith, of Mississippi.
Chuck Grassley, of Iowa.
John Thune, of South Dakota.
Kelly Loeffler, of Georgia.

Michael F. Bennet, of Colorado.
Patrick J. Leahy, of Vermont.
Amy Klobuchar, of Minnesota.
Robert P. Casey, Jr., of Pennsylvania.
Richard J. Durbin, of Illinois.

Livestock, Marketing, and Agriculture Security

Cindy Hyde-Smith, of Mississippi, *Chair*

Joni Ernst, of Iowa.
Mike Braun, of Indiana.
Chuck Grassley, of Iowa.
Deb Fischer, of Nebraska.
Kelly Loeffler, of Georgia.
Kirsten E. Gillibrand, of New York.
Patrick J. Leahy, of Vermont.
Amy Klobuchar, of Minnesota.
Robert P. Casey, Jr., of Pennsylvania.
Tina Smith, of Minnesota.

Nutrition, Agricultural Research, and Specialty Crops

Deb Fischer, of Nebraska, *Chair*

Mitch McConnell, of Kentucky.
John Boozman, of Arkansas.
John Hoeven, of North Dakota.
Joni Ernst, of Iowa.
John Thune, of South Dakota.
Robert P. Casey, Jr., of Pennsylvania.
Patrick J. Leahy, of Vermont.
Sherrod Brown, of Ohio.
Amy Klobuchar, of Minnesota.
Kirsten E. Gillibrand, of New York.

Rural Development and Energy

Joni Ernst, of Iowa, *Chair*

Mitch McConnell, of Kentucky.
John Hoeven, of North Dakota.
Mike Braun, of Indiana.
John Thune, of South Dakota.
Deb Fischer, of Nebraska.
Tina Smith, of Minnesota.
Sherrod Brown, of Ohio.
Amy Klobuchar, of Minnesota.
Michael F. Bennet, of Colorado.
Richard J. Durbin, of Illinois.

STAFF

Committee on Agriculture, Nutrition, and Forestry (SR–328A), 224–2035, fax 228–2125.

Majority Staff:
Staff Director.—James Glueck.
Chief Counsel and Policy Director.—DaNita Murray.
Senior Counsel.—Fred Clark.
Chief Economist.—Matthew Erickson.
General Counsel.—Andrew Rezendes.
Communications Director.—Meghan Cline.
Special Advisor.—CJ Mann.
Senior Professional Staff: Janae Brady, Darin Guries, Chelsie Keys, Robert Rosado, Wayne Stoskopf, Andrew Vlasaty.
Legislative Assistants: Haley Donahue, Chance Hunley.
Staff Assistants / Legislative Correspondents: Lane Coberly, Christine Rock.

Minority Staff:
Staff Director.—Joe Shultz.
Deputy Staff Director / Policy Director.—Jacqlyn Schneider.
Chief Counsel.—Mary Beth Schultz.
Senior Professional Staff: Sean Babington, Katie Naessens, Mike Schmidt, Adam Tarr.
Professional Staff: Kevin Bailey, Katie Bergh, Kyle Varner.
Special Counsel.—Susan Keith.
CFTC Detailee.—Ward Griffin.
Press Secretary.—Jess McCarron.
Policy Analyst.—Rosalyn Brummette.
Staff Assistant.—Julia Rossman.

Non-Designated:
Chief Clerk.—Jessie Williams.
Director of IT.—Bobby Mehta.
Deputy Chief Clerk.—Hans Hansen.
Archivist—Katie Salay.
GPO Detailee.—Joe Stallworth.

Appropriations

S–128 The Capitol 20510–6025, phone 224–7257

https://appropriations.senate.gov

meets upon call of the chair

Richard C. Shelby, of Alabama, *Chair*

Mitch McConnell, of Kentucky.
Lamar Alexander, of Tennessee.
Susan M. Collins, of Maine.
Lisa Murkowski, of Alaska.
Lindsey Graham, of South Carolina.
Roy Blunt, of Missouri.
Jerry Moran, of Kansas.
John Hoeven, of North Dakota.
John Boozman, of Arkansas.
Shelley Moore Capito, of West Virginia.
John Kennedy, of Louisiana.
Cindy Hyde-Smith, of Mississippi.
Steve Daines, of Montana.
Marco Rubio, of Florida.
James Lankford, of Oklahoma.

Patrick J. Leahy, of Vermont.
Patty Murray, of Washington.
Dianne Feinstein, of California.
Richard J. Durbin, of Illinois.
Jack Reed, of Rhode Island.
Jon Tester, of Montana.
Tom Udall, of New Mexico.
Jeanne Shaheen, of New Hampshire.
Jeff Merkley, of Oregon.
Christopher A. Coons, of Delaware.
Brian Schatz, of Hawaii.
Tammy Baldwin, of Wisconsin.
Christopher Murphy, of Connecticut.
Joe Manchin III, of West Virginia.
Chris Van Hollen, of Maryland.

SUBCOMMITTEES

[The chair and ranking minority member are ex officio members of all subcommittees on which they do not serve.]

Agriculture, Rural Development, Food and Drug Administration, and Related Agencies

John Hoeven, of North Dakota, *Chair*

Mitch McConnell, of Kentucky.
Susan M. Collins, of Maine.
Roy Blunt, of Missouri.
Jerry Moran, of Kansas.
Cindy Hyde-Smith, of Mississippi.
John Kennedy, of Louisiana.

Jeff Merkley, of Oregon.
Dianne Feinstein, of California.
Jon Tester, of Montana.
Tom Udall, of New Mexico.
Patrick J. Leahy, of Vermont.
Tammy Baldwin, of Wisconsin.

Commerce, Justice, Science, and Related Agencies

Jerry Moran, of Kansas, *Chair*

Lamar Alexander, of Tennessee.
Lisa Murkowski, of Alaska.
Susan M. Collins, of Maine.
Lindsey Graham, of South Carolina.
John Boozman, of Arkansas.
Shelley Moore Capito, of West Virginia.
John Kennedy, of Louisiana.
Marco Rubio, of Florida.

Jeanne Shaheen, of New Hampshire.
Patrick J. Leahy, of Vermont.
Dianne Feinstein, of California.
Jack Reed, of Rhode Island.
Christopher A. Coons, of Delaware.
Brian Schatz, of Hawaii.
Joe Manchin III, of West Virginia.
Chris Van Hollen, of Maryland.

Defense

Richard C. Shelby, of Alabama, *Chair*

Mitch McConnell, of Kentucky.
Lamar Alexander, of Tennessee.
Susan M. Collins, of Maine.
Lisa Murkowski, of Alaska.
Lindsey Graham, of South Carolina.
Roy Blunt, of Missouri.
Jerry Moran, of Kansas.
John Hoeven, of North Dakota.
John Boozman, of Arkansas.

Richard J. Durbin, of Illinois.
Patrick J. Leahy, of Vermont.
Dianne Feinstein, of California.
Patty Murray, of Washington.
Jack Reed, of Rhode Island.
Jon Tester, of Montana.
Tom Udall, of New Mexico.
Brian Schatz, of Hawaii.
Tammy Baldwin, of Wisconsin.

Energy and Water Development

Lamar Alexander, of Tennessee, *Chair*

Mitch McConnell, of Kentucky.
Richard C. Shelby, of Alabama.
Susan M. Collins, of Maine.
Lisa Murkowski, of Alaska.
Lindsey Graham, of South Carolina.
John Hoeven, of North Dakota.
John Kennedy, of Louisiana.
Cindy Hyde-Smith, of Mississippi.

Dianne Feinstein, of California.
Patty Murray, of Washington.
Jon Tester, of Montana.
Richard J. Durbin, of Illinois.
Tom Udall, of New Mexico.
Jeanne Shaheen, of New Hampshire.
Jeff Merkley, of Oregon.
Christopher A. Coons, of Delaware.

Financial Services and General Government

John Kennedy, of Louisiana, *Chair*

Jerry Moran, of Kansas.
John Boozman, of Arkansas.
Steve Daines, of Montana.
James Lankford, of Oklahoma.

Christopher A. Coons, of Delaware.
Richard J. Durbin, of Illinois.
Joe Manchin III, of West Virginia.
Chris Van Hollen, of Maryland.

Homeland Security

Shelley Moore Capito, of West Virginia, *Chair*

Richard C. Shelby, of Alabama.
Lisa Murkowski, of Alaska.
John Hoeven, of North Dakota.
John Kennedy, of Louisiana.
Cindy Hyde-Smith, of Mississippi.
James Lankford, of Oklahoma.

Jon Tester, of Montana.
Jeanne Shaheen, of New Hampshire.
Patrick J. Leahy, of Vermont.
Patty Murray, of Washington.
Tammy Baldwin, of Wisconsin.
Joe Manchin III, of West Virginia.

Interior, Environment, and Related Agencies

Lisa Murkowski, of Alaska, *Chair*

Lamar Alexander, of Tennessee.
Roy Blunt, of Missouri.
Mitch McConnell, of Kentucky.
Shelley Moore Capito, of West Virginia.
Cindy Hyde-Smith, of Mississippi.
Steve Daines, of Montana.
Marco Rubio, of Florida.

Tom Udall, of New Mexico.
Dianne Feinstein, of California.
Patrick J. Leahy, of Vermont.
Jack Reed, of Rhode Island.
Jon Tester, of Montana.
Jeff Merkley, of Oregon.
Chris Van Hollen, of Maryland.

Labor, Health and Human Services, Education, and Related Agencies

Roy Blunt, of Missouri, *Chair*

Richard C. Shelby, of Alabama.
Lamar Alexander, of Tennessee.
Lindsey Graham, of South Carolina.
Jerry Moran, of Kansas.
Shelley Moore Capito, of West Virginia.
John Kennedy, of Louisiana.
Cindy Hyde-Smith, of Mississippi.
Marco Rubio, of Florida.
James Lankford, of Oklahoma.

Patty Murray, of Washington.
Richard J. Durbin, of Illinois.
Jack Reed, of Rhode Island.
Jeanne Shaheen, of New Hampshire.
Jeff Merkley, of Oregon.
Brian Schatz, of Hawaii.
Tammy Baldwin, of Wisconsin.
Christopher Murphy, of Connecticut.
Joe Manchin III, of West Virginia.

Legislative Branch

Cindy Hyde-Smith, of Mississippi, *Chair*

Richard C. Shelby, of Alabama.
James Lankford, of Oklahoma.

Christopher Murphy, of Connecticut.
Chris Van Hollen, of Maryland.

Military Construction, Veterans Affairs, and Related Agencies

John Boozman, of Arkansas, *Chair*

Mitch McConnell, of Kentucky.
Lisa Murkowski, of Alaska.
John Hoeven, of North Dakota.
Susan M. Collins, of Maine.
Shelley Moore Capito, of West Virginia.
Marco Rubio, of Florida.
Steve Daines, of Montana.

Brian Schatz, of Hawaii.
Jon Tester, of Montana.
Patty Murray, of Washington.
Jack Reed, of Rhode Island.
Tom Udall, of New Mexico.
Tammy Baldwin, of Wisconsin.
Christopher Murphy, of Connecticut.

State, Foreign Operations, and Related Programs

Lindsey Graham, of South Carolina, *Chair*

Mitch McConnell, of Kentucky.
Roy Blunt, of Missouri.
John Boozman, of Arkansas.
Jerry Moran, of Kansas.
Marco Rubio, of Florida.
James Lankford, of Oklahoma.
Steve Daines, of Montana.

Patrick J. Leahy, of Vermont.
Richard J. Durbin, of Illinois.
Jeanne Shaheen, of New Hampshire.
Christopher A. Coons, of Delaware.
Jeff Merkley, of Oregon.
Christopher Murphy, of Connecticut.
Chris Van Hollen, of Maryland.

Transportation, Housing and Urban Development, and Related Agencies

Susan M. Collins, of Maine, *Chair*

Richard C. Shelby, of Alabama.
Lamar Alexander, of Tennessee.
Roy Blunt, of Missouri.
John Boozman, of Arkansas.
Shelley Moore Capito, of West Virginia.
Lindsey Graham, of South Carolina.
John Hoeven, of North Dakota.
Steve Daines, of Montana.

Jack Reed, of Rhode Island.
Patty Murray, of Washington.
Richard J. Durbin, of Illinois.
Dianne Feinstein, of California.
Christopher A. Coons, of Delaware.
Brian Schatz, of Hawaii.
Christopher Murphy, of Connecticut.
Joe Manchin III, of West Virginia.

STAFF

Committee on Appropriations (S–128), 224–7257.
Staff Director.—Shannon Hines (S–128).
Chief Clerk.—Robert W. Putnam (SD–114).
Deputy Staff Director.—Jonathan Graffeo.
Chief Counsel.—David Adkins.
Communications Director.—Blair Taylor (S–128).
Professional Staff: (S–128); Lucas Agnew, Jenny Winkler (SD–114).
Technical Systems Manager.—Hong Nguyen (SD–114).
Security Manager.—Clint Trocchio (SD–118).
Executive Assistant.—Mary Collins Atkinson.
Clerical Assistant.—George Castro (SD–120), 4–5433.
Minority Staff Director.—Charles E. Kieffer (S–146A), 4–7363.
Minority Deputy Staff Director.—Chanda Betourney (S–146A).
Press Secretary.—Jay Tilton (S–146A).
Senior Advisor.—Jessica Berry (S–146A).
Executive Assistant.—Teri Curtin (SH–125).
Staff Assistant.—Jean Kwon (S–146A).

Subcommittee on Agriculture, Rural Development, Food and Drug Administration, and Related Agencies (SD–127), 4–5270.
Majority Clerk.—Carlisle Clarke (SD–127).
Professional Staff: Patrick Carroll (SD–127); Elizabeth Dent (SD–127).
Staff Assistant.—Carlos Elias (SD–122).
Minority Clerk.—Jessica Arden Schulken (SD–190), 4–8090.
Professional Staff: Dianne Nellor (SD–190); Bob Ross (SD–190).
Staff Assistant.—Teri Curtin (SH–125).

Subcommittee on Commerce, Justice, Science, and Related Agencies (SD–142), 4–7277.
Majority Clerk.—Jeremy Weirich (SD–142).
Professional Staff: Amber Busby Beck (SD–142); Allen Cutler (SD–142); Matt Womble (SD–142).
Minority Clerk.—Jean Toal Eisen (SH–125), 4–5202.
Professional Staff: Jennifer Eskra (SH–125); Blaise Sheridan (SH–125).
Staff Assistant.—Jordan Stone (SH–125).

Subcommittee on Defense (SD–122), 4–7255.
Majority Clerk.—Brian Potts (SD–122).
Professional Staff: Mike Clementi (SD–122); Colleen Gaydos (SD–122); Katy Hagan (SD–122); Chris Hall (SD–122); Kate Kaufer (SD–122), Jacqui Russell (SD–122); Jennifer S. Santos (SD–122); Will Todd (SD–122).
Staff Assistant.—Carlos Elias (SD–122).
Minority Clerk.—Erik Raven (SD–117), 4–6688.
Professional Staff: David C. Gillies (SD–115); Brigid Houton (SD–115); John Lucio; Andy Vanlandingham (SD–115).

Subcommittee on Energy and Water Development (SD–142), 4–7260.
Majority Clerk.—Tyler Owens (SD–142).
Professional Staff: Jen Armstrong (SD–142); Adam DeMella (SD–142); Molly Marsh (SD–142); Meyer Seligman (SD–142).
Staff Assistant.—Rachel Littleton.
Minority Clerk.—Doug Clapp (SD–188), 4–8119.
Professional Staff: Chris Hanson (SD–188); Samantha Nelson (SD–188).

Subcommittee on Financial Services and General Government (SD–133), 4–2104.
Majority Clerk.—Andrew Newton (SD–133).
Professional Staff: Lauren Comeau; Brian Daner; LaShawnda Smith (SD–131).
Minority Clerk.—Ellen Murray (SH–125), 4–1133.
Professional Staff.—Diana Gourlay Hamilton (SH–125).
Staff Assistant.—Reeves Hart (SD–128).

Subcommittee on Homeland Security (SD–131), 4–4319.
Majority Clerk.—Adam Telle (SD–131).
Professional Staff: Peter Babb (SD–131); Chris Cook (SD–131); Christian Lee (SD–131); LaShawnda Smith (SD–131).
Minority Clerk.—Scott Nance (SD–128), 4–8244.
Professional Staff: Drenan A. Dudley (SD–128); Chip Walgren (SD–128).
Staff Assistants: Irina Bajic (SD–128); Reeves Hart (SD–128).

Subcommittee on Interior, Environment, and Related Agencies (SD–131), 4–7233.
Majority Clerk.—Leif Fonnesbeck (SD–131).
Professional Staff: Emy Lesofski (SD–131); Nona McCoy (SD–131); LaShawnda Smith (SD–131); Chris Tomassi (SD–131).
Minority Clerk.—Rachael Taylor (SH–125), 8–0774.
Professional Staff: Ryan Hunt (SH–125); Melissa Zimmerman (SH–125).
Staff Assistant.—Teri Curtin (SH–125).

Subcommittee on Labor, Health and Human Services, Education, and Related Agencies (SD–135), 4–7230.
Majority Clerk.—Laura A. Friedel (SD–135).
Professional Staff: Michael Gentile (SD–135); Ashley Palmer; Jeff Reczek (SD–135); Adam Sullivan (SD–135).
Staff Assistant.—Sophie Sando.
Minority Clerk.—Alex Keenan (SD–156).
Professional Staff: Lisa Bernhardt (SD–156); Kelly Brown (SD–156); Mark Laisch (SD–156).
Staff Assistant.—Teri Curtin (SD–156).

Subcommittee on Legislative Branch (S–128), 4–9747.
Majority Clerk.—Sarah Boliek (S–128).
Professional Staff.—Lucas Agnew (S–135).
Minority Clerk.—Melissa Zimmerman (SH–125).
Staff Assistant.—Jean Kwon (S–146A).

Subcommittee on Military Construction, Veterans Affairs, and Related Agencies (SD–125), 4–5245.
Majority Clerk.—Patrick Magnuson (SD–125).
Professional Staff: Jennifer Bastin, Joanne Hoff.
Staff Assistant.—Carlos Elias (SD–122).
Minority Clerk.—Chad Schulken (SH–125), 4–8224.
Professional Staff.—Jason McMahon (SH–125).

Subcommittee on State, Foreign Operations, and Related Programs (SD–127), 4–2104.
Majority Clerk.—Paul Grove (SD–127).
Professional Staff: Kali Matalon; LaShawnda Smith (SD–131); Jason Wheelock (SD–127); Adam Yezerski (SD–127).
Minority Clerk.—Tim Rieser (SH–125), 4–7284.
Professional Staff.—Alex Carnes (SH–125).

Subcommittee on Transportation, Housing and Urban Development, and Related Agencies (SD–184), 4–5310.
Majority Clerk.—Clare Doherty (SD–184).
Professional Staff: Gus Maples (SD–184); Rajat Mathur (SD–184); Jacob Press; Jason Woolwine (SD–184); Courtney Young.
Minority Clerk.—Dabney Hegg (SH–125), 4–7281.
Professional Staff: Christina Monroe (SH–125); Nathan Robinson (SH–125); Jordan Stone (SH–125).

Editorial and Printing (SD–126): Elmer Barnes (GPO), 4–7266; Valerie A. Hutton, 4–7267; Penny Myles; Karin Thames (GPO), 4–7217.

Armed Services

228 Russell Senate Office Building 20510–6050

phone 224–3871, https://armed-services.senate.gov

meets every Tuesday and Thursday

James M. Inhofe, of Oklahoma, *Chair*

Roger F. Wicker, of Mississippi.
Deb Fischer, of Nebraska.
Tom Cotton, of Arkansas.
Mike Rounds, of South Dakota.
Joni Ernst, of Iowa.
Thom Tillis, of North Carolina.
Dan Sullivan, of Alaska.
David Perdue, of Georgia.
Kevin Cramer, of North Dakota.
Martha McSally, of Arizona.
Rick Scott, of Florida.
Marsha Blackburn, of Tennessee.
Josh Hawley, of Missouri.

Jack Reed, of Rhode Island.
Jeanne Shaheen, of New Hampshire.
Kirsten E. Gillibrand, of New York.
Richard Blumenthal, of Connecticut.
Mazie K. Hirono, of Hawaii.
Tim Kaine, of Virginia.
ANGUS S. KING, JR., of Maine.
Martin Heinrich, of New Mexico.
Elizabeth Warren, of Massachusetts.
Gary C. Peters, of Michigan.
Joe Manchin III, of West Virginia.
Tammy Duckworth, of Illinois.
Doug Jones, of Alabama.

SUBCOMMITTEES

[The chair and the ranking minority member are ex officio (non-voting) members of all subcommittees on which they do not serve.]

Airland

Tom Cotton, of Arkansas, *Chair*

Roger F. Wicker, of Mississippi.
Thom Tillis, of North Carolina.
Dan Sullivan, of Alaska.
Kevin Cramer, of North Dakota.
Martha McSally, of Arizona.
Rick Scott, of Florida.

ANGUS S. KING, JR., of Maine.
Richard Blumenthal, of Connecticut.
Elizabeth Warren, of Massachusetts.
Gary C. Peters, of Michigan.
Tammy Duckworth, of Illinois.
Doug Jones, of Alabama.

Cybersecurity

Mike Rounds, of South Dakota, *Chair*

Roger F. Wicker, of Mississippi.
David Perdue, of Georgia.
Rick Scott, of Florida.
Marsha Blackburn, of Tennessee.

Joe Manchin III, of West Virginia.
Kirsten E. Gillibrand, of New York.
Richard Blumenthal, of Connecticut.
Martin Heinrich, of New Mexico.

Emerging Threats and Capabilities

Joni Ernst, of Iowa, *Chair*

Deb Fischer, of Nebraska.
Kevin Cramer, of North Dakota.
Marsha Blackburn, of Tennessee.
Josh Hawley, of Missouri.

Gary C. Peters, of Michigan.
Jeanne Shaheen, of New Hampshire.
Mazie K. Hirono, of Hawaii.
Martin Heinrich, of New Mexico.

Personnel

Thom Tillis, of North Carolina, *Chair*

Mike Rounds, of South Dakota.
Martha McSally, of Arizona.
Rick Scott, of Florida.
Kirsten E. Gillibrand, of New York.
Elizabeth Warren, of Massachusetts.
Tammy Duckworth, of Illinois.

Readiness and Management Support

Dan Sullivan, of Alaska, *Chair*

Deb Fischer, of Nebraska.
Joni Ernst, of Iowa.
David Perdue, of Georgia.
Martha McSally, of Arizona.
Marsha Blackburn, of Tennessee.
Tim Kaine, of Virginia.
Jeanne Shaheen, of New Hampshire.
Mazie K. Hirono, of Hawaii.
Tammy Duckworth, of Illinois.
Doug Jones, of Alabama.

Seapower

David Perdue, of Georgia, *Chair*

Roger F. Wicker, of Mississippi.
Tom Cotton, of Arkansas.
Joni Ernst, of Iowa.
Thom Tillis, of North Carolina.
Josh Hawley, of Missouri.
Mazie K. Hirono, of Hawaii.
Jeanne Shaheen, of New Hampshire.
Richard Blumenthal, of Connecticut.
Tim Kaine, of Virginia.
ANGUS S. KING, JR., of Maine.

Strategic Forces

Deb Fischer, of Nebraska, *Chair*

Tom Cotton, of Arkansas.
Mike Rounds, of South Dakota.
Dan Sullivan, of Alaska.
Kevin Cramer, of North Dakota.
Josh Hawley, of Missouri.
Martin Heinrich, of New Mexico.
ANGUS S. KING, JR., of Maine.
Elizabeth Warren, of Massachusetts.
Joe Manchin III, of West Virginia.
Doug Jones, of Alabama.

STAFF

Committee on Armed Services (SR-228), 224-3871.

Majority and Non-Designated Staff:

Staff Director.—John Bonsell.
Special Assistant.—Tyler Wilkinson.
Deputy Staff Director.—John Wason.
Policy Director.—Tom Goffus.
General Counsel.—Stephanie Barna.
Budget and Deputy Policy Director.—Diem Salmon.
Chief Clerk.—Greg Lilly.
Communications Director.—Marta Hernandez.
Professional Staff Members: Adam Barker, Augusta Binns-Berkey, Allen Edwards, Jackie Kerber, Sean O'Keefe, Tony Pankuch, Brad Patout, Jason Potter, John Riordan, Katie Sutton, Eric Trager, Dustin Walker, Robert Winkler, Gwyneth Woolwine.
Nominations and Hearings Clerk.—Leah Brewer.
Security Manager.—Debbie Chiarello.
Systems Administrator.—Gary Howard.
Defense Policy Analysts: Katie Magnus, Arthur Tellis.
Staff Assistants: John Bryant, Patty-Jane Geller, Baher Iskander, Keri Lyn Michalke, Jacqueline Modesett, Soleil Sykes.

Subcommittee on Airland

Lead.—Robert Winkler.
Staff Assistant.—Baher Iskander.

Subcommittee on Cybersecurity

Lead.—Katie Sutton.
Staff Assistant.—Patty-Jane Geller.

Subcommittee on Emerging Threats and Capabilities

Lead.—Adam Barker.
Staff Assistant.—Jacqueline Modesett.

Subcommittee on Personnel

Lead.—Allen Edwards.
Staff Assistant.—Soleil Sykes.

Subcommittee on Readiness and Management Support

Lead.—Brad Patout.
Staff Assistant.—Keri Lyn Michalke.

Subcommittee on Seapower

Lead.—Jason Potter.
Staff Assistant.—Baher Iskander.

Subcommittee on Strategic Forces

Lead.—John Riordan.
Staff Assistant.—Patty-Jane Geller.

Majority Staff Subject Areas

Acquisition.—Gwyneth Woolwine.
Ammunition.—Jackie Kerber.
Arms Control.—Augusta Binns-Berkey.
Arsenals.—Jackie Kerber.
Audit.—Jackie Kerber.
Authorization for Use of Military Force.—Stephanie Barna.
Aviation Systems (Except Rotary).—Robert Winkler.
Aviation Systems (Rotary).—Tony Pankuch.
Base Realignment and Closure (BRAC).—Brad Patout.
Budget.—Diem Salmon.
Business Systems.—Gwyneth Woolwine.
Chemical-Biological Defense.—Jackie Kerber.
Chemical Demilitarization.—Jackie Kerber.
Civilian Nominations.—Stephanie Barna.
Civilian Workforce Policy.—Sean O'Keefe.
Combatant Commands
AFRICOM.—Adam Barker.
CENTCOM.—Eric Trager.
EUCOM.—Dustin Walker.
NORTHCOM.—Eric Trager.
INDOPACOM.—Dustin Walker.
SOCOM.—Adam Barker.
SOUTHCOM.—Adam Barker.
STRATCOM.—Augusta Binns-Berkey.
TRANSCOM.—Brad Patout.
CYBERCOM.—Katie Sutton.
Combating Terrorism.—Adam Barker.
Cooperative Threat Reduction Programs.—Jackie Kerber.
Cyber.—Katie Sutton.
Defense Logistics Agency.—Jackie Kerber.
Defense Security Assistance.—Adam Barker.
Department of Energy Issues
NNSA.—Augusta Binns-Berkey.
Nuclear Cleanup.—Jackie Kerber.
Depot Maintenance Policy.—Brad Patout.
Detainee Policy.—Stephanie Barna.
Electronic Warfare.—Katie Sutton.
Environmental Issues.—Jackie Kerber.
Facilities, Sustainment, Restoration and Modernization.—Brad Patout.
Global Force Posture and Basing.—Tom Goffus.
Ground Systems.—Tony Pankuch.
Homeland Defense / Security.—Eric Trager.
Housing Construction.—Brad Patout.
Humanitarian, Disaster, and Civil Assistance.—Jackie Kerber.
Industrial Operations (Military).—Brad Patout.

Information Technology/Cloud.—Gwyneth Woolwine.
Intelligence Issues.—Adam Barker.
International Defense Cooperation.—Adam Barker.
Investigations.—Stephanie Barna.
Joint Improvised-Threat Defeat Organization (JIDO).—Jody L. Bennett.
Land Use.—Brad Patout.
Management, Business, and Data.—Gwyneth Woolwine.
Maritime Issues.—Jason Potter.
Medical Facility Construction.—Allen Edwards.
Military Construction.—Brad Patout.
Military Personnel Issues
Awards, Commemorations, Decorations, and Memorials.—Katie Magnus.
Cemeteries.—Allen Edwards.
Commissaries and Exchanges.—Allen Edwards.
Compensation.—Sean O'Keefe.
Department of Defense Schools.—Allen Edwards.
End Strength.—Sean O'Keefe.
Military Family Policy.—Katie Magnus.
Healthcare.—Allen Edwards.
Military Justice.—Stephanie Barna.
Military Nominations.—Stephanie Barna.
Morale, Welfare, and Recreation.—Allen Edwards.
POW/MIA Issues.—Allen Edwards.
Professional Military Education.—Sean O'Keefe.
Recruiting, Retention and Personnel Management.—Sean O'Keefe.
Religious Accommodation.—Stephanie Barna.
Reserve Component Personnel Policy.—Sean O'Keefe.
Service Academies.—Sean O'Keefe.
Sexual Harassment/Assault Policy.—Stephanie Barna.
Suicide Prevention.—Allen Edwards.
Wounded Warrior Issues.—Allen Edwards.
Missile Defense.—Augusta Binns-Berkey.
Munitions.—Diem Salmon.
National Defense/Military Strategy: Tom Goffus, Diem Salmon.
National Defense Stockpile.—Jackie Kerber.
Nuclear Weapons Stockpile.—Augusta Binns-Berkey.
Operational and Installation Energy.—Jackie Kerber.
Operations and Maintenance.—Brad Patout.
Readiness.—Brad Patout.
Reprogramming.—Diem Salmon.
Rotary Systems.—Tony Pankuch.
Science and Technology.—Katie Sutton.
Shipbuilding Programs.—Jason Potter.
Small Business Programs.—Gwyneth Woolwine.
Software Intensive Systems.—Gwyneth Woolwine.
Space.—John Riordan.
Special Operations Forces.—Adam Barker.
Test and Evaluation.—John Wason.
Transportation Policy.—Brad Patout.
Unmanned Aircraft Systems: Tony Pankuch, Robert Winkler.
Unmanned Surface and Undersea Systems.—Jason Potter.
War Powers.—Stephanie Barna.
Warfighting Networks: Tony Pankuch, Robert Winkler.
Working Capital Fund.—Jackie Kerber.

Minority Staff:

Staff Director.—Elizabeth L. King.
Clerk.—Mariah K. McNamara.
General Counsel.—Gerald J. Leeling.
Counsel: Jonathan D. Clark, Jonathan S. Epstein, Ozge Guzelsu, William G.P. Monahan.
Professional Staff Members: Jody L. Bennett, Carolyn A. Chuhta, Creighton Greene, Thomas K. McConnell, Mariah K. McNamara, Michael J. Noblet, John H. Quirk V, Arun A. Seraphin.
Special Assistant.—Fiona E. Tomlin.

Subcommittee on Airland

Minority Staff Members: Jody L. Bennett (lead), Creighton Greene.

Subcommittee on Cybersecurity

Minority Staff Members: Thomas K. McConnell (lead), William G.P. Monahan.

Subcommittee on Emerging Threats and Capabilities

Minority Staff Members: Michael J. Noblet (lead), Jonathan S. Epstein, Ozge Guzelsu, Thomas K. McConnell, Mariah K. McNamara, William G.P. Monahan, Arun A. Seraphin.

Subcommittee on Personnel

Minority Staff Members: Jonathan D. Clark (lead), Gerald J. Leeling.

Subcommittee on Readiness and Management Support

Minority Staff Members: John H. Quirk V (lead), Arun A. Seraphin.

Subcommittee on Seapower

Minority Staff Members: Creighton Greene (lead), Jody L. Bennett.

Subcommittee on Strategic Forces

Minority Staff Members: Jonathan S. Epstein (lead), Carolyn A. Chuhta, Creighton Greene, Thomas K. McConnell, Mariah K. McNamara.

Minority Staff Subject Areas

Acquisition Policy.—Arun A. Seraphin.
Acquisition Workforce.—Arun A. Seraphin.
Alternative Energy: John H. Quirk V, Arun A. Seraphin.
Ammunition.—John H. Quirk V.
Arms Control.—Jonathan S. Epstein.
Aviation Systems: Jonathan S. Epstein, Creighton Greene.
Base Realignment and Closure (BRAC).—John H. Quirk V.
Border Security.—Carolyn A. Chuhta.
Budget.—Carolyn A. Chuhta.
Buy America.—Arun A. Seraphin.
Chemical-Biological Defense.—Jonathan S. Epstein.
Chemical Demilitarization.—Jonathan S. Epstein.
Combatant Commands / Foreign Policy
AFRICOM.—Mariah K. McNamara.
CENTCOM: Mariah K. McNamara, Michael J. Noblet.
Central Asia.—Mariah K. McNamara.
Iraq.—Michael J. Noblet.
Middle East.—Michael J. Noblet.
CYBERCOM.—Thomas K. McConnell.
EUCOM/NATO.—William G.P. Monahan.
Israel.—Carolyn A. Chuhta.
INDOPACOM.—Ozge Guzelsu.
NORTHCOM.—Carolyn A. Chuhta.
SOCOM.—Michael J. Noblet.
SOUTHCOM.—Ozge Guzelsu.
STRATCOM.—Jonathan S. Epstein.
TRANSCOM.—Creighton Greene.
Competition Policy.—Arun A. Seraphin.
Competitive Sourcing / A-76.—Arun A. Seraphin.
Contracting (Including Service Contracts).—Arun A. Seraphin.
Cooperative Threat Reduction.—Jonathan S. Epstein.
Counternarcotics Account & Programs.—Ozge Guzelsu.
Counterterrorism Partnership Fund.—Michael J. Noblet.
Counterterrorism Policy: Ozge Guzelsu, Thomas K. McConnell, Mariah K. McNamara, Michael J. Noblet.
Cybersecurity: Creighton Greene, Thomas K. McConnell.
Defense Energy Use: John H. Quirk V, Arun A. Seraphin.
Defense Security Cooperation Agency.—William G.P. Monahan.
Defense Strategy Review.—Jody L. Bennett.
Department of Energy Issues.—Jonathan S. Epstein.
Depot Maintenance.—John H. Quirk V.
Detainee Policy.—Ozge Guzelsu.
Domestic Preparedness.—Carolyn A. Chuhta.
Embassy Security.—Ozge Guzelsu.
Environmental Issues.—John H. Quirk V.

Export Controls.—Ozge Guzelsu.
Financial Management.—Arun A. Seraphin.
Foreign Language Policy.—Mariah K. McNamara.
Global Basing.—John H. Quirk V.
Ground Systems.—Jody L. Bennett.
Homeland Defense/Security.—Carolyn A. Chuhta.
Housing Construction.—John H. Quirk V.
INDOPACOM Maritime Security Initiative.—Ozge Guzelsu.
Information Assurance: Creighton Greene, Thomas K. McConnell.
Information Management: Creighton Greene, Arun A. Seraphin.
Information Operations: Mariah K. McNamara, Michael J. Noblet.
Information Technology Systems
  IT Acquisition Policy: Thomas K. McConnell, Arun A. Seraphin.
  Business Systems.—Arun A. Seraphin.
  Tactical Systems.—Creighton Greene.
Insider Threat.—Thomas K. McConnell.
Intelligence Issues: Creighton Greene, Thomas K. McConnell, Michael J. Noblet.
Interagency Reform: Thomas K. McConnell, Michael J. Noblet.
Inventory Management.—Arun A. Seraphin.
Investigations.—Ozge Guzelsu.
Joint Improvised-Threat Defense Organization (JIDO).—Jody L. Bennett.
Land Use.—John H. Quirk V.
Laboratory Management.—Arun A. Seraphin.
Logistics Policy.—Creighton Greene.
Mergers and Acquisitions.—Arun A. Seraphin.
Military Construction.—John H. Quirk V.
Military Space.—Jonathan S. Epstein.
Military Strategy.—Jody L. Bennett.
Missile Defense.—Carolyn A. Chuhta.
National Defense Stockpile.—John H. Quirk V.
Nominations
  Civilian.—Gerald J. Leeling.
  Military.—Jonathan D. Clark.
Non-Proliferation.—Jonathan S. Epstein.
Nuclear Weapons Stockpile.—Jonathan S. Epstein.
Operation and Maintenance.—John H. Quirk V.
Overseas Humanitarian, Disaster, and Civic Aid (OHDACA) Account.—Mariah K. McNamara.
Peacekeeping.—Mariah K. McNamara.
Personnel Policy
  Civilian Personnel Policy.—Jonathan D. Clark.
  Commissaries and Exchanges.—Jonathan D. Clark.
  Education.—Jonathan D. Clark.
  End Strength.—Jonathan D. Clark.
  Health Care.—Gerald J. Leeling.
  Military Family Policy.—Gerald J. Leeling.
  Military Justice.—Gerald J. Leeling.
  Military Nominations.—Jonathan D. Clark.
  Military Personnel Policy.—Gerald J. Leeling.
  Morale, Welfare, and Recreation.—Jonathan D. Clark.
  National Guard and Reserves: Jonathan D. Clark, Gerald J. Leeling.
  Pay, Benefits, and Retirement.—Jonathan D. Clark.
  Personnel Security.—Thomas K. McConnell.
  POW/MIA Issues.—Jonathan D. Clark.
  Religious Accommodation.—Jonathan D. Clark.
  Sexual Conduct Policy.—Gerald J. Leeling.
  Suicide Prevention and Response.—Gerald J. Leeling.
  Women in Service.—Jonathan D. Clark.
  Wounded Warrior Issues.—Gerald J. Leeling.
Personnel Protective Items.—John H. Quirk V.
Readiness.—John H. Quirk V.
Reprogramming.—Carolyn A. Chuhta.
Science and Technology.—Arun A. Seraphin.
Security Assistance Programs: Ozge Guzelsu, William G.P. Monahan, Mariah K. McNamara, Michael J. Noblet.
Shipbuilding Programs.—Creighton Greene.
Small Business.—Arun A. Seraphin.

Special Operations Forces.—Michael J. Noblet.
Strategic Programs.—Jonathan S. Epstein.
Test and Evaluation.—Arun A. Seraphin.
Training.—John H. Quirk V.
Transportation Policy.—Creighton Greene.
Unified Command Plan.—Jody L. Bennett.
Unmanned Aircraft Systems: Creighton Greene, Thomas K. McConnell.
Working Capital Fund.—John H. Quirk V.

Banking, Housing, and Urban Affairs

534 Dirksen Senate Office Building 20510

phone 224–7391, https://banking.senate.gov

Mike Crapo, of Idaho, *Chair*

Richard C. Shelby, of Alabama.
Patrick J. Toomey, of Pennsylvania.
Tim Scott, of South Carolina.
Ben Sasse, of Nebraska.
Tom Cotton, of Arkansas.
Mike Rounds, of South Dakota.
David Perdue, of Georgia.
Thom Tillis, of North Carolina.
John Kennedy, of Louisiana.
Martha McSally, of Arizona.
Jerry Moran, of Kansas.
Kevin Cramer, of North Dakota.

Sherrod Brown, of Ohio.
Jack Reed, of Rhode Island.
Robert Menendez, of New Jersey.
Jon Tester, of Montana.
Mark R. Warner, of Virginia.
Elizabeth Warren, of Massachusetts.
Brian Schatz, of Hawaii.
Chris Van Hollen, of Maryland.
Catherine Cortez Masto, of Nevada.
Doug Jones, of Alabama.
Tina Smith, of Minnesota.
Kyrsten Sinema, of Arizona.

SUBCOMMITTEES

[The chair and ranking minority member are ex officio members of all subcommittees.]

Economic Policy

Tom Cotton, of Arkansas, *Chair*

Kevin Cramer, of North Dakota.
Ben Sasse, of Nebraska.
David Perdue, of Georgia.
Thom Tillis, of North Carolina.
John Kennedy, of Louisiana.

Catherine Cortez Masto, of Nevada.
Robert Menendez, of New Jersey.
Doug Jones, of Alabama.
Tina Smith, of Minnesota.
Kyrsten Sinema, of Arizona.

Financial Institutions and Consumer Protection

Tim Scott, of South Carolina, *Chair*

Mike Rounds, of South Dakota.
Thom Tillis, of North Carolina.
John Kennedy, of Louisiana.
Jerry Moran, of Kansas.
Kevin Cramer, of North Dakota.
Richard C. Shelby, of Alabama.
Patrick J. Toomey, of Pennsylvania.
Ben Sasse, of Nebraska.

Elizabeth Warren, of Massachusetts.
Jack Reed, of Rhode Island.
Jon Tester, of Montana.
Mark R. Warner, of Virginia.
Brian Schatz, of Hawaii.
Chris Van Hollen, of Maryland.
Catherine Cortez Masto, of Nevada.
Doug Jones, of Alabama.

Housing, Transportation, and Community Development

David Perdue, of Georgia, *Chair*

Richard C. Shelby, of Alabama.
Tom Cotton, of Arkansas.
Mike Rounds, of South Dakota.
Martha McSally, of Arizona.
Jerry Moran, of Kansas.
Kevin Cramer, of North Dakota.

Robert Menendez, of New Jersey.
Jack Reed, of Rhode Island.
Elizabeth Warren, of Massachusetts.
Catherine Cortez Masto, of Nevada.
Doug Jones, of Alabama.
Tina Smith, of Minnesota.

National Security and International Trade and Finance

Ben Sasse, of Nebraska, *Chair*

Martha McSally, of Arizona.
Jerry Moran, of Kansas.
Patrick J. Toomey, of Pennsylvania.
Tim Scott, of South Carolina.

Mark R. Warner, of Virginia.
Brian Schatz, of Hawaii.
Chris Van Hollen, of Maryland.
Kyrsten Sinema, of Arizona.

Securities, Insurance, and Investment

Patrick J. Toomey, of Pennsylvania, *Chair*

Richard C. Shelby, of Alabama.
Martha McSally, of Arizona.
Tim Scott, of South Carolina.
Tom Cotton, of Arkansas.
Mike Rounds, of South Dakota.
David Perdue, of Georgia.
Thom Tillis, of North Carolina.
John Kennedy, of Louisiana.

Chris Van Hollen, of Maryland.
Jack Reed, of Rhode Island.
Robert Menendez, of New Jersey.
Jon Tester, of Montana.
Mark R. Warner, of Virginia.
Elizabeth Warren, of Massachusetts.
Tina Smith, of Minnesota.
Kyrsten Sinema, of Arizona.

STAFF

Committee on Banking, Housing, and Urban Affairs (SD–534), 224–7391, fax 224–5137.

Majority Staff:
Majority Staff Director.—Gregg Richard.
Communications Director.—Amanda Critchfield.
Chief Counsel.—Joe Carapiet.
Chief Counsel, National Security Policy.—John O'Hara.
Policy Director.—Mike Quickel.
Counsel: Catherine Fuchs, Matt Jones.
Professional Staff Members: Brandon Beall, Sarah Brown, Jen Deci, James Guiliano, Lexi Hall.

Minority Staff:
Minority Staff Director.—Laura Swanson.
Deputy Staff Director.—Jeremy Hekhuis.
Chief Counsel.—Elisha Tuku.
Counsel.—Jan Singelmann.
Policy Director.—Colin McGinnis.
Press Secretary.—Ashley Lewis.
Professional Staff Members: Homer Carlisle, Megan Cheney, Beth Cooper, Corey Frayer.
Senior Legislative Assistant.—Phil Rudd.
Legislative Assistant.—Stanley Hardey.

Non-Designated Staff:
Chief Clerk.—Cameron Ricker.
IT Director.—Shelvin Simmons.
Editor.—Jim Crowell.
GPO Detailees.—Sheryl Arrington, Jason Parker.
Hearing Clerk/Staff Assistant.—Charles Moffat.
Staff Assistant.—Patrick Lally.

Subcommittee on Economic Policy
Majority Staff Director.—Kyle Hauttman.
Minority Staff Director.—Carol Wayman.

Subcommittee on Financial Institutions and Consumer Protection
Majority Staff Director.—Lila Nieves-Lee.
Minority Staff Director.—Julie Siegel.

Subcommittee on Housing, Transportation, and Community Development
Majority Staff Director.—Gerald Huang.
Minority Staff Director.—Jonathan Tsentas.

Subcommittee on National Security and International Trade and Finance
Majority Staff Director.—Katherine Duveneck.
Minority Staff Director.—Craig Radcliffe.

Subcommittee on Securities, Insurance, and Investment
Majority Staff Director.—John Crews.
Minority Staff Director.—Karolina Arias.

Budget

624 Dirksen Senate Office Building 20510–6100

phone 224–0642, https://budget.senate.gov

meets first Thursday of each month

Michael B. Enzi, of Wyoming, *Chair*

Chuck Grassley, of Iowa.
Mike Crapo, of Idaho.
Lindsey Graham, of South Carolina.
Patrick J. Toomey, of Pennsylvania.
Ron Johnson, of Wisconsin.
David Perdue, of Georgia.
Mike Braun, of Indiana.
Rick Scott, of Florida.
John Kennedy, of Louisiana.
Kevin Cramer, of North Dakota.

BERNARD SANDERS, of Vermont.
Patty Murray, of Washington.
Ron Wyden, of Oregon.
Debbie Stabenow, of Michigan.
Sheldon Whitehouse, of Rhode Island.
Mark R. Warner, of Virginia.
Jeff Merkley, of Oregon.
Tim Kaine, of Virginia.
Chris Van Hollen, of Maryland.
Kamala D. Harris, of California.

(No Subcommittees)

STAFF

Committee on the Budget (SD–624), 224–0642.
Majority Staff:
Majority Staff Director.—Elizabeth McDonnell.
Deputy Staff Director.—Matthew Giroux.
Counsel.—Thomas Fuller.
Executive Assistant and Editor.—Katherine Rossi.
Policy Director.—Thomas Borck.
Communications Director.—Joe Brenckle.
Professional Staff Members: Gable Brady, Aniela Butler, Lauren Canfield, Erich Hartman, Will Morris, Nan Swift.
Oversight Counsel.—Doug Sahmel.
Investigative Counsel: Marissa Gervasi, Ian Macbeth.
Minority Staff:
Minority Staff Director.—Warren Gunnels.
Deputy Staff Director.—Mike Jones.
Chief Counsel.—Robert Etter.
Budget Policy Director.—Josh Smith.
Senior Analyst for Social Security and Income Security.—Jeff Cruz.
Health Policy Analyst.—Marissa Barrera.
Senior Budget Analyst for National Defense.—Ethan Rosenkranz.
Budget Review Professional.—Bobby Kogan.
Policy Advisor.—Alex Beaton.
Senior Advisor on Poverty and Health.—Sophie Kasimow.
Floor Coordinator.—Ihna Mangundayao.
Budget Analyst/Agriculture Policy Advisor.—Emily Rampone.
Tax Analyst.—Richard Phillips.
Senior Education Policy Advisor.—Donnie Turner.
Research Director.—Melinda Warner.
Non-Designated Staff:
Chief Clerk.—Kim Proctor.
Deputy Chief Clerk/Archivist.—Katie Smith.
Computer Systems Administrator.—George Woodall.
Staff Assistant.—Lilly Altree.

Commerce, Science, and Transportation

512 Dirksen Senate Office Building 20510–6125

phone 224–1251, TTY / TDD 224–8418, https://commerce.senate.gov

meets Wednesday of each month

Roger F. Wicker, of Mississippi, *Chair*

John Thune, of South Dakota.
Roy Blunt, of Missouri.
Ted Cruz, of Texas.
Deb Fischer, of Nebraska.
Jerry Moran, of Kansas.
Dan Sullivan, of Alaska.
Cory Gardner, of Colorado.
Marsha Blackburn, of Tennessee.
Shelley Moore Capito, of West Virginia.
Mike Lee, of Utah.
Ron Johnson, of Wisconsin.
Todd Young, of Indiana.
Rick Scott, of Florida.

Maria Cantwell, of Washington.
Amy Klobuchar, of Minnesota.
Richard Blumenthal, of Connecticut.
Brian Schatz, of Hawaii.
Edward J. Markey, of Massachusetts.
Tom Udall, of New Mexico.
Gary C. Peters, of Michigan.
Tammy Baldwin, of Wisconsin.
Tammy Duckworth, of Illinois.
Jon Tester, of Montana.
Kyrsten Sinema, of Arizona.
Jacky Rosen, of Nevada.

SUBCOMMITTEES

[The chair and the ranking minority member are ex officio members of all subcommittees.]

Aviation and Space

Ted Cruz, of Texas, *Chair*

John Thune, of South Dakota.
Roy Blunt, of Missouri.
Jerry Moran, of Kansas.
Cory Gardner, of Colorado.
Marsha Blackburn, of Tennessee
Shelley Moore Capito, of West Virginia.
Mike Lee, of Utah.

Kyrsten Sinema, of Arizona.
Brian Schatz, of Hawaii.
Tom Udall, of New Mexico.
Gary C. Peters, of Michigan.
Tammy Duckworth, of Illinois.
Jon Tester, of Montana.
Jacky Rosen, of Nevada.

Communications, Technology, Innovation, and the Internet

John Thune, of South Dakota, *Chair*

Roy Blunt, of Missouri.
Ted Cruz, of Texas.
Deb Fischer, of Nebraska.
Jerry Moran, of Kansas.
Dan Sullivan, of Alaska.
Cory Gardner, of Colorado.
Marsha Blackburn, of Tennessee.
Shelley Moore Capito, of West Virginia.
Mike Lee, of Utah.
Ron Johnson, of Wisconsin.
Todd Young, of Indiana.
Rick Scott, of Florida.

Brian Schatz, of Hawaii.
Amy Klobuchar, of Minnesota.
Richard Blumenthal, of Connecticut.
Edward J. Markey, of Massachusetts.
Tom Udall, of New Mexico.
Gary C. Peters, of Michigan.
Tammy Baldwin, of Wisconsin.
Tammy Duckworth, of Illinois.
Jon Tester, of Montana.
Kyrsten Sinema, of Arizona.
Jacky Rosen, of Nevada.

Manufacturing, Trade, and Consumer Protection

Jerry Moran, of Kansas, *Chair*

John Thune, of South Dakota.
Deb Fischer, of Nebraska.
Dan Sullivan, of Alaska.
Marsha Blackburn, of Tennessee.
Shelley Moore Capito, of West Virginia.
Mike Lee, of Utah.
Ron Johnson, of Wisconsin.
Todd Young, of Indiana.

Richard Blumenthal, of Connecticut.
Amy Klobuchar, of Minnesota.
Brian Schatz, of Hawaii.
Edward J. Markey, of Massachusetts.
Tom Udall, of New Mexico.
Tammy Baldwin, of Wisconsin.
Kyrsten Sinema, of Arizona.
Jacky Rosen, of Nevada.

Science, Oceans, Fisheries, and Weather

Cory Gardner, of Colorado, *Chair*

Ted Cruz, of Texas.
Dan Sullivan, of Alaska.
Ron Johnson, of Wisconsin.
Rick Scott, of Florida.

Tammy Baldwin, of Wisconsin.
Richard Blumenthal, of Connecticut.
Brian Schatz, of Hawaii.
Gary C. Peters, of Michigan.

Security

Dan Sullivan, of Alaska, *Chair*

Roy Blunt, of Missouri.
Ted Cruz, of Texas.
Deb Fischer, of Nebraska.
Marsha Blackburn, of Tennessee.
Mike Lee, of Utah.
Ron Johnson, of Wisconsin.
Todd Young, of Indiana.
Rick Scott, of Florida.

Edward J. Markey, of Massachusetts.
Amy Klobuchar, of Minnesota.
Richard Blumenthal, of Connecticut.
Brian Schatz, of Hawaii.
Tom Udall, of New Mexico.
Tammy Duckworth, of Illinois.
Kyrsten Sinema, of Arizona.
Jacky Rosen, of Nevada.

Transportation and Safety

Deb Fischer, of Nebraska, *Chair*

John Thune, of South Dakota.
Roy Blunt, of Missouri.
Jerry Moran, of Kansas.
Cory Gardner, of Colorado.
Shelley Moore Capito, of West Virginia.
Todd Young, of Indiana.
Rick Scott, of Florida.

Tammy Duckworth, of Illinois.
Amy Klobuchar, of Minnesota.
Richard Blumenthal, of Connecticut.
Edward J. Markey, of Massachusetts.
Tom Udall, of New Mexico.
Gary C. Peters, of Michigan.
Tammy Baldwin, of Wisconsin.

STAFF

Committee on Commerce, Science, and Transportation (SD–512), 224–1251.
Majority Staff Director.—John Keast.
Deputy Staff Director.—Crystal Tully.
General Counsel.—Steven Wall.
Deputy Communications Director.—Brianna Manzelli.
Press Assistant.—Alexis DeJarnette.
Director of Administration.—Haley Rivero.
Staff Assistant.—Alexandra Slocum.
Minority Staff Director.—David Strickland.
Deputy Staff Director.—Melissa Porter.
Deputy Communications Director.—Peter True.
Research Assistant.—Lucy Koch.
Staff Assistant.—H. Hunter Hudspeth Blackburn.
Oversight and Investigations Staff:
Chief of Investigations.—Robert Turner.
Research Assistant.—James O'Connor.
Minority Senior Counsel and Chief of Investigations.—Christopher Day.

Aviation and Space Staff:
Policy Director.—James Mazol.
Deputy Policy Director.—Mike Reynolds.
Professional Staff: Darien Flowers, Joel Graham, Simone Perez.
NASA Detailee.—Sharmila Bhattacharya.
Minority Counsel.—Tom Chapman.
Minority Professional Staff: Alicia Brown, Mary Guenther, Laurence Wildgoose.

Communications, Technology, Innovation and the Internet Staff:
Policy Director.—Olivia Trusty.
Deputy Policy Director.—Dan Ball.
Professional Staff.—John Lin.
Research Assistant.—Reed Cook.
FCC Detailee.—Kevin Holmes.
Minority Chief Counsel.—John Branscome.
Minority Senior Counsel.—Shawn Bone.
Minority Research Assistant.—Brian McDermott.
Minority FCC Detailee.—Elizabeth McIntyre.

Manufacturing, Trade, and Consumer Protection Staff:
Policy Director.—Olivia Trusty.
Deputy Policy Director.—Gregor Chapin.
Research Assistant.—Tyler Levins.
Minority Senior Counsel.—Jared Bomberg.
Minority Counsel and Senior Technology Advisor.—Narda Jones.
Minority Research Assistant.—Hussain Altamimi.
Minority FTC Detailee.—Michael Lezaja.

Science, Oceans, Fisheries, and Weather Staff:
Policy Director.—Ellen Beares.
Deputy Policy Director.—Fern Gibbons.
Professional Staff.—Alexis Rudd.
Research Assistant.—Victoria Lombardo.
Senior Counsel.—Sara Gonzalez-Rothi.
Minority Senior Policy Advisor.—Nicole Teutschel.
Minority Professional Staff: Alicia Brown, Mary Guenther.
Minority Research Assistant.—Matthew Bobbink.

Security Staff:
Policy Director.—James Mazol.
Senior Professional Staff.—Cheri Pascoe.
Professional Staff.—Darien Flowers.
Research Assistant.—Charles Hockenbury.
Coast Guard Detailee.—Andrew Pate.
Minority Senior Professional Staff.—Nicole Teutschel.
Minority Counsel.—Tom Chapman.
Minority Professional Staff: James Bromley, Laurence Wildgoose.
Minority Coast Guard Detailee.—Nicolette Vaughan.
Minority Research Assistant.—Matthew Bobbink.

Transportation and Safety Staff:
Policy Director.—Ellen Beares.
Deputy Policy Director.—Alison Graab.
Professional Staff.—Andrew Neely.
Research Assistant.—Victoria Lombardo.
Minority Senior Counsel.—Kara Fischer.
Minority Professional Staff.—Michael Davisson.
Minority Legislative Assistant.—Stephen Stadius.

Bipartisan Staff:
Chief Clerk.—Jeffrey Johnson.
Deputy Chief Clerk.—Stephanie Gamache.
Director of Information Technology.—Jonathan Bowen.
Director of Operations.—Theresa Eugene.
Archivist.—Sarah Schmitz.
Administrative Assistant.—Lyle LaCour.
Staff Assistant.—Stephanie Lieu.
GPO Detailees: Celina Inman, Jacqueline Washington.

Energy and Natural Resources

304 Dirksen Senate Office Building 20510

phone 224–4971, fax 224–6163, https://energy.senate.gov

The Committee meets on the third Thursday of each month while the Congress is in session or upon the call of the Chair.

Lisa Murkowski, of Alaska, *Chair*

John Barrasso, of Wyoming.
James E. Risch, of Idaho.
Mike Lee, of Utah.
Steve Daines, of Montana.
Bill Cassidy, of Louisiana.
Cory Gardner, of Colorado.
Cindy Hyde-Smith, of Mississippi.
Martha McSally, of Arizona.
Lamar Alexander, of Tennessee.
John Hoeven, of North Dakota.

Joe Manchin III, of West Virginia.
Ron Wyden, of Oregon.
Maria Cantwell, of Washington.
BERNARD SANDERS, of Vermont.
Debbie Stabenow, of Michigan.
Martin Heinrich, of New Mexico.
Mazie K. Hirono, of Hawaii.
ANGUS S. KING, JR., of Maine.
Catherine Cortez Masto, of Nevada.

SUBCOMMITTEES

[The chair and the ranking minority member are ex officio members of all subcommittees.]

Energy

Bill Cassidy, of Louisiana, *Chair*

James E. Risch, of Idaho.
Mike Lee, of Utah.
Steve Daines, of Montana.
Cory Gardner, of Colorado.
Cindy Hyde-Smith, of Mississippi.
Martha McSally, of Arizona.
Lamar Alexander, of Tennessee.
John Hoeven, of North Dakota.

Martin Heinrich, of New Mexico.
Ron Wyden, of Oregon.
Maria Cantwell, of Washington.
BERNARD SANDERS, of Vermont.
Debbie Stabenow, of Michigan.
Mazie K. Hirono, of Hawaii.
ANGUS S. KING, JR., of Maine.
Catherine Cortez Masto, of Nevada.

National Parks

Steve Daines, of Montana, *Chair*

John Barrasso, of Wyoming.
Mike Lee, of Utah.
Cory Gardner, of Colorado.
Cindy Hyde-Smith, of Mississippi.
Lamar Alexander, of Tennessee.
John Hoeven, of North Dakota.

ANGUS S. KING, JR., of Maine.
BERNARD SANDERS, of Vermont.
Debbie Stabenow, of Michigan.
Martin Heinrich, of New Mexico.
Mazie K. Hirono, of Hawaii.

Public Lands, Forests, and Mining

Mike Lee, of Utah, *Chair*

John Barrasso, of Wyoming.
James E. Risch, of Idaho.
Steve Daines, of Montana.
Bill Cassidy, of Louisiana.
Cory Gardner, of Colorado.
Cindy Hyde-Smith, of Mississippi.
Martha McSally, of Arizona.
John Hoeven, of North Dakota.

Ron Wyden, of Oregon.
Maria Cantwell, of Washington.
Debbie Stabenow, of Michigan.
Martin Heinrich, of New Mexico.
Mazie K. Hirono, of Hawaii.
ANGUS S. KING, JR., of Maine.
Catherine Cortez Masto, of Nevada.

Water and Power

Martha McSally, of Arizona, *Chair*

John Barrasso, of Wyoming.
James E. Risch, of Idaho.
Bill Cassidy, of Louisiana.
Cory Gardner, of Colorado.
Lamar Alexander, of Tennessee.

Catherine Cortez Masto, of Nevada.
Ron Wyden, of Oregon.
Maria Cantwell, of Washington.
BERNARD SANDERS, of Vermont.

STAFF

Committee on Energy and Natural Resources (SD–304), 224–4971, fax 224–6163.

Majority Staff:
Majority Staff Director.—Brian Hughes.
Chief Counsel.—Kellie Donnelly.
Deputy Chief Counsel.—Lucy Murfitt.
Senior Counsel: John Crowther, Jed Dearborn.
Special Counsel.—Isaac Edwards.
Senior Writer and Advisor.—Michelle Toohey.
Senior Professional Staff Member and Energy Policy Advisor.—Brianne Miller.
Senior Professional Staff Members: Tristan Abbey, Chester Carson, Lane Dickson.
Professional Staff Members: Annie Hoefler, Michelle Lane, Nick Matiella, Spencer Nelson.
FERC Detailee.—Robert Ivanauskas.
BLM/DOI Detailee.—Stephanie Miller.
Deputy Press Secretary.—Tonya Parish.
Staff Assistant.—Chris Griffin.

Non-Designated Staff:
Chief Clerk.—Darla Ripchensky.
Staff Assistants: Abigail Hemenway, James Lai.
Systems Administrator.—Dominic Taylor.
GPO Detailee.—Cheryl Yarbrough.

Minority Staff:
Minority Staff Director.—Sarah Venuto.
Deputy Staff Director.—Lance West.
Chief Counsel.—Sam Fowler.
General Counsel: Renae Black, David Brooks.
Press Secretary.—Sam Runyon.
Senior Professional Staff Member.—Bryan Petit.
Professional Staff Members: Luke Bassett, Elliot Howard, Rory Stanley, Brie Van Cleve.
Bevinetto Fellow.—Peter Stahley.
FERC Detailee.—Nicole Buell.
Research Assistants: Adam Berry, Cam Nelson.
Press Assistant.—Cullen Tomsheck.

Environment and Public Works

410 Dirksen Senate Office Building 20510–6175

phone 224–6176, https://epw.senate.gov

John Barrasso, of Wyoming, *Chair*

James M. Inhofe, of Oklahoma.
Shelley Moore Capito, of West Virginia.
Kevin Cramer, of North Dakota.
Mike Braun, of Indiana.
Mike Rounds, of South Dakota.
Dan Sullivan, of Alaska.
John Boozman, of Arkansas.
Roger F. Wicker, of Mississippi.
Richard C. Shelby, of Alabama.
Joni Ernst, of Iowa.

Thomas R. Carper, of Delaware.
Benjamin L. Cardin, of Maryland.
BERNARD SANDERS, of Vermont.
Sheldon Whitehouse, of Rhode Island.
Jeff Merkley, of Oregon.
Kirsten E. Gillibrand, of New York.
Cory A. Booker, of New Jersey.
Edward J. Markey, of Massachusetts.
Tammy Duckworth, of Illinois.
Chris Van Hollen, of Maryland.

SUBCOMMITTEES

[The chair and the ranking minority member are ex officio (non-voting) members of all subcommittees on which they do not serve.]

Clean Air and Nuclear Safety

Mike Braun, of Indiana, *Chair*

James M. Inhofe, of Oklahoma.
Shelley Moore Capito, of West Virginia.
Kevin Cramer, of North Dakota.
Mike Rounds, of South Dakota.
Dan Sullivan, of Alaska.
John Boozman, of Arkansas.
Roger F. Wicker, of Mississippi.
Joni Ernst, of Iowa.

Sheldon Whitehouse, of Rhode Island.
Benjamin L. Cardin, of Maryland.
BERNARD SANDERS, of Vermont.
Jeff Merkley, of Oregon.
Kirsten E. Gillibrand, of New York.
Cory A. Booker, of New Jersey.
Edward J. Markey, of Massachusetts.
Tammy Duckworth, of Illinois.

Fisheries, Water, and Wildlife

Kevin Cramer, of North Dakota, *Chair*

Shelley Moore Capito, of West Virginia.
Mike Braun, of Indiana.
Dan Sullivan, of Alaska.
John Boozman, of Arkansas.
Roger F. Wicker, of Mississippi.
Richard C. Shelby, of Alabama.

Tammy Duckworth, of Illinois.
Benjamin L. Cardin, of Maryland.
BERNARD SANDERS, of Vermont.
Sheldon Whitehouse, of Rhode Island.
Jeff Merkley, of Oregon.
Chris Van Hollen, of Maryland.

Superfund, Waste Management, and Regulatory Oversight

Mike Rounds, of South Dakota, *Chair*

James M. Inhofe, of Oklahoma.
Richard C. Shelby, of Alabama.
Joni Ernst, of Iowa.

Cory A. Booker, of New Jersey.
Kirsten E. Gillibrand, of New York.
Edward J. Markey, of Massachusetts.

Transportation and Infrastructure

Shelley Moore Capito, of West Virginia, *Chair*

James M. Inhofe, of Oklahoma.
Kevin Cramer, of North Dakota.
Mike Braun, of Indiana.
Mike Rounds, of South Dakota.
Dan Sullivan, of Alaska.
John Boozman, of Arkansas.
Roger F. Wicker, of Mississippi.
Richard C. Shelby, of Alabama.

Benjamin L. Cardin, of Maryland.
BERNARD SANDERS, of Vermont.
Sheldon Whitehouse, of Rhode Island.
Jeff Merkley, of Oregon.
Kirsten E. Gillibrand, of New York.
Cory A. Booker, of New Jersey.
Edward J. Markey, of Massachusetts.
Chris Van Hollen, of Maryland.

STAFF

Committee on Environment and Public Works (SD–410), phone 224–6176; Majority fax (SD–410), 224–5167; (SH-415), 224–2322.
Majority Staff Director.—Richard Russell.
Deputy Staff Director.—Brian Clifford.
Majority Chief Counsel.—Matt Leggett.
Majority Senior Counsels: Elizabeth Horner, Justin Memmott.
Counsels: Andrew Harding, Elizabeth Olsen, James Willson.
Editorial Director.—Stephen Chapman.
Chief Clerk.—Alicia Hawkins.
Director of Information Technology.—Rae Ann Phipps.
GPO Detailees: LaVern Finks, Sonya Kunkle.
Majority Communications Director.—Mike Danylak.
Majority Press Secretary.—Sarah Durdaller.
Majority Director of Operations.—Beth Trenti.
Majority Professional Staff Members: Carl Barrick, Andrew Zach.
Majority Legislative Assistants: JR Kane, Jake Kennedy, Craig Thomas.
Majority Research Assistant.—Sam French.
Majority Staff Assistant.—Christina Rabuse.
Detailees: Steven Barnett, Lauren Diaz, Juli Huynh.
Committee on Environment and Public Works (SD–456), phone 224-8832; Minority fax (SD–456), 224–1273; (SH–508), 228–0574.
Minority Staff Director.—Mary Frances Repko.
Minority Chief Counsel.—Andrew Rogers.
Minority Senior Counsel and Policy Director.—Christophe Tulou.
Minority Director of Oversight.—Michal Freedhoff.
Minority Senior Policy Advisor for Clean Air and Climate.—Laura Haynes Gillam.
Office Manager.—Carolyn Mack.
Minority Communications Director.—Jill Farquharson.
Minority Deputy Press Secretary.—Campbell Wallace.
Minority Senior Policy Advisors: Rebecca Higgins, Elizabeth Mabry, Andrew Wishnia.
Senior Professional Staff Member.—John Kane.
Professional Staff Member.—Annie D'Amato.
Senior Policy Advisor for Infrastructure.—Kenneth Martin.
Oversight Counsel.—Brian Eiler.
Minority Legislative Aide.—Avery Mulligan.
Minority Staff Assistants: Madeline Canning, Caroline Jones.
Army Corps Detailee.—Mark Mendenhall.
Brookings Fellow.—Zach Pilchen.
Sea Grant Fellow.—Kaitlyn Pritchard.

Finance

219 Dirksen Senate Office Building 20510

phone 224–4515, fax 224–0554, https://finance.senate.gov

meets second and fourth Tuesdays of each month

Chuck Grassley, of Iowa, *Chair*

Mike Crapo, of Idaho.
Pat Roberts, of Kansas.
Michael B. Enzi, of Wyoming.
John Cornyn, of Texas.
John Thune, of South Dakota.
Richard Burr, of North Carolina.
Rob Portman, of Ohio.
Patrick J. Toomey, of Pennsylvania.
Tim Scott, of South Carolina.
Bill Cassidy, of Louisiana.
James Lankford, of Oklahoma.
Steve Daines, of Montana.
Todd Young, of Indiana.
Ben Sasse, of Nebraska.

Ron Wyden, of Oregon.
Debbie Stabenow, of Michigan.
Maria Cantwell, of Washington.
Robert Menendez, of New Jersey.
Thomas R. Carper, of Delaware.
Benjamin L. Cardin, of Maryland.
Sherrod Brown, of Ohio.
Michael F. Bennet, of Colorado.
Robert P. Casey, Jr., of Pennsylvania.
Mark R. Warner, of Virginia.
Sheldon Whitehouse, of Rhode Island.
Margaret Wood Hassan, of New Hampshire.
Catherine Cortez Masto, of Nevada.

SUBCOMMITTEES

[The chair and ranking minority member are ex officio (non-voting) members of all subcommittees on which they do not serve.]

Energy, Natural Resources, and Infrastructure

Tim Scott, of South Carolina, *Chair*

Chuck Grassley, of Iowa.
Mike Crapo, of Idaho.
Pat Roberts, of Kansas.
Michael B. Enzi, of Wyoming.
John Cornyn, of Texas.
Richard Burr, of North Carolina.
Steve Daines, of Montana.

Michael F. Bennet, of Colorado.
Ron Wyden, of Oregon.
Maria Cantwell, of Washington.
Thomas R. Carper, of Delaware.
Sheldon Whitehouse, of Rhode Island.
Margaret Wood Hassan, of New Hampshire.

Fiscal Responsibility and Economic Growth

Bill Cassidy, of Louisiana, *Chair*

Tim Scott, of South Carolina.
Ben Sasse, of Nebraska.

Margaret Wood Hassan, of New Hampshire.
Ron Wyden, of Oregon.

Health Care

Patrick J. Toomey, of Pennsylvania, *Chair*

Chuck Grassley, of Iowa.
Pat Roberts, of Kansas.
Michael B. Enzi, of Wyoming.
John Thune, of South Dakota.
Richard Burr, of North Carolina.
Tim Scott, of South Carolina
Bill Cassidy, of Louisiana.
James Lankford, of Oklahoma.
Steve Daines, of Montana.
Todd Young, of Indiana.
Ben Sasse, of Nebraska.

Debbie Stabenow, of Michigan.
Maria Cantwell, of Washington.
Robert Menendez, of New Jersey.
Thomas R. Carper, of Delaware.
Benjamin L. Cardin, of Maryland.
Sherrod Brown, of Ohio.
Robert P. Casey, Jr., of Pennsylvania.
Mark R. Warner, of Virginia.
Sheldon Whitehouse, of Rhode Island.
Margaret Wood Hassan, of New Hampshire.
Catherine Cortez Masto, of Nevada.

International Trade, Customs, and Global Competitiveness

John Cornyn, of Texas, *Chair*

Mike Crapo, of Idaho.
Pat Roberts, of Kansas.
John Thune, of South Dakota.
Rob Portman, of Ohio.
Patrick J. Toomey, of Pennsylvania.
Tim Scott, of South Carolina.
Bill Cassidy, of Louisiana.
Steve Daines, of Montana.
Todd Young, of Indiana.
Ben Sasse, of Nebraska.

Robert P. Casey, Jr., of Pennsylvania.
Ron Wyden, of Oregon.
Debbie Stabenow, of Michigan.
Maria Cantwell, of Washington.
Robert Menendez, of New Jersey.
Benjamin L. Cardin, of Maryland.
Sherrod Brown, of Ohio.
Mark R. Warner, of Virginia.
Catherine Cortez Masto, of Nevada.

Social Security, Pensions, and Family Policy

Rob Portman, of Ohio, *Chair*

Chuck Grassley, of Iowa.
Bill Cassidy, of Louisiana.
James Lankford, of Oklahoma.
Todd Young, of Indiana.

Sherrod Brown, of Ohio.
Michael F. Bennet, of Colorado.
Robert P. Casey, Jr., of Pennsylvania.
Catherine Cortez Masto, of Nevada.

Taxation and IRS Oversight

John Thune, of South Dakota, *Chair*

Mike Crapo, of Idaho.
Michael B. Enzi, of Wyoming.
John Cornyn, of Texas.
Richard Burr, of North Carolina.
Rob Portman, of Ohio.
Patrick J. Toomey, of Pennsylvania.
James Lankford, of Oklahoma.

Mark R. Warner, of Virginia.
Robert Menendez, of New Jersey.
Thomas R. Carper, of Delaware.
Benjamin L. Cardin, of Maryland.
Michael F. Bennet, of Colorado.
Sheldon Whitehouse, of Rhode Island.

STAFF

Committee on Finance (SD–219), 224–4515, fax 228–0554.

Majority Staff:

Staff Director and Chief Counsel.—Kolan Davis.
Deputy Staff Director and Chief Economist.—Jeff Wrase.
Chief Tax Counsel.—Mark Warren.
Deputy Chief Tax Policy Advisor.—Eric Oman.
Senior Advisor for Benefits and Exempt Organizations.—Vacant.
Tax Counsel: Andre Barnett, Christopher Conlin.
Tax, Infrastructure and Nominations Policy Advisor.—Nick Wyatt.
Professional Staff Member.—Alex Monie.
Chief Health Policy Director.—Karen Summar.
Deputy Health Policy Director.—Erin Dempsey.
General Counsel for Health and Chief of Special Projects.—Evelyn Fortier.
Senior Health Policy Advisor.—Brett Baker.
Senior Human Services Advisor.—Ryan Martin.
Health Policy Advisor.—Stuart Portman.
Professional Staff Member.—Kirsten Wing.
Research Assistant.—Madeleine Davidson.
Health Staff Assistant.—Brigid Ueland.
Chief International Trade Counsel.—Nasim Fussell.
International Trade Counsel: Brian Bombassaro, Mayur Patel.
International Trade Advisors: Andrew Brandt, Rory Heslington.
Professional Staff Member.—Michael Pinkerton.
Chief Investigative Counsel.—DeLisa Ragsdale.
Deputy Chief Investigative Counsel.—Joshua Flynn-Brown.
Senior Investigative Counsel.—John Shoenecker.
Investigative Counsel.—Daniel Boatright, Quinton Brady.
Oversight Counsel.—Caitlin Soto.

Investigator.—Daniel Parker.
Detailees to the Committee: Charles Pankenier, John Pias, David Timmons, Marta Wosinska.

Minority Staff:
Staff Director.—Joshua Sheinkman.
Deputy Staff Director and Chief Counsel.—Michael Evans.
Deputy Chief Counsel and Senior Health Counsel.—Beth Vrable, M.D.
Chief Tax Counsel.—Tiffany Smith.
Senior Tax and Economic Advisor.—Adam Carasso.
Senior Tax and ERISA Counsel.—Drew Crouch.
Senior Tax Counsel, International.—Jonathan Goldman.
Senior Tax Policy Advisor, Small Business and Pass-Throughs.—Sarah Schaefer.
Tax Policy Advisor.—Christopher Arneson.
Professional Staff Member.—Robert Andres.
Tax Policy Analyst.—Rachel Kauss.
Chief Health Advisor.—Elizabeth Jurinka.
Chief Human Services Advisor.—Laura Bernsten.
Senior Health Counsel.—Anne Dwyer, Arielle Woronoff.
Senior Health Advisor.—Shawn Bishop.
Senior Domestic Policy Advisor.—Thomas Klouda.
Health Policy Advisor.—Kristen Lunde.
Chief Advisor for International Competitiveness and Innovation.—Jayme White.
Senior International Trade Counsel: Sally Laing, Greta Peisch.
International Trade Counsel.—Virginia Lenahan.
Chief Investigator.—David Berick.
Investigation Counsel.—Daniel Goshorn.
Investigators: Peter Gartrell, Joshua Heath, Ian Nicholson, Michael Osborn-Grosso.
Senior Advisor for Policy Communication and Speechwriter.—Ryan Carey.
Deputy Press Secretary for Health, Spokesperson.—Taylor Harvey.

Non-Designated Staff:
Chief Clerk and Historian.—Joshua LeVasseur.
Deputy Clerk.—Jewel Harper, Susanna Segal.
Hearing Clerk.—Athena Schritz.
Archivist.—Dina Mazina.
GPO Detailees: Timothy Danowski, Mark Moore.
IT Director.—Joseph Carnucci.
Assistant to the Systems Administrator.—Mark Blair.
Staff Assistants: Samin Mirfakharai, Eliza Smith.

Foreign Relations

423 Dirksen Senate Office Building 20510–6225

phone: (202) 224–4651, https://foreign.senate.gov

James E. Risch, of Idaho, *Chair*

Marco Rubio, of Florida.
Ron Johnson, of Wisconsin.
Cory Gardner, of Colorado.
Mitt Romney, of Utah.
Lindsey Graham, of South Carolina.
John Barrasso, of Wyoming.
Rob Portman, of Ohio.
Rand Paul, of Kentucky.
Todd Young, of Indiana.
Ted Cruz, of Texas.
David Perdue, of Georgia.

Robert Menendez, of New Jersey.
Benjamin L. Cardin, of Maryland.
Jeanne Shaheen, of New Hampshire.
Christopher A. Coons, of Delaware.
Tom Udall, of New Mexico.
Christopher Murphy, of Connecticut.
Tim Kaine, of Virginia.
Edward J. Markey, of Massachusetts.
Jeff Merkley, of Oregon.
Cory A. Booker, of New Jersey.

SUBCOMMITTEES

[The chair and ranking minority member are ex officio (non-voting) members of all subcommittees on which they do not serve.]

Africa and Global Health Policy

Lindsey Graham, of South Carolina, *Chair*

David Perdue, of Georgia.
Rob Portman, of Ohio.
Ron Johnson, of Wisconsin.
Ted Cruz, of Texas.

Tim Kaine, of Virginia.
Christopher A. Coons, of Delaware.
Cory A. Booker, of New Jersey.
Christopher Murphy, of Connecticut.

East Asia, the Pacific, and International Cybersecurity Policy

Cory Gardner, of Colorado, *Chair*

Marco Rubio, of Florida.
Ron Johnson, of Wisconsin.
David Perdue, of Georgia.
Todd Young, of Indiana.

Edward J. Markey, of Massachusetts.
Christopher A. Coons, of Delaware.
Jeff Merkley, of Oregon.
Tom Udall, of New Mexico.

Europe and Regional Security Cooperation

Ron Johnson, of Wisconsin, *Chair*

John Barrasso, of Wyoming.
Rob Portman, of Ohio.
Rand Paul, of Kentucky.
Mitt Romney, of Utah.

Jeanne Shaheen, of New Hampshire.
Christopher Murphy, of Connecticut.
Benjamin L. Cardin, of Maryland.
Christopher A. Coons, of Delaware.

Multilateral International Development, Multilateral Institutions, and International Economic, Energy, and Environmental Policy

Todd Young, of Indiana, *Chair*

Mitt Romney, of Utah.
Rand Paul, of Kentucky.
David Perdue, of Georgia.
...dsey Graham, of South Carolina.

Jeff Merkley, of Oregon.
Tom Udall, of New Mexico.
Edward J. Markey, of Massachusetts.
Cory A. Booker, of New Jersey.

Near East, South Asia, Central Asia, and Counterterrorism

Mitt Romney, of Utah, *Chair*

Ted Cruz, of Texas.
Lindsey Graham, of South Carolina.
Cory Gardner, of Colorado.
Rand Paul, of Kentucky.
Christopher Murphy, of Connecticut.
Benjamin L. Cardin, of Maryland.
Jeanne Shaheen, of New Hampshire.
Tim Kaine, of Virginia.

State Department and USAID Management, International Operations, and Bilateral International Development

John Barrasso, of Wyoming, *Chair*

Todd Young, of Indiana.
Rand Paul, of Kentucky.
Rob Portman, of Ohio.
Marco Rubio, of Florida.
Cory A. Booker, of New Jersey.
Edward J. Markey, of Massachusetts.
Jeff Merkley, of Oregon.
Tom Udall, of New Mexico.

Western Hemisphere, Transnational Crime, Civilian Security, Democracy, Human Rights, and Global Women's Issues

Marco Rubio, of Florida, *Chair*

Rob Portman, of Ohio.
Ted Cruz, of Texas.
Cory Gardner, of Colorado.
John Barrasso, of Wyoming.
Benjamin L. Cardin, of Maryland.
Tom Udall, of New Mexico.
Jeanne Shaheen, of New Hampshire.
Tim Kaine, of Virginia.

STAFF

Committee on Foreign Relations (SD–423), 224–4651.

Majority Staff:

Chief of Staff.—Chris Socha.
Deputy Staff Director and Treaty Counsel.—Andy Olson.
Director of Operations.—Emily Cottle.
Communications Director.—Suzanne Wrasse.
Senior Professional Staff Members: Joan Condon, Hannah Thoburn.
Professional Staff Members: Colin Brooks, Victor Cervino, Joan Condon, Brian Cullen, Maggie Dougherty, Robert Hunter, John Tomaszewski (JT).
Counsel: Scott Richardson, Matt Sullivan.
Nominations Counsel.—Kateri Dahl.
Policy Analysts/Assistants.—Lara Crouch, Clay Huddleston, Molly Lazio, Cate Sadler.
Director of Special Projects.—Skiffington Holderness.
Special Projects Assistant.—Joe Biegun.
Fellow–Cybersecurity.—Tricia Schulz.

Minority Staff:

Staff Director.—Jessica Lewis.
Director of Operations.—Brandon Jacobsen.
Chief Counsel/Deputy Staff Director.—Andrew Keller.
Deputy Chief Counsel.—John Ryan.
Chief Investigative Counsel.—Megan Bartley.
Policy Director.—Sarah Arkin.
Communications Director.—Juan Pachon.
Senior Advisor/Counselor.—Michael Schiffer.
Research/Legislative Assistants: Chris Barr, Nury Gambarrotti, Margot Hecht, Doug Levinson, Nadhika Ramachandran, Danny Ricchetti, Jon Tsentas.
Senior Professional Staff Members: David Fite, Heather Flynn, Jim Greene, Josh Klein, Damian Murphy, Charlotte Oldham-Moore, Lowell Schwartz, Judith Williams, Brandon Yoder.
Senior Professional Staff Member on Europe.—Damian Murphy.
Policy Analysts: Terell Henry, Nina Russell, Jasmine Wyatt.
Legislative Fellow.—Laura Truitt.
Fellows: Yelda Kazimi, Adrian Mathura.

Non-Designated Staff:
Chief Clerk.—John Dutton.
Deputy Chief Clerk.—Samantha Hamilton.
Hearing Coordinator.—Bertie Bowman.
Executive Clerk.—Lexie Simpson.
Chief of Protocol/Foreign Travel.—Meg Murphy.
Protocol Assistant.—Logan Jolley.
Staff Assistants: Paul Burdette, Laurie Williams.

Health, Education, Labor, and Pensions

428 Dirksen Senate Office Building 20510–6300

phone 224–6770, https://help.senate.gov

Lamar Alexander, of Tennessee, *Chair*

Michael B. Enzi, of Wyoming.
Richard Burr, of North Carolina.
Rand Paul, of Kentucky.
Susan M. Collins, of Maine.
Bill Cassidy, of Louisiana.
Pat Roberts, of Kansas.
Lisa Murkowski, of Alaska.
Tim Scott, of South Carolina
Mitt Romney, of Utah.
Mike Braun, of Indiana.
Kelly Loeffler, of Georgia.

Patty Murray, of Washington.
BERNARD SANDERS, of Vermont.
Robert P. Casey, Jr., of Pennsylvania.
Tammy Baldwin, of Wisconsin.
Christopher Murphy, of Connecticut.
Elizabeth Warren, of Massachusetts.
Tim Kaine, of Virginia.
Margaret Wood Hassan, of New Hampshire.
Tina Smith, of Minnesota.
Doug Jones, of Alabama.
Jacky Rosen, of Nevada.

SUBCOMMITTEES

[The chair and ranking minority member are ex officio members of all subcommittees on which they do not serve.]

Children and Families

Rand Paul, of Kentucky, *Chair*

Lisa Murkowski, of Alaska.
Richard Burr, of North Carolina.
Bill Cassidy, of Louisiana.
Tim Scott, of South Carolina.
Mitt Romney, of Utah.
Kelly Loeffler, of Georgia.

Robert P. Casey, Jr., of Pennsylvania.
BERNARD SANDERS, of Vermont.
Christopher Murphy, of Connecticut.
Tim Kaine, of Virginia.
Margaret Wood Hassan, of New Hampshire.
Tina Smith, of Minnesota.

Employment and Workplace Safety

Susan M. Collins, of Maine, *Chair*

Tim Scott, of South Carolina.
Rand Paul, of Kentucky.
Mitt Romney, of Utah.
Mike Braun, of Indiana.
Bill Cassidy, of Louisiana.
Kelly Loeffler, of Georgia.

Tammy Baldwin, of Wisconsin.
Robert P. Casey, Jr., of Pennsylvania.
Elizabeth Warren, of Massachusetts.
Tina Smith, of Minnesota.
Doug Jones, of Alabama.
Jacky Rosen, of Nevada.

Primary Health and Retirement Security

Michael B. Enzi, of Wyoming, *Chair*

Richard Burr, of North Carolina.
Bill Cassidy, of Louisiana.
Pat Roberts, of Kansas.
Mitt Romney, of Utah.
Mike Braun, of Indiana.
Lisa Murkowski, of Alaska.
Tim Scott, of South Carolina.
Kelly Loeffler, of Georgia.

BERNARD SANDERS, of Vermont.
Tammy Baldwin, of Wisconsin.
Christopher Murphy, of Connecticut.
Elizabeth Warren, of Massachusetts.
Tim Kaine, of Virginia.
Margaret Wood Hassan, of New Hampshire.
Doug Jones, of Alabama.
Jacky Rosen, of Nevada.

STAFF

Committee on Health, Education, Labor, and Pensions, SD–428, 224–6770.
Staff Director.—David P. Cleary, SD–455, 4–6770.
Deputy Staff Director.—Lindsey Ward Seidman, SH–132, 4–6770.

Deputy Chief of Staff for Operations.—Misty Marshall, SH–835, 4–6770.
General Counsel.—Peter Oppenheim, SH–725, 4–6770.
Labor Research Assistant.—Grant English, SH–835, 4–6770.
Health Policy Office, SH–725, 4–0623.
Health Policy Director.—Grace Stuntz Graham, SH–725, 4–0623.
Health and Oversight Counsel.—Aliza Fishbein Silver, SH–404, 4–0623.
Senior Health Policy Advisors: Jennifer Boyer, SH–404, Margaret Coulter, Beth Nelson, SH–725, 4–0623.
Health Policy Advisor.—Virginia McMillin, SH–725, 4–0623.
Professional Staff.—Andy Vogt, SH–725, 4–0623.
Health Staff Assistants: Anna Catherine Feaster (4–0623), Meghan McCully, SH–725, 4–7675.
Health Research Assistants: Charlie Brereton, Tyler Shrive, SH–725, 4–0623.
Education Office, SH–615, 4–8484.
Education Policy Director.—Robert Moran, SH–615, 4–8484.
Education Policy Advisors: Lauren Davies, Andrew LaCasse, SH–615, 4–8484.
Education Professional Staff: Jake Baker, Jordan Hynes, Matt Stern, SH–615, 4–8484.
Education Research Assistant.—Mary Catherine Cook, SH–615, 4–8484.
Education Staff Assistant.—Jones Hussey, SH–615, 4–8484.
Labor Policy Office, SH–835, 4–6770.
Labor and Pensions Policy Director.—Andy Banducci, SH–835, 4–6770.
Labor and Pensions Counsel.—Greg Proseus, SH–835, 4–6770.
Labor and Pensions Professional Staff.—Will Campbell, SH–835, 4–3077.
Chief Counsel of Oversight.—Kristin Nelson Spiridon, SD–615, 4–6770.
Oversight Counsel.—Sandra Sawan, SD–424, 4–6770.
Oversight Staff Assistant.—Jeremy Boshwit, SD–424, 4–6770.
Communications Office, SH–132, 4–6770.
Press Secretary and Speechwriter.—Elizabeth Gibson, SH–132, 4–6770.
Deputy Press Secretary and Digital Media Director.—Evan Dixon, SH–132, 4–6770.
Subcommittee on Children and Families, SH–404, 4–0121.
Subcommittee on Employment and Workplace Safety, SH–828, 4–5800.
Subcommittee on Primary Health and Retirement Security, SH–828, 4–5406.

Minority Staff:

Staff Director.—Evan Schatz, SD–648, 4–0767.
Deputy Staff Director.—John Righter, SD–648, 4–0767.
Special Assistant.—Michelle Sanchez, SD–648, 4–0767.
Staff Assistant.—Tiffany Haas, SD–648, 4–0767.
Senior Press Secretary.—Madeleine Russak, SD–648, 4–0767.
Press Secretary.—Anali Algeria, SD–648, 4–0767.
Deputy Press Secretary.—Ryan Myers, SD–648, 4–0767.
Health Policy Office, 4–7675.
Health Policy Director.—Nick Bath, SH–525, 4–7675.
Deputy Director, Health Policy.—Andi Fristedt, SH–525, 4–7675.
Senior Health Policy Advisor.—Colin Goldfinch, SH–525, 4–7675.
Senior FDA Advisor.—Katlin Backfield, SH–525, 4–7675.
Senior Health Counsel.—Laurel Sakai, SH–525, 4–7675.
Staff Assistant.—Esther Yoon, SH–525, 4–7675.
Labor Policy Office, 4–5441.
Labor Policy Director.—Nikki McKinney, SH–622B, 4–5441.
Senior Disability Policy Advisor.—Kimberly Knackstedt, SH–440, 4–4369.
Labor Counsel: Joseph Shantz, Lafe Solomon, SH–622B, 4–5441.
Senior Pensions and Retirement Counsel.—Kendra Isaacson, SH–440, 4–4369.
Education Policy Office, 4–5501.
Education Policy Director.—Kara Marchione, SH–632, 4–5501.
Deputy Education Policy Director.—Amanda Beaumont, SH–632, 4–5501.
Policy Advisors: Mary Barry, Manuel Contreras, Bryce McKibben, SH–632, 4–5501.
Oversight and Investigation Office, 4–6403.
General Counsel and Chief Investigator.—Carly Rush, SH–833, 4–0767.
Oversight Counsel.—Lizzy Letter, SH–832A, 4–0767.
Oversight Counsel/Special Counsel.—Kathleen Borschow, SH–833, 4–0767.
Counsel.—Matt Huggins, SH–833, 4–6770.

Subcommittee on Children and Families, 4–0121.
Staff Director.—Sara Maskornick, SH–143, 8–1455.
Legislative Aides: Stephanie DeLuca, Doug Hartman, SH–143, 8–1455.
Subcommittee on Employment and Workplace Safety, 4–5800.
Senior Policy Advisor.—Michael Waske, SH–143, 4–9243.
Subcommittee on Primary Health and Retirement Security, 4–5406.
Subcommittee Staff Director.—Britt Weinstock, SH–622A, 4–5480.

Homeland Security and Governmental Affairs

340 Dirksen Senate Office Building 20510,

phone 224–4751, fax 224–9603, https://hsgac.senate.gov

Hearing Room—SD–342 Dirksen Senate Office Building

Meets first Wednesday of each month

Ron Johnson, of Wisconsin, *Chair*

Rob Portman, of Ohio.
Rand Paul, of Kentucky.
James Lankford, of Oklahoma.
Mitt Romney, of Utah.
Rick Scott, of Florida.
Michael B. Enzi, of Wyoming.
Josh Hawley, of Missouri.

Gary C. Peters, of Michigan.
Thomas R. Carper, of Delaware.
Margaret Wood Hassan, of New Hampshire.
Kamala D. Harris, of California.
Kyrsten Sinema, of Arizona.
Jacky Rosen, of Nevada.

SUBCOMMITTEES

[The chair and the ranking minority member are ex officio members of all subcommittees.]

Federal Spending Oversight and Emergency Management

Rand Paul, of Kentucky, *Chair*

Rick Scott, of Florida.
Michael B. Enzi, of Wyoming.
Josh Hawley, of Missouri.

Margaret Wood Hassan, of New Hampshire.
Kamala D. Harris, of California.
Kyrsten Sinema, of Arizona.

Permanent Subcommittee on Investigations

Rob Portman, of Ohio, *Chair*

Rand Paul, of Kentucky.
James Lankford, of Oklahoma.
Mitt Romney, of Utah.
Josh Hawley, of Missouri.

Thomas R. Carper, of Delaware.
Margaret Wood Hassan, of New Hampshire.
Kamala D. Harris, of California.
Jacky Rosen, of Nevada.

Regulatory Affairs and Federal Management

James Lankford, of Oklahoma, *Chair*

Rob Portman, of Ohio.
Mitt Romney, of Utah.
Rick Scott, of Florida.
Michael B. Enzi, of Wyoming.

Kyrsten Sinema, of Arizona.
Thomas R. Carper, of Delaware.
Jacky Rosen, of Nevada.

STAFF

Committee on Homeland Security and Governmental Affairs (SD–340), 224–4751.
Staff Director.—Gabrielle D'Adamo Singer.
Chief Counsel.—Joe Folio.
Chief Clerk.—Laura W. Kilbride.
Chief Counsel for Governmental Affairs.—Patrick Bailey.
Deputy Chief Counsel for Governmental Affairs.—Courtney Allen.
Co-Director & Chief Counsel for Homeland Security.—Michael Lueptow.
Co-Director & Chief Policy Advisor for Homeland Security.—Michelle Woods.
Senior Policy Advisors: Jerry Markon, Lydia Westlake.
Chief Economist.—Satya Thallam.
Senior Investigator.—Brian Downey.

Senior Counsel.—Mike Flynn.
Counsel.—Clark Hedrick.
Senior Professional Staff: Helen Heiden, Brian Kennedy, Josh McLeod, Scott Wittmann.
Professional Staff: Colleen Berny, Christopher Boness, Melissa Egred, Barrett Percival, Jennifer Selde, Daniel Spino, Andrew Timm.
Press Secretary.—Austin Altenburg.
Research Assistants: Maggie Frankel, William Sacripanti.
Staff Assistants: Caroline Bender, Roland Hernandez, Jr.
Fellow.—William Rhodes.
Publications Clerk.—Joyce Ward.
Financial Clerk.—Rachel Mairella.
Systems Administrator.—Dan Muchow.
Minority Staff Director.—David Weinberg (SH–442), 224–6553.
Chief Counsel.—Zachary Schram.
Communications Director.—Allison Green.
Director of Homeland Security.—Alexa Noruk.
Director of Governmental Affairs and Senior Counsel.—Ashley Poling.
Senior Investigative Counsel.—Alan Kahn.
Senior Counsel for Technology.—Sue Ramanathan.
Senior Counsel.—Michelle Benecke.
Investigative Counsel: Claudine Brenner, Charles Shaw.
Counsel.—Roy Awabdeh.
National Security Advisor.—Julie Klein.
Professional Staff Members: Annika Christensen, Katie Conle, Yogin Kothari, Samuel Rodarte, Yelena Tsilker, Jackson Voss.
Deputy Press Secretary.—David McGonigal.
Press Assistant.—Ashanée Gardner.
Office Manager.—April Beasley.
Staff Assistants: Corban Ryan, Marie Talarico.
GAO Detailee.—Chris Mulkins.
Fellows: Chelsea Davis, Anne Nelson, Jeffrey Rothblum.

Permanent Subcommittee on Investigations (PSI), (SR–199), 224–3721.
Majority Staff Director and Chief Counsel.—Andrew Dockham.
Subcommittee Clerk.—Kate Kielceski.
Deputy Chief Counsel.—Amanda Neely.
Chief Investigator and Counsel.—Andrew Polesovsky.
Counsel: Kathleen Shannon, Patrick Warren.
Investigator.—Will Dargusch.
Professional Staff Members: Adam Henderson, Cara Mumford.
Special Investigator/DHS HSI Detailee.—Brian Davis.
VA Detailee.—Jennifer Deen.
Minority Staff Director.—John Kilvington (SR–199), 224–9505.
Chief Counsel.—Brandon Reavis.
Counsel: Meeran Ahn, Roberto Berrios.
Special Investigator/ODNI Detailee.—Monica Hayes.
Special Investigator/SEC Detailee.—Kevin Stemp.

Subcommittee on Federal Spending Oversight and Emergency Management (FSO), (SH–439), 224–2254.
Majority Staff Director.—Greg McNeill.
Subcommittee Clerk.—Kate Kielceski.
Deputy Director of Homeland Security.—Adam Salmon.
Professional Staff Member.—Aaron Gottesman.
Legislative Assistant.—Jim Webb.
Minority Staff Director and Senior Cybersecurity and Counterterrorism Advisor.—Harlan Geer (SH–432), 228–0641.
Counsel for Governmental Affairs.—Allison Tinsey.
Professional Staff Member.—Jillian Joyce.
Senior Policy NCTC Detailee.—Erin Wilson.

Subcommittee on Regulatory Affairs and Federal Management (RAFM), (SH–601), 224–4551.
Majority Staff Director and General Counsel.—Chris White.
Subcommittee Clerk.—Mallory Nersesian.
Deputy Staff Director.—Amanda Hill.
Senior Counsel.—James Mann.

Minority Staff Director.—Eric Bursch (SH–605), 224–3682.
Senior Professional Staff Member.—Anthony Papian.
Policy Advisor.—Jackie Maffuci.
CBP Detailee.—Dean Williams.

Judiciary

224 Dirksen Senate Office Building 20510–6275

phone 224–5225, fax 224–9102, https://judiciary.senate.gov

meets upon call of the chair

Lindsey Graham, of South Carolina, *Chair*

Chuck Grassley, of Iowa.
John Cornyn, of Texas.
Mike Lee, of Utah.
Ted Cruz, of Texas.
Ben Sasse, of Nebraska.
Josh Hawley, of Missouri.
Thom Tillis, of North Carolina.
Joni Ernst, of Iowa.
Mike Crapo, of Idaho.
John Kennedy, of Louisiana.
Marsha Blackburn, of Tennessee.

Dianne Feinstein, of California.
Patrick J. Leahy, of Vermont.
Richard J. Durbin, of Illinois.
Sheldon Whitehouse, of Rhode Island.
Amy Klobuchar, of Minnesota.
Christopher A. Coons, of Delaware.
Richard Blumenthal, of Connecticut.
Mazie K. Hirono, of Hawaii.
Cory A. Booker, of New Jersey.
Kamala D. Harris, of California.

SUBCOMMITTEES

Antitrust, Competition Policy and Consumer Rights

Mike Lee, of Utah, *Chair*

Chuck Grassley, of Iowa.
Josh Hawley, of Missouri.
Mike Crapo, of Idaho.
Marsha Blackburn, of Tennessee.

Amy Klobuchar, of Minnesota.
Patrick J. Leahy, of Vermont.
Richard Blumenthal, of Connecticut.
Cory A. Booker, of New Jersey.

Border Security and Immigration

John Cornyn, of Texas, *Chair*

Lindsey Graham, of South Carolina.
Chuck Grassley, of Iowa.
Mike Lee, of Utah.
Ted Cruz, of Texas.
Josh Hawley, of Missouri.
Thom Tillis, of North Carolina.
Joni Ernst, of Iowa.
John Kennedy, of Louisiana.

Richard J. Durbin, of Illinois.
Dianne Feinstein, of California.
Patrick J. Leahy, of Vermont.
Amy Klobuchar, of Minnesota.
Christopher A. Coons, of Delaware.
Richard Blumenthal, of Connecticut.
Mazie K. Hirono, of Hawaii.
Cory A. Booker, of New Jersey.

The Constitution

Ted Cruz, of Texas, *Chair*

John Cornyn, of Texas.
Mike Lee, of Utah.
Ben Sasse, of Nebraska.
Mike Crapo, of Idaho.
Marsha Blackburn, of Tennessee.

Mazie K. Hirono, of Hawaii.
Richard J. Durbin, of Illinois.
Sheldon Whitehouse, of Rhode Island.
Christopher A. Coons, of Delaware.
Kamala D. Harris, of California.

Crime and Terrorism

Josh Hawley, of Missouri, *Chair*

Lindsey Graham, of South Carolina.
John Cornyn, of Texas.
Ted Cruz, of Texas.
Thom Tillis, of North Carolina.
Joni Ernst, of Iowa.
John Kennedy, of Louisiana.

Sheldon Whitehouse, of Rhode Island.
Dianne Feinstein, of California.
Richard J. Durbin, of Illinois.
Amy Klobuchar, of Minnesota.
Christopher A. Coons, of Delaware.
Cory A. Booker, of New Jersey.

Intellectual Property

Thom Tillis, of North Carolina, *Chair*

Lindsey Graham, of South Carolina.
Chuck Grassley, of Iowa.
John Cornyn, of Texas.
Mike Lee, of Utah.
Ben Sasse, of Nebraska.
Mike Crapo, of Idaho.
Marsha Blackburn, of Tennessee.
Christopher A. Coons, of Delaware.
Patrick J. Leahy, of Vermont.
Richard J. Durbin, of Illinois.
Sheldon Whitehouse, of Rhode Island.
Richard Blumenthal, of Connecticut.
Mazie K. Hirono, of Hawaii.
Kamala D. Harris, of California.

Oversight, Agency Action, Federal Rights and Federal Courts

Ben Sasse, of Nebraska, *Chair*

Chuck Grassley, of Iowa.
Thom Tillis, of North Carolina.
Joni Ernst, of Iowa.
Mike Crapo, of Idaho.
John Kennedy, of Louisiana.
Richard Blumenthal, of Connecticut.
Patrick J. Leahy, of Vermont.
Sheldon Whitehouse, of Rhode Island.
Amy Klobuchar, of Minnesota.
Mazie K. Hirono, of Hawaii.

STAFF

Committee on the Judiciary (SD–224), 224–5225.
Chief Clerk.—Heather Vachon.
Deputy Chief Clerk.—Michelle Heller.
Hearings Clerk.—Jason Covey.
Law Librarian.—Charles Papirmeister.
Legislative Calendar Clerk.—Alberta Easter.
Majority Office (SD–224), 224–5225, fax 224–9102.
Majority Chief Counsel and Staff Director.—Lee Holmes.
Deputy Staff Director and General Counsel.—Joe Keeley.
Chief Counsel for National Security and Crime.—Richard DiZinno.
Chief Counsel for Nominations and Constitutional Law.—Mike Fragoso.
Chief Investigative Counsel.—Zachary Somers.
Chief Counsel for Antitrust and Bankruptcy.—Ryan Datillo.
Chief Counsel for Liberty and Values.—Brad Kehr.
Chief Counsel for Immigration and Visa Security.—Katherine Nikas.
Senior Investigative Counsel.—Arthur Baker.
Investigative Counsel: Gabrielle Michalak, Elliot Walden.
Counsel: Brendan Chestnut, Raija Churchill, Lindsey Keiser, Kristina Sesek.
Associate Counsel: Watson Horner, Tim Rodriguez, Chris Ventura.
Senior Counsel.—Lauren Mehler.
Policy Advisor for Justice Programs.—Blair Bjellos.
Professional Staff Member.—Barbara Ledeen.
Communications Director.—Taylor Reidy.
Deputy Communications Director.—Carlee Tousman.
Legislative Aide.—Michael Perkins.
Staff Assistants: Bentley Olson, Julian Wilson.
Archivist.—Stuart Paine.
Director of Information Systems.—Steve Kirkland.
Minority Office (SD–152), 224–7703, fax 224–9516.
Minority Staff Director and Chief Counsel.—Jennifer Duck.
General Counsel.—Heather Sawyer.
Senior Counsel: Phil Brest, Nick Xenakis.
Counsel: Rachel Appleton, Sarah Bauer, Christina Calce, Patrick Day, Lindsay Erickson, Alex Haskell, Gabe Kader, Anant Raut, Sunil Varghese.
Assistant to the Staff Director.—Elizabeth Bernal.
Legislative Aide.—Matthew Halek.
Legislative Staff Assistants: Sebastian Alarcon, John Lowry, Oliver Mittelstaedt.
Staff Assistants: Hayley Aguayo, Katherine Kazmin.
Research Assistant.—Jeany Larsen.
Archivist.—Mary Ferranti.
Systems Administrator.—Lane Giardina.

Subcommittee on Antitrust, Competition Policy and Consumer Rights
Majority Chief Counsel.—Phil Alito.
Minority Chief Counsel.—Ajay Kundaria.

Subcommittee on Border Security and Immigration
Majority Chief Counsel.—Carter Burwell.
Minority Chief Counsel.—Joseph Zogby.

Subcommittee on the Constitution
Majority Chief Counsel.—Judd Stone.
Minority Chief Counsel.—Helaine Greenfeld.

Subcommittee on Crime and Terrorism
Majority Special Counsel.—Sean Cooksey.
Minority Chief Counsel.—Joe Gaeta.

Subcommittee on Intellectual Property
Majority Chief Counsel.—Brad Watts.
Minority Chief Counsel.—Erica Songer.

Subcommittee on Oversight, Agency Action, Federal Rights and Federal Courts
Majority Chief Counsel.—William Payne.
Minority Chief Counsel.—Sam Simon.

Senator Grassley Judiciary Staff
Chief Counsel.—Rita Lari.
Senior Counsel.—Kyle McCollum.
Counsel: Drew Robinson, Rachel Wright.

Senator Ernst Judiciary Staff
Chief Counsel.—Corey Becker.

Senator Crapo Judiciary Staff
Legislative Assistants: Rebecca Alcorn, Colin St. Maxens.

Senator Kennedy Judiciary Staff
Counsel.—Nick Hawatmeh.

Senator Blackburn Judiciary Staff
Chief Counsel.—Jessica Vu.

Senator Leahy Judiciary Staff
Chief Counsel.—David Pendle.

Senator Booker Judiciary Staff
Chief Counsel.—Tona Boyd.

Senator Harris Judiciary Staff
General Counsel.—Lauren Moore.

Rules and Administration

305 Russell Senate Office Building 20510–6325

phone 224–6352, https://rules.senate.gov

[Legislative Reorganization Act of 1946]

meets second and fourth Wednesday of each month

Roy Blunt, of Missouri, *Chair*

Mitch McConnell, of Kentucky.
Lamar Alexander, of Tennessee.
Pat Roberts, of Kansas.
Richard C. Shelby, of Alabama.
Ted Cruz, of Texas.
Shelley Moore Capito, of West Virginia.
Roger F. Wicker, of Mississippi.
Deb Fischer, of Nebraska.
Cindy Hyde-Smith, of Mississippi.

Amy Klobuchar, of Minnesota.
Dianne Feinstein, of California.
Charles E. Schumer, of New York.
Richard J. Durbin, of Illinois.
Tom Udall, of New Mexico.
Mark R. Warner, of Virginia.
Patrick J. Leahy, of Vermont.
ANGUS S. KING, JR., of Maine.
Catherine Cortez Masto, of Nevada.

(No Subcommittees)

STAFF

Committee on Rules and Administration (SR–305), 224–6352.
Majority Staff Director.—Fitzhugh Elder IV.
Deputy Staff Director.—Rachelle Schroeder.
Chief Counsel.—Jackie Barber.
Counsel.—Wendy Smith.
Senior Professional Staff.—Nichole Kotschwar.
Professional Staff: Molly McCarty, Kasey Shelly.
Minority Staff Director and Chief Counsel.—Lindsey Kerr.
Deputy Staff Director.—Travis Talvitie.
Operations Director.—Dustin Brandenburg.
Counsel.—Vincent Brown.
Professional Staff.—Greta Bedekovics.
Fellow.—Eric Mill.
Non-Designated Staff:
Chief Clerk.—Cindy Qualley.
Archivist.—Katie Salay.
Auditors: Lesya Eppes, Kacie Jones, Alex Stoddard.
Systems Administrator.—James Ferenc.
Staff Assistants: Robert Ninness, Lina Lenis.
GPO Detailee.—Eve Hiers.

Small Business and Entrepreneurship

428A Russell Senate Office Building 20510

phone 224–5175, fax 224–5619, https://sbc.senate.gov

[Created pursuant to S. Res. 58, 81st Congress]

meets first Thursday of each month

Marco Rubio, of Florida, *Chair*

James E. Risch, of Idaho.
Rand Paul, of Kentucky.
Tim Scott, of South Carolina.
Joni Ernst, of Iowa.
James M. Inhofe, of Oklahoma.
Todd Young, of Indiana.
John Kennedy, of Louisiana.
Mitt Romney, of Utah.
Josh Hawley, of Missouri.

Benjamin L. Cardin, of Maryland.
Maria Cantwell, of Washington.
Jeanne Shaheen, of New Hampshire.
Edward J. Markey, of Massachusetts.
Cory A. Booker, of New Jersey.
Christopher A. Coons, of Delaware.
Mazie K. Hirono, of Hawaii.
Tammy Duckworth, of Illinois.
Jacky Rosen, of Nevada.

(No Subcommittees)

STAFF

Committee on Small Business and Entrepreneurship (SR–428A), 224–5175, fax 224–5619.
Majority Staff Director.—Meredith West.
Professional Staff Members: Renee Bender, Maggie Moore, Eleni Valanos.
Senior Policy Advisor.—Chris Griswold.
Policy Analyst.—Phillip Todd.
Counsel.—Christina Salazar.
Project Director.—Caleb Orr.
Deputy Press Secretary and Policy Aide.—Samantha Scoca.
Research Assistant.—Josh Duncan.
Staff Assistant.—Gabriela Rodriguez.

Non-Designated Staff:
Chief Clerk.—Kathryn Eden.
Systems Administrator.—Steve Gingerich.

Minority Committee Main Office (SR–471), 224–4291, fax 228–1128.
Democratic Staff Director.—Sean Moore.
Tax and Economic Policy Advisor.—Ron Storhaug.
Deputy Staff Director.—Kevin Wheeler.
Counsel.—Therese Meers.
Communications Director.—Fabian Seaton.
Policy and Press Aide.—Olivia Nutter.
Staff Assistant.—Kate Landers.

Veterans' Affairs

SR–412 Russell Senate Office Building

phone 224–9126, https://veterans.senate.gov

meets first Wednesday of each month

Jerry Moran, of Kansas, *Chair*

John Boozman, of Arkansas.
Bill Cassidy, of Louisiana.
Mike Rounds, of South Dakota.
Thom Tillis, of North Carolina.
Dan Sullivan, of Alaska.
Marsha Blackburn, of Tennessee.
Kevin Cramer, of North Dakota.
Kelly Loeffler, of Georgia.

Jon Tester, of Montana.
Patty Murray, of Washington.
BERNARD SANDERS, of Vermont.
Sherrod Brown, of Ohio.
Richard Blumenthal, of Connecticut.
Mazie K. Hirono, of Hawaii.
Joe Manchin III, of West Virginia.
Kyrsten Sinema, of Arizona.

(No Subcommittees)

STAFF

Committee on Veterans' Affairs Majority Staff (SR–412), 224–9126, fax 224–8908.
Majority Staff Director.—Adam Reece.
Deputy Staff Director.—Leslie Campbell.
Professional Staff: Emily Blair, Lindsay Dearing, Patrick McGuigan, Brian Newbold, David Shearman, Jillian Workman.
Counsel.—Annabell McWherter.
Legislative Aides: Asher Allman, John Ashley.
Deputy Press Secretary.—Anna Devanny.
Senior Staff Assistant.—Thomas Coleman.
Staff Assistant.—Rieder Grunseth.
Committee on Veterans' Affairs Minority Staff (SH–825A), 224–2074, fax 228–1852.
Minority Staff Director.—Tony McClain.
Deputy Staff Director and General Counsel.—Dahlia Melendrez.
Director of Oversight.—Janko Mitric.
Professional Staff Members: Simon Coon, Sophia Friedl, JC Henry, Amy Smith.
Deputy Press Secretary.—Olya Voytovich.
Staff Assistant.—Tess Wrzesinki.
Committee on Veterans' Affairs Non-Designated Staff (SR-412), 224–9126, fax 224–8908.
Chief Clerk.—Barry Walker.
Systems Administrator.—DeKisha Williams.
Publications Printer.—Pauline Schmitt.

SELECT AND SPECIAL COMMITTEES OF THE SENATE

Committee on Indian Affairs

838 Hart Senate Office Building 20510–6450

phone 224–2251, https://indian.senate.gov

[Created pursuant to S. Res. 4, 95th Congress; amended by S. Res. 71, 103d Congress]

meets every Wednesday of each month

John Hoeven, of North Dakota, *Chair*
Tom Udall, of New Mexico, *Vice Chair*

John Barrasso, of Wyoming.
Lisa Murkowski, of Alaska.
James Lankford, of Oklahoma.
Steve Daines, of Montana.
Martha McSally, of Arizona.
Jerry Moran, of Kansas.

Maria Cantwell, of Washington.
Jon Tester, of Montana.
Brian Schatz, of Hawaii.
Catherine Cortez Masto, of Nevada.
Tina Smith, of Minnesota.

(No Subcommittees)

STAFF

Majority Staff Director / Chief Counsel.—Mike Andrews.
Deputy Staff Director.—Brandon Ashley.
Counsel: Chase Goodnight, Holmes Whelan.
Policy Advisors: Jacqueline Bisille, John Simermeyer.
Special Assistant.—Jim Robertson.
Minority Staff Director / Chief Counsel.—Jennifer Romero.
Senior Counsel.—Josh Mahan.
Counsel.—Concetta Tsosie de Haro.
Senior Policy Advisors: Kim Moxley, Anthony Sedillo.
Policy Advisor.—Ray Martin.
Staff Assistant.—Manu Tupper.
Administrative Director.—Jim Eismeier.
Hearing Clerk.—Avis Dubose.
Systems Administrator.—Dasan Fish.
Staff Assistant.—Zachary Spencer.
GPO Detailee.—Jack Fulmer.

Select Committee on Ethics

220 Hart Senate Office Building 20510

phone 224–2981, fax 224–7416

[Created pursuant to S. Res. 338, 88th Congress; amended by S. Res. 110, 95th Congress]

James Lankford, of Oklahoma, *Chair*
Christopher A. Coons, of Delaware, *Vice Chair*

Pat Roberts, of Kansas.
James E. Risch, of Idaho.

Brian Schatz, of Hawaii.
Jeanne Shaheen, of New Hampshire.

STAFF

Staff Director and Chief Counsel.—Deborah Sue Mayer.
Deputy Chief Counsel.—Karen Gorman.
Chief Clerk.—Cami Morrison.
Senior Counsel and Director of Education and Training.—Geoff Turley.
Counsel: Madeline Dang, Shane Kelly, Katharine Quaglieri, Kelly Selesnick, Charlotte Underwood.
Director of Information Technology.—Danny Remington.
Financial Disclosure Specialist.—Katie Jordan.
Special Assistant.—Brittany Prager.
Staff Assistants: Joseph Lenz, Gabrielle Quintana, Mary Yuengert.

Select Committee on Intelligence

211 Hart Senate Office Building 20510–6475

phone 224–1700, https://intelligence.senate.gov

[Created pursuant to S. Res. 400, 94th Congress]

Marco Rubio, of Florida, *Chair*
Mark R. Warner, of Virginia, *Vice Chair*

Richard Burr, of North Carolina.
James E. Risch, of Idaho.
Susan M. Collins, of Maine.
Roy Blunt, of Missouri.
Tom Cotton, of Arkansas.
John Cornyn, of Texas.
Ben Sasse, of Nebraska.
Dianne Feinstein, of California.
Ron Wyden, of Oregon.
Martin Heinrich, of New Mexico.
Angus S. King, Jr., of Maine.
Kamala D. Harris, of California.
Michael F. Bennet, of Colorado.

Ex Officio

Mitch McConnell, of Kentucky.
James M. Inhofe, of Oklahoma.
Charles E. Schumer, of New York.
Jack Reed, of Rhode Island.

STAFF

Majority Staff Director.—Christopher A. Joyner.
Minority Staff Director.—Michael Casey.
Chief Clerk.—Kelsey Stroud Bailey.

Special Committee on Aging

G–31 Dirksen Senate Office Building 20510

phone 224–5364, https://aging.senate.gov

[Reauthorized pursuant to S. Res. 4, 95th Congress]

Susan M. Collins, of Maine, *Chair*

Tim Scott, of South Carolina.
Richard Burr, of North Carolina.
Martha McSally, of Arizona.
Marco Rubio, of Florida.
Josh Hawley, of Missouri.
Mike Braun, of Indiana.
Rick Scott, of Florida.
Robert P. Casey, Jr., of Pennsylvania.
Kirsten E. Gillibrand, of New York.
Richard Blumenthal, of Connecticut.
Elizabeth Warren, of Massachusetts.
Doug Jones, of Alabama.
Kyrsten Sinema, of Arizona.
Jacky Rosen, of Nevada.

STAFF

Majority Deputy Staff Director.—Sarah Khasawinah.

Chief Counsel.—Mark LeDuc.
Health Policy Director.—Amy Pellegrino.
Professional Staff: Maria Olson, Lara Rosner.
Legislative Correspondent.—Jake Lynch.
Legislative Aide.—Owen Mahan.
Research Assistant.—Jacob Towle.
Staff Assistant.—James Erwin.

Non-Designated:
Chief Clerk/System Administrator.—Matt Lawrence.
GPO Detailee.—Ruby Ahmed.

Minority Staff (SH–628), 224–8710, fax 224–9926.
Staff Director.—Kate Mevis.
Deputy Staff Director.—Stacy Sanders.
Disability Policy Director.—Michael Gamel-McCormick.
Deputy Chief Counsel.—Rashage Green.
Special Counsel and Director of Oversight and Investigation.—Caitlin Warner.
Senior Policy Advisor.—Keith Miller.
Senior Policy Aide.—Samantha Koehler.
Policy Aide.—Joshua Dubensky.
Legislative Correspondent.—Madison West.
Staff Assistant.—Nigel Stinson.

Democratic Senatorial Campaign Committee

120 Maryland Avenue, NE., Washington, DC 20002
phone 224–2447

Catherine Cortez Masto, of Nevada, *Chair*
Charles E. Schumer, of New York, *Democratic Leader*

STAFF

Executive Director.—Scott Fairchild.
Deputy Executive Director and Chief Operating Officer.—Brynn Palmen.
Senior Advisors: Justin Barasky, Christie Roberts.
Finance Director.—Eben DuRoss.
Chief Digital Officer.—Kati Card.
Digital Director.—Marina Orcutt.
Communications Director.—Lauren Passalacqua.
Research Director.—Megan Hughes.
Policy Director.—Hazeen Ashby.
Chief Information Security Officer.—Jude Meche.
Comptroller/Treasurer.—Allison Wright.

Democratic Policy and Communications Center

419 Hart Senate Office Building, phone 224–3232

Charles E. Schumer, of New York, *Democratic Leader*

Debbie Stabenow, of Michigan, *Chair*
Joe Manchin III, of West Virginia, *Vice Chair*

STAFF

Staff Director.—Vacant.
Communications Director.—Matthew Williams.
Policy Director.—Vacant.
Counsel and Policy Advisor.—Vacant.
Senior Policy Advisor.—Aaron Suntag.

Policy Advisors: Gabrielle Borg, Cristina Shoffner.
Senior Vote Analyst.—Douglas Connolly.
Votes Director.—Mike Mozden.
Junior Investigator.—John B. Donnelly.

Democratic Steering and Outreach Committee

712 Hart Senate Office Building, phone 224–9048

Amy Klobuchar, of Minnesota, *Chair*

Jeanne Shaheen, of New Hampshire, *Vice Chair*

Charles E. Schumer, of New York, *Democratic Leader*

Richard J. Durbin, of Illinois, *Democratic Whip*

Christopher A. Coons, of Delaware, *Chair of Business Outreach*

Robert Menendez, of New Jersey, *Chair of the Hispanic Task Force*

Cory A. Booker, of New Jersey, *Chair of Metropolitan Area Outreach*

Patrick J. Leahy, of Vermont.
Kirsten E. Gillibrand, of New York.
Christopher A. Coons, of Delaware.
Robert P. Casey, Jr., of Pennsylvania.
Jon Tester, of Montana.
Brian Schatz, of Hawaii.
Tammy Baldwin, of Wisconsin.
Christopher Murphy, of Connecticut.

STAFF

Staff Director.—Laura Schiller.
Director of Outreach.—Noel Perez.
Associate Director.—Amira Hassan.
Assistant Director.—Nicole Lam.

Senate Democratic Conference

154 Russell Senate Office Building, phone 224–2621, fax 224–0238

Secretary.—*Tammy Baldwin,* of Wisconsin.
Chief of Staff.—Bill Murat.

Senate Democratic Media Center

619 Hart Senate Office Building, phone 224–1430

Charles E. Schumer, of New York, *Chair*

STAFF

Director of Digital Media.—Ken Meyer.
Deputy Director of Digital Media.—Jasmine Harris.
Creative Director.—Quinn Bowman.
Digital Producer.—Abele Tuwafie.
Engineer.—Tushar Dayal.
Video Editors: Ezra Deutsch-Feldman, Hayley Gray-Hoehn.
Videographer.—Dave Cooke.
Digital Assistant (Video).—Tinae Bluitt.
Graphic Designer.—Lindsay Dirienzo.
Production Coordinator (Photo).—Rah Foard.
Production Coordinator (Video).—Nora Younkin.
Writer.—Leah Juliett.
Project Manager.—Joel Geertsma.

National Republican Senatorial Committee

425 Second Street, NE., Washington, DC 20002

phone 675–6000, fax 675–6058

Todd Young, of Indiana, *Chair*

STAFF

Executive Director.—Kevin McLaughlin.
Director of:
Communications.—Jesse Hunt.
Finance.—Anna Rogers Duncan.
Legal Counsel.—Ryan Dollar.
Political Director.—Betsy Ankney.
Research.—Jeff Snow.
Digital.—Ashley Isaac.
Senior Advisor.—Matt Whitlock.

Senate Republican Policy Committee

347 Russell Senate Office Building

phone 224–2946 fax 224–1235, https://rpc.senate.gov

Roy Blunt, of Missouri, *Chair*

STAFF

Staff Director.—Stacy McBride.
Policy Director.—Tracy Henke.
Communications Director.—Katie Boyd.
Administrative Director.—Craig Cheney.
Analysts:
Agriculture, Energy, and Environment.—Jack Thorlin.
Budget, Tax, Appropriations, Senate Procedure.—Tori Gorman.
Health Care.—Whitney Jones.
Judiciary/Immigration, Trade.—Jack Thorlin.
Education, Labor, Banking, Transportation.—Emily Goff.
Defense, Foreign Affairs, Intelligence, Veterans Affairs.—Jeremy Hayes.
Commerce, Cybersecurity, Technology.—Troy Stock.
Professional Staff:
Editorial Director.—John Mitchell.
System Administrator/RVA Editor.—Thomas Pulju.
Station Manager/Special Projects.—Carolyn Laird.
Station Operator/Projects Assistant.—Daniel Noonan.
Creative Director.—Jesica Leonard.

Senate Republican Conference

405 Hart Senate Office Building

phone 224–2764, https://src.senate.gov

John Barrasso, of Wyoming, *Chair*

Joni Ernst, of Iowa, *Vice Chair*

STAFF

Conference of the Majority (SH–405), 224–2764.
Staff Director.—Dan Kunsman.
Deputy Staff Director.—Jeff Grappone.
Radio Services Director.—Dave Hodgdon.
Administrative Director.—Amber Moyerman.
Speechwriter.—Elizabeth Keys.

Creative & Member Services Director.—Christy Lewis.
Deputy Creative and Member Services Director.—Caleb Fisher.
Production Manager.—Cyrus Pearson.
Videographer/Editor.—Lane Marshall.
Digital Strategist.—Ruben Verastigui.
Creative Director.—Joe Colby.
Deputy Video Producers: Evan Dernberger, Josiah Lindquist.
Systems Engineer.—Nic Budde.
Floor Monitor.—Samantha Ryals.
Staff Assistant.—Tim Corley.

OFFICERS AND OFFICIALS OF THE SENATE

Capitol Telephone Directory, phone 224–3121

Senate room prefixes:
Capitol—S, Russell Senate Office Building—SR
Dirksen Senate Office Building—SD, Hart Senate Office Building—SH

PRESIDENT OF THE SENATE

Vice President of the United States and President of the Senate.—Mike Pence.

The Office of the Vice President is S–212 in the Capitol. The Vice President has offices in the Dirksen Senate Office Building, the Eisenhower Executive Office Building (EEOB), and the White House (West Wing).

phone (202) 456–1414

Assistant to the President and Chief of Staff to the Vice President.—Marc Short.
Assistant to the President and National Security Advisor to the Vice President.—Keith Kellogg.
Deputy Assistant to the President and Deputy Chief of Staff & Counsel to the Vice President.—Matthew Morgan.
Deputy Assistant to the President and Chief of Staff to Mrs. Karen Pence.—Jana Toner.
Deputy Assistant to the President and Deputy National Security Advisor to the Vice President.—Stephen Pinkos.
Deputy Assistant to the President and Director of Advance to the Vice President.—Aaron Chang.
Deputy Assistant to the President and Director of Policy for the Vice President.—John Gray.
Deputy Assistant to the President and Director of Public Liaison and Intergovernmental Affairs for the Vice President.—Sarah Makin.
Special Assistant to the President and Deputy Director of Public Liaison and Intergovernmental Affairs.—Andeliz Castillo.
Special Assistant to the President and Press Secretary to the Vice President.—Katie Waldman.
Assistant to the Vice President and Director of Legislative Affairs.—Christopher Hodgson.
Deputy Director of Legislative Affairs.—Benjamin Cantrell.
Deputy Assistant to the Vice President and Director of Administration and Finance.—Katherine Purucker.
Director of Advance.—Saibatu Mansaray.
Deputy Assistant to the Vice President and Director of Scheduling.—Bethany Scully.
Special Assistant to the Vice President.—Zach Bauer.

PRESIDENT PRO TEMPORE

S–125 The Capitol, phone 224–9400

President Pro Tempore of the Senate.—Chuck Grassley.
Chief of Staff.—Aaron Cummings.
Administrative Director.—Penne Barton.
Special Assistant.—Veronica Francis.

MAJORITY LEADER

S–230 The Capitol, phone 224–3135, fax 228–1264

Majority Leader.—Mitch McConnell.
Chief of Staff.—Sharon Soderstrom.

Deputy Chief of Staff for Operations.—Stefanie Muchow.
Deputy Chief of Staff for Policy.—Scott Raab.
Executive Assistant and Director of Scheduling.—Sarah Fairchild.
Office Manager.—Alexandra Jenkins.
Chief Counsel.—Andrew Ferguson.
National Security Advisor.—Robert Karem.
Communications Director.—David Popp.
Chief Economic Policy Counsel.—Jay Khosla.
Policy Advisors: Steve Donaldson, Jennifer Kuskowski, Jane Lee, Jim Neill, Erica Suares, Terry Van Doren, Jody Wright.
Speechwriter.—Andrew Quinn.
Deputy Speechwriter.—Dylan Vorbach.
Press Secretary.—Douglas Andres.
Deputy Press Secretary.—Georgeanna Sullivan.
Systems Administrator.—Elmamoun Sulfab.
Scheduling Assistant and Special Assistant to the Chief of Staff.—Hannah Wardell.
Staff Assistant.—Victoria Mason.

REPUBLICAN COMMUNICATIONS CENTER

S–230 The Capitol, phone 228–6397

Communications Staff Director.—Scott Sloofman.
Research Director.—Robert Utsey.
Research Advisor.—David Hauptmann.
Broadcast Communications Advisor.—Valerie Chicola.
Creative Director.—Anang Mittal.
Staff Assistant.—Emily Hauck.

OFFICE OF THE MAJORITY WHIP

S–208 The Capitol, phone 224–2708, fax 228–1507

Majority Whip.—John Thune.
Chief of Staff.—Nick Rossi.
Policy Director and Counsel.—Geoffrey Antell.
Policy Advisor for Budget and Appropriations.—Cynthia Herrle.
General Counsel.—Jason van Beek.
Whip Liaisons: David Cole, Scarlet Samp.
Director of Operations.—Daffnei Riedel.
Deputy Communications Director.—Dominique McKay.
Speechwriter.—Mary Katherine Ascik.
Digital Director.—Kristina Reese.
Floor Assistant.—Alex Charown.
Press Assistant.—Ellie Brecht.

DEMOCRATIC LEADER

S–221 The Capitol, phone 224–2158, fax 224–7362

Democratic Leader.—Charles E. Schumer.
Chief of Staff.—Mike Lynch.
Deputy Chief of Staff.—Erin Sager Vaughn.
Executive Assistant.—Raisa Shah.
Director of Scheduling.—Michelle Mittler.
Scheduling Assistant.—Emily Sweda.
Policy Director.—Gerry Petrella.
Legislative Director.—Meghan Taira.
Communications Director.—Justin Goodman.
Director of Engagement.—Cietta Kiandoli.
Chief Speechwriter.—Josh Molofsky.
General Counsel.—Mark Patterson.
Director of Operations.—Amy Mannering.

Director of Information Technology.—Scott Rodman.
Capitol Staff Assistant.—Grace Magaletta.
Capitol Staff Assistant/Room Coordinator.—Jordon Marshall.

DEMOCRATIC WHIP

S–321 The Capitol, phone 224–9447

Democratic Whip.—Richard J. Durbin.
Chief of Staff.—Pat Souders.
Deputy Chief of Staff.—Sally Brown-Shaklee.
Director of Scheduling.—Claire Reuschel.
Communications Director.—Emily Hampsten.
Deputy Communications Director.—Joe LaPaille.
Floor Director.—Reema Dodin.
Floor Assistant.—Maalik Simmons.
Staff Assistants: Riley Foti, Mady Reno.

ASSISTANT DEMOCRATIC LEADER

SR–154, phone 224–2621

Assistant Democratic Leader.—Patty Murray.
Chief of Staff.—Mindi Lindquist.
Leadership Staff Director.—Stacy Rich.
Communications Director.—Helen Hare.
Senior Leadership Advisor.—Jacqueline Usyk.

OFFICE OF THE SECRETARY

S–312 The Capitol, phone 224–3622

JULIE E. ADAMS, Secretary of the Senate; elected and sworn in as the 33rd Secretary of the Senate on January 6, 2015; native of Iowa; bachelor's degree in political science from Luther College, Decorah, IA; master's degree in education from the University of Iowa; Director of Administration, Majority Leader Mitch McConnell; spokesperson, First Lady Laura Bush; Deputy Communications Director, then-Senate Majority Whip Mitch McConnell.

Secretary of the Senate.—Julie E. Adams (S–312), 224–3622.
Assistant Secretary of the Senate.—Mary Suit Jones (S–333), 224–3622.
Chief of Staff.—Rachel Creviston (S–414C), 224–3895.
Deputy Chief of Staff.—Sydney G. Butler (S–333), 224–9461.
General Counsel.—Dan Schwager (S–414D), 224–0634.
Executive Accounts Administrator.—Zoraida Torres (S–414B), 224–7099.
Executive Assistant.—Vanessa VandeHey (S–312), 224–9278.
Capitol Offices Liaison.—Robert Braggs III (SB–36C), 224–1483.

ADMINISTRATIVE SERVICES

Chief Counsel for Employment.—Claudia A. Kostel (SH–103), 224–5424.
Conservation and Preservation.—Beverly Adams (S–416), 224–4550.
Curator.—Melinda K. Smith (S–411), 224–2955.
Gift Shop.—Neil Schwartz (SD–G42), 224–7308.
Historian.—Betty K. Koed (SH–201), 224–6900.
Human Resources.—John McIlveen (SH–231B), 224–3625.
Information Systems.—Dan Kulnis (S–422), 224–4883.
Interparliamentary Services.—Sally Walsh (SH–808), 224–3047.
Joint Office of Training and Development.—Megan Daly (SD–180), 224–7628.
Legislative Info Systems (LIS) Project.—John Pollock (SD–B44A), 224–9419.
Library.—Leona Faust (SR–B15), 224–7106.
Page School.—Josh Dorsey (Webster Hall), 224–3927.
Printing and Document Services.—Laura Rush (SH–B04), 224–0205.
Public Records.—Dana McCallum (SH–232), 224–0322.

Senate Security.—Michael P. DiSilvestro (SVC–217), 224–5632.
Stationery Room.—Terri Keller (SD–B42), 224–4771.
Web Technology.—Arin Shapiro (PSQ 6960), 224–2020.

FINANCIAL SERVICES

Disbursing Office.—Ted Ruckner (SH–127), 224–3205.

LEGISLATIVE SERVICES

Bill Clerk.—Sara Schwartzman (S–123), 224–2120.
Captioning Services.—Sandra Schumm (SVC–111), 224–4321.
Daily Digest, Editor.—Elizabeth Tratos (S–421), 224–2658.
Enrolling Clerk.—Cassandra Byrd (S–139), 224–7108.
Executive Clerk.—Jennifer Gorham (S–138), 224–4341.
Journal Clerk.—William Walsh (S–135), 224–4650.
Legislative Clerk.—John J. Merlino (S–134), 224–4350.
Official Reporters of Debates.—Dorothy Rull (S–410A), 224–3152.
Parliamentarian.—Elizabeth C. MacDonough (S–133), 224–6128.

OFFICE OF THE CHAPLAIN

S–332 The Capitol, phone 224–2510, fax 224–9686

BARRY C. BLACK, Chaplain, U.S. Senate; born in Baltimore, MD, on November 1, 1948; education: bachelor of arts, theology, Oakwood College, 1970; master of divinity, Andrews Theological Seminary, 1973; master of arts, counseling, North Carolina Central University, 1978; doctor of ministry, theology, Eastern Baptist Seminary, 1982; master of arts, management, Salve Regina University, 1989; doctor of philosophy, psychology, United States International University, 1996; military service: U.S. Navy, 1976–2003; rising to the rank of Rear Admiral; Chief of Navy Chaplains, 2000–03; awards: Navy Distinguished Service Medal; Legion of Merit Medal; Defense Meritorious Service Medal; Meritorious Service Medals (two awards); Navy and Marine Corps Commendation Medals (two awards); 1995 NAACP Renowned Service Award; family: married to Brenda; three children: Barry II, Brendan, and Bradford.

Chaplain of the Senate.—Barry C. Black.
Chief of Staff.—Lisa Schultz, 224–3849.
Communications Director.—Jody Bogoslavski, 224–2048.
Staff Scheduler/Executive Assistant.—Suzanne Chapuis, 224–7456.

OFFICE OF THE SERGEANT AT ARMS

S–151 The Capitol, phone 224–2341, fax 224–7690

MICHAEL C. STENGER was nominated as the 41st Sergeant at Arms under Senate Resolution 465, on April 16, 2018. Michael C. Stenger has served as the Chief of Staff for the U.S. Senate Sergeant as Arms since January 2015. He began working for the Senate Sergeant at Arms in 2011, serving as Assistant Sergeant at Arms for the Office of Protective Services and Continuity until his appointment as Deputy Sergeant at Arms in May 2014.

As Assistant Sergeant at Arms, Mr. Stenger was charged with overseeing security and continuity of operations policies and programs, and providing strategic and analytical assistance. Mr. Stenger is a 35-year veteran of the United States Secret Service (USSS), appointed in 2008 as Assistant Director for the USSS Office of Government and Public Affairs, where he administered USSS liaison activities with the United States Congress, Department of Homeland Security, other federal agencies, and members of the media and general public.

During his career with the USSS, he served in Newark, New York City, and Washington, D.C., in protective, investigative, and staff assignments. Mr. Stenger served as the senior official overseeing the agency's investigations as Assistant Director for the Office of Investigations. In this capacity, he developed and implemented investigative policies for cyber- and fraud-related crimes. He also served as Assistant Director of the Office of Protective Research, Special Agent in Charge of the Washington Field Office, Deputy Assistant Director of the Office of Investigations, and Special Agent in Charge of the Financial Crimes Division.

Mr. Stenger was selected in 2004 as a Presidential Meritorious Rank Award recipient. He has also received the Vice President's Award for Excellence in Financial Crimes Management and the Department of the Treasury Secretary's Annual Award for Outstanding Performance in the Area of Financial Crimes.

Mr. Stenger received his Bachelor of Arts degree from Farleigh Dickinson University in New Jersey and attained the rank of Captain in the United States Marine Corps.

Sergeant at Arms.—Michael C. Stenger, S–151, 224–2341.
Deputy Sergeant at Arms.—Jennifer Hemingway, S–151, 224–2341.
Chief of Staff.—Dick Attridge, S–151, 224–2341.
Chief Learning Officer Training and Development.—Megan Daly, SD–180, 224–7588.
Employee Assistance Program Director.—Kristin Welsh-Simpson, SH–627B, 224–3902.
Executive Advisor.—Kelly Fado, S–151, 224–6031.
General Counsel.—Terence Liley, S–151, 224–2341.
Page Program Director.—Elizabeth Roach, Page School, 228–1291.
Protocol Officer.—Becky Schaaf, S–147, 224–2341.

HUMAN RESOURCES

Director.—Tammy Buckingham, SH–142, 4–8199.
Placement Office Manager.—Brian Bean, SH–142, 4–9167.
Human Resources Managers: Anne Lyles, SH–142, 4–4909; Nicole Wojahn, SH–142, 4–9442.
Safety Program.—Taurus Moore, SH–142, 4–5717.

CAPITOL OPERATIONS

Assistant Sergeant at Arms.—Krista Beal, SVC–103, 4–4281.
Capitol Operations Special Assistant.—Bryan Huus, 4–3372.
Senate Recording Studio Manager.—Bob Swanner, SVC–160, 4–5080.
Appointment Desk Director.—Mele Williams, 4–6302.
Director of Doorkeepers.—Garrett Burns, S–213, 4–6067.

MEDIA GALLERIES

Director of the Daily Press Gallery.—Laura Lytle, S–316, 4–0241.
Director of the Periodical Press Gallery.—Justin Wilson, S–320, 4–0265.
Director of the Press Photographers Gallery.—Jeff Kent, S–317, 4–6548.
Director of the Radio and Television Gallery.—Michael Mastrian, S–325, 4–6421.

CHIEF INFORMATION OFFICER

Assistant Sergeant at Arms and Chief Information Officer.—Chris Jordan, PSB 6245, 4–1391.
Chief Technology Officer.—Ed Jankus, PSB 6250, 4–7780.
Deputy Sergeant at Arms and Chief Information Officer.—Lynden Armstrong, PSB 6614,4–7078.

COMMUNICATION AND TECHNOLOGY INTEGRATION

Director of Communication and Technology Integration.—Kenny Meadows, SH–121, 8–5650.

CYBERSECURITY

Director of Cybersecurity.—Linus Barloon, PSB 6215, 4–6454.
Information Assurance Manager.—Tim Craig, PSB 6405, 8–0472.
Cyber Operations Manager.—Bennie Martin, Site A, 8–0297.

IT SUPPORT SERVICES

Director of IT Support Services.—Robert Harris, PSB 6735, 8–3499.
Technology and Help Desk Services Manager.—Tim Dean, PSB 6280, 4–3564.
Equipment and Capitol Exchange Services Manager.—Win Grayson, SR–B59, 4–8065.
Secure and Mobile Communications Manager.—Lynette Anderson, PSB 6985, 4–1609.

Telecom Assistance Center Supervisor.—Katie Miller, SH–121, 8–6365.
Capitol Telephone Exchange Manager.—Mary Ann Williams, PSB 6115, 4–3431.

PROCESS MANAGEMENT AND INNOVATION

Director of Process Management and Innovation.—John Pino (acting), PSB 6620, 4–6685.
Identity Management Manager.—Dianne LaVanway, PSB 6950, 4–8654.
IT Research and Deployment Manager.—Andy Guyer (acting), PSB 6945, 4–8371.
Systems Design, Development and Implementation Manager.—Joe Eckert, PSB 6240, 4–2982.

TECHNOLOGY DEVELOPMENT

Director of Technology Development.—Bryan Steward (acting), PSB 6611, 4–9703.
Network Engineering and Management Manager.—Bill Hill, PSB 6610, 4–9380.
Enterprise IT Operations Manager.—Joe LaPalme, PSB 6375, 8–4451.
Systems Development Manager.—Laura Robertson, PSB 6612, 4–1831.
Enterprise Infrastructure Services Manager.—Chad Torres (acting), PSB 6391, 4–4154.
LAN Administration Supervisor.—Tony Skarlatos, PSB 6370, 4–6338.

FINANCIAL MANAGEMENT

Chief Financial Officer.—Robin Gallant, PSB 6607, 4–6292.
Accounts Payable Manager.—David Salem, PSB 6604, 4–8844.
Controller.—Mary Ann Sifford, PSB 6605, 4–1035.
Budget Manager.—Jingquing ''Christie'' Wu, PSB 6360, 4–4886.
Procurement Manager.—David Baker, PSB 6603, 4–2547.
Internal Control Manager.—Sheetal Jenkins, PSB 6606, 4–6374.

OFFICE OF SECURITY AND EMERGENCY PREPAREDNESS

Assistant Sergeant at Arms.—Brian McGinty, SVC–305, 8–9788.
Deputy Assistant Sergeant at Arms.—Stephen Klopp, SVC–305, 8–3618.
Director for Security Planning and Police Operations.—Ronda Stewart, SVC–305, 4–7173.
Director for Emergency Preparedness.—David Kayea, PSB 6015, 8–0637.
Director for Intelligence and Protective Services.—Gordon ''Scott'' Lipscomb, SVC–305, 4–0288.

CENTRAL OPERATIONS

Director.—Mike Brown, SD–150, 4–4035.
ID Office Manager.—Luke Hendrixson, SD–G58, 4–8938.
Parking Office Manager.—Robert Brindle, SD–G84, 4–7054.

OPERATIONS

Assistant Sergeant at Arms.—Michael L. Chandler, SD–G61, 8–0635.
Deputy Assistant Sergeant at Arms.—Doug White, SD–G61, 8–4877.

CAPITOL FACILITIES

Director of Capitol Facilities.—Grace Ridgeway, SC–5, 4–5524.
Facilities Systems Manager.—Vacant, SC–5, 4–4656.
Events Coordinator.—Delice Tavernier, SC–5, 4–2563.
Furnishings and Design Coordinator.—Monique Beckford, SC–5, 4–1457.

CONTINGENCY PROGRAMS

Director.—Bill Flinter, SVC–305, 8–4346.
Plans Division Chief.—Jillian Lerda, SVC–305, 4–6894.

PRINTING, GRAPHICS, AND DIRECT MAIL

Director.—Brian Trott, SD–G82, 4–9443.

Capitol Hill Operations Manager.—George Thompson, SD–G82, 4–6664.
Landover Operations Manager.—Mike Peterson, Printing and Mailing Facility, 4–9568.
Senate Support Facility Supervisor.—Mike Wilson, Senate Support Facility, 4–1970.

SENATE POST OFFICE

Postmaster.—Donnie Cook, SD–B23, 4–3731.
Retail Services Superintendent.—Lisa Cain, SD–B17, 4–5330.
Mail Processing Facility Superintendent.—Lee Reynolds, SD–B28, 4–9096.
Senate Screening Facility Superintendent.—LaToya Freeman, Senate Mail Facility, 4–0078.

STATE OFFICE OPERATIONS

State Office Liaison Director.—Kate Summers, PSB 6225, 4–9576.
Project Management.—Lauren Suranno, PSB 6295, 4–7723.
State Office Readiness Manager.—Mark Peterson, PSB 6310–B2, 4–3725.

SUPPORT SERVICES

Director.—Sam Jacobs, PSB 6455, 4–9927.
Facilities Manager.—Amy York, PSB 6235, 4–1507.
Fleet and Transportation Manager.—Shawn Fretz, SR–G06, 8–0346.
Hair Care Manager.—Cindi Brown, SR–B70, 4–4560.
Office of Communications Manager.—Terrica Gibson, PSB 6010 / C2, 4–8091.
Photo Studio Manager.—Jeff McEvoy, SD–G85 4–8570.
Photo Services Supervisor.—David Rogowski, SD–G85, 4–6000.
Lab Manager.—Lynn Dunigan, PSB 6820, 4–6634.

OFFICE OF THE SECRETARY FOR THE MAJORITY

S–337 The Capitol, phone 224–3835, fax 224–2860

Secretary for the Majority.—Robert M. Duncan (S–337).
Assistant Secretary for the Majority.—Chris Tuck (S–335).
Administrative Assistant.—Noelle Busk Ringel (S–337).
Senior Floor Assistant.—Megan Mercer (S–335), 224–6191.
Floor Assistant.—Tony Hanagan (S–335), 224–6191.

S–226 Majority Cloakroom, phone 224–6191

Senior Cloakroom Assistant.—Katherine Foster.
Cloakroom Assistants: Abigail Baker, Brian Canfield.

OFFICE OF THE SECRETARY FOR THE MINORITY

S–309 The Capitol, phone 224–3735

Secretary for the Minority.—Gary Myrick.
Assistant Secretary for the Minority.—Tricia Engle (S–118), 224–5551.
Administrative Assistant to the Secretary.—Amber Huus.

S–118 The Capitol, phone 224–5551

Senior Floor Staff.—Dan Tinsley.
Floor Staff.—Brad Watt.
Executive Assistant to the Floor Staff.—Terri Taylor.

S–225 Minority Cloakroom, phone 224–4691

Cloakroom Assistants: Rachel Jackson, Nathan Oursler, Stephanie Paone, Liza Patterson.

OFFICE OF THE LEGISLATIVE COUNSEL

668 Dirksen Senate Office Building, phone 224–6461, fax 224–0567

Legislative Counsel.—William R. Baird.

Deputy Legislative Counsel.—Elizabeth Aldridge King.

Senior Counsel: Charles E. Armstrong, Ruth Ann Ernst, John A. Goetcheus, Heather L. Burnham.

Assistant Counsel: Kimberly D. Albrecht-Taylor, John W. Baggaley, Margaret A. Bomba, Kathryne G. Bonander, Maureen C. Contreni, Kevin M. Davis, Deanna E. Edwards, Evan H. Frank, Vincent J. Gaiani, Amy E. Gaynor, John A. Henderson, Thomas B. Heywood, Christina J. Kennelly, Heather A. Lowell, Philip B. Lynch, Matthew D. McGhie, Mark M. McGunagle, Christine E. Miranda, James L. Ollen-Smith, Allison M. Otto, Kristin K. Romero, Margaret A. Rose, Patrick N. Ryan, Robert F. Silver, Kimberly A. Tamber, Kelly M. Thornburg.

Staff Attorneys: Katherine-Marie P. Canales, Molly K. Dunlop, Larissa Eltsefon, Carol L. Lewis, Mark L. Mazzone, Christopher S. Patterson.

Systems Integrator.—Thomas E. Cole.

Office Manager.—Donna L. Pasqualino.

Senior Staff Assistants: Kimberly R. Bourne-Goldring, Rebekah J. Musgrove, Daniela A. Navia, Diane E. Nesmeyer, Patricia H. Olsavsky.

OFFICE OF SENATE LEGAL COUNSEL

642 Hart Senate Office Building, phone 224–4435, fax 224–3391

Senate Legal Counsel.—Patricia Mack Bryan.

Deputy Senate Legal Counsel.—Morgan J. Frankel.

Assistant Senate Legal Counsel: Thomas E. Caballero, Grant R. Vinik.

Systems Administrator/Legal Assistant.—Jenny H. Smith.

Administrative Assistant.—Kathleen M. Parker.

STANDING COMMITTEES OF THE HOUSE

[Democrats in roman; Republicans in *italic*; Resident Commissioner and Delegates in **boldface**]

[Room numbers beginning with H are in the Capitol, with CHOB in the Cannon House Office Building, with LHOB in the Longworth House Office Building, with RHOB in the Rayburn House Office Building, with H1 in O'Neill House Office Building, and with H2 in the Ford House Office Building]

Agriculture

1301 Longworth House Office Building, phone 225–2171

https://agriculture.house.gov

Collin C. Peterson, of Minnesota, *Chair*

Alma S. Adams, of North Carolina, *Vice Chair*

David Scott, of Georgia.
Jim Costa, of California.
Marcia L. Fudge, of Ohio.
James P. McGovern, of Massachusetts.
Filemon Vela, of Texas.
Stacey E. Plaskett, of Virgin Islands.
Abigail Davis Spanberger, of Virginia.
Jahana Hayes, of Connecticut.
Antonio Delgado, of New York.
TJ Cox, of California.
Angie Craig, of Minnesota.
Anthony Brindisi, of New York.
Josh Harder, of California.
Kim Schrier, of Washington.
Chellie Pingree, of Maine.
Cheri Bustos, of Illinois.
Sean Patrick Maloney, of New York.
Salud O. Carbajal, of California.
Al Lawson, Jr., of Florida.
Tom O'Halleran, of Arizona.
Jimmy Panetta, of California.
Ann Kirkpatrick, of Arizona.
Cynthia Axne, of Iowa.
Xochitl Torres Small, of New Mexico.

K. Michael Conaway, of Texas.
Glenn Thompson, of Pennsylvania.
Austin Scott, of Georgia.
Eric A. ''Rick'' Crawford, of Arkansas.
Scott DesJarlais, of Tennessee.
Vicky Hartzler, of Missouri.
Doug LaMalfa, of California.
Rodney Davis, of Illinois.
Ted S. Yoho, of Florida.
Rick W. Allen, of Georgia.
Mike Bost, of Illinois.
David Rouzer, of North Carolina.
Ralph Lee Abraham, of Louisiana.
Trent Kelly, of Mississippi.
Roger W. Marshall, of Kansas.
Don Bacon, of Nebraska.
Neal P. Dunn, of Florida.
Dusty Johnson, of South Dakota.
James R. Baird, of Indiana.
Jim Hagedorn, of Minnesota.
Chris Jacobs, of New York.
Troy Balderson, of Ohio.

SUBCOMMITTEES

[The chair and ranking minority member are ex officio (voting) members of all subcommittees on which they do not serve.]

Biotechnology, Horticulture, and Research

Stacey E. Plaskett, of Virgin Islands, *Chair*

Antonio Delgado, of New York.
TJ Cox, of California.
Josh Harder, of California.
Anthony Brindisi, of New York.
Kim Schrier, of Washington.
Chellie Pingree, of Maine.
Salud O. Carbajal, of California.
Jimmy Panetta, of California.
Sean Patrick Maloney, of New York.
Al Lawson, Jr., of Florida.
Xochitl Torres Small, of New Mexico.

Neal P. Dunn, of Florida.
Glenn Thompson, of Pennsylvania.
Vicky Hartzler, of Missouri.
Doug LaMalfa, of California.
Rodney Davis, of Illinois.
Ted S. Yoho, of Florida.
Mike Bost, of Illinois.
James R. Baird, of Indiana.
Chris Jacobs, of New York.

Commodity Exchanges, Energy, and Credit

David Scott, of Georgia, *Chair*

Filemon Vela, of Texas.
Stacey E. Plaskett, of Virgin Islands.
Abigail Davis Spanberger, of Virginia.
Antonio Delgado, of New York.
Angie Craig, of Minnesota.
Sean Patrick Maloney, of New York.
Ann Kirkpatrick, of Arizona.
Cynthia Axne, of Iowa.
Vacant.

Austin Scott, of Georgia.
Eric A. "Rick" Crawford, of Arkansas.
Mike Bost, of Illinois.
David Rouzer, of North Carolina.
Roger W. Marshall, of Kansas.
Neal P. Dunn, of Florida.
Dusty Johnson, of South Dakota.
James R. Baird, of Indiana.

Conservation and Forestry

Abigail Davis Spanberger, of Virginia, *Chair*

Marcia L. Fudge, of Ohio.
Tom O'Halleran, of Arizona.
Chellie Pingree, of Maine.
Cynthia Axne, of Iowa.

Doug LaMalfa, of California.
Rick W. Allen, of Georgia.
Ralph Lee Abraham, of Louisiana.
Trent Kelly, of Mississippi.

General Farm Commodities and Risk Management

Filemon Vela, of Texas, *Chair*

Angie Craig, of Minnesota.
David Scott, of Georgia.
Al Lawson, Jr., of Florida.
Salud O. Carbajal, of California.
Xochitl Torres Small, of New Mexico.

Glenn Thompson, of Pennsylvania.
Austin Scott, of Georgia.
Eric A. "Rick" Crawford, of Arkansas.
Rick W. Allen, of Georgia.
Ralph Lee Abraham, of Louisiana.

Livestock and Foreign Agriculture

Jim Costa, of California, *Chair*

Anthony Brindisi, of New York.
Jahana Hayes, of Connecticut.
TJ Cox, of California.
Angie Craig, of Minnesota.
Josh Harder, of California.
Filemon Vela, of Texas.
Stacey E. Plaskett, of Virgin Islands.
Salud O. Carbajal, of California.
Cheri Bustos, of Illinois.
Jimmy Panetta, of California.

David Rouzer, of North Carolina,
Glenn Thompson, of Pennsylvania.
Scott DesJarlais, of Tennessee.
Vicky Hartzler, of Missouri.
Trent Kelly, of Mississippi.
Roger W. Marshall, of Kansas.
Don Bacon, of Nebraska.
Jim Hagedorn, of Minnesota.
Vacant.

Nutrition, Oversight, and Department Operations

Marcia L. Fudge, of Ohio, *Chair*

James P. McGovern, of Massachusetts.
Alma S. Adams, of North Carolina.
Jahana Hayes, of Connecticut.
Kim Schrier, of Washington.
Al Lawson, Jr., of Florida.
Jimmy Panetta, of California.
Vacant.

Dusty Johnson, of South Dakota.
Scott DesJarlais, of Tennessee.
Rodney Davis, of Illinois.
Ted S. Yoho, of Florida.
Don Bacon, of Nebraska.
Jim Hagedorn, of Minnesota.
Chris Jacobs, of New York.

STAFF

Committee on Agriculture (1301 LHOB), 225–2171.
Majority Staff.
Staff Director.—Anne Simmons.
Deputy Staff Director.—Troy Phillips.
Chief Counsel.—Kellie Adesina.
Senior Counsel.—Matthew MacKenzie, Prescott Martin III, Isabel Rosa.
Senior Professional Staff: Keith Jones, Lisa Shelton.
Professional Staff.—Carlton Bridgeforth.
Communications Director.—Patrick Delaney.
Digital Outreach Specialist.—Ross Hettervig.
Economist.—Katie Zenk.
Legislative Policy Director.—Melinda Cep.
Member Relations Coordinator.—Lyron Blum-Evitts.
Press Secretary.—Tommy Mattocks.
Outreach Coordinator.—Mickeala Carter.
Legislative Assistants: Emily German, Alison Titus.
Staff Assistant.—Grayson Haynes.
Committee Administrator.—Faye Thomas.
Legislative Fellow.—Malikha Daniels.
Deputy Clerk.—Jennifer Yezak.
Staff Directors:
Biotechnology, Horticulture, and Research Subcommittee.—Brandon Honeycutt.
Commodity Exchanges, Energy, and Credit Subcommittee.—Ashley Smith.
Conservation and Forestry Subcommittee.—Félix Muñiz, Jr.
General Farm Commodities and Risk Management Subcommittee.—Mike Stranz.
Livestock and Foreign Agriculture Subcommittee.—Katie Zenk.
Nutrition, Oversight, and Department Operations Subcommittee.—Jasmine Dickerson.
Non-Partisan Staff:
Chief Clerk.—Dana Sandman.
Financial Administrator.—Margaret Wetherald.
Information Technology and Policy Director.—John Konya.
Systems Administrator.—Faisal Siddiqui.
Minority Staff (1010 LHOB), 225–0317.
Staff Director.—Matt Schertz.
Deputy Staff Director and Chief Economist.—Bart Fischer.
Chief Counsel.—Patricia Straughn.
Senior Professional Staff: Paul Balzano, Josh Maxwell, Jennifer Tiller.
Professional Staff: Trevor White, Jeremy Witte.
Deputy Chief Economist.—Callie McAdams.
Communications Director.—Rachel Millard.
Legislative Assistant and Member Services Coordinator.—Ricki Schroeder.

Appropriations

H–305 The Capitol, phone 225–2771

https://appropriations.house.gov

Nita M. Lowey, of New York, *Chair*

Pete Aguilar, of California, *Vice Chair*

Marcy Kaptur, of Ohio.
Peter J. Visclosky, of Indiana.
José E. Serrano, of New York.
Rosa L. DeLauro, of Connecticut.
David E. Price, of North Carolina.
Lucille Roybal-Allard, of California.
Sanford D. Bishop, Jr., of Georgia.
Barbara Lee, of California.
Betty McCollum, of Minnesota.
Tim Ryan, of Ohio.
C. A. Dutch Ruppersberger, of Maryland.
Debbie Wasserman Schultz, of Florida.
Henry Cuellar, of Texas.
Chellie Pingree, of Maine.
Mike Quigley, of Illinois.
Derek Kilmer, of Washington.
Matt Cartwright, of Pennsylvania.
Grace Meng, of New York.
Mark Pocan, of Wisconsin.
Katherine M. Clark, of Massachusetts.
Lois Frankel, of Florida.
Cheri Bustos, of Illinois.
Bonnie Watson Coleman, of New Jersey.
Brenda L. Lawrence, of Michigan.
Norma J. Torres, of California.
Charlie Crist, of Florida.
Ann Kirkpatrick, of Arizona.
Ed Case, of Hawaii.

Kay Granger, of Texas.
Harold Rogers, of Kentucky.
Robert B. Aderholt, of Alabama.
Michael K. Simpson, of Idaho.
John R. Carter, of Texas.
Ken Calvert, of California.
Tom Cole, of Oklahoma.
Mario Diaz-Balart, of Florida.
Tom Graves, of Georgia.
Steve Womack, of Arkansas.
Jeff Fortenberry, of Nebraska.
Charles J. ''Chuck'' Fleischmann, of Tennessee.
Jaime Herrera Beutler, of Washington.
David P. Joyce, of Ohio.
Andy Harris, of Maryland.
Martha Roby, of Alabama.
Mark E. Amodei, of Nevada.
Chris Stewart, of Utah.
Steven M. Palazzo, of Mississippi.
Dan Newhouse, of Washington.
John R. Moolenaar, of Michigan.
John H. Rutherford, of Florida.
Will Hurd, of Texas.

SUBCOMMITTEES

[The chair and ranking minority member are ex officio (voting) members of all subcommittees on which they do not serve.]

Agriculture, Rural Development, Food and Drug Administration, and Related Agencies

Sanford D. Bishop, Jr., of Georgia, *Chair*

Rosa L. DeLauro, of Connecticut, *Vice Chair*

Chellie Pingree, of Maine.
Mark Pocan, of Wisconsin.
Barbara Lee, of California.
Betty McCollum, of Minnesota.
Henry Cuellar, of Texas.

Jeff Fortenberry, of Nebraska.
Robert B. Aderholt, of Alabama.
Andy Harris, of Maryland.
John R. Moolenaar, of Michigan.

Commerce, Justice, Science, and Related Agencies

José E. Serrano, of New York, *Chair*

Matt Cartwright, of Pennsylvania, *Vice Chair*

Grace Meng, of New York.
Brenda L. Lawrence, of Michigan.
Charlie Crist, of Florida.
Ed Case, of Hawaii.
Marcy Kaptur, of Ohio.

Robert B. Aderholt, of Alabama.
Martha Roby, of Alabama.
Steven M. Palazzo, of Mississippi.
Tom Graves, of Georgia.

Defense

Peter J. Visclosky, of Indiana, *Chair*

Betty McCollum, of Minnesota, *Vice Chair*

Tim Ryan, of Ohio.
C. A. Dutch Ruppersberger, of Maryland.
Marcy Kaptur, of Ohio.
Henry Cuellar, of Texas.
Derek Kilmer, of Washington.
Pete Aguilar, of California.
Cheri Bustos, of Illinois.
Charlie Crist, of Florida.
Ann Kirkpatrick, of Arizona.

Ken Calvert, of California.
Harold Rogers, of Kentucky.
Tom Cole, of Oklahoma.
Steve Womack, of Arkansas.
Robert B. Aderholt, of Alabama.
John R. Carter, of Texas.
Mario Diaz-Balart, of Florida.

Energy and Water Development, and Related Agencies

Marcy Kaptur, of Ohio, *Chair*

Peter J. Visclosky, of Indiana, *Vice Chair*

Debbie Wasserman Schultz, of Florida.
Ann Kirkpatrick, of Arizona.
Derek Kilmer, of Washington.
Mark Pocan, of Wisconsin.
Lois Frankel, of Florida.

Michael K. Simpson, of Idaho.
Ken Calvert, of California.
Charles J. ''Chuck'' Fleischmann, of Tennessee.
Dan Newhouse, of Washington.

Financial Services and General Government

Mike Quigley, of Illinois, *Chair*

José E. Serrano, of New York, *Vice Chair*

Matt Cartwright, of Pennsylvania.
Sanford D. Bishop, Jr., of Georgia.
Norma J. Torres, of California.
Charlie Crist, of Florida.
Ann Kirkpatrick, of Arizona.

Tom Graves, of Georgia.
Mark E. Amodei, of Nevada.
Chris Stewart, of Utah.
David P. Joyce, of Ohio.

Homeland Security

Lucille Roybal-Allard, of California, *Chair*

Henry Cuellar, of Texas, *Vice Chair*

C. A. Dutch Ruppersberger, of Maryland.
David E. Price, of North Carolina.
Debbie Wasserman Schultz, of Florida.
Grace Meng, of New York.
Pete Aguilar, of California.

Charles J. ''Chuck'' Fleischmann, of Tennessee.
Steven M. Palazzo, of Mississippi.
Dan Newhouse, of Washington.
John H. Rutherford, of Florida.

Interior, Environment, and Related Agencies

Betty McCollum, of Minnesota, *Chair*

Chellie Pingree, of Maine, *Vice Chair*

Derek Kilmer, of Washington.
José E. Serrano, of New York.
Mike Quigley, of Illinois.
Bonnie Watson Coleman, of New Jersey.
Brenda L. Lawrence, of Michigan.

David P. Joyce, of Ohio.
Michael K. Simpson, of Idaho.
Chris Stewart, of Utah.
Mark E. Amodei, of Nevada.

Labor, Health and Human Services, Education, and Related Agencies

Rosa L. DeLauro, of Connecticut, *Chair*

Lucille Roybal-Allard, of California, *Vice Chair*

Barbara Lee, of California.
Mark Pocan, of Wisconsin.
Katherine M. Clark, of Massachusetts.
Lois Frankel, of Florida.
Cheri Bustos, of Illinois.
Bonnie Watson Coleman, of New Jersey.
Tom Cole, of Oklahoma.
Andy Harris, of Maryland.
Jaime Herrera Beutler, of Washington.
John R. Moolenaar, of Michigan.
Tom Graves, of Georgia.

Legislative Branch

Tim Ryan, of Ohio, *Chair*

C. A. Dutch Ruppersberger, of Maryland, *Vice Chair*

Katherine M. Clark, of Massachusetts.
Ed Case, of Hawaii.
Jaime Herrera Beutler, of Washington.
Dan Newhouse, of Washington.

Military Construction, Veterans Affairs, and Related Agencies

Debbie Wasserman Schultz, of Florida, *Chair*

Sanford D. Bishop, Jr., of Georgia, *Vice Chair*

Ed Case, of Hawaii.
Tim Ryan, of Ohio.
Chellie Pingree, of Maine.
Matt Cartwright, of Pennsylvania.
Cheri Bustos, of Illinois.
John R. Carter, of Texas.
Martha Roby, of Alabama.
John H. Rutherford, of Florida.
Will Hurd, of Texas.

State, Foreign Operations, and Related Programs

Nita M. Lowey, of New York, *Chair*

Barbara Lee, of California, *Vice Chair*

Grace Meng, of New York.
David E. Price, of North Carolina.
Lois Frankel, of Florida.
Norma J. Torres, of California.
Harold Rogers, of Kentucky.
Jeff Fortenberry, of Nebraska.
Martha Roby, of Alabama.

Transportation, and Housing and Urban Development, and Related Agencies

David E. Price, of North Carolina, *Chair*

Mike Quigley, of Illinois, *Vice Chair*

Katherine M. Clark, of Massachusetts.
Bonnie Watson Coleman, of New Jersey.
Brenda L. Lawrence, of Michigan.
Norma J. Torres, of California.
Pete Aguilar, of California.
Mario Diaz-Balart, of Florida.
Steve Womack, of Arkansas.
John H. Rutherford, of Florida.
Will Hurd, of Texas.

STAFF

Committee on Appropriations (H–307), 225–2771.
Majority Staff Director.—Shalanda Young.
Deputy Staff Director.—Christopher Bigelow.
Chief Counsel.—Adam Berg.
Communications Director.—Evan Hollander.
Deputy Communications Director.—Michael Burns.
Digital Director.—Ian Mariani.
Administrative Assistant.—Anna Hansen.
Administrative Aide.—Catherine Edwards.
Editor.—Jim Cahill 5–2851.
Financial Administrator.—Amber Allen.

Systems Administrators: Eric Jackson, Lonnie Johnson (2005 RHOB), 5–2718.
Director of Information Technology.—Cathy Little.
Director of Operations.—Tom Tucker.
Professional Staff Members: Jason Gray, Adam Wilson.
Scorekeepers: Matthew Anderson, Lori Hamlin Bias.
Minority Staff Director.—Anne Marie Chotvacs (1016 LHOB), 5–3481.
Deputy Staff Director.—Johnnie Kaberle.
Communications Director.—Sarah Flaim.
Deputy Communications Director.—Alexander Attebery.
National Security Advisor.—Brian Potts.
Administrative Assistants: Graydon Daubert, Sofia Herring, John Muscolini.
Member Services Directors: Alyssa Hinman, Michelle Reinshuttle.
Parliamentarian and Policy Director.—Alec Davis.

Surveys and Investigation Staff (H307), 5–3881.
Director of Investigations.—Kevin Linskey.
Professional Staff Members: Pam Curtin, Dana Ervin, Melissa Garcia, Natasha Garcia, Diana Glod, Monica Goldie, Amy Hall, Wandafa Hollingsworth, Tim Ireland, Meagen LaGraffe, Daniel McGarry, John Needham, Andrea Rambow, Brian Shortly, Renee Simpson, Jennifer Smith.
Administrative Assistants: Tracey Russell, Connor Smith.

Subcommittee on Agriculture, Rural Development, Food and Drug Administration, and Related Agencies (2362–A RHOB), 5–2638.
Majority Clerk.—Martha Foley.
Professional Staff Members: Diem-Linh Jones, Joseph Layman, Justin Masucci, Perry Yates.
Administrative Assistant.—Randall Staples.
Minority Professional Staff Member: Tom O'Brien (1001 LHOB), 5–3481.

Subcommittee on Commerce, Justice, Science, and Related Agencies (H–310), 5–3351.
Majority Clerk.—Robert Bonner.
Professional Staff Members: Jeff Ashford, TJ Lowdermilk, Shannon McCully, Matthew Smith, BG Wright.
Administrative Assistant.—Trisha Castaneda.
Minority Professional Staff Members: Stephanie Gadbois, Kristin Richmond (1001 LHOB), 5–3481.

Subcommittee on Defense (H–405), 5–2847.
Majority Clerk.—Rebecca Leggieri.
Professional Staff Members: William Adkins, David Bortnick, Matthew Bower, Brooke Boyer, Jennifer Chartrand, Walter Hearne, Paul Kilbride, Hayden Milberg, Shannon Richter, Jackie Ripke, Ariana Sarar.
Administrative Aide.—Sherry Young.
Minority Professional Staff Members: Leslie Albright, Kiyalan Batmanglidj, Jamie McCormick (1040A LHOB), 5–3481.

Subcommittee on Energy and Water Development, and Related Agencies (2362–B RHOB), 5–3421.
Majority Clerk.—Jaime Shimek.
Majority Professional Staff Members: Mark Arnone, Michael Brain, Scott McKee, Farouk Ophaso.
Administrative Assistant.—Marcel Caldwell.
Minority Professional Staff Members: Angie Giancarlo (1001 LHOB), 5–3481.

Subcommittee on Financial Services and General Government (2000 RHOB), 5–7245.
Majority Clerk.—Lisa Molyneux.
Professional Staff Members: Laura Cylke, Elliot Doomes, Aalok Mehta, Marybeth Nassif.
Administrative Assistant.—Parker Van de Water.
Minority Professional Staff Member.—John Martens (1016 LHOB), 5–3481.

Subcommittee on Homeland Security (2006 RHOB), 5–5834.
Majority Clerk.—Darek Newby.
Professional Staff Members: Michael Herman, Robert Joachim, Kris Mallard, Karyn Richman.
Administrative Aide.—Elizabeth Lapham.
Minority Professional Staff Member.—Dena Baron (1016 LHOB), 5–3481.

Subcommittee on Interior, Environment, and Related Agencies (2007 RHOB), 5–3081.
Majority Clerk.—Rita Culp.
Professional Staff Members: Janet Erickson, Jocelyn Hunn, Peter Kiefhaber, Kusai Merchant, Donna Shahbaz.
Administrative Assistant.—Tyler Coe.

Minority Professional Staff Members: Darren Benjamin (1001 LHOB), 5–3481.

Subcommittee on Labor, Health and Human Services, Education, and Related Agencies (2358-B RHOB), 5–3508.

Majority Clerks: Robin Juliano, Stephen Steigleder.

Professional Staff Members: Jared Bass, Jennifer Cama, Jaclyn Kilroy, Laurie Mignone, Philip Tizzani.

Administrative Aide.—Brad Allen.

Minority Professional Staff Members: Susan Ross, Kathryn Salmon (1016 LHOB), 5–3481.

Subcommittee on Legislative Branch (H306), 6–7252.

Majority Clerk.—Sue Quantius (acting).

Professional Staff Members: Faye Cobb, Sue Quantius.

Minority Professional Staff Member.—Jennifer Holmes (1001 LHOB), 5–3481.

Subcommittee on Military Construction, Veterans Affairs, and Related Agencies (HT–2), 5-3047.

Majority Clerk.—Matt Washington.

Professional Staff Members: Nicole Cohen, Jennifer Hollrah, Sarah Young.

Administrative Assistant.—Keihysha Cenord.

Minority Professional Staff Members: Kiyalan Batmanglidj, Betsy Bina.

Subcommittee on State, Foreign Operations, and Related Programs (HT–2), 5–2041.

Majority Clerk.—Steve Marchese.

Professional Staff Members: Craig Higgins, Erin Kolodjeski, Dean Koulouris, Jean Kwon, Marin Stein, Jason Wheelock.

Administrative Aide.—Clelia Alvarado.

Minority Professional Staff Members: Susan Adams, James McCormick, 5–3481.

Subcommittee on Transportation, and Housing and Urban Development, and Related Agencies (2358A RHOB), 5–2141.

Majority Clerk.—Joe Carlile.

Professional Staff Members: Winnie Chang, Josephine Eckert, Angela Ohm, Sarah Puro, Rebecca Salay.

Administrative Assistant.—Gladys Barcena.

Minority Professional Staff Member.—Douglas Disrud (1001 LHOB), 5–3481.

Armed Services

2216 Rayburn House Office Building, phone 225–4151, fax 225–9077

https://armedservices.house.gov

Adam Smith, of Washington, *Chair*

Anthony G. Brown, of Maryland, *Vice Chair*

Susan A. Davis, of California.
James R. Langevin, of Rhode Island.
Rick Larsen, of Washington.
Jim Cooper, of Tennessee.
Joe Courtney, of Connecticut.
John Garamendi, of California.
Jackie Speier, of California.
Tulsi Gabbard, of Hawaii.
Donald Norcross, of New Jersey.
Ruben Gallego, of Arizona.
Seth Moulton, of Massachusetts.
Salud O. Carbajal, of California.
Ro Khanna, of California.
William R. Keating, of Massachusetts.
Filemon Vela, of Texas.
Andy Kim, of New Jersey.
Kendra S. Horn, of Oklahoma.
Gilbert Ray Cisneros, Jr., of California.
Chrissy Houlahan, of Pennsylvania.
Jason Crow, of Colorado.
Xochitl Torres Small, of New Mexico.
Elissa Slotkin, of Michigan.
Mikie Sherrill, of New Jersey.
Veronica Escobar, of Texas.
Debra A. Haaland, of New Mexico.
Jared F. Golden, of Maine.
Lori Trahan, of Massachusetts.
Elaine G. Luria, of Virginia.
Anthony Brindisi, of New York.

Mac Thornberry, of Texas.
Joe Wilson, of South Carolina.
Rob Bishop, of Utah.
Michael R. Turner, of Ohio.
Mike Rogers, of Alabama.
K. Michael Conaway, of Texas.
Doug Lamborn, of Colorado.
Robert J. Wittman, of Virginia.
Vicky Hartzler, of Missouri.
Austin Scott, of Georgia.
Mo Brooks, of Alabama.
Paul Cook, of California.
Bradley Byrne, of Alabama.
Sam Graves, of Missouri.
Elise M. Stefanik, of New York.
Scott DesJarlais, of Tennessee.
Ralph Lee Abraham, of Louisiana.
Trent Kelly, of Mississippi.
Mike Gallagher, of Wisconsin.
Matt Gaetz, of Florida.
Don Bacon, of Nebraska.
Jim Banks, of Indiana.
Liz Cheney, of Wyoming.
Paul Mitchell, of Michigan.
Jack Bergman, of Michigan.
Michael Waltz, of Florida.

SUBCOMMITTEES

Intelligence and Emerging Threats and Capabilities

James R. Langevin, of Rhode Island, *Chair*

Jason Crow, of Colorado, *Vice Chair*

Rick Larsen, of Washington.
Jim Cooper, of Tennessee.
Tulsi Gabbard, of Hawaii.
Anthony G. Brown, of Maryland.
Ro Khanna, of California.
William R. Keating, of Massachusetts.
Andy Kim, of New Jersey.
Chrissy Houlahan, of Pennsylvania.
Elissa Slotkin, of Michigan.
Lori Trahan, of Massachusetts.

Elise M. Stefanik, of New York.
Sam Graves, of Missouri.
Ralph Lee Abraham, of Louisiana.
K. Michael Conaway, of Texas.
Austin Scott, of Georgia.
Scott DesJarlais, of Tennessee.
Mike Gallagher, of Wisconsin.
Michael Waltz, of Florida.
Don Bacon, of Nebraska.
Jim Banks, of Indiana.

Military Personnel

Jackie Speier, of California, *Chair*

Gilbert Ray Cisneros, Jr., of California, *Vice Chair*

Susan A. Davis, of California.
Ruben Gallego, of Arizona.
Veronica Escobar, of Texas.
Debra A. Haaland, of New Mexico.
Lori Trahan, of Massachusetts.
Elaine G. Luria, of Virginia.

Trent Kelly, of Mississippi.
Ralph Lee Abraham, of Louisiana.
Liz Cheney, of Wyoming.
Paul Mitchell, of Michigan.
Jack Bergman, of Michigan.
Matt Gaetz, of Florida.

Readiness

John Garamendi, of California, *Chair*

Andy Kim, of New Jersey, *Vice Chair*

Tulsi Gabbard, of Hawaii.
Kendra S. Horn, of Oklahoma.
Chrissy Houlahan, of Pennsylvania.
Jason Crow, of Colorado.
Xochitl Torres Small, of New Mexico.
Elissa Slotkin, of Michigan.
Veronica Escobar, of Texas.
Debra A. Haaland, of New Mexico.

Doug Lamborn, of Colorado.
Austin Scott, of Georgia.
Joe Wilson, of South Carolina.
Rob Bishop, of Utah.
Mike Rogers, of Alabama.
Mo Brooks, of Alabama.
Elise M. Stefanik, of New York.
Jack Bergman, of Michigan.

Seapower and Projection Forces

Joe Courtney, of Connecticut, *Chair*

Elaine G. Luria, of Virginia, *Vice Chair*

James R. Langevin, of Rhode Island.
Jim Cooper, of Tennessee.
Donald Norcross, of New Jersey.
Seth Moulton, of Massachusetts.
Filemon Vela, of Texas.
Gilbert Ray Cisneros, Jr., of California.
Mikie Sherrill, of New Jersey.
Jared F. Golden, of Maine.
Anthony Brindisi, of New York.

Robert J. Wittman, of Virginia.
K. Michael Conaway, of Texas.
Mike Gallagher, of Wisconsin.
Jack Bergman, of Michigan.
Michael Waltz, of Florida.
Vicky Hartzler, of Missouri.
Paul Cook, of California.
Bradley Byrne, of Alabama.
Trent Kelly, of Mississippi.

Strategic Forces

Jim Cooper, of Tennessee, *Chair*

Kendra S. Horn, of Oklahoma, *Vice Chair*

Susan A. Davis, of California.
Rick Larsen, of Washington.
John Garamendi, of California.
Jackie Speier, of California.
Seth Moulton, of Massachusetts.
Salud O. Carbajal, of California.
Ro Khanna, of California.
William R. Keating, of Massachusetts.

Michael R. Turner, of Ohio.
Joe Wilson, of South Carolina.
Rob Bishop, of Utah.
Mike Rogers, of Alabama.
Mo Brooks, of Alabama.
Bradley Byrne, of Alabama.
Scott DesJarlais, of Tennessee.
Liz Cheney, of Wyoming.

Tactical Air and Land Forces

Donald Norcross, of New Jersey, *Chair*

Xochitl Torres Small, of New Mexico, *Vice Chair*

James R. Langevin, of Rhode Island.
Joe Courtney, of Connecticut.
Ruben Gallego, of Arizona.
Salud O. Carbajal, of California.
Anthony G. Brown, of Maryland.
Filemon Vela, of Texas.
Mikie Sherrill, of New Jersey.
Jared F. Golden, of Maine.
Anthony Brindisi, of New York.

Vicky Hartzler, of Missouri.
Paul Cook, of California.
Matt Gaetz, of Florida.
Don Bacon, of Nebraska.
Jim Banks, of Indiana.
Paul Mitchell, of Michigan.
Michael R. Turner, of Ohio.
Doug Lamborn, of Colorado.
Robert J. Wittman, of Virginia.

STAFF

Committee on Armed Services (2216 RHOB), 225–4151, fax 225–9077.
Staff Director.—Paul Arcangeli.
Deputy Staff Director.—Douglas Bush.
General Counsel.—Spencer Johnson.
Deputy General Counsel.—Jamie Jackson.
Communications Directors: Monica Matoush, Caleb Randall-Bodman.
Director, Legislative Operations.—Zach Steacy.
Professional Staff: Chidi Blyden, Heath R. Bope, Jessica Carroll, Glen Diehl, Bess Dopkeen, Elizabeth Drummond, Brian Garrett, David Giachetti, Kelly Goggin, Shannon Green, Craig Greene, Brian Greer, Stephanie Halcrow, Melanie Harris, Michael Hermann, Jamie Jackson, Will T. Johnson, Kim Lehn, Jonathan Lord, Phil MacNaughton, Sarah Mineiro, Mark Morehouse, John Muller, Halimah Najieb-Locke, Katy Quinn, Laura Rauch, Matthew Rhoades, Rebecca A. Ross, Jason Schmid, Grant Schneider, Daniel Sennott, Sapna Sharma, David Sienicki, Eric Snelgrove, Joshua Stiefel, William Sutey, Jesse D. Tolleson, Leonor Tomero, Jr., Maria Vastola, Peter Villano, Jeanine Womble, Barron Youngsmith, Carla Zeppieri.
Minority Staff Director.—Jennifer Stewart.
Communications Director.—Claude Chafin.
Security Manager.—Kathryn Thompson.
Executive Assistants: Betty B. Gray, Alexis Hasty.
Clerks: Sean Falvey, Megan Handal, Caroline Kehrli, Emma Morrison, Danielle Steitz, Zachary Taylor, Shenita White.
Staff Assistant.—John N. Johnson.

Budget

204E Cannon House Office Building 20515–6065, phone 226–7200, fax 226–9905

https://budget.house.gov

John A. Yarmuth, of Kentucky, *Chair*

Seth Moulton, of Massachusetts, *Vice Chair*

Hakeem S. Jeffries, of New York.
Brian Higgins, of New York.
Brendan F. Boyle, of Pennsylvania.
Rosa L. DeLauro, of Connecticut.
Lloyd Doggett, of Texas.
David E. Price, of North Carolina.
Janice D. Schakowsky, of Illinois.
Daniel T. Kildee, of Michigan.
Jimmy Panetta, of California.
Joseph D. Morelle, of New York.
Steven Horsford, of Nevada.
Robert C. ''Bobby'' Scott, of Virginia.
Sheila Jackson Lee, of Texas.
Barbara Lee, of California.
Pramila Jayapal, of Washington.
Ilhan Omar, of Minnesota.
Albio Sires, of New Jersey.
Scott H. Peters, of California.
Jim Cooper, of Tennessee.
Ro Khanna, of California.

Steve Womack, of Arkansas.
Rob Woodall, of Georgia.
Bill Johnson, of Ohio.
Jason Smith, of Missouri.
Bill Flores, of Texas.
George Holding, of North Carolina.
Chris Stewart, of Utah.
Ralph Norman, of South Carolina.
Kevin Hern, of Oklahoma.
Chip Roy, of Texas.
Daniel Meuser, of Pennsylvania.
Dan Crenshaw, of Texas.
Tim Burchett, of Tennessee.
Chris Jacobs, of New York.

(No Subcommittees)

STAFF

Committee on Budget (204E CHOB), 226–7200, fax 226–9905.
Majority Staff Director.—Ellen J. Balis.
Deputy Staff Director.—Diana Meredith.
General Counsel.—Raquel Spencer.
Counsel/Budget Analyst.—Jocelyn Harris.
Budget Analyst/Coalition and Member Services Coordinator.—Erika Appel.
Budget Analysts: Edward Etzkorn, Emily King, Sarah Lee, Kimberly Overbeek, Scott R. Russell, Gregory Waring, Jennifer Wheelock, Ted E. Zegers.
Budget Assistant.—Laura Santos.
Communications Director.—Alexandra Weinroth.
Digital Director.—Samantha Carter.
Economist.—Gabrielle Elul.
Financial Administrator.—Patrick Baugh.
Office Manager.—Sheila A. McDowell.
Press Assistant.—Katherine Raymond.
Systems Administrator.—Jose Guillen.
Minority Staff Director.—Dan Keniry (507 CHOB), 226–7270, fax 226–7174).
Deputy Staff Director.—Becky Relic.
Policy Director.—Jenna Spealman.
General Counsel.—Mary Popadiuk.
Director of Budget Review.—Brad Watson.
Policy Advisors: Eric Davis, Gary Haglund, Colin Hayes, Adam Steinmetz.
Communications Director.—Emily Taylor.
Digital Director.—Vacant.
Member Services/Outreach Advisor.—Samantha Bopp.
Executive Assistant.—Benjamin Gardenhour.

Education and Labor

2176 Rayburn House Office Building, phone 225–3725, fax 225–2350

https://edlabor.house.gov

Robert C. ''Bobby'' Scott, of Virginia, *Chair*

Andy Levin, of Michigan, *Vice Chair*

Susan A. Davis, of California.
Raúl M. Grijalva, of Arizona.
Joe Courtney, of Connecticut.
Marcia L. Fudge, of Ohio.
Gregorio Kilili Camacho Sablan, of Northern Mariana Islands.
Frederica S. Wilson, of Florida.
Suzanne Bonamici, of Oregon.
Mark Takano, of California.
Alma S. Adams, of North Carolina.
Mark DeSaulnier, of California.
Donald Norcross, of New Jersey.
Pramila Jayapal, of Washington.
Joseph D. Morelle, of New York.
Susan Wild, of Pennsylvania.
Josh Harder, of California.
Lucy McBath, of Georgia.
Kim Schrier, of Washington.
Lauren Underwood, of Illinois.
Jahana Hayes, of Connecticut.
Donna E. Shalala, of Florida.
Ilhan Omar, of Minnesota.
David J. Trone, of Maryland.
Haley M. Stevens, of Michigan.
Susie Lee, of Nevada.
Lori Trahan, of Massachusetts.
Joaquin Castro, of Texas.

Virginia Foxx, of North Carolina.
David P. Roe, of Tennessee.
Glenn Thompson, of Pennsylvania.
Tim Walberg, of Michigan.
Brett Guthrie, of Kentucky.
Bradley Byrne, of Alabama.
Glenn Grothman, of Wisconsin.
Elise M. Stefanik, of New York.
Rick W. Allen, of Georgia.
Lloyd Smucker, of Pennsylvania.
Jim Banks, of Indiana.
Mark Walker, of North Carolina.
James Comer, of Kentucky.
Ben Cline, of Virginia.
Russ Fulcher, of Idaho.
Ron Wright, of Texas.
Daniel Meuser, of Pennsylvania.
Dusty Johnson, of South Dakota.
Fred Keller, of Pennsylvania.
Gregory F. Murphy, of North Carolina.
Jefferson Van Drew, of New Jersey.
Vacant.

SUBCOMMITTEES

Civil Rights and Human Services

Suzanne Bonamici, of Oregon, *Chair*

Raúl M. Grijalva, of Arizona.
Marcia L. Fudge, of Ohio.
Kim Schrier, of Washington.
Jahana Hayes, of Connecticut.
David J. Trone, of Maryland.
Susie Lee, of Nevada.

James Comer, of Kentucky.
Glenn Thompson, of Pennsylvania.
Elise M. Stefanik, of New York.
Dusty Johnson, of South Dakota.

Early Childhood, Elementary, and Secondary Education

Gregorio Kilili Camacho Sablan, of Northern Mariana Islands, *Chair*

Kim Schrier, of Washington.
Jahana Hayes, of Connecticut.
Donna E. Shalala, of Florida.
Susan A. Davis, of California.
Frederica S. Wilson, of Florida.
Mark DeSaulnier, of California.
Joseph D. Morelle, of New York.

Rick W. Allen, of Georgia.
Glenn Thompson, of Pennsylvania.
Glenn Grothman, of Wisconsin.
Fred Keller, of Pennsylvania.
Jefferson Van Drew, of New Jersey.

Health, Employment, Labor, and Pensions

Frederica S. Wilson, of Florida, *Chair*

Donald Norcross, of New Jersey.
Joseph D. Morelle, of New York.
Susan Wild, of Pennsylvania.
Lucy McBath, of Georgia.
Lauren Underwood, of Illinois.
Haley M. Stevens, of Michigan.
Joe Courtney, of Connecticut.
Marcia L. Fudge, of Ohio.
Josh Harder, of California.
Donna E. Shalala, of Florida.
Andy Levin, of Michigan.
Lori Trahan, of Massachusetts.
Robert C. ''Bobby'' Scott, of Virginia.

Tim Walberg, of Michigan.
David P. Roe, of Tennessee.
Rick W. Allen, of Georgia.
Jim Banks, of Indiana.
Russ Fulcher, of Idaho.
Ron Wright, of Texas.
Daniel Meuser, of Pennsylvania.
Dusty Johnson, of South Dakota.
Fred Keller, of Pennsylvania.
Jefferson Van Drew, of New Jersey.
Vacant.

Higher Education and Workforce Investment

Susan A. Davis, of California, *Chair*

Joe Courtney, of Connecticut.
Mark Takano, of California.
Pramila Jayapal, of Washington.
Josh Harder, of California.
Andy Levin, of Michigan.
Ilhan Omar, of Minnesota.
David J. Trone, of Maryland.
Susie Lee, of Nevada.
Lori Trahan, of Massachusetts.
Joaquin Castro, of Texas.
Raúl M. Grijalva, of Arizona.
Gregorio Kilili Camacho Sablan, of Northern Mariana Islands.
Suzanne Bonamici, of Oregon.
Alma S. Adams, of North Carolina.
Donald Norcross, of New Jersey.

Lloyd Smucker, of Pennsylvania.
Brett Guthrie, of Kentucky.
Glenn Grothman, of Wisconsin.
Elise M. Stefanik, of New York.
Jim Banks, of Indiana.
Mark Walker, of North Carolina.
James Comer, of Kentucky.
Ben Cline, of Virginia.
Russ Fulcher, of Idaho.
Daniel Meuser, of Pennsylvania.
Gregory F. Murphy, of North Carolina.
Vacant.

Workforce Protections

Alma S. Adams, of North Carolina, *Chair*

Mark DeSaulnier, of California.
Mark Takano, of California.
Pramila Jayapal, of Washington.
Susan Wild, of Pennsylvania.
Lucy McBath, of Georgia.
Ilhan Omar, of Minnesota.
Haley M. Stevens, of Michigan.

Bradley Byrne, of Alabama.
Mark Walker, of North Carolina.
Ben Cline, of Virginia.
Ron Wright, of Texas.
Gregory F. Murphy, of North Carolina.

STAFF

Committee on Education and Labor (2176 RHOB), 225–3725.
Majority Staff (2176 RHOB), 5–3725.
Staff Director.—Veronique Pluviose.
General Counsel: Ilanna Brunner, Christian Haines.
Associate General Counsel.—Katelyn Walker.
Director of Personnel and Office Administration.—Liz Hollis.
Chief Clerk.—Tylease Alli.
Clerk/Special Assistant to the Staff Director.—Jaria Martin.
Staff Assistants: Mariah Mowbray, Eli Hovland, Ariel Jona, Andre Lindsay, Max Moore.
Communications Director.—Joshua Weisz.
Deputy Communications Director.—Stephanie Lalle.
Digital Manager.—Merrick Nelson.
Director of Labor Policy.—Richard Miller.
Director of Labor Oversight.—Cathy Yu.

Oversight Counsel.—Janice Nsor.
Director of Health and Human Services.—Carrie Hughes.
Civil Rights Counsel.—Carolyn Ronis.
Health and Labor Counsel.—Daniel Foster.
Labor Policy Counsel: Kyle DeCant, Udochi Onwubiko.
Senior Labor Policy Advisors: Jordan Barab, Kevin McDermott.
Labor Policy Advisor.—Eunice Ikene.
Financial Administrator.—Nekea Brown.
Senior Economic Policy Advisor.—Rachel West.
Director of Education Oversight.—Benjamin Sinoff.
Oversight Counsel.—Kia Hamadanchy.
Director of Education Policy.—Jacque Chevalier Mosely.
Education Policy Counsel.—Loredana Valtierra.
Senior Education Policy Advisor.—Katherine Valle.
Disability Counsel.—Phoebe Ball.
Director of Information Technology.—Sheila Havenner.
Deputy Director Information Technology.—Banyon Vassar.
Systems Administrator.—Everett Winnick (2051A RHOB) (shared).
Professional Staff: Katie Berger, Paula Daneri, Alison Hard, Katherine McClelland, Lakeisha Steele, Theresa Thompson, Claire Viall.
Press Assistant.—Emma Eatman.
Staff Writer.—Kota Mizutani.

Shared Employees (1201 LHOB), 5–8351.
Counsel to the Chairman.—David Dailey.
Special Assistant to the Chairman.—Randi-Joanne A. Estes-Petty.

Minority Staff (2101 RHOB), 5–4527.
Minority Staff Director.—Cyrus Artz.
Director of Education and Human Services Policy.—Amy Jones.
Chief Counsel and Deputy Director of Education.—Amanda Schaumburg.
Director of Workforce Policy.—Rob Green.
Director of Operations.—Hannah Matesic.
Director of Member Services and Coalitions.—Courtney Butcher.
Communications Director.—Audra McGeorge.
Press Secretary.—Carlton Norwood.
Senior Education Policy Advisor.—Brad Thomas.
Workforce Policy Counsel.—John Martin.
Professional Staff Members—Education: Jake Middlebrooks, Alex Ricci.
Professional Staff Members—Workforce: Akash Chougule, Alexis Murray, Benjamin Ridder, Kelly Tyroler.
Legislative Assistant—Education.—Chance Russell.
Legislative Assistant—Workforce.—Jeanne Kuehl.
Press Assistant.—Kelli Liegel.
Staff Assistants: Gabriel Bisson, Georgie Littlefair.

Energy and Commerce

2125 Rayburn House Office Building, phone 225–2927

https://energycommerce.house.gov

Frank Pallone, Jr., of New Jersey, *Chairman*

Yvette D. Clarke, of New York, *Vice Chair*

Bobby L. Rush, of Illinois.
Anna G. Eshoo, of California.
Eliot L. Engel, of New York.
Diana DeGette, of Colorado.
Michael F. Doyle, of Pennsylvania.
Janice D. Schakowsky, of Illinois.
G. K. Butterfield, of North Carolina.
Doris O. Matsui, of California.
Kathy Castor, of Florida.
John P. Sarbanes, of Maryland.
Jerry McNerney, of California.
Peter Welch, of Vermont.
Ben Ray Luján, of New Mexico.
Paul Tonko, of New York.
David Loebsack, of Iowa.
Kurt Schrader, of Oregon.
Joseph P. Kennedy III, of Massachusetts.
Tony Cárdenas, of California.
Raul Ruiz, of California.
Scott H. Peters, of California.
Debbie Dingell, of Michigan.
Marc A. Veasey, of Texas.
Ann M. Kuster, of New Hampshire.
Robin L. Kelly, of Illinois.
Nanette Diaz Barragán, of California.
A. Donald McEachin, of Virginia.
Lisa Blunt Rochester, of Delaware.
Darren Soto, of Florida.
Tom O'Halleran, of Arizona.

Greg Walden, of Oregon.
Fred Upton, of Michigan.
John Shimkus, of Illinois.
Michael C. Burgess, of Texas.
Steve Scalise, of Louisiana.
Robert E. Latta, of Ohio.
Cathy McMorris Rodgers, of Washington.
Brett Guthrie, of Kentucky.
Pete Olson, of Texas.
David B. McKinley, of West Virginia.
Adam Kinzinger, of Illinois.
H. Morgan Griffith, of Virginia.
Gus M. Bilirakis, of Florida.
Bill Johnson, of Ohio.
Billy Long, of Missouri.
Larry Bucshon, of Indiana.
Bill Flores, of Texas.
Susan W. Brooks, of Indiana.
Markwayne Mullin, of Oklahoma.
Richard Hudson, of North Carolina.
Tim Walberg, of Michigan.
Earl L. ''Buddy'' Carter, of Georgia.
Jeff Duncan, of South Carolina.
Greg Gianforte, of Montana.

SUBCOMMITTEES

Communications and Technology

Michael F. Doyle, of Pennsylvania, *Chairman*

Doris O. Matsui, of California, *Vice Chair*

Jerry McNerney, of California.
Yvette D. Clarke, of New York.
David Loebsack, of Iowa.
Marc A. Veasey, of Texas.
A. Donald McEachin, of Virginia.
Darren Soto, of Florida.
Tom O'Halleran, of Arizona.
Anna G. Eshoo, of California.
Diana DeGette, of Colorado.
G. K. Butterfield, of North Carolina.
Peter Welch, of Vermont.
Ben Ray Luján, of New Mexico.
Kurt Schrader, of Oregon.
Tony Cárdenas, of California.
Debbie Dingell, of Michigan.
Frank Pallone, Jr., of New Jersey.

Robert E. Latta, of Ohio.
John Shimkus, of Illinois.
Steve Scalise, of Louisiana.
Pete Olson, of Texas.
Adam Kinzinger, of Illinois.
Gus M. Bilirakis, of Florida.
Bill Johnson, of Ohio.
Billy Long, of Missouri.
Bill Flores, of Texas.
Susan W. Brooks, of Indiana.
Tim Walberg, of Michigan.
Greg Gianforte, of Montana.
Greg Walden, of Oregon.

Consumer Protection and Commerce

Janice D. Schakowsky, of Illinois, *Chairwoman*

Tony Cárdenas, of California, *Vice Chair*

Kathy Castor, of Florida.
Marc A. Veasey, of Texas.
Robin L. Kelly, of Illinois.
Tom O'Halleran, of Arizona.
Ben Ray Luján, of New Mexico.
Lisa Blunt Rochester, of Delaware.
Darren Soto, of Florida.
Bobby L. Rush, of Illinois.
Doris O. Matsui, of California.
Jerry McNerney, of California.
Debbie Dingell, of Michigan.
Frank Pallone, Jr., of New Jersey.

Cathy McMorris Rodgers, of Washington.
Fred Upton, of Michigan.
Michael C. Burgess, of Texas.
Robert E. Latta, of Ohio.
Brett Guthrie, of Kentucky.
Larry Bucshon, of Indiana.
Richard Hudson, of North Carolina.
Earl L. ''Buddy'' Carter, of Georgia.
Greg Gianforte, of Montana.
Greg Walden, of Oregon.

Energy

Bobby L. Rush, of Illinois, *Chairman*

Jerry McNerney, of California, *Vice Chair*

Scott H. Peters, of California.
Michael F. Doyle, of Pennsylvania.
John P. Sarbanes, of Maryland.
Paul Tonko, of New York.
David Loebsack, of Iowa.
G. K. Butterfield, of North Carolina.
Peter Welch, of Vermont.
Kurt Schrader, of Oregon.
Joseph P. Kennedy III, of Massachusetts.
Marc A. Veasey, of Texas.
Ann M. Kuster, of New Hampshire.
Robin L. Kelly, of Illinois.
Nanette Diaz Barragán, of California.
A. Donald McEachin, of Virginia.
Tom O'Halleran, of Arizona.
Lisa Blunt Rochester, of Delaware.
Frank Pallone, Jr., of New Jersey.

Fred Upton, of Michigan.
Robert E. Latta, of Ohio.
Cathy McMorris Rodgers, of Washington.
Pete Olson, of Texas.
David B. McKinley, of West Virginia.
Adam Kinzinger, of Illinois.
H. Morgan Griffith, of Virginia.
Bill Johnson, of Ohio.
Larry Bucshon, of Indiana.
Bill Flores, of Texas.
Richard Hudson, of North Carolina.
Tim Walberg, of Michigan.
Jeff Duncan, of South Carolina.
Greg Walden, of Oregon.

Environment and Climate Change

Paul Tonko, of New York, *Chairman*

Raul Ruiz, of California, *Vice Chair*

Yvette D. Clarke, of New York.
Scott H. Peters, of California.
Nanette Diaz Barragán, of California.
A. Donald McEachin, of Virginia.
Lisa Blunt Rochester, of Delaware.
Darren Soto, of Florida.
Diana DeGette, of Colorado.
Janice D. Schakowsky, of Illinois.
Doris O. Matsui, of California.
Jerry McNerney, of California.
Debbie Dingell, of Michigan.
Frank Pallone, Jr., of New Jersey.

John Shimkus, of Illinois.
Cathy McMorris Rodgers, of Washington.
David B. McKinley, of West Virginia.
Bill Johnson, of Ohio.
Billy Long, of Missouri.
Bill Flores, of Texas.
Markwayne Mullin, of Oklahoma.
Earl L. ''Buddy'' Carter, of Georgia.
Jeff Duncan, of South Carolina.
Greg Walden, of Oregon.

Health

Anna G. Eshoo, of California, *Chairwoman*

G. K. Butterfield, of North Carolina, *Vice Chair*

Eliot L. Engel, of New York.
Doris O. Matsui, of California.
Kathy Castor, of Florida.
John P. Sarbanes, of Maryland.
Ben Ray Luján, of New Mexico.
Kurt Schrader, of Oregon.
Joseph P. Kennedy III, of Massachusetts.
Tony Cárdenas, of California.
Peter Welch, of Vermont.
Raul Ruiz, of California.
Debbie Dingell, of Michigan.
Ann M. Kuster, of New Hampshire.
Robin L. Kelly, of Illinois.
Nanette Diaz Barragán, of California.
Lisa Blunt Rochester, of Delaware.
Bobby L. Rush, of Illinois.
Frank Pallone, Jr., of New Jersey.

Michael C. Burgess, of Texas.
Fred Upton, of Michigan.
John Shimkus, of Illinois.
Brett Guthrie, of Kentucky.
H. Morgan Griffith, of Virginia.
Gus M. Bilirakis, of Florida.
Billy Long, of Missouri.
Larry Bucshon, of Indiana.
Susan W. Brooks, of Indiana.
Markwayne Mullin, of Oklahoma.
Richard Hudson, of North Carolina.
Earl L. ''Buddy'' Carter, of Georgia.
Greg Gianforte, of Montana.
Greg Walden, of Oregon.

Oversight and Investigations

Diana DeGette, of Colorado, Chairwoman

Joseph P. Kennedy III, of Massachusetts, *Vice Chair*

Janice D. Schakowsky, of Illinois.
Raul Ruiz, of California.
Ann M. Kuster, of New Hampshire.
Kathy Castor, of Florida.
John P. Sarbanes, of Maryland.
Paul Tonko, of New York.
Yvette D. Clarke, of New York.
Scott H. Peters, of California.
Frank Pallone, Jr., of New Jersey.

Brett Guthrie, of Kentucky.
Michael C. Burgess, of Texas.
David B. McKinley, of West Virginia.
H. Morgan Griffith, of Virginia.
Susan W. Brooks, of Indiana.
Markwayne Mullin, of Oklahoma.
Jeff Duncan, of South Carolina.
Greg Walden, of Oregon.

STAFF

Majority Staff Director.—Jeff Carroll (2125 RHOB) 225–2927.
Deputy Committee Staff Director.—Tiffany Guarascio.
Director of Communications, Member Services and Outreach.—Andrew Souvall.
Chief Clerk.—Sharon E. Davis.
Chief Counsel.—Timothy R. Robinson.
Deputy Chief Counsel.—Waverly Gordon.
Senior Advisor/Staff Director for Energy and Environment.—Rick Kessler.
Oversight Staff Director.—Christopher Knauer.
Chief Counsel, Communications and Consumer Protection.—Alex Hoehn-Saric.
Chief Health Counsel.—Una Lee.
Chief Health Advisor.—Kimberlee Trzeciak.
Chief Oversight Counsel.—Kevin S. Barstow.
Chief Environment Counsel.—Jacqueline Cohen.
Energy and Environment Policy Advisors: Jean Fruci, Tuley Wright.
Senior Counsel: Lisa Goldman, Gerald Leverich.
Air and Climate Counsel.—Dustin Maghamfar.
Health Counsel: Stephen Holland, Richard A. Van Buren.
Counsel: Mohammad Aslami, AJ Brown, Jacquelyn Bolen, Jennifer Epperson, Manmeet Kaur Dhindsa, Judith B. Harvey, Jon Monger, Peter Rechter.
Oversight Investigator.—Kevin McAloon.
Professional Staff Members: Joseph Banez, Jesseca Boyer, Daniel M. Greene, Amy Gutierrez, Caitlin Haberman, Saha Khaterzai, Samantha Satchell, Anna Yu.
Office Manager.—Elizabeth Ertel.
Director of Technology.—Edward Walker.
Systems Administrator.—William C. Benjamin.
Outreach and Member Services Coordinator.—Zachary L. Kahan.

Policy Analysts: Adam Fischer, Omar A. Guzman-Toro, Meghan Mullon, Chloe V. Rodriquez, Benjamin S. Tabor.
Senior Policy Analyst.—Daniel Miller.
Policy Coordinators: Brendan Larkin, Jourdan M. Lewis, Aisling McDonough, Philip H. Murphy, Nikki Roy, Roberto Sada, Sydney Terry.
Press Secretaries: Elysa Montfort, CJ Young.
Deputy Press Secretary.—Evan Gilbert.
Digital Director.—Kaitlyn D. Peel.
Press Assistant.—Alivia Roberts.
Executive Assistant.—Joseph S. Orlando.
Staff Assistants: Austin J. Flack, Lino Pena Martinez, Rebecca J. Tomilchik.

Minority Staff Director.—Michael Bloomquist (2322 RHOB) 225–3641.
Deputy Staff Director.—Ryan Long.
General Counsel.—Peter Kielty.
Senior Advisor.—Jordan Davis.
Director, Communications.—Zach Roday.
Chief Counsel:
Subcommittee on Communications and Technology.—Robin Colwell.
Subcommittee on Consumer Protection and Commerce.—Tim Kurth.
Subcommittee on Energy, Subcommittee on Environment and Climate Change.—Mary Martin.
Subcommittee on Health.—JP Paluskiewicz.
Subcommittee on Oversight and Investigations.—Jennifer Barblan.
Coalitions Director/Deputy Chief Counsel, Subcommittee on Health.—Adam Buckalew.
Deputy Chief Counsel.—Gerald Couri, Brandon Mooney.
Senior Investigative Counsel.—Alan Slobodin.
Counsel: Bijan Koohmaraie, Natalie Sohn, Danielle Steele.
Senior Professional Staff Member.—Peter Spencer.
Professional Staff: Caleb Graff, Brittany Havens, Kristen Shatynski.
Press Secretary.—Sarah Matthews.
Policy Advisor.—Nolan Ahern.
Policy Coordinator.—Lorissa Bounds, Mark Ratner.
Director, Information Technology.—Everett Winnick.
Human Resources Specialist and Office Administrator.—Theresa Gambo.
Legislative Clerk/Press Assistant.—Margaret Tucker Fogarty.
Legislative Clerk.—Brannon Rains.
Communications and Technology Subcommittee Professional Staff Member.—Evan Viau.

Ethics

1015 Longworth House Office Building, phone 225–7103, fax 225–7392

Theodore E. Deutch, of Florida, *Chair*

Grace Meng, of New York.
Susan Wild, of Pennsylvania.
Dean Phillips, of Minnesota.
Anthony G. Brown, of Maryland.

Kenny Marchant, of Texas.
George Holding, of North Carolina.
Jackie Walorski, of Indiana.
Michael Guest, of Mississippi.
Vacant.

(No Subcommittees)

STAFF

Staff Director/Chief Counsel.—Tom Rust.
Counsel to the Chairman.—David Arrojo.
Counsel to the Ranking Member.—Chris Donesa.
Director of:
Administration.—Donna Herbert.
Advice and Education.—Tonia Smith.
Financial Disclosure.—Tonya Sloans.
Investigations.—Brittney Pescatore.
Senior Counsel: Kathryn Donahue, Tamar Nedzar.
Counsel: Jessica Baker, Janet Foster, Sarah Myers-Mutschall, Mark Opachan, Zeke Ross, Michelle Seo, John Szabo, Kent Walker, Tanisha Wilburn.
Professional Staff.—Adam Wambold.
Investigator.—Danielle Appleman.
Senior Financial Disclosure Manager.—Deborah Bethea.
Investigative Clerk.—Caroline Taylor.
Advice and Education Clerk.—Matt Jansen.
Financial Disclosure Clerk.—George Korn.
Staff Assistants: Steve Boursalian, Melissa Epstein, Ryan Eseppi, Trent Windes.

Financial Services

2129 Rayburn House Office Building, phone 225–4247

https://house.gov/financialservices

Maxine Waters, of California, *Chair*

Carolyn B. Maloney, of New York.
Nydia M. Velázquez, of New York.
Brad Sherman, of California.
Gregory W. Meeks, of New York.
Wm. Lacy Clay, of Missouri.
David Scott, of Georgia.
Al Green, of Texas.
Emanuel Cleaver, of Missouri.
Ed Perlmutter, of Colorado.
James A. Himes, of Connecticut.
Bill Foster, of Illinois.
Joyce Beatty, of Ohio.
Denny Heck, of Washington.
Juan Vargas, of California.
Josh Gottheimer, of New Jersey.
Vicente Gonzalez, of Texas.
Al Lawson Jr., of Florida.
Michael F. Q. San Nicolas, of Guam.
Rashida Tlaib, of Michigan.
Katie Porter, of California.
Cynthia Axne, of Iowa.
Sean Casten, of Illinois.
Ayanna Pressley, of Massachusetts.
Ben McAdams, of Utah.
Alexandria Ocasio-Cortez, of New York.
Jennifer Wexton, of Virginia.
Stephen F. Lynch, of Massachusetts.
Tulsi Gabbard, of Hawaii.
Alma S. Adams, of North Carolina.
Madeleine Dean, of Pennsylvania.
Jesús G. "Chuy" García, of Illinois.
Sylvia R. Garcia, of Texas.
Dean Phillips, of Minnesota.

Patrick T. McHenry, of North Carolina.
Frank D. Lucas, of Oklahoma.
Bill Posey, of Florida.
Blaine Luetkemeyer, of Missouri.
Bill Huizenga, of Michigan.
Steve Stivers, of Ohio.
Ann Wagner, of Missouri.
Andy Barr, of Kentucky.
Scott R. Tipton, of Colorado.
Roger Williams, of Texas.
J. French Hill, of Arkansas.
Tom Emmer, of Minnesota.
Lee M. Zeldin, of New York.
Barry Loudermilk, of Georgia.
Alexander X. Mooney, of West Virginia.
Warren Davidson, of Ohio.
Ted Budd, of North Carolina.
David Kustoff, of Tennessee.
Trey Hollingsworth, of Indiana.
Anthony Gonzalez, of Ohio.
John W. Rose, of Tennessee.
Bryan Steil, of Wisconsin.
Lance Gooden, of Texas.
Denver Riggleman, of Virginia.
William R. Timmons IV, of South Carolina.
Van Taylor, of Texas.

SUBCOMMITTEES

Consumer Protection and Financial Institutions

Gregory W. Meeks, of New York, *Chair*

David Scott, of Georgia.
Nydia M. Velázquez, of New York.
Wm. Lacy Clay, of Missouri.
Denny Heck, of Washington.
Bill Foster, of Illinois.
Al Lawson Jr., of Florida.
Rashida Tlaib, of Michigan.
Katie Porter, of California.
Ayanna Pressley, of Massachusetts.
Ben McAdams, of Utah.
Alexandria Ocasio-Cortez, of New York.
Jennifer Wexton, of Virginia.

Blaine Luetkemeyer, of Missouri.
Frank D. Lucas, of Oklahoma.
Bill Posey, of Florida.
Andy Barr, of Kentucky.
Scott R. Tipton, of Colorado.
Roger Williams, of Texas.
Barry Loudermilk, of Georgia.
Ted Budd, of North Carolina.
David Kustoff, of Tennessee.
Denver Riggleman, of Virginia.

Diversity and Inclusion

Joyce Beatty, of Ohio, *Chair*

Wm. Lacy Clay, of Missouri.
Al Green, of Texas.
Josh Gottheimer, of New Jersey.
Vicente Gonzalez, of Texas.
Al Lawson Jr., of Florida.
Ayanna Pressley, of Massachusetts.
Tulsi Gabbard, of Hawaii.
Alma S. Adams, of North Carolina.
Madeleine Dean, of Pennsylvania.
Sylvia R. Garcia, of Texas.
Dean Phillips, of Minnesota.

Ann Wagner, of Missouri.
Frank D. Lucas, of Oklahoma.
Alexander X. Mooney, of West Virginia.
Ted Budd, of North Carolina.
David Kustoff, of Tennessee.
Trey Hollingsworth, of Indiana.
Anthony Gonzalez, of Ohio.
Bryan Steil, of Wisconsin.
Lance Gooden, of Texas.

Housing, Community Development, and Insurance

Wm. Lacy Clay, of Missouri, *Chair*

Nydia M. Velázquez, of New York.
Emanuel Cleaver, of Missouri.
Brad Sherman, of California.
Joyce Beatty, of Ohio.
Al Green, of Texas.
Vicente Gonzalez, of Texas.
Carolyn B. Maloney, of New York.
Denny Heck, of Washington.
Juan Vargas, of California.
Al Lawson Jr., of Florida.
Rashida Tlaib, of Michigan.
Cynthia Axne, of Iowa.

Steve Stivers, of Ohio.
Bill Posey, of Florida.
Blaine Luetkemeyer, of Missouri.
Bill Huizenga, of Michigan.
Scott R. Tipton, of Colorado.
Lee M. Zeldin, of New York.
David Kustoff, of Tennessee.
John W. Rose, of Tennessee.
Bryan Steil, of Wisconsin.
Lance Gooden, of Texas.

Investor Protection, Entrepreneurship, and Capital Markets

Brad Sherman, of California, *Chair*

Carolyn B. Maloney, of New York.
David Scott, of Georgia.
James A. Himes, of Connecticut.
Bill Foster, of Illinois.
Gregory W. Meeks, of New York.
Juan Vargas, of California.
Josh Gottheimer, of New Jersey.
Vicente Gonzalez, of Texas.
Michael F. Q. San Nicolas, of Guam.
Katie Porter, of California.
Cynthia Axne, of Iowa.
Sean Casten, of Illinois.
Alexandria Ocasio-Cortez, of New York.

Bill Huizenga, of Michigan.
Steve Stivers, of Ohio.
Ann Wagner, of Missouri.
J. French Hill, of Arkansas.
Tom Emmer, of Minnesota.
Alexander X. Mooney, of West Virginia.
Warren Davidson, of Ohio.
Trey Hollingsworth, of Indiana.
Anthony Gonzalez, of Ohio.
Bryan Steil, of Wisconsin.

National Security, International Development, and Monetary Policy

Emanuel Cleaver, of Missouri, *Chair*

Ed Perlmutter, of Colorado.
James A. Himes, of Connecticut.
Denny Heck, of Washington.
Brad Sherman, of California.
Juan Vargas, of California.
Josh Gottheimer, of New Jersey.
Michael F. Q. San Nicolas, of Guam.
Ben McAdams, of Utah.
Jennifer Wexton, of Virginia.
Stephen F. Lynch, of Massachusetts.
Tulsi Gabbard, of Hawaii.
Jesús G. ''Chuy'' García, of Illinois.

J. French Hill, of Arkansas.
Frank D. Lucas, of Oklahoma.
Roger Williams, of Texas.
Tom Emmer, of Minnesota.
Anthony Gonzalez, of Ohio.
John W. Rose, of Tennessee.
Denver Riggleman, of Virginia.
William R. Timmons IV, of South Carolina.
Van Taylor, of Texas.

Oversight and Investigations

Al Green, of Texas, *Chair*

Joyce Beatty, of Ohio.
Stephen F. Lynch, of Massachusetts.
Nydia M. Velázquez, of New York.
Ed Perlmutter, of Colorado.
Rashida Tlaib, of Michigan.
Sean Casten, of Illinois.
Madeleine Dean, of Pennsylvania.
Sylvia R. Garcia, of Texas.
Dean Phillips, of Minnesota.

Andy Barr, of Kentucky.
Lee M. Zeldin, of New York.
Barry Loudermilk, of Georgia.
Warren Davidson, of Ohio.
John W. Rose, of Tennessee.
William R. Timmons IV, of South Carolina.
Van Taylor, of Texas.
Vacant.

STAFF

Committee on Financial Services (2129 RHOB), 225–4247.
Majority Staff:
Staff Director.—Charla Ouertatani.
Deputy Staff Director.—Kristofor Erickson.
Chief Counsel.—Lisa Peto.
General Counsel and Parliamentarian.—David Abramowitz.
Clerk.—Petrina Thomas.
Member Services and Outreach Coordinator.—Clement Abonyi.
Chief Oversight Counsel.—Kevin Burris.
Deputy Chief Oversight Counsel.—Bruce Johnson.
Senior Counsel: Carolyn Hahn, Avy Mallik, Yana Miles, Elayne Weiss.
Counsel: Devron Brown, David Fernandez, John Heinemann, Lauri Ng, Jennifer Read.
Paralegal.—Christine Baltazar.
Director of Consumer Protection and Financial Policy.—Glen Sears.
Systems Administrator.—Alfred J. Forman, Jr.
Director of Housing Policy.—Esther Kahng.
Director of Investor Protection and Capital Markets Policy.—Katelynn Bradley.
Director of Diversity and Inclusion Policy.—Erica Miles.
Financial and Administrative Officer.—Denise Scott.
Director of International Affairs.—Daniel P. McGlinchey.
Special Investigator and Counsel.—Bob Roach.
Director of National Security.—Danielle Lindholm.
Communications Director.—Eric Hersey.
Deputy Communications Director.—Erica Loewe.
Digital Director.—Marcos F. Manosalvas.
Press Assistant.—Eden Harris.
Professional Staff: Alia Fierro, Janae Ladet, Pierre Whatley.
Editor.—Terisa L. Allison.
Research Assistant.—Laura Vossler.
Staff Assistant.—Justin ''Franklin'' Thornton.
Minority Staff:
Staff Director.—Steve Cote.
Chief Oversight Counsel.—Jon Skladany.
Deputy Staff Director.—Matt Mulder.
Senior Professional Staff: Anthony E. Chang, Edward G. Skala.
Professional Staff: Connor Dunn, Kathleen Palmer.
General Counsel.—Kim Betz.
Press Secretary.—Laura Peavey.
Press Assistant.—William Barry.
Counsels: Brighton Haslett, Charlie Schreiber.
Systems Administrator.—Stacy Baker.
Legislative Assistants: McArn Bennett, Francesco Castella.
Director of Member Services and Coalitions.—Collin McCune.
Director of Operations.—Lindsey Shackelford.
Policy Assistant.—Phil Poe.
Staff Assistants: Dwayne Clark, Meg Shannon.

Foreign Affairs

2170 Rayburn House Office Building, phone 225–5021

https://foreignaffairs.house.gov

Eliot L. Engel, of New York, *Chair*

Brad Sherman, of California.
Gregory W. Meeks, of New York.
Albio Sires, of New Jersey.
Gerald E. Connolly, of Virginia.
Theodore E. Deutch, of Florida.
Karen Bass, of California.
William R. Keating, of Massachusetts.
David N. Cicilline, of Rhode Island.
Ami Bera, of California.
Joaquin Castro, of Texas.
Dina Titus, of Nevada.
Adriano Espaillat, of New York.
Ted Lieu, of California.
Susan Wild, of Pennsylvania.
Dean Phillips, of Minnesota.
Ilhan Omar, of Minnesota.
Colin Z. Allred, of Texas.
Andy Levin, of Michigan.
Abigail Davis Spanberger, of Virginia.
Chrissy Houlahan, of Pennsylvania.
Tom Malinowski, of New Jersey.
David J. Trone, of Maryland.
Jim Costa, of California.
Juan Vargas, of California.
Vicente Gonzalez, of Texas.

Michael T. McCaul, of Texas.
Christopher H. Smith, of New Jersey.
Steve Chabot, of Ohio.
Joe Wilson, of South Carolina.
Scott Perry, of Pennsylvania.
Ted S. Yoho, of Florida.
Adam Kinzinger, of Illinois.
Lee M. Zeldin, of New York.
F. James Sensenbrenner, Jr., of Wisconsin.
Ann Wagner, of Missouri.
Brian J. Mast, of Florida.
Francis Rooney, of Florida.
Brian K. Fitzpatrick, of Pennsylvania.
John R. Curtis, of Utah.
Ken Buck, of Colorado.
Ron Wright, of Texas.
Guy Reschenthaler, of Pennsylvania.
Tim Burchett, of Tennessee.
Greg Pence, of Indiana.
Michael Guest, of Mississippi.
Mark E. Green, of Tennessee.
Vacant.

SUBCOMMITTEES

Africa, Global Health, Global Human Rights, and International Organizations

Karen Bass, of California, *Chair*

Susan Wild, of Pennsylvania.
Dean Phillips, of Minnesota.
Ilhan Omar, of Minnesota.
Chrissy Houlahan, of Pennsylvania.

Christopher H. Smith, of New Jersey.
F. James Sensenbrenner, Jr., of Wisconsin.
Ron Wright, of Texas.
Tim Burchett, of Tennessee.

Asia, the Pacific, and Nonproliferation

Ami Bera, of California, *Chair*

Dina Titus, of Nevada.
Chrissy Houlahan, of Pennsylvania.
Gerald E. Connolly, of Virginia.
Brad Sherman, of California.
Andy Levin, of Michigan.
Abigail Davis Spanberger, of Virginia.

Ted S. Yoho, of Florida.
Scott Perry, of Pennsylvania.
Ann Wagner, of Missouri.
Brian J. Mast, of Florida.
John R. Curtis, of Utah.

Europe, Eurasia, Energy, and the Environment

William R. Keating, of Massachusetts, *Chair*

Abigail Davis Spanberger, of Virginia.
Gregory W. Meeks, of New York.
Albio Sires, of New Jersey.
Theodore E. Deutch, of Florida.
David N. Cicilline, of Rhode Island.
Ami Bera, of California.
Dina Titus, of Nevada.
Susan Wild, of Pennsylvania.
David J. Trone, of Maryland.
Jim Costa, of California.
Vicente Gonzalez, of Texas.

Adam Kinzinger, of Illinois.
Joe Wilson, of South Carolina.
Ann Wagner, of Missouri.
F. James Sensenbrenner, Jr., of Wisconsin.
Francis Rooney, of Florida.
Brian K. Fitzpatrick, of Pennsylvania.
Greg Pence, of Indiana.
Ron Wright, of Texas.
Michael Guest, of Mississippi.
Tim Burchett, of Tennessee.

Middle East, North Africa, and International Terrorism

Theodore E. Deutch, of Florida, *Chair*

Gerald E. Connolly, of Virginia.
David N. Cicilline, of Rhode Island.
Ted Lieu, of California.
Colin Z. Allred, of Texas.
Tom Malinowski, of New Jersey.
David J. Trone, of Maryland.
Brad Sherman, of California.
William R. Keating, of Massachusetts.
Juan Vargas, of California.

Joe Wilson, of South Carolina.
Steve Chabot, of Ohio.
Adam Kinzinger, of Illinois.
Lee M. Zeldin, of New York.
Brian J. Mast, of Florida.
Brian K. Fitzpatrick, of Pennsylvania.
Guy Reschenthaler, of Pennsylvania.
Vacant.

Oversight and Investigations

Joaquin Castro, of Texas, *Chair*

Ilhan Omar, of Minnesota.
Adriano Espaillat, of New York.
Ted Lieu, of California.
Tom Malinowski, of New Jersey.
David N. Cicilline, of Rhode Island.

Lee M. Zeldin, of New York.
Scott Perry, of Pennsylvania.
Ken Buck, of Colorado.
Guy Reschenthaler, of Pennsylvania.

Western Hemisphere, Civilian Security, and Trade

Albio Sires, of New Jersey, *Chair*

Gregory W. Meeks, of New York.
Joaquin Castro, of Texas.
Adriano Espaillat, of New York.
Dean Phillips, of Minnesota.
Andy Levin, of Michigan.
Vicente Gonzalez, of Texas.
Juan Vargas, of California.

Francis Rooney, of Florida.
Christopher H. Smith, of New Jersey.
Ted S. Yoho, of Florida.
John R. Curtis, of Utah.
Ken Buck, of Colorado.
Michael Guest, of Mississippi.

STAFF

Committee on Foreign Affairs (2170 RHOB), 225–5021, fax 225–5394.
Majority Staff:
Staff Director.—Jason Steinbaum.
Deputy Staff Director.—Doug Campbell.
Chief Counsel.—Janice Kaguyutan.
Deputy Chief Counsel.—Mark Iozzi.
Communications Director.—Tim Mulvey.
Deputy Communications Director/Policy Advisor.—Rachel Levitan.
Senior Professional Staff Members: Laura Carey, Katy Crosby, Sajit Gandhi, Jennifer Hendrixson-White, Jacqueline Ramos, Mira Resnick, Edmund B. Rice, Kimberly Stanton, Lesley Warner.
Digital Communications Manager.—Jacqueline Colvett.
Senior Policy Advisor.—Eric Jacobstein.

Professional Staff Members: Brian Skretny, Sahil Chaudhary.
Professional Staff Member/Security Officer.—George Ritchey.
Director of Operations.—Samantha Stiles.
Counsel.—Jaclyn Cahan.
Senior Counsel for Oversight & Investigations.—Jamie Bair.
Executive Director, House Democracy Partnership.—Derek Luyten.
Policy Analysts: Peter Billerbeck, Theresa Lou, Michael Matlaga, Taylor Redick, Alex Sadler, Harry Smerdijan.
Staff Associates: Raven Bellamy, Evan Bursey, Matthew Finkel, Sophie Jones.
Financial Officer.—John Gleason.
Information Resource Manager.—Vlad Cerga.
Assistant Systems Administrator.—Danny Marca.
Printing Manager/Web Assistant.—Letitia Fletcher.

Minority Staff (B-360 RHOB), 226–8467.
Staff Director.—Brendan Shields.
Deputy Staff Director.—Laura Fullerton.
Communications Director.—Kaylin Minton.
Special Assistant to the Staff Director.—Lauren Gillespie.
General Counsel.—Doug Anderson.
Senior Professional Staff Members: Samia Brahimi, John Stapleton, Jessica Steffens, Gabriella Zach.
Professional Staff Members: Bryan Burack, Katherine Curtis, Chris Farrar, Megan Gallagher, Dan Markus, Juan Carlos Monje, Thomas Rice, James Walsh.
Senior Counsel.—Grant Mullins.
Member Services and Coalitions Director.—Caroline Campbell.
Director of Operations/Parliamentarian.—Jennifer Gorski.
Staff Associate.—Sarah Markley.

Subcommittee on Africa, Global Health, Global Human Rights, and International Organizations (5190 O'Neill FOB), 226–1500.
Majority Staff:
Subcommittee Staff Director.—Janette Yarwood.
Professional Staff Member.—Corey Holmes.
Staff Associate.—Naomia Suggs-Brigety.

Subcommittee on Asia, the Pacific, and Nonproliferation (5197 O'Neill FOB), 226–7825.
Majority Staff:
Subcommittee Staff Director.—Don MacDonald.
Professional Staff Member.—Zachary Keck.

Subcommittee on Europe, Eurasia, Energy and the Environment (5193 O'Neill FOB), 226–3111.
Majority Staff:
Subcommittee Staff Director.—Gabrielle Gould.
Professional Staff Member.—Leah Nodvin.
Staff Associate.—Shestin Thomson.

Subcommittee on Middle East, North Africa, and International Terrorism (5211 O'Neill FOB), 225–7812.
Majority Staff:
Subcommittee Staff Director.—Casey Kustin.
Professional Staff Member.—Ryan Doherty.
Staff Associate.—Aviva Abusch.

Subcommittee on Oversight and Investigations
Majority Staff:
Subcommittee Staff Director.—Nikole Burroughs.
Professional Staff Member.—Ryan Uyehara.

Subcommittee on Western Hemisphere, Civilian Security, and Trade (5222 O'Neill FOB), 225–3345.
Majority Staff:
Subcommittee Staff Director.—Alexander Brockwehl.
Professional Staff Member.—Mariana Cruz Munoz.
Staff Associate.—Ricardo Martinez.

Homeland Security

176 Ford House Office Building, phone 226–2616

Bennie G. Thompson, of Mississippi, *Chair*

Sheila Jackson Lee, of Texas.
James R. Langevin, of Rhode Island.
Cedric L. Richmond, of Louisiana.
Donald M. Payne, Jr., of New Jersey.
Kathleen M. Rice, of New York.
J. Luis Correa, of California.
Xochitl Torres Small, of New Mexico.
Max Rose, of New York.
Lauren Underwood, of Illinois.
Elissa Slotkin, of Michigan.
Emanuel Cleaver, of Missouri.
Al Green, of Texas.
Yvette D. Clarke, of New York.
Dina Titus, of Nevada.
Bonnie Watson Coleman, of New Jersey.
Nanette Diaz Barragán, of California.
Val Butler Demings, of Florida.

Mike Rogers, of Alabama.
Peter T. King, of New York.
Michael T. McCaul, of Texas.
John Katko, of New York.
Mark Walker, of North Carolina.
Clay Higgins, of Louisiana.
Debbie Lesko, of Arizona.
Mark E. Green, of Tennessee.
John Joyce, of Pennsylvania.
Dan Crenshaw, of Texas.
Michael Guest, of Mississippi.
Dan Bishop, of North Carolina.
Jefferson Van Drew, of New Jersey.
Mike Garcia, of California.

SUBCOMMITTEES

[The chair and ranking minority member are ex officio members of all subcommittees on which they do not serve.]

Border Security, Facilitation, and Operations

Kathleen M. Rice, of New York, *Chair*

Donald M. Payne, Jr., of New Jersey.
J. Luis Correa, of California.
Xochitl Torres Small, of New Mexico.
Al Green, of Texas.
Yvette D. Clarke, of New York.

Clay Higgins, of Louisiana.
Debbie Lesko, of Arizona.
John Joyce, of Pennsylvania.
Michael Guest, of Mississippi.

Cybersecurity, Infrastructure Protection, and Innovation

Cedric L. Richmond, of Louisiana, *Chair*

Sheila Jackson Lee, of Texas.
James R. Langevin, of Rhode Island.
Kathleen M. Rice, of New York.
Lauren Underwood, of Illinois.
Elissa Slotkin, of Michigan.

John Katko, of New York.
Mark Walker, of North Carolina.
Mark E. Green, of Tennessee.
John Joyce, of Pennsylvania.

Emergency Preparedness, Response, and Recovery

Donald M. Payne, Jr., of New Jersey, *Chair*

Cedric L. Richmond, of Louisiana.
Max Rose, of New York.
Lauren Underwood, of Illinois.
Al Green, of Texas.
Yvette D. Clarke, of New York.

Peter T. King, of New York.
Dan Crenshaw, of Texas.
Michael Guest, of Mississippi.
Dan Bishop, of North Carolina.

Intelligence and Counterterrorism

Max Rose, of New York, *Chair*

Sheila Jackson Lee, of Texas.
James R. Langevin, of Rhode Island.
Elissa Slotkin, of Michigan.

Mark Walker, of North Carolina.
Peter T. King, of New York.
Mark E. Green, of Tennessee.

Oversight, Management, and Accountability

Xochitl Torres Small, of New Mexico, *Chair*

Dina Titus, of Nevada.
Bonnie Watson Coleman, of New Jersey.
Nanette Diaz Barragán, of California.
Dan Crenshaw, of Texas.
Clay Higgins, of Louisiana.
Jefferson Van Drew, of New Jersey.

Transportation and Maritime Security

J. Luis Correa, of California, *Chair*

Emanuel Cleaver, of Missouri.
Dina Titus, of Nevada.
Bonnie Watson Coleman, of New Jersey.
Nanette Diaz Barragán, of California.
Val Butler Demings, of Florida.
Debbie Lesko, of Arizona.
John Katko, of New York.
Dan Bishop, of North Carolina.
Jefferson Van Drew, of New Jersey.

STAFF

Committee on Homeland Security (H2–176 Ford House Office Building) phone 226–2616.
Majority Staff Director.—Hope Goins, FHOB / H2–176, 226–2616.
Chief Counsel.—Rosaline Cohen.
Oversight Director.—Alison B. Northrop.
Communications Director.—Adam M. Comis.
Subcommittee on Border Security, Facilitation, and Operations Staff Director.—Alexandra Carnes.
Subcommittee on Cybersecurity, Infrastructure Protection, and Innovation Staff Director/ Counsel.—Moira Bergin.
Subcommittee on Emergency Preparedness, Response, and Recovery Staff Director.—Lauren McClain.
Subcommittee on Oversight, Management and Accountability Director.—Lisa Canini.
Subcommittee on Transportation and Maritime Security Staff Director.—Alexander Marston.
Counsel: Nzinga Dyson, Laura Kupe, Jonathan Parnes, Sandeep Prasanna, Alicia Smith, Jack Solano.
Professional Staff Members: Melissa Alvarado, Charles Carithers, Wendy Clerinx, Naveed Jazayeri, Brittany Lynch, Devin Lynch, Joel Walsh, G. Stephen Williams.
Parliamentarian.—Ethan McClelland.
Security Director.—Marcus Clark.
Office Manager.—Amanda Mims.
Legislative Assistants: Jenna Hopkins, Camisha Johnson.
Digital Coordinator.—Emmanuel Vega.
Executive Assistant.—Christian Hollowell.
Staff Assistant.—Geremiah Lofton.
Subcommittee Clerk.—Taylor Jones.

Shared Staff:
Chief Administrative Officer.—Natalie Nixon.
Clerks: Marc Johnson, Nicholas Johnson.
GPO Detailee.—Heather Crowell.

Minority Staff Director.—Christopher Vieson (FHOB–117).
Deputy Staff Directors: Geoff Gosselin, Kathy Loden, Michael Kirlin.
General Counsel.—Forrest McConnell.
Staff Directors:
Subcommittee on Border Security, Facilitation, and Operations.—Emily Trapani.
Subcommittee on Cybersecurity, Infrastructure Protection, and Innovation.—Sarah Moxley.
Subcommittee on Emergency Preparedness, Response, and Communications.—Diana Bergwin.
Subcommittee on Intelligence and Counterterrorism.—Mandy Bowers.
Subcommittee on Oversight, Management, and Accountability.—Kathleen Flynn.
Subcommittee on Transportation and Maritime Security.—Kyle Klein.
Members Services.—Katherine Pointer.
Communications Director.—Nicole Hager.
Press / Staff Assistant.—Emily Bondi.
Professional Staff: Kyle Noyes, Joshua Ronk.
Research Assistant.—Colin Meehan.
Staff Assistant.—Meagan Devlin.

House Administration

1309 Longworth House Office Building, phone 225–2061, fax 226–2774

https://cha.house.gov

Zoe Lofgren, of California, *Chairperson*

Jamie Raskin, of Maryland, *Vice Chairman*

Susan A. Davis, of California.
G. K. Butterfield, of North Carolina.
Marcia L. Fudge, of Ohio.
Pete Aguilar, of California.

Rodney Davis, of Illinois.
Mark Walker, of North Carolina.
Barry Loudermilk, of Georgia.

Elections

Marcia L. Fudge, of Ohio, *Chair*

G. K. Butterfield, of North Carolina.
Pete Aguilar, of California.

Rodney Davis, of Illinois.

STAFF

Committee on House Administration (1309 LHOB), 5–2061.
Majority Staff:
Staff Director.—Jamie Fleet (1309 LHOB), 5–2061.
Deputy Staff Directors: Khalil Abboud, Teri Morgan.
Chief Clerk.—Eddie Flaherty.
Chief Counsel.—Daniel Taylor.
Director of Members Services.—Robert Henline.
Communications Director.—Peter Whippy.
Senior Elections Counsel.—Stephen Spaulding.
Elections Counsel: Georgina Cannan, Sarah Nasta, Giancarlo Pellegrini.
Legislative Clerk.—Sean Jones.
Parliamentarian.—David Tucker.
Press Secretary.—Mannal Haddad.
Oversight Counsel: Kemba Hendrix, Aaron LaSure, Matthew Schlesinger.
Staff Assistants: Hector Arias, Hannah Carr, Mariam Malik.
Minority Staff:
Staff Director.—Jennifer Daulby (1316 LHOB), 5–8281.
Director, Oversight.—Timothy Monahan.
General Counsel.—Cole Felder.
Director of:
Administrative Operations.—Mary Sue Englund.
Member Services.—Brittany Randall.
Communications Director.—Courtney Parella.
Counsel.—Jesse Roberts.
Professional Staff: Nicholas Crocker, Janet Schwalb.
Staff Assistant.—Roberto Estrada Lobo.

Commission on Congressional Mailing Standards (1307 LHOB), 5–9337.
Staff Director.—Matthew DeFreitas.
Minority Staff Director.—Timothy Sullivan.

Judiciary

2138 Rayburn House Office Building, phone 225–3951

https://judiciary.house.gov

Jerrold Nadler, of New York, *Chair*

Zoe Lofgren, of California.
Sheila Jackson Lee, of Texas.
Steve Cohen, of Tennessee.
Henry C. ''Hank'' Johnson, Jr., of Georgia.
Theodore E. Deutch, of Florida.
Karen Bass, of California.
Cedric L. Richmond, of Louisiana.
Hakeem S. Jeffries, of New York.
David N. Cicilline, of Rhode Island.
Eric Swalwell, of California.
Ted Lieu, of California.
Jamie Raskin, of Maryland.
Pramila Jayapal, of Washington.
Val Butler Demings, of Florida.
J. Luis Correa, of California.
Mary Gay Scanlon, of Pennsylvania.
Sylvia R. Garcia, of Texas.
Joe Neguse, of Colorado.
Lucy McBath, of Georgia.
Greg Stanton, of Arizona.
Madeleine Dean, of Pennsylvania.
Debbie Mucarsel-Powell, of Florida.
Veronica Escobar, of Texas.

Jim Jordan, of Ohio.
Doug Collins, of Georgia.
F. James Sensenbrenner, Jr., of Wisconsin.
Steve Chabot, of Ohio.
Louie Gohmert, of Texas.
Ken Buck, of Colorado.
Martha Roby, of Alabama.
Matt Gaetz, of Florida.
Mike Johnson, of Louisiana.
Andy Biggs, of Arizona.
Tom McClintock, of California.
Debbie Lesko, of Arizona.
Guy Reschenthaler, of Pennsylvania.
Ben Cline, of Virginia.
Kelly Armstrong, of North Dakota.
W. Gregory Steube, of Florida.
Thomas P. Tiffany, of Wisconsin.

SUBCOMMITTEES

[The chair and the ranking minority member are ex officio (non-voting) members of all subcommittees on which they do not serve.]

Antitrust, Commercial, and Administrative Law

David N. Cicilline, of Rhode Island, *Chair*

Henry C. ''Hank'' Johnson, Jr., of Georgia.
Jamie Raskin, of Maryland.
Pramila Jayapal, of Washington.
Val Butler Demings, of Florida.
Mary Gay Scanlon, of Pennsylvania.
Joe Neguse, of Colorado.
Lucy McBath, of Georgia.

F. James Sensenbrenner, Jr., of Wisconsin.
Ken Buck, of Colorado.
Matt Gaetz, of Florida.
Kelly Armstrong, of North Dakota.
W. Gregory Steube, of Florida.

The Constitution, Civil Rights, and Civil Liberties

Steve Cohen, of Tennessee, *Chair*

Jamie Raskin, of Maryland.
Eric Swalwell, of California.
Mary Gay Scanlon, of Pennsylvania.
Madeleine Dean, of Pennsylvania.
Sylvia R. Garcia, of Texas.
Veronica Escobar, of Texas.
Sheila Jackson Lee, of Texas.

Mike Johnson, of Louisiana.
Louie Gohmert, of Texas.
Doug Collins, of Georgia.
Guy Reschenthaler, of Pennsylvania.
Ben Cline, of Virginia.
Kelly Armstrong, of North Dakota.

Courts, Intellectual Property, and the Internet

Henry C. ''Hank'' Johnson, Jr., of Georgia, *Chair*

Theodore E. Deutch, of Florida.
Cedric L. Richmond, of Louisiana.
Hakeem S. Jeffries, of New York.
Ted Lieu, of California.
Greg Stanton, of Arizona.
Zoe Lofgren, of California.
Steve Cohen, of Tennessee.
Karen Bass, of California.
Eric Swalwell, of California.
J. Luis Correa, of California.

Martha Roby, of Alabama.
Steve Chabot, of Ohio.
Doug Collins, of Georgia.
Matt Gaetz, of Florida.
Mike Johnson, of Louisiana.
Andy Biggs, of Arizona.
Guy Reschenthaler, of Pennsylvania.
Ben Cline, of Virginia.
Thomas P. Tiffany, of Wisconsin.

Crime, Terrorism, and Homeland Security

Karen Bass, of California, *Chair*

Sheila Jackson Lee, of Texas.
Val Butler Demings, of Florida.
Lucy McBath, of Georgia.
Theodore E. Deutch, of Florida.
Cedric L. Richmond, of Louisiana.
Hakeem S. Jeffries, of New York.
David N. Cicilline, of Rhode Island.
Ted Lieu, of California.
Madeleine Dean, of Pennsylvania.
Debbie Mucarsel-Powell, of Florida.
Steve Cohen, of Tennessee.

F. James Sensenbrenner, Jr., of Wisconsin.
Steve Chabot, of Ohio.
Louie Gohmert, of Texas.
Tom McClintock, of California.
Debbie Lesko, of Arizona.
Guy Reschenthaler, of Pennsylvania.
Ben Cline, of Virginia.
W. Gregory Steube, of Florida.
Thomas P. Tiffany, of Wisconsin.
Vacant.

Immigration and Citizenship

Zoe Lofgren, of California, *Chair*

Pramila Jayapal, of Washington.
J. Luis Correa, of California.
Sylvia R. Garcia, of Texas.
Joe Neguse, of Colorado.
Debbie Mucarsel-Powell, of Florida.
Veronica Escobar, of Texas.
Sheila Jackson Lee, of Texas.
Mary Gay Scanlon, of Pennsylvania.

Ken Buck, of Colorado.
Andy Biggs, of Arizona.
Tom McClintock, of California.
Debbie Lesko, of Arizona.
Kelly Armstrong, of North Dakota.
W. Gregory Steube, of Florida.

STAFF

Committee on the Judiciary (2138 RHOB), 225–3951.
Majority Chief Counsel and Staff Director.—Perry Apelbaum, 2142 Rayburn, 225–6504.
Chief of Staff.—Amy Rutkin.
Senior Counsel: David Greengrass, Keenan Keller.
Deputy Chief Counsel, Oversight.—Aaron Hiller.
Oversight Counsel: Charles Gayle, Arya Hariharan.
Administrative Operations Director.—Kingsley Animley.
Member Services/Outreach Advisor.—Moh Sharma.
Communications Director.—Shadawn Reddick-Smith.
Strategic Communications Director.—Daniel Schwarz.
Senior Advisor.—John Doty.
Staff Assistant.—Julian Gerson.
Financial Administrator.—Patrick Baugh.
Chief Clerk.—Madeline Strasser.
Publications Clerk.—Tim Pearson.

Antitrust, Commercial and Administrative Law Subcommittee 6240 O'Neill, 226–7680.
Majority Chief Counsel.—Slade Bond.
Majority Counsel.—Lina Khan.
Majority Professional Staff: Joe Ehrenkrantz, Joseph Van Wye.
Minority Chief Counsel.—Daniel Flores.
Constitution, Civil Rights, and Civil Liberties Subcommittee H2–362 Ford, 225–2825.
Majority Chief Counsel.—James Park.
Majority Counsel: Sophia Brill, Matthew Morgan.
Majority Professional Staff.—Jordan Dashow, William Emmons.
Minority Chief Counsel.—Paul Taylor.
Courts, Intellectual Property, and the Internet Subcommittee 6310 O'Neill, 225–5741.
Majority Chief Counsel.—Jamie Simpson.
Majority Professional Staff.—Rosalind Jackson.
Minority Counsel.—Thomas Stoll.
Minority Clerk.—Andrea Woodard.
Crime, Terrorism, and Homeland Security Subcommittee 6340 O'Neill, 225–5727, fax 225–3672.
Majority Chief Counsel.—Joe Graupensperger.
Majority Deputy Chief Counsel.—Monalisa Dugue.
Majority Counsel.—Benjamin Hernandez-Stein, Rachel Rossi.
Majority Professional Staff: Veronica Eligan.
Minority Chief Counsels: Ryan Breitenbach, Jason Cervenak.
Immigration and Citizenship Subcommittee 6320 O'Neill, 225–3926, fax 225–3737.
Majority Chief Counsel.—David Shahoulian.
Majority Counsel: Joshua Breisblatt, Betsy Lawrence, Ami Shah.
Majority Professional Staff.—Rachel Calanni.
Minority Chief Counsel.—Andrea Loving.

IT Office 2451 Rayburn.
Majority Director of Information Technology.—Janna Pinckney.
Majority Deputy Director of Information Technology.—Faisal Siddiqui.
Minority Director of Information Technology.—Stacy Baker.

Minority Offices B–2035 Rayburn, H2–252 Ford, and H2–189 Ford, 225–6906, fax 225–7682.
Minority Staff Director.—Brendan Belair.
Deputy Staff Director.—Robert Parmiter.
Policy Advisor.—Sally Larson.
Chief Oversight Counsel.—Carlton Davis.
Counsel and Senior Advisor.—Ashley Callen.
Counsel and Parliamentarian.—Jonathan Ferro.
Chief Legislative Clerk.—Erica Barker.
Communications Director.—Jessica Andrews.
Digital Director.—Anne Richardson.
Member Services and Coalitions Director.—Ella Yates.
Counsel.—Daniel Ashworth.
Investigative Counsel.—Daniel Johnson.
Press Secretary.—Amy Hasenberg.

Natural Resources

1324 Longworth House Office Building, phone 225–6065

https://naturalresources.house.gov

Raúl M. Grijalva, of Arizona, *Chair*

Grace F. Napolitano, of California.
Jim Costa, of California.
Gregorio Kilili Camacho Sablan, of Northern Mariana Islands.
Jared Huffman, of California.
Alan S. Lowenthal, of California.
Ruben Gallego, of Arizona.
TJ Cox, of California.
Joe Neguse, of Colorado.
Mike Levin, of California.
Debra A. Haaland, of New Mexico.
Joe Cunningham, of South Carolina.
Nydia M. Velázquez, of New York.
Diana DeGette, of Colorado.
Wm. Lacy Clay, of Missouri.
Debbie Dingell, of Michigan.
Anthony G. Brown, of Maryland.
A. Donald McEachin, of Virginia.
Darren Soto, of Florida.
Ed Case, of Hawaii.
Steven Horsford, of Nevada.
Michael F. Q. San Nicolas, of Guam.
Matt Cartwright, of Pennsylvania.
Paul Tonko, of New York.
Jesús G. ''Chuy'' García, of Illinois.
Vacant.

Rob Bishop, of Utah.
Don Young, of Alaska.
Louie Gohmert, of Texas.
Doug Lamborn, of Colorado.
Robert J. Wittman, of Virginia.
Tom McClintock, of California.
Paul A. Gosar, of Arizona.
Paul Cook, of California.
Bruce Westerman, of Arkansas.
Garret Graves, of Louisiana.
Jody B. Hice, of Georgia.
Aumua Amata Coleman Radewagen, of American Samoa.
Daniel Webster, of Florida.
Liz Cheney, of Wyoming.
Mike Johnson, of Louisiana.
Jenniffer González-Colón, of Puerto Rico.
John R. Curtis, of Utah.
Kevin Hern, of Oklahoma.
Russ Fulcher, of Idaho.
Pete Stauber, of Minnesota.

SUBCOMMITTEES

[The chair and ranking minority member are ex officio (non-voting) members of all subcommittees on which they do not serve.]

Energy and Mineral Resources

Alan S. Lowenthal, of California, *Chair*

Mike Levin, of California.
Joe Cunningham, of South Carolina.
A. Donald McEachin, of Virginia.
Diana DeGette, of Colorado.
Anthony G. Brown, of Maryland.
Jared Huffman, of California.
Matt Cartwright, of Pennsylvania.

Paul A. Gosar, of Arizona.
Doug Lamborn, of Colorado.
Bruce Westerman, of Arkansas.
Garret Graves, of Louisiana.
Liz Cheney, of Wyoming.
Kevin Hern, of Oklahoma.

Indigenous Peoples of the United States

Ruben Gallego, of Arizona, *Chair*

Darren Soto, of Florida.
Michael F. Q. San Nicolas, of Guam.
Debra A. Haaland, of New Mexico.
Ed Case, of Hawaii.
Matt Cartwright, of Pennsylvania.
Jesús G. ''Chuy'' García, of Illinois.
Vacant.

Paul Cook, of California.
Don Young, of Alaska.
Aumua Amata Coleman Radewagen, of American Samoa.
John R. Curtis, of Utah.
Kevin Hern, of Oklahoma.
Vacant.

National Parks, Forests, and Public Lands

Debra A. Haaland, of New Mexico, *Chair*

Joe Neguse, of Colorado.
Diana DeGette, of Colorado.
Debbie Dingell, of Michigan.
Steven Horsford, of Nevada.
Jared Huffman, of California.
Ruben Gallego, of Arizona.
Alan S. Lowenthal, of California.
Ed Case, of Hawaii.
Paul Tonko, of New York.
Jesús G. "Chuy" García, of Illinois.

Don Young, of Alaska.
Louie Gohmert, of Texas.
Tom McClintock, of California.
Paul Cook, of California.
Bruce Westerman, of Arkansas.
Jody B. Hice, of Georgia.
Daniel Webster, of Florida.
John R. Curtis, of Utah.
Russ Fulcher, of Idaho.

Oversight and Investigations

TJ Cox, of California, *Chair*

Debbie Dingell, of Michigan.
A. Donald McEachin, of Virginia.
Michael F. Q. San Nicolas, of Guam.
Raúl M. Grijalva, of Arizona.

Louie Gohmert, of Texas.
Paul A. Gosar, of Arizona.
Mike Johnson, of Louisiana.
Jenniffer González-Colón, of Puerto Rico.

Water, Oceans, and Wildlife

Jared Huffman, of California, *Chair*

Grace F. Napolitano, of California.
Jim Costa, of California.
Gregorio Kilili Camacho Sablan, of Northern Mariana Islands.
Nydia M. Velázquez, of New York.
Anthony G. Brown, of Maryland.
Ed Case, of Hawaii.
Alan S. Lowenthal, of California.
TJ Cox, of California.
Joe Neguse, of Colorado.
Mike Levin, of California.
Joe Cunningham, of South Carolina.
Debbie Dingell, of Michigan.

Tom McClintock, of California.
Doug Lamborn, of Colorado.
Robert J. Wittman, of Virginia.
Garret Graves, of Louisiana.
Jody B. Hice, of Georgia.
Aumua Amata Coleman Radewagen, of American Samoa.
Daniel Webster, of Florida.
Mike Johnson, of Louisiana.
Jenniffer González-Colón, of Puerto Rico.
Russ Fulcher, of Idaho.

STAFF

Committee on Natural Resources (1324 LHOB) 5–6065.
Majority Staff Director.—David Watkins, 5–6065.
Deputy Staff Directors: Steve Feldgus, Chris Kaumo.
Director of Operations.—Ilene Clauson.
Staff Assistant.—Carlyn LeGrant.
Calendar Clerk.—Joycelyn Coleman.
Information Technology Director.—David DeMarco.
Information Technology Deputy Director.—Everett Winnick.
Chief Counsel.—Sarah Lim.
Deputy Chief Counsel.—Luis Urbina.
Senior Policy Advisor.—Glenn Miller.
Chief Clerk.—Nancy Locke.
Director of Investigations.—Vic Edgerton.
Director of Community Relations.—Chris Espinosa.
Content and Multimedia Producer.—David Shen.
Member Services and Outreach Coordinator.—Tariq Zahran.
Scheduler.—Cristina Villa.
Minority Staff Director.—Parish Braden (1329 LHOB) 5–2761.
Chief Counsel.—Lisa Pittman.
Senior Advisor.—Tanner Hanson.
Communications (1334 LHOB) 5–6065.
Majority Communications Director.—Adam Sarvana, 5–6065.

Deputy Communications Director.—Monica Sanchez.
Digital Director.—Katy Schafer.
Minority Director of Communications.—Kristina Baum (1329 LHOB), 5–2761.
Minority Deputy Press Secretary.—Austin Hacker.
Office of Insular Affairs (186 FHOB) 5–6065.
Director.—Brian Modeste.
Professional Staff: Johnathan Garza, Margarita Varela-Rosa.
Subcommittee on Energy and Mineral Resources (1522 LHOB) 5–6065.
Majority Staff Director.—Steve Feldgus, 5–6065.
Professional Staff: Becky Cairns, Peter Gallagher.
Policy Aide.—Sarina Weiss.
Minority Professional Staff: Rebecca Konolige, Ashley Nichols (4120 LHOB) 5–2761.
Subcommittee for Indigenous Peoples of the United States (1331 LHOB) 5–6065.
Majority Staff Director.—Chris Kaumo (1413A LHOB) 5–6065.
Professional Staff Member.—Naomi Miguel.
Policy Aide.—Ariana Romeo.
Minority Staff Director.—Chris Fluhr (4450 OHOB) 5–2761.
Professional Staff.—Ken Degenfelder.
Subcommittee on National Parks, Forests, and Public Lands (1328 LHOB) 5–6065.
Majority Staff Director.—Brandon Bragato.
Professional Staff: Chris Rackins, Henry Wykowski.
Policy Aide.—Lily Wang.
Minority Staff Director.—Steven Petersen (4170 OHOB) 5–2761.
Professional Staff: Terry Camp, Brandon Miller.
Subcommittee on Oversight and Investigations (186 FHOB) 5–6065.
Majority Staff Director.—Vic Edgerton (186 FHOB) 5–6065.
Policy Aide.—Auburn Bell.
Professional Staff.—Lindsay Gressard.
Minority Staff Director.—Sang Yi (4170 LHOB) 5–2761.
Subcommittee on Water, Oceans, and Wildlife (1332 LHOB) 5–6065.
Majority Staff Director (Water).—Matthew Muirragui.
Professional Staff Members: Carlee Brown, Marnie Kremer.
Majority Staff Director (Oceans and Wildlife).—Lora Snyder.
Professional Staff.—Rachel Gentile.
Minority Staff Director.—William Ball (4120 OHOB) 5–2761.
Professional Staff: Marc Alberts, Mary Youpel.

Oversight and Reform

2157 Rayburn House Office Building, phone 225–5051, fax 225–4784, TTY 225–6852

https://oversight.house.gov

Carolyn B. Maloney, of New York, *Chair*

Eleanor Holmes Norton, of District of Columbia.
Wm. Lacy Clay, of Missouri.
Stephen F. Lynch, of Massachusetts.
Jim Cooper, of Tennessee.
Gerald E. Connolly, of Virginia.
Raja Krishnamoorthi, of Illinois.
Jamie Raskin, of Maryland.
Harley Rouda, of California.
Ro Khanna, of California.
Kweisi Mfume, of Maryland.
Debbie Wasserman Schultz, of Florida.
John P. Sarbanes, of Maryland.
Peter Welch, of Vermont.
Jackie Speier, of California.
Robin L. Kelly, of Illinois.
Mark DeSaulnier, of California.
Brenda L. Lawrence, of Michigan.
Stacey E. Plaskett, of Virgin Islands.
Jimmy Gomez, of California.
Alexandria Ocasio-Cortez, of New York.
Ayanna Pressley, of Massachusetts.
Rashida Tlaib, of Michigan.
Katie Porter, of California.

James Comer, of Kentucky.
Jim Jordan, of Ohio.
Paul A. Gosar, of Arizona.
Virginia Foxx, of North Carolina.
Thomas Massie, of Kentucky.
Jody B. Hice, of Georgia.
Glenn Grothman, of Wisconsin.
Gary J. Palmer, of Alabama.
Michael Cloud, of Texas.
Bob Gibbs, of Ohio.
Clay Higgins, of Louisiana.
Ralph Norman, of South Carolina.
Chip Roy, of Texas.
Carol D. Miller, of West Virginia.
Mark E. Green, of Tennessee.
Kelly Armstrong, of North Dakota.
W. Gregory Steube, of Florida.
Fred Keller, of Pennsylvania.

SUBCOMMITTEES

[The chair and ranking minority member are ex officio (voting) members of all subcommittees.]

Civil Rights and Civil Liberties

Jamie Raskin, of Maryland, *Chair*

Wm. Lacy Clay, of Missouri.
Debbie Wasserman Schultz, of Florida.
Robin L. Kelly, of Illinois.
Jimmy Gomez, of California.
Alexandria Ocasio-Cortez, of New York.
Ayanna Pressley, of Massachusetts.
Eleanor Holmes Norton, of District of Columbia.
Vacant.

Chip Roy, of Texas.
Thomas Massie, of Kentucky.
Jody B. Hice, of Georgia.
Michael Cloud, of Texas.
Carol D. Miller, of West Virginia.
Fred Keller, of Pennsylvania.
Vacant.

Economic and Consumer Policy

Raja Krishnamoorthi, of Illinois, *Chair*

Mark DeSaulnier, of California.
Ro Khanna, of California.
Ayanna Pressley, of Massachusetts.
Rashida Tlaib, of Michigan.
Gerald E. Connolly, of Virginia.
Katie Porter, of California.

Michael Cloud, of Texas.
Glenn Grothman, of Wisconsin.
James Comer, of Kentucky.
Chip Roy, of Texas.
Carol D. Miller, of West Virginia.

Environment

Harley Rouda, of California, *Chair*

Rashida Tlaib, of Michigan.
Raja Krishnamoorthi, of Illinois.
Jackie Speier, of California.
Jimmy Gomez, of California.
Alexandria Ocasio-Cortez, of New York.
Eleanor Holmes Norton, of District of Columbia.
Mark E. Green, of Tennessee.
Paul A. Gosar, of Arizona.
Bob Gibbs, of Ohio.
Kelly Armstrong, of North Dakota.
Fred Keller, of Pennsylvania.

Government Operations

Gerald E. Connolly, of Virginia, *Chair*

Eleanor Holmes Norton, of District of Columbia.
John P. Sarbanes, of Maryland.
Jackie Speier, of California.
Brenda L. Lawrence, of Michigan.
Stacey E. Plaskett, of Virgin Islands.
Ro Khanna, of California.
Stephen F. Lynch, of Massachusetts.
Jamie Raskin, of Maryland.
Jody B. Hice, of Georgia.
Thomas Massie, of Kentucky.
Glenn Grothman, of Wisconsin.
Gary J. Palmer, of Alabama.
Ralph Norman, of South Carolina.
W. Gregory Steube, of Florida.
Vacant.

National Security

Stephen F. Lynch, of Massachusetts, *Chair*

Jim Cooper, of Tennessee.
Peter Welch, of Vermont.
Harley Rouda, of California.
Debbie Wasserman Schultz, of Florida.
Robin L. Kelly, of Illinois.
Mark DeSaulnier, of California.
Stacey E. Plaskett, of Virgin Islands.
Brenda L. Lawrence, of Michigan.
Glenn Grothman, of Wisconsin.
Paul A. Gosar, of Arizona.
Virginia Foxx, of North Carolina.
Michael Cloud, of Texas.
Mark E. Green, of Tennessee.
Clay Higgins, of Louisiana.
Vacant.

Select Subcommittee on the Coronavirus Crisis

James E. Clyburn, of South Carolina, *Chair*

Maxine Waters, of California.
Carolyn B. Maloney, of New York.
Nydia M. Velázquez, of New York.
Bill Foster, of Illinois.
Jamie Raskin, of Maryland.
Andy Kim, of New Jersey.
Steve Scalise, of Louisiana.
Jim Jordan, of Ohio.
Blaine Luetkemeyer, of Missouri.
Jackie Walorski, of Indiana.
Mark E. Green, of Tennessee.

STAFF

Oversight and Government Reform (2157 RHOB) (202) 225–5051.
Majority Staff Director.—Dave Rapallo.
Deputy Staff Director/Chief Counsel.—Susanne Grooms.
Administrative Director.—Jaron Bourke.
General Counsel.—Krista Boyd.
Deputy General Counsel.—Jason Powell.
Communications Director.—Aryele Bradford.
Chief Clerk, Operations Director.—Elisa LaNier.
Deputy Chief Clerk.—Amy Stratton.
Assistant Clerk.—Joshua Zucker.
Financial Administrative Manager.—Robin Butler.
Executive Assistant.—Trinity Goss.
Legislative Directors: Yvette Badu-Nimako, Mark Stephenson.
Chief Oversight Counsel.—Russell Anello.
Parliamentarian/Senior Counsel.—Kellie Larkin.
Senior Counsel.—Courtney French.
Chief Health Counsel.—Alexandra Golden.
Chief Counsel for Investigations.—Janet Kim.
Chief Investigative Counsel.—Peter Kenny.
Counsel/Policy Advisor.—Jordan Blumenthal.
Counsel: Tori Anderson, Aaron Blacksberg, Theresa Chalhoub, Kadeem Cooper, Cassandra Fields, Greta Gao, Jennifer Gaspar, Jessica Heller, Keith Kiles, Gina Kim, Amish Shah, Bradley Truding, Laura Waters.
Chief Advisor for Policy, Strategy, and Communications.—Tyler Grimm.
Senior Policy Advisor.—Christina Parisi.
Policy Advisor.—Kelly Hennessy.
Press Secretaries: Jamitress Bowden, Andrew Eichar.
Senior Advisor.—Maxwell Whitcomb.
Senior Executive Counselor.—Chioma Chukwu.
Senior Counselor.—Benjamin Harney.
Professional Staff Members: Bruce Fernandez, Miles Lichtman.
Systems Administrator.—William Benjamin.
Technology Director.—Eddie Walker.

2105 Rayburn House Office Building (2471 RHOB) 225–5074, fax 225–3974.
Minority Staff Director.—Christopher Hixon.
Deputy Staff Director.—David Brewer.
General Counsel.—Steve Castor.
Senior Counsel.—Betsy Ferguson.
Counsel: Mitchell Benzine, Deep Buddharaju, Kenneth David, Lauren Holmes, James Lesinski, Caroline Nabity, Kyle Smithwick.
Director of Information Technology.—Stacy Baker.
Oversight Director.—Mark Marin.
Policy Director.—Katy Rother.
Deputy Policy Director.—Christian Hoehner.
Communications Counsel.—Russell Dye.
Press Secretary.—Charli Huddleston.
Clerk.—Kiley Bidelman.
Senior Professional Staff Member.—Ellen Johnson.
Professional Staff Members: Michael Koren, Stephen Gordon.
Outreach Director/Senior Professional Staff Member.—Sarah Vance.
Executive Assistant.—Sarah Feeney.
Press Assistant.—Adeline Perkins.
Staff Assistant.—Brandon Jacobs.

Civil Rights and Civil Liberties Subcommittee.
Staff Director.—Candyce Phoenix.
Chief Counsel/Senior Policy Advisor.—Valerie Shen.

Economic and Consumer Policy Subcommittee.
Staff Director.—Richard Trumka.
Chief Counsel/Senior Policy Advisor.—William Cunningham.

Environment Subcommittee.
Staff Director.—Britteny Jenkins.
Government Operations Subcommittee.
Staff Director.—Wendy Ginsberg.
Deputy Staff Director.—Kristine Lam.
National Security Subcommittee.
Staff Director.—Daniel Rebnord.
Deputy Staff Director.—Bruce Fernandez.

Rules

H–312 The Capitol, phone 225–9091

https://rules.house.gov

James P. McGovern, of Massachusetts, *Chair*

Alcee L. Hastings, of Florida.
Norma J. Torres, of California.
Ed Perlmutter, of Colorado.
Jamie Raskin, of Maryland.
Mary Gay Scanlon, of Pennsylvania.
Joseph D. Morelle, of New York.
Donna E. Shalala, of Florida.
Doris O. Matsui, of California.

Tom Cole, of Oklahoma.
Rob Woodall, of Georgia.
Michael C. Burgess, of Texas.
Debbie Lesko, of Arizona.

SUBCOMMITTEES

Expedited Procedures

Jamie Raskin, of Maryland, *Chair*

Donna E. Shalala, of Florida, *Vice Chair*

Norma J. Torres, of California.
James P. McGovern, of Massachusetts.
Vacant.

Michael C. Burgess, of Texas.
Debbie Lesko, of Arizona.

Legislative and Budget Process

Alcee L. Hastings, of Florida, *Chair*

Joseph D. Morelle, of New York, *Vice Chair*

Mary Gay Scanlon, of Pennsylvania.
Donna E. Shalala, of Florida.
James P. McGovern, of Massachusetts.

Rob Woodall, of Georgia.
Michael C. Burgess, of Texas.

Rules and Organization of the House

Norma J. Torres, of California, *Chair*

Ed Perlmutter, of Colorado, *Vice Chair*

Mary Gay Scanlon, of Pennsylvania.
Joseph D. Morelle, of New York.
James P. McGovern, of Massachusetts.

Debbie Lesko, of Arizona.
Rob Woodall, of Georgia.

STAFF

Committee on Rules (H–312 The Capitol), 225–9091.
Majority Staff Director.—Don Sisson.
Deputy Staff Director.—Liz Pardue.
Policy Director.—Caitlin Hodgkins.
Director of Legislative Operations.—Nate Perkins.
Communications Director.—Jeff Gohringer.
Senior Advisors: Kim Corbin, Dan Turton.
Professional Staff: Eric Delaney, Lori Ismail, Rose Laughlin, Matt Price.
Deputy Clerk.—Jessica Suh.
Digital Manager.—Mary Lieb.
Staff Assistants: Ana Martinez, Sam Russell.
Minority Staff Director.—Kelly Dixon.
Policy Director.—Matthew Diller.
Communications Director.—Sarah Corley.
Director of Operations.—Chris Erb.
Senior Professional Staff: Jennifer Belair, James Fitzella, Steve Waskiewicz.
Professional Staff: Hannah Gill, Eric Shepard.
Research Associate.—Drew Roberts.

Science, Space, and Technology

2321 Rayburn House Office Building, phone 225–6375, fax 225–3895

https://science.house.gov

Eddie Bernice Johnson, of Texas, *Chair*

Ami Bera, of California, *Vice Chair*

Zoe Lofgren, of California.
Daniel Lipinski, of Illinois.
Suzanne Bonamici, of Oregon.
Lizzie Fletcher, of Texas.
Haley M. Stevens, of Michigan.
Kendra S. Horn, of Oklahoma.
Mikie Sherrill, of New Jersey.
Brad Sherman, of California.
Steve Cohen, of Tennessee.
Jerry McNerney, of California.
Ed Perlmutter, of Colorado.
Paul Tonko, of New York.
Bill Foster, of Illinois.
Donald S. Beyer, Jr., of Virginia.
Charlie Crist, of Florida.
Sean Casten, of Illinois.
Ben McAdams, of Utah.
Jennifer Wexton, of Virginia.
Conor Lamb, of Pennsylvania.
Vacant.

Frank D. Lucas, of Oklahoma.
Mo Brooks, of Alabama.
Bill Posey, of Florida.
Randy K. Weber, Sr., of Texas.
Brian Babin, of Texas.
Andy Biggs, of Arizona.
Roger W. Marshall, of Kansas.
Ralph Norman, of South Carolina.
Michael Cloud, of Texas.
Troy Balderson, of Ohio.
Anthony Gonzalez, of Ohio.
Michael Waltz, of Florida.
James R. Baird, of Indiana.
Francis Rooney, of Florida.
Gregory F. Murphy, of North Carolina.
Mike Garcia, of California.
Thomas P. Tiffany, of Wisconsin.

SUBCOMMITTEES

[The chair and ranking minority member are ex officio (voting) members of all subcommittees on which they do not serve.]

Energy

Lizzie Fletcher, of Texas, *Chair*

Daniel Lipinski, of Illinois.
Haley M. Stevens, of Michigan.
Kendra S. Horn, of Oklahoma.
Jerry McNerney, of California.
Bill Foster, of Illinois.
Sean Casten, of Illinois.
Conor Lamb, of Pennsylvania.

Randy K. Weber, Sr., of Texas.
Andy Biggs, of Arizona.
Ralph Norman, of South Carolina.
Michael Cloud, of Texas.
James R. Baird, of Indiana.

Environment

Mikie Sherrill, of New Jersey, *Chair*

Suzanne Bonamici, of Oregon.
Lizzie Fletcher, of Texas.
Paul Tonko, of New York.
Charlie Crist, of Florida.
Sean Casten, of Illinois.
Ben McAdams, of Utah.
Conor Lamb, of Pennsylvania.

Roger W. Marshall, of Kansas.
Brian Babin, of Texas.
Anthony Gonzalez, of Ohio.
Francis Rooney, of Florida.
Gregory F. Murphy, of North Carolina.

Investigations and Oversight

Bill Foster, of Illinois, *Chair*

Suzanne Bonamici, of Oregon.
Steve Cohen, of Tennessee.
Donald S. Beyer, Jr., of Virginia.
Jennifer Wexton, of Virginia.

Ralph Norman, of South Carolina.
Andy Biggs, of Arizona.
Michael Waltz, of Florida.

Research and Technology

Haley M. Stevens, of Michigan, *Chair*

Daniel Lipinski, of Illinois.
Mikie Sherrill, of New Jersey.
Brad Sherman, of California.
Paul Tonko, of New York.
Ben McAdams, of Utah.
Steve Cohen, of Tennessee.
Bill Foster, of Illinois.

James R. Baird, of Indiana.
Roger W. Marshall, of Kansas.
Troy Balderson, of Ohio.
Anthony Gonzalez, of Ohio.
Thomas P. Tiffany, of Wisconsin.

Space and Aeronautics

Kendra S. Horn, of Oklahoma, *Chair*

Zoe Lofgren, of California.
Ami Bera, of California.
Ed Perlmutter, of Colorado.
Donald S. Beyer, Jr., of Virginia.
Charlie Crist, of Florida.
Jennifer Wexton, of Virginia.
Vacant.

Brian Babin, of Texas.
Mo Brooks, of Alabama.
Bill Posey, of Florida.
Michael Waltz, of Florida.
Mike Garcia, of California.

STAFF

Committee on Science, Space, and Technology (2321 RHOB), 225–6375, fax 225–3895.

Majority Staff:

Chief of Staff.—Richard Obermann.

Administration:

Administrative and Member Services Director.—Kristin Kopshever.
Communications Director.—Rebekah Eskandani.
Systems Administrator.—Larry Whittaker.
Clerk.—Kendra Wood.
Policy & Executive Assistant.—Emily McAuliffe.
Staff Assistant.—Jona Koka.
Press Assistant.—Cassie Anderson.

Counsel:

Chief Counsel.—John Piazza.
Deputy Chief Counsel.—Stanton Johnson.

Energy Subcommittee

Staff Director.—Adam Rosenberg.
Professional Staff.—Tanya Das.
Research Assistants: James Green, Sangina Wright.

Environment Subcommittee

Staff Director.—Priyanka Hooghan.
Professional Staff.—Lauren Linsmayer.
Research Assistant.—Aria Kovalovich.

Investigations and Oversight Subcommittee

Staff Director.—Janie Thompson.
Professional Staff: Sara Palasits, Joshua Schneider.

Research and Technology Subcommittee

Staff Director.—Dahlia Sokolov.
Professional Staff: Sara Barber, Brystol English.
Research Assistant.—Benjamin Berger.

Space and Aeronautics Subcommittee

Staff Director.—Pam Whitney.

Professional Staff.—Ashlee Wilkins.
Research Assistant.—Griffin Reinicke.

Minority Staff:

Staff Director.—Josh Mathis.
Professional Staff Members: Daniel Dziadon, Cate Johnson, Hillary O'Brien.
Senior Policy Advisors: Brent Blevins, Emily Domenech, Tom Hammond, Jenn Wickre.
Counsel.—Tom Connally.
Communications Director.—Heather Vaughan.
Policy Assistant.—Anna Ferrara.
Staff Assistant.—Kelli Liegel.

Small Business

2361 Rayburn House Office Building, phone 225–4038, fax 226–7209

https://smallbusiness.house.gov

Nydia M. Velázquez, of New York, *Chair*

Abby Finkenauer, of Iowa.
Jared F. Golden, of Maine.
Andy Kim, of New Jersey.
Jason Crow, of Colorado.
Sharice Davids, of Kansas.
Kweisi Mfume, of Maryland.
Judy Chu, of California.
Dwight Evans, of Pennsylvania.
Bradley Scott Schneider, of Illinois.
Adriano Espaillat, of New York.
Antonio Delgado, of New York.
Chrissy Houlahan, of Pennsylvania.
Angie Craig, of Minnesota.

Steve Chabot, of Ohio.
Aumua Amata Coleman Radewagen, of American Samoa.
Troy Balderson, of Ohio.
Kevin Hern, of Oklahoma.
Jim Hagedorn, of Minnesota.
Pete Stauber, of Minnesota.
Tim Burchett, of Tennessee.
Ross Spano, of Florida.
John Joyce, of Pennsylvania.
Dan Bishop, of North Carolina.

SUBCOMMITTEES

Contracting and Infrastructure

Jared F. Golden, of Maine, *Chair*

Judy Chu, of California.
Vacant.
Vacant.
Vacant.
Vacant.

Pete Stauber, of Minnesota.
Jim Hagedorn, of Minnesota.
Troy Balderson, of Ohio.
Vacant.

Economic Growth, Tax, and Capital Access

Andy Kim, of New Jersey, *Chair*

Sharice Davids, of Kansas.
Bradley Scott Schneider, of Illinois.
Adriano Espaillat, of New York.
Antonio Delgado, of New York.
Jason Crow, of Colorado.

Kevin Hern, of Oklahoma.
Ross Spano, of Florida.
Aumua Amata Coleman Radewagen, of American Samoa.
Pete Stauber, of Minnesota.

Innovation and Workforce Development

Jason Crow, of Colorado, *Chair*

Chrissy Houlahan, of Pennsylvania.
Abby Finkenauer, of Iowa.
Andy Kim, of New Jersey.
Sharice Davids, of Kansas.
Vacant.

Troy Balderson, of Ohio.
Tim Burchett, of Tennessee.
Kevin Hern, of Oklahoma.
John Joyce, of Pennsylvania.

Investigations, Oversight, and Regulations

Judy Chu, of California, *Chair*

Dwight Evans, of Pennsylvania.
Angie Craig, of Minnesota.
Vacant.
Vacant.
Vacant.

Ross Spano, of Florida.
Tim Burchett, of Tennessee.
Vacant.
Vacant.

Rural Development, Agriculture, Trade and Entrepreneurship

Abby Finkenauer, of Iowa, *Chair*

Jared F. Golden, of Maine.
Jason Crow, of Colorado.
Angie Craig, of Minnesota.
Vacant.
Vacant.

John Joyce, of Pennsylvania.
Aumua Amata Coleman Radewagen, of American Samoa.
Jim Hagedorn, of Minnesota.
Dan Bishop, of North Carolina.

STAFF

Committee on Small Business (2361 RHOB).
Majority Staff:
Staff Director.—Adam Minehardt.
Deputy Staff Director/Chief Counsel.—Melissa Jung.
Office Manager.—Mory Garcia.
Clerk.—Lauren Finks.
Senior Advisors: Alex Haurek, Justin Pelletier.
Senior Economic Advisor.—Gerardo Bonilla.
Communications Director.—Evelyn Quartz.
DC Scheduler.—Richard Bruno.
Counsel.—Matthew Gomez.
Deputy Policy Director.—Ellen Harrington.
Staff Assistant.—Tracy Ennesser.
Professional Staff Member.—Matthew Bowman.
Digital Director/Deputy Press Secretary.—Michael McGinnis.
Policy Director/General Counsel.—Naveen Parmar.
Investigations and Oversight Counsel.—Peter Rechter.
Procurement Counsel.—Irene Rivera Goyco.
Professional Staff Members: Michael Stein, Meagan Sunn.
Minority Staff:
Staff Director.—Kevin Fitzpatrick.
Deputy Staff Director and Chief Counsel.—Jan Oliver.
Policy Director.—Joe Hartz.
Counsel.—Vivian Ling.
Senior Professional Staff.—Robert Yavor.
Professional Staff/Minority Clerk.—Delia Barr.
Staff Assistant/Policy Assistant.—Allison Kerman.
Staff Assistant/Press Assistant.—Rachel Emmons.

Transportation and Infrastructure

2165 Rayburn House Office Building, phone 225–4472

https://transportation.house.gov

Majority (202) 225–4472, Room 2165 RHOB

Minority (202) 225–9446, Room 2163 RHOB

Peter A. DeFazio, of Oregon, *Chair*

Salud O. Carbajal, of California, *Vice Chair*

Eleanor Holmes Norton, of District of Columbia.
Eddie Bernice Johnson, of Texas.
Rick Larsen, of Washington.
Grace F. Napolitano, of California.
Daniel Lipinski, of Illinois.
Steve Cohen, of Tennessee.
Albio Sires, of New Jersey.
John Garamendi, of California.
Henry C. ''Hank'' Johnson, Jr., of Georgia.
André Carson, of Indiana.
Dina Titus, of Nevada.
Sean Patrick Maloney, of New York.
Jared Huffman, of California.
Julia Brownley, of California.
Frederica S. Wilson, of Florida.
Donald M. Payne, Jr., of New Jersey.
Alan S. Lowenthal, of California.
Mark DeSaulnier, of California.
Stacey E. Plaskett, of Virgin Islands.
Stephen F. Lynch, of Massachusetts.
Anthony G. Brown, of Maryland.
Adriano Espaillat, of New York.
Tom Malinowski, of New Jersey.
Greg Stanton, of Arizona.
Debbie Mucarsel-Powell, of Florida.
Lizzie Fletcher, of Texas.
Colin Z. Allred, of Texas.
Sharice Davids, of Kansas.
Abby Finkenauer, of Iowa.
Jesús G. ''Chuy'' García, of Illinois.
Antonio Delgado, of New York.
Chris Pappas, of New Hampshire.
Angie Craig, of Minnesota.
Harley Rouda, of California.
Conor Lamb, of Pennsylvania.

Sam Graves, of Missouri.
Don Young, of Alaska.
Eric A. ''Rick'' Crawford, of Arkansas.
Bob Gibbs, of Ohio.
Daniel Webster, of Florida.
Thomas Massie, of Kentucky.
Scott Perry, of Pennsylvania.
Rodney Davis, of Illinois.
Rob Woodall, of Georgia.
John Katko, of New York.
Brian Babin, of Texas.
Garret Graves, of Louisiana.
David Rouzer, of North Carolina.
Mike Bost, of Illinois.
Randy K. Weber, Sr., of Texas.
Doug LaMalfa, of California.
Bruce Westerman, of Arkansas.
Lloyd Smucker, of Pennsylvania.
Paul Mitchell, of Michigan.
Brian J. Mast, of Florida.
Mike Gallagher, of Wisconsin.
Gary J. Palmer, of Alabama.
Brian K. Fitzpatrick, of Pennsylvania.
Jenniffer González-Colón, of Puerto Rico.
Troy Balderson, of Ohio.
Ross Spano, of Florida.
Pete Stauber, of Minnesota.
Carol D. Miller, of West Virginia.
Greg Pence, of Indiana.
Mike Garcia, of California.

SUBCOMMITTEES

Aviation

Rick Larsen, of Washington, *Chair*

André Carson, of Indiana.
Stacey E. Plaskett, of Virgin Islands.
Stephen F. Lynch, of Massachusetts.
Eleanor Holmes Norton, of District of Columbia.
Daniel Lipinski, of Illinois.
Steve Cohen, of Tennessee.
Henry C. ''Hank'' Johnson, Jr., of Georgia.
Dina Titus, of Nevada.
Julia Brownley, of California.
Anthony G. Brown, of Maryland.
Greg Stanton, of Arizona.
Colin Z. Allred, of Texas.
Jesús G. ''Chuy'' García, of Illinois.
Eddie Bernice Johnson, of Texas.
Sean Patrick Maloney, of New York.
Donald M. Payne, Jr., of New Jersey.
Sharice Davids, of Kansas.
Angie Craig, of Minnesota.
Grace F. Napolitano, of California.
Salud O. Carbajal, of California.

Garret Graves, of Louisiana.
Don Young, of Alaska.
Daniel Webster, of Florida.
Thomas Massie, of Kentucky.
Scott Perry, of Pennsylvania.
Rob Woodall, of Georgia.
John Katko, of New York.
David Rouzer, of North Carolina.
Lloyd Smucker, of Pennsylvania.
Paul Mitchell, of Michigan.
Brian J. Mast, of Florida.
Mike Gallagher, of Wisconsin.
Brian K. Fitzpatrick, of Pennsylvania.
Troy Balderson, of Ohio.
Ross Spano, of Florida.
Pete Stauber, of Minnesota.

Coast Guard and Maritime Transportation

Sean Patrick Maloney, of New York, *Chair*

Rick Larsen, of Washington.
Stacey E. Plaskett, of Virgin Islands.
John Garamendi, of California.
Alan S. Lowenthal, of California.
Anthony G. Brown, of Maryland.
Chris Pappas, of New Hampshire.
Conor Lamb, of Pennsylvania.

Bob Gibbs, of Ohio.
Don Young, of Alaska.
Randy K. Weber, Sr., of Texas.
Brian J. Mast, of Florida.
Mike Gallagher, of Wisconsin.
Carol D. Miller, of West Virginia.

Economic Development, Public Buildings, and Emergency Management

Dina Titus, of Nevada, *Chair*

Debbie Mucarsel-Powell, of Florida.
Sharice Davids, of Kansas.
Eleanor Holmes Norton, of District of Columbia.
Henry C. ''Hank'' Johnson, Jr., of Georgia.
John Garamendi, of California.
Anthony G. Brown, of Maryland.
Lizzie Fletcher, of Texas.

John Katko, of New York.
Gary J. Palmer, of Alabama.
Jenniffer González-Colón, of Puerto Rico.
Carol D. Miller, of West Virginia.
Greg Pence, of Indiana.
Mike Garcia, of California.

Highways and Transit

Eleanor Holmes Norton, of District of Columbia, *Chair*

Eddie Bernice Johnson, of Texas.
Steve Cohen, of Tennessee.
John Garamendi, of California.
Henry C. ''Hank'' Johnson, Jr., of Georgia.
Jared Huffman, of California.
Julia Brownley, of California.
Frederica S. Wilson, of Florida.
Alan S. Lowenthal, of California.
Mark DeSaulnier, of California.
Salud O. Carbajal, of California.
Anthony G. Brown, of Maryland.
Adriano Espaillat, of New York.
Tom Malinowski, of New Jersey.
Greg Stanton, of Arizona.
Colin Z. Allred, of Texas.
Sharice Davids, of Kansas.
Abby Finkenauer, of Iowa.
Jesús G. ''Chuy'' García, of Illinois.
Antonio Delgado, of New York.
Chris Pappas, of New Hampshire.
Angie Craig, of Minnesota.
Harley Rouda, of California.
Grace F. Napolitano, of California.
Albio Sires, of New Jersey.
Sean Patrick Maloney, of New York.
Donald M. Payne, Jr., of New Jersey.
Daniel Lipinski, of Illinois.
Dina Titus, of Nevada.
Stacey E. Plaskett, of Virgin Islands.

Rodney Davis, of Illinois.
Don Young, of Alaska.
Eric A. ''Rick'' Crawford, of Arkansas.
Bob Gibbs, of Ohio.
Daniel Webster, of Florida.
Thomas Massie, of Kentucky.
Rob Woodall, of Georgia.
John Katko, of New York.
Brian Babin, of Texas.
David Rouzer, of North Carolina.
Mike Bost, of Illinois.
Doug LaMalfa, of California.
Bruce Westerman, of Arkansas.
Lloyd Smucker, of Pennsylvania.
Paul Mitchell, of Michigan.
Mike Gallagher, of Wisconsin.
Gary J. Palmer, of Alabama.
Brian K. Fitzpatrick, of Pennsylvania.
Troy Balderson, of Ohio.
Ross Spano, of Florida.
Pete Stauber, of Minnesota.
Carol D. Miller, of West Virginia.
Greg Pence, of Indiana.
Mike Garcia, of California.

Railroads, Pipelines, and Hazardous Materials

Daniel Lipinski, of Illinois, *Chair*

Albio Sires, of New Jersey.
Donald M. Payne, Jr., of New Jersey.
Lizzie Fletcher, of Texas.
André Carson, of Indiana.
Frederica S. Wilson, of Florida.
Mark DeSaulnier, of California.
Stephen F. Lynch, of Massachusetts.
Tom Malinowski, of New Jersey.
Grace F. Napolitano, of California.
Steve Cohen, of Tennessee.
Jesús G. ''Chuy'' García, of Illinois.
Eleanor Holmes Norton, of District of Columbia.
Eddie Bernice Johnson, of Texas.
Alan S. Lowenthal, of California.
Colin Z. Allred, of Texas.
Angie Craig, of Minnesota.
Conor Lamb, of Pennsylvania.

Eric A. ''Rick'' Crawford, of Arkansas.
Scott Perry, of Pennsylvania.
Rodney Davis, of Illinois.
Brian Babin, of Texas.
Mike Bost, of Illinois.
Randy K. Weber, Sr., of Texas.
Doug LaMalfa, of California.
Lloyd Smucker, of Pennsylvania.
Paul Mitchell, of Michigan.
Brian K. Fitzpatrick, of Pennsylvania.
Troy Balderson, of Ohio.
Ross Spano, of Florida.
Pete Stauber, of Minnesota.
Greg Pence, of Indiana.

Water Resources and Environment

Grace F. Napolitano, of California, *Chair*

Debbie Mucarsel-Powell, of Florida.
Eddie Bernice Johnson, of Texas.
John Garamendi, of California.
Jared Huffman, of California.
Alan S. Lowenthal, of California.
Salud O. Carbajal, of California.
Adriano Espaillat, of New York.
Lizzie Fletcher, of Texas.
Abby Finkenauer, of Iowa.
Antonio Delgado, of New York.
Chris Pappas, of New Hampshire.
Angie Craig, of Minnesota.
Harley Rouda, of California.
Frederica S. Wilson, of Florida.
Stephen F. Lynch, of Massachusetts.
Tom Malinowski, of New Jersey.

Bruce Westerman, of Arkansas.
Daniel Webster, of Florida.
Thomas Massie, of Kentucky.
Rob Woodall, of Georgia.
Brian Babin, of Texas.
Garret Graves, of Louisiana.
David Rouzer, of North Carolina.
Mike Bost, of Illinois.
Randy K. Weber, Sr., of Texas.
Doug LaMalfa, of California.
Brian J. Mast, of Florida.
Gary J. Palmer, of Alabama.
Jenniffer González-Colón, of Puerto Rico.

STAFF

Committee on Transportation and Infrastructure (2165 RHOB) 225–4472.
Majority Staff:
Staff Director.—Katherine W. Dedrick.
General Counsel.—Mohsin Syed.
Director of Administration.—James Harrell.
Investigations Director.—Douglas Pasternak.
Legislative Assistant.—Alexa Old Crow.
Director of Budget/Deputy Counsel.—Jill Harrelson.
Director of Outreach and Member Services.—Madeline Pike.
Finance and Personnel Advisor.—Margaret Wetherald.
Professional Staff: Edward McGlone, Matthew Weisman.
Director of Travel, Security, and Facilities.—Larnell Exum.
Minority Staff:
Staff Director.—Paul Sass.
Deputy Staff Director.—Jack Ruddy.
General Counsel.—Fred Miller.
Deputy General Counsel.—Corey Cooke.
Director of Coalitions.—Abigail Camp.
Coalitions and Member Services Director.—Nick Christensen.
Research Assistant.—Victor Sarmiento.
Staff Assistants: Shawn Bloch, Jamie Hopkins, Tyler Micheletti.
Information Systems:
Systems Administrator.—Larry Whittaker.
Assistant Systems Administrator.—Scott Putz.
Communications:
Majority Communications Director.—Kerry Arndt.
Deputy Communications Director.—Bayley Sandy.
Digital Director.—Marcus Frias.
Minority Communications Director.—Justin Harclerode.
Deputy Communications Director.—Suzanne Youngblood.
Clerk's Office:
Clerk.—Michael S. Twinchek.
Printer.—Jean Paffenback.
Oversight and Investigations:
Majority Director of Oversight and Investigations.—Doug Pasternak.
Majority Professional Staff.—Matthew Weisman.
Majority Counsel.—Lauren Dudley.
Subcommittee on Aviation
Majority Staff:
Staff Director/Senior Counsel.—Alex Burkett.
Senior Counsels: Brian Bell, Dan Ngo, Michael Tien.
Legislative Assistant.—Michael Hudspith.

Minority Staff:
Staff Director and Senior Counsel.—Holly E. Woodruff Lyons.
Professional Staff.—Hunter Presti.

Subcommittee on Coast Guard and Maritime Transportation
Majority Staff:
Staff Director.—Dave Jansen.
Professional Staff: Cheryl Barnes, Matthew Dwyer, Rennie Meyers.
Legislative Assistant.—Cheryl Barnes.
Minority Staff:
Staff Director.—John C. Rayfield.

Subcommittee on Economic Development, Public Buildings, and Emergency Management
Majority Staff:
Staff Director.—Aaron Davis.
Professional Staff.—Ann Jacobs.
Legislative Assistant.—Brett Fulcer.
Minority Staff:
Staff Director.—Johanna Hardy.
Counsels: Elliot Doomes, Janet Erickson.

Subcommittee on Highways and Transit
Majority Staff:
Staff Director.—Helena Zyblikewycz.
Policy Analyst.—Brittany Lundberg.
Professional Staff: Brittany Lundberg, Auke Mahar-Piersma.
Senior Policy Advisor.—David Napoliello.
Legislative Assistant.—Chris Bell.
Minority Staff:
Staff Director.—Murphie Barrett.
Senior Professional Staff.—Cheryle Tucker.

Subcommittee on Railroads, Pipelines, and Hazardous Materials
Majority Staff:
Staff Director.—Liz Hill.
Professional Staff.—Andrea Wohleber.
Legislative Assistant.—Andrew Bridson.
Minority Staff:
Staff Director.—Michael Falencki.

Subcommittee on Water Resources and Environment
Majority Staff:
Staff Director / Senior Counsel.—Ryan Seiger.
Professional Staff: Navis Bermudez, Camille Touton.
Legislative Assistant.—Alexa Williams.
Minority Staff:
Staff Director.—Ian Bennitt.
Senior Counsel.—Jonathan R. Pawlow.

Veterans' Affairs

B234 Longworth House Office Building, phone 225–9756

https://veterans.house.gov

Mark Takano, of California, *Chair*

Julia Brownley, of California.
Kathleen M. Rice, of New York.
Conor Lamb, of Pennsylvania.
Mike Levin, of California.
Max Rose, of New York.
Anthony Brindisi, of New York.
Gilbert Ray Cisneros, Jr., of California.
Susie Lee, of Nevada.
Lauren Underwood, of Illinois.
Joe Cunningham, of South Carolina.
Elaine G. Luria, of Virginia.
Chris Pappas, of New Hampshire.
Colin Z. Allred, of Texas.
Collin C. Peterson, of Minnesota.
Gregorio Kilili Camacho Sablan, of Northern Mariana Islands.

David P. Roe, of Tennessee.
Gus M. Bilirakis, of Florida.
Aumua Amata Coleman Radewagen, of American Samoa.
Mike Bost, of Illinois.
Neal P. Dunn, of Florida.
Jack Bergman, of Michigan.
Jim Banks, of Indiana.
Andy Barr, of Kentucky.
Daniel Meuser, of Pennsylvania.
Chip Roy, of Texas.
W. Gregory Steube, of Florida.
Vacant.

SUBCOMMITTEES

Disability Assistance and Memorial Affairs

Elaine G. Luria, of Virginia, *Chair*

Gilbert Ray Cisneros, Jr., of California.
Gregorio Kilili Camacho Sablan, of Northern Mariana Islands.
Colin Z. Allred, of Texas.
Lauren Underwood, of Illinois.

Mike Bost, of Illinois.
Gus M. Bilirakis, of Florida.
W. Gregory Steube, of Florida.
Vacant.

Economic Opportunity

Mike Levin, of California, *Chair*

Kathleen M. Rice, of New York.
Anthony Brindisi, of New York.
Chris Pappas, of New Hampshire.
Elaine G. Luria, of Virginia.
Susie Lee, of Nevada.
Joe Cunningham, of South Carolina.

Gus M. Bilirakis, of Florida.
Jack Bergman, of Michigan.
Jim Banks, of Indiana.
Andy Barr, of Kentucky.
Daniel Meuser, of Pennsylvania.

Health

Julia Brownley, of California, *Chair*

Conor Lamb, of Pennsylvania.
Mike Levin, of California.
Anthony Brindisi, of New York.
Max Rose, of New York.
Gilbert Ray Cisneros, Jr., of California.
Gregorio Kilili Camacho Sablan, of Northern Mariana Islands.

Neal P. Dunn, of Florida.
Aumua Amata Coleman Radewagen, of American Samoa.
Andy Barr, of Kentucky.
Daniel Meuser, of Pennsylvania.
W. Gregory Steube, of Florida.

Oversight and Investigations

Chris Pappas, of New Hampshire, *Chair*

Kathleen M. Rice, of New York.
Max Rose, of New York.
Gilbert Ray Cisneros, Jr., of California.
Collin C. Peterson, of Minnesota.
Jack Bergman, of Michigan.
Aumua Amata Coleman Radewagen, of American Samoa.
Mike Bost, of Illinois.
Chip Roy, of Texas.

Technology Modernization

Susie Lee, of Nevada, *Chair*

Julia Brownley, of California.
Conor Lamb, of Pennsylvania.
Joe Cunningham, of South Carolina.
Jim Banks, of Indiana.
Chip Roy, of Texas.
Vacant.

STAFF

Committee on Veterans' Affairs (B234 LHOB), 225–9756, fax 225–2034.
Majority Staff Director.—Raymond Kelley (B3204 LHOB), 225–9756.
Deputy Staff Director.—Matt Reel.
General Counsel.—Grace Rodden.
Communications Director.—Miguel Salazar.
Financial Administrator/Printing Clerk.—Bernadine Dotson.
Legislative Assistant.—Daria Berstell.
Press Assistant.—Jenni Geurink.
Digital Communications Assistant.—Madison Scillian.
Chief Clerk.—Rasheedah Hasan.
Full Committee Legislative Coordinator/Office Manager.—Carol Murray.
Senior Advisor.—Yuri Beckelman.
Minority Staff Director.—Jon Towers (3460 OHOB), 225–3527.
Deputy Staff Director/General Counsel.—Chris McNamee.
Member Services Associate.—Matt Meyer.
Minority Full Committee Legislative Coordinator/Professional Staff Member.—Grayson Westmoreland.

Subcommittee on Disability Assistance and Memorial Affairs (B234 LHOB), 225–9756.
Majority Subcommittee Staff Director/Counsel.—Julie Turner.
Senior Policy Advisor/Investigator.—Sam Franco.
Minority Subcommittee Staff Director.—Maria Tripplaar (3460 OHOB).
Professional Staff Member.—Katherine Smith.

Subcommittee on Economic Opportunity (B234 LHOB), 225–9756.
Majority Staff Director.—Justin Vogt.
Professional Staff Members: Chris Bennett (3470 OHOB), Julian Purdy (B234 LHOB).
Minority Staff Director.—Jon Clark (3460 OHOB).

Subcommittee on Health (B234 LHOB), 225–9756.
Majority Staff Director.—Elizabeth Austin-Mackenzie.
Senior Professional Staff Member.—Megan Bland.
Professional Staff Member.—Sarah Dean.
Women Veterans Task Force Policy Advisor.—Andrea Goldstein.
Policy Clerk.—Stephon Bradberry.
Minority Staff Director.—Christine Hill (3460 OHOB).
Senior Professional Staff Member.—Samantha Gonzalez (3460 OHOB).

Subcommittee on Oversight and Investigations (B234 LHOB), 225–9756.
Majority Staff Director.—Peter Tyler.
Professional Staff Member.—Alexis MacDonald.
Senior Investigative Counsel.—Pal K. Shiek.
Minority Staff Director.—Chris McNamee.
Minority Professional Staff Member.—Alex Large.
Minority Legislative Aide.—Parker Chapman.

Subcommittee on Technology Modernization

Majority Staff Director.—Sarah Garcia (B234 LHOB), 225–9756.

Professional Staff Members: John Harry, Matthew Horowitz.

Minority Staff Director.—Bill Mallison (3460 OHOB), 225–1900.

Minority Professional Staff Member.—Alex Large.

Minority Legislative Aide.—Parker Chapman.

Ways and Means

1102 Longworth House Office Building, phone 225–3625

https://waysandmeans.house.gov

Richard E. Neal, of Massachusetts, *Chair*

Lloyd Doggett, of Texas.
Mike Thompson, of California.
John B. Larson, of Connecticut.
Earl Blumenauer, of Oregon.
Ron Kind, of Wisconsin.
Bill Pascrell, Jr., of New Jersey.
Danny K. Davis, of Illinois.
Linda T. Sánchez, of California.
Brian Higgins, of New York.
Terri A. Sewell, of Alabama.
Suzan K. DelBene, of Washington.
Judy Chu, of California.
Gwen Moore, of Wisconsin.
Daniel T. Kildee, of Michigan.
Brendan F. Boyle, of Pennsylvania.
Donald S. Beyer, Jr., of Virginia.
Dwight Evans, of Pennsylvania.
Bradley Scott Schneider, of Illinois.
Thomas R. Suozzi, of New York.
Jimmy Panetta, of California.
Stephanie N. Murphy, of Florida.
Jimmy Gomez, of California.
Steven Horsford, of Nevada.
Vacant.

Kevin Brady, of Texas.
Devin Nunes, of California.
Vern Buchanan, of Florida.
Adrian Smith, of Nebraska.
Kenny Marchant, of Texas.
Tom Reed, of New York.
Mike Kelly, of Pennsylvania.
George Holding, of North Carolina.
Jason Smith, of Missouri.
Tom Rice, of South Carolina.
David Schweikert, of Arizona.
Jackie Walorski, of Indiana.
Darin LaHood, of Illinois.
Brad R. Wenstrup, of Ohio.
Jodey C. Arrington, of Texas.
A. Drew Ferguson IV, of Georgia.
Ron Estes, of Kansas.

SUBCOMMITTEES

[The chair and ranking minority member are ex officio (non-voting) members of all subcommittees.]

Health

Lloyd Doggett, of Texas, *Chair*

Mike Thompson, of California.
Ron Kind, of Wisconsin.
Earl Blumenauer, of Oregon.
Brian Higgins, of New York.
Terri A. Sewell, of Alabama.
Judy Chu, of California.
Dwight Evans, of Pennsylvania.
Bradley Scott Schneider, of Illinois.
Jimmy Gomez, of California.
Steven Horsford, of Nevada.

Devin Nunes, of California.
Vern Buchanan, of Florida.
Adrian Smith, of Nebraska.
Kenny Marchant, of Texas.
Tom Reed, of New York.
Mike Kelly, of Pennsylvania.
George Holding, of North Carolina.

Oversight

Vacant, *Chair*

Suzan K. DelBene, of Washington.
Linda T. Sánchez, of California.
Thomas R. Suozzi, of New York.
Judy Chu, of California.
Gwen Moore, of Wisconsin.
Brendan F. Boyle, of Pennsylvania.

Mike Kelly, of Pennsylvania.
Jackie Walorski, of Indiana.
Darin LaHood, of Illinois.
Brad R. Wenstrup, of Ohio.

Select Revenue Measures

Mike Thompson, of California, *Chair*

Lloyd Doggett, of Texas.
John B. Larson, of Connecticut.
Linda T. Sánchez, of California.
Suzan K. DelBene, of Washington.
Gwen Moore, of Wisconsin.
Brendan F. Boyle, of Pennsylvania.
Donald S. Beyer, Jr., of Virginia.
Thomas R. Suozzi, of New York.

Adrian Smith, of Nebraska.
Tom Rice, of South Carolina.
David Schweikert, of Arizona.
Darin LaHood, of Illinois.
Jodey C. Arrington, of Texas.
A. Drew Ferguson IV, of Georgia.

Social Security

John B. Larson, of Connecticut, *Chair*

Bill Pascrell, Jr., of New Jersey.
Linda T. Sánchez, of California.
Daniel T. Kildee, of Michigan.
Brendan F. Boyle, of Pennsylvania.
Bradley Scott Schneider, of Illinois.
Brian Higgins, of New York.

Tom Reed, of New York.
Jodey C. Arrington, of Texas.
A. Drew Ferguson IV, of Georgia.
Ron Estes, of Kansas.

Trade

Earl Blumenauer, of Oregon, *Chair*

Bill Pascrell, Jr., of New Jersey.
Ron Kind, of Wisconsin.
Danny K. Davis, of Illinois.
Brian Higgins, of New York.
Daniel T. Kildee, of Michigan.
Jimmy Panetta, of California.
Stephanie N. Murphy, of Florida.
Terri A. Sewell, of Alabama.
Suzan K. DelBene, of Washington.
Donald S. Beyer, Jr., of Virginia.

Vern Buchanan, of Florida.
Devin Nunes, of California.
George Holding, of North Carolina.
Tom Rice, of South Carolina.
Kenny Marchant, of Texas.
Jason Smith, of Missouri.
David Schweikert, of Arizona.

Worker and Family Support

Danny K. Davis, of Illinois, *Chair*

Terri A. Sewell, of Alabama.
Judy Chu, of California.
Gwen Moore, of Wisconsin.
Dwight Evans, of Pennsylvania.
Stephanie N. Murphy, of Florida.
Jimmy Gomez, of California.

Jackie Walorski, of Indiana.
Brad R. Wenstrup, of Ohio.
Ron Estes, of Kansas.
Tom Reed, of New York.

STAFF

Committee on Ways and Means (1102 LHOB), 225–3625, fax 225–2610.
Staff Director.—Brandon Casey.
Assistant to the Staff Director.—Erika Poitevien.
Deputy Staff Director.—Lizzy O'Hara.
Communications Director.—Dan Rubin.
General Counsel, Parliamentarian.—Danielle Brown.
Systems Administrator.—Wuan Perkins.
Committee Administrator.—Jennifer O'Connor.
Staff Assistants: Victoria Cruz-De Jesus, Scott Larochelle.
Digital Director.—Cara Koontz.
Director of Outreach and Member Services.—Lee Slater.
Clerk.—Carrie Breidenbach.
Technology Director.—Antoine Walker.
Press Secretary.—Erin Hatch.
Counselor to the Chairman.—Kara Getz.

Minority Staff Director.—Gary Andres.
Digital Director.—Kristi Reese.
Finance and Payroll Administrator.—Mary Ellen Ruhlen.
Parliamentarian/General Counsel.—Molly Fromm.
Coalitions and Member Services Director.—Paige Decker.
Clerk.—Caroline Jones.
Assistant Clerk.—Gregory Warren.
Press Secretary.—Jesse Solis.
Staff Assistant.—Jacob Walker.

Subcommittee on Health
Majority Staff Director.—Amy Hall.
Deputy Staff Director.—Melanie Egorin.
Professional Staff: Rachel Dolin, Sarah Levin.
Legislative Assistant/Subcommittee Clerk.—Neil Patil.
Minority Staff Director.—Stephanie Parks.
Professional Staff: Devin Gerzof, Alyene Mlinar.

Subcommittee on Oversight
Majority Staff Director.—Karen McAfee.
Counsel: Zachary Baron, Isabella More.
Tax Counsel.—Susan Athy.
Clerk/Legislative Assistant.—Moyer McCoy.
Minority Staff Director.—Rachel Kaldahl.
Professional Staff.—Lindsay Steward.
Legislative Assistant.—Liz Navin.

Subcommittee on Select Revenue Measures
Majority Staff Director/Deputy Chief Counsel.—Aruna Kalyanam.
Chief Tax Counsel.—Andrew Grossman.
Senior Counsel.—Peg McGlinch.
Tax Counsel: Beth Bell, Ji Prichard, Daniel Winnick.
Minority Chief Tax Counsel.—Randy Gartin.
Tax Counsel: Aharon Friedman, Karin Hope.

Subcommittee on Social Security
Majority Staff Director.—Kathryn Olson.
Professional Staff.—TJ Sutcliffe.
Clerk.—Andrew Seddighi.
Minority Staff Director.—Amy Shuart.
Professional Staff.—Lara Rosner.

Subcommittee on Trade
Majority Chief Counsel.—Katherine Tai.
Trade Counsel: Keigan Mull, Katie White, Alexandra Whittaker.
Counsel.—Julia Friedman.
Clerk//Legislative Assistant.—John Catalfamo.
Minority Staff Director/Chief Trade Counsel.—Angela Ellard.
Professional Staff.—David Giordano.
Trade Counsel: Blake Harden, Josh Snead.

Subcommittee on Worker and Family Support
Majority Staff Director.—Morna Miller.
Legislative Assistant/Subcommittee Clerk.—Taylor Downs.
Professional Staff: Jason Kanter, Kimberly Meinert.

SELECT AND SPECIAL COMMITTEES OF THE HOUSE

Permanent Select Committee on Intelligence

HVC–304 The Capitol, phone 225–4121

[Created pursuant to H. Res. 658, 95th Congress]

Adam B. Schiff, of California, *Chair*

James A. Himes, of Connecticut.
Terri A. Sewell, of Alabama.
André Carson, of Indiana.
Jackie Speier, of California.
Mike Quigley, of Illinois.
Eric Swalwell, of California.
Joaquin Castro, of Texas.
Denny Heck, of Washington.
Peter Welch, of Vermont.
Sean Patrick Maloney, of New York.
Val Butler Demings, of Florida.
Raja Krishnamoorthi, of Illinois.

Devin Nunes, of California.
K. Michael Conaway, of Texas.
Michael R. Turner, of Ohio.
Brad R. Wenstrup, of Ohio.
Chris Stewart, of Utah.
Eric A. ''Rick'' Crawford, of Arkansas.
Elise M. Stefanik, of New York.
Will Hurd, of Texas.

SUBCOMMITTEES

[The Speaker and Minority Leader are ex officio (non-voting) members of the committee.]

Central Intelligence Agency

André Carson, of Indiana, *Chair*

Jackie Speier, of California.
Mike Quigley, of Illinois.
Joaquin Castro, of Texas.
Peter Welch, of Vermont.
Sean Patrick Maloney, of New York.

Eric A. ''Rick'' Crawford, of Arkansas.
K. Michael Conaway, of Texas.
Brad R. Wenstrup, of Ohio.
Chris Stewart, of Utah.

Defense Intelligence and Warfighter Support

Terri A. Sewell, of Alabama, *Chair*

James A. Himes, of Connecticut.
Denny Heck, of Washington.
Peter Welch, of Vermont.
Sean Patrick Maloney, of New York.
Val Butler Demings, of Florida.

Brad R. Wenstrup, of Ohio.
Michael R. Turner, of Ohio.
K. Michael Conaway, of Texas.
Will Hurd, of Texas.

Intelligence Modernization and Readiness

Eric Swalwell, of California, *Chair*

Terri A. Sewell, of Alabama.
Jackie Speier, of California.
Joaquin Castro, of Texas.
Val Butler Demings, of Florida.
Raja Krishnamoorthi, of Illinois.

Will Hurd, of Texas.
K. Michael Conaway, of Texas.
Elise M. Stefanik, of New York.

Strategic Technologies and Advanced Research

James A. Himes, of Connecticut, *Chair*

André Carson, of Indiana.
Mike Quigley, of Illinois.
Denny Heck, of Washington.
Eric Swalwell, of California.
Raja Krishnamoorthi, of Illinois.
Chris Stewart, of Utah.
Elise M. Stefanik, of New York.
Michael R. Turner, of Ohio.

STAFF

Majority Staff Director.—Timothy Bergreen.
Deputy Staff Director.—Carly Blake.
General Counsel.—Maher Bitar.
Deputy General Counsel.—Wells Bennett.
Senior Advisor and Director of Investigations.—Daniel Goldman.
Senior Counsel for Investigations.—Shannon Green.
Investigative Counsel.—Nicolas Mitchell.
Oversight Counsel.—William Evans.
Director of Budget.—William Wu.
Communications Director.—Patrick Boland.
Professional Staff: Linda Cohen, Thomas Eager, Abigail Grace, Diana Pilipenko, Amanda Rogers Thorpe, Rheanne Wirkkala.
Operations Director.—Brandon Smith.
Security Director.—Kristin Jepson.
Director of Information Management.—Kim Kerr.
Research Assistant.—Conrad Stosz.
Congressional Fellow.—Scott Miller.

Minority Staff Director.—Allen Souza.
Senior Advisor for Analysis.—Derek Harvey.
Member Services Senior Advisor.—George Pappas.
Budget Director and Investigation Coordinator.—Nick Ciarlante.
Communications Director.—Jack Langer.
Counsel.—Meghan Green.
Professional Staff: Bill Flanigan, Andrew House, Steve Keith, Lisa Major, Marissa Skaggs.
Staff Assistant.—Betsy Hulme.

Select Committee on the Climate Crisis

359 Ford House Office Building, phone 225–1107

Kathy Castor, of Florida, *Chair*

Ben Ray Luján, of New Mexico.
Suzanne Bonamici, of Oregon.
Julia Brownley, of California.
Jared Huffman, of California.
A. Donald McEachin, of Virginia.
Mike Levin, of California.
Sean Casten, of Illinois.
Joe Neguse, of Colorado.
Garret Graves, of Louisiana.
H. Morgan Griffith, of Virginia.
Gary J. Palmer, of Alabama.
Earl L. ''Buddy'' Carter, of Georgia.
Carol D. Miller, of West Virginia.
Kelly Armstrong, of North Dakota.

NO SUBCOMMITTEES

STAFF

Majority Staff Director.—Ana Unruh Cohen.
Deputy Staff Director.—Alison Cassady.
Communications Director.—Melvin Felix.
Senior Counsel: Fatima Ahmad, Samantha Medlock.
Counsel.—Mackenzie Landa.
Professional Staff.—Abigail Regitsky.

Clerk.—Dana Gansman.
Policy Assistant.—Ebadullah Ebadi.
Digital Production Specialist.—Mariah Morrison.
Minority Staff Director.—Marty Hall.
Chief Strategist.—George David Banks.
Communications Director.—Michael Lehmann.
Professional Staff Members: Maggie Ayrea, Dustin Davidson, Marcie Smith.
Staff Assistant.—Adele Born.

Select Committee on the Modernization of Congress

226 Cannon House Office Building, Washington, DC 20515, phone 225–1530

Derek Kilmer, of Washington, *Chair*
Tom Graves, of Georgia, *Vice Chair*

Suzan K. DelBene, of Washington.
Zoe Lofgren, of California.
Mark Pocan, of Wisconsin.
Mary Gay Scanlon, of Pennsylvania.

Rob Woodall, Georgia.
Susan W. Brooks, of Indiana.
Rodney Davis, of Illinois.
Dan Newhouse, of Washington.
William R. Timmons IV, of South Carolina.

NO SUBCOMMITTEES

STAFF

Staff Director.—Allie Neill.
Deputy Staff Director.—Jake Olson.
Communications Director.—Danielle Stewart.
Digital Director.—Alyssa Innis.
Clerk.—Mariah Harding.
Chief Fellow.—Marian Currinder.

National Republican Congressional Committee

320 First Street, SE, 20003, phone 479–7000

Tom Emmer, of Minnesota, *Chair*

Deputy Chairs:
West: Ken Calvert, of California.
Central and Great Lakes: Jodey C. Arrington, of Texas.
Northeast and Southeast: Earl L. ''Buddy'' Carter, of Georgia.
Vice Chair of:
Finance.—Richard Hudson, of North Carolina.
Recruitment.—Susan W. Brooks, of Indiana.
Patriots.—John Katko, of New York.
Member Services.—Jackie Walorski, of Indiana.
Redistricting.—Mario Diaz-Balart, of Florida.
Audit.—K. Michael Conaway, of Texas.
Outreach.—Anthony Gonzalez, of Ohio.
116th Class Representative.—Kelly Armstrong, of North Dakota.

STAFF

Executive Director.—Parker Poling.
Deputy Executive Director.—Robert Boland.
General Counsel.—Erin Clark.
Political Director.—Justin Richards.
Communications Director.—Chris Pack.
Data Director.—Nick Hoffnagle.
Finance Director.—Dana Klein.

Digital Director.—Lyman Munschauer.
Member Services Director.—Minyet Palich.
Policy Director.—Yvette Wissmann.
Research Director.—Matt Wall.

House Republican Policy Committee

207 Cannon House Office Building, phone 225–4921

https://policy.house.gov

meets at the call of the Chair

Gary J. Palmer, of Alabama, Chair

House Leadership:
Republican Leader.—Kevin McCarthy, of California.
Republican Whip.—Steve Scalise, of Louisiana.
Conference Chair.—Liz Cheney, of Wyoming.
Conference Vice Chair.—Mark Walker, of North Carolina.
Conference Secretary.—Jason Smith, of Missouri.
NRCC Chair.—Tom Emmer, of Minnesota.

STAFF

Executive Director.—Cameron Smith.
Senior Policy Advisor.—Kelsey Wall.

House Republican Conference

1420 Longworth House Office Building, phone 225–5107, fax 226–0154

Liz Cheney, of Wyoming, *Chair*
Mark Walker, of North Carolina, *Vice Chair*
Jason Smith, of Missouri, *Secretary*

STAFF

Chief of Staff.—Kara Ahern.
Special Assistant to the Chair.—William Henderson.
Legislative Assistant.—Ryan Hofmann.
Staff Assistant.—Kevin Sun.
Director of Member Services.—Caroline Boothe.
Member Services Assistant.—Megan Porter.
Policy Director.—John Drzewicki.
Deputy Policy Director.—Jenna Lifhits.
Director of Coalitions.—Paul Guaglianone.
Digital Director.—Morgan Anderson.
Communications Director.—Jeremy Adler.
National Press Secretary.—Steven Smith.
Press Secretary.—Natalie Johnson.
Information Technology Director.—Dray Thorne.
Operations Director.—Brian Plaut.
Rapid Response Director.—Michael Sullivan.
Scheduling Director.—Elizabeth Pearce.

Democratic Congressional Campaign Committee

430 South Capitol Street, SE., 20003, phone (202) 863–1500

Executive Committee:
Nancy Pelosi, of California, *Speaker of the House.*
Cheri Bustos, of Illinois, *Chair.*

STAFF

Executive Director.—Lucinda Guinn.
Deputy Executive Director and Director of Campaigns.—Danny Kazin.
Deputy Executive Director for Finance.—Mike Smith.
Deputy Executive Director and Chief Operating Officer.—Jacqui Newman.
Chief Financial Officer.—Jackie Forte-Mackay.
Chief Administrative Officer.—Jillian Shweiki.
Chief of Staff.—Alexandra Smith.
National Political Director.—Kory Kozloski.
Battlefield Director.—Gabrielle Quintana Greenfield.
Candidate Fundraising Director.—Alonso Salas.
National Press Secretary.—Cole Leiter.
Managing Director, Member Services.—Charles Benton.
Director of Member Engagement and Political Strategy.—Brenna Marron.
Director of Research.—Samantha McClain.
Chief Digital Officer.—Ryan Thompson.
Digital Director for Campaigns.—Kelley Hardon.
National Finance Director.—Dan Boysen.
Battleground Fundraising Director.—Ashley Coleman.
Director of Direct Marketing.—Nicole Titus.
National Field Director.—Alex Edelman.
Policy Director.—Joon Suh.
Targeting and Data Director.—Dennis Raj.
National Strategic Analytics Director.—Megan Crowe.

Democratic Steering and Policy Committee

H–204 The Capitol, phone 225–0100

Steering and Policy Chair.—Nancy Pelosi, of California, *Speaker of the House.*
Steering Co-Chair.—Rosa L. DeLauro, of Connecticut.
Policy Co-Chair.—Eric Swalwell, of California.
Vice Chair.—Katherine M. Clark, of Massachusetts.
Parliamentarian.—Donald Norcross, of New Jersey.

STAFF

Steering: George Kundanis, Michael Long.
Policy: George Kundanis, Richard Meltzer.

Democratic Caucus

1420 Longworth House Office Building, phone 225–1400, fax 226–4412

https://dems.gov

Hakeem S. Jeffries, of New York, *Chair*
Katherine M. Clark, of Massachusetts, *Vice Chair*

STAFF

Chief of Staff.—Tasia Jackson.
Executive Director.—Gideon Bragin.
Policy Director.—Lakecia Foster Stickney.
Senior Policy Advisor.—Wayne Williams.
Policy Advisor.—Meseret Araya.
Policy Associate.—Jacob Nelson.
Director of Communications, Senior Advisor.—Michael Hardaway.
Press Secretary.—Christina Stephenson.
Deputy Press Secretary.—Zach Leibell.
Digital Director.—Earnestine Dawson.

Digital Assistant.—Fiona Byon.
Director of Operations.—Manuel Joe Carrillo.
Caucus Assistant.—Alex Scheuer.
Director of Member Services.—Emily Noriega-May.
Deputy Director of Member Services.—Andrew Sachse.
Vice Chair Chief of Staff.—Brooke Scannell.
Vice Chair Director of Member Services & Counsel.—Diana Rudd.
Vice Chair Director of Outreach.—Xenia Ruiz.
Vice Chair Outreach Associate.—Wendy Hamilton.

OFFICERS AND OFFICIALS OF THE HOUSE

OFFICE OF THE SPEAKER

H–232 The Capitol, phone 225–0600, fax 225–4188

https://speaker.gov

Office of the Speaker.—Hon. Nancy Pelosi.
Chief of Staff.—Terri McCullough.
Deputy Chiefs of Staff: Diane Dewhirst, Drew Hammill, George Kundanis.
Director of Operations.—Emily Berret.
Special Assistant to the Speaker.—Alisa La.
Special Assistant to the Executive Office.—Steph Wong.
Director of Scheduling and Advance.—Kelsey Smith.
Deputy Director of Scheduling and Advance.—Nathaniel Holmes.
Deputy Director of Scheduling.—Savanna Polzin.
Scheduling and Advance Coordinator.—Shane Smith.
Policy Director.—Dick Meltzer.
Senior Policy Advisors: Michael Tecklenburg, Kenneth DeGraff, Katherine Monge, Wyndee Parker, Wendell Primus, Jaime Lizarraga, Patricia Ross.
Senior Communications and Policy Advisor.—Margaret Capron.
Policy Associate.—Sarah Swig.
Director of Member Services.— Michael Long.
Member Services Staff Assistant.—Samuel Iacobellis.
Director of Interparliamentary Affairs.—Kate Knudson.
Deputy Director of Protocol and Special Events.—Kristina Jeter.
Protocol Associate.—Claudia Marconi.
IT Director.—Wil Haynes, HB–13, The Capitol, 225–0100.
Deputy IT Director.—Kamilah Keita, HB–13, The Capitol, 225–0100.
Director of Outreach.—Reva Price.
Outreach Advisor.—Matthew Ramirez.
Staff Assistant.—Montana Miller.

SPEAKER'S PRESS OFFICE

H–2132 The Capitol, phone 226–7616

Deputy Chief of Staff.—Drew Hammill.
Communications Director.—Ashley Etienne.
Deputy Communications Director.—Henry Connelly.
Senior Advisor.—Jesse Lee.

OFFICE OF THE MAJORITY LEADER

H–107 The Capitol, phone 225–3130, fax 226–0663

Majority Leader.—Steny H. Hoyer.
Chief of Staff.—Alexis Covey-Brandt.
Deputy Chief of Staff.—Brian Romick.
Director of Legislative Operations.—Shuwanza Goff.
Deputy Floor Director.—Ray Salazar.
Floor Assistant.—Deborah Rowe.
Director of Member Services.—Courtney Fry.
Deputy Director of Member Services and Outreach Advisor.—Claudia Urrabazo.
Communications Director.—Katie Grant.
Deputy Communications Director.—Mariel Saez.

Press and Research Assistant.—Myra Valentine.
Speechwriter.—Adam Weissmann.
Policy Director.—Tom Mahr.
Senior Policy Advisors: Keith Abouchar, Trent Bauserman, James Leuschen, Daniel Silverberg, Rachel Snyder.
Senior Advisor.—Julie Merz.
Executive Assistant/Office Manager.—Jake Bayer.
Director of Scheduling.—Bridget Brennan.
Special Assistant.—Jacob Trauberman.
Digital Director and Policy Advisor.—Steve Dwyer.
Staff Assistants: Harleigh Bean, Michael Spak.

OFFICE OF THE MAJORITY WHIP

H–329 The Capitol, phone 226–3210

https://majoritywhip.gov

Majority Whip.—James E. Clyburn.
Chief of Staff.—Yelberton R. Watkins.
Communications Director.—Hope Derrick.
Deputy Communications Director.—Ryan Daniels.
Digital Director.—Morgan Butler.
Policy Director.—Wintta Woldemariam.
Deputy Policy Director.—Matthew Ellison.
Senior Advisors: Michael Hacker, Lindy Kelly.
Floor Director.—Craig Link.
Deputy Floor Directors: Nd Ubezonu, Jessica Vallejo.
Technology Director.—Tamika Mason.

OFFICE OF THE ASSISTANT SPEAKER

H–132 The Capitol, phone 225–2020, fax 225–5117

Assistant Speaker of the House of Representatives.—Ben Ray Luján.
Chief of Staff.—Angela Ramirez.
Communications Director.—Lauren French.
Member Services Director.—Hans Goff.
Senior Advisors: Ashley Jones, Carlos Sanchez.

OFFICE OF THE SENIOR CHIEF DEPUTY MAJORITY WHIP

2367 Rayburn House Office Building, phone 225–2111

Senior Chief Deputy Majority Whip.—Janice D. Schakowsky.
Legislative Director.—Syd Terry.

OFFICE OF THE REPUBLICAN LEADER

H–204 The Capitol, phone 225–4000, fax 225–0781

https://republicanleader.gov

Republican Leader.—Kevin McCarthy.
Chief of Staff.—Dan Meyer.
Deputy Chief of Staff.—James Min.
Deputy Chief of Staff for Policy.—Will Dunham.
Deputy Chief of Staff for Member Services.—Natalie Joyce.
Head of Communications.—Matthew Sparks.
Digital Communications Director.—Caleb Smith.
Director of Floor Operations.—John Leganski.
General Counsel.—Machalagh Carr.
Director of Operations and Scheduling.—Alexandra Gourdikian.
Senior Policy Advisors: Emily Domenech, Steven Giaier, Katherine Meyer, Brittan Specht.

Communications Director.—Michele Exner.
Director of Strategic Communications and Spokesman.—Mark Bednar.
California Press Secretary.—Brittany Martinez.
Media Affairs Advisor.—Christina Cameron.
Deputy Floor Director.—Christopher Bien.
Cloakroom Floor Director.—Ryan O'Toole.
Cloakroom Floor Assistant.—Sarah Coyle.
Floor Assistant.—Cullen Murphy.
Deputy Member Services Director.—Max Engling.
Member Services Coordinator.—Allie Humes.
Speechwriter.—Charles Correll.
National Security Advisor.—Luke Murry.
Policy Advisor.—Preston Hill.
Communications Advisor.—Hanna Bogorowski.
Digital Communications Advisor.—Keenan Hochschild.
Communications Aide.—Zachary Houston.
Scheduler.—Lee Bonner.
Special Assistant to the Leader.—Jack Rosemond.
Staff Assistants: Savannah Chaffee, Jordan Dayer.

OFFICE OF THE REPUBLICAN WHIP

H–148 The Capitol, phone 225–0197

Republican Whip.—Steve Scalise.
Chief of Staff.—Brett Horton.
Chief Deputy Whip.—A. Drew Ferguson IV.
Chief of Staff to the Chief Deputy Whip.—Bobby Saparow.
Policy Director.—Bill Hughes.
Member Services Director.—Bart Reising.
Floor Director.—Ben Napier.
Communications Director.—Lauren Fine.
Digital Director.—Michael Comer.
Director of Operations.—Ellen Gosnell.
Deputy Policy Director.—Marty Reiser.
Deputy Floor Director.—Annie Wolf.
Counsel.—Jeff Wieand.
Policy Advisor.—Dan Sadlosky.
Coalitions Coordinator.—Eric Schmitz.
Floor Assistant.—Dennis Nalls.
Speechwriter.—Sean Satterthwaite.
Scheduler.—Jacqueline Battaglia.
Special Assistant.—John Clarke.
Staff Assistants: Robyn Krieger, Chase Walker.

OFFICE OF THE CLERK

H–154 The Capitol, phone 225–7000

CHERYL L. JOHNSON, Clerk of the House of Representatives; Cheryl L. Johnson was sworn in as Clerk of the U.S. House of Representatives for the 116th Congress by Speaker Nancy Pelosi on February 25, 2019. Ms. Johnson is the 36th individual to serve as Clerk.

Before becoming Clerk, Ms. Johnson worked for nearly 20 years in the House followed by 10 years at the Smithsonian Institution. Most recently, Ms. Johnson served as Director of the Smithsonian's Office of Government Relations. In that role, she worked with Smithsonian leadership and the Board of Regents to build and maintain strong relationships with Congress, specifically with the congressional committees with jurisdiction over Smithsonian programs and appropriations. She also developed strategic legislative objectives, policies, and funding opportunities for the Smithsonian.

In her time on Capitol Hill, Ms. Johnson was the Chief Education and Investigative Counsel for the House Committee on Education and the Workforce, where she served as a principal policy advisor and spokesperson for the Committee. Ms. Johnson also served as Director and Counsel for the Committee on House Administration's Subcommittee on Libraries and Memorials. In this capacity, she worked with the Subcommittee chair to exercise oversight and legislative responsibility over the Library of Congress and the Smithsonian.

Ms. Johnson earned her bachelor's degree in journalism and mass communication from the University of Iowa and her law degree from Howard University. She is also a graduate of the senior management program at Harvard University's John F. Kennedy School of Government. Born in New Orleans, she lives with her husband and son in Chevy Chase, Maryland.

Clerk.—Cheryl Johnson.
Deputy Clerks: Gloria Lett, Robert F. Reeves.
Chief of:
Legislative Computer Systems.—Scott Kim, 2401 RHOB, 225–1182.
Legislative Operations.—Kevin McCumber, HT–13, 225–7925.
Legislative Resource Center.—Ronald Dale Thomas, B–81 CHOB, 226–5200.
Art and Archives.—Farar Elliott, Thomas Jefferson Bldg.-Attic, 226–1300.
Communications.—Catherine Cooke, 293 CHOB, 225–1908.
House Employment Counsel.—Ann Rogers, 4300 OFOB, 225–7075.
Official Reporter.—Damien Jackson, HT–59, The Capitol, 225–5621.

CHIEF ADMINISTRATIVE OFFICER

HB–28 The Capitol, phone 225–5555

PHILIP G. KIKO, Chief Administrative Officer of the House of Representatives, is a native of Canton, Ohio, was nominated by Speaker Paul Ryan, and elected to serve as the Chief Administrative Officer effective August 1, 2016. As CAO, Mr. Kiko is responsible for the information technology, financial, logistical, human resources, and procurement services provided to Members of the U.S. House and their staff. Mr. Kiko began his service on Capitol Hill with Representative Jim Sensenbrenner (WI-5) as Legislative Director and later served as his Chief of Staff. Mr. Kiko has also worked in the Executive Branch at the Department of Education's Office for Civil Rights and at the Department of Interior's Office of Legislative Affairs, Office of Budget and Program Resources Management, and Office of Hearings and Appeals. In 1995, he returned to Capitol Hill as Associate Administrator of Procurement and Purchasing at the newly formed CAO. Mr. Kiko was called again to serve then-Chairman Jim Sensenbrenner as Deputy Staff Director for the House Committee on Science and then as General Counsel and Chief of Staff for the House Committee on the Judiciary. He has also served as Staff Director and General Counsel of the Committee on House Administration and the House Select Committee on Benghazi.

In addition to his extensive Capitol Hill experience, Mr. Kiko served as ''Of Counsel'' at the Washington, DC law firm Foley & Lardner, LLC and Vice Chairman of the Smith-Free Group. He is a graduate of Mount Union College in Alliance, Ohio and George Mason University School of Law. Mr. Kiko is a Member of the D.C. Bar, the Virginia State Bar, and the United States Court of Appeals for both the Federal Circuit and the D.C. circuit.

Chief Administrative Officer.—Philip Kiko.
Deputy Chief Administrative Officer.—John Clocker, HB-28, The Capitol.
Chief of Staff.—Anne Binsted, HB–28, The Capitol.
Chief Customer Officer.—Richard Cappetto, B–227, OHOB.
Chief Financial Officer.—Leonard Puzzuoli, 3140, OHOB.
Chief Human Resources Officer.—John Salamone, H2–102, FHOB.
Chief Information Officer.—Catherine Szpindor, H2–631, FHOB.
Chief Logistics Officer.—Tom Coyne, WA–34, RHOB.
Chief Procurement Officer.—Lisa Grant, 5110, OHOB.
Chief Risk Officer.—Susan Simpson, H2–217, FHOB.
Administrative Counsel.—Christopher Brewster, H2–217, FHOB.

CHAPLAIN

HB–25 The Capitol, phone 225–2509, fax 226–4928

PATRICK J. CONROY, S.J., Chaplain, House of Representatives, residence, Portland, OR; a Jesuit of the Oregon Province of the Society of Jesus, graduated from Claremont McKenna College in CA in 1972, attended Gonzaga University Law School for one year before entering the Jesuit Order in 1973. Earned an M.A. in philosophy from Gonzaga University, a J.D. from St. Louis University, an M.Div. from the Jesuit School of Theology at Berkeley (CA), and an STM from Regis College of the University of Toronto in missiology. Practiced law for the Colville Confederated Tribes in Omak, WA, and the U.S. Conference of Catholic

Bishops, representing Salvadoran refugees in San Francisco. Ordained a priest in 1983. From 1984 to 1989, pastored four villages on the Colville and Spokane Indian Reservations. Worked for the national Jesuit Office of Social Ministries in Washington, DC, then began a career of university chaplaincy at Georgetown University and Seattle University. In 2003 transferred to Jesuit High School in Portland, OR, to teach freshman theology and coach the mighty JV II girls' softball team. Also served as the Oregon Province's Provincial Assistant for Formation and as superior of the Jesuit community at Jesuit High School in Portland. Sworn in as 60th House Chaplain on May 25, 2011.

Chaplain of the House.—Patrick J. Conroy, S.J.
Assistant to the Chaplain/Liaison to Staff.—Karen Bronson.

OFFICE OF INSPECTOR GENERAL

H2–386 Ford House Office Building, phone 226–1250

Inspector General.—Michael T. Ptasienski.
Deputy Inspector General.—Joseph C. Picolla.
Director of Support Services.—R. Terry Upshur.
Assistant Director, Technology and Quality Assurance.—Steven Johnson.
Assistant Director, Finance and Administration.—Susan Kozubski.
Administrative Assistant.—Deborah E. Jones.
Director, Performance and Financial Audits, and Investigative Services.—Larry R. Price, Jr.
Assistant Director, Performance Audits and Investigative Services.—Julie Poole.
Assistant Director, Performance and Financial Audits.—Vacant.
Auditors: Kevin Cornell, Nicole Loutsenhizer, Tamara Solomon, Rosario Torres.
Director, Information Systems Audits.—Saad Patel.
Assistant Directors, Information Systems Audits: Michael Howard, Clifton Persaud.
Auditors: Emmanuel Akowuah, Peter Lee, Kimberly McClellan.
Director, Management and Advisory Services.—Christen Stevenson.
Assistant Directors: Keith Sullenberger, Donna Wolfgang.
Management Analyst.—David DeMarco.

OFFICE OF THE LAW REVISION COUNSEL

H2–308 Ford House Office Building, 20515–6711, phone 226–2411, fax 225–0010

Law Revision Counsel.—Ralph V. Seep.
Deputy Counsel.—Robert M. Sukol.
Senior Counsels: Brian Lindsey, Kenneth I. Paretzky, John F. Wagner, Jr.
Assistant Counsels: Michelle Evans, Katrina M. Hall, Katherine L. Lane, Deborah Letz, Edward T. Mulligan, Michele K. Skarvelis, Lindsey Skouras.
Staff Assistants: Sylvia Tahirkheli, Monica Thompson.
Printing Editor.—Vacant.
GPO Detailee.—Andrea Sabaliauskas.
Senior Systems Engineer.—Eric Loach.
Systems Engineer.—Kenneth Thomas.

OFFICE OF THE LEGISLATIVE COUNSEL

H2–337 Ford House Office Building, phone 225–6060

Legislative Counsel.—Ernest Wade Ballou, Jr.
Deputy Legislative Counsel.—Noah L. Wofsy.
Senior Counsel: Warren Burke, Paul Callen, Henry Christrup, Lisa Daly, Mathew Eckstein, Susan Fleishman, James Grossman, Jean Harmann, Hadley Ross, Jessica Shapiro, Mark Synnes, Robert Weinhagen, Brady Young.
Counsel: Karen Anderson, Marshall Barksdale, Hallet Brazelton, Thomas Cassidy, Megan Chasnoff, Brendan Gallagher, Justin Gross, Alison Hartwich, Fiona Heckscher, Kakuti Lin, Molly Lothamer, Christopher Osborne, Scott Probst, Anthony Sciascia, Anna Shpak, Veena Srinivasa, Kathryn Swiss, Michelle Vanek, Sally Walker.
Assistant Counsel: Michael Ambinder, Thomas Anderson, Eric Bernstein, Lisa Castillo, Robert Casturo, Kenneth Cox, Casey Ebner, Brenna Gautam, Allison Gilley, Stephen Hagenbuch, Karl Hagnauer, Megan Hawkins, Ebony Holder, Paul Kubicki, Amanda

Molina, Keith Nemeth, Kalyani Parthasarathy, Sarah Rens, Donalene Roberts, Adam Schilt, Brandon Senger, Adrienne Thomas.

Office Administrator.—Nancy McNeillie.

Assistant Office Administrator.—Debra Birch.

Human Resources Administrator.—Thomas Dillon.

Director, Information Systems.—Willie Blount.

Senior Systems Analyst.—Peter Szwec.

Assistant Systems Administrator.—David Topper.

Publications Coordinator.—Craig Sterkx.

Legislative Research Analyst.—Alex Swindle.

Office Managerial Assistant.—Ashley Anderson.

Staff Assistants/Paralegals: Lauren Anderson, Elonda Blount, Mairead Crotty, Kevin Hauff, Kelly Meryweather, Tom Meryweather.

Staff Assistants: Joseph Birch, Rachel Davis, Monique Ducksworth, Miekl Joyner, Matthew Loggie, Angelina Plater.

OFFICE OF THE SERGEANT AT ARMS

H–124 The Capitol, phone 225–2456

PAUL D. IRVING, was sworn in as the 36th Sergeant at Arms of the U.S. House of Representatives on January 17, 2012, during the 2nd session of the 112th Congress. Prior to serving as Sergeant at Arms, Mr. Irving was an Assistant Director of the U.S. Secret Service from 2001 to 2008. Paul Irving was born August 21, 1957, in Tampa, Florida. He received a Bachelor of Science degree in Justice from American University in Washington, DC, and a Juris Doctorate from Whittier Law School in Los Angeles, California. He began his law enforcement career in 1980 as a clerk for the Federal Bureau of Investigation in Los Angeles, California; was appointed a Special Agent at the Secret Service's Los Angeles Field Office; was transferred to Washington, DC, where he served as the head legal instructor for constitutional law, statutory authority, and criminal procedure at the Secret Service Training Academy; and was assigned to the Presidential Protective Division at the White House during the administrations of George H.W. Bush and William Jefferson Clinton, where he rose to a supervisory position. Subsequent to his White House duty, Mr. Irving served as Deputy Assistant Director for Congressional Affairs, Assistant Director for Government and Public Affairs, Assistant Director for Homeland Security, and Assistant Director for Administration.

Mr. Irving is the recipient of numerous awards and commendations during his distinguished law enforcement career, among them the Senior Executive Service Presidential Rank Award for Meritorious Service, and the Presidential Rank Award for Distinguished Service in the Senior Executive Service; he has been a member of the California State Bar since 1982, the U.S. District Court for the Central District of California, the U.S. Court of Appeals for the Ninth Circuit, the District of Columbia Bar, and the Supreme Court Bar; Irving resides in Washington, DC.

Sergeant at Arms.—Paul D. Irving.

Deputy Sergeant at Arms.—Tim Blodgett.

Chief of Staff.—Kelle Strickland.

Assistant Sergeant at Arms, Administration.—Kathleen Joyce.

Assistant Sergeant at Arms, Protocol and Chamber Operations.—Ted Daniel.

Assistants to the Sergeant at Arms, Floor Security: Joyce Hamlett, Rick Villa.

Assistant Sergeant at Arms, Emergency Management.—Erik Speranza.

Deputy Assistant Sergeant at Arms, Police Services.—Robert Fitzpatrick.

Chief Operating Officer.—Bob Dohr.

Chief Information Officer.—Jim Kaelin.

Counsel.—Bob Sensenbrenner.

Directors:

Division of Garage and Parking Security.—Jim Abbott.

Division of House Security.—William McFarland.

Division of Identification Services.—LaShon Bethea.

Protocol & Special Events.—Catherine Huddleston.

Deputy Assistant Sergeant at Arms:

Appointments Desk.—Teresa Johnson.

Chamber Security.—Jack Looney.

Chamber Support Services.—Andrew Burns.

Assistants: LaKeisha Commodore, Lorraine Foreman, Carmelitta Riley, Ruby Tavernier.

JOINT COMMITTEES

Joint Economic Committee

G01 Dirksen Senate Office Building, 20510–6432, phone 224–5171

[Created pursuant to sec. 5(a) of Public Law 304, 79th Congress]

Mike Lee, Senator from Utah, *Chairman*

Donald S. Beyer, Jr., Representative from Virginia, *Vice Chair*

SENATE

Tom Cotton, of Arkansas.
Rob Portman, of Ohio.
Bill Cassidy, of Louisiana.
Ted Cruz, of Texas.
Kelly Loeffler, of Georgia.

Martin Heinrich, of New Mexico.
Amy Klobuchar, of Minnesota.
Gary C. Peters, of Michigan.
Margaret Wood Hassan, of New Hampshire.

HOUSE

Carolyn B. Maloney, of New York.
Denny Heck, of Washington.
David J. Trone, of Maryland.
Joyce Beatty, of Ohio.
Lois Frankel, of Florida.

David Schweikert, of Arizona.
Darin LaHood, of Illinois.
Kenny Marchant, of Texas.
Jaime Herrera Beutler, of Washington.

STAFF

Joint Economic Committee (G–01), 224–5171, fax 224–0240.
Republican Staff:
Executive Director.—Scott Winship.
Deputy Director.—Vanessa Brown Calder.
Senior Policy Advisors: Patrick Brown, Rachel Sheffield.
Senior Economists: Alan Cole, Christina King, Beila Leboeuf.
Policy Advisors: Robert Bellafiore, Wells King, Vijay Menon.
Communications Director.—Amalia Halikias.
Financial Director.—Colleen Healy.
System Administrator.—Barry Dexter.
Digital Media Director.—Kyle Treasure.
House Republican Staff Director.—Ron Donado.
House Republican Communications Director.—Grace White.
Democratic Staff:
Staff Director.—Harry Gural.
Senior Policy Advisor.—Jim Whitney.
Senior Policy Analysts: Sol Espinoza, Leyla Mocan, Kyle Moore.
Senior Economists: Owen Haaga, John Tepper Marlin.
Research Analyst.—Melanie Ackerman.
Research Assistants: Michael Pearson, Hope Sheils.
Communications Director.—Randy Woods.

Joint Committee of Congress on the Library

305 Russell Senate Office Building, 20510, phone 224–6352

Roy Blunt, Senator from Missouri, *Chair*

Zoe Lofgren, Representative from California, *Vice Chair*

SENATE

Pat Roberts, of Kansas.
Richard C. Shelby, of Alabama.
Amy Klobuchar, of Minnesota.
Patrick J. Leahy, of Vermont.

HOUSE

Tim Ryan, of Ohio.
G. K. Butterfield, of North Carolina.
Rodney Davis, of Illinois.
Barry Loudermilk, of Georgia.

Joint Committee on Printing

1309 Longworth House Office Building, 20510, phone 225–2061

[Created by act of August 3, 1846 (9 Stat. 114); U.S. Code 44, Section 101]

Zoe Lofgren, Representative from California, *Chairperson*

Roy Blunt, Senator from Missouri, *Vice Chair*

HOUSE

Jamie Raskin, of Maryland.
Susan A. Davis, of California.
Rodney Davis, of Illinois.
Barry Loudermilk, of Georgia.

SENATE

Pat Roberts, of Kansas.
Roger F. Wicker, of Mississippi.
Amy Klobuchar, of Minnesota.
Tom Udall, of New Mexico.

Joint Committee on Taxation

H2–502 Ford House Office Building, 20515, phone 225–3621

SD–G18, Senate Dirksen Office Building, 20510, phone 224–5561

https://jct.gov

[Created by Public Law 20, 69th Congress]

Chuck Grassley, Senator from Iowa, *Chair*

Richard E. Neal, Representative from Massachusetts, *Vice Chair*

SENATE

Mike Crapo, of Idaho.
Michael B. Enzi, of Wyoming.
Ron Wyden, of Oregon.
Debbie Stabenow, of Michigan.

HOUSE

Lloyd Doggett, of Texas.
Vacant.
Kevin Brady, of Texas.
Devin Nunes, of California.

NON-DESIGNATED STAFF

Joint Committee on Taxation

Chief of Staff.—Thomas Barthold.

Deputy Chief of Staff.—Robert Harvey.

Office Administrator.—Pamela Williams.

Administrative Specialist.—Frank Shima.

Senior Legislation Counsel: Gordon Clay, Adam Gropper, Harold Hirsch, Deirdre James, Cecily Rock, Kristine Roth, Kashi Way.

Legislation Counsel: Jeffrey Arbeit, Vivek Chandrasekhar, Clare Diefenbach, Jared Hermann, Andrew Lai, Shelley Leonard, Paul McLaughlin, Rhonda Migdail.

Senior Refund Counsel.—Norman Brand.

Refund Counsel: Chase Gibson, Robert Gotwald.

Senior Economists: Nicholas Bull, James Cilke, Tim Dowd, Chris Giosa, Thomas Holtmann, Kathleen Mackie, James McGuire, Christopher Overend, Zachary Richards, Brent Trigg.

Economists: Chia Chang, James Elwell, Sameh Habib, Sally Kwak, Paul Landefeld, Joseph LeCates, Bert Lue, Rachel Moore, Brandon Pecoraro, Heidi Schramm, David Splinter, Lin Xu.

Legislation Tax Accountants: Ross Margelefsky, Natalie Tucker.

Chief Statistical Analyst.—Melani Houser.

Statistical Analyst.—Tanya Butler.

Document Production Specialist.—Chris Simmons.

Tax Resource Specialist.—Melissa O'Brien.

Legal Research Analyst.—Katie Mikulka.

Economic Research Analyst.—Elena Derby.

Economic Research Assistants: Michael Pavlak, Thomas Willingham.

Director of Information Technology.—Damion Jedlicka.

Director of Information Security.—Merrick Munday.

Information Technology Specialists: Mark High, Jonathan Newton.

Desktop Support Specialist.—Dennis Ortega.

Executive Assistants: Kristine Means, Jayne Northern, Lucia Rogers.

Senior Staff Assistant.—Debra McMullen.

Staff Assistant.—Sylvester Gunn.

ASSIGNMENTS OF SENATORS TO COMMITTEES

[Republicans in roman (53); Democrats in *italic* (45); Independents in SMALL CAPS (2); total, 100]

Senator	Committees (Standing, Joint, Select, and Special)
Alexander	Health, Education, Labor, and Pensions, *chair*. Appropriations. Energy and Natural Resources. Rules and Administration.
Baldwin	Appropriations. Commerce, Science, and Transportation. Health, Education, Labor, and Pensions.
Barrasso	Environment and Public Works, *chair*. Energy and Natural Resources. Foreign Relations. Indian Affairs.
Bennet	Agriculture, Nutrition, and Forestry. Finance. Select Committee on Intelligence.
Blackburn	Armed Services. Commerce, Science, and Transportation. Judiciary. Veterans' Affairs.
Blumenthal	Armed Services. Commerce, Science, and Transportation. Judiciary. Veterans' Affairs. Special Committee on Aging.
Blunt	Rules and Administration, *chair*. Joint Committee on the Library, *chair*. Joint Committee on Printing, *vice chair*. Appropriations. Commerce, Science, and Transportation. Select Committee on Intelligence.
Booker	Environment and Public Works. Foreign Relations. Judiciary. Small Business and Entrepreneurship.
Boozman	Agriculture, Nutrition, and Forestry. Appropriations. Environment and Public Works. Veterans' Affairs.
Braun	Agriculture, Nutrition, and Forestry. Budget. Environment and Public Works. Health, Education, Labor, and Pensions. Special Committee on Aging.
Brown	Agriculture, Nutrition, and Forestry. Banking, Housing, and Urban Affairs. Finance. Veterans' Affairs.

Senator	Committees (Standing, Joint, Select, and Special)
Burr	Finance. Health, Education, Labor, and Pensions. Select Committee on Intelligence. Special Committee on Aging.
Cantwell	Commerce, Science, and Transportation. Energy and Natural Resources. Finance. Indian Affairs. Small Business and Entrepreneurship.
Capito	Appropriations. Commerce, Science, and Transportation. Environment and Public Works. Rules and Administration.
Cardin	Environment and Public Works. Finance. Foreign Relations. Small Business and Entrepreneurship.
Carper	Environment and Public Works. Finance. Homeland Security and Governmental Affairs.
Casey	Agriculture, Nutrition, and Forestry. Finance. Health, Education, Labor, and Pensions. Special Committee on Aging.
Cassidy	Energy and Natural Resources. Finance. Health, Education, Labor, and Pensions. Veterans' Affairs. Joint Economic Committee.
Collins	Special Committee on Aging, *chair.* Appropriations. Health, Education, Labor, and Pensions. Select Committee on Intelligence.
Coons	Select Committee on Ethics, *vice chair.* Appropriations. Foreign Relations. Judiciary. Small Business and Entrepreneurship.
Cornyn	Finance. Judiciary. Select Committee on Intelligence.
Cortez Masto	Banking, Housing, and Urban Affairs. Energy and Natural Resources. Finance. Indian Affairs. Rules and Administration.
Cotton	Armed Services. Banking, Housing, and Urban Affairs. Joint Economic Committee. Select Committee on Intelligence.
Cramer	Armed Services. Banking, Housing, and Urban Affairs. Budget. Environment and Public Works. Veterans' Affairs.

Senator	Committees (Standing, Joint, Select, and Special)
Crapo	Banking, Housing, and Urban Affairs, *chair.* Budget. Finance. Judiciary. Joint Committee on Taxation.
Cruz	Commerce, Science, and Transportation. Foreign Relations. Judiciary. Rules and Administration. Joint Economic Committee.
Daines	Appropriations. Energy and Natural Resources. Finance. Indian Affairs.
Duckworth	Armed Services. Commerce, Science, and Transportation. Environment and Public Works. Small Business and Entrepreneurship.
Durbin	Agriculture, Nutrition, and Forestry. Appropriations. Judiciary. Rules and Administration.
Enzi	Budget, *chair.* Finance. Health, Education, Labor, and Pensions. Homeland Security and Governmental Affairs. Joint Committee on Taxation.
Ernst	Agriculture, Nutrition, and Forestry. Armed Services. Environment and Public Works. Judiciary. Small Business and Entrepreneurship.
Feinstein	Appropriations. Judiciary. Rules and Administration. Select Committee on Intelligence.
Fischer	Agriculture, Nutrition, and Forestry. Armed Services. Commerce, Science, and Transportation. Rules and Administration.
Gardner	Commerce, Science, and Transportation. Energy and Natural Resources. Foreign Relations.
Gillibrand	Agriculture, Nutrition, and Forestry. Armed Services. Environment and Public Works. Special Committee on Aging.
Graham	Judiciary, *chair.* Appropriations. Budget. Foreign Relations.
Grassley	Finance, *chair.* Joint Committee on Taxation, *chair.* Agriculture, Nutrition, and Forestry. Budget. Judiciary.

Senator	Committees (Standing, Joint, Select, and Special)
Harris	Budget. Homeland Security and Governmental Affairs. Judiciary. Select Committee on Intelligence.
Hassan	Finance. Health, Education, Labor, and Pensions. Homeland Security and Governmental Affairs. Joint Economic Committee.
Hawley	Armed Services. Homeland Security and Governmental Affairs. Judiciary. Small Business and Entrepreneurship. Special Committee on Aging.
Heinrich	Armed Services. Energy and Natural Resources. Joint Economic Committee. Select Committee on Intelligence.
Hirono	Armed Services. Energy and Natural Resources. Judiciary. Small Business and Entrepreneurship. Veterans' Affairs.
Hoeven	Indian Affairs, *chair.* Agriculture, Nutrition, and Forestry. Appropriations. Energy and Natural Resources.
Hyde-Smith	Agriculture, Nutrition, and Forestry. Appropriations. Energy and Natural Resources. Rules and Administration.
Inhofe	Armed Services, *chair.* Environment and Public Works. Small Business and Entrepreneurship. Select Committee on Intelligence.
Johnson	Homeland Security and Governmental Affairs, *chair.* Budget. Commerce, Science, and Transportation. Foreign Relations.
Jones	Armed Services. Banking, Housing, and Urban Affairs. Health, Education, Labor, and Pensions. Special Committee on Aging.
Kaine	Armed Services. Budget. Foreign Relations. Health, Education, Labor, and Pensions.
Kennedy	Appropriations. Banking, Housing, and Urban Affairs. Budget. Judiciary. Small Business and Entrepreneurship.
KING	Armed Services. Energy and Natural Resources. Rules and Administration. Select Committee on Intelligence.

Senator	Committees (Standing, Joint, Select, and Special)
Klobuchar	Agriculture, Nutrition, and Forestry. Commerce, Science, and Transportation. Judiciary. Rules and Administration. Joint Committee on Printing. Joint Committee on the Library. Joint Economic Committee.
Lankford	Select Committee on Ethics, *chair*. Appropriations. Finance. Homeland Security and Governmental Affairs. Indian Affairs.
Leahy	Agriculture, Nutrition, and Forestry. Appropriations. Judiciary. Rules and Administration. Joint Committee on the Library.
Lee	Joint Economic Committee, *chair*. Commerce, Science, and Transportation. Energy and Natural Resources. Judiciary.
Loeffler	Agriculture, Nutrition, and Forestry. Health, Education, Labor, and Pensions. Veterans' Affairs. Joint Economic Committee.
Manchin	Appropriations. Armed Services. Energy and Natural Resources. Veterans' Affairs.
Markey	Commerce, Science, and Transportation. Environment and Public Works. Foreign Relations. Small Business and Entrepreneurship.
McConnell	Agriculture, Nutrition, and Forestry. Appropriations. Rules and Administration. Select Committee on Intelligence.
McSally	Armed Services. Banking, Housing, and Urban Affairs. Energy and Natural Resources. Indian Affairs. Special Committee on Aging.
Menendez	Banking, Housing, and Urban Affairs. Finance. Foreign Relations.
Merkley	Appropriations. Budget. Environment and Public Works. Foreign Relations.
Moran	Veterans' Affairs, *chair*. Appropriations. Banking, Housing, and Urban Affairs. Commerce, Science, and Transportation. Indian Affairs.
Murkowski	Energy and Natural Resources, *chair*. Appropriations. Health, Education, Labor, and Pensions. Indian Affairs.

Senator	Committees (Standing, Joint, Select, and Special)
Murphy	Appropriations. Foreign Relations. Health, Education, Labor, and Pensions.
Murray	Appropriations. Budget. Health, Education, Labor, and Pensions. Veterans' Affairs.
Paul	Foreign Relations. Health, Education, Labor, and Pensions. Homeland Security and Governmental Affairs. Small Business and Entrepreneurship.
Perdue	Armed Services. Banking, Housing, and Urban Affairs. Budget. Foreign Relations.
Peters	Armed Services. Commerce, Science, and Transportation. Homeland Security and Governmental Affairs. Joint Economic Committee.
Portman	Finance. Foreign Relations. Homeland Security and Governmental Affairs. Joint Economic Committee.
Reed	Appropriations. Armed Services. Banking, Housing, and Urban Affairs.
Risch	Foreign Relations, *chair.* Energy and Natural Resources. Small Business and Entrepreneurship. Select Committee on Ethics. Select Committee on Intelligence.
Roberts	Agriculture, Nutrition, and Forestry, *chair.* Finance. Health, Education, Labor, and Pensions. Rules and Administration. Joint Committee on Printing. Joint Committee on the Library. Select Committee on Ethics.
Romney	Foreign Relations. Health, Education, Labor, and Pensions. Homeland Security and Governmental Affairs. Small Business and Entrepreneurship.
Rosen	Commerce, Science, and Transportation. Health, Education, Labor, and Pensions. Homeland Security and Governmental Affairs. Small Business and Entrepreneurship. Special Committee on Aging.
Rounds	Armed Services. Banking, Housing, and Urban Affairs. Environment and Public Works. Veterans' Affairs.
Rubio	Small Business and Entrepreneurship, *chair.* Select Committee on Intelligence, *chair.* Appropriations. Foreign Relations. Special Committee on Aging.

Senator	Committees (Standing, Joint, Select, and Special)
SANDERS	Budget. Energy and Natural Resources. Environment and Public Works. Health, Education, Labor, and Pensions. Veterans' Affairs.
Sasse	Banking, Housing, and Urban Affairs. Finance. Judiciary. Select Committee on Intelligence.
Schatz	Appropriations. Banking, Housing, and Urban Affairs. Commerce, Science, and Transportation. Indian Affairs. Select Committee on Ethics.
Schumer	Rules and Administration.
Scott of Florida	Armed Services. Budget. Commerce, Science, and Transportation. Homeland Security and Governmental Affairs. Special Committee on Aging.
Scott of South Carolina	Banking, Housing, and Urban Affairs. Finance. Health, Education, Labor, and Pensions. Small Business and Entrepreneurship. Special Committee on Aging.
Shaheen	Appropriations. Armed Services. Foreign Relations. Small Business and Entrepreneurship. Select Committee on Ethics.
Shelby	Appropriations, *chair.* Banking, Housing, and Urban Affairs. Environment and Public Works. Rules and Administration. Joint Committee on the Library.
Sinema	Banking, Housing, and Urban Affairs. Commerce, Science, and Transportation. Homeland Security and Governmental Affairs. Veterans' Affairs. Special Committee on Aging.
Smith	Agriculture, Nutrition, and Forestry. Banking, Housing, and Urban Affairs. Health, Education, Labor, and Pensions. Indian Affairs.
Stabenow	Agriculture, Nutrition, and Forestry. Budget. Energy and Natural Resources. Finance. Joint Committee on Taxation.
Sullivan	Armed Services. Commerce, Science, and Transportation. Environment and Public Works. Veterans' Affairs.

Senator	Committees (Standing, Joint, Select, and Special)
Tester	Appropriations. Banking, Housing, and Urban Affairs. Commerce, Science, and Transportation. Indian Affairs. Veterans' Affairs.
Thune	Agriculture, Nutrition, and Forestry. Commerce, Science, and Transportation. Finance.
Tillis	Armed Services. Banking, Housing, and Urban Affairs. Judiciary. Veterans' Affairs.
Toomey	Banking, Housing, and Urban Affairs. Budget. Finance.
Udall	Indian Affairs, *vice chair.* Appropriations. Commerce, Science, and Transportation. Foreign Relations. Rules and Administration. Joint Committee on Printing.
Van Hollen	Appropriations. Banking, Housing, and Urban Affairs. Budget. Environment and Public Works.
Warner	Select Committee on Intelligence, *vice chair.* Banking, Housing, and Urban Affairs. Budget. Finance. Rules and Administration.
Warren	Armed Services. Banking, Housing, and Urban Affairs. Health, Education, Labor, and Pensions. Special Committee on Aging.
Whitehouse	Budget. Environment and Public Works. Finance. Judiciary.
Wicker	Commerce, Science, and Transportation, *chair.* Armed Services. Environment and Public Works. Rules and Administration. Joint Committee on Printing.
Wyden	Budget. Energy and Natural Resources. Finance. Select Committee on Intelligence. Joint Committee on Taxation.
Young	Commerce, Science, and Transportation. Finance. Foreign Relations. Small Business and Entrepreneurship.

ASSIGNMENTS OF REPRESENTATIVES, RESIDENT COMMISSIONER, AND DELEGATES TO COMMITTEES

[Democrats in roman (232); Republicans in *italic* (198); Libertarians in SMALL CAPS (1); Vacancies (4); Resident Commissioner and Delegates in **boldface** (6); total, 441.]

Representative	Committees (Standing, Joint, and Select)
Abraham	Agriculture. Armed Services.
Adams	Agriculture. Education and Labor. Financial Services.
Aderholt	Appropriations.
Aguilar	Appropriations. House Administration.
Allen	Agriculture. Education and Labor.
Allred	Foreign Affairs. Transportation and Infrastructure. Veterans' Affairs.
AMASH	[No committee assignments at press time.]
Amodei	Appropriations.
Armstrong	Judiciary. Oversight and Reform. Select Committee on the Climate Crisis.
Arrington	Ways and Means.
Axne	Agriculture. Financial Services.
Babin	Science, Space, and Technology. Transportation and Infrastructure.
Bacon	Agriculture. Armed Services.
Baird	Agriculture. Science, Space, and Technology.
Balderson	Science, Space, and Technology. Small Business. Transportation and Infrastructure.
Banks	Armed Services. Education and Labor. Veterans' Affairs.
Barr	Financial Services. Veterans' Affairs.
Barragán	Energy and Commerce. Homeland Security.
Bass	Foreign Affairs. Judiciary.
Beatty	Financial Services.
Bera	Foreign Affairs. Science, Space, and Technology.

Representative	Committees (Standing, Joint, and Select)
Bergman	Armed Services. Veterans' Affairs.
Beyer	Science, Space, and Technology. Ways and Means.
Biggs	Judiciary. Science, Space, and Technology.
Bilirakis	Energy and Commerce. Veterans' Affairs.
Bishop, Dan, of North Carolina ..	Homeland Security. Small Business.
Bishop, Rob, of Utah	Armed Services. Natural Resources.
Bishop, Sanford D., Jr., of Georgia	Appropriations.
Blumenauer	Ways and Means.
Blunt Rochester	Energy and Commerce.
Bonamici	Education and Labor. Science, Space, and Technology. Select Committee on the Climate Crisis.
Bost	Agriculture. Transportation and Infrastructure. Veterans' Affairs.
Boyle, Brendan F., of Pennsylvania	Budget. Ways and Means.
Brady	Ways and Means.
Brindisi	Agriculture. Armed Services. Veterans' Affairs.
Brooks, Mo, of Alabama	Armed Services. Science, Space, and Technology.
Brooks, Susan W., of Indiana	Energy and Commerce. Select Committee on the Modernization of Congress.
Brown, Anthony G., of Maryland	Armed Services. Ethics. Natural Resources. Transportation and Infrastructure.
Brownley, Julia, of California	Transportation and Infrastructure. Veterans' Affairs. Select Committee on the Climate Crisis.
Buchanan	Ways and Means.
Buck	Foreign Affairs. Judiciary.
Bucshon	Energy and Commerce.
Budd	Financial Services.
Burchett	Budget. Foreign Affairs. Small Business.
Burgess	Energy and Commerce. Rules.

Representative	Committees (Standing, Joint, and Select)
Bustos	Agriculture. Appropriations.
Butterfield	Energy and Commerce. House Administration.
Byrne	Armed Services. Education and Labor.
Calvert	Appropriations.
Carbajal	Agriculture. Armed Services. Transportation and Infrastructure.
Cárdenas	Energy and Commerce.
Carson, André, of Indiana	Transportation and Infrastructure. Permanent Select Committee on Intelligence.
Carter, Earl L. ''Buddy'', of Georgia	Energy and Commerce. Select Committee on the Climate Crisis.
Carter, John R., of Texas	Appropriations.
Cartwright	Appropriations. Natural Resources.
Case	Appropriations. Natural Resources.
Casten, Sean, of Illinois	Financial Services. Science, Space, and Technology. Select Committee on the Climate Crisis.
Castor, Kathy, of Florida	Select Committee on the Climate Crisis, *chair.* Energy and Commerce.
Castro, Joaquin, of Texas	Education and Labor. Foreign Affairs. Permanent Select Committee on Intelligence.
Chabot	Foreign Affairs. Judiciary. Small Business.
Cheney	Armed Services. Natural Resources.
Chu, Judy, of California	Small Business. Ways and Means.
Cicilline	Foreign Affairs. Judiciary.
Cisneros	Armed Services. Veterans' Affairs.
Clark, Katherine M., of Massachusetts	Appropriations.
Clarke, Yvette D., of New York	Energy and Commerce. Homeland Security.
Clay	Financial Services. Natural Resources. Oversight and Reform.
Cleaver	Financial Services. Homeland Security. Select Committee on the Modernization of Congress.
Cline	Education and Labor. Judiciary.

Representative	Committees (Standing, Joint, and Select)
Cloud	Oversight and Reform. Science, Space, and Technology.
Clyburn	Majority Whip.
Cohen	Judiciary. Science, Space, and Technology. Transportation and Infrastructure.
Cole	Rules, *ranking member.* Appropriations.
Collins	Judiciary.
Comer	Agriculture. Education and Labor. Oversight and Reform.
Conaway	Agriculture. Armed Services. Permanent Select Committee on Intelligence.
Connolly	Foreign Affairs. Oversight and Reform.
Cook	Armed Services. Natural Resources.
Cooper	Armed Services. Budget. Oversight and Reform.
Correa	Homeland Security. Judiciary.
Costa	Agriculture. Foreign Affairs. Natural Resources.
Courtney	Armed Services. Education and Labor.
Cox, TJ, of California	Agriculture. Natural Resources.
Craig	Agriculture. Small Business. Transportation and Infrastructure.
Crawford	Agriculture. Transportation and Infrastructure. Permanent Select Committee on Intelligence.
Crenshaw	Budget. Homeland Security.
Crist	Appropriations. Science, Space, and Technology.
Crow	Armed Services. Small Business.
Cuellar	Appropriations.
Cunningham	Natural Resources. Veterans' Affairs.
Curtis	Foreign Affairs. Natural Resources.
Davids	Small Business. Transportation and Infrastructure.
Davidson, Warren, of Ohio	Financial Services.
Davis, Danny K., of Illinois	Ways and Means.

Representative	Committees (Standing, Joint, and Select)
Davis, Rodney, of Illinois	House Administration, *ranking member.* Agriculture. Transportation and Infrastructure. Select Committee on the Modernization of Congress.
Davis, Susan A., of California	Armed Services. Education and Labor. House Administration.
Dean	Financial Services. Judiciary.
DeFazio	Transportation and Infrastructure, *chair.*
DeGette	Energy and Commerce. Natural Resources.
DeLauro	Appropriations. Budget.
DelBene	Ways and Means. Select Committee on the Modernization of Congress.
Delgado	Agriculture. Small Business. Transportation and Infrastructure.
Demings	Homeland Security. Judiciary. Permanent Select Committee on Intelligence.
DeSaulnier	Education and Labor. Oversight and Reform. Rules. Transportation and Infrastructure.
DesJarlais	Agriculture. Armed Services.
Deutch	Ethics, *chair.* Foreign Affairs. Judiciary.
Diaz-Balart	Appropriations.
Dingell	Energy and Commerce. Natural Resources.
Doggett	Budget. Ways and Means.
Doyle, Michael F., of Pennsylvania	Energy and Commerce.
Duncan	Energy and Commerce.
Dunn	Agriculture. Veterans' Affairs.
Emmer	Financial Services.
Engel	Foreign Affairs, *chair.* Energy and Commerce.
Escobar	Armed Services. Judiciary.
Eshoo	Energy and Commerce.
Espaillat	Foreign Affairs. Small Business. Transportation and Infrastructure.
Estes	Ways and Means.

Representative	Committees (Standing, Joint, and Select)
Evans	Small Business. Ways and Means.
Ferguson	Ways and Means.
Finkenauer	Small Business. Transportation and Infrastructure.
Fitzpatrick	Foreign Affairs. Transportation and Infrastructure.
Fleischmann	Appropriations.
Fletcher	Science, Space, and Technology. Transportation and Infrastructure.
Flores	Budget. Energy and Commerce.
Fortenberry	Appropriations.
Foster	Financial Services. Science, Space, and Technology.
Foxx, Virginia, of North Carolina	Education and Labor. Oversight and Reform.
Frankel	Appropriations.
Fudge	Agriculture. Education and Labor. House Administration.
Fulcher	Education and Labor. Natural Resources.
Gabbard	Armed Services. Financial Services.
Gaetz	Armed Services. Judiciary.
Gallagher	Armed Services. Transportation and Infrastructure.
Gallego	Armed Services. Natural Resources.
Garamendi	Armed Services. Transportation and Infrastructure.
García, Jesús G. ''Chuy'', of Illinois	Financial Services. Natural Resources. Transportation and Infrastructure.
Garcia, Mike, of California	Homeland Security. Science, Space, and Technology. Transportation and Infrastructure.
Garcia, Sylvia R., of Texas	Financial Services. Judiciary.
Gianforte	Energy and Commerce.
Gibbs	Oversight and Reform. Transportation and Infrastructure.
Gohmert	Judiciary. Natural Resources.
Golden	Armed Services. Small Business.
Gomez	Oversight and Reform. Ways and Means.

Representative	Committees (Standing, Joint, and Select)
Gonzalez, Anthony, of Ohio	Financial Services. Science, Space, and Technology.
Gonzalez, Vicente, of Texas	Financial Services. Foreign Affairs.
González-Colón, Jenniffer, of Puerto Rico	Natural Resources. Transportation and Infrastructure.
Gooden	Financial Services.
Gosar	Natural Resources. Oversight and Reform.
Gottheimer	Financial Services.
Granger	Appropriations.
Graves, Garret, of Louisiana	Natural Resources. Transportation and Infrastructure. Select Committee on the Climate Crisis.
Graves, Sam, of Missouri	Armed Services. Transportation and Infrastructure.
Graves, Tom, of Georgia	Select Committee on the Modernization of Congress, *vice chair.* Appropriations.
Green, Al, of Texas	Financial Services. Homeland Security.
Green, Mark E., of Tennessee	Homeland Security. Oversight and Reform.
Griffith	Energy and Commerce. Select Committee on the Climate Crisis.
Grijalva	Natural Resources, *chair.* Education and Labor.
Grothman	Education and Labor. Oversight and Reform.
Guest	Ethics. Foreign Affairs. Homeland Security.
Guthrie	Education and Labor. Energy and Commerce.
Haaland	Armed Services. Natural Resources.
Hagedorn	Agriculture. Small Business.
Harder, Josh, of California	Agriculture. Education and Labor.
Harris	Appropriations.
Hartzler	Agriculture. Armed Services.
Hastings	Rules.
Hayes	Agriculture. Education and Labor.
Heck	Financial Services. Permanent Select Committee on Intelligence.
Hern, Kevin, of Oklahoma	Budget. Natural Resources. Small Business.

Representative	Committees (Standing, Joint, and Select)
Herrera Beutler	Appropriations.
Hice, Jody B., of Georgia	Natural Resources. Oversight and Reform.
Higgins, Brian, of New York	Budget. Ways and Means.
Higgins, Clay, of Louisiana	Homeland Security. Oversight and Reform.
Hill	Financial Services.
Himes	Financial Services. Permanent Select Committee on Intelligence.
Holding	Budget. Ethics. Ways and Means.
Hollingsworth	Financial Services.
Horn, Kendra S., of Oklahoma	Armed Services. Science, Space, and Technology.
Horsford	Budget. Natural Resources. Ways and Means.
Houlahan	Armed Services. Foreign Affairs. Small Business.
Hoyer	Majority Leader.
Hudson	Energy and Commerce.
Huffman	Natural Resources. Transportation and Infrastructure. Select Committee on the Climate Crisis.
Huizenga	Financial Services.
Hurd, Will, of Texas	Appropriations. Permanent Select Committee on Intelligence.
Jackson Lee	Budget. Homeland Security. Judiciary.
Jacobs	Agriculture. Budget.
Jayapal	Budget. Education and Labor. Judiciary.
Jeffries	Budget. Judiciary.
Johnson, Bill, of Ohio	Budget. Energy and Commerce.
Johnson, Dusty, of South Dakota	Agriculture. Education and Labor.
Johnson, Eddie Bernice, of Texas	Science, Space, and Technology, *chair*. Transportation and Infrastructure.
Johnson, Henry C. ''Hank'', Jr., of Georgia.	Judiciary. Transportation and Infrastructure.
Johnson, Mike, of Louisiana	Judiciary. Natural Resources.

Representative	Committees (Standing, Joint, and Select)
Jordan	Judiciary. Oversight and Reform.
Joyce, David P., of Ohio	Appropriations.
Joyce, John, of Pennsylvania	Homeland Security. Small Business.
Kaptur	Appropriations.
Katko	Homeland Security. Transportation and Infrastructure.
Keating	Armed Services. Foreign Affairs.
Keller	Education and Labor. Oversight and Reform.
Kelly, Mike, of Pennsylvania	Ways and Means.
Kelly, Robin L., of Illinois	Energy and Commerce. Oversight and Reform.
Kelly, Trent, of Mississippi	Agriculture. Armed Services.
Kennedy	Energy and Commerce.
Khanna	Armed Services. Budget. Oversight and Reform.
Kildee	Budget. Ways and Means.
Kilmer	Select Committee on the Modernization of Congress, *chair*. Appropriations.
Kim	Armed Services. Small Business.
Kind	Ways and Means.
King, Peter T., of New York	Homeland Security.
King, Steve, of Iowa	[No committee assignments at press time.]
Kinzinger	Energy and Commerce. Foreign Affairs.
Kirkpatrick	Agriculture. Appropriations.
Krishnamoorthi	Oversight and Reform. Permanent Select Committee on Intelligence.
Kuster, Ann M., of New Hampshire	Energy and Commerce.
Kustoff, David, of Tennessee	Financial Services.
LaHood	Ways and Means.
LaMalfa	Agriculture. Transportation and Infrastructure.
Lamb	Science, Space, and Technology. Transportation and Infrastructure. Veterans' Affairs.
Lamborn	Armed Services. Natural Resources.
Langevin	Armed Services. Homeland Security.

Representative	Committees (Standing, Joint, and Select)
Larsen, Rick, of Washington	Armed Services. Transportation and Infrastructure.
Larson, John B., of Connecticut ..	Ways and Means.
Latta	Energy and Commerce.
Lawrence	Appropriations. Oversight and Reform.
Lawson, Al, Jr., of Florida	Agriculture. Financial Services.
Lee, Barbara, of California	Appropriations. Budget.
Lee, Susie, of Nevada	Education and Labor. Veterans' Affairs.
Lesko	Homeland Security. Judiciary. Rules.
Levin, Andy, of Michigan	Education and Labor. Foreign Affairs.
Levin, Mike, of California	Natural Resources. Veterans' Affairs. Select Committee on the Climate Crisis.
Lieu, Ted, of California	Foreign Affairs. Judiciary.
Lipinski	Science, Space, and Technology. Transportation and Infrastructure.
Loebsack	Energy and Commerce.
Lofgren	House Administration, *chairperson.* Judiciary. Science, Space, and Technology. Select Committee on the Modernization of Congress.
Long	Energy and Commerce.
Loudermilk	Financial Services. House Administration.
Lowenthal	Natural Resources. Transportation and Infrastructure.
Lowey	Appropriations, *chair.*
Lucas	Science, Space, and Technology, *ranking member.* Financial Services.
Luetkemeyer	Financial Services.
Luján	Assistant Speaker. Energy and Commerce. Select Committee on the Climate Crisis.
Luria	Armed Services. Veterans' Affairs.
Lynch	Financial Services. Oversight and Reform. Transportation and Infrastructure.
Malinowski	Foreign Affairs. Transportation and Infrastructure.
Maloney, Carolyn B., of New York	Oversight and Reform, *chairwoman.* Financial Services.

Representative	Committees (Standing, Joint, and Select)
Maloney, Sean Patrick, of New York	Agriculture. Transportation and Infrastructure. Permanent Select Committee on Intelligence.
Marchant	Ethics. Ways and Means.
Marshall	Agriculture. Science, Space, and Technology.
Massie	Oversight and Reform. Transportation and Infrastructure.
Mast	Foreign Affairs. Transportation and Infrastructure.
Matsui	Energy and Commerce. Rules.
McAdams	Financial Services. Science, Space, and Technology.
McBath	Education and Labor. Judiciary.
McCarthy	Republican Leader.
McCaul	Foreign Affairs. Homeland Security.
McClintock	Judiciary. Natural Resources.
McCollum	Appropriations.
McEachin	Energy and Commerce. Natural Resources. Select Committee on the Climate Crisis.
McGovern	Rules, *chair.* Agriculture.
McHenry	Financial Services.
McKinley	Energy and Commerce.
McNerney	Energy and Commerce. Science, Space, and Technology.
Meeks	Financial Services. Foreign Affairs.
Meng	Appropriations. Ethics.
Meuser	Budget. Education and Labor. Veterans' Affairs.
Mfume	Oversight and Reform. Small Business.
Miller	Oversight and Reform. Transportation and Infrastructure. Select Committee on the Climate Crisis.
Mitchell	Armed Services. Transportation and Infrastructure.
Moolenaar	Appropriations.
Mooney, Alexander X., of West Virginia	Financial Services.
Moore	Ways and Means.

Representative	Committees (Standing, Joint, and Select)
Morelle	Budget. Education and Labor. Rules.
Moulton	Armed Services. Budget.
Mucarsel-Powell	Judiciary. Transportation and Infrastructure.
Mullin	Energy and Commerce.
Murphy, Gregory F., of North Carolina	Education and Labor. Science, Space, and Technology.
Murphy, Stephanie N., of Florida	Ways and Means.
Nadler	Judiciary, *chair.*
Napolitano	Natural Resources. Transportation and Infrastructure.
Neal	Ways and Means, *chair.*
Neguse	Judiciary. Natural Resources. Select Committee on the Climate Crisis.
Newhouse	Appropriations. Select Committee on the Modernization of Congress.
Norcross	Armed Services. Education and Labor.
Norman	Budget. Oversight and Reform. Science, Space, and Technology.
Norton	Oversight and Reform. Transportation and Infrastructure.
Nunes	Ways and Means. Permanent Select Committee on Intelligence.
Ocasio-Cortez	Financial Services. Oversight and Reform.
O'Halleran	Agriculture. Energy and Commerce.
Olson	Energy and Commerce.
Omar	Budget. Education and Labor. Foreign Affairs.
Palazzo	Appropriations.
Pallone	Energy and Commerce, *chair.* Oversight and Reform.
Palmer	Transportation and Infrastructure. Select Committee on the Climate Crisis. Oversight and Reform.
Panetta	Agriculture. Budget. Ways and Means.
Pappas	Transportation and Infrastructure. Veterans' Affairs.
Pascrell	Ways and Means.

Representative	Committees (Standing, Joint, and Select)
Payne	Homeland Security. Transportation and Infrastructure.
Pelosi	The Speaker.
Pence	Foreign Affairs. Transportation and Infrastructure.
Perlmutter	Financial Services. Rules. Science, Space, and Technology.
Perry	Foreign Affairs. Transportation and Infrastructure.
Peters	Budget. Energy and Commerce.
Peterson	Agriculture, *chair.* Veterans' Affairs.
Phillips	Ethics. Financial Services. Foreign Affairs.
Pingree	Agriculture. Appropriations.
Plaskett	Agriculture. Oversight and Reform. Transportation and Infrastructure.
Pocan	Appropriations. Select Committee on the Modernization of Congress.
Porter	Financial Services. Oversight and Reform.
Posey	Financial Services. Science, Space, and Technology.
Pressley	Financial Services. Oversight and Reform.
Price, David E., of North Carolina	Appropriations. Budget.
Quigley	Appropriations. Permanent Select Committee on Intelligence.
Radewagen	Natural Resources. Small Business. Veterans' Affairs.
Raskin	House Administration. Judiciary. Oversight and Reform. Rules.
Reed	Ways and Means.
Reschenthaler	Foreign Affairs. Judiciary.
Rice, Kathleen M., of New York	Homeland Security. Veterans' Affairs.
Rice, Tom, of South Carolina	Ways and Means.
Richmond	Homeland Security. Judiciary.
Riggleman	Financial Services.

Representative	Committees (Standing, Joint, and Select)
Roby	Appropriations. Judiciary.
Rodgers, Cathy McMorris, of Washington	Energy and Commerce.
Roe, David P., of Tennessee	Veterans' Affairs, ranking member. Education and Labor.
Rogers, Harold, of Kentucky	Appropriations.
Rogers, Mike, of Alabama	Armed Services. Homeland Security.
Rooney, Francis, of Florida	Foreign Affairs. Science, Space, and Technology.
Rose, John W., of Tennessee	Financial Services.
Rose, Max, of New York	Homeland Security. Veterans' Affairs.
Rouda	Oversight and Reform. Transportation and Infrastructure.
Rouzer	Agriculture. Transportation and Infrastructure.
Roy	Budget. Oversight and Reform. Veterans' Affairs.
Roybal-Allard	Appropriations.
Ruiz	Energy and Commerce.
Ruppersberger	Appropriations.
Rush	Energy and Commerce.
Rutherford	Appropriations.
Ryan	Appropriations.
Sablan	Education and Labor. Natural Resources. Veterans' Affairs.
Sánchez	Ways and Means.
San Nicolas	Financial Services. Natural Resources.
Sarbanes	Energy and Commerce. Oversight and Reform.
Scalise	Republican Whip. Energy and Commerce.
Scanlon	Judiciary. Rules. Select Committee on the Modernization of Congress.
Schakowsky	Senior Chief Deputy Majority Whip. Budget. Energy and Commerce.
Schiff	Permanent Select Committee on Intelligence, *chairman.*
Schneider	Small Business. Ways and Means.
Schrader	Energy and Commerce.
Schrier	Agriculture. Education and Labor.
Schweikert	Ways and Means.

Representative	Committees (Standing, Joint, and Select)
Scott, Austin, of Georgia	Agriculture. Armed Services.
Scott, David, of Georgia	Agriculture. Financial Services.
Scott, Robert C. "Bobby", of Virginia	Education and Labor, *chair.* Budget.
Sensenbrenner	Foreign Affairs. Judiciary.
Serrano	Appropriations.
Sewell, Terri A., of Alabama	Ways and Means. Permanent Select Committee on Intelligence.
Shalala	Education and Labor. Rules.
Sherman	Financial Services. Foreign Affairs. Science, Space, and Technology.
Sherrill	Armed Services. Science, Space, and Technology.
Shimkus	Energy and Commerce.
Simpson	Appropriations.
Sires	Budget. Foreign Affairs. Transportation and Infrastructure.
Slotkin	Armed Services. Homeland Security.
Smith, Adam, of Washington	Armed Services, *chair.*
Smith, Adrian, of Nebraska	Ways and Means.
Smith, Christopher H., of New Jersey	Foreign Affairs.
Smith, Jason, of Missouri	Budget. Ways and Means.
Smucker	Education and Labor. Transportation and Infrastructure.
Soto	Energy and Commerce. Natural Resources.
Spanberger	Agriculture. Foreign Affairs.
Spano	Small Business. Transportation and Infrastructure.
Speier	Armed Services. Oversight and Reform. Permanent Select Committee on Intelligence.
Stanton	Judiciary. Transportation and Infrastructure.
Stauber	Small Business. Transportation and Infrastructure.
Stefanik	Armed Services. Education and Labor. Permanent Select Committee on Intelligence.
Steil	Financial Services.

Representative	Committees (Standing, Joint, and Select)
Steube	Judiciary. Oversight and Reform. Veterans' Affairs.
Stevens	Education and Labor. Science, Space, and Technology.
Stewart	Appropriations. Budget. Permanent Select Committee on Intelligence.
Stivers	Financial Services.
Suozzi	Ways and Means.
Swalwell, Eric, of California	Judiciary. Permanent Select Committee on Intelligence.
Takano	Veterans' Affairs, *chair.* Education and Labor.
Taylor	Financial Services.
Thompson, Bennie G., of Mississippi	Homeland Security, *chair.*
Thompson, Glenn, of Pennsylvania	Agriculture. Education and Labor.
Thompson, Mike, of California	Ways and Means.
Thornberry	Armed Services.
Tiffany	Judiciary. Science, Space, and Technology.
Timmons	Financial Services. Select Committee on the Modernization of Congress.
Tipton	Financial Services.
Titus	Foreign Affairs. Homeland Security. Transportation and Infrastructure.
Tlaib	Financial Services. Oversight and Reform.
Tonko	Energy and Commerce. Natural Resources. Science, Space, and Technology.
Torres, Norma J., of California	Appropriations. Rules.
Torres Small, Xochitl, of New Mexico	Agriculture. Armed Services. Homeland Security.
Trahan	Armed Services. Education and Labor.
Trone	Education and Labor. Foreign Affairs.
Turner	Armed Services. Permanent Select Committee on Intelligence.
Underwood	Education and Labor. Homeland Security. Veterans' Affairs.
Upton	Energy and Commerce.

Representative	Committees (Standing, Joint, and Select)
Van Drew	Education and Labor. Homeland Security.
Vargas	Financial Services. Foreign Affairs.
Veasey	Energy and Commerce.
Vela	Agriculture. Armed Services.
Velázquez	Small Business, *chair.* Financial Services. Natural Resources.
Visclosky	Appropriations.
Wagner	Financial Services. Foreign Affairs.
Walberg	Education and Labor. Energy and Commerce.
Walden	Energy and Commerce.
Walker	Education and Labor. Homeland Security. House Administration.
Walorski	Ethics. Ways and Means.
Waltz	Armed Services. Science, Space, and Technology.
Wasserman Schultz	Appropriations. Oversight and Reform.
Waters	Financial Services, *chair.*
Watkins	Education and Labor. Foreign Affairs. Veterans' Affairs.
Watson Coleman	Appropriations. Homeland Security.
Weber, Randy K., Sr., of Texas	Science, Space, and Technology. Transportation and Infrastructure.
Webster, Daniel, of Florida	Natural Resources. Transportation and Infrastructure.
Welch	Energy and Commerce. Oversight and Reform. Permanent Select Committee on Intelligence.
Wenstrup	Ways and Means. Permanent Select Committee on Intelligence.
Westerman	Natural Resources. Transportation and Infrastructure.
Wexton	Financial Services. Science, Space, and Technology.
Wild	Education and Labor. Ethics. Foreign Affairs.
Williams	Financial Services.
Wilson, Frederica S., of Florida	Education and Labor. Transportation and Infrastructure.

Representative	Committees (Standing, Joint, and Select)
Wilson, Joe, of South Carolina	Armed Services. Foreign Affairs.
Wittman	Armed Services. Natural Resources.
Womack	Appropriations. Budget.
Woodall	Budget. Rules. Transportation and Infrastructure. Select Committee on the Modernization of Congress.
Wright	Education and Labor. Foreign Affairs.
Yarmuth	Budget, *chair.*
Yoho	Agriculture. Foreign Affairs.
Young	Natural Resources. Transportation and Infrastructure.
Zeldin	Financial Services. Foreign Affairs.

CONGRESSIONAL ADVISORY BOARDS, COMMISSIONS, AND GROUPS

UNITED STATES AIR FORCE ACADEMY BOARD OF VISITORS

[Title 10, U.S.C., Section 9355(a)]

Board Member	**Year Appointed**
Appointed by the President:	
Roel Campos	2016
Linda Cubero	2016
Benjamin Drew	2016
Edward Rice (Chair)	2016
David Ehrhart	2018
Robert Gleason	2018
Appointed by the Vice President or the Senate President Pro Tempore:	
Senator *Mazie K. Hirono,* of Hawaii	2015
Senator *Tom Udall,* of New Mexico	2015
Senator Steve Daines, of Montana	2017
Appointed by the Speaker of the House of Representatives:	
Representative *Doug Lamborn,* of Colorado	2009
Gina Maria Ortiz Jones	2019
Appointed by the Chairman, Senate Armed Services Committee:	
Senator Cory Gardner, of Colorado	2015
Appointed by the Chairman, House Armed Services Committee:	
Representative *Don Bacon,* of Nebraska	2017

UNITED STATES MILITARY ACADEMY BOARD OF VISITORS

[Title 10, U.S.C., Section 4355(a)]

Members of Congress

Senate

Richard Burr, of North Carolina.
Jerry Moran, of Kansas.
Tammy Duckworth, of Illinois.
Joe Manchin III, of West Virginia.

House

Anthony Brindisi, Representative of New York.
Stephanie N. Murphy, Representative of Florida.
Steve Womack, Representative of Arkansas, Chair.
K. Michael Conaway, Representative of Texas.
Warren Davidson, Representative of Ohio.

Presidential Appointees:

Brenda Sue Fulton, of New Jersey.
Guy C. Swan III, of Virginia.

Frederick H. Black, Sr., of North Carolina.
SEC R. James Johnson, of Virginia, Vice Chair.
Mrs. Meaghan Mobbs, of Virginia.
David J. Urban, of Washington, DC.

UNITED STATES NAVAL ACADEMY BOARD OF VISITORS

[Title 10, U.S.C., Section 6968(a)]

Appointed by the President:

Ms. Christine Fox (Chairwoman).
ADM James Winnefeld, USN (Ret.), former Vice Chairman of the Joint Chiefs of Staff.
Ms. Matice J. Wright.
RDML Ronny L. Jackson, USN.
Mr. George Gould.
Mr. Anthony W. Parker.

Appointed by the Vice President:

Senator *Benjamin L. Cardin,* of Maryland.
Senator James Lankford, of Oklahoma.
Senator *Jeanne Shaheen,* of New Hampshire.

Designees of the Chairmen, SASC/HASC:

Representative Elaine G. Luria, of Virginia.
Senator Dan Sullivan, of Alaska.

Appointed by the Speaker of the House:

Representative *Jim Banks,* of Indiana.
Representative *Steven M. Palazzo,* of Mississippi.
Representative C. A. Dutch Ruppersberger, of Maryland (Vice Chairman).

UNITED STATES COAST GUARD ACADEMY BOARD OF VISITORS

[Title 14 U.S.C., Section 194(a)]

Roger F. Wicker, of Mississippi.
Dan Sullivan, of Alaska.
Richard Blumenthal, of Connecticut.
Maria Cantwell, of Washington.
Peter A. DeFazio, of Oregon.
Joe Courtney, of Connecticut.
Joe Cunningham, of South Carolina.
John H. Rutherford, of Florida.

BRITISH-AMERICAN PARLIAMENTARY GROUP

Senate Hart Building, Room 808, phone 224–3047

[Created by Public Law 98–164]

Senate Delegation:
Chair.—John Boozman, Senator from Arkansas.
Vice Chair.—*Patrick J. Leahy,* Senator from Vermont.

CANADA-UNITED STATES INTERPARLIAMENTARY GROUP

Senate Hart Building, Room 808, phone 224–3047

[Created by Public Law 86–42, 22 U.S.C., 1928a–1928d, 276d–276g]

Senate Delegation:
Chair.—Vacant.
Vice Chair.—Vacant.

House Delegation:
Chair.—*Bill Huizenga,* Representative of Michigan.
Vice Chair.—Vacant.

CHINA-UNITED STATES INTERPARLIAMENTARY GROUP

Senate Hart Building, Room 808, phone 224–3047

[Created by Public Law 108–199, Section 153]

Senate Delegation:
Chair.—Vacant.
Vice Chair.—Vacant.

KOREA-UNITED STATES INTERPARLIAMENTARY GROUP

House Delegation:
Chair.—Vacant.

MEXICO-UNITED STATES INTERPARLIAMENTARY GROUP

Senate Hart Building, Room 808, phone 224–3047

[Created by Public Law 82–420, 22 U.S.C. 276h–276k]

Senate Delegation:
Chair.—Vacant.
Vice Chair.—Vacant.

House Delegation:
Chair.—Henry Cuellar, Representative of Texas.
Vice Chair.—Vacant.

NATO PARLIAMENTARY ASSEMBLY

Headquarters: Place du Petit Sablon 3, B–1000 Brussels, Belgium

[Created by Public Law 84–689, 22 U.S.C., 1928z]

Senate Delegation:
Chair.—Vacant.
Vice Chair.—Vacant.

House Delegation:
Chair.—Gerald E. Connolly, Representative of Virginia.
Vice Chair.—Vacant.

STAFF

Secretary, Senate Delegation.—Julia Hart Reed, Interparliamentary Services, SH–808, 224–3047.
Secretary, House Delegation.—Jeff Dressler.

COMMISSION ON CONGRESSIONAL MAILING STANDARDS

1307 Longworth House Office Building, phone 225–9337

[Created by Public Law 93–191]

Chair.—Susan A. Davis, of California.
Brad Sherman, of California.
Debra A. Haaland, of New Mexico.
Bryan Steil, of Wisconsin.
Robert E. Latta, of Ohio.
Mark Walker, of North Carolina.

STAFF

Majority Staff Director.—Matt DeFreitas, 225–9337.
Professional Staff: Kylie Carpenter, Arwa Dubad.
Staff Assistant.—Hector Arias.
Republican Staff Director.—Tim Sullivan, 226–0647.
Republican Professional Staff.—Elizabeth Conklin.
Republican Staff Assistant.—Roberto Estrada.

COMMISSION ON SECURITY AND COOPERATION IN EUROPE

234 Ford House Office Building, phone 225–1901, fax 226–4199

https://csce.gov

Alcee L. Hastings, Representative from Florida, *Chair*

Roger F. Wicker, Senator from Mississippi, *Co-Chair*

LEGISLATIVE BRANCH COMMISSIONERS

House

Emanuel Cleaver, of Missouri.
Steve Cohen, of Tennessee.
Gwen Moore, of Wisconsin.
Marc A. Veasey, of Texas.

Joe Wilson, of South Carolina, Ranking Member.
Robert B. Aderholt, of Alabama.
Brian K. Fitzpatrick, of Pennsylvania.
Richard Hudson, of North Carolina.

Senate

John Boozman, of Arkansas.
Cory Gardner, of Colorado.
Marco Rubio, of Florida.
Thom Tillis, of North Carolina.

Benjamin L. Cardin, of Maryland, Ranking Member.
Jeanne Shaheen, of New Hampshire.
Tom Udall, of New Mexico.
Sheldon Whitehouse, of Rhode Island.

EXECUTIVE BRANCH COMMISSIONERS

Department of State.—Vacant.
Department of Commerce.—Vacant.
Department of Defense.—Vacant.

COMMISSION STAFF

Chief of Staff.—Alex T. Johnson.
Senior Senate Staff Representative.—Kyle Parker.
Senior State Department Senior Advisor.—Mark Toner.
Senior Policy Advisor; Secretary of the U.S. Delegation to the OSCE Parliamentary Assembly.—Robert Hand.
Representative of the Helsinki Commission to the USOSCE, Senior Policy Advisor.—Shannon Simrell.
Director of Global Partner Partnerships, Policy, and Innovation, Senior Policy Advisor.—Mischa Thompson.
Director of Communications.—Stacy L. Hope.
Senior Policy Advisors: Janice Helwig, Nathaniel Hurd, Everett Price, Alex Tiersky.
Policy Advisors: Rachel Bauman, A. Paul Massaro III, Jordan Warlick.
Counsel for International Law.—Erika B. Schlager.
Staff Associate.—François Hernandez.

CONGRESSIONAL AWARD FOUNDATION

379 Ford House Office Building, phone (202) 226–0130, fax 226–0131

[Created by Public Law 96–114]

Chair.—Paxton K. Baker, Washington Nationals Baseball.
Vice Chairs:
Hon. Rodney E. Slater, Squire Patton Boggs, LLP.
Shawn Whitman, FMC Corporation.
Secretary.—Laura O'Connor, Utah. Congressional Award Medalist.
Treasurer.—Lee Klumpp, BDO.

Members:

Marc Baer, Blue Cross Blue Shield of Minnesota.
Ed Blansitt, Montgomery County Inspector General Office.
Romero Brown, Georgia.
Anne Oswalt Bruce, Johnson & Johnson.
Nick Cannon, New York.
Edward Cohen, Lerner Enterprises.
Anthony Crowell, New York Law School. Congressional Award Medalist.
Kathy Didawick, BlueCross BlueShield Association.
Hon. Debbie Dingell, U.S. House of Representatives.
Mitch Draizin, New York.
Larry Duncan, Lockheed Martin Corporation.
Melissa Cortese Foxman, Entertainment Software Association.
Beverly Gilyard, AARP.
Patrick Gliha, Celgene.
George B. Gould, Washington, DC.
Raymond Hall, Miller Management Corporation.
J. Steven Hart, Esq., Williams and Jensen, P.C.
Jonathan Heafitz, PCMA.
Erica Wheelan Heyse, National Director.
Jesse Hill, Edward Jones.
Hon. Richard Hudson, U.S. House of Representatives.
David W. Hunt, Esq., Nexant.
Hon. Sheila Jackson Lee, U.S. House of Representatives.
Raymond F. Kerins Jr., Bayer U.S. LLC.
Bradley Knox, Esq. Aflac.
Karlos LaSane, Caesars Entertainment.
Christopher Leahy, Intuit.
Raul Magdaleno, Magdaleno Consulting Group.
Hon. Joe Manchin III, U.S. Senate.
Lance Mangum, FedEx Corporation.
Dr. Linda Mitchell, North Mississippi Research & Extension Center.
Michael Pitts, Wisconsin.
Steven Roberts, The Roberts Companies.
Molly Ryan, Otsuka America Pharmaceutical Inc.
David Schiappa, The Duberstein Group.
Chris Spear, American Trucking Associations.
Kim Talley, G2 Secure Staff.
Chiling Tong, National Ace.
Kelsey Troy, KinderCare Education.
Jason Van Pelt, Crossroads Strategies.
Rita Vaswani, Nevada State Bank.
Kathryn Weeden, United States Senate Page School.
Ben Zandi, Fraport USA.
Vacant, U.S. Senate.

Advisory Board Members:

Simeon Banister, New York.
David Falk, FAME.
Dr. Larry Green, Maryland.
Adrian Harpool, Adrian Harpool Associates.
Dr. Brian Johnson, Advance Higher Ed.
Beth Ann Ruoff, Washington, DC.
Will Stute, Washington, DC.

CONGRESSIONAL CLUB

2001 New Hampshire Avenue, NW., Washington, DC 20009

phone (202) 332–1155

Executive Board
President.—Patricia Engel.
Vice Presidents:
(1st) Charles Capito, Jr.
(2d) Patricia Garamendi.
(3d) Vikki Watkins.
(4th) Pat O'Halleran.
(5th) Leah Dunn.
(6th) Billie Gingrey.
Treasurer.—Martha Brooks.
Recording Secretary.—Lorena Saenz-Gonzalez.
Corresponding Secretary.—Karmen Walker-Brown.
Executive Director.—Beth Harvey.

CONGRESSIONAL EXECUTIVE COMMISSION ON CHINA

243 Ford House Office Building, phone 226–3766, fax 226–3804

[Created by Public Law 106–286]

James P. McGovern, Representative of Massachusetts, *Chair*
Marco Rubio, Senator from Florida, Co-Chair

LEGISLATIVE BRANCH COMMISSIONERS

House

Marcy Kaptur, of Ohio.
Tom Malinowski, of New Jersey.
Ben McAdams, of Utah.
Thomas R. Suozzi, of New York.
Vicky Hartzler, of Missouri.
Brian J. Mast, of Florida.
Christopher H. Smith, of New Jersey.
Vacant.

Senate

James Lankford, of Oklahoma.
Tom Cotton, of Arkansas.
Steve Daines, of Montana.
Todd Young, of Indiana.
Dianne Feinstein, of California.
Jeff Merkley, of Oregon.
Gary C. Peters, of Michigan.
ANGUS S. KING, JR., of Maine.

EXECUTIVE BRANCH COMMISSIONERS

Vacant, U.S. Department of Labor.
Vacant, U.S. Department of State.
Vacant, U.S. Department of Commerce.
Vacant, U.S. Department of State.
Vacant, U.S. Department of State.

COMMISSION STAFF

Staff Director.—Jonathan Stivers.
Deputy Staff Director.—Peter Mattis.
Director of Administration, Budget, and Contracts.—Judy Wright.
Senior Advisor and Prisoner Database Program Director.—Jen Salen.
Counsel: Steve Andrews, Andy Wong.
Research Associates: Luke Adams, Sophie Jin, John Lindblom, David Petrick, Amy Reger.
Research Associate and Manager of Annual Report Production.—Megan Fluker.
Director of Communications and Policy.—Scott Flipse.

HOUSE DEMOCRACY PARTNERSHIP (HDP)

327A Cannon House Office Building, phone 225–1784, fax 225–2014

House_Democracy_Partnership@mail.house.gov, https://democracy.house.gov

[Created by H. Res. 5, 112th Congress]

Chair.—David E. Price, of North Carolina.
Ranking Member.—*Vern Buchanan,* of Florida.

COMMISSIONERS

Gwen Moore, of Wisconsin.
Susan A. Davis, of California.
Dina Titus, of Nevada.
Gerald E. Connolly, of Virginia.
Ted Lieu, of California.
Norma J. Torres, of California.
Robin L. Kelly, of Illinois.
Terri A. Sewell, of Alabama.
Diana DeGette, of Colorado.
Barbara Lee, of California.
Jeff Fortenberry, of Nebraska.
K. Michael Conaway, of Texas.
Adrian Smith, of Nebraska.
Steve Womack, of Arkansas.
Bill Flores, of Texas.
Jackie Walorski, of Indiana.
Tom Rice, of South Carolina.
Markwayne Mullin, of Oklahoma.

Executive Director.—Derek Luyten.
Chief of Staff for Chairman Price.—Justin Wein.
Deputy Chief of Staff for Ranking Member Buchanan.—Sean Brady.

HOUSE OFFICE BUILDING COMMISSION

H–232 The Capitol, phone 225–0600

[Title 40, U.S.C. 175–176]

Chair.—Nancy Pelosi, Speaker of the House of Representatives.
Steny H. Hoyer, House Majority Leader.
Kevin McCarthy, House Minority Leader.

JAPAN-UNITED STATES FRIENDSHIP COMMISSION

1201 15th Street, NW., Suite 330, Washington, DC 20005

phone (202) 653–9800, fax 653–9802

[Created by Public Law 94–118]

Chair.—Harry A. Hill, President and CEO, Oaklawn Marketing, Inc.
Vice-Chair.—Dr. Sheila Smith, Senior Fellow for Japan Studies, Council on Foreign Relations (CFR).
Executive Director.—Paige Cottingham-Streater.
Assistant Executive Director.—Niharika C. Joe.
Assistant Executive Director, CULCON.—Pamela L. Fields.
Executive Assistant.—Sylvia L. Dandridge.
Members:
Assistant Secretary of State for East Asian and Pacific Affairs, U.S. Department of State.
Assistant Secretary of State for Educational and Cultural Affairs, U.S. Department of State.
Dr. Deanna Marcum, Managing Director, Ithaka.
Dr. Patricia Maclachlan, Associate Professor of Government and Asian Studies, University of Texas.
Dr. Edward Lincoln, Professorial Lecturer, George Washington University.
David Sneider, Simpson Thacher & Bartlett, LLP.
Mary Anne Carter, Chair, National Endowment for the Arts.
National Endowment for the Humanities.
Hon. Mark Takano, U.S. House of Representatives.
Dr. Anne Nishimura Morse, Curator of Japanese Art, Museum of Fine Arts, Boston.
Hon. Lisa Murkowski, U.S. Senate.

U.S. Department of Education.
Dr. T.J. Pempel, Professor of Political Science, University of California, Berkeley.
Vacant, U.S. House of Representatives.
Dr. Leonard J. Schoppa, Jr., Director, Woodrow Wilson Department of Politics, The University of Virginia.
Vacant, U.S. Senate.

MIGRATORY BIRD CONSERVATION COMMISSION

5275 Leesburg Pike, Falls Church, VA 22041
phone (703) 358–1716, fax (703) 358–2234
[Created by act of February 18, 1929, 16 U.S.C. 715a]

Chair.—David Bernhardt, Secretary of the Interior.
John Boozman, Senator from Arkansas.
Martin Heinrich, Senator from New Mexico.
Robert J. Wittman, Representative from Virginia.
Mike Thompson, Representative from California.
Sonny Perdue, Secretary of Agriculture.
Andrew Wheeler, Administrator of Environmental Protection Agency.
Secretary.—A. Eric Alvarez.

PERMANENT COMMITTEE FOR THE OLIVER WENDELL HOLMES DEVISE FUND

Library of Congress, 101 Independence Avenue, SE., Washington, DC 20540
phone 707–5383
[Created by act of Congress approved August 5, 1955 (Public Law 246, 84th Congress), to administer Oliver Wendell Holmes Devise Fund, established by same act]

Chairman ex officio.—Carla Hayden.
Administrative Officer for the Devise.—Janice Ruth (acting).

UNITED STATES-CHINA ECONOMIC AND SECURITY REVIEW COMMISSION

444 North Capitol Street, NW., Suite 602, Washington, DC 20001
phone 624–1407, fax 624–1406
[Created by Public Law 106–398, 114 STAT]

COMMISSIONERS

Chair.—Carolyn Bartholomew.
Vice Chair.—Robin Cleveland.

Members:
Andreas Borgeas, Ph.D.
Jeffrey L. Fiedler.
Hon. Carte P. Goodwin.
Roy D. Kamphausen.
Thea Mei Lee.
Kenneth Lewis.
Hon. James M. Talent.
Michael A. McDevitt.
Michael R. Wessel.
Larry M. Wortzel, Ph.D.

COMMISSION STAFF

Executive Director.—Daniel W. Peck.
Director, Economics and Trade.—Nargiza Salidjanova.
Economics and Trade Analysts: Virgilio Bisio, Charles Horne, Kye Malden, Leyton Nelson, Suzanna Stephens.
Director, Security and Foreign Affairs.—Benjamin Frohman.

Senior Policy Analyst, Security and Foreign Affairs.—Kristien T. Bergerson.
Security and Foreign Affairs Analysts: Alexander Bowe, Will Green, Ethan S. Meick, Matthew O. Southerland.
Policy Fellow, Security and Foreign Affairs.—Anastasya Lloyd-Damnjanovic.
Research Assistant, Security and Foreign Affairs.—Alec Blivas.
Director of Operations and Administration.—Christopher P. Fioravante.
Operations Support Specialist.—Erik Castillo.
Administrative and Human Resources Assistant.—Kerry Sutherland.
Congressional Liaison and Communications Director.—Leslie Tisdale Reagan.
Congressional Fellow.—Brittney Washington.

SENATE NATIONAL SECURITY WORKING GROUP

311 Hart Senate Office Building, 20510, phone 228–6425

Administrative Co-Chair.—Marco Rubio, Senator from Florida.
Administrative Co-Chair.—*Dianne Feinstein,* Senator from California.
Republican Leader.—Mitch McConnell, Senator from Kentucky.
Democratic Leader.—*Charles E. Schumer,* Senator from New York.
Co-Chair.—Deb Fischer, Senator from Nebraska.
Co-Chair.—Cory Gardner, Senator from Colorado.
Co-Chair.—Ben Sasse, Senator from Nebraska.
Co-Chair.—*Robert Menendez,* Senator from New Jersey.
Co-Chair.—*Jack Reed,* Senator from Rhode Island.

Members:
Roy Blunt, Senator from Missouri.
Lindsey Graham, Senator from South Carolina.
James M. Inhofe, Senator from Oklahoma.
James E. Risch, Senator from Idaho.
Mitt Romney, Senator from Utah.
Richard J. Durbin, Senator from Illinois.
Benjamin L. Cardin, Senator from Maryland.
Robert P. Casey, Jr., Senator from Pennsylvania.
Tammy Duckworth, Senator from Illinois.
Margaret Wood Hassan, Senator from New Hampshire.
Kyrsten Sinema, Senator from Arizona.

STAFF

Democratic Staff Director.—Rachel Bombach, 224–3841.
Republican Staff Director.—Mike Needham, 224–3041.

UNITED STATES ASSOCIATION OF FORMER MEMBERS OF CONGRESS

1401 K Street, NW., Suite 901, Washington, DC 20005
phone (202) 222–0972, https://usafmc.org

The bipartisan United States Association of Former Members of Congress (FMC) was founded in 1970 as a nonprofit, educational, research, and social organization. It has been chartered by the U.S. Congress and has approximately 600 members who represented American citizens in both the U.S. Senate and House of Representatives. FMC works to strengthen the Congress in the conduct of its Constitutional responsibility through promoting a collaborative approach to policymaking. FMC seeks to deepen the understanding of our democratic system, domestically and internationally, and to engage the citizenry through civic education about Congress and public service.

President.—Martin Frost, of Texas.
Vice President.—Charles Boustany, of Louisiana.
Treasurer.—Anne Marie Buerkle, of New York.
Secretary.—L.F. Payne, of Virginia.
Immediate Past President.—Cliff Stearns, of Florida.
Honorary Co-Chair.—Norm Mineta, of California.
Chief Executive Officer.—Peter M. Weichlein.
Presidents Emeritus Council: Jack Buechner, of Missouri; Dennis Hertel, of Michigan; Barbara Kennelly, of Connecticut; Larry LaRocco, of Idaho; Connie Morella, of Maryland; Matt McHugh, of New York; Jim Slattery, of Kansas; Cliff Stearns, of Florida.

U.S. CAPITOL HISTORICAL SOCIETY

200 Maryland Avenue, NE., Washington, DC 20002

phone (202) 543–8919, fax (202) 525–2790

[Congressional Charter, October 20, 1978, Public Law 95–493, 95th Congress, 92 Stat. 1643]

Chair of the Board.—Donald G. Carlson.
Vice Chair of the Board.—Connie Tipton.
President.—Hon. Jane L. Campbell.

BOARD OF TRUSTEES

Hon. Roy Blunt
Jean P. Bordewich
Kenneth Bowling, Ph.D.
Marc Cadin
Hon. *Robert P. Casey, Jr.*
Hon. Tom Cole
Hon. Gerald E. Connolly
Jeanne deCervens
Joseph W. Dooley
Ron Elving
Hon. *Virginia Foxx*
Anthony Greenberg
Mary Moore Hamrick
Betsy Wright Hawkings
Mark Hopkins
Hon. John B. Larson
Shannon McGahn
Joyce Meyer
Lorraine Miller
Niel Naraine
Hon. Edward A. Pease
Craig Purser
Michael C. Quinn
David Regan
Robert A. Rusbuldt
Anna Schneider
Jan Schoonmaker
Robert H. Schwengel, M.D.
Dontai Smalls
James A. Thurber, Ph.D.
Mark Tyndall
Brigadier General Tim White

STAFF

Vice President of:
Development and Key Initiatives.—Laura McCulty Stepp.
Merchandising.—Diana E. Wailes.
Chief Historian.—William G. diGiacomantonio.
Director of:
Corporate Giving.—Jennifer Romberg.
Historical Programs.—Lauren Borchard.
Public Programs and Chief Guide.—Steve Livengood.
Strategic Engagement.—Bee Barnett.
Manager of:
Communications and Administration.—Samuel Holliday.
Program Support and Board Liaison.—Charlotte Cummins.
Operations.—Vince Scott.
Receiving.—Mike Lawson.

U.S. CAPITOL PRESERVATION COMMISSION

[Created pursuant to Public Law 100–696]

Co-Chairs:
Nancy Pelosi, Speaker of the House.
Chuck Grassley, Senate President Pro Tempore.

MEMBERS

Senate

Mitch McConnell, Majority Leader.
Charles E. Schumer, Democratic Leader.
Roy Blunt.
Amy Klobuchar.
Deb Fischer.
John Hoeven.
Richard J. Durbin.
Vacant.

House

Steny H. Hoyer, Majority Leader.
Kevin McCarthy, Republican Leader.
Zoe Lofgren.
Rodney Davis.
Vacant.
Vacant.
Vacant.

Ex-Officio Member/Architect of the Capitol.—J. Brett Blanton.

U.S. HOUSE OF REPRESENTATIVES FINE ARTS BOARD

1309 Longworth House Office Building, phone 225–8281

[Created by Public Law 101–696]

Chair.—Zoe Lofgren, of California.

Members:
Tim Ryan, of Ohio.
G. K. Butterfield, of North Carolina.
Rodney Davis, of Illinois.
Barry Loudermilk, of Georgia.

U.S. SENATE COMMISSION ON ART

S–411 The Capitol, phone 224–2955

[Created by Public Law 100–696]

Chair.—Mitch McConnell, of Kentucky.
Vice Chair.—*Charles E. Schumer,* of New York.

Members:
Chuck Grassley, of Iowa.
Roy Blunt, of Missouri.
Amy Klobuchar, of Minnesota.

STAFF

Executive Secretary.—Julie E. Adams.
Curator.—Melinda K. Smith.
Associate Curator.—Alexander ''Sasha'' Lourie.
Administrator.—Scott M. Strong.
Historic Preservation Officer.—Kelly Steele.
Collections Manager.—Jennifer Krafchik.
Assistant Curator.—Vacant.
Registrar.—Theresa Malanum.
Collections Specialist.—Megan Hipsley.
Museum Specialist.—Richard L. Doerner.
Executive Assistant.—Phillip Rokus.

OTHER CONGRESSIONAL OFFICIALS AND SERVICES

ARCHITECT OF THE CAPITOL

ARCHITECT'S OFFICE

SB–16, U.S. Capitol, phone 228–1793, fax 228–1893, https://aoc.gov

Architect of the Capitol.—J. Brett Blanton.
Assistant Architect of the Capitol.—Michael G. Turnbull.
Chief Operating Officer.—Thomas J. Carroll III (acting).
Inspector General.—Christopher Failla.
Director of:
Communications and Congressional Relations.—Erin Courtney (acting).
Safety, Fire and Environmental Programs.—Patricia Williams.
Chief Administrative Officer.—William O'Donnell.
Chief Financial Officer.—Jonathan Kraft (acting).
Communications Officer.—Laura Condeluci.
General Counsel.—Jason Baltimore.
Executive Officer, U.S. Botanic Garden.—Saharah Moon Chapotin.
Curator.—Michele Cohen.

U.S. CAPITOL

HT–42, Capitol Superintendent's Service Center, phone 228–8800, fax 225–1957

[The Center provides Facility Services for the Capitol and CVC.]

Superintendent.—Mark Reed.
Deputy Superintendent.—Vacant.
Assistant Superintendents: Luis Rosaro, John Deubler, Jason McIntyre.

U.S. CAPITOL VISITOR CENTER

U.S. Capitol Visitor Center, Room SVC–101, 20515, phone 593–1816

Reservations, Visitor Services, and General Tour Questions, phone 593–1762
Accessibility Services, phone 224–4048, TTY 224–4049

CEO for Visitor Services.—Beth Plemmons.
Deputy CEO for Visitor Services.—Nik Apostolides.
Director of Communications and Marketing.—Tom Casey.
Exhibits and Education.—Carol Beebe.
Director of Retail.—Mark Tilghman.
Visitor Services.—Tina Pearson.
Volunteer Coordinator.—Wayne Kehoe.
Special Events.—Sherita Holt.
Director of E-Commerce and Retail Projects.—Susan Sisk.

SENATE OFFICE BUILDINGS

G–45 Dirksen Senate Office Building, phone 224–3141, fax 224–0652

Superintendent.—Lawrence Barr (acting).
Deputy Superintendent.—Eric Swanson (acting).
Assistant Superintendents: Jean Gilles, Paul Kirkpatrick, Michael Shirven.

HOUSE OFFICE BUILDINGS

2046 Rayburn House Office Building, phone 225–4141, fax 225–3003

Superintendent.—Michelle Kayon (acting), RA, LEED AP.
Assistant Superintendents: Ryan Columbo, Barron Dill, Daniel Murphy.

CAPITOL TELEPHONE EXCHANGE

6110 Postal Square Building, phone 224–3121, 225–3121

Supervisors: Debra Morgan, Joan Sartori.

CHILD CARE CENTERS

HOUSE OF REPRESENTATIVES CHILD CARE CENTER

147 Ford House Office Building & 1100 O'Neill House Office Building, 20515
phone 225–2800, fax 225–6908

Director.—Paige Beatty.
Administrative Director.—Monica Barnabae.

SENATE EMPLOYEES' CHILD CARE CENTER

United States Senate, 20510
phone 224–1461, fax 228–3686

Director.—Shannon Mara.
Assistant Director.—Bridgette Waters.

COMBINED AIRLINES TICKET OFFICES (CATO)

344 Maple West, Suite 224, Vienna, VA 22180
phone (703) 522–8664, 1 (888) 205–4482

General Manager.—Susan Willis.

SENATE AND HOUSE

B–222 Longworth House Office Building
phone (703) 522–2286, fax (202) 226–5992

Manager.—Misty Conner.

CONGRESSIONAL RECORD DAILY DIGEST

HOUSE SECTION

HT–13 The Capitol, phone 225–2868 (committees), 225–1501 (chamber)

Editors for—
Committee Meetings.—Jessica M. Rager.
Chamber Action.—Glennis Webb.

SENATE SECTION

S–421 The Capitol, phone 224–2658, fax 224–1220

Editor.—Elizabeth Tratos.
Assistant Editor.—Joseph Johnston.

CONGRESSIONAL RECORD INDEX OFFICE

U.S. Government Publishing Office, Room C–738
North Capitol and H Streets, NW., Washington, DC 20401
phone 512–0275

Chief.—Philip Hart, 512–2010, ext. 3–1975.

Manager.—Vacant.
Historian of Bills.—Barbre A. Brunson, 512–2010, ext. 3–1957.
Editors: Grafton J. Daniels, Jason Parsons.
Indexers: Joel K. Church, Kathleen M. Cooper, Jennifer E. Jones, Jane M. Wallace.

OFFICE OF CONGRESSIONAL ACCESSIBILITY SERVICES

S–156 Crypt of the Capitol, 20510, phone 224–4048, TTY 224–4049

Director.—David Hauck.

LIAISON OFFICES

AIR FORCE

2024 Rayburn House Office Building
phone 225–6656, 685–4530, DSN 325–4530, fax 685–2592

Chief.—Col. Bill Kale.
Deputy Chief.—Lt. Col. Sean Hanlen.
Liaison Officers: SMSgt Clara Burciaga, Maj. Matt Gorsuch, Maj. John Rayho.
Budget and Appropriations Liaison Officer.—Maj. David Bates.
Legislative Assistant.—MSgt Miguel Rosario.
Office Manager/Scheduler.—Ms. Shawn Baldy.

182 Russell Senate Office Building, phone 224–2481, 685–2573

Chief.—Col. Neil Richardson.
Deputy Chief.—Lt. Col. Joe Wall.
Liaison Officers: Maj. JD Frazier, Maj. Mike Gutierrez, Maj. Chris Ryan.
Appropriations Liaison Officer.—Lt. Col. Pete Shinn.
Office Manager/Scheduler.—Charlotte ''Charli'' Kiley.

ARMY

2024 Rayburn House Office Building, phone (202) 685–2676, fax 685–2674

Chief.—COL Norb Menendez.
Deputy Chief.—Jodi Mitchell.
Liaison Officers: MAJ Andrew Crowe, MAJ Tarik Jones, SGM Carlos Magwood, MAJ Devin Millson, CPT John Powell, MAJ Eric Yost.

183 Russell Senate Office Building, phone 224–2881, fax (703) 693–4574

Chief.—COL Nathan ''Nate'' Cook II.
Deputy Chief.—Michele Abell.
Liaison Officers: MAJ Stuart Anderson, Mr. Edgar ''Ed'' Dogan, MAJ David Engelman, SGM Derek Gondek, MAJ Douglas Hill, MAJ David Judson, CPT D.K. Morris, MAJ Patrick Naughton, CPT Jeffrey Tolbert.

COAST GUARD

2024 Rayburn House Office Building, phone 225–4775

House Liaison.—CDR Breanna Knutson.
Deputy House Liaison.—LCDR Taylor Kellog.
Assistant House Liaison.—LT Joe Sullivan-Springhetti.
Senior Enlisted House Liaison.—MECS William Kelly.

183 Russell Senate Building, phone 224–2913

Senate Liaison.—CDR Jack Souders.
Deputy Senate Liaison.—LCDR Jill Lamb.
Senior Enlisted House Liaison.—CSCS Sean Fullwood.

NAVY/MARINE CORPS

2024 Rayburn House Office Building, phone: Navy 225–7126, Marine Corps 225–7124

Director, USN.—CAPT Scott Farr, USN.

Deputy Director USN.—CAPT Kati Hill, USN.
USN Liaison Officers: LT Katie Calhoun, USN; LT James Lyons, USN; LT Cameron McCord, USN; LNC Andrew Shea, USN; LT James Van Kirk, USN.
Director, USMC.—Col. William McCullough, USMC.
Deputy Director USMC.—Maj. Kelly Repair, USMC.
USMC Liaison Officer.—Maj. John Pettibone, USMC.
Office Manager/Administrative Clerks: SSgt. Katherine Torres, USMC; Sgt. Christian Cepeda-Bedoya, USMC.

182 Russell Senate Office Building, phone: Navy 685–6003, Marine Corps 685–6010

Director.—CAPT Scott Sciretta, USN.
Deputy Director.—CAPT Mark Burns, USN.
USN Liaison Officers: LT Lara Bzik, USN; LT Chris Hanley, USN; LT Andrew Keene, USN; LT Jon Kokot, USN; LT Joel Robbins, USN; LT Jenn Abbott, USN.
Director, USMC.—Col. Jon Lauder, USMC.
Deputy Director.—Lt. Col. Khalilah Thomas, USMC.
USMC Liaison Officers: Capt. Sam Burke, USMC; Capt. Jeremy Alexander, USMC.
Liaison Staff Non-Commissioned Officers: GySgt. Jon Manzifortich, USMC; Sgt. Alex Ruiz, USMC.

GOVERNMENT ACCOUNTABILITY OFFICE

441 G Street, NW., Room 7125, Washington, DC 20548
phone 512–4400, fax 512–7919 or 512–4641

Managing Director, Congressional Relations.—Orice Williams Brown, 512–4400.
Executive Assistant.—Tanisha Hoaney, 512–7326.
Legislative Advisers: Patrick Dibattista, 512–6787; Carlos Diz, 512–8256; Rosa Harris, 512–9492; David Lewis, 512–7176; Tim Minelli, 512–8443; Tina Sherman, 512–8461; Chuck Wilson, 512–6891.
Associate Legislative Adviser.—Martene Rhed, 512–5414.
Congressional Information Systems Specialist.—Jane Lusby, 512–4378.
Engagement and Administrative Operations Assistant.—Theodora Guardado-Gallegos, 512–6224.

OFFICE OF PERSONNEL MANAGEMENT

2030 Rayburn House Office Building, phone 225–4955

Director of Constituent Services.—Christiana Frazee.
Constituent Services Officers: Marina Golovkina, Sarita Swan, Carlos Tingle, Carina Vazquez, Melony Witherspoon.

SOCIAL SECURITY ADMINISTRATION

RG1C2, Rayburn House Office Building, phone 225–3133, fax 225–3144

Director.—Robert Forrester.
Congressional Relations Liaisons: Sylvia Taylor-Mackey, Latrice Wingo.

STATE DEPARTMENT LIAISON OFFICES

2028 Rayburn House Office Building

For all Consular issues email: ConsularOnTheHill@state.gov.
For all other issues email: House@state.gov.
Phone: (202) 226–4642.

Director.—Kem Anderson (acting), 228–1603.
Consular Officer.—Carrie Flinchbaugh, 226–4641.

189 Russell Senate Office Building

For all Consular issues email: ConsularOnTheHill@state.gov.

For all other issues email: Senate@state.gov.
Phone: (202) 228–1602.

Director.—Leaksmy Norin (acting), 228–1602.
Consular Officer.—Ian Hillman, 228–1605.

VETERANS' AFFAIRS

2026 Rayburn House Office Building, phone 225–2280, fax 273–9988

Director.—Annmarie Amaral.
Deputy Director.—Richard Armstrong.
Representatives: Alma Bourne, Jeremy Dillard, Christina Smith.
Outreach: Brendon Gehrke, Bailey Jackson, Amanda Neumann.

189 Russell Senate Office Building, phone 224–5351, fax 273–9988

Director.—Annmarie Amaral.
Representatives: Thomas Garloch, Geisela Wimberly.
Outreach: Nikki Barnes, Michelle Myers, Alex Ware.

UNITED STATES SENATE PAGE SCHOOL

United States Senate, Washington, DC 20510–7248, fax 224–1838

Principal.—Joshua Dorsey, 224–3926.
Executive Assistant.—Nikita Thompson, 224–3927.
English Instructor.—Frances Owens, 228–1024.
Mathematics Instructor.—Louise Malik, 228–1018.
Science Instructor.—Dr. Ashley Johnson, 228–1025.
Social Studies Instructor.—Mark Fiorill, 228–1012.

U.S. CAPITOL POLICE

119 D Street, NE., Washington, DC 20510–7218

Office of the Chief: 224–9806.
Command Center: 224–0908.
Communications: 224–5151.
Emergency: 224–0911.

U.S. CAPITOL POLICE BOARD

Sergeant at Arms, U.S. House of Representatives.—Paul D. Irving.
Sergeant at Arms, U.S. Senate.—Michael C. Stenger.
Architect of the Capitol.—J. Brett Blanton.

OFFICE OF THE CHIEF

Chief of Police.—Steven A. Sund.
Chief of Staff.—William M. Goldman.
Office of:
General Counsel.—Gretchen DeMar.
Professional Responsibility.—Insp. Patrick Herrle.
Public Information.—Eva Malecki.
Office of Accountability and Improvement.—Deputy Chief Eric C. Waldow.

CHIEF OF OPERATIONS

Assistant Chief of Police.—Chad Thomas (acting).
Executive Officer.—Vacant.

COMMAND AND COORDINATION BUREAU

Bureau Commander.—Deputy Chief Yogananda D. Pittman.
Command Center: Insp. Timothy Bowen, Capt. Michael Spochart.
Communications.—Capt. Darrin Bloxson.
Emergency Planning Section.—Capt. Sean Patton.
Special Events.—Lt. Darrell Staton.

OPERATIONAL SERVICES BUREAU

Bureau Commander.—Insp. Timothy Bowen (acting).
Hazardous Incident Response Division.—Capt. Kathleen McBride.
Patrol/Mobile Response Division.—Insp. John Erickson.

PROTECTIVE SERVICES BUREAU

Bureau Commander.—Deputy Chief Sean Gallagher (acting).
Dignitary Protection Division.—Insp. Kimberley Schneider.
Investigations Division.—Insp. Wesley Mahr.

SECURITY SERVICES BUREAU

Bureau Commander.—Robert Ford.

UNIFORMED SERVICES BUREAU

Bureau Commander.—Deputy Chief Richard Rudd.
Capitol Division Commander.—Insp. Thomas Loyd.
House Division Commander.—Insp. Kimberlie Bolinger.
Library Division Commander.—Insp. Donald Rouiller.
Senate Division Commander.—Insp. Jeffrey Pickett.

CHIEF ADMINISTRATIVE OFFICER

Chief Administrative Officer.—Richard Braddock.
Deputy Chief Administrative Officer.—Dominic Storelli.
Director, Office of:
Employment Counsel.—Frederick Herrera.
Office of Inclusion, Diversity, Equity, and Action.—Natalie Holder.
Facilities and Logistics.—Thomas Madigan.
Financial Management.—Cherry Clipper.
Office of Acquisition Management.—Brett Blake.
Human Resources.—Heath Anderson.
Policy and Management Systems.—Jerome Boerste.
Training Services Bureau Commander.—Capt. Monique Moore (acting).
Office of Background Investigations and Credentialing.—Capt. Jessica Baboulis.

STATISTICAL INFORMATION

VOTES CAST FOR SENATORS IN 2014, 2016, AND 2018

[Compiled from official statistics obtained by the Clerk of the House. Figures in the last column, for the 2018 election, may include totals for more candidates than the ones shown.]

State	Vote						Total vote cast in 2018
	2014		2016		2018		
	Republican	Democrat	Republican	Democrat	Republican	Democrat	
Alabama	795,606	......	1,335,104	748,709	......	......	......
Alaska	135,445	129,431	138,149	36,200	......	......	......
Arizona	......	......	1,359,267	1,031,245	1,135,200	1,191,100	2,384,308
Arkansas	478,819	334,174	661,984	400,602	......	......	......
California	......	......	......	12,244,170	......	11,113,364	11,113,364
Colorado	983,891	944,203	1,215,318	1,370,710	......	......	......
Connecticut	......	......	552,621	920,766	545,717	787,685	1,386,840
Delaware	98,823	130,655	......	......	137,127	217,385	362,606
Florida	......	......	4,835,191	4,122,088	4,099,505	4,089,472	8,190,005
Georgia	1,358,088	1,160,811	2,135,806	1,599,726	......	......	......
Hawaii	98,006	246,827	92,653	306,604	112,035	276,316	398,657
Idaho	285,596	151,574	449,017	188,249	......	......	......
Illinois	1,538,522	1,929,637	2,184,692	3,012,940	......	......	......
Indiana	......	......	1,423,991	1,158,947	1,158,000	1,023,553	2,282,565
Iowa	588,575	494,370	926,007	549,460	......	......	......
Kansas	460,350	......	732,376	379,740	......	......	......
Kentucky	806,787	584,698	1,090,177	813,246	......	......	......
Louisiana	929,108 ([1])	581,041	1,239,489	705,271	......	......	......
Maine	413,505	190,254	......	......	223,502	66,268	646,064
Maryland	......	......	972,557	1,659,907	697,017	1,491,614	2,299,889
Massachusetts	791,950	1,289,944	......	......	979,210	1,633,371	2,752,665
Michigan	1,290,199	1,704,936	......	......	1,938,818	2,214,478	4,237,271
Minnesota	850,227	1,053,205	......	......	940,437	1,566,174	2,596,879
Mississippi	378,481	239,439	......	......	547,619	369,567	936,215
Missouri	......	......	1,378,458	1,300,200	1,254,927	1,112,935	2,442,289
Montana	213,709	148,184	......	......	235,963	253,876	504,384
Nebraska	347,636	170,127	......	......	403,151	269,917	698,883
Nevada	......	......	495,079	521,994	441,202	490,071	972,132
New Hampshire	235,347	251,184	353,632	354,649	......	......	......
New Jersey	791,297	1,043,866	......	......	1,357,355	1,711,654	3,169,310
New Mexico	229,097	286,409	......	......	212,813	376,998	697,012
New York	......	......	1,723,927	4,784,220	1,730,439	3,775,489	6,250,886
North Carolina	1,423,259	1,377,651	2,395,376	2,128,165	......	......	......
North Dakota	......	......	268,788	58,116	179,720	144,376	326,138
Ohio	......	......	3,118,567	1,996,908	2,053,963	2,355,932	4,410,898
Oklahoma	1,115,168	472,230	980,892	355,911	......	......	......
Oregon	538,847	814,537	651,106	1,105,119	......	......	......
Pennsylvania	......	......	2,951,702	2,865,012	2,134,848	2,792,437	5,009,400
Rhode Island	92,684	223,675	......	......	144,421	231,477	376,738
South Carolina	1,430,156	916,309	1,241,609	704,540	......	......	......
South Dakota	140,741	82,456	265,516	104,140	......	......	......
Tennessee	850,087	437,848	......	......	1,227,483	985,450	2,243,740
Texas	2,861,531	1,597,387	......	......	4,260,553	4,045,632	8,371,655
Utah	......	......	760,220	301,858	665,215	328,541	1,062,897
Vermont	......	......	103,637	192,243	74,815	......	278,230
Virginia	1,055,940	1,073,667	......	......	1,374,313	1,910,370	3,351,373
Washington	......	......	1,329,338	1,913,979	1,282,804	1,803,364	3,086,168
West Virginia	281,820	156,360	......	......	271,113	290,510	586,034
Wisconsin	......	......	1,479,471	1,380,335	1,184,885	1,472,914	2,660,763
Wyoming	121,554	29,377	......	......	136,210	61,227	205,275

[1] This vote count is from Louisiana's December 6, 2014, general (runoff) election, which was held because neither candidate received a majority of the vote in Louisiana's open (nonpartisan) primary on November 4, 2014. Bill Cassidy received 603,048 votes in the primary, and Mary L. Landrieu received 619,402.

VOTES CAST FOR REPRESENTATIVES, RESIDENT COMMISSIONER, AND DELEGATES IN 2014, 2016, and 2018

[The figures, compiled from official statistics obtained by the Clerk of the House, show the votes for the Republican and Democratic nominees, except as otherwise indicated. Figures in the last column, for the 2018 election, may include totals for more candidates than the ones shown.]

State and district	Vote cast in 2014		State and district	Vote cast in 2016		State and district	Vote cast in 2018		Total vote cast in 2018
	Republican	Democrat		Republican	Democrat		Democrat	Republican	
AL:			AL:			AL:			
1st	103,758	48,278	1st	208,083	....	1st	89,226	153,228	242,617
2d	113,103	54,692	2d	134,886	112,089	2d	86,931	138,879	226,230
3d	103,558	52,816	3d	192,164	94,549	3d	83,996	147,770	231,915
4th	132,831	....	4th	235,925	....	4th	46,492	184,255	230,969
5th	115,338	....	5th	205,647	102,234	5th	101,388	159,063	260,673
6th	135,945	42,291	6th	245,313	83,709	6th	85,644	192,542	278,328
7th	....	133,687	7th	....	229,330	7th	185,010	....	189,163
AK:			AK:			AK:			
At large	142,572	114,602	At large	155,088	111,019	At large	131,199	149,779	282,166
AZ:			AZ:			AZ:			
1st	87,723	97,391	1st	121,745	142,219	1st	143,240	122,784	266,089
2d	109,704	109,543	2d	179,806	135,873	2d	161,000	133,083	294,152
3d	46,185	58,192	3d	....	148,973	3d	114,650	64,868	179,518
4th	122,560	45,179	4th	203,487	81,296	4th	84,521	188,842	277,035
5th	124,867	54,596	5th	205,184	114,940	5th	127,027	186,037	313,064
6th	129,578	70,198	6th	201,578	122,866	6th	140,559	173,140	313,699
7th	....	54,235	7th	39,286	119,465	7th	113,044	....	132,051
8th	128,710	....	8th	204,942	....	8th	135,569	168,835	304,417
9th	67,841	88,609	9th	108,350	169,055	9th	159,583	101,662	261,245
AR:			AR:			AR:			
1st	124,139	63,555	1st	183,866	....	1st	57,907	138,757	201,245
2d	123,073	103,477	2d	176,472	111,347	2d	116,135	132,125	253,453
3d	151,630	....	3d	217,192	....	3d	74,952	148,717	229,568
4th	110,789	87,742	4th	182,885	....	4th	63,984	136,740	204,892
CA:			CA:			CA:			
1st	132,052	84,320	1st	185,448	128,588	1st	131,548	160,046	291,594
2d	54,400	163,124	2d	76,572	254,194	2d	243,081	72,576	315,657
3d	71,036	79,224	3d	104,453	152,513	3d	134,875	97,376	232,251
4th	211,134	....	4th	220,133	130,845	4th	156,253	184,401	340,654
5th	....	129,613	5th	67,565	224,526	5th	205,860	....	261,018
6th	36,448	97,008	6th	57,848	177,565	6th	201,939	....	201,939
7th	91,066	92,521	7th	145,168	152,133	7th	155,016	126,601	281,617
8th	77,480	37,056	8th	136,972	83,035	8th	....	170,785	170,785
9th	57,729	63,475	9th	98,992	133,163	9th	113,414	87,349	200,763
10th	70,582	55,123	10th	124,671	116,470	10th	115,945	105,955	221,900
11th	57,160	117,502	11th	83,341	214,868	11th	204,369	71,312	275,681
12th	32,197	160,067	12th	....	274,035	12th	275,292	41,780	317,072
13th	21,940	168,491	13th	29,754	293,117	13th	260,580	....	294,837
14th	34,757	114,389	14th	54,817	231,630	14th	211,384	55,439	266,823
15th	43,150	99,756	15th	70,619	198,578	15th	177,989	65,940	243,929
16th	44,943	46,277	16th	70,483	97,473	16th	82,266	60,693	142,959
17th	....	134,408	17th	....	233,192	17th	159,105	52,057	211,162
18th	63,326	133,060	18th	93,470	230,460	18th	225,142	77,096	302,238
19th	....	127,788	19th	64,061	181,802	19th	162,496	57,823	220,319
20th	....	106,034	20th	74,811	180,980	20th	183,677	....	225,721
21st	45,907	33,470	21st	75,126	57,282	21st	57,239	56,377	113,616
22d	96,053	37,289	22d	158,755	76,211	22d	105,136	117,243	222,379
23d	100,317	33,726	23d	167,116	74,468	23d	74,661	131,113	205,774
24th	95,566	103,228	24th	144,780	166,034	24th	166,550	117,881	284,431
25th	114,072	....	25th	138,755	122,406	25th	113,209	111,813	245,022
26th	82,653	87,176	26th	111,059	169,248	26th	158,216	97,210	255,426
27th	51,852	75,728	27th	81,655	168,977	27th	202,636	....	202,636
28th	....	91,996	28th	59,526	210,883	28th	196,662	54,272	250,934
29th	17,045	50,096	29th	....	171,824	29th	124,697	29,995	154,692
30th	45,315	86,568	30th	77,325	205,279	30th	191,573	69,420	260,993
31st	48,162	51,622	31st	94,866	121,070	31st	110,143	77,352	187,495
32d	34,053	50,353	32d	....	186,646	32d	121,759	55,272	177,031
33d	74,700	108,331	33d	110,822	219,397	33d	219,091	93,769	312,860
34th	....	61,621	34th	....	159,156	34th	110,195	....	151,906
35th	....	62,255	35th	47,309	124,044	35th	103,420	45,604	149,024
36th	61,457	72,682	36th	88,269	144,348	36th	122,169	84,839	207,008
37th	18,051	96,787	37th	....	237,272	37th	210,555	25,823	236,378
38th	40,288	58,192	38th	68,524	163,590	38th	139,188	62,968	202,156
39th	91,319	41,906	39th	150,777	112,679	39th	126,002	118,391	244,393
40th	....	49,379	40th	....	106,554	40th	93,938	....	121,449
41st	35,936	46,948	41st	69,159	128,164	41st	108,227	58,021	166,248
42d	74,540	38,850	42d	149,547	104,689	42d	100,892	131,040	231,932
43d	28,521	69,681	43d	52,499	167,017	43d	152,272	43,780	196,052
44th	....	59,670	44th	....	178,413	44th	143,322	....	143,322
45th	106,083	56,819	45th	182,618	129,231	45th	156,906	146,383	305,289
46th	33,577	49,738	46th	....	164,593	46th	102,278	45,638	147,916
47th	54,309	69,091	47th	88,109	154,759	47th	143,354	77,682	221,036
48th	112,082	62,713	48th	178,701	127,715	48th	157,837	136,899	294,736
49th	98,161	64,981	49th	155,888	154,267	49th	166,453	128,577	295,030

VOTES CAST FOR REPRESENTATIVES, RESIDENT COMMISSIONER, AND DELEGATES IN 2014, 2016, and 2018—CONTINUED

[The figures, compiled from official statistics obtained by the Clerk of the House, show the votes for the Republican and Democratic nominees, except as otherwise indicated. Figures in the last column, for the 2018 election, may include totals for more candidates than the ones shown.]

State and district	Vote cast in 2014		State and district	Vote cast in 2016		State and district	Vote cast in 2018		Total vote cast in 2018
	Repub-lican	Demo-crat		Repub-lican	Demo-crat		Demo-crat	Repub-lican	
50th	111,997	45,302	50th	179,937	103,646	50th	125,448	134,362	259,810
51st	25,577	56,373	51st	54,362	145,162	51st	109,527	44,301	153,828
52d	92,746	98,826	52d	139,403	181,253	52d	188,992	107,015	296,007
53d	60,940	87,104	53d	97,968	198,988	53d	185,667	83,127	268,794
CO:			CO:			CO:			
1st	80,682	183,281	1st	105,030	257,254	1st	272,886	85,207	369,715
2d	149,645	196,300	2d	170,001	260,175	2d	259,608	144,901	430,765
3d	163,011	100,364	3d	204,220	150,914	3d	146,426	173,205	336,201
4th	185,292	83,727	4th	248,230	123,642	4th	145,544	224,038	369,621
5th	157,182	105,673	5th	225,445	111,676	5th	126,848	184,002	322,716
6th	143,467	118,847	6th	191,626	160,372	6th	187,639	148,685	346,822
7th	120,918	148,225	7th	144,066	199,758	7th	204,260	119,734	338,067
CT:			CT:			CT:			
1st	78,609	127,430	1st	105,674	187,021	1st	116,155	96,024	274,140
2d	80,837	131,294	2d	111,149	186,210	2d	167,659	102,483	289,114
3d	69,454	130,009	3d	95,786	192,274	3d	163,211	95,667	270,239
4th	88,209	101,401	4th	120,653	187,811	4th	168,726	103,175	275,651
5th	92,404	106,256	5th	124,900	163,499	5th	142,901	115,146	270,664
DE:			DE:			DE:			
At large	85,146	137,251	At large	172,301	233,554	At large	227,353	125,384	353,814
FL:			FL:			FL:			
1st	165,086	54,976	1st	255,107	114,079	1st	106,199	216,189	322,388
2d	123,262	126,096	2d	231,163	102,811	2d	96,233	199,335	295,568
3d	148,691	73,910	3d	193,843	136,338	3d	129,880	176,616	306,496
4th	177,887	....	4th	287,509	113,088	4th	123,351	248,420	381,249
5th	59,237	112,340	5th	108,325	194,549	5th	180,527	89,799	270,326
6th	166,254	99,563	6th	213,519	151,051	6th	145,758	187,891	333,649
7th	144,474	73,011	7th	171,583	182,039	7th	183,113	134,285	317,398
8th	180,728	93,724	8th	246,483	127,127	8th	145,415	218,112	360,527
9th	74,963	93,850	9th	144,450	195,311	9th	172,172	124,565	296,737
10th	143,128	89,426	10th	107,498	198,491	10th	[1]	....	[1]
11th	181,508	90,786	11th	258,016	124,713	11th	128,053	239,395	367,506
12th	[1]	....	12th	253,559	116,110	12th	132,844	194,564	334,918
13th	168,172	....	13th	171,149	184,693	13th	182,717	134,254	316,971
14th	....	[1]	14th	121,088	195,789	14th	[1]	....	[1]
15th	128,750	84,832	15th	182,999	135,475	15th	134,132	151,380	285,532
16th	169,126	105,483	16th	230,654	155,262	16th	164,463	197,483	361,946
17th	141,493	82,263	17th	209,348	115,974	17th	117,194	193,326	310,520
18th	101,896	151,478	18th	201,488	161,918	18th	156,454	185,905	342,359
19th	159,354	80,824	19th	239,225	123,812	19th	128,106	211,465	339,607
20th	28,968	128,498	20th	54,646	222,914	20th	202,659	....	202,824
21st	....	153,395	21st	118,038	210,606	21st	[1]	....	[1]
22d	90,685	125,404	22d	138,737	199,113	22d	184,634	113,049	297,683
23d	61,519	103,269	23d	130,818	183,225	23d	161,611	99,446	276,366
24th	15,239	129,192	24th	....	[1]	24th	[1]	....	[1]
25th	[1]	....	25th	157,921	95,319	25th	84,173	128,672	212,845
26th	83,031	78,306	26th	148,547	115,493	26th	119,797	115,678	235,475
27th	[1]	....	27th	157,917	129,760	27th	130,743	115,588	252,586
GA:			GA:			GA:			
1st	95,337	61,175	1st	210,243	....	1st	105,942	144,741	250,683
2d	66,537	96,363	2d	94,056	148,543	2d	136,699	94,742	229,171
3d	156,277	....	3d	207,218	95,969	3d	101,010	191,996	293,006
4th	....	161,211	4th	70,593	220,146	4th	227,717	61,092	288,809
5th	....	170,326	5th	46,768	253,781	5th	275,406	....	275,406
6th	139,018	71,486	6th	201,088	124,917	6th	160,139	156,875	317,032
7th	113,557	60,112	7th	174,081	114,220	7th	140,011	140,430	280,441
8th	129,938	....	8th	173,983	83,225	8th	....	198,152	198,716
9th	146,059	34,988	9th	256,535	....	9th	57,912	224,661	282,578
10th	130,703	65,777	10th	243,725	....	10th	112,339	190,396	302,735
11th	161,532	....	11th	217,935	105,383	11th	118,653	191,887	310,540
12th	91,336	75,478	12th	159,492	99,420	12th	101,503	148,986	250,492
13th	....	159,445	13th	....	252,833	13th	223,157	69,760	293,010
14th	118,782	....	14th	216,743	....	14th	53,981	175,743	229,724
HI:			HI:			HI:			
1st	86,454	93,390	1st	45,958	145,417	1st	134,650	42,498	191,667
2d	33,630	142,010	2d	39,668	170,848	2d	153,271	44,850	206,990
ID:			ID:			ID:			
1st	143,580	77,277	1st	242,252	113,052	1st	96,922	197,719	315,069
2d	131,492	82,801	2d	205,292	95,940	2d	110,381	170,274	280,655
IL:			IL:			IL:			
1st	59,749	162,268	1st	81,817	234,037	1st	189,560	50,960	257,885
2d	43,799	160,337	2d	59,471	235,051	2d	190,684	44,567	235,251
3d	64,091	116,764	3d	....	225,320	3d	163,053	57,885	223,334
4th	22,278	79,666	4th	....	171,297	4th	143,895	22,294	166,189

VOTES CAST FOR REPRESENTATIVES, RESIDENT COMMISSIONER, AND DELEGATES IN 2014, 2016, and 2018—CONTINUED

[The figures, compiled from official statistics obtained by the Clerk of the House, show the votes for the Republican and Democratic nominees, except as otherwise indicated. Figures in the last column, for the 2018 election, may include totals for more candidates than the ones shown.]

State and district	Vote cast in 2014		State and district	Vote cast in 2016		State and district	Vote cast in 2018		Total vote cast in 2018
	Republican	Democrat		Republican	Democrat		Democrat	Republican	
5th	56,350	116,364	5th	86,222	212,842	5th	213,992	65,134	279,131
6th	160,287	78,465	6th	208,555	143,591	6th	169,001	146,445	315,446
7th	27,168	155,110	7th	46,882	250,584	7th	215,746	30,497	246,243
8th	66,878	84,178	8th	103,617	144,954	8th	130,054	67,073	197,127
9th	72,384	141,000	9th	109,550	217,306	9th	231,368	76,983	290,351
10th	95,992	91,136	10th	135,535	150,435	10th	156,540	82,124	238,664
11th	81,335	93,436	11th	108,995	166,578	11th	145,407	82,358	227,765
12th	110,038	87,860	12th	169,976	124,246	12th	118,724	134,884	261,543
13th	123,337	86,935	13th	187,583	126,811	13th	134,458	136,516	270,981
14th	145,369	76,861	14th	200,508	137,589	14th	156,035	141,164	297,199
15th	166,274	55,652	15th	274,554	....	15th	74,309	181,294	255,608
16th	153,388	63,810	16th	259,722	....	16th	104,569	151,254	255,825
17th	88,785	110,560	17th	113,943	173,125	17th	142,659	87,090	229,749
18th	184,363	62,377	18th	250,506	96,770	18th	95,486	195,927	291,413
IN:			IN:			IN:			
1st	51,000	86,579	1st	....	207,515	1st	159,611	85,594	245,209
2d	85,583	55,590	2d	164,355	102,401	2d	103,363	125,499	228,889
3d	97,892	39,771	3d	201,396	66,023	3d	86,610	158,927	245,537
4th	94,998	47,056	4th	193,412	91,256	4th	87,824	156,539	244,363
5th	105,277	49,756	5th	221,957	123,849	5th	137,142	180,035	317,177
6th	102,187	45,509	6th	204,920	79,135	6th	79,430	154,260	241,726
7th	46,887	61,443	7th	94,456	158,739	7th	141,139	76,457	217,596
8th	103,344	61,384	8th	187,702	93,356	8th	86,895	157,396	244,291
9th	101,594	55,016	9th	174,791	130,627	9th	118,090	153,271	271,361
IA:			IA:			IA:			
1st	147,762	141,145	1st	206,903	177,403	1st	170,342	153,442	334,243
2d	129,455	143,431	2d	170,933	198,571	2d	171,446	133,287	312,913
3d	148,814	119,109	3d	208,598	155,002	3d	175,642	167,933	356,241
4th	169,834	105,504	4th	226,719	142,993	4th	147,246	157,676	313,045
KS:			KS:			KS:			
1st	138,764	65,397	1st	169,992	....	1st	71,558	153,082	224,640
2d	128,742	87,153	2d	181,228	96,840	2d	123,859	126,098	264,688
3d	134,493	89,584	3d	176,022	139,300	3d	170,518	139,762	318,301
4th	138,757	69,396	4th	166,998	81,495	4th	98,445	144,248	242,693
KY:			KY:			KY:			
1st	173,022	63,596	1st	216,959	81,710	1st	78,849	172,167	251,016
2d	156,936	69,898	2d	251,825	....	2d	79,964	171,700	257,345
3d	87,981	157,056	3d	122,093	212,401	3d	173,002	101,930	278,720
4th	150,464	71,694	4th	233,922	94,065	4th	90,536	162,946	261,812
5th	171,350	47,617	5th	221,242	....	5th	45,890	172,093	218,017
6th	147,404	98,290	6th	202,099	128,728	6th	114,736	154,468	302,888
LA:			LA:			LA:			
1st	189,250	46,047	1st	243,645	63,785	1st	71,521	192,555	269,325
2d	....	190,006	2d	....	284,269	2d	190,182	....	235,982
3d	207,926	....	3d	220,621	56,215	3d	74,713	168,263	245,943
4th	152,683	....	4th	216,540	46,579	4th	72,934	139,326	216,872
5th	247,211	75,006	5th	255,662	....	5th	67,118	149,018	223,946
6th	234,200	95,127	6th	241,075	79,202	6th	76,716	186,553	268,525
ME:			ME:			ME:			
1st	94,751	186,674	1st	164,569	227,546	1st	201,195	111,188	349,963
2d	133,320	118,568	2d	192,878	159,081	2d	142,440	138,931	281,371
MD:			MD:			MD:			
1st	176,342	73,843	1st	242,574	103,622	1st	116,631	183,662	306,186
2d	70,411	120,412	2d	102,577	192,183	2d	167,201	77,782	253,302
3d	87,029	128,594	3d	115,048	214,640	3d	202,407	82,774	292,880
4th	54,217	134,628	4th	68,670	237,501	4th	209,642	53,327	268,583
5th	80,752	144,725	5th	105,931	242,989	5th	213,796	82,361	304,209
6th	91,930	94,704	6th	133,081	185,770	6th	163,346	105,209	227,084
7th	55,860	144,639	7th	69,556	238,838	7th	202,345	56,266	264,710
8th	87,859	136,722	8th	124,651	220,657	8th	217,679	96,525	319,330
MA:			MA:			MA:			
1st	....	167,612	1st	....	235,803	1st	211,790	....	275,066
2d	....	169,640	2d	....	275,487	2d	191,332	93,391	293,163
3d	81,638	139,104	3d	107,519	236,713	3d	173,175	93,445	286,583
4th	....	184,158	4th	113,055	265,823	4th	245,289	....	322,127
5th	....	182,100	5th	....	285,606	5th	236,243	74,856	323,836
6th	111,989	149,638	6th	....	308,923	6th	217,703	104,798	343,765
7th	....	142,133	7th	....	253,354	7th	216,557	....	249,375
8th	....	200,644	8th	102,744	271,019	8th	259,159	....	327,380
9th	114,971	140,413	9th	127,803	211,790	9th	192,347	131,463	331,370
MI:			MI:			MI:			
1st	130,414	113,263	1st	197,777	144,334	1st	145,246	187,251	332,497
2d	135,568	70,851	2d	212,508	110,391	2d	131,254	168,970	305,463
3d	125,754	84,720	3d	203,545	128,400	3d	134,185	169,107	310,740

VOTES CAST FOR REPRESENTATIVES, RESIDENT COMMISSIONER, AND DELEGATES IN 2014, 2016, and 2018—CONTINUED

[The figures, compiled from official statistics obtained by the Clerk of the House, show the votes for the Republican and Democratic nominees, except as otherwise indicated. Figures in the last column, for the 2018 election, may include totals for more candidates than the ones shown.]

State and district	Vote cast in 2014		State and district	Vote cast in 2016		State and district	Vote cast in 2018		Total vote cast in 2018
	Repub-lican	Demo-crat		Repub-lican	Demo-crat		Demo-crat	Repub-lican	
4th	123,962	85,777	4th	194,572	101,277	4th	106,540	178,510	285,050
5th	69,222	148,182	5th	112,102	195,279	5th	164,502	99,265	276,413
6th	116,801	84,391	6th	193,259	119,980	6th	134,082	147,436	293,438
7th	119,564	92,083	7th	184,321	134,010	7th	136,330	158,730	295,060
8th	132,739	102,269	8th	205,629	143,791	8th	172,880	159,782	341,593
9th	81,470	136,342	9th	128,937	199,661	9th	181,734	112,123	304,563
10th	157,069	67,143	10th	215,132	110,112	10th	106,061	182,808	303,064
11th	140,435	101,681	11th	200,872	152,461	11th	181,912	158,463	350,901
12th	64,716	134,346	12th	96,104	211,378	12th	200,588	85,115	294,628
13th	27,234	132,710	13th	40,541	198,771	13th	165,355		196,299
14th	41,801	165,272	14th	58,103	244,135	14th	214,334	45,899	264,994
MN:			MN:			MN:			
1st	103,536	122,851	1st	166,524	169,071	1st		146,200	291,661
2d	137,778	95,565	2d	173,970		2d		159,344	337,968
3d	167,515	101,846	3d	223,075		3d		160,839	363,949
4th	79,492	147,857	4th	121,033	203,299	4th	216,865	97,747	328,614
5th	56,577	167,079	5th	80,660	249,957	5th		74,440	343,358
6th	133,328	90,926	6th	235,385		6th		192,931	315,726
7th	109,955	130,546	7th	156,944	173,572	7th	146,672	134,668	281,509
8th	125,358	129,090	8th	177,088	179,097	8th		159,364	314,211
MS:			MS:			MS:			
1st	102,622	43,713	1st	206,455	83,947	1st	76,601	158,245	236,521
2d		100,688	2d	83,542	192,343	2d	158,921		221,379
3d	117,771	47,744	3d	209,490	96,101	3d	94,461	160,284	257,271
4th	108,776	37,869	4th	181,323	77,505	4th	68,787	152,633	223,732
MO:			MO:			MO:			
1st	35,273	119,315	1st	62,714	236,993	1st	219,781	45,867	274,375
2d	148,191	75,384	2d	241,954	155,689	2d	177,611	192,477	376,066
3d	130,940	52,021	3d	249,865	102,891	3d	106,589	211,243	324,608
4th	120,014	46,464	4th	225,348	92,510	4th	95,968	190,138	293,316
5th	69,071	79,256	5th	123,771	190,766	5th	175,019	101,069	283,785
6th	124,616	55,157	6th	238,388	99,692	6th	97,660	199,796	305,409
7th	104,054	47,282	7th	228,692	92,756	7th	89,190	196,343	296,455
8th	106,124	38,721	8th	229,792	70,009	8th	66,151	194,042	264,399
MT:			MT:			MT:			
At large	203,871	148,690	At large	285,358	205,919	At large	233,284	256,661	504,421
NE:			NE:			NE:			
1st	123,219	55,838	1st	189,771	83,467	1st	93,069	141,712	234,781
2d	78,157	83,872	2d	141,066	137,602	2d	121,770	126,715	248,485
3d	139,440	45,524	3d	226,720		3d	49,654	163,650	213,304
NV:			NV:			NV:			
1st	30,413	45,643	1st	54,174	116,537	1st	100,707	46,978	152,201
2d	122,402	52,016	2d	182,676	115,722	2d	120,102	167,435	287,537
3d	88,528	52,644	3d	142,926	146,869	3d	148,501	122,566	286,168
4th	63,466	59,844	4th	118,328	128,985	4th	121,962	102,748	234,868
NH:			NH:			NH:			
1st	125,508	116,769	1st	157,176	162,080	1st	155,884	130,996	291,939
2d	106,871	130,700	2d	158,825	174,371	2d	155,358	117,990	279,705
NJ:			NJ:			NJ:			
1st	64,073	93,315	1st	112,388	183,231	1st	169,628	87,617	263,418
2d	108,875	66,026	2d	176,338	110,838	2d	136,685	116,866	258,363
3d	100,471	82,537	3d	194,596	127,526	3d	153,473	149,500	306,875
4th	118,826	54,415	4th	211,992	111,532	4th	126,766	163,065	294,348
5th	104,678	81,808	5th	157,690	172,587	5th	169,546	128,255	301,823
6th	46,891	72,190	6th	91,908	167,895	6th	140,752	80,443	221,195
7th	104,287	68,232	7th	185,850	148,188	7th	166,985	150,785	322,742
8th	15,141	61,510	8th	32,337	134,733	8th	119,881	28,725	153,455
9th	36,246	82,498	9th	65,376	162,642	9th	140,832	57,854	200,416
10th	14,154	95,734	10th	26,450	190,856	10th	175,253	20,191	200,159
11th	109,455	65,477	11th	194,299	130,162	11th	183,684	136,322	323,574
12th	54,168	90,430	12th	92,407	181,430	12th	173,334	79,041	252,375
NM:			NM:			NM:			
1st	74,558	105,474	1st	96,879	181,088	1st	147,336	90,507	249,162
2d	95,209	52,499	2d	143,515	85,232	2d	101,489	97,767	199,256
3d	70,775	113,249	3d	102,730	170,612	3d	155,201	76,427	244,893
NY:			NY:			NY:			
1st	77,062	68,387	1st	158,409	126,635	1st	124,213	121,562	274,427
2d		41,814	2d		102,270	2d	108,803	112,565	245,926
3d	63,219	80,393	3d	133,954	171,775	3d	149,937	98,716	273,130
4th	67,811	83,772	4th	111,246	181,861	4th	156,728	90,306	267,191
5th		75,712	5th	26,791	197,852	5th	160,500		186,325
6th		49,227	6th	43,770	131,463	6th	104,293		149,540
7th	5,713	47,142	7th	14,941	165,819	7th	134,125		164,835
8th		70,469	8th		203,235	8th	170,850		204,768

VOTES CAST FOR REPRESENTATIVES, RESIDENT COMMISSIONER, AND DELEGATES IN 2014, 2016, and 2018—CONTINUED

[The figures, compiled from official statistics obtained by the Clerk of the House, show the votes for the Republican and Democratic nominees, except as otherwise indicated. Figures in the last column, for the 2018 election, may include totals for more candidates than the ones shown.]

State and district	Vote cast in 2014		State and district	Vote cast in 2016		State and district	Vote cast in 2018		Total vote cast in 2018
	Republican	Democrat		Republican	Democrat		Democrat	Republican	
9th	....	70,997	9th	....	198,886	9th	167,269	18,702	207,844
10th	....	73,945	10th	46,275	180,117	10th	162,131	33,692	216,272
11th	48,291	41,429	11th	122,606	85,257	11th	96,850	80,440	195,100
12th	19,564	78,440	12th	49,398	230,153	12th	205,858	30,446	256,239
13th	....	63,437	13th	13,129	207,194	13th	171,341	9,535	197,200
14th	....	45,370	14th	26,891	138,367	14th	110,318	19,202	146,272
15th	....	53,128	15th	6,129	165,688	15th	122,007	4,566	133,913
16th	....	90,088	16th	....	198,811	16th	172,815	....	226,338
17th	63,549	89,295	17th	....	193,819	17th	159,923	....	257,221
18th	66,523	76,235	18th	111,117	140,951	18th	126,368	96,345	261,321
19th	102,118	60,533	19th	135,905	125,956	19th	135,582	112,304	293,570
20th	61,820	103,437	20th	83,328	188,428	20th	161,330	89,058	277,066
21st	79,615	53,140	21st	152,597	75,965	21st	93,394	116,433	239,125
22d	113,574	....	22d	113,287	102,734	22d	116,001	110,125	255,100
23d	94,375	60,233	23d	136,964	106,600	23d	100,914	114,722	245,899
24th	93,881	72,631	24th	150,330	110,550	24th	115,902	113,538	265,156
25th	75,990	87,264	25th	113,840	168,660	25th	147,949	91,342	275,641
26th	38,477	100,648	26th	56,930	195,322	26th	156,968	61,488	242,371
27th	109,171	50,939	27th	175,509	107,832	27th	128,167	114,506	293,095
NC:			NC:			NC:			
1st	55,990	154,333	1st	101,567	240,661	1st	190,457	82,218	272,675
2d	122,128	85,479	2d	221,485	169,082	2d	151,977	170,072	331,704
3d	139,415	66,182	3d	217,531	106,170	3d	....	187,901	187,901
4th	57,416	169,946	4th	130,161	279,380	4th	247,067	82,052	341,403
5th	139,279	88,973	5th	207,625	147,887	5th	120,468	159,917	280,385
6th	147,312	103,758	6th	207,983	143,167	6th	123,651	160,709	284,360
7th	134,431	84,054	7th	211,801	135,905	7th	120,838	156,809	282,312
8th	121,568	65,854	8th	189,863	133,182	8th	114,119	141,102	255,521
9th	163,080	....	9th	193,452	139,041	9th	....	....	....
10th	133,504	85,292	10th	220,825	128,919	10th	113,259	164,969	278,228
11th	144,682	85,342	11th	230,405	129,103	11th	116,508	178,012	300,666
12th	42,568	130,096	12th	115,185	234,115	12th	203,974	75,164	279,138
13th	153,991	114,718	13th	199,443	156,049	13th	130,402	147,570	286,136
ND:			ND:			ND:			
At large	138,100	95,678	At large	233,980	80,377	At large	....	193,568	321,532
OH:			OH:			OH:			
1st	124,779	72,604	1st	210,014	144,644	1st	141,118	154,409	300,871
2d	132,658	68,453	2d	221,193	111,694	2d	119,333	166,714	289,661
3d	51,475	91,769	3d	91,560	199,791	3d	181,575	65,040	246,677
4th	125,907	60,165	4th	210,227	98,981	4th	89,412	167,993	257,405
5th	134,449	58,507	5th	244,599	100,392	5th	99,655	176,569	283,617
6th	111,026	73,561	6th	231,975	88,780	6th	76,716	172,774	249,490
7th	143,959	....	7th	198,221	89,638	7th	107,536	153,117	260,653
8th	126,539	51,534	8th	223,833	87,794	8th	87,281	173,852	261,133
9th	51,704	108,870	9th	88,427	193,966	9th	157,219	74,670	231,937
10th	130,752	63,249	10th	215,724	109,981	10th	118,785	157,554	281,726
11th	35,461	137,105	11th	59,769	242,917	11th	206,138	44,486	250,660
12th	150,573	61,360	12th	251,266	112,638	12th	161,251	175,677	341,647
13th	55,233	120,230	13th	99,377	208,610	13th	153,323	98,047	251,370
14th	135,736	70,856	14th	219,191	130,907	14th	137,549	169,809	307,358
15th	128,496	66,125	15th	222,847	113,960	15th	116,112	170,593	292,443
16th	132,176	75,199	16th	225,794	119,830	16th	129,681	170,029	299,710
OK:			OK:			OK:			
1st	(3)	....	1st	(3)	....	1st	103,042	150,129	253,171
2d	110,925	38,964	2d	189,839	62,387	2d	65,021	140,451	216,002
3d	133,335	36,270	3d	227,525	63,090	3d	61,152	172,913	234,065
4th	117,721	40,998	4th	204,143	76,472	4th	78,088	149,227	236,638
5th	95,632	57,790	5th	160,184	103,273	5th	121,149	117,811	238,960
OR:			OR:			OR:			
1st	96,245	160,038	1st	139,756	225,391	1st	231,198	116,446	363,249
2d	202,374	73,785	2d	272,952	106,640	2d	145,298	207,597	368,709
3d	57,424	211,748	3d	....	274,687	3d	279,019	76,187	384,326
4th	116,534	181,624	4th	157,743	220,628	4th	208,710	152,414	372,893
5th	110,332	150,944	5th	160,443	199,505	5th	197,187	149,887	358,469
PA:			PA:			PA:			
1st	27,193	131,248	1st	53,219	245,791	1st	160,745	169,053	329,798
2d	25,397	181,141	2d	35,131	322,514	2d	159,600	42,382	201,982
3d	113,859	73,931	3d	244,893	....	3d	287,610	20,387	307,997
4th	147,090	50,250	4th	220,628	113,372	4th	211,524	121,467	332,991
5th	115,018	65,839	5th	206,761	101,082	5th	198,639	106,075	304,714
6th	119,643	92,901	6th	207,469	155,000	6th	177,704	124,124	301,828
7th	145,869	89,256	7th	225,678	153,824	7th	140,813	114,437	263,261
8th	137,731	84,767	8th	207,263	173,555	8th	135,603	112,563	248,166
9th	110,094	63,223	9th	186,580	107,985	9th	100,204	148,723	248,927
10th	112,851	44,737	10th	211,282	89,823	10th	141,668	149,365	291,033

VOTES CAST FOR REPRESENTATIVES, RESIDENT COMMISSIONER, AND DELEGATES IN 2014, 2016, and 2018—CONTINUED

[The figures, compiled from official statistics obtained by the Clerk of the House, show the votes for the Republican and Democratic nominees, except as otherwise indicated. Figures in the last column, for the 2018 election, may include totals for more candidates than the ones shown.]

State and district	Vote cast in 2014		State and district	Vote cast in 2016		State and district	Vote cast in 2018		Total vote cast in 2018
	Repub-lican	Demo-crat		Repub-lican	Demo-crat		Demo-crat	Repub-lican	
11th	122,464	62,228	11th	199,421	113,800	11th	113,876	163,708	277,584
12th	127,993	87,928	12th	221,851	137,353	12th	82,825	161,047	243,872
13th	60,549	123,601	13th	....	239,316	13th	74,733	178,533	253,266
14th	....	148,351	14th	87,999	255,293	14th	110,051	151,386	261,437
15th	128,285	....	15th	190,618	124,129	15th	78,327	165,245	243,572
16th	101,722	74,513	16th	168,669	134,586	16th	124,109	135,348	262,396
17th	71,371	93,680	17th	135,430	157,734	17th	183,162	142,417	325,579
18th	166,076	....	18th	293,684	....	18th	231,472	....	231,472
RI:			RI:			RI:			
1st	58,877	87,060	1st	71,023	130,534	1st	116,099	57,567	174,083
2d	63,844	105,716	2d	70,301	133,108	2d	126,476	72,271	199,197
SC:			SC:			SC:			
1st	119,392	....	1st	190,410	110,539	1st	145,455	141,473	287,433
2d	121,649	68,719	2d	183,746	105,306	2d	109,199	144,642	257,139
3d	116,741	47,181	3d	196,325	72,933	3d	70,046	153,338	226,204
4th	126,452	....	4th	198,648	91,676	4th	89,182	145,321	243,950
5th	103,078	66,802	5th	161,669	105,772	5th	103,129	141,757	248,579
6th	44,311	125,747	6th	70,099	177,947	6th	144,765	58,282	206,433
7th	102,833	68,576	7th	176,468	103,454	7th	96,564	142,681	239,554
SD:			SD:			SD:			
At large	183,834	92,485	At large ..	237,163	132,810	At large ..	121,033	202,695	335,965
TN:			TN:			TN:			
1st	115,533	....	1st	198,293	39,024	1st	47,138	172,835	224,282
2d	120,883	37,612	2d	212,455	68,401	2d	86,668	172,856	262,134
3d	97,344	53,983	3d	176,613	76,727	3d	84,731	156,512	245,765
4th	84,815	51,357	4th	165,796	89,141	4th	78,065	147,323	232,451
5th	55,078	96,148	5th	102,433	171,111	5th	177,923	84,317	262,248
6th	115,231	37,232	6th	202,234	61,995	6th	70,370	172,810	248,740
7th	110,534	42,280	7th	200,407	65,226	7th	81,661	170,071	254,384
8th	122,255	42,433	8th	194,386	70,925	8th	74,755	168,030	248,345
9th	27,173	87,376	9th	41,123	171,631	9th	145,139	34,901	181,476
TX:			TX:			TX:			
1st	115,084	33,476	1st	192,434	62,847	1st	61,263	168,165	232,720
2d	101,936	44,462	2d	168,692	100,231	2d	119,992	139,188	263,392
3d	113,404	....	3d	193,684	109,420	3d	138,234	169,520	312,358
4th	115,085	....	4th	216,643	....	4th	57,400	188,667	249,245
5th	88,998	....	5th	155,469	....	5th	78,666	130,617	209,507
6th	92,334	55,027	6th	159,444	106,667	6th	116,350	135,961	256,042
7th	90,606	49,478	7th	143,542	111,991	7th	127,959	115,642	243,601
8th	125,066	....	8th	236,379	....	8th	67,930	200,619	273,170
9th	....	78,109	9th	36,491	152,032	9th	136,256	....	153,001
10th	109,726	60,243	10th	179,221	120,170	10th	144,034	157,166	307,827
11th	107,939	....	11th	201,871	....	11th	40,631	176,603	220,377
12th	113,186	41,757	12th	196,482	76,029	12th	90,994	172,557	268,491
13th	110,842	16,822	13th	199,050	....	13th	35,083	169,027	207,285
14th	90,116	52,545	14th	160,631	99,054	14th	92,212	138,942	234,528
15th	39,016	48,708	15th	66,877	101,712	15th	98,333	63,862	164,802
16th	21,324	49,338	16th	....	150,228	16th	124,437	49,127	181,754
17th	85,807	43,049	17th	149,417	86,603	17th	98,070	134,841	237,351
18th	26,249	76,097	18th	48,306	150,157	18th	138,704	38,368	184,332
19th	90,160	21,458	19th	176,314	....	19th	50,039	151,946	201,985
20th	....	66,554	20th	....	149,640	20th	139,038	....	171,963
21st	135,660	....	21st	202,967	129,765	21st	168,421	177,654	353,617
22d	100,861	47,844	22d	181,864	123,679	22d	138,153	152,750	297,405
23d	57,459	55,037	23d	110,577	107,526	23d	102,359	103,285	210,069
24th	93,712	46,548	24th	154,845	108,389	24th	125,231	133,317	263,418
25th	107,120	64,463	25th	180,988	117,073	25th	136,385	163,023	304,553
26th	116,944	....	26th	211,730	94,507	26th	121,938	185,551	312,505
27th	83,342	44,152	27th	142,251	88,329	27th	75,929	125,118	207,421
28th	....	62,508	28th	57,740	122,086	28th	117,494	....	139,226
29th	....	41,321	29th	31,646	95,649	29th	88,188	28,098	117,494
30th	....	93,041	30th	41,518	170,502	30th	166,784	....	183,174
31st	91,607	45,715	31st	166,060	103,852	31st	136,362	144,680	286,007
32d	96,495	55,325	32d	162,868	....	32d	144,067	126,101	275,620
33d	....	43,769	33d	33,222	93,147	33d	90,805	26,120	119,224
34th	30,811	47,503	34th	62,323	104,638	34th	85,825	57,243	143,068
35th	32,040	60,124	35th	62,384	124,612	35th	138,278	50,553	194,067
36th	101,663	29,543	36th	193,675	....	36th	60,908	161,048	221,956
UT:			UT:			UT:			
1st	84,231	36,422	1st	182,925	73,380	1st	63,308	156,692	254,333
2d	88,915	47,585	2d	170,534	93,778	2d	105,051	151,489	270,044
3d	102,952	32,059	3d	209,589	75,716	3d	70,686	174,856	258,858
4th	74,936	67,425	4th	147,597	113,413	4th	134,964	134,270	269,271
VT:			VT:			VT:			
At large	59,432	123,349	At large ..	....	264,414	At large ..	188,547	70,705	278,230

VOTES CAST FOR REPRESENTATIVES, RESIDENT COMMISSIONER, AND DELEGATES IN 2014, 2016, and 2018—CONTINUED

[The figures, compiled from official statistics obtained by the Clerk of the House, show the votes for the Republican and Democratic nominees, except as otherwise indicated. Figures in the last column, for the 2018 election, may include totals for more candidates than the ones shown.]

State and district	Vote cast in 2014		State and district	Vote cast in 2016		State and district	Vote cast in 2018		Total vote cast in 2018
	Repub-lican	Demo-crat		Repub-lican	Demo-crat		Demo-crat	Repub-lican	
VA:			VA:			VA:			
1st	131,861	72,059	1st	230,213	140,785	1st	148,464	183,250	332,101
2d	101,558	71,178	2d	190,475	119,440	2d	139,571	133,458	273,400
3d	....	139,197	3d	103,289	208,337	3d	198,615	....	217,722
4th	120,684	75,270	4th	145,731	200,136	4th	187,642	107,706	299,854
5th	124,735	73,482	5th	207,758	148,339	5th	145,040	165,339	310,926
6th	133,898	....	6th	225,471	112,170	6th	113,133	167,957	281,377
7th	148,026	89,914	7th	218,057	160,159	7th	176,079	169,295	349,803
8th	63,810	128,102	8th	98,387	246,653	8th	247,137	76,899	324,748
9th	117,465	....	9th	212,838	87,877	9th	85,833	160,933	246,980
10th	125,914	89,957	10th	210,791	187,712	10th	206,356	160,841	367,795
11th	75,796	106,780	11th	....	247,818	11th	219,191	83,023	308,250
WA:			WA:			WA:			
1st	101,428	124,151	1st	155,779	193,619	1st	197,209	135,534	332,743
2d	79,518	122,173	2d	117,094	208,314	2d	210,187	....	294,833
3d	124,796	78,018	3d	193,457	119,820	3d	145,407	161,819	307,226
4th	153,079	....	4th	229,919	....	4th	83,785	141,551	225,336
5th	135,470	87,772	5th	192,959	130,575	5th	144,925	175,422	320,347
6th	83,025	141,265	6th	126,116	201,718	6th	206,409	116,677	323,086
7th	47,921	203,954	7th	....	378,754	7th	329,800	64,881	394,681
8th	125,741	73,003	8th	193,145	127,720	8th	164,089	....	313,057
9th	48,662	118,132	9th	76,317	205,165	9th	240,567	....	240,567
10th	82,213	99,279	10th	120,104	170,460	10th	166,215	103,860	270,075
WV:			WV:			WV:			
1st	92,491	52,109	1st	163,469	73,534	1st	70,217	127,997	198,214
2d	72,619	67,687	2d	140,807	101,207	2d	88,011	110,504	204,792
3d	77,713	62,688	3d	140,741	49,708	3d	76,340	98,645	174,985
WI:			WI:			WI:			
1st	182,316	105,552	1st	230,072	107,003	1st	137,508	177,492	325,317
2d	103,619	224,920	2d	124,044	273,537	2d	309,116	....	317,295
3d	119,540	155,368	3d	....	257,401	3d	187,888	126,980	314,989
4th	68,490	179,045	4th	....	220,181	4th	206,487	59,091	273,087
5th	231,160	101,190	5th	260,706	114,477	5th	138,385	225,619	364,288
6th	169,767	122,212	6th	204,147	133,072	6th	144,536	180,311	325,065
7th	169,891	112,949	7th	223,418	138,649	7th	124,307	194,061	322,840
8th	188,553	101,345	8th	227,892	135,682	8th	119,265	209,410	328,774
WY:			WY:			WY:			
At large	113,038	37,803	At large ..	156,176	75,466	At large ..	59,903	127,963	205,275

[1] According to Florida law, the names of those with no opposition are not printed on the ballot.
[2] According to Louisiana law, the names of those with no opposition are not printed on the ballot.
[3] According to Oklahoma law, the names of those with no opposition are not printed on the ballot.

VOTES CAST FOR REPRESENTATIVES, RESIDENT COMMISSIONER, AND DELEGATES IN 2014, 2016, and 2018—CONTINUED

[The figures, compiled from official statistics obtained by the Clerk of the House, show the votes for the Republican and Democratic nominees, except as otherwise indicated. Figures in the last column, for the 2018 election, may include totals for more candidates than the ones shown.]

Commonwealth of Puerto Rico	Vote						Total vote cast in 2018
	2014		2016		2018		
	Popular Democrat	Democrat	New Progressive	Popular Democrat	Popular Democrat	Democrat	
Resident Commissioner .... (4-year term)	....	....	718,591	695,073	....	....	....

District of Columbia	Vote						Total vote cast in 2018
	2014		2016		2018		
	Republican	Democrat	Democrat	Libertarian	Democrat	Republican	
Delegate	11,673	14,923	265,178	18,713	199,124	9,700	228,769

Guam	Vote						Total vote cast in 2018
	2014		2016		2018		
	Republican	Democrat	Republican	Democrat	Democrat	Republican	
Delegate	14,956	20,693	15,617	18,345	19,193	15,398	37,386

Virgin Islands	Vote						Total vote cast in 2018
	2014		2016		2018		
	Republican	Democrat	Democrat	Write-in	Democrat	Write-in	
Delegate	1,964	21,224	14,531	371	16,341	264	16,605

American Samoa	Vote						Total vote cast in 2018
	2014		2016		2018		
	Republican	Democrat	Republican	No Party	Democrat	Republican	
Delegate	4,306	3,157	8,924	2,911	659	7,979	8,638

Northern Mariana Islands	Vote					Total vote cast in 2018
	2014		2016	2018		
	Independent	Democrat	Independent	Democrat	Republican	
Delegate	8,549	4,547	10,605	9,150	5,199	14,349

SESSIONS OF CONGRESS, 1st–116th CONGRESSES, 1789–2020

[Closing date for this table was July 22, 2020.]

MEETING DATES OF CONGRESS: Pursuant to a resolution of the Confederation Congress in 1788, the Constitution went into effect on March 4, 1789. From then until the 20th amendment took effect in January 1934, the term of each Congress began on March 4th of each odd-numbered year; however, Article I, section 4, of the Constitution provided that ''The Congress shall assemble at least once in every Year, and such Meeting shall be on the first Monday in December, unless they shall by law appoint a different day.'' The Congress therefore convened regularly on the first Monday in December until the 20th amendment became effective, which changed the beginning of Congress's term as well as its convening date to January 3rd. So prior to 1934, a new Congress typically would not convene for regular business until 13 months after being elected. One effect of this was that the last session of each Congress was a ''lame duck'' session. After the 20th amendment, the time from the election to the beginning of Congress's term as well as when it convened was reduced to two months. Recognizing that the need might exist for Congress to meet at times other than the regularly scheduled convening date, Article II, section 3 of the Constitution provides that the President ''may, on extraordinary occasions, convene both Houses, or either of them''; hence these sessions occur only if convened by Presidential proclamation. Except as noted, these are separately numbered sessions of a Congress, and are marked by an E in the session column of the table. Until the 20th amendment was adopted, there were also times when special sessions of the Senate were convened, principally for confirming Cabinet and other executive nominations, and occasionally for the ratification of treaties or other executive business. These Senate sessions were also called by Presidential proclamation (typically by the outgoing President, although on occasion by incumbents as well) and are marked by an S in the session column. MEETING PLACES OF CONGRESS: Congress met for the first and second sessions of the First Congress (1789 and 1790) in New York City. From the third session of the First Congress through the first session of the Sixth Congress (1790 to 1800), Philadelphia was the meeting place. Congress has convened in Washington since the second session of the Sixth Congress (1800).

Congress	Session	Convening Date	Adjournment Date	Length in days[1]	Recesses[2]		President pro tempore of the Senate[3]	Speaker of the House of Representatives
					Senate	House of Representatives		
1st	1	Mar. 4, 1789	Sept. 29, 1789	210			John Langdon, of New Hampshire	Frederick A.C. Muhlenberg, of Pennsylvania.
	2	Jan. 4, 1790	Aug. 12, 1790	221			...do.	
	3	Dec. 6, 1790	Mar. 3, 1791	88			...do.	
2d	S	Mar. 4, 1791	Mar. 4, 1791	1			...do.	
	1	Oct. 24, 1791	May 8, 1792	197			Richard Henry Lee, of Virginia	Jonathan Trumbull, of Connecticut.
	2	Nov. 5, 1792	Mar. 2, 1793	119			John Langdon, of New Hampshire.	
3d	S	Mar. 4, 1793	Mar. 4, 1793	1			...do.	
	1	Dec. 2, 1793	June 9, 1794	190			John Langdon, of New Hampshire; Ralph Izard, of South Carolina.	Frederick A.C. Muhlenberg, of Pennsylvania.
	2	Nov. 3, 1794	Mar. 3, 1795	121			Henry Tazewell, of Virginia.	
4th	S	June 8, 1795	June 26, 1795	19			...do.	
	1	Dec. 7, 1795	June 1, 1796	177			Henry Tazewell, of Virginia; Samuel Livermore, of New Hampshire.	Jonathan Dayton, of New Jersey.
	2	Dec. 5, 1796	Mar. 3, 1797	89			William Bingham, of Pennsylvania.	
5th	S	Mar. 4, 1797	Mar. 4, 1797	1				
	1–E	May 15, 1797	July 10, 1797	57			William Bradford, of Rhode Island	Do.
	S	July 17, 1798	July 19, 1798	3				
	2	Nov. 13, 1797	July 16, 1798	246			Jacob Read, of South Carolina; Theodore Sedgwick, of Massachusetts.	
	3	Dec. 3, 1798	Mar. 3, 1799	91			John Laurance, of New York; James Ross, of Pennsylvania.	
6th	1	Dec. 2, 1799	May 14, 1800	164			Samuel Livermore, of New Hampshire; Uriah Tracy, of Connecticut.	Theodore Sedgwick, of Massachusetts.
	2	Nov. 17, 1800	Mar. 3, 1801	107	Dec. 23–Dec. 30, 1800	Dec. 24–Dec. 29, 1800	John E. Howard, of Maryland; James Hillhouse, of Connecticut.	
7th	S	Mar. 4, 1801	Mar. 5, 1801	2				
	1	Dec. 7, 1801	May 3, 1802	148			Abraham Baldwin, of Georgia	Nathaniel Macon, of North Carolina.

	2	Dec. 6, 1802	Mar. 3, 1803	88			Stephen R. Bradley, of Vermont.	
8th	1–E	Oct. 17, 1803	Mar. 27, 1804	163			John Brown, of Kentucky; Jesse Franklin, of North Carolina.	Do.
	2	Nov. 5, 1804	Mar. 3, 1805	119			Joseph Anderson, of Tennessee.	
9th	1	Dec. 2, 1805	Apr. 21, 1806	141			Samuel Smith, of Maryland	Do.
	2	Dec. 1, 1806	Mar. 3, 1807	93			...do.	
10th	1–E	Oct. 26, 1807	Apr. 25, 1808	182			...do	Joseph B. Varnum, of Massachusetts.
	2	Nov. 7, 1808	Mar. 3, 1809	117			Stephen R. Bradley, of Vermont; John Milledge, of Georgia.	
11th	S	Mar. 4, 1809	Mar. 7, 1809	4				
	1–E	May 22, 1809	June 28, 1809	38			Andrew Gregg, of Pennsylvania	Do.
	2	Nov. 27, 1809	May 1, 1810	156			John Gaillard, of South Carolina.	
	3	Dec. 3, 1810	Mar. 3, 1811	91			John Pope, of Kentucky.	
12th	1–E	Nov. 4, 1811	July 6, 1812	245			William H. Crawford, of Georgia	Henry Clay, of Kentucky.
	2	Nov. 2, 1812	Mar. 3, 1813	122			...do.	
13th	1	May 24, 1813	Aug. 2, 1813	71			...do	Do.[4]
	2	Dec. 6, 1813	Apr. 18, 1814	134			Joseph B. Varnum, of Massachusetts; John Gaillard, of South Carolina.	Langdon Cheves, of South Carolina.[4]
	3–E	Sept. 19, 1814	Mar. 3, 1815	166			John Gaillard, of South Carolina.	
14th	1	Dec. 4, 1815	Apr. 30, 1816	148			...do	Henry Clay, of Kentucky.
	2	Dec. 2, 1816	Mar. 3, 1817	92			...do.	
15th	S	Mar. 4, 1817	Mar. 6, 1817	3			...do.	
	1	Dec. 1, 1817	Apr. 20, 1818	141	Dec. 24–Dec. 29, 1817	Dec. 25–Dec. 28, 1817	...do	Do.
	2	Nov. 16, 1818	Mar. 3, 1819	108			James Barbour, of Virginia.	
16th	1	Dec. 6, 1819	May 15, 1820	162			James Barbour, of Virginia; John Gaillard, of South Carolina.	Do.[5]
	2	Nov. 13, 1820	Mar. 3, 1821	111			John Gaillard, of South Carolina	John W. Taylor, of New York.[5]
17th	1	Dec. 3, 1821	May 8, 1822	157			...do	Philip P. Barbour, of Virginia.
	2	Dec. 2, 1822	Mar. 3, 1823	92			...do.	
18th	1	Dec. 1, 1823	May 27, 1824	178			...do	Henry Clay, of Kentucky.
	2	Dec. 6, 1824	Mar. 3, 1825	88			...do.	
19th	S	Mar. 4, 1825	Mar, 9, 1825	6			...do.	
	1	Dec. 5, 1825	May 22, 1826	169			Nathaniel Macon, of North Carolina	John W. Taylor, of New York.
	2	Dec. 4, 1826	Mar. 3, 1827	90			...do.	
20th	1	Dec. 3, 1827	May 26, 1828	175			Samuel Smith, of Maryland	Andrew Stevenson, of Virginia.
	2	Dec. 1, 1828	Mar. 3, 1829	93	Dec. 24–Dec. 29, 1828	Dec. 25–Dec. 28, 1828	...do.	
21st	S	Mar. 4, 1829	Mar. 17, 1829	14			...do.	
	1	Dec. 7, 1829	May 31, 1830	176			...do	Do.
	2	Dec. 6, 1830	Mar. 3, 1831	88			...do.	
22d	1	Dec. 5, 1831	July 16, 1832	225			Littleton Waller Tazewell, of Virginia	Do.
	2	Dec. 3, 1832	Mar. 2, 1833	91			Hugh Lawson White, of Tennessee.	
23d	1	Dec. 2, 1833	June 30, 1834	211			Hugh Lawson White, of Tennessee; George Poindexter, of Mississippi.	Do.[6]
	2	Dec. 1, 1834	Mar. 3, 1835	93			John Tyler, of Virginia	John Bell, of Tennessee.[6]
24th	1	Dec. 7, 1835	July 4, 1836	211			William R. King, of Alabama	James K. Polk, of Tennessee.
	2	Dec. 5, 1836	Mar. 3, 1837	89			...do.	
25th	S	Mar. 4, 1837	Mar. 10, 1837	7			...do.	
	1–E	Sept. 4, 1837	Oct. 16, 1837	43			...do	Do.
	2	Dec. 4, 1837	July 9, 1838	218			...do.	
	3	Dec. 3, 1838	Mar. 3, 1839	91			...do.	
26th	1	Dec. 2, 1839	July 21, 1840	233			...do	Robert M.T. Hunter, of Virginia.
	2	Dec. 7, 1840	Mar. 3, 1841	87			...do.	
27th	S	Mar. 4, 1841	Mar. 15, 1841	12			William R. King, of Alabama; Samuel L. Southard, of New Jersey.	

SESSIONS OF CONGRESS, 1st–116th CONGRESSES, 1789–2020—CONTINUED

[Closing date for this table was July 22, 2020.]

MEETING DATES OF CONGRESS: Pursuant to a resolution of the Confederation Congress in 1788, the Constitution went into effect on March 4, 1789. From then until the 20th amendment took effect in January 1934, the term of each Congress began on March 4th of each odd-numbered year; however, Article I, section 4, of the Constitution provided that "The Congress shall assemble at least once in every Year, and such Meeting shall be on the first Monday in December, unless they shall by law appoint a different day." The Congress therefore convened regularly on the first Monday in December until the 20th amendment became effective, which changed the beginning of Congress's term as well as its convening date to January 3rd. So prior to 1934, a new Congress typically would not convene for regular business until 13 months after being elected. One effect of this was that the last session of each Congress was a "lame duck" session. After the 20th amendment, the time from the election to the beginning of Congress's term as well as when it convened was reduced to two months. Recognizing that the need might exist for Congress to meet at times other than the regularly scheduled convening date, Article II, section 3 of the Constitution provides that the President "may, on extraordinary occasions, convene both Houses, or either of them"; hence these sessions occur only if convened by Presidential proclamation. Except as noted, these are separately numbered sessions of a Congress, and are marked by an E in the session column of the table. Until the 20th amendment was adopted, there were also times when special sessions of the Senate were convened, principally for confirming Cabinet and other executive nominations, and occasionally for the ratification of treaties or other executive business. These Senate sessions were also called by Presidential proclamation (typically by the outgoing President, although on occasion by incumbents as well) and are marked by an S in the session column. MEETING PLACES OF CONGRESS: Congress met for the first and second sessions of the First Congress (1789 and 1790) in New York City. From the third session of the First Congress through the first session of the Sixth Congress (1790 to 1800), Philadelphia was the meeting place. Congress has convened in Washington since the second session of the Sixth Congress (1800).

Congress	Session	Convening Date	Adjournment Date	Length in days[1]	Recesses[2]		President pro tempore of the Senate[3]	Speaker of the House of Representatives
					Senate	House of Representatives		
	1–E	May 31, 1841	Sept. 13, 1841	106			Samuel L. Southard, of New Jersey	John White, of Kentucky.
	2	Dec. 6, 1841	Aug. 31, 1842	269			Willie P. Mangum, of North Carolina.	
	3	Dec. 5, 1842	Mar. 3, 1843	89			...do.	
28th	1	Dec. 4, 1843	June 17, 1844	196			...do	John W. Jones, of Virginia.
	2	Dec. 2, 1844	Mar. 3, 1845	92			...do.	
29th	S	Mar. 4, 1845	Mar. 20, 1845	17				
	1	Dec. 1, 1845	Aug. 10, 1846	253			Ambrose H. Sevier; David R. Atchison, of Missouri.	John W. Davis, of Indiana.
	2	Dec. 7, 1846	Mar. 3, 1847	87			David R. Atchison, of Missouri.	
30th	1	Dec. 6, 1847	Aug. 14, 1848	254			...do	Robert C. Winthrop, of Massachusetts.
	2	Dec. 4, 1848	Mar. 3, 1849	90			...do.	
31st	S	Mar. 5, 1849	Mar. 23, 1849	19			...do.	
	1	Dec. 3, 1849	Sept. 30, 1850	302			William R. King, of Alabama	Howell Cobb, of Georgia.
	2	Dec. 2, 1850	Mar. 3, 1851	92			...do.	
32d	S	Mar. 4, 1851	Mar. 13, 1851	10				
	1	Dec. 1, 1851	Aug. 31, 1852	275			...do	Linn Boyd, of Kentucky.
	2	Dec. 6, 1852	Mar. 3, 1853	88			David R. Atchison, of Missouri.	
33d	S	Mar. 4, 1853	Apr. 11, 1853	39			...do.	
	1	Dec. 5, 1853	Aug. 7, 1854	246			...do	Do.
	2	Dec. 4, 1854	Mar. 3, 1855	90			Lewis Cass, of Michigan; Jesse D. Bright, of Indiana.	
34th	1	Dec. 3, 1855	Aug. 18, 1856	260			Charles E. Stuart, of Michigan; Jesse D. Bright, of Indiana.	Nathaniel P. Banks, of Massachusetts.
	2–E	Aug. 21, 1856	Aug. 30, 1856	10			Jesse D. Bright, of Indiana.	
	3	Dec. 1, 1856	Mar. 3, 1857	93			James M. Mason, of Virginia.	
35th	S	Mar. 4, 1857	Mar. 14, 1857	11			James M. Mason, of Virginia; Thomas J. Rusk, of Texas.	
	1	Dec. 7, 1857	June 14, 1858	189	Dec. 23, 1857–Jan. 4, 1858	Dec. 24, 1857–Jan. 3, 1858	Benjamin Fitzpatrick, of Alabama	James L. Orr, of South Carolina.

	S	June 15, 1858	June 16, 1858	2				
	2	Dec. 6, 1858	Mar. 3, 1859	88	Dec. 23, 1858–Jan. 4, 1859	Dec. 24, 1858–Jan. 3, 1859	...do.	
36th	S	Mar. 4, 1859	Mar. 10, 1859	7			...do.	
	1	Dec. 5, 1859	June 25, 1860	202			Benjamin Fitzpatrick, of Alabama; Jesse D. Bright, of Indiana.	William Pennington, of New Jersey.
	S	June 26, 1860	June 28, 1860	3			Benjamin Fitzpatrick, of Alabama.	
	2	Dec. 3, 1860	Mar. 3, 1861	93			Solomon Foot, of Vermont.	
37th	S	Mar. 4, 1861	Mar. 28, 1861	25			...do.	
	1–E	July 4, 1861	Aug. 6, 1861	34			...do	Galusha A. Grow, of Pennsylvania.
	2	Dec. 2, 1861	July 17, 1862	228			...do.	
	3	Dec. 1, 1862	Mar. 3, 1863	93	Dec. 23, 1862–Jan. 5, 1863	Dec. 24, 1862–Jan. 4, 1863	...do.	
38th	S	Mar. 4, 1863	Mar. 14, 1863	11			...do.	
	1	Dec. 7, 1863	July 4, 1864	209	Dec. 23, 1863–Jan. 5, 1864	Dec. 24, 1863–Jan. 4, 1864	Solomon Foot, of Vermont; Daniel Clark, of New Hampshire.	Schuyler Colfax, of Indiana.
	2	Dec. 5, 1864	Mar. 4, 1865	89	Dec. 22, 1864–Jan. 5, 1865	Dec. 22, 1864–Jan. 4, 1865	Daniel Clark, of New Hampshire.	
39th	S	Mar. 4, 1865	Mar. 11, 1865	8			Lafayette S. Foster, of Connecticut.	
	1	Dec. 4, 1865	July 28, 1866	237	Dec. 6–Dec. 11, 1865	Dec. 7–Dec. 10, 1865	...do	Do.
					Dec. 21, 1865–Jan. 5, 1866	Dec. 23, 1865–Jan. 4, 1866		
	2	Dec. 3, 1866	Mar. 3, 1867	91	Dec. 20, 1866–Jan. 3, 1867	Dec. 20, 1866–Jan. 3, 1867	Benjamin F. Wade, of Ohio.	
40th	1–E	Mar. 4, 1867	Dec. 1, 1867	273	Mar. 30–July 3, 1867	Mar. 31–July 2, 1867	...do	Do.[7]
					July 20–Nov. 21, 1867	July 21–Nov. 20, 1867		
	S	Apr. 1, 1867	Apr. 20, 1867	20				
	2	Dec. 2, 1867	Nov. 10, 1868	345	Dec. 20, 1867–Jan. 6, 1868	Dec. 21, 1867–Jan. 5, 1868		
					July 27–Sept. 21, 1868	July 26–Sept. 20, 1868		
					Sept. 21–Oct. 16, 1868	Sept. 22–Oct. 15, 1868		
					Oct. 16–Nov. 10, 1868	Oct. 17–Nov. 9, 1868		
	3	Dec. 7, 1868	Mar. 3, 1869	87	Dec. 21, 1868–Jan. 5, 1869	Dec. 22, 1868–Jan. 4, 1869	...do	Theodore M. Pomeroy, of New York.[7]
41st	1	Mar. 4, 1869	Apr. 10, 1869	38			Henry B. Anthony, of Rhode Island	James G. Blaine, of Maine.
	S	Apr. 12, 1869	Apr. 22, 1869	11				
	2	Dec. 6, 1869	July 15, 1870	222	Dec. 22, 1869–Jan. 10, 1870	Dec. 23, 1869–Jan. 9, 1870	...do.	
	3	Dec. 5, 1870	Mar. 3, 1871	89	Dec. 23, 1870–Jan. 4, 1871	Dec. 23, 1870–Jan. 3, 1871	...do.	
42d	1–E	Mar. 4, 1871	Apr. 20, 1871	48			...do	Do.
	S	May 10, 1871	May 27, 1871	18			...do.	
	2	Dec. 4, 1871	June 8, 1872	190	Dec. 21, 1871–Jan. 8, 1872	Dec. 22, 1871–Jan. 7, 1872	...do.	
	3	Dec. 2, 1872	Mar. 3, 1873	92	Dec. 20, 1872–Jan. 6, 1873	Dec. 21, 1872–Jan. 5, 1873	...do.	
43d	S	Mar. 4, 1873	Mar. 26, 1873	23			Matthew H. Carpenter, of Wisconsin.	
	1	Dec. 1, 1873	June 23, 1874	204	Dec. 19, 1873–Jan. 5, 1874	Dec. 20, 1873–Jan. 4, 1874	...do	Do.
	2	Dec. 7, 1874	Mar. 3, 1875	87	Dec. 23, 1874–Jan. 5, 1875	Dec. 24, 1874–Jan. 4, 1875	Matthew H. Carpenter, of Wisconsin; Henry B. Anthony, of Rhode Island.	
44th	S	Mar. 5, 1875	Mar. 24, 1875	20			Thomas W. Ferry, of Michigan.	
	1	Dec. 6, 1875	Aug. 15, 1876	254	Dec. 20, 1875–Jan. 5, 1876	Dec. 21, 1875–Jan. 4, 1876	...do	Michael C. Kerr, of Indiana.[8]
	2	Dec. 4, 1876	Mar. 3, 1877	90			...do	Samuel J. Randall, of Pennsylvania.[8]
45th	S	Mar. 5, 1877	Mar. 17, 1877	13			...do.	
	1–E	Oct. 15, 1877	Dec. 3, 1877	50			...do	Do.
	2	Dec. 3, 1877	June 20, 1878	200	Dec. 15, 1877–Jan. 10, 1878	Dec. 16, 1877–Jan. 10, 1878	...do.	
	3	Dec. 2, 1878	Mar. 3, 1879	92	Dec. 20, 1878–Jan. 7, 1879	Dec. 21, 1878–Jan. 6, 1879	...do.	
46th	1–E	Mar. 18, 1879	July 1, 1879	106			Allen G. Thurman, of Ohio	Do.
	2	Dec. 1, 1879	June 16, 1880	199	Dec. 19, 1879–Jan. 6, 1880	Dec. 20, 1879–Jan. 5, 1880	...do.	
	3	Dec. 6, 1880	Mar. 3, 1881	88	Dec. 23, 1880–Jan. 5, 1881	Dec. 23, 1880–Jan. 4, 1881	...do.	
47th	S	Mar. 4, 1881	May. 20, 1881	78				
	S	Oct. 10, 1881	Oct. 29, 1881	20			Thomas F. Bayard, of Delaware; David Davis, of Illinois.	
	1	Dec. 5, 1881	Aug. 8, 1882	247	Dec. 22, 1881–Jan. 5, 1882	Dec. 22, 1881–Jan. 4, 1882	David Davis, of Illinois	J. Warren Keifer, of Ohio.

SESSIONS OF CONGRESS, 1st–116th CONGRESSES, 1789–2020—CONTINUED

[Closing date for this table was July 22, 2020.]

MEETING DATES OF CONGRESS: Pursuant to a resolution of the Confederation Congress in 1788, the Constitution went into effect on March 4, 1789. From then until the 20th amendment took effect in January 1934, the term of each Congress began on March 4th of each odd-numbered year; however, Article I, section 4, of the Constitution provided that ''The Congress shall assemble at least once in every Year, and such Meeting shall be on the first Monday in December, unless they shall by law appoint a different day.'' The Congress therefore convened regularly on the first Monday in December until the 20th amendment became effective, which changed the beginning of Congress's term as well as its convening date to January 3rd. So prior to 1934, a new Congress typically would not convene for regular business until 13 months after being elected. One effect of this was that the last session of each Congress was a ''lame duck'' session. After the 20th amendment, the time from the election to the beginning of Congress's term as well as when it convened was reduced to two months. Recognizing that the need might exist for Congress to meet at times other than the regularly scheduled convening date, Article II, section 3 of the Constitution provides that the President ''may, on extraordinary occasions, convene both Houses, or either of them''; hence these sessions occur only if convened by Presidential proclamation. Except as noted, these are separately numbered sessions of a Congress, and are marked by an E in the session column of the table. Until the 20th amendment was adopted, there were also times when special sessions of the Senate were convened, principally for confirming Cabinet and other executive nominations, and occasionally for the ratification of treaties or other executive business. These Senate sessions were also called by Presidential proclamation (typically by the outgoing President, although on occasion by incumbents as well) and are marked by an S in the session column. MEETING PLACES OF CONGRESS: Congress met for the first and second sessions of the First Congress (1789 and 1790) in New York City. From the third session of the First Congress through the first session of the Sixth Congress (1790 to 1800), Philadelphia was the meeting place. Congress has convened in Washington since the second session of the Sixth Congress (1800).

Congress	Session	Convening Date	Adjournment Date	Length in days [1]	Recesses [2]		President pro tempore of the Senate [3]	Speaker of the House of Representatives
					Senate	House of Representatives		
	2	Dec. 4, 1882	Mar. 3, 1883	90			George F. Edmunds, of Vermont.	J. Warren Keifer, of Ohio.
48th	1	Dec. 3, 1883	July 7, 1884	218	Dec. 24, 1883–Jan. 7, 1884	Dec. 25, 1883–Jan. 6, 1884	...do	John G. Carlisle, of Kentucky.
	2	Dec. 1, 1884	Mar. 3, 1885	93	Dec. 24, 1884–Jan. 5, 1885	Dec. 25, 1884–Jan. 4, 1885	...do.	
49th	S	Mar. 4, 1885	Apr. 2, 1885	30				
	1	Dec. 7, 1885	Aug. 5, 1886	242	Dec. 21, 1885–Jan. 5, 1886	Dec. 22, 1885–Jan. 4, 1886	John Sherman, of Ohio	Do.
	2	Dec. 6, 1886	Mar. 3, 1887	88	Dec. 22, 1886–Jan. 4, 1887	Dec. 23, 1886–Jan. 3, 1887	John J. Ingalls, of Kansas.	
50th	1	Dec. 5, 1887	Oct. 20, 1888	321	Dec. 22, 1887–Jan. 4, 1888	Dec. 23, 1887–Jan. 3, 1888	...do	Do.
	2	Dec. 3, 1888	Mar. 3, 1889	91	Dec. 21, 1888–Jan. 2, 1889	Dec. 22, 1888–Jan. 1, 1889	...do.	
51st	S	Mar. 4, 1889	Apr. 2, 1889	30			...do.	
	1	Dec. 2, 1889	Oct. 1, 1890	304	Dec. 21, 1889–Jan. 6, 1890	Dec. 22, 1889–Jan. 5, 1890	...do	Thomas B. Reed, of Maine.
	2	Dec. 1, 1890	Mar. 3, 1891	93			Charles F. Manderson, of Nebraska.	
52d	1	Dec. 7, 1891	Aug. 5, 1892	251			...do	Charles F. Crisp, of Georgia.
	2	Dec. 5, 1892	Mar. 3, 1893	89	Dec. 22, 1892–Jan. 4, 1893	Dec. 23, 1892–Jan. 3, 1893	...do.	
53d	S	Mar. 4, 1893	Apr. 15, 1893	43			Charles F. Manderson, of Nebraska; Isham G. Harris, of Tennessee.	
	1–E	Aug. 7, 1893	Nov. 3, 1893	89			Isham G. Harris, of Tennessee	Do.
	2	Dec. 4, 1893	Aug. 28, 1894	268		Dec. 22, 1893–Jan. 2, 1894	...do.	
	3	Dec. 3, 1894	Mar. 4, 1895	97		Dec. 23, 1894–Jan. 2, 1895	Matt W. Ransom, of North Carolina; Isham G. Harris, of Tennessee.	
54th	1	Dec. 2, 1895	June 11, 1896	193			William P. Frye, of Maine	Thomas B. Reed, of Maine.
	2	Dec. 7, 1896	Mar. 3, 1897	87	Dec. 22, 1896–Jan. 5, 1897	Dec. 23, 1896–Jan. 4, 1897	...do.	
55th	S	Mar. 4, 1897	Mar. 10, 1897	11			...do.	
	1–E	Mar. 15, 1897	July 24, 1897	131			...do	Do.
	2	Dec. 6, 1897	July 8, 1898	215	Dec. 18, 1897–Jan. 5, 1898	Dec. 19, 1897–Jan. 4, 1898	...do.	
	3	Dec. 5, 1898	Mar. 4, 1899	89	Dec. 21, 1898–Jan. 4, 1899	Dec. 20, 1898–Jan. 3, 1899	...do.	
56th	1	Dec. 4, 1899	June 7, 1900	186	Dec. 20, 1899–Jan. 3, 1900	Dec. 21, 1899–Jan. 2, 1900	...do	David B. Henderson, of Iowa.
	2	Dec. 3, 1900	Mar. 3, 1901	91	Dec. 20, 1900–Jan. 3, 1901	Dec. 22, 1900–Jan. 2, 1901	...do.	
57th	S	Mar. 4, 1901	Mar. 9, 1901	6			...do.	

	1	Dec. 2, 1901	July 1, 1902	212	Dec. 19, 1901–Jan. 6, 1902	Dec. 20, 1901–Jan. 5, 1902	...do	Do.
	2	Dec. 1, 1902	Mar. 3, 1903	93	Dec. 20, 1902–Jan. 5, 1903	Dec. 21, 1902–Jan. 4, 1903	...do.	
58th	S	Mar. 5, 1903	Mar. 19, 1903	15			...do.	
	1–E	Nov. 9, 1903	Dec. 7, 1903	29			...do	Joseph G. Cannon, of Illinois.
	2	Dec. 7, 1903	Apr. 28, 1904	144	Dec. 19, 1903–Jan. 4, 1904	Dec. 19, 1903–Jan. 4, 1904	...do.	
	3	Dec. 5, 1904	Mar. 3, 1905	89	Dec. 21, 1904–Jan. 4, 1905	Dec. 22, 1904–Jan. 3, 1905	...do.	
59th	S	Mar. 4, 1905	Mar. 18, 1905	15			...do.	
	1	Dec. 4, 1905	June 30, 1906	209	Dec. 21, 1905–Jan. 4, 1906	Dec. 22, 1905–Jan. 3, 1906	...do	Do.
	2	Dec. 3, 1906	Mar. 3, 1907	91	Dec. 20, 1906–Jan. 3, 1907	Dec. 21, 1906–Jan. 2, 1907	...do.	
60th	1	Dec. 2, 1907	May 30, 1908	181	Dec. 21, 1907–Jan. 6, 1908	Dec. 22, 1907–Jan. 5, 1908	...do	Do.
	2	Dec. 7, 1908	Mar. 3, 1909	87	Dec. 19, 1908–Jan. 4, 1909	Dec. 20, 1908–Jan. 3, 1909	...do.	
61st	S	Mar. 4, 1909	Mar. 6, 1909	3			...do.	
	1–E	Mar. 15, 1909	Aug. 5, 1909	144			...do	Do.
	2	Dec. 6, 1909	June 23, 1910	202	Dec. 21, 1909–Jan. 4, 1910	Dec. 22, 1909–Jan. 3, 1910	...do.	
	3	Dec. 5, 1910	Mar. 3, 1911	89	Dec. 21, 1910–Jan. 5, 1911	Dec. 22, 1910–Jan. 4, 1911	...do.	
62d	1–E	Apr. 4, 1911	Aug. 22, 1911	141			...do.[9]	Champ Clark, of Missouri.
	2	Dec. 4, 1911	Aug. 26, 1912	267	Dec. 21, 1911–Jan. 3, 1912	Dec. 22, 1911–Jan. 2, 1912	Charles Curtis, of Kansas; Augustus O. Bacon, of Georgia; Jacob H. Gallinger, of New Hampshire; Henry Cabot Lodge, of Massachusetts; Frank B. Brandegee, of Connecticut.	
	3	Dec. 2, 1912	Mar. 3, 1913	92	Dec. 19, 1912–Jan. 2, 1913	Dec. 20, 1912–Jan. 1, 1913	Augustus O. Bacon, of Georgia; Jacob H. Gallinger, of New Hampshire.	
63d	S	Mar. 4, 1913	Mar. 17, 1913	14			James P. Clarke, of Arkansas.	
	1–E	Apr. 7, 1913	Nov. 29, 1913	239			...do	Do.
	2	Dec. 1, 1913	Oct. 24, 1914	328	Dec. 23, 1913–Jan. 12, 1914	Dec. 24, 1913–Jan. 11, 1914	...do.	
	3	Dec. 7, 1914	Mar. 3, 1915	87	Dec. 23–Dec. 28, 1914	Dec. 24–Dec. 28, 1914	...do.	
64th	1	Dec. 6, 1915	Sept. 8, 1916	278	Dec. 17, 1915–Jan. 4, 1916	Dec. 18, 1915–Jan. 3, 1916	...do[10]	Do.
	2	Dec. 4, 1916	Mar. 3, 1917	90	Dec. 22, 1916–Jan. 2, 1917	Dec. 23, 1916–Jan. 1, 1917	Willard Saulsbury, of Delaware[10]	
65th	S	Mar. 5, 1917	Mar. 16, 1917	12			...do.	
	1–E	Apr. 2, 1917	Oct. 6, 1917	188			...do	Do.
	2	Dec. 3, 1917	Nov. 21, 1918	354	Dec. 18, 1917–Jan. 3, 1918	Dec. 19, 1917–Jan. 2, 1918	...do.	
	3	Dec. 2, 1918	Mar. 3, 1919	92			...do.	
66th	1–E	May 19, 1919	Nov. 19, 1919	185	July 1–July 8, 1919	July 2–July 7, 1919	Albert B. Cummins, of Iowa	Frederick H. Gillett, of Massachusetts.
	2	Dec. 1, 1919	June 5, 1920	188	Dec. 20, 1919–Jan. 5, 1920	Dec. 21, 1919–Jan. 4, 1920	...do.	
	3	Dec. 6, 1920	Mar. 3, 1921	88			...do.	
67th	S	Mar. 4, 1921	Mar. 15, 1921	12			...do.	
	1–E	Apr. 11, 1921	Nov. 23, 1921	227	Aug. 24–Sept. 21, 1921	Aug. 25–Sept. 20, 1921	...do	Do.
	2	Dec. 5, 1921	Sept. 22, 1922	292	Dec. 22, 1921–Jan. 3, 1922	Dec. 23, 1921–Jan. 2, 1922 July 1–Aug. 14, 1922	...do.	
	3–E	Nov. 20, 1922	Dec. 4, 1922	15			...do.	
	4	Dec. 4, 1922	Mar. 3, 1923	90			...do.	
68th	1	Dec. 3, 1923	June 7, 1924	188	Dec. 20, 1923–Jan. 3, 1924	Dec. 21, 1923–Jan. 2, 1924	...do	Do.
	2	Dec. 1, 1924	Mar. 3, 1925	93	Dec. 20–Dec. 29, 1924	Dec. 21–Dec. 28, 1924	...do.	
69th	S	Mar. 4, 1925	Mar. 18, 1925	15			Albert B. Cummins, of Iowa; George H. Moses, of New Hampshire.	
	1	Dec. 7, 1925	July 3, 1926	209	Dec. 22, 1925–Jan. 4, 1926	Dec. 23, 1925–Jan. 3, 1926	...do	Nicholas Longworth, of Ohio.
	2	Dec. 6, 1926	Mar. 4, 1927	88	Dec. 22, 1926–Jan. 3, 1927	Dec. 23, 1926–Jan. 2, 1927	...do.	
70th	1	Dec. 5, 1927	May 29, 1928	177	Dec. 21, 1927–Jan. 4, 1928	Dec. 22, 1927–Jan. 3, 1928	...do	Do.
	2	Dec. 3, 1928	Mar. 3, 1929	91	Dec. 22, 1928–Jan. 3, 1929	Dec. 23, 1928–Jan. 2, 1929	...do.	
71st	S	Mar. 4, 1929	Mar. 5, 1929	2			...do.	
	1–E	Apr. 15, 1929	Nov. 22, 1929	222	June 19–Aug. 19, 1929	June 20–Sept. 22, 1929	...do	Do.
	2	Dec. 2, 1929	July 3, 1930	214	Dec. 21, 1929–Jan. 6, 1930	Dec. 22, 1929–Jan. 5, 1930	...do.	

SESSIONS OF CONGRESS, 1st–116th CONGRESSES, 1789–2020—CONTINUED

[Closing date for this table was July 22, 2020.]

MEETING DATES OF CONGRESS: Pursuant to a resolution of the Confederation Congress in 1788, the Constitution went into effect on March 4, 1789. From then until the 20th amendment took effect in January 1934, the term of each Congress began on March 4th of each odd-numbered year; however, Article I, section 4, of the Constitution provided that "The Congress shall assemble at least once in every Year, and such Meeting shall be on the first Monday in December, unless they shall by law appoint a different day." The Congress therefore convened regularly on the first Monday in December until the 20th amendment became effective, which changed the beginning of Congress's term as well as its convening date to January 3rd. So prior to 1934, a new Congress typically would not convene for regular business until 13 months after being elected. One effect of this was that the last session of each Congress was a "lame duck" session. After the 20th amendment, the time from the election to the beginning of Congress's term as well as when it convened was reduced to two months. Recognizing that the need might exist for Congress to meet at times other than the regularly scheduled convening date, Article II, section 3 of the Constitution provides that the President "may, on extraordinary occasions, convene both Houses, or either of them"; hence these sessions occur only if convened by Presidential proclamation. Except as noted, these are separately numbered sessions of a Congress, and are marked by an E in the session column of the table. Until the 20th amendment was adopted, there were also times when special sessions of the Senate were convened, principally for confirming Cabinet and other executive nominations, and occasionally for the ratification of treaties or other executive business. These Senate sessions were also called by Presidential proclamation (typically by the outgoing President, although on occasion by incumbents as well) and are marked by an S in the session column. MEETING PLACES OF CONGRESS: Congress met for the first and second sessions of the First Congress (1789 and 1790) in New York City. From the third session of the First Congress through the first session of the Sixth Congress (1790 to 1800), Philadelphia was the meeting place. Congress has convened in Washington since the second session of the Sixth Congress (1800).

Congress	Session	Convening Date	Adjournment Date	Length in days[1]	Recesses[2]		President pro tempore of the Senate[3]	Speaker of the House of Representatives
					Senate	House of Representatives		
	S	July 7, 1930	July 21, 1930	15			do.	
	3	Dec. 1, 1930	Mar. 4, 1931	93	Dec. 20, 1930–Jan. 5, 1931	Dec. 21, 1930–Jan. 4, 1931	George H. Moses, of New Hampshire	Nicholas Longworth, of Ohio.
72d	1	Dec. 7, 1931	July 16, 1932	223	Dec. 22, 1931–Jan. 4, 1932	Dec. 23, 1931–Jan. 3, 1932	do	John N. Garner, of Texas.
	2	Dec. 5, 1932	Mar. 4, 1933	89			do.	
73d	S	Mar. 4, 1933	Mar. 6, 1933	3			do.	
	1–E	Mar. 9, 1933	June 16, 1933	99			Key Pittman, of Nevada	Henry T. Rainey, of Illinois.
	2	Jan. 3, 1934	June 18, 1934	167			do.	
74th	1	Jan. 3, 1935	Aug. 26, 1935	236			do	Joseph W. Byrns, of Tennessee.[11]
	2	Jan. 3, 1936	June 20, 1936	170	June 8–June 15, 1936	June 9–June 14, 1936	do	William B. Bankhead, of Alabama.[11]
75th	1	Jan. 5, 1937	Aug. 21, 1937	229			do	Do.
	2–E	Nov. 15, 1937	Dec. 21, 1937	37			do.	
	3	Jan. 3, 1938	June 16, 1938	165			do.	
76th	1	Jan. 3, 1939	Aug. 5, 1939	215			do	Do.[12]
	2–E	Sept. 21, 1939	Nov. 3, 1939	44			do.	
	3	Jan. 3, 1940	Jan. 2, 1941	366	July 11–July 22, 1940	June 23–June 30, 1940 July 12–July 21, 1940	Key Pittman, of Nevada;[13] William H. King, of Utah.[13]	Sam Rayburn, of Texas.[12]
77th	1	Jan. 3, 1941	Jan. 2, 1942	365			Pat Harrison, of Mississippi;[14] Carter Glass, of Virginia.[14]	Do.
	2	Jan. 5, 1942	Dec. 16, 1942	346			Carter Glass, of Virginia.	
78th	1	Jan. 6, 1943	Dec. 21, 1943	350	July 8–Sept. 14, 1943	Apr. 23–May 2, 1943 July 8–Sept. 13, 1943	do	Do.
	2	Jan. 10, 1944	Dec. 19, 1944	345	Apr. 1–Apr. 12, 1944 June 23–Aug. 1, 1944 Sept. 21–Nov. 14, 1944	Apr. 2–Apr. 11, 1944 June 24–June 31, 1944 Sept. 22–Nov. 13, 1944	do.	
79th	1	Jan. 3, 1945	Dec. 21, 1945	353	Aug. 1–Sept. 5, 1945	July 22–Sept. 4, 1945	Kenneth McKellar, of Tennessee	Do.
	2	Jan. 14, 1946	Aug. 2, 1946	201		Apr. 19–Apr. 29, 1946	do.	
80th	[15] 1	Jan. 3, 1947	Dec. 19, 1947	351	July 27–Nov. 17, 1947	July 28–Nov. 16, 1947	Arthur H. Vandenberg, of Michigan	Joseph W. Martin, Jr., of Massachusetts.

	[15]2	Jan. 6, 1948	Dec. 31, 1948	361	June 20–July 26, 1948 Aug. 7–Dec. 31, 1948	June 21–July 25, 1948 Aug. 8–Dec. 30, 1948	...do.	
81st	1	Jan. 3, 1949	Oct. 19, 1949	290	Apr. 15–May 2, 1949		Kenneth McKellar, of Tennessee	Sam Rayburn, of Texas.
	2	Jan. 3, 1950	Jan. 2, 1951	365		Apr. 6–Apr. 18, 1950 Sept. 23–Nov. 27, 1950	...do.	
82d	1	Jan. 3, 1951	Oct. 20, 1951	291		Mar. 23–Apr. 1, 1951 Aug. 24–Sept. 11, 1951	...do	Do.
	2	Jan. 8, 1952	July 7, 1952	182		Apr. 11–Apr. 21, 1952	...do.	
83d	1	Jan. 3, 1953	Aug. 3, 1953	213		Apr. 3–Apr. 12, 1953	Styles Bridges, of New Hampshire	Joseph W. Martin, Jr., of Massachusetts.
	2	Jan. 6, 1954	Dec. 2, 1954	331	Aug. 20–Nov. 8, 1954 Nov. 18–Nov. 29, 1954	Apr. 16–Apr. 25, 1954 Adjourned sine die Aug. 20, 1954	...do.	
84th	1	Jan. 5, 1955	Aug. 2, 1955	210	Apr. 4–Apr. 13, 1955	Apr. 5–Apr. 12, 1955	Walter F. George, of Georgia	Sam Rayburn, of Texas.
	2	Jan. 3, 1956	July 27, 1956	207	Mar. 29–Apr. 9, 1956	Mar. 30–Apr. 8, 1956	...do.	
85th	1	Jan. 3, 1957	Aug. 30, 1957	239	Apr. 18–Apr. 29, 1957	Apr. 19–Apr. 28, 1957	Carl Hayden, of Arizona	Do.
	2	Jan. 7, 1958	Aug. 24, 1958	230	Apr. 3–Apr. 14, 1958	Apr. 4–Apr. 13, 1958	...do.	
86th	1	Jan. 7, 1959	Sept. 15, 1959	252	Mar. 26–Apr. 7, 1959	Mar. 27–Apr. 6, 1959	...do	Do.
	2	Jan. 6, 1960	Sept. 1, 1960	240	Apr. 14–Apr. 18, 1960 May 27–May 31, 1960 July 3–Aug. 8, 1960	July 4–Aug. 14, 1960	...do.	
87th	1	Jan. 3, 1961	Sept. 27, 1961	268		Mar. 31–Apr. 9, 1961	...do	Do.[16]
	2	Jan. 10, 1962	Oct. 13, 1962	277		Apr. 20–Apr. 29, 1962	...do	John W. McCormack, of Massachusetts.[16]
88th	1	Jan. 9, 1963	Dec. 30, 1963	356		Apr. 11–Apr. 21, 1963	...do	Do.
	2	Jan. 7, 1964	Oct. 3, 1964	270	July 10–July 20, 1964 Aug. 21–Aug. 31, 1964	Mar. 27–Apr. 5, 1964 July 3–July 19, 1964 Aug. 22–Aug. 30, 1964	...do.	
89th	1	Jan. 4, 1965	Oct. 23, 1965	293			...do	Do.
	2	Jan. 10, 1966	Oct. 22, 1966	286	Apr. 7–Apr. 13, 1966 June 30–July 11, 1966	Apr. 8–Apr. 17, 1966 June 1–June 10, 1966	...do.	
90th	1	Jan. 10, 1967	Dec. 15, 1967	340	Mar. 23–Apr. 3, 1967 June 29–July 10, 1967 Aug. 31–Sept. 11, 1967 Nov. 22–Nov. 27, 1967	Mar. 24–Apr. 2, 1967 June 30–July 9, 1967 Sept. 1–Sept. 10, 1967 Nov. 23–Nov. 26, 1967	...do	Do.
	2	Jan. 15, 1968	Oct. 14, 1968	274	Apr. 11–Apr. 17, 1968 May 29–June 3, 1968 July 3–July 8, 1968 Aug. 2–Sept. 4, 1968	Apr. 12–Apr. 21, 1968 May 30–June 2, 1968 July 4–July 7, 1968 Aug. 3–Sept. 3, 1968	...do.	
91st	1	Jan. 3, 1969	Dec. 23, 1969	355	Feb. 7–Feb. 17, 1969 Apr. 3–Apr. 14, 1969 July 2–July 7, 1969 Aug. 13–Sept. 3, 1969 Nov. 26–Dec. 1, 1969	Feb. 8–Feb. 16, 1969 Apr. 4–Apr. 13, 1969 May 29–June 1, 1969 July 3–July 6, 1969 Aug. 14–Sept. 2, 1969 Nov. 7–Nov. 11, 1969 Nov. 27–Nov. 30, 1969	Richard B. Russell, of Georgia	Do.

SESSIONS OF CONGRESS, 1st–116th CONGRESSES, 1789–2020—CONTINUED

[Closing date for this table was July 22, 2020.]

MEETING DATES OF CONGRESS: Pursuant to a resolution of the Confederation Congress in 1788, the Constitution went into effect on March 4, 1789. From then until the 20th amendment took effect in January 1934, the term of each Congress began on March 4th of each odd-numbered year; however, Article I, section 4, of the Constitution provided that ''The Congress shall assemble at least once in every Year, and such Meeting shall be on the first Monday in December, unless they shall by law appoint a different day.'' The Congress therefore convened regularly on the first Monday in December until the 20th amendment became effective, which changed the beginning of Congress's term as well as its convening date to January 3rd. So prior to 1934, a new Congress typically would not convene for regular business until 13 months after being elected. One effect of this was that the last session of each Congress was a ''lame duck'' session. After the 20th amendment, the time from the election to the beginning of Congress's term as well as when it convened was reduced to two months. Recognizing that the need might exist for Congress to meet at times other than the regularly scheduled convening date, Article II, section 3 of the Constitution provides that the President ''may, on extraordinary occasions, convene both Houses, or either of them''; hence these sessions occur only if convened by Presidential proclamation. Except as noted, these are separately numbered sessions of a Congress, and are marked by an E in the session column of the table. Until the 20th amendment was adopted, there were also times when special sessions of the Senate were convened, principally for confirming Cabinet and other executive nominations, and occasionally for the ratification of treaties or other executive business. These Senate sessions were also called by Presidential proclamation (typically by the outgoing President, although on occasion by incumbents as well) and are marked by an S in the session column. MEETING PLACES OF CONGRESS: Congress met for the first and second sessions of the First Congress (1789 and 1790) in New York City. From the third session of the First Congress through the first session of the Sixth Congress (1790 to 1800), Philadelphia was the meeting place. Congress has convened in Washington since the second session of the Sixth Congress (1800).

Congress	Session	Convening Date	Adjournment Date	Length in days [1]	Recesses [2]		President pro tempore of the Senate [3]	Speaker of the House of Representatives
					Senate	House of Representatives		
	2	Jan. 19, 1970	Jan. 2, 1971	349	Feb. 10–Feb. 16, 1970 .... Mar. 26–Mar. 31, 1970 Sept. 2–Sept. 8, 1970 Oct. 14–Nov. 16, 1970 Nov. 25–Nov. 30, 1970 Dec. 22–Dec. 28, 1970	Feb. 11–Feb. 15, 1970 .... Mar. 27–Mar. 30, 1970 May 28–May 31, 1970 July 2–July 5, 1970 Aug. 15–Sept. 8, 1970 Oct. 15–Nov. 15, 1970 Nov. 26–Nov. 29, 1970 Dec. 23–Dec. 28, 1970	...do.	
92d ...	1	Jan. 21, 1971	Dec. 17, 1971 ...	331	Feb. 11–Feb. 17, 1971 .... Apr. 7–Apr. 14, 1971 May 26–June 1, 1971 June 30–July 6, 1971 Aug. 6–Sept. 8, 1971 Oct. 21–Oct. 26, 1971 Nov. 24–Nov. 29, 1971	Feb. 11–Feb. 16, 1971 .... Apr. 8–Apr. 18, 1971 May 28–May 31, 1971 July 2–July 5, 1971 Aug. 7–Sept. 7, 1971 Oct. 8–Oct. 11, 1971 Oct. 22–Oct. 25, 1971 Nov. 20–Nov. 28, 1971	Richard B. Russell, of Georgia;[17] Allen J. Ellender, of Louisiana.[17]	Carl B. Albert, of Oklahoma.
	2	Jan. 18, 1972	Oct. 18, 1972 ...	275	Feb. 9–Feb. 14, 1972 .... Mar. 30–Apr. 4, 1972 May 25–May 30, 1972 June 30–July 17, 1972 Aug. 18–Sept. 5, 1972	Feb. 10–Feb. 15, 1972 .... Mar. 30–Apr. 9, 1972 May 25–May 29, 1972 June 1–July 16, 1972 Aug. 19–Sept. 4, 1972	Allen J. Ellender, of Louisiana;[18] James O. Eastland, of Mississippi.[18]	

93d ...	1	Jan. 3, 1973	Dec. 22, 1973 ...	354	Feb. 8–Feb. 15, 1973 .... Apr. 18–Apr. 30, 1973 May 23–May 29, 1973 June 30–July 9, 1973 Aug. 3–Sept. 5, 1973 Oct. 18–Oct. 23, 1973 Nov. 21–Nov. 26, 1973	Feb. 9–Feb. 18, 1973 .... Apr. 20–Apr. 29, 1973 May 25–May 28, 1973 July 1–July 9, 1973 Aug. 4–Sept. 4, 1973 Oct. 5–Oct. 8, 1973 Oct. 19–Oct. 22, 1973 Nov. 16–Nov. 25, 1973	James O. Eastland, of Mississippi	Do.
	2	Jan. 21, 1974	Dec. 20, 1974 ...	334	Feb. 8–Feb. 18, 1974 .... Mar. 13–Mar. 19, 1974 Apr. 11–Apr. 22, 1974 May 23–May 28, 1974 Aug. 22–Sept. 4, 1974 Oct. 17–Nov. 18, 1974 Nov. 26–Dec. 2, 1974	Feb. 8–Feb. 12, 1974 .... Apr. 12–Apr. 21, 1974 May 24–May 27, 1974 July 4–July 8, 1974 Aug. 23–Sept. 10, 1974 Oct. 18–Nov. 17, 1974 Nov. 27–Dec. 2, 1974	...do.	
94th ..	1	Jan. 14, 1975	Dec. 19, 1975 ...	340	Mar. 26–Apr. 7, 1975 .... May 22–June 2, 1975 June 27–July 7, 1975 Aug. 1–Sept. 3, 1975 Oct. 9–Oct. 20, 1975 Oct. 23–Oct. 28, 1975 Nov. 20–Dec. 1, 1975	Mar. 27–Apr. 6, 1975 .... May 23–June 1, 1975 June 27–July 7, 1975 Aug. 2–Sept. 2, 1975 Oct. 10–Oct. 19, 1975 Oct. 24–Oct. 27, 1975 Nov. 21–Nov. 30, 1975	...do	Do.
	2	Jan. 19, 1976	Oct. 1, 1976	257	Feb. 6–Feb. 16, 1976 .... Apr. 14–Apr. 26, 1976 May 28–June 2, 1976 July 2–July 19, 1976 Aug. 10–Aug. 23, 1976 Sept. 1–Sept. 7, 1976	Feb. 12–Feb. 15, 1976 .... Apr. 15–Apr. 25, 1976 May 28–May 31, 1976 July 3–July 18, 1976 Aug. 11–Aug. 22, 1976 Sept. 3–Sept. 7, 1976	...do.	
95th ..	1	Jan. 4, 1977	Dec. 15, 1977 ...	346	Feb. 11–Feb. 21, 1977 .... Apr. 7–Apr. 18, 1977 May 27–June 6, 1977 July 1–July 11, 1977 Aug. 6–Sept. 7, 1977	Feb. 10–Feb. 15, 1977 .... Apr. 7–Apr. 17, 1977 May 27–May 31, 1977 July 1–July 10, 1977 Aug. 6–Sept. 6, 1977 Oct. 7–Oct. 10, 1977	...do	Thomas P. O'Neill, Jr., of Massachusetts.
	2	Jan. 19, 1978	Oct. 15, 1978 ...	270	Feb. 10–Feb. 20, 1978 .... Mar. 23–Apr. 3, 1978 May 26–June 5, 1978 June 29–July 10, 1978 Aug. 25–Sept. 6, 1978	Feb. 10–Feb. 13, 1978 .... Mar. 23–Apr. 2, 1978 May 26–May 30, 1978 June 30–July 9, 1978 Aug. 18–Sept. 5, 1978	...do.	
96th ..	1	Jan. 15, 1979	Jan. 3, 1980	354	Feb. 9–Feb. 19, 1979 .... Apr. 10–Apr. 23, 1979 May 24–June 4, 1979 June 27–July 9, 1979 Aug. 3–Sept. 5, 1979 Nov. 20–Nov. 26, 1979 Adjourned sine die, Dec. 20, 1979	Feb. 9–Feb. 12, 1979 .... Apr. 11–Apr. 22, 1979 May 25–May 29, 1979 June 30–July 8, 1979 Aug. 3–Sept. 4, 1979 Nov. 21–Nov. 25, 1979	Warren G. Magnuson, of Washington ...	Do.

SESSIONS OF CONGRESS, 1st–116th CONGRESSES, 1789–2020—CONTINUED

[Closing date for this table was July 22, 2020.]

MEETING DATES OF CONGRESS: Pursuant to a resolution of the Confederation Congress in 1788, the Constitution went into effect on March 4, 1789. From then until the 20th amendment took effect in January 1934, the term of each Congress began on March 4th of each odd-numbered year; however, Article I, section 4, of the Constitution provided that "The Congress shall assemble at least once in every Year, and such Meeting shall be on the first Monday in December, unless they shall by law appoint a different day." The Congress therefore convened regularly on the first Monday in December until the 20th amendment became effective, which changed the beginning of Congress's term as well as its convening date to January 3rd. So prior to 1934, a new Congress typically would not convene for regular business until 13 months after being elected. One effect of this was that the last session of each Congress was a "lame duck" session. After the 20th amendment, the time from the election to the beginning of Congress's term as well as when it convened was reduced to two months. Recognizing that the need might exist for Congress to meet at times other than the regularly scheduled convening date, Article II, section 3 of the Constitution provides that the President "may, on extraordinary occasions, convene both Houses, or either of them"; hence these sessions occur only if convened by Presidential proclamation. Except as noted, these are separately numbered sessions of a Congress, and are marked by an E in the session column of the table. Until the 20th amendment was adopted, there were also times when special sessions of the Senate were convened, principally for confirming Cabinet and other executive nominations, and occasionally for the ratification of treaties or other executive business. These Senate sessions were also called by Presidential proclamation (typically by the outgoing President, although on occasion by incumbents as well) and are marked by an S in the session column. MEETING PLACES OF CONGRESS: Congress met for the first and second sessions of the First Congress (1789 and 1790) in New York City. From the third session of the First Congress through the first session of the Sixth Congress (1790 to 1800), Philadelphia was the meeting place. Congress has convened in Washington since the second session of the Sixth Congress (1800).

Congress	Session	Convening Date	Adjournment Date	Length in days [1]	Recesses [2]		President pro tempore of the Senate [3]	Speaker of the House of Representatives
					Senate	House of Representatives		
	2	Jan. 3, 1980	Dec. 16, 1980	349	Apr. 3–Apr. 15, 1980 May 22–May 28, 1980 July 2–July 21, 1980 Aug. 6–Aug. 18, 1980 Aug. 27–Sept. 3, 1980 Oct. 1–Nov. 12, 1980 Nov. 25–Dec. 1, 1980	Jan. 18–21, 1980 Feb. 14–Feb. 18, 1980 Apr. 3–Apr. 14, 1980 May 23–May 27, 1980 July 3–July 20, 1980 Aug. 2–Aug. 17, 1980 Aug. 29–Sept. 2, 1980 Oct. 3–Nov. 11, 1980 Nov. 22–Nov. 30, 1980	Warren G. Magnuson, of Washington; Milton Young, of North Dakota;[19] Warren G. Magnuson, of Washington.[19]	
97th	1	Jan. 5, 1981	Dec. 16, 1981	347	Feb. 6–Feb. 16, 1981 Apr. 10–Apr. 27, 1981 June 25–July 8, 1981 Aug. 3–Sept. 9, 1981 Oct. 7–Oct. 14, 1981 Nov. 24–Nov. 30, 1981	Feb. 7–Feb. 16, 1981 Apr. 11–Apr. 26, 1981 June 27–July 7, 1981 Aug. 5–Sept. 8, 1981 Oct. 8–Oct. 12, 1981 Nov. 24–Nov. 29, 1981	Strom Thurmond, of South Carolina	Do.
	2	Jan. 25, 1982	Dec. 21, 1982	333	Feb. 11–Feb. 22, 1982 Apr. 1–Apr. 13, 1982 May 27–June 8, 1982 July 1–July 12, 1982 Aug. 20–Sept. 8, 1982 Oct. 1–Nov. 29, 1982	Feb. 11–Feb. 21, 1982 Apr. 7–Apr. 19, 1982 May 29–June 1, 1982 July 2–July 11, 1982 Aug. 21–Sept. 7, 1982 Oct. 3–Nov. 28, 1982	...do	
98th	1	Jan. 3, 1983	Nov. 18, 1983	320	Jan. 3–Jan. 25, 1983 Feb. 3–Feb. 14, 1983 Mar. 24–Apr. 5, 1983 May 26–June 6, 1983 June 29–July 11, 1983 Aug. 4–Sept. 12, 1983 Oct. 7–Oct. 17, 1983	Jan. 7–Jan. 24, 1983 Feb. 18–Feb. 21, 1983 Mar. 25–Apr. 4, 1983 May 27–May 31, 1983 July 1–July 10, 1983 Aug. 5–Sept. 11, 1983 Oct. 7–Oct. 16, 1983	Strom Thurmond, of South Carolina	Thomas P. O'Neill, Jr., of Massachusetts.

	2	Jan. 23, 1984	Oct. 12, 1984	264	Feb. 9–Feb. 20, 1984 Apr. 12–Apr. 24, 1984 May 24–May 31, 1984 June 29–July 23, 1984 Aug. 10–Sept. 5, 1984	Feb. 10–Feb. 20, 1984 Apr. 13–Apr. 23, 1984 May 25–May 29, 1984 June 30–July 22, 1984 Aug. 11–Sept. 4, 1984	...do.	
99th	1	Jan. 3, 1985	Dec. 20, 1985	352	Jan. 7–Jan. 21, 1985 Feb. 7–Feb. 18, 1985 Apr. 4–Apr. 15, 1985 May 9–May 14, 1985 May 24–June 3, 1985 June 27–July 8, 1985 Aug. 1–Sept. 9, 1985 Nov. 23–Dec. 2, 1985	Jan. 8–Jan. 20, 1985 Feb. 8–Feb. 18, 1985 Mar. 8–Mar. 18, 1985 Apr. 5–Apr. 14, 1985 May 24–June 2, 1985 June 28–July 7, 1985 Aug. 2–Sept. 3, 1985 Nov. 22–Dec. 1, 1985	...do	Do.
	2	Jan. 21, 1986	Oct. 18, 1986	278	Feb. 7–Feb. 17, 1986 Mar. 27–Apr. 8, 1986 May 21–June 2, 1986 June 26–July 7, 1986 Aug. 15–Sept. 8, 1986	Feb. 7–Feb. 17, 1986 Mar. 25–Apr. 7, 1986 May 23–June 2, 1986 June 27–July 13, 1986 Aug. 17–Sept. 7, 1986	...do.	
100th	1	Jan. 6, 1987	Dec. 22, 1987	351	Jan. 6–Jan. 12, 1987 Feb. 5–Feb. 16, 1987 Apr. 10–Apr. 21, 1987 May 21–May 27, 1987 July 1–July 7, 1987 Aug. 7–Sept. 9, 1987 Nov. 20–Nov. 30, 1987	Jan. 9–Jan. 19, 1987 Feb. 12–Feb. 17, 1987 Apr. 10–Apr. 20, 1987 May 22–May 26, 1987 July 2–July 6, 1987 July 16–July 19, 1987 Aug. 8–Sept. 9, 1987 Nov. 11–Nov. 15, 1987 Nov. 21–Nov. 29, 1987	John C. Stennis, of Mississippi	James C. Wright, Jr., of Texas.
	2	Jan. 25, 1988	Oct. 22, 1988	272	Feb. 4–Feb. 15, 1988 Mar. 4– Mar. 14, 1988 Mar. 31–Apr. 11, 1988 Apr. 29–May 9, 1988 May 27–June 6, 1988 June 29–July 6, 1988 July 14–July 25, 1988 Aug. 11–Sept. 7, 1988	Feb. 10–Feb. 15, 1988 Apr. 1–Apr. 10, 1988 May 27–May 31, 1988 July 1–July 5, 1988 July 15–July 25, 1988 Aug. 12–Sept. 6, 1988	...do.	
101st	1	Jan. 3, 1989	Nov. 22, 1989	324	Jan. 4–Jan. 20, 1989 Jan. 20–Jan. 25, 1989 Feb. 9–Feb. 21, 1989 Mar. 17–Apr. 4, 1989 Apr. 19–May 1, 1989 May 18–May 31, 1989 June 23–July 11, 1989 Aug. 4–Sept. 6, 1989	Jan. 5–Jan. 18, 1989 Feb. 10–Feb. 20, 1989 Mar. 24–Apr. 2, 1989 Apr. 19–Apr. 24, 1989 May 26–May 30, 1989 June 30–July 9, 1989 Aug. 6–Sept. 5, 1989	Robert C. Byrd, of West Virginia	James C. Wright, Jr., of Texas;[20] Thomas S. Foley, of Washington.[20]
	2	Jan. 23, 1990	Oct. 28, 1990	260	Feb. 8–Feb. 20, 1990 Mar. 9–Mar. 20, 1990 Apr. 5–Apr. 18, 1990 May 24–June 5, 1990 June 28–July 10, 1990 Aug. 4–Sept. 10, 1990	Feb. 8–Feb. 19, 1990 Apr. 5–Apr. 17, 1990 May 26–June 4, 1990 June 29–July 9, 1990 Aug. 5–Sept. 4, 1990	...do.	

SESSIONS OF CONGRESS, 1st–116th CONGRESSES, 1789–2020—CONTINUED

[Closing date for this table was July 22, 2020.]

MEETING DATES OF CONGRESS: Pursuant to a resolution of the Confederation Congress in 1788, the Constitution went into effect on March 4, 1789. From then until the 20th amendment took effect in January 1934, the term of each Congress began on March 4th of each odd-numbered year; however, Article I, section 4, of the Constitution provided that ''The Congress shall assemble at least once in every Year, and such Meeting shall be on the first Monday in December, unless they shall by law appoint a different day.'' The Congress therefore convened regularly on the first Monday in December until the 20th amendment became effective, which changed the beginning of Congress's term as well as its convening date to January 3rd. So prior to 1934, a new Congress typically would not convene for regular business until 13 months after being elected. One effect of this was that the last session of each Congress was a ''lame duck'' session. After the 20th amendment, the time from the election to the beginning of Congress's term as well as when it convened was reduced to two months. Recognizing that the need might exist for Congress to meet at times other than the regularly scheduled convening date, Article II, section 3 of the Constitution provides that the President ''may, on extraordinary occasions, convene both Houses, or either of them''; hence these sessions occur only if convened by Presidential proclamation. Except as noted, these are separately numbered sessions of a Congress, and are marked by an E in the session column of the table. Until the 20th amendment was adopted, there were also times when special sessions of the Senate were convened, principally for confirming Cabinet and other executive nominations, and occasionally for the ratification of treaties or other executive business. These Senate sessions were also called by Presidential proclamation (typically by the outgoing President, although on occasion by incumbents as well) and are marked by an S in the session column. MEETING PLACES OF CONGRESS: Congress met for the first and second sessions of the First Congress (1789 and 1790) in New York City. From the third session of the First Congress through the first session of the Sixth Congress (1790 to 1800), Philadelphia was the meeting place. Congress has convened in Washington since the second session of the Sixth Congress (1800).

Congress	Session	Convening Date	Adjournment Date	Length in days [1]	Recesses [2]		President pro tempore of the Senate [3]	Speaker of the House of Representatives
					Senate	House of Representatives		
102d	1	Jan. 3, 1991	Jan. 3, 1992	366	Feb. 7–Feb. 19, 1991 Mar. 22–Apr. 9, 1991 Apr. 25–May 6, 1991 May 24–June 3, 1991 June 28–July 8, 1991 Aug. 2–Sept. 10, 1991 Nov. 27, 1991–Jan. 3, 1992	Feb. 7–Feb. 18, 1991 Mar. 23–Apr. 8, 1991 May 24–May 28, 1991 June 28–July 8, 1991 Aug. 3–Sept. 10, 1991 Nov. 28, 1991–Jan. 2, 1992	...do	Thomas S. Foley, of Washington.
	2	Jan. 3, 1992	Oct. 9, 1992	281	Jan. 3–Jan. 21, 1992 Apr. 10–Apr. 28, 1992 May 21–June 1, 1992 July 2–July 20, 1992 Aug. 12–Sept. 8, 1992	Jan. 4–Jan. 21, 1992 Apr. 11–Apr. 27, 1992 May 22–May 25, 1992 July 3–July 6, 1992 July 10–July 20, 1992 Aug. 13–Sept. 8, 1992	...do.	
103d	1	Jan. 5, 1993	Nov. 26, 1993	326	Jan. 7–Jan. 20, 1993 Feb. 4–Feb. 16, 1993 Apr. 7–Apr. 19, 1993 May 28–June 7, 1993 July 1–July 13, 1993 Aug. 7–Sept. 7, 1993 Oct. 7–Oct. 13, 1993 Nov. 11–Nov. 16, 1993	Jan. 7–Jan. 19, 1993 Jan. 28–Feb. 1, 1993 Feb. 5–Feb. 15, 1993 Apr. 8–Apr. 18, 1993 May 28–June 7, 1993 July 2–July 12, 1993 Aug. 7–Sept. 7, 1993 Sept. 16–Sept. 20, 1993 Oct. 8–Oct. 11, 1993 Nov. 11–Nov. 14, 1993	Robert C. Byrd, of West Virginia	Thomas S. Foley, of Washington.

	2	Jan. 25, 1994	Nov. 29, 1994	311	Feb. 11–Feb. 22, 1994 Mar. 26–Apr. 11, 1994 May 25–June 7, 1994 July 1–July 11, 1994 Aug. 25–Sept. 12, 1994 Oct. 8–Nov. 30, 1994	Jan. 27–Jan. 31, 1994 Feb. 12–Feb. 21, 1994 Mar. 25–Apr. 11, 1994 May 27–June 7, 1994 July 1–July 11, 1994 Aug. 27–Sept. 11, 1994 Oct. 8–Nov. 28, 1994	...do.	
104th.	1	Jan. 4, 1995	Jan. 3, 1996	365	Feb. 16–Feb. 22, 1995 Apr. 7–Apr. 24, 1995 May 26–June 5, 1995 June 30–July 10, 1995 Aug. 11–Sept. 5, 1995 Sept. 29–Oct. 10, 1995 Nov. 20–Nov. 27, 1995	Feb. 17–Feb. 20, 1995 Mar. 17–Mar. 20, 1995 Apr. 8–Apr. 30, 1995 May 4–May 8, 1995 May 26–June 5, 1995 July 1–July 9, 1995 Aug. 5–Sept. 5, 1995 Sept. 30–Oct. 5, 1995 Nov. 21–Nov. 27, 1995	Strom Thurmond, of South Carolina	Newt Gingrich, of Georgia.
	2	Jan. 3, 1996	Oct. 4, 1996	276	Jan. 10–Jan. 22, 1996 Mar. 29–Apr. 15, 1996 May 24–June 3, 1996 June 28–July 8, 1996 Aug. 2–Sept. 3, 1996	Jan. 10–Jan. 21, 1996 Mar. 30–Apr. 14, 1996 May 24–May 28, 1996 June 29–July 7, 1996 Aug. 3–Sept. 3, 1996	...do.	
105th.	1	Jan. 7, 1997	Nov. 13, 1997	311	Jan. 9–Jan. 21, 1997 Feb. 13–Feb. 24, 1997 Mar. 21–Apr. 7, 1997 June 27–July 7, 1997 July 31–Sept. 2, 1997 Oct. 9–Oct. 20, 1997	Jan. 10–Jan. 19, 1997 Jan. 22–Feb. 3, 1997 Feb. 14–Feb. 24, 1997 Mar. 22–Apr. 7, 1997 June 27–July 7, 1997 Aug. 2–Sept. 2, 1997 Oct. 10–Oct. 20, 1997	...do	Do.
	2	Jan. 27, 1998	Dec. 19, 1998	327	Feb. 13–Feb. 23, 1998 Apr. 3–Apr. 20, 1998 May 22–June 1, 1998 June 26–July 6, 1998 July 31–Aug. 31, 1998 Adjourned sine die, Oct. 21, 1998.	Jan. 29–Feb. 2, 1998 Feb. 6–Feb. 10, 1998 Feb. 13–Feb. 23, 1998 Apr. 2–Apr. 20, 1998 May 23–June 2, 1998 June 25–July 13, 1998 Aug. 8–Sept. 8, 1998 Oct. 22–Dec. 16, 1998	...do.	
106th.	1	Jan. 6, 1999	Nov. 22, 1999	321	Feb. 12–Feb. 22, 1999 Mar. 25–Apr. 12, 1999 May 27–June 7, 1999 July 1–July 12, 1999 Aug. 5–Sept. 8, 1999	Jan. 7–Jan. 18, 1999 Jan. 20–Feb. 1, 1999 Feb. 13–Feb. 22, 1999 Mar. 26–Apr. 11, 1999 May 28–June 6, 1999 July 2–July 11, 1999 Aug. 7–Sept. 7, 1999	...do	J. Dennis Hastert, of Illinois.
	2	Jan. 24, 2000	Dec. 15, 2000	326	Feb. 10–Feb. 22, 2000 Mar. 9–Mar. 20, 2000 Apr. 13–Apr. 25, 2000 May 25–June 6, 2000 June 30–July 10, 2000 July 27–Sept. 5, 2000 Nov. 2–Nov. 14, 2000 Nov. 14–Dec. 5, 2000	Feb. 17–Feb. 28, 2000 Apr. 14–May 1, 2000 May 26–June 5, 2000 July 1–July 9, 2000 July 28–Sept. 5, 2000 Nov. 4–Nov. 12, 2000 Nov. 15–Dec. 3, 2000	...do.	

SESSIONS OF CONGRESS, 1st–116th CONGRESSES, 1789–2020—CONTINUED

[Closing date for this table was July 22, 2020.]

MEETING DATES OF CONGRESS: Pursuant to a resolution of the Confederation Congress in 1788, the Constitution went into effect on March 4, 1789. From then until the 20th amendment took effect in January 1934, the term of each Congress began on March 4th of each odd-numbered year; however, Article I, section 4, of the Constitution provided that "The Congress shall assemble at least once in every Year, and such Meeting shall be on the first Monday in December, unless they shall by law appoint a different day." The Congress therefore convened regularly on the first Monday in December until the 20th amendment became effective, which changed the beginning of Congress's term as well as its convening date to January 3rd. So prior to 1934, a new Congress typically would not convene for regular business until 13 months after being elected. One effect of this was that the last session of each Congress was a "lame duck" session. After the 20th amendment, the time from the election to the beginning of Congress's term as well as when it convened was reduced to two months. Recognizing that the need might exist for Congress to meet at times other than the regularly scheduled convening date, Article II, section 3 of the Constitution provides that the President "may, on extraordinary occasions, convene both Houses, or either of them"; hence these sessions occur only if convened by Presidential proclamation. Except as noted, these are separately numbered sessions of a Congress, and are marked by an E in the session column of the table. Until the 20th amendment was adopted, there were also times when special sessions of the Senate were convened, principally for confirming Cabinet and other executive nominations, and occasionally for the ratification of treaties or other executive business. These Senate sessions were also called by Presidential proclamation (typically by the outgoing President, although on occasion by incumbents as well) and are marked by an S in the session column. MEETING PLACES OF CONGRESS: Congress met for the first and second sessions of the First Congress (1789 and 1790) in New York City. From the third session of the First Congress through the first session of the Sixth Congress (1790 to 1800), Philadelphia was the meeting place. Congress has convened in Washington since the second session of the Sixth Congress (1800).

Congress	Session	Convening Date	Adjournment Date	Length in days[1]	Recesses[2]		President pro tempore of the Senate[3]	Speaker of the House of Representatives
					Senate	House of Representatives		
107th.	1	Jan. 3, 2001	Dec. 20, 2001	352	Jan. 8–Jan. 20, 2001 Feb. 15–Feb. 26, 2001 Apr. 6–Apr. 23, 2001 May 26–June 5, 2001 June 29–July 9, 2001 Aug. 3–Sept. 4, 2001 Oct. 18–Oct. 23, 2001 Nov. 16–Nov. 27, 2001	Jan. 7–Jan. 19, 2001 Jan. 21–Jan 29, 2001 Feb. 1–Feb. 5, 2001 Feb. 15–Feb. 25, 2001 Apr. 5–Apr. 23, 2001 May 27–June 4, 2001 June 29–July 9, 2001 Aug. 3–Sept. 4, 2001 Oct. 18–Oct. 22, 2001 Nov. 20–Nov. 26, 2001	Robert C. Byrd, of West Virginia;[21] Strom Thurmond, of South Carolina;[21] Robert C. Byrd, of West Virginia.[21]	Do.
	2	Jan. 23, 2002	Nov. 22, 2002	304	Jan. 29–Feb. 4, 2002 Feb. 15–Feb. 25, 2002 Mar. 22–Apr. 8, 2002 May 23–June 3, 2002 June 28–July 8, 2002 Aug. 1–Sept. 3, 2002	Jan. 30–Feb. 3, 2002 Feb. 15–Feb. 25, 2002 Mar. 21–Apr. 8, 2002 May 25–June 3, 2002 June 29–July 7, 2002 July 28–Sept. 3, 2002	Robert C. Byrd, of West Virginia.	
108th.	1	Jan. 7, 2003	Dec. 8, 2003	337	Feb. 14–Feb. 24, 2003 Apr. 11–Apr. 28, 2003 May 23–June 2, 2003 June 27–July 7, 2003 Aug. 1–Sept 2, 2003 Oct. 3–Oct. 14, 2003 Nov. 25–Dec. 9, 2003	Jan. 9–Jan. 26, 2003 Feb. 14–Feb. 24, 2003 Apr. 13–Apr. 28, 2003 May 24–June 1, 2003 June 28–July 6, 2003 July 30–Sept. 2, 2003 Nov. 26–Dec. 7, 2003	Ted Stevens, of Alaska	J. Dennis Hastert, of Illinois.

	2	Jan. 20, 2004	Dec. 7, 2004	324	Feb. 12–Feb. 23, 2004 Mar. 12–Mar. 22, 2004 Apr. 8–Apr. 19, 2004 May 21–June 1, 2004 June 9–June 14, 2004 June 25–July 6, 2004 July 22–Sept. 7, 2004 Oct. 11–Nov. 16, 2004 Nov. 24–Dec. 7, 2004	Feb. 12–Feb. 23, 2004 Apr. 3–Apr. 19, 2004 May 21–May 31, 2004 June 10–June 13, 2004 June 26–July 5, 2004 July 23–Sept. 6, 2004 Oct. 10–Nov. 15, 2004 Nov. 25–Dec. 5, 2004	...do.	
109th.	1	Jan. 4, 2005	Dec. 22, 2005	353	Jan. 6–Jan. 20, 2005 Jan. 26–Jan. 31, 2005 Feb. 18–Feb. 28, 2005 Mar. 20–Apr. 4, 2005 Apr. 29–May 9, 2005 May 26–June 6, 2005 July 1–July 11, 2005 July 29–Sept. 1, 2005 Sept. 1–Sept. 6, 2005 Oct. 7–Oct. 17, 2005 Nov. 18–Dec. 12, 2005	Jan. 7–Jan. 19, 2005 Jan. 21–Jan. 24, 2005 Jan. 27–Jan. 31, 2005 Feb. 3–Feb. 7, 2005 Feb. 18–Feb. 28, 2005 Mar. 22–Apr. 4, 2005 May 27–June 6, 2005 July 1–July 8, 2005 July 30–Sept. 1, 2005 Oct. 8–Oct. 16, 2005 Nov. 19–Dec. 5, 2005	...do	Do.
	2	Jan. 3, 2006	Dec. 9, 2006	341	Jan. 3–Jan. 18, 2006 Feb. 17–Feb. 27, 2006 Mar. 16–Mar. 27, 2006 Apr. 7–Apr. 24, 2006 May 26–June 5, 2006 June 29–July 10, 2006 Aug. 4–Sept. 5, 2006 Sept. 30–Nov. 9, 2006 Nov. 16–Dec. 4, 2006	Jan. 4–Jan. 30, 2006 Feb. 2–Feb. 6, 2006 Feb. 9–Feb. 13, 2006 Feb. 17–Feb. 27, 2006 Mar. 17–Mar. 27, 2006 Apr. 7–Apr. 24, 2006 May 26–June 5, 2006 June 30–July 9, 2006 Aug. 3–Sept. 5, 2006 Oct. 1–Nov. 8, 2006 Nov. 16–Dec. 3, 2006	...do.	
110th.	1	Jan. 4, 2007	Dec. 19, 2007	362	Feb. 17–Feb. 26, 2007 Mar. 29–Apr. 10, 2007 May 25–June 4, 2007 June 29–July 9, 2007 Aug. 3–Sept. 4, 2007 Oct. 5–Oct. 15, 2007	Jan. 25–Jan. 28, 2007 Feb. 1–Feb. 4, 2007 Feb. 17–Feb. 26, 2007 Mar. 31–Apr. 15, 2007 May 25–June 4, 2007 June 29–July 9, 2007 Aug. 6–Sept. 3, 2007 Nov. 16–Dec. 3, 2007	Robert C. Byrd, of West Virginia	Nancy Pelosi, of California.
	2	Jan. 3, 2008	Jan. 3, 2009	367	June 27–July 7, 2008	Jan. 4–Jan. 14, 2008 Jan. 24–Jan. 27, 2008 Jan. 30–Feb. 5, 2008 Mar. 15–Mar. 30, 2008 May 23–June 2, 2008 June 27–July 7, 2008 Aug. 2–Sept. 7, 2008 Oct. 4–Nov. 18, 2008 Nov. 21–Dec. 8, 2008 Dec. 11, 2008–Jan. 3, 2009	...do.	

SESSIONS OF CONGRESS, 1st–116th CONGRESSES, 1789–2020—CONTINUED

[Closing date for this table was July 22, 2020.]

MEETING DATES OF CONGRESS: Pursuant to a resolution of the Confederation Congress in 1788, the Constitution went into effect on March 4, 1789. From then until the 20th amendment took effect in January 1934, the term of each Congress began on March 4th of each odd-numbered year; however, Article I, section 4, of the Constitution provided that ''The Congress shall assemble at least once in every Year, and such Meeting shall be on the first Monday in December, unless they shall by law appoint a different day.'' The Congress therefore convened regularly on the first Monday in December until the 20th amendment became effective, which changed the beginning of Congress's term as well as its convening date to January 3rd. So prior to 1934, a new Congress typically would not convene for regular business until 13 months after being elected. One effect of this was that the last session of each Congress was a ''lame duck'' session. After the 20th amendment, the time from the election to the beginning of Congress's term as well as when it convened was reduced to two months. Recognizing that the need might exist for Congress to meet at times other than the regularly scheduled convening date, Article II, section 3 of the Constitution provides that the President ''may, on extraordinary occasions, convene both Houses, or either of them''; hence these sessions occur only if convened by Presidential proclamation. Except as noted, these are separately numbered sessions of a Congress, and are marked by an E in the session column of the table. Until the 20th amendment was adopted, there were also times when special sessions of the Senate were convened, principally for confirming Cabinet and other executive nominations, and occasionally for the ratification of treaties or other executive business. These Senate sessions were also called by Presidential proclamation (typically by the outgoing President, although on occasion by incumbents as well) and are marked by an S in the session column. MEETING PLACES OF CONGRESS: Congress met for the first and second sessions of the First Congress (1789 and 1790) in New York City. From the third session of the First Congress through the first session of the Sixth Congress (1790 to 1800), Philadelphia was the meeting place. Congress has convened in Washington since the second session of the Sixth Congress (1800).

Congress	Session	Convening Date	Adjournment Date	Length in days [1]	Recesses [2]		President pro tempore of the Senate [3]	Speaker of the House of Representatives
					Senate	House of Representatives		
111th.	1	Jan. 6, 2009	Dec. 23, 2009	353	Apr. 2–Apr. 20, 2009 May 21–June 1, 2009 June 25–July 6, 2009 Nov. 10–Nov. 16, 2009 Nov. 21–Nov. 30, 2009	Jan. 29–Feb. 1, 2009 Feb. 5–Feb. 8, 2009 Feb. 14–Feb. 22, 2009 Apr. 3–Apr. 20, 2009 May 22–June 1, 2009 June 27–July 6, 2009 Aug. 1–Sept. 7, 2009 Nov. 8–Nov. 15, 2009 Nov. 20–Nov. 30, 2009	...do	Do.
	2	Jan. 5, 2010	Dec. 22, 2010	352	Feb. 11–Feb. 23, 2010 Mar. 26–Apr. 12, 2010 May 28–June 7, 2010 June 30–July 12, 2010 Aug. 5–Aug. 12, 2010 Aug. 12–Sept. 13, 2010 Nov. 19–Nov. 29, 2010	Jan. 6–Jan. 11, 2010 Feb. 10–Feb. 21, 2010 Mar. 26–Apr. 12, 2010 May 29–June 7, 2010 July 2–July 12, 2010 July 31–Aug. 8, 2010 Aug. 11–Sept. 13, 2010 Oct. 1–Nov. 14, 2010 Nov. 19–Nov. 28, 2010	Robert C. Byrd, of West Virginia;[22] Daniel K. Inouye, of Hawaii.[22]	
112th.	1	Jan. 5, 2011	Jan. 3, 2012	360	Jan. 5 –Jan. 25, 2011 Feb. 17–Feb. 28, 2011 Mar. 17–Mar. 28, 2011 Apr. 14–May 2, 2011	Jan. 13–Jan. 17, 2011 Jan. 27–Feb. 7, 2011 Feb. 20–Feb. 27, 2011 Mar. 18–Mar. 28, 2011 Apr. 16–May 1, 2011 May 14–May 22, 2011	Daniel K. Inouye, of Hawaii	John A. Boehner, of Ohio.

	2	Jan. 3, 2012	Jan. 3, 2013	367	Aug. 3–Sept. 10, 2012	Mar. 31–Apr. 15, 2012 Apr. 28–May 6, 2012 June 30–July 8, 2012 Aug. 8–Sept. 9, 2012 Nov. 17–Nov. 26, 2012	Daniel K. Inouye, of Hawaii;[23] Patrick J. Leahy, of Vermont.[23]	
113th.	1	Jan. 3, 2013	Jan. 3, 2014	356	Jan. 4–Jan. 22, 2013 Feb. 15–Feb. 25, 2013 Mar. 22–Apr. 8, 2013 May 23–June 3, 2013 June 28–July 8, 2013 Aug. 2–Aug. 12, 2013 Aug. 12–Sept. 6, 2013	Jan. 5–Jan. 13, 2013 Feb. 16–Feb. 24, 2013 Mar. 26–Apr. 8, 2013 May 25–June 2, 2013 June 29–July 7, 2013 Aug. 3–Sept. 5, 2013 Oct. 31–Nov. 11, 2013 Nov. 23–Dec. 1, 2013 Dec. 27, 2013–Jan. 2, 2014	Patrick J. Leahy, of Vermont	Do.
	2	Jan. 3, 2014	Jan. 2, 2015	365	Apr. 11–Apr. 28, 2014 Aug. 8–Sept. 8, 2014 Sept. 18–Oct. 15, 2014 Oct. 15–Nov. 12, 2014	Apr. 11–Apr. 27, 2014 Aug. 5–Sept. 7, 2014 Sept. 20–Nov. 11, 2014 Nov. 21–Nov. 30, 2014 Dec. 17–Jan. 1, 2015	...do	Do.
114th.	1	Jan. 6, 2015	Dec. 18, 2015	347	Mar. 26–Apr. 13, 2015 June 25–July 7, 2015 Aug. 6–Sept. 8, 2015 Nov. 19–Nov. 30, 2015	Mar. 27–Apr. 12, 2015 June 26–July 6, 2015 Aug. 5–Sept. 7, 2015 Nov. 6–Nov. 15, 2015 Nov. 20–Nov. 29, 2015	Orrin Hatch, of Utah	John A. Boehner, of Ohio[24] Paul D. Ryan, of Wisconsin[24]
	2	Jan. 4, 2016	Jan. 3, 2017	366	Feb. 12–Feb. 22, 2016	Jan. 14–Jan 24, 2016 Feb. 13–Feb. 22, 2016 Mar. 24–April 10, 2016 July 26–Sep. 5, 2016 Sep. 29–Nov. 13, 2016	...do	...Do.
115th.	1	Jan. 3, 2017	Jan. 2, 2018	365			Orrin Hatch, of Utah	...Do.
	2	Jan. 3, 2018	Jan. 2, 2019				...do	...Do.
116th.	1	Jan. 3, 2019	Jan. 2, 2020	365			Chuck Grassley, of Iowa	Nancy Pelosi, of California
	2	Jan. 3, 2020					...do	...Do.

[1] For the purposes of this table, a session's "length in days" is defined as the total number of calendar days from the convening date to the adjournment date, inclusive. It does not mean the actual number of days that Congress met during that session.

[2] For the purposes of this table, a "recess" is defined as a break in House or Senate proceedings of three or more days, excluding Sundays. According to Article I, section 5 of the U.S. Constitution, neither house may adjourn for more than three days without the consent of the other.

[3] The election and role of the President pro tempore has evolved considerably over the Senate's history. "*Pro tempore* is Latin for 'for the time being'; thus, the post was conceived as a temporary presiding officer. In the eighteenth and nineteenth centuries, the Senate frequently elected several Presidents pro tempore during a single session. Since Vice Presidents presided routinely, the Senate thought it necessary to choose a President pro tempore only for the limited periods when the Vice President might be ill or otherwise absent." Since no provision was in place (until the 25th amendment was adopted in 1967) for replacing the Vice President if he died or resigned from office, or if he assumed the Presidency, the President pro tempore would continue under such circumstances to fill the duties of the chair until the next Vice President was elected. Since Mar. 12, 1890, however, Presidents pro tempore have served until "the Senate otherwise ordered." Since 1949, while still elected, the position has gone to the most senior member of the majority party (see footnote 19 for a minority party exception). To gain a more complete understanding of this position, see Robert C. Byrd's *The Senate 1789–1989: Addresses on the History of the United States Senate*, vol. 2, ch. 6 "The President Pro Tempore," pp. 167–183, from which the quotes in this footnote are taken. Also, a complete listing of the dates of election of the Presidents pro tempore is in vol. 4 of the Byrd series (*The Senate 1789–1989: Historical Statistics, 1789–1992*), table 6–2, pp. 647–653.

[4] Henry Clay resigned as Speaker on Jan. 19, 1814. He was succeeded by Langdon Cheves who was elected on that same day.

[5] Henry Clay resigned as Speaker on Oct. 28, 1820, after the sine die adjournment of the first session of the 16th Congress. He was succeeded by John W. Taylor who was elected at the beginning of the second session.

[6] Andrew Stevenson resigned as Speaker on June 2, 1834. He was succeeded by John Bell who was elected on that same day.

[7] Speaker Schuyler Colfax resigned as Speaker on the last day of the 40th Congress, Mar. 3, 1869, in preparation for becoming Vice President of the United States on the following day. Theodore M. Pomeroy was elected Speaker on Mar. 3, and served for only that one day.

[8] Speaker Michael C. Kerr died on Aug. 19, 1876, after the sine die adjournment of the first session of the 44th Congress. Samuel J. Randall was elected Speaker at the beginning of the second session.

[9] William P. Frye resigned as President pro tempore on Apr. 27, 1911.

[10] President pro tempore James P. Clarke died on Oct. 1, 1916, after the sine die adjournment of the first session of the 64th Congress. Willard Saulsbury was elected President pro tempore during the second session.

[11] Speaker Joseph W. Byrns died on June 4, 1936. He was succeeded by William B. Bankhead who was elected Speaker on that same day.

[12] Speaker William B. Bankhead died on Sept. 15, 1940. He was succeeded by Sam Rayburn who was elected Speaker on that same day.

[13] President pro tempore Key Pittman died on Nov. 10, 1940. He was succeeded by William H. King who was elected President pro tempore on Nov. 19, 1940.

[14] President pro tempore Pat Harrison died on June 22, 1941. He was succeeded by Carter Glass who was elected President pro tempore on July 10, 1941.

[15] President Harry S. Truman called the Congress into extraordinary session twice, both times during the 80th Congress. Each time Congress had essentially wrapped up its business for the year, but for technical reasons had not adjourned sine die, so in each case the extraordinary session is considered an extension of the regularly numbered session rather than a separately numbered one. The dates of these extraordinary sessions were Nov. 17 to Dec. 19, 1947, and July 26 to Aug. 7, 1948.

[16] Speaker Sam Rayburn died on Nov. 16, 1961, after the sine die adjournment of the first session of the 87th Congress. John W. McCormack was elected Speaker at the beginning of the second session.

[17] President pro tempore Richard B. Russell died on Jan. 21, 1971. He was succeeded by Allen J. Ellender who was elected to that position on Jan. 22, 1971.

[18] President pro tempore Allen J. Ellender died on July 27, 1972. He was succeeded by James O. Eastland who was elected President pro tempore on July 28, 1972.

[19] Milton Young was elected President pro tempore for one day, Dec. 5, 1980, which was at the end of his 36-year career in the Senate. He was a Republican, which was the minority party at that time. Warren G. Magnuson resumed the position of President pro tempore on Dec. 6, 1980.

[20] James C. Wright, Jr., resigned as Speaker on June 6, 1989. He was succeeded by Thomas S. Foley who was elected on that same day.

[21] The 2000 election resulted in an even split in the Senate between Republicans and Democrats. From the date the 107th Congress convened on Jan. 3, 2001, until Inauguration Day on Jan. 20, 2001, Vice President Albert Gore's tie breaking vote resulted in a Democratic majority, hence Robert C. Byrd served as President pro tempore during this brief period. When Vice President Richard B. Cheney took office on Jan. 20, the Republicans became the majority party, and Strom Thurmond was elected President pro tempore. On June 6, 2001, Republican Senator James Jeffords became an Independent, creating a Democratic majority, and Robert C. Byrd was elected President pro tempore on that day.

[22] President pro tempore Robert C. Byrd died on June 28, 2010. He was succeeded by Daniel K. Inouye who was elected President pro tempore on that same day.

[23] President pro tempore Daniel K. Inouye died on December 17, 2012. He was succeeded by Patrick J. Leahy who was elected President pro tempore on that same day.

[24] John A. Boehner, resigned as Speaker on Oct. 29, 2015. He was succeeded by Paul D. Ryan who was elected on that same day.

CEREMONIAL MEETINGS OF CONGRESS

The following ceremonial meetings of Congress occurred on the following dates, at the designated locations, and for the reasons indicated. Please note that Congress was not in session on these occasions.

-July 16, 1987, 100th Congress, Philadelphia, Pennsylvania, Independence Hall and Congress Hall—In honor of the bicentennial of the Constitution, and in commemoration of the Great Compromise of the Constitutional Convention which was agreed to on July 16, 1787.

-September 6, 2002, 107th Congress, New York City, New York, Federal Hall—In remembrance of the victims and heroes of September 11, 2001, and in recognition of the courage and spirit of the City of New York.

JOINT SESSIONS AND MEETINGS, ADDRESSES TO THE SENATE OR THE HOUSE, AND INAUGURATIONS

1st–116th CONGRESSES, 1789–2020 [1]

The parliamentary difference between a joint session and a joint meeting has evolved over time. In recent years the distinctions have become clearer: a joint session is more formal, and occurs upon the adoption of a concurrent resolution; a joint meeting occurs when each body adopts a unanimous consent agreement to recess to meet with the other legislative body. Joint sessions typically are held to hear an address from the President of the United States or to count electoral votes. Joint meetings typically are held to hear an address from a foreign dignitary or visitors other than the President.

The Speaker of the House of Representatives usually presides over joint sessions and joint meetings; however, the President of the Senate does preside over joint sessions where the electoral votes are counted, as required by the Constitution.

In the earliest years of the Republic, 1789 and 1790, when the national legislature met in New York City, joint gatherings were held in the Senate Chamber in Federal Hall. In Philadelphia, when the legislature met in Congress Hall, such meetings were held in the Senate Chamber, 1790–1793, and in the Hall of the House of Representatives, 1794–1799. Once the Congress moved to the Capitol in Washington in 1800, the Senate Chamber again was used for joint gatherings through 1805. Since 1809, with few exceptions, joint sessions and joint meetings have occurred in the Hall of the House.

Presidential messages on the state of the Union were originally known as the ''Annual Message,'' but since the 80th Congress, in 1947, have been called the ''State of the Union Address.'' After President John Adams's Annual Message on November 22, 1800, these addresses were read by clerks to the individual bodies until President Woodrow Wilson resumed the practice of delivering them to joint sessions on December 2, 1913.

In some instances more than one joint gathering has occurred on the same day. For example, on January 6, 1941, Congress met in joint session to count electoral votes for President and Vice President, and then met again in joint session to receive President Franklin Delano Roosevelt's Annual Message.

Whereas in more recent decades, foreign dignitaries invited to speak before Congress have typically done so at joint meetings, in earlier times (and with several notable exceptions), such visitors were received by the Senate and the House separately, or by one or the other singly, a tradition begun with the visit of General Lafayette of France in 1824. At that time a joint committee decided that each body would honor Lafayette separately, establishing the precedent. (See footnote 7 for more details.) Not all such occasions included formal addresses by such dignitaries (e.g., Lafayette's reception by the Senate in their chamber, at which he did not speak before they adjourned to greet him), hence the ''occasions'' listed in the third column of the table include not only addresses, but also remarks (defined as brief greetings or off-the-cuff comments often requested of the visitor at the last minute) and receptions. Relatively few foreign dignitaries were received by Congress before World War I.

Congress has hosted inaugurations since the first occasion in 1789. They always have been formal joint gatherings, and sometimes they also were joint sessions. Inaugurations were joint sessions when both houses of Congress were in session, and they processed to the ceremony as part of the business of the day. In many cases, however, one or both houses were not in session or were in recess at the time of the ceremony. In this table, inaugurations that were not joint sessions are listed in the second column. Those that were joint sessions are so identified and described in the third column.

JOINT SESSIONS AND MEETINGS, ADDRESSES TO THE SENATE OR THE HOUSE, AND INAUGURATIONS

[See notes at end of table]

Congress and Date	Type	Occasion, topic, or inaugural location	Name and position of dignitary (where applicable)
		NEW YORK CITY	
1st CONGRESS			
Apr. 6, 1789	Joint session	Counting electoral votes	N.A.
Apr. 30, 1789	...do	Inauguration and church service [2]	President George Washington; Right Reverend Samuel Provoost, Senate-appointed Chaplain.
Jan. 8, 1790	...do	Annual Message	President George Washington.
		PHILADELPHIA	
Dec. 8, 1790	...do	...do	Do.
2d CONGRESS			
Oct. 25, 1791	...do	...do	Do.
Nov. 6, 1792	...do	...do	Do.
Feb. 13, 1793	...do	Counting electoral votes	N.A.
3d CONGRESS			
Mar. 4, 1793	Inauguration	Senate Chamber	President George Washington.
Dec. 3, 1793	Joint session	Annual Message	Do.
Nov. 19, 1794	...do	...do	Do.
4th CONGRESS			
Dec. 8, 1795	...do	...do	Do.
Dec. 7, 1796	...do	...do	Do.
Feb. 8, 1797	...do	Counting electoral votes	N.A.
5th CONGRESS			
Mar. 4, 1797	Inauguration	Hall of the House	President John Adams.
May 16, 1797	Joint session	Relations with France	Do.
Nov. 23, 1797	...do	Annual Message	Do.
Dec. 8, 1798	...do	...do	Do.
6th CONGRESS			
Dec. 3, 1799	...do	...do	Do.
Dec. 26, 1799	...do	Funeral procession and oration in memory of George Washington.[3]	Representative Henry Lee.
		WASHINGTON	
Nov. 22, 1800	...do	Annual Message	President John Adams.
Feb. 11, 1801	...do	Counting electoral votes [4]	N.A.
7th CONGRESS			
Mar. 4, 1801	Inauguration	Senate Chamber	President Thomas Jefferson.
8th CONGRESS			
Feb. 13, 1805	Joint session	Counting electoral votes	N.A.
9th CONGRESS			
Mar. 4, 1805	Inauguration	Senate Chamber	President Thomas Jefferson.
10th CONGRESS			
Feb. 8, 1809	Joint session	Counting electoral votes	N.A.
11th CONGRESS			
Mar. 4, 1809	Inauguration	Hall of the House	President James Madison.
12th CONGRESS			
Feb. 10, 1813	Joint session	Counting electoral votes	N.A.
13th CONGRESS			
Mar. 4, 1813	Inauguration	Hall of the House	President James Madison.
14th CONGRESS			
Feb. 12, 1817	Joint session	Counting electoral votes [5]	N.A.
15th CONGRESS			
Mar. 4, 1817	Inauguration	In front of Brick Capitol	President James Monroe.
16th CONGRESS			
Feb. 14, 1821	Joint session	Counting electoral votes [6]	N.A.
17th CONGRESS			
Mar. 5, 1821	Inauguration	Hall of the House	President James Monroe.
18th CONGRESS			
Dec. 9, 1824	Senate	Reception	General Gilbert du Motier, Marquis de Lafayette, of France.
Dec. 10, 1824	House [7]	Address	Speaker Henry Clay; General Gilbert du Motier, Marquis de Lafayette, of France.
Feb. 9, 1825	Joint session	Counting electoral votes [8]	N.A.
19th CONGRESS			
Mar. 4, 1825	Inauguration	Hall of the House	President John Quincy Adams.
20th CONGRESS			
Feb. 11, 1829	Joint session	Counting electoral votes	N.A.

JOINT SESSIONS AND MEETINGS, ADDRESSES TO THE SENATE OR THE HOUSE, AND INAUGURATIONS—CONTINUED

[See notes at end of table]

Congress and Date	Type	Occasion, topic, or inaugural location	Name and position of dignitary (where applicable)
21st CONGRESS			
Mar. 4, 1829	Inauguration	East Portico [9]	President Andrew Jackson.
22d CONGRESS			
Feb. 13, 1833	Joint session	Counting electoral votes	N.A.
23d CONGRESS			
Mar. 4, 1833	Inauguration	Hall of the House [10]	President Andrew Jackson.
Dec. 31, 1834	Joint session	Lafayette eulogy	Representative and former President John Quincy Adams; ceremony attended by President Andrew Jackson.
24th CONGRESS			
Feb. 8, 1837	...do	Counting electoral votes	N.A.
25th CONGRESS			
Mar. 4, 1837	Inauguration	East Portico	President Martin Van Buren.
26th CONGRESS			
Feb. 10, 1841	Joint session	Counting electoral votes	N.A.
27th CONGRESS			
Mar. 4, 1841	Inauguration	East Portico	President William Henry Harrison.
28th CONGRESS			
Feb. 12, 1845	Joint session	Counting electoral votes	N.A.
29th CONGRESS			
Mar. 4, 1845	Inauguration	East Portico	President James Knox Polk.
30th CONGRESS			
Feb. 14, 1849	Joint session	Counting electoral votes	N.A.
31st CONGRESS			
Mar. 5, 1849	Inauguration	East Portico	President Zachary Taylor.
July 10, 1850	Joint session	Oath of office to President Millard Fillmore.[11]	N.A.
32d CONGRESS			
Jan. 5, 1852	Senate	Reception	Louis Kossuth, exiled Governor of Hungary.
Jan. 7, 1852	House	Remarks and Reception	Do.
Feb. 9, 1853	Joint session	Counting electoral votes	N.A.
33d CONGRESS			
Mar. 4, 1853	Inauguration	East Portico	President Franklin Pierce.
34th CONGRESS			
Feb. 11, 1857	Joint session	Counting electoral votes	N.A.
35th CONGRESS			
Mar. 4, 1857	Inauguration	East Portico	President James Buchanan.
36th CONGRESS			
Feb. 13, 1861	Joint session	Counting electoral votes	N.A.
37th CONGRESS			
Mar. 4, 1861	Inauguration	East Portico	President Abraham Lincoln.
Feb. 22, 1862	Joint session	Reading of Washington's farewell address.	John W. Forney, Secretary of the Senate.
38th CONGRESS			
Feb. 8, 1865	...do	Counting electoral votes	N.A.
39th CONGRESS			
Mar. 4, 1865	Inauguration	East Portico	President Abraham Lincoln.
Feb. 12, 1866	Joint session	Memorial to Abraham Lincoln	George Bancroft, historian; ceremony attended by President Andrew Johnson.
40th CONGRESS			
June 9, 1868	House	Address	Anson Burlingame, Envoy to the U.S. from China, and former Representative.
Feb. 10, 1869	Joint session	Counting electoral votes	N.A.
41st CONGRESS			
Mar. 4, 1869	Inauguration	East Portico	President Ulysses S. Grant.
42d CONGRESS			
Mar. 6, 1872	House	Address	Tomomi Iwakura, Ambassador from Japan.
Feb. 12, 1873	Joint session	Counting electoral votes [12]	N.A.
43d CONGRESS			
Mar. 4, 1873	Inauguration	East Portico	President Ulysses S. Grant.
Dec. 18, 1874	Joint meeting	Reception and Remarks	Speaker James G. Blaine; David Kalakaua, King of the Hawaiian Islands.[13]

JOINT SESSIONS AND MEETINGS, ADDRESSES TO THE SENATE OR THE HOUSE, AND INAUGURATIONS—CONTINUED

[See notes at end of table]

Congress and Date	Type	Occasion, topic, or inaugural location	Name and position of dignitary (where applicable)
44th CONGRESS			
Feb. 1, 1877	Joint session	Counting electoral votes [14]	N.A.
Feb. 10, 1877			
Feb. 12, 1877			
Feb. 19, 1877			
Feb. 20, 1877			
Feb. 21, 1877			
Feb. 24, 1877			
Feb. 26, 1877			
Feb. 28, 1877			
Mar. 1, 1877			
Mar. 2, 1877			
45th CONGRESS			
Mar. 5, 1877	Inauguration	East Portico	President Rutherford B. Hayes.
46th CONGRESS			
Feb. 2, 1880	House	Address	Charles Stewart Parnell, member of Parliament from Ireland.
Feb. 9, 1881	Joint session	Counting electoral votes	N.A.
47th CONGRESS			
Mar. 4, 1881	Inauguration	East Portico	President James A. Garfield.
Feb. 27, 1882	Joint session	Memorial to James A. Garfield	James G. Blaine, former Speaker, Senator, and Secretary of State; ceremony attended by President Chester A. Arthur.
48th CONGRESS			
Feb. 11, 1885	...do	Counting electoral votes	N.A.
Feb. 21, 1885	...do	Completion of Washington Monument	Representative John D. Long; Representative-elect John W. Daniel,[15] ceremony attended by President Chester A. Arthur.
49th CONGRESS			
Mar. 4, 1885	Inauguration	East Portico	President Grover Cleveland.
50th CONGRESS			
Feb. 13, 1889	Joint session	Counting electoral votes	N.A.
51st CONGRESS			
Mar. 4, 1889	Inauguration	East Portico	President Benjamin Harrison.
Dec. 11, 1889	Joint session	Centennial of George Washington's first inauguration.	Melville W. Fuller, Chief Justice of the United States; ceremony attended by President Benjamin Harrison.
52d CONGRESS			
Feb. 8, 1893	...do	Counting electoral votes	N.A.
53d CONGRESS			
Mar. 4, 1893	Inauguration	East Portico	President Grover Cleveland.
54th CONGRESS			
Feb. 10, 1897	Joint session	Counting electoral votes	N.A.
55th CONGRESS			
Mar. 4, 1897	Inauguration	In front of original Senate Wing of Capitol.	President William McKinley.
56th CONGRESS			
Dec. 12, 1900	Joint meeting	Centennial of the Capital City	Representatives James D. Richardson and Sereno E. Payne, and Senator George F. Hoar; ceremony attended by President William McKinley.
Feb. 13, 1901	Joint session	Counting electoral votes	N.A.
57th CONGRESS			
Mar. 4, 1901	Inauguration	East Portico	President William McKinley.
Feb. 27, 1902	Joint session	Memorial to William McKinley	John Hay, Secretary of State; ceremony attended by President Theodore Roosevelt and Prince Henry of Prussia.
58th CONGRESS			
Feb. 8, 1905	...do	Counting electoral votes	N.A.
59th CONGRESS			
Mar. 4, 1905	Inauguration	East Portico	President Theodore Roosevelt.
60th CONGRESS			
Feb. 10, 1909	Joint session	Counting electoral votes	N.A.
61st CONGRESS			
Mar. 4, 1909	Inauguration	Senate Chamber [16]	President William Howard Taft.

JOINT SESSIONS AND MEETINGS, ADDRESSES TO THE SENATE OR THE HOUSE, AND INAUGURATIONS—CONTINUED

[See notes at end of table]

Congress and Date	Type	Occasion, topic, or inaugural location	Name and position of dignitary (where applicable)
Feb. 9, 1911	House	Address	Count Albert Apponyi, Minister of Education from Hungary.
62d CONGRESS			
Feb. 12, 1913	Joint session	Counting electoral votes	N.A.
Feb. 15, 1913	...do	Memorial for Vice President James S. Sherman.[17]	Senators Elihu Root, Thomas S. Martin, Jacob H. Gallinger, John R. Thornton, Henry Cabot Lodge, John W. Kern, Robert M. LaFollette, John Sharp Williams, Charles Curtis, Albert B. Cummins, George T. Oliver, James A. O'Gorman; Speaker Champ Clark; President William Howard Taft.
63d CONGRESS			
Mar. 4, 1913	Inauguration	East Portico	President Woodrow Wilson.
Apr. 8, 1913	Joint session	Tariff message	Do.
June 23, 1913	...do	Currency and bank reform message	Do.
Aug. 27, 1913	...do	Mexican affairs message	Do.
Dec. 2, 1913	...do	Annual Message	Do.
Jan. 20, 1914	...do	Trusts message	Do.
Mar. 5, 1914	...do	Panama Canal tolls	Do.
Apr. 20, 1914	...do	Mexico message	Do.
Sept. 4, 1914	...do	War tax message	Do.
Dec. 8, 1914	...do	Annual Message	Do.
64th CONGRESS			
Dec. 7, 1915	...do	...do	Do.
Aug. 29, 1916	...do	Railroad message (labor-management dispute).	Do.
Dec. 5, 1916	...do	Annual Message	Do.
Jan. 22, 1917	Senate	Planning ahead for peace	Do.
Feb. 3, 1917	Joint session	Severing diplomatic relations with Germany.	Do.
Feb. 14, 1917	...do	Counting electoral votes	N.A.
Feb. 26, 1917	...do	Arming of merchant ships	President Woodrow Wilson.
65th CONGRESS			
Mar. 5, 1917	Inauguration	East Portico	Do.
Apr. 2, 1917	Joint session	War with Germany	Do.
May 1, 1917	Senate	Address	René Raphaël Viviani, Minister of Justice from France; Jules Jusserand, Ambassador from France; address attended by Marshal Joseph Jacques Césaire Joffre, member of French Commission to U.S.
May 3, 1917	House	...do	Do.
May 5, 1917	...do	...do	Arthur James Balfour, British Secretary of State for Foreign Affairs.
May 8, 1917	Senate	...do	Do.
May 31, 1917	...do	...do	Ferdinando di'Savoia, Prince of Udine, Head of Italian Mission to U.S.
June 2, 1917	House	...do	Ferdinando di'Savoia, Prince of Udine, Head of Italian Mission to U.S.; Guglielmo Marconi, member of Italian Mission to U.S.
June 22, 1917	Senate	Address	Baron Moncheur, Chief of Political Bureau of Belgian Foreign Office at Havre.
June 23, 1917	House	...do	Boris Bakhmetieff, Ambassador from Russia.[18]
June 26, 1917	Senate	...do	Do.
June 27, 1917	House	...do	Baron Moncheur, Chief of Political Bureau of Belgian Foreign Office at Havre.
Aug. 30, 1917	Senate	...do	Kikujirō Ishii, Ambassador from Japan.
Sept. 5, 1917	House	...do	Do.
Dec. 4, 1917	Joint session	Annual Message/War with Austria-Hungary.	President Woodrow Wilson.
Jan. 4, 1918	...do	Federal operation of transportation systems.	Do.
Jan. 5, 1918	Senate	Address	Milenko Vesnic, Head of Serbian War Mission.
Jan. 8, 1918	House	...do	Do.
Do	Joint session	Program for world's peace	President Woodrow Wilson.
Feb. 11, 1918	...do	Peace message	Do.
May 27, 1918	...do	War finance message	Do.
Sept. 24, 1918	Senate	Address and Reception[19]	Jules Jusserand, Ambassador from France; Vice President Thomas R. Marshall.
Sept. 30, 1918	...do	Support of woman suffrage	President Woodrow Wilson.
Nov. 11, 1918	Joint session	Terms of armistice signed by Germany	Do.

JOINT SESSIONS AND MEETINGS, ADDRESSES TO THE SENATE OR THE HOUSE, AND INAUGURATIONS—CONTINUED

[See notes at end of table]

Congress and Date	Type	Occasion, topic, or inaugural location	Name and position of dignitary (where applicable)
Dec. 2, 1918	...do	Annual Message	Do.
Feb. 9, 1919	...do	Memorial to Theodore Roosevelt	Senator Henry Cabot Lodge, Sr.; ceremony attended by former President William Howard Taft.
66th CONGRESS			
June 23, 1919	Senate	Address	Epitácio da Silva Pessoa, President-elect of Brazil.
July 10, 1919	...do	Versailles Treaty	President Woodrow Wilson.
Aug. 8, 1919	Joint session	Cost of living message	Do.
Sept. 18, 1919	...do	Address	President pro tempore Albert B. Cummins; Speaker Frederick H. Gillett; Representative and former Speaker Champ Clark; General John J. Pershing.
Oct. 28, 1919	Senate	...do	Albert I, King of the Belgians.
Do	House	...do	Do.
Feb. 9, 1921	Joint session	Counting electoral votes	N.A.
67th CONGRESS			
Mar. 4, 1921	Inauguration	East Portico	President Warren G. Harding.
Apr. 12, 1921	Joint session	Federal problem message	Do.
July 12, 1921	Senate	Adjusted compensation for veterans of the World War [20].	Do.
Dec. 6, 1921	Joint session	Annual Message	Do.
Feb. 28, 1922	...do	Maintenance of the merchant marine	Do.
Aug. 18, 1922	...do	Coal and railroad message	Do.
Nov. 21, 1922	...do	Promotion of the American merchant marine.	Do.
Dec. 8, 1922	...do	Annual Message [21]	Do.
Feb. 7, 1923	...do	British debt due to the United States	Do.
68th CONGRESS			
Dec. 6, 1923	...do	Annual Message	President Calvin Coolidge.
Feb. 27, 1924	...do	Memorial to Warren G. Harding	Charles Evans Hughes, Secretary of State; ceremony attended by President Calvin Coolidge.
Dec. 15, 1924	...do	Memorial to Woodrow Wilson	Dr. Edwin Anderson Alderman, President of the University of Virginia; ceremony attended by President Calvin Coolidge.
Feb. 11, 1925	...do	Counting electoral votes	N.A.
69th CONGRESS			
Mar. 4, 1925	Inauguration	East Portico	President Calvin Coolidge.
Feb. 22, 1927	Joint session	George Washington birthday message	Do.
70th CONGRESS			
Jan. 25, 1928	House	Reception and Address	William Thomas Cosgrave, President of Executive Council of Ireland.
Feb. 13, 1929	Joint session	Counting electoral votes	N.A.
71st CONGRESS			
Mar. 4, 1929	Inauguration	East Portico	President Herbert Hoover.
Oct. 7, 1929	Senate	Address	James Ramsay MacDonald, Prime Minister of the United Kingdom.
Jan. 13, 1930	...do	Reception	Jan Christiaan Smuts, former Prime Minister of South Africa.
72d CONGRESS			
Feb. 22, 1932	Joint session	Bicentennial of George Washington's birth.	President Herbert Hoover.
May 31, 1932	Senate	Emergency character of economic situation in U.S..	Do.
Feb. 6, 1933	Joint meeting	Memorial to Calvin Coolidge	Arthur Prentice Rugg, Chief Justice of the Supreme Judicial Court of Massachusetts; ceremony attended by President Herbert Hoover.
Feb. 8, 1933	Joint session	Counting electoral votes	N.A.
73d CONGRESS			
Mar. 4, 1933	Inauguration	East Portico	President Franklin Delano Roosevelt.
Jan. 3, 1934	Joint session	Annual Message	Do.
May 20, 1934	...do	100th anniversary, death of Lafayette	André de Laboulaye, Ambassador of France; President Franklin Delano Roosevelt; ceremony attended by Count de Chambrun, great-grandson of Lafayette.
74th CONGRESS			
Jan. 4, 1935	...do	Annual Message	President Franklin Delano Roosevelt.
May 22, 1935	...do	Veto message	Do.
Jan. 3, 1936	...do	Annual Message	Do.

JOINT SESSIONS AND MEETINGS, ADDRESSES TO THE SENATE OR THE HOUSE, AND INAUGURATIONS—CONTINUED

[See notes at end of table]

Congress and Date	Type	Occasion, topic, or inaugural location	Name and position of dignitary (where applicable)
75th CONGRESS			
Jan. 6, 1937	...do	Counting electoral votes	N.A.
Do	...do	Annual Message	President Franklin Delano Roosevelt.
Jan. 20, 1937	Inauguration	East Portico	President Franklin Delano Roosevelt; Vice President John Nance Garner.[22]
Apr. 1, 1937	Senate	Address	John Buchan, Lord Tweedsmuir, Governor General of Canada.
Do	House	...do	Do.
Jan. 3, 1938	Joint session	Annual Message	President Franklin Delano Roosevelt.
76th CONGRESS			
Jan. 4, 1939	...do	...do	Do.
Mar. 4, 1939	...do	Sesquicentennial of the 1st Congress	Do.
May 8, 1939	Senate	Address	Anastasio Somoza Garcia, President of Nicaragua.
Do	House	...do	Do.
June 9, 1939	Joint meeting	Reception[23]	George VI and Elizabeth, King and Queen of the United Kingdom.
Sept. 21, 1939	Joint session	Neutrality address	President Franklin Delano Roosevelt.
Jan. 3, 1940	...do	Annual Message	Do.
May 16, 1940	...do	National defense message	Do.
77th CONGRESS			
Jan. 6, 1941	...do	Counting electoral votes	N.A.
Do	...do	Annual Message	President Franklin Delano Roosevelt.
Jan. 20, 1941	...do	Inauguration, East Portico	President Franklin Delano Roosevelt; Vice President Henry A. Wallace.
Dec. 8, 1941	...do	War with Japan	President Franklin Delano Roosevelt.
Dec. 26, 1941	Joint meeting[24]	Address	Winston Churchill, Prime Minister of the United Kingdom.
Jan. 6, 1942	Joint session	Annual Message	President Franklin Delano Roosevelt.
May 11, 1942	Senate	Address	Manuel Prado, President of Peru.
Do	House	...do	Do.
June 2, 1942	...do	...do	Manuel Luis Quezon, President of the Philippines.[25]
June 4, 1942	Senate	...do	Do.
June 15, 1942	...do	...do	George II, King of Greece.[26]
Do	House	...do	Do.
June 25, 1942	Senate	...do	Peter II, King of Yugoslavia.[26]
Do	House	...do	Do.
Aug. 6, 1942	Senate[27]	...do	Wilhelmina, Queen of the Netherlands.[26]
Nov. 24, 1942	House	...do	Carlos Arroyo del Río, President of Ecuador.
Nov. 25, 1942	Senate	...do	Do.
Dec. 10, 1942	House	...do	Fulgencio Batista, President of Cuba.
78th CONGRESS			
Jan. 7, 1943	Joint session	Annual Message	President Franklin Delano Roosevelt.
Feb. 18, 1943	Senate	Remarks	Madame Chiang Kai-shek, of China.
Do	House	Address	Do.
May 6, 1943	Senate	Address	Enrique Peñaranda, President of Bolivia.
Do	House	...do	Do.
May 13, 1943	Senate	...do	Edvard Beneš, President of Czechoslovakia.[26]
Do	House	...do	Do.
May 19, 1943	Joint meeting	...do	Winston Churchill, Prime Minister of the United Kingdom.
May 27, 1943	Senate	Remarks	Edwin Barclay, President of Liberia.
Do	House	Address	Do.
June 10, 1943	Senate	...do	President Hininio Moríñigo M., President of Paraguay.
Do	House	...do	Do.
Oct. 15, 1943	Senate	...do	Elie Lescot, President of Haiti.
Nov. 18, 1943	Joint meeting	Moscow Conference	Cordell Hull, Secretary of State.
Jan. 20, 1944	Senate	Address	Isaías Medina Angarita, President of Venezuela.
Do	House	...do	Do.
79th CONGRESS			
Jan. 6, 1945	Joint session	Counting electoral votes	N.A.
Do	...do	Annual Message	President Roosevelt was not present. His message was read before the Joint Session of Congress.
Jan. 20, 1945	Inauguration	South Portico, The White House[28]	President Franklin Delano Roosevelt; Vice President Harry S. Truman.
Mar. 1, 1945	Joint session	Yalta Conference	President Franklin Delano Roosevelt.
Apr. 16, 1945	...do	Prosecution of the War	President Harry S. Truman.
May 21, 1945	...do	Bestowal of Congressional Medal of Honor on Tech. Sgt. Jake William Lindsey.	General George C. Marshall, Chief of Staff, U.S. Army; President Harry S. Truman.

JOINT SESSIONS AND MEETINGS, ADDRESSES TO THE SENATE OR THE HOUSE, AND INAUGURATIONS—CONTINUED

[See notes at end of table]

Congress and Date	Type	Occasion, topic, or inaugural location	Name and position of dignitary (where applicable)
June 18, 1945	Joint meeting	Address	General Dwight D. Eisenhower, Supreme Commander, Allied Expeditionary Force.
July 2, 1945	Senate	United Nations Charter	President Harry S. Truman.
Oct. 5, 1945	Joint meeting	Address	Admiral Chester W. Nimitz, Commander-in-Chief, Pacific Fleet.
Oct. 23, 1945	Joint session	Universal military training message	President Harry S. Truman.
Nov. 13, 1945	Joint meeting	Address	Clement R. Attlee, Prime Minister of the United Kingdom.
May 25, 1946	Joint session	Railroad strike message	President Harry S. Truman.
July 1, 1946	...do	Memorial to Franklin Delano Roosevelt	John Winant, U.S. Representative on the Economic and Social Council of the United Nations; ceremony attended by President Harry S. Truman and Mrs. Franklin Delano Roosevelt.
80th CONGRESS			
Jan. 6, 1947	...do	State of the Union Address [29]	President Harry S. Truman.
Mar. 12, 1947	...do	Greek-Turkish aid policy	Do.
May 1, 1947	Joint meeting	Address	Miguel Alemán, President of Mexico.
Nov. 17, 1947	Joint session	Aid to Europe message	President Harry S. Truman.
Jan. 7, 1948	...do	State of the Union Address	Do.
Mar. 17, 1948	...do	National security and conditions in Europe.	Do.
Apr. 19, 1948	...do	50th anniversary, liberation of Cuba	President Harry S. Truman; Guillermo Belt, Ambassador of Cuba.
July 27, 1948	...do	Inflation, housing, and civil rights	President Harry S. Truman.
81st CONGRESS			
Jan. 5, 1949	...do	State of the Union Address	Do.
Jan. 6, 1949	...do	Counting electoral votes	N.A.
Jan. 20, 1949	...do	Inauguration, East Portico	President Harry S. Truman; Vice President Alben W. Barkley.
May 17, 1949	House	Reception	General Lucius D. Clay.
Do	Senate	Address	Do.
May 19, 1949	Joint meeting	...do	Eurico Gaspar Dutra, President of Brazil.
Aug. 9, 1949	House	...do	Elpidio Quirino, President of the Philippines.
Do	Senate	...do	Do.
Oct. 13, 1949	...do	...do	Jawaharlal Nehru, Prime Minister of India.
Do	House	...do	Do.
Jan. 4, 1950	Joint session	State of the Union Address	President Harry S. Truman.
Apr. 13, 1950	Senate	Address	Gabriel González-Videla, President of Chile.
May 4, 1950	...do	...do	Liaquat Ali Khan, Prime Minister of Pakistan.
Do	House	...do	Do.
May 31, 1950	Joint meeting	...do	Dean Acheson, Secretary of State.
July 28, 1950	Senate	Address	Chōjirō Kuriyama, member of Japanese Diet.
July 31, 1950	House	...do	Tokutarō Kitamura, member of Japanese Diet.
Aug. 1, 1950	...do	...do	Robert Gordon Menzies, Prime Minister of Australia.
Do	Senate	...do	Do.
82d CONGRESS			
Jan. 8, 1951	Joint session	State of the Union Address	President Harry S. Truman.
Feb. 1, 1951	Joint meeting [30]	North Atlantic Treaty Organization	General Dwight D. Eisenhower.
Apr. 2, 1951	...do	Address	Vincent Auriol, President of France.
Apr. 19, 1951	...do	Return from Pacific Command	General Douglas MacArthur.
June 21, 1951	...do	Address	Galo Plaza, President of Ecuador.
July 2, 1951	Senate	Addresses	Tadao Kuraishi, and Aisuke Okamoto, members of Japanese Diet.
Aug. 23, 1951	...do	Address	Zentarō Kosaka, member of Japanese Diet.
Sept. 24, 1951	Joint meeting	...do	Alcide de Gasperi, Prime Minister of Italy.
Jan. 9, 1952	Joint session	State of the Union Address	President Harry S. Truman.
Jan. 17, 1952	Joint meeting	Address	Winston Churchill, Prime Minister of the United Kingdom.
Apr. 3, 1952	...do	...do	Juliana, Queen of the Netherlands.
May 22, 1952	...do	Korea	General Matthew B. Ridgway.
June 10, 1952	Joint session	Steel industry dispute	President Harry S. Truman.
83d CONGRESS			
Jan. 6, 1953	...do	Counting electoral votes	N.A.
Jan. 20, 1953	...do	Inauguration, East Portico	President Dwight D. Eisenhower; Vice President Richard M. Nixon.
Feb. 2, 1953	...do	State of the Union Address	President Dwight D. Eisenhower.

JOINT SESSIONS AND MEETINGS, ADDRESSES TO THE SENATE OR THE HOUSE, AND INAUGURATIONS—CONTINUED

[See notes at end of table]

Congress and Date	Type	Occasion, topic, or inaugural location	Name and position of dignitary (where applicable)
Jan. 7, 1954	...do	...do	Do.
Jan. 29, 1954	Joint meeting	Address	Celal Bayar, President of Turkey.
May 4, 1954	...do	...do	Vincent Massey, Governor General of Canada.
May 28, 1954	...do	...do	Haile Selassie I, Emperor of Ethiopia.
July 28, 1954	...do	...do	Syngman Rhee, President of South Korea.
Nov. 12, 1954	Senate	Remarks	Shigeru Yoshida, Prime Minister of Japan.
Nov. 17, 1954	..do	Address [31]	Sarvepalli Radhakrishnan, Vice President of India.
Nov. 18, 1954	...do	Remarks	Pierre Mendès-France, Premier of France.
84th CONGRESS			
Jan. 6, 1955	Joint session	State of the Union Address	President Dwight D. Eisenhower.
Jan. 27, 1955	Joint meeting	Address	Paul E. Magliore, President of Haiti.
Mar. 16, 1955	Senate	...do	Robert Gordon Menzies, Prime Minister of Australia.
Do	House	...do	Do.
Mar. 30, 1955	Senate	...do	Mario Scelba, Prime Minister of Italy.
Do	House	...do	Do.
May 4, 1955	Senate	...do	P. Phibunsongkhram, Prime Minister of Thailand.
Do	House	...do	Do.
June 30, 1955	Senate	...do	U Nu, Prime Minister of Burma.
Do	House	...do	Do.
Jan. 5, 1956	Senate	...do	Juscelino Kubitschek de Oliverira, President-elect of Brazil.
Feb. 2, 1956	...do	...do	Anthony Eden, Prime Minister of the United Kingdom.
Do	House	...do	Do.
Feb. 29, 1956	Joint meeting	...do	Giovanni Gronchi, President of Italy.
Mar. 15, 1956	Senate	...do	John Aloysius Costello, Prime Minister of Ireland.
Do	House	...do	Do.
Apr. 30, 1956	Senate	...do	João Goulart, Vice President of Brazil.
May 17, 1956	Joint meeting	...do	Sukarno, President of Indonesia.
85th CONGRESS			
Jan. 5, 1957	Joint session	Middle East message	President Dwight D. Eisenhower.
Jan. 7, 1957	...do	Counting electoral votes	N.A.
Jan. 10, 1957	...do	State of the Union Address	President Dwight D. Eisenhower.
Jan. 21, 1957	...do	Inauguration, East Portico	President Dwight D. Eisenhower; Vice President Richard M. Nixon.
Feb. 27, 1957	House	Address	Guy Mollet, Premier of France.
Do	Senate	...do	Do.
May 9, 1957	Joint meeting	...do	Ngo Dinh Diem, President of Vietnam.
May 28, 1957	House	Address	Konrad Adenauer, Chancellor of West Germany.
Do	Senate	...do	Do.
June 20, 1957	...do	...do	Nobusuke Kishi, Prime Minister of Japan.
Do	House	...do	Do.
July 11, 1957	Senate	...do	Husseyn Shaheed Suhrawardy, Prime Minister of Pakistan.
Jan. 9, 1958	Joint session	State of the Union Address	President Dwight D. Eisenhower.
June 5, 1958	Joint meeting	Address	Theodor Heuss, President of West Germany.
June 10, 1958	Senate	...do	Harold Macmillan, Prime Minister of the United Kingdom.
June 18, 1958	Joint meeting	...do	Carlos F. Garcia, President of the Philippines.
June 25, 1958	House	...do	Muhammad Daoud Khan, Prime Minister of Afghanistan.
Do	Senate	...do	Do.
July 24, 1958	...do	...do	Kwame Nkrumah, Prime Minister of Ghana.
July 25, 1958	House	...do	Do.
July 29, 1958	Senate	...do	Amintore Fanfani, Prime Minister of Italy.
Do	House	...do	Do.
86th CONGRESS			
Jan. 9, 1959	Joint session	State of the Union Address	President Dwight D. Eisenhower.
Jan. 21, 1959	Joint meeting	Address	Arturo Frondizi, President of Argentina.
Feb. 12, 1959	Joint session	Sesquicentennial of Abraham Lincoln's birth.	Fredric March, actor; Carl Sandburg, poet.
Mar. 11, 1959	Joint meeting	Address	Jose Maria Lemus, President of El Salvador.
Mar. 18, 1959	...do	...do	Sean T. O'Kelly, President of Ireland.
May 12, 1959	...do	...do	Baudouin, King of the Belgians.
Jan. 7, 1960	Joint session	State of the Union Address	President Dwight D. Eisenhower.

JOINT SESSIONS AND MEETINGS, ADDRESSES TO THE SENATE OR THE HOUSE, AND INAUGURATIONS—CONTINUED

[See notes at end of table]

Congress and Date	Type	Occasion, topic, or inaugural location	Name and position of dignitary (where applicable)
Mar. 30, 1960	Senate	Address	Harold Macmillan, Prime Minister of the United Kingdom.
Apr. 6, 1960	Joint meeting	...do	Alberto Lleras-Camargo, President of Colombia.
Apr. 25, 1960	...do	...do	Charles de Gaulle, President of France.
Apr. 28, 1960	...do	...do	Mahendra, King of Nepal.
June 29, 1960	...do	...do	Bhumibol Adulyadej, King of Thailand.
87th CONGRESS			
Jan. 6, 1961	Joint session	Counting electoral votes	N.A.
Jan. 20, 1961	...do	Inauguration, East Portico	President John F. Kennedy; Vice President Lyndon B. Johnson.
Jan. 30, 1961	...do	State of the Union Address	President John F. Kennedy.
Apr. 13, 1961	Senate	Remarks	Konrad Adenauer, Chancellor of West Germany.
Apr. 18, 1961	House	Address	Constantine Karamanlis, Prime Minister of Greece.
May 4, 1961	Joint meeting	...do	Habib Bourguiba, President of Tunisia.
May 25, 1961	Joint session	Urgent national needs: foreign aid, defense, civil defense, and outer space.	President John F. Kennedy.
June 22, 1961	Senate	Remarks	Hayato Ikeda, Prime Minister of Japan.
Do	House	Address	Do.
July 12, 1961	Joint meeting	...do	Mohammad Ayub Khan, President of Pakistan.
July 26, 1961	House	...do	Abubakar Tafawa Balewa, Prime Minister of Nigeria.
Sept. 21, 1961	Joint meeting	...do	Manuel Prado, President of Peru.
Jan. 11, 1962	Joint session	State of the Union Address	President John F. Kennedy.
Feb. 26, 1962	Joint meeting	Friendship 7: 1st United States orbital space flight.	Lt. Col. John H. Glenn, Jr., USMC; Friendship 7 astronaut.
Apr. 4, 1962	...do	Address	João Goulart, President of Brazil.
Apr. 12, 1962	...do	...do	Mohammad Reza Shah Pahlavi, Shahanshah of Iran.
88th CONGRESS			
Jan. 14, 1963	Joint session	State of the Union Address	President John F. Kennedy.
May 21, 1963	Joint meeting	Flight of Faith 7 Spacecraft	Maj. Gordon L. Cooper, Jr., USAF, Faith 7 astronaut.
Oct. 2, 1963	Senate	Address	Haile Selassie I, Emperor of Ethiopia.
Nov. 27, 1963	Joint session	Assumption of office	President Lyndon B. Johnson.
Jan. 8, 1964	...do	State of the Union Address	Do.
Jan. 15, 1964	Joint meeting	Address	Antonio Segni, President of Italy.
May 28, 1964	...do	...do	Eamon de Valera, President of Ireland.
89th CONGRESS			
Jan. 4, 1965	Joint session	State of the Union Address	President Lyndon B. Johnson.
Jan. 6, 1965	Joint session	Counting electoral votes	N.A.
Jan. 20, 1965	...do [32]	Inauguration, East Portico	President Lyndon B. Johnson; Vice President Hubert H. Humphrey.
Mar. 15, 1965	...do	Voting rights	President Lyndon B. Johnson.
Sept. 14, 1965	Joint meeting	Flight of Gemini 5 Spacecraft	Lt. Col. Gordon L. Cooper, Jr., USAF; and Charles Conrad, Jr., USN; Gemini 5 astronauts.
Jan. 12, 1966	Joint session	State of the Union Address	President Lyndon B. Johnson.
Sept. 15, 1966	Joint meeting	Address	Ferdinand E. Marcos, President of the Philippines.
90th CONGRESS			
Jan. 10, 1967	Joint session	State of the Union Address	President Lyndon B. Johnson.
Apr. 28, 1967	Joint meeting	Vietnam policy	General William C. Westmoreland.
Aug. 16, 1967	Senate	Address	Kurt George Kiesinger, Chancellor of West Germany.
Oct. 27, 1967	Joint meeting	...do	Gustavo Diaz Ordaz, President of Mexico.
Jan. 17, 1968	Joint session	State of the Union Address	President Lyndon B. Johnson.
91st CONGRESS			
Jan. 6, 1969	...do	Counting electoral votes [33]	N.A.
Jan. 9, 1969	Joint meeting	Apollo 8: 1st flight around the moon	Col. Frank Borman, USAF; Capt. James A. Lowell, Jr., USN; Lt. Col. William A. Anders, USAF; Apollo 8 astronauts.
Jan. 14, 1969	Joint session	State of the Union Address	President Lyndon B. Johnson.
Jan. 20, 1969	...do [32]	Inauguration, East Portico	President Richard M. Nixon; Vice President Spiro T. Agnew.
Sept. 16, 1969	Joint meeting	Apollo 11: 1st lunar landing	Neil A. Armstrong; Col. Edwin E. Aldrin, Jr., USAF; and Lt. Col. Michael Collins, USAF; Apollo 11 astronauts.
Nov. 13, 1969	House	Executive-Legislative branch relations and Vietnam policy.	President Richard M. Nixon.
Do	Senate	...do	Do.
Jan. 22, 1970	Joint session	State of the Union Address	Do.

JOINT SESSIONS AND MEETINGS, ADDRESSES TO THE SENATE OR THE HOUSE, AND INAUGURATIONS—CONTINUED

[See notes at end of table]

Congress and Date	Type	Occasion, topic, or inaugural location	Name and position of dignitary (where applicable)
Feb. 25, 1970	Joint meeting	Address	Georges Pompidou, President of France.
June 3, 1970	...do	...do	Rafael Caldera, President of Venezuela.
Sept. 22, 1970	...do	Report on prisoners of war	Col. Frank Borman, Representative to the President on Prisoners of War.
92d CONGRESS			
Jan. 22, 1971	Joint session	State of the Union Address	President Richard M. Nixon.
Sept. 9, 1971	...do	Economic policy	Do.
Do	Joint meeting	Apollo 15: lunar mission	Col. David R. Scott, USAF; Col. James B. Irwin, USAF; and Lt. Col. Alfred M. Worden, USAF; Apollo 15 astronauts.
Jan. 20, 1972	Joint session	State of the Union Address	President Richard M. Nixon.
June 1, 1972	...do	European trip report	Do.
June 15, 1972	Joint meeting	Address	Luis Echeverria Alvarez, President of Mexico.
93d CONGRESS			
Jan. 6, 1973	Joint session	Counting electoral votes	N.A.
Jan. 20, 1973	Inauguration	East Portico	President Richard M. Nixon; Vice President Spiro T. Agnew.
Dec. 6, 1973	Joint meeting	Oath of office to, and Address by Vice President Gerald R. Ford.	Vice President Gerald R. Ford; ceremony attended by President Richard M. Nixon.
Do	Senate	Remarks and Reception	Vice President Gerald R. Ford.
Jan. 30, 1974	Joint session	State of the Union Address	President Richard M. Nixon.
Aug. 12, 1974	...do	Assumption of office	President Gerald R. Ford.
Oct. 8, 1974	...do	Economy	Do.
Dec. 19, 1974	Senate	Address [34]	Vice President Nelson A. Rockefeller.
94th CONGRESS			
Jan. 15, 1975	Joint session	State of the Union Address	President Gerald R. Ford.
Apr. 10, 1975	...do	State of the World message	Do.
June 17, 1975	Joint meeting	Address	Walter Scheel, President of West Germany.
Nov. 5, 1975	...do	...do	Anwar El Sadat, President of Egypt.
Jan. 19, 1976	Joint session	State of the Union Address	President Gerald R. Ford.
Jan. 28, 1976	Joint meeting	Address	Yitzhak Rabin, Prime Minister of Israel.
Mar. 17, 1976	...do	...do	Liam CosgrAvenue, Prime Minister of Ireland.
May 18, 1976	...do	...do	Valery Giscard d'Estaing, President of France.
June 2, 1976	...do	...do	Juan Carlos I, King of Spain.
Sept. 23, 1976	Joint meeting	Address	William R. Tolbert, Jr., President of Liberia.
95th CONGRESS			
Jan. 6, 1977	Joint session	Counting electoral votes	N.A.
Jan. 12, 1977	...do	State of the Union Address	President Gerald R. Ford.
Jan. 20, 1977	Inauguration	East Portico	President Jimmy Carter; Vice President Walter F. Mondale.
Feb. 17, 1977	House	Address	José López Portillo, President of Mexico.
Feb. 22, 1977	Joint meeting	...do	Pierre Elliot Trudeau, Prime Minister of Canada.
Apr. 20, 1977	Joint session	Energy	President Jimmy Carter.
Jan. 19, 1978	...do	State of the Union Address	Do.
Sept. 18, 1978	...do	Middle East Peace agreements	President Jimmy Carter; joint session attended by Anwar El Sadat, President of Egypt, and by Menachem Begin, Prime Minister of Israel.
96th CONGRESS			
Jan. 23, 1979	...do	State of the Union Address	Do.
June 18, 1979	...do	Salt II agreements	Do.
Jan. 23, 1980	...do	State of the Union Address	Do.
97th CONGRESS			
Jan. 6, 1981	...do	Counting electoral votes	N.A.
Jan. 20, 1981	...do [32]	Inauguration, West Front	President Ronald Reagan; Vice President George Bush.
Feb. 18, 1981	...do	Economic recovery	President Ronald Reagan.
Apr. 28, 1981	...do	Economic recovery—inflation	Do.
Jan. 26, 1982	...do	State of the Union Address	Do.
Jan. 28, 1982	Joint meeting	Centennial of birth of Franklin Delano Roosevelt.	Dr. Arthur Schlesinger, historian; Senator Jennings Randolph; Representative Claude Pepper; Averell Harriman, former Governor of New York [35]; former Representative James Roosevelt, son of President Roosevelt.
Apr. 21, 1982	...do	Address	Beatrix, Queen of the Netherlands.

JOINT SESSIONS AND MEETINGS, ADDRESSES TO THE SENATE OR THE HOUSE, AND INAUGURATIONS—CONTINUED

[See notes at end of table]

Congress and Date	Type	Occasion, topic, or inaugural location	Name and position of dignitary (where applicable)
98th CONGRESS			
Jan. 25, 1983	Joint session	State of the Union Address	President Ronald Reagan.
Apr. 27, 1983	...do	Central America	Do.
Oct. 5, 1983	Joint meeting	Address	Karl Carstens, President of West Germany.
Jan. 25, 1984	Joint session	State of the Union Address	President Ronald Reagan.
Mar. 15, 1984	Joint meeting	Address	Dr. Garett FitzGerald, Prime Minister of Ireland.
Mar. 22, 1984	...do	...do	François Mitterand, President of France.
May 8, 1984	...do	Centennial of birth of Harry S. Truman	Representatives Ike Skelton and Alan Wheat; former Senator Stuart Symington; Margaret Truman Daniel, daughter of President Truman; and Senator Mark Hatfield.
May 16, 1984	...do	Address	Miguel de la Madrid, President of Mexico.
99th CONGRESS			
Jan. 7, 1985	Joint session	Counting electoral votes	N.A.
Jan. 21, 1985	Inauguration	Rotunda [36]	President Ronald Reagan; Vice President George Bush.
Feb. 6, 1985	Joint session	State of the Union Address	President Ronald Reagan.
Feb. 20, 1985	Joint meeting	Address	Margaret Thatcher, Prime Minister of the United Kingdom.
Mar. 6, 1985	...do	...do	Bettino Craxi, President of the Council of Ministers of Italy.
Mar. 20, 1985	...do	...do	Raul Alfonsin, President of Argentina.
June 13, 1985	...do	...do	Rajiv Gandhi, Prime Minister of India.
Oct. 9, 1985	...do	...do	Lee Kuan Yew, Prime Minister of Singapore.
Nov. 21, 1985	Joint session	Geneva Summit	President Ronald Reagan.
Feb. 4, 1986	...do	State of the Union Address	Do.
Sept. 11, 1986	Joint meeting	Address	Jose Sarney, President of Brazil.
Sept. 18, 1986	...do	...do	Corazon C. Aquino, President of the Philippines.
100th CONGRESS			
Jan. 27, 1987	Joint session	State of the Union Address	President Ronald Reagan.
Nov. 10, 1987	Joint meeting	Address	Chaim Herzog, President of Israel.
Jan. 25, 1988	Joint session	State of the Union Address	President Ronald Reagan.
Apr. 27, 1988	Joint meeting	Address	Brian Mulroney, Prime Minister of Canada.
June 23, 1988	Joint meeting	Address	Robert Hawke, Prime Minister of Australia.
101st CONGRESS			
Jan. 4, 1989	Joint session	Counting electoral votes	N.A.
Jan. 20, 1989	Inauguration	West Front	President George Bush; Vice President Dan Quayle.
Feb. 9, 1989	Joint session	Building a Better America	President George Bush.
Mar. 2, 1989	Joint meeting	Bicentennial of the 1st Congress	President Pro Tempore Robert C. Byrd; Speaker James C. Wright, Jr.; Representatives Lindy Boggs, Thomas S. Foley, and Robert H. Michel; Senators George Mitchell and Robert Dole; Howard Nemerov, Poet Laureate of the United States; David McCullough, historian; Anthony M. Frank, Postmaster General; former Senator Nicholas Brady, Secretary of the Treasury.
Apr. 6, 1989	Senate [37]	Addresses on the 200th anniversary commemoration of Senate's first legislative session.	Former Senators Thomas F. Eagleton and Howard H. Baker, Jr.
June 7, 1989	Joint meeting	Address	Benazir Bhutto, Prime Minister of Pakistan.
Oct. 4, 1989	...do	...do	Carlos Salinas de Gortari, President of Mexico.
Oct. 18, 1989	...do	...do	Roh Tae Woo, President of South Korea.
Nov. 15, 1989	...do	...do	Lech Walesa, chairman of Solidarność labor union, Poland.
Jan. 31, 1990	Joint session	State of the Union Address	President George Bush.
Feb. 21, 1990	Joint meeting	Address	Vaclav Hável, President of Czechoslovakia.
Mar. 7, 1990	...do	...do	Giulio Andreotti, President of the Council of Ministers of Italy.

JOINT SESSIONS AND MEETINGS, ADDRESSES TO THE SENATE OR THE HOUSE, AND INAUGURATIONS—CONTINUED

[See notes at end of table]

Congress and Date	Type	Occasion, topic, or inaugural location	Name and position of dignitary (where applicable)
Mar. 27, 1990	...do	Centennial of birth of Dwight D. Eisenhower.	Senator Robert Dole; Walter Cronkite, television journalist; Winston S. Churchill, member of British Parliament and grandson of Prime Minister Churchill; Clark M. Clifford, former Secretary of Defense; James D. Robinson III, chairman of Eisenhower Centennial Foundation; Arnold Palmer, professional golfer; John S.D. Eisenhower, former Ambassador to Belgium and son of President Eisenhower; Representatives Beverly Byron, William F. Goodling, and Pat Roberts.
June 26, 1990	...do	Address	Nelson Mandela, Deputy President of the African National Congress, South Africa.
Sept. 11, 1990	Joint session	Invasion of Kuwait by Iraq	President George Bush.
102d CONGRESS			
Jan. 29, 1991	...do	State of the Union Address	Do.
Mar. 6, 1991	...do	Conclusion of Persian Gulf War	Do.
Apr. 16, 1991	Joint meeting	Address	Violeta B. de Chamorro, President of Nicaragua.
May 8, 1991	House [38]	...do	General H. Norman Schwarzkopf.
May 16, 1991	Joint meeting	...do	Elizabeth II, Queen of the United Kingdom; joint meeting also attended by Prince Philip.
Nov. 14, 1991	...do	...do	Carlos Saul Menem, President of Argentina.
Jan. 28, 1992	Joint session	State of the Union Address	President George Bush.
Apr. 30, 1992	Joint meeting	Address	Richard von Weizsäcker, President of Germany.
June 17, 1992	...do	...do	Boris Yeltsin, President of Russia.
103d CONGRESS			
Jan. 6, 1993	Joint session	Counting electoral votes	N.A.
Jan. 20, 1993	Inauguration	West Front	President William J. Clinton; Vice President Albert Gore.
Feb. 17, 1993	Joint session	Economic Address [39]	President William J. Clinton.
Sept. 22, 1993	...do	Health care reform	Do.
Jan. 25, 1994	...do	State of the Union Address	Do.
May 18, 1994	Joint meeting	Address	Narasimha Rao, Prime Minister of India.
July 26, 1994	...do	Addresses	Hussein I, King of Jordan; Yitzhak Rabin, Prime Minister of Israel.
Oct. 6, 1994	...do	Address	Nelson Mandela, President of South Africa.
104th CONGRESS			
Jan. 24, 1995	Joint session	State of the Union Address	President William J. Clinton.
July 26, 1995	Joint meeting	Address	Kim Yong-sam, President of South Korea.[40]
Oct. 11, 1995	...do	Close of the Commemoration of the 50th Anniversary of World War II.	Speaker Newt Gingrich; Vice President Albert Gore; President Pro Tempore Strom Thurmond; Representatives Henry J. Hyde and G.V. "Sonny" Montgomery; Senators Daniel K. Inouye and Robert Dole; former Representative Robert H. Michel; General Louis H. Wilson (ret.), former Commandant of the Marine Corps.
Dec. 12, 1995	...do	Address	Shimon Peres, Prime Minister of Israel.
Jan. 30, 1996	Joint session	State of the Union Address	President William J. Clinton.
Feb. 1, 1996	Joint meeting	Address	Jacques Chirac, President of France.
July 10, 1996	...do	...do	Binyamin Netanyahu, Prime Minister of Israel.
Sept. 11, 1996	...do	...do	John Bruton, Prime Minister of Ireland.
105th CONGRESS			
Jan. 9, 1997	Joint session	Counting electoral votes	N.A.
Jan. 20, 1997	Inauguration	West Front	President William J. Clinton; Vice President Albert Gore.
Feb. 4, 1997	Joint session	State of the Union Address [41]	President William J. Clinton.
Feb. 27, 1997	Joint meeting	Address	Eduardo Frei, President of Chile.
Jan. 27, 1998	Joint session	State of the Union Address	President William J. Clinton.
June 10, 1998	Joint meeting	Address	Kim Dae-jung, President of South Korea.
July 15, 1998	...do	...do	Emil Constantinescu, President of Romania.
106th CONGRESS			
Jan. 19, 1999	Joint session	State of the Union Address	President William J. Clinton.
Jan. 27, 2000	...do	...do	Do.

JOINT SESSIONS AND MEETINGS, ADDRESSES TO THE SENATE OR THE HOUSE, AND INAUGURATIONS—CONTINUED

[See notes at end of table]

Congress and Date	Type	Occasion, topic, or inaugural location	Name and position of dignitary (where applicable)
Sept. 14, 2000	Joint meeting	Address	Atal Bihari Vajpayee, Prime Minister of India.
107th CONGRESS			
Jan. 6, 2001	Joint session	Counting electoral votes	N.A.
Jan. 20, 2001	Inauguration	West Front	President George W. Bush; Vice President Richard B. Cheney.
Feb. 27, 2001	Joint session	Budget message [39]	President George W. Bush.
Sept. 6, 2001	Joint meeting	Address	Vicente Fox, President of Mexico.
Sept. 20, 2001	Joint session	War on terrorism	President George W. Bush; joint session attended by Tony Blair, Prime Minister of the United Kingdom, by Tom Ridge, Governor of Pennsylvania, by George Pataki, Governor of New York, and by Rudolph Giuliani, Mayor of New York City.
Jan. 29, 2002	...do	State of the Union Address	President George W. Bush; joint session attended by Hamid Karzai, Chairman of the Interim Authority of Afghanistan.
June 12, 2002	Joint meeting	Address [42]	John Howard, Prime Minister of Australia.
108th CONGRESS			
Jan. 28, 2003	Joint session	State of the Union Address	President George W. Bush.
July 17, 2003	Joint meeting	Address	Tony Blair, Prime Minister of the United Kingdom; joint meeting attended by Mrs. George W. Bush.
Jan. 20, 2004	Joint session	State of the Union Address	President George W. Bush.
Feb. 4, 2004	Joint meeting	Address	Jose Maria Aznar, President of the Government of Spain.
June 15, 2004	...do	...do	Hamid Karzai, President of Afghanistan.
Sept. 23, 2004	...do	...do	Ayad Allawi, Interim Prime Minister of Iraq.
109th CONGRESS			
Jan. 6, 2005	Joint session	Counting electoral votes [43]	N.A.
Jan. 20, 2005	Inauguration	West Front	President George W. Bush; Vice President Richard B. Cheney.
Feb. 2, 2005	Joint session	State of the Union Address	President George W. Bush.
Apr. 6, 2005	Joint meeting	Address	Viktor Yushchenko, President of Ukraine.
July 19, 2005	...do	...do	Dr. Manmohan Singh, Prime Minister of India.
Jan. 31, 2006	Joint session	State of the Union Address	President George W. Bush.
Mar. 1, 2006	Joint meeting	Address	Silvio Berlusconi, Prime Minister of Italy.
Mar. 15, 2006	Joint meeting	Address	Ellen Johnson Sirleaf, President of Liberia.
May 24, 2006	...do	...do	Ehud Olmert, Prime Minister of Israel.
June 7, 2006	...do	...do	Dr. Vaira Vike-Freiberga, President of Latvia.
July 26, 2006	...do	...do	Nouri Al-Maliki, Prime Minister of Iraq.
110th CONGRESS			
Jan. 23, 2007	Joint session	State of the Union Address	President George W. Bush.
Mar. 7, 2007	Joint meeting	Address	Abdullah II Ibn Al Hussein, King of Jordan.
Nov. 7, 2007	...do	...do	Nicolas Sarkozy, President of France.
Jan. 28, 2008	Joint session	State of the Union Address	President George W. Bush.
Apr. 30, 2008	Joint meeting	Address	Bertie Ahern, Prime Minister of Ireland.
111th CONGRESS			
Jan. 8, 2009	Joint session	Counting electoral votes	N.A.
Jan. 20, 2009	Inauguration	West Front	President Barack H. Obama; Vice President Joseph R. Biden, Jr.
Feb. 24, 2009	Joint session	Economic Address	President Barack H. Obama.
Mar. 4, 2009	Joint meeting	...do	Gordon Brown, Prime Minister of the United Kingdom.
Sept. 9, 2009	Joint session	Health care reform	President Barack H. Obama.
Nov. 2, 2009	Joint meeting	Address	Angela Merkel, Chancellor of Germany.
Jan. 27, 2010	Joint session	State of the Union Address	President Barack H. Obama.
May 20, 2010	Joint meeting	Address	Felipe Calderon Hinojosa, President of Mexico.
112th CONGRESS			
Jan. 25, 2011	Joint session	State of the Union Address	President Barack H. Obama.
Mar. 9, 2011	Joint meeting	Address	Julia Gillard, Prime Minister of Australia.
May 24, 2011	...do	...do	Binyamin Netanyahu, Prime Minister of Israel.
Sept. 8, 2011	Joint session	American Jobs Act	President Barack H. Obama.
Oct. 13, 2011	Joint meeting	Address	Lee Myung-bak, President of the Republic of Korea.

JOINT SESSIONS AND MEETINGS, ADDRESSES TO THE SENATE OR THE HOUSE, AND INAUGURATIONS—CONTINUED

[See notes at end of table]

Congress and Date	Type	Occasion, topic, or inaugural location	Name and position of dignitary (where applicable)
Jan. 24, 2012	Joint session	State of the Union Address	President Barack H. Obama.
113th CONGRESS			
Jan. 4, 2013	...do	Counting electoral votes	N.A.
Jan. 21, 2013	Inauguration	West Front	President Barack H. Obama; Vice President Joseph R. Biden, Jr.
Feb. 12, 2013	Joint session	State of the Union Address	President Barack H. Obama.
May 8, 2013	Joint meeting	Address	Park Geun-hye, President of the Republic of Korea.
Jan. 28, 2014	Joint session	State of the Union Address	President Barack H. Obama.
Sept. 18, 2014	Joint meeting	Address	Petro Poroshenko, President of Ukraine.
114th CONGRESS			
Jan. 20, 2015	Joint session	State of the Union Address	President Barack H. Obama.
Mar. 3, 2015	Joint meeting	Address	Binyamin Netanyahu, Prime Minister of Israel.
Mar. 25, 2015	...do	...do	Mohammad Ashraf Ghani, President of the Islamic Republic of Afghanistan.
Apr. 29, 2015	...do	...do	Shinzo Abe, Prime Minister of Japan.
Sept. 24, 2015	...do	...do	Pope Francis of the Holy See.
Jan. 12, 2016	Joint session	State of the Union Address	President Barack H. Obama.
June 12, 2016	Joint meeting	Address	Narendra Modi, Prime Minister of the Republic of India.
115th CONGRESS			
Jan. 6, 2017	Joint session	Counting electoral votes	N.A.
Jan. 20, 2017	Inauguration	West Front	President Donald J. Trump; Vice President Mike Pence.
Feb. 28, 2017	Joint meeting	Address	President Donald J. Trump.
Jan. 30, 2018	Joint Session	State of the Union Address	President Donald J. Trump.
Apr. 25, 2018	Joint Meeting	Address	Emmanuel Macron, President of France.
116th CONGRESS			
Feb. 5, 2019	Joint Session	State of the Union Address	President Donald J. Trump.
Apr. 3, 2019	Joint Meeting	Address	Secretary General Jens Stoltenberg, North Atlantic Treaty Organization (NATO).
Feb. 4, 2020	Joint Session	State of the Union Address	President Donald J. Trump.

[1] Closing date for this table was July 22, 2020.

[2] The oath of office was administered to George Washington outside on the gallery in front of the Senate Chamber, after which the Congress and the President returned to the chamber to hear the inaugural address. They then proceeded to St. Paul's Chapel for the "divine service" performed by the Chaplain of the Congress. Adjournment of the ceremony did not occur until the Congress returned to Federal Hall.

[3] Funeral oration was delivered at the German Lutheran Church in Philadelphia.

[4] Because of a tie in the electoral vote between Thomas Jefferson and Aaron Burr, the House of Representatives had to decide the election. Thirty-six ballots were required to break the deadlock, with Jefferson's election as President and Burr's as Vice President on February 17. The Twelfth Amendment was added to the Constitution to prevent the 1800 problem from recurring.

[5] During most of the period while the Capitol was being reconstructed following the fire of 1814, the Congress met in the "Brick Capitol," constructed on the site of the present Supreme Court building. This joint session took place in the Representatives' chamber on the 2d floor of the building.

[6] The joint session to count electoral votes was dissolved because the House and Senate disagreed on Missouri's status regarding statehood. The joint session was reconvened the same day and Missouri's votes were counted.

[7] While this occasion has historically been referred to as the first joint meeting of Congress, the Journals of the House and Senate indicate that Lafayette actually addressed the House of Representatives, with some of the Senators present as guests of the House (having been invited at the last minute to attend). Similar occasions, when members of the one body were invited as guests of the other, include the Senate address by Queen Wilhelmina of the Netherlands on Aug. 6, 1942, and the House address by General H. Norman Schwarzkopf on May 8, 1991.

[8] Although Andrew Jackson won the popular vote by a substantial amount and had the highest number of electoral votes from among the several candidates, he did not receive the required majority of the electoral votes. The responsibility for choosing the new President therefore devolved upon the House of Representatives. As soon as the Senators left the chamber, the balloting proceeded, and John Quincy Adams was elected on the first ballot.

[9] The ceremony was moved outside to accommodate the extraordinarily large crowd of people who had come to Washington to see the inauguration.

[10] The ceremony was moved inside because of cold weather.

[11] Following the death of President Zachary Taylor, Vice President Millard Fillmore took the Presidential oath of office in a special joint session in the Hall of the House.

[12] The joint session to count electoral votes was dissolved three times so that the House and Senate could resolve several electoral disputes.

[13] Because of a severe cold and hoarseness, the King could not deliver his speech, which was read by former Representative Elisha Hunt Allen, then serving as Chancellor and Chief Justice of the Hawaiian Islands.

[14] The contested election between Rutherford B. Hayes and Samuel J. Tilden created a constitutional crisis. Tilden won the popular vote by a close margin, but disputes concerning the electoral vote returns from four states deadlocked the proceedings of the joint session. Anticipating this development, the Congress had created a special commission of five Senators, five Representatives, and five Supreme Court Justices to resolve such disputes. The Commission met in the Supreme Court Chamber (the present Old Senate Chamber) as each problem arose. In each case, the Commission accepted the Hayes electors, securing his election by one electoral vote. The joint session was convened on 15 occasions, with the last on March 2, just three days before the inauguration.

[15] The speech was written by former Speaker and Senator Robert C. Winthrop, who could not attend the ceremony because of ill health.

[16] Because of a blizzard, the ceremony was moved inside, where it was held as part of the Senate's special session. President William Howard Taft took the oath of office and gave his inaugural address after Vice President James S. Sherman's inaugural address and the swearing-in of the new senators.

[17] Held in the Senate Chamber.

[18] Bakhmetieff represented the provisional government of Russia set up after the overthrow of the monarchy in March 1917 and recognized by the United States. The Bolsheviks took over in November 1917.

[19] The address and reception were in conjunction with the presentation to the Senate by France of two Sèvres vases in appreciation of the United States' involvement in World War I. The vases are today in the Senate lobby, just off the Senate floor. Two additional Sèvres vases were given without ceremony to the House of Representatives, which today are in the Rayburn Room, not far from the floor of the House.

[20] Senators later objected to President Harding's speech (given with no advance notice to most of the Senators) as an unconstitutional effort to interfere with the deliberations of the Senate, and Harding did not repeat visits of this kind.

[21] This was the first Annual Message broadcast live on radio.

[22] This was the first inauguration held pursuant to the Twentieth Amendment, which changed the date from March 4 to January 20. The Vice Presidential oath, which previously had been given earlier on the same day in the Senate Chamber, was added to the inaugural ceremony as well, but the Vice Presidential inaugural address was discontinued.

[23] A joint reception for the King and Queen of the United Kingdom was held in the Rotunda, authorized by Senate Concurrent Resolution 17, 76th Congress. Although the concurrent resolution was structured to establish a joint meeting, the Senate, in fact, adjourned rather than recessed as called for by the resolution.

[24] Held in the Senate Chamber.

[25] At this time, the Philippines was still a possession of the United States, although it had been made a self-governing commonwealth in 1935, in preparation for full independence in 1946. From 1909 to 1916, Quezon had served in the U.S. House of Representatives as the resident commissioner from the Philippines.

[26] In exile.

[27] For this Senate Address by Queen Wilhelmina, the members of the House of Representatives were invited as guests. This occasion has sometimes been mistakenly referred to as a joint meeting.

[28] The oaths of office were taken in simple ceremonies at the White House because the expense and festivity of a Capitol ceremony were thought inappropriate because of the war. The Joint Committee on Arrangements of the Congress was in charge, however, and both the Senate and the House of Representatives were present.

[29] This was the first time the term "State of the Union Address" was used for the President's Annual Message. Also, it was the first time the address was shown live on television.

[30] This was an informal meeting in the Coolidge Auditorium of the Library of Congress.

[31] Presentation of new ivory gavel to the Senate.

[32] According to the Congressional Record, the Senate adjourned prior to the inaugural ceremonies, even though the previously adopted resolution had stated the adjournment would come immediately following the inauguration. The Senate Journal records the adjournment as called for in the resolution, hence this listing as a joint session.

[33] The joint session to count electoral votes was dissolved so that the House and Senate could each resolve the dispute regarding a ballot from North Carolina. The joint session was reconvened the same day and the North Carolina vote was counted.

[34] Rockefeller was sworn in as Vice President by Chief Justice Warren E. Burger, after which, by unanimous consent, he was allowed to address the Senate.

[35] Because the Governor had laryngitis, his speech was read by his wife, Pamela.

[36] The ceremony was moved inside because of extremely cold weather.

[37] These commemorative addresses were given in the Old Senate Chamber during a regular legislative session.

[38] For this House Address by General Schwarzkopf, the members of the Senate were invited as guests.

[39] This speech was mislabeled in many sources as a State of the Union Address.

[40] President Kim Yong-sam was in Washington for the dedication of the Korean Veterans' Memorial, held the day after this joint meeting.

[41] This was the first State of the Union Address carried live on the Internet.

[42] Prime Minister Howard was originally scheduled to address a joint meeting on September 12, 2001, but because of the attack on the United States on September 11, 2001, the event was postponed until this occasion.

[43] The joint session to count electoral votes was dissolved so that the House and Senate could each discuss the dispute regarding the ballots from Ohio. The joint session was reconvened the same day and the Ohio votes were counted.

REPRESENTATIVES UNDER EACH APPORTIONMENT

The original apportionment of Representatives was assigned in 1787 in the Constitution and remained in effect for the 1st and 2d Congresses. Subsequent apportionments based on the censuses over the years have been figured using several different methods approved by Congress, all with the goal of dividing representation among the states as equally as possible. After each census up to and including the thirteenth in 1910, Congress would enact a law designating the specific changes in the actual number of Representatives as well as the increase in the ratio of persons-per-Representative. After having made no apportionment after the Fourteenth census in 1920, Congress by statute in 1929 fixed the total number of Representatives at 435 (the number attained with the apportionment after the 1910 census), and since that time, only the ratio of persons-per-Representative has continued to increase, in fact, significantly so. Since the total is now fixed, the specific number of Representatives per state is adjusted after each census to reflect its percentage of the entire population. Since the Sixteenth Census in 1940, the "equal proportions" method of apportioning Representatives within the 435 total has been employed. A detailed explanation of the entire apportionment process can be found in *The Historical Atlas of United States Congressional Districts, 1789–1983*. Kenneth C. Martis, The Free Press, New York, 1982.

State	Constitutional apportionment	First Census, 1790	Second Census, 1800	Third Census, 1810	Fourth Census, 1820	Fifth Census, 1830	Sixth Census, 1840	Seventh Census, 1850	Eighth Census, 1860	Ninth Census, 1870	Tenth Census, 1880	Eleventh Census, 1890	Twelfth Census, 1900	Thirteenth Census, 1910	Fifteenth Census, 1930 [1]	Sixteenth Census, 1940	Seventeenth Census, 1950	Eighteenth Census, 1960	Nineteenth Census, 1970	Twentieth Census, 1980	Twenty-First Census, 1990	Twenty-Second Census, 2000	Twenty-Third Census, 2010
AL	...	...	...	[2]	3	5	7	7	6	8	8	9	9	10	9	9	9	8	7	7	7	7	7
AK	...	...	...	...	...	...	...	...	...	...	...	...	...	...	...	...	[2,3]	1	1	1	1	1	1
AZ	...	...	...	...	...	...	...	...	...	...	...	...	[2]	[4]1	1	2	2	3	4	5	6	8	9
AR	...	...	...	...	...	[2]	1	2	3	4	5	6	7	7	7	7	6	4	4	4	4	4	4
CA	...	...	...	...	...	...	[2]	[4]2	3	4	6	7	8	11	20	23	30	38	43	45	52	53	53
CO	...	...	...	...	...	...	...	...	...	[2]	1	2	3	4	4	4	4	4	5	6	6	7	7
CT	5	7	7	7	6	6	4	4	4	4	4	4	5	5	6	6	6	6	6	6	6	5	5
DE	1	1	1	2	1	1	1	1	1	1	1	1	1	1	1	1	1	1	1	1	1	1	1
FL	...	...	...	...	...	...	[2]	1	1	2	2	2	3	4	5	6	8	12	15	19	23	25	27
GA	3	2	4	6	7	9	8	8	7	9	10	11	11	12	10	10	10	10	10	10	11	13	14
HI	...	...	...	...	...	...	...	...	...	...	...	...	...	...	...	...	[2,3]	2	2	2	2	2	2
ID	...	...	...	...	...	...	...	...	...	...	[2]	1	1	2	2	2	2	2	2	2	2	2	2
IL	...	...	...	[2]	1	3	7	9	14	19	20	22	25	27	27	26	25	24	24	22	20	19	18
IN	...	...	...	[2]	3	7	10	11	11	13	13	13	13	13	12	11	11	11	11	10	10	9	9
IA	...	...	...	...	...	...	[2]	2	6	9	11	11	11	11	9	8	8	7	6	6	5	5	4
KS	...	...	...	...	...	...	...	[2]	[4]1	3	7	8	8	8	7	6	6	5	5	5	4	4	4
KY	[2]	[4]2	6	10	12	13	10	10	9	10	11	11	11	11	9	9	8	7	7	7	6	6	6
LA	...	...	...	[2]	3	3	4	4	5	6	6	6	7	8	8	8	8	8	8	8	7	7	6
ME	...	...	...	[5]	7	8	7	6	5	5	4	4	4	4	3	3	3	2	2	2	2	2	2
MD	6	8	9	9	9	8	6	6	5	6	6	6	6	6	6	6	7	8	8	8	8	8	8
MA	8	14	17	[5]20	13	12	10	11	10	11	12	13	14	16	15	14	14	12	12	11	10	10	9
MI	...	...	...	...	...	[2]	3	4	6	9	11	12	12	13	17	17	18	19	19	18	16	15	14
MN	...	...	...	...	...	...	...	[2]	2	3	5	7	9	10	9	9	9	8	8	8	8	8	8
MS	...	...	...	[2]	1	2	4	5	5	6	7	7	8	8	7	7	6	5	5	5	5	4	4
MO	...	...	...	[2]	[4]1	2	5	7	9	13	14	15	16	16	13	13	11	10	10	9	9	9	8
MT	...	...	...	...	...	...	...	...	...	...	[2]	1	1	2	2	2	2	2	2	2	1	1	1
NE	...	...	...	...	...	...	...	...	[2]	1	3	6	6	6	5	4	4	3	3	3	3	3	3
NV	...	...	...	...	...	...	...	...	[2]	1	1	1	1	1	1	1	1	1	1	2	2	3	4
NH	3	4	5	6	6	5	4	3	3	3	2	2	2	2	2	2	2	2	2	2	2	2	2
NJ	4	5	6	6	6	6	5	5	5	7	7	8	10	12	14	14	14	15	15	14	13	13	12
NM	...	...	...	...	...	...	...	...	...	...	...	...	[2]	[4]1	1	2	2	2	2	3	3	3	3
NY	6	10	17	27	34	40	34	33	31	33	34	34	37	43	45	45	43	41	39	34	31	29	27
NC	5	10	12	13	13	13	9	8	7	8	9	9	10	10	11	12	12	11	11	11	12	13	13
ND	...	...	...	...	...	...	...	...	...	...	[2]	1	2	3	2	2	2	2	1	1	1	1	1
OH	...	...	[2]	6	14	19	21	21	19	20	21	21	21	22	24	23	23	24	23	21	19	18	16
OK	...	...	...	...	...	...	...	...	...	...	...	...	[2]	8	9	8	6	6	6	6	6	5	5
OR	...	...	...	...	...	...	...	[2]	1	1	1	2	2	3	3	4	4	4	4	5	5	5	5
PA	8	13	18	23	26	28	24	25	24	27	28	30	32	36	34	33	30	27	25	23	21	19	18
RI	1	2	2	2	2	2	2	2	2	2	2	2	2	3	2	2	2	2	2	2	2	2	2
SC	5	6	8	9	9	9	7	6	4	5	7	7	7	7	6	6	6	6	6	6	6	6	7
SD	...	...	...	...	...	...	...	...	...	...	[2]	2	2	3	2	2	2	2	2	1	1	1	1
TN	...	[2]	3	6	9	13	11	10	8	10	10	10	10	10	9	10	9	9	8	9	9	9	9
TX	...	...	...	...	...	...	[2]	2	4	6	11	13	16	18	21	21	22	23	24	27	30	32	36
UT	...	...	...	...	...	...	...	...	...	...	...	[2]	1	2	2	2	2	2	2	3	3	3	4
VT	[2]	[4]2	4	6	5	5	4	3	3	3	2	2	2	2	1	1	1	1	1	1	1	1	1
VA	10	19	22	23	22	21	15	13	[6]11	9	10	10	10	10	9	9	10	10	10	10	11	11	11
WA	...	...	...	...	...	...	...	...	...	...	[2]	2	3	5	6	6	7	7	7	8	9	9	10
WV	...	...	...	...	...	...	...	...	[6]	3	4	4	5	6	6	6	6	5	4	4	3	3	3
WI	...	...	...	...	...	...	[2]	3	6	8	9	10	11	11	10	10	10	10	9	9	9	8	8
WY	...	...	...	...	...	...	...	...	...	...	[2]	1	1	1	1	1	1	1	1	1	1	1	1
Total	65	105	141	181	213	240	223	234	241	292	325	356	386	435	435	435	435	435	435	435	435	435	435

NOTE: Information for table obtained from the U.S. Census Bureau.

[1] No apportionment was made after the 1920 census.

[2] The following Representatives were added after the indicated apportionments when these states were admitted in the years listed. The number of these additional Representatives for each state remained in effect until the next census's apportionment (with the exceptions of California and New Mexico, as explained in footnote 4). They are not included in the total for each column. In reading this table, please remember that the apportionments made after each census took effect with the election two years after the census date. As a result, in the table footnote 2 is placed for several states under the decade preceding the one in which it entered the Union, since the previous decade's apportionment was still in effect at the time of statehood. *Constitutional:* Vermont (1791), 2; Kentucky (1792), 2; *First:* Tennessee (1796), 1; *Second:* Ohio (1803), 1; *Third:* Louisiana (1812), 1; Indiana (1816), 1; Mississippi (1817), 1; Illinois (1818), 1; Alabama (1819), 1; Missouri (1821), 1; *Fifth:* Arkansas (1836), 1; Michigan (1837), 1; *Sixth:* Florida (1845), 1; Texas (1845), 2; Iowa (1846), 2; Wisconsin (1848), 2; California (1850), 2; *Seventh:* Minnesota (1858), 2; Oregon (1859), 1; Kansas (1861), 1; *Eighth:* Nevada (1864), 1; Nebraska (1867), 1; *Ninth:* Colorado (1876), 1; *Tenth:* North Dakota (1889), 1; South Dakota (1889), 2; Montana (1889), 1; Washington (1889), 1; Idaho (1890), 1; Wyoming (1890), 1; *Eleventh:* Utah (1896), 1; *Twelth:* Oklahoma (1907), 5; New Mexico (1912), 2; Arizona (1912), 1; *Seventeenth:* Alaska (1959), 1; Hawaii (1959), 1.

[3] When Alaska and then Hawaii joined the Union in 1959, the law was changed to allow the total membership of the House of Representatives to increase to 436 and then to 437, apportioning one new Representative for each of those states. The total returned to 435 in 1963, when the 1960 census apportionment took effect.

[4] Even though the respective censuses were taken before the following states joined the Union, Representatives for them were apportioned either because of anticipation of statehood or because they had become states in the period between the census and the apportionment, hence they are included in the totals of the respective columns. *First:* Vermont (1791); Kentucky (1792); *Fourth:* Missouri (1821); *Seventh:* California (1850); *Eighth:* Kansas (1861); *Thirteenth:* New Mexico (1912); Arizona (1912). (Please note: These seven states are also included in footnote 2 because they became states while the previous decade's apportionment was still in effect for the House of Representatives.) California's situation was unusual. It was scheduled for inclusion in the figures for the 1850 census apportionment; however, when the apportionment law was passed in 1852, California's census returns were still incomplete so Congress made special provision that the state would retain "the number of Representatives [two] prescribed by the act of admission * * * into the Union until a new apportionment [i.e., after the 1860 census]" would be made. The number of Representatives from California actually increased before the next apportionment to three when Congress gave the state an extra Representative during part of the 37th Congress, from 1862 to 1863. Regarding New Mexico, the 1911 apportionment law, passed by the 62d Congress in response to the 1910 census and effective with the 63d Congress in 1913, stated that "if the Territor[y] of * * * New Mexico shall become [a State] in the Union before the apportionment of Representatives under the next decennial census [it] shall have one Representative * * *." When New Mexico became a state in 1912 during the 62d Congress, it was given two Representatives. The number was decreased to one beginning the next year in the 63d.

[5] The "Maine District" of Massachusetts became a separate state during the term of the 16th Congress, in 1820. For the remainder of that Congress, Maine was assigned one "at large" Representative while Massachusetts continued to have 20 Representatives, the number apportioned to it after the 1810 census. For the 17th Congress (the last before the 1820 census apportionment took effect), seven of Massachusetts's Representatives were reassigned to Maine, leaving Massachusetts with 13.

[6] Of the 11 Representatives apportioned to Virginia after the 1860 census, three were reassigned to West Virginia when that part of Virginia became a separate state in 1863. Since the Virginia seats in the House were vacant at that time because of the Civil War, all of the new Representatives from West Virginia were able to take their seats at once. When Representatives from Virginia reentered the House in 1870, only eight members represented it.

IMPEACHMENT PROCEEDINGS

The provisions of the United States Constitution which apply specifically to impeachments are as follows: Article I, section 2, clause 5; Article I, section 3, clauses 6 and 7; Article II, section 2, clause 1; Article II, section 4; and Article III, section 2, clause 3.

For the officials listed below, the date of impeachment by the House of Representatives is followed by the dates of the Senate trial, with the result of each listed at the end of the entry.

WILLIAM BLOUNT, a Senator of the United States from Tennessee; impeached July 7, 1797; tried Monday, December 17, 1798, to Monday, January 14, 1799; charges dismissed for want of jurisdiction.

JOHN PICKERING, judge of the United States District Court for the District of New Hampshire; impeached March 2, 1803; tried Thursday, March 3, 1803, to Monday, March 12, 1804; removed from office.

SAMUEL CHASE, Associate Justice of the Supreme Court of the United States; impeached March 12, 1804; tried Friday, November 30, 1804, to Friday, March 1, 1805; acquitted.

JAMES H. PECK, judge of the United States District Court for the District of Missouri; impeached April 24, 1830; tried Monday, April 26, 1830, to Monday, January 31, 1831; acquitted.

WEST H. HUMPHREYS, judge of the United States District Court for the Middle, Eastern, and Western Districts of Tennessee; impeached May 6, 1862; tried Wednesday, May 7, 1862, to Thursday, June 26, 1862; removed from office and disqualified from future office.

ANDREW JOHNSON, President of the United States; impeached February 24, 1868; tried Tuesday, February 25, 1868, to Tuesday, May 26, 1868; acquitted.

MARK DELAHAY, judge of the United States District Court of Kansas; impeached February 28, 1873; resigned office Friday, December 12, 1873, before the Senate trial was held, with no further action taken by the Senate.

WILLIAM W. BELKNAP, Secretary of War; impeached March 2, 1876; tried Friday, March 3, 1876, to Tuesday, August 1, 1876; acquitted.

CHARLES SWAYNE, judge of the United States District Court for the Northern District of Florida; impeached December 13, 1904; tried Wednesday, December 14, 1904, to Monday, February 27, 1905; acquitted.

ROBERT W. ARCHBALD, associate judge, United States Commerce Court; impeached July 11, 1912; tried Saturday, July 13, 1912, to Monday, January 13, 1913; removed from office and disqualified from future office.

GEORGE W. ENGLISH, judge of the United States District Court for the Eastern District of Illinois; impeached April 1, 1926; tried Friday, April 23, 1926, to Monday, December 13, 1926; resigned office Thursday, November 4, 1926; Court of Impeachment adjourned to December 13, 1926, when, on request of House managers, the proceedings were dismissed.

HAROLD LOUDERBACK, judge of the United States District Court for the Northern District of California; impeached February 24, 1933; tried Monday, May 15, 1933, to Wednesday, May 24, 1933; acquitted.

HALSTED L. RITTER, judge of the United States District Court for the Southern District of Florida; impeached March 2, 1936; tried Monday, April 6, 1936, to Friday, April 17, 1936; removed from office.

HARRY E. CLAIBORNE, judge of the United States District Court of Nevada; impeached July 22, 1986; tried Tuesday, October 7, 1986, to Thursday, October 9, 1986; removed from office.

ALCEE L. HASTINGS, judge of the United States District Court for the Southern District of Florida; impeached August 3, 1988; tried Wednesday, October 18, 1989, to Friday, October 20, 1989; removed from office.

WALTER L. NIXON, judge of the United States District Court for the Southern District of Mississippi; impeached May 10, 1989; tried Wednesday, November 1, 1989, to Friday, November 3, 1989; removed from office.

WILLIAM JEFFERSON CLINTON, President of the United States; impeached December 19, 1998; tried Thursday, January 7, 1999, to Friday, February 12, 1999; acquitted.

SAMUEL B. KENT, judge of the United States District Court for the Southern District of Texas; impeached June 19, 2009; resigned office effective Tuesday, June 30, 2009; Court of Impeachment convened on Wednesday, July 22, 2009, when, on request of House managers, proceedings were dismissed.

G. THOMAS PORTEOUS, Jr., judge of the United States District Court for the Eastern District of Louisiana; impeached March 11, 2010; tried Tuesday, December 7, 2010, to Wednesday, December 8, 2010; removed from office and disqualified from future office.

DONALD J. TRUMP, President of the United States; impeached December 18, 2019; tried Thursday, January 16, 2020, to Wednesday, February 5, 2020; acquitted.

REPRESENTATIVES, SENATORS, DELEGATES, AND RESIDENT COMMISSIONERS SERVING IN THE 1st–116th CONGRESSES *

Since the U.S. Congress convened on March 4, 1789, 12,351 individuals have served as Representatives, Senators, or in both capacities. There have been 10,366 Members who served only as Representatives, 1,307 Members who served only in the Senate, and 677 Members with service in both chambers. The total number of Representatives (including individuals serving in both bodies) is 11,040. The total number of Senators (including individuals serving in both bodies) is 1,984.

These numbers do not include statutory representatives: Resident Commissioners and Delegates. An additional 145 people have served only as Territorial Delegates in the House and 33 people have served only as Resident Commissioners from Puerto Rico or the Philippines.

State/Territory	Date Became a U.S. Territory	Date Entered the Union	Delegates (Only)	Resident Commis-sioners [1]	Representatives (Only) [2]	Representa-tives and Delegates	Senators (Only) [3]	Senators and Representa-tives [4]	Senators and Delegates	Senators, Representa-tives, and Delegates	Total House Members
Alabama	Mar. 3, 1817	Dec. 14, 1819 (22d)	0	0	169	1	29	13	0	0	183
Alaska	Aug. 24, 1912	Jan. 3, 1959 (49th)	7	0	4	0	7	0	1	0	12
American Samoa	Apr. 17, 1900		3	0	0	0	0	0	0	0	3
Arizona	Feb. 24, 1863	Feb. 14, 1912 (48th)	10	0	36	0	5	6	2	0	54
Arkansas	Mar. 2, 1819	June 15, 1836 (25th)	2	0	87	0	22	12	1	0	102
California		Sept. 9, 1850 (31st)	0	0	369	0	35	9	0	0	378
Colorado	Feb. 28, 1861	Aug. 1, 1876 (38th)	2	0	61	0	23	10	2	1	76
Connecticut		Jan. 9, 1788 (5th)	0	0	210	0	29	26	0	0	236
Delaware		Dec. 7, 1787 (1st)	0	0	63	0	37	14	0	0	77
District of Columbia	July 16, 1790		3	0	0	0	0	0	0	0	3
Florida	Mar. 20, 1822	Mar. 3, 1845 (27th)	4	0	145	0	28	6	1	0	156
Georgia		Jan. 2, 1788 (4th)	0	0	287	0	40	22	0	0	309
Guam	Apr. 11, 1899		5	0	0	0	0	0	0	0	5
Hawaii	June 14, 1900	Aug. 21, 1959 (50th)	10	0	10	0	3	4	0	0	24
Idaho	Mar. 3, 1863	July 3, 1890 (43d)	8	0	28	0	19	6	1	0	43
Illinois	Feb. 3, 1809	Dec. 3, 1818 (21st)	3	0	456	0	31	20	0	0	479
Indiana	May 7, 1800	Dec. 11, 1816 (19th)	2	0	304	1	28	19	0	0	326
Iowa	June 12, 1838	Dec. 28, 1846 (29th)	1	0	173	0	22	11	1	0	186
Kansas	May 30, 1854	Jan. 29, 1861 (34th)	2	0	112	0	24	9	0	0	123
Kentucky		June 1, 1792 (15th)	0	0	313	0	38	28	0	0	341
Louisiana [5]	Mar. 4, 1804	Apr. 30, 1812 (18th)	2	0	151	0	36	14	0	0	167
Maine		Mar. 15, 1820 (23d)	0	0	136	0	22	15	0	0	151
Mariana Islands	Apr. 11, 1899		1	0	0	0	0	0	0	0	1
Maryland		Apr. 28, 1788 (7th)	0	0	282	0	29	28	0	0	310
Massachusetts		Feb. 6, 1788 (6th)	0	0	406	0	24	29	0	0	435
Michigan	Jan. 11, 1805	Jan. 26, 1837 (26th)	5	0	267	0	23	14	1	1	288
Minnesota	Mar. 3, 1849	May 11, 1858 (32d)	2	0	128	0	29	10	1	0	141
Mississippi	Apr. 17, 1798	Dec. 10, 1817 (20th)	3	0	112	0	30	14	0	1	130
Missouri	June 4, 1812	Aug. 10, 1821 (24th)	2	0	293	1	36	10	0	0	306
Montana	May 26, 1864	Nov. 8, 1889 (41st)	5	0	27	0	15	6	0	1	39

Nebraska	May 30, 1854	Mar. 1, 1867 (37th)	5	0	88	0	31	6	1	0	100
Nevada	Mar. 2, 1861	Oct. 31, 1864 (36th)	2	0	33	0	20	7	0	0	42
New Hampshire		June 21, 1788 (9th)	0	0	138	0	38	26	0	0	164
New Jersey		Dec. 18, 1787 (3d)	0	0	329	0	51	15	0	0	344
New Mexico	Sept. 9, 1850	Jan. 6, 1912 (47th)	16	0	25	1	11	5	1	0	48
New York		July 26, 1788 (11th)	0	0	1,454	0	36	23	0	0	1,477
North Carolina		Nov. 21, 1789 (12th)	0	0	336	0	37	18	0	0	354
North Dakota[6]	Mar. 2, 1861	Nov. 2, 1889 (39th)	9	0	14	0	17	7	0	0	30
Ohio		Mar. 1, 1803 (17th)	2	0	634	0	36	19	0	1	656
Oklahoma	May 2, 1890	Nov. 16, 1907 (46th)	3	0	77	1	12	6	0	0	87
Oregon	Aug. 14, 1848	Feb. 14, 1859 (33d)	1	0	57	0	32	4	1	0	63
Pennsylvania		Dec. 12, 1787 (2d)	0	0	1,065	0	33	21	0	0	1,086
Philippines[7]	Apr. 11, 1899		0	13	0	0	0	0	0	0	13
Puerto Rico[7]	Apr. 11, 1899		0	20	0	0	0	0	0	0	20
Rhode Island		May 29, 1790 (13th)	0	0	78	0	38	10	0	0	88
South Carolina		May 23, 1788 (8th)	0	0	228	0	39	17	0	0	245
South Dakota[6]	Mar. 2, 1861	Nov. 2, 1889 (40th)	9	0	15	1	16	10	1	0	36
Tennessee		June 1, 1796 (16th)	1	0	249	0	40	19	0	0	269
Texas		Dec. 29, 1845 (28th)	0	0	261	0	23	9	0	0	270
Utah	Sept. 9, 1850	Jan. 4, 1896 (45th)	5	0	35	0	12	3	2	0	45
Vermont		Mar. 4, 1791 (14th)	0	0	80	0	24	16	0	0	96
Virgin Islands	Mar. 31, 1917		5	0	0	0	0	0	0	0	5
Virginia		June 25, 1788 (10th)	0	0	424	0	27	27	0	0	451
Washington	Mar. 2, 1853	Nov. 11, 1889 (42d)	12	0	74	0	12	10	1	0	97
West Virginia		June 20, 1863 (35th)	0	0	88	0	24	9	0	0	97
Wisconsin	Apr. 20, 1836	May 29, 1848 (30th)	4	0	175	1	19	8	1	0	189
Wyoming	July 25, 1868	July 10, 1890 (44th)	6	0	16	0	17	3	1	0	26

* State Representation March 4, 1789 to July 22, 2020.

[1] Includes 3 members who served as Representatives and 2 members who served as Senators from a different state.

[2] Includes 3 members who served as Delegates and 18 members who served as Senators from a different state.

[3] Includes 18 members who served as Representatives from a different state. One Senator served from two states and one Senator served from three states.

[4] Includes only those members who served as both a Representative and a Senator from the same state. Eighteen members served as a Senator from one state and a Representative from a different state.

[5] Designated Orleans Territory before attaining statehood in 1812.

[6] Dakota Territory became North and South Dakota in 1889. The nine Delegates from this territory are included in counts for both states. The two Delegates who became Representatives from South Dakota are included only in that state's count.

[7] Resident Commissioners served the Philippines (1902–1946) and continue to serve Puerto Rico (1900 to present). Floor and committee privileges granted to statutory representatives (Territorial Delegates and Resident Commissioners) have changed over time; however, they have never been permitted to vote on the final passage of a bill. The Resident Commissioner's duties vary from that of a Delegate in that he has diplomatic privileges as well as most of those of a Member of Congress. The Puerto Rican Resident Commissioner has served a four-year term since 1917. For more information, see "Status of Delegates and Resident Commissioner," Deschler's Precedents, H.Doc. 94–661, Volume 2, Chapter 7, Section 3.

SOURCE: Biographical Directory of the United States Congress.

POLITICAL DIVISIONS OF THE SENATE AND HOUSE FROM 1855 TO 2020

[All Figures Reflect Immediate Results of Elections. Figures Supplied by the Clerk of the House]

Congress	Years	SENATE					HOUSE OF REPRESENTATIVES				
		No. of Senators	Democrats	Republicans	Other parties	Vacancies	No. of Representatives	Democrats	Republicans	Other parties	Vacancies
34th	1855–1857	62	42	15	5	....	234	83	108	43	....
35th	1857–1859	64	39	20	5	....	237	131	92	14	....
36th	1859–1861	66	38	26	2	....	237	101	113	23	....
37th	1861–1863	50	11	31	7	1	178	42	106	28	2
38th	1863–1865	51	12	39	....	....	183	80	103	....	....
39th	1865–1867	52	10	42	....	....	191	46	145	....	....
40th	1867–1869	53	11	42	....	....	193	49	143	....	1
41st	1869–1871	74	11	61	....	2	243	73	170	....	....
42d	1871–1873	74	17	57	....	....	243	104	139	....	....
43d	1873–1875	74	19	54	....	1	293	88	203	....	2
44th	1875–1877	76	29	46	....	1	293	181	107	3	2
45th	1877–1879	76	36	39	1	....	293	156	137	....	....
46th	1879–1881	76	43	33	....	....	293	150	128	14	1
47th	1881–1883	76	37	37	2	....	293	130	152	11	....
48th	1883–1885	76	36	40	....	....	325	200	119	6	....
49th	1885–1887	76	34	41	....	1	325	182	140	2	1
50th	1887–1889	76	37	39	....	....	325	170	151	4	....
51st	1889–1891	84	37	47	....	....	330	156	173	1	....
52d	1891–1893	88	39	47	2	....	333	231	88	14	....
53d	1893–1895	88	44	38	3	3	356	220	126	10	....
54th	1895–1897	88	39	44	5	....	357	104	246	7	....
55th	1897–1899	90	34	46	10	....	357	134	206	16	1
56th	1899–1901	90	26	53	11	....	357	163	185	9	....
57th	1901–1903	90	29	56	3	2	357	153	198	5	1
58th	1903–1905	90	32	58	....	....	386	178	207	....	1
59th	1905–1907	90	32	58	....	....	386	136	250	....	....
60th	1907–1909	92	29	61	....	2	386	164	222	....	....
61st	1909–1911	92	32	59	....	1	391	172	219	....	....
62d	1911–1913	92	42	49	....	1	391	228	162	1	....
63d	1913–1915	96	51	44	1	....	435	290	127	18	....
64th	1915–1917	96	56	39	1	....	435	231	193	8	3
65th	1917–1919	96	53	42	1	....	435	[1] 210	216	9	....
66th	1919–1921	96	47	48	1	....	435	191	237	7	....
67th	1921–1923	96	37	59	....	....	435	132	300	1	2
68th	1923–1925	96	43	51	2	....	435	207	225	3	....
69th	1925–1927	96	40	54	1	1	435	183	247	5	....
70th	1927–1929	96	47	48	1	....	435	195	237	3	....
71st	1929–1931	96	39	56	1	....	435	163	267	1	4
72d	1931–1933	96	47	48	1	....	435	[2] 216	218	1	....
73d	1933–1935	96	59	36	1	....	435	313	117	5	....
74th	1935–1937	96	69	25	2	....	435	322	103	10	....
75th	1937–1939	96	75	17	4	....	435	333	89	13	....
76th	1939–1941	96	69	23	4	....	435	262	169	4	....
77th	1941–1943	96	66	28	2	....	435	267	162	6	....
78th	1943–1945	96	57	38	1	....	435	222	209	4	....
79th	1945–1947	96	57	38	1	....	435	243	190	2	....
80th	1947–1949	96	45	51	....	....	435	188	246	1	....
81st	1949–1951	96	54	42	....	....	435	263	171	1	....
82d	1951–1953	96	48	47	1	....	435	234	199	2	....
83d	1953–1955	96	46	48	2	....	435	213	221	1	....
84th	1955–1957	96	48	47	1	....	435	232	203	....	....
85th	1957–1959	96	49	47	....	....	435	234	201	....	....
86th	1959–1961	98	64	34	....	....	[3] 436	283	153	....	....
87th	1961–1963	100	64	36	....	....	[4] 437	262	175	....	....
88th	1963–1965	100	67	33	....	....	435	258	176	....	1
89th	1965–1967	100	68	32	....	....	435	295	140	....	....
90th	1967–1969	100	64	36	....	....	435	248	187	....	....
91st	1969–1971	100	58	42	....	....	435	243	192	....	....
92d	1971–1973	100	54	44	2	....	435	255	180	....	....
93d	1973–1975	100	56	42	2	....	435	242	192	1	....
94th	1975–1977	100	61	37	2	....	435	291	144	....	....
95th	1977–1979	100	61	38	1	....	435	292	143	....	....
96th	1979–1981	100	58	41	1	....	435	277	158	....	....
97th	1981–1983	100	46	53	1	....	435	242	192	1	....
98th	1983–1985	100	46	54	....	....	435	269	166	....	....
99th	1985–1987	100	47	53	....	....	435	253	182	....	....
100th	1987–1989	100	55	45	....	....	435	258	177	....	....
101st	1989–1991	100	55	45	....	....	435	260	175	....	....
102d	1991–1993	100	56	44	....	....	435	267	167	1	....
103d	1993–1995	100	57	43	....	....	435	258	176	1	....
104th	1995–1997	100	48	52	....	....	435	204	230	1	....
105th	1997–1999	100	45	55	....	....	435	207	226	2	....
106th	1999–2001	100	45	55	....	....	435	211	223	1	....
107th	2001–2003	100	50	50	....	....	435	212	221	2	....
108th	2003–2005	100	48	51	1	....	435	204	229	1	1
109th	2005–2007	100	44	55	1	....	435	202	232	1	....
110th	2007–2009	100	49	49	2	....	435	233	202	....	....
111th	2009–2011	100	55	41	2	2	435	256	178	....	1
112th	2011–2013	100	51	47	2	....	435	193	242	....	....
113th	2013–2015	100	53	45	2	....	435	200	234	....	1
114th	2015–2017	100	44	54	2	....	435	188	246	....	1
115th	2017–2019	100	47	51	2	....	435	193	236	....	6
116th	2019–2021	100	45	53	2	....	435	232	198	1	4

[1] Democrats organized House with help of other parties.
[2] Democrats organized House due to Republican deaths.
[3] Proclamation declaring Alaska a State issued January 3, 1959.
[4] Proclamation declaring Hawaii a State issued August 21, 1959.

GOVERNORS OF THE STATES, COMMONWEALTH, AND TERRITORIES—2020

State, Commonwealth, or Territory	Capital	Governor	Party	Term of service	Expiration of term
STATE				*Years*	
Alabama	Montgomery	Kay Ivey	Republican	[c] 4	Jan. 2023
Alaska	Juneau	Mike Dunleavy	Republican	[f] 4	Dec. 2022
Arizona	Phoenix	Doug Ducey	Republican	[f] 4	Jan. 2023
Arkansas	Little Rock	Asa Hutchinson	Republican	[c] 4	Jan. 2023
California	Sacramento	Gavin Newsom	Democrat	[c] 4	Jan. 2023
Colorado	Denver	Jared Polis	Democrat	[c] 4	Jan. 2023
Connecticut	Hartford	Ned Lamont	Democrat	[b] 4	Jan. 2023
Delaware	Dover	John Carney	Democrat	[c] 4	Jan. 2021
Florida	Tallahassee	Ron DeSantis	Republican	[f] 4	Jan. 2023
Georgia	Atlanta	Brian Kemp	Republican	[f] 4	Jan. 2023
Hawaii	Honolulu	David Ige	Democrat	[c] 4	Dec. 2022
Idaho	Boise	Brad Little	Republican	[b] 4	Jan. 2023
Illinois	Springfield	JB Pritzker	Democrat	[b] 4	Jan. 2023
Indiana	Indianapolis	Eric Holcomb	Republican	[f] 4	Jan. 2021
Iowa	Des Moines	Kim Reynolds	Republican	[b] 4	Jan. 2023
Kansas	Topeka	Laura Kelly	Democrat	[c] 4	Jan. 2023
Kentucky	Frankfort	Andy Beshear	Democrat	[c] 4	Dec. 2023
Louisiana	Baton Rouge	John Bel Edwards	Democrat	[f] 4	Jan. 2024
Maine	Augusta	Janet Mills	Democrat	[f] 4	Jan. 2023
Maryland	Annapolis	Larry Hogan	Republican	[f] 4	Jan. 2023
Massachusetts	Boston	Charlie Baker	Republican	[b] 4	Jan. 2023
Michigan	Lansing	Gretchen Whitmer	Democrat	[b] 4	Jan. 2023
Minnesota	St. Paul	Tim Walz	Democrat	[b] 4	Jan. 2023
Mississippi	Jackson	Tate Reeves	Republican	[c] 4	Jan. 2024
Missouri	Jefferson City	Mike Parson	Republican	[c] 4	Jan. 2021
Montana	Helena	Steve Bullock	Democrat	[g] 4	Jan. 2021
Nebraska	Lincoln	Pete Ricketts	Republican	[c] 4	Jan. 2023
Nevada	Carson City	Steve Sisolak	Democrat	[c] 4	Jan. 2023
New Hampshire	Concord	Chris Sununu	Republican	[b] 2	Jan. 2021
New Jersey	Trenton	Phil Murphy	Democrat	[c] 4	Jan. 2022
New Mexico	Santa Fe	Michelle Lujan Grisham	Democrat	[c] 4	Jan. 2023
New York	Albany	Andrew Cuomo	Democrat	[b] 4	Jan. 2023
North Carolina	Raleigh	Roy Cooper	Democrat	[c] 4	Jan. 2021
North Dakota	Bismarck	Doug Burgum	Republican	[b] 4	Dec. 2020
Ohio	Columbus	Mike DeWine	Republican	[c] 4	Jan. 2023
Oklahoma	Oklahoma City	Kevin Stitt	Republican	[c] 4	Jan. 2023
Oregon	Salem	Kate Brown	Democrat	[f] 4	Jan. 2023
Pennsylvania	Harrisburg	Tom Wolf	Democrat	[c] 4	Jan. 2023
Rhode Island	Providence	Gina Raimondo	Democrat	[c] 4	Jan. 2023
South Carolina	Columbia	Henry McMaster	Republican	[c] 4	Jan. 2023
South Dakota	Pierre	Kristi Noem	Republican	[c] 4	Jan. 2023
Tennessee	Nashville	Bill Lee	Republican	[c] 4	Jan. 2023
Texas	Austin	Greg Abbott	Republican	[b] 4	Jan. 2023
Utah	Salt Lake City	Gary R. Herbert	Republican	[b] 4	Jan. 2021
Vermont	Montpelier	Phil Scott	Republican	[b] 2	Jan. 2021
Virginia	Richmond	Ralph Northam	Democrat	[a] 4	Jan. 2022
Washington	Olympia	Jay Inslee	Democrat	[d] 4	Jan. 2021
West Virginia	Charleston	Jim Justice	Republican	[c] 4	Jan. 2021
Wisconsin	Madison	Tony Evers	Democrat	[b] 4	Jan. 2023
Wyoming	Cheyenne	Mark Gordon	Republican	[c] 4	Jan. 2023
COMMONWEALTH OF					
Puerto Rico	San Juan	Wanda Vázquez	PNP [h]	[b] 4	Jan. 2021
TERRITORIES					
Guam	Agana	Lou Leon Guerrero	Democrat	[c] 4	Jan. 2023
Virgin Islands	Charlotte Amalie	Albert Bryan	Democrat	[c] 4	Jan. 2023
American Samoa	Pago Pago	Lolo Matalasi Moliga	Independent	[c] 4	Jan. 2021
Northern Mariana Islands.	Saipan	Ralph Deleon Guerrero Torres	Republican	[i] 5	Jan. 2023

[a] Cannot succeed himself. [b] No limit. [c] Can serve 2 consecutive terms. [d] Can serve 3 consecutive terms. [e] Can serve 4 consecutive terms. [f] Can serve no more than 8 years in a 12-year period. [g] Can serve no more than 8 years in a 16-year period. [h] New Progressive Party of Puerto Rico/Democrat. [i] Absolute two-term limitation.

NOTE: Information for table obtained from the National Governors Association.

PRESIDENTS AND VICE PRESIDENTS AND THE CONGRESSES COINCIDENT WITH THEIR TERMS [1]

President	Vice President	Service	Congresses
George Washington	John Adams	Apr. 30, 1789–Mar. 3, 1797	1, 2, 3, 4.
John Adams	Thomas Jefferson	Mar. 4, 1797–Mar. 3, 1801	5, 6.
Thomas Jefferson	Aaron Burr	Mar. 4, 1801–Mar. 3, 1805	7, 8.
Do	George Clinton	Mar. 4, 1805–Mar. 3, 1809	9, 10.
James Madison	...do. [2]	Mar. 4, 1809–Mar. 3, 1813	11, 12.
Do	Elbridge Gerry [3]	Mar. 4, 1813–Mar. 3, 1817	13, 14.
James Monroe	Daniel D. Tompkins	Mar. 4, 1817–Mar. 3, 1825	15, 16, 17, 18, 19.
John Quincy Adams	John C. Calhoun	Mar. 4, 1825–Mar. 3, 1829	19, 20.
Andrew Jackson	...do. [4]	Mar. 4, 1829–Mar. 3, 1833	21, 22.
Do	Martin Van Buren	Mar. 4, 1833–Mar. 3, 1837	23, 24.
Martin Van Buren	Richard M. Johnson	Mar. 4, 1837–Mar. 3, 1841	25, 26.
William Henry Harrison [5]	John Tyler	Mar. 4, 1841–Apr. 4, 1841	27.
John Tyler		Apr. 6, 1841–Mar. 3, 1845	27, 28.
James K. Polk	George M. Dallas	Mar. 4, 1845–Mar. 3, 1849	29, 30.
Zachary Taylor [5]	Millard Fillmore	Mar. 5, 1849–July 9, 1850	31.
Millard Fillmore		July 10, 1850–Mar. 3, 1853	31, 32.
Franklin Pierce	William R. King [6]	Mar. 4, 1853–Mar. 3, 1857	33, 34.
James Buchanan	John C. Breckinridge	Mar. 4, 1857–Mar. 3, 1861	35, 36.
Abraham Lincoln	Hannibal Hamlin	Mar. 4, 1861–Mar. 3, 1865	37, 38.
Do. [5]	Andrew Johnson	Mar. 4, 1865–Apr. 15, 1865	39.
Andrew Johnson		Apr. 15, 1865–Mar. 3, 1869	39, 40.
Ulysses S. Grant	Schuyler Colfax	Mar. 4, 1869–Mar. 3, 1873	41, 42.
Do	Henry Wilson [7]	Mar. 4, 1873–Mar. 3, 1877	43, 44.
Rutherford B. Hayes	William A. Wheeler	Mar. 4, 1877–Mar. 3, 1881	45, 46.
James A. Garfield [5]	Chester A. Arthur	Mar. 4, 1881–Sept. 19, 1881	47.
Chester A. Arthur		Sept. 20, 1881–Mar. 3, 1885	47, 48.
Grover Cleveland	Thomas A. Hendricks [8]	Mar. 4, 1885–Mar. 3, 1889	49, 50.
Benjamin Harrison	Levi P. Morton	Mar. 4, 1889–Mar. 3, 1893	51, 52.
Grover Cleveland	Adlai E. Stevenson	Mar. 4, 1893–Mar. 3, 1897	53, 54.
William McKinley	Garret A. Hobart [9]	Mar. 4, 1897–Mar. 3, 1901	55, 56.
Do. [5]	Theodore Roosevelt	Mar. 4, 1901–Sept. 14, 1901	57.
Theodore Roosevelt		Sept. 14, 1901–Mar. 3, 1905	57, 58.
Do	Charles W. Fairbanks	Mar. 4, 1905–Mar. 3, 1909	59, 60.
William H. Taft	James S. Sherman [10]	Mar. 4, 1909–Mar. 3, 1913	61, 62.
Woodrow Wilson	Thomas R. Marshall	Mar. 4, 1913–Mar. 3, 1921	63, 64, 65, 66, 67.
Warren G. Harding [5]	Calvin Coolidge	Mar. 4, 1921–Aug. 2, 1923	67.
Calvin Coolidge		Aug. 3, 1923–Mar. 3, 1925	68.
Do	Charles G. Dawes	Mar. 4, 1925–Mar. 3, 1929	69, 70.
Herbert C. Hoover	Charles Curtis	Mar. 4, 1929–Mar. 3, 1933	71, 72.
Franklin D. Roosevelt	John N. Garner	Mar. 4, 1933–Jan. 20, 1941	73, 74, 75, 76, 77.
Do	Henry A. Wallace	Jan. 20, 1941–Jan. 20, 1945	77, 78, 79.
Do. [5]	Harry S. Truman	Jan. 20, 1945–Apr. 12, 1945	79.
Harry S. Truman		Apr. 12, 1945–Jan. 20, 1949	79, 80, 81.
Do	Alben W. Barkley	Jan. 20, 1949–Jan. 20, 1953	81, 82, 83.
Dwight D. Eisenhower	Richard M. Nixon	Jan. 20, 1953–Jan. 20, 1961	83, 84, 85, 86, 87.
John F. Kennedy [5]	Lyndon B. Johnson	Jan. 20, 1961–Nov. 22, 1963	87, 88, 89.
Lyndon B. Johnson		Nov. 22, 1963–Jan. 20, 1965	88, 89.
Do	Hubert H. Humphrey	Jan. 20, 1965–Jan. 20, 1969	89, 90, 91.
Richard M. Nixon	Spiro T. Agnew [11]	Jan. 20, 1969–Dec. 6, 1973	91, 92, 93.
Do. [13]	Gerald R. Ford [12]	Dec. 6, 1973–Aug. 9, 1974	93.
Gerald R. Ford		Aug. 9, 1974–Dec. 19, 1974	93.
Do	Nelson A. Rockefeller [14]	Dec. 19, 1974–Jan. 20, 1977	93, 94, 95.
James Earl "Jimmy" Carter	Walter F. Mondale	Jan. 20, 1977–Jan. 20, 1981	95, 96, 97.
Ronald Reagan	George Bush	Jan. 20, 1981–Jan. 20, 1989	97, 98, 99, 100, 101.
George Bush	Dan Quayle	Jan. 20, 1989–Jan. 20, 1993	101, 102, 103.
William J. Clinton	Albert Gore	Jan. 20, 1993–Jan. 20, 2001	103, 104, 105, 106, 107.
George W. Bush	Richard B. Cheney	Jan. 20, 2001–Jan. 20, 2009	107, 108, 109, 110, 111.
Barack H. Obama	Joseph R. Biden, Jr.	Jan. 20, 2009–Jan. 20, 2017	111, 112, 113, 114.
Donald J. Trump	Mike Pence	Jan. 20, 2017–	115, 116.

[1] From 1789 until 1933, the terms of the President and Vice President and the term of the Congress coincided, beginning on March 4 and ending on March 3. This changed when the 20th amendment to the Constitution was adopted in 1933. Beginning in 1934 the convening date for Congress became January 3, and beginning in 1937 the starting date for the Presidential term became January 20. Because of this change, the number of Congresses overlapping with a Presidential term increased from two to three, although the third only overlaps by a few weeks.

[2] Died Apr. 20, 1812.

[3] Died Nov. 23, 1814.

[4] Resigned Dec. 28, 1832, to become a United States Senator from South Carolina.

[5] Died in office.

[6] Died Apr. 18, 1853.

[7] Died Nov. 22, 1875.

[8] Died Nov. 25, 1885.

[9] Died Nov. 21, 1899.

[10] Died Oct. 30, 1912.

[11] Resigned Oct. 10, 1973.

[12] Nominated to be Vice President by President Richard M. Nixon on Oct. 12, 1973; confirmed by the Senate on Nov. 27, 1973; confirmed by the House of Representatives on Dec. 6, 1973; took the oath of office on Dec. 6, 1973 in the Hall of the House of Representatives. This was the first time a Vice President was nominated by the President and confirmed by the Congress pursuant to the 25th amendment to the Constitution.

[13] Resigned from office.

[14] Nominated to be Vice President by President Gerald R. Ford on Aug. 20, 1974; confirmed by the Senate on Dec. 10, 1974; confirmed by the House of Representatives on Dec. 19, 1974; took the oath of office on Dec. 19, 1974, in the Senate Chamber.

CAPITOL BUILDINGS AND GROUNDS

UNITED STATES CAPITOL

Overview of the Building and its Function

The United States Capitol is among the most architecturally impressive and symbolically important buildings in the world. It has housed the chambers of the Senate and the House of Representatives for more than two centuries. Begun in 1793, the Capitol has been built, burnt, rebuilt, extended, and restored; today, it stands as a monument not only to its builders but also to the American people and their government.

As the focal point of the government's legislative branch, the Capitol is the centerpiece of the Capitol complex, which includes the six principal congressional office buildings and three Library of Congress buildings constructed on Capitol Hill in the 19th and 20th centuries.

In addition to its active use by Congress, the Capitol is a museum of American art and history. Each year, it is visited by millions of people from around the world.

A fine example of 19th-century neoclassical architecture, the Capitol combines function with aesthetics. Its design was derived from ancient Greece and Rome and evokes the ideals that guided the nation's founders as they framed their new republic. As the building was expanded from its original design, harmony with the existing portions was carefully maintained.

Today, the Capitol covers a ground area of 175,170 square feet, or about 4 acres, and has a floor area of approximately 16½ acres. Its length, from north to south, is 751 feet 4 inches; its greatest width, including approaches, is 350 feet. Its height above the base line on the east front to the top of the Statue of Freedom is 288 feet; from the basement floor to the top of the dome is an ascent of 365 steps.

The building is divided into five levels. The first, or ground, floor is occupied chiefly by committee rooms and the spaces allocated to various congressional officers. The areas accessible to visitors on this level include the Hall of Columns, the restored Old Supreme Court Chamber, and the Crypt beneath the Rotunda.

The second floor holds the chambers of the House of Representatives (in the south wing) and the Senate (in the north wing). This floor also contains three major public areas. In the center under the dome is the Rotunda, a circular ceremonial space that also serves as a gallery of paintings and sculpture depicting significant people and events in the nation's history. The Rotunda is 96 feet in diameter and rises 180 feet 3 inches to the canopy. The semicircular chamber south of the Rotunda served as the Hall of the House until 1857; now designated National Statuary Hall, it houses part of the Capitol's collection of statues donated by the states in commemoration of notable citizens. The Old Senate Chamber northeast of the Rotunda, which was used by the Senate until 1859, has been returned to its mid-19th-century appearance.

The third floor allows access to the galleries from which visitors to the Capitol may watch the proceedings of the House and the Senate when Congress is in session. The rest of this floor is occupied by offices, committee rooms, and press galleries.

The fourth floor and the basement/terrace level of the Capitol are occupied by offices, machinery rooms, workshops, and other support areas.

Located beneath the East Front plaza, the newest addition to the Capitol is the Capitol Visitor Center (CVC). Preparatory construction activities began in 2002, and the CVC was opened to the public on December 2, 2008. This date was chosen for its significance in the Capitol's history: it was on December 2, 1863, that the Statue of Freedom was placed atop the Capitol. The CVC occupies 580,000 square feet of space on three levels and includes an Exhibition Hall, a restaurant, orientation theaters, gift shops, and other visitor amenities as well as meeting space for the House and Senate.

Location of the Capitol

The Capitol is located at the eastern end of the Mall on a plateau 88 feet above the level of the Potomac River, commanding a westward view across the Capitol Reflecting

Pool to the Washington Monument 1.4 miles away and the Lincoln Memorial 2.2 miles away.

Before 1791, the Federal Government had no permanent site. The early Congresses met in eight different cities: Philadelphia, Baltimore, Lancaster, York, Princeton, Annapolis, Trenton, and New York City. The subject of a permanent capital for the Government of the United States was first raised by Congress in 1783; it was ultimately addressed in Article I, Section 8 of the Constitution (1787), which gave the Congress legislative authority over "such District (not exceeding ten Miles square) as may, by Cession of Particular States, and the Acceptance of Congress, become the Seat of the Government of the United States. . . ."

In 1788, the State of Maryland ceded to Congress "any district in this State, not exceeding ten miles square," and in 1789 the State of Virginia ceded an equivalent amount of land. In accordance with the "Residence Act" passed by Congress in 1790, President Washington in 1791 selected the area that is now the District of Columbia from the land ceded by Maryland (private landowners whose property fell within this area were compensated by a payment of £25 per acre); that ceded by Virginia was not used for the capital and was returned to Virginia in 1846. Also under the provisions of that Act, he selected three commissioners to survey the site and oversee the design and construction of the capital city and its government buildings. The commissioners, in turn, selected the French-American engineer Pierre Charles L'Enfant to plan the new city of Washington. L'Enfant's plan, which was influenced by the gardens at Versailles, arranged the city's streets and avenues in a grid overlaid with baroque diagonals; the result is a functional and aesthetic whole in which government buildings are balanced against public lawns, gardens, squares, and paths. The Capitol itself was located at the elevated east end of the Mall, on the brow of what was then called Jenkins' Hill. The site was, in L'Enfant's words, "a pedestal waiting for a monument."

Selection of a Plan

L'Enfant was expected to design the Capitol and to supervise its construction. However, he refused to produce any drawings for the building, claiming that he carried the design "in his head"; this fact and his refusal to consider himself subject to the commissioners' authority led to his dismissal in 1792. In March of that year, the commissioners announced a competition, suggested by Secretary of State Thomas Jefferson, that would award $500 and a city lot to whoever produced "the most approved plan" for the Capitol by mid-July. None of the 17 plans submitted, however, was wholly satisfactory. In October, a letter arrived from Dr. William Thornton, a Scottish-trained physician living in Tortola, British West Indies, requesting an opportunity to present a plan even though the competition had closed. The commissioners granted this request.

Thornton's plan depicted a building composed of three sections. The central section, which was topped by a low dome, was to be flanked on the north and south by two rectangular wings (one for the Senate and one for the House of Representatives). President Washington commended the plan for its "grandeur, simplicity and convenience," and on April 5, 1793, it was accepted by the commissioners; Washington gave his formal approval on July 25.

Brief Construction History

1793–1829

The cornerstone was laid by President Washington in the building's southeast corner on September 18, 1793, with Masonic ceremonies. Work progressed under the direction of three architects in succession. Stephen H. Hallet (an entrant in the earlier competition) and George Hadfield were eventually dismissed by the commissioners because of inappropriate design changes that they tried to impose; James Hoban, the architect of the White House, saw the first phase of the project through to completion.

Construction was a laborious and time-consuming process: the sandstone used for the building had to be ferried on boats from the quarries at Aquia, Virginia; workers had to be induced to leave their homes to come to the relative wilderness of Capitol Hill; and funding was inadequate. By August 1796, the commissioners were forced to focus the entire work effort on the building's north wing so that it at least could be ready for government occupancy as scheduled. Even so, some third-floor rooms were still unfinished when the Congress, the Supreme Court, the Library of Congress, and the courts of the District of Columbia occupied the Capitol in late 1800.

In 1803, Congress allocated funds to resume construction. A year earlier, the office of the Commissioners had been abolished and replaced by a superintendent of the city of Washington. To oversee the renewed construction effort, Benjamin Henry Latrobe was appointed surveyor of public buildings. The first professional architect and engineer to work in America, Latrobe modified Thornton's plan for the south wing to include space for offices and committee rooms; he also introduced alterations to simplify the construction work. Latrobe began work by removing a squat, oval, temporary building known as "the Oven," which had been erected in 1801 as a meeting place for the House of Representatives. By 1807, construction on the south wing was sufficiently advanced that the House was able to occupy its new legislative chamber, and the wing was completed in 1811.

In 1808, as work on the south wing progressed, Latrobe began the rebuilding of the north wing, which had fallen into disrepair. Rather than simply repair the wing, he redesigned the interior of the building to increase its usefulness and durability; among his changes was the addition of a chamber for the Supreme Court. By 1811, he had completed the eastern half of this wing, but funding was being increasingly diverted to preparations for a second war with Great Britain. By 1813, Latrobe had no further work in Washington and so he departed, leaving the north and south wings of the Capitol connected only by a temporary wooden passageway.

The War of 1812 left the Capitol, in Latrobe's later words, "a most magnificent ruin": on August 24, 1814, British troops set fire to the building, and only a sudden rainstorm prevented its complete destruction. Immediately after the fire, Congress met for one session in Blodget's Hotel, which was at Seventh and E Streets, NW. From 1815 to 1819, Congress occupied a building erected for it on First Street, NE., on part of the site now occupied by the Supreme Court Building. This building later came to be known as the Old Brick Capitol.

Latrobe returned to Washington in 1815, when he was rehired to restore the Capitol. In addition to making repairs, he took advantage of this opportunity to make further changes in the building's interior design (for example, an enlargement of the Senate Chamber) and introduce new materials (for example, marble discovered along the upper Potomac). However, he came under increasing pressure because of construction delays (most of which were beyond his control) and cost overruns; finally, he resigned his post in November 1817.

On January 8, 1818, Charles Bulfinch, a prominent Boston architect, was hired to succeed Latrobe. Continuing the restoration of the north and south wings, he was able to make the chambers for the Supreme Court, the House, and the Senate ready for use by 1819. Bulfinch also redesigned and supervised the construction of the Capitol's central section. The copper-covered wooden dome that topped this section was made higher than Bulfinch considered appropriate to the building's size (at the direction of President James Monroe and Secretary of State John Quincy Adams). After completing the last part of the building in 1826, Bulfinch spent the next few years on the Capitol's decoration and landscaping. In 1829, his work was done and his position with the government was terminated. In the 38 years following Bulfinch's tenure, the Capitol was entrusted to the care of the commissioner of public buildings.

1830–1868

The Capitol was by this point already an impressive structure. At ground level, its length was 351 feet 7½ inches and its width was 282 feet 10½ inches. Up to the year 1827—records from later years being incomplete—the project cost was $2,432,851.34. Improvements to the building continued in the years to come (running water in 1832, gas lighting in the 1840s), but by 1850 its size could no longer accommodate the increasing numbers of Senators and Representatives from newly admitted states. The Senate therefore voted to hold another competition, offering a prize of $500 for the best plan to extend the Capitol. Several suitable plans were submitted, some proposing an eastward extension of the building and others proposing the addition of large north and south wings. However, Congress was unable to decide between these two approaches, and the prize money was divided among five architects. Thus, the tasks of selecting a plan and appointing an architect fell to President Millard Fillmore.

Fillmore's choice was Thomas U. Walter, a Philadelphia architect who had entered the competition. On July 4, 1851, in a ceremony whose principal oration was delivered by Secretary of State Daniel Webster, the president laid the cornerstone in the northeast corner of the House wing. Over the next 14 years, Walter supervised the construction of the extension, ensuring their compatibility with the architectural style of the existing building. However, because the Aquia Creek sandstone used earlier had deteriorated noticeably, he chose to use marble for the exterior. For the veneer, Walter selected marble quarried at Lee, Massachusetts, and for the columns he used marble from Cockeysville, Maryland.

Walter faced several significant challenges during the course of construction. Chief among these was the steady imposition by the government of additional tasks without additional pay. Aside from his work on the Capitol extension, Walter designed the wings of the Patent

Office building, extensions to the Treasury and Post Office buildings, and the Marine barracks in Pensacola and Brooklyn. When the Library of Congress in the Capitol's west central section was gutted by a fire in 1851, Walter was commissioned to restore it. He also encountered obstacles in his work on the Capitol extensions. His location of the legislative chambers was changed in 1853 at the direction of President Franklin Pierce, based on the suggestions of the newly appointed supervising engineer, Captain Montgomery C. Meigs. In general, however, the project progressed rapidly; the House of Representatives was able to meet in its new chamber on December 16, 1857, and the Senate first met in its present chamber on January 4, 1859. The old House chamber was later designated National Statuary Hall. In 1861 most construction was suspended because of the Civil War, and the Capitol was used briefly as a military barracks, hospital, and bakery. In 1862 work on the entire building was resumed.

As the new wings were constructed, more than doubling the length of the Capitol, it became apparent that the dome erected by Bulfinch no longer suited the building's proportions. In 1855, Congress voted for its replacement based on Walter's design for a new, fireproof cast-iron dome. The old dome was removed in 1856, and 5,000,000 pounds of new masonry was placed on the existing rotunda walls. Iron used in the dome construction had an aggregate weight of 8,909,200 pounds and was lifted into place by steam-powered derricks.

In 1859, Thomas Crawford's plaster model for the Statue of Freedom, designed for the top of the dome, arrived from the sculptor's studio in Rome. With a height of 19 feet 6 inches, the statue was almost 3 feet taller than specified, and Walter was compelled to make revisions to his design for the dome. When cast in bronze by Clark Mills at his foundry on the outskirts of Washington, it weighed 14,985 pounds. The statue was lifted into place atop the dome in 1863, its final section being installed on December 2 to the accompaniment of gun salutes from the forts around the city.

The work on the dome and the extension was completed under the direction of Edward Clark, who had served as Walter's assistant and was appointed Architect of the Capitol in 1865 after Walter's resignation. In 1866, the Italian-born artist Constantino Brumidi finished the canopy fresco, a monumental painting entitled *The Apotheosis of George Washington*. The Capitol extension was completed in 1868.

1869–1902

Clark continued to hold the post of Architect of the Capitol until his death in 1902. During his tenure, the Capitol underwent considerable modernization. Steam heat was gradually installed in the old Capitol. In 1874, the first elevator was installed, and in the 1880s electric lighting began to replace gas lights.

Between 1884 and 1891, the marble terraces on the north, west, and south sides of the Capitol were constructed. As part of the landscape plan devised by Frederick Law Olmsted, these terraces not only added over 100 rooms to the Capitol but also provided a broader, more substantial visual base for the building.

On November 6, 1898, a gas explosion and fire in the original north wing dramatically illustrated the need for fireproofing. The roofs over the Statuary Hall wing and the original north wing were reconstructed and fireproofed, the work being completed in 1902 by Clark's successor, Elliott Woods. In 1901, the space in the west central front vacated by the Library of Congress was converted to committee rooms.

1903–1970

During the remainder of Woods's service, which ended with his death in 1923, no major structural work was required on the Capitol. The activities performed in the building were limited chiefly to cleaning and refurbishing the interior. David Lynn, the Architect of the Capitol from 1923 until his retirement in 1954, continued these tasks. Between July 1949 and January 1951, the corroded roofs and skylights of both wings and the connecting corridors were replaced with new roofs of concrete and steel, covered with copper. The cast-iron and glass ceilings of the House and Senate chambers were replaced with ceilings of stainless steel and plaster, with a laylight of carved glass and bronze in the middle of each. The House and Senate chambers were completely redecorated, modern lighting was added, and acoustical problems were solved. During this renovation program, the House and Senate vacated their chambers on several occasions so that the work could progress.

The next significant modification made to the Capitol was the east front extension. This project was carried out under the supervision of Architect of the Capitol J. George Stewart, who served from 1954 until his death in 1970. Begun in 1958, it involved the construction of a new east front 32 feet 6 inches east of the old front, faithfully reproducing the sandstone structure in marble. The old sandstone walls were not destroyed; rather, they were left in place to become a part of the interior wall and are now buttressed by the addition. The marble columns of the connecting corridors were also moved and reused. Other elements of this project included repairing the dome, constructing a subway terminal under the Senate steps, reconstructing those steps, cleaning both wings, birdproofing the building, providing furniture and furnishings for 90 new rooms created by the extension, and improving the lighting throughout the building. The project was completed in 1962.

1971–Present

During the nearly 25-year tenure (1971–1995) of Architect of the Capitol George M. White, FAIA, the building was both modernized and restored. Electronic voting equipment was installed in the House chamber in 1973; facilities were added to allow television coverage of the House and Senate debates in 1979 and 1986, respectively; and improved climate control, electronic surveillance systems, and new computer and communications facilities have been added to bring the Capitol up-to-date. The Old Senate Chamber, National Statuary Hall, and the Old Supreme Court Chamber, on the other hand, were restored to their mid-19th-century appearance in the 1970s.

In 1983, work began on the strengthening, renovation, and preservation of the west front of the Capitol. Structural problems had developed over the years because of defects in the original foundations, deterioration of the sandstone facing material, alterations to the basic building fabric (a fourth-floor addition and channeling of the walls to install interior utilities), and damage from the fires of 1814 and 1851 and the 1898 gas explosion.

To strengthen the structure, over 1,000 stainless steel tie rods were set into the building's masonry. More than 30 layers of paint were removed, and damaged stonework was repaired or replicated. Ultimately, 40 percent of the sandstone blocks were replaced with limestone. The walls were treated with a special consolidant and then painted to match the marble wings. The entire project was completed in 1987.

A related project, completed in January 1993, effected the repair of the Olmsted terraces, which had been subject to damage from settling, and converted the terrace courtyards into several thousand square feet of meeting space.

As the Capitol enters its third century, restoration and modernization work continues. Alan M. Hantman, FAIA, was appointed in February 1997 to a 10-year term as Architect of the Capitol. Projects under his direction included rehabilitation of the Capitol dome; conservation of murals; improvement of speech-reinforcement, electrical, and fire-protection systems in the Capitol and the Congressional office buildings; work on security improvements within the Capitol complex; restoration of the U.S. Botanic Garden Conservatory; the design and construction of the National Garden adjacent to the Botanic Garden Conservatory; renovation of the building systems in the Dirksen Senate Office Building; publication of the first comprehensive history of the Capitol to appear in a century; and construction of the Capitol Visitor Center. At the end of Mr. Hantman's term in February 2007, Stephen T. Ayers, FAIA, LEED AP, assumed the position of Acting Architect of the Capitol. On February 24, 2010, President Barack Obama nominated Mr. Ayers to serve as the 11th Architect of the Capitol. On May 12, 2010, the United States Senate, by unanimous consent, confirmed Mr. Ayers, and on May 13, 2010, the President officially appointed Mr. Ayers to a 10-year term as Architect of the Capitol. On December 9, 2019, President Donald J. Trump nominated J. Brett Blanton to serve as the 12th Architect of the Capitol. On December 20, 2019, the United States Senate confirmed Mr. Blanton, and on January 16, 2020, he was sworn in as Architect of the Capitol by Supreme Court Chief Justice John Roberts, Jr.

HOUSE OFFICE BUILDINGS

Cannon House Office Building

An increased membership of the Senate and House resulted in a demand for additional rooms for the accommodations of the Senators and Representatives. On March 3, 1903, the Congress authorized the erection of a fireproofed office building for the use of the House. It was designed by the firm of Carrere & Hastings of New York City in the Beaux Arts style. The first brick was laid July 5, 1905, in square No. 690, and formal exercises were held at the laying of the cornerstone on April 14, 1906, in which President Theodore

Roosevelt participated. The building was completed and occupied January 10, 1908. A subsequent change in the basis of congressional representation made necessary the building of an additional story in 1913–14. The total cost of the building, including site, furnishings, equipment, and the subway connecting it with the U.S. Capitol, amounted to $4,860,155. This office building contains about 500 rooms, and was considered at the time of its completion fully equipped for all the needs of a modern building for office purposes. A garage was added in the building's courtyard in the 1960s.

Pursuant to authority in the Second Supplemental Appropriations Act, 1955, and subsequent action of the House Office Building Commission, remodeling of the Cannon Building began in 1966. The estimated cost of this work was $5,200,000. Pursuant to the provisions of Public Law 87–453, approved May 21, 1962, the building was named in honor of Joseph G. Cannon of Illinois, who was Speaker at the time the building was constructed.

Longworth House Office Building

Under legislation contained in the Authorization Act of January 10, 1929, and in the urgent deficiency bill of March 4, 1929, provisions were made for an additional House office building, to be located on the west side of New Jersey Avenue (opposite the first House office building). The building was designed by the Allied Architects of Washington in the Neoclassical Revival style.

The cornerstone was laid June 24, 1932, and the building was completed on April 20, 1933. It contains 251 two-room suites and 16 committee rooms. Each suite and committee room is provided with a storeroom. Eight floors are occupied by members. The basement and subbasement contain shops and mechanical areas needed for the maintenance of the building. A cafeteria was added in the building's courtyard in the 1960s. The cost of this building, including site, furnishings, and equipment, was $7,805,705. Pursuant to the provisions of Public Law 87–453, approved May 21, 1962, the building was named in honor of Nicholas Longworth of Ohio, who was Speaker when the second House office building was constructed.

Rayburn House Office Building and Other Related Changes and Improvements

Under legislation contained in the Second Supplemental Appropriations Act, 1955, provision was made for construction of a fireproof office building for the House of Representatives.

All work was carried forward by the Architect of the Capitol under the direction of the House Office Building Commission at a cost totaling $135,279,000.

The Rayburn Building is connected to the Capitol by a subway. Designs for the building were prepared by the firm of Harbeson, Hough, Livingston & Larson of Philadelphia, Associate Architects. The building contains 169 congressional suites; full-committee hearing rooms for 9 standing committees, 16 subcommittee hearing rooms, committee staff rooms, and other committee facilities; a large cafeteria and other restaurant facilities; an underground garage; and a variety of liaison offices, press and television facilities, maintenance and equipment shops or rooms, and storage areas. This building has nine stories and a penthouse for machinery.

The cornerstone was laid May 24, 1962, by John W. McCormack, Speaker of the House of Representatives. President John F. Kennedy participated in the cornerstone laying and delivered the address.

A portion of the basement floor was occupied beginning March 12, 1964, by House of Representatives personnel moved from the George Washington Inn property. Full occupancy of the Rayburn Building, under the room-filing regulations, was begun February 23, 1965, and completed April 2, 1965. Pursuant to the provisions of Public Law 87–453, approved May 21, 1962, the building was named in honor of Sam Rayburn of Texas.

House Office Building Annex No. 2, named the "Gerald R. Ford House of Representatives Office Building," was acquired in 1975 from the General Services Administration. The structure, located at Second and D Streets, SW., was built in 1939 for the Federal Bureau of Investigation as a fingerprint file archives. This building has approximately 432,000 square feet of space.

SENATE OFFICE BUILDINGS

Richard Brevard Russell Senate Office Building

In 1891, the Senate provided itself with office space by the purchase of the Maltby Building, then located on the northwest corner of B Street (now Constitution Avenue) and New Jersey Avenue, NW. When it was condemned as an unsafe structure, Senators needed safer and more commodious office space. Under authorization of the Act of April 28, 1904, square 686 on the northeast corner of Delaware Avenue and B Street, NE., was purchased as a site for the Senate Office Building. The plans for the House Office Building were adapted for the Senate Office Building by the firm of Carrere & Hastings, with the exception that the side of the building fronting on First Street, NE., was temporarily omitted. The cornerstone was laid without special exercises on July 31, 1906, and the building was occupied March 5, 1909. In 1931, the completion of the fourth side of the building was commenced. In 1933, it was completed, together with alterations to the C Street facade and the construction of terraces, balustrades, and approaches. The cost of the completed building, including the site, furnishings, equipment, and the subway connecting it with the United States Capitol, was $8,390,892.

The building was named the ''Richard Brevard Russell Senate Office Building'' by Senate Resolution 296, 92nd Congress, agreed to October 11, 1972, as amended by Senate Resolution 295, 96th Congress, agreed to December 3, 1979.

Everett McKinley Dirksen Senate Office Building

Under legislation contained in the Second Deficiency Appropriations Act, 1948, Public Law 80–785, provision was made for an additional office building for the United States Senate with limits of cost of $1,100,000 for acquisition of the site and $20,600,000 for constructing and equipping the building.

The construction cost limit was subsequently increased to $24,196,000. All work was carried forward by the Architect of the Capitol under the direction of the Senate Office Building Commission. The New York firm of Eggers & Higgins served as the consulting architect.

The site was acquired and cleared in 1948–49 at a total cost of $1,011,492.

A contract for excavation, concrete footings, and mats for the new building was awarded in January 1955, in the amount of $747,200. Groundbreaking ceremonies were held January 26, 1955.

A contract for the superstructure of the new building was awarded September 9, 1955, in the amount of $17,200,000. The cornerstone was laid July 13, 1956.

As a part of this project, a new underground subway system was installed from the Capitol to both the Old and New Senate Office Buildings.

An appropriation of $1,000,000 for furniture and furnishings for the new building was provided in 1958. The building was accepted for beneficial occupancy on October 15, 1958.

The building was named the ''Everett McKinley Dirksen Senate Office Building'' by Senate Resolution 296, 92nd Congress, agreed to October 11, 1972, and Senate Resolution 295, 96th Congress, agreed to December 3, 1979.

Philip A. Hart Senate Office Building

Construction as an extension to the Dirksen Senate Office Building was authorized on October 31, 1972; legislation enacted in subsequent years increased the scope of the project and established a total cost ceiling of $137,700,400. The firm of John Carl Warnecke & Associates served as Associate Architect for the project.

Senate Resolution 525, passed August 30, 1976, amended by Senate Resolution 295, 96th Congress, agreed to December 3, 1979, provided that upon completion of the extension it would be named the ''Philip A. Hart Senate Office Building'' to honor the Senator from Michigan.

The contract for clearing of the site, piping for utilities, excavation, and construction of foundation was awarded in December 1975. Groundbreaking took place January 5, 1976. The contract for furnishing and delivery of the exterior stone was awarded in February 1977, and the contract for the superstructure, which included wall and roof systems and the erection of all exterior stonework, was awarded in October 1977. The contract for the first portion of the interior and related work was awarded in December 1978. A contract for interior finishing was awarded in July 1980. The first suite was occupied on November

22, 1982. Alexander Calder's mobile/stabile *Mountains and Clouds* was installed in the building's atrium in November 1986.

CAPITOL POWER PLANT

During the development of the plans for the Cannon and Russell Buildings, the question of heat, light, and power was considered. The Senate and House wings of the Capitol were heated by separate heating plants. The Library of Congress also had a heating plant for that building. It was determined that needs for heating and lighting and electrical power could be met by a central power plant.

A site was selected in Garfield Park. Since this park was a Government reservation, an appropriation was not required to secure title. The determining factors leading to the selection of this site were its proximity to the tracks of what is now the Penn Central Railroad and to the buildings to be served.

The dimensions of the Capitol Power Plant, which was authorized on April 28, 1904, and completed in 1910, were 244 feet 8 inches by 117 feet.

The buildings originally served by the Capitol Power Plant were connected to it by a reinforced-concrete steam tunnel.

In September 1951, when the demand for electrical energy was reaching the maximum capacity of the Capitol Power Plant, arrangements were made to purchase electrical service from the local public utility company and to discontinue electrical generation. The heating and cooling functions of the Capitol Power Plant were expanded in 1935, 1939, 1958, 1973, and 1980. A new refrigeration plant modernization and expansion project was completed in 2007.

U.S. CAPITOL GROUNDS

A Description of the Grounds

Originally a wooded wilderness, the U.S. Capitol Grounds today provide a park-like setting for the Nation's Capitol, offering a picturesque counterpoint to the building's formal architecture. The grounds immediately surrounding the Capitol are bordered by a stone wall and cover an area of 58.8 acres. Their boundaries are Independence Avenue on the south, Constitution Avenue on the north, First Street, NE./SE., on the east, and First Street, NW./SW., on the west. Over 100 varieties of trees and bushes are planted around the Capitol, and thousands of flowers are used in seasonal displays. In contrast to the building's straight, neoclassical lines, most of the walkways in the grounds are curved. Benches along the paths offer pleasant spots for visitors to appreciate the building, its landscape, and the surrounding areas, most notably the Mall to the west.

The grounds were designed by Frederick Law Olmsted (1822–1903), who planned the landscaping of the area that was performed from 1874 to 1892. Olmsted, who also designed New York's Central Park, is considered the greatest American landscape architect of his day. He was a pioneer in the development of public parks in America, and many of his designs were influenced by his studies of European parks, gardens, and estates. In describing his plan for the Capitol Grounds, Olmsted noted that, ''The ground is in design part of the Capitol, but in all respects subsidiary to the central structure.'' Therefore, he was careful not to group trees or other landscape features in any way that would distract the viewer from the Capitol. The use of sculpture and other ornamentation has also been kept to a minimum.

Many of the trees on the Capitol Grounds have historic or memorial associations. Over 30 states have made symbolic gifts of their state trees to the Capitol Grounds. Many of the trees on the grounds bear plaques that identify their species and their historic significance.

At the East Capitol Street entrance to the Capitol plaza are two large rectangular stone fountains. Six massive red granite lamp piers topped with light fixtures in wrought-iron cages, and 16 smaller bronze light fixtures, line the paved plaza. Three sets of benches are enclosed with wrought-iron railings and grilles; the roofed bench was originally a shelter for streetcar passengers.

The northern part of the grounds offers a shaded walk among trees, flowers, and shrubbery. A small, hexagonal brick structure, named the Summer House, may be found in the northwest corner of the grounds. This structure contains shaded benches, a central ornamental fountain, and three public drinking fountains. In a small grotto on the eastern side of the Summer House, a stream of water flows and splashes over rocks to create a pleasing sound and cool the summer breezes.

A Brief History of the Grounds Before Olmsted

The land on which the Capitol stands was first occupied by the Manahoacs and the Monacans, who were subtribes of the Algonquin Indians. Early settlers reported that these tribes occasionally held councils not far from the foot of the hill. This land eventually became a part of Cerne Abbey Manor, and at the time of its acquisition by the Federal Government it was owned by Daniel Carroll of Duddington.

The "Residence Act" of 1790 provided that the Federal Government should be established in a permanent location by the year 1800. In early March 1791, the commissioners of the city of Washington, who had been appointed by President George Washington, selected the French engineer Pierre Charles L'Enfant to plan the new federal city. L'Enfant decided to locate the Capitol at the elevated east end of the Mall (on what was then called Jenkins' Hill); he described the site as "a pedestal waiting for a monument."

At this time, the site of the Capitol was a relative wilderness partly overgrown with scrub oak. Oliver Wolcott, a signer of the Declaration of Independence, described the soil as an " *exceedingly stiff* clay, becoming dust in dry and mortar in rainy weather."

In 1825, a plan was devised for imposing order on the Capitol Grounds, and it was carried out for almost 15 years. The plan divided the area into flat, rectangular grassy areas bordered by trees, flower beds, and gravel walks. The growth of the trees, however, soon deprived the other plantings of nourishment, and the design became increasingly difficult to maintain in light of sporadic and small appropriations. John Foy, who had charge of the grounds during most of this period, was "superseded for political reasons," and the area was then maintained with little care or forethought. Many rapidly growing but short-lived trees were introduced and soon depleted the soil; a lack of proper pruning and thinning left the majority of the area's vegetation ill-grown, feeble, or dead. Virtually all was removed by the early 1870s, either to make way for building operations during Thomas U. Walter's enlargement of the Capitol or as required by changes in grading to accommodate the new work on the building or the alterations to surrounding streets.

The Olmsted Plan

The mid-19th-century extension of the Capitol, in which the House and Senate wings and the new dome were added, also required that the Capitol Grounds be enlarged, and in 1874 Frederick Law Olmsted was commissioned to plan and oversee the project. As noted above, Olmsted was determined that the grounds should complement the building. In addition, he addressed an architectural problem that had persisted for some years: from the west (the growth of the city had nothing to do with the terraces)—the earthen terraces at the building's base made it seem inadequately supported at the top of the hill. The solution, Olmsted believed, was to construct marble terraces on the north, west, and south sides of the building, thereby causing it to "gain greatly in the supreme qualities of stability, endurance, and repose." He submitted his design for these features in 1875, and after extensive study, it was approved.

Work on the grounds began in 1874, concentrating first on the east side and then progressing to the west, north, and south sides. First, the ground was reduced in elevation. Almost 300,000 cubic yards of earth and other material were eventually removed, and over 200 trees were removed. New sewer, gas, and water lines were installed. The soil was then enriched with fertilizers to provide a suitable growth medium for new plantings. Paths and roadways were graded and laid.

By 1876, gas and water service was completed for the entire grounds, and electrical lamp-lighting apparatuses had been installed. Stables and workshops had been removed from the northwest and southwest corners. A streetcar system north and south of the west grounds had been relocated farther from the Capitol, and ornamental shelters were in place at the north and south car-track termini. The granite and bronze lamp piers and ornamental bronze lamps for the east plaza area were completed.

Work accelerated in 1877. By this time, according to Olmsted's report, "altogether 7,837 plants and trees [had] been set out." However, not all had survived: hundreds were stolen or destroyed by vandals, and, as Olmsted explained, "a large number of cattle [had] been caught trespassing." Other work met with less difficulty. Foot-walks were laid with artificial stone, a mixture of cement and sand, and approaches were paved with concrete. An ornamental iron trellis had been installed on the northern east-side walk, and another was under way on the southern walk.

The 1878 appointment of watchmen to patrol the grounds was quite effective in preventing further vandalism, allowing the lawns to be completed and much shrubbery to be added. Also in that year, the roads throughout the grounds were paved.

Most of the work required on the east side of the grounds was completed by 1879, and effort thus shifted largely to the west side. The Pennsylvania Avenue approach was virtually finished, and work on the Maryland Avenue approach had begun. The stone walls on the west side of the grounds were almost finished, and the red granite lamp piers were placed at the eastward entrance from Pennsylvania Avenue.

In the years 1880–1882, many features of the grounds were completed. These included the walls and coping around the entire perimeter, the approaches and entrances, and the Summer House. Work on the terraces began in 1882, and most work from this point until 1892 was concentrated on these structures.

In 1885, Olmsted retired from superintendency of the terrace project; he continued to direct the work on the grounds until 1889. Landscaping work was performed to adapt the surrounding areas to the new construction, grading the ground and planting shrubs at the bases of the walls, as the progress of the masonry work allowed. Some trees and other types of vegetation were removed, either because they had decayed or as part of a careful thinning-out process.

In 1888, the wrought-iron lamp frames and railings were placed at the Maryland Avenue entrance, making it the last to be completed. In 1892, the streetcar track that had extended into grounds from Independence Avenue was removed.

The Grounds After Olmsted

In the last years of the 19th century, work on the grounds consisted chiefly of maintenance and repairs as needed. Trees, lawns, and plantings were tended, pruned, and thinned to allow their best growth. This work was quite successful: by 1894, the grounds were so deeply shaded by trees and shrubs that Architect of the Capitol Edward Clark recommended an all-night patrol by watchmen to ensure public safety. A hurricane in September 1896 damaged or destroyed a number of trees, requiring extensive removals in the following year. Also in 1897, electric lighting replaced gas lighting in the grounds.

Between 1910 and 1935, 61.4 acres north of Constitution Avenue were added to the grounds. Approximately 100 acres was added in subsequent years, bringing the total area to 274 acres. Late in 2011, care for the Grant Memorial and the reflecting pool at the eastern end of the National Mall was transferred from the National Park Service to the Architect of the Capitol.

Since 1983, increased security measures have been put into effect; however, the area still functions in many ways as a public park, and visitors are welcome to use the walks to tour the grounds. Demonstrations and ceremonies are often held on the grounds. In the summer, a series of evening concerts by the bands of the Armed Forces is offered free of charge on the west front plaza. On various holidays, concerts by the National Symphony Orchestra are held on the west front lawn.

LEGISLATIVE BRANCH

CONGRESSIONAL BUDGET OFFICE

Ford House Office Building

Second and D Streets, SW., H2–405, Washington, DC 20515

phone (202) 226–2600, https://cbo.gov

[Created by Public Law 93–344]

Director.—Phillip Swagel, 226–2700.
Chief Operating Officer and General Counsel.—Mark P. Hadley, 226–2700.
Director of:
Budget Analysis.—Theresa Gullo, 226–2800.
Communications.—Deborah Kilroe, 226–2602.
Financial Analysis.—Sebastien Gay, 226–3579.
Health, Retirement, and Long-Term Analysis.—Vacant, 226–2666.
Legislative Affairs.—Leigh Angres, 226–2701.
Macroeconomic Analysis.—Jeffrey Werling, 226–2750.
Management, Business and Information Services.—Joseph E. Evans, Jr., 226–2600.
Microeconomic Studies.—Joseph Kile, 226–2940.
National Security.—David E. Mosher, 226–2900.
Research.—Jeffrey Kling, 226–2700.
Tax Analysis.—John McClelland, 226–2680.

GOVERNMENT ACCOUNTABILITY OFFICE

441 G Street, NW., Washington, DC 20548

phone (202) 512–3000, https://gao.gov

Comptroller General of the United States.—Gene L. Dodaro, 512–5500, fax 512–5507.
Chief Operating Officer.—Katherine ''Kate'' Siggerud, 512–5600.
Chief Administrative Officer/Chief Financial Officer.—Karl Maschino, 512–5800.
General Counsel.—Thomas ''Tom'' Armstrong, 512–5400.
Deputy General Counsel and Ethics Counselor.—Edda Emmanuelli Perez, 512–2853.
Deputy Ethics Counselor.—James Lager, 512–8170.
Managing Director, Opportunity and Inclusiveness.—Kate Lenare, 512–2792.

TEAMS

Acquisition and Sourcing Management.—Michele Mackin, 512–4841.
Applied Research and Methods.—Nancy Kingsbury, 512–2700.
Defense Capabilities and Management.—Cathleen A. Berrick, 512–4300.
Education Workforce and Income Security.—Barbara D. Bovbjerg, 512–7215.
Financial Management and Assurance.—Gary Engel, 512–2600.
Financial Markets and Community Investments.—Lawrance L. Evans, 512–4802.
Forensic Audits and Investigative Services.—Johana Ayers, 512–6722.
Health Care.—Angela ''Nikki'' Clowers, 512–7114.
Homeland Security and Justice.—Charles M. Johnson, Jr., 512–7331.
Information Technology.—Valerie Melvin, 512–7351.
International Affairs and Trade.—Tom Melito, 512–9601.
Natural Resources and Environment.—Mark Gaffigan, 512–3841.
Physical Infrastructure.—Dan Bertoni, 512–2834.
Strategic Issues.—J. Christopher Mihm, 512–6806.

SUPPORT FUNCTIONS

Audit Policy and Quality Assurance.—Tim Bowling, 512–6100.
Congressional Relations.—Orice Williams Brown, 512–4400.
Legislative Advisers: Patrick Dibattista, 512–6576; Carlos Diz, 512–8256; Rosa Harris, 512–9492; David Lewis, 512–7176; Tim Minelli, 512–8443; Tina Sherman, 512–8461; Chuck Wilson, 512–6891.
Associate Legislative Adviser.—Martene Rhed, 512–5414.
Field Operations.—Linda Calbom (206) 287–4809.
Inspector General.—Adam Trzeciak, 512–8110.
Opportunity and Inclusiveness.—Edda Emmanuelli Perez, 512–2853.
Personnel Appeals Board.—Richard Ugelow, 512–7841.
Public Affairs.—Charles "Chuck" Young, 512–3823.
Strategic Planning and External Liaison.—James-Christian Blockwood, 512–2639.

MISSION SUPPORT OFFICES

Chief Human Capital Officer.—William "Bill" White, 512–5811.
Chief Information Officer.—Howard Williams, Jr., 512–5589.
Controller/Deputy Chief Financial Officer.—William Anderson, 512–2908.
Infrastructure Operations.—Terry Dorn, 512–6923.
Professional Development Program.—Terri Russell, 512–5649.

U.S. GOVERNMENT PUBLISHING OFFICE

732 North Capitol Street, NW., Washington, DC 20401

phone (202) 512–0000, https://gpo.gov

Director.—Hugh Nathanial Halpern, 512–1000, hhalpern@gpo.gov.
Deputy Director.—Patricia S. Collins, 512–1000, pcollins@gpo.gov.
Chief of Staff.—Richard G. Davis (acting), 512–1000, rdavis@gpo.gov.
General Counsel.—Kerry L. Miller, 512–0033, kmiller@gpo.gov.
Managing Director, Equal Employment Opportunity.—Mark A. "Tony" Paras, 512–2331, mparas@gpo.gov.
Chief Financial Officer.—William L. Boesch, Jr., 512–2073, wboesch@gpo.gov.
Chief Administrative Officer.—Lyle L. Green (acting), 512–2010 ext. 30799, llgreen@gpo.gov.
Superintendent of Documents.—Laurie B. Hall, 512–1114, lhall@gpo.gov.
Inspector General.—Michael P. Leary, 512–0039, mleary@gpo.gov.

CHIEF OF STAFF

Chief of Staff.—Richard G. Davis (acting), 512–1622, rdavis@gpo.gov.

COMMUNICATIONS

Congressional Relations Officer.—James McCarthy (acting), 512–1968, jmccarthy@gpo.gov.
Chief Public Relations Officer.—Gary G. Somerset, 512–1957, gsomerset@gpo.gov.

PROGRAMS, STRATEGY, AND TECHNOLOGY

Chief Technology Officer.—Richard G. Davis, 512–1622, rdavis@gpo.gov.

GENERAL COUNSEL

General Counsel.—Kerry L. Miller, 512–0033, kmiller@gpo.gov.
Associate General Counsel, Labor Relations.—Melissa S. Hatfield, 512–0064, mhatfield@gpo.gov.

EQUAL EMPLOYMENT OPPORTUNITY

Managing Director, Equal Employment Opportunity Programs.—Mark A. "Tony" Paras, 512–2331, mparas@gpo.gov.
Assistant Managing Director, Equal Employment Opportunity Programs.—S. Denise Hendricks, 512–2331, shendricks@gpo.gov.

FINANCE

Chief Financial Officer.—William L. Boesch, Jr., 512–2073, wboesch@gpo.gov.
Deputy Chief Financial Officer.—Vacant, 512–2073.

CHIEF ADMINISTRATIVE OFFICER

Chief Administrative Officer.—Lyle L. Green (acting), 512–2010 ext. 30799, llgreen@gpo.gov.

HUMAN CAPITAL

Chief Human Capital Officer.—Dan M. Mielke, 512–1182, dmielke@gpo.gov.
Human Capital Operations Manager.—Lyvette Wallace, 512–1182, lwallace@gpo.gov.
Human Capital Strategy, Policy, Communications and Data Manager.—Terri Leeds, 512–1182, tleeds@gpo.gov.
Chief of Workforce Development, Education and Training.—Stewart Lane, 512–1144, slane@gpo.gov.
Medical Officer.—Telisha D. Anthony, FNP–BC, 512–2061, tanthony@gpo.gov.

INFORMATION TECHNOLOGY

Chief Information Officer.—Sam Musa, 512–1040, wmusa@gpo.gov.
Deputy Chief Information Officer.—Vacant, 512–1040.
Chief of:
Applications Development and Management Division.—Layton F. Clay, 512–2001, lclay@gpo.gov.
Information Technology Operations Division.—Nadeem Sahibzada, 512–1406, nsahibzada@gpo.gov.
Information Technology Security Division.—John L. Hannan, 512–1021, jhannan@gpo.gov.

SECURITY SERVICES

Chief Security Officer.—LaMont R. Vernon, 512–1103, lvernon@gpo.gov.
Commander, Uniformed Police Branch.—Paul D. Epley, 512–1084, pepley@gpo.gov.
Chief of:
Physical Security.—Gresham Harkless, 512–0872, gharkless@gpo.gov.
Product Security.—Aaron P. Williams, 512–2041, apwilliams@gpo.gov.
Safety Branch.—Lonny Beal, 512–0537, lbeal@gpo.gov.

ACQUISITION SERVICES

Managing Director, Chief Acquisition Officer.—Lorna Baptiste-Jones, 512–0351, lbaptistejones@gpo.gov.
Chief, Acquisition Services.—Ricky L. Clark, 512–0346, rclark@gpo.gov.
Supervisor of:
Team #1.—Reginald Walker, 512–2010, ext. 31500, rwalker@gpo.gov.
Team #2.—Ronald Ortega, 512–0803, rortega@gpo.gov.
Team #3.—Beverly J. Williams, 512–2010, ext. 31200, bwilliams@gpo.gov.

DEPUTY DIRECTOR OF THE GOVERNMENT PUBLISHING OFFICE

Deputy Director.—Patricia S. Collins, 512–1000, pcollins@gpo.gov.

OFFICIAL JOURNALS OF GOVERNMENT

Managing Director.—Lyle L. Green, 512–0224, llgreen@gpo.gov.
Chief of:
Congressional Publishing Services.—Cathy DeVinney, 512–0224, mdevinney@gpo.gov.
Congressional Record Index Office.—Philip Hart, 512–0275, pchart@gpo.gov.
Office of Federal Register Publishing Services Manager.—Jeffrey D. MacAfee, 512–2100, jmacafee@gpo.gov.

PLANT OPERATIONS

Managing Director.—John W. Crawford, 512–0707, jcrawford@gpo.gov.

Deputy Managing Director.—Gregory E. Estep, 512–0707, gestep@gpo.gov.
Chief, Engineering Services.—Michael Dietz, 512–1976, mdietz@gpo.gov.
Production Manager (shift 1).—Vacant, 512–1407.
Assistant Production Manager.—Ibrahim N. ''Abe'' Sussan, 512–0589, isussan@gpo.gov.
Production Manager (shift 3).—Vacant, 512–0625.
Manager of:
Prepress Operations.—Francine R. ''Renee'' Rosa, 512–1651, frosa@gpo.gov.
Press and Bindery.—Ravinder Birdi, 512–0707.
Production Engineering.—David J. Robare, 512–1370, drobare@gpo.gov.
Production Planning and Control.—Robert M. Martein, 512–1470, rmartein@gpo.gov.
Quality Control and Inventory Management.—Michael P. Mooney, 512–0766, mmooney@gpo.gov.

SECURITY AND INTELLIGENT DOCUMENTS

Managing Director.—Stephen G. LeBlanc, 512–2285, sleblanc@gpo.gov.
Operations Manager.—David H. Ford, 512–1194, dford@gpo.gov.
Manager of Business Development.—Gerald Egan, 512–2010, gegan@gpo.gov.
New Product and Program Development.—Scott Stole, 512–0697, sstole@gpo.gov.
Secure Production (DC).—Daniel R. Wilson, 512–1485, dwilson@gpo.gov.
Secure Production (Stennis).—David Spiers (228) 813–1716, dspiers@gpo.gov.

CUSTOMER SERVICES

Managing Director.—Sandra K. MacAfee, 512–0320, smacafee@gpo.gov.
Deputy Managing Director.—Vacant, 512–2213.
Chief of:
DC Agency Procurement Services.—Julie A. Hasenfus, 512–0655, jhasenfus@gpo.gov.
Regional Agency Procurement Services.—Teddy J. Priebe, 512–2015, tpriebe@gpo.gov.
Sales and Publishing Support.—Kirk D. Knoll, 512–1147, kknoll@gpo.gov.
Manager, Creative and Digital Media Services.—Ronald J. Keeney, 512–2012, rkeeney@gpo.gov.

GPO REGIONAL PRINTING PROCUREMENT OFFICES

Atlanta: 3715 Northside Parkway, Suite 4–305, Atlanta, GA 30327 (404) 605–9160, fax 605–9185, infoatlanta@gpo.gov.
Manager.—Elizabeth A. Rich.

Boston: John F. Kennedy Federal Building, 15 New Sudbury Street, E270, Boston, MA 02203–0002 (617) 565–1370, fax 565–1385, infoboston@gpo.gov.
Manager.—Michael J. Sommer (acting).

Charleston: 2154 North Center Street, Suite D401, North Charleston, SC 29406–1819 (843) 743–2036, fax 743–2068, infocharleston@gpo.gov.
Manager.—Richard W. Gilbert.

Chicago: 200 North LaSalle Street, Suite 810, Chicago, IL 60601–1055 (312) 353–3916, fax 886–3163, infochicago@gpo.gov.
Manager.—Clint J. Mixon.

Columbus: 1335 Dublin Road, Suite 112–B, Columbus, OH 43215–7034 (614) 488–4616, fax 488–4577, infocolumbus@gpo.gov.
Manager.—Michael J. Sommer.
Assistant Manager.—Bill Lansky.

Dallas: Federal Office Building, 1100 Commerce Street, Room 731, Dallas, TX 75242–1027 (214) 767–0451, fax 767–4101, infodallas@gpo.gov.
Manager.—Elizabeth A. Rich.
Assistant Manager.—Jermaine Berryman.

Denver: 12345 West Alameda Parkway, Suite 208, Lakewood, CO 80228–2842 (303) 236–5292, fax 236–5304, infodenver@gpo.gov.
Manager.—Diane L. Abeyta.

Philadelphia: 928 Jaymore Road, Suite A190, Southampton, PA 18966–3820 (215) 364–6465, fax 364–6476, infophiladelphia@gpo.gov.
Manager.—Michael J. Sommer (acting).

San Antonio: 1320 Truemper Street, Building 9122, Room 2707, Lackland AFB, TX 78236–5515 (210) 675–1480, fax 675–2429, infosanantonio@gpo.gov.
Manager.—Elizabeth A. Rich.
Assistant Manager.—Jermaine Berryman.

San Diego: 8880 Rio San Diego Drive, 8th Floor, San Diego, CA 92108–3609 (619) 209–6178, fax 209–6179, infosandiego@gpo.gov.
Manager.—Michael A. Barnes.

San Francisco: 536 Stone Road, Suite 1, Benicia, CA 94510–1170 (707) 748–1970, fax 748–1980, infosanfran@gpo.gov.
Manager.—Michael A. Barnes.

Seattle: Federal Center South, 4735 East Marginal Way South, Seattle, WA 98134–2397 (206) 764–3726, fax 764–3301, infoseattle@gpo.gov.
Manager.—Roland Whitehurst.

Virginia Beach: 291 Independence Boulevard, Suite 401, Virginia Beach, VA 23462 (757) 490–7940, fax 490–7950, infovirginiabeach@gpo.gov.
Manager.—Richard W. Gilbert.

SUPERINTENDENT OF DOCUMENTS

Superintendent of Documents.—Laurie B. Hall, 512–1114, lhall@gpo.gov.

LIBRARY SERVICES AND CONTENT MANAGEMENT

Managing Director.—Laurie B. Hall, 512–1114, lhall@gpo.gov.
Chief of:
Federal Depository Support Services.—Katherine Pitcher, kpitcher@gpo.gov.
Library Technical Services.—Fang H. Gao, 512–1966, fgao@gpo.gov.
Projects and Systems.—Vacant.

PUBLICATION AND INFORMATION SALES

Managing Director.—Vacant.
Chief, Publication Sales and Marketing.—Vacant, 512–1065.
Content Acquisitions and Contact Center.—Vacant, 512–1065.

TO ORDER SUBSCRIPTIONS AND PUBLICATIONS

Outside the Washington, DC Area: phone (866) 512–1800.
Washington, DC: phone (202) 512–1800, fax (202) 512–2104.
Mail Orders: Superintendent of Documents, P.O. Box 371954, Pittsburgh, PA 15250–7954.
Online from the U.S. Government Bookstore: https://bookstore.gpo.gov.
GPO Customer Support: ContactCenter@gpo.gov.

DISTRIBUTION SERVICES AND OUTREACH

Chief, Publication and Information Sales.—Lisa L. Williams, 512–1065, llwilliams@gpo.gov.

LAUREL FACILITY

Operations Manager.—Robert E. Mitchell, 8660 Cherry Lane, Mail Stop: SSR, Laurel, MD 20707–4982 (202) 512–2317, remitchell@gpo.gov.

CONGRESSMAN FRANK EVANS GOVERNMENT PUBLISHING OFFICE DISTRIBUTION CENTER

Operations Manager.—Thomas L. Hunt, P.O. Box 4007, Pueblo, CO 81003 (719) 295–2678, fax 948–3315, thunt@gpo.gov.

LIBRARY OF CONGRESS

The James Madison Memorial Building (LM)
101 Independence Avenue, SE., Washington, DC 20540

The Thomas Jefferson Building (LJ)
10 First Street, SE., Washington, DC 20540

The John Adams Building (LA)
102 Second Street, SE., Washington, DC 20002

phone (202) 707–5000, https://loc.gov

OFFICE OF THE LIBRARIAN

phone (202) 707–5205

The Librarian of Congress.—Carla Hayden (202) 707–5205.
Confidential Assistant to the Librarian of Congress.—Terri Humphries, LM 608, 707–5205.
Principal Deputy Librarian of Congress.—J. Mark Sweeney, 707–1323.
Confidential Assistant to the Principal Deputy Librarian of Congress.—Nicole L. Marcou, LM 608, 707–7159.
General Counsel.—Elizabeth Pugh, LM 601, 707–6316.
Senior Advisor for Organizational Performance.—Dianne Houghton, LM 608, 707–3096.

OFFICE OF THE CHIEF OF STAFF

phone (202) 707–5205

Chief of Staff.—Ryan Ramsey, LM 608 (202) 707–5205.
Director, Congressional Relations Office.—Sarah Boliek, LM 611, 707–6577.
Director, Development Office.—Jane McAuliffe, LM 605, 707–0636.
Chief, Office of EEO and Diversity Programs.—Vicki Magnus, LM 612, 707–6024.
Supervisory Program Specialist for Administration, Office of the Librarian and Centers Administration.—Erika White, LM 608, 707–1502.

OFFICE OF COMMUNICATIONS AND EXTERNAL RELATIONS

Chief Communications Officer.—Roswell Encina, LM 608 (202) 707–5205.
Director, Office of Communications.—Bill Ryan (acting), LM 106, 707–2905.
Chief, Multimedia Group.—Jim Cannady, LM G51, 707–4595.

CENTER FOR EXHIBITS AND INTERPRETATION

Director.—David Mandel, LM 608 (202) 707–3689.
Director, Publishing Office.—Rebecca Brasington Clark, LA 5159, 707–1520.
Head, Design Office.—Michael Munshaw, LM G56, 707–9596.
Deputy Chief, Exhibits Office.—Karen Werth, LA G25, 707–2642.

CENTER FOR LEARNING, LITERACY AND ENGAGEMENT

Director.—Shari Rosenstein Werb, LM 608 (202) 707–9042.
Director, Center for the Book.—Vacant, LA 300, 707–4543.
Head, Poetry and Literature Center.—Rob Casper, LJ A02, 707–1308.
Director of Educational Outreach, Learning and Innovation Office.—Lee Ann Potter, LA 300, 707–8735.
Head, Young Readers Center.—Vacant, LJ G29, 707–1950.
Director, Library Events Office.—Mary Eno, LM 623, 707–5574.
Director, Signature Programs Office.—Jarrod MacNeil, LM 629, 707–6385.
Visitor Services Officer, Visitor Engagement Office.—Giulia Adelfio, LJ G59, 707–2153.

LIBRARY COLLECTIONS AND SERVICES GROUP (LCSG)

Deputy Librarian for Library Collections and Services.—Jane Sánchez, LM 642 (202) 707–9825.
Assistant Deputy Librarian for Library Collections and Services.—Colleen Shogan, LM 642, 707–8231.

Confidential Assistant to the Deputy and Assistant Deputy Librarians.—Timothy Robbins, LM 642, 707–0303.

Director, National Library Service for the Blind and Print Disabled.—Karen Keninger, TSA, 707–5104.

Chief, Internship and Fellowship Programs.—Kimberly Powell, LA 209, 707–8976.

Director, The John W. Kluge Center.—John Haskell, LJ 120, 707–3302.

Director, LCSG Operations.—Joe Cappello, LM 637, 707–3411.

LAW LIBRARY OF CONGRESS

Law Librarian of Congress.—Jane Sánchez, LM 240 (202) 707–9825.

Special Assistant to the Law Librarian of Congress.—Mirela Savic-Fleming, LM 240, 707–8923.

Deputy Law Librarian for Collections, Global Legal Collection Directorate.—Vacant, LM 240.

Assistant Law Librarian for Research, Global Legal Research Directorate.—Peter Roudik, LM 240, 707–9861.

Assistant Law Librarian for Operations and Planning, Office of Administrative Operations.—Roberto Salazar, LM 240, 707–0947.

Chief of:

Collection Services Division.—Kurt Carroll, LM 232, 707–1494.

Digital Resources Division.—Vacant, LM 240.

Foreign, Comparative, and International Law Division I.—Hanibal Goitom, LM 235, 707–9117.

Foreign, Comparative, and International Law Division II.—Luis Acosta, LM 235, 707–9131.

Public Services Division.—Debbie Keysor, LM 235, 707–3164.

LIBRARY SERVICES

phone (202) 707–5325

Associate Librarian for Library Services.—Robin L. Dale, LM 642 (202) 707–2774.

Administrative Specialist.—Darlene Foster, LM 642, 707–9778.

Collection Development Officer.—Joseph Puccio, LJ Deck A, 707–1413.

Chief, National Audio-Visual Conservation Center/Motion Picture, Broadcasting, and Recorded Sound Division.—Gregory Lukow, PC 2013, 707–5709.

Chief Operating Officer.—Alvert ''Al'' Banks, LM 637, 707–9562.

Chief, Digital Collection Management and Services Division.—Steve Morris, LA G04, 707–5212.

Chief, Integrated Library System Program Office.—Ann Della Porta, LA 301, 707–4761.

Director, Acquisitions and Bibliographic Access.—Beacher Wiggins, LM 642, 707–5137.

Chief of:

Acquisitions, Fiscal, and Overseas Support Division.—Beacher Wiggins (acting), LM B42/B46, 707–5137.

African, Latin American, and Western European Division.—Angela Kinney, LM 542, 707–5572.

Asian and Middle Eastern Division.—Jessalyn Zoom, LM 511, 707–4264.

Cooperative and Instructional Programs Division.—Judith Cannan, LA 305, 707–2031.

Germanic and Slavic Division.—Lucy Barron (acting), LM 523, 707–6326.

Network Development and MARC Standards Office.—Sally H. McCallum, LA 309, 707–5119.

Policy and Standards Division.—Judith Cannan, LA 305, 707–2031.

U.S./Anglo Division.—Diana Snigurowicz, LM G35, 707–2855.

U.S. Arts, Sciences, and Humanities Division.—Vera Clyburn, LM 515, 707–3943.

U.S. Programs, Law, and Literature Division.—Karl Debus-López, LM 501, 707–6641.

Director of Special Collections Directorate.—Michelle Light, LM 642, 707–3343.

Director, Veterans History Project.—Karen Lloyd, LA 1143, 707–6074.

American Folklife Center.—Elizabeth Peterson, LJ G49, 707–1745.

Chief of:

Geography and Map Division.—Paulette Hasier, LM B02, 707–3400.

Manuscript Division.—Janice Ruth (acting), LM 102, 707–5383.

Music Division.—Susan H. Vita, LM 113, 707–5503.

Prints and Photographs Division.—Helena Zinkham, LM 339, 707–2922.

Rare Book and Special Collections Division.—Mark G. Dimunation, LJ 230, 707–2025.

Director, Preservation.—Jacob Nadal, LM 642, 707–2068.

Chief of:

Binding and Collections Care Division.—Jeanne Drewes, LM G21, 707–5330.

Collections Management Division.—Steven J. Herman, LJ G02, 707–1410.

Conservation Division.—Elmer Eusman, LM G38, 707–5838.

Preservation Reformatting Division.—Adrija Henley, LA 230, 707–0788.

Preservation Research and Testing Division.—Fenella France, LM G38, 707–5525.

Director of General and International Collections.—Eugene Flanagan, LM 642, 707–8203.

Chief of:

African and Middle Eastern Division.—Joan Weeks (acting), LJ 220, 707–3657.

Asian Division.—Dongfang Shao, LJ 149, 707–5919.

European Division.—Grant Harris, LJ 250, 707–5859.

Hispanic Division.—Suzanne Schadl, LJ 240, 707–9167.

Researcher and Reference Services Division.—Kimberley Bugg, LJ 139A, 707–5530.

Science, Technology, and Business Division.—Ronald S. Bluestone, LA 5203, 707–0948.

Serial and Government Publications Division.—Teresa V. Sierra, LM 133, 707–5277.

CHIEF OPERATING OFFICER

Chief Operating Officer.—Edward R. Jablonski, LM 643 (202) 707–8397.

Chief Acquisition Officer, Contracts and Grants Directorate.—Ronald W. Backes, LA 322, 707–0833.

Chief Financial Officer, Financial Services Directorate.—Mary Klutts, LM 613, 707–2418.

Chief Human Capital Officer, Human Capital Directorate.—Rachel A. Bouman, LM 645, 707–7364.

Director of:

Integrated Support Services Directorate.—Elizabeth Scheffler, LM 327, 707–6042.

Security and Emergency Preparedness Directorate.—Kenneth Lopez, LM G03, 707–9410.

Library Enterprises Directorate.—Greg Abraham, LM 643, 707–3569.

Chief, Business Enterprises Division.—Deirdre Scott, LA 130, 707–1421.

Chief, Federal Research Division.—Kristian Hassinger, LA 5282, 707–0038.

Executive Director, FEDLINK.—Laurie Neider, LA 217, 707–8425.

OFFICE OF THE CHIEF INFORMATION OFFICER

phone (202) 707–3300

Chief Information Officer.—Bernard A. ''Bud'' Barton, Jr., LM 635 (202) 707–3300.

Confidential Assistant to the CIO.—Kim Barnhart, LM 635, 707–6530.

Deputy Chief Information Officer.—Judith Conklin, LM 635, 707–3165.

Director of:

Digital Strategy.—Kate Zwaard, LM 635, 707–5242.

IT Design and Development.—Jim Karamanis, LM 635, 707–2732.

IT Financial Management.—Molly Johnson, 707–3300.

IT Governance.—Kristin Laurente, LM 635, 707–5068.

IT Partner Engagement.—John Rutledge, LM 635, 707–0442.

IT Quality and Performance Management.—Vanley Bucknor, LM 635, 707–5456.

IT Service Operations.—Timothy Daugherty, LM 635, 707–8355.

CONGRESSIONAL RESEARCH SERVICE

phone (202) 707–5700

Director.—Mary B. Mazanec, LM 203 (202) 707–5775.

Head, Administrative Operations.—Rosslyn Richardson, LM 203, 707–5484.

Deputy Director.—TJ Halstead, LM 203, 707–7981.

Counselor to the Director.—Catherine Hurst Weber, LM 203, 707–0903.

Congressional Programs and Communications.—Stephen Dagadakis, LM 204, 707–0822.

Associate Director, Office of Administrative Operations.—Francois A. DiFolco, LM 209, 707–2877.

Associate Director, Office of Congressional Information and Publishing.—Clifford T. Cohen, LM 215, 707–1858.

Assistant Director, Division of:

American Law.—Karen J. Lewis, LM 227, 707–7460.

Domestic Social Policy.—Laura B. Shrestha, LM 323, 707–7046.

Foreign Affairs, Defense and Trade.—Michael L. Moodie, LM 315, 707–8470.

Government and Finance.—Jeffrey W. Seifert, LM 304, 707–0781.

Knowledge Services Group.—Lillian W. Gassie, LM 215, 707–7573.
Resources, Science and Industry.—Dana A. Shea, LM 419, 707–6844.

U.S. COPYRIGHT OFFICE

phone (202) 707–8350

Register of Copyrights and Director.—Karyn A. Temple, LM 403, 707–8128.
Special Assistant to the Register.—Terri Vincent, LM 403, 707–8128.
Associate Register of Copyrights and Director of Registration Policy and Practice.—Robert J. Kasunic, LM 443, 707–0229.
General Counsel and Associate Register of Copyrights.—Regan A. Smith, LM 403, 707–0214.
Associate Register of Copyrights and Director of Public Information and Education.—Catherine Zaller Rowland, LM 403, 707–0956.
Associate Register of Copyrights and Director of Policy and International Affairs.—Maria Strong, LM 403, 707–8390.
Director of Public Records and Repositories.—Denise Wofford, LM 433, 707–2638.
Director of the Copyright Modernization Office.—Ricardo Farraj-Feijoo, LM 560, 707–0110.
Chief Financial Officer.—Jody A. Harry, LM 403, 707–8772.
Chief of Operations.—Jody A. Harry (acting), LM 403, 707–8772.
Deputy Director of:
General Counsel.—Kevin R. Amer, LM 403, 707–1434.
Office of Public Information and Education.—George Thuronyi, LM 453, 707–6866.
Registration Policy and Practice.—Erik Bertin, LM 443, 707–7566.
Director of Policy and International Affairs.—Vacant.
Director of Copyright Modernization Office.—Gustave Schlesier, LM 560, 707–7451.
Chief Financial Officer.—Chris Fredericks, LM 403, 707–2784.
Chief of:
Acquisitions Division.—Stephen D. Want, LM 526, 707–6781.
Administrative Services Office.—Bruce J. McCubbin, LM 458, 707–8395.
Licensing Division.—James B. Enzinna, LM 504, 707–6801.
Literary Division.—Charles Bubeck, LM 438, 707–7526,
Performing Arts Division.—Laura Lee Fischer, LM 443, 707–5751.
Receipt Analysis and Control Division.—Craig R. Taylor, LM 424, 707–2830.
Visual Arts Division.—John H. Ashley, LM 433, 707–8223.

OFFICE OF THE INSPECTOR GENERAL

phone (202) 707–6314

Inspector General.—Kurt Hyde, LM 630.
Deputy Inspector General.—John Mech, LM 630, 707–6314.

UNITED STATES BOTANIC GARDEN

245 First Street, SW., Washington, DC 20515

phone (202) 225–8333 (information), 226–8333 (administration)

https://usbg.gov

Director.—J. Brett Blanton, Architect of the Capitol, 228–1793.
Executive Director.—Saharah Moon Chapotin, Ph.D., 225–6670.
Deputy Executive Director.—Susan K. Pell, Ph.D., 225–1269.
Business Operations Manager.—Vacant, 225–5002.
Horticulture Division Manager.—James R. Adams, 695–5232.
Operations Division Manager.—Patrick Andriuk, 225–6646.
Public Programs Division Manager.—Amy Bolton, 262–4148.

THE CABINET

Vice President of the United States	MICHAEL R. PENCE.
Secretary of State	MIKE POMPEO.
Secretary of the Treasury	STEVEN T. MNUCHIN.
Secretary of Defense	MARK ESPER.
Attorney General	WILLIAM BARR.
Secretary of the Interior	DAVID BERNHARDT.
Secretary of Agriculture	SONNY PERDUE.
Secretary of Commerce	WILBUR L. ROSS, JR.
Secretary of Labor	EUGENE SCALIA.
Secretary of Health and Human Services	ALEX AZAR.
Secretary of Housing and Urban Development	BENJAMIN S. CARSON, SR.
Secretary of Transportation	ELAINE L. CHAO.
Secretary of Energy	DAN BROUILLETTE.
Secretary of Education	ELISABETH PRINCE DEVOS.
Secretary of Veterans Affairs	ROBERT WILKIE.
Secretary of Homeland Security	CHAD WOLF (acting).
White House Chief of Staff	MARK MEADOWS.
Administrator of the Environmental Protection Agency	ANDREW WHEELER.
U.S. Trade Representative	ROBERT LIGHTHIZER.
Director of National Intelligence	JOHN RATCLIFFE.
Director of the Central Intelligence Agency	GINA HASPEL.
Director of the Office of Management and Budget	RUSS VOUGHT.
Administrator of the Small Business Administration	JOVITA CARRANZA.

EXECUTIVE BRANCH

THE PRESIDENT

DONALD J. TRUMP, 45th President of the United States; born in Queens, NY, June 14, 1946; graduated from New York Military Academy in Cornwall, NY, in 1964; received a bachelor of science degree in economics in 1968 from the Wharton School of the University of Pennsylvania in Philadelphia, PA; joined Trump Management Company in 1968; became president of the Trump Organization in 1971 until 2016, when elected President of the United States; family: married to Melania; five children: Donald Jr., Ivanka, Eric, Tiffany, and Barron; nine grandchildren; elected as President of the United States on November 8, 2016, and took the oath of office on January 20, 2017.

EXECUTIVE OFFICE OF THE PRESIDENT

1600 Pennsylvania Avenue, NW., Washington, DC 20500

Eisenhower Executive Office Building (EEOB), 17th Street and Pennsylvania Avenue, NW., Washington, DC 20500

phone (202) 456–1414, https://whitehouse.gov

The President of the United States.—Donald J. Trump.
Deputy Assistant to the President and Director of Oval Office Operations.—Nicholas F. Luna.
Executive Assistant to the President.—Molly A. Michael.

OFFICE OF THE VICE PRESIDENT

phone (202) 456–1414

The Vice President.—Mike Pence.
Assistant to the President and Chief of Staff to the Vice President.—Marc Short.
Assistant to the President and National Security Advisor to the Vice President.—Keith Kellogg.
Deputy Assistant to the President and Deputy Chief of Staff and Counsel to the Vice President.—Gregory Jacob.
Deputy Assistant to the President and Chief of Staff to Mrs. Karen Pence.—Jana Toner.
Deputy Assistant to the President and Deputy National Security Advisor to the Vice President.—Stephen Pinkos.
Deputy Assistant to the President and Director of Advance to the Vice President.—Aaron Chang.
Deputy Assistant to the President and Director of Policy for the Vice President.—John Gray.
Deputy Assistant to the President and Director of Public Liaison and Intergovernmental Affairs for the Vice President.—Paul Teller.
Special Assistant to the President and Deputy Director of Public Liaison and Intergovernmental Affairs.—Andeliz Castillo.
Special Assistant to the President and Press Secretary to the Vice President.—Katie Waldman.
Assistant to the Vice President and Director of Legislative Affairs.—Christopher Hodgson.
Deputy Director of Legislative Affairs.—Benjamin Cantrell.
Deputy Assistant to the Vice President and Director of Administration and Finance.—Katherine Purucker.
Deputy Assistant to the Vice President and Director of Scheduling.—Bethany Scully.
Special Assistant to the Vice President.—Zach Bauer.

COUNCIL OF ECONOMIC ADVISERS

1650 Pennsylvania Avenue, NW., Room 360, Washington, DC 20006

phone (202) 456–4779, https://whitehouse.gov/cea/staff

Chair.—Tyler Goodspeed (acting).
Vice Chair.—Tyler Goodspeed.
Chief of Staff.—Rachel Slobodien.
Member.—Richard Burkhauser.

COUNCIL ON ENVIRONMENTAL QUALITY

730 Jackson Place, NW., Washington, DC 20503

phone (202) 456–6224, https://www.whitehouse.gov/ceq

Chair.—Vacant.
Chief of Staff.—Mary Neumayr.
Special Assistant.—Katherine Smith.
Speechwriter.—David Sorensen.
General Counsel.—Vacant.
Deputy General Counsel.—Viktoria Seale.
Attorney Advisors: Philip Bristol, Caroline Gignoux, Beverly Li, Thomas Sharp, Howard Sun.
Director of Finance and Administration.—Angela Matos.
Administrative Officer.—Essence Tillett.
Administrative Assistants: Mary Green, Juschelle McLaurin.
Associate Director for NEPA.—Edward ''Ted'' Boling.
Deputy Associate Directors for NEPA: Michael Drummond, Karen Hanley, Sarah Shattuck, Sara Upchurch.
Associate Director for Infrastructure.—Alexander ''Alex'' Herrgott.
Senior Advisors on Infrastructure: Michael Harkins, April Marchese, Michael Patella.
Deputy Advisors on Infrastructure: Allison Rusnak, Mark Wingate.
Associate Director for Natural Resources.—Christopher ''Chris'' Prandoni.
Deputy Associate Director for Ecosystems.—Tabitha Cale.
Associate Director for Regulatory Reform.—Mario Loyola.
Deputy Chief Sustainability Officer.—Bernice ''Dee'' Siegel.
Senior Sustainability Officers: Mark Ackiewicz, Caroline D'Angelo.

PRESIDENT'S INTELLIGENCE ADVISORY BOARD

phone (202) 456–2352

Chair.—Steve Feinberg.
Executive Director.—Vacant.

NATIONAL SECURITY COUNCIL

EEOB, 17th Street and Pennsylvania Avenue, NW., Washington, DC 20500

phone (202) 456–1414, https://whitehouse.gov/nsc

MEMBERS

The President.—Donald J. Trump.
The Vice President.—Mike Pence.
The Secretary of State.—Mike Pompeo.
The Secretary of Defense.—Mark Esper.

STATUTORY ADVISERS

Director of National Intelligence.—John Ratcliffe.
Chair, Joint Chiefs of Staff.—Gen. Mark A. Milley.

STANDING PARTICIPANTS

The Secretary of the Treasury.—Steven T. Mnuchin.

Chief of Staff to the President.—Mark R. Meadows.
Counsel to the President.—Pasquale Cipollone.
National Security Adviser.—Robert O'Brien.
Assistant to the President for Economic Policy.—Larry Kudlow.

OFFICIALS

Assistant to the President for National Security Affairs.—Robert O'Brien.
Assistant to the President for National Security Affairs and Deputy National Security Adviser.—Matthew Pottinger.

OFFICE OF ADMINISTRATION

EEOB, 17th Street and Pennsylvania Avenue, NW., Washington, DC 20500

phone (202) 395–5555

Director of White House Management and Administration and Director of the Office of Administration.—Monica J. Block.
Special Assistant to the President and Deputy Director of White House Management and Administration.—Alexandra E. Stone.

OFFICE OF MANAGEMENT AND BUDGET

EEOB, 17th Street and Pennsylvania Avenue, NW., Washington, DC 20500

phone (202) 395–4840

Director.—Russell Vought.
Deputy Director.—Tom Reilly (acting).
Deputy Director for Management.—Dustin Brown (acting).
General Counsel.—Mark Paoletta.
Administrator, Office of:
Federal Chief Information Officer.—Suzette Kent.
Federal Financial Management/Controller.—Tim Soltis (acting).
Federal Procurement Policy.—Michael Wooten.
Information and Regulatory Affairs.—Dominc J. Mancini (acting).
Assistant Director for—
Budget.—Kelly Kinneen.
Legislative Reference.—Matthew Vaeth.
Associate Director for—
Communications.—Vacant.
Economic Policy.—Vacant.
Education, Income Maintenance, and Labor Programs.—John Gray.
General Government Programs.—Kathy Kraninger.
Health Programs.—Greg D'Angelo.
Intergovernmental Affairs and Strategic Initiatives.—Vacant.
Legislative Affairs.—Vacant.
National Security Programs.—Vacant.
Natural Resources, Energy, and Science Programs.—Vacant.
Performance and Personnel Management.—Dustin Brown (acting).

OFFICE OF NATIONAL DRUG CONTROL POLICY

750 17th Street, NW., Washington, DC 20500

phone (202) 395–6700, fax 395–6711

Director.—James Carroll, Room 810, 395–6700.
Chief of Staff.—Kayla Tonnessen (acting), Room 518, 395–6601.
Deputy Chief of Staff.—Taylor P. Weyeneth, Room 805, 395–7336.
Deputy Director.—Vacant, Room 810, 395–6700.
Assistant Deputy Director, Office of:
Policy, Research, and Budget.—Terry W. Zobeck, Room 609, 395–5503.
Supply Reduction.—Vacant, Room 825, 395–5535.

General Counsel.—Lawrence L. Muir, Room 518, 395–6601.
Associate Director, Office of:
Cocaine Task Force.—Eric Talbot, Room 756, 395–6885.
Heroin Task Force.—Kemp Chester, Room 731, 395–5615.
Intelligence.—Gerard Burns, Room 755, 395–6764.
Legislative Affairs.—Kayla Tonnessen, Room 825, 395–4693.
Management and Administration.—Michele C. Marx, Room 326, 395–6883.
Policy, Research, and Budget.—Jon E. Rice, Room 661, 395–6791.
Programs.—Michael Gottlieb, Room 836, 395–4868.
Public Affairs.—Vacant.

OFFICE OF SCIENCE AND TECHNOLOGY POLICY

EEOB, 17th Street and Pennsylvania Avenue, NW., Washington, DC 20500

phone (202) 456–4444, fax 456–6021, https://whitehouse.gov/ostp

Director.—Kelvin Droegemeier.
Chief of Staff.—Sean Bonyun.
U.S. Chief Technology Officer, Deputy Assistant to the President for Technology Policy.—Michael Kratsios.
Principal Assistant Director for—
National Security and Senior Policy Advisor.—Aaron Miles.
Oceans and Environment.—Deerin Babb-Brott.
Physical Sciences and Engineering.—John Looney.
General Counsel.—Rob Bernstein.
Assistant Director for Legislative Affairs.—Neil Canfield.
Director of Strategic Communications.—Kristina Baum.
Executive Director, National Science and Technology Council.—Chloe Kontos.

OFFICE OF THE UNITED STATES TRADE REPRESENTATIVE

600 17th Street, NW., Washington, DC 20508

phone (202) 395–6890, https://ustr.gov

United States Trade Representative.—Robert E. Lighthizer.
Deputy United States Trade Representatives: Jeff Gerrish, C.J. Mahoney.
Deputy United States Trade Representative and Chief of Mission, Geneva.—Dennis Shea.
Chief Agricultural Negotiator.—Gregg Doud.
Chief Innovation and Intellectual Property Negotiator.—Vacant.
Chief of Staff.—Kevin Garvey.
General Counsel.—Joseph L. Barloon.
Deputy General Counsel.—Maria Pagan.
Assistant United States Trade Representatives (AUSTR) for—
Administration.—Fred Ames.
Africa.—Constance Hamilton.
Agricultural Affairs and Commodity Policy.—Julie Callahan.
China Affairs.—Terrence J. McCartin.
Congressional Affairs.—Christopher Jackson.
Environment and Natural Resources.—Kelly Milton (acting).
Europe and the Middle East.—L. Daniel Mullaney.
Innovation and Intellectual Property.—Daniel Lee (acting).
Intergovernmental Affairs and Public Engagement.—Vacant.
Japan, Korea, and APEC.—Michael Beeman.
Labor.—Lewis Karesh.
Monitoring and Enforcement.—Juan A. Millan.
Public and Media Affairs.—Jeff Emerson.
Services and Investment.—Daniel Bahar.
Small Business, Market Access, and Industrial Competitiveness.—Jim Sanford.
South and Central Asia.—Christopher Wilson.
Southeast Asia and the Pacific.—Karl Ehlers.
Textiles.—Bill Jackson.
Trade Policy and Economics.—Edward Gresser.
Western Hemisphere.—Daniel Watson (acting).
WTO (World Trade Organization) and Multilateral Affairs.—Dawn Shackleford.

THE WHITE HOUSE OFFICE

CABINET AFFAIRS

Deputy Assistant to the President and Cabinet Secretary.—Kristan K. Nevins.

CHIEF OF STAFF

Assistant to the President and Chief of Staff.—Mark R. Meadows.
Assistant to the President and Deputy Chief of Staff for Operations.—Anthony M. Ornato.
Assistant to the President and Deputy Chief of Staff for Policy.—Chris Liddell.

COMMUNICATIONS AND PRESS

Assistant to the President and Director of Strategic Communications.—Alyssa A. Farah.
Assistant to the President and Press Secretary.—Kayleigh McEnany.
Assistant to the President and Deputy Chief of Staff for Communications.—Daniel Scavino.
Deputy Assistant to the President and Principal Deputy Press Secretary.—John H. Gidley.
Deputy Assistant to the President and Deputy Director for Communications.—Julia A. Hahn.
Deputy Director for Communications and Deputy Press Secretary.—Brian Morgenstern.
Deputy Assistant to the President and Senior Advisor to the Chief of Staff and Senior Communications Advisor.—Benjamin D. Williamson.

OFFICE OF DIGITAL STRATEGY

Deputy Assistant to the President and Deputy Chief Digital Officer.—Katlyn L. Pamitzke.

OFFICE OF AMERICAN INNOVATION

Assistant to the President and Senior Advisor.—Jared Kushner.
Assistant to the President and Counselor to the President.—Hope Hicks.
Assistant to the President and Special Representative for International Negotiations.—Avrahm J. Berkowitz.
Deputy Assistant to the President for Strategic Initiatives.—John N. Rader.

DOMESTIC POLICY COUNCIL

Assistant to the President and Director of the Domestic Policy Council.—Brooke L. Rollins (acting).

OFFICE OF THE SENIOR ADVISOR FOR POLICY

Assistant to the President and Senior Advisor for Policy.—Stephen Miller.
Deputy Assistant to the President and Director of Intergovernmental Affairs.—Douglas L. Hoelscher.
Deputy Assistant to the President and Advisor for Policy, Strategy, and Speechwriting.—Vincent Haley.

OFFICE OF ECONOMIC INITIATIVES AND ENTREPRENEURSHIP

Advisor to the President.—Ivanka Trump.
Deputy Assistant to the President and Chief of Staff to the Advisor.—Julie Radford.

OFFICE OF THE FIRST LADY

Assistant to the President and Chief of Staff to the First Lady and Spokesperson.—Stephanie A. Grisham.

Assistant to the President and Deputy Chief of Staff for Policy to the First Lady.—Emma K. Doyle.
Senior Advisor to the First Lady.—Marcia L. Kelly.

OFFICE OF LEGISLATIVE AFFAIRS

Assistant to the President and Director, Office of Legislative Affairs.—Amy Swonger (acting).
Deputy Assistant to the President for Legislative Affairs.—Christopher C. Cox.
Special Assistants to the President for Legislative Affairs: Thomas S. Andrews, Jeffrey K. Freeland, Virginia D. McMillin, David M. Planning, Sean M. Riley, Alec L. Sugarman, Adam R. Telle.

OFFICE OF MANAGEMENT AND ADMINISTRATION

Deputy Assistant to the President and Director of White House Management and Administration (and Director of the Office of Administration).—Monica J. Block.

NATIONAL ECONOMIC COUNCIL

Assistant to the President for Economic Policy.—Larry Kudlow.
Assistant to the President for Trade and Manufacturing Policy.—Peter Navarro.
Deputy Assistant to the President for Economic Policy and Deputy Director of the National Economic Council.—Francis J. Brooke, Jr.
Special Assistant to the President for Economic Policy and Chief of Staff to the Director of the National Economic Council.—Susan C. Varga.

PRESIDENTIAL PERSONNEL OFFICE

Assistant to the President and Director of Presidential Personnel.—John D. McEntee II.
Special Assistant to the President and Associate Directors of Presidential Personnel: Matthew A. Buckham, Spencer J. Chretien.

OFFICE OF INTERGOVERNMENTAL AFFAIRS

Deputy Assistant to the President and Director of Intergovernmental Affairs.—Douglas L. Hoelscher.

OFFICE OF POLITICAL AFFAIRS

Deputy Assistant to the President and Director of Political Affairs.—Brian T. Jack.

OFFICE OF PUBLIC LIASION

Deputy Assistant to the President and Director of the Office of Public Liaison.—Timothy A. Pataki.

OFFICE OF PRESIDENTIAL APPOINTMENTS AND SCHEDULING

Deputy Assistant to the President and Director for Scheduling and Advance.—Michael Haidet.

OFFICE OF PRESIDENTIAL ADVANCE

Deputy Assistant to the President and Director of Presidential Advance.—Max L. Miller.

OFFICE OF THE SENIOR COUNSELOR

Assistant to the President and Senior Counselor.—Kellyanne Conway.
Deputy Assistant to the President and Chief of Staff to the Senior Counselor.—Hope Renee Hudson.

OFFICE OF THE STAFF SECRETARY

Assistant to the President and Counselor to the President.—Derek Lyons.
Deputy Assistant to the President and Deputy Staff Secretary.—Catherine Bellah Keller.

WHITE HOUSE COUNSEL

Counsel to the President.—Pasquale A. Cipollone.
Deputy Assistant to the President and Advisor to White House Counsel.—Sylvia M. Davis.
Deputy Assistant to the President and Deputy Counsel to the President for National Security Affairs and Legal Advisor to the National Security Council.—John Eisenberg.
Deputy Counsel to the President: Scott F. Gast, Patrick F. Philbin, Michael M. Purpura, Kathryn L. Todd.

DEPARTMENT OF STATE

2201 C Street, NW., Washington, DC 20520

phone (202) 647–4000

MIKE POMPEO, Secretary of State; born in Orange, CA, December 30, 1963; education: B.S., mechanical engineering, United States Military Academy at West Point, NY, 1986, graduated first in his class; J.D., Harvard Law School, Cambridge, MA, 1994; editor of *Harvard Law Review*; professional: owner / founder, Thayer Aerospace; president, Sentry International; religion: Presbyterian; married: Susan Pompeo of Wichita, KS; children: Nick; elected to the 112th Congress, from the 4th District of Kansas, on November 2, 2010, and reelected to the three succeeding Congresses; Director, Central Intelligence Agency (CIA), January 2017 to April 2018; nominated by President Donald Trump to become the 70th Secretary of State on March 13, 2018, and was sworn in on April 26, 2018.

OFFICE OF THE SECRETARY

Secretary of State.—Mike Pompeo, Room 7226 (202) 647–9572.
Deputy Secretary.—Stephen Biegun, Room 7220, 647–8636.

UNDER SECRETARY FOR MANAGEMENT AND RESOURCES

Under Secretary.—Brian Bulatao, Room 7207, 647–1500.

OFFICE OF GLOBAL CRIMINAL JUSTICE

Ambassador-at-Large.—Morse H. Tan, Room 7806, 647–5072.
Deputy.—Kelly Eckels-Currie, 647–5072.

OFFICE OF THE CHIEF OF PROTOCOL

Chief of Protocol.—Katherine C. Henderson, Room 1238, 647–4543.
Deputy Chief of Protocol.—Mary-Kate Fisher, 647–1144.

OFFICE OF CIVIL RIGHTS

Director.—Gregory B. Smith, Room 5806, 647–9294.
Deputy Director.—Glenn Budd (acting).

BUREAU OF COUNTERTERRORISM

Coordinator.—Nathan Sales, Room 2509, 647–9892.
Principal Deputy Coordinator.—Alina Romanowski, 647–9892.

BUREAU OF CONFLICT AND STABILIZATION OPERATIONS

Assistant Secretary.—Denise Natali, Room SW 3565 HST (202) 647–7068.

BUREAU OF ENERGY RESOURCES (ENR)

Assistant Secretary.—Francis R. ''Frank'' Fannon, Room 4428 (202) 647–8543.

EXECUTIVE SECRETARIAT

Special Assistant and Executive Secretary.—Lisa Kenna, Room 7224, 647–8448.
Deputy Executive Secretaries: Karen Enstrom, 647–5302; Roopa Rangaswamy, 647–5302; Norman Thatcher Scharpf, 647–5302.

OFFICE OF THE INSPECTOR GENERAL

1700 North Moore Street, Arlington, VA 22209

Inspector General.—Steve Linick, Room 800 SA–39 (571) 349–9262.
Deputy Inspector General.—Vacant.

BUREAU OF INTELLIGENCE AND RESEARCH

Assistant Secretary.—Ellen McCarthy, Room 6468, 647–9177.
Principal Deputy Assistant Secretary.—Kin Moy, 647–7826.
Deputy Assistant Secretaries: Victor Raphael, 647–9633; Annette Redmond (acting), 647–7754.

OFFICE OF THE LEGAL ADVISER

Legal Adviser.—Marik String, Room 6805, 647–9598.
Principal Deputy Legal Adviser.—Richard Visek, 647–8460.
Deputy Legal Advisers: Joshua Dorosin, 647–7942; Steve Fabry, 647–7942; Kathleen Hooke, 647–7942.

BUREAU OF LEGISLATIVE AFFAIRS

Assistant Secretary.—Mary Elizabeth Taylor, Room 7805, 647–1807.
Principal Deputy Assistant Secretary.—Ryan Kaldahl, 647–1050.
Deputy Assistant Secretary (Global, Regional, and Functional).—Daniel Stoian, 647–1050.
Deputy Assistant Secretary (Senate).—Colleen Donnelly, 647–2623.
Deputy Assistant Secretary (House).—Jessica Moore, 647–2071.

POLICY PLANNING STAFF

Director.—Peter Berkowitz, Room 7311, 647–2972.
Principal Deputy Director.—Vacant.

OFFICE OF THE U.S. GLOBAL AIDS COORDINATOR

Coordinator.—Dr. Deborah Birx, Room SA–22, 663–2579.
Principal Deputy U.S. Global AIDS Coordinator.—Angeli Achrekar, 663–2802.

UNDER SECRETARY FOR POLITICAL AFFAIRS

Under Secretary.—David Hale, Room 7250, 647–2471.
Executive Assistant.—Jonathan Pratt, 647–1598.

AFRICAN AFFAIRS

Assistant Secretary.—Tibor Nagy, Room 6234A, 647–2530.
Principal Deputy Assistant Secretary.—Geeta Pasi, 647–2447.

EAST ASIAN AND PACIFIC AFFAIRS

Assistant Secretary.—David R. Stilwell, 647–9596.
Principal Deputy Assistant Secretary.—Atul Keshap, 647–8929.
Deputy Assistant Secretaries: Walter Douglas, 647–7234; Jonathan Fritz, 647–6910; Marc Knapper, 736–4393; Sandra Oudkirk, 647–6904; Alex Wong, 647–3137.

EUROPEAN AND EURASIAN AFFAIRS

Assistant Secretary.—Philip T. Reeker (acting), Room 6226, 647–9626.
Principal Deputy Assistant Secretary.—Maureen E. Cormack (acting), 647–6233.
Deputy Assistant Secretaries: Matthew Boyse, 647–6323; Julie Fisher, 647–9450; George Kent, 647–0907; Michael Murphy, 647–6402; Matthew Palmer, 647–5170; Christopher Robinson, 647–5146.

NEAR EASTERN AFFAIRS

Assistant Secretary.—David Schenker, Room 6242, 647–7207.
Principal Deputy Assistant Secretary.—Vacant, 647–7209.
Deputy Assistant Secretaries: Chris Backemeyer, 647–7166; Amanda Pilz, 647–3672; Joel Rayburn, 736–7901; Andrew Reek, 647–7168.

SOUTH AND CENTRAL ASIAN AFFAIRS

Assistant Secretary.—Alice Wells (acting), Room 6254, 736–4325.
Acting Principal Deputy Assistant Secretary.—Greta Holtz, 736–4315.
Executive Director.—Elizabeth Aubin, 647–3269.
Deputy Assistant Secretaries: Michael Adler (acting), 647–6708; Jonathan Henick (acting), 647–1312; Ervin Massinga (acting), 647–5058; Thomas Vajda (acting), 647–1114.

WESTERN HEMISPHERE AFFAIRS

Assistant Secretary.—Michael G. Kozak (acting), Room 6262, 647–5780.
Principal Deputy Assistant Secretary.—Julie Chung, 647–8387.
Deputy Assistant Secretaries: Carrie Filipetti, 647–7337; Cynthia Kierscht, 647–9510; Kevin O'Reilly, 647–8563; Jon Piechowski, 647–9921; Hugo Rodriguez, 647–6755.

INTERNATIONAL NARCOTICS AND LAW ENFORCEMENT AFFAIRS

Assistant Secretary.—Kirsten Dawn Madison, Room 7826, 647–8464.
Principal Deputy Assistant Secretary.—James A. Walsh, 647–9822.
Deputy Assistant Secretaries: Jorgan Andrews, 647–6054; Richard Glenn, 647–6054; Heather Merritt, 647–9822.

INTERNATIONAL ORGANIZATION AFFAIRS

Assistant Secretary.—Jonathan Moore (acting), Room 6323, 647–9600.
Principal Deputy Assistant Secretary.—Jonathan Moore, 647–9602.
Deputy Assistant Secretaries: Nerissa J. Cook, 647–5798; Joseph Manso, 647–9604; Katherine Wright, 647–6117.

UNDER SECRETARY FOR ECONOMIC GROWTH, ENERGY, AND THE ENVIRONMENT

Under Secretary.—Keith Krach, Room 7256, 647–7575.
Executive Assistant.—Vacant, 647–7674.
Acting Chief Of Staff.—Stephen Akard, 647–7674.

ECONOMIC AND BUSINESS AFFAIRS

Assistant Secretary.—Manisha Singh, Room 4932 / 4934, 647–7971.
Principal Deputy Assistant Secretary.—Peter Haas, 647–9496.
Deputy Assistant Secretaries: Roland De Marcelus (acting); David Meale; Robert L. Strayer, 647–5858; Hugo Yon.

UNDER SECRETARY FOR ARMS CONTROL AND INTERNATIONAL SECURITY

Under Secretary.—Vacant, Room 7208, 647–1049.

Chief Of Staff.—Maureen Tucker, 647–0302.

INTERNATIONAL SECURITY AND NONPROLIFERATION

Assistant Secretary.—Dr. Christopher A. Ford, Room 3932, 647–5999.
Principal Deputy Assistant Secretary.—Eliot Kang, Room 3932, 647–9612.
Deputy Assistant Secretary For Non-Nuclear Encounter For Proliferation.—Ann Ganzer (acting), Room 3932, 647–6977.
Deputy Assistant Secretary For Nonproliferation Programs.—Phillip Dolliff (acting), 647–9612.

POLITICAL-MILITARY AFFAIRS

Assistant Secretary.—R. Clarke Cooper, Room 6212, 647–9022.
Principal Deputy Assistant Secretary.—Stanley L. Brown (acting), 647–9023.
Deputy Assistant Secretaries: Vacant; Kevin O'Keefe (acting), 663–3450; Vacant, 647–9023.

ARMS CONTROL, VERIFICATION AND COMPLIANCE

Assistant Secretary.—Vacant, Room 5950, 647–5875.
Principal Deputy Assistant Secretary.—Bruce Turner, 647–9399.
Deputy Assistant Secretaries: Bruce Turner (acting), 647–9399; Vacant, 647–5315.
Senior Business Official.—Thomas Dinanno, 647–5315.

UNDER SECRETARY FOR PUBLIC DIPLOMACY AND PUBLIC AFFAIRS

Under Secretary.—Michelle Giuda (acting), Room 6634, 647–6088.
Executive Assistant/Chief Of Staff.—Jennifer Hall Godfrey, 647–7017.

EDUCATIONAL AND CULTURAL AFFAIRS

Assistant Secretary.—Marie Thérèse Royce, 632–6066.
Principal Deputy Assistant Secretary.—Rick Ruth (acting), 632–6442.
Deputy Assistant Secretaries: Caroline Casagrande, Susan Crystal, Aleisha Woodward.
Managing Directors: Mariane Craven, 632–9331; Chris Miner, 632–6446; Kevin Saba, 634–4722.

PUBLIC AFFAIRS

Assistant Secretary.—Michelle Giuda, Room 6634, 647–6088.
Principal Deputy Assistant Secretary.—Nicole Chulich, 647–6088.
Spokesperson.—Morgan Ortagus, 647–6088.
Deputy Assistant Secretaries: Benjamin Friedmann, 647–8232; Katie Martin, 647–6088; Amanda Milius (acting), 647–9701; Robert Palladino, 647–7611; Lucas Peterson, 647–7721.

UNDER SECRETARY FOR MANAGEMENT

Under Secretary.—Brian Bulatao, Room 7207, 647–1500.
Executive Assistant.—Michael Lampel, 647–1501.

ADMINISTRATION

Assistant Secretary.—Carrie Cabelka, Room 6529, 647–4421.
Deputy Assistant Secretaries: Keith Hanran, 647–2967; Vacant (703) 875–6956; John Sullivan (202) 663–2215.

CONSULAR AFFAIRS

Assistant Secretary.—Carl Risch, Room 6826, (202) 485–8961.

Principal Deputy Assistant Secretary.—Ian Brownlee, 485–8961.
Deputy Assistant Secretaries: Rachel Arndt, 485–6378; Karen King, 485–6040; Edward Ramotowski, 647–6947.

DIPLOMATIC SECURITY

Assistant Secretary.—Michael T. Evanoff, Room 6316, 647–6290.
Principal Deputy Assistant Secretary.—Todd J. Brown (571) 345–3818.
Deputy Assistant Secretaries: Assyia Ashras-Miller (571) 345–3841; Wendy Bashnan (acting), (571) 226–9761; Ricardo Colon, 345–3785; John Fitzsimmons (acting), (571) 345–3835; Carlos Matus (acting), (571) 345–3809; Lonnie Price (571) 345–7675; Greg Sherman (571) 345–3388.

DIRECTOR GENERAL OF THE FOREIGN SERVICE AND
DIRECTOR OF HUMAN RESOURCES

Director General.—Carol Perez, Room 6218, 647–9898.
Principal Deputy Assistant Secretary.—Kenneth Merten, 647–5942.
Deputy Assistant Secretaries: Jeanne Juliano, 647–9438; Philippe Lussier, 647–5152; Mirembe Nantongo, 647–9442.

FOREIGN SERVICE INSTITUTE

Director.—Amb. Daniel Smith, Room F2101 (703) 302–6703.
Deputy Director.—Julieta Noyes, 302–6707.

INFORMATION RESOURCE MANAGEMENT

Chief Information Officer.—Stuart McGuigan, 647–2889.
Deputy CIO For Operations.—Glen Johnson, 634–3683.
Deputy CIO For Business Management And Planning.—Kenneth Rogers (acting), 634–3083.
Chief Information Security Officer of Information Assurance.—Alford Bowden, 634–3690.

MEDICAL SERVICES

Medical Director.—Mark Cohen (acting), 663–1649.
Principal Deputy Medical Director.—Larry Padget, 663–1641.

OVERSEAS BUILDINGS OPERATIONS

Director.—Addison ''Tad'' Davis IV (703) 875–6361.
Principal Deputy Director.—Henry V. Jardine, 875–6351.

UNDER SECRETARY OF STATE FOR CIVILIAN SECURITY, DEMOCRACY, AND HUMAN RIGHTS

Under Secretary.—Vacant, Room 7261, 647–1189.
Executive Assistant.—Ian Boyd (acting), 647–7818.

DEMOCRACY, HUMAN RIGHTS, AND LABOR

Assistant Secretary.—Robert A. Destro, Room 7827, 647–3273.
Senior Bureau Official.—Amb. Michael G. Kozak, 647–8714.
Principal Deputy Assistant Secretary.—Vacant, 647–3273.

OCEANS AND INTERNATIONAL ENVIRONMENTAL AND SCIENTIFIC AFFAIRS

Assistant Secretary.—Vacant, Room 3880, 647–6950.
Principal Deputy Assistant Secretary.—Amb. Marcia S. Bernicat, 647–1554.

Deputy Assistant Secretaries: Vacant, 647–2396; Jonathan Margolis, 647–3584; Vacant, 647–2232.

POPULATION, REFUGEES, AND MIGRATION

Assistant Secretary.—Carol T. O'Connell (acting), Room 7817, 647–5822.
Principal Deputy Assistant Secretary.—Carol T. O'Connell, 647–5822.
Deputy Assistant Secretaries: Richard Albright, 647–5822; Nancy I. Jackson, 647–5822; Andrew Veprek, 647–5822.

U.S. MISSION TO THE UNITED NATIONS

Representative of the U.S. to the United Nations.—Amb. Kelly Knight Craft, Room 2112 (212) 415–4444.
Deputy to the Representative of the U.S. to the United Nations.—Vacant, Room 6633 HST (202) 736–7578.

OFFICE OF U.S. FOREIGN ASSISTANCE RESOURCES

Director.—James Richardson, Room 5923, 647–2608.
Chief Of Staff.—Lisa Greene, 647–3690.

UNITED STATES DIPLOMATIC OFFICES—FOREIGN SERVICE

(C = Consular Office, N = No Embassy or Consular Office)

https://usembassy.state.gov

LIST OF CHIEFS OF MISSION

AFGHANISTAN, ISLAMIC REPUBLIC OF (Kabul).
Ross L. Wilson (Charge d'Affaires).
ALBANIA, REPUBLIC OF (Tirana).
Hon. Yuri Kim.
ALGERIA, DEMOCRATIC AND POPULAR REPUBLIC OF (Algiers).
Hon. John Desrocher.
ANDORRA (Andorra La Vella) (N).
Richard Duke Buchan III (Also U.S. Ambassador to Spain).
ANGOLA, REPUBLIC OF (Luanda).
Hon. Nina Maria Fite.
ARGENTINA (Buenos Aires).
Hon. Edward C. Prado.
ARMENIA, REPUBLIC OF (Yerevan).
Lynne M. Tracy.
ASSOCIATION OF SOUTHEAST ASIAN NATIONS (ASEAN).
Melissa Brown (Chief of Mission) (Charge d'Affaires).
AUSTRALIA (Canberra).
Arthur B. Culvahouse, Jr.
AUSTRIA, REPUBLIC OF (Vienna).
Trevor D. Traina.
AZERBAIJAN, REPUBLIC OF (Baku).
Hon. Earle D. "Lee" Litzenberger.
BAHAMAS, THE COMMONWEALTH OF THE (Nassau).
Vacant.
BAHRAIN, STATE OF (Manama).
Hon. Justin Siberell.
BANGLADESH, PEOPLE'S REPUBLIC OF (Dhaka).
Hon. Earl Robert Miller.
BARBADOS (Bridgetown).
Hon. Linda Taglialatela.
BELARUS, REPUBLIC OF (Minsk).
Jennifer H. Moore (Charge d'Affaires).
BELGIUM (Brussels).
Hon. Ronald Gidwitz.
BELIZE (Belmopan).
Keith R. Gilges (Charge d'Affaires).
BENIN, REPUBLIC OF (Cotonou).
Hon. Patricia Mahoney.
BOLIVIA, REPUBLIC OF (La Paz).
Bruce Williamson (Charge d'Affaires).
BOSNIA-HERZEGOVINA (Sarajevo).
Hon. Eric George Nelson.
BOTSWANA, REPUBLIC OF (Gaborone).
Hon. Craig Lewis Cloud.
BRAZIL, FEDERATIVE REPUBLIC OF (Brasilia).
Hon. Todd C. Chapman.
BRUNEI DARUSSALAM (Bandar Seri Begawan).
Hon. Matthew John Matthews.
BULGARIA, REPUBLIC OF (Sofia).
Hon. Herro Mustafa.
BURKINA FASO (Ouagadougou).
Hon. Andrew Young.
BURMA, UNION OF (Rangoon).
Hon. Scot Marciel.
BURUNDI, REPUBLIC OF (Bujumbura).
Eunice S. Reddick (Charge d'Affaires).
CABO VERDE.
Hon. John Jefferson Daigle.
CAMBODIA, KINGDOM OF (Phnom Penh).

Hon. W. Patrick Murphy.
CAMEROON, REPUBLIC OF (Yaounde).
Hon. Peter Barlerin.
CANADA (Ottawa).
Vacant.
CENTRAL AFRICAN REPUBLIC (Bangui).
Hon. Lucy Tamlyn.
CHAD, REPUBLIC OF (N'Djamena).
Vacant.
CHILE, REPUBLIC OF (Santiago).
Baxter Hunt (Charge d'Affaires).
CHINA, PEOPLE'S REPUBLIC OF (Beijing).
Hon. Terry Branstad.
COLOMBIA, REPUBLIC OF (Bogota).
Hon. Philip Goldberg.
COMOROS, UNION OF (Moroni) (N).
Hon. Michael Peter Pelletier (Also Ambassador to the Republic of Madagascar).
CONGO, DEMOCRATIC REPUBLIC OF THE (Kinshasa).
Hon. Mike Hammer.
CONGO, REPUBLIC OF THE (Brazzaville).
Hon. Todd Haskell.
COSTA RICA, REPUBLIC OF (San Jose).
Hon. Sharon Day.
COTE D'IVOIRE, REPUBLIC OF (Abidjan).
Hon. Richard K. Bell.
CROATIA, REPUBLIC OF (Zagreb).
Hon. W. Robert Kohorst.
CUBA (Havana).
Mara Tekach (Charge d'Affaires).
CURACAO and ARUBA (Consul General).
Allen Greenberg (Chief of Mission).
CYPRUS, REPUBLIC OF (Nicosia).
Hon. Judith G. Garber.
CZECH REPUBLIC (Prague).
Hon. Stephen B. King.
DENMARK (Copenhagen).
Hon. Carla Sands.
DJIBOUTI, REPUBLIC OF (Djibouti).
Hon. Larry André.
DOMINICAN REPUBLIC (Santo Domingo).
Hon. Robin Bernstein.
ECUADOR, REPUBLIC OF (Quito).
Hon. Michael J. Fitzpatrick.
EGYPT, ARAB REPUBLIC OF (Cairo).
Hon. Johnathan R. Cohen.
EL SALVADOR, REPUBLIC OF (San Salvador).
Hon. Ronald D. Johnson.
EQUATORIAL GUINEA, REPUBLIC OF (Malabo) (N).
Hon. Susan Stevenson.
ERITREA, STATE OF (Asmara).
Natalie Brown (Chief of Mission).
ESTONIA.
Hon. James Melville.
ESWATINI, KINGDOM OF (Mbabane).
Hon. Lisa Peterson.
ETHIOPIA, FEDERAL DEMOCRATIC REPUBLIC OF (Addis Ababa).
Hon. Michael Arthur Raynor.
EUROPEAN UNION.
Vacant.
FIJI ISLANDS, REPUBLIC OF THE (Suva).
Hon. Joseph Cella.
FINLAND, REPUBLIC OF (Helsinki).
Hon. Robert F. Pence.
FRANCE (Paris).
Hon. Jamie D. McCourt.
GABONESE REPUBLIC (Libreville).
Robert Whitehead (Charge d'Affaires) (Also Charge d'Affaires to the Democratic Republic of Sao Tome and Principe).
GAMBIA, REPUBLIC OF THE (Banjul).
Hon. Richard Carlton Paschall III.
GEORGIA (Tbilisi).
Hon. Kelly C. Degnan.
GERMANY, FEDERAL REPUBLIC OF (Berlin).
Hon. Richard A. Grenell.
GHANA, REPUBLIC OF (Accra).
Hon. Stephanie Sullivan.
GREECE (Athens).
Hon. Geoffrey Pyatt.
GUATEMALA, REPUBLIC OF (Guatemala).
Hon. Luis E. Arreaga.
GUINEA, REPUBLIC OF (Conakry).
Hon. Simon Henshaw.
GUINEA-BISSAU, REPUBLIC OF (Bissau) (N).
Hon. Tulinabo Salama Mushingi (Also Ambassador to the Republic of Senegal).
GUYANA, CO-OPERATIVE REPUBLIC OF (Georgetown).
Hon. Sarah-Ann Lynch.
HAITI, REPUBLIC OF (Port-au-Prince).
Hon. Michele Jeanne Sison.
HOLY SEE (Vatican City).
Hon. Callista L. Gingrich.
HONDURAS, REPUBLIC OF (Tegucigalpa).
Vacant.
HONG KONG (Hong Kong) (C).
Hon. Hanscom Smith (Consul General).
HUNGARY, REPUBLIC OF (Budapest)
Hon. David Cornstein.
ICELAND, REPUBLIC OF (Reykjavik).
Hon. Jeffrey Ross Gunter.
INDIA (New Delhi).
Hon. Kenneth I. Juster.
INDONESIA, REPUBLIC OF (Jakarta).
James R. Dayringer (Deputy Chief of Mission).
IRAN.
No Diplomatic Relations.
IRAQ, REPUBLIC OF (Baghdad).
Hon. Matthew Tueller.
IRELAND (Dublin).

Hon. Edward F. Crawford.
ISRAEL, STATE OF (Tel Aviv).
Hon. David Friedman.
ITALY (Rome).
Hon. Lewis Eisenberg.
JAMAICA (Kingston).
Hon. Donald Tapia.
JAPAN (Tokyo).
Vacant.
JORDAN, HASHEMITE KINGDOM OF (Amman).
Mike Hankey (Deputy Chief of Mission).
KAZAKHSTAN, REPUBLIC OF (Almaty).
Hon. William Moser.
KENYA, REPUBLIC OF (Nairobi).
Hon. Kyle McCarter.
KOSOVO (Pristina).
Hon. Philip Kosnett.
KUWAIT, STATE OF (Kuwait City).
Hon. Alina L. Romanowski.
KYRGYZ REPUBLIC (Bishkek).
Hon. Donald Lu.
LAO PEOPLE'S DEMOCRATIC REPUBLIC (Vientiane).
Hon. Peter M. Haymond.
LATVIA, REPUBLIC OF (Riga).
Hon. John Leslie Carwile.
LEBANON, REPUBLIC OF (Beirut).
Hon. Dorothy Shea.
LESOTHO, KINGDOM OF (Maseru).
Hon. Rebecca E. Gonzales.
LIBERIA, REPUBLIC OF (Monrovia).
Hon. Christine Elder.
LIBYA (Tripoli).
Hon. Richard B. Norland.
LIECHTENSTEIN, PRINCIPALITY OF (Vaduz) (N).
Hon. Edward McMullen, Jr. (Also Ambassador to the Swiss Confederation).
LITHUANIA, REPUBLIC OF (Vilnius).
Hon. Robert S. Gilchrist.
LUXEMBOURG, GRAND DUCHY OF (Luxembourg).
Hon. Randy Evans.
MACEDONIA, REPUBLIC OF (Skopje).
Hon. Kate Marie Byrnes.
MADAGASCAR, REPUBLIC OF (Antananarivo).
Hon. Michael P. Pelletier (Also Ambassador to Union of Comoros).
MALAWI, REPUBLIC OF (Lilongwe).
Hon. Robert K. Scott.
MALAYSIA (Kuala Lumpur).
Hon. Kamala Lakhdhir.
MALI, REPUBLIC OF (Bamako).
Hon. Dennis Hankins.
MALTA, REPUBLIC OF (Valletta).
Vacant.
MARSHALL ISLANDS, REPUBLIC OF THE (Majuro).
Hon. Roxanne Cabral.
MAURITANIA, ISLAMIC REPUBLIC OF (Nouakchott).
Hon. Michael J. Dodman.
MAURITIUS, REPUBLIC OF (Port Louis).
Hon. David Reimer (Also Ambassador to the Republic of the Seychelles).
MEXICO (Mexico City).
Hon. Christopher Landau.
MICRONESIA, FEDERATED STATES OF (Kolonia).
Hon. Carmen G. Cantor.
MOLDOVA, REPUBLIC OF (Chisinau).
Hon. Derek J. Hogan.
MONACO (Monaco).
Hon. Jamie D. McCourt (Also Ambassador to the French Republic).
MONGOLIA (Ulaanbaatar).
Hon. Michael S. Klecheski.
MONTENEGRO, REPUBLIC OF (Podgorica).
Hon. Judy Rising Reinke.
MOROCCO, KINGDOM OF (Rabat).
Hon. David T. Fischer.
MOZAMBIQUE, REPUBLIC OF (Maputo).
Hon. Dennis W. Hearne.
NAMIBIA, REPUBLIC OF (Windhoek).
Hon. Lisa Johnson.
NEPAL, KINGDOM OF (Kathmandu).
Hon. Randy W. Berry.
NETHERLANDS, KINGDOM OF THE (The Hague).
Hon. Peter Hoekstra.
NEW ZEALAND (Wellington).
Hon. Scott P. Brown (Also Ambassador to the State of Samoa).
NICARAGUA, REPUBLIC OF (Managua).
Hon. Kevin K. Sullivan.
NIGER, REPUBLIC OF (Niamey).
Hon. Eric Whitaker.
NIGERIA, FEDERAL REPUBLIC OF (Abuja).
Hon. Mary Beth Leonard.
NORTH ATLANTIC TREATY ORGANIZATION (NATO).
Hon. Kay Bailey Hutchison.
NORTH KOREA.
No Diplomatic Relations.
NORWAY (Oslo).
Hon. Kenneth J. Braithwaite.
OMAN, SULTANATE OF (Muscat).
Hon. Leslie Meredith Tsou.
ORGANIZATION FOR SECURITY AND COOPERATION IN EUROPE (OSCE).
Harry Kamian (Chief of Mission).
ORGANIZATION OF AMERICAN STATES (OAS).
Hon. Carlos Trujillo (Permanent Representative).
PAKISTAN, ISLAMIC REPUBLIC OF (Islamabad).
Paul W. Jones (Charge d'Affaires).
PALAU, REPUBLIC OF (Koror).
Hon. John Hennessey-Niland.
PANAMA, REPUBLIC OF (Panama).

Philip Laidlaw (Charge d'Affaires).
PAPUA NEW GUINEA (Port Moresby).
Hon. Erin E. McKee.
PARAGUAY, REPUBLIC OF (Asuncion).
Hon. Lee McClenny.
PERU, REPUBLIC OF (Lima).
Hon. Krishna R. Urs.
PHILIPPINES, REPUBLIC OF THE (Manila).
Hon. Sung Kim.
POLAND, REPUBLIC OF (Warsaw).
Hon. Georgette Mosbacher.
PORTUGAL, REPUBLIC OF (Lisbon).
Hon. George Glass.
QATAR, STATE OF (Doha).
William Grant (Charge d'Affaires).
ROMANIA (Bucharest).
Hon. Adrian Zuckerman.
RUSSIAN FEDERATION (Moscow).
Hon. John J. Sullivan.
RWANDA, REPUBLIC OF (Kigali).
Hon. Peter Vrooman.
SAN MARINO, REPUBLIC OF (San Marino) (N).
Hon. Lewis Eisenberg (Also Ambassador to the Italian Republic).
SAO TOME AND PRINCIPE, DEMOCRATIC REPUBLIC OF (Sao Tome) (N).
Robert Whitehead (Charge d'Affaires) (Also Ambassador to Gabonese Republic).
SAUDI ARABIA, KINGDOM OF (Riyadh).
Hon. John P. Abizaid.
SENEGAL, REPUBLIC OF (Dakar).
Hon. Tulinabo Salama Mushingi (Also Ambassador to the Republic of Guinea-Bissau).
SERBIA (Belgrade).
Hon. Anthony F. Godrey.
SEYCHELLES, REPUBLIC OF (Victoria) (N).
David Reimer (Also Ambassador to the Republic of Mauritius).
SIERRA LEONE, REPUBLIC OF (Freetown).
Hon. Maria Brewer.
SINGAPORE, REPUBLIC OF (Singapore).
Rafik Mansour (Charge d'Affaires).
SLOVAK REPUBLIC (Bratislava).
Hon. Bridget A. Brink.
SLOVENIA, REPUBLIC OF (Ljubljana).
Hon. Lynda Blanchard.
SOLOMON ISLANDS (Honiara) (N).
Hon. Erin E. McKee (Also Ambassador to Papua New Guinea and Republic of Vanuatu).
SOMALIA.
Hon. Donald Y. Yamamoto.
SOUTH AFRICA, REPUBLIC OF (Pretoria).
Hon. Laura J. Marks.
SOUTH KOREA.
Hon. Harry B. Harris, Jr.
SOUTH SUDAN, REPUBLIC OF (Juba).
Hon. Thomas J. Hushek.
SPAIN (Madrid).
Hon. Richard Duke Buchan III (Also Ambassador to the Principality of Andorra).
SRI LANKA, DEMOCRATIC SOCIALIST REPUBLIC OF (Colombo).
Hon. Alaina Teplitz (Also Ambassador to the Republic of Maldives).
SUDAN, REPUBLIC OF THE (Khartoum).
Brian Shukan (Chief of Mission).
SURINAME, REPUBLIC OF (Paramaribo).
Hon. Karen L. Williams.
SWEDEN (Stockholm).
Hon. Kenneth A. Howery.
SWITZERLAND (Bern).
Hon. Edward McMullen, Jr. (Also Ambassador to the Principality of Liechtenstein).
SYRIAN ARAB REPUBLIC (Damascus).
(No relations with U.S.).
TAJIKISTAN, REPUBLIC OF (Dushanbe).
Hon. John Mark Pommersheim.
TANZANIA, UNITED REPUBLIC OF (Dar es Salaam).
Inmi Patterson (Charge d'Affaires).
THAILAND, KINGDOM OF (Bangkok).
Hon. Michael G. DeSombre.
TIMOR-LESTE.
Hon. Kathleen M. Fitzpatrick.
TOGO.
Hon. Eric Williams Stromayer.
TRINIDAD AND TOBAGO, REPUBLIC OF (Port-of-Spain).
Hon. Joseph N. Mondello.
TUNISIA, REPUBLIC OF (Tunis).
Hon. Donald A. Blome.
TURKEY, REPUBLIC OF (Ankara).
Hon. David Satterfield.
TURKMENISTAN (Ashgabat).
Hon. Matthew Klimow.
U.S. MISSION TO UNESCO.
Vacant.
U.S. MISSION TO THE AFRICAN UNION (AU).
Hon. Jessica E. Lapenn.
UGANDA, REPUBLIC OF (Kampala).
Hon. Christopher Krafft.
UKRAINE (Kyiv).
Kristina Kvien (Charge d'Affaires a.i.).
UNITED ARAB EMIRATES (Abu Dhabi).
Hon. John Rakolta, Jr.
UNITED KINGDOM OF GREAT BRITAIN AND NORTHERN IRELAND (London).
Hon. Robert Wood Johnson, IV.
UNITED NATIONS HUMAN RIGHTS COUNCIL.
Vacant.

UNITED NATIONS IN GENEVA.
Hon. Andrew P. Bremberg.
UNITED NATIONS IN ROME.
Hon. Kip E. Tom.
UNITED NATIONS IN VIENNA.
Hon. Jackie Wolcott (Also International Atomic Energy Agency (IAEA)).
UNITED NATIONS.
Hon. Kelly Knight Craft.
URUGUAY, ORIENTAL REPUBLIC OF (Montevideo).
Hon. Kenneth S. George.
UZBEKISTAN, REPUBLIC OF (Tashkent).
Hon. Daniel N. Rosenblum.
VANUATU, REPUBLIC OF (Port Vila) (N).
Hon. Erin E. McKee (Also Ambassador to Solomon Islands and Papua New Guinea).
VENEZUELA, BOLIVARIAN REPUBLIC OF (Caracas).
Christopher Lambert (Deputy Chief of Mission) (acting).
VIETNAM, SOCIALIST REPUBLIC OF (Hanoi).
Hon. Daniel J. Kritenbrink.
YEMEN, REPUBLIC OF (Sanaa).
Hon. Christopher Paul Henzel.
ZAMBIA, REPUBLIC OF (Lusaka).
Martin A. Dale (Deputy Chief of Mission) (Charge d'Affaires).
ZIMBABWE, REPUBLIC OF (Harare).
Hon. Brian A. Nichols.

UNITED STATES PERMANENT DIPLOMATIC MISSIONS TO INTERNATIONAL ORGANIZATIONS

ASSOCIATION OF SOUTHEAST ASIAN NATIONS (Jakarta).
Melissa Brown (Deputy Chief of Mission).
AFRICAN UNION (Addis Ababa).
Hon. Jessica E. Lapenn.
NORTH ATLANTIC TREATY ORGANIZATION (Brussels).
Hon. Kay Bailey Hutchison.
ORGANIZATION FOR ECONOMIC COOPERATION AND DEVELOPMENT (Paris).
Andrew Haviland (Charge d'Affaires).
ORGANIZATION FOR SECURITY AND COOPERATION IN EUROPE (Vienna).
Hon. James S. Gilmore.
ORGANIZATION OF AMERICAN STATES (Washington, DC).
Hon. Carlos Trujillo.

DEPARTMENT OF THE TREASURY

1500 Pennsylvania Avenue, NW., Washington, DC 20220
phone (202) 622–2000, https://ustreas.gov

STEVEN T. MNUCHIN, Secretary of the Treasury; nominated by President Donald J. Trump January 20, 2017, to become the 77th Secretary of the Treasury and confirmed by the U.S. Senate on February 13, 2017.

OFFICE OF THE SECRETARY

Secretary of the Treasury.—Steven T. Mnuchin, Room 3330, 622–1100.
Executive Assistant.—Shirley E. Gathers, 622–1100.
Confidential Assistant.—Vacant.

OFFICE OF THE DEPUTY SECRETARY

Deputy Secretary.—Justin Muzinich, Room 3326, 622–1080.
Executive Assistant.— Pat Griffin, Room 3326, 622–7588.

OFFICE OF THE CHIEF OF STAFF

Chief of Staff.—Vacant, Room 3408, 622–1135.
Deputy Chief of Staff.—Zachary McEntee, Room 3330, 622–1501.
White House Liaison/Deputy Chief of Staff.—Baylor Myers, Room 3420, 622–0987.
Special Assistant to the Chief of Staff.—Jackson Miles, Room 3408, 622–1906.

OFFICE OF THE GENERAL COUNSEL

General Counsel.—Brian Callanan, Room 3000 (202) 622–0283.
Deputy General Counsel.—Brian Morrissey, 622–0283.
Staff Assistant.—Kim Wilson, 622–0283.
Confidential Assistant.—Arianne Minks, 622–9714.
Counselors to the General Counsel: Joseph R. Clark, Room 3020, 622–0351; James Stern, Room 3014, 622–1147.
Assistant General Counsel for Banking and Finance.—Eric Froman, Room 3023, 622–1942.
Principal Deputy Assistant General Counsel for Banking and Finance.—Paul Wolfteich, 504–3705.
Deputy Assistant General Counsel for Banking and Finance.—Stephen Milligan, Room 2028B, 622–4051.
Assistant General Counsel for Enforcement and Intelligence.—Paul Ahern, Room 2000, 622–3108.
Deputy Assistant General Counsel for Enforcement and Intelligence.—Heather Trew, Room 2000, 622–0348.
Assistant General Counsel for General Law, Ethics, and Regulation.—Brian Sonfield, Room 2312, 622–9804.
Deputy Assistant General Counsel for General Law, Ethics, and Regulation.—Mike Briskin, Room 2020, 622–6966.
Deputy Assistant General Counsel for General Law, Ethics, and Regulation (Ethics).—Hanoi Veras, Room 2209B, 622–1181.
Assistant General Counsel for International Affairs.—David Sullivan, Room 2308, 622–7148.
Deputy Assistant General Counsel for International Affairs.—Jeffrey Klein, Room 2306, 622–2122.
Chief Counsel, Foreign Assets Control.—Charles Steele, 622–6037.
Assistant Chief Counsel: Andrea L. Delisi, Room 3138, 622–1404; Sara F. Liebschutz, Room 3031, 622–8948.

OFFICE OF THE INSPECTOR GENERAL

Inspector General.—Richard K. Delmar (acting), Room 4436 (202) 622–1090.
Deputy Inspector General.—Vacant.
Counsel to the Inspector General.—Richard K. Delmar, Suite 400 (202) 927–0650.
Assistant Inspector General for—
Audit.—Deborah Harker, Suite 300, 927–5400.
Investigations.—Vacant, Suite 400, 927–5260.
Management Services.—Vacant, Suite 200, 927–5200.
Deputy Assistant Inspector General for—
Audits: Pauletta Battle, Suite 300, 927–5400; Lisa Carter, Suite 300, 927–5400; Donna Joseph, Suite 300, 927–5400.
Investigation.—Vacant, Suite 400, 927–5260.
Management.—Jeffrey Lawrence, Suite 200, 927–5200.

OFFICE OF THE UNDER SECRETARY FOR DOMESTIC FINANCE

Under Secretary.—Vacant (202) 622–1703.

OFFICE OF THE ASSISTANT SECRETARY FOR FINANCIAL INSTITUTIONS

Assistant Secretary.—Bimal Patel (202) 622–2850.
Deputy Assistant Secretary, Office of:
Community and Economic Development.—Vacant.
Cybersecurity and Critical Infrastructure Protection.—David Lacquement.
Financial Institutions Policy.—Tyler Williams.
Director, Office of:
Community and Economic Development.—Vacant.
Community Development Financial Institutions Fund.—Jodie Harris.
Cybersecurity and Critical Infrastructure Protection.—Brian Peretti.
Federal Insurance Office.—Steven Seitz.
Financial Institutions Policy.—Moses Kim.
Financial Stability.—Danielle Johnson-Kutch.
Small Business Lending Fund.—Sally Phillips.
Terrorism Risk Insurance Program.—Vacant.
Deputy Director, Office of:
Community and Economic Development.—Mary Ellen Mitchell-Whisnant.
Federal Insurance Office.—Vacant.
Financial Institutions Policy.—Natalia Li.

OFFICE OF THE ASSISTANT SECRETARY FOR FINANCIAL MARKETS

Assistant Secretary.—Vacant (202) 622–0481.
Principal Deputy Assistant Secretary.—Kipp Kranbuhl.
Deputy Assistant Secretary, Office of:
Capital Markets.—Peter Phelan.
Federal Finance.—Brian Smith.
Public Finance.—Gary Grippo.
Director, Office of:
Capital Markets.—Daniel Harty.
Debt Management.—Fred Pietrangeli.
Federal Lending.—Christopher Tuttle.
Federal Program Finance.—Jeffrey Stout.
State and Local Finance.—Melissa Moye.

OFFICE OF THE FISCAL ASSISTANT SECRETARY

Assistant Secretary.—Dàve A. Lebryk (202) 622–0560.
Deputy Assistant Secretary, Office of:
Accounting Policy and Financial Transparency.—Amy Edwards.
Fiscal Operations and Policy.—Gregory Till.
Director, Office of:
Fiscal Projections.—Chris Kubeluis.
Grants and Asset Management.—Theodore Kowalsky.
Program Manager, Office of:

Gulf Coast Restoration.—Laurie McGilvray.
Housing and Energy.—Ellen Neubauer.
Supervisory Financial Analyst, Office of Financial Agents.—Alex Abawi.

FINANCIAL STABILITY OVERSIGHT COUNCIL

Deputy Assistant Secretary.—Howard Adler.
Independent Member with Insurance Expertise.—Thomas Workman.

BUREAU OF THE FISCAL SERVICE

401 14th Street, SW., Washington, DC 20227

phone (202) 504–3535, fax 874–7016

Commissioner.—Timothy Gribben.
Chief Counsel.—Paul Wolfteich.
Deputy Commissioner for—
Accounting and Shared Services.—Matt Miller.
Finance and Administration.—Steven Manning.
Financial Services and Operations.—Jeff Schramek.
Assistant Commissioner for—
Debt Management Services.—Daniel Vavasour.
Fiscal Accounting.—Mike Linder.
Information and Security Services (Chief Information Officer).—Doug Anderson.
Office of Financial Innovation and Transformation.—John Hill.
Office of Legislative and Public Affairs.—Marshall Kofler (acting).
Office of Management (Chief Financial Officer).—Theresa Kohler.
Office of Shared Services.—David Copenhaver.
Payment Management (Chief Disbursing Officer).—Ronda Kent.
Retail Securities Services.—Jan Draber.
Revenue Collections Management.—Corvelli McDaniel.
Wholesale Securities Services.—Dara Seaman.
Executive Director for Government Securities Regulations.—Lori Santamorena.

OFFICE OF THE UNDER SECRETARY FOR INTERNATIONAL AFFAIRS

Under Secretary.—Brent McIntosh, Room 3436 MT (202) 622–1270.
Staff Assistant.—Karen DeLaBarre Chase, Room 3432A MT, 622–0060.
Special Assistant.—John Poulson, Room 3432B MT, 622–1166.
Senior Advisors: Elizabeth Horning, Room 3041A MT, 622–3381; Cherrica Li, Room 3202 MT, 622–0123.
Counselor to the Under Secretary.—Ashok Pinto, Room 3224 MT, 622–3381.
Director, IA Business and Programs Operations.—Diane Klopack, Room 3037 MT, 662–6405.

OFFICE OF INTERNATIONAL AFFAIRS TRAVEL OFFICE

Deputy Assistant Secretary and Director of:
Africa, Africa and Middle East.—Joanne Crane.
ECC, New Employee Registration.—Yvonne Moore.
Europe and Eurasia, Asian Nations, and International Development Policy.—Barbara Rollins.
International Financial Markets.—Mark Chambers.
International Monetary and Financial Policy (including Markets Room), and Trade and Environment.—Shaunte Sams.
Investment, Energy and Infrastructure, and Western Hemisphere.—Alice Brown.

OFFICE OF THE ASSISTANT SECRETARY FOR INTERNATIONAL AFFAIRS

Assistant Secretary for International Finance and Development.—Geoffrey ''Geoff'' W.S. Okamoto, Room 3428 MT, 622–3890.
Senior Advisor.—Marina Rose Best, Room 3034 MT, 622–4620.
Staff Assistant.—Samantha Heyrich, Room 3430A MT, 622–6016.
Deputy Assistant Secretary for—
Africa and the Middle East.—Eric Meyer, Room 3036 MT, 622–2156.

Asian Nations.—Robert Kaproth, Room 3217 MT, 622–0132.
Europe and Eurasia.—Vacant.
International Development Finance and Policy.—Mathew Haarsager, Room 3205 MT, 622–5052.
International Monetary and Financial Policy.—Andy Baukol, Room 3216 MT, 622–2129.
Western Hemisphere.—Michael Kaplan, Room 3221 MT, 622–4262.

Assistant Secretary for International Markets.—Mitchell "Mitch" Silk (acting), Room 3428 MT, 622–0496.
Senior Advisor.—Daniel Katz, Room 3041B MT, 622–0020.
Staff Assistant.—Talia Rubin, Room 3430B MT, 622–2273.

Deputy Assistant Secretary for—
International Financial Markets.—Sharon Yang, Room 3209 MT, 622–1707.
Investment, Energy and Environment.—Devesh B. Ashra, Room 3204 MT, 622–7016.
Technical Assistance Policy.—W. Larry McDonald, Room 3208 MT, 622–5504.
Trade and Investment Policy.—Lailee Moghtader, Room 3213 MT, 622–1819.

Assistant Secretary for Investment Security.—Thomas "Tom" Feddo, Room 4138A MT, 622–7222.
Senior Advisor.—Kyle Hathaway, Room 4138C MT, 622–3010.
Staff Assistant.—Isabella Brooks, Room 4464 MT, 622–2241.

Deputy Assistant Secretary Investment Security.—J. Tyler McGaughey, Room 4222 MT, 622–6019.
Staff Assistant.—Isabella Brooks, Room 4464 MT, 622–2241.

Directors for Investment Security:
Investment Review and Investigation.—Brian Reissaus, Room 5008 MT, 622–0182.
Mitigation Monitoring & Enforcement.—Joseph Ludvigson, Room 4441 MT, 622–1588.
Policy and International Relations.—Laura Black, Room 5221A MT, 622–0060.

Directors for International Affairs:
Africa (INN).—Patrick Stuart (acting), Room 1064D, 622–1219.
Development Results and Accountability (R or ODRA).—C. Alex Severens, Room 1320R MT, 622–7741.
East Asia (ISA).—Shannon Ding, Room 4456 MT, 622–0716.
Europe and Eurasia (ICN).—Brian McCauley, Room 4138D MT, 622–5921.
Global Economics and Debt (IMG).—Peter Wisner, Room 1054A MT, 622–9885.
International Debt Policy (IDD).—Elizabeth Lien, Room 1320Q MT, 622–6997.
International Financial Markets (IFM).—Matthew Swinehart, Room 5310 MT, 622–1022.
International Monetary Policy (IMP).—Elizabeth Shortino, Room 5326 MT, 622–6407.
Markets Room (IMR).—Albert Lee, Room 1328G MT, 622–0368.
Middle East and North Africa (INM).—Anthony Marcus, Room 1024A MT, 622–6565.
Multilateral Development Banks (IDB).—Charles Moravec, Room 5313M MT, 622–3831.
Office of Trade and Investment Policy (ITT).—Mirea Lynton Grotz, Room 5204A MT, 622–0406.
South and Southeast Asia (ISS).—Seth Bleiweis, Room 4440M MT, 622–4262.
Technical Assistance.—Jason Orlando, 1750 Pennsylvania Avenue, NW., Room 8026, 622–5792.
Trade Finance and Debt (ITF).—Anthony Ieronimo, Room 5419J MT, 622–1747.
Western Hemisphere (IWH).—Alejandro Mares, Room 1446A MT, 622–1251.

U.S. Executive Director of:
African Development Bank and Fund (Cote d'Ivoire).—Joseph Steven Dowd, 011–225–20–26–2010.
Asian Development Bank (Manila, Philippines).—Vacant.
European Bank for Reconstruction and Development (London, England).—Vacant.
Inter-American Development Bank.—Eliot Pedrosa (202) 623–3959.
International Monetary Fund.—Mark Rosen (acting), 623–7719.
World Bank.—D.J. Nordquist, 458–0291.

U.S. Alternate Executive Director of:
Asian Development Bank (Manila, Philippines).—Jason Chung, 011–63–2-632–6051.
European Bank for Reconstruction and Development (London, England).—Colin Mahoney, 011–44–77–4132–1129.

Advisor, European Bank for Reconstruction and Development (London, England).—John Kriegsman, 011–44–20–7338–6459.

UNDER SECRETARY FOR TERRORISM AND FINANCIAL INTELLIGENCE

Under Secretary.—Justin Muzinich (acting), MT Room 4326 (202) 622–8260.

ASSISTANT SECRETARY FOR TERRORIST FINANCING AND FINANCIAL CRIMES

Assistant Secretary.—Vacant, MT Room 4316, 622–1943.
Deputy Assistant Secretary for Terrorist Financing and Financial Crimes.—Paul Ahern (acting), MT Room 4304 (inside Room 4000), 622–3108.
Director, Office of:
Global Affairs.—Anna Morris (acting), MT Room 4001 (inside Room 4000), 622–5790.
Strategic Policy.—Scott Rembrandt, MT Room 4308, 622–9926.

ASSISTANT SECRETARY FOR INTELLIGENCE AND ANALYSIS

Assistant Secretary.—Isabel M. Patelunas, Room 4332 (202) 622–1835.
Principal Deputy Assistant Secretary for Analysis and Production.—A. Daniel McGlynn, Room 2441 (202) 622–1841.
Deputy Assistant Secretary for Support and Technology.—Michael Neufeld, Room 2441, 622–1841.
Deputy Assistant Secretary for Security.—Thomas Wolverton (acting), Room 2441, 622–1841.

OFFICE OF FOREIGN ASSETS CONTROL

Director.—Andrea Gacki, Room 2240 (202) 622–2510.

EXECUTIVE OFFICE FOR ASSET FORFEITURE

1341 G Street, NW., Suite 900, Washington, DC 20005, phone (202) 622–9600

Director.—John M. Farley.

FINANCIAL CRIMES ENFORCEMENT NETWORK (FINCEN)

P.O. Box 39, Vienna, VA 22183

Director.—Kenneth A. Blanco (703) 839–4185.
Deputy Director.—Jamal El-Hindi (703) 839–4185.
Chief of Staff.—Kim Donovan (202) 354–6034.
Senior Advisor, Legislative Affairs.—Kelly M. Whitney (703) 839–4131.

OFFICE OF THE ASSISTANT SECRETARY FOR ECONOMIC POLICY

Assistant Secretary.—Michael Faulkender, Room 3460 (202) 622–2200.
Special Assistant.—Stephen Sandora, Room 3454–A, 622–0181.
Deputy Assistant Secretary for Macroeconomic Analysis.—Vacant.
Director, Office of Macroeconomic Analysis.—Samuel Brown (acting), Room 2464–B, 622–2293.
Deputy Assistant Secretary for Microeconomic Analysis.—Vacant.
Director, Office of Microeconomic Analysis.—Chris Soares, Room 4426, 622–2656.

OFFICE OF THE ASSISTANT SECRETARY FOR LEGISLATIVE AFFAIRS

Assistant Secretary for Legislative Affairs.—Brian McGuire, Room 3134.
Senior Advisor.—J. Brady Howell, Room 3464, 622–1900.
Special Assistant.—Kelsey Hayes, Room 3134–A.
Executive Assistant.—Linda L. Powell, Room 3453–D, 622–1900.
Special Advisors: William Dargusch, 3134–B, 622–0202; Julia Prus, Room 3124–A, 622–0010.
Deputy Assistant Secretary for—
Appropriations and Management.—Lauren Nunnally, Room 3122, 622–1900.
Banking and Finance.—Jon Blum, Room 3132, 622–1900.
International Affairs.—Michael DiRoma, Room 3421–B, 622–1900.
Oversight.—Frederick Vaughan, Room 3128, 622–2678.
Tax and Budget.—Kimberly Pinter, Room 3124–B, 622–1900.
TFI.—Andrew Eck, Room 3421–C, 622–1900.

OFFICE OF THE ASSISTANT SECRETARY FOR MANAGEMENT

Assistant Secretary for Management.—David F. Eisner, Room 2438, Main Treasury (202) 622–2014.

Executive Assistant.—Danielle Dixon, 927–0398.
Principal Senior Advisor.—Mike Lewis, 622–3068.
Senior Advisor.—Daniel Brandt, 622–6240.
Program Analyst.—Samantha Upwright, 622–1870.
Deputy Assistant Secretary for Management and Budget.—Robert Mahaffie, 622–1497.
Departmental Budget Director.—William Sessions, 622–3539.
Conference Events and Meeting Services.—Lucinda Gooch, 622–2071.
Strategic Planning and Performance Improvement.—Lenora Stiles, 622–1020.
Director, Office of Budget and Travel.—Tonya Burton, 622–1220.
Deputy Assistant Secretary for Treasury Operations.—Michael Thomas, 622–2195.
Environmental Safety and Health.—Jonathan Weeda, 662–6771.
Facilities Management.—Polly Dietz, 622–7067.
Deputy Assistant Secretary for Information Systems and Chief Information Officer.—Eric Olson, 622–2015.
Deputy Assistant Secretary for Human Resources and Chief Human Capital Officer.—Trevor Norris, 622–1282.
Equal Opportunity and Diversity.—Mariam Harvey, 622–0316.
Deputy Assistant Secretary for Privacy, Transparency, and Records.—Ryan Law, 622–0494.
Deputy Chief Financial Officer.—Carole Banks, 622–0818.
Director, Financial Reporting and Policy.—Kawan Taylor, 622–7899.
Senior Procurement Executive.—Michelle Sharpe (acting), 622–0248.
Director, General and Special Entity Accounting.—Stephen Cotter, 622–4279.
Director, Office of Emergency Programs.—J. Michael Thomas, 927–9213.
Director, Office of Minority and Women Inclusion.—Lorraine Cole, 927–8181.

OFFICE OF THE ASSISTANT SECRETARY FOR PUBLIC AFFAIRS

Assistant Secretary.—Monica Crowley, Room 3438 MT (202) 622–2910.

Deputy Assistant Secretary, Public Affairs for International Affairs.—Rebecca Miller, Room 3111 MT.
Deputy Assistant Secretary for TFI.—Patricia McLaughlin (acting), Room 3111 MT.
Senior Advisor, Public Affairs.—Kaelan Dorr.
Deputy Assistant Secretary/Domestic Finance/Public Liaison.—Brian Morgenstern.
Director of Public Affairs, TFI.—Zachary Isakowitz, Room 3111 MT.
Review Analyst and Scheduling Coordinator.—Traci Altman, Room 3442 MT, 622–7483.
Media Coordinator.—Vacant.
Media Affairs Specialist.—William Upton.
Confidential Assistant.—Hunter Ihrman.
Special Assistant.—Katherine McCarthy.
Press Assistant.—Vacant.

OFFICE OF THE ASSISTANT SECRETARY FOR TAX POLICY

Assistant Secretary.—David J. Kautter, Room 3120 MT (202) 622–0050.

Deputy Assistant Secretary for—
International Tax Affairs.—L. ''Chip'' Harter, Room 3108 MT, 622–1317.
Tax Analysis.—Vacant.
Tax Policy.—Vacant.
Tax, Trade and Tariff Policy.—Timothy Skud, Room 3104 MT, 622–0220.
Senior Advisor.—Jeffrey Van Hove, Room 3112 MT, 622–0140.
Tax Legislative Counsel.—Krishna Vallabhaneni, Room 3040 MT, 622–0835.
Deputy Tax Legislative Counsel: Hannah Hawkins, Room 4224 MT, 622–3351; Brent York, Room 3060 MT, 622–1285.
International Tax Counsel.—Douglas Poms, Room 3054 MT, 622–1754.
Deputy International Tax Counsel.—Kevin Nichols, Room 5064 MT, 622–9461.
Deputy International Tax Counsel for Treaty Affairs.—Quyen Huynh, Room 5064 MT, 622–1791.
Benefits Tax Counsel.—Carol Weiser, Room 3050 MT, 622–0869.
Deputy Benefits Tax Counsel.—Vacant.
Director, Office of Tax Analysis.—Janet McCubbin, Room 4116 MT, 622–0589.
Director, Division of:

Business and International Taxation.—Edith Brashares, Room 4221 MT, 622–0463.
Economic Modeling and Computer Applications.—Robert Gillette, Room 4039 MT, 622–0852.
Individual Taxation.—Adam Cole, Room 4104A MT, 622–1779.
Revenue and Receipts Forecasting/Business Revenue Division.—Curtis Carlson, Room 4112 MT, 622–0130.
Revenue and Receipts Forecasting/Individual Revenue Division.—Scott Jaquette, Room 4064 MT, 622–1319.

BUREAU OF ENGRAVING AND PRINTING

14th and C Streets, SW., Washington, DC 20228, phone (202) 874–2000

[Created by act of July 11, 1862; codified under U.S.C. 31, section 303]

Director.—Leonard R. Olijar, 874–2016.
Deputy Director, Chief Operating Officer.—Charlene Williams (817) 847–3880.
Deputy Director, Chief Administrative Officer.—Marty Greiner, 874–4532.
Chief Counsel.—Heather Book, 874–2306.
Associate Directors:
Chief Financial Officer.—Steven Fisher, 874–2020.
Chief Information Officer.—Harry Singh, 874–3000.
Management.—Frank Freeman III, 874–2040.
Product Design and Development.—Justin Draheim, 874–1239.
Quality.—Richard Clark, 874–0045.
Deputy Associate Directors:
Manufacturing DCF.—David Hatch, 874–2385.
Manufacturing WCF.—Ron Voelker (817) 847–3979.

OFFICE OF THE COMPTROLLER OF THE CURRENCY

400 7th Street, SW., Washington, DC 20219, phone (202) 649–6800

Comptroller.—Brian P. Brooks (acting), 649–6400.
Public Affairs Operations.—Bryan Hubbard, 649–6870.
Senior Deputy Comptroller and Chief Counsel.—Jonathan Gould, 649–5566.
Senior Deputy Comptrollers for—
Bank Supervision Policy and Chief National Bank Examiner.—Grovetta Gardineer, 649–6994.
Economics.—Michael Sullivan, 649–5472.
Large Bank Supervision.—Maryann Kennedy, 649–6786.
Management and Chief Financial Officer.—Kathy Murphy, 649–6993.
Midsize and Community Bank Supervision.—Toney Bland, 649–5420.
Director for Congressional Liaison.—Carrie Moore, 649–6737.
Senior Deputy Comptroller EG and Ombudsman.—Larry Hattix, 649–6857.

INTERNAL REVENUE SERVICE

1111 Constitution Avenue, NW., Washington, DC 20224, phone (202) 622–5000

[Created by act of July 1, 1862; codified under U.S.C. 26, section 7802]

Commissioner.—Charles P. Rettig, 317–7070.
Chief of Staff.—Lia Colbert, 317–7070.
Deputy Commissioner, Services and Enforcement.—Kirsten Wielobob, 317–4263.
Commissioner of:
Large Business and International Division.—Douglas O'Donnell, 317–8954.
Small Business/Self-Employed.—Mary Beth Murphy, 317–6500.
Tax Exempt and Government Entities.—Sunita Lough, 317–8400.
Wage and Investment.—Kenneth Corbin, 317–7060.
Chief, Criminal Investigation.—Don Fort, 317–3200.
Directors:
Office of Professional Responsibility.—Elizabeth Kastenberg, 317–6487.
Return Preparer Office.—Carol A. Campbell, 317–7063.
Whistleblower Office.—Lee Martin, 317–3500.
Deputy Commissioner, Operations Support.—Jeffrey Tribiano, 317–3950.
Chief:

Appeals.—Donna Hansberry, 317–8975.
Communications and Liaison.—Terry Lemons, 317–6849.
Equity, Diversity and Inclusion.—Elita Christiansen, 317–5400.
Facilities Management and Security Services.—Richard Rodriguez, 317–4070.
Financial Officer.—Ursula Gillis, 317–6400.
Information Officer.—Nancy Sieger, 317–5000.
IRS Human Capital Officer.—Robin D. Bailey, Jr., 317–7600.
Office of Privacy, Governmental Liaison and Disclosure.—Edward Killen, 317–6449.
Procurement.—Shanna R. Webbers, 317–3473.
Risk Officer.—Tom Brandt, 317–6988.
Chief Counsel.—Michael Desmond, 317–3300.
National Taxpayer Advocate.—Bridget Roberts, 317–6100.
Director, Office of Research, Analysis and Statistics.—Barry Johnson, 317–4276.
Office of Legislative Affairs.—Leonard Oursler, 317–4316.

INSPECTOR GENERAL FOR TAX ADMINISTRATION (TIGTA)

1401 H Street, NW., Suite 469, Washington, DC 20005

phone (202) 622–6500, fax 927–0001

Inspector General.—J. Russell George.
Principal Deputy Inspector General.—Vacant.
Congressional Liaison.—David Barnes (acting), 622–3062.
Chief Counsel.—Gladys M. Hernandez, 622–3103.
Deputy Inspector General for Audit.—Michael E. McKenney, 622–5916.
Assistant Inspector General for—
Compliance and Enforcement Operations.—Matthew A. Weir, 622–3837.
Management Planning and Workforce Development.—Nancy A. LaManna, 927–7076.
Management Services and Organizations.—Heather Hill (acting), 927–7084.
Returns Processing and Accounts Services.—Russell Martin (978) 809–0296.
Security and Information Technology Services.—Danny Verneuille (901) 546–3111.
Deputy Inspector General for Investigations.—James S. Jackson, 927–0029.
Assistant Inspectors General for Investigations: Ruben Florez, 927–7234; Jeff Long, 927–7214; Trevor Nelson, 927–0150.
Deputy Assistant Inspector General for Investigations.—Susan Moats (acting), 927–7188.
Deputy Inspector General for—
Inspections and Evaluations.—Greg D. Kutz, 622–4946.
Mission Support.—Mervin Hyndman (acting), 622–7586.

OFFICE OF THE TREASURER OF THE UNITED STATES

Treasurer.—Vacant (202) 622–0100.
Senior Advisor.—Kelsey Kats.
Executive Assistant.—Gail Harris-Berry (detail).
Director, Office of Consumer Policy.—Vacant.

UNITED STATES MINT

801 9th Street, NW., Washington, DC 20220

phone (202) 354–7200, fax 756–6160

Director.—David J. Ryder, 354–7200.
Executive Assistant to the Director.—Lori Avant, 354–7200.
Deputy Director.—Patrick Hernandez (acting), 354–7200.
Executive Assistant to the Deputy Director.—Vacant, 354–7200.
Chief Counsel.—John Schorn, 354–7200.
Director, Legislative and Intergovernmental Affairs.—Jennifer Warren, 354–7200.
Deputy Director, Legislative and Intergovernmental Affairs.—Betty Birdsong, 354–7770.
Chief, Corporate Communications.—Thomas Johnson, 354–7718.
Chief, Office of Protection.—Dennis O'Connor, 354–7300.
Deputy Chief, Office of Protection.—Bill R. Bailey, 354–7300.
Associate Director, Chief Information Officer.—Joe Jankauskas, 354–7780.
Deputy Associate Director.—DeAnna Wynn, 354–6749.
Associate Director, Chief Financial Officer.—Kristie McNally, 354–6706.
Deputy Associate Director.—Kenyatta Fletcher, 354–7899.

Associate Directors of:
Human Capital.—Vacant, 354–8431.
Manufacturing.—David Croft, 354–7411.
Sales and Marketing.—Matthew Holben, 354–8315.
Deputy Associate Directors of:
Human Capital.—Kirk Carter, 354–8431.
Manufacturing.—Don Bennett, 354–6777.
Sales and Marketing.—Greg Dawson, 354–8417.

DEPARTMENT OF DEFENSE

The Pentagon, Washington, DC 20301

phone (703) 545–6700

DR. MARK T. ESPER, Secretary of Defense; born in Uniontown, Pennsylvania, April 26, 1964; education: United States Military Academy—received commission in the Infantry, 1986. Upon completion of Ranger and Pathfinder training, he served in the 101st Airborne Division and participated in the 1990–91 Gulf War with the ''Screaming Eagles.'' He later commanded a Rifle Company in the 3–325 Airborne Battalion Combat Team in Vicenza, Italy. He retired from the U.S Army in 2007 after spending 10 years on active duty and 11 years in the National Guard and Army Reserve. After leaving active duty, he served as Chief of Staff at the Heritage Foundation think tank, followed by service as legislative director and senior policy advisor to former Senator Chuck Hagel. He was a senior professional staff member on the Senate Foreign Relations and Senate Government Affairs committees, policy advisor for former Senate Majority Leader Bill Frist. During the President George W. Bush administration, he served as the Deputy Assistant Secretary of Defense for Negotiations Policy at the Pentagon. From 2006–07, Dr. Esper was the Chief Operating Officer and Executive Vice President of Defense and International Affairs at Aerospace Industries Association. He was the national policy director to Senator Fred Thompson for his 2008 Presidential campaign, and was a Senate-appointed commissioner on the U.S.-China Economic and Security Review Commission. Dr. Esper later served concurrently as the Executive Vice President for Europe and Eurasian Affairs from 2008–10. Before being nominated as the Secretary of the Army in 2017, Dr. Esper was the Vice President for Government Relations at the Raytheon Company. Dr. Esper is a recipient of the Department of Defense Medal for Distinguished Public Service. Among his many military awards and decorations are the Legion of Merit, Bronze Star Medal, the Kuwait Liberation Medal, Kuwait Liberation Medal Saudi-Arabia, and the Combat Infantryman Badge. Dr. Esper holds a Master Degree of Public Administration degree from John F. Kennedy School of Government, and a doctorate in Public Policy from George Washington University. Dr. Esper and his wife, Leah, have been married for 30 years and have three adult children. The Honorable Mark T. Esper was sworn in as the 27th Secretary of Defense July 23, 2019. He served as Acting Secretary of Defense from June 24, 2019, to July 15, 2019. Dr. Esper served as the Secretary of the Army from Nov. 20, 2017, to June 24, 2019, and from July 15, 2019, to July 23, 2019.

OFFICE OF THE SECRETARY

1000 Defense Pentagon, Room 3E880, Washington, DC 20301–1000

phone (703) 692–7100, fax (703) 571–8951

Secretary of Defense.—Dr. Mark T. Esper.

OFFICE OF THE DEPUTY SECRETARY

1010 Defense Pentagon, Room 3E944, Washington, DC 20301–1010

phone (703) 692–7150

Deputy Secretary of Defense.—David L. Norquist.

EXECUTIVE SECRETARIAT

1000 Defense Pentagon, Room 3E880, Washington, DC 20301–1000

phone (703) 692–7120, fax 571–8951

Executive Secretary.—CAPT Oliver Lewis.

GENERAL COUNSEL

Pentagon, Room 3E788, Washington, DC 20301–1600

phone (703) 695–3341, fax 693–7278

General Counsel.—Hon. Paul C. Ney, Jr.
Principal Deputy.—William S. Castle.

OPERATIONAL TEST AND EVALUATION

Pentagon, Room 3E1088, Washington, DC 20301–1700

phone (703) 697–3655, fax 614–9103

Director.—Hon. Robert F. Behler.

INSPECTOR GENERAL

4800 Mark Center Drive, Alexandria, VA 22350–1500

phone (703) 604–8300

DoD Hotline (800) 424–9098, DoD Hotline fax (703) 604–8567

Inspector General.—Sean O'Donnell (acting).
Principal Deputy Inspector General (acting) and Chief of Staff.—Steven A. Stebbins.
Deputy Inspector General for—
Administrative Investigations.—Marguerite C. Garrison.
Audit.—Jacqueline L. Wicecarver.
Evaluations.—Michael J. Roark.
Investigations.—Dermot F. O'Reilly.
Overseas Contingency Operations.—Michael S. Child, Sr.
General Counsel to the Inspector General.—Paul Hadjiyane.
Assistant Inspector General for Legislative Affairs and Communications.—Michael C. Zola.
Director, DoD Hotline.—Patrick W. Gookin.

UNDER SECRETARY OF DEFENSE FOR ACQUISITION AND SUSTAINMENT

Pentagon, Room 3E1010, Washington, DC 20301

phone (703) 697–7021

Under Secretary.—Ellen M. Lord.
Deputy Under Secretary.—Alan R. Shaffer.
Assistant Secretary for—
Acquisition.—Kevin M. Fahey.
Nuclear, Chemical, and Biological Defense Programs.—Vacant.
Sustainment.—Robert H. McMahon.
Deputy Assistant Secretary for Industrial Policy.—Jennifer S. Santos.

JOINT STRIKE FIGHTER PROGRAM OFFICE

200 12th Street South, Suite 600, Arlington, VA 22202–5402

phone (703) 602–7640

Program Executive Officer.—Lt. Gen. Eric T. Fick, USAF.

UNDER SECRETARY OF DEFENSE (COMPTROLLER) AND CHIEF FINANCIAL OFFICER

Pentagon, Room 3E770, Washington, DC 20301–1100

phone (703) 695–3237

Under Secretary/Chief Financial Officer.—Thomas W. Harker (performing the duties of the Under Secretary of Defense (Comptroller)/Chief Financial Officer).
Deputy Under Secretary.—Elaine McCusker.

UNDER SECRETARY OF DEFENSE FOR PERSONNEL AND READINESS

Pentagon, Room 3E986, Washington, DC 20301–4000

phone (703) 697–2121

Under Secretary of Defense.—Hon. Matthew P. Donovan.
Deputy Under Secretary of Defense.—William G. Bushman (performing the duties of the Deputy Under Secretary of Defense for Personnel and Readiness), (703) 697–2121.
Assistant Secretary of Defense for—
Health Affairs.—Hon. Thomas McCaffery, 697–2111.
Manpower and Reserve Affairs.—Virginia Penrod (acting), 614–3240.
Readiness.—Thomas A. Constable (acting), 693–0466.

UNDER SECRETARY OF DEFENSE FOR POLICY

Pentagon, Room 3E806, Washington, DC 20301–2000

phone (703) 697–7200

Under Secretary.—Dr. James Anderson (acting).
Deputy Under Secretary.—Anthony J. Tata (performing the duties of Deputy Under Secretary of Defense for Policy).
Assistant Secretary of Defense for—
Homeland Defense and Global Security.—Kenneth P. Rapuano.
Indo-Pacific Security Affairs.—David Helvey (performing the duties of Assistant Secretary of Defense for Indo-Pacific Security Affairs).
International Security Affairs.—Michael Cutrone (performing the duties of Assistant Secretary of Defense for International Security Affairs).
Special Operations/Low-Intensity Conflict.—Ezra Cohen (acting).
Strategy, Plans, and Capabilities.—Vic Mercado.

DEPARTMENT OF DEFENSE CHIEF INFORMATION OFFICER (DoD CIO)

Pentagon, Room 3E1030, Washington, DC 20301–6000

phone (703) 695–0348

DoD CIO.—Dana Deasy.
Principal Deputy DoD CIO.—John Sherman

ASSISTANT SECRETARY OF DEFENSE FOR LEGISLATIVE AFFAIRS

Pentagon, Room 3E970, Washington, DC 20301–1300

phone (703) 697–6210, fax 695–5860

Assistant Secretary.—Ann Thomas ''A.T.'' Johnston (acting).
Principal Deputy.—Matthew I. Kenney (performing the duties of Principal Deputy Assistant Secretary of Defense for Legislative Affairs).
Deputy Assistant Secretary of Defense (Senate Affairs).—Andrew H. Tabler.
Deputy Assistant Secretary of Defense (House Affairs).—William E. Wolfe.

ASSISTANT TO THE SECRETARY FOR PUBLIC AFFAIRS

Pentagon, Room 2E964, Washington, DC 20301–1400

phone (703) 697–9312, fax 695–4299, public inquiries 571–3343

Assistant to the Secretary.—Johnathan Rath Hoffman.
Principal Deputy Assistant to the Secretary.—Charles E. Summers, Jr.

OFFICE OF THE CHIEF MANAGEMENT OFFICER

Pentagon, Room 3E146, Washington, DC 20301–9010

phone (703) 614–8888, fax 695–5395

Chief Management Officer.—Lisa W. Hershman.

Assistant Deputy Chief Management Officer.—Vacant.

DEPARTMENT OF DEFENSE FIELD ACTIVITIES

DEFENSE MEDIA ACTIVITY

6700 Taylor Avenue, Fort George G. Meade, MD 20755

phone (301) 222–6000, https://dma.mil/

Director.—COL Paul R. Haverstick (acting).
Deputy Director.—Gene Brink (acting).

DEPARTMENT OF DEFENSE EDUCATION ACTIVITY

4800 Mark Center Drive, Arlington, VA 22350–1400

School Information (571) 372–0590

Director.—Thomas M. Brady, 372–0590.
Chief Academic Officer.—Beth Schiavino-Narvaez, 372–1893.
Associate Director for Finance and Business Operations.—Robert Brady, 372–1901.
Chief of Staff.—Jay M. Burcham, 372–5820.

DEPARTMENT OF DEFENSE HUMAN RESOURCES ACTIVITY

4800 Mark Center Drive, Suite 06J25–01, Alexandria, VA 22350–4000

Director.—William Booth.
Deputy Director.—Jeffrey Register.
Executive Assistant.—Katherine Roddy.

OFFICE OF ECONOMIC ADJUSTMENT

2231 Crystal Drive, Suite 520, Arlington, VA 22202

phone (703) 697–2130

Director.—Patrick J. O'Brien, 697–2123.
Deputy Director for—
Compliance.—James P. Holland, 697–2188.
Integration.—Doug Brown, 697–2015.
Programs.—Dan Glasson, 697–2162.

WASHINGTON HEADQUARTERS SERVICES

Pentagon, Washington, DC 20301

phone (703) 693–7995

Director.—Thomas M. Muir.
Deputy Director.—Vacant.
Director for—
Acquisition Directorate.—David D. Sanders, 545–0423.
Executive Services Directorate.—Darren L. Irvine (acting), 692–5473.
Facilities Services Directorate.—Paul G. McMahon (acting), 697–7241.
Financial Management Directorate.—Jae W. Lee (acting), 545–0018.
History and Library.—Dr. Erin Mahan, 697–5046.
Human Resources Directorate.—Christopher A. Kapellas (571) 256–4504.
Plans and Programs Office.—Rayford D. Nichols, 545–1001.
Raven Rock Mountain Complex.—Col. Larry Nierdringhaus (717) 878–2791.
Small Business Programs.—Mark J. Gazillo, 545–0542.
WHS General Counsel.—John S. Albanese, 697–1305.

JOINT CHIEFS OF STAFF

OFFICE OF THE CHAIR

Pentagon, Room 2E872, Washington, DC 20318–9999

phone (703) 697–9121

Chair.—GEN Mark A. Milley, USA.
Vice Chair.—Gen. John E. Hyten, USAF, Room 2E868, 695–9283.
Assistant to the Chair, Joint Chiefs of Staff.—LTG Ricky L. Waddell, USA, Room 2E858, 697–6485.

JOINT STAFF

Director.—RADM William D. Byrne (acting), USN, Room 2E936, 614–5221.
Vice Director.—RADM William D. Byrne, USN, Room 2E936, 614–5221.
Director for—
Command, Control, Communications, and Computer/Cyber, J–6.—Lt. Gen. Bradford J. Shwedo, USAF, Room 2E939, 695–4420.
Force Structure, Resources, and Assessment, J–8.—VADM Ronald A. Boxall, USN, Room 2E838, 697–6605.
Intelligence, J–2.—RADM Frank D. Whitworth, USN, Room 2D877, 697–9773.
Joint Force Development, J–7.—VADM Stuart B. Munsch, USN, Room 2D864, 697–9031.
Logistics, J–4.—Lt. Gen. Giovanni K. Tuck, USAF, Room 2D867, 697–7000.
Manpower and Personnel, J–1.—Maj. Gen. Lenny J. Richoux, USAF, Room 2D857, 697–9644.
Operations, J–3.—LTG Andrew P. Poppas, USA, Room 2D882, 614–6173.
Strategic Plans and Policy, J–5.—Lt. Gen. David W. Allvin, USAF, Room 2E800, 697–9716.

DEFENSE AGENCIES

MISSILE DEFENSE AGENCY

5700 18th Street, Fort Belvoir, VA 22060–5573

Director.—RADM Jon A. Hill, USN (571) 231–8006.
Director, Public Affairs.—Mark Wright, 231–8212.
Director, Congressional Affairs.—Kimo Hollingsworth, 231–8105.

DEFENSE ADVANCED RESEARCH PROJECTS AGENCY

675 North Randolph Street, Arlington, VA 22203

Director.—Dr. Victoria Coleman (703) 696–2402.
Deputy Director.—Dr. Peter Highnam, 248–1540.

DEFENSE COMMISSARY AGENCY

1300 E Avenue, Fort Lee, VA 23801–1800

phone (804) 734–8720/8330

Special Assistant for Commissary Operations for Manpower and Reserve Affairs (M&RA).—Robert J. Bianchi, 734–8330.
Chief Operating Officer.—Michael J. Dowling, 734–8330.

WASHINGTON OFFICE

4100 Defense Pentagon, Room 5D636, Washington, DC 20301–4100

phone (703) 571–7186/7184

Chief.—Robin Schmidt.

DEFENSE CONTRACT AUDIT AGENCY

8725 John J. Kingman Road, Suite 2135, Fort Belvoir, VA 22060

phone (703) 767–3200

Director.—Anita F. Bales, 767–3200.
Deputy Director.—Joseph P. Bentz, 767–3272.

DEFENSE COUNTERINTELLIGENCE AND SECURITY AGENCY

27130 Telegraph Road, Quantico, VA 22134

phone (703) 617–2352

Director.—William K. Lietzau.

DEFENSE FINANCE AND ACCOUNTING SERVICE

8899 East 56th Street, Indianapolis, IN 46249–0100

phone (317) 212–0714

Director.—Audrey Y. Davis.
Principal Deputy Director.—Vacant.

DEFENSE HEALTH AGENCY

7700 Arlington Boulevard, Falls Church, VA 22042–5101

phone (703) 681–8707

Director.—Lt. Gen. Ronald J. Place, M.D.
Deputy Director.—Guy T. Kiyokawa.

DEFENSE INFORMATION SYSTEMS AGENCY

P.O. Box 549, Command Building, Fort Meade, MD 20755

Director.—VADM Nancy Norton, USN (301) 225–6001.
Assistant to the Director.—MG Garrett Yee, USA, 225–6010.
Executive Deputy Director.—Anthony Montemarano, 225–6080.
Chief of Staff.—Laura Radney, 225–6020.

DEFENSE INTELLIGENCE AGENCY

200 MacDill Boulevard, Washington, DC 20340

phone (202) 231–0800

Director.—LTG Robert P. Ashley, Jr., USA.
Deputy Director.—Suzanne L. White.

DEFENSE LEGAL SERVICES AGENCY

Pentagon, Room 3E788, Washington, DC 20301–1600

phone (703) 695–3341, fax 693–7278

General Counsel.—Paul C. Ney, Jr.
Principal Deputy General Counsel.—William S. Castle, 697–7248.

DEFENSE LOGISTICS AGENCY

8725 John J. Kingman Road, Suite 2533, Ft. Belvoir, VA 22060

phone (703) 767–5264

Director.—VADM Michelle C. Skubic, USN.

Vice Director.—Michael D. Scott, SES.

DEFENSE POW / MIA ACCOUNTING AGENCY
2300 Defense Pentagon, Washington, DC 20301–2300
phone (703) 699–1102, fax 602–1890

Director.—Kelly K. McKeague.

DEFENSE SECURITY COOPERATION AGENCY
201 12th Street South, Suite 203, Arlington, VA 22202–5408
phone (703) 604–6605

Director.—Heidi Grant, 604–6604.
Deputy Director.—Cara L. Abercrombie (acting), 604–6606.

DEFENSE THREAT REDUCTION AGENCY
8725 John J. Kingman Road, Stop 6201, Ft. Belvoir, VA 22060–6201
phone (703) 767–4883

Director.—Vayl S. Oxford.
Deputy Director.—MG Antonio M. Fletcher.

NATIONAL GEOSPATIAL-INTELLIGENCE AGENCY
7500 GEOINT Drive, Springfield, VA 22150
phone (571) 557–5300

Director.—VADM Robert Sharp.
Deputy Director.—Dr. Stacey Dixon.

NATIONAL SECURITY AGENCY / CENTRAL SECURITY SERVICE
Ft. George G. Meade, MD 20755
phone (301) 688–6524

Director, NSA / Chief, CSS.—GEN Paul M. Nakasone, USA; Commander, U.S. Cyber Command.
Deputy Director, NSA.—George C. Barnes.
Deputy Chief, CSS.—Rachel "Rach" J. Velasco-Lind.

JOINT SERVICE SCHOOLS

DEFENSE ACQUISITION UNIVERSITY
9820 Belvoir Road, Ft. Belvoir, VA 22060
phone (800) 845–7606

President.—James P. Woolsey (703) 805–3360.
Vice President.—Frank L. Kelley, 805–2828.
Chief of Staff.—Joseph E. Johnson, 805–2828.

NATIONAL INTELLIGENCE UNIVERSITY

President.—J. Scott Cameron, Ph.D. (202) 231–3344.

NATIONAL DEFENSE UNIVERSITY
Fort McNair, Building 62, 300 Fifth Avenue, Washington, DC 20319
phone (202) 685–3912

President.—VADM Frederick J. "Fritz" Roegge, USN, Building 62, Room 307, 685–3936.

Senior Vice President.—Amb. Arnold Chacon, Building 62, Room 307A, 685–3923.

Provost and Vice President for Academic Affairs.—Dr. John Yaeger, Building 62, Room 309C, 685–0080.

CAPSTONE / PINNACLE / KEYSTONE

Director.—RADM Gerard ''Gerry'' M. Mauer, Jr. (Ret.), USN, Building 64, Room 3510, 685–2330.

NATIONAL WAR COLLEGE

Commandant.—RDML Cedric E. Pringle, USN, Building 61, Room 124, 685–4341.

DWIGHT D. EISENHOWER SCHOOL FOR NATIONAL SECURITY AND RESOURCE STRATEGY

Commandant.—BG Joy L. Curriera, USA, Building 64, Room 200, 685–4337.

COLLEGE OF INTERNATIONAL SECURITY AFFAIRS

Chancellor.—Amb. John Hoover (acting), Building 64, Room 2102, 685–7209.

COLLEGE OF INFORMATION AND CYBERSPACE

Chancellor/Dean of Faculty and Academic Programs.—Dr. Cassandra D. Lewis (acting), Building 62, Room 201G, 685–3886.

JOINT FORCES STAFF COLLEGE

Commandant.—Maj. Gen. William H. Seely III, USMC, 7800 Hampton Boulevard, Norfolk, VA 23511 (757) 443–6124.

UNIFORMED SERVICES UNIVERSITY OF THE HEALTH SCIENCES

4301 Jones Bridge Road, Bethesda, MD 20814

President.—Richard W. Thomas, M.D., D.D.S., F.A.C.S., Room A1019 (301) 295–3013.

DEPARTMENT OF THE AIR FORCE

1670 Air Force Pentagon, Washington, DC 20330–1670
phone (703) 697–7376, fax 695–8809

SECRETARY OF THE AIR FORCE

Secretary of the Air Force.—Hon. Barbara Barrett, Room 4E878.
Confidential Assistant.—Peggy Buchanan.
Senior Military Assistant.—Brig. Gen. David Miller.
Deputy Military Assistant.—Lt. Col. Sean Piccirilli.
Military Aid.—Lt. Col. Angela Tapia.
Executive Assistants: SMSgt Ronald Lerch, TSgt Kristen Winters.

SECAF/CSAF EXECUTIVE ACTION GROUP

Director.—Col. Deborah Lovette (703) 697–5540.
Deputy Chief.—Catherine Perro.

UNDER SECRETARY OF THE AIR FORCE

1670 Air Force Pentagon, Room 4E858, Washington, DC 20330–1670
phone (703) 697–1361

Under Secretary of the Air Force.—Hon. John Roth (acting), PTDO.
Confidential Assistant.—Rosa Ramirez.
Senior Military Assistant.—Col. Andrew Clark.
Military Assistant.—Lt. Col. Tyler Hess.
Executive Assistant.—MSgt Ivanka Vrechkov.

CHIEF OF STAFF

1670 Air Force Pentagon, Room 4E924, Washington, DC 20330–1670
phone (703) 693–7837

Chief of Staff.—Gen. Charles Q. Brown, Jr.
Confidential Assistant.—Terri Stern.
Special Assistant.—Samuel Neill, Room 4E929, 697–1930.
Executive Officer.—Col. Curtis Bass.
Vice Chief of Staff.—Gen. Stephen Wilson, Room 4E944, 695–7911.
Director of Staff.—Lt. Gen. Timothy Fay, Room 4E877, 695–7913.
Chief Master Sergeant of the Air Force.—CMSAF Joanne Bass, Room 4E941, 695–0498.

CHIEF OF SPACE OPERATIONS

1670 Air Force Pentagon, Room 4E858, Washington, DC 20330–1670
phone (703) 695–9387

Chief of Space Operations.—Gen. John Raymond.
Confidential Assistant.—Audrey Pfingston.
Executive Officer.—Lt. Col. Tammy Schlichenmaier.
Director of Staff.—Lt. Gen. Nina Armagno, 693–9513.
United States Space Force Senior Enlisted Advisor.—CMSgt Roger Towberman, 693–6276.

DEPUTY UNDER SECRETARY FOR INTERNATIONAL AFFAIRS

1080 Air Force Pentagon, Room 4E192, Washington, DC 20330–1080

Deputy Under Secretary.—Kelli L. Seybolt (703) 695–7263.

Assistant Deputy.—Maj. Gen. Stephen "Steve" Oliver, 695–7261.
Executive Officers: Lt. Col. Bethany McCarthy, 693–1941; Georgia Smothers, 695–7263.
Congressional Liaison.—Julie Birt (571) 309–9969.

1080 Air Force Pentagon, Room 4C253, Washington, DC 20330–1080

Director of Policy.—James A. Dunn (571) 256–7491.
Executive Officer.—Lt. Col. John Smith, 256–7494.
Executive Assistant.—Michelle Polk, 256–7495.

1080 Air Force Pentagon, Room 4C947, Washington, DC 20330–1080

Director of Regional Affairs.—Brig. Gen. Todd A. Dozier (703) 695–2022.
Executive Officer.—Maj. Linda Thierauf, 695–2077.
Executive Assistant.—Sanura Wade, 695–2080.

1080 Air Force Pentagon, Room 4C253, Washington, DC 20330–1080

Director of Strategy, Resources, and Integration.—Maj. Gen. Brian Neal (ANG), (571) 256–9492.
Executive Assistant.—Patricia Green, 256–9491.

ASSISTANT SECRETARY FOR ACQUISITION, TECHNOLOGY AND LOGISTICS

1060 Air Force Pentagon, Washington, DC 20330

110 Luke Avenue, Suite 200, Bolling AFB, Washington, DC 20032–6400

Assistant Secretary.—Dr. Will Roper (703) 697–6361.
Senior Military Assistant.—Col. Luke Cropsey, 697–6990.
Military Assistant.—Lt. Col. Jonathan Varoli, 697–6362.
Principal Deputy.—Darlene Costello, 697–9373.
Military Deputy.—Lt. Gen. Duke Richardson, 697–6363.
Executive Officer.—Maj. Matthew Foertsch, 695–7311.

DEPUTY ASSISTANT SECRETARY FOR ACQUISITION INTEGRATION

Deputy Assistant Secretary.—William Bailey (571) 256–0355.
Associate Deputy Assistant Secretary.—Mark Murphy, 256–0351.
Executive Officer.—Maj. Michael Huegerich, 256–0356.

DEPUTY ASSISTANT SECRETARY FOR CONTRACTING

Deputy Assistant Secretary.—Maj. Gen. Cameron Holt (571) 256–2397.
Associate Deputy Assistant Secretary.—John Cannaday, 256–2397.
Executive Officer.—Lt. Col. Mark Mizzell, 256–2397.

DEPUTY ASSISTANT SECRETARY FOR SCIENCE, TECHNOLOGY AND ENGINEERING

Deputy Assistant Secretary.—Ms. Kristen Baldwin (571) 256–0303.
Associate Deputy Assistant Secretary.—Dr. Yvette Weber, 256–0303.
Executive Officer.—Maj. Matthew Saar, 256–0303.

CAPABILITY DIRECTORATE FOR GLOBAL POWER PROGRAMS

Director.—Maj. Gen. James Dawkins, Jr. (571) 256–0191.
Deputy Director.—Col. Erik Rhylander, 256–0192.
Executive Officer.—Maj. Austin Page, 256–0196.

CAPABILITY DIRECTORATE FOR GLOBAL REACH PROGRAMS

Director.—Brig. Gen. Mark R. August (571) 256–0489.
Deputy Director.—Col. Leland A. Davis, 256–0497.
Executive Officer.—Maj. Joseph Dias, 256–0522.

CAPABILITY DIRECTORATE FOR INFORMATION DOMINANCE

Director.—Kevin Stamey (571) 256–0081.

Deputy Director.—Col. Robert Dietrick, 256–0082.
Military Assistant.—Lt. Col. Robert Thornton, 256–0085.
Executive Officer.—Maj. Nicholas DuPre, 256–0083.

CAPABILITY DIRECTORATE FOR SPACE PROGRAMS

Director.—Brig. Gen. Steven Whitney (571) 695–3423.
Deputy Director.—Col. Deven Lowman, 695–3499.
Executive Officer.—Lt. Col. David Sampayan, 695–3435.

DIRECTORATE FOR SPECIAL PROGRAMS

Director.—Col. Richard McGlamory (202) 767–3890.
Deputy Director.—Chris DiNenna (571) 256–0005.
Executive Officer.—Lt. Col. Eric Palmer (571) 256–0028.

DIRECTORATE FOR DEPARTMENT OF THE AIR FORCE RAPID CAPABILITIES

Director.—Randall Walden (202) 767–1800.
Deputy Director.—Charles Nava (acting), 767–1800.
Executive Officer.—Maj. Blaine Stewart, 767–3203.

ASSISTANT SECRETARY FOR FINANCIAL MANAGEMENT AND COMPTROLLER (SAF/FM)

1130 Air Force Pentagon, Washington, DC 20330–1130

Air Force Cost Analysis Agency, Jones Building
1500 West Perimeter Road, Joint Base Andrews, MD 20762

Assistant Secretary.—John P. Roth, Room 4E978 (703) 695–0829.
Senior Military Assistant.—Lt. Col. Phelemon T. Williams, 695–0829.
Chief, Enlisted Matters.—CMSgt. John A. Writer, 614–5429.

PRINCIPAL DEPUTY ASSISTANT SECRETARY FOR FINANCIAL MANAGEMENT

Principal Deputy Assistant Secretary.—Richard Hartley (703) 695–0837.
Military Assistant.—Maj. Ashley A. Housley, 695–0837.

DEPUTY ASSISTANT SECRETARY FOR BUDGET (SAF/FMB)

Deputy Assistant Secretary.—Maj. Gen. James D. Peccia III, Room 5D912 (703) 695–1876.
Executive Officer.—Lt. Col. Scott J. Thompson, 695–1876.
Deputy.—Carolyn M. Gleason, 697–1876.
Director of:
Budget and Appropriations Liaison.—Col. Kerry D. Britt, Room 5C949, 614–8114.
Budget Investment.—Carlos Rodgers, Room 5D912, 697–1220.
Budget Operations and Personnel.—Brig. Gen. James D. Peccia, Room 5D912, 697–0627.
Budget Programs.—Col. James R. Culpepper, Room 5C950, 614–7883.

DEPUTY ASSISTANT SECRETARY FOR COST AND ECONOMICS (SAF/FMC)

Deputy Assistant Secretary.—Pamela C. Schwenke, Room 5E975 (703) 697–5311.
Associate Deputy Assistant Secretary.—Grant McVicker, Room 5E975, 697–5313.
Executive Officer.—Lt. Col. David E. Stephens, Room 5E975, 697–5312.
Technical Director for Cost and Economics.—Ranae P. Woods, Suite 3500 (240) 612–5615.
Director, Economics and Business Management.—Dr. Anne L. Gorney, Room 4C843 (703) 693–9347.
Director, Cost Analysis Division.—Col. Davis H. Maulding, Room 4C943, 697–0288.

DEPUTY ASSISTANT SECRETARY FOR FINANCIAL OPERATIONS (SAF/FMF)

Deputy Assistant Secretary.—Fredrick E. Carr, Room 5D739 (703) 614–4180.
Associate Deputy Assistant Secretary.—Tina M. Pierce, Room 5D739, 614–4180.
Chief Information Officer.—Shirley L. Reed, Room 5D739, 614–5437.
Military Assistant.—Lt. Col. Nyree D. Lensch, 614–4180.
Director for—
Accounting Policy and Reporting.—Omolola A. Fawole, Andrews AFB, MD (240) 612–5212.
AF Financial Systems Organization.—Glena G. Gibson, Wright-Patterson AFB, OH (937) 257–2262.
AFAFO.—Eric Cuebas, JB Andrews, MD (240) 612–5600.
AF-IPPS.—Deborah Kennedy, San Antonio, TX (210) 565–4329.
DEAMS.—Todd M. Baker, Wright-Patterson AFB, OH (937) 656–8554.
FIAR.—Katrina M. Rawls, Andrews AFB, MD (240) 612–5281.
Financial Services.—Gregory Wilson, Ellsworth AFB, SD (605) 385–8682.
Information Systems and Technology.—John Koski, Andrews AFB, MD (240) 612–5283.

ASSISTANT SECRETARY FOR INSTALLATIONS, ENVIRONMENT AND ENERGY
1665 Air Force Pentagon, Washington, DC 20330–1665

Assistant Secretary.—Hon. John W. Henderson.
Principal Deputy Assistant Secretary.—Jennifer Miller.
Executive Officers: Lt. Col. William Notbalm, 697–5023; Col. Rockie Wilson.
Executive Secretary.—Vacant, 697–4936.

DEPUTY ASSISTANT SECRETARY FOR INSTALLATIONS (SAF/IEI)

Deputy Assistant Secretary.—Jennifer Miller, 695–3592.
Executive Officer.—Maj. Sean Stapler, 695–6456.
Executive Secretary/Administrative Support.—Sheenia T. Williams, 695–3592.
Deputy, Installation Planning.—Steve Arenson (571) 256–2471.
Director, Installation Planning (IEIP).—Col. Craig Rezac, 697–0997.
Director, Real Estate Policy.—Carol Ann Beda, 697–7003.
Manager, Legislative/Public Affairs.—Frank Smolinsky, 697–1980.
Cooperative, Installation Policy.—Vacant, 693–3349.
Program Managers: Tim P. Brennan, 695–5730; Ed McCarthy, 693–9339; John Smith, 693–8309; Terry Tallent, 697–6492.
AFCEC Liaison.—Robert McCann, 692–9515.
Assistant for ANG Affairs, Installations.—Col. Craig Rezac, 697–0997.

DEPUTY ASSISTANT SECRETARY FOR ENVIRONMENT, SAFETY AND INFRASTRUCTURE (SAF/IEE)

Deputy Assistant Secretary.—Mark A. Correll, 697–9297.
Principal Director, E/S/I Policy.—Christa Gunn, 697–2066.
Executive Officer.—Capt. Gina McComb, 697–9297.
Executive Secretary/Administrative Support.—Sheenia T. Williams, 695–3592.
Environment Policy and Programs.—Michelle Brown, 697–0989.
Director:
Environmental Policy and Programs.—Otis Hicks, 693–9328.
Infrastructure Policy.—Lt. Col. David Berrios, 693–2047.
Installation Energy Policy and Programs.—Douglas Tucker, 693–9544.
Occupational Health Plans and Programs.—Col. Joel Almosara (571) 256–4397.
Occupational Health Policy.—Lt. Col. Freeman Hollfield, 693–2055.
Safety Policy.—William Walkowiak, 693–7706.
Manager, Facilities Energy.—Kathleen Richardson, 693–3254.
Manager, Process Energy and Vehicles.—Andrew Morris, 571–5771.
Contract Support, ESOH Policy.—Daniel Kowalczyk, 697–1198.
Facilities Energy Analyst.—Richard Brill, 697–1018.

DEPUTY ASSISTANT SECRETARY FOR OPERATIONAL ENERGY (SAF/IEN)

Deputy Assistant Secretary.—Roberto I. Guerrero (571) 256–4711.

Principal Director, Operational Energy Policy and Chief of Staff.—Michael Penland (571) 256–3944.
Executive Officer.—Capt. Charles McDaniel (703) 697–6032.
Executive Secretary.—Ann Belfield (571) 256–4711.
Chief of Aviation Energy Logistics Policy.—Toniann Fisher, 697–0987.
Chief of Future Operations and Acquisitions Policy.—Fred Parker, 697–1113.
Contractor Lead.—Shelly Black, 697–1113.
Lead Analyst, Aviation Energy Current Operational Policy.—Jordon Eccles, 614–8279.
Energy Analyst, Strategy and Communications.—Corrie Poland, 697–1207.
Energy Analyst, Education and Training.—Lauren Dupont, 697–1207.

ASSISTANT SECRETARY OF THE AIR FORCE FOR MANPOWER AND RESERVE AFFAIRS (SAF/MR)

1660 Air Force Pentagon, Room 4E1010, Washington, DC 20330–1660

Assistant Secretary.—Shon J. Manasco (703) 697–2302.
Principal Deputy Assistant Secretary.—John A. Fedrigo, 697–2302.
Senior Military Assistant.—Col. Kelly M. Sams, 697–2302.
Confidential Assistant.—Yolanda Washington (571) 256–4405.
Military Assistant.—Lt. Col. Mary F. Wilson (703) 697–2302.
Director of Staff.—Ryan McDonald, 697–2302.
Deputy Director of Staff.—Savannah Jolly, 697–2302.
Deputy Assistant Secretary.—Tamera Nelson, 697–6588.
Reserve Mobilization Assistant.—Brig. Gen. Ellen Moore (571) 256–1317.
Guard Mobilization Assistant.—Brig. Gen. Christopher Walker (304) 341–6332.
Senior Enlisted Advisor.—CMSgt Eric Nielsen (703) 697–6583.

DEPUTY ASSISTANT SECRETARY FOR FORCE MANAGEMENT INTEGRATION (SAF/MRM)

Deputy Assistant Secretary.—Patricia Mulcahy (703) 614–4751.
Executive Secretary.—Alicia Bobbitt (703) 614–4751.
Assistant Deputy.—Col. Paul Nosek (703) 693–9764.

DEPUTY ASSISTANT SECRETARY FOR RESERVE AFFAIRS AND AIRMAN READINESS (SAF/MRR)

Deputy Assistant Secretary.—Christy Nolta (703) 697–6375.
Executive Secretary.—Vacant (703) 697–6375.
Assistant Deputy.—Col. Jason Knudsen (571) 256–4043.

AIR FORCE REVIEW BOARDS AGENCY (SAF/MRB)

1500 West Perimeter Road, Suite 3700, Joint Base Andrews NAF–Washington, MD 20762

Director.—Dr. Gerald Curry (240) 612–5400.
Executive Secretary.—Lynn Redmond, 612–5400.
Deputy Director.—Troy McIntosh, 612–5403.

AIR FORCE CIVILIAN APPELLATE REVIEW OFFICE (AFCARO)

(SAF/MRBA) (Suite 4350)

Director.—Rita S. Looney (240) 612–5330.
Assistant Director.—Cassidy Fludd, 612–5340.

AIR FORCE SECURITY PROTECTION DIRECTORATE (SAF/MRBB)

President.—Thomas Shubert (240) 612–5364.
Deputy.—Joseph Schott, 612–5350.
Executive Secretary/Attorney Advisor on Clemency/Parole Board.—Thomas Shubert (240) 612–5364.

AIR FORCE BOARD FOR CORRECTION OF MILITARY RECORDS (AFBCMR) (SAF/MRBC)

Executive Director.—John Vallario (240) 612–5392.
Associate Directors: Janet Hutson, 612–5381; Nicole Jackson, 612–5385.
Chief, Board Analysis.—Deborah Davidson, 612–5383.
Lead Examiners: Charles ''Ty'' Alston, 612–5399; Catherine Danzy, 612–5384; Michael Hayden, 612–4865.
President, Remissions Board.—Troy McIntosh, 612–5392.

DoD PHYSICAL DISABILITY BOARD OF REVIEW (PDBR) (SAF/MRBD) (Suite 4350)

President.—Gregory Johnson (240) 612–4390.
Deputy.—Phyllis Joyner, 612–4392.

AIR FORCE REVIEW BOARDS AGENCY LEGAL DIRECTORATE (SAF/MRBL)

Director.—Col. Laura Barchick (240) 612–4529.

AIR FORCE REVIEW BOARDS AGENCY MEDICAL SUPPORT DIRECTORATE (SAF/MRBM)

Director.—Col. June Cook (240) 612–4016.

SECRETARY OF THE AIR FORCE PERSONNEL COUNCIL (SAFPC) (SAF/MRBP)

Director.—Col. John Russo (240) 612–5365.
Military Deputy Director/Air Force Reserve Advisor.—Col. Edward Segura, 612–5355.
Civilian Deputy Director.—John Vallario, 612–5380.
Chief, Air Force Discharge Review Board.—Col. Edward Segura, 612–5355.
Chief, Awards/Decorations.—Col. Patricia Barr, 612–5364.
Executive Secretary, DoD Civilian/Military Service Review Board.—Col. Patricia Barr, 612–5364.

MISSION SUPPORT DIRECTORATE (SAF/MRBX)

Director.—Clifford R. Tompkins (240) 612–5402.
Resource Manager.—Timothy Nolte, 612–6269.
Human Resources.—Jameill Barksdale, 612–5357.
Information Technology Manager.—Michael Cusick, 612–5359.

CHIEF INFORMATION OFFICER

1800 Air Force Pentagon, Room 4E878, Washington, DC 20330

Chief Information Officer.—Hon. Matthew Donovan, Room 4E878 (703) 697–7376.
Deputy Chief Information Officer.—William E. ''Bill'' Marion, Room 4E226 (707) 695–6829.
Associate Deputy Chief Information Officer.—Arthur ''AG'' Hatcher, Jr., Room 4E226 (703) 695–1839.
Assistant Deputy Chief Information Officer.—Maj. Gen. Kevin Kennedy, Room 5D1068 (703) 614–2997.

DEPUTY CHIEF OF STAFF FOR INTELLIGENCE, SURVEILLANCE, RECONNAISSANCE, AND CYBER EFFECTS OPERATIONS (ISR & CEO)

1700 Air Force Pentagon, Room 4E1070, Washington, DC 20330

Deputy Chief of Staff.—Lt. Gen. Mary O'Brien (703) 695–5613.
Executive Officer.—Lt. Col. Erica Fountain, 695–5613.
Assistant Deputy Chief of Staff for CEO.—Brig. Gen. Rob Lyman, 695–5613.
Assistant Deputy Chief of Staff for ISR.—Maj. Gen. Daniel Simpson, 695–5613.
Associate Deputy Chief of Staff.—Ken Bray, 614–1049.

Director of:

Analysis, Partnerships, and Engagements.—Col. Steven Gorski, 693–1657.

Civilian Aviation Intel Integration.—Dr. Jeffrey Wooden (202) 404–3426.

Cyberspace Operations and Warfighter Communications.—Brig. Gen. (s) Eric DeLange, 695–1835.

ISR Operations.—Brig. Gen. (s) Parker Wright, 695–6240.

Readiness and Talent Management.—Theresa Sanchez, 614–3701.

RPA/Airborne ISR Capabilities.—Brig. Gen. Stewart Hammons, 695–0066.

Staff.—Col. Matthew Reilman, 697–3869.

DEPUTY CHIEF OF STAFF FOR LOGISTICS, ENGINEERING AND FORCE PROTECTION

1030 Air Force Pentagon, Washington, DC 20330

Deputy Chief of Staff.—Lt. Gen. Warren D. Berry, Room 4E154 (703) 695–5590.

Assistant Deputy Chief of Staff.—Daniel A. Fri, SES, Room 4E154, 695–2664.

Director of:

Civil Engineers.—Brig. Gen. William H. Kale, Room 4C1057, 693–4308.

Logistics.—Brig. Gen. Linda S. Hurry, Room 4C1065, 695–4900.

Resources Integration.—Edwin H. Oshiba, SES, Room 4B1088, 697–2822.

Security Forces.—Brig. Gen. Roy W. Collins, Room 5E1040, 693–5401.

DEPUTY CHIEF OF STAFF FOR MANPOWER, PERSONNEL AND SERVICES

1040 Air Force Pentagon, Room 4E168, Washington, DC 20330

Deputy Chief of Staff.—Lt. Gen. Brian T. Kelly (703) 697–6088.

Assistant Deputy Chief of Staff.—Gwendolyn DeFilippi.

Chief, AF/A1 Action Group.—Lt. Col. Matt "Jon" Hart, Room 4E169, 695–4215.

Director of:

Air Force General Officer Management.—Col. Jason Janaros, Room 4D1066, 697–1181.

Force Development.—Russell Frasz, Room 4D950, 695–2144.

Force Management Policy.—Brig. Gen. Troy Dunn, Room 4D950A, 697–1228.

Manpower, Organization, and Resources.—Brig. Gen. Gentry Boswell, Room 5B349, 692–6138.

Plans and Integration.—Gregory Parsons, Room 4D1054A, 697–5222.

Services.—Horace Larry, Room 4D1054 (571) 256–8598.

DEPUTY CHIEF OF STAFF FOR OPERATIONS

1630 Air Force Pentagon, Room 4E1024, Washington, DC 20330

Deputy Chief of Staff.—Lt. Gen. Joseph T. Gaustella, Jr. (703) 697–9991.

Assistant Deputy.—Maj. Gen. Brian Robinson, 697–9881.

Mobility Assistant.—Brig. Gen. Robert Polumbo, 697–3087.

Director of:

Current Operations.—Brig. Gen. Bradley Saltzman, Room 5D756, 697–6745.

Cyberspace Operations and Warfighting Integration.—Brig. Gen. David Gaedecke, Room 5D1068, 697–1835.

Resource Integration.—Robert Graves, Room 5E873, 697–7823.

Training and Readiness.—Maj. Gen. Scott Smith, Room 5D756, 697–9996.

DEPUTY CHIEF OF STAFF FOR STRATEGY, INTEGRATION, AND REQUIREMENTS

1070 Air Force Pentagon, Room 4E1050, Washington, DC 20330–1070

Deputy Chief of Staff.—Lt. Gen. S. Clinton Hinote (703) 697–1605.

Assistant Deputy Chief of Staff.—Michael R. Shoults, 695–4943.

Directorate of:

Air Force Warfighting Integration Capability.—Brig. Gen. David Harris, Room 5D950, 695–9223.

Electromagnetic Spectrum Superiority.—Brig. Gen. (S) Michael Manion, Room 5E682, 695–1733.

Foreign Policy Advisor to the Chief of Staff (POLAD).—Hon. Kathleen Hill, Room 4C944, 693–9652.

Operational Capability Requirements.—Maj. Gen. Dawn Dunlop, Room 5C889, 695–3018.

Strategy, Posture and Assessments.—LeeAnn Borman, Room 5D1050, 697–3117.

DIRECTORATE OF STUDIES AND ANALYSIS AND ASSESSMENTS

1570 Air Force Pentagon, Room 4E214, Washington, DC 20330–1570

Director.—Vacant (571) 256–2015.

Principal Deputy Director.—Robert C. Swallow, SES.

Military Deputy Director.—Col. Lorenzo Bradley.

Technical Director.—Dr. Angela P. Giddings, Ph.D., SL.

Chief Analyst.—Col. Michael J. Artelli.

DEPUTY CHIEF OF STAFF FOR STRATEGIC DETERRENCE AND NUCLEAR INTEGRATION (AF/A10)

1488 Air Force Pentagon, Suite 4E240, Washington, DC 20330

Deputy Chief of Staff of the Air Force.—Lt. Gen. Richard M. Clark (703) 693–9747.

Assistant Deputy Chief of Staff.—James J. Brooks, SES, 693–9747.

Associate Deputy Chief of Staff.—Dr. Billy Mullins, Ph.D., SES, 693–9747.

Air National Guard Advisor.—Brig. Gen. Gene W. Hughes, 693–9747.

Mobilization Assistant.—Col. Kenneth P. Woodcock, Ph.D., 693–9747.

Director of Staff.—Damon Franklin, GS–15, 693–9748.

Senior Executive.—Lt. Col. James Hendrickson, 693–9747.

Junior Executive.—Lt. Col. Robby Modad, 693–9746.

Action Group Chief.—Lt. Col. Mark Amendt, 614–0334.

Administrative Assistant.—Rhonda Gill, 693–9747.

Senior Enlisted Advisor.—CMSgt Tracy Wallace, 695–3178.

Division Chiefs:

Capabilities (A10C).—Col. Bob Ewers, 692–3502.

Countering WMD (A10S).—Col. LeAnne Moore, 614–6009.

Nuclear Command, Control, and Communications (A10N).—Col. John Dines, 692–7386.

Policy and Strategy (A10P).—Col. Kyle Cone, 697–1189.

ADMINISTRATIVE ASSISTANT TO THE SECRETARY

1720 Air Force Pentagon, Washington, DC 20330

Administrative Assistant.—Anthony P. Reardon, Room 4E824 (703) 695–9492.

Deputy Administrative Assistant.—Jeffery R. Shelton, 695–9492.

Director of Staff.—Jadee Purdy, 697–2717.

Executive Officer.—Maj. Christopher Joers, 695–9492.

Confidential Assistant.—Ruby Hill, 695–9492.

Executive Administrator.—TSgt Alexandria Waszmer, 695–3151.

Director of:

Concepts, Development and Management.—John Salvatori, Waples Mills (571) 256–7081 and 697–7509.

Executive Dining Facility.—Shad Glover, Room 4D869, 697–1112.

Information Management.—Winston Beauchamp, 5E915, 697–6529.

Operations.—Ralph F. Davis, Room 5D855, 697–8225.

Resources, Finance.—Daniel Sheesley, Room 4D846, 695–3148.

Resources, Personnel.—Heather Meyer, Room 4D846, 693–9503.

Security, Counterintelligence and Special Programs Oversight Division.—James Eisner (acting), Room MD779, 693–2013.

Sensitive Activities Office.—Russell Wyler (202) 404–1500.

AUDITOR GENERAL

1120 Air Force Pentagon, Washington, DC 20330

4375 Chidlaw Road, Wright-Patterson AFB, OH 45433–5066 (WPAFB)

1500 West Perimeter Road, Suite 4700, Joint Base Andrews, MD 20762 (JBA)

470 I Street East, Randolph AFB, TX 78150–4332 (RAFB)

Auditor General.—Douglas M. Bennett, Pentagon, Room 4E204 (703) 614–5626.

AIR FORCE AUDIT AGENCY

Director of Staff.—Jonathan W. Bareuther, Pentagon (703) 697–7602.
Director of Operations.—Kanisha D. Haney, JBA (240) 612–5133.
Assistant Auditor General for—
Acquisition, Logistics, and Financial Audits.—R. Todd Camden, WPAFB (937) 257–7435.
Deputy Auditor General/Field Activities Directorate.—Jacqueline R. Benningfield, Pentagon (703) 614–5626.
Operations and Support Audits.—Tony M. Ames, RAFB (210) 652–0550.

CHIEF OF CHAPLAINS

1380 Air Force Pentagon, Room 4E260, Washington, DC 20330

Chief.—Chaplain (Maj. Gen.) Steven A. Schaick (571) 256–7729.
Deputy Chief.—Chaplain (Brig. Gen.) Randall E. Kitchens, 256–7729.

AIR FORCE CHIEF OF SAFETY

1400 Air Force Pentagon, Room 4E252, Washington, DC 20330–1400

Chief of Air Force Safety/Commander, Air Force Safety Center.—Maj. Gen. John T. Rauch, Jr. (703) 693–7281.
Deputy Chief of Air Force Safety.—Vacant.
Director, Safety Issues Division.—Col. Lawrence A. Nixon, 693–3333.
Executive Officer.—Maj. Maggie Coppini, 614–3389.

AIR FORCE GENERAL COUNSEL

1740 Air Force Pentagon, Suite 4E836, Washington, DC 20330

General Counsel.—Hon. Thomas E. Ayres (703) 697–0941.
Principal Deputy.—Craig A. Smith, 697–4406.
Senior Military Assistant.—Col. Daniel J. Higgins, 693–7304.
Military Assistant.—Capt. Brian Shust, 697–4406.
Executive Assistant.—Debra R. Swanson, 697–8418.
Deputy General Counsel for—
Acquisition, Technology and Logistics.—Richard B. Clifford, Jr., Room 5B914, 693–7284.
Contractor Responsibility and Conflict Resolution.—Derek Santos, Crystal City, 604–0423.
Fiscal, Ethics and Administrative Law.—Douglas D. Sanders, Room 4C934, 693–9291.
Installations, Energy and Environment.—Jeffrey P. Luster, Room 5E773 (571) 256–4809.
Intelligence, International and Military Affairs: Vacant, Room 4C756, 695–5663; Scott R. Martin (acting), 692–5633.

AIR FORCE HISTORIAN

1190 Air Force Pentagon, Room 4E1062, Washington, DC 20330–1190

Director.—Walter Grudzinskas (703) 697–5603.
Executive Officer.—Aungelic Nelson, 697–2289.
Director, Air Force Historical Research Agency, Maxwell AFB, AL.—Dr. Mary Dysart (334) 953–2241.

INSPECTOR GENERAL

1140 Air Force Pentagon, Room 4E1040, Washington, DC 20330–1140

Inspector General.—Lt. Gen. Sami D. Said (703) 697–6733.
Deputy Inspector General.—Brig. Gen. Jeff Hurlbert, 697–4351.
Executive Officer.—Lt. Col. Laura S. DeJong, 697–4787.
Advisor for Air National Guard Matters.—Col. Kimbra Sterr, Room 5B937, 697–7811.
Advisor for Reserve Matters.—Col. Kathy Hash, Room 5B937, 695–6209.
Director of:
Complaints Resolution Directorate.—Col. Brian Hinsvark, JBAB-Building 5863, Room 150 (202) 404–5262.

Inspections.—Col. Sloan L. Hollis, Air Force Inspection Agency, Kirtland AFB, NM (505) 846–2342.
Senior Officials Inquiries.—Col. Eric Cain, Room 5B937 (703) 693–3579.
Special Investigations.—Col. Christopher Church, Room 5B919, 697–0411.

JUDGE ADVOCATE GENERAL

1420 Air Force Pentagon, Washington, DC 20330

1500 West Perimeter Road, Joint Base Andrews, MD 20762 (JBA)

The Judge Advocate General.—Lt. Gen. Jeffrey A. Rockwell, Room 4E180 (703) 614–5732.
Deputy Judge Advocate General.—Maj. Gen. Charles L. Plummer, Room 4E180, 614–5732.
Senior Paralegal Manager to The Judge Advocate General.—CMSgt Ralph E. Oliver, Room 4E180, 614–5732.
Director for—
Professional Development.—Col. Suanne M. Crowley, Room 5D116, 614–3021.
Strategic, Plans and Programs.—Col. Corea B. Smith, Room 5D116, 692–2828.
USAF Court of Criminal Appeals.—Col. J. Christopher Johnson, JBA, Suite 1900 (240) 612–5070.
USAF Trial Judiciary.—Col. Bryan D. Watson, JBA, Suite 1150 (240) 612–4570.

LEGAL OPERATIONS

Military Justice and Discipline.—Brig. Gen. Rebecca R. Vernon, JBA, Suite 1330 (240) 612–4590.
Operations and International Law.—Brig. Gen. Mitchel Neurock, Room 5D116 (703) 695–9631.
Civil Law.—Col. C. Taylor Smith, JBA, Suite 1530 (240) 612–4613.

DIRECTORATE OF LEGISLATIVE LIAISON

1160 Air Force Pentagon, Washington, DC 20330

Rayburn House Office Building, Room B–322, Washington, DC 20515 (RHOB)

Russell Senate Office Building, Room SR–182, Washington, DC 20510 (RSOB)

Director.—Maj. Gen. Christopher Finerty, Room 4E812 (703) 697–4142.
Deputy Director.—Nancy Dolan, 697–4142.
Director of Staff.—Joe Pak, 4B852, 693–0315.
Mobilization Assistant to the Director.—Brig. Gen. Vanessa Dornhoefer, 697–4142.
Executive Officer to the Director.—Maj. Daniel Naske, 697–4142.
Congressional Actions.—Col. James Suhr, Room 4B852, 692–2014.
Congressional Correspondence.—Col. Julia Sundstrom, Room 4B852, 697–3786.
House Liaison Office.—Col. Benjamin Spencer, RHOB (202) 685–4531.
Programs and Legislation.—Col. Ryan Novotny, Room 4B852 (703) 693–9111.
Senate Liaison Office.—Col. Neil Richardson, RSOB (202) 685–2573.
Weapons Systems.—Col. Patrick Weir, Room 4B852 (703) 697–3376.

NATIONAL GUARD BUREAU

1636 Defense Pentagon, Room 2E630, Washington, DC 20301

Chief.—Gen. Joseph L. Lengyel, Pentagon, Room 2E630 (703) 614–3087.
Vice Chief.—Vacant, Pentagon, Room 2E630, 614–3148.
Legislative Liaison.—Maj. Gen. Sherrie L. McCandless, Room 1D163 (571) 256–7345.
Director for Air National Guard.—Lt. Gen. L. Scott Rice, Pentagon, Room 4E126, 614–8033.
Director for Army National Guard.—Lt. Gen. Daniel R. Hokanson, Arlington Hall Readiness Center, 111 South George Mason Drive, Arlington, VA 22204 (703) 607–7005.

OFFICE OF PUBLIC AFFAIRS

Director.—Brig. Gen. Patrick S. Ryder (703) 697–6061.
Executive Officer.—Maj. Vicki Porto, 697–6061.

Director of Staff.—Col. Mark Sotallaro, 697–6061.
Chief of:
Engagement.—Todd Fleming, 695–9664.
Media Operations.—Ann Stefanek, 695–0640.
Requirements and Development.—Sherry Medders, 697–6701.
Strategy and Assessment.—Todd Sholtis, 697–6715.

AIR FORCE RESERVE

1150 Air Force Pentagon, Room 4E138, Washington, DC 20330

Chief, Air Force Reserve/Commander, Air Force Reserve Command.—Lt. Gen. Richard Scobee (703) 695–9225.
Deputy to the Chief of Air Force Reserve.—Maj. Gen. Hubert C. Hegtvedt, 695–5528.
Executive Officer.—Col. John Dobbin, 695–5528.
Assistant Executive Officer.—Lt. Col. Barbara Givens, 695–5528.
Executive SNCO.—SMSgt Kandi Costa, 614–7307.

SCIENTIFIC ADVISORY BOARD

1500 West Perimeter Road, Suite 3300, Joint Base Andrews, MD 20762

Chair.—Dr. James Chow (240) 612–5500.
Vice Chair.—Dr. Nils Sandell (240) 612–5500.
Military Director.—Lt. Gen. Duke Richardson, Pentagon, Room 4E962 (703) 697–6363.
Executive Director.—Lt. Col. Elizabeth Sorrells, Pentagon, Room 5E815 (703) 697–1109.
Administration.—MSgt Aileen Griffith (240) 612–5500.

AIR FORCE SCIENTIST

1075 Air Force Pentagon, Room 4E130, Washington, DC 20330

Chief Scientist.—Dr. Richard J. Joseph (703) 697–7842.
Military Assistant.—Col. Mario Serna.

AIR FORCE OFFICE OF SMALL BUSINESS PROGRAMS

1060 Air Force Pentagon, Room 4E268, Washington, DC 20330–1060

Director.—Scott A. Kiser.

SURGEON GENERAL

1780 Air Force Pentagon, Room 4E114, Washington, DC 20330–1780

7700 Arlington Boulevard, Suite 5152, Falls Church, VA 22042–5152

Surgeon General.—Lt. Gen. Dorothy Hogg (703) 692–6800.
Executive Officer.—Lt. Col. Tony Lawrence, 692–6990.
Deputy Surgeon General.—Maj. Gen. Sean Murphy, 681–6994.
Executive Officer.—Maj. Shanita Webb, 681–6994.
Director for—
Congressional and Public Affairs.—Tony Joyner, 681–7921.
Manpower and Personnel.—Brig. Gen. Susan Pietrykowski, 681–8157.
Medical Operations.—Maj. Gen. Robert Miller, 681–7373.
Air Force Medical Readiness Agency Commander.—Brig. Gen. Mark Koeniger, 681–8137.

DIRECTORATE OF TEST AND EVALUATION

1650 Air Force Pentagon, Room 4E276, Washington, DC 20330

Director.—Devin L. Cate (703) 697–4774.
Deputy Director.—Dr. Eileen A. Bjorkman.
Executive Assistant.—Dawniel C. Conner.

ARMY AND AIR FORCE EXCHANGE SERVICE

3911 South Walton Walker Boulevard, Dallas, TX 75236

phone (800) 527–6790

Director/Chief Executive Officer.—Thomas C. Shull.

WASHINGTON OFFICE/OFFICE OF THE BOARD OF DIRECTORS

2530 Crystal Drive, Suite 4158, 4th Floor, Arlington, VA 22202

phone (703) 602–3439

Senior Vice President, Government Affairs.—Gregg Cox.

DEPARTMENT OF THE ARMY

The Pentagon, Washington, DC 20310

phone (703) 695–2442

SECRETARY OF THE ARMY

101 Army Pentagon, Room 3E700, Washington, DC 20310–0101

phone (703) 695–1717, fax 697–8036

Secretary of the Army.—Hon. Ryan D. McCarthy.
Executive Officer.—COL Philip J. Ryan.

UNDER SECRETARY OF THE ARMY

102 Army Pentagon, Room 3E700, Washington, DC 20310–0102

phone (703) 695–4311, fax 697–8036

Under Secretary of the Army.—James E. McPherson.
Executive Officer.—COL Philip J. Ryan.

CHIEF OF STAFF OF THE ARMY (CSA)

200 Army Pentagon, Room 3E672, Washington, DC 20310–0200

phone (703) 697–0900, fax 614–5268

Chief of Staff of the Army.—GEN James C. McConville.
Vice Chief of Staff of the Army.—GEN Joseph M. Martin.
Executive Officers: COL Eric S. Strong, 697–0900; COL Andy Gainey, 695–4371.
Director of the CSA Staff Group.—COL Monte L. Rone, Room 3D654, 693–8371.
Director of the Army Staff.—LTG Walter E. Piatt, Room 3E663, 693–7707.
Sergeant Major of the Army.—SMA Michael A. Grinston, Room 3E677, 695–2150.
Director, Army Protocol.—Michele K. Fry, Room 3A532, 692–6701.
Director, Executive Communications and Control.—Thea Harvell III, Room 3D664, 695–7552.

Direct Reporting Units
Commanding General, U.S. Army Test and Evaluation Command.—BG James J. Gallivan (443) 861–9954 / 861–9989.
Superintendent, U.S. Military Academy.—LTG Darryl A. Williams (845) 938–2610.
Commanding General, U.S. Army Military District of Washington.—MG Omar J. Jones IV (202) 685–2807.
Commandant, U.S. Army War College.—MG John S. Kem (717) 245–4400.

DEPUTY UNDER SECRETARY OF THE ARMY (DUSA)

101 Army Pentagon, Room 3E650, Washington, DC 20310–0001

phone (703) 697–5075, fax 697–3145

Deputy Under Secretary of the Army.—Thomas E. Kelly III.
Executive Officer.—COL Scott Beall, 695–4392.
Executive Assistant.—Natalie S. Bosse, 697–8150.

ASSISTANT SECRETARY OF THE ARMY

(ACQUISITION, LOGISTICS, AND TECHNOLOGY) [ASA(ALT)]

103 Army Pentagon, Room 2E532, Washington, DC 20310–0103

phone (703) 693–6153, fax 693–9728

Assistant Secretary.—Dr. Bruce D. Jette.
Principal Deputy.—Jeffrey S. White, Room 2E516, 614–4372.
Principal Military Deputy.—LTG Paul A. Ostrowski, Room 2E532, 697–4278.
Chief of Staff.—COL John Reim, 695–5749.
Executive Officer.—COL Ryan A. Howell, 695–6742.
Confidential Assistant.—Anita J. Odom, 695–6153.
Executive Assistant to the Military Deputy.—Patty Shotwell, 693–3927.
Deputy Assistant Secretary of the Army (DASA):
Acquisition and Systems Management.—COL Glen A. Dean III (acting), 695–3115.
Acquisition, Policy, and Logistics.—Ray M. Gagne (acting), 697–5050.
Defense Exports and Cooperation.—Ann Castiglione-Cataldo, 614–3434.
Plans, Programs, and Resources.—John J. Daniels, 697–0387.
Procurement.—Stuart A. Hazlett, 695–2488.
Research and Technology.—Dr. Thomas P. Russell, 692–1830.
Strategy, Acquisition and Reform.—Dr. Alexis L. Ross, 695–2549.

Direct Reporting Units
Director, U.S. Army Acquisition Support Center.—Craig Spisak, 664–5606.

ASSISTANT SECRETARY OF THE ARMY (CIVIL WORKS) [ASA(CW)]

108 Army Pentagon, Room 3E446, Washington, DC 20310–0108

phone (703) 697–4672, fax 697–7401

Assistant Secretary.—Hon. R.D. James.
Principal Deputy.—Ryan A. Fisher, 695–1370.
Executive Officer.—COL Matthew Tyler, 697–9809.
Military Assistant.—LTC Christopher Berge, 695–0482.
Executive Assistant.—Regena L. Townsend-Treleaven, 697–4672.
Deputy Assistant Secretary of the Army (DASA):
Management and Budget.—Vance Stewart, Room 3E441, 695–1376.
Project Planning and Review.—David J. Leach, GAO–6S91 (202) 761–0033 / 761–0016.

ASSISTANT SECRETARY OF THE ARMY

(FINANCIAL MANAGEMENT AND COMPTROLLER) [ASA(FM&C)]

109 Army Pentagon, Room 3E320, Washington, DC 20310–0109

phone (703) 614–4356, fax 693–7584

Assistant Secretary.—Hon. John E. Whitley.
Principal Deputy.—Vacant, 614–4337.
Military Deputy for Budget.—LTG Thomas A. Horlander, 614–4104.
Executive Officer.—COL Andrew J. Hyatt, 614–5548.
Military Assistant.—LTC Heather Doran, 614–4240.
Administrative Officer.—Judy A. Gupton, 614–4034.
Deputy Assistant Secretary of the Army:
Cost and Economics.—Stephen G. Barth, Room 3E352, 614–7550.
Financial Information Management.—John M. Bergin II, Room 3A320, 692–8529.
Financial Operations.—Wesley C. Miller, Room 3A320A, 693–2758.
Director, Army Budget.—MG Paul A. Chamberlain, Room 3E336, 614–1573.
Director, U.S. Army Financial Management Command.—MG David C. Coburn (317) 212–4449.

ASSISTANT SECRETARY OF THE ARMY (INSTALLATIONS, ENERGY, AND ENVIRONMENT) [ASA(IE&E)]

110 Army Pentagon, Room 3E464, Washington, DC 20310–0110

phone (703) 692–9800, fax 692–9808

Assistant Secretary.—Hon. Alex A. Beehler.
Principal Deputy.—Bryan Gossage, 692–9802.
Executive Officer.—COL G. Shawn Wells, 692–9804.
Military Assistant.—LTC Scott Swilley, 692–9805.
Executive Assistant.—Maria A. Margary, 692–9800.
Deputy Assistant Secretary of the Army:
Energy and Sustainability.—John E. Surash (acting), Room 3D453, 692–9890.
Environment, Safety, and Occupational Health.—Amy L. Borman (acting), Room 3D453, 697–1913.
Installations, Housing, and Partnerships.—Paul D. Cramer, Room 3E475, 697–0867.
Strategic Integration.—Richard E. Kidd, Room 3D453, 692–9817.

ASSISTANT SECRETARY OF THE ARMY (MANPOWER AND RESERVE AFFAIRS) [ASA(M&RA)]

111 Army Pentagon, Room 2E460, Washington, DC 20310–0111

phone (703) 697–9253, fax 692–9000

Assistant Secretary.—Hon. E. Casey Wardynski.
Principal Deputy.—Marshall M. Williams, 692–1292.
Executive Officer.—COL Eugenia Guilmartin, 614–2850.
Executive Assistant.—Wanda L. Artis, 697–9253.
Deputy Assistant Secretary of the Army:
Army Review Boards/Director, Army Review Boards Agency.—Alexander Conyers (acting), 545–5639.
Deputy Director.—Alexander Conyers, Crystal City, 571–0542.
Military Personnel Policy and Quality of Life.—Vacant, Room 2D484, 614–1648.
Civilian Personnel / Director, Civilian Senior Leader Management Office.—Curtis K. Southern, Room 2E485, 614–8143.
Diversity and Leadership.—Semma Salter (acting), 614–5284.
Training, Readiness, and Mobilization.—Gerry L. Kitzhaber (acting), Room 2E482, 697–2631.

ARMY GENERAL COUNSEL (GC)

104 Army Pentagon, Room 2E724, Washington, DC 20310–0104

phone (703) 697–9235, fax 693–9254

General Counsel of the Army.—Michele A. Pearce (acting).
Principal Deputy General Counsel.—Michele A. Pearce, 697–9235.
Executive Officer/Special Counsel: COL Jeff Bovarnick, 697–2800; Robert Moore, 692–8252.
Executive Assistant.—Veronica H. Jacques, 692–9141.
Deputy General Counsel:
Acquisition.—Levator Norsworthy, Jr., Room 3C546, 697–5120.
Ethics and Fiscal Law.—Shelley P. Turner, Room 3C546, 695–4296.
Installations, Environment, and Civil Works.—Craig R. Schmauder, Room 3C546, 695–3024.
Operations and Personnel.—Michael Lacey, Room 3C546, 695–0562.

ADMINISTRATIVE ASSISTANT TO THE SECRETARY OF THE ARMY (AASA)

105 Army Pentagon, Room 3E733, Washington, DC 20310–0105

phone (703) 695–2442, fax 697–6194

Administrative Assistant to the Secretary of the Army.—Kathleen S. Miller.
Deputy Administrative Assistant.—Mark F. Averill, 697–7741.

Executive Officer.—Rhonda C. Shaffer (acting), 695–7444.
Executive Assistant.—Tiffany N. Christmas, 695–2442.
Director, Civilian Aides to the Secretary of the Army (CASA).—Angela K. Ritz, Room 3D742, 545–0525.
Executive Director, U.S. Army Headquarters Services.—Susan D. Tigner, Fort Belvoir, Building 1458, 545–4870.

ARMY AUDITOR GENERAL

6000 6th Street, Building 1464, Fort Belvoir, VA 22060–5609

phone (703) 545–5907, fax 806–1199

Auditor General of the Army.—Anne L. Richards.
Principal Deputy Auditor General.—Monique Ferrell, 545–5910.
Executive Officer.—Vacant, 545–5909.
Executive Assistant.—Jennifer Crick, 545–5907.
General Counsel.—Michael Hoadley, 545–5879.
Deputy Auditors General:
Acquisition, Cyber, and Logistics Audits.—William Jenkins, 545–5853.
Business Operations Audits.—Kathleen A. Nelson, 545–5903.
Forces and Infrastructure Audits.—Felix Strelsky, 545–5874.
Operations Management.—Elizabeth Catiaro, 545–5851.

ARMY NATIONAL MILITARY CEMETERIES (ANMC)

phone (703) 614–0615, fax (571) 256–3366

Executive Director.—Karen L. Durham-Aguilera.
Chief of Staff.—COL Jerry Farnsworth, 614–1062.
Executive Officer.—LTC Mark O'Brien, 614–0615.

Direct Reporting Unit
Executive Director, Arlington National Cemetery.—Karen L. Durham-Aguilera.
Superintendent, Arlington National Cemetery.—Vacant.

OFFICE OF THE DEPUTY CHIEF OF STAFF, G-9 (DCS, G-9) (Installations)

600 Army Pentagon, Room 3E484, Washington, DC 20310-0600

phone (703) 693-3233, fax 693-3507

Deputy Chief of Staff.—LTG Jason T. Evans.
Assistant Deputy Chief of Staff.—Daniel ''Dan'' M. Klippstein.
Senior Enlisted Advisor to the Deputy Chief of Staff.—SM Ulysses D. Rayford.
Director of:
Information and Technology.—Christopher Thomas.
Installation Services.—Michael E. Reheuser.
Operations.—BG Joseph Edwards.
Resource Integration.—Sally G. Pfenning.

CHIEF ARMY RESERVE (CAR)

2400 Army Pentagon, Room 3E562, Washington, DC 20310–2400

phone (703) 695–0031, fax 697–1891

Chief of Army Reserve.—LTG Charles D. Luckey.
Assistant Chief.—Stephen D. Austin, 695–0047.
Executive Officer.—LTC Clay Huffman, 695–1784.
Executive Assistant.—Brandy DiMarco, 695–0031.
Congressional Affairs Communication Officer.—COL Monica Hock, 835–3357.

CHIEF INFORMATION OFFICER, G–6 (CIO, G–6)

107 Army Pentagon, Room 3E608, Washington, DC 20310–0107

phone (703) 695–4366, fax 695–3091

Chief Information Officer.—Greg Garcia (acting).
Deputy Chief.—Greg Garcia, 695–6604.
Executive Officer.—COL Duane K. Green, 697–5503.

CHIEF LEGISLATIVE LIAISON (CLL)

1600 Army Pentagon, Room 1E416, Washington, DC 20310–1600

phone (703) 697–6767, fax 614–7599

Chief Legislative Liaison.—BG Brian S. Eifler.
Principal Deputy.—Bernard P. Ingold, 697–0278.
Deputy.—COL Justin Reese, 695–1235.
Executive Officer.—MAJ Todd Hook, 695–3524.
Enlisted Aide.—SSG Kenin Arwood, 695–1353.
Executive Assistant.—Keirsten Davis, 697–6767.
Chief of:
Congressional Inquiry.—Michele Cromwell, Room 1E423, 697–2583.
Congressional Operations Division.—LTC Alex Lee, Room 1D437 (703) 692–2235.
House Liaison Division.—COL Noberto Menendez, Room 2024, Rayburn House Office Building, Washington, DC (202) 685–2675.
Investigations and Legislative Division.—COL John Hamner, Room 1E433, 697–8218.
Management and Support Operations Division.—Harry B. Williams, Room 1E423, 692–4159.
Programs Division.—COL Lance Calvert, Room 1E385, 693–8766.
Senate Liaison Division.—COL Nathan Cook, Room SR183, Senate Russell Office Building, Washington, DC (202) 685–3633.

CHIEF NATIONAL GUARD BUREAU (CNGB)

Pentagon, Room 1E169, Washington, DC 20301–1636

phone (703) 614–3087, fax 614–0274

Chief.—GEN Daniel R. Hokanson.
Vice Chief.—Vacant, 614–3038.
Executive Officer.—COL J. R. Hoeflein, 614–3087.
Executive Assistant.—Carol Lagasse, 614–3117.
Director, Air National Guard.—Lt. Gen. Michael A. Loh, 614–8033.
Director, Army National Guard.—Lt. Gen. Jon A. Jensen, Room 2A514B, 693–8464.

CHIEF OF CHAPLAINS (CCH)

2700 Army Pentagon, Room 3E524, Washington, DC 20310–2700

phone (703) 695–1133, fax 695–9834

Chief of Chaplains.—Chaplain (MG) Thomas L. Solhjem.
Deputy Chief of Chaplains.—Chaplain (BG) William Green, 695–1133.
Executive Officer.—Chaplain (COL) Tom Helms, 695–1133.
Executive Assistant.—Caridad ''Carie'' Gelineau, 695–1135.

CHIEF OF ENGINEERS (CoE)

GAO Building, 441 G Street, NW., 20314–1000

phone (202) 761–0001, fax (202) 761–4463

Chief of Engineers.—LTG Scott A. Spellmon.
Deputy Chief of Engineers.—MG David C. Hill, 761–0002.
Director.—COL Jason Kelly, 693–4407.

Direct Reporting Unit

Commanding General, U.S. Army Corps of Engineers.—LTG Scott A. Spellmon.
Deputy.—MG David C. Hill, 761–0002.
Chief of Staff.—COL John Lloyd, 761–0761.
Executive Officer.—LTC Travis Rayfield, 761–0468.
Executive Assistant.—Christina Kearney, 761–0001.

CHIEF OF PUBLIC AFFAIRS (CPA)

1500 Army Pentagon, Room 1E484, Washington, DC 20310–1500
phone (703) 695–5135, fax 693–8362

Chief of Public Affairs.—BG Amy E. Hannah.
Principal Deputy.—Michael P. Brady, 697–1747.
Chief of Staff.—COL Richard Edwards, 693–8605.
Chief, Media Relations Division.—COL Kathleen Turner, 693–4723.
Director, U.S. Army Public Affairs Center.—COL Eric Bloom (301) 677–7270.
Executive Officer.—LTC Jennifer A. Ludwick, 697–4200.
Executive Assistant.—Vacant, 695–5135.

DEPUTY CHIEF OF STAFF, G–1 (DCS, G–1) (PERSONNEL)

300 Army Pentagon, Room 2E446, Washington, DC 20310–0300
phone (703) 697–8060

Deputy Chief of Staff.—LTG Gary Brito.
Executive Assistant.—Vacant, 697–8060.
Assistant Deputy Chief of Staff.—Roy A. Wallace, 692–1585.
Executive Officer.—COL Hope C. Rampy, 697–2893.
Military Assistant.—MAJ William Lincoln, 614–1862.
Director:
Army Resiliency.—James Helis, 571–7357.
Assistant G–1 for Civilian Personnel.—Michael Reheuser, 614–8143.
Human Systems Integration.—Michelle Sams, 695–6761.
Military Personnel Management.—BG Doug Stitt, 695–5871.
Plans and Resources.—Dr. Robert Steinrauf, 697–5263.
Sexual Harassment/Assault Response and Prevention.—James Helis, 695–5568.
Technology and Business Architecture Integration.—Terry Watson, 614–5138.

Field Operating Agencies

Commanding General, U.S. Army Human Resources Command.—MG Jason T. Evans (502) 613–8844.
Director, U.S. Army Civilian Human Resources Agency.—Carol Burton (410) 306–1701.

DEPUTY CHIEF OF STAFF, G–2 (DCS, G–2) (INTELLIGENCE)

1000 Army Pentagon, Room 2E408, Washington, DC 20310–1000
phone (703) 695–3033, fax 697–7605

Deputy Chief of Staff.—LTG Scott D. Berrier.
Assistant Deputy Chief of Staff.—Vacant.
Military Deputy.—BG Kevin C. Wulfhorst.
Executive Officer.—COL Richard Appelhans, 695–3033.
Executive Assistant.—Anne H. Fesmire, 695–3033.

Direct Reporting Unit

Commanding General, U.S. Army Intelligence and Security Command.—MG Gary Johnston, 706–1603.

DEPUTY CHIEF OF STAFF, G–3 (DCS, G–3) (OPERATIONS)

400 Army Pentagon, Room 2E670, Washington, DC 20310–0400
phone (703) 695–2904, fax 697–4660

Deputy Chief of Staff.—LTG Charles A. Flynn.

Assistant Deputy Chief.—Christopher Lowman (703) 695–0728.
Executive Officer.—COL Ryan P. O'Connor, 697–4521.
Executive Assistant.—Maureen Marshall, 695–3447.
Director:
Aviation.—BG Michael McCurry, 692–1628.
Cyber.—Vacant, 692–2224.
Joint and Defense Affairs.—COL Tom J. Robinson, Room 2D337, 614–2993.
Operations, Readiness, and Mobilization.—BG Christopher LaNeve, 695–0526.
Strategy, Plans, and Policy.—MG Bradley Gericke, 692–8805.
Training.—BG Charles Costanza, 692–7332.

Field Operating and Staff Support Agencies
Director, U.S. Army Command and Control Support Agency.—COL Chad Campfield, 697–1245.
Director, U.S. Army Force Management Support Agency.—COL William M. Fairclough, 693–3227.
Director, U.S. Army Nuclear and Combating WMD Agency.—COL John W. Weidner, 614–2670.

DEPUTY CHIEF OF STAFF, G–4 (DCS, G–4) (LOGISTICS)

500 Army Pentagon, Room 1E394, Washington, DC 20310–0500

phone (703) 695–4104, fax 692–0759

Deputy Chief of Staff.—LTG Duane A. Gamble.
Assistant Deputy Chief.—William F. Moore, 697–9138.
Assistant Deputy Chief/Operations.—MG Michel Russell, 697–5032.
Executive Officer.—COL Edward "Lee" English, 697–9039.
Executive Assistant.—Torwanna D. Herbert, 695–4102.
Director:
Enterprise Support.—Robert Thurston, Room 1E360, 695–6160.
Maintenance Policy, Programs, and Processes.—Vic Ramdass, Room 1E360, 693–1624.
Resource Management.—COL Floyd Crocker, Room 1E380, 693–1900.
Supply Policy, Programs, and Processes.—Peter B. Bechtel, Room 1E380, 692–2282.

Field Operating Agency
Director, U.S. Army Logistics Innovation Agency.—William F. Crain, 805–5440.

DEPUTY CHIEF OF STAFF, G–8 (DCS, G–8) (PROGRAMS)

700 Army Pentagon, Room 3E406, Washington, DC 20310–0700

phone (703) 697–8232, fax 697–8242

Deputy Chief of Staff.—LTG James F. Pasquerette.
Assistant Deputy Chief.—Dr. David Markowitz, 692–9099.
Executive Assistant.—Jessica M. Collins, 697–8236.
Executive Officer.—COL Andrew Cole Jr., 697–8232.
Director of:
Center for Army Analysis.—Dr. Steve A. Stoddard.
Force Development.—MG Erik C. Peterson, 692–7707.
Program Analysis and Evaluation.—MG Karl H. Gingrich, 697–1475.

Field Operating Agency
Director, U.S. Army Center for Army Analysis.—Dr. William F. Crain, 806–5510.

DIRECTOR OF THE ARMY STAFF (DAS)

202 Army Pentagon, Room 3E663, Washington, DC 20310–0202

phone (703) 693–7710, fax 695–6117

Director of the Army Staff.—LTG Walter E. Piatt.
Vice Director.—Steven J. Redmann, Room 3D644, 695–0294.
Executive Officer.—COL Jay Barholomees, 693–7710.

Executive Assistant.—Samantha Johnson, 695–6117.

Field Operating Agency

Commanding General, U.S. Army Combat Readiness/Safety Center.—BG Timothy J. Daugherty (334) 255–9360.

PROVOST MARSHAL GENERAL (PMG)

2800 Army Pentagon, Room 1E596, Washington, DC 203103–2800

phone (703) 692–6966, fax 614–5628

Provost Marshal General.—MG Donna W. Martin.
Deputy Provost Marshal General.—BG Duane R. Miller, 692–7290.
Executive Officer.—COL Noel Smart, 692–6970.
Chief of Staff.—Herman ''Tracy'' Williams III, 692–6829.
Executive Assistant.—Deborah L. Van Heest, 695–4036.

Direct Reporting Unit

Commanding General, U.S. Army Criminal Investigation Command.—MG Donna W. Martin.

Field Operating Agencies

Commanding General, U.S. Army Corrections Command.—BG Duane R. Miller.
Director, Defense Forensics and Biometrics Agency.—Glen Krizay, 571–0507.

OFFICE OF SMALL BUSINESS PROGRAMS (OSBP)

106 Army Pentagon, Room 3B514, Washington, DC 20310–0106

phone (703) 697–2868, fax 693–3898

Director.—Kimberly Diane Buehler.
Deputy/Executive Officer.—Pamela D. Callicutt, 695–5588.
Executive Assistant.—Jasmine Barrett, 806–8659.

THE INSPECTOR GENERAL (TIG)

1700 Army Pentagon, Room 3E588, Washington, DC 20310–1700

phone (703) 695–1500, fax 614–5628

The Inspector General.—LTG Leslie C. Smith.
Deputy Inspector General.—MG Donald E. Jackson, 695–1501.
Executive Officer.—COL Kevin F. Ciocca, 695–1502.
Executive Assistant.—LTC Duane Williams, 695–1500.

Field Operating Agency

Commanding General, U.S. Army Inspector General Agency.—LTG Leslie C. Smith, 695–1500.

THE JUDGE ADVOCATE GENERAL (TJAG)

2200 Army Pentagon, Room 3E542, Washington, DC 20310–2200

phone (703) 697–5151, fax 697–1059

The Judge Advocate General.—LTG Charles N. Pede.
Deputy Judge Advocate General.—MG Stewart W. Risch, 693–5112.
Executive Officer.—COL Allison Martin, 695–3786.
Executive Assistant.—Cindy G. Mitchell, 697–5151.

Field Operating Agencies

Commander, U.S. Army Legal Services Agency.—BG Susan K. Escallier, 693–1100.
Commander/Commandant, U.S. Army Judge Advocate General's Legal Center and School.—BG Joseph B. Berger III (434) 971–3301.

THE SURGEON GENERAL (TSG)

7700 Arlington Boulevard, Defense Health Headquarters (DHHQ)

Falls Church, VA 22042

phone (703) 681–3000, fax 681–3167

The Surgeon General.—LTG R. Scott Dingle.
Deputy Surgeon General.—MG Telita Crosland, 681–3002.
Chief of Staff.—Rich Beauchemin, 681–9514.
Executive Officer.—COL Michael W. Smith, 681–3010.
Executive Assistant.—Vacant, 695–1647.
Command Sergeant Major.—CSM Michael L. Gragg, 681–8046.
Operations Center.—Duty Officer-in-Charge, 681–8052.

ARMY COMMANDS

U.S. ARMY FORCES COMMAND (FORSCOM)

4700 Knox Street, Fort Bragg, NC 28310–5000

phone (910) 570–5052, fax (910) 570–1971

Commanding General.—GEN Michael X. Garrett.
Deputy Commanding General.—LTG Leopaldo Quintas Jr., 570–5001.
Chief of Staff.—MG Eugene ''Gene'' J. LeBoeuf, 570–5002.
Executive Officer.—COL Arturo Horton, 570–5051.
Command Sergeant Major.—CSM Todd Sims, 570–5045.
Secretary of the General Staff.—COL Matthew Condry, 570–5066.
Operations Center.—COL Andrew Herbst, 570–6533.
Staff Action Control Officer.—Jennifer Bhartiya. 697–2552.
Liaison Office (Washington, DC).—LTC John ''Andy'' Kerin, 697–2591.

U.S. ARMY TRAINING AND DOCTRINE COMMAND (TRADOC)

950 Jefferson Avenue, Fort Eustis, VA 23604–5700

phone (757) 501–6469, fax (757) 501–6476

Commanding General.—GEN Paul E. Funk II.
Deputy Commanding General/Chief of Staff.—LTG Theodore D. Martin, 501–6478.
Executive Officers: COL Michael Katona, 501–6472; COL Andrew Morgado, 501–6466; MAJ Richard Whitman, 501–6485.
Deputy Chief of Staff.—MG Arlen Royalty, 501–6495.
Command Sergeant Major.—CSM Daniel T. Hendrix, 501–6464.
Secretary of the General Staff.—Victor Holman, 501–5199.
Director, G–33/Operations Center.—Perry Helton, 501–5094.

Field Operating Agency
U.S. Army Center of Military History.—Charles R. Bowery, Jr., Fort McNair, Building 35, Room 147 (202) 685–2705.

U.S. ARMY MATERIEL COMMAND (AMC)

4400 Martin Road, Redstone Arsenal, AL 35898–5000

phone (256) 450–6000, fax (256) 450–8833

Commanding General.—GEN Edward M. Daly.
Deputy Commanding General.—LTG Donnie Walker, 450–6100.
Executive Deputy Commanding General.—Lisha H. Adams, 450–6200.
Chief of Staff.—MG Robert D. Harter, 450–7867.
Executive Officer.—COL Gavin J. Gardner, 450–6005.
Command Sergeant Major.—CSM Alberto Delgado, 450–6300.
Secretary of the General Staff.—MAJ Timothy P. Gibbons, 450–6440.
Operations Center.—Duty Officer-in-Charge, 450–9496.

ARMY SERVICE COMPONENT COMMANDS LIAISON OFFICES

Pentagon, Washington, DC 20310

U.S. Army Africa/Southern European Task Force (USARAF/SETAF).—Lt. Col. Ian Dinesen, 2B865 (703) 695–6450; COL Gregory S. Harkins, Room 3D513 (571) 256–1803.
U.S. Army Central (USARCENT).—Hank Foresman, Room 2B475A4 (703) 693–4033.
U.S. Army Europe (USAREUR).—Timothy C. Touzinsky, Room 1E1074 (703) 692–6886.
U.S. Army North (USARNORTH).—John D. Nelson, Room 2B485, 692–6893.
U.S. Army Pacific (USARPAC).—Robert Ralston, Room 2B485 (703) 697–6952.
U.S. Army South (USARSO).—LTC Robert Sholl, Room 2A474 (703) 692–8221.
U.S. Army Space and Missile Defense Command/Army Strategic Command (SMDC/ARSTRAT): Vacant, Room 2D831 (703) 614–9592; Col. James Zirkel, 614–9593.
Military Surface Deployment and Distribution Command (SDDC): COL Gary Cregan (703) 571–9708; Todd Wolf, Room 2B858, 571–9710.

JOINT FORCE HEADQUARTERS–NATIONAL CAPITAL REGION AND MILITARY DISTRICT OF WASHINGTON (JFHQ–NCR/MDW)

102 3rd Avenue, Building 39, Fort Lesley J. McNair, Washington, DC 20319

phone (202) 685–2807, fax 685–3481

Commanding General.—MG Omar J. Jones IV.
Executive Officer.—MAJ Meaghan Ederlee, 685–2817.
Aide de Camp.—CPT Chris Blanchard, 685–2807.
Deputy Commander.—Egon F. Hawrylak, 685–1949.
JTF Deputy.—RDML Carl Lahti, 433–2777.
Command Sergeant Major.—CSM Richard Woodring, 685–2812.
Chief of Staff.—COL Brandon Robbins, 685–2812.
Secretary of the General Staff.—Vacant, 685–0640.

U.S. ARMY SPECIAL OPERATIONS COMMAND

Fort Bragg, NC 28310–5200

phone (910) 432–3000, fax (910) 432–4243

Commanding General.—LTG Francis M. Beaudette.
Deputy Commanding General.—BG Allan M. Pepin, 432–6622.
Chief of Staff.—MG J. Marcus Hicks, 432–9861.
Command Sergeant Major.—CSM Marc Eckard, 432–0946.
Secretary of the General Staff.—Russ Vona, 432–0946.

DEPARTMENT OF THE NAVY

Pentagon, Washington, DC 20350–1000

phone (703) 695–3131

OFFICE OF THE SECRETARY OF THE NAVY

Pentagon, Room 4E686, Washington, DC 20350

phone (703) 695–3131

Secretary of the Navy.—Kenneth J. Braithwaite II.
Chief of Staff.—J. Ibrahim.
Personal and Confidential Assistant.—S. Cline, 695–3131.
Scheduler.—J. Jaramillo, 695–3131.
Administrative Aide.—Lt. Col. D. Arenas, 695–5410.
Marine Personal Aide.—Maj. R. Bergstedt, USMC, 695–3131.
Navy Personal Aide.—CDR D. Ganci, USN, 695–3131.
Special Assistant for Public Affairs.—CAPT J. Dorsey, 697–7491.
Navy Senior Military Assistant.—CAPT G. Rogeness, USN, 695–3131.
Navy Junior Military Assistant.—LCDR R. Wayland, USN, 695–3131.
Marine Senior Military Assistant.—Col. J. Ryans, USMC, 695–3131.
Marine Junior Military Assistant.—Maj. M. Walls, USMC, 695–3131.

OFFICE OF THE UNDER SECRETARY OF THE NAVY

Pentagon, Room 4E720, Washington, DC 20350

phone (703) 695–3141

Under Secretary of the Navy.—Hon. Gregory J. Slavonic (acting).
Chief of Staff.—Robert E. Love.
Military Aide (Navy).—CAPT Alexis T. Walker.
Military Aide (Marine).—Vacant.
Executive Assistant.—Johnny J. Jaramillo.
Administrative Assistants: SSgt Miguel Ramirez, YN1 Sheldon O. Serrano.

GENERAL COUNSEL

Pentagon, Room 4E782, Washington, DC 20350

phone (703) 614–1994

General Counsel.—Robert J. Sander.
Principal Deputy General Counsel.—Garrett L. Ressing, 614–8733.
Executive Assistant and Special Counsel.—CAPT Anne B. Fischer, JAGC, USN.
Associate General Counsel for Litigation.—Craig D. Jensen, Washington Navy Yard, Building 36 (202) 685–6985.
Deputy General Counsel.—Diane M. Boyle, Room 4E791, 614–6870.
Assistant General Counsel for—
Ethics.—Sara Thompson, Room 4D641, 614–7433.
Manpower and Reserve Affairs.—Mark Romano, Room 4D548, 614–1377.
Research, Development and Acquisition.—Tom Frankfurt, Room 4C682, 614–6985.
Military Assistant.—Maj. Stacy Allen, USMC, Room 4E782, 692–6164.

NAVAL INSPECTOR GENERAL

2000 Navy Pentagon, Washington, DC 20350

phone (202) 433–2000

Inspector General.—VADM Rick Snyder.
Deputy Naval Inspector General.—Catherine Donovan.
Command Master Chief.—Donald Myrick.

U.S. NAVY OFFICE OF INFORMATION (CHINFO)

1200 Navy Pentagon, Room 4B463, Washington, DC 20350

phone (703) 697–7391, CHINFO Duty Officer (703) 850–1047

Chief of Information (CI).—RDML Charlie Brown, 697–7391.
Executive Assistant to Chief of Information (EA).—CDR Courtney Hillson, 697–7392.
Vice Chief of Information (VCI).—RDML Paula Dunn, 692–7391.
Deputy, Chief of Information (DCI).—CAPT Anastasia Quanbeck, 695–0911.
Flag Aide to Chief of Information.—LT Clint Ramsden, 697–7391.
Senior Enlisted Advisor (SEA).—MCCM Michael Lewis, 692–4704.
Staff Senior Enlisted Leader (SEL).—YNC Winston Banton, 693–3570.
Flag Writer.—YN1 Shaun Hamilton, 697–7391.
Assistant Chief of Information for—
Administration and Resource Management (OI–1).—Erica Echeverry, 614–7750.
Community Outreach (OI–6).—Rob Newell, 614–1879.
Media Operations (OI–3).—CDR Clay Doss, 697–5342.
Navy Media Content Services (OI–2).—Chris Madden, 614–9341.
Requirements and Policy (OI–8).—Kyra Daley, 692–4728.
Strategy, Plans, and Integration (OI–5).—Jennifer Ivey, 693–3569.
Deputy Director of Defense Media Activity (DMA).—CDR Scott McIlnay (301) 222–6312.
Director of:
Navy Office of Community Outreach.—CDR Krin Burzynski (901) 874–5802.
Navy Office of Information, East.—LCDR Megan Shutka (212) 784–0133.
Navy Office of Information, West.—Russ Coons (310) 235–7481.

JUDGE ADVOCATE GENERAL

Pentagon, Room 4C642, Washington, DC 20350

Washington Navy Yard, 1322 Patterson Avenue, SE., Suite 3000
Washington, DC 20374–5066

phone (703) 614–7420, fax 697–4610

Judge Advocate General.—VADM John Hannink.
Executive Assistant.—CAPT Peter Koebler (703) 695–9116.
Deputy Judge Advocate General.—RADM Del Crandall, 614–7420.
Executive Assistant to the Deputy Judge Advocate General.—CDR Mary Pohanka, 693–4322.
Assistant Judge Advocate General for—
Civil Law.—CAPT Shannon Kopplin, Pentagon, Room 4D640, 693–1332.
Military Justice.—Col. David Bligh, USMC, Building 58, 3rd Floor, Washington Navy Yard, 20374–1111 (202) 685–7051.
Operations and Management.—CAPT David Wilson (202) 685–5196.
Deputy Assistant Judge Advocate General for—
Administrative Law.—CAPT Rock DeTolve, 614–0925.
Admiralty.—CAPT Al Janin (202) 685–5075.
Claims, Investigations and Tort Litigation.—Hal Dronberger (202) 685–4627, fax (202) 685–5484.
Criminal Law.—CAPT Robert Monahan, USN (202) 685–7057.
General Litigation.—Grant Lattin (202) 685–4592, fax (202) 685–5472.
International and Operational Law.—CAPT Susan McGarvey, 697–5406.
Legal Assistance.—Kathlene Somerville (202) 685–4639, fax (202) 685–5486.
Military Personnel.—CAPT David Gonzalez (202) 685–7254.
National Security Litigation and Intelligence Law.—CDR William Perdue (202) 685–5464/5481, fax (202) 685–5467.
Technology, Operations and Plans.—CDR Matthew Beran (202) 685–5213, fax (202) 685–5477.
Special Assistant to the Judge Advocate General, Command Master Chief.—LNCM (SW/AW), Brook Larkins (202) 685–5194.
Comptroller.—Dawn C. Rooney (202) 685–5274, fax 685–5455.
Inspector General.—CAPT Mark Holley, USN (619) 310–1672, fax (202) 685–5489.

U.S. NAVY OFFICE OF LEGISLATIVE AFFAIRS (OLA)

1200 Navy Pentagon, Room 4C549, Washington, DC 20350

phone (703) 697–7146

Chief of Legislative Affairs.—RADM Sara Joyner, 697–7146.
Deputy Chief of Legislative Affairs.—CAPT Jerry Miranda, 697–7146.
Deputy Chief for Strategy and Assessment.—Sandra Latta, 695–6358.
Executive Assistant.—CDR Richard Slye, 697–7146.
Deputy Executive Assistant.—LCDR Tom Roberts, 697–7146.
Flag Aide to the Chief of Legislative Affairs.—LT Kyle Stewart, 697–7146.
Flag Writer.—YN1 Robert Atutubo, 697–7146.
Director of:
Administrative and Congressional Information.—LCDR Steven Rancourt, 695–9359.
Congressional Operations and Budget.—Dee Wingfield, 693–5764.
Legislation.—CDR Matt Ivey, 697–2776.
Naval Programs.—Geno Autrey, 693–2919.
Public Affairs.—CDR Francisco ''Mags'' Magallon, APR, 695–0395.
Senate Liaison Director.—CAPT Scott Sciretta (202) 685–6006.
Senate Liaison Deputy Director.—CAPT Chase Patrick (202) 685–6007.
House Liaison Director.—CAPT Peter Schnappauf (202) 225–7808.
House Liaison Deputy Director.—CAPT Katrina Hill (202) 225–3075.
Director, Financial Management and Comptroller Appropriations Matters Office (FMBE).—CAPT David Walt, 692–6730.
Deputy Director, Financial Management and Comptroller Appropriations Matters Office (FMBE).—CAPT Charles McKissick, 692–6735.
Branch Head, Financial Management and Comptroller Appropriations Matters Office (FMBE).—Marc Hone, 692–4924.

ASSISTANT SECRETARY FOR FINANCIAL MANAGEMENT AND COMPTROLLER

Pentagon, Room 4E618, Washington, DC 20350

phone (703) 695–3378

Assistant Secretary.—Thomas W. Harker.
Executive Assistant and Naval Aide.—CAPT Rob Patrick, USN.
Military Assistant and Marine Aide.—Capt. Luis Martinez, USMC.
Deputy Assistant Secretary for Budget.—RADM Randy Crites, USN, Room 4E348, 697–7105.
Deputy Assistant Secretary for Financial Operations.—Alaleh Jenkins, Washington Navy Yard (202) 685–6701.

ASSISTANT SECRETARY FOR ENERGY, INSTALLATIONS AND ENVIRONMENT

Pentagon, Room 4E739, Washington, DC 20350

phone (703) 693–4530

Assistant Secretary.—Hon. Charles Williams.
Executive Assistant.—CAPT Wes McCall, 693–4532.
Principal Deputy Assistant Secretary of the Navy.—Todd L. Schafer, 693–4527.
Deputy Assistant Secretary for Installations, Energy and Facilities.—Jim Balocki, 695–0461.
Deputy Assistant Secretary for Environment.—Karnig Ohannessian, 614–5080.
Assistant General Counsel.—Jill Morrison, 614–1090.

ASSISTANT SECRETARY FOR MANPOWER AND RESERVE AFFAIRS

Pentagon, Room 4E598, Washington, DC 20350

phone (703) 695–4333

Assistant Secretary.—Catherine L. Kessmeier (acting), Room 4E598, 695–4333.
Principal Deputy.—Catherine L. Kessmeier, Room 4E598, 692–6162.
Executive Assistant and Naval Aide.—CAPT Putnam Browne, Room 4E590, 695–4537.
Military Assistant and Marine Aide.—Col. Coby Moran, Room 4E590, 697–0975.
Administrative Officer.—LCDR Tessa Denaro, Room 4E590, 697–2179.

Administrative Chief.—GySgt Jeremiah McCoy, Room 4E590, 614–4439.
Deputy Assistant Secretary of Civilian Human Resources.—Paige Hinkle-Bowles, Room 4D548, 695–2633.
Deputy Assistant Secretary of Manpower Personnel Policy and Reserve Matters.—Dr. Russ Beland, Room 4D548, 693–1213.

SECRETARY OF THE NAVY COUNCIL OF REVIEW BOARDS

Washington Navy Yard, 720 Kennon Street, SE., Room 309, Washington, DC 20374–5023

phone (202) 685–6408, fax 685–6610

Director.—Jeffrey Riehl.
Counsel.—Roger R. Claussen.
Office Administrator.—Christopher Philson.
Physical Evaluation Board.—Robert Powers.
Naval Clemency and Parole Board.—Randall Lamoureux.
Naval Discharge Review Board.—John D. Reeser.
Combat-Related Special Compensation Board.—Leif Larsen.
Board of Decorations and Medals.—James Nierle.

ASSISTANT SECRETARY FOR RESEARCH, DEVELOPMENT AND ACQUISITION

Pentagon, Room 4E665, Washington, DC 20350

phone (703) 695–6315

Assistant Secretary.—Hon. James F. Geurts.
Special Assistant.—Candy R. Hearn.
Executive Assistant and Naval Aide.—CAPT Seiko Okano, USN.
Military Assistant and Marine Aide.—Col. Brian Taylor, USMC.
Principal Military Deputy (PMD).—VADM Michael T. Moran, USN.
PMD Executive Assistant and Naval Aide.—CAPT David Rueter, USN.
PMD Flag Writer.—LT Latasha Griffin, USN.
Principal Civilian Deputy (PCD).—Jay Stefany, 614–6430.
PCD Executive Assistant.—Ed Foster.
Deputy Assistant Secretary of the Navy for—
Acquisition Policy and Budget.—Jaimie Reese, Room 4C681, 695–6370.
Air and Ground Programs.—Daniel L. Nega, Room 4C712, 614–7795.
C5IES.—Jane Rathbun, Room BF963, 614–6619.
International Programs.—RADM Frank D. Morley, WNY (202) 433–5900.
Procurement.—Cindy Shaver, Room BF992A, 614–9595.
Research, Engineering and Test.—William Bray, Room 4C681, 614–3591.
Ship Programs.—Bilyana Anderson, Room 4C712, 614–5299.
Sustainment.—Sean Burke, Room 4C712, 695–2496.

DEPARTMENT OF THE NAVY CHIEF INFORMATION OFFICER

Pentagon, Room 4E720, Washington, DC 20350

phone (703) 695–3141.

Chief Information Officer.—Aaron D. Weis.

CHIEF OF NAVAL OPERATIONS

Pentagon, Room 4E662, Washington, DC 20350

phone (703) 695–5664, fax 693–9408

Chief of Naval Operations.—ADM Michael Gilday.
Vice Chief of Naval Operations.—ADM William Lescher.
Judge Advocate General of the Navy.—VADM John Hannink.
Directors:
Naval Criminal Investigative Service.—Omar R. Lopez.
Naval Intelligence.—VADM Matthew Kohler.
Naval Nuclear Propulsion Program.—ADM James Caldwell.

Navy Staff.—Stephanie Easter.
Chief of:
Chaplains.—RADM Brent Scott.
Information.—RDML Charles Brown.
Legislative Affairs.—RADM Charles B. Cooper II.
Navy Reserve.—VADM Luke McCollum.
Oceanographer of the Navy.—RDML John Okon.
Surgeon General of the Navy.—RADM Bruce L. Gillingham.
Master Chief Petty Officer of the Navy.—MCPON Russel Smith.
President, Board of Inspection and Survey.—RDML Christopher Engdahl.
Commander, Naval Education and Training.—RADM Kyle Cozad.
Commander, Naval Safety Center.—RADM Mark Leavitt.
Deputy Chief of Naval Operations for—
Fleet Readiness and Logistics.—VADM Ricky Williamson.
Information Warfare.—VADM Brian Brown.
Integration of Capabilities and Resources.—VADM Bill Lescher.
Manpower, Personnel, Training, and Education.—VADM John Nowell, Jr.
Operations, Plans, and Strategy.—VADM Stuart Munsch.
Warfare Systems.—VADM James Kilby.

BUREAU OF MEDICINE AND SURGERY

7700 Arlington Boulevard, Suite 5113, Arlington, VA 22042–5113
phone (703) 681–5200, fax 681–9527

Chief.—RADM Bruce L. Gillingham, MC, USN.

MILITARY SEALIFT COMMAND

471 East C Street, Norfolk, VA 23511–2491
phone (757) 443–2839

Commander.—RADM Michael A. Wettlaufer.

WALTER REED NATIONAL MILITARY MEDICAL CENTER

4494 North Palmer Road, Bethesda, MD 20889
phone (301) 295–4000 / 5802, fax 295–5336

Director.—COL Andrew M. Barr, USA.
Chief of Staff.—COL Rodney S. Gonzalez, USA.
Command Master Chief.—Randy F. Swanson.

NAVAL AIR SYSTEMS COMMAND

47123 Buse Road, Building 2272, Suite 540, Patuxent River, MD 20670
phone (301) 757–7825

Commander.—VADM Dean Peters.

NAVAL CRIMINAL INVESTIGATIVE SERVICE HEADQUARTERS

27130 Telegraph Road, Quantico, VA 22134
phone (571) 305–9000

Director.—Omar R. Lopez.

NAVAL DISTRICT OF WASHINGTON

1343 Dahlgren Avenue, SE., Building 1, Washington, DC 20374–5001
phone (202) 433–2777, fax 433–2207

Commandant.—RDML Carl A. Lahti.

Chief of Staff.—CAPT Geoffrey Moore.

NAVAL FACILITIES ENGINEERING COMMAND

1322 Patterson Avenue, SE., Washington Navy Yard, Washington, DC 20374–5065

phone (202) 685–9499, fax 685–1463

Commander.—RADM John W. Korka, CEC, USN.

OFFICE OF NAVAL INTELLIGENCE

4251 Suitland Road, Washington, DC 20395–5720

phone (301) 669–3001, fax 669–3509

Commander.—RADM Kelly Aeschbach.

NAVAL SEA SYSTEMS COMMAND

1333 Isaac Hull Avenue, SE., Washington Navy Yard, Washington, DC 20376

phone (202) 781–0000

Commander.—VADM William Galinas.

NAVAL SUPPLY SYSTEMS COMMAND

5450 Carlisle Pike, Mechanicsburg, PA 17050–2411

phone (717) 605–3433

Commander.—RADM Peter Stamatopoulos.

NAVAL INFORMATION WARFARE SYSTEMS COMMAND (NAVWAR)

4301 Pacific Highway, San Diego, CA 92110

phone (619) 524–3433, fax (858) 537–0463

Commander.—RADM Christian Becker.
Director of Congressional and Legislative Affairs, PAO.—Steven Yuhas.

U.S. NAVAL ACADEMY

121 Blake Road, Annapolis, MD 21402

phone (410) 293–1000

Superintendent.—VADM Sean Buck.

U.S. MARINE CORPS HEADQUARTERS

Pentagon, Room 4E734, Washington, DC 20350

phone (703) 614–2500

Commandant.—Gen. D.H. Berger.
Assistant Commandant.—Gen. G.L. Thomas, 614–1201.
Aide-de-Camp.—Lt. Col. I.D. Stevens.
Chaplain.—RDML G.N. Todd, 614–4627.
Dental Officer.—CAPT R.L. Gunning.
Fiscal Director of the Marine Corps.—SES C.E. Spangler.
Inspector General of the Marine Corps.—Maj. Gen. J.W. Lukeman, 614–1533.
Judge Advocate.—Maj. Gen. D.J. Lecce, 614–8661.
Legislative Assistant.—Brig. Gen. R.C. Fulford, 614–1686.
Medical Officer.—RDML J.L. Hancock.
Military Secretary.—Col. S.D. Leonard.

Sergeant Major of the Marine Corps.—Sgt. Maj. T.E. Black, 614–8762.
Deputy Commandant of Marine Corps for—
Aviation.—Lt. Gen. S. Rudder, 614–1010.
Information.—Lt. Gen. L.E. Reynolds (571) 256–8780.
Installations and Logistics.—Lt. Gen. C.G. Chiarotti, 695–8572.
Manpower and Reserve Affairs.—Lt. Gen. M.A. Rocco, 695–1929.
Plans, Policies, and Operations.—Lt. Gen. G.W. Smith, 614–8521.
Programs and Resources.—Lt. Gen. J.M. Jansen, 614–3435.
Public Affairs.—Brig. Gen. S.M. Salene, 614–8010.
Director of Intelligence.—Brig. Gen. M.G. Carter.
Director, Marine Corps History and Museums.—Dr. E.T. Nevgloski.

MARINE BARRACKS

Eighth and I Streets, SE., Washington, DC 20390
phone (202) 433–4094

Commanding Officer.—Col. Teague A. Pastel.

TRAINING AND EDUCATION COMMAND

3300 Russell Road, Quantico, VA 22134
phone (703) 784–3730, fax 784–3724

Commanding General.—Lt. Gen. Lewis A. Craparotta.

DEPARTMENT OF JUSTICE

Robert F. Kennedy Department of Justice Building

950 Pennsylvania Avenue, NW., Washington, DC 20530

phone (202) 514–2000, https://usdoj.gov

WILLIAM P. BARR was born on May 23, 1950 in New York City. Mr. Barr received his A.B. in government from Columbia University in 1971 and his M.A. in government and Chinese studies in 1973. From 1973 to 1977, he served in the Central Intelligence Agency before receiving his J.D. with highest honors from George Washington University Law School in 1977.

In 1978, Mr. Barr served as a law clerk under Judge Malcolm Wilkey of the U.S. Court of Appeals for the District of Columbia Circuit. Following his clerkship, Mr. Barr joined the Washington, D.C. office of the law firm of Shaw, Pittman, Potts & Trowbridge as an associate. He left the firm to work in the White House under President Ronald Reagan from 1982 to 1983 on the domestic policy staff, then returned to the law firm and became a partner in 1985.

Under President George H.W. Bush, Mr. Barr served as the Deputy Attorney General from 1990 to 1991; the Assistant Attorney General of the Office of Legal Counsel from 1989 to 1990; and the 77th Attorney General of the United States from 1991 to 1993. While serving at the Department, Mr. Barr helped create programs and strategies to reduce violent crime and was responsible for establishing new enforcement policies in a number of areas including financial institutions, civil rights, and antitrust merger guidelines. Mr. Barr also led the Department's response to the Savings & Loan crisis; oversaw the investigation of the Pan Am 103 bombing; directed the successful response to the Talladega prison uprising and hostage taking; and coordinated counter-terrorism activities during the First Gulf War.

From 1994 to 2000, Mr. Barr served as Executive Vice President and General Counsel for GTE Corporation. Mr. Barr then served as Executive Vice President and General Counsel of Verizon from 2000 to 2008. At both GTE and Verizon, Mr. Barr led the legal, regulatory, and government affairs activities of the companies.

After retiring from Verizon in 2008, Mr. Barr advised major corporations on government enforcement matters, as well as regulatory litigation. Mr. Barr served as Of Counsel at Kirkland & Ellis LLP in 2009 and rejoined the firm in 2017.

President Donald Trump announced his intention to nominate Mr. Barr on December 7, 2018, and he was confirmed as the 85th Attorney General of the United States by the U.S. Senate on February 14, 2019. U.S. Supreme Court Chief Justice John Roberts administered the oath of office. Mr. Barr joins John Crittenden (1841 and 1850–53) as one of only two people in U.S. history to serve twice as Attorney General.

OFFICE OF THE ATTORNEY GENERAL

950 Pennsylvania Avenue, NW., Room 5111, Washington, DC 20530

phone (202) 514–2001

Attorney General.—William P. Barr.

Chief of Staff and Counselor to the Attorney General.—Brian Rabbitt, Room 5111, 514–3892.

Counselor to the Attorney General: Seth DuCharme, Room 5127, 514–9665; Gene Hamilton, Room 5224, 514–4969; Will Levi, Room 5116, 616–7740; John Moran, Room 5112, 616–2372; Timothy Shea, Room 5110, 514–9798; Lauren Willard, Room 5214, 305–8674.

White House Liaison.—Rachel Bissex, Room 5119, 305–7378.

Director of Advance.—Jeffrey Favitta, Room 5119, 353–4435.

Director of Scheduling.—Brittany Psyhogios-Smith, Room 5134, 514–9797.

Confidential Assistant.—Theresa Watson, Room 5111, 514–2001.

OFFICE OF THE DEPUTY ATTORNEY GENERAL

950 Pennsylvania Avenue, NW., Room 4111, Washington, DC 20530

phone (202) 514–2101

Deputy Attorney General.—Jeffrey A. Rosen, Room 4111.
Confidential Assistant to the Deputy Attorney General.—Marcia Murphy, Room 4111, 514–2101.
Principal Associate Deputy Attorney General.—Robert K. Hur, Room 4208, 514–2105.
Chief of Staff and Associate Deputy Attorney General.—James A. Crowell IV, Room 4210, 514–8699.
Deputy Chief of Staff and Associate Deputy Attorney General.—G. Zachary Terwilliger, Room 4210, 307–1045.
Chief, Professional Misconduct Review Unit.—John Geise, Room 4131, 514–0049.
Associate Deputy Attorneys General: Antoinette Bacon, Room 4110, 616–1621; Steven Cook, Room 4415, 305–0180; Tashina Gauhar, Room 4218, 514–3712; Iris Lan, Room 4311, 514–6907; Sujit Raman, Room 4222, 307–0697; Scott Schools, Room 4113, 305–7848; James Swanson, Room 4135, 305–8657; Robert Troester, Room 4224, 514–3853.
Associate Deputy Attorney General and National Criminal Discovery Coordinator.—Andrew D. Goldsmith, Room 4214, 514–5705.
Associate Deputy Attorney General and Director, OCDETF.—Bruce G. Ohr, Room 4115, 307–2510.
Senior Counsel to the Deputy Attorney General.—Amelia Medina, Room 4121, 616–0663.
Counsel to the Deputy Attorney General: Zachary Bolitho, Room 4114, 514–7473; Leah Bressack, Room 4129, 514–6753; Patrick Bumatay, Room 4226, 305–0071; Brendan Groves, Room 4304, 305–4127; John Hill, Room 4214, 353–3030; Daniel Loveland, Room 4315, 305–0620; Chad Mizelle, Room 4116, 305–3481; Michael Murray, Room 4220, 307–2090; Matthew Sheehan, Room 4119, 514–4995.
Emergency Preparedness and Crisis Response Coordinator.—Mark E. Michalic, Room 4112, 514–0438.
Senior Advisor on Forensics.—Ted Hunt, Room 4303, 514–4995.
National Coordinator for Child Exploitation Prevention and Interdiction.—Michael Frank, Room 4217, 305–0273.

OFFICE OF THE ASSOCIATE ATTORNEY GENERAL

950 Pennsylvania Avenue, NW., Room 5706, Washington, DC 20530

phone (202) 514–9500

Associate Attorney General.—Vacant.
Confidential Assistant/Office Manager.—Ashley Wilson*, Room 5706, 514–9500.
Principal Deputy Associate Attorney General.—Claire McCusker Murray.
Deputy Associate Attorneys General: Katherine Allen*, Stephen Cox, Patrick Davis, Jennifer Dickey, Taylor McConkie*, Brian Pandya, Prerak Shah.
Counsel to the Associate Attorney General.—Vacant.
Senior Counsel to the Associate Attorney General.—Vacant.
Chief of Staff and Counselor to the Associate Attorney General.—Stephen Cox (acting).
Staff Assistant.—Vacant, Room 5706, 616–0565.

Note: * Indicates detailed from other component within DOJ.

OFFICE OF THE SOLICITOR GENERAL

950 Pennsylvania Avenue, NW., Room 5143, Washington, DC 20530

phone (202) 514–2201, https://usdoj.gov/osg

Solicitor General.—Noel Francisco, Room 5143, 514–2201.
Principal Deputy Solicitor General.—Jeffrey Wall, Room 5143, 514–2206.
Executive Officer.—Valerie Hall Yancey, Room 5142, 514–3957.
Supervisory Case Management Specialist.—Charlene Goodwin, Room 5608, 514–2218.
Research and Publications Section Manager.—Jason Manuel, Room 6634, 353–4122.

ANTITRUST DIVISION

950 Pennsylvania Avenue, NW., Washington, DC 20530 (RFK)

Liberty Square Building, 450 5th Street, NW., Washington, DC 20001 (LSB)

Assistant Attorney General.—Makan Delrahim, Room 3109 (202) 514–2401.
Principal Deputy Assistant Attorney General.—Barry Nigro, Room 3208, 353–6417.
Deputy Assistant Attorneys General: Rene Augustine, Room 3216, 598–8931; Michael Murray, Room 3119, 532–4698; Bernard Nigro, Room 3212, 353–4656; Richard Powers, Room 3218, 598–2447; Jeffrey Wilder, Room 3214, 307–6665.
Director of:
Civil Enforcement.—Kathy O'Neill, Room 3115, 307–2931.
Criminal Enforcement.—Marvin N. Price, Jr., Room 3214, 307–0719.
Economics Enforcement.—Ronald Drennan, Room 3416, 9400, 307–6603.
Freedom of Information Act Officer.—Kenneth Hendricks (LSB), Room 1000, 514–2692.
Executive Officer.—Walt Cain (LSB), Room 3626, 514–7305.
Section Chiefs:
Appellate.—Daniel Haar, Room 3222, 598–2846.
Competition Policy.—David Lawrence, Room 3218, 532–4698.
Defense, Industrial, and Aerospace.—Katrina Rouse (LSB), Room 8700, 598–2459.
Economic Litigation.—Norman Familant (LSB), Room 9912, 307–6323.
Economic Regulatory.—Beth Armington (LSB), Room 3700, 307–6332.
Ethics Office, Office of the Chief Legal Advisor.—Dorothy Fountain, Room 3218, 514–3543.
Foreign Commerce.—Lynda Marshall (LSB), Room 11000, 514–2264.
Healthcare and Consumer Products.—Eric Welsh (LSB), Room 4050, 598–8881.
Media, Entertainment, and Professional Services.—Owen Kendler (LSB), Room 4000, 305–8376.
National Criminal Enforcement.—Ryan Danks (LSB), Room 11400, 307–6694.
Networks and Technology.—Aaron Hoag (LSB), Room 7700, 307–6153.
Telecommunications and Media.—Scott A. Scheele (LSB), Room 7000, 307–6132.
Transportation, Energy, and Agriculture.—Robert Lepore (LSB), Room 8100, 532–4928.

FIELD OFFICES

California: Manish Kumar, 450 Golden Gate Avenue, Room 10–0101, Box 36046, San Francisco, CA 94102 (415) 934–5333.
Illinois: Kalina Tulley, Rookery Building, 209 South LaSalle Street, Suite 600, Chicago, IL 60604 (312) 984–7211.
New York: Joseph Muoio, Jr., 26 Federal Plaza, Room 3630, New York, NY 10278–1040 (212) 824–1236.

BUREAU OF ALCOHOL, TOBACCO, FIREARMS, AND EXPLOSIVES (ATF)

99 New York Avenue, NE., Suite 5S–100, Washington, DC 20226

OFFICE OF THE DIRECTOR

Director.—Regina Lombardo (acting), (202) 648–8700.
Associate Deputy Director/Chief Operating Officer.—Marvin Richardson, 648–8710.
Chief of Staff.—Joseph J. Allen (acting), 648–7113.
Deputy Chief of Staff.—Marianna Mitchem (acting), 648–7371.
Special Assistant to the Deputy Director.—Betty L. Coleman, 648–8710.
Confidential Project Manager to the Acting Director.—Michelle A. Back, 648–8700.

OFFICE OF STRATEGIC MANAGEMENT

Chief.—Charlayne Armentrout, 648–7099.

OFFICE OF CHIEF COUNSEL

Chief Counsel.—Joel J. Roessner, 648–7058.
Deputy Chief Counsel.—Pamela J. Hicks, 648–7836.

OFFICE OF ENFORCEMENT PROGRAMS AND SERVICES

Assistant Director.—Alphonso J. Hughes, 648–7080.
Deputy Assistant Director.—Andrew R. Graham, 648–7080.

OFFICE OF EQUAL OPPORTUNITY

Chief.—Evette R. Young, 648–8760.

OFFICE OF FIELD OPERATIONS

Assistant Director.—Thomas Chittum (702) 469–4203.
Deputy Assistant Director for—
Central.—George Lauder (202) 648–7241.
East.—Marcus Watson (616) 340–1139.
Industry Operations.—Megan Bennett (202) 648–8344.
Programs.—Vacant.
West.—John Durastanti (202) 648–8227.

OFFICE OF MANAGEMENT

Assistant Director/CFO.—Francis H. Frandé, 648–7800.
Deputy Assistant Director.—Stuart Lowrey, 648–7800.

OFFICE OF OMBUDSPERSON

Ombudsperson.—Grace M. Reisling, 648–7351.

OFFICE OF PROFESSIONAL RESPONSIBILITY AND SECURITY OPERATIONS

Assistant Director/Chief Security Officer.—Celinez Nunez, 648–7500.
Deputy Assistant Director.—Mickey Leadingham, 648–8702.

OFFICE OF PUBLIC AND GOVERNMENTAL AFFAIRS

Assistant Director.—Danny Board, 648–8323.
Deputy Assistant Director.—Megan Bennett, 648–8344.
Chief, Division of:
Intergovernmental Affairs.—John Wells (acting), 648–8807.
Legislative Affairs.—Ross Arends, 648–7722.
Public Affairs.—April Langwell, 648–8686.

OFFICE OF SCIENCE AND TECHNOLOGY/CIO

Assistant Director/Chief Information Officer.—Roger Beasley, 648–8390.
Deputy Assistant Director for IT Services/Deputy CIO.—Victoria Gold, 648–8390.
Deputy Assistant Director for Forensic Services.—Greg Czarnopys, 648–6001.

OFFICE OF STRATEGIC INTELLIGENCE AND INFORMATION

Assistant Director.—James E. McDermond, 648–7600.
Deputy Assistant Director.—Dana Nichols, 648–7600.

OFFICE OF HUMAN RESOURCES AND PROFESSIONAL DEVELOPMENT

Assistant Director.—Steven L. Gerido, 648–7979.
Deputy Assistant Director, Professional Development.—Lisa Boykin, 648–7489.
Deputy Assistant Director, Human Resources.—Kelly D. Brady, 648–8415.

CIVIL DIVISION

950 Pennsylvania Avenue, NW., Washington, DC 20530 (RFK)

1100 L Street, NW., Washington, DC 20530 (L ST)

Liberty Square Building, 450 5th Street, NW., Washington, DC 20001 (LSB)

175 N Street, NE., 3 Constitution Square, Washington, DC 20002 (3CON)

Assistant Attorney General.—Joseph H. Hunt, Room 3601 (202) 514–3301.
Principal Deputy Assistant Attorney General.—Ethan P. Davis, Room 3605, 514–7830.
Chief of Staff.—Paul Perkins, Room 3611, 514–5090.

APPELLATE STAFF

Deputy Assistant Attorney General.—Hashim Mooppan, Room 3135, 353–8679.
Director.—Mark Freeman, Room 7519, 514–5714.
Deputy Director.—Dana Martin, Room 7517, 514–2541.

COMMERCIAL LITIGATION BRANCH

Deputy Assistant Attorney General.—Michael Granston, Room 3607, 307–0231.
Directors: David M. Cohen (L ST), Room 12124, 514–7300; John N. Fargo (L ST), Room 11116, 514–7223.
Deputy Directors: Jeanne Davidson (L ST), Office of Foreign Litigation, Room 12124, 616–8277; Gary Hausken (L ST), Intellectual Property, Room 8000, 307–0342; Robert Kirschman (L ST), National Courts, Room 10000, 616–8277.
Legal Officer.—Donna C. Maizel, Esq., U.S. Department of Justice, Civil Division European Office, The American Embassy, London, England, PSC 801, Box 42, FPO AE, 09498–4042, 9+011–44–20–7894–0840.
Attorney-in-Charge.—Barbara Williams, Suite 359, 26 Federal Plaza, New York, NY 10278 (212) 264–9240.

CONSUMER LITIGATION BRANCH

Deputy Assistant Attorney General.—David M. Morrell, Room 3131 (202) 514–2331.
Director.—Gustav W. Eyler (LSB), Room 6254, 307–3009.

FEDERAL PROGRAMS BRANCH

Deputy Assistant Attorney General.—James M. Burnham, Room 3137, 353–2793.
Directors: John Griffiths (L ST), Room 11100, 514–4651; Alexander K. Haas (L ST), Room 12000, 514–1259; Jennifer Ricketts (L ST), Room 11000, 514–3671.

IMMIGRATION LITIGATION

Deputy Assistant Attorney General.—Scott G. Stewart, Room 3129, 307–6482.
Directors: David McConnell (LSB), Appellate Court, Room 10000, 616–4881; William Peachey (LSB), District Court, Room 6054, 307–0871.

MANAGEMENT PROGRAMS

Executive Officer of Management Programs.—Catherine E. Emerson, Room 3140, 514–4552.

TORTS BRANCH

Deputy Assistant Attorney General.—Thomas G. Ward, Room 3133 (202) 514–7835.
Directors: Barry Benson, Aviation and Admiralty (Room 8.137, 3CON), 616–4030; Rupa Bhattacharyya, Victim Compensation Fund (Room 11708, FCB), 1099 14th Street, NW., Washington, DC 20005, 305–0008; Sal D'Alessio, Constitutional and Specialized Torts (Room 7.115, 3CON), 616–4168; James Touhey, Federal Torts Claims Act (Room 11.137, 3CON), 616–4400.

CIVIL RIGHTS DIVISION

950 Pennsylvania Avenue, NW., Washington, DC 20530 (RFK)

150 M Street, NE., 4 Constitution Square, Washington, DC 20002 (4CON)

https://usdoj.gov/crt

Assistant Attorney General.—Eric S. Dreiband, Room 5649, 353–9789.
Principal Deputy Assistant Attorney General.—John Daukas, Room 5748, 353–9430.
Deputy Assistant Attorneys General: Greg Friel, Room 5744, 353–9418; Alexander Maugeri, Room 5740, 616–5894; Cynthia McKnight, Room 5533, 616–1278; Robert Moossy, Room 5541, 514–0621.
Counsel to the Assistant Attorney General: Eric Treene (acting), Room 5531, 353–8622; Matthew Donnelly (acting), Room 5537, 353–9013/9014; Jeffrey Morrison (acting), Room 5535, 616–9617; Hilary Pinion (acting), Room 5637, 514–9879/9953; Dan Yi, Room 5539, 616–4183.
Special Assistant.—Cassandra Collins, Room 5644, 598–9038.
Director of Operational Management.—Kathleen Toomey, Room 5646, 323–0283.
Section Chiefs:
Administrative Management.—Suey Howe (4CON), Room 11.216, 514–2151.
Appellate.—Thomas Chandler (RFK), Room 3708, 307–3192.
Complaint Adjudication.—Robert Abraham (acting), (RFK), Room 3747, 305–0079.
Criminal.—James Felte (4CON), Room 711.02, 305–3963.
Disability Rights.—Rebecca Bond (4CON), Room 9.1102, 305–0748.
Educational Opportunities.—Shaheena Simons (4CON), Room 10.202, 305–3364.
Employment Litigation.—Delora Kenebrew (4CON), Room 9.1819, 514–3831.
Federal Coordination and Compliance.—Christine Stoneman (4CON), Room 7.1425, 305–3963.
Housing and Civil Enforcement.—Sameena Shina Majeed (4CON), Room 8.1102, 305–1311.
Immigrant and Employee Rights.—Alberto Ruisanchez (4CON), Room 7.1807, 616–5594.
Policy and Strategy Section.—Shelia Foran (acting), (4CON), Room 6.530, 305–0160.
Professional Development.—Jessica Ginsburg (4CON), Room 9.1805, 514–4530.
Special Litigation.—Steven Rosenbaum (4CON), Room 10.1801, 616–3244.
Voting.—Chris Herren (4CON), Room 8.1807, 514–1416.

OFFICE OF COMMUNITY ORIENTED POLICING SERVICES

145 N Street, NE., Washington, DC 20530

DIRECTOR'S OFFICE

Director.—Phil Keith, 11th Floor, 616–2888.
Deputy Director for—
Community Policing.—Rob Chapman.
Grant Operations.—Cory Randolph.
Management.—Wayne Henry.

COMMUNICATIONS DIVISION

Assistant Director.—Shannon Long, 11th Floor, 514–9079.

COMMUNITY RELATIONS SERVICE

145 N Street, NE., 2 Constitution Square, Suite 5E.300, Washington, DC 20530

phone (202) 305–2935, fax 353–2164

Director.—Vacant.
Deputy Director.—Gerri Ratliff.
General Counsel.—Antoinette Barksdale.
Associate Director.—Theresa Segovia.

REGIONAL DIRECTORS (RDs)

New England.—Mary Gorecki (acting), 408 Atlantic Avenue, Suite 222, Boston, MA 02110–1032 (617) 424–5715.
Northeast Region.—Christian Van Alstyne (acting), 26 Federal Plaza, Suite 36–118, New York, NY 10278 (212) 264–0700.
Mid-Atlantic Region.—Christian Van Alstyne (acting), 200 2nd and Chestnut Streets, Suite 208, Philadelphia, PA 19106 (215) 597–2344.
Southeast Region.—Synthia Taylor (acting), 61 Forsyth Street, SW., Suite 7B65, Atlanta, GA 30303 (404) 331–6883.
Midwest Region.—Mary Gorecki, 230 South Dearborn Street, Suite 2130, Chicago, IL 60604 (312) 353–4391.
Southwest Region.—Synthia Taylor, Hardwood Center Building, 1999 Bryan Street, Suite 2050, Dallas, TX 75201 (214) 655–8175.
Central Region.—Christian Van Alstyne, 601 East 12th Street, Suite 0802, Kansas City, MO 64106 (816) 426–7434.
Rocky Mountain Region.—Ronald Wakabayashi (acting), 1244 Speer Boulevard, Suite 650, Denver, CO 80204–3584 (303) 844–2973.
Western Region.—Ronald Wakabayashi, 888 South Figueroa Street, Suite 2010, Los Angeles, CA 90017 (213) 894–2941.
Northwest Region.—Ronald Wakabayashi (acting), 915 Second Avenue, Suite 1808, Seattle, WA 98174 (206) 220–6700.

CRIMINAL DIVISION

950 Pennsylvania Avenue, NW., Washington, DC 20530

Bond Building, 1400 New York Avenue, NW., Washington, DC 20530 (Bond)

1331 F Street, NW., Washington, DC 20530 (F ST)

Keeney Building, 1301 New York Avenue, NW., Washington, DC 20530 (1301 NYA)

145 N Street, NE., 2 Constitution Square, Washington, DC 20530 (2CON)

Mainline Telephone (202) 514–7200

Assistant Attorney General.—Brian Rabbitt (acting), Room 2107, 514–7200.
Principal Deputy Assistant Attorney General.—John P. Cronan, Room 2206, 514–7200.
Deputy Assistant Attorneys General: Richard W. Downing, Room 2119, 353–7849; Kevin Driscoll, Room 2113, 307–6465; Jennifer A. H. Hodge, Room 2115, 305–9291; Matthew S. Miner, Room 2121, 598–6206; David C. Rybicki, Room 2220, 514–9834; Bruce C. Swartz, Room 2212, 514–2333.
Chief of Staff and Counselor to the Assistant Attorney General.—Candice C. Wong (acting), Room 2208, 514–2338.
Senior Counsel to the Assistant Attorney General: Lauren Bell, Room 2214, 616–0761; Molly Braese, Room 2116, 307–5856; Samuel Nazzaro, Room 2222, 353–9989.
Administrative Officer.—Stephen M. Qureshi, Room 2215, 353–1904.
Executive Officer.—Tracy Melton (Bond), Room 5100, 305–0534.
Section Chiefs / Office Directors:
Appellate.—Patty M. Stemler (RFK), Room 1521, 514–2611.
Capital Case.—Richard Burns (F ST), Suite 600, 353–1911.
Child Exploitation and Obscenity.—Steve Grocki (Bond), Suite 6000, 616–8900.
Computer Crime and Intellectual Property.—John Lynch (1301 NYA), Suite 600, 305–8732.
Enforcement Operations.—Robert Bryden (acting), (1301 NYA), Suite 1200, 305–9206.
Fraud.—Robert Zink (Bond), Room 4100, 616–0429.
Human Rights and Special Prosecutions.—Teresa McHenry (1301 NYA), Room 215, 616–8385.
International Affairs.—Vaughn Ary (1301 NYA), Suite 900, 616–1503.
International Criminal Investigative Training Assistant Program.—Gregory Ducot (acting), (F ST), Suite 500, 353–4784.
Money Laundering and Asset Recovery.—Deborah Connor (Bond), Suite 10100, 616–2886.
Narcotic and Dangerous Drug.—Arthur Wyatt (2CON), Room 2E.200, 307–2382.
Organized Crime and Gangs.—David Jaffe (1301 NYA), Suite 700, 514–0865.
Overseas Prosecutorial Development, Assistance and Training.—Faye Ehrenstamm (F ST), Suite 700, 514–1437.

Policy and Legislation.—Jonathan Wroblewski (RFK), Room 1744, 514–4730.
Public Integrity.—Corey Amundson (F ST), Suite 300, 598–2253.

DRUG ENFORCEMENT ADMINISTRATION

Lincoln Place–1 (East), 600 Army-Navy Drive, Arlington, VA 22202 (LP–1)

Lincoln Place–2 (West), 700 Army-Navy Drive, Arlington, VA 22202 (LP–2)

Administrator.—Timothy J. Shea (acting), (202) 307–8000.
Chief of Staff.—Robyn L. Thiemann, 307–6755.
Principal Deputy Administrator.—Preston L. Grubbs, 307–7345.
Equal Employment Opportunity Officer.—Michele C. Daly, 307–6337.
Executive Assistants: Vacant.
Chief, Congressional and Public Affairs.—Dawn Dearden, 307–7363.
Section Chiefs:
Electronic and Internal Communications.—Michael Shavers, 307–2402.
Congressional Affairs.—Katie A. Laughery, 307–4899.
Community Outreach and Prevention Support.—Sean T. Fearns, 307–3479.
National Media Affairs.—Mary Brandenberger, 307–1650.
Intergovernmental Affairs.—Sean Mitchell, 307–1650.
Chief Counsel.—Dayle Elieson, 307–7322.
Deputy Chief Counsel.—Robert C. Gleason, 307–8083.
Chief, Office of Administrative Law Judges.—John Mulrooney, 307–8188.

FINANCIAL MANAGEMENT DIVISION

Chief Financial Officer.—Jeffrey Sutton, Room W–12138, 307–7330.
Deputy Assistant Administrator for—
Acquisition Management.—Jeffrey Saylor, 307–7777.
Finance.—Daniel Gillette, Room E–7397, 307–7001.
Resource Management.—Brian Horn, Room E–5156, 307–4800.
Administration.—Renaldo Prillman, Room W–9088, 307–7703.
Associate Deputy Assistant Administrator, Office of:
Acquisition Management.—Kevin Dupuis, Room E–8193, 598–8192.
Administration.—Tracy Rozier, Room W–9082, 307–1795.
Finance.—Jeff Rashap, Room E–7395, 598–8870.
Resource Management.—Stephan Faherty, Room E–5288, 307–4009.
Section Chiefs:
Acquisition Management.—Nanaesi Amoo, Room E–8359, 307–7801.
Controls and Coordination.—Bryan Parks, Room E–5384, 307–5276.
Cost Analysis.—Ashley Dalton, Room E–5334, 307–9361.
Financial Integrity.—Angela Ivy, Room E–7331, 307–5459.
Financial Operations.—Daanish Ahmed, Room E–7165, 307–7270.
Financial Policy.—Claire Hutchins, Room E–7377, 307–7064.
Financial Reports.—Sherri Woodle, Room E–7297, 307–7040.
Financial Systems.—Andrew Kenny, Room E–8001, 307–7215.
Organization and Staffing Management.—Jason Dolan, Room E–5284, 305–7097.
Policy.—Carol S. Burger, Room E–8161, 307–4732.
Program Liaison and Analysis.—Joshua Ginsburg, Room E–5003–17, 307–9361.
Statistical Services.—Gamaliel Rose, Room E–5332, 307–8276.
Transportation and Relocation.—Christopher Booker, Room E–8045, 307–7835.

HUMAN RESOURCES DIVISION

Assistant Administrator.—Sharyn J. Saunders, 307–4487.
Deputy Assistant Administrator for Human Resources.—Amanda Voight, Room W–3166, 307–4993.
Section Chiefs:
Compensation and Benefits.—John Christie, Room W–3126, 307–6487.
HR Information Systems.—Isaiah Barnwell, Room W–3240, 307–7576.
HR Policy.—Janet McMichael, Room W–3114, 307–4050.
HR Processing.—Debra Henderson, Room W–3058, 307–1219.
Suitability.—Pat Murphy, Room W–9171–17, 307–4058.
Career Board Executive Secretary.—Lawyer Wilson, Room W–2270 (202) 353–1552.

Chair, Board of Professional Conduct.—Kenneth M. Ludwig, Room E–9355, 598–8864.
Special Agent-in-Charge, Office of Training.—William J.C. Matthews (acting), 2500 Investigation Parkway, DEA Academy, Quantico, VA 22135 (703) 632–5010.
Assistant Special Agents-in-Charge:
Criminal—Diversion and Intelligence Training Section.—Karen Dorough (703) 632–5343.
Domestic Training Section.—Jason Alznauer (703) 632–5181.
International and Personnel Recovery Training Section.—Brian Townsend (703) 632–5399.
Policy and Learning Development Section.—John F. Niece (703) 632–5141.
Specialized Training Section.—Justin May (703) 632–5110.

INSPECTIONS DIVISION

Chief Inspector.—Kevin ''Scott'' McRory, Room W–12042A, 353–1032.
Deputy Chief Inspector, Office of:
Inspections.—Jeff Walsh, Room W–4250, 307–6748.
Professional Responsibility.—Gary Owen, Room W–4080, 307–6747.
Security Programs.—Sean Vereault, Room W–2350, 307–5399.

INTELLIGENCE DIVISION

Assistant Administrator.—Paul Knierim, Room W–12036–A, 307–3607.
Director/Special Agent-in-Charge, El Paso Intelligence Center.—James R. Reed (acting), Building 11339, SSG Sims Street, El Paso, TX 79908–8098 (915) 760–2011.
Deputy Assistant Administrator, Office of Intelligence.—Steven M. Towne, Room W–12036–C, 307–3607.
Executive Assistant.—Carrie Thompson, 307–3607.
Deputy Assistant Administrator, Office of:
Intelligence Programs.—Arthur A. Doty, Merrifield, VA (571) 362–0802.
National Security Intelligence.—Cheryl E. Hooper (acting), 307–6101.
OCDETF Fusion Center.—Jon S. Pickette (571) 362–5210.
Special Intelligence.—James Schrant, Merrifield, VA (571) 362–0913.
Section Chiefs:
Analysis and Production.—Lidia Lipsey, 307–8108.
Data Management.—William Barlow (571) 362–0762.
Document and Media Exploitation.—Jim Wink (571) 362–0927.
Field Support.—Arlyn Brunet, 307–6424.
Indicator Programs.—Benjamin C. Sanborn, 307–4358.
Intelligence Community Integration.—Gregg Lindskoog, 307–6644.
Investigative Support.—Christopher Wojciechowski (703) 488–4246.
Operations Support.—Daniel Palewicz (acting), (571) 362–0890.
Program Management and Budget.—Demetrice Crumley, 307–7534.
Requirements and Collection.—Gregg Lindskoog (acting), 307–6644.
Strategic Intelligence.—Jacquelyn Mazza, 353–1224.
Technical Support.—Kurt Lund, 307–3651.

OPERATIONS DIVISION

Chief of Operations.—D. Christopher Evans, Room W–12050, 307–7339.
Chief of:
Domestic Operations.—Michael T. DellaCorte, Room W–11148, 353–1164.
Foreign Operations.—Miguel Rivera, Jr. (acting), Room W–11024, 307–8696.
Operations Management.—Timothy A. Jennings, Room W–11148, 353–1164.
Special Agent-in-Charge, Special Operations Division.—Wendy C. Woolcock, Chantilly, VA (703) 488–4200.

DIVERSION CONTROL DIVISION

Deputy Assistant Administrator, Office of Diversion Control.—Tim McDermott (acting), Crystal City, 598–2605.

OPERATIONAL SUPPORT DIVISION

Assistant Administrator.—Timothy J. Plancon, Room W–12142 (571) 362–1650.

Deputy Assistant Administrator, Office of:

Forensic Sciences.—Nelson Santos, Room W–7342, 307–8866.

Information Systems.—Maura Quinn, Crystal City, 307–3653.

Investigative Technology.—Fred Smith, Lorton, VA (703) 495–6501.

Special Agent-in-Charge, Aviation Division.—Gary W. Hill, Fort Worth, TX (817) 837–2000.

Associate Deputy Assistant Administrator, Office of:

Forensic Sciences: David W. Love, W–7338, 353–1297; Scott Oulton, Room W–7344, 307–8866.

Information Systems: Jack Baxter, Sterling Park (571) 362–0108; Michelle Bower, Crystal City (571) 362–7924; Daniel Tovar, Crystal City (571) 362–4291.

Section Chiefs:

Administrative Support Section.—Marcia Fisher, Lorton, VA (703) 495–6523.

Administrative Support and Financial Management.—Stephen E. Wasem, Room W–7310, 307–7206.

Audio/Video Surveillance Section.—Dwayne Bareng (acting), Lorton, VA (703) 495–6583.

Business Program Management.—Millie Tyler, Crystal City (571) 362–7977.

Communication and Polygraph Support.—Mary Toomey, Lorton, VA (703) 495–6719.

Core Enterprise Facility Transformation.—John Bowman, Sterling Park (571) 362–5646.

Cyber Support.—Gabriel O. Bewley, W–5018, 353–1587.

Cybersecurity Services.—Carlos R. Perez, Crystal City (571) 362–0333.

Diversion IT.—Anna Pacula, Crystal City (571) 362–0101.

Finance and Administration.—Evelyn Wideman, Crystal City (571) 362–7929.

Forensic Sciences Instruction.—David G. Boyd, Quantico, VA (703) 632–5316.

Environmental Management.—Ronald A. Leadore, Room W–7118–6, 307–9501.

Engineering and Integration.—Timothy Bilbro, Sterling Park (571) 362–0102.

IT Field Services.—Tom Schlauch, Crystal City (571) 362–0431.

Laboratory Management and Operations.—Lance Kvetko, Room W–7312, 307–8880.

OCDETF Fusion Center IT Support.—Gisele Gatjanis, Merrifield, VA (571) 362–7107.

Software Engineering and Data Standardization.—Brad Shepherd, Merrifield, VA (571) 362–0900.

Software Operations.—Deborah Roberts, Crystal City (571) 362–8078.

Technology Officer.—Alex Smith, Crystal City (571) 362–4328.

Technology Support.—Edgar Remspecher, Jr., Lorton, VA (703) 495–6601.

Telecommunications/Intercept Support.—Joseph Muenchow, Lorton, VA (703) 495–6727.

Tracking and Signal Section.—Richard Rosa, Lorton, VA (703) 495–6574.

FIELD OFFICES

Special Agents-in-Charge:

Atlanta Division.—Robert Murphy, 75 Ted Turner Drive, SW., Room 800, Atlanta, GA 30303 (404) 893–7100.

Caribbean Division.—Apolonio J. Collazo, Jr., Metro Office Park, Millennium Park Plaza #15, 2nd Street, Suite 710, Guaynabo, PR 00968 (787) 277–4700.

Chicago Division.—Robert Bell, John C. Kluczynski Federal Building, 230 South Dearborn Street, Suite 1200, Chicago, IL 60604 (312) 353–7875.

Dallas Division.—Clyde E. Shelley, Jr., 10160 Technology Boulevard East, Dallas, TX 75220 (214) 366–6900.

Denver Division.—Vacant, 12154 East Easter Avenue, Centennial, CO 80112–6740 (720) 895–4040.

Detroit Division.—Keith Martin, 431 Howard Street, Detroit, MI 48226 (313) 234–4000.

El Paso Division.—Kyle Williamson, 660 Mesa Hills Drive, Suite 2000, El Paso, TX 79912 (915) 832–6000.

Houston Division.—William R. Glaspy, 1433 West Loop South, Suite 600, Houston, TX 77027–9506 (713) 693–3000.

Louisville Division.—Karen Flowers, 1006 Federal Building, 600 Martin Luther King Place, Louisville, KY 40202.

Los Angeles Division.—William Bodner, 255 East Temple Street, 17th Floor, Los Angeles, CA 90012 (213) 621–6700.

Miami Division.—Adolphus P. Wright, 2100 North Commerce Parkway, Weston, FL 33326 (954) 660–4500.

New England Division.—Brian D. Boyle, JFK Federal Building, 15 New Sudbury Street, Room E–400, Boston, MA 02203 (617) 557–2100.

New Jersey Division.—Susan Gibson, 80 Mulberry Street, 2nd Floor, Newark, NJ 07102–4206 (973) 776–1200.

New Orleans Division.—Bradford Byerley, 3 Lakeway Center, 3838 North Causeway Boulevard, Suite 1800, Metaire, LA 70002 (504) 840–1100.

New York Division.—Raymond Donovan, 99 10th Avenue, New York, NY 10011 (212) 337–3900.

Omaha Division.—Richard W. Salter, Jr., 2707 North 108th Street, Suite D–201, Omaha, NE 68167 (402) 965–3600.

Philadelphia Division.—Jonathan Wilson, William J. Green Federal Building, 600 Arch Street, Room 10224, Philadelphia, PA 19106 (215) 861–3474.

Phoenix Division.—Douglas W. Coleman, Westmount Place, 3010 North Second Street, Suite 100, Phoenix, AZ 85012 (602) 664–5600.

San Diego Division.—John Callery, 4560 Viewridge Avenue, San Diego, CA 92123–1672 (858) 616–4100.

San Francisco Division.—Daniel Comeaux, 450 Golden Gate Avenue, 14th Floor, San Francisco, CA 94102 (415) 436–7900.

Seattle Division.—Keith R. Weis, 300 Fifth Avenue, Suite 1300, Seattle, WA 98104–2398 (206) 553–5443.

St. Louis Division.—William J. Callahan III, 317 South 16th Street, St. Louis, MO 63103 (314) 538–4600.

Washington, DC Division.—Jesse Fong, 800 K Street, NW., Suite 500, Washington, DC 20001 (202) 305–8500.

OTHER DEA OFFICES

Special Agents-in-Charge:

James A. Reed, El Paso Intelligence Center, Building 11339, SSG Sims Street, El Paso, TX 79908 (915) 760–2011.

Gary W. Hill, Aviation Operations Division, 2300 Horizon Drive, Fort Worth, TX 76177 (817) 837–2000.

Wendy C. Woolcock, Special Operations Division, 14560 Avion Parkway, Chantilly, VA 20151 (703) 488–4200.

William J. C. Matthews (acting), Office of Training, P.O. Box 1475, Quantico, VA 22134 (703) 632–5010.

FOREIGN OFFICES

Ankara, Turkey: American Embassy Ankara, DEA/Justice, PSC 93, Box 5000, APO AE 09823–5000, 9–011–90–312–468–6136.

Asuncion, Paraguay: DEA/Justice, American Embassy Asuncion, Unit 4740, APO AA 34036, 9–011–595–21–210–738.

Athens, Greece: American Embassy Athens, DEA/Justice, Unit 7100, Box 14, DPO AE 09842, 9–011–30–210–720–2490.

Bangkok, Thailand: American Embassy, DEA/Justice, Unit 46164, Box 49, APO AP 96546–6164, 9–011–662–205–4984.

Beijing, China: American Embassy Beijing, DEA/Justice, Unit 7300, Box 0255, DPO AP 96521, 9–011–8610–8531–4928.

Belmopan, Belize: American Embassy Belmopan, DEA/Justice, Unit 3050, DPO AA 34025, 301–985–9387.

Bern, Switzerland: Department of State, DEA/Justice, 5110 Bern Place, Washington, DC 20521–5110, 9–011–41–31–357–7367.

Bogota, Colombia: American Embassy Bogota, DEA/Justice, Unit 5116, APO AA 34038, 9–011–571–315–2121.

Brasilia, Brazil: DEA/Justice, American Embassy Brasilia, Unit 7500, DPO AA 34030, 9–011–55–61–3312–7158.

Bridgetown, Barbados: American Embassy Bridgetown, DEA/Justice, DPO AA 34055, 9–1–246–227–4171.

Brussels, Belgium: American Embassy Brussels, DEA/Justice, Unit 7600, Box 1700, DPO AE 09710, 9–011–32–2–811–4589.

Buenos Aires, Argentina: DEA / Justice, American Embassy Buenos Aires, Unit 4309, APO AA 34034, 9–011–5411–5777–4696.

Cairo, Egypt: American Embassy Cairo, DEA / Justice, Unit 64900, Box 25, APO AE 09839–4900, 9–011–20–2–2797–2461.

Canberra, Australia: American Embassy Canberra, DEA / Justice, APO AP 96549, 9–011–61–2–6214–5903.

Caracas, Venezuela: American Embassy Caracas, DEA / Justice, Unit 4962, APO AA 34037, 9–011–582–212–975–8380 / 8443 / 8407.

Cartagena, Resident Office: American Embassy, DEA Cartagena, Unit 5141, APO AA 34038, 9–011–575–664–9369.

Chiang-Mai, Resident Office: American Embassy Chiang-Mai, Unit 46220, Box C, APO AP 96546, 9–011–66–53–908–910.

Ciudad, Resident Office: U.S. Consulate / Ciudad Juarez Resident Office, P.O. Box 17000, El Paso, TX 79917, 9–011–52–656–227–3409.

Cochabamba, Resident Office: Unit 3220, Box 211, APO AA 34032, 9–011–591–4–429–3320.

Copenhagen, Denmark: American Embassy Copenhagen, DEA / Justice, Unit 5280, DPO AE 09716, 9–011–45–3341–7289.

Curacao, Netherlands Antilles: American Consulate Curacao, DEA / Justice, Washington, DC 20521, 9–011–5999–461–6985.

Dubai, United Arab Emirates: U.S. Consulate General, DEA / Justice, 6020 Dubai Place, Dulles, VA 20189–6020, 9–011–971–4–309–4929.

Dushanbe, Tajikistan: American Embassy Dushanbe, DEA / Justice, Drug Enforcement Administration, 7090 Dushanbe Place, Dulles, VA 20189–7090, 9–011–992–37–229–2812.

Frankfurt, Resident Office: American Consulate General Frankfurt, DEA / Justice, Unit 7900, Box 1600, DPO AE 09213–0115, 9–011–49–69–7535–3770.

Freeport, Bahamas Resident Office: GPS, c/o U.S. Embassy, DEA, 5115 Northwest 17th Terrace, Hanger #39A, Ft. Lauderdale, FL 33309, 9–1–242–352–5353 / 5354.

Guadalajara, Resident Office: DEA, Guadalajara Resident Office, P.O. Box 9001, Brownsville, TX 78520, 9–011–52–33–3268–2191.

Guatemala City, Guatemala: American Embassy Guatemala City, DEA / Justice, Unit 3190, DPO AA 34024, 9–301–985–9311.

Guayaquil, Resident Office: DEA / Justice, American Embassy Guayaquil, Unit 5350, APO AA, 34039, 9–011–593–42–32–3715.

The Hague, Netherlands: American Embassy The Hague, DEA / Justice, Unit 6707, Box 8, APO AE 09715, 9–011–31–70–310–2327.

Hanoi, Vietnam: American Embassy Hanoi, DEA / Justice, Unit 45500, Box 3069, DPO AP 96504–3069, 9–011–8424–3850–5153.

Hermosillo, Resident Office: U.S. Consulate-Hermosillo, P.O. Box 1689, Nogales, AZ 85628–1689, 9–011–52–662–289–3550.

Hong Kong Special Administrative Region (SAR): U.S. Consulate General DEA / Justice, Unit 8000, DPO AP 96521, 9–011–852–2521–4536.

Islamabad, Pakistan Country Office: DEA / Justice, American Embassy Islamabad, 8100 Islamabad Place, Washington, DC 20521–8100, 9–011–92–51–201–4000 (Embassy).

Istanbul, Turkey Resident Office: American Consulate General, DEA / Justice, Unit 5030, Box 0016, DPO AE 09827, 9–011–90–212–335–9179.

Kabul, Afghanistan Country Office: DEA / Justice, American Embassy Kabul, Unit 6180, Box 0062, DPO AE 09806–0062, 301–490–1042.

Kingston, Jamaica Country Office: U.S. Embassy Kingston, 30 Munroe Road, Kingston 6, Jamaica, 9–1–876–702–6004.

Kuala Lumpur, Malaysia Country Office: American Embassy Kuala Lumpur, DEA / Justice, DPO AP 96535–1900, 9–011–603–2168–4957.

Lagos, Nigeria: Department of State, DEA / Justice, 8300 Lagos Place, Washington, DC 20521–8300, 9–011–234–1–460–3440.

La Paz, Bolivia: American Embassy La Paz, DEA / Justice, Unit 3220, DPO AA 34032, 9–011–591–2–216–8313.

Lima, Peru: American Embassy Lima, DEA / Justice, Unit 3230, DPO AA 34031, 9–011–511–618–2475.

London, England: American Embassy London, DEA / Justice, Unit 8400, DPO AE 09498–4008, 9–011–44–207–894–0826.

Madrid, Spain: American Embassy Madrid, DEA/Justice, Unit 8500, Box 0014, DPO AE 09642–8500, 9–011–34–91–587–2280.

Managua, Nicaragua: DEA, American Embassy Nicaragua, 3240 Managua Place, Washington, DC 20521–3240, 9–011–505–252–7217.

Manila, Philippines: American Embassy Manila, DEA/Justice, Unit 8600, Box 1580, DPO AP 96515–1580, 9–011–632–301–2084.

Matamoros, Mexico Resident Office: Matamoros DEA, P.O. Box 9004, Brownsville, TX 78501, 9–011–52–868–149–1285.

Mazatlan, Resident Office: DEA, Mazatlan Resident Office, P.O. Box 9006, Brownsville, TX 78520–0906, 9–011–52–669–982–1775.

Merida, Mexico: U.S. Consulate-Merida, P.O. Box 9003, Brownsville, TX 78520–0903, 9–011–52–999–942–5738.

Mexico City, Mexico: : DEA/Justice, U.S. Embassy Mexico City, P.O. Box 9000, Brownsville, TX 78520, 9–011–52–55–5080–2600.

Milan, Resident Office: American Consulate Milan, DEA/Justice, PSC 833, Box 60–M, FPO AE 09624, 9–011–39–02–2903–5422.

Monterrey, Resident Office: U.S. Consulate General, Monterrey Resident Office, P.O. Box 9002, Brownsville, TX 78520–0902, 9–011–5281–8340–1299.

Moscow, Russia: American Embassy Moscow, DEA/Justice, 5430 Moscow Place, Washington, DC 20521–5430, 9–011–7–495–728–5218.

Nassau: Nassau Country Office, DEA/Justice, American Embassy Nassau, 3370 Nassau Place, Dulles, VA 20189, 9–1–242–322–1700.

New Delhi, India: American Embassy New Delhi, Department of State, 9000 New Delhi Place, Washington, DC 20521, 9–011–91–11–2419–8046.

Nicosia, Cyprus: American Embassy Nicosia, DEA/Justice, Unit 5450, Box 1, DPO AE 09836–0001, 9–011–357–22–393–565.

Nuevo Laredo, Mexico: DEA, Nuevo Laredo Resident Office, P.O. Box 3089, Laredo, TX 78044–3089, 9–011–52–867–714–0512.

Ottawa, Canada: American Embassy Ottawa, DEA/Justice, P.O. Box 35, Ogdensburg, New York 13669, 9–1–613–238–5633.

Panama City, Panama: American Embassy Panama, DEA/Justice, 9100 Panama City Place, Washington, DC 20521–9100, 9–011–507–317–5541.

Paramaribo, Suriname: American Embassy Paramaribo, DEA/Justice, 3390 Paramaribo Place, Dulles, VA 20189–3390, 301–985–8693.

Paris, France: American Embassy Paris, DEA/Justice, Unit 9200 APO AE 09777, 9–011–33–1–4312–2732.

Peshawar, Pakistan: American Consulate Peshawar, DEA/Justice, Unit 62217, APO AE 09812–2217, 9–011–92–91–584–0424/0425.

Port-au-Prince, Haiti: U.S. Department of State, DEA, 3400 Port-au-Prince, Washington, DC 20521, 9–011–509–2–229–8413.

Port of Spain, Trinidad and Tobago: Department of State, DEA/Justice, Port of Spain Country Office, 3410 Port of Spain Place, Dulles, VA 20189, 9–1–868–628–8136.

Pretoria, South Africa: American Embassy Pretoria, Department of State, DEA/Justice, 9300 Pretoria Place, Washington, DC 20189, 9–011–27–10–141–2403.

Quito, Ecuador: DEA/Justice, American Embassy Quito, Unit 5338, APO AA 34039, 9–011–593–22–231–547.

Rangoon, Burma: American Embassy Rangoon, DEA/Justice, Box B, APO AP 96546, 9–011–95–1–536–509.

Rome, Italy: American Embassy Rome, DEA/Justice, Unit 9500, Box 22, DPO AE 09624, 9–011–39–06–4674–2225.

San Jose, Costa Rica: American Embassy San Jose, DEA/Justice, Unit 3440, Box 376, APO AA 34020–0376, 9–011–506–22–20–2433.

San Salvador, El Salvador: American Embassy San Salvador, DEA/Justice, 3450 San Salvador Place, Washington, DC 20521–3450, 9–011–503–2501–2582.

Santa Cruz, Resident Office: DEA/Justice, American Embassy, Unit 3913 (Santa Cruz), APO AA 34032, 9–011–591–332–7153.

Santiago, Chile: DEA/Justice, American Embassy Santiago, Unit 3460, Box 20, DPO AA34033, 9–011–56–2–330–3401.

Santo Domingo, Dominican Republic: American Embassy Santo Domingo, DEA/Justice, Unit 3470, DPO AA 34041, 9–1–809–368–7475.

Sao Paulo, Resident Office: DEA/Justice, U.S. Consulate Sao Paulo, 3110 Sao Paulo Place, Dulles, VA 20189–3110, 301–985–9364.

Seoul, Korea: American Embassy Seoul, DEA/Justice, 9600 Seoul Place, Washington, DC 20521–9600, 9–011–82–2–397–4260.

Singapore: American Embassy Singapore, Unit 4280, Box #30, FPO AP 96507–90030, 9–011–65–6476–9021.

Tashkent: Uzbekistan Country Office, DEA/Justice, 7110 Tashkent Place, Washington, DC 20521, 9–011–998–371–120–8924.

Tegucigalpa, Honduras: American Embassy Tegucigalpa, Tegucigalpa Country Office, Unit 3480, Box 212, DPO AA 34022, 301–985–9321.

Tijuana, Resident Office: DEA, Tijuana Resident Office, P.O. 439039, San Diego, CA 92143–9039, 9–011–619–407–7802.

Tokyo, Japan: American Embassy Tokyo, DEA/Justice, 9800 Tokyo Place, Washington, DC 20521–9800, 9–011–81–3–3224–5452.

Trinidad, Bolivia Resident Office: American Embassy La Paz, DEA/Justice, Unit 3220 TRO, DPO AA 34032, 301–985–9398.

Udorn, Thailand Resident Office: American Embassy (Udorn), Unit 46218, DPO AP 96546, 9–011–66–42–248–1666.

Vancouver Resident Office: DEA ConGen Vancouver, 701 Harrison Avenue, Unit 8200, Blaine, WA 98231, 9–1–604–694–7710.

Vienna, Austria: Vienna Country Office, DEA/Justice, American Embassy, Unit 9900, Box 0013, DPO AE 09701, 9–011–43–1–31339–7551.

Vientiane, Laos: American Embassy Vientiane, DEA/Justice, Unit 8165, Box V, APO AP 96546, 9–011–856–21–219–565.

Warsaw, Poland Country Office: DEA/Justice, American Embassy Warsaw, Unit 5010, DPO AE 09730–5010, 9–011–48–22–504–2043.

ENVIRONMENT AND NATURAL RESOURCES DIVISION

950 Pennsylvania Avenue, NW., Washington, DC 20530 (RFK)

150 M Street, NE., 4 Constitution Square, Washington, DC 20002 (4CON)

Assistant Attorney General.—Jeffrey B. Clark, Room 2143 (202) 514–2701.

Principal Deputy Assistant Attorney General (PDAAG).—Jonathan Brightbill, Room 2603, 514–2766.

Deputy Assistant Attorneys General (DAAG): Bruce Gelber, Room 2609, 514–4624; Eric Grant, Room 2611, 514–0943; Lawrence VanDyke, Room 2607, 305–0312; Jean Williams, Room 2135, 305–0228..

Counsel/Chief of Staff.—Corinne Snow, Room 2133, 514–3370.

Executive Officer.—Andrew Collier (4CON), Room 2.1142, 616–3147.

Section Chiefs:

Appellate.—James C. Kilbourne (RFK), Room 2339, 514–2748.

Environmental Crimes.—Deborah Harris (4CON), Room 4.202, 305–0347.

Environmental Defense.—Letitia J. Grishaw (4CON), Room 4.1102, 514–2219.

Environmental Enforcement.—Tom Mariani (4CON), Room 6.202, 514–4620.

Indian Resources.—Craig Alexander (4CON), Room 3.1142, 514–9080.

Land Acquisition.—Andrew Goldfrank (4CON), Room 5.202, 305–0316.

Law and Policy.—Karen Wardzinski (RFK), Room 2613, 514–0474.

Natural Resources.—Lisa Russell (4CON), Room 3.202, 305–0438.

Wildlife and Marine Resources.—Seth Barsky (4CON), Room 3.1102, 305–0210.

EXECUTIVE OFFICE FOR IMMIGRATION REVIEW (EOIR)

5107 Leesburg Pike, Suite 2600, Falls Church, VA 22041

Director.—James R. McHenry, 2600 SKYT (703) 305–0169.

Deputy Director.—Sirce E. Owen (acting).

Chief of Staff.—Kathryn D. Sheehey.

Senior Counsel to the Director.—Dimple Gupta.

Counsel to the Deputy Director.—Daniel Swanwick.
Executive Secretariat.—Sheaya Thomas.
General Counsel.—Jill Anderson (acting), 2644 SKYT, 305–0470.
Deputy General Counsel.—Jill Anderson.
Chairman, Board of Immigration Appeals.—David L. Neal, 2300 SKYT, 305–1194.
Vice Chairman, Board of Immigration Appeals.—Charles Adkins-Blanch.
Chief Judge, Office of the Chief Immigration Judge.—Christopher A. Santoro (acting), 2401 SKYT, 305–1247.
Deputy Chief Immigration Judges: Christopher A. Santoro (Principal), Mary Cheng, R. Print Maggard.
Chief, Office of the Chief Administrative Hearing Officer.—Robin M. Stutman, 2500 SKYT, 305–0864.
Counsel to the Chief Administrative Hearing Officer.—Elizabeth Vayo.
Assistant Director of Administration.—Lisa Ward, 1900 SKYT, 605–1730.
Deputy Assistant Directors of Administration: James McDaniel, Michael Porter.
Assistant Director for Policy.—Lauren Alder Reid, 2616 SKYT, 305–0701.
Chief Information Officer, Information Technology.—Edward P. So, 970 SKY6, 605–6933.
Deputy Chief Information Officer, Information Technology.—Craig Hegermann.
Telephone Directory Coordinator.—Annette Thomas, 970 SKY6, 605–1336.

EXECUTIVE OFFICE FOR UNITED STATES ATTORNEYS (EOUSA)

950 Pennsylvania Avenue, NW., Room 2245, Washington, DC 20530 (RFK)
175 N Street, NE., 3 Constitution Square, Washington, DC 20002 (3CON)
National Advocacy Center, 1620 Pendleton Street, Columbia, SC 29201 (NAC)

Office of the Director, phone (202) 252–1300

Director, Office of the Director.—Corey F. Ellis (acting), (RFK), Room 2243.
Principal Deputy Director, Office of the Director.—Norman Wong (RFK), Room 2246.
Deputy Director and Chief of Staff, Office of the Director.—Suzanne L. Bell (RFK), Room 2244.
Administrative Operations Liaison, Office of the Director.—Joy Smith (3CON), Room 6.208, 252–5553.
Attorney General's Advisory Committee (AGAC) Liaison and USA Nominations Coordinator, Office of the Director.—Karen Winzenburg (RFK), Room 2248, 252–1374.
Victims' Rights Ombudsman, Office of the Director.—Marie O'Rourke (RFK), Room 2260, 252–1317.
Chief Learning Officer, Office of Legal Education (OLE).—Mark Yancey (NAC), (803) 705–5162.
General Counsel, General Counsel's Office.—Jay Macklin (3CON), Room 5.202, 252–1600.
Assistant Directors:
Asset Recovery Staff, Legal Programs Staff.—Mark Redmiles (3CON), Room 4.206, 252–5879.
Data Integrity and Analysis, Legal Programs Staff.—Will Turner (3CON), Room 4.133, 252–5571.
Equal Employment Opportunity Staff.—Julie Lu (3CON), Room 5.132.
Evaluation and Review Staff.—Richard Durbin (3CON), Room 5.800 (210) 384–7430.
FOIA and Privacy Act Staff.—Kevin Krebs (3CON), Room 5.220, 252–6020.
Strategic Communications Staff.—David Ausiello (RFK), Room 2523, 252–5985.
Indian, Violent and Cyber Crimes Staff, Legal Programs Staff.—John Kuhn (acting), (3CON), Room 4.109, 252–5870.
Chief, Legal Initiatives, Legal Programs Staff.—David Smith (3CON), Room 4.208, 252–1326.
Assistant Director, Victim Witness Staff, Legal Programs Staff.—Kristina Neal (3CON), Room 4.204, 252–5833.
Chief, Legal Programs Staff.—Tammy Reno (3CON), Room 4.1302, 252–5877.
Assistant Director, Audit and Review, Resource Management and Planning.—Louisa McCarter-Dadzie (3CON), Room 6.101, 252–5624.
Assistant Director, Budget Execution, Resource Management and Planning.—Dorjan Short (3CON), 252–5627.

Chief Financial Officer.—Jonathan Pelletier (3CON), Room 6.202, 252–5628.

Assistant Director, Acquisitions Staff.—Stephanie Girard (3CON), Room 6.1316, 252–5407.

Assistant Director, Facilities and Support Services Staff.—Ana Indovina (3CON), Room 6.222, 252–5964.

Chief Information Officer.—Mark Fleshman (3CON), Room 3.202, 252–6246.

Assistant Directors:

Case Management Staff.—Siobhan Sperin (3CON), Room 3.222, 252–6120.

Enterprise Voice over IP (EVoIP).—Joe Pfeifer (3CON), Room 3.1328, 252–4468.

Information Systems Security Staff.—Gregory Hall (3CON), Room 3.139, 252–6090.

Office Automation Staff.—Glenn Shrieves (3CON), Room 2.202, 252–6281.

Records and Information Management Staff.—Siobhan Sperin (acting), (3CON), Room 3.222, 252–6120.

Telecommunications and Technology Development Staff.—Joe Pfeifer (acting), (3CON), Room 2.133, 252–6430.

Managing Attorney, Litigation Technology Service Center.—Marc Fulkert, ITEC (NAC), (803) 705–5422.

Chief Human Resources Officer.—Shawn Flinn (3CON), Room 7.202, 252–5310.

Administrator, Employee Assistance Program.—Ed Neunlist (3CON), Room 5.701, 252–5455.

Assistant Director, Policy and Special Programs Division, Personnel Staff.—Valerie Mulcahy (3CON), Room 7.1302, 252–5357.

Assistant Director, Operations Division, Personnel Staff.—Jewel Campos (3CON), Room 7.208, 252–5355.

Chief, Emergency Management, Security and Emergency Management Staff.—James McAtamney (3CON), Room 2.406, 252–5749.

Assistant Director, Security and Emergency Management Staff.—Timothy George (3CON), Room 2.1302, 252–5694.

EXECUTIVE OFFICE FOR UNITED STATES TRUSTEES

441 G Street, NW., Washington, DC 20530

phone (202) 307–1391, https://usdoj.gov/ust

Director.—Clifford J. White III, Suite 6150.

Deputy Directors:

Field Operations.—William T. Neary (acting), Suite 6150.

General Counsel.—Ramona D. Elliott, Suite 6150, 307–1399.

Management.—Henry Hensley, Suite 6150.

Chief Information Officer.—Barbara A. Brown, 353–8754.

Assistant Director, Office of:

Administration.—Ryan A. Higgins, Suite 6150, 353–3548.

Oversight.—Robert S. Gebhard, Suite 6150, 305–0222.

Planning and Evaluation.—Christopher Haverstock (acting), Suite 6150, 305–7827.

U.S. TRUSTEES

Region I:

Suite 1000, 5 Post Office Square, Boston, MA 02109 (617) 788–0400.

Suite 300, 537 Congress Street, Portland, ME 04101 (207) 780–3564.

14th Floor, Sovereign Tower Building, 446 Main, Worcester, MA 01608 (508) 793–0555.

Suite 2300, 53 Pleasant Street, Concord, NH 03301 (603) 226–3949.

Suite 431, One Exchange Terrace, Providence, RI 02903 (401) 528–5551.

Region II:

Suite 1006, U.S. Federal Building, 201 Varick Street, New York, NY 10014 (212) 510–0500.

Room 620, 11A Clinton Avenue, Albany, NY 12207 (518) 434–4553.

Suite 401, 300 Pearl Street, Buffalo, NY 14202 (716) 551–5541.

Suite 560, Long Island Federal Courthouse, 560 Federal Plaza, Central Islip, NY 11722–4456 (631) 715–7800.

Suite 302, 150 Court Street, New Haven, CT 06510 (203) 773–2210.
Room 609, 100 State Street, Rochester, NY 14614 (585) 263–5812.
Room 105, 10 Broad Street, Utica, NY 13501 (315) 793–8191.

Region III:
Room 229, 900 Market Street, Philadelphia, PA 19107 (215) 597–4411.
Suite 502, 200 Chestnut Street, Philadelphia, PA 19106 (215) 597–4411.
Suite 2100, One Newark Center, Newark, NJ 07102 (973) 645–3014.
Suite 970, 1001 Liberty Avenue, Pittsburgh, PA 15222 (412) 644–4756.
Suite 1190, 228 Walnut Street, Harrisburg, PA 17101 or P.O. Box 969, Harrisburg, PA 17108 (717) 221–4515.
Suite 2207, 844 King Street, Wilmington, DE 19801 (302) 573–6491.

Region IV:
Suite 953, 1835 Assembly Street, Columbia, SC 29201 (803) 765–5250.
Suite 650, 1725 Duke Street, Alexandria, VA 22314 (703) 557–7176.
Room 625, 200 Granby Street, Norfolk, VA 23510 (757) 441–6012.
Room 2025, 300 Virginia Street East, Charleston, WV 25301 (304) 347–3400.
First Campbell Square Building, 210 First Street, SW., Suite 505, Roanoke, VA 24011 (540) 857–2806.
Suite 4304, U.S. Courthouse, 701 East Broad Street, Richmond, VA 23219 (804) 771–2310.
Suite 600, 6305 Ivy Lane, Greenbelt, MD 20770 (301) 344–6216.
Suite 2625, 101 West Lombard Street, Baltimore, MD 21201 (410) 962–4300.

Region V:
Suite 2110, 400 Poydras Street, New Orleans, LA 70130 (504) 589–4018.
Suite 3196, 300 Fannin Street, Shreveport, LA 71101–3099 (318) 676–3456.
Suite 6–430, 501 East Court Street, Jackson, MS 39201 (601) 965–5241.

Region VI:
Room 976, 1100 Commerce Street, Dallas, TX 75242 (214) 767–8967.
Room 300, 110 North College Avenue, Tyler, TX 75702 (903) 590–1450.

Region VII:
Suite 3516, 515 Rusk Street, Houston, TX 77002 (713) 718–4650.
Room 230, 903 San Jacinto, Austin, TX 78701 (512) 916–5328.
Suite 533, 615 East Houston Street, San Antonio, TX 78205 (210) 472–4640.
Suite 1107, 606 North Carancahua Street, Corpus Christi, TX 78401 (361) 888–3261.

Region VIII:
Suite 400, 200 Jefferson Avenue, Memphis, TN 38103 (901) 544–3251.
Suite 512, 601 West Broadway, Louisville, KY 40202 (502) 582–6000.
Fourth Floor, 31 East 11th Street, Chattanooga, TN 37402 (423) 752–5153.
Suite 318, 701 Broadway, Nashville, TN 37203 (615) 736–2254.
Suite 500, 100 East Vine Street, Lexington, KY 40507 (859) 233–2822.

Region IX:
Suite 441, BP Building, 201 Superior Avenue East, Cleveland, OH 44114 (216) 522–7800.
Suite 200, Schaff Building, 170 North High Street, Columbus, OH 43215–2403 (614) 469–7411.
Suite 4–812, 550 Main Street, Cincinnati, OH 45202 (513) 684–6988.
Suite 700, 211 West Fort Street, Detroit, MI 48226 (313) 226–7999.
Suite 200R, 125 Ottawa Street, Grand Rapids, MI 49503 (616) 456–2002.

Region X:
Room 1000, 101 West Ohio Street, Indianapolis, IN 46204 (317) 226–6101.
Suite 1100, 401 Main Street, Peoria, IL 61602 (309) 671–7854.
Suite 555, 100 East Wayne Street, South Bend, IN 46601 (574) 236–8105.

Region XI:
Suite 873, 219 South Dearborn Street, Chicago, IL 60604 (312) 886–5785.
Suite 430, 517 East Wisconsin Avenue, Milwaukee, WI 53202 (414) 297–4499.

Suite 304, 780 Regent Street, Madison, WI 53715 (608) 264–5522.

Region XII:

Suite 2800, 111 Seventh Avenue, SE., Cedar Rapids, IA 52401 (319) 364–2211.

Suite 1015, U.S. Courthouse, 300 S. Fourth Street, Minneapolis, MN 55415 (612) 334–1350.

Room 793, 210 Walnut Street, Des Moines, IA 50309–2108 (515) 284–4982.

Suite 303, 314 South Main Avenue, Sioux Falls, SD 57104 (605) 330–4450.

Region XIII:

Suite 3440, 400 East 9th Street, Kansas City, MO 64106–1910 (816) 512–1940.

Suite 6353, 111 South 10th Street, St. Louis, MO 63102 (314) 539–2976.

Suite 1200, 200 West Capitol Avenue, Little Rock, AR 72201–3344 (501) 324–7357.

Suite 1148, 111 South 18th Plaza, Omaha, NE 68102 (402) 221–4300.

Region XIV:

Suite 204, 230 North First Avenue, Phoenix, AZ 85003 (602) 682–2600.

Region XV:

Suite 3230, 880 Front Street Third Floor, San Diego, CA 92101–8511 (619) 557–5013.

Suite 602, 1132 Bishop Street, Honolulu, HI 96813–2836 (808) 522–8150.

Region XVI:

Suite 1850, 915 Wilshire Boulevard, Los Angeles, CA 90017 (213) 894–6811.

Suite 7160, 411 West Fourth Street, Santa Ana, CA 92701–8000 (714) 338–3400.

Suite 720, 3801 University Avenue, Riverside, CA 92501 (951) 276–6990.

Region XVII:

Suite 5–0153, 450 Golden Gate Avenue, 5th Floor, San Francisco, CA 94102 (415) 705–3300.

Suite 7–500, U.S. Courthouse, 501 I Street, Sacramento, CA 95814–2322 (916) 930–2100.

Suite 1401, 2500 Tulare Street, Fresno, CA 93721 (559) 487–5002.

Oakland Office, Suite #05–0153, 450 Golden Gate Avenue, 5th Floor, San Francisco, CA 94102 (415) 252–2080.

Room 4300, 300 Las Vegas Boulevard South, Las Vegas, NV 89101 (702) 388–6600.

Suite 3009, 300 Booth Street, Reno, NV 89509 (775) 784–5335.

Room 268, 280 South First Street, San Jose, CA 95113 (408) 535–5525.

Region XVIII:

Suite 5103, 700 Stewart Street, Seattle, WA 98101 (206) 553–2000.

Suite 213, 620 Southwest Main Street, Portland, OR 97205 (503) 326–4000.

Suite 220, 720 Park Boulevard, Boise, ID 83712 (208) 334–1300.

Room 593, 920 West Riverside, Spokane, WA 99201 (509) 353–2999.

Suite 204, 301 Central Avenue, Great Falls, MT 59401 (406) 761–8777.

Anchorage Office, Suite 5103, 700 Stewart Street, Seattle, WA 98101 (206) 553–2000.

Suite 1100, 405 East Eighth Avenue, Eugene, OR 97401 (541) 465–6330.

Region XIX:

Suite 12–200, Byron G. Rogers Federal Building, 1961 Stout Street, Denver, CO 80294 (303) 312–7230.

Suite 203, 308 West 21st Street, Cheyenne, WY 82001 (307) 772–2790.

Suite 300, 405 South Main Street, Salt Lake City, UT 84111 (801) 524–5734.

Region XX:

Suite 1150, Epic Center, 301 North Main Street, Wichita, KS 67202 (316) 269–6637.

Suite 112, 421 Gold Street, SW., Albuquerque, NM 87102 (505) 248–6544.

Suite 408, 215 Northwest Dean A. McGee Avenue, Oklahoma City, OK 73102 (405) 231–5950.

Suite 225, 224 South Boulder Avenue, Tulsa, OK 74103 (918) 581–6670.

Region XXI:

Suite 362, 75 Ted Turner Drive, SW., Atlanta, GA 30303 (404) 331–4437.

Suite 301, Edificio Ochoa, 500 Tanca Street, San Juan, PR 00901 (787) 729–7444.

Suite 1204, 51 Southwest First Avenue, Miami, FL 33130 (305) 536–7285.

Suite 725, Johnson Square Business Center, 2 East Bryan Street, Savannah, GA 31401 (912) 652–4112.

Suite 1200, 501 East Polk Street, Tampa, FL 33602 (813) 228–2000.

Suite 302, 440 Martin Luther King Boulevard, Macon, GA 31201 (478) 752–3544.

Suite 128, 110 East Park Avenue, Tallahassee, FL 32301 (850) 942–1660.

Suite 1101, George C. Young Federal Building and Courthouse, 400 West Washington Street, Orlando, FL 32801 (407) 648–6301.

FEDERAL BUREAU OF INVESTIGATION

J. Edgar Hoover Building

935 Pennsylvania Avenue, NW., Washington, DC 20535–0001

phone (202) 324–3000, https://fbi.gov

Director.—Christopher A. Wray, 324–6500.
Deputy Director.—David Bowdich, 324–3316.
Associate Deputy Director.—Paul M. Abbate, 324–0308.
Chief of Staff.—Paul B. Murphy, 324–6500.
Deputy Chief of Staff.—Brandon Long, 324–6500.

OFFICE OF THE DIRECTOR / DEPUTY DIRECTOR / ASSOCIATE DEPUTY DIRECTOR

Office of:
General Counsel.—Jason A. Jones, 324–6810.
Congressional Affairs.—Jill C. Tyson, 324–5051.
Equal Employment Opportunity Affairs.—Vacant, 324–4128.
Ombudsman.—Monique Bookstein, 324–2156.
Partner Engagement.—George P. Beach II, 324–7126.
Professional Responsibility.—L. Stuart Platt, 436–7444.
Public Affairs.—Brian Hale, 324–5354.
Finance and Facilities Division.—David W. Schlendorf, 324–1345.
Information Management Division.—Arlene A. Gaylord (540) 678–7400.
Inspection Division.—Douglas A. Leff, 324–2901.
Resource Planning Office.—Caroline Otto, 324–2211.

INFORMATION AND TECHNOLOGY BRANCH

Executive Assistant Director.—Richard Haley II, 324–3907.
IT Applications and Data Division.—Michael T. Gavin, 323–5197.
IT Enterprise Services Division: Kathleen T. Mills, 324–7209; Dennis Rice, 323–0796.
IT Infrastructure Division.—Dean Phillips, 324–4507.

CRIMINAL, CYBER, RESPONSE, AND SERVICES BRANCH

Executive Assistant Director.—Terry Wade, 324–4180.
Assistant Director of:
Criminal Investigative Division.—Calvin Shivers, 324–4260.
Critical Incident Response Group.—John Selleck (703) 632–4100.
Cyber Division.—Frankland ''Matt'' M. Gorham, 324–7770.
International Operations Division.—Charles P. Spencer, 324–5904.
Office of Victim Assistance.—Regina E. Thompson, 324–1339.

HUMAN RESOURCES BRANCH

Executive Assistant Director.—Jeffrey Sallet, 324–3036.
Assistant Director of:
Human Resources Division.—Hayden Temin, 324–3514.
Security Division.—Larissa Knapp, 203–1702.
Training and Development Division.—Renee McDermott (703) 632–1100.

NATIONAL SECURITY BRANCH

Executive Assistant Director.—John A. Brown, 324–7045.

Assistant Director of:

Counterintelligence Division.—Alan Kohler, 324–4614.

Counterterrorism Division.—Jill Sanborn, 324–2770.

Weapons of Mass Destruction Directorate.—Don Alway, 324–4985.

SCIENCE AND TECHNOLOGY BRANCH

Executive Assistant Director.—Darrin Jones, 324–0805.

Assistant Director of:

Criminal Justice Information Services Division.—Michael D. DeLeon (304) 625–2700.

Laboratory Division.—G. "Gurvais" Clayton Grigg (703) 632–7002.

Operational Technology Division.—Brian Turner (703) 985–6010.

INTELLIGENCE BRANCH

Executive Assistant Director.—Stephen C. Laycock, 324–7705.

Assistant Director of Directorate of Intelligence.—Ryan Young, 324–7605.

FIELD DIVISIONS

Albany: 200 McCarty Avenue, Albany, NY 12209 (518) 465–7551.

Albuquerque: 4200 Luecking Park Avenue, NE., Albuquerque, NM 87107 (505) 224–2000.

Anchorage: 101 East 6th Avenue, Anchorage, AK 99501 (907) 258–5322.

Atlanta: 2635 Century Center Parkway, NE., Suite 400, Atlanta, GA 30345 (404) 679–9000.

Baltimore: 2600 Lord Baltimore Avenue, Baltimore, MD 21244 (410) 265–8080.

Birmingham: 1000 18th Street North, Birmingham, AL 35203 (205) 326–6166.

Boston: 201 Maple Street, Chelsea, MA 02150 (617) 742–5533.

Buffalo: 68–94 South Elwood Avenue, Buffalo, NY 14202 (716) 856–7800.

Charlotte: 7915 Microsoft Way, Charlotte, NC 28273 (704) 377–9200.

Chicago: 2111 West Roosevelt Road, Chicago, IL 60608–1128 (312) 431–1333.

Cincinnati: 2012 Ronald Reagan Drive, Cincinnati, OH 45236 (513) 421–4310.

Cleveland: 1501 Lakeside Avenue, Cleveland, OH 44114 (216) 522–1400.

Columbia: 151 Westpark Boulevard, Columbia, SC 29210 (803) 551–4200.

Dallas: J. Gordon Shanklin Building, One Justice Way, Dallas, TX 75220 (972) 559–5000.

Denver: Federal Office Building, 8000 East 36th Avenue, Denver, CO 80238 (303) 629–7171.

Detroit: P.V. McNamara Federal Office Building, 477 Michigan Avenue, 26th Floor, Detroit, MI 48226 (313) 965–2323.

El Paso: 660 South Mesa Hills Drive, Suite 3000, El Paso, TX 79912 (915) 832–5000.

Honolulu: Kalanianaole Federal Office Building, 91 Enterprise Avenue, Honolulu, HI 96850 (808) 566–4300.

Houston: 1 Justice Park Drive, Houston, TX 77092 (713) 693–5000.

Indianapolis: Federal Office Building, 8825 Nelson B Klein Parkway, Indianapolis, IN 46250 (371) 639–3301.

Jackson: Federal Office Building, 1220 Echelon Parkway, Jackson, MS 39213 (601) 948–5000.

Jacksonville: 6061 Gate Parkway, Jacksonville, FL 32256 (904) 721–1211.

Kansas City: 1300 Summit, Kansas City, MO 64105 (816) 512–8200.

Knoxville: John J. Duncan Federal Office Building, 1501 Dowell Springs Boulevard, Knoxville, TN 37909 (423) 544–0751.

Las Vegas: John Lawrence Bailey Building, 1787 West Lake Mead Boulevard, Las Vegas, NV 89106–2135 (702) 385–1281.

Little Rock: 24 Shackleford West Boulevard, Little Rock, AR 72211 (501) 221–9100.

Los Angeles: Federal Office Building, 11000 Wilshire Boulevard, Suite 1700, Los Angeles, CA 90024 (310) 477–6565.

Louisville: 12401 Sycamore Station Place, Louisville, KY 40299 (502) 583–2941.

Memphis: Eagle Crest Building, 225 North Humphreys Boulevard, Suite 3000, Memphis, TN 38120 (901) 747–4300.

Miami: 2030 Southwest 145th Avenue, Miami, FL 33027 (305) 944–9101.

Milwaukee: 3600 South Lake Drive, Milwaukee, WI 53235 (414) 276–4684.

Minneapolis: 1501 Freeway Boulevard, Brooklyn Center, MN 55430 (612) 376–3200.

Mobile: 200 North Royal Street, Mobile, AL 36602 (334) 438–3674.

New Haven: 600 State Street, New Haven, CT 06511 (203) 777–6311.

New Orleans: 2901 Leon C. Simon Boulevard, New Orleans, LA 70126 (504) 816–3122.

New York: 26 Federal Plaza, 23rd Floor, New York, NY 10278 (212) 384–1000.
Newark: Claremont Tower Building, 11 Centre Street, Newark, NJ 07102 (973) 792–3000.
Norfolk: 509 Resource Road, Chesapeake Beach, VA 23320 (757) 455–0100.
Oklahoma City: 3301 West Memorial, Oklahoma City, OK 73134 (405) 290–7770.
Omaha: 4411 South 121st Court, Omaha, NE 68137 (402) 493–8688.
Philadelphia: William J. Green, Jr. Federal Office Building, 600 Arch Street, 9th Floor, Philadelphia, PA 19106 (215) 418–4000.
Phoenix: 21711 North 7th Street, Phoenix, AZ 85024 (602) 279–5511.
Pittsburgh: Martha Dixon Building, 3311 East Carson Street, Pittsburgh, PA 15203 (412) 432–4000.
Portland: 9109 Northeast Cascades Parkway, Portland, OR 97220 (503) 224–4181.
Richmond: 1970 East Parham Road, Richmond, VA 23228 (804) 261–1044.
Sacramento: 2001 Freedom Way, Roseville, CA 95678 (916) 481–9110.
Salt Lake City: 5425 West Amelia Earhart Drive, Salt Lake City, UT 84116 (801) 579–1400.
San Antonio: 5740 University Heights Boulevard, San Antonio, TX 78249 (210) 225–6741.
San Diego: Federal Office Building, 10385 Vista Sorrento Parkway, San Diego, CA 92121 (858) 565–1255.
San Francisco: 450 Golden Gate Avenue, 13th Floor, San Francisco, CA 64102 (415) 553–7400.
San Juan: U.S. Federal Office Building, 150 Carlos East Chardon Avenue, Room 526, Hato Rey, PR 00918 (787) 754–6000.
Seattle: 1110 3rd Avenue, Seattle, WA 98101 (206) 622–0460.
Springfield: 900 East Linton Avenue, Springfield, IL 62703 (217) 522–9675.
St. Louis: 2222 Market Street, St. Louis, MO 63103 (314) 241–5357.
Tampa: 5525 West Gray Street, Tampa, FL 33609 (813) 273–4566.
Washington, DC: 601 4th Street, NW., Washington, DC 20535 (202) 278–3400.

FEDERAL BUREAU OF PRISONS (BOP)

320 First Street, NW., Washington, DC 20534

General Information Number (202) 307–3198

Director.—Michael Carvajal, Room 654, HOLC, 307–3250.
Deputy Director.—Thomas R. Kane, Room 654, HOLC, 307–3250.
Director, National Institute of Corrections.—Vacant, 2nd Floor, 500 First Street, 514–4202.
Assistant Director of:
Administration.—Bradley T. Gross, 901 D Street, SW., 307–3230.
Correctional Programs.—Andre Matevousian, Room 554, HOLC, 307–3226.
Federal Prison Industries.—Patrick T. O'Connor, 8th Floor, 400 FRST, 305–3501.
General Counsel.—Ken Hyle, Room 958C, HOLC, 307–3062.
Health Services.—N. C. English, Room 454, HOLC, 307–3055.
Human Resources Management.—L. Cristina Griffith, Room 754, HOLC, 307–3082.
Information, Policy, and Public Affairs.—Sonya D. Thompson (acting), Room 670, HOLC, 514–6537.
Program Review.—Vacant, Room 1054, HOLC, 307–1076.
Regional Director for—
Mid-Atlantic.—Darrin Harmon (301) 317–3101.
North Central.—Jeffrey E. Krueger (913) 551–1000.
Northeast.—J. Ray Ormond (215) 521–7300.
South Central.—J. Baltazar (972) 730–8800.
Southeast.—Jeff Keller (678) 686–1200.
Western.—Gene Beasley (209) 956–9700.
Telephone Directory Coordinator.—Marla Clayton, 307–3250.

FOREIGN CLAIMS SETTLEMENT COMMISSION

Government Accountability Office Building

441 G Street, NW., Room 6232, Washington, DC 20579

phone (202) 616–6975

Chair.—Vacant.
Commissioners: Sylvia M. Becker, Patrick Hovakimian.
Chief Counsel.—Brian M. Simkin.
Chief Administrative Counsel.—Jeremy R. LaFrancois.

OFFICE OF INFORMATION POLICY

1425 New York Avenue, NW., Suite 11050, Washington, DC 20530

phone (202) 514–3642

Director.—Bobby Talebian (acting).
Chief of Staff.—Sean O'Neill (acting).

OFFICE OF THE INSPECTOR GENERAL

950 Pennsylvania Avenue, NW., Room 4706, Washington, DC 20530

phone (202) 514–3435

Inspector General.—Michael E. Horowitz.
Deputy Inspector General.—William M. Blier.
Senior Counsel to the Inspector General: John S. Lavinsky, Rene R. Lee.
Counsel to the Inspector General: Adam Miles, Karen Rich.
General Counsel.—Jonathan M. Malis (RFK), Suite 4726 (202) 616–0646.
Assistant Inspectors General:
Audit.—Jason R. Malmstrom (4CON), 12th Floor, 616–1697.
Evaluations and Inspections.—Nina Pelletier (4CON), 11th Floor, 616–4620.
Investigations.—Sarah Lake (4CON), 12th Floor, 616–4760.
Management and Planning.—Gregory T. Peters (4CON), 11th Floor, 616–4550.
Oversight and Review.—M. Sean O'Neill (4CON), 12th Floor, 616–0645.

REGIONAL AUDIT OFFICES

Atlanta: Ferris B. Polk, Suite 1130, 75 Spring Street, Atlanta, GA 30303 (404) 331–5928.

Chicago: Carol S. Taraszka, Suite 3510, Citicorp Center, 500 West Madison Street, Chicago, IL 60661 (312) 353–1203.

Dallas: Fletcher Couglas, Suite 410, Box 21, 2505 State Highway 360, Grand Prairie, TX 75050 (214) 655–5000.

Denver: David M. Sheeren, Suite 1500, Chancery Building, 1120 Lincoln Street, Denver, CO 80203 (303) 864–2000.

Philadelphia: Thomas O. Puerzer, Suite 201, 701 Market Street, Philadelphia, PA 19106 (215) 580–2111.

San Francisco: David J. Gaschke, Suite 201, 1200 Bayhill Drive, San Bruno, CA 94066 (650) 876–9220.

Washington: John Manning, 1300 North 17th Street, Suite 3400, Arlington, VA 22209 (202) 616–4688.

Computer Security and Information Technology Audit Office: Reginald Allen, Room 5000 (202) 616–3801.

Financial Statement Audit Office: Mark L. Hayes, 1425 New York Avenue, NW., #13000, Washington, DC 20530 (202) 616–4660.

REGIONAL INVESTIGATIONS OFFICES

Atlanta: Eddie D. Davis, 60 Forsyth Street, SW., Room 8M45, Atlanta, GA 30303 (404) 562–1980.

Boston: Daniel Benedict, U.S. Courthouse, 1 Courthouse Way, Room 9200, Boston, MA 02210 (617) 748–3218.

Chicago: John F. Oleskowicz, P.O. Box 1802, Chicago, IL 60690 (312) 886–7050.

Denver: Sandra D. Barnes, Suite 1501, 1120 Lincoln Street, Denver, CO 80203 (303) 335–4201.

Dallas: Monte A. Cason, 2505 State Highway 360, Room 410, Grand Prairie, TX 75050 (817) 385–5200.

Detroit: Nicholas V. Candela, Suite 1402, 211 West Fort Street, Detroit, MI 48226 (313) 226–4005.

El Paso: Eric Benn, Suite 135, 4050 Rio Bravo, El Paso, TX 79902 (915) 577–0102.

Houston: Douglas B. Bruce, P.O. Box 53509, Houston, TX 77052 (713) 718–4888.

Los Angeles: James K. Cheng, Suite 655, 330 North Brand Street, Glendale, CA 91203 (818) 543–1172.

Miami: Robert Allen Bourbon, Suite 200, 510 Shotgun Road, Sunrise, FL 33326 (954) 370–8300.

New York: Ronald Gardella, One Battery Park Plaza, 29th Floor, New York, NY 10004 (212) 824–3650.

New Jersey: Kenneth R. Connaughton, Jr., 361 Scotch Road, West Trenton, NJ 08628 (609) 883–5423.

San Francisco: Michael Barranti, Suite 220, 1200 Bayhill Drive, San Bruno, CA 94066 (650) 876–9058.

Seattle: Wayne Hawney, Suite 104, 620 Kirkland Way, Kirkland, WA 98033 (253) 852–0194.

Tucson: James Greer, 405 West Congress, Room 3600, Tucson, AZ 85701 (520) 620–7389.

Washington: Michael P. Tompkins, 1425 New York Avenue, NW., Suite 7100, Washington, DC 20530 (202) 616–4760.

Fraud Detection Office.—Lewe F. Sessions, Room 7100 (202) 353–2975.

INTERPOL WASHINGTON (U.S. NATIONAL CENTRAL BUREAU)

phone (202) 616–9000

Director.—Wayne H. Salzgaber, 532–4239.

Deputy Director.—Michael A. Hughes, 616–1071.

General Counsel.—Kevin Smith, 616–4103.

Public and Congressional Affairs Officer.—Christie Dawson, 305–8602.

JUSTICE MANAGEMENT DIVISION

950 Pennsylvania Avenue, NW., Washington, DC 20530 (RFK)

145 N Street, NE., 2 Constitution Square, Washington, DC 20530 (2CON)

Liberty Square Building, 450 5th Street, NW., Washington, DC 20001 (LSB)

Assistant Attorney General for Administration.—Lee J. Lofthus, Room 1111 (202) 514–3101.

Deputy Assistant Attorney General, Policy, Management and Planning.—Michael H. Allen, Room 1113, 514–3101.

Staff Directors:

Department Ethics Office.—Cindy Shaw (2CON), Room 8E.310, 514–8196.

Facilities and Administrative Services Staff.—Scott Snell (2CON), Room 9E.204, 616–2995.

General Counsel Office.—Arthur Gary, General Counsel (2CON), Room 8E.528, 514–3452.

Internal Review and Evaluation Office.—Neil Ryder (2CON), Room 8W.1419, 616–5499.

Office of Small and Disadvantaged Business Utilization.—Robert Connolly (2CON), Room 8E.1009, 616–0521.

Deputy Director/Procurement Services Staff.—Thomas Naccarato, Room 8E.202, 307–2000.

Records Management Policy Office.—Jeanette Plante (2CON), Room 8W.1401, 514–3528.

Senior Procurement Executive.—Michael H. Allen, Room 1113, 514–3101.

Deputy Assistant Attorney General/Controller.—Jolene Lauria, Room 1117, 514–1843.

Staff Directors:

Asset Forfeiture Management.—Vacant (2CON), Room 5W.725, 616–8000.

Budget Staff.—Linda Smith, Room 2732, 514–4082.

Debt Collection Management.—Dennis Dauphin (2CON), Room 5E.103, 514–5343.

Finance.—Chris Alvarez (2CON), Room 7E.202, 616–5800.

Deputy Assistant Attorney General, Human Resources and Administration.—Monty Wilkinson, Room 1112, 514–5501.

Staff Directors:

Attorney Recruitment and Management Office.—Vacant (LSB), Suite 10200, 514–3905.

Consolidated Executive Office.—Cyntoria Carter, Room 7113, 514–5537.

DOJ Executive Secretariat.—Dana Paige, Room 4412, 514–2063.

Equal Employment Opportunity.—Richard Toscano (2CON), Room 1W.102, 616–4800.

Human Resources Staff.—Mary Lamary (2CON), Room 9W.102, 514–6788.

Library.—Dennis Feldt, Room 7535, 514–2133.

Security and Emergency Planning Staff.—James Dunlap, Room 6217, 514–2094.

Deputy Assistant Attorney General, Information Resources Management/CIO.—Joseph Klimavicz, Room 1310–A, 514–0507.

Deputy CIO.—Melinda Rogers, Room 1310, 514–7017.
Staff Directors:
Cyber Security Services Staff.—Nickolous Ward (2CON), Room 4E.206, 616–2478.
Policy and Planning.—Cynthia Sjoberg-Radway (2CON), Room 3E.202, 616–6050.
Service Delivery Staff.—Lawrence Reed (acting), (2CON), Room 4E.101, 305–9673.

OFFICE OF JUSTICE PROGRAMS (OJP)

810 7th Street, NW., Washington, DC 20531

OFFICE OF THE ASSISTANT ATTORNEY GENERAL

Assistant Attorney General.—Vacant (202) 307–5933.
Principal Deputy Assistant Attorney General.—Katherine T. Sullivan, 307–5933.
Deputy Assistant Attorney General.—Maureen Henneberg, 307–5933.
Manager, Equal Employment Opportunity.—Laura Colón-Marrero (202) 616–1998.

BUREAU OF JUSTICE ASSISTANCE

Director.—Michael Costigan (acting), 616–6500.
Principal Deputy Director.—Tracey Trautman, 616–6500.
Deputy Director of:
Policy.—Silas Darden, 616–6500.
Programs.—Kristen Mahoney, 616–6500.

BUREAU OF JUSTICE STATISTICS

Director.—Jeffrey Anderson (202) 307–0765.
Principal Deputy Director, Statistical Operations.—Vacant, 307–0765.
Deputy Directors: Doris James, 307–0765; Jinney Smith, 307–1594.

NATIONAL INSTITUTE OF JUSTICE

Director.—David Muhlhausen, 307–2942.
Principal Deputy Director.—Vacant.
Chief of Staff.—Jennifer Scherer, 307–2942.

OFFICE OF JUVENILE JUSTICE AND DELINQUENCY PREVENTION

Administrator.—Caren Harp, 307–1464.
Deputy Administrator.—Chyrl Y. Jones, 353–0798.

OFFICE FOR VICTIMS OF CRIME

Director.—Jessica Hart, 307–5983.
Principal Deputy Director.—Vacant.
Senior Advisor for Human Trafficking.—Bill Woolf, 307–5983.

OFFICE OF ADMINISTRATION

Director.—Phillip K. Merkle, 307–0087.
Deputy Director, Division of:
Acquisition Management.—Christopher Henshaw, 307–0087.
Business Resources.—Angela Noel Gantt, 305–8006.
Human Resources.—Jennifer McCarthy, 307–0730.

OFFICE OF AUDIT, ASSESSMENT, AND MANAGEMENT

Director.—Ralph Martin, 305–1802.
Deputy Director, Division of:
Audit and Review Division.—Jeff Haley, 616–2936.
Grants Management Division.—Maria Swineford, 616–0109.

Program Assessment Division.—Kathleen Mantila, 514–5185.

OFFICE OF THE CHIEF FINANCIAL OFFICER

Chief Financial Officer.—Leigh Benda, 307–0623.
Deputy Chief Financial Officer.—Rachel Johnson, 307–0623.

OFFICE OF THE CHIEF INFORMATION OFFICER

Chief Information Officer.—Brian McGrath, 305–9071.
Deputy Chief Information Officer.—David Todd, 616–1611.

OFFICE FOR CIVIL RIGHTS

Director.—Michael Alston, 307–0690.
Deputy Directors: Tammie Gregg, 616–4627; Allesandro Terenzoni, 616–1708.

OFFICE OF COMMUNICATIONS

Director.—Vacant, 307–0703.
Deputy Director.—Robert Davis, 307–0703.

OFFICE OF THE GENERAL COUNSEL

General Counsel.—Rafael A. Madan, 307–6235.
Deputy General Counsel: Rosemary Carradini, 616–3257; Rhonda Craig, 616–3233; Charlotte Grzebien, 307–2986; Matthew Scodellaro, 305–8219.

OFFICE OF SEX OFFENDER SENTENCING, MONITORING, APPREHENDING, REGISTERING, AND TRACKING

Director.—Kendel Ehrlich, 307–0886.
Deputy Director.—Dawn Doran, 514–4689.

OFFICE OF LEGAL COUNSEL

950 Pennsylvania Avenue, NW., Room 5218, Washington, DC 20530

phone (202) 514–2051

Assistant Attorney General.—Steven A. Engel, Room 5218, 514–2051.
Principal Deputy Assistant Attorney General.—Curtis Gannon, Room 5218, 514–4132.
Deputy Assistant Attorneys General: Liam Hardy, Room 5235; Daniel Koffsky, Room 5238, 514–2030; Jennifer Mascott, Room 5229; Henry Whitaker, Room 5231 (202) 305–8521.
Special Counsel: Paul P. Colborn, Room 5240, 514–2048; Rosemary Hart, Room 5242, 514–2027.
Senior Counsel.—Jeffrey Singdahlsen, Room 5262, 514–4174.

OFFICE OF LEGAL POLICY

950 Pennsylvania Avenue, NW., Room 4234, Washington, DC 20530

phone (202) 514–4601

Assistant Attorney General.—Beth A. Williams, Room 4230, 514–0624.
Principal Deputy Assistant Attorney General.—Mark Champoux, Room 4238, 514–6131.
Deputy Assistant Attorneys General: Vacant, Room 4511, 514–2456; Kevin Jones, Room 4248, 514–4604; Vacant, Room 4240, 305–4870; Robyn Thiemann, Room 4237, 514–8356.
Chief of Staff.—Katherine Crytzer, Room 4228, 353–3069.
Executive Officer.—Matrina Matthews, Room 4517, 616–0040.

OFFICE OF LEGISLATIVE AFFAIRS (OLA)

950 Pennsylvania Avenue, NW., Room 1145, Washington, DC 20530

phone (202) 514–2141

Assistant Attorney General.—Stephen E. Boyd.
Principal Deputy Assistant Attorney General.—Prim Escalona.
Deputy Assistant Attorney General.—Mary Blanche Hankey.
Chief of Staff and Counsel.—Mary Blanche Hankey.

NATIONAL SECURITY DIVISION

950 Pennsylvania Avenue, NW., Room 7339, Washington, DC 20530

phone (202) 514–1057

Assistant Attorney General.—John C. Demers.
Principal Deputy Assistant Attorney General.—David P. Burns.
Chief of Staff.—Kelli A. Andrews.
Deputy Assistant Attorneys General: Adam Hickey, Melissa MacTough, George Toscas, Brad Wiegmann.
Executive Officer.—Scott Damelin.

COUNTERINTELLIGENCE AND EXPORT CONTROL SECTION

950 Pennsylvania Avenue, NW., 6th Floor, Washington, DC 20530

phone (202) 233–0986

Chief.—Jay Bratt.

COUNTERTERRORISM SECTION

950 Pennsylvania Avenue, NW., 7th Floor, Washington, DC 20530

phone (202) 514–0849

Chief.—Jennifer Smith.

FOREIGN INVESTMENT REVIEW SECTION

175 N Street, NW., Washington, DC 20001

phone (202) 622–1860

Chief.—Sanchitha Jayaram.

OFFICE OF INTELLIGENCE

950 Pennsylvania Avenue, NW., 6th Floor, Washington, DC 20530

phone (202) 514–5600

Chief, Litigation.—John Scully.
Chief, Operations.—Gabrielle Sanz-Rexach.
Chief, Oversight.—Kevin O'Connor.

OFFICE OF LAW AND POLICY

950 Pennsylvania Avenue, NW., 6th Floor, Washington, DC 20530

phone (202) 353–4542

Chief, Policy.—Chris Hardee.
Chief, Appellate.—Steven Dunne.

OFFICE OF JUSTICE FOR VICTIMS OF OVERSEAS TERRORISM

175 N Street, NW., Washington, DC 20001

phone (202) 233–0701

Director.—Heather Cartwright.

OFFICE OF THE PARDON ATTORNEY

145 N Street, NE., 2 Constitution Square, Washington, DC 20530

phone (202) 616–6070

Pardon Attorney.—Vacant.
Deputy Pardon Attorney.—Rosalind Sargent-Burns.
Executive Officer.—William Taylor II.

OFFICE OF PROFESSIONAL RESPONSIBILITY

950 Pennsylvania Avenue, NW., Room 3266, Washington, DC 20530

phone (202) 514–3365

Director and Chief Counsel.—Jeffrey Ragsdale.
Deputy Counsel.—G. Bradley Weinsheimer.
Senior Associate Counsel.—William J. Birney.
Associate Counsel: Raymond C. ''Neil'' Hurley, Margaret McCarty.
Senior Counsel.—Lyn Hardy.
Senior Assistant Counsel: Suzanne Drouet, Frederick Leiner, Mark Masling.
Assistant Counsel: Allison Barlotta, Sarah Cable, Paul Colby, Leonard Evans, Mark G. Fraase, John ''Jack'' Geise, Gregory Gonzalez, Albert Herring, John Sciortino, James Vargason, Barbara Ward.

PROFESSIONAL RESPONSIBILITY ADVISORY OFFICE

1425 New York Avenue, NW., Washington, DC 20530

phone (202) 514–0458

Director.—Stacy M. Ludwig.
Deputy Director.—Benjamin K. Grimes.

OFFICE OF PUBLIC AFFAIRS

950 Pennsylvania Avenue, NW., Room 1220, Washington, DC 20530

phone (202) 514–2007

Director.—Kerri Kupec.
Principal Deputy Director.—Matt Lloyd.
Deputy Director.—Wyn Hornbuckle.

TAX DIVISION

950 Pennsylvania Avenue, NW., Washington, DC 20530 (RFK)

Judiciary Center Building, 555 Fourth Street, NW., Washington, DC 20001 (JCB)

Maxus Energy Tower, 7717 North Harwood Street, Suite 400, Dallas, TX 75242 (MAX)

145 M Street, NE., 4 Constitution Square, Washington, DC 20002 (4CON)

Assistant Attorney General.—Vacant (RFK), Room 4137 (202) 514–2901.
Deputy Assistant Attorneys General:
Appellate and Review.—Travis A. Greaves (RFK), Room 4607, 514–5109.
Civil Matters.—David A. Hubbert (RFK), Room 4137, 514–1958.
Criminal Matters.—Richard E. Zuckerman (Principal), (RFK), Room 4603, 514–2901.
Policy and Planning.—T. Joshua Wu (RFK), Room 4611, 305–3108.

Senior Legislative Counsel.—Eileen M. Shatz (RFK), Room 4134, 307–6419.
Civil Trial Section Chiefs:
Central Region.—R. Scott Clarke (JCB), Room 8921–B, 514–6502.
Eastern Region.—Deborah S. Meland (JCB), Room 6126, 307–6426.
Northern Region.—David M. Katinsky (JCB), Room 7804–A, 307–6435.
Southern Region.—Angelo A. Frattarelli (JCB), Room 6243–A, 307–6612.
Southwestern Region.—Cynthia Messersmith (MAX), Suite 400 (214) 880–9721.
Western Region.—Richard R. Ward (JCB), Room 7907–B, 307–6413.
Criminal Enforcement Section Chiefs:
Northern Region.—Vacant (PHB), Room 7802, 514–5150.
Southern Region.—Karen Kelly (4CON), Room 1.903 , 616–3864.
Western Region.—Larry J. Wszalek (4CON), Room 2.101, 514–5762.
Section Chiefs:
Appellate.—Francesca Ugolini (RFK), Room 4326, 514–3361.
Court of Federal Claims.—David I. Pincus (JCB), Room 8804–A, 307–6440.
Criminal Appeals and Tax Enforcement Policy.—S. Robert ''Bob'' Lyons (4CON), Room 2.220, 514–2839.
Office of Review.—Ann Carroll Reid (JCB), Room 6846–D, 514–6567.
Executive Officer.—Robert L. Bruffy (4CON), Room 1.1629, 616–8412.

UNITED STATES MARSHALS SERVICE (USMS)

Washington, DC 22202

Communications Center (202) 307–9100

Director.—Donald W. Washington (703) 740–1600.
Deputy Director.—Derrick Driscoll, 740–1600.
Chief of Staff.—John Kilgallon, 740–1642.
Chief of District Affairs.—Brent Browshow (acting), 740–1664.
Associate Director for Administration.—Katherine T. Mohan, 740–1618.
Associate Director for Operations.—Nelson Hackmaster, 740–8402.
Chief, Office of Congressional and Public Affairs.—William Delaney, 740–1603.

OFFICE OF EQUAL EMPLOYMENT OPPORTUNITY

Equal Employment Opportunity Officer.—Marcus Williams.

OFFICE OF THE GENERAL COUNSEL

General Counsel.—Gerald M. Auerbach.
Deputy General Counsel.—Lisa Dickinson.

OFFICE OF PROFESSIONAL RESPONSIBILITY

Assistant Director.—Stanley Griscavage (acting).
Deputy Assistant Director.—Ronald Carter (acting).

JUDICIAL SECURITY DIVISION

Assistant Director.—Darrell White.
Deputy Assistant Directors: Jose Soto, Larry Moltzan.

INVESTIGATIVE OPERATIONS DIVISION

Assistant Director.—Jeffrey R. Tyler.
Deputy Assistant Directors: Richard Kelly, Andrew Smith.

PRISONER OPERATIONS DIVISION

Assistant Director.—John ''Jack'' Sheehan (acting).
Deputy Assistant Directors.—Paul Detar, Aaron Sawyer (acting).

JUSTICE PRISONER AND ALIEN TRANSPORTATION SYSTEM (JPATS)

1251 Northwest Briar Cliff Parkway, Suite 300, Kansas City, MO 64116

Assistant Director.—Shannon Brown.
Deputy Assistant Director.—Harry Little (acting).

ASSET FORFEITURE DIVISION

Assistant Director.—Timothy Virtue.
Deputy Assistant Director.—Pam Bass.

WITNESS SECURITY DIVISION

Assistant Director.—Donald P. O'Hearn.
Deputy Assistant Director.—Marcus Walker.

TACTICAL OPERATIONS DIVISION

Assistant Director.—Heather Walker (acting).
Deputy Assistant Director.—Marty Hunt (acting).

FINANCIAL SERVICES DIVISION

Chief Financial Officer.—Holley O'Brien.
Deputy Assistant Director.—Mary Ellen Kline.
Procurement Executive.—Carole O'Brien.

HUMAN RESOURCES DIVISION

Assistant Director.—Dianne Campbell.
Deputy Assistant Director.—Beth Brown-Ghee.

INFORMATION TECHNOLOGY DIVISION

Assistant Director.—Karl Mathias.
Deputy Assistant Director.—Gwendolyn Miller.

MANAGEMENT SUPPORT DIVISION

Assistant Director.—Kate Hickman.
Deputy Assistant Director.—Jim Murphy.

TRAINING DIVISION

Federal Law Enforcement Training Center, Building 20, Glynco, GA 31524

Assistant Director.—Roberto Robinson.
Deputy Assistant Director.—Stephanie Creasy.

U.S. PAROLE COMMISSION

90 K Street, NE., 3rd Floor, Washington, DC 20530

phone (202) 346–7000, fax (202) 357–1085

Chair.—Patricia K. Cushwa (acting).
Vice Chair.—Charles T. Massarone (acting).
Commissioners: Patricia K. Cushwa, Charles T. Massarone.
Chief of Staff.—James E. Bacchus.
Case Operations Administrator.—Stephen J. Husk.
Case Services Administrator.—Deirdre M. McDaniel.
General Counsel.—Helen H. Krapels.
Executive Officer.—Zelia M. Carter.
Staff Assistant to the Chair.—Jacquelyn E. Graham.

OFFICE ON VIOLENCE AGAINST WOMEN (OVW)

145 N Street, NE., Suite 10W.121, Washington, DC 20530

Director.—Laura L. Rogers (acting), (202) 307–6026.
Principal Deputy Director.—Laura L. Rogers, 307–6026.
General Counsel.—Jennifer E. Kaplan, 514–0052.
Deputy Director, Tribal Affairs.—Sherriann C. Moore, 514–8804.
Deputy Director, Grant Development and Management.—Nadine M. Neufville, 307–6026
Executive Officer.—Sybil N. Barksdale, 353–7378.
Chief Financial Officer.—Vacant, 353–3982.

DEPARTMENT OF THE INTERIOR

Interior Building

1849 C Street, NW., Washington, DC 20240

phone (202) 208–3100, https://doi.gov

DAVID L. BERNHARDT, Secretary of the Interior; raised in Rifle, Colorado; education: B.A., University of Northern Colorado in Greeley; J.D., the George Washington University National Law Center; professional: solicitor, deputy solicitor, deputy chief of staff, counselor to the Secretary, and director of Congressional and Legislative Affairs, Department of the Interior, 2001–09; member of the Board of Game and Inland Fisheries for the Commonwealth of Virginia, 2012–16; chair, International Boundary Commission, 2007–08; nominated by President Donald Trump to become the 53rd Secretary of the Interior, and was confirmed by the U.S. Senate on April 11, 2019.

OFFICE OF THE SECRETARY

Secretary of the Interior.—David L. Bernhardt.
  Special Assistant to the Secretary.—Hannah Cooke.
  Executive Assistant.—Shandria Dixon.
  Chief of Staff.—Todd Willens.
  Counselors to the Secretary: Margaret Everson, Gary Lawkowski, Gregg Renkes, John Tahsuda.
  Director for Scheduling and Advance.—Samantha Hebert.
  Director of External and Intergovernmental Affairs,—Tim Williams.
  Senior Advisor for Alaska Affairs.—Steve Wackowski, Anchorage, AK.
  Advisors: John Bockmier, Rick May, William Werkheiser.

EXECUTIVE SECRETARIAT

Director.—Richard Cardinale.

CONGRESSIONAL AND LEGISLATIVE AFFAIRS

Director.—Cole Rojewski.
  Deputy Director.—Faith Vander Voort.
  Legislative Counsel.—Chris Salotti.

OFFICE OF COMMUNICATIONS

Director.—Nicholas Goodwin.
  Press Secretary.—Benjamin Goldey.

OFFICE OF THE DEPUTY SECRETARY

Deputy Secretary.—Katharine MacGregor.
    Executive Assistant to the Deputy Secretary.—Katie White.
  Associate Deputy Secretaries: James Cason, Kiel Weaver.

ASSISTANT SECRETARY FOR FISH AND WILDLIFE AND PARKS

Assistant Secretary.—Rob Wallace, Room 3160 (202) 208–4116.
  Principal Deputy Assistant Secretary.—John Tanner, Room 3154, 208–4416.

Deputy Assistant Secretary.—Ryan Hambleton, Room 3150, 208–4416.
Chief of Staff.—Maureen Foster, Room 3161, 208–5970.

U.S. FISH AND WILDLIFE SERVICE

1849 C Street, NW., Washington, DC 20240

Director.—Aurelia Skipwith (202) 208–4545.
Principal Deputy Director.—Margaret Everson, 208–4545.
Deputy Directors: Bryan Arroyo, 208–4545; Steve Guertin, 208–4545.
Associate Director.—Vacant.
Senior Advisor for Energy.—Bud Cribley, 208–4331.
Assistant Director for External Affairs.—Barbara Wainman, 208–6541.
Chief of Staff.—Charisa Morris, 208–3843.
Chief of:
Congressional and Legislative Affairs.—Marty Kodis (703) 358–2241.
National Wildlife Refuge System.—Cynthia Martinez (202) 208–5333.
Office of Law Enforcement.—Ed Grace (703) 358–2048.
Public Affairs.—Gavin Shire (703) 358–2649.
Assistant Director for:
Ecological Services.—Gary Frazer, 208–4646.
Fisheries and Habitat Conservation.—David Hoskins, 208–3517.
Information Resources and Technology Management.—Paul Gibson (703) 358–2636.
International Affairs.—Vacant.
Management and Administration.—Janine Velasco, 501–6843.
Migratory Birds.—Jerome Ford, 208–1050.
Science Applications.—Deborah Rocque (703) 358–1957.
Wildlife & Sport Fish Restoration.—Paul Rauch, 208–1050.
Regional Directors:
Interior Region 1.—Wendi Weber, 300 Westgate Center Drive, Hadley, MA 01035 (413) 253–8300, fax (413) 253–8308.
Interior Region 2/4.—Leo Miranda, 1875 Century Boulevard, Atlanta, GA 30345 (404) 679–4000, fax (404) 679–4006.
Interior Region 3.—Charlie Wooley, 5600 American Boulevard West, #990, Minneapolis, MN 55437 (612) 713–5301.
Interior Region 5/7.—Noreen Walsh, 134 Union Boulevard, #400, Lakewood, CO 80228 (303) 236–7920, fax (303) 236–8295.
Interior Region 6/8.—Amy Leuders, 500 Gold Avenue, SW., Room 1306, Albuquerque, NM 87103 (505) 248–6282, fax (503) 872–2716.
Interior Region 9/12.—Robyn Thorson, Eastside Federal Complex, 911 Northeast 11th Avenue, Portland, OR 97232 (503) 231–6118, fax (503) 872–2716.
Interior Region 10.—Paul Souza, 2800 Cottage Way, #W2606, Sacramento, CA 95825 (916) 414–6464, fax (916) 414–6484.
Interior Region 11.—Greg Siekaniec, 1011 East Tudor Road, Anchorage, AK 99503 (907) 786–3542, fax (907) 786–3306.

NATIONAL PARK SERVICE

Director.—Vacant.
Deputy Director.—David Vela (exercising the authority of the Director), Room 3311 (202) 208–4621.
Deputy Director, Operations.—Shawn Benge (acting), Room 3313, 208–4621.
Deputy Director, Management and Administration.—Lena McDowall, Room 2711, 513–7240.
Chief of Staff.—Chris Powell, Room 3312, 513–7181.
Associate Director for—
Business Services.—Vacant.
Chief Information Officer.—Shane Compton, Room 2212, 354–1820.
Cultural Resources, Partnerships, and Science.—Joy Beasley (acting), Room 3316, 354–6991.
Interpretation, Education, and Volunteers.—Tom Medema (acting), Room 3322, 354–6998.
Natural Resource Stewardship and Science.—Ray Sauvajot, Room 3320, 354–6992.
Park Planning, Facilities, and Lands.—Mike Caldwell (acting), Room 3329, 354–6996.
Visitor and Resource Protection.—Louis Rowe (acting), Room 3326, 354–6995.
Workforce and Inclusion.—Marlon Taubenheim (acting), Room 2216, 354–1990.

Comptroller.—Jessica Bowron, Room 2721, 513–7280.
Assistant Director for—
Communications.—Vacant.
Legislative and Congressional Affairs.—Charles Laudner, Room 3328, 513–7212.
Partnerships and Civic Engagement.—Reginald ''Reggie'' Chapple (acting), Room 3325, 354–6997.
NPS Interior Regional Directors:
NPS Interior Region 1: National Capital Area.—Lisa Mendelson (acting), 1100 Ohio Drive, SW., Washington, DC 20242, 619–7020.
NPS Interior Region 1: North Atlantic-Appalachian.—Gay Vietzke, 1234 Market Street, 20th Floor, Philadelphia, PA 19107 (215) 597–5814.
NPS Interior Region 2: South Atlantic-Gulf (Includes Puerto Rico and the U.S. Virgin Islands).—Bob Vogel, 100 Alabama Street, NW., 1924 Building, Atlanta, GA 30303 (404) 507–5604.
NPS Interior Regions 3, 4, and 5: Great Lakes, Mississippi Basin, and Missouri Basin.—Bert Frost, 601 Riverfront Drive, Omaha, NE 68102 (402) 661–1520.
NPS Interior Regions 6, 7, and 8: Arkansas-Rio Grande-Texas-Gulf, Upper Colorado Basin, and Lower Colorado Basin.—Kate Hammond (acting), 12795 West Alameda Parkway, P.O. Box 25287, Denver, CO 80225 (303) 969–2503.
NPS Interior Regions 9, 10, and 12: Columbia-Pacific Northwest, California-Great Basin, and Pacific Islands.—Stan Austin, 333 Bush Street, Suite 500, San Francisco, CA 94104 (415) 623–2101.
NPS Interior Region 11: Alaska.—Don Stricker (acting), 240 West Fifth Avenue, Room 114, Anchorage, AK 99501 (907) 644–3510.

ASSISTANT SECRETARY FOR INDIAN AFFAIRS

Assistant Secretary.—Tara Sweeney, Room 4160 (202) 208–7163.
Principal Deputy Assistant Secretary.—John Tahsuda, Room 4160, 208–7163.
Deputy Assistant Secretary for—
Management.—Jason Freihage, Room 4659, 219–0440.
Policy and Economic Development.—Mark Cruz, Room 4160, 208–7163.
Chief of Staff.—Richard Myers, Room 4154, 208–4723.
Director of:
Congressional Affairs.—Vacant.
Public Affairs.—Nedra Darling, Room 4140, 208–3710.

BUREAU OF INDIAN AFFAIRS

Director.—Darryl LaCounte, Room 4606, 208–5116.
Deputy Director of:
Field Operations.—James ''Jim'' James, Albuquerque (505) 563–5227.
Justice Services.—Charles Addington, Room 2603, 208–5787.
Tribal Services.—Spike Bighorn (acting), Room 3645, 208–6941.
Trust Services.—Johanna Blackhair (acting), Room 4624, 208–5968.

BUREAU OF INDIAN EDUCATION

Director.—Tony Dearman, Room 3609 (202) 208–6123.
Deputy Bureau Director, School Operations.—Sharon Pinto (505) 563–5317.
Chief of Staff.—Clint Bowers (202) 208–3479.
Special Assistant.—Juanita Mendoza (202) 208–3559.
Chief Academic Officer.—Tamarah Pfeiffer (acting), (505) 563–3020.
Associate Deputy Director of:
BIE Operated Schools.—Hankie Ortiz (505) 563–5257.
Division of Performance and Accountability.—Jeffrey Hamley (202) 208–6666.
Navajo Schools.—Charles Sherman (acting), (928) 871–5932.
Tribally Controlled Schools.—Tracia ''Keri'' Jojola (acting), (952) 851–5427.

ASSISTANT SECRETARY FOR LAND AND MINERALS MANAGEMENT

Assistant Secretary.—Casey Hammond (exercising the authority of the Assistant Secretary), Room 6614 (202) 208–6734.
Principal Deputy Assistant Secretary.—Casey Hammond, Room 6614, 208–6734.

BUREAU OF LAND MANAGEMENT

1849 C Street, NW., Room 5665, Washington, DC 20240

phone (202) 208–3801, fax 208–5242

Director.—Vacant.

Deputy Director of:

Operations.—Mike Nedd, 208–3801, fax 208–5242.

Programs and Policy.—William Perry Pendley, 208–3801, fax 208–5242.

Division Chief, Legislative Affairs.—Patrick Wilkerson, 912–7429, fax 245–0050.

Deputy Division Chief.—Jill Ralston, 912–7173, fax 245–0050.

State Directors:

Alaska.—Chad Padgett, 222 West Seventh Avenue, No. 13, Anchorage, AK 99513 (907) 271–5080, fax 271–4596.

Arizona.—Raymond Suazo, One North Central Avenue, Suite 800, Phoenix, AZ 85004 (602) 417–9500, fax 417–9398.

California.—Karen Mouritsen, 2800 Cottage Way, Suite W1623, Sacramento, CA 95825 (916) 978–4600, fax 978–4699.

Colorado.—Jamie Connell, 2850 Youngfield Street, Lakewood, CO 80215 (303) 239–3700, fax 239–3933.

Eastern States.—Vacant, 20th M Street, SE., Suite 950, Washington, DC 20003 (202) 912–7701, fax 912–7186.

Idaho.—John Ruhs, 1387 South Vinnell Way, Boise, ID 83709 (208) 373–4001, fax 373–4005.

Montana/Dakotas.—John Mehlhoff, 5001 Southgate Drive, Billings, MT 59101 (406) 896–5000, fax 896–5298.

Nevada.—John Raby, 1340 Financial Boulevard, Reno, NV 89502 (775) 861–6400, fax 861–6606.

New Mexico.—Tim Spisak, 301 Dinosaur Trail, Santa Fe, NM 87508 (505) 954–2222, fax 954–2010.

Oregon/Washington.—Jose Linares (acting), 1220 SW. 3rd Avenue, Portland, OR 97204 (503) 808–6026, fax 808–6390.

Utah.—Ed Roberson, 440 West 200 South, Suite 500, Salt Lake City, UT 84101 (801) 539–4010, fax 539–4013.

Wyoming.—Duane Spencer (acting), 5353 Yellowstone Road, Cheyenne, WY 82009 (307) 775–6001, fax 775–6003.

BUREAU OF OCEAN ENERGY MANAGEMENT

Director.—Walter D. Cruickshank (acting), (202) 208–6300.

Deputy Director/Chief Financial Officer.—Walter D. Cruickshank, 208–6300.

Chief, Office of:

Budget and Program Coordination.—James G. Anderson, 208–6264.

Congressional Affairs.—Lee Tilton, 208–3502.

Environmental Programs.—William Y. Brown, 208–6249.

Policy, Regulation and Analysis.—Deanna P. Meyer-Pietruszka, 208–6352.

Public Affairs.—Connie Gillette, 208–5387.

Renewable Energy Programs.—James F. Bennett (703) 787–1660.

Strategic Resources Programs.—L. Renee Orr, 208–3515.

Outer Continental Shelf Regional Directors:

Alaska.—James J. Kendall, Jr., 3801 Centerpoint Drive, Anchorage, AK 99503–5823 (907) 334–5200.

Gulf of Mexico.—Michael Celata, 1201 Elmwood Park Boulevard, New Orleans, LA 70123 (504) 736–2592.

Pacific.—Joan Barminski, 760 Paseo Camarillo, Camarillo, CA 93010–6002 (805) 384–6318.

BUREAU OF SAFETY AND ENVIRONMENTAL ENFORCEMENT

Director.—Scott A. Angelle (202) 208–3500.

Deputy Director.—Vacant.

Associate Director for Administration.—Scott Mabry (703) 787–1228.

Budget.—Eric Modrow (703) 787–1694.

Offshore Regulatory Programs.—Stacey Noem (acting), (703) 787–1222.

Policy and Analysis.—Molly Madden (202) 219–7271.

Congressional Affairs.—Julie Fleming, 208–3827.

Outer Continental Shelf Regional Directors:
Alaska.—Mark Fesmire, 3801 Centerpoint Drive, Suite 500, Anchorage, AK 99503 (907) 334–5300.
Gulf of Mexico.—Lars T. Herbst, 1201 Elmwood Park Boulevard, New Orleans, LA 70123 (504) 736–2589.
Pacific.—Mark Fesmire (acting), 770 Paseo Camarillo, Camarillo, CA 93010 (805) 389–7514.

OFFICE OF SURFACE MINING RECLAMATION AND ENFORCEMENT

Director.—Vacant, Room 4511 (202) 208–4006.
Deputy Director.—Glenda H. Owens, 208–4006.
Assistant Director for Finance and Administration.—Ted Woronka, 208–2546.
Congressional Contact.—Tristan Weis, 208–2838.
Regional Director for—
Appalachian Region.—Thomas D. Shope, Three Parkway Center, Pittsburgh, PA 15220 (412) 937–2828, fax 937–2903.
Mid-Continent Region.—Alfred Clayborne, 501 Belle Street, Room 216, Alton, IL 62002 (618) 463–6460, fax 463–6470.
Western Region.—David Berry, 1999 Broadway, Suite 3320, Denver, CO 80202 (303) 293–5001, fax 293–5006.

ASSISTANT SECRETARY FOR POLICY, MANAGEMENT, AND BUDGET

Assistant Secretary.—Susan Combs, Room 5113 (202) 208–1927.
Principal Deputy Assistant Secretary.—Scott J. Cameron, Room 5113, 208–1927.
Deputy Assistant Secretary for—
Administrative Services.—Jacqueline Jones, 208–1927.
Budget, Finance, Grants, and Acquisition.—Andrea Brandon, 208–1927.
Human Capital and Diversity.—Raymond Limon, 208–1927.
Natural Resources Revenue Management.—Greg Gould, 208–1927.
Policy and Environmental Management.—Michael Freeman, 208–1927.
Public Safety, Resource Protection, and Emergency Services.—Lisa Branum, 208–1927.

ASSISTANT SECRETARY FOR WATER AND SCIENCE

Assistant Secretary.—Dr. Timothy R. Petty, Room 6654 (202) 208–3186.
Senior Advisors: Aubrey Bettencourt, Room 6650, 208–3186; Ryan Nichols, Room 6653, 208–3186.
Chief of Staff.—Kerry Rae, Room 6651 (202) 513–0535.

U.S. GEOLOGICAL SURVEY

The National Center, 12201 Sunrise Valley Drive, Reston, VA 20192
phone (703) 648–7411, fax 648–4454

Director.—Jim Reilly, 648–7411.
Deputy Director.—Cynthia Lodge, 648–7412.
Chief Scientist.—Geoff Plumlee (acting), 648–6403.
Chief of Staff.—Bill Lukas (acting), 648–7406.
Office of:
Administration.—Katherine McCulloch, 648–7200.
Budget, Planning, and Integration.—Eric Reichard (acting), 648–4443.
Communications and Publishing.—Leslie Jones (acting), 648–4354.
Congressional Liaison Officer.—Jeffrey Onizuk, 648–4242.
Enterprise Information.—Tim Quinn, 648–6839
Human Capital.—Julie Wozniak, 648–7442.
International Programs.—Vic Labson, 648–6206
Public Affairs Officer.—Karen Armstrong (acting), 648–4447.
Science Quality and Integrity.—Craig Robinson, 648–6774.
Associate Director for:
Core Science Systems.—Kevin Gallagher, 648–5747.
Ecosystems.—Anne Kinsinger, 648–4050.
Energy and Minerals.—Sarah Ryker, 648–6403.

Environmental Health and National Climate Adaptation Science Center.—Anne Kinsinger (acting), 648–4050.
Land Resources.—Kevin Gallagher (acting), 648–5747.
Natural Hazards.—David Applegate, 648–6600.
Water Resources.—Donald Cline, 648–4557.
Regional Director for:
North Atlantic-Appalachian Region (DOI Region 1).—Michael Tupper, 12201 Sunrise Valley Drive, Reston, VA 20192 (703) 648–6600.
South Atlantic-Gulf-PR-USVI Region (DOI Region 2).—Holly Weyers, 1770 Corporate Drive, Suite 500, Norcross, GA 30093 (703) 715–7020.
Great Lakes Region (DOI Region 3).—Scott Morlock (acting), 5957 Lakeside Boulevard, Lakeside Phase II (317) 600–2753.
Mississippi Basin Region (DOI Region 4).—Holly Weyers, 1770 Corporate Drive, Suite 500, Norcross, GA 30093 (703) 715–7020.
Missouri Basin Region (DOI Region 5).—Scott Morlock (acting), 5957 Lakeside Boulevard, Lakeside Phase II (317) 600–2753.
Arkansas-Rio Grande-Texas-Gulf Region (DOI Region 6).—Holly Weyers, 1770 Corporate Drive, Suite 500, Norcross, GA 30093 (703) 715–7020.
Upper Colorado Basin Region (DOI Region 7).— Roseann Gonzales-Schreiner, Denver Federal Center, DFC Building 67 (303) 236–9202.
Lower Colorado Basin Region (DOI Region 8).— Mark Sogge, Modoc Hall, 3020 State University Drive East, Sacramento, CA 95819 (916) 278–9550.
Columbia-Pacific Northwest Region (DOI Region 9).— Marijke van Heeswijk (acting), 909 First Avenue, Federal Office Building (206) 220–4606.
California-Great Basin Region (DOI Region 10).—Mark Sogge, Modoc Hall, 3020 State University Drive East, Sacramento, CA 95819 (916) 278–9550.
Alaska Region (DOI Region 11).—Aimee Devaris, 4230 University Drive, Suite 201, Anchorage, AK 99508 (907) 786–7055.
Pacific Islands Region (DOI Region 12).—Marijke van Heeswijk (acting), 909 First Avenue, Federal Office Building (206) 220–4606.

BUREAU OF RECLAMATION

Commissioner.—Brenda Burman, Room 7657 (202) 513–0501.
Deputy Commissioner.—Shelby Hagenauer, Room 7653, 513–0501.
Deputy Commissioner for Operations.—David Palumbo, Room 7645, 513–0616.
Deputy Commissioner for Policy, Administration, and Budget.—Grayford Payne, Room 7650, 513–0509.
Chief of Staff.—James Hess, Room 7646, 513 0543.
Chief of:
Congressional and Legislative Affairs.—Vacant, Room 7643, 513–0570.
Public Affairs.—Theresa Eisenman, Room 7644, 513–0574.
Regional Directors:
Great Plains.—Michael Black, 2021 4th Avenue North, Billings, MT 59107 (406) 247–7795, fax 247–7793.
Lower Colorado.—Terrance Fulp, 500 Date Street, Boulder City, NV 89006 (702) 293–8000, fax 293–8333.
Mid-Pacific.—Ernest Conant, 2800 Cottage Way, Sacramento, CA 95825 (916) 978–5000, fax 978–5005.
Pacific Northwest.—Lorri Gray, 1150 North Curtis Road, Suite 100, Boise, ID 83706 (208) 378–5012, fax 378–5019.
Upper Colorado.—Brent Esplin, 125 South State Street, Room 6107, Salt Lake City, UT 84138 (801) 524–3600, fax 524–3855.

OFFICE OF INSPECTOR GENERAL

Inspector General.—Mark Greenblatt, Room 4411 (202) 208–5745.
Deputy Inspector General.—Vacant, 208–5745.
Chief of Staff.—Stephen Hardgrove, Room 4410, 208–5745.
Director for Whistleblower Protection.—Jennifer French, Room 4456.
Director for External Affairs.—Nancy DiPaolo, Room 4416.

OFFICE OF THE SOLICITOR

Solicitor.—Daniel H. Jorjani, Room 6352 (202) 208–4423.

Principal Deputy Solicitor.—Gregory Zerzan.
Deputy Solicitor for—
Energy and Mineral Resources.—Kevin O'Scannlain (acting).
General Law.—Hubbel Relat.
Indian Affairs.—Kyle Scherer.
Land Resources.—Marc Marie (acting).
Parks and Wildlife.—Karen Budd-Falen.
Water Resources.—Brandon Middleton.
Associate Solicitor for—
General Law.—Scott de la Vega, Room 6440, 208–4722.
Indian Affairs.—Eric Shepard, Room 6511, 208–3401.
Land Resources.—Aaron Moody, Room 6412, 208–4444.
Mineral Resources.—Karen Hawbecker, Room 5359, 208–3175.
Parks and Wildlife.—Peg Romanik, Room 6313, 208–4344.
Water Resources.—Carter Brown, Room 6413, 208–4379.
Administration.—Marc Smith, Room 6557, 208–6115.
Designated Agency Ethics Official.—Heather Gottry (acting), Room 5311, 208–3038.

OFFICE OF THE SPECIAL TRUSTEE FOR AMERICAN INDIANS

Principal Deputy Special Trustee.—Jerold Gidner (202) 208–3946.

DEPARTMENT OF AGRICULTURE

Jamie L. Whitten Building

1400 Independence Avenue, SW., Washington, DC 20250

phone (202) 720–3631, https://usda.gov

SONNY PERDUE, Secretary of Agriculture; education: D.V.M, University of Georgia; professional: State Senator, 1991–2001; Governor, Georgia, 2002–10; nominated by President Donald J. Trump to become the 31st Secretary of Agriculture, and was confirmed by the U.S. Senate on April 25, 2017.

OFFICE OF THE SECRETARY

Secretary of Agriculture.—Sonny Perdue, Room 200–A (202) 720–3631.
Deputy Secretary.—Stephen Censky.
Chief of Staff.—Joby Young.
Deputy Chief of Staff.—Blake Rollins.

OFFICE OF THE ASSISTANT SECRETARY FOR ADMINISTRATION

1400 Independence Avenue, SW., Room 240–W, Washington, DC 20250

phone (202) 720–3291

Assistant Secretary.—Vacant.
Executive Assistant.—Tyra Taylor.
Principal Deputy Assistant Secretary.—David Wu.
Deputy Assistant Secretary.—Donald Bice (acting).
Chief of Staff.—Dr. Johanna Briscoe.

OFFICE OF ADMINISTRATIVE LAW JUDGES

1400 Independence Avenue, SW., Stop 9202, Room 1049–S, Washington, DC 20250

phone (202) 720–8423

Chief Administrative Law Judge.—Channing D. Strother.
Administrative Management Specialist.—Marilyn T. Kennedy.
Administrative Law Judge.—Jill S. Clifton, 720–8423.
Hearing Clerk.—Caroline Hill, 720–4443.

OFFICE OF HUMAN RESOURCES MANAGEMENT

1400 Independence Avenue, SW., Room 318–W, Washington, DC 20250

phone (202) 720–3585

Chief Human Capital Officer.—Mary Pletcher Rice.
Executive Assistant.—Sharntay Harry.
Deputy Director.—Douglas Follansbee.
Chief of Staff.—Tonique Coley, 720–0027.
Management Analyst.—Darcelle Walker, 692–0263.
Directors:
Chief Learning Officer.—Dr. Karlease Kelly, Provost, 720–0185.
Employee and Labor Relations Division.—Kevin McGrath, 260–8160.
Executive Resources Management Division.—Douglas Follansbee (acting), 720–3585.
HR Enterprise Systems Management Division.—Marquette DeFillo, 302–6137.
HR Policy Division.—Michael Rafferty (acting), 603–6180.
Strategic HR, Planning and Accountability Division.—Allen Hatcher, 720–0941.

OFFICE OF THE JUDICIAL OFFICER

1400 Independence Avenue, SW., Room 1112–S, Washington, DC 20250

phone (202) 772–4820, fax (844) 332–7988, email: sm.oha.ojo@usda.gov

Judicial Officer.—Judge Bobbie J. McCartney.
Attorney Advisor.—Linda S. Ziskin.

OFFICE OF OPERATIONS

1400 Independence Avenue, SW., Room 1456–S, Washington, DC 20250

phone (202) 720–3937

Director of Operations.—Duane Williams.
Deputy Director of Operations.—Mark Rucker.
Senior Advisor.—Christopher Nelson, 690–2824.
Director of:
Executive Services.—Carmelnita Fossum, 720–8482.
Facilities Management.—Thomas Hoffman, 720–2804.
Mail and Reproduction Management.—Dennis Banks, 720–8393.
Materiel Management Service Center.—Joseph Govan (301) 394–0414.
Program and Policy and Support Staff.—Carlos Casaus, 720–4134.
Safety, Sustainability and Emergency Operations.—Gilbert Stokes, 720–6894.

OFFICE OF PROPERTY AND FLEET MANAGEMENT

1400 Independence Avenue, SW., Room 1635–S, Washington, DC 20250

phone (202) 720–4765

Director.—Scott Davis, 720–4765.
Division Director for Environmental Management.—Karen Zhang, 401–4747.
Division Director for Property Management.—Anne Anderson, 720–7283.

OFFICE OF CONTRACTING AND PROCUREMENT

1400 Independence Avenue, SW., Room 335–W, Washington, DC 20250

phone (202) 720–9448

Director.—Tiffany J. Taylor (acting), 690–5407.
Chief of Staff.—Christopher A. Corder, 720–3671.
Procurement Operations.—Richard R. Jiron (970) 295–5487.
Procurement Policy.—Crandall Watson, 720–7529.
IAS Branch Chief.—Richard Toothman, 720–9765.
Charge Card Service Center.—Veronica Nelson.

OFFICE OF HOMELAND SECURITY

Director.—Vacant.
Deputy Director.—Vacant.
Associate Director.—Mike O'Conner (202) 205–3609.
Chief of Staff.—Vacant.
Chief for—
Continuity and Planning Division.—John Aucott, 205–3587.
Emergency Programs Division.—Todd Barrett, 690–3191.
National Security Division.—Michelle Colby, 260–0106.
Personnel and Document Security Division.—Camelia Murdock, 720–7373.
Radiation Safety Division.—John Jensen (301) 504–2441.

OFFICE OF SMALL AND DISADVANTAGED BUSINESS UTILIZATION

1400 Independence Avenue, SW., Room 1085–S, Washington, DC 20250

phone (202) 720–7117

Director.—Vacant.

Deputy Director.—Michelle Warren, 720–7835.

ASSISTANT SECRETARY FOR CIVIL RIGHTS

1400 Independence Avenue, SW., Room 507–A, Washington, DC 20250

phone (202) 720–3808

Assistant Secretary.—Vacant.
Deputy Assistant Secretary.—Naomi C. Earp, Esq.

OFFICE OF BUDGET AND PROGRAM ANALYSIS

1400 Independence Avenue, SW., Room 101–A, Washington, DC 20250

phone (202) 720–3323

Director.—Erica Navarro.
Deputy Director for—
Budget Execution.—Nicole Pollard, Room 102–E, 720–6176.
Budget Formulation.—Leslie Barrack, Room 126–W.
Departmental Operations and Performance.—Paola Zuco, Room 101–A.
Legislative and Regulatory Coordination.—Andrew Perry (acting), Room 102–E.

OFFICE OF THE CHIEF ECONOMIST

1400 Independence Avenue, SW., Room 112–A, Washington, DC 20250

phone (202) 720–4164

Chief Economist.—Robert Johansson, Room 112–A, 720–4164.
Deputy Chief Economist.—Cindy Nickerson, Room 112–A, 720–5955.
Chair, World Agricultural Outlook Board.—Mark Jekanowski, Room 4419–S, 720–6030.
Chief Meteorologist.—Mark Brusberg, Room 4441C–S, 720–2012.
Director:
Office of Energy and Environmental Policy.—William Hohenstein, Room 4059–S, 720–6698.
Office of Pest Management Policy.—Sheryl Kunickis, Room 3869–S, 720–5375.
Risk Assessment and Cost Benefit Analysis.—Linda C. Abbott, Room 4032–S, 690–6056.
Sustainable Development.—Elise Golan, Room 112–A, 720–2456.

OFFICE OF THE CHIEF FINANCIAL OFFICER

1400 Independence Avenue, SW., Room 143–W, Washington, DC 20250

phone (202) 720–0727

Chief Financial Officer.—Vacant.
Principal Deputy Chief Financial Officer.—George ''Scott'' Soles, 720–7407.
Deputy Chief Financial Officer.—Lynn Moaney, 720–9427.
Associate Chief Financial Officer for—
Financial Operations and Shared Services.—Stanley McMichael, Room 3054–S, 720–0564.
Financial Policy and Planning.—Lucas Castillo, Room 3057–S, 720–1221.
Director, National Finance Center.—Calvin Turner, P.O. Box 60000, New Orleans, LA 70160 (504) 426–0120.

OFFICE OF THE CHIEF INFORMATION OFFICER

1400 Independence Avenue, SW., Room 420–W, Washington, DC 20250

phone (202) 720–8833

Chief Information Officer.—Gary S. Washington.
Deputy Chief Information Officer.—Bajinder Paul, 720–8833.
Chief of Staff.—Tonya L. Judkins.
Chief Data Officer.—Ted Kaouk.
Chief Technology Officer.—Stephen Lowe.

Executive for IT Modernization.—Telora T. Dean.
Associate Chief Information Officer for—
Client Experience Center (CEC).—Tim McCrosson, 720–4109.
Digital Infrastructure Services Center (DISC).—Victoria Turley (acting), 619–8550.
Information Resource Management Center (IRMC).—Ravoyne Payton.
Information Security Center (ISC) and Chief Information Security Officer.—Venice Goodwine, 720–8281.

OFFICE OF COMMUNICATIONS

1400 Independence Avenue, SW., Room 412–A, Washington, DC 20250
phone (202) 720–4623

Director.—Michawn Rich.
Deputy Director.—Meghan Rodgers.
Deputy Director for—
Creative Development.—Brian Mabry.
Press Operations and Press Secretary.—Alec Varsamis.
Director, Center for—
Brand Review.—Michael Illenberg (acting).
Broadcast Media and Technology.—Garth Clark.
Constituent Affairs: Kathryn Hill, Mocile Trotter.
Web Communication.—Peter Rhee.

OFFICE OF CONGRESSIONAL RELATIONS

1400 Independence Avenue, SW., Room 212–A, Washington, DC 20250
phone (202) 720–7095

Assistant Secretary.—Kenneth Steven Barbic.
Chief of Staff.—Evan Lee.

EXTERNAL AND INTERGOVERNMENTAL AFFAIRS

1400 Independence Avenue, SW., Room 211–A, Washington, DC 20250
phone (202) 720–7095

Director.—Jordan Bonfitto.
Deputy Director.—Ashley Willits.

OFFICE OF TRIBAL RELATIONS

1400 Independence Avenue, SW., Room 501–A, Washington, DC 20250
phone (202) 205–2249

Director.—Diane Cullo.
Deputy Director.—Linda Cronin.
Outreach Specialists: Jeffrey Harris, Dennis Kennedy.
Staff Assistant.—Esha Tariq.

OFFICE OF THE EXECUTIVE SECRETARIAT

1400 Independence Avenue, SW., Room 116–A, Washington, DC 20250
phone (202) 720–7100

Director.—Norbert H. Snobeck (acting).
Executive Secretary to the Department.—Jeanette Whitener.
Branch Chief.—Adrian Lindsey.

OFFICE OF THE GENERAL COUNSEL

1400 Independence Avenue, SW., Room 107–W, Washington, DC 20250
phone (202) 720–3351

General Counsel.—Stephen Alexander Vaden.

Principal Deputy General Counsel.—Richard Goeken.
Deputy General Counsel: Inga Bumbary-Langston, Tyler Clarkson.
Senior Counsel.—Karen Fletcher.
Senior Counselor.—Chris Esparza.
Advisor to the General Counsel.—Rachel H. Pick.
Associate General Counsel for—
Civil Rights, Labor, and Employment Law.—Arlean Leland, 720–1760.
General Law and Research.—Benjamin Young, 720–4814.
International Affairs, Food Assistance, and Farm and Rural Programs.—Ralph Linden, 720–6883.
Marketing, Regulatory, and Food Safety Programs.—Carrie Ricci, 720–3155.
Natural Resources and Environment.—Ron Mulach, 720–2063.
Assistant General Counsel, Division of:
Civil Rights Litigation.—Steven Brammer, 720–4375.
Civil Rights Policy, Compliance, and Counsel.—Vacant, 690–3993.
General Law and Research.—Brian Mizoguchi, 720–7219.
International Affairs, Food Assistance, and Farm and Rural Programs: Peter Bonner, 720–3569; Janet Safian, 720–2923.
Marketing, Regulatory, and Food Safety: Mai Dinh, 720–5935; Sheila Novak, 720–2670.
Natural Resources and Environment.—Beverly Li, 772–1183.
Director, Administration and Resource Management.—Charlene Buckner, 720–6324.
Resource Management Specialist.—Robyn Davis, 720–4861.

OFFICE OF INSPECTOR GENERAL

1400 Independence Avenue, SW., Room 117–W, Washington, DC 20250

phone (202) 720–8001, fax 690–1278

Inspector General.—Phyllis K. Fong.
Deputy Inspector General.—Ann Coffey.
Assistant Inspector General for—
Audit.—Gil Harden, Room 403–E, 720–6945.
Office of Data Science.—Virginia Rone, Room 44–E, 720–5168.
Office of Investigations.—Peter Paradis (acting), Room 146–W, 720–3965.
Office of Management.—Robert Hutenlocker, Room 5–E, 720–6979.

NATIONAL APPEALS DIVISION

1320 Braddock Place, 4th Floor, Alexandria, VA 22314

Director.—Frank M. Wood (703) 305–1166.

UNDER SECRETARY FOR NATURAL RESOURCES AND ENVIRONMENT

1400 Independence Avenue, SW., Room 202–W, Washington, DC 20250

phone (202) 720–7173

Under Secretary.—James E. Hubbard.
Deputy Under Secretary.—Vacant.
Chief of Staff.—Chris Marklund.

FOREST SERVICE

Sydney R. Yates Building, 201 14th Street, SW., Washington, DC 20227

phone (202) 205–1661

Chief.—Vicki Christiansen, 205–8439.
Associate Chief.—Angela Coleman (acting), 205–1779.
Director for—
International Programs.—Valdis E. Mezainis, 644–4621.
Law Enforcement and Investigations.—Tracy Perry (703) 605–4869.
Legislative Affairs.—Douglas Crandall, 205–1637.
Office of Communications.—Kathryn O'Connor, 205–1470.

BUSINESS OPERATIONS

Sydney R. Yates Building, 201 14th Street, SW., 4th Floor, Washington, DC 20227

phone (202) 205–1707

Deputy Chief.—Claudette Fernandez, 649–1160.
Associate Deputy Chiefs: Malcom Shorter (703) 605–4167; Robert Velasco, (703) 605–4726.
Chief of Staff.—Anna Briatico, 205–1668.
Senior Staff Assistants: Anton Malkowski, 205–0914; Matthews Smith (acting), 403–8961.
Deputy Area Budget Coordinator.—Tracey Hanson, 403–8975.
Director for—
Acquisition Management.—George Sears (703) 605–4662.
Enterprise.—Chris Feutrier (acting), (406) 361–9417.
Human Resources Management.—Mark Green (703) 605–4604.
Job Corps.—Jerry Ingersoll (acting), 205–1707.
Regulatory and Management Services.—Anne Goode (acting), 205–1056.
Safety and Occupational Health.—Douglas Parrish (703) 605–4482.
Strategic Program and Budget Analysis.—John Rapp, 644–4679.
Assistant Chief Information Officer.—Joseph Powers (703) 605–4814.

NATIONAL FOREST SYSTEM

Sydney R. Yates Building, 201 14th Street, SW., 5th Floor, Washington, DC 20227

phone (202) 205–1523

Deputy Chief.—Christopher B. French.
Associate Deputy Chiefs: Vacant, 205–3171; Allen Rowley, 205–0824; Tina Terrell (703) 605–4802.
Staff Director of:
Ecosystem Management Coordination.—Christine Dawe, 205–0830.
Engineering Technology and Geo-Spatial Service.—Lamont Jackson (acting), (703) 605–4616.
Forest Management.—Jacqueline Buchanan (acting), 644–4715.
Lands and Realty.—Greg Smith, 205–1769.
Minerals and Geology Management.—Kathryn Conant (acting), (703) 605–4785.
National Partnership Office.—Jacqueline Emanuel, 205–1072.
Rangeland Management Vegetation Ecology.—Jacqueline Buchanan (acting), 644–4715.
Recreation Heritage and Volunteer Resources.—Michiko Martin, 205–1240.
Watershed, Fish, Wildlife, Air, and Rare Plants.—Robert Harper, 205–1671.
Wilderness, Wild and Scenic Rivers.—Susan Spear, 644–4862.

RESEARCH AND DEVELOPMENT

Sydney R. Yates Building, 201 14th Street, SW., 2nd Floor, Washington, DC 20227

fax (202) 205–1530

Deputy Chief.—Dr. Alexander L. Friend, 205–1665.
Associate Deputy Chief.—Monica M. Lear, 205–1702.
Chief of Staff.—Deborah Bush-Butler, 649–1716.
Senior Staff Assistant.—Linda Jones, 205–1200.
Deputy Budget Coordinator.—John Rothlisberger, 205–0833.
Staff Directors:
Inventory, Monitoring, and Assessment Research.—Linda Heath (703) 605–4177.
Knowledge Management and Communications.—Tracy Hancock, 205–1724.
Landscape Restoration and Ecosystem Services Research.—Carl Lucero (703) 405–3823.
Sustainable Forest Management Research.—Toral Patel-Weynand, 205–0878.

STATE AND PRIVATE FORESTRY

Sydney R. Yates Building, 201 14th Street, SW., 3rd Floor, Washington, DC 20227

fax (202) 205–1657

Deputy Chief.—John Phipps, 205–1606.

Associate Deputy Chiefs: Jaelith Hall-Rivera, Patti Hirami.
Chief of Staff.—Alice Ewen (acting), 570–2156.
Director of:
Conservation Education.—Tinelle Bustam (acting), 205–1241.
Cooperative Forestry.—Steve Koehn, 205–1389.
Fire and Aviation Management.—Shawna Legarza, 205–1483.
Forest Health Protection.—Rick Cooksey (703) 605–5332.
Office of Tribal Relations.—Fred Clark, 205–1514.

NATURAL RESOURCES CONSERVATION SERVICE

1400 Independence Avenue, SW., Room 5105–A, Washington, DC 20250

phone (202) 720–4525

Chief.—Kevin Norton (acting).
Associate Chief.—Ron Alvarado (acting), 720–4531.

DEPUTY CHIEF FOR PROGRAMS

1400 Independence Avenue, SW., Room 5109–S, Washington, DC 20250

phone (202) 720–4527

Deputy Chief.—Jimmy Bramblett (202) 720–4630.
Director, Division of:
Conservation Technical Assistance.—Kristy Oates (acting), 720–0673.
Easement.—Jeff White (acting), 720–1882.
Financial Assistance Programs.—Maggie Rhodes, 720–1844.

HUMAN RESOURCES DIVISION

Chief Human Resources Officer.—Melissa Drummond (202) 720–7847.
Administrative and Program Specialist.—Jeffrey Henneman, 572–0495.
Director, Workforce Programs Branch Chief.—Sherry Dixon, 720–8676.
Workforce Operations Branch Chief.—Danny Sadler (816) 926–3011.
Quality Assurance and Workforce Policy Branch Chief.—Leslie Violette, 720–3042.

DEPUTY CHIEF OF SCIENCE AND TECHNOLOGY

Deputy Chief.—Diane Gelburd, Room 5113–S (202) 720–4528.
Director, Division of:
Conservation Engineering.—Noller Herbert, Room 6136–S, 720–2520.
Ecological Sciences.—Shaun McKinney (acting), Room 6160–S, 205–9434.
Soil Health Division.—Bianca Moebius-Clune, 205–7712.

DEPUTY CHIEF OF SOIL SCIENCE AND RESOURCE ASSESSMENT

Deputy Chief.—Louie Tupas, Room 1–1289GWCC (301) 504–2302.
Director, Division of:
National Geospatial Center of Excellence.—Javier Ruiz (acting), (817) 509–3420.
National Soil Survey Center.—David Hoover (402) 437–5389.
Resources Inventory and Assessment Division.—Mark Xu (acting), Room 6011–S (202) 690–1253.
Leader, Resources Assessment Branch.—Daniel Mullarkey, Room 1–1291 (301) 504–2311.

UNDER SECRETARY FOR FARM PRODUCTION AND CONSERVATION

Under Secretary.—Bill Northey.
Chief of Staff.—Jamie Clover Adams.
Special Assistants: Andrew Shaeffer, Josh Storey.
Executive Assistant.—Michael Aguerro.

FARM PRODUCTION AND CONSERVATION BUSINESS CENTER

1400 Independence Avenue, SW., Room 5110–S, Washington, DC 20250

phone (202) 692–5278

Chief Operating Officer.—Robert Stephenson.
Deputy Chief Operating Officer.—Robert Ibarra.
Chief of Staff.—Terri Meighan.
Executive Assistant.—Julie Gordon.
Acquisitions Division.—Derek Beavers, Room 6144–S, 692–0103.
Appeals and Litigation Division.—Jack Welch, Room 5969–S, 690–3297.
Budget Division.—Jim Staiert, Room 6243–S, 401–6182.
Civil Rights Division.—Emily Su, Patriot's Plaza III, 401–1919.
Customer Experience Division.—Ken Hill (acting), Patriot's Plaza III, 772–6035.
Economic and Policy Analysis Division.—Joy Harwood, Room 3741–S, 720–3451.
Environmental Activities Division.—Nell Fuller, Room 4704–S, 720–6303.
External Affairs Division.—David Warner, Room 4082–S, 720–7809.
Financial Management Division.—Margo Erny, Room 6818–S, 720–4877.
Grants and Agreements Division.—Galon Hall (acting), Raleigh, NC (919) 873–2164.
Homeland Security Division.—Scott Linsky, Room 3704–S, 720–7795.
Human Resources Division.—Melissa Drummond, Room 6205–S, 260–8062.
Information Solutions Division.—Darren Ash, Room 6644–S, 720–5320.
Management Services Division.—Stephen Schaefer, Room 6801–S, 720–6707.
Performance, Accountability, and Risk Division.—Ken Hill, Patriot's Plaza III, 772–6035.

UNDER SECRETARY FOR TRADE AND FOREIGN AGRICULTURAL AFFAIRS

Under Secretary.—Ted McKinney.
Chief of Staff.—Zhulieta Willbrand.
Executive Assistant.—Robert Perry.
Special Trade Counsel.—Jason Hafemeister.

FARM SERVICE AGENCY

1400 Independence Avenue, SW., Room 3086–S, Washington, DC 20250

phone (202) 720–3467

Administrator.—Richard Fordyce.
Deputy Administrator for Farm Loan Programs.—Bill Cobb, 720–4671.
Program Development and Economic Enhancement Division.—Nancy New, Room 4919–S, 720–3647.
Loan Making Division.—Vacant, Room 5438–S, 720–1632.
Loan Servicing and Property Management Division.—Michael Hinton, Room 5449–S, 720–4572.
Deputy Administrator for Farm Programs.—Bill Beam, Room 3612–S, 720–3175.
Assistant Deputy Administrator for Farm Programs.—Vacant, 720–2070.
Conservation and Environmental Programs Division.—Martin Bomar, Room 4714–S, 720–6221.
Price Support Division.—Dani Cooke, Room 4095–S, 720–7901.
Production, Emergencies and Compliance Division.—Lisa Berry (acting), Room 4754, 720–7641.
Deputy Administrator for Field Operations.—Peggy Browne, Room 3092, 690–2807.
Assistant Deputy Administrator for Field Operations.—Vacant, Room 8092, 690–2807.
Operations Review and Analysis Staff.—Perry Thompson, Room 2720–S, 690–2532.
Kansas City Commodity Office.—Vacant (816) 926–6301.

FOREIGN AGRICULTURAL SERVICE

1400 Independence Avenue, SW., Room 5071, Washington, DC 20250

phone (202) 720–3935, fax (202) 690–2159

Administrator.—Kenneth Isley.
Associate Administrator.—Daniel Whitley, 720–3935.
Associate Administrator/General Sales Manager.—Clay Hamilton, 690–1642.
Chief of Staff.—Barbara Chaves, 690–8064.

Deputy Chief of Staff.—Erica Summe, 720–7458.
Senior Director of:
Civil Rights.—Adriano Vasquez, 720–8907.
Communications and Executive Support.—Ellen Dougherty (acting), 720–0328.
Compliance and Security.—Kim Cash, 720–0773.
Customer Engagement.—Clay Hamilton, 690–1642.
Legislative Affairs.—Christopher Church, 720–6830.
Strategy and Organizational Performance.—Michelle Moore, 720–1341.

BUSINESS OPERATIONS

Executive Director.—Ronald Croushorn (acting), (202) 720–3038.
Managing Director.— Ronald Croushorn, 720–3038.
Budget.—Vacant.
Financial Management, Contracts and Grants.—Dennis Martin, 378–1061.
General Services.—Kenneth Vernon, 720–9285.
Human Capital Management.—Vacant.
Information Technology.—Christopher Wood (acting), 720–7741.

TRADE POLICY AND GEOGRAPHIC AFFAIRS

Deputy Administrator.—Mark Dries (202) 690–4062.
Managing Director.—Allison Thomas, 690–1850.
Senior Director, Division of:
Animal.—Laura Anderson, 720–6064.
Asia Pacific.—Sharynne Nenon, 690–3412.
Europe, Africa, and Middle East.—Emel Lyons, 720–1818.
Multilateral Affairs.—Aileen Mannix, 720–6791.
New Technologies and Production Methods.—Maria Pool, 720–8371.
Plant.—Catherine Fulton, 720–2461.
Processed Products.—Karina Ramos-Hides, 720–3736.
Western Hemisphere.—Charles Bertsch, 720–6278.

FOREIGN AFFAIRS

Deputy Administrator.—Katherine Nishiura (202) 720–7457.
Managing Director.—Mary Ellen Smith, 720–7241.
Senior Director for—
Africa and Middle East Operations.—Dwight Wilder, 720–7931.
Europe Operations.—Candice Bruce, 720–1324.
Global Services.—Vacant.
North Asia Operations.—Valerie Brown, 649–3862.
South Asia Operations.—Valerie Brown, 649–3862.
Western Hemisphere Operations.—Adam Branson, 690–2529.

GLOBAL MARKET ANALYSIS

Deputy Administrator.—Patrick Packnett (202) 720–6301.
Managing Director.—Vacant.
Director, Division of:
Global Commodity Analysis.—Richard O'Meara (acting), 720–6791.
International Production Assessment.—Ronald Frantz, 720–4056.
Trade and Economic Analysis.—Paul Trupo, 720–1335.

GLOBAL PROGRAMS

Deputy Administrator.—Mark Slupek (202) 720–9516.
Managing Directors: William Bomersheim, 720–1590; Marianne McElroy, 720–9408.
Senior Director, Division of:
Agricultural Economic Development.—Otto Gonzalez, 649–3859.
Cooperator Programs.—Corey Pickelsimer, 690–6888.
Credit Programs.—Amy Slusher (acting), 720–0775.
Fellowship Programs.—Avis Watts-Massenburg, 690–0032.
International Food Assistance.—Shane Danielson, 720–1230.

Program Monitoring, Evaluation and Strategic Planning.—Michelle Calhoun, 720–9513.
Program Operations.—Curt Alt, 690–4784.
Trade and Regulatory Capacity Building.—Betsy Baysinger, 720–1667.
Trade Missions and Shows.—Ryan Brewster, 720–9084.

RISK MANAGEMENT AGENCY

1400 Independence Avenue, SW., Room 6092–S, Washington, DC 20250

phone (202) 690–2803

Administrator.—Martin R. Barbre.
Chief of Staff.—Keith Gray.
Policy Advisor to the Administrator.—R. J. Layher.
Associate Administrator and Deputy Manager, FCIC, Board of Directors.—Vacant.
Associate Administrator.—Vacant.
Deputy Administrator for—
Compliance.—Heather Manzano, Room 6603–S, 720–0642.
Insurance Services.—Delores Dean (acting), Room 6709–S, 690–4494.
Product Management.—Richard Flournoy, Kansas City (816) 926–7394.

UNDER SECRETARY FOR RURAL DEVELOPMENT

1400 Independence Avenue, SW., Washington, DC 20250

phone (202) 720–4581

Under Secretary.—Vacant.
Deputy Under Secretary.—Bette Brand.
Chief of Staff.—Misty Giles.
Director, Office of External Affairs.—Marie Wheat, 720–1019.

BUSINESS AND COOPERATIVE PROGRAMS

1400 Independence Avenue, SW., Room 5801–S, Washington, DC 20250

phone (202) 690–4730

Administrator.—Rebeckah Freeman-Adcock.
Chief of Staff.—Stephanie Holderfield, 720–6165.
Deputy Administrator.—Mark Brodziski, 205–0903.
Chief of:
Cooperative Services Branch.—James Wadsworth, 720–3952.
Direct Programs Branch.—Amy Cavanaugh, 690–1681.
Intermediary Programs Branch.—David Chestnut, 692–5233.
Program Operations Branch.—Kelly Bogle, 720–7581.
Public Private Partnerships Branch.—Andrew Jermolowicz (acting), 720–3952.
Servicing Branch.—David Lewis, 690–0797.
Underwriting Branch.—Brenda Griffin, 720–6802.
Director of:
Business Development Division.—Andrew Jermolowicz, 690–0361.
Program Management Division.—Sami Zarour, 720–9549.
Program Processing Division.—Aaron Morris, 720–1501.

RURAL HOUSING SERVICE

1400 Independence Avenue, SW., Room 5014–S, Washington, DC 20250

phone (202) 692–0268

Administrator.—Beth Green (acting), 260–8165.
Director, Program Support Staff.—Ed Duval, 720–9619.
Deputy Administrator for Single Family Housing.—Cathy Glover, 720–5177.
Assistant Deputy Administrator for Single Family Housing.—Scott Nista (acting), 720–5177.
Deputy Administrator for Multi-Family Housing.—Nancie-Ann Bodell (acting), 720–3773.
Assistant Deputy Administrator for Multi-Family Housing.—Adam Hauptman, 720–3773.
Deputy Administrator for Community Facilities Programs.—Chad Parker, 720–1500.

Assistant Deputy Administrator for Community Facilities Programs.—Joseph Ben-Israel, 720–1500.

Director of:

Direct Loan and Grant Processing Division (CF).—Martha Torrez, 720–4072.

Family Housing Direct Loan Division (SFH).—Barry Ramsey, 720–5378.

Family Housing Guaranteed Loan Division (SFH).—Joaquin Tremols, 720–1465.

Guaranteed Loan Division (MFH).—Michael Steininger, 720–1610.

Guaranteed Loan Processing and Servicing Division (CF).—Deb Jackson, 720–8454.

Multi-Family Housing Portfolio Management Division, Direct Housing.—Jennifer Larson, 720–1615.

Preservation and Direct Loan Division (MFH).—C.B. Alonso, 720–1624.

RURAL UTILITIES SERVICE

1400 Independence Avenue, SW., Room 5135, Washington, DC 20250

phone (202) 720–9540

Administrator.—Chad Rupe, Room 5135–S, 720–9540.

Deputy Administrator.—Vacant.

Chief of Staff.—Curtis Anderson, Room 5135–S, 690–2732.

Assistant Administrator for Electric Programs.—Christopher McLean, Room 5165, 720–9545.

Deputy Assistant Administrator, Office of Operations.—James Elliott, Room 5165–S, 720–9546.

Senior Policy Advisor.—Jon Claffey, Room 5165–S, 720–9545.

Deputy Assistant Administrator, Office of Loan Origination and Approval.—Joseph Badin, Room 0221–S, 720–0409.

Deputy Assistant Administrator, Office of Portfolio Management and Risk Assessment.—Victor T. Vu, Room 0270–S, 720–1449.

Deputy Assistant Administrator, Office of Customer Service and Technical Assistance.—Luis Bernal, Room 0243–S, 205–3655.

Assistant Administrator for Telecommunications.—Laurel Leverrier (acting), Room 5151, 720–9556.

Deputy Assistant Administrator for Telecommunications.—Shawn Arner, Room 5151, 720–9556.

Deputy Assistant Administrator, Loan Origination and Approval.—Randall Millhiser (acting), Room 2808–S, 720–0800.

Deputy Assistant Administrator, Policy and Outreach Division.—Ken Kuchno, Room 2868–S, 720–0667.

Deputy Assistant Administrator, Portfolio Management and Risk Assessment.—Peter Aimable, Room 2839–S, 720–1025.

Assistant Administrator, Water and Environmental Programs (WEP).—Edna Primrose, Room 5145–S, 690–0308.

Deputy Assistant Administrator, Water and Environmental Programs (WEP).—Scott Barringer, Room 5145–S, 720–9643.

Assistant Administrator, Program Accounting and Regulatory Analysis.—Tim Frantz (acting), Room 5159–S, 720–9450.

Chief, Portfolio Management Branch.—Jim Wehrer, Room 2231–S, 720–2526.

Chief, Program Operations Branch.—Hal Nielson, 2236–S, 604–1664.

Director, Engineering and Environmental Staff.—Barbara Britton, Room 2237–S, 720–2567.

Director, Water Programs Division.—Vacant, Room 2232–S, 720–2567.

Legislative and Public Affairs Staff.—Anne Mayberry, Room 5144–S, 690–1756.

Senior Level Program and Policy Advisor, Policy Analysis and Regulatory Management.—Gary A. Bojes, Room 5150–S, 720–1256.

FOOD, NUTRITION, AND CONSUMER SERVICES

1400 Independence Avenue, SW., Room 216–E, Washington, DC 20250

Under Secretary.—Vacant (202) 720–7711.

Deputy Under Secretary.—Brandon Lipps.

Chief of Staff/Policy Advisor.—Anne DeCesaro.

FOOD AND NUTRITION SERVICE

3101 Park Center Drive, Room 906, Alexandria, VA 22302

phone (703) 305–2060

OFFICE OF THE ADMINISTRATOR

Administrator.—Pam Miller (703) 305–2060.
Executive Assistant.—Ruthie Jefferson, 305–2060.
Chief, Governmental Affairs.—Scott A. Carter, 305–2313.

OFFICE OF POLICY SUPPORT

Deputy Administrator for Policy Support.—Richard Lucas (703) 305–2119.
Assistant Deputy Administrator for Policy Support.—Melissa Abelev, 305–2209.
Special Assistant.—Karen Garcia, 305–2207.
Communications Director.—Brooke Hardison, 605–0229.
Director, SNAP Research and Analysis Division.—Kathryn Law, 305–2138.
Director, Special Nutrition Research and Analysis Division.—Kelley Scanlon, 457–7767.
Planning and Regulatory Affairs Branch Chief.—Kelly Stewart, 457–7772.

OFFICE OF MANAGEMENT TECHNOLOGY AND FINANCE

Associate Administrator and Chief Operating Officer.—Tameka Owens, Room 906 (703) 305–2060.
Director of Civil Rights.—Robert Contreras, Room 1200, 305–2195.

MANAGEMENT

Director, Division of:
Contracts Management.—Vacant.
Human Resources.—Allen Hatcher, Room 637, 457–7760.
Operations and Facilities.—Jose Avila, Room 217, 305–2625.

FINANCIAL MANAGEMENT

Deputy Administrator (Chief Financial Officer).—David Burr, Room 607 (703) 305–2191.
Director, Division of:
Accounting (Chief Accounting Officer).—Vacant.
Budget (Chief Budget Officer).—Lisa Greenwood, Room 611, 305–2172.
Funds Management and Planning.—Lisha Dorman, Room 609, 305–2754.
Grants and Fiscal Policy.—Vacant.
Director, Office of Internal Controls, Audits, and Investigations.—Vacant.

INFORMATION TECHNOLOGY

phone (703) 305–4370

Deputy Administrator.—Kimberly R. Jackson, Room 236.
Chief Information Security Officer.—Joseph Binns, Room 232.
Director, Division of Technology.—Sonja Farrell, Room 230.

REGIONAL OPERATIONS AND SUPPORT

Associate Administrator.—Tim English (acting), Room 906 (703) 305–2060.
Director, Division of Emergency Management.—Steve Hortin, Room 1134, 305–4375.
Director, Division of State Systems.—Karen Painter-Jacquess, Room 1146 (303) 844–6533.

OFFICE OF SUPPLEMENTAL NUTRITION ASSISTANCE PROGRAM

SNAP Associate Administrator.—Jessica Shahin, Suite 808 (703) 305–2026.
Director:
Office of Employment and Training.—Moira Johnston, Room 806, 305–2515.

Program Accountability and Administration Division.—Ron Ward, Room 816, 305–2523.
Program Development Division.—Sasha Gersten-Paal (acting), Room 814, 305–2507.
Retailer Policy and Management Division.—Andrea Gold, Room 424, 305–2434.

OFFICE OF CHILD NUTRITION PROGRAMS

Deputy Administrator.—Cindy Long, Room 640 (703) 305–2590.

OFFICE OF SUPPLEMENTAL NUTRITION AND SAFETY PROGRAMS

Deputy Administrator.—Diane M. Kriviski, Room 640 (703) 305–2057.

CENTER FOR NUTRITION POLICY AND PROMOTION

Executive Director.—Vacant.
Deputy Director.—Jackie Haven, Suite 1034 (703) 305–7600.
Director, Office of Nutrition Guidance and Analysis.—Colette Rihane, Suite 1034, 305–2403.
Director, Office of Marketing and Communication Division.—Vacant.
Senior Policy Advisor.—Stephenie Fu, Suite 1034, 305–2217.

UNDER SECRETARY FOR FOOD SAFETY

1400 Independence Avenue, SW., Room 210–W, Washington, DC 20250

phone (202) 720–0350, fax (202) 690–0820

Deputy Under Secretary.—Dr. Mindy Brashears.

FOOD SAFETY AND INSPECTION SERVICE

1400 Independence Avenue, SW., Room 331–E, Washington, DC 20250

phone (202) 720–7025, fax (202) 690–0550

Administrator.—Paul Kiecker.
Deputy Administrator.—Terri Nintemann.
Chief Operating Officer.—Todd Reed.

OFFICE OF FIELD OPERATIONS (OFO)

1400 Independence Avenue, SW., Room 344–E, Washington, DC 20250

phone (202) 720–8803, fax (202) 720–5439

Assistant Administrator.—Dr. Phil Bronstein.
Deputy Assistant Administrator.—Dr. Hany Sidrak.
Director, Recall Management Staff.—Barry Rhodes, 205–4284.
Executive Associates, Regulatory Operations: Jessica Pulz, Room 3161–S, 720–0272; Michael Watts, 205–0194.

OFFICE OF PLANNING, ANALYSIS, AND RISK MANAGEMENT (OPARM)

Assistant Administrator.—Janet Stevens, Room 3130–S, 720–9599, fax 690–5634.
Deputy Assistant Administrator.—Nathan Greenwell (acting), Room 3126–S, 981–6836, fax 690–5634.

OFFICE OF INTERNATIONAL COORDINATION (OIC)

International Coordination Executive.—Dr. Michelle Catlin, Room 3143–S, 708–8769.
Senior Advisor.—Mary Stanley, Room 3151–S, 720–0287.
International Program Specialist.—Shannon McMurtrey, Room 3147–S, 720–9966.

OFFICE OF MANAGEMENT (OM)

1400 Independence Avenue, SW., Room 347–E, Washington, DC 20250

phone 720–4425, fax 690–1742

Assistant Administrator.—Frank Mays.
Deputy Assistant Administrator.—C. Natalie Lui Duncan.

OFFICE OF POLICY AND PROGRAM DEVELOPMENT (OPPD)

1400 Independence Avenue, SW., Room 350–E, Washington, DC 20250

phone 205–0495, fax 720–2025

Assistant Administrator.—Rachel Edelstein.
Deputy Assistant Administrator.—April Regonlinski (acting).

OFFICE OF INVESTIGATION, ENFORCEMENT AND AUDIT (OIEA)

Assistant Administrator.—Carl Mayes, Room 3133–S, 720–8609, fax 720–9893.
Deputy Assistant Administrator.—Carl-Martin Ruiz, Room 3133–S, 708–9553, fax 720–9893.
Director, Audit and Resource Management Division.—Vincent Fayne, Room 2171–S, 690–5662, fax 690–0071.
Director, Compliance and Investigations Division.—Mark W. Crowe, Room 2149–S, 720–3781.

OFFICE OF PUBLIC AFFAIRS AND CONSUMER EDUCATION (OPACE)

Assistant Administrator.—Carol Blake, Room 3137–S, 720–3884, fax (202) 205–0158.
Deputy Assistant Administrator.—Aaron Lavallee, Room 3137–S, 720–0460.
Director, Congressional and Public Affairs Staff.—Roxanne Smith, Room 1175–S, 720–4413, fax 205–0158.
Director, Digital and Executive Correspondence Staff.—Shayla Mae Bailey (acting), Room 1152–S, 690–6188, fax 205–0158.

OFFICE OF PUBLIC HEALTH SCIENCE (OPHS)

1400 Independence Avenue, SW., Room 341–E, Washington, DC 20250

Assistant Administrator.—Dr. Denise Eblen, 720–2644, fax (202) 690–2980.
Deputy Assistant Administrator, Chief Public Health Veterinarian.—Dr. Kis Robertson-Hale, 720–4819, fax 690–2980.
Chief Scientist.—Dr. J. Emilio Esteban, Room 2129–S, 690–9058.

OFFICE OF EMPLOYEE EXPERIENCE AND DEVELOPMENT (OEED)

Assistant Administrator.—Soumaya Tohamy, Room 3171–S, 708–9554, fax 260–8061.
Executive Associate of Employee Experience.—Pete Bridgeman, Room 3807–S, 720–4432, fax 260–8061.

SIGNIFICANT INCIDENT PREPAREDNESS AND RESPONSE STAFF (SIPRS)

Director.—James Lott, Room 9–258, Patriot Plaza III, 690–6523, fax 690–6459.

UNDER SECRETARY FOR RESEARCH, EDUCATION, AND ECONOMICS

Under Secretary.—Vacant.
Deputy Under Secretary.—Dr. Scott H. Hutchins (202) 720–1542.
Chief of Staff.—Courtney Knupp, 720–1542.
Communications Director.—Vacant, 720–1375.
Executive Assistant.—Michele Simmons, 720–1542.
Staff Assistant.—Elizabeth Edmunds, 690–1254.

AGRICULTURAL RESEARCH SERVICE

1400 Independence Avenue, SW., Room 302–A, Washington, DC 20250

phone (202) 720–3656, fax 720–5427

Administrator.— Dr. Chavonda Jacobs-Young.
Associate Administrator for—
Research Operations.—Dr. Simon Liu, 720–3658.
Research Programs.—Dr. Steven Kappes (301) 504–5084.
Director of:
Budget and Program Management Staff.—Michael Arnold, Room 358–A, 720–4421.
Legislative Affairs.—Gary Mayo, 260–9494.
Office of Communications.—J.D. Wyllie (301) 504–1636.
Assistant Administrator, Research Operations and Management, Office of Technology Transfer.—Mojdeh Bahar (301) 504–6905.
Deputy Administrator, Administrative and Financial Management.—Joon Park, 690–2575.
Director, National Agricultural Library.—Paul Wester (301) 504–5248.

AREA OFFICES

Director of:
Midwest Area.—J.L. Willett, 1815 North University Street, Room 2004, Peoria, IL 61604–0000 (309) 681–6602.
Northeast Area.—Dariusz Swietlik, Building 003, Room 223, BARC-West, Beltsville, MD 20705 (301) 504–6078.
Pacific West Area.—Robert Matteri, 800 Buchanan Street, Room 2030, Albany, CA 94710 (510) 559–6060.
Plains Area.—Larry Chandler, 2150 Centre Avenue, Building D, Suite 300, Ft. Collins, CO 80525–8119 (970) 492–7057.
Southeast Area.—Archie Tucker, 141 Experiment Station Road, Stoneville, MS 38776 (662) 686–5265.

NATIONAL INSTITUTE OF FOOD AND AGRICULTURE

1400 Independence Avenue, SW., Room 305–A, Washington, DC 20250

phone (202) 720–4423, fax 720–8987

Director.—Dr. Parag Chitnis (acting).
Associate Director for Programs.—Bryan Kaphammer (acting), 445–5404.
Chief/Officer/Legislative Liaisons: William Hoffman, Room 305–A, 445–5576; Kimberly Whittet, Room 305–A, 720–8291.
Director of:
Budget Staff.—Paula Geiger, Room 332–A, 720–2675.
Communications.—Faith Peppers.
Equal Opportunity Staff.—Drenda Williams.
Planning, Accountability, and Reporting.—Michael Fitzner (acting).
Deputy Director for—
Institute of Bioenergy, Climate, and Environment.—Timothy Conner (acting).
Institute of Food Production and Sustainability.—Michael Fitzner (acting).
Institute of Food Safety and Nutrition.—Timothy Conner (acting).
Institute of Youth, Family, and Community.—Siva Sureshwaran (acting).
Office of Grants and Financial Management.—Matthew Faulkner.

ECONOMIC RESEARCH SERVICE

355 E Street, SW., Washington, DC 20024–3221

phone (202) 694–5000

Administrator.—Spiro Stefanou, Room 6–201.
Associate Administrator.—Jim Staiert, Room 6–197.
Assistant Administrator.—Kelly Maguire (acting), Room 6–142.
Civil Rights Director.—Chris Van Alstyne.
Director, Division of:
Food Economics.—Jay Variyam, Room 5–203, 694–5457.

Information Services.—Camille Haylock (acting), Room 4–197, 694–5004.
Market Trade and Economics.—Utpal Vasavada (acting), Room 5–197, 694–5626.
Resource and Rural Economics.—Robert Gibbs, Room 6–131, 694–5478.

NATIONAL AGRICULTURAL STATISTICS SERVICE

1400 Independence Avenue, SW., Room 5041A–S, Washington, DC 20250

phone (202) 720–2707

Administrator.—Hubert Hamer, Room 5041A, 720–2707.
Associate Administrator.—Kevin Barnes, Room 5041A, 720–4333.
Director of:
Census and Survey Division.—Barbara Rater, Room 6306, 720–4557.
Eastern Field Operations.—Jay Johnson, Room 5053, 720–3638.
Information Technology Division.—Paul Williams (acting), Room 5847, 720–2984.
Methodology Division.—Joe Parsons, Room 5336C, 690–8141.
National Operations Division.—Joseph Prusacki (314) 595–9501, ext. 57501.
Research and Development Division.—Dr. Linda Young, Room 6035, 690–1401.
Statistics Division.—Daniel Kerestes, Room 5435, 720–3896.
Western Field Operations.—Troy Joshua, Room 5053, 720–8220.

UNDER SECRETARY FOR MARKETING AND REGULATORY PROGRAMS

1400 Independence Avenue, SW., Room 228–W, Washington, DC 20250

phone (202) 720–4256, fax 720–5775

Under Secretary.—Greg Ibach.
Chief of Staff.—Lorren Walker.
Senior Advisor and Counsel.—Caleb Crosswhite
Policy Advisor and Special Assistant.—Turner Bridgforth.

AGRICULTURAL MARKETING SERVICE

1400 Independence Avenue, SW., Room 3069–S, Washington, DC 20250

phone (202) 720–5115, fax 692–0313

Administrator.—Bruce Summers.
Associate Administrator.—Erin Morris, 690–4024.
Associate Administrator/Chief Operations Officer.—Randall Jones, 720–0220.
Deputy Associate Administrator.—Charles Parrott, 690–9144.
Deputy Administrator for—
Commodity Procurement Program.—David Tuckwiller, Room 3522, 720–2784.
Cotton and Tobacco Program.—Darryl Earnest (901) 384–3060.
Dairy Program.—Dana Coale, Room 2968–S, 720–4392.
Fair Trade Practices Program.—Michael Durando, Room 2055–S, 720–0219.
Federal Grain Inspection Services.—Arthur Neal, Room 2043, 720–9171.
Livestock and Poultry Program.—Jennifer Porter, Room 2092–S, 720–5705.
Management and Analysis Program.—Keith Adams, Room 2095–S, 720–6766.
National Organic Program.—Jennifer Tucker, Room 2642, 720–3252.
Science and Technology Program.—Ruihong Guo, Room 3543–S, 720–8556.
Specialty Crops Program.—Sonia Jimenez, Room 2077–S, 720–4722.
Transportation and Marketing Program.—Karla Whalen (acting), Room 4543, 690–1300.
Director, Legislative and Regulatory Review Staff.—Bill Allen, Room 3943–S, 720–2468.

ANIMAL AND PLANT HEALTH INSPECTION SERVICE (APHIS)

1400 Independence Avenue, SW., Room 312–E, Washington, DC 20250

phone (202) 720–3668, fax 720–3054

OFFICE OF THE ADMINISTRATOR

Administrator.—Kevin Shea.
Associate Administrators: Dr. Mark Davidson, Dr. Jack Shere, Dr. Michael Watson.
Director, Office of Civil Rights, Diversity, and Inclusion.—Michon Oubichon, Room 1137–S, 720–7012, fax 720–2365.

ANIMAL CARE

4700 River Road, Riverdale, MD 20737

phone (301) 851–3751, fax 734–4328

Deputy Administrator.—Dr. Elizabeth Goldentyer.
Associate Deputy Administrator.—Dr. Robert Gibbens (acting).

BIOTECHNOLOGY REGULATORY SERVICES

4700 River Road, Riverdale, MD 20737

phone (301) 851–3877, fax (301) 734–6352

Deputy Administrator.—Bernadette Juarez, 851–2735.
Associate Deputy Administrator.—Ibrahim M. Shaqir, 851–3938.
Assistant Deputy Administrator.—Alan Pearson, 851–3944.

INTERNATIONAL SERVICES

1400 Independence Avenue, SW., Room 324–E, Washington, DC 20250

phone (202) 799–7132, fax 690–1484

Deputy Administrator.—Cheryle Blakely, 799–7132.
Associate Deputy Administrators: Rebecca Bech, 799–7131; Jessica Mahalingappa, 799–7121.
Chief of Staff.—Robin White, 799–7130.

LEGISLATIVE AND PUBLIC AFFAIRS

1400 Independence Avenue, SW., Room 1147–S, Washington, DC 20250

phone (202) 799–7031, fax 720–3982

Deputy Administrator.—Bethany Jones.
Associate Deputy Administrator.—Abbey Fretz.
Director of:
Executive Communications.—Christina Myers (301) 851–4111.
Freedom of Information.—Tonya Woods, 851–4102.
Public Affairs.—Ed Curlett, 851–4100.

MARKETING AND REGULATORY PROGRAMS BUSINESS SERVICES

1400 Independence Avenue, SW., Room 308–E, Washington, DC 20250

phone (202) 799–7065, fax (202) 690–0686

Deputy Administrator.—Douglas Nash, 799–7064.
Associate Deputy Administrator.—Melissa Tharp, 799–7058.

PLANT PROTECTION AND QUARANTINE

1400 Independence Avenue, SW., Room 303–E, Washington, DC 20250

phone (202) 799–7163, fax 690–0472

Deputy Administrator.—Osama El-Lissy.
Associate Deputy Administrator for—
Field Operations.—Matthew Royer (919) 855–7300.
Policy Management.—Alan Dowdy (202) 799–7163.
Science and Technology.—Ronald Sequeira (301) 851–2244.

POLICY AND PROGRAM DEVELOPMENT

4700 River Road, Riverdale, MD 20737

phone (301) 851–3095, fax (301) 734–5899

Deputy Administrator.—Christine Zakarka.

Associate Deputy Administrator.—Shannon Hamm.
Unit Chiefs:
Budget and Program Analysis.—Karen Ratzow, 851–3081.
Environmental and Risk Analysis Service.—Elizabeth Nelson, 851–3089.
Planning, Evaluation, and Decision Support.—Michelle Wenberg, 851–3143.
Policy Analysis and Development.—Parveen Setia, 851–3126.
Program Assessment and Accountability.—Erik Anderson (612) 336–3393.
Regulatory Analysis and Development.—Benjamin Kaczmarski, 851–3080.

VETERINARY SERVICES

1400 Independence Avenue, SW., Room 317–E, Washington, DC 20250

phone (202) 799–7146, fax 690–4171

Deputy Administrator.—Burke L. Healey, 799–7147.
Administrative Assistant.—Vacant, 799–7146.
Associate Deputy Administrator.—Rosemary Sifford, 799–7145.
Chief of Staff.—Ashley Levesque, 799–7151.
Associate Deputy Administrator for—
Diagnostics and Biologics.—Beth Lautner (515) 337–6161.
Field Operations.—Vacant.
Program Support Services.—Vacant.
Strategy and Policy.—Sarah Tomlinson (970) 474–7152.

WILDLIFE SERVICES

1400 Independence Avenue, SW., Room 1624, Washington, DC 20250

phone (202) 799–7095, fax 690–0053

Deputy Administrator.—Janet L. Bucknall.
Associate Deputy Administrators: Martin Mendoza, Jr., Ginger Murphy.
Director for Operational Support.—David S. Reinhold (301) 851–4009.

DEPARTMENT OF COMMERCE

Herbert C. Hoover Building

1401 Constitution Avenue, NW., Washington, DC 20230

phone (202) 482–2000, https://doc.gov

WILBUR ROSS, Secretary of Commerce; born in Weehawken, NJ, November 28, 1937; education: B.A., Yale University, New Haven, CT, 1959; M.B.A.; Harvard University, Cambridge, MA, 1961; professional: U.S. Army Adjutant General's Corps, 1961–63; president, Faulkner Dawkins and Sullivan Securities Corp., New York, NY, 1964–76; executive managing director, Rothschild, Inc. (and its predecessor, New Court Securities Corp.), New York, 1976–2000; chairman and chief strategy officer, WL Ross & Co. LLC, New York, 2000–17; named by Bloomberg Markets as one of the 50 most influential people in global finance; only person elected to both Private Equity Hall of Fame and Turnaround Management Hall of Fame; married: Hilary Geary Ross; children: Jessica Ross, Amanda Ross, Ted Geary, and Jack Geary; nominated by President Donald J. Trump to become the 39th Secretary of Commerce, and was sworn in by Vice President Mike Pence on February 28, 2017.

OFFICE OF THE SECRETARY

Secretary of Commerce.—Wilbur Ross, Room 5854 (202) 482–2112.

Deputy Secretary.—Karen Dunn Kelley, Room 5838, 482–8376.

Chief of Staff.—Michael J. Walsh, Jr., Room 5854, 482–4246.

Deputy Chief of Staff and Director of Policy.—Vacant.

Senior Advisor.—Daniel Risko, Room 5838, 482–6010.

Director, Office of Business Liaison.—W. Patrick Wilson, Room 5062, 482–1360.

Executive Secretariat, Director of Administration.—Tanika Hawkins (acting), Room 5516, 482–3934.

Public Affairs.—Caroline Tucker (acting), Room 5413, 482–2584.

Scheduling and Advance.—Teresa Davis (acting), Room 5883, 482–5129.

White House Liaison.—Peter Barrett, Room 50037, 482–4864.

Deputy Director, Office of White House Liaison.—Ryan H. Leppert, Room 50037, 482–4674.

GENERAL COUNSEL

General Counsel.—Michael J. Walsh, Jr. (performing the delegated duties of the General Counsel), Room 5870 (202) 482–4772.

ASSISTANT SECRETARY FOR LEGISLATIVE AND INTERGOVERNMENTAL AFFAIRS

Assistant Secretary.—Anthony Foti (performing the delegated duties of the Assistant Secretary), Room 5421 (202) 482–3663, fax 482–4420.

Deputy Assistant Secretary.—Lawson Kluttz (acting), Room 5421, 482–3663, fax 482–4420.

Director for Intergovernmental Affairs.—Vacant.

Associate Director for Legislative Affairs.—Harry Kumar, Room 5422, 482–8094.

Legislative Affairs Specialist.—Eileen Dombrowski, Room 5422, 482–5714.

Intergovernmental Affairs Specialist.—Diego-Christopher Lopez, Room 5421, 482–3844

Confidential Assistant.—Duncan McGaan, Room 5421, 482–3663.

CHIEF FINANCIAL OFFICER AND ASSISTANT SECRETARY FOR ADMINISTRATION

Chief Financial Officer and Assistant Secretary.—Thomas F. Gilman, Room 58038 (202) 482–2118, fax 482–3592.

Deputy Assistant Secretary for Administration.—Wynn W. Coggins, Room 58032.
Deputy Chief Financial Officer/Director for Financial Management.—Stephen Kunze, Room D203, 482–1207.
Director, Office of:
Acquisition Management.—Barry Berkowitz, Room 6422, 482–4248.
Budget.—Michael Phelps, Room C300, 482–4648, fax 482–3361.
Civil Rights.—Tinisha Agramonte, Room 6058, 482–0625, fax 482–0048.
Human Resources Management.—John Guenther (acting), Room 50003, 482–4807, fax 482–1601.
Program Evaluation.—Christine Heflin, Room 4858, 482–1705.
Risk Management.—Albert Moesle, Room 6422, 482–3760.
Security.—Richard Townsend, Room 1067, 482–4371, fax 501–6355.

CHIEF INFORMATION OFFICER

Chief Information Officer.—André Mendes, Room 38014 (202) 482–4797.
Deputy Chief Information Officer.—Terri Ware, Room 38014, 482–1888.
Deputy Chief Information Officer, Office of Solutions and Service Delivery.—Vacant.
Office of Cybersecurity and IT Risk Management:
Chief Information Security Officer.—Vacant.
Deputy Chief Information Security Officer.—Donna Bennett, Room 6889, 482–5988.
Director for—
Business and Administrative Services.—Lucas Castillo, Room 38014, 482–2337.
Enterprise Solutions and Services.—Antoinette Brown, Room 6078, 482–4444.
Enterprise Technology.—Rajeev Sharma, Room 6616, 482–8330.
FITARA.—Shirley Bowie-Dean, Room 38014, 482–0084.
National Programs.—Roger Clark, Room C234, 482–7989.
National Security Solutions and Services.—Ja'Nelle DeVore, Room 6625, 482–6443.
Policy and Guidance.—Jennifer Jessup, Room 6616, 482–0336.

INSPECTOR GENERAL

Inspector General.—Peggy E. Gustafson, Room 7898C (202) 482–4661.
Deputy Inspector General.—Roderick Anderson, Room 7898B, 482–1855.
Counsel to the Inspector General.—Wade Green, Room 7896, 482–5992.
Principal Assistant Inspector General for Audit.—Mark Zabarsky, Room 7087, 482–3884.
Assistant Inspector General, Office of Investigations.—Scott Kiefer, Room 7886B, 482–0300.

OFFICE OF THE UNDER SECRETARY FOR ECONOMIC AFFAIRS

1401 Constitution Avenue, NW., Washington, DC 20230

phone (202) 482–6607

Under Secretary for Economic Affairs.—Brian C. Moyer (performing the non-exclusive functions and duties of the Under Secretary for Economic Affairs), Room 4848, 482–3727.
Chief Counsel.—Vacant, Room 4877, 482–5394.
Chief Economist.—Vacant, Room 4860, 482–3523.
Deputy Chief Economist.—Vacant, Room 4861, 482–4871.
Director of External Affairs.—Vacant, Room 4838, 482–3331.

BUREAU OF ECONOMIC ANALYSIS

4600 Silver Hill Road, Washington, DC 20230

phone (301) 278–9004

Director.—Mary Bohman (acting), Room 8K405A, 278–9600.
Deputy Director.—Mary Bohman, Room 8K403, 278–9602.
Chief Economist.—Dennis Fixler, Room 8K417, 278–9607.
Chief Information Officer.—Brian Callahan, Room 8K126, 278–9332.
Associate Director for—
Industry Economics.—Thomas Howells, Room 6K406, 278–9612.
International Economics.—Paul Farello, Room 7K102, 278–9561.
National Economic Accounts.—Erich Strasser, Room 8K403, 278–9602.

Regional Economics.—Joel Platt, Room 7K408, 278–9605.
Chief Administrative Officer.—Kathleen James, Room 8K102, 278–9014.
Division Chiefs:
Administrative Services.—John Ingley (acting), Room 8K104, 278–9043.
Balance of Payments.—Kristy Howell, Room 7K102, 278–9561.
Communications.—Lucas Hitt, Room 8K122, 278–9223.
Direct Investment Division.—Patricia Abaroa, Room 7K136, 278–9591.
Government.—Pamela Kelly, Room K136, 278–9781.
Industry Applications Division.—Thomas Howells (acting), Room 6K411, 278–9586.
Industry Sector Division.—Ted Morgan, Room 6K403B, 278–9541.
National Income and Wealth.—David Wasshausen, Room 6K108, 278–9752.
Regional Income Division.—Mauricio Ortiz, Room 7K411, 278–9269.
Regional Product Division.—Joel Platt (acting), Room 7K207, 278–9788.

THE BUREAU OF THE CENSUS

4600 Silver Hill Road, Suitland, MD 20746

Director.—Steven Dillingham, Room 8H002 (301) 763–2135.
Deputy Director and Chief Operating Officer.—Ron S. Jarmin, Room 8H006, 763–2138.
Chief Advisor.—Enrique Lamas, Room 8H114, 763–3811.
Chief Administrative Officer.—Laura K. Furgione, Room 8H140, 763–0264.
Chief Financial Officer.—Benjamin J. Page, Room 8H128, 763–4700.
Chief Information Officer.—Kevin B. Smith, Room 8H138, 763–2117.
Deputy Chief Information Officer.—Gregg D. Bailey, Room 4K030, 763–0989.
Chief, Office of Program, Performance and Stakeholder Integration.—David R. Ziaya, Room 8H212, 763–7924.
Deputy Chief, Office of Program, Performance and Stakeholder Integration.—Douglas Clift, Room 2K124, 763–5499.
Associate Director for—
Communications.—Ali M. Ahmad, Room 8H144, 763–8789.
Decennial Census Programs.—Albert E. Fontenot, Room 8H122, 763–4668.
Demographic Programs.—Victoria A. Velkoff, Room 8H134, 763–1372.
Economic Programs.—Nick Orsini, Room 8K132, 763–6959.
Field Operations.—Timothy P. Olson, Room 8H126, 763–2072.
Research and Methodology.—John M. Abowd, Room 8H120, 763–5880.
Assistant Director for—
Communications: Stephen L. Buckner, Room 8H062, 763–3586; Burton Reist, Room 8H069, 763–4155.
Decennial Census Programs: Deborah M. Stempowski, Room 2H174, 763–1417; Michael T. Thieme, Room 2K276, 763–9062.
Demographic Programs.—Eloise K. Parker, Room 8H182, 763–1679.
Economic Programs.—Samuel C. Jones, Room 5H160, 763–2265.
Field Division.—James T. Christy, Room 5H128, (818) 267–1700.
Research and Methodology.—John L. Eltinge, Room 5K156, 763–9604.
Division and Office Chief for—
Acquisition.—Molly A. Shea, Room 2J438, 763–5590.
Administrative and Customer Services.—John T. Blanchard, Room 3J436, 763–0697.
American Community Survey Office.—Donna M. Daily, Room 4K276, 763–5258.
Applications Development and Services Division.—David J. Peters, Room 3H174, 763–9359.
Budget.—Everett G. Whiteley, Room 2K122, 763–3861.
Center for Behavioral Science Methods.—Paul C. Beatty, Room 5K418, 763–5001.
Center for Economic Studies.—Lucia S. Foster, Room 5K032, 763–6444.
Center for Enterprise Dissemination.—Robert T. Sienkiewicz, Room 5K124, 763–1234.
Center for New Media and Promotions.—Lisa Wolfisch, Room 8H484, 763–5716.
Center for Optimization and Data Science.—John Eltinge (acting), Room 5K156, 763–9604.
Center for Statistical Research and Methodology.—Tommy Wright, Room 5K108, 763–1702.
Chief Technology Office.—Vacant, Room 3H162, 763–2398.
Computer Services Division.—Kenneth R. Boyd, Bowie, 763–4341.
Customer Liaison and Marketing Services Office.—Misty L. Reed, Room 8H180, 763–0228.
Decennial Census Management Division.—Jennifer W. Reichert, Room 2H175, 763–4298.
Decennial Contracts Execution Office.—Luis J. Cano, 2K067, 763–2340.
Decennial Information Technology Division.—Michael T. Thieme (acting), Room 5K030, 763–9062.

Decennial Statistical Studies Division.—Patrick Cantwell, Room 4H464, 763–4982.
Demographic Statistical Methods Division.—Anthony G. Tersine, Jr., Room 7H162, 763–1994.
Demographic Systems Division.—Jeffery D. Sisson, Room 7H128, 763–3773.
Economic Applications Division.—Samuel C. Jones (acting), Room 5H160, 763–2265.
Economic Indicators Division.—Stephanie I. Studds, Room 7K154, 763–2633.
Economic Management Division.—Lisa Endy Donaldson, Room 6K064, 763–7296.
Economic Reimbursable Surveys Division.—Kevin E. Deardorff, Room 6H128, 763–6033.
Economic Statistical Methods Division.—Carol V. Caldwell, Room 5H174, 763–3390.
Economy Wide Statistics Division.—Kimberly P. Moore, Room 8K154, 763–7643.
Equal Employment Opportunity Office.—Joseph E. Hairston, Room 3K108, 763–9002.
Field Division.—Dale C. Kelly, Room 5H128, 763–6937.
Finance Division.—Ben J. Page (acting), Room 8H128, 763–2101.
Geography Division.—Deirdre Dalpiaz Bishop, Room 4H174, 763–1696.
Human Resources Division.—Veronica M. LeGrande, Room 2J436, 763–3721.
Information Systems Support and Review Office.—Ilene Tayman (acting), Room 3K047, 763–5070.
LAN Technology Support Office.—Patricia T. Musselman, Room 4K108, 763–5632.
National Processing Center.—Jeffrey L. Bryant (812) 215–3344.
Office of Congressional and Intergovernmental Affairs.—Christopher J. Stanley, Room 8H166, 763–4276.
Office of Information Security.—Beau Houser (acting), Room 3K133, 763–5032.
Policy Coordination Office.—David Donovan (acting), Room 8H146, 763–3449.
Population Division.—Karen Battle, Room 6H174, 763–2071.
Public Information Office.—Michael C. Cook, Room 8H060, 763–4083.
Security Office.—Robert J. Drew (acting), Room 3J231, 763–8340.
Social, Economic, and Housing Statistics.—David G. Waddington, Room 7H174, 763–3195.
Telecommunications Office.—Kenneth R. Harrison, Room 4K032, 763–1793.

BUREAU OF INDUSTRY AND SECURITY

Under Secretary.—Cordell Hull (acting), Room 3898B (202) 482–1455.
Deputy Under Secretary.—Jeremy Pelter (performing the non-exclusive functions and duties of the Deputy Under Secretary), Room 3894, 482–1427.
Deputy Chief of Staff.—Stephen Billy.
Deputy Chief of Staff for Policy.—Kevin Kurland.
Chief Counsel.—Deborah Curtis, Room 3839, 482–2315.
Office of Congressional and Public Affairs.—Michael Cys, Room 3895, 482–0097.
Chief Financial Officer and Director of Administration.—Carol Rose, Room 6622, 482–1900.
Chief Information Officer.—Vacant, Room 6092, 482–4296.
Assistant Secretary for Export Administration.—Rich Ashooh, Room 3886C, 482–5491.
Deputy Assistant Secretary.—Matthew S. Borman, Room 3886C, 482–5711.
Assistant Secretary for Export Enforcement.—P. Lee Smith (performing the non-exclusive functions and duties of the Assistant Secretary for Export Enforcement), Room 3723, 482–3618.
Deputy Assistant Secretary.—Douglas R. Hassebrock, Room 3723, 482–3618.
Operating Committee Chair.—MiYong Kim, Room 3889, 482–5863 / 5864.
Director, Office of:
Antiboycott Compliance.—Cathleen Ryan, Room 6098, 482–2381.
Enforcement Analysis.—Kevin J. Kurland, Room 4065, 482–4255.
Export Enforcement.—John Sonderman (acting), Room 4508, 482–5079.
Exporter Services.—Karen H. Nies-Vogel, Room 2099B, 482–3811.
National Security and Technology Transfer Controls.—Eileen M. Albanese, Room 2616, 482–0092.
Nonproliferation and Treaty Compliance.—Alexander Lopes, Room 2627, 482–3825.
Strategic Industries and Economic Security.—Vacant, Room 3878, 482–4506.
Technology Evaluation.—Vacant, Room 1093, 482–4933.

ECONOMIC DEVELOPMENT ADMINISTRATION

Assistant Secretary.—Dana Gartzke (delegated the authority to perform the functions and duties of the Assistant Secretary), Room 78006 (202) 482–5081.
Deputy Assistant Secretary and Chief Operating Officer.—Dennis Alvord, Room 71030, 482–3846.

Chief Counsel.—Jeff Roberson, Room 72023, 482–1315.
Chief Financial Officer and Chief Administrative Officer.—Gregory Brown, Room 70025, 482–0886.
Director, Office of:
Budget and Finance Division.—Robert White, Room 70023, 482–4740.
External Affairs.—Joel Frushone, Room 70004, 482–6395.
Innovation and Entrepreneurship.—Craig Buerstatte, Room 78018, 482–6331.
Legislative and Intergovernmental Affairs.—Angela Ewell-Madison, Room 71006, 482–2900.
Public Affairs.—John Atwood (acting), Room 71014, 482–4085.
Performance and National Programs, Trade Adjustment Assistance.—Bryan Borlik, Room 71021, 482–3901.

INTERNATIONAL TRADE ADMINISTRATION

Under Secretary.—Joseph C. Semsar (acting), Room 3850 (202) 482–2867.
Deputy Under Secretary.—Diane Farrell (acting), Room 3842, 482–3917.
Chief of Staff.—Bradley McKinney, Room 3850, 482–5142.
Legislative and Intergovernmental Affairs.—Alex Stoddard, Room 3424, 482–3015.
Public Affairs.—Vanessa Ambrosini (acting), Room 3421, 482–3809.
Trade Promotion Coordinating Committee.—Pat Kirwan, Room 3424, 482–5455.
Chief Counsel for International Commerce.—John Cobau, Room 5624, 482–0937.

ADMINISTRATION

Director of Budget, Finance and Administration.—Marcus Points, Room 3836, 482–1343.
Deputy Chief Administrative Officer.—Vacant.
Chief Information Officer.—Rona Bunn (acting), Room 48000, 482–3801.
Analysis and Reporting.—Susan Hamrock Mann, Room 41014, 482–9151.
Budget and Finance.—Tanya Smith, Room 41026, 482–5739.
Human Capital, People Division.—Ruben Pedroza, Room 20011, 482–3072.
Human Capital, Learning Division.—Brian McNamara, Room 40007, 482–0332.
Knowledge Management.—Stan Kowalski, Room 48015, 482–0123.
Management and Operations.—Victor E. Powers, Room 40003, 482–5436.

GLOBAL MARKETS AND U.S. AND FOREIGN COMMERCIAL SERVICE

Assistant Secretary for Global Markets and Director General of the U.S. and Foreign Commercial Service.—Ian Steff, Room 3868, 482–5777.
Deputy Director General.—Dale Tasharski, Room 3868, 482–5777.
Deputy Assistant Secretary for—
Asia.—Laurie Farris (acting), Room 2846, 482–0423.
China.—Alan Turley, Room 38006, 482–4527.
Domestic Operations.—Ana Guevara, Room 42030, 482–1466.
Europe.—David De Falco (acting), Room 31032, 482–2178.
The Middle East and Africa.—Robyn Kessler (acting), Room 31022, 482–1902.
Western Hemisphere.—Ian Saunders, Room 30013, 482–2689.
Executive Director, Office of:
Asia.—Valerie Dees (acting), Room 2038, 482–0477.
China.—Scott Tatlock, Room 38008, 482–5908.
Europe and Eurasia.—Maria Luisa Escudero (acting), Room 31032, 482–0431.
Middle East and Africa.—Vacant.
National Field.—Thomas McGinty, Room 48033, 482–5927.
SelectUSA.—Greg Kalbaugh, Room 30033, 482–0829.
Western Hemisphere.—Rich Steffens, Room 30017, 482–5755.
Director, Office of:
Administrative Services.—Jerome Holloway, Room 21018, 482–1594.
Advocacy Center.—Americo Tadeu (acting), Room 10020, 482–7428.
Budget.—David Tumblin, Room 21008R, 482–0823.
Digital Initiatives.—John Larsen (acting), Room 11011, 482–6432.
Foreign Service Human Capital.—Allison Smith, Room 1184, 482–5061.
Strategic Planning.—Joe Carter (acting), Room 21022, 482–2484.

ASSISTANT SECRETARY FOR ENFORCEMENT AND COMPLIANCE

Assistant Secretary.—Jeffrey I. Kessler, Room 3099B, 482–1780.
Deputy Assistant Secretary.—Christian Marsh, Room 3705, 482–2104.
Chief Counsel.—Robert Heilferty, Room 3622, 482–0082.
Deputy Assistant Secretary for—
Antidumping and Countervailing Duty Operations.—James Maeder, Room 3095, 482–5497.
Policy and Negotiations.—Carole Showers (acting), Room 3713, 482–6199.
Associate Deputy Assistant Secretary for AD/CVD Operations.—Vacant.
Executive Secretary for Foreign-Trade Zones Board.—Andrew McGilvray, Room 21013, 482–2862.
Executive Director, Office of:
Policy.—Carole Showers, Room 3713, 482–6199.
Trade Agreements Policy and Negotiations.—Steven Presing, Room 3051, 482–1672.

ASSISTANT SECRETARY FOR INDUSTRY AND ANALYSIS

Assistant Secretary.—Nazak Nikakhtar, Room 2856, 482–1461.
Deputy Assistant Secretary.—Anne Driscoll, Room 2856, 482–1112.
Deputy Assistant Secretary for—
Manufacturing.—Brian Lenihan, Room 28004, 482–1872.
Services.—James Sullivan, Room 11030, 482–5261.
Textiles, Consumer Goods, and Materials.—Lloyd E. Wood III, Room 30003, 482–3737.
Trade Policy and Analysis.—Praveen Dixit, Room 21028, 482–3177.
Travel and Tourism.—Philip Lovas, Room 10007, 482–4931.
Director, Office of:
Industry Engagement.—Kirt Gallatin, Room 2065, 482–1124.
Planning, Coordination, and Management.—Sylvia Prosak, Room 32038, 482–1976.
Trade Agreements Secretariat.—Paul Morris, Room 2061, 482–5438.

PRESIDENT'S EXPORT COUNCIL

[Authorized by Executive Order 12131, as amended]

Executive Director, Under Secretary of International Trade.—Joseph C. Semsar (acting), Room 3850, 482–2867.
Executive Secretary and Staff Director.—Tricia Van Orden, Room 3424, 482–5876.

MINORITY BUSINESS DEVELOPMENT AGENCY

National Director.—David J. Byrd, Room 5053 (202) 482–2332.
Confidential Assistant.—Ryan Sun, Room 5053, 482–6068.
National Deputy Director.—Vacant.
Chief Counsel.—Josephine Arnold, Room 5093, 482–5461.
Associate Director for Business Development.—Efrain Gonzalez, Room 5079, 482–1940.
Chief for Business Development.—Joann Hill, Room 5079, 482–1940.
Associate Director for Legislative, Education and Intergovernmental Affairs.—Vacant.
Chief of Legislative, Education and Intergovernmental Affairs.—Bridget Gonzales, Room 5089, 482–6272.
Public Affairs Supervisor.—Velicia Woods, Room 5089, 482–6272.
Associate Director for Management.—Edith McCloud, Room 5082, 482–2332.
Chief Financial Officer.—Tania White, Room 5606, 482–3341.

NATIONAL OCEANIC AND ATMOSPHERIC ADMINISTRATION

14th & Constitution Avenue, NW., Washington, DC 20230–0001 (HCHB)

1335 East-West Highway, Silver Spring, MD 20910 (SSMC1)

1325 East-West Highway, Silver Spring, MD 20910 (SSMC2)

1315 East-West Highway, Silver Spring, MD 20910 (SSMC3)

1305 East-West Highway, Silver Spring, MD 20910 (SSMC4)

Assistant Secretary of Commerce for Environmental Observation and Prediction.—Neil Jacobs, Ph.D. (performing the duties of Under Secretary of Commerce for Oceans and Atmosphere), HCHB, Room 58006 (202) 482–6236.

Assistant Secretary of Commerce for Oceans and Atmosphere/Deputy NOAA Administrator.—RDML Timothy Gallaudet, Ph.D., USN (Ret.), HCHB, Room 51030, 482–3436.
Chief Scientist.—Craig McLean (acting), SSMC3, Room 11458 (301) 713–2458.
Chief of Staff.—John Luce (acting), HCHB, Room 78026 (202) 482–4627.
Deputy Under Secretary for Operations.—Benjamin Friedman, HCHB, Room 58012, 482–4569.
Deputy Assistant Secretary for International Fisheries.—Drew Lawler, SSMC3, Room 15410 (301) 427–8061.
Director, Office of:
Acquisition and Grants.—Jeffrey Thomas (acting), SSMC1, Room 6300 (301) 713–0325.
Communications and External Affairs.—Scott Smullen, HCHB, Room 60032R (202) 482–1097.
Education.—Louisa Koch, HCHB, Room 6869, 482–3384.
Federal Coordinator for Meteorology.—Michael Bonadonna, SSMC2, Room 7130 (301) 628–0055.
International Affairs and Senior Advisor for International Affairs.—Elizabeth McLanahan, Room 68029 (202) 482–6196.
Legislative and Intergovernmental Affairs.—Wendy Lewis, HCHB, Room 60018, 482–5448.
Office of Human Capital Services.—Kimberlyn Bauhs, SSMC4, Room 12520 (301) 628–1866.
Chief Administrative Officer.—Deirdre Jones (acting), SSMC4, Room 8431 (301) 713–0836, ext. 105.
Chief Financial Officer.—Mark Seiler, HCHB, Room 62025 (202) 482–4022.
Chief Information Officer/High Performance Computing and Communications.—Zachary Goldstein, SSMC3, HCHB, Room 9651 (301) 713–9600.
General Counsel.—John Luce, HCHB, Room 78026 (202) 482–4627.

NATIONAL MARINE FISHERIES SERVICE

1315 East-West Highway, Silver Spring, MD 20910 (SSMC3)

Assistant Administrator.—Chris Oliver, Room 14636 (301) 427–8000.
Deputy Assistant Administrator for—
Operations.—Paul Doremus, Ph.D., Room 14743, 427–8000.
Regulatory Programs.—Samuel Rauch, Room 14657, 427–8000.
Chief Information Officer.—Roy Varghese, Room 3657, 427–8810.
Director, Office of:
Aquaculture Program.—David O'Brien (acting), Room 12618, 427–8337.
Habitat Conservation.—Pat Montanio, Room 14828, 427–8600.
International Affairs and Seafood Inspection.—Alexa Cole, Room 15750, 427–8286.
Law Enforcement.—Jim Landon, Room 415, 427–2300.
Management and Budget.—Brian Pawlak, Room 14450, 427–8621.
Policy.—Jennifer Lukens, Room 14451, 427–8004.
Protected Resources.—Donna Wieting, Room 13821, 427–8400.
Science and Technology.—David Detlor (acting), Room 12455, 427–8100.
Scientific Programs and Chief Science Advisor.—Francisco Werner, Ph.D., Room 14659, 427–8000.
Sustainable Fisheries.—Alan Risenhoover, Room 13362, 427–8500.

NATIONAL OCEAN SERVICE

1305 East-West Highway, Silver Spring, MD 20910 (SSMC4)

Assistant Administrator.—Nicole LeBoeuf (acting), Room 13632 (301) 713–3074.
Deputy Assistant Administrator.—Nicole LeBoeuf, Room 13632, 713–3074.
Director, Office of:
Center for Operational Oceanographic Products and Services.—Richard Edwing, Room 6650, 713–2981.
Coast Survey.—RADM Shepard Smith, Room 6147, 713–2770.
Coastal Management.—Jeff Payne, Room 10413, 713–3155.
Management and Budget.—Paul Scholz, Room 13442, 713–3056.
National Centers for Coastal Ocean Science.—Steve Thur, Room 8211, 713–3020.
National Geodetic Survey.—Juliana Blackwell, Room 8657, 713–3222.
National Marine Sanctuaries.—John Armor, Room 11523, 713–7235.
Response and Restoration.—Scott Lundgren, Room 10102 (240) 533–0408.

NATIONAL ENVIRONMENTAL SATELLITE, DATA, AND INFORMATION SERVICE

1335 East-West Highway, Silver Spring, MD 20910 (SSMC1)

Assistant Administrator.—Stephen M. Volz, Room 8268 (301) 713–3578.
Deputy Assistant Administrator.—Mark Paese, Room 8300, 713–2010.
Deputy Assistant Administrator, Systems.—Vacant.
Chief Financial Officer.—Cherish Johnson, Room 8338, 713–9476.
Deputy Chief Financial Officer.—James Donnellon, Room 8340, 713–9228.
Chief Information Officer.—Irene Parker, Room 7103, 713–9220.
International and Interagency Affairs Chief.—Charles Wooldridge, Room 7315, 713–2024.
Office of System Architecture and Advanced Planning.—Dr. Karen St. German, Room 5410, 713–7342.
Director, Office of:
Commercial Remote Sensing Regulatory Affairs.—Tahara Dawkins, Room 8260, 713–3385.
GOES–R Program.—Mark Stringer (acting), NASA GSFC, Room C100D, 286–1355.
Joint Polar Satellite System.—Greg Mandt, Room 3301, 713–4782.
National Center for Environmental Information.—Mary Wohlgemuth, Room 557–C (828) 271–4476.
Satellite and Product Operations.—Vanessa Griffin, NSOF, Room 1605 (301) 817–4000.
Satellite Applications and Research.—Harry Cikanek, Room 701, 763–8127.
Satellite Ground Services.—Steven Petersen, SS3, Room 4117, 713–7111.
Space Commercialization.—Mark Paese (acting), Room 8300, 713–2010.
Systems Development.—Dr. Karen St. German, Room 6234, 713–0100.

NATIONAL WEATHER SERVICE

1325 East-West Highway, Silver Spring, MD 20910 (SSMC2)

https://weather.gov/organization

Assistant Administrator of NOAA for Weather Services and NWS Director.—Louis W. Uccellini, Ph.D., Room 18150 (301) 713–9095.
Deputy Assistant Administrator/Deputy Director.—Mary C. Erickson, Room 18130, 713–0711.
Chief Financial/Administrative Officer.—John Potts, Room 18176, 427–6911.
Chief of Staff.—George Jungbluth, Room 18236, 427–9685.
Chief Operating Officer.—John Murphy, Room 15300, 427–9212.
Director, Congressional Affairs Division.—John Sokich, 427–9064.
Director of Planning and Programming for Service Delivery.—Kevin Cooley, Room 16212, 427–9810.

OCEANIC AND ATMOSPHERIC RESEARCH

1315 East-West Highway, Silver Spring, MD 20910 (SSMC3)

Assistant Administrator.—Craig McLean, Room 11458, (301) 713–2458.
Deputy Assistant Administrator for—
Programs and Administration.—Ko Barrett, Room 11555, 734–1167.
Science.—Gary Matlock, Room 11461, 734–1184.
Chief of Staff.—James Jenkins, Room 11462, 734–1182.
Chief Science Integrity Officer.—Dr. Cynthia Decker, Room 11230, 734–1156.
Director of:
Air Resources Laboratory.—Gary Matlock (acting), Room 11461, 734–1184.
Atlantic Oceanographic and Meteorological Laboratory (AOML).—Dr. John Cortinas, AOML (305) 361–4301.
Earth System Research Laboratory (ESRL).—Robert Webb, Ph.D., ESRL, Room 1D116 (303) 497–5942.
Division of:
Chemical Sciences.—David Fahey, Ph.D., ESRL, Room 2A125, 497–5277.
Geophysical Fluid Dynamics Laboratory (GFDL).—Venkatachalam ''Ram'' Ramaswamy, Ph.D., GFDL, Room 220 (609) 452–6510.
Global Monitoring.—James Butler, Ph.D., ESRL, Room 3D–116, 497–6898.
Global Systems.—Jennifer Mahoney, ESRL, Room 3B121, 497–4122.
Great Lakes Environmental Research Laboratory (GLERL).—Deborah H. Lee, GLERL, Room 155 (734) 741–2244.
National Severe Storms Laboratory (NSSL).—Kurt Hondl (acting), Ph.D., NSSL, Room 2409 (405) 325–6900.

Pacific Marine Environmental Laboratory (PMEL).—Michelle McClure, Ph.D., PMEL, Bldg. 3, Room 2112 (206) 526–6800.
Physical Science.—Robert Webb, Ph.D., ESRL, Room 1D116 (609) 452–6510.
Director, Office of:
Climate Program.—Wayne Higgins, Ph.D., Room 12837 (301) 427–1263.
National Sea Grant College Program.—Jonathan Pennock, Ph.D., Room 11716, 734–1089.
Ocean Acidification.—Libby Jewett, Ph.D., Room 12826, 734–1075.
Oceanic Exploration and Research.—Alan Leonardi, Ph.D., Room 10151, 734–1016.
Weather and Air Quality.—Kandis Boyd (acting), Ph.D., Room 10357, 734–1026.

OFFICE OF MARINE AND AVIATION OPERATIONS (OMAO) AND NOAA COMMISSIONED OFFICER CORPS (NOAA Corps)

8403 Colesville Road, Suite 500, Silver Spring, MD 20910

https://omao.noaa.gov

Director.—RADM Michael Silah (301) 713–7600.
Deputy Director for Operations and Deputy Director of the NOAA Commissioned Officer Corps Aircraft Operations.—RDML Nancy Hann, 713–7703.
Deputy Assistant Administrator for Programs and Administration.—Randy TeBeest, 713–7656.
Chief Financial Officer.—Dana Flower Lake, 713–7606.
Chief of Staff.—Greg Raymond, 713–7658.
Marine Operations Director.—Troy Frost (541) 867–8801.
Aircraft Operations Commanding Officer.—CDR Chris Sloan (863) 500–3999.
Diving Program Manager.—Gregory B. McFall (305) 809–4713.
Small Boat Program Manager.—LCDR Nicola VerPlanck (206) 553–0258.

UNITED STATES PATENT AND TRADEMARK OFFICE

P.O. Box 1450, 600 Dulany Street, Arlington, VA 22313–1450

phone (571) 272–8600

OFFICE OF THE UNDER SECRETARY AND DIRECTOR

Under Secretary of Commerce for Intellectual Property and Director of the United States Patent and Trademark Office.—Andrei Iancu (571) 272–8600.
Deputy Under Secretary of Commerce for Intellectual Property and Deputy Director of the United States Patent and Trademark Office.—Laura Peter, 272–8700.
Special Assistant to the Under Secretary and Deputy Under Secretary.—Nicole Grove, 272–8600.
Chief of Staff.—Chris Shipp (acting), 272–8600.
Chief of Staff to the Deputy Under Secretary of Commerce for Intellectual Property and Deputy Director of the United States Patent and Trademark Office.—Wynn Coggins, 272–8700.
Senior Legislative Advisor.—Peter Krug, 272–8600.
Senior Trademark Policy Advisor.—Kathleen Cooney-Porter, 272–8600.

REGIONAL DIRECTORS

Eastern Regional Outreach Director.—Elizabeth Dougherty (571) 272–8600.
Regional Director (Midwest).—Damian O. Porcari (313) 446–4800.
Regional Director (Rocky Mountains).—Molly Kocialski (303) 297–4600.
Regional Director (Silicon Valley).—John Cabeca (408) 918–9900.
Regional Director (Texas).—Hope Shimabuku (469) 295–9000.

PATENT TRIAL AND APPEAL BOARD

phone (571) 272–9797

Chief Administrative Patent Judge.—Scott Boalick.

Deputy Chief Administrative Patent Judge.—Jacqueline Bonilla.
Vice Chief Administrative Patent Judges: Michelle Ankenbrand (acting), William ''Tim'' Fink, Michael Tierney, Scott Weidenfeller.
Vice Chief Judge for Strategy.—Janet Gongola.
Board Executive.—David Talbott.

TRADEMARK TRIAL AND APPEAL BOARD

Chief Administrative Trademark Judge.—Gerard F. Rogers (571) 272–8500.
Deputy Chief Administrative Trademark Judge.—Mark A. Thurmon, 272–8500.

COMMISSIONER FOR PATENTS

Commissioner for Patents.—Drew Hirshfeld (571) 272–8800.
Deputy Commissioner for—
International Patent Cooperation.—Mark Powell, 272–8800.
Patent Administration.—Rick Seidel, 272–8800.
Patent Examination Policy.—Bob Bahr, 272–8800.
Patent Operations.—Andy Faile, 272–8800.
Patent Quality.—Valencia Martin-Wallace, 272–8800.
Senior Advisors for—
Administration.—Errica Miller, 272–4370.
OIPC.—Mary Hale, 272–2507.
OPQA: Jolyn Eley, 272–2546; Stefanos Karmis, 272–6744.
Patent Operations: Allana Bidder, 272–5560; Marivelisse Santiago-Cordero, 272–8800.
Senior Advisors: Alex Beck, 272–8800; Steven Griffin, 272–8800; Patricia Mallari, 272–8800.

COMMISSIONER FOR TRADEMARKS

phone (571) 272–8901

Commissioner for Trademarks.—Mary Boney-Denison.
Deputy Commissioner for—
Trademark Administration.—Greg Dodson.
Trademark Examination Policy.—Sharon R. Marsh.
Trademark Operations.—Meryl Hershkowitz.
Group Directors, Trademark Law Offices: Steve Berk, Dan Vavonese, Tomas Vlcek, Angela Wilson.
Chief of Staff.—Monita Pressey (acting).

CHIEF ADMINISTRATIVE OFFICER

phone (571) 272–9600

Chief Administrative Officer.—Fred Steckler.
Chief of Staff.—Chris Gambill.
Senior Advisor.—Jason Clark.

CHIEF FINANCIAL OFFICER

Chief Financial Officer.—Sean Mildrew (acting), (571) 272–9200.
Deputy Chief Financial Officer.—Michelle Picard (acting), 272–6354.
Senior Management and Program Analyst.—Sarah Brown, 272–8054.
Senior Program Analyst for IT.—Tori Key, 272–8054.

CHIEF INFORMATION OFFICER

Chief Information Officer.—Jamie Holcombe (571) 272–9400.
Deputy Chief Information Officer.—Debbie Stephens, 272–9410.
Chief Technology Officer.—David Chiles, 272–7001.
Chief of Staff.—Scott Williams, 272–5664.

OFFICE OF POLICY AND INTERNATIONAL AFFAIRS

Chief Policy Officer and Director for International Affairs.—Shira Perlmutter (571) 272–0991.
Deputy Chief Policy Officer.—Karin Ferriter, 272–8472.
Deputy Chief Policy Officer for Operations.—Danette Campbell (acting), 272–8472.
Chief of Staff.—Ari Leifman, 272–0991.

OFFICE OF GOVERNMENTAL AFFAIRS

Director.—Branden Ritchie (571) 272–7300.
Deputy Director.—Kimberley Alton, 272–7300.

OFFICE OF THE GENERAL COUNSEL

General Counsel.—Sarah T. Harris (571) 272–7000.
Deputy General Counsel, Office of General Law.—David M. Shewchuk, 272–3000.
Deputy General Counsel and Director, Office of Enrollment and Discipline.—William R. Covey, 272–5757.
Deputy General Counsel for IP Law and Solicitor.—Thomas W. Krause, 272–6401.
Chief of Staff.—Paulo F. Mendes, 272–5533.
Senior Legal Advisor.—Nicholas Matich, 272–9035.

OFFICE OF THE CHIEF COMMUNICATIONS OFFICER

Chief Communications Officer.—Timothy Clark (571) 272–8600.
Deputy Communications Officers: Chris Katopis, 272–8400; Paul Rosenthal, 272–8400.
Special Advisor for Communications.—Michael ''Owen'' Burgess, 270–0735.

OFFICE OF EEO AND DIVERSITY

Director.—Bismarck Myrick (571) 272–8292.
Deputy Director.—Clint Janes, 272–6311.

OFFICE OF THE OMBUDSMAN

phone (571) 270–3140

Chief Ombudsman.—Paul Sotoudeh.
Senior Ombudsman.—Karen J. Dean.
Associate Ombudsman.—Andrea Brown.

NATIONAL INSTITUTE OF STANDARDS AND TECHNOLOGY

100 Bureau Drive, Gaithersburg, MD 20899

phone (301) 975–NIST (6478)

Under Secretary for Standards and Technology and NIST Director.—Walter G. Copan (301) 975–2300.
Associate Director for—
Industry and Innovation Services.—Phillip Singerman, 975–2340.
Laboratory Programs.—Jim Olthoff, 975–2300.
Management Resources.—Del Brockett, 975–5000.
Chief of Staff.—Kevin Kimball, 975–3070.
Director of:
Acquisition and Agreements Management.—George Jenkins (acting), 975–5080.
Advanced Manufacturing.—Mike Molnar, 975–3673.
Baldrige Performance Excellence Program.—Robert Fangmeyer, 975–4781.
Civil Rights and Diversity.—Mirta-Marie M. Keys, 975–2042.
Center for Nanoscale Science and Technology.—James Kushmerick, 975–5697.
Communications Technology Laboratory.—Marla Dowell (303) 497–6700.
Congressional and Legislative Affairs.—Jim Schufreider, 975–5675.
Emergency Services.—Mark Spurrier, 975–2660.

Engineering Laboratory.—Howard Harary, 975–5900.
Fabrication Technology.—Mark Luce, 975–2159.
Facilities and Property Management.—Skip Vaughn, 975–8832.
Financial Resource Management.—George Jenkins, 975–5080.
Hollings Manufacturing Extension Partnership Program.—Carroll Thomas, 975–4676.
Human Resources Management.—Susanne Porch, 975–2487.
Human Subjects Protection.—Anne Andrews, 975–5445.
Information Services.—Rachel Glenn (acting), 975–2906.
Information Systems Management.—Susannah Schiller (acting), 975–6500.
Information Technology Laboratory.—Charles Romine, 975–2900.
International and Academic Affairs.—Claire M. Saundry, 975–2386.
Management and Organization.—Catherine Fletcher, 975–4054.
Material Measurement Laboratory.—Eric Lin, 975–6743.
NIST Center for Neutron Research.—Robert Dimeo, 975–6210.
Physical Measurement Laboratory.—Carl Williams, 975–4200.
Program Coordination.—Kevin Kimball (acting), 975–3070.
Public Affairs.—Gail J. Porter, 975–3392.
Safety, Health, and Environment.—Elizabeth Mackey, 975–5149.
Special Programs.—Richard Cavanagh, 975–4447.
Standards Coordination.—Gordon Gillerman, 975–8406.
Technology Partnerships.—Paul Zielinski, 975–4980.

NATIONAL TECHNICAL INFORMATION SERVICE

5301 Shawnee Road, Alexandria, VA 22312

Director.—Avi Bender (703) 605–6401.

NATIONAL TELECOMMUNICATIONS AND INFORMATION ADMINISTRATION

1401 Constitution Avenue, NW., Washington, DC 20230

Assistant Secretary and Administrator.—Adam Candeub (acting), Room 4898 (202) 482–1840.
Deputy Assistant Secretary.—Douglas Kinkoph (acting), 482–1830.
Chief of Staff.—Vacant.
Deputy Chief of Staff and Congressional Affairs Director.—James Wasilewski, 482–1830.
Chief Counsel.—Kathy Smith.
Director, Office of:
Institute for Telecommunication Sciences.—Sheryl Genco.
International Affairs.—Vernita Harris (acting).
Policy Analysis and Development.—Evelyn Remaley.
Public Affairs.—Vacant.
Public Safety Communications.—Michael Dame (acting).
Spectrum Management.—Charles Cooper.
Telecommunications and Information Applications.—Douglas Kinkoph.

DEPARTMENT OF LABOR

Frances Perkins Building

200 Constitution Avenue, NW., Washington, DC 20210

phone (866) 4–USA–DOL, https://dol.gov

EUGENE SCALIA, Secretary of Labor. Eugene Scalia was sworn in as Secretary of Labor on September 27, 2019. As Secretary, he oversees the enforcement and administration of more than 180 federal employment laws covering more than 150 million workers and 10 million workplaces. Laws administered by the Department include the workplace safety requirements of the Occupational Safety and Health Administration (OSHA) and Mine Safety and Health Administration, federal minimum wage and overtime protections, the anti-discrimination requirements applicable to federal contractors, and ERISA's protection of the more than $11 trillion held in employee retirement plans and health plans. The Department also administers a range of programs intended to support worker training and enhance the skills of the American workforce through grants and other funding to States, educational institutions, and other public and private sector organizations.

As Secretary, Scalia chairs the board of directors of the Pension Benefit Guaranty Corporation—which insures U.S. private pension plans—and is on the board of trustees of the Social Security and Medicare Trust Fund.

Secretary Scalia's priorities include enhancing employment opportunities for Americans by supporting economic growth through reductions in unnecessary regulatory burdens, improving the effectiveness and efficiency of the Department's enforcement programs, and bolstering worker training through apprenticeships and other business-driven programs that emphasize performance and accountability. Under his leadership, the Labor Department has supported President Trump's initiatives to promote employment for veterans and military spouses, to overcome the opioid crisis, and to help Americans exiting the criminal justice system reenter the workforce.

In addition to serving on the White House Coronavirus Task Force, Scalia guides the Labor Department as it plays a central role in overseeing the new federal programs intended to help workers and their families respond to COVID-19. The Department is also involved in implementing the U.S.-Mexico-Canada Agreement, the NAFTA replacement negotiated by President Trump that includes the strongest labor protections ever included in an international trade agreement.

Secretary Scalia graduated with distinction from the University of Virginia, and attended the University of Chicago Law School, where he graduated cum laude and served as editor-in-chief of the Law Review. He and his wife Trish have seven children. He is the son of Maureen and Antonin Scalia, the late Supreme Court Justice.

OFFICE OF THE SECRETARY

phone (202) 693–6000

Secretary of Labor.—Eugene Scalia.
Deputy Secretary.—Patrick Pizzella.
Chief of Staff.—Rachel E. Mondl.
Deputy Chief of Staff.—Catherine A. Bartley.
Counselor to the Secretary.—Andrew G. Kilberg.
Executive Secretariat Director.—Caroline Harman Robinson.
Director of Scheduling and Operations.—Abbie Sumbrum (acting).

OFFICE OF PUBLIC ENGAGEMENT

Director.—Dean Heyl (202) 693–6450.

ADMINISTRATIVE LAW JUDGES
Techworld, 800 K Street, NW., Suite 400, Washington, DC 20001–8002

Chief Administrative Law Judge.—Stephen R. Henley (202) 693–7424.
Associate Chief Judges: Paul Almanza, 693–7344; William S. Colwell, 693–7355.

ADMINISTRATIVE REVIEW BOARD

Chief and Chair.—Thomas H. Burrell (acting), Room N–5404 (202) 693–6200.
Vice Chair.—E. Cooper Brown, Room N–5404, 693–6200.

OFFICE OF THE ASSISTANT SECRETARY FOR ADMINISTRATION AND MANAGEMENT (OASAM)

Assistant Secretary.—Bryan Slater, Room S–2203 (202) 693–4040.
Deputy Assistant Secretary for—
Budget.—Geoffrey Kenyon, Room S–4020, 693–4090.
Operations.—Al Stewart, Room S–2203, 693–4040.
Policy.—David Langhaim, Room S–2203, 693–4040.
Special Assistants: Lisa Freeman, Room S–2203, 693–4040; Douglas Robins, Room S–2203, 693–4040.
Program Manager: Traci Smith, Room S–2203, 693–4040.
Senior Advisors: Mark Baker, Room S–2203, 693–4040; Edward ''Chip'' Wilkinson, Room S–2203, 693–4040.
Administrative Officer.—Braye Cloud, 693–4040.

BUSINESS OPERATIONS CENTER

Director.—Julia Tritz, Room S–1524, 693–1094.
Deputy Director.—Macaire Carroll-Gavula, Room S–1524, 693–6676.
Office of:
Administrative Services.—Phil Puckett, Room S–1521, 693–6650.
Asset and Resource Management.—Tanisha Bynum-Frazier, Room S–1519B, 693–4546.
Chief Procurement Officer.—Carl V. Campbell, Room S–1510–C, 693–7246.
Procurement Services.—Sandra Foster (acting), Room S–4307, 693–4599.
Small and Disadvantaged Business Utilization.—Gladys Bailey, Room N–6402, 693–7244.
Worker Safety and Health Services.—Stephanie Semmer, Room S–1321, 693–6678.

PERFORMANCE MANAGEMENT CENTER

Director.—Dennis Johnson, Room S–3317, 693–7124.
Deputy Director.—Vacant.

CIVIL RIGHTS CENTER

Director.—Naomi Barry-Perez, Room N–4123, 693–6500.
Associate Director for Program Operations.—Dennis Fish, Room N–4123, 693–6532.
Administrative Officer.—Aquila Branch-James, Room N–4123, 693–6519.
Office of:
Enforcement/External.—Lee Perselay (acting), 693–6519.
Enforcement/Internal.—Samuel Rhames, 693–6500.
Reasonable Accommodation Hotline.—Kim Borowicz, Room N–4123, 693–6527.

EMERGENCY MANAGEMENT CENTER
800 K Street, NW., Suite 450 North, Washington, DC 20001–8002.

Director.—Michael Smith, 693–7504.
Deputy Director.—Matt Konopka, 693–7512.

BENEFITS.GOV

Program Manager.—Myung Moon, Room S–1508, 693–4429.

HUMAN RESOURCES CENTER

Director.—Sydney Rose, Room C–5526, 693–7600.
Deputy Director.—Vacant, Room C–5526, 693–7600.
Office of:
Administration and Management Services.—Donna Childs Speight, Room C–5517, 693–7762.
Diversity and Inclusion.—Vacant, Room S–4015, 693–5840.
Employee and Labor Management Relations.—Shawn Hooper, Room N–5476, 693–7612.
Executive Resources.—Demeatric Gamble, Room N–2453, 693–7800.
Human Resources Consulting and Operations.—Vacant, Room C–5516, 693–7690.
Human Resources Policy and Accountability.—Kristin Siegfried, Room C–5526, 693–7709.
Office of HR Works and Systems Support (OHRWSS).—LaRell Faulkner, Room S–3308, 693–4320.
Training and Development.—Kimberly Lacey, Room N–5464, 693–7838.
Worklife, Leave, Benefits Policy, and Programs.—Maria Jordan, Room N–5454, 693–7610.

OFFICE OF THE CHIEF INFORMATION OFFICER

Chief Information Officer.—Gundeep Ahluwalia, Room N–1301, 693–4200.
Deputy CIO for Administration and Strategy.—Rick Kryger, Room N–1301, 693–4200.
Deputy CIO for Operations.—Lou Charlier, Room N–1301, 693–4200.
Directorate of Administration, Business Management, and Governance.—Jeff Johnson, Room N–1301, 693–4449.
Division of Administration.—Tracey Schaeffer, Room N–1301, 693–4158.
Division of Application & Platform Governance and Standards: Tim Erskine (acting), Room N–1301, 693–8128; Samson Teffera, Room N–1301, 693–4179.
Division of Architecture, Strategy, and Design.—Paul Beckham, Room N–1301, 693–4437.
Division of Client Engagement.—Atash Mehta, Room N–1301, 693–4157.
Directorate of Cybersecurity.—Paul Blahusch, Room N–1301, 693–1567.
Directorate of Information Technology Operations and Services.—Vacant, Room N–1301, 693–4147.
Enterprise Program Management.—Duane Eldridge, Room N–1301, 693–4136.
Enterprise Service Desk.—24/7, Room N–1505 (855) 522–6748, or EnterpriseServiceDesk@dol.gov.

SECURITY CENTER

Director.—Billie Jo Agambar, Room S–1229G (202) 693–7204.
Deputy Director.—Stacey Thompson, 693–7210.
Administrative Specialist.—Julie LeMon, 693–7514.

ASSISTANT SECRETARY FOR POLICY

Assistant Secretary.—Vacant, Room S–2312 (202) 693–5959.
Principal Deputy Assistant Secretary.—Jonathan Berry.
Deputy Assistant Secretaries: Alison Kilmartin, Jonathan Wolfson.
Career Deputy Assistant Secretary.—Stephanie Swirsky.
Chief of Staff.—Vacant.
Regulatory and Programmatic Policy.—Laura Dawkins.
Chief Evaluation Officer.—Christina Yancey.

BENEFITS REVIEW BOARD

Chair.—Judith S. Boggs, Room N–5101 (202) 693–6300.

BUREAU OF LABOR STATISTICS
Postal Square Building
2 Massachusetts Avenue, NE., Suite 4040, Washington, DC 20212
phone (202) 691–7800

Commissioner.—William Beach, 691–7800.

Deputy Commissioner.—William Wiatrowski, 691–6301.
Associate Commissioner, Office of:
Administration.—Nancy Ruiz de Gamboa, Suite 4060, 691–7777.
Compensation and Working Conditions.—Kristen Monaco, Suite 4130, 691–7527.
Employment and Unemployment Statistics.—Vacant.
Field Operations.—Jay Mousa, Suite 2935, 691–5800.
Prices and Living Conditions.—David Friedman, Suite 3120, 691–6960.
Productivity and Technology.—Lucy Eldridge, Suite 2150, 691–6598.
Publications and Special Studies.—Michael Levi, Suite 2850, 691–5100.
Survey Methods Research.—William Mockovak (acting), Suite 5930, 691–7414.
Technology and Survey Processing.—Wesley Chou (acting), Suite 5025, 691–7203.
Assistant Commissioner, Office of:
Compensation Levels and Trends.—Hilery Simpson, Suite 4130, 691–5184.
Consumer Prices and Price Indexes.—Vacant.
Current Employment Analysis.—Julie Hatch Maxfield, Suite 4675, 691–5473.
Industrial Prices and Price Indexes.—Jeffrey Hill, Suite 3840, 691–7156.
Industry Employment Statistics.—Kenneth Robertson, Suite 4860, 691–5440.
Occupational Statistics and Employment Projections.—Rebecca Rust, Suite 2135, 691–5701.
Director of:
Survey Processing.—Rick Kryger, Suite 5025, 691–7562.
Technology and Computing Services.—Wesley Chou, Suite 5025, 691–7203.

BUREAU OF INTERNATIONAL LABOR AFFAIRS

OFFICE OF THE DEPUTY UNDER SECRETARY

Deputy Under Secretary.—Martha Newton, Room S–2235 (202) 693–4770.
Associate Deputy Under Secretary.—Mark Mittelhauser, Room S–2235, 693–4770.
Associate Deputy Under Secretary.—Vacant.
Chief of Staff.—Grant Lebens, Room S–2235, 693–4770.
Administrative Officer.—Deborah Becker, Room S–5315, 693–4770.
Policy Advisor.—Quinn Marschik, Room S–2235, 693–4812.
Executive Assistant.—Diane Ward, Room S–2235, 693–4770.
Program and Management Analyst.—Alfreda Johnson, Room S–2235, 693–4773.
Special Assistant.—Kia Gaskins, Room S–2235, 693–4903.

OFFICE OF CHILD LABOR, FORCED LABOR, AND HUMAN TRAFFICKING

Director.—Marcia Eugenio, Room S–5315 (202) 693–4849.
Deputy Director.—Kevin Willcutts, Room S–5317, 693–4832.

OFFICE OF TRADE AND LABOR AFFAIRS

Director.—Matthew Levin, Room S–5315 (202) 693–5745.
Deputy Directors: Donna Chung, Room S–5315, 693–4861; Katy Mastman, Room S–5315, 693–4800.

OFFICE OF INTERNATIONAL RELATIONS AND ECONOMIC RESEARCH

Director.—Robert B. Shepard, Room S–5315 (202) 693–4808.
Deputy Directors: Zhao Li, Room S–5315, 693–4803; Kenneth Swinnerton, Room S–5315, 693–4916.

OFFICE OF THE CHIEF FINANCIAL OFFICER

Chief Financial Officer.—James Williams, Room S–4030 (202) 693–6800.
Deputy Chief Financial Officer.—Kevin Brown (acting), Room S–4030, 693–6800.
Associate Deputy Chief Financial Officer.—Kevin Brown, Room S–4030.
Administrative Officer.—Marella Turner, Room S–4030.
Accounts Payable (Vendor Payment).—Natasha Brown, Room S–5526.
Audit Liaison.—Neil Starzynski, Room S–4030.
Central Accounting Operations.—Westley Everette, Room S–5526.
Customer Support.—Sharnell Montgomery, Room N–2719.

E–Travel.—Sheila Alexander, Room N–2719.
Financial Performance and Payment Integrity (A–123 Compliance).—Chris Polen, Room S–4030.
Financial Reporting.—Jennifer Maurer (acting), Room S–4502.
Operations Support.—Andrew Allen, Room N–2719.
Security and Technology.—Robert Springfield, Room N–2719.
Travel/Conference Policy and A–123 Compliance.—Dylan Sacchetti, Room S–4030.

OFFICE OF CONGRESSIONAL AND INTERGOVERNMENTAL AFFAIRS

Assistant Secretary.—Vacant, Room S–2006 (202) 693–4601.
Deputy Assistant Secretary for Congressional and Intergovernmental Affairs.—Joe Wheeler, Room S–2220, 693–4601.
Chief of Staff.—John Patrick Walsh, Room S–2220, 693–4600.
Administrative Officer.—DuRon Blount, Room S–2220, 693–4600.
Staff Assistants: Glenda Manning, Room S–2006, 693–4601; Claudette Tidwell, Room S–2220, 693–4600; Tiffany Williams, Room S–2220, 693–4600; Jaunae Young, Room S–2220, 693–4600.
Deputy Assistant Secretary for Intergovernmental Affairs.—Michael Downing, S-2220, 693–4600.
Senior Advisor, Intergovernmental Affairs.—Jim Blazer, Room S–2220, 693–4600.
Senior Legislative Officer for—
Appropriations/Budget/Employee Benefits/PBGC/COBRA.—Margarita Almanza, Room S–2220, 693–4600.
BLS/ILAB/Employment and Training—Trade, OFLC.—Brian Maves, Room S–2220, 693–4600.
Labor Management Standards/OFCCP/FOIA.—Robert Rische, Room S–2220, 693–4600.
Mine Safety and Health/Occupational Safety and Health/OWCP.—Adam Turner, Room S–2220, 693–4600.
Women's Bureau/Wage and Hour Division/ODEP.—Sharon Utz, Room S–2220, 693–4600.
Legislative Officer, Employment and Training—WIOA/Apprenticeship/YouthBuild/Job Corps/VETS.—Bradley Thomas, Room S–2220, 693–4600.
Senior Legislative Officer, Casework Support.—David McFadden, Room S–2220, 693–4600.
Legislative Officer, Casework Support.—C.C. Christakos, Room S–2220, 693–4600.
Casework Officers: Joseph Gollinger, Room S–2220, 693–4600; Jacob Smith, Room S–2220, 693–4600.

REGIONAL OFFICES

Great Lakes.—Illinois, Indiana, Iowa, Michigan, Minnesota, Wisconsin.
Regional Representative.—Christopher E. Hagerup.
Heartland.—Kansas, Missouri, Nebraska.
Regional Representative.—Vacant.
Mid-Atlantic.—Delaware, District of Columbia, Maryland, Ohio, Pennsylvania, Virginia, West Virginia.
Regional Representative.—James Fitzpatrick.
New England.— Connecticut, Maine, Massachusetts, New Hampshire, Rhode Island, Vermont.
Regional Representative.—Peter Steele.
New York/New Jersey.— New Jersey, New York, Puerto Rico, Virgin Islands.
Regional Representative.—Vacant.
Pacific Northwest.—Alaska, Idaho, Oregon, Washington.
Regional Representative.—Vacant.
Rocky Mountain.—Colorado, Montana, North Dakota, South Dakota, Wyoming.
Regional Representative.—Jonathan Finer.
South-Central.—Arkansas, Louisiana, New Mexico, Oklahoma, Texas.
Regional Representative.—Aaron Krejci.
Southeast.—Alabama, Florida, Georgia, Kentucky, Mississippi, North Carolina, South Carolina, Tennessee.
Regional Representative.—Ruth Sherlock.
West Coast/Pacific.—American Samoa, Arizona, California, Guam, Hawaii, Nevada, Northern Mariana Islands, Utah.
Regional Representative.—Jeffrey Stone.

OFFICE OF DISABILITY EMPLOYMENT POLICY

Assistant Secretary.—Vacant, Room S–1303 (202) 693–7880.

Deputy Assistant Secretary.—Jennifer Sheehy.
Chief of Staff.—Patrick Mannix.
Special Assistant.—Brian Walsh.
Director of Policy Development.—Vacant.

EMPLOYEE BENEFITS SECURITY ADMINISTRATION

Assistant Secretary.—Jeanne Klinefelter Wilson (acting), Room S–2524 (202) 693–8300.
Principal Deputy Assistant Secretary.—Jeanne Klinefelter Wilson, Room S–2524, 693–8300.
Chief of Staff.—Timothy Cummings, Room S–2524, 693–8300.
Senior Policy Advisors: Rebecca Cole, Room S–2524, 693–8300; Monica McGuire, Room S–2524, 693–8300.
Policy Advisor.—Trevor Carlsen, Room S–2524, 693–8300.
Special Assistant.—Matthew Mullins, Room S–2524, 693–8300.
Deputy Assistant Secretary for National Office Operations.—Timothy Hauser, Room N–5677, 693–8315.
Deputy Assistant Secretary for Regional Office Operations.—Amy Turner, Room N–5677, 693–8315.
Executive Assistant.—Becki Marchand, Room N–5677, 693–8315.
Director of:
Enforcement.—Mabel Capolongo, 122 C Street, Suite 600, 693–8443.
Exemption Determinations.—Lyssa Hall, 122 C Street, Suite 400, 693–8540.
Health Plan Standards and Compliance Assistance.—Amber Rivers, Room N–5653, 693–8335.
Outreach, Education, and Assistance.—Mark Connor, Room N–5625, 693–8337.
Program, Planning, Evaluation, and Management.—Joel Lovelace, Room N–5668, 693–8490.
Regulations and Interpretations.—Joseph Canary, Room N–5655, 693–8500.
Technology and Information Services.—Leyla Mansur, Room N–5410, 693–8618.
Chief Accountant.—Michael Auerbach, 122 C Street, Suite 400, 693–8369.

EMPLOYEES' COMPENSATION APPEALS BOARD

Chief Judge and Chairman.—Alec Koromilas (202) 693–6403.
Deputy Chief Judge and Vice Chairman.—Christopher James Godfrey, Room N–5416, 693–6410.

EMPLOYMENT AND TRAINING ADMINISTRATION

Assistant Secretary.—John Pallasch, Room S–2307.
Deputy Assistant Secretaries: Matthew Hunter, Room S–2307, 693–2772; Nicholas Lalpuis (acting), Room S–2307, 693–2772; Nancy Rooney, Room S–2307, 693–2772.
Administrator, Office of:
Apprenticeship.—John Ladd, Room N–5311, 693–2796.
Contracts Management.—Jillian Matz (acting), Room N–4643, 693–2785.
Financial Administration.—Adrienne E. Young, Room N–4702, 693–3132.
Foreign Labor Certification.—Vacant, Patriots Plaza II, 513–7350.
Grants and Management.—Laura P. Watson, Room N–4673, 693–3333.
Job Corps.—Debra Carr, Room N–4463, 693–3000.
Management and Administrative Services.—Ryan Gilligan, Room N–4653, 693–3001.
Policy Development and Research.—Adele Gagliardi, Room N–5637, 693–3700.
Trade Adjustment Assistance.—Norris Tyler, Room C–5428, 693–3560.
Unemployment Insurance.—Gay Gilbert, Room S–4524, 693–3029.
Workforce Investment.—Kimberly Vitelli (acting), Room S–4510, 693–3980.

CENTER FOR FAITH AND OPPORTUNITY INITIATIVES

Director.—Mark Zelden (202) 693–6017.

OFFICE OF THE INSPECTOR GENERAL

Inspector General.—Larry D. Turner (acting), Room S–5502 (202) 693–5100.
Deputy Inspector General.—Larry D. Turner, Room S–5502, 693–5100.

Assistant Inspector General for—
Audit.—Elliot P. Lewis, Room S–5512, 693–5170.
Congressional and Public Relations.—Luiz Santos, Room S–5506, 693–7062.
Labor Racketeering and Fraud Investigations.—Leia Burks, Room S–5014, 693–7034.
Legal Services.—Delores Thompson, Room S–5502, 693–5116.
Management and Policy.—Thomas Williams, Room S–5028, 693–5191.
Performance and Risk Management.—Jessica Southwell, Room S–5506, 693–5208.

MINE SAFETY AND HEALTH ADMINISTRATION

201 12th Street South, Arlington, VA 22202–5452

phone (202) 693–9414, fax 693–9401, https://msha.gov

Assistant Secretary.—David G. Zatezalo, Room 5C330, 693–9402.
Deputy Assistant Secretary for Policy.—Wayne Palmer, Room 5C329, 693–9407.
Deputy Assistant Secretary for Operations.—Patricia W. Silvey, Room 5C328, 693–9642.
Director, Office of:
Assessments, Accountability, Special Enforcement, and Investigations.—Thomas Charboneau, Room 2518, 693–9700.
Program Education and Outreach Services.—David Wycinsky, Room 5C314, 693–9422.
Program Evaluation and Information Resources.—Syed Hafeez, Room 5W130, 693–9765.
Standards, Regulations, and Variances (OSRV).—Sheila McConnell, Room 5W208, 693–9440.
Technical Support.—William Francart, Room 4W210, 693–9470.

COAL MINE SAFETY AND HEALTH

Administrator.—Tim Watkins, Room 4W255, 693–9414.
Deputy Administrator.—David Weaver, Room 4C312, 693–9503.

METAL AND NONMETAL MINE SAFETY AND HEALTH

Administrator.—Tim Watkins, Room 4W255, 693–9414.
Deputy Administrator.—Brian Goepfert, Room 4C316, 693–9600.

EDUCATIONAL POLICY AND DEVELOPMENT

Director.—Vacant, Room 5W204, 693–9570.
Administration and Management (A&M).—Li-Tai Bilboa, Room 4E462, 693–9802.

OCCUPATIONAL SAFETY AND HEALTH ADMINISTRATION

Assistant Secretary.—Vacant, Room S–2315 (202) 693–2000.
Principal Deputy Assistant Secretary.—Loren Sweatt, 693–2000.
Chief of Staff.—Krisann Pearce, 693–2000.
Special Assistant.—Brian Walsh, 693–2000.
Director of:
Administrative Programs.—Kimberly A. Locey, 693–1600.
Communications.—Frank Meilinger, 693–1999.
Construction.—Scott Ketcham, 693–2100.
Cooperative and State Programs.—Doug Kalinowski, 693–2200.
Enforcement Programs.—Patrick Kapust (acting), 693–2100.
Standards and Guidance.—Bill Perry, 693–1950.
Technology Support and Emergency Management.—Amanda Edens, 693–2300.
Whistleblower Protection Programs.—Francis Yebesi (acting), 693–2199.

OFFICE OF PUBLIC AFFAIRS

Assistant Secretary.—Robert F. Bozzuto III, Room S–2514 (202) 693–4676.
Deputy Assistant Secretaries: Eric Holland, Mike Trupo.

REGIONAL OFFICES

Region I.—Boston.
Regional Director.—Edmund Fitzgerald, JFK Federal Building, Government Center, 25 New Sudbury Street, Room 525–A, Boston, MA 02203 (617) 565–2075.
Region III.—Philadelphia.
Regional Director.—Lenore Uddyback-Fortson, Curtis Center, 170 South Independence Mall West, Suite 633 East, Philadelphia, PA 19106–3306 (215) 861–5102.
Region IV.—Atlanta.
Regional Director.—Michael D'Aquino, Atlanta Federal Center, 61 Forsyth, SW., Suite 6B75, Atlanta, GA 30303 (678) 237–0630.
Region V.—Chicago.
Regional Director.—Scott Allen, 230 South Dearborn Street, Room 3194, Chicago, IL 60604 (312) 353–4727.
Region VI.—Dallas.
Regional Director.—Chauntra Rideaux, 525 Griffin Street, Room 734, Dallas, TX 75202 (972) 850–4710.
Region IX.—California.
Regional Director.—Leo Kay, 90 7th Street, Suite 2–650, San Francisco, CA 94103–1516 (415) 625–2630.

OFFICE OF SMALL AND DISADVANTAGED BUSINESS UTILIZATION

Director.—Gladys Bailey, N–6432 (202) 693–7244.

OFFICE OF THE SOLICITOR

Solicitor.—Kate O'Scannlain, Room S–2002 (202) 693–5260.
Deputy Solicitor.—Timothy Taylor, 693–5260.
Deputy Solicitor for National Operations.—Stanley Keen, 693–5260.
Deputy Solicitor for Regional Enforcement.—Katherine Bissell, 693–5260.
Senior Advisors: Jamila Gleason, Edward Sieger.
Senior Counsel: Robbie Norton, Sharon Rose, Courtney Walter.
Counsel.—Rebecca Furde.

DIVISION OF BLACK LUNG AND LONGSHORE LEGAL SERVICES

Associate Solicitor.—Barry H. Joyner, Room N–2117 (202) 693–5660.
Deputy Associate Solicitor.—Kevin Lyskowski.
Counsel for Administrative Litigation and Legal Advice.—Michael J. Rutledge.
Appellate Litigation.—Gary K. Stearman.
Enforcement and Appellate Litigation.—Sean G. Bajkowski.
Longshore.—Mark A. Reinhalter.
Regulations and Legislation.—Vacant.

DIVISION OF CIVIL RIGHTS AND LABOR-MANAGEMENT

Associate Solicitor.—Beverly Dankowitz, Room N–2474, 693–5740.
Deputy Associate Solicitor.—Consuela Pinto.
Counsel for Civil Rights and Appellate Litigation.—Eleanor Simms.
Interpretation and Advice.—Kier Bickerstaff.
Litigation and Regional Coordination.—Consuela Pinto.
LMRDA Advice.—Clinton Wolcott.
LMRDA Programs.—Radine Legum.

DIVISION OF EMPLOYMENT AND TRAINING LEGAL SERVICES

Associate Solicitor.—Matthew Bernt, Room N–2101, 693–5710.
Deputy Associate Solicitor.—Jessica Lyn.
Counsel for Employment and Training Advice.—Heather Vitale.
Immigration Programs.—Nora Carroll.
International Affairs and USERRA.—Derek Baxter.

DIVISION OF FAIR LABOR STANDARDS

Associate Solicitor.—Jennifer S. Brand, Room N–2716, 693–5555.
Deputy Associate Solicitor.—William C. Lesser.
Counsel for Appellate Litigation.—Paul L. Frieden.
Contract Labor Standards.—Jonathan T. Rees.
Legal Advice.—Lynn McIntosh.
Trial Litigation.—Jonathan M. Kronheim.
Whistleblower Programs.—Megan E. Guenther.

DIVISION OF FEDERAL EMPLOYEE AND ENERGY WORKERS COMPENSATION

Associate Solicitor.—Thomas G. Giblin (acting), Room S–4325, 693–5320.
Deputy Associate Solicitor.—Alexandra Tsiros (acting).
Counsel for Claims and Compensation.—Catherine P. Carter.
Energy Employees Compensation.—Sheldon O. Turley, Jr.
FECA Subrogation.—Jim Gordon.

DIVISION OF MANAGEMENT AND ADMINISTRATIVE LEGAL SERVICES

Associate Solicitor.—Rose Marie L. Audette, Room N–2420, 693–5405.
Deputy Associate Solicitors: Allen K. Goshi, David Koeppel.
Chief of:
Financial Management Office.—Michelle Fox.
Human Resources Office.—Michael Parrish.
Legal Technology Unit.—Denise Hoffman.
Counsel for Appropriations.—Omyra Ramsingh.
Director, Office of Information Services.—Ramona Oliver.
Employment Law.—Elizabeth L. Beason.
FOIA and Information Law.—Joseph J. Plick.
FOIA Appeals, Paperwork Reduction Act and Federal Records Act.—Ray Mitten, Jr.
Procurement and Contracts.—Peter Dickson.

DIVISION OF MINE SAFETY AND HEALTH

201 12th Street South, Suite 401, Arlington, VA 22202–5414

Associate Solicitor.—April Nelson, Suite 401, 693–9333.
Deputy Associate Solicitor.—Thomas A. Paige.
Counsel for Appellate Litigation.—Ali Beydoun.
Standards and Legal Advice.—Brad J. Mantel.
Trial Litigation.—Jason Grover.

DIVISION OF OCCUPATIONAL SAFETY AND HEALTH

Associate Solicitor.—Edmund C. Baird, Room S–4004, 693–5452.
Deputy Associate Solicitor.—Lauren Goodman.
Counsel for Appellate Litigation: Charles F. James, Heather Phillips.
Health Standards.—Ian Moar.
Regional Litigation and Legal Advice: Orlando J. Pannocchia, Robert W. Swain.
Safety Standards.—Ian Moar.
Special Litigation.—Vacant.

DIVISION OF PLAN BENEFITS SECURITY

Associate Solicitor.—William Scott, Room N–4611, 693–5600.
Deputy Associate Solicitor.—Joanne Roskey.
Counsel for Appellate and Special Litigation.—Thomas Tso.
Fiduciary Litigation.—Risa D. Sandler.
Financial Litigation.—Robert Furst.
General Litigation.—Glenn M Loos.
Regulations.—James Craig.

OFFICE OF LEGAL COUNSEL

Associate Solicitor.—Peter J. Constantine, Room N–2700, 693–5500.
Counsel for Ethics.—Robert M. Sadler.
Legislative Affairs.—Jill M. Otte.
Honors Program Director.—Susan Hutton.

VETERANS' EMPLOYMENT AND TRAINING SERVICE

Room S–1325, phone (202) 693–4700

Assistant Secretary.—John Lowry.
Deputy Assistant Secretary for Policy.—Vacant.
Deputy Assistant Secretary for Operations and Management.—J.S. Shellenberger.
Chief of Staff.—Jonathan VanderPlas.
Executive Assistant.—Rhonda McGhee.
Agency Management and Budget.—Iris Diaz.
Field Operations.—Bill Metheny.
National Programs.—Ivan Denton.
Strategic Outreach.—Mark Toal.

WOMEN'S BUREAU

Room S–3002, phone (202) 693–6710.

Director.—Laurie Todd-Smith, Ph.D.
Deputy Directors: Erica Clayton-Wright, Joan Harrigan-Farrelly.
Chief of Staff.—Jillian Rogers.
Chief, Office of:
Information and Support Services.—Paris M. Mack.
Policy and Programs.—Tiffany Boiman.

OFFICE OF WORKERS' COMPENSATION PROGRAMS

Director.—Julia K. Hearthaway, Room S–3524, (202) 343–5580.
Deputy Director.—Vacant, Room S–3524, 343–5580.
Chief of Staff.—James Blazer, Room S–3524, 343–5580.
Director of:
Division of Administration and Operations.—Vincent Alvarez, Room S–3201, 343–5580.
Division of Coal Mine Workers' Compensation.—Michael Chance, Room C–3520, 343–5580.
Division of Energy Employees Occupational Illness Compensation.—Rachel Leiton, Room C–3317, 343–5580.
Division of Federal Employees' Compensation.—Antonio Rios, Room S–3229, 343–0040.
Division of Financial Administration.—Hari Kadavath, Room 3524, 343–5580.
Division of Longshore and Harbor Workers' Compensation.—Douglas C. Fitzgerald, Room C–4319, 343–5580.
Deputy Director of:
Division of Administration and Operations.—Megan Hylton, Room S–3201, 343–5580.
Division of Financial Administration.—Shanti Ananthanayagam, Room S–3524, 343–5580.
Division of Coal Mine Workers' Compensation National Administrator of Field Operations.—Dean Woodard (214) 749–4138.
Division of Energy Employees Occupational Illness Compensation:
National Administrator of Field Operations.—Christy Long (206) 504–5104.
Deputy Administrator of Field Operations.—Annette Prindle (216) 802–1333.
Division of Federal Employees' Compensation:
National Administrator of Field Operations.—Magdalena Fernandez (904) 366–0509.
Deputy Administrators of Field Operations: Kellianne Conaway (202) 343–5580; Zev Sapir (212) 863–0870.

OFFICE OF LABOR-MANAGEMENT STANDARDS

Director.—Andrew Auerbach (acting), Room N–5603 (202) 693–0123.
Deputy Director.—Andrew Auerbach, Room N–5603, 693–0123.
Director of Field Operations.—Stephen Willertz, Room N–5119, 693–1182.

Director of Programs Operations.—Lorenzo Harrison, Room N–5609, 693–1299.
Regional Directors:
Central Region.—Daniel LaFond (414) 297–1504.
Northeastern Region.—Andriana Vamvakas (643) 264–3190.
Southern Region.—Daniel Cherry (504) 589–6174.
Western Region.—Jena de Mers Raney (720) 264–3232.
Division of:
Enforcement.—Brian Pifer, Room N–5119, 693–1204.
Interpretations and Standards.—Andrew Davis, Room N–5609, 693–1254.
Planning, Management, and Technology.—Teresa Thomas, Room N–5613, 693–0506.
Reports, Disclosure and Audits.—James Haskins, Room N–5603, 693–0829.
Statutory Programs.—Karen Torre, Room N–5119, 693–1209.

WAGE AND HOUR DIVISION

Administrator.—Cheryl Stanton, Room S–3502 (202) 693–0051.
Deputy Administrator.—Keith Sonderling, Room S–3502, 693–0051.
Chief of Staff.—Michael Stojsavljevich, Room S–3502, 693–0686.
Senior Policy Advisors: Bradford Kelley, Room S–3502, 693–0051; David McFadden, Room S–3502, 693–0051.
Deputy Administrator for Program Operations.—Patricia Davidson, Room S–3502, 693–0663.
Assistant Administrator, Office of:
Administrative Operations.—Rachel Torres, Room S–3502, 693–1252.
Government Contracts.—Vacant, Room S–3502, 693–1283.
Planning, Performance, Evaluation, and Communications.—Vacant, Room S–3502, 693–0621.
Policy.—Mary Ziegler, Room S–3502, 693–0517.

OFFICE OF FEDERAL CONTRACT COMPLIANCE PROGRAMS

Director.—Craig E. Leen, Room C–3325 (202) 693–0101.
Deputy Director.—Bob Gaglione, Room C–3325, 693–0101.
Chief of Staff.—Lissette Geán, Room C–3325, 693–0101.
Senior Policy Advisors: Valerie Maloney, Room C–3325, 693–0101; Matthew Mimnaugh, Room C–3325, 693–0101.
Special Assistant.—Lissette Geán, Room C–3325, 693–0101.
Director of:
Enforcement.—Bob LaJeunesse (acting), Room C–3325, 693–0101.
Management and Administrative Programs.—Kelley Smith, Room C–3315, 693–0101.
Policy and Program Development.—Bob Gaglione (acting), Room N–3422, 693–0105.
Program Operations.—Dr. Javaid Kaiser, Room C–3325, 693–0101.

DEPARTMENT OF HEALTH AND HUMAN SERVICES

200 Independence Avenue, SW., Washington, DC 20201

https://hhs.gov

ALEX M. AZAR II, Secretary of Health and Human Services; born in Johnstown, PA; education: B.A., *summa cum laude*, economics and government, Dartmouth College, Hanover, NH; J.D., Yale University, New Haven, CT; professional: attorney; General Counsel, 2001–05, and Deputy Secretary, 2005–07, Health and Human Services Department, Washington, DC; vice president for corporate affairs and communications, 2007–12, and president, 2012–17, Eli Lilly and Co., Indianapolis, IN; appointed by President Donald Trump to become the Secretary of Health and Human Services on November 13, 2017, confirmed by the Senate on January 24, 2018, and sworn into office on January 29, 2018.

OFFICE OF THE SECRETARY

Secretary of Health and Human Services.—Alex M. Azar II.
Executive Assistant to the Secretary.—Rose Lusi (202) 690–7000.
Deputy Secretary.—Eric D. Hargan.
Executive Secretary.—Ann Agnew, 868–9642.
Chief of Staff.—Brian Harrison, 690–7000.
Deputy Chief of Staff for Operations and Strategy.—Judy Stecker, 690–7000.
Chair, Departmental Appeals Board.—Constance B. Tobias, 565–0220.
Director, Intergovernmental and External Affairs.—Laura Trueman, 690–6060.

ASSISTANT SECRETARY FOR ADMINISTRATION

Assistant Secretary for Administration.—Scott W. Rowell (202) 690–7431.
Principal Deputy Assistant Secretary for Administration.—Catherine Bird, 690–7431.
Chief Information Officer.—Jose Arrieta, 690–6162.
Chief Operating Officer.—Shalley Kim, 260–6229.
Deputy Assistant Secretary for—
Acquisitions.—James E. Simpson, 205–9538.
Human Resources.—J. Blair Duncan, 260–2843.
Program Support.—Allen Sample (301) 443–5432.
Director, Equal Employment Opportunity, Diversity and Inclusion.—Julie Murphy, 260–6742.
Senior Advisor for National Labor Relations and Ethics Officer.—Darrell Hoffman, 205–3979.

ASSISTANT SECRETARY FOR LEGISLATION

Assistant Secretary.—Sarah Arbes (202) 690–7627.
Deputy Assistant Secretary for—
Congressional Liaison.—Sara Morse, 690–6786.
Discretionary Health.—Laura Pence, 690–7450.
Human Services.—Traci Vitek, 690–6311.
Mandatory Health.—Rebekah Armstrong, 690–7450.
Oversight and Investigations.—Vacant, 690–7627.

ASSISTANT SECRETARY FOR PLANNING AND EVALUATION

Assistant Secretary for Planning and Evaluation.—Vacant.
Deputy Assistant Secretary for Planning and Evaluation (HSP).—Brenda Destro, 690–7858.
Deputy Assistant Secretary for—
Disability and Long Term Care.—Arne Owens, 690–6443.
Health Policy.—Matthew Kiley, 690–6870.

Human Services Policy.—Brenda Destro, 690–7409.
Science and Data Policy.—Laina Bush, 690–7100.

ASSISTANT SECRETARY FOR PUBLIC AFFAIRS

Assistant Secretary.—Michael R. Caputo (202) 260–7441, fax 690–6247.
Principal Deputy Assistant Secretary.—Ryan Murphy, 260–7441, fax 690–6247.
Deputy Assistant Secretary for—
Health Care.—Ryan Murphy (acting), 260–7441, fax 690–6247.
Human Services.—Mark Weber, 260–6412, fax 690–6247.
Public Health.—Bill Hall, 690–6344, fax 690–6247.
Director, Freedom of Information/Privacy Act Division.—Brandon Gaylord, 260–7100, fax 690–6247.
Executive Officer/Deputy Agency Chief FOIA Officer.—Kim Hutchinson, 205–5839, fax 690–6247.

ASSISTANT SECRETARY FOR PREPAREDNESS AND RESPONSE

phone (202) 205–2882

Assistant Secretary.—Robert Kadlec, M.D.
Principal Deputy Assistant Secretary.—David Christian Hassell, Ph.D. (acting).
Deputy Assistant Secretary and Director, Office of Incident Command and Control.—Sally Phillips, RN, Ph.D. (acting).
Deputy Assistant Secretary and Director, Office of Biomedical Advanced Research and Development Authority.—Gary L. Disbrow, Ph.D. (acting).

ASSISTANT SECRETARY FOR FINANCIAL RESOURCES

Assistant Secretary.—Jen Moughalian (acting), (202) 690–6061.
Principal Deputy Assistant Secretary.—Jen Moughalian.
Deputy Assistant Secretary for—
Acquisitions.—David Dasher, 205–0706.
Budget.—Norris Cochran, 690–7393.
Congressional Liaison Branch.—Caitrin Shuy, 690–6883.
Finance.—Sheila Conley, 690–7084.
Grants.—Alice Bettencourt (acting), 619–0142.
Appropriations Liaison Director.—Alex Pinson, 690–6401.
Branch Chief.—Camille Sealy, 690–6639.

OFFICE FOR CIVIL RIGHTS

phone (202) 619–0403

Toll Free Voice Number (Nationwide): 1–800–368–1019

Toll Free TDD Number (Nationwide): 1–800–527–7697

Director.—Roger Severino.
Principal Deputy Director.—Robinsue Frohboese.
Chief of Staff.—March Bell.
Deputy Director for—
Civil Rights Division.—Pamela Barron.
Conscience and Religious Freedom Division—Luis Perez.
Health Information Privacy.—Timothy Noonan.
Operations and Resources Division.—Steve Novy.

OFFICE OF THE GENERAL COUNSEL

fax (202) 690–7998

General Counsel.—Robert P. Charrow, 690–7741.
Deputy General Counsel: Stacy Amin, 795–7640; Daniel J. Barry, 690–7741; William Chang, 690–7741; Kelly M. Cleary, 690–7741; Brenna Jenny, 690–0300; Sean Keveney, 690–7741; Brian R. Stimson, 690–7741.
Associate Deputy General Counsel: Kyle Brosnan, 690–7741; Carrie-Lee Early, 690–7741; Jonah Hecht, 690–7741; John Strom, 690–7741.

Assistant Deputy General Counsel.—Tyler Sanderson, 690–7741.
Senior Advisor to the General Counsel.—Elizabeth Jordan Gianturco, 690–7741.
Law Clerk.—Allison Beattie, 690–7741.
Associate General Counsel for—
Centers for Medicare and Medicaid Division.—Janice L. Hoffman, 619–0300.
Children, Family, and Aging Division.—Judith Haron, 690–8005.
Civil Rights Division.—Aaron Schuham, 619–0900.
Ethics Division/Special Counsel for Ethics.—Elizabeth J. Fischmann, 690–7258.
Food and Drug Division.—Stacy Amin (301) 796–3978.
General Law Division.—Michael Goulding, 619–0150.
Legislation Division.—Edith R. Blackwell, 690–7773.
Public Health Division.—David E. Benor (301) 443–2644.

OFFICE OF GLOBAL AFFAIRS

phone (202) 690–6174

Director.—Garrett Grigsby.
Principal Deputy Director.—Thomas Alexander.
Deputy Director.—Colin McIff.
Chief of Staff.—Kyle Zebley.

OFFICE OF THE INSPECTOR GENERAL

330 Independence Avenue, SW., Washington, DC 20201

Inspector General.—Christi Grimm (acting), (202) 619–3148.
Principal Deputy Inspector General.—Christi Grimm.
Chief Counsel to the Inspector General.—Gregory E. Demske, 619–2078.
Director, External Affairs.—Christopher Seagle, 260–7006.
Deputy Inspector for—
Audit Services.—Amy Frontz, 619–3157.
Evaluation and Inspections.—Suzanne Murrin, 619–0480.
Investigations.—Gary L. Cantrell, 205–4081.
Management and Policy.—Robert Owens, 205–9117.

OFFICE OF MEDICARE HEARINGS AND APPEALS

phone (703) 235–0635

Chief Administrative Law Judge.—C.F. Moore (acting).
Deputy Chief Administrative Law Judge.—Brian J. Haring.
Executive Director for the Office of Management.—Eileen C. McDaniel.
Executive Director for Operations.—Karen W. Ames.

OFFICE OF THE NATIONAL COORDINATOR FOR HEALTH INFORMATION TECHNOLOGY

National Coordinator for Health Information Technology.—Donald W. Rucker, M.D. (202) 969–3374.

OFFICE OF THE ASSISTANT SECRETARY FOR HEALTH

Assistant Secretary for Health.—ADM Brett P. Giroir, M.D. (202) 690–7694.
Executive Assistant to the Assistant Secretary for Health.—LCDR Katie Bante, 690–7694.
Principal Deputy Assistant Secretary for Health.—RADM Sylvia Trent-Adams, Ph.D., RN, F.A.A.N., 690–7694.
The Surgeon General.—VADM Jerome M. Adams, M.D., M.P.H., 205–0143.
Deputy Assistant Secretary for—
Communications.—Tara Broido, M.P.H., 205–1842.
Disease Prevention and Health Promotion.—Don Wright, M.D., M.P.H. (240) 453–8280.
External Affairs.—Mia Palmieri Heck, 578–6071.
Human Research Protections.—Jerry Menikoff, M.D., J.D. (240) 453–6900.
Infectious Disease and HIV/AIDS Policy.—Tammy R. Beckham, D.V.M., Ph.D., 795–7697.

Medicine and Science.—CAPT Paul Reed, M.D., 260–2873.
Minority Health.—CAPT Felicia Collins, M.D., M.P.H. (240) 453–6179.
Population Affairs.—Diane Foley, M.D., FAAP (240) 453–2805.
Research Integrity.—Elisabeth Handley, MPA (interim), (240) 453–8200.
Women's Health.—Dorothy Fink, M.D., 690–7650.

Executive Director of President's Council on Sports, Fitness, and Nutrition.—Kristina Harder (acting), (240) 276–9567.

Regional Health Administrator for—
Region I: CT, ME, MA, NH, RI, VT.—Betsy Rosenfeld, JD-C (617) 565–1505.
Region II: NJ, NY, PR, VI.—April Smith-Hirak (acting), (212) 264–2560.
Region III: DE, DC, MD, PA, VA, WV.—Dalton G. Paxman, Ph.D. (215) 861–4631.
Region IV: AL, FL, GA, KY, MS, NC, SC, TN.—Sharon Ricks (404) 562–7906.
Region V: IL, IN, MI, MN, OH, WI.—CAPT Joshua Devine, PharmD, Ph.D. (312) 353–1385.
Region VI: AR, LA, NM, OK, TX.—CAPT Mehran S. Massoudi, Ph.D., M.P.H. (214) 767–3879.
Region VII: IA, KS, MO, NE.—Catherine Lindsey Satterwhite, Ph.D., M.S.P.H., M.P.H. (816) 426–3330.
Region VIII: CO, MT, ND, SD, UT, WY.—Laurie Konsella, M.P.A. (acting), (303) 844–7860.
Region IX: AZ, CA, HI, NV, American Samoa, CNMI, FSMI, Guam, RMI, Republic of Palau.—CDR Matthew C. Johns, M.P.H. (415) 437–8096.
Region X: AK, ID, OR, WA.—Renée Bouvion, M.P.H. (206) 615–2469.

ADMINISTRATION FOR COMMUNITY LIVING

330 C Street, SW., Washington, DC 20201

Assistant Secretary for Aging and Administrator, Administration for Community Living.—Lance Allen Robertson (202) 401–4541.
Principal Deputy Administrator, Administration for Community Living.—Mary Lazare, 401–4541.
Chief of Staff.—Richard Nicholls, 795–7415.
Commissioner, Administration on Disabilities.—Julie Hocker, 401–4541.
Deputy Assistant Secretary, Administration on Aging.—Edwin L. Walker, 795–7463.
Deputy Administrator for—
Center for Innovation and Partnership.—Kelly Cronin, 795–7470.
Center for Management and Budget.—Rasheed Williams, 401–5481.
Center for Regional Operations.—Thomas Moran, Ph.D., 795–7788.
National Institute for Disability, Independent Living, and Rehabilitation Research.—Kristi Hill, Ph.D. (acting), 795–7363.
Director, Center for Policy and Evaluation.—Vicki Gottlich, 795–7352.
Director, Office of External Affairs.—Christine Phillips, 795–7419.
Deputy Chief of Staff and Legislative Affairs.—Jennifer Klocinski, 795–7377.

ADMINISTRATION FOR CHILDREN AND FAMILIES

330 C Street, SW., Washington, DC 20201

phone (202) 401–9215

Assistant Secretary.—Lynn A. Johnson (202) 401–3445.
Principal Deputy Assistant Secretary.—Scott Lekan, 401–7229.
Chief of Staff.—Bradley Wassink, 401–6984.
Deputy Assistant Secretary for—
Administration.—Ben Goldhaber, 401–3438.
External Affairs.—Vacant.
Planning, Research, and Evaluation.—Naomi Goldstein, 401–9220.
Policy.—Heidi Stirrup, 475–2478.
Commissioner for—
Administration for Native Americans.—Jeannie Hovland, 565–0165.
Administration on Children, Youth, and Families.—Elizabeth Darling, 205–7889.
Office of Child Support Enforcement.—Scott Lekan (acting), 401–7229.
Associate Commissioner, Children's Bureau.—Jerry Milner, 205–9618.
Associate Commissioner, Family and Youth Services Bureau.—Vacant.
Senior Advisors to the Assistant Secretary: Pedro Moreno, 401–4556; Anna Pilato, 401–9216; Amy Stephens, 565–0182.

Chief Information Officer.—Sebrina Blake, 818–8450.
Director, Office of:
Child Care.—Shannon Christian, 795–7610.
Communications.—Ken Wolfe (acting), 401–9215.
Community Services.—Clarence Carter (acting), 401–4830.
Early Childhood Development.—Deborah Bergeron, 205–8740.
Family Assistance.—Clarence Carter, 401–9275.
Head Start.—Deborah Bergeron, 205–9767.
Human Services Emergency Preparedness and Response.—Natalie Grant, 205–7843.
Legislative Affairs and Budget.—Amanda Barlow, 401–9223.
Refugee Resettlement.—Jonathan Hayes, 205–8244.
Regional Operations.—Mishaela Duran, 401–4605.
Trafficking in Persons.—Katherine Chon, 401–9200.

AGENCY FOR HEALTHCARE RESEARCH AND QUALITY (AHRQ)

Director.—Gopal Khanna, M.B.A. (301) 427–1200.
Deputy Director and Chief Physician.—David Meyers, M.D., 427–1634.

AGENCY FOR TOXIC SUBSTANCES AND DISEASE REGISTRY

1600 Clifton Road, NE., Atlanta, GA 30329–4027

Administrator.—Robert R. Redfield, M.D. (404) 639–7000.
Director.—Patrick Breysse, Ph.D.

CENTERS FOR DISEASE CONTROL AND PREVENTION

1600 Clifton Road, NE., Atlanta, GA 30329–4027

phone (404) 639–7000

Director.—Robert R. Redfield, M.D. (404) 639–7000.
Principal Deputy Director.—Anne Schuchat, M.D. (RADM, USPHS, Ret.).
Chief Operating Officer.—Sherri A. Berger, M.S.P.H.
Chief of Staff.—Robert "Kyle" McGowan.
Chief Medical Officer.—Mitchell Wolfe, M.D., M.P.H. (RADM, USPHS).
CDC Washington Director.—Anstice Brand Kenefick (acting).
Director, Office of:
Equal Employment Opportunity.—Reginald R. Mebane, M.S.
Minority Health and Health Equity.—Leandris Liburd, Ph.D., M.P.H., M.A.
Program Performance and Evaluation.—Sara Patterson, M.A.
Associate Director for—
Communication.—Katherine Lyon Daniel, Ph.D.
Laboratory Science and Safety.—Steve Monroe, Ph.D.
Policy and Strategy.—Robin M. Ikeda, M.D., M.P.H., (RADM, USPHS) (acting).
Deputy Director for—
Infectious Diseases.—Jay C. Butler, M.D, (CAPT, USPS, Ret.).
Non-Communicable Diseases.—Ileana Arias, Ph.D. (acting).
Public Health Service and Implementation Science.—Stephen C. Redd, M.D. (RADM, USPHS).
Public Health Science and Surveillance.—Chesley Richards, M.D., M.P.H., F.A.C.P.
Director of:
Center for Chronic Disease Prevention and Health Promotion.—Karen Hacker, M.D., M.P.H.
Center for Emerging and Zoonotic Infectious Diseases.—Rima F. Khabbaz, M.D.
Center for Environmental Health/Agency for Toxic Substances and Disease Registry.—Patrick Breysse, Ph.D., C.I.H.
Center for Global Health.—Rebecca Martin, Ph.D.
Center for Health Statistics.—Jennifer Madans, Ph.D. (acting).
Center for HIV/AIDS, Viral Hepatitis, STD, and TB Prevention.—Jonathan Mermin, M.D., M.P.H. (RADM, USPHS).
Center for Immunization and Respiratory Diseases.—Nancy Messonnier, M.D. (CAPT, USPHS, Ret.).
Center for Injury Prevention and Control.—Debra Houry, M.D., M.P.H.
Center for Preparedness and Response.—Stephen C. Redd, M.D. (RADM, USPHS, Ret.), (acting).

Center for State, Tribal, Local, and Territorial Support.—Jose T. Montero, M.D., M.H.C.D.S.
Center for Surveillance, Epidemiology and Laboratory Services.—Michael F. Iademarco, M.D., M.P.H. (RADM, USPHS).
Center on Birth Defects and Developmental Disabilities.—Coleen A. Boyle, Ph.D., M.S.Hyg.
National Institute for Occupational Safety and Health.—John Howard, M.D., M.P.H., J.D., L.L.M., M.B.A.
Office of Science.—Rebecca Bunnell, Ph.D., M.Ed.

CENTER FOR FAITH AND OPPORTUNITY INITIATIVES

(THE PARTNERSHIP CENTER)

Director.—Shannon O. Royce, Esq. (202) 260–6501.

CENTERS FOR MEDICARE AND MEDICAID SERVICES

200 Independence Avenue, SW., Washington, DC 20201

phone (202) 690–6726

Headquarters: https://cms.gov/About-CMS/Agency-Information/CMSLeadership/index.html

Regional Offices: https://cms.gov/Medicare/Coding/ICD10/CMS-Regional-Offices

Administrator.—Seema Verma (202) 619–0630.
Deputy Administrator and Chief of Staff.—Brady Brookes, 619–0630.
Principal Deputy Administrator for Policy and Operations.—Kimberly Brandt, 619–0630.
Principal Deputy Administrator for Medicare and Director, Center for Medicare.—Demetrios Kouzoukas, 619–0630.
Chief Operating Officer.—Jennifer Main (410) 786–5448.
Deputy Chief Operating Officer.—Karen Jackson, 786–3151.
Chief Actuary, Office of the Actuary.—Paul Spitalnic, 786–6374.
Deputy Administrator and Director, Center for—
Consumer Information and Insurance Oversight.—Randolph Pate (202) 690–6360.
Medicaid and CHIP Services.—Calder Lynch, 202–5682.
Medicare and Medicaid Innovation.—Brad Smith, 260–7153.
Program Integrity.—Alec Alexander (410) 786–1795.
Director and CMS Chief Medical Officer, Center for Clinical Standards and Quality.—Lee Fleisher, M.D., 786–8110.
Director, Office of:
Acquisition and Grants Management.—Melissa Starinsky, 786–1391.
Burden Reduction and Health Informatics.—Mary Greene, M.D.
Communications.—Tom Corry (202) 205–9450.
Enterprise Data and Analytics and CMS Chief Data Officer.—Allison Oelschlaeger, 690–6627.
Equal Opportunity and Civil Rights.—Anita Pinder (410) 786–5493.
Federal Coordinated Health Care.—Tim Engelhardt (202) 260–1291.
Financial Management and CMS Chief Financial Officer.—Megan Worstell (410) 786–2085.
Hearings and Inquiries.—Randy Brauer, 786–1618.
Human Capital and Chief Administrative Officer.—Tia Butler, 786–0763.
Information Technology and Chief Information Officer.—Rajiv Uppal, 786–1800.
Legislation.—Alec Aramanda (202) 690–5960.
Minority Health.—Cara James (410) 786–6842.
Program Operations and Local Engagement.—Nancy O'Connor (215) 861–4140.
Security, Facilities and Logistics Operations.—James Weber (410) 786–1051.
Strategic Operations and Regulatory Affairs.—Kathleen Cantwell (202) 690–8390.
Strategy, Performance, and Results.—Andrea Chapman (acting).
Consortium Administrator for—
Financial Management and FFS Operations.—Gregory Dill (acting), (816) 426–5233.
Medicare Health Plans Operations.—Nancy O'Conner (acting), (215) 861–4140.
Quality Improvement and Survey and Certification Operations.—Jean Moody-Williams (acting), (404) 562–7150.

FOOD AND DRUG ADMINISTRATION

10903 New Hampshire Avenue, Silver Spring, MD 20993

Commissioner.—Stephen M. Hahn, M.D. (301) 796–5000.
Principal Deputy Commissioner.—Amy Abernethy, M.D., Ph.D., 796–6700.
Chief of Staff.—Keagan Lenihan (acting), 796–8445.
The Executive Secretariat.—Martina Varnado, 796–8331.
Counselor to the Commissioner.—Vacant.
Deputy Commissioner for—
Food Policy and Response.—Frank Yiannis, 796–4500.
Medical and Scientific Affairs.—Anand Shah, M.D.
Policy, Planning, Legislation, and Analysis.—Anna Abram, 796–8770.
Chiefs:
Counsel.—Stacy Amin, J.D., 796–3978.
Financial Officer.—James Tyler, 796–4770.
Information Officer.—Amy Abernethy, M.D., Ph.D., 796–6700.
Operating Officer.—James Sigg, 796–4700.
Scientist.—RADM Denise Hinton, 796–4880.
Principal Associate Commissioner for Policy.—Lowell Schiller, J.D.
Associate Commissioner for—
External Affairs.—John Wagner, 796–8546.
Global Policy and Strategy.—Mark Abdoo, 796–8964.
Legislative Affairs.—Karas Gross, 796–8900.
Minority Health.—RADM Richardae Araojo, PharmD, M.D., 796–1152.
Planning.—CAPT Darian Tarver (acting), 796–4733.
Policy.—Lauren Roth, J.D., 796–4460.
Regulatory Affairs.—Judith A. McMeekin, PharmD., 796–8800.
Women's Health.—Kaveeta Vasisht, M.D., PharmD.
Director of:
Center for Biologics Evaluation and Research.—Peter Marks, M.D., Ph.D. (240) 402–8000.
Center for Devices and Radiological Health.—Jeffrey Shuren, M.D., J.D., 796–5900.
Center for Drug Evaluation and Research.—Janet Woodcock, M.D., 796–5400.
Center for Food Safety and Applied Nutrition.—Susan Mayne, Ph.D. (240) 402–1600.
Center for Tobacco Products.—Mitch Zeller, J.D., 796–9200.
Center for Veterinary Medicine.—Steven Solomon, D.V.M. (240) 276–9000.
National Center for Toxicological Research.—William Slikker, Jr., Ph.D. (870) 543–7517.
Oncology Center of Excellence.—Richard Pazdur, M.D.
Office of Clinical Policy and Programs.—Nicole Wolanski (acting).
Office of Safety, Security and Crisis Management.—Lionel Carter, 796–8250.
Office of Minority Health and Health Equity.—CAPT Richardae Araojo, PharmD, M.D., 796–1152.
Senior Advisor for Science, Innovation, and Policy.—Vacant, 847–3530.
Senior Advisor to the Commissioner.—Vacant, 796–7064.

HEALTH RESOURCES AND SERVICES ADMINISTRATION

5600 Fishers Lane, Rockville, MD 20857

Administrator.—Thomas J. Engels (301) 443–2216.
Deputy Administrators: Diana Espinosa, 443–2216; Brian LeClair, 443–2216.
Chief Operating Officer.—Wendy Ponton, 443–4244.
Associate Administrator for—
Federal Assistance Management.—Rimas Liogys, 945–3939.
Health Workforce.—Luis Padilla, M.D., 443–5794.
Healthcare Systems.—Cheryl Dammons, 443–3300.
HIV/AIDS.—Laura Cheever, M.D., 443–1993.
Maternal and Child Health.—Michael Warren, M.D., 443–2170.
Primary Health Care.—Jim Macrae, 594–4110.
Regional Operations.—Natasha Coulouris, 443–7070.
Rural Health Policy.—Tom Morris, 443–0835.
Director, Office of:
Civil Rights, Diversity and Inclusion.—Anthony Archeval, J.D., 443–5636.
Communications.—Martin Kramer, 443–3376.
Global Health.—Kerry Nesseler, RN, RADM, USPHS, 443–2741.

Health Equity.—Michelle Allender-Smith, RN, 443–2042.
Legislation.—Leslie Atkinson, 443–1890.
Planning, Analysis and Evaluation.—Susan Monarez, Ph.D., 443–4701.
Women's Health.—Sabrina Matoff-Stepp, Ph.D., 443–8664.

INDIAN HEALTH SERVICE

5600 Fishers Lane, Rockville, MD 20857

Director.—RADM Michael D. Weahkee, (301) 443–1083.
Deputy Director.—RADM Chris Buchanan, 443–1083.
Deputy Director for—
Field Operations.—Christopher Mandregan, 443–1083.
Intergovernmental Affairs.—Benjamin Smith, 443–1083.
Management Operations.—Randy Grinnell, 443–1083.
Quality Health Care.—Jonathan Merrell, 443–1083.
Chief Medical Officer.—RADM Michael Toedt, M.D., 443–1083.
Chief of Staff.—RADM Brandon Taylor, 443–1083.
Senior Advisor.—Vacant.
Director of:
Clinical and Preventative Services.—Darrell LaRoche, 443–4644.
Direct Service and Contracting Tribes.—Hope Johnson (acting), 443–1104.
Environmental Health and Engineering.—Gary Hartz, 443–1247.
Equal Employment Opportunity.—Sarah Nelson, 443–1108.
Executive Secretariat.—Julie Czajkowski, 443–1011.
Finance and Accounting.—Ann Church (acting), 443–1270.
Human Resources.—Lisa Gyorda, 443–6520.
Information Technology.—Mitchell Thornbrugh, 443–3408.
Legislative and Congressional Affairs.—Darren Pete, 443–7261.
Management Services.—Athena Elliott, 443–6290.
Public Affairs.—Jennifer Buschick, 443–1865.
Public Health Support.—RADM Francis Frazier, 443–0222.
Resource Access and Partnerships.—CDR John Rael, 443–3216.
Tribal Self-Governance.—Jennifer Cooper, 443–7821.
Urban Indian Health Programs.—Rose Weahkee, Ph.D. (acting), 443–4680.

NATIONAL INSTITUTES OF HEALTH

9000 Rockville Pike, Bethesda, MD 20892

Director.—Francis S. Collins, M.D., Ph.D. (301) 496–2433.
Principal Deputy Director.—Lawrence A. Tabak, D.D.S., Ph.D., 496–2433.
Deputy Director for—
Division of Program Coordination, Planning, and Strategic Initiatives.—James Anderson, M.D., Ph.D., 402–9852.
Extramural Research.—Michael S. Lauer, M.D., 496–1096.
Intramural Research.—Michael M. Gottesman, M.D., 496–1921.
Management.—Alfred C. Johnson, Ph.D., 496–3271.
Chief of Staff and Associate Director for Science Policy.—Carrie Wolinetz, Ph.D. (acting), 496–2122.
Associate Deputy Director.—Tara A. Schwetz, Ph.D., 496–2433.
Associate Director for—
Administration.—Diane Frasier, 496–4422.
AIDS Research.—Maureen M. Goodenow, Ph.D., 496–0357.
Behavioral and Social Sciences Research.—William T. Riley, Ph.D., 402–1148.
Budget.—Neil K. Shapiro, J.D., 496–9103.
Clinical Research.—John I. Gallin, M.D., 827–5428.
Communications and Public Liaison.—John T. Burklow, 496–4461.
Data Science.—Susan Gregurick, Ph.D., 827–7616.
Disease Prevention.—David Murray, Ph.D., 827–5561.
International Research.—Roger I. Glass, M.D., Ph.D., 496–1415.
Legislative Policy and Analysis.—Adrienne Hallett, 496–3471.
Management and Executive Officer, Office of the Director.—Darla Hayes (acting), 594–8231.
Research Facilities Development and Operations.—Daniel Wheeland, 594–0999.
Research on Women's Health.—Janine Clayton, M.D., 402–1770.

Research Services.—Colleen McGowan, 496–2215.
Science Policy.—Carrie Wolinetz, Ph.D., 496–2122.
Chief Information Officer and Director, Center for Information Technology.—Andrea T. Norris, 496–5703.
Chief Officer for Scientific Workforce Diversity.—Hannah A. Valantine, M.D., 451–4296.
Legal Advisor, Office of the General Counsel.—David Lankford, 496–6043.
Director, Office of:
Acquisition and Logistics Management.—Diane Frasier, 496–4422.
Equal Opportunity and Diversity Management.—Debra Chew, J.D., 496–6301.
Ethics.—Holli Beckerman Jaffe, J.D., 594–9555.
Executive Secretariat.—Patrice Allen-Gifford, 496–1461.
Federal Advisory Committee Policy.—Claire Harris, 496–2123.
Financial Management.—Glenda Conroy, 435–7995.
Human Resources.—Julie Berko, 496–3592.
Management Assessment.—Michael D. Shannon, 496–1873.
Technology Transfer.—Karen L. Rogers (acting), 435–4359.
Director of:
Center for Information Technology.—Andrea T. Norris, 496–5703.
Center for Scientific Review.—Noni Byrnes, Ph.D., 435–1111.
Eunice Kennedy Shriver National Institute of Child Health and Human Development.—Diana W. Bianchi, M.D., 496–3454.
Fogarty International Center.—Roger I. Glass, M.D., Ph.D., 496–1415.
National Cancer Institute.—Douglas R. Lowy, M.D. (acting), (240) 781–4100.
National Center for Advancing Translational Sciences.—Christopher Austin, M.D., 435–0878.
National Center for Complementary and Integrative Health.—Helene Langevin, M.D., 435–6826.
National Eye Institute.—Santa Tumminia, Ph.D. (acting), (301) 496–2234.
National Heart, Lung, and Blood Institute.—Gary Gibbons, M.D., 496–5166.
National Human Genome Research Institute.—Eric Green, M.D., Ph.D., 496–0844.
National Institute of Allergy and Infectious Diseases.—Anthony S. Fauci, M.D., 496–2263.
National Institute of Arthritis and Musculoskeletal and Skin Diseases.—Robert Carter, M.D. (acting), 496–3651.
National Institute of Biomedical Imaging and Bioengineering.—Bruce Tromberg, Ph.D., 496–8859.
National Institute of Dental and Craniofacial Research.—Martha Somerman, D.D.S., Ph.D., 496–3571.
National Institute of Diabetes and Digestive and Kidney Diseases.—Griffin P. Rodgers, M.D., M.A.C.P., 496–5741.
National Institute of Environmental Health Sciences.—Richard Woychik, Ph.D. (acting), (919) 541–3201.
National Institute of General Medical Sciences.—Jon Lorsch, Ph.D. (301) 594–2172.
National Institute of Mental Health.—Joshua Gordon, M.D., Ph.D., 443–3673.
National Institute of Neurological Disorders and Stroke.—Walter Koroshetz, M.D., 496–3167.
National Institute of Nursing Research.—Lawrence A. Tabak, D.D.S., Ph.D. (acting), 496–2433.
National Institute on Aging.—Richard J. Hodes, M.D., 496–9265.
National Institute on Alcohol Abuse and Alcoholism.—George Koob, Ph.D., 443–3885.
National Institute on Deafness and Other Communication Disorders.—Debara L. Tucci, M.D., M.S., M.B.A., 402–0900.
National Institute on Drug Abuse.—Nora D. Volkow, M.D., 443–6480.
National Institute on Minority Health and Health Disparities.—Eliseo J. Pérez-Stable, M.D., 496–7162.
National Library of Medicine.—Patricia F. Brennan, RN, Ph.D., 496–6221.
Chief Executive Officer, NIH Clinical Center.—James Gilman, M.D., 496–4114.

SUBSTANCE ABUSE AND MENTAL HEALTH SERVICES ADMINISTRATION (SAMHSA)

5600 Fishers Lane, Rockville, MD 20857

https://samhsa.gov

Assistant Secretary for Mental Health and Substance Use.—Elinore F. McCance-Katz, M.D., Ph.D., Room 18E41, (240) 276–2000.

Director, Office of:

Communications.—Daryl Kade, Room 18E31, 276–2201.

Financial Resources.—Deepa Avula, Room 17E51, 276–2200.

Management, Technology, and Operations.—Paolo del Vecchio, Room 12E41, 276–1946.

National Mental Health and Substance Use Policy Laboratory.—Thomas Clarke, Ph.D., Room 18E63, 276–0493.

Director, Center for—

Behavioral Health Statistics and Quality.—Elizabeth Lopez, Ph.D. (acting), Room 15E41, 276–2242.

Mental Health Services.—Anita Everett, M.D., Room 14E41, 276–2001.

Substance Abuse Prevention.—Johnnetta Davis-Joyce, Room 16E41, 276–1164.

Substance Abuse Treatment.—Louis Trevisan, M.D., Room 13E41, 276–1236.

DEPARTMENT OF HOUSING AND URBAN DEVELOPMENT

Robert C. Weaver Federal Building

451 Seventh Street, SW., Washington, DC 20410

phone (202) 708–1112, https://hud.gov

BENJAMIN CARSON, Secretary of Housing and Urban Development, born in Detroit, MI, September 18, 1951; education: B.A., psychology, Yale University, New Haven, CT, 1973; M.D., University of Michigan Medical School, Ann Arbor, MI, 1977; professional: in 1984, at age 33, became youngest physician to head a major division (pediatric neurosurgery) at Johns Hopkins Hospital in Baltimore, MD, where he remained until his retirement in 2013; in 1994, started Carson Scholars Fund with his wife to help fund college education and install reading rooms around the country; served on President's Council on Bioethics, 2004–08; awarded Spingarn Medal, highest honor given by NAACP (National Association for the Advancement of Colored People), 2006; awarded the Presidential Medal of Freedom, nation's highest civilian honor, 2008; married to Candy; three adult sons and three grandchildren; nominated by President Donald J. Trump to become the 17th Secretary of Housing and Urban Development on December 5, 2016; confirmed by the U.S. Senate, and was sworn in on March 2, 2017.

OFFICE OF THE SECRETARY

Secretary of Housing and Urban Development.—Dr. Benjamin Carson, Room 10000 (202) 708–0417.
Chief of Staff.—Andrew Hughes, 402–2713.
Deputy Chiefs of Staff: John Baker, 402–4825; Alfonso Costa, Jr., 402–6463; Drew McCall, 708–2713.
Executive Secretariat Senior Advisor.—Jozetta R. Robinson (acting), 708–3054.

OFFICE OF THE DEPUTY SECRETARY

Deputy Secretary.—Brian D. Montgomery, Room 10100 (202) 402–6552.
Deputy Chief of Staff.—Michael Dendas, Room 10100, 402–3761.

ASSISTANT SECRETARY FOR ADMINISTRATION

Assistant Secretary.—John Bobbitt, Room 10100 (202) 402–6552.
Principal Deputy Assistant Secretary for Administration.—Charles Cowan, Room 6100, 402–6425.

ASSISTANT SECRETARY FOR COMMUNITY PLANNING AND DEVELOPMENT

Assistant Secretary.—John Gibbs (acting), Room 7100 (202) 402–4445.
Principal Deputy Assistant Secretary.—David Woll, Room 7100, 402–7040.
General Deputy Assistant Secretary.—John Bravacos, 402–6064.
Associate Deputy Assistant Secretary for—
Grant Programs.—Steve Rawlinson, Room 7204, 402–7117.
Special Needs.—Jemine Bryon, Room 7244, 708–2404.

ASSISTANT SECRETARY FOR CONGRESSIONAL AND INTERGOVERNMENTAL RELATIONS

Assistant Secretary.—Len Wolfson, Room 10120 (202) 708–0980.
Deputy Assistant Secretary for—
Congressional Relations.—Abby Gunderson-Schwarz, Room 10120, 402–4353.

Intergovernmental Relations.—Stephanie Fila, Room 10148, 708–0005.

ASSISTANT SECRETARY FOR FAIR HOUSING AND EQUAL OPPORTUNITY

Assistant Secretary.—Anna María Farías, Room 5100.
General Deputy Assistant Secretary.—Daniel Huff (202) 402–3463.
Deputy Assistant Secretary for—
Enforcement and Programs.—David Enzel, 402–5557.
Operations and Management.—Jaime E. Forero, 402–6036.
Policy, Legislative Initiatives, and Outreach.—DeAndra Johnson-Cullen (acting), 402–4115.

ASSISTANT SECRETARY FOR HOUSING

Assistant Secretary/Federal Housing Commissioner.—Brian D. Montgomery, Room 9100 (202) 708–2601.
General Deputy Assistant Secretary.—John L. Garvin, Room 9100, 708–2601.
Associate General Deputy Assistant Secretary.—Vacant, Room 9100, 708–2601.
Deputy Assistant Secretary for—
Finance and Budget.—Susan Betts, 708–2004.
Healthcare Programs.—Roger Lukoff, Room 6264, 708–0599.
Housing Counseling.—Sarah Gerecke, Room 9224, 402–3453.
Housing Operations.—Jeffrey Little, Room 9136, 402–5649.
Multifamily Housing Programs.—C. Lamar Seats, Room 6106, 708–2495.
Risk Management and Regulatory Affairs.—Shawn Jones (acting), Room 9162, 402–2398.
Single Family Housing.—Gisele Roget, Room 9282, 708–3175.

ASSISTANT SECRETARY FOR POLICY DEVELOPMENT AND RESEARCH

Assistant Secretary.—Seth D. Appleton, Room 8100 (202) 708–1600.
General Deputy Assistant Secretary.—Todd M. Richardson, Room 8100, 708–1600.
Deputy Assistant Secretary for the Office of:
Economic Affairs.—Kurt G. Usowski, Room 8204, 708–3080.
Innovation.—Christopher Bourne, Room 7132, 708–1600.
Policy Development.—Paige J. Esterkin, Room 8106, 708–1537.
Research, Evaluation, and Monitoring.—Calvin C. Johnson, Room 8124, 708–4230.

ASSISTANT SECRETARY FOR PUBLIC AFFAIRS

Assistant Secretary for Public Affairs.—Caroline Vanvick (acting), Room 10130 (202) 708–0980.
General Deputy Assistant Secretary.—Jereon M. Brown.
Deputy Assistant Secretary.—Raphael Williams.
Communications Director.—Vacant.
Press Secretary.—Caitlin Thompson.

ASSISTANT SECRETARY FOR PUBLIC AND INDIAN HOUSING

Assistant Secretary.—R. Hunter Kurtz (202) 402–4100.
General Deputy Assistant Secretary.—Dominique G. Blom, 402–4181.
Deputy Assistant Secretary for—
Field Operations.—Felicia R. Gaither, Room 3180, 402–6009.
Native American Programs.—Heidi J. Frechette, Room 4126, 402–6321.
Public Housing and Voucher Programs.—Danielle L. Bastarache, Room 4204, 402–5264.
Public Housing Investments.—Robert E. Mulderig (acting), Room 4130, 402–4780.
Real Estate Assessment Center.—Donald J. Lavoy, Potomac Center, 475–7949.

OFFICE OF FIELD POLICY AND MANAGEMENT

Assistant Deputy Secretary.—Benjamin DeMarzo, Room 7108 (202) 708–2426.
Director of Field Policy and Management.—Timothy Smyth, Room 7108, 708–2426.
Director, Office of Davis Bacon and Labor Standards.—Pamela Glekas, Room 7122, 708–2426.

GOVERNMENT NATIONAL MORTGAGE ASSOCIATION

President, Executive Vice President, and COO.—Eric G. Blankenstein (202) 475–8808.
Principal Executive Vice President.—Seth Appleton, 402–4560.
Executive Vice President/Senior Vice President, Strategic Planning and Policy.—Michael R. Drayne (acting), 475–7836.
Senior Vice Presidents, Office of:
Capital Markets.—John F. Getchis, 475–8855.
Enterprise Data and Technology Solutions.—Barbara Cooper-Jones, 475–7817.
Enterprise Risk.—Gregory A. Keith (also Chief Risk Office), 475–4918.
Issuer and Portfolio Management.—Leslie Pordzik, 475–4934.
Management Operations.—Tawanna Preston, 475–8802.
Securities Operations.—John T. Daugherty, 475–7848.
Chief Financial Officer.—Adetokunbo (Toky) Lofinmakin, 475–7896.

CHIEF FINANCIAL OFFICER

Chief Financial Officer.—Irving L. Dennis (202) 708–1946.
Deputy Chief Financial Officer.—George J. Tomchick, 402–5911.
Assistant Chief Financial Officer for—
Accounting.—Nita Nigam, 402–6850.
Budget.—Emily Kornegay, 402–6824.
Financial Management.—MelaJo Kubacki (acting), 402–6549.
Systems.—Joseph Hungate, 402–2801.

CHIEF INFORMATION OFFICER

Chief Information Officer.—David C. Chow, Room 4160 (202) 708–0306.
Principal Deputy Chief Information Officer.—Kevin R. Cooke, Jr., Room 4160, 708–0306.
Chief Information Security Officer.—Hun Kim, Room 4282, 402–3246.
Deputy Chief Information Officer for—
Business and IT Resource Management.—Nancy Corsiglia, Room 4278, 402–4025.
Infrastructure and Operations.—Juan Sargeant, Room 4180, 402–7431.

CHIEF PROCUREMENT OFFICER

Chief Procurement Officer.—Ronald C. Flom, Room 5280 (202) 708–0600.
Deputy Chief Procurement Officer.—Jimmy Scott, Room 5256, 708–1290.

GENERAL COUNSEL

General Counsel.—J. Paul Compton, Jr., Room 10110 (202) 708–2240.
Principal Deputy General Counsel.—Joseph Grassi, Room 10110, 708–2244.
Deputy General Counsel for—
Enforcement and Fair Housing.—Timothy Petty, Room 10110, 402–5976.
Housing Programs.—Millicent B. Potts (acting), Room 9226, 402–5255.
Operations.—Gayle E. Bohling, Room 10240, 402–6519.
Associate General Counsel for—
Assisted Housing and Community Development.—Althea Forrester, Room 8166, 402–5268.
Ethics, Appeals, and Personnel Law.—Vacant, Room 2134, 402–2024.
Fair Housing.—Jeanine Worden, Room 10272, 402–5188.
Finance, Procurement, and Administrative Law.—Kevin M. Simpson, Room 8150, 402–2036.
Insured Housing.—Amy Brown, Room 9240, 402–3826.
Legislation and Regulations.—Aaron Santa Anna, Room 10282, 402–5300.
Litigation.—Dane M. Narode (acting), Room 10258, 402–7934.
Program Enforcement.—Dane M. Narode, Portals Building, 245–4141.
Director, Departmental Enforcement Center.—Craig Clemmensen, Portals Building, 245–4195.

INSPECTOR GENERAL

Inspector General.—Rae Oliver Davis, Room 8256 (202) 708–0430.
Counsel to the Inspector General.—Jeremy Kirkland, 708–1613.
Deputy Inspector General.—Chuck Jones (acting), cjones@hudoig.gov.

Assistant Inspector General for—
Audit.—Kilah White.
Evaluation.—Brian Pattison.
Investigation.—Vacant.
Management and Technology.—Vacant.
Office of Special Inquiry.—Brian Nysenbaum (acting).

OFFICE OF DEPARTMENTAL EQUAL EMPLOYMENT OPPORTUNITY

Director.—John P. Benison, Room 2102 (202) 708–3362.
Deputy Director.—Aisa K. McCullough, Room 2102, 708–5582.

OFFICE OF THE CHIEF HUMAN CAPITAL OFFICER

Chief Human Capital Officer.—Monica Matthews, Room 2254 (202) 708–0940.
Deputy Chief Human Capital Officer.—Priscilla Clark, Room 2254, 708–0940.
Chief Learning Officer, HUD LEARN.—Matisha Montgomery, Room 2250, 402–4396.
Chief Management Officer, Office of Management and Administration.—Janice Boyd, Room 2172B, 402–7605.
Chief Performance Officer, Office of Performance Management.—Joe Sullivan, Room 2150, 402–2087.
Director, Office of Human Capital Services.—Vacant.

OFFICE OF LEAD HAZARD CONTROL AND HEALTHY HOMES

Director.—Matthew Ammon, Room 8236 (202) 402–4337.
Deputy Director.—Michelle Miller, Room 8236, 402–5769.

OFFICE OF SMALL AND DISADVANTAGED BUSINESS UTILIZATION

Director.—Jean Lin Pao, Room 2200 (202) 402–5713.

HUD REGIONAL ADMINISTRATORS

Region I.—Connecticut, Maine, Massachusetts, New Hampshire, Rhode Island, Vermont.
Regional Administrator.—David E. Tille, Thomas P. O'Neill, Jr. Federal Building, 10 Causeway Street, 3rd Floor, Boston, MA 02222–1092 (617) 994–8223.

Region II.—New Jersey, New York.
Regional Administrator.—Lynne M. Patton, 26 Federal Plaza, Suite 3541, New York, NY 10278–0068 (212) 542–7109.

Region III.—Delaware, District of Columbia, Maryland, Pennsylvania, Virginia, West Virginia.
Regional Administrator.—Joseph J. DeFelice, The Wanamaker Building, 100 Penn Square East, Philadelphia, PA 19107–3380 (215) 656–0600.

Region IV.—Alabama, Florida, Georgia, Kentucky, Mississippi, North Carolina, Puerto Rico, South Carolina, Tennessee.
Regional Administrator.—Denise Cleveland-Leggett, Five Points Plaza, 40 Marietta Street, NW., 2nd Floor, Atlanta, GA 30303–2806 (687) 732–2009.

Region V.—Illinois, Indiana, Michigan, Minnesota, Ohio, Wisconsin.
Regional Administrator.—Joseph P. Galvan, Ralph Metcalfe Federal Building, 77 West Jackson Boulevard, Chicago, IL 60604–3507 (312) 353–5680.

Region VI.—Arkansas, Louisiana, New Mexico, Oklahoma, Texas.
Regional Administrator.—Vacant, 801 Cherry Street, Fort Worth, TX 76113–2905 (817) 978–5965.

Region VII.—Iowa, Kansas, Missouri, Nebraska.
Regional Administrator.—Jason Mohr, Gateway Tower II, 400 State Avenue, Room 507, Kansas City, KS 66101–2406 (913) 551–5462.

Region VIII.—Colorado, Montana, North Dakota, South Dakota, Utah, Wyoming.
Regional Administrator.—Evelyn Lim, 1670 Broadway, Denver, CO 80202–4801 (303) 672–5440.

Region IX.—American Samoa, Arizona, California, Hawaii, Nevada, Guam, Northern Mariana Islands.
Regional Administrator.—Christopher Patterson, One Sansome Street, Suite 1200, San Francisco, CA 94104–1300 (415) 489–6400.

Region X.—Alaska, Idaho, Oregon, Washington.

Regional Administrator.—Jeffrey McMorris, Seattle Federal Office Building, 909 First Avenue, Suite 200, Seattle, WA 98104–1000 (206) 220–5101.

DEPARTMENT OF TRANSPORTATION

1200 New Jersey Avenue, SE., Washington, DC 20590

phone (202) 366–4000, https://dot.gov

ELAINE L. CHAO, Secretary of Transportation; education: MBA, Harvard Business School; B.A., Mount Holyoke College, South Hadley, MA; professional: Distinguished Fellow, The Hudson Institute from 2009–17; U.S. Secretary of Labor, U.S. Department of Labor from 2001–09; Distinguished Fellow, the Heritage Foundation from 1996–2001; President and Chief Executive Officer, United Way of America from 1992–96; Director, Peace Corps from 1991–92; Deputy Secretary, U.S. Department of Transportation from 1989–91; Chairman, Federal Maritime Commission from 1988–89; Deputy Maritime Administrator, U.S. Department of Transportation from 1986–88; family: married to the Honorable Mitch McConnell, Majority Leader, United States Senate; nominated by President Donald J. Trump to become the 18th Secretary of Transportation on November 29, 2016, and was confirmed by the U.S. Senate on January 31, 2017.

OFFICE OF THE SECRETARY

[Created by the act of October 15, 1966; codified under U.S.C. 49]

Secretary of Transportation.—Elaine L. Chao, Room W91–320 (202) 366–1111.
Deputy Secretary.—Vacant, Room W91–308, 366–2222.
Chief of Staff.—J. Todd Inman, Room W90–314, 366–2165.
Under Secretary of Transportation for Policy.—Joel Szabat (acting), Room W80–308, 366–9570.
Director, Office of:
Civil Rights.—Charles James, Room W78–320, 366–8825.
Executive Secretariat.—Ruth Knouse, Room W93–324, 366–9747.
Intelligence and Security.—Rich Chavez, Room W56–308, 366–6525.
Small and Disadvantaged Business Utilization.—Willis Morris, Room W56–310, 366–1084.

ASSISTANT SECRETARY FOR ADMINISTRATION

Assistant Secretary.—Vacant, Room W80–322 (202) 366–2332.
Deputy Assistant Secretary.—Keith Washington, Room W80–320, 366–2332.
Director, Office of:
Facilities, Information and Asset Management.—Keith Szakal (acting), Room W58–336, 366–9422.
Financial Management.—Marie Petrosino-Woolverton, Room W81–306, 366–3967.
Hearings, Chief Administrative Law Judge.—Vacant, 55 M Street, 366–2137.
Human Resource Management.—Lisa Williams, Room W81–302, 366–4088.
Security.—Keith Szakal, Room W54–328, 366–9422.
Senior Procurement Executive.—Willie Smith, Room W83–306, 366–4212.

ASSISTANT SECRETARY FOR AVIATION AND INTERNATIONAL AFFAIRS

Assistant Secretary.—Joel Szabat, Room W88–314 (202) 366–8822.
Deputy Assistant Secretaries: David Short, Room W88–324; vacant, Room W88–326, 366–8822.

Director, Office of:
Aviation Analysis.—Todd Homan, Room W86–481, 366–5903.
International Aviation.—Brian Hedberg, Room W86–406, 366–2423.
International Transportation and Trade.—Julie Abraham, Room W88–306, 366–4398.

ASSISTANT SECRETARY FOR BUDGET AND PROGRAMS

Chief Financial Officer/Assistant Secretary.—John E. Kramer, Room W95–330 (202) 366–9191.
Deputy Assistant Secretary.—Lana Hurdle, Room W95–316, 366–9192.
Deputy Chief Financial Officer.—Jennifer Funk, Room W93–322, 366–9192.
Director, Office of:
Budget and Program Performance.—Laura Ziff, Room W93–308, 366–4594.
Financial Management.—Daniel King, Room W93–326, 366–5381.

ASSISTANT SECRETARY FOR GOVERNMENTAL AFFAIRS

Assistant Secretary.—Adam Sullivan, Room W85–326 (202) 366–4573.
Deputy Assistant Secretary for Congressional Affairs.— Anne Reinke.
Governmental Affairs Officers: Mira Lezell, Owen Morgan, Brett Scott.

OFFICE OF THE UNDER SECRETARY OF TRANSPORTATION FOR POLICY

Under Secretary of Transportation for Policy.—Vacant.
Assistant Secretary for Aviation and International Affairs.—Joel Szabat, 366–8822.
Deputy Assistant Secretary for Aviation and International Affairs.—David Short, 366–8822.
Assistant Secretary for Policy.—Vacant.
Deputy Assistant Secretaries for Policy: Finch Fulton, Room W82–30312, 366–8186; Loren Smith, Room W82–308, 366–2952; David Wonnenberg, Room W82–326, 366–3040.
Assistant Secretary for Research and Technology.—Vacant.
Deputy Assistant Secretary for Research and Technology.—Diana Furchtgott-Roth, Room E37–312, 366–6321.
Chief Infrastructure Funding Officer.—Dan DeBono, Room W12–405, 366–7265.

GENERAL COUNSEL

General Counsel.—Steven G. Bradbury, Room W92–300, 366–4702.
Deputy General Counsel: Christina G. Aizcorbe, Room W92–318, 366–4702; Judith S. Kaleta, Room W92–312, 366–4713.
Associate General Counsel: Gregory Cote, Room W92–320, 366–4702; Liam McKenna, Room W92–319, 366–4702.
Senior Counsel.—Jessica Conrad, Room W92–313, 366–4702.
Assistant General Counsel for—
Aviation Enforcement and Proceedings.—Blane A. Workie, Room W96–322, 366–9345.
General Law.—Terence W. Carlson, Room W94–306, 366–9152.
International Law.—Donald H. Horn, Room W98–324, 366–2972.
Legislation.—Thomas W. Herlihy, Room W96–326, 366–4687.
Litigation and Enforcement.—Paul M. Geier, Room W94–310, 366–4731.
Operations.—Ronald A. Jackson, Room W96–304, 366–4710.
Regulation.—Jonathan P. Moss, Room W94–302, 366–9314.

INSPECTOR GENERAL

Inspector General.—Calvin L. Scovel III, Room W70–300 (202) 366–1959.
Deputy Inspector General.—Mitch Behm, 366–6767.
Chief Counsel.—Omer Poirier, 366–8751.
Chief of Staff.—Amanda Seese, 366–5583.
Director of Government and Public Affairs.—Nathan Richmond, 366–8751.
Principal Assistant Inspector General for—
Auditing and Evaluation.—Joseph Comé, 366–1427.
Investigations.—Elise Chawaga, 366–1967.
Assistant Inspector General for—
Acquisition and Procurement Audits.—Mary Kay Langan Feirson, 366–5225.

Administration and Management.—Vacant, 366–1959.
Audit Operations and Special Reviews.—Charles Ward, 366–1249.
Aviation Audits.—Matthew Hampton, 366–0500.
Financial and Information Technology Audits.—Louis King, 366–1407.
Surface Transportation Audits.—Barry DeWeese, 366–5630.
Deputy Assistant Inspector General for—
Aviation Audits.—Anthony Zakel, 366–0500.
Investigations.—Susan DeYoung, 366–1967.
Surface Transportation Audits.—David Pouliott, 366–5630.

OFFICE OF PUBLIC AFFAIRS

Assistant to the Secretary and Director of Public Affairs.—Andrew Post (202) 366–0100.
Deputy Director.—Stephen Bradford, 366–7311.
Associate Director of Public Affairs.—Vacant, 366–9268.

FEDERAL AVIATION ADMINISTRATION

800 Independence Avenue, SW., Washington, DC 20591 (202) 267–3111

Administrator.—Stephen Dickson, 267–3111.
Executive Assistant to the Administrator.—Megan Bailey, 267–3111.
Deputy Administrator.—Daniel Elwell, 267–8111.
Executive Assistant to the Deputy Administrator.—Glendola Salisbury, 267–8111.
Chief of Staff.—Angela Stubblefield, 267–7416.
Senior Technical Advisor to the Deputy Administrator.—Vacant, 267–3173.
Senior Advisor to the Deputy Administrator.—Daniel Blum, 267–3370.
Executive Secretariat.—Vacant, 267–3518.
Director of Audit and Evaluation.—H. Clayton Foushee, 267–9000.
Assistant Administrator for Finance and Management.—Mark House, 267–8627.
Deputy Assistant Administrator for:
Acquisitions and Business Services.—Nathan Tash, 267–7222.
Financial Services/CFO.—Karen Gahart (acting), 267–4001.
Information Services/CIO.—Kristen Baldwin, 267–9692.
Regions and Property Operations.—Sean Torpey, 267–9011.
Director of:
Budget and Programs.—Carl Burrus, 267–8010.
Financial Analysis.—Tye White (acting), 267–5751.
Financial Management.—Allison Ritman, 267–5657.
Investment Planning and Analysis.—Josh Pepper (acting), 365–8824.
Labor Analysis.—Rich McCormick, 267–5943.
Regional Administrators:
Alaskan.—Kerry Long (907) 271–5645.
Central.—Joseph N. Miniace (816) 329–3050.
Eastern.—Jennifer Solomon (718) 553–3000.
Great Lakes.—Rebecca MacPherson (847) 294–7294.
New England.—Colleen D'Alessandro (acting) (781) 238–7020.
Northwest Mountain.—David Suomi (425) 227–2001.
Southern.—Michael O'Harra (404) 305–5000.
Southwest.—Rob Lowe (acting) (817) 222–5001.
Western-Pacific.—Raquel Girvin (424) 405–7000.
Director, Logistics Center.—Randall Burke (405) 954–4358.
Director, Mike Monroney Aeronautical Center.—Michelle Coppedge (405) 954–4521.
Assistant Administrator for Civil Rights.—John Benison, 267–3254.
Deputy Assistant Administrator for Civil Rights.—Courtney Wilkerson, 267–3254.
Assistant Administrator for Policy, International Affairs and Environment.—Bailey Edwards, 267–3927.
Deputy Assistant Administrator for Policy, International Affairs and Environment.—Jodi McCarthy (acting), 267–5178.
Executive Director of:
Aviation Policy and Plans.—David Chien (acting), 267–3274.
Environment and Energy.—Rebecca Cointin (acting), 267–3575.
International Affairs.—Christopher Rocheleau, 267–1000.
Director of:
Asia-Pacific.—Carey Fagan, 011–65–6475–9475.

Europe, Africa, and Middle East.—Tina Amereihn, 011–322–811–5159.
Western Hemisphere.—Christopher Barks, 011–507–317–5370.
Chief Counsel.—Arjun Garg, 267–3222.
Deputy Chief Counsel.—Patricia McNall, 267–3773.
Assistant Administrator for Government and Industry Affairs.—Andrew Giacini (acting), 267–3277.
Deputy Assistant Administrator for Government and Industry Affairs.—Kate Howard, 267–3277.
Assistant Administrator for Human Resource Management.—Annie Andrews, 267–3456.
Deputy Assistant Administrator for Human Resource Management.—Lisbeth Mack, 267–9341.
Director of:
Accountability Board.—Tammy Van Keuren, 267–3065.
Compensation, Benefits and Work-Life.—Elizabeth Dayan, 267–4028.
Human Resource Services.—Renee Coates, 267–2990.
Labor and Employee Relations.—Laura Glading, 267–6268.
Talent Development and Chief Learning Officer.—Thomas Langdon, 267–9041.
Assistant Administrator for Communications.—Brianna Manzelli, 267–3883.
Deputy Assistant Administrator for Public Affairs.—Laura Brown, 267–3455.
Deputy Assistant Administrator for Corporate Communications.—Jeannie Shiffer, 267–8859.
Assistant Administrator for Security and Hazardous Material Safety.—Claudio Manno, 267–7211.
Deputy Assistant Administrator for Security and Hazardous Material Safety.—Joshua Holtzman, 267–7211.
Director, Office of:
Business and Mission Services.—Don Faulkner, 267–8005.
Hazardous Materials Safety.—Janet McLaughlin, 267–9419.
Infrastructure Protection.—Patricia Pausch (847) 294–7411.
Investigations.—Michelle Root, 267–1456.
National Security Programs and Incident Response.—Brett Feddersen, 267–7980.
Personnel Security.—Gerald Moore (424) 405–7100.
Chief Operating Officer for Air Traffic Organization.—Teri Bristol, 267–1240.
Deputy Chief Operating Officer for Air Traffic Organization.—Timothy Arel, 267–7224.
Vice President for—
Air Traffic Services.—Jeffrey Vincent (acting), 267–0634.
Management Services.—Jeffrey Yarnell (acting), 267–3889.
Mission Support.—Angela McCullough, 267–8261.
Program Management.—Kristen Burnham, 267–8626.
Safety and Technical Training.—Glen Martin, 267–3341.
System Operations.—Mike Artist, 267–0753.
Technical Operations.—Jeffrey Planty, 267–3366.
Assistant Administrator for NextGen.—Pamela Whitley (acting), 267–7111.
Deputy Assistant Administrator for NextGen.—Gregory Burke (acting), 267–3520.
William J. Hughes Technical Center.—Shelley Yak (609) 485–6085.
Director of:
Chief Scientist.—Steve Bradford, 267–1218.
Interagency Planning.—Ted Mercer, 267–4544.
Management Services.—Suzanne Styc (acting), 267–0556.
NAS Systems Engineering and Integration.—Joseph Post (acting), 267–2766.
NextGen Performance and Outreach.—Mark Allen, 267–4544.
Portfolio Management and Technology Development.—Paul Fontaine, 267–9250.
Associate Administrator for Airports.—Kirk Shaffer, 267–9471.
Deputy Associate Administrator for Airports.—Winsome Lenfert, 267–9590.
Director of:
Airport Compliance and Management Analysis.—Kevin Willis, 267–8741.
Airport Planning and Programming.—Robin Hunt (acting), 267–4125.
Airport Policy.—Elliot Black, 267–8775.
Airport Safety and Standards.—John Dermody, 267–3053.
Associate Administrator for Commercial Space Transportation.—Wayne Montieth, 267–7793.
Deputy Associate Administrator for Commercial Space Transportation.—Kelvin Coleman, 267–7972.
Director of:
Operational Safety.—Lirio Liu, 267–7793.
Strategic Management.—James Hatt, 267–4156.
Associate Administrator for Aviation Safety.—Ali Bahrami, 267–3131.
Deputy Associate Administrator for Aviation Safety.—Michael O'Donnell (acting), 267–8776.
Director of:

Accident Investigation and Prevention.—Steven Gottleib, 267–9614.
Aircraft Certification Service.—Earl Lawrence, 267–8235.
Federal Air Surgeon.—Michael Berry, 267–3535.
Flight Standards Service.—Rick Domingo, 267–8237.
Office of Air Traffic Oversight.—Vacant, 267–5202.
Quality, Integration and Executive Service.—Margaret McArthur (acting), 267–3685.
Rulemaking.—Brandon Roberts (acting), 267–9688.

FEDERAL HIGHWAY ADMINISTRATION

Washington Headquarters, 1200 New Jersey Avenue, SE., Washington, DC 20590–9898
Turner-Fairbank Highway Research Center (TFHRC)
6300 Georgetown Pike, McLean, VA 22201

Administrator.—Nicole R. Nason (202) 366–2240.
Deputy Administrator.—Mala K. Parker, 366–0585.
Associate Administrator/Director of TFHRC.—Kelly Regal, 493–3999.
Associate Administrator for Administration.—Arlan Finfrock, Jr., 366–0604.
Executive Director.—Thomas D. Everett, 366–2242.
Chief Counsel.—Adrienne E. Camire, 366–0617.
Deputy Chief Counsel.—Nicolle M. Fleury, 366–1379.
Chief Financial Officer.—Brian R. Bezio, 366–0534.
Associate Administrator for—
Civil Rights.—Irene Rico, 366–8154.
Federal Lands.—Timothy Hess, 366–9472.
Infrastructure.—Hari Kalla, 366–0371.
Operations.—Martin C. Knopp, 366–8753.
Planning, Environment, and Realty.—Gloria M. Shepherd, 366–0581.
Policy & Governmental Affairs.—Alex Etchen, 366–9233.
Public Affairs.—Mike Reynard, 366–9910.
Safety.—Cheryl J. Walker, 366–6378.

FIELD SERVICES

Organizationally report to Executive Director (HOA–3), Washington, DC

Director of Technical Services.—Amy Lucero, 12300 West Dakota Avenue, Suite 340, Lakewood, CO 80228 (720) 963–3246.
Director of:
Field Services–North.—Robert E. Arnold, Leo W. O'Brien Federal Building, Suite 719, Albany, NY 12207 (518) 431–8873.
Field Services–South.—Derrell Turner, 61 Forsyth Street, SW., Suite 16T100B, Atlanta, GA 30303–3104 (404) 562–3571.
Field Services–West.—Peter W. Osborn, 12300 West Dakota Avenue, Suite 310, Lakewood, CO 80228 (720) 963–3730.
Field Services–Mid America.—John Rohlf, 4749 Lincoln Mall Drive, Suite 600, Matteson, IL 60443 (708) 283–3507.

FEDERAL MOTOR CARRIER SAFETY ADMINISTRATION

Administrator.—Jim Mullen (acting), Room W60–308 (202) 366–1927.
Deputy Administrator.—Jim Mullen, 366–1927.
Chief Safety Officer and Assistant Administrator.—John Van Steenburg, 366–1927.
Associate Administrator for Administration.—Anne L. Collins, 493–0013.
Director, Office of:
External Affairs.—Kyle Bonini, 366–9554.

FIELD OFFICES

Eastern Service Center (CT, DC, DE, MA, MD, ME, NH, NJ, NY, PA, PR, RI, VA, VT, WV).—Fallon Federal Building, 31 Hopkins Plaza, Suite 800, Baltimore, MD 21201 (443) 703–2240.
Midwestern Service Center (IA, IL, IN, KS, MI, MN, MO, NE, OH, WI).—4749 Lincoln Mall Drive, Suite 300A, Matteson, IL 60443 (708) 283–3577.

Southern Service Center (AL, AR, FL, GA, KY, LA, MS, NC, OK, SC, TN).—1800 Century Boulevard, NE., Suite 1700, Atlanta, GA 30345 (404) 327–7400.

Western Service Center (AK, American Samoa, AZ, CA, CO, Guam, HI, ID, MT, ND, NM, Northern Mariana Islands, NV, OR, SD, TX, UT, WA, WY).—Golden Hills Office Centre, 12600 West Colfax Avenue, Suite B–300, Lakewood, CO 80215 (303) 407–2350.

FEDERAL RAILROAD ADMINISTRATION

1200 New Jersey Avenue, SE., Washington, DC 20590

https://fra.dot.gov

Administrator.—Ronald Batory, Room W30–308 (202) 493–6014.
Deputy Administrator.—Quintin Kendall, Room W30–311, 493–0774.
Executive Director.—Vacant, Room W30–310, 493–6194.
Associate Administrator for—
Administration.—Tami Riggs, Room W34–332, 493–6301.
Chief Financial Officer.—Rebecca Pennington, Room W36–306, 440–2870.
Railroad Policy and Development.—Paul Nissenbaum, Room W38–328, 493–6312.
Safety.—Karl Alexy, Room W35–306, 493–6282.
Chief Counsel.—Vacant, Room W31–320, 493–6022.
Deputy Chief Counsel.—Brett Jortland (acting), Room W31–318, 493–6035.
Communications and Legislative Affairs.—George Riccardo, Room W32–204, 366–4285.
Director of:
Budget.—Scott Keene, Room W36–306, 493–0786.
Civil Rights.—Calvin Gibson, Room W33–316, 493–6010.
Financial Management.—Tiwalade Bello, Room W36–304, 493–6163.
Public Engagement.—Timothy Barkley, Room W33–320, 493–1305.

REGIONAL OFFICES (RAILROAD SAFETY)

Region 1 (Northeastern).—Connecticut, Maine, Massachusetts, New Hampshire, New Jersey, New York, Rhode Island, Vermont.
Regional Administrator.—Les Fiorenzo, Room 1077, 55 Broadway, Cambridge, MA 02142 (617) 494–3484.

Region 2 (Eastern).—Delaware, District of Columbia, Maryland, Ohio, Pennsylvania, Virginia, West Virginia.
Regional Administrator.—Dave Kannenberg, 1510 Chester Pike, Baldwin Tower, Suite 660, Crum Lynne, PA 19022 (610) 521–8200.

Region 3 (Southern).—Alabama, Florida, Georgia, Kentucky, Mississippi, North Carolina, South Carolina, Tennessee.
Regional Administrator.—Carmen Patriarca, 61 Forsyth Street, NW., Suite 16T20, Atlanta, GA 30303 (404) 562–3809.

Region 4 (Central).—Illinois, Indiana, Michigan, Minnesota, Wisconsin.
Regional Administrator.—Mike Turnbull, 200 West Adams Street, Chicago, IL 60606 (312) 353–6203.

Region 5 (Southwestern).—Arkansas, Louisiana, New Mexico, Oklahoma, Texas.
Regional Administrator.—Vence Haggard, 4100 International Plaza, Suite 450, Ft. Worth, TX 96109 (817) 862–2220.

Region 6 (Midwestern).—Colorado, Iowa, Kansas, Missouri, Nebraska.
Regional Administrator.—Steven Fender, DOT Building, 901 Locust Street, Suite 464, Kansas City, MO 64106 (816) 329–3840.

Region 7 (Western).—Arizona, California, Nevada, Utah.
Regional Administrator.—James Jordan, 801 I Street, Suite 466, Sacramento, CA 95814 (916) 498–6547.

Region 8 (Northwestern).—Alaska, Idaho, Montana, North Dakota, Oregon, South Dakota, Washington, Wyoming.
Regional Administrator.—Mark Daniels, 500 Broadway, Murdock Executive Plaza, Suite 240, Vancouver, WA 98660 (360) 696–7536.

FEDERAL TRANSIT ADMINISTRATION

Administrator.—Vacant.
Deputy Administrator.—K. Jane Williams (202) 366–4040.
Chief Counsel.—John Brennan, 366–4011.

Director, Office of Civil Rights.—Selene Dalton-Kumins, 366–5401.
Planning and Environment.—Felicia James, 366–2851.
Associate Administrator for—
Administration.—Reggie Allen, 366–0189.
Budget and Policy.—Robert Tuccillo, 366–4050.
Communications and Congressional Affairs.—Bailey Wood, 366–0842.
Program Management.—Bruce Robinson, 366–4209.
Research, Demonstration, and Innovation.—Vincent Valdes, 366–3052.
Safety and Oversight.—Henrika Buchanan, 366–5080.

MARITIME ADMINISTRATION

Administrator and Chair, Maritime Subsidy Board.—RADM Mark H. Buzby, USN (Ret.), Room W22–318 (202) 366–1719.
Deputy Administrator.—Richard A. Balzano, Room W22–314, 366–5823.
Secretary, Maritime Administration and Maritime Subsidy Board.—Vacant, 366–5746.
Chief Counsel and Member, Maritime Subsidy Board.—Douglas Burnett, Room W24–310, 366–0709.
Director, Office of Congressional and Public Affairs.—Randon Lane, Room E25–336.
Public Affairs Officer.—Kim Strong, Room W22–324, 366–5067.
Executive Director.—Vacant, Room W28–316, 366–3907.
Director of:
International Activities.—Lonnie T. Kishiyama, Room W28–312, 366–5493.
Policy and Plans.—Douglas McDonald, Room W26–326, 366–2145.
Associate Administrator for Budget and Programs/Chief Financial Officer.—Lydia Moschkin, Room W21–334, 366–3071.
Director, Office of:
Accounting.—Inga Maik, Room W25–333, 366–1947.
Budget.—Alex J. Caine, Room W26–310, 493–0362.
National Security Program/Funds Control.—Inga Maik, Room W25–333, 366–1947.
Program Performance.—Mary Grice, Room W26–308, 366–4264.
Associate Administrator for Administration.—Delia P. Davis, Room W26–312, 366–2181.
Director, Office of:
Acquisition.—Bruce Markman, Room W26–324, 366–1942.
Deputy Director.—Gregory Harris, Room W26–319.
Information Technology.—Robert Ellington, Room W26–320, 366–2531.
Management and Information Services.—Steve Snipes, Room W26–302, 366–2811.
Personnel.—Sandra Ambrose, Room W26–319, 366–0619.
Associate Administrator for Environment and Compliance.—Michael Carter (acting), Room W25–302, 366–9431.
Director, Office of:
Environment.—Daniel Yuska, Room W28–228, 366–0714.
Safety.—Kevin Kohlman, Room W25–302, 366–5126.
Security.—Cameron Naron, Room W28–340, 366–1883.
Associate Administrator for Intermodal System Development.—Vacant, Room W21–320, 366–7057.
Deputy.—William Paape, Room W21–307, 366–5005.
Director, Office of:
Deepwater Ports and Offshore Activities.—Yvette Fields, Room W21–309, 366–0926.
Gateway Offices.—William Paape, Room W21–307, 366–5005.
Infrastructure Development and Congestion Mitigation.—Robert Bouchard, Room W21–308, 366–5076.
Marine Highways and Passenger Services.—Timothy Pickering, Room W21–312, 366–0704.
Associate Administrator for Sealift.—Kevin M. Tokarski, Room W25–332, 366–5400.
Deputy Associate Administrator for Commercial Sealift.—Anthony Fisher, Room W23–316, 366–1875.
Deputy Associate Administrator for Federal Sealift/Director of Ship Operations.—Douglas Harrington, Room W25–336, 366–2628.
Director, Office of Emergency Response.—Russell Krause, Room W23–304, 366–5909.
Deputy Ship Operations.—Melinda Simmons-Healy, Room W25–340, 366–9750.
Division of Maintenance and Repair.—Joseph McElhinney, Room W23–304, 366–1742.
Sealift Operations and Emergency Response.—Russell Krause, Room W23–302, 366–1031.
Division of Logistics.—Channing Jones, Room W23–310, 366–4447.
Office of Ship Disposal.—Shawn Ireland, Room W25–334, 366–0688.
Cargo Preference and Commercial Sealift.—Tony Padilla, Room W23–316, 366–7045.

Sealift Support.—William McDonald, Room W25–310, 366–0688.
Deputy Associate Administrator for Marine Education and Training.—Shasi Kumar, Room W21–326, 366–2105.
Emory S. Land Chair of Maritime Affairs.—Christopher McMahon (Rhode Island).
Program Excellence and Quality Assurance Advisor.—Nuns Jain (757) 322–5801.
Office of Maritime Labor and Training.—Christopher Wahler, Room W23–314, 366–5469.
Associate Administrator for Business and Finance Development.—David Heller, Room W23–324, 366–1850.
Office of Marine Insurance.—Michael Yarrington, Room W23–312, 366–1915.
Office of Financial Approvals.—Daniel Ladd, Room W23–321, 366–1859.
Director, Office of Marine Finance.—Dave Gilmore, Room W23–321, 366–2118.
Maritime Workforce Development.—Anne Wehde, Room W23–314, 366–5469.
Shipyards and Marine Engineering.—David Heller, Room W23–324, 366–1850.

FIELD ACTIVITIES

Director for:
Great Lakes and Upper Inland Waterways Region.—Floyd Miras, Suite 185, 2860 South River Road, Des Plaines, IL 60018 (847) 905–0122.
North Atlantic Region.—Jeffrey Flumignan, 1 Bowling Green, Room 418, New York, NY 10004 (212) 668–2064.
Northern California/Hawaii Region.—John Hummer, Suite 2200, 201 Mission Street, San Francisco, CA 94105 (415) 744–3125.
South Atlantic Region.—Frances Bohnsack, Building 4D, Room 211, 7737 Hampton Boulevard, Norfolk, VA 23505 (757) 441–6393.

U.S. MERCHANT MARINE ACADEMY

Superintendent.—RADM Jack Bono, Kings Point, NY 11024 (516) 773–5000.
Deputy Superintendent for Academic Affairs (Academic Dean).—RDML Susan Dunlap, Kings Point, NY 11024 (516) 726–5814.

NATIONAL HIGHWAY TRAFFIC SAFETY ADMINISTRATION

Administrator.—Vacant, Room W42–302 (202) 366–1836.
Executive Assistant to the Administrator.—Mackenzie Praytor, 366–1836.
Coordinator, External Meetings and Events.—Belinda Rawls, 366–5964.
Deputy Administrator.—James C. Owens, 366–1836.
Director, Communications.—Sean Rushton, 366–1836.
Director, Governmental Affairs, Policy and Strategic Planning.—Steven Bayless, 366–1836.
Deputy Director, Governmental Affairs, Policy and Strategic Planning.—Sara Peters, 366–8849.
Chief Counsel.—Jonathan Morrison, 366–9511.
Deputy Chief Counsel.—John Donaldson, 366–9511.
Chief Safety Scientist.—Joseph Kolly, 366–5664.
Executive Director.—Jack Danielson, 366–1836.
Associate Administrator for—
Administrative Management.—Anne Collins, 493–0013.
Communications and Consumer Information.—Julie Vallese, 366–2712.
Enforcement.—Jeffrey Giuseppe, 366–5756.
National Center for Statistics and Analysis.—Chou-Lin Chen, 366–1048.
Regional Operations and Program Delivery.—Jamie Pfister, 366–5424.
Research and Program Development.—Nanda Srinivasan, 366–0179.
Rulemaking.—Ryan Posten, 366–1810.
Vehicle Safety Research Program.—Cem Hatipoglu, 366–0812.
Chief Financial Officer.—Cynthia Parker, 366–2255.
Chief Technology Officer.—Vacant, 366–1199.
Director, Office of Civil Rights.—Regina Morgan, 366–8046.
Director, Office of International Policy, Fuel Economy, and Consumer Standards.—Jane Doherty, 366–7272.
Supervisor, Executive Correspondence.—Julie Korkor, 366–5470.

REGIONAL OFFICES

Region 1.—Maine, Massachusetts, New Hampshire, Rhode Island, Vermont.
Regional Administrator.—Art Kinsman, Volpe National Transportation Center, 55 Broadway, Kendall Square, Code RTV–8E, Cambridge, MA 02142 (617) 494–3427.

Region 2.—Connecticut, New Jersey, New York, Pennsylvania, Puerto Rico, Virgin Islands.
Regional Administrator.—Richard Simon, 245 Main Street, Suite 210, White Plains, NY 10601 (914) 682–3445.

Region 3.—Delaware, District of Columbia, Kentucky, Maryland, North Carolina, Virginia, West Virginia.
Regional Administrator.—Stephanie Hancock, George H. Fallon Federal Building, 31 Hopkins Plaza, Room 902, Baltimore, MD 21201 (410) 962–0063.

Region 4.—Alabama, Florida, Georgia, South Carolina, Tennessee.
Regional Administrator.—Carmen Hayes, Atlanta Federal Center, 61 Forsyth Street, SW., Suite 17T30, Atlanta, GA 30303–3106 (404) 562–3739.

Region 5.—Illinois, Indiana, Michigan, Minnesota, Ohio, Wisconsin.
Regional Administrator.—Jonlee Anderle, 4749 Lincoln Mall Drive, Suite 3008, Matteson, IL 60443 (202) 266–7297.

Region 6.—Indian Nations, Louisiana, Mississippi, New Mexico, Oklahoma, Texas.
Regional Administrator.—Maggi Gunnels, 819 Taylor Street, Room 8A38, Fort Worth, TX 76102–6177 (817) 978–4032.

Region 7.—Arkansas, Iowa, Kansas, Missouri, Nebraska.
Regional Administrator.—Susan DeCourcy, 901 Locust Street, Room 466, Kansas City, MO 64106 (816) 329–3900.

Region 8.—Colorado, North Dakota, Nevada, South Dakota, Utah, Wyoming.
Regional Administrator.—Gina Espinosa-Salcedo, 12300 West Dakota Avenue, Suite 140, Lakewood, CO 80228–2583 (720) 963–3100.

Region 9.—American Samoa, Arizona, California, Guam, Mariana Islands, Hawaii.
Regional Administrator.—Chris Murphy, John E. Moss Federal Building, 650 Capitol Mall, Suite 5–400, Sacramento, CA 95814 (916) 498–5058.

Region 10.—Alaska, Idaho, Montana, Oregon, Washington.
Regional Administrator.—Greg T. Fredericksen, Federal Building, 915 Second Avenue, Suite 3140, Seattle, WA 98174 (206) 220–7641.

Vehicle Research and Testing Center, 10820 State Route 347, East Liberty, OH 43319.
Director.—Timothy Johnson (937) 666–4511.

PIPELINE AND HAZARDOUS MATERIALS SAFETY ADMINISTRATION

Administrator.—Howard ''Skip'' Elliott, Room E27–300 (202) 366–4433.
Deputy Administrator.—Drue Pearce, Room E27–300, 366–4433.
Executive Director.—Howard ''Mac'' McMillan, Room E27–325, 366–4433.
Chief Counsel.—Paul Roberti, Room E26–320, 366–4400.
Director, Office of Civil Rights.—Rosanne Goodwill, Room E27–334, 366–9638.
Chief Financial Officer.—Tami Perriello, Room E22–312, 366–4433.
Associate Administrator for—
Governmental, International, and Public Affairs.—Bobby Fraser, Director, Room E27–300, 366–4831.
Hazardous Materials Safety.—William Schoonover, Room E21–316, 366–4488.
Management and Administration.—Audrey Farley, Room E32–330, 366–4831.
Pipeline Safety.—Alan Mayberry, Room E22–321, 366–4595.
Planning and Analytics.—Vacant, Room E25–336, 366–4433.

HAZARDOUS MATERIALS SAFETY OFFICES

Director of:
Eastern Region.—Vincent Mercandante, 820 Bear Tavern Road, Suite 306, West Trenton, NJ 08628 (609) 989–2256.
Central Region.—Tyler Patterson, Suite 478, 2350 East Devon Avenue, Des Plaines, IL 60018 (847) 294–8580.
Western Region.—Marc Nichols, 3401 Centre Lake Drive, Suite 550–B, Ontario, CA 91761 (909) 937–3279.
Southern Region.—John Heneghan, 233 Peachtree Street, NE., Suite 602, Atlanta, GA 30303 (404) 832–1140.

Southwest Region.—Matt Ripley, 8701 South Gessner Road, Suite 1110, Houston, TX 77004 (713) 272–2820.

PIPELINE SAFETY OFFICES

Director of:

Eastern Region.—Robert Burroughs, 820 Bear Tavern Road, Suite 103, West Trenton, NJ 08628 (609) 989–2171.

Central Region.—Alan Beshore, 901 Locust Street, Room 462, Kansas City, MO 64106 (816) 329–3800.

Western Region.—Dustin Hubbard, 12300 West Dakota Avenue, Suite 110, Lakewood, CO 80228 (720) 963–3160.

Southwest Region.—Mary McDaniels, 8701 South Gessner, Suite 1110, Houston, TX 77074 (713) 272–2859.

Southern Region.—James Urisko, 233 Peachtree Street, NE., Suite 600, Atlanta, GA 30303 (404) 832–1140.

OFFICE OF THE ASSISTANT SECRETARY FOR RESEARCH AND TECHNOLOGY (OST–R)

https://transportation.gov/new-and-emerging-technologies

Assistant Secretary.—Vacant.

Deputy Assistant Secretary.—Diana Furchtgott-Roth, Room E37–312 (202) 366–6321.

Public Affairs Contact, Bureau of Transportation Statistics.—David Smallen, Room E36–328, 366–5568; OST–R.—Nancy Wilochka, Room E36–332, 366–5128.

Director for—

Bureau of Transportation Statistics.—Patricia Hu, Room E34–314, 366–6268.

Intelligent Transportation Systems.—Kenneth M. Leonard, Room E86–322, 366–9536.

Positioning, Navigation and Timing & Spectrum Management.—Karen Van Dyke, Room E33–312, 366–3180.

Research, Development, and Technology (RD&T).—Vacant.

Technology Policy and Outreach.—Timothy A. Klein, Room E36–334, 366–0075.

Transportation Safety Institute.—Dr. Troy Jackson (acting), 6500 South MacArthur Boulevard, Oklahoma City, OK 73169 (405) 954–7312.

Volpe National Transportation Systems Center.—Anne Aylward, Room 1240, 55 Broadway, Kendall Square, Cambridge, MA 02142 (617) 494–2191.

SAINT LAWRENCE SEAWAY DEVELOPMENT CORPORATION–U.S. DOT

https://greatlakes-seaway.com/en

Administrator.—Vacant (202) 366–0091, fax 366–7147.

Deputy Administrator.—Craig H. Middlebrook, 366–0105.

Chief of Staff.—Wayne A. Williams, 366–0107.

Director, Office of:

Budget and Economic Development.—Kevin P. O'Malley, 366–8982.

Congressional and Public Relations.—Nancy T. Alcalde, 366–6114.

SEAWAY OPERATIONS

180 Andrews Street, Massena, NY 13662–0520

phone (315) 764–3200, fax 764–3235

Associate Administrator.—Thomas A. Lavigne.

Deputy Associate Administrator.—Vacant.

Chief Counsel.—Carrie Mann Lavigne.

Director, Office of:

Engineering and Maintenance.—Jeffrey W. Scharf.

Financial Management and Administration and CFO.—Nancy C. Scott.

Lock Operations and Marine Services.—Christopher L. Guimond.

DEPARTMENT OF ENERGY

James Forrestal Building

1000 Independence Avenue, SW., Washington, DC 20585

phone (202) 586–5000, https://energy.gov

DAN BROUILLETTE, Secretary of Energy; born on August 18, 1962, in Paincourtville, LA; education: B.A., University of Maryland. Secretary Brouillette has three decades of experience in both the public and private sector. Most recently he was the Deputy Secretary of Energy.

He also served as the Senior Vice President and head of public policy for USAA, the Nation's leading provider of financial services to the military community. Before joining USAA, Secretary Brouillette was a Vice President of Ford Motor Company, where he led the automaker's domestic policy teams and served on its North American Operating Committee.

At Ford and USAA, he was part of senior management teams that helped bring to market innovative technologies like auto collision avoidance and remote deposit capture, a technology invented by USAA that allows the use of smart devices to deposit funds into our banking accounts.

Before his transition into the private sector, Secretary Brouillette held numerous positions in government. He was Chief of Staff to the U.S. House of Representatives Committee on Energy and Commerce, which has broad jurisdictional and oversight authority over five Cabinet-level Federal agencies. He also served as Assistant Secretary of Energy for Congressional and Intergovernmental Affairs from 2001 to 2003. In addition, he is a former state energy regulator, having served as a member of the Louisiana State Mineral and Energy Board from 2013 to 2016.

Secretary Brouillette and his wife, Adrienne, are both U.S. Army veterans and have been married for 28 years. They hail from San Antonio, TX, and have nine children.

OFFICE OF THE SECRETARY

Secretary of Energy.—Dan Brouillette (202) 586–5000.
Deputy Secretary.—Vacant.
Chief of Staff.—James Colgary, 586–5500.
Inspector General.—Teri Donaldson, 586–0034.
Assistant Secretary for Congressional and Intergovernmental Affairs.—Melissa Burnison, 586–5450.
Assistant Secretary for International Affairs.—Theodore Garrish, 586–1145.
General Counsel.—William Cooper, 586–5281.
Chief Financial Officer.—Randall Hendrickson (acting), 586–4171.
Chief Human Capital Officer.—Steven Erhart, 586–2666.
Chief Information Officer.—Rocky Campione, 586–0166.
Director, Office of:
Economic Impact and Diversity.—James Campos, 586–8383.
Enterprise Assessments.—Nathan Martin, 586–4360.
Hearings and Appeals.—Poli Marmolejos, 287–1566.
Intelligence and Counterintelligence.—Steve Black, 586–1352.
Management.—Ingrid Kolb, 586–2550.
Public Affairs.—Dirk Vande Beek, 586–1760.
Small and Disadvantaged Business Utilization.—Charles Smith, 586–9259.
Administrator for Energy Information Administration.—Linda Capuano, 586–4361.
Director, Advanced Research Projects Agency-Energy.—Lane Genatowski, 586–8321.

UNDER SECRETARY OF ENERGY

Under Secretary of Energy.—Mark Menezes.

Assistant Secretary for—

Cybersecurity, Energy Security, and Emergency Response.—Vacant (202) 287–1849.

Electricity Delivery and Energy Reliability.—Bruce Walker, 586–1411.

Energy Efficiency and Renewable Energy.—Daniel Simmons, 586–9220.

Fossil Energy.—Steven Winberg, 586–6660.

Nuclear Energy.—Rita Baranwal, 586–6630.

Director, Office of:

Indian Energy Policy and Programs.—Kevin Frost, 287–6566.

Policy.—Cathleen Tripodi, 586–5050.

Project Management Oversight and Assessments.—Paul Bosco, 586–3524.

Associate Under Secretary for Environment, Health, Safety and Security.—Matthew Moury, 586–1285.

Executive Director of the Loan Programs Office.—Dong Kim, 586–7707.

UNDER SECRETARY FOR SCIENCE

Under Secretary for Science.—Paul M. Dabbar (202) 586–0505.

Assistant Secretary for Environmental Management.—Vacant.

Director, Office of:

Artificial Intelligence and Technology.—Dimitri Kusnezov (acting), 586–1800.

Legacy Management.—Carmelo Melendez, 586–4882.

Science.—Christopher Fall, 287–5102.

Technology Transitions.—Connor Prochaska, 586–2000.

NATIONAL NUCLEAR SECURITY ADMINISTRATION

Administrator for National Nuclear Security Administration/Under Secretary for Nuclear Security.—Lisa E. Gordon-Hagerty (202) 586–5555.

Principal Deputy Administrator.—William Bookless, 586–5555.

Deputy Administrator for—

Defense Nuclear Nonproliferation.—Dr. Brent Park, 586–0645.

Defense Programs.—Charles Verdon, 586–1877.

Naval Reactors.—ADM James Caldwell, USN, 781–6174.

Deputy Under Secretary for Counterterrorism.—Jay A. Tilden, 586–1734.

Associate Administrator for—

Acquisition and Project Management.—Robert Raines, 586–5627.

Defense Nuclear Security.—Jeffrey Johnson, 586–8900.

Emergency Operations.—Charles Hopkins, 586–9892.

External Affairs.—Nora Khalil, 586–8343.

Information Management.—Wayne Jones, 586–9728.

Management and Budget.—Frank Lowery, 586–0101.

Office of the General Counsel.—Bruce Diamond, 586–6946.

Safety, Infrastructure, and Operations.—James J. McConnell, 586–4379.

MAJOR FIELD ORGANIZATIONS

OPERATIONS OFFICES

Managers:

Golden Field Office (EERE).—Derek Passarelli (720) 356–1742.

Richland (EM).—Brian Vance (509) 302–3228.

Office of River Protection (ORP).—Brian Vance (509) 302–3228.

Savannah River (EM).—Michael Budney (803) 952–7243.

Carlsbad Field Office (EM).—Kirk Lachman (575) 234–7303.

Los Alamos (EM).—Douglas Hintze (505) 257–7920.

Oak Ridge Office (EM).—John Mullis (865) 241–3706.

Portsmouth and Paducah Project Office (EM).—Robert Edwards (859) 219–4002.

Idaho (NE).—Robert Boston (208) 526–7300.

Ames Office (SC).—Samuel Bigger (515) 294–8037.

Argonne Office (SC).—Joanna Livengood (630) 252–2366.

Fermi (SC).—Michael Weis (630) 840–3281.

Bay Area (SC).—Paul Golan (650) 926–3208.

Princeton (SC).—Peter Johnson (609) 243–3706.

Pacific Northwest (SC).—Roger Snyder (509) 372–4005.
Thomas Jefferson (SC).—Joseph Arango (757) 269–5094.
Brookhaven (SC).—Robert Gordon (631) 344–3346.
Oak Ridge National Laboratory Site Office (SC).—Johnny Moore (865) 576–3536.
Naval Reactors Laboratory (NNSA).—Matthew Brott (412) 476–7251.
Sandia (NNSA).—Jeffrey Harrell (505) 845–6036.
Kansas City (NNSA).—Mark Holecek (816) 488–3920.
Los Alamos (NNSA).—Gabriel Pugh (acting) (505) 665–7124.
Nevada (NNSA).—Steven Lawrence (702) 295–3211.
Livermore (NNSA).—Peter Rodrik (925) 423–4339.
Savannah River (NNSA).—Nicole Nelson-Jean (803) 208–3689.

INTEGRATED SUPPORT / BUSINESS CENTERS

Managers:
EM Consolidated Business Center.—John Zimmerman (513) 246–1050.
NNSA Production Office.—Geoffrey Beausoleil (505) 845–4392.
SC Consolidated Service Center.—Kenneth Tarcza (865) 576–4444.

POWER MARKETING ADMINISTRATIONS

Administrator, Power Marketing Administration:
Bonneville.—Elliott Mainzer (503) 230–4175.
Southeastern Area.—Kenneth Legg (706) 213–3800.
Southwestern Area.—Michael Wech (417) 891–2626.
Western Area.—Mark Gabriel (720) 962–7705.

NATIONAL ENERGY TECHNOLOGY LABORATORY

Director, National Energy Technology Laboratory.—Brian Anderson (304) 285–2043.

STRATEGIC PETROLEUM RESERVE PROJECT OFFICE

Project Manager.—Paul Oosterling (504) 734–4339.

FEDERAL ENERGY REGULATORY COMMISSION

888 First Street, NE., Washington, DC 20426

Chair.—Neil Chatterjee (202) 502–8000.
Commissioners: James Danly, 502–6477; Richard Glick, 502–6530; Bernard McNamee, 502–8510.
Chief Administrative Law Judge.—Carmen A. Cintron, 502–8500.
Executive Director.—Anton C. Porter, 502–8300.
General Counsel.—David L. Morenoff, 502–6000.
Secretary, Office of the Secretary.—Kimberly Bose, 502–8400.
Director, Office of:
Administrative Litigation.—John Kroeger, 502–6100.
Electric Reliability.—Andrew Dodge, 502–8600.
Energy Infrastructure Security.—Joseph McClelland, 502–8867.
Energy Market Regulation.—Anna V. Cochrane, 502–6700.
Energy Policy and Innovation.—Jignasa Gadani, 502–8850.
Energy Projects.—Terry Turpin, 502–8700.
Enforcement.—Larry R. Parkinson, 502–8100.
External Affairs.—Leonard Tao, 502–8004.

DEPARTMENT OF EDUCATION

400 Maryland Avenue, SW., Washington, DC 20202

phone (202) 401–3000, fax 260–7867, https://ed.gov

BETSY DEVOS, Secretary of Education, born in Holland, MI, January 8, 1958; education: B.A., business economics, Calvin College, Grand Rapids, MI, 1979; professional: chairwoman, The Windquest Group; organizations: the Kennedy Center for the Performing Arts; Kids Hope USA; ArtPrize; Mars Hill Bible Church; Kendall College of Art and Design; married: Dick DeVos; four children; six grandchildren; nominated by President Donald Trump to become the 11th Secretary of Education on November 23, 2016; confirmed by the U.S. Senate on February 7, 2017.

OFFICE OF THE SECRETARY

Room 7W301, phone (202) 401–3000, fax 260–7867

Secretary of Education.—Betsy DeVos.
Deputy Secretary.—Mitchell Zais, Ph.D.
Chief of Staff.—Nathan Bailey.
Deputy Chief of Staff, Operations.—Dougie Simmons.
Deputy Chief of Staff, Policy.—Vacant.

OFFICE OF THE UNDER SECRETARY

Room 7E307, phone (202) 401–0429

Under Secretary.—Diane Jones (delegated the duties of the Under Secretary).
Deputy Under Secretaries: Vacant.
Chief of Staff.—Michael Brickman.

OFFICE OF FINANCE AND OPERATIONS

400 Maryland Avenue, SW., Washington, DC 20202, phone (202) 401–5848

Assistant Secretary and Chief Financial Officer.—Denise L. Carter (acting), Room 200–02, 401–5848.
Principal Deputy Assistant Secretary.—Denise L. Carter, Room 200–02, 401–0330.
Chief of Staff.—Richard Smith, Room 200–00, 260–8987.
Executive Officer.—Ayesha Edwards-Kemp, Room 206–32, 453–6055.
Director, Alternative Dispute Resolution Center.—Anthony Cummings, Room PCP–10089, 245–7185.
Service Director of Equal Employment Opportunity Services.—Michael Chew, Room 1E–110–D, 401–0691, fax 205–5760.
Director, Office of Hearings and Appeals.—Anthony Cummings, Room PCP–10089, 245–7185, fax 245–6931.
Deputy Assistant Secretary, Office of:
Acquisition Management/DCAO/SPE.—Jim Stader (acting), Room PCP–6056, 245–6036.
Budget Service.—Larry Kean, Room 200–72, 401–0330.
Business Support Services.—Penny Mefford, Room PCP–9151, 245–7056.
Financial Management.—Gary Wood, Room PCP–6089, 245–8118.
Grants Administration.—Jim Stader, Room PCP–6056, 245–6036.
Human Resources.—Antonia Harris, Room 210–04, 401–5931, fax 401–0520.
Security, Facilities and Logistics Services.—Jim Hairfield, Room 218–02, 245–6219.
Director, Office of Small and Disadvantaged Business Utilization.—Phillip Juengst, Room PCP–6125, 245–8030.

OFFICE FOR CIVIL RIGHTS

400 Maryland Avenue, SW., Room 4E340, Washington, DC 20202–1100

phone (202) 423–5900, fax 423–6010

Assistant Secretary for Civil Rights.—Kenneth Marcus, Room 4E313, 453–7723.
Principal Deputy Assistant Secretary.—Kimberly Richey, Room 4E314, 453–7800.
Confidential Assistant to the Assistant Secretary for Civil Rights.—Chelsea Henderson, Room 4E319, 453–5799.
Confidential Assistant to the Principal Deputy Assistant Secretary.—Lauren Roppolo, Room 4E326, 453–5617.
Senior Counsel to the Assistant Secretary.—Christian Corrigan, Room 4E309, 453–7035.
Counsel to the Assistant Secretary.—Samantha Scheuler, Room 4E305, 453–5568.
Deputy Assistant Secretary for Policy and Development.—David Tryon, Room 4E348, 453–7024.
Senior Counsel to the Deputy Assistant Secretary for Policy and Development.—Meir Katz, Room 4E342, 453–5748.
Deputy Assistant Secretary for Management and Operations.—Donald Salo, Room 4E311, 453–5607.
Special Assistant to the Deputy Assistant Secretary for Management and Operations.—Anna Kasior, Room 4E317, 453–6613.
Executive Officer.—Will Young, Room 4E105, 453–6075.
Deputy Assistant Secretary for Enforcement.—Randolph Wills, Room 4E329, 453–5956.
Enforcement Directors: Carol Ashley, Room 4E312, 453–6790; Lisa Chang, Room 4E330, 453–6849; Mia Karvonides, Room 4E310, 453–7070.
Executive Assistant to the Deputy Assistant Secretary for Enforcement.—Marvida Scarbrough, Room 4E328, 453–5749.
Director, Program Legal Group.—Alejandro Reyes, Room 4E308, 453–6639.
Senior Counsel/Litigation.—Joshua Shopf, Room 4E344, 453–7078.
Senior Counsel.—Vincent Mulloy, Room 4E332, 453–5618.
Human Resources Team Supervisor.—Nichelle Boone, Room 4W106, 401–3710.
Budget and Planning Support Team Lead.—Crystal Foster, Room 4W104, 453–6454.
Customer Service and Technology Team Supervisor.—Anna Kasior (acting), Room 4E317, 453–6613.

OFFICE OF CAREER, TECHNICAL, AND ADULT EDUCATION

550 12th Street, SW., 11th Floor, Washington, DC 20202

phone (202) 245–7700, fax 245–7171

Assistant Secretary.—Scott Stump.
Deputy Assistant Secretary.—Casey Sacks, casey.sacks@ed.gov.
Staff Assistant.—Francine Sinclair, francine.sinclair@ed.gov.

OFFICE OF COMMUNICATIONS AND OUTREACH

Information Resource Center

400 Maryland Avenue, SW., Washington, DC 20202, phone (202) 401–2000

Assistant Secretary.—Liz Hill (acting), Room 7W101, LBJ, 453–7877.
Press Secretary.—Angela Morabito, Room 7W103, 453–5576, LBJ, press@ed.gov.
Deputy Assistant Secretaries:
Communications.—Liz Hill, Room 7W101, LBJ, 453–7877.
Outreach.—Daniela Garcia, Room 7W107, LBJ, 453–5576.
Management and Planning.—Daniel J. Miller, Room 7E206, LBJ, 453–6435.

OFFICE OF ELEMENTARY AND SECONDARY EDUCATION

Room 3W300, phone (202) 401–0113, fax 205–0303

Assistant Secretary.—Frank T. Brogan, Room 3W315, 401–0113.
Principal Deputy Assistant Secretary.—Aimee Viana, Room 3W307, 401–0113.
Deputy Assistant Secretary for the Office of Administration.—Mark Washington, Room 3W314, 205–0167.
Deputy Assistant Secretary for Discretionary Grants.—Christopher Rinkus (acting), Room 3W313, 401–0113.

Deputy Assistant Secretary for Formula Grants.—Ruth Ryder, Room 3W224, 401–0113.
Executive Officer.—Tina Hunter, Room 3W308, 205–8527.
Director for Management Support Unit.—Kim Okahara, Room 3W330, 453–6930.
Program Directors:
Charter School Program.—Ellen Safranek, Room 3E120, 453–7660.
Disaster Recovery Group.—Meredith Miller, Room 3W311, 401–8368.
Effective Educator Development Program.—Venitia Richardson (acting), Room 3C139, 260–2614.
Effective Teaching and Social Emotional Learning.—Venitia Richardson, Room 3C139, 260–2614.
Expanding Student Choice and High-Quality Schools.—Anna Hinton, Room 3E231, 260–1816.
High Quality Assessments and Accountability Systems.—Victoria Hammer, Room 3W103, 260–1438.
Impact Aid Program.—Marilyn Hall, Room 3C105, 205–8724.
Innovation and Early Learning Programs.—Jamila Smith, Room 3E304, 453–6360.
Migrant Education.—Lisa Gillette, Room 3E317, 260–1426.
Office of Indian Education.—Angeline Boulley, Room 3W101, 453–7042.
Program and Grantee Support Services.—David Cantrell, Room 3E206, 453–5990.
Rural, Insular and Native Achievement Programs.—Ruth Ryder (acting), Room 3W224, 401–0113.
Safe and Supportive Schools.—Paul Kesner, Room 3E330, 453–6727.
School Choice and Improvement Programs.—Norris Dickard, Room 3C140, 453–6723.
School Support and Accountability.—Patrick Rooney, Room 3W202, 453–5514.
State and Grantee Relations.—Tara Ramsey, Room 3W203, 260–2063.
Well-Rounded Education Programs.—Sylvia Lyles, Room 3E314, 260–2551.

OFFICE OF ENGLISH LANGUAGE ACQUISITION

400 Maryland Avenue, SW., Washington, DC 20202

phone (202) 401–4300, fax 401–8452

Assistant Deputy Secretary and Director.—Jose Viana, Room 4W202, 453–6781.
Deputy Director.—Supreet Anand, Ph.D., Room 4W230, 401–9795.

OFFICE OF FEDERAL STUDENT AID

830 First Street, NE., Washington, DC 20202

phone (202) 377–3000, fax 275–5000

Chief Operating Officer.—Mark A. Brown, Room 112E1, 377–4145.
Principal Deputy Chief Operating Officer.—Joe Lindsey, Room 112C1, 377–4023.
Deputy Chief Operating Officers:
Deputy COO for Strategy, Innovation and Transformation.—Dave Albers, Room 112J1, 377–3707.
Partner Participation and Oversight.—Robin Minor, Room 112E1, 377–3717.
Strategic Measures and Outcomes.—Dr. Michael Dean, Room 112D1, 377–4132.
Student Experience and Aid Delivery.—Chris Greene, Room 112F1, 377–4141.
Chiefs:
Administration Officer.—Quasette Crowner, Room 21A5, 377–3064.
Financial Officer.—Alison Doone, Room 54E1, 377–4124.
Information Officer.—Wanda Broadus (acting), Room 102E3, 377–3539.
Executive Director, Acquisitions.—James E. Davis, Room 91J1, 377–4782.
Director, Policy Liaison and Implementation.—Jeff Appel, Room 113C1, 377–3936.
Director, Strategic Communications.—Marianna O'Brien, Room 402, 377–4155.
Ombudsman.—Joyce DeMoss, Room 41I1, 377–3992.

OFFICE OF THE GENERAL COUNSEL

Room 6E313, phone (202) 401–6000, fax 205–2689

General Counsel.—Vacant.
Principal Deputy General Counsel.—Reed D. Rubinstein (delegated the authority to perform the functions and duties of the General Counsel).

Confidential Assistant.—Patrick Shaheen (202) 453–6339.
Deputy General Counsel: Jedediah Brinton, Hilary Malawer, Philip H. Rosenfelt.
Chief of Staff.—Rob Wexler (acting).
Senior Counsel.—''Bucky'' Methfessel, Ron Petracca, Rob Wexler.
Executive Officer.—Liza Araujo (202) 260–4008.
Assistant General Counsel: Kathryn Ellis, Marcella Keller-Goodridge, Dennis Koeppel, Paul Riddle, Tracey Sasser, Brian Siegel (acting).

OFFICE OF INSPECTOR GENERAL

Potomac Center Plaza (PCP), 8th Floor, Washington, DC 20024

phone (202) 245–6900, fax 245–6993

Inspector General.—Vacant.
Deputy Inspector General.—Sandra D. Bruce (delegated the duties of the Inspector General).
Counsel to the Inspector General.—Antigone Potamianos, 245–8322.
Assistant Inspector General for—
Audit Services.—Byron Gordon, 245–6051.
Investigations.—Aaron Jordan, 245–7829.
IT Audit and Computer Crimes Investigations.—Robert Mancuso, 245–7330.
Management Services.—David Morris, 245–6369.

INTERNATIONAL AFFAIRS OFFICE

Room 6W108, phone (202) 401–0430

Senior Advisor to the Secretary and Director.—Maureen McLaughlin.
International Affairs Specialists: JoAnne Livingston, Rebecca Miller, Rafael Nevarez, Sambia Shivers-Barclay.
Staff Assistant.—Veronica Tahir.

INSTITUTE OF EDUCATION SCIENCES

550 12th Street, SW., 4th Floor, Washington, DC 20004

phone (202) 245–7095, fax 245–6752

Director.—Mark Schneider, 245–6909.
Deputy Director for—
Administration and Policy.—Craig Stanton, 245–6605.
Science.—Anne Riccuiti, 245–8455.
National Center for—
Education Evaluation and Regional Assistance.—Matthew Soldner, 245–8385.
Education Research.—Elizabeth Albro, 245–8495.
Education Statistics.—James ''Lynn'' Woodworth, 245–7291.
Special Education Research.—Joan McLaughlin, 245–8201.

OFFICE OF LEGISLATION AND CONGRESSIONAL AFFAIRS

Room 6W301, phone (202) 401–0020, email: OLCAinquiries@ed.gov

Assistant Secretary.—Jordan Harding (acting), 401–0020.
Deputy Assistant Secretary.—Anna Bartlett, 453–6786.
Confidential Assistant.—Madeleine Huizinga, 543–6966.
Director of Legislative Affairs.—Molly Petersen, 453–5707.

OFFICE OF PLANNING, EVALUATION, AND POLICY DEVELOPMENT

Room 4W333, phone (202) 205–9765

Assistant Secretary.—James Blew, Room 4W317.
Senior Advisor/Acting Principal Deputy Assistant Secretary.—Erin McHugh, Room 4W314, 401–1304.
Chief Data Officer.—Gregory Fortelny, Room 6W231, 401–1270.
Deputy Director of the Office of Educational Technology.—Jake Steel, Room 4W307, 453–6973.

Director of Grants Policy Office.—Jessica Ramakis, Room 4W313, 738–0872.
Director of Student Privacy Policy Office.—Vacant.
Executive Officer.—Ann Margaret Owens, Room 4W333, 205–9765.

OFFICE OF POSTSECONDARY EDUCATION

400 Maryland Avenue, SW., Washington, DC 20202, phone (202) 453–6914

Assistant Secretary.—Robert King, 453–5924.
Deputy Assistant Secretary for—
Higher Education Programs.—Christopher McCaghren, 453–7337.
International and Foreign Language Education.—Cheryl Gibbs (Senior Director), 453–5690.
Management and Planning.—Phil Maestri, 453–7377.
Policy, Planning, and Innovation.—Lynn Mahaffie, 453–7862.
Executive Officer.—John Woodard, 245–6248.

OFFICE OF SPECIAL EDUCATION AND REHABILITATIVE SERVICES

Potomac Center Plaza (PCP), 550 12th Street, SW., 5th Floor, Washington, DC 20202

phone (202) 245–7468, fax 245–7638

Assistant Secretary.—Mark Schultz (delegated the authority to perform the functions and duties of the Assistant Secretary for Special Education and Rehabilitative Services), Room 5107, 245–7408.
Deputy Assistant Secretary.—Vacant.
Director of the Office of Special Education Programs.—Laurie VanderPloeg, Room 5139, 245–6180.
Deputy Director of the Office of Special Education Programs.—David Cantrell, Room 5138B.
Commissioner of the Rehabilitation Services Administration.—Mark Schultz, Room 5107, 245–7408.
Deputy Commissioner of the Rehabilitation Services Administration.—Vacant.
Executive Officer.—Melanie Winston, Room 5148–1, 245–7419.

DEPARTMENT OF VETERANS AFFAIRS

Mail should be addressed to 810 Vermont Avenue, NW., Washington, DC 20420

https://va.gov

ROBERT L. WILKIE, Secretary of Veterans Affairs; born August 6, 1962, Frankfurt, Germany; education: B.A., Wake Forest University, Winston-Salem, NC, 1985; J.D., Loyola University School of Law, New Orleans, LA, 1988; LLM, Georgetown University Law School, Washington, DC, 1992; M.S.S., U.S. Army War College, Carlisle Barracks, PA, 2002; professional: Counsel, Office of Senate Majority Leader Trent Lott, 1997–2003; Special Assistant to the President, National Security Council, 2003–05; Principal Deputy Assistant Secretary of Defense (Legislative Affairs), Department of Defense, 2005–06; Assistant Secretary of Defense (Legislative Affairs), 2006–09; Under Secretary of Defense for Personnel and Readiness, 2017–18; Acting Secretary of Veterans Affairs Department, March–May, 2018; military: U.S. Air Force Reserve, U.S. Navy Reserve; nominated by President Donald J. Trump to serve as the tenth Secretary of the Department of Veterans Affairs on May 18, 2018, confirmed on July 23, 2018, and sworn in on July 30, 2018.

OFFICE OF THE SECRETARY

Secretary of Veterans Affairs.—Robert L. Wilkie (202) 461–4800.
- *Deputy Secretary of Veterans Affairs.*—Vacant, 461–4817.
- *Chief of Staff.*—Pamela Powers, 461–4808.
- *Deputy Chief of Staff.*—Christopher D. Syrek, 461–4808.
- *Veterans Service Organization Liaison.*—Jason Beardsley, 461–4884.
- *White House Liaison.*—Darren J. Bossie, 461–4868.
- *Executive Secretary.*—Carrie McVicker, 461–4869.
- *Director, Center for—*
  - *Minority Veterans.*—Stephen Dillard, 461–6191.
  - *Women Veterans.*—Jacquelyn Hayes-Byrd, 461–6193.
- *Director of:*
  - *Employment Discrimination and Complaint Adjudication.*—Maxanne R. Witkin, 1575 I Street, NW., 461–4050.
  - *Mission Operations.*—Katherine Childress, 461–4836.
  - *Office of Survivors Assistance.*—Ann Duff, 266–4524.
  - *Protocol.*—Heine Rivera, 461–7726.
  - *Regulation Policy and Management.*—Michael Shores, 461–4921.
  - *Strategic Communications.*—Traci Scott, 461–4812.
  - *Strategic Partnerships.*—Deborah Scher, 461–0325.
- *VA Chief Historian.*—Michael Visconage, 1717 H Street, NW., 461–4842.
- *Committee Management Officer.*—Jeffrey Moragne, 1717 H Street, NW., 266–4660.
- *Executive Director of:*
  - *Small and Disadvantaged Business Utilization.*—Ruby Harvey, 801 I Street, NW., 461–4600.
  - *Electronic Health Record Modernization.*—John H. Windom, 811 Vermont Avenue, NW., 461–5820.

BOARD OF VETERANS' APPEALS

Chairman.—Cheryl L. Mason, 425 I Street, NW. (202) 632–5710.
- *Vice Chairman.*—David C. Spickler, 632–5591.
- *Chief of Staff.*—Nicholas A. Uchalik, 461–6482.

OFFICE OF GENERAL COUNSEL

General Counsel.—William A. Hudson, Jr. (acting), (202) 461–4995.
- *Principal Deputy General Counsel.*—William A. Hudson, Jr.
- *Senior Counsel.*—Catherine Mitrano, 578–7585.

Deputy General Counsel for—
General Law.—Michael R. Hogan, 461–7713.
Legal Operations.—D. Brent Pope, 461–0678.
Veterans' Programs.—Vacant.

OFFICE OF INSPECTOR GENERAL

Inspector General.—Michael Missal, 801 I Street, NW., 461–4720.
Deputy Inspector General.—David T. Case, 461–4720.

OFFICE OF ACQUISITIONS, LOGISTICS, AND CONSTRUCTION

Principal Executive Director.—Karen Brazell (202) 632–4606.
Deputy Executive Director.—Phillip Christy, 632–5224.
Chief of Staff.—Iris Hall (acting), 632–6906.
Executive Director for—
Acquisition and Logistics.—Angela Billups, Ph.D., 461–6920.
Business Operations Center.—Todd Hunter, 461–4202.
Construction and Facilities.—Anthony Costa, 632–4607.
Procurement, Acquisition, and Logistics.—Vacant.

ASSISTANT SECRETARY FOR ACCOUNTABILITY AND WHISTLEBLOWER PROTECTION

Assistant Secretary.—Dr. Tamara Bonzato (202) 461–4119.

ASSISTANT SECRETARY FOR CONGRESSIONAL AND LEGISLATIVE AFFAIRS

Assistant Secretary.—Brooks D. Tucker (202) 461–6490.
Principal Deputy Assistant Secretary.—Glenn Johnson (acting), 461–5707.
Deputy Assistant Secretary for Congressional Affairs.—David Balland, 461–6493.
Director of:
Operations.—Richard Roa, 461–5914.
Congressional Affairs.—David Balland, 461–6493.
Health Team.—Angela Prudhomme (acting), 461–6471.
Benefits Team.—Lesia Mandzia (acting), 461–6177.
Legislative Team.—David Ballenger, 461–6493.
Outreach Team.—Annmarie Amaral, 225–2280.
Corporate Enterprise Legislative Affairs Service.—Lesia Mandzia, 461–6177.

ASSISTANT SECRETARY FOR PUBLIC AND INTERGOVERNMENTAL AFFAIRS

Assistant Secretary.—James Hutton (202) 461–7500.
Principal Deputy Assistant Secretary.—John E. Wagner, 461–5722.
Chief of Staff.—Lyndon B. Johnson, 461–6448.
Press Secretary.—Christina M. Mandreucci, 461–5120.
Deputy Press Secretary.—William J. Eason, 461–7458.
Executive Director for—
Intergovernmental Affairs.—Thayer Verschoor, 461–7385.
Strategic Planning and Veterans Outreach.—Gary C. Tallman, 461–7478.
Tribal Government Relations.—Stephanie Birdwell, 461–4851.
Director, State and Local Government Affairs.—John Fish, 461–7486.
Deputy Director, Center for Faith and Opportunity Initiative.—Conrad Washington, 461–7865.

ASSISTANT SECRETARY FOR ENTERPRISE INTEGRATION

Assistant Secretary.—Melissa S. Glynn, Ph.D. (202) 461–5800.
Principal Deputy Assistant Secretary.—Dat P. Tran, 461–5800.
Chief of Staff.—Shana Love-Holmon, 632–5285.
Deputy Assistant Secretary for Planning and Performance Management.—Mike Frueh, 461–8784.

Executive Director for—
Data Governance and Analytics.—Kshemndra Paul, 461–1052.
Office of Modernization.—Surafeal Asgedom, 461–5817.
Policy and Interagency Collaboration.—John Medve, 461–5626.
VA Innovations Center.—Michael Akinyele (acting), 897–6940.

ASSISTANT SECRETARY FOR MANAGEMENT

Assistant Secretary/Chief Financial Officer.—Jon J. Rychalski (202) 461–6703.
Principal Deputy Assistant Secretary for Management/Deputy Chief Financial Officer.—Edward J. Murray, 461–6703.
Executive Director of Financial Planning and Analysis.—Vacant.
Chief of Staff.—Nealie Page, 461–6703.
Deputy Assistant Secretary for—
Budget.—Andrew McIlroy, 461–7790.
Finance.—Joanne Choi, 461–6180.
Financial Management Business Transformation Services.—Terry Riffel, 461–6154.
Executive Director of:
Actuarial Services.—Margot Kaplan, 461–0256.
Asset Enterprise Management.—Edward Bradley III, 461–7778.
Business Oversight.—Roberta R. Lowe (512) 460–5726.
Revolving Fund.—Vacant.

ASSISTANT SECRETARY FOR INFORMATION AND TECHNOLOGY

Assistant Secretary and Chief Information Officer.—James P. Gfrerer (202) 461–6910.
Principal Deputy Assistant Secretary for Information Technology.—Dominic A. Cussatt, 461–0044.
Chief of Staff.—Susan Perez, 461–6552.
Deputy Assistant Secretary for—
Development and Operations.—Bill James, 705–6275.
Information Security and Chief Information Security Officer.—Paul Cunningham, 382–9261.
Deputy Chief Information Officer for—
Account Management.—Alan Constantian, 430–0046.
Officer, Quality, Performance, and Risk.—Martha Orr, 461–5139.
Strategic Sourcing.—LuWanda Jones, 461–7198.
Resource Management.—John Oswalt, 461–7200.

ASSISTANT SECRETARY FOR HUMAN RESOURCES AND ADMINISTRATION/ OPERATIONS, SECURITY AND PREPAREDNESS

Assistant Secretary.—Daniel R. Sitterly (202) 461–7750.
Principal Deputy Assistant Secretary.—Jeffrey R. Mayo, 461–7750.
Chief of Staff.—Laura H. Eskenazi, 632–4881.
Chief Human Capital Officer.—Tracey Therit, 461–0235.
Deputy Assistant Secretary for—
Administration.—Roy Hurndon, 461–5000.
Diversity and Inclusion.—Harvey Johnson, 461–4064.
Resolution Management.—Harvey Johnson, 1575 I Street, NW., 461–4064.
Executive Director of:
Human Resources Enterprise Center/Chief Learning Officer.—Amy Parker, 461–5369.
Labor-Management Relations.—Tracy Schulberg, 461–4009.
Corporate Senior Executive Management Office.—Carrie Johnson-Clarke, 632–5181.
Management, Planning and Analysis.—Catherine Biggs-Silvers, 632–7160.

OFFICE OF OPERATIONS, SECURITY, AND PREPAREDNESS

Principal Deputy Assistant Secretary for Operations, Security and Preparedness.—Kevin T. Hanretta, 461–4980.
Director, Operations, Security, and Preparedness Resource Management.—Sylvia B. Dunn, DM, 461–4984.
Deputy Assistant Secretary for Emergency Management and Resilience.—Lewis R. Ratchford, Jr., 461–5930.

Executive Director of:
Security and Law Enforcement.—Frederick R. Jackson, 461–5500.
Identity, Credential, and Access Management.—Daniel Galilk, 461–0075.

NATIONAL CEMETERY ADMINISTRATION

Under Secretary for Memorial Affairs.—Randy C. Reeves (202) 461–6112.
Principal Deputy Under Secretary.—Ronald E. Walters, 461–6013.
Chief of Staff.—Thomas C. Howard, 461–6013.
Deputy Under Secretary for—
Field Programs and Cemetery Operations.—Glenn R. Powers, 461–5723.
Finance and Planning / CFO.—Matthew Sullivan, 461–7334.
Management.—Richard C. Chandler, 461–7898.
Executive Director of:
Cemetery Operations.—Lisa Pozzebon, 461–8352.
Field Programs.—Amerophan Callahan (314) 416–6304.
Engagement and Memorial Innovation.—Daniel Devine, 461–1803.
Strategy and Analysis.—Gina Farrisee, 461–7730.
Human Capital Management.—Dr. Lisa Thomas, 461–7006.
Director of:
Budget Service.—Kathleen McManaman, 632–8841.
Congressional Affairs and Correspondence Service.—Patricia ''Tish'' Tyson, 461–6307.
Contracting Service.—Robert Capers (540) 658–7206.
Design and Construction Service.—Michael Roth, 632–4691.
Legislative and Regulatory Service.—Patricia Watts, 461–5950.
Transformation, Technology, and Data Management.—Bill Barnes (703) 441–3099.
Veterans Cemetery Grants Program.—George Eisenbach, 632–7369.
Deputy Director, Memorial Products Service.—Eric Powell, 632–8670.

VETERANS BENEFITS ADMINISTRATION

Under Secretary for Benefits.—Paul R. Lawrence, Ph.D., 1800 G Street, NW. (202) 461–9300.
Principal Deputy Under Secretary.—Margarita Devlin, 461–9300.
Chief of Staff.—Andrea Lee, 461–9300.
Deputy Chief of Staff.—Brandye Terrell, 461–9300.
Deputy Under Secretary for Field Operations.—Willie Clark, 461–9340.
Chief Financial Officer.—Charles A. Tapp, II, 461–9900.
Executive Director of:
Administration and Facilities.—Jeffrey M. Smith, 461–9197.
Appeals Management Office.—David McLenachen, 530–9455.
Business Process Integration.—Brad Houston, 461–9797.
Compensation.—Beth Murphy, 461–9700.
Education.—Charmain Bogue, 461–9800.
Insurance.—Vincent Markey, (215) 381–3029.
Loan Guaranty.—Jeffrey London, 632–8862.
Pension and Fiduciary.—Ronald Burke, 461–9165.
Performance Analysis and Integrity.—Mark Seastrom, 461–9040.
Talent Management.—Terri A. Beer, 461–9450.
Transition and Economic Development.—Cheryl Rawls, 632–8863.
Vocational Rehabilitation and Employment.—William Streitberger, 461–9600.

VETERANS HEALTH ADMINISTRATION

Executive in Charge.—Richard A. Stone, M.D. (202) 461–7000.
Principal Deputy Under Secretary for Health.—Steven Lieberman, M.D. (acting), 461–7008.
Chief of Staff.—Lawrence Connell, 461–7016.
Deputy Chief of Staff.—Jon Jensen (acting), 461–7016.
Deputy Under Secretary for Health for—
Community Care.—Kameron Matthews, M.D. (acting), 461–4240.
Discovery, Education and Affiliate Networks.—Carolyn Clancy, M.D., 461–0370.
Operations and Management.—Renee Oshinski (acting), 461–7026.
Organizational Excellence.—Gerard Cox, M.D., 461–7571.
Policy and Services.—Lucille Beck, Ph.D., 461–7590.

Assistant Deputy Under Secretary for Health for—
Administrative Operations.—Tammy Czarnecki, M.S.O.L., 461–7026.
Access to Care.—Susan R. Kirsch, M.D. (acting), 461–7107.
Clinical Operations and Management.—Theresa Boyd, M.D., 461–0474.
Community Care.—Mark Upton, M.D., 461–7459.
Informatics and Information Governance.—Chuck Hume, FACHE, 461–5834.
Integrity.—David B. Chiesa, DDS, 461–7786.
Patient Care Services.—Rachel McArdle, Ph.D. (acting), 461–7590.
Policy and Planning.—Valerie Mattison-Brown, 461–7115.
Quality, Safety, and Value.—Joel A. Ross, M.D., 461–1009.
Workforce Services.—Jessica Bonjorni (acting), 461–6720.
Chief:
Employee Education System.—Volney ''Jim'' Warner, 461–4019.
Finance Officer.—Laura Dupke, MPP, 461–7790.
Nursing Officer.—Beth Taylor, RN, 461–7250.
Readjustment Counseling Officer.—Michael Fisher, M.S.W., 461–6525.
Director of Member Services.—Garth Miller (678) 924–6480.
Research and Development.—Rachel Ramoni, D.M.D., 461–1700.
Medical Inspector.—Erica Scavalla, M.D., 461–1075.
Academic Affiliations.—Marjorie Bowman, 461–9490.
Connected Care.—Neil C. Evans, M.D., 461–0157.
Improvement & Analytics.—Joseph Francis, M.D. (acting), 302–3110.
Executive Director of:
National Center for Ethics.—Virginia ''Ashby'' Sharpe (acting), 632–8452.
National Center for Patient Safety.—William Gunnar, M.D. (734) 930–5916.
Office of Patient Advocacy.—Ann E. Doran, 461–7607.
Office of Research Oversight.—Doug Bannerman, Ph.D., 632–6122.
Patient Centered Care and Cultural Transformation.—Tracy Gaudet, M.D., 266–4670.
Veterans Health Administrations Communications.—Gina Screen (acting), 461–7221.

DEPARTMENT OF HOMELAND SECURITY

2707 Martin Luther King Jr. Avenue, SE., Washington, DC 20528

phone (202) 282–8000

CHAD F. WOLF was designated as the Acting Secretary of Homeland Security by President Donald J. Trump and was also confirmed as the first Under Secretary of the U.S. Department of Homeland Security's (DHS) Office of Strategy, Policy, and Plans (PLCY). Previously, he served as the Acting Under Secretary.

As the senior official for PLCY, Mr. Wolf leads the Department's policymaking process to develop and coordinate strategies and policies that advance the homeland security mission and protect the American public.

Since his selection by the President, Mr. Wolf has advanced many of the Administration's critical priorities across the entire homeland security mission. Mr. Wolf oversaw the completion of the recently released DHS Strategic Plan, which establishes the Department's long-term strategic goals and objectives to inform key leadership decisions. Additionally, he led several significant initiatives to counter international and domestic terrorism, prevent terrorist travel, safeguard the U.S. electoral process, and protect American trade interests. As part of his duties, Mr. Wolf led and coordinated the Department's engagement with international partners to protect American homeland security interests at home and abroad.

During his tenure, Mr. Wolf has made significant progress to strengthen U.S. border security, address the humanitarian crisis on the U.S. Southwest Border, and improve the integrity of the U.S. immigration system. As a result of these efforts, Mr. Wolf and his staff have implemented policies that protect American communities from transnational criminal organizations and safeguard American workers.

With over 20 years of policy development and management experience in both the public and private sectors, Mr. Wolf is an effective leader and policymaker on a variety of complex issues. During the Trump Administration, he served as the Chief of Staff for the Transportation Security Administration (TSA), Deputy Chief of Staff and Chief of Staff for the Department. For his leadership and management of complex national issues, Mr. Wolf received the U.S. Secretary of Homeland Security Distinguished Service Medal. Shortly after the terrorist attack on September 11, 2001, Mr. Wolf served as the Assistant Administrator of Transportation Security Policy in which he played a leading role in establishing the Transportation Security Administration.

Beyond his service in the executive branch, Mr. Wolf served as Vice President and Senior Director at Wexler & Walker, a bipartisan public policy consultancy, and held staff positions in the U.S. Senate.

Mr. Wolf earned his Bachelor of Arts in History from Southern Methodist University, and holds a Master's Certificate in Government Contract Management from Villanova University.

OFFICE OF THE SECRETARY

Secretary of Homeland Security.—Chad F. Wolf (acting).

Deputy Secretary.—Ken Cuccinelli (senior official performing the duties of the Deputy Secretary).

Chief of Staff.—John Gountanis (acting).

Director, U.S. Citizenship and Immigration Services.—Ken Cuccinelli (senior official performing the duties of the Director, U.S. Citizenship and Immigration Services).

Deputy Director, U.S. Citizenship and Immigration Services.—Mark Koumans.

Ombudsman.—Michael Dougherty.

CIVIL RIGHTS AND CIVIL LIBERTIES

phone (202) 401–1474, toll free 1–866–644–8360

Officer for Civil Rights and Civil Liberties.—Cameron Quinn.

EXECUTIVE SECRETARIAT

phone (202) 282–8221

Executive Secretary.—Juliana Blackwell (acting).

OFFICE OF THE GENERAL COUNSEL

phone (202) 282–8137

General Counsel.—Chad Mizelle (acting).

OFFICE OF INSPECTOR GENERAL

phone (202) 254–4100

Inspector General.—Joseph V. Cuffari.

OFFICE OF INTELLIGENCE AND ANALYSIS

phone (202) 282–9690

Under Secretary and Chief Intelligence Officer.—Brian J. Murphy (acting).
Principal Deputy Under Secretary.—Brian J. Murphy.
Chief of Staff.—Matthew Hanna.
Deputy Chief of Staff.—Adam Luke.
Deputy Under Secretary for Intelligence Enterprise Operations.—Horace Jen.
Deputy Under Secretary for Intelligence Enterprise Readiness.—Melissa Smislova.

OFFICE OF PARTNERSHIP AND ENGAGEMENT

phone (202) 282–9310

Assistant Secretary.—John H. Hill.

OFFICE OF LEGISLATIVE AFFAIRS

phone (202) 447–5890

Assistant Secretary.—Beth Spivey.
Deputy Assistant Secretaries: Natalie McGarry (Senate), Aaron Calkins (House).

MILITARY ADVISOR'S OFFICE

phone (202) 282–8245

Military Advisor.—Rear Admiral Brendan C. McPherson.

PRIVACY OFFICE

phone (202) 343–1717

Chief Privacy Officer.—Dena Kozanas.

OFFICE OF PUBLIC AFFAIRS

phone (202) 282–8069

Assistant Secretary.—Dirk J. Vande Beek.

CYBERSECURITY AND INFRASTRUCTURE SECURITY AGENCY

phone (703) 235–2080

Director.—Christopher C. Krebs.

Deputy Director.—Matthew Travis.
Chief of Staff.—Emily Early.
Assistant Director for—
Cybersecurity.—Bryan Ware.
Emergency Communication.—Vince DeLaurentis (acting).
Infrastructure Security.—Brian Harrell.
Integrated Operations.—John Felker.
National Risk Management Center.—Robert Kolasky.
Stakeholder Engagement.—Bradford Willke (acting).

SCIENCE AND TECHNOLOGY DIRECTORATE

phone (202) 254–6033

Under Secretary.—William Bryan (senior official performing the duties of the Under Secretary).
Deputy Under Secretary.—Andre Hentz (acting).
Chief of Staff.—Kathryn Coulter.
Deputy Chief of Staff.—Gail Miller.
Director of:
Finance and Budget.—Rachel Lewis (acting).
Homeland Security Advanced Research Projects Agency.—Dan Cotter.

MANAGEMENT DIRECTORATE

phone (202) 447–3400

Under Secretary.—Vacant.
Deputy Under Secretary.—R. D. Alles.
Chief of Staff.—Janene Corrado (acting).
Chief:
Human Capital Officer.—Angela Bailey.
Information Officer.—Elizabeth Capello (acting).
Procurement Officer.—Soraya Correa.
Readiness Support Officer.—Tom Chaleki.
Security Officer.—Rich McComb.
Deputy Chief Financial Officer.—Stacy Marcott.
Executive Director, Office of Program Accountability and Risk Management.—Debra Cox.

OFFICE OF POLICY

phone (202) 282–9708

Under Secretary, Office of Strategy, Policy, and Plans.—Scott Glabe (senior official performing the duties of the Under Secretary).
Deputy Under Secretary.—James W. McCament.
Chief of Staff, Office of Strategy, Policy, and Plans.—David R. Dorey.
Assistant Secretary, International Affairs.—Valerie S. Boyd.
Deputy Assistant Secretary, International Affairs.—Robert Paschall.
Deputy Assistant Secretary, Western Hemisphere.—David Cloe.
Assistant Secretary, Threat Prevention and Security Policy.—Elizabeth Neumann.
Deputy Assistant Secretary, Counterterrorism and Threat Prevention Policy.—Nate Blumenthal (acting).
Deputy Assistant Secretary, Screening and Vetting Policy.—Alex Zemek.
Assistant Secretary, Border, Immigration, and Trade Policy.—Scott Glabe.
Deputy Assistant Secretary, Foreign Investment and Trade Policy.—Christa Brzozowski.
Deputy Assistant Secretary, Immigration Policy.—Sarah Rehberg.
Deputy Assistant Secretary, Immigration Statistics.—Marc Rosenblum.
Assistant Secretary, Cyber Policy.—Sam Kaplan.
Deputy Assistant Secretary, Cyber Policy.—Thomas McDermott.
Assistant Secretary, Strategy, Planning, Analysis & Risk.—Vacant.
Deputy Assistant Secretary, Integration.—Drew Kuepper.
Deputy Assistant Secretary, Strategic Planning.—Patrick Kearney (acting).

FEDERAL EMERGENCY MANAGEMENT AGENCY (FEMA)

500 C Street, SW., Washington, DC 20472, phone (202) 646–2500

Administrator.—Pete Gaynor.

Deputy Administrator.—Vacant.
Chief of Staff.—Eric Heighberger.
Senior Law Enforcement Advisor to the Administrator.—Roberto L. Hylton.
Director, Office of:
Center of Faith-Based and Neighborhood Partnerships.—Kevin Smith.
Congressional and Intergovernmental Affairs Divisions.—Robby Wehagen.
Disability Integration and Coordination.—Linda Mastrandea.
Equal Rights.—Jo Linda Johnson.
Executive Operations.—Marcia Hodges.
Executive Secretariat.—Nicole Dyson.
External Affairs.—Jessica Nalepa.
National Advisory Council.—Jasper Cooke.
National Capital Region Coordination.—Kim Kadesch.
Regional Operations.—Elizabeth Edge.
Chief Counsel.—Adrian Sevier.
Chief Financial Officer.—Mary Comans (acting).
Associate Administrator for Policy, Program Analysis and International Affairs.—Joel Doolin.
Deputy Administrator, Protection and National Preparedness.—Chad Gorman (acting).
Assistant Administrators:
Grant Programs.—Bridget Bean (acting).
National Continuity Programs.—William Zito, Jr.
National Preparedness.—Alex Amparo.
Administrator, U.S. Fire Administration.—G. Keith Bryant.
Deputy Associate Administrator, Mission Support.—Traci L. Clever.
Chiefs, Mission Support:
Administrative Officer.—Tracey Showman.
Component Human Capital Officer.—Karen Filipponi.
Information Officer.—Lytwaive Hutchinson.
Procurement Officer.—Bobby McCane.
Security Officer.—Michael Apodaca (acting).
Associate Administrator, Response and Recovery.—Jeff Byard.
Deputy Associate Administrator, Response and Recovery.—David Bibo.
Assistant Administrators:
Field Operations.—John Rabin.
Logistics.—Jeffrey Dorko.
Recovery.—Keith Turi (acting).
Response.—Damon Penn.
Deputy Associate Administrator for Insurance and Mitigation, Federal Insurance and Mitigation Administration.—David Maurstad.

COUNTERING WEAPONS OF MASS DESTRUCTION (CWMD)

phone (202) 254–8866

Assistant Secretary.—David Richardson.
Chief of Staff.—Charles Cook (acting).

TRANSPORTATION SECURITY ADMINISTRATION (TSA)

601 South 12th Street, Arlington, VA 20598–6001

Administrator/Assistant Secretary.—David P. Pekoske.
Deputy Administrator.—Patricia Cogswell.
Chief of Staff.—Ryan Propis.

UNITED STATES CUSTOMS AND BORDER PROTECTION (CBP)

1300 Pennsylvania Avenue, NW., Washington, DC 20229

Commissioner.—Mark Alan Morgan (acting), (202) 344–2001.
Deputy Commissioner.—Robert E. Perez, 344–2001.
Chief of Staff.—Debbie W. Seguin (acting), 344–2001.
Deputy Chief of Staff.—Steve Schorr, 344–2001.
Deputy Chief of Staff (Policy).—John J. Yap (acting), 344–2369.
Chief Counsel.—Scott Falk, 344–2940.
Executive Assistant Commissioner of:

Air and Marine.—Edward E. Young, 344–3950.
Enterprise Services.—Benjamine ''Carry'' Huffman, 344–2300.
Field Operations.—Todd C. Owen 202–344–1620.
Operations Support.—William Ferrara, 344–2230.
Trade.—Brenda Brockman Smith, 325–6000.
Chief, United States Border Patrol.—Rodney S. Scott, 325–1596.
Assistant Commissioner of:
Congressional Affairs.—Stephanie Talton (acting), 344–1760.
International Affairs.—E. Erik Moncayo (acting), 344–3000.
Professional Responsibility.—Matthew Klein, 344–1800.
Public Affairs.—Casey Durst, 344–1137.
Executive Director, Office of:
Intergovernmental Public Liaison.—Tim Quinn, 325–0871.
Policy.—Marty P. Chavers (acting), 325–1395.
Privacy and Diversity.—Rebekah A. Salazar, 344–1610.
Trade Relations.—Valarie M. Neuhart (acting), 344–1440.
Director, Executive Secretariat.—Wayne Winterling, 344–1684.

UNITED STATES IMMIGRATION AND CUSTOMS ENFORCEMENT (ICE)

Director.—Matthew T. Albence (acting), (202) 732–3000.
Deputy Director.—Derek N. Benner (acting), 732–3000.
Chief of Staff.—Christopher S. Kelly, 732–3000.
Assistant Director of:
Congressional Relations.—Raymond Kovacic, 732–4200.
Professional Responsibility.—Waldemar Rodriguez, 732–8300.
Public Affairs.—Charissa Pallas, 732–4251.
Principal Legal Advisor.—Tracy Short, 732–5001.
Executive Secretariat.—Corey Mayberry, 732–4307.
Executive Associate Director, Enforcement and Removal Operations.—Timothy Robbins, 732–3100.
Deputy Executive Associate Director, Enforcement and Removal Operations.—Henry Lucero, 732–3100.
Assistant Director of:
Custody Management.—Tae D. Johnson, 732–3100.
Enforcement.—Chris Cronen, 732–4546.
Field Operations.—Gregory Archambeault (acting), 732–3111.
ICE Health Service Corps.—Dr. Steward D. Smith, 732–3100.
Operational Support.—Jacki B. Klopp, 732–3100.
Repatriation.—Marlen Piñeiro, 732–3100.
Executive Associate Director, Homeland Security Investigations.—Alysa D. Erichs, 732–5110.
Deputy Executive Associate Director, Homeland Security Investigations.—Matthew Allen, 732–5100.
Assistant Director for—
Domestic Operations.—Debra Parker, 732–3907.
Intelligence.—Peter J. Hatch, 732–3101.
International Affairs.—Patrick J. Lechleitner, 732–5100.
Mission Support.—Katrina Berger, 732–5100.
National Security Investigations Division.—David Shaw, 732–5100.
Programs.—Greg Nevano, 732–5100.
Executive Associate Director, Management and Administration.—Staci Barrera, 732–3000.
Director, Acquisition Management.—Albert Dainton, 732–3000.
Assistant Director, Diversity Officer and Civil Rights.—Scott F. Lanum, 732–0125.
Director, Chief Financial Officer.—Stephen Roncone, 732–6208.
Chief Information Officer.—Irfan Malik, 732–1045.
Freedom of Information Act Officer.—Catrina Pavlik Keenan, 732–6259.
Human Capital Officer.—Susan Cullen, 732–3100.
Assistant Director, Office of Leadership and Career Development.—Sandra Walker, 732–3100.
Assistant Director, Office of Policy.—Debbie Seguin, 732–5323.
Assistant Director, Information Governance and Privacy Officer.—Kenneth Clark, 732–3300.

FEDERAL LAW ENFORCEMENT TRAINING CENTERS

1131 Chapel Crossing Road, Glynco, GA 31524

Director.—Thomas J. Walters (912) 267–2070.
Deputy Director.—William Fallon, 267–2070.
Chief of Staff.—Bryan Lemons, 267–2070.
Deputy Chief of Staff.—David Christy, 267–2070.
Associate Director for Training Operations.—James R. Gregorius, 554–4284.
Assistant Director for—
Mission Readiness and Support Directorate.—Marcus L. Hill, 267–2231.
National Capital Region Training Operations.—Darren Cruzan (202) 233–0260.
Assistant Director/Chief Financial Officer.—Donald R. Lewis (912) 267–2999.
Assistant Director/Chief Information Officer.—Michael L. Vesta, 267–2014.
Core Training Operations Directorate.—Richard Deasey, 280–5326.
Assistant Director/Chief Counsel.—Michael Bunker, 554–4487.
Training Management Operations Directorate.—Ariana Roddini (acting), 554–4456.
Technical Training Operations Directorate.—Dominic D. Braccio, 267–2040.
Chief for—
Office of Organizational Health.—Brenda M. Lloyd, 267–2280.
Office of Security and Professional Responsibility.—Kaizad Munshi, 267–3027.
Protocol and Communications Office.—Christa Thompson (acting), 267–2447.

UNITED STATES CITIZENSHIP AND IMMIGRATION SERVICES

20 Massachusetts Avenue, NW., Washington, DC 20529, phone (202) 272–1000

Director.—Kenneth T. Cuccinelli (acting).
Deputy Director.—Mark Koumans.
Chief of Staff.—Lora Ries.
Chief Information Officer.—Bill McElhaney.
Associate Director for—
Fraud Detection and National Security Directorate.—Matthew Emrich.
Refugee, Asylum and International Operations Directorate.—Jennifer Higgins.
Service Center Operations Directorate.—Donald Neufeld.
Chief, Office of:
Administration.—Michael Gibbs.
Administrative Appeals.—Barbara Velarde.
Chief Counsel.—Joseph Edlow.
Chief Financial Officer.—Kika Scott.
External Affairs Directorate.—Kathryn Rexrode (Legislative and Intergovernmental Affairs, Public Affairs, and Citizenship and Applicant Information Services fall under this directorate).
Policy and Strategy.—Kathy Nuebel-Kovarik.

UNITED STATES COAST GUARD

2703 Martin Luther King Jr. Avenue, SE., Washington, DC 20593

phone (202) 372–4400

Commandant.—ADM Karl Schultz.
Vice Commandant.—ADM Charles W. Ray.
Deputy Commandant for—
Mission Support.—VADM Michael F. McAllister.
Operations.—VADM Daniel B. Abel.
Chief Administrative Law Judge.—Hon. Walter Brudzinski.
Judge Advocate General/Chief Counsel.—RADM Steven J. Anderson.
Deputy Judge Advocate General/Deputy Chief Counsel.—Calvin Lederer.
Director of Governmental and Public Affairs.—RADM Melissa Bert.
Senior Military Advisor to the Secretary of Homeland Security.—RDML Brendan C. McPherson.

UNITED STATES SECRET SERVICE

245 Murray Drive, SW., Building T–5, Washington, DC 20223

Director.—James M. Murray.

Deputy Director.—Leonza Newsome III.

Special Agent in Charge, Congressional Affairs Program.—Benjamin P. Kramer (202) 406–5676, fax 406–5740.

INDEPENDENT AGENCIES, COMMISSIONS, BOARDS

ADVISORY COUNCIL ON HISTORIC PRESERVATION

401 F Street, NW., Suite 308, Washington, DC 20001

phone (202) 517–0200, https://achp.gov

[Created by Public Law 89–665, as amended]

Chair.—Aimee K. Jorjani, Falls Church, Virginia.
Vice Chair.—Leonard A. Forsman, Suquamish, Washington.
Expert Members:
Terry Guen-Murray, Chicago, Illinois.
Dorothy Lippert, Washington, District of Columbia.
Robert G. Stanton, Fairfax Station, Virginia.
Luis G. Hoyos, Los Angeles County, California.
Citizen Members:
Bradford J. White, Evanston, Illinois.
Jordan E. Tannenbaum, Fairfax, Virginia.
Native American Member.—Reno Keoni Franklin, Santa Rosa, California.
Governor.—Vacant.
Mayor.—Vacant.
Architect of the Capitol.—Hon. J. Brett Blanton.
Secretary, Department of:
Agriculture.—Hon. Sonny Perdue.
Defense.—Hon. Mark Esper.
Education.—Hon. Elisabeth DeVos.
Homeland Security.—Hon. Chad F. Wolf (acting).
Housing and Urban Development.—Hon. Benjamin Carson, M.D.
Interior.—Hon. David Bernhardt.
Transportation.—Hon. Elaine L. Chao.
Veterans Affairs.—Robert Wilkie.
Administrator of General Services Administration.—Emily W. Murphy.
National Conference of State Historic Preservation Officer.—Mark Wolfe, Austin, Texas.
National Association of Tribal Historic Preservation Officer.—Shasta Gaughen, Pala, California.
National Trust for Historic Preservation.—Timothy P. Whalen, Los Angeles, California.
Staff:
Executive Director.—John M. Fowler.
Manager, Office of:
Administration.—Ismail Ahmed.
Communications, Education, and Outreach.—Susan A. Glimcher.
Federal Agency Programs.—Reid J. Nelson.
General Counsel.—Javier Marqués.
Information Technology.—Rezaur Rahman.
Native American Affairs.—Valerie Hauser.
Preservation Initiatives.—Druscilla Null.

AMERICAN BATTLE MONUMENTS COMMISSION

2300 Clarendon Boulevard, Suite 500, Arlington, VA 22201–3367

phone (703) 696–6902

[Created by Public Law 105–225]

(Note: Public law changed to 105–225, August 1998; H.R. 1085.)

Chair.—David J. Urban.

Members:

Hon. Jennifer Carroll.
Hon. Benjamin Cassidy.
Hon. Dorothy Gray.
Hon. Thomas Hicks.
Hon. John McGoff.
Hon. Robert Ord.
Hon. Luis Quinonez.
Hon. Evans Spiceland.
Hon. Robert Wefald.

Secretary.—William M. Matz, Jr.
Deputy Secretary.—Robert J. Dalessandro.
Chief of Staff.—Michael Conley.
Chief Engineer & Strategy, Plans, and Policy.—Thomas Sole.
Chief Financial Officer.—Christine Philpot.
Chief Human Resources and Administration.—Jamilyn Smyser.
Chief Information Officer.—Jennifer Li.
Director of Public Affairs.—Alison Bettencourt.

AMERICAN NATIONAL RED CROSS

National Headquarters, 430 17th Street, NW., Washington, DC 20006

phone (202) 303–5000

Government Relations, phone (202) 303–4371

HONORARY OFFICERS

Honorary Chair.—Donald J. Trump, President of the United States.

CORPORATE OFFICERS

Chair.—Bonnie McElveen-Hunter.
President/CEO.—Gail J. McGovern.
General Counsel.—Phyllis Harris.
Chief Financial Officer.—Brian J. Rhoa.
Corporate Secretary.—Jennifer L. Hawkins.

BOARD OF GOVERNORS

Jennifer Bailey
Ajay Banga
Afsaneh Beschloss
Brent Briggs
David Brandon
Herman Bulls
David Clark
Steven Collis
Enrique A. Conterno
Y. Michele Kang
Joseph E. Madison
Bonnie McElveen-Hunter
Gail J. McGovern
Johnny Taylor
David Thomas, Ph.D.
Kirt Walker
Dennis Woodside

EXECUTIVE LEADERSHIP

Chief Diversity Officer.—Floyd Pitts.
Chief Human Resources Officer.—Melissa B. Hurst.
Chief Innovation Officer.—Sajit Joseph.
Chief Marketing Officer.—Neal Litvack.
Chief Public Affairs Officer.—Suzanne C. DeFrancis.
Chief Operating Officer.—Cliff Holtz.
Chief Transformation Officer.—Shaun P. Gilmore.
Corporate Ombudsman.—Jacqueline Villafañe.
President Biomedical Services.—James ''Chris'' Hrouda.
President Humanitarian Services.—Harvey Johnson.
President Training Services.—Jack McMaster.

GOVERNMENTAL RELATIONS

Senior Vice President for Government Relations.—Cherae L. Bishop.
Manager, Government Relations.—Jacqueline G. Bassermann.
Legislative Specialist, Government Relations.—Tiffany Del Rio.
Director, Government Relations.—Julie Manes.
Legislative Consultant, Government Relations.—Eric Mondero.
Director, Government Relations.—Christina McWilson Thomas.

APPALACHIAN REGIONAL COMMISSION

1666 Connecticut Avenue, NW., Washington, DC 20009

phone (202) 884–7660, fax 884–7693

Federal Co-Chair.—Tim Thomas.
Alternate Federal Co-Chair.—Vacant.
States' Washington Representative.—James Hyland.
Executive Director.—Charles Howard.
Chief of Staff.—Andrew Howard.

ARMED FORCES RETIREMENT HOME

3700 North Capitol Street, NW., Box 1303, Washington, DC 20011–8400

phone (202) 541–7532, fax 541–7506

Chief Operating Officer.—Lt. Col. James M. Branham, U.S. Army (Ret.).
Managing Director of Finance & Administration/CFO.—Nancy Anne Baugher.
Chief Information Officer.—Vacant.

ARMED FORCES RETIREMENT HOME—WASHINGTON

phone (202) 541–7536, fax 541–7588 or 7615

Administrator.—Susan Bryhan.

ARMED FORCES RETIREMENT HOME—GULFPORT

1800 Beach Drive, Gulfport, MS 39507

phone (228) 897–4408, fax 897–4488

Administrator.—Jeff Eads.

BOARD OF GOVERNORS OF THE FEDERAL RESERVE SYSTEM

Constitution Avenue and 20th Street, NW., Washington, DC 20551

phone (202) 452–3000

Chair.—Jerome H. Powell.
Vice Chair.—Randal K. Quarles.
Member.—Lael Brainard.

OFFICE OF BOARD MEMBERS

Assistant to the Board and Division Director.—Michelle A. Smith.
Assistants to the Board: Lucretia M. Boyer, Linda L. Robertson, David W. Skidmore.
Special Assistant to the Board.—Jennifer C. Gallagher.
Senior Special Adviser to the Chair.—Trevor A. Reeve.

DIVISION OF BANKING SUPERVISION AND REGULATION

Director.—Michael S. Gibson.
Deputy Directors: Jennifer Burns, Maryann F. Hunter.

Senior Associate Directors: Mary Aiken, Barbara J. Bouchard, Arthur W. Lindo, Steve Merriett, Todd Vermilyea.

Associate Directors: Kevin M. Bertsch, Sean Campbell, Nida Davis, Christopher Finger, Jeffery W. Gunther, Anna L. Hewko, Mike Hsu, Richard A. Naylor, Lisa H. Ryu, Michael Solomon, Thomas Sullivan.

Deputy Associate Directors: John Beebe, Constance M. Horsley, Ryan Lordos, David Lynch, Molly Mahar, Kirk Odegard, Catherine Piche, Laurie Priest, Suzanne L. Williams.

Assistant Directors: Robert Ashman, James Diggs, Kathleen Johnson, Keith Ligon, Susan Motyka, Steve Spurry, Catherine Tilford, Joanne Wakim, Donna Webb.

Senior Adviser.—Norah M. Barger.

Advisers: Ann McKeehan, William F. Treacy, Sarkis D. Yoghourtdjian.

DIVISION OF CONSUMER AND COMMUNITY AFFAIRS

Director.—Eric S. Belsky.

Deputy Director.—V. Nicole Bynum.

Senior Associate Directors: Anna Alvarez Boyd, Suzanne G. Killian.

Associate Directors: Carol A. Evans, Allen J. Fishbein, Phyllis L. Harwell, James A. Michaels.

Deputy Associate Directors: David E. Buchholz, Joseph Firschein, Marisa A. Reid.

DIVISION OF FEDERAL RESERVE BANK OPERATIONS AND PAYMENT SYSTEMS

Director.—Matthew J. Eichner.

Deputy Directors: Jeffrey C. Marquardt, David P. Sidari.

Senior Associate Directors: Marta Chaffee, Gregory L. Evans, Susan V. Foley.

Associate Directors: Michael J. Lambert, Lawrence Mize.

Deputy Associate Directors: Jennifer Chang, Jennifer A. Lucier, David C. Mills, Stuart E. Sperry.

Assistant Directors: Timothy W. Maas, Travis Nesmith, Mark Olechowski, Rebecca Royer, Jeffrey D. Walker.

Assistant Director.—Amy Burr (acting).

DIVISION OF INFORMATION TECHNOLOGY

Director.—Sharon L. Mowry.

Deputy Directors: Lisa Bell, Raymond Romero, Kofi Sapong.

Associate Directors: Glenn S. Eskow, Sheryl L. Warren, Rajasekhar R. Yelisetty.

Deputy Associate Directors: William K. Dennison, Marietta Murphy, Theresa C. Palya, Charles B. Young.

Assistant Directors: Tom Nguyen, Deborah Prespare, Jonathan Shrier, Eric Turner, Virginia M. Wall, Edgar Wang, Ivan Wun.

Adviser.—Tillena G. Clark.

DIVISION OF INTERNATIONAL FINANCE

Director.—Steve B. Kamin.

Deputy Directors: Thomas A. Connors, Beth Anne Wilson.

Senior Associate Director.—Christopher J. Erceg.

Associate Directors: Shaghil Ahmed, David H. Bowman, Mark S. Carey, Brian M. Doyle, Joseph W. Gruber, Charles P. Thomas.

Deputy Associate Directors: James A. Dahl, Sally M. Davies.

Assistant Directors: Carol Bertaut, Stephanie Curcuru, Matteo Iacoviello, Paul Wood.

Senior Adviser.—John H. Rogers.

DIVISION OF MONETARY AFFAIRS

Director.—Thomas Laubach.

Deputy Directors: James A. Clouse, Brian Madigan, Stephen A. Meyer.

Senior Associate Director.—Gretchen C. Weinbach.

Associate Directors: Margaret DeBoer, Jane E. Ihrig, David Lopez-Salido.

Deputy Associate Directors: Mary T. Hoffman, Matthew M. Luecke, Min Wei.

Assistant Directors: Christopher Gust, Elizabeth Klee, Laura Lipscomb, Jason Wu.
Senior Advisers: Antulio Bomfim, Ellen Meade, Edward Nelson, Robert Tetlow, Egon Zakrajsek, Joyce K. Zickler.
Advisers: Eric C. Engstrom, Don Kim.

DIVISION OF RESEARCH AND STATISTICS

Director.—David Wilcox.
Deputy Directors: Jeff Campione, Daniel Covitz, William L. Wascher III.
Senior Associate Directors: Eric M. Engen, Joshua H. Gallin, Diana Hancock, David E. Lebow, Michael G. Palumbo.
Associate Directors: Elizabeth K. Kiser, John J. Stevens, Stacey M. Tevlin.
Deputy Associate Directors: Timothy Mullen, Steven A. Sharpe.
Assistant Directors: Stephanie Aaronson, Burcu Duygan-Bump, J. Andrew Figura, Glenn Follette, Erik Heitfield, Normin Morin, Karen M. Pence, John Sabelhaus, Shane M. Sherlund, Lillian Sewmaker, Paul Smith.
Senior Advisers: S. Wayne Passmore, Robin Prager, Jeremy Rudd.
Advisers: Eric C. Engstrom, Patrick McCabe, John M. Roberts.

INSPECTOR GENERAL

Inspector General.—Mark Bialek.
Deputy Inspector General.—J. Anthony Ogden.
Associate Inspectors General: Jacqueline M. Becker, Melissa Heist, Alberto Rivera-Journier, Lawrence Valett.
Assistant Inspectors General: Gerald Maye, Peter Sheridan.

LEGAL DIVISION

General Counsel.—Mark Van Der Weide.
Deputy General Counsels.—Richard M. Ashton.
Associate General Counsels: Stephanie Martin, Laurie S. Schaffer, Katherine H. Wheatley.
Assistant General Counsels: Jean C. Anderson, Patrick M. Bryan, Alye S. Foster, Benjamin McDonough, Alison M. Thro, Cary K. Williams.

MANAGEMENT DIVISION

Director.—Michell C. Clark.
Deputy Directors: Steven Miranda, Winona Varnon.
Senior Associate Directors: Tameika Pope, Marie S. Savoy.
Deputy Associate Director.—Reginald V. Roach.
Associate Directors: Curtis Eldridge, Catherine Jack, Tara Tinsley Pelitere.
Assistant Directors: Keith F. Bates, Ann Buckingham, Timothy E. Markey, Jeffrey Martin, Stephen Pearson, Katherine Perez-Grines, Theresa A. Trimble.

OFFICE OF THE SECRETARY

Secretary.—Ann E. Misback.
Deputy Secretary.—Margaret M. Shanks.
Associate Secretaries: Yao-Chin Chao, Michele T. Fennell.

DIVISION OF FINANCIAL STABILITY POLICY AND RESEARCH

Director.—Andreas W. Lehnert.
Deputy Director.—Michael T. Kiley.
Assistant Directors: William Bassett, Rochelle M. Edge, John Schindler.
Deputy Associate Director.—Luca Guerrieri.
Assistant Directors: Andrew Cohen, Jennifer Roush, Skander Van den Heuvel.

OFFICE OF THE CHIEF OPERATING OFFICER

Chief Operating Officer.—Donald V. Hammond.
Chief Data Officer.—Michael J. Kraemer.
ODI Program Director.—Sheila Clark.
Assistant Directors: Philip Daher, Todd A. Glissman, Jeff Monica.

DIVISION OF FINANCIAL MANAGEMENT

Director.—Ricardo A. Aguilera.
Deputy Director.—Stephen J. Bernard.
Associate Director.—Christine M. Fields.
Deputy Associate Directors: Jeffret R. Peirce, Karen Vassallo.
Senior Adviser.—Andrew Leonard.

CENTRAL INTELLIGENCE AGENCY

phone (703) 482–1100

Director.—Gina C. Haspel.
Deputy Director.—Vaughn Bishop.
Chief Operating Officer.—Andrew Markridis.
General Counsel.—Courtney S. Elwood.
Director of:
Analysis.—Cynthia ''Didi'' Rapp.
Congressional Affairs.—Jaime Cheshire.
Public Affairs.—Brittany Bramell.
Science and Technology.—Dawn C. Meyerriecks.
Support.—Elizabeth ''Betsy'' Davis.

COMMISSION OF FINE ARTS

National Building Museum, 401 F Street, NW., Suite 312, Washington, DC 20001–2728

phone (202) 504–2200, fax 504–2195, https://cfa.gov

Commissioners:
Earl A. Powell III, Washington, DC, *Chair.*
Elizabeth K. Meyer, Charlottesville, VA.
Alex Krieger, Boston, MA.
Liza Gilbert, Washington, DC.
Edward D. Dunson, Jr., Washington, DC.
Toni L. Griffin, New York, NY.
Justin Shubow, Silver Spring, MD.

Secretary.—Thomas Luebke, FAIA.
Assistant Secretary.—Frederick J. Lindstrom.

BOARD OF ARCHITECTURAL CONSULTANTS FOR THE OLD GEORGETOWN ACT

H. Alan Brangman, AIA, *Chair.*
Richard Williams, FAIA.
Mary Katherine Lanzillotta, FAIA.

COMMITTEE FOR PURCHASE FROM PEOPLE WHO ARE BLIND OR SEVERELY DISABLED

1401 S. Clark Street, Suite 715, Arlington, VA 22202–3259

phone (703) 603–2100, fax 603–0655

[Operating as U.S. AbilityOne Commission]

Chair.—Thomas D. Robinson.
Vice Chair.—Robert T. Kelly, Jr.
Executive Director.—Tina Ballard.
Members:

Vacant, Department of Education.
Vacant, Department of Veterans Affairs.
Stuart Hazlett, Department of Army.
Vacant, Department of Defense.
Thomas D. Robinson, Department of the Air Force.
Vacant, General Services Administration.
Vacant, Department of Agriculture.
Virna L. Winters, Department of Commerce.
Vacant, Department of the Navy.
James M. Kesteloot, Private Citizen (Obstacles to Employment of People Who Are Blind).
Vacant, (Nonprofit Agency Employees Who Are Blind).
Vacant, (Nonprofit Agency Employees with Other Severe Disabilities).
Robert T. Kelly, Jr., Private Citizen (Obstacles to Employment of People with Other Severe Disabilities).
Vacant, Department of Justice.
Jennifer Sheehy, Department of Labor.

COMMODITY FUTURES TRADING COMMISSION

Three Lafayette Centre, 1155 21st Street, NW., Washington, DC 20581

phone (202) 418–5000, fax 418–5521, https://cftc.gov

Chair.—Heath P. Tarbert, 418–5030, fax 418–5533.
Chief of Staff.—Michael Gill, 418–5713.
Senior Counsel.—Marcia Blasé, 418–5138.
Special Advisor.—Richard Danker, 418–5609.
Market Intelligence Advisor.—Andrew Busch (312) 596–0598.
Executive Assistant.—Shonneice Jones (202) 418–5770.
Commissioners: Rostin Behnam, 418–5575, fax 418–5067; Dan K. Berkovitz; Brian D. Quintenz, 418–5010, fax 418–5072; Dawn DeBerry Stump.
Special Counsel: John Dunfee, 418–5575; Laura Gardy, 418–5575.
Executive Assistant.—Kyndra Burke, 418–5575.
Chief of Staff.—Kevin Webb, 418–5010.
Executive Assistant.—Andrea Owens, 418–5010.
Director, Division of:
Clearing and Intermediary Oversight.—Eileen Flaherty (312) 596–0600.
Enforcement.—Jamie McDonald (202) 418–5637, fax 418–5523.
Market Oversight.—Amir Zaidi, 418–6770, fax 418–5527.
Executive Director.—Anthony C. Thompson, 418–5697, fax 418–5541.
Chief Economist.—Sayee Srinivasan, 418–5309, fax 418–5660.
General Counsel.—Daniel Davis, 418–5649, fax 418–5524.
Inspector General.—A. Roy Lavik, 418–5110, fax 418–5522.
Data and Technology Chief Information Officer.—John Rogers, 418–5240.
Director, Office of:
Diversity and Inclusion.—Lorena McElwain, 418–5935, fax 418–5546.
International Affairs.—Eric Pan, 418–5559, fax 418–5548.
Legislative Affairs.—Charlie Thornton, 418–5145, fax 418–5525.
Public Affairs.—Erica Elliott Richardson, 418–5382, fax 418–5525.
Office of the Secretariat, Secretary of the Commission.—Chris Kirkpatrick, 418–5100, fax 418–5521.

REGIONAL OFFICES

Central Region: 525 West Monroe Street, Suite 1100, Chicago, IL 60601 (312) 596–0700, fax 596–0716, TTY 596–0565.
Southwestern Region: 4900 Main Street, Suite 500, Kansas City, MO 64112 (816) 960–7700, fax 960–7750, TTY 960–7704.
Eastern Region: 140 Broadway, Nineteenth Floor, New York, NY 10005 (646) 746–9700, fax 746–9938, TTY 746–9820.

CONSUMER PRODUCT SAFETY COMMISSION

4330 East West Highway, Bethesda, MD 20814

phone (301) 504–7923, fax 504–0124, https://cpsc.gov

[Created by Public Law 92–573]

Chair.—Robert ''Bob'' Adler (acting), (301) 504–7731.

Commissioners: Dana Baiocco, 504–7338; Peter Feldman, 504–7892; Elliot Kaye, 504–7900.

Executive Director.—Mary Boyle, 504–7582.

Deputy Executive Director for Operations Support.—Monica Summit, 504–7691.

Deputy Executive Director for Safety Operations.—DeWane Ray, 504–7547.

Director, Office of the Secretariat.—Abioye Moshiem, 504–7454.

Director, Office of Legislative Affairs.—Christopher Hudgins, 504–7853.

General Counsel.—John ''Gib'' Mullan (acting), 504–7066.

CORPORATION FOR NATIONAL AND COMMUNITY SERVICE

250 E Street, SW., Washington, DC 20525

phone (202) 606–5000, https://cns.gov

[Executive Order 11603, June 30, 1971; codified in 42 U.S.C., section 4951]

Chief Executive Officer.—Barbara Stewart.

Chief of Staff.—Brian Finch (acting).

Chief Financial Officer.—Robert McCarty, 606–6652.

Director of:

AmeriCorps National Civilian Community Corps.—Gina Cross (acting), 606–3233.

AmeriCorps State and National.—Chester Spellman, 606–6991.

AmeriCorps VISTA.—Desiree Tucker-Sorini, 606–6992.

Office of Government Relations.—Bo Bryant, 606–6707.

Senior Corps.—Deborah Cox-Roush, 606–6634.

General Counsel.—Tim Noelker, 606–6985.

DEFENSE NUCLEAR FACILITIES SAFETY BOARD

625 Indiana Avenue, NW., Suite 700, Washington, DC 20004

phone (202) 694–7000, fax 208–6518, https://dnfsb.gov

Chair.—Bruce Hamilton.

Vice Chair.—Vacant.

Members: Joyce Connery, Jessie Roberson.

General Counsel.—Joseph Gilman (acting).

General Manager.—Glenn Sklar.

Technical Director.—Christopher Roscetti.

DELAWARE RIVER BASIN COMMISSION

25 Cosey Road, P.O. Box 7360, West Trenton, NJ 08628–0360

phone (609) 883–9500, fax 883–9522, https://drbc.net

[Created by Public Law 87–328]

FEDERAL REPRESENTATIVES

Federal Commissioner.—Brig. Gen. Thomas J. Tickner, Commanding General and Division Engineer, U.S. Army Corps of Engineers, North Atlantic Division (347) 370–4501.

First Alternate.—LTC David C. Park, Philadelphia District Commander, U.S. Army Corps of Engineers, Philadelphia (215) 656–6501.

Second Alternate.—Alternate Pending, Regional Director of Programs, U.S. Army Corps of Engineers, North Atlantic Division, 370–4629.

Third Alternate.—Henry W. Gruber, Deputy Chief, Civil Planning and Project Formulation Center, Planning and Policy Division, U.S. Army Corps of Engineers, North Atlantic Division, 370–4566.

STAFF

Executive Director.—Steven J. Tambini, ext. 200.

Commission Secretary/Assistant General Counsel.—Pamela M. Bush, J.D., M.R.P., ext. 203.
External Affairs and Communications Director.—Peter Eschbach, ext. 208.

DELAWARE REPRESENTATIVES

State Commissioner.—John C. Carney, Governor (302) 744–4101.
First Alternate.—Shawn M. Garvin, Secretary, Delaware Department of Natural Resources and Environmental Control (DNREC), 739–9000.
Second Alternate.—Alternate Pending, Deputy Secretary, Division of Water Resources (DNREC), 739–9949.
Third Alternate.—Virgil R. Holmes, Director, Division of Water Management Section (DNREC), 739–9949.
Fourth Alternate.—Bryan A. Ashby, Program Manager, Surface Water Section (DNREC), 739–9946.

NEW JERSEY REPRESENTATIVES

State Commissioner.—Philip D. Murphy, Governor (609) 292–6000.
First Alternate.—Catherine R. McCabe, Commissioner, New Jersey Department of Environmental Protection (NJDEP), 292–2885.
Second Alternate.—Michele M. Putnam, Assistant Commissioner, Water Resource Management (NJDEP), 292–4543.
Third Alternate.—Jeffrey L. Hoffman, P.G., State Geologist, New Jersey Geological and Water Survey, Division of Water Supply and Geoscience (NJDEP), 292–1185.

NEW YORK REPRESENTATIVES

State Commissioner.—Andrew M. Cuomo, Governor (518) 474–8390.
First Alternate.—Basil Seggos, Commissioner, New York State Department of Environmental Conservation (NYSDEC), (518) 402–8540.
Second Alternate.—Mark Klotz, P.E., Director, Division of Water (NYSDEC), 402–8233.
Third Alternate.—Vacant.
Fourth Alternate.—Kenneth Kosinski, P.E., Chief, Watershed Implementation Section (NYSDEC), 402–8110.

PENNSYLVANIA REPRESENTATIVES

State Commissioner.—Tom Wolf, Governor (717) 787–2500.
First Alternate.—Patrick McDonnell, Secretary, Pennsylvania Department of Environmental Protection (PADEP), 787–2814.
Second Alternate.—Aneca Y. Atkinson, Deputy Secretary, Office of Water Programs (PADEP), 783–2950.
Third Alternate.—Vacant.

ENVIRONMENTAL PROTECTION AGENCY

1200 Pennsylvania Avenue, NW., Washington, DC 20460

phone (202) 564–4700, https://epa.gov

Administrator.—Andrew Wheeler, 564–4700.
Deputy Administrator.—Vacant, 564–4700.
Chief of Staff.—Ryan Jackson, 564–6999.
Deputy Chief of Staff.—Kevin Debell (acting), 566–1931.
White House Liaison.—Kaitlyn Shimmin, 564–4108.
Environmental Appeals Board: Mary Kay Lynch, 233–0122.
Associate Administrator for—
Congressional and Intergovernmental Relations.—Joseph Brazauskas, 564–5200.
Homeland Security.—Ted Stanich, 564–5484
Policy.—Brittany Bolen, 564–4332
Public Affairs.—Corry Schiermeyer, 564–6782.
Public Engagement and Environmental Education/Agricultural Advisor.—Tate Bennett, 564–1785.
Director, Office of:
Children's Health Protection.—Jeanne Briskin, 564–2188.
Civil Rights.—Vicki Simons, 564–7272.

Cooperative Environmental Management.—Vacant.
Executive Secretariat.—Elizabeth White, 564–7311.
Executive Services.—Lance McCluney (acting), 564–0444.
Science Advisory Board.—Thomas Brennan, 564–2221.
Small and Disadvantaged Business Utilization.—Denise Benjamin-Sirmons, 564–2075.
Director of Management, Office of Administrative Law Judges.—Susan Biro, 564–6255.

OFFICE OF MISSION SUPPORT

Assistant Administrator.—Vacant, 564–4600.
Principal Deputy Assistant Administrator.—Donna Vizian, 564–4600.

AIR AND RADIATION

Assistant Administrator.—Anne Idsal (acting), 564–7404.
Deputy Assistant Administrator for Policy.—Karl Moor, 564–7400.
Deputy Assistant Administrator.—Betsy Shaw, 564–7400.

ENFORCEMENT AND COMPLIANCE ASSURANCE

Assistant Administrator.—Susan Bodine, 564–2440.
Principal Deputy Assistant Administrator.—Larry Starfield, 564–2440.
Deputy Assistant Administrator.—John Irving, 564–2440.

CHIEF FINANCIAL OFFICER

Chief Financial Officer.—David Bloom (acting), 564–1151.
Associate Chief Financial Officer.—Carol Terris, 564–1152.

GENERAL COUNSEL

General Counsel.—Matthew Z. Leopold, 564–8040.
Principal Deputy General Counsel.—David Fotouhi, 564–8064.

INSPECTOR GENERAL

Inspector General.—Sean O'Donnell, 566–0847.
Deputy Inspector General.—Charles Sheehan, 566–0847.

INTERNATIONAL AFFAIRS

Assistant Administrator.—William ''Chad'' McIntosh 564–6600.
Deputy Assistant Administrator.—Jane Nishida, 564–6600.

CHEMICAL SAFETY AND POLLUTION PREVENTION

Assistant Administrator.—Alexandra ''Alex'' Dunn, 564–2910.
Deputy Assistant Administrator.—David Fisher, 564–2910.

RESEARCH AND DEVELOPMENT

Assistant Administrator.—Vacant, 564–6620.
Deputy Assistant Administrator of Science.—Jennifer Orme-Zavaleta, 564–6620.
Deputy Assistant Administrator of Science Policy.—David Dunlap, 564–6620.

LAND AND EMERGENCY RESPONSE

Assistant Administrator.—Peter Wright, 566–0200.
Principal Deputy Assistant Administrator.—Barry Breen, 566–0200.
Deputy Assistant Administrator.—Steven Cook, 566–0200.

WATER

Assistant Administrator.—Dave Ross, 564–5700.

Principal Deputy Assistant Administrator.—Anna Wilderman, 564–5700.
Deputy Assistant Administrator.—Lee Forsgren, 564–5700.

REGIONAL ADMINISTRATION

Region I, Boston.—Connecticut, Maine, New Hampshire, Rhode Island, Vermont.
Regional Administrator.—Dennis Deziel, One Congress Street, Suite 1100, Boston, MA 02114 (617) 918–1011.
Public Affairs.—Doug Gutro (617) 918–1011.

Region II, New York City.—New Jersey, New York, Puerto Rico, Virgin Islands.
Regional Administrator.—Pete Lopez, 290 Broadway, New York, NY 10007 (212) 637–5000.
Public Affairs.—Mary Mears (212) 637–3660.

Region III, Philadelphia.—Delaware, Washington DC, Maryland, Pennsylvania, Virginia, West Virginia.
Regional Administrator.—Cosmo Servidio, 1650 Arch Street, Philadelphia, PA 19103–2029 (215) 814–2900.
Public Affairs.—Chad Nitsch, (215) 814–2900.

Region IV, Atlanta.—Alabama, Florida, Georgia, Kentucky, Mississippi, North Carolina, South Carolina, Tennessee.
Regional Administrator.—Mary Walker, 61 Forsyth Street, SW., Atlanta, GA 30303–8960 (404) 562–8357.
Public Affairs.—Brandi Jenkins, (404) 562–8327.

Region V, Chicago.—Illinois, Indiana, Michigan, Minnesota, Ohio, Wisconsin.
Regional Administrator.—Kurt Thiede, 77 West Jackson Boulevard, Chicago, IL 60604–3507 (312) 886–3000.
Public Affairs.—Jeff Kelley (312) 886–3000.

Region VI, Dallas.—Arkansas, Louisiana, New Mexico, Oklahoma, Texas.
Regional Administrator.—Kenley ''Ken'' McQueen, 1201 Elm Street, Dallas, TX 75270–2102 (214) 665–2100.
Public Affairs.—Jeffrey ''Jeff'' McAtee (214) 665–2200.

Region VII, Kansas City.—Iowa, Kansas, Missouri, Nebraska.
Regional Administrator.—Jim Gulliford, 901 North 5th Street, Kansas City, MO 66101 (913) 551–7006.
Public Affairs.—Curtis Carey (913) 551–7003.

Region VIII, Denver.—Colorado, Montana, North Dakota, South Dakota, Utah, Wyoming.
Regional Administrator.—Gregory E. Sopkin, 999 18th Street, Suite 300, Denver, CO 80202–2466 (303) 312–6407.
Public Affairs.—Andrew Mutter (303) 312–6448.

Region IX, San Francisco.—Arizona, California, Hawaii, Nevada, American Samoa, Guam.
Regional Administrator.—Mike Stoker, 75 Hawthorne Street, San Francisco, CA 94105 (415) 947–8702.
Public Affairs.—Michael ''Mike'' Alpern, (415) 947–8702.

Region X, Seattle.—Alaska, Idaho, Oregon, Washington.
Regional Administrator.—Chris Hladick, 1200 Sixth Avenue, Seattle, WA 98101 (206) 553–1234.
Public Affairs.—Marianne Holsman (206) 553–1234.

EQUAL EMPLOYMENT OPPORTUNITY COMMISSION

131 M Street, NE., Washington, DC 20507

phone (202) 663–4900

Chair.—Janet Dhillon, Suite 6NW20C, 663–4001, fax 663–4110.
Chief Operating Officer.—Vacant.
Deputy Chief Operating Officer.—Mona Papillon, Suite 6NW12B, 663–4001.
Confidential Assistant.—Vacant.
Commissioners: Charlotte A. Burrows, Suite 6NE27B, 663–4052, fax 663–4108; Victoria Lipnic, Suite 6NE37B, 663–4099, fax 663–7086; Vacant; Vacant.
General Counsel.—Sharon Gustafon, 5th Floor, 663–4702, fax 663–4196.
Legal Counsel.—Kean Bhirud, 5th Floor, 663–4637, fax 663–4679.
Director, Office of:
Chief Financial Officer.—Grace Zhao, 4th Floor, 663–4200, fax 663–7068.

Communications and Legislative Affairs.—Brett Brenner (acting), 6th Floor, 663–4191, fax 663–4912.
Equal Opportunity.—Stan Pietrusiak (acting), 6th Floor, 663–7081, fax 663–7003.
Executive Secretariat/Executive Secretary.—Bernadette Wilson, 6th Floor, 663–4070, fax 663–4114.
Field Operations.—Carlton Hadden, 5th Floor, 663–4599, fax 663–7022.
Field Programs.—Nicholas Inzeo, 5th Floor, 663–4801, fax 663–7190.
Human Resources.—Kevin Richardson, 4th Floor, 663–4059, fax 663–4324.
Information Technology.—Bryan Burnett, 4th Floor, 663–4447, fax 663–4451.
Inspector General.—Milton Mayo, 6th Floor, 663–4327, fax 663–7204.
Research, Information, and Planning.—Chris Haffer, 4th Floor, 663–4953, fax 663–4093.

EXPORT-IMPORT BANK OF THE UNITED STATES

811 Vermont Avenue, NW., Washington, DC 20571

phone (202) 565–3230, fax (202) 565–3236

https://exim.gov, OCIA@exim.gov

President and Chairman of Board.—Kimberly A. Reed, 565–3500.
First Vice President and Vice Chair of Board.—Vacant.
Board of Directors Members: Spencer Bachus, III, 565–3540; Judith Pryor, 565–3520; Vacant.
Senior Vice President and:
Chief of Staff.—David Fogel.
Chief Banking Officer.—Stephen Renna.
Chief Ethics Officer.—Lisa V. Terry.
Chief Financial Officer.—Inci Tonguch-Murray (acting).
Chief Management Officer.—Adam Martinez (acting).
Chief Risk Officer.—Kenneth M. Tinsley.
General Counsel.—David Slade.
Senior Vice President of:
Board Authorized Finance.—David M. Sena.
Communications and Marketing.—Jennifer Hazelton.
Congressional and Intergovernmental Affairs.—Ross Branson.
External Engagement.—Luke Lindberg.
Information Management and Technology and Chief Information Officer.—Howard Spira.
Strategy and Performance.—Michele A. Kuester.
Policy Analysis and International Relations.—James C. Cruse.
Resource Management.—Vacant.
Small Business.—James G. Burrows.
Senior Advisor to the President and Chairman.—Lauren Fuller.
Senior Advisor for National Security.—Jamal Ware.

OFFICE OF INSPECTOR GENERAL

Inspector General.—Jennifer L. Fain (acting) (202) 565–3908.
Deputy Inspector General.—Vacant, 565–3908.

FARM CREDIT ADMINISTRATION

1501 Farm Credit Drive, McLean, VA 22102–5090

phone (703) 883–4000, fax 734–5784

[Reorganization pursuant to Public Law 99–205, December 23, 1985]

Board Chair and Chief Executive Officer.—Glen R. Smith.
Board Member.—Jeffery S. Hall.
Secretary to the Board.—Dale L. Aultman, 883–4009, fax 883–4181.
Chief Financial Officer.—Stephen G. Smith, 883–4275, fax 883–4151.
Chief Human Capital Officer.—Vonda K. Bell, 883–4200, fax 883–4151.
Chief Information Officer.—Jerald Golley, 883–4444, fax 734–1950.
Chief Operating Officer.—Samuel R. Coleman, 883–4340, fax 883–4246.
Director, Office of:
Agency Services.—Vonda K. Bell, 883–4200, fax 883–4151.

Congressional and Public Affairs.—Michael A. Stokke, 883–4056, fax 790–3260.
Equal Employment Opportunity and Inclusion.—Thais Burlew, 883–4290, fax 790–3260.
Examination.—Roger Paulsen, 883–4160, fax 893–2978.
Regulatory Policy.—David Grahn, 883–4414, fax 883–4477.
Secondary Market Oversight.—Laurie Rea, 883–4280, fax 790–3260.
General Counsel.—Charles R. Rawls, 883–4020, fax 790–0052.
Inspector General.—Wendy LaGuarda, 883–4030, fax 883–4059.

FEDERAL COMMUNICATIONS COMMISSION

445 12th Street, SW., Washington, DC 20554

phone (202) 418–0200, https://fcc.gov

FCC National Consumer Center: 1 (888) 225–5322 / 1 (888) 835–5322 (TTY)

Chair.—Ajit Pai.
Confidential Assistant to the Chairman.—Montana Hyde.
Chief of Staff.—Matthew Berry.
Senior Counselor to the Chair.—Nicholas Degani.
Special Counsel.—Michael Carowitz.
Policy Advisor.—Nathan Leamer.
Legal Advisors: Aaron Goldberger, Zenji Nakazawa, Niral Patel, Alexander Sanjenis, Preston Wise.
Executive Assistants: Deanne Erwin, Andi Roane.
Staff Assistant.—Carlos Minnix.
Commissioner.—Michael P. O'Rielly.
Chief of Staff, Media Legal Advisor.—Joel Miller.
Wireless Legal Advisors: Erin McGrath, Arielle Roth.
Confidential Assistant.—Susan Fisenne.
Staff Assistant.—Ovonda Walker.
Commissioner.—Brendan Carr.
Chief of Staff.—Vacant.
Legal Advisors: Will Adams, Evan Swarztrauber.
Confidential Assistant.—Drema Johnson.
Commissioner.—Jessica Rosenworcel.
Chief of Staff.—Travis Litman.
Legal Advisor.—Umair Javed.
Policy Advisor.—Kate Black.
Special Advisor.—Jessica Martinez.
Staff Assistant.—Aurelle Porter.
Commissioner.—Geoffrey Starks.
Chief of Staff and Legal Advisor.—Bill Davenport.
Legal Advisors: Randy Clarke (acting), Mike Scurato (acting).
Special Advisor.—Alisa Valintin.
Staff Assistant.—Rhonda Hill.

OFFICE OF ADMINISTRATIVE LAW JUDGES

Administrative Law Judge.—Jane Halprin, Room 1–C768, 418–1716.

OFFICE OF COMMUNICATIONS BUSINESS OPPORTUNITIES

Director.—Sanford Williams, Room 4–A760, 418–1508.

CONSUMER AND GOVERNMENTAL AFFAIRS BUREAU

Chief.—Patrick Webre, Room 5–C758, 418–0952.
Deputy Bureau Chiefs: Diane Burstein, Room 5–C755, 418–2388; Barbara Esbin, Room 5–A848, 418–0535; Mark Stone, Room 5–C754, 418–0816.
Associate Bureau Chief.—Eduard Bartholme, Room 5–A864, 418–1035.
Chief of Staff.—Zachary Champ, Room 5–C831, 418–1495.
Assistant Bureau Chief for Management.—Tamika Jackson, Room 5–A847, 418–0159.
Chief, Division of:
Consumer Affairs and Outreach.—Lyle Ishida, Room 4–A525, 418–0743.

Consumer Inquiries and Complaints.—Sharon Wright, Room 5–C818, 418–2898.
Consumer Policy.—Kurt Schroeder, Room 5–A844, 418–0966.
Web and Print Publishing.—Howard Parnell, Room 4–C456, 418–7280.
Chief, Office of:
Disability Rights.—Suzanne Singleton, Room 3–B431 (202) 510–9446.
Intergovernmental Affairs.—Gregory Cooke, Room 5–A630, 418–2351.
Office of Native Affairs and Policy.—Matthew Duchesne, Room 4–C763, 202–418–3629.
Reference Information Center.—Melissa Askew, Room CY–C203D, 418–0292.

ENFORCEMENT BUREAU

Chief.—Rosemary Harold, Room 3–C252, 418–7450.
Deputy Bureau Chiefs: Lisa Gelb, Room 3–C254, 418–7450; Christopher Killion, Room 3–C342, 418–1711; Keith Morgan, Room 3–C255, 418–7450; Phillip Rosario, Room 3–C250, 418–7450.
Assistant Bureau Chiefs: Pamela Gallant, Room 2–A622, 418–0614; Jeremy Marcus, Room 3–C163, 418–0059.
Chief, Division of:
Investigations and Hearings.—Jeffrey Gee, Room 4–C322, 418–7479.
Market Disputes Resolutions.—Rosemary McEnery, Room 4–C324, 418–7336.
Spectrum Enforcement.—Elizabeth Mumaw, Room 3–C366, 418–1381.
Telecommunications.—Kristi Thompson, Room 4–C220, 418–1318.
Field Director.—Ronald Ramage (acting), 678–293–3194.
Deputy Field Director.—Janet Moran, Room 4–A336, 418–7923.

OFFICE OF ECONOMICS AND ANALYTICS

Chief.—Giulia McHenry (acting), Room 7–C450, 418–2105.
Associate Chiefs: Patrick DeGraba, Room 7–C360, 418–0948; Eric Ralph, Room 7–A669, 418–0771; Andrew Wise, Room 7–A761, 418–7026.
Chief of Staff.—Rachel Kazan (acting), Room 7–C452, 418–0651.
Chief Economist.—Jeff Prince, Room 7–C410, 418–0219.
Deputy Chief Economist.—Jonathan Levy, Room 7–C362, 418–2048.
Chief Technology Officer.—Eric Burger, Room 7–C247, 418–0267.
Chief, Division of:
Auctions.—Margaret Wiener, Room 6–A466, 418–2176.
Data.—Steven Rosenberg (Acting), Room 5–C356, 418–3614.
Economic Analysis.—Emily Talaga, Room 7–A760, 418–7396.
Industry Analysis.—Kenneth Lynch, Room 6–A462, 418–7356.
Assistant Office Chief.—Michael Janson (acting), Room 6–A361, 418–0627.
Assistant Bureau Chief, Administration.—Larry Shields (acting), Room 1–A265, 418–7537.

OFFICE OF ENGINEERING AND TECHNOLOGY

Chief.—Julius P. Knapp, Room 7–C155, 418–2470.

OFFICE OF GENERAL COUNSEL

General Counsel.—Thomas Johnson, Jr., Room 8–C750, 418–1744.
Deputy General Counsel: Ashley Boizelle, Room 8–C755, 418–1736; Michael Carlson, Room 8–C830, 418–2792; Michele Ellison, Room 8–C712, 418–1718; David Gossett, Room 8–C758, 418–0980.
Associate General Counsel.—Karen Onyeije, Room 8–C758, 418–1757.
Senior Counsel.—James R. Bird, Room 8–C862, 418–7802.
Senior Counsel to the General Counsel.—John Williams, Room 8–C860, 418–1747.

OFFICE OF INSPECTOR GENERAL

Inspector General.—David L. Hunt, Room 2–C347, 418–0470.

INTERNATIONAL BUREAU

Chief.—Thomas P. Sullivan, Room 6–C750, 418–0437.

Deputy Chiefs: Nese Guendelsberger, Roon 6–C746, 418–0634; Jim Schlichting, Room 6–C752, 418–1547; Troy Tanner, Room 6–C475, 418–1475.
Chief, Division of:
Telecommunications and Analysis Division.—Denise Coca, Room 7–A760, 418–0574.
Satellite Division.—Jose Albuquerque, Room 6–A665, 418–2288.
Strategic Analysis and Negotiations Division.—Olga Madruga Forti, Room 6–A763, 418–2489.

OFFICE OF LEGISLATIVE AFFAIRS

Director.—Timothy Strachan, Room 8–C453, 418–2242.
Deputy Director.—James ''Jim'' Balaguer, Room 8–C464, 418–1915.

OFFICE OF MANAGING DIRECTOR

Managing Director.—Mark Stephens, Room 1–C152, 418–0817.
Deputy Managing Director.—Mindy Ginsburg, Room 1–C154, 418–0983.
Associate Managing Directors:
Chief Administrative Officer.—MaryKay Mitchell, Room 1–C402, 418–2173.
Financial Operations.—James Lyons (acting), 418–7749.
Information Technology.—John Skudlarek (acting), Room 1–C261, 418–0859.
Performance Evaluations and Records Management.—Vanessa Lamb, Room 1–C804, 418–7044.
Secretary.—Marlene Dortch, Room TW–B204, 418–0300.
Chief, Human Capital Office.—Tom Green, Room 1–A100, 418–0293, TTY 202–481–0150 (employment verification).

OFFICE OF MEDIA RELATIONS

Director.—Brian Hart, Room CY–C314B, 418–0505.
Deputy Director.—Mark Wigfield, Room CY–C314C, 418–0253.

MEDIA BUREAU

Chief.—Michelle Carey, Room 3–C486, 418–7200.
Deputy Bureau Chiefs: Holly Sauer, Room 3–C742, 418–7200, Sarah Whitesell, Room 3–C740, 418–7200.
Chief of Staff.—Thomas Horan, Room 3–C478, 418–7200.
Assistant Bureau Chief for Management.—India Malcolm, Room 3–C838, 418–7200.
Chief, Division of:
Audio Division.—Albert Shuldiner, Room 2–A360, 418–2700.
Engineering Division.—John Wong, Room 4–C838, 418–7012.
Industry Analysis Division.—Brendan Holland, Room 2–C360, 418–2330.
Policy Division.—Martha Heller, Room 4–A766, 418–2120.
Video Division.—Barbara A. Kreisman, Room 2–A666, 418–1600.

PUBLIC SAFETY AND HOMELAND SECURITY BUREAU

Chief.—Lisa M. Fowlkes, Room 7–C485, 418–7452.
Deputy Chiefs: David Furth, Room 7–C753, 418–0632; Debra Jordan, Room 7–C751, 418–0676; Nicole McGinnis, Room 7–C745, 418–2877.
Chief of Staff.—Lauren Kravetz, Room 7–C737, 418–7944.
Associate Chiefs: Jeffery Goldthorp, Room 7–A325, 418–1096; Anita Patankar-Stoll, Room 7–C749, 418–7121.
Chief Technologist.—Kenneth Carlberg, Room 7–C841, 418–0214.
Senior Counsel.—Erika Olsen, Room 7–B443, 418–2868.
Special Counsel.—Renee Roland, Room 3–A232, 418–2357.
Media Director.—Rochelle Cohen, Room 7–C747, 418–1162.
Assistant Bureau Chief for Management.—Ronnie Banks, Room 7–A630, 418–1099.
Chief, Division of:
Cybersecurity and Communications Reliability.—Austin Randazzo, Room 7–A325, 418–1462.
Operations and Emergency Management.—Chris Anderson, Room 7–C838, 418–1104.

Policy and Licensing.—Michael Wilhelm, Room 7–A848, 418–0870.

WIRELESS TELECOMMUNICATIONS BUREAU

Bureau Chief.—Donald Stockdale, Room 6–C160, 418–0600.
Deputy Bureau Chief and Chief of Staff.—Dana Shaffer, Room 6–C140, 418–0832.
Deputy Bureau Chiefs: Jean Kiddoo, Room 7–C252, 418–7757; Joel Taubenblatt, Room 6–C260, 418–1513; Suzanne Tetreault, Room 6–C164, 418–1769.
Associate Bureau Chiefs: Aaron Goldberger, Room 6–C120, 418–2607; Charles Mathias, Room 6–C110, 418–7147.
Assistant Bureau Chief.—Matthew Pearle, Room 6–C120, 418–2607.
Assistant Bureau Chief for Management.—Johnny Drake, Room 6–A223, 418–7328.
Chief Engineer.—Kenneth Baker, Room 6–C210, 418–0585.
Chief, Division of:
Broadband.—Blaise Scinto, Room 3–C124, 418–2487.
Competition and Infrastructure Policy.—Garnet Hanly, Room 6–A160, 418–0995.
Mobility.—Roger Noel, Room 2–B554, 418–0698.
Technology, Systems, and Innovation.—Diane Dupert, Gettysburg, PA (717) 338–2512.

WIRELINE COMPETITION BUREAU

Chief.—Kris Monteith, Room 5–C450, 418–1500.
Deputy Bureau Chief.—Lisa Hone, Room 5–C356, 418–1500; Trent Harkrader, Room 5–C352, 418–1500.
Associate Bureau Chiefs: Daniel Kahn, Room 5–C413, 418–1500; Sue McNeil, Room 5–C441, 418–1500; Terri Natoli, Room 5–C360, 418–1500; D'wana Terry, Room 5–C441, 418–1500.
Chief of Staff.—Kirk Burgee, Room 5–C354, 418–1500.
Legal Advisors: Irina Asoskov, Room 5–C453, 418–1500, Justin Fauth, Room 5–C434, 418–1500, Jese Jachman, Room 5–B451, 418–1500.
Economic Advisor.—Allison Baker, Room 5–C330, 418–0119.

OFFICE OF WORKPLACE DIVERSITY

Director.—Larry Hudson, Room 1–C861, 418–0591.
Deputy Director.—Ramona Mann, Room 1–C764, 418–7298.

REGIONAL AND FIELD OFFICES

Region 1: David Dombrowski, Columbia Office, Columbia, MD; Boston Office, Quincy, MA; Chicago Office, Park Ridge, IL; New York Office, New York, NY.
Region 2: Ronald Ramage, Powder Springs, GA; Atlanta Office, Duluth, GA; Dallas Office, Dallas, TX; Miami Office, Sunrise, FL; New Orleans Office, Metairie, LA.
Region 3: Lark Hadley, Los Angeles Offices, Cerritos, CA; Denver Office, Lakewood, CO.

FEDERAL DEPOSIT INSURANCE CORPORATION

550 17th Street, NW., Washington, DC 20429

phone (877) 275–3342, https://fdic.gov

Chair.—Jelena McWilliams, 898–3888.
Deputy to the Chair and Chief Operating Officer.—Arleas Upton Kea (703) 562–2100.
Deputy to the Chair and Chief Financial Officer.—Bret Edwards, 898–6525.
Vice Chair.—Vacant.
Deputy to the Vice Chair.—Vacant.
Director (Appointive).—Martin J. Gruenberg, 898–3888.
Deputy to the Director (Appointive).—Kym Copa, 898–8832.
Director (OCC).—Brian P. Brooks, 874–4900.
Deputy to the Director (OCC).—William Rowe, 898–6960.
Director (CFPB).—Kathleen Laura Kraninger, 435–9637.
Deputy to the Director (CFPB).—Stephanie Richo, 435–9307.
Director, Office of Legislative Affairs.—M. Andy Jiminez, 898–6761, fax 898–3745.

FEDERAL ELECTION COMMISSION

999 E Street, NW., Washington, DC 20463

phone (202) 694–1000, Toll Free (800) 424–9530, fax 219–3880

https://fec.gov

Chair.—James E. ''Trey'' Trainor III, 694–1035.
Vice Chairman.—Steven T. Walther.
Commissioners: Ellen L. Weintraub, 694–1045; Vacant, 694–1055.
Staff Director.—D. Alec Palmer, 694–1007, fax 219–2338.
Deputy Staff Director for—
Communications.—Vacant.
Compliance / Chief Compliance Officer.—Patricia C. Orrock, 694–1150.
Information Technology / Chief Information Officer.—D. Alec Palmer, 694–1250.
Management and Administration.—Katie Higginbothom, 694–1007.
Assistant Staff Director for Public Disclosure and Media Relations.—Judith Ingram, 694–1220.
Assistant Staff Director for Information Division.—Greg J. Scott, 694–1100.
Director for Congressional, Legislative, and Intergovernmental Affairs.—J. Duane Pugh, 694–1006.
Director Human Resources.—Lauren Lien, 694–1080.
Administrative Officer.—India K. Robinson, 694–1240.
EEO Director.—Kevin Salley, 694–1229.
General Counsel.—Lisa J. Stevenson (acting), 694–1650.
Deputy General Counsel for Administration.—Gregory R. Baker, 694–1650.
Deputy General Counsel for Law.—Lisa J. Stevenson, 694–1650.
Associate General Counsel for—
Enforcement.—Charles Kitcher (acting), 694–1650.
Litigation.—Kevin Deeley, 694–1650.
Policy.—Neven F. Stipanovic, 694–1650.
Library Director (Law).—Vacant.
Chief Financial Officer.—Jon Quinlan, 694–1217.
Deputy Chief Financial Officer / Budget Director.—Gilbert Ford, 694–1216.
Director of Accounting.—Nida Awan (acting), 694–1639.
Inspector General.—Christopher L. Skinner, 694–1015.
Deputy Inspector General.—Vacant.

FEDERAL HOUSING FINANCE AGENCY

400 7th Street, NW., Washington, DC 20024

phone (202) 649–3800, fax 649–1017, https://fhfa.gov

[Created by Housing and Economic Recovery Act of 2008, 122 Stat. 2654, Public Law 110–289—July 30, 2008]

Director.—Mark A. Calabria, 649–3001.
Chief of Staff.—John Roscoe, 649–3001.
Principal Deputy Director.—Adolfo Marzol, 649–3001.
Deputy Director, Division of:
Bank Regulation.—Andre Galeano, 649–3500.
Enterprise Regulation.—Nina Nichols, 649–3265.
Housing, Mission and Goals.—Sandra Thompson, 649–3384.
General Counsel.—Alfred Pollard, 649–3050.
Senior Deputy General Counsel.—Christopher Curtis, 649–3051.
Senior Associate Director, Conservatorship.—Robert Fishman, 649–3527.

OFFICE OF CONGRESSIONAL AFFAIRS AND COMMUNICATIONS

Director of External Relations.—Sheila Greenwood, 649–3017.
Director of Legislative Affairs.—Sarah Merchak, 649–3688.
Congressional Affairs Staff: Gabriel Bitol, 649–3506; Julian Colbert, 649–3318; Matthew Grinney, 649–3021; Jeannine Schroeder, 649–3029; Dion Spencer, 649–3207.
Supervisory Communications Specialist.—Cynthia Adcock, 649–3753.
Public Affairs Staff: Stefanie Johnson, 649–3030; Corinne Russell, 649–3032.

Executive Advisor for Consumer Communications.—Dion Spencer (acting), 649–3207.
Ombudsman.—John Roscoe (acting), (888) 665–1474.
Associate Director for the Office of Minority and Women Inclusion.—Sharron Levine, 649–3496.
Chief Operating Officer.—Lawrence Stauffer (acting), 649–3402.
Chief Information Officer.—Kevin Winkler, 649–3600.
Inspector General.—Laura S. Wertheimer (800) 793–7724.

FEDERAL LABOR RELATIONS AUTHORITY

1400 K Street, NW., Washington, DC 20424–0001

phone (202) 218–7770, fax 482–6778

FLRA Agency Head.—Colleen Duffy Kiko, 218–7900.
Executive Director.—Michael W. Jeffries, 218–7982.
Director of Legislative Affairs.—Richard P. Burkard, 218–7927.
Solicitor.—Noah B. Peters, 218–7908.
Inspector General.—Dana Rooney, 218–7970.
Foreign Service Impasse Disputes Panel (FSIDP).—Mark A. Carter, Chairman, 218–7790.
Foreign Service Labor Relations Board Chairman.—Colleen Duffy Kiko, 218–7900.

AUTHORITY

Chairman.—Colleen Duffy Kiko, 218–7900.
Chief Counsel.—Anna Molpus, 218–7900.
Member.—Ernest DuBester, 218–7920.
Chief Counsel.—Kurt Rumsfeld, 218–7920.
Member.—James T. Abbott, 218–7930.
Chief Counsel.—Tabitha Mack, 218–7930.
Chief, Case Intake and Publication.—Emily Sloop, 218–7740.

GENERAL COUNSEL OF THE FLRA

General Counsel.—Vacant, 218–7910.
Deputy General Counsel.—Charlotte A. Dye, 218–7910.
Assistant General Counsel for Advice and Legal Policy.—Vacant, 218–7910.
Assistant General Counsel for Appeals.—Cabrina S. Smith, 218–7910.

OFFICE OF ADMINISTRATIVE LAW JUDGES

Chief Judge.—David Welch, 218–7950.

FEDERAL SERVICE IMPASSES PANEL (FSIP)

FSIP Chairman.—Mark A. Carter, 218–7790.
Executive Director.—Kimberly Moseley, 218–7790.

REGIONAL OFFICES

Regional Directors:
Atlanta.—Richard S. Jones, 225 Peachtree Street, Suite 1950, Atlanta, GA 30303 (404) 331–5300, fax: (404) 331–5280.
Chicago.—Sandra LeBold, 224 S. Michigan Avenue, Suite 445, Chicago, IL 60604 (312) 886–3465, fax: (312) 886–5977.
Denver.—Timothy ''Tim'' Sullivan, 1244 Speer Boulevard, Suite 446, Denver, CO 80204 (303) 844–5224, fax: (303) 844–2774.
San Francisco.—John R. Pannozzo, Jr., 901 Market Street, Suite 470, San Francisco, CA 94103 (415) 356–5000, fax: (415) 356–5017.
Washington, DC.—Jessica S. Bartlett, 1400 K Street, N.W., 2nd Flr., Washington, DC 20424 (202) 357–6029, fax: (202) 482–6724.

FEDERAL MARITIME COMMISSION

800 North Capitol Street, NW., Washington, DC 20573
phone (202) 523–5725, fax 523–0014

OFFICE OF THE CHAIR

Chair.—Michael A. Khouri, Room 1000, 523–5911.
Chief of Staff.—Mary T. Hoang.
Counsel.—John A. Moran.
Commissioner.—Carl W. Bentzel, 523–5723.
Counsel.—John Young.
Commissioner.—Rebecca F. Dye, Room 1038, 523–5715.
Counsel.—Robert M. Blair.
Commissioner.—Daniel B. Maffei, Room 1032, 523–5721.
Counsel.—Katharine Primosch.
Commissioner.—Louis E. Sola, Room 1044 (202) 523–5712.
Counsel.—Cory Cinque.

OFFICE OF THE SECRETARY

Secretary.—Rachel E. Dickon, Room 1046, 523–5725.

OFFICE OF EQUAL EMPLOYMENT OPPORTUNITY

Director.—Ebony Jarrett, Room 1052, 523–5859.

OFFICE OF THE GENERAL COUNSEL

General Counsel.—Tyler J. Wood, Room 1018, 523–5740.

OFFICE OF CONSUMER AFFAIRS AND DISPUTE RESOLUTION

Director.—Rebecca A. Fenneman, Room 932, 523–5807.

OFFICE OF ADMINISTRATIVE LAW JUDGES

Chief Judge.—Erin M. Wirth, Room 1088, 523–5750.

OFFICE OF THE INSPECTOR GENERAL

Inspector General.—Jonathan Hatfield, Room 1054, 523–5863.

OFFICE OF THE MANAGING DIRECTOR

Managing Director.—Karen V. Gregory, Room 1082, 523–5800.
Deputy Managing Director.—Peter J. King.
Area Representatives:
Houston.—Adam Sinko (281) 386–8211.
Los Angeles: John Clausen 310–514–8618; Gabriel Padilla 310–514–4905.
New York: Matthew D. Forst (732) 283–2497; Erin Tasova (732) 283–2496.
Seattle: Diane Rebollo (732) 731–7319; Shadrack Scheirman (253) 922–7622.
South Florida: Yeseira Diaz 954–963–5284; Eric O. Mintz (954) 954–963–5362.
Director, Office of:
Budget and Finance.—Bruce Rayno, Room 916, 523–5770.
Human Resources.—William T. Cole, Room 924, 523–5773.
Information Technology.—Edward D. Anthony, Room 904, 523–5835.
Management Services.—Katona Bryan-Wade, Room 926, 523–5900.

BUREAU OF CERTIFICATION AND LICENSING

Director.—Sandra L. Kusumoto, Room 970, 523–5787.

Special Assistant.—Clifford R. Johnson.
Director, Office of:
Passenger Vessels and Information Processing.—Tajuanda L. Singletary, 523–5818.
Transportation Intermediaries.—Aline A. Hull, 523–5843.

BUREAU OF ENFORCEMENT

Director.—Benjamin K. Trogdon, Room 900, 523–5783 or 523–5860.

BUREAU OF TRADE ANALYSIS

Director.—Florence A. Carr, Room 940 (202) 523–5796.
Director, of:
Competition Analysis.—Anthony Homan, 523–5845.
Economic Studies.—Grace Wang, 523–5796.
Service Contracts.—Tanga S. FitzGibbon.

FEDERAL MEDIATION AND CONCILIATION SERVICE

250 E Street, SW., Washington, DC 20427

phone (202) 606–8100, fax 606–4251

[Codified under 29 U.S.C. 172]

Director.—Richard Giacolone.
Deputy Director/National Representative.—Scot L. Beckenbaugh.
Chief of Staff.—Gregory Goldstein, 606–8100.
General Counsel.—Dawn Starr, 606–8090.
Director for—
Administrative Services.—Cynthia Washington, 606–5477.
ADR/International.—Eileen Hoffman, 606–5447.
Arbitration Services.—Arthur Pearlstein, 606–5111.
Budget and Finance.—Will Shields, 606–3660.
Finance.—Nicole Wallace, 606–3660.
Grants.—Linda Gray-Broughton, 606–8181.
Human Resources.—Angela Titcombe, 606–3689.
Information Systems.—Doug Jones, 606–5483.
Deputy Director, Field Operations.—D. Scott Blakeal.

FEDERAL MINE SAFETY AND HEALTH REVIEW COMMISSION

1331 Pennsylvania Avenue, NW., Suite 520N, Washington, DC 20004

phone (202) 434–9900, fax 434–9944

[Created by Public Law 95–164]

Chair.—Marco M. Rajkovich, Jr., 434–9912.
Commissioners: William I. Althen, 434–9951; Mary Lu Jordan, Room 548, 434–9925; Arthur R. Traynor III, 434–9921; Michael G. Young, 434–9914.
Executive Director.—Lisa M. Boyd, 434–9905.
Chief Administrative Law Judge.—Glynn F. Voisin, 434–9943.
General Counsel.—Michael McCord, 434–9920.

FEDERAL RETIREMENT THRIFT INVESTMENT BOARD

77 K Street, NE., Washington, DC 20002

phone (202) 942–1600, fax 942–1676

[Authorized by 5 U.S.C. 8472]

Executive Director.—Ravindra Deo, 942–1601.
Office of Chief Operating Officer, Deputy Executive Director.—Suzanne Tosini, 942–1440.
General Counsel.—Megan Grumbine, 942–1670.
Director, Office of:

Communications and Education.—Jim Courtney, 942–1600.
Enterprise Planning.—Renee Wilder, 942–1600..
Enterprise Risk Management.—Jay Ahuja, 942–1600.
External Affairs.—Kimberly Weaver, 942–1641.
Financial Management.—Susan Crowder, 942–1620.
Investments.—Sean McCaffery, 942–1600.
Participant Operations.—Tee Ramos, 942–1600.
Resource Management.—Gisile Goethe, 942–1600.
Technology Services.—Vijay Desai, 639–3847.
Chair.—David A. Jones (acting), 942–1661.
Board Members:
Dana K. Bilyeu.
Ronald D. McCray.
David A. Jones.
William Jasien.

FEDERAL TRADE COMMISSION

600 Pennsylvania Avenue, NW., Washington, DC 20580

phone (202) 326–2222, https://ftc.gov

Chairman.—Joseph S. Simons, Room 438, 326–3400.
Executive Assistant.—Shawnee Parker, Room 438, 326–3264.
Chief of Staff.—Tara Koslov, Room 446, 326–2386.
Commissioners: Rohit Chopra, Room 328, 326–3886; Noah Phillips, Room 338, 326–3776; Rebecca Slaughter, Room 538, 326–2144; Christine Wilson, Room 526, 326–3217.
Director, Office of:
Competition.—Ian Conner (acting), Room 370, 326–3300.
Congressional Relations.—Jeanne Bumpus, Room 408, 326–2195.
Consumer Protection.—Andrew Smith, Room 470, 326–3240.
Economics.—Bruce H. Kobayashi, Room 270, 326–3419.
Policy Planning.—Bilal Sayyed, Room 392, 326–2004.
Public Affairs.—Cathy MacFarlane, Room 423, 326–2180.
International Affairs.—Randolph W. Tritell, Room 492, 326–3051.
Executive Director.—David B. Robbins, Room 426, 326–2748.
General Counsel.—Alden Abbott, Room 570, 326–2424.
Secretary.—April Tabor (acting), Room 172, 326–2514.
Inspector General.—Andrew Katsaros (acting), Room CC-5216, 326–3527.
Chief Administrative Law Judge.—D. Michael Chappell, Room 111, 326–3637.

REGIONAL DIRECTORS

East Central Region: Jon M. Steiger, 1111 Superior Avenue, Suite 200, Cleveland, OH 44114 (216) 263–3455.
Midwest Region: Todd Kossow, 230 South Dearborn Street, Room 3030, Chicago, IL 60604 (312) 960–5634.
Northeast Region: William Efron, One Bowling Green, Suite 318, New York, NY 10004 (212) 607–2829.
Northwest Region: Charles Harwood, 915 Second Avenue, Suite 2896, Seattle, WA 98174 (206) 220–6350.
Southeast Region: Cindy A. Liebes, 225 Peachtree Street, NE., Suite 1500, Atlanta, GA 30303 (404) 656–1390.
Southwest Region: Dama J. Brown, 1999 Bryan Street, Suite 2150, Dallas, TX 75201 (214) 979–9350.
Western Region—Los Angeles: Tom Dahdouh, 10990 Wilshire Boulevard, Suite 400, Los Angeles, CA 90024–3679 (310) 824–4300.
Western Region—San Francisco: Tom Dahdouh, 901 Market Street, Suite 570, San Francisco, CA 94103 (415) 848–5100.

FOREIGN-TRADE ZONES BOARD

1401 Constitution Avenue, NW., Room 21013, Washington, DC 20230

phone (202) 482–2862, fax 482–0002

Chair.—Wilbur L. Ross, Jr., Secretary of Commerce.

Member.—Steven T. Mnuchin, Secretary of the Treasury.
Executive Secretary.—Andrew McGilvray.

GENERAL SERVICES ADMINISTRATION

1800 F Street, NW., Washington, DC 20405

phone (202) 501–0800, https://gsa.gov

OFFICE OF THE ADMINISTRATOR

Administrator.—Emily W. Murphy.
Deputy Administrator.—Allison F. Brigati.
Chief of Staff.—Robert Borden.
Deputy Chief of Staff.—LaFondra Lynch.

NATIONAL SERVICES

PUBLIC BUILDING SERVICE

Commissioner.—Dan Matthews (202) 501–1100.
Deputy Commissioner.—Allison Azevedo.
Chief of Staff.—Dawn Stalter.
Assistant Commissioner, Office of:
Acquisition Management.—Tracy Marcinowski.
Design and Construction.—Brett Wallen (acting).
Facilities Management.—Andrew Heller.
Leasing.—John Thomas (acting).
Portfolio Management and Customer Engagement.—Stuart Burns.
Real Property Utilization and Disposal.—Flavio Peres.
Chief Architect.—David Insinga.

FEDERAL ACQUISITION SERVICE

Commissioner.—Julie Dunne (acting).
Deputy Commissioner.—Tom Howder (acting).
Deputy Commissioner (Director, Technology Transformation Services).—Anil Cheriyan.
Chief of Staff.—Karen Link (acting).
Assistant Commissioner, Office of:
Assisted Acquisition Services.—Christopher Bennethum (acting).
Customer and Stakeholder Engagement.—Erv Koehler.
Enterprise Strategy Management.—Crystal Philcox.
General Supplies and Services.—Bob Noonan.
Information Technology Category.—William Zielinski.
Policy and Compliance.—Mark Lee.
Professional Services and Human Capital Categories.—Tiffany T. Hixson.
Systems Management.—Judith Zawatsky.
Travel, Transportation, and Logistics.—William Toth (acting).

STAFF OFFICES

OFFICE OF THE CHIEF FINANCIAL OFFICER

Chief Financial Officer.—Gerard Badorrek (202) 501–1721.
Deputy Chief Financial Officer.—Evan Farley.
Chief of Staff.—Matthew Watt.
Director of:
Analytics, Performance and Improvement.—Stephen Brockelman (acting).
Budget.—Mehul Parekh.
Financial Operations.—Lisa Ziehmann.
Regional Financial Operations.—Steven Varnum (acting).

OFFICE OF CONGRESSIONAL AND INTERGOVERNMENTAL AFFAIRS

Associate Administrator.—Jeffrey A. Post, (202) 501–0563.
Deputy Associate Administrator.—Vacant.
Senior Policy Advisor.—Saul Japson.

Director of Congressional Operations.—Erin Mewhirter.
Director of Congressional Support Services.—Michael Gurgo.

OFFICE OF STRATEGIC COMMUNICATIONS

Associate Administrator.—Mark McHale.
Deputy Associate Administrator of Communications and Marketing.—Donna Garland.
Deputy Associate Administrator of Operations.—Justin Ward.
Press Secretary.—Pam Dixon.
Senior Communications Advisor.—Chris Godbey.

OFFICE OF GOVERNMENTWIDE POLICY

Associate Administrator.—Jessica Salmoiraghi (202) 501–8880.
Deputy Associate Administrator.—Beth Angerman.
Deputy Associate Administrator, Office of:
Asset and Transportation Management.—Alexander Kurien.
Acquisition Policy.—Jeff Koses.
Evaluation Sciences.—Kelly Bidwell.
Evidence and Analysis.—Todd Coleman.
High Performance Federal Buildings.—Kevin Kampschroer.
Information, Integrity, and Access.—Vacant.
Shared Solutions and Performance Management.—Earl Pinto.
Chief of Staff.—David Frye.
Chief Acquisition Officer.—Jessica Salmoiraghi.
Senior Procurement Executive.—Jeff Koses.

OFFICE OF THE GENERAL COUNSEL

General Counsel.—Jack St. John (202) 501–2200.
Deputy General Counsel.—Lennard S. Loewentritt.
Associate General Counsel for:
General Law.—Eugenia D. Ellison.
Personal Property.—Janet Harney.
Real Property.—Barry Segal.

OFFICE OF THE CHIEF INFORMATION OFFICER

Chief Information Officer.—David Shive (202) 501–1000.
Deputy Chief Information Officer.—Beth Anne Killoran.
Chief of Staff.—Vanessa Ros.
Chief Data Officer.—Kris Rowley.
Chief Technology Officer.—Navin Vembar.
Chief Information Security Officer.—Kurt Garbars.
Associate Chief Information Officer, Office of:
Acquisition IT Services.—Sagar Samant.
Corporate IT Services.—Elizabeth DelNegro.
Enterprise Infrastructure Operations.—David Harrity.
Enterprise Planning and Governance.—Lesley Briante.
Public Building IT Services.—Philip Klokis.
Deputy Associate Chief Information Officer, Office of Corporate IT Services.—Daryle "Mike" Seckar.
Director, Management Services Division.—Erika Dinnie.

OFFICE OF SMALL BUSINESS UTILIZATION

Associate Administrator.—Charles Manger (202) 501–1021.
Deputy Associate Administrator.—Amy L. Lineberry.
Chief of Staff.—Daniel Walczyk.

OFFICE OF HUMAN RESOURCES MANAGEMENT

Chief Human Capital Officer.—Antonia T. Harris (202) 501–0398.
Deputy Chief Human Capital Officer.—Merrick Krause.
Chief of Staff.—Autumn Jones.

OFFICE OF CIVIL RIGHTS

Associate Administrator.—Mary Gilbert (202) 501–0767.
Deputy Associate Administrator.—Aluanda Drain.
Chief of Staff.—Vacant.

OFFICE OF MISSION ASSURANCE

Associate Administrator.—Robert J. Carter (202) 219–0291.
Deputy Associate Administrator.—Robert D. Shaw.
Chief of Staff.—Maggie Dugan.

OFFICE OF ADMINISTRATIVE SERVICES

Chief Administrative Services Officer.—Bob Stafford (202) 357–9697.
Deputy Chief Administrative Services Officer.—Dan Miller.
Chief of Staff.—Matthew Watt.

REGIONAL OFFICES

National Capital Region (NCR 11): 17th and D Street, SW., Washington, DC 20407 (202) 708–9100.
Regional Administrator.—Scott Anderson.
Regional Commissioner for Federal Acquisition Service.—Houston Taylor.
Regional Commissioner for Public Buildings Service.—Darren Blue.
New England Region I: Thomas P. O'Neill Federal Building, 10 Causeway Street, Boston, MA 02222 (617) 565–5860.
Regional Administrator.—Glenn Rotondo (acting).
Regional Commissioner for Federal Acquisition Service.—Joe Nickerson.
Regional Commissioner for Public Buildings Service.—Glenn Rotondo.
Northeast and Caribbean Region 2: 26 Federal Plaza, New York, NY 10278 (212) 264–2600.
Regional Administrator.—John A. Sarcone III (acting).
Regional Commissioner for Federal Acquisition Service.—Jeff Lau.
Regional Commissioner for Public Buildings Service.—Michael Gelber.
Mid-Atlantic Region 3: The Strawbridge's Building, 20 North Eight Street, Philadelphia, PA 19107 (215) 446–4900.
Regional Administrator.—Joyce C. Haas.
Regional Commissioner for Federal Acquisition Service.—Dena McLaughlin.
Regional Commissioner for Public Buildings Service.—Joanna Rosato.
Southeast Sunbelt Region 4: 77 Forsyth Street, Suite 600, Atlanta, GA 30303 (404) 331–3200.
Regional Administrator.—Brian Stern.
Regional Commissioner for Federal Acquisition Service.—Thomas Meiron (acting).
Regional Commissioner for Public Buildings Service.—Kevin Kerns.
Great Lakes Region 5: 230 South Dearborn, Chicago, IL 60604 (312) 353–5395.
Regional Administrator.—Brad Hansher.
Regional Commissioner for Federal Acquisition Service.—Kim Brown.
Regional Commissioner for Public Buildings Service.—John Cooke.
Heartland Region 6: 1500 East Bannister Road, Kansas City, MO 64131 (816) 926–7201.
Regional Administrator.—Michael Copeland.
Regional Commissioner for Federal Acquisition Service.—Mary Ruwwe.
Regional Commissioner for Public Buildings Service.—Kevin Rothmier (acting).
Great Southwest Region 7: 819 Taylor Street, Fort Worth, TX 76102 (817) 978–2321.
Regional Administrator.—Robert Babcock.
Regional Commissioner for Federal Acquisition Service.—George Prochaska.
Regional Commissioner for Public Buildings Service.—Giancarlo Brizzi.
Rocky Mountain Region 8: Building 41, Denver Federal Center, Denver, CO 80225 (303) 236–7329.
Regional Administrator.—Timothy Horne (acting).
Regional Commissioner for Federal Acquisition Service.—Penny Grout (acting).
Regional Commissioner for Public Buildings Service.—Timothy Horne.
Pacific Mountain Region 9: 450 Golden Gate Avenue, Room 5–2690, San Francisco, CA 94102 (415) 522–3001.
Regional Administrator.—Tom Scott.
Regional Commissioner for Federal Acquisition Service.—Casey Kelley.

Regional Commissioner for Public Buildings Service.—Daniel Brown.

Northwest / Arctic Region 10: GSA Center, 400 15th Street, SW., Auburn, WA 98001 (253) 931–7000.

Regional Administrator.—Chaun Benjamin (acting).

Regional Commissioner for Federal Acquisition Service.—Tiffany Hixson.

Regional Commissioner for Public Buildings Service.—Chaun Benjamin.

INDEPENDENT OFFICES

OFFICE OF THE INSPECTOR GENERAL

Inspector General.—Carol F. Ochoa (202) 501–0450.

Deputy Inspector General.—Robert C. Erickson.

Assistant Inspector General for:

Administration.—Larry Gregg.

Auditing.—Vacant.

Inspections.—Patricia Sheenan.

Investigations.—Vacant.

Congressional Relations Officer.—Robert Preiss.

General Counsel.—Ed Martin.

CIVILIAN BOARD OF CONTRACT APPEALS

Chair.—Jeri K. Somers (202) 606–8820.

Vice Chair.—Erica S. Beardsley.

Chief Counsel.—J. Gregory Parks, 606–8787.

Clerk.—Cheryl L. Hilton, 606–8800.

Board Judges:

Jeri K. Somers, Chair
Erica S. Beardsley, Vice Chair
Kyle E. Chadwick
Jerome M. Drummond
Allan H. Goodman
Catherine B. Hyatt
Harold C. Kullberg
Harold D. ''Harv'' Lester, Jr.
Kathleen J. O'Rourke
Beverly M. Russell
Patricia J. Sheridan
Marian E. Sullivan
Joseph A. Vergilio
Jonathan D. Zischkau

HARRY S. TRUMAN SCHOLARSHIP FOUNDATION

712 Jackson Place, NW., Washington, DC 20006

phone (202) 395–4831, fax 395–6995

[Created by Public Law 93–642]

BOARD OF TRUSTEES

President.—Hon. Madeleine K. Albright.

Vice President.—Hon. Max Sherman.

Treasurer.—Hon. Frederick Slabach.

Secretary.—Clifton Truman Daniel.

General Counsel.—Westbrook Murphy.

Members:

Terry Babcock-Lumish, Executive Secretary, Harry S. Truman Scholarship Foundation.
Hon. Roy Blunt, Senator from Missouri.
Steven H. Cohen, Attorney, Cohen Law Group.
Hon. Laura Cordero, Associate Judge, D.C. Superior Court.
Hon. Theodore E. Deutch, Representative of Florida.
Hon. Betsy DeVos, U.S. Secretary of Education.
Hon. Kay Granger, Representative of Texas.
Ingrid Gregg, President, the Philadelphia Society.

Michael W. Hail, Professor of Government, Morehead State University.
Hon. Brian Schatz, Senator from Hawaii.
Chief Information Officer.—Tonji Wade.
Executive Secretary.—Terry Babcock-Lumish.
Deputy Executive Secretary.—Tara Yglesias.
Program Manager.—Kelsea Cooper.
Program Assistant.—Ellen Dunlavey.
Resident Scholar.—Rachael Johnson.

INTER-AMERICAN FOUNDATION

1331 Pennsylvania Avenue, NW., Suite 1200, North Washington, DC 20004

phone (202) 360–4530

Chair, Board of Directors.—Eddy Arriola.
Vice Chair, Board of Directors.—Juan Carlos Iturregui.
President and Chief Executive Officer.—Paloma Adams-Allen.
Chief Operating Officer.—Lesley Duncan.
General Counsel.—Vacant.
Managing Director of:
External and Government Affairs.—Daniel Friedman.
Grant-Making and Portfolio Management.—Marcy Kelley.
Learning and Impact.—Raquel Gomes.

JAMES MADISON MEMORIAL FELLOWSHIP FOUNDATION

1613 Duke Street, Alexandria, VA 22314

phone (571) 858–4200, fax (703) 838–2180

[Created by Public Law 99–591]

BOARD OF TRUSTEES

Members Appointed by the President of the United States:

John Cornyn, Senator from Texas, Chair.
Benjamin L. Cardin, Senator from Maryland.
Betsy DeVos, U.S. Secretary of Education (ex officio).

Foundation Staff:
President Emeritus.—Admiral Paul A. Yost, Jr.
President.—Lewis F. Larsen.
Director of Academics.—Dr. Jeffry Morrison.
Management and Program Analysis Officer.—Elizabeth G. Ray.
Academic Advisor.—Sheila Osbourne.
Director of Development.—Kimberly A. Alldredge.
Director of Special Programs.—Katie Robison.
Support Services Assistant.—Oliver Alwes.

THE JOHN F. KENNEDY CENTER FOR THE PERFORMING ARTS

2700 F Street, NW., Washington, DC 20566

phone (202) 416–8000, fax 416–8205

BOARD OF TRUSTEES

Honorary Chairs:
Mrs. Melania Trump
Mrs. Michelle Obama
Mrs. Laura Bush
Hon. Hillary Rodham Clinton
Mrs. George Bush †
Mrs. Ronald Reagan †
Mrs. Jimmy Carter

Officers:
Chair.—David M. Rubenstein.
President.—Deborah F. Rutter.
Secretary.—Jacqueline Badger Mars.
Treasurer.—Michael F. Neidorff.

General Counsel.—Maria C. Kersten.

Members Appointed by the President of the United States:

Adrienne Arsht
Fred Eychaner
Sakurako Fisher
John Goldman
Janet Hill
Michael Huckabee
Valerie Jarrett
Victoria Reggie Kennedy
Michele Kessler
Karen Tucker LeFrak
Carl H. Lindner III
Michael Lombardo
Andrés W. López
Bryan Lourd
Amalia Perea Mahoney
Barbara Goodman Manilow
Alyssa Mastromonaco
W. James McNerney, Jr.
Charles B. Ortner
Susan Rice
Laura Ricketts
Kelly Roberts
Daryl Roth
David M. Rubenstein
Margaret Russell
Susan S. Sher
Marc I. Stern
Bryan Traubert
Ranvir Trehan
Walter F. Ulloa
Reginald Van Lee
Jon Voight
Kelcy Warren
Heather Washburne
Phyllis J. Washington
Ann Marie Wilkins

Members Ex Officio Designated by Act of Congress

Alex Azar II, Secretary of Health and Human Services.
Dr. Carla Hayden, Librarian of Congress.
Mike Pompeo, Secretary of State.
Earl A. Powell III, Chair of the Commission of Fine Arts.
Muriel E. Bowser, Mayor, District of Columbia.
Lewis Ferebee, Chancellor, D.C. Public Schools.
Margaret Everson, Acting Director, National Park Service.
Betsy DeVos, Secretary of Education.
Lonnie G. Bunch III, Secretary, Smithsonian Institution.
Nancy Pelosi, Speaker of the House of Representatives from California.
Kevin McCarthy, Republican Leader of the House of Representatives from California.
Peter DeFazio, Representative from Oregon.
Sam Graves, Representative from Missouri.
Joseph P. Kennedy III, Representative from Massachusetts.
Joyce Beatty, Representative from Ohio.
Jason Smith, Representative from Missouri.
Mitch McConnell, Senate Majority Leader from Kentucky.
Charles E. Schumer, Senate Democratic Leader from New York.
John Barrasso, Senator from Wyoming.
Thomas R. Carper, Senator from Delaware.
Mark R. Warner, Senator from Virginia.
Roy Blunt, Senator from Missouri.
John Cornyn, Senator from Texas.

Senior Counsel.—Robert Barnett.
Founding Chair.—Roger L. Stevens. †
Chair Emeriti: James A. Johnson, Stephen A. Schwarzman, James D. Wolfensohn.
President Emeritus.—Michael M. Kaiser.

Honorary Trustees:

Buffy Cafritz
Kenneth M. Duberstein
Alma Gildenhorn
Melvin R. Laird †
Leonard L. Silverstein †
Jean Kennedy Smith

† *Deceased*

LEGAL SERVICES CORPORATION

3333 K Street, NW., 3rd Floor, Washington, DC 20007–3522

phone (202) 295–1500, fax 337–6797

BOARD OF DIRECTORS

John G. Levi, *Board Chair*
Rev. Joseph Pius Pietrzyk, *Board Vice Chair*
Robert J. Grey, Jr.
Matthew Keenan
Abigail Lawlis Kuzma
Victor B. Maddox
Laurie I. Mikva
Julie A. Reiskin
Gloria Valencia-Weber

President.—James J. Sandman.
General Counsel, Corporate Secretary, and Vice President for Legal Affairs.—Ronald Flagg.
Vice President for Grants Management.—Lynn A. Jennings.
Vice President, Government Relations and Public Affairs.—Carol A. Bergman.

Chief Financial Officer and Treasurer.—Deborah Moore.
Inspector General.—Jeffrey E. Schanz.
Director of Communications and Media Relations.—Carl Rauscher.

NATIONAL AERONAUTICS AND SPACE ADMINISTRATION

300 E Street, SW., Washington, DC 20546

phone (202) 358–0000, https://nasa.gov

OFFICE OF THE ADMINISTRATOR

Suite 9F44, phone 358–1010

Administrator.—Jim Bridenstine.
Executive Assistant.—Megan Wenrich, 358–1808.
Deputy Administrator.—Jim Morhard.
Associate Administrator.—Steve Jurczyk.
Chief of Staff.—Gabe Sherman.
Deputy Associate Administrator.—Melanie Saunders, 358–3858.
Associate Administrator for Strategy and Plans.—Thomas E. Cremins, 358–1747.
Chiefs:
Financial Officer.—Jeff DeWitt, 358–0978.
Information Officer.—Renee Wynn, 358–1824.
Engineer.—Ralph Roe (757) 864–2400.
Health and Medical Officer.—Dr. James Polk, 358–1959.
Safety and Mission Assurance.—Terrence Wilcutt (281) 244–8715.
Scientist.—Jim Green, 358–4580.
Technologist.—Dr. Douglas Terrier, (281) 483–0903.

OFFICE OF THE GENERAL COUNSEL

Suite 9V39, phone 358–2450

General Counsel.—Sumara Thompson-King.
Deputy General Counsel.—Tom McMurray.

OFFICE OF INSPECTOR GENERAL

Suite 8U79, phone 358–1220

Inspector General.—Paul K. Martin.
Deputy Inspector General.—George Scott.

OFFICE OF COMMUNICATIONS

Suite 5S87, phone 358–1898

Associate Administrator.—Bettina Inclan, 358–1898.
Deputy Associate Administrator.—Robert Jacobs, 358–1600.

OFFICE OF DIVERSITY AND EQUAL OPPORTUNITY PROGRAMS

Suite 6J81, phone 358–2167

Associate Administrator.—Stephen T. Shih.

OFFICE OF STEM ENGAGEMENT

Suite 4V76, phone 358–0103

Associate Administrator.—Mike Kincaid.
Deputy Associate Administrator.—Kristi Brown.
Deputy Associate Administrator for Programs.—Elaine Ho.

OFFICE OF INTERNATIONAL AND INTERAGENCY RELATIONS

Suite 5V16, phone 358–0450

Associate Administrator.—Mike Gold (acting).

Deputy Associate Administrator.—Karen Feldstein.

OFFICE OF LEGISLATIVE AND INTERGOVERNMENTAL AFFAIRS

Code VA000, Room 9K24, phone 358–1948

Associate Administrator.—Suzanne Gillum.
Deputy Associate Administrator.—Chris Flaherty (acting).

OFFICE OF SMALL BUSINESS PROGRAMS

Suite 4F22, phone 358–2088

Associate Administrator.—Glenn A. Delgado.

AERONAUTICS RESEARCH MISSION DIRECTORATE

Suite 6J39–A, phone 358–4700

Associate Administrator.—Bob Pearce.
Deputy Associate Administrator for Policy.—John Montgomery.
Deputy Associate Administrator for Programs.—Edgar Waggoner.

HUMAN EXPLORATION AND OPERATIONS MISSION DIRECTORATE

Suite 7K22, phone 358–2015

Associate Administrator.—Kenneth Bowersox (acting).
Deputy Associate Administrator for Technical.—Kenneth Bowersox.

SCIENCE MISSION DIRECTORATE

Suite 3K20, phone 358–3889

Associate Administrator.—Dr. Thomas H. Zurbuchen.
Deputy Associate Administrator.—Sandra Connelly (acting).

SPACE TECHNOLOGY MISSION DIRECTORATE

Associate Administrator.—James Reuter, 358–5212.

MISSION SUPPORT DIRECTORATE

Suite 4J19, phone 358–2789

Associate Administrator.—Robert Gibbs.
Deputy Associate Administrator.—Lisa Ziehmann, 358–3861.

OFFICE OF HUMAN CAPITAL MANAGEMENT

Suite 4V85, phone 358–0100 or 4400

Associate Administrator.—Jane Datta.
Deputy Associate Administrator.—Brady Pyle.

OFFICE OF PROCUREMENT

Suite 5O16, phone 358–2090

Assistant Administrator.—Monica Manning.
Deputy Assistant Administrator.—William Roets.

OFFICE OF PROTECTIVE SERVICES

Suite 6T26, phone 358–3752

Assistant Administrator.—Joseph Mahaley.
Deputy Associate Administrator.—Charles Lombard.

OFFICE OF STRATEGIC INFRASTRUCTURE

Suite 2Z88, phone 358–2800

Assistant Administrator.—Calvin F. Williams.
Deputy Assistant Administrator.—Richard L. Marrs.

NASA MANAGEMENT OFFICE

Phone (818) 354–5359

Director.—Marcus Watkins.

NASA NATIONAL OFFICES

Air Force Space Command / XPX (NASA): Peterson Air Force Base, CO 80914.
NASA Senior Representative.—Thomas Plumb (719) 554–4900.
Ames Research Center: Moffett Field, CA 94035.
Director.—Dr. Eugene Tu (650) 604–5062.
Deputy Center Director.—Carol Carroll.
Armstrong Flight Research Center: P.O. Box 273, Edwards, CA 93523.
Director.—David McBride (661) 276–3101.
Deputy Center Director.—Patrick Stoliker.
Glenn Research Center at Lewisfield: 21000 Brookpark Road, Cleveland, OH 44135.
Director.—Marla E. Perez-Davis, Ph.D. (216) 433–5835.
Goddard Institute for Space Studies: Goddard Space Flight Center, 2880 Broadway, New York, NY 10025.
Chief.—Dr. Gavin A. Schmidt (212) 678–5500.
Goddard Space Flight Center: 8800 Greenbelt Road, Greenbelt, MD 20771.
Director.—Dennis Andrucyk (301) 286–5122.
Center Associate Deputy Director.—Raymond Rubilotta.
Jet Propulsion Laboratory: 4800 Oak Grove Drive, Pasadena, CA 91109.
Director.—Dr. Michael M. Watkins (818) 354–4321.
Lyndon B. Johnson Space Center: 2101 NASA Parkway Houston, TX 77058–3696.
Director.—Mark Geyer (281) 483–3622.
John F. Kennedy Space Center: Kennedy Space Center, FL 32899.
Director.—Robert Cabana (321) 867–5000.
Langley Research Center: Hampton, VA 23681.
Director.—Clayton Turner (757) 864–4111.
George C. Marshall Space Flight Center: Marshall Space Flight Center, AL 35812.
Director.—Jody Singer (256) 544–1915.
Michoud Assembly Facility: P.O. Box 29300, New Orleans, LA 70189.
Director.—Robert Champion (256) 544–0478.
NASA IV and V Facility: NASA Independent Verification and Validation Facility, 100 University Drive, Fairmont, WV 26554.
Director.—Gregory D. Blaney (304) 367–8200.
NASA Management Office: Jet Propulsion Laboratory, 4800 Oak Grove Drive, Pasadena, CA 91109.
Director.—Marcus Watkins (818) 354–5359.
John C. Stennis Space Center: Stennis Space Center, MS 39529.
Director.—Dr. Richard Gilbrech (228) 688–2121.
Deputy Director.—Vanessa Wyche (281) 483–7343.
Vandenberg AFB: P.O. Box 425, Lompoc, CA 93438.
Manager.—Ted L. Oglesby (805) 866–5859.
Wallops Flight Facility: Goddard Space Flight Center, Wallops Island, VA 23337.
Director.—David Pierce (757) 824–1201.
White Sands Test Facility: Johnson Space Center, P.O. Drawer MM, Las Cruces, NM 88004.
Manager.—Robert Cort (575) 524–5771.

NASA OVERSEAS REPRESENTATIVES

Europe: U.S. Embassy, Paris, Unit 9200, Box 1653, DPO, AE 09777, 011–33–1–4312–7070.
NASA Representative.—Timothy Tawney.
Japan: U.S. Embassy, Tokyo, 1–10–5 Akasaka, Minato-ku, Tokyo, Japan 107–8420 81–3–3224–5000.

NASA Representative.—Garvey McIntosh.
Russia: U.S. Embassy, 5433 Moscow Place, Apt 35, Dulles, VA 20189 (256) 961–6333.
NASA Representatives: Jon Shearer, Patrick Finley.

NATIONAL ARCHIVES AND RECORDS ADMINISTRATION

700 Pennsylvania Avenue, NW., Washington, DC 20408–0001

8601 Adelphi Road, College Park, MD 20740–6001

https://archives.gov

[Created by Public Law 98–497]

Archivist of the United States.—David Ferriero (202) 357–5900, (301) 837–1600, fax (202) 357–5901.
Deputy Archivist of the United States.—Debra S. Wall (202) 357–5900, (301) 837–1600, fax (202) 357–5901.
Chief Officers:
Chief of Staff.—Maria Stanwich (202) 357–5900, fax 357–5901.
Operating.—William J. Bosanko (301) 837–3604, fax 837–3217.
Management and Administration.—Micah Cheatham (301) 837–2992, fax 837–3224.
Human Capital.—Valorie Findlater (acting) (301) 837–3710, fax 837–3195.
Innovation.—Pamela Wright (301) 837–2029, fax 837–0312.
Records.—Lawrence Brewer (301) 837–1539, fax 837–3697.
Information Services.—Swarnali Haldar (301) 837–1583.
Financial.—Colleen Murphy, (301) 837–1723, fax 837–0312.
Executive for—
Agency Services.—Jay Trainer (301) 837–3064.
Business Support Services.—Donna Forbes (301) 837–1719, fax 837–3657.
Legislative Archives, Presidential Libraries, and Museum Services.—Susan Donius (acting) (202) 357–5472, fax 357–5939.
Research Services.—Ann Cummings (301) 837–3110, fax 837–3633.
Director for—
Communications and Marketing.—John Valceanu (202) 357–5300, fax 357–6809.
Congressional Affairs.—John O. Hamilton (202) 357–5100, fax 357–5959.
Equal Employment Opportunity and Diversity Office.—Erica Pearson (301) 837–1849, fax 837–0869.
External Affairs.—Meg Phillips (202) 837–3111.
Federal Register.—Oliver A. Potts (202) 741–6100, fax 741–6012.
General Counsel.—Gary M. Stern (301) 837–3025, fax 837–0293.
Government Information Services.—Alina Semo (202) 741–5770, fax 741–5769.
Information Security Oversight Office.—Mark Bradley (202) 357–5250, fax 357–5907.
Inspector General.—James Springs (301) 837–3000, fax 837–3197.
National Historical Publications and Records Commission.—Christopher Eck (202) 357–5263, fax 357–5914.

Presidential Libraries.—Susan K. Donius (301) 837–3250, fax 837–3199.
Director for—
Herbert Hoover Library.—Thomas Schwartz, West Branch, IA 52358–0488 (319) 643–5301.
Franklin D. Roosevelt Library.—Paul M. Sparrow, Hyde Park, NY 12538–1999 (845) 486–7770.
Harry S. Truman Library.—Kurt K. Graham, Independence, MO 64050–1798 (816) 268–8200.
Dwight D. Eisenhower Library.—Dawn D. Hammatt, Abilene, KS 67410–2900 (785) 263–6700.
John F. Kennedy Library.—Alan Price, Boston, MA 02125–3398 (617) 514–1600.
Lyndon Baines Johnson Library.—Patrick X. Mordente (acting), Austin, TX 78705–5737 (512) 721–0200.
Richard Nixon Library.—Michael D. Ellzey, Yorba Linda, CA 92886 (714) 983–9120.
Gerald R. Ford Library.—Elaine K. Didier, Ann Arbor, MI 48109–2114 (734) 205–0555.
Gerald R. Ford Museum.—Elaine K. Didier, Grand Rapids, MI 49504–5353 (616) 254–0400.
Jimmy Carter Library.—Meredith R. Evans, Atlanta, GA 30307–1498 (404) 865–7100.
Ronald Reagan Library.—R. Duke Blackwood, Simi Valley, CA 93065–0699 (800) 410–8354.

George Bush Library.—Warren L. Finch, College Station, TX 77845 (979) 691–4000.
William J. Clinton Library.—Terri T. Garner, Little Rock, AR 72201 (501) 374–4242.
George W. Bush Library.—Patrick X. Mordente, Dallas, TX 75205–2300 (214) 346–1650.
Barack Obama Library.—Brooke L. Clement, Hoffman Estates, IL 60169–1114, (847) 252–5714.

ADMINISTRATIVE COMMITTEE OF THE FEDERAL REGISTER

7 G Street, NW., Suite A–734, 20401, phone (202) 741–6000

Mailing Address: 8601 Adelphi Road, College Park, MD 20740

Members:
David Ferriero, Archivist of the United States, *Chair.*
Hugh Halpern, Director of the U.S. Government Publishing Office.
Rosemary Hart, Senior Counsel, Department of Justice.
Secretary.—Oliver A. Potts, Director of the Federal Register, National Archives and Records Administration.

NATIONAL ARCHIVES TRUST FUND BOARD

phone (301) 837–3550, fax 837–3191

Members:
David Ferriero, Archivist of the United States, *Chair.*
Jon Parrish Peede, Chair, National Endowment for the Humanities.
David Lebryk, Fiscal Assistant Secretary, Department of the Treasury.
Secretary.—Lawrence Post.

NATIONAL HISTORICAL PUBLICATIONS AND RECORDS COMMISSION

700 Pennsylvania Avenue, NW., 20408

phone (202) 357–5010, fax 357–5914

https://archives.gov/nhprc

Members:
David S. Ferriero, Archivist of the United States, National Archives and Records Administration, *Chair.*
John S. Cooke, Deputy Director, Federal Judicial Center, Judicial Branch.
Daniel Sullivan, member of the U.S. Senate, Alaska.
Vacant, U.S. House of Representatives.
Naomi Nelson, Associate University Librarian, Duke University, Presidential Appointee.
Rebecca Hankins, Associate Professor, Curator, and Librarian for Africana Studies, Women's and Gender Studies, and Arabic Language, Texas A&M University, Presidential Appointee.
Keren F. Meyers, Director of the Executive Services, Department of Defense.
Nicole Saylor, Head, American Folklife Center Archive, Library of Congress.
Adam Howard, Director, Office of the Historian, Department of State.
Michael Stevens, State Historian of Wisconsin Emeritus, Association for Documentary Editing.
W. Eric Emerson, Director, South Carolina Department of Archives and History, American Association for State and Local History.
William G. Thomas III, Chair, Department of History, University of Nebraska-Lincoln, American Historical Association.
Kaye Lanning Minchew, former Director, Troup County Archives (GA), National Association of Government Archives and Records Administrators.
George A. Miles, Curator, Western Americana Collection at the Bienecke Rare Book and Manuscript Library, Yale University, Organization of American Historians.
Dennis Meissner, former Deputy Director, Minnesota Historical Society and past President of the Society of American Archivists.
Executive Director.—Christopher Eck (202) 357–5010.

NATIONAL CAPITAL PLANNING COMMISSION

401 9th Street, NW., North Lobby, Suite 500, Washington, DC 20004

phone (202) 482–7200, fax 482–7272

https://ncpc.gov, info@ncpc.gov

APPOINTIVE MEMBERS

Presidential Appointees:
Beth White.
Thomas Gallas.
Vacant.
Mayoral Appointees:
Arrington Dixon.
Linda Argo.
Ex Officio Members:
Dr. Mark T. Esper, Secretary of Defense.
First Alternate.—Paul McMahon Jr.
Second Alternate.—Thomas Muir.
Third Alternate.—Sajeel S. Ahmed.
David Bernhardt, Secretary of the Interior.
First Alternate.—Paul Daniel ''Dan'' Smith.
Second Alternate.—Lisa Mendelson-Ielmini.
Third Alternate.—Peter May.
Emily W. Murphy, Administrator of General Services.
First Alternate.—Daniel Mathews.
Second Alternate.—Darren Blue.
Third Alternate.—Scott Anderson.
Fourth Alternate.—Mina Wright.
Fifth Alternate.—Kristi Tunstall.
Ron Johnson, Chair, Senate Committee on Homeland Security and Governmental Affairs.
Alternate.—Patrick Bailey.
Alternate.—Daniel Spino.
Carolyn B. Maloney, Chair, House Committee on Oversight and Government Reform.
First Alternate.—Wendy Ginsberg.
Second Alternate.—Kristine Lam.
Muriel E. Bowser, Mayor of the District of Columbia.
First Alternate.—Andrew Trueblood.
Second Alternate.—Jennifer Steingasser.
Phil Mendelson, Chair, Council of the District of Columbia.
First Alternate.—Evan Cash.

EXECUTIVE STAFF

Executive Director.—Marcel C. Acosta, 482–7221.
Secretariat.—Julia A. Koster, 482–7211.
General Counsel.—Anne R. Schuyler, 482–7223.
Director, Office of:
Administration.—Debra Dickson, 482–7229.
Physical Planning.—Elizabeth Miller, 482–7246.
Policy and Research.—Michael A. Sherman, 482–7254.
Public Engagement.—Julia A. Koster, 482–7211.
Urban Design and Plan Review.—Diane Sullivan, 482–7244.

NATIONAL COUNCIL ON DISABILITY

1331 F Street, NW., Suite 850, Washington, DC 20004

phone (202) 272–2004, TTY 272–2074, fax 272–2022

Chair.—Neil Romano, New York, NY.
Vice Chair.—James Brett, Boston, MA.

Members:
Billy Altom, Little Rock, AR.
Jim Baldwin, Bakersfield, CA.
Rabia Belt, Stanford, CA.
Andrés Gallegos, Chicago, IL.
Wendy Harbour, Minneapolis, MN.
Benro Ogunyipe, Chicago, IL.
Clyde Terry, Concord, NH.

NATIONAL CREDIT UNION ADMINISTRATION

1775 Duke Street, Alexandria, VA 22314–3428
phone (703) 518–6300, fax 518–6319

Chair.—Rodney E. Hood.
Board Members: Todd M. Harper, J. Mark McWatters.
Secretary to the Board.—Gerard Poliquin.
Executive Director.—Larry Fazio, 518–6320, fax 518–6661.
Deputy Executive Director.—Rendell Jones, 518–6320.
Inspector General.—Jim Hagen, 518–6350.
Chief Financial Officer.—Vacant, 518–6570, fax 518–6664.
Chief Information Officer.—Robert Foster, 518–6440, fax 518–6669.
National Examinations and Supervision.—Scott Hunt, 518–6640, fax 518–6665.
Minority and Women Inclusion.—Monica Davy, 518–1650.
Examination and Insurance.—Vacant, 518–6360, fax 518–6666.
General Counsel.—Frank Kressman (acting), 518–6540, fax 518–6667.
Deputy General Counsel.—Linda Dent (acting).
Human Resources.—Towanda Brooks, 518–6510, fax 518–6668.
External Affairs and Communications.—Gisele Roget, 518–6330.
Credit Union Resources and Expansion—Martha Ninichuk, 518–6610.

REGIONAL OFFICES

Director, Office of:
Eastern Region I (Alexandria).—John Kutchey, 519–4600, fax 519–4620.
Southern Region (Austin).—C. Keith Morton, 4807 Spicewood Springs Road, Suite 5200, Austin, TX 78759–8490 (512) 342–5600, fax 342–5620.
Western Region (Tempe).—Cherie Freed, 1230 West Washington Street, Suite 301, Tempe, AZ 85281 (602) 302–6000, fax 302–6024.
President, Asset Management and Assistance Center (Austin).—C. Keith Morton, 4807 Spicewood Springs Road, Suite 5100, Austin, TX 78759–8490 (512) 231–7900, fax 231–7920.

NATIONAL FOUNDATION ON THE ARTS AND THE HUMANITIES

400 7th Street, SW., Washington, DC 20506

NATIONAL ENDOWMENT FOR THE ARTS

https://arts.gov

Chair.—Mary Anne Carter.
Senior Deputy Chair.—Vacant.
Deputy Chair for Management and Budget.—Ann Eilers, 682–5534.
Chief of Staff.—Mike Griffin, 682–5773.
Congressional Liaison.—Nick Abramczyk, 682–5582.
Senior Adviser to the Chair.—Bill O'Brien, 682–5550.
Director of Research and Analysis.—Sunil Iyengar, 682–5654.
General Counsel.—India Pinkney, 682–5418.
Inspector General.—Ronald Stith, 682–5774.

THE NATIONAL COUNCIL ON THE ARTS

Chair.—Mary Anne Carter.

Members:

Bruce Carter, Ph.D.
Aaron Dworkin
Lee Greenwood
Deepa Gupta
Paul Hodes
Maria Rosario Jackson, Ph.D.
Emil J. Kang
Charlotte Kessler
María López De León
Rick Lowe
David "Mas" Masumoto
Barbara Ernst Prey
Ranee Ramaswamy
Diane Rodriguez
Tim Rothman
Olga Viso

Ex Officio Members:

Tammy Baldwin, Senator
Chellie Pingree, Representative
Glenn Thompson, Representative

NATIONAL ENDOWMENT FOR THE HUMANITIES

phone 1–800–NEH–1121, or (202) 606–8446

https://neh.gov, questions@neh.gov

Chair.—Jon Parrish Peede, 606–8310.
Deputy Chair.—Carlos Díaz-Rosillo, 606–8310.
Director of:
Communications.—Carmen Covelli-Ingwell, 606–8255.
Planning and Budget.—David Dohanic (acting), 606–8444.
White House and Congressional Affairs.—Timothy Robison, 606–8273.
General Counsel.—Michael McDonald, 606–8322.
Inspector General.—Laura M.H. Davis, 606–8574.
Public Information Officer.—Christopher Flynn, 606–8440.

NATIONAL COUNCIL ON THE HUMANITIES

Members:

Katie Albrecht
Francine Berman
Russell Berman
Allison Blakely
Keegan F. Callanan
Constance M. Carroll
Armand DeKeyser
William English
Marjorie Fisher
John Fonte
Claire McCaffery Griffin
Kim Holmes
Phyllis Kaminsky
Dorothy M. Kosinski
Shelly C. Lowe
Joyce Malcolm
Adair Margo
Matthew Rose
Ramón Saldívar
William Schneider, Jr.
Katherine H. Tachau
Noel Valis
Jean Yarbrough

FEDERAL COUNCIL ON THE ARTS AND THE HUMANITIES

Federal Council Members:

Mary Anne Carter, Chair, National Endowment for the Arts.
Jon Parrish Peede, Chair, National Endowment for the Humanities.
Betsy DeVos, Secretary, Department of Education.
Lonnie Bunch, Secretary, Smithsonian Institution.
France A. Córdova, Director, National Science Foundation.
Carla Hayden, Librarian of Congress, Library of Congress.
Kaywin Feldman, Director, National Gallery of Art.
Earl A. Powell III, Chair, Commission of Fine Arts.
David Ferriero, Archivist of the United States, National Archives and Records Administration.
Daniel Mathews, Commissioner, Public Buildings Service, General Services Administration.
Marie Royce, Assistant Secretary of State, Bureau of Educational and Cultural Affairs, Department of State.
Julie E. Adams, Secretary, United States Senate.
Wilbur Ross, Secretary, Department of Commerce.
Elaine L. Chao, Secretary, Department of Transportation.
Kathryn K. Matthew, Chair, National Museum and Library Services Board; Director, Institute of Museum and Library Services.
Ben Carson, Secretary, Department of Housing and Urban Development.
Emily W. Murphy, Administrator, General Services Administration.
Patrick Pizzella (acting), Secretary, Department of Labor.
Robert Wilkie, Secretary, Department of Veterans Affairs.

Lance Allen Robertson, Assistant Secretary for Aging, Department of Health and Human Services.

INSTITUTE OF MUSEUM AND LIBRARY SERVICES

phone (202) 653–4657, fax 653–4625, https://imls.gov

[The Institute of Museum and Library Services was created by the Museum and Library Services Act of 1996, Public Law 104–208]

Director.—Crosby Kemper III, 653–4644.
Deputy Director for Library Services.—Cyndee Landrum, 653–4650.
Deputy Director for Museum Services.—Paula Gangopadhyay, 653–4717.
Chief Information Officer.—Scott Carey, 653–4690.
Chief Operating Officer.—Chris Catignani (acting), 653–4672.
General Counsel.—Nancy Weiss, 653–4640.
Communications Manager.—Elizabeth Holtan, 653–4630.

National Museum And Library Services Board
Chair.— Crosby Kemper III, IMLS *
Members:

Sayeed Choudhury
Lisa Funderburke Hoffman
Paula Gangopadhyay, IMLS *
Luis Herrera
Lynne M. Ireland
Tammie Kahn
George Kerscher
Cyndee Landrum, IMLS *
Mary Minow
Homa Naficy
Tey Marianna Nunn
Sylvia Orozco
Jane Pickering
Mort Sajadian
Kenneth J. Schutz
Annette Evans Smith
Jacquelyn K. Sundstrand
Beth Takekawa
Deborah Taylor
Suzanne Thorin
Robert Wedgeworth
Nancy Weiss, IMLS *
Jonathan L. Zittrain

* Nonvoting member

NATIONAL GALLERY OF ART

6th Street and Constitution Avenue, NW., Washington, DC 20565
(Mailing Address: 2000B South Club Drive, Landover, MD 20785)
phone (202) 737–4215, https://nga.gov

[Under the direction of the Board of Trustees of the National Gallery of Art]

The National Gallery of Art is governed by a nine-member board of trustees, composed of five general trustees, who are appointed to staggered ten-year terms, and four *ex officio* trustees.

BOARD OF TRUSTEES

General Trustees:
Sharon Percy Rockefeller, Chair.
Mitchell P. Rales, President.
David M. Rubenstein.
David Walker.
Trustees Emeriti:
Frederick W. Beinecke.
Julian Ganz, Jr.
Alexander M. Laughlin.
David O. Maxwell.
Andrew M. Saul.
John Wilmerding.
Ex Officio Trustees:
John G. Roberts, Jr., Chief Justice of the United States.
Michael R. Pompeo, Secretary of State.
Steven T. Mnuchin, Secretary of the Treasury.
Lonnie G. Bunch III, Secretary of the Smithsonian Institution.

The board of trustees appoints the National Gallery of Art director and five executive officers, who manage the day-to-day operations of the museum.

Executive Officers:

Director.—Kaywin Feldman.
Deputy Director and Chief Curator.—Franklin Kelly.
Administrator.—Darrell R. Willson.
Treasurer.—William W. McClure.
Secretary and General Counsel.—Nancy Robinson Breuer.
Dean, Center for Advanced Study in the Visual Arts.—Elizabeth Cropper.

NATIONAL LABOR RELATIONS BOARD

1099 14th Street, NW., Washington, DC 20570–0001
Personnel Locator (202) 273–1000

Chair.—John F. Ring, 273–1790, fax 273–4270. (Term expires December 16, 2022.)
Chief of Staff.—Christine B. Lucy.
Chief Counsel.—Peter J. Carlton.
Deputy Chief Counsel.—Grant Kraus.
Members:
Board Member.—William J. Emanuel, 273–1740.
Chief Counsel.—Douglas Free (acting).
Deputy Chief Counsel.—Lara Zick.
Board Member.—Marvin E. Kaplan, 273–1770.
Chief Counsel.—James R. Murphy.
Deputy Chief Counsel.—Rachel G. Lennie.
Board Member.—Lauren McGarity McFerran, 273–1700.
Chief Counsel.—John F. Colwell.
Deputy Chief Counsel.—Andrew J. Krafts.
Board Member.—Vacant, 273–1790.
Chief Counsel.—Vacant.
Deputy Chief Counsel.—Elicia Watts.
Executive Secretary.—Roxanne Rothchild, 273–1940, fax 273–4270.
Deputy Executive Secretary.—Vacant, 273–2917.
Associate Executive Secretaries: Farah Qureshi, 273–1949; Leigh Reardon, 273–1736.
Solicitor.—Fred Jacob, 273–1711, fax 273–1962.
Inspector General.—David P. Berry, 273–1960, fax 273–2344.
Director, Representation Appeals; Assistant Chief Counsel.—Terence Schoone-Jongen, 273–1971, fax 273–1962.
Director, Office of Congressional and Public Affairs.—Edwin Egee, 273–1991, fax 273–1789.
Chief Information Officer, Office of the Chief Information Officer.—Prem Aburvasamy, 273–3925, fax 273–2850.

DIVISION OF JUDGES

Chief Administrative Law Judge.—Robert A. Giannasi, 501–8800, fax 501–8686.
Deputy Chief Administrative Law Judge.—Arthur Amchan, 501–8800.
Associate Chief Administrative Law Judges: Vacant; Gerald Etchingham, 901 Market Street, Suite 300, San Francisco, CA 94103–1779 (415) 356–5255, fax 356–5254; Vacant, 120 West 45th Street, 11th Floor, New York, NY 10036–5503 (212) 944–2941, fax 944–4904.
General Counsel.—Peter B. Robb, 273–3700, fax 273–4483.
Deputy General Counsel.—Alice B. Stock, 273–3700.
Associate General Counsel, Ethics.—Lori Ketcham, 273–2939.
Special Counsel and Labor Relations; Senior Special Counsel.—Barry F. Smith, 273–2998.
Director, Division of Administration.—Lasharn Hamilton, 273–3936, fax 273–2928.
Chief Financial Officer, Office of the Chief Financial Officer.—Isabel McConnell, 273–3726, fax 273–2928.

DIVISION OF OPERATIONS MANAGEMENT

Associate General Counsel.—Beth Tursell, 273–2900, fax 273–4274.
Deputy Associate General Counsel.—John Doyle.
Assistant General Counsels: Joseph Baniszewski, 273–2897; Yvette Hatfield, 273–3798; Emily Hunt, 273–4253; Aaron Karsh, 273–3828; David A. Kelly, 273–2878; Elizabeth Kilpatrick, 273–0058; Joan A. Sullivan, 273–3742; Miguel Rodriguez, (602) 416–4777; Rick Wainstein, 273–2931.

DIVISION OF ADVICE

Associate General Counsel.—Richard Bock, 273–3800, fax 273–4275.
Deputy Associate General Counsel.—Vacant.
Assistant General Counsel.—Miriam Szapiro, 273–0998.
Assistant General Counsel, Injunction.—Elinor Merberg, 273–3833.
Deputy Assistant General Counsel, Injunction.—Laura Vazquez, 273–3832.

DIVISION OF ENFORCEMENT LITIGATION

Associate General Counsel.—Vacant, 273–2950, fax 273–4244.
Deputy Associate General Counsel.—Vacant.
Appellate and Supreme Court Litigation Branch:
Deputy Associate General Counsel.—David Habenstreit (acting), 273–0979.
Assistant General Counsel.—David Habenstreit, 273–0979.
Deputy Assistant General Counsels: Ruth E. Burdick, 273–7958; Meredith Jason, 273–2945.

DIVISION OF LEGAL COUNSEL

Associate General Counsel.—Vacant, 273–2958.
Deputy Associate General Counsel.—Nancy Platt, 273–2937.
Contempt Litigation and Compliance Branch:
Assistant General Counsel.—William Mascioli, 273–3746.
Deputy Assistant General Counsel.—Dawn Goldstein, 273–2936.
Freedom of Information Act Branch:
FOIA Officer/Assistant General Counsel.—Synta Keeling, 273–2995.

NATIONAL MEDIATION BOARD

1301 K Street, NW., Suite 250 East, Washington, DC 20005

phone (202) 692–5000, fax 692–5081

Chair.—Kyle Fortson, 692–5017.
Board Members: Gerald W. Fauth III, 692–5023; Linda Puchala, 692–5020.
Chief of Staff.—Vacant.
General Counsel and Director, Office of Legal Affairs.—Mary L. Johnson, 692–5040.
Chief Financial Officer and Director, Office of Fiscal Services.—Michael Jerger, 692–5047.
Chief Information Officer and Director, Office of Information Services.—William Fumey, 692–5048.
Director, Office of:
Administration.—Samantha T. Jones, 692–5010.
Arbitration Services.—Terri Brown.
Mediation Services.—Patricia Sims, 692–5066.

THE NATIONAL ACADEMIES OF SCIENCES, ENGINEERING, AND MEDICINE

2101 Constitution Avenue, NW., Washington, DC 20418

(Mailing address: 500 Fifth Street, NW., Washington, DC 20001)

phone (202) 334–2000

The National Academies of Sciences, Engineering, and Medicine serve as an independent adviser to the Federal Government on scientific and technical questions of national importance. Although operating under a congressional charter granted to the National Academy of Sciences in 1863, the three organizations are private organizations, not agencies of the Federal Government, and receive no appropriations from Congress.

NATIONAL ACADEMY OF SCIENCES

President.—Marcia McNutt, 334–2101.
Vice President.—Diane E. Griffin, Johns Hopkins Bloomberg School of Public Health.
Home Secretary.—Susan R. Wessler, University of California, Riverside.

Foreign Secretary.—John Hildebrand, University of Arizona.
Treasurer.—William H. Press, The University of Texas.
Chief Program Officer.—Gregory Symmes, 334–3000.
Chief Operating Officer.—James F. Hinchman, 334–3000.
Executive Director, Office of Congressional Affairs, National Academies of Sciences, Engineering, and Medicine.—Christopher J. King, 334–1601.

NATIONAL ACADEMY OF ENGINEERING

President.—John L. Anderson, 334–3201.
Chair.—Gordon R. England, Chair, PFP Cybersecurity.
Vice President.—Corale L. Brierley, Principal, Brierley Consultancy LLC.
Home Secretary.—Julia M. Phillips, retired Vice President and CTO, Sandia National Laboratories.
Foreign Secretary.—James Tien, Distinguished Professor and Dean Emeritus, College of Engineering, University of Miami.
Executive Officer.—Alton D. Romig, Jr., 334–3677.
Treasurer.—Martin B. Sherwin (Ret.), W.R. Grace.

NATIONAL ACADEMY OF MEDICINE

President.—Victor J. Dzau, M.D., 334–3300.
The Leonard D. Schaeffer Executive Officer.—J. Michael McGinnis, M.D.
Home Secretary.—Jane E. Henney, M.D.
Foreign Secretary.—Margaret Hamburg, M.D.

NATIONAL SCIENCE FOUNDATION

2415 Eisenhower Avenue, Alexandria, VA 22314

phone (703) 292–8000, https://nsf.gov

Director.—Sethuraman Panchanathan (703) 292–8000.
Deputy Director.—Vacant.
Chief Financial Officer and Director, Office of Budget, Finance, & Award Management.—Teresa A. Grancorvitz (acting), 292–8200.
Chief Human Capital Officer and Director, Office of Information & Resource Management.—Wonzie L. Gardner, 292–8100.
Chief Information Officer.—Dorothy Aaronson, 292–4299.
Chief Operating Officer.—F. Fleming Crim.
Assistant Director for—
Biological Sciences.—Joanne S. Tornow, 292–8400.
Computer and Information Science and Engineering.—Erwin Gianchandani (acting), 292–8900.
Education and Human Resources.—Karen A. Marrongelle, 292–8600.
Engineering.—Dawn Tillbury, 292–8300.
Geosciences.—William E. Easterling, 292–8500.
Mathematical and Physical Sciences.—Anne Kinney, 292–8800.
Social, Behavioral, and Economic Sciences.—Arthur W. Lupia, 292–8700.
Director, Office of:
Diversity and Inclusion.—Rhonda J. Davis, 292–8020.
General Counsel.—Lawrence Rudolph, 292–8060.
Inspector General.—Allison C. Lerner, 292–7100.
Integrative Activities.—Suzanne Iacono, 292–8040.
International Science and Engineering.—Rebecca S. Keiser, 292–8710.
Legislative and Public Affairs.—Amanda Hallberg Greenwell, 292–8070.

NATIONAL SCIENCE BOARD

Chair.—Diane L. Souvaine, 292–7000.
Vice Chair.—.Ellen Ochoa.

MEMBERS

John L. Anderson
Roger N. Beachy
Arthur Bienenstock
Vicki L. Chandler
Maureen L. Condic
W. Kent Fuchs
Suresh V. Garimella
Robert M. Groves
James S. Jackson
Steven Leath
W. Carl Lineberger
Victor R. McCrary
Emilio F. Moran
Ellen Ochoa
Sethuraman Panchanathan
G.P. ''Bud'' Peterson
Julia M. Phillips
Daniel A. Reed
Geraldine L. Richmond
Anneila I. Sargent
Diane L. Souvaine
S. Alan Stern
Stephen H. Willard
Maria T. Zuber

NATIONAL TRANSPORTATION SAFETY BOARD

490 L'Enfant Plaza, SW., Washington, DC 20594

phone (202) 314–6000

Chair.—Robert L. Sumwalt III, 314–6021.
Vice Chair.—Bruce Landsberg, 314–6072.
Members: Michael E. Graham, 314–6073; Thomas B. Chapman, 314–6073; Jennifer Homendy, 314–6073.
Managing Director.—Sharon Bryson, 314–6188.
Deputy Managing Director.—Paul Sledzik, 314–6134.
General Counsel.—Kathleen Silbaugh, 314–6016.
Chief Administrative Law Judge.—Alfonso Montano, Jr., 314–6150.
Chief Financial Officer.—Edward Benthall, 314–6241.
Director, Office of:
Aviation Safety.—Dana Schulze, 314–6323.
Government and Industry Affairs.—Christopher Wallace, 314–6007.
Highway Safety.—Robert Molloy, 314–6471.
Marine Safety.—Brian Curtis, 314–6456.
Media Relations.—Christopher O'Neil, 314–6100.
Railroad, Pipeline and Hazardous Materials Investigations.—Robert Hall, 314–6463.
Research and Engineering.—James Ritter, 314–6502.
Safety Advocacy.—Nicholas Worrell, 314–6608.
Safety Recommendations and Communications.—Dolline Hatchett, 314–6057.
Transportation Disaster Assistance.—Elias Kontanis, 314–6187.

NEIGHBORHOOD REINVESTMENT CORPORATION

(Doing business as NeighborWorks America)

999 North Capitol Street, NE., Suite 900, Washington, DC 20002

phone (202) 760–4000, fax 376–2600

BOARD OF DIRECTORS

Chair.—Hon. Martin Gruenberg, Appointive Director, Federal Deposit Insurance Corporation
Vice Chair.—Hon. Michelle W. Bowman, Member, Board of Governors, Federal Reserve System
Members:
Hon. Grovetta Gardineer, Senior Deputy Comptroller for Compliance and Community Affairs, Office of the Comptroller.
Hon. Mark McWatters, Board Member, National Credit Union Administration Board.
Hon. Brian D. Montgomery, Assistant Secretary for Housing, Federal Housing Commissioner, U.S. Department of Housing and Urban Development.
President and Chief Executive Officer.—Marietta Rodriquez, 524–9946.
Executive Vice President and General Counsel/Corporate Secretary.—Rutledge Simmons, 760–4105.
Executive Vice President and Chief Operating Officer.—Susan Ifill, 760–4070.
Executive Vice President and Chief Financial Officer.—Rebecca Bond, 760–4088.
Senior Vice President for—
Resource Development.—Valerie Navy-Daniels, 760–4038.
Public Relations.—Michelle Hudgins, 760–4058.
Field Operations.—Kathryn Watts, 683–6659.
Controller.—Yonas Tessema, 760–4092.
Chief Audit Executive.—Frederick Udochi, 524–9937.

Public Policy and Legislative Affairs.—Kirsten Johnson-Obey, 760–4139.
Training.—Randy Gordon, 760–4197.

NUCLEAR REGULATORY COMMISSION

Washington, DC 20555–0001

phone (301) 415–7000, https://nrc.gov

[Authorized by 42 U.S.C. 5801 and U.S.C. 1201]

OFFICE OF THE CHAIR

Chair.—Kristine L. Svinicki, 415–1855.
Chief of Staff.—Alan Frazier, 415–1855.
Administrative Assistant.—Janet L. Lepre, 415–1855.

COMMISSIONERS

Jeff Baran, 415–1839.
Chief of Staff.—Amy Powell, 415–1839.
Administrative Assistant.—Stacy Schumann, 415–1839.
Annie Caputo, 415–1855.
Chief of Staff.—Steven G. Cade, 415–1867.
Administrative Assistant.—Nicole D. Riddick, 415–1855.
Christopher T. Hanson, 415–0566.
Chief of Staff.—Molly Marsh, 415–0566.
Administrative Assistant.—Kathleen Blake, 415–0566.
David A. Wright, 415–1758.
Chief of Staff.—Catherine E. Kanatas, 415–2896.
Administrative Assistant.—Kimberly G. Lora, 415–1759.

STAFF OFFICES OF THE COMMISSION

Secretary.—Annette L. Vietti-Cook, 415–1969, fax 415–1672.
Chief Financial Officer.—Maureen Wylie, 415–7322, fax 415–4236.
Commission Appellate Adjudication.—Andrew Averbach, 415–2653, fax 415–3200.
Congressional Affairs.—Eugene Dacus, 415–1776, fax 415–2162.
General Counsel.—Marian L. Zobler, 415–1743, fax 415–3086.
Inspector General.—David Lee (acting), 415–5930, fax 415–5091.
International Programs.—Nader L. Mamish (301) 287–9056.
Public Affairs.—David Castelveter, 415–8200, fax 415–2234.

ADVISORY COMMITTEE ON MEDICAL USES OF ISOTOPES

Chair.—Darlene F. Metter.

ADVISORY COMMITTEE ON REACTOR SAFEGUARDS

Executive Director.—Scott Moore, 415–7360, fax 415–5589.

ATOMIC SAFETY AND LICENSING BOARD PANEL

Chief Administrative Judge.—E. Roy Hawkens, 415–7454, fax 415–5599.

OFFICE OF THE EXECUTIVE DIRECTOR FOR OPERATIONS

Executive Director for Operations.—Margaret M. Doane, 415–1700, fax 415–2700.
Deputy Executive Director for:
Materials, Waste, Research, State, Tribal, Compliance, Administration, and Human Capital Programs.—K. Steve West, 415–1705, fax 415–2700.
Reactor and Preparedness Programs.—Daniel H. Dorman, 415–1713, fax 415–2700.

Director, Office of:
Administration.—Jennifer M. Golder, 415–8747, fax 415–5352.
Enforcement.—George A. Wilson (301) 287–9527, fax (301) 287–3325.
Chief Human Capital Officer.—Miriam L. Cohen (301) 287–0747, fax (301) 287–9343.
Information Services.—David J. Nelson, 415–8700, fax 415–4246.
Investigations.—Edward Shuttleworth, 415–2373, fax 415–2370.
Nuclear Material Safety and Safeguards.—John Lubinski, 415–0595, fax 492–3360.
Nuclear Regulatory Research.—Ray V. Furstenau, 415–1914, fax 415–6671.
Nuclear Reactor Regulation.—Ho Nieh (301) 415–1270, fax (301) 415–8333.
Nuclear Security and Incident Response.—Brian Holian (301) 287–3734, fax (301) 287–9351.
Small Business and Civil Rights.—Vonna L. Ordaz, 415–7380, fax 415–5953.

REGIONAL OFFICES

Region I: David C. Lew, 2100 Renaissance Boulevard, Suite 100, King of Prussia, PA 19406 (610) 337–5299, fax (610) 337–5241.
Region II: Laura Dudes, 245 Peachtree Center Avenue, NE., Suite 1200, Atlanta, GA 30303 (404) 997–4411, fax (404) 997–4901.
Region III: Darrell J. Roberts, 2443 Warrenville Road, Suite 210, Lisle, IL 60532 (630) 829–9657, fax (630) 515–1096.
Region IV: Scott A. Morris, 1600 East Lamar Boulevard, Arlington, TX 76011 (817) 200–1225, fax (817) 200–1122.

OCCUPATIONAL SAFETY AND HEALTH REVIEW COMMISSION

1120 20th Street, NW., 9th Floor, Washington, DC 20036–3457

phone (202) 606–5100

[Created by Public Law 91–596]

Chair.—James J. Sullivan Jr., 606–5373.
Chief Counsel to the Chair.—Vacant, 606–5736.
Confidential Assistant to the Chair (Public Affairs Officer).—Kelly L. Tyroler, 606–5723.
Commissioner.—Amanda Wood Laihow.
Chief Counsel to the Commissioner.—Vacant.
Commissioner.—Cynthia L. Attwood.
Chief Counsel to the Commissioner.—Vacant.
Confidential Assistant to the Commissioner.—Vacant.
Administrative Law Judges:
Patrick B. Augustine, U.S. Custom House, 721 19th Street, Room 407, Denver, CO 80202–2517.
Peggy S. Ball, U.S. Custom House, 721 19th Street, Room 407, Denver, CO 80202–2517.
Carol A. Baumerich, 1120 20th Street, NW., 9th Floor, Washington, DC 20036–3457.
Keith E. Bell, 1120 20th Street, NW., 9th Floor, Washington, DC 20036–3457.
Sharon D. Calhoun, 100 Alabama Street, SW., Building 1924, Room 2R90, Atlanta, GA 30303–3104.
William S. Coleman, 1120 20th Street, NW., 9th Floor, Washington, DC 20036–3457.
Brian A. Duncan, U.S. Custom House, 721 19th Street, Room 407, Denver, CO 80202–2517.
John B. Gatto, 100 Alabama Street, SW., Building 1924, Room 2R90, Atlanta, GA 30303–3104.
Christopher D. Helms, U.S. Custom House, 721 19th Street, Room 407, Denver, CO 80202–2517.
Heather A. Joys, 100 Alabama Street, SW., Building 1924, Room 2R90, Atlanta, GA 30303–3104.
Dennis L. Phillips, 1120 20th Street, NW., 9th Floor, Washington, DC 20036–3457.
Covette Rooney, 1120 20th Street, NW., 9th Floor, Washington, DC 20036–3457.
General Counsel.—Nadine N. Mancini.
Executive Secretary.—John X. Cerveny.
Executive Director.—Debra A. Hall.

OFFICE OF GOVERNMENT ETHICS

1201 New York Avenue, NW., Suite 500, Washington, DC 20005

phone (202) 482–9300, https://oge.gov

[Created by Act of October 1, 1989; codified in 5 U.S.C. app., section 401]

Director.—Emory A. Rounds III.
Chief of Staff and Program Counsel.—Shelley K. Finlayson.
General Counsel.—David J. Apol.
Deputy Director for Compliance.—Dale A. Christopher.

OFFICE OF PERSONNEL MANAGEMENT

Theodore Roosevelt Building, 1900 E Street, NW., Washington, DC 20415

phone (202) 606–1800, https://opm.gov

OFFICE OF THE DIRECTOR

Director.—Michael J. Rigas (acting), 606–1000.
Special Assistant.—Mary E. Anderson.
Deputy Director.—Michael J. Rigas.
Senior Advisor to the Director.—Vacant.
Chief of Staff.—Jonathan Blyth (acting).
Executive Assistant.—Vacant.
Deputy Chief of Staff.—Vacant.
Counselor to the Director.—Vacant.
White House Liaison.—Kathleen M. Bullock, 606–1000.
Executive Assistant.—Torlanda Young, 606–1467.
Chief Management Officer.—Kathleen McGettigan, 606–2938.
Executive Assistant.—Delicia T. Harrell, 606–2732.
Senior Advisor.—Basil Parker.
Chief Privacy Officer.—Kelly C. Riley.
Executive Director, Chief Human Capital Officers (CHCO) Council.—Sara B. Ratcliff.

OFFICE OF THE EXECUTIVE SECRETARIAT

Director.—Vacant, 606–1000.
Deputy Director.—Stephen Hickman, 606–1973.
International Affairs.—Jill Feldman, 606–5099.
Regulatory Affairs.—Alexys Stanley, 606–1183.

CHIEF FINANCIAL OFFICER

Chief Financial Officer.—Dennis D. Coleman, 606–2938.
Deputy Chief Financial Officer.—Daniel K. Marella, 606–2638.
Executive Officer/Resource Management.—Katina P. Cotton, 606–4725.
OPM Projects and Initiatives.—Teresa F. Williams, 606–1414.
Associate Chief Financial Officer:
Policy and Internal Control.—Thomas Moschetto, 418–3149.
Budget and Performance.—Margaret P. Pearson, 606–0087.
Financial Services.—Tonya R. Johnson, 606–1531.
Financial Operations Management.—Rochelle S. Bayard, 606–4366.

OFFICE OF COMMUNICATIONS

Director.—Dean Hunter (acting), 606–2402.
Deputy Director.—LaShonne Williams, 606–2402.
Administrative Assistant.—Jean Smith, 606–2402.
Speechwriter.—Lauren R. Westcott, 606–2402.
Press Secretary.—Vacant.
Digital Director.—Briana Kaya, 606–2402.

CONGRESSIONAL, LEGISLATIVE, AND INTERGOVERNMENTAL AFFAIRS (CLIA)

Director.—Jonathan Blyth, 606–1300.

Executive Assistant.—Vacant.
Deputy Director.—Vacant.
Congressional Relations Officer.—Vacant, 606–5197.
Chief, Legislative Analysis Group.—Kristine Prentice.
Legislative Analysts: Timothy Duffy, 606–2367; Darin Gibbons, 606–8230; Andrew Moore, 606–5197.
Correspondence Analyst.—Jerson Matias, 418–4360.
Chief, Constituent Services, Capitol Hill.—Christiana Frazee, B332 Rayburn House Office Building, 225–4955, FAX: 225–4974.
Constituent Services Representatives: Marina Golovkina, Sarita Swan, Carlos E. Tingle, Carina Vazquez, Melony Witherspoon.

MERIT SYSTEM ACCOUNTABILITY AND COMPLIANCE

Associate Director.—Mark W. Lambert, 606–2980.
Deputy Associate Director.—Ana Mazzi, 606–2980.
Director, Combined Federal Campaign (CFC) Operations.—Keith Willingham, 606–2564.
Director, Internal Oversight and Compliance.—Janet L. Barnes, 606–3207.
Program Manager, Voting Rights and Resource Management.—Jeremy J. Leahy (acting), 606–5290.
Administrative Assistant.—Kimberlin C. Chaney, 606–3207.

CHIEF INFORMATION OFFICER

Chief Information Officer.—David A. Garcia, 606–2150.
Deputy Chief Information Officer.—Robert M. Leahy, 606–2150.
Resource Management.—Vacant.
Chief Information Security Officer.—Cord Chase, 606–6210.
IT Security/Security Operations Center.—Jeffrey Wagner, 606–2571.
Chief Technology Officer.—Vacant.
IT Strategy and Policy:
Associate Chief Information Officer.—Dovarius L. Peoples, 606–2150.
Strategic Planning.—Vacant.
IT Enterprise Architect.—Vacant.
IT Investment Management.—Stephen L. Schultz, 606–8089.
Information Management.—Vacant.
Quality Assurance.—Huy Le, 606–1384.
Freedom of Information and Privacy Act.—Vacant.
Federal Data Solutions:
Associate CIO.—Dovarius L. Peoples, 606–2150.
Data Management.—Vacant.
Data Warehouse.—Victor A. Karcher, Jr. (724) 794–2005, ext. 3209.
Enterprise Infrastructure Solutions (EIS):
Associate Chief Information Officer.—Jeffrey Wagner (acting), 606–2571.
Web Services.—Linzie T. Oliver (acting), 606–2445.
Network Management.—Vacant.
Data Center.—Heather Kowalski, 606–1893.
Program Office Support IT PMO.—Oliver Linzie, 606–2445.
Federal IT Business Solutions:
Associate Chief Information Officer.—Lawrence L. Anderson, 606–2150.
Retirement Services IT PMO.—May T. Cheng, 606–7009.
Federal Investigative Services IT PMO.—Vacant.
Human Resources Solutions IT PMO.—MC Price (478) 744–2051.
Employee Services IT PMO.—Michelle Gilder Early, 606–2641.
Healthcare and Insurance and *Merit System Accountability and Compliance IT PMO.*—Juan C. García Rolón, 418–4362.
Federal Applications IT PMO.—MC Price (acting), (478) 744–2051.

HUMAN RESOURCES SOLUTIONS (HRS)

Associate Director.—Joseph S. Kennedy, 606–0900.
Principal Deputy Associate Director.—Reginald M. Brown (acting), 606–1332.
Executive Assistant.—Shirl Sibley, 606–1304.
Deputy Associate Directors:
Center for Leadership Development, and Director, Federal Executive Institute.—Susan G. Logann (434) 980–6220.

Center for Leadership Development, and Innovation Lab.—Sydney Smith-Heimborck, 606–2762.
Center for Management Services.—Reginald M. Brown, 606–1332.
Federal Staffing Group.—Dianna M. Saxman (215) 362–3154.
HR Strategy and Evaluation Solutions.—Leslie Pollack, 606–1426.
Training and Management Assistance Program.—James McPherson, 606–4667.

RETIREMENT SERVICES

Associate Director.—Kenneth J. Zawodny, Jr. (724) 794–7759.
Deputy Associate Director (Boyers).—Nicholas Ashenden, 794–2005 ext. 3214.
Executive Assistant.—Christy Bernhart, 794–7760.
Deputy Associate Director (DC).—Tia N. Butler (202) 606–4168.
Executive Assistant.—Arminta Thompson-Smith, 606–3803.

OFFICE OF THE GENERAL COUNSEL

General Counsel.—Ted M. Cooperstein, 606–1700.
Deputy General Counsels: Steven D. Dillingham, 606–1700; Kathie Ann Whipple, 606–1700.
Special Counsel and Senior Advisor.—Vacant.
Special Counsel.—Amy W. Apostol, 606–5206.
Associate General Counsel (Compensation, Benefits, Products and Services).—Jason C. Foster, 606–1700.
Assistant General Counsel (Merit Systems and Accountability).—Steven E. Abow.
Chief, Administrative Operations.—Paul J. Carr, 606–4018.

OFFICE OF THE INSPECTOR GENERAL

Inspector General.—Norbert E. Vint (acting), 606–1200.
Deputy Inspector General.—Norbet E. Vint, 606–1200.
Executive Assistant.—A. Paulette Berry, 606–3807.
Counsel to the Inspector General.—Robin M. Richardson, 606–2037.
Assistant Inspector General for Audits.—Michael R. Esser, 606–1200.
Deputy Assistant Inspectors General for Audits: Melissa D. Brown, 606–4714; Lewis F. Parker, 606–4738.
Assistant Inspector General for Investigations.—Drew M. Grimm, 606–1200.
Deputy Assistant Inspector General for Investigations.—Thomas Sourth, 606–4730.
Assistant Inspector General for Legal Affairs.—Vacant.
Assistant Inspector General for Management.—James L. Ropelewski, 606–0846.
Deputy Assistant Inspector General for Management.—Nicholas E. Hoyle, 606–2156.
Chief Information Technology Officer.—Gopala Seelamneni.

OFFICE OF SMALL AND DISADVANTAGED BUSINESS UTILIZATION (OSDBU)

Director.—Desmond Brown, 606–2862.

OFFICE OF PROCUREMENT OPERATIONS (OPO)

Senior Procurement Executive.—Juan Arratia, 606–1984.
Executive Assistant.—Eva X. Lopez, 606–7933.
Director, Contracting.—Elijah Anderson (acting), 606–6429.
Division Director, Procurement Policy and Innovation.—Gregory F. Blaszko (215) 861–3112.

FACILITIES, SECURITY, AND EMERGENCY MANAGEMENT (FSEM)

Director.—Dean Hunter, 606–3130.
Executive Assistant.—Eva X. Lopez, 606–7933.
Director, Administrative Operations.—Mark A. Anderson, 418–3214.
Facilities Management:

Director.—Mariano Aquino, 606–4590.
Facility Services and Logistics.—Marla Neustadt, 606–2502.
Building Operations.—Timothy J. Allman, 606–1457.
Safety and Occupational Health.—Victoria Pearson, 606–2220.
Security Services:
Director.—Kevin McCombs, 418–0201.
Physical Security.—Elvis Chase, 606–2872.
Security Assessment.—Dairel L. Rawson (724) 794–7137.
Personnel Security.—Melinda M. Davis (724) 794–7112.
Adjudication and Compliance.—Patricia Neiderhiser (724) 794–7171.
Adjudication and Clearance Processing.—Michael Price (724) 794–7110.
Special Agreements and Identity Processing.—Scott Kaminski (724) 794–7128.
Emergency Management:
Director.—Sandra L. Hawthorne, 606–5068.
SitRoom Operations.—Dwayne Butler, 606–7016.
Emergency Actions.—Brien Gibney, 418–9920.

EQUAL EMPLOYMENT OPPORTUNITY

Director.—LaShonn M. Woodland, 606–2460.
Lead EEO Specialist.—Yasmin A. Rosa, 606–2460.

HUMAN RESOURCES

Director, OPM Human Resources and Chief Human Capital Officer.—Andrea J. Bright, 606–3590.
Deputy Director, Human Resources and OPM Learning.—Tyshawn J. Thomas, 606–2646.

DIVERSITY AND INCLUSION

Director.—Zina B. Sutch, 606–0020.
Deputy Director.—Nicole Lassiter (acting), 606–2267.

HEALTHCARE AND INSURANCE

Director.—Alan P. Spielman, 606–4995.
Deputy Director.—Laurie Bodenheimer, 606–1572.
Staff Assistant.—Lorraine Waller, 606–4017.
Chief Medical Officer.—Christine Hunter, 606–4653.
Assistant Director, Federal Employee Insurance Operations.—Edward DeHarde, 606–0522.
Deputy Assistant Director, Federal Employee Insurance Operations.—Deputy Assistant Director.—Cindy Butler, 606–7019.
Assistant Director, Program Development Support.—Lori H. Amos, 606–0277.
Deputy Assistant Director, Program Development Support.—Holly Schumann, 606–7112.

PLANNING AND POLICY ANALYSIS

Director.—Anne Easton (acting), 606–2213.
Deputy Director.—Vacant.
Senior Advisor, Research and Evaluation.—Kimya Lee, 606–6428.
Program Management Office.—Dennis Hardy, 606–4182.
Office of Actuaries.—Steve Niu, 606–1578.
Data Analysis.—Lance Harris, 606–1449.
Survey Analysis.—Kim Wells, 606–9088.
Policy Analysis.—Jodi Miller, 418–3398.
Human Resources Line of Business.—David Vargas, 418–3236.

EMPLOYEE SERVICES

Associate Director.—Mark Reinhold, 606–2520.
Principal Deputy Associate Director.—Veronica Villalobos, 606–7992.
Deputy Associate Directors:

Outreach, Diversity, and Inclusion.—Zina B. Sutch, 606–2433.
Partnership and Labor Relations.—Tim F. Curry, 606–2402.
Pay and Leave.—Brenda Roberts, 606–2858.
Recruitment and Hiring.—Kimberly Holden, 418–3218.
Senior Executive Service and Performance Management.—Vacant.
Strategic Workforce Planning.—Veronica Villalobos (acting), 606–7992.
Veterans Services.—Hakeem Basheerud-Deen, 606–3602.

OFFICE OF THE SPECIAL COUNSEL

1730 M Street, NW., Suite 300, Washington, DC 20036–4505

phone (202) 804–7000

[Authorized by 5 U.S.C. 1101 and 5 U.S.C. 1211]

Special Counsel.—Henry Kerner.
Principal Deputy Special Counsel.—Ellen Chubin Epstein.

PEACE CORPS

1275 First Street, NE., Washington, DC 20526

phone (202) 692–2000, Toll-Free Number (855) 855–1961

https://peacecorps.gov

[Created by Public Law 97–113]

OFFICE OF THE DIRECTOR

phone (202) 962–2100, fax 692–2101

Director.—Jody Olsen.
Deputy Director.—Vacant.
Chief of Staff.—Michelle Brooks.
Deputy Chief of Staff/White House Liaison.—Matthew McKinney.
Senior Advisors: Sheila Crowley, Maura Fulton, Maryann Minutillo, Heather Schwenk, Carl Sosebee.
Executive Secretary.—Vacant.
Chief Administrative Officer.—Amaka Okafor.
Chief Compliance Officer.—Anne Hughes.

OFFICE OF VICTIM ADVOCACY

Director.—Da Shawnna Townsend.

OFFICE OF CIVIL RIGHTS AND DIVERSITY

Director.—John Burden.

OFFICE OF COMMUNICATIONS

Director of Press Relations.—Matthew Sheehey.

OFFICE OF CONGRESSIONAL RELATIONS

Director.—Nancy Herbolsheimer.
Deputy Director.—Scott Rausch.

OFFICE OF THE GENERAL COUNSEL

General Counsel.—Robert Shanks.

OFFICE OF STRATEGIC PARTNERSHIPS AND INTERGOVERNMENTAL AFFAIRS

Director.—Shannon Kendrick.

OFFICE OF EXTERNAL AFFAIRS

Associate Director.—Rachel Kahler.

OFFICE OF GIFTS AND GRANTS MANAGEMENT

Director.—Karen Roberts.
Deputy Director.—Charlotte Kea.

OFFICE OF STRATEGIC INFORMATION, RESEARCH, AND PLANNING

Director.—Vacant.
Deputy Director.—Jeff Kwiecinski.

OFFICE OF THIRD GOAL AND RETURNED VOLUNTEER SERVICES

Director.—Keith Honda.

OFFICE OF GLOBAL OPERATIONS

Associate Director.—Patrick Young.
Senior Advisor.—Diana Schmidt.

Africa Region:

Regional Director.—Johnathan Miller.
Chief of Operations.—Tim Hartman.

Europe / Mediterranean / Asia Region:

Regional Director.—Jeannette Windon.
Chief of Operations.—Mark Vander Vort.

Inter-America and Pacific Region:

Regional Director.—Gregory Huger.
Chief of Operations.—Mary Kate Lowndes.

OFFICE OF OVERSEAS PROGRAMMING AND TRAINING SUPPORT

Director.—Stephanie Rust.

PEACE CORPS RESPONSE

Director.—Kweku Boafo.
Chief of Operations.—Alex Garcia.

OFFICE OF GLOBAL HEALTH AND HIV

Director.—Marie McLeod.

OFFICE OF MANAGEMENT

Associate Director.—Clark Presnell (acting).
Chief Administrative Officer.—Clark Presnell.
FOIA / Privacy Act Officer.—Virginia Burke.

OFFICE OF HUMAN RESOURCE MANAGEMENT

Director.—Vacant.

OFFICE OF THE INSPECTOR GENERAL

Inspector General.—Kathy Buller.
Deputy Inspector General.—Joaquin Ferrao.

OFFICE OF THE CHIEF FINANCIAL OFFICER

Chief Financial Officer.—Richard Swarttz.
Deputy Chief Financial Officer.—Andrew Pierce.

OFFICE OF THE CHIEF INFORMATION OFFICER

Chief Information Officer.—Scott Knell.
Deputy Chief Information Officer.—Michael Terry.

OFFICE OF VOLUNTEER RECRUITMENT AND SELECTION

Associate Director.—David Walker.
Chief of Operations.—Tina Williams.
Chief Administrative Officer.—Debra Booker (acting).
Director of:
Placement.—Christine O'Neill.
Recruitment and Diversity.—Brad Merryman.
University Programs.—La'Teashia Sykes.
Analysis and Evaluations.—Erin Krizay.

REGIONAL OFFICES

Central Region (Alabama, Arkansas, Illinois, Indiana, Iowa, Kansas, Kentucky, Louisiana, Michigan, Minnesota, Mississippi, Missouri, Nebraska, North Dakota, Ohio, Oklahoma, South Dakota, Tennessee, Texas, West Virginia, Wisconsin)
Regional Recruitment Supervisor.—Jessica Vig, 230 South Dearborn Street, Suite 2020, Chicago, IL 60604 (312) 353–4990.
East Region (Connecticut, Delaware, District of Columbia, Florida, Georgia, Maine, Maryland, Massachusetts, New Hampshire, New Jersey, New York, North Carolina, Pennsylvania, Rhode Island, South Carolina, Vermont, Virginia, Puerto Rico, U.S. Virgin Islands)
Regional Recruitment Supervisor.—Katrina Bowser, 201 Varick Street, Suite 1025, New York, NY 10014 (212) 352–5440.
West Region (Alaska, Arizona, California, Colorado, Hawaii, Idaho, Montana, Nevada, New Mexico, Oregon, Utah, Washington, Wyoming)
Regional Recruitment Supervisor.—Sarah Kassel, 1301 Clay Street, Suite 620N, Oakland, CA 94612 (510) 452–8444.

OFFICE OF SAFETY AND SECURITY

Associate Director.—Shawn Bardwell.
Physical Security Specialist.—John McIntire.

OFFICE OF HEALTH SERVICES

Associate Director.—Karen Becker.
Director of:
Counseling and Outreach.—Jill Carty.
Medical Services.—Vacant.

PENSION BENEFIT GUARANTY CORPORATION

1200 K Street, Washington, DC 20005–4026

phone (202) 326–4000

BOARD OF DIRECTORS

Chair.—Eugene Scalia, Secretary of Labor.
Members:
Steven T. Mnuchin, Secretary of the Treasury.
Wilbur Ross, Secretary of Commerce.

OFFICIALS

Director.—Gordon Hartogensis, 326–4010.

Chief Policy Officer.—Andy Banducci, 326–4010.
Deputy Chief Policy Officer.—Michael Rae, 326–4010.
Chief Officers for—
Benefits Administration.—David Foley, 326–4000.
Finance.—Patricia Kelly, 326–4170.
General Counsel.—Judith Starr, 326–4020.
Information Technology.—Robert Scherer, 326–4000.
Management.—Alice Maroni, 326–4000.
Negotiations and Restructuring.—Karen Morris, 326–4000.
Department Director for—
Budget.—Kimberly Mayo, 326–4000.
Communications Outreach and Public Affairs.—Martha Threatt, 326–3727.
Contracts and Controls Review.—Franklin Pace, 326–4161.
Corporate Finance and Restructuring.—Adi Berger, 326–4000.
Financial Operations.—Theodore Winter, 326–4060.
Human Resources.—Arrie Etheridge, 326–4110.
Information Technology Infrastructure Operations.—Joshua Kossoy, 326–4130.
Business Innovation Services.—Srividhya Shyamsunder, 326–4130.
Policy, Research and Analysis.—Ted Goldman, 326–4000.
Workplace Solutions.—Alisa Cottone, 326–4150.

POSTAL REGULATORY COMMISSION

901 New York Avenue, NW., Suite 200, Washington, DC 20268–0001

phone (202) 789–6800, fax 789–6891

Chair.—Robert Taub, 789–6897.
Vice Chair.—Michael Kubayanda, 789–6810.
Commissioners:
Mark Acton, 789–6866.
Ann Fisher, 789–6893.
Ashley Poling, 789–6807.
Chief Administrative Officer and Secretary.—Darcie Tokioka (acting), 789–6842.
Director, Public Affairs and Government Relations.—Jennifer Warburton, 789–6803.
General Counsel.—David Trissell, 789–6818.
Director, Office of Accountability and Compliance.—Margaret Cigno, 789–6855.

SECURITIES AND EXCHANGE COMMISSION

100 F Street, NE., Washington, DC 20549

Phone (202) 551–6000, TTY Relay Service 1–800–877–8339

https://sec.gov

THE COMMISSION

Chairman.—Jay Clayton, 551–2100, chairmanoffice@sec.gov, fax 772–9200.
Chief of Staff.—Sean Memon.
Deputy Chief of Staff.—Bryan Wood.
Chief Counsel and Senior Policy Advisor for Market and Activities-Based Risk.—Jeffrey Dinwoodie.
Chief Counsel and Senior Policy Advisor.—Kimberly Hamm.
Senior Advisors to the Chairman: Sebastian Gomez Abero, Aleah Borghard, Eric Diamond, Kay Smith, Kevin Zerrusen.
Commissioners:
Hester M. Peirce, 551–5080, CommissionerPeirce@sec.gov.
Elad Roisman, 551–2700, CommissionerRoisman@sec.gov.
Allison Herren Lee, 551–2800, CommissionerLee@sec.gov.

OFFICE OF THE SECRETARY

Secretary.—Vanessa Countryman, 551–5400.
Deputy Secretary.—Eduardo Aleman, 551–5400.
Assistant Secretaries: Jill Peterson; J. Lynn Taylor, 551–5400.

OFFICE OF LEGISLATIVE AND INTERGOVERNMENTAL AFFAIRS

Director.—Holli Heiles Pandol, 551–2010, fax 772–9200.

OFFICE OF THE CHIEF OPERATING OFFICER

Chief Operating Officer.—Kenneth Johnson, 551–2200.
Chief Risk Officer.—Gabriel Benincasa, 551–2200.

OFFICE OF INVESTOR EDUCATION AND ADVOCACY

Director.—Lori J. Schock, 551–6500, fax 772–9295.
Deputy Director.—Mary S. Head, 551–6500.

OFFICE OF SUPPORT OPERATIONS

Director/Chief FOIA Officer.—Barry D. Walters, 551–8400.
FOIA Officer.—John Livornese, 551–3831, fax 772–9336/9337.

OFFICE OF EQUAL EMPLOYMENT OPPORTUNITY

Director.—Peter Henry, 551–6040, fax 772–9316.

OFFICE OF MINORITY AND WOMEN INCLUSION

Director.—Pamela Gibbs, 551–6046.
Deputy Director.—John Moses, 551–6046.

OFFICE OF THE CHIEF ACCOUNTANT

Chief Accountant.—Sagar S. Teotia, 551–5300, fax 772–9253.
Chief Counsel.—Giles Cohen (acting), 551–5300.

OFFICE OF COMPLIANCE INSPECTIONS AND EXAMINATIONS

Director.—Peter Driscoll, 551–6200, fax 772–9184.
Deputy Directors: Daniel Kahl; Kristin Snyder, 551–6200.
Associate Director/Chief Counsel.—Daniel Kahl, 551–6730.
Associate Directors:
Broker-Dealer.—John Polise.
Clearance and Settlement.—Dan Gregus.
FINRA Securities Industry Oversight.—Kevin Goodman.
Investment Adviser/Investment Company: Marshall Gandy, Kristin Snyder.
Risk and Strategy.—James Reese.
Technology Controls Program.—Keith Cassidy.

DIVISION OF ECONOMIC AND RISK ANALYSIS

Director and Chief Economist.—S.P. Kothari, 551–6600, DERA@sec.gov.
Deputy Director and Deputy Chief Economist.—Chyhe Becker, 551–6600.

OFFICE OF THE GENERAL COUNSEL

General Counsel.—Robert B. Stebbins, 551–5100.
Deputy General Counsel: Jeffrey Finnell, 551–5100; Elizabeth McFadden, 551–5100; Meredith Mitchell, 551–5100.
Associate General Counsel for Adjudication.—Benjamin Schiffrin, 551–5003.
Solicitor, Appellate Litigation and Bankruptcy.—Michael Conley, 551–5100.
Deputy Solicitor.—John Avery, 551–5100.
Associate General Counsel for Legal Policy 1.—Lori Price, 551–5196.
Associate General Counsel for Legal Policy 2.—Laura Jarsulic, 551–4873.
Associate General Counsel for Litigation and Administrative Practice.—Richard M. Humes, 551–5140.

OFFICE OF ETHICS COUNSEL

Ethics Counsel and Designated Ethics Officer.—Danae Serrano, 551–5170.

DIVISION OF INVESTMENT MANAGEMENT

Director.—Dalia Blass, 551–6720, fax 772–9234.
Deputy Director / Chief Counsel.—Paul Cellupica, 551–6720.
Associate Director / Senior Policy Advisor.—Susan Nash, 551–6720.
Associate Director, Office of Analytics.—Timothy Husson, 551–6720.
Chief Counsel: David Bartels, 551–6720; Sara Cortes, 551–6720.
Disclosure Review and Accounting.—Brent Fields, 551–6720.
Rulemaking.—Sarah ten Siethoff, 551–6720.
Chief Accountant.—Alison Staloch, 551–6720.

DIVISION OF CORPORATION FINANCE

Director.—William Hinman, 551–3100.
Managing Executive.—Charlene Arietti, 551–3822.
Deputy Director.—Shelley E. Parratt, 551–3540.
Chief Accountant.—Kyle Moffatt, 551–3836.
Chief Counsel.—David Fredrickson, 551–5144.

DIVISION OF ENFORCEMENT

Co-Directors: Stephanie Avakian, 551–4500; Steven Peikin, 551–4500, fax 772–9279.
Managing Executive.—Victor Valdez, 551–4500.
Associate Directors: Anita Bandy, Antonia Chion, Melissa Hodgman, Carolyn Welshhans.
Chief, Market Intelligence.—Jennifer Diamantis, 551–4500.
Chief Counsel.—Joseph Brenner, 551–4500.
Chief Litigation Counsel.—Bridget Fitzpatrick, 551–4500.
Deputy Chief Litigation Counsel.—David Gottesman, 551–4500.
Chief Accountant.—Matthew Jacques, 551–6150.
Senior Associate Chief Accountants: Dwayne Brown, Kristen Dieter, David Estabrook, Peter Rosario, 551–4647.
Office of Collections: Gordon Brumback, 551–4500; Marsha Massey, 551–4500.
Office of Whistleblower, Chief.—Jane Norberg, 551–4411.

DIVISION OF TRADING AND MARKETS

Director.—Brett Redfearn, 551–5500.
Deputy Directors: Christian Sabella, Elizabeth Baird, 551–5500.
Associate Director, Chief Counsel.—Emily Westerberg Russell, 551–5576.
Associate Directors:
Analytics and Research.—David Saltiel, 551–7422.
Broker-Dealer Finances.—Michael Macchiaroli, 551–5510; Thomas McGowan, 551–5521.
Clearance and Settlement.—Jeffrey Mooney, 551–5712.
Derivatives Policy and Trading Practices.—Mark Wolfe, 551–5730.
Market Supervision.—John Roeser, 551–5630; David Shillman, 551–5668.

OFFICE OF CREDIT RATINGS

Director.—Jessica Kane, (212) 336–9080.

OFFICE OF MUNICIPAL SECURITIES

Director.—Rebecca Olsen, 551–5680.

OFFICE OF ADMINISTRATIVE LAW JUDGES

Chief Administrative Law Judge.—Carol Fox Foelak (acting), 551–6030, fax 777–1031.
Administrative Law Judges: James Grimes, Jason S. Patil.

OFFICE OF INTERNATIONAL AFFAIRS

Director.—Raquel Fox, 551–6690.

OFFICE OF THE INVESTOR ADVOCATE

Investor Advocate.—Rick Fleming, 551–3302.

OFFICE OF THE INSPECTOR GENERAL

Inspector General.—Carl W. Hoecker, 551–6061, fax 772–9265.
Counsel to the IG/Deputy Inspector General.—Roderick Fillinger, 551–6061.
Deputy Inspector General for Audits, Evaluations, and Special Projects.—Rebecca Sharek, 551–6061.
Deputy Inspector General for Operations and Management.—Helen Albert, 551–6061.
Deputy Inspector General for Investigations.—Nicholas Padilla, 551–6001.

OFFICE OF PUBLIC AFFAIRS

Director.—John Nester, 551–4120, news@sec.gov.
Deputy Directors: Florence Harmon, 551–4120; Chandler Costello, 551–4120.

OFFICE OF FINANCIAL MANAGEMENT

Chief Financial Officer.—Caryn Kauffman, 551–7840, fax 756–0473.

OFFICE OF INFORMATION TECHNOLOGY

Director/Chief Information Officer.—Charles Riddle (acting), 551–8800.
Deputy Director/Chief Technology Officer.—Todd Mauzy (acting), 551–8800.

OFFICE OF ACQUISITIONS

Director.—Vance Cathell, 551–8385, fax 572–1386.

OFFICE OF HUMAN RESOURCES

Director/Chief Human Capital Officer.—James McNamara, 551–7500.
Deputy Chief Human Capital Officer.—Dennis Truskey (acting), 551–7500.

EDGAR BUSINESS OFFICE

Director/EDGAR Business Office.—Jed Hickman, 551–8600.

OFFICE OF THE ADVOCATE FOR SMALL BUSINESS CAPITAL FORMATION

Small Business Advocate.—Martha Legg Miller, 551–5407.

REGIONAL OFFICES

Atlanta Regional Office: 950 East Paces Ferry Road, NE., Suite 900, Atlanta, GA 30326–1382 (404) 842–7600, fax 842–7633 (Enforcement, Administration), fax 842–5752 (Examination).
Regional Director.—Richard Best.
Associate Regional Director, Director, Enforcement.—Justin Jeffries.
Associate Regional Director, Examinations.—Donna Esau.
Boston Regional Office: 33 Arch Street, 24th Floor, Boston, MA 02110–1424 (617) 573–8900, fax 573–4590.
Regional Director.—Paul Levenson.
Associate Regional Director, Enforcement.—John T. Dugan.

Associate Regional Director, Examinations.—Kevin Kelcourse.

Chicago Regional Office: 175 West Jackson Boulevard, Suite 1450, Chicago, IL 60604 (312) 353–7390, fax 353–7398.

Regional Director.—Joel R. Levin.

Senior Associate Regional Director, Enforcement.—Robert J. Burson.

Associate Regional Director, Enforcement.—Kathryn A. Pyszka.

Associate Regional Director, Examinations: Daniel Gregus, Steven Levine.

Denver Regional Office: Byron G. Rogers Federal Building, 1961 Stout St., Suite 1700, Denver, CO 80294–1961 (303) 844–1000, fax 297–1730.

Regional Director.—Kurt L. Gottschall.

Associate Regional Directors:

Enforcement.—Jason Burt.

Examinations.—Thomas M. Piccone.

Operations.—Christopher P. Friedman.

Fort Worth Regional Office: 801 Cherry Street, Suite 1900, Unit 18, Fort Worth, TX 76102 (817) 978–3821, fax 978–4096.

Regional Director.—David Peavler.

Associate Regional Director, Enforcement.—Eric R. Werner.

Associate Regional Director, Examinations.—Marshall Gandy.

Regional Trial Counsel.—David Fraser.

Los Angeles Regional Office: 444 South Flower Street, Suite 900, Los Angeles, CA 90071 (323) 965–3998, fax 443–1902.

Regional Director.—Michele Wein Layne.

Associate Regional Directors, Enforcement: Alka Patel, Katharine Zoladz.

Associate Regional Director, Examinations.—Bryan Bennett.

Supervisory Regional Trial Counsel.—Amy Longo.

Miami Regional Office: 801 Brickell Avenue, Suite 1800, Miami, FL 33131 (305) 982–6300, fax 536–4120.

Regional Director.—Eric I. Bustillo.

Associate Regional Director, Enforcement.—Glenn S. Gordon.

Associate Regional Director, Examination.—John C. Mattimore.

New York Regional Office: 200 Vesey Street, Suite 400, New York, NY 10281–1022, (212) 336–1100, fax 336–1323.

Regional Director.—Marc P. Berger.

Associate Regional Directors:

Broker-Dealer.—Robert A. Sollazzo.

Enforcement: Lara Mehraban, Sanjay Wadhwa.

Investment Management.—Thomas Butler, Maurya Keating.

Philadelphia Regional Office: One Penn Center, 1617 John F. Kennedy Boulevard, Suite 520, Philadelphia, PA 19103–1844 (215) 597–3100, fax 597–1036.

Regional Director.—G. Jeffrey Boujoukos.

Associate Regional Director, Enforcement.—Kelly Gibson.

Associate Regional Director, Examinations.—Joy G. Thompson.

Salt Lake Regional Office: 351 S. West Temple, Suite 6.100, Salt Lake City, UT 84101 (801) 524–5796, fax 524–3558.

Regional Director.—Daniel J. Wadley.

San Francisco Regional Office: 44 Montgomery Street, Suite 2800, San Francisco, CA 94104 (415) 705–2500, fax 705–2501.

Regional Director.—Erin Schneider.

Associate Regional Director, Enforcement.—Monique Winkler.

Associate Regional Director, Examinations.—Kristin Snyder.

SELECTIVE SERVICE SYSTEM

1515 Wilson Boulevard, 5th Floor, Arlington, VA 22209–2425

phone (703) 605–4100, fax 605–4106, https://sss.gov

Data Management Center, P.O. Box 94638, Palatine, IL 60094–4638

phone (847) 688–6888, fax 688–2860

Director.—Donald M. Benton, 605–4010.

Director for—

Financial Management.—Roderick R. Hubbard, 605–4022.

Operations.—Craig T. Brown, 605–4080.

Public and Intergovernmental Affairs.—Wadi A. Yakhour (acting), 605–4057, fax 605–4106.

SMITHSONIAN INSTITUTION

Smithsonian Institution Building—The Castle (SIB)
1000 Jefferson Drive, SW., Washington, DC 20560
phone (202) 633–1000, https://si.edu

The Smithsonian Institution is an independent trust instrumentality created in accordance with the terms of the will of James Smithson of England who in 1826 bequeathed his property to the United States of America "to found at Washington under the name of the Smithsonian Institution an establishment for the increase and diffusion of knowledge among men." Congress pledged the faith of the United States to carry out the trust in 1836 (Act of July 1, 1836, C. 252, 5 Stat. 64), and established the Institution in its present form in 1846 (August 10, 1846, C. 178, 9 Stat. 102), entrusting the management of the institution to its independent Board of Regents.

THE BOARD OF REGENTS

ex officio

Chief Justice of the United States.—John G. Roberts, Jr., Chancellor.
Vice President of the United States.—Mike Pence.

Appointed by the President of the Senate
Hon. Patrick J. Leahy
Hon. David Perdue
Hon. John Boozman

Appointed by the Speaker of the House
Hon. Lucille Roybal-Allard
Hon. John Shimkus
Hon. Doris Matsui

Appointed by Joint Resolution of Congress

Roger W. Ferguson, Jr.
Michael Govan
John W. McCarter, Jr.
David M. Rubenstein
Steve Case
John Fahey
Risa J. Lavizzo-Mourey
Michael M. Lynton

Chief of Staff to the Regents.—Porter Wilkinson, 633–8899.

OFFICE OF THE SECRETARY

Secretary.—Lonnie G. Bunch, III, 633–1846.
Chief of Staff.—Greg Bettwy, 633–6287.
Inspector General.—Cathy Helm, 633–7095.
General Counsel.—Judith Leonard, 633–5115.
Director of Government Relations.—Vacant.
Director of the Smithsonian Institution Traveling Exhibition Service.—Myriam Springuel, 633–3137.
Assistant Secretary for Communications and External Affairs.—Julissa Marenco, 633–2371.
Assistant Secretary for Education and Access.—Patricia Bartlett, 633–1869.
Smithsonian Affiliations Program.—Harold Closter, 408–1990.
Smithsonian Associates Program.—Frederica Adelman, 633–8628.
Smithsonian Center for Learning and Digital Access.—Stephanie L. Norby, 633–5297.
Smithsonian Science Education Center.—Carol O'Donnell, 633–3004.

OFFICE OF THE UNDER SECRETARY FOR FINANCE AND ADMINISTRATION

Under Secretary and CFO.—Mike McCarthy (acting), 633–6148.
Director of:
Accessibility Program.—Elizabeth Ziebarth, 633–2946.
Special Events and Protocol.—Vacant.
Director, Office of:
Equal Employment and Minority Affairs.—Era Marshall, 633–6414.
Facilities Engineering and Operations.—Nancy Bechtol, 633–5687.
Human Resources.—Dana Moreland, 633–4923.
Information Technology and CIO.—Deron Burba, 633–4901.
Ombudsman.—Dania Palosky, 633–2008.

OFFICE OF THE PROVOST

Provost.—John Davis, 633–5240.

Director of:

Anacostia Community Museum.—Melanie Adams, 633–4839.

Archives of American Art.—Kate Haw, 633–7969.

Asian Pacific American Program.—Lisa Sasaki, 633–3590.

Center for Folklife and Cultural Heritage.—Michael Mason, 633–1141.

Cooper Hewitt, Smithsonian Design Museum.—Caroline Baumann (212) 849–8320.

Freer and Sackler Galleries.—Chase Robinson, 633–0454.

Hirshhorn Museum and Sculpture Garden.—Melissa Chiu, 633–2824.

National Museum of African American History and Culture.—Spencer Crew (acting), 633–4751.

National Museum of African Art.—Augustus Casely-Hayford, 633–4604.

National Museum of American History.—Anthea Hartig, 633–3766.

National Museum of the American Indian.—Kevin Gover, 633–6700.

National Portrait Gallery.—Kim Sajet, 633–8276.

National Postal Museum.—Elliot Gruber, 633–5501.

Smithsonian American Art Museum.—Stephanie Stebich, 633–8409.

Smithsonian Latino Center.—Eduardo Diaz, 633–0978.

Smithsonian Institution Archives.—Anne Van Camp, 633–5908.

Smithsonian Institution Libraries.—Vacant, 633–2236.

Director of:

International Relations.—Aviva Rosenthal (acting), 633–1849.

National Air and Space Museum.—Ellen Stofan, 633–2352.

National Museum of Natural History.—Kirk Johnson, 633–2661.

National Zoological Park.—Steven Monfort, 633–4442.

Office of Sponsored Projects.—Tracey Fraser, 633–3763.

Smithsonian Astrophysical Observatory.—Charles Alcock (617) 495–7100.

Smithsonian Environmental Research Center.—Anson Hines (443) 482–2208.

Smithsonian Museum Conservation Institute.—Robert Koestler (301) 238–1205.

Smithsonian Tropical Research Institute.—Matt Larsen, 633–4700.

SMITHSONIAN ENTERPRISES

President.—Carol LeBlanc, 633–5558.

Publisher, Smithsonian Magazine.—Vacant.

Editor, Smithsonian Magazine.—Vacant.

SOCIAL SECURITY ADMINISTRATION

Annex Building, 6401 Security Boulevard, Baltimore, MD 21235 (ANXB)

East High Rise Building, 6401 Security Boulevard, Baltimore, MD 21235 (EHRB)

Joseph P. Addabbo Federal Building, 155–10 Jamaica Avenue, Jamaica, NY 11432 (JAFB)

Meadows East Building, 6300 Security Boulevard, Baltimore, MD 21235 (MEB)

One Independence Square Building, 250 E Street, SW., Washington, DC 20219 (OISB)

One Skyline Tower, 5107 Leesburg Pike, Falls Church, VA 22041 (SKY)

Perimeter East Building, 6201 Security Boulevard, Baltimore, MD 21235 (PEB)

Robert M. Ball Building, 6401 Security Boulevard, Baltimore, MD 21235 (RMBB)

Security West Tower, 1500 Woodlawn Drive, Baltimore, MD 21241 (SWT)

West High Rise Building, 6401 Security Boulevard, Baltimore, MD 21235 (WHRB)

West Low Rise Building, 6401 Security Boulevard, Baltimore, MD 21235 (WLRB)

https://socialsecurity.gov

OFFICE OF THE COMMISSIONER

Commissioner.—Andrew Saul, RMBB, Suite 2600 (410) 965–3120 or OISB, Suite 8002 (202) 358–6000.

Deputy Commissioner.—David F. Black.

Chief of Staff.—Beatrice Disman (acting), RMBB, Suite 2600 (410) 965–0386 or OISB, Suite 8002 (202) 358–6000.

Deputy Chief of Staff.—Stephanie Hall, RMBB, Suite 2600 (410) 965–9704 or OISB, Suite 8002 (202) 358–6000.

Executive Counselor to the Commissioner.—Jay Ortis, RMBB, Suite 2600 (410) 966–8994.
Press Officer.—Mark Hinkle (acting), RMBB, Suite 2600 (410) 966–4091.
Executive Secretary.—Vacant.
Director for Executive Operations.—Kimberly L. Duncan, RMBB, Suite 2600 (410) 966–1156.

OFFICE OF ANALYTICS, REVIEW AND OVERSIGHT

Deputy Commissioner.—B. Chad Bungard, WHRB, Room 7160–C (410) 965–1890.
Assistant Deputy Commissioner.—Brad Flick, WHRB, Room 7160–B (410) 965–8980.
Executive Director of Appellate Operations.—Judge Florence Felix-Lawson (acting), SKY, Room 1400 (703) 605–7100.
Associate Commissioner, Office of:
Analytics and Improvements.—Daryl Wise, WHRB, Room 4138 (410) 965–4557.
Anti-Fraud Programs.—Mark Majestic, RMBB, Room 1513 (410) 965–1461.
Quality Review.—Vera Bostick-Borden, JAFB, Room 1110 (718) 557–5346.

OFFICE OF BUDGET, FINANCE, AND MANAGEMENT

Deputy Commissioner.—Michelle A. King, RMBB, Room 2710–B (410) 965–7748.
Assistant Deputy Commissioner.—Seth P. Binstock (acting), RMBB, Room 2710D (410) 965–9538.
Associate Commissioner, Office of:
Acquisition and Grants.—Christian Hellie (acting), RMBB, Room 1540 (410) 965–9511.
Budget.—Tiffany Flick (acting), WHRB, Room 2126 (410) 965–3501.
Facilities and Supply Management.—Marc Mason, RMBB, Room 2719 (410) 966–2772.
Financial Policy and Operations.—Joanne Gasparini (acting), EHRB, Room 2154 (410) 965–7340.
Security and Emergency Preparedness.—Joe Sliwka, RMBB, Room 1600 (410) 965–9616.
Director, Systems Support Staff.—Jim Guidry, EHRB, Room 5139 (410) 965–9794.

OFFICE OF THE CHIEF ACTUARY

Chief Actuary.—Stephen C. Goss, RMBB, Room 2409 (410) 965–3000.
Deputy Chief Actuary for—
Long Range.—Karen P. Glenn, RMBB, Room 2408 (410) 965–3002.
Short Range.—Vacant.

OFFICE OF COMMUNICATIONS

Deputy Commissioner.—Mike Korbey, WHRB, Room 1126 (410) 965–9608.
Assistant Deputy Commissioner.—Darlynda Bogle, WHRB, Room 1126 (410) 965–3906.
Associate Commissioner, Office of:
Public Inquiries and Communications Support.—Steven L. Patrick, WHRB, Room 1100 (410) 965–0709.
Strategic and Digital Communications.—Darlynda Bogle (acting), WHRB, Room 1126 (410) 965–3906.

OFFICE OF THE GENERAL COUNSEL

General Counsel.—Royce Min (acting), RMBB, Suite 2415 (410) 965–0600.
Deputy General Counsel.—Daniel F. Callahan, RMBB, Suite 2416 (410) 965–0644.
Associate General Counsel for—
General Law.—Mitchell Chitwood, WHRB, Room G300 (410) 965–4660.
Program Law.—Jeffrey C. Blair, WHRB, Room G400–J (410) 965–3157.
Executive Director, Office of Privacy and Disclosure.—Matthew Ramsey, WHRB, Room G400–F (410) 965–6247.
Regional Chief Counsels for—
Atlanta.—Christopher Harris, Atlanta Federal Center, 61 Forsyth Street, SW., Suite 20T45, Atlanta, GA 30303 (404) 562–1010.
Boston.—Michael Pelgro, JFK Federal Building, 15 New Sudbury Street, Room 625, Boston, MA 02203 (617) 565–1844.

Chicago.—Kathryn Caldwell, 200 West Adams Street, 30th Floor, Chicago, IL 60606 (877) 800–7578, ext. 19110.

Dallas.—Ben Harrison, 1301 Young Street, Room A–702, Dallas, TX 75202–5433 (214) 767–3462.

Denver.—John J. Lee, 1961 Stout Street, Suite 4169, Denver, CO 80294 (303) 844–0013.

Kansas City.—Lisa Thomas, Richard Bolling Federal Building, 601 East 12th Street, Room 965, Federal Office Building, Kansas City, MO 64106 (816) 936–5754.

New York.—Ellen Sovern (acting), 26 Federal Plaza, Suite 3904, New York, NY 12078 (212) 264–2216.

Philadelphia.—Eric Kressman, 300 Spring Garden Street, 6th Floor, Philadelphia, PA 19123 (215) 597–4642.

San Francisco.—Deborah Stachel, 160 Spear Street, Suite 800, San Francisco, CA 94105 (415) 977–8968.

Seattle.—Mathew Pile (acting), 701 Fifth Avenue, Columbia Tower, Suite 2900, M/S 221A, Seattle, WA 98104 (206) 615–3760.

OFFICE OF HEARINGS OPERATIONS

Deputy Commissioner.—Theresa Gruber, WLRB, Suite 2108 (410) 965–6006, or SKY, Suite 1600 (703) 605–8200.

Assistant Deputy Commissioner.—Elaine Garrison-Daniels, WLRB, Suite 2108 (410) 965–6006, or SKY, Suite 1600 (703) 605–8200.

Chief Administrative Law Judge.—Patrick Nagle, SKY, Suite 1608 (703) 605–8500.

Associate Commissioner, Office of:

Budget, Facilities and Security.—Dean Landis, WLRB, Room 2134 (703) 605–8989.

Electronic Services and Systems Integration.—Joe Lopez, WLRB, Room 2123 (410) 965–6006 or SKY, Suite 1509 (703) 605–8970.

Executive Operations and Human Resources.—Joe Lytle, WLRB, Room 2132 (410) 965–4530 or SKY, Suite 1700 (703) 605–8543.

Regional Chief Administrative Law Judges:

Atlanta.—Sheila Lowther, 61 Forsyth Street, SW., Suite 20T10, Atlanta, GA 30303 (404) 562–1182.

Boston.—Aaron Morgan, 10 Causeway Street, Suite 565, Boston, MA 02222 (888) 870–7578.

Chicago.—Sherry Thompson, 600 W. Madison Street, 4th Floor, Chicago, IL 60661 (877) 800–7576.

Dallas.—Joan Parks Saunders, 1301 Young Street, Suite 460, Dallas, TX 75202 (214) 767–9401.

Denver.—Michael S. Kidd, 1244 North Speer Boulevard, Suite 600, Denver, CO 80204 (888) 397–9803.

Kansas City.—Sherianne Laba, 2300 Main Street, Suite 600, Kansas City, MO 64108 (888) 238–7975.

New York.—Aaron Morgan, 26 Federal Plaza, Room 34–102, New York, NY 10278 (212) 264–4036.

Philadelphia.—Tamara Turner-Jones, 300 Spring Garden Street, 4th Floor, Philadelphia, PA 19123 (215) 597–9980.

San Francisco.—Jennifer Horne, 555 Battery Street, 5th Floor, San Francisco, CA 94111 (866) 964–7584.

Seattle.—Michael S. Kidd, 701 5th Avenue, Suite 2900 M/S 904, Seattle, WA 98104 (206) 615–2236.

OFFICE OF HUMAN RESOURCES

Deputy Commissioner.—Marianna LaCanfora, ANXB, Suite 2570 (410) 965–5514.

Assistant Deputy Commissioner.—Bonnie Doyle, ANXB, Suite 2570 (410) 965–4463.

Associate Commissioner, Office of:

Civil Rights and Equal Opportunity.—Claudia Postell, WHRB, Room 3350 (410) 966–3635.

Labor Management and Employee Relations.—James Julian, ANXB, Room 2170 (410) 965–5806.

Strategy, Learning, and Workforce Development.—Kristen Medley-Proctor, EHRB, Room 1130 (410) 965–1037.

Personnel.—Lydia Marshall, ANXB, Room 2570 (410) 966–9916.

Director, Office of:

Executive and Special Services.—Sarah Rohde, ANXB, Room 2510 (410) 965–8473.
Information Technology for Human Resources.—David R. Bacon, EHRB, Room G–140 (410) 594–2099.

OFFICE OF THE INSPECTOR GENERAL

Inspector General.—Gail Ennis, MEB, Room 3–ME–5 (410) 966–2850.
Deputy Inspector General.—Benjamin Alpert (acting), MEB, Room 3–ME–5 (410) 965–1689.
Chief of Staff.—Steve Schaeffer, MEB, Room 3–ME–5 (410) 965–9701.
Chief Counsel to the Inspector General.—Joe Gangloff, MEB, Room 3–ME–1 (410) 965–6263.
Assistant Inspector General, Office of:
Audit.—Rona Lawson, MEB, Room 3–ME–2 (410) 965–8701.
Counsel for Investigations and Enforcement.—Joscelyn Funnie, MEB, Room 2–ME–5 (410) 594–0126.
Investigations.—Jennifer Walker, MEB, Room 3–ME–3 (410) 965–2657.
Resource Management.—Andrew Cannarsa, MEB, Room 2–ME–4 (410) 966–1375.

OFFICE OF LEGISLATION AND CONGRESSIONAL AFFAIRS

Deputy Commissioner.—Eric Skidmore (acting), OISB, Room 8029 (202) 358–6030, or RMBB, Room 2404 (410) 597–1833.
Assistant Deputy Commissioner.—Vacant.
Associate Commissioner, Office of:
Congressional Affairs.—Suzanne Payne, OISB, Room 8028 (202) 358–6046.
Legislative Development and Operations.—Erik Hansen, WHRB, Room 3103–A (410) 965–3112.
Director for—
Disability Insurance.—Nitin Jagdish (acting), WHRB, Room 3109 (410) 965–2649.
Legislative and Constituent Services Staff.—Robert J. Forrester, WHRB, Room 3105 (410) 966–6706.
Program Administration and Financing Staff.—Jenni Greenlee (acting), WHRB, Room 3102 (410) 965–4725.
Regulations and Reports Clearance.—Faye Lipsky, WHRB, Room 3104 (410) 965–8783.
Retirement and Survivors Insurance Benefits.—Chris Tino (acting), WHRB, Room 3107 (410) 965–3313.

OFFICE OF OPERATIONS

Deputy Commissioner.—Grace M. Kim, WHRB, Room 1204 (410) 965–3877.
Assistant Deputy Commissioners.—Erik Jones, WHRB, Room 1204 (410) 965–0130; Fred Maurin, WHRB, Room 1204 (410) 965–5190.
Chief Business Officer for IT Modernization and Digital Services.—Kim Baldwin Sparks, WHRB, Room 1312 (410) 966–3224.
Associate Commissioner, Office of:
Central Operations.—Christopher Goble, SWT, Room 7000 (410) 966–7000.
Customer Service.—Cynthia Bennett, ANXB, Room 4845 (410) 965–7507.
Disability Determinations.—John Owen, ANXB, Room 3570 (410) 966–6111.
Electronic Services and Technology.—Jeremiah Schofield (acting), ANXB, Room 4705 (410) 965–9885.
Public Service and Operations Support.—Janet Walker, ANXB, Room 1540 (410) 965–4599.
Regional Commissioner for—
Atlanta.—Rose Mary Buehler, Sam Nunn Federal Center, 61 Forsyth Street, SW., Suite 23T30, Atlanta, GA 30303 (404) 562–5600.
Boston.—Linda M. Dorn, JFK Federal Building, 15 New Sudbury Street, Room 1900, Boston, MA 02203 (617) 565–2870.
Chicago.—Phyllis Smith, Harold Washington Social Security Center, 600 West Madison Street, Chicago, IL 60661 (312) 575–4000.
Dallas.—Sheila Everett, 1301 Young Street, Suite 130, Dallas, TX 75202–5433 (214) 767–4207.
Denver.—Mary Lisa Lewandowski, Byron G. Rogers Federal Building, 1961 Stout Street, Suite 06–145, Denver, CO 80294 (303) 844–2388.
Kansas City.—Linda Kerr-Davis, Federal Office Building, 601 East 12th Street, Room 1016, Kansas City, MO 64106 (816) 936–5700.

New York.—Raymond Egan, 26 Federal Plaza, Room 40–100, New York, NY 10278 (212) 264–1166.

Philadelphia.—Terry M. Stradtman, 300 Spring Garden Street, Philadelphia, PA 19123 (215) 597–5157.

San Francisco.—Steve Breen, 1221 Nevin Avenue, Richmond, CA 94801 (510) 970–8400.

Seattle.—Mary Lisa Lewandowski, 701 5th Avenue, Suite 2900, M/S 301, Seattle, WA 98104–7075 (206) 615–2100.

OFFICE OF RETIREMENT AND DISABILITY POLICY

Deputy Commissioner.—Mark Warshawsky, RMBB, Room 3718 (410) 966–3579.

Assistant Deputy Commissioner.—Stephen Evangelista, RMBB, Room 3719 (410) 965–6522.

Associate Commissioner, Office of:

Data Exchange, Policy Publications, and International Negotiations.—Laura Train, ANXB, Room 4701 (410) 966–9223.

Disability Programs.—Gina Clemmons, ANXB, Room 4555 (410) 966–9897.

Income Security Programs.—Dawn Wiggins (acting), RMBB, Room 2512B (410) 966–6580.

Research, Demonstration, and Employment Support.—Susan Wilschke (acting), ANXB, Room 4170–A (410) 966–8906.

Research, Evaluation, and Statistics.—Katherine Bent (acting), MEB, Room 4700–C (410) 966–9038.

Retirement Policy.—Natalie Lu, ALTMB, Room 118 (410) 965–3327.

OFFICE OF SYSTEMS / OFFICE OF THE CHIEF INFORMATION OFFICER

Deputy Commissioner and Chief Information Officer.—Rajive Mathur, RMBB, Room 3005 (410) 965–3941.

Assistant Deputy Commissioner and Deputy Chief Information Officer, IT Modernization.—Sean Brune, RMBB, Room 3105 (410) 966–2762.

Assistant Deputy Commissioner and Deputy Chief Information Officer, IT Operations.—Jim Borland, RMBB, Room 3001 (410) 966–2030.

Assistant Deputy Commissioner for IT Business Support.—Sylviane Haldiman, RMBB, Room 3103 (410) 966–8040.

Assistant Deputy Commissioner for Software Engineering.—Diana Andrews, RMBB, Room 3003 (410) 965–7641.

Chief Technology Officer.—John Morenz, RMBB, Room 3101 (410) 966–4205.

Associate Commissioner, Office of:

Benefit Information Systems.—Wayne Lemon, RMBB, Room 4700 (410) 965–5617.

Disability Information Systems.—Rachel Dumser, RMBB, Room 3613 (410) 965–6398.

Enterprise Information Systems.—Ann Amrhein, RMBB, Room 2101 (410) 965–9019.

Hardware Engineering.—Dave Thomas, PEB, Room 550A (410) 966–5372.

Information Security.—Robert Collins, PEB, Room 3493 (410) 966–9693.

IT Financial Management and Support.—Lester Diamond, RMBB, Room 3111 (410) 965–3429.

IT Programmatic Business Support.—William Martinez, RMBB, Room 2204 (410) 965–5122.

Systems Architecture.—Dan Parry, RMBB, Room 4100 (410) 965–0778.

Systems Operations.—Tom Fellona, PEB, Room 450A (410) 965–4090.

Product & Project Management.—Vacant.

STATE JUSTICE INSTITUTE

11951 Freedom Drive, Suite 1020, Reston, VA 20190

phone (571) 313–8843, https://sji.gov

BOARD OF DIRECTORS

Chair.—John D. Minton, Jr.

Vice Chair.—Daniel J. Becker.

Secretary.—Gayle A. Nachtigal.

Treasurer.—David V. Brewer.

Members:
Jonathan Lippman.
Wilfredo Martinez.
Marsha J. Rabiteau.
Hernan D. Vera.
Isabel Framer.

Officer:
Executive Director.—Jonathan D. Mattiello.

SURFACE TRANSPORTATION BOARD

395 E Street, SW., Washington, DC 20423–0001

phone (202) 245–0238, https://stb.dot.gov

Chairman.—Ann D. Begeman, 245–0203.
Vice Chairman.—Martin J. Oberman, 245–0210.
Office of the Managing Director.—Rachel Campbell, 245–0357.
General Counsel.—Craig Keats, 245–0264.
Director, Office of:
Economics.—William Brennan, 245–0321.
Environmental Analysis.—Victoria Rutson, 245–0295.
Proceedings.—Allison Davis, 245–0386.
Public Assistance, Governmental Affairs, and Compliance.—Lucille Marvin, 245–0238.

SUSQUEHANNA RIVER BASIN COMMISSION

COMMISSIONERS AND ALTERNATES

Federal Government:
Commissioner.—Brig. Gen. Thomas J. Tickner, U.S. Army Corps of Engineers.
Alternate.—COL John T. Litz, U.S. Army Corps of Engineers.
2nd Alternate.—Amy M. Guise.

New York:
Commissioner.—Basil Seggos.
Alternate.—James M. Tierney.
2nd Alternate.—Paul D'Amato.

Pennsylvania:
Commissioner.—Patrick McDonnell.
Alternate.—Aneca Atkinson.
2nd Alternate.—Jennifer Orr-Greene.

Maryland:
Commissioner.—Ben Grumbles.
Alternate.—Saeid Kasraei.
2nd Alternate.—Suzanne Dorsey.

STAFF

4423 North Front Street, Harrisburg, PA 17110

phone (717) 238–0423, https://srbc.net, srbc@srbc.net

Executive Director.—Andrew D. Dehoff.
Deputy Executive Director.—Andrew G. Gavin.
Director of Administration and Finance.—Marcia E. Hutchinson.
Secretary to the Commission.—Jason E. Oyler.

TENNESSEE VALLEY AUTHORITY

500 North Capitol Street, NW., Suite 220, Washington, DC 20001 (202) 898–2999

400 West Summit Hill Drive, Knoxville, TN 37902 (865) 632–2101

1101 Market Street, Chattanooga, TN 37402 (423) 751–0011

BOARD OF DIRECTORS

Chair.—John L. Ryder.
Directors: Kenneth E. Allen, A. D. Frazier, William B. Kilbride, Jeff W. Smith.

EXECUTIVE OFFICERS:

President and Chief Executive Officer.—Jeffrey L. Lyash (865) 632–2366.
Executive Vice Presidents:
External Relations Officer.—Vacant (423) 751–2555.
Chief Financial Officer.—John M. Thomas III, (423) 751–8919.
Chief Nuclear Officer.—Timothy Rausch (423) 751–8682.
Chief Operating Officer.—Michael D. Skaggs (865) 632–6503.
General Counsel.—Sherry A. Quirk (865) 632–4131.
Senior Vice President and Chief Human Resources Officer.—Susan E. Collins (423) 751–8584.

WASHINGTON OFFICE:

Director, Federal Government Relations.—Bevin Taylor (202) 898–2999, fax: (202) 898–2998.

U.S. ADVISORY COMMISSION ON PUBLIC DIPLOMACY

301 4th Street, SW., SA–44, M–04, 20547

phone (202) 203–7386, fax 203–7886

[Created by Executive Order 12048 and Public Law 96–60]

Chair.—Sim Farar.
Members:
William J. Hybl, *Vice-Chair.*
Amb. Lyndon Olson, Jr., *Vice-Chair.*
Amb. Penne K. Peacock.
Anne Terman Wedner.
Lezlee Westine.
Executive Director.—Vivian S. Walker.

U.S. AGENCY FOR GLOBAL MEDIA

330 Independence Avenue, SW., Suite 3300, Washington, DC 20237

phone (202) 203–4545, fax 203–4568

The U.S. Agency for Global Media (formerly Broadcasting Board of Governors) oversees the operation of the IBB and provides yearly funding grants approved by Congress to three non-profit grantee corporations: Radio Free Europe/Radio Liberty, Radio Free Asia, and the Middle East Broadcasting Networks.

Chair.—Kenneth Weinstein (acting).

UNITED STATES AGENCY FOR GLOBAL MEDIA (USAGM)

[Created by Public Law 103–236]

The U.S. Agency for Global Media (USAGM) is composed of the Voice of America and Office of Cuba Broadcasting, Radio and TV Marti.

Chief Executive Officer and Director.—Michael Pack (202) 203–4545, fax 203–4568.
Director of:
Office of Cuba Broadcasting.—Emilio J. Vazquez (interim) (305) 437–7026, fax 437–7016.
Voice of America.—Vacant (202) 203–4500, fax 203–4513.
President, Radio Free Asia.—Bay Fang (202) 530–4900, fax 530–7795.
President, Radio Free Europe.—Jamie Fly (202) 457–6900, fax 457–6933.
President, Middle East Broadcasting Networks.—Alberto Fernandez (703) 852–9000, fax 991–1250.

U.S. AGENCY FOR INTERNATIONAL DEVELOPMENT

1300 Pennsylvania Avenue, NW., Washington, DC 20523

phone (202) 712–0000, https://usaid.gov

Administrator.—John Barsa (acting), Room 6.09, 712–4040, fax 216–3445.

Deputy Administrator.—Bonnie Glick, Room 6.09, 712–4040, fax 216–3445.
Counselor.—Chris Milligan, Room 6.08, 712–5010.
Chief of Staff.—William R. Steiger, Room 6.09, 712–4040.
Assistant Administrator for the Bureau for—
Africa.—Ramsey Day, Room 4.08–031, 712–0500.
Asia.—Gloria Steele (acting), Room 4.09–034, 712–0200.
Europe and Eurasia.—Brock Bierman, SA44, 247-J 567–4020
Latin America and the Caribbean.—John Barsa, Room 5.09–012, 712–4800.
Middle East.—Michael T. Harvey, Room 4.09–005, 712–0300.
Economic Growth, Education and Environment.—Michelle Bekkering, 1717 Pennsylvania Ave, Room 1106, 712–0670.
Food Security.—Beth Dunford, Room 3.09–008, 712–0550.
Global Health.—Alma Crumm Golden, 500 D Street, SW., 07.8.0G, 916–2392.
Legislative and Public Affairs.—Richard Parker, Room 6.10–107, 712–4300.
Management.—Frederick Nutt, USAID Annex, 12.8.0F, 921–5200.
Policy, Planning and Learning.—Ramsey Day, Room 7.09–304, 712–0880.
Senior Deputy Assistant Administrator for the Bureau for Humanitarian Assistance.—Max Primorac, Room 8.06–084, 712–0100.
Executive Director, U.S. Global Development Lab.—Harry Bader (acting), Room 7.08–250, 712–1331.
Director, Office of:
Civil Rights and Diversity.—Ismael Martinez (acting).
Security.—John Voorhees, Room 2.06–008, 712–0990.
Small and Disadvantaged Business Utilization.—Mauricio Vera, USAID Annex, 10.2.0A, 567–4730.
General Counsel.—Craig Wolf, Room 6.06–125, 712–0900.
Inspector General.—Ann Calvaresi Barr, Room 6.06–113, 712–1150.

U.S. COMMISSION ON CIVIL RIGHTS

1331 Pennsylvania Avenue, NW., Suite 1150, Washington, DC 20425

phone (202) 376–8371, fax 376–7672

(Codified in 42 U.S.C., section 1975)

Chair.—Catherine E. Lhamon.
Vice Chair.—Vacant.
Commissioners: Debo Adegbile, Stephen Gilchrist, Gail Heriot, Peter N. Kirsanow, David Kladney, Michael Yaki.
Staff Director.—Mauro A. Morales.

U.S. ELECTION ASSISTANCE COMMISSION

1335 East-West Highway, Suite 4300, Silver Spring, MD 20910

phone (301) 563–3919, (866) 747–1471, fax (301) 734–3108

https://eac.gov

[Created by Public Law 107–252]

Commissioners:
Christy McCormick (301) 960–1306.
Ben Hovland (301) 960–1316.
Don Palmer (301) 960–1324.
Thomas Hicks (301) 960–1310.

OFFICE OF THE EXECUTIVE DIRECTOR

Executive Director.—Mona Harrington (acting) (301) 960–1888.

OFFICE OF THE GENERAL COUNSEL

Associate General Counsel.—Amanda Joiner (301) 960–1253.

OFFICE OF COMMUNICATIONS

Director of Communications.—Kristen Muthig (acting) (301) 960–1897.

OFFICE OF THE INSPECTOR GENERAL

Inspector General.—Patricia Layfield (301) 734–3104.

U.S. HOLOCAUST MEMORIAL COUNCIL

The United States Holocaust Memorial Museum

100 Raoul Wallenberg Place, SW., Washington, DC 20024

phone (202) 488–0400, fax (202) 314–7881

Officials:

Chair.—Howard M. Lorber, New York, NY.

Vice Chair.—Allan M. Holt, Washington, DC.

Director.—Sara J. Bloomfield, Washington, DC.

Members:

Walter Ray Allen, Jr., Coral Gables, FL.
Lawrence M. Baer, San Francisco, CA.
Daniel Benjamin, Hanover, NH.
Tom A. Bernstein, New York, NY.
Joshua B. Bolten, Washington, DC.
Michael S. Bosworth, New York, NY.
Ethel C. Brooks, Metuchen, NJ.
Jonathan W. Burkan, Harrison, NY.
Andrew M. Cohn, Scottsdale, AZ.
Sara Darehshori, New York, NY.
Sam M. Devinki, Kansas City, MO.
Norman L. Eisen, Washington, DC.
Jeffrey P. Feingold, Fort Lauderdale, FL.
Lee A. Feinstein, Bloomington, IN.
Helene "Haiki" Feldman, New York, NY.
David M. Flaum, Rochester, NY.
Raffi M. Freedman-Gurspan, Washington, DC.
Jordan T. Goodman, Chicago, IL.
Samuel N. Gordon, Wilmette, IL.
Jeremy Halpern, Livingston, NJ.
Sarah K. Hurwitz, Washington, DC.
Pricilla Levine Kersten, Chicago, IL.
Murray J. Laulicht, Bar Harbour, FL.
Jonathan S. Lavine, Boston, MA.
Edward P. Lazarus, Bethesda, MD.
Stuart A. Levey, London, England.
Eric A. LeVine, Seattle, WA.
Susan G. Levine, Paradise Valley, AZ.
Susan E. Lowenberg, San Francisco, CA.
David M. Marchick, Washington, DC.
Tamar Newberger, Chicago, IL.
Deborah A. Oppenheimer, Los Angeles, CA.
Eric P. Ortner, Los Angeles, CA.
Michael P. Polsky, Chicago, IL.
Michael H. Posner, New York, NY.
Richard S. Price, Chicago, IL.
Ronald Ratner, Shaker Heights, OH.
Benjamin J. Rhodes, Venice, CA.
Melissa Rogers, Falls Church, VA.
Daniel J. Rosen, New York, NY.
Menachem Z. Rosensaft, New York, NY.
Elliot J. Schrage, Menlo Park, CA.
Maureen Schulman, Chicago, IL.
Betty Pantirer Schwartz, Livingston, NJ.
Irvin N. Shapell, Anna Maria, FL.
Cindy Simon Skjodt, Carmel, IN.
Howard D. Unger, Briarcliff Manor, NY.
Clemantine Wamariya, San Francisco, CA.
Andrew J. Weinstein, Coral Springs, FL.
Jeremy M. Weinstein, Stanford, CA.
Daniel G. Weiss, Los Angeles, CA.
Bradley D. Wine, Bethesda, MD.
Fred S. Zeidman, Houston, TX.

Congressional Members:

U.S. House of Representatives:

Theodore E. Deutch, of Florida.
David Kustoff, of Tennessee.
Bradley Scott Schneider, of Illinois.
Lee M. Zeldin, of New York.

U.S. Senate:

Benjamin L. Cardin, of Maryland.
Marco Rubio, of Florida.
BERNARD SANDERS, of Vermont.
Tim Scott, of South Carolina.

Ex Officio Members:

U.S. Department of:

Education.—Philip H. Rosenfelt.
Interior.—Vacant.
State.—Cherrie Daniels.

Council Staff:

General Counsel.—Gerard Leval.
Secretary of the Council.—Jessica Viggiano.

Former Chairs:

Tom A. Bernstein, 2010–2017.
Fred S. Zeidman, 2002–2010.
Irving Greenberg, 2000–2002.
† Miles Lerman, 1993–2000.
Harvey M. Meyerhoff, 1987–1993.
† Elie Wiesel, 1980–1986.

Former Vice Chairs:

Joshua B. Bolten, 2010–2015.
Joel M. Geiderman, 2005–2010.
† Ruth B. Mandel, 1993–2005.
† William J. Lowenberg, 1986–1993.
Mark E. Talisman, 1980–1986.

† *Deceased*

U.S. INSTITUTE OF PEACE

2301 Constitution Avenue, NW., Washington, DC 20037

phone (202) 457–1700, fax 429–6063

BOARD OF DIRECTORS

Public Members:
Chair.—Stephen J. Hadley.
Vice Chair.—George E. Moose.
Members:
Judith A. Ansley
Eric E. Edelman
Joseph T. Eldridge
Kerry Kennedy
Ikram U. Khan
Stephen D. Krasner
John A. Lancaster
Jeremy A. Rabkin
J. Robinson West
Nancy M. Zirkin
Ex Officio:
Department of Defense.—Secretary Mark T. Esper (or his Senate-confirmed designee).
Department of State.—Secretary Mike Pompeo (or his Senate-confirmed designee).
National Defense University.—Vice Admiral Fritz Roegge, USN.
United States Institute of Peace.—President Nancy Lindborg (non-voting).
Officials:
President.—Nancy Lindborg.
Chief Administrative Officer.—Kathleen Ross.
Chief Financial Officer.—Joe Lataille.
Vice President for External Relations.—Jill Welch.
Congressional Relations.—Anne Hingeley.

U.S. INTERNATIONAL TRADE COMMISSION

500 E Street, SW., Washington, DC 20436

phone (202) 205–2000, fax 205–2798, https://usitc.gov

COMMISSIONERS

Chair.—Jason E. Kearns.
Vice Chair.—Randolph J. Stayin.
Commissioners:
Rhonda K. Schmidtlein.
David S. Johanson.
Amy A. Karpel.
Vacant.
Vacant.
Director, Office of External Relations / Executive Liaison.—Jennifer Andberg, 205–3141.
Congressional Relations Officer.—Laura Bloodgood, 205–3151.
Public Affairs Officer.—Margaret O'Laughlin.
General Counsel.—Dominic Bianchi.
Secretary to the Commission.—Lisa Barton.
Inspector General.—Philip M. Heneghan.
Director, Office of:
Operations.—Catherine DeFilippo.
Economics.—William Powers.
Industries.—Jonathan Coleman.
Tariff Affairs and Trade Agreements.—James Holbein.

U.S. MERIT SYSTEMS PROTECTION BOARD

1615 M Street, NW., Washington, DC 20419

phone (202) 653–7200, toll-free (800) 209–8960, fax 653–7130

[Created by Public Law 95–454]

Chair.—Vacant.
Vice Chair.—Vacant.
Member.—Vacant.

Executive Director.—William D. Spencer (acting).
General Counsel.—Tristan Leavitt.
Deputy General Counsel.—Katherine M. Smith.
Appeals Counsel.—Susan Swafford.
Legislative Counsel.—Rosalyn L. Coates, 653–7171.
Clerk of the Board.—Jennifer Everling (acting), 653–7200.

REGIONAL OFFICES

Regional Directors / Chief Administrative Judges:

Atlanta Regional Office: Covering Alabama, Florida, Georgia, Mississippi, South Carolina, Tennessee.—Thomas J. Lanphear, 401 West Peachtree Street, NW., 10th Floor, Atlanta, GA 30308–3519 (404) 730–2751, fax 730–2767.

Central Regional Office: Covering Illinois, Iowa, Kansas City, Kansas, Kentucky, Indiana, Michigan, Minnesota, Missouri, Ohio, Wisconsin.—Michele Schroeder, 230 South Dearborn Street, 31st Floor, Chicago, IL 60604–1669 (312) 353–2923, fax 886–4231.

Dallas Regional Office: Covering Arkansas, Louisiana, Oklahoma, Texas.—Laura Albornoz, 1100 Commerce Street, Room 620, Dallas, TX 75242–9979 (214) 767–0555, fax 767–0102.

Northeastern Regional Office: Covering Connecticut, Delaware, Maine, Maryland (except Montgomery and Prince Georges counties), Massachusetts, New Hampshire, New Jersey (except the counties of Bergen, Essex, Hudson, and Union), Pennsylvania, Rhode Island, Vermont, West Virginia.—William L. Boulden, 1601 Market Street, Suite 1700, Philadelphia, PA 19103–2310 (215) 597–9960, fax 597–3456.

Western Regional Office: Covering Alaska, California, Hawaii, Idaho, Nevada, Oregon, Washington, and Pacific Overseas.—Sara Snyder, 1301 Clay Street, Suite 1380N, Oakland, CA 94612–5217 (510) 273–7022, fax 273–7136.

Washington Regional Office: Covering Washington, DC, Maryland (counties of Montgomery and Prince Georges), North Carolina, Virginia, all overseas areas not otherwise covered.—Jeremiah Cassidy, 1811 Diagonal Road, Suite 205, Alexandria, VA 22314–2840 (703) 756–6250, fax 756–7112.

New York Field Office: Covering New York, Puerto Rico, Virgin Islands, the following counties in New Jersey: Bergen, Essex, Hudson, Union.—Arthur Joseph, Chief Administrative Judge, 26 Federal Plaza, Room 3137–A, New York, NY 10278–0022 (212) 264–9372, fax 264–1417.

Denver Field Office: Covering Arizona, Colorado, Kansas (except Kansas City), Montana, Nebraska, New Mexico, North Dakota, South Dakota, Utah, Wyoming.—Stephen Mish, Chief Administrative Judge, 165 South Union Boulevard, Suite 318, Lakewood, CO 80228–2211 (303) 969–5101, fax 969–5109.

U.S. OVERSEAS PRIVATE INVESTMENT CORPORATION

1100 New York Avenue, NW., Washington, DC 20527

phone (202) 336–8400

President and CEO.—Ray W. Washburne.
Executive Vice President.—David Bohigian.
Chief of Staff.—Douglas Sellers (acting).
Vice President and General Counsel.—William Doffermyre.
Vice President, Investment Funds.—Lynn Nguyen (acting).
Vice President, Office of Investment Policy.—Ryan Brennan.
Managing Director for Global Women's Initiatives.—Kathryn C. Kaufman.
Vice President, Office of External Affairs.—Edward A. Burrier.
Vice Presidents:
Small and Medium Enterprise Finance.—James Polan.
Structured Finance and Insurance.—Tracey Webb.
Human Resources Management.—Dr. Paula Molloy.
Financial and Portfolio Management.—Mildred Callear.
Department of Management and Administration.—Michele Perez.
Special Assistant for Congressional and Intergovernmental Affairs.—James W. Morrison.

BOARD OF DIRECTORS

Government Directors:
R. Alexander Acosta, Secretary, U.S. Department of Labor.
Ambassador Mark Green, Administrator, U.S. Agency for International Development.
Ambassador Robert E. Lighthizer, U.S. Trade Representative.
David R. Malpass, Under Secretary for International Affairs, U.S. Department of the Treasury.
Wilbur L. Ross, Jr., Secretary, U.S. Department of Commerce.
John J. Sullivan, Deputy Secretary, U.S. Department of State.
Ray W. Washburne, President and Chief Executive Officer, OPIC.
Private Sector Directors:
James Demers, President, Demers and Blaisdell, Inc.
Todd Fisher, CAO, Kohlberg Kravis Roberts & Co.
Roberto Herencia, President and CEO, BXM Holdings, Inc.
Matthew Maxwell Taylor Kennedy, Director, Kennedy Enterprises.
Terry Lewis, Principal, LIA Advisors, LLC.
Deven Parekh, Managing Director, Insight Venture Partners.
Michael J. Warren, Principal, Albright Stonebridge Group, LLC.

U.S. POSTAL SERVICE

475 L'Enfant Plaza, SW., Washington, DC 20260–0010

phone (202) 268–2000

BOARD OF GOVERNORS

Postmaster General and Chief Executive Officer.—Louis DeJoy.
Deputy Postmaster General and Chief Government Relations Officer.—Vacant.

OFFICERS OF THE BOARD OF GOVERNORS

Chairman.—Robert M. Duncan.
Vice Chairman.—David C. Williams.
Members: John M. Barger, Ron A. Bloom, Roman Martinez IV, Donald L. Moak, William D. Zollars.
Secretary to the Board of Governors.—Michael J. Elston (acting), 268–4800.

OFFICERS OF THE POSTAL SERVICE

Postmaster General and Chief Executive Officer.—Louis DeJoy, 268–2550.
Deputy Postmaster General and Chief Government Relations Officer.—Vacant, 268–2519.
Judicial Officer.—Hon. Alan Caramella (acting), 2101 Wilson Boulevard, Suite 600, Arlington, VA 22201–3078 (703) 812–1904.
Chief Customer & Marketing Officer and Executive Vice President.—Steve Monteith (acting).
Vice President of:
Customer Experience.—Kelly Sigmon.
Marketing.—Vacant.
Product Innovation.—Gary Reblin.
Sales.—Tim Costello (acting).
Chief Commerce & Business Solutions Officer and Executive Vice President.—Jakki Krage Strako, 268–5710.
Vice President of:
Business Development.—Vacant.
Business Solutions.—Vacant.
Facilities.—Tom Samra.
Transportation Strategy.—Kelly Abney (acting).
Chief Financial Officer and Executive Vice President.—Joseph Corbett.
Senior Vice President of Finance and Strategy.—Luke Grossman.
Vice President, Controller.—Cara Green.
Vice President of:
Pricing and Costing.—Sharon Owens.

Supply Management.—Mark Guilfoil.
Chief Human Resources Officer and Executive Vice President.—Isaac Cronkhite, 268–4010.
Vice President of:
Employee Resource Management.—Simon Storey.
Labor Relations.—Douglas Tulino.
Chief Information Officer and Executive Vice President.—Pritha Mehra (acting).
Vice President and Chief Information Security Officer.—Gregory Crabb.
Vice President of:
Information Technology.—Marc McCrery (acting).
Mail Entry and Payment Technology.—Randy Workman (acting).
Chief Logistics & Processing Operations Officer and Executive Vice President.—David Williams.
Vice President of:
Logistics.—Robert Cintron, 268–3250.
Processing and Maintenance Operations.—Mike Barber.
Regional Processing Operations (Eastern).—Dane Coleman.
Regional Processing Operations (Western).—Larry Munoz.
Chief Retail & Delivery Officer and Executive Vice President.—Kristin Seaver, 268–5571.
Vice President of:
Area Retail and Delivery Operations (Atlantic).—Salvatore Vacca.
Area Retail and Delivery Operations (Central).—Krista Finazzo (acting).
Area Retail and Delivery Operations (Southern).—Shaun Mossman.
Area Retail and Delivery Operations (Western Pacific).—Greg Graves.
Delivery Operations.—Joshua Colin.
Retail and Post Office Operations.—Angela Curtis.
Chief Technology Officer and Executive Vice President.—Scott Bombaugh (acting).
Vice President of:
Engineering Systems.—Linda Malone (acting).
Enterprise Analytics.—Jeff Johnson.
General Counsel and Executive Vice President.—Thomas Marshall, 268–2951.

U.S. RAILROAD RETIREMENT BOARD

844 North Rush Street, Chicago, IL 60611

phone (312) 751–4777, fax 751–7154

Office of Legislative Affairs, 1310 G Street, NW., Suite 500, Washington, DC 20005

phone (202) 272–7742, fax 272–7728

https://rrb.gov, ola@rrb.gov

Chairman.—Erhard R. Chorlé, 751–4900.
Assistant to the Chairman.—Kimberley M. Cameron.
Counsel to the Chairman.—Amal S. Amin.
Labor Member.—Johnathan D. Bragg, 751–4905, fax 751–7194.
Assistants to the Labor Member: Geraldine L. Clark, Brigitte A. Munoz, Michele L. Neuendorf, Mark L. Thomson.
Counsel to the Labor Member.—Nancy V. Russell.
Management Member.—Thomas R. Jayne, 751–4910, fax 751–7189.
Assistants to the Management Member: Ann L. Chaney, Natasha L. Marx.
Counsel to the Management Member.—Robert M. Perbohner.
Inspector General.—Martin J. Dickman, 751–4690, fax 751–4342.
General Counsel.—Ana M. Kocur, 751–4984, fax 751–7102.
Secretary to the Board.—Stephanie D. Hillyard, 751–4920, fax 751–4923.
Director of:
Administration.—Keith B. Earley, 751–4990, fax 751–7197.
Disability Benefits.—Sherita Boots, 751–4740, fax 751–7167.
Equal Opportunity.—Pamela M. Tate, 751–4943, fax 751–7179.
Hearings and Appeals.—Rachel L. Simmons, 751–4946, fax 751–7159.
Human Resources.—Marguerite V. Daniels, 751–4384, fax 751–7164.
Legislative Affairs.—Beverly Britton Fraser, (202) 272–7742, fax 272–7728.
Policy and Systems.—Kimberly A. Price, 751–4383, fax 751–4650.
Program Evaluation and Management Services.—Janet M. Hallman, 751–4543, fax 751–7190.
Programs.—Crystal Coleman, 751–3310, fax 751–4333.
Public Affairs.—Michael P. Freeman, 751–4777, fax 751–7154.

Retirement and Survivor Benefits.—Valerie F. Allen, 751–3323, fax 751–7104.
Unemployment and Programs Support.—Micheal T. Pawlak, 751–4708, fax 751–7157.
Supervisor of Congressional Inquiry.—Lori A. Winn, 751–4747, fax 751–7154.
Chief of:
Acquisition Management.—Paul T. Ahern, 751–7130, fax 751–4923.
Actuary.—Frank J. Buzzi, 751–4915, fax 751–7129.
Benefit and Employment Analysis.—Michael J. Rizzo, 751–4771, fax 751–7129.
Finance.—Shawna R. Weekley, 751–4930, fax 751–4931.
Information.—Terryne F. Murphy, 751–4851, fax 751–7169.
Librarian.—Anne C. Mentkowski, 751–4926, fax 751–4924.
SEO/Director of Field Service.—Daniel J. Fadden, 751–4627, fax 751–3360.

U.S. SENTENCING COMMISSION

One Columbus Circle, NE., Suite 2–500, South Lobby, Washington, DC 20002–8002

phone (202) 502–4500, fax 502–4699

Chair.—Vacant.
Commissioners: Judge Charles R. Breyer, Judge Danny C. Reeves.
Commissioners ex officio: Patricia K. Cushwa, Candice C. Wong.
Staff Director.—Kenneth P. Cohen, 502–4523.
General Counsel.—Kathleen C. Grilli, 502–4563.
Director of Legislative and Public Affairs.—Christine M. Leonard, 502–4519.
Director of:
Administration.—Susan M. Brazel, 502–4587.
Research and Data.—Glenn R. Schmitt, 502–4531.
Education and Sentencing Practice.—Raquel K. Wilson, 502–4526.
Senior Publishing and Public Affairs Specialist.—Jennifer Dukes Jordan, 502–4593.

U.S. SMALL BUSINESS ADMINISTRATION

409 Third Street, SW., Washington, DC 20416

phone (202) 205–6600, fax 205–7064, https://sba.gov

Administrator.—Jovita Carranza.
Deputy Administrator.—Althea Coetzee Leslie, 205–6605.
Chief of Staff.—Pradeep Belur, 205–6605.
Director of Executive Secretariat.—Kim Bradley, 205–2410.
General Counsel.—Chris Pilkerton, 619–1848.
Deputy General Counsel: Steve Lancellotta, Nina Levine.
Chief Counsel for Advocacy.—Major L. Clark III (acting), 205–6804.
Inspector General.—Hannibal ''Mike'' Ware, 205–6586.
Assistant Inspector General for Management and Operations.—Sheldon Shoemaker.
Assistant Inspector General for Audits.—Andrea Deadwyler.
Assistant Administrator, Office of Inter-Governmental Affairs.—George Brown.
Assistant Administrator, Office of Performance Management and Chief Financial Officer.—Dorrice Roth (acting), 205–7420.
Associate Administrator, Office of Disaster Assistance.—James Rivera, 205–6734.
Deputy Associate Administrator, Office of Disaster Assistance.—Rafaela Monchek.
Field Operations.—Jason Simmons, 205–6411.
Associate Administrator, Office of Communications and Public Liaison.—Jill Billimoria.
Deputy Associate Administrator, Office of Communications and Public Liaison.—Erin McCracken.
Deputy Associate Administrator, Office of Communications and Public Liaison (Operations).—Terry Sutherland.
Associate Administrator, Office of Congressional and Legislative Affairs.—Michael Hershey, 205–6634.
Associate Administrator, Office of Diversity, Inclusion and Civil Rights.—Gaye Walker (acting).
Assistant Administrator, Office of Hearings and Appeals.—Delorice Price Ford (202) 401–8200.
Chief Operating Officer.—Stephen Kong (acting), 205–6340.
Chief Information Officer.—Maria Roat, 205–6708.
Deputy Chief Information Officer.—Guy Cavallo.
Chief Human Capital Officer.—Elias Hernandez, 205–6749.
Deputy Chief Human Capitol Officer.—Julie Brill.

Associate Administrator, Office of Capital Access.—William Manger, 205–6663.
Deputy Associate Administrator, Office of Capital Access.—John Miller.
Associate Administrator, Office of Entrepreneurial Development.—Allen Gutierrez.
Deputy Associate Administrator, Office of Entrepreneurial Development.—Adriana Menchaca-Gendron.
Associate Administrator, Office of Field Operations.—Michael Vallante.
Deputy Associate Administrator, Office of Field Operations.—Victor Parker.
Director of Entrepreneurship Education.—Donald Malcolm Smith, 205–6665.
Director of Financial Assistance.—Dianna Seaborn (acting), 205–3645.
Associate Administrator, Office of Investment and Innovation.—Joseph Shepard, 205–6513.
The National Ombudsman.—Stephanie Wehagen.
Deputy National Ombudsman.—Mina Wales.
Assistant Administrator, Office of Native American Affairs.—Shawn Pensoneau.
Assistant Administrator, Office of Technology.—Edsel Brown, 205–7343.
Director of Credit Risk Management.—Linda Rusche, 205–6538.
Associate Administrator, Office of Small Business Development Centers.—George Koklanaris.
Director of Surety Guarantees.—Frank Lalumiere, 205–6540.
Associate Administrator, Office of International Trade.—David M. Glaccum.
Deputy Associate Administrator, Office of International Trade.—Michele Schimpp.
Associate Administrator, Office of Veterans Business Development.—Larry Stubblefield.
Deputy Associate Administrator, Office of Veterans Business Development.—Timothy Green.
Assistant Administrator, Office of Women's Business Ownership.—Kathleen McShane, 205–6774.
Deputy Associate Administrator, Office of Business Development.—Jackie Robinson-Burnette, 205–7026.
Deputy Associate Administrator, Office of Government Contracting and Business Development.—Barbara E. Carson.
Director of Government Contracting.—Sean Crean, 205–6933.
Office of Size Standards.—Khem Sharma, 205–7189.

U.S. TRADE AND DEVELOPMENT AGENCY

1101 Wilson Boulevard, Suite 1600, Arlington, VA 22209

phone (703) 875–4357

Director.—Thomas R. Hardy (acting).
Deputy Director.—Todd Abrajano (acting).
General Counsel.—Sarah Fandell.
Chief of Staff.—Vacant.
Director for Congressional and Public Affairs.—Thomas R. Hardy.
Chief of Acquisitions Management.—Garth Hibbert.
Director of Finance.—Bedir Memmedli.
Chief Information Officer.—Benjamin Bergersen.
Program Director for—
Latin America and the Caribbean.—Nathan Younge.
Middle East, North Africa, Europe and Eurasia.—Carl B. Kress.
Indo-Pacific.—Verinda Fike.
Sub-Saharan Africa.—Heather Lanigan.
Global Programs.—Andrea Lupo.
Program Monitoring and Evaluations.—Sarah Randolph.
Partnerships and Innovation.—Paul A. Marin.

WASHINGTON METROPOLITAN AREA TRANSIT AUTHORITY

600 Fifth Street, NW., Washington, DC 20001

phone (202) 962–1234

General Manager and Chief Executive Officer.—Paul J. Wiedefeld.
General Counsel.—Patricia Lee.
Chief Financial Officer and Executive Vice President.—Dennis Anosike.
Chief Operating Officer and Executive Vice President.—Joe Leader.
Chief Safety Officer and Executive Vice President.—Theresa Impastato.
Senior Vice President for Bus Service.—Robert Potts.
Senior Vice President for Customer Service, Communications and Marketing.—Lynn Bowersox.

Vice President for the Office of Government Relations.—Regina Sullivan.
Chief Communications Officer.—Dan Stessel.
Chief, Metro Transit Police Department.—Ronald Pavlik.

WASHINGTON NATIONAL MONUMENT SOCIETY

[Organized 1833; chartered 1859; amended by Acts of August 2, 1876, October, 1888]

President Ex Officio.—Donald J. Trump, President of the United States.
First Vice President.—Outerbridge Horsey, AIA, 1632 32nd Street, NW., Washington, DC 20007 (202) 714–4826.
Treasurer.—Henry Ravenel, Jr.
Secretary.—Karen Cucurullo, Acting Superintendent, National Mall and Memorial Parks, 900 Ohio Drive, SW., Washington, DC 20024–2000 (202) 485–9875.

Members:
Christopher Addison
Neil C. Folger
James M. Goode
Gilbert M. Grosvenor
Outerbridge Horsey, AIA
Henry Ravenel, Jr.
Hon. James W. Symington
John A. Washington
Robert Vogel, Regional Director of the National Capital Region, National Park Service.

Member Emeritus:
Harry F. Byrd, Jr. †

† *Deceased*

WOODROW WILSON INTERNATIONAL CENTER FOR SCHOLARS

One Woodrow Wilson Plaza

1300 Pennsylvania Avenue, NW., Washington, DC 20004–3027

phone (202) 691–4000, fax 691–4001

[Under the direction of the Board of Trustees of Woodrow Wilson International Center for Scholars]

Director/President/CEO.—Hon. Jane Harman, 691–4202.
Senior Vice President and Director of International Security Studies.—Robert S. Litwak, 691–4179.
Chief Operating Officer.—Bruce Blakeman.
Strategic and National Security Advisor to the Wilson Center's CEO and President.—Meg King, 691–4104.
Vice President for External Relations.—Linda Roth, 691–4122.
Director of Congressional Relations.—Aaron C. Jones, 691–4140.
Deputy Director of Development.—Nora Shuler, 691–4162.
Human Resources Director.—Vickki G. Johnson, 691–4018.
Director Support Operations.—Prince Palmer.
Chief Information Officer.—Dennis Reimer.
Chief Technology Officer.—Bruce Griffith.
Chief Financial Officer.—Susan Howard (interim).

Board of Trustees:
Chair.—Vacant.
Vice Chair.—Drew Maloney, President and CEO, American Investment Council.

Private Members:
Peter J. Beshar, Executive Vice President and General Counsel, Marsh & McLennan Companies, Inc.
Thelma Duggin, President, The AnBryce Foundation.
Barry S. Jackson, Managing Director, The Lindsey Group, and Strategic Advisor, Brownstein Hyatt Farber Schreck.
David C. Jacobson, Former U.S. Ambassador to Canada and Vice Chair, BMO Financial Group.
Nathalie Rayes, President and CEO, Latino Victory.
Earl W. Stafford, Chief Executive Officer, The Wentworth Group, LLC.
Hon. Louis Susman, Former U.S. Ambassador to the United Kingdom; Senior Advisor, Perella Weinberg Partners.

Public Members:

Elisabeth DeVos, Secretary, U.S. Department of Education.
David Ferriero, Archivist of the United States.
Carla Hayden, Librarian of Congress.
Jon Parrish Peede, Chairman, National Endowment for the Humanities.
Lonnie Bunch, Secretary, Smithsonian Institution.
Michael Pompeo, Secretary, U.S. Department of State.
Alex Azar, Secretary, U.S. Department of Health and Human Services.

Designated Appointee of the President from within the Federal Government:
Vacant.

JUDICIAL BRANCH

SUPREME COURT OF THE UNITED STATES

One First Street, NE., Washington, DC 20543

phone (202) 479–3000

JOHN G. ROBERTS, JR., Chief Justice of the United States, was born in Buffalo, NY, January 27, 1955. He married Jane Marie Sullivan in 1996 and they have two children, Josephine and Jack. He received an A.B. from Harvard College in 1976 and a J.D. from Harvard Law School in 1979. He served as a law clerk for Judge Henry J. Friendly of the United States Court of Appeals for the Second Circuit from 1979–80 and as a law clerk for then Associate Justice William H. Rehnquist of the Supreme Court of the United States during the 1980 term. He was Special Assistant to the Attorney General, U.S. Department of Justice from 1981–82, Associate Counsel to President Ronald Reagan, White House Counsel's Office from 1982–86, and Principal Deputy Solicitor General, U.S. Department of Justice from 1989–93. From 1986–89 and 1993–2003, he practiced law in Washington, DC. He was appointed to the United States Court of Appeals for the District of Columbia Circuit in 2003. President George W. Bush nominated him as Chief Justice of the United States, and he took his seat September 29, 2005.

CLARENCE THOMAS, Associate Justice, was born in the Pin Point community near Savannah, Georgia on June 23, 1948. He attended Conception Seminary from 1967–68 and received an A.B., *cum laude*, from Holy Cross College in 1971 and a J.D. from Yale Law School in 1974. He was admitted to law practice in Missouri in 1974, and served as an Assistant Attorney General of Missouri, 1974–77; an attorney with the Monsanto Company, 1977–79; and Legislative Assistant to Senator John Danforth, 1979–81. From 1981–82, he served as Assistant Secretary for Civil Rights, U.S. Department of Education, and as Chairman of the U.S. Equal Employment Opportunity Commission, 1982–90. From 1990–91, he served as a Judge on the United States Court of Appeals for the District of Columbia Circuit. President Bush nominated him as an Associate Justice of the Supreme Court and he took his seat October 23, 1991. He married Virginia Lamp on May 30, 1987 and has one child, Jamal Adeen, by a previous marriage.

† RUTH BADER GINSBURG, Associate Justice, was born in Brooklyn, NY, March 15, 1933. She married Martin D. Ginsburg in 1954, and has a daughter, Jane, and a son, James. She received her B.A. from Cornell University, attended Harvard Law School, and received her LL.B. from Columbia Law School. She served as a law clerk to the Honorable Edmund L. Palmieri, Judge of the United States District Court for the Southern District of New York, from 1959–61. From 1961–63, she was a research associate and then Associate Director of the Columbia Law School Project on International Procedure. She was a Professor of Law at Rutgers University School of Law from 1963–72, and Columbia Law School from 1972–80, and a fellow at the Center for Advanced Study in the Behavioral Sciences in Stanford, CA, from 1977–78. In 1971, she was instrumental in launching the Women's Rights Project of the American Civil Liberties Union, and served as the ACLU's General Counsel from 1973–80, and on the National Board of Directors from 1974–80. She was appointed a Judge of the United States Court of Appeals for the District of Columbia Circuit in 1980. President Clinton nominated her as an Associate Justice of the Supreme Court, and she took her seat August 10, 1993.

† Died after closing date of this directory.

STEPHEN G. BREYER, Associate Justice, was born in San Francisco, CA, August 15, 1938. He married Joanna Hare in 1967, and has three children, Chloe, Nell, and Michael. He received an A.B. from Stanford University, a B.A. from Magdalen College, Oxford, and an LL.B. from Harvard Law School. He served as a law clerk to Justice Arthur Goldberg of the Supreme Court of the United States during the 1964 term, as a Special Assistant to the Assistant U.S. Attorney General for Antitrust, 1965–67, as an Assistant Special Prosecutor of the Watergate Special Prosecution Force, 1973, as Special Counsel of the U.S. Senate Judiciary Committee, 1974–75, and as Chief Counsel of the committee, 1979–80. He was an Assistant Professor, Professor of Law, and Lecturer at Harvard Law School, 1967–94, a Professor at the Harvard University Kennedy School of Government, 1977–80, and a Visiting Professor at the College of Law, Sydney, Australia, and at the University of Rome. From 1980–90, he served as a Judge of the United States Court of Appeals for the First Circuit, and as its Chief Judge, 1990–94. He also served as a member of the Judicial Conference of the United States, 1990–94, and of the United States Sentencing Commission, 1985–89. President Clinton nominated him as an Associate Justice of the Supreme Court, and he took his seat August 3, 1994.

SAMUEL A. ALITO, JR., Associate Justice, was born in Trenton, NJ, April 1, 1950. He married Martha-Ann Bomgardner in 1985, and has two children, Philip and Laura. He served as a law clerk for Leonard I. Garth of the United States Court of Appeals for the Third Circuit from 1976–77. He was Assistant U.S. Attorney, District of New Jersey, 1977–81, Assistant to the Solicitor General, U.S. Department of Justice, 1981–85, Deputy Assistant Attorney General, U.S. Department of Justice, 1985–87, and U.S. Attorney, District of New Jersey, 1987–90. He was appointed to the United States Court of Appeals for the Third Circuit in 1990. President George W. Bush nominated him as an Associate Justice of the Supreme Court, and he took his seat January 31, 2006.

SONIA SOTOMAYOR, Associate Justice, was born in Bronx, NY, June 25, 1954. She earned a B.A. in 1976 from Princeton University, graduating *summa cum laude* and receiving the university's highest academic honor. In 1979, she earned a J.D. from Yale Law School where she served as an editor of the *Yale Law Journal.* She served as Assistant District Attorney in the New York County District Attorney's Office from 1979–84. She then litigated international commercial matters in New York City at Pavia & Harcourt, where she served as an associate and then partner from 1984–92. In 1991, President George H.W. Bush nominated her to the U.S. District Court Southern District of New York, and she served in that role from 1992–98. She served as a judge on the United States Court of Appeals for the Second Circuit from 1998–2009. President Barack Obama nominated her as an Associate Justice of the Supreme Court on May 26, 2009, and she assumed this role August 8, 2009.

ELENA KAGAN, Associate Justice, was born in New York, New York, on April 28, 1960. She received an A.B. from Princeton in 1981, an M.Phil. from Oxford in 1983, and a J.D. from Harvard Law School in 1986. She clerked for Judge Abner Mikva of the U.S. Court of Appeals for the D.C. Circuit from 1986–87 and for Justice Thurgood Marshall of the U.S. Supreme Court during the 1987 Term. After briefly practicing law at a Washington, DC, law firm, she became a law professor, first at the University of Chicago Law School and later at Harvard Law School. She also served for four years in the Clinton Administration, as Associate Counsel to the President and then as Deputy Assistant to the President for Domestic Policy. Between 2003 and 2009, she served as the Dean of Harvard Law School. In 2009, President Obama nominated her as the Solicitor General of the United States. A year later, the President nominated her as an Associate Justice of the Supreme Court on May 10, 2010. She took her seat on August 7, 2010.

NEIL M. GORSUCH, Associate Justice, was born in Denver, CO, August 29, 1967. He and his wife Louise have two daughters. He received a B.A. from Columbia University, a J.D. from Harvard Law School, and a D.Phil. from Oxford University. He served as a law clerk to Judge David B. Sentelle of the United States Court of Appeals for the District of Columbia Circuit, and as a law clerk to Justice Byron White and Justice Anthony M. Kennedy of the Supreme Court of the United States. From 1995–2005, he was in private practice, and from 2005–06 he was Principal Deputy Associate Attorney General at the U.S. Department of Justice. He was appointed to the United States Court of Appeals for the Tenth Circuit in 2006. He served on the Standing Committee on Rules for Practice and Procedure of the U.S. Judicial Conference, and as chairman of the Advisory Committee on Rules of Appellate Procedure. He taught at the University of Colorado Law School. President Donald J. Trump nominated him as an Associate Justice of the Supreme Court, and he took his seat on April 10, 2017.

BRETT M. KAVANAUGH, Associate Justice, was born in Washington, DC, on February 12, 1965. He married Ashley Estes in 2004, and they have two daughters—Margaret and Liza. He received a B.A. from Yale College in 1987 and a J.D. from Yale Law School in 1990. He served as a law clerk for Judge Walter Stapleton of the U.S. Court of Appeals for the Third Circuit from 1990–91, for Judge Alex Kozinski of the U.S. Court of Appeals for the Ninth Circuit from 1991–92, and for Justice Anthony M. Kennedy of the U.S. Supreme Court during the 1993 Term. In 1992-1993, he was an attorney in the Office of the Solicitor General of the United States. From 1994–97 and for a period in 1998, he was Associate Counsel in the Office of Independent Counsel. He was a partner at a Washington, DC, law firm from 1997–98 and again from 1999–2001. From 2001–03, he was Associate Counsel and then Senior Associate Counsel to President George W. Bush. From 2003–06, he was Assistant to the President and Staff Secretary for President Bush. He was appointed a Judge of the United States Court of Appeals for the District of Columbia Circuit in 2006. President Donald J. Trump nominated him as an Associate Justice of the Supreme Court, and he took his seat on October 6, 2018.

RETIRED ASSOCIATE JUSTICES

ANTHONY M. KENNEDY (Retired), Associate Justice, was born in Sacramento, CA, July 23, 1936. He married Mary Davis and has three children. He received his B.A. from Stanford University and the London School of Economics, and his LL.B. from Harvard Law School. He was in private practice in San Francisco, CA, from 1961–63, as well as in Sacramento, CA, from 1963–75. From 1965–88, he was a Professor of Constitutional Law at the McGeorge School of Law, University of the Pacific. He has served in numerous positions during his career, including a member of the California Army National Guard in 1961, the board of the Federal Judicial Center from 1987–88, and two committees of the Judicial Conference of the United States: the Advisory Panel on Financial Disclosure Reports and Judicial Activities, subsequently renamed the Advisory Committee on Codes of Conduct, from 1979–87, the Committee on Pacific Territories from 1979–90, which he chaired from 1982–90. He was appointed to the United States Court of Appeals for the Ninth Circuit in 1975. President Reagan nominated him as an Associate Justice of the Supreme Court, and he took his seat February 18, 1988. Justice Kennedy retired from the Supreme Court on July 31, 2018.

SANDRA DAY O'CONNOR (Retired), Associate Justice, was born in El Paso, TX, March 26, 1930. She married John Jay O'Connor III in 1952 and has three sons, Scott, Brian, and Jay. She received her B.A. and LL.B. from Stanford University. She served as Deputy County Attorney of San Mateo County, CA, from 1952–53 and as a civilian attorney for Quartermaster Market Center, Frankfurt, Germany, from 1954–57. From 1958–60, she practiced law in Maryvale, AZ, and served as Assistant Attorney General of Arizona from 1965–69. She was appointed to the Arizona State Senate in 1969 and was subsequently reelected to two two-year terms. In 1975, she was elected Judge of the Maricopa County Superior Court and served until 1979, when she was appointed to the Arizona Court of Appeals. President Reagan nominated her as an Associate Justice of the Supreme Court, and she took her seat September 25, 1981. Justice O'Connor retired from the Supreme Court on January 31, 2006.

DAVID H. SOUTER (Retired), Associate Justice, was born in Melrose, MA, September 17, 1939. He graduated from Harvard College, from which he received his A.B. After two years as a Rhodes Scholar at Magdalen College, Oxford, he received an A.B. in Jurisprudence from Oxford University and an M.A. in 1989. After receiving an LL.B. from Harvard Law School, he was an associate at Orr and Reno in Concord, NH, from 1966 to 1968, when he became an Assistant Attorney General of New Hampshire. In 1971, he became Deputy Attorney General and in 1976, Attorney General of New Hampshire. In 1978, he was named an Associate Justice of the Superior Court of New Hampshire, and was appointed to the Supreme Court of New Hampshire as an Associate Justice in 1983. He became a Judge of the United States Court of Appeals for the First Circuit on May 25, 1990. President Bush nominated him as an Associate Justice of the Supreme Court, and he took his seat October 9, 1990. Justice Souter retired from the Supreme Court on June 29, 2009.

OFFICERS OF THE SUPREME COURT

Counselor to the Chief Justice.—Jeffrey P. Minear.
Clerk.—Scott S. Harris.
Librarian.—Linda Maslow.
Marshal.—Pamela Talkin.
Reporter of Decisions.—Christine L. Fallon.
Court Counsel.—Ethan V. Torrey.
Curator.—Catherine E. Fitts.
Director of Information Technology.—Robert J. Hawkins.
Public Information Officer.—Kathleen L. Arberg.

UNITED STATES COURTS OF APPEALS

First Judicial Circuit (Districts of Maine, Massachusetts, New Hampshire, Puerto Rico, and Rhode Island)

Chief Judge.—Jeffrey R. Howard.
Circuit Judges: Juan R. Torruella, Sandra L. Lynch, O. Rogeriee Thompson, William J. Kayatta, Jr., David J. Barron.
Senior Circuit Judges: Bruce M. Selya, Michael Boudin, Norman H. Stahl, Kermit V. Lipez.
Circuit Executive.—Susan J. Goldberg (617) 748–9614.
Clerk.—Maria Hamilton (617) 748–9053, John Joseph Moakley U.S. Courthouse, One Courthouse Way, Suite 2500, Boston, MA 02210.

Second Judicial Circuit (Districts of Connecticut, New York [Eastern, Northern, Southern, and Western], and Vermont)

Chief Judge: Robert A. Katzmann.
Circuit Judges: Joseph F. Bianco, José A. Cabranes, Susan L. Carney, Denny Chin, Peter W. Hall, Debra A. Livingston, Raymond J. Lohier, Jr., Michael H. Park, Rosemary S. Pooler, Reena Raggi, Richard J. Sullivan, William J. Nardini, Steven J. Menashi.
Senior Circuit Judges: Guido Calabresi, Dennis Jacobs, Amalya L. Kearse, Pierre N. Leval, Gerard E. Lynch, Jon O. Newman, Barrington D. Parker, Jr., Robert D. Sack, Chester J. Straub, John M. Walker, Jr., Richard C. Wesley, Ralph K. Winter.
Circuit Executive.—Karen Greve Milton.
Clerk.—Catherine O'Hagan Wolfe (212) 857–8700, Thurgood Marshall United States Courthouse, 40 Foley Square, New York, NY 10007–1581.

Third Judicial Circuit (Districts of Delaware, New Jersey, Pennsylvania, and Virgin Islands)

Chief Judge.—D. Brooks Smith.
Circuit Judges: Theodore A. McKee, Thomas L. Ambro, Michael A. Chagares, Kent A. Jordan, Thomas M. Hardiman, Joseph A. Greenaway, Jr., Patty Shwartz, Cheryl Ann Krause, L. Felipe Restrepo, Stephanos Bibas, David J. Porter, Paul B. Matey, Peter J. Phipps.
Senior Circuit Judges: Walter K. Stapleton, Morton I. Greenberg, Anthony J. Scirica, Robert E. Cowen, Richard L. Nygaard, Jane R. Roth, Marjorie O. Rendell, Julio M. Fuentes, D. Michael Fisher.
Circuit Executive.—Margaret A. Wiegand (215) 597–0718, U.S. Courthouse, 601 Market Street, Room 22409, Philadelphia, PA 19106.
Clerk.—Patricia S. Dodszuweit (215) 597–2995, U.S. Courthouse, 601 Market Street, Room 21400, Philadelphia, PA 19106.

Fourth Judicial Circuit (Districts of Maryland, North Carolina, South Carolina, Virginia, and West Virginia)

Chief Judge: Roger L. Gregory.
Circuit Judges: J. Harvie Wilkinson III, Paul V. Niemeyer, Diana Gribbon Motz, Robert B. King, G. Steven Agee, Barbara Milano Keenan, James A. Wynn, Jr., Albert Diaz, Henry F. Floyd, Stephanie D. Thacker, Pamela A. Harris, Julius N. Richardson, A. Marvin Quattlebaum, Jr., Allison J. Rushing.
Senior Circuit Judges: William B. Traxler, Jr., Dennis W. Shedd.
Circuit Executive.—James N. Ishida (804) 916–2184.
Clerk.—Patricia S. Connor (804) 916–2700, Lewis F. Powell, Jr., U.S. Courthouse Annex, 1100 E. Main Street, Richmond, VA 23219.

Fifth Judicial Circuit (Districts of Louisiana, Mississippi, and Texas)

Chief Judge.—Priscilla R. Owen.
Circuit Judges: Edith H. Jones, Jerry E. Smith, Carl E. Stewart, James L. Dennis, Jennifer Walker Elrod, Leslie H. Southwick, Catharina Haynes, James E. Graves, Jr., Stephen

A. Higginson, Gregg J. Costa, Don R. Willett, James C. Ho, Andew S. Oldham, Stuart Kyle Duncan, Kurt D. Engelhardt, Cory T. Wilson.

Senior Circuit Judges: Thomas M. Reavley, Carolyn Dineen King, E. Grady Jolly, Patrick E. Higginbotham, W. Eugene Davis, John M. Duhé, Jr., Jacques L. Wiener, Jr., Rhesa H. Barksdale, Fortunato P. Benavides, Edith Brown Clement.

Circuit Executive.—Ted Cominos (504) 310–7777, John Minor Wisdom U.S. Court of Appeals Building, 600 Camp Street, New Orleans, LA 70130–3425.

Clerk.—Lyle W. Cayce (504) 310–7700, 600 S. Maestri Place, New Orleans, LA 70130.

Sixth Judicial Circuit (Districts of Kentucky, Michigan, Ohio, and Tennessee)

Chief Judge.—R. Guy Cole, Jr.

Circuit Judges: Karen Nelson Moore, Eric Lee Clay, Julia Smith Gibbons, Jeffrey S. Sutton, Richard Allen Griffin, Raymond M. Kethledge, Helene N. White, Jane B. Stranch, Bernice Bouie Donald, Amul R. Thapar, John Kenneth Bush, Joan Louise Larsen, John B. Nalbandian, Chad A. Readler, Eric E. Murphy.

Senior Circuit Judges: Gilbert S. Merritt, Ralph B. Guy, Danny J. Boggs, Alan E. Norris, Richard F. Suhrheinrich, Eugene E. Siler, Jr., Alice M. Batchelder, Martha Craig Daughtrey, Ronald Lee Gilman*, John M. Rogers, Deborah L. Cook, David W. McKeague.

Circuit Executive.—Clarence Maddox (513) 564–7200.

Clerk.—Deborah Hunt (513) 564–7000, Potter Stewart U.S. Courthouse, 100 E. Fifth Street, Cincinnati, OH 45202.

Seventh Judicial Circuit (Districts of Illinois, Indiana, and Wisconsin)

Chief Judge.—Diane S. Sykes.

Circuit Judges: Joel M. Flaum, Frank H. Easterbrook, Michael S. Kanne, Ilana Diamond Rovner, Diane P. Wood, David F. Hamilton, Amy Coney Barrett, Michael B. Brennan, Michael Y. Scudder, Jr., Amy J. St. Eve.

Senior Circuit Judges: William J. Bauer, Kenneth F. Ripple, Daniel A. Manion.

Circuit Executive.—Collins T. Fitzpatrick (312) 435–5803.

Clerk.—Gino J. Agnello (312) 435–5850, 2722 U.S. Courthouse, 219 S. Dearborn Street, Chicago, IL 60604.

Eighth Judicial Circuit (Districts of Arkansas, Iowa, Minnesota, Missouri, Nebraska, North Dakota, and South Dakota)

Chief Judge.—Lavenski R. Smith.

Circuit Judges: James B. Loken, Steven M. Colloton, Raymond W. Gruender, Duane Benton, Bobby E. Shepherd, Jane L. Kelly, Ralph R. Erickson, L. Steven Grasz, David R. Stras, Jonathan A. Kobes.

Senior Circuit Judges: Pasco M. Bowman II, Roger L. Wollman, C. Arlen Beam, Morris S. Arnold, Michael J. Melloy.

Circuit Executive.—Millie Adams (314) 244–2600.

Clerk.—Michael E. Gans (314) 244–2400, 111 S. Tenth Street, Suite 24.329, St. Louis, MO 63102.

Ninth Judicial Circuit (Districts of Alaska, Arizona, California [Central, Eastern, Northern, and Southern], Guam, Hawaii, Idaho, Montana, Nevada, Northern Mariana Islands, Oregon, Eastern Washington, Western Washington)

Chief Judge.—Sidney R. Thomas.

Circuit Judges: Susan P. Graber, M. Margaret McKeown, Kim McLane Wardlaw, William A. Fletcher, Ronald M. Gould, Richard A. Paez, Marsha L. Berzon, Johnnie B. Rawlinson, Consuelo M. Callahan, Milan D. Smith, Jr., Sandra S. Ikuta, Mary H. Murguia, Morgan Christen, Jacqueline H. Nguyen, Paul J. Watford, Andrew D. Hurwitz, John B. Owens, Michelle T. Friedland, Mark J. Bennett, Ryan Nelson, Eric D. Miller, Bridget S. Bade, Daniel P. Collins, Kenneth Lee, Daniel A. Bress, Danielle Hunsaker.

Senior Circuit Judges: Alfred T. Goodwin, J. Clifford Wallace, Mary M. Schroeder, Jerome Farris, Dorothy W. Nelson, William C. Canby, Jr., Edward Leavy, Stephen S. Trott, Ferdinand F. Fernandez, Andrew J. Kleinfeld, Michael D. Hawkins, A. Wallace Tashima, Diarmuid F. O'Scannlain, Barry G. Silverman, Richard C. Tallman, N. Randy Smith, Richard R. Clifton, Jay S. Bybee, Carlos T. Bea.

Circuit Executive.—Elizabeth A. Smith (415) 355–8800.

Clerk.—Molly C. Dwyer (415) 355–8000, P.O. Box 193939, San Francisco, CA 94119–3939.

Tenth Judicial Circuit (Districts of Colorado, Kansas, New Mexico, Oklahoma, Utah, and Wyoming)

Chief Judge.—Timothy M. Tymkovich.
Circuit Judges: Mary Beck Briscoe, Carlos F. Lucero, Harris L. Hartz, Jerome A. Holmes, Scott M. Matheson, Jr., Robert E. Bacharach, Gregory A. Phillips, Carolyn B. McHugh, Nancy L. Moritz, Allison H. Eid, Joel Carson.
Senior Circuit Judges: Stephanie K. Seymour, John C. Porfilio, Bobby R. Baldock, David M. Ebel, Paul J. Kelly, Jr., Michael R. Murphy, Terrence L. O'Brien.
Circuit Executive.—David Tighe (303) 844–2067.
Clerk.—Betsy Shumaker (303) 844–3157, Byron White United States Courthouse, 1823 Stout Street, Denver, CO 80257.

Eleventh Judicial Circuit (Districts of Alabama, Florida, and Georgia)

Chief Judge.—William H. Pryor, Jr.
Circuit Judges: Charles R. Wilson, Beverly B. Martin, Adalberto Jordán, Robin S. Rosenbaum, Jill A. Pryor, Kevin C. Newsom, Elizabeth L. Branch, Britt C. Grant, Robert J. Luck, Barbara Lagoa, Andrew L. Brasher.
Senior Circuit Judges: James C. Hill, Peter T. Fay, Phyllis A. Kravitch, R. Lanier Anderson III, J. L. Edmondson, Emmett R. Cox, Joel F. Dubina, Susan H. Black, Ed Carnes, Frank M. Hull, Julie E. Carnes, Gerald B. Tjoflat, Stanley Marcus.
Circuit Executive.—James P. Gerstenlauer (404) 335–6535.
Clerk.—David J. Smith (404) 335–6100, 56 Forsyth Street, NW., Atlanta, GA 30303.

UNITED STATES COURT OF APPEALS FOR THE DISTRICT OF COLUMBIA CIRCUIT

333 Constitution Avenue, NW., Washington, DC 20001
phone (202) 216–7300

MERRICK BRIAN GARLAND, chief circuit judge; born in Chicago, IL, 1952; A.B., Harvard University, 1974, *summa cum laude*, Phi Beta Kappa, Paul Revere Frothingham Award and Richard Perkins Parker Award; J.D., Harvard Law School, 1977, *magna cum laude*, articles editor, *Harvard Law Review*; law clerk to Judge Henry J. Friendly, U.S. Court of Appeals for the 2d Circuit, 1977–78; law clerk to Justice William J. Brennan, Jr., U.S. Supreme Court, 1978–79; Special Assistant to the Attorney General, 1979–81; associate then partner, Arnold and Porter, Washington, DC, 1981–89; Assistant U.S. Attorney, Washington, DC, 1989–92; partner, Arnold and Porter, 1992–93; Deputy Assistant Attorney General, Criminal Division, U.S. Department of Justice, 1993–94; Principal Associate Deputy Attorney General, 1994–97; Lecturer on Law, Harvard Law School, 1985–86. Edmund J. Randolph Award, U.S. Department of Justice, 1997. Admitted to the bars of the District of Columbia; U.S. District Court; Court of Appeals, District of Columbia Circuit; U.S. Courts of Appeals for the 4th, 9th, and 10th Circuits; and U.S. Supreme Court. Author: Antitrust and State Action, 96 Yale Law Journal 486 (1987); Antitrust and Federalism, 96 Yale Law Journal 1291 (1987); *Deregulation and Judicial Review*, 98 Harvard Law Review 505 (1985); co-chair, Administrative Law Section, District of Columbia Bar, 1991–94; President, Board of Overseers, Harvard University, 2009–10, member, 2003–09; American Law Institute; U.S. Judicial Conference Executive Committee, 2013–present, Committee on Judicial Security, 2008–13, Committee on the Judicial Branch, 2001–05; appointed to the U.S. Court of Appeals for the District of Columbia Circuit on April 9, 1997.

KAREN LECRAFT HENDERSON, circuit judge. [Biographical information not supplied, per Judge Henderson's request.]

JUDITH W. ROGERS, circuit judge; born in New York, NY; A.B. (with honors), Radcliffe College, 1961; Phi Beta Kappa honors member; LL.B., Harvard Law School, 1964; LL.M., University of Virginia School of Law, 1988; law clerk, D.C. Juvenile Court, 1964–65; assistant U.S. Attorney for the District of Columbia, 1965–68; trial attorney, San Francisco Neighborhood Legal Assistance Foundation, 1968–69; Attorney, U.S. Department of Justice, Office of the Associate Deputy Attorney General and Criminal Division, 1969–71; General Counsel, Congressional Commission on the Organization of the D.C. Government, 1971–72; legislative assistant to D.C. Mayor Walter E. Washington, 1972–79; Corporation Counsel for the District of Columbia, 1979–83; trustee, Radcliffe College, 1982–90; member of Visiting Committee to Harvard Law School, 1984–90 and 2006–11; appointed by President Reagan to the District of Columbia Court of Appeals as an Associate Judge on September 15, 1983; served as Chief Judge, November 1, 1988 to March 17, 1994; appointed by President Clinton to the U.S. Court of Appeals for the District of Columbia Circuit on March 18, 1994, and entered on duty March 21, 1994; member of Executive Committee, Conference of Chief Justices, 1993–94; member, U.S. Judicial Conference Committee on the Codes of Conduct, 1998–2004.

DAVID S. TATEL, circuit judge; born in Washington, D.C., March 16, 1942; son of Molly and Dr. Howard Tatel (both deceased); married to Edith Tatel, née Bassichis, 1965; children: Rebecca, Stephanie, Joshua, and Emily; grandchildren: Olivia, Maya, Olin, Reuben, Rae, Cameron, Ozzie, and Daria; B.A., University of Michigan, 1963; J.D., University of Chicago Law School, 1966; instructor, University of Michigan Law School, 1966–67; associate, Sidley, Austin, Burgess & Smith, 1967–69, 1970–72; director, Chicago Lawyers' Committee for Civil Rights Under Law, 1969–70; director, National Lawyers' Committee for Civil Rights Under Law, 1972–74, and co-chair, 1989–91; director, Office for Civil Rights, U.S. Department of Health, Education and Welfare, 1977–79; associate and partner, Hogan and Hartson, 1974–77, 1979–94; lecturer, Stanford University Law School, 1991–92; board of directors, Spencer

Foundation, 1987–97, and chair, 1990–97; board of directors, National Board for Professional Teaching Standards, 1997–2000; board of directors, Carnegie Foundation for the Advancement of Teaching, and chair, 2005–09; co-chair, the National Academy of Sciences Committee on Science, Technology and Law, 2014-present; board member, Associated Universities, Inc., 2019-present; board of advisors, American Society of International Law; advisory board member, Federal Judicial Center; member, the American Philosophical Society; member, the American Academy of Arts and Sciences; admitted to practice law in Illinois in 1966 and the District Columbia in 1970; appointed to the U.S. Court of Appeals for the District of Columbia Circuit by President Clinton on October 7, 1994, and entered on duty October 11, 1994.

GREGORY G. KATSAS, circuit judge; born in Boston, MA, 1964; son of George and Clara Katsas; married to Simone Mele Katsas; two daughters; A.B., Princeton University, 1986, cum laude; J.D., Harvard Law School, cum laude, executive editor, Harvard Law Review; law clerk to Judge Edward Becker, U.S. Court of Appeals for the Third Circuit, 1989–90; law clerk to Judge Clarence Thomas, U.S. Court of Appeals for the D.C. Circuit, 1990–91; law clerk to Justice Clarence Thomas, Supreme Court of the United States, 1991–92; associate then partner, Jones Day, 1992–2001; Deputy Assistant Attorney General, Civil Division, U.S. Department of Justice, 2001–06; Principal Deputy Associate Attorney General, 2006–08; Acting Associate Attorney General, 2007–08; Assistant Attorney General, Civil Division, 2008–09; partner, Jones Day, 2009–17; Deputy Assistant to the President and Deputy Counsel to the President, 2017; Edmund J. Randolph award, U.S. Department of Justice, 2009; Member, Advisory Committee on Civil Rules, 2008–09; Member, Advisory Committee on Appellate Rules, 2013–17. Appointed to the U.S. Court of Appeals for the D.C. Circuit on December 8, 2018.

THOMAS B. GRIFFITH, circuit judge; born in Yokohama, Japan, July 5, 1954; B.A., Brigham Young University, 1978; J.D., University of Virginia School of Law, 1985; editor, *Virginia Law Review*; associate, Robinson, Bradshaw and Hinson, Charlotte, NC, 1985–89; associate and then a partner, Wiley, Rein and Fielding, Washington, DC, 1989–95 and 1999–2000; Senate Legal Counsel of the United States, 1995–99; Assistant to the President and General Counsel, Brigham Young University, Provo, UT, 2000–05; appointed to the United States Court of Appeals for the District of Columbia Circuit on June 14, 2005 and sworn in on July 1, 2005.

NEOMI RAO, circuit judge; was appointed to the United States Court of Appeals for the District of Columbia Circuit in March 2019. She graduated from Yale College in 1995 and the University of Chicago Law School in 1999. Following graduation, she served as a law clerk to Judge J. Harvie Wilkinson III of the U.S. Court of Appeals for the Fourth Circuit and, in the 2001 October Term, as law clerk to Justice Clarence Thomas of the U.S. Supreme Court. Between her clerkships, Judge Rao served as counsel for nominations and constitutional law to the U.S. Senate Committee on the Judiciary. In 2002, she joined the international arbitration group of Clifford Chance LLP in London, England. From 2005 to 2006, she served as Special Assistant and Associate White House Counsel to President George W. Bush. From 2006 to 2017, Judge Rao was a professor at the Antonin Scalia Law School at George Mason University, where she taught constitutional law, legislation and statutory interpretation, and the history and foundations of the administrative state. In 2014, she founded the Center for the Study of the Administrative State, a non-profit Center that promotes academic scholarship and public policy debates about administrative law. In July 2017, she was appointed to serve as the Administrator of the Office of Information and Regulatory Affairs in the Office of Management Budget. She served in this position until her appointment to the D.C. Circuit.

SRI SRINIVASAN, circuit judge; born in Chandigarh, India, February 23, 1967; son of Saroja and T.P. Srinivasan; two children; B.A. Stanford University, 1989; J.D. Stanford Law School, 1995; M.B.A. Stanford Graduate School of Business, 1995; law clerk to Judge J. Harvie Wilkinson III of the U.S. Court of Appeals for the Fourth Circuit, 1995–96; Bristow Fellow, Office of the Solicitor General of the United States, 1996–97; law clerk to Associate Justice Sandra Day O'Connor of the U.S. Supreme Court, 1997–98; associate, O'Melveny & Myers LLP, 1998–2002; Assistant to the Solicitor General, 2002–07; partner, O'Melveny & Myers LLP, 2007–11; Lecturer on Law, Harvard Law School, 2009–10; Principal Deputy Solicitor General, 2011–13; Adjunct Professor of Law, Georgetown University Law Center, 2015–present; member, U.S. Judicial Conference Committee on Rules of Practice and Procedure, 2017–present; appointed to the U.S. Court of Appeals for the District of Columbia Circuit on May 24, 2013.

PATRICIA A. MILLETT, circuit judge; born in Dexter, MA, 1963; B.A., *summa cum laude*, University of Illinois at Urbana-Champaign, 1985; Harvard Law School, 1988, *magna cum laude*; litigation associate, Miller and Chevalier, 1988–90; law clerk, Judge Thomas Tang, U.S. Court of Appeals for the 9th Circuit, 1990–92; appellate staff, U.S. Department of Justice Civil Division, 1992–96; Assistant U.S. Solicitor General, 1996–2007; partner, Akin Gump Strauss Hauer and Feld, 2007–13; appointed by President Obama to the United States Court of Appeals for the District of Columbia Circuit on December 10, 2013.

CORNELIA T.L. PILLARD, circuit judge; born in Cambridge, MA, 1961; B.A. Yale College, *magna cum laude*, with distinction in History; J.D., Harvard Law School, *magna cum laude*, Editor, *Harvard Women's Law Journal*, 1984–85; Book Review and Commentary Editor, *Harvard Law Review*; law clerk to Judge Louis H. Pollak, U.S. District Court for the Eastern District of Pennsylvania, 1987–88; Marvin M. Karpatkin Fellowship, American Civil Liberties Union, 1988–89; member of the Bars of New York (1989), Massachusetts (1989), D.C. (1990); Assistant Counsel, NAACP Legal Defense and Education Fund, Inc., 1989–94; Assistant to the Solicitor General of the United States, 1994–97; Assistant Professor, then Professor, Georgetown University Law Center, 1997–2013; Deputy Assistant Attorney General, Office of Legal Counsel, 1998–2000; Chair, American Bar Association Scholars' Reading Group, Standing Committee on the Federal Judiciary, 2005–06; Visiting Scholar, Institute for Advanced Legal Studies (London, U.K.), 2006; Academic Co-Director and Professor, Center for Transnational Legal Studies (London, U.K.), 2008–09; Advisory Board (2003–11) and Faculty Co-Director (2011–13) Georgetown Law Supreme Court Institute; member, Board of Directors, American Arbitration Association, 2005–13; Fellow, Woodrow Wilson International Center for Scholars, 2012–13; member, American Law Institute; appointed to the United States Court of Appeals for the District of Columbia Circuit on December 2013.

ROBERT L. WILKINS, circuit judge; born in Muncie, IN, 1963, B.S., Rose-Hulman Institute of Technology, 1986, *cum laude*, Herman A. Moench Distinguished Senior Commendation; J.D., Harvard Law School, 1989, executive editor and comments editor of the *Civil Rights-Civil Liberties Law Review*; law clerk to Judge Earl B. Gilliam of the U.S. District Court for the Southern District of California, 1989–90; staff attorney, Public Defender Service for the District of Columbia, 1990–95; chief, Special Litigation and Programs Division of Public Defender Service for the District of Columbia, 1995–2000; president, National African American Museum and Cultural Complex, Inc., 2000–02; partner, Venable LLP, 2002–11; selected one of the ''90 Greatest Washington Lawyers of the Last 30 Years'' by the *Legal Times* in 2008; selected one of the ''40 under 40 most successful young litigators in America'' by the *National Law Journal* in 2002; named one of ''Washington's Top Lawyers: Criminal Defense,'' 2004, *Washingtonian* magazine; named one of ''Washington's Top Lawyers: Education,'' 2007, *Washingtonian* magazine; Honor Alumni Award, 2005, Rose-Hulman Institute of Technology; Henry W. Edgerton Civil Liberties Award, 2001, American Civil Liberties Union Fund of the National Capital Area; Pro Bono Attorney of the Year, 2001, American Civil Liberties Union of Maryland; ''Practitioner of the Year'' Award, 1999, University of Maryland Black Law Students Association; Nominee, ''Roger Baldwin Medal of Liberty'' Award, 1999, American Civil Liberties Union of Maryland; District of Columbia Access to Justice Commission (2005–08); Board of Trustees, Public Defender Service for the District of Columbia (2002–08); National Museum of African American History and Culture Plan for Action Presidential Commission (chairman of the Site and Building Committee) (2002–03); member, District of Columbia Advisory Commission on Sentencing (1998–2000); member, District of Columbia Truth-In-Sentencing Commission (1997–98); District of Columbia Juvenile Justice Advisory Group (1998–2000); *Federal Influence on Sentencing Policy in the District of Columbia: An Oppressive and Dangerous Experiment*, 11 Fed. Sent. Rptr. 143–148 (Nov./Dec. 1998); *The South African Legal System: Black Lawyer's Views*, 7 TransAfrica Forum 9 (Fall 1990); *Black Neighborhoods Becoming Black Cities: Group Empowerment, Local Control and the Implications of Being Darker than Brown*, 23 Harv. C.R.—C.L. L. Rev. 415 (1988) (co-author); admitted to the bars of the District of Columbia; Massachusetts; U.S. Supreme Court, U.S. Court of Appeals for the D.C. Circuit, U.S. Court of Appeals for the Federal Circuit, U.S. District Court for the District of Columbia, U.S. District Court for the District of Maryland, and U.S. District Court for the Eastern District of Wisconsin; member, Judicial Conference of the United States, Committee on Judicial Security, 2013–present; appointed to the U.S. District Court for the District of Columbia on December 27, 2010; appointed to the U.S. Court of Appeals for the District of Columbia Circuit on January 13, 2014.

SENIOR JUDGES

HARRY T. EDWARDS, senior circuit judge; born in New York, NY, November 3, 1940; son of George H. Edwards and Arline (Ross) Lyle; married to Pamela Carrington-Edwards;

children: Brent and Michelle; B.S., Cornell University, 1962; J.D. (with distinction), University of Michigan Law School, 1965; associate with Seyfarth, Shaw, Fairweather and Geraldson, 1965–70; professor of law, University of Michigan, 1970–75 and 1977–80; professor of law, Harvard University, 1975–77; visiting professor of law, Free University of Brussels, 1974; arbitrator of labor/management disputes, 1970–80; vice president, National Academy of Arbitrators, 1978–80; member (1977–79) and chairman (1979–80), National Railroad Passenger Corporation (Amtrak); Executive Committee of the Association of American Law Schools, 1979–80; public member of the Administrative Conference of the United States, 1976–80; International Women's Year Commission, 1976–77; American Bar Association Commission of Law and the Economy; co-author of five books: *Labor Relations Law in the Public Sector, The Lawyer as a Negotiator, Higher Education and the Law*, and *Collective Bargaining and Labor Arbitration*; and, most recently, Edwards and Ellliot, *Federal Standards of Review* (3rd ed. 2018), recipient of the Judge William B. Groat Alumni Award, 1978, given by Cornell University; the Society of American Law Teachers Award (for ''distinguished contributions to teaching and public service''); the Whitney North Seymour Medal presented by the American Arbitration Association for outstanding contributions to the use of arbitration; Recipient of the 2004 Robert J. Kutak Award, presented by the American Bar Association Section of Legal Education and Admission to the Bar ''to a person who meets the highest standards of professional responsibility and demonstrates substantial achievement toward increased understanding between legal education and the active practice of law'', and several Honorary Doctor of Laws degrees; Professor of Law at NYU School of Law (member of faculty since 1990); has also taught part-time at Duke, Georgetown, Michigan, Harvard Law, Pennsylvania, and University of California Irvine Schools of Law; co-chair of the Forensics Science Committee established by the National Academy of Sciences, 2006–09; member of the Committee on Science, Technology, and Law at the National Academy of Sciences; appointed to the U.S. Court of Appeals, February 20, 1980; served as chief judge September 15, 1994 to July 16, 2001.

LAURENCE HIRSCH SILBERMAN, senior circuit judge; recipient of the Presidential Medal of Freedom, June 19, 2008; born in York, PA, October 12, 1935; son of William Silberman and Anna (Hirsch); married to Rosalie G. Gaull on April 28, 1957 (deceased), married Patricia Winn on January 5, 2008; children: Robert Stephen Silberman, Katherine DeBoer Balaban, and Anne Gaull Otis; B.A., Dartmouth College, 1957; LL.B., Harvard Law School, 1961; admitted to Hawaii Bar, 1962; District of Columbia Bar, 1973; associate, Moore, Torkildson and Rice, 1961–64; partner (Moore, Silberman and Schulze), Honolulu, 1964–67; attorney, National Labor Relations Board, Office of General Counsel, Appellate Division, 1967–69; Solicitor, Department of Labor, 1969–70; Under Secretary of Labor, 1970–73; partner, Steptoe and Johnson, 1973–74; Deputy Attorney General of the United States, 1974–75; Ambassador to Yugoslavia, 1975–77; President's Special Envoy on ILO Affairs, 1976; senior fellow, American Enterprise Institute, 1977–78; visiting fellow, 1978–85; managing partner, Morrison and Foerster, 1978–79 and 1983–85; executive vice president, Crocker National Bank, 1979–83; lecturer, University of Hawaii, 1962–63; board of directors, Commission on Present Danger, 1978–85, Institute for Educational Affairs, New York, NY, 1981–85, member: General Advisory Committee on Arms Control and Disarmament, 1981–85; Defense Policy Board, 1981–85; vice chairman, State Department's Commission on Security and Economic Assistance, 1983–84; American Bar Association (Labor Law Committee, 1965–72, Corporations and Banking Committee, 1973, Law and National Security Advisory Committee, 1981–85); Hawaii Bar Association Ethics Committee, 1965–67; Council on Foreign Relations, 1977–present; Judicial Conference Committee on Court Administration and Case Management, 1994; member, U.S. Foreign Intelligence Surveillance Act Court of Review, 1996–2003; Adjunct Professor of Law (Administrative Law and Labor Law) Georgetown Law Center, 1987–94; 1997; Adjunct Professor of Law, New York University Law School, 1995–96; Distinguished Visitor from the Judiciary, Georgetown Law Center, 2003–present; co-chairman of the President's Commission on The Intelligence Capabilities of the United States Regarding Weapons of Mass Destruction, 2004–05; appointed to the U.S. Court of Appeals for the District of Columbia Circuit by President Reagan on October 28, 1985.

STEPHEN F. WILLIAMS, senior circuit judge; born in New York, NY, September 23, 1936; son of Charles Dickerman Williams and Virginia (Fain); married to Faith Morrow, 1966; children: Susan, Geoffrey, Sarah, Timothy, and Nicholas; B.A., Yale, 1958, J.D., Harvard Law School, 1961; U.S. Army Reserves, 1961–62; associate, Debevoise, Plimpton, Lyons and Gates, 1962–66; Assistant U.S. Attorney, Southern District of New York, 1966–69; associate professor and professor of law, University of Colorado School of Law, 1969–86; visiting professor of law, UCLA, 1975–76; visiting professor of law and fellow in law and economics, University Chicago Law School, 1979–80; visiting George W. Hutchison Professor of Energy Law, SMU, 1983–84; consultant to: Administrative Conference of the United States, 1974–76; Federal Trade Commission on energy-related issues, 1983–85; member, American Law

Institute; appointed to the U.S. Court of Appeals for the District of Columbia Circuit by President Reagan, June 16, 1986.

DOUGLAS HOWARD GINSBURG, circuit judge; born in Chicago, IL, May 25, 1946; diploma, Latin School of Chicago, 1963; B.S., Cornell University, 1970 (Phi Kappa Phi, Ives Award); J.D., University of Chicago, 1973 (Mecham Prize Scholarship 1970–73, Casper Platt Award, 1973, Order of Coif, Articles and Book Rev. Ed., 40 U. Chi. L. Rev.); bar admissions: Illinois (1973), Massachusetts (1982), U.S. Supreme Court (1984), U.S. Court of Appeals for the Ninth Circuit (1986); member: Mont Pelerin Society, American Economic Association, American Law and Economics Association, Honor Society of Phi Kappa Phi, American Bar Association, Antitrust Section, Council, 1985–86 (ex officio), judicial liaison (2000–03 and 2009–12); advisory boards: Competition Policy International; Harvard Journal of Law and Public Policy; *Journal of Competition Law and Economics*; Law and Economics Center, George Mason University School of Law; *Supreme Court Economic Review; University of Chicago Law Review*; Board of Directors: Foundation for Research in Economics and the Environment, 1991–2004; Rappahannock County Conservation Alliance, 1998–2004; Rappahannock Association for Arts and Community, 1997–99; Committees: Judicial Conference of the United States, 2002–08, Budget Committee, 1997–2001, Committee on Judicial Resources, 1987–96; Boston University Law School, Visiting Committee, 1994–97; University of Chicago Law School, Visiting Committee, 1985–88; law clerk to: Judge Carl McGowan, U.S. Court of Appeals for the District of Columbia Circuit, 1973–74; Associate Justice Thurgood Marshall, U.S. Supreme Court, 1974–75; previous positions: assistant professor, Harvard University Law School, 1975–81; Professor 1981–83; Deputy Assistant Attorney General, Antitrust Division, U.S. Department of Justice, 1983–84; Administrator for Information and Regulatory Affairs, Executive Office of the President, Office of Management and Budget, 1984–85; Assistant Attorney General, Antitrust Division, U.S. Department of Justice, 1985–86; lecturer in law, Columbia University, New York City, 1987–88, 2009–11; lecturer in law, Harvard University, Cambridge, MA, 1988–89; distinguished professor of law, George Mason University, Arlington, VA, 1988–present; senior lecturer, University of Chicago Law School, 1990–present; lecturer on law, New York Law School, 2005–09; Visiting Professor, Faculty of Laws, University College, London, 2010–15; appointed to U.S. Court of Appeals for the District of Columbia Circuit by President Reagan on October 14, 1986, taking the oath of office on November 10, 1986, Chief Judge, 2001–08.

DAVID BRYAN SENTELLE, circuit judge, born in Canton, NC, February 12, 1943; son of Horace and Maude Sentelle; married to Jane LaRue Oldham; three daughters and four granddaughters; B.A., University of North Carolina at Chapel Hill, 1965; J.D. with honors, University of North Carolina School of Law, 1968; associate, Uzzell and Dumont, Asheville, 1968–70; Assistant U.S. Attorney, Charlotte, 1970–74; North Carolina State District Judge, 1974–77; partner, Tucker, Hicks, Sentelle, Moon and Hodge, Charlotte, 1977–85; U.S. District Judge for the Western District of North Carolina, 1985–87. Adjunct professor, University of North Carolina, Florida State, George Mason University, and University of Georgia. Appointed to the U.S. Court of Appeals by President Reagan in October 1987; Chief Judge, 2008–13; assumed senior status February 12, 2013. Appointed to the Foreign Intelligence Surveillance Court of Review, May 19, 2018–present; Member, U.S. Judicial Conference Committee on Court Administration and Case Management, 1992; Presiding Judge, Special Division of the Court for the Appointment of Independent Counsels, 1992–2006; Member, Judicial Conference Committee on Code of Conduct, 2004–05; Chair, Judicial Conference Committee on Judicial Security, 2005–08; Member, Judicial Conference Executive Committee, 2008–13 (Chair 2010–13); past President, Edward Bennett Williams Inn of the American Inns of Court. Recipient, 2008 American Inns of Court Professionalism Award in the DC Circuit.

A. RAYMOND RANDOLPH, senior circuit judge; born in Riverside, NJ, November 1, 1943; son of Arthur Raymond Randolph, Sr. and Marile (Kelly); two children: John Trevor and Cynthia Lee Randolph; married to Eileen Janette O'Connor, May 18, 1984. B.S., Drexel University, 1966; J.D., University of Pennsylvania Law School, 1969, *summa cum laude;* managing editor, *University of Pennsylvania Law Review*; Order of the Coif. Admitted to Supreme Court of the United States; Supreme Court of California; District of Columbia Court of Appeals; U.S. Courts of Appeals for the First, Second, Fourth, Fifth, Sixth, Seventh, Ninth, Eleventh, and District of Columbia Circuits. Memberships: American Law Institute. Law clerk to Judge Henry J. Friendly, U.S. Court of Appeals for the Second Circuit, 1969–70; Assistant to the Solicitor General, 1970–73; adjunct professor of law, Georgetown University Law Center, 1974–78; George Mason School of Law, 1992; Deputy Solicitor General, 1975–77; Special Counsel, Committee on Standards of Official Conduct, House of Representatives, 1979–80; special assistant attorney general, State of Montana (honorary), 1983–July 1990; special assistant attorney general, State of New Mexico, 1985–July 1990; special assistant attorney general, State of Utah, 1986–July 1990; advisory panel, Federal Courts Study Committee, 1989–July 1990; partner, Pepper, Hamilton and Scheetz, 1987–July 1990; chairman, Committee on Codes of Conduct, U.S. Judicial Conference, 1995–98; distinguished professor of law, George Mason Law School, 1999–present; recipient, Distinguished Alumnus Award, University of Pennsylvania Law School, 2002; appointed to the U.S. Court of Appeals for the District of Columbia Circuit by President George H.W. Bush on July 16, 1990, and took oath of office on July 20, 1990.

OFFICERS OF THE UNITED STATES COURT OF APPEALS FOR THE DISTRICT OF COLUMBIA CIRCUIT

Circuit Executive.—Betsy Paret (202) 216–7340.
Clerk.—Mark J. Langer, 216–7300.
Chief Deputy Clerk.—Marilyn R. Sargent, 216–7300.
Director, Legal Division.—Melissa McKenney Ryan, 216–7500.

UNITED STATES COURT OF APPEALS FOR THE FEDERAL CIRCUIT

717 Madison Place, NW., Washington, DC 20439
phone (202) 275–8000

SHARON PROST, Chief Judge, was appointed by President George W. Bush in 2001 and assumed the duties of Chief Circuit Judge on May 31, 2014. Prior to her appointment, Judge Prost served as Minority Chief Counsel, Deputy Chief Counsel, and Chief Counsel of the Committee on the Judiciary, United States Senate from 1993 to 2001. She also served as Chief Labor Counsel (Minority), Senate Committee on Labor and Human Resources from 1989 to 1993. She was Assistant Solicitor, Associate Solicitor, and Acting Solicitor of the National Labor Relations Board from 1984 to 1989. She was an Attorney at the Internal Revenue Service from 1983 to 1984, and Field Attorney at the Federal Labor Relations Authority from 1980 to 1983. Judge Prost also served as Labor Relations Specialist/Auditor at the United States General Accounting Office from 1976 to 1980 and Labor Relations Specialist at the United States Civil Service Commission from 1973 to 1976. Judge Prost received a B.S. from Cornell University in 1973, an M.B.A. from George Washington University in 1975, a J.D. from the Washington College of Law, American University in 1979, and an LL.M. from George Washington University School of Law in 1984.

PAULINE NEWMAN, Circuit Judge, was appointed by President Ronald Reagan in 1984. From 1982 to 1984, Judge Newman was Special Adviser to the United States Delegation to the Diplomatic Conference on the Revision of the Paris Convention for the Protection of Industrial Property. She served on the advisory committee to the Domestic Policy Review of Industrial Innovation from 1978 to 1979 and on the State Department Advisory Committee on International Intellectual Property from 1974 to 1984. From 1969 to 1984, Judge Newman served as director, Patent, Trademark and Licensing Department, FMC Corp. From 1961 to 1962 she worked for the United Nations Educational, Scientific and Cultural Organization as a science policy specialist in the Department of Natural Sciences. She served as patent attorney and house counsel of FMC Corp. from 1954 to 1969 and as research scientist, American Cyanamid Co. from 1951 to 1954. Judge Newman received a B.A. from Vassar College in 1947, an M.A. from Columbia University in 1948, a Ph.D. from Yale University in 1952 and an LL.B. from New York University School of Law in 1958.

ALAN D. LOURIE, Circuit Judge, was appointed to the United States Court of Appeals for the Federal Circuit on April 6, 1990, by President George H.W. Bush. He was formerly Vice President, Corporate Patents and Trademarks, and Associate General Counsel of SmithKline Beecham Corporation. Born in Boston, Massachusetts, on January 13, 1935, Judge Lourie received his Bachelor's degree from Harvard University (1956), his Master's degree in organic chemistry from the University of Wisconsin (1958), and his Ph.D. in chemistry from the University of Pennsylvania (1965). He received his J.D. degree from Temple University in 1970. Before being appointed to the court, Judge Lourie had been President of the Philadelphia Patent Law Association, a member of the Board of Directors of the American Intellectual Property Law Association (formerly American Patent Law Association), treasurer of the Association of Corporate Patent Counsel, and a member of the board of directors of the Intellectual Property Owners Association. He was also Vice Chairman of the Industry Functional Advisory Committee on Intellectual Property Rights for Trade Policy Matters (IFAC 3) for the Department of Commerce and the Office of the U.S. Trade Representative. He was a member of the U.S. delegation to the Diplomatic Conference on the Revision of the Paris Convention for the Protection of Industrial Property, held in Geneva in October and November 1982, and in March 1984. He was chairman of the Patent Committee of the Law Section of the Pharmaceutical Manufacturers Association from 1980 to 1985. Judge Lourie was awarded the Jefferson Medal of the New Jersey Intellectual Property Law Association for extraordinary contributions to the field of intellectual property law in 1998; was a recipient of the Intellectual Property Owners Education Foundation Distinguished Intellectual

Property Professional Award for extraordinary leadership in the intellectual property community and a lifetime commitment to invention and innovation in 2008; was a recipient of the Philadelphia Intellectual Property Law Association's Award for outstanding IP achievement in 2010; was a recipient of the Boston Patent Law Association's Distinguished Public Service Award in 2011; was a recipient of a ''lifetime achievement'' award from The Sedona Conference in 2011; and recently was a recipient of NYIPLA's 10th Annual Outstanding Public Service Award in 2012. He was a member of the Judicial Conference Committee on Financial Disclosure from 1990 to 1998 and has been a member of the Committee on Codes of Conduct since 2005. He is a member of the American Intellectual Property Law Association, the American Chemical Society, the Cosmos Club, and the Harvard Club of Washington. Judge Lourie is married and has two daughters and four grandchildren.

TIMOTHY B. DYK, Circuit Judge, was appointed by President William J. Clinton in 2000. Prior to his appointment, Judge Dyk was Partner and Chair, Issues and Appeals Practice Area, at Jones, Day, Reavis and Pogue from 1990 to 2000. He was Adjunct Professor at Yale Law School from 1986 to 1987 and 1989, at the University of Virginia Law School in 1984 and 1985, and from 1987 to 1988, and at the Georgetown University Law Center in 1983, 1986, 1989 and 1991. Judge Dyk was Associate and Partner, Wilmer Cutler and Pickering from 1964 to 1990. From 1963 to 1964, Judge Dyk served as Special Assistant to Assistant Attorney General Louis F. Oberdorfer. He also served as Law Clerk to Chief Justice Warren from 1962 to 1963, and to Justices Reed and Burton (retired) from 1961 to 1962. Judge Dyk received an A.B. from Harvard College in 1958 and an LL.B. from Harvard Law School in 1961. He was First President of the Edward Coke Appellate Inn of Court from 2000 to 2001 and President of the Giles Sutherland Rich Inn of Court from 2006 to 2007. He was the recipient of the 2012 American Inns of Court Professionalism Award for the Federal Circuit. Judge Dyk is the co-author of the Chapter on Patents in the Third Edition of the treatise, Business and Commercial Litigation in Federal Courts.

KIMBERLY A. MOORE, Circuit Judge, was appointed by President George W. Bush in 2006. Prior to her appointment, Judge Moore was a Professor of Law from 2004–06 and Associate Professor of Law from 2000 to 2004 at the George Mason University School of Law. She was an Assistant Professor of Law at the University of Maryland School of Law from 1999 to 2000. She served both as an Assistant Professor of Law from 1997 to 1999 and the Associate Director of the Intellectual Property Law Program from 1998 to 1999 at the Chicago-Kent College of Law. Judge Moore clerked from 1995 to 1997 for the Honorable Glenn L. Archer, Jr., Chief Judge of the United States Court of Appeals for the Federal Circuit, and was an Associate at Kirkland and Ellis from 1994 to 1995. From 1988 to 1992, Judge Moore was employed in electrical engineering with the Naval Surface Warfare Center. Judge Moore received her B.S.E.E. in 1990, M.S. in 1991, both from the Massachusetts Institute of Technology, and her J.D., *cum laude* from the Georgetown University Law Center in 1994. Judge Moore has written and presented widely on patent litigation. She co-authored a legal casebook entitled Patent Litigation and Strategy and served as the Editor of The Federal Circuit Bar Journal from 1998 to 2006.

KATHLEEN M. O'MALLEY, Circuit Judge, was appointed to the United States Court of Appeals for the Federal Circuit by President Barack Obama in 2010. Prior to her elevation to the Federal Circuit, Judge O'Malley was appointed to the United States District Court for the Northern District of Ohio by President William J. Clinton on October 12, 1994. Judge O'Malley served as First Assistant Attorney General and Chief of Staff for Ohio Attorney General Lee Fisher from 1992–94, and Chief Counsel to Attorney General Fisher from 1991–92. From 1985–91, she worked for Porter, Wright, Morris and Arthur, where she became a partner. From 1983–84, she was an associate at Jones, Day, Reavis and Pogue. During her sixteen years on the district court bench, Judge O'Malley presided over in excess of 100 patent and trademark cases and sat by designation on the United States Circuit Court for the Federal Circuit. As an educator, Judge O'Malley has regularly taught a course on Patent Litigation at Case Western Reserve University Law School; she is a member of the faculty of the Berkeley Center for Law and Technology's program designed to educate Federal Judges regarding the handling of intellectual property cases. Judge O'Malley serves as a board member of the Sedona Conference; as the judicial liaison to the Local Patent Rules Committee for the Northern District of Ohio; and as an advisor to national organizations publishing treatises on patent litigation (Anatomy of a Patent Case, Complex Litigation Committee of the American College of Trial Lawyers; Patent Case Management Judicial Guide, Berkeley Center for Law and Technology). Judge O'Malley began her legal career as a law clerk to the Honorable Nathaniel R. Jones, Sixth Circuit Court of Appeals in 1982–83. She received her J.D. degree from Case Western Reserve University School of Law, Order of the Coif, in 1982, where she served on Law Review and was a member of the National Mock Trial Team. Judge O'Malley attended Kenyon College in Gambier, Ohio where she graduated *magna cum laude* and Phi Beta Kappa in 1979.

JIMMIE V. REYNA, Circuit Judge, was appointed to the United States Court of Appeals for the Federal Circuit by President Barack Obama in 2011. Prior to his appointment, Judge Reyna was an international trade attorney and shareholder at Williams Mullen, where, from 1998 to 2011, he directed the firm's Trade and Customs Practice Group and its Latin America Task Force, and served on its board of directors (2006–08, 2009–11). He was an associate and partner at the law firm of Stewart and Stewart (1986–98). From 1981 to 1986, Judge Reyna was a solo practitioner in Albuquerque, New Mexico and, prior to that, an associate at Shaffer, Butt, Thornton and Baehr, also in Albuquerque, New Mexico. Judge Reyna served on the U.S. roster of dispute settlement panelists for trade disputes under Chapter 19 of the North American Free Trade Agreement, and the U.S. Indicative List of Non-Governmental Panelists for the World Trade Organization, Dispute Settlement Mechanism, for both trade in goods and trade in services. Judge Reyna is the author of two books, Passport to North American Trade: Rules of Origin and Customs Procedures Under the NAFTA (Shepards 1995), and The GATT Uruguay Round, A Negotiating History: Services, 1986–92 (Kluwer 1993) and numerous articles on international trade and customs issues. He was the founder and Senior Co-Editor of the Hispanic National Bar Association *Journal of Law and Policy*. Judge Reyna is a recipient of the Ohtli Award (the highest honor bestowed by the Mexican Government for non-Mexican citizens). Other awards include: 100 Influentials, *Hispanic Business Magazine*, 2011; 101 Latino Leaders in America, *Latino Leaders Magazine*, 2011 and 2012; Minority Business Leader, *Washington Business Journal*; Extraordinary Leadership, Hispanic National Bar Association (HNBA); Lifetime Honorary Membership, Society of Hispanic Professional Engineers; Distinguished Citizen Award, Military Airlift Command, U.S. Air Force; Spirit of Excellence Award, Albuquerque Hispano Chamber of Commerce. Judge Reyna served over a decade of leadership in the HNBA, including as National President (2006–07). He served in various leadership positions in the ABA Sections on International Law and Dispute Settlement. He was a founder and member of the board of directors of the U.S. Mexico Law Institute, and the Community Services for Autistic Adults and Children Foundation. He currently serves on the Nationwide Hispanic Advisory Council of Big Brothers Big Sisters of America. He received a B.A. from the University of Rochester in 1975 and a J.D. from the University of New Mexico School of Law in 1978.

EVAN J. WALLACH, Circuit Judge, was appointed to the United States Court of Appeals for the Federal Circuit by President Barack Obama in 2011, confirmed by the Senate on November 9, 2011, and assumed the duties of his office on November 18, 2011. Prior to his appointment, he served for sixteen years as a judge of the United States Court of International Trade, having been appointed to that court by President William J. Clinton in 1995. Judge Wallach worked as a general litigation partner with an emphasis on media representation at the law firm of Lionel Sawyer and Collins in Las Vegas, Nevada from 1982 to 1995. He was an associate at the same firm from 1976 to 1982. While working with the firm, Judge Wallach took a leave of absence to serve as General Counsel and Public Policy Advisor to Senator Harry Reid from 1987 to 1988. From 1989 to 1995, he served in the Nevada National Guard as a Judge Advocate. In 1991, while on leave from his firm, he served as an Attorney/Advisor in the International Affairs Division of the Judge Advocate of the Army at the Pentagon. Judge Wallach, a recognized expert in the law of war, has taught at a number of law schools, including Brooklyn Law School, New York Law School, George Mason University School of Law, and the University of Münster in Münster, Germany. Judge Wallach has received a number of awards, including: the ABA Liberty Bell Award in 1993; the Nevada Press Association President's Award in 1994; and the Clark County School Librarians Intellectual Freedom Award in 1995. Judge Wallach served on active duty in the Army of the United States from 1969 to 1971. During his military career, he was awarded the Bronze Star, the Air Medal, the Good Conduct Medal, the Meritorious Service Medal, the Nevada Medal of Merit, the Valorous Unit Citation, a Vietnam Campaign Medal, and the RVN Cross of Gallantry with Palm. Judge Wallach received his B.A. in Journalism from the University of Arizona in 1973, his J.D. from the University of California, Berkeley in 1976, and an LLB with honors in International Law from Cambridge University in 1981.

RICHARD G. TARANTO, Circuit Judge, was appointed to the United States Court of Appeals for the Federal Circuit by President Barack H. Obama, in 2013, confirmed by the Senate on March 11, 2013 and assumed the duties of his office on March 15, 2013. Judge Taranto practiced law with the firm of Farr and Taranto from 1989 to 2013, where he specialized in appellate litigation. From 1986 to 1989, he served as an Assistant to the Solicitor General, representing the United States in the Supreme Court. He was in private practice from 1984 to 1986 with the law firm of Onek, Klein and Farr. Judge Taranto served as a law clerk at all three levels of the federal court system. He clerked for Justice Sandra Day O'Connor of the Supreme Court of the United States from 1983 to 1984; for Judge Robert Bork of the United States Court of Appeals for the District of Columbia Circuit from 1982 to 1983; and for Judge Abraham Sofaer of the United States District Court for the Southern District of New York from 1981 to 1982. Judge Taranto received a J.D. from Yale Law School in 1981 and a B.A. from Pomona College in 1977.

RAYMOND T. CHEN, Circuit Judge, was appointed to the United States Court of Appeals for the Federal Circuit by President Barack H. Obama in 2013, confirmed by the Senate on August 1, 2013 and assumed his office on August 5, 2013. Judge Chen served as Deputy General Counsel for Intellectual Property Law and Solicitor at the United States Patent and Trademark Office from 2008 to 2013. He was an Associate Solicitor in that office from 1998 to 2008. From 1996 to 1998, Judge Chen served as a Technical Assistant at the United States Court of Appeals for the Federal Circuit. Before joining the court staff, Judge Chen was an associate with Knobbe, Martens, Olson and Bear from 1994 to 1996. Before entering law school, Judge Chen worked as a scientist at the law firm of Hecker and Harriman from 1989 to 1991. Judge Chen received his J.D. from the New York University School of Law in 1994 and his B.S. in Electrical Engineering from the University of California, Los Angeles in 1990.

TODD M. HUGHES, Circuit Judge, was appointed to the United States Court of Appeals for the Federal Circuit by President Barack H. Obama in 2013, confirmed by the Senate on September 24, 2013 and assumed the duties of his office on September 30, 2013. Judge Hughes served as Deputy Director of the Commercial Litigation Branch of the Civil Division of the United States Department of Justice from 2007 to 2013. He was the Assistant Director in that office from 1999 to 2007 and a Trial Attorney from 1994 to 1999. From 1992 to 1994, Judge Hughes served as a Law Clerk to Circuit Judge Robert Krupansky of the United States Court of Appeals for the Sixth Circuit. He was an Adjunct Lecturer in Law at Cleveland-Marshall College of Law during the Spring, 1994 semester. Judge Hughes received a J.D. from Duke Law School in 1992, an M.A. from Duke University in 1992, and an A.B. from Harvard College in 1989.

KARA FARNANDEZ STOLL, Circuit Judge, was appointed to the United States Court of Appeals for the Federal Circuit by President Barack H. Obama on November 12, 2014, was confirmed unanimously by the United States Senate on July 7, 2015, and assumed her duties on July 17, 2015. Judge Stoll practiced law with the firm of Finnegan, Henderson, Farabow, Garrett and Dunner from 1998 to 2015, and became a partner at the firm in 2006. While in private practice, Judge Stoll specialized in patent litigation with an emphasis on appeals. Judge Stoll was an adjunct professor at George Mason University Law School from 2008 to 2015 and at the Howard University School of Law from 2004 to 2008. From 1997 to 1998, Judge Stoll served as a law clerk to The Honorable Alvin A. Schall of the United States Court of Appeals for the Federal Circuit. Judge Stoll worked as a patent examiner at the United States Patent and Trademark Office from 1991 to 1997. Judge Stoll received a J.D. from the Georgetown University School of Law in 1997, where she received the Leon Robin Patent Award, and a B.S.E.E. from Michigan State University in 1991.

SENIOR JUDGES

HALDANE ROBERT MAYER, Circuit Judge, has been a member of the court since 1987. He served as Chief Judge from 1997 to 2004. Born in Buffalo, Judge Mayer was educated in the public schools of Lockport, New York, before attending the United States Military Academy at West Point, from which he graduated with a Bachelor of Science degree in 1963. He earned a law degree in 1971 at the Marshall-Wythe School of Law of The College of William and Mary, where he was editor-in-chief of the *William and Mary Law Review* as well as a member of Omicron Delta Kappa National Leadership Society. He has served as a director of the William and Mary Law School Association. Judge Mayer served on active duty in the Army of the United States from 1963 until 1975 in the Infantry and the Judge Advocate General's Corps. He was awarded the Bronze Star Medal, the Meritorious Service Medal, the Army Commendation Medal with Oak Leaf Cluster, the Combat Infantryman Badge, Parachutist Badge, Ranger Tab, RVN Ranger Combat Badge, and several campaign and service ribbons. He resigned his Regular Army commission to take an Army Reserve commission, retiring in 1985 as a lieutenant colonel. In 1971, Judge Mayer served as a law clerk for Judge John D. Butzner, Jr., of the United States Court of Appeals for the Fourth Circuit in Richmond, VA. He practiced law in Charlottesville, VA, in the mid-1970's, simultaneously serving as an adjunct at the University of Virginia School of Law, as he did again in the 1990's. He has also been an adjunct at George Washington University National Law Center. From 1977 through 1980, Judge Mayer was the Special Assistant to the Chief Justice of the United States, Warren E. Burger, after which he returned to private law practice in Washington, DC, until he became Deputy and Acting Special Counsel (by designation of the President). President Ronald Reagan appointed Judge Mayer to what is now the United States Court of Federal Claims in 1982, and to the United States Court of Appeals for the Federal Circuit in 1987. He assumed senior status on June 30, 2010.

S. JAY PLAGER, Circuit Judge, was appointed Judge by President George H.W. Bush in 1989. Prior to his appointment, Judge Plager served in the Executive Office of the President from 1987 to 1989, as Associate Director of OMB and as Administrator, OIRA. He served as Counselor to the Under Secretary, Department of Health and Human Services from 1986 to 1987. Judge Plager was Dean and Professor, Indiana University School of Law from 1977 to 1984. He was Professor, Faculty of Law, University of Illinois from 1964 to 1977, and from 1958 to 1964 was Professor, Faculty of Law, University of Florida. Judge Plager was Visiting Scholar, Stanford University Law School from 1984 to 1985, Visiting Fellow, Trinity College, and Visiting Professor, Cambridge University in 1980, and Visiting Research Professor of Law, University of Wisconsin from 1967 to 1968. Judge Plager served on active duty in the United States Navy during the Korean Conflict. Judge Plager grew up in New Jersey, where he attended public schools. In 1952, he received an A.B. degree from the University of North Carolina, a J.D. in 1958 from the University of Florida, with high honors, where he was editor-in-chief of the *Florida Law Review*, and in 1961 an LL.M. from Columbia University. He has three children. Judge Plager assumed senior status in 2000.

RAYMOND C. CLEVENGER III, Circuit Judge, was appointed by President George H.W. Bush in 1990. Judge Clevenger received a B.A. from Yale University in 1959. As a Carnegie Teaching Fellow, he taught European History at Yale College in the 1959–60 academic year. From 1960 to 1963, he was employed by the Morgan Guaranty Trust Company in New York City. He received an LL.B. from Yale University in 1966. Judge Clevenger served as a law clerk to Mr. Justice White in October Term 1966. Judge Clevenger joined Wilmer, Cutler and Pickering in 1967, serving as a partner in the firm from 1974 until his appointment to the bench. Judge Clevenger assumed senior status on February 1, 2006.

ALVIN A. SCHALL, Circuit Judge, was appointed by President George H.W. Bush in 1992. Prior to his appointment, Judge Schall served as Assistant to the Attorney General of the United States from 1988 to 1992. He was a member of the Washington, DC law firm of Perlman and Partners from 1987 to 1988. He served as Trial Attorney and Senior Trial Counsel, Civil Division, United States Department of Justice, from 1978 to 1987. Judge Schall was an Assistant United States Attorney, Office of the United States Attorney for the Eastern District of New York, from 1973 to 1978, and served as Chief of the Appeals Division from 1977 to 1978. From 1969 to 1973, Judge Schall was in private practice with the New York City law firm of Shearman and Sterling. Judge Schall received a B.A. degree from Princeton University in 1966 and a J.D. degree from Tulane Law School in 1969. Judge Schall assumed senior status on October 5, 2009.

WILLIAM C. BRYSON, Circuit Judge, was appointed by President William J. Clinton in 1994. Prior to his appointment, Judge Bryson was with the United States Department of Justice from 1978 to 1994. During that period, he served as an Assistant to the Solicitor General [1978–79], Chief of the Appellate Section of the Criminal Division [1979–83], Counsel to the Organized Crime and Racketeering Section [1983–86], Deputy Solicitor General [1986–94], Acting Solicitor General [1989 and 1993], and Acting Associate Attorney General [1994]. He was an Associate at the Washington, DC law firm of Miller, Cassidy, Larroca and Lewin from 1975 to 1978. Judge Bryson served as Law Clerk to the Honorable Henry J. Friendly, United States Court of Appeals for the Second Circuit from 1973 to 1974, and as Law Clerk to the Honorable Thurgood Marshall, Supreme Court of the United States, from 1974 to 1975. Judge Bryson received an A.B. from Harvard College in 1969 and a J.D. from the University of Texas School of Law in 1973.

RICHARD LINN, Circuit Judge, was appointed by President William J. Clinton in 1999. Prior to his appointment, Judge Linn was a Partner and Practice Group Leader at the Washington, DC law firm of Foley and Lardner from 1997 to 1999. He was a Partner and head of the intellectual property department at Marks and Murase, LLP from 1977 to 1997. Judge Linn served as Patent Advisor, United States Naval Air Systems Command from 1971 to 1972, was a Patent Agent at the United States Naval Research Laboratory from 1968 to 1969, and served as a Patent Examiner at the United States Patent Office from 1965 to 1968. He was a member of the founding Board of Governors of the Virginia Bar Section on Patent, Trademark, and Copyright Law and served as Chairman in 1975. In 2000, Judge Linn received the Rensselaer Alumni Association Fellows Award. He was honored in 2006 for dedication, service, and devotion to justice by the Austin Intellectual Property Law Association. Judge Linn was awarded the 2009 New York Intellectual Property Law Association Leadership Award. He also received the 2009 Jefferson Medal from the New Jersey Intellectual Property Law Association ''in recognition of meritorious and outstanding contributions in support of the Constitution of the United States of America and furtherance of a fundamental principle thereof—'to promote the progress of Science and useful Arts.''' In 2010, Judge Linn received the Outstanding Public Service Award from the New York Intellectual Property Law Association. In 2011, he was awarded the inaugural Mark Banner Award by the American Bar Association for his contributions to intellectual property law and the A. Sherman Christensen Award by the American Inns of Court Foundation for distinguished, exceptional and significant leadership to the American Inns of Court movement. He served as an Adjunct Professor and Professorial Lecturer in Law at George Washington University Law School from 2001 to 2003, and currently serves on the Law School's Intellectual Property Advisory Board. Judge Linn is a past president of the Giles Sutherland Rich American Inn of Court, a member of the Richard Linn American Inn of Court, a visiting member of the Hon. William C. Conner American Inn of Court, and an honorary lifetime member of the Benjamin Franklin American Inn of Court. He received a B.E.E. from Rensselaer Polytechnic Institute in 1965, and a J.D. from Georgetown University Law Center in 1969.

Officers of the United States Court of Appeals for the Federal Circuit

Circuit Executive and Clerk of Court.—Peter R. Marksteiner (202) 275–8020.
Deputy Circuit Executive and Operations Officer.—Dale Bosley, 275–8141.
General Counsel.—J. Douglas Steere, 275–8000.
Circuit Librarian.—John D. Moore, 275–8403.
Chief Deputy Clerk.—Jarrett B. Perlow, 275–8021.
Director of Information Technology.—Riley Toussaint, 275–8421.

UNITED STATES DISTRICT COURT FOR THE DISTRICT OF COLUMBIA

E. Barrett Prettyman U.S. Courthouse

333 Constitution Avenue, NW., Room 2002, Washington, DC 20001
phone (202) 354–3320, fax 354–3412

BERYL A. HOWELL, chief judge; born in Fort Benning, GA; daughter of Col. (Ret.) Leamon and Ruth Howell; Killeen High School, Killeen, TX, 1974; B.A. with honors in philosophy, Bryn Mawr College (President and Member, Honor Board, 1976–78); J.D., Columbia University School of Law, 1983 (Harlan Fiske Stone Scholar, 1981–82; International Fellows Program, 1982–83, *Transnational Law Journal*, Notes Editor); law clerk to Hon. Dickinson R. Debevoise, District of New Jersey, 1983–84; litigation associate, Schulte, Roth and Zabel, 1985–87; Assistant United States Attorney, United States District Court for the Eastern District of New York, 1987–93; Deputy Chief, Narcotics Section, 1990–93; Senior Counsel, U.S. Senate Committee on the Judiciary Subcommittee on Technology and the Law, 1993–94; Senior Counsel, U.S. Senate Committee on the Judiciary Subcommittee on Antitrust, Business Rights and Competition, 1995–96; General Counsel, U.S. Senate Committee on the Judiciary, 1997–2003; Executive Managing Director and General Counsel, Stroz Friedberg, 2003–09; Commissioner, United States Sentencing Commission, 2004–11; Member, Commission on Cyber Security for the 44th Presidency, 2008; Adjunct Professor of Law, American University's Washington College of Law, 2010; appointed judge, U.S. District Court for the District of Columbia by President Obama on December 27, 2010, took oath of office on January 21, 2011; became Chief Judge in March 2016; appointed by Chief Justice Roberts to serve on the Judicial Conference of the U.S. Committee on Information Technology, 2013–16, and to the Judicial Conference, 2016–present. Awards include U.S. Attorney's Special Achievement Award for Sustained Superior Performance, 1990, 1991; Drug Enforcement Administration Commendations, 1990, 1992, 1993; Attorney General's Director's Award for Superior Performance, 1991; Federal Bureau of Investigation Award and New York City Department of Investigation Award for public corruption investigation and prosecution, 1992; Freedom of Information Hall of Fame, 2001; First Amendment Award, Society of Professional Journalists, 2004; Federal Bureau of Investigation Director's Award, 2006; Book chapters and law review article publications include Seven Weeks: The Making of the USA PATRIOT Act, *The George Washington Law Review*, 2004; FISA's Fruits in Criminal Cases: An Opportunity for Improved Accountability, UCLA Journal of International Law and Foreign Affairs, 2007; Book Chapters include: Real World Problems of Virtual Crime, in Cybercrime: Digital Cops in a Networked Environment, 2007; Foreign Intelligence Surveillance Act: Has the Solution Become the Problem, in Protecting What Matters: Technology, Security, and Liberty Since 9/11, 2006; and articles in the *New York Law Journal, Journal of Internet Law, Vermont Bar Journal*, and *Yale Journal of Law and Technology.*

EMMET G. SULLIVAN, judge; son of Emmet A. Sullivan and Eileen G. Sullivan; born in Washington, DC; graduated McKinley High School, 1964; B.A., Howard University, 1968; J.D., Howard University Law School, 1971; recipient of Reginald Heber Smith Fellowship, assigned to the Neighborhood Legal Services Program in Washington, DC, 1971–72; law clerk to Judge James A. Washington, Jr., 1972–73; joined the law firm of Houston and Gardner, 1973–80, became a partner; thereafter, was a partner with Houston, Sullivan and Gardner; board of directors of the DC Law Students in Court Program; DC Judicial Conference Voluntary Arbitration Committee; Nominating Committee of the Bar Association of the District of Columbia; U.S. District Court Committee on Grievances; adjunct professor at Howard University School of Law; adjunct professor at American University, Washington College of Law; member: National Bar Association, Washington Bar Association, Bar Association of the District of Columbia; appointed by President Reagan to the Superior Court of the District of Columbia as an associate judge, 1984; deputy presiding judge and presiding judge of the probate and tax division; chairperson of the rules committees for the probate and tax divisions; member: Court Rules Committee and the Jury Plan Committee; appointed by President George H.W. Bush to serve as an associate judge of the District of Columbia Court of Appeals, 1991; chairperson for the nineteenth annual judicial conference of the District of Columbia, 1994 (the Conference theme was ''Rejuvenating Juvenile Justice—Responses to the Problems of Juvenile Violence in the District of Columbia''); appointed by chief judge Wagner to chair the ''Task Force on Families and Violence for the District of Columbia Courts''; nominated to the U.S. District Court by President Clinton on March 22, 1994; and confirmed by the U.S. Senate on June 15, 1994; appointed by Chief Justice Rehnquist to serve on the Judicial Conference of the U.S. Committee on Criminal Law 1998–2005; District of Columbia Judicial Disabilities and Tenure Commission, 1996–2001; chair of the District of Columbia Judicial Nomination Commission since 2005; appointed by Chief Justice Roberts to serve on the Judicial Conference of the U.S. Committee on Space and Facilities, 2012, re-appointed by the Chief Justice in 2015; only person in the District of Columbia to have been appointed to three judicial positions by three different U.S. Presidents; recipient of the Ollie May Cooper Award, awarded by the Washington Bar Association; the Thurgood Marshall Award of Excellence, awarded by the Howard University Alumni Association; the Howard University Distinguished Alumni Award, awarded by the President and Board of Trustees of Howard University; American Inns of Court Professionalism Award for the District of Columbia Circuit for 2015; the National Bar Association's Gertrude E. Rush Award; the Charles Hamilton Houston Medallion of Merit, awarded by the Washington Bar Association; named Judge of the Year for 2017 by the Bar Association of the District of Columbia; founder and current director of the Frederick B. Abramson Scholarship Foundation.

COLLEEN KOLLAR-KOTELLY, judge; born in New York, NY; daughter of Konstantine and Irene Kollar; attended bilingual schools in Mexico, Ecuador, and Venezuela and Georgetown Visitation Preparatory School in Washington, DC; received B.A. degree in English at Catholic University (Delta Epsilon Honor Society); received J.D. at Catholic University's Columbus School of Law (Moot Court Board of Governors); law clerk to Hon. Catherine B. Kelly, District of Columbia Court of Appeals, 1968–69; attorney, United States Department of Justice, Criminal Division, Appellate Section, 1969–72; chief legal counsel, Saint Elizabeths Hospital, Department of Health and Human Services, 1972–84; received Saint Elizabeths Hospital Certificate of Appreciation, 1981; Meritorious Achievement Award from Alcohol, Drug Abuse and Mental Health Administration (ADAMHA), Department of Health and Human Services, 1981; appointed judge, Superior Court of the District of Columbia by President Reagan, October 3, 1984, took oath of office October 21, 1984; served as Deputy Presiding Judge, Criminal Division, January 1996–April 1997; received Achievement Recognition Award, Hispanic Heritage CORO Awards Celebration, 1996; appointed judge, U.S. District Court for the District of Columbia by President Clinton on March 26, 1997, took oath of office May 12, 1997; appointed by Chief Justice Rehnquist to serve on the Financial Disclosure Committee, 2000–02; presiding judge of the United States Foreign Intelligence Surveillance Court, 2002–09; appointed by Chief Justice John Roberts to the Judicial Resources Committee of the Judicial Conference, 2009–16; appointed by Chief Judge Beryl A. Howell to the District of Columbia Commission on Judicial Disabilities and Tenure, 2017.

JAMES E. BOASBERG, judge; born in San Francisco, CA, 1963; son of Emanuel Boasberg III and Sarah Szold Boasberg; graduated St. Albans School, Washington, DC, 1981; B.A., *magna cum laude*, in history from Yale College, 1985; M.St. in modern European history from Oxford University, 1986; J.D. from Yale Law School, 1990; law clerk to Judge Dorothy W. Nelson on the U.S. Court of Appeals for the Ninth Circuit, 1990–91; associate, Keker and Van Nest in San Francisco, CA, 1991–94; associate, Kellogg, Huber, Hansen, Todd and Evans in Washington, DC, 1995–96; Assistant United States Attorney for the District of Columbia, 1996–2002; visiting lecturer, George Washington Law School, 2003; Associate Judge, District of Columbia Superior Court, 2002–11; United States District Judge for the District of Columbia, 2011–present; appointed to the U.S. Foreign Intelligence Surveillance Court, May 2014.

AMY BERMAN JACKSON, judge; appointed March of 2011; prior to joining the Court, engaged in private practice in Washington, DC, as a member of Trout Cacheris, specializing in complex criminal and civil trials and appeals; earlier, partner at Venable, Baetjer, Howard, and Civiletti; Assistant United States Attorney for the District of Columbia, 1980–86; received Department of Justice Special Achievement Awards for work on murder and sexual assault cases; J.D., *cum laude*, Harvard Law School, 1979; A.B. *cum laude*, Harvard College, 1976; law clerk to the Honorable Harrison L. Winter of the United States Court of Appeals for the Fourth Circuit; lectured on corporate criminal investigations and has been a regular teacher at the National Institute of Trial Advocacy, the Georgetown University Law Center CLE Intensive Session in Trial Advocacy Skills, and the Harvard Law School Trial Advocacy workshop; while in private practice, was elected to serve as a DC Bar delegate to the ABA House of Delegates; active in the ABA Litigation Section, the ABA Criminal Justice Section White Collar Crime Committee, and DC Bar and Women's Bar Association committee activities; member of the Parent Steering Committee of the Interdisciplinary Council on Developmental and Learning Disorders; served on the Board of the DC Rape Crisis Center and other educational and community organizations.

RUDOLPH CONTRERAS, judge, appointed to the District Court in March 2012. In April 2016, Chief Justice John Roberts appointed Contreras to the United States Foreign Intelligence Surveillance Court for a term starting May 19, 2016. Prior to joining the District Court, Judge Contreras served from 2006 to 2012 as the Chief of the Civil Division of the United States Attorney's Office of the District of Columbia. In that capacity, he supervised 39 Assistant United States Attorneys who defend and bring civil cases on behalf of the United States. Judge Contreras was awarded his Bachelor of Science degree from Florida State University in 1984 and his Juris Doctor degree, *cum laude*, from the University of Pennsylvania Law School in 1991, where he was a member of the Order of the Coif and Editor of the *University of Pennsylvania Law Review*. Following law school, Judge Contreras joined the law firm of Jones, Day, Reavis and Pogue, where he was an Associate in the General Litigation Group. In 1994, Judge Contreras joined the United States Attorney's Office for the District of Columbia as an Assistant United States Attorney in the Civil Division, where he was responsible for a wide array of cases, including employment, Federal Tort Claims Act, Administrative Procedure Act, Bivens and Affirmative Civil Enforcement matters. In 2003, Judge Contreras left the DC Office to become the Chief of the Civil Division for the United States Attorney's Office in Delaware, where he oversaw that civil program and personally handled a wide variety of matters, including environmental and health care fraud cases.

KETANJI BROWN JACKSON, judge, received her commission as a United States District Judge in March 2013. Until December 2014, she also served as a Vice Chair and Commissioner on the United States Sentencing Commission, and she taught a seminar on Sentencing Policy at the George Washington University Law School as an adjunct professor. Prior to her service on the Commission, Judge Jackson was Of Counsel at Morrison and Foerster LLP for three years, with a practice that focused on criminal and civil appellate litigation in both state and federal courts, as well as cases in the Supreme Court of the United States. From 2005 until 2007, prior to joining Morrison and Foerster LLP, Judge Jackson served as an assistant federal public defender in the Appeals Division of the Office of the Federal Public Defender in the District of Columbia. Before that appointment, Judge Jackson worked as an assistant special counsel at the United States Sentencing Commission and as an associate with two law firms: one, specializing in white collar criminal defense; the other, focusing on the negotiated settlement of mass-tort claims. Judge Jackson also served as a law clerk to three federal judges: Associate Justice Stephen G. Breyer of the Supreme Court of the United States (October Term 1999), Judge Bruce M. Selya of the U.S. Court of Appeals for the First Circuit (1997–98), and Judge Patti B. Saris of the U.S. District Court for the District of Massachusetts (1996–97). In 2017, Chief Justice Roberts appointed Judge Jackson to serve a three-year term on the Judicial Conference of the U.S. Committee on Defender Services. Judge Jackson is currently a member of the Board of Overseers of Harvard University, the American Law Institute's Council, the Supreme Court Fellows Commission, and the board of the DC Circuit Historical Society. She received an A.B., *magna cum laude*, in Government from Harvard-Radcliffe College in 1992, and, in 1996, a J.D., *cum laude*, from Harvard Law School, where she served as a supervising editor of the *Harvard Law Review*.

CHRISTOPHER R. COOPER, judge; born in Mobile, Alabama, 1966; son of Paulette Reid Cooper and William Madison Cooper; graduated Trinity Preparatory School, Winter Park, Florida, 1984; B.A., *summa cum laude*, in economics and political science, Yale University, 1988, and member of Phi Beta Kappa; Research Analyst, Strategic Planning Associates, Washington, DC, 1988–90; J.D., with distinction, Stanford Law School, 1993; President, Volume 45, *Stanford Law Review*, 1992–93; Board Member, East Palo Alto Community Law Project, 1992–93; law clerk to then-Chief Judge Abner J. Mikva, United States Court of Appeals for the D.C. Circuit, 1993–94; United States Department of Justice, Special Assistant to the Deputy Attorney General, Washington, DC, 1994–96; Associate (1996–2000) and Partner (2000), Miller, Cassidy, Larroca and Lewin LLC, Washington, DC; Partner, Baker Botts LLP, Washington, DC (2000–10) and London (2010–12); Partner, Covington and Burling LLP, London (2012–13) and Washington, DC (2013–14); appointed to the United States District Court for the District of Columbia on March 28, 2014.

TANYA S. CHUTKAN, judge; born in Kingston, Jamaica; daughter of Dr. Winston Chutkan and Noelle Chutkan, Esq.; B.A., George Washington University, 1983; J.D., University of Pennsylvania Law School, 1987 (Associate Editor, *Law Review*; Arthur Littleton Legal Writing Fellow); Associate, Hogan and Hartson LLP, 1987–90; Associate, Donovan, Leisure, Rogovin, Huge and Schiller, 1990–91; Staff Attorney and Supervisor, Public Defender Service for the District of Columbia, 1991–2002; Counsel and Partner, Boies, Schiller and Flexner LLP, 2002–14; Steering Committee, Criminal Law and Individual Rights Section of the District of Columbia Bar, 2000–03; member of Visiting Faculty, Harvard Law School Trial Advocacy Workshop; nominated judge, U.S. District Court for the District of Columbia by President Obama; confirmed by the Senate on June 4, 2014; took the oath of office on July 25, 2014.

RANDOLPH D. MOSS, judge, born in Springfield, Ohio 1961; son of Dr. Howard A. Moss and Adrienne Moss. A.B., *summa cum laude*, phi beta kappa, philosophy, from Hamilton College in 1983; J.D., Yale Law School, 1986. Law clerk to Judge Pierre Leval, United States District Court for the Southern District of New York, 1986–87. Law clerk to Justice John Paul Stevens, United States Supreme Court, 1988–89. Private practice at Wilmer, Cutler and Pickering, first as associate then as partner, 1989–96. Department of Justice Office of Legal Counsel, 1996–2001; Deputy Assistant Attorney General, 1996–98; Acting Assistant Attorney General, 1998–2000; Assistant Attorney General, 2000–01. Partner, Wilmer, Cutler, Pickering Hale and Dorr, 2001–14; chair of the firm's Regulatory and Government Affairs Department. Confirmed to the bench November 2014.

AMIT MEHTA, judge; born in Patan, India; son of Priyavadan and Ragini Mehta. B.A., *magna cum laude* and Phi Beta Kappa in political science and economics from Georgetown University, 1993; J.D., Order of the Coif, University of Virginia, 1997; Law Clerk to Judge Susan P. Graber, United States Court of Appeals for the Ninth Circuit, 1998–1999; Associate, Counsel and Partner, Zuckerman Spaeder, LLP, 1999–2002, 2007–14; Staff Attorney, Public Defender Service for the District of Columbia, 2002–07; Judge, U.S. District Court for the District of Columbia, 2014–present.

TIMOTHY J. KELLY, judge; born in Glen Cove, NY, 1969; son of Timothy Noel Kelly and Helen Ann Kelly (Stevens); graduated Delbarton School, Morristown, NJ, 1987; A.B., *cum laude*, Duke University, 1991; J.D., Georgetown University, 1997; Senior Associate Editor, *American Criminal Law Review*, 1996–97; Associate, Arnold & Porter, Washington, DC, 1997–2001, 2002–03; Loaned Associate to the Legal Aid Society of the District of Columbia, 1999–2000; Law Clerk to the Honorable Ronald L. Buckwalter, United States District Court for the Eastern District of Pennsylvania, 2001–02; Assistant United States Attorney for the District of Columbia, 2003–07; Trial Attorney, Public Integrity Section, Criminal Division, United States Department of Justice, 2007–13; Recipient of the Assistant Attorney General's Award for Distinguished Service, 2012; Treasurer, District of Columbia Bar's Criminal Law and Individual Rights Section Steering Committee, 2013–16; Chief Counsel for National Security and Senior Crime Counsel to Ranking Member (2013–14) and Chairman (2015–17) of the Senate Judiciary Committee Charles E. Grassley; Staff Director to Co-Chairman of the Senate Caucus on International Narcotics Control, Charles E. Grassley, 2013–17; appointed to the United States District Court for the District of Columbia on September 8, 2017.

TREVOR N. McFADDEN, judge; born in Alexandria, VA, 1978; son of William J. and Carol (Prester) McFadden. Attended the American School in London and Robinson Secondary School, Fairfax, VA. B.A., *magna cum laude*, in English and political science, from Wheaton College, IL, 2001; J.D., Order of the Coif and *Virginia Law Review*, University of Virginia, 2006; Law Clerk to Judge Steven M. Colloton, United States Court of Appeals for the Eighth Circuit, 2006–07; Counsel to the Deputy Attorney General, United States Department of Justice, 2007–09; Assistant United States Attorney, District of Columbia, 2009–13; Associate and Partner, Baker & McKenzie, LLP, Washington, DC, 2013–17; Acting Principal Deputy Assistant Attorney General and Deputy Assistant Attorney General, United States Department of Justice Criminal Division, 2017. Confirmed to the bench October 2017.

DABNEY L. FRIEDRICH, judge; B.A., *magna cum laude*, Phi Beta Kappa, economics, from Trinity University, 1988; Diploma in Legal Studies from University College, Oxford University, 1989; J.D. from Yale Law School, 1992; law clerk to Judge Thomas F. Hogan of the United States District Court for the District of Columbia, 1992–94; associate, Latham & Watkins in San Diego, CA, 1994–95; Assistant United States Attorney for the Southern District of California, 1995–98; Assistant United States Attorney for the Eastern District of Virginia, 1998–2002; counsel to Ranking Member and Chairman Orrin G. Hatch of the United States Senate Committee on the Judiciary, 2002–03; associate counsel to President George W. Bush, 2003–06; member, United States Sentencing Commission, 2006–17; adjunct law professor, George Washington Law School, 2014; United States District Judge for the District of Columbia, December 2017–present.

CARL J. NICHOLS, judge; B.A., *cum laude* and with high honors in Philosophy, Dartmouth College, 1992; J.D., with high honors and Order of the Coif, The University of Chicago Law School, 1996; law clerk to Judge Laurence H. Silberman of the U.S. Court of Appeals for the District of Columbia, 1996–97; law clerk to Clarence Thomas of the Supreme Court of the United States, 1997–98; associate and partner, Boies, Schiller & Flexner LLP, 1998–2005; Deputy Assistant Attorney General, Civil Division, U.S. Department of Justice, 2005–08; Principal Deputy Associate Attorney General, U.S. Department of Justice, 2008–09; partner, Wilmer Cutler Pickering Hale & Dorr LLP, 2010–19; U.S. District Judge for the District of Columbia, June 2019–present.

SENIOR JUDGES

THOMAS F. HOGAN, senior judge; born in Washington, DC, 1938; son of Adm. Bartholomew W. (MC) (USN) Surgeon Gen., USN, 1956–62, and Grace (Gloninger) Hogan; Georgetown Preparatory School, 1956; A.B., Georgetown University (classical), 1960; master's program, American and English literature, George Washington University, 1960–62; J.D., Georgetown University, 1965–66; Honorary Degree, Doctor of Laws, Georgetown University Law Center, May 1999; St. Thomas More Fellow, Georgetown University Law Center, 1965–66; American Jurisprudence Award: Corporation Law; member, bars of the District of Columbia and Maryland; law clerk to Hon. William B. Jones, U.S. District Court for the District of Columbia, 1966–67; counsel, Federal Commission on Reform of Federal Criminal Laws, 1967–68; private practice of law in the District of Columbia and Maryland, 1968–82; adjunct professor of law, Potomac School of Law, 1977–79; adjunct professor of law, Georgetown University Law Center, 1986–88; public member, officer evaluation board, U.S. Foreign Service, 1973; member: American Bar Association, State Chairman, Maryland Drug Abuse Education Program, Young Lawyers Section (1970–73), District of Columbia Bar Association, Bar Association of the District of Columbia, Maryland State Bar Association, Montgomery County Bar Association, National Institute for Trial Advocacy, Defense Research Institute, The Barristers, The Lawyers Club; chairman, board of directors, Christ Child Institute for Emotionally Ill Children, 1971–74; served on many committees; USDC Executive Committee; Conference Committee on Administration of Federal Magistrates System, 1988–91; chairman, Inter-Circuit Assignment Committee, 1990–96; appointed judge of the U.S. District Court for the District of Columbia by President Reagan on October 4, 1982; chief judge, June 19, 2001; member: Judicial Conference of the United States, 2001–08; Executive Committee, U.S. District Court for the District of Columbia 873 of the Judicial Conference, July 2001–08, Chair 2005–08; Edward J. Devitt Distinguished Service to Justice Award, 2011; Director of the Administrative Office of the United States Courts, 2011–13; member, Foreign Intelligence Surveillance Court, 2009–16, Presiding Judge, 2014–16.

ROYCE C. LAMBERTH, senior judge; born in San Antonio, TX, 1943; son of Nell Elizabeth Synder and Larimore S. Lamberth, Sr.; South San Antonio High School, 1961; B.A., University of Texas at Austin, 1966; LL.B., University of Texas School of Law, 1967; permanent president, class of 1967, University of Texas School of Law; U.S. Army (Captain, Judge Advocate General's Corps, 1968–74; Vietnam Service Medal, Air Medal, Bronze Star with Oak Leaf Cluster, Meritorious Service Medal with Oak Leaf Cluster); Assistant U.S. Attorney, District of Columbia, 1974–87 (chief, Civil Division, 1978–87); President's Reorganization Project, Federal Legal Representation Study, 1978–79; honorary faculty, Army Judge Advocate General's School, 1976; Attorney General's Special Commendation Award; Attorney General's John Marshall Award, 1982; vice chairman, Armed Services and Veterans Affairs Committee, Section on Administrative Law, American Bar Association, 1979–82, chairman, 1983–84; chairman, Professional Ethics Committee, 1989–91; co-chairman, Committee of Article III Judges, Judiciary Section 1989–present; chairman, Federal Litigation Section, 1986–87; chairman, Federal Rules Committee, 1985–86; deputy chairman, Council of the Federal Lawyer, 1980–83; chairman, Career Service Committee, Federal Bar Association, 1978–80; appointed judge, U.S. District Court for the District of Columbia by President Reagan, November 16, 1987; appointed by Chief Justice Rehnquist to be presiding judge of the United States Foreign Intelligence Surveillance Court, 1995–2002.

PAUL L. FRIEDMAN, senior judge; born in Buffalo, NY, 1944; son of Cecil A. and Charlotte Wagner Friedman; B.A., political science, Cornell University, 1965; J.D., *cum laude*, School of Law, State University of New York at Buffalo, 1968; admitted to the bars of the District of Columbia, New York, U.S. Supreme Court, and U.S. Courts of Appeals for the D.C., Federal, Fourth, Fifth, Sixth, Seventh, Ninth and Eleventh Circuits; Law Clerk to Judge Aubrey E. Robinson, Jr., U.S. District Court for the District of Columbia, 1968–69; Law Clerk to Judge Roger Robb, U.S. Court of Appeals for the District of Columbia Circuit, 1969–70; Assistant U.S. Attorney for the District of Columbia, 1970–74; assistant to the Solicitor General of the United States, 1974–76; associate independent counsel, Iran-Contra investigation, 1987–88; private law practice, White and Case, partner, 1979–94; associate, 1976–79; member: American Bar Association, Commission on Multidisciplinary Practice 1998–2000, District of Columbia Bar (president, 1986–87), American Law Institute (1984) and ALI Council, 1998–present (member of Executive Committee as Secretary, 2013–present), American Academy of Appellate Lawyers, Bar Association of the District of Columbia, Women's Bar Association of the District of Columbia, Washington Bar Association, Hispanic Bar Association, Assistant United States Attorneys Association of the District of Columbia (president, 1976–77), Civil Justice Reform Act Advisory Group (chair, 1991–94), District of Columbia Judicial Nomination Commission (member, 1990–94; chair, 1992–94), Advisory Committee on Procedures, U.S. Court of Appeals for the D.C. Circuit (1982–88), Grievance Committee; U.S. District Court for the District of Columbia (member, 1981–87; chair, 1983–85); fellow, American College of Trial Lawyers; fellow, American Bar Foundation; board of directors: Frederick B. Abramson Memorial Foundation (president, 1991–94), Washington Area Lawyers for the Arts (1988–92), Washington Legal Clinic for the Homeless (member, 1987–92; vice-president, 1988–91), Stuart Stiller Memorial Foundation (1980–94), American Judicature Society (1990–94); board of trustees, District of Columbia Public Defender Service (1989–92); member: Cosmos Club, Lawyers Club of Washington; recipient of Distinguished Alumnus Award, the University at Buffalo Law Alumni Association (1998); Civil Justice Award, Academy of Court Appointed Masters (2007); Judicial Honoree, the 138th Annual Banquet of the Bar Association of the District of Columbia (2009); Buffalo Law Review Award, the University at Buffalo Law Review (2016); Judge Charles R. Richey Equal Justice Award, the George Washington University Law School (2016); appointed 874 *Congressional Directory judge, U.S. District Court for the District of Columbia by President Clinton, June 16, 1994, and took oath of office August 1, 1994; U.S. Judicial Conference Advisory Committee on Federal Criminal Rules.*

ELLEN SEGAL HUVELLE, senior judge; born in Boston, MA, 1948; daughter of Robert M. Segal, Esq., and Sharlee Segal; B.A., Wellesley College, 1970; Masters in City Planning, Yale University, 1972; J.D., *magna cum laude*, Boston College Law School, 1975 (Order of the Coif; Articles Editor of the *Law Review*); law clerk to Chief Justice Edward F. Hennessey, Massachusetts Supreme Judicial Court, 1975–76; associate, Williams and Connolly, 1976–84; partner, Williams and Connolly, 1984–90; associate judge, Superior Court of the District of Columbia, 1990–99; appointed judge, U.S. District Court for the District of Columbia by President Clinton in October 1999, and took oath of office on February 25, 2000. Member: American Bar Association, District of Columbia Bar, Women's Bar Association; Fellow of the American Bar Foundation; Master in the Edward Bennett Williams Inn of Court and member of the Inn's Executive Committee; instructor of Trial Advocacy at the University of Virginia Law School; member of Visiting Faculty at Harvard Law School's Trial Advocacy Workshop; Boston College Law School Board of Overseers; seminar instructor at the Peking University School of Transnational Law in Shenzhen, 2010; faculty, CEELI Institute for training Tunisian judges, 2012; appointed by the Chief Justice of the United States to Judicial Conference Committee on Judicial Resources, 2002–09, Judicial Conference Committee on Criminal Law, 2011–17, Judicial Panel on Multidistrict Litigation, 2013–present; American Inns of Court Professionalism Award for the District of Columbia Circuit for 2017; Board Member for the Frederick B. Abramson Scholarship Foundation.

REGGIE B. WALTON, judge; born in Donora, PA, 1949; son of the late Theodore and Ruth (Garard) Walton; B.A., West Virginia State College, 1971; J.D., American University, Washington College of Law, 1974; admitted to the bars of the Supreme Court of Pennsylvania, 1974; United States District Court for the Eastern District of Pennsylvania, 1975; District of Columbia Court of Appeals, 1976; United States Court of Appeals for the District of Columbia Circuit, 1977; Supreme Court of the United States, 1980; United States District Court for the District of Columbia; Staff Attorney, Defender Association of Philadelphia, 1974–76; Assistant United States Attorney for the District of Columbia, 1976–80; Chief, Career Criminal Unit, Assistant United States Attorney for the District of Columbia, 1979–80; Executive Assistant United States Attorney for the District of Columbia, 1980–81; Associate Judge, Superior Court of the District of Columbia, 1981–89; deputy presiding judge of the Criminal Division, Superior Court of the District of Columbia, 1986–89; Associate Director, Office of National Drug Control Policy, Executive Office of the President, 1989–91; Senior White House Advisor for Crime, The White House, 1991; Associate Judge, Superior Court of the District of Columbia, 1991–2001; Presiding Judge of the Domestic Violence Unit, Superior Court of the District of Columbia, 2000; Presiding Judge of the Family Division, Superior Court of the District of Columbia, 2001; Instructor: National Judicial College, Reno,

Nevada, 1999–present; Harvard University Law School, Trial Advocacy Workshop, 1994–present; National Institute of Trial Advocacy, Georgetown University Law School, 1983–present; co-author, Pretrial Drug Testing—An Essential Component of the National Drug Control Strategy, *Brigham Young University Journal of Public Law* (1991); co-author, Business and Commercial Litigation in Federal Courts (4th ed. 2016); co-author, Tough Cases (2018); Distinguished Alumnus Award, American University, Washington College of Law (1991); The William H. Hastie Award, The Judicial Council of the National Bar Association (1993); Commissioned as a Kentucky Colonel by the Governor (1990, 1991); Governor's Proclamation declaring April 9, 1991, Judge Reggie B. Walton Day in the State of Louisiana; The West Virginia State College National Alumni Association James R. Waddy Meritorious Service Award (1990); Secretary's Award, United States Department of Veterans Affairs (1990); Outstanding Alumnus Award, Ringgold High School (1987); Director's Award for Superior Performance as an Assistant United States Attorney (1980); Profiled in book entitled *Black Judges on Justice: Perspectives From The Bench* by Linn Washington (1995); appointed district judge, United States District Court for the District of Columbia by President George W. Bush, September 24, 2001, and took oath of office October 29, 2001; appointed by President Bush in 2004 to serve as the Chairperson of the National Prison Rape Reduction Commission, a two-year commission created by the United States Congress tasked with the mission of identifying methods to curb the incidents of prison rape; appointed by former Chief Justice Rehnquist to serve on Judicial Conference Criminal Law Committee, 2005–11; member, United States Foreign Intelligence Surveillance Court, 2007–14; Presiding Judge, 2013–14; appointed by Chief Justice Roberts to serve on Judicial Conference Committee on Court Administration and Management, 2014–present; appointed by Secretary of Defense James Mattis to serve on Defense Advisory Committee on Investigations, Prosecution and Defense of Sexual Assault in the Armed Forces, 2017–present; sitting by designation, United States District Court for the Western District of Pennsylvania, 2016–present; assisted in creation of and presides over reentry court in United States District Court for the District of Columbia, 2016–present; serves on American Law Institute Committee on the Model Penal Code for Sexual Assault and Related Offenses, 2013–present; active youth mentor and participant in Big Brother program.

JOHN D. BATES, senior judge; born in Elizabeth, NJ, 1946; son of Richard D. and Sarah (Deacon) Bates; B.A., Wesleyan University, 1968; J.D., University of Maryland School of Law, 1976; U.S. Army (1968–71, 1st Lt., Vietnam Service Medal, Bronze Star); law clerk to Hon. Roszel Thomsen, U.S. District Court for the District of Maryland, 1976–77; Assistant U.S. Attorney, District of Columbia, 1980–97 (Chief, Civil Division, 1987–97); Director's Award for Superior Performance (1983); Attorney General's Special commendation Award (1986); Deputy Independent Counsel, Whitewater Investigation, 1995–97; private practice of law, Miller and Chevalier (partner, 1998–2001), Chair of Government Contracts Litigation Department and member of Executive Committee), Steptoe and Johnson (associate, 1977–80); District of Columbia Circuit Advisory Committee for Procedures, 1989–93; Civil Justice Reform Committee of the U.S. District Court for the District of Columbia, 1996–2001; Treasurer, D.C. Bar, 1992–93; Publications Committee, D.C. Bar (1991–97, Chair 1994–97); D.C. Bar Special Committee on Government Lawyers, 1990–91; D.C. Bar Task Force on Civility in the Profession, 1994–96; D.C. Bar Committee on Examination of Rule 49, 1995–96; Chair, Litigation Section, Federal Bar Association, 1986–89; Board of Directors, Washington Lawyers Committee for Civil Rights and Urban Affairs, 1999–2001; appointed to the U.S. District Court for the District of Columbia in December, 2001; member, Court Administration and Case Management Committee of the Judicial Conference, 2003–09; member, United States Foreign Intelligence Surveillance Court, 2006–13, presiding judge, 2009–13; Director, Administrative Office of United States Courts, 2013–14; Chairman, Advisory Committee on Federal Rules of Civil Procedure, 2015–present.

RICHARD J. LEON, judge; born in South Natick, MA, 1949; son of Silvano B. Leon and Rita (O'Rorke) Leon; A.B., Holy Cross College, 1971, J.D., *cum laude*, Suffolk Law School, 1974; LL.M., Harvard Law School, 1981; Law Clerk to Chief Justice McLaughlin and the Associate Justices, Superior Court of Massachusetts, 1974–75; Law Clerk to Hon. Thomas F. Kelleher, Supreme Court of Rhode Island, 1975–76; admitted to the bar, Rhode Island, 1975, and District of Columbia, 1991; Special Assistant U.S. Attorney, Southern District of New York, 1977–78; Assistant Professor of Law, St. John's Law School, New York, 1979–83; Senior Trial Attorney, Criminal Section, Tax Division, U.S. Department of Justice, 1983–87; Deputy Chief Minority Counsel, U.S. House Select "Iran-Contra" Committee, 1987–88; Deputy Assistant U.S. Attorney General, Environment Division, 1988–89; Partner, Baker and Hostetler, Washington, DC, 1989–99; Commissioner, The White House Fellows Commission, 1990–92; Chief Minority Counsel, U.S. House Foreign Affairs Committee "October Surprise" Task Force, 1992–93; Special Counsel, U.S. House Banking Committee "Whitewater" Investigation, 1994; Special Counsel, U.S. House Ethics Reform Task Force,

1997; Adjunct Professor, Georgetown University Law Center, 1997–present; Partner, Vorys, Sater, Seymour and Pease, Washington, DC, 1999–2002; Commissioner, Judicial Review Commission on Foreign Asset Control, 2000–01; Master, Edward Bennett Williams Inn of Court; appointed U.S. District Judge for the District of Columbia by President George W. Bush on February 19, 2002; took oath of office on March 20, 2002.

ROSEMARY M. COLLYER, judge; born in White Plains, NY, 1945; daughter of Thomas C. and Alice Henry Mayers; educated in parochial and public schools in Stamford, Connecticut; B.A., Trinity College, Washington, DC, 1968; J.D., University of Denver College of Law, 1977; practiced with Sherman and Howard, Denver, Colorado, 1977–81; Chairman, Federal Mine Safety and Health Review Commission, 1981–84, by appointment of President Ronald Reagan with Senate confirmation; General Counsel, National Labor Relations Board, 1984–89, by appointment of President Reagan with Senate confirmation; private practice with Crowell and Moring LLP, Washington, DC, 1989–2003; member and chairman of the firm's Management Committee; appointed U.S. District Judge for the District of Columbia by President George W. Bush and took oath of office on January 2, 2003. Member, Foreign Intelligence Surveillance Court, 2013–present. Presiding Judge, Foreign Intelligence Surveillance Court, 2016–present. Chief Judge, Alien Terrorist Removal Court, 2016–present.

Officers of the United States District Court for the District of Columbia

Bankruptcy Judge.—S. Martin Teel, Jr.

United States Magistrate Judges: G. Michael Harvey, Robin M. Meriweather, Deborah A. Robinson.

Clerk of Court.—Angela D. Caesar.

Administrative Assistant to the Chief Judge.—Lisa J. Klem.

UNITED STATES COURT OF INTERNATIONAL TRADE

One Federal Plaza, New York, NY 10278–0001
phone (212) 264–2800

TIMOTHY C. STANCEU, chief judge; born in Canton, OH; A.B., Colgate University, 1973; J.D., Georgetown University Law Center, 1979; appointed to the U.S. Court of International Trade by President George W. Bush and began serving on April 15, 2003; prior to appointment, private practice for 13 years in Washington, DC, with the law firm Hogan and Hartson, LLP, during which he represented clients in a variety of matters involving customs and international trade law; Deputy Director, Office of Trade and Tariff Affairs, U.S. Department of the Treasury; where his responsibilities involved the regulatory and enforcement matters of the U.S. Customs Service and other agencies; Special Assistant to the Assistant Secretary of the Office of Enforcement, U.S. Department of the Treasury; Program Analyst and Environmental Protection Specialist, U.S. Environmental Protection Agency, where he concentrated on the development and review of regulations on various environmental subjects.

MARK A. BARNETT, judge; graduated *magna cum laude*, Phi Beta Kappa from Dickinson College; studied at the Dickinson Center for European Studies; J.D., *cum laude* from the University of Michigan Law School; member of the Bars of Pennsylvania and the District of Columbia and admitted to practice before the U.S. Court of International Trade and the U.S. Court of Appeals for the Federal Circuit; practiced in the international trade group at Steptoe and Johnson; joined the Office of Chief Counsel for Import Administration at the U.S. Department of Commerce as a staff attorney, served as a senior counsel, and subsequently served as the Deputy Chief Counsel for Import Administration; member of the U.S. negotiating teams for the U.S.-Morocco Free Trade Agreement, the World Trade Organization's Doha Round Rules Negotiating Group, and the Trans-Pacific Partnership; represented the United States before dispute settlement panels and the Appellate Body of the World Trade Organization and binational panels composed under the North American Free Trade Agreement; detailed to the U.S. House of Representatives, Committee on Ways and Means, Subcommittee on Trade as a Trade Counsel; served two terms as a member of the board of directors of the International Model United Nations Association, Inc., including Vice-Chairman and Chairman; nominated to the U.S. Court of International Trade by President Obama on July 12, 2012, and confirmed by the U.S. Senate on May 23, 2013.

CLAIRE R. KELLY, judge; born in New York, NY. Married to Joseph A DiBartolo. Child: Joseph J. DiBartolo. Attended Sacred Heart Academy, Hempstead, NY; Barnard College, B.A. 1987, *cum laude*; and Brooklyn Law School, J.D., 1993, *magna cum laude*. Professional experience: Coudert Brothers (1993–97) associated; Brooklyn Law School (1997–2013), Legal Writing Instructor, Associate Professor of Law and Professor of Law and Co-Director of the Dennis J. Block Center for the Study of International Business Law. Elected Member of the American Law Institute, 2011; nominated to the U.S. Court of International Trade by President Obama on November 14, 2012, and confirmed by the U.S. Senate on May 23, 2013.

JENNIFER CHOE-GROVES, judge; born in Chicago, IL; A.B., Princeton University; J.D., Rutgers School of Law-Newark; LL.M., Columbia Law School; Juilliard School, Pre-College Degree (Piano and Composition). Nominated by the President of the United States on July 30, 2015 and confirmed unanimously by the United States Senate on June 6, 2016. Judge Choe-Groves served as an Assistant District Attorney in the Manhattan District Attorney's Office, as Senior Director for Intellectual Property and Innovation and Chair of the Special 301 Committee for the Office of the United States Trade Representative (USTR) under Presidents George W. Bush and Barack Obama. Prior to her appointment to the United States Court of International Trade, Judge Choe-Groves was a partner in private practice.

GARY S. KATZMANN, judge; born in New York, NY. New York City public schools; A.B., *summa cum laude*, Phil Beta Kappa, Columbia, 1973; M.Litt, Oxford, 1976; J.D., Yale Law School, 1979; Editor, Yale Law Journal; M.P.P.M., Yale School of Management, 1979. Law Clerk, Judge Leonard B. Sand, United States District Court for the Southern

District of New York, 1979–80; Law Clerk, Judge Stephen G. Breyer, United States Court of Appeals for the First Circuit, 1980–81. Research Associate, Center for Criminal Justice, Harvard Law School, 1981–83; special investigator, Administrative Board, Harvard Law School, 1982–83. Assistant United States Attorney, District of Massachusetts, 1983–2004 (variously trial and appellate litigator in the criminal and civil divisions, Chief Appellate Attorney, Deputy Chief of the Criminal Division, Chief Legal Counsel to the United States Attorney). Associate Deputy Attorney General, Washington, D.C., 1993–94 (on detail from U.S. Attorney's Office); Office of the Director, Federal Bureau of Investigation (1995) (on detail). Recipient, Director's Awards, Department of Justice, for excellence in appellate advocacy (1993) and for successful terrorism prosecution (2003). Associate Justice, Massachusetts Appeals Court, 2004–16 (appointed by Governor Mitt Romney). Judge, United States Court of International Trade, 2016–present (appointed by President Barack Obama, sworn in on September 16, 2016). Lecturer on Law, Harvard Law School, 1990–94, 1997; John F. Kennedy School of Government, Harvard University, 1993–2003; research fellow and project director, 1997–2001; Fellow, 2002–03. Governance Institute, Washington, D.C., 1997–2003, research fellow and project director, 1997–2001; Fellow, 2002–03. Yale Law School, 1999, participant in course on sentencing. Faculty, Institute for Judicial Administration, NYU Law School, Seminar for New Appellate Judges, 2013–present. Author, Inside the Criminal Process (1990) (W.W. Norton, publisher); Editor and Contributing Author, Securing Our Children's Future: New Approaches to Juvenile Justice and Youth Violence (2004) (Brookings/Governance, publisher). Author, various articles.

TIMOTHY M. REIF, judge. From 2017 to 2019, Judge Reif served as Senior Advisor to the United States Trade Representative. From 2009 to 2017, he was the General Counsel for the Office of the United States Trade Representative. As General Counsel, Judge Reif was responsible for compliance with and enforcement of all U.S. trade and investment agreements, and for providing legal counsel on all U.S. trade negotiations. From 1998 to 2009, Judge Reif served as Chief International Trade Counsel for the Committee on Ways and Means in the U.S. House of Representatives, where he advised on the regulation of all international trade, investment, regulatory and economic matters, and related legislation. Prior to this appointment, Judge Reif worked as Special International Trade Counsel at Dewey Ballantine, LLP. From 1993 to 1995, Judge Reif served as Trade Counsel to the Ways and Means Committee. From 1989 to 1993, Judge Reif served as Associate General Counsel in the Office of the U.S. Trade Representative, where he was lead USTR negotiator for key provisions of the Uruguay Round Agreements and the North American Free Trade Agreement (NAFTA), as well as a number of bilateral agreements such as the U.S.-Japan Semiconductor Agreement (1991). Judge Reif also litigated or supervised the litigation of numerous disputes under the General Agreement on Tariffs and Trade (GATT). From 1987 to 1989, Judge Reif served as Attorney-Advisor with the U.S. International Trade Commission. From 1985 to 1987, he served as an associate with the Washington office of Milbank Tweed Hadley & McCloy. Since 2015, Judge Reif has been Lecturer in Law at Columbia Law School and has also served as Visiting Lecturer at the Woodrow Wilson School of Public and International Affairs at Princeton University (2017, 2012, 2008, 2004) and at Georgetown Law School (1995–2007). Mr. Reif received his JD from Columbia Law School and his MPA and AB degrees from Princeton University. He is married to Desiree Green and they are the parents of Paul, Anna, Sarah and Clare. They live with their Airedales, Winston and Clementine.

M. MILLER BAKER, judge. Appointed as a Judge of the United States Court of International Trade on December 18, 2019, by President Donald J. Trump. Judge Baker entered on duty on December 20, 2019. A native of Terrebonne Parish, Louisiana, Judge Baker grew up in Louisiana and Wyoming and attended Louisiana State University. Judge Baker thereafter earned his J.D. from Tulane University Law School and was admitted to the Louisiana bar in 1984 at age 22. After graduating from Tulane, he served as a law clerk to Judge John Malcolm Duhé, Jr., of the United States District Court for the Western District of Louisiana and then for Judge Thomas Gibbs Gee of the United States Court of Appeals for the Fifth Circuit. Following his judicial clerkships, from 1986 until the end of the Reagan Administration on January 20, 1989, Judge Baker served in the Justice Department under Attorneys General Edwin Meese III and Richard Thornburgh, first as an attorney-advisor in the Office of Legal Policy, and later as a special assistant to the Assistant Attorney General for Civil Rights. Judge Baker then entered private practice in Washington, D.C., until 1991. From 1991 to 1993 he served as counsel to Senator Orrin G. Hatch on the staff of the Senate Judiciary Committee. Following his service on the Judiciary Committee staff, Judge Baker returned to private practice in Washington, D.C., focusing on complex civil litigation involving a wide range of subjects at the law firms of Carr Goodson Warner (1993–2000) and McDermott Will & Emery LLP (2000–19). At McDermott, Judge Baker co-chaired the firm's appellate practice group. When he was in private practice, Judge Baker argued before the Supreme Court, nine of the thirteen federal courts of appeals, and appellate courts in three states and the District of Columbia. In 2009, The American Lawyer named Judge Baker as "Litigator of the Week" for one of his Supreme Court wins. In addition to his appellate practice, Judge Baker litigated in state and federal trial courts in seventeen states and the District of Columbia. From 1986 to 1995, Judge Baker served as a naval reserve intelligence officer and received an honorable discharge. His duties included serving with an anti-terrorist unit, on the battle staff of an admiral commanding a carrier battle group operating in the North Atlantic during a large NATO exercise in the Cold War, and as a watch officer in the Navy Command Center in the Pentagon during the Persian Gulf War. In the aftermath of 9/11, Judge Baker testified before the House and Senate Judiciary Committees on constitutional and policy issues associated with continuity of government. He also testified before the Continuity of Government Commission, a bipartisan study commission established by the American Enterprise Institute and the Brookings Institution. Judge Baker and his wife Margaret have five children, two of whom are active duty military officers.

SENIOR JUDGES

JANE A. RESTANI, senior judge; born in San Francisco, CA, 1948; parents: Emilia C. and Roy J. Restani; husband: Ira Bloom; B.A., University of California at Berkeley, 1969; J.D., University of California at Davis, 1973; law review staff writer, 1971–72; articles editor, 1972–73; member, Order of the Coif; elected to Phi Kappa Phi Honor Society; admitted to the bar of the Supreme Court of the State of California, 1973; joined the civil division of the Department of Justice under the Attorney General's Honor Program in 1973 as a trial attorney; assistant chief commercial litigation section, civil division, 1976–80; director, commercial litigation branch, civil division, 1980–83; recipient of the John Marshall Award of outstanding legal achievement in 1983; Judicial Improvements Committee (now Committee on Court Administration and Case Management) of the Judicial Conference of the United States, 1987–94; Judicial Conference Advisory Committee on the Federal Rules of Bankruptcy Procedure, and liaison to the Advisory Committee on the Federal Rules of Civil Procedure, 1994–96; member, Judicial Conference of the United States, 2003–10; Executive Committee of the Judicial Conference, 2010; ABA Standing Committee on Customs Laws, 1990–93; and the Board of Directors, New York State Association of Women Judges, 1992–present; nominated to the United States Court of International Trade on November 2, 1983 by President Reagan; entered upon the duties of that office on November 25, 1983; Chief Judge, 2003–10.

THOMAS J. AQUILINO, JR., senior judge; born in Mount Kisco, NY, December 7, 1939; son of Thomas J. and Virginia B. (Doughty) Aquilino; married to Edith Berndt Aquilino; children: Christopher Thomas, Philip Andrew, Alexander Berndt; attended Cornell University, 1957–59; B.A., Drew University, 1959–60, 1961–62; University of Munich, Germany, 1960-61; Free University of Berlin, Germany, 1965–66; J.D., Rutgers University School of Law, 1966–69; research assistant, Prof. L.F.E. Goldie (Resources for the Future-Ford Foundation), 1967–69; administrator, Northern Region, 1969 Jessup International Law Moot Court Competition; served in the U.S. Army, 1962–65; law clerk, Hon. John M. Cannella, U.S. District Court for the Southern District of New York, 1969–71; attorney with Davis Polk and Wardwell, New York, NY, 1971–85; admitted to practice New York, U.S. Supreme Court, U.S. Court of Appeals for Second and Third Circuits, U.S. Court of International Trade, U.S. Court of Claims, U.S. District Courts for Eastern, Southern and Northern Districts of New York, Interstate Commerce Commission; adjunct professor of law, Benjamin N. Cardozo School of Law, 1984–95; Mem., Drew University Board of Visitors, 1997–present; appointed to the U.S. Court of International Trade by President Reagan on February 22, 1985; confirmed by U.S. Senate, April 3, 1985.

RICHARD W. GOLDBERG, senior judge; born in Fargo, ND, September 23, 1927; married; two children, a daughter and a son; J.D., University of Miami, 1952; served on active duty as an Air Force Judge Advocate, 1953–56; admitted to Washington, DC Bar, Florida Bar and North Dakota Bar; from 1959 to 1983, owned and operated a regional grain processing firm in North Dakota; served as State Senator from North Dakota for eight years; taught military law for the Army and Air Force ROTC at North Dakota State University; was vice-chairman of the board of Minneapolis Grain Exchange; joined the Reagan Administration in 1983 in Washington at the U.S. Department of Agriculture; served as Deputy Under Secretary for International Affairs and Commodity Programs and later as Acting Under Secretary; in 1990 joined the Washington, DC law firm of Anderson, Hibey and Blair; appointed judge of the U.S. Court of International Trade in 1991; assumed senior status in 2001.

RICHARD K. EATON, senior judge; born in Walton, NY; married to Susan Henshaw Jones; two children: Alice and Elizabeth; attended Walton public schools; B.A., Ithaca College, J.D., Union University Albany Law School, 1974; professional experience: Eaton and Eaton, partner; Mudge Rose Guthrie Alexander and Ferdon, New York, NY, associate and partner; Stroock and Stroock and Lavan, partner; served on the staff of Senator Daniel Patrick Moynihan; confirmed by the United States Senate to the U.S. Court of International Trade on October 22, 1999.

LEO M. GORDON, senior judge; graduate of Newark Academy in Livingston, NJ; University of North Carolina-Chapel Hill, Phi Beta Kappa, 1973; J.D., Emory University School of Law, 1977; member of the Bars of New Jersey, Georgia and the District of Columbia; Assistant Counsel at the Subcommittee on Monopolies and Commercial Law, Committee on the Judiciary, U.S. House of Representatives, 1977–81; in that capacity, Judge Gordon was the principal attorney responsible for the Customs Courts Act of 1980 that created the U.S. Court of International Trade; for 25 years, Judge Gordon was on the staff at the Court, serving first as Assistant Clerk from 1981–99, and then Clerk of the Court from 1999–2006; appointed to the U.S. Court of International Trade in March 2006.

INACTIVE SENIOR JUDGES

GREGORY W. CARMAN, inactive senior judge; born in Farmingdale, Long Island, NY; son of Nassau County District Court Judge Willis B. and Marjorie Sosa Carman; B.A., St. Lawrence University, Canton, NY, 1958; J.D., St. John's University School of Law (honors program), 1961; University of Virginia Law School, JAG (with honors), 1962; admitted to New York Bar, 1961; practiced law with firm of Carman, Callahan and Sabino, Farmingdale, NY; admitted to practice: U.S. Court of Military Appeals, 1962, U.S. District Courts, Eastern and Southern Districts of New York, 1965, Second Circuit Court of Appeals, 1966, Supreme Court of the United States, 1967, U.S. Court of Appeals, District of Columbia, 1982; Councilman Town of Oyster Bay, 1972–80; member, U.S. House of Representatives, 97th Congress; member, Banking, Finance and Urban Affairs Committee and Select Committee on Aging; member, International Trade, Investment, and Monetary Policy Subcommittee; U.S. Congressional Delegate to International I.M.F. Conference; nominated by President Reagan, confirmed and appointed Judge of the U.S. Court of International Trade, March 2, 1983; Acting Chief Judge, 1991; Chief Judge, 1996–2003; Statutory Member, Judicial Conference of United States; member, Executive Committee, Judicial Branch Committee, and Subcommittees on Long Range Planning, Benefits, Civic Education, and Seminars; Captain, U.S. Army, 1958–64; awarded Army Commendation Medal for Meritorious Service, 1964; member, Rotary International, 1964–present; named Paul Harris Fellow of the Rotary Foundation of Rotary International; member, Holland Society, and recipient of its 1999 Gold Medal for Distinguished Achievement in Jurisprudence; member, Federal Bar Association, American Bar Association, Fellow of American Bar Foundation, New York State Bar Association; member, and former Chair, New York State Bar Association's Committee on Courts and the Community, and recipient of its 1996 Special Recognition Award; Doctor of Laws, honoris causa, Nova Southeastern University, 1999; Distinguished Jurist in Residence, Touro College Law Center, 2000; Doctor of Laws, honoris causa, St. John's University, 2002; Inaugural Lecturer, DiCarlo U.S. Court of International Trade Lecture, John Marshall Law School, 2003; Distinguished Alumni Citation, St. Lawrence University, 2003; Italian Board of Guardians Public Service Award, 2003; director and member, Respect for Law Alliance, Inc.; Recipient of Respect for Law Alliance, 2010, Judiciary Leader Award; Executive Committee member and past president, Theodore Roosevelt American Inn of Court; past president, Protestant Lawyers Association of Long Island; member, Vestry, St. Thomas's Episcopal Church, Farmingdale, NY; married to Nancy Endruschat (deceased); children: Gregory Wright, Jr., John Frederick, James Matthew, and Mira Catherine; married to Judith L. Dennehy.

R. KENTON MUSGRAVE, inactive senior judge; born in Clearwater, FL, September 7, 1927; married May 7, 1949 to former Ruth Shippen Hoppe, of Atlanta, GA; three children: Laura Marie Musgrave (deceased), Ruth Shippen Musgrave, Esq., and Forest Kenton Musgrave; attended Augusta Academy (Virginia); B.A., University of Washington, 1948; editorial staff, Journal of International Law, Emory University; J.D., with distinction, Emory University, 1953; assistant general counsel, Lockheed Aircraft and Lockheed International, 1953–62; vice president and general counsel, Mattel, Inc., 1963–71; director, Ringling Bros. and Barnum and Bailey Combined Shows, Inc., 1968–72; commissioner, BSA (Atlanta), 1952–55; partner, Musgrave, Welbourn and Fertman, 1972–75; assistant general counsel, Pacific Enterprises, 1975–81; vice president, general counsel and secretary, Vivitar Corporation, 1981–85; vice president and director, Santa Barbara Applied Research Corp., 1982–87; trustee, Morris Animal Foundation, 1981–94; director Emeritus, Pet Protection Society, 1981–present; director, Dolphins of Shark Bay (Australia) Foundation, 1985–present; trustee, The Dian Fossey Gorilla

Fund, 1987–present; trustee, The Ocean Conservancy, 2000–present; vice president and director, South Bay Social Services Group, 1963–70; director, Palos Verdes Community Arts Association, 1973–79; member, Governor of Florida's Council of 100, 1970–73; director, Orlando Bank and Trust, 1970–73; counsel, League of Women Voters, 1964–66; member, State Bar of Georgia, 1953–present; State Bar of California, 1962–present; Los Angeles County Bar Association, 1962–87 and chairman, Corporate Law Departments Section, 1965–66; admitted to practice before the U.S. Supreme Court, 1962; Supreme Court of Georgia, 1953; California Supreme Court, 1962; U.S. Customs Court, 1967; U.S. Court of International Trade, 1980; nominated to the U.S. Court of International Trade by President Reagan on July 1, 1987; confirmed by the Senate on November 9, and took oath of office on November 13, 1987.

JUDITH M. BARZILAY, inactive senior judge; born in Russell, KS, January 3, 1944; husband, Sal (Doron) Barzilay; children, Ilan and Michael; parents, Arthur and Hilda Morgenstern; B.A., Wichita State University, 1965; M.L.S., Rutgers University School of Library and Information Science, 1971; J.D., Rutgers University School of Law, 1981, Moot Court Board, 1980–81; trial attorney, U.S. Department of Justice (International Trade Field Office), 1983–86; litigation associate, Siegel, Mandell and Davidson, New York, NY, 1986–88; Sony Corporation of America, 1988–98; customs and international trade counsel, 1988–89; vice-president for import and export operations, 1989–96; vice-president for government affairs, 1996–98; executive board of the American Association of Exporters and Importers, 1993–98; appointed by Treasury Secretary Robert Rubin to the Advisory Committee on Commercial Operations of the United States Customs Service, 1995–98; nominated for appointment on January 27, 1998 by President Clinton; sworn in as judge June 3, 1998.

DELISSA A. RIDGWAY, inactive senior judge; born in Kirksville, MO, June 28, 1955; B.A. (honors), University of Missouri-Columbia, 1975; graduate work, University of Missouri-Columbia, 1975–76; J.D., Northeastern University School of Law, 1979; Duke University School of Law, LL.M. in Judicial Studies-2014; Shaw Pittman Potts and Trowbridge (Washington, DC), 1979–94; Chair, Foreign Claims Settlement Commission of the U.S., 1994–98; Adjunct Professor of Law, Cornell Law School, 1999–present; Adjunct Professor of Law /Lecturer, Washington College of Law /The American University, 1992–94; District of Columbia Bar, Secretary, 1991–92; Board of Governors, 1992–98; President, Women's Bar Association, 1992–93; American Bar Association, Standing Committee on Federal Judicial Improvements (2008–11); Co-Chair, Section of Litigation Task Force on Implicit Bias (2010–13); Commission on Women in the Profession, 2002–05; Federal Bar Association, National Council, 1993–2002, 2003–present; Government Relations Committee, 1996–2008, Public Relations Committee Chair, 1998–99; Board of Directors, Federal Bar Building Corporation; Executive Committee, National Conference of Federal Trial Judges, 2004–11; Chair, National Conference of Federal Trial Judges, 2009–10; Board of Directors, American Judicature Society (2010–present); Founding Member of Board, D.C. Conference on Opportunities for Minorities in the Legal Profession, 1992–93; Chair, D.C. Bar Summit on Women in the Legal Profession, 1995–98; Fellow, American Bar Foundation; Member, American Law Institute; Fellow, Federal Bar Foundation; Earl W. Kintner Award of the Federal Bar Association (2000); Woman Lawyer of the Year, Washington, DC (2001); Distinguished Visiting Scholar-in-Residence, University of Missouri-Columbia (2003); sworn in as a judge to the U.S. Court of International Trade in May 1998.

OFFICER OF THE UNITED STATES COURT OF INTERNATIONAL TRADE

Clerk.—Mario Toscano (212) 264–2814.

UNITED STATES COURT OF FEDERAL CLAIMS

Lafayette Square, 717 Madison Place, NW., Washington, DC 20439

phone (202) 357–6406

MARGARET M. SWEENEY, chief judge; born in Baltimore, MD; B.A. in history, Notre Dame of Maryland, 1977; J.D., Delaware Law School, 1981; Delaware Family Court Master, 1981–83; litigation associate, Fedorko, Gilbert, and Lanctot, Morrisville, PA, 1983–85; law clerk to Hon. Loren A. Smith, Chief Judge of the U.S. Court of Federal Claims, 1985–87; trial attorney in the General Litigation Section of the Environment and Natural Resources Division of the United States Department of Justice, 1987–99; president, U.S. Court of Federal Claims Bar Association, 1999; attorney advisor, United States Department of Justice Office of Intelligence Policy and Review, 1999–2003; special master, U.S. Court of Federal Claims, 2003–05; member of the Bars of the Supreme Court of Pennsylvania and the District of Columbia Court of Appeals; appointed to the U.S. Court of Federal Claims by President George W. Bush on October 24, 2005, and entered duty on December 14, 2005. Designated chief judge by President Donald J. Trump on July 13, 2018.

THOMAS C. WHEELER, judge; born in Chicago, IL, March 18, 1948; married; two grown children; B.A., Gettysburg College, 1970; J.D., Georgetown University Law School, 1973; private practice in Washington, DC, 1973–2005; associate and partner, Pettit and Martin until 1995; partner, Piper and Marbury (later Piper Marbury Rudnick and Wolfe, and then DLA Piper Rudnick Gray Cary); member of the District of Columbia Bar; American Bar Association's Public Contracts and Litigation Sections; appointed to the U.S. Court of Federal Claims on October 24, 2005.

PATRICIA E. CAMPBELL-SMITH, judge; born in Baltimore, MD, 1966; B.S.E.E., Duke University, 1987; J.D., Tulane Law School, 1992; admitted to the Bar of Louisiana; judicial extern to Hon. John Minor Wisdom, U.S. Court of Appeals for the Fifth Circuit, 1991; law clerk to Hon. Martin L. C. Feldman, U.S. District Court for Eastern District of Louisiana, 1992–93; associate, Liskow and Lewis, 1993–96, 1997–98; law clerk to Hon. Sarah S. Vance (Chief Judge), U.S. District Court for Eastern District of Louisiana, 1996–97; senior law clerk to Hon. Emily C. Hewitt (Chief Judge), U.S. Court of Federal Claims, 1998–2005; special master, U.S. Court of Federal Claims, 2005–11; chief special master, U.S. Court of Federal Claims, 2011–13; appointed to the U.S. Court of Federal Claims by President Obama on September 19, 2013; chief judge from October 21, 2013-March 13, 2017.

ELAINE D. KAPLAN, judge; born in Brooklyn, New York, December 18, 1955; B.A., State University of New York at Binghamton, 1976; J.D., Georgetown University, 1979; Office of the Solicitor General, Department of Labor, 1979–83; Attorney, State and Local Legal Center, 1983–84; Attorney and Deputy General Counsel, National Treasury Employees Union, 1984–98; Special Counsel, Office of Special Counsel, 1998–03; Of Counsel, Bernabei and Katz, 2003–04; Senior Deputy General Counsel, National Treasury Employees Union, 2004–09; General Counsel, U.S. Office of Personnel Management, 2009–13; Acting Director, U.S. Office of Personnel Management, 2013; appointed to the U.S. Court of Federal Claims by President Barack Obama on September 17, 2013.

LYDIA KAY GRIGGSBY, judge; born in Baltimore, MD, January 16, 1968; educated at the Park School, Brooklandville, MD, 1980–86; B.A., University of Pennsylvania, 1990; J.D., Georgetown University Law Center, 1993; member, Bar of Maryland and Bar of the District of Columbia; private practice of law, DLA Piper, 1993–95; Trial Attorney, United States Department of Justice, Civil Division, Commercial Litigation Branch, 1995–98; Assistant United States Attorney, United States Attorney's Office for the District of Columbia, 1998–2004; Counsel, United States Senate Select Committee on Ethics, 2004–06; Privacy Counsel, United States Senate Committee on the Judiciary, 2006–08; Chief Counsel for Privacy and Information Policy, United States Senate Committee on the Judiciary 2008–14; appointed by President Obama to the U.S. Court of Federal Claims on December 5, 2014; entered duty on December 15, 2014.

RICHARD A. HERTLING, judge; confirmed by the Senate and sworn in as a judge of the United States Court of Federal Claims in June 2019. Born and raised in New York City, he graduated from Brown University and received his law degree from the University of Chicago Law School. He is admitted to practice in New York and the District of Columbia. Upon graduating from law school, Judge Hertling clerked for Judge Henry A. Politz of the United States Court of Appeals for the Fifth Circuit in 1985–86. Following his clerkship, he was hired through the Attorney General's Honors Program and served as a Trial Attorney in the Federal Programs Branch of the Civil Division of the U.S. Department of Justice, litigating constitutional and regulatory cases, from 1986 until January 1990. In January 1990, Judge Hertling began his Capitol Hill career, serving on the staff of the Senate Judiciary Committee as minority chief counsel of the Subcommittee on the Constitution and the Subcommittee on Technology and the Law, and as chief counsel of the Subcommittee on Terrorism, Technology and Government Information, while also serving as chief counsel to Senator Arlen Specter (R-PA). Subsequently, Judge Hertling became senior counsel to the Senate Governmental Affairs Committee, while also handling Judiciary Committee and other legal issues for its chairman, Senator Fred Thompson (R-TN). Following that position, he became chief of staff to newly elected Senator Peter Fitzgerald (R-IL), and then returned to the Governmental Affairs Committee as minority staff director. Upon the retirement of Senator Thompson, Judge Hertling served as deputy chief of staff and legislative director to newly elected Senator Lamar Alexander (R-TN). In July 2003, Judge Hertling was appointed Deputy Assistant Attorney General for Legal Policy at the Department of Justice and in 2005 was named the Principal Deputy Assistant Attorney General for Legal Policy. In 2007, he was appointed Acting Assistant Attorney General for Legislative Affairs at the Department of Justice. Judge Hertling was appointed minority deputy chief of staff and policy director of the House Judiciary Committee in 2008, becoming the committee's staff director and chief counsel in 2012. In 2013, Judge Hertling joined a prominent Washington law firm as of counsel in its public policy group and practiced at the firm until his appointment to the court.

RYAN T. HOLTE judge; confirmed by the United States Senate in June 2019 and sworn in as a judge on the United States Court of Federal Claims in July 2019. Prior to confirmation he served as the David L. Brennan Professor of Law and Director of the Center for Intellectual Property Law and Technology at The University of Akron School of Law (2017–19) and an assistant professor of law at Southern Illinois University School of Law (2013–17). He was the recipient of multiple research fellowships on patent law topics, including awards from the George Mason University School of Law and Case Western Reserve University School of Law. As an academic, Judge Holte taught a wide variety of courses, including all intellectual property subjects and property law. Judge Holte has written and presented widely on patent law subjects and empirical legal studies of Federal Circuit and district court patent law cases. His most recent articles were published in the Iowa Law Review (2019), George Mason Law Review (2018), and Washington Law Review (2017). In practice, Judge Holte served for six years as general counsel and partner of an electrical engineering technology company and is co-inventor of two patents related to Systems and Methods for Countering Satellite-Navigated Munitions (originally held under U.S. Army Secrecy Order until June 2016). Prior to entering academia, Judge Holte practiced as a litigation attorney at the Federal Trade Commission, an associate in the Intellectual Property Practice Group at Jones Day, and a patent prosecutor at Finnegan. Prior to practice, he served as a law clerk to Judge Stanley F. Birch, Jr. on the United States Court of Appeals for the Eleventh Circuit and as a law clerk to Judge Loren A. Smith on the United States Court of Federal Claims. While in practice, Judge Holte represented numerous pro bono clients on IP matters and served as lead court-appointed habeas corpus counsel in the United States Court of Appeals for the Sixth Circuit. Judge Holte also served in intellectual property bar leadership positions on the Atlanta IP Inn of Court (Executive Committee), and the State Bar of Georgia (IP Section Trademark Committee Chair). Before law practice, Judge Holte owned a car dealership in the San Francisco Bay Area specializing in biodiesel vehicles and worked as an engineer for Agilent Technologies/Hewlett Packard in Sonoma County, California. Judge Holte received his JD from the University of California Davis School of Law where he served as a staff editor of the *UC Davis Business Law Journal.* He received his BS, *magna cum laude*, in engineering from the California Maritime Academy where he was a First Class graduate of the Corps of Cadets Third Engineering Division and sailed as a U.S. Merchant Marine oiler. Judge Holte is the recipient of the 2018 California Maritime Academy Distinguished Alumnus award. Judge Holte is married and the proud father of two young children. He has been active for many years in various church and community organizations and his outside interests include classic car and truck restoration, motorcycle riding, and chasing after his kids.

DAVID AUSTIN TAPP, judge; confirmed on November 5, 2019 by the U.S. Senate as Judge of the U.S. Court of Federal Claims. Prior to confirmation, Judge Tapp served 15 years as Judge of the 28th Circuit and District of the Kentucky Court of Justice. He holds a Juris Doctorate from the University of Louisville Brandeis School of Law, a Master of Science from Chaminade University of Honolulu, and a Bachelor of Arts from Morehead State University. Judge Tapp is a frequent presenter and author on a wide variety of civil and criminal issues including court culture, judicial stress, court-targeted acts of violence, evidence, electronically stored information, and civil and criminal procedure. He previously served as a law enforcement officer, prosecutor, private counsel, and adjunct professor of law. Judge Tapp's efforts on a variety of justice-related issues have been well-recognized. In 2011, Judge Tapp received the "All Rise" Award from the National Association of Drug Court Professionals for his efforts related to funding issues for substance abuse treatment courts. Most recently, Judge Tapp's drug court team became one of only 15 drug courts (out of 2,700 worldwide) to receive the NADCP's Community Transformation Award for his team's continuing efforts to provide meaningful substance abuse treatment. Judge Tapp was also the lead judge for Kentucky's efforts to explore the use of extended-release injectable naltrexone as part of a comprehensive opiate treatment strategy. Judge Tapp currently serves as a policy advisor to the 2020 RX Drug and Heroin Abuse Summit, the nation's largest conference addressing opioid-related issues. Until his confirmation, he served on the U.S. Coordinating Council on Juvenile Justice and Delinquency Prevention which reports to the President and Congress through the U.S. Department of Justice and provides advice regarding programming and intervention strategies for the nation's justice-involved children. Judge Tapp previously served six years as Chairperson of Kentucky's Circuit Judges Education Committee where he directed the continuing education of all general jurisdiction and family court judges within Kentucky. He also acted as Kentucky's Co-Chairperson of the Judicial Child Fatality Task Force which focused on awareness issues surrounding fatal and near-fatal events involving children within the judicial and child protective system, and as a member of Kentucky's Criminal Justice Policy Assessment Council, a statewide group tasked with evaluation of the Commonwealth's justice practices.

MATTHEW H. SOLOMSON judge; confirmed by the U.S. Senate in January 2020, and entered on duty at the court on February 4, 2020. The son of a retired U.S. Army colonel, Judge Solomson lived in eight states before starting high school in Maryland, where he currently resides with his family. He completed a B.A. in Economics, cum laude, from Brandeis University. In 2002, Judge Solomson graduated, with honors and Order of the Coif, from the University of Maryland Francis King Carey School of Law, and earned an M.B.A. (with a concentration in accounting) from the University of Maryland Robert H. Smith School of Business. Judge Solomson is the author of *Court of Federal Claims: Jurisdiction, Practice, and Procedure*, a legal treatise first published by Bloomberg BNA in 2016. Prior to joining the court, Judge Solomson served as Chief Legal & Compliance Officer for an $11B federal contracting business unit of a Fortune 50 healthcare company. In that role, Judge Solomson managed a team of attorneys, compliance professionals, and internal auditors. He also previously led the government contracts practice group within the in-house law department of Booz Allen Hamilton, while serving as the principal government contracts counsel to the company's intelligence business unit. Judge Solomson's private practice experience includes having served as Counsel in the government contracts and litigation practice groups of Sidley Austin LLP, and as an Associate with Arnold & Porter LLP, both in Washington, DC. In addition to his private sector experience, Judge Solomson was a Trial Attorney with the Commercial Litigation Branch of the U.S. Department of Justice, where he represented a variety of military and civilian agencies as counsel of record in dozens of cases before the National Courts, which include the U.S. Court of Federal Claims, the U.S. Court of International Trade, and the U.S. Court of Appeals for the Federal Circuit. Following law school, Judge Solomson served as a law clerk to Judge Francis M. Allegra of the U.S. Court of Federal Claims. Since 2008, Judge Solomson has served as Adjunct Professor at the University of Maryland Francis King Carey School of Law, where he teaches government contracts law. He is a member of the Maryland and DC bars, and previously was an officer of the Court of Federal Claims Bar Association. Judge Solomson enjoys studying Talmud, playing tennis, and spending time at the beach with his family.

ELENI M. ROUMEL, judge; appointed Judge of the United States Court of Federal Claims on February 24, 2020. She previously served as the Deputy Counsel to Vice President Mike Pence from 2018–20. Prior to her tenure at the White House, she served from 2012–18 as Assistant General Counsel in the U.S. House of Representatives Office of General Counsel.

While serving in the House Office of General Counsel she advised and represented the U.S. House of Representatives, Members of Congress, and congressional staff in federal trial and appellate courts across the country. Judge Roumel previously was a partner with Nelson Mullins Riley & Scarborough, LLP, in Charleston, South Carolina, and before that practiced at Wilmer Cutler Pickering Hale and Dorr, LLP and Skadden Arps Slate Meagher & Flom, LLP in New York City. She also was an adjunct professor at the Charleston School of Law, where she taught intellectual property law. Judge Roumel served as a law clerk to the Honorable William H. Pauley III, United States District Judge for the Southern District of New York, from 2002–04. Judge Roumel has practiced before 26 different federal and state courts during her nearly 20 years of law practice. A native of Maryland, Judge Roumel received her J.D., *magna cum laude*, in 2000 from Tulane Law School, where she graduated Order of the Coif and was an editor of the Tulane Law Review. Judge Roumel also received her M.B.A. from Tulane University's A.B. Freeman School of Business in 2000. She earned her bachelor of arts degree, *cum laude*, from Wake Forest University in 1996.

SENIOR JUDGES

JOHN PAUL WIESE, senior judge; born in Brooklyn, NY, April 19, 1934; son of Gustav and Margaret Wiese; B.A., cum laude, Hobart College, 1962, Phi Beta Kappa; LL.B., University of Virginia School of Law, 1965; married to Alice Mary Donoghue, June, 1961; one son, John Patrick; served U.S. Army, 1957–59; law clerk: U.S. Court of Claims, trial division, 1965–66, and Judge Linton M. Collins, U.S. Court of Claims, appellate division, 1966–67; private practice in District of Columbia, 1967–74 (specializing in government contract litigation); trial judge, U.S. Court of Claims, 1974–82; admitted to the Bar of the District of Columbia, 1966; admitted to practice in the U.S. Supreme Court, the U.S. Court of Appeals for the Federal Circuit, the U.S. Court of Federal Claims; member: District of Columbia Bar Association and American Bar Association; designated in Federal Courts Improvement Act of 1982 as judge, U.S. Court of Federal Claims and reappointed by President Reagan to 15-year term on October 14, 1986.

LOREN A. SMITH, senior judge; born in Chicago, IL, 1944; married to Catherine Yore Smith; two sons; attended Northwestern University (BA 1966) and Northwestern University School of Law (JD 1969); admitted to practice Supreme Court of Illinois, federal courts in Washington, DC; consultant at Sidley & Austin, Chicago (1972–73); general attorney, Federal Communications Commission (1973), assistant to the special counsel to the president (1973–74); special assistant U.S. attorney for the District of Columbia (1974–75); professor of law, Delaware Law School (1976–84); deputy director of the Executive Branch Management Office of Presidential Transition (1980–81); chairman of the Administrative Conference of the United States (1981–1985); adjunct professor of law at George Mason University School of Law; Washington College of Law, American University; Georgetown University Law Center; Columbus School of Law, The Catholic University of America; nominated to the U.S. Court of Federal Claims by President Reagan on May 15, 1985; and assumed duties of the office on July 11, 1985; served as chief judge from January 14, 1986-July 11, 2000.

MARIAN BLANK HORN, senior judge; born in New York, NY, 1943; daughter of Werner P. and Mady R. Blank; married to Robert Jack Horn; three daughters; attended Fieldston School, New York, NY, Barnard College, Columbia University, and Fordham University School of Law; admitted to practice U.S. Supreme Court, 1973, Federal and State courts in New York, 1970, and Washington, DC, 1973; assistant district attorney, Deputy Chief Appeals Bureau, Bronx County, NY, 1969–72; attorney, Arent, Fox, Kintner, Plotkin and Kahn, 1972–73; adjunct professor of law, Washington College of Law, American University, 1973–76; litigation attorney, Federal Energy Administration, 1975–76; senior attorney, Office of General Counsel, Strategic Petroleum Reserve Branch, Department of Energy, 1976–79; deputy assistant general counsel for procurement and financial incentives, Department of Energy, 1979–81; deputy associate solicitor, Division of Surface Mining, Department of the Interior, 1981–83; associate solicitor, Division of General Law, Department of the Interior, 1983–85; principal deputy solicitor and acting solicitor, Department of Interior, 1985–86; adjunct professor of law, George Washington University National Law Center, 1991–present; Woodrow Wilson Visiting Fellow, 1994; assumed duties of judge, U.S. Court of Federal Claims in 1986 and confirmed for a second term in 2003.

ERIC G. BRUGGINK, senior judge; born in Kalidjati, Indonesia, September 11, 1949; naturalized U.S. citizen, 1961; married to Melinda Harris Bruggink; sons: John and David; B.A., cum laude (sociology), Auburn University, AL, 1971; M.A. (speech), 1972; J.D., University of Alabama, 1975; Hugo Black Scholar and Note and Comments Editor of Alabama

Law Review; member, Alabama State Bar and District of Columbia Bar; served as law clerk to chief judge Frank H. McFadden, Northern District of Alabama, 1975–76; associate, Hardwick, Hause and Segrest, Dothan, AL, 1976–77; assistant director, Alabama Law Institute, 1977–79; director, Office of Energy and Environmental Law, 1977–79; associate, Steiner, Crum and Baker, Montgomery, AL, 1979–82; Director, Office of Appeals Counsel, Merit Systems Protection Board, 1982–86; appointed to the U.S. Court of Federal Claims on April 15, 1986.

LYNN J. BUSH, senior judge; born in Little Rock, AR, December 30, 1948; daughter of John E. Bush III and Alice (Saville) Bush; one son, Brian Bush Ferguson; B.A., Antioch College, 1970, Thomas J. Watson Fellow; J.D., Georgetown University Law Center, 1976; admitted to the Arkansas Bar in 1976 and to the District of Columbia Bar in 1977; trial attorney, Commercial Litigation Branch, Civil Division, U.S. Department of Justice, 1976–87; senior trial attorney, Naval Facilities Engineering Command, Department of the Navy, 1987–89; counsel, Engineering Field Activity Chesapeake, Naval Facilities Engineering Command, Department of the Navy, 1989–96; administrative judge, U.S. Department of Housing and Urban Development Board of Contract Appeals, 1996–98; nominated by President Clinton to the U.S. Court of Federal Claims, June 22, 1998; and assumed duties of the office on October 26, 1998.

EDWARD J. DAMICH, senior judge; born in Pittsburgh, PA, June 19, 1948; son of John and Josephine (Lovrencic) Damich; A.B., St. Stephen's College, 1970; J.D., Catholic University, 1976; professor of law at Delaware School of Law of Widener University, 1976–84; served as a Law and Economics Fellow at Columbia University School of Law, where he earned his L.L.M. in 1983 and his J.S.D. in 1991; professor of law at George Mason University, 1984–98; appointed by President George H.W. Bush to be a Commissioner of the Copyright Royalty Tribunal, 1992–93; Chief Intellectual Property Counsel for the Senate Judiciary Committee, 1995–98; admitted to the Bar of the District of Columbia; member of the District of Columbia Bar Association, American Bar Association, Supreme Court of the United States, the Federal Circuit and Association litteraire et artistique internationale; president of the National Federation of Croatian Americans, 1994–95; appointed by President Clinton as judge, U.S. Court of Federal Claims, October 22, 1998; served as chief judge May 13, 2002 to March 11, 2009.

NANCY B. FIRESTONE, senior judge; born in Manchester, NH, October 17, 1951; B.A., Washington University, 1973; J.D., University of Missouri, Kansas City, 1977; one child; attorney, Appellate Section and Environmental Enforcement Section, U.S. Department of Justice, Washington, DC, 1977–84; assistant chief, Policy Legislation and Special Litigation, Environment and Natural Resources Division, Department of Justice, Washington, DC, 1984–85; Deputy Chief, Environmental Enforcement Section, Department of Justice, Washington, DC, 1985–89; associate deputy administrator, Environmental Protection Agency, Washington, DC, 1989–92; judge, Environmental Appeals Board, Environmental Protection Agency, Washington, DC, 1992–95; Deputy Assistant Attorney General, Environment and Natural Resources Division, Department of Justice, Washington, DC, 1995–98; adjunct professor, Georgetown University Law Center, 1985–present; appointed to the U.S. Court of Federal Claims by President Clinton on October 22, 1998.

CHARLES F. LETTOW, senior judge; born in Iowa Falls, IA, 1941; son of Carl F. and Catherine Lettow; B.S.Ch.E., Iowa State University, 1962; LL.B., Stanford University, 1968, Order of the Coif; M.A., Brown University, 2001; Note Editor, Stanford Law Review; children: Renee Burnett, Carl Frederick II, John Stangland, and Paul Vorbeck; served U.S. Army, 1963–65; law clerk to Judge Ben C. Duniway, U.S. Court of Appeals for the Ninth Circuit, 1968–69, and Chief Justice Warren E. Burger, Supreme Court of the United States, 1969–70; counsel, Council on Environmental Quality, Executive Office of the President, 1970–73; associate (1973–76) and partner (1976–2003), Cleary, Gottlieb, Steen and Hamilton, Washington, DC; admitted to practice before the U.S. Supreme Court, the U.S. Courts of Appeals for the D.C., Second, Third, Fourth, Fifth, Sixth, Eighth, Ninth, Tenth, and Federal Circuits, the U.S. District Courts for the District of Columbia, the Northern District of California, and the District of Maryland, and the U.S. Court of Federal Claims; member: American Law Institute, the American Bar Association, the D.C. Bar, the California State Bar, the Iowa State Bar Association, and the Maryland State Bar; nominated by President George W. Bush to the U.S. Court of Federal Claims in 2001 and confirmed and took office in 2003.

MARY ELLEN COSTER WILLIAMS, senior judge; born in Flushing, NY, April 3, 1953; married with two children; B.A. summa cum laude (Greek and Latin) and M.A. (Latin),

The Catholic University of America, 1974; J.D., Duke University, 1977; Editorial Board, Duke Law Journal, 1976–77; admitted to the District of Columbia Bar; associate, Fulbright and Jaworski, 1977–79; associate, Schnader, Harrison, Segal and Lewis, 1979–83; Assistant U.S. Attorney, Civil Division, District of Columbia, 1983–87; partner, Janis, Schuelke and Wechsler, 1987–89; administrative judge, General Services Board of Contract Appeals, March 1989-July 2003; secretary, District of Columbia Bar, 1988–89; Fellow, American Bar Foundation, elected 1985; Board of Directors, Bar Association of the District of Columbia, 1985–88; Chairman, Young Lawyers Section, Bar Association of the District of Columbia, 1985–86; Chair, Public Contract Law Section of the American Bar Association, 2002–03; Chair-Elect, Vice-Chair, Secretary, Council, 1995–2002; Delegate, Section of Public Contract Law, ABA House of Delegates, 2003–08 and 2014–present; ABA Board of Governors, 2010–13; Adjunct Professor, Johns Hopkins University, 2006–present; Adjunct Professor, The Catholic University of America Columbus School of Law, 2004–06; appointed to the U.S. Court of Federal Claims on July 21, 2003.

VICTOR JOHN WOLSKI, senior judge; born in New Brunswick, NJ, November 14, 1962; son of Vito and Eugenia Wolski; B.A., B.S., University of Pennsylvania, 1984; J.D., University of Virginia School of Law, 1991; married to Lisa Wolski; admitted to Supreme Court of the United States, 1995; California Supreme Court, 1992; Washington Supreme Court, 1994; Oregon Supreme Court, 1996; District of Columbia Court of Appeals, 2001; U.S. Court of Appeals for the Ninth Circuit, 1993; U.S. Court of Appeals for the Federal Circuit, 2001; U.S. District Court for the Eastern District of California, 1993; U.S. District Court for the Northern District of California, 1995; U.S. Court of Federal Claims, 2001; U.S. District Court for the District of Columbia, 2002; research assistant, Center for Strategic and International Studies, 1984–85; research associate, Institute for Political Economy, 1985–88; confidential assistant and speechwriter to the Secretary, U.S. Department of Agriculture, 1988; paralegal specialist, Office of the general counsel, U.S. Department of Energy, 1989; law clerk to Judge Vaughn R. Walker, U.S. District Court for the Northern District of California, 1991–92; attorney, Pacific Legal Foundation, 1992–97; general counsel, Sacramento County Republican Central Committee, 1995–97; counsel Senator Connie Mack, Vice-Chairman of the Joint Economic Committee, U.S. Congress, 1997–98; general counsel and chief tax adviser, Joint Economic Committee, U.S. Congress, 1999–2000; associate, Cooper, Carvin and Rosenthal, 2000–01; associate, Cooper and Kirk, 2001–03; associate editor, Public Contract Law Journal, 2006–present; appointed by President George W. Bush to the U.S. Court of Federal Claims on July 14, 2003.

UNITED STATES TAX COURT

400 Second Street, NW., Washington, DC 20217
phone (202) 521–0700

MAURICE B. FOLEY, chief judge; Born in Illinois; Received a Bachelor of Arts degree from Swarthmore College, a Juris Doctor from University of California, Berkeley School of Law, and a Masters of Law in Taxation from Georgetown University Law Center. Prior to the appointment to the Court was an attorney for the Legislation and Regulations Division of the Internal Revenue Service, Tax Counsel for the United States Senate Committee on Finance, and Deputy Tax Legislative Counsel in the U.S. Treasury's Office of Tax Policy. Appointed by President Clinton as Judge, United States Tax Court, on April 9, 1995, for a term ending April 8, 2010. Reappointed on November 25, 2011, for a term ending November 24, 2026. Elected as Chief Judge fora two-year term effective June 1, 2018.

JOSEPH H. GALE, judge; born in Virginia; A.B., Philosophy, Princeton University, Princeton, NJ, 1976; J.D., University of Virginia School of Law, Charlottesville, VA, Dillard Fellow, 1980; practiced law as an Associate Attorney, Dewey Ballantine, Washington, DC, and New York, 1980–83; Dickstein, Shapiro and Morin, Washington, DC, 1983–85; served as Tax Legislative Counsel for Senator Daniel Patrick Moynihan, (D-NY), 1985–88; Administrative Assistant and Tax Legislative Counsel, 1989; Chief Counsel, 1990–93; Chief Tax Counsel, Committee on Finance, U.S. Senate, 1993–95; minority Chief Tax Counsel, Senate Finance Committee, January 1995-July 1995; minority Staff Director and Chief Counsel, Senate Finance Committee, July 1995-January 1996; admitted to District of Columbia Bar; member of American Bar Association, Section of Taxation. Appointed by President Clinton as Judge, United States Tax Court, February 6, 1996, for a term ending February 5, 2011. Reappointed on October 18, 2011, for a term ending October 17, 2026.

MICHAEL B. THORNTON, judge; born in Mississippi; University of Southern Mississippi, B.S., in Accounting, summa cum laude, 1976; M.S., in Accounting, 1977; M.A., in English Literature, University of Tennessee, 1979; J.D., with distinction, Duke University School of Law, 1982; Order of the Coif, Duke Law Journal Editorial Board. Admitted to District of Columbia Bar, 1982. Served as Law Clerk to the Honorable Charles Clark, Chief Judge, U.S. Court of Appeals for the Fifth Circuit, 1983–84. Practiced law as an Associate Attorney, Sutherland, Asbill and Brennan, Washington, DC, 1982–83, and summer 1981; Miller and Chevalier, Chartered, Washington, DC, 1985–88. Served as Tax Counsel, U.S. House Committee on Ways and Means, 1988–94; Chief Minority Tax Counsel, U.S. House Committee on Ways and Means, January 1995; Attorney-Adviser, U.S. Treasury Department, February-April 1995; Deputy Tax Legislative Counsel in the Office of Tax Policy, United States Treasury Department, April 1995-February 1998. Recipient of Treasury Secretary's Annual Award, U.S. Department of the Treasury, 1997; Meritorious Service Award, U.S. Department of the Treasury, 1998. Appointed by President Clinton as Judge, United States Tax Court, on March 8, 1998, for a term ending March 7, 2013. Served as Chief Judge from June 1, 2012, to March 7, 2013. Reappointed by President Obama on August 7, 2013, for a term ending August 6, 2028, and served again as Chief Judge from August 7, 2013, until May 31, 2016.

DAVID GUSTAFSON, judge; born in Greenville, South Carolina; Bob Jones University, B.A. summa cum laude, 1978. Duke University School of Law, J.D. with distinction, 1981. Order of the Coif (1981). Executive Editor of the Duke Law Journal (1980–81). Admitted to the District of Columbia Bar, 1981. Associate at the law firm of Sutherland, Asbill and Brennan, in Washington, D.C., 1981–83. Trial Attorney (1983–89), Assistant Chief (1989–2005), and Chief (2005–08) in the Court of Federal Claims Section of the Tax Division in the U.S. Department of Justice; and Coordinator of Tax Shelter Litigation for the entire Tax Division (2002–06). Tax Division Outstanding Attorney Awards, 1985, 1989, 1997, 2001–05. Federal Bar Association's Younger Attorney Award, 1991. President of the Court of

Federal Claims Bar Association (2001). Appointed by President George W. Bush as Judge, United States Tax Court, on July 29, 2008, for a term ending July 29, 2023.

ELIZABETH CREWSON PARIS, judge; born in Oklahoma; B.S., University of Tulsa, 1980; J.D., University of Tulsa College of Law, 1987; LL.M., Taxation, University of Denver College of Law, 1993. Admitted to the Supreme Court of Oklahoma and U.S. District Court for the District of Oklahoma, 1988; U.S. Tax Court, U.S. Court of Federal Claims, U.S. Court of Appeals for the Tenth Circuit, 1993; Supreme Court of Colorado, 1994. Former partner, Brumley Bishop and Paris, 1992; Senior Associate, McKenna and Cueno, 1994; Tax Partner, Reinhart, Boerner, Van Deuren, Norris and Rieselbach, 1998. Tax Counsel to the United States Senate Finance Committee, 2000–08. Member of the American Bar Association, Section of Taxation and Real Property and Probate Sections, formerly served as Vice Chair to both Agriculture and Entity Selection Committees. Member of Colorado and Oklahoma Bar Associations. Recognized as Distinguished Alumnus by the University of Tulsa School of law. Author of numerous tax, estate planning, real property, agriculture articles and chapters. Former Adjunct Professor, Georgetown University Law Center, LL.M. Taxation Program, and University of Tulsa College of Law. Appointed by President George W. Bush as Judge, United States Tax Court, on July 30, 2008, for a term ending July 29, 2023.

RICHARD T. MORRISON, judge; born in Hutchinson, Kansas; B.A., B.S., University of Kansas, 1989; visiting student at Mansfield College, Oxford University, 1987–88; J.D., University of Chicago Law School, 1993; Member, University of Chicago Law Review; Associate Editor, University of Chicago Legal Forum; M.A., University of Chicago, 1994. Clerk to Judge Jerry E. Smith, United States Court of Appeals for the Fifth Circuit, 1993–94. Associate, Baker & McKenzie, Chicago, Illinois, 1994–96. Associate, Mayer Brown & Platt, Chicago, Illinois 1996–2001. Deputy Assistant Attorney General for Review and Appellate Matters, Tax Division, United States Department of Justice, from 2001–08 (except for term as Acting Assistant Attorney General, from July 2007 to January 2008). Appointed by President George W. Bush as Judge, United States Tax Court, on August 28, 2008, for a term ending August 27, 2023.

KATHLEEN KERRIGAN, judge; born in Springfield, Massachusetts; B.S., Boston College 1985; J.D., University of Notre Dame Law School, 1990. Admitted to Massachusetts Bar, 1991 and District Columbia Bar, 1992. Legislative Director for Congressman Richard E. Neal, Member of the Ways and Means Committee, 1990 to 1998. Associate and partner at Baker & Hostetler LLP, Washington, D.C. 1998–2005. Tax Counsel for Senator John F. Kerry, Member of Senate Finance Committee, 2005–12. Appointed by President Barack Obama as Judge United States Tax Court, on May 4, 2012, for a term ending on May 3, 2027.

RONALD L. BUCH, judge; Born in Flint, Michigan. Northwood Institute, B.B.A., 1987. Detroit College of Law, J.D. with Taxation Concentration, 1993. Capital University Law School, LL.M. in Taxation, 1994. Research Editor of the Detroit College of Law Review, 1992–93. Ohio Tax Review Fellow, 1993–94. Admitted to the bars of Michigan, inactive (1993), Ohio, inactive (1994), Florida (1994), and the District of Columbia (1995). Consultant at KPMG Washington National Tax (1995–97). Attorney-Advisor (1997–2000) and Senior Legal Counsel (2000–01) at the IRS Office of Chief Counsel. Associate (2001–05) and Partner (2005–09) at McKee Nelson LLP. Partner at Bingham McCutchen LLP (2009–13). James E. Markham Attorney of the Year Award, 1999. Chair of the DC Bar Tax Audits and Litigation Committee, 2006–08. Chair of the ABA Tax Section's Administrative Practice Committee, 2008–09. Appointed by President Barack H. Obama as Judge, United States Tax Court, on January 14, 2013, for a term ending January 13, 2028.

JOSEPH W. NEGA, judge; born in Illinois; DePaul University, B.S.C. in Accounting, 1981; DePaul University School of Law, J.D., 1984; Georgetown University School of Law, M.L.T., 1986. Admitted to the Illinois Bar 1984. On staff of the Joint Committee on Taxation of the United States Congress: Legislation Attorney, 1985–89; Legislation Counsel, 1989–2009; and Senior Legislation Counsel, 2009–13. Appointed by President Barack H. Obama as Judge, United States Tax Court, on September 4, 2013, for a term ending September 3, 2028.

CARY DOUGLAS PUGH, judge; born in Virginia; B.A., in Political Science and Russian, magna cum laude, Duke University, 1987; M.A., in Russian and East European Studies, Stanford University, 1988; J.D., University of Virginia School of Law, 1994; Order of the

Coif, Virginia Law Review Executive Editor. Admitted to Virginia State Bar, 1994, District of Columbia Bar, 1995, United States Supreme Court Bar, 1997. Served as Law Clerk to the Honorable Jackson L. Kiser, Chief Judge, U.S. District Court, Western District of Virginia, 1994–95. Practiced law as an Associate, Vinson & Elkins LLP, Washington, DC, 1995–99. Served as Minority Tax Counsel and Majority Tax Counsel, Committee on Finance, United States Senate, 1999–2002. Served as Special Counsel to the Chief Counsel, 2002–05. Recipient of the Chief Counsel's Award 2003. Practiced law as Counsel, Skadden, Arps, Slate, Meagher & Flom LLP, 2005–14. Member of American Bar Association, Section of Taxation; named John S. Nolan Tax Law Fellow, 2001–02; served as Chair, Tax Shelter Committee and Government Relations Committee and as Council Director. Fellow, American College of Tax Counsel. Former Adjunct Professor, Georgetown University Law Center, LL.M. Taxation Program. Appointed by President Obama as Judge, United States Tax Court, on December 16, 2014, for a term ending December 15, 2029.

TAMARA W. ASHFORD, judge; born in Boston, Massachusetts; B.A., in public policy studies, Duke University (1991); J.D., Vanderbilt University Law School (1994); LL.M., Master of Laws in Taxation, with an honors certificate of specialization in international tax, University of Miami School of Law (1997). Admitted to the Bars of North Carolina; District of Columbia; United States Tax Court; United States Courts of Appeals for the District of Columbia, First, Second, Fourth, Fifth, Sixth, Ninth and Tenth Circuits; United States Supreme Court. Served as Law Clerk to the Honorable John C. Martin, North Carolina Court of Appeals (1994–96). Practiced law as a Trial Attorney in the Appellate Section, Tax Division, United States Department of Justice (1997–2001). Practiced law as a Senior Associate, Miller & Chevalier, Chartered (2001–04). Served as Assistant to the Commissioner (2004–07) and U.S. Director for the Joint International Tax Shelter Information Centre/Senior Advisor to the Commissioner, Large and Mid-Size Business Division (2007–08) in the Internal Revenue Service. Recipient of the Sheldon S. Cohen National Outstanding Support to the Office of Chief Counsel Award (2006). Practiced law as Counsel, Dewey & LeBoeuf, LLP (2008–11). Recognized for Tax Controversy by the 2010 edition of The Legal 500. Served as Deputy Assistant Attorney General for Appellate and Review (2011–14), Principal Deputy Assistant Attorney General and Acting Deputy Assistant Attorney General for Policy and Planning (2013–14), and Acting Assistant Attorney General (June 2014-December 2014) in the Tax Division, United States Department of Justice. Named a 2012 Person of the Year by Tax Analysts. Appointed by President Obama as Judge, United States Tax Court, on December 19, 2014, for a term ending December 18, 2029.

ELIZABETH A. COPELAND, judge; born in Colorado; Bachelor of Business Administration from the University of Texas at Austin, cum laude, and Juris Doctor from the University of Texas School of Law. Certified Public Accountant (Texas, 1988); admitted to the State Bar of Texas (1992). Ernst & Whinney (1986–89); Law Clerk to Justice Cook of the Texas Supreme Court; Attorney-Adviser to Judge Mary Ann Cohen of the US Tax Court (1992–93); Adjunct Professor at Our Lady of the Lake University (1997–99); Partner with Clark Hill PLC. Recipient of the American Bar Association Section of Taxation's Janet Spragens Pro Bono Award (2009); Tax Person of the Year by Tax Analysts (2012); San Antonio Tax Lawyer of the Year (2011, 2017, 2018). Chair, State Bar of Texas Tax Section for the 2013–14 term. Appointed by President Trump as Judge, United States Tax Court, on October 12, 2018, for a term ending October 11, 2033.

COURTNEY D. JONES, judge; B.S., Hampton University, magna cum laude (2000), recipient of the President's Award for Exceptional Achievement; J.D., Harvard Law School (2004). Editor-in-Chief of the Harvard BlackLetter Law Journal. Admitted to the District of Columbia Bar. Practiced law as a Senior Attorney, Tax-Exempt and Government Entities Division, Office of Chief Counsel of the Internal Revenue Service (2011–19); as an Associate with Caplin & Drysdale, Chartered, Washington, D.C. (2008–11); and as an Associate with Bird, Loechl, Brittain & McCants, Atlanta, Georgia (2004–08). Served on the Board of Trustees of Hampton University (2015–18). Appointed by President Trump as Judge, United States Tax Court, on August 9, 2019, for a term ending in 2034.

EMIN TORO, judge; born in Albania; Received a Bachelor of Arts degree from Palm Beach Atlantic College and a Juris Doctor with highest honors from the University of North Carolina School of Law (Order of the Coif). Prior to appointment to the Court served as a Law Clerk to Judge Karen LeCraft Henderson of the U.S. Court of Appeals for the District of Columbia Circuit, served as a Law Clerk to Associate Justice Clarence Thomas of the Supreme Court of the United States, and was a Partner at Covington & Burling

LLP. Appointed by President Trump as Judge of the United States Tax Court; sworn in on October 18, 2019 for a term ending October 17, 2034.

PATRICK J. URDA, judge; born in Indiana; Received a Bachelor of Arts degree, summa cum laude, from the University of Notre Dame and a Juris Doctor from Harvard Law School. Prior to appointment to the Court practiced law with McDermott Will & Emery and with Maciorowski, Sackmann & Ulrich; served as a Law Clerk to Judge Daniel A. Manion of the U.S. Court of Appeals for the Seventh Circuit; and held several positions with the U.S. Department of Justice's Tax Division, including details as Counsel to the Deputy Assistant Attorney General for Appellate and Review and to the Criminal Division's Office of Overseas Prosecutorial Development Assistance and Training. Former Adjunct Professor of Law at American University Washington College of Law. Appointed by President Trump as Judge of the United States Tax Court; sworn in on September 27, 2018 for a term ending September 26, 2033.

TRAVIS A. GREAVES, judge; born in Texas. Received a Bachelor of Arts degree from the University of Tennessee; a Juris Doctor, cum laude, from South Texas College of Law; and a Masters of Law in Taxation, with distinction, from Georgetown University Law Center. Immediately before appointment served as Deputy Assistant Attorney General for Appellate and Review in the U.S. Department of Justice's Tax Division. Before joining the Department of Justice, was an attorney with Greaves Wu LLP; Caplin & Drysdale, Chartered; and Reed Smith, LLP. Previously served as Tax & Economic Policy Advisor for the Office of Governor Bobby Jindal of the State of Louisiana. Appointed by President Trump as Judge of the United States Tax Court and sworn in on March 9, 2020 for a term ending March 8, 2035.

SENIOR JUDGES

MARY ANN COHEN, senior judge; born in New Mexico; Attended public schools in Los Angeles, CA; B.S., University of California, at Los Angeles, 1964; J.D., University of Southern California School of Law, 1967. Practiced law in Los Angeles, member in law firm of Abbott & Cohen. American Bar Association, Section of Taxation, and Continuing Legal Education activities. Received Dana Latham Memorial Award from Los Angeles County Bar Association Taxation Section, May 30, 1997; Jules Ritholz Memorial Merit Award from ABA Tax Section Committee on Civil and Criminal Tax Penalties, 1999; and Joanne M. Garvey Award from California Bar Taxation Section on November 7, 2008. Appointed by President Reagan as Judge, United States Tax Court, on September 24, 1982, for a term ending September 23, 1997. Served as Chief Judge from June 1, 1996 to September 23, 1997. Reappointed on November 7, 1997, for a term ending November 6, 2012, and served again as Chief Judge from November 7, 1997, to May 31, 2000. Assumed senior status on October 1, 2012.

THOMAS B. WELLS, senior judge; born in Ohio; B.S., Miami University, Oxford, OH, 1967; J.D., Emory University Law School, Atlanta, GA, 1973; LL.M., Taxation, New York University Law School, New York, 1978. Supply Corps Officer, U.S. Naval Reserve, active duty 1967–70, Morocco and Vietnam, received Joint Service Commendation Medal. Admitted to practice law in Georgia; member of law firm of Graham and Wells, P.C.; County Attorney for Toombs County, GA; City Attorney, Vidalia, GA, until 1977; member of law firm of Hurt, Richardson, Garner, Todd and Cadenhead, Atlanta, until 1981; law firm of Shearer and Wells, P.C., until 1986; member of American Bar Association, Section of Taxation; State Bar of Georgia, member of Board of Governors; Board of Editors, Georgia State Bar Journal; member Atlanta Bar Association; Editor of the Atlanta Lawyer; active in various tax organizations, such as Atlanta Tax Forum, presently, Honorary Member; Director, Atlanta Estate Planning Council; Director, North Atlanta Tax Council; American College of Tax Counsel, Honorary Fellow; Emory Law Alumni Association's Distinguished Alumnus Award, 2001; Life Member, National Eagle Scout Association, Eagle Scout, 1960. Member, Metropolitan Club; Chevy Chase Club, Vidalia Kiwanis Club, President, recipient Distinguished President Award. Appointed by President Reagan as Judge, United States Tax Court, on October 13, 1986, for a term ending October 12, 2001. Reappointed by President Bush on October 10, 2001, for a term ending October 9, 2016. Served as Chief Judge from September 24, 1997, to November 6, 1997, and from June 1, 2000, to May 31, 2004. Assumed senior status on January 1, 2011.

ROBERT PAUL RUWE, senior judge; born in Ohio; Roger Bacon High School, St. Bernard, OH, 1959; Xavier University, Cincinnati, OH, 1963; J.D., Salmon P. Chase College of Law (graduated first in class), 1970; admitted to Ohio Bar, 1970; Special Agent, Intelligence Division, Internal Revenue Service, 1963–70; joined Office of Chief Counsel, Internal Revenue Service in 1970, and held the following positions: Trial Attorney (Indianapolis), Director, Criminal Tax Division, Deputy Associate Chief Counsel (Litigation), and Director, Tax Litigation Division. Appointed by President Reagan as Judge, United States Tax Court, on November 20, 1987, for a term ending November 19, 2002. Retired on November 20, 2002, but continues to perform judicial duties as Senior Judge on recall.

JOHN O. COLVIN, senior judge; born in Ohio; A.B., University of Missouri, 1968; J.D., 1971; LL.M., Taxation, Georgetown University Law Center, 1978. During college and law school, employed by Niedner, Niedner, Nack and Bodeux, St. Charles, MO; Missouri Attorney General John C. Danforth and Missouri State Representative Richard C. Marshall, Jefferson City, MO; and U.S. Senator Mark O. Hatfield and Congressman Thomas B. Curtis, Washington, DC. Admitted to practice law in Missouri, 1971, and District of Columbia, 1974. Office of the Chief Counsel, U.S. Coast Guard, Washington, D.C., 1971–75. Served as Tax Counsel, Senator Bob Packwood, 1975–84; Chief Counsel, 1985–87, and Chief Minority Counsel, 1987–88, U.S. Senate Finance Committee; Officer, Tax Section, Federal Bar Association, since 1978; Adjunct Professor of Law, Georgetown University Law Center, since 1987. Numerous civic and community activities. Appointed by President Reagan as Judge, United States Tax Court, on September 1, 1988, for a term ending August 31, 2003. Reappointed on August 12, 2004, for a term ending August 11, 2019. Elected as Chief Judge fortwo-year terms effective June 1, 2006, June 1, 2008, and June 1, 2010; and for the interim period March 8 through August 6, 2013. Retired on November 16, 2016, but continues to perform judicial duties as Senior Judge on recall.

JAMES S. HALPERN, senior judge; born in New York; Hackley School, Tarrytown, NY, 1963; Wharton School, B.S., University of Pennsylvania, 1967; J.D., University of Pennsylvania Law School, 1972; LL.M., Taxation, New York University Law School, 1975; Associate Attorney, Mudge, Rose, Guthrie and Alexander, New York City, 1972–74; assistant professor of law, Washington and Lee University, 1975–76; assistant professor of law, St. John's University, New York City, 1976–78, visiting professor, Law School, New York University, 1978–79; associate attorney, Roberts and Holland, New York City, 1979–80; Principal Technical Advisor, Assistant Commissioner (Technical) and Associate Chief Counsel (Technical), Internal Revenue Service, Washington, DC, 1980–83; partner, Baker and Hostetler, Washington, DC, 1983–90; Adjunct Professor, Law School, George Washington University, Washington, DC, 1984-present; Colonel, U.S. Army Reserve (retired). Appointed by President George H.W. Bush as Judge, United States Tax Court, on July 3, 1990, for a term ending July 2, 2005. Reappointed on November 2, 2005, for a term ending November 1, 2020. Retired on October 16, 2015, but continues to perform judicial duties as Senior Judge on recall.

JOSEPH ROBERT GOEKE, senior judge; born in Kentucky; B.S., cum laude, Xavier University, 1972; J.D., University of Kentucky, College of Law, 1975, Order of the Coif. Admitted to Illinois and Kentucky Bar, U.S. District Court for the Northern District of Illinois (Trial Bar), U.S. Court of Federal Claims. Trial Attorney, Chief Counsel's Office, Internal Revenue Service, New Orleans, LA, 1975–80. Senior Trial Attorney, Chief Counsel's Office, Internal Revenue Service, Cincinnati, OH, 1980–85. Special International Trial Attorney, Chief Counsel's Office, Internal Revenue Service, Cincinnati, OH, 1985–88. Partner, Law Firm of Mayer, Brown, Rowe & Maw, Chicago, IL, 1988 to 2003. Appointed by President Bush as Judge, United States Tax Court, on April 22, 2003, for a term ending April 21, 2018. Retired on April 21, 2018, but continues to perform judicial duties as Senior Judge on recall.

JUAN F. VASQUEZ, senior judge; born in Texas; Attended Fox Tech High School and San Antonio Junior College, A.D. (Data Processing); received B.B.A. (Accounting), University of Texas, Austin, 1972; attended State University of New York, Buffalo in 1st year law school, 1975; J.D., University of Houston Law Center, 1977; LL.M., Taxation, New York University Law School, 1978. Admitted to Texas Bar, 1977. Certified in Tax Law by Texas Board of Legal Specialization, 1984; Certified Public Accountant Certificate from Texas, 1976, and California, 1974. Admitted to United States District Court, Southern District of Texas, 1982, and Western District of Texas, 1985, U.S. Court of Appeals for the Fifth Circuit, 1982; private practice of tax law, in San Antonio, TX, 1987-April 1995; partner, Leighton, Hood and Vasquez, 1982–87, San Antonio, TX; Trial Attorney, Office of Chief Counsel, Internal Revenue Service, Houston, TX, 1978–82; accountant, Coopers and Lybrand,

Los Angeles, CA., 1972–74. Member of American Bar Association, Tax Section; Texas State Bar, Tax and Probate Section; Fellow of Texas and San Antonio Bar Foundations, Mexican American Bar Association (MABA) of San Antonio (Treasurer); Houston MABA; Texas MABA (Treasurer); National Association of Hispanic CPA's; San Antonio Chapter (founding member); College of State Bar of Texas, National Hispanic Bar Association; member of Greater Austin Tax Litigation Association; served on Austin Internal Revenue Service District Director's Practitioner Liaison Committee, 1990–91, chairman, 1991. Appointed by President Clinton as Judge, United States Tax Court, on May 1, 1995, for a term ending April 30, 2010. Reappointed by President Barack Obama on October 13, 2011, for a term ending October 12, 2026. Retired on June 24, 2018, but continues to perform judicial duties as Senior Judge on recall.

MARK V. HOLMES, senior judge; born in New York; B.A. Harvard College, 1979; J.D. University of Chicago Law School, 1983. Admitted to New York and District of Columbia Bars; U.S. Supreme Court; DC, Second, Fifth and Ninth Circuits; Southern and Eastern Districts of New York, Court of Federal Claims. Practiced in New York as an Associate, Cahill Gordon & Reindel, 1983–85; Sullivan & Cromwell, 1987–91; served as Clerk to the Hon. Alex Kozinski, Ninth Circuit, 1985–87; and in Washington as Counsel to Commissioners, United States International Trade Commission, 1991–96; Counsel, Miller & Chevalier, 1996–2001; Deputy Assistant Attorney General, Tax Division, 2001–03. Member, American Bar Association (Litigation and Tax Sections). Appointed by President George W. Bush as Judge, United States Tax Court, on June 30, 2003, for a term ending June 29, 2018.

L. PAIGE MARVEL, judge; born in Maryland; B.A., magna cum laude, 1971; College of Notre Dame, Baltimore, MD; J.D. with honors, University of Maryland School of Law, Baltimore, MD, 1974 (awarded Order of the Coif). Garbis & Schwait, P.A., associate 1974–76, and shareholder 1976–85; Garbis, Marvel & Junghans, P.A., shareholder 1985–86; Melnicove, Kaufman, Weiner, Smouse & Garbis, P.A., shareholder 1986–88; Venable, Baetjer & Howard L.L.P., partner, 1988–98. Member, American Bar Association, Section of Taxation, Vice-Chair, Committee Operations, 1993–95; Council Director, 1989–92; Chair, Court Procedure Committee, 1985–87; Maryland State Bar Association, Board of Governors, 1988–90, and 1996–98; Chair, Taxation Section, 1982–83. Fellow, American Bar Foundation; Fellow, Maryland Bar Foundation; Fellow and former Regent, 1996–98, American College of Tax Counsel; Member, American Law Institute; Advisor, ALI Restatement of Law Third-The Law Governing Lawyers 1988–98; University of Maryland Law School Board of Visitors, 1995–2001; Loyola/Notre Dame Library, Inc. Board of Trustees, 1996–2003; Co-editor, Procedure Department, The Journal of Taxation 1990–98. Member, Commissioner's Review Panel on IRS Integrity, 1989–91; Member and Chair, Procedure Subcommittee, Commission to Revise the Annotated Code of Maryland, (Tax Provisions), 1981–87; Member, Advisory Commission to the Maryland State Department of Economic and Community Development, 1978–81. Appointed by President Clinton as Judge, United States Tax Court, on April 6, 1998, for a term ending April 5, 2013. Reappointed by President Obama on December 3, 2014, for a term ending December 2, 2029. Served as Chief Judge from June 1, 2016 to May 31, 2018.

ALBERT G. LAUBER, judge; born in Bronxville, New York; Education: Yale College (B.A., summa cum laude, 1971); Clare College, Cambridge University (M.A., Classics, 1974); Yale Law School (J.D., 1977). Phi Beta Kappa; Woodrow Wilson Fellow; Mellon Fellow; Note Editor, Yale Law Journal; Moot Court Prize Argument; Cardozo Prize, Best Moot Court Brief. Employment: Law Clerk to Malcolm R. Wilkey, U.S. Court of Appeals for the D.C. Circuit (1977–78); Law Clerk to Justice Harry A. Blackmun, U.S. Supreme Court (1978–79). Associate Attorney, Caplin & Drysdale, Chtd., Washington D.C. (1979–83); Tax Assistant to the Solicitor General, U.S. Department of Justice (1983–86); Deputy Solicitor General, U.S. Department of Justice (1986–87); Partner, Caplin & Drysdale, Chtd., Washington, D.C. (1988–2005); Visiting Professor and Director, Graduate Tax & Securities Programs, Georgetown University Law Center (2006–13). Professorial Lecturer, George Washington University Law School (1983–84); Lecturer, University of Virginia Law School (1988–90); Adjunct Professor, Georgetown University Law Center (2013-present); Board of Trustees, The Studio Theatre (1993-present); Member, District of Columbia Alcoholic Beverage Control Board (2004–08). Admitted to the Bars of the District of Columbia (1978); U.S. Supreme Court (1983); U.S. Court of Appeals, D.C. Circuit (1983); U.S. Court of Appeals, Federal Circuit (1994); Connecticut (inactive). Member, American Bar Association, Section of Taxation. Appointed by President Barack H. Obama as Judge, United States Tax Court, on January 31, 2013, for a term ending January 30, 2028.

SPECIAL TRIAL JUDGES OF THE COURT

Lewis R. Carluzzo (Chief Special Trial Judge), Daniel A. Guy, Diana L. Leyden, Peter J. Panuthos.

COURT STAFF

Clerk.—Stephanie A. Servoss.
Deputy Clerk/Case Services Officer.—Jessica F. Marine.
Deputy Clerk/Chief Information Officer.—Michael C. McVicker.
General Counsel.—Patricia L. Levy.
Public Affairs Counsel.—Jennifer E. Siegel.
Legislative Counsel.—Anita Horn Rizek.
Court Administrator.—Fig Ruggieri.
Case Services Director.—Tina Buckler.
Facilities Management Director.—Byron L. Tindall.
Financial Management Director.—Joseph L. Hardy, Jr.
Human Resources Director.—Janet L. Boyer.
Librarian.—Nancy A. Ciliberti.
Reporter of Decisions.—Sheila A. Murphy.

UNITED STATES COURT OF APPEALS FOR THE ARMED FORCES[1]

450 E Street, NW., Washington, DC 20442–0001

phone (202) 761–1448, fax 761–4672

SCOTT W. STUCKY, chief judge; born in Hutchinson, KS; B.A. *summa cum laude*, Wichita State University, 1970; J.D., Harvard Law School, 1973; M.A., Trinity University, 1980; LL.M. with highest honors, George Washington University, 1983; Federal Executive Institute, 1988; Harvard Program for Senior Officials in National Security, 1990; National War College, 1993; admitted to bar, Kansas and District of Columbia; U.S. Air Force, judge advocate, 1973–78; U.S. Air Force Reserve, 1982–2003 (retired as colonel); married to Jean Elsie Seibert of Oxon Hill, MD, August 18, 1973; children: Mary-Clare and Joseph; private law practice, Washington, DC, 1978–82; branch chief, U.S. Nuclear Regulatory Commission, 1982–83; legislative counsel and principal legislative counsel, U.S. Air Force, 1983–96; General Counsel, Committee on Armed Services, U.S. Senate, 1996–2001 and 2003–06; Minority Counsel, 2001–03; National Commander-in-Chief, Military Order of the Loyal Legion of the United States, 1993–95; Board of Directors, Adoption Service Information Agency, 1998–2002 and 2004–07; Board of Directors, Omicron Delta Kappa Society, 2006–10; member, Federal Bar Association (Pentagon Chapter), Judge Advocates Association, the District of Columbia Bar; OPM LEGIS Fellow, office of Senator John Warner (R–VA), 1986–87; member and panel chairman, Air Force Board for Correction of Military Records, 1989–96; nominated by President George W. Bush to serve on the U.S. Court of Appeals for the Armed Forces on November 15, 2006; confirmed by the Senate, December 9, 2006; began service on December 20, 2006, and became Chief Judge on August 1, 2017.

MARGARET A. RYAN, judge; born in Chicago, IL; B.A. cum laude, Knox College; J.D., *summa cum laude*, University of Notre Dame Law School; recipient of the William T. Kirby Legal Writing Award and the Colonel William J. Hoynes Award for Outstanding Scholarship; active duty in the U.S. Marine Corps, 1986–99, serving as a communications officer, staff officer, company commander, platoon commander, and operations officer in units within the II and III Marine Expeditionary Forces and as a judge advocate in Okinawa, Japan, and Quantico, VA; also served as Aide de Camp to General Charles C. Krulak, the 31st Commandant of the Marine Corps; law clerk to the Honorable J. Michael Luttig, U.S. Court of Appeals for the Fourth Circuit, and law clerk to the Honorable Clarence Thomas, Associate Justice of the Supreme Court of the United States; litigation partner at the law firm of Bartlik Beck Herman Palenchar and Scott LLP and partner in litigation and appellate practices at the law firm Wiley Rein Fielding LLP; nominated by President George W. Bush to serve on the U.S. Court of Appeals for the Armed Forces on November 15, 2006; confirmed by the Senate on December 9, 2006; began service on December 20, 2006.

KEVIN A. OHLSON, judge; born in Sterling, MA; B.A., Washington and Jefferson College, 1982; four-year Army R.O.T.C. scholarship; Phi Beta Kappa; Air Assault training with the 101st Airborne Division at Fort Campbell, Kentucky, 1980; J.D., University of Virginia School of Law, 1985; Airborne training at Fort Benning, GA, 1986; administrative law officer and trial counsel at Fort Bragg, NC, 1986–89; federal prosecutor in Washington, D.C., 1989–97; volunteered to return to active duty and served as a legal advisor to the XVIII Airborne Corps Command Staff during Operation Desert Storm, 1990–91; awarded the Bronze Star; returned to the United States Attorney's Office for the District of Columbia and resumed duties as a federal prosecutor; Chief of Staff to the Deputy Attorney General, 1997–2001; member of the Board of Immigration Appeals, 2001–03; deputy director, and then the director, of the Executive Office for Immigration Review, 2003–09; Chief of Staff and Counselor to the Attorney General of the United States, 2009–2011; chief of the Professional Misconduct

[1] Prior to October 5, 1994, United States Court of Military Appeals.

Review Unit at the Department of Justice, 2011–13; nominated by the President and confirmed by the Senate to serve on the U.S. Court of Appeals for the Armed Forces; began service on November 1, 2013.

JOHN E. SPARKS, Jr., judge; born in Mount Holly, NJ; B.S., U.S. Naval Academy, 1976; J.D., University of Connecticut School of Law, 1986; Military Service, U.S. Navy 1971; U.S. Marine Corps 1976–98, as an Infantry Officer, and a variety of legal positions including military prosecutor, defense counsel, legal adviser to a naval hospital, military judge, Military Assistant and Special Counsel to the General Counsel of the Navy, and in the White House as a Deputy Legal Adviser to the National Security Council; Special Assistant for Civil Rights to the Secretary of Agriculture, 1998; Principal Deputy General Counsel of the Navy, 1999–2000; senior legal advisor to then Judge and later Chief Judge James E. Baker, United States Court of Appeals for the Armed Forces, 2000–15; nominated by President Barack Obama and confirmed by the Senate to serve on the United States Court of Appeals for the Armed Forces; began service on April 8, 2016.

GREGORY E. MAGGS, judge; born in Cambridge, MA; raised in Urbana, IL; son of Professor Peter B. Maggs and Dr. Barbara A. Maggs; married to Janice Calabresi of Barrington, RI, June 5, 1993; B.A. summa cum laude, Harvard College, 1985; J.D. magna cum laude, Harvard Law School, 1988; M.S.S. U.S. Army War College; law clerk to the late Honorable Joseph T. Sneed, Judge of the U.S. Court of Appeals for the Ninth Circuit, 1988–89; law clerk to the Honorable Anthony M. Kennedy, 1989–90, and the Honorable Clarence Thomas, 1991–92, Associate Justices of the Supreme Court of the United States; faculty member at The George Washington University Law School, 1993–2018, Interim Dean, 2010–11 and 2013–14, Senior Associate Dean for Academic Affairs, 2008–10, Co-director of the National Security and U.S. Foreign Relations LL.M. program, 2011–18, the Arthur Selwyn Miller Research Professor of Law, 2017–18; U.S. Army Reserve, Judge Advocate General's Corps, 1990–2018 (retired in the rank of colonel); special master for the Supreme Court of the United States, 2001–04; consultant to Independent Counsel Kenneth Starr in the Whitewater Investigation; assistant professor of law at the University of Texas at Austin School of Law, 1991–93; assistant to the late Judge Robert H. Bork in private practice and research, 1990–91; admitted to practice law in the District of Columbia, New York, and Massachusetts; nominated by President Donald J. Trump to serve on the U.S. Court of Appeals for the Armed Forces on September 28, 2018; confirmed by the Senate, February 1, 2018; began service on February 2, 2018.

SENIOR JUDGES

WALTER THOMPSON COX III, senior judge; born in Anderson, SC; son of Walter T. Cox and Mary Johnson Cox; married to Vicki Grubbs of Anderson, SC, February 8, 1963; children: Lisa and Walter; B.S., Clemson University, 1964; J.D., *cum laude*, University of South Carolina School of Law, 1967; graduated Defense Language Institute (German), 1969; graduated basic course, the Judge Advocate General's School, Charlottesville, VA, 1967; studied procurement law at that same school, 1968; active duty, U.S. Army judge advocate general's corps, 1964–72 (1964–67, excess leave to U.S.C. Law School); private law practice, 1973–78; elected resident judge, 10th Judicial Circuit, South Carolina, 1978–84; also served as acting associate justice of South Carolina supreme court, on the judicial council, on the circuit court advisory committee, and as a hearing officer of the judicial standards commission; member: bar of the Supreme Court of the United States; bar of the U.S. Court of Military Appeals; South Carolina Bar Association; Anderson County Bar Association; the American Bar Association; the South Carolina Trial Lawyers Association; the Federal Bar Association; and the Bar Association of the District of Columbia; has served as a member of the House of Delegates of the South Carolina Bar, and the Board of Commissioners on Grievances and Discipline; nominated by President Reagan, as judge of U.S. Court of Military Appeals, June 28, 1984, for a term of 15 years; confirmed by the Senate, July 26, 1984; sworn-in and officially assumed his duties on September 6, 1984; retired on September 30, 1999 and immediately assumed status of Senior Judge on October 1, 1999 and returned to full active service until September 19, 2000.

EUGENE R. SULLIVAN, senior judge; born in St. Louis, MO; son of Raymond V. and Rosemary K. Sullivan; married to Lis U. Johansen of Ribe, Denmark, June 18, 1966; children: Kim A. and Eugene R. II; B.S., U.S. Military Academy, West Point, 1964; J.D., Georgetown Law Center, Washington, DC, 1971; active duty with the U.S. Army, 1964–69; service included duty with the 3rd Armored Division in Germany, and the 4th Infantry Division in Vietnam; R&D assignments with the Army Aviation Systems Command; one year as an instructor at the Army Ranger School, Ft. Benning, GA; decorations include: Bronze Star, Air Medal, Army Commendation Medal, Ranger and Parachutist Badges, Air Force Exceptional Civilian Service Medal; following graduation from law school, clerked with U.S. Court of Appeals (8th Circuit), St. Louis, 1971–72; private law practice, Washington, DC, 1972–74; assistant special counsel, White House, 1974; trial attorney, U.S. Department of Justice, 1974–82; deputy general counsel, Department of the Air Force, 1982–84; general counsel of the Department of Air Force, 1984–86; Governor of Wake Island, 1984–86; presently serves on the Board of Governors for the West Point Society of the District of Columbia; the American Cancer Society (Montgomery County Chapter); nominated by President Reagan, as judge, U.S. Court of Military Appeals on February 25, 1986, and confirmed by the Senate on May 20, 1986, and assumed his office on May 27, 1986; President George H.W. Bush named him the chief judge of the U.S. Court of Military Appeals, effective October 1, 1990, a position he held for five years; he retired on September 30, 2001 and immediately assumed status of Senior Judge and returned to full active service until Sept. 30, 2002.

SUSAN J. CRAWFORD, senior judge; born in Pittsburgh, PA; daughter of William E. and Joan B. Crawford; married to Roger W. Higgins of Geneva, NY, September 8, 1979; one child, Kelley S. Higgins; B.A., Bucknell University, Pennsylvania, 1969; J.D., *cum laude*, Dean's Award, Arthur McClean Founder's Award, New England School of Law, Boston, MA, 1977; history teacher and coach of women's athletics, Radnor High School, Pennsylvania, 1969–74; associate, Burnett and Eiswert, Oakland, MD, 1977–79; Assistant State's Attorney, Garrett County, Maryland, 1978–80; partner, Burnett, Eiswert and Crawford, 1979–81; instructor, Garrett County Community College, 1979–81; deputy general counsel, 1981–83, and general counsel, Department of the Army, 1983–89; special counsel to Secretary of Defense, 1989; inspector general, Department of Defense, 1989–91; member: bar of the Supreme Court of the United States; bar of the U.S. Court of Military Appeals, Maryland Bar Association, District of Columbia Bar Association, American Bar Association, Federal Bar Association, and the Edward Bennett Williams American Inn of Court; member: board of trustees, 1989–present, and Corporation, 1992–present, of New England School of Law; board of trustees, 1988–present, Bucknell University; nominated by President Bush as judge, U.S. Court of Military Appeals, February 19, 1991, for a term of 15 years; confirmed by the Senate on November 14, 1991, sworn in and officially assumed her duties on November 19, 1991; on October 1, 1999, she became the Chief Judge for a term of five years; retired on September 30, 2006 and assumed the status of Senior Judge on October 1, 2006.

ANDREW S. EFFRON, senior judge; born in Stamford, CT; A.B., Harvard College, 1970; J.D., Harvard Law School, 1975; The Judge Advocate General's School, U.S. Army, 1976, 1983; legislative aide to the late Representative William A. Steiger, 1970–76 (two years full-time, the balance between school semesters); judge advocate, Office of the Staff Judge Advocate, Fort McClellan, Alabama, 1976–77; attorney-adviser, Office of the General Counsel, Department of Defense, 1977–87; Counsel, General Counsel, and Minority Counsel, Committee on Armed Services, U.S. Senate, 1987–96; nominated by President Clinton to serve on the U.S. Court of Appeals for the Armed Forces, June 21, 1996; confirmed by the Senate, July 12, 1996; took office on August 1, 1996; assumed his duties on August 1, 1996. On October 1, 2006, he became Chief Judge for a five year term, and immediately assumed status as Senior Judge on October 1, 2011.

JAMES E. BAKER, senior judge; born in New Haven, CT; education: BA., Yale University, 1982; J.D., Yale Law School, 1990; Attorney, Department of State, 1990–93; Counsel, President's Foreign Intelligence Advisory Board/Intelligence Oversight Board, 1993–94; Deputy Legal Advisor, National Security Council, 1994–97; Special Assistant to the President and Legal Advisor, National Security Council, 1997–2000; military service: U.S. Marine Corps and U.S. Marine Corp Reserve; nominated by President Clinton to serve on the U.S. Court of Appeals for the Armed Forces; began service on September 19, 2000, and became Chief Judge on October 1, 2011; became a Senior Judge on August 1, 2015.

CHARLES E. ERDMANN, senior judge; born in Great Falls, MT; B.A., Montana State University, 1972; J.D., University of Montana Law School, 1975; Air Force Judge Advocate Staff Officers Course, 1981; Air Command and Staff College, 1992; Air War College, 1994; Military Service: U.S. Marine Corps, 1967–70; Air National Guard, 1981–2002 (retired as a Colonel); Assistant Montana Attorney General, 1975–76; Chief Counsel, Montana State Auditor's Office, 1976–78; Chief Staff Attorney, Montana Attorney General's Office, Antitrust Bureau; Bureau Chief, Montana Medicaid Fraud Bureau, 1980–82; General Counsel, Montana School Boards Association, 1982–86; private practice of law, 1986–95; Associate Justice, Montana Supreme Court, 1995–97; Office of High Representative of Bosnia and Herzegovina, Judicial Reform Coordinator, 1998–99; Office of High Representative of Bosnia and

Herzegovina, Head of Human Rights and Rule of Law Department, 1999; Chairman and Chief Judge, Bosnian Election Court, 2000–01; Judicial Reform and International Law Consultant, 2001–02; appointed by President George W. Bush to serve on the U.S. Court of Appeals for the Armed Forces on October 9, 2002, commenced service on October 15, 2002 and became Chief Judge on August 1, 2015; became a Senior Judge on August 1, 2017.

OFFICERS OF THE U.S. COURT OF APPEALS FOR THE ARMED FORCES

Clerk of the Court.—Joseph R. Perlak.
Chief Deputy Clerk of the Court.—David A. Anderson.
Deputy Clerk for Opinions.—Patricia Mariani.
Court Executive.—Keith Roberts.
Librarian.—Agnes Kiang.

UNITED STATES COURT OF APPEALS FOR VETERANS CLAIMS

625 Indiana Avenue, NW., Suite 900, Washington, DC 20004
phone (202) 501–5970

MARGARET BARTLEY, chief judge; was nominated to the United States Court of Appeals for Veterans Claims by President Barack Obama on June 22, 2011, confirmed by the United States Senate on May 24, 2012, appointed by the President on June 25, 2012, and took the judicial oath on June 28, 2012, for a term of fifteen years. She became Chief Judge of the Veterans Court on December 4, 2019. For over 17 years prior to her appointment, Chief Judge Bartley served as a veterans advocate, working as staff attorney and then senior staff attorney for National Veterans Legal Services Program (NVLSP), a veterans service organization. In that capacity, she advised and trained staff and service officers for The American Legion, Military Order of the Purple Heart, Vietnam Veterans of America, and other veterans service organizations and State departments of veterans affairs, on issues related to veterans benefits and veterans preference in Federal employment. She also represented veterans and survivors of veterans in their pursuit of VA benefits before the USCAVC and the U.S. Court of Appeals for the Federal Circuit. From 2004 to 2012, Chief Judge Bartley served as editor of the NVLSP veterans' law quarterly, *The Veterans Advocate.* She also testified before Congress concerning federal agency failure to apply veterans preference laws and appeared on behalf of amici curiae in several significant veterans preference cases. From 2005 until her appointment to the bench, Chief Judge Bartley also served as Director of Outreach and Education for the Veterans Consortium Pro Bono Program. In that capacity, she organized nationwide training classes for lawyers interested in providing pro bono representation to veterans and their survivors before the USCAVC. Prior to her career as a veterans advocate, Chief Judge Bartley served as a judicial law clerk to the late Judge Jonathan R. Steinberg of the USCAVC. Chief Judge Bartley earned a Bachelor of Arts degree, cum laude, from Pennsylvania State University in 1981 and a juris doctor degree, cum laude, from the American University Washington College of Law in 1993. Aside from her many articles on veterans law published in *The Veterans Advocate*, Chief Judge Bartley is co-author, co-editor, or contributing author of several other articles and publications, including the *Veterans Benefits Manual* (LexisNexis) (co-author 1999–2010, co-editor 2011–12); *American Veterans' and Servicemembers' Survival Guide* (Veterans for America, 2008) (contributing author); *VA Benefits for Low-Income Veterans* (Clearinghouse Review, Sept–Oct 2006) (co-author); *VA's Obligations Toward Claimants: Analysis of the Veterans Claims Assistance Act of 2000* (Clearinghouse Review, July–August 2001) (co-author); *The Elderlaw Portfolio Series: Veterans Benefits for the Elderly* (Little, Brown and Company, 1996) (co-author); and *Consideration of Pain and Other Factors in Rating Disabilities* (Clearinghouse Review, July-August 1996) (co-author).

CORAL WONG-PIETSCH, judge; born in Waterloo, IA, Judge Pietsch has a distinguished career in public service, both in the military and as a civilian. She was commissioned in the U.S. Army Judge Advocate General's Corps and served six years on active duty. Judge Pietsch continued her service in the U.S. Army Reserve and rose to the rank of Brigadier General. She became the first woman to be promoted to the rank of Brigadier General in the U.S. Army Judge Advocate General's Corps and the first woman of Asian ancestry to be promoted to Brigadier General in the Army. Until her appointment to the bench, Judge Pietsch held the position of Senior Attorney and Special Assistant at Headquarters, U.S. Army Pacific located in Honolulu, Hawaii. In this position, she provided and managed legal services in support of the U.S. Army Pacific's mission to train Army Forces for military operations and peacetime engagements aimed at promoting regional stability. As part of the 2007 "surge" in Iraq, Judge Pietsch volunteered as a Department of Defense civilian to deploy to Iraq for a year, where she was seconded to the U.S. Department of State to serve as the Deputy Rule of Law Coordinator for the Baghdad Provincial Reconstruction Team. During her deployment to Iraq, Judge Pietsch assisted with numerous civil society projects involving a variety of Rule of Law partners, including the Iraqi Jurist Union, Iraqi

Bar Association, law schools, and international rights, women's rights, and human rights organizations. She evaluated and sought funding for numerous projects aimed at building capacity within the Iraqi legal community to include the establishment, in close collaboration with the Iraqi Bar Association, of a Legal Aid Clinic at one of Iraq's largest detention facilities. In 2006 Judge Pietsch was appointed by the Governor of Hawaii to the Hawaii Civil Rights Commission where she served for seven years. Shortly after the appointment, the Governor selected Judge Pietsch as its Chair. Earlier in her civilian legal career, Judge Pietsch had been appointed a Deputy Attorney General for the State of Hawaii, advising the State Department of Health, State Department of Agriculture, and the State Criminal History Records Division. Judge Pietsch's academic degrees include a bachelor of arts, master of arts, and a juris doctor degree. She was also a Senior Executive Fellow at the Harvard University Kennedy School of Government, is a graduate of the Defense Leadership and Management Program, and a graduate of the Army War College. Her awards and decorations include the Distinguished Service Medal, Legion of Merit, Meritorious Service Medal, Joint Service Commendation Medal, Decoration for Exceptional Civilian Service, the Meritorious Civilian Service Medal, Superior Civilian Performance Medal, and the Global War on Terrorism Medal. She has been the recipient of the Organization of Chinese Americans Pioneer Award, the Hawaii Women Lawyers Attorney of the Year Award, the Honolulu YWCA Achievement in Leadership Award, the Catholic University Alumni Achievement Award, the Federal Executive Board Award for Excellence, the U.S. Army Pacific Community Service Award and recognized for lifetime accomplishments by the Women Veterans Igniting the Spirit of Entrepreneurship. Judge Pietsch is admitted to the bars of the United States Supreme Court, the Ninth Circuit Court of Appeals, U.S. District Court of the District of Hawaii, State Bar of Hawaii, State Bar of Iowa, and the United States Court of Appeals for the Armed Forces; nominated by President Barack Obama and subsequently appointed a Judge of the U.S. Court of Appeals for Veterans Claims on May 24, 2012 and sworn in June 2012.

WILLIAM S. GREENBERG, judge; Judge Greenberg was a partner of McCarter and English, LLP. He initially joined the firm as an associate following a judicial clerkship in 1968, then returned as a partner in 1993. The majority of his career has involved litigation in Federal and state courts. Judge Greenberg had been a Certified Civil Trial Attorney by the Supreme Court of New Jersey since 1983. He served as Chairman of the Judicial and Prosecutorial Appointments Committee of the New Jersey State Bar Association, which considers all candidates to be a judge or prosecutor submitted by the Governor of New Jersey. He was President of the Association of Trial Lawyers of America, New Jersey, (The New Jersey Association for Justice) and has served as Trustee of the New Jersey State Bar Association and of the New Jersey State Bar Foundation. He also served as a member of the New Jersey Supreme Court Committee on the Admission of Foreign Attorneys. He established and chaired the New Jersey State Bar Association (public service/pro bono) program of military legal assistance for members of the Reserve Components called to active duty after September 11, 2001. He was a member of the New Jersey Supreme Court Civil Practice Committee. With the approval of the Secretary of Defense, on the recommendation of the White House, Judge Greenberg became Chairman of the Reserve Forces Policy Board in 2009, a Board established by the Secretary of Defense in 1951 and by Act of Congress in 1952. On July 26, 2011, Judge Greenberg was awarded the Secretary of Defense Medal for Outstanding Public Service, the second highest civilian award in the Defense Department, at a public ceremony in the Pentagon, and completed his term in August 2011. In 2006 his *Civil Trial Handbook*, Volume 47 of the *New Jersey Practice Series*, was published by Thomson/West. A special 20th anniversary issue was published in 2009, to commemorate the 1989 publication of its predecessor, *Trial Handbook for New Jersey Lawyers*. A retired Brigadier General, he served as a member of the New Jersey World War II Memorial Commission. In June 2009 he received the highest honor granted by the New Jersey State Bar Foundation, its medal of honor for his work in establishing the military legal assistance program, and especially in his public service representation of soldiers at Walter Reed Army Medical Center during their Physician Disability Hearings. His article in the June 2007 issue of *New Jersey Lawyer Magazine* describes the program in detail. He has served as special litigation counsel to the Adjutants General Association of the United States and was special litigation counsel *pro bono* to the National Guard Association of the United States. Judge Greenberg was a Commissioner of the New Jersey State Commission of Investigation. He also served as Assistant Counsel to the Governor of New Jersey and as Commissioner of the New Jersey State Scholarship Commission. Professor Greenberg served as the first Adjunct Professor of Military Law at the Seton Hall University School of Law. He was chosen the New Jersey Lawyer of the Year for 2009 by the *New Jersey Law Journal*. He received the Distinguished Alumnus Award from the Johns Hopkins University in 2010, and the Rutgers Law School Public Service Award in 2010 for his work in developing and leading the efforts to represent wounded and injured soldiers at Walter Reed. Judge Greenberg is admitted in New Jersey, New York, and the District of Columbia. He is a member of the bar of the Supreme Court of the United States, and of the Third, Fourth, and Federal Circuits, the Southern District of New York, and the United States Court of Appeals for the Armed Forces. Judge Greenberg is a graduate of the Johns Hopkins University (A.B., 1964) and Rutgers University Law School (J.D., 1967). He is married to the former Betty Kaufmann Wolf of Pittsburgh. They have three children, Katherine of New York, Anthony of Baltimore, and Elizabeth of New York; nominated to the United States Court of Appeals for Veterans Claims by President Barack Obama on November 15, 2012, confirmed by the United States Senate on December 21, 2012, appointed by the President on December 27, 2012, and took the judicial oath on December 28, 2012, for a term of fifteen years.

MICHAEL P. ALLEN, judge; Judge Allen was nominated by the President of the United States in June 2017. He was confirmed by the United States Senate, and appointed a Judge of the United States Court of Appeals for Veterans Claims in August 2017. United States District Judge Elizabeth Kovachevich of the Middle District of Florida administered the judicial oath to Judge Allen on August 11, 2017. For 16 years before his judicial appointment, Judge Allen was a tenured full professor of law at Stetson University College of Law in Gulfport, Florida. He was also the director of Stetson's Veterans Law Institute, and he spent four years as the College of Law's associate dean. Judge Allen also served as a visiting professor of law at the University of Illinois College of Law. Before entering teaching, Judge Allen practiced law for nine years in the litigation department of the Boston-based international law firm Ropes & Gray. Judge Allen graduated summa cum laude from the University of Rochester earning bachelor's degrees in American history and political science. He received his juris doctor from Columbia Law School, where he was a Harlan Fiske Stone Scholar during his final two years. As a professor, Judge Allen taught courses in constitutional law, civil procedure, federal courts, remedies, and veterans' benefits law. He has been a prolific author, co-writing two books and more than 25 articles and essays. Judge Allen also received numerous awards for his scholarship and teaching including the Stetson University Award for Excellence in Scholarship, the Brown-Dickerson Award for Excellence in Scholarship, the Stetson University Award for Excellence in Teaching, and the Stetson University Award for Excellence in Professionalism and Career Development. He also received the Stetson's Golden Apple Award for teaching and was twice named the best all-around professor. Judge Allen was also a frequent speaker at community and professional groups while in legal education. Among his speaking engagements were featured roles at the judicial conferences of the Court of Appeals for Veterans Claims and the United States Court of Appeals for the Federal Circuit. In addition, Judge Allen testified before the Veterans' Affairs Committees of both the United States Senate and the United States House of Representatives. Before taking the bench, Judge Allen was active in professional associations. He served on the Board of Trustees of the Southeastern Association of Law Schools and was the Chair of the American Association of Law Schools' sections on Remedies and New Law Teachers. He is also active in his synagogue where, along with his wife, he received the Shofar Award for community service. Judge Allen is married to Debra Brown Allen and has two sons, Ben and Noah.

AMANDA L. MEREDITH, judge; Judge Meredith was nominated by the President of the United States in June 2017. She subsequently was confirmed by the United States Senate and appointed a Judge of the United States Court of Appeals for Veterans Claims in August 2017. For more than 12 years prior to her appointment, Judge Meredith worked for the Republican staff of the United States Senate Committee on Veterans' Affairs. Most recently, she served from 2015 to 2017 as the Deputy Staff Director and General Counsel for Chairman Johnny Isakson. She served as General Counsel from 2008 to 2015 and as Benefits Counsel from 2005 to 2008 under Ranking Member Richard Burr and Chairman/Ranking Member Larry Craig. During this time, she was responsible for legislative and oversight activities regarding a wide range of veterans' issues and assisted Members of Congress in enacting numerous laws to help improve the benefits and services for our nation's veterans. Prior to joining the staff of the Committee on Veterans' Affairs, Judge Meredith worked for the United States Court of Appeals for Veterans Claims for more than seven years. While at the Court, she served from 2004 to 2005 as the Director of the Court's Task Force for Backlog Reduction, a team of experienced attorneys dedicated to reducing the inventory of pending appeals. From 2000 to 2004, she was the Executive Attorney to Chief Judge Kenneth Kramer, serving as the principal legal advisor to the Chief Judge regarding all judicial functions; supervising the chambers law clerks; and managing the chambers caseload. She served from 1997 to 2000 as a judicial law clerk to Judge Kramer. Judge Meredith graduated summa cum laude from the University at Buffalo with a Bachelor of Science degree in accounting and graduated magna cum laude from the University at Buffalo Law School, where she was a member of the Buffalo Law Review.

JOSEPH L. TOTH, judge; Judge Toth was nominated by the President of the United States in June 2017. He was subsequently confirmed by the United States Senate and was appointed a Judge of the United States Court of Appeals for Veterans Claims in August 2017. Judge Toth is a veteran of the Judge Advocate General (JAG) Corps of the United States Navy, where he served as Senior Defense Counsel in Pearl Harbor, Hawaii, and provided legal assistance to veterans, service members, and their families. In 2011, Judge Toth was deployed to the Zhari district of Afghanistan where he served as a Field Officer for the Rule of Law Field Force Afghanistan (ROLFF-A) and was stationed with the Army's 10th Mountain Division. He received the Joint Service Commendation Medal for his service in Afghanistan. After leaving active duty, Judge Toth served as Associate Federal Defender in Milwaukee, Wisconsin, with a focus on appellate litigation and motions practice. Judge Toth has served on or appeared before several federal and military courts, including the United States Court of Appeals for the Seventh Circuit and the United States Court of Appeals for the Fourth Circuit. Judge Toth clerked for Judge Daniel A. Manion of the United States Court of Appeals for the Seventh Circuit and Judge Robert J. Conrad of the United States District Court for the Western District of North Carolina. Additionally, he worked as an Associate Counsel at Drinker Biddle & Reath, LLP in the commercial litigation group. Judge Toth received his Bachelor of Arts degree from the University of Chicago and his juris doctor from the Ave Maria School of Law, where he was the managing editor of the Ave Maria Law Review.

JOSEPH L. FALVEY, Jr., judge; Judge Falvey was nominated by President Donald J. Trump, confirmed by the Senate, and appointed a Judge of the United States Court of Appeals for Veterans Claims in May 2018. Before his judicial appointment, Judge Falvey was the District Counsel, Detroit District, U.S. Army Corps of Engineers. As District Counsel, Judge Falvey supervised the District legal staff and was responsible for resolving issues related to statutory and regulatory compliance, government contracting and fiscal law, labor and employment law, environmental law, claims, real property, standards of conduct/ethics, procurement fraud, and litigation. Previously, Judge Falvey served as an Assistant United States Attorney, in the United States Attorney's Office for the Eastern District of Michigan. As a member of the National Security Unit, he was responsible for investigating and prosecuting matters involving national security including matters involving individuals and organizations that engage in foreign counter-intelligence, espionage, and those who plan, financially support, or carry out international and domestic terrorist activities. Before joining the United States Attorney's Office, Judge Falvey was a Professor of Law at Ave Maria School of Law from 1999 to 2007 and the University of Detroit School of Law from 1994 to 1998, where he taught evidence, trial advocacy, military law, national security law, and criminal law and procedure. Judge Falvey is also a retired Marine Corps officer who began his military career as an Armor Officer in 1981 and served as a Tank Platoon Commander, Battalion Adjutant, and Anti-Tank (TOW) Company Executive Officer. From 1984 to 1987, he attended law school through the Marine Corps's Funded Legal Education Program. Certified as a Judge Advocate in 1987, Judge Falvey was initially assigned to Camp Pendleton, California, where he served as a prosecutor or defense counsel in more than 250 courts-martial. He also served as the Senior Judge Advocate for the 11th Marine Expeditionary Unit (Special Operations Capable). In 1990, Judge Falvey attended The Judge Advocate General's School of the Army, and he was subsequently assigned as the Deputy Head, Military Law Branch, Judge Advocate Division, Headquarters Marine Corps. In 1994, Judge Falvey left active duty and continued to serve in the U. S. Marine Corps Reserve. From 1994 to 1998, Judge Falvey was a Special Courts-Martial Judge and presided over more than 100 courts-martial. In 1998, he was assigned as an Assistant Staff Judge Advocate for Operational Law at U.S. Central Command, and he was mobilized in support of Operation Enduring Freedom in the aftermath of the 9/11 terrorist attacks. In this capacity, he worked closely with various agencies of the U.S. Government on matters related to the Global War on Terrorism and he deployed to Afghanistan in 2002. Judge Falvey subsequently served as an Appellate Judge for the U.S. Navy-Marine Corps Court of Criminal Appeals. From 2008 to 2010, Judge Falvey served as the Commanding Officer, Marine Forces Reserve, Legal Services Support Section. Judge Falvey retired in 2011 having attained the rank of Colonel. His decorations include the Legion of Merit (with star), Defense Meritorious Service Medal, Meritorious Service Medal, Navy-Marine Corps Commendation Medal, Joint Service Achievement Medal, and Navy-Marine Corps Achievement Medal. Judge Falvey was selected as both the ABA Outstanding Young Military Lawyer (1990) and the Judge Advocate Association Outstanding Career Judge Advocate (2011). Judge Falvey holds a Bachelor of Arts in economics from the University of Notre Dame, a juris doctor, cum laude, from Notre Dame Law School, and a master of laws, Distinguished Graduate, from The Judge Advocate General's School. Judge Falvey and his wife, Anne, have nine children and they are licensed foster parents who have opened their home to more than a dozen abused and neglected children.

OFFICERS OF THE U.S. COURT OF APPEALS
FOR VETERANS CLAIMS

Clerk of the Court.—Gregory O. Block, 501–5970.
Chief Deputy Clerk Operations Manager.—Anne P. Stygles.
Counsel to the Clerk.—Cary P. Sklar.
Senior Staff Attorney, Central Legal Staff.—Cynthia Brandon-Arnold.
Deputy Executive Officer.—Patrick H. Barnwell.
Librarian.—Allison Fentress.

UNITED STATES JUDICIAL PANEL ON MULTIDISTRICT LITIGATION

Thurgood Marshall Federal Judiciary Building

One Columbus Circle, NE., Room G–255, North Lobby, Washington, DC 20002

phone (202) 502–2800, fax 502–2888

(National jurisdiction to centralize related cases pending in multiple circuits and districts under 28 U.S.C. §§ 1407 & 2112)

Chairman.—Karen K. Caldwell, U.S. District Judge, Eastern District of Kentucky.

Judges:

Ellen Segal Huvelle, U.S. District Judge, District of Columbia.
R. David Proctor, U.S. District Judge, Northern District of Alabama.
Catherine D. Perry, U.S. District Judge, Eastern District of Missouri.
Nathaniel M. Gorton, U.S. District Judge, District of Massachusetts.
Matthew F. Kennelly, U.S. District Judge, Northern District of Illinois.
David C. Norton, U.S. District Judge, District of South Carolina.

Panel Executive.—Thomasenia P. Duncan.

Clerk.—John W. Nichols.

ADMINISTRATIVE OFFICE OF THE UNITED STATES COURTS

Thurgood Marshall Federal Judiciary Building

One Columbus Circle, NE., Washington, DC 20544

phone (202) 502–2600

Director.—James C. Duff, 502–3000.
Deputy Director.—Lee Ann Bennett, 502–3015.
Chief of Staff.—Brian Lynch, 502–1300.
Judicial Integrity Officer, Office of Judicial Integrity.—Jill B. Langley (303) 335–2962.
Audit Officer, Office of Audit.—Veleda T. Henderson, 502–1000.
Fair Employment Practices Officer, Office of Fair Employment Practices.—Amaal Scroggins (acting), 502–3080.
General Counsel, Office of the General Counsel.—Sheryl L. Walter, 502–1100.
Deputy General Counsel.—William E. Meyers, 502–1100.
Ethics Staff.—Sheryl L. Walter, 502–1100.
Chief, Rules Committee Support Staff.—Rebecca Womeldorf, 502–1820.
Judicial Conference Secretariat Officer, Judicial Conference Secretariat.—Katherine Hord Simon, 502–2400.
Public Affairs Officer, Office of Public Affairs.—David A. Sellers, 502–2600.
Legislative Affairs Officer, Office of Legislative Affairs.—David Best, 502–1700.
Deputy Legislative Affairs Officer.—Peter Owen, 502–1700.
Chief, Defender Services Office.—Cait T. Clarke, 502–3030.
Associate Director, Department of Administrative Services.—James R. Baugher, 502–2000.
Chief of Staff.—Michael Culver, 502–2000.
Chief:
Administrative Systems Office.—Joseph W. Bossi, 502–2200.
Facilities and Security Office.—Melanie F. Gilbert, 502–1200.
Finance and Procurement Office.—Michael Milby, 502–2000.
Financial Liaison and Analysis Staff.—Edward O'Kane, 502–2000.
Judiciary Budget Officer, Budget Division.—Kevin A. Lee (acting), 502–2100.
Judiciary Procurement Executive, Procurement Division.—Francis Sullivan, 502–1330.
Human Resources Officer, Human Resources Office.—Cindy Roth, 502–1170.
Associate Director, Department of Program Services.—Mary Louise Mitterhoff, 502–3500.
Chief of Staff.—Leeann Yufanyi, 502–3500.
Chief:
Case Management Systems Office.—Ronald E. Blankenship, 502–2500.
Court Services Office.—Robert Lowney, 502–1500.
Judiciary Data and Analysis Office.—Gary Yakimov, 502–3900.
Judicial Services Office.—Michele E. Reed, 502–1800.
Probation and Pretrial Services Office.—John J. Fitzgerald, 502–1600.
Associate Director, Department of Technology Services.—Joseph R. Peters, Jr., 502–2300.
Chief of Staff.—Elena Simms, 502–2300.
Chief:
AO Technology Office.—John C. Chang, 502–2830.
Cloud Hosting and Networks Office.—Roch J. Turco (acting), 502–2377.
Enterprise Operations Office.—Joann H. Swanson (acting), 502–2640.
IT Security Office.—Bethany De Lude, 502–2350.
Systems and Development and Support Office.—Constance P. Porzucek (acting), 502–2700.
Technology Solutions Office.—Prabhjot Bajwa, 502–2730.

FEDERAL JUDICIAL CENTER

One Columbus Circle, NE., Washington, DC 20002–8003

phone (202) 502–4160

Director.—John S. Cooke, 502–4060, fax 502–4099.
Deputy Director.—Clara Altman, 502–4162, fax 502–4099.
Director of:
Editorial and Information Services Office.—Michelle Slavin, 502–4263, fax 502–4077.
Education Division.—Dana Chapman, 502–4257, fax 502–4099.
Federal Judicial History Office.—Vacant, 502–4181, fax 502–4099.
Information Technology Office.—Esther DeVries, 502–4195, fax 502–4288.
International Judicial Relations Office.—Mira Gur-Arie, 502–4191, fax 502–4099.
Research Division.—James B. Eaglin, 502–4071, fax 502–4199.

DISTRICT OF COLUMBIA COURTS

500 Indiana Avenue, NW., Washington, DC 20001

phone (202) 879–1010

Executive Officer.—Cheryl R. Bailey (acting), 879–1700.
Deputy Executive Officer.—Herb Rouson (acting), 879–1700.
Director, Media and Public Relations.—Leah Gurowitz, 879–1700.
Manager, Government Relations.—Callie Coffman, 879–1700.

DISTRICT OF COLUMBIA COURT OF APPEALS

Historic Courthouse, 430 E Street, NW., Washington, DC 20001

phone (202) 879–1010

Chief Judge.—Anna Blackburne-Rigsby.

Associate Judges:
Stephen H. Glickman.
John R. Fisher.
Phyllis D. Thompson.
Corinne Beckwith.
Cathàrine F. Easterly.
Roy W. McLeese.

Senior Judges:
Frank Q. Nebeker.
John M. Steadman.
John M. Ferren.
Vanessa Ruiz.
Eric T. Washington.

Clerk.—Julio Castillo, 879–2725.
Chief Deputy Clerk.—Marie Robertson (acting), 879–1717.
Director of:
Administration.—Reginald Turner, 879–2755.
Admissions.—Shela Shanks, 879–2710.
Public Office Operations.—Terry Lambert, 879–2702.
Staff Counsel.—Rosanna Mason, 879–2718.

SUPERIOR COURT OF THE DISTRICT OF COLUMBIA

Moultrie Courthouse, 500 Indiana Avenue, NW., Washington, DC 20001

phone (202) 879–1010

Chief Judge.—Robert E. Morin.
Associate Judges:

Jennifer M. Anderson.
Ronna L. Beck.
Julie Becker.
Steven Berk.
Patricia A. Broderick.
John M. Campbell.
Erik P. Christian.
Laura A. Cordero.
Carol Dalton.
Danya A. Dayson.
Marisa Demeo.
Jennifer A. DiToro.
Todd E. Edelman.
Anthony Epstein.
Gerald I. Fisher.
Wendell P. Gardner, Jr.
Alfred S. Irving.
Craig Iscoe.
Kelly Higashi.
William M. Jackson.
Anita Josey-Herring.
Kimberley S. Knowles.
Peter Krauthamer.
Neal E. Kravitz.
Milton C. Lee.
Lynn Leibowitz.
José M. López.
John McCabe.
Juliet J. McKenna.
Carmen McLean.
William Nooter.
Michael R. O'Keefe.
Robert D. Okun.
Florence Y. Pan.
Heidi Pasichow.
Jonathan Pittman.
Hiram E. Puig-Lugo.
Maribeth Raffinan.
Robert Rigsby.
Maurice Ross.
Michael J. Ryan.
Fern Flanagan Saddler.
Robert Salerno.
Judith Smith.
Darlene M. Soltys.
Steven Wellner.
Yvonne Williams.
Elizabeth Wingo.

Magistrate Judges:
Janet Albert.
Errol Arthur.
Joseph E. Beshouri.
Tanya Jones Bosier.
Rahkel Bouchet.
Rainey R. Brandt.
Diane M. Brenneman.
Julie Breslow.
Tyrona DeWitt.
Tara Fentress.
Heide Herrmann.
Noel Johnson.
Diane Lepley.
Kenia Seoane Lopez.
Shana Frost Matini.
Shelly A. Mulkey.
Lloyd U. Nolan.
Adrienne Noti.
Renee Raymond.
Mary Grace Rook.
Sean Staples.
Sherry Trafford.
Jorge Vila.
Katherine M. Wiedmann.

Senior Judges:
Geoffrey M. Alprin.
John H. Bayly.
Zoe Bush.
Russell F. Canan.
Kaye R. Christian.
Jeanette Clark.
Natalia Combs-Greene.
Harold Cushenberry, Jr.
Linda Kay Davis.
Herbert B. Dixon, Jr.
Stephanie Duncan-Peters.
Stephen F. Eilperin.
Henry F. Greene.
Gregory Jackson.
Ann O'Regan Keary.
Cheryl M. Long.
Judith N. Macaluso.
Bruce S. Mencher.
Zinora Mitchell-Rankin.
Gregory E. Mize.
Truman A. Morrison III.
Thomas Motley.
John Mott.
Robert I. Richter.
Lee F. Satterfield.
Nan R. Shuker.
Robert S. Tignor.
Linda D. Turner.
Curtis Von Kann.
Frederick H. Weisberg.
Ronald P. Wertheim.
Rhonda Reid Winston.
Peter H. Wolf.
Melvin R. Wright.
Patricia A. Wynn.
Joan Zeldon.

Clerk of the Court.—Zabrina Dempson, 879–1400.

GOVERNMENT OF THE DISTRICT OF COLUMBIA

John A. Wilson Building, 1350 Pennsylvania Avenue, NW., Washington, DC 20004

phone (202) 724–8000

[All area codes within this section are (202) unless stated otherwise.]

COUNCIL OF THE DISTRICT OF COLUMBIA

Council Chairman.—Phil Mendelson, Suite 504, 724–8032.
Council Members (at-Large):
Anita D. Bonds, Suite 404, 724–8064.
David Grosso, Suite 402, 724–8105.
Elissa Silverman, Suite 408, 724–7772.
Robert J. White, Jr., Suite 107, 724–8174.
Council Members:
Brianne Nadeau, Ward 1, Suite 102, 724–8181.
Brooke Pinto, Ward 2, Suite 106, 724–8058.
Mary M. Cheh, Ward 3, Suite 108, 724–8062.
Brandon T. Todd, Ward 4, Suite 105, 724–8052.
Kenyan McDuffie, Ward 5, Suite 506, 724–8028.
Charles Allen, Ward 6, Suite 110, 724–8072.
Vincent C. Gray, Ward 7, Suite 406, 724–8068.
Trayon White, Sr., Ward 8, Suite 400, 724–8045.
Council Officers:
Secretary to the Council.—Nyasha Smith, Suite 5, 724–8080.
Budget Director.—Jennifer Budoff, Suite 508, 724–8544.
General Counsel.—Nicole L. Streeter, Suite 4, 724–8026.
Chief Technology Officer.—Christopher Warren, Suite 13, 724–8018.

EXECUTIVE OFFICE OF THE MAYOR

Suite 300, phone 727–6263, fax 727–6561

Mayor of the District of Columbia.—Hon. Muriel E. Bowser.
Assistant to the Mayor.—Tonya Poindexter, Suite 300, 727–2643, fax 727–7743.
Chief of Staff.—John Falcicchio.
Deputy Chief of Staff.—Tomás Talamante, 741–0922.
City Administrator.—Rashad Young, Suite 513, 478–9200, fax 727–9878.
Senior Advisor.—Beverly Perry, Suite 324, 724–7173.
Legal Counsel.—Ronald Ross, Suite 407, 727–8812.
General Counsel.—Betsy Cavendish, Suite 300, 727–7681, fax 724–7743.
Deputy Mayor for—
Education.—Paul Kihn, Suite 307, 727–3636, fax 727–8198.
Health and Human Services.—Wayne Turnage, Suite 223, 727–7973, fax 442–5066.
Operations and Infrastructure.—Lucinda Babers, Suite 533, 724–5400.
Planning and Economic Development.—John Falcicchio (interim), Suite 317, 727–6365, fax 727–6703.
Public Safety and Justice.—Kevin Donahue, Suite 533, 724–5400.
Director of:
Budget and Performance Management.—Jennifer Reed, Suite 513, 478–9206.
Communications.—LaToya Foster, Suite 311, 727–5011, fax 727–8527.
Community Affairs.—Lamont Akins, Suite 327, 442–8150, fax 727–2357.
Federal and Regional Affairs.—Eugene Kinlow, Suite 356, 724–5333.
Inspector General.—Daniel Lucas, 717 14th Street, NW., 5th Floor, 727–2540, fax 727–9846.
Secretary of Washington, DC.—Kimberly Bassett, Suite 419, 727–6306, fax 727–3582.

OFFICE OF THE CITY ADMINISTRATOR

Suite 513, phone 478–9200, fax 727–9878

City Administrator.—Rashad Young.
Executive Assistant to City Administrator.—Timothy Banner.

COMMISSIONS

Arts and Humanities, 200 I (Eye) Street, SE., Suite 1400, Washington, DC 20003, 724–5613, fax 727–4135, https://dcarts.dc.gov/DC/DCARTS.
Executive Director.—Heran Serene-Brhan (interim).
Chairperson.—Judith F. Terra.

Judicial Disabilities and Tenure, 515 5th Street, NW., Building A, Room 246, Washington, DC 20001, 727–1363, fax 727–9718, https://cjdt.dc.gov/DC/CJDT.
Executive Director.—Cathaee Hudgins.
Chairperson.—Hon. Gladys Kessler.

Judicial Nominations, 515 5th Street, NW., Suite 235, Washington, DC 20001, 879–0478, fax 879–0755, https://jnc.dc.gov/DC/JNC.
Executive Director.—Kim M. Whatley.
Chairperson.—Hon. Emmet G. Sullivan.

Serve DC, Frank D. Reeves Municipal Center, 2000 14th Street, NW., Suite 101, Washington, DC 20009, 727–7200, fax 727–9942, https://serve.dc.gov/page/about-serve-dc.
Executive Director.—Ayris Scales.
Chairperson.—Peter Brusoe.

Washington Metropolitan Area Transit, 8701 Georgia Avenue, Suite 808, Silver Spring, MD 20910–3700 (301) 427–0140, fax 588–5262, https://www.wmatc.gov.
Executive Director / General Counsel.—William S. Morrow, Jr.
Chairperson.—Lawrence Brenner.

DEPARTMENTS

Behavioral Health, 64 New York Avenue, NE., 4th Floor, 20002, 673–7440, fax 673–3433.
Director.—Barbara Bazron.

Child and Family Services Agency, 400 6th Street, SW., 5th Floor, 20024, 442–6100, fax 727–6505.
Director.—Brenda Donald.

Consumer and Regulatory Affairs, 941 North Capitol Street, NE., 20002, 442–4400, fax 442–9445.
Director.—Ernest Chrappah.

Corrections, 1923 Vermont Avenue, NW., Room 207 North, 20001, 673–7316, fax 671–2043.
Director.—Quincy Booth.

Employment Services, 4058 Minnesota Avenue, NE., 20019, 724–7000, fax 673–6993.
Director.—Unique Morris-Hughes.

Energy and the Environment, 1200 First Street, NE., 5th Floor, 20002, 535–2600, fax 673–6993.
Director.—Tommy Wells.

Fire and Emergency Medical Services, 1923 Vermont Avenue, NW., Suite 201, 20001, 673–3320, fax 462–0807.
Fire Chief.—Gregory Dean.

For-Hire Vehicles, 2235 Shannon Place, SE., Client Services Suite 2001 / Executive Offices Suite 3001, 20020, 645–7300, fax 889–3604.
Director.—David Do.

General Services, 2000 14th Street, NW., 8th Floor, 20009, 724–4400, fax 727–9877.
Director.—Keith Anderson.

Health, 899 North Capitol Street, NE., 5th Floor, 20002, 442–5955, fax 442–4795.
Director.—LaQuandra Nesbitt.

Housing and Community Development, 1800 Martin Luther King Jr. Avenue, SE., 20020, 442–7200, fax 645–6730.
Director.—Polly Donaldson.

Human Resources, 441 4th Street, NW., Suite 330 South, 20001, 442–9600, fax 727–6827.
Director.—Ventris Gibson.

Human Services, 64 New York Avenue, NE., 6th Floor, 20002, 671–4200, fax 671–4325.
Director.—Laura Zeilinger.

Insurance, Securities and Banking, 810 1st Street, NE., Suite 701, 20002, 727–8000, fax 535–1196.
Commissioner.—Stephen Taylor.

Metropolitan Police, 300 Indiana Avenue, NW., 20001, phone 311 or (202) 737–4404 if calling from outside DC, fax 727–9524.
Police Chief.—Peter Newsham.

Motor Vehicles, 301 C Street, NW., 20001, 727–5000, fax 727–4653.
Director.—Gabriel Robinson.

Parks and Recreation, 3149 16th Street, NW., 20010, 673–7647, fax 673–2087.
Director.—Delano Hunter.

Public Works, 2000 14th Street, NW., 6th Floor, 20009, 673–6833, fax 671–0642.
Director.—Christopher Geldart.

Small and Local Business Development, 441 4th Street, NW., Suite 970 North, 20001, 727–3900, fax 724–3786.
Director.—Kristi Whitfield.

Transportation, 55 M Street, SE., Suite 400, 20003, 673–6813, fax 671–0650.
Director.—Jeffrey Marootian.

Youth Rehabilitation Services, 450 H Street, NW., 10th Floor, 20001, 576–8175, fax 727–4434.
Director.—Clinton Lacey.

OFFICES

Administrative Hearings, One Judiciary Square, 441 4th Street, NW., 20001, 442–9091, fax 442–9451.
Chief Judge.—Eugene Adams.

Aging and Community Living, 441 4th Street, NW., Suite 900 South, 20001, 724–5622, fax 724–4979.
Director.—Laura Newland.

Asian and Pacific Islander Affairs, 441 4th Street, NW., Suite 721 North, 20001, 727–3120, fax 727–9655.
Executive Director.—Ben de Guzman.

Attorney General, 441 4th Street, NW., Suite 400 South, 20001, 727–3400, fax 347–8922.
Attorney General.—Karl Racine.

Talent and Appointments, 1350 Pennsylvania Avenue, NW., Suite 600, 20004, 727–1372, fax 727–2359.
Director.—Steven Walker.

Cable Television and Telecommunications, 3007 Tilden Street, NW., Pod P, 20008, 671–0066, fax 332–7020.
Director.—Angie Gates.

Chief Financial Officer, 1350 Pennsylvania Avenue, NW., Suite 203, 20004, 727–2476, fax 727–1643.
Chief Financial Officer.—Jeffrey DeWitt.

Chief Medical Examiner, 1910 Massachusetts Avenue, SE., Building 27, 20003, 698–9000, fax 698–9100.
Chief Medical Examiner.—Dr. Roger Mitchell.

Chief Technology Officer, 441 4th Street, NW., Suite 930 South, 20001, 727–2277, fax 727–6857.
Chief Technology Officer.—Lindsey Parker.

Communications Office, 1350 Pennsylvania Avenue, NW., Suite 310, 20004, 727–5011, fax 727–8527.
Director.—Michael Czin.

Office of Community Affairs, 1350 Pennsylvania Avenue, NW., Suite 327, 20004, 442–8150, fax 727–5931.
Director.—Lamont Akins.

Contracting and Procurement, 441 4th Street, NW., Suite 700 South, 20001, 727–0252, fax 727–0245.
Chief Procurement Officer.—George Schutter.

Emergency Management Agency, 2720 Martin Luther King Jr. Avenue, SE., 20032, 727–6161, fax 715–7288.
Director.—Chris Geldart.

Employee Appeals, 1100 4th Street, SW., Suite 620 East, 20024, 727–0004, fax 727–5631.
Executive Director.—Sheila Barfield, Esq.

Finance and Resource Management, 441 4th Street, NW., Suite 890 North, 20001, 727–0333, fax 727–0659.
Director of Finance Operations.—Mohamed Mohamed.

Human Rights, 441 4th Street, NW., Suite 570 North, 20001, 727–4559, fax 727–9589.
Director.—Michelle Garcia (interim).

Labor Relations and Collective Bargaining, 441 4th Street, NW., Suite 820 North, 20001, 724–4953, fax 727–6887.
Director.—Lindsey Maxwell.

Latino Affairs, 2000 14th Street, NW., 2nd Floor, 20009, 671–2825, fax 673–4557.
Director.—Jackie Reyes.

Lesbian, Gay, Bisexual and Transgender Affairs, 1350 Pennsylvania Avenue, NW., Suite 327, 20004, 727–9493, fax 727–5931.
Director.—Sheila Alexander-Reid.

Motion Picture and Television Development, 3007 Tilden Street, NW., 4th Floor, 20008, 727–6608, fax 727–3246.
Director.—Angie Gates.

Planning, 1100 4th Street, SW., Suite E650, 20024, 442–7600, fax 442–7638.
Director.—Andrew Trueblood.

Policy and Legislative Affairs, 1350 Pennsylvania Avenue, NW., Suite 533, 20004, 727–6979, fax 727–3765.
Director.—Vacant.

Risk Management, 441 4th Street, NW., Suite 800 South, 20001, 727–8600, fax 727–8319.
Director.—Jed Ross.

State Superintendent of Education, 810 First Street, NE., 9th Floor, 20002, 727–6436, fax 727–2019.
Superintendent.—Hanseul Kang.

Unified Communications, 2720 Martin Luther King Jr. Avenue, SE., 20032, 730–0524, fax 730–1425.
Director.—Karima Holmes.

Veterans Affairs, 441 4th Street, NW., Suite 570 South, 20001, 724–5454, fax 727–7117.
Director.—Tammi Lambert (interim).

Victim Services and Justice Grants Administration, 441 4th Street, NW., Suite 700, 20004, 727–3934, fax 727–1617.
Director.—Michelle Garcia.

Zoning, 441 4th Street, NW., Suite 200 South, 20001, 727–6311, fax 727–6072.
Director.—Sara Benjamin Bardin.

INDEPENDENT AGENCIES

Advisory Neighborhood Commissions, 1350 Pennsylvania Avenue, NW., Room 8, 20004, 727–9945, fax 727–0289.
Executive Director.—Gottlieb Simon.

Alcoholic Beverage Regulation Administration, 2000 14th Street, NW., Suite 400 South, 20009, 442–4423, fax 442–9563.
Director.—Fred Moosally.

Board of Elections and Ethics, 441 4th Street, NW., Suite 250 North, 20001, 727–2525, fax 347–2648.
Chairperson of the Board.—Cliff Tatum.

Criminal Justice Coordinating Council, 441 4th Street, NW., Suite 727 North, 20001, 442–9283, fax 724–3691.
Executive Director.—Mannone Butler.

Destination DC, 1212 New York Avenue, NW., Suite 600, 20005, 904–0616 or 249–3012, fax 789–7037.
President and CEO.—Elliot Ferguson.

District of Columbia Court of Appeals, 430 E Street, Room 115, 20001, 879–2701, fax 626–8840.
Chief Judge.—Eric T. Washington.

District of Columbia Housing Authority, 1133 North Capitol Street, NE., 20001, 535–1500, fax 535–1740.
Executive Director.—Adrianne Todman.

District of Columbia Public Defender Service, 633 Indiana Avenue, NW., 20001, 628–1200, fax 824–2784.
Director.—Avis Buchanan.

District of Columbia Public Library, 901 G Street, NW., Suite 400, 20001, 727–1101, fax 727–1129.
Director.—Richard Reyes-Gavilan.

District of Columbia Public Schools, 825 North Capitol Street, NW., Suite 9026, 20002, 442–4226, fax 442–5026.
Chancellor.—Dr. Lewis Ferebee.

District of Columbia Retirement Board, 900 7th Street, NW., 2nd Floor, 20001, 343–3200, fax 566–5000.
Executive Director.—Sheila Morgan-Johnson.

District of Columbia Sentencing and Criminal Code Revision Commission, 441 4th Street, NW., Suite 830 South, 20001, 727–8822, fax 727–7929.
Executive Director.—Barbara Tombs-Souvey.

District Lottery and Charitable Games Control Board, 2101 Martin Luther King Jr. Avenue, SE., 20020, 645–8000, fax 645–7914.
Executive Director.—Tracey Cohen.

Housing Finance Agency, 815 Florida Avenue, NW., 20001, 777–1600, fax 986–6705.
Executive Director.—Todd Lee.

Metropolitan Washington Council of Governments, 777 North Capitol Street, NE., 20002, 962–3200, fax 962–3201.
Executive Director.—Dave Robertson.

People's Counsel, 1133 15th Street, NW., Suite 500, 20005, 727–3071, fax 727–1014.
People's Counsel.—Sandra Mattavous-Frye, Esq.

Police Complaints, 1400 I Street, NW., Suite 700, 20005, 727–3838, fax 727–9182.
Executive Director.—Philip K. Eure.

Public Charter School Board, 3333 14th Street, NW., Suite 210, 20010, 328–2660, fax 328–2661.
Executive Director.—Scott Pearson.

Public Employee Relations Board, 1100 4th Street, SW., Suite E630, 20024, 727–1822, fax 727–9116.
Executive Director.—Clarene Phyllis Martin.

Public Service Commission, 1333 H Street, NW., Suite 200, West Tower, 20005, 626–5100, fax 393–1389.
Chairperson.—Willie Phillips.

Superior Court of the District of Columbia, H. Carl Moultrie I Courthouse, 500 Indiana Avenue, NW., 20001, 879–1010.
Chief Judge.—Lee F. Satterfield.

Washington Convention and Sports Authority, 801 Mount Vernon Place, NW., 20001, 249–3012, fax 249–3133.
President and CEO.—Greg O'Dell.

Water and Sewer Authority, 5000 Overlook Avenue, SW., 20032, 787–2000, fax 787–2210.
Chairman.—William M. Walker.
General Manager.—George S. Hawkins.

Workforce Investment Council, 4058 Minnesota Avenue, NE., 20009, 671–1900, fax 673–6993.
Chairperson.—Vacant.

OTHER

Board of Real Property Assessments and Appeals, 441 4th Street, NW., Suite 430, 20001, 727–6860, fax 727–0392.
Chairperson.—Towanda Paul-Bryant.

Contract Appeals Board, 441 4th Street, NW., Suite N350, 727–6597, fax 727–3993.
Chief Administrative Judge.—Marc D. Loud, Sr.

Justice Grants Administration, 1350 Pennsylvania Avenue, NW., Suite 327A, 20004, 727–6239, fax 727–1617.
Director.—Josh Weber.

Rehabilitation Services Administration, 1125 15th Street, NW., 20005, 730–1700, fax 730–1516.
Administrator.—Vacant.

DISTRICT OF COLUMBIA POST OFFICE LOCATIONS

900 Brentwood Road, NE., Washington, DC 20066–9998, General Information 636–1200

Postmaster.—Gerald A. Roane.

CLASSIFIED STATIONS

Station	Phone	Location / Zip Code
Anacostia	(301) 423–9091 / 9092	3719 Branch Ave., Temple Hills, MD 20748
Ben Franklin	523–2386	1200 Pennsylvania Ave., NW., 20004
B.F. Carriers	636–2289	900 Brentwood Rd., NE., 20004
Benning	523–2391	3937½ Minnesota Ave., NE., 20029
Bolling AFB	767–4419	Bldg. 10, Brookley Ave., 20332
Brightwood	726–8119	6323 Georgia Ave., NW., 20011
Brookland	523–2126	3401 12th St., NE., 20017
Calvert	523–2908	2336 Wisconsin Ave., NW., 20007
Cleveland Park	523–2396	3430 Connecticut Ave., NW., 20008
Columbia Heights	636–1549	900 Brentwood Road, NE., 20010
Congress Heights	523–2112	400 Southern Ave., SE., 20032
Customs House	523–2195	3178 Bladensburg Rd., NE., 20018
Dulles	(703) 471–9497	Dulles International Airport, 20041
Farragut	523–2507	1145 19th St., NW., 20033
Fort Davis	842–4964	3843 Pennsylvania Ave., SE., 20020
Fort McNair	523–2144	300 A St., SW., 20319
Frederick Douglass	842–4959	Alabama Ave., SE., 20020
Friendship	523–2130	4005 Wisconsin Ave., NW., 20016
Georgetown	523–2406	1215 31st St., NW., 20007
Government Mail	523–2138 / 2139	3300 V Street, NE., 20018–9998
Headsville	357–3029	Smithsonian Institute, 20560
Kalorama	523–2906	2300 18th St., NW., 20009
Lamond Riggs	523–2041	6200 North Capitol St., NW., 20011
LeDroit Park	483–0973	416 Florida Ave., NW., 20001
L'Enfant Plaza	268–4970	458 L'Enfant Plaza, SW., 20026
Main Office Window	636–2130	Curseen / Morris P&DC, 900 Brentwood Rd., NE., 20066–9998

CLASSIFIED STATIONS—CONTINUED

Station	Phone	Location / Zip Code
Martin L. King Jr.	523–2001	1400 L St., NW., 20043
McPherson	842–1229	1750 Pennsylvania Ave., NW., 20038
Mid City	....	Temporarily Closed
NASA	358–0235	600 Independence Ave., SW., 20546
National Capitol	523–2368	2 Massachusetts Ave., NE., 20002
Naval Research Lab	767–3426	4565 Overlook Ave., 20390
Navy Annex	(703) 920–0815	1668 D Street, 20335
Northeast	388–5216	1563 Maryland Ave., NE., 20002
Northwest	523–2570	5632 Connecticut Ave., NW., 20015
Palisades	842–2291	5136 MacArthur Blvd., NW., 20016
Pavilion Postique	523–2571	1100 Pennsylvania Ave., NW., 20004
Pentagon	(703) 695–6835	Concourse Pentagon (Army-20301 / 20310; Air Force-20330; Navy-20350)
Petworth	523–2681	4211 9th St., NW., 20011
Postal Museum	523–2022	2 Massachusetts Ave., NW., 20002
Randle	584–6807	2341 Pennsylvania Ave., SE., 20023
River Terrace	523–2988	3621 Benning Rd., NE., 20019
Section 2	636–1010 / 4497	Section 2, Curseen / Morris P&DC, 900 Brentwood Rd., NE., 20002–9998
Southeast	523–2174	327 7th St., SE., 20003
Southwest	523–2597	45 L St., SW., 20024
State Department	523–2574	2201 C St., NW., 20520
14th/T Street	232–6301	2000 14th St., NW., 20009
Tech World	523–2019	800 K St., NW., 20001
Temple Heights	523–2563	1921 Florida Ave., NW., 20009
22nd Street	523–2411	1255 22nd St., NW., 20037
U.S. Naval	433–2216	940 M St., SE., 20374
V Street	523–2138 / 2139	3300 V St., NE., 20018
Walter Reed	....	6800 Georgia Ave., NW., 20012
Ward Place	523–2109	2121 Ward Place, NW., 20037
Washington Square	523–3632	1050 Connecticut Ave., NW., 20035
Watergate	965–6278	2512 Virginia Ave., NW., 20037
Woodridge	523–2195	2211 Rhode Island Ave., NE., 20018

INTERNATIONAL ORGANIZATIONS

EUROPEAN SPACE AGENCY (E.S.A.)

Headquarters: 24 Rue De General Bertrand, CS 30798, 75345 Paris Cedex 07, France

phone 011–33–1–5369–7654, fax 011–33–1–5369–7560

Director General.—Johann-Dietrich Woerner.

Member Countries:

Austria
Belgium
Denmark
Estonia
Finland
France
Germany
Greece
Hungary
Ireland
Italy
Luxembourg
Netherlands
Norway
Poland
Portugal
Romania
Spain
Sweden
Switzerland
United Kingdom
Czech Republic

Associate Member Countries.—Slovenia.

Cooperative Agreement.—Canada.

European Space Operations Center (ESOC), Robert-Bosch-Str. 5, D–64293 Darmstadt, Germany, phone 011–49–6151–900, fax 011–49–6151–90495.

European Space Research and Technology Center (ESTEC), Keplerlaan 1, NL–2201, AZ Noordwijk, ZH, The Netherlands, phone 011–31–71–565–6565, Telex: 844–39098, fax 011–31–71–565–6040.

European Space Research Institute (ESRIN), Via Galileo Galilei, Casella Postale 64, 00044 Frascati, Italy, phone 011–39–6–94–18–01, fax 011–39–6–9418–0280.

European Space Astronomy Centre (ESAC), P.O. Box, E–28691 Villanueva de la Cañada, Madrid, Spain, phone 011–34 91 813 11 00, fax: 011–34 91 813 11 39.

European Astronaut Centre (EAC), Linder Hoehe, 51147 Cologne, Germany, phone 011–49–220360–010, fax 011–49–2203–60–1103.

European Centre for Space Applications and Telecommunications (ECSAT), Atlas Building, Harwell Science & Innovation Campus, Didcot, Oxfordshire, OX11 0QX, United Kingdom, phone 011–44 1235 567900.

European Space Security and Education Centre (ESEC), 1 Place de l'ESA, B–6890, Redu, Belgium, phone 011–32 61 229511, fax 011–32 61 229544.

European Space Agency Washington Office (EWO), 1201 F Street, NW., Suite 470, Washington, DC 20004.
Head of Office.—Micheline Tabache (202) 488–4158, micheline.tabache@esa.int.

INTER-AMERICAN DEFENSE BOARD

2600 16th Street, NW., 20441, phone (202) 939–6041, fax 319–2791

Chairman.—General de División Luciano José Penna, Brazil.
Vice Chairman.—General de Brigada Carlos Humberto Castañeda Nassi, Peru.
Chairman's Chefe de Cabinet.—Coronel Julio Cesar Belaguarda Nagy de Oliveira, Brazil.
Director General.—General de Brigada Juan José Gómez Ruiz, México.
Deputy Secretary for Administration.—Coronel Darren Dodd Lynn, United States.
Director Conferences.—Capitán de Navio Valinei Ciola, Brazil.

CHIEFS OF DELEGATION

Antigua and Barbuda.—Consejera Guilliam Ingrid Joseph.
Argentina.—Comodoro de Marina Enrique Antonio Balbi.
Barbados.—Embajador Noel Anderson Lynch.
Belize.—Embajador Francisco Daniel Gutierez.
Bolivia.—General de División Ramiro Hugo Mojica Aparicio.
Brazil.—Contraalmirante Nelson Nunes da Rosa.
Canada.—General de División Paul Ormsby.
Chile.—General de Brigada Luis Claudio Weber Orellana.
Colombia.—Coronel Ricardo Roque.
Dominican Republic.—General de Brigada Pedro René Valenzuela Quiroz.
Ecuador.—Coronel Diego Hernández Guijarro.
El Salvador.—Coronel Walter Jacobo Lovato Villatoro.
Grenada.—Comisionado Michael Francois.
Guatemala.—Vacant.
Guyana.—Coronel Trevor E. Bowman.
Haiti.—Embajador Leon Charles.
Honduras.—Coronel José Munguía Díaz.
Jamaica.—Embajadora Audrey P. Marks.
Mexico.—General de Brigada Guillermo Almazán Bertotto.
Nicaragua.—Coronel Mario Alberto Miranda Jaime.
Panama.—Comisionado Máximo Emilio Ruíz Peña.
Paraguay.—General de Brigada Mario Osvaldo Centurión Marecos.
Peru.—Mayor General Luis Alberto Gonzalez Buttgenbach.
Saint Kitts and Nevis.—Embajador Everson Hull.
Suriname.—Vacant.
Trinidad and Tobago.—Coronel Roger Glen Carter.
United States.—Brigadier General Richard Heitkamp.
Uruguay.—Major General Gerardo Daniel Fregossi Alvarez.
Venezuela.—Vacant.

INTER-AMERICAN DEFENSE COLLEGE

Director.—Major General James E. Taylor, United States.
Vice Director.—Contra-Almirante Sílvio Luis dos Santos, Brazil.
Chief of Studies.—General de Brigada Rubén Darío Díaz Esparza, Mexico.

INTER-AMERICAN DEVELOPMENT BANK

1300 New York Avenue, NW., 20577, phone (202) 623–1000

https://iadb.org

OFFICERS

President.—Luis Alberto Moreno.
Chief of Staff, Office of the President.—Luis Alberto Giorgio.
Executive Vice President.—John Scott (United States), a.i.
Chief Advisor of the Office of the Executive Vice President.—José Jorge Seligmann-Silva.
Ethics Officer.—Alberto Rivera-Fournier.
Chief Economist and General Manager of the Research Department.—Eric Parrado Herrera.
Executive Auditor.—Jorge Da Silva.
Secretary of the Bank.—Martin Bès.
Manager, Office of Outreach and Partnerships.—Bernardo Guillamon.
Chief Risk Officer.—Federico Galizia.
Chief Executive Officer, IDB Lab.—Irene Arias Hofman.
Manager, Office of Strategic Planning and Development Effectiveness.—Luis Miguel Castilla Rubio.
Chief, Office of Institutional Integrity.—Laura Profeta.
Vice-President for Countries.—Alexandre Meira da Rosa.
Country Manager, Office of:
Manager, Andean Country Group.—Rafael de la Cruz.

General Manager, Country Department Caribbean Group.—Therese Turner-Jones.
Manager, Central America, Haiti, Mexico, Panama, and Dominican Republic and Country Representative in Panama.—Verónica Zavala.
Manager, Southern Cone Country Department.—José Luis Lupo.
Vice President for Sectors and Knowledge.—Ana María Rodriguez-Ortiz.
Manager of:
Climate Change and Sustainable Development Sector.—Juan Pablo Bonilla.
Knowledge, Innovation and Communication Sector.—Federico Basañes.
Infrastructure and Energy Sector.—José Agustin Aguerre.
Institutions for Development.—Moisés J. Schwartz.
Integration and Trade Sector.—Fabrizio Opertti.
Social Sector.—Marcelo Cabrol.
Vice President for Finance and Administration.—Claudia Bock-Valotta.
General Manager, Budget and Administrative Services Department.—Diego Murguiondo.
General Manager, Finance Department and Chief Financial Officer.—Gustavo De Rosa.
General Manager, Human Resources Department.—Carolina Serra.
Chief Information Officer and General Manager, Department of Information Technology.—Nuria Simo Vila.
General Counsel and General Manager, Legal Department.—Diego Buchara, a.i.

IDB INVEST

Chief Executive Officer.—James P. Scriven.
Chief Investment Officer.—Gema Sacristan.
Chief Strategy Officer and Chief Finance and Administration Officer.—Orlando Ferreira, a.i.
General Counsel.—H. Rosemary Jeronimides.
Chief Risk Officer.—Rachel Robboy.

MULTILATERAL INVESTMENT FUND

General Manager.—Brigit Helms.

BOARD OF EXECUTIVE DIRECTORS

Argentina and Haiti.—Guillermo Alberto Francos.
Alternate.—Jorge Eduardo Srur.
Austria, Denmark, Finland, France, Norway, Spain, and Sweden.—Alicia Montalvo Santamaria.
Alternate.—Patrick Jean Hervé.
Bahamas, Barbados, Guyana, Jamaica, and Trinidad and Tobago.—Selwin Charles Hart.
Alternate.—Vacant.
Belgium, China, Germany, Israel, Italy, The Netherlands, and Switzerland.—Christine Elisabeth Bogemann-Hagedorn.
Alternate.—Adolfo Di Carluccio.
Belize, Costa Rica, El Salvador, Guatemala, Honduras, and Nicaragua.—Francisco José Mayorga Balladares.
Alternate.—Edna Gabriela Camacho.
Bolivia, Paraguay, and Uruguay.—Germán Hugo Rojas Irigoyen.
Alternate.—Marcelo Bisogno.
Brazil and Suriname.—José Gullherme Amelda dos Reis.
Alternate.—Sergio Savino Portugal.
Canada.—Donald John Boblash.
Alternate.—Eric Daniel Madueño.
Chile and Ecuador.—Alex Foxley.
Alternate.—Bernardo Acosta.
Colombia and Peru.—Gerardo M. Corrochano.
Alternate.—Sergio Diaz Granados.
Croatia, Japan, Korea, Portugal, Slovenia, and United Kingdom.—Toshiyuki Yasui.
Alternate.—Malcolm Geere.
Dominican Republic and Mexico.—Juan Bosco Marti Ascencio.
Alternate.—Carlos Augusto Pared Vidal.
Panama and Venezuela.—Gina Montiel.
Alternate.—Fernando Ernesto de Leon de Alba.
United States of America.—Elliot Pedrosa.
Alternate.—Vacant.

INTER-AMERICAN TROPICAL TUNA COMMISSION

8901 La Jolla, Shores Drive, La Jolla, CA 92037–1508

phone (858) 546–7100, fax (858) 546–7133, https://iattc.org

Director.—Guillermo A. Compeán.

Commissioners:

Belize:

Valerie Lanza, Ministry of Finance / Belize High Seas Fisheries Unit, Marina Towers, Suite 204, Newtown Barracks, Belize City, Belize, phone (501) 223–4918, fax (501) 223–5087; e-mail: director@bhsfu.gov.bz.

Delice Pinkard, Ministry of Finance / Belize High Seas Fisheries Unit, Marina Towers, Suite 204, Newtown Barracks, Belize City, Belize, phone (501) 223–4918, fax (501) 223–5087; e-mail: sr.fishofficer@bhsfu.gov.bz.

Robert Robinson, Ministry of Finance / Belize High Seas Fisheries Unit, Marine Towers, Suite 204, Newtown Barracks, Belize City, Belize, phone (501) 223–4918, fax (501) 223–5048; e-mail: deputydirector@bhsfu.gov.bz.

Canada:

Estelle Couture, Fisheries and Oceans Canada, 200 Kent Street, Station 8E240, Ottawa, ONT K1A 0E6, Canada, phone (613) 991–6135, fax (613) 993–5995; e-mail: Estelle.Couture@dfo-mpo.gc.ca.

China:

Liming Liu, Ministry of Agriculture / Bureau of Fisheries, No. 11 Nongzhanguan Nanli, Beijing 100125, People's Republic of China, phone (86–10) 5919–3056, fax (86–10) 5919–2951; e-mail: fishcngov@126.com.

Zhao Liling, Ministry of Agriculture / Bureau of Fisheries, No. 11 Nongzhanguan Nanli, Beijing, 100125, People's Republic of China, phone (86–10) 5919–2928, fax (86–10) 5919–2951; e-mail: bofdwf@agri.gov.cn.

Colombia:

Elsa Ardila, Ministerio de Comercio, Industria y Turismo, Calle 28 n 13A-15, Bogota, DC, Colombia, phone (57–1) 606–7676; e-mail: emardila@mincit.gov.co.

Luis Humberto Guzman Vergara, Ministerio de Agricultura y Desarrollo Rural, Avenida Jimenez 7–65, Bogota, DC 001, Colombia, phone (57–1) 334–1199 ext. 310 (57–1) 283–3977, fax (57–1) 334–1199; e-mail: luis.guzman@minagricultura.gov.co.

Andrea Ramirez Martinez, Ministerio de Ambiente y Desarrollo Sostenible, Calle 35 No. 24–48, Bogota, Colombia, phone (57–1) 288–2132, (57–1) 332–3400; e-mail: ARamirez@minambiente.gov.co.

Carolina Díaz Acosta, Ministerio de Relaciones Exteriores, Calle 10 No. 5–51 Palacio de San Carlos, Bogota, DC, Colombia, phone (57–1) 381–4265, fax (57–1) 381–4747; e-mail: carolina.diaz@cancilleria.gov.co.

Costa Rica:

Bernardo Antonio Jaén Hernández, Ministerio de Agricultura y Ganadería, Sabana Sur, antiguo Colegio La Salle, San Jose, Costa Rica, phone (506) 2231–2344, fax: (506) 2232–2103; e-mail: bjaen@mag.go.cr.

Daniel Carrasco, INCOPESCA, Frente a las Instalaciones del Instituto Nacional de Aprendizaje, El Cocal, Puntarenas 5400, Costa Rica, phone (506) 8726–0876, fax (506) 2630–0636; e-mail: dcarrasco@incopesca.go.cr.

Marco Antonio Quesada Alpizar, Conservación Internacional, Contiguo a Correos de Costa Rica, San Jose, 113–2010, Costa Rica, phone (506) 2223–5311, fax (506) 2258–2103; e-mail: mquesada@conservation.org.

Ecuador:

Ricardo Perdomo, Ministerio de Acuacultura y Pesca, Puerto Pesquero Artesanal de San Mateo, Manta, Ecuador, phone (593–5) 266–6109; e-mail: jperdomo@produccion.gob.ec.

Nicolas Brando, Ministerio de Acuacultura y Pesca, Puerto Pesquero Artesanal de San Mateo, Manta, Ecuador, phone (593–5) 262–7930, fax (593–5) 262–7911; e-mail: nbrando@produccion.gob.ec.

Roberto Viteri, Ministerio de Acuacultura y Pesca, Puerto Pesquero Artesanal de San Mateo, Manta, Ecuador, phone (593–5) 262–6360, e-mail: rviteri@produccion.gob.ec.

El Salvador:

Juan Osorio, CENDEPESCA, Final 1a. Ave. Norte y Ave. Manuel Gallardo, Santa Tecla, La Libertad, El Salvador, phone (503) 2210–6108, fax (503) 2534–9885; e-mail: juan.osorio@mag.gob.sv.

Rigoberto Soto, Ministerio de Agricultura y Ganadería, Final 1a. Av. Norte y Av. Manuel Gallardo, Santa Tecla, El Salvador, phone (503) 2534–9882; e-mail: rigoberto.soto@mag.gob.sv.

Norma Lobo, CENDEPESCA, Final 1a. Avenida Norte y Avenida Manuel Gallardo, Santa Tecla, La Libertad, El Salvador, phone (503) 2210–1700, fax (503) 2534–9885; e-mail: norma.lobo@mag.gob.sv.

Numa Rafael Hernández Rodríguez, CENDEPESCA, Final 1a. Avenida Norte y Avenida Manuel Gallardo, Santa Tecla, La Libertad, El Salvador, phone (503) 7749–0756; e-mail: numa.hernandez@mag.gob.sv.

European Union:

Angela Martini, European Commission, Rue Joseph II, 99, Brussels, 1049, Belgium, phone (32–2) 299–4276, fax (32–2) 299–5570; e-mail: Angela.MARTINI@ec.europa.eu.

Luis Molledo, European Commission, Rue Joseph II, 99, Brussels, 1049, Belgium, phone (32–2) 299–3765, fax (32–2) 299–5570; e-mail: Luis.MOLLEDO@ec.europa.eu.

France:

Marie-Sophie Dufau-Richet, Secretariat d'Etat a la Mer, 16 Boulevard Raspail, Paris, 75700, France, phone (33–1) 5363–4153, fax (33–1) 5363–4178; e-mail: marie.sophie.dufau-richet@pm.gouv.fr.

Christiane Laurent-Monpetit, Ministere de l'Interieur, de l'Outre-Mer et des Collectivites T., 27, rue Oudinot, Paris, 75358 F SPO7, France, phone (33–1) 5369–2466, fax (33–1) 5369–2065; e-mail: christiane.laurent-monpetit@outre-mer.gouv.fr.

Anne-France Mattlet, Ministere de l'Ecologie, du Developpement durable et de l'Energie, Direction des peches maritimes et de l'aquaculture, 1 Place Carpeaux, Paris, 92055, France, phone (33–1) 6313–4235; e-mail: anne-france.mattlet@developpement-durable.gouv.fr.

Michel Sallenave, Haut Commissariat de la Republique Francaise en Polynesie, 43 Avenue Bruat. BP 115, Papeete, 98713, French Polynesia, phone (689) 549–525, fax (689) 434–390; e-mail: affmar@affaires-maritimes.pf.

Guatemala:

Byron Omar Acevedo Cordon, Ministerio de Agricultura, Ganadería y Alimentación, 7ma. Avenida 12–90 Zona 13, Guatemala, Guatemala, phone (502) 2413–7035, fax (502) 2413–7036; e-mail: bacevedo@maga.gob.gt.

Daniel Harold Vasquez Lainez, Ministerio de Agricultura, Ganadería y Alimentación, Km. 22 Carretera al Pacifico, Edif. La Ceiba, 3er. Nivel, Villa Nueva, Guatemala, phone (502) 2413–7000; e-mail: davlainez@yahoo.es.

Nancy Yezenia Sandoval Reyes, Ministerio de Agricultura, Ganadería y Alimentación, 7a. Ave. 12–90 zona 13, Guatemala, Guatemala, phone (502) 6640–9329 e-mail: dipescaguatemala@gmail.com.

Japan:

Tatsuo Hirayama, Ministry of Foreign Affairs, 2–2–1 Kasumigaseki 2–2–1, Chiyodaku, Tokyo, Japan, phone (81–3) 5501–8338, fax (81–3) 5501–8332; e-mail: tatsuo.hirayama@mofa.go.jp.

Takumi Fukuda, Fisheries Agency of Japan, 1–2–1 Kasumigaseki, Chiyoda-ku, Tokyo, 100–8907, Japan, phone (81–3) 3502–8460; e-mail: kengotanaka880@maff.go.jp.

Jun Yamashita, Japan Tuna Fisheries Cooperative Association, 2–3–22 Kudankita, Tokyo, 102, Japan, phone (81–3) 5646–2380, fax (81–3) 5646–2651; e-mail: takumi_fukuda720@maff.go.jp.

Kiribati: (Contacts, not appointed Commissioners)

Naomi Biribo, Ministry of Fisheries and Marine Resources Development, P.O. Box 64 Bairiki, Tarawa, Kiribati, phone (686) 21099, fax: (686) 21120; e-mail: naomib@mfmrd.gov.ki.

Aketa Tanga, Ministry of Fisheries and Marine Resources Development, P.O. Box 64 Bairiki, Tarawa, Kiribati, phone (686) 21099, fax: (686) 21120; e-mail: aketat@mfmrd.gov.ki.

Korea:

Anna Jo, Ministry of Oceans and Fisheries, Government Complex Bldg. #5, 94, Dasom2-ro, Sejong-City, Sejong, 339–012 Republic of Korea, phone (82–44) 2005397, fax (82–44) 2005349; e-mail: anna.jo@korea.kr.

Dongyeob Yang, Ministry of Oceans and Fisheries, Government Complex Bldg. #5, 94, Dasom2-ro, Sejong-City, Sejong, 339–012 Republic of Korea, phone (82–44) 200–5397; e-mail: dyyang@korea.kr.

Hyuntae Kim, Ministry of Oceans and Fisheries, Government Complex, 94, Damason2-ro, Sejong-City, Republic of Korea, phone (82–44) 200–5397; e-mail: khtrhw@korea.kr.

Seung Lyong Kim, Ministry of Oceans and Fisheries, Government Complex Bldg. #5, 94, Dasom2-ro, Sejong-City, Sejong, 339–012 Republic of Korea, phone (82–44) 2005368, fax (82–44) 2005379; e-mail: kpoksl5686@korea.kr.

Mexico:

Raul de Jesus Elenes Angulo, Comisión Nacional de Pesca y Acuacultura, Av. Camarón Sábalo S/N, Mazatlán, Sin 82100, Mexico, phone (52–669) 915–6900, fax (52–669) 915–6904; e-mail: raul.elenes@conapesca.gob.mx.

Pablo Roberto Arenas Fuentes, Instituto Nacional de la Pesca, Pitagoras #1320, Piso 8vo. Col. Sta Cruz Atoyac, Mexico, D.F. 03310 Mexico, phone (52–55) 3781–9501 (52–55) 3871–9502, fax (52–55) 3626–8421; e-mail: pablo.arenas@inapesca.gob.mx.

Bernardino Jesus Muñoz Resendez, Comisión Nacional de Pesca y Acuacultura, Av. Camarón Sábalo S/N, Mazatlán, Sin 82100, Mexico, phone (52–669) 915–6900, fax (52–669) 915–6904; e-mail: bernardino.munoz@conapesca.gob.mx.

Luis Fleischer, Instituto Nacional de la Pesca, Km 1 carretera Pichilingue s/n Col. Esterito, La Paz 23020, Baja California Sur, Mexico, phone (612) 122–1367; e-mail: lfleischer21@hotmail.com.

Nicaragua:

Julio Cesar Guevara, Industrial Atunera de Nicaragua, Balboa Ancon, Panama City, 0843–02264, Panama, phone (507) 6997–5100, fax (507) 204–4651; e-mail: juliocgq@hotmail.com.

Edward Jackson, Instituto Nicaraguense de la Pesca y Acuicultura, Km. 3.5 Carretera Norte, Managua, Nicaragua, phone (505) 2244–2460, fax (505) 2244–2552; e-mail: ejackson@inpesca.gob.ni.

Armando Segura Espinoza, Camara de la Pesca de Nicaragua, Av. 27 de Mayo, Managua, Nicaragua, phone (505) 2266–6704, fax (505) 2222–5818; e-mail: capenic@ibw.com.ni.

Panama:

Raul Delgado, Autoridad de los Recursos Acuaticos de Panama Edificio La Riviera, Avenida Justo Arosemena y Calle 46 Bella Vista, diagonal a Estacion el Arbol, Panama City, Panama, phone (507) 511–6057, fax (507); e-mail: rdelgado@arap.gob.pa.

Arnulfo Franco, FIPESCA, Corozal, Zona Libre de Proceso, Edif. 319, Panama, phone (507) 317–3644, fax (507) 317–3862; e-mail: arnulfofranco@fipesca.com.

Lucas Pacheco, Autoridad de los Recursos Acuaticos de Panama Edificio La Riviera, Avenida Justo Arosemena y Calle 45 Bella Vista, diagonal a Estacion el Arbol, Panama City, Panama, phone (507) 511–6000; e-mail: lpacheco@arap.gob.pa.

Zuleika Pinzon, Autoridad de los Recursos Acuaticos de Panama, Edificio La Riviera, Avenida Justo Arosemena y Calle 45 Bella Vista, diagonal a Estacion el Arbol, Panama City, 0819–05850, Panama, phone (507) 511–6000, fax (507) 511–6071; e-mail: administraciongeneral@arap.gob.pa.

Peru:

Gladys Cardenas, Instituto del Mar del Peru, Esquina de Gamarra y General Valle s/n Chucuito-Callao Lima, Peru, phone (51–1) 208–8650, fax (51–1) 420–0144; email: gcardenas@imarpe.gob.pe.

Rossy Yesenia Chumbe Cedeño, Ministerio de Produccion, Calle 1 Oeste #066, San Isidro, Lima 27, Peru, phone (51–1) 988004419; e-mail: rchumbe@produce.gob.pe.

Andres Martin Garrido Sanchez, Ministerio de Relaciones Exteriores, Jiron Lampa 545, Cercado de Lima, Peru, phone (51–1) 204–3244; e-mail: agarrido@rree.gob.pe.

Omar Ricardo Rios Bravo de Rueda, Ministerio de Produccion, Calle 1 Oeste #066, San Isidro, Lima 27, Peru, phone (51–1) 616–2222; e-mail: orios@produce.gob.pe.

Chinese Taipei:

Hong-Yen Huang, Fisheries Agency, No. 2 Chaozhou St. Zhongzheng Dist., Taipei City, Taiwan, 100, phone (886–7) 823–9828, fax (886–7) 815–8278; e-mail: hangyen@ms1.fa.gov.tw.

Chi-Chao Liu, Fisheries Agency, Council of Agriculture, 6F No. 100, Sec. 2 Heping W. Rd Zhongzheng Dist., Taipei, 100, Taiwan, phone (886–2) 2383–5882; e-mail: chichao@ms1.fa.gov.tw.

Ted Tien-Hsiang Tsai, Fisheries Agency, No. 2, Chaozhou St. Zhongzheng Dist., Taipei City, Taiwan, phone (886–2) 3343–6045, fax (886–2) 3343–6128, e-mail: ted@ms1.fa.gov.tw.

USA:

William Fox, U.S. Commissioner-IATTC, P.O. Box 60633, San Diego, CA 92166, USA, phone (202) 495–4397, fax (619) 222–2489; e-mail: bill.fox@wwfus.org.

Drew Lawler, NOAA/National Marine Fisheries Service, 1315 East-West Highway, Silver Spring, MD 20910 , USA, phone (301) 427–8000; e-mail: andrew.lawler@noaa.gov.

Barry Thom, NOAA/National Marine Fisheries Service, 1201, NE., Lloyd Blvd., Suite 1100, Portland, OR 97232, USA, phone (503) 231–6266, fax (503) 230–5441; email: barry.thom@noaa.gov.

Michael Thompson, U.S. Commissioner-IATTC, 26032 Via del Rey, San Juan Capristano, CA 92675 , USA, phone (949) 500–5901; e-mail: mthompson041@cox.net.

Vanuatu:

Christophe Emelee, Vanuatu Government, P.O. Box 1640, Port Vila, Vanuatu, phone (678) 774–0219; e-mail: tunafishing@vanuatu.com.vu, c.emelee@yahoo.co.nz.

Roy M. Joy, Embassy of Vanuatu, Avenue de Tervueren 380 Chemin de Ronde, Brussels 1150, Belgium, phone (32–2) 771–7494, fax (32–2) 771–7494; e-mail: rjoy@vanuatuembassy.net, joyroymickey@gmail.com.

Dimitri Malvirlani, Vanuatu IATTC Commissioner, Marine Quay, P.O. Box 320, Port-Vila, Vanuatu, phone (678) 23128, fax (678) 22949; e-mail: vma@vanuatu.com.vn.

Laurent Parente, Vanuatu IATTC Commissioner, P.O. Box 1435, Port Vila Vanuatu, phone (447–55) 438–0005; e-mail: laurentparente-vanuatu-imo@hotmail.com.

Venezuela:

Alvin Delgado Martínez, FUNDATUN-PNOV, Urb. La Floresta Calle B I22, Cumana, Sucre, 6101, Venezuela, phone (58–293) 433–0431, fax (58–293) 433–0431; e-mail: fundatunpnov@gmail.com.

Dante Rivas, Ministerio del Poder Popular de Pesca y Acuicultura, Avenida Lecuna, Parque Central, Torre Este, Piso 17, Caracas, Venezuela, phone (58–212) 573–1055; e-mail: ori@insopesca.gob.ve.

Miguel Carpio, Ministerio del Poder Popular de Pesca y Acuicultura, Avenida Lecuna, Parque Central, Torre Este, Piso 17, Caracas, Venezuela, phone (58–212) 573–1055; e-mail: vicepropesca@gmail.com.

Rodger Gutierrez, Ministerio del Poder Popular de Pesca y Acuicultura, Avenida Lecuna, Parque Central, Torre Este, Piso 17, Caracas, Venezuela, phone (58–212) 573–1055; e-mail: rodgerleonardo2@gmail.com.

INTERNATIONAL BOUNDARY AND WATER COMMISSION, UNITED STATES AND MEXICO

UNITED STATES SECTION

4191 North Mesa, El Paso, TX 79902–1441

phone (915) 832–4100, https://ibwc.gov

Commissioner.—Jayne Harkins, 832–4101.
Foreign Affairs Secretary.—Sally Spencer, 832–4175.
Principal Engineer.—Jose Nuñez, 832–4749.
Human Resources Director.—Fred Graf, 832–4114.
General Counsel/Legal Advisor.—Matt Myers, 832–4728.

MEXICAN SECTION

Avenida Universidad, No. 2180, Zona de El Chamizal, A.P. 1612–D, C.P. 32310

Ciudad Juarez, Chihuahua, Mexico

P.O. Box 10525, El Paso, TX 79995

phone 011–52–16–13–7311 or 011–52–16–13–7363 (Mexico)

Commissioner.—Roberto F. Salmon Castello.
Foreign Affairs Secretary.—Jose de Jesus Luevano Grano.
Principal Engineers: Gilberto Elizalde Hernandez, L. Antonio Rascon Mendoza.

INTERNATIONAL BOUNDARY COMMISSION, UNITED STATES AND CANADA

UNITED STATES SECTION

1717 H Street, NW., Suite 845, Washington, DC 20006, phone (202) 736–9100

Commissioner.—Kyle K. Hipsley.
Deputy Commissioner.—John T. Moore, Jr.
Administrative Officer.—Tracy Morris.

CANADIAN SECTION

588 Booth Street, Suite 210, Ottawa, ON, Canada K1A 0Y7, phone (613) 944–4515

Commissioner.—Jean Gagnon.
Deputy Commissioner.—Vacant.

INTERNATIONAL COTTON ADVISORY COMMITTEE

Headquarters: 1629 K Street, NW., Suite 702, 20006, secretariat@icac.org
phone (202) 463–6660, https://icac.org

(Permanent Secretariat of the Organization)

MEMBER COUNTRIES

Argentina
Australia
Bangladesh
Brazil
Burkina Faso
Cameroon
Chad
Côte d'Ivoire
Egypt
European Union
India
Kazakhstan
Kenya
Korea, Republic of
Mali
Mozambique
Nigeria
Pakistan
Russia
South Africa
Sudan
Switzerland
Taiwan
Togo
Turkey
Uganda
United States
Uzbekistan
Zimbabwe

Executive Director.—Kai Hughes.
Statistician.—Lihan Wei.
Director of Trade Analysis.—Andrei Guitchounts.
Economist.—Lorena Ruíz.
Head of Technical Information Section.—Keshava Raj Kranthi.

INTERNATIONAL JOINT COMMISSION, UNITED STATES AND CANADA

UNITED STATES SECTION

1717 H Street, NW., Suite 835, 20006

phone (202) 736–9000, fax 632–2006, https://ijc.org

Chair.—Jane Corwin.
Commissioners: Robert Sisson, Lance Yohe.
Secretary.—Charles A. Lawson.
Legal Advisor.—Susan Daniel.
Engineering Advisors: Mark Colosimo, Mark Gabriel.
Public Information Officer.—Frank Bevacqua.
Ecologist.—Victor Serveiss.
GIS Coordinator.—Michael Laitta.
Senior Advisor.—Caron Demars.

CANADIAN SECTION

234 Laurier Avenue West, Ottawa, ON, Canada K1P 6K6

phone (613) 995–2984, fax 993–5583

Chairman.—Pierre Beland.
Commissioners: Henry Lickers, Merrell-Ann Phare.
Secretary.—Camille Mageau.
Legal Advisors: Christine Blanchet, Shane Zurbrigg.
Public Affairs Advisor.—Sarah Lobrichon.
Director, Science and Engineering.—Pierre Yves Caux.
Engineering Advisors: David Fay, Wayne Jenkinson, Erika Klyszejko.
Ecosystem Advisor.—Robert Phillips.
Environmental Officer.—Catherine Lee-Johnston.

Director, Policy and Programs.—Paul Allen.
Senior Communications Advisor.—Michele D'Amours.

GREAT LAKES REGIONAL OFFICE

100 Ouellette Avenue, 8th Floor, Windsor, ON, Canada N9A 6T3

phone (519) 257–6700 (Canada), (313) 226–2170 (U.S.)

Director.—David Burden.
Public Affairs Officer.—Sally Cole-Misch.
Physical Scientists: Antonette Arvai, Raj Bejankiwar, Jennifer Boehme, Mark Burrows, Matthew Child, Lizhu Wang, John E. Wilson.

INTERNATIONAL LABOR ORGANIZATION

Headquarters: 4, route des Morillons, CH–1211, Geneva 22, Switzerland

phone 41–22–799–6111, https://ilo.org

ILO USA Office, 900 19th Street, NW., Suite 300, 20006

phone (202) 617–3952, fax 617–3960, https://ilo.org/washington

Liaison Office with the United Nations

One Dag Hammarskjöld Plaza, 885 Second Avenue, 30th Floor, New York, NY 10017

phone (212) 697–0150, fax 697–5218, https://ilo.org/newyork

International Labor Office (Permanent Secretariat of the Organization)
Headquarters Geneva:
Director-General.—Guy Ryder.
Washington:
Director.—Kevin Cassidy.
New York:
Director.—Vinicius Pinheiro.
Deputy Director.—Vacant.

INTERNATIONAL MONETARY FUND

700 19th Street, NW., 20431, phone (202) 623–7000

https://imf.org

MANAGEMENT AND SENIOR OFFICERS

Managing Director.—Kristalina Georgieva.
First Deputy Managing Director.—David Lipton.
Deputy Managing Director and Chief Administrative Officer.—Carla Grasso.
Deputy Managing Directors: Mitsuhiro Furusawa, Tao Zhang.
Economic Counselor.—Gita Gopinath.
Financial Counselor.—Tobias Adrian.
Legal Department General Counsel.—Rhoda Weeks-Brown.
Departmental Directors:
African.—Abebe Aemro Selassie.
Asia and Pacific.—Changyong Rhee.
Budget and Planning.—Daniel Citrin.
European.—Poul Mathias Thomsen.
Communications.—Gerard T. Rice.
Finance.—Andrew Tweedie.
Fiscal Affairs.—Vitor Gaspar.
Human Resources.—Kalpana Kochhar.
Internal Audit and Inspection.—Nancy Onyango.
Middle East and Central Asia.—Jihad Azour.
Monetary and Capital Markets.—Tobias Adrian.
Strategy, Policy, and Review.—Martin Muhleisen.
Research.—Gita Gopinath.
Secretary.—Jianhai Lin.

Statistics.—Louis Marc Ducharme.
Information Technology.—Ed Anderson.
Western Hemisphere.—Alejandro Werner.
Director, Regional Office for Asia and the Pacific.—Chikahisa Sumi.
Director, Europe Offices.—Jeffrey Franks.
Director and Special Representative to the United Nations.—Chris Lane.
Independent Evaluations Office.—Charles Collyns.
Institute for Capacity Development.—Sharmini A. Coorey.
Legal and General Counsel.—Rhoda Weeks-Brown.

EXECUTIVE DIRECTORS AND ALTERNATES

Executive Directors:

Maher Mouminah, represents Saudi Arabia.

Herve M. Jodon de Villeroche, represents France.

Thomas Ostros, represents Denmark, Estonia, Finland, Iceland, Latvia, Lithuania, Norway, Sweden.

Bruno Saraiva, represents Brazil, Cabo Verde, Dominican Republic, Ecuador, Guyana, Haiti, Nicaragua, Panama, Suriname, Timor-Leste, Trinidad and Tobago.

Louise Levonian, represents Antigua and Barbuda, the Bahamas, Barbados, Belize, Canada, Dominica, Grenada, Ireland, Jamaica, St. Kitts and Nevis, St. Lucia, St. Vincent and the Grenadines.

Dumisani Herbert Mahlinza, represents Angola, Botswana, Burundi, Eritrea, Ethiopia, The Gambia, Kenya, Lesotho, Liberia, Malawi, Mozambique, Namibia, Nigeria, Sierra Leone, Somalia, South Africa, South Sudan (Republic of), Sudan, Eswantini, Tanzania, Uganda, Zambia, Zimbabwe.

Mahinda Siriwardana, represents Bangladesh, Bhutan, India, Sri Lanka.

Alisara Mahasandana, represents Brunei Darussalam, Cambodia, Fiji, Indonesia, Lao People's Democratic Republic, Malaysia, Myanmar, Nepal, Philippines, Singapore, Thailand, Tonga, Vietnam.

Paul Inderbinen, represents Azerbaijan, Kazakhstan, Kyrgyz Republic, Poland, Serbia, Switzerland, Tajikistan, Turkmenistan, and Uzbekistan.

Leonardo Villar, represents Colombia, Costa Rica, El Salvador, Guatemala, Honduras, Mexico, Spain, Venezuela (Republica Bolivariana de Venezuela).

Raci Kaya, represents Austria, Belarus, Czech Republic, Hungary, Kosovo, Slovak Republic, Slovenia, Turkey.

Mohamed-Lemine Raghani, represents Benin, Burkina Faso, Cameroon, Central African Republic, Chad, Comoros, Congo (Democratic Republic of), Congo (Republic of), Cote d'Ivoire, Djibouti, Equatorial Guinea, Gabon, Guinea, Guinea-Bissau, Madagascar, Mali, Mauritania, Mauritius, Niger, Rwanda, Sao Tome and Principe, Senegal, Togo.

Domenico Fanizza, represents Albania, Greece, Italy, Malta, Portugal, San Marino.

Mark Rosen, represents United States.

Takuji Tanaka, represents Japan.

Jafar Mojarrad, represents Afghanistan (Islamic Republic of), Algeria, Ghana, Iran (Islamic Republic of), Morocco, Pakistan, Tunisia.

Gabriel Lopetegui, represents Argentina, Bolivia, Chile, Paraguay, Peru, Uruguay.

Ruediger von Kleist, represents Germany.

Hazem Beblawi Elbeblawi, represents Bahrain, Egypt, Iraq, Jordan, Kuwait, Lebanon, Libya, Maldives, Oman, Qatar, Syrian Arab Republic, United Arab Emirates, Yemen (Republic of).

Aleksei V. Mozhin, represents Russian Federation.

Nigel Ray, represents Australia, Kiribati, Korea, Marshall Islands, Micronesia (Federated States of), Mongolia, Nauru, New Zealand, Palau, Papua New Guinea, Samoa, Seychelles, Solomon Islands, Tuvalu, and, Vanuatu.

Anthony De Lannoy, represents Armenia, Belgium, Bosnia and Herzegovina, Bulgaria, Croatia, Cyprus, Georgia, Israel, Luxembourg, Macedonia (former Yugoslav Republic of), Moldova, Republic of North Montenegro, Netherlands, Romania, Ukraine.

Zhongxia Jin, represents China.

Shona Riach, represents United Kingdom.

INTERNATIONAL ORGANIZATION FOR MIGRATION

Geneva Headquarters: 17 Route Des Morillons (P.O. Box 71), CH1211
Geneva 19, Switzerland, phone +41.22.798.61.50
Washington Mission: 1752 N Street, NW., Suite 600
Washington, DC 20036, phone (202) 862–1826
New York Mission: 122 East 42nd Street, 48th Floor
New York, NY 10168–1610, phone (212) 681–7000

HEADQUARTERS

Director General.—António Vitorino (Portugal).
Deputy Director General.—Laura Thompson (Costa Rica).
Washington Chief of Mission.—Luca Dall'Oglio (Italy).
Director of Office to the United Nations.—Ashraf El Nour (South Sudan).

MEMBER STATES

Afghanistan
Albania
Algeria
Angola
Antigua and Barbuda
Argentina
Armenia
Australia
Austria
Azerbaijan
Bahamas
Bangladesh
Belarus
Belgium
Belize
Benin
Bolivia (Plurinational State of)
Bosnia and Herzegovina
Botswana
Brazil
Bulgaria
Burkina Faso
Burundi
Cabo Verde
Cambodia
Cameroon
Canada
Central African Republic
Chad
Chile
China
Colombia
Comoros
Congo
Cook Islands
Costa Rica
Cote d'Ivoire
Croatia
Cuba
Cyprus
Czech Republic
Democratic Republic of the Congo
Denmark
Djibouti
Dominica
Dominican Republic
Ecuador
Egypt
El Salvador
Eritrea
Estonia
Eswatini
Ethiopia
Fiji
Finland
France
Gabon
Gambia
Georgia
Germany
Ghana
Greece
Grenada
Guatemala
Guinea
Guinea-Bissau
Guyana
Haiti
Holy See
Honduras
Hungary
Iceland
India
Iran (Islamic Republic of)
Ireland
Israel
Italy
Jamaica
Japan
Jordan
Kazakhstan
Kenya
Kiribati
Kyrgyzstan
Lao People's Democratic Republic
Latvia
Lesotho
Liberia
Libya
Lithuania
Luxembourg
Madagascar
Malawi
Maldives
Mali
Malta
Marshall Islands
Mauritania
Mauritius
Mexico
Micronesia (Federated States of)
Mongolia
Montenegro
Morocco
Mozambique
Myanmar
Namibia
Nauru
Nepal
Netherlands
New Zealand
Nicaragua
Niger
Nigeria
North Macedonia
Norway
Pakistan
Palau
Panama
Papua New Guinea
Paraguay
Peru
Philippines
Poland
Portugal
Republic of Korea
Republic of Moldova
Romania
Rwanda
Saint Kitts and Nevis
Saint Lucia

Saint Vincent and the Grenadines
Samoa
Sao Tome and Principe
Senegal
Serbia
Seychelles
Sierra Leone
Slovakia
Slovenia
Solomon Islands
Somalia
South Africa
South Sudan
Spain
Sri Lanka
Sudan
Suriname
Sweden
Switzerland
Tajikistan
Thailand
Timor-Leste
Togo
Tonga
Trinidad and Tobago
Tunisia
Turkey
Turkmenistan
Tuvalu
Uganda
Ukraine
United Kingdom of Great Britain and Northern Ireland
United Republic of Tanzania
United States of America
Uruguay
Uzbekistan
Vanuatu
Venezuela (Bolivarian Republic of)
Viet Nam
Yemen
Zambia
Zimbabwe

OBSERVER STATES (8)

Bahrain
Bhutan
Indonesia
Kuwait
Qatar
Russian Federation
San Marino
Saudi Arabia

INTERNATIONAL GOVERNMENTAL AND NON-GOVERNMENTAL ORGANIZATIONS

Organs and Organizations of the United Nations System

United Nations
Economic and Social Commission for Asia and the Pacific (ESCAP)
Economic Commission for Africa (ECA)
Economic Commission for Latin America and the Caribbean (ECLAC)
Food and Agriculture Organization of the United Nations (FAO)
International Labour Organization (ILO)
International Maritime Organization (IMO)
Office for the Coordination of Humanitarian Affairs (OCHA)
Office of the United Nations High Commissioner for Human Rights (OHCHR)
Office of the United Nations High Commissioner for Refugees (UNHCR)
United Nations Children's Fund (UNICEF)
United Nations Conference on Trade and Development (UNCTAD)
United Nations Development Programme (UNDP)
United Nations Educational, Scientific and Cultural Organization (UNESCO)
United Nations Entity for Gender Equality and the Empowerment of Women (UN–WOMEN)
United Nations Environment Programme (UNEP)
United Nations Human Settlements Programme (UN–HABITAT)
United Nations Industrial Development Organization (UNIDO)
United Nations Population Fund (UNFPA)
United Nations Research Institute for Social Development (UNRISD)
Universal Postal Union (UPU)

World Bank
World Food Programme (WFP)
World Health Organization (WHO)
World Intellectual Property Organization (WIPO)
World Meteorological Organization (WMO)
Intergovernmental organizations and other entities

African Union
African, Caribbean and Pacific Group of States (ACP Group)
Asian-African Legal Consultative Organization (AALCO)
Common Market for Eastern and Southern Africa (COMESA)
Community of Portuguese Speaking Countries (CPLP)
Community of Sahel-Saharan States (CEN–SAD)

Council of Europe
East African Community (EAC)
Economic Community of Central African States (ECCAS)

Economic Community of West African States Commission (ECOWAS)

European Union (EU)
Ibero-American General Secretariat (SEGIB)
Inter-American Development Bank (IADB)
Intergovernmental Authority on Development (IGAD)
International Centre for Migration Policy Development (ICMPD)
International Committee of the Red Cross
International Federation of Red Cross and Red Crescent Societies
Islamic Educational, Scientific and Cultural Organization (ISESCO)
Italian-Latin American Institute

League of Arab States
Organisation internationale de la Francophonie
Organization for Economic Co-operation and Development
Organization of American States
Organization of the Islamic Cooperation
Parliamentary Assembly of the Union for the Mediterranean
Sovereign Order of Malta
Southeast European Cooperative Initiative (SECI) - Regional Center for Combating Transborder Crime
Southern African Development Community Secretariat (SADC)
Union du Maghreb Arabe (UMA)

OTHER ORGANIZATIONS WITH OBSERVER STATUS

Africa Humanitarian Action (AHA)
Africa Recruit
African and Black Diaspora Global Network on HIV and AIDS (ABDGN)
African Foundation for Development
American Jewish Joint Distribution Committee (JDC) - Center for International Migration and Integration (CIMI)
Amnesty International
Assistance pédagogique internationale (API)
Australian Catholic Migrant and Refugee Office (ACMRO)
CARAM Asia
CARE International
Caritas Internationalis
Catholic Relief Services
Center for Migration Studies of New York (CMS)
Danish Refugee Council
December 18
Episcopal Migration Ministries
European Youth Forum (YFJ)
Federation of Ethnic Communities' Councils of Australia, Inc.
Femmes Africa Solidarité (FAS)
FOCSIV-Volontari Nel Mondo (Federation of Christian Organizations for International Volunteer Service)
Food for the Hungry International
Friends World Committee for Consultation (FWCC)
Hassan II Foundation for Moroccans Residing Abroad
HIAS, Inc.
Human Rights Watch
Internal Displacement Monitoring Centre
International Catholic Migration Commission
International Council of Voluntary Agencies
International Council on Social Welfare
International Institute of Humanitarian Law (IIHL)
International Islamic Relief Organisation
International Medical Corps
International Organisation of Employers
International Rescue Committee
International Social Service
International Trade Union Confederation (ITUC)
INTERSOS
Islamic Relief
Japan International Friendship and Welfare Foundation
Jesuit Refugee Service (JRS)
"La Caixa" Foundation
Lutheran World Federation
Migrant Help
Migrants Rights International (MRI)
NGO Committee on Migration
Niwano Peace Foundation
Norwegian Refugee Council
Partage avec les enfants du tiers monde
Paulino Torras Doménech Foundation
Qatar Charity
Refugee Council of Australia
Refugee Education Trust (RET)
Sasakawa Peace Foundation
Save the Children
Scalabrini International Migration Network (SIMN)
Solidar
Terre des Hommes International Federation
The Hague Institute for Global Justice
Tolstoy Foundation, Inc.
United Ukrainian American Relief Committee
World Council of Churches
World Vision International

DUTY STATIONS 2015

Afghanistan 2
Herat
Kabul

Albania 1
Tirana

Algeria 1
Algiers

Angola 3
Luanda
Maquela d Zombo
Uige

Argentina 1
Buenos Aires

Armenia 2
Gyumri
Yerevan

Australia 6
Brisbane
Canberra
Darwin
Melbourne
Perth
Sydney

Austria 2
Vienna CO
Vienna RO

Azerbaijan 2
Baku
Mingachevir

Bangladesh 3
Chittagong
Dhaka
Sylhet

Belarus 1
Minsk

Belgium 1
Brussels

Benin 1
Cotonou

Bolivia (Plurinational State of) 1
La Paz

Bosnia and Herzegovina 2
Banja Luka
Sarajevo

Botswana 1
Gaborone

Bulgaria 2
Burgas
Sofia

Burkina Faso 1
Ouagadougou

Burundi 3
Bujumbura
Rutana
Ruyigi

Cabo Verde 1
Praia

Cambodia 1
Phnom Penh

Cameroon 1
Yaounde

Canada 1
Ottawa

Central African Republic 3
Bangui
Boda
Kabo

Chad 8
Abeche
Farchana
Faya
Gore
Mao
Moussoro
N'Djamena
Tissi

Chile 1
Santiago

China 2
Beijing
Hong Kong SAR

Colombia 31
Arauca
Armenia
Barranquilla
Bogota
Bucaramanga
Buenaventura
Cali
Cartagena
Cauca Valley
Cucuta
Florencia
Guajira
Ibagué
Manizales
Medellin
Mitu
Mocoa
Monteria
Nariño
Neiva
Pasto
Pereira
Popayan
Quibdo
Santa Marta
Sincelejo
SJ de Guaviare
Tumaco
Tunja
Valledupar
Villavicencio

Congo 1
Brazzaville

Costa Rica 1
San Jose

Côte d'Ivoire 4
Abidjan
Danane
Tabou
Toulepleu

Croatia 1
Zagreb

Cyprus 1
Nicosia

Czech Republic 1
Prague

Democratic Republic of the Congo (the) 7
Bukavu
Bunia
Goma
Kasindi
Kimpese
Kinshasa
Lubumbashi

Denmark 1
Copenhagen

Djibouti 1
Djibouti

Dominican Republic 1
Santo Domingo

Ecuador 1
Quito

Egypt 1
Cairo

El Salvador 1
San Salvador

Estonia 1

Tallinn

Ethiopia 9
Addis Ababa
Assosa
Dollo Addo
Gambella
Jijiga
Moyale
Semera
Shimelba
Shire Endaselas

Finland 1
Helsinki

France 2
Marseille
Paris

Gabon 1
Libreville

Gambia 1
Banjul

Georgia 5
Batumi
Gori
Kutaisi
Tbilisi
Telavi

Germany 2
Berlin
Nuremberg

Ghana 1
Accra

Greece 1
Athens

Guatemala 1
Guatemala City

Guinea 2
Conakry
Nzerekore

Guyana 1
Georgetown

Haiti 3
Gonaives
Ouanaminthe
Port-au-Prince

Honduras 1
Tegucigalpa

Hungary 1
Budapest

India 1
New Delhi

Indonesia 25
Aceh Selatan
Aceh Timur
Aceh Utara
Ambon
Balikpapan
Banda Aceh
Batam
Bener Meriah
Jakarta
Jayapura
Jimbaran
Kupang
Langsa
Lhokseumawe
Makassar
Medan
Menado
Merauke
Pekanbaru
Pontianak
Semarang
Surabaya
Takengon
Tanjung Pinang
Yogyakarta

Iran 1
Teheran

Iraq 6
Al Basrah
Ar Ramadi
Baghdad
Dohuk
Erbil
Sulaymaniah

Ireland 1
Dublin

Italy 2
Rome
Turin

Jamaica 1
Kingston

Japan 1
Tokyo

Jordan 1
Amman

Kazakhstan 2
Almaty
Astana

Kenya 8
Dadaab
Eldoret
Garissa
Kakuma
Lodwar
Marsabit
Nairobi
Wajir

Korea (Republic of) 1
Seoul

Kuwait 1
Kuwait City

Kyrgyzstan 2
Bishkek
Osh

Lao People's Democratic Republic 1
Vientiane

Latvia 1
Riga

Lebanon 1
Beirut

Lesotho 1
Maseru

Liberia 4
Buchanan
Monrovia
Sinje
Tubmanburg

Libya 2
Benghazi
Tripoli

Lithuania 1
Vilnius

Madagascar 1
Antananarivo

Malawi 1
Lilongwe

Malaysia 1
Kuala Lumpur

Maldives 1
Male

Mali 4
Bamako
Gao
Mopti
Tombouctou

Malta 1
Valletta

Marshall Islands 1
Majuro

Mauritania 1
Nouakchott

Mauritius 1
Port Louis

Mexico 3
Mexico City
Tapachula
Tuxtla

Micronesia (Federated States of) 4
Chuuk
Kosrae
Pohnpei
Yap

Mongolia 1
Ulaanbaatar

Montenegro 1
Podgorica

Morocco 4
Khouribga
Rabat
Tangier
Tetouan

Mozambique 3
Maputo
Quelimane
Xai-Xai

Myanmar 12
Mon
Ayeyarwady Delt
Bogalay
Hpa-an
Loikaw
Mawlamyinegyun
Myawaddy
Myitkyina
Sittwe
Thaton
Yangon
Ye

Namibia 1
Windhoek

Nepal 4
Chautara
Damak
Gorkha
Kathmandu

Netherlands 3
Schiphol Airp.
The Hague
Zwolle

Nicaragua 1
Managua

Niger 4
Arlit
Diffa
Niamey
Zinder

Nigeria 3
Abuja
Lagos
Yola

Norway 1
Oslo

Pakistan 5
Islamabad
Karachi
Lahore
Mirpur
Peshawar

Panama 1
Panama City

Papua New Guinea 6
Buka
Kimbe
Lae
Manus
Popondetta
Port Moresby

Paraguay 1
Asuncion

Peru 1
Lima

Philippines 8
Cebu
Cotabato City
Guiuan
Manila
Ormoc
Roxas
Tacloban
Zamboanga

Poland 1
Warsaw

Portugal 1
Lisbon

Republic of Moldova 1
Chisinau

Romania 1
Bucharest

Russian Federation 2
Krasnodar
Moscow

Rwanda 1
Kigali

Saudi Arabia 1
Riyadh

Senegal 1
Dakar

Serbia 2
Belgrade
Pristina

Sierra Leone 1
Freetown

Slovakia 2
Bratislava
Kosice

Slovenia 1
Ljubljana

Somalia 4
Bossaso
Garowe
Hargeisa-Somali
Mogadishu

South Africa 1
Pretoria

South Sudan 8
Bentiu
Bor
Juba
Maban
Malakal
Malualkon
Renk
Wau

Spain 1
Madrid

Sri Lanka 6
Ampara
Batticaloa
Colombo
Jaffna
Kilinochchi
Vavuniya

Sudan 8
Abyei
El Fasher
El Fula
Geneina
Kadugli
Kassala
Khartoum
Nyala

Switzerland 5
Altstatten
Basel
Bern
Geneva
Kreuzlingen

Syrian Arab Republic 11

Al Hasakah
Aleppo
Damascus
Deirezzor
Dera'a
Homs
Idleb
Latakia
Quneitra
Sweida
Tartus

Tajikistan 1
Dushanbe

Thailand 10
Bangkok
Chanthaburi
Chiang Mai
Chiang Rai
Mae Hong Son
Mae Sariang
Mae Sot
Phang Nga
Ranong
Songkhla

The former Yugoslav Republic of Macedonia 1
Skopje

Timor-Leste 1
Dili

Togo 1
Lome

Trinidad and Tobago 1
Port of Spain

Tunisia 2
Tunis
Zarzis

Turkey 3
Ankara
Gaziantep
Istanbul

Turkmenistan 1
Ashgabad

Uganda 1
Kampala

Ukraine 3
Kharkiv
Kiev
Odessa

United Arab Emirates 1
Dubai

United Kingdom of Great Britain and Northern Ireland 1
London

United Republic of Tanzania 3
Dar-es-Salaam
Kigoma
Moshi

United States of America 10
Chicago
Guantanamo Bay
Irvine
Los Angeles
Miami
New York
New York-JFK
Newark
SLO New York
Washington

UNSC resolution 1244-administered, Kosovo 3
Mitrovica
Peje
Pristina

Uruguay 1
Montevideo

Uzbekistan 1
Tashkent

Vanuatu 1
Port Vila

Venezuela (Bolivarian Republic of) 2
Caracas
San Cristobal

Viet Nam 2
Hanoi
Ho Chi Minh City

Yemen 3
Aden
Harad
Sana'a

Zambia 1
Lusaka

Zimbabwe 3
Beitbridge
Harare
Mutare

Grand Total 401

INTERNATIONAL PACIFIC HALIBUT COMMISSION
UNITED STATES AND CANADA

Headquarters / Mailing address:

2320 West Commodore Way, Suite 300, Seattle, WA 98199–1287

phone (206) 634–1838, fax 632–2983

American Commissioners:

Robert Alverson, Fishing Vessel Owners' Association, 4005–20th Avenue West, Room 232, Seattle, WA 98199 (206) 283–7735.

Chris Oliver, NOAA Fisheries, 1305 East West Highway, Silver Spring, MD 20910 (301) 713–2065.

Richard Yamada, 2320 West Commodore Way, Suite 300, Seattle, WA 98199–1287.

Canadian Commissioners:

Paul Ryall, Fisheries and Oceans Canada, 401 Burrard Street, Suite 200, Vancouver, BC V6C 3S4, Canada (604) 666–0115.

Neil Davis, Fisheries and Oceans Canada, 401 Burrard Street, Suite 200, Vancouver, BC V6C 3R2, Canada.

Peter DeGreef, 2320 West Commodore Way, Suite 300, Seattle, WA 98199–1287.

Director and Secretary (ex officio).—Dr. David Wilson, 2320 West Commodore Way, Suite 300, Seattle, WA 98199–1287.

ORGANIZATION OF AMERICAN STATES

17th Street and Constitution Avenue, NW., Washington, DC 20006

phone (202) 370–5000, fax 458–3967

PERMANENT MISSIONS TO THE OAS

Antigua and Barbuda.—Ambassador Sir Ronald Sanders, Permanent Representative, 3234 Prospect Street, NW., 20007, phone 362–5122 / 5166 / 5211, fax 362–5225.

Argentina.—Ambassador Paula Maria Bertol, Permanent Representative, 1816 Corcoran Street, NW., 20009, phone 387–4142 / 4146 / 4170.

The Bahamas.—Ambassador Sydnie Stanley Collie, Permanent Representative, 2220 Massachusetts Avenue, NW., 20008, phone 319–2660 / 2667, fax 319–2668.

Barbados.—Ambassador Noel Anderson Lynch, Permanent Representative, 2144 Wyoming Avenue, NW., 20008, phone 939–9200 / 9201 / 9202, fax 332–7467.

Belize.—Ambassador Francisco Daniel Gutierez, Permanent Representative, 2535 Massachusetts Avenue, NW., 20008–3098, phone 332–9636, ext. 228, fax 332–6888.

Bolivia.—Ambassador Jose Alberto Gonzales, Permanent Representative, 1710 Rhode Island Ave., NW., Suite 400, 20036, phone 785–0218 / 0219 / 0224.

Brazil.—Ambassador Fernando Simas Magalhaes, Permanent Representative, 2600 Virginia Avenue, NW., Suite 412, 20037, phone 333–4224 / 4225 / 4226, fax 333–6610.

Canada.—Mr. Francois Jubinville, Interim Representative, 501 Pennsylvania Avenue, NW., 20001, phone 682–1768, fax 682–7624.

Chile.—Ambassador Hernan Salinas Burgos, Permanent Representative, 2175 K Street, NW., Suite 350, 20037, phone 887–5475 / 5476 / 5477 / 5478, fax 775–0713.

Colombia.—Ambassador Alejandro Ordoñez Maldonado, Permanent Representative, 1724 Massachusetts Ave., NW., 7th Floor, 20036, phone 332–8003 / 8004, fax 234–9781.

Costa Rica.—Ambassador Montserrat Solano Carboni, Permanent Representative, 2112 S Street, NW., Suite 300, 20008, phone 234–9280 / 9281, fax 986–2274.

Dominica.—Ambassador Dr. Vince Henderson, Permanent Representative, 1001 North 19th Street, Suite 1200, Arlington, VA 22209, phone (202) 364–6781 / 6782.

Dominican Republic.—Ambassador Gedeon Santos, Permanent Representative, 1715 22nd Street, NW., 20008, phone 332–9142 / 0616 / 0772, fax 232–5038.

Ecuador.—Ambassador Carlos Alberto Játiva Naranjo, Permanent Representative, 1889 F St., NW., 2nd Floor, 20006, phone 551–9160 / 9161.

El Salvador.—Ambassador Wendy Acevedo Castillo, Interim Representative, 2308 California Street, NW., 20008, phone 595–7546, fax 232–4806.

Grenada.—Ambassador Yoland Yvonne Smith, Permanent Representative, 1701 New Hampshire Avenue, NW., 20009, phone 265–2561, fax 265–2468.

Guatemala.—Ambassador Rita Claverie de Sciolli, Permanent Representative, 1507 22nd Street, NW., 20037, phone 833–4015, fax 833–4011.

Guyana.—Ambassador Dr. Riyad Insanally, Permanent Representative, 2490 Tracy Place, NW., 20008, phone 265–6900 / 6901, fax 232–1297.

Haiti.—Ambassador Leon Charles, Interim Representative, 2311 Massachusetts Avenue, NW., 20008, phone 742–1970 / 1975, fax 518–8742.

Honduras.—Ambassador Leonidas Rosa Bautista, Permanent Representative, 1250 Connecticut Ave., NW., Suite 700, 20008, phone 966–0812 / 7702.

Jamaica.—Ambassador Audrey Marks, Permanent Representative, 1520 New Hampshire Avenue, NW., 20036, phone 986–0121 / 0123, fax 452–9395.

Mexico.—Ambassador Luz Elena Baños Rivas, Permanent Representative, 2440 Massachusetts Avenue, NW., 20008, phone 332–3663 / 328–5300, fax 234–0602.

Nicaragua.—Ambassador Denis Ronaldo Moncada Colindres, Permanent Representative, 1627 New Hampshire Avenue, NW., 20009, phone 939–6536, fax 745–0710.

Panama.—Mrs. Juana de Dios Mudarra de Morales, Interim Representative, 2201 Wisconsin Avenue, NW., Suite 350, 20007, phone 506–7910.

Paraguay.—Ambassador Elisa Ruiz Diaz Bareiro, Permanent Representative, 2022 Connecticut Avenue, NW., 20008, phone 232–8020 / 8021 / 8022, fax 244–3005.

Peru.—Ambassador José Manuel Boza Orozco, Permanent Representative, 1901 Pennsylvania Avenue, NW., Suite 775, 20006, phone 232–2281, fax 466–3068.

Saint Kitts and Nevis.—Ambassador Dr. Everson Hull, Permanent Representative, 1627 K Street, NW., Suite 1200, Washington, DC 20006, phone 686–2636 / (571) 527–1360, fax 686–5740.

Saint Lucia.—Ambassador Anton E. Edmunds, Permanent Representative, 1629 K Street, NW., Suite 1250, Washington, DC 20006, phone 364–6792, fax 364–6723.

Saint Vincent and The Grenadines.—Ambassador Lou-Anne Gaylene Christ, Permanent Representative, 1627 K Street, Suite 1202, Washington, DC 20006, phone 364–6730, fax 364–6736.
Suriname.—Ambassador Niermala Badrising, Permanent Representative, 4201 Connecticut Ave., NW., Suite 400, 20008, phone 629–4302 / 4401 / 4392, fax 629–4769.
Trinidad and Tobago.—Ambassador Anthony Phillips-Spencer, Permanent Representative, 1708 Massachusetts Avenue, NW., 20036, phone 467–6490, fax 785–3130.
United States of America.—Ambassador Carlos Trujillo, Permanent Representative, WHA / USOAS Bureau of Western Hemisphere Affairs, Department of State, Room 5914, 20520–6258, phone 647–9376, fax 647–0911 / 6973.
Uruguay.—Ambassador Hugo Cayrus, Permanent Representative, 1913 I (Eye) Street, NW., 4th Floor, 20006, phone 223–1961, fax 223–1966.
Venezuela.—Ambassador Gustavo Tarre Briceño, National Assembly's designated Permanent Representative, 1099 30th Street, NW., Second Floor, 20007, phone 483–0285.

GENERAL SECRETARIAT

Secretary General.—Luis Almagro (202) 370–5000.
Chief of Staff to the Secretary General.—Gonzalo Koncke, 370–0300.
Assistant Secretary General.—Nestor Mendez, 370–0195, fax 458–3011.
Chief of Staff to the Assistant Secretary General.—Ambassador La Celia Prince, 370–0195.
Executive Secretary for—
Integral Development.—Kim Hurtault-Osborne, 370–9014.
Inter-American Commission on Human Rights.—Paulo Abrão, 370–9000.
Secretary for—
Administration and Finance.—Charles H. Grover, 370–5401.
Multidimensional Security.—Farah Diva Urrutia, 370–9959.
Strengthening Democracy.—Francisco Guerrero, 370–9962.
Access to Rights and Equity.—Gastão Alves de Toledo, 370–5513.
Hemispheric Affairs.—James M. Lambert, 370–4448.
Legal Affairs.—Jean Michel Arrighi, 370–0741.
Director for—
Summits Secretariat.—(Appointment pending), 370–0281.
Press and Communications.—Gonzalo Espariz (acting), 370–5437.

ORGANIZATION FOR ECONOMIC CO-OPERATION AND DEVELOPMENT

Headquarters: Paris, France, https://oecd.org

Washington Center, 1776 Eye Street, NW., Suite 450, 20006

phone (202) 785–6323, fax 785–0350

Washington.contact@oecd.org, https://oecd.org/washington

PARIS HEADQUARTERS

Secretary-General.—Angel Gurría.
Deputy Secretaries-General: Masamichi Kono, Ulrick Vestergaard Knudsen, Jeffrey Schlangenhauf, Ludger Schuknecht.
Chief Economist.—Laurence Boone.

WASHINGTON CENTER

Head of Center.—Will Davis.
Member Countries:

Australia	France	Korea
Austria	Germany	Latvia
Belgium	Greece	Lithuania
Canada	Hungary	Luxembourg
Chile	Iceland	Mexico
Czech Republic	Ireland	Netherlands
Denmark	Israel	New Zealand
Estonia	Italy	Norway
Finland	Japan	Poland

Portugal
Slovak Republic
Slovenia
Spain
Sweden
Switzerland
Turkey
United Kingdom
United States

OECD WASHINGTON CENTER

1776 Eye Street, NW., Suite 450, 20006, phone (202) 785–6323, fax 315–2508
https://oecd.org/washington

Head of Center.—Will Davis.

PAN AMERICAN HEALTH ORGANIZATION (PAHO) REGIONAL OFFICE OF THE WORLD HEALTH ORGANIZATION

525 23rd Street, NW., 20037, phone (202) 974–3000
fax 974–3663

Director.—Dr. Carissa F. Etienne, 974–3408.
Deputy Director.—Dr. Isabella Danel, 974–3178.
Assistant Director.—Dr. Jarbas Barbosa, 974–3404.
Director of Administration.—Gerald Anderson, 974–3412.

PAHO / WHO FIELD OFFICES

OPS / WHO OFICINAS DE LOS REPRESENTANTES EN LOS PAISES

Barbados and Eastern Caribbean Countries (ECC serves the following countries, territories, and departments: Antigua and Barbuda, Barbados, Dominica, Grenada, St. Kitts and Nevis, Saint Lucia, St. Vincent and the Grenadines. Overseas Territories: Anguilla, British Virgin Islands, Montserrat).—Dr. Jean Marie Rwangabwoba a.i., Dayralls and Navy Garden Roads, Christ Church, (P.O. Box 508), Bridgetown, Barbados, phone (246) 426–3860 / 435–9263, fax 228–5402, e-mail: ECC@paho.org, https://paho.org/ecc.

Office of Caribbean Program Coordination, OCPC.—Mrs. Jessie Schutt-Aine, Caribbean Program Coordinator, Dayralls and Navy Garden Roads, Christ Church, Bridgetown, Barbados (P.O. Box 508), (French Antilles: Guadaloupe, Martinique, St. Martin and St. Bartholomew, French Guiana), phone (246) 434–5200 / 3865 427–9434, fax 436–9779, e-mail: CPC@paho.org, https://cpc.paho.org.

PAHO / WHO Representatives:

Argentina.—Dra. Maureen Birmingham, Marcelo T. de Alvear 684, 4o. piso, 1058 Buenos Aires, Argentina, phone (54–11) 4319–4200, fax (54–11) 4319–4201, e-mail: pwr-arg@paho.org, https://paho.org/arg.

Bahamas (Also serves Turks and Caicos).—Dr. Esther de Gourville, 2nd Floor, Grosvenor Medical Centre, off Shirley Street, Nassau, Bahamas, phone (242) 326–7299 / 326–7390 / 325–0121, fax (242) 326–7012, e-mail: E-mail@bah.paho.org, https://paho.org/bah.

Belize.—Dr. Noreen Jack, 4792 Coney Drive, Coney Drive Business Plaza, 3rd Floor, (P.O. Box 1834), Belize City, Belize, phone (501–2) 2448–85 / 2339–46, fax 2309–17, e-mail: admin@blz.paho.org, https://paho.org/blz.

Bolivia.—Dr. Alfonso Tenorio Gnecco, a.i., Calle 18 No. 8022, Edificio Parque 18 Piso 2 y 3, Zona Calacoto, La Paz, Bolivia, phone (591–2) 2412–313 / fax 2412–598, e-mail: contacto@paho.org, https://paho.org/bol/, e-mail: pwrbol@bol.ops-oms.org, https://ops.org.bo.

Brazil.—Dr. Socorro Gross, Setor de Embaixadas Norte, Lote 19, 70800–400, Brasilia, (Caixa Postal 08–629, 70312–970, Brasilia, D.F., Brasil), phone (55–61) 3251–9455 / 9549 / 9500, fax 3223–0269, e-mail: email@bra.ops-oms.org, https://opas.org.br/.

Chile.—Dr. Fernando Leanes, Av. Dag Hammarskjold 3269, Vitacura, Santiago, Chile. Phone (56–2) 2437–4600 / 4605, fax 207–4717, e-mail: email@chi.ops-oms.org, https://chi.ops-oms.org.

Colombia.—Dra. Gina Tambini, Calle 66 No. 11–50, Piso 6 y 7, Edificio Villorio, Bogota, D.C., Colombia, phone (57–1) 314–4141 / 254–7050, fax 254–7070, e-mail: opscol@latino.net.co, https://col.ops-oms.org/.

Costa Rica.—Dra. Maria Dolores Perez-Rosales, Calle 16, Avenida 6 y 8, Distrito Hospital, (Apartado 3745), San Jose, Costa Rica, phone (506) 2521–7045 / 2258–5810, fax 2258–5830, e-mail: email@cor.ops-oms.org, https://cor.ops-oms.org.

Cuba.—Dr. Jose Moya, Calle 4 No. 407, entre 17 y 19 Vedado, (Casilla diplomatica 68), La Habana, Cuba C.P. 10400, phone (53–7) 831–8944 / 837–5808, fax 833–2075 /

66–2075, e-mail: pwr@cub.ops-oms.org or cruzmari@cub.ops-oms.org, https://cub.ops-oms.org.

Dominican Republic.—Dra. Alma Morales, Edificio OPS / OMS, y Defensa Civil, Calle Pepillo Salcedo-Recta Final, Plaza de la Salud, Ensanche La Fe, (Apartado Postal 1464), Santo Domingo, Republica Dominicana, phone (809) 562–1519 / 544–3241 / 542–6177, fax 544–0322, e-mail: email@dor.ops-oms.org, https://dor.ops-oms.org.

Ecuador.—Dra. Gina Watson, Amazonas N. 2889 y Mariana de Jesus, Quito, Ecuador, phone (593–2) 2460–330 / 296 / 215, fax 2460–325, e-mail: email@ecu.ops-oms.org, https://opsecu.org.ec.

El Salvador.—Dr. Carlos Garzon, 73 Avenida Sur No. 135, Colonia Escalon, (Apartado Postal 1072, Sucursal Centro), San Salvador, El Salvador, phone (503) 2511–9500 / 9504 / 9501, fax 2511–9555, e-mail: email@els.ops-oms.org, https://ops.org.sv/.

Guatemala.—Dr. Oscar Barreneche, Diagonal 6, 10–15 zona 10, Edificio Interamericas, torre norte, cuarto nivel, (Apartado Postal 383), Guatemala, Guatemala, phone (502) 2329–4200 / 2336–7426 / 2336–7425, fax 2334–3804, https://ops.org.gt.

Guyana.—Dr. William Adu-Know, Lot 8 Brickdam Stabroek, (P.O. Box 10969), Georgetown, Guyana, phone (592) 225–3000 / 227–5159, fax 226–6654 / 227–4205, e-mail: email@guy.paho.org.

Haiti.—Dr. Luis Codina, No. 295 Avenue John Brown, (Boite Postale 1330), Port-au-Prince, Haiti, phone (509) 2814–3000 / 3001 / 3002 / 3005, fax 2814–3089, e-mail: email@hai.ops-oms.org.

Honduras.—Mrs. Piedad Huerta, Edificio Imperial, 6o.y 7o.piso, Avenida Republica de Panama, Frente a la Casa de Naciones Unidas, Tegucigalpa M.D.C., Honduras, phone (504) 2221–6091 / 6098 / 6102, fax 2221–6103, e-mail: pwr@hon.ops-oms.org, https://paho-who.hn.

Jamaica (also serves Bermuda and Cayman).—Dr. Bernadette Theodore-Gandi, 8 Gibraltar Way, University of the West Indies, Mona Campus, Kingston 7, Jamaica, (P.O. Box 384, Cross Roads, P.O., Kingston 5) phone (876) 970–0016, fax 927–2657, e-mail: email@jam.ops-oms.org.

Mexico.—Econ. Christian Morales, a.i., Horacio No. 1855, 3er. Piso, Of. 305, Colonia Los Morales, Polanco, Del. Miguel Hidalgo, Mexico D.F., 11510, Mexico, phone (52–55) 5980–0880 / 0871, fax 5395–5681, e-mail: e-mail@mex.ops-oms.org, https://mex.opsoms.org.

Nicaragua.—Ing. Ana Solis-Ortega Treasure, Complejo Nacional de Salud, Camino a la Sabana, Apartado Postal 1309, Managua, Nicaragua, phone (505) 2289–4200 / 4800, fax 2289–4999, e-mail: email@nic.ops-oms.org, https://ops.org.ni.

Panama.—Dr. Gerardo Alfaro, Ministerio de Salud de Panama, Ancon, Avenida Gorgas, Edificio 261, 2o piso, (Casilla Postal 0843–3441), Panama, Panama, phone (507) 262–0030 / 1996, fax 262–4052, e-mail: email@pan.ops-oms.org, https://opsoms.org.pa.

Paraguay.—Dr. Luis Roberto Escoto, Edificio ''Faro del Rio'' Mcal Lopez 957 Esq. Estados Unidos, (Casilla de Correo 839), Asuncion, Paraguay, (Casilla de Correo 839) phone (595–21) 450–495 / 449–864, fax 450–498, e-mail: email@par.ops-oms.org, https://par.ops-oms.org.

Peru.—Dr. Rubén Mayorga-Sagastume, Los Pinos 251, Urbanizacion Camacho, La Molina, Lima 12, Peru, phone (51–1) 319–5700 / 5781, fax 437–8289, e-mail: email@per.opsoms.org, https://per.ops.oms.org.

Puerto Rico.—Dr. Raul Castellanos Bran, P.O. Box 70184, San Juan, Puerto Rico 00936, phone (787) 274–7608, fax 250–6547 / 767–8341.

Suriname.—Dr. Yitades Gebre, Burenstraat #33, (P.O. Box 1863), Paramaribo, Suriname, phone (597) 471–676 / 425–355, fax 471–568, e-mail: email@sur.paho.org.

Trinidad and Tobago.—Dr. Erica Wheeler, Sweet Briar Place, First Floor, 10–12 Sweet Briar Road, St. Clair, Trinidad, phone (868) 624–7524 / 4376 / 2078 / 625–4492, fax 624–5643, email: email@trt.paho.org.

Uruguay.—Dr. Giovanni Escalante, Ave. Brasil 2697, Aptos. 5, 6 y 8, Esquina Coronel Alegre, Codigo Postal 11300, (Casilla de Correo 1821), Montevideo, Uruguay, phone (598–2) 707–3590 / 2589, fax 707–3530, e-mail: pwr@uru.ops-oms.org, https://ops.org.uy/.

Venezuela (Also serves Netherlands Antilles).—Dr. Gerardo De Cosio, a.i., Avenida Sexta entre 5a y 6a, Transversal No. 43, Quinta OPS / OMS, Urbanizacion Altamira, Caracas 1060, Venezuela, (Apartado 6722–Carmelitas, Caracas 1010, Venezuela) phone (58–212) 206–5022 / 5000, 265–0403, fax 261–6069, e-mail: email@ven.ops-oms.org, https://opsoms.org.ve/.

CENTERS

Latin American and Caribbean Center on Health Sciences Information (BIREME).—Dr. Diego Gonzalez, Rua Vergueiro 1,759, 12th floor, Paraiso, CEP 04101–000, Sao Paulo, SP, Brasil, phone (55–11) 5576–9800, e-mail: birdir@paho.org.

Latin American Center for Perinatology and Human Development (CLAP).—Dr. Suzanne Jacob Serruya, Av. Brasil 2697–Ap. 4 CP 11300, Montevideo, Uruguay, phone (598–2) 487–2929, (598–2) 706–3020; fax 598–2 487–2593, e-mail: postmasterCLAP@clap.ops-oms.org.

Pan American Foot-and-Mouth Disease Center (PANAFTOSA).—Dr. Ottorino Cosivi, Av. Governador Leonel de Moura Brizola 7778, (antigua Av. Presidente Kennedy), São Bento, Duque de Caxias, 25045–002, Duque de Caixias, RJ, Brasil, (55–21) 3661–9000; fax (55–21) 3661–9001.

PERMANENT JOINT BOARD ON DEFENSE, CANADA-UNITED STATES

CANADIAN SECTION

National Defence Headquarters, MG George R. Pearkes Building, Ottawa, ON Canada K1A OK2, phone (613) 992–4423

Members:

Canadian Co-Chairman.—Hon. Laurie Hawn, P.C., C.D., M.P.

Military Policy.—Cmdre Bob Auchterlonie, Director, of General Plans.

Defence Policy.—Gordon Venner, Assistant Deputy, Minister Policy.

Foreign Affairs.—David Drake, DFATD Director General, Security and Intelligence Bureau.

Canada Strategic Joint Staff.—MGen Charles Lamarre, Director of Staff.

NORAD.—LGen Pierre St-Amand, Deputy Commander NORAD.

Public Safety.—Megan Nichols, Director General, Border Policy and International Affairs.

Military Secretary.—LCol Michael Ward, Directorate of Western Hemisphere Policy.

Political Secretary.—Yasemin Heinbecker, DFADT Directorate of International Defence Relations, (613) 867–1234.

UNITED STATES SECTION

JCS, J–5, Western Hemisphere Directorate, Pentagon, Room 2E773, 20318

phone (703) 695–4955

Members:

U.S. Co-Chair.—Elissa Slotkin, Principal Deputy Assistant Secretary of Defense for International Security Affairs.

Military Policy (Joint Staff).—BG Joseph Whitlock, Deputy Director for Western Hemisphere.

Defense Policy (OSD).—Dr. Rebecca Chavez, Deputy Assistant Secretary of Defense for Western Hemisphere.

State Department.—Karen Choe-Fichte, Deputy Director, Office of Canadian Affairs.

National Security Council.—Denison Offutt, Director of North American Affairs.

USNORTHCOM.—RADM Richard P. Snyder, Director of Strategy, Policy, and Plans.

NORAD.—RADM Richard P. Snyder, Director of Strategy, Policy, and Plans.

DHS.—RDML Joanna Nunan, Military Advisor to the Secretary of DHS.

Military Secretary.—Maj. Francis Marino, Canada Desk Officer on the Joint Staff, 695–4955.

Political Secretary.—Keith Gilges, Political Affairs, Office of Canadian Affairs, 202–647–2228.

SECRETARIAT OF THE PACIFIC COMMUNITY

B.P. D5, 98848 Noumea Cedex, New Caledonia, phone (687) 26.20.00, fax 26.38.18

spc@spc.int, https://spc.int

Director-General.—Dr. Stuart Minchin.

Deputy Director General (Noumea).—Cameron Diver.

Deputy Director General (Suva).—Dr. Audrey Aumua.
Director:
Public Health Division.—Dr. Paula Vivili.
Fisheries, Aquaculture, and Marine Ecosystems Division.—Neville Smith.
Land Resources Division.—Jan Helsen.
Geoscience, Energy and Maritime Division.—Dr. Andrew Jones.
Social Development Programme.—Leituala Kuiniselani Toelupe Tago-Elisara.
Regional Rights Resource Team (Human Rights Programme).—Miles Young.
Statistics for Development Division.—Epeli Waqavonovono.
Strategy, Performance and Learning.—Emily Sharp.
Communications.—Peter Foster.
Human Resources.—Craig Parker.
Finance.—Subhash Gupta.
Climate Change and Environmental Sustainability.—Sylvie Goyet.
Educational Quality and Assessment Programme.—Michelle Belisle.
Information Service.—Johan Sebastiaan ''Bas'' Berghoef.
Melanesia Region.—Mia Rimon.
Micronesia (Pohnpei) Region.—Lara Studzinski.

U.S. Contact: Bureau of East Asian and Pacific Affairs, Office of Australia, New Zealand and Pacific Island Affairs, Department of State, Washington, DC 20520, phone (202) 736–4741, fax 647–0118

Member Countries and Territories of the SPC:

American Samoa
Australia
Cook Islands
Federated States of Micronesia
Fiji
France
French Polynesia
Guam
Kiribati
Marshall Islands
Nauru
New Caledonia
Niue
New Zealand
Northern Mariana Islands
Palau
Papua New Guinea
Pitcairn Islands
Samoa
Solomon Islands
Tokelau
Tonga
Tuvalu
United States
Vanuatu
Wallis and Futuna

SECRETARIAT OF THE PACIFIC REGIONAL ENVIRONMENT PROGRAMME

P.O. Box 240, Apia, Samoa, phone (685) 21929, fax (685) 20231

E-mail: sprep@sprep.org, https://sprep.org

Director General.—Kosi Latu.
Deputy Director.—Roger Cornforth.
Director of:
Island and Ocean Ecosystems.—Stuart Chape.
Climate Change Resilience.—Tagaloa Cooper-Halo.
Environmental Monitoring and Governance.—Easter Galuvao.
Waste Management and Pollution Control.—Vicki Hall.

U.S. Contact: Bureau of Oceans and International Environmental and Scientific Affairs, Office of Ocean and Polar Affairs, Department of State, Washington, DC 20520
phone (202) 647–3262

Member Countries and Territories of SPREP:

- American Samoa
- Australia
- Cook Islands
- Federated States of Micronesia
- Fiji
- France
- French Polynesia
- Guam
- Kiribati
- Marshall Islands
- Nauru
- New Caledonia
- New Zealand
- Niue
- Northern Mariana Islands
- Palau
- Papua New Guinea
- Samoa
- Solomon Islands
- Tokelau
- Tonga
- Tuvalu
- United Kingdom
- United States
- Vanuatu
- Wallis and Futuna

UNITED NATIONS

GENERAL ASSEMBLY

The General Assembly is composed of all 193 United Nations Member States.

SECURITY COUNCIL

The Security Council has 15 members. The United Nations Charter designates five States as permanent members, and the General Assembly elects ten other members for two-year terms. The term of office for each non-permanent member of the Council ends on 31 December of the year indicated in parentheses next to its name.

The five permanent members of the Security Council are China, France, Russian Federation, United Kingdom, and the United States.

The ten non-permanent members of the Council in 2019 are Belgium (2020), Côte d'Ivoire (2019), Dominican Republic (2020), Equatorial Guinea (2019), Germany (2020), Indonesia (2020), Kuwait (2019), Peru (2019), Poland (2019), and South Africa (2020).

ECONOMIC AND SOCIAL COUNCIL

The Economic and Social Council has 54 members, elected for three-year terms by the General Assembly. The term of office for each member expires on 31 December of the year indicated in parentheses next to its name. Voting in the Council is by simple majority; each member has one vote. In 2019, the Council is composed of the following 54 States:

- Andorra (2019)
- Angola (2021)
- Armenia (2021)
- Azerbaijan (2019)
- Belarus (2020)
- Benin (2019)
- Brazil (2021)
- Cambodia (2019)
- Cameroon (2019)
- Canada (2021)
- Chad (2019)
- China (2019)
- Colombia (2019)
- Denmark (2019)
- Ecuador (2020)
- Egypt (2021)
- El Salvador (2020)
- Eswatini (2019)
- France (2020)
- Germany (2020)
- Ghana (2020)
- India (2020)
- Iran (Islamic Republic of) (2021)
- Ireland (2020)
- Jamaica (2021)
- Japan (2020)
- Kenya (2021)
- Luxembourg (2021)
- Malawi (2020)
- Mali (2021)
- Malta (2020)
- Mexico (2020)
- Morocco (2020)
- Netherlands (2021)
- Norway (2019)
- Pakistan (2021)
- Paraguay (2021)
- Philippines (2020)
- Republic of Korea (2019)
- Romania (2019)
- Russian Federation (2019)
- Saint Vincent and the Grenadines (2019)
- Saudi Arabia (2021)
- Sudan (2020)
- Togo (2020)
- Turkey (2020)

Turkmenistan (2021)
Ukraine (2021)
United Kingdom of Great Britain and Northern Ireland (2019)
United States of America (2021)
Venezuela (Bolivarian Republic of) (2019)
Yemen (2019)

TRUSTEESHIP COUNCIL

The Trusteeship Council has five members: China, France, Russian Federation, United Kingdom, and the United States. With the independence of Palau, the last remaining United Nations trust territory, the Council formally suspended operation on 1 November 1994. By a resolution adopted on that day, the Council amended its rules of procedure to drop the obligation to meet annually and agreed to meet as occasion required—by its decision or the decision of its President, or at the request of a majority of its members or the General Assembly or the Security Council.

INTERNATIONAL COURT OF JUSTICE

The International Court of Justice has 15 members, elected by both the General Assembly and the Security Council. Judges hold nine-year terms. The term of office for each member expires on February 5th of the year indicated in parentheses next to its name. The current composition of the court is as follows:

President Abdulqawi Ahmed Yusuf (Somalia 2027)
Vice-President Xue Hanqin (China 2021)
Judge Peter Tomka (Slovakia 2021)
Judge Ronny Abraham (France 2027)
Judge Mohamed Bennouna (Morocco 2024)
Judge Antônio Augusto Cançado Trindade (Brazil 2027)
Judge Joan E. Donoghue (USA 2024)
Judge Giorgio Gaja (Italy 2021)
Judge Julia Sebutinde (Uganda 2021)
Judge Dalveer Bhandari (India 2027)
Judge Patrick Lipton Robinson (Jamaica 2024)
Judge James Richard Crawford (Australia 2024)
Judge Kirill Gevorgian (Russian Federation 2024)
Judge Nawaf Salam (Lebanon 2027)
Judge Yuji Iwasawa (Japan 2021)

UNITED NATIONS SECRETARIAT

One United Nations Plaza, New York, NY 10017, (212) 963–1234, https://un.org.

Secretary-General.—Antonio Guterres (Portugal).
Deputy Secretary-General.—Amina J. Mohammed (Nigeria).

EXECUTIVE OFFICE OF THE SECRETARY-GENERAL

Chief of Staff.—Maria Luiza Ribeiro Viotti (Brazil).
Spokesman.—Stephane Dujarric.
Special Adviser to the Secretary-General, Policy.—Ana Maria Menendez Perez (Spain).
Principal Officer.—David Vennett (United States).

OFFICE OF INTERNAL OVERSIGHT SERVICES

Under-Secretary-General.—Heidi Mendoza (Philippines).
Assistant Secretary-General.—David Kanja (Kenya).

OFFICE OF LEGAL AFFAIRS

Under-Secretary-General and Legal Counsel.—Miguel de Serpa Soares (Portugal).
Assistant Secretary-General.—Stephen Mathias (United States).

DEPARTMENT OF POLITICAL AND PEACEBUILDING AFFAIRS

Under-Secretary-General.—Rosemary DiCarlo (United States).
Assistant Secretary-General for Peacebuilding Support.—Oscar Fernandez-Taranco (Argentina).

DEPARTMENT OF PEACE OPERATIONS

Under-Secretary-General.—Jean-Pierre Lacroix (France).

Assistant Secretary-General/Military Adviser.—Lieutenant General Carlos Humberto Loitey (Uruguay).

Assistant Secretary-General of the Office of Rule of Law and Security Institutions.—Alexandre Zouev (Russian Federation).

DEPARTMENT OF POLITICAL AND PEACEBUILDING AFFAIRS AND DEPARTMENT OF PEACE OPERATIONS

Assistant Secretary-General for Africa.—Bintou Keita (Guinea).

Assistant Secretary-General for Europe, Central Asia and the Americas.—Jenča Miroslav (Slovakia).

Assistant Secretary-General for Middle East, Asia and the Pacific.—Khaled Khiari (Tunisia).

DEPARTMENT OF OPERATIONAL SUPPORT

Under-Secretary-General.—Atul Khare (India).

Assistant Secretary-General for Support Operations.—Lisa Buttenheim (United States).

Assistant Secretary-General for Supply Chain Management.—Christian Saunders (United Kingdom).

OFFICE FOR THE COORDINATION OF HUMANITARIAN AFFAIRS (OCHA)

Under-Secretary-General, Humanitarian Affairs and Emergency Relief Coordinator.—Mark Lowcock (United Kingdom).

Assistant Secretary-General/Deputy Emergency Relief Coordinator.—Ursula Mueller (Germany).

DEPARTMENT OF ECONOMIC AND SOCIAL AFFAIRS

Under-Secretary-General.—Liu Zhenmin (China).

Assistant Secretary-General, Policy Coordination and Inter-Agency Affairs.—Maria Francesca Spatolisano (Italy).

Assistant Secretary-General, Economic Development.—Elliott Harris.

DEPARTMENT OF GENERAL ASSEMBLY AND CONFERENCE MANAGEMENT

Under-Secretary-General.—Movses Abelian (Armenia).

DEPARTMENT OF GLOBAL COMMUNICATIONS

Under-Secretary-General.—Melissa Fleming (United States).

DEPARTMENT OF SAFETY AND SECURITY

Under-Secretary-General.—Gilles Michaud (Canada).

Assistant Secretary-General.—Noirin O' Sullivan (Ireland).

DEPARTMENT OF MANAGEMENT

Under-Secretary-General.—Catherine Pollard (Guyana).

Assistant Secretary-General, Human Resources Management.—Martha Helena Lopez (Colombia).

Assistant Secretary-General, Office of Enterprise Resource Planning & Controller.—Chandramouli Ramanathan (India).

Assistant Secretary-General, Information and Communications Technology.—Atefeh Riazi (United States).

OFFICE FOR DISARMAMENT AFFAIRS

Assistant Secretary-General, High Representative for Disarmament Affairs.—Izumi Nakamitsu (Japan).

UNITED NATIONS COUNTER TERRORISM OFFICE

Under-Secretary-General.—Vladimir Voronkov (Russian Federation).

UNITED NATIONS OFFICE FOR PARTNERSHIPS

United Nations Democracy Fund (UNDEF) Executive Head.—Annika Savill.

United Nations Fund for International Partnerships (UNFIP) Executive Director.—Robert Skinner (United States).

UNITED NATIONS DEVELOPMENT COORDINATION OFFICE

Assistant Secretary-General.—Robert Piper (Australia).

UNITED NATIONS AT GENEVA (UNOG)

Palais des Nations, 1211 Geneva 10, Switzerland, phone (41–022) 917–1234

Director-General of UNOG.—Tatiana Valovaya (Russian Federation).

UNITED NATIONS AT VIENNA (UNOV)

Vienna International Centre, P.O. Box 500, 1400 Vienna, Austria, phone (43–1) 26060

Director-General.—Yury Fedotov (Russian Federation).

UNITED NATIONS AT NAIROBI (UNON)

P.O. Box 67578, Nairobi, Kenya 00200, phone: +254 20 7621234

Director-General.—Workneh Gebeyehu Negewo (Ethiopia).

UNITED NATIONS INFORMATION CENTRE

1775 K Street, NW., Suite 500, Washington, DC 20006

phone: (202) 331–8670, email: unicdc@unic.org

https://unicwash.org

Director.—Mary Waters (United States).

REGIONAL ECONOMIC COMMISSIONS

Economic Commission for Africa (ECA), Menelik II Ave., P.O. Box 3001, Addis Ababa, Ethiopia, phone 251–11–544 4999, fax 251–11–551–4416.
Executive Secretary.—Vera Songwe (Cameroon).

Economic Commission for Europe (ECE) Palais des Nations, 1211 Geneva 10, Switzerland, phone (41–22) 917–1234 (switchboard).
Executive Secretary.—Olga Algayerova (Slovakia).

Economic Commission for Latin America and the Caribbean (ECLAC), Casilla 179–D, Santiago, Chile, Postal code: 7630412, phone (56–2) 2471 2000, 2210 2000, fax (56–2) 208–0252.
Executive Secretary.—Alicia Barcena (Mexico).

ECLAC Washington Office: 1825 K Street, NW., Washington, DC, phone (202) 596–3713.
Director.—Ines Bustillo.

Economic and Social Commission for Asia and the Pacific (ESCAP), United Nations Building, Rajadamnern Nok Avenue, Bangkok, Thailand, phone (66–2) 288–1234, fax (66–2) 288–1000.
Executive Secretary.—Armida Salsiah Alisjahbana (Indonesia).

Economic and Social Commission for Western Asia (ESCWA), P.O. Box 11–8575, Riad El-Solh Square, Beirut, Lebanon, phone 9611–981301, fax 9611–981510.
Executive Secretary.—Rola Dashti (Kuwait).

Regional Commissions, New York Office, (ECE, ESCAP, ECLAC, ECA, ESCWA), phone (212) 963–8088.
Director.—Amr Nour (Egypt).

FUNDS AND PROGRAMS

United Nations High Commissioner for Refugees (UNHCR), Case Postale 2500, CH–1211 Geneve 2 Depot, Switzerland, phone (41–22) 739–8111.

High Commissioner.—Filippo Grandi (Italy).

United Nations High Commissioner for Refugees (UNHCR), Regional Office for the United States and the Caribbean, 1800 Massachusetts Avenue, NW., Suite 500, Washington, DC 20036, phone (202) 296–5191.
Regional Representative.—Matthew Reynolds (United States).

United Nations Children's Fund (UNICEF), UNICEF House, 3 United Nations Plaza, New York, NY 10017, phone (212) 326–7000.
Executive Director.—Henrietta Fore (United States).

United Nations Children's Fund (UNICEF), Representation Office, 1775 K Street, NW., Suite 360, Washington, DC 20006, phone (212) 824–6463.
Public Partnerships Manager.—Sean Snyder (United States).

United Nations Conference on Trade and Development (UNCTAD), Palais des Nations, 8–14 Avenue de la Paix, 1211 Geneva 10, Switzerland, phone (41–22) 917–1234.
Secretary General.—Mukhisa Kituyi (Kenya).

International Trade Centre (ITC), Palais des Nations, 1211 Geneva 10, Switzerland, phone (41–22) 730 01 11.
Executive Director.—Maria Aranzuzu Gonzalez Laya (Spain).

United Nations Development Programme (UNDP), 1 United Nations Plaza, New York, NY 10017, phone (212) 906–5000.
Administrator.—Achim Steiner (Germany).

United Nations Development Programme (UNDP), Representation Office, 1775 K Street, NW., Suite 500, Washington, DC 20006, phone (202) 331–9130.
Director.—Paul Clayman (United States).

UN Women (United Nations Entity for Gender Equality and the Empowerment of Women), 220 East 42nd Street, New York, NY 10017, phone (646) 781–4400.
Executive Director.—Phumzile Mlambo-Ngcuka (South Africa).

United Nations Volunteers Programme (UNV), Postfach 260 111, D–53153 Bonn, Germany, phone (49–228) 815–2000.
Executive Coordinator.—Olivier Adam (France).

United Nations Environment Programme (UNEP), United Nations Avenue, Gigiri, P.O. Box 30552, 00100, Nairobi, Kenya, phone (254–20) 762–1234.
Executive Director.—Inger Andersen (Denmark).

United Nations Environment Programme, Regional Office for North America, 900 17th Street, NW., Suite 506, Washington, DC 20006, phone (202) 785–0465.
Regional Director.—Barbara Hendrie (United States).

United Nations Human Settlements Programme (UN-HABITAT), United Nations Office at Nairobi, United Nations Avenue, Gigiri, P.O. Box 30030, Nairobi, 00100, Kenya, phone (254–20) 762–1234.
Executive Director.—Maimunah Mohd Sharif (Malaysia).

United Nations Office on Drugs and Crime (UNODC), Vienna International Centre, P.O. Box 500, A–1400 Vienna, Austria, phone (43–1) 26060.
Executive Director.—Yury Fedotov (Russian Federation).

United Nations Population Fund (UNFPA), 605 Third Avenue, New York, NY 10158, phone (212) 297–5000.
Executive Director.—Natalia Kanem (Panama).

UNFPA Liaison Office, 1717 K Street, NW., Suite 900, Washington, DC 20037, phone (202) 653–1155.
Director.—Sarah Craven (United States).

United Nations Relief and Works Agency for Palestine Refugees in the Near East (UNRWA), Headquarters Amman, Bayader Wadi Seer, P.O. Box 140157, Amman 11814, Jordan, phone (+ 962 6) 580–8100. Headquarters Gaza, P.O. Box 338, IL 78100, Ashqelon, Israel, P.O. Box 371 Gaza City, Palestinian Territory, phone (+ 972 8) 288–7701.
Commissioner-General.—Pierre Krahenbuhl (Switzerland).

UNRWA Representative Office, 1901 Pennsylvania Avenue, NW., Suite 804, Washington, DC 20006, phone (202) 847–4350.
Director.—Elizabeth Campbell (United States).

World Food Programme (WFP), Via Cesare Giulio Viola 68, Parco dei Medici, 00148 Rome, Italy, phone (39–6) 65131.
Executive Director.—David Beasley (United States).

WFP U.S. Relations Office, 2121 K Street, NW., Suite 800–A, Washington, DC 20037, phone (202) 653–0010.
Senior Director.—Gresham Barrett (United States).
Managing Director.—Jon Brause (United States).

OTHER UNITED NATIONS ENTITIES

Office of the United Nations High Commissioner for Human Rights (OHCHR), Palais des Nations, CH–1211 Geneva 10, Switzerland, phone (41–022) 917–9220.
High Commissioner for Human Rights.—Michelle Bachelet (Chile).

Office of the United Nations High Commissioner for Human Rights (OHCHR), New York Office.

Assistant Secretary-General.—Andrew Gilmour (United Kingdom).

United Nations Non-Governmental Liaison Office (NGLS), New York Office, United Nations Building DC1, Room 1106, New York, NY 10017, phone (212) 963–3125; Geneva Office, Room A1–50, Palais des Nations, 1211 Geneva 10, Switzerland, phone (41 22) 917–2076.
Officer-in-Charge, New York.—Susan Alzner.
Officer-in-Charge, Geneva.—Hamish Jenkins.

United Nations Office for Project Services (UNOPS), Marmorvej 51, P.O. Box 2695, 2100 Copenhagen, Denmark, phone (45–4) 533–7500.
Executive Director.—Grete Faremo (Norway).

UNOPS Liaison Office, 1775 K Street, NW., Suite 500, Washington, DC, phone (917) 200–8248.
Head of Office.—Nicholas George.

United Nations System Chief Executives Board (CEB) for Coordination, Geneva Office, C–553, Palais des Nations, CH–1211 Geneve 10, Switzerland, phone (41–22) 917–3276; New York Office, DC2–0610, 2 United Nations Plaza, New York, NY 10017, phone (212) 963–8138.

United Nations System Staff College (UNSSC), Viale Maestri del Lavoro 10, 10127 Torino, Italy, phone (39 011) 653–5911.
Director.—Dr. Jafar Javan.

United Nations University (UNU), 5–53–70 Jingumae, Shibuya-ku, Tokyo 150–8925, Japan, phone (81–3) 5467–1212.
Director.—David Malone (Canada).

International Computing Centre (ICC), Palais des Nations, 1211 Geneva 10, Switzerland, phone (41–22) 929–1444.
Director.—Sameer Chauhan.

Joint United Nations Programme on HIV/AIDS (UNAIDS), 20, Avenue Appia, CH–1211 Geneva 27, Switzerland, phone (41–22) 791–3666.
Executive Director.—Winnie Byanyima (Uganda).

UNAIDS Washington Liaison Office, 1889 F Street, NW., 3rd Floor, Washington, DC 20006, phone (202) 223–7611.
Director.—Regan Hofmann, a.i.

RESEARCH AND TRAINING INSTITUTES

United Nations Institute for Disarmament Research (UNIDIR), Palais des Nations, 1211 Geneva 10, Switzerland, phone (41–22) 917–3186/1583.
Director.—Renata Dwan.

United Nations Institute for Training and Research (UNITAR), UNITAR, International Environment House, Chemin des Anemones 11–13, CH–1219 Chatelaine, Geneva-Switzerland, phone (41–22) 917–8400.
Executive Director.—Nikhil Seth (India).

United Nations International Research and Training Institute for the Advancement of Women (INSTRAW), Part of UN Women as July 2010.

United Nations Interregional Crime and Justice Research Institute (UNICRI), Viale Maestri del Lavoro, 10, 10127 Turin, Italy, phone (39–011) 6537–111.
Director.—Bettina Tucci Bartsiotas, a.i (Uruguay/United States).

United Nations Research Institute for Social Development (UNRISD), Palais des Nations, 1211 Geneva 10, Switzerland, phone (41–22) 917–3060.
Director.—Paul Ladd.

SPECIALIZED AGENCIES

Food and Agriculture Organization (FAO), Viale delle Terme di Caracalla, 00153 Rome, Italy, phone (39–6) 57051.
Director-General.—Qu Dongyu (China).

Food and Agriculture Organization, Liaison Office for North America, Suite 800–B, 2121 K Street, NW., Washington, DC 20037, phone (1–202) 653–2400.
Director.—Vimlendra Sharan (India).

International Civil Aviation Organization (ICAO), 999 University Street, Montreal, Quebec H3C 5H7, Canada, phone (1–514) 954–8219.
Secretary-General.—Dr. Fang Liu (China).

International Fund for Agricultural Development (IFAD), Via Paolo di Dono, 44, 00142 Rome, Italy, phone (39–6) 54591.

President.—Gilbert F. Houngbo (Togo).

External Affairs Department, IFAD North American Liaison Office, 1775 K Street, NW., Suite 500, Washington, DC 20006, phone (1–202) 331–9099.

Chief.—Joanna Veltri (United States).

International Labour Organization (ILO), 4, Routes des Morillons, CH–1211 Geneva 22, Switzerland, phone (41–22) 799–6111.

Director-General.—Guy Ryder (United Kingdom).

ILO Washington Branch Office, 1801 I Street, NW., 9th Floor, Washington, DC 20006, phone (1–202) 617–3952.

Director.—Kevin Cassidy (United States).

International Maritime Organization (IMO), 4 Albert Embankment, London SE1 7SR, United Kingdom, phone (44–20) 7735–7611.

Secretary-General.—Kitack Lim (Republic of Korea).

International Monetary Fund (IMF), 700 19th Street, NW., Washington, DC 20431, phone (1–202) 623–7000.

Managing Director.—David Lipton (acting).

International Telecommunications Union (ITU), Palais des Nations, 1211 Geneva 20, Switzerland, phone (41–22) 730–5111.

Secretary-General.—Houlin Zhao (China).

United Nations Educational, Scientific, and Cultural Organization (UNESCO), 7 Place de Fontenoy, 75352 Paris 07 SP, France, phone (33–01) 4568–1000.

Director-General.—Audrey Azoulay (France).

United Nations Industrial Development Organization (UNIDO), Vienna International Centre, Wagramerstr. 5, P.O. Box 300, A–1400 Vienna, Austria, phone (43–1) 26026–0.

Director-General.—Li Yong (China).

Universal Postal Union (UPU), International Bureau, Case Postale 312, 3015 Berne, Switzerland, phone (41–31) 350–3111.

Director-General.—Bishar Abdirahman Hussein (Kenya).

World Bank Group, 1818 H Street, NW., Washington, DC 20433, phone (1–202) 473–1000.

President.—David Malpass (United States).

World Health Organization (WHO), 20 Avenue Appia, 1211 Geneva 27, Switzerland, phone (41–22) 791–2111.

Director-General.—Tedros Adhanom Ghebreyesus (Ethiopia).

Pan American Health Organization/World Health Organization Regional Office for the Americas (PAHO), 525 23rd Street, NW., Washington, DC 20037, phone (1–202) 974–3000.

Director.—Carissa F. Etienne (Dominica).

World Intellectual Property Organization (WIPO), 34, chemin des Colombettes, CH–1211 Geneva 20, Switzerland, phone (41–22) 338–9111.

Director General.—Francis Gurry (Australia).

World Meteorological Organization (WMO), 7bis, avenue de la Paix, Case Postale 2300, CH–1211 Geneva 2, Switzerland, phone (41–22) 730–8111.

Secretary-General.—Petteri Taalas (Finland).

RELATED BODY

International Atomic Energy Agency (IAEA), Vienna International Centre, P.O. Box 100 A–1400 Vienna, Austria, phone (431) 2600–0.

Director General.—Cornel Feruta (acting).

IAEA Washington Office, 1629 K Street, NW., Suite 450, Washington, DC 20006, phone (202) 293–8580. (The IAEA is an independent intergovernmental organization under the aegis of the UN).

Consultant.—Andrew Semmel (United States).

SPECIAL AND PERSONAL REPRESENTATIVES AND ENVOYS OF THE SECRETARY-GENERAL

AFRICA

Africa:

Emergency Ebola Response Coordinator.—David Gressly (United States).

Special Envoy of the Secretary-General to lead and coordinate the political efforts of the United Nations in Burundi.—Michel Kafando (Burkina Faso).

Special Adviser to the Secretary-General on Africa, OSAA.—Bience Gawanas (Namibia).

High Representative for the Least Developed Countries, Landlocked Developing Countries and Small Island Developing States, UN-OHRLLS.—Fekitamoeloa Katoa 'Utoikamanu (Tonga).

African Union:

Special Representative of the Secretary-General to the African Union, UNOAU.—Hanna Serwaa Tetteh (Ghanaz).

Central Africa:

Special Representative of the Secretary-General and Head of UNOCA.—François Louncény Fall (Guinea).

Central African Republic:

Special Representative of the Secretary-General and Head of the United Nations Integrated Peacebuilding Office in the Central African Republic.—Mankeur Ndiaye (Senegal).

Deputy Special Representative of the Secretary-General and Deputy Head of Mission, MINUSCA.—Kenneth Gluck (United States).

Deputy Special Representative of the Secretary-General in the Central African Republic and UN Resident Coordinator and Resident Representative, MINUSCA.—Denise Brown (Canada).

Democratic Republic of the Congo:

Special Representative of the Secretary-General for the Democratic Republic of the Congo and Head of MONUSCO.—Leila Zerrougui (Algeria).

United Nations Emergency Ebola Response Coordinator.—David Gressly (United States).

Deputy Special Representative of the Secretary-General for Protection and Operations, MONUSCO.—François Grignon (France), a.i.

Deputy Special Representative ad interim, MONUSCO, and United Nations Resident Coordinator and Humanitarian Coordinator.—David McLachlan-Karr (Australia).

Great Lakes Region:

Special Representative of the Secretary-General for the Great Lakes Region.—Huang Xia (China).

Guinea-Bissau:

Special Representative of the Secretary-General and Head of UNOGBIS.—Rosine Sori-Coulibaly (Burkina Faso).

Horn of Africa:

Special Envoy of the Secretary-General for the Horn of Africa.—Parfait Onanga-Anyanga (Gabon).

Mali:

Special Representative of the Secretary-General and Head of Mission, MINUSMA.—Mahamat Saleh Annadif (Chad).

Deputy Special Representative of the Secretary-General (Political), MINUSMA.—Joanne Adamson (United Kingdom).

Deputy Special Representative of the Secretary-General, MINUSMA and UN Resident Coordinator, Humanitarian Coordinator and Resident Representative of UNDP.—Mbaranga Gasarabwe (Rwanda).

Sahel:

United Nations Office for West Africa (UNOWA) and the Office of the Special Envoy for the Sahel (OSES) have merged into a single entity, UNOWAS.

Somalia:

Special Representative of the Secretary-General for Somalia and Head of Mission, UNSOM.—James Swan (United States).

Deputy Special Representative of the Secretary-General for Somalia.—Raisedon Zenenga (Zimbabwe).

Deputy Special Representative, Resident and Humanitarian Coordinator in Somalia.—Adam Abdelmoula (Sudan/United States).

Head of the United Nations Support Office in Somalia (UNSOS).—Lisa Filipetto (Australia).

South Sudan:

Special Representative of the Secretary-General and Head of UNMISS.—David Shearer (New Zealand).

Deputy Special Representative of the Secretary-General (Political), UNMISS.—Moustapha Soumaré (Mali).

Deputy Special Representative of the Secretary-General, Resident Coordinator, Humanitarian Coordinator and Resident Representative, UNMISS.—Alain Noudéhou (Benin).

Sudan / Abyei:

Head of Mission and Force Commander, UNISFA.—Major General Mehari Zewde Gebremariam (Ethiopia).

Sudan / Darfur:

Joint African Union-United National Special Representative for Darfur, Head of UNAMID.—Jeremiah Nyamane Kingsley Mamabolo (South Africa).

Deputy Joint Special Representative, UNAMID.—Anita Kokui Gbeho (Ghana).

West Africa:

Special Representative of the Secretary-General and Head of UNOWAS.—Mohammed Ibn Chambas (Ghana).

Deputy Special Representative of the United Nations Secretary-General for West Africa and the Sahel.—Ruby Sandhu-Rojon (United States).

Western Sahara:

Special Representative of the Secretary-General for Western Sahara and Head of MINURSO.—Colin Stewart (Canada).

Personal Envoy of the Secretary-General for Western Sahara.—Vacant.

THE AMERICAS

Colombia:

Special Representative for Colombia and Head of the United Nations Verification Mission in Colombia.—Carlos Ruiz Massieu (Mexico).

Deputy Special Representative and Deputy Head of the United Nations Verification Mission in Colombia.—Karla Gabriela Samayoa Recari (Guatemala).

El Salvador:

Special Envoy to the Secretary-General to Facilitate Dialogue in El Salvador.—Benito Andion (Mexico).

Haiti:

Special Representative of the Secretary-General and Head of Mission, MINUJUSTH.—Helen Meagher La Lime (United States).

Deputy Special Representative of the Secretary-General and United Nations Resident Coordinator and Humanitarian Coordinator, MINUJUSTH.—Mamadou Diallo (Guinea).

Special Adviser to the Secretary-General for Community-based Medicine and Lessons from Haiti.—Paul Farmer (United States).

Deputy Special Representative of the United Nations Mission for Justice Support in Haiti.—Mamadou Diallo (Guinea).

Special Envoy of the Secretary-General for Haiti.—Josette Sheeran (United States).

ASIA AND THE PACIFIC

Afghanistan:

Special Representative of the Secretary-General for Afghanistan and Head of UNAMA.—Tadamichi Yamamoto (Japan).

Deputy Special Representative of the Secretary-General, UN Resident Coordinator and UN Humanitarian Coordinator for Afghanistan, UNAMA.—Toby Lanzer (United Kingdom).

Deputy Special Representative of the Secretary-General (Political) for UNAMA.—Ingrid Hayden (Australia).

Central Asia:

Special Representative of the Secretary-General and Head of the UN Regional Centre for Preventive Diplomacy for Central Asia (UNRCCA).—Natalia Gherman (Republic of Moldova).

India-Pakistan:

Chief Military Observer and Head of Mission, UNMOGIP.—José Eladio Alcaín (Uruguay).

Myanmar:

Special Envoy of the Secretary-General for Myanmar.—Christine Schraner Burgener (Switzerland).

EUROPE

Cyprus:

Special Representative of the Secretary-General and Head of Mission, UNFICYP.—Elizabeth Spehar (Canada).

Special Adviser to the Secretary-General on Cyprus.—Jane Holl Lute (United States).

Geneva International Discussions (UNRGID):

United Nations Representative.—Ayşe Cihan Sultanoğlu (Turkey).

Kosovo:

Special Representative of the Secretary-General and Head of Mission, UNMIK.—Zahir Tanin (Afghanistan).

Deputy Special Representative of the Secretary-General, UNMIK.—Christopher Coleman (United States).

MIDDLE EAST

Middle East:

Special Coordinator for the Middle East Peace Process and Personal Representative of the Secretary-General to the Palestine Liberation Organization and the Palestinian Authority.—Nickolay Mladenov (Bulgaria).

Deputy Special Coordinator for the Middle East Peace Process/United Nations Coordinator for Humanitarian Aid and Development Activities in the Occupied Palestinian Territory.—Jamie McGoldrick (Ireland).

Head of Mission and Chief of Staff of UN Truce Supervision Organization (UNTSO).—Major General Kristin Lund (Norway).

Afghanistan:

Special Representative of the Secretary-General for Afghanistan and Head of UNAMA.—Tadamichi Yamamoto (Japan).

Deputy Special Representative of the Secretary-General, UN Resident Coordinator and UN Humanitarian Coordinator for Afghanistan, UNAMA.—Toby Lanzer (United Kingdom).

Deputy Special Representative of the Secretary-General (Political) for UNAMA.—Ingrid Hayden (Australia).

Iraq (UNAMI):

Special Representative of the Secretary-General for Iraq and Head of Mission, UNAMI.—Jeanine Hennis-Plasschaert (Netherlands).

Deputy Special Representative of the Secretary-General for Political Affairs and Electoral Assistance, UNAMI.—Alice Walpole (United Kingdom).

Deputy Special Representative of the Secretary-General (Development and Humanitarian Support) and Resident Coordinator/Humanitarian Coordinator for Iraq, UNAMI.—Marta Ruedas (Spain).

Kuwait:

Humanitarian Envoy of the Secretary-General.—Ahmed Al Meraikhi (Qatar).

Lebanon:

Special Coordinator of the Secretary-General for Lebanon.—Ján Kubiš (Slovakia).

Deputy Special Coordinator of the Secretary-General for Lebanon, UN Resident Coordinator, Humanitarian Coordinator and Resident Representative.—Philippe Lazzarini (Switzerland).

Head of Mission and Force Commander of UNIFIL.—Major General Stefano Del Col (Italy).

Libya:

Special Representative of the Secretary-General and Head of Mission, UNSMIL.—Ghassan Salame (Lebanon).

Deputy Special Representative and Deputy Head of the United Nations Support Mission in Libya, UNSMIL (Political).—Stephanie T. Williams (United States).

Deputy Special Representative in Libya, United Nations Resident Coordinator and Humanitarian Coordinator.—Yacoub El Hillo (Sudan).

Syria:

Special Envoy of the Secretary-General for Syria.—Geir O. Pedersen (Norway).

Deputy Special Envoy of the Secretary-General for Syria.—Khawla Matar (Bahrain).

Syria Golan Heights:

Head of Mission and Force Commander of the UN Disengagement Observer Force (UNDOF).—Major General Shivaram Kharel (acting) (Nepal).

Yemen:

Special Envoy of the Secretary-General for Yemen.—Martin Griffiths (United Kingdom).

Resident and Humanitarian Coordinator for Yemen.—Lise Grande (United States).

OTHER HIGH LEVEL APPOINTMENTS

Alliance of Civilizations:

High Representative.—Miguel Ángel Moratinos Cuyaubé (Spain).

Children and Armed Conflict:

Special Representative.—Virginia Gamba (Argentina).

Cities and Climate Change:

Special Envoy.—Michael Bloomberg (United States).

Special Adviser to the Secretary-General on Climate Change.—Robert Orr (United States).

Disability and Accessibility:

Special Envoy on Disability and Accessibility.—Maria Soledad Cisternas Reyes (Chile).

Disaster Reduction:

Special Representative.—Mami Mizutori (Japan).

Disaster Risk Reduction and Water:

Special Envoy.—Han Seung-soo (Republic of Korea).

Global Education:

Special Representative.—Gordon Brown (United Kingdom).

Prevention of Genocide:

Special Adviser.—Adama Dieng (Senegal).

Responsibility to Protect:

Special Adviser.—Karen Smith (South Africa).

Road Safety:

Special Envoy.—Jean Todt (France).

Improving United Nations Response to Sexual Exploitation and Abuse:

Special Coordinator.—Jane Holl Lute (United States).

Sexual Violence in Conflict:

Special Representative.—Pramila Patten (Mauritius).

South-South Cooperation:

Special Envoy.—Jorge Chediek (Argentina).

Sustainable Energy for All:

Special Representative.—Rachel Kyte (United Kingdom).

Violence Against Children:

Special Representative.—Najat Maalla M'jid (Morocco).

Youth:

Envoy.—Jayathma Wickramanayake (Sri Lanka).

WORLD BANK GROUP

The World Bank Group comprises five organizations: the International Bank for Reconstruction and Development (IBRD), the International Development Association (IDA), the International Finance Corporation (IFC), the Multilateral Investment Guarantee Agency (MIGA), and the International Centre for the Settlement of Investment Disputes (ICSID).

Headquarters: 1818 H Street, NW., Washington, DC 20433 (202) 473–1000

INTERNATIONAL BANK FOR RECONSTRUCTION AND DEVELOPMENT

President.—David Malpass.

Managing Director and World Bank Group Chief Administrative Officer.—Shaolin Yang.

Managing Director and World Bank Group Chief Financial Officer.—Bernard Lauwers (acting).

Chief Executive Officer.—Axel van Trotsenburg (acting).

Chairperson, Inspection Panel.—Imrana Jalal.

Senior Vice President and World Bank Group General Counsel, Vice President, Compliance.—Sandie Okoro.
World Bank Group Chief Economist.—Pinelopi Koujianou Goldberg.
Senior Vice President for the 2030 Development Agenda, United Nations Relations, and Partnerships Operations.—Mahmoud Mohieldin.
Vice President, Human Development Vice Presidency.—Annette Dixon.
World Bank Group Vice President Information and Technology Solutions and WBG Chief Information Officer.—Denis Robitaille.
Vice President and World Bank Group Controller.—Jorge Familiar Calderon.
Vice President, Budget, Performance Review and Strategic Planning.—Antonella Bassani.
Vice President and Corporate Secretary.—Yvonne Tsikata.
Vice President and Treasurer.—Jingdong Hua.
Vice President of:
Africa.—Hafez Ghanem.
East Asia and Pacific.—Victoria Kwakwa.
South Asia.— Hartwig Schafer.
Vice President, World Bank Group External and Corporate Relations.—Sheila Redzepi.
North American Affairs (External and Corporate Relations) Special Representative.—William C. Danvers.
Europe (External and Corporate Relations) Special Representative and Director.—Mario Alexander Sander von Torklus.
Japan-External and Corporate Relations, Special Representative.—Masato Miyazaki.
Human Resources.—Ousmane Diagana.
Latin America and the Caribbean.—Axel van Trotsenburg.
Middle East and North Africa.—Ferid Belhaj.
Vice President of Europe and Central Asia.—Cyril Muller.
Vice President and Network Head, Operations Policy and Country Services.—Manuela Ferro.
Vice President, Institutional Projects.—Bernard Lauwers.
Vice President, Equitable Growth, Finance and Institutions.—Ceyla Pazarbasioglu.
Vice President, Sustainable Development Vice Presidency.—Laura Tuck.
Vice President, Infrastructure.—Makhtar Diop.
Vice President, Development Finance.—Akihiko Nishio.
Vice President and Bank Group Risk Officer.—Lakshmi Shyam-Sunder.
Vice President, Compliance Advisor / Ombudsman.—Osvaldo Luis Gratacós.
Director-General, Independent Evaluation.—Alison Evans.
Vice President and Auditor-General.—Anke D'Angelo.
Vice President, Institutional Integrity.—Pascale Helene Dubois.
Vice President and World Bank Group Chief Ethics Officer.—Jorge Dajani Gonzalez.

OTHER WORLD BANK OFFICES

London: Millbank Tower, 12th Floor, 21–24 Millbank, London SW1P 4QP.
Geneva: 3, Chemin Louis Dunant, CP 66, CH 1211, Geneva 10, Switzerland.
Paris: 66, Avenue d'Iena, 75116 Paris, France.
Brussels: Avenue Marnix 17, 2nd Floor, 1000 Brussels, Belgium.
Tokyo: Fukoku Seimei Building, 10th Floor, 2–2–2 Uchisawai-cho, Chiyoda-Ku, Tokyo 100, Japan.
Sydney: CML Building Level 19–14, Martin Place, Sydney, NSW 2000, Australia.
Berlin: Reichpietschufer 20, 10785 Berlin, Germany.

BOARD OF EXECUTIVE DIRECTORS

Bahrain, Egypt (Arab Republic of), Iraq, Jordan, Kuwait, Lebanon, Libya, Maldives, Oman, Qatar, United Arab Emirates, Yemen (Republic of).
Executive Director.—Merza H. Hasan (Kuwait).
Alternate.—Ragui El-Etreby (Arab Republic of Egypt).
Saudi Arabia.
Executive Director.—Hesham Fahad Alogeel.
Alternate.—Abdulmuhsen Saad Alkhalaf.
Austria, Belarus, Belgium, Czech Republic, Hungary, Kazakhstan, Luxembourg, Slovak Republic, Slovenia, Turkey.
Executive Director.—Guenther Schoenleitner (Austria).
Alternate.—Nathalie Marie-Louise J. Francken (Belgium).
Australia, Cambodia, Kiribati, Korea (Republic of), Marshall Islands, Micronesia (Federated States of), Mongolia, New Zealand, Palau, Papua New Guinea, Samoa, Solomon Islands, Vanuatu.

Executive Director.—Kunil Hwang (Republic of Korea).
Alternate.—Gerard Antioch (Australia).
Albania, Greece, Italy, Malta, Portugal, San Marino, Timor-Leste.
Executive Director.—Patrizio Pagano (Italy).
Alternate.—Paulo Pedroso (Portugal).
United States.
Executive Director.—Jennifer D. Nordquist.
Alternate.—Erik Bethel.
Brazil, Colombia, Dominican Republic, Ecuador, Haiti, Panama, Philippines, Suriname, Trinidad and Tobago.
Executive Director.—Fabio Kanczuk (Brazil).
Alternate.—Rommel Salazar Herrera (Philippines).
Germany.
Executive Director.—Juergen Zattler.
Alternate.—Claus Happe.
Afghanistan, Algeria, Ghana, Iran (Islamic Republic of), Morocco, Pakistan, Tunisia.
Executive Director.—Shahid Ashraf Tarar (Pakistan).
Alternate.—Omar Bougara (Algeria).
France.
Executive Director.—Herve M. Jodon de Villeroche.
Alternate.—Pierre-Olivier Chotard.
Benin, Burkina Faso, Cameroon, Cape Verde, Central African Republic, Chad, Comoros, Congo (Democratic Republic of), Congo (Republic of), Côte d'Ivoire, Djibouti, Equatorial Guinea, Gabon, Guinea, Guinea-Bissau, Madagascar, Mali, Mauritania, Mauritius, Niger, Rwanda, Sao Tome and Principe, Senegal, Togo.
Executive Director.—Jean-Claude Tchatchouang (Cameroon).
Alternate.—Alphonse Ibi Kouagou (Benin).
Fiji, Indonesia, Lao People's Democratic Republic, Malaysia, Myanmar, Nepal, Singapore, Thailand, Tonga, Vietnam.
Executive Director.—Kulaya Tantitemit (Thailand).
Alternate.—Parjiono (Indonesia).
Denmark, Estonia, Finland, Iceland, Latvia, Lithuania, Norway, Sweden.
Executive Director.—Geir H. Haarde (Iceland).
Alternate.—Lasse Antero Klemola (Finland).
Russian Federation, Syrian Arab Republic.
Executive Director.—Roman Marshavin.
Alternate.—Konstantin Panov.
Costa Rica, El Salvador, Guatemala, Honduras, Mexico, Nicaragua, Spain, Venezuela (Republica Bolivariana de).
Executive Director.—Jorge Alejandro Chavez Presa (Mexico).
Alternate.—Fernando Jimenez (Spain).
Antigua and Barbuda, Bahamas (The), Barbados, Belize, Canada, Dominica, Grenada, Guyana, Ireland, Jamaica, St. Kitts and Nevis, St. Lucia, St. Vincent and the Grenadines.
Executive Director.—Christine Hogan (Canada).
Alternate.—Donna Oretha Harris (Guyana).
Armenia, Bosnia and Herzegovina, Bulgaria, Croatia, Cyprus, Georgia, Israel, Macedonia (former Yugoslav Republic of), Moldova, Netherlands, Romania, Ukraine.
Executive Director.—Koen Davidse (Netherlands).
Alternate.—Florin Vodita (Romania).
Japan.
Executive Director.—Masanori Yoshida.
Alternate.—Kenichi Nishikata.
Argentina, Bolivia, Chile, Paraguay, Peru, Uruguay.
Executive Director.—Adrian Fernandez (Uruguay).
Alternate.—Daniel Pierini (Argentina).
United Kingdom.
Executive Director.—Richard Montgomery.
Alternate.—David Kinder.
Angola, Nigeria, South Africa.
Executive Director.—Vacant.
Alternate.—Armando Manuel (Angola).
Botswana, Burundi, Eritrea, Ethiopia, Gambia (The), Kenya, Lesotho, Liberia, Malawi, Mozambique, Namibia, Seychelles, Sierra Leone, Sudan, Swaziland, Tanzania, Uganda, Zambia, Zimbabwe.
Executive Director.—Anne Kabagambe (Uganda).
Alternate.—Taufila Nyamadzabo (Botswana).
Bangladesh, Bhutan, India, Sri Lanka.

Executive Director.—Aparna Subramani (India).
Alternate.—Muhammad Bhuiyan (Bangladesh).

Azerbaijan, Serbia and Montenegro, Kyrgyz Republic, Poland, Switzerland, Tajikistan, Turkmenistan, Uzbekistan, Yugoslavia (Fed. Rep. of), Switzerland, Yemen, (Republic of).
Executive Director.—Werner Gruber (Switzerland).
Alternate.—Katarzyna Zajdel-Kurowska (Poland).

China.
Executive Director.—Yingming Yang.
Alternate.—Minwen Zhang.

INTERNATIONAL DEVELOPMENT ASSOCIATION

[The officers, executive directors, and alternates are the same as those of the International Bank for Reconstruction and Development.]

INTERNATIONAL FINANCE CORPORATION

President.—David Malpass.
Executive Vice President and Chief Executive Officer.—Philippe Le Houérou.
Vice President and Corporate Secretary.—Yvonne Tsikata.
Chief Operating Officer.—Stephanie von Friedeburg.
Director-General, Independent Evaluation.—Alison Evans.
Compliance Advisor/Ombudsman (IFC/ICC and MIGA).—Osvaldo Luis Gratacos.
Vice President and General Counsel, Legal & Compliance Risk.—Ethiopis Tafara.
Vice President:
Human Resource.—Ousmane Diagana.
Risk and Finance.—Mohamed Gouled.
Treasury and Syndications.—John Gandolfo.
Economics and Private Sector Development.—Hans Peters Lankes.
Corporate Strategy and Resources.—Monish Mahurkar.
Partnerships, Communication and Outreach.—Karin Finkelston.
Asset Management Company Services and CEO, IFC Asset Management Company.—Marcos Brujis.
South Asia, East Asia & Pacific.—Snezana Stoiljkovic.
Middle East & Africa.—Sergio Pimenta.
Latin America & Caribbean, Europe & Central Asia.—Georgina Baker.
Director, Office of:
Budget and Business Administration.—Elizabeth Kibirige Namugenyi.
Blended Finance.—Martin Spicer.
Climate Business.—Alzbeta Klein.
Disruptive Technology and Funds.—Shannon Wells Atkeson (acting).
Corporate Strategy and Operational Policies and Procedures.—Aisha Elaine Williams.
Information and Technology.—Sekkappa Nagappan (acting).
Legal.—Leslie Sturtevant.
Business Risk and Compliance.—Ceri Wyn Lawley.
Environment, Social and Governance Sustainability Advice and Solutions.—Mary Porter Peschka.
Human Resources.—Davide Bonzano.
Financial Institutions Group.—Paulo de Bolle.
IFC Controller.—Paul B. Bravery.
Infrastructure and Natural Resources.—Morgan J. Landy.
Portfolio Management.—Deema Fakhoury.
PPP and Corporate Finance.—Emmanuel Damian Bahizi Nyirinkindi.
Country Economics and Engagement.—Mona E. Haddad.
Sector Economics and Development Impact.—Issa Faye.
Global Macro and Market Research.—Jean Pierre Lacombe.
Corporate Risk Management.—Tarek S. Himmo.
Investment and Credit Risk.—Khawaja Aftab Ahmed.
Special Operations.—Eric J. Jourdanet.
Manufacturing, Agribusiness and Services.—Tomasz Telma.
Energy and Mining.—Bertrand Heysch de la Borde.
East Asia and the Pacific.—Vivek Pathak.
Eastern Africa.—Jumoke Jagun-Dokunmu.
Southern Africa.—Kevin Njiraini.
West and Central Africa.—Aliou Maiga.

Europe and Central Asia.—Wiebke Schloemer.
South Asia.—Mengistu Alemayehu.
Middle East and North Africa.—Mouayed Makhlouf.
Latin America and the Caribbean.—Gabriel B. Goldschmidt.
Telecom, Media, Tech and Venture Investing.—Atul Mehta.
Treasury Market Operations.—Tom Maurice Valentine Ceusters.
Treasury Client Solutions.—Keshav Gaur.
Treasury Quantitative Analysis.—Takehisa Eguchi.
Syndicated Loans and Mobilization.—Sabrina M. Borlini.
Tokyo.—Toshitake Kurosawa.
Western Europe.—Ousseynou Nakoulima.
Manager, Office of:
Global Internal Engagement.—Audrey Sibusisiwe Mpunzwana.
Global Engagement and Outreach.—Thomas Michael Kerr.
Campaigns and Content.—Riham Mustafa.
Global Business Partners.—Rapti A. Goonesekere.
External Relations.—Mame Annan-Brown.
Gender Secretariat.—Henriette Kolb.
FIG Europe and Central Asia.—Vittorio Di Bello.
FIG Latin America and the Caribbean.—Allen Nanglefack Agandie Forlemu.
FIG Middle East and Africa.—Manuel Reyes-Retana.
FIG South Asia, East Asia and the Pacific.—Rosy Khanna.
INR Latin America and the Caribbean.—Adil Marghub.
INR Europe and Central Asia.—Cheryl Edleson Hanway.
INR Middle East and Africa.—Rudo Linda Munyengeterwa.
INR South Asia, East Asia and the Pacific.—Isabel Chatterton.
MAS Latin America and the Caribbean.—Tania Kaddeche.
MAS Europe and Central Asia.—Tatiana Bogatyreva.
MAS Middle East and Africa.—Mary-Jean Lindile Moyo.
MAS South Asia, East Asia and the Pacific.—Rana Karadsheh.

MULTILATERAL INVESTMENT GUARANTEE AGENCY

President.—David Malpass.
Executive Vice President and Chief Executive Officer.—Keiko Honda.
Director and General Counsel, Legal Affairs and Claims Group.—Aradhana Kumar-Capoor.
Compliance Advisor/Ombudsman (IFC/ICC and MIGA).—Osvaldo Luis Gratacos.
Vice President and Chief Operating Officer.—Subramaniam Vijay Iyer.
Director, Operations Group.—Sarvesh Suri.
Chief Underwriter, Operations Group.—Muhamet Fall.
Director, Economics and Sustainability Group.—Merli Margaret Baroudi.
Director, Corporate Risk.—Santiago Assalini.
Head, MIGA Africa Hub.—Hoda Moustafa.
Head, MIGA Europe Hub.—Christopher Millward.
Head, MIGA North Asia.—Jae Hyung Kwon.
Head, MIGA Singapore Office.—Timothy Histed.

FOREIGN DIPLOMATIC OFFICES IN THE UNITED STATES

AFGHANISTAN

Embassy of Afghanistan
2341 Wyoming Avenue, NW., Washington, DC 20008
phone (202) 483–6410, fax 483–6488
Her Excellency Roya Rahmani
Ambassador Extraordinary and Plenipotentiary
Consular Offices:
California, Los Angeles
New York, New York

AFRICAN UNION

Delegation of the African Union Mission
1640 Wisconsin Avenue, NW., Washington, DC 20007
Embassy of the African Union
phone (202) 342–1100, fax 342–1101
Mr. Tarek Ben Youssef
Counselor (Chargé d'Affaires)

ALBANIA

Embassy of the Republic of Albania
2100 S Street, NW., Washington, DC 20008
phone (202) 223–4942, fax 628–7342
Her Excellency Floreta Faber
Ambassador Extraordinary and Plenipotentiary
Consular Offices:
Connecticut, Stamford
Georgia, Avondale Estates
Louisiana, New Orleans
Michigan, West Bloomfield
Missouri, Blue Springs
New York, New York
North Carolina, Pinehurst
Ohio, Cleveland
Texas, Houston

ALGERIA

Embassy of the People's Democratic Republic of Algeria
2118 Kalorama Road, NW., Washington, DC 20008
phone (202) 265–2800, fax 252–986–5906
His Excellency Madjid Bougerra
Ambassador Extraordinary and Plenipotentiary
Consular Office: New York, New York

ANDORRA

Embassy of the Principality of Andorra
2 United Nations Plaza, 27th Floor, New York, NY 10017
phone (212) 750–8064, fax 750–6630
Her Excellency Elisenda Vives Balmaña
Ambassador Extraordinary and Plenipotentiary
Consular Office: California, San Diego

ANGOLA

Embassy of the Republic of Angola
2100–2108 16th Street, NW., Washington, DC 20009
phone (202) 785–1156, fax 822–9049
His Excellency Joaquim do Espirito Santo
Ambassador Extraordinary and Plenipotentiary
Consular Offices:
New York, New York
Texas, Houston

ANTIGUA AND BARBUDA

Embassy of Antigua and Barbuda
3234 Prospect Street, NW., Washington, DC 20007
phone (202) 362–5122, fax 362–5225
His Excellency Ronald Sanders
Ambassador Extraordinary and Plenipotentiary
Consular Office: New York, New York

ARGENTINA

Embassy of the Argentine Republic
1600 New Hampshire Avenue, NW., Washington, DC 20009
phone (202) 238–6400, fax 332–3171
His Excellency Jorge Martin Arturo Argüello
Ambassador Extraordinary and Plenipotentiary
Consular Offices:
California, Los Angeles
Florida, Miami
Georgia, Atlanta
Illinois, Chicago
New York, New York
Texas, Houston

ARMENIA

Embassy of the Republic of Armenia
2225 R Street, NW., Washington, DC 20008
phone (202) 319–1976, fax 319–2982
His Excellency Varuzhan Vazgeni Nerseyan
Ambassador Extraordinary and Plenipotentiary
Consular Office: California, Glendale

AUSTRALIA

Embassy of the Commonwealth of Australia
1601 Massachusetts Avenue, NW., Washington, DC 20036

phone (202) 797–3000, fax 797–3168
His Excellency Arthur Sinodinos
Ambassador Extraordinary and Plenipotentiary
Consular Offices:
California:
Los Angeles
San Francisco
District of Columbia, Washington
Hawaii, Honolulu
Illinois, Chicago
New York, New York
Texas, Houston

AUSTRIA

Embassy of the Republic of Austria
3524 International Court, NW., Washington, DC 20008
phone (202) 895–6700, fax 895–6750
His Excellency Martin Weiss
Ambassador Extraordinary and Plenipotentiary
Consular Offices:
California, Los Angeles
New York, New York

AZERBAIJAN

Embassy of the Republic of Azerbaijan
2741 34th Street, NW., Washington, DC 20008
phone (202) 337–3500, fax 337–5911
His Excellency Elin Emin Oglu Suleymanov
Ambassador Extraordinary and Plenipotentiary

BAHAMAS

Embassy of the Commonwealth of The Bahamas
2220 Massachusetts Avenue, NW., Washington, DC 20008
phone (202) 319–2660, fax 319–2668
His Excellency Sidney Stanley Collie
Ambassador Extraordinary and Plenipotentiary
Consular Offices:
District of Columbia, Washington
Florida, Miami
New York, New York

BAHRAIN

Embassy of the Kingdom of Bahrain
3502 International Drive, NW., Washington, DC 20008
phone (202) 342–1111, fax 362–2192
His Excellency Abdulla Rashed Abdulla Alkhalifa
Ambassador Extraordinary and Plenipotentiary
Consular Offices:
District of Columbia, Washington
New York, New York

BANGLADESH

Embassy of the People's Republic of Bangladesh
3510 International Drive, NW., Washington, DC 20008
phone (202) 244–0183, fax 244–2771
His Excellency Mohammad Ziauddin
Ambassador Extraordinary and Plenipotentiary
Consular Offices:
California, Los Angeles
District of Columbia, Washington
New York, New York

BARBADOS

Embassy of Barbados
2144 Wyoming Avenue, NW., Washington, DC 20008
phone (202) 939–9200, fax 332–7467
His Excellency Noel Anderson Lynch
Ambassador Extraordinary and Plenipotentiary
Consular Offices:
District of Columbia, Washington
Florida, Miami
New York, New York

BELARUS

Embassy of the Republic of Belarus
1619 New Hampshire Avenue, NW., Washington, DC 20009
phone (202) 986–1606, fax 986–1805
Mr. Dmitry Basik
Counselor (Chargé d'Affaires)
Consular Offices:
District of Columbia, Washington
New York, New York

BELGIUM

Embassy of the Kingdom of Belgium
1430 K Street, NW., Unit 1000, Washington, DC 20005
phone (202) 333–6900, fax 338–4960
His Excellency Dirk Jozef M. Wouters
Ambassador Extraordinary and Plenipotentiary
Consular Offices:
California, Los Angeles
District of Columbia, Washington
Georgia, Atlanta
New York, New York

BELIZE

Embassy of Belize
2535 Massachusetts Avenue, NW., Washington, DC 20008
phone (202) 332–9636, fax 332–6888
His Excellency Francisco Daniel Gutierez
Ambassador Extraordinary and Plenipotentiary
Consular Offices:
California, Los Angeles
District of Columbia, Washington
North Carolina, Wilmington

BENIN

Embassy of the Republic of Benin
2124 Kalorama Road, NW., Washington, DC 2008
phone (202) 232–6656, fax (202) 265–1996

Mr. Gafari Nadey Dango
Counselor (Chargé d'Affaires)

BOLIVIA

Embassy of the Plurinational State of Bolivia
3014 Massachusetts Avenue, NW., Washington, DC 20008
phone (202) 483–4410, fax 328–3712
Mr. Walter Oscar Serrate Cuellar
Chargé d'Affaires
Consular Offices:
California, Los Angeles
District of Columbia, Washington
Florida, Miami
New York, New York
Puerto Rico, San Juan
Texas, Houston

BOSNIA AND HERZEGOVINA

Embassy of Bosnia and Herzegovina
2109 E Street, NW., Washington, DC 20037
phone (202) 337–1500, fax 337–1502
His Excellency Bojan Vujić
Ambassador Extraordinary and Plenipotentiary
Consular Offices:
District of Columbia, Washington
Illinois, Chicago

BOTSWANA

Embassy of the Republic of Botswana
1531 New Hampshire Avenue, NW., Washington, DC 20036
phone (202) 244–4990, fax 244–4164
His Excellency David John Newman
Ambassador Extraordinary and Plenipotentiary
Consular Offices:
District of Columbia, Washington

BRAZIL

Embassy of the Federative Republic of Brazil
3006 Massachusetts Avenue, NW., Washington, DC 20008
phone (202) 238–2700, fax 238–2827
Mr. Nestor José Forster Júnior
Minister Counselor (Chargé d'Affaires)
Consular Offices:
California:
Los Angeles
San Francisco
Connecticut, Hartford
District of Columbia, Washington
Florida, Miami
Georgia, Atlanta
Illinois, Chicago
Massachusetts, Boston
New York, New York
Texas, Houston

BRUNEI

Embassy of Brunei Darussalam
3520 International Court, NW., Washington, DC 20008
phone (202) 237–1838, fax 885–0560
His Excellency Serbini Ali
Ambassador Extraordinary and Plenipotentiary
Consular Offices:
District of Columbia, Washington
New York, New York

BULGARIA

Embassy of the Republic of Bulgaria
1621 22nd Street, NW., Washington, DC 20008
phone (202) 387–0174, fax 234–7973
His Excellency Tihomir Anguelov Stoytchev
Ambassador Extraordinary and Plenipotentiary
Consular Offices:
California, Los Angeles
District of Columbia, Washington
Illinois, Chicago
New York, New York

BURKINA FASO

Embassy of Burkina Faso
2340 Massachusetts Avenue, NW., Washington, DC 20008
phone (202) 332–5577, fax 667–1882
His Excellency Seydou Kabore
Ambassador Extraordinary and Plenipotentiary
Consular Offices:
District of Columbia, Washington
New York, New York

BURMA

Embassy of the Union of Burma
2300 S Street, NW., Washington, DC 20008
phone (202) 332–3344, fax 332–4351
His Excellency Aung Lynn
Ambassador Extraordinary and Plenipotentiary

BURUNDI

Embassy of the Republic of Burundi
2233 Wisconsin Avenue, NW., Suite 408, Washington, DC 20007
phone (202) 342–2574, fax 342–2578
His Excellency Gaudence Sindayigaya
Ambassador Extraordinary and Plenipotentiary
Consular Office: District of Columbia, Washington

CABO VERDE

Embassy of the Republic of Cabo Verde
3415 Massachusetts Avenue, NW., Washington, DC 20007
phone (202) 965–6820, fax 965–1207
Mr. Antonio Joao Nascimento
Minister (Deputy Chief of Mission)
Consular Offices:
District of Columbia, Washington
Massachusetts, Boston

CAMBODIA

Embassy of the Kingdom of Cambodia
4530 16th Street, NW., Washington, DC 20011
phone (202) 726–7742, fax 726–8381
His Excellency Sounry Chum
Ambassador Extraordinary and Plenipotentiary
Consular Office: District of Columbia, Washington

CAMEROON

Embassy of the Republic of Cameroon
2349 Massachusetts Ave., NW., Washington, DC 20008
phone (202) 285–8790, fax 387–3826
His Excellency Essomba Etoundi
Ambassador Extraordinary and Plenipotentiary
Consular Office: District of Columbia, Washington

CANADA

Embassy of Canada
501 Pennsylvania Avenue, NW., Washington, DC 20001
phone (202) 682–1740, fax 682–7726
Ms. Kirsten Andrea Hillman
Minister (Chargé d'Affaires)
Consular Offices:
California:
Los Angeles
San Francisco
Colorado, Denver
District of Columbia, Washington
Florida, Miami
Georgia, Atlanta
Illinois, Chicago
Massachusetts, Boston
Michigan, Detroit
Minnesota, Minneapolis
New York, New York
Texas, Dallas
Washington, Seattle

CENTRAL AFRICAN REPUBLIC

Embassy of the Central African Republic
2704 Ontario Road, NW., Washington, DC 20009
phone (202) 483–7800, fax 332–9893
His Excellency Martial Ndoubou
Ambassador Extraordinary and Plenipotentiary
Consular Office: District of Columbia, Washington

CHAD

Embassy of the Republic of Chad
2401 Massachusetts Avenue, NW., Washington, DC 20008
phone (202) 652–1312
His Excellency Koutou Ngote Gali
Ambassador Extraordinary and Plenipotentiary
Consular Office: District of Columbia, Washington

CHILE

Embassy of the Republic of Chile
1732 Massachusetts Avenue, NW., Washington, DC 20036
phone (202) 785–1746, fax 887–5579
His Excellency Oscar Alfonso Sebastian Silva Navarro
Ambassador Extraordinary and Plenipotentiary
Consular Offices:
California:
Los Angeles
San Francisco
District of Columbia, Washington
Florida, Miami
Illinois, Chicago
New York, New York
Texas, Houston

CHINA

Embassy of the People's Republic of China
3505 International Place, NW., Washington, DC 20008
phone (202) 495–2266, fax 495–2138
His Excellency Tiankai Cui
Ambassador Extraordinary and Plenipotentiary
Consular Offices:
California:
Los Angeles
San Francisco
Illinois, Chicago
New York, New York

COLOMBIA

Embassy of the Republic of Colombia
1724 Massachusetts Ave., NW., Washington, DC 20036
phone (202) 387–8338, fax 232–8643
His Excellency Francisco Santos Calderón
Ambassador Extraordinary and Plenipotentiary
Consular Offices:
California:
Beverly Hills
San Francisco
District of Columbia, Washington
Florida:
Miami
Orlando
Georgia, Atlanta
Illinois, Chicago
Massachusetts, Boston
New Jersey, Newark
New York, New York
Puerto Rico, San Juan
Texas, Houston

COMOROS

Embassy of the Union of the Comoros
866 United Nations Plaza, Suite 418, New York, NY 10017
phone (212) 750–1637, fax 750–1657

His Excellency Mohamed Soilihi Soilih
Ambassador Extraordinary and Plenipotentiary

CONGO, DEMOCRATIC REPUBLIC OF THE

Embassy of the Democratic Republic of the Congo
1800 New Hampshire Ave., NW., Washington, DC 20009
phone (202) 234–7690
His Excellency François Nkuna Balumuene
Ambassador Extraordinary and Plenipotentiary
Consular Office: District of Columbia, Washington

CONGO, REPUBLIC OF THE

Embassy of the Republic of the Congo
1720 16th Street, NW., Washington, DC 20009
phone (202) 726–5500, fax 726–1860
His Excellency Serge Mombouli
Ambassador Extraordinary and Plenipotentiary
Consular Office: District of Columbia, Washington

COSTA RICA

Embassy of the Republic of Costa Rica
2114 S Street, NW., Washington, DC 20008
phone (202) 480–2200, fax 265–4795
His Excellency Fernando Llorca Castro
Ambassador Extraordinary and Plenipotentiary
Consular Offices:
California, Los Angeles
District of Columbia, Washington
Florida, Miami
Georgia, Atlanta
New York, New York
Texas, Houston

COTE D'IVOIRE

Embassy of the Republic of Cote d'Ivoire
2424 Massachusetts Avenue, NW., Washington, DC 20008
phone (202) 797–0300, fax 462–9444
His Excellency Mamadou Haidara
Ambassador Extraordinary and Plenipotentiary
Consular Offices:
District of Columbia, Washington

CROATIA

Embassy of the Republic of Croatia
2343 Massachusetts Avenue, NW., Washington, DC 20008
phone (202) 588–5899, fax 588–8937
His Excellency Pjer Šimunović
Ambassador Extraordinary and Plenipotentiary
Consular Offices:
California, Los Angeles
District of Columbia, Washington
Illinois, Chicago
New York, New York

CUBA

Embassy of the Republic of Cuba
2630 16th Street, NW., Washington, DC 20009
phone (202) 797–8518
His Excellency José Ramón Cabañas Rodríguez
Ambassador Extraordinary and Plenipotentiary
Consular Office: District of Columbia, Washington

CYPRUS

Embassy of the Republic of Cyprus
2211 R Street, NW., Washington, DC 20008
phone (202) 462–5772, fax 483–6710
His Excellency Marios Lysiotis
Ambassador Extraordinary and Plenipotentiary
Consular Offices:
District of Columbia, Washington
New York, New York

CZECHIA

Embassy of the Czech Republic
3900 Spring of Freedom Street, NW., Washington, DC 20008
phone (202) 274–9100, fax 966–8540
His Excellency Hynek Kmoníček
Ambassador Extraordinary and Plenipotentiary
Consular Offices:
California, Los Angeles
Illinois, Chicago
New York, New York

DENMARK

Embassy of the Kingdom of Denmark
3200 Whitehaven Street, NW., Washington, DC 20008
phone (202) 234–4300, fax 328–1470
Her Excellency Lone Dencker Wisborg
Ambassador Extraordinary and Plenipotentiary
Consular Offices:
District of Columbia, Washington
Illinois, Chicago
New York, New York

DJIBOUTI

Embassy of the Republic of Djibouti
1156 15th Street, NW., Suite 515, Washington, DC 20005
phone (202) 331–0270, fax 331–0302
His Excellency Mohamed Said Doualeh
Ambassador Extraordinary and Plenipotentiary

DOMINICA

Embassy of the Commonwealth of Dominica
1001 North 19th Street, Suite 1200, Arlington, VA 22209
phone (571) 527–1370, fax 384–7916
His Excellency Vince Henderson
Ambassador Extraordinary and Plenipotentiary

Consular Offices:
District of Columbia, Washington
New York, New York

DOMINICAN REPUBLIC

Embassy of the Dominican Republic
1715 22nd Street, NW., Washington, DC 20008
phone (202) 332–6280, fax 265–8057
His Excellency José Tomás Pérez Vázquez
Ambassador Extraordinary and Plenipotentiary
Consular Offices:
California, Glendale
District of Columbia, Washington
Florida, Miami
Illinois, Chicago
Louisiana, New Orleans
Massachusetts, Boston
New York, New York
Puerto Rico:
Mayaguez
San Juan

ECUADOR

Embassy of the Republic of Ecuador
2535 15th Street, NW., Washington, DC 20009
phone (202) 234–7200, fax 234–3497
Her Excellency Ivonne Leila Juez de a Baki
Ambassador Extraordinary and Plenipotentiary
Consular Offices:
Arizona, Phoenix
California, Los Angeles
Connecticut, New Haven
District of Columbia, Washington
Florida, Miami
Georgia, Atlanta
Illinois, Chicago
Minnesota, Minneapolis
New Jersey, Newark
New York, New York
Puerto Rico, San Juan
Texas, Houston

EGYPT

Embassy of the Arab Republic of Egypt
3521 International Court, NW., Washington, DC 20008
phone (202) 895–5400, fax 244–4319
His Excellency Yasser Reda Abdalla Ali Said
Ambassador Extraordinary and Plenipotentiary
Consular Offices:
California, Los Angeles
Illinois, Chicago
New York, New York
Texas, Houston

EL SALVADOR

Embassy of the Republic of El Salvador
1400 16th Street, NW., Suite 100, Washington, DC 20036
phone (202) 595–7500
Mr. Werner Matias Romero Guerra
Minister (Chargé d'Affaires)
Consular Offices:
California:
Los Angeles
San Francisco
District of Columbia, Washington
Florida:
Miami
Tampa
Georgia, Atlanta
Illinois, Chicago
Nevada, Las Vegas
New Jersey, Elizabeth
New York:
Brentwood
New York
Texas, Dallas
Virginia, Woodbridge
Washington, Seattle

EQUATORIAL GUINEA

Embassy of the Republic of Equatorial Guinea
2020 16th Street, NW., Washington, DC 20009
phone (202) 518–5700, fax 518–5252
His Excellency Miguel Ntutumu Evuna Andeme
Ambassador Extraordinary and Plenipotentiary
Consular Office: District of Columbia, Washington

ERITREA

Embassy of the State of Eritrea
1708 New Hampshire Avenue, NW., Washington, DC 20009
phone (202) 319–1991, fax 319–1304
Mr. Berhane Gebrehiwet Solomon
Counselor (Chargé d'Affaires)
Consular Office: District of Columbia, Washington

ESTONIA

Embassy of the Republic of Estonia
2131 Massachusetts Avenue, NW., Washington, DC 20008
phone (202) 588–0101, fax 588–0108
His Excellency Jonatan Vseviov
Ambassador Extraordinary and Plenipotentiary
Consular Offices:
California, San Francisco
New York, New York

ESWATINI

Embassy of the Kingdom of Eswatini
1712 New Hampshire Ave., NW., Washington, DC 20009
Phone: 202–234–5002, fax 234–8254
Her Excellency Njabuliso Busiswe Sikhulile Gwebu
Ambassador Extraordinary and Plenipotentiary

ETHIOPIA

Embassy of the Federal Democratic Republic of Ethiopia
3506 International Drive, NW., Washington, DC 20008
phone (202) 364–1200, fax 587–0195
His Excellency Fitsum Arega Gebrekidan
Ambassador Extraordinary and Plenipotentiary
Consular Offices:
California, Los Angeles
District of Columbia, Washington

EUROPEAN UNION

Delegation of the European Union
2175 K Street, NW., Floor 1, 6–11, Washington, DC 20037
His Excellency Stavros Lambrinidis
Ambassador (Head of Delegation)

FIJI

Embassy of the Republic of the Fiji
1707 L Street, NW., Suite 200, Washington, DC 20036
phone (202) 466–8320, fax 466–8325
Mr. Akuila Kamanalagi Vuira
First Secretary (Chargé d'Affaires)
Consular Office: New York, New York

FINLAND

Embassy of the Republic of Finland
3301 Massachusetts Avenue, NW., Washington, DC 20008
phone (202) 298–5800, fax 298–6030
Her Excellency Kirsti Helena Kauppi
Ambassador Extraordinary and Plenipotentiary
Consular Offices:
California, Los Angeles
New York, New York

FRANCE

Embassy of the French Republic
4101 Reservoir Road, NW., Washington, DC 20008
phone (202) 944–6000, fax 944–6166
His Excellency Philippe Noel Marie Marc Etienne
Ambassador Extraordinary and Plenipotentiary
Consular Offices:
California:
Los Angeles
San Francisco
District of Columbia, Washington
Florida, Miami
Georgia, Atlanta
Illinois, Chicago
Louisiana, New Orleans
Massachusetts, Boston
New York, New York
Texas, Houston

GABON

Embassy of the Gabonese Republic
2034 20th Street, NW., Washington, DC 20009
phone (202) 797–1000, fax (301) 332–0668
His Excellency Michael Moussa Adamo
Ambassador Extraordinary and Plenipotentiary

THE GAMBIA

Embassy of The Gambia
5630 16th Street, NW., Washington, DC 20011
phone (202) 785–1399
His Excellency Dawda D. Fadera
Ambassador Extraordinary and Plenipotentiary

GEORGIA

Embassy of Georgia
1824–1826 R Street, NW., Washington, DC 20009
phone (202) 387–2390, fax 387–0864
His Excellency David Bakradze
Ambassador Extraordinary and Plenipotentiary
Consular Office: New York, New York

GERMANY

Embassy of the Federal Republic of Germany
4645 Reservoir Road, NW., Washington, DC 20007
phone (202) 298–4000, fax 298–4249
Her Excellency Emily Margarethe Haber
Ambassador Extraordinary and Plenipotentiary
Consular Offices:
California:
Los Angeles
San Francisco
Florida, Miami
Georgia, Atlanta
Illinois, Chicago
Massachusetts, Boston
New York, New York
Texas, Houston

GHANA

Embassy of the Republic of Ghana
3512 International Drive, NW., Washington, DC 20008
phone (202) 686–4520, fax 686–4527
His Excellency Barfuor Adjei Barwuah
Ambassador Extraordinary and Plenipotentiary
Consular Offices:
New York, New York
Texas, Houston

GREECE

Embassy of the Hellenic Republic
2217 Massachusetts Avenue, NW., Washington, DC 20008
phone (202) 939–1300, fax 939–1324
Her Excellency Alexandra Papadopoulou
Ambassador Extraordinary and Plenipotentiary
Consular Offices:
California:

Los Angeles
San Francisco
Florida, Tampa
Georgia, Atlanta
Illinois, Chicago
Massachusetts, Boston
New York, New York
Texas, Houston

GRENADA

Embassy of Grenada
1701 New Hampshire Avenue, NW., Washington, DC 20009
phone (202) 265–2561, fax 265–2468
Her Excellency Yolande Yvonne Smith
Ambassador Extraordinary and Plenipotentiary

GUATEMALA

Embassy of the Republic of Guatemala
2220 R Street, NW., Washington, DC 20008
phone (202) 745–4953, fax 745–1908
Mr. José Gabriel Lambour Penalonzo
Minister Counselor (Chargé d'Affaires)
Consular Offices:
Alabama, Montgomery
Arizona:
Phoenix
Tucson
California:
Los Angeles
San Bernardino
San Francisco
Colorado, Denver
Florida, Miami
Georgia, Atlanta
Illinois, Chicago
Maryland, Silver Spring
New York, New York
Rhode Island, Providence
Texas:
Del Rio
Houston
McAllen

GUINEA

Embassy of the Republic of Guinea
2112 Leroy Place, NW., Washington, DC 20008
phone (202) 986–4300
His Excellency Kerfalla Yansane
Ambassador Extraordinary and Plenipotentiary
Consular Office: New York, New York

GUYANA

Embassy of the Cooperative Republic of Guyana
2490 Tracy Place, NW., Washington, DC 20008
phone (202) 265–6900, fax 232–1297
His Excellency Sheik Riyad David Insanally
Ambassador Extraordinary and Plenipotentiary
Consular Office: New York, New York

HAITI

Embassy of the Republic of Haiti
2311 Massachusetts Avenue, NW., Washington, DC 20008
phone (202) 332–4090, fax 745–7215
Mr. Hervé Denis
Minister (Chargé d'Affaires)
Consular Offices:
District of Columbia, Washington
Florida:
Miami
Orlando
Georgia, Atlanta
Illinois, Chicago
Massachusetts, Boston
New York, New York

HOLY SEE

Apostolic Nunciature
3339 Massachusetts Avenue, NW., Washington, DC 20008
phone (202) 333–7121, fax 337–4036
His Excellency Christophe Pierre
Apostolic Nuncio
Ambassador Extraordinary and Plenipotentiary

HONDURAS

Embassy of the Republic of Honduras
1220 19th Street, NW., Suite 320, Washington, DC 20036
phone (202) 966–7702
His Excellency Marlon Ramsses Tabora Munoz
Ambassador Extraordinary and Plenipotentiary
Consular Offices:
California:
Los Angeles
San Francisco
Florida, Miami
Georgia, Atlanta
Illinois, Chicago
Louisiana, New Orleans
New York, New York
Texas:
Dallas
Houston

HUNGARY

Embassy of Hungary
3910 Shoemaker Street, NW., Washington, DC 20008
phone (202) 362–6730, fax 966–8135
The Honorable Mr. Zsolt Gabor Hetesy
Minister (Deputy Chief of Mission)
Consular Offices:
California, Los Angeles
District of Columbia, Washington
New York, New York

ICELAND

Embassy of the Republic of Iceland
2900 K Street, NW., Suite 509, Washington, DC 20007
phone (202) 265–6653, fax 265–6656
Her Excellency Bergdís Ellertsdóttir
Ambassador Extraordinary and Plenipotentiary
Consular Office: New York, New York

INDIA

Embassy of the Republic of India
2107 Massachusetts Avenue, NW., Washington, DC 20008
phone (202) 939–7000, fax 265–4351
His Excellency Taranjit Singh Sandhu
Ambassador Extraordinary and Plenipotentiary
Consular Offices:
- California, San Francisco
- District of Columbia, Washington
- Georgia, Atlanta
- Illinois, Chicago
- New York, New York
- Texas, Houston

INDONESIA

Embassy of the Republic of Indonesia
2020 Massachusetts Avenue, NW., Washington, DC 20036
phone (202) 775–5200, fax 775–5365
Mr. Iwan Freddy Hari Susanto
Minister (Chargé d'Affaires)
Consular Offices:
- California:
  - Los Angeles
  - San Francisco
- District of Columbia, Washington
- Illinois, Chicago
- New York, New York
- Texas, Houston

IRAQ

Embassy of the Republic of Iraq
3421 Massachusetts Avenue, NW., Washington, DC 20008
phone (202) 742–1600, fax 333–1129
His Excellency Fareed Mustafa Kamil Yasseen Yasseen
Ambassador Extraordinary and Plenipotentiary
Consular Offices:
- California, Los Angeles
- District of Columbia, Washington
- Michigan, Detroit

IRELAND

Embassy of Ireland
2234 Massachusetts Avenue, NW., Washington, DC 20008
phone (202) 462–3939, fax 232–5993
His Excellency Daniel Gerard Mulhall
Ambassador Extraordinary and Plenipotentiary
Consular Offices:
- California, San Francisco
- District of Columbia, Washington
- Georgia, Atlanta
- Illinois, Chicago
- Massachusetts, Boston
- New York, New York

ISRAEL

Embassy of the State of Israel
3514 International Drive, NW., Washington, DC 20008
phone (202) 364–5500, fax 364–5607
His Excellency Ron Dermer
Ambassador Extraordinary and Plenipotentiary
Consular Offices:
- California:
  - Los Angeles
  - San Francisco
- District of Columbia, Washington
- Florida, Miami
- Georgia, Atlanta
- Illinois, Chicago
- Massachusetts, Boston
- New York, New York
- Pennsylvania, Philadelphia
- Texas, Houston

ITALY

Embassy of the Italian Republic
3000 Whitehaven Street, NW., Washington, DC 20008
phone (202) 612–4400, fax 518–2152
His Excellency Armando Varricchio
Ambassador Extraordinary and Plenipotentiary
Consular Offices:
- California:
  - Los Angeles
  - San Francisco
- Florida, Miami
- Illinois, Chicago
- Massachusetts, Boston
- Michigan, Detroit
- New York, New York
- Pennsylvania, Philadelphia
- Texas, Houston

JAMAICA

Embassy of Jamaica
1520 New Hampshire Avenue, NW., Washington, DC 20036
phone (202) 452–0660, fax 452–0036
Her Excellency Audrey Patrice Marks
Ambassador Extraordinary and Plenipotentiary

Consular Offices:
District of Columbia, Washington
Florida, Miami
New York, New York

JAPAN

Embassy of Japan
2520 Massachusetts Avenue, NW., Washington, DC 20008
phone (202) 238–6700, fax 328–2187
His Excellency Shinsuke Sugiyama
Ambassador Extraordinary and Plenipotentiary
Consular Offices:
Alaska, Anchorage
California:
Los Angeles
San Francisco
Colorado, Denver
District of Columbia, Washington
Florida, Miami
Georgia, Atlanta
Guam, Hagatna
Hawaii, Honolulu
Illinois, Chicago
Massachusetts, Boston
Michigan, Detroit
New York, New York
Northern Mariana Islands, Saipan
Oregon, Portland
Tennessee, Nashville
Texas, Houston
Washington, Seattle

JORDAN

Embassy of the Hashemite Kingdom of Jordan
3504 International Drive, NW., Washington, DC 20008
phone (202) 966–2664, fax 966–3110
Her Excellency Dina Khalil Tawfiq Kawar
Ambassador Extraordinary and Plenipotentiary

KAZAKHSTAN

Embassy of the Republic of Kazakhstan
1401 16th Street, NW., Washington, DC 20036
phone (202) 232–5488, fax 232–5845
His Excellency Erzhan Kazykhanov
Ambassador Extraordinary and Plenipotentiary
Consular Offices:
District of Columbia, Washington
New York, New York

KENYA

Embassy of the Republic of Kenya
2249 R Street, NW., Washington, DC 20008
phone (202) 387–6101, fax 462–3829
Mr. David Kahiro Gacheru
Minister (Chargé d'Affaires)
Consular Offices:
California, Los Angeles
New York, New York

KIRIBATI

Embassy of the Republic of Kiribati
800 Second Avenue, Suite 400A, New York, NY 10017
phone (212) 867–3310, fax 867–3320
His Excellency Teburoro Tito
Ambassador Extraordinary and Plenipotentiary
Consular Office: Hawaii, Honolulu

KOREA (SOUTH)

Embassy of the Republic of Korea
2450 Massachusetts Avenue, NW., Washington, DC 20008
phone (202) 939–5600, fax 797–0595
His Excellency Soo Hyuck Lee
Ambassador Extraordinary and Plenipotentiary
Consular Offices:
Alaska, Anchorage
California:
Los Angeles
San Francisco
District of Columbia, Washington
Georgia, Atlanta
Guam, Hagatna
Hawaii, Honolulu
Illinois, Chicago
Massachusetts, Boston
New York, New York
Texas:
Dallas
Houston
Washington, Seattle

KOSOVO

Embassy of the Republic of Kosovo
2175 K Street, NW., Suite 300, Washington, DC 20037
phone (202) 450–2130, fax 735–0609
Her Excellency Vlora Citaku
Ambassador Extraordinary and Plenipotentiary
Consular Office: New York, New York

KUWAIT

Embassy of the State of Kuwait
2940 Tilden Street, NW., Washington, DC 20008
phone (202) 966–0702, fax 966–0517
His Excellency Salem Abdullah Jaber Alsabah
Ambassador Extraordinary and Plenipotentiary
Consular Offices:
California, Los Angeles
District of Columbia, Washington
New York, New York

KYRGYZSTAN

Embassy of the Kyrgyz Republic
2360 Massachusetts Avenue, NW., Washington, DC 20008

phone (202) 449–9822, fax 386–7550
His Excellency Bolot Otunbaev
Ambassador Extraordinary and Plenipotentiary
Consular Office: District of Columbia, Washington

LAOS

Embassy of the Lao People's Democratic Republic
2222 S Street, NW., Washington, DC 20008
phone (202) 332–6416, fax 332–4923
His Excellency Khamphan Anlavan
Ambassador Extraordinary and Plenipotentiary
Consular Office: District of Columbia, Washington

LATVIA

Embassy of the Republic of Latvia
2306 Massachusetts Avenue, NW., Washington, DC 20008
phone (202) 328–2840, fax 328–2860
His Excellency Māris Selga
Ambassador Extraordinary and Plenipotentiary
Consular Offices:
District of Columbia, Washington
New York, New York

LEBANON

Embassy of the Lebanese Republic
2560 28th Street, NW., Washington, DC 20008
phone (202) 939–6300, fax 939–6324
His Excellency Gabriel Issa
Ambassador Extraordinary and Plenipotentiary
Consular Offices:
California, Los Angeles
District of Columbia, Washington
Massachusetts, Boston
Michigan, Detroit
New York, New York

LESOTHO

Embassy of the Kingdom of Lesotho
2511 Massachusetts Avenue, NW., Washington, DC 20008
phone (202) 797–5533, fax 234–6815
His Excellency Sankatana Gabriel Maja
Ambassador Extraordinary and Plenipotentiary
Consular Office: District of Columbia, Washington

LIBERIA

Embassy of the Republic of Liberia
5201 16th Street, NW., Washington, DC 20011
phone (202) 723–0437, fax 723–0436
His Excellency George S.W. Patten Sr.
Ambassador Extraordinary and Plenipotentiary
Consular Offices:
District of Columbia, Washington
New York, New York

LIBYA

Embassy of Libya
1460 Dahlia Street, NW., Washington, DC 200
phone (202) 944–9601, fax 944–9606
Her Excellency Wafa M. T. Bughaighis
Ambassador Extraordinary and Plenipotentiary
Consular Offices:
District of Columbia, Washington
New York, New York

LIECHTENSTEIN

Embassy of the Principality of Liechtenstein
2900 K Street, NW., Suite 602B, Washington, DC 20007
phone (202) 331–0590, fax 331–3221
His Excellency Kurt Jaeger
Ambassador Extraordinary and Plenipotentiary
Consular Office: New York, New York

LITHUANIA

Embassy of the Republic of Lithuania
2622 16th Street, NW., Washington, DC 20009
phone (202) 234–5860, fax 328–0466
His Excellency Rolandas Krisciunas
Ambassador Extraordinary and Plenipotentiary
Consular Offices:
Illinois, Chicago
New York, New York

LUXEMBOURG

Embassy of the Grand Duchy of Luxembourg
2200 Massachusetts Avenue, NW., Washington, DC 20008
phone (202) 265–4171, fax 328–8270
His Excellency Gaston Pierre Jean Stronck
Ambassador Extraordinary and Plenipotentiary
Consular Offices:
California, San Francisco
New York, New York

MACEDONIA (NORTH)

Embassy of the Republic of North Macedonia
2129 Wyoming Avenue, NW., Washington, DC 20008
phone (202) 667–0501, fax 667–2131
Ms. Vilma Petkovski
Minister Counselor (Chargé d'Affaires)
Consular Offices:
Illinois, Chicago
Michigan, Southfield
New York, New York

MADAGASCAR

Embassy of the Republic of Madagascar
2374 Massachusetts Avenue, NW., Washington, DC 20008
phone (202) 265–5525, fax 265–3034
Ms. Amielle Pelenne Niriniavisoa Marceda
Minister Counselor (Chargé d'Affaires)
Consular Office: New York, New York

MALAWI

Embassy of the Republic of Malawi
2408 Massachusetts Avenue, NW., Washington, DC 20008
phone (202) 721–0270, fax 721–0288
His Excellency Edward Yakobe Sawerengera
Ambassador Extraordinary and Plenipotentiary
Consular Office: New York, New York

MALAYSIA

Embassy of Malaysia
3516 International Court, NW., Washington, DC 20008
phone (202) 572–9700, fax 572–9882
His Excellency Azmil Bin Mohd Zabidi
Ambassador Extraordinary and Plenipotentiary
Consular Office: New York, New York

MALDIVES

Embassy of the Republic of Maldives
800 Second Avenue, Suite 400E, New York, NY 10017
phone (212) 599–6195, fax 661–6405
Her Excellency Thilmeeza Hussain
Ambassador Extraordinary and Plenipotentiary

MALI

Embassy of the Republic of Mali
2130 R Street, NW., Washington, DC 20008
phone (202) 332–2249, fax 332–6603
His Excellency Mahamadou Nimaga
Ambassador Extraordinary and Plenipotentiary

MALTA

Embassy of Malta
2017 Connecticut Avenue, NW., Washington, DC 20008
phone (202) 462–3611, fax 387–5470
His Excellency Keith Azzopardi
Ambassador Extraordinary and Plenipotentiary
Consular Offices:
  District of Columbia, Washington
  New York, New York

MARSHALL ISLANDS

Embassy of the Republic of the Marshall Islands
2433 Massachusetts Avenue, NW., Washington, DC 20008
phone (202) 234–5414, fax 232–3236
His Excellency Gerald M. Zackios
Ambassador Extraordinary and Plenipotentiary

MAURITANIA

Embassy of the Islamic Republic of Mauritania
2129 Leroy Place, NW., Washington, DC 20008
phone (202) 232–5700, fax 319–2623
His Excellency Samba Ba
Ambassador Extraordinary and Plenipotentiary
Consular Office: New York, New York

MAURITIUS

Embassy of the Republic of Mauritius
1709 N Street, NW., Washington, DC 20036
phone (202) 244–1491, fax 966–0983
Mr. Vikash Neethalia
First Secretary (Chargé d'Affaires)
Consular Office: District of Columbia, Washington

MEXICO

Embassy of the United Mexican States
1911 Pennsylvania Avenue, NW., Washington, DC 20006
phone (202) 728–1600, fax 728–1698
Her Excellency Martha Elena Federica Barcena Coqui
Ambassador Extraordinary and Plenipotentiary
Consular Offices:
- Arizona:
  - Douglas
  - Nogales
  - Phoenix
  - Tucson
  - Yuma
- Arkansas, Little Rock
- California:
  - Calexico
  - Fresno
  - Los Angeles
  - Oxnard
  - Sacramento
  - San Bernardino
  - San Diego
  - San Francisco
  - San Jose
  - Santa Ana
- Colorado, Denver
- District of Columbia, Washington
- Florida:
  - Miami
  - Orlando
- Georgia, Atlanta
- Idaho, Boise
- Illinois, Chicago
- Indiana, Indianapolis
- Louisiana, New Orleans
- Massachusetts, Boston
- Michigan, Detroit
- Minnesota, St. Paul
- Missouri, Kansas City
- Nebraska, Omaha
- Nevada, Las Vegas
- New Mexico, Albuquerque
- New York, New York
- North Carolina, Raleigh
- Oregon, Portland
- Pennsylvania, Philadelphia
- Puerto Rico, San Juan
- Texas:

Austin
Brownsville
Dallas
Del Rio
Eagle Pass
El Paso
Houston
Laredo
McAllen
Presidio
San Antonio
Utah, Salt Lake City
Washington, Seattle
Wisconsin, Milwaukee

MICRONESIA, FEDERATED STATES OF

Embassy of the Federated States of Micronesia
1725 N Street, NW., Washington, DC 20036
phone (202) 223–4383, fax 223–4391
His Excellency Akillino Harris Susaia
Ambassador Extraordinary and Plenipotentiary

MOLDOVA

Embassy of the Republic of Moldova
2101 S Street, NW., Washington, DC 20008
phone (202) 667–1130, fax 667–2624
Ms. Carolina Perebinos
Minister Counselor (Chargé d'Affaires)
Consular Office: District of Columbia, Washington

MONACO

Embassy of the Principality of Monaco
888 17th Street, NW., Suite 501, Washington, DC 20006
Her Excellency Maguy Maccario Doyle
Ambassador Extraordinary and Plenipotentiary
Consular Office: New York, New York

MONGOLIA

Embassy of Mongolia
2833 M Street, NW., Washington, DC 20007
phone (202) 333–7117, fax 298–9227
His Excellency Otgonbayar Yondon
Ambassador Extraordinary and Plenipotentiary
Consular Offices:
California, San Francisco
District of Columbia, Washington
New York, New York

MONTENEGRO

Embassy of Montenegro
1610 New Hampshire Avenue, NW., Washington, DC 20009
phone (202) 234–6108, fax 234–6109
His Excellency Nebojsa Kaludjerovic
Ambassador Extraordinary and Plenipotentiary
Consular Office: New York, New York

MOROCCO

Embassy of the Kingdom of Morocco
3508 International Drive, NW., Washington, DC 20008
phone (202) 499–1052, fax 457–0053
Her Excellency Lalla Joumala Alaoui
Ambassador Extraordinary and Plenipotentiary
Consular Office: New York, New York

MOZAMBIQUE

Embassy of the Republic of Mozambique
1525 New Hampshire Avenue, NW., Washington, DC 20036
phone (202) 293–7146, fax 835–0245
His Excellency Carlos Dos Santos
Ambassador Extraordinary and Plenipotentiary
Consular Office: New York, New York

NAMIBIA

Embassy of the Republic of Namibia
1605 New Hampshire Avenue, NW., Washington, DC 20009
phone (202) 986–0540, fax 986–0443
Her Excellency Monica Ndiliawike Nashandi
Ambassador Extraordinary and Plenipotentiary
Consular Office: District of Columbia, Washington

NAURU

Embassy of the Republic of Nauru
300 E. 42nd Street, Suite 1601, New York, NY 10017
phone (212) 937–0074, fax 937–0079
Her Excellency Marlene Inemwin Moses
Ambassador Extraordinary and Plenipotentiary

NEPAL

Embassy of the Federal Democratic Republic of Nepal
2730 34th Place, NW., Washington, DC 20007
phone (202) 667–4550, fax 667–5534
His Excellency Arjun Kumar Karki
Ambassador Extraordinary and Plenipotentiary
Consular Office: District of Columbia, Washington

NETHERLANDS

Embassy of the Kingdom of the Netherlands
4200 Linnean Avenue, NW., Washington, DC 20008
phone (202) 244–5300, fax 362–3430
His Excellency Andre Haspels
Ambassador Extraordinary and Plenipotentiary
Consular Offices:
California, San Francisco
District of Columbia, Washington
Florida, Miami
Illinois, Chicago
New York, New York

NEW ZEALAND

Embassy of New Zealand

37 Observatory Circle, NW., Washington, DC 20008
phone (202) 328–4800, fax 667–5227
Her Excellency Rosemary Banks
Ambassador Extraordinary and Plenipotentiary
Consular Offices:
California, Los Angeles
District of Columbia, Washington

NICARAGUA

Embassy of the Republic of Nicaragua
1627 New Hampshire Avenue, NW., Washington, DC 20009
phone (202) 939–6570, fax 939–6545
His Excellency Francisco Obadiah Campbell Hooker
Ambassador Extraordinary and Plenipotentiary
Consular Offices:
California:
Los Angeles
San Francisco
District of Columbia, Washington
Florida, Miami
New York, New York
Texas, Houston

NIGER

Embassy of the Republic of Niger
2204 R Street, NW., Washington, DC 20008
phone (202) 483–4224, fax 483–3169
His Excellency Abdallah Wafy
Ambassador Extraordinary and Plenipotentiary

NIGERIA

Embassy of the Federal Republic of Nigeria
3519 International Court, NW., Washington, DC 20008
phone (202) 986–8400, fax 362–6541
His Excellency Sylvanus Adiewere Nsofor
Ambassador Extraordinary and Plenipotentiary
Consular Office: Georgia, Atlanta

NORWAY

Embassy of the Kingdom of Norway
2720 34th Street, NW., Washington, DC 20008
phone (202) 333–6000, fax 469–3990
His Excellency Kaare Reidar Aas
Ambassador Extraordinary and Plenipotentiary
Consular Offices:
California, San Francisco
District of Columbia, Washington
New York, New York
Texas, Houston

OMAN

Embassy of the Sultanate of Oman
2535 Belmont Road, NW., Washington, DC 20008
phone (202) 387–1980, fax 745–4933
Her Excellency Hunaina Sultan Ahmed Al Mughairy
Ambassador Extraordinary and Plenipotentiary
Consular Office: District of Columbia, Washington

PAKISTAN

Embassy of the Islamic Republic of Pakistan
3517 International Court, NW., Washington, DC 20008
phone (202) 243–6500, fax 686–1534
His Excellency Asad Majeed Khan
Ambassador Extraordinary and Plenipotentiary
Consular Offices:
California, Los Angeles
District of Columbia, Washington
Illinois, Chicago
New York, New York
Texas, Houston

PALAU

Embassy of the Republic of Palau
1701 Pennsylvania Avenue, NW., Suite 300, Washington, DC 20006
phone (202) 452–6814, fax 452–6281
His Excellency Hersey Kyota
Ambassador Extraordinary and Plenipotentiary
Consular Office: District of Columbia, Washington

PANAMA

Embassy of the Republic of Panama
2862 McGill Terrace, NW., Washington, DC 20007
phone (202) 483–1407, fax 483–8413
His Excellency Juan Ricardo de Dianous Henriquez
Ambassador Extraordinary and Plenipotentiary
Consular Offices:
District of Columbia, Washington
Florida:
Miami
Tampa
Louisiana, New Orleans
New York, New York
Pennsylvania, Philadelphia
Puerto Rico, San Juan
Texas, Houston

PAPUA NEW GUINEA

Embassy of the Independent State of Papua New Guinea
1825 K Street, NW., Suite 1010, Washington, DC 20006
phone (202) 745–3680, fax 745–3679
Mr. Cephas Kayo
Minister (Chargé d'Affaires)

PARAGUAY

Embassy of Paraguay
2209 Massachusetts Avenue, NW., Washington, DC 20008
phone (202) 483–6960, fax 234–4508
His Excellency Manuel Maria Caceres Cardozo
Ambassador Extraordinary and Plenipotentiary

Consular Offices:
California, Los Angeles
District of Columbia, Washington
Florida, Miami
New York, New York

PERU

Embassy of the Republic of Peru
1700 Massachusetts Avenue, NW., Washington, DC 20036
phone (202) 833–9860, ext. 9869; fax 659–8124
His Excellency Hugo Claudio de Zela Martinez
Ambassador Extraordinary and Plenipotentiary
Consular Offices:
California:
Los Angeles
San Francisco
Colorado, Denver
Connecticut, Hartford
District of Columbia, Washington
Florida, Miami
Georgia, Atlanta
Illinois, Chicago
Massachusetts, Boston
New Jersey, Paterson
New York, New York
Texas:
Dallas
Houston

PHILIPPINES

Embassy of the Republic of the Philippines
1600 Massachusetts Avenue, NW., Washington, DC 20036
phone (202) 467–9300, fax 467–9417
His Excellency Jose Manuel del Gallego Romualdez
Ambassador Extraordinary and Plenipotentiary
Consular Offices:
California:
Los Angeles
San Francisco
District of Columbia, Washington
Guam, Hagatna
Hawaii, Honolulu
Illinois, Chicago
New York, New York

POLAND

Embassy of the Republic of Poland
2640 16th Street, NW., Washington, DC 20009
phone (202) 499–1700, fax 588–0565
His Excellency Piotr Antoni Wilczek
Ambassador Extraordinary and Plenipotentiary
Consular Offices:
California, Los Angeles
District of Columbia, Washington
Illinois, Chicago
New York, New York

PORTUGAL

Embassy of the Portuguese Republic
2012 Massachusetts Avenue, NW., Washington, DC 20036
phone (202) 350–5400, fax 223–3926
His Excellency Domingos Teixeira De Abreu Fezas Vital
Ambassador Extraordinary and Plenipotentiary
Consular Offices:
California, San Francisco
District of Columbia, Washington
Massachusetts:
Boston
New Bedford
New Jersey, Newark
New York, New York
Rhode Island, Providence
Texas, Houston

QATAR

Embassy of the State of Qatar
2555 M Street, NW., Washington, DC 20037
phone (202) 274–1600, fax 237–0061
His Excellency Meshal Hamad M.J. Al Thani
Ambassador Extraordinary and Plenipotentiary
Consular Office:
New York, New York
Texas, Houston

ROMANIA

Embassy of Romania
1607 23rd Street, NW., Washington, DC 20008
phone (202) 332–4846, fax 232–4748
His Excellency George Cristian Maior
Ambassador Extraordinary and Plenipotentiary
Consular Offices:
California, Los Angeles
District of Columbia, Washington
Illinois, Chicago
New York, New York

RUSSIA

Embassy of the Russian Federation
2650 Wisconsin Avenue, NW., Washington, DC 20007
phone (202) 298–5700, fax (202) 298–5735
His Excellency Anatoly Ivanovich Antonov
Ambassador Extraordinary and Plenipotentiary
Consular Offices:
District of Columbia, Washington
New York, New York
Texas, Houston

RWANDA

Embassy of the Republic of Rwanda
1875 Connecticut Avenue, NW., Suite 540, Washington, DC 20009
phone (202) 232–2882
Her Excellency Mathilde Mukantabana

Ambassador Extraordinary and Plenipotentiary
Consular Offices:
District of Columbia, Washington
New York, New York

SAINT KITTS AND NEVIS

Embassy of the Federation of St. Kitts and Nevis
1627 K Street, NW., 12th Floor, Washington, DC 20006
phone (202) 686–2636
Her Excellency Thelma Patricia Phillip Browne
Ambassador Extraordinary and Plenipotentiary
Consular Office: New York, New York

SAINT LUCIA

Embassy of St. Lucia
1629 K Street, NW., Suite 1250, Washington, DC 20006
phone (202) 364–6792, fax (202) 364–6723
His Excellency Anton Edsel Edmunds
Ambassador Extraordinary and Plenipotentiary
Consular Offices:
Florida, Miami
New York, New York

SAINT VINCENT AND THE GRENADINES

Embassy of St. Vincent and the Grenadines
1627 K Street, NW., 12th Floor, Washington, DC 20006
phone (202) 364–6730, fax 364–6736
Her Excellency LouAnne Gaylene Gilchrist
Ambassador Extraordinary and Plenipotentiary
Consular Office: New York, New York

SAMOA

Embassy of the Independent State of Samoa
685 Third Avenue, Suite 1102, New York, NY 10017
phone (212) 599–6196, fax 599–0797
His Excellency Ali'ioaiga Feturi Elisaia
Ambassador Extraordinary and Plenipotentiary

SAN MARINO

Embassy of the Republic of San Marino
327 E. 50th Street, New York, NY 10022
phone (202) 223–2418
His Excellency Damiano Beleffi
Ambassador Extraordinary and Plenipotentiary
Consular Offices:
District of Columbia, Washington
New York, New York

SÃO TOMÉ AND PRÍNCIPE

Embassy of São Tomé and Príncipe
675 Third Avenue, Suite 1807 New York, NY 10017
phone (212) 651–8116, fax 651–8117
His Excellency C. Azevedo Agostinho Das Neves
Ambassador Extraordinary and Plenipotentiary

SAUDI ARABIA

Embassy of the Kingdom of Saudi Arabia
601 New Hampshire Avenue, NW., Washington, DC 20037
phone (202) 342–3800, fax (202) 337–3233
His Excellency Reema Bint Bandar bin Sultan Al Saud
Ambassador Extraordinary and Plenipotentiary
Consular Offices:
California, Los Angeles
District of Columbia, Washington
New York, New York
Texas, Houston

SENEGAL

Embassy of the Republic of Senegal
2215 M Street, NW., Washington, DC 20007
phone (202) 234–0540, fax 629–2961
His Excellency Mansour Kane
Ambassador Extraordinary and Plenipotentiary
Consular Offices:
California, Burlingame
District of Columbia, Washington
New York, New York
Texas, Houston

SERBIA

Embassy of the Republic of Serbia
2233 Wisconsin Ave., NW., Suite 410, Washington, DC 20007
phone (202) 332–0333, fax 332–3933
His Excellency Derd Matkovic
Ambassador Extraordinary and Plenipotentiary
Consular Offices:
District of Columbia, Washington
Illinois, Chicago
New York, New York

SEYCHELLES

Embassy of the Republic of Seychelles
685 Third Avenue, Suite 1107, New York, NY 10017
His Excellency Ronald Jean Jumeau
Ambassador Extraordinary and Plenipotentiary

SIERRA LEONE

Embassy of the Republic of Sierra Leone
1701 19th Street, NW., Washington, DC 20009
phone (202) 939–9261, fax 483–1793
His Excellency Sidique Abou Bakarr Wai
Ambassador Extraordinary and Plenipotentiary

SINGAPORE

Embassy of the Republic of Singapore
3501 International Place, NW., Washington, DC 20008
phone (202) 537–3100, fax 537–0876

His Excellency Ashok Kumar
Ambassador Extraordinary and Plenipotentiary
Consular Offices:
California, San Francisco
New York, New York

SLOVAKIA

Embassy of the Slovak Republic
3523 International Court, NW., Washington, DC 20008
phone (202) 237–1054, fax 237–6438
Mr. Jozef Polakovic
Counselor (Deputy Chief of Mission)
Consular Offices:
District of Columbia, Washington
New York, New York

SLOVENIA

Embassy of the Republic of Slovenia
2410 California Street, NW., Washington, DC 20008
phone (202) 386–6601, fax 386–6633
His Excellency Stanislav Vidovic
Ambassador Extraordinary and Plenipotentiary
Consular Offices:
New York, New York
Ohio, Cleveland

SOMALIA

Embassy of the Federal Republic of Somalia
1705 Desales Street, NW., Suite 300, Washington, DC 20036
202–296–0570
His Excellency Ali Sharif Ahmed
Ambassador Extraordinary and Plenipotentiary
Consular Office: New York, New York

SOUTH AFRICA

Embassy of the Republic of South Africa
3051 Massachusetts Avenue, NW., Washington, DC 20008
phone (202) 232–4400, fax 265–1607
Her Excellency Nomaindiya Cathleen Mfeketo
Ambassador Extraordinary and Plenipotentiary
Consular Offices:
California, Los Angeles
District of Columbia, Washington
Illinois, Chicago
New York, New York

SOUTH SUDAN

Embassy of the Republic of South Sudan
1015 31st Street, NW., Floor 3, Washington, DC 20007
Phone (202) 293–7940, fax 293–7941
His Excellency Philip Jada Natana
Ambassador Extraordinary and Plenipotentiary

SPAIN

Embassy of the Kingdom of Spain
2375 Pennsylvania Avenue, NW., Washington, DC 20037
phone (202) 452–0100, fax 833–5670
His Excellency Santiago Cabanas Ansorena
Ambassador Extraordinary and Plenipotentiary
Consular Offices:
California:
Los Angeles
San Francisco
District of Columbia, Washington
Florida, Miami
Illinois, Chicago
Massachusetts, Boston
New York, New York
Puerto Rico, San Juan
Texas, Houston

SRI LANKA

Embassy of the Democratic Socialist Republic of Sri Lanka
3025 Whitehaven Street, NW., Washington, DC 20008
phone (202) 483–4025, fax 232–7181
His Excellency Eluppiti Mudiyanselage Rodney Man Perera
Ambassador Extraordinary and Plenipotentiary
Consular Offices:
California, Los Angeles
District of Columbia, Washington
New York, New York

SUDAN

Embassy of the Republic of the Sudan
2210 Massachusetts Avenue, NW., Washington, DC 20008
phone (202) 338–8565, fax 667–2406
Ms. Amira Abdalla Mohamed Agarib
Minister (Chargé d'Affaires)
Consular Office: New York, New York

SURINAME

Embassy of the Republic of Suriname
4201 Connecticut Avenue, NW., Suite 400, Washington, DC 20008
phone (202) 629–4302, fax 629–4769
Her Excellency Niermala Sakoentala Badrising
Ambassador Extraordinary and Plenipotentiary
Consular Office: Florida, Miami

SWEDEN

Embassy of the Kingdom of Sweden
2900 K Street, NW., Washington, DC 20007
phone (202) 467–2600, fax 467–2699
Her Excellency Karin Ulrika Olofsdotter
Ambassador Extraordinary and Plenipotentiary
Consular Offices:
California:
San Diego
San Francisco

District of Columbia, Washington
New York, New York

SWITZERLAND

Embassy of the Swiss Confederation
2900 Cathedral Avenue, NW., Washington, DC 20008
phone (202) 745–7900, fax 387–2564
His Excellency Jacques Henri Pitteloud
Ambassador Extraordinary and Plenipotentiary
Consular Offices:
California:
Los Angeles
San Francisco
District of Columbia, Washington
Georgia, Atlanta
Massachusetts, Boston
New York, New York

TAJIKISTAN

Embassy of the Republic of Tajikistan
1005 New Hampshire Avenue, NW., Washington, DC 20037
phone (202) 223–6090, fax 223–6091
His Excellency Farhod Salim
Ambassador Extraordinary and Plenipotentiary
Consular Office: District of Columbia, Washington

TANZANIA

Embassy of the United Republic of Tanzania
1232 22nd Street, NW., Washington, DC 20037
phone (202) 884–1080, fax 797–7408
His Excellency Wilson Mutagaywa Masilingi
Ambassador Extraordinary and Plenipotentiary

THAILAND

Embassy of the Kingdom of Thailand
1024 Wisconsin Avenue, NW., Washington, DC 20007
phone (202) 944–3600, fax 944–3611
His Excellency Thani Thongphakdi
Ambassador Extraordinary and Plenipotentiary
Consular Offices:
California, Los Angeles
District of Columbia, Washington
Illinois, Chicago
New York, New York

TIMOR-LESTE

Embassy of the Democratic Republic of Timor-Leste
4201 Connecticut Avenue, NW., Suite 504, Washington, DC 20008
phone (202) 966–3202, fax 966–3205
His Excellency Isilio Antonio de Fatima Coelho da Silva
Ambassador Extraordinary and Plenipotentiary
Consular Offices:
District of Columbia, Washington
New York, New York

TOGO

Embassy of the Togolese Republic
2208 Massachusetts Avenue, NW., Washington, DC 20008
phone (202) 234–4212, fax 232–3190
His Excellency Frederic Edem Hegbe
Ambassador Extraordinary and Plenipotentiary
Consular Office: District of Columbia, Washington

TRINIDAD AND TOBAGO

Embassy of the Republic of Trinidad and Tobago
1708 Massachusetts Avenue, NW., Washington, DC 20036
phone (202) 467–6490, fax 785–3130
His Excellency Anthony Wayne Jerome Phillips Spencer
Ambassador Extraordinary and Plenipotentiary
Consular Offices:
Florida, Miami
New York, New York

TUNISIA

Embassy of the Tunisian Republic
1515 Massachusetts Avenue, NW., Washington, DC 20005
phone (202) 862–1850, fax 862–1858
His Excellency Faycal Gouia
Ambassador Extraordinary and Plenipotentiary
Consular Office: District of Columbia, Washington

TURKEY

Embassy of the Republic of Turkey
2525 Massachusetts Avenue, NW., Washington, DC 20008
phone (202) 612–6700, fax 612–6744
His Excellency Serdar Kilic
Ambassador Extraordinary and Plenipotentiary
Consular Offices:
California, Los Angeles
District of Columbia, Washington
Florida, Miami
Illinois, Chicago
Massachusetts, Boston
New York, New York
Texas, Houston

TURKMENISTAN

Embassy of Turkmenistan
2207 Massachusetts Avenue, NW., Washington, DC 20008
phone (202) 588–1500, fax 288–1003
His Excellency Meret Orazov
Ambassador Extraordinary and Plenipotentiary

TUVALU

Embassy of Tuvalu
685 Third Avenue, Suite 1104, New York, NY 10017

phone (212) 490–0534, fax 808–4975
His Excellency Samuelu Laloniu
Ambassador Extraordinary and Plenipotentiary

UGANDA

Embassy of the Republic of Uganda
5911 16th Street, NW., Washington, DC 20011
phone (202) 726–0416, fax 726–1727
His Excellency Sebujja Mull Katende
Ambassador Extraordinary and Plenipotentiary

UKRAINE

Embassy of Ukraine
3350 M Street, NW., Washington, DC 20007
phone (202) 349–2920, fax 333–0817
His Excellency Volodymyr Yelchenko
Ambassador Extraordinary and Plenipotentiary
Consular Offices:
California, San Francisco
District of Columbia, Washington
Illinois, Chicago
New York, New York

UNITED ARAB EMIRATES

Embassy of the United Arab Emirates
3522 International Court, NW., Washington, DC 20008
phone (202) 243–2400, fax 243–2432
His Excellency Yousif Mana Saeed Ahmed Alotaiba
Ambassador Extraordinary and Plenipotentiary
Consular Office: California, Los Angeles

UNITED KINGDOM

Embassy of the United Kingdom of Great Britain and Northern Ireland
3100 Massachusetts Avenue, NW., Washington, DC 20008
phone (202) 588–6500, fax 588–7866
Her Excellency Karen Elizabeth Roxburgh
Ambassador Extraordinary and Plenipotentiary
Consular Offices:
California:
Los Angeles
San Francisco
District of Columbia, Washington
Florida, Miami
Georgia, Atlanta
Illinois, Chicago
Massachusetts, Boston
New York, New York
Texas, Houston

URUGUAY

Embassy of the Oriental Republic of Uruguay
1913 I Street, NW., Washington, DC 20006
phone (202) 331–1313, fax 331–8645
His Excellency Carlos Alberto Gianelli Derois
Ambassador Extraordinary and Plenipotentiary
Consular Offices:
California, Los Angeles
District of Columbia, Washington
Florida, Miami
Illinois, Chicago
New York, New York

UZBEKISTAN

Embassy of the Republic of Uzbekistan
1746 Massachusetts Avenue, NW., Washington, DC 20036
phone (202) 887–5300, fax 293–6804
His Excellency Javlon Vakhabov
Ambassador Extraordinary and Plenipotentiary
Consular Offices:
District of Columbia, Washington
New York, New York

VANUATU

Embassy of the Republic of Vanuatu
685 Third Avenue, Suite 1103, New York, NY 10017
Phone (212) 661–4303, fax 661–5544
His Excellency Odo Tevi
Ambassador Extraordinary and Plenipotentiary

VENEZUELA

Embassy of the Bolivarian Republic of Venezuela
1099 30th Street, NW., Washington, DC 20007
phone (202) 342–2214, fax 342–6820
His Excellency Carlos Alfredo Vecchio
Ambassador Extraordinary and Plenipotentiary
Consular Offices:
California, San Francisco
Florida, Miami
Illinois, Chicago
Louisiana, New Orleans
Massachusetts, Boston
New York, New York
Puerto Rico, San Juan
Texas, Houston

VIETNAM

Embassy of the Socialist Republic of Vietnam
1233 20th Street, NW., Suite 400, Washington, DC 20036
phone (202) 861–0737, fax 861–0917
His Excellency Kim Ngoc Ha
Ambassador Extraordinary and Plenipotentiary
Consular Offices:
California, San Francisco
New York, New York

YEMEN

Embassy of the Republic of Yemen
2319 Wyoming Avenue, NW., Washington, DC 20008
phone (202) 337–2017, fax 337–2017

His Excellency Ahmed Awad Ahmed BinMubarak
Ambassador Extraordinary and Plenipotentiary
Consular Office: District of Columbia, Washington

ZAMBIA

Embassy of the Republic of Zambia
2200 R Street, NW., Washington, DC 20008
phone (202) 265–9717, fax 332–0826
His Excellency Lazarous Kapambwe
Ambassador Extraordinary and Plenipotentiary
Consular Offices:
District of Columbia, Washington
New York, New York

ZIMBABWE

Embassy of the Republic of Zimbabwe
1608 New Hampshire Avenue, NW., Washington, DC 20009
phone (202) 332–7100, fax 483–9326
His Excellency Ammon Mutembwa
Ambassador Extraordinary and Plenipotentiary

The following is a list of countries with which diplomatic relations have been severed:

After each country, in parenthesis, is the name of the country's protecting power in the United States.

IRAN (Pakistan)

PRESS GALLERIES *

SENATE PRESS GALLERY

The Capitol, Room S–316, phone 224–0241

https://dailypress.senate.gov

Director.—Laura Lytle.
Deputy Director.—Christopher Bois.

Senior Media Relations Coordinators:
Amy H. Gross
John E. Mulligan III
Kristyn K. Socknat

Media Relations Coordinators:
Laura E. Reed
Samantha J. Yeider

HOUSE PRESS GALLERY

The Capitol, Room H–315, phone 225–3945

https://pressgallery.house.gov

Superintendent.—Annie Tin.
Deputy Superintendent.—Justin J. Supon.
Assistant Superintendents:
Ric Anderson
Edward Kachinske
Kristine Michalson
Jill Ornitz

STANDING COMMITTEE OF CORRESPONDENTS

Sarah Wire, Los Angeles Times, *Chair*
Jonathan Tamari, Philadelphia Inquirer, *Secretary*
Rachel Oswald, Congressional Quarterly
Jonathan Salant, New Jersey Advance Media
Andrew Taylor, Associated Press

RULES GOVERNING PRESS GALLERIES

1. Administration of the press galleries shall be vested in a Standing Committee of Correspondents elected by accredited members of the Galleries. The Committee shall consist of five persons elected to serve for terms of two years. Provided, however, that at the election in January 1951, the three candidates receiving the highest number of votes shall serve for two years and the remaining two for one year. Thereafter, three members shall be elected in odd-numbered years and two in even-numbered years. Elections shall be held in January. The Committee shall elect its own chairman and secretary. Vacancies on the Committee shall be filled by special election to be called by the Standing Committee.

2. Persons desiring admission to the press galleries of Congress shall make application in accordance with Rule VI of the House of Representatives, subject to the direction and

*Information is based on data furnished and edited by each respective Gallery.

control of the Speaker and Rule 33 of the Senate, which rules shall be interpreted and administered by the Standing Committee of Correspondents, subject to the review and an approval by the Senate Committee on Rules and Administration.

3. The Standing Committee of Correspondents shall limit membership in the press galleries to bone fide correspondents of repute in their profession, under such rules as the Standing Committee of Correspondents shall prescribe.

4. An applicant for press credentials through the Daily Press Galleries must establish to the satisfaction of the Standing Committee of Correspondents that he or she is a fulltime, paid correspondent who requires on-site access to congressional members and staff.

Correspondents must be employed by a news organization:

(a) with General Publication periodicals mailing privileges under U.S. Postal Service rules, and which publishes daily; or

(b) whose principal business is the daily dissemination of original news and opinion of interest to a broad segment of the public, and which has published continuously for 18 months.

The applicant must reside in the Washington, D.C. area, and must not be engaged in any lobbying or paid advocacy, advertising, publicity or promotion work for any individual, political party, corporation, organization, or agency of the U.S. Government, or in prosecuting any claim before Congress or any federal government department, and will not do so while a member of the Daily Press Galleries.

Applicants' publications must be editorially independent of any institution, foundation or interest group that lobbies the federal government, or that is not principally a general news organization.

Failure to provide information to the Standing Committee for this determination, or misrepresenting information, can result in the denial or revocation of credentials.

5. Members of the families of correspondents are not entitled to the privileges of the Galleries.

6. The Standing Committee of Correspondents shall propose no changes in these rules except upon petition in writing signed by not less than 100 accredited members of the galleries. The above rules have been approved by the Committee on Rules and Administration.

NANCY PELOSI,
Speaker of the House of Representatives.

ROY BLUNT,
Chair, Senate Committee on Rules and Administration.

MEMBERS ENTITLED TO ADMISSION

PRESS GALLERIES

Abbott, Charles: FERN's Ag Insider by Charles Abbott
Abe, Mineko: Yomiuri Shimbun
Abott, Richard: Defense Daily
Abutaleb, Yasmeen: Washington Post
Achenbach, Joel: Washington Post
Ackerman, Andrew: Wall Street Journal / Dow Jones
Adams, Rebecca: CQ / Roll Call
Adams, T. Becket: Washington Examiner
af Kleen, Bjorn: Dagens Nyheter
Ahmann, Timothy: Thomson Reuters
Ahmed, Akbar Shahid: Huffington Post
Alandete Ballester, David: ABC Newspaper
Albaqami, Hamad: Saudi Press Agency
Albaqami, Hindi: Saudi Press Agency
Alemany, Jacqueline: Washington Post
Alexander, Keith: Washington Post
Alexis, Alexei: CQ / Roll Call
Alfaro Martinez, Mariana: Washington Post
Ali, Idrees: Thomson Reuters
Allahverdi, Safvan: Anadolu News Agency
Allassan, Fadel: Axios
Allen, Michael: Axios
Allen, Nicholas: London Daily Telegraph
Allison, William: Bloomberg News
Alltucker, Kenneth: USA Today
Almubarak, Haifaa: Saudi Press Agency
Alonso, Ricardo: Associated Press
Alonso, Hernan Martin: EFE News Services
Alper, Alexandra: Thomson Reuters
Ampolsk, Sarah: Kyodo News
Anders Hagstrom, Anders: Daily Caller
Anderson, Greta: Inside Higher Ed
Anderson, Mark: Wall Street Journal / Dow Jones
Anderson, Nicholas: Washington Post
Andrews, Natalie: Wall Street Journal / Dow Jones
Aoyama, Naoatsu: Asahi Shimbun
Appelbaum, Binyamin: New York Times
Appleby, Julie: Kaiser Health News
Arai, Takuya: Kyodo News
Aratani, Lori: Washington Post
Armour, Stephanie: Wall Street Journal / Dow Jones
Arnsdorf, Isaac: ProPublica
Arundel, Kara: LRP Publications
Ashizuka, Tomoko: Nikkei
Asseo, Laurie: Bloomberg News
Aubourg, Lucie: Agence France-Presse
Aukofer, Frank: Artists & Writers Syndicate
Austin, Emily: Wall Street Journal / Dow Jones
Ayesh, Rashaan: Axios
Bacon, Erin: CQ / Roll Call
Bade, Rachael: Washington Post
Badger, Emily: New York Times
Bailey, Holly: Washington Post
Bain, Benjamin: Bloomberg News
Baird, Addy: Buzzfeed
Baker, Samuel: Axios
Baker, Brian: MLEX US
Baker, Peter: New York Times
Baldor, Lolita: Associated Press
Ball, Michael: Argus Media
Ballhaus, Rebecca: Wall Street Journal / Dow Jones
Balsamo, Michael: Associated Press
Balz, Daniel: Washington Post
Banco, Erin: Daily Beast
Banerjee, Neela: Inside Climate News
Banks, Adelle: Religion News Service
Barker, Jeffrey: Baltimore Sun
Barnes, Julian: New York Times
Barnes, Robert: Washington Post
Baron, Martin: Washington Post
Barone, Michael: Washington Examiner
Barr, Cameron: Washington Post
Barrett, John: Washington Post
Barros Cantillo, Laura: EFE News Services
Bartash, Jeffry: MarketWatch
Bartz, Diane: Thomson Reuters
Basu, Zachary: Axios
Batz, Jurgen: German Press Agency–DPA
Baykan, Dildar: Anadolu News Agency
Beattie, Anita: Agence France-Presse
Beattie, Jeffrey: Energy Daily
Becker, Amanda: Thomson Reuters
Beckett, Paul: Wall Street Journal / Dow Jones
Beckwith, Ryan: Bloomberg News
Bedard, Paul: Washington Examiner
Beech, Eric: Thomson Reuters
Beene, Ryan: Bloomberg News
Beg, Sajeer: CQ / Roll Call
Behrmann, Savannah: USA Today
Beinart, Matthew: Defense Daily
Belaiba, Ines: Agence France-Presse
Bell, Alistair: Thomson Reuters
Bell, Jarrett: USA Today
Benac, Nancy: Associated Press
Bender, Michael: Wall Street Journal / Dow Jones
Bendery, Jennifer: Huffington Post
Benjaminson, Wendy: Bloomberg News
Benner, Katie: New York Times
Benning, Thomas: Dallas Morning News

MEMBERS ENTITLED TO ADMISSION—Continued

Benning, Victoria: Washington Post
Benyon, Steven: Stars and Stripes
Berg, Kirsten: ProPublica
Berkowitz, Steven: USA Today
Berley, Max: Bloomberg News
Berman, Mark: Washington Post
Berner, Anna Sofia: Helsingin Sanomat
Berry, Lynn: Associated Press
Berry, Deborah: Gannett Washington Bureau
Bever, Kathleen: CQ / Roll Call
Bidgood, Jessica: Boston Globe
Bierman, Noah: Los Angeles Times
Biesecker, Michael: Associated Press
Bilski, Christina: Nikkei
Bing, Christopher: Thomson Reuters
Black, William: Asahi Shimbun
Blanc, Sebastien: Agence France-Presse
Bland, Melissa: Thomson Reuters
Blokker, Bastiaan: NRC Handelsblad
Blum, Justin: Bloomberg News
Blumenthal, Paul: Huffington Post
Boak, Joshua: Associated Press
Bobic, Igor: Huffington Post
Bocchetti, Mark: CQ / Roll Call
Bohan, Caren: USA Today
Booker, Janet: Wall Street Journal / Dow Jones
Bordelon, Brendan: National Journal
Borenstein, Seth: Associated Press
Borger, Julian: Guardian US,
Bose, Nandita: Thomson Reuters
Boshart, Glen: S & P Global
Bouchard, Mikayla: New York Times
Bowden, Ebony: New York Post
Bowers, Becky: Wall Street Journal / Dow Jones
Bowers, Jeremy: Washington Post
Boyer, Antoine: Agence France-Presse
Boyer, David: Washington Times
Brandt, Martin: Wall Street Journal / Dow Jones
Braun, Stephen: Associated Press
Bravin, Jess: Wall Street Journal / Dow Jones
Brodbeck, Scott: LocalNews Now
Broderick, Timothy: Christian Science Monitor
Brodey, Sam: Daily Beast
Brody, Ben: Bloomberg News
Brooks, David: La Jornada
Brooks, David: New York Times
Brown, Emma: Washington Post
Brune, Thomas: Newsday
Brunnstrom, David: Thomson Reuters
Bufkin, Elizabeth: Washington Examiner
Bull, Alister: Bloomberg News
Bulla, Beatriz: O Estado De S. Paulo
Bumiller, Elisabeth: New York Times
Burgess, Jeffrey: New York Times
Burk, Ginger: Thomson Reuters
Burke, Melissa: Detroit News
Burley, Tahirah: New York Times
Burnett, Mark: CQ / Roll Call
Burns, Robert: Associated Press
Burr, Thomas: Salt Lake Tribune
Burton, Thomas: Wall Street Journal / Dow Jones
Buskirk, Howard: Communications Daily
Bykowicz, Julie: Wall Street Journal / Dow Jones
Calmes, Jackie: Los Angeles Times
Camdessus, Camille: Agence France-Presse
Cameron, Christopher: New York Times
Campbell, Alexia: Center for Public Integrity
Cannon, Carl: Real Clear Politics
Capaccio, Anthony: Bloomberg News
Caplan, Abby: Argus Media
Capps, Kriston: Bloomberg News
Caralle, Katelyn: DailyMail.com
Cardenas, Teresa: CQ / Roll Call
Carey, Dominic: Bloomberg News
Carey, Mary Agnes: Kaiser Health News
Carney, Timothy: Washington Examiner
Carter, Charlene: CQ / Roll Call
Cartillier, Jerome: Agence France-Presse
Cassata, Donna: Washington Post
Cassidy, Alan: Tages Anzeiger
Catanese, David: McClatchy
Celik, Can: MLEX US
Cha, Joniel: S & P Global
Cha, Ariana: Washington Post
Chabanas, Julie: Agence France-Presse
Chaffee, Conrad: Tokyo Chunichi Shimbun
Chambers, Francesca: McClatchy
Chaney, Sarah: Wall Street Journal / Dow Jones
Chang, Chia: United Daily News
Chang, Carolyn: World Journal
Charlton, Emma: Agence France-Presse
Charter, David: Times of London
Chavez, Aida: The Intercept
Cheng, Tsung-Shen: Taiwan Central News Agency
Chiacu, Doina: Thomson Reuters
Chiang, Chinyeh: Taiwan Central News Agency
Chiantaretto, Mariuccia: WolfNews
Chinni, Dante: Wall Street Journal / Dow Jones
Chinyeh, Chiang: Central News Agency
Cho, Yi Jun: Chosun Ilbo
Chong, Christina: Korea Times
Chorus, Jutta: NRC Handelsblad
Christian, Molly: S & P Global
Christian, Rodney: Wall Street Journal / Dow Jones
Cimmino, Jeffrey: Washington Examiner
Cirilli, Kevin: Bloomberg News
Clark, Colin: Breaking Defense
Clark, L. Kareema: Wall Street Journal / Dow Jones
Clason, Lauren: CQ / Roll Call
Clearfield, Alex: National Journal
Clevenger, Andrew: CQ / Roll Call
Clift, Eleanor: Daily Beast
Cloud, David: Los Angeles Times
Cochrane, Emily: New York Times

MEMBERS ENTITLED TO ADMISSION—Continued

Codrea, George: CQ / Roll Call
Cohen, Ian: International Trade Today
Cohen, Zachary: National Journal
Cohn, Peter: CQ / Roll Call
Collins, Margaret: Bloomberg News
Collins, Michael: Gannett Washington Bureau
Collins, Eliza: Wall Street Journal / Dow Jones
Colvin, Jill: Associated Press
Colvin, Ross: Thomson Reuters
Condon, Christopher: Bloomberg News
Condon, George: National Journal
Conlon, Charles: CQ / Roll Call
Cooke, Anthony: MLEX US
Cooney, Peter: Thomson Reuters
Copley, Michael: S & P Global
Copp, Tara: McClatchy
Copur, Hakan: Anadolu News Agency
Corchado, Alfredo: Dallas Morning News
Cornwell, Susan: Thomson Reuters
Correll, Diana: Washington Examiner
Corrigan, John: Wall Street Journal / Dow Jones
Corse, Alexa: Wall Street Journal / Dow Jones
Costa, Robert: Washington Post
Cottle, Michelle: New York Times
Couronne, Ivan: Agence France-Presse
Covey, Erin: National Journal
Cowan, Richard: Thomson Reuters
Cox, Matthew: Military.com
Crabtree, Susan: Real Clear Politics
Craig, Tim: Washington Post
Cramer, Harrison: National Journal
Crane, Marcy: S & P Global
Crilly, Robert: Washington Examiner
Crisp, Elizabeth: Baton Rouge Advocate
Cross, Miriam: American Banker
Crowley, Michael: New York Times
Crutsinger, Martin: Associated Press
Cullison, Alan: Wall Street Journal / Dow Jones
Cullum, James: LocalNews Now
Cummings, William: USA Today
Cummings, Jeanne: Wall Street Journal / Dow Jones
Cunningham, Stephen: Bloomberg News
Cunningham, Paige: Washington Post
Curtis, Laura: Bloomberg News
Cuzin, Elodie: Agence France-Presse
Dabbs, Brian: National Journal
Daly, Matthew: Associated Press
Daly, Kyle: Axios
Daneman, Matthew: Communications Daily
D'Angelo, Christopher: Huffington Post
Daniel, Douglass: Associated Press
Daniel, Annie: New York Times
D'Anna, John: USA Today
Dasgupta, Shirsho: McClatchy
Date, Shirish: Huffington Post
Datoc, Christian: Daily Caller
Daugherty, Alex: McClatchy
Davenport, Coral: New York Times
Davenport, Christian: Washington Post
Davidson, Julie: LRP Publications
Davidson, Joseph: Washington Post
Davidson Choma, Kate: Wall Street Journal / Dow Jones
Davis, Julie: New York Times
Davis, Robert: Wall Street Journal / Dow Jones
Davis, Aaron: Washington Post
Davison, Laura: Bloomberg News
Dawsey, Joshua: Washington Post
Day, James: Energy Daily
Day, Chad: Wall Street Journal / Dow Jones
DeBonis, Michael: Washington Post
DeChalus, Camila: CQ / Roll Call
Decker, Susan: Bloomberg News
Decker, Cathleen: Washington Post
DeFrank, Andrew: National Journal
Dei, Ryota: Jiji Press
Delaney, Arthur: Huffington Post
Delgado-Robles, Jose: El Nuevo Dia
Demirjian, Karoun: Washington Post
Dennis, Steven: Bloomberg News
Dennis, Brady: Washington Post
Depillis, Lydia: ProPublica
Dexheimer, Elizabeth: Bloomberg News
DeYoung, Karen: Washington Post
Dias, Marina: Folha de Sao Paulo
Dias, Elizabeth: New York Times
Diaz-Briseno, Jose: Reforma Newspaper
Dickstein, Corey: Stars and Stripes
Dieste Markl, Alina: Agence France-Presse
Dinan, Stephen: Washington Times
Dlouhy, Jennifer: Bloomberg News
Dmitrieva, Ekaterina: Bloomberg News
Dobrik, Adam: Global Investigations Review
Doemens, Karl: RND News Network
Dolan, Christopher: Washington Times
Dolley, Steven: S & P Global
Donati-Bourne, Jessica: Wall Street Journal / Dow Jones
Donnelly, John: CQ / Roll Call
Dorning, Michael: Bloomberg News
Douglas, Leah: FERN's Ag Insider by Charles Abbott
Dowd, Maureen: New York Times
Downing, James: Power Markets Today
Doyle, Katherine: Washington Examiner
Drogin, Robert: Los Angeles Times
Drucker, David: Washington Examiner
du Lac, Joshua: Washington Post
Duehren, Andrew: Wall Street Journal / Dow Jones
Dufour, Jeff: National Journal
Dumain, Emma: McClatchy
Duncan, Ian: Washington Post
Dunham, William: Thomson Reuters
Dunleavy, Jeremiah: Washington Examiner
Dunlop, William: Agence France-Presse

MEMBERS ENTITLED TO ADMISSION—Continued

Dunsmuir, Lindsay: Thomson Reuters
Durkin, Erin: National Journal
Dusseau, Brigitte: Agence France-Presse
Duval, Sebastien: Agence France-Presse
Earle, Geoffrey: DailyMail.com
Eaton, Sabrina: Cleveland Plain Dealer
Ebersole Vaino, Jenna: MLEX US
Edgerton, Anna: Bloomberg News
Edmondson, Catie: New York Times
Edwards-Levy, Ariel: Huffington Post
Egan, Casey: S & P Global
Egbame, Assima: Bloomberg News
Egkolfopoulou, Misyrlena: Bloomberg News
Eichelberger, Curtis: MLEX US
Eilperin, Juliet: Washington Post
Eisler, Peter: Thomson Reuters
Elfin, David: LRP Publications
Ellis, Isobel: National Journal
Emerson, Lars: CQ / Roll Call
Emmons, Alexander: The Intercept
Engblom, Andrew: S & P Global
Epstein, Edward: Argus Media
Epstein, Jennifer: Bloomberg News
Epstein, Reid: New York Times
Epstein, Ethan: Washington Times
Facher, Lev: STAT
Fadulu, Lolade: New York Times
Fahrenthold, David: Washington Post
Fain, Paul: Inside Higher Ed
Fallor, Evan: S & P Global
Fandos, Nicholas: New York Times
Fang, Marina: Huffington Post
Fang, Lee: The Intercept
Faries, William: Bloomberg News
Fears, Darryl: Washington Post
Fedor, Lauren: Financial Times
Felder, Rafi: MLEX US
Feldman, Carole: Associated Press
Feldmann, Linda: Christian Science Monitor
Felker, Edward: CQ / Roll Call
Feltman, Peter: CQ / Roll Call
Ferguson, Ellyn: CQ / Roll Call
Fernandez, Marisa: Axios
Fernandez, Alfonso: EFE News Services
Ferrechio, Susan: Washington Examiner
Ferriss, Susan: Center for Public Integrity
Figueroa Hernandez, Laura: Newsday
Fillion, Maxwell: MLEX US
Fineman, Howard: Real Clear Politics
Fingerhut, Hannah: Associated Press
Finn, Teaganne: Bloomberg News
Finney, Maranda: Daily Caller
Firozi, Paulina: Washington Post
Firth, Shannon: MedPage Today
Fischer, Sara: Axios
Fischer-Baum, Reuben: Washington Post
Fisher, Marc: Washington Post
FitzGerald, Drew: Wall Street Journal / Dow Jones
Fitzmartin, Tara: Asahi Shimbun
Flaherty, Mary: Washington Post
Flatley, Daniel: Bloomberg News
Flavelle, Christopher: New York Times
Florko, Nicholas: STAT
Foley, Elise: Huffington Post
Fontelo, Paul: CQ / Roll Call
Fontemaggi, Francesco: Agence France-Presse
Forden, Sara: Bloomberg News
Forrest, Brett: Wall Street Journal / Dow Jones
Fouriezos, Nicholas: Ozy Media
Fox, Benjamin: Associated Press
Fram, Alan: Associated Press
Francis, Theodore: Wall Street Journal / Dow Jones
Frankel, Todd: Washington Post
Freebairn, William: S & P Global
Freedberg, Sydney: Breaking Defense
Freedman, Andrew: Washington Post
Freking, Kevin: Associated Press
Frieden, Joyce: MedPage Today
Friedman, Lisa: New York Times
Fritze, John: USA Today
Fry, Madeline: Washington Examiner
Fryer-Biggs, Zachary: Center for Public Integrity
Fuchino, Shinichi: Kyodo News
Fujiwara, Akihiro: Kyodo News
Fuller, Matthew: Huffington Post
Funakoshi, Sho: Yomiuri Shimbun
Furlow, Robert: Associated Press
Furumoto, Yoso: Mainichi Shimbun
Gaither, Ronald: McClatchy
Galewitz, Philip: Kaiser Health News
Gallu, Joshua: Bloomberg News
Gambino, Lauren: Guardian US,
Gamm, Colin: Yomiuri Shimbun
Ganesh, Janan: Financial Times
Gardner, Timothy: Thomson Reuters
Gardner, Amy: Washington Post
Gardner Whyte, Elizabeth: Washington Post
Gearan, Anne: Washington Post
Gehrke, Joel: Washington Examiner
Geman, Benjamin: Axios
George, Justin: Washington Post
Ghani, Saleha: Bloomberg News
Ghosh, Nirmal: Singapore Straits Times
Giaritelli, Anna: Washington Examiner
Gibbons-Neff, Thomas: New York Times
Gibney, James: Bloomberg News
Gilbert, Craig: Milwaukee Journal Sentinel
Gillman, Todd: Dallas Morning News
Gillum, Jack: ProPublica
Ginsberg, Steven: Washington Post
Givens, David: Argus Media
Glazier, Kyle: Bond Buyer
Glenn, Michael: Washington Times
Gnoffo, Anthony: CQ / Roll Call

MEMBERS ENTITLED TO ADMISSION—Continued

Goba, Kadia: Buzzfeed
Gold, Shabtai: German Press Agency–DPA
Gold, Matea: Washington Post
Golden, Rodrek: Thomson Reuters
Goldhamer Sherry, Marisha: Agence France-Presse
Goldman, Adam: New York Times
Goldstein, Amy: Washington Post
Golle, Henry: Bloomberg News
Golshan, Tara: Huffington Post
Gomez, Sergio: El Tiempo
Gonzalez, Miguel: Wall Street Journal / Dow Jones
Good, Allison: S & P Global
Goodin, Emily: DailyMail.com
Goodman, Alana: Washington Examiner
Goodnough, Abigail: New York Times
Goodwin, Liz: Boston Globe
Gordon, Marcy: Associated Press
Gordon, D. Craig: Bloomberg News
Gordon, Meghan: S & P Global
Gordon, Michael: Wall Street Journal / Dow Jones
Gouveia Monteiro, Ana: Bloomberg News
Grady, Anne: CQ / Roll Call
Grandoni, Dino: Washington Post
Grant, Paul: Thomson Reuters
Graves, Lucia: Guardian US,
Greber, Jacob: Australian Financial Review
Greeley, Brendan: Financial Times
Green, Justin: Axios
Green, Joshua: Bloomberg News
Greenberg, Jonathan: PolitiFact
Greene, Ronnie: Thomson Reuters
Gregg, Aaron: Washington Post
Gresko, Jessica: Associated Press
Greve, Joan: Guardian US,
Greve, Joan: Washington Post
Grier, Peter: Christian Science Monitor
Griffiths, Brent: Washington Post
Grim, Ryan: The Intercept
Grimaldi, James: Wall Street Journal / Dow Jones
Groer, Anne L.: Annie Groer Writer At Large
Groppe, Maureen: Gannett Washington Bureau
Grube, Nicholas: Honolulu Civil Beat
Guevara, Tomas: El Diario de Hoy
Gugarats, Haik: Argus Media
Guggenheim, Kenneth: Associated Press
Gunerigok, Servet: Anadolu News Agency
Gurman, Sadie: Wall Street Journal / Dow Jones
Gustin, Georgina: Inside Climate News
Haberkorn, Jennifer: Los Angeles Times
Hackman, Michelle: Wall Street Journal / Dow Jones
Haggerty, Cornelius: American Banker
Hahn, Dorothea: Die Tageszeitung
Halaschak, Zachary: Washington Examiner
Hale, Zachary: S & P Global
Hall, Eileen: Buzzfeed
Hall, Kevin: McClatchy
Halper, Evan: Los Angeles Times
Halsey, Ashley: Washington Post
Hamann, Carlos: Agence France-Presse
Hamburger, Thomas: Washington Post
Hamby, Chris: New York Times
Hamilton, Jesse: Bloomberg News
Hancock, James: Kaiser Health News
Handley, Paul: Agence France-Presse
Hanrahan, Timothy: Wall Street Journal / Dow Jones
Harder, Amy: Axios
Harkins, Gina: Military.com
Harper, Jennifer: Washington Times
Harras, Steven: CQ / Roll Call
Harris, Shane: Washington Post
Harrison, David: Wall Street Journal / Dow Jones
Harte, Julia: Thomson Reuters
Harwell, Andrew: Washington Post
Hatch, David: Daily Deal
Hauser, Ryan: Market News International
Hautkapp, Dirk: Funke Mediengruppe
Hayashi, Yuka: Wall Street Journal / Dow Jones
Hayes, Christal: USA Today
Hazell, Dino: Associated Press
Heath, Bradford: Thomson Reuters
Heavey, Susan: Thomson Reuters
Heflin, Jay: Washington Examiner
Heim, Joseph: Washington Post
Helderman, Rosalind: Washington Post
Heltman, John: American Banker
Henderson, Nell: Wall Street Journal / Dow Jones
Hensley-Clancy, Molly: Buzzfeed
Hepinstall, Sonya: Thomson Reuters
Herchenroeder, Karl: Communications Daily
Heredia Rodriguez, Carmen: Kaiser Health News
Hermann, Peter: Washington Post
Hernandez, Michael: Anadolu News Agency
Hernandez, Arelis: Washington Post
Herrmann, Frank: Rheinische Post
Hesson, Theodore: Thomson Reuters
Higgins, Sean: Washington Examiner
Himori, Shiro: Kyodo News
Hinckley, Story: Christian Science Monitor
Hirji, Zahra: Buzzfeed
Hitchens, Theresa: Breaking Defense
Hogan, Monica: Communications Daily
Hohmann, James: Washington Post
Holan, Angie: PolitiFact
Holden, Emily: Guardian US,
Holland, Benjamin: Bloomberg News
Holland, William: S & P Global
Holland, Steve: Thomson Reuters
Holmes, Allan: Center for Public Integrity
Holzman, Jacob: S & P Global
Hood, David: S & P Global
Hook, Janet: Los Angeles Times
Hopkins, Jamie: Center for Public Integrity
Horwitz, Sari: Washington Post
Hosenball, Mark: Thomson Reuters

MEMBERS ENTITLED TO ADMISSION—Continued

House, Billy: Bloomberg News
Howard, Megan: Bloomberg News
Howell, Thomas: Washington Times
Hoyama, Taisei: Nikkei
Hsu, Stacy: Central News Agency
Hsu, Spencer: Washington Post
Hu, Zexi: China People's Daily
Hudson, Clara: Global Investigations Review
Hudson, Jasmin: S & P Global
Hudson, John: Washington Post
Huetteman, Emmarie: Kaiser Health News
Hughes, Siobhan: Wall Street Journal / Dow Jones
Hulac, Benjamin: CQ / Roll Call
Hulse, Carl: New York Times
Hurley, Lawrence: Thomson Reuters
Hurt, Henry: Washington Times
Ignatiou, Michail: Phileleftheros Cyprus
Ikeda, Susumu: Akahata
Ikeda, Kai: Kyodo News
Ip, Gregory: Wall Street Journal / Dow Jones
Irby, Kate: McClatchy
Ishibashi, Miki: Kyodo News
Ishigaki ,Hideyuki: Jiji Press
Isikoff, Michael: Yahoo News
Ismay, John: New York Times
Ivanovich, David: Argus Media
Iwata, Nakahiro: Tokyo Chunichi Shimbun
Jacke, Christiane: German Press Agency–DPA
Jackson, Herbert: CQ / Roll Call
Jackson, David: USA Today
Jacobs, Jennifer: Bloomberg News
Jacobson, Louis: PolitiFact
Jaffe, Alexandra: Associated Press
Jakes-Jason, Lara: New York Times
Jalonick, Mary Clare: Associated Press
Jameel, Maryam: ProPublica
Jamerson, Joshua: Wall Street Journal / Dow Jones
Jamieson, Dave: Huffington Post
Jan, Tracy: Washington Post
Jansen, Bart: USA Today
Jaulmes, Adrien: Le Figaro
Jenkins, John: Religion News Service
Jenks, Paul: CQ / Roll Call
Jha, Lalit: India Press Trust
Johnson, Ted: Deadline
Johnson, Akilah: ProPublica
Johnson, Katanga: Thomson Reuters
Johnson, Kevin: USA Today
Johnson, Jenna: Washington Post
Johnston, Nicholas: Axios
Jonson Hart, Kimberly: Axios
Jordan, David: CQ / Roll Call
Jordan, Alethea: Gannett Washington Bureau
Jordan, Mary: Washington Post
Judkis, Maura: Washington Post
Julien, Cyril: Agence France-Presse
Jung, Hyosik: Joongang Ilbo
Jung, Jae Young: Segye Times
Kagubare, Ines: Global Investigations Review
Kaiya, Michitaka: Yomiuri Shimbun
Kaminishikawara, Jun: Kyodo News
Kampeas, Ronald: Jewish Telegraphic Agency
Kanasugi, Takao: Tokyo Chunichi Shimbun
Kane, Paul: Washington Post
Kaneya, Rui: Center for Public Integrity
Kang, Insun: Chosun Ilbo
Kang, Cecilia: New York Times
Kanno-Youngs, Zolan: New York Times
Kaplan, Sheila: New York Times
Kaplan, Thomas: New York Times
Kaplan, Sophie: Washington Times
Karam, Joyce: National (The),
Karanth, Sanjana: Huffington Post
Katori, Keisuke: Asahi Shimbun
Kawachi, Motoko: Nikkei
Kawanami, Takeshi: Nikkei
Kearns, Jeffrey: Bloomberg News
Keating, Daniel: Washington Post
Keefe, Stephen: Nikkei
Keenan, Edward: Toronto Star
Kehaulani Goo, Sara: Axios
Kelley, Patrick: CQ / Roll Call
Kellman Blazar, Laurie: Associated Press
Kelly, Kimbrielle: Los Angeles Times
Kelly, Christopher: Tokyo Chunichi Shimbun
Kendall, Brent: Wall Street Journal / Dow Jones
Kennedy, Elizabeth: Associated Press
Kenney, Caitlin: Stars and Stripes
Kenyon, Henry: CQ / Roll Call
Kerr, Jennifer: Associated Press
Kertes, Noella: CQ / Roll Call
Kessler, Glenn: Washington Post
Kesten, Louis: Associated Press
Khalil, Ashraf: Associated Press
Kiernan, Paul: Wall Street Journal / Dow Jones
Kim, Anne: CQ / Roll Call
Kim, Eun: CQ / Roll Call
Kim, Jaejoong: Kyunghyang Daily News
Kim, Soyoung: Thomson Reuters
Kim, Seung Min: Washington Post
Kindy, Kimberly: Washington Post
Kinery, Emma: Bloomberg News
King, Ledyard: Gannett Washington Bureau
Kirchgaessner, Stephanie: Guardian US,
Kleiner, Sarah: Center for Public Integrity
Klimasinska, Katarzyna: Bloomberg News
Klimkeit, Lena: German Press Agency–DPA
Knickmeyer, Ellen: Associated Press
Knight, Christopher: Argus Media
Knight, Victoria: Kaiser Health News
Knott, Matthew: Sydney Morning Herald
Knutson, Jacob: Axios
Kodjak, Alison: Associated Press
Koffler, Keith: White House Dossier

MEMBERS ENTITLED TO ADMISSION—Continued

Komori, Yoshihisa: Sankei Shimbun
Kondo, Masaki: Jiji Press
Konishi, Jiro: Jiji Press
Kopan, Tal: San Francisco Chronicle
Kopp, Emily: CQ / Roll Call
Korte, Gregory: Bloomberg News
Kosova, Weston: Bloomberg News
Kovacheva, Iva: Mainichi Shimbun
Krantz, Laura: Boston Globe
Krasny, Rosalind: Bloomberg News
Krawczak, Paul: CQ / Roll Call
Krishan, Nihal: Washington Examiner
Kucinich, Jackie: Daily Beast
Kurose, Yoshinari: Sankei Shimbun
Lackey, Katharine: CQ / Roll Call
LaFraniere, Sharon: New York Times
Laing, Keith: Detroit News
Lake, Eli: Bloomberg News
Lakshman, Sriram: "Hindu, The"
Lambert, Lisa: Thomson Reuters
Landay, Jonathan: Thomson Reuters
Lang, Hannah: American Banker
Lang, Marissa: Washington Post
Langan, Michael: Agence France-Presse
Langberg, Oystein: Aftenposten
Lange, Jason: Thomson Reuters
Lanman, Scott: Bloomberg News
Lanne, Makini: Thomson Reuters
Lanteaume, Sylvie: Agence France-Presse
Laping, Karen: S & P Global
Lardner, Richard: Associated Press
Larimer, Sarah: Washington Post
Laris, Michael: Washington Post
Larsen, Poul: Jyllands-Posten
Larsen, Emily: Washington Examiner
Lauter, David: Los Angeles Times
Lavelle, Marianne: Inside Climate News
Lawder, David: Thomson Reuters
Lawler, David: Axios
Lawler, Joseph: Washington Examiner
Lawrence, Katharine: USA Today
Layton, Lyndsey: Washington Post
Lazo, Luz: Washington Post
Leal, Lucia: EFE News Services
Leary, Alex: Wall Street Journal / Dow Jones
Lee, Matthew: Associated Press
Lee, Ariel: Dong-A Ilbo
Lee, Mara: International Trade Today
Lee, Chang Yul: Korea Times
Lee, Jong Kook: Korea Times
Lee, Dong: Los Angeles Times
Lee, Michelle: Washington Post
Lefkow, David: Agence France-Presse
Leibovich, Mark: New York Times
Lemus, Katherina: Thomson Reuters
Leonard, Jennifer: Bloomberg News
Lerer, Lisa: New York Times
Lerman, David: CQ / Roll Call
Lester, William: Associated Press
Leubsdorf, Carl: Dallas Morning News
Lever, Robert: Agence France-Presse
Levey, Noam: Los Angeles Times
Levin, Alan: Bloomberg News
Levine, Carrie: Center for Public Integrity
Levinthal, David: Center for Public Integrity
Levy, Rachel: Wall Street Journal / Dow Jones
Lewis, Gregory: CQ / Roll Call
Lewis, Herbert: CQ / Roll Call
Lewis, Matthew: Daily Beast
Lewis, Philip: Huffington Post
Li, Zhiwei: China People's Daily
Liebert, Larry: Bloomberg News
Lightman, David: McClatchy
Lim, Naomi: Washington Examiner
Lind, Dara: ProPublica
Linderman, Juliet: Associated Press
Linskey, Anne: Washington Post
Liptak, Adam: New York Times
Lipton, Eric: New York Times
Litvan, Laura: Bloomberg News
Livingston, Abby: Texas Tribune
Livni, Ephrat: Quartz
Lobsenz, George: Energy Daily
Lockwood, Frank: Arkansas Democrat-Gazette
Londres, Eduardo: Bloomberg News
Long, Colleen: Associated Press
Long, Heather: Washington Post
Loop, Emma: Buzzfeed
Lovelace, Ryan: Washington Times
Lowry, Bryan: McClatchy
Lubold, Gordon: Wall Street Journal / Dow Jones
Luce, Edward: Financial Times
Lucero, Kat: MLEX US
Luo, Xiaoyuan: World Journal
Lustig, Michael: S & P Global
Luthra, Shefali: Kaiser Health News
Lynch, Suzanne: Irish Times
Lynch, Sarah: Thomson Reuters
Lynch, David: Washington Post
Macagnone, Michael: CQ / Roll Call
Machi, Vivienne: Defense Daily
Madhani, Aamer: Associated Press
Magner, Michael: CQ / Roll Call
Make, Jonathan: Communications Daily
Makieli, Justine: New York Times
Makita, Kazuhiko: Yomiuri Shimbun
Maler, Sandra: Thomson Reuters
Mandato, Brian: McClatchy
Mann, Jason: CQ / Roll Call
Mann, Edward: Wall Street Journal / Dow Jones
Mannion, James: Agence France-Presse
Manson, Katrina: Financial Times
Marfil, Jude: Wall Street Journal / Dow Jones
Marino, Kim Ben: Financial Times

MEMBERS ENTITLED TO ADMISSION—Continued

Mark, David: Washington Examiner
Markay, Lachlan: Daily Beast
Marks, Joseph: Washington Post
Mars, Amanda: El Pais
Martin, Lawrence: Globe and Mail
Martin, Gary: Las Vegas Review-Journal
Martin, Jonathan: New York Times
Mascaro, Lisa: Associated Press
Mashie, Abraham: Washington Examiner
Mason, Jeffrey: Thomson Reuters
Masterson, Lauren: Argus Media
Mastio, David: USA Today
Mathes, Michael: Agence France-Presse
Matthews, Samuel: Yahoo News
Mauldin, William: Wall Street Journal / Dow Jones
Mauriello, Tracie: Pittsburgh Post-Gazette
Mayes, Brittany: Washington Post
McAuliff, Michael: New York Daily News
McBride, Courtney: Wall Street Journal / Dow Jones
McCabe, David: New York Times
McCammond, Alexi: Axios
McCarten, James: Canadian Press
McCarthy, William: PolitiFact
McCartney, Robert: Washington Post
McCreesh, Shawn: New York Times
McGill, Margaret: Axios
McGinley, Mary: Washington Post
McGough, Michael: Los Angeles Times
McIntire, Mary Ellen: CQ / Roll Call
McIntyre, Michelle: Washington Post
McKenzie, Lindsay: Inside Higher Ed
McKinnon, John: Wall Street Journal / Dow Jones
McLaughlin, David: Bloomberg News
McLaughlin, Seth: Washington Times
McLaughlin, Jenna: Yahoo News
McLeary, Paul: Breaking Defense
McLeod, Paul: Buzzfeed
McManus, Doyle: Los Angeles Times
McSwane, J. David: ProPublica
Meadows, Clifton: New York Times
Meckler, Laura: Washington Post
Meehan, Brian: Bloomberg News
Megerian, Christopher: Los Angeles Times
Meier, Lauren: Washington Times
Meiritz, Annett: Handelsblatt
Mellnik, Ted: Washington Post
Mendoza, Jessica: Christian Science Monitor
Mercer, Marsha: Mercer Media
Merey, Can: German Press Agency–DPA
Merle, Renae: Washington Post
Mersereau, Anson: Asahi Shimbun
Mershon, Erin: STAT
Metz, Jacob: CQ / Roll Call
Michaels, David: Wall Street Journal / Dow Jones
Middleton, Christopher : Bloomberg News
Migdon, Brooke: Market News International
Milbank, Dana: Washington Post
Miller, Zeke: Associated Press
Miller, Kathleen: Bloomberg News
Miller, Richard: Bloomberg News
Miller, Jonathan: CQ / Roll Call
Miller, Gregory: Washington Post
Miller, S.A.: Washington Times
Milliken, Mary: Thomson Reuters
Mills-Gregg, Dorothy: Military.com
Mimms, Sarah: Buzzfeed
Minkoff, Michelle: Associated Press
Mir De Francia, Ricardo: El Periodico
Misra, Tanvi: CQ / Roll Call
Mitchell, Tia: Atlanta Journal Constitution
Moday, Todd: Bloomberg News
Mohammed, Arshad: Thomson Reuters
Montague, Zachary: New York Times
Montgomery, David: Washington Post
Montgomery, Lori: Washington Post
Monyak, Frederick: Associated Press
Moore, Daniel: Pittsburgh Post-Gazette
Moran, Catherine: LocalNews Now
Morath, Eric: Wall Street Journal / Dow Jones
Mordock, Jeffrey: Washington Times
Morello, Carol: Washington Post
Morgan, Jonathan: Bloomberg News
Morgan, David: Thomson Reuters
Morin, Rebecca: USA Today
Morrison, Cassidy: Washington Examiner
Morrow, Adrian: Globe and Mail
Morton, Joseph: Omaha World-Herald
Mott, Gregory: Bloomberg News
Mouren, Leo: Agence France-Presse
Mufson, Steven: Washington Post
Mullins, Broderick: Wall Street Journal / Dow Jones
Muñoz, Gabriella: Washington Times
Munson, Emilie: Hearst Newspapers
Murakami, Kery: Inside Higher Ed
Murray, Kieran: Thomson Reuters
Mutikani, Lucia: Thomson Reuters
Myers, Marcia: CQ / Roll Call
Myers, Jim: Tulsa World
Naganuma, Aki: Nikkei
Nagasawa, Tsuyoshi: Nikkei
Nakai, Daisuke: Kyodo News
Nakai, Masahiro: Mainichi Shimbun
Nakamura, Ryo: Nikkei
Nakamura, David: Washington Post
Nakashima, Ellen: Washington Post
Nasaw, Daniel: Wall Street Journal / Dow Jones
Nather, David: Axios
Natter, Ari: Bloomberg News
Navarro, Beatriz: La Vanguardia
Navarro Morales, Ariela: Agence France-Presse
Nawaguna, Elvina: CQ / Roll Call
Naylor, Sean: Yahoo News
Nazaryan, Aleksandr: Yahoo News
Neergaard, Lauran: Associated Press

MEMBERS ENTITLED TO ADMISSION—Continued

Nelson, Steven: New York Post
Newkumet, Christopher: S & P Global
Newmyer, Tory: Washington Post
Nicholas, Andrew: Kyodo News
Nickol, Alexander: Yomiuri Shimbun
Nix, Naomi: Bloomberg News
Nixon, Ron: Associated Press
Nocera, Kate: Buzzfeed
Nuckols, Benjamin: Associated Press
O'Toole, Molly: Los Angeles Times
O'Brien, Lawrence: Huffington Post
O'Connell, Jonathan: Washington Post
O'Donnell, Paul: Religion News Service
O'Harrow, Robert: Washington Post
Ohlemacher, Stephen: Associated Press
Ohlheiser, Abigail: Washington Post
O'Keeffe, Kate: Wall Street Journal / Dow Jones
Oliphant, James: Thomson Reuters
Olson, Laura: Allentown Morning Call
Omeokwe, Amara: Wall Street Journal / Dow Jones
O'Reilly, Eileen: Axios
O'Reilly, Cary: CQ / Roll Call
Orol, Ronald: Daily Deal
Osborne, James: Houston Chronicle
Oswald, Rachel: CQ / Roll Call
Ota, Alan: Law 360
Ott, Matthew: Associated Press
Otton, Christian: Agence France-Presse
Ourlian, Robert: Wall Street Journal / Dow Jones
Overberg, Paul: Wall Street Journal / Dow Jones
Owens, Caitlin: Axios
Pace, Julie: Associated Press
Page, Clarence: Chicago Tribune
Page, Susan: USA Today
Page, Paul: Wall Street Journal / Dow Jones
Pager, Tyler: Bloomberg News
Paletta, Damian: Washington Post
Pamuk, Humeyra: Thomson Reuters
Pandey, Erica: Axios
Pandi, Nicolas: Jiji Press
Paris, Gilles: Le Monde
Park, Hyun Young: Joongang Ilbo
Parker, Mario: Bloomberg News
Parker, Ashley: Washington Post
Parlapiano, Alicia: New York Times
Parschalk, William: Jiji Press
Pascual Macias, Beatriz: EFE News Services
Patel, Anjali: LRP Publications
Patterson, Scott: Wall Street Journal / Dow Jones
Paul, Corey: S & P Global
Pavlova, Uliana: MLEX US
Pawlyk, Oriana: Military.com
Peake, Daniel: CQ / Roll Call
Pearce, Timothy: Washington Examiner
Pedersen, Brendan: American Banker
Perano, Ursula: Axios
Perera, David: MLEX US
Perrone, Matthew: Associated Press
Perry, Kati: Associated Press
Peterson, Kristina: Wall Street Journal / Dow Jones
Pexton, Patrick: CQ / Roll Call
Philbrick, Ian: New York Times
Phillips, Anna: Los Angeles Times
Phillips, Kristine: USA Today
Phillips, Michael: Wall Street Journal / Dow Jones
Phillips, James: Warren Communications
Phillips, Amber: Washington Post
Pickert, Reade: Bloomberg News
Picket, Kerry: Washington Examiner
Plantive, Charlotte: Agence France-Presse
Plott, Elaina: New York TImes
Plumer, Brad: New York Times
Politi, James: Financial Times
Pollard, Sonya: Bloomberg News
Poon, Linda: Bloomberg News
Portnoy, Jenna: Washington Post
Postell, Elliot: Washington Post
Potter, Ellie: S & P Global
Powers, Martine: Washington Post
Pradhan, Rachana: Kaiser Health News
Prakash, Nidhi: Buzzfeed
Prentice, Christine: Thomson Reuters
Press, Robert: Bloomberg News
Price, Michelle: Thomson Reuters
Psaledakis, Daphne: Thomson Reuters
Puente, Maria: USA Today
Puko, Timothy: Wall Street Journal / Dow Jones
Purce, Melinda: Associated Press
Putman, Eileen: Associated Press
Puzzanghera, James: Boston Globe
Qiu, Linda: New York Times
Quinn, Melissa: Washington Examiner
Quintana, Christopher: USA Today
Rabinowitz, Kate: Washington Post
Radelat, Ana: Connecticut Mirror
Radnofsky, Louise: Wall Street Journal / Dow Jones
Rajghatta, Chidanand: Times of India
Raman, Sandhya: CQ / Roll Call
Rappeport, Alan: New York Times
Ratnam, Gopal: CQ / Roll Call
Rau, Jordan: Kaiser Health News
Recio, Maria: Austin American-Statesman
Reiley, Laura: Washington Post
Reilly, Caitlin: CQ / Roll Call
Reilly, Ryan: Huffington Post
Rein, Lisa: Washington Post
Reinbold, Fabian: T-Online.de
Reinhard, Beth: Washington Post
Reklaitis, Victor: MarketWatch
Renner, Nausicaa: The Intercept
Resnick, Gabrielle: Kyodo News
Restuccia, Andrew: Wall Street Journal / Dow Jones
Ricci, Andrea: Thomson Reuters
Rice, Carter: Asahi Shimbun

MEMBERS ENTITLED TO ADMISSION—Continued

Rich, Gillian: Investor's Business Daily
Riechmann-Kepler, Debra: Associated Press
Riley, Michael: Bloomberg News
Riley-Smith, Benedict: London Daily Telegraph
Risen, James: The Intercept
Rives, Karin: Energy Daily
Rizzo, Salvador: Washington Post
Roarty, Alexander: McClatchy
Robb, Gregory: MarketWatch
Roberts, Catalina: CQ / Roll Call
Robertson, Jordan: Bloomberg News
Robillard, Kevin: Huffington Post
Robinson, John: Defense Daily
Robinson, Eugene: Washington Post
Rocha, Polo: S & P Global
Rodgers, Henry: Daily Caller
Rogan, Thomas: Washington Examiner
Rogers, Katie: New York Times
Rogin, Joshua: Washington Post
Roig-Franzia, Manuel: Washington Post
Rojas, Daxia: Agence France-Presse
Romm, Anthony: Washington Post
Rosenberg, Matthew: New York Times
Rosenwald, Michael: Washington Post
Roston, Aram: Thomson Reuters
Rotella, Sebastian: ProPublica
Rothschild, Neal: Axios
Rouach, Herve: Agence France-Presse
Rovner, Julia: Kaiser Health News
Rowland, Christopher: Washington Post
Rowley, James: Bloomberg News
Rubin, Gabriel: Wall Street Journal / Dow Jones
Rubin, Richard: Wall Street Journal / Dow Jones
Rucker, Philip: Washington Post
Ruf, Renzo: Aargauer Zeitung
Rugaber, Christopher: Associated Press
Ruger, Todd: CQ / Roll Call
Rummler, Ivy: Axios
Ryan, Timothy: Thomson Reuters
Ryser, Evan: Market News International
Ryu, Jewon: Korea Times
Sabur, Rozina: London Daily Telegraph
Sagalow, Zoe: CQ / Roll Call
Saito, Kaori: Kyodo News
Saksa, James: CQ / Roll Call
Salant, Jonathan: NJ Advance Media
Salcedo, Michele: Axios
Saleh, Maryam: The Intercept
Salfeety, Stephen: CQ / Roll Call
Sallah, Michael: Buzzfeed
Salmeron, Marvin: Bloomberg News
Salvalaggio, Claudio: ANSA,
Samhan Arias, Susana: EFE News Services
Samuels, Lexier: CQ / Roll Call
Samuels, Robert: Washington Post
Sancho, Victor: El Universal
Sanders, Edmund: Los Angeles Times
Sanders, Chris: Thomson Reuters
Sands, Darren: Buzzfeed
Sands, David: Washington Times
Sanger, David: New York Times
Sanger-Katz, Margot: New York Times
Santucci, Jeanine: USA Today
Sapsford, Jathon: Wall Street Journal / Dow Jones
Sarcina, Giuseppe: Corriere Della Sera
Sargent, Ann: Washington Post
Sattar, Majid: Frankfurter Allgemeine Zeitung
Satter, Raphael: Thomson Reuters
Saunders, Debra: Las Vegas Review-Journal
Savage, David: Los Angeles Times
Savage, Charles: New York Times
Savitsky, Shane: Axios
Sawamura, Wataru: Asahi Shimbun
Scarborough, Rowan: Washington Times
Schaeuble, Juliane: Der Tagesspiegel
Schaul, Kevin: Washington Post
Schectman, Joel: Thomson Reuters
Scheid, Brian: S & P Global
Scherer, Michael: Washington Post
Scheuble, Kristy: Bloomberg News
Schlesinger, Jacob: Wall Street Journal / Dow Jones
Schlisserman, Courtney: Argus Media
Schluter, Fabian: Agence France-Presse
Schmidt, Robert: Bloomberg News
Schmidt, Michael: New York Times
Schmitt, Eric: New York Times
Schneider, Gabriel: MinnPost
Schneider, Howard: Thomson Reuters
Schoenberg, Thomas: Bloomberg News
Schram, Martin: Tribune Content Agency
Schroeder, Robert: MarketWatch
Schroeder, Peter: Thomson Reuters
Schulte, Fred: Kaiser Health News
Schutt, Bryan: S & P Global
Schwab, Nikki: DailyMail.com
Scott-Molleda, Heather: Agence France-Presse
Scully, Megan: CQ / Roll Call
Sebenius, Alyza: Bloomberg News
Seck, Hope: Military.com
Seib, Gerald: Wall Street Journal / Dow Jones
Seibel, Mark: Washington Post
Seiki, Yasuyiki: Kyodo News
Selk, Avi: Washington Post
Seltzer, Rick: Inside Higher Ed
Selway, William: Bloomberg News
Sertic, Kylie: Kyodo News
Sevastopulo, Demetri: Financial Times
Shaban, Hamza: Washington Post
Shalal, Andrea: Thomson Reuters
Shankar, Vivek: Bloomberg News
Shanker, Thomas: New York Times
Shaw, Michael: CQ / Roll Call
Shear, Michael: New York Times
Shepard, Michael: Bloomberg News

MEMBERS ENTITLED TO ADMISSION—Continued

Shepardson, David: Thomson Reuters
Sheperd, Brittany: Yahoo News
Sherfinski, David: Washington Times
Sherman, Mark: Associated Press
Shesgreen, Deirdre: Gannett Washington Bureau
Shields, Todd: Bloomberg News
Shields, Mark: Creators Syndicate
Shiffman, John: Thomson Reuters
Shiobara, Nagahisa: Sankei Shimbun
Shiraishi, Wataru: Tokyo Chunichi Shimbun
Shorey, Rachel: New York Times
Shubber, Kadhim: Financial Times
Shutt, Jennifer: CQ / Roll Call
Sichelman, Lew: United Media
Siciliano, John: Washington Examiner
Siddiqui, Sabrina: Wall Street Journal / Dow Jones
Siddons, Andrew: CQ / Roll Call
Siegel, Joshua: Washington Examiner
Simao, Paul: Thomson Reuters
Simon, Caroline: CQ / Roll Call
Simon, Erica: New York Times
Simonson, Joseph: Washington Examiner
Sink, Justin: Bloomberg News
Sisk, Richard: Military.com
Slack, Donovan: USA Today
Slater, James: Agence France-Presse
Sloan, Steven: Associated Press
Slodysko, Brian: Associated Press
Smalley, Suzanne: Yahoo News
Smialek, Jeanna: New York Times
Smietana, Robert: Religion News Service
Smith, Sebastian: Agence France-Presse
Smith, David: Guardian US,
Smith, Sarah: S & P Global
Smith, Abby: Washington Examiner
Snyder, Alison: Axios
Sobczyk, Joseph: Bloomberg News
Somashekhar, Sandhya: Washington Post
Sommer, William: Daily Beast
Sonmez, Felicia: Washington Post
Sonne, Paul: Washington Post
Sonoda, Koji: Asahi Shimbun
Sorcher, Sara: Washington Post
Spang, Thomas: US Report (Germany),
Spangler, Todd: Detroit Free Press
Spencer, James: Minneapolis Star Tribune
Spetalnick, Matthew: Thomson Reuters
Stacey, Kiran: Financial Times
Stanfield, Jeff: S & P Global
Stanley-Becker, Isaac: Washington Post
Stapleton, Stephanie: Kaiser Health News
Stech Ferek, Katy: Wall Street Journal / Dow Jones
Stein, Chris: Agence France-Presse
Stein, Samuel: Daily Beast
Stein, Jeffrey: Washington Post
Steinhauer, Jennifer: New York Times
Sternberg, William: USA Today
Stevenson, Richard: New York Times
Stewart, Cameron: Australian Newspaper
Stewart, B Scott: Sankei Shimbun
Stewart, Phillip: Thomson Reuters
Stewart, Martina: USA Today
Stiehm, Jamie: Creators Syndicate
Stoddard, A.B.: Real Clear Politics
Stohr, Gregory: Bloomberg News
Stokols, Eli: Los Angeles Times
Stolberg, Sheryl: New York Times
Stone, Michael: Thomson Reuters
Strauss, Daniel: Guardian US,
Stricherz, Mark: CQ / Roll Call
Strobel, Warren: Wall Street Journal / Dow Jones
Strohm, Christopher: Bloomberg News
Strong, Thomas: Associated Press
Stubbs, Kathleen: Asahi Shimbun
Stumme, Susan: Agence France-Presse
Sturm, Daniel: Die Welt
Subramanian, Courtney: USA Today
Suebsaeng, Asawin: Daily Beast
Sugeno, Mikio: Nikkei
Sullivan, Gregory: Bloomberg News
Sullivan, Eileen: New York Times
Sullivan, Sean: S & P Global
Sullivan, Andrew: Thomson Reuters
Sullivan, Kevin: Washington Post
Sullivan, Patricia: Washington Post
Sullivan, Sean: Washington Post
Sumii, Kyosuke: Sankei Shimbun
Sun, Lena: Washington Post
Superville, Darlene: Associated Press
Svrluga, Susan: Washington Post
Swan, Jonathan: Axios
Swanson, Emily: Associated Press
Swanson, Ana: New York Times
Sweet, Lynn: Chicago Sun-Times
Sword, Doug: CQ / Roll Call
Swoyer, Alex: Washington Times
Szep, Jason: Thomson Reuters
Tackett, Michael: Associated Press
Taggart, Francis: Agence France-Presse
Takamoto, Kota: Mainichi Shimbun
Takemoto, Atsushi: Kyodo News
Talev, Margaret: Axios
Talley, Ian: Wall Street Journal / Dow Jones
Tamari, Jonathan: Philadelphia Inquirer
Tan, Shen Wu: Washington Times
Tanaka, Yumi: Jiji Press
Tanaka, Mitsuya: Kyodo News
Tanaka, Miya: Kyodo News
Tandon, Shaun: Agence France-Presse
Tanfani, Joseph: Thomson Reuters
Tankersley, James: New York Times
Tanner, Caroline: CQ / Roll Call
Tanzi, Alex: Bloomberg News
Tau, Byron: Wall Street Journal / Dow Jones

MEMBERS ENTITLED TO ADMISSION—Continued

Taylor, Andrew: Associated Press
Taylor, William: Communications Daily
Taylor, Marisa: Thomson Reuters
Taylor, Guy: Washington Times
Teitelbaum, Michael: CQ / Roll Call
Terkel, Amanda: Huffington Post
Terris, Benjamin: Washington Post
Tharoor, Ishaan: Washington Post
Thebault, Reis: Washington Post
Thomas, Ashley: Associated Press
Thomas, Richard: Voterama in Congress
Thomas, Kenneth: Wall Street Journal / Dow Jones
Thomason, Robert: MLEX US
Thrush, Glenn: New York Times
Tillman, Zoe: Buzzfeed
Timberlake, Ian: Agence France-Presse
Timiraos, Nicolas: Wall Street Journal / Dow Jones
Timmons, Heather: Thomson Reuters
Tomasky, Michael: Daily Beast
Tomkin, Robert: CQ / Roll Call
Torbati, Yeganeh: ProPublica
Torres, Craig: Bloomberg News
Torry, Harriet: Wall Street Journal / Dow Jones
Touitou, Delphine: Agence France-Presse
Tourial, Gregory: CQ / Roll Call
Tracy, Ryan: Wall Street Journal / Dow Jones
Traver, Albert: EFE News Services
Treene, Alayna: Axios
Tribble, Sarah: Kaiser Health News
Trudo, Hanna: Daily Beast
Trumbull, Mark: Christian Science Monitor
Tsao, Stephanie: S & P Global
Tsuchiya, Konomi: Kyodo News
Tucker, Eric: Associated Press
Tumulty, Brian: Bond Buyer
Tumulty, Karen: Washington Post
Uhrmacher, Kevin: Washington Post
Ulloa, Jazmine: Boston Globe
Urano, Eri: Tokyo Chunichi Shimbun
Valbrun, Marjorie: Inside Higher Ed
Van Buren, Eleanor: CQ / Roll Call
Vanden Brook, Thomas: USA Today
Velez, Kimberly: Bloomberg News
Vergano, Daniel: Buzzfeed
Viebeck, Elise: Washington Post
Vineys, Kevin: Associated Press
Viser, Matthew: Washington Post
Viswanatha, Aruna: Wall Street Journal / Dow Jones
Vogel, Kenneth: New York Times
Vogt, Patrick: Agence France-Presse
Volcovici, Valerie: Thomson Reuters
Volz, Dustin: Wall Street Journal / Dow Jones
Vondracek, Christopher: Washington Times
Wadhams, Nicholas: Bloomberg News
Wagner, John: Washington Post
Waldron, Bryan: Huffington Post
Walker, Mark: New York Times
Walker, Hunter: Yahoo News
Wallsten, Peter: Washington Post
Walsh, Bryan: Axios
Wang, Amy: Washington Post
Ward, Emily: Washington Examiner
Ward, Jonathan: Yahoo News
Warrick, Joby: Washington Post
Wasko, Stephanie: Axios
Wasserman, Elizabeth: Bloomberg News
Wasson, Erik: Bloomberg News
Watanabe, Takashi: Asahi Shimbun
Watanabe, Kensaku: Jiji Press
Watkins, Thomas: Agence France-Presse
Wax, Emily: Washington Post
Wayne, Alexander: Bloomberg News
Weaver, Dustin: Associated Press
Weaver, Courtney: Financial Times
Webber, Caitlin: Bloomberg News
Weber, Maya: S & P Global
Weekes, Michael: Thomson Reuters
Wegmann, Philip: Real Clear Politics
Wehrman, Jessica: CQ / Roll Call
Weigel, David: Washington Post
Weiland, Noah: New York Times
Weinberger, Sharon: Yahoo News
Weiner, Mark: Syracuse Post-Standard
Weiner, Rachel: Washington Post
Weinger, Mackenzie: National Journal
Weisman, Jonathan: New York Times
Weiss, Miles: Bloomberg News
Weiss, Laura: CQ / Roll Call
Weissert, William: Associated Press
Wentling, Nikki: Stars and Stripes
Wermund, Benjamin: Houston Chronicle
Werner, Erica: Washington Post
Wertz, Joseph: Center for Public Integrity
Westbrook, Jesse: Bloomberg News
Whalen, Jeanne: Washington Post
Whieldon, Esther: S & P Global
White, Keith: CQ / Roll Call
White, Dina: Los Angeles Times
White, Gordon: Washington Telecommunications Services
Whitelaw, Kevin: Bloomberg News
Whitesides, John: Thomson Reuters
Whitlock, Craig: Washington Post
Whoriskey, Peter: Washington Post
Whyte, Elizabeth: Center for Public Integrity
Wieder, Benjamin: McClatchy
Wieneke, Charles: Bloomberg News
Wilber, Del: Los Angeles Times
Wilkinson, Tracy: Los Angeles Times
Williams, Khari: CQ / Roll Call
Williams, Aime: Financial Times
Williams, Clarence: Washington Post
Williams, Vanessa: Washington Post
Williamson, Elizabeth: New York Times
Willis, Daniel: CQ / Roll Call

MEMBERS ENTITLED TO ADMISSION—Continued

Willis, Derek: ProPublica
Wilner, Michael: McClatchy
Wilson, Scott: Washington Post
Wines, Stephen: New York Times
Wingrove, Joshua: Bloomberg News
Wire, Sarah: Los Angeles Times
Wise, Lindsay: Wall Street Journal / Dow Jones
Wiseman, Paul: Associated Press
Wolf, Richard: USA Today
Wolfe, Jan: Thomson Reuters
Wolfgang, Benjamin: Washington Times
Wollner, Adam: McClatchy
Wong, Edward: New York Times
Woodall, Hunter: Daily Beast
Woodward, Calvin: Associated Press
Woodward, Robert: Washington Post
Woolls, Daniel: Agence France-Presse
Wooten, Casey: National Journal
Wootson, Cleve: Washington Post
Wright, Christopher: CQ / Roll Call
Wu, Lejun: China People's Daily
Wu, Nicholas: USA Today
Wynn, Sarah: Bond Buyer
Yadidi, Noa: Axios
Yadoo, Jordan: Bloomberg News
Yamauchi, Ryosuke: Yomiuri Shimbun
Yamazaki, Yosuke: Sekai Nippo
Yang, Tia: CQ / Roll Call
Yen, Hope: Associated Press
Yerardi, Joseph: Center for Public Integrity
Yilek, Caitlin: Washington Examiner
Yoder, Eric: Washington Post
Yokobori, Yuya: Yomiuri Shimbun
Yoon, Yanghee: Korea Times
York, Byron: Washington Examiner
Young, Donna: S & P Global
Youssef, Nancy: Wall Street Journal / Dow Jones
Yu, Donghui: China Review News Agency
Yung, Jean: Market News International
Zak, Daniel: Washington Post
Zakaria, Toby: McClatchy
Zakrzewski, Cat: Washington Post
Zapotosky, Matthew: Washington Post
Zargham, Mohammad: Thomson Reuters
Zeffman, Henry: Times of London
Zeller, Kate: CQ / Roll Call
Zeller, Shawn: CQ / Roll Call
Zengerle, Patricia: Thomson Reuters
Zengin, Dilara: Anadolu News Agency
Zezima, Katie: Washington Post
Zhang, Mengxu: China People's Daily
Zhang, Niansheng: China People's Daily
Zheng, Qi: China People's Daily
Zipp, Richard: S & P Global
Zitner, Aaron: Wall Street Journal / Dow Jones
Zornick, George: Huffington Post
Zoroya, Gregg: USA Today
Zoupaniotis, Apostolos: Cyprus News Agency
Zremski, Jerry: Buffalo News
Zumbrun, Joshua: Wall Street Journal / Dow Jones

NEWSPAPERS REPRESENTED IN PRESS GALLERIES

House Gallery, phone 225–3945   Senate Gallery, phone 224–0241

AARGAUER ZEITUNG—(202) 403–7115; Neumattstrasse 1, Aarau 05001 Switzerland: Renzo Ruf.

ABC NEWSPAPER—(202) 344–0856; Juan Ignacio Luca de Tena 7 Madrid, Madrid 20005 Spain: David Alandete Ballester.

AFTENPOSTEN—(917) 615–7321; 2000 M Street,, NW., Suite 890 Washington, DC 20036: Oystein Langberg.

AGENCE FRANCE-PRESSE—(202) 414–0604; 1500 K Street, NW., Suite 600 Washington, DC 20005: Lucie Aubourg, Anita Beattie, Ines Belaiba, Sebastien Blanc, Antoine Boyer, Camille Camdessus, Jerome Cartillier, Julie Chabanas, Emma Charlton, Ivan Couronne, Elodie Cuzin, Alina Dieste Markl, William Dunlop, Brigitte Dusseau, Sebastien Duval, Francesco Fontemaggi, Marisha Goldhamer Sherry, Carlos Hamann, Paul Handley, Cyril Julien, Michael Langan, Sylvie Lanteaume, David Lefkow, Robert Lever, James Mannion, Michael Mathes, Leo Mouren, Ariela Navarro Morales, Christian Otton, Charlotte Plantive, Daxia Rojas, Herve Rouach, Fabian Schluter, Heather Scott-Molleda, James Slater, Sebastian Smith, Chris Stein, Susan Stumme, Francis Taggart, Shaun Tandon, Ian Timberlake, Delphine Touitou, Patrick Vogt, Thomas Watkins, Daniel Woolls.

AKAHATA—(202) 393–5238; 978 National Press Building, Washington, DC 20045: Susumu Ikeda.

ALLENTOWN MORNING CALL—(610) 820–6500; 101 North 6th Street, Allentown, PA 18105: Laura Olson.

AMERICAN BANKER—(212) 803–8200; 1410 Wilson Boulevard, Suite 1002; Arlington, VA 22209: Miriam Cross, Cornelius Haggerty, John Heltman, Hannah Lang, Brendan Pedersen.

ANADOLU NEWS AGENCY—(202) 662–7437; 529 14th Street, NW., Suite 1131, Washington, DC 20045: Safvan Allahverdi, Dildar Baykan, Hakan Copur, Servet Gunerigok, Michael Hernandez, Dilara Zengin.

ANNIE GROER WRITER AT LARGE—(202) 489–4044: Anne L. Groer.

ANSA—(202) 662–7195; 529 14th Street, NW., Suite 1200, Washington, DC 20045: Claudio Salvalaggio.

ARGUS MEDIA—(202) 775–0240; 1667 K Street, NW., Suite 1150, Washington, DC 20006: Michael Ball, Abby Caplan, Edward Epstein, David Givens, Haik Gugarats, David Ivanovich, Christopher Knight, Lauren Masterson, Courtney Schlisserman.

ARKANSAS DEMOCRAT-GAZETTE—(501) 399–3691; 960A National Press Building, Washington, DC 20045: Frank Lockwood.

ARTISTS & WRITERS SYNDICATE—(703) 965–7296: Frank Aukofer.

ASAHI SHIMBUN—(202) 783–1000; 1022 National Press Building, Washington, DC 20045: Naoatsu Aoyama, William Black, Tara Fitzmartin, Keisuke Katori, Anson Mersereau, Carter Rice, Wataru Sawamura, Koji Sonoda, Kathleen Stubbs, Takashi Watanabe.

ASSOCIATED PRESS—(202) 641–9000; 1100 13th Street, NW., Suite 500 Washington, DC 20005: Ricardo Alonso, Lolita Baldor, Michael Balsamo, Nancy Benac, Lynn Berry, Michael Biesecker, Joshua Boak, Seth Borenstein, Stephen Braun, Robert Burns, Jill Colvin, Martin Crutsinger, Matthew Daly, Douglass Daniel, Carole Feldman, Hannah Fingerhut, Benjamin Fox, Alan Fram, Kevin Freking, Robert Furlow, Marcy Gordon, Jessica Gresko, Kenneth Guggenheim, Dino Hazell, Alexandra Jaffe, Mary Clare Jalonick, Laurie Kellman Blazar, Elizabeth Kennedy, Jennifer Kerr, Louis Kesten, Ashraf Khalil, Ellen Knickmeyer, Alison Kodjak, Richard Lardner, Matthew Lee, William Lester, Juliet Linderman, Colleen Long, Aamer Madhani, Lisa Mascaro, Zeke Miller, Michelle Minkoff, Frederick Monyak, Lauran Neergaard, Ron Nixon, Benjamin Nuckols, Stephen Ohlemacher, Matthew Ott, Julie Pace, Matthew Perrone, Kati Perry, Melinda Purce, Eileen Putman, Debra Riechmann-Kepler, Christopher Rugaber, Mark Sherman, Steven Sloan, Brian Slodysko, Thomas Strong, Darlene Superville, Emily Swanson, Michael Tackett, Andrew Taylor, Ashley Thomas, Eric Tucker, Kevin Vineys, Dustin Weaver, William Weissert, Paul Wiseman, Calvin Woodward, Hope Yen.

ATLANTA JOURNAL CONSTITUTION—(404) 526–2373; 444 North Capitol Street, NW., Suite 750, Washington, DC 20001: Tia Mitchell.

AUSTIN AMERICAN-STATESMAN—(301) 933–0387; 400 North Capitol Street, NW., Suite 750, Washington, DC 20001: Maria Recio.

AUSTRALIAN FINANCIAL REVIEW—(202) 770–7600; 1310 G Street, NW., Suite 750, Washington, DC 20009: Jacob Greber.

AUSTRALIAN NEWSPAPER—(202) 710 1006; 1025 Connecticut Avenue, NW., Suite 800, Washington, DC 20036: Cameron Stewart.

AXIOS—3100 Clarendon Boulevard, Arlington, VA 22201: Fadel Allassan, Michael Allen, Rashaan Ayesh, Samuel Baker, Zachary Basu, Kyle Daly, Marisa Fernandez, Sara Fischer, Benjamin Geman, Justin

NEWSPAPERS REPRESENTED—Continued

Green, Amy Harder, Nicholas Johnston, Kimberly Jonson Hart, Sara Kehaulani Goo, Jacob Knutson, David Lawler, Alexi McCammond, Margaret McGill, David Nather, Eileen O'Reilly, Caitlin Owens, Erica Pandey, Ursula Perano, Neal Rothschild, Ivy Rummler, Michele Salcedo, Shane Savitsky, Alison Snyder, Jonathan Swan, Margaret Talev, Alayna Treene, Bryan Walsh, Stephanie Wasko, Noa Yadidi.

BALTIMORE SUN—(410) 332–6000; 1090 Vermont Avenue, NW., Suite 1000, Washington, DC 20005: Jeffrey Barker.

BATON ROUGE ADVOCATE—(225) 383–1111; 10705 Rieger Road, Baton Rouge, LA 70809: Elizabeth Crisp.

BLOOMBERG NEWS—(202) 624–1820; 1101 New York Avenue, NW., 9th Floor, Washington, DC 20005: William Allison, Laurie Asseo, Benjamin Bain, Ryan Beckwith, Ryan Beene, Wendy Benjaminson, Max Berley, Justin Blum, Ben Brody, Alister Bull, Anthony Capaccio, Kriston Capps, Dominic Carey, Kevin Cirilli, Margaret Collins, Christopher Condon, Stephen Cunningham, Laura Curtis, Laura Davison, Susan Decker, Steven Dennis, Elizabeth Dexheimer, Jennifer Dlouhy, Ekaterina Dmitrieva, Michael Dorning, Anna Edgerton, Assima Egbame, Misyrlena Egkolfopoulou, Jennifer Epstein, William Faries, Teaganne Finn, Daniel Flatley, Sara Forden, Joshua Gallu, Saleha Ghani, James Gibney, Henry Golle, D. Craig Gordon, Ana Gouveia Monteiro, Joshua Green, Jesse Hamilton, Benjamin Holland, Billy House, Megan Howard, Jennifer Jacobs, Jeffrey Kearns, Emma Kinery, Katarzyna Klimasinska, Gregory Korte, Weston Kosova, Rosalind Krasny, Eli Lake, Scott Lanman, Jennifer Leonard, Alan Levin, Larry Liebert, Laura Litvan, Eduardo Londres, David McLaughlin, Brian Meehan, Christopher Middleton, Kathleen Miller, Richard Miller, Todd Moday, Jonathan Morgan, Gregory Mott, Ari Natter, Naomi Nix, Tyler Pager, Mario Parker, Reade Pickert, Sonya Pollard, Linda Poon, Robert Press, Michael Riley, Jordan Robertson, James Rowley, Marvin Salmeron, Kristy Scheuble, Robert Schmidt, Thomas Schoenberg, Alyza Sebenius, William Selway, Vivek Shankar, Michael Shepard, Todd Shields, Justin Sink, Joseph Sobczyk, Gregory Stohr, Christopher Strohm, Gregory Sullivan, Alex Tanzi, Craig Torres, Kimberly Velez, Nicholas Wadhams, Elizabeth Wasserman, Erik Wasson, Alexander Wayne, Caitlin Webber, Miles Weiss, Jesse Westbrook, Kevin Whitelaw, Charles Wieneke, Joshua Wingrove, Jordan Yadoo.

BOND BUYER—(212) 803–8200; 1401 Wilson Boulevard, Suite 1002, Arlington, VA 22209: Kyle Glazier, Brian Tumulty, Sarah Wynn.

BOSTON GLOBE—(617) 929–2000; 1130 Connecticut Avenue, NW., Suite 725, Washington, DC 20036: Jessica Bidgood, Liz Goodwin, James Puzzanghera, Laura Krantz, Jazmine Ulloa.

BREAKING DEFENSE—1440 G Street, NW., Washington, DC 20005: Colin Clark, Sydney Freedberg, Theresa Hitchens, Paul McLeary.

BUFFALO NEWS—(716) 842–1111; One News Plaza, P.O. Box 100 Buffalo, NY 14240: Jerry Zremski.

BUZZFEED—1630 Connecticut Avenue, NW., 7th floor, Washington, DC 20009: Addy Baird, Kadia Goba, Eileen Hall, Molly Hensley-Clancy, Zahra Hirji, Emma Loop, Paul McLeod, Sarah Mimms, Kate Nocera, Nidhi Prakash, Michael Sallah, Darren Sands, Zoe Tillman, Daniel Vergano.

CANADIAN PRESS—(202) 641–9734; 1100 13th Street, NW., Suite 500 Washington, DC 20005: James McCarten.

CENTER FOR PUBLIC INTEGRITY—(202) 466–1300; 910 17th Street, NW., Suite 700, Washington, DC 20006: Alexia Campbell, Susan Ferriss, Zachary Fryer-Biggs, Allan Holmes, Jamie Hopkins, Rui Kaneya, Sarah Kleiner, Carrie Levine, David Levinthal, Joseph Wertz, Elizabeth Whyte, Joseph Yerardi.

CENTRAL NEWS AGENCY—1173 National Press Building, Washington, DC 20045: Chiang Chinyeh, Stacy Hsu.

CHICAGO SUN-TIMES—(312) 321–3000; 30 North Racine Avenue, 3rd Floor, Chicago, IL 60607: Lynn Sweet.

CHICAGO TRIBUNE—(312) 222–3232; 160 North Stetson Avenue, Chicago, IL 60601: Clarence Page.

CHINA PEOPLE'S DAILY—(202) 661–8185; 529 14th Street, NW., Washington, DC 20045: Zexi Hu, Zhiwei Li, Lejun Wu, Mengxu Zhang, Niansheng Zhang, Qi Zheng.

CHINA REVIEW NEWS AGENCY—(703) 725–0720; 20 Westlands Road, Room 201, Quarry Bay Hong Kong: Donghui Yu.

CHOSUN ILBO—(571) 289–7735; 1291 National Press Building, Washington, DC 20045: Yi Jun Cho, Insun Kang.

CHRISTIAN SCIENCE MONITOR—(617) 450–2300; 1615 L Street, NW., Suite 800, Washington, DC 20036: Timothy Broderick, Linda Feldmann, Peter Grier, Story Hinckley, Jessica Mendoza, Mark Trumbull.

CLEVELAND PLAIN DEALER—(216) 999–6000; 1801 Superior Avenue East, Suite 100, Cleveland, OH 44114: Sabrina Eaton.

COMMUNICATIONS DAILY—(202) 872–9200; 2115 Ward Court, NW., Washington, DC 20037: Howard Buskirk, Matthew Daneman, Karl Herchenroeder, Monica Hogan, Jonathan Make, William Taylor.

CONNECTICUT MIRROR—(860) 218–6380; 1049 Aslyum Avenue, Hartford, CT 06105: Ana Radelat.

CORRIERE DELLA SERA—(646) 752–0422; 2600 Pennsylvania Avenue, NW., Washington, DC 20037: Giuseppe Sarcina.

NEWSPAPERS REPRESENTED—Continued

CQ/ROLL CALL—(202) 793–5300; 1201 Pennsylvania Avenue, NW., 6th Floor Washington, DC 20004: Rebecca Adams, Alexei Alexis, Erin Bacon, Sajeer Beg, Kathleen Bever, Mark Bocchetti, Mark Burnett, Teresa Cardenas, Charlene Carter, Lauren Clason, Andrew Clevenger, George Codrea, Peter Cohn, Charles Conlon, Camila DeChalus, John Donnelly, Lars Emerson, Edward Felker, Peter Feltman, Ellyn Ferguson, Paul Fontelo, Anthony Gnoffo, Anne Grady, Steven Harras, Benjamin Hulac, Herbert Jackson, Paul Jenks, David Jordan, Patrick Kelley, Henry Kenyon, Noella Kertes, Anne Kim, Eun Kim, Emily Kopp, Paul Krawczak, Katharine Lackey, David Lerman, Gregory Lewis, Herbert Lewis, Michael Macagnone, Michael Magner, Jason Mann, Mary Ellen McIntire, Jacob Metz, Jonathan Miller, Tanvi Misra, Marcia Myers, Elvina Nawaguna, Cary O'Reilly, Rachel Oswald, Daniel Peake, Patrick Pexton, Sandhya Raman, Gopal Ratnam, Caitlin Reilly, Catalina Roberts, Todd Ruger, Zoe Sagalow, James Saksa, Stephen Salfeety, Lexier Samuels, Megan Scully, Michael Shaw, Jennifer Shutt, Andrew Siddons, Caroline Simon, Mark Stricherz, Doug Sword, Caroline Tanner, Michael Teitelbaum, Robert Tomkin, Gregory Tourial, Eleanor Van Buren, Jessica Wehrman, Laura Weiss, Keith White, Khari Williams, Daniel Willis, Christopher Wright, Tia Yang, Kate Zeller, Shawn Zeller.

CREATORS SYNDICATE—(310) 337–7003, 737 3rd Street, Hermosa Beach, CA 90254: Mark Shields, Jamie Stiehm.

CYPRUS NEWS AGENCY—(202) 462–5772; 21 Akademias Avenue, 2107 Agiantzia, Nicosia Cyprus: Apostolos Zoupaniotis.

DAGENS NYHETER—(202) 704–7996: Björn af Kleen.

DAILY BEAST—1825 Connecticut Avenue, NW., Suite 620, Washington, DC 20001: Erin Banco, Sam Brodey, Eleanor Clift, Jackie Kucinich, Matthew Lewis, Lachlan Markay, William Sommer, Samuel Stein, Asawin Suebsaeng, Michael Tomasky, Hanna Trudo, Hunter Woodall.

DAILY CALLER—(202) 506–2027; 1920 L Street, NW., Suite 200, Washington, DC 20036: Christian Datoc, Anders Anders Hagstrom, Maranda Finney, Henry Rodgers.

DAILY DEAL—444 North Capitol Street, NW., Suite 413, Washington, DC 20001: David Hatch, Ronald Orol.

DAILYMAIL.COM—51 Astor Place, 9th Floor, New York, NY 10003: Katelyn Caralle, Geoffrey Earle, Emily Goodin, Nikki Schwab.

DALLAS MORNING NEWS—(214) 745–8383, 930 National Press Building, Washington, DC 20045: Thomas Benning, Alfredo Corchado, Todd Gillman, Carl Leubsdorf.

DEADLINE—(310) 484–2548; 11175 Santa Monica Boulevard, Los Angeles, CA 90025: Ted Johnson.

DEFENSE DAILY—(703) 522–5655; 1911 North Ft. Myer Drive, Suite 705, Arlington, VA 22209: Richard Abott, Matthew Beinart, Vivienne Machi, John Robinson.

DER TAGESSPIEGEL—(202) 819–9190; Askanischer Platz 3, 10963 Berlin Germany: Juliane Schaeuble.

DETROIT FREE PRESS—(202) 906–9993; 1575 Eye Street, NW., Suite 350 Washington, DC 20005: Todd Spangler.

DETROIT NEWS—1100 13th Street, NW., Suite 500 Washington, DC 20005: Melissa Burke, Keith Laing.

DIE TAGESZEITUNG—(202) 569–5369: Dorothea Hahn.

DIE WELT—(202) 550–1021: Daniel Sturm.

DONG-A ILBO—(571) 217–4922; 837 National Press Building, Washington, DC 20045: Ariel Lee.

EFE NEWS SERVICES—(202) 745–7692; 1220 National Press Building, Washington, DC 20045: Hernan Martin Alonso, Susana Samhan Arias, Laura Barros Cantillo, Alfonso Fernandez, Lucia Leal, Beatriz Pascual Macias, Albert Traver.

EL DIARIO DE HOY—(202) 361–8005: Tomas Guevara.

EL NUEVO DIA—(202) 662–7360; 960d National Press Building, Washington, DC 20045: Jose Delgado-Robles.

EL PAIS—(202) 735–6380; 1134 National Press Building, Washington, DC 20045: Amanda Mars.

EL PERIODICO—(202) 679–8656: Ricardo Mir De Francia.

EL TIEMPO—(202) 607–5929: Sergio Gomez.

EL UNIVERSAL—(202) 531–8538; 1201 National Press Building, Washington, DC 20045: Victor Sancho.

ENERGY DAILY—(202) 431–3748; 1300 Connecticut Avenue, NW., Suite 700, Washington, DC 20036: Jeffrey Beattie, James Day, George Lobsenz, Karin Rives.

FERN'S AG INSIDER BY CHARLES ABBOTT—(646) 248–6014; 576 5th Avenue, Suite 903, New York, NY 10036: Charles Abbott, Leah Douglas.

FINANCIAL TIMES—1667 K Street, NW., Suite 825, Washington, DC 20006: Lauren Fedor, Janan Ganesh, Brendan Greeley, Edward Luce, Katrina Manson, Kim Ben Marino, James Politi, Demetri Sevastopulo, Kadhim Shubber, Kiran Stacey, Courtney Weaver, Aime Williams.

FOLHA DE SAO PAULO—(202) 549–6845: Marina Dias.

FRANKFURTER ALLGEMEINE ZEITUNG—(202) 492–7591: Majid Sattar.

FUNKE MEDIENGRUPPE—(202) 244–4845: Dirk Hautkapp.

GANNETT WASHINGTON BUREAU—(703) 854–6000; 1575 Eye Street, NW., Suite 350, Washington, DC 20005: Deborah Berry, Michael Collins, Maureen Groppe, Alethea Jordan, Ledyard King, Deirdre Shesgreen.

GERMAN PRESS AGENCY-DPA—(202) 662–1220; 1112 National Press Building, Washington, DC 20045: Jurgen Batz, Shabtai Gold, Christiane Jacke, Lena Klimkeit, Can Merey.

NEWSPAPERS REPRESENTED—Continued

GLOBAL INVESTIGATIONS REVIEW—(202) 831–4651; 2122 P Street, NW., Washington, DC 20037: Adam Dobrik, Clara Hudson, Ines Kagubare.

GLOBE AND MAIL—1333 H Street, NW., Suite 700, Washington, DC 20005: Lawrence Martin, Adrian Morrow.

GUARDIAN US—900 17th Street, NW., Suite 250, Washington, DC 20006: Julian Borger, Lauren Gambino, Lucia Graves, Joan Greve, Emily Holden, Stephanie Kirchgaessner, David Smith, Daniel Strauss.

HANDELSBLATT—(202) 413–2743: Annett Meiritz.

HEARST NEWSPAPERS—1100 13th Street, NW., Suite 950, Washington, DC 20005: Emilie Munson.

HELSINGIN SANOMAT—(301) 907–0080: Anna Sofia Berner.

HINDU, THE—(917) 587–2444: Sriram Lakshman.

HONOLULU CIVIL BEAT—(808) 377–0246; 3465 Waialae Avenue, Suite 20, Honolulu, HI 968156: Nicholas Grube.

HOUSTON CHRONICLE—(713) 362–7211; 1100 13th Street, NW., Suite 950, Washington, DC 20005: James Osborne, Benjamin Wermund.

HUFFINGTON POST—1750 Pennsylvania Avenue, NW., Suite 600, Washington, DC 20006: Akbar Shahid Ahmed, Jennifer Bendery, Paul Blumenthal, Igor Bobic, Christopher D'Angelo, Shirish Date, Arthur Delaney, Ariel Edwards-Levy, Marina Fang, Elise Foley, Matthew Fuller, Tara Golshan, Dave Jamieson, Sanjana Karanth, Philip Lewis, Lawrence O'Brien, Ryan Reilly, Kevin Robillard, Amanda Terkel, Bryan Waldron, George Zornick.

INDIA PRESS TRUST—PTI Building 4 Parliament Street, New Delhi India: Lalit Jha.

INSIDE CLIMATE NEWS—16 Court Street, Suite 2307, Brooklyn, NY 11241: Neela Banerjee, Georgina Gustin, Marianne Lavelle.

INSIDE HIGHER ED—(202) 659–9208; 1150 Connecticut Avenue, NW., Suite 400, Washington, DC 20036: Greta Anderson, Paul Fain, Lindsay McKenzie, Kery Murakami, Rick Seltzer, Marjorie Valbrun.

INTERCEPT, THE—Aida Chavez, Alexander Emmons, Lee Fang, Ryan Grim, Nausicaa Renner, James Risen, Maryam Saleh.

INTERNATIONAL TRADE TODAY—(202) 872–9200; 2115 Ward Court, NW., Washington, DC 20037: Ian Cohen, Mara Lee.

INVESTOR'S BUSINESS DAILY—(800) 831–2525; 1200 18th Street, NW., Washington, DC 20036: Gillian Rich.

IRISH TIMES—(202) 431–4636; 1235 Independence Avenue, SE., Washington, DC 20003: Suzanne Lynch.

JEWISH TELEGRAPHIC AGENCY—(571) 723–2027; PO Box 5401, Arlington, VA 22207: Ronald Kampeas.

JIJI PRESS—(202) 783–4330; 550 National Press Building, Washington, DC 20045: Ryota Dei, Hideyuki Ishigaki, Masaki Kondo, Jiro Konishi, Nicolas Pandi, William Parschalk, Yumi Tanaka, Kensaku Watanabe.

JOONGANG ILBO—(202) 347–0122; 997 National Press Building, Washington, DC 20045: Hyosik Jung, Hyun Young Park.

JYLLANDS-POSTEN—1700 Lanier Place, NW., Washington, DC 20009: Poul Larsen.

KAISER HEALTH NEWS—(202) 347–5270/(703) 941–8001; 1330 G Street, NW., Washington, DC 20005: Julie Appleby, Mary Agnes Carey, Philip Galewitz, James Hancock, Carmen Heredia Rodriguez, Emmarie Huetteman, Victoria Knight, Shefali Luthra, Rachana Pradhan, Jordan Rau, Julia Rovner, Fred Schulte, Stephanie Stapleton, Sarah Tribble.

KOREA TIMES—(703) 941–8001; 7601 Little River Turnpike, Annandale, VA 22003: Christina Chong, Chang Yul Lee, Jong Kook Lee, Jewon Ryu, Yanghee Yoon.

KYODO NEWS—(202) 347–5767; 1310 G Street, NW., Suite 690, Washington, DC 20005: Sarah Ampolsk, Takuya Arai, Shinichi Fuchino, Akihiro Fujiwara, Shiro Himori, Kai Ikeda, Miki Ishibashi, Jun Kaminishikawara, Daisuke Nakai, Andrew Nicholas, Gabrielle Resnick, Kaori Saito, Yasuyiki Seiki, Kylie Sertic, Atsushi Takemoto, Mitsuya Tanaka, Miya Tanaka, Konomi Tsuchiya.

KYUNGHYANG DAILY NEWS—(571) 882–0196: Jaejoong Kim.

LA JORNADA—(202) 669–7760: David Brooks.

LA VANGUARDIA—(202) 290–2727: Beatriz Navarro.

LAS VEGAS REVIEW-JOURNAL—(702) 383–0211; 1111 West Bonanza Road, Las Vegas, NV 89106: Gary Martin, Debra Saunders.

LAW 360—(202) 439–8609: Alan Ota.

LE FIGARO—(202) 846–7774: Adrien Jaulmes.

LE MONDE—(202) 248–2836: Gilles Paris.

LOCALNEWS NOW—4075 Wilson Boulevard, 8th Floor, Arlington, VA 22203: Scott Brodbeck, James Cullum, Catherine Moran.

LONDON DAILY TELEGRAPH—1310 G Street, NW., Suite 750, Washington, DC 20005: Nicholas Allen, Benedict Riley-Smith, Rozina Sabur.

LOS ANGELES TIMES—1100 Vermont Avenue, NW., Suite 900, Washington, DC 20005: Noah Bierman, Jackie Calmes, David Cloud, Robert Drogin, Jennifer Haberkorn, Evan Halper, Janet Hook, Kimbrielle Kelly, David Lauter, Dong Lee, Noam Levey, Michael McGough, Doyle McManus, Christopher Megerian, Molly O'Toole, Anna Phillips, Edmund Sanders, David Savage, Eli Stokols, Dina White, Del Wilber, Tracy Wilkinson, Sarah Wire.

NEWSPAPERS REPRESENTED—Continued

LRP PUBLICATIONS—(561) 622–6520; 360 Hiatt Drive, Palm Beach Gardens, FL 33418: Kara Arundel, Julie Davidson, David Elfin, Anjali Patel.

MAINICHI SHIMBUN—(202) 737–2817; 1114 National Press Building, Washington, DC 20045: Yoso Furumoto, Iva Kovacheva, Masahiro Nakai, Kota Takamoto.

MARKET NEWS INTERNATIONAL—(202) 371–2121; 1100 National Press Building, Washington, DC 20045: Ryan Hauser, Brooke Migdon, Evan Ryser, Jean Yung.

MARKETWATCH—1025 Connecticut Avenue, NW., Suite 800, Washington, DC 20036: Jeffry Bartash, Victor Reklaitis, Gregory Robb, Robert Schroeder.

McCLATCHY—700 12th Street, NW., Suite 1000, Washington, DC 20005: David Catanese, Francesca Chambers, Tara Copp, Shirsho Dasgupta, Alex Daugherty, Emma Dumain, Ronald Gaither, Kevin Hall, Kate Irby, David Lightman, Bryan Lowry, Brian Mandato, Alexander Roarty, Benjamin Wieder, Michael Wilner, Adam Wollner, Toby Zakaria.

MEDPAGE TODAY—(646) 728–9500; 345 Hudson Street, 16th Floor, New York, NY 10014: Shannon Firth, Joyce Frieden.

MERCER MEDIA—(202) 834–1261: Marsha Mercer.

MILITARY.COM—555 12th Street, NW., Suite 610, Washington, DC 20004: Matthew Cox, Gina Harkins, Dorothy Mills-Gregg, Oriana Pawlyk, Hope Seck, Richard Sisk.

MILWAUKEE JOURNAL SENTINEL—(202) 841–2028; 1575 Eye Street, NW., Suite 350 Washington, DC 20005: Craig Gilbert.

MINNEAPOLIS STAR TRIBUNE—(202) 408–2752; 969 National Press Building, Washington, DC 20045: James Spencer.

MINNPOST—(818) 281–5907; 900 6th Avenue, SE., Minneapolis, MN 55414: Gabriel Schneider.

MLEX US—1776 Eye Street, NW., Suite 260, Washington, DC 20006: Brian Baker, Can Celik, Anthony Cooke, Jenna Ebersole Vaino, Curtis Eichelberger, Rafi Felder, Maxwell Fillion, Kat Lucero, Uliana Pavlova, David Perera, Robert Thomason.

NATIONAL (THE)—(202) 588–0106; PO Box 73121, Washington, DC 20056: Joyce Karam.

NATIONAL JOURNAL—(202) 266–7849; 600 New Hampshire Avenue, NW., 4th Floor, Washington, DC 20037: Brendan Bordelon, Alex Clearfield, Zachary Cohen, George Condon, Erin Covey, Harrison Cramer, Brian Dabbs, Andrew DeFrank, Jeff Dufour, Erin Durkin, Isobel Ellis, Mackenzie Weinger, Casey Wooten.

NEW YORK DAILY NEWS—(917) 85–3111; 1050 Thomas Jefferson Street, Second Floor, Washington, DC 20007: Michael McAuliff.

NEW YORK POST—(212) 930–8288; 1025 Connecticut Avenue, NW., Suite 800, Washington, DC 20036: Ebony Bowden, Steven Nelson.

NEW YORK TIMES—(202) 862–0300; 1627 Eye Street, NW., Suite 700, Washington, DC 20006: Binyamin Appelbaum, Emily Badger, Peter Baker, Julian Barnes, Katie Benner, Mikayla Bouchard, David Brooks, Elisabeth Bumiller, Jeffrey Burgess, Tahirah Burley, Christopher Cameron, Emily Cochrane, Michelle Cottle, Michael Crowley, Annie Daniel, Coral Davenport, Julie Davis, Elizabeth Dias, Maureen Dowd, Catie Edmondson, Reid Epstein, Lolade Fadulu, Nicholas Fandos, Christopher Flavelle, Lisa Friedman, Thomas Gibbons-Neff, Adam Goldman, Abigail Goodnough, Chris Hamby, Carl Hulse, John Ismay, Lara Jakes-Jason, Cecilia Kang, Zolan Kanno-Youngs, Sheila Kaplan, Thomas Kaplan, Sharon LaFraniere, Mark Leibovich, Lisa Lerer, Adam Liptak, Eric Lipton, Justine Makieli, Jonathan Martin, David McCabe, Shawn McCreesh, Clifton Meadows, Zachary Montague, Alicia Parlapiano, Ian Philbrick, Elaina Plott, Brad Plumer, Linda Qiu, Alan Rappeport, Katie Rogers, Matthew Rosenberg, David Sanger, Margot Sanger-Katz, Charles Savage, Michael Schmidt, Eric Schmitt, Thomas Shanker, Michael Shear, Rachel Shorey, Erica Simon, Jeanna Smialek, Jennifer Steinhauer, Richard Stevenson, Sheryl Stolberg, Eileen Sullivan, Ana Swanson, James Tankersley, Glenn Thrush, Kenneth Vogel, Mark Walker, Noah Weiland, Jonathan Weisman, Elizabeth Williamson, Stephen Wines, Edward Wong.

NEWSDAY—1001 National Press Club, Washington, DC 20045: Thomas Brune, Laura Figueroa Hernandez.

NIKKEI—(202) 393–1388; 815 Connecticut Avenue, NW., Suite 310, Washington, DC 20006: Tomoko Ashizuka, Christina Bilski, Taisei Hoyama, Motoko Kawachi, Takeshi Kawanami, Stephen Keefe, Aki Naganuma, Tsuyoshi Nagasawa, Ryo Nakamura, Mikio Sugeno.

NJ ADVANCE MEDIA—(301) 770–3813; 485 Route 1S, Building E Suite 300, Iselin, NJ 08830: Jonathan Salant.

NRC HANDELSBLAD—(202) 899–0712: Bastiaan Blokker, Jutta Chorus.

O ESTADO DE S. PAULO—(347) 698–0479: Beatriz Bulla.

OMAHA WORLD-HERALD—(202) 997–9787; 836 National Press Building, Washington, DC 20045: Joseph Morton.

OZY MEDIA—(470) 233–2949; 444 Castro Street, Suite 303, Mountain View, CA 94041: Nicholas Fouriezos.

PHILADELPHIA INQUIRER—(215) 854–2000; 801 Market Street, Suite 300, Philadelphia, PA 19107: Jonathan Tamari.

PHILELEFTHEROS CYPRUS—(202) 408–0109: Michail Ignatiou.

PITTSBURGH POST-GAZETTE—(800) 228–6397; 358 North Shore Drive, Suite 300, Pittsburgh, PA 15212: Tracie Mauriello, Daniel Moore.

NEWSPAPERS REPRESENTED—Continued

POLITIFACT—(727) 821–9494; 1100 Connecticut Avenue, NW., Suite 1300-B, Washington, DC 20036: Jonathan Greenberg, Angie Holan, Louis Jacobson, William McCarthy.

POWER MARKETS TODAY—(301) 769–6903; 4908 Hornbeam Drive, Rockville, MD 20853: James Downing.

PROPUBLICA—(212) 514–5250; 5335 Wisconsin Avenue, NW., Suite 440, Washington, DC 20015: Isaac Arnsdorf, Kirsten Berg, Lydia Depillis, Jack Gillum, Maryam Jameel, Akilah Johnson, Dara Lind, J. David McSwane, Sebastian Rotella, Yeganeh Torbati, Derek Willis.

QUARTZ—(202) 266–6000; 600 New Hampshire Avenue, NW., Washington, DC 20037: Ephrat Livni.

REAL CLEAR POLITICS—1725 Desales Street, NW., Suite 700 Washington, DC 20036: Carl Cannon, Susan Crabtree, Howard Fineman, A.B. Stoddard, Philip Wegmann.

REFORMA NEWSPAPER—(202) 341–3255; 1009 New Hampshire Avenue, NW., Suite 700, Washington, DC 20037: Jose Diaz-Briseno.

RELIGION NEWS SERVICE—(844) 767–6397; 1009 National Press Building, Washington, DC 20045: Adelle Banks, John Jenkins, Paul O'Donnell, Robert Smietana.

RHEINISCHE POST—(202) 966–2393: Frank Herrmann.

RND NEWS NETWORK—(202) 330–1962: Karl Doemens.

S & P GLOBAL—(877) 863–1306; 1200 G Street, NW., Suite 1000, Washington, DC 20005: Glen Boshart, Joniel Cha, Molly Christian, Michael Copley, Marcy Crane, Steven Dolley, Casey Egan, Andrew Engblom, Evan Fallor, William Freebairn, Allison Good, Meghan Gordon, Zachary Hale, William Holland, Jacob Holzman, David Hood, Jasmin Hudson, Karen Laping, Michael Lustig, Christopher Newkumet, Corey Paul, Ellie Potter, Polo Rocha, Brian Scheid, Bryan Schutt, Sarah Smith, Jeff Stanfield, Sean Sullivan, Stephanie Tsao, Maya Weber, Esther Whieldon, Donna Young, Richard Zipp.

SALT LAKE TRIBUNE—(202) 662–8732: Thomas Burr.

SAN FRANCISCO CHRONICLE—(202) 263–6573; 1100 13th Street, NW., Suite 950, Washington, DC 20005: Tal Kopan.

SANKEI SHIMBUN—(202) 347–2842; 330 National Press Building, Washington, DC 20045: Yoshihisa Komori, Yoshinari Kurose, Nagahisa Shiobara, B. Scott Stewart, Kyosuke Sumii.

SAUDI PRESS AGENCY—(202) 944–3890; 601 New Hampshire Avenue, NW., Washington, DC 20037: Hamad Albaqami, Hindi Albaqami, Haifaa Almubarak.

SEGYE TIMES—(571) 302–0609; 909 National Press Building, Washington, DC 20045: Jae Young Jung.

SEKAI NIPPO—(571) 459–2542: Yosuke Yamazaki.

SINGAPORE STRAITS TIMES—(202) 680–3303: Nirmal Ghosh.

STARS AND STRIPES—(202) 886–0003; 633 3rd Street, NW., Suite 116, Washington, DC 20001: Corey Dickstein, Steven Benyon, Caitlin Kenney, Nikki Wentling.

STAT—(617) 929–3333; 1130 Connecticut Avenue, NW., Suite 735, Washington, DC 20036: Lev Facher, Nicholas Florko, Erin Mershon.

SYDNEY MORNING HERALD—(917) 775–2243; 1310 G Street, NW., Suite 750, Washington, DC 20005: Matthew Knott.

SYRACUSE POST-STANDARD—(315) 440–1163: Mark Weiner.

TAGES ANZEIGER—(202) 813–7678: Alan Cassidy.

TAIWAN CENTRAL NEWS AGENCY—1173 National Press Building, Washington, DC 20045: Tsung-Shen Cheng, Chinyeh Chiang.

TEXAS TRIBUNE—(512) 716–8600; 19 Congress Avenue, The Sixth Floor, Austin, Texas 78701: Abby Livingston.

THOMSON REUTERS—(646) 223–4000; 1333 H Street, NW., Suite 700, Washington, DC 20005: Timothy Ahmann, Idrees Ali, Alexandra Alper, Diane Bartz, Amanda Becker, Eric Beech, Alistair Bell, Christopher Bing, Melissa Bland, Nandita Bose, David Brunnstrom, Ginger Burk, Doina Chiacu, Ross Colvin, Peter Cooney, Susan Cornwell, Richard Cowan, William Dunham, Lindsay Dunsmuir, Peter Eisler, Timothy Gardner, Rodrek Golden, Paul Grant, Ronnie Greene, Julia Harte, Bradford Heath, Susan Heavey, Sonya Hepinstall, Theodore Hesson, Steve Holland, Mark Hosenball, Lawrence Hurley, Katanga Johnson, Soyoung Kim, Lisa Lambert, Jonathan Landay, Jason Lange, Makini Lanne, David Lawder, Katherina Lemus, Sarah Lynch, Sandra Maler, Jeffrey Mason, Mary Milliken, Arshad Mohammed, David Morgan, Kieran Murray, Lucia Mutikani, James Oliphant, Humeyra Pamuk, Christine Prentice, Michelle Price, Daphne Psaledakis, Andrea Ricci, Aram Roston, Timothy Ryan, Chris Sanders, Raphael Satter, Joel Schectman, Howard Schneider, Peter Schroeder, Andrea Shalal, David Shepardson, John Shiffman, Paul Simao, Matthew Spetalnick, Phillip Stewart, Michael Stone, Andrew Sullivan, Jason Szep, Joseph Tanfani, Marisa Taylor, Heather Timmons, Valerie Volcovici, Michael Weekes, John Whitesides, Jan Wolfe, Mohammad Zargham. Patricia Zengerle.

TIMES OF INDIA—(301) 495–9548: Chidanand Rajghatta.

TIMES OF LONDON—1101 17th Street, NW., Suite 601, Washington, DC 20045: David Charter. Henry Zeffman.

TOKYO CHUNICHI SHIMBUN—(202) 783–9479; 1012 National Press Building, Washington, DC 20045: Conrad Chaffee, Nakahiro Iwata, Takao Kanasugi, Christopher Kelly, Wataru Shiraishi. Eri Urano.

NEWSPAPERS REPRESENTED—Continued

T-ONLINE.DE—(202) 299–9508: Fabian Reinbold.
TORONTO STAR—(301) 320–6360: Edward Keenan.
TRIBUNE CONTENT AGENCY—(202) 494–1189: Martin Schram.
TULSA WORLD—(703) 623–4397: Jim Myers.
UNITED DAILY NEWS—(202) 655–8268: Chia Chang.
UNITED MEDIA—(301) 494–0430: Lew Sichelman.
USA TODAY—(703) 854–6000; 1575 Eye Street, NW., Suite 350, Washington, DC 20005: Kenneth Alltucker, Savannah Behrmann, Jarrett Bell, Steven Berkowitz, Caren Bohan, William Cummings, John D'Anna, John Fritze, Christal Hayes, David Jackson, Bart Jansen, Kevin Johnson, Katharine Lawrence, David Mastio, Rebecca Morin, Susan Page, Kristine Phillips, Maria Puente, Christopher Quintana, Jeanine Santucci, Donovan Slack, William Sternberg, Martina Stewart, Courtney Subramanian, Thomas Vanden Brook, Richard Wolf, Nicholas Wu. Gregg Zoroya.
US REPORT (GERMANY)—(301) 299–5777: Thomas Spang.
VOTERAMA IN CONGRESS—(202) 332–0857: Richard Thomas.
WALL STREET JOURNAL / DOW JONES—(202) 862–9200; 1025 Connecticut Avenue, NW., Suite 800, Washington, DC 20036: Andrew Ackerman, Mark Anderson, Natalie Andrews, Stephanie Armour, Emily Austin, Rebecca Ballhaus, Paul Beckett, Michael Bender, Janet Booker, Becky Bowers, Martin Brandt, Jess Bravin, Thomas Burton, Julie Bykowicz, Sarah Chaney, Dante Chinni, Rodney Christian, L. Kareema Clark, Eliza Collins, John Corrigan, Alexa Corse, Alan Cullison, Jeanne Cummings, Kate Davidson Choma, Robert Davis, Chad Day, Jessica Donati-Bourne, Andrew Duehren, Drew FitzGerald, Brett Forrest, Theodore Francis, Miguel Gonzalez, Michael Gordon, James Grimaldi, Sadie Gurman, Michelle Hackman, Timothy Hanrahan, David Harrison, Yuka Hayashi, Nell Henderson, Siobhan Hughes, Gregory Ip, Joshua Jamerson, Brent Kendall, Paul Kiernan, Alex Leary, Rachel Levy, Gordon Lubold, Edward Mann, Jude Marfil, William Mauldin, Courtney McBride, John McKinnon, David Michaels, Eric Morath, Broderick Mullins, Daniel Nasaw, Kate O'Keeffe, Amara Omeokwe, Robert Ourlian, Paul Overberg, Paul Page, Scott Patterson, Kristina Peterson, Michael Phillips, Timothy Puko, Louise Radnofsky, Andrew Restuccia, Gabriel Rubin, Richard Rubin, Jathon Sapsford, Jacob Schlesinger, Gerald Seib, Sabrina Siddiqui, Katy Stech Ferek, Warren Strobel, Ian Talley, Byron Tau, Kenneth Thomas, Nicolas Timiraos, Harriet Torry, Ryan Tracy, Aruna Viswanatha, Dustin Volz, Lindsay Wise, Nancy Youssef, Aaron Zitner. Joshua Zumbrun.
WARREN COMMUNICATIONS—(202) 872–9202; 2115 Ward Court, NW.. Washington, DC 20037: James Phillips.
WASHINGTON EXAMINER—(202) 496–3345; 1152 15th Street, NW., Suite 200, Washington, DC 20005: T. Becket Adams, Michael Barone, Paul Bedard, Elizabeth Bufkin, Timothy Carney, Jeffrey Cimmino, Diana Correll, Robert Crilly, Katherine Doyle, David Drucker, Jeremiah Dunleavy, Susan Ferrechio, Madeline Fry, Joel Gehrke, Anna Giaritelli, Alana Goodman, Zachary Halaschak, Jay Heflin, Sean Higgins, Nihal Krishan, Emily Larsen, Joseph Lawler, Naomi Lim, David Mark, Abraham Mashie, Cassidy Morrison, Timothy Pearce, Kerry Picket, Melissa Quinn, Thomas Rogan, John Siciliano, Joshua Siegel, Joseph Simonson, Abby Smith, Emily Ward, Caitlin Yilek. Byron York.
WASHINGTON POST—(202) 334–6000; 1301 K Street, NW., Washington, DC 20071: Yasmeen Abutaleb, Joel Achenbach, Jacqueline Alemany, Keith Alexander, Mariana Alfaro Martinez, Nicholas Anderson, Lori Aratani, Rachael Bade, Holly Bailey, Daniel Balz, Robert Barnes, Martin Baron, Cameron Barr, John Barrett, Victoria Benning, Mark Berman, Jeremy Bowers, Emma Brown, Donna Cassata, Ariana Cha, Robert Costa, Tim Craig, Paige Cunningham, Christian Davenport, Joseph Davidson, Aaron Davis, Joshua Dawsey, Michael DeBonis, Cathleen Decker, Karoun Demirjian, Brady Dennis, Karen DeYoung, Joshua du Lac, Ian Duncan, Juliet Eilperin, David Fahrenthold, Darryl Fears, Paulina Firozi, Reuben Fischer-Baum, Marc Fisher, Mary Flaherty, Todd Frankel, Andrew Freedman, Amy Gardner, Elizabeth Gardner Whyte, Anne Gearan, Justin George, Steven Ginsberg, Matea Gold, Amy Goldstein, Dino Grandoni, Aaron Gregg, Joan Greve, Brent Griffiths, Ashley Halsey, Thomas Hamburger, Shane Harris, Andrew Harwell, Joseph Heim, Rosalind Helderman, Peter Hermann, Arelis Hernandez, James Hohmann, Sari Horwitz, Spencer Hsu, John Hudson, Tracy Jan, Jenna Johnson, Mary Jordan, Maura Judkis, Paul Kane, Daniel Keating, Glenn Kessler, Seung Min Kim, Kimberly Kindy, Marissa Lang, Sarah Larimer, Michael Laris, Lyndsey Layton, Luz Lazo, Michelle Lee, Anne Linskey, Heather Long, David Lynch, Joseph Marks, Brittany Mayes, Robert McCartney, Mary McGinley, Michelle McIntyre, Laura Meckler, Ted Mellnik, Renae Merle, Dana Milbank, Gregory Miller, David Montgomery, Lori Montgomery, Carol Morello, Steven Mufson, David Nakamura, Ellen Nakashima, Tory Newmyer, Jonathan O'Connell, Robert O'Harrow, Abigail Ohlheiser, Damian Paletta, Ashley Parker, Amber Phillips, Jenna Portnoy, Elliot Postell, Martine Powers, Kate Rabinowitz, Laura Reiley, Lisa Rein, Beth Reinhard, Salvador Rizzo, Eugene Robinson, Joshua Rogin, Manuel Roig-Franzia, Anthony Romm, Michael Rosenwald, Christopher Rowland, Philip Rucker, Robert Samuels, Ann Sargent, Kevin Schaul, Michael Scherer, Mark Seibel, Avi Selk, Hamza Shaban, Sandhya Somashekhar, Felicia Sonmez, Paul Sonne, Sara Sorcher, Isaac Stanley-Becker, Jeffrey Stein, Kevin Sullivan, Patricia Sullivan, Sean Sullivan, Lena Sun, Susan Svrluga, Benjamin Terris, Ishaan Tharoor, Reis Thebault, Karen Tumulty, Kevin Uhrmacher, Elise Viebeck, Matthew Viser, John Wagner, Peter Wallsten, Amy Wang, Joby

NEWSPAPERS REPRESENTED—Continued

Warrick, Emily Wax, David Weigel, Rachel Weiner, Erica Werner, Jeanne Whalen, Craig Whitlock, Peter Whoriskey, Clarence Williams, Vanessa Williams, Scott Wilson, Robert Woodward, Cleve Wootson, Eric Yoder, Daniel Zak, Cat Zakrzewski, Matthew Zapotosky. Katie Zezima.

WASHINGTON TELECOMMUNICATIONS SERVICES—(804) 695–4628: Gordon White.

WASHINGTON TIMES—(202) 636–3000; 3600 New York Avenue, NE., Washington, DC 20002: David Boyer, Stephen Dinan, Christopher Dolan, Ethan Epstein, Michael Glenn, Jennifer Harper, Thomas Howell, Henry Hurt, Sophie Kaplan, Ryan Lovelace, Seth McLaughlin, Lauren Meier, S.A. Miller, Jeffrey Mordock, Gabriella Muñoz, David Sands, Rowan Scarborough, David Sherfinski, Alex Swoyer, Shen Wu Tan, Guy Taylor, Christopher Vondracek. Benjamin Wolfgang.

WHITE HOUSE DOSSIER—(202) 277–5416: Keith Koffler.

WOLFNEWS—Mariuccia Chiantaretto.

WORLD JOURNAL—954 National Press Building, Washington, DC 20045: Carolyn Chang. Xiaoyuan Luo.

YAHOO NEWS—701 First Avenue, Sunnyvale, CA 94089: Michael Isikoff, Samuel Matthews, Jenna McLaughlin, Sean Naylor, Aleksandr Nazaryan, Brittany Sheperd, Suzanne Smalley, Hunter Walker, Jonathan Ward. Sharon Weinberger.

YOMIURI SHIMBUN—(202) 783–2050; 802 National Press Building, Washington, DC 20045: Mineko Abe, Sho Funakoshi, Colin Gamm, Michitaka Kaiya, Kazuhiko Makita, Alexander Nickol, Ryosuke Yamauchi. Yuya Yokobori.

PRESS PHOTOGRAPHERS' GALLERY*

The Capitol, Room S–317, phone 224–6548

https://pressphotographers.senate.gov

Director.—Jeffrey S. Kent.
Deputy Director.—Mark A. Abraham.
Senior Assistant Director.—Tricia Munro.
Assistant Director.—Matthew Grant.

STANDING COMMITTEE OF PRESS PHOTOGRAPHERS

J. Scott Applewhite, Associated Press, *Chair*
Win McNamee, Getty Images, *Secretary-Treasurer*
Jim Bourg, Reuters News Pictures
Tom Williams, CQ / Roll Call
Melina Mara, Washington Post
Gabriella Demczuk, Independent

RULES GOVERNING PRESS PHOTOGRAPHERS' GALLERY

1. (a) Administration of the Press Photographers' Gallery is vested in a Standing Committee of Press Photographers consisting of six persons elected by accredited members of the Gallery. The Committee shall be composed of one member each from Associated Press Photos; Reuters News Pictures or AFP Photos; magazine media; local newspapers; agency or freelance member; and one at-large member. The at-large member may be, but need not be, selected from media otherwise represented on the Committee; however no organization may have more than one representative on the Committee.

(b) Elections shall be held as early as practicable in each year, and in no case later than March 31. A vacancy in the membership of the Committee occurring prior to the expiration of a term shall be filled by a special election called for that purpose by the Committee.

(c) The Standing Committee of the Press Photographers' Gallery shall propose no change or changes in these rules except upon petition in writing signed by not less than 25 accredited members of the Gallery.

2. Persons desiring admission to the Press Photographers' Gallery of the Senate shall make application in accordance with Rule 33 of the Senate, which rule shall be interpreted and administered by the Standing Committee of Press Photographers subject to the review and approval of the Senate Committee on Rules and Administration.

3. The Standing Committee of Press photographers shall limit membership in the photographers' gallery to bona fide news photographers of repute in their profession and Heads of Photographic Bureaus under such rules as the Standing Committee of Press Photographers shall prescribe.

4. Provided, however, that the Standing Committee of Press Photographers shall admit to the Gallery no person who does not establish to the satisfaction of the Committee all of the following:

(a) That any member is not engaged in paid publicity or promotion work or in prosecuting any claim before Congress or before any department of the Government, and will not become so engaged while a member of the Gallery.

*Information is based on data furnished and edited by each respective Gallery.

(b) That he or she is not engaged in any lobbying activity and will not become so engaged while a member of the Gallery.

The above rules have been approved by the Committee on Rules and Administration.

NANCY PELOSI,
Speaker, House of Representatives.

ROY BLUNT,
Chair, Senate Committee on Rules and Administration.

MEMBERS ENTITLED FOR ADMISSION

PRESS PHOTOGRAPHERS' GALLERY

Abraham, Mark: Freelance
Abramson, Mark: Freelance
Ake, John David: Associated Press Photos
Andrew, Jason: Freelance
Angerer, Andrew: Getty Images
Applewhite, J. Scott: Associated Press Photos
Ashley, Douglas: Suburban Communications Corp.
Augustino, Jocelyn: Freelance
Barouh, Stanford: Freelance
Barrett, Stephen: Freelance
Barria Moraga, Carlos: Reuters News Pictures
Barrick, Matthew: Freelance
Benic, Patrick: United Press International
Berglie, James: Zuma Press
Bernstein, Aaron: Freelance
Binks, Porter: Sports Illustrated
Bivera, Johnny: Freelance
Boal, John: Freelance
Bongioanni, Carlos: Stars and Stripes
Botsford, Jabin: Washington Post
Bourg, James: Reuters News Pictures
Bowe, Diane: ImageCatcher News
Brack, William: Black Star
Brandon, James: Associated Press Photos
Brenner, Thomas: Freelance
Bulbin, Lauren: Washingtonian
Butow, David: Freelance
Caballero-Reynolds, Andrew: Agence France-Presse
Calvert, Mary: Freelance
Carioti, Richard: Washington Post
Cedeno, Kenneth: Freelance
Ceneta, Manuel: Associated Press Photos
Chebbine, Lina: U.S. News & World Report
Chen, Meng Tong: China News Service
Chikwendiu, Jahi: Washington Post
Christian, Douglas: Freelance
Chung, Andre: Freelance
Clark, William: CQ/Roll Call
Cohen, Marshall: Bigmarsh News Photos
Coleman, Chloe: Washington Post
Connor, Kristopher: Freelance
Contreras Cruz, Oliver: Freelance
Coppage, Gary: Photo Press International
Corum, Samuel: Freelance
Crowley, Stephen: Freelance
Demczuk, Gabriella: Freelance
Dietsch, Kevin: United Press International
Domb-Sadof, Karly: Washington Post
Douliery, Olivier: AbacaPress Photo Agency
Drago, Alexander: Freelance
Duggan, James: Freelance
Edelman, Alexander: Freelance
Elkins, Jeffrey: Washingtonian
Elswick, Jonathan: Associated Press Photos
Ernst, Jonathan: Reuters News Pictures
Falk, Steven: Philadelphia Inquirer
Frey, Katherine: Washington Post
Gail, Carl: Washington Post
Galietta, Wendy: Washington Post
Georges, Salwan: Washington Post
Gibson, Zachary: Freelance
Golon, MaryAnne: Washington Post
Gripas, Yuri: Freelance
Gromelski, Joseph: Stars and Stripes
Gruber, Jack: USA Today
Gupta, Avijit: U.S. News & World Report
Gurbuz, Sait: Freelance
Guzy, Carol: Freelance
Hambach, Eva: Agence France-Presse
Harnik, Andrew: Associated Press Photos
Harrer, Andrew: Bloomberg News Photo
Harrington, John: Black Star
Helber, Stephen: Associated Press Photos
Hill, Robert: Freelance
Hockstein, Evelyn: Freelance
Hosefros, Paul: Freelance
Jackson, Lawrence: Freelance
Jennings, Graeme: Washington Examiner
Jimenez-Stuard, Olga: Washington Post
Jones, Leah: Freelance
Joseph, Marvin: Washington Post
Kahn, Gregory: Freelance
Kahn, Nikki: Freelance
Kamm, Nicholas: Agence France-Presse
Kaster, Carolyn: Associated Press Photos
Katopodis, Anastasios: Freelance
Katz, Martin: Chesapeake News Service
Kennedy, Charles: Freelance
Kennerly, David: Freelance
Key, Michael: Washington Blade
Kirkpatrick, Nicholas: Washington Post
Kirkpatrick, Thomas Jay: Freelance
Kittner, Samuel: Freelance
Kleponis, Christopher: Freelance
Kruszewski, Eric: Freelance
Lamarque, Kevin: Reuters News Pictures
Lamkey, Rodney Arthur, Jr.: Freelance
Lane, Keith: Freelance
Lanham, Yuko: Asahi Shimbun
Latimer, Bronwen: Washington Post
LaVor, Martin: Freelance
Lawidjaja, Rudy: Freelance

MEMBERS ENTITLED FOR ADMISSION—Continued

Lesser, Erik: European Pressphoto Agency
Lewis, Roy: Washington Informer
Liu, Jie: Xinhua News Agency
Loeb, Saul: Agence France-Presse
Loehrke, Timothy: USA Today
LoScalzo, James: European Pressphoto Agency
Lynch, Mary: Freelance
Lyttle, Melissa: Freelance
Magana-oceja, Jose Luis: Freelance
Mages, Evy: Freelance
Mahaskey, Michael: Politico
Makela, Mark: Freelance
Malet, Jeffrey: Freelance
Mallin, Jay: Freelance
Mara, Melina: Washington Post
Markel, Bradley: Capri
Marks, Donovan: Freelance
Marovich, Peter: Freelance
Martin, Jacquelyn: Associated Press Photos
Martinez Monsivais, Pablo: Associated Press Photos
Mathieson, Gregory: MAI Photo Agency
May, Cheriss: Freelance
McClain, Matthew: Washington Post
McCoy, Michael: Freelance
McDonnell, John: Washington Post
McKoy, Kirk: Los Angeles Times
McNamee, Bruce: Getty Images
Meyer, Cheryl: Freelance
Miller, Mark: Washington Post
Miller, Robert: Washington Post
Millis, Leah: Reuters News Pictures
Mills, Douglas: New York Times
Mohammed, Eman: Freelance
Moneymaker, Anna: Freelance
Morigi, Paul: Freelance
Morones, Michael: The Freelance-Star
Mount, Bonnie: Washington Post
Nash, Gregory: The Hill
Newton, Jonathan: Washington Post
Ngan, Mandel: Agence France-Presse
Nipp, Lisa: Freelance
Nolly Araujo, Angel: Notimex
Nordby, Leslie: Freelance
O'Leary, William: Washington Post
Owen, Clifford: Freelance
Ozturk, Yasin: Anadolu Agency
Palu, Luigino: Zuma Press
Panagos, Dimitrios: Greek American News Agency
Partlow, Wayne: Associated Press Photos
Patterson, Kathryn: Freelance
Peterson, Mark: Freelance
Petros, Vasilios: Freelance
Philippi, Joy: Freelance
Plowman, William: Freelance
Purcell, Steven: Freelance
Radzinschi, Diego: National Law Journal
Reinhard, Richard: Impact Digitals
Reynolds, Michael: European Pressphoto Agency
Reynolds, Stefani: The Hill
Riecken, Astrid: Freelance
Roberts, Joshua: Freelance
Robinson-Chavez, Michael: Washington Post
Rolfe, Judith: Freelance
Ryan, Patrick: Freelance
Sachs, Ronald: Consolidated News Pictures
Samperio, Aurora: Freelance
Sandys, Toni: Washington Post
Savi, Riccardo: Freelance
Schaeffer-Hopkins, Sandra: MAI Photo Agency
Schaff, Erin: New York Times
Schmalz, Julia: Chronicle of Higher Education
Schmidt, Roberto: Freelance
Scott, Andrew: USA Today
Scott, Erin: Polaris Images
Semansky, Patrick: Associated Press Photos
Sha, Hanting: China News Service
Shelley, Allison: Freelance
Shen, Ting: Freelance
Shipman-Singleton, Paulette: Freelance
Simon, Martin: Redux Pictures
Simonetti, Thomas: Washington Post
Slim, Daniel: Agence France-Presse
Smialowski, Brendan: Agence France-Presse
Somodevilla, Kenneth: Getty Images
Squires, Derek: Tax Analysts'
Swall, Lexey: Freelance
Sweets, Fredric: St. Louis American
Sykes, Jack: Professional Pilot Magazine
Tatlow, Dermot: Panos Pictures
Taylor, Marisa: New York Times
Thayer, Eric: Freelance
Theiler, Michael: Freelance
Thew, Shawn: European Pressphoto Agency
Tripplaar, Kristoffer: Freelance
Usher, Christopher: Freelance
Van Houten, Carolyn: Washington Post
Varias, Stelios: Reuters News Pictures
Vick, Vanessa: Freelance
Vogel, Leigh: Freelance
Voisard, Amanda: Freelance
Voisin, Sarah: Washington Post
Voss, Stephen: Freelance
Vucci, Evan: Associated Press Photos
Walsh, Susan: Associated Press Photos
Watkins, Frederick: Freelance
Watson, James: Agence France-Presse
Wells, Jonathan: Sipa Press, Inc.
Whitehouse, Raymond: Freelance
Wiegold, David: 1105 Media
Williams, Thomas: CQ/Roll Call
Williamson, Michael: Washington Post
Wilson, Mark: Getty Images
Winter, Damon: New York Times
Wolf, Kevin: Freelance

MEMBERS ENTITLED FOR ADMISSION—Continued

Wolf, Lloyd: Freelance
Wong, Alex: Getty Images
Wroblewski, Alex: Freelance
Yim, Heesoon: Hana
Young, James: Reuters News Pictures
Ziegler, Brett: U.S. News & World Report

SERVICES REPRESENTED

(Service and telephone number, office address, and name of representative)

1105 MEDIA—8609 Westwood Center Drive, Vienna, VA 22182–2215: Wiegold, David.

ABACA USA—989 6th Avenue, New York City, NY 10018: Douliery, Oliver.

AGENCE FRANCE PRESSE—(202) 289–0700; 1500 K Street, NW., Suite 600, Washington, DC 20005: Cahellero-Reynolds, Andrew; Hambach, Eva; Kamm, Nicholas; Loeb, Saul; Ngan, Mandel; Slim, Daniel; Smialowski, Brendan; Watson, James.

ANADOLU—National Press Building, 529 14th Street NW., Suite 1131, Washington, DC 20045: Corum, Samuel; Ozturk, Yasin.

ASAHI SHIMBUN—(202) 783–1000; National Press Building, 529 14th Street NW., Suite 1022, Washington, DC 20045: Lanham, Yuko.

ASSOCIATED PRESS PHOTOS—(202) 641–9520; 1100 13th Street, NW., Suite 700, Washington, DC 20005: Ake, David; Applewhite, J. Scott; Brandon, James Alex; Ceneta, Manuel B.; Elswick, Jon; Harnik, Andrew; Helber, Stephen; Kaster, Carolyn; Martin, Jacquelyn; Martinez Monsivas, Pablo; Partlow, Wayne; Semansky, Patrick; Vucci, Evan; Walsh, Susan.

BIGMARSH NEWS PHOTOS—(202) 364–8332; 5131 52nd Street, NW., Washington, DC 20016: Cohen, Marshall.

BLACK STAR—(703) 547–1176; 7704 Tauxemont Road, Alexandria, VA 22308: Brack, William; Harrington, John.

BLOOMBERG GOVERNMENT—(202) 654–7300; 1801 South Bell Street, Arlington, VA 22202: Harrer, Andrew.

CAPRI—Markel, Bradley.

CHESAPEAKE NEWS SERVICE—(410) 484–3500; 619 Oakwood Drive, Seven Valleys, PA 17360: Katz, Marty.

CHINA NEWS SERVICE—(703) 536–3657: Chen, Meng Tong; Sha, Hanting.

CHRONICLE OF HIGHER EDUCATION—(202) 466–1728; 1255 23rd Street, NW., Suite 700, Washington, DC, 20037: Schmaltz, Julia.

CONSOLIDATED NEWS PICTURES—(202) 543–3203; 10305 Leslie Street, Silver Spring, MD 20902: Sachs, Ronald.

CONTACT PRESS IMAGES—341 West 38th Street, New York City, NY, 10018.

CORBIS—710 2nd Avenue, Suite 200, Seattle, Washington, 98104: Simon, Martin.

CQ/Roll Call—(202) 650–6500; 1625 Eye St. NW Washington, DC 20006: Clark, Bill; Williams, Tom.

EUROPEAN PRESS PHOTO—(202) 347–4694; 529 14th Street, NW., Suite 1122, Washington, DC 20045: Lesser, Erik; LoScalzo, Jim; Reynolds, Michael; Thew, Shawn.

GETTY IMAGES—(202) 347–2050; National Press Building, 529 14th Street, NW., Suite 1125, Washington, DC 20045: Angerer, Drew; McNamee, Win; Somodevilla, Kenneth; Wilson, Mark L.; Wong, Alex.

GREEK AMERICAN NEWS AGENCY—(516) 931–2333; 35–0723 Avenue, Astoria, NY, 11105: Panagos, Dimitrios.

HANA—(202) 262–4541; 3505 International Place, NW., Washington, DC 20008: Yim, Heesoon.

IMAGE CATCHER NEWS—(301) 652–2774; 4911 Hampden Lane, Bethesda, MD 20815: Bowe, Diane.

IMPACT DIGITALS—(212) 614–8406; 32 6th Avenue, Suite 1, New York City, NY 10013: Reinhard, Rick.

LOS ANGELES TIMES—(213) 283–2274; 1025 F Street NW, Suite 700, Washington, DC 20004: McKoy, Kirk.

MAI PHOTO AGENCY—(703) 968–0030; 10856 Caraway Circle, Manassas, VA 20109: Mathieson, Greg; Schaeffer-Hopkins, Sandra.

MCCLATCHY WASHINGTON BUREAU—(202) 383–6126; 700 12th Street, NW., Suite 1000, Washington, DC 20005: Meyer, Cheryl.

NATIONAL JOURNAL—(202) 739–8400; 600 New Hampshire Avenue, NW., Washington, DC 20037: Lynch, Liz.

NATIONAL LAW JOURNAL—(202) 828–0336; 1100 M Street NW., Washington, DC 20036: Radzinschi, Diego.

NOTIMEX—(202) 347–5227; 529 14th Street, NW., Suite 425, Washington, DC 20045–1401: Nolly Araujo, Angel.

PANOS—(617) 710–7413; Unit K, Reliance Wharf Hertford Road, London, N15EW, UK: Tatlow, Dermott.

PHILADELPHIA INQUIRER—400 N Broad St., Philadelphia, PA 19130: Falk, Stephen.

PHOTO PRESS INTERNATIONAL—(540) 286–1045; P.O. Box 190, Goldvein, VA 22720: Coppage, Gary.

SERVICES REPRESENTED—Continued

POLARIS IMAGES—259 West 30th Street, 13th Floor, New York, NY 10001: Hockstein, Evelyn; Scott, Erin.

POLITICO—(703) 647–7694: 1100 Wilson Boulevard, 8th Floor, Arlington, VA: Shinkle, John.

PROFESSIONAL PILOT MAGAZINE—30 South Quaker Lane, Unit 300, Alexandria, VA, 22314: Sykes, Jack.

REUTERS NEWS PICTURES—(202) 898–8333; 1333 H Street, NW., Suite 500, Washington, DC 20005: Barria, Carlos; Bourg, Jim; Ernst, Jonathan; Lamarque, Kevin; Millis, Leah; Varias, Stelios; Young, James.

SAINT LOUIS AMERICAN—(314) 533–8000; 2315 Pine Street, St. Louis, MO 63103: Sweets, Frederic.

SIPA PRESS—(212) 463–0150; 307 7th Avenue, Suite 807, New York, NY 10001: Triplar, Kristoffer: Wells, Jonathan.

SPORTS ILLUSTRATED—135 West 50th Street, New York City, NY 10020: Binks, Porter.

STARS AND STRIPES—529 14th St., NW., Suite 350, Washington, DC 20045: Bongioanni, Carlos; Gromelski, Joseph.

SUBURBAN COMMUNICATIONS CORP—(248) 568–0006; 331 East Bell Street, Camden, MI 44232: Ashley, Douglas.

TAX ANALYSTS'—(703) 533–4476; 400 South Maple Ave., Suite 400, Falls Church, VA 22046: Squires, Derek.

THE FREELANCE-STAR—(540) 368–5053; 1340 Central Park Blvd., Suite 100, Fredericksburg, VA 22401: Morones, Mike.

THE HILL—(202) 628–8525; 1625 K Street, Suite 900, Washington, DC 20006: Nash, Greg; Reynolds, Stefani.

THE NEW YORK TIMES—1627 Eye Street, NW., Washington, DC 20005: Crowley, Stephen; Mills, Doug; Schaff, Erin; Taylor, Marisa; Winter, Damon.

THE WASHINGTON BLADE—1712 14th Street, NW., Washington, DC 20009: Key, Michael.

THE WASHINGTON EXAMINER—(202) 903–2000; 1015 15th Street, NW., Suite 500, Washington, DC 20005: Jennings, Graeme.

THE WASHINGTON INFORMER—(202) 561–4100; 3117 Martin L. King Avenue, SE., Washington, DC 20032: Lewis, Roy.

THE WASHINGTON POST—(202) 334–7380; 1150 17th Street, NW., Washington, DC 20071: Botsford, Jabin; Carioti, Richard; Chikwendiu, Jahi; Coleman, Chloe; Domb-Sadof, Karly; Frey, Katherine; Gail, Carl; Galieta, Wendy; Golon, MaryAnne; Jimenez-Stuard, Olga; Joseph, Marvin; Kirkpatrick, Nick; Latimer, Bronwen; Mara, Melina; McClain, Matt; McDonnell, John; Miller, Mark; Miller, Robert; Mount, Bonnie; Newton, Jonathan; O'Leary, William; Robinson-Chavez, Michael; Georges, Salwan; Sandys, Toni; Simonetti, Thomas; Van Houten, Carolyn; Voisin, Sarah; Williamson, Michael.

UNITED PRESS INTERNATIONAL—(202) 898–8071; 1133 19th Street, Suite 800, Washington, DC 20036: Benic, Patrick T.; Dietsch, Kevin.

US NEWS AND WORLD REPORT—(202) 955–2000; 1050 Thomas Jefferson St. NW, Washington, DC 20007: Chebbine, Lina; Gupta, Avijit; Ziegler, Brett.

USA/ TODAY—(703) 854–5216; 1575 I Street, NW., Suite 350, Washington, DC 20005: Gruber, Jack; Loehrke, Tim; Scott, Andrew.

WASHINGTONIAN—(202) 296–3600; 1828 L Street NW, Suite 200, Washington, DC 20036: Bulbin, Lauren; Elkins, Jeffrey.

XINHUA NEWS AGENCY—(703) 875–0082; 1740 N. 14th Street, Arlington, VA 22209: Liu, Jie.

ZUMA PRESS—408 North El Camino Road, San Clemente, CA 92672: Berglie, James; Palu, Luigino.

FREELANCE

Freelance—Abraham, Mark; Abramson, Mark; Andrew, Jason; Augustino, Jocelyn; Barouh, Stanford; Barrett, Stephen; Barrick, Matthew; Bernstein, Aaron; Bivera, Johnny; Boal, John; Brenner, Thomas; Butow, David; Calvert, Mary; Cedeno, Kenneth; Christian, Douglas; Chung, Andre; Connor, Kristopher; Contreras Cruz, Oliver; Corum, Samuel; Crowley, Stephen; Demczuk, Gabriella; Drago, Alexander; Duggan, James; Edelman, Alexander; Gibson, Zachary; Gripas, Yuri; Gurbuz, Sait; Guzy, Carol; Hill, Robert; Hockstein, Evelyn; Hosefros, Paul; Jackson, Lawrence; Jones, Leah; Kahn, Gregory; Kahn, Nikki; Katopodis, Anastasios; Kennedy, Charles; Kennerly, David; Kirkpatrick, Thomas Jay; Kittner, Samuel; Kleponis, Christopher; Kruszewski, Eric; Lamkey, Jr., Rodney Arthur; Lane, Keith; LaVor, Martin; Lawidjaja, Rudy; Lynch, Mary; Lyttle, Melissa; Magana-oceja, Jose Luis; Mages, Evy; Makela, Mark; Malet, Jeffrey; Mallin, Jay; Marks, Donovan; Marovich, Peter; May, Cheriss; McCoy, Michael; Meyer, Cheryl; Mohammed, Eman; Moneymaker, Anna; Morigi, Paul; Nipp, Lisa; Nordby, Leslie; Owen, Clifford; Patterson, Kathryn; Peterson, Mark; Petros, Vasilios; Philippi, Joy; Plowman, William; Purcell, Steven; Riecken, Astrid; Roberts, Joshua; Rolfe, Judith; Ryan, Patrick; Samperio, Aurora; Savi, Riccardo; Schmidt, Roberto; Shelley, Allison; Shen, Ting; Shipman-Singleton, Paulette; Swall, Lexey; Thayer, Eric; Theiler, Michael; Tripplaar, Kristoffer; Usher, Christopher; Vick, Vanessa; Vogel, Leigh; Voisard, Amanda; Voss, Stephen; Watkins, Frederick; Whitehouse, Raymond; Wolf, Kevin; Wolf, Lloyd; Wroblewski, Alex.

WHITE HOUSE NEWS PHOTOGRAPHERS' ASSOCIATION

P.O. Box 7119, Ben Franklin Station, Washington, DC 20044–7119

https://whnpa.org

OFFICERS

Whitney Shefte, WTTG–TV, *President*
Jim Bourg, Reuters, *Vice President*
Jessica Koscielniak, McClatchy, *Secretary*
Jonathan Elswick, Associated Press, *Treasurer*

EXECUTIVE BOARD

Jonathan Ernst (Reuters)
Pablo Martinez Monsivais (Associated Press)
Carol Guzy (Freelance)
McKenna Ewen (CNN)
David Postovit (Hearst TV)
Whitney Leaming (The Washington Post)
Andrew Harnik, Contest Chair, Still (The Associated Press)
Pege Gilgannon, Contest Co-Chair, Broadcast (WJLA–TV) (retired)
Doug Wilkes, Contest Co-Chair, Broadcast (WTTG–TV)
Whitney Leaming, Contest Chair, Digital Storytelling (Freelance)
Al Drago, Contest Chair, Student (Freelance)
Bethany Swain, Contest Co-Chair, Student (University of Maryland)
Pablo Martinez Monsivais, Education Chair (Associated Press)

MEMBERS REPRESENTED

Abdallah, Khalil: CNN
Abraham, Mark: Freelance
Adlerblum, Robin: Freelance
Ake, J. David: Associated Press
Alamiri, Yasmeen: CGTN America
Albert, Christopher: CBS News, Freelance
Alberter, William Jr.: CNN
Allard, Marc: freelance
Allen, Tom: The Washington Post (retired)
Anderson, Kristina: AWPS News
Angerer, Drew: Getty Images
Applewhite, J. Scott: Associated Press
Apt Johnson, Roslyn: CBS News
Arcuri, Bronson: NPR
Ashley, Douglas: Suburban News Group & ABC TV
Assaf, Christopher: Academic
Auth, William: Freelance
Bahler, Barry: Images and News Creations
Barlow, Joshua: CGTN America
Barria, Carlos: Reuters
Barrick, Matthew: Freelance
Batten, Rodney: NBC News
Beattie, Sam: Freelance
Beiser, H. Darr: USA Today (retired)
Benic, Patrick: UPI
Bennett, Ronald T.: Executive Branch (retired)
Bennett, Donald: The Washington Post
Berkman, Eliezer (Elie): Freelance
Biddle, Susan: The Washington Post (retired)
Bing, Bonita: Freelance
Bivera, Johnny: Freelance
Boal, John: Freelance
Bodnar, John: CNN
Botsford, Jabin: The Washington Post
Bourg, James: Reuters
Bowe, Christy: ImageCatcher News
Brack, Dennis: Black Star
Brandon, Alex: Associated Press
Brantley, James R.: Freelance
Brehman, Caroline: CQ Roll Call
Brochstein, Michael: Freelance
Brown, Beth: WRC–TV
Brown, Stephen: Freelance
Brusk, Steven: CNN
Bryan, Beverly: (retired)

MEMBERS REPRESENTED—Continued

Buell, Hal: AP (retired)
Burgess, Robert: Freelance
Burke, Geoffrey: USA Today Sports
Burke, William C., Jr.: (retired)
Burnett, David: Contact Press Images
Butow, David: (retired)
Caballero-Reynolds, Andrew: AFP
Calvert, Mary: Washington Times
Cameron, Gary: Reuters News Pictures (retired)
Carioti, Ricky: The Washington Post
Carr, Robert: Getty Images
Carter, David: NBC4 WRC–TV
Cedeno, Ken: Freelance
Ceneta, Manuel: Associated Press
Chikwendiu, Jahi: The Washington Post
Chiu, Lisa: CGTN America
Chowdhury, Maureen: McClatchy
Chung, Andre: Freelance
Cirace, Robert: CNN (retired)
Clark, Bill: Roll Call
Cobb, Jodi: Freelance
Cohen, Marshall H.: Big Marsh News Photos
Cohen, Stuart: Freelance
Colburn, James: Freelance
Cole, Adam: NPR
Cole, Bryan: Fox News Channel
Collins, Maxine: BBC TV
Colvin, Rhonda: The Washington Post
Conger, Dean: (retired)
Conner, Eric: Fox News Network
Contreras, Oliver: Freelance
Cortez, Julio: The Associated Press
Costello, Thomas, II: Asbury Park Press
Courtney, Eric: CGTN America
Criswell, Daniel, Jr.: CGTN America
Daugherty, Bob: Associated Press (retired)
Demark, Michael: Fox News Channel
Demczuk, Gabriella: Freelance
Devorah, Carrie: Freelance (retired)
Diaz Meyer, Cheryl: Freelance
DiBartolo, Melissa: Nikon
Dietsch, Kevin: UPI
Doane, Martin: WJLA–TV
Douliery, Oliver: Abaca Press
Downing, Larry: Reuters (retired)
Drago, Al: Roll Call
Drapkin, Arnold: TIME Magazine
Du, Yubin: CGTN America
Dukehart, Thomas, Jr.: WUSA–TV (retired)
Dunmire, John: WTTG–TV (retired)
Eaves, Ed: NBC News
Edelman, Alex: Freelance
Edmonds, Ron: Associated Press
Edrington, Michael: DMIOC (retired)
Elswick, Jonathan: Associated Press
Epstein, Linda: IIPP, Department of State
Ernst, Jonathan: Reuters
Ewen, McKenna: The Washington Post
Farmer, Sharon: Freelance
Fertig, Natalie: McClatchy
Fine, Paul: Fine Films
Fine, Holly: Fine Films
Folwell, Frank: Freelance
Ford, Nancy: IFPO / American International News
Forrest, James: WRC (retired)
Forte, BJ: NBC4 WRC–TV
Foss, Philip: Speed Graphic
Foster, William: Freelance
Frame, John: WTTG–TV
Frame, Kara: NPR
Frey, Katherine: The Washington Post
Fridrich, George: Brighter Images Productions LLC
Friedman, David: Portable Productions
Gail, Mark: Freelance
Galdabini, Christian: Fox News Network
Geissinger, Michael: Freelance
Gentilo, Richard: Associated Press
Georges, Salwan: The Washington Post
Gerberg, Jon: The Washington Post
Gilgannon, Pege: WJLA (retired)
Gillis, Elizabeth: NPR
Goldman, Judy-Anne: (retired)
Goldman, Mark: Goldmine Photos
Goodman, Jeffrey: NBC / Freelance
Gorman, James: Associated Press
Goyal, Raghubir: Asia Today & India Globe / ATN News
Grace, Arthur: Freelance
Greenblatt, William: UPI
Griggs, Kendall: WJLA–TV
Grile, Sarah: Mesa7Media
Gripas, Yuri: Reuters
Grudovich, Daniel: WTTG–TV
Guzy, Carol: Freelance
Haefeli, Brian: ABC
Halstead, Dirck: The Digital Journalist
Happe, Mackenzie: CNN
Harbage, Claire: NPR
Harlan, Rebecca: NPR
Harley, Tonia: Freelance
Harnik, Andrew: The Associated Press
Harrer, Andrew: Bloomberg
Harrington, John: Freelance
Harrity, Chick: Whimsy Works
Heilemann, Tami: Department of Interior
Hillian, Vanessa: The Washington Post (retired)
Hopkins, Brian: WJLA–TV
Horan, Michael: WTTG–TV
Huff, Daniel: Associated Press
Ing, Lance: WTTG–TV
Ingalls, Bill: NASA e Management
Jette, Patricia: Freelance
Johnson, Kenneth: ABC–TV
Johnston, Frank: The Washington Post
Jones, Donnamarie: DCTV

MEMBERS REPRESENTED—Continued

Jones, Nelson: WTTG–TV
Joplin, Ashleigh: The Washington Post
Judge, Michel: NBC News / Comcast
Kahn, Nikki: Independent Photographer
Kanicka, Stephen: Fox News Network
Kapustin, Doug: Freelance
Kaster, Carolyn: Associated Press
Katopodis, Anastasios: Freelance
Katz, Marty: Chesapeake News Service
Kellman, Ryan: NPR
Kennerly, David Hume: Eagles Roar Inc.
Kessler, Calla: Freelance
Kirkpatrick, TJ : Freelance
Kittner, Sam: Freelance
Koppelman, Mitch: Reuters Television
Koscielniak, Jessica: McClatchy
Kossoff-Nordby, Leslie: LK Photos
Lamarque, Kevin: Reuters
Lamkey, Rod, Jr.: Freelance
Lanham, Yuko: The Asahi Shimbun
Larsen, Gregory: Freelance
Lavies, Bianca: Freelance
LaVor, Marty: Freelance
Lawrence, Jeffrey: Freelance
Leaming, Whitney: The Washington Post
Lee, Joyce: The Washington Post
Lenihan, Niall: Australian Broadcasting Corp.
Lesser, Erik: European Pressphoto Agency
Levine, Lewis: Costal News Service
Li, Alice: The Washington Post
Lo Scalzo, James: EPA
Loeb, Saul: AFP
Love, Diane: Tribal Cultures Productions
Lowman, Wayne: Fox News Channel
Luna, Nathan: ABC News
Lynaugh, Mike: Freelance
Lynch, Patricia: Freelance
Lyons, Paul: NET (retired)
MacDonald, Charles: C Mac Fido Productions
Magana, Jose Luis: Freelance / AP
Mager, Dickon: Sky News
Mahaskey, Michael Scott: Politico
Mallin, Jay: Freelance
Mara, Melina: The Washington Post
Marovich, Peter, Jr.: Freelance / Corbis
Martin, Ben: ITN
Martin, Gina: National Geographic
Martin, Jacquelyn: AP
Martinez Monsivais, Pablo: Associated Press
Mason, Thomas: WTTG–TV (retired)
May, Cheriss: Noemay Media Group
Mazariegos, Mark: CBS News
Maze, Stephanie: Moonstone Press LLC
Mazer Field, Joni: Freelance
Mazzatenta, O. Louis: Freelance
McCarthy, Edward, III: Hudson Valley Black Press (retired)
McCarty, Dennis Page: CBS News
McClain, Matthew: The Washington Post
McDermott, Richard: NBC
McDonnell, John: The Washington Post
McGreevy, Allen: Freelance
McKiernan, Scott: Zuma Press
McKinless, Thomas: CQ Roll Call
McNamee, Win: Getty Images
McNay, James: Senior editor Kobre guide (retired)
Mees, John: CTV
Michael, Nicholas: NPR
Millis, Leah: Reuters
Mills, Doug: New York Times
Mohammed, Eman: Freelance
Mole, Robert: NBC (retired)
Moorhead, Jeremy: CNN
Morones, Michael: The Free Lance Star
Morris, Larry: The Washington Post (retired)
Morris, Peter: CNN
Murphy, Richard: CGTN America
Murphy, Zoeann: The Washington Post
Murtaugh, Peter: Murtaugh Productions, LLC
Natoli, Sharon: freelance
Newton, Jonathan: The Washington Post
Nguyen, Phi: US House of Representatives
Nighswander, Marcia: Ohio University
Nikpour, Javad: Metropole Photo
Norling, Richard: Freelance
O'Connor, Erix: The Washington Post
O'Leary, William: The Washington Post
O'Molloy, Colm: Freelance / BBC
Orenstein, Jayne Winsten: The Washington Post
Palu, Louie: Zuma Press
Panzer, Chester: NBC–WRC
Parcell, James: The Washington Post (retired)
Partlow, Wayne: Associated Press
Peterson, Brittany: McClatchy
Petrilli, Daniel: Fox News Channel
Petros, Bill: Freelance
Pinczuk, Murray: Freelance
Pinczuk, Samuel: Student
Plowman, William: Freelance
Polich, John: (retired)
Pope, Kolin: The Washington Post
Popper, Andrew: Business Week
Postovit, David: Hearst Television WNB
Powell, Lee: The Washington Post
Ratner, Moriah: Student
Ribas, Jorge Luis: The Washington Post
Ribeiro, Luiz: Freelance
Richardson, Charlotte: Freelance
Riecken, Astrid: Freelance
Riley, Molly: Freelance
Rizzo, Meredith: NPR
Roberts, Joshua: Freelance
Robinson, Clyde, Sr.: (retired)
Roth, Johnie, Jr.: NBC (retired)
Rothschild, Anna: The Washington Post

MEMBERS REPRESENTED—Continued

Russek, Ronald, II: UPI
Ruwe, Renee Lyn: Hudson Valley News & Entertainment
Sachs, Ronald: Consolidated News Photos
Sandys, Toni: The Washington Post
Sardari, Kaveh: Sardari Group, Inc.
Savage, Craig: FOX News Channel
Schaff, Erin: Freelance
Schneider, Jack: NBC–TV (retired)
Semansky, Patrick: Associated Press
Sharp, Duncan: SKY News
Shefte, Whitney: The Washington Post
Shelley, Allison: Freelance
Shepherd, Ray: Defense Media Activity
Sheras, Michael: Canon USA, Inc. (retired)
Shlemon, Christopher: Independent TV News
Sierra, Joann: CNN
Sikes, Laura: Laura Sikes Photography
Silbiger, Sarah: Freelance
Silverberg, James: The Intellectual Property Group, PLLC
Skeans, Ronald, Jr.: BBC
Smialowski, Brendan: Freelance
Smith, Andrew: CGTN America
Smith, Jason: WTTG–TV
Smith, Patrick: Getty Images
Smyth, Christopher: Hearst
Somodevilla, Kenneth: Getty Images
Spodak, Cassandra: CNN
Stein, Norman: (retired)
Stewart, Charles, Jr.: Hudson Valley Press
Stoddard, Mark: Freelance
Stolz, Peter: CGTN America
Stonington, Joel: AJ+
Strasser, Franz: BBC News
Suban, Mark: Freelance
Sun, Xiaolu: CGTN America
Swain, Bethany Anne: Educator
Swenson, Gordon: ABC (retired)
Sykes, Jack: Harris Corp.
Taherimoghaddam, Kamran: CGTN America
Taylor, Daron: The Washington Post
Thomas, Margaret: (retired), Washington Post
Thorp, Frank, V: NBC News
Tolbert, George Dalton, IV: Freelance / U.S. Senate (retired)
Trippett, Robert: Freelance (retired)
Uhl, Kim: CNN
Usher, Chris: Freelance
Valeri, Charlene: National Geographic
van Duyne, Marty: Freelance
Van Houten, Carolyn: The Washington Post
Viers, Meta: McClatchy
Vineys, Kevin: Associated Press
Voisard, Amanda: Freelance
Voisin, Sarah: The Washington Post
Voss, Stephen: Freelance
Vucci, Evan: Associated Press
Vurnis, Ambrose: NBC News / WRC–TV
Walker, Diana: Freelance
Wallace, Elliott: CGTN America
Wallace, Jim: Smithsonian Institution (retired)
Walsh, Susan: Associated Press
Watkins, Duane: Media Links CCTV
Watrud, Donald: WTTG–TV
Watson, James: AFP
Wells, Jonathan: SIPA Press
Werbeck, Nicole: NPR
Whitehouse, Ray: Freelance
Wilkes, Douglas: WTTG–TV
Williams, Milton: Freelance (retired)
Williams, Robert: NABET 31
Williams, Thomas: Roll Call Newspaper
Williams Babic, Indira: Newseum
Wilson, Mark: Getty Images
Wong, Alex: Getty Images
Woolfolk, Daniel: Sightline Media Group
Wuls, Jakub: CGTN America
Young, Jim: Reuters
Zervos, Stratis: Freelance–Zervos Video Productions, LLC

RADIO AND TELEVISION CORRESPONDENTS' GALLERIES*

SENATE RADIO AND TELEVISION GALLERY

The Capitol, Room S–325, phone 224–6421

Director.—Michael J. Mastrian.
Deputy Director.—Ellen Eckert.
Senior Media Coordinators: Michael Lawrence, Erin Yeatman.
Media Coordinators: Charles Moxley, Tamara Robinson.

HOUSE RADIO AND TELEVISION GALLERY

The Capitol, Room H–320, phone 225–5214

Director.—Olga Ramirez Kornacki.
Deputy Director.—Andy Elias.
Senior Media Logistics Coordinator.—Kim Oates.
Media Logistics Coordinators: Ryan Dahl, Kinsey Harvey, Makenna Sievertson.

EXECUTIVE COMMITTEE OF THE RADIO AND TELEVISION CORRESPONDENTS' GALLERIES

Jason Donner, Fox News, *Chair*
Greta Brawner, C–SPAN, *Vice Chair*
Jared Halpern, Fox News Radio, *Treasurer*
Paul Courson, Sinclair Broadcasting
Ben Siegel, ABC News
Kelsey Snell, NPR

RULES GOVERNING RADIO AND TELEVISION CORRESPONDENTS' GALLERIES

1. Persons desiring admission to the Radio and Television Galleries of Congress shall make application to the Speaker, as required by Rule 34 of the House of Representatives, as amended, and to the Committee on Rules and Administration of the Senate, as required by Rule 33, as amended, for the regulation of the Senate wing of the Capitol. Applicants shall state in writing the names of all radio stations, television stations, systems, or newsgathering organizations by which they are employed and what other occupation or employment they may have, if any. Applicants shall further declare that they are not engaged in the prosecution of claims or the promotion of legislation pending before Congress, the Departments, or the independent agencies, and that they will not become so employed without resigning from the Galleries. They shall further declare that they are not employed in any legislative or executive department or independent agency of the Government, or by any foreign government or representative thereof; that they are not engaged in any lobbying activities; that they do not and will not, directly or indirectly, furnish special information

*Information is based on data furnished and edited by each respective Gallery.

to any organization, individual, or group of individuals for the influencing of prices on any commodity or stock exchange; that they will not do so during the time they retain membership in the Galleries. Holders of visitors' cards who may be allowed temporary admission to the Galleries must conform to all the restrictions of this paragraph.

2. It shall be a prerequisite to membership that the radio station, television station, system, or news-gathering agency which the applicant represents shall certify in writing to the Radio and Television Correspondents' Galleries that the applicant conforms to the foregoing regulations.

3. The applications required by the above rule shall be authenticated in a manner that shall be satisfactory to the Executive Committee of the Radio and Television Correspondents' Galleries who shall see that the occupation of the Galleries is confined to bona fide news gatherers and/or reporters of reputable standing in their business who represent radio stations, television stations, systems, or news-gathering agencies engaged primarily in serving radio stations, television stations, or systems. It shall be the duty of the Executive Committee of the Radio and Television Correspondents' Galleries to report, at its discretion, violation of the privileges of the Galleries to the Speaker or to the Senate Committee on Rules and Administration, and pending action thereon, the offending individual may be suspended.

4. Persons engaged in other occupations, whose chief attention is not given to—or more than one-half of their earned income is not derived from—the gathering or reporting of news for radio stations, television stations, systems, or news-gathering agencies primarily serving radio stations or systems, shall not be entitled to admission to the Radio and Television Galleries. The Radio and Television Correspondents' List in the Congressional Directory shall be a list only of persons whose chief attention is given to or more than one-half of their earned income is derived from the gathering and reporting of news for radio stations, television stations, and systems engaged in the daily dissemination of news, and of representatives of news-gathering agencies engaged in the daily service of news to such radio stations, television stations, or systems.

5. Members of the families of correspondents are not entitled to the privileges of the Galleries.

6. The Radio and Television Galleries shall be under the control of the Executive Committee of the Radio and Television Correspondents' Galleries, subject to the approval and supervision of the Speaker of the House of Representatives and the Senate Committee on Rules and Administration.

Approved.

NANCY PELOSI,
Speaker, House of Representatives.

ROY BLUNT,
Chair, Senate Committee on Rules and Administration.

MEMBERS ENTITLED TO ADMISSION

RADIO AND TELEVISION CORRESPONDENTS' GALLERIES

Aaron, John: WTOP Radio
Abamu, Jenny: WAMU
Abarca, Gonzalo: Voice of America
Abbott, Stacey: National Public Radio
Abdalla, Hebah: German TV (ZDF)
Abdallah, Khalil: CNN
Abdalwahab, Yamen: TRT World
Abdi, Mona: ABC News
Abdu, Grace: Voice of America
Abdul-Mateen, Yasin: Fox News
Abdulrazzaq, Ahmed: Al Jazeera International
Abe, Takaaki: Nippon TV Network
Abed, Morad: Al Jazeera International
Abeshouse, Robert: Al Jazeera English
Abo-Issa, Abdul Hadi: Al Jazeera English
Abowd, Paul: Al Jazeera English
Abrahams, Natalia: NBC News
Abrams, Chanel: CBN News
Abtar, Rana: AP–Broadcast
Abu Diab, Naser: AP–Broadcast
Abu-Kwaik, Biesan: Al Jazeera International
Aburahma, Eyad: Al Jazeera International
Acevedo, Enrique: Univision
Acevedo, Juan: WFDC–TV Univision
Acosta, Abilo: CNN
Adamjee, Zohreen: ABC News
Adams, Angelyn: Al Arabiya TV
Adams, Douglas: NBC News
Adams, Lori: Fox News
Adeboyejo, Oluwatomike: NBC News
Adkins, Lenore: Al Arabiya TV
Adkinson, Nicholas: ABC News
Adlerblum, Robin: NBC News
Adly, Jill: CNN
Adragna, Richard: Fox News
Adrian, Yaridis: Caracol Radio
Adridge, Dawin: Morningside Partners, LLC
Advani, Reena: National Public Radio
Agnew, Robert: SRN News (Salem)
Agobian, Faiez: AP–Broadcast
Agobian Villegas, Jorge: Voice of America
Agredo Vasquez, Jose: Caracol Television
Ahmed, Ali: Middle East Broadcasting Networks (MBN)
Ahmed, Amir: CNN
Ahmed, Aziz: AP–Broadcast
Ahmed, Faiza: TRT World
Ahmed, Lukman: BBC
Ahn, Soyoung: Voice of America
Ahn, Joo Sik: Korean Broadcasting Systems
Aiello, Augustine: National Public Radio
Aigner-Treworgy, Adam: CBS News
Ainsley, Julia: NBC News
Ajaka, Nadine: Washingtonpost.com
Ake, Gabrielle: CBS News
Akey, Zackary: CBS News
Akhoun, Laura: Agence France Presse (AFP–TV)
Akhtar, Monica: Washingtonpost.com
Akiyama, Rihoko: TV Tokyo
Akkad, Reem: Washingtonpost.com
Aklilu, Simret: CNN
Akman-Duffy, Timur: National Public Radio
Alami, Mohammed: Al Jazeera International
Alarian, Laila: Al Jazeera English
Alazawi, Mohammed: Al Arabiya TV
Alba, Carmen: NBC News
Albano, Thomas: CBS News
Albert, Christopher: CBS News
Albert, Mark: Hearst Television Inc.
Alberter, William: CNN
Albright, Mary: Washingtonpost.com
Alcindor, Yamiche: PBS NewsHour
Aldag, Jason: Washingtonpost.com
Alderman, Carol: Washingtonpost.com
Alegret, Gustau: NTN24
Alesse, Elizabeth: ABC News
Alexander, Clinton: CBS News
Alexander, Kenneth: C–SPAN
Alexander, Peter: NBC News
Alexander, Robert: WTTG–Fox Television
Alexander, Sophie: Independent Television News (ITN)
Alfarone, Debra: CBS News
Alff, Emily: CBS News
Alfin Johnson, Emily: WAMU
Alhafiz, Samer: Al Jazeera International
Alhazeem, Ahmed: Al Jazeera International
Al Hmoud, Mounira: I24 News
Ali, Amber: CBS News
Ali, Ammar: National Public Radio
Ali, Mohammad: WETA
Ali, Omar: Sky News Arabia
Aliakbar, Nihad: Fox News
Aliakbar, Nihad: Middle East Broadcasting Networks (MBN)
Aljasheme, Mohaimen: Sky News Arabia
Al Juboori, Haitham: Al Jazeera International
Alkadiri, Faisal: ABC News
Al Khirsan, Fatima: Vice News
Al-Lami, Ziadoon: Berkeley Studios International
Allard, Fanny: France 24
Allard, John: ABC News

MEMBERS ENTITLED TO ADMISSION—Continued

Allbritton, David: CNN
Alldredge, Thomas: C–SPAN
Allen, Abigail: CBN News
Allen, Brian: Voice of America
Allen, Christopher: Voice of America
Allen, Ciara: Now This News
Allen, Darrell: Voice of America
Allen, Jonathan: NBC News
Allen, Lisa: Gray Television
Allen, Vadim: Voice of America
Allman, Bryan: Fox News
Allman, Mark: CNN
Allman, Robert: CBN News
Allmond, Scott: ABC News
Alqarni, Ahmed: AP–Broadcast
Alrajjal, Tala: CNN
Alrawi, Khaldoun: AP–Broadcast
Al Rawi, Khalid: Al Arabiya TV
Alshaer, Sohail: Sky News Arabia
Alston, Leslie: Deutsche Welle TV
Alva, Mitchell: ABC News
Alvarenga, Adan: Agence France Presse (AFP–TV)
Alvarenga, Daniel: Al Jazeera International
Alvarez, Alayna: Stateline
Alvarez, Alejandro: News2Share
Alvarez-Ibarra, Angelica: Sinclair Broadcast Group
Alvey, Jay: WRC–TV / NBC–4
Aly, Noureldin: Feature Story News
Amaya, Miguel: Voice of America
Ambriz-Mendez, Elizabeth: CNN
Ament, Jennifer: Politico.com
Amin, Ahmad: CBS News
Amirault-Michel, Theresa: C–SPAN
Ammerman, Stuart: CBS News
Amon, Whitney: CNN
Amon, Whitney: WUSA–TV
Amos, George: WJLA–TV / Newschannel 8
Anastasi, Patrick: CNBC
Anderson, Alice: Feature Story News
Anderson, Kimberly: Fox News
Anderson, Patrick: Swiss Broadcasting
Andree, Eric: AP–Broadcast
Andress, Jeannie: AP–Broadcast
Aneiva, Roberto: NBC News
Angeline, Jillian: Gray Television
Angeloni, Benjamin: Al Jazeera International
Anglim, John: CNN
Anopchenko, Dmytro: Inter TV
Ansell, Anna: Fox News
Anthony, Tony: Morningside Partners, LLC
Antoun, Charbel: Middle East Broadcasting Networks (MBN)
Anwar, Sohail: National Public Radio
Anyse, Alana: CBS News
Anzur, Matthew: Scripps News
Ao, Siqiao: Voice of America
Applegate, Van: WTTG–Fox Television
Arabasadi, Arash: Voice of America
Arai, Masaki: NHK
Aral, Drew: NHK
Arbogast, Vincent: Fox News
Ardono, Herdiyanto: Voice of America
Arena, Bruno: AP–Broadcast
Arenas, William: The Real News Network
Arensberg, Chloe: NBC News
Argueta Colina, Alvaro: Hispanic Communications Network
Argyri, Eleni: Hellenic Public TV
Aridi, Sal: NBC News
Arke, Raymond: CNN
Arkhipov, Viacheslav: Channel One Russian TV
Armstrong, Patricia: NBC News
Armstrong, Thomas: ABC News
Arnholz, John: ABC News
Arnold, Jessica: WUSA–TV
Arnold, Noah: One America
Arnum, Gerard: FedNet
Aronson, David: NBC News
Aronson, Victoria: PBS NewsHour
Arrieta, Rolando: National Public Radio
Arroyo, Raymond: EWTN
Arroyo Valles, Lorena: Univision
Art, Jeremiah: C–SPAN
Arter, Melanie: Cnsnews.com
Artesona, Eva: BBC
Arthur-Asmah, Ama: WTTG–Fox Television
Aryankalavil, Babu: Middle East Broadcasting Networks (MBN)
Arzoumanov, Abigail: CNN
Asaad, Ahmad: Al Jazeera International
Asberg, Stefan: Swedish Broadcasting
Ash, Audrey: CNN
Asmael, Hussein: Berkeley Studios International
Atalaya, Amandine: TF1–French TV
Atchison, Tyler: One America
Atkins, Chloe: NBC News
Atkins, Kimberly: WBUR
Attkisson, Sharyl: Sinclair Broadcast Group
Atwood, Kylie: CNN
Augenstein, Neal: WTOP Radio
Aulenkamp, Jan: German TV (ARD)
Ault, Trevor: ABC News
Auresto, John: AP–Broadcast
Austermuhle, Martin: WAMU
Austin, Alana: Gray Television
Austin, Gail: National Public Radio
Austin, Jason: Fox News Radio
Austin, Jonathan: CTV Canadian TV
Austin, Kenneth: NBC News
Austin, Tiane: CNN
Avner, Philip: AP–Broadcast
Avrutine, Matthew: CNN
Awada, Adam: Sky News Arabia
Ayala, Jorge: Telesur
Ayats, Guillem: TV3–Televisio de Catalunya
Ayaz, Faruk: TRT

MEMBERS ENTITLED TO ADMISSION—Continued

Ayhan, Sally: TRT World
Ayoub, Betty: Voice of America
Azais, Jean-Pascal: Swiss Broadcasting
Aziz, Khawar: Fox News
Baber, Qazafi: Voice of America
Baca, Nathan: WUSA–TV
Bacallao, Alexandra: NBC News
Bagnall, Thomas: Voice of America
Baharaeen, Renee: CNN
Baier, William: Fox News
Bailey, Blayne: NBC Newschannel
Bailey, Jordan: NBC News
Bailor, Michelle: C–SPAN
Bainer, Rebecca: Hearst Television Inc.
Baker, Elizabeth: National Public Radio
Baker, Leslie: Fox News
Baker, Sarah: NBC News
Balderas Iglesias, Veronica: Voice of America
Baldwin, Travis Renee: ABC News
Baldwin III, Robert: National Public Radio
Balinovic, Daniel: Reuters Radio & TV
Ball, George: WJLA–TV / Newschannel 8
Ball, Krystal: The Hill
Ballard, Hitomi: NHK
Ballou, Jeff: Al Jazeera English
Balot, Andrew: Spectrum News
Baltimore, Dennis: Middle East Broadcasting Networks (MBN)
Banks, Joshua: Fox News
Banks, Laquasha: CBS News
Banks, Mark: ABC News
Banks, Morris: CBS News
Bannigan, Michael: Fox Business Network
Bannister, Craig: Cnsnews.com
Baragona, Steve: Voice of America
Baratta, Christine: Bloomberg Radio & TV
Barber, Ellison: Fox News
Barber, Timothy: WJLA–TV / Newschannel 8
Barghouty, Phoebe: Al Jazeera International
Barillas, Mariana: Sinclair Broadcast Group
Barker, Edward: AP–Broadcast
Barker, Timothy: Vice News
Barker-Singh, Serena: Independent Television News (ITN)
Barnard, Robert: WTTG–Fox Television
Barnes, Daniel: NBC News
Barnes, David: CTV–Community TV of PG County
Barnett, Errol: CBS News
Barondess, Rose: NBC News
Barr, Alice: NBC Newschannel
Barr, Bryan: Sinclair Broadcast Group
Barr, Luke: ABC News
Barrett, Barbara: Stateline
Barrett, Calvin: Fox News
Barrett, Edward: CNN
Barringer, Reginald: CBS News
Barros, Aline: Voice of America
Barss, Kyle: Washingtonpost.com
Barthel, Margaret: WAMU
Bartiromo, Maria: Fox Business Network
Bartlam, Tyler: C–SPAN
Barua, Satarupa: Voice of America
Basch, Michelle: WTOP Radio
Bash, Dana: CNN
Bash, David: WETA
Basinger, Stuart: Fox News
Baskin, Morgan: Vice News
Bates, Jeffrey: WETA
Batten, Rodney: NBC News
Battistella, Marilisa: CBS News
Bauer, Matthew: NBC News
Baumel, Susan: Voyage Productions
Baumel-Lamonica, Ely: Voyage Productions
Bautista, Mark: CBN News
Bautista, Veronica: CNN
Baynard, Robert: Now This News
Bays, James: Al Jazeera English
Beahn, James: WTTG–Fox Television
Beal, Robin: Fox News
Bearne, Adam: Eurovision Americas, Inc.
Beattie, Sam: BBC
Beck, Tomoko: Nippon TV Network
Becker, Bruce: Fox Business Network
Becker, Christopher: Fox News
Becker, Farrel: CBS News
Becker, Frank: WJLA–TV / Newschannel 8
Beckett, Paul: Wall Street Journal
Beckner, Steven: National Public Radio
Beesch, Courtney: C–SPAN
Behnam, Babak: Vice News
Behnke, Camille: NBC News
Behrmann, Savannah: CNN
Beigarten, Stacey: C–SPAN
Bejarano, Mark: National Public Radio
Belanger, Jean-Francois: CBC (Canadian Broadcasting Corporation)
Belgraver, Jet: Al Jazeera English
Belha, Nickouszha: Small House Productions
Belhadj, Salima: Agence France Presse (AFP–TV)
Bell, Bradley: WJLA–TV / Newschannel 8
Bell, Kennedey: ABC News
Belton, Jasmine: NBC News
Belton, Jordan: NBC News
Bena, John: Diversified Communications, Inc. (DCI)
Bendeck, Michael: Al Jazeera International
Bender, Jason: C–SPAN
Benetato, Michael: NBC News
Benezra, Shani: CBS News
Benincasa, Robert: National Public Radio
Bennett, Abbie: Connecting Vets
Bennett, Dalton: Washingtonpost.com
Bennett, Geoffrey: NBC News
Bennett, Justin: NBC News
Bennett, Kate: CNN
Bennett, Shepard: SRN News (Salem)
Bennewitz, Alexa: CNN

MEMBERS ENTITLED TO ADMISSION—Continued

Bensen, Jackie: WRC–TV / NBC–4
Benson, James: CBS News
Bentwila, Kalyl: Middle East Broadcasting Networks (MBN)
Bentz, Leslie: CNN
Berdiel, Daniel: Sirius XM Satellite Radio
Berg, Rebecca: CNN
Bergal, Jenni: Stateline
Berger, Catherine: Al Jazeera English
Berger, Judson: Fox News
Berger Fox, Deborah: CNN
Bergfeldt, Barbro Carina: Swedish Broadcasting
Berman, Daniel: CNN
Bernal, Maria: CNN
Bernardini, Laura: CNN
Bernice, Emily: National Public Radio
Bernknopf, David: Sinclair Broadcast Group
Bernstein, Howard: WUSA–TV
Bernstein, Leandra: Sinclair Broadcast Group
Berrai, Hanane: Al Jazeera International
Berry, Christopher: National Public Radio
Betsill, Brett: C–SPAN
Bevington, Ben: BBC
Bey, Maher: Middle East Broadcasting Networks (MBN)
Beyer, Kenneth: GPI TV
Beyer, William: WTTG–Fox Television
Bharania, Anoopam: Reuters Radio & TV
Bhatti, Ahad: Al Jazeera English
Bica Vieira Guerreiro, Ricardo: RTP Portuguese Public Television
Bidar, Musadiq: CBS News
Biddle, Kristina: Fox News
Biello, Mark: CNN
Bikkers, Remco: Dutch TV & Radio (NOS)
Billings, Ashley: CNN
Bills, Lindzie: CNN
Bintrim, Tim: WETA
Bird, Lauren: WTTG–Fox Television
Bishop, Benjamin: Vice News
Biskupic, Joan: CNN
Black, Phillip: ABC News
Blackman, Jay: NBC News
Blackman, John: NBC News
Blackwill, Sarah: NBC News
Blaine, Adrienne: Al Jazeera International
Blair, Adam: Independent Television News (ITN)
Blakey, Leona: C–SPAN
Blakley, Kevin: CNN
Blanchard, David: National Public Radio
Blanchard, Lauren: Fox News
Blanco, Hugo: AP–Broadcast
Bleiker, Carla: Deutsche Welle TV
Blitzer, Wolf: CNN
Block, Eliana: WUSA–TV
Block, Melissa: National Public Radio
Bloom, Daniel: Scripps News
Blooston, Victoria: NBC News
Blum-Dostie, Jacqueline: AP–Broadcast
Boag, Keith: CBC (Canadian Broadcasting Corporation)
Boazman, Simon: Al Jazeera English
Bobadilla-Marino, Anna: CBS News
Boccagno, Julia: CBS News
Bodlander, Gerald: Westwood One
Bodnar, John: CNN
Boesche, Jan: German Public Radio (ARD)
Bogan, Raymond: Fox News
Boglind, Kajsa: Swedish Broadcasting
Bohannon, Joseph: NBC News
Bohn, Kevin: CNN
Bolden, Bailey: Bloomberg Radio & TV
Bolf, Daniele: WPLG–TV10
Bolling, Eric: Sinclair Broadcast Group
Bond, Larry: Voice of America
Bonewald, Jason: Fox News Radio
Boney, Stephen: Imagination Media
Bonin, Richard: CBS News
Booker, Brakkton: National Public Radio
Booker, Cory: NBC News
Borak, Donna: CNN
Borger, Gloria: CNN
Borland, Karen: Fox News
Bos, Emiliano: Swiss Broadcasting
Bost, Mark: WUSA–TV
Boston, Tyrone: CNN
Boughton, Bryan: Fox News
Bourar, Hicham: Middle East Broadcasting Networks (MBN)
Bourogaa, Lamia: Al Jazeera International
Bouvier-Auclair, Raphael: CBC (Canadian Broadcasting Corporation)
Bowen, Timothy: WETA
Bowman, Michael: Voice of America
Boyd, Patrick: National Public Radio
Boyd, Sophia: National Public Radio
Boyle, Molly: EWTN
Bozek, Walter: CBN News
Bradford, Janece: NBC News
Bradner, Eric: CNN
Brady, Marianna: BBC
Bragale, Charles: WRC–TV / NBC–4
Brain, Jonathan: TRT World
Branch, Natasha: National Public Radio
Brand, Katrin: German Public Radio (ARD)
Brand, Natalie: CBS News
Brandkamp, Jonathan: Voice of America
Brandus, Paul: West Wing Reports
Brangham, William: PBS NewsHour
Brannon, Timothy: Voice of America
Bransford, Neill: Fox News
Brantley-Jones, Kiara: CNN
Brashear, Graelyn: Al Jazeera International
Braun, Joshua: CNN
Brawner, Donald: WETA
Brawner, Greta: C–SPAN

MEMBERS ENTITLED TO ADMISSION—Continued

Bream, Shannon: Fox News
Breiterman, Charles: ABC News
Brennan, Margaret: CBS News
Bretschneider, John: Sightline Media Group
Breuner, Bonnie: One America
Breuninger, Kevin: CNBC
Brewer, Carl: Spectrum News
Brewer, Georgina: Independent Television News (ITN)
Brewster, Adam: CBS News
Brickhouse, Ayana: Al Jazeera English
Brieger, Annette: German TV (ZDF)
Bright, Whitney: CBS News
Britch, Raymond: CNN
Brock, Robert: Reuters Radio & TV
Broder, Noah: CNN
Brody, David: CBN News
Broffman, Craig: AP–Broadcast
Broleman, Michael: NBC Newschannel
Bronstein, Scott: CNN
Bronston, Sally: NBC News
Brooke, Sarah: NBC News
Brooks, David: CNN
Brooks, Kurt: WUSA–TV
Broom, William: WUSA–TV
Browder, Jenna: CBN News
Brower, Brooke: CNN
Brown, Ashley: National Public Radio
Brown, Beth: WRC–TV / NBC–4
Brown, Donald: C–SPAN
Brown, Elizabeth: ABC News
Brown, Elizabeth: Al Jazeera English
Brown, Erica: CBS News
Brown, James: ABC News
Brown, Kenneth: Verizon
Brown, Kimberly: CBS News
Brown, Kristin: Fox News
Brown, Lauretta: EWTN
Brown, Malcolm: Feature Story News
Brown, Paul: C–SPAN
Brown, Tracy: AP–Broadcast
Brown, Zachary: Washingtonpost.com
Browne, Ryan: CNN
Browning, Robert: C–SPAN
Bruce, Mary: ABC News
Bruce, Susan: EWTN
Bruggeman, Lucien: ABC News
Brumfiel, Geoffrey: National Public Radio
Bruns, David: Washingtonpost.com
Brusk, Steven: CNN
Brust, Amelia: Federal News Radio 1500 AM
Bryan, Ellen: WUSA–TV
Bryant, Aubrey: WUSA–TV
Bryant, Nicholas: BBC
Bua, Jon-Christopher: Talk Media News
Buble, Courtney: NBC News
Buchholz, Jenny: Fox News
Buck, Kenneth: C–SPAN
Buckenmaier, Claudia: German TV (ARD)
Buckhorn, Burke: CNN
Buckler, Christopher: BBC
Buckley, Daniel: WRC–TV / NBC–4
Buddenhagen, Kristina: C–SPAN
Buenten, Verena: German TV (ARD)
Bugash, Eric: GPI TV
Bullard, John: ABC News
Bullard Harmon, Susan: CBS News
Bullock, Peter: Reuters Radio & TV
Bullock, Tiffany: CNN
Bun, Agnes: Agence France Presse (AFP–TV)
Bundock, Susan: C–SPAN
Bundy, Austen: CNN
Bunson, Matthew: EWTN
Burdick, Leslie: C–SPAN
Burgard, Jan Philipp: German TV (ARD)
Burger, Todd: EWTN
Burgess, David: CNN
Burk, Penny: NBC News
Burke, Kathleen: EWTN
Burke, Michael: Voice of America
Burkett-Hall, Jesse: WUSA–TV
Burkett-Hall, Lorenzo: WUSA–TV
Burles, Jason: CBC (Canadian Broadcasting Corporation)
Burlij, Terence: CNN
Burman, Blake: Fox Business Network
Burns, Mary: Cox Broadcasting
Burton, Matthew: ABC News
Bush, Daniel: PBS NewsHour
Butler, James: Diversified Communications, Inc. (DCI)
Butler, Norman: NBC News
Buttler, Martina: German Public Radio (ARD)
Butts, Keshia: CTV–Community TV of PG County
Byers, Jennifer: Al Jazeera International
Byrd, Crystal: Al Jazeera English
Byrd, Haley: CNN
Byrnes, Dennis: National Public Radio
Cabral Pichardo, Juan: CNN
Cadigan, William: CNN
Cahill, Kathy: C–SPAN
Caifa, Karin: CNN
Cala, Ivonne: National Public Radio
Calcaterra, James: Blaze Media
Caldwell, Leigh Ann: NBC News
Caldwell-Rafferty, Noah: National Public Radio
Calfat, Marcel: CBC (Canadian Broadcasting Corporation)
Callahan, Michael: CNN
Calo-Christianson, Nancy: C–SPAN
Calvi, Jason: EWTN
Camah, Malik: Al Jazeera English
Camarda, Timothy: CBS News
Campbell, Elizabeth: CBS News
Campbell, Evan: CQ / Roll Call
Canalichio, Timothy: NBC News

MEMBERS ENTITLED TO ADMISSION—Continued

Candia, Kirsten: German TV (ZDF)
Cannon, Catherine: CBS News
Caperton, Katherine: Sirius XM Satellite Radio
Capion, Toby: EWTN
Caplan, Craig: C–SPAN
Capra, Anthony: NBC News
Capucci, Michael: Eye–To–Eye Video
Cardno, Christopher: EWTN
Caren, Allison: Washingtonpost.com
Carey, Julie: WRC–TV / NBC–4
Carlson, Brett: Global TV Canada
Carlson, Frank: PBS NewsHour
Carlson, Tucker: Fox News
Carmean, Kyle: WTTG–Fox Television
Carney, Keith: FedNet
Carpeaux, Emily: PBS NewsHour
Carr, Evan: WRC–TV / NBC–4
Carr, Martin: WETA
Carrero Alvarez, Ney: Al Jazeera International
Carrick, Kenneth: C–SPAN
Carroll, Joshua: Washingtonpost.com
Carson, Cheryl: Sinclair Broadcast Group
Carson, Christopher: FedNet
Carswell, Diana: ABC News
Carter, Catherine: CNN
Carter, David: WRC–TV / NBC–4
Carter, Walter, Jr.: Fox News
Carvajal, Nicole: CNN
Casas, Angelica: BBC
Casenco, Anatolie: Voice of America
Casey, Elizabeth: Washingtonpost.com
Casey, Sean: WRC–TV / NBC–4
Cassano, Joseph: WRC–TV / NBC–4
Castiel, Carol: Voice of America
Castillejo Carrasco, Esther: ABC News
Castro, Pablo: Hispanic Communications Network
Castro Jaramillo, William: Al Jazeera English
Cathey, Elizabeth: ABC News
Catrett, David: CNN
Causey, Mike: Federal News Radio 1500 AM
Cecchini, Reginald: Global TV Canada
Chacon, Brian: Al Jazeera English
Chadbourn, Margaret: Spectrum News
Chadha-Kaye, Stephanie: C–SPAN
Chakraborty, Barnini: Fox News
Chalian, David: CNN
Chamberlain, Richard: WJLA–TV / Newschannel 8
Chan, Enoch: WETA
Chance, Bradleigh: NBC News
Chandler, Alexander: Independent Television News (ITN)
Chang, Ailsa: National Public Radio
Chang, Ching-Yi: AP–Broadcast
Chang, Darzen: WETA
Chantrait, Marie: TF1–French TV
Chapman, Irwin: Bloomberg Radio & TV
Chapman, Michael: Cnsnews.com
Charles, Daniel: National Public Radio
Charley, Peter: Al Jazeera English
Charlip, Louis: Fox News
Charters, Nadia: Al Arabiya TV
Chase, David: Cox Broadcasting
Chase, Spencer: Agri–Pulse
Chatelain, Gabrielle: Agence France Presse (AFP–TV)
Chatterjee, Ryan: Australian Broadcasting Corporation
Chaytor, David: Diversified Communications, Inc. (DCI)
Chekuru, Kavitha: Al Jazeera English
Chen, Chieh-Yuan: Hong Kong Phoenix Satellite Television
Chen, Han: Radio Free Asia
Chen, Joie: Medill News Service
Chen, Lingnan: Hong Kong Phoenix Satellite Television
Chen, Nancy: WJLA–TV / Newschannel 8
Chen, Natasha: CNN
Chen, Yi Qiu: Hong Kong Phoenix Satellite Television
Chen, Zheng: Shenzhen Media Group (SZMG)
Chenevey, Stephen: WTTG–Fox Television
Cheng, Tsung-Shen: Radio Free Asia
Cherneff, Elizabeth: Voice of America
Cherouny, Robert: German TV (ARD)
Cherrie, Sarah: Independent Television News (ITN)
Cherry, Jayk: WAMU
Cheslow, Daniella: WAMU
Chevez, Carlos: National Public Radio
Chour, David: National Public Radio
Chick, Jane: CBS News
Childs, Lete: CBS News
Chipak, John: EWTN
Chirinos Vasquez, Carlos: Univision
Cho, Aimee: WRC–TV / NBC–4
Cho, Hans: Voice of America
Choe, Jaywon: PBS NewsHour
Choi, Hannah: JTBC
Chopra, Namita: Sinclair Broadcast Group
Choto, Raymond: Voice of America
Chowdhury, Sarmat: FedNet
Chrea, Vanrith: Radio Free Asia
Christ, Jacqueline: Fox News
Christman, Andrew: CNN
Chuku, Onyinyechi: CTV–Community TV of PG County
Chung, E–Ting: Voice of America
Chunko, April: Hearst Television Inc.
Ciammachilli, Esther: WAMU
Cilesizoglu, Ali: TRT
Cima, Roseann: Scripps News
Cinque, Vicente: TV Globo International
Cione, Ciara: NBC News
Ciridon, Robert: NBC News
Cirilli, Kevin: Bloomberg Radio & TV
Ciuffetelli, Gabriella: Fox News

MEMBERS ENTITLED TO ADMISSION—Continued

Claar, Matthew: C–SPAN
Clancy, Julia: NBC News
Clancy, Kevin: Scripps News
Clarenne, Gilles: Agence France Presse (AFP–TV)
Clark, James: C–SPAN
Clarke, Casey: Fox News
Clarke, John: Feature Story News
Clary, Gregory: CNN
Claudet, Marie: CBC (Canadian Broadcasting Corporation)
Clemons, Bobby: CNN
Clifford, Jordan: One America
Cloherty, Megan: WTOP Radio
Clottey, Peter: Voice of America
Clugston, Gregory: SRN News (Salem)
Coates, Avron: CNN
Cobb, Benjamin: Scripps News
Cochran, Carrie: Scripps News
Cockerham, Richard: Fox News
Cockey, William: WTTG–Fox Television
Coffee, Mel: Capital News Service TV–U of MD
Coffin, Cori: WTTG–Fox Television
Cofske, Harvey: Diversified Communications, Inc. (DCI)
Cohen, Marshall: CNN
Cohen, Zachary: CNN
Cohencious, Robert: Native American TV (NATV)
Coil, Holley: Nexstar Media Group
Coker, Edward: WTTG–Fox Television
Cole, Bryan: Fox News
Colella, Anthony: WTTG–Fox Television
Coleman, Thomas: NBC News
Coleman, Youman: CNN
Coleman, Zachary: National Public Radio
Coles, David: PBS NewsHour
Coley, Adam: The Real News Network
Colimore, Eric: Fox News
Collette, Matthew: Washingtonpost.com
Collins, Bruce: C–SPAN
Collins, Kaitlan: CNN
Collins, Maxine: BBC
Collins, Michael: C–SPAN
Collins, Patrick: WRC–TV / NBC–4
Collinson, Stephen: CNN
Colombo-Abdullah, Andrea: AP–Broadcast
Colonna, Micaela: NBC News
Colt, Jasper: USA Today
Colvin, Rhonda: Washingtonpost.com
Conant, Caitlin: CBS News
Concaugh, Joseph, Jr.: Diversified Communications, Inc. (DCI)
Conciatori, Tess: PBS NewsHour
Condon, Edward: EWTN
Coney, Carol: CBS News
Conlin, Sheila: NBC Newschannel
Connelly, Phoebe: Washingtonpost.com
Conner, Eric: CBS News
Conrad, Jacob: National Public Radio
Conte, Michael: CNN
Contreras, Glenda: Telemundo Network
Contreras, Gustavo: National Public Radio
Contreras, Jorge: Univision
Contreras, Marvin: WFDC–TV Univision
Cook, James: C–SPAN
Cook, Jeffery: ABC News
Cook, Joseph: NBC News
Cook, Samuel: WUSA–TV
Cook, Sara: CBS News
Coomarasamy, James: BBC
Coon, Janice: WUSA–TV
Coonce, Stephen: Al Jazeera English
Cooney, Daniel: PBS NewsHour
Cooper, Kyle: WTOP Radio
Cooper, Nero, Jr.: NBC News
Copeland, Natasha: WRC–TV / NBC–4
Coppin, Stephen: CNN
Cordes, Nancy: CBS News
Corke, Kevin: Fox News
Cornejo Castelforte, Andrea: Washingtonpost.com
Corner, Howard: C–SPAN
Cornish Emery, Audie: National Public Radio
Corpet, Anne: Radio France Internationale
Correa, Lina: Voice of America
Correa, Pedro: Telemundo Network
Corripio, Michael: Al Jazeera English
Cortes, Gerard: Caracol Television
Cortes, William: Telemundo Network
Costa, Christian: Fox News
Costantini, Robert: Westwood One
Costello, Thomas: NBC News
Cote, Timothy: NBC News
Cotterill, Rebecca: Sky News
Couger, Charles: Fox News
Coughlan, Victoria: CBS News
Courson, Paul: Sinclair Broadcast Group
Courtney, Eric: Diversified Communications, Inc. (DCI)
Cousins, Bria: CNBC
Couture, Denise: WAMU
Cox, Jerry: This Is America With Dennis Wholey
Cozzolino, Ashley: Fox News
Craca, Thomas: NBC News
Craft, Carl: National Public Radio
Craig, John: Diversified Communications, Inc. (DCI)
Craig, William: National Public Radio
Crane, Stephen: Cronkite News Service
Crawford, James: CNN
Crawford, Robert: CBS News
Crawford, Shannon: ABC News
Crawford, Woody: Voice of America
Criales, Ricardo: Agence France Presse (AFP–TV)
Cridland, Jeffrey: WRC–TV / NBC–4
Crim, Lorraine: Fox News
Crisafulli, Melanie: WTTG–Fox Television
Crocker, Octavia: Hearst Television Inc.

MEMBERS ENTITLED TO ADMISSION—Continued

Crombe, Laura: CBN News
Crosby, Kevin: Hearst Television Inc.
Crosdale, Natalia: CNN
Cross, Christopher: CNN
Crowther, Philip: AP–Broadcast
Crum, John: CBS News
Crupi, Nicolas: Voice of America
Crutchfield, Curtis: CTV–Community TV of PG County
Cruz, Abigail: ABC News
Csapo, Jonathan: BBC
Cucchiara, Natalie: NBC News
Cuddy, Matthew: CNBC
Cuesta-Roca, Carmen: Agence France Presse (AFP–TV)
Cui, Han: Sinovision
Culhane, Patricia: Al Jazeera English
Cullen, Michael: National Public Radio
Cullen, Ryan: NBC News
Cullinan, Charlotte: Bloomberg Radio & TV
Culver, David: WRC–TV / NBC–4
Cumber, Erika: CTV–Community TV of PG County
Cunanan, Rene: NBC News
Cunha, John: CNN
Cunningham, Megan: ABC News
Cuozzo, Rebecca: Fox News
Curiel, Claudia: WRC–TV / NBC–4
Currier, Liam: C–SPAN
Curry, Jessica: Fox News
Curtis, Alexander: C–SPAN
Curtis, Jodie: Fox News
Cusson, Zachary: Scripps News
Cutler-Mason, Anne: WTTG–Fox Television
Czaplinski, Michael: National Public Radio
Czys, Janet: National Public Radio
Czzowitz, Gregory: C–SPAN
Daborowski, Karen: Gray Television
Dakin, Carla: NBC News
Dale, Daniel: CNN
Dale, Jordan: The Hill
Daley, James: The Real News Network
Dalgetty, Audrey: ABC News
Dalton, Benjamin: TV Tokyo
Daly, John: CBS News
Danahar, Paul: BBC
Daniel, Zoe: Australian Broadcasting Corporation
Danielian, Edward: Fox Business Network
Daniels, Donnell: ABC News
Daniels, Eugene: Politico.com
Daniels, Peter: C–SPAN
Dann, Caroline: NBC News
Dao, Thao: Vietv Network
Dargakis, Minas: Voice of America
Daschle, Kelly: AP–Broadcast
Dashevsky, Arik: Fox News
Datcher, Phillip: Voice of America
Date, Ajinkya: ABC News
Datil, Ariane: WUSA–TV
Dauchess, Matthew: C–SPAN
Daugherty, Jeffery: Voice of America
Davalos Macdonald, Anna: NBC Newschannel
Dave, Jagruti: Feature Story News
Davey, Mark: Independent Television News (ITN)
Davis, Anthony: C–SPAN
Davis, Jackson: Now This News
Davis, Ray: NBC Newschannel
Davis, Susan: National Public Radio
Davis, Tiffani: Vice News
Davydov, Denis: Russian State TV and Radio (RTR)
Dawood, Mohammed: APTVS–American Press & TV Services
Dawson, Wendy: Fox News
Day, Kara: CNN
Deahl, Jessica: National Public Radio
Deal, Larry: Sinclair Broadcast Group
Dean, Sarah: NBC News
Dean Rutherford, Jessica: CNN
De Chagas, Bridget: National Public Radio
Decker, Jonathan: Fox News Radio
Dede, Mehmet: Al Jazeera International
De Diego, Javier: CNN
De Franceschi, Jela: Voice of America
Defrank, Debra: Fox News
Dejene, Abinet: ABC News
De La Cuetara, Ines: ABC News
Del Aguila, Andres: Fox News
Delany, Kevin: Westwood One
Delawala, Imtiyaz: ABC News
D'elia, Alexandra: PBS NewsHour
Del Pino, Javier: Cadena Ser
Delshad, Carmel: WAMU
Del Toro, Natasha: Al Jazeera English
Deluca, Joan: Voice of America
De Luce, Daniel: NBC News
Del Vado Chicharro, Marta: Cadena Ser
Demarco, Nicole: Washingtonpost.com
Demaria, Edward: NBC News
Demark, Michael: Fox News
Demas, William: ABC News
Demilio, Paul: Sirius XM Satellite Radio
Demoss, Gary: CBS News
Dennert, Mary Pat: Fox News
Densmore, Steven: Voice of America
Depenbrock, Julie: WAMU
De Poilloue De Saint Perier, Charles: Groupe TVA
Dermody, Kevin: Nexstar Media Group
Derose, Adam: The Hill
Derrien, Mathieu: TF1–French TV
De Schaetzen, Emilie: Eurovision Americas, Inc.
Desjardins, Lisa: PBS NewsHour
Desta, Benyam: C–SPAN
Detrow, Scott: National Public Radio
De Vasconcelos Albino Da Silva, Joao: RTP Portuguese Public Television
De Vogue, Ariane: CNN
De Vries, Marieke: Dutch TV & Radio (NOS)

MEMBERS ENTITLED TO ADMISSION—Continued

Dezell, Maureen: Washington Bureau News Service
Dezenski, Lauren: CNN
Dhonden, Passang: Radio Free Asia
Dhue, Stephanie: CNBC
Dhuy, Hans: Finnish Broadcasting Company (YLE)
Dia, Abdourahmane: Voice of America
Diamond, Jeremy: CNN
Diantonio, Nicole: WUSA–TV
Diao, Alexis: Washingtonpost.com
Diaz, Daniella: CNN
Diaz, Juan Carlos: Small House Productions
Diaz Morales, Aixa: Hearst Television Inc.
Dibartolo, Danielle: Fox News
Dibella, Richard: Fox News
Dickyi, Tenzin: Radio Free Asia
Difonzo, Thomas: Wall Street Journal
Diggs, Bridget: C–SPAN
Diieguts, Daria: Voice of America
Dilanian, Kenneth: NBC News
Dill, Daniel: C–SPAN
Dillard, Juanita: ABC News
Dipaola, Marcus: Dailymail.com
Dipietro, Annamaria: Sinclair Broadcast Group
Diss, Kathryn: Australian Broadcasting Corporation
Dixon, Jarmel: C–SPAN
Dixson, Charles: CBS News
Doan, Laura: CBS News
Doane, Martin C.: WJLA–TV / Newschannel 8
Dobal, Michael: NBC Newschannel
Dockett, Sakina: CTV–Community TV of PG County
Doernen, Daniel: German TV (ARD)
Doherty, Brian: Fox News
Doherty, Peter: ABC News
Doherty, Susan: Scripps News
Dohr-Grill, Karin: German TV (ARD)
Doi, Kazuo: Tokyo Broadcasting System
Dolce, Stephen: CNN
Dolma, Nordhey: Radio Free Asia
Domen, John: WTOP Radio
Dominick, Katherine: CBS News
Donahue, Edward: AP–Broadcast
Donald, William: Eye–To–Eye Video
Donato, Christopher: ABC News
Donevan, Connor: National Public Radio
Donner, Jason: Fox News
Donovan, Lionel: TRT World
Donovan, Maria: Fox News Radio
Donzel, Thomas: France 2 Television
Doocy, Peter: Fox News
Doody, Sean: C–SPAN
Dooms, Roberta: WUSA–TV
Dore, Margaret: CBS News
Dorf-Dolce, Heather: German TV (ARD)
Dorsey, Steven: CBS News
Dossantos, Christopher: CNN
Doty, Mitchell: Al Jazeera English
Dougherty, David: Al Jazeera International
Dougherty, Paul: ABC News
Dove, Nicholas: Al Jazeera English
Dowdell, Kristofer: Fox News
Dowhaluk, Sonya: CNN
Doyle, John: C–SPAN
Drabo, Aboubacar: National Public Radio
Dragsted, Stine: Danish Broadcasting Corporation
Dreher, Sydni: PBS NewsHour
Drennen, Kevin: ABC News
Drewenskus, Alex: National Public Radio
Dridi, Sonia: AP–Broadcast
Dries, William: CBS News
Drimmer, Ilana: NBC News
Drory, Sarah: NBC News
Druce, Ian: BBC
Druker, Bonnie: CNN
Drummond, Mallory: C–SPAN
Du, Haipeng: New Tang Dynasty TV
Duarte, Alfredo: WRC–TV / NBC–4
Duarte, Alina: Telesur
Dubinin, Sergii: Inter TV
Dubose, Michael: Diversified Communications, Inc. (DCI)
Dubose, Kadesh: Diversified Communications, Inc. (DCI)
Dubose, Michael: EWTN
Duchardt, Kilmeny: TRT World
Duckham, Justin: Talk Media News
Dudar, Hasan: TRT World
Duffy, Cecilia: Fox News
Duffy, Conor: Australian Broadcasting Corporation
Dugan, William: CTV Canadian TV
Duggeli, Peter: Swiss Broadcasting
Dukakis, Alexandra: ABC News
Duncan, Victoria: NBC News
Duncombe, Lyndsay: CBC (Canadian Broadcasting Corporation)
Dunlop, William: Eurovision Americas, Inc.
Dunn, Lisa: WAMU
Dupree, James: Cox Broadcasting
Durak, Kadir: TRT World
Durham, Deborah: Univision
Durkin, John: Cheddar
Dutcher, Mizumi: Fuji TV Japan
Duwaji, Omar: Al Jazeera International
Dwyer, Devin: ABC News
Dwyer-Shapiro, Lisa: AP–Broadcast
Dyer, Lois: CBS News
Dziarkach, Andrei: Voice of America
Eastham, James: NBC News
Eastin, Yi-Pei: C–SPAN
Ebbs, Stephanie: ABC News
Ebel, Thomas: CNN
Ebersohl, Kevin: WTTG–Fox Television
Ebrahimi, Mehrnoosh: BBC
Echevarria, Pedro: C–SPAN
Echols, Jerry: Fox News
Eck, Christina: German Press Agency

MEMBERS ENTITLED TO ADMISSION—Continued

Eckardt, Julia: Blaze Media
Edem, Ariel: To The Contrary (Persephone Productions)
Eder, Teresa: German TV (ZDF)
Edmondson, William: Fox News
Edson, Richard: Fox News
Edwards, Brian: CBN News
Edwards, Christopher: EWTN
Edwards, Courtney: CNN
Edwards, Destry: Blaze Media
Edwards, Windsor: National Public Radio
Egan, Lauren: NBC News
Einarsen, Jonathan: NBC Newschannel
Eiras, Arlene: Reuters Radio & TV
Eizeldin, Sam: APTVS–American Press & TV Services
Ejedepang-Koge, Nkwenten: Middle East Broadcasting Networks (MBN)
Ejiochi, Azubuike: WTTG–Fox Television
Elahmed, Mouhamed: Al Jazeera International
Elamrani, Abdelmounim: Al Jazeera English
Elfers, Stephen: USA Today
Elgazar, Hosny: Middle East Broadcasting Networks (MBN)
Elgin, John: Middle East Broadcasting Networks (MBN)
Elhag, Areig: Middle East Broadcasting Networks (MBN)
Elias, Jonathan: WJLA–TV / Newschannel 8
Elizondo, Gabriel: Al Jazeera English
Elker, Jonathan: Washingtonpost.com
Elkhalili, Sari: Al Jazeera International
El-Khamissi, Elian: APTVS–American Press & TV Services
Elkomi, Dalia: AP–Broadcast
Ellard, Nancy: NBC Newschannel
Ellenwood, Gary: C–SPAN
Ellingham, Morgan: NBC News
Ellis, Nicole: Washingtonpost.com
Elrashidi, Adam: Scripps News
El Sabawi, Yasmine: TRT World
Elving, Ronald: National Public Radio
Elvington, Daniel Glenn: ABC News
Emanuel, Michael: Fox News
Enders, David: TRT World
Engel, Mariam: Al Jazeera English
Engel, Seth: C–SPAN
English, Elizebeth: CNN
Enjeti, Saagar: The Hill
Ensign, Ernie: WJLA–TV / Newschannel 8
Epstein, Steven: CBS News
Erbe-Leckar, Bonnie: To The Contrary (Persephone Productions)
Erdogan, Abdulmuttalip: TRT World
Erickson, Bo: CBS News
Ernst, Manuel: German TV (ARD)
Escobedo, Richard: CBS News
Esfahani, Lara: German TV (ZDF)
Eskalis, Ryan: WJLA–TV / Newschannel 8
Esquivel, Patricia: C–SPAN
Essamuah, Zinhle: Now This News
Estes, Diane: PBS NewsHour
Estrada, Rodolfo: AP–Broadcast
Estulin, Shayna: I24 News
Eubanks, Olivia: ABC News
Eustace, Colin: One America
Eustis, Robert: ABC News
Eversden, Andrew: CBS News
Ewall-Wice, Sarah: CBS News
Ewart, Esther: Voice of America
Ewen, McKenna: CNN
Fabian, Geoffrey: Voice of America
Fabian, Kathleen: Al Jazeera English
Fabic, Gregory: C–SPAN
Facchinei, Bianca: Scripps News
Fahey, Mark: Scripps News
Fahs, Mohamed: Al Jazeera International
Faison, Alfred: EWTN
Fakhry Khane, Ghida: TRT World
Falls, John: CBS News
Fancy, Stephen: ABC News
Fantacone, John: CBS News
Fantis, Patricia: WRC–TV / NBC–4
Farkas, Daniel: Middle East Broadcasting Networks (MBN)
Farkas, Mark: C–SPAN
Farmer, Robert: CNN
Farooq, Faizan: National Public Radio
Farrell, John: C–SPAN
Farrell, Kathryn: BBC
Farzaneh, Sam: BBC
Fatih, Artun: Sky News Arabia
Fattahi, Kambiz: BBC
Faulders, Katherine: ABC News
Fauqueux-Veit, Hannelore: Austrian Radio & TV (ORF)
Favela Munoz, Cecilia: Voice of America
Faw, Caitlin: Wall Street Journal
Feeney, Joseph: C–SPAN
Feezer, Cory: EWTN
Feinstein, Jared: ABC News
Feist, Samuel: CNN
Fekadu, Salem: Voice of America
Felan, Mitchell: NBC News
Feldman, Leonardo: Voice of America
Feldman, Randy: Viewpoint Communications
Felix, Tsitsiki: WFDC–TV Univision
Fell, Jacqueline: Cox Broadcasting
Fendrick, Anne-Marie: NHK
Fenston, Jacob: WAMU
Fenton, Amy: Fox News
Ferder, Bruce: Voice of America
Ferguson, Amber: Washingtonpost.com
Ferguson, Johnnie: ABC News
Ferguson, Patrick: CBC (Canadian Broadcasting Corporation)

MEMBERS ENTITLED TO ADMISSION—Continued

Feria, Elizabeth: Reuters Radio & TV
Ferran, Lee: ABC News
Ferrell, Regan: FedNet
Ferrise, Patrick: Sirius XM Satellite Radio
Fertig, Natalie: Sinclair Broadcast Group
Fessler, Pamela: National Public Radio
Fetzer, Robert: Fox News
Feudner, Eric: C–SPAN
Fiegel, Eric: CNN
Field, Andrew: ABC News
Fifield, Paul: Diversified Communications, Inc. (DCI)
Filali, Rabah: Middle East Broadcasting Networks (MBN)
Finch, Justin: WRC–TV / NBC–4
Finch, Mark: Fox News
Fink, Kathryn: WAMU
Finkel, Benjamin: Viewpoint Communications
Finn, Sean: ABC News
Finney, Maranda: The Daily Caller
Finney, Richard: Radio Free Asia
Finney, Sara Shannon: WTOP Radio
Fioraliso, Theodore: Gray Television
Fischer, Andrew: News2Share
Fischer, Richard: WUSA–TV
Fischer, Tanya: Eurovision Americas, Inc.
Fischoff, Michael: WTTG–Fox Television
Fishel, Justin: ABC News
Fisher, Kathryn: Feature Story News
Fisher, Siobhan: ABC News
Fisher, Thomas: Al Jazeera English
Fitzgerald, Meagan: WRC–TV / NBC–4
Fitzgerald, Thomas: WTTG–Fox Television
Fitzke, Karl: National Public Radio
Flack, Eric: WUSA–TV
Flaherty, Anne: ABC News
Fleeson, Richard: C–SPAN
Fleischer, Jodie: WRC–TV / NBC–4
Fleischer Belmar, Heidi: German TV (ZDF)
Fletcher, Lisa: WJLA–TV / Newschannel 8
Flood, Joseph: ABC News
Flood, Randolph: Native American TV (NATV)
Florance, Benjamin: Fox News
Flores, Cesar: Fox News
Flores, Karla: WRC–TV / NBC–4
Flores, Reena: Washingtonpost.com
Flowers, Alexandra: NBC News
Floyd, Jessica: Sinclair Broadcast Group
Flynn, Ann: CBS News
Flynn, Maureen: NBC News
Foellmer, Kristin: German TV (ZDF)
Foerg, Maximilan: Deutsche Welle TV
Fogarty, J. Kevin: Reuters Radio & TV
Fogel, Golda: NTN24
Fok, Leung: Radio Free Asia
Foley, Rita: AP–Broadcast
Foley Elias, Pablo: Deutsche Welle TV
Foran, Clare: CNN
Foran, Laura: CBS News
Forbes, Latoya: CNN
Forcier, Vincent: WETA
Ford, Patrick: CNN
Ford, Samuel: WJLA–TV / Newschannel 8
Forehand, Kristin: Fox News
Foreman, Thomas: CNN
Forgotson, Edward: CBS News
Forman, David: NBC News
Fornicola, Jason: Federal News Radio 1500 AM
Forte, Bernard: WRC–TV / NBC–4
Forte, Douglas: Now This News
Fortner, Amanda: C–SPAN
Fortney, Daniel: Voice of America
Fortunato, Robert: CBS News
Fossum, Samuel: CNN
Foster, Carl: C–SPAN
Foster, Rebecca: Feature Story News
Foster, Scott: NBC News
Foster Mathewson, Lesli: WUSA–TV
Foty, Thomas: CBS News
Fougere, Fabien: France 2 Television
Foukara, Abderrahim: Al Jazeera International
Fowler, Scott: NBC News
Fox, Darren: Voice of America
Fox, Lauren: CNN
Fox, Michael: Al Jazeera International
Fox, Peggy: WUSA–TV
Fox, Stacey: NBC News
Frail, Marie: Reuters Radio & TV
Fraley, Jason: WTOP Radio
Frandino, Nathaniel: Reuters Radio & TV
Frank, Noah: WTOP Radio
Frankel, Jillian: NBC News
Frankel, Kendrick: FedNet
Frankel, Melissa: NBC News
Franklin, Jonathan: WUSA–TV
Fraser, Kristin: Vice News
Frasier, Jordan: NBC News
Frates, Christopher: Sirius XM Satellite Radio
Frazee, Gretchen: PBS NewsHour
Frazier, Leslie: C–SPAN
Frazier, Robert: Feature Story News
Frazier, William: C–SPAN
Fredman, Nathaniel: The Hill
Fredrickson, Drew: NBC News
Freeland, Charla: Sirius XM Satellite Radio
Freeman, Ariana: CBS News
Freitag-Schmitt, Christina: German TV (ARD)
French, Francis: ABC News
Frey, Kevin: Spectrum News
Friden, Elizabeth: Fox News
Friedman, David: Fox News
Friedman, Mathew: AP–Broadcast
Friedrich, Michael: Cox Broadcasting
Fritz, Michael: PBS NewsHour
Froneberger, Lauryn: WUSA–TV

MEMBERS ENTITLED TO ADMISSION—Continued

Froom, Leroy: SRN News (Salem)
Fry, Deanna: Hearst Television Inc.
Frydman, Melissa: CNN
Fuglesang, Anna Lisa: Independent Television News (ITN)
Fuhr, Michael: WUSA–TV
Fukuda, Haruyo: Tokyo Broadcasting System
Fulton, Bradley: ABC News
Fung, Brian: CNN
Furlow, Tony: CBS News
Furman, Hal: CBS News
Fuse, Satoru: TV Asahi
Fuss, Brian: CBS News
Futrowsky, David: Voice of America
Gaber Saletan, Hannah: USA Today
Gabriel, Oscar: AP–Broadcast
Gaffney, John: NBC News
Gaffney, Morgan: NBC News
Gains, Mosheh: NBC News
Galarce Crain, Teresita: CNN
Galdabini, Christian: Fox News
Galey, Melinda: Fox News
Galey, Travis: CBS News
Galindo Pena, Raul: Telesur
Gallacher, Andy: Al Jazeera English
Gallagher, Fallon: NBC News
Gallagher, John: C–SPAN
Gallagher, William: C–SPAN
Gallasch, Hillery: German TV (ARD)
Galowin, Craig: C–SPAN
Galperovich, Danila: Voice of America
Gamboa, Suzanne: NBC News
Gangel, Jamie: CNN
Ganslmeier, Martin: German Public Radio (ARD)
Gantz, Jordan: Vice News
Gaouette, Katherine: CNN
Garay, Gavino: Reuters Radio & TV
Garbitt, Devin: ABC News
Garcia, Danelle: CNN
Garcia, Elizabeth: WUSA–TV
Garcia, Jon: ABC News
Garcia, Juan: Fox News
Garcia, July: CBS News
Garcia, Manny: CBS News
Gardella, Richard: NBC News
Gardinier, Elizabeth: PBS NewsHour
Gardner, Evan: Fox News
Garifo, Stephen: WUSA–TV
Garlock, Tracy: C–SPAN
Garner, Dave: WTOP Radio
Garnier, Terace: Scripps News
Garofalo, Elise: CNN
Garratt, Jonathan: Al Jazeera English
Garraty, Timothy: CNN
Garrett, Christopher: CNN
Garrett, Major: CBS News
Garrett Scott, Amina: CNN
Garrott, Jennifer: C–SPAN
Gary, Garney: C–SPAN
Gaskin, Keith: NBC News
Gasparello, Linda: White House Chronicle
Gassot, Philippe: I24 News
Gato, Pablo: Univision
Gatza, Fabian: German TV (ZDF)
Gaudino, Ralph: NBC News
Gaur, Girish: One America
Gauthier, Arthur: ABC News
Gawad, Atef: AP–Broadcast
Gayle, Anna-Lysa: WJLA–TV / Newschannel 8
Gayon Granell, Fernando: TVE–Spanish Public Television
Gazis, Olivia: CBS News
Gebremariam, Solomon: Voice of America
Gee, Alexander: CNN
Gehlen, Robert: ABC News
Geller, Laura: WUSA–TV
Gelman, Micah: Washingtonpost.com
Gembara, Deborah: Reuters Radio & TV
Gentilo, Richard: AP–Broadcast
Gentzler Miller, Doreen: WRC–TV / NBC–4
Geoghegan, Thomas: BBC
George, Charles: C–SPAN
George, Pavithra: Reuters Radio & TV
Gerberg, Jonathan: Washingtonpost.com
Gerhiser, James: National Public Radio
Geriquiji, Geri: Radio Free Asia
Gerondidakis, Dimitrios: NBC News
Gessner, Brian: NBC News
Gestoso, Jorge: Telesur
Getachew, Eden: CNN
Getter, Thomas: Westwood One
Geyelin, Philip: CBS News
Ghandour, Michel: Middle East Broadcasting Networks (MBN)
Ghanem, Pierre: Al Arabiya TV
Giaimo, Melissa: CNN
Giammetta, Massimo: WTTG–Fox Television
Giannakopoulos, Sarah: CNN
Gibson, Giles: Feature Story News
Gibson, Jake: Fox News
Gibson, Jenna: CBS News
Gibson, Karlee: Washington Examiner
Gibson, Sheri Lynn: NBC Newschannel
Gibson, Teneille: WRC–TV / NBC–4
Giebel, Amy: ABC News
Gilbert, Jennifer: CBN News
Gilchrist, Aaron: WRC–TV / NBC–4
Gile, Charles: NBC News
Gilles, Elizabeth: National Public Radio
Gillis, Gary: Fox News
Gilmore, Elizabeth: NBC News
Gilpin-Green, Justice: NBC News
Ginebra, Nelson: NBC Newschannel
Gingrich, Laura: Blaze Media
Ginsburg, Benson: CBS News
Ginsburg, Franklyn: Al Jazeera English

MEMBERS ENTITLED TO ADMISSION—Continued

Girard, David: ABC News
Girdusky, Ryan: One America
Girdwood, Barton: National Public Radio
Gisholt Minard, Morgan: BBC
Gittlen, Jason: WRC–TV / NBC–4
Gittleson, Benjamin: ABC News
Giunta, Meg: EWTN
Given, Margaret: CNN
Gjorgjievska, Milena: Voice of America
Gladden, Dwayne: The Real News Network
Glassman, Matt: WRC–TV / NBC–4
Glenday, James: Australian Broadcasting Corporation
Glennon, John: ABC News
Glor, Jeffrey: CBS News
Gloria, Catherine: CNN
Glover, Aronica: CBN News
Goddard, Andre: CNN
Godfrey, Autria: WJLA–TV / Newschannel 8
Godin, Jake: Scripps News
Godsick, Andrew: NBC Newschannel
Godwin, Ross: Washingtonpost.com
Gold, Emily: NBC News
Gold, Lawrence: AP–Broadcast
Gold, Peter: Fuji TV Japan
Golden, Amanda: CNN
Golden, Rodrek: Reuters Radio & TV
Golden, Vaughn: Laslo Congressional Bureau
Goldrick, Michael: WRC–TV / NBC–4
Gomes, Christer: CNN
Gomez, Justin: ABC News
Gomez, Serafin: CBS News
Goncalves De Oliveira, Alexandra: The Hill
Goncalves Perry, Delia: WUSA–TV
Gongadze, Myroslava: Voice of America
Gonyea, Donald: National Public Radio
Gonzalez, Dennis: Fox News
Gonzalez, John: WJLA–TV / Newschannel 8
Gonzalez, Mario: NTN24
Gonzalez Homs, Roberto: WRC–TV / NBC–4
Gonzalez Martinez, Cesar: NBC News
Gonzalez-Ramirez, Liliana: WRC–TV / NBC–4
Goodall, Samuel: CBS News
Goodknight, Charles: WRC–TV / NBC–4
Goodman, David: Bloomberg Radio & TV
Goodman, Jeffrey: NBC News
Goolsby, Wyatt: EWTN
Gorap, Pema: Voice of America
Gordemer, Barry: National Public Radio
Gordon, Candace: NBC Newschannel
Gordon, Herbert: WRC–TV / NBC–4
Gordon, Robert: ABC News
Gordon, Tamara: National Public Radio
Gore, Celina: CBS News
Gorham, Glenn: ABC News
Gorjestani, Kethevane: France 24
Gorman, James: AP–Broadcast
Goryashko, Sergey: BBC
Gottbrath, Laurin-Whitney: Al Jazeera International
Gottlieb, Brian: CBS News
Gough, Sarah: Independent Television News (ITN)
Gould, Robert: C–SPAN
Gourley, Hugh: WJLA–TV / Newschannel 8
Gracey, David: CNN
Gracia, Michael: AP–Broadcast
Gradison, Robin: NBC News
Graef, Aileen: CNN
Graesvik, Fredrik: TV2–Norway
Graf, Heather: WJLA–TV / Newschannel 8
Graff, Valentin: Agence France Presse (AFP–TV)
Graham, Taya: The Real News Network
Granadino, Cameron: The Real News Network
Grand, Raphael: Swiss Broadcasting
Granda-Murillo, Marco: NTN24
Granitz, Peter: National Public Radio
Granville, Samantha: BBC
Grasso, Neil: CBS News
Graumann, Eva: German Public Radio (ARD)
Gray, Cameron: Westwood One
Gray, Justin: Cox Broadcasting
Gray, Noah: CNN
Graydon, James: CNN
Grayer, Anne: CNN
Green, Jessie J.: WTOP Radio
Green, Molette: WRC–TV / NBC–4
Green, Myra: ABC News
Green, Richard: Voice of America
Greenbaum, Adamson: Voice of America
Greenberger, Jonathan: ABC News
Greenberger, Scott: Stateline
Greenblatt, Larry: Viewpoint Communications
Greenblatt, Mark: Scripps News
Greenburg, Jan: CBS News
Greene, David: National Public Radio
Greene, Gus: CNN
Greene, James: NBC News
Greene, Trevor: Fox News
Gregory, Matthew: WUSA–TV
Greiner, Nicholas: ABC News
Greisiger, Stephen: The Hill
Griffin, Jennifer: Fox News
Griffin, Julia: PBS NewsHour
Griffin, Kevin: NBC News
Griffith, Paul: FedNet
Griffitts, William: WELT N24 German TV
Griggs, Kendall: WJLA–TV / Newschannel 8
Grigsby, Lee: Eurovision Americas, Inc.
Grim, Natalie: Gray Television
Grimaldi, Angelica: CNN
Grimes, Sanford: Fox News
Gringlas, Samuel: National Public Radio
Grisales, Claudia: National Public Radio
Grishkoff Rockell, Kira: Al Jazeera English
Grose, Jessica: The Hill
Gross, Andrew: NBC News

MEMBERS ENTITLED TO ADMISSION—Continued

Gross, Eddie: CNN
Gross, Joshua: CBS News
Grossheim, Jessica: Nexstar Media Group
Grossman, David: BBC
Grover, Esha: Voice of America
Grudovich, Daniel: WTTG–Fox Television
Grumbach, Garrett: NBC News
Grumke, Kathryn: PBS NewsHour
Guastadisegni, Richard: WJLA–TV / Newschannel 8
Guerouani, Fayrouz: AP–Broadcast
Guerrero, Bertha: ABC News
Guevara Medrano, Paul Henry: NTN24
Guez, Bertrand: CBC (Canadian Broadcasting Corporation)
Guild, Blair: Washingtonpost.com
Guise, Gregory: Al Jazeera English
Gunnery, Mark: WAMU
Guo, Yina: Xinhua
Guray, Geoffrey Lou: PBS NewsHour
Gurbanzada, Rafig: Caspian Broadcasting TV
Gutierrez Riveros, Diego: WRC–TV / NBC–4
Gutmann, Hanna: Washington Radio And Press Service
Guttman, Nathan: Israel Television And Radio
Guzman, Armando: Azteca America
Guzman, Joseph: NBC News Radio
Guzman, Wilber: Telemundo Network
Gypson, Katherine: Voice of America
Haake, Garrett: NBC News
Habib, Elias: Al Arabiya TV
Haddad, Karim: Al Jazeera English
Haddad, Tamara: Feature Story News
Hadro, Catherine: EWTN
Hadro, Matthew: EWTN
Haefeli, Brian: ABC News
Hagan, Caroline: Fox News
Hager, Mary: CBS News
Hager, Nathan: Bloomberg Radio & TV
Hagerty, Colleen: BBC
Haggerty, Patrick: This WEEK In Agribusiness
Hahn, Jay: Eurovision Americas, Inc.
Haidari, Aws: TRT World
Haider, Zahra: Now This News
Haji Kakol, Aso: AP–Broadcast
Halkett, Kimberly: Al Jazeera English
Hall, Andrew: Sinclair Broadcast Group
Hall, Dwight: C–SPAN
Hall, Glenn: C–SPAN
Hall, Richard: C–SPAN
Haller, Sylvia: NBC News
Haller, Thomas: EWTN
Halpern, Jared: Fox News Radio
Halpern, Lacey: Fox News
Hamberg, Steven: Viewpoint Communications
Hamby, Bo: National Public Radio
Hamilton, James: Al Jazeera English
Hamilton, Lawan: Scripps News
Hammond, Jennifer: Sirius XM Satellite Radio
Hammond, Joe: WTTG–Fox Television
Hampton, Brian: CNN
Han, Duk In: Radio Free Asia
Han, Kyuseok: Korean Broadcasting Systems
Han, Sung Soo: Seoul Broadcasting System (SBS)
Handly, Jim: WRC–TV / NBC–4
Haney, Taylor: National Public Radio
Hanna, Michael: Al Jazeera English
Hannah, Daniel: ABC News
Hannan, Lori: Deutsche Welle TV
Hanson, Christopher: C–SPAN
Happe, Mackenzie: CNN
Harada, Kathryn: Nippon TV Network
Harbage, Claire: National Public Radio
Harding, Tomas: Diversified Communications, Inc. (DCI)
Harding, William: CBS News
Hardymon, Barrie: National Public Radio
Harf, Marie: Fox News
Harkness, Stephen: C–SPAN
Harleston, Robert: C–SPAN
Harper, Averi: ABC News
Harper, Steven: CBS News
Harper, Sydney: National Public Radio
Harrington, Candice: NBC News
Harrington, Joshua: WJLA–TV / Newschannel 8
Harris, James: Metro Teleproductions
Harris, Heather: WETA
Harris, Kristen: WUSA–TV
Harris, Mikayla: NBC News
Harris, Richard: National Public Radio
Harris, Rodney: EWTN
Harris, Roy: Diversified Communications, Inc. (DCI)
Harrison, Brandon: Fox News
Harrison, Byron: CTV–Community TV of PG County
Harrison, Mary Jean: C–SPAN
Hartman, Christopher: NBC News
Harton, Marcus: Voice of America
Hartwig, Ralf: German TV (ZDF)
Harwood, John: CNBC
Haselton, Brennan: WTOP Radio
Hash, James: WUSA–TV
Hashemi, Sarah: Washingtonpost.com
Hashmi, Siraj: Washington Examiner
Haslett, Cheyenne: ABC News
Hassanein, Gamal: APTVS–American Press & TV Services
Hastings-Jones, Kirsty: Hearst Television Inc.
Hatch, Edmund: NBC News
Hatfield, William: NBC News
Hauser, Amanda: WUSA–TV
Hawkins, Arielle: Gray Television
Hawkins, Shonty: WJLA–TV / Newschannel 8
Hawley, Alison: CBS News
Hawthorne, Dave: CBS News
Hayes, Monique: WRC–TV / NBC–4

MEMBERS ENTITLED TO ADMISSION—Continued

Hayes, Owen: NBC News
Haynes, Darren: WUSA–TV
Haynes, Laine: WUSA–TV
Haynes, Maurice: C–SPAN
Haynes, Oscar: Voice of America
Hays, Guerin: Fox News
Haywood, Barry: ABC News
He, Alan: CBS News
Headington, Brady: Hearst Television Inc.
Healey, Sean: CBS News
Healy, Gabrielle: WAMU
Hebden, David: The Real News Network
Hebden, Taylor: The Real News Network
Hecht, Barry: Diversified Communications, Inc. (DCI)
Hecker, Jenna: Sirius XM Satellite Radio
Heckman, Jory: Federal News Radio 1500 AM
Heffley, William: C–SPAN
Heina, Martin: Fox News
Heinbaugh, Jack: WRC–TV / NBC–4
Heiner, Stephen: Middle East Broadcasting Networks (MBN)
Helaoua, Yona: France 24
Helke, Michael: Voice of America
Helman, Jonathan: NBC News
Helskog, Gerhard: TV2–Norway
Hempen, Michael: AP–Broadcast
Hemphill, Anjali: WTTG–Fox Television
Henderson, Jarrad: USA Today
Henderson, Susan: AP–Broadcast
Henderson, Thomas: Stateline
Hendren, John: Al Jazeera English
Hendry, Erica: PBS NewsHour
Hennecke, Saskia: Spectrum News
Hennemuth, Maren: German TV (ARD)
Henriquez Maldonado, Rafael: WFDC–TV Univision
Henry, Christopher: NBC News
Henry, Edward: Fox News
Henry, John: WUSA–TV
Henry, Jonelle: C–SPAN
Henry, Robert: Sirius XM Satellite Radio
Henry, Shirley: National Public Radio
Henry, Skyler: CBS News
Hentunen, Mika: Finnish Broadcasting Company (YLE)
Herb, Jeremy: CNN
Herbas, Francis: C–SPAN
Herber, Massimiliano: Swiss Broadcasting
Herbert, Andrew: BBC
Heritage, Robert: NBC News
Herkner, Michael: CNN
Hermelijn, Ryan: Dutch TV & Radio (NOS)
Hernandez, Jinitzail: CQ / Roll Call
Hernandez, Linda: Washington Examiner
Hernandez Orellana, Angel: Univision
Hernandez Wood, Caridad: WUSA–TV
Hernon, Louise: NBC News
Herrera, Francisco-Ruben: German TV (ZDF)
Herridge, Catherine: CBS News
Herring, Charles: One America
Herring, Dawn: One America
Hersher, Rebecca: National Public Radio
Hess, Ione: CNN
Hesse, Alicia: Blaze Media
Hesse-Kastein, Sebastian: German Public Radio (ARD)
Hickman, Stacy: Fox News
Hicks, Samuel: Cheddar
Hidayat, Rafki: Voice of America
Higgins, Ricardo: NBC News
Hildebrand, Kristen: EWTN
Hill, Angela: Scripps News
Hill, Ashley: C–SPAN
Hill, Charles: ABC News
Hill, Christen: ABC News
Hill, Dallas: C–SPAN
Hill, Jarred: Hearst Television Inc.
Hill, Jonquilyn: WAMU
Hill, Martin: Fox News
Hillmann, Melanie: German TV (ZDF)
Hillyard, Vaughn: NBC News
Hindes, Walter: SRN News (Salem)
Hines, Andrea: ABC News
Hines, John: One America
Hirten, Kevin: Al Jazeera English
Hishchynsky, James: NBC News
Ho, King: Radio Free Asia
Hoar McGibbon, Adrienne: C–SPAN
Hobaica Santa Cruz, Melissa: NTN24
Hodge, Darnley: Imagination Media
Hodges, Lauren: National Public Radio
Hoffman, Brian: AP–Broadcast
Hoffman, Charles: NBC News
Hoffman, Jason: CNN
Hoja, Gulchehra: Radio Free Asia
Holbert, William: CNN
Holland, Faith: CNN
Holland, Tashick: National Public Radio
Hollenbeck, Paul: Bt Video Productions
Hollingsworth, Conor: Gray Television
Holmes, Horace: WJLA–TV / Newschannel 8
Holmes, Kristen: CNN
Holmes, Regina: Talk Media News
Hong, Albert: Radio Free Asia
Hong, Paula: BBC
Hooper, Molly: CBS News
Hopkins, Brian: WJLA–TV / Newschannel 8
Hopkins, Michael: CBS News
Hopper, David: NBC News
Horacek, Eric: C–SPAN
Hormuth, Thomas: WJLA–TV / Newschannel 8
Horn, Caroline: CBS News
Horn, Charles: Viewpoint Communications
Hornish, Cory: WETA
Horrigan, Derek: CNN

MEMBERS ENTITLED TO ADMISSION—Continued

Horsley, Scott: National Public Radio
Horton, Harry: Feature Story News
Horton, Robert: ABC News
Hosford, Matthew: ABC News
Hoshi, Mariko: Nippon TV Network
Hossain, Selim: Voice of America
Howard, Charles: NBC News
Howard, Kevin: ABC News
Howell, Emily: CNN
Howell, Kellan: Scripps News
Howell, Melissa: WTOP Radio
Hoye, Matthew: CNN
Hristova, Rozalia: BBC
Hssaini, Nasreddine: Al Jazeera International
Hsu, Andrea: National Public Radio
Hu, Yousong: Xinhua
Huaiquil, Enrique: Al Jazeera International
Huang, Paris: Voice of America
Huang, Zhuo: Hong Kong Phoenix Satellite Television
Hubert, Jason: ABC News
Hudak, Lara: FedNet
Hudak, Zackary: CBS News
Hudock, Richard: NBC News
Huether, Andrew: National Public Radio
Huey-Burns, Caitlin: CBS News
Huff, Daniel: AP–Broadcast
Huff, Priscilla: Fox News
Hughes, James: NBC News
Hughes, Jillian: CBS News
Hughes, Katherine: C–SPAN
Hughes, Mary: Fox News
Hughes, Maxine: TRT World
Hughes Hemmerlein, Megan: ABC News
Hume, Alexander: Fox News
Humeau, Thierry: Al Jazeera English
Hummelsheim, Scott: C–SPAN
Humphrey, Helena: Deutsche Welle TV
Hunsicker, Thomas: WUSA–TV
Hunt, Kasie: NBC News
Hunter, Alison: BBC
Hunter, Joshua: NBC News
Hunter, Paul: CBC (Canadian Broadcasting Corporation)
Hunter, Tracy: C–SPAN
Huraimi, Nadia: BBC
Hurst, Nathan: C–SPAN
Hurt, James: NBC Newschannel
Hurtado, Eugenia: Bloomberg Radio & TV
Hussain, Iftikhar: Voice of America
Hussin, Utami: Voice of America
Hutchinson, Heather: WRC–TV / NBC–4
Hwang, Song: TVBS
Hyman, Brett: Fox News
Hyman, Mark: Sinclair Broadcast Group
Hymes, Clare: CBS News
Hynds, Margaret: CBS News
Iacone, Michael: NBC News
Iannelli, Nick: WTOP Radio
Iannuzzi, John: ABC News
Iarmolenko, Iuliia: Voice of America
Ibarra, Adolfo: CNN
Ibrahim, Heind: AP–Broadcast
Ibrahim, Mohamed: German TV (ZDF)
Ibrahim, Zena: AP–Broadcast
Ichikawa, Masatoshi: Tokyo Broadcasting System
Ide, Charles: WETA
Ikushima, Shinichiro: Tokyo Broadcasting System
Iman, Falastine: Voice of America
Imparato, Walter: CNN
Ing, Lance: WRC–TV / NBC–4
Ingber, Alexandra: Scripps News
Ingle, Cynthia: C–SPAN
Inguanzo, Fidel: Bloomberg Radio & TV
Inman, Willie: Scripps News
Innes, Michael: BBC
Inoue, Yukimasa: Nippon TV Network
Insignares, Giovanni: WUSA–TV
Inskeep, Steven: National Public Radio
Inzaurralde, Bastien: Agence France Presse (AFP–TV)
Irons, Mark: EWTN
Isdale, Danielle: Independent Television News (ITN)
Isella, Elena: EWTN
Isgro, Ernest: WJLA–TV / Newschannel 8
Isham, Christopher: CBS News
Ishibashi, Yuki: Fuji TV Japan
Ishibe, Shun: NHK
Ishii, Yusaku: NHK
Islam, Saqib: Voice of America
Islam, Towhidul: Voice of America
Ivey, Michael: Voice of America
Iwata, Natsuya: Tokyo Broadcasting System
Jaakson, Uelle-Mall: Austrian Radio & TV (ORF)
Jackson, Clifton: Rural TV News
Jackson, George: WJLA–TV / Newschannel 8
Jackson, Hallie: NBC News
Jackson, Katharine: Reuters Radio & TV
Jackson, Kaylah: Connecting Vets
Jackson, Roberta: C–SPAN
Jackson, Ryan: ABC News
Jackson, Samuel: WJLA–TV / Newschannel 8
Jacobi, Isabelle: Swiss Broadcasting
Jacobi, Steven: CBN News
Jacobs, Adia: CNN
Jacobson, William: CNN
Jaconi, Michelle: Washingtonpost.com
Jaeger, Britta: German TV (ZDF)
Jaffe, Gary: Voice of America
Jaklitsch, Vanessa: Antena 3 TV
Jalawan, Wagma: Voice of America
James, Acacia: NBC News
James Sloan, Karen: CNBC
Jamison, Dennis: CBS News
Jamshidi, Kaveh: Voice of America

MEMBERS ENTITLED TO ADMISSION—Continued

Janis, Stephen: The Real News Network
Janney, Oliver: CNN
Janney, Renata: TV Asahi
Jansen, Eric: WUSA–TV
Janssen, Simon-Laslo: German Public Radio (ARD)
Japaridze, Nunu: Fox News
Jarboe, Brian: National Public Radio
Jarrett, Laura: CNN
Jarrett, Ricky: National Public Radio
Jarrett, Tracy: Vice News
Jarvis, Julie: NBC Newschannel
Javadi, Afshin: EWTN
Javers, Eamon: CNBC
Jay, Paul: The Real News Network
Jefferson, Rickey: CBS News
Jeffrey, Terence: Cnsnews.com
Jegisman, Valeria: Voice of America
Jenkins, David: CNN
Jenkins, Lee: Sinclair Broadcast Group
Jenkins, Tiara: C–SPAN
Jenkins, William: Fox News
Jennings, Alicia: NBC News
Jennings, Edward, Jr.: ABC News
Jensen, Heidi: ABC News
Jentile De Canecaude, Catherine: TF1–French TV
Jermin, Ede: WRC–TV / NBC–4
Jeroro, Ewholomeyovwi: CNN
Jessen, Peder: Diversified Communications, Inc. (DCI)
Jessup, John: CBN News
Jester, William: ABC News
Jeswani, Geet: NBC News
Jewell, Hannah: Washingtonpost.com
Jewsevskyj, George: Fox News
Ji, Yewon: Radio Free Asia
Jiang, Weijia: CBS News
Jibai, Wafaa: Middle East Broadcasting Networks (MBN)
Jimenez, Cecilia: ABC News
Jimenez, Christopher: Fox News
Jimenez, Omar: CNN
Jin, Ho Sung: Korean Broadcasting Systems
Jin, Yuelei: Xinhua
Joannides, Jihan: Agence France Presse (AFP–TV)
Joehnk, Astrid: German Public Radio (ARD)
Johannes, Wilhelm: Voice of America
Johns, David: Sinclair Broadcast Group
Johns, Joseph: CNN
Johnson, Aiden: BBC
Johnson, Carrie: National Public Radio
Johnson, Chester: WUSA–TV
Johnson, Christopher: Radio One
Johnson, Daniel: BBC
Johnson, Irene: WRC–TV / NBC–4
Johnson, Joshua: WAMU
Johnson, Katherine: CBS News
Johnson, Kevin: Cox Broadcasting
Johnson, Kia: Reuters Radio & TV
Johnson, Mahreon: Fox News
Johnson, Mansa: Imagination Media
Johnson, Mary Jennifer: NBC Newschannel
Johnson, Monique: CNN
Johnson, William: WJLA–TV / Newschannel 8
Johnston, Jeffrey: CBS News
Johnston, Vanessa: Reuters Radio & TV
Jonas, Gerald: Agence France Presse (AFP–TV)
Joneidi, Majid: BBC
Jones, Andrew: Al Jazeera English
Jones, Arthur: CBS News
Jones, Athena: CNN
Jones, Douglas: CNN
Jones, Gwyneth: NBC News
Jones, Katerra: CTV–Community TV of PG County
Jones, Kellianne: Fox News
Jones, Kenneth: WETA
Jones, Lorna: CBS News
Jones, Lyrone: WRC–TV / NBC–4
Jones, Matthew: NBC News
Jones, Nelson: WTTG–Fox Television
Jones, Phelix: C–SPAN
Jones, Stephen: Fox News
Jones, Torrance: Fox News
Jones Jackson, Andreia: Nexstar Media Group
Joost, Nathalie: Fox News
Joplin, Ashleigh: Washingtonpost.com
Jordan, Rosiland: Al Jazeera English
Jordan, Tracey: CNN
Jorgenson, David: Washingtonpost.com
Joseph, Akilah: Al Jazeera English
Joseph, Cameron: Vice News
Joslyn, James: WJLA–TV / Newschannel 8
Joy, Richard: Ventana Productions
Joyner, Arcelious: CNN
Joynt, Carol: CBS News
Judd, Donald: CNN
Juhasz, Aubri: National Public Radio
Juma, Mamatjan: Radio Free Asia
Jung, Joonhyung: Seoul Broadcasting System (SBS)
Jussim, Roderick: AP–Broadcast
Kades, Cathy: NBC News
Kady, Matt: WJLA–TV / Newschannel 8
Kaji, Mina: ABC News
Kalman, Nicholas: Fox News
Kamal, Hufsa: Fox News
Kamisar, Benjamin: NBC News
Kane, Jason: PBS NewsHour
Kanicka, Stephen: Fox News
Kanneth, Polson: CNN
Kaplan, William: Metro Teleproductions
Kapp, Bonney: CNN
Karacam, Serra: TRT World
Karamehmedovic, Almin: ABC News
Karasu, Oguz: TRT World
Karl, Jonathan: ABC News
Karp, James: NBC Newschannel

MEMBERS ENTITLED TO ADMISSION—Continued

Karson, Kendall: ABC News
Kasap, Bunyamin: TRT World
Kaseko, Omary: Voice of America
Kashfi, Monna: WAMU
Kashgary, Jilil: Radio Free Asia
Kasper, Kristin: Gray Television
Kastein, Julia: German Public Radio (ARD)
Kastens, Katharine: ABC News
Katcef, Susan: Capital News Service TV–U of Md
Katmer, Elvan: Fox News
Kato, Atsushi: NHK
Katz, Drew: CBS News
Kauffman, Don: Nexstar Media Group
Kaufman, Elena: CNN
Kavanagh, Peter: CNN
Kavi, Aishvarya: CNN
Kay, Katharine: BBC
Kaye, Matthew: The Berns Bureau, Inc.
Kealy, Courtney: TRT World
Keator, John: National Public Radio
Keedy, Matthew: CBN News
Keegan, Ashley: CNN
Kehayias Farhi, Arden: CBS News
Kehoe, Steven: C–SPAN
Kehs, Robert: NBC News
Kelemen, Michele: National Public Radio
Kellam, Brandi: CBS News
Kelley, Colleen: Fox News
Kelley, Jonathan: C–SPAN
Kellum, Gail: New Tang Dynasty TV
Kelly, Caroline: CNN
Kelly, Cristina: EWTN
Kelly, Margaret: Washingtonpost.com
Kelly, Mary: National Public Radio
Kelly, Shannon: CTV Canadian TV
Kelly, Terence: NBC News
Kelly, William: WJLA–TV / Newschannel 8
Kelsey, Adam: ABC News
Kendall, Halle: BBC
Kennedy, Andrew: Radio Free Asia
Kennedy, Benjamin: CBN News
Kennedy, Miranda: National Public Radio
Kennedy, Siobhan: Independent Television News (ITN)
Kenney, Colleen: Fox News
Kenny, Caroline: CNN
Kent, Peter: NBC News
Kenyon, Linda: Westwood One
Keo, Sovannarith: Radio Free Asia
Kepnes, Jeffrey: NBC News
Keppler, Kristin: CNN
Kerbs, Kenneth: CBS News
Kerchner, Eric: CBS News
Kerley, Paul: ABC News
Kerr, Roxane: C–SPAN
Kerwin, Christopher: WRC–TV / NBC–4
Kerwin, Kristin: Cox Broadcasting
Kesbeh, Dina: Al Jazeera International
Kessler, Aaron: CNN
Kessler, Jonathan: CBS News
Kettlewell, Christian: AP–Broadcast
Keum, Chul Young: Korean Broadcasting Systems
Key, Kayla Nicole: C–SPAN
Keyes, Allison: CBS News
Khairy, Khaled: AP–Broadcast
Khalaf, Lina: Al Jazeera International
Khaleefah, Basheer: Middle East Broadcasting Networks (MBN)
Khalil, Joseph: Nexstar Media Group
Khaliq, Mohammad: Al Jazeera International
Khamidov, Sandzhar: Voice of America
Khan, Javaria: NBC News
Khan, Junaid: National Public Radio
Khan, Mariam: ABC News
Khan, Saba: Voice of America
Khan, Saher: PBS NewsHour
Khan, Saliqa: WUSA–TV
Khananayev, Grigory: Fox News
Kharel, Nilu: Sagarmatha Television
Kharel, Ram: Sagarmatha Television
Khdr, Kawa: AP–Broadcast
Khimm, Suzy: NBC News
Khizder, Anastasia: NBC News
Khristenko, Alexander: Russian State TV and Radio (RTR)
Kianpour, Suzanne: BBC
Kidd, Sally: Hearst Television Inc.
Kieffer, Vivian: Radio Free Asia
Kiernan, Ryan: NBC News
Kilaru, Vandana: Fox News
Kill, Adrian: CBS News
Killion Boykin, Nikole: CBS News
Killough, Ashley: CNN
Kim, Annie: WUSA–TV
Kim, April: NHK
Kim, Caitlyn: Colorado Public Radio
Kim, Diana: NBC News
Kim, Hyunki: JTBC
Kim, Jin Kuik: Radio Free Asia
Kim, Jiyeon: Voice of America
Kim, Kyung Hyun: Korean Broadcasting Systems
Kim, Lauren: Yonhap News TV
Kim, Rosa: CBS News
Kim, Seon Myung: Voice of America
Kim, Soohyung: Seoul Broadcasting System (SBS)
Kim, Soo Rin: ABC News
Kim, Soyoung: Radio Free Asia
Kim, Woong Kyu: Korean Broadcasting Systems
Kimani, Julia: CBS News
Kimmel, Corey: ABC News
King, Elizabeth: ABC News
King, Erica: ABC News
King, Jennifer: AP–Broadcast
King, John: CNN
King, Kevin G.: Al Jazeera English
King, Kevin N.: C–SPAN

MEMBERS ENTITLED TO ADMISSION—Continued

King, Llewellyn: White House Chronicle
Kinoshita, Takahiro: TV Asahi
Kirby, Kevin: Fox News
Kirby, Michael: FedNet
Klapper, Henry: Fox News
Klass, Reed: CBN News
Klayman, Elliot: Eye–To–Eye Video
Kleim, Peter: N–TV German News Channel
Klein, Kent: Sirius XM Satellite Radio
Klein, Mary: CNN
Klein, Richard: ABC News
Klein, Robert: Diversified Communications, Inc. (DCI)
Klein, Shawn: Spectrum News
Kleinhenz, Stefan: One America
Kleinman, Avery: WAMU
Klos, Daniel: CBS News
Knapp, Brandon: CNN
Knapp, Timothy: Gray Television
Knier, Rebecca: WUSA–TV
Knigge, Michael: Deutsche Welle TV
Knight, Danielle: WAMU
Knighton, David: C–SPAN
Knoedler, Matthew: Lilly Broadcasting
Knoller, Mark: CBS News
Knox, Olivier: Sirius XM Satellite Radio
Koch, William: NBC News
Kodjak, Alison: National Public Radio
Koenig, Lauren: CNN
Koenig-Muenster, Kailani: NBC News
Koerber Moir, Ashley: Fox News
Koessler, Thilo: German Public Radio (ARD)
Koh, Joyce: Washingtonpost.com
Kohl, Christoph: Austrian Radio & TV (ORF)
Kohno, Kenji: NHK
Kolinovsky, Sarah: ABC News
Kompaore, Arzouma: Voice of America
Kono, Torao: NHK
Konsmo, Sarah: WUSA–TV
Kook, Heekyung: Voice of America
Koprowicz, Tatiana: Voice of America
Kor, Mehmet: TRT World
Kordares, Molly: CBS News
Korff, Jay: WJLA–TV / Newschannel 8
Korte, Cara: CBS News
Kos, Martin: Bt Video Productions
Kosinski, Michelle: CNN
Koskin, Nikolay: Russian State TV and Radio (RTR)
Koslof, Evan: WUSA–TV
Kosnar, Michael: NBC News
Koster, Jesse: Voice of America
Kotke, Wolfgang: German TV (ZDF)
Kotuby, Stephanie: PBS NewsHour
Kouddous, Sharif: Al Jazeera English
Koura, Bagassi: Voice of America
Kovach, Robert: CBS News
Koval, Sergii: Inter TV
Kozlov, Petr: BBC
Krahenbuhl, Raquel: TV Globo International
Krall, Jenica: Fox News
Kramer, Kent: Radio One
Kraus, Melissa: Fox News Radio
Kraus, Nick: Al Jazeera English
Krawchenko, Katiana: CBS News
Kreinbihl, Mary: Fox Business Network
Kretz, Lillian: Danish Broadcasting Corporation
Kretz, Steffen: Danish Broadcasting Corporation
Krieg, Gregory: CNN
Krieger, Barbara: Fox News
Kriegleder, David: Austrian Radio & TV (ORF)
Kroker, Florian: German TV (ARD)
Kroll, Donald: ABC News
Krolowitz, Benjamin: CNN
Krupin, David: The Hill
Krupnik, Kathryn: CBS News
Kube, Courtney: NBC News
Kubota, Samantha: WUSA–TV
Kuhn, Gaspard: Swiss Broadcasting
Kunitz, Danielle: Washingtonpost.com
Kurihara, Takeshi: NHK
Kurtz, Howard: Fox News
Kurtzleben, Danielle: National Public Radio
Kurtzman, Alison: I24 News
Kurzius, Rachel: WAMU
Kusmez, Kevin: TRT World
Kvarnkullen, Tomas: Expressen TV
Kwan, Chi Hai: Shenzhen Media Group (SZMG)
Kwong, Matthew: CBC (Canadian Broadcasting Corporation)
Kyaw, Nayrein: Radio Free Asia
Kyi, Tsering: Voice of America
Labella, Michael: Al Jazeera English
Laboy, Felix: C–SPAN
Lacey, Donna: Fox News
Lafever, April: Fox News
Lamb, Brian: C–SPAN
Lamb, Deborah: C–SPAN
Lamb-Atkinson, Grace: CBS News
Lambert, Guy: WTTG–Fox Television
Lambert-McMichael, Evan: WTTG–Fox Television
Lamonica, John: CBN News
Landers, Elizabeth: Vice News
Landis, Austin: Scripps News
Landwehr, Arthur: German Public Radio (ARD)
Landy, Ekaterina: Al Jazeera English
Landy, John: BBC
Lane, Christopher: WETA
Lane, Keith: Voice of America
Lane, Samuel: PBS NewsHour
Langille, Sean: Fox News
Langley, Kevin: National Public Radio
Lanningham, Kyle: Eurovision Americas, Inc.
Lanningham, Sarah: Eurovision Americas, Inc.
Lantry, Lauren: ABC News
Lanzano, Dario: Fox News

MEMBERS ENTITLED TO ADMISSION—Continued

Lanzendoerfer, Nancy: WELT N24 German TV
Larade, Darren: C–SPAN
Larsen, Gregory: CBS News
Larson, Benjamin: CBS News
Larson, Lauren: Federal News Radio 1500 AM
La Rue, Corryn: Rural TV News
Laslo, Matthew: Laslo Congressional Bureau
Latendresse, Richard: Groupe TVA
Latreille, Christian: CBC (Canadian Broadcasting Corporation)
Latremoliere, France: NBC News
Lattie, Winston: FedNet
Laudiero, Anna: EWTN
Laughlin, Ara: CTV–Community TV of PG County
Laville, Molly: C–SPAN
Lawrence, Michael: Senate Radio–TV Gallery
Lazar, Robert: C–SPAN
Le, Viet: National Public Radio
Le, Yen Phuong: Vietv Network
Leach, Matthew: Fox News
Leahigh, Pamela: WRC–TV / NBC–4
Leake, Lindsey: Sinclair Broadcast Group
Leaming, Whitney: Washingtonpost.com
Lebedeva, Natasha: NBC News
Leblanc, Paul: CNN
Lebreton, Anne: Agence France Presse (AFP–TV)
Leclair, Matthew: GPI TV
Lecroy, Lillian: Fox News
Lecroy, Philip: Fox News
Leddon, Jerome: C–SPAN
Lederman, Joshua: NBC News
Lee, Carol: NBC News
Lee, Daniel: Voice of America
Lee, David: BBC
Lee, Donald: CBS News
Lee, Ji: CNN
Lee, Jo Eun: Voice of America
Lee, Joseph: JTBC
Lee, Kyu Sang: Radio Free Asia
Lee, Meredith: PBS NewsHour
Lee, Min: CNN
Lee, Sangdo: MBC–TV Korea (Munhwa)
Lee, Sanghoon: Voice of America
Lee, Sangmin: Radio Free Asia
Lee, So-Hyun: Washingtonpost.com
Lee, Xin-Yi: Tokyo Broadcasting System
Lee, Yihua: Voice of America
Lee, Jae Won: Korean Broadcasting Systems
Lefrak, Mikaela: WAMU
Legare, Robert: CBS News
Legro, Thomas: Washingtonpost.com
Leidelmeyer, Ronald: WRC–TV / NBC–4
Leidsmar, George: Small House Productions
Leimbach, Nicholas: WRC–TV / NBC–4
Lenchner, Charles: The Real News Network
Lenghi, Abdul-Mola: CBS News
Lenihan, Niall: Australian Broadcasting Corporation
Lent, David: GPI TV
Leon, Erika: WRC–TV / NBC–4
Leong, Dexter: CBS News
Leong, Hsiu: WJLA–TV / Newschannel 8
Leshan, Bruce: WUSA–TV
Lesiw, Victoria: Vice News
Leslie, Katie: WRC–TV / NBC–4
Lesser, Howard: Washington Radio And Press Service
Lester, Paul: WTTG–Fox Television
Leventhal, Jamie: PBS NewsHour
Levine, Adam: CNN
Levine, Michael: ABC News
Levine, Indira: WTTG–Fox Television
Levinson, James: Fox News
Levkovich, Denis: Feature Story News
Levy, Adam: CNN
Levy, Rebecca: CBS News
Lewis, Darrell: CBS News
Lewis, Edward: Fox News
Lewis, John B.: WJLA–TV / Newschannel 8
Lewis, Kevin: WJLA–TV / Newschannel 8
Lewis, Kimberly: Voice of America
Lewis, Latavia: CNN
Lewis, Misha: CNN
Lewis, Tisha: WTTG–Fox Television
Lewnes, Lisa: Reuters Radio & TV
Li, Alice: Washingtonpost.com
Li, Jingxun: Voice of America
Li, Yunjin: American Chinese Television (ACT)
Liao, Xiaoqiang: Radio Free Asia
Liasson, Mara: National Public Radio
Libin, Louis: Sinclair Broadcast Group
Lien, Arthur: NBC News
Lien, Christine: CNN
Lien, Jonathan: CBS News
Liffiton, Bruce: CBS News
Lilleston, Kristi-Sue: WTOP Radio
Lilling, David: Metro Teleproductions
Lim, Jong Ju: JTBC
Lim, Lister: Al Jazeera English
Lim, Sang: MBC–TV Korea (Munhwa)
Lim, Dongsoo: Korean Broadcasting Systems
Lin, Chuan: New Tang Dynasty TV
Linares, Moises: WRC–TV / NBC–4
Lindsey, Melvin: ABC News
Lipman, Melissa: CNN
Lipson, David: Australian Broadcasting Corporation
Liptak, Kevin: CNN
Lisker, Samuel: Spectrum News
Lisko, Lisa: Sinclair Broadcast Group
Little, Craig: WTTG–Fox Television
Littler, Caryn: NBC News
Littleton, Philip: CNN
Liu, Libo: Voice of America
Liu, Senhao: Hong Kong Phoenix Satellite Television
Livermore, Erin: ABC News
Ljung, Erik: Al Jazeera English

MEMBERS ENTITLED TO ADMISSION—Continued

Llargues, Anna: WRC–TV / NBC–4
Lloyd, Brian: C–SPAN
Lloyd, Ian: WJLA–TV / Newschannel 8
Lo, Wai: Radio Free Asia
Lobianco, Tomas: Laslo Congressional Bureau
Lobosco, Katherine: CNN
Lochstampfor, Eric: Scripps News
Locke, Alexandra: Al Jazeera International
Lockhart, Kathleen: NBC News
Loebach, Joseph: NBC News
Loeschke, Paul: C–SPAN
Loffman, Matthew: PBS NewsHour
Logan, Charles: C–SPAN
Loganathan, Sonikka: CNN
Lohr, Christopher: Washington Examiner
Loiaconi, Stephen: Sinclair Broadcast Group
Lokay, James: WTTG–Fox Television
Loker, Jessica: Fox News
Londono, Cristina: Telemundo Network
Long, James: NBC News
Long-Higgins, Hannah: BBC
Longo, Adam: WUSA–TV
Lonsdorf, Katherine: National Public Radio
Lopez Bolanos, Jazmin: Voice of America
Lopez-Capera, Dario: WRC–TV / NBC–4
Lopez-Pulido, Clara: CNN
Lopez Reyes, Edwing: Telemundo Network
Lopez Ruiz, Juan Carlos: CNN
Lopez Zamorano, Jose: Hispanic Communications Network
Lora, Edwin: CNN
Lorenzen, Elizabeth: Native American TV (NATV)
Lorenzen, Jacob: Danish Broadcasting Corporation
Lormand, John: SRN News (Salem)
Low, Harry: BBC
Low, Scott: Fox News
Lowery, Stephen: Nexstar Media Group
Lowie, Zachary: Fox News
Lowman, Wayne: Fox News
Lowther, Jason: CBC (Canadian Broadcasting Corporation)
Lozada Salgado, Edith: WRC–TV / NBC–4
Lozano Villo, Maria Eugenia: TV3-Televisio de Catalunya
Lu, Liyuan: Voice of America
Lu, Lucy: Radio Free Asia
Lu, Tao: Hong Kong Phoenix Satellite Television
Lucas, Christina: German TV (ARD)
Lucas, David: WJLA–TV / Newschannel 8
Lucas, Mary Grace: Vice News
Lucas, Ryan: National Public Radio
Lucchini, Maria: Univision
Luhby, Tami: CNN
Lujan, Brianna: CNN
Lukas, Jayne: Global TV Canada
Luke, Colette: Reuters Radio & TV
Luna, Nathan: ABC News
Luqman, Jacqueline: The Real News Network
Lussenhop, Jessica: BBC
Lutan, Albert: CNN
Lutterbeck, Deborah: Reuters Radio & TV
Luviano, Janette: WRC–TV / NBC–4
Luzader, Douglas: Fox News
Luzi, Iacopo: Voice of America
Luzquinos, Julio: NBC News
Lybrand, John: CNN
Lydick, Sarah: WUSA–TV
Lyles, Darius: Imagination Media
Lyn, Brendan: FedNet
Lynch, Cordelia: Sky News
Lynch, Shannon: Sirius XM Satellite Radio
Lynch, Thomas: WRC–TV / NBC–4
Lynn, Emily: Fox News
Lynn, Gary: NBC News
Lynn, Kellye: WJLA–TV / Newschannel 8
Lyon, Daniel: Sinclair Broadcast Group
Lysak, Michael: Bloomberg Radio & TV
Ma, Moqiu: TV Tokyo
Maass, Allison: Gray Television
Mabin, Matthieu: France 24
Macaluso, Michelle: Sinclair Broadcast Group
Macaya, Melissa: Washingtonpost.com
Macchi, Victoria: Voice of America
Macfarlane, Scott: WRC–TV / NBC–4
Macgillivray, Graham: CQ / Roll Call
Machalek, Steven: CNN
Machles, Maren: Scripps News
Macholz, Wolfgang: German TV (ZDF)
Macias, Amanda: CNBC
Macias, Mitzi: Voice of America
Macneil, Lachlan Murdoch: ABC News
Madan, Richard: CTV Canadian TV
Madden Iv, Nathaniel: Blaze Media
Madigan, Tracey: Groupe TVa
Mager, Dickon: Sky News
Magnus, Anders: Norwegian Broadcasting
Mague, Anthony: WRC–TV / NBC–4
Mahdi, Ahmed: Al Arabiya TV
Mahdi, Ali: Middle East Broadcasting Networks (MBN)
Mahtani, Dhanesh: Radio Free Asia
Maier, Timothy: Talk Media News
Maile, Amanda: ABC News
Main, Alison: CNN
Maina, Njuwa: I24 News
Maisler, Aaron: Fuji TV Japan
Majeed, Alicia: NBC News
Mak, Timothy: National Public Radio
Makori, Vincent: Voice of America
Malbon, Joy: CTV Canadian TV
Malik, Osman: Washingtonpost.com
Mallin, Alexander: ABC News
Mallonee, Mary: CNN
Malloy, Allison: CNN
Malone, Connor: German TV (ARD)
Malone, Hannah: NBC News

MEMBERS ENTITLED TO ADMISSION—Continued

Malone, James: Voice of America
Maltas, Michael: Fox News
Malveaux, Suzanne: CNN
Mammadli, Aytan: Caspian Broadcasting TV
Mamonov, Roman: Voice of America
Mancini, Anthony: Bloomberg Radio & TV
Mandelson, Adam: Eurovision Americas, Inc.
Manduley, Christina: CNN
Manley, Nicole: CNN
Manning, Samantha: Cox Broadcasting
Mansour, Fadi: Al Jazeera International
Maqbool, Aleem: BBC
Marcello, Michele: NBC News
March, Stephanie: Australian Broadcasting Corporation
Marchitto, John: National Public Radio
Marcucci, John: WRC–TV / NBC–4
Marcum, James: WJLA–TV / Newschannel 8
Maresco, Brian: One America
Marfil, Judy Grace: Wall Street Journal
Marin Arteaga, Jesus: WFDC–TV Univision
Marion, Marvin: Voice of America
Marks, Benjamin: NHK
Marks, Simon: Feature Story News
Marno, Michael: Middle East Broadcasting Networks (MBN)
Marquardt, Alexander: CNN
Marques, Antonio: CBS News
Marquez, Maria: Al Jazeera English
Marquez Marquez, Jessica: EWTN
Marquis, Melissa: National Public Radio
Marraco, Marina: WTTG–Fox Television
Marriott, Marc: NBC News
Marsh, Mary: ABC News
Marsh, Michelle: WJLA–TV / Newschannel 8
Marsh, Rene: CNN
Marshall, Colin: National Public Radio
Marshall, Miri: WUSA–TV
Marshall, Serena: ABC News
Marshall, Steven: CBS News
Marsic, Mathew: Australian Broadcasting Corporation
Martin, Ben: Independent Television News (ITN)
Martin, Bianca: WAMU
Martin, David: CBS News
Martin, Gregory: NBC News
Martin, Jeffrey: Sightline Media Group
Martin, Jon: ABC News
Martin, Joseph: NBC News
Martin, Michel: National Public Radio
Martin, Patrick: Washingtonpost.com
Martin, Rachel: National Public Radio
Martin, Raquel: Nexstar Media Group
Martin, Wisdom: WTTG–Fox Television
Martin Ewing, Samara: WUSA–TV
Martinez, Angelica: WRC–TV / NBC–4
Martinez, Carlos: WRC–TV / NBC–4
Martinez, Daniel: CNN
Martinez, Joseph: WRC–TV / NBC–4
Martinez, Luis: ABC News
Martinez, Mercedes: Al Jazeera English
Martinez Fierro, Juan: Cope Radio (Spain)
Martino, Jeffrey: CBC (Canadian Broadcasting Corporation)
Martone, James: Sky News Arabia
Mason, Pamela: CBS News
Massarelli, Valeria: NTN24
Massimo, Richard: WTOP Radio
Masters, Chase: CNN
Mastrangelo, Dominick: Washington Examiner
Mastromarino, James: National Public Radio
Mathis, James: NBC Newschannel
Mathurin, Jean Michel: Voice of America
Matkosky, Timothy: Cox Broadcasting
Matsuyama, Toshiyuki: Fuji TV Japan
Matthews, Andre: CTV–Community TV of PG County
Matthews, Christopher: NBC News
Matthews, Lisa: AP–Broadcast
Matthews, Samuel: Yahoo News
Matthews, Valerie: C–SPAN
Mattingly, Philip: CNN
Mattout, Charlotte: France 2 Television
Matza, Max: BBC
Matzka, Jeffrey: SRN News (Salem)
Maucione, Scott: Federal News Radio 1500 AM
Mauro, Ellen: CBC (Canadian Broadcasting Corporation)
Maxwell, Chloe: C–SPAN
May, Ashley: Al Jazeera English
Mayk, Lauren: WRC–TV / NBC–4
Mazariegos, Luis: To The Contrary (Persephone Productions)
Mazariegos, Mark: CBS News
Mazrieva, Eva: Voice of America
Mazza, Mathieu: German TV (ZDF)
McAleese, Kevin: Feature Story News
McAlpine, David: Fox News
McArdle, John: C–SPAN
McCabe, Neil: One America
McCabe, Valerie: NBC News
McCagg, David: NHK
McCalister, Sharon: National Public Radio
McCammon, Sarah: National Public Radio
McCann, Michael: WTTG–Fox Television
McCann, Sean: C–SPAN
McCarren, Christian: C–SPAN
McCarthy, Jacqueline: Gray Television
McCarthy, Kevin: WTTG–Fox Television
McCarty, Dennis: CBS News
McCarty, Donald Jay: CBS News
McClam, Herbert: Al Jazeera English
McClam, Kevin: EWTN
McClelland, Brianna: Fox News
McCloskey, George: Fox News

MEMBERS ENTITLED TO ADMISSION—Continued

McClure, Tipp: Diversified Communications, Inc. (DCI)
McConnell, Dave: WTOP Radio
McCoo, Cynthia: ABC News
McCray, Ronnie: CNN
McCrory, Sarah: Fox News Radio
McCulloch, Lauren: NBC News
McCullough, Colin: CNN
McDaniel, Eric: National Public Radio
McDermott, Richard: Australian Broadcasting Corporation
McDevitt, Lauren: Bloomberg Radio & TV
McDonald, Joel: WUSA–TV
McDonnell, Brigid Mary: Fox News
McDonough, Constance: Fox News
McDougald, Tomika: C–SPAN
McDougall, Ian: NBC News
McEachern, Cheryl: Fox News
McEachern, Terrance: Fox News
McEwan, Erin: Fox News
McFall, Caitlin: The Daily Caller
McGarrity, Gerard: C–SPAN
McGee, Ebony: CNN
McGehee, Alyssa: EWTN
McGinniss, Richard: The Daily Caller
McGonagle, Paul: WTTG–Fox Television
McGrath, Megan: WRC–TV / NBC–4
McGraw, Meridith: ABC News
McGreevy, Allen: BBC
McGregor, Jeanavive: Australian Broadcasting Corporation
McGuire, Gitte: Danish Broadcasting Corporation
McGuire, James: ABC News
McHenry, Robert: ABC News
McIntyre, Colin: Al Jazeera English
McKee, Caroline: Fox News
McKee, Michael: Bloomberg Radio & TV
McKelvey, Tara: BBC
McKelway, Douglas: Fox News
McKend, Eva: Spectrum News
McKinless, Thomas: CQ / Roll Call
McKinley, Douglas: CNN
McKinney, Lee: NBC News
McLaughlin, Elizabeth: ABC News
McLellan, Daniel: CBS News
McLellan, Jennifer: Sirius XM Satellite Radio
McLennan, Bradley: Independent Television News (ITN)
McManus, Maureen: Spectrum News
McManus, Nicole: NBC Newschannel
McMenamin, Angelique: ABC News
McMichael, Samuel: CNN
McMinn, Nan Hee: AP–Broadcast
McMorris-Santoro, Evan: Vice News
McNamara, Cassie: CNN
McNeil, Tiffany: WUSA–TV
McPherson, Cecile: Eurovision Americas, Inc.
McQuade, Kathryn: ABC News
McShane, Connell: Fox Business Network
Meadows, Jennifer: NBC News
Mears, William: Fox News
Mebane, Martinez: ABC News
Meech, James: CNN
Meek, James: ABC News
Mees, John: Australian Broadcasting Corporation
Megginson, Abigail: C–SPAN
Meghani, Sagar: AP–Broadcast
Meier, Markus: Austrian Radio & TV (ORF)
Melendez-Vela, Milagros: WRC–TV / NBC–4
Mellman, Ira: Voice of America
Memoli, Michael: NBC News
Men, Kimseng: Voice of America
Mercado, D'Juan: TV Asahi
Meredith, Mark: Fox News
Merica, Daniel: CNN
Meriwether, Brooks: WRC–TV / NBC–4
Merkel, Joseph: Scripps News
Merlano, Juan: Caracol Television
Mesmer, Nardos: Fox News
Mesner-Hage, Jesse: Washingtonpost.com
Metcalfe, Rhoda: CBC (Canadian Broadcasting Corporation)
Metelerkamp, Florian: N–TV German News Channel
Metjian, Julia: NBC News
Metzger, Justin: C–SPAN
Meyer, Kellie: Nexstar Media Group
Meyer, Kerry: Diversified Communications, Inc. (DCI)
Meza-Martinez, Cecily: National Public Radio
Mi, Tra: Voice of America
Mich, Daniel: Washingtonpost.com
Michael, Nicholas: National Public Radio
Michaels, Allison: Washingtonpost.com
Michaud, Robert: Al Jazeera English
Michel de la Morvonnais, Loiq: France 2 Television
Michell, Erenia: Fox News
Micklas, Kelsey: CBS News
Micklos, Gregg: EWTN
Middleton, Simone: Fox News
Midura, Kyle: Gray Television
Mielec, Antonio: Bloomberg Radio & TV
Mikols, Glenn: Eurovision Americas, Inc.
Mikutsky, David: NBC News
Milam, Greg: Sky News
Miles, Jon: WETA
Milford, Robert: WELT N24 German TV
Millar, Christopher: NBC News
Miller, Alexandra: Scripps News
Miller, Andrew: C–SPAN
Miller, Anna: CNN
Miller, Avery: ABC News
Miller, Blair: Cox Broadcasting
Miller, Jason: Federal News Radio 1500 AM
Miller, Jon: WTOP Radio
Miller, Jonathan: Blaze Media

MEMBERS ENTITLED TO ADMISSION—Continued

Miller, Larry: WUSA–TV
Miller, Lawrence: European Pressphoto Agency
Miller, Paul: CNN
Miller, Timothy: Middle East Broadcasting Networks (MBN)
Miller, William: CBS News
Millington, Takiha: NBC News
Mills, Joseph: National Public Radio
Mills, Katherine: C–SPAN
Millward, Craig: Cnsnews.com
Milton Steinfort, Patricia: CBS News
Minas, Marina: Fox News
Minott, Gloria: National Scene News
Minters, Camille: Politico.com
Mir, Mashaal: Al Jazeera International
Miran, Alec: CNN
Miranda, Alexa: CNN
Miranda Salazar, Juan: Telesur
Mirsaeedi, Guita: Voice of America
Mirza, Atthar: Washingtonpost.com
Mitchell, Adrienne: Bloomberg Radio & TV
Mitchell, Alexander: NBC News
Mitchell, Andrea: NBC News
Mitchell, Benjamin: CBS News
Mitchell, Lacrai: CBS News
Mitchell, Min: Radio Free Asia
Mitnick, Steven: NBC News
Mizelle, Shawna: CNN
Mizroch, Marissa: NBC News
Mizukami, Takashi: NHK
Mock, Sarah: Rural TV News
Mohall, Christopher: Spectrum News
Mohammed, Linah: Washingtonpost.com
Moise, Joseph: WTTG–Fox Television
Molina, Emiliana: NTN24
Mollaoglu, Muhammed: TRT World
Moller, Jeffrey: CNN
Mollet, Melissa: WRC–TV / NBC–4
Molnar, George: WTOP Radio
Moloney, Mary: CNN
Monack, David: C–SPAN
Monange, Arielle: France 2 Television
Mondora, William: Nexstar Media Group
Monier, Emmanuelle: Agence France Presse (AFP–TV)
Monroe, Brian: Washingtonpost.com
Monsalve, Lizeth Juliana: Telemundo Network
Montague, William: Fox News
Montanaro, Domenico: National Public Radio
Montenegro, Lorestina: Telemundo Network
Montgomery, Tamara: Fox News
Montoro, Victor: C–SPAN
Montoya-Galvez, Camilo: CBS News
Mooar, Brian: NBC Newschannel
Moore, Andrew: WTOP Radio
Moore, Elena: National Public Radio
Moore, Garrett: C–SPAN
Moore, Jacob: CBN News
Moore, Oddessey: Fox News
Moore, Robert: Independent Television News (ITN)
Moore, Terrence: NBC News Radio
Moore, William: Middle East Broadcasting Networks (MBN)
Moorer, Willie: Voice of America
Moorhead, Jeremy: CNN
Morada, Raymond: NBC News
Morales, Davone: NBC News
Morales, Isabel: CNN
Moran, Jane: BBC
Moran, Terence: ABC News
Morano, Edward: CBN News
Moreno Gomez, Jaime: Caracol Television
Moreno Vargas, Julio: NTN24
Morgan, Nancy: WETA
Moriizumi, Saori: Tokyo Broadcasting System
Morley, Gillian: CBS News
Morris, Amy: Bloomberg Radio & TV
Morris, Holly: WTTG–Fox Television
Morris, Julie Asher: TF1–French TV
Morris, Kylie: Independent Television News (ITN)
Morris, Michael: Cnsnews.com
Morris, Peter: CNN
Morrison, Donald: BBC
Morrison, James: WAMU
Morrison, Nadine: Agence France Presse (AFP–TV)
Morrison, Vaughn: AP–Broadcast
Morse, Julie: CBS News
Morse, Richard: Fox News
Mortman, Howard: C–SPAN
Morton, Daniel: C–SPAN
Mortreux, Vincent: TF1–French TV
Mosk, Matthew: ABC News
Mosley, Matthew: Fuji TV Japan
Moton, Kenneth: ABC News
Moutsatsos Morales, Basilio: Televisa News Network
Movit, Lisa: The Hill
Moxley, Charles: Senate Radio–TV Gallery
Moynihan, Mark: Fox News
Mozaffari, Shaheen: NBC News
Mozgovaya, Natalia: Voice of America
Mucha, Sarah: CNN
Muhammad, Amjad: Al Jazeera International
Muhammad, Askia: National Scene News
Muhammad, Seleena: Fox News
Mui McClintock, Ylan: CNBC
Muir, Breanna: Washingtonpost.com
Muir, David: ABC News
Mulcahy, Bridget: NBC News
Muldavin, Julia: Al Jazeera International
Muldoon, Edward: Washingtonpost.com
Mulholland, Kristopher: WUSA–TV
Mulligan, Robert: WTTG–Fox Television
Mullis, Steven, Jr.: National Public Radio
Mullon, Tiffany: NBC News

MEMBERS ENTITLED TO ADMISSION—Continued

Muncy, Christopher: Dailymail.com
Munford, Corey: Radio Free Asia
Munneke, Amy: Fox News
Munoz, Luis: Middle East Broadcasting Networks (MBN)
Muntean, Peter: WUSA–TV
Muong, Nareth: Radio Free Asia
Muriithi, Jonathan: Voice of America
Murillo, Michael: WTOP Radio
Murphy, James: Diversified Communications, Inc. (DCI)
Murphy, John: CBS News
Murphy, Susan: WRC–TV / NBC–4
Murphy, Terence: C–SPAN
Murphy, Tim: Fox News
Murphy, Zoeann: Washingtonpost.com
Murray, Benjamin: Sightline Media Group
Murray, Douglas: Cheddar
Murray, Mark: NBC News
Murray, Matthew: WRC–TV / NBC–4
Murray, Megan: Fox News
Murray, Sara: CNN
Murray, Timothy: Ventana Productions
Murry, Rosetta: NBC News
Murtaugh, Peter: BBC
Muskat, Steven: NBC Newschannel
Musurlian, Peter: One America
Mutesa, Mirembe: CNN
Mwakalyelye, Ndimyake: Voice of America
Myers, Megan: Fox News
Myers, Nile: One America
Mylroie, Laurie: AP–Broadcast
Myo, July: Radio Free Asia
Myre, John: National Public Radio
Nado, Jill: Fox News Radio
Nagle, Molly: ABC News
Nagy, Ashraf: Al Jazeera International
Nagy, Leah: PBS NewsHour
Naing, Thet: Voice of America
Najarian, Sarkis: Radio Free Asia
Najjar, Ruqaiyah: Fox Business Network
Nalesnick, Brian: CBS News
Nam, Sooji: NBC News
Namling, Dondhon: Voice of America
Nania, Rachel: WTOP Radio
Nannes, Steven: CNN
Narahari, Priya: Eurovision Americas, Inc.
Narancio, Federica: AP–Broadcast
Narayan, Vivek: Scripps News
Narisi, Stephen: WELT N24 German TV
Nascimento, Aurea: Voice of America
Nasir, Labib: Reuters Radio & TV
Nason, Andrew: C–SPAN
Nasr, Hiba: Sky News Arabia
Nasser, Mohamed: AP–Broadcast
Natour, Rhana: PBS NewsHour
Navarro, Aaron: CBS News
Naylor, Brian: National Public Radio
Naylor, Robert: Voice of America
Neal, Jason: NBC News
Neal, Michelle: NBC News
Neary, Sean: Voice of America
Neel, Joe: National Public Radio
Neely, Brett: National Public Radio
Neff, Blake: Fox News
Neff, William: Washingtonpost.com
Neill, Tara: BBC
Neloms, Nia: FedNet
Nelson, Glenn: C–SPAN
Nelson, James: Fox News
Nelson, Joseph: Washington Bureau News Service
Nelson, Marie: ABC News
Nelson-Schneider, Donna: NBC News
Neme Garrido, Chaid: WFDC–TV Univision
Nerska, Alexander: Fox Business Network
Neto, Joaquim: WJLA–TV / Newschannel 8
Nettles, Meredith: ABC News
Neubauer, Kristin: Reuters Radio & TV
Neunan, Megan: Fox News
Nevel, Paul: WETA
Neville, Nicholas: CNN
Nevins, Elizabeth: NBC News
Newberry, William: NBC Newschannel
Newell, Carla: Voice of America
Newhauser, Daniel: Vice News
Newman, Mary: Politico.com
Newton, Robin: C–SPAN
Nguyen, Anh: Fox News
Nguyen, Anh: Radio Free Asia
Nguyen, Minh Tuyen: Spectrum News
Nguyen, Trung: Voice of America
Nha, Kevin: Voice of America
Ni, Chia-Hui: TVBS
Nicci, Nicholette: ABC News
Nichols, Hans: NBC News
Nicolaidis, Virginia: Fox News
Niemann, Stefan: German TV (ARD)
Nikuradze, David: Rustavi 2 Broadcasting Company
Niliahmadabadi, Hadi: BBC
Ninh, Trang: C–SPAN
Nishikawa, Atsutoshi: NHK
Nishimoto, Momoca: NHK
Niv, Ohad: Bloomberg Radio & TV
Nixon, Adam: Middle East Broadcasting Networks (MBN)
Niyazi, Kuerban: Radio Free Asia
Nneji, Nkechi: NBC News
Nobles, Ryan: CNN
Noh, Jung: Radio Free Asia
Nolan, Bridget: CNN
Nolasco, Maira: Scripps News
Nolen, John: CBS News
Noor, Dharna: The Real News Network
Norins, Jamie: Diversified Communications, Inc. (DCI)
Norling, Richard: ABC News

MEMBERS ENTITLED TO ADMISSION—Continued

Norman, Jeffrey: CNN
Norris, Courtney: PBS NewsHour
Norris, Donna: C–SPAN
Norris, Elise: Fox News
Norris, James: Middle East Broadcasting Networks (MBN)
Northam, Jackie: National Public Radio
Novosel, James: NBC News
Nunez, Jorge: ABC News
Nunez, Shoshannah: CBN News
Oakes, Alena: WTTG–Fox Television
Oat, Michael: CNN
O'Beirne, Jonathan: CNN
O'Berry, Donald: Fox News
Oberti, Ralf: NHK
O'Brien, Benen: C–SPAN
O'Brien, David: NBC News
O'Brien, Lindsey: WJLA–TV / Newschannel 8
O'Brien-Hosein, Alexi-Noelle: TRT World
O'Connell, Benjamin: C–SPAN
O'Connell, Michael: NBC Newschannel
O'Connell, Rosalie: Voice of America
O'Connor, Erin: Washingtonpost.com
O'Day, Andrew: Bloomberg Radio & TV
Odendahl, Eric: CNN
Odom, Quillie: Fox News
O'Donnell, Kelly: NBC News
O'Donnell, Norah: CBS News
O'Donnell, Patrick: Eye–To–Eye Video
O'Donoghue, Gary: BBC
O'Donovan, Brian: RTE–Irish Radio & TV
Offermann, Claudia: German TV (ZDF)
O'Gara, Patrick: ABC News
O'Grady, Andrea: Fox News
Ogrysko, Nicole: Federal News Radio 1500 AM
Ogunfolaju, Babatunde: The Real News Network
Oh, Esther: NHK
Oh, Jung S.: Seoul Broadcasting System (SBS)
O'Hara, Jessica: Fox News
Okada, Takamori: TV Asahi
O'Keefe, Kitty: CNN
O'Keefe, Edward: CBS News
Olazagasti, Carlos: Hearst Television Inc.
Olds, Katie: Feature Story News
Olea Fernandez, Cristina: TVE–Spanish Public Television
Olick, Diana: CNBC
Oliger, Brian: WTOP Radio
Olkhovskaia, Iuliia: Channel One Russian TV
Ollove, Michael: Stateline
Olmstead, Charles: NBC News
Olmstead, Craig: Al Jazeera International
Olmsted, Alan: C–SPAN
Olson, Christopher: Vice News
Olson, Emily: Australian Broadcasting Corporation
Olson, Kendra: Fox News
Omar, Ammad: National Public Radio
Omar, Angie: France 24
Omeokwe-Davis, Amarachukwu: National Public Radio
O'Neil, Jennifer: NBC News
Oni, Jesusemen: Voice of America
Onsanit, Rattaphol: Voice of America
Oo, Thar: Voice of America
Oo, Thein: Voice of America
Orchard, Mark: Sinclair Broadcast Group
Ordonez, Francisco: National Public Radio
O'Regan Schroeder, Deirdra: Washingtonpost.com
Orellana Canas, Luis: Azteca America
Orenstein, Jayne: Washingtonpost.com
Orgel, Paul: C–SPAN
Orlov, Arkadiy: Voice of America
Ormiston, Susan: CBC (Canadian Broadcasting Corporation)
Ortiz, Fabien: TV3-Televisio de Catalunya
Os, Lars: Norwegian Broadcasting
Osburn, Lesley: WAMU
O'Shea, Daniel: ABC News
Osmani, Woria: AP–Broadcast
Ostermann, Torben: German Public Radio (ARD)
Ota, Yusuke: NHK
Ouafi, Mohamed Said: AP–Broadcast
Ouellette, Nathan: CQ / Roll Call
Overby, Peter: National Public Radio
Overton, Kathi: Diversified Communications, Inc. (DCI)
Overzat, Gregory: NBC News
Owen, Andrea: ABC News
Owen, Quinton: ABC News
Ozol, Bernard: CBS News
Ozug, Matthew: National Public Radio
Pacuraru, Denis: CBN News
Padial, Maribel: Gray Television
Padilla, Mercy: Hispanic Communications Network
Padilla Alvarado, Ivenneth: Univision
Pagan, Louis: AP–Broadcast
Page, Paige: Fox News
Palca, Joseph: National Public Radio
Palka Minukas, Liz: WUSA–TV
Pallone, Frank: Fuji TV Japan
Palmer, Hope: NBC News
Palmeri, Tara: ABC News
Palombo, Russell: WPLG–TV10
Pamias Reichard, Alexandra: Fox News
Pande, Arunima: Voice of America
Panetta, Alexander: CBC (Canadian Broadcasting Corporation)
Panzer, Chester: WRC–TV / NBC–4
Papinashvili, Aleksandre: Rustavi 2 Broadcasting Company
Pappas, Raymond: Fox News
Parangot, Ann: CNN
Parenti, Alisa: Bloomberg Radio & TV
Park, Calvin: National Public Radio
Park, Edward: Seoul Broadcasting System (SBS)
Park, Elizabeth: Fox Business Network

MEMBERS ENTITLED TO ADMISSION—Continued

Park, Hanbyul: JTBC
Park, Ji Hee: Eurovision Americas, Inc.
Park, Jung-Woo: Radio Free Asia
Park, Sungho: MBC–TV Korea (Munhwa)
Parker, Andre: CNN
Parker, Glenn: CBC (Canadian Broadcasting Corporation)
Parker, Marley: CTV Canadian TV
Parker, Robert: CNN
Parkinson, John: ABC News
Parks, John: Washingtonpost.com
Parks, MaryAlice: ABC News
Parks, Miles: National Public Radio
Parnass, Sarah: Washingtonpost.com
Parr, Stephanie: Fox News
Parresol, Alexandra: Nexstar Media Group
Parsell, Robert: Voice of America
Partsinevelos, Kristina: Fox Business Network
Pascale, Jordan: WAMU
Pasha, Firoze: National Public Radio
Pathammavong, Kingsavanh: Voice of America
Patience, Keenan: Verizon
Patrickis, Caroline: WJLA–TV / Newschannel 8
Patruznick, Michael: C–SPAN
Patsko, Daniel: ABC News
Patterson, Stephen: CNN
Paxton, Bradford: Fox News
Payam, Amir: BBC
Paylor, Eddie: CNN
Paz-Goldenheart, Beni: Hispanic Communications Network
Peaches, Sandra: CTV–Community TV of PG County
Peacock, Grant: GPI TV
Peaks, Gershon: Reuters Radio & TV
Pearson, Christopher: Sky News
Pearson, Leonard: WUSA–TV
Peck, Christina: National Public Radio
Pecoraro, Vincent: Spectrum News
Pecorin, Allison: ABC News
Peebles, Daniel: CBS News
Pegues, Jeffrey: CBS News
Pellerin, Roch: Eurovision Americas, Inc.
Pellish, Aaron: CNN
Peltier, Anthony: AP–Broadcast
Pena, Alexander: C–SPAN
Pena, Maria: Telemundo Network
Pendorf, Felicia: NBC News
Penman, Margaret: Washingtonpost.com
Pennell, Elizabeth: Morningside Partners, LLC
Pennington, Craig: Al Jazeera English
Pepino, Jason: Al Jazeera English
Peppers, Gregory: AP–Broadcast
Pereira, Julia: National Public Radio
Perera, Katryna: CBS News
Perez, Anna: Blaze Media
Perez, Evan: CNN
Perez, Simone: Vice News
Pergram, Chad: Fox News
Peries, Sharmini: The Real News Network
Perkins, Douglas: Fox News
Perkins, Vernon: C–SPAN
Perl, Drora: Galei–Tzahal (Israel Army Radio)
Perlmutter-Gumbiner, Elyse: NBC News
Perlow, Rebecca: ABC News
Perrell, Thomas: WJLA–TV / Newschannel 8
Perry, Clayton: CNN
Perry, Jessica: Yahoo News
Perry, Timothy: CBS News
Persinko, Timothy: Viewpoint Communications
Persons, Sally: Fox News
Peruga-Martinez, Alejandro: CNN
Pessin, Don: Reuters Radio & TV
Peterson, Beatrice: ABC News
Peterson, Robert: CBS News
Petraitis, Gerald: AP–Broadcast
Petrilli, Daniel: Fox News
Petrillo, Nicholas: WUSA–TV
Petrimoulx, Drew: Nexstar Media Group
Petroka, Katelyn: CNN
Petromelis, Nicholas: FedNet
Petrychka, Ruslan: Voice of America
Pettingell, Dolia: Proyecto Puente
Pexton, Kenneth: Ventana Productions
Peyton, Michael: CBS News
Pezenik, Alexandra: ABC News
Pfeiffer, Alexander: Fox News
Phares, Kelly: Fox News
Phelps, Jordyn: ABC News
Philipps, Gregory: Radio France
Philips, Eric: CBN News
Phillip, Abigail: CNN
Phillips, Kathryn: ABC News
Picht, Matthew: Scripps News
Picket, Kerry: Sirius XM Satellite Radio
Pickup, Michael: ABC News
Pierce, Nanako: Al Jazeera International
Pierre-Louis, Guillaume: The Daily Caller
Pimienta Hernandez, Alberto: WRC–TV / NBC–4
Pinczuk, Murray: NHK
Pinczuk, Sam: GPI TV
Pinto, Susanna: EWTN
Pinzon, Wingel: Small House Productions
Pinzon-Contreras, Henry: Small House Productions
Piotrowski, Luke: Scripps News
Piper, Allan: Now This News
Piper, Jeffrey: WRC–TV / NBC–4
Pisczek, Scott: CNN
Pisnia-Bystriakova, Nataliia: Voice of America
Pitney, Nicholas: Now This News
Pitocco, Nickolas: C–SPAN
Pitti, Edwin: WFDC–TV Univision
Pizarro, Fernando: Univision
Plater, Christopher: ABC News
Plaza, Elizabeth: EWTN

MEMBERS ENTITLED TO ADMISSION—Continued

Pliszak, Kevin: ABC News
Ploss, Sarah: NBC News
Plotnick, Ariel: Washingtonpost.com
Plummer, Shonequa: Fox News
Poarch, David: CNN
Poch, Reasey: Voice of America
Poindexter, Zoe: CBS News
Pointer, Jack: WTOP Radio
Polantz, Katelyn: CNN
Poley, Michelle: CNN
Pollock, Richard: One America
Pollock, Ryan: CNN
Polmer, Brendan: Bloomberg Radio & TV
Ponnudurai, Parameswaran: Radio Free Asia
Ponsard, Adrien: TF1–French TV
Poole, John: National Public Radio
Pope, Kolin: Washingtonpost.com
Pope, Michael: Virginia Public Radio
Popielarz, Taylor: Spectrum News
Porter, Almon: C–SPAN
Portnoy, Steven: CBS News
Posey, Mahlia: Washingtonpost.com
Posobiec, John: One America
Post, Megan: Colorado Public Radio
Postovit, David: Hearst Television Inc.
Potts, Nina-Maria: Feature Story News
Potts, Tracie: NBC Newschannel
Pouladi Najafabadi, Farhad: Voice of America
Pourshariati, Shapoor: ABC News
Povich, Elaine: Stateline
Pov Sok, Khemara: Voice of America
Powell, Brian: Radio Free Asia
Powell, Lee: Washingtonpost.com
Powell-Escobar, Alesia: CBS News
Powers, Kristen: WJLA–TV / Newschannel 8
Pratapas, Lauren: CNN
Pratz, Megan: Cheddar
Pray, Thomas: The Hill
Preloh, Anne: C–SPAN
Prescott, Willa: CNN
Preston, Christopher: Vice News
Preston, Mark: CNN
Presutti Davison, Carolyn: Voice of America
Pretorius, Marthinus: NBC News
Price, Amanda: Al Jazeera English
Prichard, Matthew: Hearst Television Inc.
Prifti, Ilir: Al Jazeera English
Prince, Todd: Radio Free Europe
Privot, Benjamin: WAMU
Prokupecz, Shimon: CNN
Pronko, Anthony: C–SPAN
Prophet, Ike: ABC News
Proskow, Jackson: Global TV Canada
Pruitt, Claude: Scripps News
Przybyla, Heidi: NBC News
Pugliese, Pat: CNBC
Pula, Dardan: Bloomberg Radio & TV
Puljic, Ivica: Al Jazeera English
Purbaugh, Michael: ABC News
Purser, Emily: Sky News
Purvis, Haleigh: WUSA–TV
Pyatt, Kyle: Scripps News
Quadrani, Federico: CNN
Quander, Michael: WUSA–TV
Quarry, Ralph: CBS News
Quijano Jovel, Jackeline: WFDC–TV Univision
Quinn, Clare: C–SPAN
Quinn, Diana: CBS News
Quinn, Jason: NBC News
Quinn, John: Voice of America
Quinn, Mary: ABC News
Quinnette, John: NBC News
Quinonez, Omar: CBS News
Quiñonez Silva, Rosbelis: WFDC–TV Univision
Quinton, Sophie: Stateline
Quiroga, Juan: AP–Broadcast
Rabbe, George: NBC News
Rabiee, Mana: Reuters Radio & TV
Rabin, Mark: CBS News
Rabin Aber, Carrie: CBS News
Rad, Ali: Fox News
Radke, Jason: ABC News
Raffaele, Robert: Voice of America
Rafferty, Andrew: Scripps News
Rager, Bryan: CNBC
Rahn, Richard: CBS News
Raju, Manu: CNN
Rama, Padmananda: AP–Broadcast
Ramanathan, Rajeshwari: Al Jazeera International
Ramirez, Edwin: Small House Productions
Ramirez, Marisela: The Hill
Ramirez, Stephanie: CBS News
Ramos, Raul: WFDC–TV Univision
Ramos-Tomeoni, Stephanie: ABC News
Randle, James: Voice of America
Rangel, Corey: Scripps News
Rapela, Daniel: WTTG–Fox Television
Rashid, Kutaba: Al Jazeera International
Rashidi, Rahim: AP–Broadcast
Rathner, Jeffrey: WETA
Ratliff, Rikki: Blaze Media
Ratliff, Walter: AP–Broadcast
Rattansi, Shihab: Al Jazeera English
Raval, Nikhil: C–SPAN
Raviv, Daniel: I24 News
Rawls, Dejah: CTV–Community TV of PG County
Ray, Alonzo: NBC News
Ray, Douglas: Fox News
Read, Russel George: Sinclair Broadcast Group
Reber, Susanne: Scripps News
Reddy, Pallavi: CNN
Redisch, Stuart: Voice of America
Redmon, Jonathan: WTTG–Fox Television
Redmond Morgan, Kuren: C–SPAN

MEMBERS ENTITLED TO ADMISSION—Continued

Redpath, Julia: National Public Radio
Rees, Annie: Politico.com
Reeves, Alea: Al Jazeera English
Reeves, Austin: WTTG–Fox Television
Reeves, Tracy: ABC News
Reffes, Melanie: NHK
Rego, Alexandra: Fox News
Rehkopf, George: CBS News
Reid, Charles: CBS News
Reid, Paula: CBS News
Reid, Samuel: Voice of America
Reidy, Matthew: Fox News
Reilly, Robert: C–SPAN
Reinhard, Irvin: CBS News
Reinsel, Edward: Fox News
Reis, Chester: NBC News
Reis, Sylvia: WETA
Reische, Erin: CNN
Reiss, John: NBC News
Remillard, Michele: C–SPAN
Ren, Meixing: AP–Broadcast
Renaud, Jean: CNN
Renbaum, Bryan: Talk Media News
Renfro, Owen: Fox News
Renken, David: Fox News
Renner, Solape: Independent Television News (ITN)
Replogle, Joshua: CNN
Resnick, Jonathan: Fox Business Network
Reston, Maeve: CNN
Reuter, Cynthia: C–SPAN
Revaz, Philippe: Swiss Broadcasting
Reverter Baquer, Francesc: TV3-Televisio de Catalunya
Reyes, Joel: Reuters Radio & TV
Reynolds, Catherine: CBS News
Reynolds, Kathleen: WUSA–TV
Reynolds, Robert: Al Jazeera English
Reynolds, Talesha: NBC News
Rhee, Kyung: Radio Free Asia
Rhoades, Alexandra: I24 News
Rhodes, Nevin: Morningside Partners, LLC
Ribas, Jorge: Washingtonpost.com
Ricalde, Katheryn: Fox'News
Ricciardella, William: Washington Examiner
Rice, John: WJLA–TV / Newschannel 8
Rice, Shannon: C–SPAN
Rice, Rodney, Jr.: Verizon
Richard, Sylvain: CBC (Canadian Broadcasting Corporation)
Richardson, Grace: Fox News
Richardson, Young: One America
Rickard, Michael: WTTG–Fox Television
Ricker, Jeffrey: Vice News
Rico, Jorge: WRC–TV / NBC–4
Riddle, Casey: CNN
Ridley, Lakisha: Eurovision Americas, Inc.
Rieger, John Michael: Washingtonpost.com
Rieger, Wendy: WRC–TV / NBC–4
Riera Parera, Julia: Voice of America
Riess, Steffanie: German TV (ZDF)
Riggs, James: NBC News
Rigizadeh, Stephanie: NBC News
Rigney, Paul: NBC News
Riha, Anne Marie: Fox News
Riley, Justin: Voice of America
Rion, Chanel: One America
Rios, Delia: C–SPAN
Rios-Hernandez, Raul: CNN
Ritter, Dana: CBN News
Ritterpusch, Matthew: Vice News
Rivara, Kayla: The Real News Network
Rivas, Ivan: Agence France Presse (AFP–TV)
Rivera, Matthew: NBC News
Rivera, Michelle: WRC–TV / NBC–4
Rivera Garcia, Katherine: WFDC–TV Univision
Rivera Trinidad, Carlos Daniel: WRC–TV / NBC–4
Rizzo, John: AP–Broadcast
Robbins, Christina: Fox News
Robbins, Diana: German Public Radio (ARD)
Robbins, Francisco: CBS News
Robbins, Michael: Fox News
Robert, Olivier: Eye–To–Eye Video
Roberts, Bryan: WTTG–Fox Television
Roberts, Corinne: ABC News
Roberts, Jean Pierre: Eurovision Americas, Inc.
Roberts, William: Al Jazeera International
Robertson, Dominique Genevieve: CNN
Robertson, Gregory: CNN
Robertson, John: Fox News
Robertson, Marcella: WUSA–TV
Robertson, Patrick: CBN News
Robinson, Adia: ABC News
Robinson, David: CNN
Robinson, Emerald: One America
Robinson, John: CNN
Robinson, Kelvin: NBC News
Robinson, Laura: CNN
Robinson, Ralph: Voice of America
Roby, Erin: WUSA–TV
Roca, Xavier: Swiss Broadcasting
Rocha, Juan: Ventana Productions
Rockovich, John: Blaze Media
Rocque, Tiffany: C–SPAN
Rodeffer, Mark: C–SPAN
Rodriguez, Eduardo: AP–Broadcast
Rodriguez, Janet: Univision
Rodriguez, Lissette: ABC News
Rodriguez, Martine: C–SPAN
Rodriguez, Micaela: CQ / Roll Call
Rodriguez, Valdemar: NTN24
Rodriguez, Maya: Scripps News
Rodriguez Lopez, Marcela: WFDC–TV Univision
Rogers, David: CNN
Rogin, Ali: PBS NewsHour
Rogosin, Joshua: National Public Radio

MEMBERS ENTITLED TO ADMISSION—Continued

Rohrbaugh, Randolph: C–SPAN
Rohrbeck, Douglas: Fox News
Rokus, Brian: CNN
Rolfes, Ellen: Scripps News
Roman, Kaitlyn: CBS News
Romero, Latrice Nadia: CNN
Romero Juarez, Walter: WFDC–TV Univision
Rondeau, Micha: Bloomberg Radio & TV
Roof, Peter: NBC Newschannel
Root, Pathik: Scripps News
Root, Sean: The Hill
Root, Thomas: Fox News Radio
Rosario, Eduardo: Eurovision Americas, Inc.
Rosborough, Tiffany: ABC News
Rosche, Jedd: CNN
Rose, Art: WTOP Radio
Rose, Victoria: WJLA–TV / Newschannel 8
Rosen, James: Sinclair Broadcast Group
Rosen, Shari: CNBC
Rosenberg, Gary: ABC News
Rosenberg, Howard: CBS News
Rosenthal, Joshua: WTTG–Fox Television
Ross, Chloe: Australian Broadcasting Corporation
Rossetti-Meyer, Misaele: Diversified Communications, Inc. (DCI)
Ross Taylor, Allyson: CBS News
Rotella, Audrey: NBC News
Roth, Samantha-Jo: Spectrum News
Roth, Theodore: CBS News
Rothschild, Anna: Washingtonpost.com
Rousselle, Christine: EWTN
Roussey, Thomas: WJLA–TV / Newschannel 8
Rowe, Tom: Reuters Radio & TV
Rowls, Megan: C–SPAN
Royce-Bartlett, Lindy: CNN
Royster, Meredith: WRC–TV / NBC–4
Rubashkin, Jacob: NBC News
Rubin, Olivia: ABC News
Rudd, Michael: WJLA–TV / Newschannel 8
Ruff, Jennifer: C–SPAN
Ruffini, Christina: CBS News
Ruffini, Joseph: CBS News
Ruggiero, Diane: CNN
Rushing, Ian: CBN News
Rushing, Joshua: Al Jazeera English
Ruskin, Elizabeth: Alaska Public Radio Network / Alaska Public Media
Russell, Carmen: The Real News Network
Russell, Eugene: WTTG–Fox Television
Russell, James: Voice of America
Rwema, Edward: Voice of America
Ryan, April: Aurn
Ryan, Bruce: WRC–TV / NBC–4
Ryan, Kate: WTOP Radio
Rydell, Mary Kate: CBS News
Ryntjes, Daniel: Feature Story News
Rysak, Francis: WTTG–Fox Television
Saakov, Rafael: Voice of America
Saavedra, Tupac: Al Jazeera International
Sabol, Tracy: EWTN
Sadighi, Shahla: Voice of America
Saeed, Sana: Al Jazeera International
Saenz, Katherine: CNN
Sagalyn, Daniel: PBS NewsHour
Said, Samira: CBS News
Saine-Spang, Cynthia: Voice of America
Sajaia, Nana: Voice of America
Sakamoto, Rex: Now This News
Sakowska, Magdalena: TV Polsat
Saks, Lauren: Washingtonpost.com
Salazar, Sulema: WRC–TV / NBC–4
Salenetri, Mia: WUSA–TV
Salim, Yuni: Voice of America
Sallet, Oliver: Deutsche Welle TV
Salman, Sara: Al Jazeera International
Saloomey, Kristen: Al Jazeera English
Salvatierra, Rodrigo: Vice News
Sammon, William: Fox News
Sampaio, Carlos: C–SPAN
Sampson, Thomas: AP–Broadcast
Sampy, David: Independent Television News (ITN)
Samuel, Charles: Verizon
Samuel, Stacey: National Public Radio
Samuels, Elyse: Washingtonpost.com
Samuels, Genienne: CTV–Community TV of PG County
Sanchez, Boris: CNN
Sanchez, George: ABC News
Sanchez, Pablo: Univision
Sanchez, Stephen: CBS News
Sanchez-Bonmati, Damian: Al Jazeera International
Sanchez Cruz, Rafael: WFDC–TV Univision
Sanders, Molly: C–SPAN
Sanders-Smith, Sherry: C–SPAN
Sandiford, Michele: C–SPAN
Sandoval, Hillary: Fox Business Network
Sands-Sadowitz, Geneva: CNN
Sandza, Allison: NBC News
Sanfuentes, Jose: CNN
Sanfuentes, Lisa: CNBC
Sanli, Tuna: TRT
Sansone, Amanda: CNN
Santa-Rita, Joad: Voice of America
Santayana, Michelle: CNN
Santucci, John: ABC News
Saracho De Meraz, Dinah Luis: Grupo Radio Centro
Sargeant, Nancy: Bloomberg Radio & TV
Sargis, Joseph: Fox News
Sarlin, Benjamin: NBC News
Sasaki, Tomoaki: ABC News
Satchell, David: WUSA–TV
Satterfield, John: WETA
Satterfield, Kolbie: WUSA–TV
Saunders, Alexis: NBC News
Saunders, John: Eurovision Americas, Inc.
Savage, Craig: Fox News

MEMBERS ENTITLED TO ADMISSION—Continued

Savage, Hamid: Fox News
Savchenko, Yulia: Voice of America
Savchuk, Dmitriy: Voice of America
Savoy, Gregory: Reuters Radio & TV
Say, Mony: Voice of America
Sayed, Amr: Al Jazeera International
Sayilgan, Barbaros: TRT World
Scanlan, Quinn: ABC News
Scanlan, William: C–SPAN
Scanlon, Bridget: C–SPAN
Scanlon, Katherine: EWTN
Scannell, Kara: CNN
Scarbrough, Dominique: WAMU
Scarnato, David: WUSA–TV
Schachtel, Jordan: Blaze Media
Schantz, Douglas: CNN
Schantz, Kristine: Scripps News
Schapitl, Lexie: National Public Radio
Scharf, Jason: Eurovision Americas, Inc.
Scheimer, Dorey: Cox Broadcasting
Schelfhout, Cosima: BBC
Scheuer, John: CNN
Schick, Camilla: CBS News
Schiff, Brian: Voice of America
Schifrin, Nicholas: PBS NewsHour
Schlegel, Barry: ABC News
Schlenker, Aungthu: Radio Free Asia
Schloemer, Hans-Peter: German TV (ZDF)
Schmerling, Stacey: NBC News
Schmidt, Harlan: CNN
Schmidt, Matthew: Fox News Radio
Schmitz, Leonard: CBS News
Schneider, Amy: WJLA–TV / Newschannel 8
Schneider, Edward: Voice of America
Schneider, James: WETA
Schneider, Jessica: CNN
Schoenmann, Donald: Eye–To–Eye Video
Schoenmann, Jacob: WJLA–TV / Newschannel 8
Scholer, Mee: ABC News
Schonberger, Jennifer: Fox Business Network
Schottle, John: WETA
Schreiber, Sebastian: German Public Radio (ARD)
Schrobsdorff, Ingalisa: WAMU
Schrum, Bart: Voice of America
Schubauer, Katharine: Agence France Presse (AFP–TV)
Schular, Elizabeth: Blaze Media
Schultz, Kyley: WUSA–TV
Schultz, Marisa: Fox News
Schultze, Emily: ABC News
Schuster, Mark: CBS News
Schwartz, Brian: CNBC
Schwartz, Chad: Morningside Partners, LLC
Schwarzkopf, Steffen: WELT N24 German TV
Schweiger, Ellen: C–SPAN
Schweitzer, Allison: WAMU
Sciacca, Joseph: Fox News
Sciutto, James: CNN
Scott, Beth: NBC News
Scott, Gurnal: Fox News Radio
Scott, Rachel: ABC News
Scott, Raquel: CNN
Scritchfield, Andrew: NBC News
Scruggs, Wesley: NBC News
Sculletti, Justin: Washingtonpost.com
Scully, Steven: C–SPAN
Seabrook, Willliam: WETA
Seaby, Gregory: CNN
Seales, Chance: Scripps News
Searles, David: ABC News
Sears, Carl: NBC News
See, Patrice: German TV (ZDF)
Seem, Thomas: CBS News
Segears, Leon: EWTN
Segers, Grace: CBS News
Segovia Reche, Bricio: Voice of America
Segraves, Mark: WRC–TV / NBC–4
Seib, Gerald: Wall Street Journal
Seidman, Jesse: Vice News
Seidman, Joel: NBC News
Seifert, Jan: German TV (ZDF)
Seipel, Arnold: National Public Radio
Seitz-Wald, Alexander: NBC News
Seium, Michael: Small House Productions
Sejima, Ryutaro: Fuji TV Japan
Seldin, Jeffrey: Voice of America
Selyukh Pickeral, Alina: National Public Radio
Semler, Ashley: BBC
Sen, Shreya: TRT World
Sens, Eleonore: Agence France Presse (AFP–TV)
Seo, Hye Jun: Korean Broadcasting Systems
Seo, Ja Ryen: Korean Broadcasting Systems
Seo, Jiyoung: Korean Broadcasting Systems
Serbu, Jared: Federal News Radio 1500 AM
Serfaty, Sunlen: CNN
Sergi, Samantha: ABC News
Serrano, Randy: Telemundo Network
Serrano Quintero, Monica: CNN
Setsang, Pema: Voice of America
Severson, Theodore: CNN
Sevilla, Maria: NBC News
Sevilla Garcia, Francisco: TVE–Spanish Public Television
Sexton, James: The Hill
Seyler, Matthew: ABC News
Seytoff, Alim: Radio Free Asia
Sganga, Nicole: CBS News
Shabad, Rebecca: NBC News
Shaffir, Gregory: CBS News
Shaffir, Kimberlee: CBS News
Shalhoup, Joseph: NBC News
Shammo, Hakim: Voice of America
Shannon, Michael: ABC News
Shapiro, Ari: National Public Radio
Sharief, Islam: Middle East Broadcasting Networks (MBN)

MEMBERS ENTITLED TO ADMISSION—Continued

Sharma, Bhupinder: WJLA–TV / Newschannel 8
Sharp, Duncan: Sky News
Shaw, David: Politico.com
Shaw, Joseph: Reuters Radio & TV
Shaw, Lawrence: ABC News
Shawley, Garrett: Blaze Media
Shaylor, John: CNN
Sheerin, Jude: BBC
Shefte, Whitney: Washingtonpost.com
Sheikh, Ayan: Al Arabiya TV
Shelton, Nina: C–SPAN
Shelton, Steven: Fox News
Shepard, Ryan: ABC News
Sheppard, Markette: WUSA–TV
Sheridan, Chris: Al Jazeera English
Sherman, Roger: Voice of America
Sherwin, Travis: Hearst Television Inc.
Sherzai, Magan: PBS NewsHour
Shibaki, Tomokazu: Fuji TV Japan
Shields, Daniel: Fox News Radio
Shihab-Eldin, Ahmed: Al Jazeera International
Shikaki, Muna: Al Arabiya TV
Shimabukuro, Albert: WTOP Radio
Shimizu, Jumpei: Nippon TV Network
Shine, Tom: ABC News
Shire, Robert: German TV (ARD)
Shirley, Trevor: Nexstar Media Group
Shitama, Colby: CBS News
Shivaram, Deepa: NBC News
Shlemon, Christopher: Independent Television News (ITN)
Shoffner, Harry: NHK
Shoichet, Catherine: CNN
Shore, Zachary: WTOP Radio
Shortell, David: CNN
Shull, Roger: Reuters Radio & TV
Shure, Michael: I24 News
Shutt, Charles: WUSA–TV
Sicile, James: ABC News
Sidi, Mawal: CNN
Sieg, Setareh: Voice of America
Siegel, Benjamin: ABC News
Siegel, David: CNN
Siegfriedt, Anita: Fox News
Sikka, Madhulika: Washingtonpost.com
Sills, Cecil John: NBC Newschannel
Silva Llancaleo, Juan: TRT World
Silva-Pinto, Daniel: TV Globo International
Silva-Pinto, Luis: TV Globo International
Silver, Quentin: NBC News
Silverman, Arthur: National Public Radio
Simkins, George: Voice of America
Simmons, Jamal: The Hill
Simmons, Sarah: WTTG–Fox Television
Simmons-Duffin, Selena: National Public Radio
Simms, Jeffery: CNN
Simon, Matthew: Scripps News
Simons, Sasha-Ann: WAMU
Simons, Stefan: German TV (ZDF)
Simpson, April: Stateline
Simpson, Janet: ABC News
Simpson, Jennifer: CNN
Simpson, Kathryn: CBC (Canadian Broadcasting Corporation)
Sinclair, Caitlin: One America
Sinderbrand, Rebecca: NBC News
Sinn, Rebecca: WJLA–TV / Newschannel 8
Sipos, Joseph: Voice of America
Sitz, Lindsey: Washingtonpost.com
Siu, Benjamin: ABC News
Skeans, Ronald: BBC
Skeele, Erin: Hearst Television Inc.
Skokowski, Christopher: NBC Newschannel
Skomal, Paul: Eurovision Americas, Inc.
Skopek, Aaron: NBC News
Slansky, Heike: German TV (ZDF)
Slater, Edward: ABC News
Slavica, Branka: HRT / Croatian Radio Television
Sleiman, William: Fox News
Slen, Peter: C–SPAN
Slie, Charles: NBC News
Sliman, Mostafa: APTVS–American Press & TV Services
Sloan, David: Regional News Network (RNN)
Sloane, Ward: CBS News
Small, Matthew: AP–Broadcast
Small, Taurean: Spectrum News
Smalley, Suzanne: Yahoo News
Smit, Cristina: Voice of America
Smith, Aaron: WTOP Radio
Smith, Andrew: CNN
Smith, Anthony: Diversified Communications, Inc. (DCI)
Smith, Brian: WETA
Smith, Cassano: NBC News
Smith, Christie: NBC Newschannel
Smith, Cory: WRC–TV / NBC–4
Smith, Cynthia: ABC News
Smith, Ethan: Fox News
Smith, Felicia: AP–Broadcast
Smith, James: ABC News
Smith, Jason: Fox News
Smith, Jordan-Marie: Washingtonpost.com
Smith, Kristin: Sinclair Broadcast Group
Smith, Lindley: C–SPAN
Smith, Megan: Scripps News
Smith, Michelle: CNN
Smith, Nicholas: WTTG–Fox Television
Smith, Oliver: BBC
Smith, Phillip: CNBC
Smith, Sara: NBC News
Smith, Scott: WJLA–TV / Newschannel 8
Smith, Terrance: NBC News
Smith, Tyler: Gray Television
Smoot, Kelly: CNN
Smysom, Osamah: Sky News Arabia

MEMBERS ENTITLED TO ADMISSION—Continued

Smyth, Christopher: Hearst Television Inc.
Sneed, Kimberly: NBC News
Snell, Kelsey: National Public Radio
So, Linda: Reuters Radio & TV
Sobocinski, Matthew: USA Today
Soe, Khin Maung: Radio Free Asia
Soete, Koen: Dutch TV & Radio (NOS)
Sohn, Seokmin: Seoul Broadcasting System (SBS)
Sokolov, Sergey: Voice of America
Soley, Joan: BBC
Solorzano, Gilbert: NBC News
Soltani, Leili: Voice of America
Soltis, David: CNBC
Sonmez, Zumrut: TRT World
Sonn, Courtney: Hearst Television Inc.
Sonnheim, Jon: Cox Broadcasting
Sopel, Jonathan: BBC
Sorenson, Benjamin: C–SPAN
Sotomayor, Marianna: NBC News
Soucy, Peggy: Eurovision Americas, Inc.
Southee, Haley: C–SPAN
Spaht, Erin: WUSA–TV
Spangenberg, Andrew: EWTN
Spears, John: FedNet
Speck, Bruce Alan: C–SPAN
Spector, Teresa: Fox News
Speer, John: National Public Radio
Speiser, Matthew: PBS NewsHour
Speiser, Tess: NBC News
Spencer, Kim Darcy: WRC–TV / NBC–4
Spevak, Joseph: WTTG–Fox Television
Spiegler, Theodore: CBS News
Spodak, Cassandra: CNN
Sprunt, Barbara: National Public Radio
Spunt, David: Fox News
Squitieri, Thomas: Talk Media News
Sreng, Leakhena: Voice of America
Stanczyk, Rafal: TVP Polish Television
Stanczyk-Pinkwart, Joanna: TVP Polish Television
Stang, Annette: NBC News
Stansfield, John: Sinclair Broadcast Group
Starddard, Donna: AP–Broadcast
Starikoff, Gary: C–SPAN
Stark, Elizabeth: CNN
Starr, Barbara: CNN
Starrs, Jennifer: Washingtonpost.com
Statler, James: C–SPAN
Staton, Montre: WTTG–Fox Television
Staton, Thomas: ABC News
Stead, Scott: CNN
Steakin, William: ABC News
Steck, Emily: CNN
Stein, Cari: To The Contrary (Persephone Productions)
Stein, Rob: National Public Radio
Steinberger, Daniel: Sinclair Broadcast Group
Stephens, Mark: WRC–TV / NBC–4
Stevens, Seneca: Fox News
Stevenson, John: CNN
Stevenson, Peter: Washingtonpost.com
Stewart, Andrew: SRN News (Salem)
Stewart, Briana: ABC News
Stewart, Ian: National Public Radio
Stewart, Kyle: NBC News
Stewart, Robin: Ventana Productions
Stiles, Victoria: EWTN
Stirewalt, Christopher: Fox News
Stix, Gabriel: CBS News
St. James, Greg: C–SPAN
St. Jean, Johnny: C–SPAN
St. John, Jonathan: Fox Business Network
Stockert, Natalie: Austrian Radio & TV (ORF)
Stoddard, Mark: ABC News
Stoddard, Richard: C–SPAN
Stoddart, Michelle: ABC News
Stone, Evie: National Public Radio
Stone Evans, Jessica: Fox Business Network
St. Onge, Derek: CNN
St-Onge Fleurant, Paul: CBC (Canadian Broadcasting Corporation)
Stopar, Andrej: RTV Slovenija
Storkel, Scott: Voice of America
Storms, Leslie: NBC News
Stout, Matthew: Fox News
Stracqualursi, Veronica: CNN
Strain, Eric: Fox News
Strand, Paul: CBN News
Strasser, Franz: BBC
Straub, Noelle: Stateline
Street, Eileen: NBC News
Streeter, Rodney: ABC News
Strickland, Kenneth: NBC News
Strickler, Laura: NBC News
Stringer, Ashley: CNBC
Strissel, Timothy: ABC News
Strolle, Margaret: C–SPAN
Strong, Amber: Scripps News
Strong, David: CBS News
Stuard, Christopher: WJLA–TV / Newschannel 8
Stubbs, James: NBC News
Stuhlmacher, Steven: WJLA–TV / Newschannel 8
Stumpf, Kaitlin: EWTN
Styles, Hannah: One America
Styles, Julian: AP–Broadcast
Suarez, Fernando: CBS News
Suarez, Sara: WFDC–TV Univision
Subramaniam, Tara: CNN
Subramanian, Courtney: BBC
Sucherman, David: Bloomberg Radio & TV
Suddeth, James: Fox News
Suddeth, Richard: Fox News
Sugg, Anna: CBS News
Suiters, Katherine: Cox Broadcasting
Sullivan, Katherine: CNN
Sullivan, Laura: National Public Radio
Sullivan, Rebecca: National Public Radio

MEMBERS ENTITLED TO ADMISSION—Continued

Summers, Kelly: Fox News
Summers, Patrick: Fox News
Sun, Ding: Xinhua
Suner, Rebecca: France 2 Television
Sung, Shenghua: New Tang Dynasty TV
Suphaphon, Songphot: Voice of America
Sutherland, Rachel: Fox News Radio
Suto, Ena: TV Asahi
Svahn, Nina: Finnish Broadcasting Company (YLE)
Svoboda, Sarah: BBC
Swain, Susan: C–SPAN
Swalec, Andrea: WRC–TV / NBC–4
Swanson, Carl: Voice of America
Sway, Aung: Voice of America
Sweeney, Robert: WRC–TV / NBC–4
Sweeney, Sam: WJLA–TV / Newschannel 8
Sweet, David: Fox News
Swezey, Christian: EWTN
Swicord, Jeffrey: Voice of America
Swinhart, Amanda: CNN
Sylvester, John: Fox News Radio
Symanski, Mary: C–SPAN
Szypulski, Tom: Al Jazeera English
Tabet, Joseph: Middle East Broadcasting Networks (MBN)
Tadelman, Samantha: Cheddar
Takaba, Yusuke: TV Asahi
Takahashi, Yoshiyuki: TV Tokyo
Talbot, Haley: NBC News
Tam, Ruth: WAMU
Tamary, Gil: Channel 10 Israel
Tamerlani, George: Reuters Radio & TV
Tan, Yixiao: Xinhua
Tanaka, Hikari: Nippon TV Network
Tanaka, Kentaro: NHK
Tanis, Fatma: National Public Radio
Tanner, Dustin: CNN
Tanno, Kiyoshi: NHK
Tapper, Jacob: CNN
Tarhan, Erkan: TRT
Tartaglia, Louis: Fox News
Tashi, Yeshi: Radio Free Asia
Tate, Simon: Al Jazeera English
Tatum, Samuel: Radio One
Tatum, Sophia: ABC News
Tausche, Kayla: CNBC
Tavana, Kambiz: Voice of America
Tavcar, Erik: Spectrum News
Tawfik, Nada: BBC
Tayier, Hamuti: Radio Free Asia
Taylor, Christina: C–SPAN
Taylor, Daron: Washingtonpost.com
Taylor, Jacqueline: Fox News
Taylor, Jessica: National Public Radio
Taylor, Kimberly: CBN News
Taylor, Russell: CNN
Taylor, Scott: WJLA–TV / Newschannel 8
Tea, Brandon: CBS News
Teasdale, Millicent: Independent Television News (ITN)
Teeples, Joseph: C–SPAN
Teichmann, Torsten: German Public Radio (ARD)
Tejera, Richard: ABC News
Tejerina, Pilar: Al Jazeera English
Temin, Thomas: Federal News Radio 1500 AM
Tennant, Gerald: National Public Radio
Tenney, Garrett: Fox News
Terpstra, Patrick: Scripps News
Terrel, Michael: NBC News
Terrelonge-Stone, Shomari: WRC–TV / NBC–4
Tessler, Barton: Westwood One
Tetrashvili, Alexander: Channel One Russian TV
Tevault, Neil David: National Public Radio
Tha, Kyaw: Voice of America
Thalman, Mark: Ventana Productions
Theisen, Michael: Voice of America
Theodorou, Christine: ABC News
Thevessen, Andrea: German TV (ZDF)
Thevessen, Elmar: German TV (ZDF)
Thoman, Eric: C–SPAN
Thomas, Bert: NBC News
Thomas, Christopher: Spectrum News
Thomas, Elizabeth: ABC News
Thomas, Haley: BBC
Thomas, James: Now This News
Thomas, Pierre: ABC News
Thomas, Sharahn: National Public Radio
Thomas, Shari: ABC News
Thomas, Shawna: Vice News
Thomas, Stephanie: Federal News Radio 1500 AM
Thompson, Joseph: One America
Thompson, Mallory: CNN
Thompson, Ronald: Radio One
Thorne, Clifford: Washington Bureau News Service
Thornes, Troy: CBS News
Thornton, David: Federal News Radio 1500 AM
Thornton, Thomas: ABC News
Thorp, Frank: NBC News
Thorp, Tamara: CNN
Thueringer, Tamara: C–SPAN
Thuman, Scott: Sinclair Broadcast Group
Tichawonna, Sowande: Imagination Media
Tidmarsh, Kevin: National Public Radio
Tikare, Olutayo: One America
Tiller, Arthur: C–SPAN
Tillett, Emily: CBS News
Tillman, Zeplyn: Radio One
Tilman, Brandon: C–SPAN
Tilve, Priyanka: Al Jazeera International
Tin, Alexander: CBS News
Tinaz, Baybora: TRT
Titus, Rhea: WUSA–TV
Tobianski, Sarah: Fox News
Tobias Delgado, Gessel: Voice of America
Todd, Charles: NBC News
Tolliver, Terri: WTTG–Fox Television

MEMBERS ENTITLED TO ADMISSION—Continued

Tomlinson, Lucas: Fox News
Tomy, Serge: WJLA–TV / Newschannel 8
Tone, Joseph: Vice News
Toombs, Zachary: Scripps News
Torres, Mari: CNN
Torres-Garcia, Armando: ABC News
Totenberg, Nina: National Public Radio
Touhey, Noel: C–SPAN
Tracey, Bree: Fox News
Tracy, Benjamin: CBS News
Trainor, Thomas: Eurovision Americas, Inc.
Tram, Thanh: CNN
Trammell, Michael: WUSA–TV
Trams, Ines: German TV (ZDF)
Tran, Hoa Ai: Radio Free Asia
Travers, Karen: ABC News
Travis, Alexandra: Scripps News
Traynham, Peter: CBS News
Trevelyan, Laura: BBC
Triantafillides, Demetrea: NBC News
Triay, Andres P.: CBS News
Trice, Ayesha: National Public Radio
Trindade, Angelica: CNN
Trujillo, Ashlee: NBC News
Tsao, Yufen: Radio Free Asia
Tserenbaljid, Uyanga: German TV (ZDF)
Tsirkin, Julia: NBC News
Tucker, Caroline: WRC–TV / NBC–4
Tucker, Elke: German TV (ZDF)
Tucker, William: Washingtonpost.com
Tulachom, Pinitkarn: Voice of America
Tull, Cameron: NBC News
Tunnard, Frederica: NBC News
Tuohey, Kenneth: CNN
Turman, Jack: CBS News
Turner, Christopher: CNN
Turner, Geoff: CBS News
Turner, Gillian: Fox News
Turner, Hayley: Fox News
Turner, James: AP–Broadcast
Turner, Melanie: NBC News
Turner, Mikea: WUSA–TV
Turner, Patricia: ABC News
Turner, Taylor: Washingtonpost.com
Turner, Tyrone: WAMU
Turrell, Elizabeth: CNN
Tuss, Adam: WRC–TV / NBC–4
Tyler, Brett: CNN
Ubeda-Carulla, Anna Maria: TVE–Spanish Public Television
Ucciardo, Frank: TRT World
Uceda, Claudia: Univision
Uhl, Kim: CNN
Uitz-Dallinger, Robert: Austrian Radio & TV (ORF)
Ulbrich-Strothe, Sabine: WELT N24 German TV
Uliano, Dick: WTOP Radio
Ulloa Ramirez, Victor: CBS News
Umeh, Maureen: WTTG–Fox Television
Umrani, Anthony: CNN
Uprety, Sharmila: Sagarmatha Television
Upton, Emily: Sky News
Urbanski, Tina: NBC News
Urbina, Luis: WJLA–TV / Newschannel 8
Ure, Laurie: CNN
Uribe, Juvenal: Morningside Partners, LLC
Usero, Adriana: Washingtonpost.com
Usher, Barbara: BBC
Utz, Anthony: National Public Radio
Vaeth-Levin, Benjamin: Viewpoint Communications
Vahramian, Agnes: France 2 Television
Vakil, Caroline: NBC News
Valdez, Ariel: WAMU
Valencia, Eric: CBN News
Valentine, Catherine: CNN
Valentine, Michael: WUSA–TV
Valerio, Michael: WUSA–TV
Vales, Tara: CNN
Valladares Perez, Carolina: Voice of America
Vallice, Christina: Wall Street Journal
Vance, Denise: AP–Broadcast
Van Cleave, Kristopher: CBS News
Vandercook, Rebecca: CBS News
Van Der Horst, Arjen: Dutch TV & Radio (NOS)
Vander Veen, Paul: WETA
Van Haren, Joel: Al Jazeera English
Vanlaere, Kathryn: Fox News
Vann, Matthew: ABC News
Van Susteren, Greta: Voice of America
Varelas, Thalia: WFDC–TV Univision
Vargas, Carlos: AP–Broadcast
Vargas, Julia: Univision
Varner, Jesse: WUSA–TV
Vasilogambros, Matthew: Stateline
Vasquez, Jennifer: WRC–TV / NBC–4
Vasquez Ramirez, Cristobal: Caracol Radio
Vaughan, Scott: Reuters Radio & TV
Vaughn, Michael: WJLA–TV / Newschannel 8
Vazquez, Maegan: CNN
Vega Urreta, Javier: Telemundo Network
Vega Yudico, Andrea: NHK
Velarde, Luis: Washingtonpost.com
Vera, Dennis: CBS News
Vera Rojas, Jaime: AP–Broadcast
Verdugo, Adam: CBS News
Verhovek, John: ABC News
Vermaak, Dawid: CNN
Ververs, Vaughn: NBC News
Vestal, Christine: Stateline
Viers, Dana: ABC News
Vigil, Marcos: ABC News
Vilas Delgado, Carlos: European Pressphoto Agency
Vilen, Paula: Finnish Broadcasting Company (YLE)
Villone, Patricia: CTV–Community TV of PG County
Vinson, Bryce: Fox News
Viqueira, Michael: NBC News

MEMBERS ENTITLED TO ADMISSION—Continued

Virji, Anar: Al Jazeera English
Visioli, Christopher: Fox News
Visley, Andrew: AP–Broadcast
Vitale, Joseph: Voice of America
Vitali, Alexandra: NBC News
Vitka, William: WTOP Radio
Vitorovich, Susan: NBC News
Vittal, Jeevan: Spectrum News
Vittert, Leland: Fox News
Vizcarra Coloma, Mario: Univision
Vodopivec, Tamara: RTV Slovenija
Vogel, Philip: Fox News
Vollmer, Charles: Bloomberg Radio & TV
Von Bonsdorff, Juri: Eurovision Americas, Inc.
Von Nahmen, Alexandra: Deutsche Welle TV
Vossekuil, Matthew: CNN
Vosti, Andrea: Swiss Broadcasting
Vowell, Nicole: Scripps News
Vu, Doanh: Vietv Network
Vu, Tu: CNN
Vuokko, Mikko: Deutsche Welle TV
Vurnis, Ambrose: WRC–TV / NBC–4
Wagener, Joseph: WTTG–Fox Television
Wagner, Paul: WTTG–Fox Television
Wait, Kevin: National Public Radio
Wakeam, Kira: PBS NewsHour
Waldenberg, Samantha: CNN
Walker, Amanda: Sky News
Walker, Jackie Lyn: ABC News
Walker, James: WJLA–TV / Newschannel 8
Walker, William: CBS News
Wallace, Christopher: Fox News
Wallace, Gregory: CNN
Wallace, John: Fox News
Wallace, Neil: Fox News
Walsh, Deirdre: National Public Radio
Walsh, Kelsey: ABC News
Walsh, Mary: CBS News
Walter, Charles: Eurovision Americas, Inc.
Walters, Amy: Al Jazeera International
Walters, Gregory: Vice News
Walters, Taylor: Fox News
Walz, Julia: WELT N24 German TV
Walz, Mark: CNN
Wang, Bingru: Hong Kong Phoenix Satellite Television
Wang, Jianying: Radio Free Asia
Wang, Taofeng: AP–Broadcast
Wang, Tianyi: Hong Kong Phoenix Satellite Television
Wang, Xiaoquan: Radio Free Asia
Wang, Yang: New Tang Dynasty TV
Wang, Youyou: Hong Kong Phoenix Satellite Television
Wangchuk, Tamdin: Radio Free Asia
Wangchuk, Tashi: Radio Free Asia
Waqfi, Wajd: Al Jazeera International
Ward, Derrick: WRC–TV / NBC–4
Ward, Donald: Fox News
Ward, Kevin: CBS News
Ward, Melissa: WUSA–TV
Warfield, Marcel: WUSA–TV
Warner, Quinn: NBC News
Warner, Tarik: WRC–TV / NBC–4
Warren, Michael: CNN
Washburn, Kevin: C–SPAN
Washington, Erick: CBS News
Washington, Ervin: CNBC
Washington-Anderson, Robert: WJLA–TV / Newschannel 8
Waters, Carlos: Wall Street Journal
Watkins, Eli: CNN
Watkins, Nicholas: Tokyo Broadcasting System
Watrud, Donald: WTTG–Fox Television
Watson, Eleanor: CBS News
Watson, Kathryn: CBS News
Watson, Owen: Al Jazeera English
Watson, Warren: GPI TV
Watters, Gemma: National Public Radio
Watts, Elizabeth: Al Jazeera International
Watts, Lindsay: WTTG–Fox Television
Webster, Aaron: Fox News
Webster, Ferlon: WUSA–TV
Wee, Misha: NBC News
Weekes, Michael: Reuters Radio & TV
Wehinger, Amy: Fox News
Wei, Chang: Hong Kong Phoenix Satellite Television
Weinbloom, Henry: Fox News Radio
Weiner, Cydney: NBC News
Weinstein, Richard: C–SPAN
Weinstock, Roy: WRC–TV / NBC–4
Weir, John: NBC News
Weiss, Ellen: Scripps News
Welch, Emily: CNN
Welker, Kristen: NBC News
Weller, George: NBC News
Wellford, Rachel: PBS NewsHour
Wellons, Mary: CNBC
Wells, Dylan: CNN
Welna, David: National Public Radio
Welsh, Meghan: Fox News
Werdel, Amna: PBS NewsHour
Werner, Katharina: BBC
Werner, Michaela: German TV (ARD)
Werschkul, Benjamin: Yahoo News
Wessinger, Kelli: National Public Radio
Westerman, Ashley: National Public Radio
Westfall, Richard: CBN News
Westhrin, Veronica: Norwegian Broadcasting
Westin, David: Bloomberg Radio & TV
Westwood, Sarah: CNN
Wexler, Casey: NBC Newschannel
Wheeler, Brian: Vice News
Whelan, Catherine: National Public Radio
Whitaker, Ginger: WTOP Radio

MEMBERS ENTITLED TO ADMISSION—Continued

White, Bria: WUSA–TV
White, Eric: Federal News Radio 1500 AM
White, Jennifer: NHK
White, Mark: CBS News
Whiteman, Caroline: Fox News
Whitfield, Christopher: Westwood One
Whitley, John: CBS News
Whitley, Walter: Fox News
Whitley-Berry, Victoria: National Public Radio
Whitney, Michael: Washington Bureau News Service
Whitson, Ricardo: CBS News
Whittington, Christopher: NBC News
Whong, Eugene: Radio Free Asia
Whyte, Scarlette: CBS News
Wick, Jeffrey: Scripps News
Widmer, Christopher: CBS News
Wiener, Jamie: CNN
Wiernicki, Anna: Nexstar Media Group
Wiersema, Alisa: ABC News
Wiggins, Christopher: NBC Newschannel
Wiggins, Dion: WUSA–TV
Wik, Snorre: Vice News
Wilde, Winston: NBC News
Wiley, Robert: GPI TV
Wilk, Wendy: Hearst Television Inc.
Wilkes, Douglas: WTTG–Fox Television
Wilkie Sumner, Christina: CNBC
Wilkins, Tracee: WRC–TV / NBC–4
Wilkins, Dikembe: BBC
Willetts, James: National Public Radio
Willey, Anna: Fox News
Williams, Abigail: NBC News
Williams, Algernon: CTV–Community TV of PG County
Williams, Amanda: WAMU
Williams, Brenna: CNN
Williams, David: Fox News
Williams, Jeffrey: Cox Broadcasting
Williams, John: Fox News
Williams, Louis: NBC News
Williams, Roxanne: NBC News
Williams, Steven: WTTG–Fox Television
Williams, Tom: Al Jazeera English
Williams, Tonya: Fox News Radio
Williams, Valeska: CNN
Williamson, Calum: NBC News
Williamson, Christopher: NBC News
Williams Vyas, Colleen: Fox News
Willis, Anne Marie: Fox News
Willis, Carl: WJLA–TV / Newschannel 8
Wilpert, Bernhard Gregory: The Real News Network
Wilson, Adrian: Al Jazeera English
Wilson, Donna: The Hill
Wilson, Jeffrey: Radio One
Wilson, Mark: CBS News
Wilson, Stephanie: WUSA–TV
Wiltz, Teresa: Stateline
Winborn, Tracy: Fox News
Windham, Ronald: CBS News
Wines, Karen: EWTN
Wing, Terry: Federal News Radio 1500 AM
Winston, Adrienne: CNN
Winston, Natalie: National Public Radio
Winters, Latonya: CBS News
Winters, Ronald: CBS News
Wise, Alana: WAMU
Wise, Michael: WUSA–TV
Wiseman, Frederick: CNN
Wishingrad, Emily: Hearst Television Inc.
Witkin, Rachel: NBC News
Wohlrab, Ezekial: NBC News
Wolf, Philip: Blaze Media
Wolf, Zachary: CNN
Wolfe, Lisa: Federal News Radio 1500 AM
Wolff, Timothy: Washington Examiner
Wollmann, Corinna: Al Jazeera International
Wood, Owen: WETA
Wood, Zachary: Vice News
Woodall, Crystal: CBN News
Woodruff, Joel: NBC News
Woodsome, Kathleen: Washingtonpost.com
Woolbright, Melinda: WRC–TV / NBC–4
Woolfolk, Daniel: Sightline Media Group
Wordock, Colleen: Spectrum News
Worthington, Barry: White House Chronicle
Wotshela, Sicelo: BBC
Wright, Cindy: Capital News Service TV–U of Md
Wright, Dale: WJLA–TV / Newschannel 8
Wright, David: CNN
Wright, David J.: ABC News
Wright, Jasmine: CNN
Wright, Malissa: CTV–Community TV of PG County
Wright, Morgan: Nexstar Media Group
Wright, Pamela: CNN
Wrona, Marcin: TVN Poland
Wu, Wei: New Tang Dynasty TV
Wudarczyk, Pawel: TV Polsat
Wurm, Christina: Fox News
Wyszogrodzki, Marcin: TVN Poland
Xu, Chuanqi: Voice of America
Yager, Joshua: CBS News
Yaklyvich, Brian: ABC News
Yamamoto, Yuta: Tokyo Broadcasting System
Yamasaki, Takeshi: NHK
Yancy, Shawn: WTTG–Fox Television
Yanevskyy, Oleksandr: Voice of America
Yang, Daniel: PBS NewsHour
Yang, Eun: WRC–TV / NBC–4
Yang, Guofu: Voice of America
Yang, Hee: Radio Free Asia
Yang, John: PBS NewsHour
Yang, Lianhua: American Chinese Television (ACT)
Yang, Lixin: New Tang Dynasty TV

MEMBERS ENTITLED TO ADMISSION—Continued

Yang, Zhuoqin: One America
Yang, Ziyi: New Tang Dynasty TV
Yaoka, Ryoichiro: Nippon TV Network
Yaqub, Nadeem: Voice of America
Yar, Dan: Al Jazeera International
Yarborough, Richard: WRC–TV / NBC–4
Yarmuth, Floyd: ABC News
Yates, Mark: Swiss Broadcasting
Ybarra, Jose: ABC News
Yee Gaffney, Suzanne: AP–Broadcast
Yeo, Hong Gyu: MBC–TV Korea (Munhwa)
Yeung Yam, Raymond: Voice of America
Yi, Joy: Washingtonpost.com
Yianopoulos, Karen: Middle East Broadcasting Networks (MBN)
Yimam, Bofta: Cox Broadcasting
Ying, Francis: Kaiser Health News
Yokoyama, Takahisa: CNN
Yoo, Jacqueline: ABC News
Yoon, Seokyee: Yonhap News TV
Yoshitake, Yosuke: NHK
Young, Jeremy: Al Jazeera English
Young, Melissa: ABC News
Young, Robert: C–SPAN
Young, Simone: New Tang Dynasty TV
Young, Victor: NBC News
Young, Jerome, Jr.: CBN News
Yu, Elly: WAMU
Yu, Mallory: National Public Radio
Yui, Hideki: NHK
Yun, Samean: Radio Free Asia
Yurtseven, Aydin: TRT World
Zagorski, Artur: TVP Polish Television
Zahn, Jamie: CNN
Zajko, Robert: Diversified Communications, Inc. (DCI)
Zak, Lana: ABC News
Zaman, Pias: National Public Radio
Zamora, Alban: WRC–TV / NBC–4
Zamora, Michael: National Public Radio
Zampa, Peter: Gray Television
Zang, Guohua: CTI–TV (Taiwan)
Zaru, Deena: ABC News
Zaslav, Alison: CNN
Zeffler, Markus: Swiss Broadcasting
Zelaya, Laura: NTN24
Zeledon, Marlon: Morningside Partners, LLC
Zeleny, Jeffrey: CNN
Zeliger, Robert: NBC News
Zernell, Ove Erik Andreas: Swedish Broadcasting
Zervos, Stratis: ABC News
Zhang, Bilei: Fox News
Zhang, Hangda: Al Jazeera International
Zheng, Ren: WTOP Radio
Zhou-Castro, Heidi: Al Jazeera English
Ziegenbein, Darren: WRC–TV / NBC–4
Zients, Sasha: CNN
Zimerman, Ariel: I24 News
Zosso, Elizabeth: Middle East Broadcasting Networks (MBN)
Zschieschang, Marion: German TV (ARD)
Zucconi, Anthony: Fox News
Zuckerman, Alexandra: Scripps News
Zuker, Karen: CNN
Zumbado, Joaquin: NBC News
Zurcher, Anthony: BBC
Zurita, Pablo: CNN

NETWORKS, STATIONS, AND SERVICES REPRESENTED

Senate Gallery, phone 224–6421 House Gallery, phone 225–5214

ABC NEWS—(202) 222–7700; 1717 DeSales Street, NW., Washington, DC 20036: Mona Abdi, Zohreen Adamjee, Elizabeth Alesse, Faisal Alkadiri, John Allard, Scott Allmond, Mitchell Alva, John Arnholz, Trevor Ault, Luke Barr, Kennedey Bell, Phillip Black, Elizabeth Brown, James Brown, Mary Bruce, Lucien Bruggeman, Matthew Burton, Diana Carswell, Esther Castillejo Carrasco, Elizabeth Cathey, Jeffery Cook, Shannon Crawford, Abigail Cruz, Megan Cunningham, Audrey Dalgetty, Donnell Daniels, Ajinkya Date, Abinet Dejene, Ines de La Cuetara, Imtiyaz Delawala, Christopher Donato, Kevin Drennen, Alexandra Dukakis, Devin Dwyer, Daniel Glenn Elvington, Olivia Eubanks, Robert Eustis, Stephen Fancy, Katherine Faulders, Jared Feinstein, Johnnie Ferguson, Lee Ferran, Justin Fishel, Siobhan Fisher, Anne Flaherty, Bradley Fulton, Devin Garbitt, Jon Garcia, Robert Gehlen, Amy Giebel, Benjamin Gittleson, Justin Gomez, Robert Gordon, Myra Green, Jonathan Greenberger, Bertha Guerrero, Brian Haefeli, Daniel Hannah, Averi Harper, Christen Hill, Robert Horton, Matthew Hosford, Kevin Howard, Megan Hughes Hemmerlein, Heidi Jensen, William Jester, Cecilia Jimenez, Mina Kaji, Almin Karamehmedovic, Jonathan Karl, Katharine Kastens, Adam Kelsey, Paul Kerley, Mariam Khan, Soo Rin Kim, Elizabeth King, Erica King, Richard Klein, Sarah Kolinovsky, Donald Kroll, Lauren Lantry, Michael Levine, Erin Livermore, Nathan Luna, Lachlan Murdoch MacNeil, Amanda Maile, Mary Marsh, Serena Marshall, Luis Martinez, Cynthia McCoo, Meridith McGraw, James McGuire, Elizabeth McLaughlin, Angelique McMenamin, Kathryn McQuade, Martinez Mebane, James Meek, Avery Miller, Terence Moran, Matthew Mosk, Kenneth Moton, David Muir, Molly Nagle, Marie Nelson, Meredith Nettles, Nicholette Nicci, Jorge Nunez, Patrick O'Gara, Andrea Owen, Tara Palmeri, John Parkinson, MaryAlice Parks, Allison Pecorin, Rebecca Perlow, Beatrice Peterson, Alexandra Pezenik, Jordyn Phelps, Kathryn Phillips, Michael Pickup, Kevin Pliszak, Ike Prophet, Jason Radke, Stephanie Ramos-Tomeoni, Tracy Reeves, Corinne Roberts, Adia Robinson, Lissette Rodriguez, Tiffany Rosborough, Olivia Rubin, George Sanchez, John Santucci, Mee Scholer, Rachel Scott, David Searles, Samantha Sergi, Matthew Seyler, Michael Shannon, Lawrence Shaw, Ryan Shepard, Tom Shine, Benjamin Siegel, Janet Simpson, Benjamin Siu, James Smith, William Steakin, Briana Stewart, Michelle Stoddart, Sophia Tatum, Richard Tejera, Christine Theodorou, Elizabeth Thomas, Pierre Thomas, Armando Torres-Garcia, Karen Travers, Patricia Turner, Matthew Vann, John Verhovek, Dana Viers, Kelsey Walsh, Alisa Wiersema, David Wright, Jose Ybarra, Jacqueline Yoo, Melissa Young, Lana Zak, Deena Zaru.

AGENCE FRANCE PRESSE (AFP-TV)—1500 K Street, NW., Washington, DC 20005: Laura Akhoun, Adan Alvarenga, Salima Belhadj, Agnes Bun, Gabrielle Chatelain, Ricardo Criales, Carmen Cuesta-Roca, Valentin Graff, Bastien Inzaurralde, Jihan Joannides, Gerald Jonas, Anne Lebreton, Emmanuelle Monier, Nadine Morrison, Ivan Rivas, Katharine Schubauer, Eleonore Sens.

AGRI–PULSE—1111 Belle Pre Way 22314, #103, Alexandria, VA 22314: Spencer Chase.

AL ARABIYA TV—(202) 355 6614; 1620 I Street, NW., 10th floor, Washington, DC 20006: Angelyn Adams, Lenore Adkins, Mohammed Alazawi, Khalid Al Rawi, Nadia Charters, Pierre Ghanem, Elias Habib, Basheer Khaleefah, Ahmed Mahdi, Ayan Sheikh, Muna Shikaki.

ALASKA PUBLIC RADIO NETWORK/ALASKA PUBLIC MEDIA—140 13th Street, SE., Washington, DC 20003: Elizabeth Ruskin.

AL JAZEERA ENGLISH—1200 New Hampshire Avenue, NW., 2nd Floor, Washington, DC 20036: Robert Abeshouse, Abdul Hadi Abo-Issa, Paul Abowd, Laila Alarian, Jeff Ballou, James Bays, Jet Belgraver, Catherine Berger, Ahad Bhatti, Simon Boazman, Ayana Brickhouse, Elizabeth Brown, Crystal Byrd, Malik Camah, William Castro Jaramillo, Brian Chacon, Peter Charley, Kavitha Chekuru, Stephen Coonce, Michael Corripio, Patricia Culhane, Natasha Del Toro, Mitchell Doty, Nicholas Dove, Abdelmounim ElAmrani, Gabriel Elizondo, Mariam Engel, Kathleen Fabian, Thomas Fisher, Andy Gallacher, Jonathan Garratt, Franklyn Ginsburg, Kira Grishkoff Rockell, Gregory Guise, Karim Haddad, Kimberly Halkett, James Hamilton, Michael Hanna, John Hendren, Kevin Hirten, Thierry Humeau, Andrew Jones, Rosiland Jordan, Akilah Joseph, Kevin King, Nick Kraus, Michael LaBella, Ekaterina Landy, Lister Lim, Erik Ljung, Maria Marquez, Mercedes Martinez, Ashley May, Herbert McClam, Colin McIntyre, Robert Michaud, Craig Pennington, Jason Pepino, Amanda Price, Ilir Prifti, Ivica Puljic, Shihab Rattansi, Alea Reeves, Robert Reynolds, Joshua Rushing, Kristen Saloomey, Chris Sheridan, Tom Szypulski, Simon Tate, Pilar Tejerina, Joel Van Haren, Anar Virji, Owen Watson, Tom Williams, Adrian Wilson, Jeremy Young, Heidi Zhou-Castro.

AL JAZEERA INTERNATIONAL—(202) 689–3600; 1200 New Hampshire Ave., NW., 2nd Floor, Washington, DC 20036: Ahmed Abdulrazzaq, Morad Abed, Biesan Abu-Kwaik, Eyad Aburahma, Mohammed Alami, Samer Alhafiz, Ahmed Alhazeem, Haitham Al Juboori, Daniel Alvarenga, Benjamin Angeloni, Ahmad Asaad, Phoebe Barghouty, Michael Bendeck, Hanane Berrai, Adrienne Blaine, Lamia Bourogaa,

NETWORKS, STATIONS, AND SERVICES REPRESENTED—Continued

Graelyn Brashear, Jennifer Byers, Ney Carrero Alvarez, Mehmet Dede, David Dougherty, Omar Duwaji, Mouhamed Elahmed, Sari Elkhalili, Mohamed Fahs, Abderrahim Foukara, Michael Fox, Laurin-Whitney Gottbrath, Nasreddine Hssaini, Enrique Huaiquil, Dina Kesbeh, Lina Khalaf, Mohammad Khaliq, Alexandra Locke, Fadi Mansour, Mashaal Mir, Amjad Muhammad, Julia Muldavin, Ashraf Nagy, Craig Olmstead, Nanako Pierce, Rajeshwari Ramanathan, Kutaba Rashid, Tupac Saavedra, Sana Saeed, Sara Salman, Damian Sanchez-Bonmati, Ahmed Shihab-Eldin, Priyanka Tilve, Amy Walters, Wajd Waqfi, Corinna Wollmann, Dan Yar, Hangda Zhang.

AMERICAN CHINESE TELEVISION (ACT)—(240) 988–4660; 722 Ridgemont Avenue, Rockville, MD 20850: Yunjin Li, Lianhua Yang.

ANTENA 3 TV—4901 Seminary Road, #1513, Alexandria, VA 22311: Vanessa Jaklitsch.

AP-BROADCAST—(202) 641–9000; 1100 13th St, NW., Suite 500, Washington, DC 20005: Khaldoun Alrawi, Eric Andree, Jeannie Andress, John Auresto, Philip Avner, Edward Barker, Hugo Blanco, Jacqueline Blum-Dostie, Craig Broffman, Tracy Brown, Andrea Colombo-Abdullah, Kelly Daschle, Edward Donahue, Lisa Dwyer-Shapiro, Rita Foley, Mathew Friedman, Oscar Gabriel, Richard Gentilo, Lawrence Gold, James Gorman, Michael Gracia, Michael Hempen, Susan Henderson, Brian Hoffman, Daniel Huff, Roderick Jussim, Christian Kettlewell, Jennifer King, Lisa Matthews, Nan Hee McMinn, Sagar Meghani, Vaughn Morrison, Federica Narancio, Woria Osmani, Louis Pagan, Gregory Peppers, Gerald Petraitis, Padmananda Rama, Walter Ratliff, John Rizzo, Matthew Small, Felicia Smith, Donna Starddard, Julian Styles, James Turner, Denise Vance, Carlos Vargas, Andrew Visley, Suzanne Yee Gaffney.

APTVS—AMERICAN PRESS & TV SERVICES—(202) 601–2284; 1445 New York Avenue, NW., Suite 500, Washington, DC 20005: Mohammed Dawood, Sam Eizeldin, Elian El-khamissi, Gamal Hassanein, Mostafa Sliman.

AURN—938 Penn Avenue, Suite 701, Pittsburgh, PA 15222: April Ryan.

AUSTRALIAN BROADCASTING CORPORATION—(202) 466–8575; 2000 M Street, NW., Suite 660, Washington, DC 20036: Ryan Chatterjee, Zoe Daniel, Kathryn Diss, Conor Duffy, James Glenday, Niall Lenihan, David Lipson, Stephanie March, Mathew Marsic, Richard McDermott, Jeanavive McGregor, John Mees, Emily Olson, Chloe Ross.

AUSTRIAN RADIO & TV (ORF)—1206 Eton Court, NW., Washington, DC 20007: Hannelore Fauqueux-Veit, Uelle-Mall Jaakson, Christoph Kohl, David Kriegleder, Markus Meier, Natalie Stockert, Robert Uitz-Dallinger.

AZTECA AMERICA—400 North Capitol, NW., Suite 361, Washington, DC 20001: Armando Guzman, Luis Orellana Canas.

BBC—(202) 223–2050; 2000 M Street, NW., #800, Washington, DC 20009: Lukman Ahmed, Ben Bevington, Marianna Brady, Nicholas Bryant, Christopher Buckler, Angelica Casas, Maxine Collins, James Coomarasamy, Jonathan Csapo, Paul Danahar, Ian Druce, Mehrnoosh Ebrahimi, Kathryn Farrell, Sam Farzaneh, Kambiz Fattahi, Thomas Geoghegan, Morgan Gisholt Minard, Sergey Goryashko, Samantha Granville, David Grossman, Colleen Hagerty, Andrew Herbert, PAULA HONG, Rozalia Hristova, Alison Hunter, Nadia Huraimi, Michael Innes, Daniel Johnson, Majid Joneidi, Katharine Kay, Halle Kendall, Suzanne Kianpour, Petr Kozlov, John Landy, David Lee, Hannah Long-Higgins, Harry Low, Jessica Lussenhop, Aleem Maqbool, Max Matza, Tara McKelvey, Donald Morrison, Tara Neill, Hadi Niliahmadabadi, Gary O'Donoghue, Amir Payam, Cosima Schelfhout, Ashley Semler, Jude Sheerin, Ronald Skeans, Oliver Smith, Joan Soley, Jonathan Sopel, Franz Strasser, Courtney Subramanian, Sarah Svoboda, Nada Tawfik, Haley Thomas, Laura Trevelyan, Barbara Usher, Dikembe Wilkins, Anthony Zurcher.

BERKELEY STUDIOS INTERNATIONAL—50 F Street, NW., Suite C150, Washington, DC 20001: Ziadoon Al-lami, Hussein Asmael.

BLAZE MEDIA—(802) 777–5516; 601 New Jersey Avenue, NW., Suite 240, Washington, DC 20001: James Calcaterra, Julia Eckardt, Destry Edwards, Laura Gingrich, Alicia Hesse, Nathaniel Madden IV, Jonathan Miller, Anna Perez, Rikki Ratliff, John Rockovich, Jordan Schachtel, Elizabeth Schular, Garrett Shawley, Philip Wolf.

BLOOMBERG RADIO & TV—1399 NY Avenue, NW., 11th Floor, Washington, DC 20005: Christine Baratta, Bailey Bolden, Irwin Chapman, Kevin Cirilli, Charlotte Cullinan, David Goodman, Nathan Hager, Eugenia Hurtado, Fidel Inguanzo, Michael Lysak, Anthony Mancini, Lauren McDevitt, Michael McKee, Antonio Mielec, Adrienne Mitchell, Amy Morris, Ohad Niv, Andrew O'Day, Alisa Parenti, Brendan Polmer, Dardan Pula, Micha Rondeau, Nancy Sargeant, David Sucherman, Charles Vollmer, David Westin.

BT VIDEO PRODUCTIONS—7117 Wolftree Lane, Rockville, MD 20852: Paul Hollenbeck, Martin Kos.

CADENA SER—(202) 596 6969; 4520 Cumberland Avenue, Chevy Chase, MD 20815: Javier del Pino, Marta Del Vado Chicharro.

CAPITAL NEWS SERVICE TV—U OF MD—Philip Merrill College of Journalism, 1100 Knight Hall—University of Maryland, College Park, MD 20742: Mel Coffee, Susan Katcef, Cindy Wright.

CARACOL RADIO—1320 Fairmont Street, #103, Washington, DC 20009: Yaridis Adrian, Cristobal Vasquez Ramirez.

NETWORKS, STATIONS, AND SERVICES REPRESENTED—Continued

CARACOL TELEVISION—(202) 615–3899; 400 North Capitol Street, NW., Suite 361, Washington, DC 20001: Jose Agredo Vasquez, Gerard Cortes, Juan Merlano, Jaime Moreno Gomez.

CASPIAN BROADCASTING TV—1319 18th Street, NW., Washington, DC 20036: Rafig Gurbanzada, Aytan Mammadli.

CBC / CANADIAN BROADCASTING CORPORATION—(202) 383–2900; National Press Building 529 14th Street, NW., Suite 510, Washington, DC 20045: Jean-Francois Belanger, Keith Boag, Raphael Bouvier-Auclair, Jason Burles, Marcel Calfat, Marie Claudet, Lyndsay Duncombe, Patrick Ferguson, Bertrand Guez, Paul Hunter, Matthew Kwong, Christian Latreille, Jason Lowther, Ellen Mauro, Susan Ormiston, Alexander Panetta, Glenn Parker, Sylvain Richard, Kathryn Simpson, Paul St-Onge Fleurant.

CBN NEWS—(202) 833 2707; 1919 M Street, NW., Suite 100, Washington, DC 20036: Chanel Abrams, Abigail Allen, Robert Allman, Mark Bautista, Walter Bozek, David Brody, Jenna Browder, Laura Crombe, Brian Edwards, Jennifer Gilbert, Aronica Glover, Mario Gonzalez, Steven Jacobi, John Jessup, Matthew Keedy, Benjamin Kennedy, Reed Klass, John LaMonica, Jacob Moore, Edward Morano, Shoshannah Nunez, Denis Pacuraru, Eric Philips, Dana Ritter, Patrick Robertson, Ian Rushing, Paul Strand, Kimberly Taylor, Eric Valencia, Richard Westfall, Crystal Woodall, Jerome Young Jr.

CBS NEWS—(202) 457–4444; 2020 M Street, NW., Washington, DC 20036: Adam Aigner-Treworgy, Gabrielle Ake, Zackary Akey, Thomas Albano, Clinton Alexander, Debra Alfarone, Emily Alff, Amber Ali, Alana Anyse, Laquasha Banks, Morris Banks, Errol Barnett, Reginald Barringer, Farrel Becker, Shani Benezra, James Benson, Musadiq Bidar, Anna Bobadilla-Marino, Julia Boccagno, Richard Bonin, Natalie Brand, Margaret Brennan, Adam Brewster, Whitney Bright, Erica Brown, Kimberly Brown, Susan Bullard Harmon, Timothy Camarda, Elizabeth Campbell, Catherine Cannon, Jane Chick, Lete Childs, Caitlin Conant, Carol Coney, Eric Conner, Sara Cook, Nancy Cordes, Victoria Coughlan, John Crum, John Daly, Charles Dixson, Laura Doan, Katherine Dominick, Margaret Dore, Steven Dorsey, William Dries, Lois Dyer, Bo Erickson, Richard Escobedo, Andrew Eversden, Sarah Ewall-Wice, John Falls, John Fantacone, Ann Flynn, Laura Foran, Edward Forgotson, Robert Fortunato, Tony Furlow, Hal Furman, Brian Fuss, Travis Galey, July Garcia, Manny Garcia, Major Garrett, Olivia Gazis, Jenna Gibson, Benson Ginsburg, Jeffrey Glor, Serafin Gomez, Celina Gore, Brian Gottlieb, Neil Grasso, Jan Greenburg, Joshua Gross, Mary Hager, William Harding, Alison Hawley, Dave Hawthorne, Alan He, Skyler Henry, Catherine Herridge, Molly Hooper, Michael Hopkins, Caroline Horn, Zackary Hudak, Caitlin Huey-Burns, Jillian Hughes, Clare Hymes, Margaret Hynds, Christopher Isham, Dennis Jamison, Rickey Jefferson, Weijia Jiang, Jeffrey Johnston, Arthur Jones, Lorna Jones, Carol Joynt, Arden Kehayias Farhi, Brandi Kellam, Kenneth Kerbs, Jonathan Kessler, Adrian Kill, Nikole Killion Boykin, Rosa Kim, Julia Kimani, Daniel Klos, Mark Knoller, Molly Kordares, Cara Korte, Robert Kovach, Katiana Krawchenko, Kathryn Krupnik, Grace Lamb-Atkinson, Benjamin Larson, Donald Lee, Robert Legare, Abdul-Mola Lenghi, Rebecca Levy, Steven Marshall, David Martin, Pamela Mason, Mark Mazariegos, Dennis McCarty, Donald Jay McCarty, Kelsey Micklas, William Miller, Patricia Milton Steinfort, Benjamin Mitchell, LaCrai Mitchell, Camilo Montoya-Galvez, Gillian Morley, Julie Morse, John Murphy, Brian Nalesnick, Aaron Navarro, John Nolen, Norah O'Donnell, Edward O'Keefe, Jeffrey Pegues, Katryna Perera, Timothy Perry, Michael Peyton, Zoe Poindexter, Steven Portnoy, Alesia Powell-Escobar, Diana Quinn, Omar Quinonez, Carrie Rabin Aber, Richard Rahn, Stephanie Ramirez, George Rehkopf, Charles Reid, Paula Reid, Irvin Reinhard, Catherine Reynolds, Francisco Robbins, Kaitlyn Roman, Howard Rosenberg, Allyson Ross Taylor, Christina Ruffini, Mary Kate Rydell, Samira Said, Stephen Sanchez, Camilla Schick, Leonard Schmitz, Mark Schuster, Thomas Seem, Grace Segers, Nicole Sganga, Gregory Shaffir, Kimberlee Shaffir, Colby Shitama, Ward C. Sloane, Gabriel Stix, David Strong, Fernando Suarez, Anna Sugg, Brandon Tea, Emily Tillett, Alexander Tin, Benjamin Tracy, Peter Traynham, Andres P. Triay, Jack Turman, Geoff Turner, Victor Ulloa Ramirez, Kristopher Van Cleave, Rebecca Vandercook, Dennis Vera, Adam Verdugo, William Walker, Mary Walsh, Kevin Ward, Erick Washington, Eleanor Watson, Kathryn Watson, Mark White, John Whitley, Ricardo Whitson, Scarlette Whyte, Christopher Widmer, Ronald Windham, Joshua Yager.

CHANNEL 10 ISRAEL—(202) 460–0223; 195 Hardy Place, Rockville, MD 20852: Gil Tamary.

CHANNEL ONE RUSSIAN TV—2000 M Street, NW., Suite 324, Washington, DC 20036: Viacheslav Arkhipov, Iuliia Olkhovskaia, Alexander Tetrashvili.

CHEDDAR—601 New Jersey Avenue, NW., Washington, DC 20001: John Durkin, Samuel Hicks, Douglas Murray, Megan Pratz, Samantha Tadelman.

CNBC—(202) 776–7405; 400 North Capitol Street, NW., Suite 850, Washington, DC 20001: Patrick Anastasi, Kevin Breuninger, Bria Cousins, Matthew Cuddy, Stephanie Dhue, John Harwood, Karen James Sloan, Eamon Javers, Amanda Macias, Ylan Mui McClintock, Diana Olick, Pat Pugliese, Shari Rosen, Lisa Sanfuentes, Brian Schwartz, David Soltis, Ashley Stringer, Kayla Tausche, Ervin Washington, Mary Wellons, Christina Wilkie Sumner.

CNN—(202) 898–7900; 820 1st Street, NE., Washington, DC 20002: Khalil Abdallah, Abilo Acosta, Jill Adly, Amir Ahmed, Simret Aklilu, William Alberter, David Allbritton, Mark Allman, Tala Alrajjal, Elizabeth Ambriz-Mendez, Whitney Amon, John Anglim, Raymond Arke, Abigail Arzoumanov, Audrey Ash, Kylie Atwood, Tiane Austin, Matthew Avrutine, Renee Baharaeen, Edward Barrett, Dana Bash, Veronica Bautista, Savannah Behrmann, Kate Bennett, Alexa Bennewitz, Leslie Bentz, Rebecca Berg,

NETWORKS, STATIONS, AND SERVICES REPRESENTED—Continued

Deborah Berger Fox, Daniel Berman, Maria Bernal, Laura Bernardini, Mark Biello, Ashley Billings, Lindzie Bills, Joan Biskupic, Kevin Blakley, Wolf Blitzer, John Bodnar, Kevin Bohn, Donna Borak, Gloria Borger, Tyrone Boston, Eric Bradner, Kiara Brantley-Jones, Kiara Brantley-Jones, Joshua Braun, Raymond Britch, Noah Broder, Scott Bronstein, David Brooks, Brooke Brower, Ryan Browne, Steven Brusk, Burke Buckhorn, Tiffany Bullock, Austen Bundy, David Burgess, Terence Burlij, Haley Byrd, Juan Cabral Pichardo, William Cadigan, Karin Caifa, Michael Callahan, Catherine Carter, Nicole Carvajal, David Catrett, David Chalian, Natasha Chen, Andrew Christman, Gregory Clary, Bobby Clemons, Avron Coates, Marshall Cohen, Zachary Cohen, Youman Coleman, Kaitlan Collins, Stephen Collinson, Michael Conte, Stephen Coppin, James Crawford, Natalia Crosdale, Christopher Cross, John Cunha, Daniel Dale, Patrick Davis, Kara Day, Jessica Dean Rutherford, Javier de Diego, Ariane de Vogue, Lauren Dezenski, Jeremy Diamond, Daniella Diaz, Stephen Dolce, Christopher DosSantos, Sonya Dowhaluk, Bonnie Druker, Thomas Ebel, Courtney Edwards, Elizebeth English, McKenna Ewen, Robert Farmer, Samuel Feist, Eric Fiegel, Clare Foran, Latoya Forbes, Patrick Ford, Thomas Foreman, Samuel Fossum, Lauren Fox, Melissa Frydman, Brian Fung, Teresita Galarce Crain, Jamie Gangel, Katherine Gaouette, Danelle Garcia, Elise Garofalo, Timothy Garraty, Christopher Garrett, Amina Garrett Scott, Alexander Gee, Eden Getachew, Melissa Giaimo, Sarah Giannakopoulos, Margaret Given, Catherine Gloria, Andre Goddard, Amanda Golden, Christer Gomes, David Gracey, Aileen Graef, Noah Gray, James Graydon, Anne Grayer, Gus Greene, Angelica Grimaldi, Eddie Gross, Brian Hampton, Mackenzie Happe, Jeremy Herb, Michael Herkner, Ione Hess, Jason Hoffman, William Holbert, Faith Holland, Kristen Holmes, Derek Horrigan, Emily Howell, Matthew Hoye, Adolfo Ibarra, Walter Imparato, Adia Jacobs, William Jacobson, Oliver Janney, Laura Jarrett, David Jenkins, Ewholomeyovwi Jeroro, Omar Jimenez, Joseph Johns, Monique Johnson, Athena Jones, Douglas Jones, Tracey Jordan, Arcelious Joyner, Donald Judd, Polson Kanneth, Bonney Kapp, Elena Kaufman, Peter Kavanagh, Aishvarya Kavi, Ashley Keegan, Caroline Kelly, Caroline Kenny, Kristin Keppler, Aaron Kessler, Ashley Killough, John King, Mary Klein, Brandon Knapp, Lauren Koenig, Michelle Kosinski, Gregory Krieg, Benjamin Krolowitz, Paul LeBlanc, Ji Lee, Min Lee, Adam Levine, Adam Levy, Latavia Lewis, Misha Lewis, Christine Lien, Melissa Lipman, Kevin Liptak, Philip Littleton, Katherine Lobosco, Sonikka Loganathan, Clara Lopez-Pulido, Juan Carlos Lopez Ruiz, Edwin Lora, Tami Luhby, Brianna Lujan, Albert Lutan, John Lybrand, Steven Machalek, Alison Main, Mary Mallonee, Allison Malloy, Suzanne Malveaux, Christina Manduley, Nicole Manley, Alexander Marquardt, Rene Marsh, Daniel Martinez, Chase Masters, Philip Mattingly, Ronnie McCray, Colin McCullough, Ebony McGee, Douglas McKinley, Samuel McMichael, Cassie McNamara, James Meech, Daniel Merica, Anna Miller, Paul Miller, Alec Miran, Alexa Miranda, Shawna Mizelle, Jeffrey Moller, Mary Moloney, Jeremy Moorhead, Isabel Morales, Peter Morris, Sarah Mucha, Sara Murray, Mirembe Mutesa, Steven Nannes, Nicholas Neville, Ryan Nobles, Bridget Nolan, Jeffrey Norman, Michael Oat, Jonathan O'Beirne, Eric Odendahl, Kitty OKeefe, Ann Parangot, Andre Parker, Robert Parker, Stephen Patterson, Eddie Paylor, Aaron Pellish, Evan Perez, Clayton Perry, Alejandro Peruga-Martinez, Katelyn Petroka, Abigail Phillip, Scott Pisczek, David Poarch, Katelyn Polantz, Michelle Poley, Ryan Pollock, Lauren Pratapas, Willa Prescott, Mark Preston, Shimon Prokupecz, Federico Quadrani, Manu Raju, Pallavi Reddy, Erin Reische, Jean Renaud, Joshua Replogle, Maeve Reston, Casey Riddle, Raul Rios-Hernandez, Dominique Genevieve Robertson, Gregory Robertson, David Robinson, John Robinson, David Rogers, Brian Rokus, Latrice Nadia Romero, Jedd Rosche, Lindy Royce-Bartlett, Diane Ruggiero, Katherine Saenz, Boris Sanchez, Geneva Sands-Sadowitz, Jose Sanfuentes, Amanda Sansone, Michelle Santayana, Kara Scannell, Douglas Schantz, John Scheuer, Harlan Schmidt, Jessica Schneider, James Sciutto, Raquel Scott, Gregory Seaby, Sunlen Serfaty, Monica Serrano Quintero, Theodore Severson, John Shaylor, Catherine Shoichet, David Shortell, Mawal Sidi, David Siegel, Jeffery Simms, Jennifer Simpson, Andrew Smith, Michelle Smith, Kelly Smoot, Cassandra Spodak, Elizabeth Stark, Barbara Starr, Scott Stead, Emily Steck, John Stevenson, Derek St. Onge, Veronica Stracqualursi, Tara Subramaniam, Katherine Sullivan, Amanda Swinhart, Dustin Tanner, Jacob Tapper, Russell Taylor, Mallory Thompson, Tamara Thorp, Mari Torres, Thanh Tram, Angelica Trindade, Kenneth Tuohey, Christopher Turner, Elizabeth Turrell, Brett Tyler, Kim Uhl, Anthony Umrani, Catherine Valentine, Tara Vales, Maegan Vazquez, Dawid Vermaak, Matthew Vossekuil, Tu Vu, Samantha Waldenberg, Gregory Wallace, Mark Walz, Michael Warren, Eli Watkins, Emily Welch, Dylan Wells, Sarah Westwood, Jamie Wiener, Brenna Williams, Valeska Williams, Adrienne Winston, Frederick Wiseman, Zachary Wolf, David Wright, Jasmine Wright, Pamela Wright, Takahisa Yokoyama, Jamie Zahn, Alison Zaslav, Jeffrey Zeleny, Sasha Zients, Karen Zuker, Pablo Zurita.

CNSNEWS.COM—(571) 267–3500; 1900 Campus Commons Drive, Suite 600, Reston, VA 20191: Melanie Arter, Craig Bannister, Michael Chapman, Terence Jeffrey, Craig Millward, Michael Morris.

COLORADO PUBLIC RADIO—Washington, DC 20510: Caitlyn Kim, Megan Post.

CONNECTING VETS—(202) 971–8050; 1015 Half Street, SE., Suite 200, Washington, DC 20003: Abbie Bennett, Kaylah Jackson.

COPE RADIO (SPAIN)—4904 Bett Road, NW., Washington, DC 20016: Juan Martinez Fierro.

COX BROADCASTING—(202) 777–7000; 400 North Capitol Street, NW., #635, Washington, DC 20001: David Chase, James Dupree, Jacqueline Fell, Michael Friedrich, Justin Gray, Kevin Johnson, Kristin

NETWORKS, STATIONS, AND SERVICES REPRESENTED—Continued

Kerwin, Samantha Manning, Blair Miller, Dorey Scheimer, Jon Sonnheim, Katherine Suiters, Jeffrey Williams, Bofta Yimam.

CQ/ROLL CALL—(202) 650–6500; 1201 Pennsylvania Avenue, NW., 7th Floor, Washington, DC 20004: Evan Campbell, Jinitzail Hernandez, Graham MacGillivray, Thomas McKinless, Nathan Ouellette, Micaela Rodriguez.

CRONKITE NEWS SERVICE—(202) 684–2400; 1800 I Street, NW., Washington, DC 20006: Stephen Crane.

C–SPAN—(202) 737–3220; 400 North Capitol Street, NW., #650, Washington, DC 20001: Kenneth Alexander, Thomas Alldredge, Theresa Amirault-Michel, Jeremiah Art, Michelle Bailor, Tyler Bartlam, Courtney Beesch, Stacey Beigarten, Jason Bender, Brett Betsill, Leona Blakey, Greta Brawner, Donald Brown, Paul Brown, Robert Browning, Kenneth Buck, Kristina Buddenhagen, Susan Bundock, Leslie Burdick, Kathy Cahill, Nancy Calo-Christianson, Craig Caplan, Kenneth Carrick, Stephanie Chadha-Kaye, Matthew Claar, James Clark, Bruce Collins, Michael Collins, James Cook, Howard Corner, Liam Currier, Alexander Curtis, Gregory Czzowitz, Peter Daniels, Matthew Dauchess, Anthony Davis, Benyam Desta, Bridget Diggs, Daniel Dill, Jarmel Dixon, Sean Doody, John Doyle, Mallory Drummond, Yi-Pei Eastin, Pedro Echevarria, Gary Ellenwood, Seth Engel, Patricia Esquivel, Gregory Fabic, Mark Farkas, John Farrell, Joseph Feeney, Eric Feudner, Richard Fleeson, Amanda Fortner, Carl Foster, Leslie Frazier, William Frazier, John Gallagher, William Gallagher, Craig Galowin, Tracy Garlock, Jennifer Garrott, Garney Gary, Charles George, Robert Gould, Dwight Hall, Glenn Hall, Richard Hall, Christopher Hanson, Stephen Harkness, Robert Harleston, Mary Jean Harrison, Maurice Haynes, William Heffley, Jonelle Henry, Francis Herbas, Ashley Hill, Dallas Hill, Adrienne Hoar McGibbon, Eric Horacek, Katherine Hughes, Scott Hummelsheim, Tracy Hunter, Nathan Hurst, Cynthia Ingle, Roberta Jackson, Tiara Jenkins, Phelix Jones, Steven Kehoe, Jonathan Kelley, Roxane Kerr, Kayla Nicole Key, Kevin King, David Knighton, Felix Laboy, Brian Lamb, Deborah Lamb, Darren Larade, Molly Laville, Robert Lazar, Jerome Leddon, Brian Lloyd, Paul Loeschke, Charles Logan, Graham MacGillivray, Valerie Matthews, Chloe Maxwell, John McArdle, Sean McCann, Christian McCarren, Tomika McDougald, Gerard McGarrity, Abigail Megginson, Justin Metzger, Andrew Miller, Katherine Mills, David Monack, Victor Montoro, Garrett Moore, Howard Mortman, Daniel Morton, Terence Murphy, Andrew Nason, Glenn Nelson, Robin Newton, Trang Ninh, Donna Norris, Benen O'Brien, Benjamin O'Connell, Alan Olmsted, Paul Orgel, Michael Patruznick, Alexander Pena, Vernon Perkins, Nickolas Pitocco, Almon Porter, Anne Preloh, Anthony Pronko, Clare Quinn, Nikhil Raval, Kuren Redmond Morgan, Robert Reilly, Michele Remillard, Cynthia Reuter, Shannon Rice, Delia Rios, Tiffany Rocque, Mark Rodeffer, Martine Rodriguez, Randolph Rohrbaugh, Megan Rowls, Jennifer Ruff, Carlos Sampaio, Molly Sanders, Sherry Sanders-Smith, Michele Sandiford, William Scanlan, Bridget Scanlon, Ellen Schweiger, Steven Scully, Nina Shelton, Peter Slen, Lindley Smith, Benjamin Sorenson, Haley Southee, Bruce Alan Speck, Gary Starikoff, James Statler, Greg St. James, Johnny St. Jean, Richard Stoddard, Margaret Strolle, Susan Swain, Mary Symanski, Christina Taylor, Joseph Teeples, Eric Thoman, Tamara Thueringer, Arthur Tiller, Brandon Tilman, Noel Touhey, Kevin Washburn, Richard Weinstein, Robert Young.

CTI–TV (TAIWAN)—(301) 792–8883; 7 Monona Court, Derwood, MD 20855: Guohua Zang.

CTV CANADIAN TV—(202) 775–0356; 1717 DeSales Street, NW., Suite 354, Washington, DC 20036: Jonathan Austin, William Dugan, Shannon Kelly, Richard Madan, Joy Malbon, Marley Parker.

CTV–COMMUNITY TV OF PG COUNTY—(202) 383–6061; 9475 Lottsford Road, Largo, MD 20774: David Barnes, Keshia Butts, Onyinyechi Chuku, Curtis Crutchfield, Erika Cumber, Sakina Dockett, Ara Laughlin, Sandra Peaches, Dejah Rawls, GeNienne Samuels, Patricia Villone, Algernon Williams, Malissa Wright.

DAILYMAIL.COM—5941 Oak Leather Drive, Burke, VA 22015: Marcus DiPaola, Christopher Muncy.

DANISH BROADCASTING CORPORATION—(202) 785–1957; 2000 M Street, NW., Suite 890, Washington, DC 20036: Stine Dragsted, Lillian Kretz, Steffen Kretz, Jacob Lorenzen, Gitte McGuire.

DEUTSCHE WELLE TV—(202) 785–5730; 2000 M Street, NW., Suite 335, Washington, DC 20036: Leslie Alston, Carla Bleiker, Maximilan Foerg, Pablo Foley Elias, Lori Hannan, Helena Humphrey, Michael Knigge, Oliver Sallet, Alexandra von Nahmen, Mikko Vuokko.

DIVERSIFIED COMMUNICATIONS, INC. (DCI)—2000 M Street, NW., 3rd Floor, Washington, DC 20036: John Bena, James Butler, Joseph Concaugh Jr., Michael Dubose, Paul Fifield, Peder Jessen, Robert Klein, Tipp McClure, James Murphy, Jamie Norins, Kathi Overton, Robert Zajko.

DUTCH TV & RADIO (NOS)—2000 M Street, NW., #365, Washington, DC 20036: Marieke De Vries, Arjen van der Horst.

EUROPEAN PRESSPHOTO AGENCY—(202) 347–4694; 1122 National Press Building, Washington, DC 20045: Lawrence Miller, Carlos Vilas Delgado.

EUROVISION AMERICAS, INC.—2000 M Street, NW., Suite 300, Washington, DC 20036: Adam Bearne, Emilie de Schaetzen, William Dunlop, Tanya Fischer, Lee Grigsby, Jay Hahn, Kyle Lanningham, Sarah Lanningham, Adam Mandelson, Cecile McPherson, Glenn Mikols, Priya Narahari, Ji Hee Park, Roch Pellerin, Lakisha Ridley, Jean Pierre Roberts, Eduardo Rosario, John Saunders, Jason Scharf, Peggy Soucy, Thomas Trainor, Juri von Bonsdorff, Charles Walter.

NETWORKS, STATIONS, AND SERVICES REPRESENTED—Continued

EWTN—(202) 909–2900; 750 First Street, NE., Suite 1115, Washington, DC 20002: Raymond Arroyo, Lauretta Brown, Susan Bruce, Matthew Bunson, Todd Burger, Kathleen Burke, Jason Calvi, Toby Capion, Christopher Cardno, John Chipak, Edward Condon, Michael DuBose, Christopher Edwards, Meg Giunta, Wyatt Goolsby, Catherine Hadro, Matthew Hadro, Thomas Haller, Rodney Harris, Kristen Hildebrand, Mark Irons, Elena Isella, Afshin Javadi, Cristina Kelly, Anna Laudiero, Jessica Marquez Marquez, Alyssa McGehee, Gregg Micklos, Susanna Pinto, Elizabeth Plaza, Christine Rousselle, Tracy Sabol, Katherine Scanlon, Leon Segears, Victoria Stiles, Kaitlin Stumpf, Christian Swezey, Karen Wines.

EXPRESSEN TV—(202) 227–8322; 1772 Church Street, #503, Washington, DC 20036: Tomas Kvarnkullen.

EYE-TO-EYE VIDEO—4614 Chevy Chase Boulevard, Chevy Chase, MD 20815: Michael Capucci, Elliot Klayman, Patrick O'Donnell.

FEATURE STORY NEWS—(202) 296–9012; 1730 Rhode Island Avenue Ste. 405, Washington, DC 20036: Noureldin Aly, Alice Anderson, Malcolm Brown, John Clarke, Jagruti Dave, Kathryn Fisher, Rebecca Foster, Robert Frazier, Giles Gibson, Tamara Haddad, Harry Horton, Harry Horton, Denis Levkovich, Simon Marks, Kevin McAleese, Katie Olds, Nina-Maria Potts, Daniel Ryntjes.

FEDERAL NEWS RADIO 1500 AM—5425 Wisconsin Ave., Chevy Chase, DC 20815: Amelia Brust, Mike Causey, Jason Fornicola, Jory Heckman, Lauren Larson, Scott Maucione, Jason Miller, Nicole Ogrysko, Jared Serbu, Thomas Temin, Stephanie Thomas, David Thornton, Terry Wing, Lisa Wolfe.

FEDNET—50 F Street, NW., Suite 1C, Washington, DC 20001: Gerard Arnum, Keith Carney, Christopher Carson, Sarmat Chowdhury, Regan Ferrell, Kendrick Frankel, Paul Griffith, Lara Hudak, Michael Kirby, Winston Lattie, Brendan Lyn, Nia Neloms, Nicholas Petromelis, John Spears.

FINNISH BROADCASTING COMPANY (YLE)—2000 M Street, NW., Suite 890, Washington, DC 20036: Hans Dhuy, Mika Hentunen, Paula Vilen.

FOX BUSINESS NETWORK—(202) 684–4000; 400 North Capitol Street, NW., Washington, DC 20001: Michael Bannigan, Maria Bartiromo, Bruce Becker, Blake Burman, Edward Danielian, Mary Kreinbihl, Connell McShane, Alexander Nerska, Elizabeth Park, Kristina Partsinevelos, Jonathan Resnick, Hillary Sandoval, Jennifer Schonberger, Jonathan St. John, Jessica Stone Evans.

FOX NEWS—(202) 824–6300; 400 North Capitol Street, NW., Washington, DC 20001: Yasin Abdul-Mateen, Lori Adams, Richard Adragna, Nihad Aliakbar, Bryan Allman, Kimberly Anderson, Anna Ansell, Vincent Arbogast, Khawar Aziz, William Baier, Leslie Baker, Joshua Banks, Ellison Barber, Calvin Barrett, Stuart Basinger, Robin Beal, Christopher Becker, Judson Berger, Kristina Biddle, Lauren Blanchard, Raymond Bogan, Bryan Boughton, Neill Bransford, Shannon Bream, Kristin Brown, Jenny Buchholz, Tucker Carlson, Walter Carter, Jr., Barnini Chakraborty, Louis Charlip, Jacqueline Christ, Gabriella Ciuffetelli, Casey Clarke, Richard Cockerham, Bryan Cole, Eric Colimore, Eric Conner, Kevin Corke, Christian Costa, Charles Couger, Ashley Cozzolino, Lorraine Crim, Rebecca Cuozzo, Jessica Curry, Jodie Curtis, Wendy Dawson, Debra DeFrank, Andres del Aguila, Michael Demark, Mary Pat Dennert, Danielle DiBartolo, Richard DiBella, Brian Doherty, Jason Donner, Peter Doocy, Kristofer Dowdell, Cecilia Duffy, Jerry Echols, William Edmondson, Richard Edson, Michael Emanuel, Amy Fenton, Robert Fetzer, Mark Finch, Benjamin Florance, Kristin Forehand, Elizabeth Friden, Christian Galdabini, Melinda Galey, Juan Garcia, Evan Gardner, Jake Gibson, Gary Gillis, Dennis Gonzalez, Trevor Greene, Jennifer Griffin, Sanford Grimes, Caroline Hagan, Lacey Halpern, Marie Harf, Brandon Harrison, Guerin Hays, Edward Henry, Stacy Hickman, Martin Hill, Priscilla Huff, Mary Hughes, Alexander Hume, Brett Hyman, Nunu Japaridze, William Jenkins, George Jewsevskyj, Christopher Jimenez, Mahreon Johnson, Kellianne Jones, Stephen Jones, Torrance Jones, Nathalie Joost, Nicholas Kalman, Hufsa Kamal, Stephen Kanicka, Elvan Katmer, Colleen Kelley, Colleen Kenney, Grigory Khananayev, Vandana Kilaru, Kevin Kirby, Henry Klapper, Ashley Koerber Moir, Jenica Krall, Barbara Krieger, Howard Kurtz, Donna Lacey, April LaFever, Sean Langille, Dario Lanzano, Matthew Leach, Lillian LeCroy, Philip LeCroy, James Levinson, Edward Lewis, Jessica Loker, Scott Low, Zachary Lowie, Wayne Lowman, Mary Lucas, Douglas Luzader, Emily Lynn, Michael Maltas, David McAlpine, Brianna McClelland, George McCloskey, Brigid Mary McDonnell, Constance McDonough, Cheryl McEachern, Erin McEwan, Caroline McKee, Douglas McKelway, William Mears, Mark Meredith, Nardos Mesmer, Erenia Michell, Simone Middleton, Marina Minas, Tamara Montgomery, Oddessey Moore, Richard Morse, Mark Moynihan, Seleena Muhammad, Amy Munneke, Tim Murphy, Megan Myers, Blake Neff, James Nelson, Megan Neunan, Virginia Nicolaidis, Elise Norris, Quillie Odom, Andrea O'Grady, Jessica O'Hara, Kendra Olson, Paige Page, Alexandra Pamias Reichard, Raymond Pappas, Stephanie Parr, Bradford Paxton, Chad Pergram, Sally Persons, Daniel Petrilli, Alexander Pfeiffer, Kelly Phares, Shonequa Plummer, Ali Rad, Alexandra Rego, Matthew Reidy, Owen Renfro, David Renken, Katheryn Ricalde, Grace Richardson, Anne Marie Riha, Christina Robbins, Michael Robbins, John Robertson, Douglas Rohrbeck, William Sammon, Joseph Sargis, Craig Savage, Hamid Savage, Marisa Schultz, Joseph Sciacca, Steven Shelton, Anita Siegfriedt, William Sleiman, Ethan Smith, Jason Smith, Teresa Spector, David Spunt, Seneca Stevens, Christopher Stirewalt, Matthew Stout, Eric Strain, James Suddeth, Kelly Summers, Patrick Summers, David Sweet, Louis Tartaglia, Garrett Tenney, Sarah Tobianski, Lucas Tomlinson, Bree Tracey, Gillian Turner, Hayley Turner, Kathryn VanLaere, Bryce Vinson, Christopher Visioli, Leland Vittert, Philip Vogel, Christopher Wallace, John

NETWORKS, STATIONS, AND SERVICES REPRESENTED—Continued

Wallace, Neil Wallace, Taylor Walters, Donald Ward, Amy Wehinger, Meghan Welsh, Caroline Whiteman, Walter Whitley, Anna Willey, John Williams, Colleen Williams Vyas, Anne Marie Willis, Tracy Winborn, Christina Wurm, Bilei Zhang, Anthony Zucconi.

FOX NEWS RADIO—(212) 301–5800; 400 North Capitol Street, NW., Washington, DC 20001: Jason Austin, Jason Bonewald, Jonathan Decker, Maria Donovan, Jared Halpern, Melissa Kraus, Sarah McCrory, Jill Nado, Thomas Root, Matthew Schmidt, Gurnal Scott, Daniel Shields, Rachel Sutherland, John Sylvester, Henry Weinbloom, Tonya Williams.

FRANCE 24—(703) 340–5577; 9506 Blarney Stone Drive, Springfield, VA 22152: Angie Omar, Fanny Allard, Kethevane Gorjestani, Yona Helaoua, Matthieu Mabin.

FRANCE 2 TELEVISION—(202) 833–1818; 1620 I St, NW., Washington, DC 20006: Thomas Donzel, Fabien Fougere, Charlotte Mattout, Loic Michel de la Morvonnais, Arielle Monange, Rebecca Suner, Agnes Vahramian.

FUJI TV JAPAN—(202) 347–1600; 529 14th Street, NW., Suite 330, Washington, DC 20045: Mizumi Dutcher, Peter Gold, Yuki Ishibashi, Aaron Maisler, Toshiyuki Matsuyama, Matthew Mosley, Frank Pallone, Ryutaro Sejima, Tomokazu Shibaki.

GALEI–TZAHAL (ISRAEL ARMY RADIO)—(301) 520–2503; 112 Shaw Avenue Silver Spring, MD 20904: Drora Perl.

GERMAN PRESS AGENCY—(202) 662–1220; 1112 National Press Building, Washington, DC 20045: Christina Eck.

GERMAN PUBLIC RADIO (ARD)—(202) 342–1730; 3132 M Street, NW., Washington, DC 20007: Jan Boesche, Katrin Brand, Martina Buttler, Martin Ganslmeier, Eva Graumann, Sebastian Hesse-Kastein, Simon-Laslo Janssen, Astrid Joehnk, Julia Kastein, Thilo Koessler, Arthur Landwehr, Torben Ostermann, Diana Robbins, Sebastian Schreiber, Torsten Teichmann.

GERMAN TV (ARD)—(202) 298–6535; 3132 M Street, NW., Washington, DC 20007: Jan Aulenkamp, Claudia Buckenmaier, Verena Buenten, Jan Philipp Burgard, Robert Cherouny, Daniel Doernen, Karin Dohr-Grill, Christina Freitag-Schmitt, Hillery Gallasch, Maren Hennemuth, Florian Kroker, Christina Lucas, Connor Malone, Stefan Niemann, Robert Shire, Michaela Werner, Marion Zschieschang.

GERMAN TV (ZDF)—(202) 333–3909; 1077 31st Street, NW., Washington, DC 20007: Hebah Abdalla, Annette Brieger, Kirsten Candia, Teresa Eder, Lara Esfahani, Heidi Fleischer Belmar, Fabian Gatza, Ralf Hartwig, Francisco-Ruben Herrera, Melanie Hillmann, Britta Jaeger, Wolfgang Kotke, Wolfgang Macholz, Claudia Offermann, Steffanie Riess, Hans-Peter Schloemer, Patrice See, Jan Seifert, Stefan Simons, Heike Slansky, Andrea Thevessen, Elmar Thevessen, Ines Trams, Uyanga Tserenbaljid, Elke Tucker.

GLOBAL TV CANADA—(202) 824–6771; 400 North Capitol Street, NW., #850, Washington, DC 20001: Jackson Proskow.

GPI TV—P.O. Box 218, Garrett Park, MD 20896: Kenneth Beyer, Matthew LeClair, Sam Pinczuk, Robert Wiley.

GRAY TELEVISION—(202) 910–8644; 500 New Jersey Avenue, Suite 350, Washington, DC 20001: David Ade, Lisa Allen, Jillian Angeline, Alana Austin, Karen Daborowski, Theodore Fioraliso, Natalie Grim, Arielle Hawkins, Conor Hollingsworth, Kristin Kasper, Timothy Knapp, Allison Maass, Jacqueline McCarthy, Kyle Midura, Maribel Padial, Tyler Smith, Peter Zampa.

GROUPE TVA—(202) 822–4588; 820 1st Street, NE., Washington, DC 20002: Charles De Poilloue De Saint Perier, Richard Latendresse, Tracey Madigan.

GRUPO RADIO CENTRO—12319 Houser Drive, Clarksburg, MD 20871: Dinah Luis Saracho de Meraz.

HEARST TELEVISION INC—(202) 457–0220; 1100 13th Street, NW., #950, Washington, DC 20005: Mark Albert, Rebecca Bainer, April Chunko, Octavia Crocker, Kevin Crosby, Aixa Diaz Morales, Deanna Fry, Kirsty Hastings-Jones, Brady Headington, Jarred Hill, Sally F. Kidd, Carlos Olazagasti, David Postovit, Matthew Prichard, Travis Sherwin, Erin Skeele, Christopher Smyth, Courtney Sonn, Wendy Wilk, Emily Wishingrad.

HELLENIC PUBLIC TV—(202) 413–9219; 2742 Thornbrook Court, Odenton, MD 21113: Eleni Argyri.

HISPANIC COMMUNICATIONS NETWORK—(202) 360–4112; 529 14th Street, NW., Suite 827, Washington, DC 20045: Alvaro Argueta Colina, Pablo Castro, Jose Lopez Zamorano, Mercy Padilla, Beni Paz-Goldenheart.

HONG KONG PHOENIX SATELLITE TELEVISION—101 Constitution Avenue, NW., #920 East, Washington, DC 20001: Chieh-Yuan Chen, Lingnan Chen, Yi Qiu Chen, Zhuo Huang, Senhao Liu, Tao Lu, Bingru Wang, Tianyi Wang, Youyou Wang, Chang Wei.

HRT/CROATIAN RADIO TELEVISION—1230 23rd Street, Washington, DC 20037: Branka Slavica.

I24 NEWS—(202) 641–9289; 1100 13th Street, NW., Suite 400, Washington, DC 20005: Mounira Al Hmoud, Shayna Estulin, Philippe Gassot, Alison Kurtzman, Njuwa Maina, Daniel Raviv, Alexandra Rhoades, Michael Shure, Ariel Zimerman.

IMAGINATION MEDIA—(301) 567–2222; 810 Broderick Drive, Oxon Hill, MD 20745: Stephen Boney, Darnley Hodge, Mansa Johnson, Darius Lyles, Sowande Tichawonna.

INDEPENDENT TELEVISION NEWS (ITN)—400 North Capitol Street, NW., #899, Washington, DC 20008: Sophie Alexander, Serena Barker-Singh, Adam Blair, Georgina Brewer, Alexander Chandler,

NETWORKS, STATIONS, AND SERVICES REPRESENTED—Continued

Sarah Cherrie, Mark Davey, Anna Lisa Fuglesang, Sarah Gough, Danielle Isdale, Siobhan Kennedy, Ben Martin, Bradley McLennan, Robert Moore, Kylie Morris, Solape Renner, David Sampy, Christopher Shlemon, Millicent Teasdale.

INTER TV—(202) 415–8624; 801 15th Street, #802, Arlington, VA 22202: Dmytro Anopchenko, Sergii Dubinin, Sergii Koval.

ISRAEL TELEVISION AND RADIO—3412 Woolsey Drive, Chevy Chase, MD 20815: Nathan Guttman.

JTBC—529 14th Street, NW., Suite 997, Washington, DC 20045: Hannah Choi, Hyunki Kim, Joseph Lee, Jong Ju Lim, Hanbyul Park.

KAISER HEALTH NEWS—(202) 654–1466; 1330 G Street, NW., Washington, DC 20005: Francis Ying.

KOREAN BROADCASTING SYSTEMS—(202) 662–7345; 529 14th Street, NW., Suite 1055, Washington, DC 20045: Joo Sik Ahn, Kyuseok Han, Ho Sung Jin, Chul Young Keum, Kyung Hyun Kim, Woong Kyu Kim, Yeong Seon Kim, Jae Won Lee, Dongsoo Lim, Hye Jun Seo, Ja Ryen Seo, Jiyoung Seo.

LASLO CONGRESSIONAL BUREAU—(202) 510–4331; 1705 East West Highway, #519, Silver Spring, MD 20910: Vaughn Golden, Matthew Laslo, Tomas LoBianco.

LILLY BROADCASTING—(202) 440–3831; 400 North Capitol Street, NW., Washington, DC 22201: Matthew Knoedler.

MBC–TV KOREA (MUNHWA)—529 14th Street, NW., #1131, Washington, DC 20045: SangDo Lee, Sang Lim, Sungho Park, Hong Gyu Yeo.

MEDILL NEWS SERVICE—1325 G Street, NW., #730, Washington, DC 20005: Joie Chen.

METRO TELEPRODUCTIONS—(301) 608–9077; 2500 Virginia Avenue, NW., 416 S, Washington, MD 20037: James Harris, William Kaplan, David Lilling.

MIDDLE EAST BROADCASTING NETWORKS (MBN)—7600–D Boston Boulevard, Springfield, VA 22153: Ali Ahmed, Nihad Aliakbar, Charbel Antoun, Babu Aryankalavil, Dennis Baltimore, Kalyl Bentwila, Maher Bey, Hicham Bourar, Nkwenten Ejedepang-Koge, Hosny Elgazar, John Elgin, Areig Elhag, Daniel Farkas, Rabah Filali, Michel Ghandour, Stephen Heiner, Wafaa Jibai, Basheer Khaleefah, Ali Mahdi, Michael Marno, Timothy Miller, William Moore, Luis Munoz, Adam Nixon, James Norris, Islam Sharief, Joseph Tabet, Karen Yianopoulos, Elizabeth Zosso.

MORNINGSIDE PARTNERS, LLC—4200 Forbes Road Suite 200, Lanham, MD 20706: Dawin Adridge, Tony Anthony, Elizabeth Pennell, Nevin Rhodes, Chad Schwartz, Juvenal Uribe, Marlon Zeledon.

NATIONAL PUBLIC RADIO—(202) 513–2073; 1111 North Capitol Street, NE., Washington, DC 20002: Stacey Abbott, Reena Advani, Augustine Aiello, Timur Akman-Duffy, Ammar Ali, Sohail Anwar, Rolando Arrieta, Gail Austin, Elizabeth Baker, Robert Baldwin III, Mark Bejarano, Robert Benincasa, Emily Bernice, Christopher Berry, David Blanchard, Melissa Block, Brakkton Booker, Patrick Boyd, Sophia Boyd, Natasha Branch, Ashley Brown, Geoffrey Brumfiel, Dennis Byrnes, Ivonne Cala, Noah Caldwell-Rafferty, Ailsa Chang, Daniel Charles, Carlos Chevez, David Chhour, Zachary Coleman, Jacob Conrad, Gustavo Contreras, Audie Cornish Emery, Carl Craft, William Craig, Michael Cullen, Michael Czaplinski, Janet Czys, Susan Davis, Jessica Deahl, Bridget De Chagas, Scott Detrow, Connor Donevan, Aboubacar Drabo, Alex Drewenskus, Windsor Edwards, Ronald Elving, Faizan Farooq, Pamela Fessler, Karl Fitzke, James Gerhiser, Elizabeth Gilles, Barton Girdwood, Donald Gonyea, Barry Gordemer, Tamara Gordon, Peter Granitz, David Greene, Samuel Gringlas, Claudia Grisales, Bo Hamby, Taylor Haney, Claire Harbage, Barrie Hardymon, Sydney Harper, Richard Harris, Shirley Henry, Rebecca Hersher, Lauren Hodges, TaShick Holland, Scott Horsley, Andrea Hsu, Andrew Huether, Steven Inskeep, Brian Jarboe, Ricky Jarrett, Carrie Johnson, Aubri Juhasz, John Keator, Michele Kelemen, Mary Kelly, Miranda Kennedy, Junaid Khan, Caitlyn Kim, Alison Kodjak, Danielle Kurtzleben, Kevin Langley, Viet Le, Mara Liasson, Katherine Lonsdorf, Ryan Lucas, Timothy Mak, John Marchitto, Melissa Marquis, Colin Marshall, Michel Martin, Rachel Martin, James Mastromarino, Sharon McCalister, Sarah McCammon, Eric McDaniel, Cecily Meza-Martinez, Nicholas Michael, Joseph Mills, Domenico Montanaro, Elena Moore, Steven Mullis Jr., John Myre, Brian Naylor, Joe Neel, Brett Neely, Jackie Northam, Ammad Omar, Amarachukwu Omeokwe-Davis, Francisco Ordonez, Peter Overby, Matthew Ozug, Joseph Palca, Calvin Park, Miles Parks, Firoze Pasha, Christina Peck, Julia Pereira, John Poole, Julia Redpath, Joshua Rogosin, Stacey Samuel, Lexie Schapitl, Arnold Seipel, Alina Selyukh Pickeral, Ari Shapiro, Arthur Silverman, Selena Simmons-Duffin, Kelsey Snell, John Speer, Barbara Sprunt, Rob Stein, Ian Stewart, Evie Stone, Laura Sullivan, Rebecca Sullivan, Fatma Tanis, Jessica Taylor, Gerald Tennant, Neil David Tevault, Sharahn Thomas, Kevin Tidmarsh, Nina Totenberg, Ayesha Trice, Anthony Utz, Kevin Wait, Deirdre Walsh, Gemma Watters, David Welna, Kelli Wessinger, Ashley Westerman, Catherine Whelan, Victoria Whitley-Berry, James Willetts, Natalie Winston, Mallory Yu, Pias Zaman, Michael Zamora.

NATIONAL SCENE NEWS—1030 15th Street, NW., Suite 333-UB, Washington, DC 20005: Gloria Minott, Askia Muhammad.

NATIVE AMERICAN TV (NATV)—17690 Old Waterford Road, Leesburg, VA 20176: Robert Cohencious, Randolph Flood, Elizabeth Lorenzen.

NBC NEWS—(202) 885–4200; 4001 Nebraska Avenue, NW., Washington, DC 20016: Natalia Abrahams, Douglas Adams, Oluwatomike Adeboyejo, Julia Ainsley, Carmen Alba, Peter Alexander, Jonathan

NETWORKS, STATIONS, AND SERVICES REPRESENTED—Continued

Allen, Roberto Aneiva, Chloe Arensberg, Sal Aridi, David Aronson, Chloe Atkins, Kenneth Austin, Alexandra Bacallao, Jordan Bailey, Sarah Baker, Daniel Barnes, Rodney Batten, Matthew Bauer, Camille Behnke, Jasmine Belton, Jordan Belton, Geoffrey Bennett, Justin Bennett, Jay Blackman, John Blackman, Sarah Blackwill, Victoria Blooston, Joseph Bohannon, Cory Booker, Sally Bronston, Sarah Brooke, Courtney Buble, Norman Butler, Leigh Ann Caldwell, Timothy Canalichio, Anthony Capra, Bradleigh Chance, Ciara Cione, Robert Ciridon, Julia Clancy, Micaela Colonna, Joseph Cook, Nero Cooper Jr., Thomas Costello, Natalie Cucchiara, Ryan Cullen, Rene Cunanan, Caroline Dann, Sarah Dean, Daniel De Luce, Edward Demaria, Kenneth Dilanian, Ilana Drimmer, Sarah Drory, Victoria Duncan, James Eastham, Lauren Egan, Morgan Ellingham, Mitchell Felan, Alexandra Flowers, Maureen Flynn, David Forman, Scott Foster, Scott Fowler, Stacey Fox, Jillian Frankel, Melissa Frankel, Jordan Frasier, Drew Fredrickson, John Gaffney, Morgan Gaffney, Mosheh Gains, Fallon Gallagher, Suzanne Gamboa, Richard Gardella, Keith Gaskin, Dimitrios Gerondidakis, Brian Gessner, Charles Gile, Elizabeth Gilmore, Justice Gilpin-Green, Emily Gold, Cesar Gonzalez Martinez, Robin Gradison, James Greene, Andrew Gross, Garrett Grumbach, Garrett Haake, Sylvia Haller, Candice Harrington, Mikayla Harris, Christopher Hartman, Edmund Hatch, William Hatfield, Owen Hayes, Jonathan Helman, Christopher Henry, Robert Heritage, Ricardo Higgins, Vaughn Hillyard, Charles Hoffman, Charles Howard, Richard Hudock, James Hughes, Kasie Hunt, Joshua Hunter, Michael Iacone, Hallie Jackson, Acacia James, Alicia Jennings, Geet Jeswani, Gwyneth Jones, Carol Joynt, Benjamin Kamisar, Terence Kelly, Jeffrey Kepnes, Javaria Khan, Suzy Khimm, Anastasia Khizder, Ryan Kiernan, Diana Kim, William Koch, Kailani Koenig-Muenster, Michael Kosnar, Courtney Kube, Natasha Lebedeva, Joshua Lederman, Carol Lee, Arthur Lien, Caryn Littler, Kathleen Lockhart, Joseph Loebach, James Long, Gary Lynn, Hannah Malone, Marc Marriott, Gregory Martin, Joseph Martin, Christopher Matthews, Valerie McCabe, Lauren McCulloch, Lee McKinney, Jennifer Meadows, Michael Memoli, Julia Metjian, David Mikutsky, Christopher Millar, Alexander Mitchell, Andrea Mitchell, Steven Mitnick, Marissa Mizroch, Raymond Morada, Davone Morales, Shaheen Mozaffari, Bridget Mulcahy, Tiffany Mullon, Mark Murray, Rosetta Murry, Sooji Nam, Jason Neal, Michelle Neal, Donna Nelson-Schneider, Elizabeth Nevins, Hans Nichols, Nkechi Nneji, David O'Brien, Kelly O'Donnell, Charles Olmstead, Jennifer O'Neil, Gregory Overzat, Hope Palmer, Elyse Perlmutter-Gumbiner, Sarah Ploss, Heidi Przybyla, John Quinnette, George Rabbe, Alonzo Ray, Chester Reis, John Reiss, Talesha Reynolds, Stephanie Rigizadeh, Paul Rigney, Matthew Rivera, Kelvin Robinson, Audrey Rotella, Jacob Rubashkin, Allison Sandza, Benjamin Sarlin, Alexis Saunders, Stacey Schmerling, Andrew Scritchfield, Wesley Scruggs, Carl Sears, Joel Seidman, Alexander Seitz-Wald, Maria Sevilla, Rebecca Shabad, Joseph Shalhoup, Deepa Shivaram, Rebecca Sinderbrand, Aaron Skopek, Charles Slie, Cassano Smith, Terrance Smith, Kimberly Sneed, Gilbert Solorzano, Marianna Sotomayor, Tess Speiser, Annette Stang, Kyle Stewart, Eileen Street, Kenneth Strickland, Laura Strickler, Haley Talbot, Michael Terrel, Frank Thorp, Charles Todd, Demetrea Triantafillides, Ashlee Trujillo, Julia Tsirkin, Frederica Tunnard, Tina Urbanski, Caroline Vakil, Vaughn Ververs, Alexandra Vitali, Susan Vitorovich, Quinn Warner, Misha Wee, Cydney Weiner, John Weir, Kristen Welker, Christopher Whittington, Winston Wilde, Abigail Williams, Louis Williams, Roxanne Williams, Calum Williamson, Christopher Williamson, Rachel Witkin, Ezekial Wohlrab, Joel Woodruff, Victor Young, Robert Zeliger, Joaquin Zumbado.

NBC NEWSCHANNEL—(202) 783–2615; 400 North Capitol Street, Suite 850, Washington, DC 20001: Blayne Bailey, Alice Barr, Sheila Conlin, Ray Davis, Michael Dobal, Jonathan Einarsen, Nancy Ellard, Sheri Lynn Gibson, Nelson Ginebra, Andrew Godsick, Candace Gordon, James Hurt, Julie Jarvis, Mary Jennifer Johnson, James Karp, Nicole McManus, Brian Mooar, Steven Muskat, William Newberry, Michael O'Connell, Tracie Potts, Cecil John Sills, Christopher Skokowski, Casey Wexler, Christopher Wiggins.

NBC NEWS RADIO—(602) 374–6100; 1801 Rockville Pike, 5th Floor, Rockville, MD 20852: Joseph Guzman, Terrence Moore.

NEWS2SHARE—5453 30th Place, NE., Washington, DC 20015: Alejandro Alvarez, Andrew Fischer.

NEW TANG DYNASTY TV—(202) 449–9480; 529 14th Street, NW., Suite 446, Washington, MD 20045: Haipeng Du, Gail Kellum, Chuan Lin, Shenghua Sung, Yang Wang, Wei Wu, Lixin Yang, Ziyi Yang, Simone Young.

NEXSTAR MEDIA GROUP—(202) 570–5610; 400 North Capitol Street, NW., Washington, DC 20001: Holley Coil, Kevin Dermody, Jessica Grossheim, Andreia Jones Jackson, Don Kauffman, Joseph Khalil, Stephen Lowery, Raquel Martin, Kellie Meyer, William Mondora, Alexandra Parresol, Drew Petrimoulx, Trevor Shirley, Anna Wiernicki, Morgan Wright.

NHK—(202) 828–5180; 2030 M Street, NW., #706, Washington, DC 20006: Masaki Arai, Drew Aral, Hitomi Ballard, Shun Ishibe, Yusaku Ishii, April Kim, Kenji Kohno, Torao Kono, Takeshi Kurihara, Benjamin Marks, David McCagg, Atsutoshi Nishikawa, Momoca Nishimoto, Esther Oh, Yusuke Ota, Kentaro Tanaka, Kiyoshi Tanno, Andrea Vega Yudico, Jennifer White, Takeshi Yamasaki, Yosuke Yoshitake, Hideki Yui.

NIPPON TV NETWORK—(202) 638–0890; 529 14th Street, NW., #1036, Washington, DC 20045: Takaaki Abe, Tomoko Beck, Kathryn Harada, Mariko Hoshi, Yukimasa Inoue, Jumpei Shimizu, Hikari Tanaka, Ryoichiro Yaoka.

NETWORKS, STATIONS, AND SERVICES REPRESENTED—Continued

NORWEGIAN BROADCASTING—(202) 785–1460; 2000 M Street, NW., #890, Washington, DC 20036: Anders Magnus, Veronica Westhrin.

NOW THIS NEWS—Discovery Networks c/o NowThis, One Discovery Place, Silver Spring, MD 20910: Ciara Allen, Robert Baynard, Jackson Davis, Zinhle Essamuah, Douglas Forte, Zahra Haider, Allan Piper, Nicholas Pitney, Rex Sakamoto, James Thomas.

NTN24—1333 H Street, NW., Washington, DC 20005: Gustau Alegret, Alfredo Duarte, Golda Fogel, Mario Gonzalez, Marco Granda-Murillo, Paul Henry Guevara Medrano, Melissa Hobaica Santa Cruz, Valeria Massarelli, Emiliana Molina, Julio Moreno Vargas, Valdemar Rodriguez, Carolina Valladares Perez, Laura Zelaya.

N–TV GERMAN NEWS CHANNEL—1100 13th Street, NW., Suite 400, Washington, DC 20005: Peter Kleim, Florian Metelerkamp.

ONE AMERICA—(858) 270–690; 101 Constitution Avenue, NW., Washington, DC 20001: Noah Arnold, Tyler Atchison, Bonnie Breuner, Jordan Clifford, Colin Eustace, Girish Gaur, Ryan Girdusky, Charles Herring, Dawn Herring, John Hines, Stefan Kleinhenz, Brian Maresco, Neil McCabe, Peter Musurlian, Nile Myers, Richard Pollock, John Posobiec, Young Richardson, Chanel Rion, Emerald Robinson, Caitlin Sinclair, Hannah Styles, Joseph Thompson, Olutayo Tikare, Zhuoqin Yang.

PBS NEWSHOUR—3620 S. 27th Street, Arlington, VA 22206: Yamiche Alcindor, Victoria Aronson, William Brangham, Frank Carlson, Emily Carpeaux, Jaywon Choe, David Coles, Tess Conciatori, Daniel Cooney, Alexandra D'Elia, Lisa Desjardins, Sydni Dreher, Diane Estes, Gretchen Frazee, Michael Fritz, Elizabeth Gardinier, Julia Griffin, Kathryn Grumke, Geoffrey Lou Guray, Erica Hendry, Jason Kane, Saher Khan, Stephanie Kotuby, Samuel Lane, Meredith Lee, Jamie Leventhal, Matthew Loffman, Leah Nagy, Rhana Natour, Courtney Norris, Ali Rogin, Daniel Sagalyn, Nicholas Schifrin, Magan Sherzai, Matthew Speiser, Kira Wakeam, Rachel Wellford, Amna Werdel, Daniel Yang, John Yang.

POLITICO.COM—(703) 842–1791; 1100 Wilson Boulevard, Suite 601, Arlington, VA 22209: Jennifer Ament, Eugene Daniels, Camille Minters, Mary Newman, Annie Rees, David Shaw.

PROYECTO PUENTE—2300 Darius Lane, Reston, VA 20191: Dolia Pettingell.

RADIO FRANCE—3126 Dumbarton Street, NW., Washington, DC 20007: Gregory Philipps.

RADIO FRANCE INTERNATIONALE—4509 Ellicott Street, NW., Washington, DC 20016: Anne Corpet.

RADIO FREE ASIA—(202) 530–4900; 2025 M Street, NW., #300, Washington, DC 20036: Han Chen, Tsung-shen Cheng, Vanrith Chrea, Passang Dhonden, Tenzin Dickyi, Nordhey Dolma, Richard Finney, Leung Fok, Geri Geriquiji, Duk In Han, King Ho, Gulchehra Hoja, Albert Hong, Yewon Ji, Mamatjan Juma, Jilil Kashgary, Andrew Kennedy, Sovannarith Keo, Vivian Kieffer, Jin Kuk Kim, Soyoung Kim, Nayrein Kyaw, Kyu Sang Lee, Sangmin Lee, Xiaoqiang Liao, Wai Lo, Lucy Lu, Dhanesh Mahtani, Min Mitchell, Corey Munford, Nareth Muong, July Myo, Sarkis Najarian, Anh Nguyen, Kuerban Niyazi, Jung Noh, Jung-Woo Park, Parameswaran Ponnudurai, Brian Powell, Kyung Rhee, Aungthu Schlenker, Alim Seytoff, Khin Maung Soe, Yeshi Tashi, Hamuti Tayier, Hoa Ai Tran, Yufen Tsao, Jianying Wang, Xiaoquan Wang, Tamdin Wangchuk, Tashi Wangchuk, Eugene Whong, Hee Yang, Samean Yun.

RADIO FREE EUROPE—(202) 457–6900; 1201 Connecticut Avenue, NW., Washington, DC 20036: Todd Prince.

RADIO ONE—(301) 565–8182; 8515 Georgia Avenue, Silver Spring, MD 20910: Christopher Johnson, Kent Kramer, Samuel Tatum, Ronald Thompson, Zeplyn Tillman, Jeffrey Wilson.

REGIONAL NEWS NETWORK (RNN)—400 North Capitol Street, NW., #775, Washington, DC 20001: David Sloan.

REUTERS RADIO & TV—(202) 898–0056; 1333 H Street, NW., 6th Floor, Washington, DC 20005: Daniel Balinovic, Anoopam Bharania, Robert Brock, Peter Bullock, Arlene Eiras, Elizabeth Feria, J. Kevin Fogarty, Marie Frail, Nathaniel Frandino, Gavino Garay, Deborah Gembara, Pavithra George, Rodrek Golden, Katharine Jackson, Kia Johnson, Vanessa Johnston, Lisa Lewnes, Deborah Lutterbeck, Labib Nasir, Kristin Neubauer, Gershon Peaks, Don Pessin, Mana Rabiee, Joel Reyes, Tom Rowe, Joseph Shaw, Roger Shull, Linda So, George Tamerlani, Scott Vaughan, Michael Weekes.

RTE–IRISH RADIO & TV—(202) 467–5933; 2000 M Street, NW., #315, Washington, DC 20036: Brian O'Donovan.

RTP PORTUGUESE PUBLIC TELEVISION—(202) 774–8608; 2400 16th Street, NW., Apt 15, Washington, DC 20008: Ricardo Bica Vieira Guerreiro, Joao de Vasconcelos Albino da Silva.

RTV SLOVENIJA—(202) 604–2268; 1841 Columbia Road, NW., Washington, DC 20009: Andrej Stopar, Tamara Vodopivec.

RURAL TV NEWS—(202) 554–0514; 611 Pennsylvania Avenue, SE., Suite 397, Washington, DC 20003: Clifton Jackson, Corryn La Rue, Sarah Mock.

RUSSIAN STATE TV AND RADIO (RTR)—(202) 262–2595; 2000 N Street, NW., Suite 810, Washington, DC 20007: Denis Davydov, Alexander Khristenko, Nikolay Koskin.

RUSTAVI 2 BROADCASTING COMPANY—1111 Army Navy Drive Unit 127, Arlington, VA 22202: Aleksandre Papinashvili.

SAGARMATHA TELEVISION—(703) 926–9530; 9655 Hawkshead Drive, Lorton, VA 22079: Nilu Kharel, Ram Kharel, Sharmila Uprety.

NETWORKS, STATIONS, AND SERVICES REPRESENTED—Continued

SCRIPPS NEWS—1100 13th Street, NW. Suite 450, Suite 450, Washington, DC 20005: Matthew Anzur, Daniel Bloom, Roseann Cima, Kevin Clancy, Benjamin Cobb, Carrie Cochran, Zachary Cusson, Susan Doherty, Adam Elrashidi, Bianca Facchinei, Mark Fahey, Terace Garnier, Jake Godin, Mark Greenblatt, Lawan Hamilton, Angela Hill, Kellan Howell, Alexandra Ingber, Willie Inman, Austin Landis, Eric Lochstampfor, Maren Machles, Joseph Merkel, Alexandra Miller, Vivek Narayan, Maira Nolasco, Matthew Picht, Luke Piotrowski, Claude Pruitt, Kyle Pyatt, Andrew Rafferty, Corey Rangel, Susanne Reber, Maya Rodriguez, Ellen Rolfes, Pathik Root, Kristine Schantz, Chance Seales, Matthew Simon, Megan Smith, Amber Strong, Patrick Terpstra, Zachary Toombs, Alexandra Travis, Nicole Vowell, Ellen Weiss, Jeffrey Wick, Alexandra Zuckerman.

SEOUL BROADCASTING SYSTEM (SBS)—(202) 637–9850; 529 14th Street, NW., #979, Washington, DC 20045: Sung Soo Han, Joonhyung Jung, Soohyung Kim, Jung S. Oh, Edward Park, Seokmin Sohn.

SHENZHEN MEDIA GROUP (SZMG)—(202) 815–6463; 1330S Fair Street, Apt. 1101, Arlington, VA 22202: Zheng Chen, Chi Hai Kwan.

SIGHTLINE MEDIA GROUP—(703) 750–7479; 1919 Gallows Road, Vienna, VA 22182: John Bretschneider, Jeffrey Martin, Benjamin Murray, Daniel Woolfolk.

SINCLAIR BROADCAST GROUP—(410) 568–1500; 10706 Beaver Dam Rd., Cockeysville, MD 21030: Angelica Alvarez-Ibarra, Sharyl Attkisson, Mariana Barillas, Bryan Barr, David Bernknopf, Leandra Bernstein, Eric Bolling, Cheryl Carson, Namita Chopra, Paul Courson 3rd, Larry Deal, AnnaMaria DiPietro, Natalie Fertig, Jessica Floyd, Andrew Hall, Mark Hyman, Lee Jenkins, David Johns, Lindsey Leake, Louis Libin, Lisa Lisko, Stephen Loiaconi, Daniel Lyon, Michelle Macaluso, Mark Orchard, Russel George Read, James Rosen, Kristin Smith, John Stansfield, Daniel Steinberger, Scott Thuman.

SINOVISION—2111 Jefferson Davis Highway, #202N, Arlington, VA 22202: Han Cui.

SIRIUS XM SATELLITE RADIO—(202) 380–4000; 1500 Eckington Place, NE., Washington, DC 20002: Daniel Berdiel, Katherine Caperton, Paul DeMilio, Patrick Ferrise, Christopher Frates, Charla Freeland, Jennifer Hammond, Jenna Hecker, Robert Henry, Olivier Knox, Shannon Lynch, Jennifer McLellan, Kerry Picket.

SKY NEWS—400 North Capitol Street, NW., #550, Washington, DC 20001: Rebecca Cotterill, Cordelia Lynch, Dickon Mager, Greg Milam, Christopher Pearson, Emily Purser, Duncan Sharp, Emily Upton, Amanda Walker.

SKY NEWS ARABIA—400 North Capitol, Suite 770, Washington, DC 20001: Omar Ali, Mohaimen Aljasheme, Sohail Alshaer, Adam Awada, Artun Fatih, James Martone, Hiba Nasr, Osamah Smysom.

SMALL HOUSE PRODUCTIONS—10304 Royal Woods Court, Montgomery Village, MD 20886: Nickouszha Belha, Juan Carlos Diaz, George Leidsmar, Wingel Pinzon, Henry Pinzon-Contreras, Edwin Ramirez.

SPECTRUM NEWS—(202) 783–0565; 400 North Capitol Street, NW., Suite G–95, Washington, DC 20001: Andrew Balot, Carl Brewer, Margaret Chadbourn, Kevin Frey, Saskia Hennecke, Shawn Klein, Samuel Lisker, Eva McKend, Maureen McManus, Christopher Mohall, Minh Tuyen Nguyen, Vincent Pecoraro, Taylor Popielarz, Samantha-Jo Roth, Taurean Small, Erik Tavcar, Christopher Thomas, Jeevan Vittal, Colleen Wordock.

SRN NEWS (SALEM)—(703) 528–6213; 1901 North Moore Street, #201, Arlington, VA 22209: Robert Agnew, Shepard Bennett, Gregory Clugston, LeRoy Froom, Walter Hindes, John Lormand, Jeffrey Matzka, Andrew Stewart.

STATELINE—901 E Street, NW., Washington, DC 20004: Alayna Alvarez, Barbara Barrett, Jenni Bergal, Scott Greenberger, Thomas Henderson, Michael Ollove, Elaine Povich, Sophie Quinton, April Simpson, Noelle Straub, Matthew Vasilogambros, Christine Vestal, Teresa Wiltz.

SWEDISH BROADCASTING—(202) 785 1727; 2000 M Street, NW., Suite 890, Washington, DC 20036: Stefan Asberg, Barbro Carina Bergfeldt, Kajsa Boglind, Ove Erik Andreas Zernell.

SWISS BROADCASTING—(202) 429 9668; 2000 M Street, NW., Suite 370, Washington, DC 20036: Emiliano Bos, Peter Duggeli, Raphael Grand, Massimiliano Herber, Isabelle Jacobi, Gaspard Kuhn, Philippe Revaz, Andrea Vosti, Mark Yates, Markus Zeffler.

TALK MEDIA NEWS—(202) 337–5322; 300 New Jersey Avenue, NW., Suite 974, Washington, DC 20002: Regina Holmes, Timothy Maier, Bryan Renbaum, Thomas Squitieri.

TELEMUNDO NETWORK—400 North Capitol Street, NW., Suite 850, Washington, DC 20001: Glenda Contreras, William Cortes, Wilber Guzman, Cristina Londono, Edwing Lopez Reyes, Lizeth Juliana Monsalve, Lorestina Montenegro, Maria Pena, Randy Serrano, Javier Vega Urreta.

TELESUR—(202) 420 5560; 1100 13th Street, NW., Washington, DC 20005: Jorge Ayala, Alina Duarte, Raul Galindo Pena, Jorge Gestoso, Juan Miranda Salazar.

TELEVISA NEWS NETWORK—1730 Rhode Island Avenue, NW., Suite 405, Washington, DC 20036: Basilio Moutsatsos Morales.

TF1-FRENCH TV—2000 M Street, NW., Suite 870, Washington, DC 20036: Amandine Atalaya, Marie Chantrait, Mathieu Derrien, Catherine Jentile de Canecaude, Julie Asher Morris, Vincent Mortreux, Adrien Ponsard.

THE BERNS BUREAU, INC.—Washington, DC 20510: Matthew Kaye.

THE HILL—1625 K Street, NE., Suite 900, Washington, DC 20006: Krystal Ball, Jordan Dale, Adam Derose, Saagar Enjeti, Nathaniel Fredman, Alexandra Goncalves De Oliveira, Stephen Greisiger, Jessica

NETWORKS, STATIONS, AND SERVICES REPRESENTED—Continued

Grose, David Krupin, Lisa Movit, Thomas Pray, Marisela Ramirez, Sean Root, James Sexton, Jamal Simmons, Donna Wilson.

THE REAL NEWS NETWORK—(410) 500–5235; 231 Holliday Street, Baltimore, MD 21202: William Arenas, Adam Coley, James Daley, Dwayne Gladden, Taya Graham, Cameron Granadino, David Hebden, Taylor Hebden, Stephen Janis, Paul Jay, Charles Lenchner, Jacqueline Luqman, Dharna Noor, Babatunde Ogunfolaju, Sharmini Peries, Kayla Rivara, Carmen Russell, Bernhard Gregory Wilpert.

THIS IS AMERICA WITH DENNIS WHOLEY—1333 H Street, NW., Washington, DC 20005: Jerry Cox.

THIS WEEK IN AGRIBUSINESS—(301) 466–7403; 9915 Hillridge Drive, Kensington, MD 20895: Patrick Haggerty.

TOKYO BROADCASTING SYSTEM—The National Press Bldg., Washington, DC 20045: Kazuo Doi, Haruyo Fukuda, Masatoshi Ichikawa, Shinichiro Ikushima, Natsuya Iwata, Xin-Yi Lee, Saori Moriizumi, Nicholas Watkins, Yuta Yamamoto.

TO THE CONTRARY (PERSEPHONE PRODUCTIONS)—1819 L Street, NW., 7th Floor, Washington, DC 20036: Ariel Edem, Bonnie Erbe-Leckar, Luis Mazariegos, Cari Stein.

TRT—(703) 401–6482; 529 14th Street, NW., #1085, Washington, DC 20045: Faruk Ayaz, Ali Cilesizoglu, Tuna Sanli, Erkan Tarhan, Baybora Tinaz.

TRT WORLD—(202) 800–5734; 1819 L Street, NW., Suite 700, Washington, DC 20036: Faiza Ahmed, Jonathan Brain, Kilmeny Duchardt, Hasan Dudar, Kadir Durak, Yasmine El Sabawi, David Enders, Abdulmuttalip Erdogan, Ghida Fakhry Khane, Aws Haidari, Maxine Hughes, Serra Karacam, Oguz Karasu, Bunyamin Kasap, Courtney Kealy, Mehmet Kor, Kevin Kusmez, Muhammed Mollaoglu, Alexi-Noelle O'Brien-Hosein, Barbaros Sayilgan, Shreya Sen, Juan Silva Llancaleo, Zumrut Sonmez, Frank Ucciardo, Elif Yediyildiz, Aydin Yurtseven.

TV2-NORWAY—2000 M Street, Suite 380, Washington, DC 20036: Fredrik Graesvik, Gerhard Helskog.

TV3-TELEVISIO DE CATALUNYA—(202) 785–0580; 2000 M Street, NW., Suite 830, Washington, DC 20036: Guillem Ayats, Maria Eugenia Lozano Villo, Fabien Ortiz, Francesc Reverter Baquer.

TV ASAHI—529 14th Street, NW., #1280, Washington, DC 20045: Satoru Fuse, Renata Janney, Takahiro Kinoshita, D'Juan Mercado, Takamori Okada, Yusuke Takaba.

TVBS—2500 Wisconsin Avenue, Washington, DC 20007: Song Hwang, Chia-Hui Ni.

TVE—SPANISH PUBLIC TELEVISION—(202) 785–1813; 2000 M Street, NW., #325, Washington, DC 20036: Fernando Gayon Granell, Cristina Olea Fernandez, Francisco Sevilla Garcia, Anna Maria Ubeda-Carulla.

TV GLOBO INTERNATIONAL—(202) 429–2525; 2141 Wisconsin Avenue, NW., Suite L, Washington, DC 20007: Vicente Cinque, Raquel Krahenbuhl, Daniel Silva-Pinto, Luis Silva-Pinto.

TVN POLAND—7429 Chummley Court, Falls Church, VA 22043: Marcin Wrona, Marcin Wyszogrodzki.

TV POLSAT—5550 Columbia Pike, #764, Arlington, VA 22204: Magdalena Sakowska, Pawel Wudarczyk.

TVP POLISH TELEVISION—(202) 765–7717; 3024 O Street, NW., #2, Washington, DC 20007: Rafal Stanczyk, Joanna Stanczyk-Pinkwart, Artur Zagorski.

TV TOKYO—1333 H Street, NW., 5th Floor, Washington, DC 20005: Rihoko Akiyama, Benjamin Dalton, Moqiu Ma, Yoshiyuki Takahashi.

UNIVISION—(202) 682–6160; 101 Constitution Avenue, NW., Suite 800W, Washington, DC 20001: Enrique Acevedo, Lorena Arroyo Valles, Carlos Chirinos Vasquez, Jorge Contreras, Deborah Durham, Pablo Gato, Angel Hernandez Orellana, Ivenneth Padilla Alvarado, Fernando Pizarro, Janet Rodriguez, Pablo Sanchez, Claudia Uceda, Julia Vargas, Mario Vizcarra Coloma.

USA TODAY—7950 Jones Branch Drive, McLean, VA 22107: Jasper Colt, Stephen Elfers, Hannah Gaber Saletan, Jarrad Henderson, Matthew Sobocinski.

VENTANA PRODUCTIONS—(202) 785–5112; 1819 L Street, NW., Washington, DC 20036: Richard Joy, Timothy Murray, Juan Rocha, Robin Stewart, Mark Thalman.

VERIZON—Kenneth Brown, Keenan Patience, Rodney Rice Jr., Charles Samuel.

VICE NEWS—U.S. Capitol, Room S–325, Washington, DC 20510: Fatima Al Khirsan, Timothy Barker, Morgan Baskin, Babak Behnam, Benjamin Bishop, Tiffani Davis, Kristin Fraser, Jordan Gantz, Tracy Jarrett, Cameron Joseph, Elizabeth Landers, Victoria Lesiw, Mary Grace Lucas, Evan McMorris-Santoro, Daniel Newhauser, Simone Perez, Jeffrey Ricker, Jesse Seidman, Joseph Tone, Gregory Walters, Brian Wheeler.

VIETV NETWORK—(215) 883–9738; 1604 Spring Hill Road, Suite 150, Vienna, VA 22182: Thao Dao, Yen Phuong Le, Doanh Vu.

VIEWPOINT COMMUNICATIONS—(301) 565–1650; 8607 2nd Avenue, Suite 402, Silver Spring, MD 20910: Randy Feldman, Benjamin Finkel, Larry Greenblatt, Steven Hamberg, Charles Horn.

VIRGINIA PUBLIC RADIO—703 South Royal Street, Alexandria, VA 22314: Michael Pope.

VOICE OF AMERICA—330 Independence Avenue, SW., Washington, DC 20237: Gonzalo Abarca, Grace Abdu, Soyoung Ahn, Brian Allen, Christopher Allen, Darrell Allen, Vadim Allen, Miguel Amaya, Arash Arabasadi, Herdiyanto Ardono, Betty Ayoub, Qazafi Baber, Thomas Bagnall, Steve Baragona, Aline Barros, Larry Bond, Michael Bowman, Jonathan Brandkamp, Timothy Brannon, Michael Burke, Carol Castiel, Elizabeth Cherneff, Raymond Choto, Peter Clottey, Lina Correa, Woody Crawford,

NETWORKS, STATIONS, AND SERVICES REPRESENTED—Continued

Nicolas Crupi, Minas Dargakis, Jeffery Daugherty, Jela de Franceschi, Joan Deluca, Steven Densmore, Abdourahmane Dia, Esther Ewart, Geoffrey Fabian, Cecilia Favela Munoz, Salem Fekadu, Leonardo Feldman, Bruce Ferder, Darren Fox, David Futrowsky, Solomon Gebremariam, Myroslava Gongadze, Pema Gorap, Richard Green, Adamson Greenbaum, Esha Grover, Katherine Gypson, Marcus Harton, Michael Helke, Rafki Hidayat, Selim Hossain, Paris Huang, Iftikhar Hussain, Utami Hussin, Iuliia Iarmolenko, Saqib Islam, Towhidul Islam, Michael Ivey, Gary Jaffe, Wagma Jalawan, Kaveh Jamshidi, Valeria Jegisman, Wilhelm Johannes, Sandzhar Khamidov, Saba Khan, Seon Myung Kim, Arzouma Kompaore, Tatiana Koprowicz, Jesse Koster, Bagassi Koura, Tsering Kyi, Daniel Lee, Sanghoon Lee, YiHua Lee, Kimberly Lewis, Jingxun Li, Libo Liu, Jazmin Lopez Bolanos, Liyuan Lu, Victoria Macchi, Mitzi Macias, Vincent Makori, James Malone, Marvin Marion, Jean Michel Mathurin, Eva Mazrieva, Ira Mellman, Kimseng Men, Tra Mi, Guita Mirsaeedi, Jaime Moreno Gomez, Natalia Mozgovaya, Jonathan Muriithi, Ndimyake Mwakalyelye, Thet Naing, Dondhon Namling, Aurea Nascimento, Robert Naylor, Sean Neary, Carla Newell, Trung Nguyen, Rosalie O'Connell, Jesusemen Oni, Rattaphol Onsanit, Thar Oo, Thein Oo, Arkadiy Orlov, Arunima Pande, Robert Parsell, Kingsavanh Pathammavong, Ruslan Petrychka, Reasey Poch, Khemara Pov Sok, Carolyn Presutti Davison, John Quinn, Robert Raffaele, James Randle, Stuart Redisch, Samuel Reid, Julia Riera Parera, Justin Riley, Ralph Robinson, James Russell, Edward Rwema, Rafael Saakov, Shahla Sadighi, Cynthia Saine-Spang, Nana Sajaia, Yuni Salim, Joad Santa-Rita, Yulia Savchenko, Mony Say, Brian Schiff, Edward Schneider, Bart Schrum, Bricio Segovia Reche, Jeffrey Seldin, Pema Setsang, Roger Sherman, Setareh Sieg, George Simkins, Joseph Sipos, Leili Soltani, Leakhena Sreng, Scott Storkel, Songphot Suphaphon, Carl Swanson, Aung Sway, Jeffrey Swicord, Kyaw Tha, Michael Theisen, Gessel Tobias Delgado, Pinitkarn Tulachom, Greta Van Susteren, Joseph Vitale, Chuanqi Xu, Oleksandr Yanevskyy, Guofu Yang, Raymond Yeung Yam.

VOYAGE PRODUCTIONS—(202) 276–2848; 565 Pennsylvania Avenue, NW., #302, Washington, DC 20001: Susan Baumel, Ely Baumel-Lamonica.

Wall STREET JOURNAL—1025 Connecticut Avenue, Washington, DC 20036: Paul Beckett, Thomas DiFonzo, Caitlin Faw, Judy Grace Marfil, Gerald Seib, Christina Vallice, Carlos Waters.

WAMU—4000 Brandywine Street, NW., Washington, DC 20016: Jenny Abamu, Emily Alfin Johnson, Martin Austermuhle, Margaret Barthel, Jayk Cherry, Daniella Cheslow, Esther Ciammachilli, Denise Couture, Carmel Delshad, Julie Depenbrock, Lisa Dunn, Jacob Fenston, Kathryn Fink, Mark Gunnery, Gabrielle Healy, Jonquilyn Hill, Joshua Johnson, Monna Kashfi, Avery Kleinman, Danielle Knight, Rachel Kurzius, Mikaela Lefrak, Bianca Martin, James Morrison, Lesley Osburn, Jordan Pascale, Benjamin Privot, Dominique Scarbrough, Ingalisa Schrobsdorff, Allison Schweitzer, Sasha-Ann Simons, Ruth Tam, Tyrone Turner, Ariel Valdez, Amanda Williams, Alana Wise, Elly Yu.

WASHINGTON BUREAU NEWS SERVICE—7425 Savan Point Way, Columbia, MD 21045: Maureen Dezell, Joseph Nelson, Clifford Thorne, Michael Whitney.

WASHINGTON EXAMINER—(202) 459–4943; 1152 15th Street, NW., Suite 200, Washington, DC 20005: Karlee Gibson, Siraj Hashmi, Linda Hernandez, Christopher Lohr, Dominick Mastrangelo, William Ricciardella, Timothy Wolff.

WASHINGTONPOST.COM—1301 K Street, NW., Washington, DC 20071: Nadine Ajaka, Monica Akhtar, Reem Akkad, Mary Albright, Jason Aldag, Carol Alderman, Kyle Barss, Dalton Bennett, Zachary Brown, David Bruns, Allison Caren, Joshua Carroll, Elizabeth Casey, Matthew Collette, Rhonda Colvin, Phoebe Connelly, Andrea Cornejo Castelforte, Nicole DeMarco, Alexis Diao, Jonathan Elker, Nicole Ellis, Amber Ferguson, Reena Flores, Micah Gelman, Jonathan Gerberg, Ross Godwin, Blair Guild, Sarah Hashemi, Michelle Jaconi, Hannah Jewell, Ashleigh Joplin, David Jorgenson, Margaret Kelly, Joyce Koh, Danielle Kunitz, Whitney Leaming, So-Hyun Lee, Thomas Legro, Alice Li, Melissa Macaya, Osman Malik, Patrick Martin, Jesse Mesner-Hage, Daniel Mich, Allison Michaels, Atthar Mirza, Linah Mohammed, Brian Monroe, Breanna Muir, Edward Muldoon, Zoeann Murphy, William Neff, Erin O'Connor, Deirdra O'Regan Schroeder, Jayne Orenstein, John Parks, Sarah Parnass, Margaret Penman, Ariel Plotnick, Kolin Pope, Mahlia Posey, Lee Powell, Jorge Ribas, John Michael Rieger, Anna Rothschild, Lauren Saks, Elyse Samuels, Justin Scuiletti, Whitney Shefte, Madhulika Sikka, Lindsey Sitz, Jordan-Marie Smith, Jennifer Starrs, Peter Stevenson, Daron Taylor, William Tucker, Taylor Turner, Adriana Usero, Luis Velarde, Kathleen Woodsome, Joy Yi.

WASHINGTON RADIO AND PRESS SERVICE—(301) 229–2576; 6702 Pawtucket Road, Bethesda, MD 20817: Hanna Gutmann, Howard Lesser.

WBUR—1401 S Joyce Street, #1012, Arlington, VA 22202: Kimberly Atkins.

WELT N24 GERMAN TV—1620 I Street, NW., Suite 1000, Washington, DC 20006: William Griffitts, Robert Milford, Steffen Schwarzkopf, Sabine Ulbrich-Strothe.

WEST WING REPORTS—11614 Old Brookville Court, Reston, VA 20194: Paul Brandus.

WESTWOOD ONE—202 457–7991; 2020 M Street, NW., Washington, DC 20036: Robert Costantini, Kevin DeLany, Thomas Getter, Cameron Gray, Linda Kenyon, Barton Tessler, Christopher Whitfield.

WETA—(703) 998–1800; 3939 Campbell Avenue, Arlington, VA 22206: Mohammad Ali, David Bash, Jeffrey Bates, Timothy Bowen, Donald Brawner, Martin Carr, Enoch Chan, Darzen Chang, Vincent Forcier, Heather Harris, Cory Hornish, Charles Ide, Kenneth Jones, Christopher Lane, Jon Miles,

NETWORKS, STATIONS, AND SERVICES REPRESENTED—Continued

Nancy Morgan, Paul Nevel, Jeffrey Rathner, Sylvia Reis, John Satterfield, James Schneider, John Schottle, Willliam Seabrook, Brian Smith, Paul Vander Veen, Owen Wood.

WFDC–TV UNIVISION—101 Constitution Avenue, NW., Suite L–100, Washington, DC 20001: Juan Acevedo, Marvin Contreras, Tsitsiki Felix, Rafael Henriquez Maldonado, Jesus Marin Arteaga, Chaid Neme Garrido, Edwin Pitti, Jackeline Quijano Jovel, Rosbelis Quiñonez Silva, Raul Ramos, Katherine Rivera Garcia, Marcela Rodriguez Lopez, Walter Romero Juarez, Rafael Sanchez Cruz, Sara Suarez, Thalia Varelas.

WHITE HOUSE CHRONICLE—1042 Wisconsin Avenue, NW., Washington, DC 20007: Linda Gasparello, Llewellyn King, Barry Worthington.

WJLA–TV / NEWSCHANNEL 8—(703) 239–9480; 1100 Wilson Boulevard, Arlington, VA 22209: George Amos, George Ball, Timothy Barber, Frank Becker, Bradley Bell, Cheryl Carson, Richard Chamberlain, Nancy Chen, Larry Deal, Martin C. Doane, Jonathan Elias, Ernie Ensign, Ryan Eskalis, Lisa Fletcher, Samuel Ford, Anna-Lysa Gayle, Autria Godfrey, John Gonzalez, Hugh Gourley, Heather Graf, Kendall Griggs, Richard Guastadisegni, Joshua Harrington, Shonty Hawkins, Horace Holmes, Brian Hopkins, Thomas Hormuth, Ernest Isgro, George Jackson, Samuel Jackson, William Johnson, James Joslyn, Matt Kady, Don Kauffman, William Kelly, Jay Korff, Hsiu Leong, John B. Lewis, Kevin Lewis, Ian Lloyd, David Lucas, Kellye Lynn, James Marcum, Michelle Marsh, Joaquim Neto, Lindsey O'Brien, Caroline Patrickis, Thomas Perrell, Kristen Powers, John Rice, Victoria Rose, Thomas Roussey, Michael Rudd, Amy Schneider, Jacob Schoenmann, Bhupinder Sharma, Rebecca Sinn, Scott Smith, Christopher Stuard, Steven Stuhlmacher, Sam Sweeney, Scott Taylor, Serge Tomy, Luis Urbina, Michael Vaughn, James Walker, Robert Washington-Anderson, Carl Willis, Dale Wright.

WPLG–TV10—1717 DeSales, Washington, DC 20036: Daniele Bolf, Russell Palombo.

WRC–TV / NBC–4—4001 Nebraska Avenue, NW., Washington DC, 20016: Jay Alvey, Jackie Bensen, Charles Bragale, Beth Brown, Daniel Buckley, Julie Carey, David Carter, Sean Casey, Joseph Cassano, Aimee Cho, Patrick Collins, Natasha Copeland, David Culver, Claudia Curiel, Alfredo Duarte, Patricia Fantis, Justin Finch, Meagan Fitzgerald, Jodie Fleischer, Karla Flores, Bernard Forte, Doreen Gentzler Miller, Teneille Gibson, Aaron Gilchrist, Jason Gittlen, Matt Glassman, Michael Goldrick, Roberto Gonzalez Homs, Liliana Gonzalez-Ramirez, Charles Goodknight, Herbert Gordon, Molette Green, Diego Gutierrez Riveros, Jim Handly, Monique Hayes, Jack Heinbaugh, Lance Ing, Ede Jermin, Lyrone Jones, Christopher Kerwin, Pamela Leahigh, Ronald Leidelmeyer, Nicholas Leimbach, Erika Leon, Katie Leslie, Moises Linares, Anna Llargues, Dario Lopez-Capera, Edith Lozada Salgado, Janette Luviano, Thomas Lynch, Scott MacFarlane, Anthony Mague, John Marcucci, Angelica Martinez, Carlos Martinez, Joseph Martinez, Lauren Mayk, Megan McGrath, Milagros Melendez-Vela, Susan Murphy, Matthew Murray, Chester Panzer, Alberto Pimienta Hernandez, Jeffrey Piper, Jorge Rico, Wendy Rieger, Michelle Rivera, Carlos Daniel Rivera Trinidad, Meredith Royster, Bruce Ryan, Sulema Salazar, Mark Segraves, Cory Smith, Kim Darcy Spencer, Mark Stephens, Andrea Swalec, Shomari Terrelonge-Stone, Caroline Tucker, Adam Tuss, Jennifer Vasquez, Ambrose Vurnis, Roy Weinstock, Tracee Wilkins, Melinda Woolbright, Eun Yang, Richard Yarborough, Alban Zamora, Darren Ziegenbein.

WTOP RADIO—3400 Idaho Avenue, NW., Washington, DC 20016: John Aaron, Neal Augenstein, Michelle Basch, Megan Cloherty, John Domen, Jason Fraley, Noah Frank, Dave Garner, Jessie J. Green, Brennan Haselton, Melissa Howell, Nick Iannelli, Kristi-Sue Lilleston, Richard Massimo, Dave McConnell, Jon Miller, George Molnar, Andrew Moore, Michael Murillo, Rachel Nania, Brian Oliger, Jack Pointer, Art Rose, Kate Ryan, Albert Shimabukuro, Zachary Shore, Aaron Smith, Dick Uliano, William Vitka, Ginger Whitaker, Ren Zheng.

WTTG–FOX TELEVISION—5151 Wisconsin Avenue, NW., Washington, DC 20016: Robert Alexander, Van Applegate, Ama Arthur-Asmah, Robert Barnard, James Beahn, William Beyer, Lauren Bird, Kyle Carmean, Stephen Chenevey, William Cockey, Cori Coffin, Edward Coker, Anthony Colella, Melanie Crisafulli, Anne Cutler-Mason, Kevin Ebersohl, Azubuike Ejiochi, Michael Fischoff, Thomas Fitzgerald, Massimo Giammetta, Daniel Grudovich, Joe Hammond, Anjali Hemphill, Nelson Jones, Guy Lambert, Evan Lambert-McMichael, Paul Lester, Indira LeVine, Tisha Lewis, Craig Little, James Lokay, Marina Marraco, Wisdom Martin, Michael McCann, Kevin McCarthy, Ronnie McCray, Paul McGonagle, Joseph Moise, Holly Morris, Robert Mulligan, Alena Oakes, Daniel Rapela, Jonathan Redmon, Michael Rickard, Bryan Roberts, Joshua Rosenthal, Eugene Russell, Francis Rysak, Sarah Simmons, Nicholas Smith, Joseph Spevak, Montre Staton, Terri Tolliver, Maureen Umeh, Joseph Wagener, Paul Wagner, Donald Watrud, Lindsay Watts, Douglas Wilkes, Steven Williams, Shawn Yancy.

WUSA–TV—(202) 895–5588; 4100 Wisconsin Avenue, NW., Washington, DC 20016: Whitney Amon, Jessica Arnold, Nathan Baca, Howard Bernstein, Eliana Block, Mark Bost, Kurt Brooks, William Broom, Ellen Bryan, Aubrey Bryant, Jesse Burkett-Hall, Lorenzo Burkett-Hall, Samuel Cook, Janice Coon, Ariane Datil, Nicole DiAntonio, Roberta Dooms, Richard Fischer, Eric Flack, Lesli Foster Mathewson, Peggy Fox, Jonathan Franklin, Lauryn Froneberger, Michael Fuhr, Elizabeth Garcia, Stephen Garifo, Laura Geller, Delia Goncalves Perry, Matthew Gregory, Kristen Harris, James Hash, Amanda Hauser, Darren Haynes, Laine Haynes, John Henry, Caridad Hernandez Wood, Thomas Hunsicker, Giovanni Insignares, Eric Jansen, Chester Johnson, Saliqa Khan, Annie Kim, Rebecca Knier, Sarah

NETWORKS, STATIONS, AND SERVICES REPRESENTED—Continued

Konsmo, Evan Koslof, Samantha Kubota, Bruce Leshan, Adam Longo, Sarah Lydick, Miri Marshall, Samara Martin Ewing, Joel McDonald, Tiffany McNeil, Larry Miller, Kristopher Mulholland, Peter Muntean, Liz Palka Minukas, Leonard Pearson, Nicholas Petrillo, Haleigh Purvis, Michael Quander, Kathleen Reynolds, Marcella Robertson, Erin Roby, Mia Salenetri, David Satchell, Kolbie Satterfield, David Scarnato, Kyley Schultz, Markette Sheppard, Charles Shutt, Erin Spaht, Rhea Titus, Michael Trammell, Mikea Turner, Michael Valentine, Michael Valerio, Jesse Varner, Melissa Ward, Marcel Warfield, Ferlon Webster, Bria White, Dion Wiggins, Stephanie Wilson, Michael Wise.

XINHUA—1740 North 14th Street, Arlington, VA 22209: Yina Guo, Yousong Hu, Yuelei Jin, Ding Sun, Yixiao Tan.

YAHOO NEWS—1717 DeSales Street, NW., 3rd Floor, Washington, DC 20036: Samuel Matthews, Jessica Perry, Suzanne Smalley, Benjamin Werschkul.

YONHAP NEWS TV—529 14th Street, NW., Washington, DC 20045: Lauren Kim, Seokyee Yoon.

FREELANCE

Freelancers: Rana Abtar, Naser Abu Diab, Nicholas Adkinson, Robin Adlerblum, Faiez Agobian, Jorge Agobian Villegas, Aziz Ahmed, Christopher Albert, Ahmed Alqarni, Ahmad Amin, Stuart Ammerman, Patrick Anderson, Siqiao Ao, Bruno Arena, Patricia Armstrong, Thomas Armstrong, Eva Artesona, Sally Ayhan, Jean-Pascal Azais, Veronica Balderas Iglesias, Travis Renee Baldwin, Mark Banks, Rose Barondess, Satarupa Barua, Marilisa Battistella, Sam Beattie, Steven Beckner, Michael Benetato, Remco Bikkers, Tim Bintrim, Gerald Bodlander, Karen Borland, JaNece Bradford, Charles Breiterman, Michael Broleman, Jon-Christopher Bua, Eric Bugash, John Bullard, Penny Burk, Mary Burns, Daniel Bush, Brett Carlson, Evan Carr, Anatolie Casenco, Reginald Cecchini, Ching-Yi Chang, David Chaytor, Hans Cho, Eting Chung, Gilles Clarenne, Harvey Cofske, Thomas Coleman, Kyle Cooper, Pedro Correa, Pedro Correa, Timothy Cote, Eric Courtney, Thomas Craca, John Craig, Robert Crawford, Jeffrey Cridland, Philip Crowther, Carla Dakin, Arik Dashevsky, Phillip Datcher, William Demas, Gary DeMoss, Daria Diieguts, Juanita Dillard, Peter Doherty, William Donald, Lionel Donovan, Heather Dorf-Dolce, Paul Dougherty, Sonia Dridi, Kadesh DuBose, Andrei Dziarkach, Stephanie Ebbs, Hosny Elgazar, Dalia Elkomi, Steven Epstein, Manuel Ernst, Rodolfo Estrada, Alfred Faison, Cory Feezer, Anne-Marie Fendrick, Andrew Field, Paul Fifield, Sean Finn, Sara Shannon Finney, Joseph Flood, Cesar Flores, Kristin Foellmer, Daniel Fortney, Thomas Foty, Ariana Freeman, Francis French, David Friedman, Danila Galperovich, Ralph Gaudino, Arthur Gauthier, Atef Gawad, Philip Geyelin, David Girard, Milena Gjorgjievska, John Glennon, Samuel Goodall, Jeffrey Goodman, Glenn Gorham, Nicholas Greiner, Kevin Griffin, Fayrouz Guerouani, Aso Haji Kakol, Tomas Harding, Steven Harper, Roy Harris, Byron Harrison, Cheyenne Haslett, Oscar Haynes, Barry Haywood, Sean Healey, Barry Hecht, Martin Heina, Ryan Hermelijn, Louise Hernon, Charles Hill, Andrea Hines, James Hishchynsky, Darnley Hodge, David Hopper, Jason Hubert, Heather Hutchinson, John Iannuzzi, Heind Ibrahim, Mohamed Ibrahim, Zena Ibrahim, Falastine Iman, Ryan Jackson, Edward Jennings, Jr., Wafaa Jibai, Aiden Johnson, Irene Johnson, Katherine Johnson, Katerra Jones, Matthew Jones, Cathy Kades, Kendall Karson, Omary Kaseko, Atsushi Kato, Drew Katz, Robert Kehs, Peter Kent, Eric Kerchner, Allison Keyes, Khaled Khairy, Basheer Khaleefah, Kawa Khdr, Jiyeon Kim, Corey Kimmel, Kent Klein, Heekyung Kook, Sharif Kouddous, Keith Lane, Nancy Lanzendoerfer, Gregory Larsen, France Latremoliere, Jo Eun Lee, David Lent, Dexter Leong, Darrell Lewis, Jonathan Lien, Bruce Liffiton, Melvin Lindsey, Maria Lucchini, Jayne Lukas, Colette Luke, Iacopo Luzi, Julio Luzquinos, Anna Davalos MacDonald, Ahmed Mahdi, Alicia Majeed, Alexander Mallin, Roman Mamonov, Michele Marcello, Antonio Marques, Jon Martin, Jeffrey Martino, James Mathis, Timothy Matkosky, Andre Matthews, Mathieu Mazza, Kevin McClam, Ian McDougall, Terrance McEachern, Allen McGreevy, Robert McHenry, Daniel McLellan, Brooks Meriwether, Rhoda Metcalfe, Kerry Meyer, Takiha Millington, Takashi Mizukami, Melissa Mollet, William Montague, Willie Moorer, Jane Moran, Megan Murray, Peter Murtaugh, Laurie Mylroie, Ruqaiyah Najjar, Stephen Narisi, Mohamed Nasser, Anh Nguyen, Kevin Nha, Richard Norling, James Novosel, Donald O'Berry, Ralf Oberti, Christopher Olson, Lars Os, Daniel O'Shea, Mohamed Said Ouafi, Quinton Owen, Bernard Ozol, Daniel Patsko, Grant Peacock, Daniel Peebles, Anthony Peltier, Felicia Pendorf, Douglas Perkins, Timothy Persinko, Robert Peterson, Kenneth Pexton, Murray Pinczuk, Nataliia Pisnia-Bystriakova, Christopher Plater, Farhad Pouladi Najafabadi, Shapoor Pourshariati, Christopher Preston, Marthinus Pretorius, Michael Purbaugh, Ralph Quarry, Jason Quinn, Mary Quinn, Juan Quiroga, Mark Rabin, Bryan Rager, Rahim Rashidi, Douglas Ray, Austin Reeves, Melanie Reffes, Edward Reinsel, Meixing Ren, James Riggs, Matthew Ritterpusch, Olivier Robert, William Roberts, Laura Robinson, Xavier Roca, Eduardo Rodriguez, Peter Roof, Gary Rosenberg, Misaele Rossetti-Meyer, Theodore Roth, Joseph Ruffini, Rodrigo Salvatierra, Thomas Sampson, Tomoaki Sasaki, Dmitriy Savchuk, Gregory Savoy, Amr Sayed, Quinn Scanlan, Barry Schlegel, Donald Schoenmann, Emily Schultze, Beth Scott, Michael Seium, Hakim Shammo, Harry Shoffner, James Sicile, Quentin Silver, Paul Skomal, Edward Slater, Cristina Smit, Anthony Smith, Christie Smith, Cynthia Smith, Phillip Smith, Sara Smith, Koen Soete, Sergey Sokolov, Andrew Spangenberg, Theodore Spiegler, Thomas Staton, Mark Stoddard, Leslie Storms, Rodney Streeter, Timothy Strissel,

NETWORKS, STATIONS, AND SERVICES REPRESENTED—Continued

James Stubbs, Richard Suddeth, Ena Suto, Nina Svahn, Robert Sweeney, Kambiz Tavana, Jacqueline Taylor, Bert Thomas, Shari Thomas, Troy Thornes, Thomas Thornton, Cameron Tull, Melanie Turner, Laurie Ure, Benjamin Vaeth-Levin, Carolina Valladares Perez, Jaime Vera Rojas, Marcos Vigil, Michael Viqueira, Jackie Lyn Walker, Julia Walz, Taofeng Wang, Derrick Ward, Tarik Warner, Warren Watson, Elizabeth Watts, Aaron Webster, George Weller, Katharina Werner, Eric White, Snorre Wik, David Williams, Mark Wilson, LaTonya Winters, Ronald Winters, Zachary Wood, Sicelo Wotshela, Brian Yaklyvich, Nadeem Yaqub, Floyd Yarmuth, Stratis Zervos.

PERIODICAL PRESS GALLERIES*

HOUSE PERIODICAL PRESS GALLERY

The Capitol, H–304, phone 225–2941

Director.—Robert M. Zatkowski.
Deputy Director.—Gerald Rupert, Jr.
Assistant Directors: Jenn Walters, Ryan Hamel.

SENATE PERIODICAL PRESS GALLERY

The Capitol, S–320, phone 224–0265

Director.—Justin Wilson.
Deputy Director.—Vacant.
Assistant Director.—Nick Mead.

EXECUTIVE COMMITTEE OF CORRESPONDENTS

Leo Shane III, Sightline Media Group, *Chairman*
Stephen Cooper, Tax Notes, *Secretary*
Alexander Bolton, The Hill, *Treasurer*
Jason Dick, Roll Call
Philip Elliott, Time Magazine
Burgess Everett, Politico
Jack Fitzpatrick, BNA News

RULES GOVERNING PERIODICAL PRESS GALLERIES

1. Persons eligible for admission to the Periodical Press Galleries must be bona fide resident correspondents of reputable standing, giving their chief attention to the gathering and reporting of news. They shall state in writing the names of their employers and their additional sources of earned income; and they shall declare that, while a member of the Galleries, they will not act as an agent in the prosecution of claims, and will not become engaged or assist, directly or indirectly, in any lobbying, promotion, advertising, or publicity activity intended to influence legislation or any other action of the Congress, nor any matter before any independent agency, or any department or other instrumentality of the Executive Branch; and that they will not act as an agent for, or be employed by the Federal, or any State, local or foreign government or representatives thereof; and that they will not, directly or indirectly, furnish special or ''insider'' information intended to influence prices or for the purpose of trading on any commodity or stock exchange; and that they will not become employed, directly or indirectly, by any stock exchange, board of trade or other organization or member thereof, or brokerage house or broker engaged in the buying and selling of any security or commodity. Applications shall be submitted to the Executive Committee of the Periodical Correspondents' Association and shall be authenticated in a manner satisfactory to the Executive Committee.

2. Applicants must be employed by periodicals that regularly publish a substantial volume of news material of either general, economic, industrial, technical, cultural, or trade character. The periodical must require such Washington coverage on a continuing basis and must be owned and operated independently of any government, industry, institution, association, or lobbying organization. Applicants must also be employed by a periodical that is published for profit and is supported chiefly by advertising or by subscription, or by a periodical meeting the conditions in this paragraph but published by a nonprofit organization that, first, operates independently of any government, industry, or institution and, second, does

*Information is based on data furnished and edited by each respective Gallery.

not engage, directly or indirectly, in any lobbying or other activity intended to influence any matter before Congress or before any independent agency or any department or other instrumentality of the Executive Branch. House organs are not eligible.

3. Members of the families of correspondents are not entitled to the privileges of the Galleries.

4. The Executive Committee may issue temporary credentials permitting the privileges of the Galleries to individuals who meet the rules of eligibility but who may be on short-term assignment or temporarily residing in Washington.

5. Under the authority of Rule 6 of the House of Representatives and of Rule 33 of the Senate, the Periodical Galleries shall be under the control of the Executive Committee, subject to the approval and supervision of the Speaker of the House of Representatives and the Senate Committee on Rules and Administration. It shall be the duty of the Executive Committee, at its discretion, to report violations of the privileges of the Galleries to the Speaker or the Senate Committee on Rules and Administration, and pending action thereon, the offending correspondent may be suspended. The committee shall be elected at the start of each Congress by members of the Periodical Correspondents' Association and shall consist of seven members with no more than one member from any one publishing organization. The committee shall elect its own officers and a majority of the committee may fill vacancies on the committee. The list in the Congressional Directory shall be a list only of members of the Periodical Correspondents' Association.

NANCY PELOSI,
Speaker, House of Representatives.

ROY BLUNT,
Chair, Senate Committee on Rules and Administration.

MEMBERS ENTITLED TO ADMISSION

PERIODICAL PRESS GALLERIES

Abarinova, Mariya: Broadband Census
Abbott, Ryan: Courthouse News Service
Abel, Allen: Maclean's
Abramson, Alana: Time Magazine
Adragna, Anthony: Politico
Aftab, Mirza: BNA News
Akan, Emel: Epoch Times
Akin, Stephanie: Roll Call
Albergo, Paul: BNA News
Alberta, Timothy: Politico
Albon, Courtney: Inside Washington Publishers
Albright, Nicole: Politico
Alder, Madison: BNA News
Alexander, Ayanna: BNA News
Alexander, Madison: BNA News
Alexis, Alexei: BNA News
Al-Faruque, Ferdous: Informa
Allington, Adam: BNA News
Alphonse, Lylah: U.S. News & World Report
Al-Sadi, Amena: Vox Media
Altscher, Judy: The Hill
Ambrosio, Patrick: BNA News
Anchondo, Carlos: E&E News
Antonides, David: Tax Notes
Anzalotta, Nicholas: BNA News
Appelbaum, Yonatan: Atlantic Monthly
Arkin, James: Politico
Arrieta-Kenna, Ruairi: Politico
Ashworth, Jerry: Thompson Information Services
Askarinam, Leah: Inside Elections
Astill, James: Economist
Athey, Philip: E&E News
Atkins, Pamela: BNA News
Atkinson, Khorri: Law360
Aton, Adam: E&E News
Atwood, John: CCH Inc.
August, Melissa: Time Magazine
Aulino, Margaret: BNA News
Axelrod, Joshua: Sightline Media Group
Ayala, Christine: The Hill
Ayers, Carl: Regulatory Compliance Watch
Babbage, Sarah: BNA News
Bacon, Perry, Jr.: FiveThirtyEight
Bade, Gavin: Politico
Bagchi, Aysha: BNA News
Baker, Rebecca: BNA News
Baksh, Mariam: Inside Washington Publishers
Ball, Emily: Time Magazine
Bancroft, John: Inside Mortgage Finance
Barash, Martina: BNA News
Barber, Charles: National Law Journal
Barber, Ernest: Exchange Monitor Publications
Barnes, Denise: Washington Informer
Barron-Lopez, Laura: Politico
Basu, Kaustuv: BNA News
Bauer-Wolf, Jeremy: Industry Dive
Bauman, Valerie: BNA News
Baumann, Jeannie: BNA News
Beasley, Stephanie: Politico
Beauchamp, Zachary: Vox Media
Beaven, Lara: Inside Washington Publishers
Beavers, Olivia: The Hill
Becker, Bernard, II: Politico
Beckman, Katie Howell: E&E News
Behr, Peter: E&E News
Behsudi, Adam: Politico
Beitsch, Rebecca: The Hill
Bell, Kevin: BNA News
Belles, Carina: AIS Health
Bennett, Brian: Time Magazine
Bennett, Cory: Politico
Bennett, Jennifer: BNA News
Bennett, John: Roll Call
Benton, Nicholas: Falls Church News Press
Berenson, Tessa: Time Magazine
Bergengruen Sapelli, Vera: Time Magazine
Berger, Mary: Washington Trade Daily
Berman-Gorvine, Martin: CEO Update
Bernal, Rafael: The Hill
Bernard, Roger: IEG Policy
Bernardini, Matthew: Law360
Bernhardt, Sonya: The Georgetowner
Bertrand, Natasha: Atlantic Monthly
Bertuca, Anthony, IV: Inside Washington Publishers
Bettelheim, Adriel: Politico
Beynon, Steven: BNA News
Beyoud, Lydia: BNA News
Bice, Alexandra: Politico
Birnbaum, Emily: The Hill
Blad, Evie: Education Week
Bliss, Jeffrey: Capitol Forum
Blumenstyk, Goldie: Chronicle of Higher Education
Bogardus, Kevin: E&E News
Bolton, Alexander: The Hill
Bomster, Mark: Education Week
Bonaquist, Maria: Law360
Bottemiller, Helena: Politico
Boudreau, Catherine: Politico
Bowman, Bridget: Roll Call
Boyanton, Megan: BNA News

MEMBERS ENTITLED TO ADMISSION, PERIODICAL PRESS GALLERIES—Continued

Boyd, Aaron: Government Executive
Bracken, Matthew: Morning Consult
Bradford, Hazel: Crain Communications
Brady, Mary Shaffrey: E&E News
Brady, Michael: Modern Healthcare
Brasher, Philip: Agri-Pulse
Bresnahan, John: Politico
Brevetti, Rossella: BNA News
Brittain, Steven: BNA News
Britton, Kathryn: BNA News
Broder, Jonathan: Newsweek
Brooks, George: Inside Mortgage Finance
Brooks, Michael: RTO Insider
Brooks, Michael: U.S. News & World Report
Brown, Dylan: E&E News
Brown, Kathleen: Industry Dive
Brownstein, Ronald: Atlantic Monthly
Bruce, Dylan: BNA News
Bruenig, Matthew: Capitol Forum
Brufke, Julia Grace: The Hill
Brugger, Kelsey: E&E News
Bruninga, Susan: BNA News
Bruno, Michael: Aviation Week
Brusoe, Peter: BNA News
Bryant, Lori: CEO Update
Buble, Courtney: Government Executive
Buchman, Brandi: Courthouse News Service
Bur, Jessica: Sightline Media Group
Burnette, Daarel, II: Education Week
Burns, Caroline: Roll Call
Burns, Mark: Morning Consult
Byrnes, Jesse: The Hill
Cahlink, George: E&E News
Cai, Cynthia: Epoch Times
Calabresi, Massimo: Time Magazine
Callahan, Madelyn: BNA News
Cama, Timothy: E&E News
Camera, Lauren: U.S. News & World Report
Campisi, Jessica: Industry Dive
Cancryn, Adam: Politico
Capps, Kriston: Atlantic Monthly
Cardoza, Kavitha: Education Week
Carey, William, Jr.: Aviation Week
Carignan, Sylvia: BNA News
Carlile, Amy: E&E News
Carlson, Jeffrey: Research Institute of America Group
Carney, Jordain: The Hill
Carpenter, Zoe: Nation
Carr, Jennifer: Tax Notes
Cassella, Megan: Politico
Catanese, David: U.S. News & World Report
Cauterucci, Christina: Slate
Cavanagh, Sean: Education Week
Chalfant, Morgan: The Hill
Chamseddine, Jad: Tax Notes
Chappellet-Lanier, Tajha: FedScoop
Chemnick, Jean: E&E News
Chen, Jinghong: AIS Health
Cheney, Kyle: Politico
Chibbaro, Louis, Jr.: Washington Blade
Childers, Andrew: BNA News
Chile, Patricio: BNA News
Choi, Matthew: Politico
Chong, Sei Hee: Morning Consult
Cioffi, Christopher: Roll Call
Cipriano, Michael: Informa
Cirruzzo, Chelsea: Inside Washington Publishers
Clark, Andrew: Broadband Census
Clark, Charles: Government Executive
Clark, James: Task & Purpose
Clarke, Sara: U.S. News & World Report
Coaston, Jane: Vox Media
Coffin, James: Public Lands News
Cohen, Ariel: Inside Washington Publishers
Cohen, Matthew: Washington City Paper
Cohen, Richard: FCW
Cohen, Zachary: National Journal
Cohn, Amelia: Government Executive
Cohrs, Rachel: Modern Healthcare
Colbert, Madeleine: Atlantic Monthly
Cole, Christopher: Law360
Coleman, Emma: Government Executive
Colman, Zachary: Politico
Connolly, Griffin: Roll Call
Connolly, Paul: BNA News
Cook, Nancy: Politico
Cook, Steven: BNA News
Cooke, Stephanie: Energy Intelligence
Coomes, Jessica: BNA News
Cooper, Perry: BNA News
Cooper, Stephen: Law360
Corrigan, John: Government Executive
Courtney, Shaun: BNA News
Covey, Erin: National Journal
Cox, Bowman: Informa
Craft, Lauren: Energy Intelligence
Cramer, Harrison: National Journal
Crampton, Elizabeth: Politico
Craver, Martha: Kiplinger Washington Editors
Crawley, John: BNA News
Croce, Brian: Crain Communications
Crowley, Michael: Politico
Cullen, Anne: Law360
Cumings, Stephanie: Tax Notes
Curry, Jonathan: Tax Notes
Cusack, Robert: The Hill
Custer, Anne: World Magazine
Cuthbertson, Charlotte: Epoch Times
Daniels, Alexander: Chronicle of Philanthropy
Darcey, Susan: Informa
Datlowe, Nicholas: BNA News
Davenport, Lydia: BNA News
Davidson, Mark: Energy Intelligence
Davies, Stephen: Agri-Pulse

MEMBERS ENTITLED TO ADMISSION, PERIODICAL PRESS GALLERIES—Continued

Davis, Aaron: Tax Notes
Davis, Sylvia Diane: BNA News
Demko, Paul: Politico
DeSanctis, Alexandra: National Review
Desiderio, Andrew: Politico
Devaney, Robert: The Georgetowner
Diamond, Daniel: Politico
Diaz, Jaclyn: BNA News
DiBiagio, Marcia: National Law Journal
Dick, Jason: Roll Call
DiCosmo, Bridget: Energy Intelligence
Dillon, Jeremy: E&E News
DiMascio, Jennifer: Aviation Week
DiMento, Maria: Chronicle of Philanthropy
DiSciullo, Joseph: Tax Notes
Divis, Dee: Inside GNSS
Dixon, Darius: Politico
Dong, Zhaoxia: Epoch Times
Dorrian, Patrick: BNA News
Doubleday, Justin: Inside Washington Publishers
Douglas, Genevieve: BNA News
Dovere, Edward-Isaac: Atlantic Monthly
Downey, Theodore: Capitol Forum
Doyle, Kenneth: BNA News
Doyle, Michael: E&E News
Dreid, Nadia: Law360
Duggan, Loren, IV: BNA News
Dugyala, Rishika: Politico
Duran, Nicole: Kiplinger Washington Editors
Eakin, Britain: Law360
Easley, Cameron: Morning Consult
Easley, Jonathan: The Hill
Eborn, Katrice: BNA News
Eckert, Toby: Politico
Edney, Hazel: Trice Edney Newswire
Ege, Konrad: Freitag
Ehart, William: CEO Update
Ehley, Brianna: Politico
Elfin, Dana: Industry Dive
Elis, Niv: The Hill
Elliott, Philip: Time Magazine
Ellis, Isobel: National Journal
Emma, Caitlin: Politico
Engleman, Eric: Politico
Entous, Adam: New Yorker
Ertel, Karen: BNA News
Erwin, Sandra: Space News
Esquivel, Jesus: Proceso
Everett, Burgess: Politico
Eversden, Andrew: Sightline Media Group
Fabian, Jordan: The Hill
Faler, Brian: Politico
Fasman, Jonathan: Economist
Feinberg, Andrew: Broadband Census
Ferguson, Andrew: Atlantic Monthly
Ferguson, Brett: Tax Notes
Ferguson, Hugh: Politico
Ferris, Sarah: Politico
Fertig, Natalie: Politico
Feuerberg, Gary: Epoch Times
Figueroa, Ariana: E&E News
Fingerhuth, Michael: U.S. News & World Report
Finn, Teaganne: BNA News
Fitzpatrick, Jack: BNA News
Flood, Brian: BNA News
Forgey, Burl, V: Politico
Fortnam, Brett: Inside Washington Publishers
Foster, Emily: Tax Notes
Foust, Jeffrey: Space News
Francis, Laura: BNA News
Frank, Thomas: E&E News
Franklin, Daniel: Economist
Franklin Volpe, Mary Beth: InvestmentNews
Frazin, Rachel: The Hill
Freed, Benjamin: FedScoop
Fribush, Rebecca: BNA News
Friedman, Sara: FCW
Galvin, Maria: U.S. News & World Report
Gangitano, Alexandra: The Hill
Gardner, Eric: Hollywood Reporter
Gardner, Lauren: Politico
Gatrone, Allison: BNA News
Gatz, Nicholas: Falls Church News Press
Geller, Eric: Politico
Gerber, Drew: National Journal
Gheorghiu, Iulia: Industry Dive
Giangreco, Leigh: Capitol Forum
Gibb, Steven: BNA News
Giglio, Michael: Atlantic Monthly
Gilbert, Lindsey: Roll Call
Gill, Daniel: BNA News
Gill, Jaspreet: Inside Washington Publishers
Gilmer, Ellen: BNA News
Gilpin-Green, Justice: National Journal
Gilsinan, Kathleen: Atlantic Monthly
Gilston, Meredith: Gilston-Kalin Communications
Gingery, Derrick: Informa
Giroux, Gregory: BNA News
Gizzi, John: NewsMax
Glancy, Joshua: Sunday Times
Glass, Andrew: Politico
Glasser, Susan: New Yorker
Glover, Asha: Tax Notes
Godfrey, Elaine: Atlantic Monthly
Goindi, Geeta: India This Week
Gold, Ashley: The Information
Golden, Ryan: Industry Dive
Goldstein, Benjamin: Aviation Week
Golshan, Tara: Vox Media
Gonzales, Nathan: Inside Elections
Goslin, JoAnn: BNA News
Gottlieb, Isabel: BNA News
Gould, Joseph: Sightline Media Group
Goyal, Raghubir: Asia Today

MEMBERS ENTITLED TO ADMISSION, PERIODICAL PRESS GALLERIES—Continued

Graham, David: Atlantic Monthly
Graham, Victoria: BNA News
Gramer, Robert: Foreign Policy
Gray, William: Synopsis
Green, Emma: Atlantic Monthly
Green, Micha: Afro-American Newspapers
Green, Miranda: The Hill
Greenwood, Kristopher: The Hill
Gregory, Patrick: BNA News
Gregory, Stephen: Epoch Times
Greiling Keane, Angela: Politico
Grena Manley, Mary Ann: BNA News
Griffis, Kelcee: Law360
Gruenberg, Mark: Press Associates
Guida, Victoria: Politico
Guillen, Alexander: Politico
Gunter, William: FCW
Gurciullo, Brianna: Politico
Hagen, Lisa: U.S. News & World Report
Hagstrom, Jerry: National Journal
Hainsfurther, Adam: The Hill
Hale, Christian: Roll Call
Hale, Conor: FierceMarkets
Halvorsen, Morgan: Morning Consult
Hamilton, Amy: Tax Notes
Hamrick, Mark: Bankrate.com
Hansard, Sara: BNA News
Hansen, Claire: U.S. News & World Report
Haq, Masooma: Epoch Times
Harrington, Jeffrey: BNA News
Harris, Adam: Atlantic Monthly
Harris, Hamil: Washington Informer
Hassenfeld, Noam: Vox Media
Hayes, Peter: BNA News
Hefling, Kimberly: Politico
Hegstad, Maria: Inside Washington Publishers
Heidorn, Richard, Jr.: RTO Insider
Heikkinen, Niina: E&E News
Heissler, Philipp: WirtschaftsWoche
Heitin, Liana: Education Week
Heller, Marc: E&E News
Hellmann, Jessie: The Hill
Helton, John: Roll Call
Hendel, John: Politico
Henderson, Gregory: BNA News
Hendin, Robert: Atlantic Monthly
Hendrie, Paul: BNA News
Herckis, Mitchel: Government Executive
Hess, Ryan: MII Publications
Hesson, Theodore, III: Politico
Hiar, Corbin: E&E News
Hijazi, Jennifer: E&E News
Hillman, G. Robert: Politico
Ho, Soyoung: Research Institute of America Group
Hoagland, Isabelle: Inside Washington Publishers
Hobbs, Matthew Nielsen: Informa
Hoffman, Rebecca: BNA News
Hoffman, William, III: Tax Notes
Hollier, Dennis: Inside Mortgage Finance
Hoover, James: Law360
Horwood, Rachel: Economist
Hotakainen, Robert: E&E News
Housiaux, Matthew: Kiplinger Washington Editors
Howard, Megan: BNA News
Hudson, Elizabeth: Aviation Week
Hussain, Irfan: BNA News
Hussein, Fatima: BNA News
Hyland, Terence: BNA News
Iacone, Amanda: BNA News
Ichniowski, Thomas: Engineering News-Record
Insinna, Valerie: Sightline Media Group
Irfan, Umair: Vox Media
Jackson, Brianna: BNA News
Jackson, Julie: Global Competition Review
Jagoda, Naomi: The Hill
Jahner, Kyle: BNA News
Janifer, Salina: Research Institute of America Group
Jaworski, Thomas: Tax Notes
Jeane, Jessica: CCH Inc.
Jekielek, Jan: Epoch Times
Jin, Yan: Caijing Magazine
Jing, Hui: Epoch Times
Johnson, Alisa: BNA News
Johnson, Christopher: Washington Blade
Johnson, Eliana: Politico
Johnson, Fawn: BNA News
Johnson, Hannah: Inside Washington Publishers
Jones, Caroline: Washington City Paper
Jones, Paige: Tax Notes
Jordan, George: Afro-American Newspapers
Joselow, Maxine: E&E News
Jost, Kenneth: CQ Researcher
Jowers, Karen: Sightline Media Group
Judson, Jennifer: Sightline Media Group
Kamens, Jessie: BNA News
Kanu, Hassan: BNA News
Karem, Brian: Playboy
Karlin-Smith, Sarah: Politico
Kash, Wyatt: FedScoop
Kassam, Sonia: BNA News
Katz, Eric: Government Executive
Katz, Justin: Inside Washington Publishers
Kaut, David: Capitol Forum
Kelly, Catherine: Informa
Kelly, Laura: The Hill
Kelly, Lauren: AIS Health
Kenen, Joanne: Politico
Kern, Rebecca: BNA News
Kessler, Aaron: BNA News
Kheel, Rebecca: The Hill
Kim, Ellis: National Law Journal
Kim, Yujin: Industry Dive
King, Pamela: E&E News
King, Peter: Politico

MEMBERS ENTITLED TO ADMISSION, PERIODICAL PRESS GALLERIES—Continued

King, Robert: FierceMarkets
Kirby, Paul: Telecommunications Reports
Klar, Rebecca: The Hill
Klein, Alyson: Education Week
Kliff, Sarah: Vox Media
Klimas, Jacqueline: Politico
Klingst, Martin: Die Zeit
Koenig, Bryan: Law360
Kohnert-Gross, Natalie: Sightline Media Group
Koren, Marina: Atlantic Monthly
Koss, Geoffrey: E&E News
Kovski, Alan: Oil & Gas Journal
Kragie, Andrew: Law360
Kramer, Alexis: BNA News
Kraushaar, Joshua: National Journal
Kreighbaum, Andrew: BNA News
Kroll, Andrew: Rolling Stone
Kruse, Michael: Politico
Kruzel, John: The Hill
Kubetin, William: BNA News
Kuckro, Rod: E&E News
Kuehne, Joseph: BNA News
Kuldell, Heather: Government Executive
Kullgren, Ian: Politico
Kumar, Anita: Politico
Kumar, Vikas: Capitol Forum
Kushin, Philip: BNA News
LaBrecque, Louis: BNA News
Lacey, Anthony: Inside Washington Publishers
Lane, Sylvan: The Hill
LaRoss, David: Inside Washington Publishers
Larsen, Kathryn: BNA News
Lassiter, Shevry: Washington Informer
Lavers, Michael: Washington Blade
Lee, Brandon: BNA News
Lee, Jane: Nature
Lee, Julia: BNA News
Lee, Mary: Politico
Lee, Robert: BNA News
Lee, Steve: BNA News
Lefebvre, Benjamin: Politico
Leins, Casey: U.S. News & World Report
Lengell, Sean: Kiplinger Washington Editors
Leonard, Matthew: Industry Dive
Leonard, Michael: BNA News
Leone, Daniel: Exchange Monitor Publications
Lesesne, William: Research Institute of America Group
Lesniewski, Niels: Roll Call
Levine, Alexandra: Politico
LeVine, Marianne: Politico
LeVines, George: Roll Call
Lienhard, Kelly: Inside Washington Publishers
Lillis, Michael: The Hill
Lim, David: Industry Dive
Lim, David: Politico
Lima, Cristiano: Politico
Lind, Dara: Vox Media
Lippman, Daniel: Politico
Lira-Guerra, Alvin: BNA News
Lithwick, Dahlia Hannah: Slate
Lloyd, Richard: IAM Magazine
Lopez, Ian: BNA News
Lorenzo, Aaron: Politico
Lorenzo, Heather: Politico
Loricchio, Lauren: Tax Notes
Losey, Stephen: Sightline Media Group
Lovelace, Ryan: National Law Journal
Luccioli, Colleen: E&E News
Lunney, Kellie: E&E News
Luthi, Susannah: Politico
Lyngaas, Sean: FedScoop
Maas, Angela: AIS Health
Macagnone, Michael: Law360
Macaluso, Nora: BNA News
MacNeal, Caitlin: Talking Points Memo
Macri, Giuseppe: BNA News
Magill, Robert: BNA News
Maine, Amanda: CCH Inc.
Mak, Aaron: Slate
Malhi, Sabrina: The Hill
Manchester, Julia: The Hill
Mandel, Jennifer: E&E News
Manzo, Kathleen: Education Week
Marcos, Cristina: The Hill
Marcy, Steven: BNA News
Marshall, Christa: E&E News
Martel, Catherine: The Hill
Martin, Emily: Inside Washington Publishers
Martin, Jill: E&E News
Martinson, Erica: E&E News
Marx, Claude: FTCWatch
Mathur, Vandana: BNA News
Matishak, Martin: Politico
Matthews, Mark, Jr.: E&E News
Mauro, Anthony: National Law Journal
Mayer, Jane: New Yorker
Maza, Cristina: Newsweek
Mazmanian, Adam: FCW
McCaskill, Nolan: Politico
McConnell, William, IV: Law360
McCormack, John: National Review
McCrimmon, Ryan: Politico
McCutcheon, Charles: BNA News
McDonald, Natashka: Hispanic Link News Service
McGann, Laura: Vox Media
McGill, Margaret: Politico
McGowan, Mary Frances: National Journal
McGraw, Meridith: Politico
McLoughlin, Jennifer: Tax Notes
McManus, Erin: BNA News
McNeal, Abigail: BNA News
McPherson, Lindsey: Roll Call
McQuillan, Samuel: BNA News
Mears, Megan: BNA News

MEMBERS ENTITLED TO ADMISSION, PERIODICAL PRESS GALLERIES—Continued

Mehta, Aaron: Sightline Media Group
Mejdrich, Kellie: Politico
Menard, Courtney: BNA News
Mendoza, Carmen: Chronicle of Higher Education
Menezes, Andrew: Roll Call
Meredith, Emily: Energy Intelligence
Merken, Sara: BNA News
Meszoly, Robin: BNA News
Meyer, Robinson: Atlantic Monthly
Miessler, James: FDAnews
Miley, John: Kiplinger Washington Editors
Milhiser, Ellen: Synopsis
Miller, Margaret: The Hill
Millhiser, Ian: Vox Media
Milligan, Susan: U.S. News & World Report
Millman, Jason: Politico
Mills Rodrigo, Christopher: The Hill
Mineiro, Megan: Courthouse News Service
Minemyer, Paige: FierceMarkets
Mintz, Samuel: Politico
Mitchell, Charles: Inside Washington Publishers
Mitchell, Corey: Education Week
Mitchell, Ellen: The Hill
Mitchell, William, III: FedScoop
Modan, Naaz: Industry Dive
Mokhiber, Russell: Corporate Crime Reporter
Monastersky, Richard: Nature
Montellaro, Zachary: Politico
Moore, Miles: Crain Communications
Morehouse, Catherine: Industry Dive
Morello, Lauren: Nature
Moroses, Dylan: Law360
Morrison, Richard: IEG Policy
Muchmore, Shannon: Industry Dive
Mueller, Marion: Politico
Mulvaney, Erin: BNA News
Muolo, Paul: Inside Mortgage Finance
Murad, Yusra: Morning Consult
Murphy, Colleen: BNA News
Murphy, Joan: IEG Policy
Murphy, Patricia: Roll Call
Muse, Andrea: Tax Notes
Mutnick, Allison: The Hotline
Myers, Meghann: Sightline Media Group
Myers, William: Regulatory Compliance Watch
Narea, Nicole: Vox Media
Nayak, Malathi: BNA News
Neidig, Harper: The Hill
Nelles, Roland: Der Spiegel
Nelson, Jill: Pharmaceutical Executive
Nerbovig, Ariel: BNA News
Neuhauser, Alan: U.S. News & World Report
Newell, James: Slate
Newkumet, Patrick: OPIS
Newman, Katelyn: U.S. News & World Report
Nguyen, Thien-Nga: Politico
Nicholas, Peter: Atlantic Monthly
Nicholson, Jonathan: BNA News
Nilsen, Ella: Vox Media
Noah, Timothy: Politico
Noble, Andrea: Government Executive
Northey, Hannah: E&E News
Nuelle, Benjamin: Agri-Pulse
Nwanevu, Ositadinma: New Republic
Nyczepir, David, Jr.: Government Executive
Obey, Douglas: Inside Washington Publishers
O'Brien, Connor: Politico
O'Brien, Cortney: Townhall
O'Donnell, Katherine: Politico
Ognanovich, Nancy: BNA News
Okun, Eli: Politico
Ollstein, Alice: Politico
O'Mahony, Olivier: Paris Match
O'Neal, Lydia: BNA News
Opfer, Christopher: BNA News
Oprysko, Caitlin: Politico
Orchowski, Margaret: Hispanic Outlook
Osnos, Evan: New Yorker
Otterbein, Holly: Politico
Overly, Steven: Politico
Owermohle, Sarah: Politico
Pagel, Hannah: Agri-Pulse
Pak, Kum: USA Journal
Palmer, Anna: Politico
Palmer, Douglas: Politico
Panetta, Alexander: Politico
Parillo, Kristen: Tax Notes
Parker, Alexander: Law360
Parker, Stuart: Inside Washington Publishers
Parts, Spencer: Global Competition Review
Pathe, Simone: Roll Call
Patterson, James: Kiplinger Washington Editors
Patton, Adrienne: Broadband Census
Pavlich, Catherine: Townhall
Payne, David: Kiplinger Washington Editors
Pazanowski, Bernard: BNA News
Pazanowski, Mary Anne: BNA News
Pearson, Samuel: BNA News
Pekow, Charles: American Brewer Media
Penn, Benjamin: BNA News
Perez, Juan, Jr.: Politico
Perine, Keith: BNA News
Perks, Ashley: The Hill
Perlman, Matthew: Law360
Pfister, Rene: Der Spiegel
Phillips, Ariella: Chronicle of Philanthropy
Piacenza, Joanna: Morning Consult
Pickrell, Ryan: Business Insider
Pifer, Rebecca: Industry Dive
Plott, Elaina: Atlantic Monthly
Pollak, Suzanne: Montgomery County Sentinel
Polunina, Valentyna: Der Spiegel
Pomerleau, Mark: Sightline Media Group
Ponnuru, Ramesh: National Review

MEMBERS ENTITLED TO ADMISSION, PERIODICAL PRESS GALLERIES—Continued

Pradhan, Rachana: Politico
Press, William: The Hill
Prete, Ryan: BNA News
Prokop, Andrew: Vox Media
Prude, Harvest: World Magazine
Pugh, Anthony: BNA News
Pulsford, Michael: Capitol Forum
Quilantan, Bianca: Politico
Quinones Ramos, Manuel: E&E News
Raghunathan, Nicola: BNA News
Rainey, Rebecca: Politico
Ramonas, Andrew: BNA News
Raycheva, Margarita: IEG Policy
Reardon, Sarah: Nature
Reddy, Sudeep: Politico
Reeves, Dawn: Inside Washington Publishers
Reid, Jonathan: BNA News
Reilly, Amanda: E&E News
Reilly, Sean: E&E News
Reishus, Mark: Thompson Information Services
Remaly, Benjamin: Global Competition Review
Rempfer, Kyle: Sightline Media Group
Restuccia, Andrew: Politico
Reynolds, David: Inside Washington Publishers
Rich, Elizabeth: Education Week
Richards, Heather: E&E News
Richardson, Tyrone: BNA News
Richman, Nathan: Tax Notes
Riley, John: Metro Weekly
Rizzuto, Denise: BNA News
Roberts, Edward: CTFN
Robinson, Kimberly: BNA News
Robinson, Melissa: BNA News
Rockwell, Lawrence: FCW
Rodgers, John, III: Courthouse News Service
Rodriguez, Sabrina: Politico
Rogers, David: Politico
Rojas, Warren: BNA News
Rolfsen, Bruce: BNA News
Rosas, Julio: Townhall
Rosenbaum, Claudia: Billboard Magazine
Rosenberg, Joshua: Law360
Ross, Garrett: Politico
Ross, Michaela: BNA News
Rothenberg, Stuart: Inside Elections
Rothman, Heather: BNA News
Roubein, Rachel: Politico
Roza, David: Inside Washington Publishers
Rozen, Courtney: BNA News
Rubin, Jordan: BNA News
Rudig, Stephanie: Washington City Paper
Ruf, Jessica: Diverse: Issues in Higher Education
Rund, Jacob: BNA News
Ruoff, Alexander: BNA News
Russell, Lia: FCW
Ryan, Timothy: Courthouse News Service
Sabin, Samantha: Morning Consult
Saenz, Cheryl: BNA News
Saiyid, Amena: BNA News
Salpini, Cara: Industry Dive
Salzano, Carlo: Professional Mariner
Samuels, Brett: The Hill
Samuels, Christina: Education Week
Samuelsohn, Darren: Politico
Saunders, Karen: BNA News
Savoie, Andre: Aviation Week
Savoy Lyles, Mahogany: BNA News
Sawchuk, Stephen: Education Week
Scarcella, Michael: National Law Journal
Schaffer, Michael: Washingtonian
Schatz, Joseph: Politico
Scherman, Robert: Satellite Business News
Scheu, Katherine: Industry Dive
Scheuermann, Christoph: Der Spiegel
Schneider, Elena: Politico
Schoeff, Mark, Jr.: InvestmentNews
Scholtes, Jennifer: Politico
Schomisch, Jeffrey: Thompson Information Services
Schoof, Renee: BNA News
Schreckinger, Benjamin: Politico
Schultz, David: BNA News
Schwartz, David: BNA News
Schwartz, Paul: Montgomery County Sentinel
Schwartz, Sarah: Education Week
Scola, Nancy: Politico
Scott, Dean: BNA News
Scott, Dylan: Vox Media
Scott, Katherine: BNA News
Seddiq, Oma: Politico
Seiden, Daniel: BNA News
Seligman, Lara: Foreign Policy
Sellers, Steven: BNA News
Semones, Evan: Politico
Shafer, Jack: Politico
Shane, Leo, III: Sightline Media Group
Shapiro, Walter: Roll Call
Sheets, Scott: Tax Notes
Shelbourne, Mallory: Inside Washington Publishers
Shepard, Steven: Politico
Shepherd, Brittany: Washingtonian
Sherman, Jacob: Politico
Sherwood, Daniel: Capitol Forum
Sherwood, Zachary: BNA News
Shevenock, Sarah: Morning Consult
Shinkman, Paul: U.S. News & World Report
Shreve, Margaret: BNA News
Simendinger, Alexis: The Hill
Siripurapu, Anshuman: Inside Washington Publishers
Sirota, Sara: Inside Washington Publishers
Skolnik, Samuel: BNA News
Sloan, Tina: FierceMarkets
Small, Leslie: AIS Health
Smelson, Cheryl: BNA News
Smith, Abigail: BNA News

MEMBERS ENTITLED TO ADMISSION, PERIODICAL PRESS GALLERIES—Continued

Smith, Paige: BNA News
Sneed, Tierney: Talking Points Memo
Snider, Ann: Politico
Snow, Nicholas: Oil & Gas Journal
Snyder, Tanya: Politico
Sobczak, Blake: E&E News
Sobczyk, Nicholas, II: E&E News
Sobieraj-Westfall, Sandra: People Magazine
Sodergreen, John: Scudder Publishing
Soderstrom, Nathan: Capitol Forum
Somerville, Glenn: Kiplinger Washington Editors
South, Todd: Sightline Media Group
Sparks, Sarah: Education Week
Spicer, Malcolm: Informa
Sprackland, Teri: Tax Notes
Sprague, John: Budget & Program
Stahl, Jeremy: Slate
Stam, John: BNA News
Stanage, Niall: The Hill
Stanton, Lynn: Telecommunications Reports
Stanzione, Melissa: BNA News
Stark, Lisa: Education Week
Starks, Timothy, II: Politico
Starr, Beth: BNA News
Stecker, Tiffany: BNA News
Steiger, Kay: Vox Media
Stein, Michelle: Inside Washington Publishers
Stein, Shira: BNA News
Steinberg, Julie: BNA News
Stern, Christopher: The Information
Stokeld, Frederick: Tax Notes
Stoller, Daniel: BNA News
Stratford, Michael: Politico
Strauss, Daniel: Politico
Strickler, Andrew: Law360
Strout, Nathaniel: Sightline Media Group
Stubbs, Kathleen: Montgomery County Sentinel
Sturdza, Gina: Epoch Times
Sullivan, Peter: The Hill
Sultan, Michael: Energy Intelligence
Sun, Yujia: BNA News
Superville, Denisa: Education Week
Sutter, Susan: Informa
Swann, James: BNA News
Tahir, Darius: Politico
Tamborrino, Kelsey: Politico
Tan, Anjelica: The Hill
Tang, Chia Chieh: Sina News
Tapscott, Stanley: Epoch Times
Taylor, Joy: Kiplinger Washington Editors
Taylor, Thomas: BNA News
Teale, Christopher: Industry Dive
Temple-West, Patrick: Politico
Theis, Michael: Chronicle of Philanthropy
Thomas, Alexander: Playboy
Thompson, Wenoka: DC Spotlight Newspaper
Thomsen, Jacqueline: National Law Journal
Timms, Edward: Roll Call
Tiron, Roxana: BNA News
Toloken, Steven: Crain Communications
Tomson, William, Jr.: Agri-Pulse
Toobin, Jeffrey: New Yorker
Toosi, Nahal: Politico
Tosh, Dennis: Thompson Information Services
Touchberry, Ramsey: Newsweek
Townsend, Rachael: BNA News
Tressel, Ashley: Inside Washington Publishers
Tricchinelli, Robert: BNA News
Trimarchi, Michael: BNA News
Trimble, Stephen: Aviation Week
Tritten, Travis: BNA News
Trudo, Hanna: The Hotline
Trygstad, Kyle: The Hotline
Tucker, Brian: Industry Dive
Tucker, Charlotte: BNA News
Tully-McManus, Katherine: Roll Call
Twachtman, Gregory: Frontline Medical Communications
Ujifusa, Andrew: Education Week
Unglesbee, Benjamin: Industry Dive
van den Berg, David: Law360
Vargas, Carolina: BNA News
Vavra, Shannon: FedScoop
Velarde, Andrew: Tax Notes
Velgot, Stephen: CTFN
Versprille, Allyson: BNA News
Vesoulis, Abigail: Time Magazine
Vespa, Matthew: Townhall
Viadero-Rogers, Debra: Education Week
Victor, Kirk: FTCWatch
Villa Huerta, Lissandra: Time Magazine
Vincent, Brandi: Government Executive
Vissiere, Helene: Le Point
Vittorio, Andrea: BNA News
Waddell Diab, Melanie: Investment Advisor Magazine
Wagner, Erich: Government Executive
Waldman, Scott: E&E News
Walker, Molly: FierceMarkets
Wallender, Andrew: BNA News
Walsh, Kenneth: U.S. News & World Report
Walsh, Mark: Education Week
Wang, Beth: Inside Washington Publishers
Ward, Alexander: Vox Media
Ward, Molly: BNA News
Ward-Lucas, Tamara: E&E News
Warmbrodt, Zachary: Politico
Warminsky, Joseph, III: FedScoop
Weaver, Allen, Jr.: The Hill
Weber, Ricky: Inside Washington Publishers
Webster, James: Agri-Pulse
Weinberger, Evan: BNA News
Weinger, Mackenzie: National Journal
Weisgerber, Marcus: Defense One
Weixel, Nathaniel: The Hill

MEMBERS ENTITLED TO ADMISSION, PERIODICAL PRESS GALLERIES—Continued

Wells, Porter: BNA News
Wermund, Benjamin: Politico
Weyl, Benjamin: Politico
Whitaker, Joel: Whitaker & Company, Publishers, Inc.
White, Molly: OPIS
Whitford, Emma: Politico
Wilhelm, Colin: BNA News
Wilkerson, John: Inside Washington Publishers
Wilkins, Emily: BNA News
Will, Madeline: Education Week
Wille, Jacklyn: BNA News
Williams, Claire: Morning Consult
Williams, John: Capitol Forum
Williams, Jordan: FDAnews
Williams, Katherine: Defense One
Williams, Lauren: FCW
Williams, Michael: Capitol Forum
Williams, Walter: CEO Update
Wilson, Megan: BNA News
Wilson, Reid: The Hill
Winters, Conor: Capitol Forum
Wise, Sara: Roll Call
Witt, Emily: New Yorker
Wittenberg, Ariel: E&E News
Wofford, Benjamin: Washingtonian
Wolfe, Kathryn: Politico
Wolff, Eric: Politico
Wong, Scott: The Hill
Worland, Justin: Time Magazine
Wright, James, Jr.: Washington Informer
Wyant Johnson, Sara: Agri-Pulse
Xiao, Bowen: Epoch Times
Yachnin, Jennifer: E&E News
Yamazaki, Kazutami: Washington Watch
Yang, Yemeng: Inside Mortgage Finance
Yermal, Brian, Jr.: Morning Consult
Yokley, Eli: Morning Consult
Yukhananov, Anna: BNA News
Yurkovic, Janet: BNA News
Zaneski, Cyril: E&E News
Zanona, Melanie: Politico
Zapler, Michael: Politico
Zeng, Zheng: Epoch Times
Zhang, Mona: Politico
Zhang, Qi: Caixin Media
Zhou, Li: Vox Media
Zoettl, Ines: Capital

PERIODICALS REPRESENTED IN PRESS GALLERIES

House Gallery 225–2941 Senate Gallery 224–0265

AFRO-AMERICAN NEWSPAPERS—(410) 554–8257; 1140 3rd Street NE, 2nd Floor, Washington, DC 20002: Micha Green, George Jordan.

AGRI-PULSE—(202) 488–0185; 1400 Independence Avenue SW, Suite 1639, Washington, MO 20250: Philip Brasher, Stephen Davies, Benjamin Nuelle, Hannah Pagel, William Tomson Jr, James Webster, Sara Wyant Johnson.

AIS HEALTH—(202) 775–9008; 2101 L St NW., Suite 400, Washington, DC 20037: Carina Belles, Jinghong Chen, Lauren Kelly, Angela Maas, Leslie Small.

AMERICAN BREWER MEDIA—(301) 493–6926; 5225 Pooks Hill Road, #1118N, Bethesda, MD 20814: Charles Pekow.

ASIA TODAY—(202) 271–1100; 27025 McPherson Square Street, Washington, DC 20038: Raghubir Goyal.

ATLANTIC MONTHLY—(202) 266–6000; 600 New Hampshire Avenue NW., Washington, DC 20037: Yonatan Appelbaum, Natasha Bertrand, Ronald Brownstein, Kriston Capps, Madeleine Colbert, Edward-Isaac Dovere, Andrew Ferguson, Michael Giglio, Kathleen Gilsinan, Elaine Godfrey, David Graham, Emma Green, Adam Harris, Robert Hendin, Marina Koren, Robinson Meyer, Peter Nicholas, Elaina Plott.

AVIATION WEEK—(202) 517–1064; 2121 K Street, Suite 210, Washington, DC 20037: Michael Bruno, William Carey Jr, Jennifer DiMascio, Benjamin Goldstein, Elizabeth Hudson, Andre Savoie, Stephen Trimble.

BANKRATE.COM—(202) 450–4465; National Press Building, Suite 841, Washington, DC 20045: Mark Hamrick.

BILLBOARD MAGAZINE—(323) 594–0250: Claudia Rosenbaum.

BNA NEWS—(703) 341–3000; 1801 South Bell Street, Arlington, VA 22202: Mirza Aftab, Paul Albergo, Madison Alder, Ayanna Alexander, Madison Alexander, Alexei Alexis, Adam Allington, Patrick Ambrosio, Nicholas Anzalotta, Pamela Atkins, Margaret Aulino, Sarah Babbage, Aysha Bagchi, Rebecca Baker, Martina Barash, Kaustuv Basu, Valerie Bauman, Jeannie Baumann, Kevin Bell, Jennifer Bennett, Steven Beynon, Lydia Beyoud, Megan Boyanton, Rossella Brevetti, Steven Brittain, Kathryn Britton, Dylan Bruce, Susan Bruninga, Peter Brusoe, Madelyn Callahan, Sylvia Carignan, Andrew Childers, Patricio Chile, Paul Connolly, Steven Cook, Jessica Coomes, Perry Cooper, Shaun Courtney, John Crawley, Nicholas Datlowe, Lydia Davenport, Sylvia Diane Davis, Jaclyn Diaz, Patrick Dorrian, Genevieve Douglas, Kenneth Doyle, Loren Duggan IV, Katrice Eborn, Karen Ertel, Teaganne Finn, Jack Fitzpatrick, Brian Flood, Laura Francis, Rebecca Fribush, Allison Gatrone, Steven Gibb, Daniel Gill, Ellen Gilmer, Gregory Giroux, JoAnn Goslin, Isabel Gottlieb, Victoria Graham, Patrick Gregory, Mary Ann Grena Manley, Sara Hansard, Jeffrey Harrington, Peter Hayes, Gregory Henderson, Paul Hendrie, Rebecca Hoffman, Megan Howard, Irfan Hussain, Fatima Hussein, Terence Hyland, Amanda Iacone, Brianna Jackson, Kyle Jahner, Alisa Johnson, Fawn Johnson, Jessie Kamens, Hassan Kanu, Sonia Kassam, Rebecca Kern, Aaron Kessler, Alexis Kramer, Andrew Kreighbaum, William Kubetin, Joseph Kuehne, Philip Kushin, Louis LaBrecque, Kathryn Larsen, Brandon Lee, Julia Lee, Robert Lee, Steve Lee, Michael Leonard, Alvin Lira-Guerra, Ian Lopez, Nora Macaluso, Giuseppe Macri, Robert Magill, Steven Marcy, Vandana Mathur, Charles McCutcheon, Erin McManus, Abigail McNeal, Samuel McQuillan, Megan Mears, Courtney Menard, Sara Merken, Robin Meszoly, Erin Mulvaney, Colleen Murphy, Malathi Nayak, Ariel Nerbovig, Jonathan Nicholson, Nancy Ognanovich, Lydia O'Neal, Christopher Opfer, Bernard Pazanowski, Mary Anne Pazanowski, Samuel Pearson, Benjamin Penn, Keith Perine, Ryan Prete, Anthony Pugh, Nicola Raghunathan, Andrew Ramonas, Jonathan Reid, Tyrone Richardson, Denise Rizzuto, Kimberly Robinson, Melissa Robinson, Warren Rojas, Bruce Rolfsen, Michaela Ross, Heather Rothman, Courtney Rozen, Jordan Rubin, Jacob Rund, Alexander Ruoff, Cheryl Saenz, Amena Saiyid, Karen Saunders, Mahogany Savoy Lyles, Renee Schoof, David Schultz, David Schwartz, Dean Scott, Katherine Scott, Daniel Seiden, Steven Sellers, Zachary Sherwood, Margaret Shreve, Samuel Skolnik, Cheryl Smelson, Abigail Smith, Paige Smith, John Stam, Melissa Stanzione, Beth Starr, Tiffany Stecker, Shira Stein, Julie Steinberg, Daniel Stoller, Yujia Sun, James Swann, Thomas Taylor, Roxana Tiron, Rachael Townsend, Robert Tricchinelli, Michael Trimarchi, Travis Tritten, Charlotte Tucker, Carolina Vargas, Allyson Versprille, Andrea Vittorio, Andrew Wallender, Molly Ward, Evan Weinberger, Porter Wells, Colin Wilhelm, Emily Wilkins, Jacklyn Wille, Megan Wilson, Anna Yukhananov, Janet Yurkovic.

BROADBAND CENSUS—(202) 329–9517; 1750 K Street NW., Suite 1200, Washington, DC 20006: Mariya Abarinova, Andrew Clark, Andrew Feinberg, Adrienne Patton.

PERIODICALS REPRESENTED IN PRESS GALLERIES—Continued

BUDGET & PROGRAM—(202) 628–3860; 1408 Teal Court, Frederick, MD 21703: John Sprague.

BUSINESS INSIDER—(770) 286–4053: Ryan Pickrell.

CAIJING MAGAZINE—(202) 525–2117; 3133 Connecticut Avenue NW., 110A, Washington, DC 20008: Yan Jin.

CAIXIN MEDIA—(202) 375–9744; 708 15th Street South, #5, Arlington, VA 22202: Qi Zhang.

CAPITAL—(202) 262–4470; 605 8th Street NE, Washington, DC 20002: Ines Zoettl.

CAPITOL FORUM—(202) 601–2300; 1200 New Hampshire Ave NW., Suite 750, Washington, DC 20036: Jeffrey Bliss, Matthew Bruenig, Theodore Downey, Leigh Giangreco, David Kaut, Vikas Kumar, Michael Pulsford, Daniel Sherwood, Nathan Soderstrom, John Williams, Michael Williams, Conor Winters.

CCH INC.—(202) 842–7355; 1015 15th Street NW., 10th Floor, Washington, DC 20005: John Atwood, Jessica Jeane, Amanda Maine.

CEO UPDATE—(202) 721–7656; 1725 I Street NW., Suite 200, Washington, DC 20006: Martin Berman-Gorvine, Lori Bryant, William Ehart, Walter Williams.

CHRONICLE OF HIGHER EDUCATION—(202) 466–1000; 1255 23rd Street NW., Suite 700, Washington, DC 20037: Goldie Blumenstyk, Carmen Mendoza.

CHRONICLE OF PHILANTHROPY—(202) 466–1200; 1255 23rd Street NW., Washington, DC 20037: Alexander Daniels, Maria DiMento, Ariella Phillips, Michael Theis.

CORPORATE CRIME REPORTER—(202) 737–1680; 1209 National Press Building, Washington, DC 20045: Russell Mokhiber.

COURTHOUSE NEWS SERVICE—(443) 783–1463; 125 Chester Avenue, Annapolis, MD 21403: Ryan Abbott, Brandi Buchman, Megan Mineiro, John Rodgers III, Timothy Ryan.

CQ RESEARCHER—(202) 729–1800; 2600 Virginia Avenue, NW., Suite 600, Washington, DC 20037: Kenneth Jost.

CRAIN COMMUNICATIONS—(202) 662–7200; 1200 G Street NW., Suite 859, Washington, DC 20005: Hazel Bradford, Brian Croce, Miles Moore, Steven Toloken.

CTFN—(202) 243–8714; 7905 Bounding Bend Court, Rockville, MD 20855: Edward Roberts, Stephen Velgot.

DC SPOTLIGHT NEWSPAPER—(301) 288–7997; P.O. Box 673, Gaithersburg, MD 20884: Wenoka Thompson.

DEFENSE ONE—(202) 739–8501; 600 New Hampshire Avenue NW., Washington, DC 20037: Marcus Weisgerber, Katherine Williams.

DER SPIEGEL—(202) 347–5222; 1202 National Press Building, Washington, DC 20045: Roland Nelles, Rene Pfister, Valentyna Polunina, Christoph Scheuermann.

DIE ZEIT—(301) 312–8453; 4701 Willard Avenue, #1214, Chevy Chase, MD 20815: Martin Klingst.

DIVERSE: ISSUES IN HIGHER EDUCATION—(703) 385–2981; 10520 Warwick Avenue, Suite B-8, Fairfax, VA 22030: Jessica Ruf.

ECONOMIST—(202) 429–0890; 1730 Rhode Island Avenue NW., Suite 1210, Washington, DC 20036: James Astill, Jonathan Fasman, Daniel Franklin, Rachel Horwood.

EDUCATION WEEK—(301) 280–3100; 6935 Arlington Road, Suite 100, Bethesda, MD 20814: Evie Blad, Mark Bomster, Daarel Burnette II, Kavitha Cardoza, Sean Cavanagh, Liana Heitin, Alyson Klein, Kathleen Manzo, Corey Mitchell, Elizabeth Rich, Christina Samuels, Stephen Sawchuk, Sarah Schwartz, Sarah Sparks, Lisa Stark, Denisa Superville, Andrew Ujifusa, Debra Viadero-Rogers, Mark Walsh, Madeline Will.

E&E NEWS—(202) 628–6500; 122 C Street NW., Suite 722, Washington, DC 20001: Carlos Anchondo, Philip Athey, Adam Aton, Katie Howell Beckman, Peter Behr, Kevin Bogardus, Mary Shaffrey Brady, Dylan Brown, Kelsey Brugger, George Cahlink, Timothy Cama, Amy Carlile, Jean Chemnick, Jeremy Dillon, Michael Doyle, Ariana Figueroa, Thomas Frank, Niina Heikkinen, Marc Heller, Corbin Hiar, Jennifer Hijazi, Robert Hotakainen, Maxine Joselow, Pamela King, Geoffrey Koss, Rod Kuckro, Colleen Luccioli, Kellie Lunney, Jennifer Mandel, Christa Marshall, Jill Martin, Erica Martinson, Mark Matthews Jr, Hannah Northey, Manuel Quinones Ramos, Amanda Reilly, Sean Reilly, Heather Richards, Blake Sobczak, Nicholas Sobczyk II, Scott Waldman, Tamara Ward-Lucas, Ariel Wittenberg, Jennifer Yachnin, Cyril Zaneski.

ENERGY INTELLIGENCE—(202) 662–0700; 1401 K Street NW., Suite 1000, Suite 602, Washington, DC 20005: Stephanie Cooke, Lauren Craft, Mark Davidson, Bridget DiCosmo, Emily Meredith, Michael Sultan.

ENGINEERING NEWS-RECORD—(301) 649–3508; 10408 Huntley Avenue, Silver Spring, MD 20902: Thomas Ichniowski.

EPOCH TIMES—(202) 662–7160; 529 14th Street NW., Suite 446, Washington, MD 20045: Emel Akan, Cynthia Cai, Charlotte Cuthbertson, Zhaoxia Dong, Gary Feuerberg, Stephen Gregory, Masooma Haq, Jan Jekielek, Hui Jing, Gina Sturdza, Stanley Tapscott, Bowen Xiao, Zheng Zeng.

EXCHANGE MONITOR PUBLICATIONS—(571) 527–1407; 1911 North Fort Meyer Drive, Suite 705, Arlington, VA 22209: Ernest Barber, Daniel Leone.

FALLS CHURCH NEWS PRESS—(703) 532–3267; 200 Little Falls Street, Suite 508, Falls Church, VA 22046: Nicholas Benton, Nicholas Gatz.

PERIODICALS REPRESENTED IN PRESS GALLERIES—Continued

FCW—(703) 876–5100; 8251 Greensboro Drive, Suite 510, McLean, VA 22102: Richard Cohen, Sara Friedman, William Gunter, Adam Mazmanian, Lawrence Rockwell, Lia Russell, Lauren Williams.

FDANEWS—(703) 538–7600; 300 North Washington Street, Suite 200, Falls Church, VA 22046: James Miessler, Jordan Williams.

FEDSCOOP—(202) 887–8001; 2001 K Street NW., Suite 1411, Washington, DC 20006: Tajha Chappellet-Lanier, Benjamin Freed, Wyatt Kash, Sean Lyngaas, William Mitchell III, Shannon Vavra, Joseph Warminsky III.

FIERCEMARKETS—(202) 628–8778; 1900 L St NW., Suite 400, Washington, DC 20036: Conor Hale, Robert King, Paige Minemyer, Tina Sloan, Molly Walker.

FIVETHIRTYEIGHT—(202) 210–8387; 3430 Brown Street, Washington, DC 20010: Perry Bacon Jr.

FOREIGN POLICY—(202) 728–7300; 1750 Pennsylvania Avenue NW., Suite 200, Washington, DC 20006: Robert Gramer, Lara Seligman.

FREITAG—(301) 699–3908; 4506 32nd Street, Mt. Rainier, MD 20712: Konrad Ege.

FRONTLINE MEDICAL COMMUNICATIONS 635 Fishers Lane, Suite 6000, Rockville, MD 20852: Gregory Twachtman.

FTCWATCH—(703) 684–7171; 1776 I Street NW., Suite 260, Washington, DC 20006: Claude Marx, Kirk Victor.

THE GEORGETOWNER—(202) 338–4833; 1050 30th Street NW., Washington, DC 20007: Sonya Bernhardt, Robert Devaney.

GILSTON-KALIN COMMUNICATIONS—(301) 460–3060; P.O. Box 5325, Rockville, MD 20848–5325: Meredith Gilston.

GLOBAL COMPETITION REVIEW—(202) 831–4660; 2122 P Street NW., Suite 201, Washington, DC 20037: Julie Jackson, Spencer Parts, Benjamin Remaly.

GOVERNMENT EXECUTIVE—(202) 739–8501; 600 New Hampshire Avenue NW., Washington, DC 20037: Aaron Boyd, Courtney Buble, Charles Clark, Amelia Cohn, Emma Coleman, John Corrigan, Mitchel Herckis, Eric Katz, Heather Kuldell, Andrea Noble, David Nyczepir Jr, Brandi Vincent, Erich Wagner.

THE HILL—(202) 628–8500; 1625 K Street NW., Suite 900, Washington, DC 20006: Judy Altscher, Christine Ayala, Olivia Beavers, Rebecca Beitsch, Rafael Bernal, Emily Birnbaum, Alexander Bolton, Julia Grace Brufke, Jesse Byrnes, Jordain Carney, Morgan Chalfant, Robert Cusack, Jonathan Easley, Niv Elis, Jordan Fabian, Rachel Frazin, Alexandra Gangitano, Miranda Green, Kristopher Greenwood, Adam Hainsfurther, Jessie Hellmann, Naomi Jagoda, Laura Kelly, Rebecca Kheel, Rebecca Klar, John Kruzel, Sylvan Lane, Michael Lillis, Sabrina Malhi, Julia Manchester, Cristina Marcos, Catherine Martel, Margaret Miller, Christopher Mills Rodrigo, Ellen Mitchell, Harper Neidig, Ashley Perks, William Press, Brett Samuels, Alexis Simendinger, Niall Stanage, Peter Sullivan, Anjelica Tan, Allen Weaver Jr, Nathaniel Weixel, Reid Wilson, Scott Wong.

HISPANIC LINK NEWS SERVICE—(202) 234–0280; 1420 N Street NW., Washington, DC 20005: Natashka McDonald.

HISPANIC OUTLOOK—(202) 236–5595; 2627 O Street NW., Washington, DC 20007: Margaret Orchowski.

HOLLYWOOD REPORTER—(646) 729–4824; 806 Charles James Circle, Ellicott City, MD 21043: Eric Gardner.

THE HOTLINE—(202) 739–8400; 600 New Hampshire Avenue NW., Washington, DC 20037: Allison Mutnick, Hanna Trudo, Kyle Trygstad.

IAM MAGAZINE—(202) 316–4965; 1346 Rittenhouse Street, NW., Washington, DC 20011: Richard Lloyd.

IEG POLICY—(703) 595–2255; 2121 K Street NW., Suite 300, Washington, DC 20037: Roger Bernard, Richard Morrison, Joan Murphy, Margarita Raycheva.

INDIA THIS WEEK—(703) 599–6623; 1541 Wellingham Court, Vienna, VA 22182: Geeta Goindi.

INDUSTRY DIVE—(202) 331–2480; 1575 I Street NW., 4th Floor, Washington, DC 20005: Jeremy Bauer-Wolf, Kathleen Brown, Jessica Campisi, Dana Elfin, Iulia Gheorghiu, Ryan Golden, Yujin Kim, Matthew Leonard, David Lim, Naaz Modan, Catherine Morehouse, Shannon Muchmore, Rebecca Pifer, Cara Salpini, Katherine Scheu, Christopher Teale, Brian Tucker, Benjamin Unglesbee.

INFORMA—(240) 221–4500; 2121 K Street NW., Suite 300, Washington, DC 20037: Ferdous Al-Faruque, Michael Cipriano, Bowman Cox, Susan Darcey, Derrick Gingery, Matthew Nielsen Hobbs, Catherine Kelly, Malcolm Spicer, Susan Sutter.

THE INFORMATION—1140 3rd Street NE, 2nd Floor, Washington, DC 20002: Ashley Gold, Christopher Stern.

INSIDE ELECTIONS—(202) 546–2822; 810 7th Street NE, Washington, DC 20002: Leah Askarinam, Nathan Gonzales, Stuart Rothenberg.

INSIDE GNSS—(703) 920–9041; 1014 17th Street South, Arlington, VA 22202: Dee Divis.

INSIDE MORTGAGE FINANCE—(301) 951–1240; 7910 Woodmont Avenue, Suite 1000, Bethesda, MD 20814: John Bancroft, George Brooks, Dennis Hollier, Paul Muolo, Yemeng Yang.

INSIDE WASHINGTON PUBLISHERS—(703) 416–8500; 1919 South Eads Street, Suite 201, Arlington, VA 22202: Courtney Albon, Mariam Baksh, Lara Beaven, Anthony Bertuca IV, Chelsea Cirruzzo, Ariel Cohen, Justin Doubleday, Brett Fortnam, Jaspreet Gill, Maria Hegstad, Isabelle Hoagland, Hannah

PERIODICALS REPRESENTED IN PRESS GALLERIES—Continued

Johnson, Justin Katz, Anthony Lacey, David LaRoss, Kelly Lienhard, Emily Martin, Charles Mitchell, Douglas Obey, Stuart Parker, Dawn Reeves, David Reynolds, David Roza, Mallory Shelbourne, Anshuman Siripurapu, Sara Sirota, Michelle Stein, Ashley Tressel, Beth Wang, Ricky Weber, John Wilkerson.

INVESTMENT ADVISOR MAGAZINE 202) 370–4810; 1301 Connecticut Avenue NW., Suite 300, Washington, DC 20036: Melanie Waddell Diab.

INVESTMENTNEWS—(202) 991–0230; 601 13th Street NW., Suite 900 South, Washington, DC 20005: Mary Beth Franklin Volpe, Mark Schoeff Jr.

KIPLINGER WASHINGTON EDITORS—(202) 887–6400; 1100 13th Street NW., Suite 750, Washington, DC 20005: Martha Craver, Nicole Duran, Matthew Housiaux, Sean Lengell, John Miley, James Patterson, David Payne, Glenn Somerville, Joy Taylor.

LAW360—(646) 783–7100; 1150 18th Street NW., Suite 600, Washington, DC 20036: Khorri Atkinson, Matthew Bernardini, Maria Bonaquist, Christopher Cole, Stephen Cooper, Anne Cullen, Nadia Dreid, Britain Eakin, Kelcee Griffis, James Hoover, Bryan Koenig, Andrew Kragie, Michael Macagnone, William McConnell IV, Dylan Moroses, Alexander Parker, Matthew Perlman, Joshua Rosenberg, Andrew Strickler, David van den Berg.

LE POINT—(202) 244–6656; 3234 McKinley Street NW., Washington, DC 20015: Helene Vissiere.

MACLEAN'S—(703) 534–1283; 6316 24th Street North, Arlington, VA 22207: Allen Abel.

METRO WEEKLY—(202) 638–6830; 1775 I Street NW., Suite 1150, Washington, DC 20006: John Riley.

MII PUBLICATIONS—(202) 830–7985; 4920 Niagara Road, Suite 322, College Park, MD 20740: Ryan Hess.

MODERN HEALTHCARE—(877) 812–1581: Michael Brady, Rachel Cohrs.

MONTGOMERY COUNTY SENTINEL—(301) 838–0788; 22 West Jefferson Street, Suite 309, Rockville, MD 20850: Suzanne Pollak, Paul Schwartz, Kathleen Stubbs.

MORNING CONSULT—(202) 506–1957; 729 15th Street NW., Washington, DC 20005: Matthew Bracken, Mark Burns, Sei Hee Chong, Cameron Easley, Morgan Halvorsen, Yusra Murad, Joanna Piacenza, Samantha Sabin, Sarah Shevenock, Claire Williams, Brian Yermal Jr, Eli Yokley.

NATION—(212) 209–5400: Zoe Carpenter.

NATIONAL JOURNAL—(202) 739–8400; 600 New Hampshire Avenue NW., Washington, DC 20037: Zachary Cohen, Erin Covey, Harrison Cramer, Isobel Ellis, Drew Gerber, Justice Gilpin-Green, Jerry Hagstrom, Joshua Kraushaar, Mary Frances McGowan, Mackenzie Weinger.

NATIONAL LAW JOURNAL—(202) 457–0686; 1100 G Street NW., Suite 900, Washington, DC 20005: Charles Barber, Marcia DiBiagio, Ellis Kim, Ryan Lovelace, Anthony Mauro, Michael Scarcella, Jacqueline Thomsen.

NATIONAL REVIEW—(212) 679–7330: Alexandra DeSanctis, John McCormack, Ramesh Ponnuru.

NATURE—(202) 737–2355; 968 National Press Building, Washington, DC 20045: Jane Lee, Richard Monastersky, Lauren Morello, Sarah Reardon.

NEW REPUBLIC—(202) 508–4482; 1620 L Street NW., Suite 300C, Washington, DC 20036: Ositadinma Nwanevu.

NEWSMAX—(202) 465–8730; 1900 K Street NW., Suite 1120, Washington, DC 20006: John Gizzi.

NEWSWEEK—(202) 626–2000; 1750 Pennsylvania Avenue NW., Suite 1220, Washington, DC 20006: Jonathan Broder, Cristina Maza, Ramsey Touchberry.

NEW YORKER—(202) 955–0960; 1730 Rhode Island Avenue NW., Suite 603, Washington, DC 20036: Adam Entous, Susan Glasser, Jane Mayer, Evan Osnos, Jeffrey Toobin, Emily Witt.

OIL & GAS JOURNAL—(703) 533–1552; 7013 Jefferson Avenue, Falls Church, VA 22042: Alan Kovski, Nicholas Snow.

OPIS—(301) 284–2000; 2099 Gaither Road, 5th Floor, Rockville, MD 20850: Patrick Newkumet, Molly White.

PARIS MATCH—(202) 721–9501: Olivier O'Mahony.

PEOPLE MAGAZINE—(202) 861–4000; 1130 Connecticut Avenue NW., Suite 900, Washington, DC 20036: Sandra Sobieraj-Westfall.

PHARMACEUTICAL EXECUTIVE—(301) 656–3339; 7715 Rocton Avenue, Chevy Chase, MD 20815: Jill Nelson.

PLAYBOY—(310) 424–1884: Brian Karem, Alexander Thomas.

POLITICO—(703) 647–7999; 1100 Wilson Boulevard, 6th Floor, Arlington, VA 22209: Anthony Adragna, Timothy Alberta, Nicole Albright, James Arkin, Ruairi Arrieta-Kenna, Gavin Bade, Laura Barron-Lopez, Stephanie Beasley, Bernard Becker II, Adam Behsudi, Cory Bennett, Adriel Bettelheim, Alexandra Bice, Helena Bottemiller, Catherine Boudreau, John Bresnahan, Adam Cancryn, Megan Cassella, Kyle Cheney, Matthew Choi, Zachary Colman, Nancy Cook, Elizabeth Crampton, Michael Crowley, Paul Demko, Andrew Desiderio, Daniel Diamond, Darius Dixon, Rishika Dugyala, Toby Eckert, Brianna Ehley, Caitlin Emma, Eric Engleman, Burgess Everett, Brian Faler, Hugh Ferguson, Sarah Ferris, Natalie Fertig, Burl Forgey V, Lauren Gardner, Eric Geller, Andrew Glass, Angela Greiling Keane, Victoria Guida, Alexander Guillen, Brianna Gurciullo, Kimberly Hefling, John Hendel, Theodore Hesson III, G. Robert Hillman, Eliana Johnson, Sarah Karlin-Smith, Joanne Kenen, Peter King, Jacqueline Klimas, Michael Kruse, Ian Kullgren, Anita Kumar, Mary Lee, Benjamin Lefebvre, Alexandra Levine,

PERIODICALS REPRESENTED IN PRESS GALLERIES—Continued

Marianne LeVine, David Lim, Cristiano Lima, Daniel Lippman, Aaron Lorenzo, Heather Lorenzo, Susannah Luthi, Martin Matishak, Nolan McCaskill, Ryan McCrimmon, Margaret McGill, Meridith McGraw, Kellie Mejdrich, Jason Millman, Samuel Mintz, Zachary Montellaro, Marion Mueller, Thien-Nga Nguyen, Timothy Noah, Connor O'Brien, Katherine O'Donnell, Eli Okun, Alice Ollstein, Caitlin Oprysko, Holly Otterbein, Steven Overly, Sarah Owermohle, Anna Palmer, Douglas Palmer, Alexander Panetta, Juan Perez Jr, Rachana Pradhan, Bianca Quilantan, Rebecca Rainey, Sudeep Reddy, Andrew Restuccia, Sabrina Rodriguez, David Rogers, Garrett Ross, Rachel Roubein, Darren Samuelsohn, Joseph Schatz, Elena Schneider, Jennifer Scholtes, Benjamin Schreckinger, Nancy Scola, Oma Seddiq, Evan Semones, Jack Shafer, Steven Shepard, Jacob Sherman, Ann Snider, Tanya Snyder, Timothy Starks II, Michael Stratford, Daniel Strauss, Darius Tahir, Kelsey Tamborrino, Patrick Temple-West, Nahal Toosi, Zachary Warmbrodt, Benjamin Wermund, Benjamin Weyl, Emma Whitford, Kathryn Wolfe, Eric Wolff, Melanie Zanona, Michael Zapler, Mona Zhang.

PRESS ASSOCIATES—(312) 806–4825; 4000 Cathedral Avenue NW., Washington, DC 20016: Mark Gruenberg.

PROCESO—(202) 737–1538; 529 14th Street NW., Suite 1117, Washington, DC 20045: Jesus Esquivel.

PROFESSIONAL MARINER—(207) 772–2466: Carlo Salzano.

PUBLIC LANDS NEWS—(703) 553–0552; 133 South Buchanan Street, Arlington, VA 22204: James Coffin.

REGULATORY COMPLIANCE WATCH—(202) 908–6194; 9737 Washingtonian Boulevard, Suite 502, Gaithersburg, MD 20877: Carl Ayers, William Myers.

RESEARCH INSTITUTE OF AMERICA GROUP—(202) 842–1240; 1275 K Street NW., Suite 875, Washington, DC 20005: Jeffrey Carlson, Soyoung Ho, Salina Janifer, William Lesesne.

ROLL CALL—(202) 650–6000; 77 K Street NE, 8th Floor, Washington, DC 20002: Stephanie Akin, John Bennett, Bridget Bowman, Caroline Burns, Christopher Cioffi, Griffin Connolly, Jason Dick, Lindsey Gilbert, Christian Hale, John Helton, Niels Lesniewski, George LeVines, Lindsey McPherson, Andrew Menezes, Patricia Murphy, Simone Pathe, Walter Shapiro, Edward Timms, Katherine Tully-McManus, Sara Wise.

ROLLING STONE—(202) 695–2563: Andrew Kroll.

RTO INSIDER—(202) 577–9221; 10837 Deborah Drive, Potomac, MD 20854: Michael Brooks, Richard Heidorn Jr.

SATELLITE BUSINESS NEWS—(202) 785–0505; 5614 Connecticut Avenue NW., #300, Washington, DC 20015: Robert Scherman.

SCUDDER PUBLISHING—(410) 923–0688; 1145 Generals Highway, Crownsville, MD 21032: John Sodergreen.

SIGHTLINE MEDIA GROUP—(703) 750–7400; 1919 Gallows Road, Suite 400, Vienna, VA 22182: Joshua Axelrod, Jessica Bur, Andrew Eversden, Joseph Gould, Valerie Insinna, Karen Jowers, Jennifer Judson, Natalie Kohnert-Gross, Stephen Losey, Aaron Mehta, Meghann Myers, Mark Pomerleau, Kyle Rempfer, Leo Shane III, Todd South, Nathaniel Strout.

SINA NEWS—(347) 659–9327; 1415 North Oak Street, Arlington, VA 22209: Chia Chieh Tang.

SLATE—(202) 261–2066; 1350 Connecticut Avenue, Suite 400, Washington, DC 20036: Christina Cauterucci, Dahlia Hannah Lithwick, Aaron Mak, James Newell, Jeremy Stahl.

SPACE NEWS—(571) 356–9532; 1414 Prince Street, Suite 300, Alexandria, VA 22314: Sandra Erwin, Jeffrey Foust.

SUNDAY TIMES—(917) 547–5348: Joshua Glancy.

SYNOPSIS—(307) 728–4988; 20312 Aspenwood Lane, Montgomery Village, MD 20886: William Gray, Ellen Milhiser.

TALKING POINTS MEMO—(202) 758–3048; 1615 L Street NW., Suite 310, Washington, DC 20036: Caitlin MacNeal, Tierney Sneed.

TASK & PURPOSE—(831) 428–6204; 218 9th Street NE, Apartment 1, Washington, DC 20002: James Clark.

TAX NOTES—(703) 533–4400; 400 South Maple Avenue, Suite 400, Falls Church, VA 22046: David Antonides, Jennifer Carr, Jad Chamseddine, Stephanie Cumings, Jonathan Curry, Aaron Davis, Joseph DiSciullo, Brett Ferguson, Emily Foster, Asha Glover, Amy Hamilton, William Hoffman III, Thomas Jaworski, Paige Jones, Lauren Loricchio, Jennifer McLoughlin, Andrea Muse, Kristen Parillo, Nathan Richman, Scott Sheets, Teri Sprackland, Frederick Stokeld, Andrew Velarde.

TELECOMMUNICATIONS REPORTS—(202) 842–8923; 1015 15th Street NW., 10th Floor, Washington, DC 20005: Paul Kirby, Lynn Stanton.

THOMPSON INFORMATION SERVICES—800–677–3789; 1560 Wilson Boulevard, Suite 825, Arlington, VA 22209: Jerry Ashworth, Mark Reishus, Jeffrey Schomisch, Dennis Tosh.

TIME MAGAZINE—(202) 861–4000; 1130 Connecticut Avenue NW., Suite 900, Washington, DC 20036: Alana Abramson, Melissa August, Emily Ball, Brian Bennett, Tessa Berenson, Vera Bergengruen Sapelli, Massimo Calabresi, Philip Elliott III, Abigail Vesoulis, Lissandra Villa Huerta, Justin Worland.

TOWNHALL—(703) 294–6046; 1901 North Moore Street, Suite 701, Arlington, VA 22209: Cortney O'Brien, Catherine Pavlich, Julio Rosas, Matthew Vespa.

PERIODICALS REPRESENTED IN PRESS GALLERIES—Continued

TRICE EDNEY NEWSWIRE—(202) 291–9310; 6817 Georgia Avenue NW., Suite 218, Washington, DC 20012: Hazel Edney.

USA JOURNAL—(202) 714–7330; P.O. Box 714, Washington, DC 20044: Kum Pak.

U.S. NEWS & WORLD REPORT—(202) 955–2000; 1050 Thomas Jefferson Street NW., 4th Floor, Washington, DC 20007: Lylah Alphonse, Michael Brooks, Lauren Camera, David Catanese, Sara Clarke, Michael Fingerhuth, Maria Galvin, Lisa Hagen, Claire Hansen, Casey Leins, Susan Milligan, Alan Neuhauser, Katelyn Newman, Paul Shinkman, Kenneth Walsh.

VOX MEDIA—(202) 591–1170; 1201 Connecticut Avenue NW., Suite 1100, Washington, DC 20036: Amena Al-Sadi, Zachary Beauchamp, Jane Coaston, Tara Golshan, Noam Hassenfeld, Umair Irfan, Sarah Kliff, Dara Lind, Laura McGann, Ian Millhiser, Nicole Narea, Ella Nilsen, Andrew Prokop, Dylan Scott, Kay Steiger, Alexander Ward, Li Zhou.

WASHINGTON BLADE—(202) 747–2077; 1712 14th Street NW., Washington, DC 20009: Louis Chibbaro Jr, Christopher Johnson, Michael Lavers.

WASHINGTON CITY PAPER—(202) 650–6939; 734 15th Street NW., Suite 400, Washington, DC 20005: Matthew Cohen, Caroline Jones, Stephanie Rudig.

WASHINGTONIAN—(202) 296–3600; 1828 L Street NW., Suite 200, Washington, DC 20036: Michael Schaffer, Brittany Shepherd, Benjamin Wofford.

WASHINGTON INFORMER—(202) 561–4100; 3117 Martin Luther King Jr. Avenue SE., Washington, DC 20032: Denise Barnes, Hamil Harris, Shevry Lassiter, James Wright Jr.

WASHINGTON TRADE DAILY—(301) 946–0817; P.O. Box 1802, Wheaton, MD 20915: Mary Berger.

WASHINGTON WATCH—(301) 263–9023; 5923 Onondaga Road, Bethesda, MD 20816: Kazutami Yamazaki.

WHITAKER & COMPANY, PUBLISHERS, INC.—(240) 583–0280; P.O. Box 224, Spencerville, MD 20868: Joel Whitaker.

WIRTSCHAFTSWOCHE—(202) 509–4651: Philipp Heissler.

WORLD MAGAZINE—(202) 744–8987: Anne Custer, Harvest Prude.

CONGRESSIONAL DISTRICT MAPS

ALABAMA—Congressional Districts—(7 Districts)

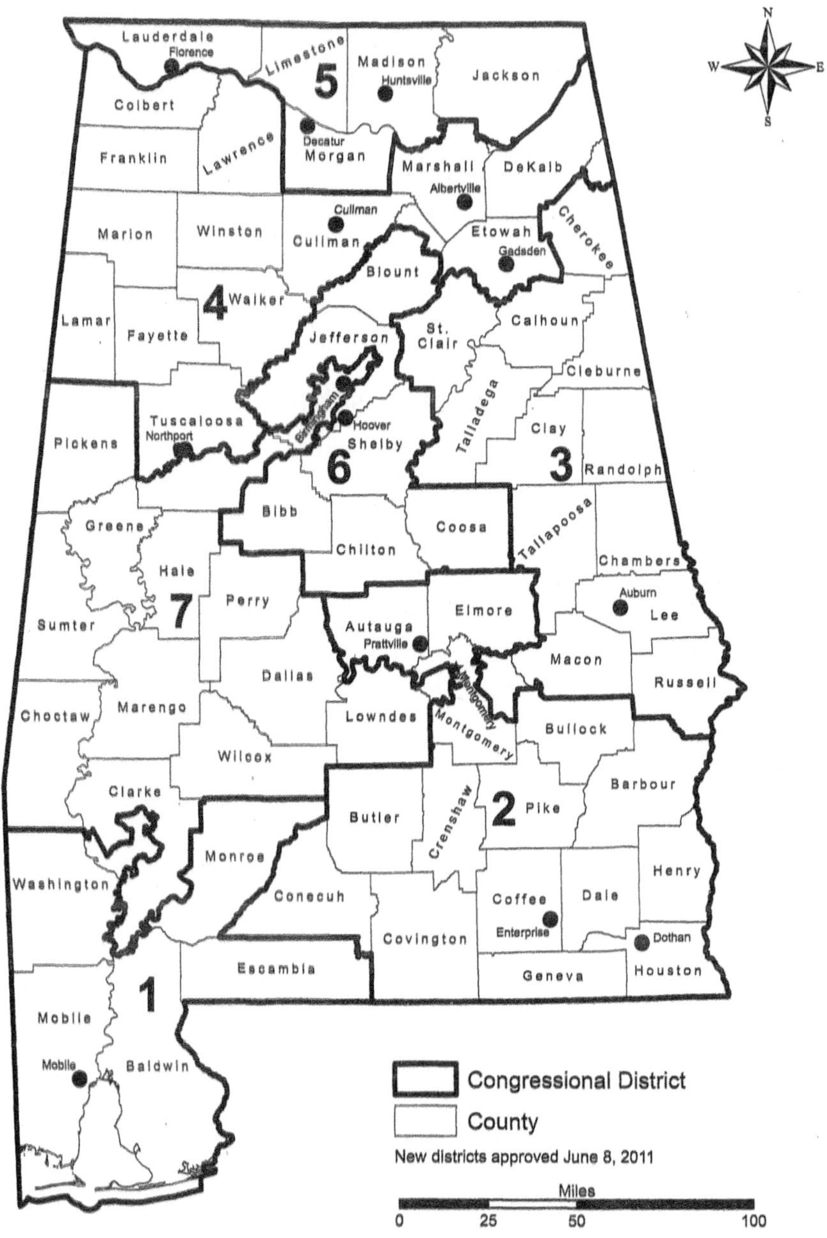

ALASKA—Congressional District—(1 District At Large)

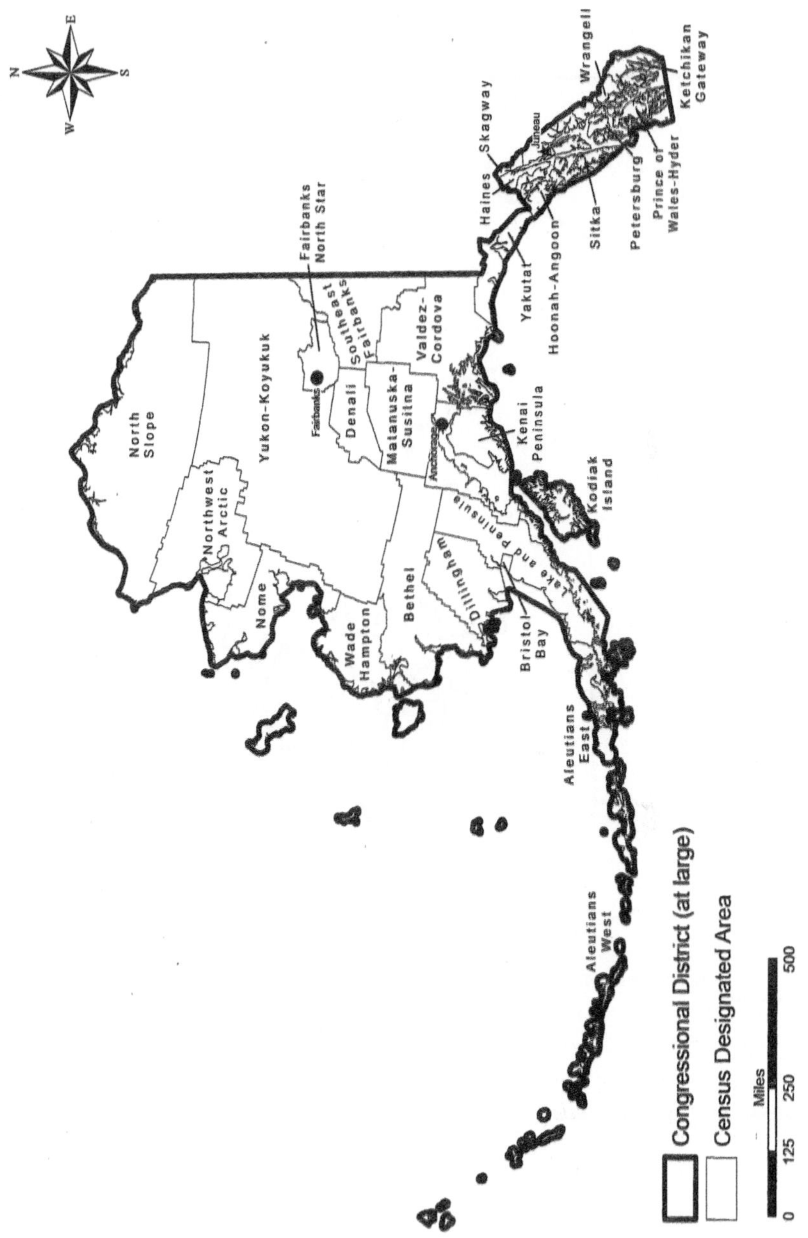

ARIZONA—Congressional Districts—(9 Districts)

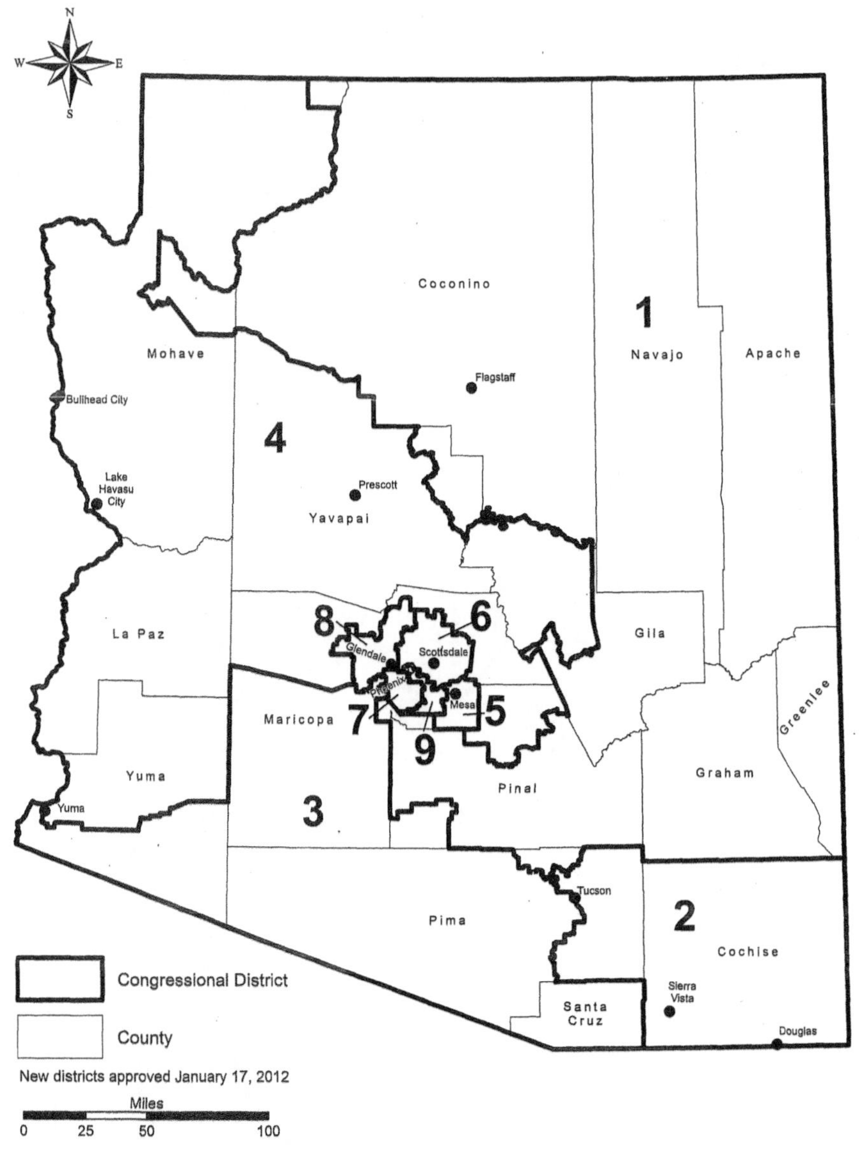

ARKANSAS—Congressional Districts—(4 Districts)

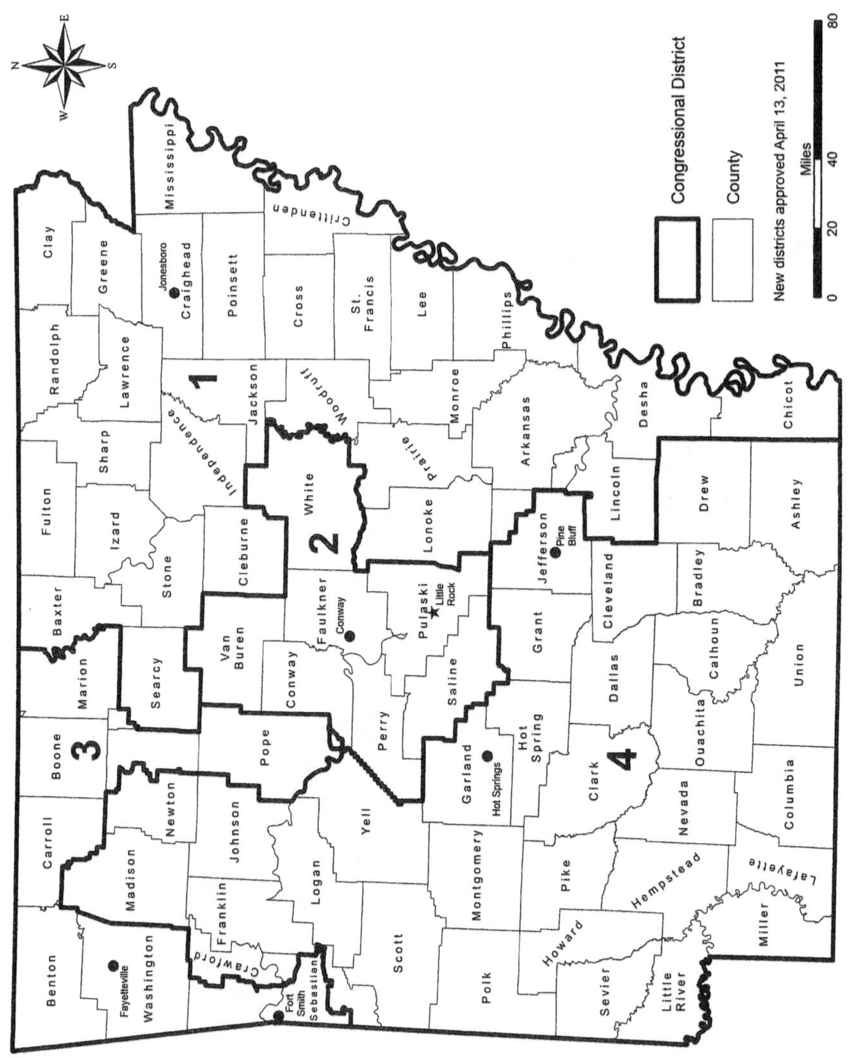

CALIFORNIA—Congressional Districts—(53 Districts)

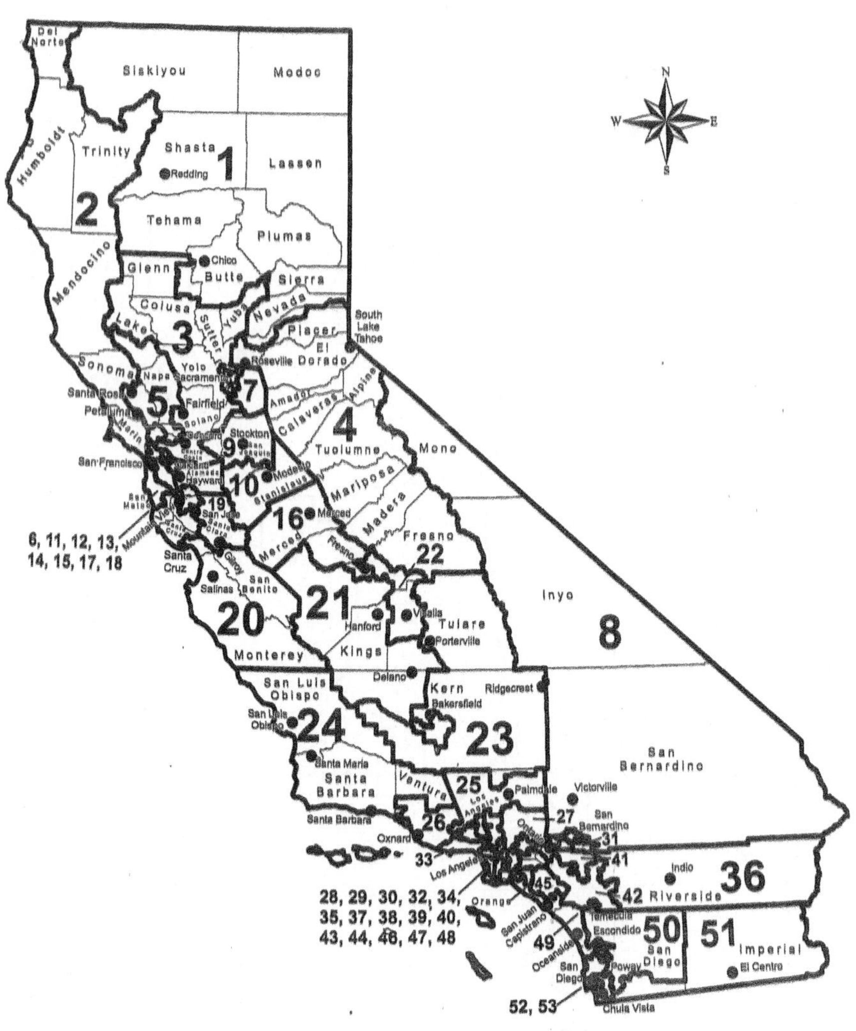

COLORADO—Congressional Districts—(7 Districts)

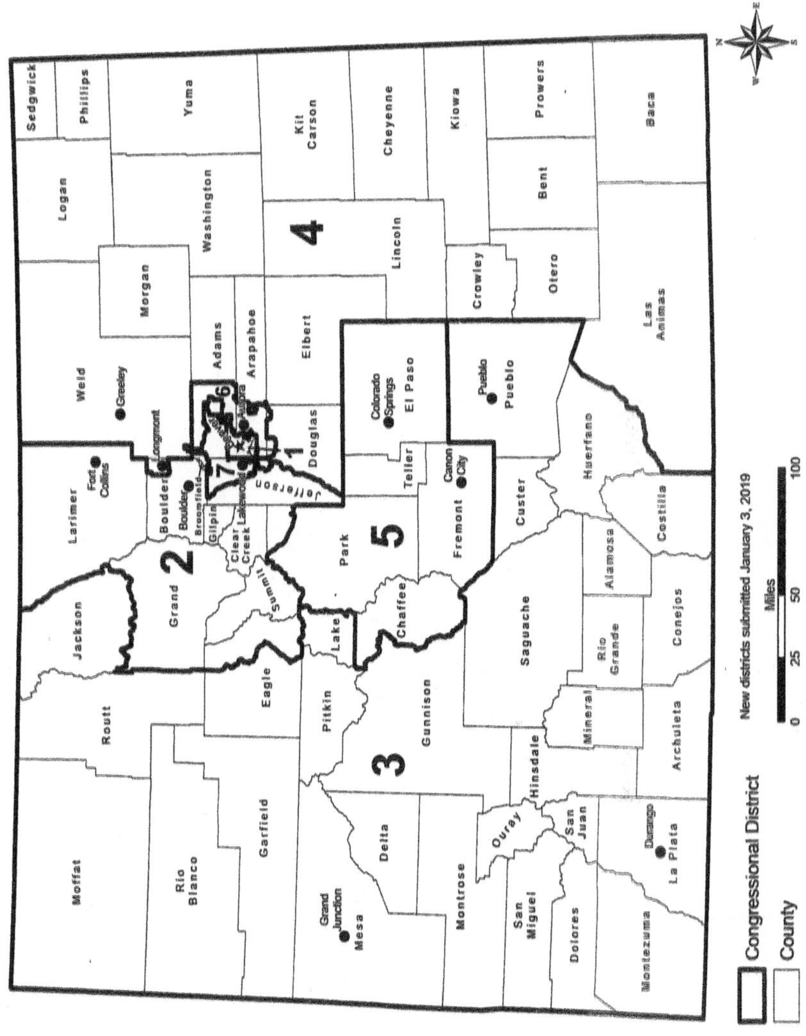

CONNECTICUT—Congressional Districts—(5 Districts)

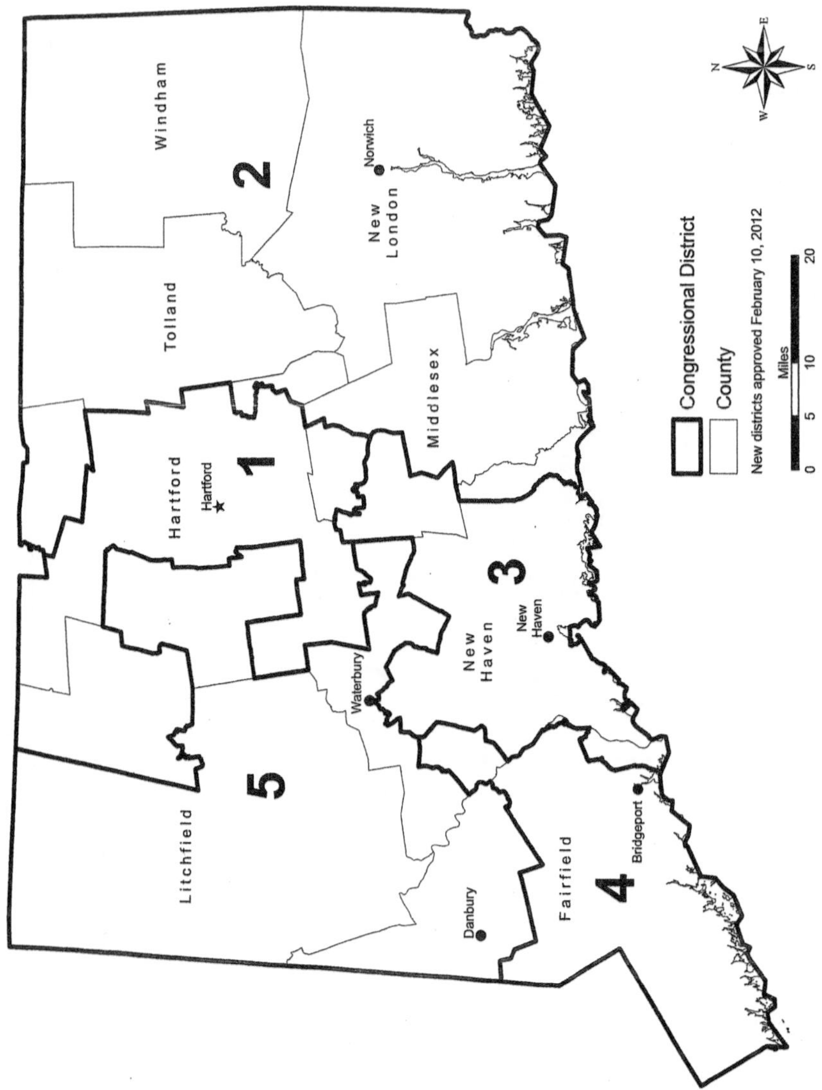

DELAWARE—Congressional District—(1 District At Large)

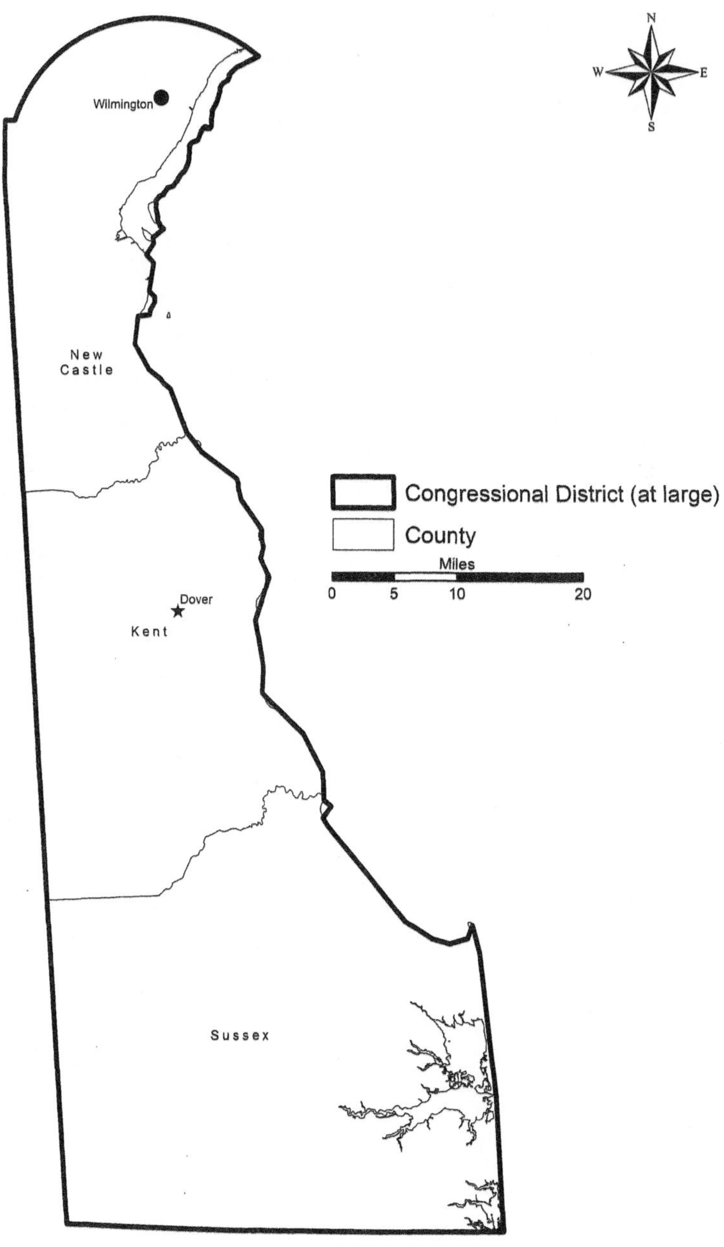

FLORIDA—Congressional Districts—(27 Districts)

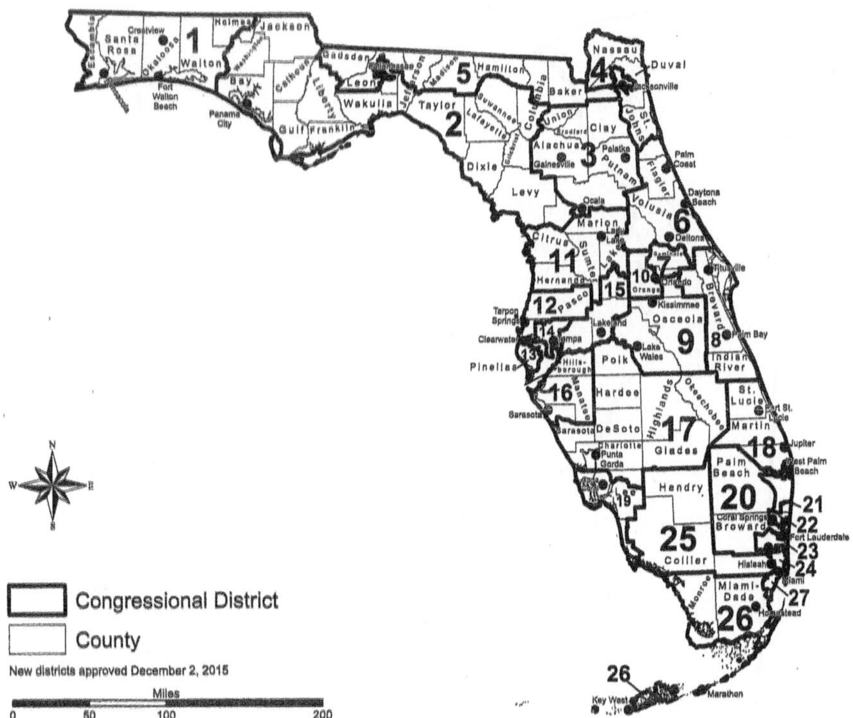

GEORGIA—Congressional Districts—(14 Districts)

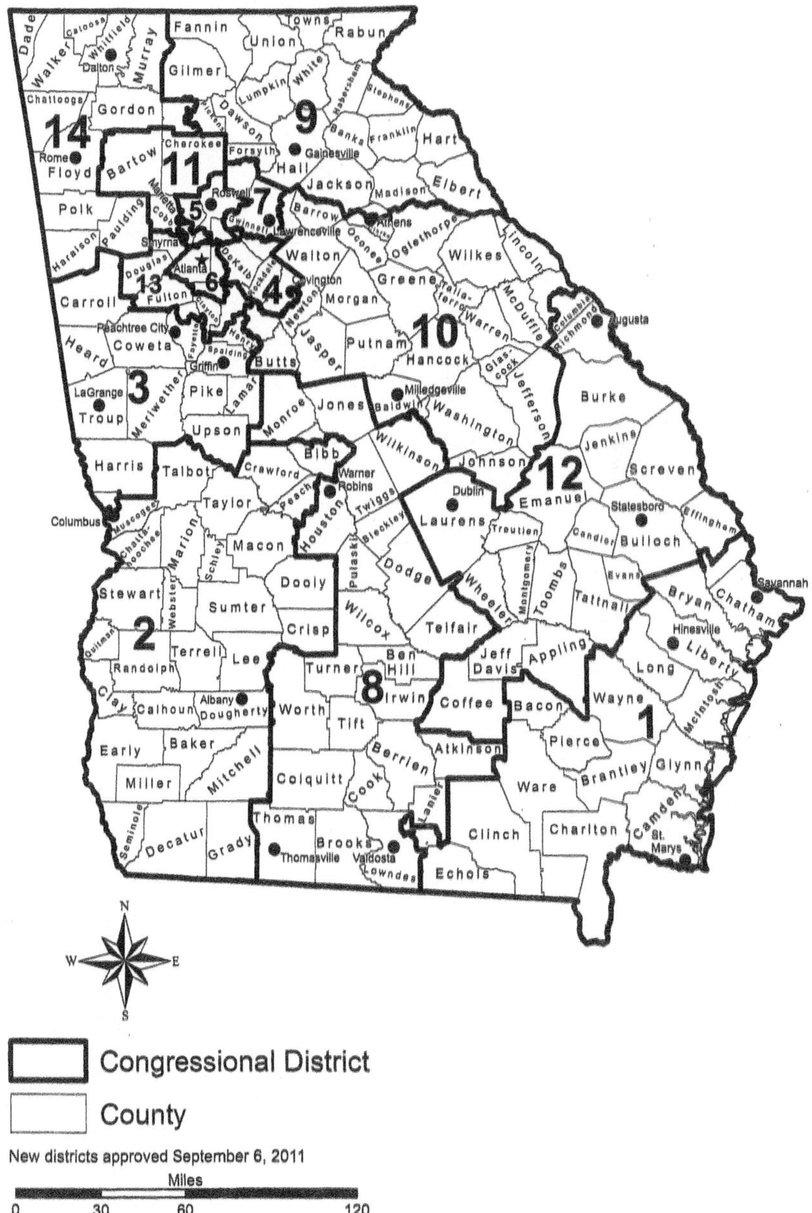

HAWAII—Congressional Districts—(2 Districts)

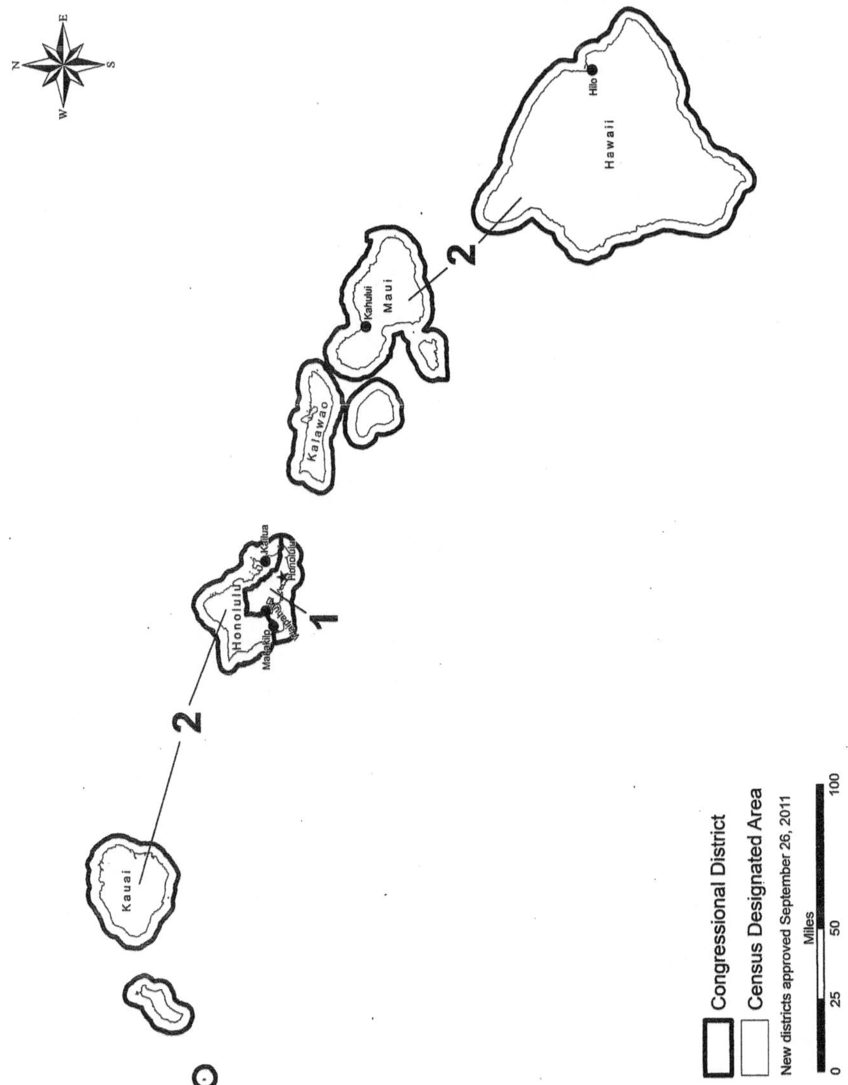

IDAHO —Congressional Districts—(2 Districts)

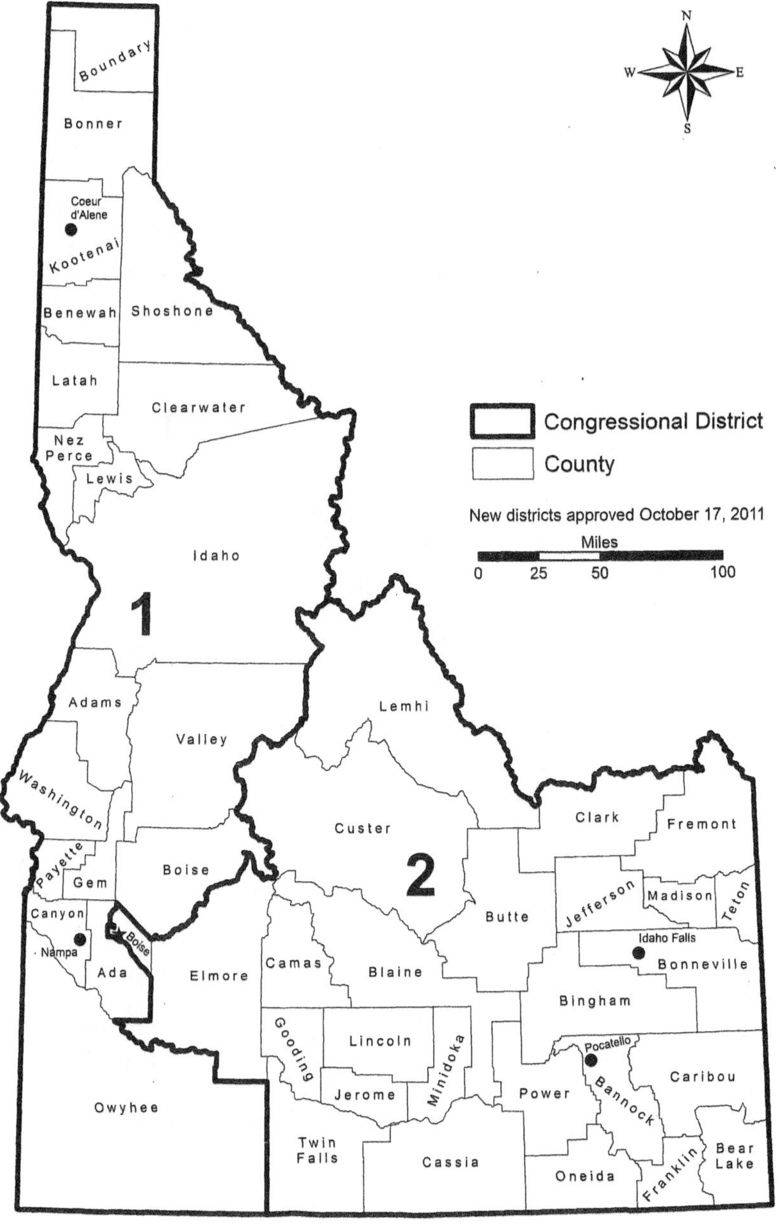

ILLINOIS—Congressional Districts—(18 Districts)

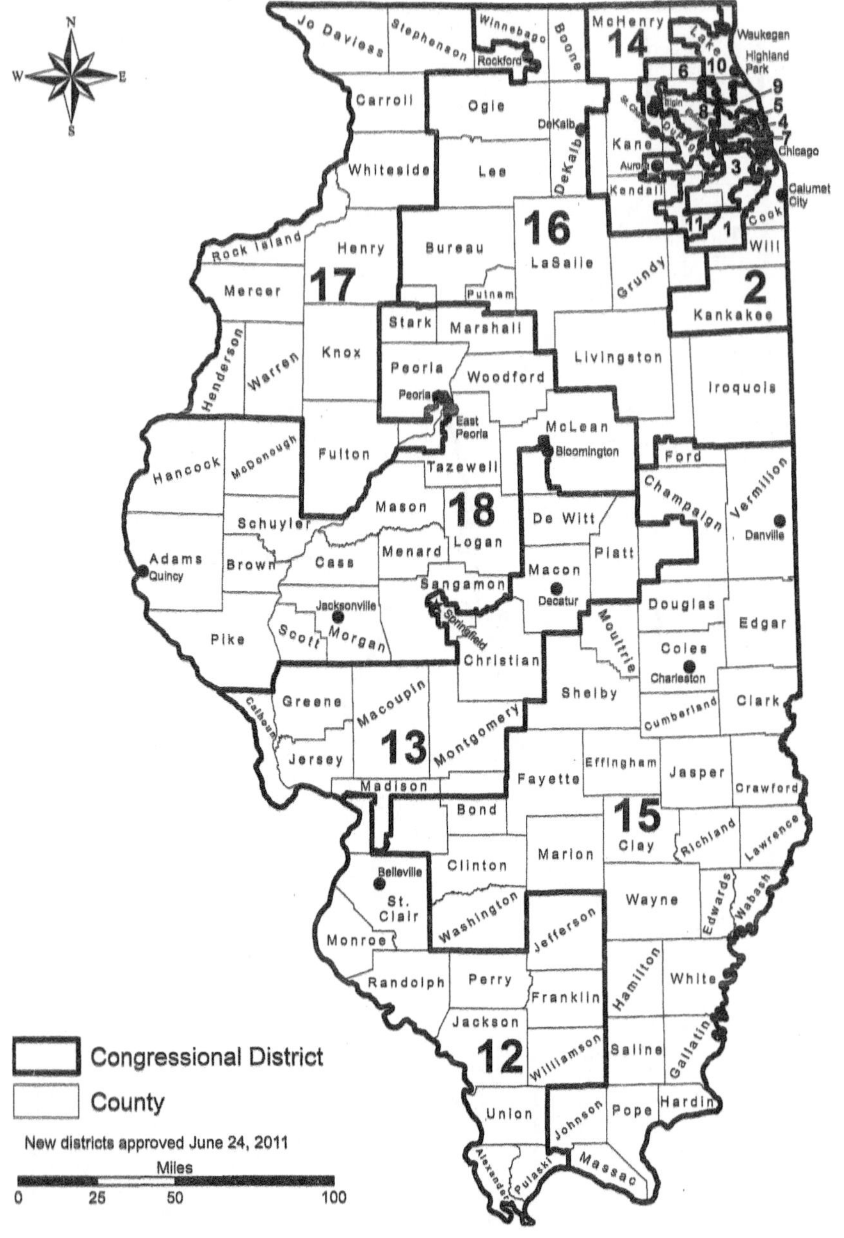

INDIANA—Congressional Districts—(9 Districts)

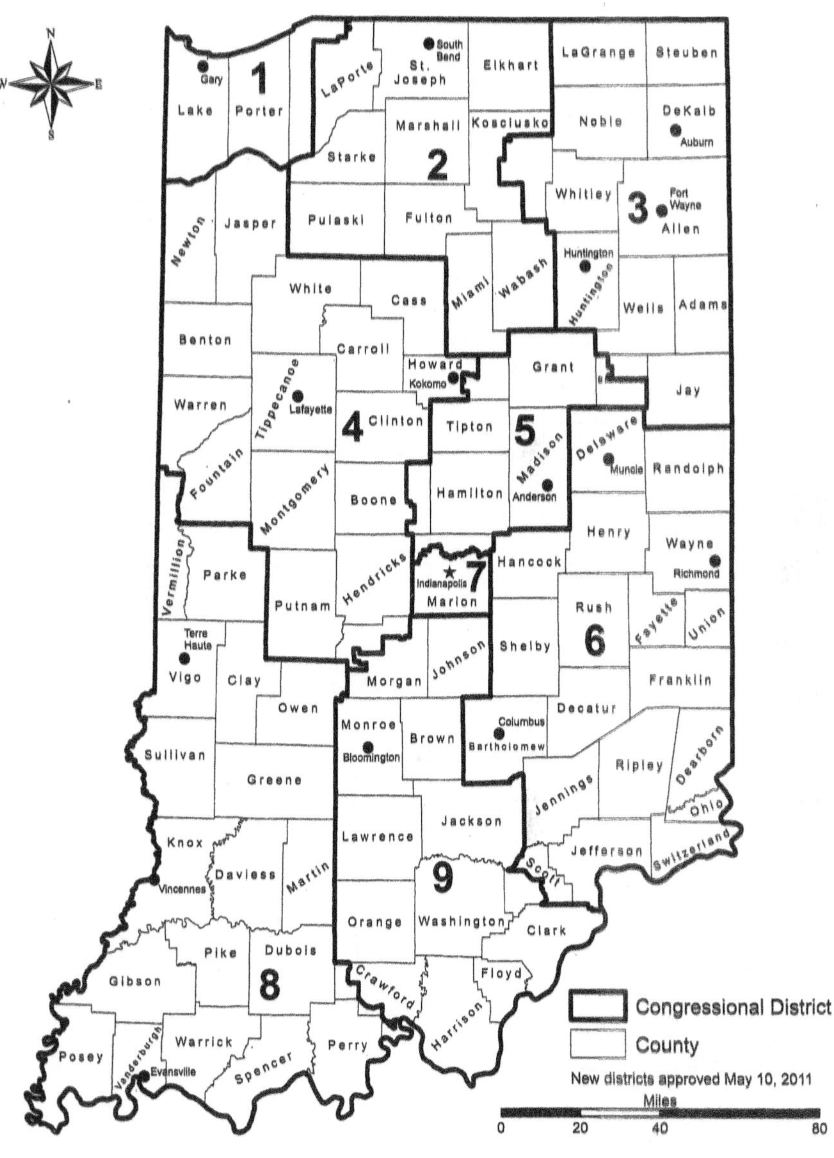

IOWA—Congressional Districts—(4 Districts)

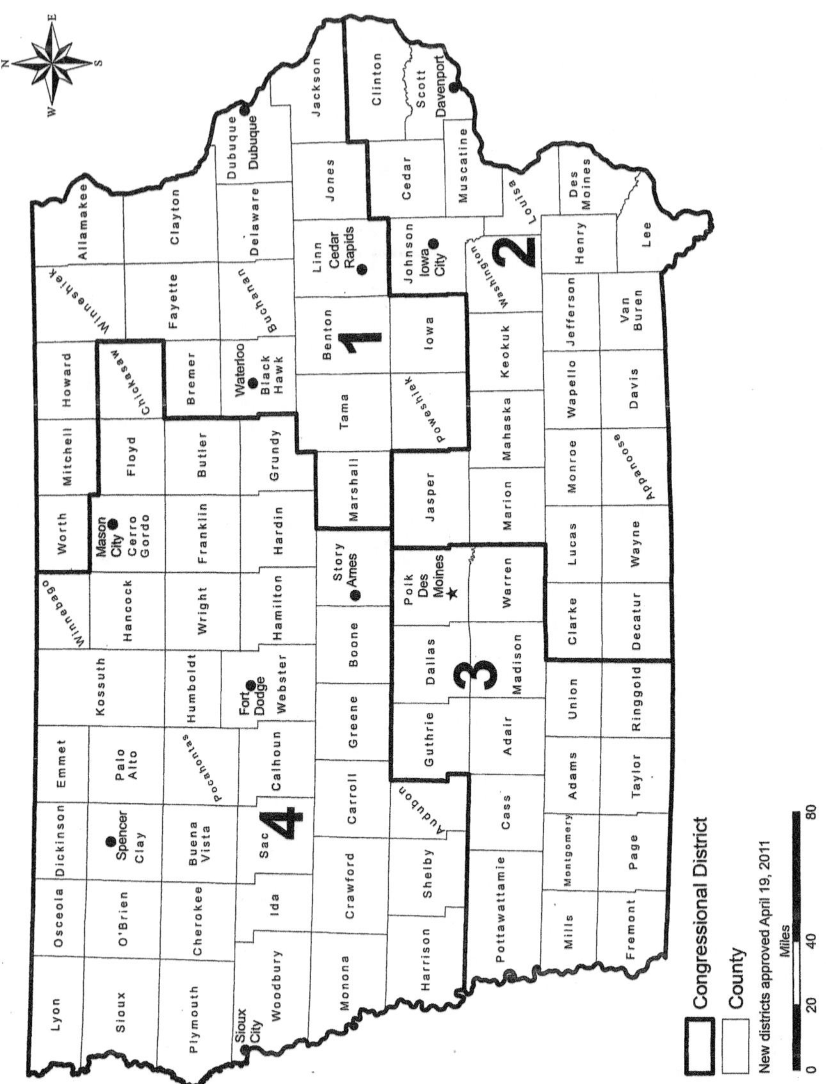

KANSAS—Congressional Districts—(4 Districts)

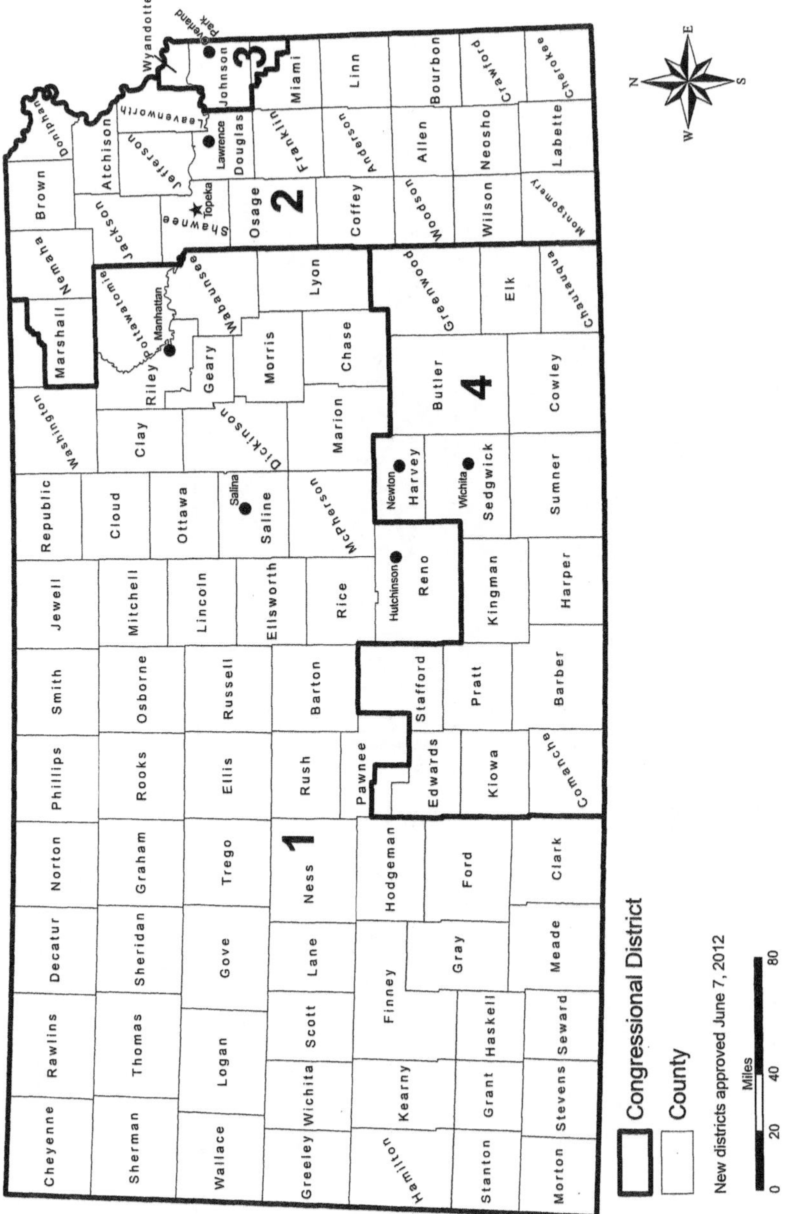

KENTUCKY—Congressional Districts—(6 Districts)

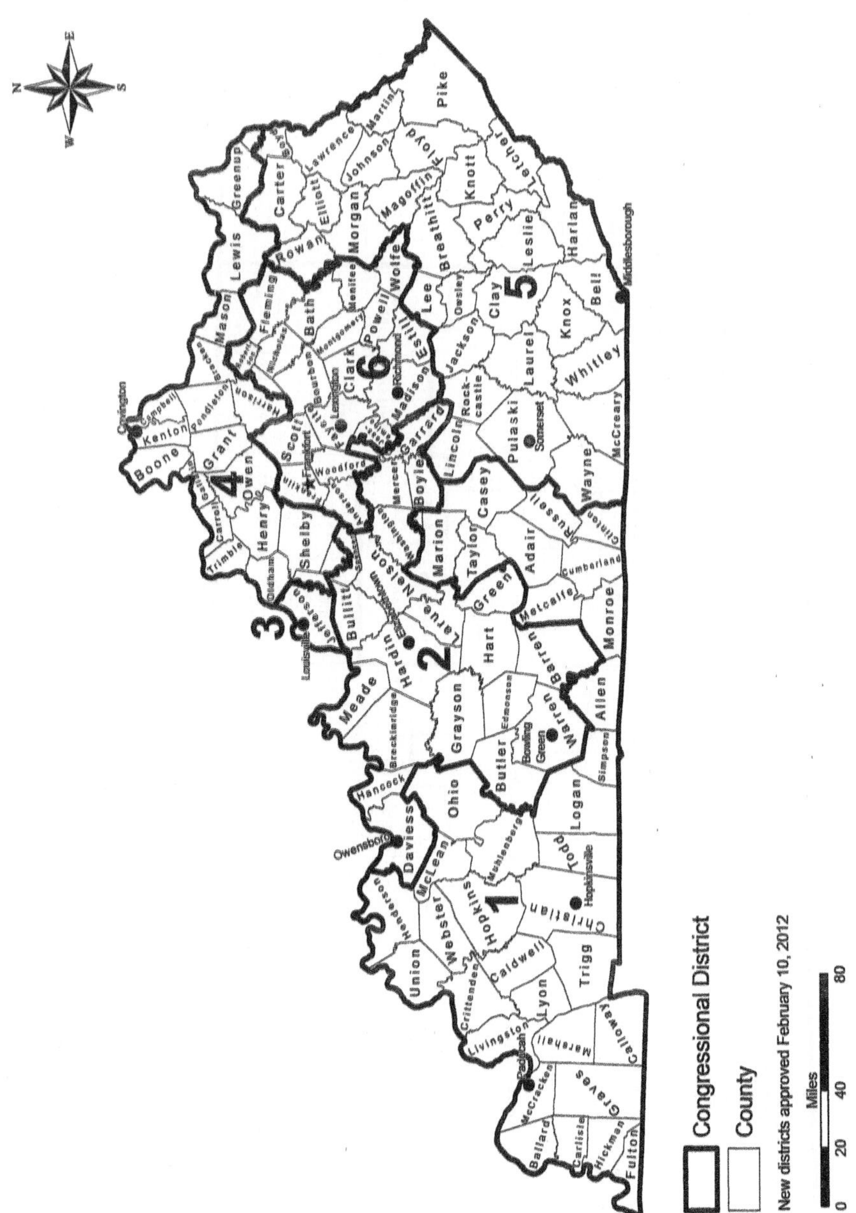

LOUISIANA—Congressional Districts—(6 Districts)

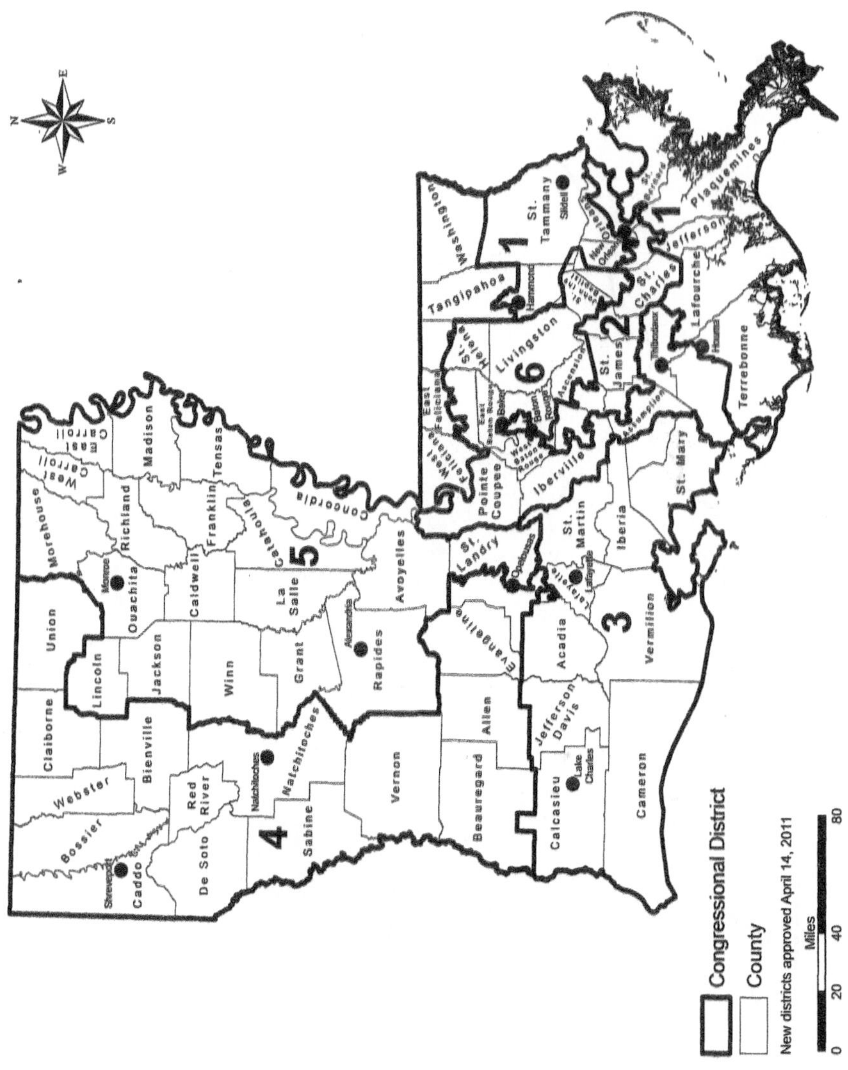

MAINE—Congressional Districts—(2 Districts)

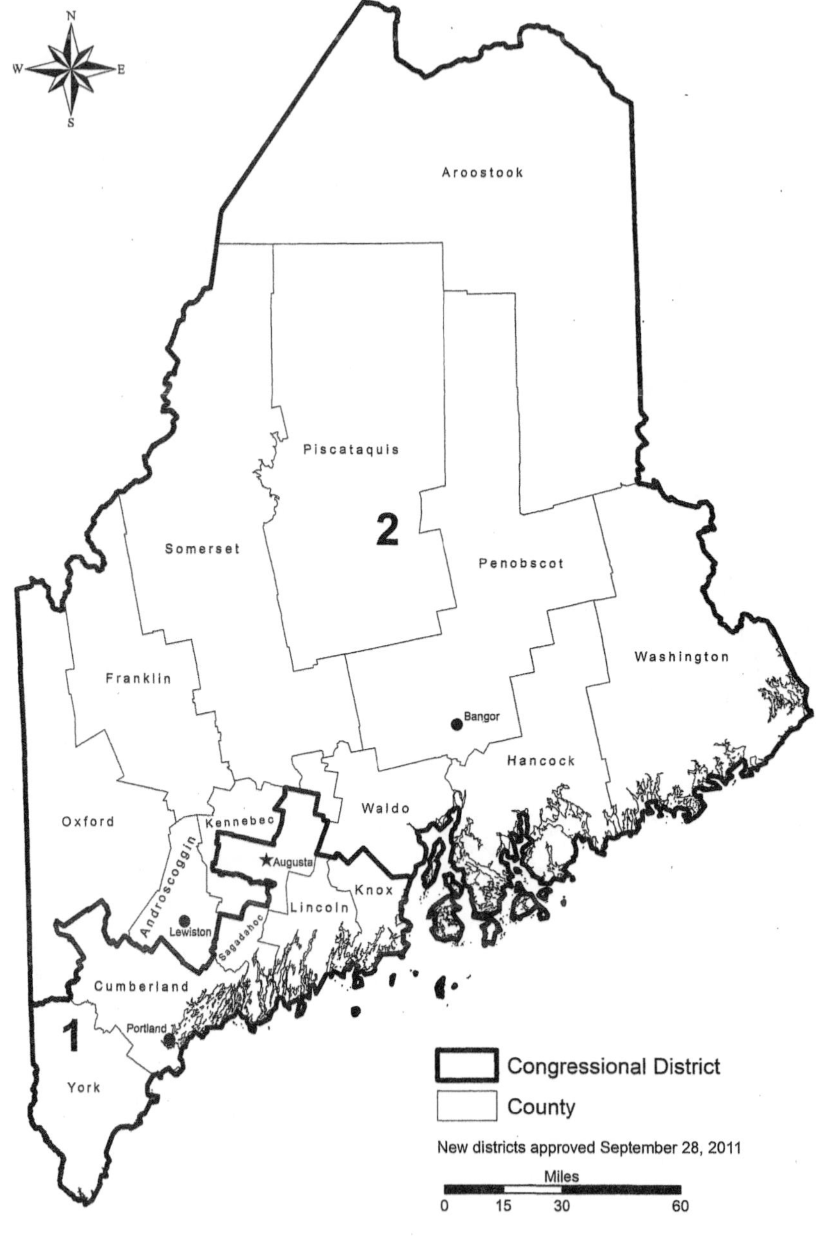

MARYLAND—Congressional Districts—(8 Districts)

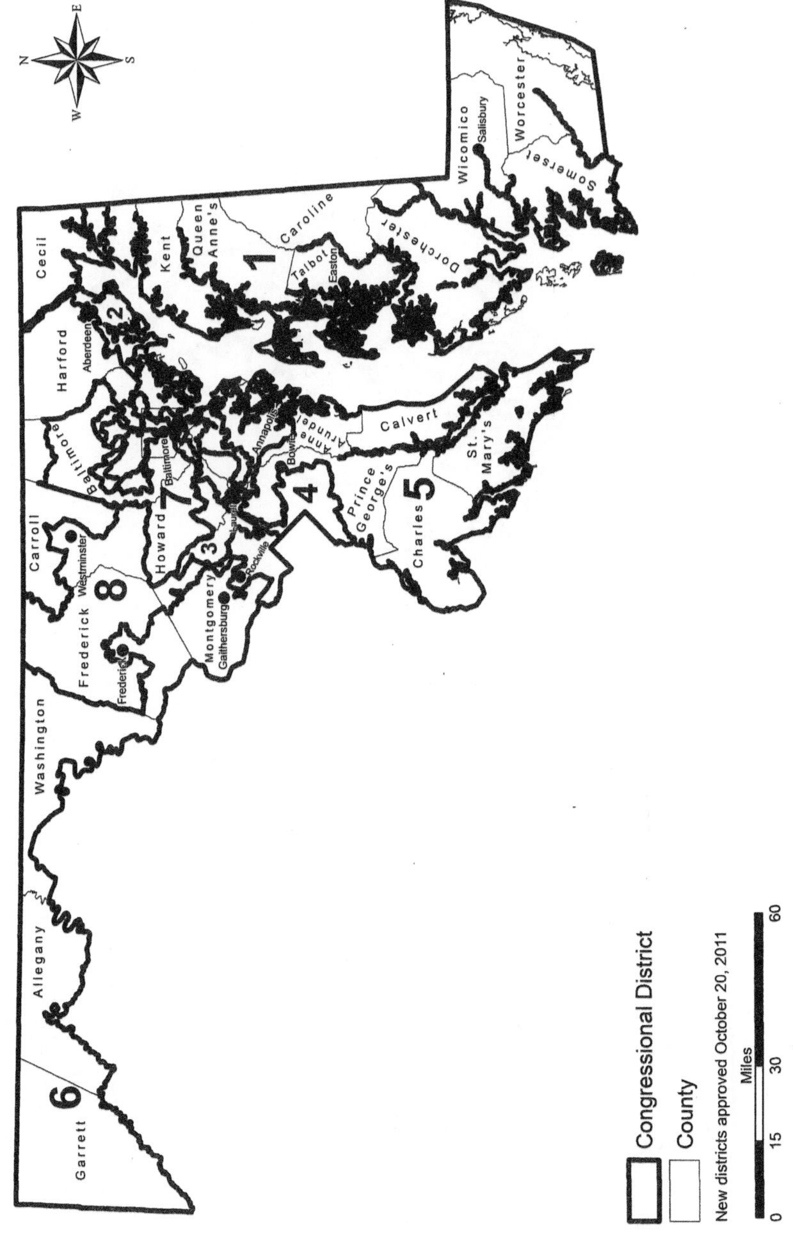

MASSACHUSETTS—Congressional Districts—(9 Districts)

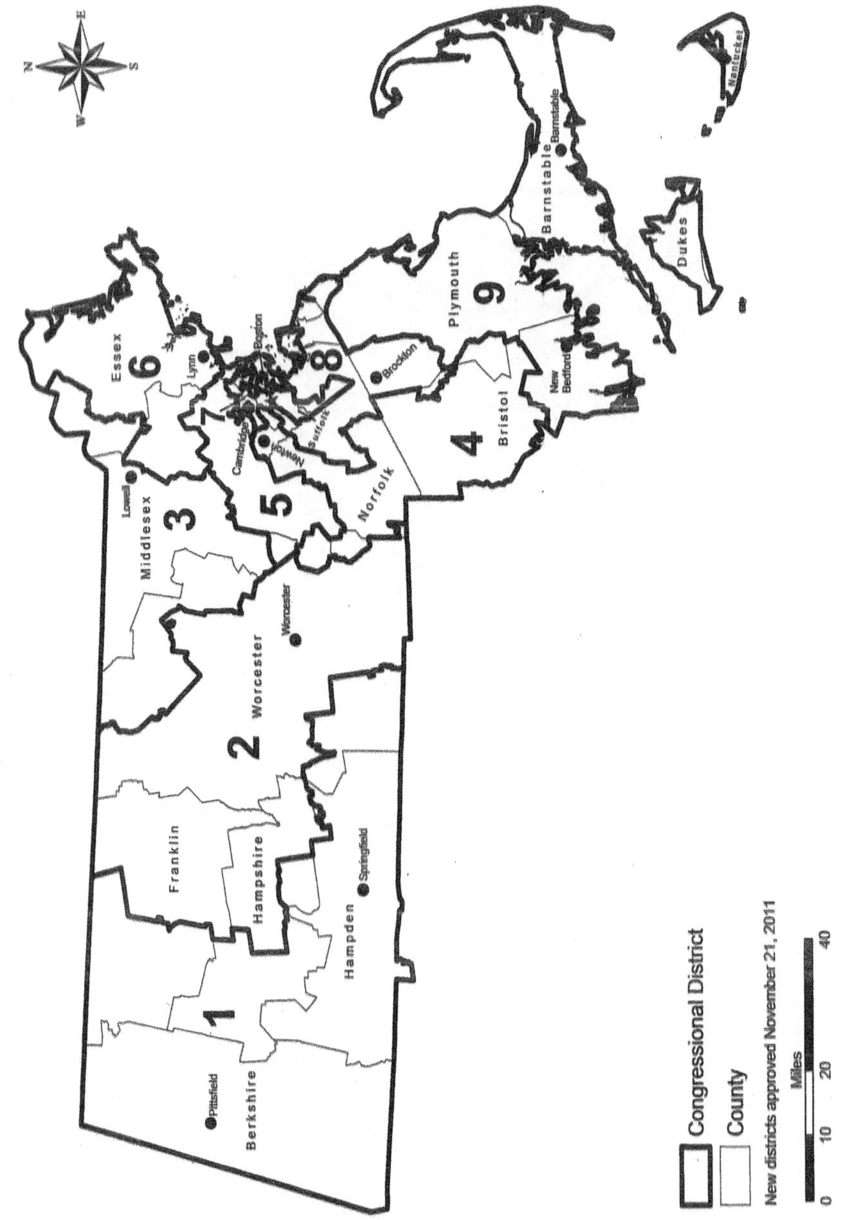

MICHIGAN—Congressional Districts—(14 Districts)

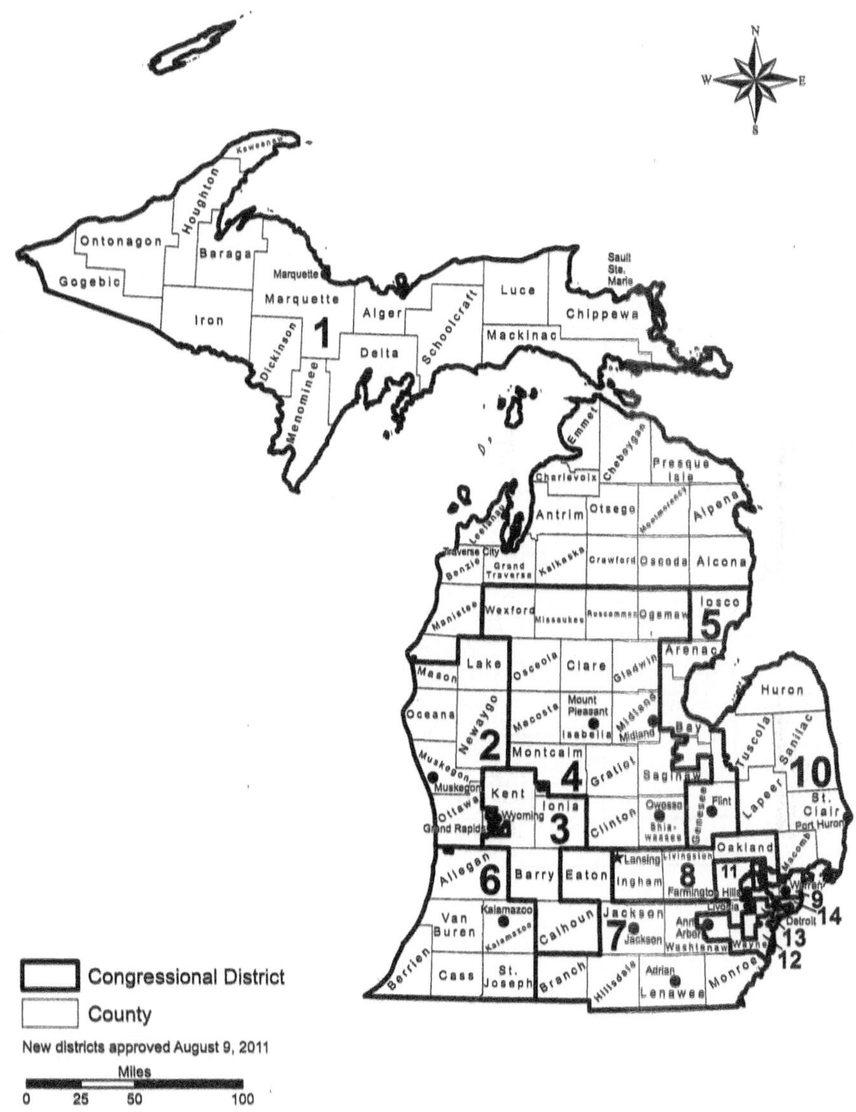

MINNESOTA—Congressional Districts—(8 Districts)

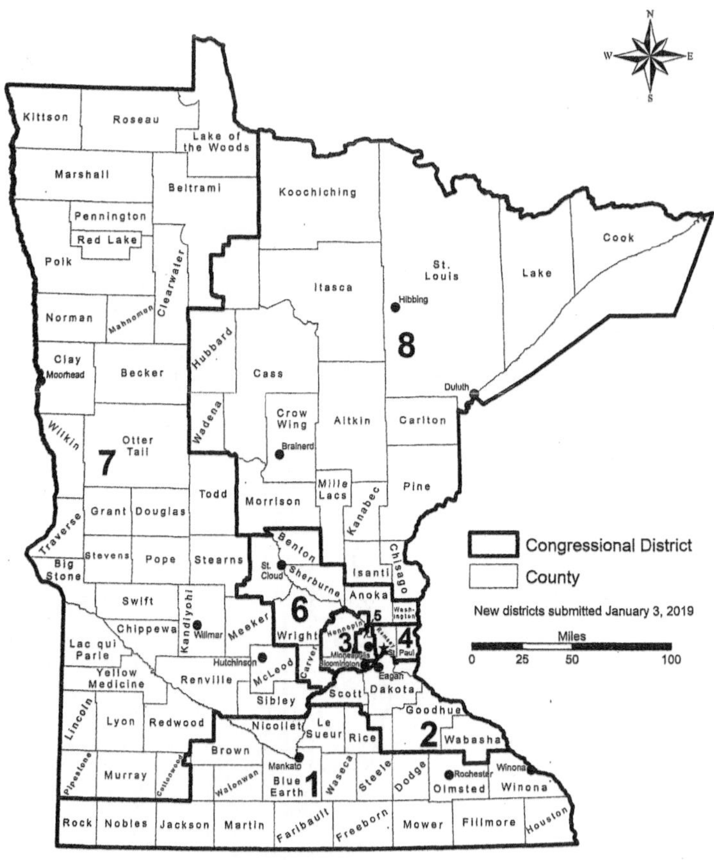

MISSISSIPPI—Congressional Districts—(4 Districts)

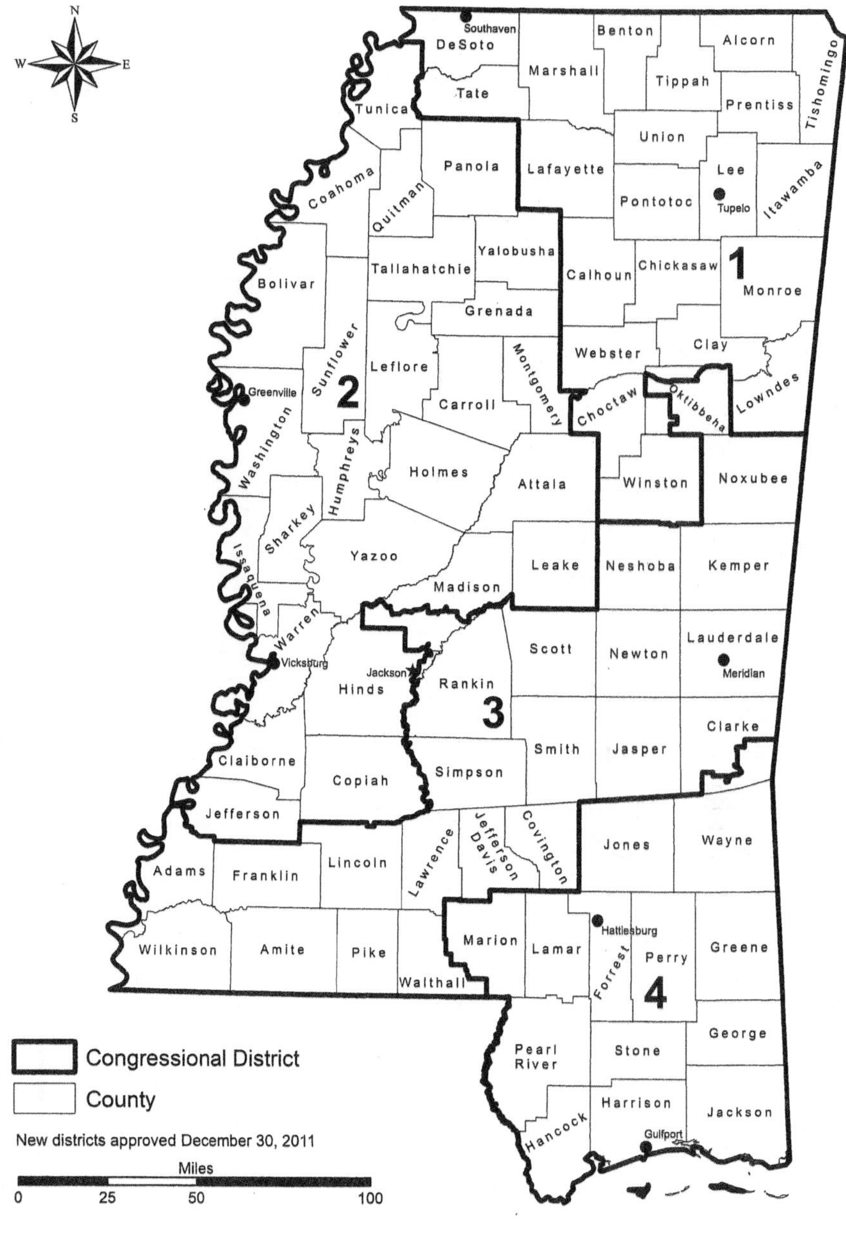

MISSOURI—Congressional Districts—(8 Districts)

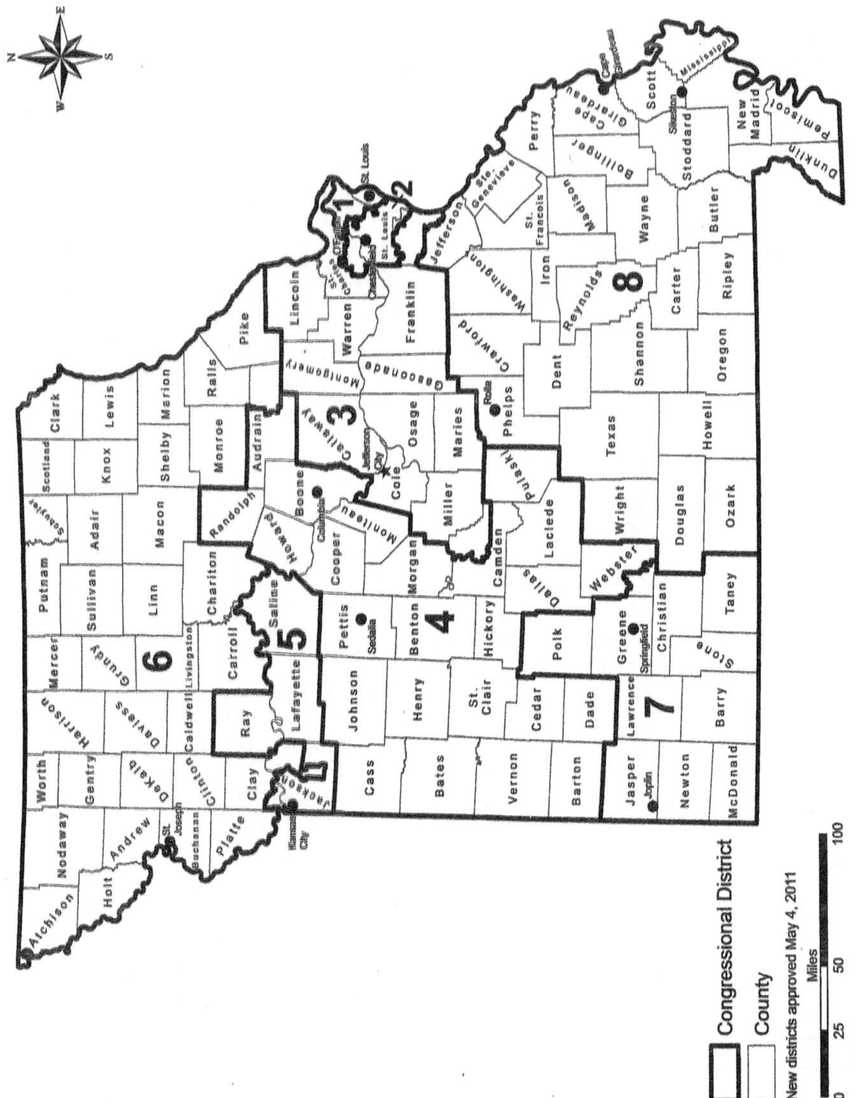

MONTANA—Congressional District—(1 District At Large)

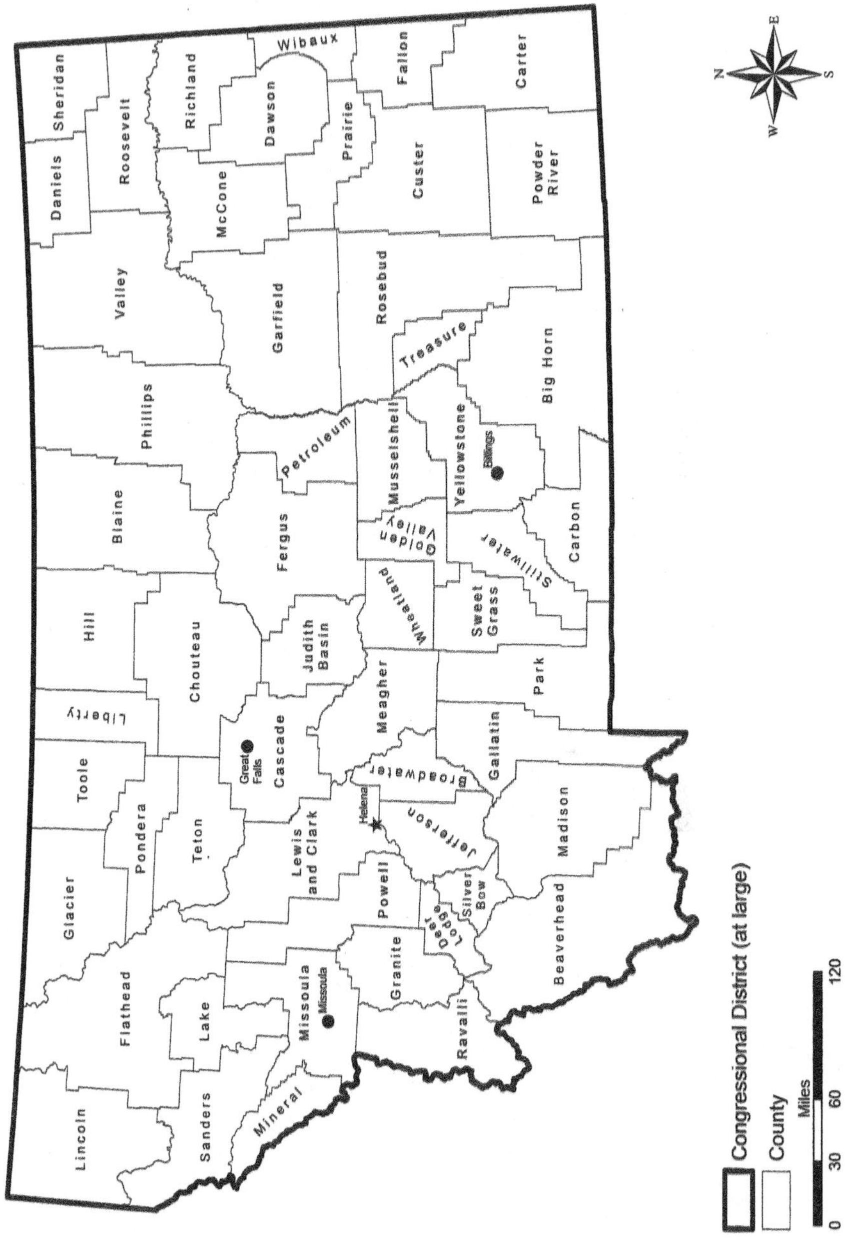

NEBRASKA—Congressional Districts—(3 Districts)

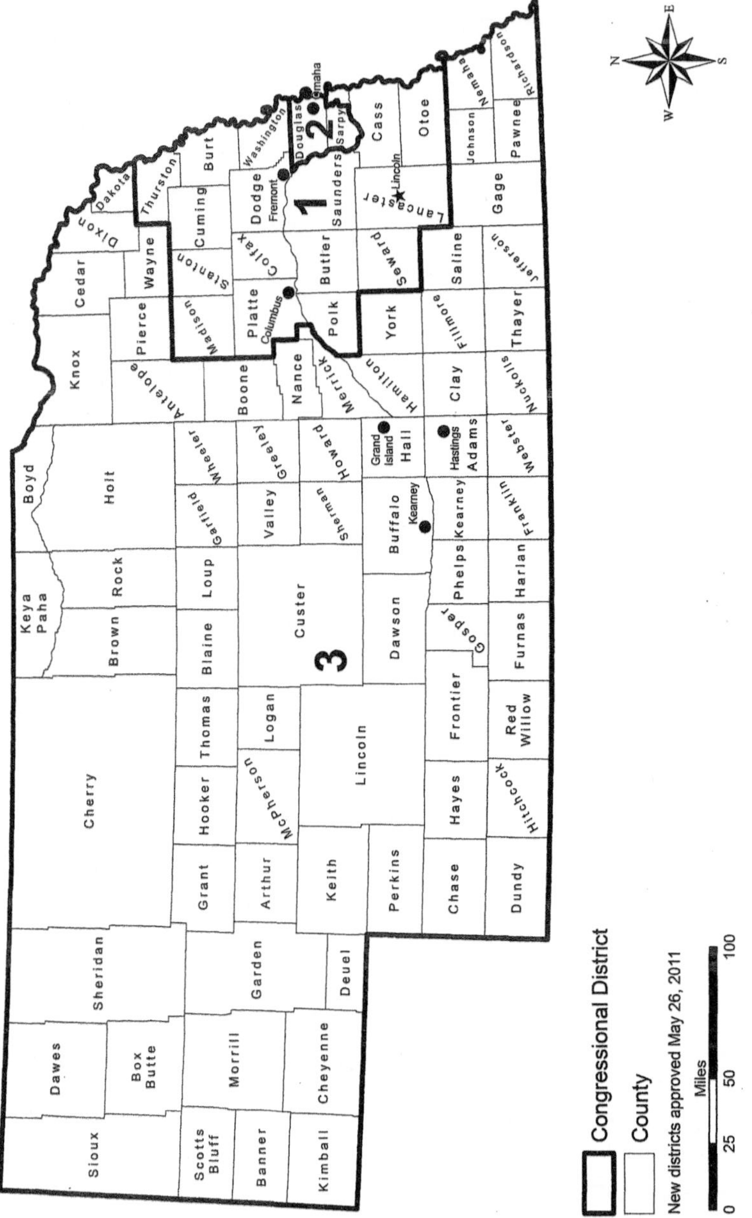

NEVADA—Congressional Districts—(4 Districts)

NEW HAMPSHIRE—Congressional Districts—(2 Districts)

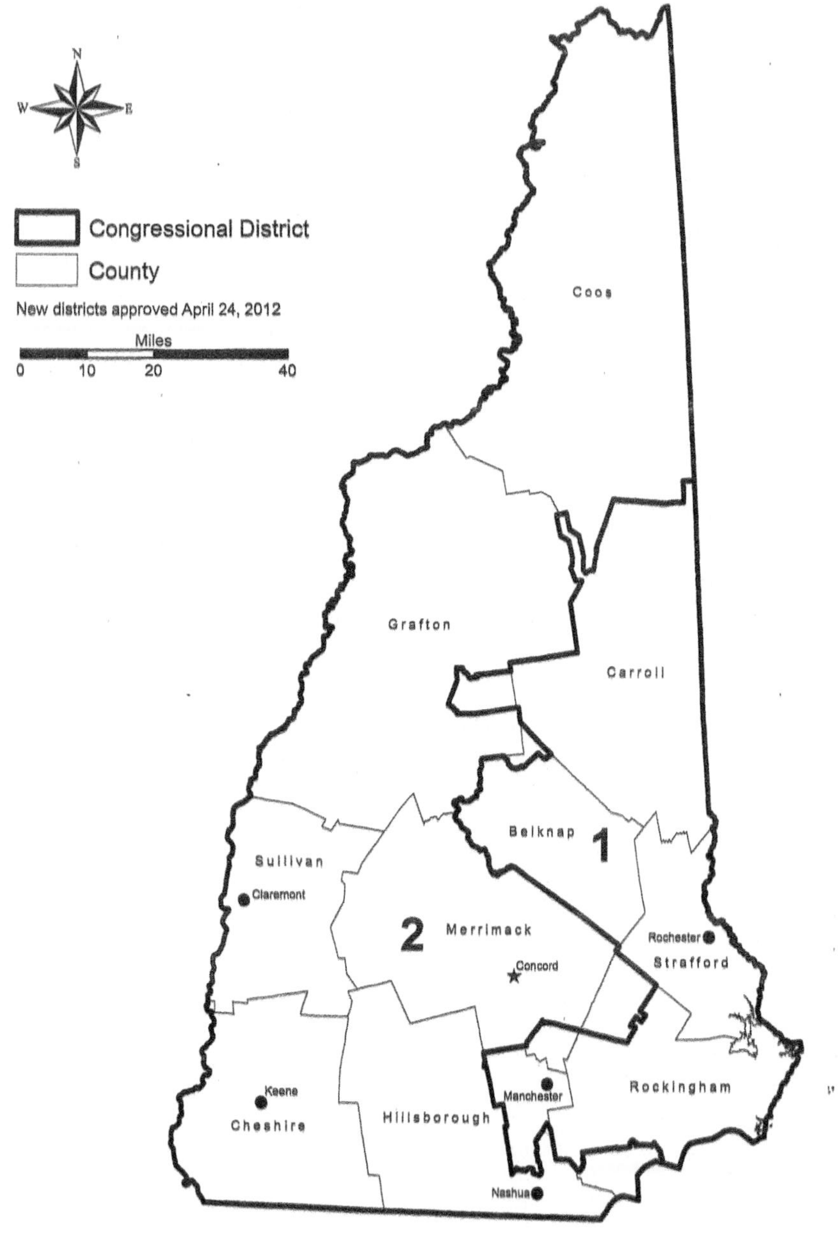

NEW JERSEY—Congressional Districts—(12 Districts)

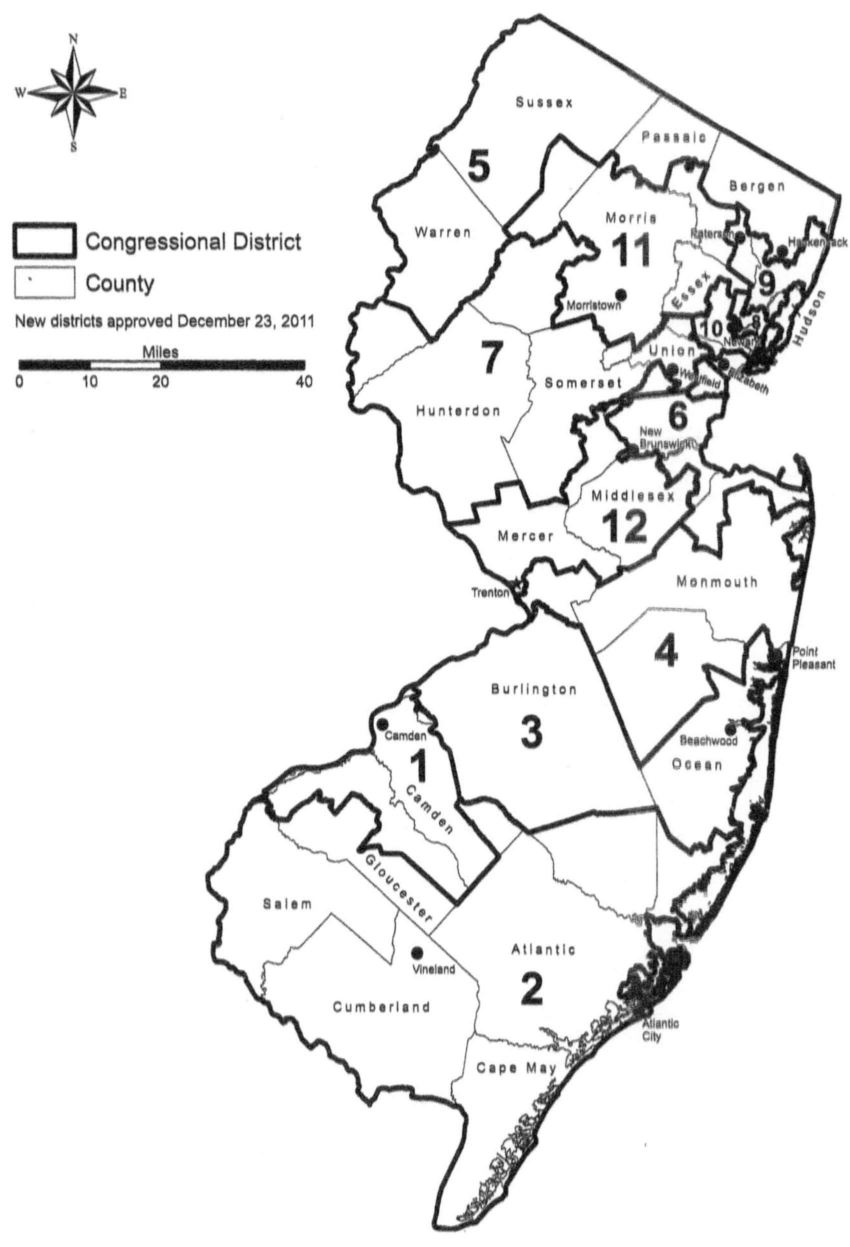

NEW MEXICO—Congressional Districts—(3 Districts)

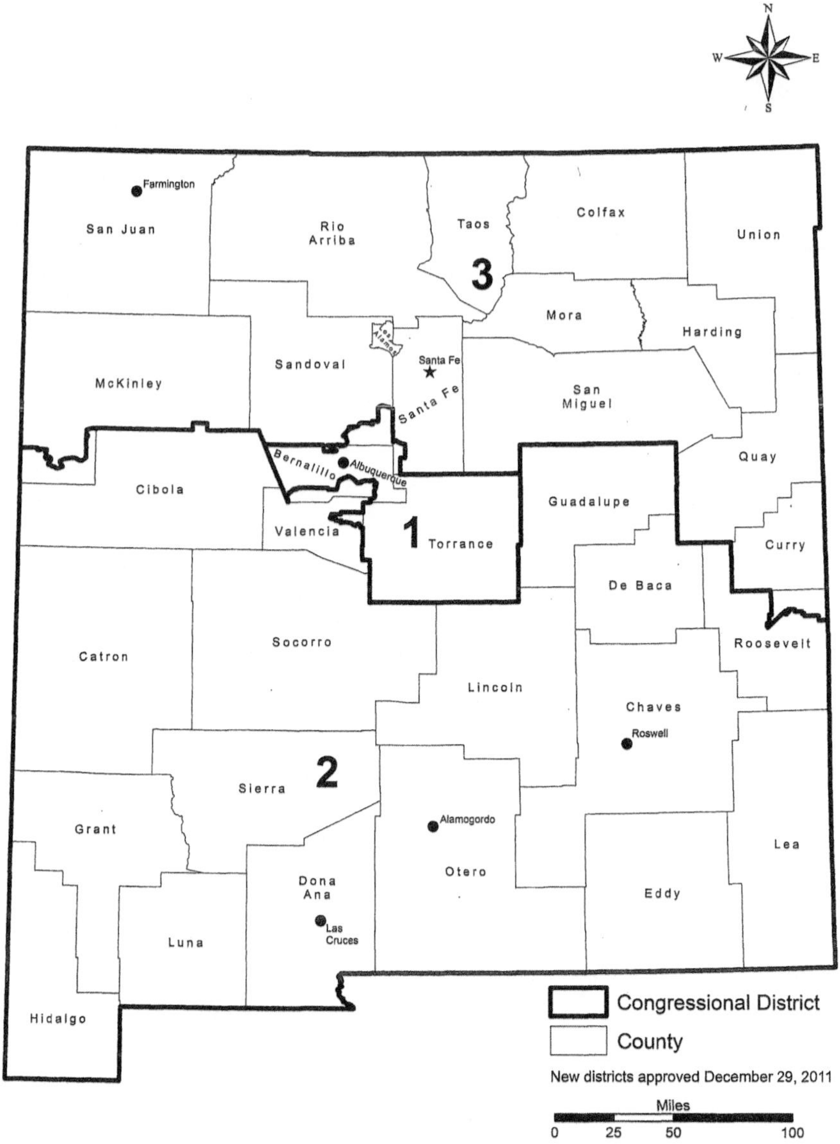

NEW YORK—Congressional Districts—(27 Districts)

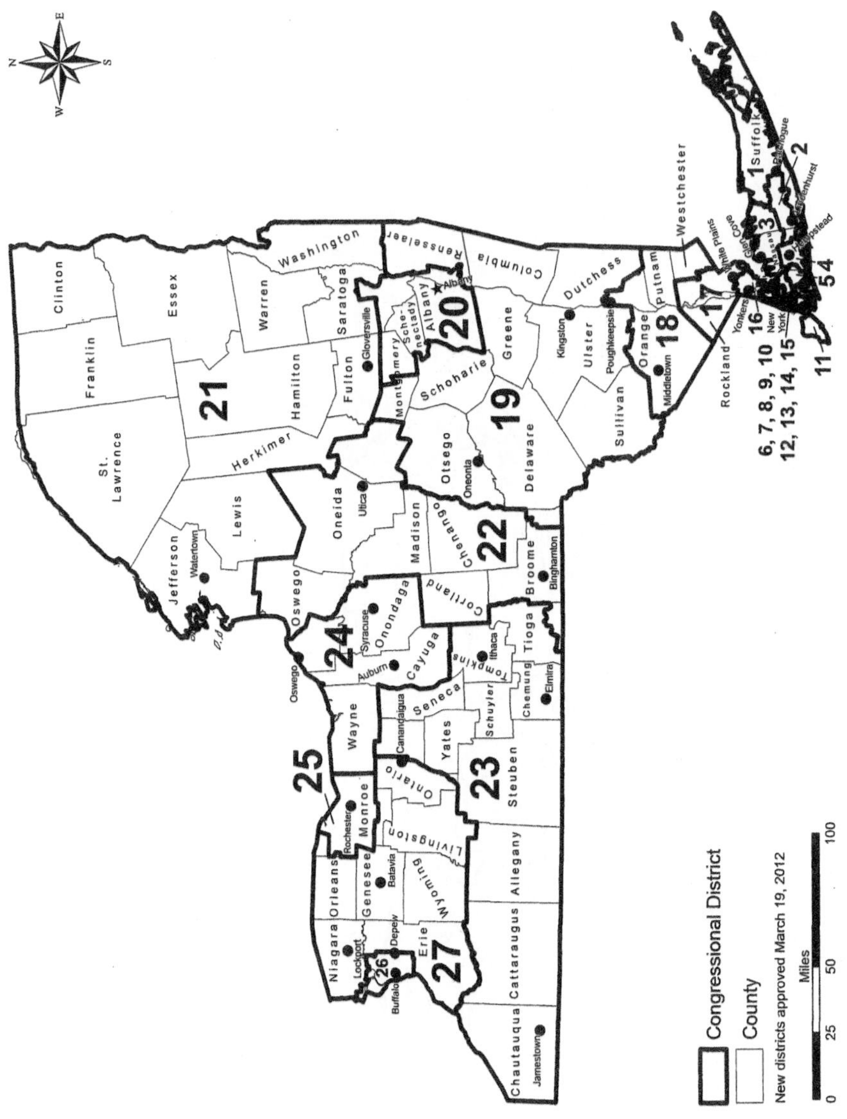

NORTH CAROLINA—Congressional Districts—(13 Districts)

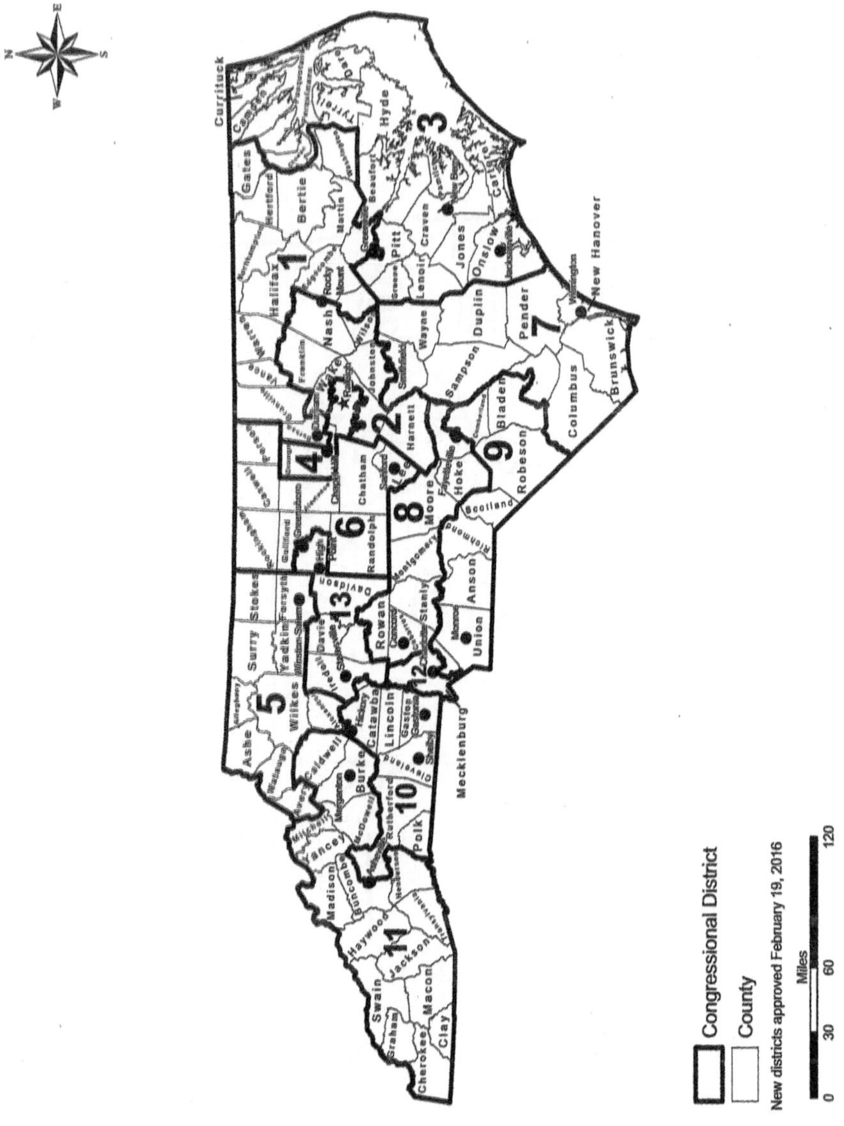

Congressional District

County

New districts approved February 19, 2016

Miles

0 30 60 120

NORTH DAKOTA—Congressional District—(1 District At Large)

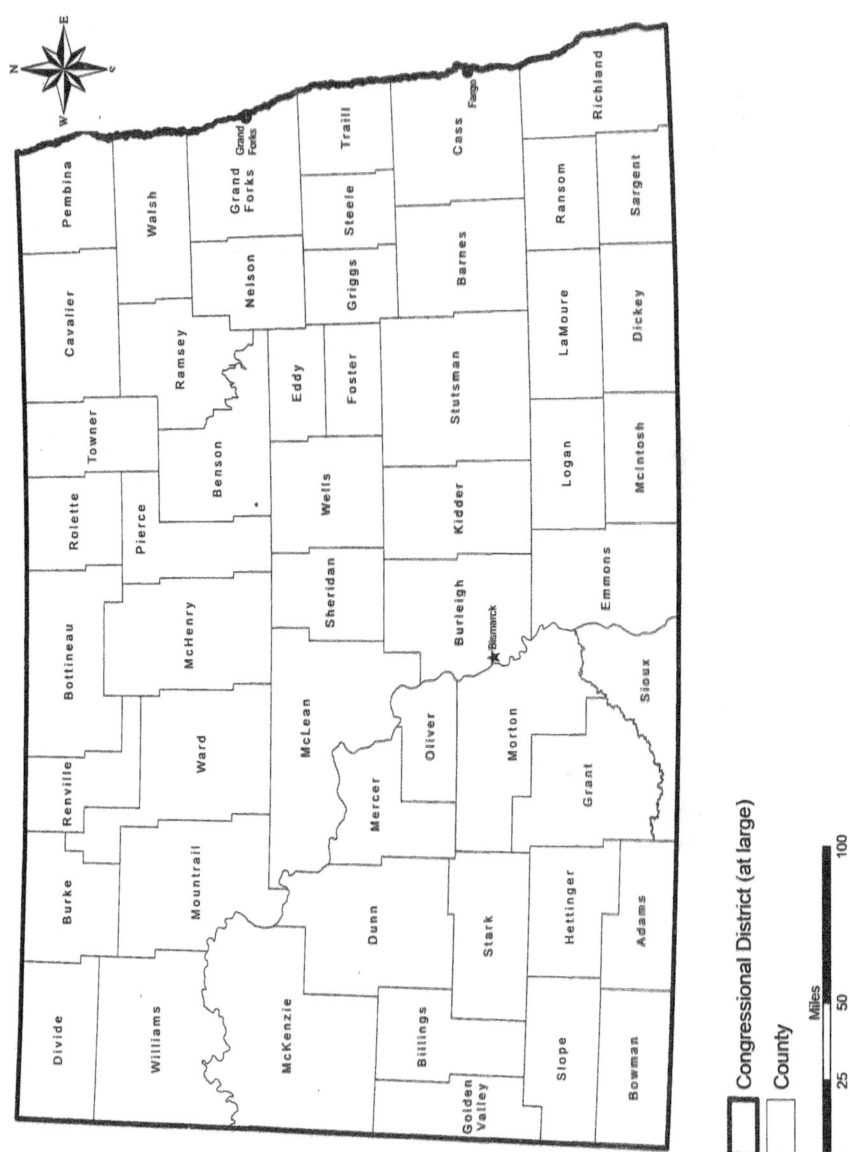

OHIO—Congressional Districts—(16 Districts)

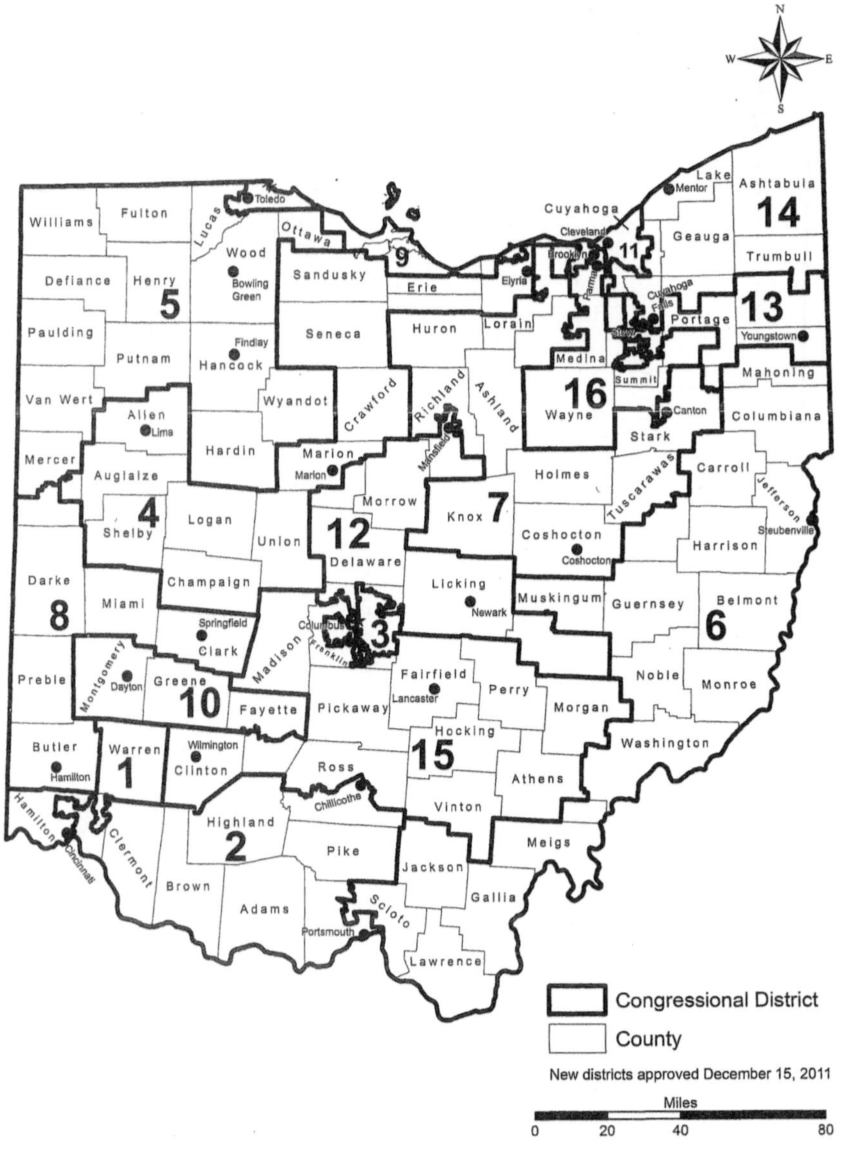

OKLAHOMA—Congressional Districts—(5 Districts)

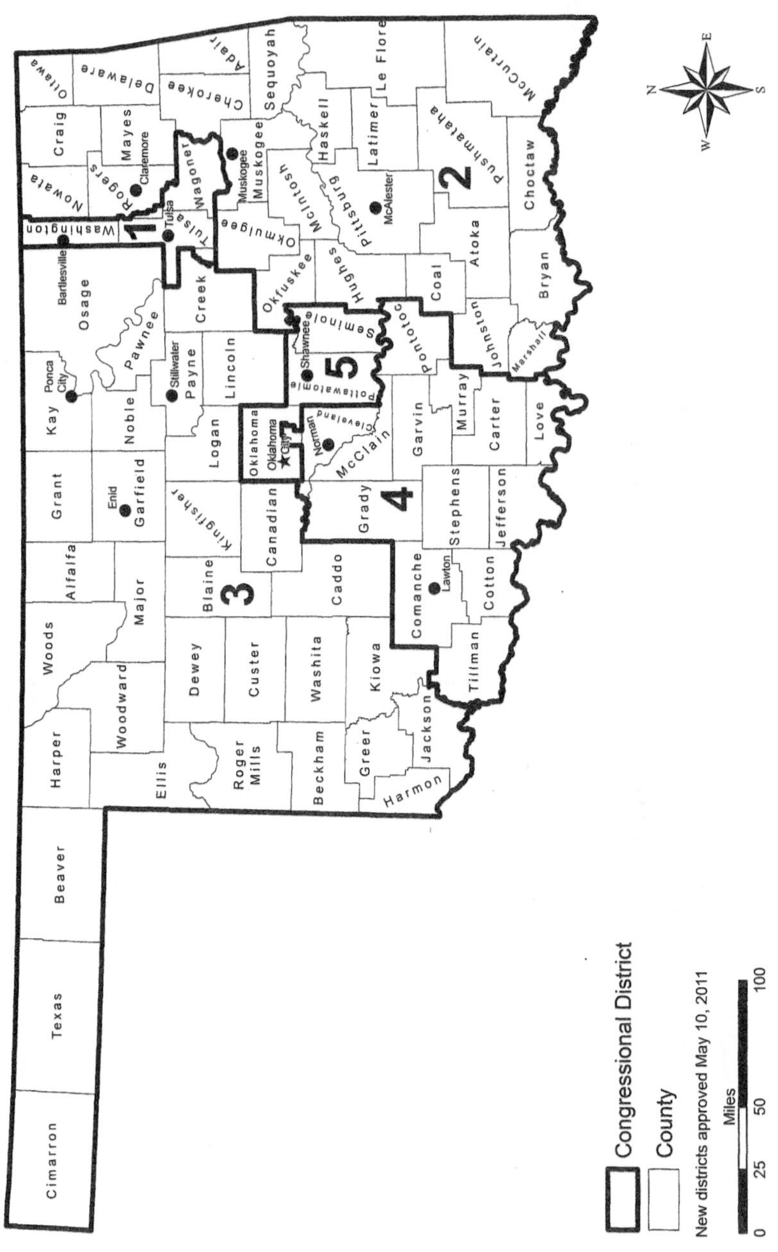

OREGON—Congressional Districts—(5 Districts)

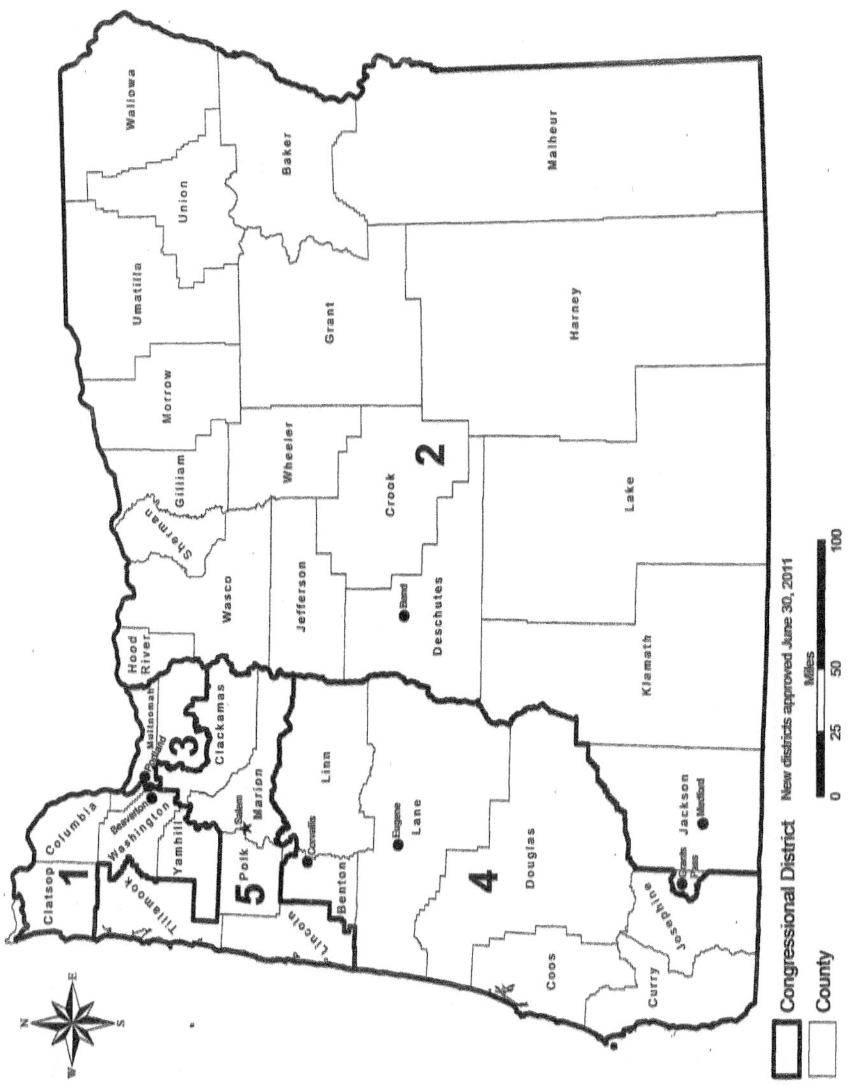

PENNSYLVANIA—Congressional Districts—(18 Districts)

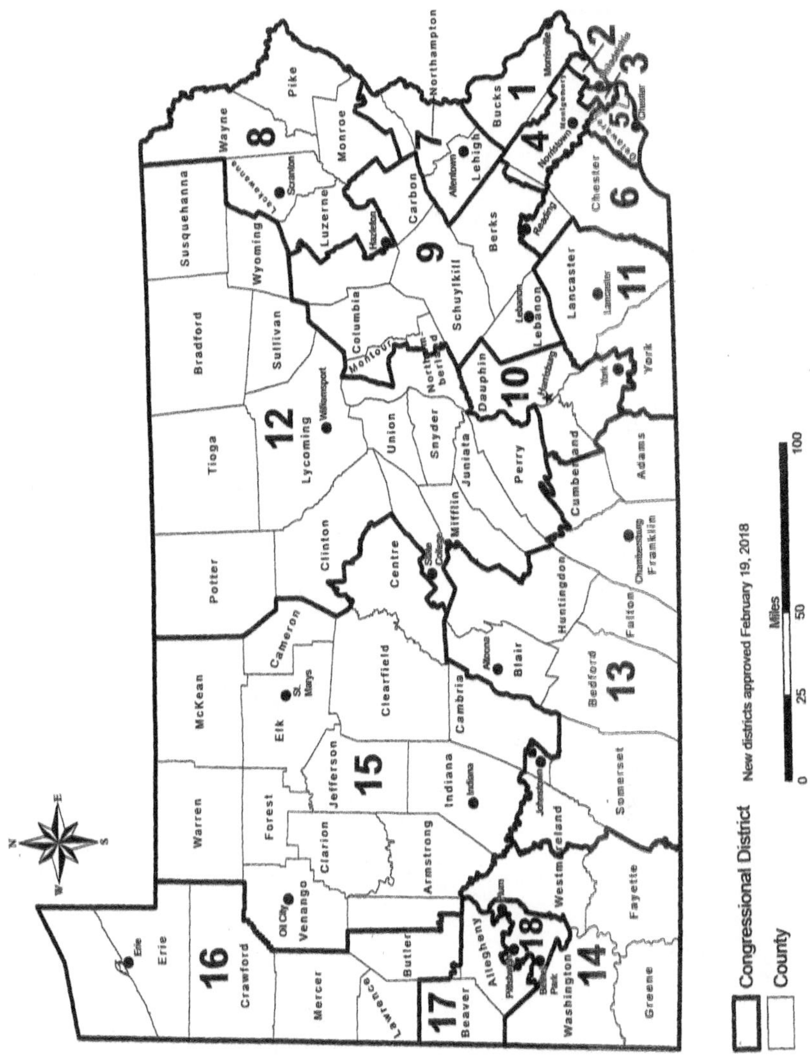

RHODE ISLAND—Congressional Districts—(2 Districts)

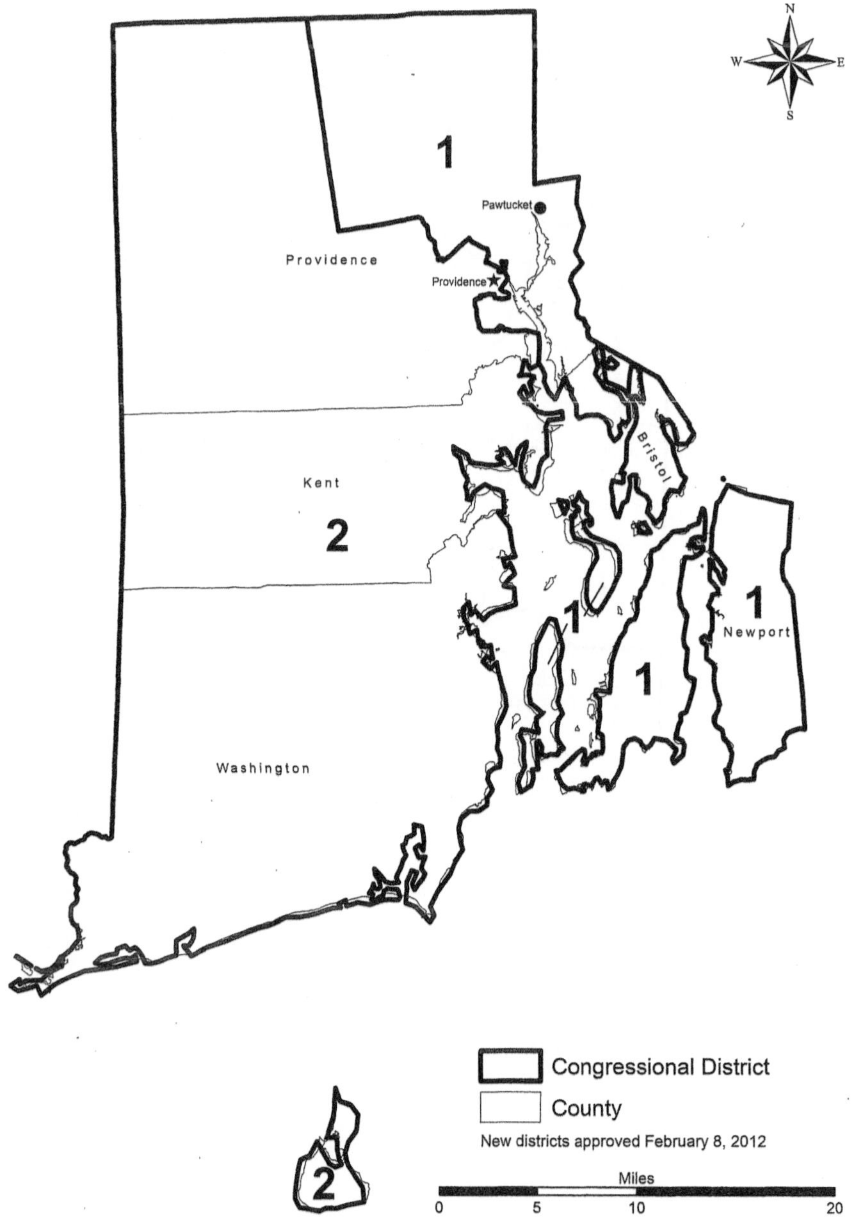

SOUTH CAROLINA—Congressional Districts—(7 Districts)

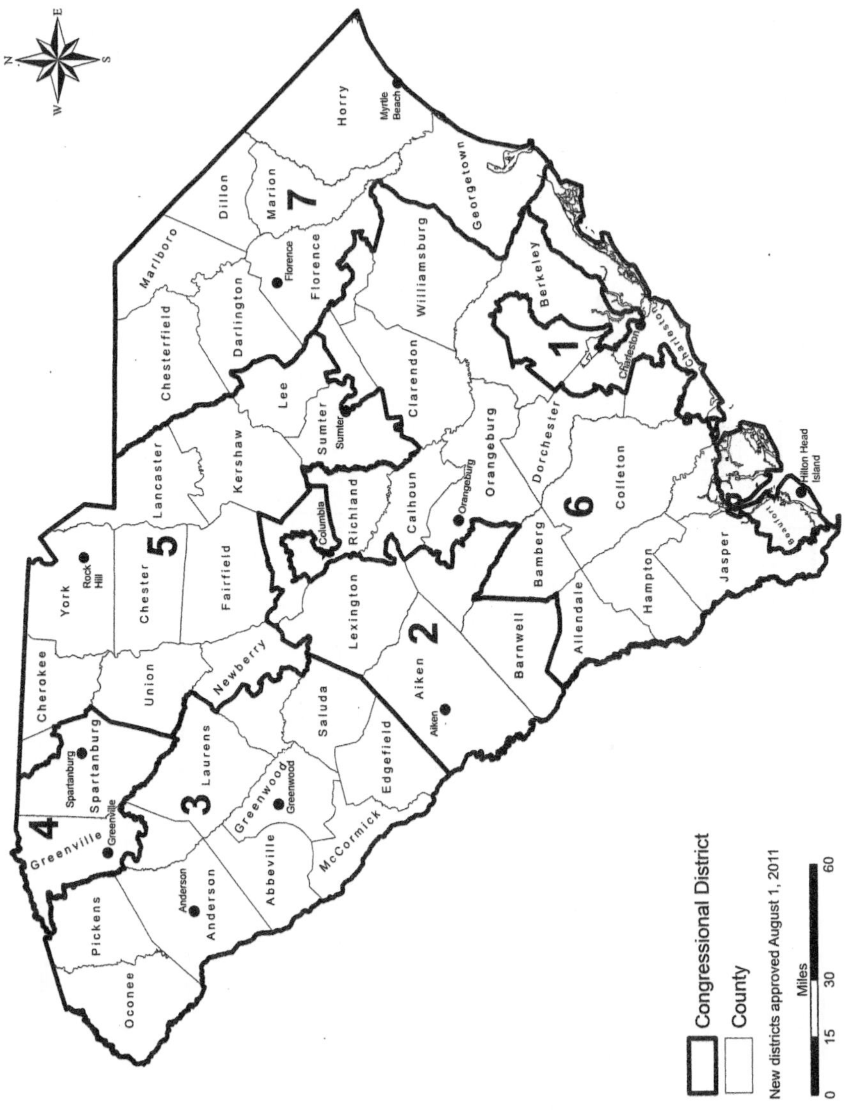

SOUTH DAKOTA—Congressional District—(1 District At Large)

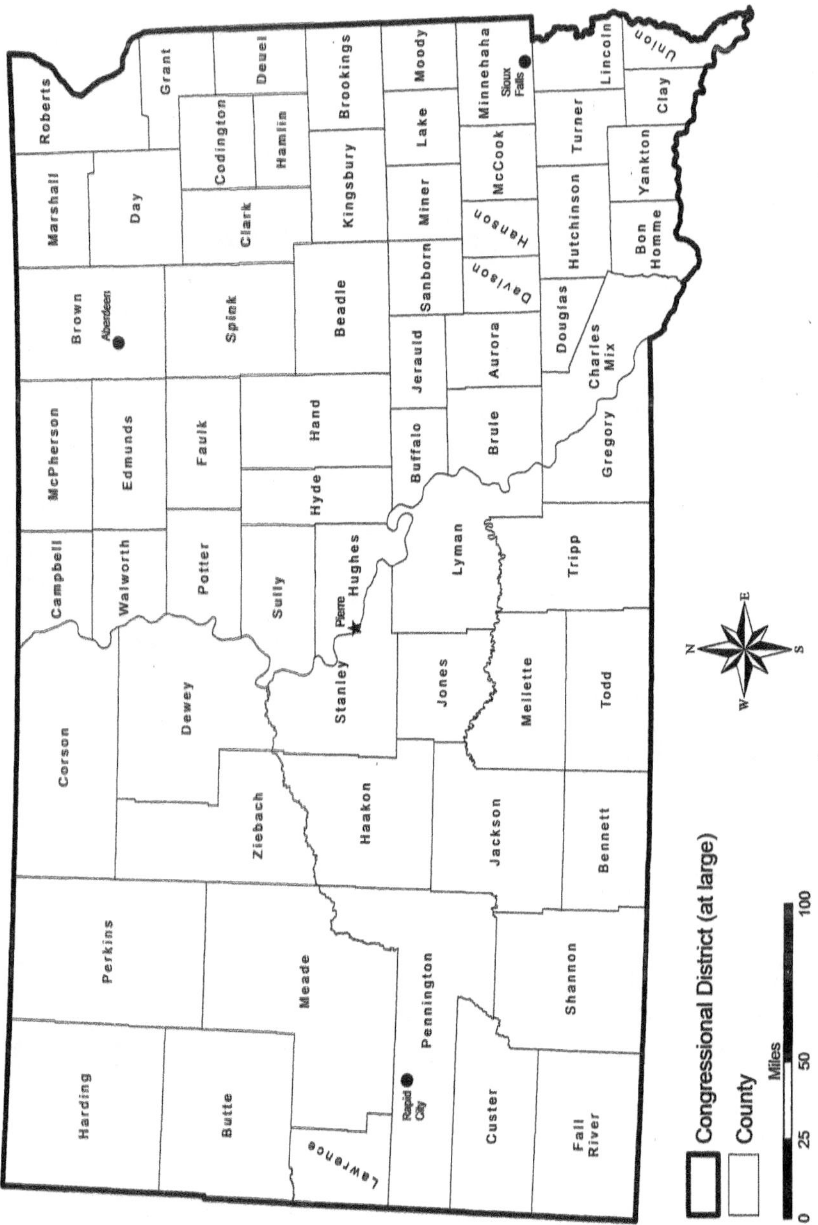

TENNESSEE—Congressional Districts—(9 Districts)

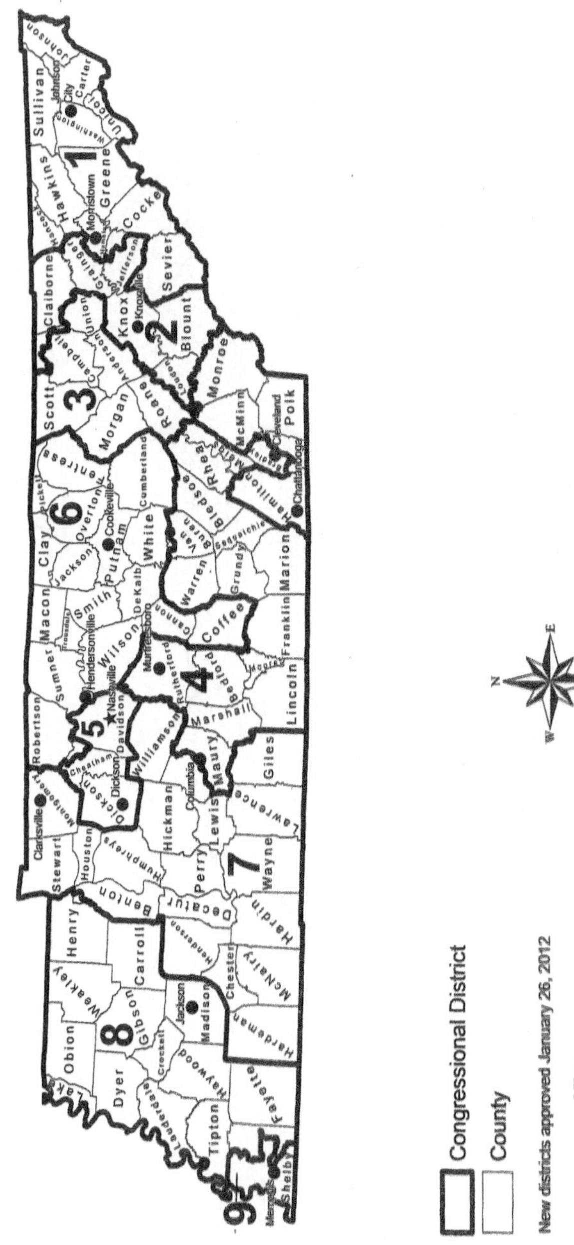

TEXAS—Congressional Districts—(36 Districts)

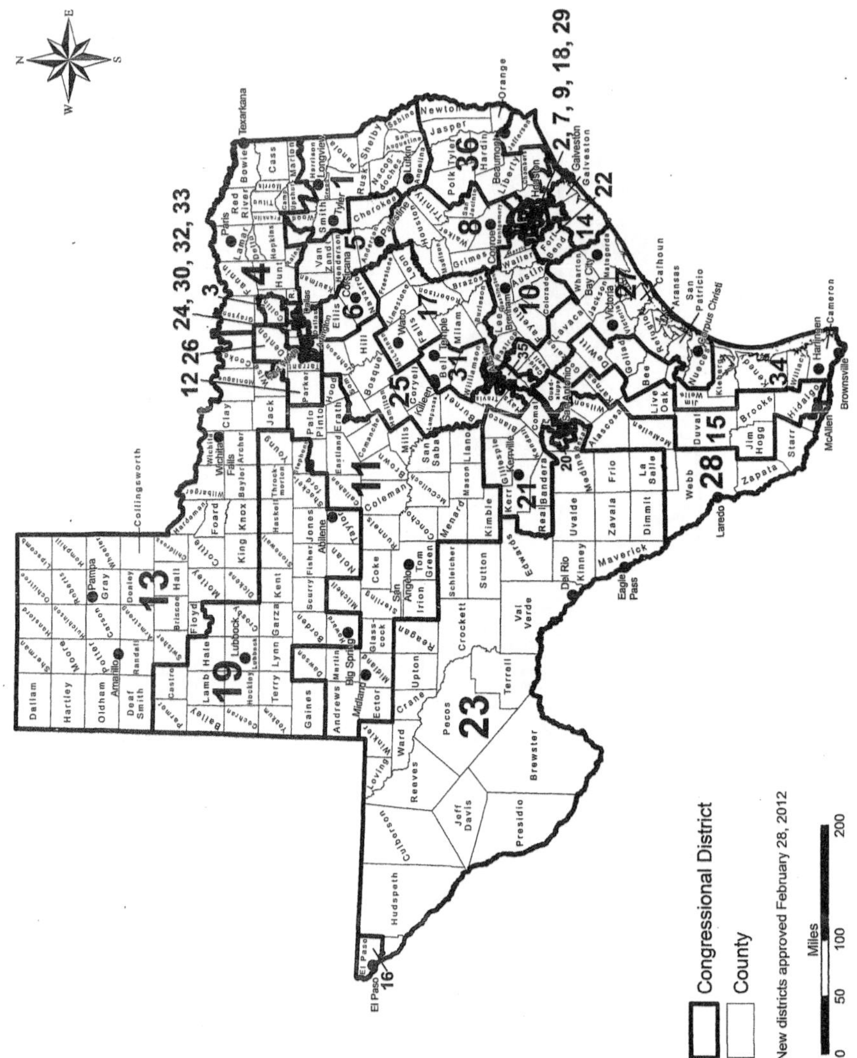

UTAH—Congressional Districts—(4 Districts)

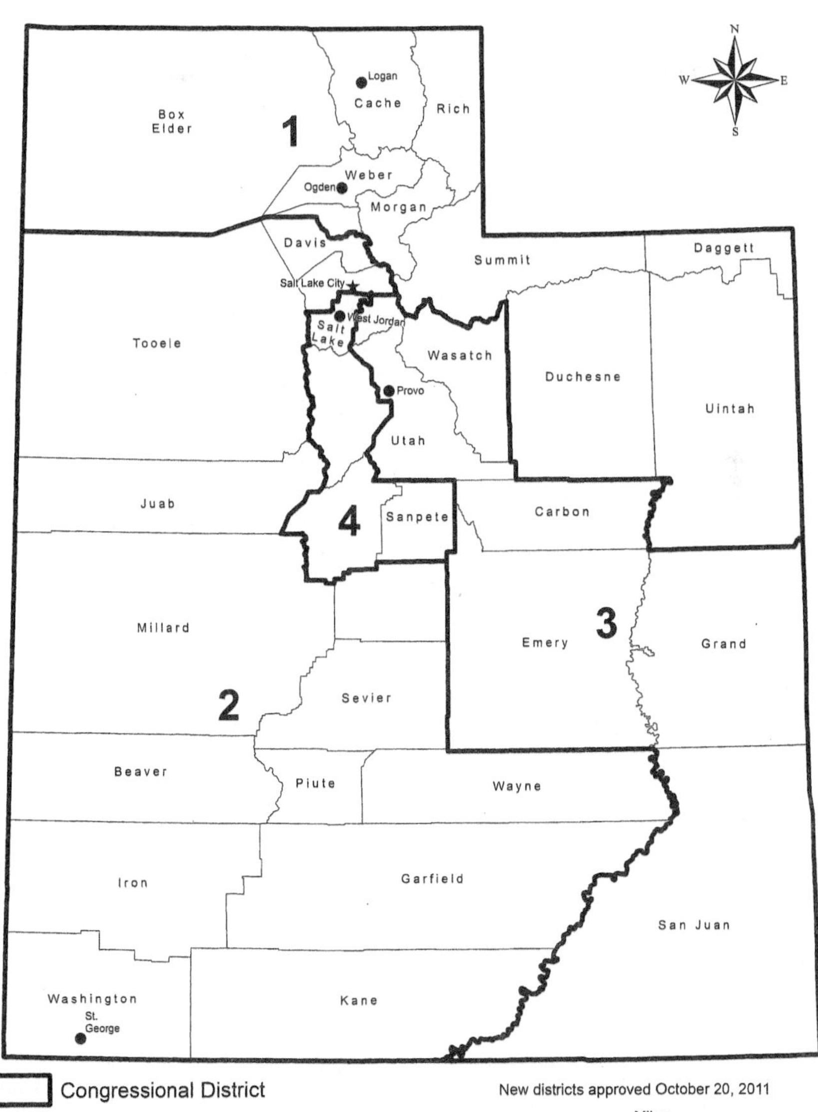

VERMONT —Congressional District—(1 District At Large)

VIRGINIA—Congressional Districts—(11 Districts)

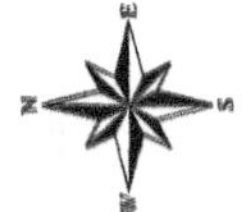

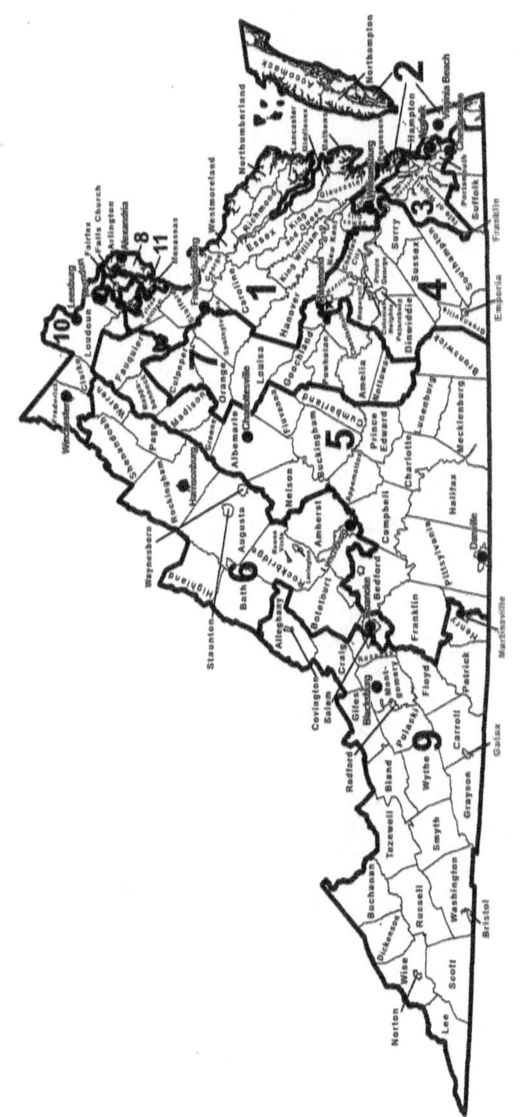

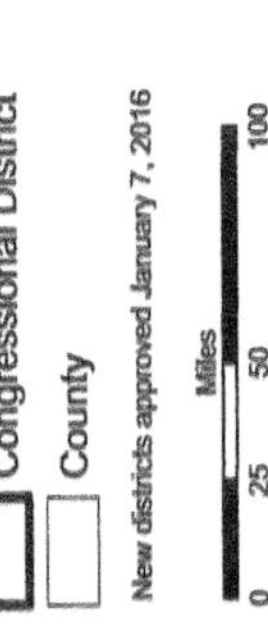

WASHINGTON—Congressional Districts—(10 Districts)

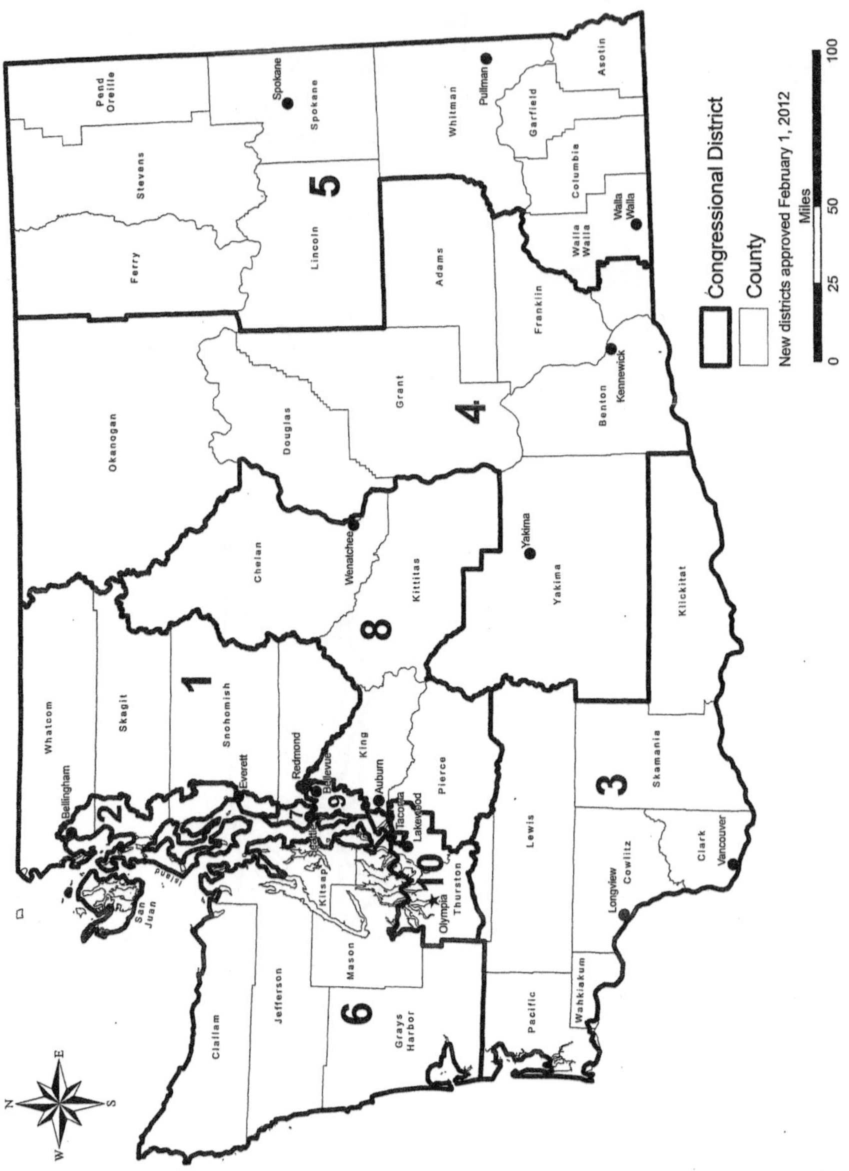

WEST VIRGINIA—Congressional Districts—(3 Districts)

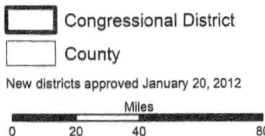

Congressional District

County

New districts approved January 20, 2012

Miles

0 20 40 80

WISCONSIN—Congressional Districts—(8 Districts)

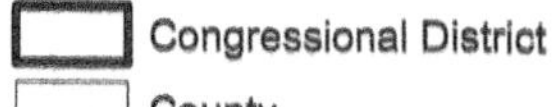

New districts approved August 9, 2011

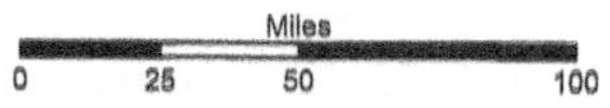

WYOMING—Congressional District—(1 District At Large)

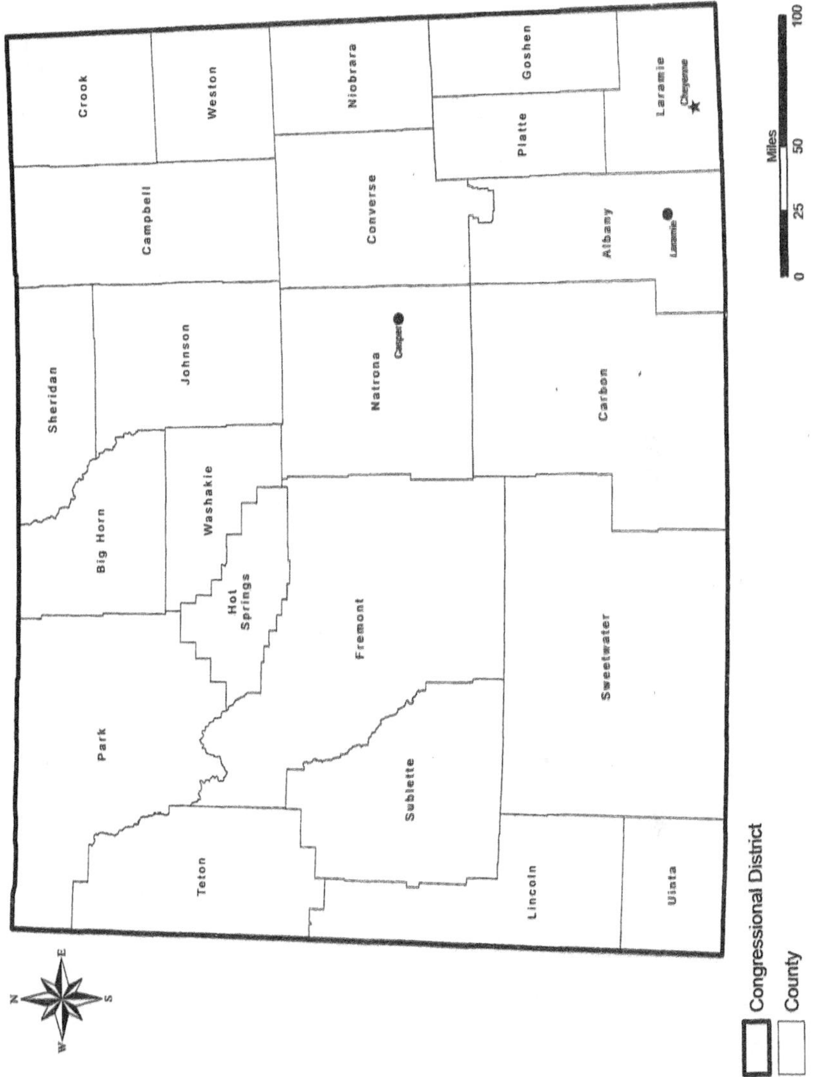

AMERICAN SAMOA —(1 Delegate At Large)

Swains Island

Eastern

Western

Manu'a

Rose Island

Islands

Miles

0 20 40 80

DISTRICT OF COLUMBIA—(1 Delegate At Large)

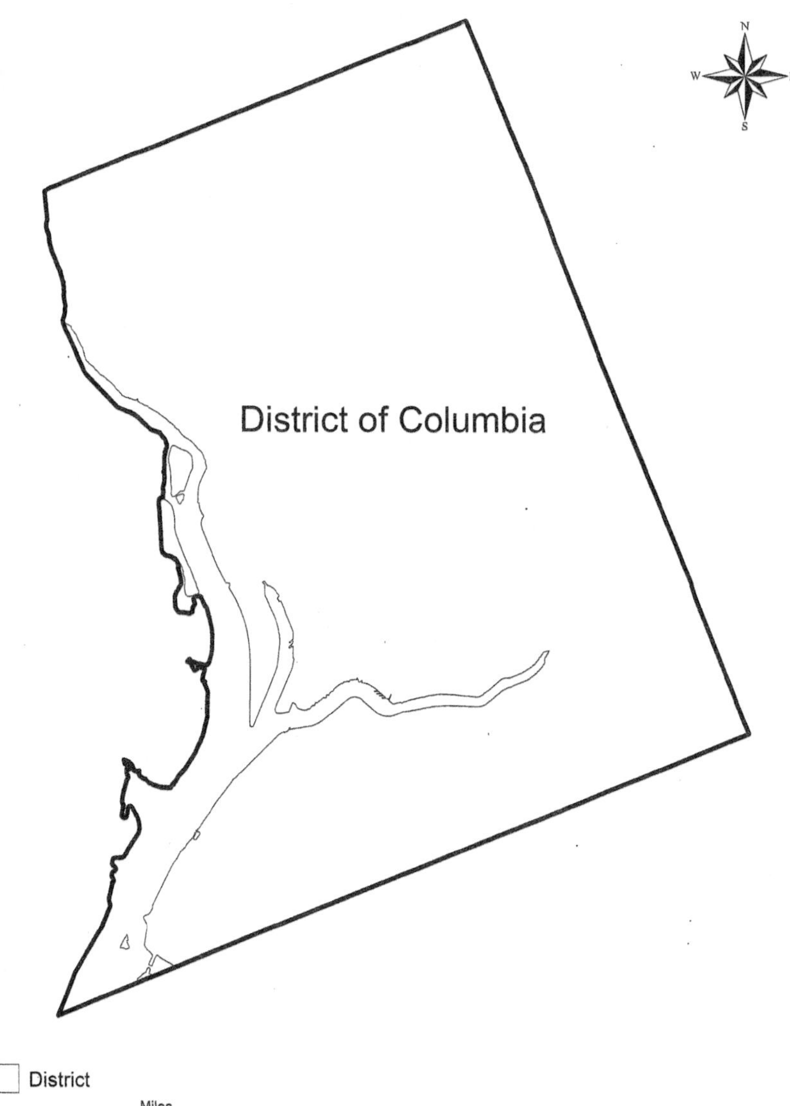

GUAM —(1 Delegate At Large)

NORTHERN MARIANA ISLANDS—(1 Delegate At Large)

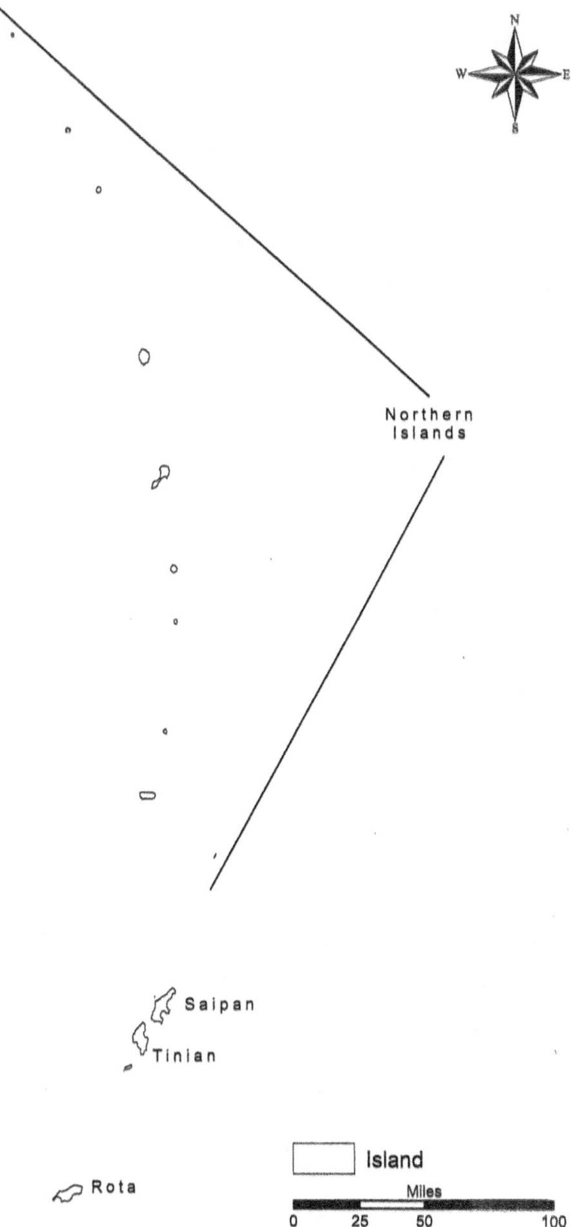

PUERTO RICO —(1 Resident Commissioner At Large)

THE VIRGIN ISLANDS OF THE UNITED STATES—(1 Delegate At Large)

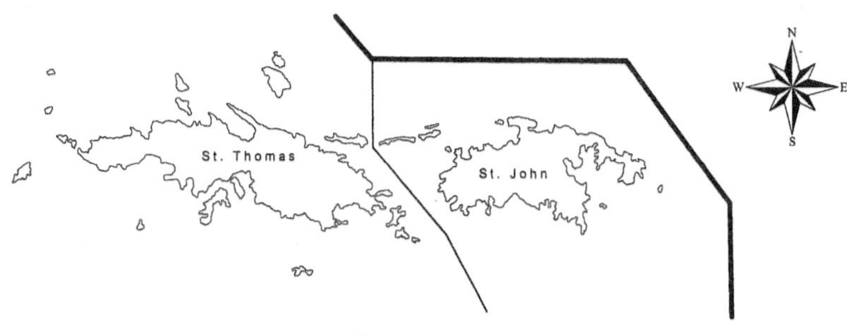

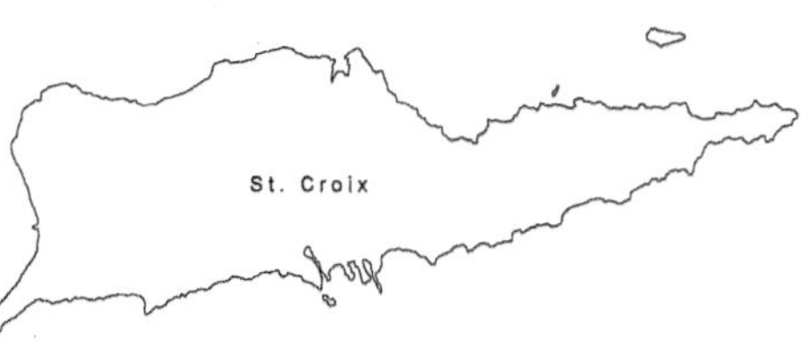

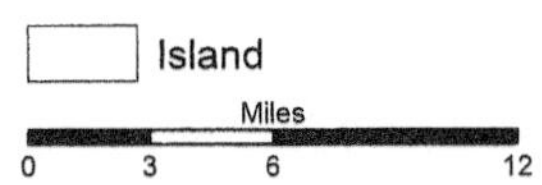

NAME INDEX

I

J

L

M

O

U